ॐ सर्व्वमङ्गल मङ्गल्ये शिवे सर्व्वार्थसाधिके।
शरण्ये त्रम्वके गौरि नारायणि नमोऽस्तुते॥

Dedicated to

THE GODDESS KALI

The DIVINE MOTHER

who is the source of inspiration and strength behind this work

FINANCIAL ACCOUNTING

Volume I

FINANCIAL ACCOUNTING

Volume I

[For Part I BCom (Hons) and General New Syllabus, Calcutta University; also for MCom, CA (PCE), ICWA, CS]

Dr S Kr Paul MCom, PhD, MBIM (London)

Principal (Retd)
Reader and Head, Department of Accountancy
South City College, Kolkata

Prof. Chandrani Paul MCom, MBA (WBUT)

Jogamaya Devi College, Kolkata
And, South City College
(Prafulla Chandra College)
Formerly Faculty Member, Sikkim Manipal University
and Asia Pacific Institute of Hospitality Management

New Central Book Agency (P) Ltd

LONDON

HYDERABAD ERNAKULAM BHUBANESWAR

NEW DELHI KOLKATA PUNE GUWAHATI

NCBA

REGD OFFICE

8/1 Chintamoni Das Lane, Kolkata 700 009, India
email: ncbapvtltd@eth.net

OVERSEAS

NCBA (UK) Ltd, 149 Park Avenue North, Northampton, NN3 2HY, UK
email: ncbauk@yahoo.com

EXPORT

NCBA Exports Pvt. Ltd, 212 Shahpur Jat, New Delhi 110 049
email: ncbaexports@ncbapvtltd.com

BRANCHES

212 Shahpur Jat
New Delhi 110 049
email: ncbadel@ncbapvtltd.com

Shop Nos. 3 & 4, Vinayak Towers
681/B Budhwar Peth, Appa Balwant Chowk
Pune 411 002
email: ncbapune@ncbapvtltd.com

Shop No. 15, Bharati Towers, Ground Floor
Forest Park, **Bhubaneswar** 751 001
email: ncbabub@ncbapvtltd.com

House No. 3-1-315, 1st Floor
Nimboliadda, Kachiguda, **Hyderabad** 500 027
email: ncbahydb@ncbapvtltd.com

GSS Shopping Complex, 1st Floor
Opposite College Post Office, Convent Road
Ernakulam 682 035
0484-4021054/53

Radhamayee Complex (Second Floor)
Opp. SBI, Panbazar, Jaswanta Road
Guwahati 781 001
email: ncbaguwahati@ncbapvtltd.com

FINANCIAL ACCOUNTING [Vol. I] • Dr S Kr Paul and Chandrani Paul

First Published: September 1989
Thoroughly Revised and Enlarged Sixth Edition: July 2011
Revised Reprint: January 2015

PUBLISHER AND TYPESETTER
New Central Book Agency (P) Ltd
8/1 Chintamoni Das Lane, Kolkata 700 009

PRINTER
New Central Book Agency (P) Ltd
Web-Offset Division, Dhulagarh, Sankrail, Howrah

COVER DESIGNER
Soumen Paul

COVER PRINTER
Biswanath Studio, Kolkata

TECHNICAL EDITOR
Subas Maitra

PROJECT TEAM
Pradip Das, Ashoke Das, Pradip Biswas, Prodip Baidya and Prabhat Jas

ISBN: 978 81 7381 668 0

Price: ₹ 465.00

CONTENTS

PREFACE TO THE SIXTH EDITION

It gives us great pleasure to present the sixth edition of Financial Accounting. The book has been updated, revised, and enlarged thoroughly.

The dimension of Financial Accounting is changing day by day due to diversifications in business and economic activities in the country, as also in the world, as a whole. As a result, academic and professional bodies of accountancy, as well as various corporate entities, are all trying to incorporate such changes in their accounting literature. For this, various Accounting Standards framed by the Institute of Chartered Accountants of India, SEBI Guidelines, Companies Act, etc. have framed various rules and regulations to incorporate corporate transactions.

This fresh volume has incorporated thoroughly and meticulously all such rules, regulations, laws, and by-laws framed by the above authorities. By the perusal of this book, the students can be well-versed and highly acclaimed 'citizens' of the modern 'world' of Financial Accounting.

The book is primarily meant for the Calcutta University General and Honours students who are preparing themselves for appearing at the BCom Part I (Honours and General). Some chapters are presented in this volume which are very important for acquiring the knowledge of accounting although they are excluded from the syllabus (viz. Bank Reconciliation Statement, Negotiable Instruments, Joint Venture, etc.). All the chapters have been thoroughly re-written.

For the problems presented in this title, we have drawn heavily on the undergraduate and postgraduate current question papers of different Indian Universities as also those of the CA, ICWA, CS, and other examinations so as to make the problems widely representative and up-to-date in character. Moreover, a large number of problems in all the chapters have been formulated by us. We are indebted to all the standard works on the various aspects of the subject for ideas and thoughts from which we have borrowed freely.

Problems have been solved as per latest SEBI Guidelines, and the Accounting Standards are as per the directives of the Companies Act.

Illustrations have been presented with solutions and detailed working notes. Similarly, unsolved problems are given at the end of each chapter under the head "Assignment Materials" for revision and further practice.

We shall be failing in our duty if we do not acknowledge the help extended to us by Prof. Shymalesh Maity, Head of the Dept. of Commerce, Jogamaya Devi College, Kolkata; Prof. Chiranjib Das, MCom, ACA, AICWA, Deputy Director of Studies, Institute of Cost and Works Accountants of India; and Prof. Soumya Banerjee, MCom (1st Class), SET, NET Qualified, Lecturer, St. Xavier's College, in preparing this book.

We are thankful to Sri Amitabha Sen, Director, New Central Book Agency (P) Ltd, for his active cooperation and support. We also express our appreciation for the cooperation of Sri Subas Maitra, Sri Prabhat Jas, Sri Pradip Kr Das and Sri Ashoke Kr Das of New Central for bringing out the book within the shortest possible time.

In spite of our best efforts, some shadowy areas may have remained. If any anomaly is found, please e-mail to author ***santoshkumarpaul@47.gmail.com***. We also welcome suggestions and criticisms from teachers and students which will help us to make the title more student-friendly in the forthcoming editions.

April 2011

Authors

187B Lake Town, Block B, Kolkata 700 089
Ph. : (033) 2534 6405

PREFACE TO THE FIRST EDITION

In a career spanning almost three decades as a College Lecturer and Examiner in various public and professional examinations, I have observed that most students enter the examination ill-prepared for the work they are expected to perform to the reasonable satisfaction of the examiner due to lack of consistent and comprehensive guidance in the subject. Practically, there is no such book in the market which provides clear instructions through theories and application of the same through practice although a good number of standard textbooks on the subject are available in the market. This volume will, no doubt, serve the said purposes.

Accountancy, in its wider term, has been widely covered in this title. It also includes the preliminary topics of Book-keeping in such a fashion as even a neophite can easily grasp its fundamental principles and practice. Moreover, this volume explains the theoretical part in a very lucid style and, after the theoretical discussion, a 'Ruling' of the account concerned (wherever necessary) is shown so as to enable the students to follow the principles and their practical applications with ease. In fact, this title is a wonderful blend of theory and practice.

For the problems presented in this title, I have drawn heavily on the undergraduate and postgraduate question papers of different Indian Universities, as also those of the CA, ICWA, CS, CAIIB and other examinations, so as to make the problems widely representative and up-to-date in character. Moreover, a large number of problems in all the chapters have been formulated by me.

I am indebted to all the standard works on the various aspects of the subject for ideas and thoughts from which I have borrowed freely.

I shall be failing in my duty If I do not acknowledge the help extended to me by my students Sri Sanat Chandra Chandra, BCom (1st Class), ACA; and Sri Anjan Sen, ACA, AICWA, in preparing this volume.

I also take the opportunity of expressing my gratitude to Sri J. N. Sen and affection to Sri Amitabha Sen and Sri Arunabha Sen of New Central Book Agency (P) Ltd without whose active cooperation this book would never have seen the light of day.

Despite my best efforts some grey areas may remain and an opportunity to revise the title in the near future will enable the author to make it less imperfect than it is in its first print.

Last, but not the least, I will consider my labour amply rewarded if the book proves useful to all those for whom it is intended. I also welcome suggestions for its improvement from all quarters.

S Kr Paul

City College (South Calcutta)
23/49 Gariahat Road, Calcutta 700 029
Mahalaya
The 29th September 1989

CHAPTER 1

FUNDAMENTALS OF ACCOUNTING

Learning Objectives

Meaning of Accounting

Accounting—a means, not an end

Accounting—as the language of Business

Brief History and Evolution of Accounting

—Pre-Development Period (Up to 1494)

—Development during 19th Century

—Development during the 1st Half of 20th Century

—Middle of 20th Century (1950) to the Present

Recent trends in the Development of Accounting

Accounting Cycle

Functions of Accounting

Steps in Accounting Process

Objectives of Accounting

Advantages of Accounting

Limitation of Accounts

Division of Accounts

Classification of Accounts

Difference between—

—Book-keeping and Accounting

Accounting and other Disciplines

—Accountancy and Law

—Accountancy and Economics

—Accountancy and Statistics

—Accountancy and Engineering.

Users of Accounting Information

Types of Accounting Information

Qualitative Characteristics of Accounting Information

Accounting as Management Information System (MIS)

Role of Accountants in Society

MEANING OF ACCOUNTING

According to AICPA, Accounting is "......... the art of recording, classifying, and summarising in a significant manner and in terms of money, transactions and events which are, in part at least, of a financial character, and interpreting the results thereof."1

From the above, Accounting refers to:

i. A procedure of writing financial transactions; and

ii. A system of recording, classifying, summarising, reporting periodically, in terms of money, which provides necessary financial information.

The said financial information is used for taking necessary and proper decisions about the allocation of economic resources. Besides, Accounting refers to a set of practices and a systematised body of knowledge.[2]

No doubt Accounting plays a very significant role in recording financial transactions in the field of financial activities. It has been stated above that it provides necessary financial information by preparing reports and statements since it keeps proper accounts of all the financial transactions which have occurred. Therefore, the general function of accounting includes:

(i) Measuring the resources held by an entity; (ii) Ascertaining the claims and interests in the said entity; (iii) Measuring changes in those resources; (iv) Assigning the changes to specified period(s) of time, in terms of money; and (v) Communicating information about the entity.

From the above; it becomes clear that Accounting accumulates data systematically and supplies the necessary information to the users of financial statements by which the users can take proper economic decisions and also may make proper predictions, i.e., in short, it conveys financial information about an entity for a specified period.

Besides the above, in order to solve the day-to-day financial problems, it becomes necessary to have a knowledge and/or information about the past and present economic events. Accounting is developed out of the need for communicating necessary information about the events. Maintenance of accounts would become unnecessary if a person (viz.,. decision-maker) could remember and observe all the relevant financial events personally.

That is not possible due to the following facts:

i. since it is not possible for a human being to remember all the events which occur at different places and times;

ii. he may be interested in the subsequent facts (to its happening) which may not have any connection with the earlier ones;

iii. all attributes of an event are not equally useful and important to the users.

However, the events are to be recorded in such a manner as they could easily be comprehended and, at the same time, such records may also be used as evidences of the events in future.

It should be remembered that all recorded economic information and/or events are not accounts (i.e., mere statement of facts is not an account).[3] At first, subject matters are to be classified and divided according to their needs in such a way that desired information can easily be collected. But care should be exercised before such classification, otherwise it will be of no use. Besides, in order to avoid ambiguity of the recorded evidences, clear-cut explanation becomes necessary. As it is impossible to present all sorts of recorded information at a time, events should be explained as far as possible so that they serve the needs of the users.

Now, from the foregoing discussion, it is evident that the main function of accounting is to represent economic events in a significant way. In case of a trading concern, accounts are maintained for the purpose of: (i) ascertaining the result of the operation with the help of Profit and Loss Account or Income Statement; and (ii) ascertaining the financial position at the end of the year with the help of the Balance Sheet.

---

1 *Accounting Terminology Bulletin,* No. 1, American Institute of Certified Public Accountants, Committee on Terminology—New York, The Institute, 1953, P. 9

2 Whenever we use the term 'Accounting' it usually refers to Financial Accounting—the oldest form where accounting first emerged and thereafter gradually developed. The other branches of accounting (viz., Cost Accounting, Management Accounting etc.), which are of very recent origin, are very close to it

3 Account may be defined as: It is a collated but classified statement prepared in monetary figures in combination with language in a systematic way to present the economic events of an economic unit

Similarly, in case of a non-profit seeking concern, accounts are prepared for the purpose of ascertaining the deficit/surplus and position of assets and liabilities at a particular date without, however, creating any utility through purchasing or selling goods or manufac-turing products or generating services. In such a case, mere keeping of accounts can neither generate any profit nor render any service to society. In other words, the entities are not created with the primary object of keeping accounts although there is an exception, viz.,. Chartered and Cost Accounting firms who prepare accounts on behalf of their clients, i.e., business houses.

Accounting—a means and not an end

After analysing properly the information supplied by the accounting statements, the users of the same take decisions for future activities. Since accounting supplies the necessary information, it performs a service function and, at the same time, it is used to represent the economic position of an entity. On the contrary, the primary objective is to take decision(s) on the basis of financial facts presented by accounting statements. Thus, the understanding of accounts is not the basic objective, it only helps to realise a specific objective. As such, *accounting is not an end in itself but a means to an end.* It is essentially a service function designed to provide relevant information concerning an entity for those who are interested in interpreting and using that information.

Accounting—as the language of business

We express ourselves through our language. Similarly, the results of the business activities are expresed through accouting with the help of finncial statements. Accounting measures the performances of the business, i.e., profitability position financial and position at a particular date. Thus, the language of accounting expresss the whole story of the undertaking through the various processes of accounting. It also presents various valuable information to the users of financial statement in various ways.

In other words, the progress or development— or otherwise, of the firm can easily be compared and seen with the help of various accounting data.

Brief History and Evolution of Accounting

It is the opinion of many esteemed and learned authors/people that the word ***account*** comes from the word 'count'. Because, we know that there was no existence of accountancy in ancient times—neither in the theoretical field of studies nor in the practical part of trading activities. The study of Accountancy was gradually needed as a result of complexities and economic activities—both in the field of social and economic life of society. The importance of Accountancy is constantly increasing from its very inception. Nowadays, Accountancy is regarded as an accounting aid to personal life, society, business, nation, and also internationally.

We will highlight the development and evolution of accounting in the following stages of development:

Pre-Development Period (up to 1494)

This period is taken from the beginning of human civilisation which continues up to the last decade of the 15th century i.e., up to 1494 when an Italian clergyman, Luca Pacioli, explained in details the principles of Double Entry System in his book ***"Summa De Arithmetica Geometrica Proportionet Proportionalita"***. Before that period, i.e., at the primitive age, people collected food from various sources (e.g., hunting, etc.) and the surplus of food/animals were stored for future consumption or loaned to their neighbours after meeting their own consumption. Thus, it became necessary to keep records of their food (animals, and others) resources/belongings. They formed a society ultimately for their own interest and lived a social life for various purposes. They tried to save the surplus of resources which were utilised for their future development. Gradually, they needed to maintain assets properly although barter system was in use. As a result, the progress of accounting system was introduced in place of barter system—which had many drawbacks. Division of labour among the people was also introduced. Goods and services were exchanged with the help of money among the people—this also needed a sound accounting system. Before that, people used various symbols for keeping records of the day-to-day activities or events although these were totally cumbersome and confusing.

Thus, as a result of the increased activities of the various transactions in the societies, both trading and non-trading, through the monetary system, accounting spread rapidly in society. Gradually, in order to keep records properly for various purposes or results, (viz., buying and selling transaction, receipts and payments, assets and liabilities etc.), it becames necessary to maintain accounts. In short, accounting procedure developed to record correctly and systematically the details of creation, development and maintenance of resources. Moreover, at that time, the size and nature of business was very small and limited since these were controlled/governed by a sole-proprietor or by the members of the family. The owners kept the records of their business transactions. Gradually, the size, nature, types and complexities of business changed thoroughly and were converted into partnership or joint stock company. It is interesting to note that, irrespective of the forms of business, accounting played a very significant role. In short, accounting was introduced in each and every step of human life—even in religious institutions.

It has already been stated above that the primitive people used to keep accounts by introducing various symbols. At a later stage—before introducing the Double Entry System—accounting was kept as mere notes.

We must remember that by the end of 15th century, i.e., after 1494, accounting was introduced and applied in various fields but was not developed much. A new development in accounting took place between 1559-1795 when profit and loss account was first drawn up at the end of each year to know the results of the business. (First suggestion came in 1605). Thereafter, Balance Sheet was drawn up at periodical intervals—after another 50 years. By that time, a very new and popular concept in accounting came up i.e., **Going Concern Concept**.

Developments during the 19th Century

The so-called mechanical system of book-keeping was developed into a sound theory of accounting. During this period, many authors on the subject, all from European countries, tried to establish a general theory of accounting which was applied under Double Entry Principles. During this period, the Proprietorship Theory of Accounting was developed. It was explained with the help of the following equation:

Proprietorship = Assets – Liabilities

During the second half of the 19th century, another accounting theory was developed—**Entity Theory of Accounting**, which suggested that the firm and the owner are absolutely different. Accounts should be maintained on behalf of the business. This theory explains that

Assets = Capital + Liabilities

Developments during the 1st half of the 20th Century

During this period a large number of complex General Explanatory Accounting Theories were developed and published by some of the researchers and accounting scholars and authors. These theories of accounting helped to increase the level of knowledge of contemporary accounting practice.

Some of the General Explanatory Accounting Theories are:

1.	**Postulates of Business Entity**—	Balance Sheet Equity, Going Concern Concept, Balance Sheet, Costing and Valuation etc.
	Author: W. A. Paton	*"Accounting Theory"*—Published in 1922.
2.	**General Accounting Principles**—	Income Statement, Balance Sheet etc.
	Author: Sanders, Hatfield and Moore	*"A Statement of Accounting Principles"*—Published in 1938
3.	**Doctrines**—	Consistency, Conservatism, Disclosures and Materiality etc.
	Author: Stephen Gilman	**"Accounting Concept of Profit"**—Published in 1939
4.	**Concepts**—	Verifiable Evidence and Objective Evidence etc.
	Author: W. A. Paton & A. C. Littleton	**"An Introduction to Corporate Accounting Standard"** —Published in 1940

Middle of 20th Century (1950) to the Present

This is the "Golden Period" when new accounting principles, systems and procedures were evolved in order to keep records and to analyse and interpret financial events along with their results. This period is known as the **Modern Period of Accounting**. Now, the entire society is considered as economic unit with the exceptions of trading concerns. In other words, the accounting information relating to business is required not only by the owners but also by various people from their respective angle, e.g., Creditors,

Bankers, Investors, Government, Employees, Researchers, etc. Each one is interested from his own angle, e.g., creditors' interest lie in the ultimate solvency and liquidity position of a firm etc. i.e., the so-called objects of accounting are changed. In order to understand the present position and development of accounting, the students are advised to pursue the **"Recent Trends in the Development of Accounting"** which are presented next:

Recent Trends in the Development of Accounting

It has already been stated in an earlier paragraph that accounting, at its initial stage, tried to meet the need of historical and stewardship functions. But, in recent times, it provides a means of collecting, classifying, processing and presenting principles and practices which prove to be sufficient. That is why, at present accounting plays a significant and important role while forecasting and directing the future course of action, evaluating the performance, controlling cost, fixing the responsibility of the employees among others. That is, it has now become a very dynamic subject. Moreover, various new branches of accounting and new methodologies have also been developed in order to cope with the changing needs of the users. At present, some of the important specialised branches of accounting which have developed are: Cost Accounting, Management Accounting, Responsibility Accounting, Social Accounting or Macro-Accounting, Government Accounting, Inflation Accounting, Current Cost Accounting, Mechanised Accounting, Human Resource Accounting, Environmental Accounting etc. Needless to mention that some of the said techniques are Standard Costing, Marginal Costing, Budgetary Control, Statistical and Quantitative techniques, Ratio Accounting, Funds, and Cash Flow Analysis. Thus, the above-mentioned specialised branches of accounting—along with the said improved techniques—have made the present accounting a dynamic information, measurement and reporting system which are very useful for decision-makers. That is why accounting at present undertakes the responsi-bility of measuring, interpreting, guiding, controlling and communicating the results of various economic activities.

Accounting Cycle

The accounting cycle is a complete sequence of accounting procedure which is frequently repeated in the same direction during an accounting period.

Various Phases of Accounting Cycle

(i) Recording transactions in subsidiary books; (ii) Classifying the data through posting from subsidiary books to the ledger accounts; (iii) Balancing the accounts at the end of the accounting year; (iv) Preparing a Trial Balance from the ledger accounts balances; and (v) Preparation of Profit and Loss Account, and (vi) Preparation of Balance Sheet.

These are explained below :

(i) Recording Transactions

The first phase of accounting cycle is to record all transactions in Subsidiary Books i.e.,, preparation of Journal.

(ii) Classifying the Data

The next phase is to classify the data through posting from Subsidiary Books to various ledger accounts. i.e., posting from Journal to Ledger.

(iii) Balancing of Accounts

All the ledger accounts should be balanced at the end of the period in order to prepare a Trial Balance i.e., to ascertain the closing balances of all ledger accounts for the preparation of Trial Balance.

(iv) Preparation of Trial Balance

By taking all the closing balances of various heads of ledger accounts, a Trial Balance is prepared at the end of the period for the purpose of preparing the final accounts (i.e., Profit and Loss Account and Balance Sheet) of a firm i.e., preparation of Trial Balance for preparing final accounts.

(v) Preparation of Profit and Loss Account (Income Statement)

In order to ascertain the result of the operations a Profit and Loss Account or, an Income Statement is prepared by taking all the nominal accounts from the Trial Balance at the end of the period.

(vi) Preparation of Balance Sheet (or Position Statement)

Preparation of Balance Sheet is the last phase of the accounting cycle. It is prepared to show the financial position at the end of the period. The accounting cycle may be depicted as:

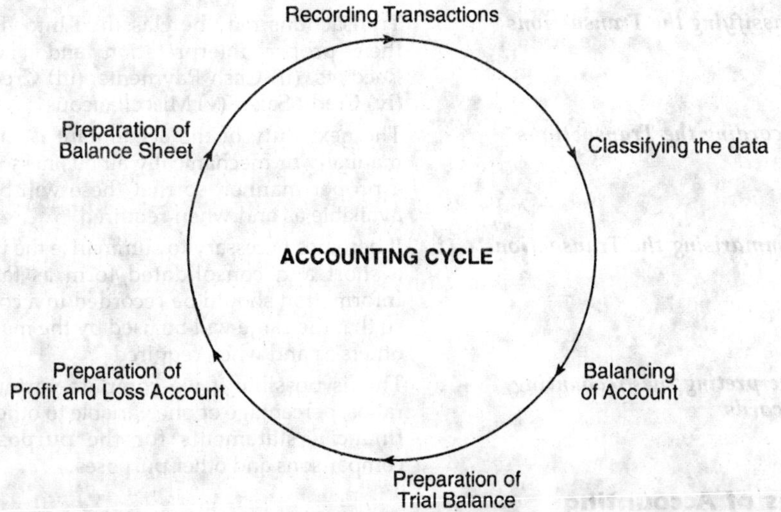

Fig. 1.1 : Accounting Cycle

Functions of Accounting

It has already been highlighted above that the primary or basic function of accounting is to supply the necessary information to the users and analysts for taking decisions which will be formulated in future.

The other functions, however, are:

i. It provides necessary information about the financial activities to the interested parties.
ii. It provides necessary information about the efficiency or otherwise of the management, regarding the proper utilisation of the scarce resources.
iii. It provides necessary information for predictions (financial forecasting).
iv. It helps to evaluate the earning capacity of the firm by supplying a statement of financial position, a statement of periodical earnings together with a statement of financial activities to the various interested persons.
v. It facilitates decisions regarding the changes in the manner of acquisition, utilisation, preservation and distribution of the scarce resources.

Other Functions of Accounting

The users of accounting information may not be interested in information about the present and past transactions but are interested about the future transactions as well, i.e., they require good services from accounting for taking financial and managerial decisions which are presented by a financial statement. Thus, accounting has two-fold functions, viz.

(a) **Stewardship or Historical Function**, and (b) **Management Function.**

(a) **Stewardship or Historical Function,**

It includes recording, classifying, summarising and interpreting past transactions about an enterprise. The reporting of performance is done with the help of Profit and Loss Account and Balance Sheet, at a regular intervals, for the owners, managers and other interested parties.

(b) **Management Function**

It supplies information to managers of all levels for the purpose of planning, co-ordinating, controlling day-to-day activities or appraising the result between the actual and the predetermined standards, which, in other words, help to secure maximum efficiency by avoiding the chances of fraud and errors, wastage and pilferage, misappropriation, etc.

Steps in Accounting Process

The steps of accounting process may be summarised as:

(a) *Analysing the Transactions* : Each and every business transaction must be analysed so that their role for ascertaining profit or loss or preparation of Balance Sheet can be achieved

(b) *Classifying the Transactions* : Transactions may be classified into five groups for their proper interpretation and analysis: (i) Cash Receipts, (ii) Cash Payments, (iii) Credit Purchases, (iv) Credit Sales, (v) Miscellaneous

(c) *Recording the Transactions* : The next duty of the accountant is to record either manually or mechanically all business transactions in a proper manner, so that these will be fruitful and available as and when required

(d) *Summarising the Transactions* : It becomes necessary to summarise the transac-tions in a short and consolidated form as far as possible. Information should be recorded in a condensed form so that the same will be used by the management and others as and when required

(e) *Interpreting the Accounting Records* : This is possible if we compute various accounting ratios, percentage of one variable to other etc. from the financial statements for the purpose of making comparisons and other purposes.

Objectives of Accounting

The primary objectives of accounting are:

(a) To maintain records of business
(b) To calculate profit or loss
(c) To depict the financial position, and
(d) To make the information available to various groups and users.

These objectives are explained in brief:

(a) ***To maintain records of business*** : We know that it is impossible for humans to keep in memory all the day-to-day transactions. In order to overcome this difficulty various methods of accounting are followed. After analysing and scrutinising the accounting data from the financial statement(s), an analyst can take proper decision, prepare budget for the future, help the management to take right decision(s) at right 'time. All these are possible if proper books and records are maintained. It is the primary duty of the accountant to maintain records always up-to-date so that the correct decision(s) may be taken.

(b) ***To calculate profit or loss*** : Next duty of the accountant is to ascertain the profit Account, or loss i.e., the result of the operation, by preparing Trading, and Profit and Loss Account under Double Entry Principle. Thus, it is also one of the most important objectives of accounting. Naturally, in order to prepare the Income Statement (i.e., Trading Account, and Profit and Loss Account), the accountant must prepare other necessary ledger accounts. Calculations and ascertainment of profit will be impossible if the accountants do not properly maintain the subsidiary books of account and other necessary ledger accounts. For this purpose, various ledger accounts, preparation of Cash Book, and Trial Balance are absolutely necessary.

(c) ***To depict the financial position*** : Financial position can only be depicted correctly if the accounts are maintained under Double Entry Principle. It means the accountant is to prepare the Balance Sheet which will exhibit the true and fair position of the state of affairs of the company. But the preparation of Balance Sheet depends on the sound application of accounting principles while preparing Income Statement. We know that the Balance Sheet exhibits the real or true financial position or 'health' of an enterprise at a particular date. Moreover, while preparing Balance Sheet, the Accountant must remember the various valuation modes of assets. Thus, it is also a major objective of accountants to depict financial information to the users of accounting. An accounting information helps us to proceed further. Various accounting ratios may also be computed from the financial statement.

(d) *To make the informatio n available to various groups and users* : It is known to all that financial information helps various people interested in various fields. For example, owners will look after the rate of return on capital employed, long-term solvency of the business, whereas creditors' interest will lie on the liquidity position and, ultimately, solvency of the firm. Similarly, investors will be interested to study the investment opportunities, and management of the firm will be interested about profitability and efficiency of the business. Thus, various people are interested to have the accounting information for various purposes.

Advantages of Accounting

The following benefits and advantages may be derived from accounting:

(i) *Assistance of management* : Accounting helps the management in the following manner: (a) it provides the required information which enables a firm to do its operation efficiently and properly; (b) The infor-mation which is supplied by the accountant helps the management in decision-making, planning, budgeting and controlling the firm.

(ii) *Comparative study* : Accounting facilitates comparative study of the current year's profit, sales, expenses, incomes etc. with those of the past years.

(iii) *Maintenance of records* : Since it is impossible for human beings to remember all business transactions, it becomes necessary to record the transactions as soon as they occur and that is done by accounting.

(iv) *Compliance with legal formalities* : Accounting helps a firm to maintain books of accounts up-to-date as per current legal formalities by which filling of Income-tax Return or Sales Tax Returns etc. become very easy.

(v) *Presenting financial information* : An analyst can easily analyse the financial position after scrutinising and analysing the Income Statement and Balance Sheet which are prepared by the accountant.

(vi) *Other advantages* : (a) **Evidence in Court:** If accounts are maintained properly, the same can be produced before a court of law in order to settle a dispute.

(b) **Sale of Business:** If a businessman wants to sell his business, he can claim the proper price if he maintains his accounts properly.

(c) **Help to the Insolvent:** It also helps an insolvent owner. Because, in a court of law, if he can produce properly maintained accounts the same will be accepted in order to furnish his assets and liabilities position.

Disadvantages/Limitations of Accounting

Accounting is not free from snags. Some of them are:

(i) *Non-monetary information is excluded* : We know that accounting presents its information in monetary terms. But, there are some factors which are non-monetary but have a direct bearing on financial status of a firm although accounting is silent about it. For example, it does not take into consideration the labour trouble or strike in the factory/office in its reports.

(ii) *Ignoring present money value* : Accounting does not recognise the difference between the present value or price levels and the past ones. For example, a plant which was acquired 30 years back is not recorded at its written-down value on the basis of historical cost. But the other current assets are presented in the same Balance Sheet at present value basis which, rather, may mislead us. Thus, financial statement actually does not exhibit a true position.

(iii) *Comparison of financial statements may be misleading* : We know that there are many alterations in accounting principles. Thus comparison of two similar firms becomes meaningless if both of them do not follow the same method of accounting. For example, one firm follows the Straight Line Method of depreciation in the case of a plant whereas the other one has followed the Diminishing Balance Method, or someone has followed FIFO method for valuation of unsold stock but the other has followed thc LIFO method. Thus, a dissimilar comparison proves to be misleading.

(iv) ***Limitation of range*** : Everyone will accept the fact that the range of area of financial accounting is very limited at present in the various fields of modern business. For the purpose, advanced sections of accounting—viz., Cost Accounting, Management Accounting—have been evolved.

(v) ***Personal bias and discretion of the accountant*** : It is unfortunately true that an accountant has a number of scopes for applying his own bias and discretion in the field of accounting. Accounting is, no doubt, subjective (particularly, accrual basis of accounting) in valuation of closing stock, choice of method for depreciation etc. which vitiate the Balance Sheet valuation.

Division of Accounting

Generally, accounting can be subdivided into:

(i) Book-keeping; (ii) Accounting, and; (iii) Auditing.

Accounting function may be performed in two ways:

(i) Manual Accounting; (ii) Mechanised Accounting.

Moreover, accounting may be of two specified types:

(i) **Micro Accounting:** It relates to accounts of any individual, any firm or an association or any government.

(ii) **Macro Accounting:** It relates to accounts of National Income, National Input and Output, Balance of Trade, Cash Flow, etc.

Classification of Accounting

The accounting system is the principal quantitative information system in any organisation. It can broadly be classified into:

(a) Financial Accountancy; (b) Cost Accountancy; (c) Management Accountancy, and; (d) Social Accountancy.

(a) **Financial Accountancy:** It is primarily concerned with the provisions of information for managers and for outside parties including shareholders, suppliers, customers, employees, government departments, and the general public as well. The outsiders must accept the information that the business chooses to provide. The presentation of information, while accurate, shows only broad movements of income and expenditure over a comparatively long period of time.

The information is expressed in two main types of financial statements:

(i) The Profit and Loss Account (the income and expenditure attributable to activities undertaken by the firm during the period);

(ii) The Balance Sheet (the final position at a particular date).[1]

(b) **Cost Accountancy:** It is that branch of accounting which deals with classification, recording, allocation, summarisation and reporting of current and prospective costs. It includes the design and operation of cost systems and procedures, the determination of costs by departments, functions, responsibilities, activities, products, territories, periods and other units, and forecasting future costs and standard cost as well as historical costs. In other words, it deals with a group of accounts constituting the records of production and distribution activities as well.

(c) **Management Accountancy:** Management Accounting is the presentation of accounting information in order to formulate the policies to be adopted by the management and assists its day-to-day activities. In other words, it helps the management to perform all its functions including planning, organising, staffing, directing and controlling. It actually presents to the management the accounting information in the form of processed data which it collects from Financial Accounting and Cost Accounting including Statistics so that it will be very helpful on the part of the management to take proper decisions in a scientific manner as and when necessary.

(d) **Social Accountancy:** It is concerned with the application of double entry system of book-keeping to socio-economic analyses, with the calculation, estimation and analyses of national and international income, national or international balance sheet.

1 At present another statement is also to be prepared, viz., the Statement of Sources and Application of Funds (the flow of funds arising from activities during the period covered by the statement)

Differences between Book-keeping and Accounting

Although, in practical life, Book-keeping and Accounting are terms which are used inter-changeably, there are some differences between the two. Because, Book-keeping is concerned with the recording of business transactions in a significant and orderly manner which is mechanical and repetitive in character. As such, this work is usually entrusted to junior employees of the accounts department—the book-keepers.

Accounting, on the other hand, is used in a broader sense of the term and is more analytical. Needless to mention that accounting includes the design of accounting system, preparation of financial statements and audits, development of forecasts, cost studies, income-tax calculations, analysis and interpretation of accounting information for internal as well as external end in users as an aid to making business decisions which, in other words, require some skill, experience and imagination. The persons who are engaged with these works are known as **Accountants.** That is why it is rightly said that *when book-keeping ends accounting starts.* Book-keeping supplies the basis for accounting. But this distinction is particularly meaningful only in case of big enterprises since in small business-houses both these works are performed by the same staff.

Accounting and other Disciplines

(a) **Accountancy and Law:** These two subjects are closely related to each other. Particularly, without sufficient knowledge in law, an accountant cannot prove his efficiency in his profession. We know that accounting function must be performed in accordance with the internal and external affairs of a firm. Therefore, an accountant should possess sufficient knowledge about the Partnership Act if he wants to be an accountant of such a firm or if he wants to maintain proper books of accounts of such a firm. Same principle is also being followed in case of company accounts since there is the Companies Act, i.e., he must know thoroughly the Companies Act while preparing company accounts, otherwise his accounting work may not be valid or sufficient. For this purpose, an accountant should know, particularly, commercial law in details—and that is why Commercial Law has been prescribed by different universities and the institutes as a compulsory subject for commerce students.

An accountant should know the various commercial laws, viz., Company Law, Partnership Law, Sale of Goods Act, Sales Tax Act, Income-tax Act etc.; otherwise, he will not be able to solve the problems that may arise relating to laws or he will be unable to help his employer in legal affairs.

On the contrary, a lawyer should possess adequate knowledge in accountancy, since, in most cases, disputes are created out of transactions and tax-matters. Thus, in order to perform his duties or to solve the accounting problems or to understand the monetary matters relating to accounts, a lawyer should possess sufficient knowledge in accountancy. That is why it can be stated that Accountancy and Law are related to each other. They are the obverse and reverse of the same coin.

(b) **Accountancy and Economics:** It is the primary objective of an economist to enquire about the money that one can earn and its application in various sources as well. An accountant, on the other hand, maintains all the records of transactions of an individual (firm/association etc.). That is why it can rightly be said that both the economist and the accountant should know each other's subject to perform their respective duties in an efficient manner. Although accountancy is related with the problems of production unit and economics is related with the problems of scarce resources in the economic life of a man, an accountant will understand his own subject better if he can understand the different economic concepts like value, cost, production-cost, etc. On the contrary, an economist may also perform his duties better provided he knows the concepts and conventions of different accounting principles and procedures. When an economist acquires sufficient knowledge in accountancy in addition to the various branches of economics—viz., production, consumption, exchange, distribution, etc.—his knowledge proves to be concrete. Same principle is also applicable in case of an accountant. For this purpose a significant role is being played by various branches of economics in the study of accountancy. Thus both economics and accountancy are related to each other.

(c) **Accountancy and Statistics:** The service function of Accountancy and Statistics is also same. Both the Accountant and the Statistician collect data and present the collected data in a table, analyse them, and finally, present the same to the related parties. For this purpose both the Accountant and the Statistician use diagrams and charts (viz., Bar Chart, Pie Chart, Histogram, etc.). The only difference between the two is that the Accountant is interested in data relating to money or data which are expressed in terms of money only, whereas the Statistician is not interested in the limited data—since his areas are wide. Therefore, it can be stated that the Accountant and the Statistician should cooperate and help each other to serve their respective functions.

(d) **Accountancy and Engineering:** In an engineering firm the accountant of a production unit—particularly the Cost Accountant and an Engineer who is associated with the planning and production of such unit—are to work simultaneously in order to solve the day-to-day problems. The figures and values which an engineer uses for preparing his statements, designs etc., are presented frequently in different accounting reports and statements which are prepared by the accountant. Thus, it is clear that, in order to perform his duty efficiently, an engineer should possess some knowledge of accountancy and, on the contrary, an accountant should possess sufficient knowledge of different machinery, its effective working life etc. Otherwise he will not be able to perform his duties in an efficient manner. Thus, it can be stated that there should be harmony and cooperation between the accountant and the engineer for the purpose of efficient management of an engineering firm, for taking any decision and to maintain the efficiency of the firm as a whole.

Users of Accounting Information

People in various walks of life need accounting information which are supplied by the accounting process for various purposes. Some of the groups who use this information are:

No.	Users	For the respective interest
1.	*Owners/Proprietors and Partners*	They are interested to know the rates of return on Capital employed, the long-term solvency of the firm and the rates of dividends, among others. These information are available from the published financial statements.
2.	*Creditors, Bankers and other Lending Institutions*	Their interest lies in the ultimate solvency and liquidity position of a firm and in the interest cover. These they can read from the analysis of financial statements.
3.	*Potential Investors*	Investors use accounting information while determining the relative merits of various investment opportunities. They are interested to know the profitability and safety of their investment which are presented by the financial statements.
4.	*Management*	Management is interested about profitability and efficiency in financial management which are supplied by the accounting information in a number of ways.
5.	*Government*	Government is interested in profit-earning capacity and in the effective utilisation of a firm's capacity which are also supplied by the accounting statements.
6.	*Regulatory Agencies*	Various government departments and agencies (i.e., Company Law Board, Registrar of Companies, including tax authorities) use accounting reports for the purpose of tax assessment and to evaluate the business operation under the regulatory legislations.
7.	*Employees*	They are interested in the earning capacity of the firm since their remuneration depends on it. At present, trade unions are using accounting reports and statements to support their demand for increasing the rate of wages.
8.	*Researchers*	Research scholars use the accounting data in their research work.
9.	*M.P.s, Members of Public Accounts Committee and Estimate Committee*	They analyse and interpret the functions of state enterprises to see whether efficient working system is being used or not, which are supplied by the accounting reports and statements.

Types of Accounting Information

Accounting information may be presented in various ways and forms. It depends on its purposes and uses. The main purpose or basic/primary objective of the accounting information is to supply the financial information at a particular date (i.e., by presenting Income Statement and Balance Sheet) which will help the users and the analysts of accounting information. Thus, types of accounting information may be represented as :

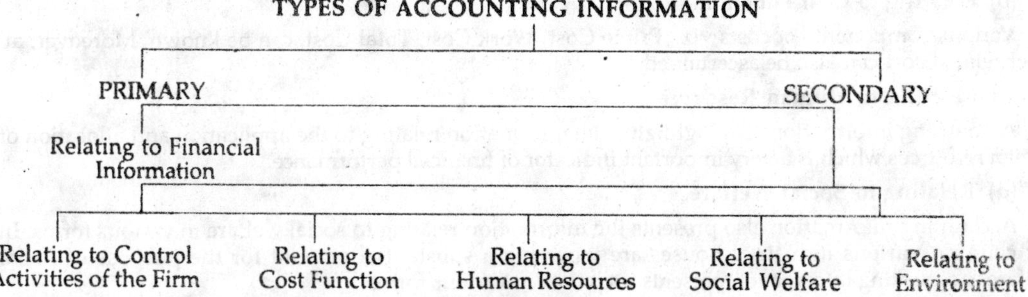

PRIMARY

Relating to Financial Information : It has already been stated above that the primary objective of accounting information is to supply the financial performances with the help of two financial statements viz., Income Statement and Balance Sheet. The financial statements help us to know the various aspects of financial performances, e.g., liquidity and solvency position, Working Capital position, position of Capital Structure, position of fixed assets, etc.

They also give us information relating to the **utilisations of economic resources** by which the operating performances of an enterprise can be measured for the purpose of assessing the rate of return on Capital employed.

The accounting information also highlights the financial structure, assets structure and capital structure as well from which the composition of various assets and liabilities are known which directly help us to assess the financial position as a whole.

It also helps us to measure the liquidity and solvency position of an enterprise by the application of various accounting ratios as accounting ratios are very important tools for measuring financial control.

Income Statement

An Income Statement which is prepared at the end of the period presents accounting information relating to its profit earning capacity, rate of return on Capital Employed, EPS, etc. which directly helps the users of accounting information for assessing the financial performances as a whole, i.e., profitability position can easily be estimated and analysed.

Balance Sheet

The financial position of an enterprise can be assessed from its Balance Sheet as it exhibits the real financial position through the presentation of assets and liabilities at a particular date. Practically, it presents the changes that are made in comparison with the last year, whether economic resources have properly been utilised or not, possibility to generate more cash flows, proper employment of additional resources, utilisation of human sources etc.

Funds Flow Statement

A Funds Flow Statement presents the various sources (e.g., issue of shares, sale of assets etc.) of funds and their applications (e.g., payment of Dividend and Tax, purchase of assets etc.). It also presents the changes in Working Capital.

Cash Flow Statement

Cash Flow Statement highlights the financial information relating to: (i) ***operating activities***; (ii) ***Investing Activities***; (iii) ***Financing Activities of a firm***. This is a very useful device to asses the circulating movement of cash and cash position to assess the ability of the firm to generate cash and cash equivalent and the proper application for the same.

SECONDARY

(a) **Relating to Control Activities of a firm**

It includes the various aspects of information relating to:

(i) Production Function; (ii) Finance Function; (iii) Personnel Function; (iv) Marketing Function; (v) Operating Function; (vi) Investing Function.

(b) **Relating to Cost Function**

Various components of costs viz., Prime Cost, Work Cost, Total Cost, can be known. Moreover, all other related cost can also be ascertained.

(c) **Relating to Human Resource**

Accounting information also highlights the information relating to the application and allocation of human resources which is a very important indicator of financial performance.

(d) **Relating to Social Welfare**

Accounting information also presents the information relating to social welfare in various forms. In our country, various industrial houses are incurring a substantial amount for the purpose of social welfare. Accounting information presents such data in various forms.

(e) **Relating to environment**

Accounting information also helps us to know the various aspects of environment in various way.

Qualitative Characteristics of Accounting Information

The financial information are very useful to the users due to its qualitative characteristics. Such qualitative characteristics of accounting information may be represented as :

(a) **Reliability;** (b) **Relevance;** (c) **Understandability**; and (d) **Comparability**.

(a) **Reliability**

The first part of Qualitative Characteristics is **Reliability**. In other words, information so received must be reliable. If the same is not reliable, it will mislead the users. The same cannot be used as a faithful, reliable, dependable source of accounting information. For example, if the value of closing stock is window-dressed, the Balance Sheet will not exhibit True and Fair View financial position of an enterprise. So, if any decision is taken on the basis of such window-dressed figure, that will simply mislead us. Thus, the data which are presented must be reliable and dependable. However, the reliability of accounting information depends on the following:

(i) **Dependable/Faithful Representation**

The accounting information must be dependable and faithful in nature. The events or transactions which occur must be represented properly as per accounting principle. Because, there remains always a risk of recording transactions which should have been represented faithfully. It does not mean that accountants record the transactions having being biased, but the same may be recorded otherwise.

(ii) **Bias-less**

The accounting information must be bias-less in order to be a reliable and dependable one. The financial statements which are prepared and presented to the users of accounting must not be based on biased decision-oriented facts, i.e., Personal or Individual judgement must not reflect in accounts.

(iii) **Prudence**

While preparing financial statements some undesirable elements may appear which may distort the facts or transactions that ultimately affect the accounts. Those elements, uncertainties must be tackled with care by the exercise of prudence at the time of preparing the financial statements. While making the various estimated figures care must be taken after applying proper judgement and principles. The exercise of pundence will help us to ascertain the value of assets and liabilities accurately so that no undervaluation or overvaluation of assets and liabilities is made. In other words, the financial statements must not be window-dressed. Question of Secret Reserve or making excessive provision will not appear at all. Thus, the users of accounting information will consider it a reliable and dependable one.

(iv) **Completeness**

The accounting information must be complete i.e., incomplete information is of no use. If any transaction is omitted, the financial statements based on such omission will be a wrong and misleading and the same will not be useful to the users. Thus, unreliable and incomplete accounting information will be of no use.

(b) **Relevance**

The accounting information must be relevant to the users. In other words, it must contain qualitative information so that the users, after careful consideration, will take their decisions on the basis of such information available to them. In short, information will help them to understand and evaluate the present, past and future transactions. It may also be considered from another standpoint. The accounting information must be **material**. It should be remembered that no material information is left out or omitted. Because, Ommission of a material fact/information may influence the economic or financial decisions of the users of accounting information. If any material information is omitted from the accounts, the financial statements so prepared will not exhibit a real picture. As such, the same will not be reliable.

(c) **Understandability**

The accounting information will be prepared in such a manner so that a neophite can understand its meaning, preparation and interpretation although it is expected that the users should have at least a minimum knowledge about the subject as accounting is a highly technical subject. It may so happen that some complex matters appear in the financial statements as a matter of relevance. However, it may generally be stated that the accounting information as a whole must be understandable.

(d) **Comparability**

The accounting information must be comparable by the users so that, after proper comparison, they can take the right decision about the financial health of an enterprise. They must compare their financial statements with that of other comparable firms to evaluate the financial performance and ascertain the changes in financial position in different phases. But users must remember that comparison is meaningful only when the basis of valuation of the two comparable firms are same. For exempla, if Firm A values the closing stock as per FIFO method while Firm B values the same as per LIFO method, proper comparison. in this case, is not possible about the valuation of closing stock. Thus, comparison, will be meaningful only when the same is done (i) between the two firms of the same group; (ii) between two accounting periods of the same firm, etc. That is why while considering any accounting principles, various accounting conventions should be taken into consideration, i.e., the theory of Consistency, Conservatism, Materiality, and Disclosure. Because, accounting policy must be consistent, otherwise, if it varies from year to year, proper comparison is not possible. Thus, the users must compare the accounting information for the purpose of assessing the financial health of an enterprise.

Accounting as MIS

A Management Information System (MIS) is nothing but an integrated user-machine system which provides information to support the operations, management, analysis and decision- making functions in an organisation. MIS produces information products which support many of the day-to-day decision-making needs of management. The system utilises hardware and software, manual procedure, models for analysis, planning, control and decision-making and/or database.

We know that the accounting work is to some extent repetitive in nature and it also involves routine work for some common purposes. This routine work—which is also repetitive to some extent—can better be performed faster and accurately by a computer. Large or medium scale organisations need the help of a computer for its multipurpose activities, since, with the help of computer, it becomes possible to know comparative analysis of cost/cost reduction by past data which are stored in a computer. In addition to that, processing of payroll, preparation of bills and invoices, and maintenance of stock records are effectively performed by a computer for which the same is used widely in the commercial world. Various accounting reports in the form of Cash Book, Ledger, Trial Balance, Profit and Loss Account and also the Balance Sheet are available after proper processing and clarifying the accounting jobs.

Accounting function, no doubt, can better be presented by a computer neatly in systematic and summarised form than manual performance. Thus, various accounting works are effectively and efficiently done at present by a computer. Its areas of application are:

(i) Preparation of various bills and invoices
(ii) Preparation and maintenance of stock and records
(iii) Preparation and recording of business transactions
(iv) Preparation of payroll accounting
(v) Preparation of individual records viz., Creditors' and Debtors' Ledgers, etc.
(vi) Preparation of purchase and sales ledger along with other ledgers
(vii) Preparation of various budgets
(viii) Preparation of performance appraisal through final statement of account
(ix) Preparation of comparative analysis of the statement of accounts, etc.

Computers, in effect, can do the same work much faster and much more accurately than done by several hundred clerks in the Accounts Department, namely:

(i) copying details (say, date, number, particulars, quantity, rates, amount, etc.) from one record (usually original vouchers) to another, i.e., Book of prime entry and ledger

(ii) analysing and consolidating figures (through adding, subtracting, etc.) so as to provide meaningful information relating to each account

(iii) proving the accuracy of work (through the trial balance), and

(iv) summarising information for preparation of final statements and for review.

Role of Accountants in Society

The Accountant, basically being a professional person, is to serve sometimes some vocational activities, that is what he does actually in practice. No doubt his primary function is to prepare the financial statements, interpret and analyse such statements and audit at the end. At present, they also take part in the matters relating to company law, corporated legislations, taxation laws, and general problems of the management and/or administration. As such, their area of functions should be discussed critically.

Areas of Service

It includes

(a) Maintaining books of accounts; (b) Taxation laws; (c) Statutory and Internal Audit; (d) Advices relating to financial problems; (e) Management Accounting; (f) Management Consultancy Services; (g) Miscellaneous.

Among all professions, accounting is one which is highly esteemed in our society. No doubt it is the 'fairest invention of the human mind'. However, an accountant is to provide multiple service to our ever-growing society in order to complete the basic financial requirements with the help of his education and knowledge, training and analytical mind. At present, an accountant is not only concerned with the problems relating to accounts, taxation, laws, costing, management accounting but also to provide for the necessary information about the financial policies, budgeting, economic policies, and so on. Thus, the areas of service of an accountant is practically unlimited.

The following services are rendered by the accountants to society:

(a) *Maintaining Books of Accounts*

The primary function of an accountant is to exhibit the financial position at a particular date after proper recording of the financial transactions in order to find out the result of the operation of the business undertakings. That is, an accountant may assist the management in the following manner :

(i) **Service to the Management :**

Accounting performs many significant roles in addition to accounting activities relating to financial results in the following manner :

(a) **Planning :** With the help of the accounting and information data, management may make out an estimate relating to sales, expenses, profit, flow of cash, expected rate of return etc. for future date, i.e., subsequent years.

(b) **Controlling :** Accounting also helps the management to see that the cost which has been incurred is reasonable and the work which has been done is also according to plan.

(c) **Decision Making :** Accounting helps the management to forecast, i.e., helps to take the decisions which will be formulated in future on the basis of data prepared by the Financial Accountant.

(d) **Budgeting :** It also helps to prepare budgets on the basis of financial data for the future by which the management can take proper action.

(ii) **Comparative Study :**

Proper comparison can be made between the actual and the budgeted figures, current year and the previous year, etc., so that the management can understand the real position relating to results.

(iii) **Taxation Liability :**

Accounting provides necessary information data to the Government for taking proper decisions relating to Income-tax, Sales tax, other duties etc.

(iv) **Evaluating the Earning Capacity :**

Accounting also helps to evaluate the earning capacity of the firm by supplying a statement of financial position, a statement of periodical earnings together with a statement of financial activities to various interested persons.

(v) It also provides necessary data and information to the managers for internal reporting and formulation of overall policies.

(b) *Taxation Laws*

It has already been stated earlier that an accountant can help the business about the taxation laws or can represent himself as a representative of a business or a person before the tax authorities and, consequently, settle the tax liabilities according to the prevailing rates of tax. He can also suggest a proper tax planning by which a businessman can reduce his tax burden. Moreover, an accountant can express his views on tax policies of the country which is considered accordingly.

(c) ***Statutory and Internal Audit***

We know that every company must appoint a Chartered Accountant as a statutory auditor who will prepare his report every year about the financial position, i.e., whether, according to him, the Balance Sheet and Profit and Loss Account show a true and fair view of the state of affairs on the Balance Sheet date and true and fair view of the profit or loss.

Similarly, an internal auditor examines the accounting transactions thoroughly and also the system of accounting by which he can reassure the management that the accounts are properly maintained. It also helps to detect any fraud committed by a firm. An internal auditor really helps the management towards improving the operational efficiency.

(d) ***Advices relating to Financial Problems***

An accountant who has a sound knowledge about finance, taxation and accounts can render valuable assistance to the society in various ways. Some of them are :

(i) **Investment Opportunities**

An accountant can assist a person regarding investment in different ways. He can suggest how, when and where an investment should be made so that the investor will earn a maximum return.

(ii) **Expansion of the Undertaking**

When the existing undertaking is expanded or developed, accountants, by interpreting accounts, making suggestions relating to schemes for cost and financial matters, can render a valuable advice. Accountants can also advice the directors on problems relating to issue of shares and their allotment and also to the borrowing of money if so needed.

(iii) **Financial Investigations**

An accountant can assist the management about the financial investigation which is extremely desired in the following manner :

(a) to determine the financial position for the interested parties relating to issue of shares, amalgamation/merger, reconstruction etc.; (b) to ascertain the reason of decreasing profit or increasing losses—if so happened; (c) to detect fraud, if occurred, and necessary suggestions to avoid it in future; (d) to assist the management when a particular product will be manufactured or will be purchased from outside; (e) to assess the value of investment — if so made.

Moreover, if we find any problems relating to finance, investigation should be made immediately by the experienced accountant.

(iv) **Insurance**

We know that there are different kinds of insurance policies. An accountant can help which policy should be more appropriate to a particular business unit.

(e) *Management Accounting*

It helps the management in the following manner :

(i) It measures the actual performance in comparison with the budget; (ii) it helps the management in such a way that the latter can maximise the rate of return on capital employed; (iii) it helps to increase the efficiency of the business; (iv) it helps the mana-gement to chalk out future plan of action on the basis of past result; (v) it also helps to improve the relation between the management and the labourer.

(f) Management Consultancy Services

It can be presented in the following manner :

(i) **Organisation and Method**

Accountants can give valuable advice to the management relating to principles of organisation and methods which can be formulated for effective delegation.

(ii) **Control of Expenditure**

In order to ascertain the measure for the effective utilisation of resources, an application of appraisal techniques for new investments, accountants can assist properly. Moreover, they can design cost control techniques and budgetary control system for capital and revenue expenditures.

(iii) **Working Capital Requirements**

Proper requirement of working capital and its efficient use improve productivity, inventory control, credit control, cash management, source and application of funds, etc. which can properly be ascertained by an accountant.

(iv) **Corporate Planning**

Assisting management for long-term planning and advising management regarding amalgamation/ mergers, reconstruction etc. He can also assist in financial planning and see whether effective utilisation of resources is made or not.

(v) **Data Processing**

An accountant can also advice the benefits of mechanised accounting together with the computer applications for accounting activities in order to reduce the clerical costs and to improve the procedure of data processing for management decision and action.

(vi) **Selection of Executives**

While selecting the executives for various management affairs, e.g., accounts, production, marketing etc., accountants can assist the management on the basis of requirements.

(vii) **Business Problems**

Accountants can render valuable services while solving business problems like decisions relating to prices, representation to government on different matters, etc.

(viii) **Selection of Personnel, Placement and Training**

Accountants can review the salary structure (including retirement benefit) of the employees, appraise the personnel policies and their practices. They, also can provide general introduction on management accounting courses, training courses, etc.

(g) **Miscellaneous**

There are certain activities which are duly performed by the accountants frequently :

(i) Formation of Company

Accountants play at present a significant role while forming a company in addition to legal advice for registration of companies. They are, no doubt, a very helping hand to the promoters.

(ii) Secretarial Duty

Accountants also perform secretarial duty in almost all organisations like club, association, company, etc.

(iii) Receivership etc.

When a company is being wound up, or, when a debentureholder and/or a loan creditor exercises his right to recover his claim, accountants have to perform such duty as a liquidator/receiver.

(iv) Registering Share Transfer

Sometimes the accountants are also engaged for registering share transfer or issue of new shares in the market.

(v) Arbitration

Sometimes the accountants are requested to act as arbitrators to settle disputes between the parties.

ASSIGNMENT MATERIALS
THEORETICAL

Multiple Choice Questions

1. (a) Pre-Development Period of Accounting is considered up to:

   (i) 1594; (ii) 1494; (iii) 1694; (iv) None of these

   (b) Number of phases of Accounting Cycle is:

   (i) Five; (ii) Six; (iii) Seven; (iv) Ten

   (c) Qualitative Characteristics in accounting information are:

   (i) Three; (ii) Two; (iii) Four; (iv) Ten

(d) Double Entry System was introduced at first by:
(i) Luca Pacioli; (ii) W.A. Paton; (iii) A.C. Littletion; (iv) None of these

(e) Going Concern Concept was introduced by:
(i) S. Gilman; (ii) A.C. Littleton; (iii) W.A. Paton; (iv) None of these

(f) Proprietorship:
(i) Assets – Liabilities; (ii) Fixed Assets – Current Liabilities;
(iii) Total Assets – Long-term Liability; (iv) None of these

(g) Assets:
(i) Capital + Current Assets; (ii) Total Liabilities – Current Liabilities;
(iii) Capital + Liabilities; (iv) None of these

(h) Creditors are interested to know:
(i) Liquidity and Solvency Positions; (ii) Working Capital Position;
(iii) Financial Position; (iv) None of these.

[Ans. (a) (ii); (b) (ii); (c) (iii); (d) (i); (e) (iii); (f) (i); (g) (iii); (h) (i)]

Short-Answer Type Questions

2. What is Accounting Cycle?
3. Mention the Functions of Accountancy.
4. State any two advantages and disadvantages of accounting.
5. What are the objectives of Accounting?
6. State the Divisions of Accounting.
7. How do you classify Accounting?
8. Distinguish between Accounting and Economies?
9. State any five advantags of Accounting

Long-Answer Type Questions

10. Explain the role of accountants in Society.
11. Explain the Qualitative Characteristics of Accounting Information.
12. What is MIS? Explain it in detail.
13. Mention the difference between Book-keeping and Accounting.
14. Distinguish between.
    (a) Accountancy and Statistics
    (b) Accountancy and Law
15. How do the users use accounting information? Do you think that all of them use the same information?
16. Explain the Objectives of Accounting.
17. Explain the recent trend in the development of Accounting.
18. Explain the different types of Accounting Information.
19. Explain
    (a) Accounting - a means and not an end
    (b) Accounting—as the language of business.
20. Explain the development of accounting during the middle of 20th century to the present.

CHAPTER 2

THEORY BASE OF ACCOUNTING

Learning Objectives

ACCOUNTING PRINCIPLES

Accounting Principles and Postulates

Characteristics of Accounting Principles

A. ***Basic Assumptions***
   - *(a) Accounting Entity*
   - *(b) Going Concerns*
   - *(c) Money Measurement*
   - *(d) Accounting Period*

B. ***Basic Principles***
   - *(a) Revenue Realisation*
   - *(b) Expenses*
   - *(c) Matching*
   - *(d) Full Disclosure*
   - *(e) Dual Aspect*
   - *(f) Verifiable Objective Evidence*
   - *(g) Cost*
   - *(h) Balance Sheet Equation*

C. ***Modifying Principles***
   - *(a) Materiality*
   - *(b) Consistency*
   - *(c) Prudence/Conservatism*
   - *(d) Timeliness*
   - *(e) Industry Practice*

GENERALLY ACCEPTED ACCOUNTING PRINCIPLES (GAAP)

Introduction

Concepts—Conventions—Principles—Rules

Advantages of GAAP

Limitations of GAAP

Inadequacy of GAAP

ACCOUNTING STANDARDS

Meaning

Need for Accounting Standards (IASC)

International Accounting Standard Committee (IASC)

Indian Accounting Standards

Accounting Principles and Postulates

Principle means the fundamental truth implying uniformity of acceptance everywhere. However, the word 'Principle', when applied in accounting, may have different meanings in different contexts. It is rarely used in the sense of a fundamental accounting truth—it connotes a guiding influence or an accepted rule of action or conduct.[1] Accounting principles have been defined as the body of doctrine, commonly associated with the theory and procedure of accounting, serving as an explanation of current practices, and as a guide for the selection of conventions or procedures where alternatives exist. Rules governing the formation of accounting axioms and the principles derived from them have arisen from common experiences, historical precedent, statements by individuals and professional bodies and regulations of governmental agencies.[2] At present, recommendations of the accounting principles have emanated from the professional bodies, such as The Institute of Chartered Accountants of England and Wales, The American Accounting Association, The American Institute of Certified Public Accountants, The Institute of Chartered Accountants of India, and so on. As such, The American, Institute of Certified Public Accountants (AICPA), in their Accounting Terminology Bulletin, defines the principles as a "general law or rule adopted or proposed as a guide to action, a settled ground or basis of conduct or practice'. Paton and Littleton, however, prefer to use the term 'Standard' in place of principles. The International Federation of Accountants have constituted the 'International Accounting Standards Committee' which lays down the various accounting principles that are in practice. These principles, of course, have been named as 'Standards' in order to avoid the confusion which may arise from the term 'Principles'.

Accounting Principles, i.e., a 'Standard', should always satisfy the following three rules :

(i) *Usefulness (Relevance)* : The 'Standards' must cater to the carefulness of the accounting statements. In short, the statements must be meaningful to the users of the same.

(ii) *Objectivity* : The 'Standards' should have objectivity, i.e., they must be supported and supplemented by basic facts or data and not by the whims of the individuals who prepare the statements.

(iii) *Feasibility* : The 'Standards' must be practicable or feasible to attain. For example, inventory should be valued at cost price or market price/realisable value, whichever is lower. This is determined on the basis of feasibility and practicability for ascertaining the costs from cost records and market/realisable value from the past sales or future trend.

Generally, the above three factors are found in accounting standards. But exceptions are there, where a compromise is made and an optimum balance of the three is struck.

Characteristics of Accounting Principles

The characteristics of Accounting Principles are:

(a) Accounting principles are made and developed by men (accountants) and, as such, they do not have the authoritativeness of universal principles, like other natural sciences, viz., Physics, Chemistry, Mathematics etc., since they cannot be validated/proved by reference to natural laws—as in the case of physical sciences. They are the best possible suggestions based on practical experiences, reasons and observations which have been developed by the accountants.

(b) Accounting principles are developed for common usage to ensure uniformity and understandablity. They also enhance the usefulness of facts and figures relating to economic activities of the firm.

(c) The principles are not specifically made or enhanced by any authority.

(d) The principles are in the process of evolution, i.e., are not in their finished form. On the other hand, they are fast developing.

(e) They are not rigid.

(f) The principles should generally be acceptable and, for the purpose, the three criteria (referred to above)—viz., usefulness, objectivity and feasibility—must be fulfilled.

---

1 Kohler, E.L.—*A Dictionary for Accounts*—Prentice Hall, Inc. New Jersey, 1960, P. 12
2 Canadian Institute of Chartered Accountants (1957)

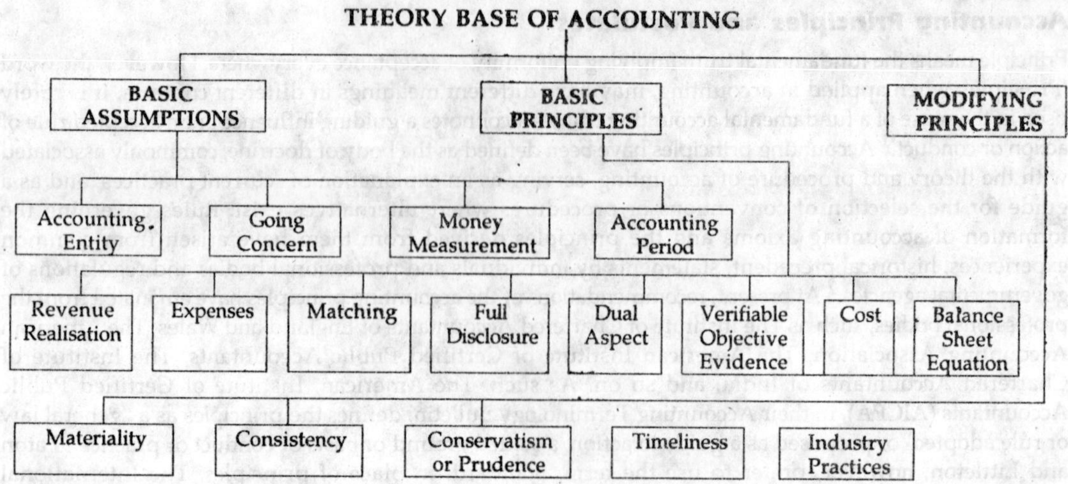

A. Basic Assumptions

(a) **Accounting Equity :** Under this concept, it is assumed that the business unit is distinct and completely separate from its owners (including employees, officers, creditors and others who are associated with it). For accounting purposes, the business enterprise exists in its own right. As a result, transactions should be recorded in the books of accounts with such persons and individuals together with the owners. It becomes necessary that accounting records of the business must be maintained in a manner which is free from any bias to any particular section of people related to it. As such, accounts are maintained for business entity as distinguished from all categories of persons related to it. For recording transactions the pertinent question which arises is that how far such transactions affect the business itself and not how do they affect the people associated with it. When the owner introduces cash to the business as capital, it simply means an inflow of cash to the business which is recorded in business books. But actually, to an owner, it is a shift from personal cash to business cash.

However, some practical difficulties may arise by defining a business entity for which accounts are kept, specially in case of sole proprietorship and partnership business and that of the people who own it. That is, a sole trader is personally liable for his business debts and may be required to use non-business (Personal) assets in order to pay-off the business debts. On the contrary, business assets of the Sole-Proprietor may be utilised for paying-off the personal obligation of the Proprietor, i.e., in the eyes of law, business and non-business (Personal) assets and liabilities are treated alike in the case of a Sole-Proprietor. Same principle is, however, applicable in case of a partnership firm, i.e., after paying-off the business liabilities, if any surplus remains, the same can also be used in order to pay-off the personal obligations of the partners.

In case of a company, however, the entity of the business is legally separated from that of the owners. The application of the concept becomes relatively easier in this case. Practical difficulties arise by identifying business affairs of a group of companies under common management. Thus, if eight companies, under the same management, utilised common services like accommodation, office and administration service etc. the proper allocation of such common services among all the eight companies would not be an easy task. Besides, at its initial stage, accounting has the basic stewardship function. Consequently, the manager of the firm was supplied with the necessary funds by the owners and the lenders. It was the duty of the management to utilise such funds properly and the reports of the financial accounting were designed to project how best the management discharged this stewardship function. The origin of this concept can be traced from this stewardship function.

Thus accounting, in this concept, suggests the affairs of the business must not be mixed up with the private affairs of owners or other persons associated with it. As such, this concept helps to give a true picture of the financial conditions of a business enterprise.

(b) **Going Concern :** This concept assumes that the business entity has a continuity of life or the future of a business enterprise is to be prolonged or extended indefinitely, i.e., continuance of the activity and not the dissolution/liquidation is the normal business process. In other words, a business is viewed as a mechanism for continuous additions of value to the resources or utility used by such unit. The success or failure of the business is measured by the difference between the value of its output sale and/or services and the cost of such output.

It has been stated above that the business entity has a continuity of life. Since there is some degree of continuity of every entity and no one can accurately predict the future of an entity due to the possibility of cessation of its life, it is more convenient to treat the same as a *going concern*. But this does not mean that the business entity has a perpetual life.

This concept recognises the value of the assets and liabilities of the business enterprises on the basis of their productivity and not on the basis of their current realisable value on the assumption that they are to be disposed-off. Since they are held in a 'going concern' for earning revenue and not for resale, there is no such utility to show the expected realisble values in the Balance Sheet. Besides, under this concept, prepaid expenses are recognised as assets since the benefits will be utilised in future when the business entity will continue. Going Concern Concept helps other business undertakings to make contracts with specific business unit for business dealings in future. It also stresses more emphasis on the earning capacity in judging the overall performance of the business.

(c) **Money Measurement (Monetary Expression) :** In accounting, all transactions are expressed and interpreted in terms of money. The benefit of this expression is that it provides a common denominator or unit of measurement by means of which heterogeneous facts about a business can be expressed in terms of quantifies which can either be added or subtracted. Since different transactions occur, they are recorded and interpreted in various accounts in monetary terms. So, accounting helps to express heterogeneous economic activities in terms of money. Actually, the basic purpose of using money is to implement an element of uniformity among diversity. Therefore, fixed assets—like Land, Furniture and Fixtures—are expressed in terms of money and not in terms of area (for land) or quantity (Furniture and Fixtures) for recording in accounts properly, like other assets, e.g. Cash in hand and Cash at Bank (which are always expressed in monetary terms).

But this method suffers from the following limitations:

(i) It does not recognise the changes in the purchasing power of the monetary unit.

(ii) It fails to keep any record of such matters which cannot be expressed in terms of money— e.g., human genius, which may be highly productive, is not considered in accounting as there is no acceptable value in exchange. But intellectual property rights are accepted under international law and can be patented.

In other words, a fact or an event which cannot be expressed in terms of money cannot be recorded in the books of accounts. Yet, for accounting purposes, it is the best means for measuring varied transactions, e.g. goods, service, natural resources etc.

(d) **Accounting Period Concept :** A business is assumed to continue indefinitely in order to ascertain the state of affairs of the business at different intervals. We are to choose the intervals for ascertaining the financial position and the operational results at each such interval which, in other words, is known as Accounting Period. Usually, a period of 365 days or 52 weeks is considered as the accounting period. Sometimes half-yearly or quarterly period is also taken into consideration. Besides, the interested parties (viz., Shareholders, Creditors, Investors etc.) need periodical reports about accounting of business activities at specific intervals of time for understanding the business performances and for making necessary decisions which will be formulated in the near future. However, this concept is particularly applicable to : (i) The valuation of assets and liabilities, (ii) Costs between expired and unexpired, (iii) Analytical description of financial transactions, (iv) The estimation of profits, (v) The presentation of the True and Fair View of the financial position etc.

Besides, this method helps to measure the income generated during the specific accounting period which also helps to distribute the same periodically. The accounting period concept recognises division and appropriation of accounting records into specific periods. It recognises the measurements of the operating results of each such period. This method also reveals a clear demarcation of accrued or deferred items of incomes and expenses. The performance of a period is measured by matching cost with revenue. Therefore, total costs and expenses pertaining to the generation of such revenue together with the expenses and cost incurred for the specific accounting period are matched against the revenue for the said period. As such, Accrual System or Mercantile System of accounting is of fundamental importance in accounting.

The segregation of expenditure between capital and revenue arises from this concept. That is, whether a particular item of expenditure will appear in the income/revenue statement (i.e., P & L A/c) or will appear in the Balance Sheet is to be determined by the accountants on the basis of this concept. Because, a capital expenditure may be treated as revenue, if the period is taken for a decade instead of a year. That is why accounting period concept plays a very significant role in accounting.

B. Basic Principles

(a) **Revenue Realisation :** According to this concept, revenue is considered as earned on the date when it is realised. In other words, revenue realised (either by sale of goods or by rendering services) during an accounting period should only be taken in the income statement (Profit and Loss Account). Unearned/Unrealised revenue should not be taken into account. The revenue is treated as earned on some specific matters or transactions. For example, when goods are sold to customers, they are legally liable to pay, i.e., as soon as the title of property or goods passes from the seller to the buyer. In short, when an order is simply received from a customer, it does not mean that the revenue is earned or realised. On the other hand, when an advance payment is made by a customer, the same cannot be treated as revenue realised or earned. In case of hire-purchase transactions, however, the title or ownership of the goods is not transferred from the seller to the buyer till the last instalment is paid. As such, the down payments and the instalment received or due should be treated as actual sale, i.e., revenue earned.

(b) **Expenses** : The term 'expense' is a flow concept. It represents both favourable and unfavourable changes made in an accounting period. The favourable one represents revenue, where as the unfavourable one represents the expense. In short, the consumption or use of goods and services in order to earn revenue is the expense. Thus, Hendriksen opines: 'Expenses are the using or consuming of goods and services in the process of obtaining revenues'.

American Accounting Association, Committee on Concepts and Standards, defines : 'Expense is the expired cost, directly or indirectly related to given fiscal period, of the flow of goods or services into the market and of related operations'. The primary objective of all costs is to earn revenue from the customers—in exchange of goods and services produced by the firm at a given period. As such, the amount which is spent in anticipation of earning revenue, no doubt, constitute cost.

All sacrifices are not expenses. The sacrifices which are directly or indirectly related to the production are included in expenses. At the same time, such sacrifices are losses against which neither any benefit has been realised nor is there any chance of realising the same in future. Thus, the benefits which are received in excess of the sacrifices are incomes which accrue to the proprietors.

(c) **Matching** : This concept recognises that the determination of profit or loss on a particular accounting period is a problem of matching the expired cost allocated to an activity period. In other words, the expenses which are actually incurred during a specific activity period, in order to earn revenue for the said period, must be matched against the revenue which is realised for that period. For these purposes, expenses which are specially incurred for earning the revenue of the related period are to be considered. In short, all expenses incurred during the activity period must not be taken. Only relevant costs should be deducted from the revenue of a period for periodic income statement, i.e., the expenses that are related to the accounting period shall be considered for the purpose of matching. This process of relating costs to revenue is called Machine Process. It should be remembered that cost of fixed assets is not taken but only the depreciation on such fixed assets related to the accounting period is taken (for the purpose of machine, prepaid expenses are excluded from the total costs but outstanding expenses are added to the total costs for ascertaining the cost related to the period). Like costs, all revenues earned during the period are not taken, but revenues which are related to the accounting period are considered.

Application of matching concept creates some problems:

(i) Some special items of expenses—e.g., preliminary expenses, in connection with the issue of shares and debentures, advertisement expenses, etc.—cannot be easily identified and matched against revenues of a particular period.

(ii) Another problem is that how much of the capital expenditure should be written-off by way of depreciation for a particular period; for matching against revenue creates the problem of finding out the expected life of the asset. As such, accurate matching is not possible.

(iii) In case of long-term contracts, usually, the amount is not received in proportion to the work done. As a result, expenditures which are carried forward and not related to the income received may create some problems.

(d) **Full Disclosure :** The doctrine of disclosure suggests that all accounting statements should be honest, and, to that end, full disclosure of all significant information must be made. It involves proper classification, summarisation, aggregation and explanation of accounting data in the published financial statements which are of material interest to the users—proprietors, creditors, investors, etc. This doctrine actually gives emphasis on the actuality, materiality, objectivity and consistency of accounting data in order to disclose fully the true and fair view of the economic activities of a firm for a particular period. The doctrine is becoming more popular at present since most of the business units are in the form of joint stock companies. For this purpose, the Companies Act, 1956, has prescribed the forms and schedules of accounts in which financial statements are to be prepared. Since the Companies Act makes proper provisions for the disclosure of essential information relating to accounting data, concealment of material information is practically limited.

Besides the above, the reporting or accounting information is made by means of comments, footnotes, descriptive capitals, supplementary schedules, etc. in periodical statements which may also require further clarification. However, this doctrine does not express that the trade secrets or other necessary information should also be disclosed. It should reveal simply the full disclosure of all essential or significant material information to the users of financial statement. In 1945, the Cohen Committee—an enquiring company that practised in England—made the following statements regarding this accounting doctrine:

"We are in favour of as much disclosure as practicable. It is also important in our opinion to ensure that there should be adequate disclosure and publication of the results of companies so as to create confidence in the financial management of industry and to dispute any suggestion that hidden profits are being accumulated by industrial concerns to the determinant of consumers and those who work for industry. . . On the other hand, if there is no detailed disclosure in the Profit and Loss Account, undisclosed reserve accumulated in the past period, may be used to swell the profits in years when the company is faring badly, and the shareholders may be misled into thinking that the company is making profits when such is not the case."

(e) **Dual Aspect :** This is, no doubt, the basic concept in accounting. Under this concept, every transaction has a twofold aspect—(i) yielding to or receiving of benefit, and (ii) giving of that benefit. For instance, when a firm acquires an asset (receiving of the benefit) it must pay cash (giving of the benefit). Therefore, two accounts are to be passed in the books of accounts, one—for receiving the benefit, and the other—for giving the benefit. Thus, there will be a double entry for every transaction—Debit for receiving the benefit and Credit for giving the benefit. So, for each and every Debit, there must be a corresponding Credit, and *vice versa*. This is nothing but the principle of Double Entry System of Accounting which, in other words, is known as the 'Dual Aspect Concept'.

The Accounting Equation, i.e., *Assets* = *Equities* (or, *Liabilities* + *Capital*) is based on this concept.

(f) **Verifiable and Objective Evidence Concept :** It expresses that accounting data are subject to verification by independent experts, i.e., there must be documentary evidences of transactions which are capable of verification. Otherwise, the same will neither be verifiable nor realisable or dependable. In other words, accounting data must be free from any bias. Because verifiability and objectivity imply reliability, trustworthiness, dependability,—which are all very useful for conveying the accounting data and information furnished in periodical accounting reports and statements—there should always be some documentary evidences in establishing the truth reflected in the said reports or statements. Entries which are recorded in accounting from the transactions and data which are reported in financial statements must be based on objectively determined evidence. The confidence of users of the financial statement cannot be maintained until there is a close adherence to this principle. Invoices and vouchers for purchases, sales and expenses, physical checking of stock in hand, etc. are examples of objective evidence which are capable of verification. Therefore, it must be said that every entry must be supported by some objective evidence, as far as possible, and, as such, it will minimise the possibility of errors and frauds. But, evidence does not always play the most significant role since there are different occasions where significant role is being played by other factors, e.g., personal opinions and judgement, provision for bad debts, valuation of inventories, etc.

(g) **Cost :** Accounting is a historical record (on a monetary basis) of the transaction of a business entity. From the historical record of cost, one can ascertain the progress—or otherwise—of the accounting unit with the help of financial statements. **According to this concept, an asset is recorded at its cost in the books of accounts**, i.e. the price which is paid at the time of acquiring it. When an asset is acquired or purchased, its cost price is the only source by which the basis for all subsequent accounting in relation to the same can be made. The asset, when it is acquired, is originally recorded at its cost price and gradually reduced by way of depreciation. Amount of depreciation is to be calculated on the basis of its cost price and the effective life of the asset. The market value of the asset is not to be taken into consideration for the purpose of valuation or depreciation of such asset. This method is closely related to the 'Going Concern Concept' method.

This concept, however, has an advantage. Since the valuation of asset does not depend on the market value, which, again, depends on the subjective views of accountants, accounts are maintained properly, i.e. without any personal bias of the accountants. But this concept also suffers from one limitation. That is, as the cost concept ignores the effect of excessive inflation in the present economy it becomes irrelevant for the purpose of valuation of assets. In order to overcome this shortcoming, inflation accounting and current values of the assets are advocated. Since there are a number of practical difficulties, Cost Concept Method still serves as a fair and adequate basis for the valuation of assets.

(h) **Balance Sheet Equation :** The Historical Cost Concept needs support of two other concepts for practical purposes : (i) The Money Measurement Concept (already discussed above), (ii) The Balance Sheet Equation Concept. Accounting process, however, conforms to an algebraic equation which, in other words, is involved in two laws of nature, i.e. the law of constancy of matter, and the law that every effect originates from a cause.

In relation to the former, it may be deduced that **all that has been received by us must be equal to (=) all that has been given by us.** (In accounts, **receipts are classified as debits and giving or sacrifices are classified as credits**). Here, the basic equation comes :

Debit = Credit

(That is, in other words, **every debit must have corresponding equal credit, and/or vice versa).** All receipts (referred to above) may again be classified into : (i) Benefits/services received and totally consumed (which are known as Expenses), (ii) Benefits or services received but not used properly or misused (which are known as Losses), and (iii) Benefits or services received but kept to be used in future (which are known as Assets). Similarly, in the opposite case, all that has been given by others may also be classified into : (i) What has been given to us but are not to be repaid (which are known as Incomes or Gains), and (ii) What has been given by the others but has to be repaid at a later date (which are known as Liabilities).

Therefore, the above equation may again be rewritten as :

Expenses + Loss + Assets = Incomes + Gains + Liabilities

However, if expenses and losses are set-off against incomes and gains the same equation will be reproduced in the following form :

Assets = Incomes + Gains + Liabilities – Expenses – Losses

OR, ***Assets = Net Profit (–) Net Loss + Liabilities***

Liabilities become due either to outsider or to the owner, viz. the proprietors; in that case :

Assets = Net Profits or (–) Net Losses + External Liabilities + Dues to Proprietors

We know that the proprietor's due increases with the amount of net profit whereas decreases with the amount of net loss. The same is known as Equity in the business. So, the above equation comes down to :

Assets = Equity + External Liabilities

Again, from the proprietor's point of view, the equation can also be rewritten as :

Proprietor's Fund or Equity = Assets – Liabilities

E = A – L

From the above, it may be said that the entire accounting process depends on the above accounting equation.

C. Modifying Principles

The **Basic Assumptions** and the **Basic Principles** which have been highlighted in earlier paragraphs are **primarily used** as operating guidelines in order to make financial statements of an enterprise. It is needless to mention that the accounting information must be concise, intelligible, useful and practical from the standpoint of practical applications. That is, any accounting information should possess some important qualities, viz., primary qualities (Reliability and Relevance) and secondary qualities (Comparability and Consistency). It has already been stated earlier that accounting information must be relevant, dependable, reliable, comparable, consistent etc. That is why the Basic Assumptions and the **Basic Principles** should be modified to achieve properly.

Accountants at present apply the modifying principles as : (a) Materiality, (b) Consistency, (c) Conservatism, (d) Timeliness, and (e) Industry Practices which are explained below :

(a) **Materiality** : Materiality means 'relative importance'. In other words, whether a matter should be disclosed or not in the financial statements depend on its materiality, i.e., whether it is material or not (immaterial).

American Accounting Association (AAA) defines 'Materiality' as:

"An item should be regarded as material if there is reason to believe that knowledge of it would influence the decision of informed investors." But E. L. Kohler described it as : The characteristic attaching to a statement of fact or item where by its disclosure or the method of giving it expression would be likely to influence the judgment of reasonable persons. In this regard, the accountant is vitally concerned with the following two important matters:

(i) Materiality of **information**; and

(ii) Materiality of **amounts**.

Of course, an accountant cannot ignore the consideration of materiality of *procedures*. The term itself is a subjective term. As such, an accountant should record an item of material even though it is of small amount if the same influences the decisions of the users, viz., proprietors, auditors or investors etc. On the other hand, if it is found that an information is not sufficiently important to influence the quality of periodical financial statements, the same should be treated as 'immaterial' and, hence, should be avoided.

It has been stated above that materiality depends on the amounts involved and the account so affected. As a result, whether a particular item is material or immaterial depends on the amount and nature of the same. Because, the material information helps the management to avoid unnecessary wastage of time and money on principal materials. It should be noted that this doctrine of materiality refers to separate disclosure of information in the published financial statements for the user of the same. In short, material items should separately be disclosed whereas immaterial items may not be disclosed separately but may be combined in a consolidated form in the published financial statements.

(b) **Consistency** : This doctrine implies that accounting rules, practices and conventions should be continuously observed and applied. In other words, these should not be changed from year to year. Comparison of result among different years is meaningful and significant only when the accounting rules, procedures and practices are continuously adhered to from year to year. For example, the principle of valuing *stock at cost or market price, whichever is lower*, should be followed every year for making proper comparison, i.e., the method adopted should be consistent for all the years. If there is any uncertainty regarding accounting procedures the same is considerably offset by a consistent method adopted from one accounting period to another. Consistency serves to eliminate personal bias but it must not become a fetish so as to ignore changed conditions or the need for improvements in technique.

It should be stressed that the doctrine of consistency does not preclude changes if these changes are desirable and the effects of them are made known.[1]

E. L. Kohler analyses consistency into three types:

(a)	*Vertical Consistency*	:	Where the same principle, methods, practice are adopted within the interrelated financial statements of the same date.
(b)	*Horizontal Consistency*	:	It helps to make a proper comparison of the operation of a company from one period to another.
(c)	*Third Dimensional Consistency*	:	It helps to make a proper comparison of the operation between two firms within the same industry.

[1] Ibid

However, the doctrine of consistency helps in the following manner:

(i) It helps to eliminate the personal bias of an accountant since he is not allowed to change any accounting method or principle according to his own opinion and desire from one year to another.

(ii) It helps a accountant to use his own judgement.

(iii) It also helps to prepare a periodical financial statement which is more dependable and comparable.

(c) **Conservatism :** Conservatism refers to the principles and practices which are established by way of tradition, reluctance to change from such established principles and practices, and an inclination to play safe. In short, it is a policy of caution or playing safe and has its origin as safeguard against possible losses in a business world of uncertainty.

The accountant wants to play safe, particularly in the determination of income or profit or loss and in the process of valuation which he is associated with in the accounting literature. He is inclined not to assess any gain or income until the same has been realised or converted into money, i.e., until there is actual sale or realisation of income or gains actually accrues. In other words, there seems to be no objective indication of the emergence of income or gain. This arises due to the keen inclination of the accountant to the doctrine of objectivity. But at the time of estimating expenses or losses, the accountant goes beyond the purview of objectivity and makes a subjective estimate of a possibility. And for this reason, in accounting, proper provisions are always made against current profit for future losses and contingencies.

Therefore, the common accounting practices are:

(i) Do not consider any income or gain till the same is realised in cash.

(ii) Create or make a provision for future expected losses and contingencies on the basis of past performance. This aspect of the doctrine of conservatism has been particularly meaningful and significant with the growth of limited companies.

Practically, this doctrine helps to keep the human desire to be on the safe side as a matter of prudence. In order to protect the interest of the different parties the net profits and net assets must not be overstated but may be understated. Because, conservatism refers to deliberate understatement where uncertainties lie. Of course this doctrine does not recognise the unnecessary deliberate understatement(s) in order to make a manipulation in accounting data, e.g., the inventory valuation rule—cost prices or market prices, whichever is lower.

The excessive application of conservatism could result in the creation of secret reserve which directly contradicts the Convention of Disclosure. Conservatism carried beyond what is warranted by reasonable doubt distorts earning in as much as net profit in one period may be declared at less than it should be. As such, current accounting thought shifted somewhat from the principles of conservatism.

(d) **Timeliness :** The principles of timeliness means each and every business transaction should be recorded in proper time/appropriate time. Usually, as soon as a transaction takes place, the same should be recorded in the proper books of accounts, i.e., the transactions should be recorded date-wise or first-come-first-served basis. For example, if a transaction has happened on 1st April, the same must be recorded in the books before 2nd April. In short, accounting records must be performed as early as possible. Delay in recording the transactions may result in misplacement of vouchers, manipulations, misappropriations or embezzlement of cash/goods etc. Moreover, finalisation of accounts are not possible at the proper time when they are urgently needed by the decision-makers or other interested group of people.

This principle is urgently needed while verifying day-to-day cash balance, i.e., principle of timeliness must be followed here. Otherwise, there may be some misappropriation of cash. Banks verify their day-to-day cash balance with their Cash Book, i.e., it must be completed within the day.

If the quarterly reports are presented on half-yearly basis (i.e., if accounting year closes on 31st March but the accounts are made on 30th June), it will be of no use or little value to the decision-makers since that period is already over. Thus, principle of Timeliness is very important while recording business transactions.

(e) **Industry Practices** : It is known to us that every business enterprise possesses its own characteristics. Similarly, every industry has its own features, type of work, requirement, specialities, etc. Even there may be seasonal industries among the industries. Again, industries include large, medium and small-scale industries. Thus, each and every industry has to follow the accounting principles and assumptions in order to perform its accounting activities. In practice, they follow the norms sometimes in a modified way, although a particular industry follows the accounting practice which prevails in the industry itself. Following examples may be cited here:

Electric Supply Companies maintain separate type of accounts. Insurance Companies prepare their 'Revenue Account' to ascertain Profit or Loss and not to prepare Profit and Loss Account that are ordinarily prepared by other industries. Non-trading organisations prepare Receipts and Payments Account and Income and Expenditure Account etc.

GENERALLY ACCEPTED ACCOUNTING PRINCIPLES (GAAP)

We know that the accounting work is a practical activity of an accountant. While accomplishing such activities, the accountants usually do not consider the theoretical aspects in greater details as the theoretical part sometimes differs from practical work. However, the accountants prepare the accounts and present the same to the users of accounting information for their respective uses. In order to defend and justify themselves, they prepare the accounts which are generally acceptable. Naturally, to accomplish their activities, the accountant must consider rules, principles and conventions of accounting and prepare their reports and statements and present the same to the users of accounting information and to the management for taking decision and future courses of action. In short, the accountants must maintain some GAAP (Generally Accepted Accounting Principles) for maintaining and presenting accounts.

The view of AICPA (American Institute of Certified Public Accountants) in this regard is:

". . . Generally Accepted Accounting Principles incorporate the consensus at a particular time as to which economic resource and obligations should be recorded as assets and liabilities by financial accounting, which changes in assets and liabilities should be recorded, when these changes should be recorded, how the assets and liabilities and changes in them should be measured, what information should be disclosed and how it should be disclosed, and which financial statements should be prepared. It also states that GAAP encompass the conventions, rules and procedures necessary to define accepted accounting practice at a particular time . . . include not only broad guidelines of general application, but also detailed practice and procedures."

However, the Accounting Principle Board (APB), USA, states that "GAAP are conventional —that is, they become generally accepted by agreement (often tacit agreement) rather than by formal derivation from a set of postulates or basic concepts. The principles have been developed on the basis of experience, reason, custom, usage, and to a significant extent, practical necessity."[1]

Concepts—Conventions—Principles—Rules

The principles, concepts and conventions of Accounting create a lot of confusion among the readers of the subject. As it is not used as an uniform basis it is difficult for the accountants to present and prepare the accounts as per rules, principles, concepts, conventions etc. simply because a lot of snags lies therein. Practically there is no hard and fast rules which can uniformly be used irrespective of caste and creed in accounting. In other words, how Generally Accepted Accounting Principles (GAAP) is to be ascertained which can uniformly be applied in accounting.

In order to overcome the said difficulty the International Accounting Standard Committee (IASC) was formed on 29th June 1973 to maintain uniformity in accounting principle throughout all the countries in the world. The primary objective of IASC is to formulate and publish the International Accounting Standard (IAS) to be maintained while preparing financial statements and to promote their worldwide acceptance.

Similarly, the Institute of Chartered Accountants of India (ICAI), being the premier accounting body in India, has set up an "Accounting Standards Board" (ASB) on 21.8.1977 in order to harmonise the

---

1 Statement No. 4, Accounting Principle Board, AICPA, 1970, PP. 45-55
Ibid

diverse accounting policies and practice in our country. The objective and function of Accounting Standards Board (ASB) is to formulate accounting standards for our country. The so-called Standard may be established by the ICAI. While formulating the accounting standards, the ASB must consider the customs, usage, applicable laws of the land and the business environment bearing in mind the provisions of IAS.[1]

Thus, the accounting standard will help the accountants to prepare and present the accounts of a corporate body. That is why some of the Accounting Standards are treated as mandatory. It is expected that, in the near future, there will be a significant improvement about the accounting principles and policies.

However, Prof. R. N. Anthony and Prof. Reece[2] mentioned 11 (eleven) basic concepts of Accounting out of which 5 concepts are applicable for preparing Balance Sheet and 6 concepts are applicable for preparing Profit and Loss Account:

1. **Concepts Relating to Balance Sheet**
   - (a) Entity Concept
   - (b) Money Measurement Concept
   - (c) Going Concern Concept
   - (d) Cost Concept
   - (e) Dual Aspect Concept.

2. **Concepts Relating to Profit and Loss Account**
   - (a) Realisation Concept
   - (b) Matching Concept
   - (c) Accounting Period Concept
   - (d) Conservatism
   - (e) Materiality
   - (f) Consistency.

However, Professor L. S. Porwal[3] suggested the whole matter as:

- (a) Four Accounting Postulates
- (b) Five Theoretical Concepts
- (c) Five Basic Accounting Principles
- (d) Four Modifying Principles.

He mentioned details of such postulates, concepts and principles as :

(a) The Accounting Postulates

- (i) The Entity Postulate
- (ii) The Going Concern Postulate
- (iii) The Monetary Unit Postulate
- (iv) The Accounting Period Postulate.

(b) The Theoretical Concepts

- (i) The Proprietary Theory
- (ii) The Entity Theory
- (iii) The Residual Entity Theory
- (iv) The Enterprise Theory
- (v) The Fund Theory.

(c) Basic Accounting Principles

- (i) The Revenue Principle
- (ii) The Cost Principle
- (iii) The Matching Principle
- (iv) The Objectivity Principle
- (v) The Full Disclosure Principle.

(d) The Modifying Principles

- (i) Materiality
- (ii) Consistency
- (iii) Conservatism
- (iv) Timeliness.

In this respect we may mention another view expressed by Ian Tilley[4] in order to remove the conclusion about GAAP. A structure of GAAP was suggested by him as:

---

1 However, the ASB seeks the views and guidance of various industrial houses, Government and other interested parties etc. The members of the ASB are: Members of the Council of the Institute, representatives of industry, banks, Central Board of Direct Tax, UGC and Educational and Professional Institutions, the Company Law Board, Central Board of Excise and Customs, Controller General of Accounts, the Controller and Auditor General of India, and SEBI

2 Anthony R. N., *Accounting Principles*, 1989, P. 221

3 Porwal, L. S., *Accounting Theory, An Introduction*; Tata McGraw Hill (P) Ltd, 1989, PP. 69-84

4 Ian Tilley, 'A Critique of Historical Record Accounting' in *Studies in Accounting Theory*, Edited by Ghosh, Maheswari and Goyale, 1985, P. 114

A. Conventions
B. Doctrines
C. Principles
D. Rules.

Subdivisions of the above are:

A. Conventions

(i) Entity Convention
(ii) Continuity Convention
(iii) Period Convention
(iv) Monetary Convention
(v) Cost of Economic Significance Convention
(vi) Cost Cohesion Convention
(vii) Constant Value of Money Convention
(viii) Historical Record Convention
(ix) Historical Cost Convention.

B. Doctrines

(i) Conservatism
(ii) Consistency
(iii) Verifiable Objective Evidence
(iv) Full Disclosure
(v) Materiality.

C. Principles

(i) Matching Principle
(ii) Expense Recognition Principle
(iii) Revenue Recognition Principle.

D. Rules

The host of procedures and techniques are used by accountants' recognition in their day-to-day activities, e.g., FIFO, LIFO etc.

From the discussion made so far, it becomes quite clear that practically there is no wide variation or a very little variation among the various accounting concepts, assumptions, conventions and principles. For example, the term Entity is a convention as per Ian Tilley, the same is a Postulate to L. S. Porwal, and it is a concept as per Anthony and Reece. However, an accountant must maintain the concept, convention, postulate, and principle of accounting at the time of preparing the financial statement what should be disclosed as True and Fair irrespective of the variation while classifying a particular term as concept, convention, postulate and principle.

Advantages of GAAP

GAAP has the following advantages:

(a) **Helpful for maintaining day-to-day accounts**

GAAP helps the accountants who prepare day-to-day accounting activities and records them. Since they are following the various treatments in accounting according to the guidance or principles formulated in GAAP, no doubt discrepancies arise regarding the accounting treatment of various types of transactions. Practically, it helps the accountants to maintain accounts properly.

(b) **Harmonisation of accounting principles and practices**

Since various types of principles and techniques are followed by various firms while preparing financial statements no consistency is made and, as such, proper comparison is not possible. GAAP helps to maintain such harmonisation in accounting principles and practices and, as such, consistency in such principles for maintaining accounts is possible. Thus, accounts which are prepared on the basis of GAAP can be compared significantly. That is, intra-firm comparison and inter-firm comparison become possible.

(c) **Effect of window dressing**.

Window dressing in Balance Sheet which are done by the accountants presents a distorted picture to the analyst. The same can be stopped or avoided showing the application of GAAP in maintaining accounts.

(d) **Acceptance of qualitative work in accounting**

The accounting principles which are formulated in GAAP are the product of collective knowledge and experience of experts in the professional line. As such, GAAP presents qualitative improvement while maintaining accounts.

(e) **Reduces fraud and manipulation**

Since accounts are maintained as per the directives/principles of GAAP, possibility of community fraud is less and manipulation of accounts is difficult. Thus, GAAP helps the accounting world to make proper accounts which satisfy the accounting community as a whole.

(f) **Acceptability of accounts**

If accounts are maintained by the accountants as per the principles and practices of GAAP, the same is acceptable by all concerned. Needless to say that if accounts are maintained as per the principles of International Accounting Standards, they are widely accepted all over the world for the purpose of analysing the financial statements on which the financing decision depends.

(g) **Helpful in stock-exchange transactions**

If accounts are maintained as per accounting standards, it becomes helpful in dealing with stock exchange transactions for the purpose of valuation of various securities/shares. At the same time, if the accounts are maintained as per the International Accounting Standards, its acceptance is widely recognised all over the world.

Limitations of GAAP

Even the GAAP is not free from snags. Some are:

(a) **Difficult to apply**

It is not very easy to apply GAAP in day-to-day accounting practice since it is not only costly but also requires a lot of time for its applications. Small firms cannot afford it.

(b) **Non-comparable in certain cases**

GAAP is not applicable in all cases irrespective of 'caste and creed'. Firms differ among themselves according to their size, style, capacity etc. So, a particular principle cannot be properly applied in all cases. Even a firm within the same group may also differ. Thus, GAAP has got little effect on those firms who differ in various forms among themselves for the purpose of making proper comparison.

(c) **Fixed standard principles**

We know that while setting up a GAAP some fixed standard principles are taken into consideration which should strictly be followed by the firms. But the so-called fixed standard principles do not have any bearing as the business world is constantly changing. So how can a rigid principle be applied in this changing world for the purpose of making comparison?

(d) **Not possible to ignore personal judgment**

The necessity of applying personal judgment for the purpose of preparing financial statements cannot be ignored by the accounting standards set in a GAAP. For example, valuation of stock.

(e) **Proper interpretation not always possible**

The GAAP which are set by a group of people/experts for proper evaluation of performances may create confusion regarding its meaning and this proper interpretation cannot be made under such circumstances, i.e., proper interpretation is not always possible.

(f) **Knowledge of accounting not developed by the accountants**

Since accountants are to follow the standard principles and practices for maintaining accounts they do not find any interest in developing their knowledge of accounting in a better way. That is, personal knowledge and judgment are not improved.

(g) **Standards set up purposely for a group of people**

Sometimes standards are set up to satisfy the needs of a particular group of people, i.e., they are not always set up for better accounting performances. It may also be found that some useful or logical standards are waived or amended only to satisfy the interest of a group of people.

Inadequacy of GAAP

It has already been stated earlier that GAAP encompasses the conventions, rules and procedures necessary to define accepted accounting practice at a particular time and includes not only broad guidelines of general application but also detailed practice and procedures[1]. The principles of accounting

1 Statement No. 4, Accounting Principle Board, AICPA, 1970, PP. 45-55

which have been developed to set up GAAP are considered on the basis of experience, reason, customs, usages etc. GAAP also contains the forms and contents of financial statements which should be followed by a firm. GAAP is followed in order to product the interest of creditors, investors and other stakeholders. However, the GAAP is found to be quite inadequate in some areas. Such inadequacies distort the financial performances of an enterprise. Some of them are:

(a) **Even Professional bodies not free from unscrupulous activities**

Usually, the GAAPs are prepared by professional bodies some of even whom are not free from unscrupulous activities and act with the management in order to avoid the various provisions of GAAP which are formulated. It has even been found in the past that famous auditors prepared the cooked accounts and violated the principles of GAAP.

(b) **Useless in inflationary situations**

GAAP does not consider the effect of inflation. As such, it considers the historical cost basis of accounting and does not give due emphasis on market values, i.e., it presents distorted financial statements at the time of changing price level. In order to make the financial statements more meaningful, the same should be prepared as per market value basis, i.e., figures are understated in financial statements during periods of inflation.

(c) **Possibility of misinterpretation**

The various accounting principles/standards are framed by the various accounting bodies (viz., FASB, APB, IAS etc.). As such, possibility of misinterpretation about the principles among them arises as they are not concise or short.

(d) **Not applicable for specific users**

Usually GAAPs are prepared for the analysis of general purposes and, as such, they cannot satisfy the needs of specific users. GAAPs are applied in all business enterprises irrespective of 'caste and creed' on uniformity basis. But in real-world situation, firms vary among themselves both in nature, types, sizes. Thus, proper comparison is not possible.

(e) **Silent about the format of income statement**

No standardised classification of expenses and incomes are made by GAAP—which is a very important one—i.e., it is silent about the format of Income Statement. As such, various enterprises prepare this statement according to their choice.

(f) **Not useful for all categories of users**

GAAPs are not useful for all categories of users. For example, one stakeholder is interested to analyse the liquidity position of a firm whereas another is interested in the profit-earning capacity of a firm, i.e., rate of profitability, or, someone is interested in long-term solvency of a firm. GAAPs cannot satisfy all of them—as it is meant for some general use.

(g) **No comprehensive set is made**

GAAPs are compiled by various accounting bodies derived from their practical experiences and, as such, no basic set of GAAP is prepared.

(h) **Non-financial factors are neglected**

GAAPs do not consider the non-financial factors while setting-up principles or standards although they have direct bearing for setting-up such principles or standards. At present, some advanced countries (UK, USA etc.) direct the companies to present comments at their annual report about the financial resources which are excluded from the Balance Sheet, which, in other words, is known as MD&A (Management Decision and Analysis).

(i) **Not mandatory**

Since it is not a mandatory one for the Indian companies to follow the accounting standards and no penalty is imposed for non-compliance with the same, in the absence of legal provisions, Indian companies try to escape from this issue. Although, Sec., 211, sub-section (3A) and (3B), as prômulgated by the Companies (Amendment) Ordinance of 1998 include the same (i.e., Indian companies are required to prepare financial statements as per accounting standards, i.e., they must comply with the same). But it is interesting to note that no penal process is made for non-compliance with the accounting standards.

(j) **Not considering the latest areas of accounting**

A notable development has been made in the various areas of accounting in the last century, particularly after the second half, e.g., Human Resource Accounting, Brand Accounting, Social Accounting, Value Added Reporting, etc. But GAAP did not consider them as yet. So the GAAP, which has been set up earlier, is quite inadequate in the present-day accounting world.

Steps may be taken to Improve the Inadequacies

When the users of financial statements find the GAAP is inadequate, the various regulatory bodies, after negotiating opinions, take some steps to improve the inadequacies of GAAP. Some of them are:

(i) Various Regulatory bodies may pass relevant/adequate laws, rules and regulations in order to meet the challenges against the inadequacies of GAAP.

(ii) As per the requirement of the users, the principles or standards may be revised or changed or may be withdrawn if it thinks so.

(iii) Current Purchasing Power (CPP) Method and Current Cost Account (CCA) Method may be applied to set-up the principles of GAAP against the inflationary effect.

(iv) Non-financial matters should also be given due importance.

ACCOUNTING STANDARDS

Accounting is the language of business. It may also be stated that accounting is the language of communication of all organisations. All financial information (i.e., nature of financial activities, financial position, financial results, present trend and further prospects etc.) are available through accounting. The so-called financial information are communicated to the users (both internal as well as external) of accounting information by preparing and presenting the financial statements. As such, it becomes necessary to develop some GAAP (Generally Accepted Accounting Principles) while preparing the financial statements by which the language of the business can be communicated to the users. In addition, there must not be any ambiguity and uncertainty relating to the facts, figures and terms which are contained in the financial statements which will be presented to the users of accounting information. In recent years, due to the growth of multinational corporations, certain international standards are required in order to avoid confusion relating to financial status and operating results. Thus, the principles which are formulated or developed in this regard and which are approved by the specialised bodies are known as "**Accounting Standards**." Practically, it will help us to assess the progress or otherwise of a firm after comparing the actual performances with the standard.

According to some authorities like Yorston, Smyth and Brown: 'a standard is a performance target or goal or an agreed criterion of what is proper practice in a particular situation.' There are some other authorities who prefer to use the term "Accounting Principles" in place of "Accounting Standards".

In short, Accounting Standard may be defined as the accounting principles and rules which are to be followed for various accounting treatments while preparing financial statements on uniform basis and which will reveal the same meaning to all the interested groups who will use the same. Thus, the Standards are considered as a guide for maintaining and preparing accounts.

Need of Accounting Standards

Practically speaking, in order to avoid the variance which may arise between the accounting principles and accounting practice and also to find a uniformity among diversity among the various underlying principles of accounting, we emphasise the Accounting Standards framed by the IASC or IAS (Indian Accounting Standard, based on IASC) for maintaining accounting practice in our country.

However, the reasons for setting the Standards are:

(a) Comparison between two firms is possible if both of them maintain the same principle, otherwise proper comparison is not possible. For example, if Firm A follows the FIFO method of valuation of stock whereas Firm B follows the LIFO method for valuing stock, the comparison between the two firms becomes useless. The same is possible only when both of them follow identical method of valuing closing stock.

(b) The firms are not allowed to maintain and present their accounts according to their own will or choice or cannot prepare report of financial statements for various interested groups. The same is possible only when there is some fixed standard for setting practice.

(c) The Accounting Standards recognise the principle of equity applicable for different users of accounting information, viz., creditors, investors, shareholders, etc.

Thus the purpose of setting Accounting Standards is nothing but to find a uniformity in accounting practice while formulating financial reports and make consistent and proper comparison of data which are contained in financial statements for the users of accounting information. Practically, Accounting Standards have been presented in order to maintain fairness, consistency and transparency in accounting practice which will satisfy the users of accounting.

Objectives and Features

The objectives of IASC which are set out in its revised agreement and constitution are:

(i) to formulate and publish in the public interest Accounting Standards to be observed in the presentation of financial statements and to promote their worldwide acceptance and observation; and

(ii) to work for the improvement and harmonisation of regulation of Accounting Standards and procedures relating to the presentation of financial statements.

In regard to the objective (i) stated above—i.e. worldwide acceptance and operation—the statement of J. L. Kirkparick, Chairman of the Board of IASC, delivered to the members of the Institute of Chartered Accountants, Ireland, is quite significant. According to him : "When we sit round the IASC Board table and in the steering committee which creates the standard, we do so in our capacity as experts in Accounting and certainly not as auditors. It is irrelevant whether we are practitioners or not." Therefore the Standards which are set/issued by ISAC are meant for universal acceptance.

DEVELOPMENT OF ACCOUNTING STANDARDS

A. INTERNATIONAL ACCOUNTING STANDARDS (IAS)

International Accounting Standard Committee (IASC)

It came into being on 29th June 1973 when 16 accounting bodies (viz., The Institute of Chartered Accountants from 10 nations i.e., USA, Canada, UK and Ireland, Australia, France, Germany, Japan, Mexico and Netherlands) signed the constitution for its formation. Its headquarters is situated at London. The Objectives of IAS is to develop accounting standards which are to be observed in the presentation of audited financial statements and to promote their worldwide acceptance. Moreover, its other responsibility is to keep member bodies informed of the latest development and standards by issuing exposure drafts form time to time. Needless to mention that the Institute of Chartered Accountants of India and the Institute of Cost Accountants of India are Members of the International Accounting Standards Committee.[1]

The objectives of IASC, which are set out in its revised agreement and constitution (Nov. 1982), are :

(i) to formulate and publish in the public interest accounting standards to be observed in the presentation of financial statements and to promote their worldwide acceptance and observation, and

(ii) to work for the improvement and harmonisation of regulating accounting standards and procedures relating to the presentation of financial statements.

Moreover, The International Federation of Accountants (IFAC)—which was held at the IXth International Congress of Accountants in October 1977—had been set up in order to harmonise accounting, auditing and reporting practices in an area which will see growing interdependence of the commercial and industrial systems of the world. In order to formalise their relationship, International Accounting Standards Committee (IASC) and International Federation of Accountants (IFAC) constituted a working group which has, in the meantime, issued a statement of 'Mutual Commitments'. Practically, this statement, inter alia, accepts IASC as the sole body responsible for issuing pronouncements on international accounting standards. The Council of IFAC has approved it on May 1981.

At regional level, 'International Cooperation in Accountancy' was actually the theme of the Confederation of Asian and Pacific Accountants (CAPA) conference held in 1979 in recognition of the universality of accounting and the consolidation of efforts of accounting organisations throughout the

1 The Council of the Institute of Chartered Accountants of India established an Accounting Standard Board on 22.4.1977 for formulating accounting standards The Accounting Standard Board takes into consideration the accounting standards developed by IASC which develops accounting standards from time to time

world. Similarly, the Financial Accounting Standards Board (FASB) of USA has recently issued a number of Statements on conceptual framework for financial accounting and reporting in order to develop the respective standards.

Till 1st January 2004, International Accounting Standards have been issued by IASC. Some standards have been withdrawn and some were revised. The standards are :

IAS 1 : Presentation of Financial Statements
IAS 2 : .Valuation and Presentation of Inventories
IAS 7 : Cash Flow Statement
***IAS 8 : Net Profit or Loss for the Period—Fundamental Errors and Changes in Accounting Policies**
IAS 10 : Events occurring after Balance Sheet Date
IAS 11 : Accounting for Construction Contracts
IAS 12 : Accounting for Taxes on Income
***IAS 14 : Reporting Financial Information by Segments**
***IAS 15 : Information reflecting the effects of Changing Prices**
IAS 16 : Accounting for Property, Plant and Equipment
IAS 17 : Accounting for Leases
IAS 18 : Revenue Recognition
IAS 19 : Accounting for Retirement Benefits of Employees in the Financial Statements of Employers
IAS 20 : Accounting for Government Grants and Disclosure of Government Assistance
IAS 21 : Accounting for Effects of Changes in Foreign Exchange Rates
***IAS 22 : Accounting for Business Combinations**
IAS 23 : Capitalisations of Borrowing Costs
IAS 24 : Disclosure of Related Party Transactions
IAS 26 : Accounting and Reporting by Retirement Benefits Plans
IAS 27 : Consolidated Financial Statements and Accounting for Investments
IAS 28 : Accounting for Investments in Associates
IAS 29 : Financial Reporting by Hyperinflationary Economics
***IAS 30 : Disclosure of Financial Statement and Banks and Similar Financial Institutions**
IAS 31 : Financial Reporting of Interests in Joint Ventures
IAS 32 : Financial Instruments—Disclosure and Presentations
IAS 33 : Earning per Share
IAS 34 : Accounting for Interim Financials Reporting
***IAS 35 : Discontinuing Operations**
IAS 36 : Impairment of Assets
IAS 37 : Provisions, Contingent Liabilities and Contingent Assets
IAS 38 : Intangible Assets
IAS 39 : Financial Investments—Recognition and Measurement
IAS 40 : Investment Property
IAS 41 : Accounting for Agriculture.

B. INTERNATIONAL FINANCIAL REPORTING STANDARDS (IFRS) (Standards Issued after 2001)

Introduction

International Financial Reporting Standards (IFRS) are practically principle-based standards, interpretations and the framework which were adapted by the International Accounting Standards Board. Some International Accounting Standards (IAS) which were issued between 1973 and 2001 by the IASC (International Accounting Standards Committee) form a part of International Financial Reporting

* These Standards have been withdrawn

Standards (IFRS). Needless to say that the International Accounting Standards Board (IASB) took the responsibility to set the various International Accounting Standards on 1st April 2001 from the IASC. The International Accounting Standards Board will continue to develop various needed standards which are popularly known as IFRS. In short, IFRS are nothing but a set of accounting standards which are developed by the IASB. These standards are global standards in order to prepare the financial statements of public companies.

At present, about 120 nations require IFRS for their domestic companies which are listed. Of them, 90 countries have totally conformed with IFRS which are promulgated by IASB. It includes a statement acknowledging such conformity in their audit reports. India has adopted IFRS in Apriil 2011. As such, Indian listed companies are trying to achieve the important milestones while adopting various clauses of the regulations of IFRSs. The European Securities Committee (ESC) needs 'EU adopted IFRSs equivalence' from those companies who are following the Third World Countries. Naturally, those companies would have to fill financial reports as per the 'EU adopted IFRSs' for the purpose of using and listing securities in the absence of equivalence. Presently the EC (European Commission) has notified that Indian Accounting Standards must be treated at par with EU adopted IFRSs for the time being which are applicable for those companies that are incorporated in US, Mexico, Canada, Japan, South Korea, and China. These companies must follow the requirements of IFRSs within the next three years. For example, Mexico will adopt IFRSs to be standard from 2012 for all listed companies whereas Canada and Korea are expected to introduce by 2011. Japan is expected to adopt by 2015 or 2016 although it permits certain domestic companies to introduce IFRSs after 31st March 2010. Many countries have their respective plans to introduce IFRSs as early as possible.

Advantages of IFRS

For the conversion from IAS to IFRS, the following advantage are advocated :

(a) IFRS helps to raise Capital abroad since both the countries use IFRS for their allocating standards, i.e., the basis is the same.

(b) IFRS helps to present its financial statement on the identical basis of its foreign competitors, i.e., comparisons become easy.

(c) Subsidiary of a foreign company must use IFRS if its parent company follows the same.

(d) It helps the foreign investors who are using IFRS.

(e) One uniform accounting language may be applied in case of a foreign company having subsidiary to some other countries.

Disadvantages of IFRS

Even the IFRS is not free from snags. Some of them are :

(a) There are certain use–issuers who will resist IFRS as they do not have any market incentive for the preparation of IFRS financial statements.

(b) Adopting IFRS is costly.

Adoption of IFRS

It has already been stated that many countries of the world have already accepted IFRS and some are trying to implements the IFRS as early as possible (e.g., all European Union, Hong Kong, Australia, Malaysia, India, Pakistan, Russia, South Africa, Singapore, Turkey, etc.). Many countries require IFRS reporting for all domestic listed companies. The United States of America is also progressing towards IFRS. For this purpose, they are shifting from US GAAP to accept IFRS. General acceptance of IFRS will, no doubt, help the investors as well as the other users of financial statements. It will improve and increase the quality of information and will also reduce the cost of comparing alternative investments. Since the investors will be more interested to provide financing, companies are also expected to take the advantage of adequate financing.

Structures of IFRS

IFRSs are basically 'principle-based set of Standards' which frame results and various specific treatments of financial statements.

It computes :

(a) Framework for the preparation and presentation of Financial Statement 1989

(b) Standing Interpretation Committee (SIC) issued before 2001

(c) International Accounting Standards (IAS) issued before 2001

(d) Interpretations originate from the International Financial Reporting Interpretations Committee (IFRIC)— issued after 2001

(e) International Financial Reporting Standards (IFRS) —Issued after 2000.

List of IFRS

The list of IFRS comprises :

IFRS 1 : **First Time Adoptions of IFRS**

IFRS 2 : **Share-Based Payments**

IFRS 3 : **Business Combination**

IFRS 4 : **Insurance Contracts**

IFRS 5 : **Non-Current Assets held for Sale and Discontinued Operations**

IFRS 6 : **Exploration for and Evaluation of Mineral Resources**

IFRS 7 : **Financial Instruments; Disclosures**

IFRS 8 : **Operating Segments**

IFRS 9 : **Financial Instruments.**

C. INDIAN ACCOUNTING STANDARDS (OLD)

ACCOUNTING STANDARD BOARD OF INDIA

On 21st April 1977, The Institute of Chartered Accountants of India, as the premier accounting body in our country, set up the "Accounting Standard Board" (ASB) to harmonise the diverse accounting policies and practice prevalent in our country. The primary duty of ASB is to formulate the accounting standards for India. These standards may be established by the Council of the Institute in India. During formulation of accounting standards, the ASB considered the applicable laws, usages, customs and the business environment existing in our country. For this purpose ASB took the valued views and guidelines of various industrial houses, the Government, and other interested parties.

The body consists of the following members: Company Law Board, CBDT, Central Board of Excise and Customs, Controller General of Accounts, SEBI, Comptroller & Auditor General of India, UGC, Educational and Professional Institutions, Council of the Institute, and representatives of Industry, Banks.

The Accounting Standards will, however, be issued under the guidance of the Council. As such, ASB has given the authority of propagating the Accounting Standards and instituing the parties to prepare and present the accounts on the basis of Accounting Standards. ASB will explain the basic concepts on which accounting principles should be oriented and will also explain the accounting principles on which the practice and procedures should conform while performing its functions.

However, this Council of the Institute of Chartered Accountants of India (ICAI) has issued 32 Accounting Standards (AS) so far. These Accounting Standards are presented:

ACCOUNTING STANDARDS (Old)

AS No.	Title/Head
1.	**Disclosure of Accounting Policies**
2.	**Valuation of Inventories**
3.	**Cash Flow Statement**

4. Contingencies and Events Occurring After Balance Sheet Date
5. Net Profit or Loss for the Prior Period Items and Changes in Accounting Policies—Revised
6. Depreciation Accounting—Revised
7. Construction Contract—Revised
8. Accounting for Research and Development [Withdrawn from 1.4.2003]
9. Revenue Recognition
10. Accounting for Fixed Assets
11. Accounting for the Effects of Changes in Foreign Exchange Rates—Revised
12. Accounting for Government Grants
13. Accounting for Investments
14. Accounting for Amalgamation
15. Accounting for Employee Benefits
16. Borrowing Costs
17. Segment Reporting
18. Related Party Disclosures
19. Leases
20. Earning per Share
21. Consolidated Financial Statements
22. Accounting for Taxes on Income
23. Accounting for Investments in Associates in Consolidated Financial Statement
24. Discounting Operations
25. Interim Financial Reporting
26. Intangible Assets
27. Financial Reporting of Interest in Joint Ventures
28. Impairment of Assets
29. Provisions, Contingent Liabilities and Contingent Assets
30. Financial Instruments: Recognition and Measurement
31. Financial Instruments: Presentations
32. Financial Instruments: Disclosures.

D. INDIAN ACCOUNTING STANDARDS (NEW)

The then Hon. Minister for State, Ministry of Corporate Affairs, Mr. Salman Khursheed, had said that the ministry had met its commitments of starting IFRS-Compliant reporting by 2011. According to him, the next revolution after the software revolution will be in the world of Accountancy with the convergence of IFRS where we would be contributing the best and largest number of young accountants. For this, the Government of India is firm on the transition of Indian Companies from GAAP to IFRS. We were on schedule for convergence with IFRS from 2011. Accordingly, new Indian Accounting Standards (Ind AS) have been introduced from April 2011.

Phase Approach

Mr. S. Khursheed had announced a three phase convergence schedule in Jan. 2011 :

In First Phase : The listed companies, including those on overseas exchanges and with a Net Worth of Rs. 1,000 crores, will adopt IFRS Standards in April 2011.

In Second Phase : It includes companies having a Net Worth of Rs. 500 crores to Rs. 1,000 crores—which will move to IFRS standing from April 2013.

In Third Phase : Listed companies having a Net Worth of Rs. 500 crores or less will adopt it in April 2014.

NEW 35 INDIAN ACCOUNTING STANDARDS

(Ind AS)	1 :	**Presentation of Financial Statements**
(Ind AS)	2 :	**Valuation of Inventories**
(Ind AS)	7 :	**Statement of Cash Flow**
(Ind AS)	8 :	**Accounting Policies, Changes in Accounting Estimates and Errors**
(Ind AS)	10 :	**Events After the Reporting Period**
(Ind AS)	11 :	**Construction Contracts**
(Ind AS)	12 :	**Income-Taxes**
(Ind AS)	16 :	**Property, Plant and Equipment**
(Ind AS)	17 :	**Leases**
(Ind AS)	18 :	**Revenue**
(Ind AS)	19 :	**Employee Benefits**
(Ind AS)	20 :	**Accounting for Govemmnent Grants and Disclosure of Govemmnent Assistance**
(Ind AS)	21 :	**The Effect of Changes in Foreign Exchange Rates**
(Ind AS)	23 :	**Borrowing Costs**
(Ind AS)	24 :	**Related Party Disclosures**
(Ind AS)	27 :	**Consolidated and Separate Financial Statements**
(Ind AS)	28 :	**Investments in Associates**
(Ind AS)	29 :	**Financial Reporting in Hyperinflationary Economics**
(Ind AS)	31 :	**Interests in Joint Ventures**
(Ind AS)	32 :	**Financial Instruments : Presentation**
(Ind AS)	33 :	**Earning per Share**
(Ind AS)	34 :	**Interim Financial Reporting**
(Ind AS)	36 :	**Impairment of Assets**
(Ind AS)	37 :	**Provisions, Contingent Liabilities and Contingent Assets**
(Ind AS)	38 :	**Intangible Assets**
(Ind AS)	39 :	**Financial Instruments: Recognition and Measurement**
(Ind AS)	40 :	**Investment Property**
(Ind AS)	101 :	**First-Time Adoption of Indian Accounting Standards**
(Ind AS)	102 :	**Share-based Payment**
(Ind AS)	103 :	**Business Combination**
(Ind AS)	104 :	**Insurance Contract**
(Ind AS)	105 :	**Non-Current Assets held for Sale and Discontinued Operations**
(Ind AS)	106 :	**Exploration for and Evaluation of Mineral Resources**
(Ind AS)	107 :	**Financial Instruments : Disclosure**
(Ind AS)	108 :	**Operating Segments**

COMPARATIVE STUDY AT A GLANCE

A.	International Accounting Standards—IAS	B.	International Financial Reporting Standards—IFRS	C.	Indian Accounting Standards—Ind AS (Old)	D.	Indian Accounting Standards—Ind AS (New)
IAS 1 :	Presentation of Financial Statements	IFRS 1 :	First Time Adoption of IFRS	AS 1 :	Disclosure of Accounting Policies	Ind AS 1 :	Presentations of Financial Statement
2 :	Inventories	2 :	Share-Based Payments	2 :	Valuations of Inventories	2 :	Inventories
7 :	Statement of Cash Flow	3 :	Business Combination	3 :	Cash Flow Statement	7 :	Statement of Cash Flow
8 :	Net Profit or Loss for the Period—Fundamental Errors and Changes in Accounting Policy	4 :	Insurance Contract	4 :	Contingencing and Events Occurring After Balance Sheet Date	8 :	Accounting Policies Changes in Accounting Estimates and Errors
10 :	Events After the Reporting Period	5 :	Non-Current Assets held for Sales and Discontinued Operations	5 :	Net Profit or Loss for the period, Prior Period Items and Changes in Accounting Policies	10 :	Events After the Reporting Date
11 :	Construction Contracts	6 :	Exploration of Mineral Resources	6 :	Depreciation Accounting	11 :	Construction Contracts
12 :	Income Taxes	7 :	Financial Instruments —Disclosure	7 :	Construction Contracts	12 :	Income Taxes
16 :	Property, Plant and Equipment	8 :	Operating Segments	8 :	Accounting for Research and Development (Withdrawn on and from 1.4.2003)	16 :	Property, Plant and Equipment
17 :	Leases	9 :	Financial Instruments	9 :	Revenue Recognition	17 :	Leases
18 :	Revenue			10 :	Accounting for Fixed Asset	18 :	Revenue
19 :	Employee Benefits			11 :	Accounting for Effects of Changes in Foreign Exchange Rates	19 :	Employee Benefits
20 :	Accounting for Govt Grants and Disclosure of Govt Assistance			12 :	Accounting for Govt Grants	20 :	Accounting for Govt Grants and Disclosure of Govt Assistance
21 :	The Effects of Changes in Foreign Exchange			13 :	Accounting for Investment	21 :	The effect of Change in Foreign Exchange
23 :	Borrowing Costs			14 :	Accounting for Amalgamation	23 :	Borrowing Cost
24 :	Related Party Disclosure					24 :	Related Partly Disclosures
26 :	Accounting and Reporting by Retirement Benefits Plans					27 :	Consolidated and Separate Financial Statement
						28 :	Investments in Associates
						29 :	Financial Reporting in Hyperinflationary Economies

Contd.

A. International Accounting Standards—IAS	B. International Financial Reporting Standards—IFRS	C. Indian Accounting Standards—Ind AS (Old)	D. Indian Accounting Standards—Ind AS (New)
27 : Consolidated and Separate Financial Statements		15 : Accounting for Employees' Benefit	31 : Interest in Joint Venture
28 : Investments in Associates		16 : Borrowing Costs	32 : Financial Interest —Presentation
29 : Financial Reporting in Hyperinflationary Economies		17 : Segment Reporting	33 : Earning Per Share
31 : Interest in Joint Venture		18 : Related Party Disclosure	34 : Interim Financial Reporting
32 : Financial Instruments : —Presentation		19 : Leases	36 : Impairment of Assets
33 : Earning Per Share		20 : Earning Per Share	37 : Provision, Contingent Liabilities and Contingent Assets
34 : Interim Financial Reporting		21 : Consolidated Financial Statement	38 : Intangible Assets
36 : Impairment of Assets		22 : Accounting for Taxes on Income	39 : Financial Investment —Recognition and Measurement
37 : Provisions, Contingent Liabilities and Contingent Assets		23 : Accounting for Investments	40 : Investment Property
38 : Intangible Assets		24 : Discontinuing Operations	101 : First Time Adoption of Indian Accounting Standard
39 : Financial Instruments: —Recognition and Measurement		25 : Interim Finance Reporting	102 : Share Based Payment
40 : Investment Property		26 : Intangible Assets	103 : Business Combination
41 : Agriculture		27 : Financial Reporting of Interest in Joint Venture	104 : Insurance Contract
		28 : Impairment of Assets	105 : Non-Current Assets Held for Sale and Discontinued Operation
		29 : Provision, Contingent Liabilities and Contingent Assets	106 : Exploration for and Evaluation of Mineral Resources
		30 : Financial Instruments —Recognition and Measurement	107 : Financial Instruments —Disclosure
		31 : Financial Instruments —Presentations	108 : Operating Segments
		32 : Financial Instruments —Disclosure	

ASSIGNMENT MATERIALS

THEORETICAL

Short Answer-Type Questions

1. What is Accounting Principle?
2. Define : (a) Dual Aspect Concept; (b) Accounting Period Concept.
3. What is GAAP? What are its limitations?
4. What do you mean by Accounting Convention?
5. Define : (a) Convention of Disclosure; (b) Convertion of Consistency.
6. Discuss the importance of Accounting Standards.
7. Is there any differences between Accounting Principle and Accounting Standard? If so, explain.
8. Is there any difference between 'Concepts' and 'Conventions '?
9. What do you mean by Disclosure of Accounting Policy as per AS 1?
10. Principles, Concepts and Standards are same. Do you agree? State, with reasons.

ASSIGNMENT MATERIAL

THEORETICAL

Short Answer Type Questions

1. What is Accounting Principle?
2. Define (a) Dual Aspect Concept; (b) Accounting Period Concept.
3. What is GAAP? What are its limitations?
4. What do you mean by Accounting Convention?
5. Define (a) Convention of Disclosure; (b) Convention of Consistency.
6. Discuss the importance of Accounting Standards.
7. Is there any difference between Accounting Principle and Accounting Standard? If so, explain.
8. Is there any difference between Concepts and Conventions?
9. What do you mean by Dual Aspect or Accounting Entry [illegible]
10. Principles, Concepts and Standards are same. Do you agree? State with reasons.

CHAPTER 3

PRACTICAL BASE OF ACCOUNTING

Learning Objectives

TRANSACTIONS

Meaning
Features
Transactions relating to Goods
Effect of Transactions
Classification of Transactions
Modern Concept of Transactions
Events
Transactions vs. Events
Vouchers
Source Document

RULES FOR DEBIT AND CREDIT

Rules

1. **American Approach/Modern Approach**
   A. *Assets Account*
   B. *Liabilities Account*
   C. *Capital Account*
   D. *Revenue or Income or Profit*
   E. *Expenses or Losses*
2. **British Approach/Traditional Approach or Double Entry System**
   Double Entry System
   Advantages
   Accounts
   Classification of Accounts
   Rules for Debit and Credit

ACCOUNTING EQUATION

Meaning
Method of Computation

CASH AND ACCRUAL BASIS OF ACCOUNTING

1. *Cash Basis of Accounting*
2. *Accrual or Mercantile Basis of Account*
3. *Mixed or Hybrid Basis of Accounting—Conversion of* ***Cash Basis of Accounting*** *into Accrual Basis of Accounting.*

JOURNAL

Definition
Classification of Journal

—General
—Special
—Cash Book
—Purchases Day Book
—Sales Day Book
—Returns Inward Book
—Returns Outward Book
—Bills Receivable Book
—Bills Payable Book
Function of Journal
Advantages
Why Journal is called Original Book
Subdivision of Journal
—Advantages
—Necessities
Recording of Transactions in a Journal
Compound Journal

LEDGER

Definition
Advantages
Subdivisions of Ledger
—Advantages
Relation between the Books of Original Entry and Books of Final Entry
Process of Ledger Posting from Journal
Balancing of Account
Arrangement of Accounts in the Ledger
Closing Balance and Opening Balance
Standard T-Form of Ledger Account
Cross-Balancing

TRIAL BALANCE

Meaning and Objective
Preparation of Trial Balance
Advantages
Objectives and Functions
Features of a Trial Balance
Is Trial Balance Indispensable?

ERRORS

Errors which are not disclosed by a Trial Balance
—Errors of Omission;
—Errors of Commission;
—Errors of Principles;
—Errors of Misposting
—Compensating Errors
Errors which do not affect the agreement of Trial Balance
Errors which affect the agreement of Trial Balance
Errors which are disclosed by a Trial Balance
Procedure to locate errors
Pre-closing or Adjusted Trial Balance
Post Closing Trial Balance.

TRANSACTIONS

Transaction means to deal in money or money's worth. As soon as a business event occurs which can be measured and expressed in terms of money it must be recorded in the books of accounts. It is called a transaction. Transactions may be explained from another angle. The events which make some change in assets or equities' i.e., either increase or decrease of an enterprise—may also be termed as transaction. In short, any increase in asset with increase in liability or decrease in asset with decrease in liability is the effect of a transaction.

From the discussion so far it becomes crystal clear that, in a transaction, there must be some monetary change between the parties. In other words, the meaning of a transaction is **to receive** and to **give**, viz., one party receives and the other party gives or sacrifices the benefit.

For example, if Mr. X gives Rs. 400 to Mr. Y, Y is receiving the benefit Rs. 400 and X is giving or sacrificing Rs. 400. Thus, there is a monetary change between the parties. So, ***a transaction also means a change in affairs that alters the financial state in any way.***

Features of a Transaction

The following are the features of a transaction:

(a) A transaction must bring some monetary change between the parties;

(b) It must be measured in terms of money or money's worth;

(c) The effect of a transaction is either to increase the assets with increase in liabilities or decrease the assets with decrease in liabilities;

(d) It has direct bearing on the accounting equation;

(e) A transaction has two sides— 'Receiving the benefit' and 'Sacrificing the benefit';

(f) Application of Double Entry principle depends on it.

Two Aspects

It has already been highlighted above that a transaction has two sides, viz., 'Receiving' the benefit i.e., 'Receiving'; or 'Giving the benefit' or 'Sacrificing'. It is the basic principle of Double Entry System that a **transaction must be recorded in the two sides with equal amount.** The 'receiving side' or the left hand side is called the debit side, the 'giving side' or the right hand side is called the credit side.

In short, a transaction has got two sides—debit side and credit side; that is why it is said that ***every debit has a corresponding credit, and vice versa.***

Transactions relating to Goods

There are a number of transactions which affect goods; as such, it is not worthy to open a single Goods Account for all purposes. Because, the balance of Goods Account, if it is at all opened—will not reveal any specific or correct information to the users of the subjects. As we know, Goods Account is affected by (i) the amount of purchases, (ii) the amount of sales, (iii) the amount of returns inward, and (iv) the amount of returns outward—each one will express its own story, which is completely different from the other.

As a result, Goods Account is divided into several accounts. These are done in the following manner:

(a) **Increase in Goods/Stock**

Goods/Stock can be increased either: (i) when goods are purchased, or (ii) when goods are returned from customers. For this purpose, two different accounts are to be maintained, viz., Purchase Account (for recording goods which are purchased), and Returns Inwards Account (for recording goods which are returned by customers).

(b) **Decrease in Goods/Stock**

Goods or stock can be decreased either: (i) when goods are sold, or (ii) when goods are returned to suppliers. For recording these transactions also two separate accounts are to be maintained, viz., Sales Account (for recording goods which are sold), and Returns Outwards Account (for recording goods which are returned to suppliers).

Effects of Transaction

Illustration 1

Ascertain the account that will be debited and credited from the following transactions on the basis of Double Entry principle explained in the previous chapter:

(i) Bought goods for cash.
(ii) Bought goods from A and Co. on credit.
(iii) Returned goods to A and Co.
(iv) Sold goods for cash.
(v) Sold goods to B and Co. on credit.
(vi) B and Co. returned goods to us.

Solution

	Effects of Transaction	Account	To Be
(i)	Increase in Stock	Purchase A/c	Dr.
	Decrease in Cash	Cash A/c	Cr.
(ii)	Increase in Stock	Purchase A/c	Dr.
	Increase in Liability	A and Co. A/c	Cr.
(iii)	Decrease in Stock	Returns Outwards A/c	Cr.
	Decrease in Liability	A and Co. A/c	Dr.
(iv)	Decrease in Stock	Sales A/c	Cr.
	Increase in Cash	Cash A/c	Dr.
(v)	Decrease in Stock	Sales A/c	Cr.
	Increase in Assets (i.e., Debtors)	B and Co. A/c	Dr.
(vi)	Increase in Stock	Returns Inward A/c	Dr.
	Decrease in Assets (i.e., owing by customer)	B and Co. A/c	Cr.

Purchases Account and Sales Account—Application

The term 'purchase' means the acquisition of goods for the purpose of resale, either in the same form or after taking some required benefit, or after performing some activities. That is, if a furniture dealer purchases furniture for resale, furniture in this case will be treated as 'goods', but when the same dealer purchases furniture for his office decoration, the same will not appear in purchase account since the furniture is not used for resale purpose.

Same principle is, however, applicable in case of sales, viz., Sale Account must not be used for disposal of any other item or Sales Account should be recorded only when goods (which are acquired for resale) are sold; in short, if any asset or any other goods are sold, (not acquired for resale purpose), the particular item or asset account should be credited.

In short, the commodities which are purchased for normal buying and selling transactions are known as 'goods'.

Classification of Transactions

Transactions may be classified as:

(a) Simple transactions;
(b) Compound transactions;
(c) Complex transactions;
(d) Cash transactions;
(e) Non-cash transactions;
(f) External and internal transactions.

They are explained below one by one:

(a) **Simple Transactions**

When two aspects of a transaction can easily be formed showing debit in one account and credit in the other, the same is known as Simple Transaction.

Illustration 2

Bought goods for cash for Rs. 1,000. Here, the two aspects of the transaction are purchase account and cash account, i.e., purchase account Rs. 1,000 and cash account Rs. 1,000, i.e., one account will show a **debit** and the other account will show a **credit**.

(b) **Compound Transactions**

A transaction is a compound one where it has more than one account either in debit or in credit.

Illustration 3

Started business with a capital of Cash Rs. 1,000; Bank Rs. 3,000; Plant Rs. 10,000; Stock Rs. 5,000.

Here, the transaction affects more than one debit, i.e., Cash Account Rs. 1,000; Bank Account Rs. 3,000; Plant Account Rs. 10,000 and Stock Account Rs. 5,000, and the total is Capital Account Rs. 19,000.

In other words, in this illustration, Cash, Bank, Plant and Stock are one aspect, whereas Capital Account alone represents one aspect.

(c) Complex Transactions

When it becomes necessary to find out the two aspects of a transaction after making some necessary adjustments, the same is known as complex transaction.

Illustration 4

Good sold to X Enterprises as under: 1,000 ladies shawl @ Rs. 500 each at a trade discount of 10%, followed by a cash discount of another 10%.

In the present problem, the net selling price is calculated as:

		Rs.
	Goods Sold 1,000 × Rs. 500	5,00,000
Less:	Trade Discount @ 10%	50,000
		4,50,000
Less:	Cash Discount @ 10%	45,000
		4,05,000

Thus, Sales Account is considered as Rs. 4,05,000, whereas cash discount and cash realisation should be considered as Rs. 45,000 and Rs. 4,05,000, respectively.

(d) Cash Transactions

Cash Transactions: When any transaction involves immediate and physical movement of cash or bank, the same is known as cash transaction.

Illustration 5

X sold goods to Y for Rs. 1,000 in cash. It is a cash transaction because it involves money. In short, when the transaction affects cash or bank the same is known as cash transaction.

(e) Non-cash Transactions

It is needless to say that the transactions which are not cash transactions may be treated as non-cash transactions.

Illustration 6

Goods returned by our customers, return of goods to our creditors, or purchase and sale of goods without receiving or giving cash or cash equivalent or outstanding or prepaid expenses etc. are some of the examples of non-cash transactions.

(f) External and Internal Transactions

External Transaction—also known as Business Transaction is one when it is related with an outside person.

Illustration 7

B. Banerjee and Co. bought goods from P. Paul and Co. for Rs. 3,000 in cash, or, B. Banerjee, the proprietor of B. Banerjee and Co., took goods for his own use. These are also external transactions since, in accounting, B. Banerjee and B. Banerjee and Co. are not the same (applying entity concept).

Internal Transactions—also known as Accounting Transactions—arise when a transaction comes out from the expiration of cost or from the adjustment made or allocation of increase or expenses or transfer. In short, these transactions are made within the firm itself, i.e., they do not have any relation with outsiders.

Example: Prepaid salaries, outstanding expenses, depreciation of fixed assets, transfer from one account to another, etc. are examples of internal transactions.

Modern Concept of Transactions

Modern writers on accounting explain the term transaction as a financial event which results in exchange—either in the asset or in the equities of a firm.

Equities are divided into two:

i.e., Proprietorship (Internal Equities), and Liabilities (External Equities).

We all also know that **the sum total of the assets must always be equal to the sum total of the liabilities**. Thus, we can further write:

(A) Assets = P (Proprietorship) + L (Liabilities)

It is nothing but the Accounting Equation which we have highlighted in page No. 3.18

Events

According to Yorston, Smyth and Brown "A transaction is an event involving transfer of money or money's worth, the recognition of which gives rise to records in the books of account." In other words, it may be stated as any monetary change in the affairs of a trading/non-trading firm.

Example: S. Sen & Co.:

(i) Introduced further capital Rs. 3,000;
(ii) Bought goods for cash Rs. 1,000;
(iii) Sold goods for cash Rs. 5,000;
(iv) Paid salary Rs. 1,000;
(v) Lost 3 files @ Rs. 30 each;
(vi) Mr. X, the manager of S. Sen & Co., retires and he was paid Rs. 30,000 as gratuity.

All these are events to S. Sen & Co. as there are monetary changes. But the accountant of S. Sen & Co. accepts the events only from: (i) to (iv) and not (v) and (vi) for accounting purpose—although there were money changes.

Thus, in order to be considered an event, the following conditions must be satisfied:

(a) Accounting evidence; (b) Measurement in terms of money; (c) Accrual concept; (d) Actual cost of fixed asset; (e) Actual account of liabilities; (f) Basis of accounting (i.e., cash basis or accrual basis), and (g) Materiality concept.

We have explained events which are considered as transactions.

Now, we are going to highlight the events which represent the whole accounting process:

According to E. L. Kohler: "An event is a process (e.g., accounting process) or a part of process (e.g., a transaction or a group of transactions) having a particular moment or place or occurrence". Thus, it may be stated that an accountant must perform with a number of transactions which occurred during an accounting period which represents the whole accounting process. Anyone may have the accounting information. In other words, collecting, measuring and presenting the accounting data, recording the same after proper classification, and preparing a summary statement is treated as Event.

So, the financial statements (i.e., Profit and Loss Account and Balance Sheet) so prepared present some valuable accounting information about the firm to the users of financial statement.

Again, we will explain another aspect of an event, viz., processing of a group of related transactions.

"Event" means the processing of a group of related transactions. The same may be explained with the help of the following:

Sen Bros. had the following particulars:

(i) on 1.2.2009 Goods sold to Mr. D on credit for Rs. 10,000;
(ii) on 18.2.2009 Mr. D returned goods valued Rs. 1,000;
(iii) on 1.3.2009 Mr. D returned goods for Rs. 500;
(iv) on 18.3.2009 Mr. D paid Rs. 5,000 in cash.

From the above information if we prepare Mr. D's Account in the books of Sen Bros. the same will be represented as:

Mr. D's Account

Dr. Cr.

Date	Particulars	L.F.	V.N.	Amount	Date	Particulars	L.F.	V.N.	Amount
2009				Rs.	2009				Rs.
Feb. 1	To Sales A/c			10,000	Feb. 18	By Returns Inward A/c			1,000
					Mar. 01	" Returns Inward A/c			500
					18	" Cash A/c			5,000
					31	" Balance c/d			3,500
				10,000					10,000
Apr. 1	To Balance b/d			3,500					

It is quite clear from the above that after recording the transactions in the form of Journal and posting them in Mr. D's Account in the ledger and balancing the account (i.e., after the whole accounting process) the accountant supplies the information about the customer Mr. D that Mr. D is indebted to Sen Bros. for Rs. 3,500 on April 1, 2009. On the basis of the above information, Sen Bros. will send a reminder to pay-off their dues at an early date.

The above example reveals that an event may also be introduced in the whole accounting process.

Thus, from the foregoing discussion it may be stated that an event is the entire accounting process completed by an accountant which happens during an accounting period with a bundle of transactions— i.e., they are a bundle of transactions of financial activities which end with the end of the purpose for which the same is made to occur. In other words, it may be stated that ***the monetary transactions that happen during the performance of a short period non-profit activity is called an Event.***

Transaction vs Event

From the discussion made so far it is evident that ***"every transaction may be an event, but every event may not be a transaction"***. The events which satisfy the various concepts and conventions of accounting may be treated as transactions. However, the difference between the two is from the theoretical point of view, yet some of the differences may be noted:

Transaction	Event
1. A transaction may change the financial activities of an enterprise.	1. An event cannot make such change in financial activities of an enterprise.
2. A transaction is an event.	2. An event is not a transaction.
3. A transaction deals with the economic or financial activities of a firm.	3. An event deals with the financial and non-financial activities of a firm.
4. An accountant records only the transactions in the books of accounts.	4. An accountant does not record all the events.
5. Transaction is used in a narrower sense of the term.	5. Event is used in a broader sense of the term.
6. A transaction requires an exchange of goods or services between two or more parties.	6. An event does not require such exchange of goods or services.
7. A transaction must be expressed in terms of money.	7. An event may not always be expressed in terms of money.
8. A transaction always arises out of business documents and papers.	8. An event may happen out of business documents and papers.
9. A transaction is recorded as per accounting principles.	9. There is no such accounting principle for an event.
10. A transaction is complete in itself.	10. An event may be an incomplete action, i.e., it may have happened, is happening, or/and (continue) happening in future.

Voucher

A voucher is a piece of evidence or a written document serving as a proof. It is a paper which confirms the truth of anything as a receipt or a certificate of correctness. In short, a voucher is a document which witnesses an entity recorded in a primary book of account, i.e., ***a voucher is a documentary evidence in support of a transaction.*** Thus, there must be a documentary evidence in order to establish the monetary transactions or accounts for which the same is recorded in the books of accounts as each transaction has an effect on the business undertaking as a whole. The transaction should also be authorised. It serves as **Source Document.**

Source Document

Source documents are the evidence of business transactions. It has been stated above that vouchers are the documentary evidences which supply the necessary information about the transaction. Practically, the source documents are the basis on which the entries are recorded in subsidiary books of account. However, different source documents are:

	Name of the Book		Source Documents
(a)	Cash Book	:	Cash Memos, Cash Receipts and Issue Vouchers.
(b)	Purchases Book	:	Inward Invoice Received from the Creditors of goods.
(c)	Sales Book	:	Outward Invoice issued to Debtors.
(d)	Returns Inward Book	:	Credit Notes issued to Debtors and Debit Notes received from Debtors.
(e)	Returns Outward Book	:	Debit Notes issued to Creditors and Credit Notes Issued to Creditors.

Types of Voucher

Vouchers are of two types : (i) Primary or Accounting Vouchers, and (ii) Supporting Vouchers. The types of vouchers are depicted as :

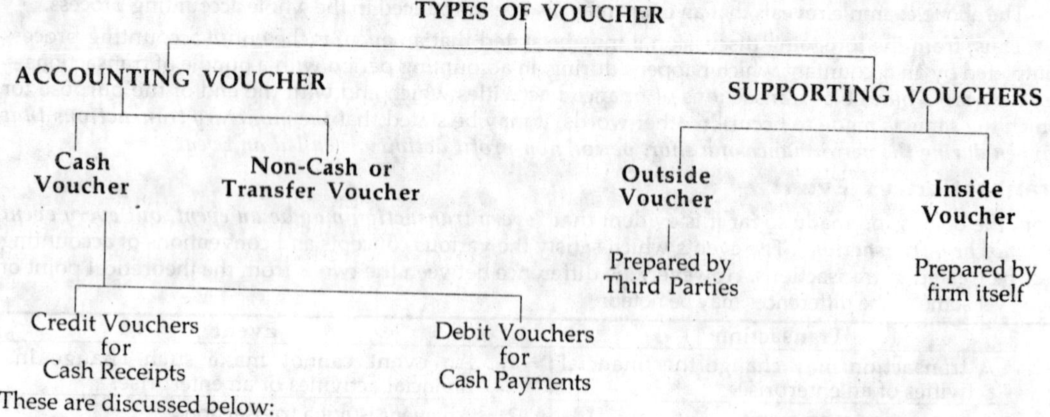

These are discussed below:

Accounting Voucher

These vouchers are prepared on the basis of supporting vouchers by the accounts clerk or the accountant of the organisation and which are countersigned by an authorsed signatory. As soon as it is signed the same is recorded in the books of accounts. These vouchers are made both for cash and non-cash transactions. Thus, accounting Vouchers are of two types, —(a) Cash Voucher and (b) Non-Cash Voucher or Transfer Voucher.

(a) **Cash Voucher**

Cash vouchers are the doucmentary evidence of both cash receipts and cash payments. Again, Cash Vouchers are of two following types, (i) Debit Voucher, and (ii) Credit Voucher.

(i) **Debit Voucher**

Debit vouchers are the documentary evidence of cash payments. These vouchers are prepared to keep records of various cash payments relating to the business including capital and revenue payments. For example, payment of Wages and Salaries, purchase of Plant by cash; Purchase of goods for cash, etc.

Contents of Debit Vouchers

The followng information are normally available from a debit voucher.

(a) Names and Addresses of the Parties; (b) Date of preparing the voucher; (c) Voucher Number; (d) Amount of the transaction; (e) Head of Account; (f) Signature of the person who is preparing the voucher; (g) Authorised signatory; (h) Narration i.e., short description of the transaction; (i) Number of supporting Vouchers.

The format of a Debit Voucher is presented:

Debit Voucher

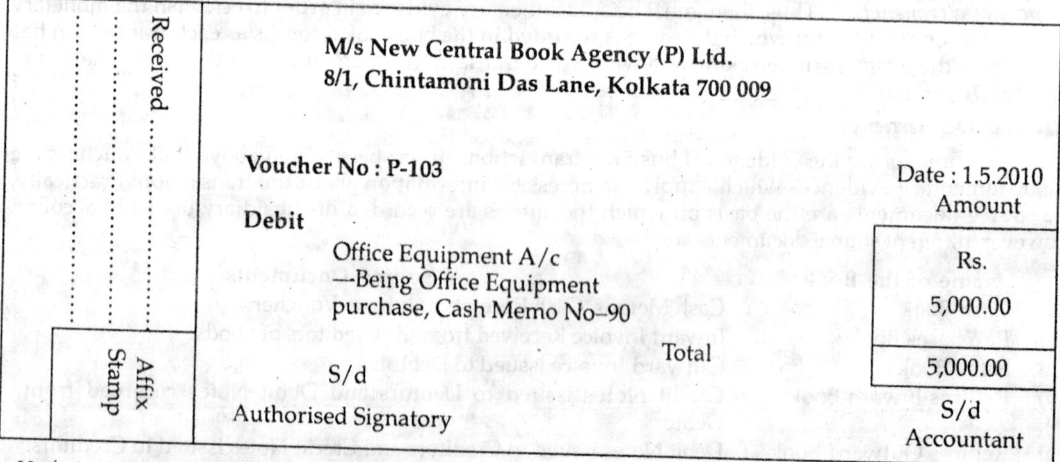

Note. 1. If the amount of transaction exceeds Rs. 500 a revenue stamp valued Re 1. should be affixed.

2. As the supporting voucher (i.e., Cash Memo No 90) is available, hence, the receipt portion of the debit voucher is not required.

(ii) **Credit Voucher**

Credit vouchers are the documentary evidence of Cash receipts. These vouchers are prepared to record various cash receipts relating to the business. Examples of credit vouchers: Sale of Goods for cash; Sale of fixed assets or investment for cash; Cash received from Debtors, etc.

Contents of Credit Voucher

The following information are usually available from a credit voucher:

(a) Names and address of the parties; (b) Date of preparing the voucher; (c) Voucher Number; (d) Amount of the transaction; (e) Heads of account; (f) Signature of the person who is preparing the voucher; (g) Authorised Signatory; (h) Narrations, i.e., short description of the transaction, and (i) Number of Supporting Voucher.

The format of a Credit Voucher is presented:

Credit Voucher

M/s New Central Book Agency 8/1 Chintamoni Das Lane, Kolkata 700 009	
Voucher No. 358	Date : 1.5.2010
Credit	Amount
Interest A/c Being the interest received in cash Vide Bill No. 458	1,000.00
Total	1,000.00
S/d Authorised Signatory	S/d Accountant

Non-Cash or Transfer Voucher

Non-Cash or Transfer vouchers are the documentary evidence of non-cash transactions. These vouchers are prepared to record the non-cash transactions of the business. Examples of non-cash vouchers are : Goods sold on Credit; Sale of Fixed Assets or Investment on Credit; Writing-off depreciation or Bad Debts, Returns Inward, etc.

Contents of Non-Cash Vouchers

(a) Name and Address of the parties; (b) Date of preparing the voucher; (c) Voucher Number; (d) Amount of the transaction; (e) Heads of Account; (f) Signature of the person who is preparing it; (g) Authorised Signatory; (h) Narration, i.e., short description of the transaction; (i) Number of Supporting Vouchers.

The format of a Non-Cash or Transfer Voucher is given:

Non-Cash or Transfer Voucher

M/s New Central Book Agency 8/1 Chintamoni Das Lane, Kolkata 700 009	
	Date : 1.5.2010
Voucher No. 255 **Debit**	Amount Rs.
Plant A/c	25,000.00
	25,000.00
Credit	
Ratna A/c —Being the Plant purchased Cash Memo No. 444	25,000.00
Total	25,000.00
S/d Authorised Signatory	S/d Accountant

Supporting Vouchers

Supporting Vouchers are the documentary evidence of business transactions which have happened. They are of two types : (i) External Supporting Vouchers; and

(ii) Internal Supporting Vouchers.

(i) **External Supporting Vouchers**

These vouchers are prepared by the third parties who are associated with the firm. For example:

(a) Debit Note Received; (b) Credit Note Received; (c) Purchase Invoice Received from the Supplier of Goods, etc. (d) Cash Memo Received from the Sellers, etc.

The format of a Supporting Voucher is presented:

Supporting Voucher
Stationery Receipt

		SRI KRISHNA STORES 185 Lake Town, Kolkata 700 089			
	Sl.	Descriptions	Quantity	Rate	Amount
	1. 2. 3.	5 copies of Binding Khata 1 Dozen Ball Pen 100 Pcs Executive Bond Paper	5 1 dozen 100	20 60 1	100.00 60.00 100.00
		Total			260.00
		Rs. 260.00	S/d Signature		

(ii) **Internal Supporting Vouchers**

These vouchers are prepared by the internal staff on behalf of the firm which are accepted by the third parties for the transaction so happened. For example: (a) Counterfoil of Challan for payment of income-tax to a bank; (b) Counterfoil of pay-in-slip when money is deposited into bank, etc.

RULES FOR DEBIT AND CREDIT

The very word **Debit** is derived from the Latin word *debitum* or 'who owes', which reveals 'what is due or owed'. But, technically, to debit an account means to write on the left hand side of an account which is called the **Debit side**. It is written in short form 'Dr.'. Similarly, the word **'Credit'** is derived from the Latin word *creditum* (loan), from *credere* (to believe) or 'who trust' which reveals 'what is trusted'. But, to credit an account means to write on the right hand side of an account which is called the **'Credit side'**. In short, it is written as **'Cr.'**.

Practically, these two terms are the two sides of an account, the left hand side is called the **Debit side** and the right hand side is called the **Credit side**.

Rules

Whether a transaction should be recorded on the **Debit side** or **Credit side** of an account depends on the two following approaches:

1. **American Approach or Modern Approach, and**
2. **British Approach or Traditional Approach (also known as Double Entry System).**

1. AMERICAN APPROACH OR MODERN APPROACH

This is nothing but the Accounting Equation Approach. Thus the rules for **Debit** and **Credit** depend on the nature of an account. All accounts are classified under the following heads:

A. **Assets Accounts**
B. **Liabilities Account**
C. **Capital Account or Owners' Equity Account**
D. **Revenue or Income Account**
E. **Expenses or Losses Account.**

We know that an increase in one account means decrease in another account, or vice versa.

A. Assets Account

We know that assets directly help the business to earn revenue or profit. We also know that as a result of various accounting transactions, the value of assets are constantly changing. So the increase or decrease of such assets must be recorded systematically to know the real financial position of an enterprise. As soon as a transaction relating to asset occurs, we are to think whether the asset is coming i.e., increasing, or going, i.e., decreasing. If there is an increase in assets, such an increase must be recorded on the **Debit side** of the asset account; and if there is a reduction (i.e., lost/sold) in the amount of an asset, the same must be recorded on the **Credit side** of the asset account.

Example: Purchase a plant for cash Rs. 10,000.

In this case, since the plant is coming, it increases the value of the plant, it will appear in the **Debit side** of the Plant Account. Similarly, if any plant is sold, the same must appear in the **Credit side** of the Plant Account as the Plant is going out or is reduced in value.

Dr. **Assets Account** Cr.

Particulars	Amount	Particulars	Amount
	Rs.		Rs.
Increase in Assets		Decrease in Assets	

∴ **Increase in Assets = Debit** **Decrease in Assets = Credit**

The following illustration also will help us to understand the principle clearly:

Transactions	Accounts involved	Change		To	Do
		Increase	Decrease	Dr.	Cr.
(i) Purchase of Plant for Cash	Plant A/c	Plant	—	Dr.	—
	Cash A/c	—	Cash		Cr.
(ii) Sale of Furniture for Cash	Cash A/c	Cash A/c	—	Dr.	—
	Furniture A/c	—	Furniture A/c	—	Cr.
(iii) Received from Customers in Cash	Cash A/c	Cash A/c	—	Dr.	—
	Customers A/c	—	Customers A/c	—	Cr.

B. Liabilities Account

Needless to mention here that, like assets, liabilities of the business also are constantly changing. We know that if the liabilities of the business are increased, proprietor's claim also increases as the money **borrowed** increases proprietor's equity. In other words, if there is an increase in liabilities, such an increase will be recorded in the credit side of the liabilities account. At the same time, if the amount of liabilities are reduced, the same will appear on the debit side of the liabilities account.

Example: Bought goods on credit from Mr. X for Rs. 5,000.

Under the circumstances, it will appear on the **Credit side** of Creditors' Account as the liabilities to them are increased, i.e., the firm is owing to the creditors. But when the creditors will be paid, the same will appear in the **Debit side** of the Creditors' Account as the amount of borrowing is reduced.

Dr. **Liabilities Account** Cr.

Particulars	Amount	Particulars	Amount
	Rs.		Rs.
Decrease in Liabilities		Increase in Liabilities	

∴ **Decrease in Liabilities = Debit** **Increase in Liabilities = Credit**

C. Capital Account

Capital means amount/s which is contributed by the owner in the business which represents Proprietor's Account. Naturally, when he introduces money to the business his claims increase. Similarly, when the proprietor withdraws money from the business his claims reduce. Thus, when there is an increase in capital, the same will appear in the **Credit side** of Capital Account and when there is a decrease in capital (in case of drawings) the same will appear in the **Debit side** of the account.

Example: Further Capital is contributed to the business for Rs. 50,000.

In this case, liability of the firm is increased to the owner, so, the same will appear in the **Credit side** of Capital Account. But if the owner withdraws Rs. 10,000, the same will appear in the **Debit side** of the account as the liabilities of the firm decrease.

Dr. **Capital Account** Cr.

Particulars	Amount	Particulars	Amount
	Rs.		Rs.
Decrease in Capital		Increase in Capital	

∴ **Decrease in Capital = Debit** **Increase in Capital = Credit**

D. Revenue or Income or Profit

Increase in revenue will increase proprietor's claims to the business and will be credited. Similarly, decrease in revenue will reduce proprietor's claim and will be debited with the amount of decrease. In short, an increase in revenue/income/profit is recorded in the Credit side of the account as it increases capital.

On the other hand, if the same is reduced, it will appear in the **Debit side** of the account.

Example: Received interest for Rs. 1,000.

The same will appear in the Credit side of interest account as it is an income which increases the amount of capital. But if interest is paid to others, the same will appear in the Debit side of the interest account as it reduces the amount of capital.

In short, an **increase** in revenue will be recorded on the **Credit side**, and a **decrease** in revenue will appear in the **Debit side**.

Dr. **Revenue/Income Account** *Cr.*

Particulars	Amount Rs.	Particulars	Amount Rs.
Decrease in Revenue/Gains/Income		Increase in Revenue/Gains/Income	

∴ **Decrease in Revenue = Debit** **Increase in Revenue = Credit**

E. Expenses/Loss Account

An increase in expense means reduction in capital as it reduces the amount of profit. Similarly, decrease in expenses increases the amount of profit vis-a-vis capital. Thus, increase in expenses will appear in the **Debit side** of the account whereas decrease in expenses will appear in the **Credit side**, and vice versa in the opposite case.

Example: Paid Rent to landlord Rs. 5,000. Since Rent which is paid to the landlord is an expense, it will reduce the amount of profit as well as capital. Thus, it will appear in the **Debit side**, and vice versa in the opposite case.

Dr. **Expenses/Loss Account** *Cr.*

Particulars	Amount Rs.	Particulars	Amount Rs.
Increase in Expenses/Loss		Decrease in Expenses/Loss	

∴ **Increase in Expenses/Loss = Debit** **Decrease in Expenses/Loss = Credit**

To sum-up:

(i)	Increase in Assets	=	Dr.	(iv)	Decrease in Income or Profit	=	Dr.
	Decrease in Assets	=	Cr.		Increase in Income or Profit	=	Cr.
(ii)	Decrease in Liabilities	=	Dr.	(v)	Increase in Expenses or Loss	=	Dr.
	Increase in Liabilities	=	Cr.		Decrease in Expenses or Loss	=	Cr.
(iii)	Decrease in Capital	=	Dr.	(vi)	Increase in Stock/Goods	=	Dr.
	Increase in Capital	=	Cr.		Decrease in Stock/Goods	=	Cr.

Illustration 8

(a) The following accounts have been increased. State in which side they will be recorded. State also the nature of account:

(i) Plant
(ii) Debtors
(iii) Creditors
(iv) Rent received
(v) Insurance paid
(vi) Cash
(vii) Capital.

(b) The following accounts have been decreased. State on which side they will appear:

(i) Plant
(ii) Outstanding salary
(iii) Ram—a customer
(iv) Bank Overdraft
(v) Rent paid.

Solution

(a)	(i) Plant	= Assets	= Debit
	(ii) Debtors	= Assets	= Debit
	(iii) Creditors	= Liabilities	= Credit

	(iv)	Rent Received	= Income	= Credit
	(v)	Insurance Paid	= Expenses	= Debit
	(vi)	Cash	= Assets	= Debit
	(vii)	Capital	= Liabilities	= Credit
(b)	(i)	Plant	= Assets	= Credit
	(ii)	Outstanding Salary	= Liabilities	= Debit
	(iii)	Ram—a customer	= Assets	= Credit
	(iv)	Bank Overdraft	= Liabilities	= Debit
	(v)	Rent Paid	= Expenses	= Credit

2. BRITISH APPROACH OR TRADITIONAL APPROACH OR DOUBLE ENTRY SYSTEM

This system was invented by an Italian merchant named Luca Pacioli in 1494 in Venice. According to this system, every transaction has twofold aspects, i.e., one party giving the benefit and the other receiving the benefit. Also, ***every transaction is divided into two sides,* debit** and **credit**. In short, one account is to be debited and another account is to be credited for every transaction in order to have a complete record of the same. Therefore, every transaction affects two accounts in opposite direction. For example, if **goods** are sold to Mr. A on credit, the same will affect goods/sales account and A's account; and entries will be made in opposite direction in these two accounts. This system is called ***Double Entry System since it keeps records for every transaction in two accounts.*** Therefore, the basic principle, under this system, is that ***for every debit there must be a corresponding credit, and vice versa.***

Advantages of Double Entry System

(a) Under this system, both personal and impersonal accounts are to be opened in order to keep a complete record of business transactions.

(b) It reveals the result of the operations, i.e., profit or loss of the business, through Trading Account and Profit and Loss Account.

(c) It provides full information including properties and assets or losses and gains of the business.

(d) It also provides a check on the arithmetical accuracy with the help of a Trial Balance. Since every debit has a corresponding credit, **the total of debit balances must be equal to the total of the credit balances.**

(e) Financial position can be known under this system through the preparation of Balance Sheet.

(f) Since errors and frauds can be detected under this system, it reduces the chance of committing fraud.

(g) Comparisons between the two heads of accounts can be made which indicate the reasons for changing the net results of the business between two years.

Account

It has already been stated above that every transaction must be recorded in two accounts in the ledger. This is done after proper classification of all transactions. Complete records are also to be made by posting the transactions in different accounts which, in other words, supply all information to the management. Therefore, it may be stated that *Account* is the code or language of the accountant, and that is why it has been rightly said—**An Account is the code or language in which accountancy records and supplies information.**

An account has two sides, viz., **Debit—the left hand side, and Credit—the right hand side.**

Classification of Accounts

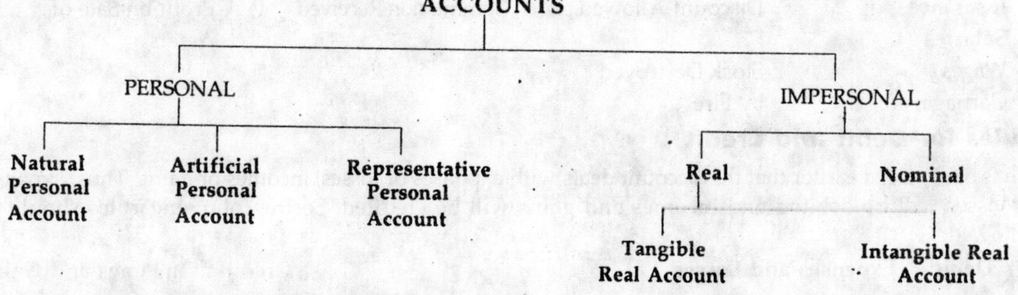

Personal Account

It deals with the accounts relating to persons and takes the following forms:

(i) *Natural Personal Account:* Natural person, i.e., human being, or the name of an individual e.g., Ram, Shyam, Jadu, etc.

(ii) *Artificial Personal Account:* Artificial persons do not have physical existence like human beings but they work like personal account, e.g., the name of any firm, club, association etc.,—State Bank of India, Calcutta University, Calcutta Police Academy, etc.

(iii) *Representative Personal Account:* They represent either a particular person or a group of persons, e.g., Outstanding Salaries, Rent, etc.

Rules for Debit and Credit

Whenever we deal with Personal Accounts, they either receive something or give something. When we sell goods to our customers on credit or we pay to our creditors, they are receiving goods/cash. So their accounts should be debited since they take the benefit or take something. Similarly, when we receive something from our customers, their accounts should be credited. Thus the standing rules come as:

∴ **Debit = the Receiver** **Credit = the Giver**

Impersonal Account

All the accounts other than personal accounts are called Impersonal Accounts. They relate to: (i) Properties and Assets, or (ii) Expenses and Losses, or Incomes and Gains, i.e., to: (a) Real Accounts, and (ii) Nominal Accounts.

(a) **Real Accounts** : It relates to properties and assets. It is, again, subdivided into (i) Tangible Real Accounts, and (ii) Intangible Real Accounts.

(i) **Tangible Real Accounts:** They are related to properties and assets, i.e., relate to those assets which exist. In other words, the assets which can be seen, touched, have physical existence, shape, form and size are known as Tangible Real Accounts, e.g., Plant and Machinery, Furniture and Fixtures, Land and Buildings, etc.

(ii) **Intangible Real Accounts:** They are intangibles in the sense that they do not have shape, form, size and also do not have any physical existence, e.g., Goodwill, Patent Rights, Trade-marks, etc.

Rules for Debit and Credit

It has been stated earlier that Real Accounts involve **Properties and Assets**. So these assets are either acquired or purchased or sold, i.e., either they come (in case of purchase) or they go (in case of **sales**).

On that basis we are to remember:

∴ **Debit = What comes in** **Credit = What goes out**

In short, as soon as the business will purchase any asset, this **same will be debited, and, when the assets** are sold, the same will be credited.

(b) **Nominal Accounts/Fictitious Accounts/Revenue Accounts:** Nominal accounts are those which do not have any physical existence like **Real** Accounts. These are always related to **Expenses and Losses and Incomes and Gains. All the** Nominal Accounts are closed at the end of the Financial Year by **transferring to either** Trading Account or Profit and Loss Account.

Example:

Expenses	**Losses**	**Incomes**	**Gains**
Rent	Bad Debts	Interest Received	Discount Received
Insurance	Discount Allowed	Commission Received	Profit on Sale of Assets
Salaries			
Wages	Stock Destroyed by Fire		
Carriage, etc.			

Rules for Debit and Credit

It has been stated earlier that this account deals with expenses or losses, incomes or gains. Thus, expenses or losses will be debited and incomes and gains will be credited. So the following rules should be followed:

∴ **Debit = Expenses and Losses** **Credit = Incomes and Gains**

Illustration 9

Classify the following accounts into Personal, Real and Nominal:

(a) Cash Account
(b) Wages Account
(c) Building Account
(d) Calcutta Tramways Co. A/c
(e) East Bengal Club Account
(f) Rent Account
(g) Capital Account
(h) Drawings Account
(i) Interest Account
(j) Trademark Account
(k) Dividend Account
(l) Land Account
(m) Goodwill Account
(n) Patent Account
(o) Bad Debts Account
(p) Bank Account
(q) Discount Allowed Account
(r) Interest Received Account
(s) Discount Received Account

Solution

(a) Cash Account = Real
(b) Wages Account = Nominal
(c) Building Account = Real
(d) Calcutta Tramways Co. A/c = Personal
(e) East Bengal Club Account = Personal
(f) Rent Account = Nominal
(g) Capital Account = Personal
(h) Drawings Account = Personal
(i) Interest Account = Nominal
(j) Trademark Account = Real
(k) Dividend Account = Nominal
(l) Land Account = Real
(m) Goodwill Account = Real
(n) Patent Account = Real
(o) Bad Debts Account = Nominal
(p) Bank Account = Real
(q) Discount Allowed Account = Nominal
(r) Interest Received Account = Nominal
(s) Discount Received Account = Nominal

Form of an Account:

Dr. *Cr.*

Date	Particulars	L.F.	Amount	Date	Particulars	L.F.	Amount

To Sum Up

Application of Golden Rule (i.e., Rules for ascertaining 'Debit' and 'Credit'):

Personal Account
- Debit = The Receiver/The person who takes the benefit.
- Credit = The Giver/The person who sacrifices the benefit

Real Account
- Debit = What comes in.
- Credit = What goes out.

Nominal Account
- Debit = All Expenses/Losses.
- Credit = All Incomes/Gains.

Besides the above, for ascertaining 'debit' and 'credit', the following principles should also carefully be applied:

1. **Increase in Asset** = Dr.
   Decrease in Asset = Cr.
2. **Increase in Liability** = Cr.
   Decrease in Liability = Dr.
3. **Increase in Expenses or Loss** = Dr.
   Decrease in Expenses or Loss = Cr.
4. **Increase in Income or Profit** = Cr.
   Decrease in Income or Profit = Dr.
5. **Increase in Capital** = Cr.
   Decrease in Capital = Dr.
6. **Increase in Stock/Goods** = Dr.
   Decrease in Stock/Goods = Cr.

Illustration 10

Find out the **Debit** and **Credit** from the following particulars (I) As per Traditional Approach, and (II) As per Modern Approach.

(i) Started business with a Capital.
(ii) Deposited cash into bank.
(iii) Bought goods for cash.
(iv) Bought goods from Mr. X on credit.
(v) Sold goods for cash.
(vi) Paid salary to Mr. Y.
(vii) Paid to Mr. X by cheque.
(viii) Paid rent out of personal cash.

Solution

I. As per Traditional Approach

The **Debit** and **Credit** may be ascertained as:

Before finding out the **Debit and Credit**, we are to follow the following four steps:

Step I : Find out the two accounts from the transactions.
Step II : Classify them into Personal, Real, or Nominal Account.
Step III : Write down the characteristics of the three Accounts.
Step IV : Ascertain **Debit or Credit** according to the **Golden Rule**.

Following the principle laid down above, we may prepare:

	Step I	Step II	Step III	Step IV
(i)	Cash A/c	Real	Comes in	Dr.
	Capital A/c	Personal	Giver	Cr.
(ii)	Bank A/c	Real	Comes in	Dr.
	Cash A/c	Real	Goes out	Cr.
(iii)	Goods/Purchase A/c	Real	Comes in	Dr.
	Cash A/c	Real	Goes out	Cr.
(iv)	Goods/Purchase A/c	Real	Comes in	Dr.
	Mr. X A/c	Personal	Giver	Cr.
(v)	Cash A/c	Real	Comes in	Dr.
	Goods/Sales A/c	Real	Goes out	Cr.
(vi)	Salary A/c	Nominal	Expenses	Dr.
	Cash A/c	Real	Goes out	Cr.
(vii)	Mr. X A/c	Personal	Receiver	Dr.
	Bank A/c	Real	Goes out	Cr.
(viii)	Rent A/c	Nominal	Expenses	Dr.
	Capital A/c	Personal	Giver	Cr.

II. Alternative Approach—As per Modern Approach

	Effect of Transaction	Account	To Do
(i)	Increase in Cash	Cash A/c	Dr.
	Increase in Capital	Capital A/c	Cr.
(ii)	Increase in Bank	Bank A/c	Dr.
	Decrease in Cash	Cash A/c	Cr.
(iii)	Increase in Stock	Purchase A/c	Dr.
	Decrease in Cash	Cash A/c	Cr.
(iv)	Increase in Stock	Purchase A/c	Dr.
	Increase in Liability	Mr. X A/c	Cr.
(v)	Increase in Cash	Cash A/c	Dr.
	Decrease in Stock	Sales A/c	Cr.
(vi)	Increase in Expenses	Salary A/c	Dr.
	Decrease in Cash	Cash A/c	Cr.
(vii)	Decrease in Liability	Mr. X A/c	Dr.
	Decrease in Bank	Bank A/c	Cr.
(viii)	Increase in Expenses	Rent A/c	Dr.
	Increase in Capital/Liability	Capital A/c	Cr.

ACCOUNTING EQUATION

Accounting Equation Approach, known as Modern Approach (also called Balance Sheet Equation), is **one on which the entire financial accounting depends.** We know that a firm requires resources to run a business unit. These resources are supplied by the proprietors to the firm. The resources which are possessed by the firms are called **assets** of the business. Needless to mention that the assets which are possessed by the firm has a simultaneous claim to these assets of the related proprietor. Thus, the equation is

Asset = Claims to Assets/Claims to Assets or Equities.

Thus, it can be rewritten as:

Assets = Equities

It must be mentioned here that some of the assets of the business may also be supplied by some other people known as creditors or outsiders. Thus, the indebtedness of the business to these people other than the proprietor is called **Liabilities** or **External Equities** or **External Liabilities** and the indebtedness of this business to its owner is called **Internal Equities** or **Internal Liabilities.**

Since there is a legal distinction between the claims of the owner or proprietors and those of the creditors/outsiders, the above equation may also be rewritten as:

Assets = Liabilities + Proprietorship

Now, before explaining further about the Accounting Equation, we are to **explain** the above three terms,— Assets, Liabilities, and Proprietorship:

(a) **Assets:** Practically, assets are the valuable things which are owned by a firm for its normal operational activities. These are acquired not for sale but for utilising the earning capacity of the business. Some of them are used for a long period of time. The assets are classified into various groups: viz., Fixed Assets, Current Assets, Liquid Assets, Fictitious Assets, etc.

Thus, the assets include:

Land and Building, Plant and Machinery, Furniture and Fixtures, Investment, Closing Stock, Sundry Debtors, Bills Receivable, Prepaid Expenses, Cash at Bank, Cash in hand etc., i.e., **which are owned by a firm.**

(b) **Liabilities:** Practically, liabilities are the claims of the creditors/outsiders and owners against the assets of the firms. In short, to whom the business is **liable to pay** is called liabilities. It may be in the form of outsider which is known as creditors, and when the claims of owners are considered, the same is known as Proprietors' Fund/Proprietors' Claim or Capital. The classification of liabilities have already been explained in **Chapter 20.**

Thus, the liabilities include:

Creditors (for goods, for expenses), Bills Payable, Bank Overdraft, Bank Loan, etc.

(c) **Capital or Proprietorship:** It has already been stated above that the owners of the business have claims against the assets of the business—the same is known as Capital or Proprietor's Fund (also called Internal Capital). Owners contribute capital towards the business and they earn profit. Sometimes a part of profit is transferred to Reserve Fund or any other fund which is also included in Proprietors' Fund.

Thus, it includes:

Capital + Reserves and Surplus + Net Profit

From the above discussion, it is quite clear that at each and every stage of operation **the assets of any unit must be equal to its equities** (i.e., internal and external) in terms of money. In short

Assets = Equities

To sum-up, the equations stand as

(i) **A = L + P** (where, A = Assets; L = External Equities)

(ii) **P = A – L** (where, P = Internal Equities/Capital)

or (iii) **L = A – P**

Method of Computation

From the discussion made so far it is absolutely clear that Assets, Liabilities, and Capital are the basic terms used in every business transaction and their respective relationship do not make any change (which is shown in above equations). Thus it is obvious that a change in one element must change the other, i.e., if there is a change in assets, there must be a corresponding change in liabilities also.

Consider the following examples one by one:

(i) Increase in Assets with corresponding Increase in Capital

Example: Started business with a capital of Rs. 50,000. It will take the following form:

Accounting Equation

Transactions	Assets	=	Liabilities	+	Capital
	A	=	L	+	P
Started business with Cash	50,000	=	–	+	50,000

At this point, the Balance Sheet takes the following form:

Balance Sheet

as at ....

Liabilities	Amount	Assets	Amount
	Rs.		Rs.
Capital	50,000	Cash	50,000
Liabilities	—	Other Assets	—
	50,000		50,000

(ii) Increase in Assets with corresponding Increase in Liabilities

Example : Purchased goods on credit for Rs. 10,000.

It will increase the assets through the increase of goods/stocks and, similarly, increase the amount of liabilities, viz., creditors.

Thus, it will take the following form:

Transactions	Assets	=	Liabilities	+	Capital
	Rs.		Rs.		Rs.
Started business with Cash Rs. 50,000	50,000	=	—	+	50,000
	50,000	=	—		50,000
Purchased goods on credit for Rs. 10,000	+ 10,000	=	+ 10,000	+	—
New Equation	60,000	=	10,000	+	50,000

(iii) Increase in Assets with corresponding Decrease in Assets

Example: Bought a plant for cash Rs. 20,000.

It will increase the asset by increasing the plant and also will decrease the amount of assets, viz., Cash.

Thus, it will stand as:

Transactions	Assets	=	Liabilities	+	Capital
	Rs.		Rs.		Rs.
Started business with Capital in Cash Rs. 50,000	50,000	=	—	+	50,000
	50,000	=	—		50,000
Purchased goods on credit for Rs. 10,000	+ 10,000	=	+ 10,000	+	—
	60,000	=	10,000		50,000
Bought a Plant for cash Rs. 20,000	+ 20,000 – 20,000		—	+	—
New Equation	60,000	=	10,000	+	50,000

(iv) Decrease in Assets with corresponding Decrease in Liabilities

Example: Paid to creditors Rs. 5,000.

As soon as the creditors are paid, both assets and liabilities are reduced. It will be deducted from Assets (since cash is going out) and also will be deducted from Creditors (since amount of creditors is reduced).

Thus, it takes the following form:

Transactions	Assets	=	Liabilities	+	Capital
	Rs.		Rs.		Rs.
Previous Equation	60,000	=	10,000	+	50,000
Paid to Creditors	(–) 5,000	=	(–) 5,000	+	—
New Equation	55,000	=	5,000	+	50,000

(v) Increase and Decrease in Liabilities

Example: A bill drawn by a creditor for Rs. 8,000 accepted for 1 month.

When a bill is drawn up by a creditor and the same is accepted by a Debtor, Creditors' account is reduced i.e., a reduction in liability. But when a new bill is accepted, liability is increased.

Thus, it will be represented as:

Transactions	Assets Rs.	=	Liabilities Rs.	+	Capital Rs.
Previous Equation	55,000	=	5,000	+	50,000
Bill accepted by a Creditor for Rs. 8,000	—	=	8,000	+	—
	—		(–) 8,000		—
New Equation	55,000	=	5,000	+	50,000

(vi) Decrease in Liabilities with corresponding Increase in Capital

Example: Creditors are paid by issuing equity shares amounting to Rs. 3,000 only.

Under the circumstances, creditors' account will be reduced and, at the same time, capital account will be increased.

Thus, the position is:

Transactions	Assets Rs.	=	Liabilities Rs.	+	Capital Rs.
Previous Equation	55,000	=	5,000	+	50,000
Creditors are paid by issuing equity shares for Rs. 3,000	—	=	(–) 3,000	+	3,000
New Equation	55,000	=	2,000	+	53,000

Consider the following illustration:

Illustration 11

Miss Sampa starts a business under the name Sampa and Co. The details of the transactions are presented:

		Rs.
1.	Invested capital in her firm	10,000
2.	Purchased goods on credit from B. Das	1,000
4.	Bought Furniture for Cash	3,000
7.	Purchased goods for Cash	2,000
10.	Sold goods for Cash (Cost Rs. 3,000 + Profit Rs. 1,000)	4,000
16.	Paid to B. Das in Cash	500
18.	Received from A. Sen	1,000
22.	Paid Salary	500
30.	Received Interest	400

Solution

In the books of
Miss Sampa
Effect of Transactions on Assets, Liabilities and Capital

No.	*Transactions*		*Assets* A Rs.	=	*Liabilities* L Rs.	+	*Capital* P Rs.
1.	Started business with Cash Rs. 10,000		10,000	=	0	+	10,000
2.	Purchased goods on Credit from B. Das Rs. 1,000		1,000	=	1,000	+	0
	New Equation		11,000	=	1,000	+	10,000
4.	Bought Furniture for Cash Rs. 3,000	+	3,000				
		–	3,000	=	0	+	0
	New Equation		11,000	=	1,000	+	10,000
7.	Purchased goods for Cash Rs. 2,000	+	2,000				
		–	2,000	=	0	+	0
			11,000	=	1,000	+	10,000

Contd.

			Rs.		Rs.		Rs.
10.	Sold goods for Cash Rs. 4,000 (Cost Rs. 3,000 + Profit Rs. 1,000)		+ 4,000 − 3,000	=	0	+	1,000
		New Equation	12,000	=	1,000	+	11,000
16.	Paid to B. Das Rs. 500		− 500	=	−500		
		New Equation	11,500	=	500	+	11,000
18.	Received from A. Sen Rs. 1,000		+ 1,000 − 1,000	=	0	+	0
		New Equation	11,500	=	500	+	11,000
22.	Paid Salary Rs. 500		− 500	=	0	−	− 500
		New Equation	11,000	=	500	+	10,500
30.	Received Interest Rs. 400		+ 400	=	0	+	400
		New Equation	11,400	=	500	+	10,900

CASH AND ACCRUAL BASIS OF ACCOUNTING

We know that one of the most significant functions of the accountants is to supply information to the proprietor—relating to profit earned by a business enterprise for a particular period. Needless to say that the term 'profit' is used by the economists and the general public in different senses. However, in accounting, the term Profit means and includes 'Net Income' or 'Net Profit'. ***Profit denotes an increase in assets or decrease in liability or increase in owner's equity or capital,*** which results from the business operations. That is, it is measured by matching; setting-off expense against revenue.

Usually, there are two accounting methods by which profit or income is measured in accounts : (1) **Cash Basis**, or (2) **Accrual** or **Mercantile Basis.**

1. Cash Basis of Accounting

Under this method, all incomes are considered to be earned only when they are actually received in Cash. Similarly, expenses are deemed to be incurred only when they are actually paid in Cash. As such, the difference between the total incomes so received in cash and the total expenses so paid in cash, i.e., actual outlay of cash, represents the profit or loss of a firm for a particular accounting period. Needless to say that all the adjustments, viz., outstanding and accrued income or income received in advance, are not considered at all—under this method of accounting.

Practical Applications

This method is particularly followed by individuals like Doctors, Lawyers, Auditors, Engineers, Brokers, i.e., professional people, and some small traders.

Advantages and Disadvantages

The only advantage of this method of accounting is that it is very simple since it does not require adjustment entries on periodical account at closing date. But the great disadvantages is that it fails to express profit or loss accurately since it does not incorporate the necessary adjustments. At the same time, this method is found unsuitable where there are numerous transactions.

Illustration 12

Dr. S. K. Dasgupta furnishes the following particulars for the year ended 31st Dec. 2008 :

	Rs.
Fees received in cash in 2008	80,000
Rent of chamber paid in 2008	6,000
Salary paid to staff in 2008	12,000
Magazine and Journal for 2008	2,000
Subscription to Medical Association paid in 2008	1,000
Conveyance paid in 2008	2,000
Miscellaneous Expenses (including Stationery) paid in 2008	800

Additional Information

(i) Fees include Rs. 5,000 in respect of 2007 and Rs. 3,000 was due but not yet received for 2008.

(ii) Chamber rent includes Rs. 2,000 in respect of 2007 and outstanding rent, i.e., not yet paid for 2008, Rs. 1,000.

(iii) Subscription to Medical Association includes Rs. 400, in respect of 2009, i.e., paid in advance.

Compute his net income for the year 2008, under cash basis of accounting.

Solution

Dr. S. K. Dasgupta
Statement of Income : Under Cash Basis
for the year ended 31st Dec. 2008

		Rs.	Rs.
	Fees received in 2008		80,000
Less :	*Expenses in 2008*		
	Rent of chamber	6,000	
	Salary paid to staff	12,000	
	Magazine and Journal	2,000	
	Subscription to Medical Association	1,000	
	Conveyance paid	2,000	
	Miscellaneous expenses	800	23,800
	Net income for the year		56,200

2. Accrual or Mercantile Basis of Accounting

Under this method, Incomes are recorded or credited to the period in which they are earned irrespective of the fact that whether the same has actually been received or not. Similarly, expenses are charged to the period in which they relate, irrespective of the fact that they have actually been paid or not. As such, ***the difference between the total income earned and the total expenses incurred represents the profits or loss for the period.*** Under this basis all adjustments, i.e., outstanding and prepaid expenses, accrued income, etc. are to be adjusted accordingly for ascertaining the correct result of the operation.

Practical Application

This method is actually followed everywhere. **The accrual basis is a generally accepted accounting convention in business accounting**—McCuller Daniker. It is commonly known as Mercantile System of Accounting.

Advantages

The most significant advantage of this system of accounting is that income which is measured by a firm under this method is measured accurately. That is, **Profit and Loss Account and Balance Sheet exhibit a true and fair view of the state of affairs.**

Illustration 13

From the data contained in the previous illustration, ascertain the income under accrual basis of accounting.

Solution

Dr. S. K. Dasgupta
Statement of Income : Under Accrual Basis
for the year ended 31st Dec. 2008

		Rs.	Rs.	Rs.
	Fees Received in 2008		80,000	
Add :	Accrued fees for 2008		3,000	
			83,000	
Less :	Fees for 2007		5,000	78,000
Less :	*Expenses*			
	Rent paid	6,000		
Add :	Outstanding for 2008	1,000		
		7,000		
Less :	For 2007	2,000		
			5,000	
	Salary paid		12,000	
	Magazine & Journal		2,000	
	Subscription to Medical Association	1,000		
Less :	Prepaid	400		
			600	
	Conveyance paid		2,000	
	Miscellaneous Expenses		800	22,400
	Net Income for the year			55,600

There is another basis of accounting which is known as **Mixed Basis or Hybrid Basis.**

Mixed or Hybrid Basis of Accounting

Under this method, ***revenues are accounted for Cash Basis, whereas expenses for Accrual Basis.*** This basis of accounting is not widely used in actual practice since it fails to measure accurate income.

Illustration 14

From data contained in the previous illustration, ascertain the income under Mixed Basis of Accounting.

Solution

Dr. S. K. Dasgupta
Statement of Income : Under Mixed Basis
for the year ended 31st Dec. 2008

		Rs.	Rs.	Rs.
	Fees Received in 2008			80,000
Less :	Expenses			
	Rent paid	6,000		
Add :	Outstanding for 2008	1,000		
		7,000		
Less :	For 2007	2,000		
			5,000	
	Salary paid		12,000	
	Magazine & Journal		2,000	
	Subscription to Medical Association	1,000		
Less :	Prepaid	400		
			600	
	Conveyance paid		2,000	
	Miscellaneous expenses		800	22,400
	Net income for the year			57,600

Differences between Cash Basis and Accrual Basis of Accounting

Differences between the Cash Basis of Accounting and Accrual Basis of Accounting, may be presented as under :

No.	Points of Difference	Cash Basis	Accrual Basis
1.	*Users*	Professional people ascertain their profit or loss under Cash Basis, or some institutions with service motive.	A business unit with profit motive ascertains profit or loss under Accrual Basis.
2.	*Nature of transactions*	Units with mostly cash transactions prefer this basis.	Units with Cash and Credit transactions prefer this basis.
3.	*Accurate Result*	Accurate profit or loss cannot actually be ascertained under this basis.	Profit or loss can be ascertained correctly, if this basis is followed.
4.	*Size of the Accounting Unit*	Professional people, small ventures of temporary nature, some non-trading organisations prefer to use this method due to its simplicity.	Large-scale organisations (i.e., going concern with profit motive) where there is a credit transaction and non-trading concerns prefer to use this basis.
5.	*Technicality*	This basis does not require any technical knowledge.	This basis is highly technical since it involves the adjustments of accounts for preparing final accounts.
6.	*True and Fair view*	This basis does not help to ascertain profit as true and fair view of state of affairs is not available.	This basis helps to ascertain true and fair view of profit and true state of affairs is available.

Conversion of Cash Basis of Accounting into Accrual Basis

When accounting is done under Cash Basis and the final accounts are prepared, the same can be converted into Accrual Basis from the beginning of the next financial period. The following procedure should be carefully observed for the purpose:

(a) At first ascertain the amount of outstanding and prepaid expenses and, at the same time, accrued incomes and income received in advance.

(b) Thereafter, following journal entries should be made :

(i) Accrued Income A/c Dr.
Prepaid Expenses A/c Dr.
To Profit and Loss Adjustment A/c
(The entry made for bringing into account the accrued income, prepaid expenses for converting the Cash Basis of Accounting into Accrual Basis.)

(ii) Profit and Loss Adjustment A/c Dr.
To Income Received in Advance A/c
To Outstanding Expenses A/c
(The entry made for bringing into account the income and received in advance and outstanding expenses for converting the Cash Basis of Accounting into Accrual Basis.)

(iii) If there is a profit as a result of the above adjustment
Profit and Loss Adjustment A/c Dr.
To Capital A/c
(Profit transferred to capital accounts as a result of conversion from Cash Basis to Accrual Basis.)

If there is a loss as a result of the above adjustment
Capital A/c Dr.
To Profit and Loss Adjustment A/c
(Loss transferred to Capital Account as a result of conversion from Cash Basis to Accrual Basis).

Illustration 15

Good and Bad are partners sharing profits and losses in the ratio of 2 : 1. They prepare their accounts on Cash Basis. They earned a profit of Rs. 50,000 in the year 2012, which was transferred to their Capital Accounts. There were, however, the following accruals and deferrals on 31st December 2012, when they decided to convert the Cash Basis of Accounting in to Accrual Basis :

		Rs.
Outstanding expenses	on 31.12.2012	1,000
Prepaid expenses	on 31.12.2012	400
Outstanding fees	on 31.12.2012	2,000
Fees received in advance	on 31.12.2012	500

Show the entry (Narrations are not required).

Solution

Journal (Without Narration)

Date	Particulars		L.F.	Debit	Credit
				Rs.	Rs.
2012	Outstanding Fees A/c	Dr.		2,000	
Dec. 31	Prepaid Expenses A/c	Dr.		400	
	To Profit and Loss Adjustment A/c				2,400
	Profit and Loss Adjustment A/c	Dr.		1,500	
	To Outstanding Expenses A/c				1,000
	To Fees Received in Advance A/c				500
	Profit and Loss Adjustment A/c	Dr.		900	
	To Good's Capital A/c				600
	To Bad's Capital A/c				300

JOURNAL (Book of Original Entry)

Definition

In order to provide a chronological record of business transactions where each transaction is set down with relevant supplementary information, it becomes necessary to have some preliminary book. This book is known as 'journal', i.e., the process of recording transactions is called 'journal'. Various ledger accounts are recorded and/or posted from this book. That is why journal is called the **'book of original or prime entry'** and the ledger 'the book of final entry'.

Journal is a subsidiary book which provides chronological records and the ledger is a main book which provides analytical records. As transactions are recorded first in the journal, it is also called Book of First Entry, Preliminary Entry or Original Entry. It is also called a Subsidiary Book as it serves the Principal Book—Ledger.

Classification of Journal

Journal is divided into (a) General Journal and (b) Special Journal.

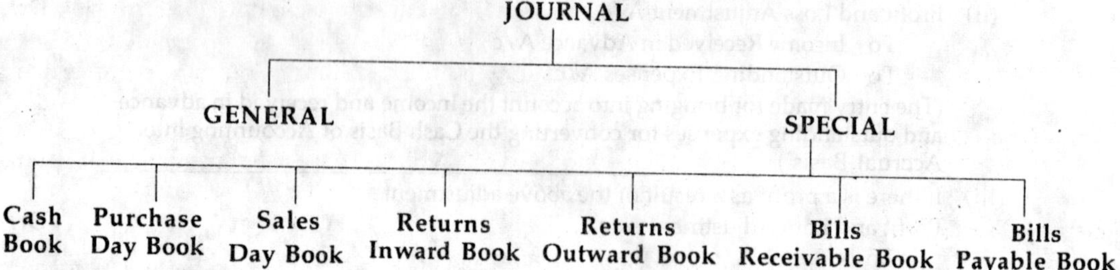

General Journal

It is easier type of Journal which keeps records of transactions. The outline of general journal is given:

Specimen of a Journal

Journal

Date	Particulars	L.F.	Amount	
			Debit	Credit

Explanation

(i) **Date Column** : This column contains the date of recording the transaction. It is subdivided into year, month and date; year is written at the top, then month and then the date.

(ii) **Particulars Column** : This column is the Explanation column or Description column. This column contains the account which is debited and the account which is credited using debit as 'Dr.' and credit as 'Cr.' But the account to be credited is written on the next line in this column, leaving some space on the left-hand side using the word 'To' prefixed. After recording the accounts debited or credited, a short explanation of the transaction is written on the next line in this column which is known as 'Narration'.

(iii) **L.F. (Ledger Folio) Column** : This column contains the page number of the ledger.

(iv) **Amount Column** : There must be two 'Amount Columns'—one for the debit and the other for the credit. The debit amount is entered on the column headed 'Dr.' amount just opposite the debit entry, whereas the credit amount is entered on the column headed 'Cr.' Amount, just opposite the credit entry.

Functions of Journal

The functions/objects/purposes or utilities of a journal are:

(a) ***Analytical Functions*** : Each transaction affects ledger accounts and the amount which is debited or credited are first analysed into debit or credit in the journal.

(b) ***Recording Functions*** : Journal is also supported by narration. Any reference of a transaction can be obtained from the journal with the help of narration.

(c) ***Historical Functions*** : Some journal entries are recorded in the books as soon as they occur in a chronological way, i.e., a journal provides a chronological record or diary of the transactions.

Advantages of Journal

The following advantages can be obtained from a journal:

(a) *Chronological record* : Journal is the chronological record of all transactions in a firm. Thus, it provides a date-wise information to us.

(b) *Reducing the possibility of errors* : As soon as a transaction takes place, it is debited and credited side by side here which helps us to compare whether the total of both sides are equal or not.

(c) *Narration* : Journal is always supported by narration which helps us to know the date of the transaction and the transaction itself, i.e., the history of each transaction can be known.

(d) *Minimising errors of omission* : Errors of omission are minimised if transactions are recorded in a journal.

(e) *Helps to prepare final accounts* : From journal we prepare ledger, and from ledger we prepare a Trial Balance and from a Trial Balance we prepare the final account of a firm. Thus, journal helps to prepare the final accounts.

Special Journals

It is subdivided into Cash Book, Day Book, Sales Day Book, Returns Inwards Book, Returns Outwards Book, Bills Receivable Book and Bills Payable Book. These books are called Subsidiary Books (These are discussed in a subsequent chapter).

Why Journal or Day Book is called Original Book?

The word 'original' is very significant here. Because, as soon as a transaction occurs in financial accounting, the same is recorded at first in the journal systematically. **Since the transactions are recorded at first in the journal it is called the Original Book.** From journal, the transaction are posted into the ledger chronologically after a certain period. With the help of journal and ledger various accounting information can be obtained which help decision-making in financial affairs. Journal is the original source of accounting infor-mation. Moreover, from journal we can prepare ledger, from ledger we can prepare a Trial Balance and, consequently, from a Trial Balance we can prepare the Final Accounts'—the ultimate requirement of the concern. That is why journal is called the Original Book.

Subdivisions of Journal

Since there are numerous transactions in a business unit, it becomes necessary to use a number of subsidiary journals instead of a single journal although one journal is used for maintaining one particular class of transaction. That is why, in all business houses, a number of original entries for recording the different types of transactions are used.

Cash Book is the most important Day Book. It contains all cash transactions.

Cash Book contains all cash transactions. Therefore, the following subsidiary books are maintained for credit and other types of transactions:

1. **Purchases Day Book** (meant for recording all credit purchases of goods).
2. **Sales Day Books** (meant for recording all credit sales of goods).
3. **Returns Inwards Book** (meant for recording goods returned by the customers).
4. **Returns Outwards Book** (meant for recording goods returned to suppliers).
5. **Bills Receivable Book** (meant for recording all transactions relating to Bills Receivable).
6. **Bills Payable Book** (meant for recording all transactions relating to Bills Payable).
7. **Cash Book** (meant for recording all Cash transactions).

Subdivisions of Journal—Advantages

The following advantages may be derived from the subdivisions of a journal:

(i) Subdivision of journal helps us to record the special type of journal with the help of specialised people. Because, it is not always possible for an ordinary accountant to record all types of transactions in the journal.

(ii) Since all cash transactions are recorded in cash book, it becomes very helpful on the part of the accountant to maintain records.

(iii) Since all transactions are recorded in the journal at first, it becomes very helpful to post the transactions in the ledger chronologically.

(iv) We know that there occurs a large number of transactions in a firm and, since there are different ledgers for different purposes, no one ledger becomes voluminous—this helps the accountant to detect the errors, if any.

(v) Since all the transactions are recorded on the basis of Double Entry Principle, no difficulty will arise on the part of the accountant to record the same.

Subdivisions of Journal—Necessities

It is needless to mention here that the necessities of subdivisions of journal actually depends upon the volume and nature of the transactions of the firm. In other words, in a small business enterprise, where transactions are few in number, it is sufficient to maintain records with the help of journal and ledger. But in the case of a big/large business, it is not enough in order to maintaining records properly with the help of journal and ledger. Because, it is impossible to handle them. That is why the journal is subdivided. The necessities for this purpose are:

(i) ***As a result of increased number of transactions:*** : If there are large number of transactions and they are to be recorded in the journal, it would not be possible to record them by one employee. The same is possible only when journals are subdivided as per requirement.

(ii) ***As a result of increased volume of journal*** : It would not be possible to move that voluminous journal if all the transactions are recorded.

(iii) ***Possibility of committing errors*** : It is needless to say that if all the transactions are recorded in a journal, there will be the possibility of maximum errors.

(iv) ***Special transactions to be posted in a separate ledger*** : If the summary of special types of transactions are recorded from a special journal, then, after proper subdivision of journal, the same may be well-placed.

(v) ***Special information available from special transactions.*** : The special types of transactions are recorded in each type of transaction if journals are subdivided according to the needs of the users.

The following illustration will help us to understand better the principle:

Illustration 16

2011 Miss Piu Sen:

Jan. 1 Started business with a capital of Rs. 10,000
2 Bought goods for Cash Rs. 3,000
4 Sold goods to Mr. X on credit Rs. 8,000
5 Paid salaries to the staff Rs. 4,000
6 Purchased a plant for cash Rs. 3,000
7 Paid Advertisement Rs. 1,000

Show the entries.

Solution

In the books of Miss Piu Sen
Journal

Date	*Particulars*		*L.F.*	*Debit*	*Credit*
2011				Rs.	Rs.
Jan. 1	Cash A/c	Dr.		10,000	
	To Capital				10,000
	(Business started with a capital of Rs. 10,000)				
2	Purchase A/c	Dr.		3,000	
	To Cash A/c				3,000
	(Goods purchased for cash)				
4	Mr. X A/c	Dr.		8,000	
	To Sales A/c				8,000
	(Goods sold to Mr. X on credit)				
5	Salaries A/c	Dr.		4,000	
	To Cash A/c				4,000
	(Salaries paid)				
6	Plant A/ct	Dr.		3,000	
	To Cash A/c				3,000
	(Plant purchased for cash)				

Contd.

				Rs.	Rs.
7	Advertisement A/c To Cash A/c (Advertisement paid)	Dr.		1,000	1,000

So long we have explained some basic theoretical aspects of Journal. In the present study we will highlight only the recording aspect of Journal and Ledger.

Before explaining further about the journal and ledger we are to explain the following:

Entry = The record of a transaction in a journal is called an Entry.

There are two types of entry:

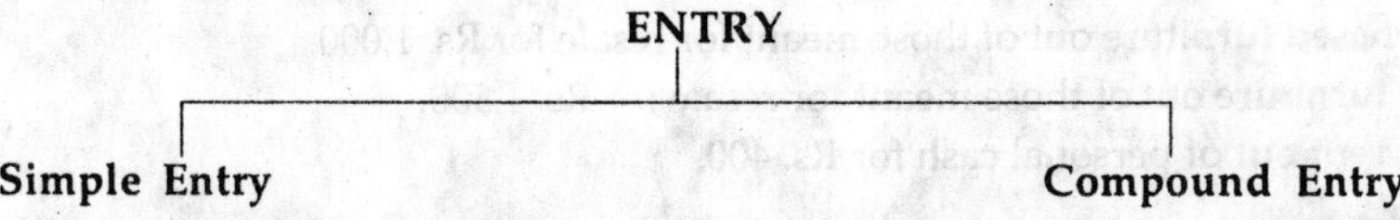

Simple Entry : When there are only two accounts that arise from a transaction, the same is known as Simple Entry, e.g., Started business with a capital of Rs. 5,000. Here, the entry being:

		Rs.	Rs.
Cash A/c	Dr.	5,000	
To Capital A/c			5,000

Compound Entry : Where there are more than two accounts that arise from a transaction the same is known as Compound Entry, e.g., Received cash from Mr. X Rs. 950 in full settlement of Rs. 1,000. Here, the entry being:

		Rs.	Rs.
Cash A/c	Dr.	950	
Discount Allowed A/c		50	
To X A/c			1,000

Recording of Transactions in a Journal

In the preceding pages we have highlighted journal and its subdivisions in details. In the present study, however, we will highlight how the transactions are recorded in journal.

We know that as soon as a transaction takes place, the same is immediately recorded in the journal chronologically. The two accounts of every transaction should be determined first, i.e., which account will be debited and which account will be credited as per Double Entry System. It is better to follow the under-mentioned principles for recording transactions in a journal:

Step I : At first, write the date of the transaction in the left-hand side under the column 'Date'.

Step II : Ascertain the **Debit** and **Credit** from the transaction.

Step III : Write the Debit amount in 'Dr.' amount column and Credit amount in 'Cr.' amount column.

Step IV : Write the page number of the account in L.F. column.

Step V : Write the short/brief history of the transaction, i.e., Narration, under the journal.

The details of the column and their explanation have already been explained in the previous chapter while discussing journal.

Illustration 17

Journalise the following transactions as per (a) American Approach, and (b) as per British Approach:

(i) Started business with a capital of Rs. 7,500.

(ii) Opened a bank account with State Bank of India for Rs. 2,000.

(iii) Paid commission to X for Rs. 300.

(iv) Purchased goods from K and Co. for cash Rs. 1,000.

(v) Purchased goods from Mr. Z for Rs. 2,000.

(vi) Goods returned to Mr. Z for Rs. 500.

(vii) Paid to Mr. Z in full settlement of Rs. 1,400.

(viii) Received interest on Investments for Rs. 400.
(ix) Paid rent to landlord Mr. Y for Rs. 500.
(x) Withdrew cash for household expenses amounting to Rs. 600.
(xi) Sold goods to Mr. L for cash Rs. 2,500.
(xii) Sold goods to Mr. D on credit for Rs. 1,000.
(xiii) Goods returned by Mr. D for Rs. 250.
(xiv) Received cash from Mr. D in full settlement for Rs. 700.
(xv) Paid carriage on goods purchased for Rs. 350.
(xvi) Paid carriage on goods sold for Rs. 800.
(xvii) Purchased furniture for office decoration for cash amounted Rs. 1,000.
(xviii) Purchased furniture out of those meant for resale for Rs. 1,000.
(xix) Sold furniture out of those meant for resale for Rs. 1,500.
(xx) Paid rent out of personal cash for Rs. 400.

Solution

(a) As per American Approach

Before preparing 'Journal', let us examine the double entry concept stated above:

	Effect of Transactions	To Do	
(i)	Increase in Cash	Cash A/c	Dr.
	Increase in Capital	Capital A/c	Cr.
(ii)	Increase in Bank	Bank A/c	Dr.
	Decrease in Cash	Cash A/c	Cr.
(iii)	Increase in Expenses	Commission A/c	Dr.
	Decrease in Cash	Cash A/c	Cr.
(iv)	Increase in Stock	Purchase A/c	Dr.
	Decrease in Cash	Cash A/c	Cr.
(v)	Increase in Stock	Purchase A/c	Dr.
	Increase in Liability	Z A/c	Cr.
(vi)	Decrease in Liability	Z A/c	Dr.
	Decrease in Stock	Returns Outwards A/c	Cr.
(vii)	Decrease in Liability	Z A/c	Dr.
	Decrease in Cash	Cash A/c	Cr.
(viii)	Increase in Cash	Cash A/c	Dr.
	Increase in Income	Interest A/c	Cr.
(ix)	Increase in Expenses	Rent A/c	Dr.
	Decrease in Cash	Cash A/c	Cr.
(x)	Decrease in Liability	Drawing A/c	Dr.
	Decrease in Cash	Cash A/c	Cr.
(xi)	Increase in Cash	Cash A/c	Dr.
	Decrease in Stock	Sales A/c	Cr.
(xii)	Increase in Asset (i.e., Debtors)	D A/c	Dr.
	Decrease in Stock	Sales A/c	Cr.
(xiii)	Increase in Stock	Returns Inwards A/c	Dr.
	Decrease in Asset (i.e., Owing by Creditors)	D A/c	Cr.
* (xiv)	Increase in Cash	Cash A/c	Dr.
	Decrease in Asset	D A/c	Cr.
(xv)	Increase in Expenses	Carriage Inwards A/c	Dr.
	Decrease in Cash	Cash A/c	Cr.
(xvi)	Increase in Expenses	Carriage Outwards A/c	Dr.
	Decrease in Cash	Cash A/c	Cr.
(xvii)	Increase in Furniture	Furniture A/c	Dr.
	Decrease in Cash	Cash A/c	Cr.
(xviii)	Increase in Cash	Cash A/c	Dr.
	Decrease in Stock	Sales A/c	Cr.

* Question of discount received and allowed are not considered here temporarily

(xix)	Increase in Cash	Cash A/c	Dr.
	Decrease in Stock	Sales A/c	Cr.
(xx)	Increase in Expenses	Rent A/c	Dr.
	Increase in Capital	Capital A/c	Cr.

(b) **As per British Approach**

Journal can also be recorded with the help of the following:

Step I : Find out the two accounts from the transaction.
Step II : Classify them into Personal, Real or Nominal Accounts.
Step III : Write down the characteristics of the three accounts.
Step IV : Ascertain debit or credit according to the Golden Rule.

Consider the first five transactions stated above:

	Step I	Step II	Step III	Step IV
(i)	Cash A/c	Real	Comes in	Dr.
	Capital A/c	Personal	Giver	Cr.
(ii)	Bank A/c	Real	Comes in	Dr.
	Cash A/c	Real	Goes out	Cr.
(iii)	Commission A/c	Nominal	Expenses	Dr.
	Cash A/c	Real	Goes out	Cr.
(iv)	Goods/Purchase A/c	Real	Comes in	Dr.
	Cash	Real	Goes out	Cr.
(v)	Goods/Purchase A/c	Real	Comes in	Dr.
	Z A/c	Personal	Giver	Cr.

Note : The students may follow any method they prefer. Alternative approach is comparatively easy.

In the books of ....
Journal

Date	Particulars		L.F.	Debit Rs.	Credit Rs.
	(i) Cash A/c	Dr.		7,500	
	To Capital A/c				7,500
	(Cash taken to start business)				
	(ii) Bank A/c	Dr.		2,000	
	To Cash A/c				2,000
	(Cash deposited into Bank)				
	(iii) Commission A/c	Dr.		300	
	To Cash A/c				300
	(Commission paid in Cash)				
	(iv) Purchase A/c	Dr.		1,000	
	To Cash A/c				1,000
	(Goods purchased from K and Co. for cash)				
	(v) Purchase A/c	Dr.		2,000	
	To Z A/c				2,000
	(Goods purchased from Z on credit)				
	(vi) Z A/c	Dr.		500	
	To Returns Outward A/c				500
	(Goods returned to Z)				
	(vii) Z A/c	Dr.		1,500	
	To Cash A/c				1,400
	To Discount Received A/c				100
	(Cash paid to Z and received discount)				
	(viii) Cash A/c	Dr.		400	
	To Interest on Investment A/c				400
	(Interest received in cash)				
	(ix) Rent A/c	Dr.		500	
	To Cash A/c				500
	(Rent paid in cash)				
	(x) Drawing A/c	Dr.		600	
	To Cash A/c				600
	(Cash withdrawn for household expenses)				

Contd.

	Particulars		Rs.	Rs.
(xi)	Cash A/c To Sales A/c (Goods sold to L for cash)	Dr.	2,500	2,500
(xii)	D A/c To Sales A/c (Goods sold to D on credit)	Dr.	1,000	1,000
(xiii)	Returns Inwards A/c To D A/c (Goods returned by D)	Dr.	250	250
(xiv)	Cash A/c Discount Allowed A/c To D A/c (Cash received from D and allowed him discount)	Dr. Dr.	700 50	750
(xv)	Carriage Inwards A/c To Cash A/c (Carriage paid for goods purchased)	Dr.	350	350
(xvi)	Carriage Outwards A/c To Cash A/c (Carriage paid for goods Sold)	Dr.	800	800
(xvii)	Furniture A/c To Cash A/c (Furniture purchased for cash)	Dr.	1,000	1,000
(xviii)	Purchase A/c To Cash A/c (Furniture purchased for resale)	Dr.	1,000	1,000
(xix)	Cash A/c To Sales A/c (Furniture out of those meant for resale sold for cash)	Dr.	1,500	1,500
(xx)	Rent A/c To Capital A/c (Rent paid out of personal cash)	Dr.	400	400

Compound Journal

From a single transaction—when one account is debited and the other account is credited—it is known as Simple Journal. But when the transaction requires more than one debit or more than one credit, or both, the same is known as Compound Journal. Usually, the compound journal is used only when the transaction takes place on the same day and there are at least more than two accounts. In fact, it is the combination of two or more simple journals.

The following illustration will make the principle clear:

Illustration 18

2011 Jan. Started business with a capital of:
1 Cash Rs. 3,000, Bank Rs. 5,000, and Plant Rs. 10,000
8 Sold goods for cash Rs. 1,000 and credit Rs. 7,000 to Mr. X
10 Received Cash from Mr. X Rs. 6,500 in full settlement.

Solution **In the books of ....**

Journal

Date	*Particulars*		*L.F.*	*Debit*	*Credit*
2011				Rs.	Rs.
Jan. 1	Cash A/c Bank A/c Plant A/c To Capital A/c (Business started with a capital of Rs. 18,000)	Dr. Dr. Dr.		3,000 5,000 10,000	18,000
8	Cash A/c X A/c To Sales A/c Goods sold for cash and credit to X)	Dr. Dr.		1,000 7,000	8,000
10	Cash A/c Discount Allowed A/c To X A/c (Received cash from Mr. X in full settlement)	Dr. Dr.		6,500 500	7,000

Illustration 19

Pass journal entries in the books of Miss Anindita Paul for the year ended 31st Dec. 2010:

2010

Dec. 1 Started business with a capital of:
Cash Rs. 3,000; Bank Rs. 4,000; Plant Rs. 12,000; Creditors Rs. 4,000 and Debtors Rs. 8,000.

3 Purchased a plant for Rs. 50,000, Cost of Carriage Rs. 500; and installation expenses being paid for Rs. 1,500.

4 Purchased furniture for resale from X Ltd. Rs. 3,000.

5 Purchased furniture for office decoration Rs. 8,000.

8 Sold furniture out of those meant for resale Rs. 4,000.

10 Returned a part of furniture out of those meant for resale to X Ltd. for Rs. 400.

14 Goods drawn by the proprietor for her own use for Rs. 1,000.

18 Goods distributed as free samples Rs. 500.

19 Paid Rs. 4,000 into business bank account from private cash.

22 A table purchased for Rs. 500 for the personal use of Miss Paul.

25 Withdrawn Cash from business for private use Rs. 1,000.

27 Paid Salary to Mr. X Rs. 3,000.

29 Paid advertisement to Anandabazar Patrika for Rs. 500.

30 Miss Paul encashed her Savings Deposit certificates and deposited the amount into her business for Rs. 3,000.

31 Life Insurance Premium paid by Miss Paul for Rs. 1,000.

Solution

In the books of Miss Anindita Paul

Journal

Date	Particulars		L.F.	Debit Rs.	Credit Rs.
2010 Dec. 1	Cash A/c	Dr.		3,000	
	Bank A/c	Dr.		4,000	
	Plant A/c	Dr.		12,000	
	Debtors A/c	Dr.		8,000	
	To Creditors A/c				4,000
	To Capital A/c *(bal. fig.)*				23,000
	(Business started with a capital of Rs. 23,000 consisting of Cash, Bank, Plant, Debtors and Creditors)				
3	Plant A/c	Dr.		52,000	
	To Cash A/c				52,000
	(Plant purchased for Cash Rs. 50,000, carriage paid Rs. 500 and installation expenses being Rs. 1,500)				
4	Purchase A/c	Dr.		3,000	
	To X Ltd. A/c				3,000
	(Purchase of furniture meant for resale)				
5	Furniture A/c	Dr.		8,000	
	To Cash A/c				8,000
	(Furniture purchased for office decoration)				
8	Cash A/c	Dr.		4,000	
	To Sales A/c				4,000
	(Sold part of furniture meant for resale)				
10	X Ltd. A/c	Dr.		400	
	To Returns Outward A/c				400
	(A part of furniture, meant for resale, returned to X Ltd.)				
14	Drawing A/c	Dr.		1,000	
	To Purchase A/c				1,000
	(Goods taken by the proprietor for her own use)				
18	Advertisement A/c	Dr.		500	
	To Purchase A/c				500
	(Goods distributed as free sample)				

Contd.

				Rs.	Rs.
19	Bank A/c Dr. To Capital A/c (Further capital introduced in the business)			4,000	4,000
22	Drawing A/c Dr. To Cash A/c (A table purchased for personal use)			500	500
25	Drawings A/c Dr. To Cash A/c (Cash withdrawn from business for private use)			1,000	1,000
27	Salary A/c Dr. To Cash A/c (Salary paid for cash)			3,000	3,000
29	Advertisement A/c Dr. To Cash A/c (Advertisement paid for cash)			500	500
30	Bank A/c Dr. To Capital A/c (Further capital introduced in the business)			3,000	3,000
31	Drawings A/c Dr. To Cash A/c (Life Insurance premium paid)			1,000	1,000

Reasons

1 Cash, Bank, Plant and Debtors are real account which come in, so these are to be debited and creditors will be credited, the balance is treated as capital.

3 When any plant/machinery is acquired its installation expenses or carriage expenses are also treated as capital expenditure, so, instead of debiting installation expenses or carriage, plant account will be debited, i.e. not the nominal account but the real account.

4 When any asset is acquired/purchased for resale, the same is treated as goods. As such, when it is sold, sales account will be credited and when it is purchased, purchase account will be debited, i.e. it should be treated like goods.

5 When any asset is acquired not for sale, but for use, the same is treated as an asset.

8 Same as 4.

10 Same as 4.

14 When goods are taken by the proprietor for her own use, Drawings Account should be debited and Purchase or Stock Account should be credited.

18 When goods are distributed as free samples, the same is treated as advertisement.

19 It is nothing but further introduction in the business.

22 It is nothing but drawing, that is, every drawing account should be debited, not the furniture account.

25 It is nothing but drawings.

27 When we pay salary to the employee, personal account cannot be debited (since we receive the service from the employees and against service, we pay) and that is why nominal account will be debited.

29 Same as 27.

30 Same as 19.

31 It is treated as drawings since life insurance premium is related with the life of the proprietor and not for business. It is not business expense.

LEDGER

Ledger

When the transactions are recorded from the primary books of accounts on permanent basis under double entry system in a summarised and classified form in different accounts and the same is posted in separate pages, it is called a Ledger (i.e., a book which contains records of all transactions permanently in a summarised and classified form). Since all the transac-tions are recorded in this book on permanent basis, it is called the Book of Final Entry. Practically, Ledger is the principal book of accounts. As a result, all the necessary information relating to any account is available from the ledger. This is the most important book of the business and, hence, is rightly called the King of all Books. It should be remembered that a group of particular class of transactions recorded in the different folios of the ledger is called an account, e.g., Rent Account, Salary Account, Plant Account, etc.

The specimen form of Ledger Account is presented:

Dr. *Cr.*

Date	*Particulars*	*L.F.*	*V.N.*	*Amount*	*Date*	*Particulars*	*L.F.*	*V.N.*	*Amount*
				Rs.					Rs.
	To					By			

Advantages of Ledger

It has been stated earlier that ledger is called the book of final entry. Ledger has many advantages, both direct and indirect. The advantages are:

Direct Advantages

(i) ***Preparation of Trial Balance*** : It is not possible to prepare a Trial Balance without ledgers. Because, a Trial Balance is prepared by taking up the ledger accounts balance. Moreover, arithmetical accuracy is not possible.

(ii) ***Presenting Final position*** : We know that final account can only be prepared from a Trial Balance (i.e., Trading Account, Profit and Loss Account and Balance Sheet). Thus, if we do not get the ledger accounts balance from a Trial Balance, it is impossible for us to prepare final accounts.

(iii) ***Application of Double Entry System*** : Double Entry System is completed only when we post the journals to different ledger accounts.

(iv) ***Determining results of each account*** : The results of each account can be obtained from the ledger on the basis of Double Entry principles.

(v) ***Maintaining classified Accounts*** : The particulars of classified accounts may be revealed after recording in ledger account properly.

Indirect Advantages

(i) ***Presenting Statistical information*** : The ledger accounts with their respective balances are the sources of statistical information which are used by the management while decision-making.

(ii) ***Collecting information*** : The ledger may be called the collection or storeroom of various transactions.

(iii) ***Present Financial position*** : The financial position of an enterprise (i.e., after preparing final account) can only be known if we maintain ledger account properly.

Subdivisions of Ledger

When transactions are extensive and numerous it becomes necessary to subdivide ledger into separate books, although it varies from firm to firm—depending on the nature and size of the business unit. The ledgers are subdivided into (a) Personal ledger, (b) Impersonal ledger.

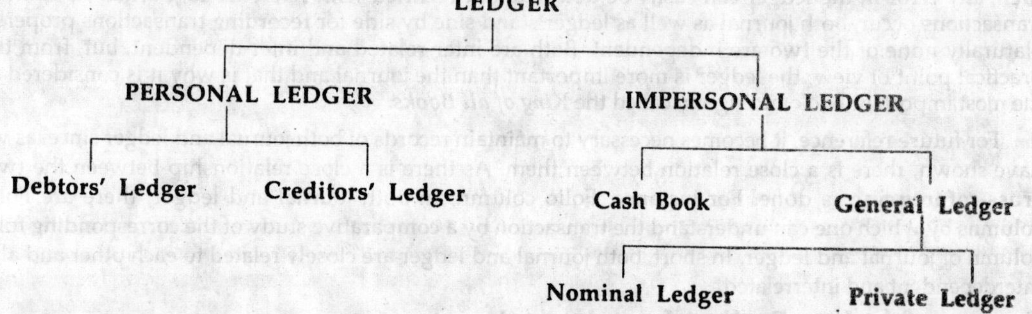

The personal ledger may again be subdivided into (a) Debtors' Ledger and (b) Creditors' Ledger, whereas the impersonal ledger may be subdivided into: (a) Cash Book, and (b) General Ledger. The

General Ledger, again, may be subdivided into (i) Nominal Ledger and 'Private' Ledger. Now, the whole subdivision of ledger may be depicted as :

Debtors' Ledger : It contains the accounts of those customers or debtors to whom goods were sold on credit, i.e., for credit sales. It is also called Sold Ledger, Sales Ledger etc.

Creditors' Ledger : It contains the accounts of those suppliers or creditors from whom goods were purchased on credit, i.e., for credit purchases. It is also called Bought Ledger, Purchases Ledger, etc.

General/Nominal Ledger : It contains the ledger relating to Real and Nominal Accounts as well as the totals of Debtors' and Creditors' Ledger Accounts.

Sometimes the ledger is subdivided into two:

(a) Nominal Ledger : It contains transactions relating to various expenses and losses, incomes and gains.

(b) Private Ledger : It contains transactions that are usually confidential in nature, i.e., Capital Account, Drawings Account, Investment Account etc.

Subdivisions of Ledger—Advantages

The advantages of subdivision of ledger may be presented:

(i) *Easy to handle* : If the ledger is subdivided, the size and volume of the same will be decreased which can easily be movable from one place to another.

(ii) *Easy to minimise change of errors and frauds* : It is needless to say that errors, mistakes and frauds will be minimised if ledgers are subdivided.

(iii) *Easy to complete the accounting work* : The final accounts may easily be completed if ledgers are subdivided.

(iv) *Easy to accountable responsibility* : If ledgers are subdivided, it becomes possible to allot various types of work to the particular/respective employees so that responsibility may be fixed and accountable.

(v) *Easy to divide work* : Division of work is possible if ledgers are subdivided. The employees of the accounts department may efficiently use their talent to maintain accounts.

(vi) *Easy for collecting information* : If ledgers are subdivided, the particular type of transac-tions may be located without any difficulty.

(vii) *Easy to reconcile* : If ledgers are subdivided, the arithmetical accuracy can easily be checked under self-balancing ledger system.

Relation between the Books of Original Entry and Books of Final Entry (i.e., between Journal and Ledger)

As per Double Entry System, each transaction is recorded at first in the journal and thereafter they are posted to the ledger permanently. No doubt journal is the basis of ledger. The transactions cannot correctly be recorded without recording in journals. Journal provides the detailed description of the transactions whereas ledger provides the short description of the transactions. Both of them supply the same information. Close relation may be maintained between the two with the help of cross-reference. As such, any error in the ledger can easily be detected and rectified with reference to journal. As soon as transactions occur, both journal as well as ledger stand side by side for recording transactions properly. Naturally none of the two are independent. Both are inter-related and inter-dependent, but, from the practical point of view, the ledger is more important than the journal and that is why it is considered as the most important Book and rightly called the *King of all Books.*

For future reference, it becomes necessary to maintain records of both journal and ledger since, as we have shown, there is a close relation between them. As there is a close relationship between the two, **cross-referencing** is done. For instance, Folio column: In both journal and ledger, there are Folio columns by which one can understand the transaction by a comparative study of the corresponding folio column of journal and ledger. In short, both journal and ledger are closely related to each other and also interdependent and interrelated.

Process of Ledger Posting from Journal

The following procedure should carefully be followed while posting the entries into the ledger:

First part of the Account

(i) Write the date of the transaction in the date column—one date of one account in the left-hand side (Debit side) while the date of other related account in the right-hand side (Credit side) of the account.

(ii) Take the first entry from the journal entry and open the two accounts accordingly.

(iii) Write on the debit side of one account, in particular column, the name of the account credited along with the prefix 'To'.

(iv) Write on the folio column of the left-hand side of the account the page number of the journal.

(v) Write also on the debit column of the account the amount/value as per journal.

(vi) Similarly, write the ledger's page number in the folio column of the journal.

Second part of the other Account

(i) Take the name of the second account, from the journal which is credited.

(ii) Write the date of the transaction in the date column.

(iii) Write on the debit side of that account, under head Particulars, the name of the first account which is debited.

(iv) Write on the folio column of the right-hand of the account the page number of the journal.

(v) Write also on the credit column of the account the amount/value as per journal.

(vi) Write also the ledger's page number in the folio column of the journal.

Ledger Posting from Journal

As soon as a transaction takes place, the same is recorded in the journal in the form of a journal entry. This entry is posted again in the respective ledger accounts under double entry principle from the journal. This is called ledger posting. The following example will make the principle clear:

Example: On 1.1.2011, X started business with a capital of Rs. 4,000.

Journal
(without narration)

Date	*Particulars*		*L.F.*	*Amount*	*Amount*
2011				Rs.	Rs.
Jan. 1	Cash A/c	Dr.	10	4,000	
	To Capital A/c		10		4,000

Ledger Posting

LEDGER

Dr. **Cash Account** *Cr.*

Date	*Particulars*	*L.F.*	*Amount*	*Date*	*Particulars*	*L.F.*	*Amount*
2011			Rs.	2011			Rs.
Jan. 1	To Capital A/c	7	4,000				

Dr. **Capital Account** *Cr.*

Date	*Particulars*	*L.F.*	*Amount*	*Date*	*Particulars*	*L.F.*	*Amount*
2011			Rs.	2011			Rs.
				Jan. 1	By Cash A/c	7	4,000

Balancing of Account—Debit Balance and Credit Balance

It is already been stated that the left-hand side of an account is called its debit side and the right-hand side of an account is known as the credit side. Naturally, debit entry means an entry which is posted on the left-hand side of an account and a credit entry means an entry which is posted on the right-hand side of an account. The difference between the total debit and the total credit sides of an account is called the 'balancing'. If debit side of an account is greater than the credit side of the same, it is called a debit balance, and vice versa.

The following steps should carefully be followed for the purpose:

(a) At first add up the greater side of the account.

(b) Ascertain the amount of difference of both the sides.

(c) If debit total is more than the credit total, put the difference in the credit side (so that the total of both sides become equal) and write the words *"By Balance c/d"* in Particulars column. On the contrary, if credit total is more than the debit total, put the difference on the debit side of the account and write the words *"To Balance c/d"* in Particulars Column.

(d) Close the account by rules, above and below the total of both sides of the account.

(e) Put the debit balance on the debit side of the account and write *"To Balance b/d"* in the Particulars Column.

Consider the following example:

Example:

Dr. **Cash Account** *Cr.*

Date	*Particulars*	*L.F.*	*V.N.*	*Amount*	*Date*	*Particulars*	*L.F.*	*V.N.*	*Amount*
2011				Rs.	2011				Rs.
Jan. 1	To Capital A/c			5,000	Jan. 5	By Salary A/c			1,000
8	" Sales A/c			3,000	12	" Purchases A/c			2,000
18	" X and Co. A/c			6,000	22	" Y and Co. A/c			4,000
					28	" Rent A/c			1,000
					31	" Balance c/d			6,000
				14,000					14,000
Feb. 1	To Balance b/d			6,000					

Arrangement of Accounts in the Ledger

Accounts in the ledger must be arranged systematically. Some business houses maintain their accounts in the ledger in an alphabetical order while others prefer to show the Personal Accounts at the beginning of the ledger, followed by Real Account and Nominal Account.

The primary object of arranging the accounts is that it helps the accountant to find out a particular account quickly when required.

Closing Balance and Opening Balance

The debit or credit balance of an account—what we get at the end of the accounting period—is known as Closing Balance of that account. It is interesting to note that the balance of the nominal accounts is closed by transferring to Trading and Profit and Loss Account, the result of which (i.e., net profit or net loss) is transferred to Capital Account (in case of proprietorship business) whereas the closing balance of assets, liabilities and proprietorship accounts are carried forward to the next accounting period. These closing balances of such accounts become the opening balances in the succeeding accounting period. For this purpose, we are to use the abbreviations while casting and balancing.

Some common terms used while Balancing of an account:

Carried Down (c/d) : It means carried down, (i.e., the amount is carried down). It is just used for recording a balance on the same page either for carrying down the balance to the next date or after the expiry of a fixed period (say Dec. 31).

Brought Down (b/d) : It means brought down (i.e., the amount is brought down). It is the opposite of carried down (c/d). That is, it is used for recording a balance on the same page either for bringing down the balance to the next date or after the expiry of a fixed period (say, Dec. 31) in opposite side of the account.

Carried Forward (c/f) : It means carried forward at a later stage. It is used either to transfer the balance of an account from one ledger to another, or from one period to the period immediately succeeding, or to transfer the total of a column of figures to another column or to another page, particularly where a column or a page has been filled with entries on posting.

Brought Forward (b/f) : It is the opposite of carried forward (c/f). That is, it is used to record the balance of an account to be written on any page at the beginning of the account.

Carried Over (c/o; : It means the amount is taken over to another page. It is used when the balance of the total of an account is carried over.

Brought Over (b/o) : It is the opposite of carried over (c/o). That is, it is used to record the balance at the beginning of the account brought to a next page from the previous page.

Standard T-Form of Ledger Account

Modern writers on accounting call the usual form of ledger account Standard T-Account or, simply, T-Account. Practically, it is short form or simplest form of account. Like ordinary ledger account, it also has two sides (Debit and Credit), and each side is subdivided into (i) Date, (ii) Particulars, (iii) Folio No., and (iv) Account.

The outline of such an account is given:

..............Account

Dr. Cr.

Date	Particulars	L.F.	Amount	Date	Particulars	L.F.	Amount
			Rs.				Rs.
	To				By		

Ledger Account maintained by a Bank

In this case, the format is quite different than the ledger account discussed earlier. This form is particularly followed by banks. The columns are divided into seven headings viz., (1) Date, (2) Particulars, (3) Cheque No., (4) Folio No., (5) Withdrawal (Dr.) Amount, (6) Deposit (Cr.) Amount, and (7) Balance.

The outlines of such a ledger account is given:

Pass Book

Date	Particulars	Cheque No.	Folio No.	Debit (Withdrawal)	Credit (Deposits)	Balance

PREPARATION OF JOURNAL AND LEDGER

Illustration 20

Record the following transactions and post them into ledgers:

(i) Started business with a capital of Rs. 5,000.
(ii) Sold goods to Mr. X for Rs. 500.
(iii) Received cash from Mr. X for Rs. 450 in full settlement.
(iv) Purchased goods from Mr. T for Rs. 1,500.
(v) Paid to Mr. T in full in cash Rs. 1,450.
(vi) Paid salary to Mr. Z Rs. 300.
(vii) Purchased a plant for Rs. 1,000.
(viii) Sold goods for cash Rs. 1,300.
(ix) Received interest Rs. 50.
(x) Deposited cash into bank Rs. 1,000.
(xi) Paid wages Rs. 100.
(xii) Withdrew cash from bank for personal use Rs. 200.

Solution

In the books of ....

Journal

Date	Particulars		L.F.	Debit	Credit
				Rs.	Rs.
(i)	Cash A/c	Dr.		5,000	
	To Capital A/c				5,000
	(Business started with a capital of Rs. 5,000)				
(ii)	X A/c	Dr.		500	
	To Sales A/c				500
	(Goods sold to Mr. X)				
(iii)	Cash A/c	Dr.		450	
	Discount Allowed A/c	Dr.		50	
	To X A/c				500
	(Cash received from Mr. X for Rs. 450 in full settlement)				
(iv)	Purchases A/c	Dr.		1,500	
	To T A/c				1,500
	(Goods purchased from T)				
(v)	T A/c	Dr.		1,500	
	To Cash A/c				1,450
	To Discount Received A/c				50
	(Cash paid to T for Rs. 1,450 in full settlement)				

Contd.

			Rs.	Rs.
(vi)	Salary A/c Dr. To Cash A/c (Salary paid in cash)		300	300
(vii)	Plant A/c Dr. To Cash A/c (Plant purchased for cash)		1,000	1,000
(viii)	Cash A/c Dr. To Sales A/c (Goods sold for cash)		1,300	1,300
(ix)	Cash A/c Dr. To Interest A/c (Interest received in cash)		50	50
(x)	Bank A/c Dr. To Cash A/c (Cash deposited into Bank)		1,000	1,000
(xi)	Wages A/c Dr. To Cash A/c (Wages paid in cash)		100	100
(xii)	Drawings A/c Dr. To Bank A/c (Cash withdrawn from bank for personal use)		200	200

LEDGER

Cash Account

Dr. Cr.

Date	Particulars	L.F.	Amount	Date	Particulars	L.F.	Amount
?			Rs.	?			Rs.
	To Capital A/c		5,000		By T A/c		1,450
	" X A/c		450		" Sales A/c		300
	" Sales A/c		1,300		" Plant A/c		1,000
	" Interest A/c		50		" Bank A/c		1,000
					" Wages A/c		100
					" Balance c/d		2,950
			6,800				6,800
	To Balance b/d		2,950				

Capital Account

Dr. Cr.

Date	Particulars	L.F.	Amount	Date	Particulars	L.F.	Amount
			Rs.				Rs.
?	To Bal. c/d		5,000	?	By Cash A/c		5,000
			5,000				5,000
					By Bal. b/d		5,000

X Account

Dr. Cr.

Date	Particulars	L.F.	Amount	Date	Particulars	L.F.	Amount
			Rs.				Rs.
?	To Sales A/c		500		By Cash A/c		450
					" Discount Allowed A/c		50
			500				500

Sales Account

Dr. Cr.

Date	Particulars	L.F.	Amount	Date	Particulars	L.F.	Amount
			Rs.				Rs.
?	To Bal. c/d		1,800	?	By X A/c		500
					" Cash A/c		1,300
			1,800				1,800
					By Bal. b/d		1,800

Discount Allowed Account

Dr. Cr.

Date	Particulars	L.F.	Amount	Date	Particulars	L.F.	Amount
			Rs.				Rs.
?	To XA/c		50	?	By Bal. c/d		50
			50				50
	To Bal. b/d		50				

Purchase Account

Dr. Cr.

Date	Particulars	L.F.	Amount	Date	Particulars	L.F.	Amount
			Rs.				Rs.
?	To T A/c		1,500	?	By Bal. c/d		1,500
			1,500				1,500
	To Bal. b/d		1,500				

T Account

Dr. Cr.

Date	Particulars	L.F.	Amount	Date	Particulars	L.F.	Amount
			Rs.				Rs.
?	To Cash A/c		1,450	?	By Pur. A/c		1,500
	" Discount		50				
			1,500				1,500

Dr. **Discount Received Account** Cr.

Date	Particulars	L.F.	Amount	Date	Particulars	L.F.	Amount
			Rs.				Rs.
?	To Bal. c/d		50	?	By T A/c		50
			50				50
					By Bal. b/d		50

Dr. **Salary Account** Cr.

Date	Particulars	L.F.	Amount	Date	Particulars	L.F.	Amount
			Rs.				Rs.
?	To Cash A/c		300	?	By Bal. c/d		300
			300				300
	To Bal. b/d		300				

Dr. **Plant Account** Cr.

Date	Particulars	L.F.	Amount	Date	Particulars	L.F.	Amount
			Rs.				Rs.
?	To Cash A/c		1,000	?	By Bal. c/d		1,000
			1,000				1,000
	To Bal. b/d		1,000				

Dr. **Interest Account** Cr.

Date	Particulars	L.F.	Amount	Date	Particulars	L.F.	Amount
			Rs.				Rs.
?	To Bal. c/d		50	?	By Cash A/c		50
			50				50
					By Bal. b/d		50

Dr. **Bank Account** Cr.

Date	Particulars	L.F.	Amount	Date	Particulars	L.F.	Amount
			Rs.				Rs.
?	To Cash A/c		1,000	?	By Drawings A/c		200
					" Bal. c/d		800
			1,000				1,000
	To Bal. b/d		800				

Dr. **Wages Account** Cr.

Date	Particulars	L.F.	Amount	Date	Particulars	L.F.	Amount
			Rs.				Rs.
?	To Cash A/c		100	?	By Bal. c/d		100
			100				100
	To Bal. b/d		100				

Dr. **Drawings Account** Cr.

Date	Particulars	L.F.	Amount	Date	Particulars	L.F.	Amount
			Rs.				Rs.
?	To Bank A/c		200	?	By Balance c/d		200
			200				200
	To Balance b/d		200				

Illustration 21

From the following information, given by Naresh, write-up in his books the personal account of Ramala:

(i) On 10.4.2012 Sold to Ramala goods on credit for Rs. 3,000 gross and allowed her a trade discount at 10% on that price.

(ii) On 12.4.2012 Ramala returned defective goods for Rs. 500 gross.

(iii) On 15.4.2012 Ramala settled her account in full by paying only a cheque for Rs. 2,200.

(iv) On 20.4.2012 Cheque received from Ramala was returned dishonoured by the Bank.

(v) On 29.4.2012 Ramala paid Rs. 1,500 in cash in lieu of the dishonoured cheque as part payment.

(vi) On 31.5.2012 Ramala's business was dissolved and, as it became impossible to recover the dues from her, the account was closed.

Solution

In the books of Naresh
Ramala Account

Dr. Cr.

Date	Particulars	L.F.	V.N.	Amount	Date	Particulars	L.F.	V.N.	Amount
2012				Rs.	2012				Rs.
Apr. 10	To Sales A/c (3,000 – 300)			2,700	Apr. 12	By Returns Inward A/c (500 – 50)			450

Contd.

				Rs.					Rs.
20	To	Bank A/c		2,200	15	By	Bank A/c		2,200
	"	Discount A/c		50		"	Dis. Allowed A/c		50
					29	"	Cash A/c		1,500
					31	"	Bad Debts A/c		750
				4,950					4,950

Cross-Balancing

When both the debit and the credit balances are shown in the same account, it is said Cross- Balancing .

Illustration 22

2011, Jan. 8 Rs. 800 is received by X & Co. through telegraphic money-order although the name of the customer is not known.

" 20 Rs. 2,000 is paid by X & Co. to the lawyer for expenses relating to a law suit, but the particular of the expenses is not yet received form the lawyer.

Solution

From the above two transactions, it would be practically wrong if we show the difference between the two amounts Rs. 1,200 (i.e., Rs. 2000 – Rs. 800) in the Suspense Account as simply "By Balance c/d" Rs. 1,200, since the items belong to two different types. And, although the debit and the credit entries are in the same account the balancing figure amounting to Rs. 1,200 must not be shown as an asset in the Balance Sheet. Instead of that, such entries should be shown by way of cross-balancing as under:

In the books of X & Co.

Dr. **Suspense Account** *Cr.*

Date	*Particulars*	*L.F.*	*Amount*	*Date*	*Particulars*	*L.F.*	*Amount*
2011			Rs.	2011			Rs.
Jan. 20	To Cash A/c		2,000	Jan. 8	By Cash A/c		800
31	" Balance c/d		800	31	" Balance c/d		2,000
			2,800				2,800
Feb. 1	To Balance b/d		2,000	Feb. 1	" Balance b/d		800

Needless to say, the above two balances must be show separately as asset and liability, respectively, in the Balance Sheet since they are quite different.

Note : Cross Balancing is also applicable i case of Self-Balancing ledger.

TRIAL BALANCE

Meaning and Objectives

Trial Balance is a statement which is prepared in a separate set of papers by taking up all the ledger account balances on a particular date in order to verify the arithmetical accuracy of the accounts in the ledger and putting the debits on one side and the credits on the other.

No doubt, it is a useful device and it helps to prepare the final account, since it contains all the Personal, Real and Nominal accounts' balances. As it is prepared by taking up the ledger accounts' balances, both debit and credit side of a Trial Balance must always be equal. In other words, it assures that (a) the balances (debit or credit) which are taken from different accounts are arithmetically correct; (b) The balances are taken and posted in the Trial Balance correctly, and (c) Debits and credits of all transactions are recorded.

One is to remember that Trial Balance is not a part of an account but a statement which is prepared only to verify the arithmetical accuracy of ledger accounts.

Preparation of Trial Balance

At first, close each of the individual accounts one by one, by taking up their respective differences which will either show a debit balance (i.e., if the debit total is greater than the credit total) or a credit balance (i.e., if credit total is greater than the debit total).

The debit balances of the accounts are to be written in debit column whereas the credit balances of the accounts are to be written in the credit column. The total of both the columns must be equal.

Advantages or Utilities of Drawing-up a Trial Balance

The Advantages of a Trial Balance are:

(i) It proves the arithmetical accuracy of the book-keeping work done during the period which is covered by a Trial Balance.

(ii) It supplies ready reference of all the balances of the ledger accounts which help us to avoid trouble for opening of different ledger accounts again and again.

(iii) It is a basis on which the final accounts of a firm (i.e., Trading Accounts, Profit and Loss Account and a Balance Sheet) can be prepared.

(iv) It summarises the results of all transactions during a period. That is why it supplies same useful information to the management before preparing the Final Accounts of the firm.

(v) If any error is found out by preparing a Trial Balance, the same can be rectified before preparing the final accounts.

Objectives and Functions of Trial Balance

The following are the objectives or functions of a Trial Balance:

(i) To test the arithmetical accuracy;
(ii) To help in locating/detecting errors;
(iii) To summarise information about ledger accounts;
(iv) To help in preparing final accounts.

(i) **To test the arithmetical accuracy:** No doubt a Trial Balance provides the arithmetical accuracy of transactions. That is why, if the Trial Balance agrees, it may be assumed that the posting of various accounts and casting and balancing are correct. But if it does not agree, there must be some errors (which should be located/detected) for which the Trial Balance does not agree. After careful scrutiny the accountant locates the errors which are known as 'Errors disclosed by a Trial Balance' or 'Errors which affect the agreement of Trial Balance.'

(ii) **To help in locating/detecting errors:** It has been pointed out in an earlier paragraph that if the Trial Balance does not agree, the accountant must locate such errors. The accountant must give equal emphasis or weightage to both small and wide differences found in a Trial Balance. Because, there may be a number of errors which have practically compensated the effect of one another producing a small difference.

The following steps may be advocated to locate the errors:

(a) Check the posting, casting of various ledger accounts from journal—one by one.
(b) Divide the difference by 2 and see if the said figures appear on the correct side or not.
(c) Check the additions of subsidiary books, ledger accounts and their respective balances.
(d) Check the opening balances to see if they are brought forward correctly or not.
(e) At last, if the Trial Balance still does not agree, checking should be started again from journal and subsidiary books and tick (√) marks put.

(iii) **To summarise information about ledger accounts:** Since a Trial Balance contains all the ledgers accounts' balances, summarised information about the ledgers, i.e., whether a particular account shows a debit balance or a credit balance, can easily be seen at a glance.

(iv) **To help in preparing final accounts:** It is practically impossible to prepare the final accounts of a firm in the absence of Trial Balance. The various ledger accounts that we get from a Trial Balance are transformed to Trading and Profit and Loss Account and also to the Balance Sheet in order to know the result of the operation and also the financial position—as a whole.

Features of a Trial Balance

From the definition and objectives presented above, a Trial Balance has the following salient features:

(a) *Statement only* : A Trial Balance is merely a statement and not at all an account.

(b) *Proof of arithmetical accuracy* : A Trial Balance proves the arithmetical accuracy of transactions so posted/recorded. In addition, financial result (i.e., from Profit and Loss Account and the Balance Sheet) can also be prepared from it.

(c) *Prepared in a separate sheet* : It is prepared in a sheet of paper since it is neither a journal nor a ledger.

(d) *Prepared at the end of the period* : Usually, a Trial Balance is prepared at the end of a certain period—say, monthly, quarterly, biannually, annually.

(e) *Contains list of balances* : A Trial Balance contains the balances of different ledger accounts for the particular period as per requirements of the users.

(f) *Helps to prepare final accounts* : It is not possible to prepare the final accounts of a concern without a Trial Balance, since the balances of all ledger accounts are contained in it.

Is Trial Balance Indispensable?

We know that in the practical field of accounting the preparation of Trial Balance is of great help to the accountants although it is neither an account in itself nor an essential part of the formation of accounting system, nor a part of ledger accounts. It is merely a statement prepared by the accountants for convenience and, if it agrees, we may be satisfied or assume that at least arithmetical accuracy has been done—although there may be a lot of errors. But, Trial Balance helps us to prepare the financial accounts of a firm—whether trading or non-trading.

Example :

State in which side of a Trial balance the following terms will appear :

Capital, Drawings, Opening Stock, Purchases, Sales, Returns Inward, Returns Outward, Wages, Carriage Inward, Freight, Royalty on Production, Gas and Fuel, Discount Received, Discount Allowed, Bad Debts, Reserve for Bad Debts, Commission Received, Repairs, Rent, Salaries, Loan Secured, Interest Received, Interest Paid, Insurance, Carriage Outwards, Advertisement, Sundry Expenses, Trade Charges, Miscellaneous Receipts, Income-tax, Office Expenses, Import Duty, Allowances, Sales-tax, Provision for Discount on Debtors, Provision for Discount on Creditors, Sundry Creditors (Purchase Ledger Balances); Sundry Debtors (Sales Ledger Balances), Goodwill, Plant and Machinery, Land and Buildings, Furniture, Fixtures and Fittings, Investments, 5% G. P. Notes, Cash in Hand, Cash at Bank, Reserve Fund, Loan Advanced, Horses and Carts, Export Duty, Deposit with Mr. A. Roy, Sinking Fund, General Reserve, Bills Receivable, Bills Payable, Advance Payment of Income-tax, Depreciation, Accrued Rent, Bank Overdraft, Outstanding Salaries, Prepaid Insurance, Income-tax refunded, Bad Debts Recovered, Patents and Trademarks, Accrued Income, Rent Received in Advance, Motor Cycle, Apprentice Premium Received.

Solution

The following items will appear on the **Debit** side of a Trial Balance :

Drawings, Opening Stock, Purchases, Returns Inward, Wages, Carriage Inwards, Freight, Royalty on Production, Gas and Fuel, Discount Allowed, Bad Debts, Repairs, Rent, Salaries, Interest Paid, Insurance, Carriage Outwards, Advertisement, Sundry Expenses, Trade Charges, Income-tax, Office Expenses, Import Duty, Allowances, Sales tax, Provision for Discount on Creditors, Sundry Debtors (Sales Ledger Balances), Goodwill, Plant and Machinery, Land and Building, Furniture, Fixtures and Fitting, Investments, 5% G. P. Notes, Cash in Hand, Cash at Bank, Loan Advanced, Horses and Carts, Export Duty, Deposit with Mr. A. Roy, Bills Receivable, Advance Payment of Income-Tax, Depreciation, Accrued Rent, Prepaid Insurance, Patents and Trademarks, Accrued Income, and Motor Cycle.

The following items will appear on the **Credit** side of a Trial balance:

Capital, Sales, Returns Outward, Discount Received, Reserve for Bad Debts, Commission Received, Interest Received, Miscellaneous Receipts, Provision for Discount on Debtors, Sundry Creditors (Purchase Ledger Balances), Reserve Fund, Sinking Fund, General Reserve, Bills Payable, Bank Overdraft, Outstanding Salaries, Income-tax Refunded, Bad Debts Recovered, Rent Received in Advance and Apprentice Premium Received.

Hints for preparation of a Trial Balance :

Reasons for ascertaining *Debit* or *Credit* applying

Golden Rule

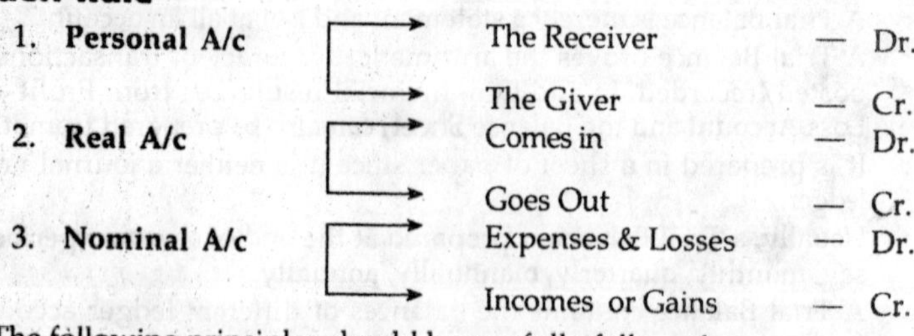

The following principles should be carefully followed :

(i)	DEBIT SIDE	=	(i) ***Assets, (ii) Expenses; (iii) Losses; (iv) Drawings; (v) Debtors.***
(ii)	CREDIT SIDE	=	(i) ***Liabilities; (ii) Incomes; (iii) Gains; (iv) Creditors.***

Methods of Preparation

The following three methods may be followed at the time of Trial Balance prepara-tion: viz., 1. Total Method; 2. Balance Method; and 3. Compound Method.

(a) **Total Method** : Under this method, Trial Balance is prepared by taking up the total of both debits and credits of all ledger accounts.

(b) **Balance Method** : Under this method, Trial Balance is prepared by taking up the balance of each ledger account only.

(c) **Compound Method** : It is the combination of the above two methods. It is also known as Total-cum-Balance Method.

Illustration 23

Take Illustration 20 and prepare a Trial Balance under each of the above methods.

Method I: Total Method

Trial Balance
as at..........

Heads of Accounts	*L.F.*	*Debit*	*Credit*
		Rs.	Rs.
Cash Account		6,800	3,850
Capital Account		—	5,000
X Account		500	500
Sales Account		—	1,800
Discount Allowed Account		50	—
Purchases Account		1,500	—
T Account		1,500	1,500
Discount Received Account			50
Salary Account		300	—
Plant Account		1,000	—
Interest Account		—	50
Bank Account		1,000	200
Wages Account		100	—
Drawings Account		200	—
		12,950	12,950

Method II: Balance Method

Trial Balance
as at/on ....

Heads of Accounts	*L.F.*	*Debit*	*Credit*
		Rs.	Rs.
Cash Account		2,950	—
Capital Account		—	5,000
Sales Account			1,800
Discount Allowed Account		50	—
Purchases Account		1,500	—
Discount Received Account		—	50
Salary Account		300	—
Plant Account		1,000	—
Interest Account		—	50
Bank Account		800	—
Wages Account		100	—
Drawings Account		200	—
		6,900	6,900

Method III: Compound Method

Trial Balance
as at/on ....

Heads of Accounts	*L.F.*	*Total*		*Balance*	
		Debit	*Credit*	*Debit*	*Credit*
		Rs.	Rs.	Rs.	Rs.
Cash Account		6,800	3,850	2,950	—
Capital Account		—	5,000	—	5,000
X Account		500	500	—	—
Sales Account		—	1,800	—	1,800
Discount Allowed Account		50	—	50	—
Purchases Account		1,500	—	1,500	—
T Account		1,500	1,500	—	—
Discount Received Account		—	50	—	50
Salary Account		300	—	300	—
Plant Account		1,000	—	1,000	—
Interest Account		—	50	—	50
Bank Account		1,000	200	800	—
Wages Account		100	—	100	—
Drawings Account		200	—	200	—
		12,950	12,950	6,900	6,900

ERRORS

For recording transactions in the books of accounts, it is quite natural that certain errors may arise either due to: (i) Carelessness of the accountants, or (ii) Lack of adequate knowledge of the accounts clerks and/or, accountants. The errors may arise in the form of: (i) Arithme-tical inaccuracy, (ii) Inability to apply the principles of accounting properly, and (iii) Absence of certain information. It is not possible to ascertain the correct profit or loss if any error exists in the accounts. That is why it becomes necessary to rectify the errors. If the detection and rectification of errors take time, the Trial Balance can be prepared by taking the difference to a newly opened Suspense Account for the time being and, at a subsequent date, when the errors are located, the Suspense Account is to be automatically closed.

Errors which are not disclosed by a Trial Balance

The following errors are not detected by a Trial Balance:

(a) Errors of Omission; (b) Errors of Commission; (c) Errors of Principles; (d) Errors of Misposting; (e) Compensating Errors.

(a) Errors of Omission

(i) *Partial Omission*

This type of error arises particularly where the transaction is recorded in the subsidiary books but the same is not correspondingly posted to the ledger.

Examples:

(a) Goods sold to the customers but not debited to Customers Account.

(b) Goods returned to creditors but not debited to Creditors Account.

(ii) *Complete Omission*

When the transaction is not at all recorded in the books of accounts, i.e., totally omitted or, neither in the debit side nor in the credit side of the account, it is called Errors of Complete Omission.

Examples:

(a) Goods sold to Mr. X for Rs. 500, not at all recorded in the books.

(b) Interest and commission received in Cash, for Rs. 1,000, not recorded at all in the books of accounts.

(b) Errors of Commission

These errors arise due to ignorance or absent-mindedness of the accounts clerks.

They are relating to subsidiary books.

These arise from:

(a) Wrong figure to be recorded in subsidiary books :

Ex: Goods sold to Mr. D for Rs. 800, wrongly recorded as Rs. 80 in the books of accounts.

(b) Transactions to be recorded in wrong subsidiary books:

Ex: Purchase goods for Mr. X, wrongly passed through Sales Account.

(c) Wrong casting in subsidiary books:

Ex: Sales Day Book was overcast/undercast by Rs. 1,000.

This will affect only one account, e.g., undercasting/overcasting in sales account affect only sales account, and so on.

(c) Errors of Misposting

When wrong posting is made to a wrong account instead of a correct one, although amount is correctly recorded:

Ex: Sold goods to Mr. B for Rs. 100 wrongly debited to D's Account.

(d) Errors of Principles

When wrong posting is made in the books of accounts, i.e., amounts are prepared not according to double entry principles. These errors arise due to:

(i) Capital expenditures to be treated as revenue expenditure:

Ex: Purchased a plant for Rs. 1,000, wrongly passed through the Purchase Account.

(ii) Revenue Expenditure to be treated as capital expenditure:

Ex: Repairs made to Building wrongly debited to Building Account.

(iii) Capital receipts to be treated as revenue receipts:

Ex: Sold a plant for Rs. 3,000, wrongly passed through Sales Account.

(iv) Revenue Receipts to be treated as Capital Receipts.

(e) Compensating Errors

When one error is compensated by another error, i.e., one error is compensated by another error or errors in a opposite way.

Ex: Discount allowed Rs. 100, not debited to discount allowed account whereas, Commission received Rs. 100, but not credited to Commission Account.

Before discussing the errors with their rectification, it becomes necessary to know:

(i) Errors which do not affect the agreement of Trial Balance;

(ii) Errors which affect the agreement of Trial Balance.

A. Errors which do not affect the agreement of Trial balance

The following errors do not actually affect the Trial Balance

(i) If any complete omission of a transaction exists from the books of accounts, i.e., neither debit nor credit—Trial Balance will agree.

(ii) If wrong posting is made to a wrong account instead of a correct one, although the amount is correctly recorded, Trial Balance will agree, since it keeps only the figure work for its agreement, e.g., sold goods to B, wrongly debited to D's A/c.

(iii) If wrong posting is made in the books of accounts according to accounting principles—Trial Balance will agree, e.g., purchase of a Plant wrongly debited to Purchase Account.

(iv) If any variation of figure/amount exists—Trial Balance will agree, e.g., purchased goods from P, for Rs. 1,000, but recorded only Rs. 100, in both the accounts, viz, P and Purchases.

(v) If any compensating error arises—Trial Balance will agree, e.g., discount allowed overcast by Rs. 100, whereas, carriage outward undercast by Rs. 100.

B. Errors which affect the agreement of Trial Balance

There are a number of errors which affect the agreement of Trial Balance. Some of them are:

(i) If only one aspect of an account is recorded, i.e., either debit or credit is omitted. (ii) If transactions are recorded in the wrong side of an account. (iii) If different figures are recorded to debit and credit sides, respectively, i.e., one figure is recorded on the debit side while another figure is recorded on the credit side. (iv) If any error arises while casting total in books of original entry or in ledger accounts.

Errors which are Disclosed by a Trial Balance

It has already been stated earlier that Trial Balance is a way to test the arithmetical accuracy of the records in the books of accounts. If any error, whether clerical or otherwise, exists in the book of accounts, the same will cause disagreement of a Trial Balance.

The following errors may be noted:

(i) ***Wrong Posting*** — Posting on the wrong side of an account and posting of a wrong amount in a ledger account will cause disagreement of Trial balance.

(ii) ***Omission of Posting*** — Omission of posting of an entry from the subsidiary book will cause disagreement.

(iii) ***Errors in Casting or Totalling*** — Errors in casting or totalling of subsidiary books or accounts will cause disagreement.

(iv) ***Errors in Balancing*** — If any error arises as a result of balancing of an account, the same will cause disagreement.

(v) ***Double Posting*** — If any item is posted twice in a ledger account from a subsidiary book, the same will create disagreement.

(vi) ***Incomplete Double Entry*** — If the double entry principle is not completed, i.e., either debit or credit side of an account is not recorded the same will invite disagreement.

(vii) ***Balance carried forward wrongly*** — If the debit balance of an account is shown or posted as a credit balance in the Trial Balance it would fail to agree, e.g., Rent Account shows a debit balance as per ledger but posted on the credit side of the Trial Balance.

(viii) ***Variation in amount*** — If different amount is entered in the two different accounts it will cause disagreement e.g., Rent Account is debited by Rs. 500 whereas Cash Account is credited by Rs. 50.

(ix) ***Wrong Total in Trial Balance*** — If the total of both the columns of the Trial balance is not correctly added up, it will cause disagreement.

Procedure to locate Errors, or, Steps to be taken if the Trial Balance does not agree

If the Trial Balance does not agree, the following procedure should carefully be followed:

(i) At first, check the extraction and listing of the ledger account balances—one by one.

(ii) Check the addition of both the columns (debit and credit) of the Trial Balance and ascertain the amount of difference.

(iii) Divide the difference by 2 and see whether the said figure appears on the correct side or not.

(iv) Check the additions of the subsidiary books.

(v) Check the additions of the ledger accounts and also the balances of each account.

(vi) Check the posting from subsidiary books to the ledger.

(vii) Check that balance of the account which is exactly equal to the difference of Trial Balance, if any.

(viii) Check the opening balances of all accounts—whether brought forward correctly or not.

(ix) Up to the level, if the errors are not even deleted, checking and re-checking must be done by other staffs following the same principle.

(x) If the trial balance is still not agreed, checking should be started again from the journal and book of original entry—using tick mark (√) against each and every transaction.

In order to locate the causes of disagreement of a Trial Balance, a thorough checking is necessary in the books of account. After several checking and re-checking, if the Trial Balance does not agree, put the difference to Suspense Account. This account will be automatically closed when the error or errors in Trial Balance are subsequently discovered or rectified.

Illustration 24

The undermentioned balances were extracted from the books of Sri Atash Banerjee as on 31. 3.2012. You are asked to prepare a Trial Balance as on that date.

	Rs.
Capital	78,000
Stock on 1.4.2011	5,000
Leasehold Premises	46,000
Furniture & Fixtures	13,500
Plant & Machinery	35,000
Purchases	78,900
Sales	1,30,620
Discount Received	470
Discount Allowed	540
Carriage Outwards	120
Carriage Inwards	230
Returns Inwards	1,500
Returns Outwards	380
Wages and Salaries	17,680
Rates & Taxes	1,370
Rent Received	530
Sundry Expenses	1,660
Trade Creditors	22,760
Book Debts	34,000
Drawings	3,000
Bills Payable	1,140
Cash in hand	1,200
Bank Loan	5,800
Closing Stock	3,900

Solution

In the books of Sri Atash Banerjee
Trial Balance as at 31st March 1012

Heads of Accounts	*L.F.*	*Debit*	*Credit*
		Rs.	Rs.
Capital A/c		—	78,000
Stock (1.4.1992)		5,000	—
Leasehold Premises A/c		46,000	—
Furniture & Fixtures A/c		13,500	—
Plant and Machinery A/c		35,000	—
Purchase A/c		78,900	—
Sales A/c		—	1,30,620
Discount Received A/c		—	470
Discount Allowed A/c		540	—
Carriage Outwards A/c		120	—
Carriage Inwards A/c		230	—
Returns Inwards A/c		1,500	—
Returns Outwards A/c			380
Wages and Salaries A/c		17,680	—
Rates & Taxes A/c		1,370	—
Rent Received A/c		—	530
Sundry Expenses A/c		1,660	—
Trade Creditors A/c			22,760
Book Debts A/c		34,000	—
Drawings A/c		3,000	—
Bills Payable A/c			1,140
Cash in hand		1,200	—
Bank Loan A/c		—	5,800
		2,39,700	2,39,700

TRIAL BALANCE OF A NON-TRADING CONCERN

Under the circumstances, we are to prepare the Trial Balance just like trading concern. There is practically no difference between the two in accounting principles; of course, there are some unusual items, viz., Donation, Entrance Fees, Legacies etc. According to their nature they will come under the head 'Debit' or 'Credit' according to the Double Entry principle.

Consider the following illustration :

Illustration 25

From the following ledger balances prepare a 'Trial Balance of Sports Club' for the year ended 31st Dec. 2011 :

	Rs.		Rs.
Cash in hand	1,000	Gardening	500
Cash at Bank	4,000	Cleaning	300
Furniture & Fixture	5,000	General Expenses	1,700
8% Govt. Securities	2,500	Newspapers and Magazines	800
Buildings	8,000	Sports Materials (1.1.2011)	4,000
Library	5,000	Purchase of Sports Materials	8,000
Other Investments	3,000	Sports Materials (31.12.2011)	3,000
Building Fund Investment	5,000	Outstanding Subscription (Dr.)	1,000
Donation	8,000	Sub. Received in Advance (Cr.)	500
Subscription from Members	10,000	Accrued Interest (Dr.)	500
Entrance Fees	12,000	Building Fund	5,000
Locker Rent	4,000	Hire of Hall (Income)	1,000
Interest on Investment	1,000	Grants from Govts.	3,000
Misc. Receipts	1,000	Travelling Expenses	500
Printing & Stationery	500	Refreshments	1,000
Electricity Charges	1,000	Accumulated Fund	7,800

Solution

In the books of 'Sports Club'
Trial Balance
As at 31st December 2011

Heads of Accounts	*L.F.*	*Debit* Rs.	*Credit* Rs.
Cash in hand		1,000	—
Cash at bank		4,000	—
Furniture & Fixtures		5,000	—
8% Govt. Securities		2,500	—
Building		8,000	—
Library		5,000	—
Other Investments		3,000	—
Building Fund Investments		5,000	—
Donation		—	8,000
Subscription from Members		—	10,000
Entrance Fees		—	12,000
Locker Rent		—	4,000
Interest on Investments		—	1,000
Miscellaneous Receipts		—	1,000
Printing and Stationery		500	—
Electric Charges		1,000	—
Gardening		500	—
Cleaning		300	—
General Expenses		1,700	—
Newspapers and Magazines		800	—
Sports Material (1.1.2011)		4,000	—
Purchase of Sports Materials		8,000	—
Outstanding Subscriptions		1,000	—
Subscription Received in Advance		—	500
Accrued Interest		500	—

Contd.

	Rs.	Rs.
Building Fund	—	5,000
Hire of Hall	—	1,000
Grants from Govts.	—	3,000
Travelling Expenses	500	—
Refreshments	1,000	—
Accumulated Fund	—	7,800
	53,300	53,300

Trial Balance of an Individual

Illustration 26

In this case also, the procedure of preparing a trial balance is the same as that of a trading concern.

From the following ledger balances of a family available on 31st Dec. 2012, prepare trial balance as on that date :

	Rs.
Expenses for fish, meat, eggs etc.	1,250
Expenses for foodgrains	2,100
Newspaper subscriptions	70
Expenses for pulses	300
Expenses for mustard oil	250
Expenses for spices	280
Expenses for vegetables	650
Cost of Almirah and Dinner Table	5,200
Cash in hand (31.12.2012)	300
Income from House Property	5,400
Income from Salary	4,200
Income from Agriculture	800

Solution

In the books of ......

Trial Balance

As at 31st Dec. 2012

Heads of Accounts	*L.F.*	*Debit* Rs.	*Credit* Rs.
Expenses for fish, meat, eggs, etc.		1,250	—
Expenses for foodgrains		2,100	—
Newspaper subscription		70	—
Expenses for pulses		300	—
Expenses for mustard oil		250	—
Expenses for spices		280	—
Expenses for vegetables		650	—
Cost of Almirah & Dinner Table		5,200	—
Cash in hand		300	—
Income from House Property		—	5,400
Income from Salary		—	4,200
Income from Agriculture		—	800
		10,400	10,400

GENERAL ILLUSTRATIONS

Illustration 27

The Trial Balance of X Ltd was extracted on 30th Nov. 2012, which is given below although the accounting year ends on 30th Dec. 2012 :

Trial Balance

Heads of Accounts	Dr. Rs.	Cr. Rs.
Equity Share Capital A/c	—	1,00,000
Plant and Machinery at Cost	60,000	—
Purchases	50,000	—

Contd.

	Rs.	Rs.
Sales		90,000
Sundry Debtors	30,000	—
Sundry Creditors	—	10,000
Salaries	12,000	—
Wages	8,000	—
Rent	10,000	—
Misc. Expenses	5,000	—
Cash in Hand	13,000	—
Bank Overdraft	—	1,000
Furniture and Fixture	6,000	—
Investments	7,000	—
	2,01,000	2,01,000

The following transactions took place during Dec. 2012 :

Dec. 2012

2. Sold goods to Y for Rs. 10,000 on credit.
3. Sold goods for Cash Rs. 8,000.
6. Y returned goods valued Rs. 1,000.
9. Purchased goods from Z for Rs. 8,000 on credit.
12. Returned goods to Z for Rs. 1,000.
17. Purchased goods for Cash Rs. 4,000.
19. Paid Rent by cheque Rs. 1,000.
21. Received cash from Y for Rs. 7,000. Allowed him discount Rs. 1,000.
24. Paid to Z for Rs. 5,000. Discount Received Rs. 1,000.
27. Bought a new machine for Rs. 10,000 for cash.
31. Deposited all cash in excess of Rs. 3,000 into the bank.

Prepare the necessary journal entries (without narration, ledger accounts for the month of Dec. 2011, and a Trial balance as on 31st Dec. 2012.

Solution

In the books of X Ltd.

Sales Day Book

Date	Name of the Customers	L. F.	Details	Total	Remarks
2012			Rs.	Rs.	
Dec. 2	Y		10,000		
				10,000	

Purchases Day Book

Date	Name of the Customers	L. F.	Details	Total	Remarks
2012			Rs.	Rs.	
Dec. 9	Z		8,000		
				8,000	

Returns Inward Book

Date	Name of the Customers	Credit Note No.	L. F.	Details	Total	Remarks
2012				Rs.	Rs.	
Dec. 6	Y			1,000		
					1,000	

Returns Outward Book

Date	Name of the Creditors	Credit Note No.	L. F.	Details	Total	Remarks
2012				Rs.	Rs.	
Dec. 12	Z			1,000		
					1,000	

Journal
(Without Narration)

Date	Particulars	L.F.	Debit	Credit
2012			Rs.	Rs.
Dec. 2	Debtors (Y) A/c ... Dr.		10,000	
	To Sales A/c			10,000
3	Cash A/c ... Dr.		8,000	
	To Sales A/c			8,000
6	Returns Inward A/c ... Dr.		1,000	
	To Debtors (Y) A/c			1,000
9	Purchases A/c ... Dr.		8,000	
	To Creditors (Z) A/c			8,000
12	Creditors (Z) A/c ... Dr.		1,000	
	To Returns Outward A/c			1,000
17	Purchases A/c ... Dr.		4,000	
	To Cash A/c			4,000
19	Rent A/c ... Dr.		1,000	
	To Bank A/c			1,000
21	Cash A/c ... Dr.		7,000	
	To Debtors (Y) A/c			7,000
21	Discount Allowed A/c ... Dr.		1,000	
	To Debtors (Y) A/c			1,000
24	Creditors (Z) A/c ... Dr.		5,000	
	To Cash A/c			5,000
24	Creditors (Z) A/c ... Dr.		1,000	
	To Discount Received A/c			1,000
27	Machinery A/c ... Dr.		10,000	
	To Cash A/c			10,000
31	Bank A/c ... Dr.		6,000	
	To Cash A/c			6,000

Dr. **Equity Share Capital A/c** Cr.

Date	Particulars	Amount	Date	Particulars	Amount
2012		Rs.	2012		Rs.
31	To Balance c/d	1,00,000	Dec. 1	By Balance b/d	1,00,000
		1,00,000			1,00,000
			2013		
			Jan. 1	By Balance b/d	1,00,000

Dr. **Plant and Machinery A/c** Cr.

Date	Particulars	Amount	Date	Particulars	Amount
2012		Rs.	2012		Rs.
Dec. 1	To Balance b/d	60,000	Dec. 31	By Balance c/d	70,000
27	" Cash A/c	10,000			
		70,000			70,000
2013					
Jan. 1	To Balance b/d	70,000			

Dr. **Purchases A/c** Cr.

Date	Particulars	Amount	Date	Particulars	Amount
2012		Rs.	2012		Rs.
Dec. 1	To Balance b/d	50,000	Dec. 31	By Balance c/d	62,000
" 9	" Creditors A/c	8,000			
" 17	" Cash A/c	4,000			
		62,000			62,000
2013					
Jan. 1	To Balance b/d	62,000			

Sales A/c

Dr. Date	Particulars	Amount	Date	Particulars	Cr. Amount
2012		Rs.	2012		Rs.
Dec. 31	To Balance c/d	1,08,000	Dec. 1	By Balance b/d	90,000
			2	" Debtors A/c	10,000
			3	" Cash A/c	8,000
		1,08,000			1,08,000
			2013		
			Jan. 1	By Balance b/d	1,08,000

Sundry Debtors A/c

Dr. Date	Particulars	Amount	Date	Particulars	Cr. Amount
2012		Rs.	2012		Rs.
Dec. 1	To Balance b/d	30,000	Dec. 6	By Returns Inward A/c	1,000
2	" Sales A/c	10,000	21	" Cash A/c	7,000
				" Discount Allowed A/c	1,000
			21	" Balance c/d	31,000
		40,000			40,000
2013					
Jan. 1	To Balance b/d	31,000			

Sundry Creditors A/c

Dr. Date	Particulars	Amount	Date	Particulars	Cr. Amount
2012		Rs.	2012		Rs.
Dec. 12	To Ret. Outward A/c	1,000	Dec. 1	By Balance b/d	10,000
" 14	" Cash A/c	5,000	9	" Purchase A/c	8,000
" 14	" Dis. Received A/c	1,000			
" 31	" Balance c/d	11,000			
		18,000			18,000
			2013		
			Jan. 1	By Balance b/d	11,000

Salaries A/c

Dr. Date	Particulars	Amount	Date	Particulars	Cr. Amount
2012		Rs.	2012		Rs.
Dec. 31	To Balance b/d	12,000	Dec. 31	By Balance c/d	12,000
		12,000			12,000
2013					
Jan. 1	To Balance b/d	12,000			

Wages A/c

Dr. Date	Particulars	Amount	Date	Particulars	Cr. Amount
2012		Rs.	2012		Rs.
Dec. 31	To Balance b/d	8,000	Dec. 31	By Balance c/d	8,000
		8,000			8,000
2013					
Jan. 1	To Balance b/d	8,000			

Rent A/c

Dr. Date	Particulars	Amount	Date	Particulars	Cr. Amount
2012		Rs.	2012		Rs.
Dec. 1	To Balance b/d	10,000	Dec. 31	By Balance c/d	11,000
19	" Bank A/c	1,000			
		11,000			11,000
2013					
Jan. 1	To Balance b/d	11,000			

Dr. Misc. Expenses A/c Cr.

Date	Particulars	Amount	Date	Particulars	Amount
2012		Rs.	2012		Rs.
Dec. 1	To Balance b/d	5,000	Dec. 31	By Balance c/d	5,000
		5,000			5,000
2013					
Jan. 1	To Balance b/d	5,000			

Dr. Furniture and Fixtures A/c Cr.

Date	Particulars	Amount	Date	Particulars	Amount
2012		Rs.	2012		Rs.
Dec. 31	To Balance b/d	6,000	Dec. 31	By Balance c/d	6,000
		6,000			6,000
2013					
Jan. 1	To Balance b/d	6,000			

Dr. Investment A/c Cr.

Date	Particulars	Amount	Date	Particulars	Amount
2012		Rs.	2012		Rs.
Dec. 31	To Balance b/d	7,000	Dec. 31	By Balance c/d	7,000
		7,000			7,000
2013					
Jan. 1	To Balance b/d	7,000			

Dr. Cash A/c Cr.

Date	Particulars	Amount	Date	Particulars	Amount
2012		Rs.	2012		Rs.
Dec. ?	To Balance b/d	13,000	Dec. 17	By Purchase A/c	4,000
Dec. 3	" Sales A/c	8,000	Dec. 24	" Creditors A/c	5,000
Dec. 21	To Debtors A/c	7,000	Dec. 27	By Machinery A/c	10,000
			31	" Bank A/c (*bal. fig.*)	6,000
			31	By Balance c/d	3,000
		28,000			28,000
2013					
Jan. 1	To Balance b/d	3,000			

Dr. Bank A/c Cr.

Date	Particulars	Amount	Date	Particulars	Amount
2012		Rs.	2012		Rs.
Dec. 31	To Cash A/c	6,000	Dec. 1	By Balance b/d	1,000
			19	" Rent A/c	1,000
			31	By Balance c/d	4,000
		6,000			6,000
2013					
Jan. 1	To Balance b/d	6,000			

Dr. Returns Inward A/c Cr.

Date	Particulars	Amount	Date	Particulars	Amount
2012		Rs.	2012		Rs.
Dec. 6	To Sundry Debtors A/c	1,000	Dec. 31	By Balance c/d	1,000
		1,000			1,000
2013					
Jan. 1	To Balance b/d	1,000			

Dr. Returns Outward A/c Cr.

Date	Particulars	Amount	Date	Particulars	Amount
2012		Rs.	2012		Rs.
Dec. 31	To Balance c/d	1,000	Dec. 12	By Creditors A/c	1,000
		1,000			1,000
			2013		
			Jan. 1	By Balance b/d	1,000

Dr. Discount Allowed A/c Cr.

Date	Particulars	Amount	Date	Particulars	Amount
2012		Rs.	2012		Rs.
Dec. 21	To Debtors A/c	1,000	Dec. 31	By Balance c/d	1,000
		1,000			1,000
2013					
Jan. 1	To Balance b/d	1,000			

Dr. Discount Received A/c Cr.

Date	Particulars	Amount	Date	Particulars	Amount
2012		Rs.	2012		Rs.
Dec. 31	To Balance c/d	1,000	Dec. 24	By Creditors A/c	1,000
		1,000			1,000
			2013		
			Jan. 1	To Balance b/d	1,000

Trial Balance
as at 31st Dec. 2012

Heads of Accounts	L.F.	Debit	Credit
		Rs.	Rs.
Equity Share Capital A/c		—	1,00,000
Plant and Machinery A/c		70,000	—
Purchases A/c		62,000	—
Sales A/c		—	1,08,000
Sundry Debtors A/c		31,000	—
Sundry Creditors A/c		—	11,000
Salaries A/c		12,000	—
Wages A/c		8,000	—
Rent A/c		11,000	—
Misc. Expenses A/c		5,000	—
Furniture and Fixtures A/c		6,000	—
Investment A/c		7,000	—
Cash A/c		3,000	—
Bank A/c		4,000	—
Returns Outward A/c		—	1,000
Returns Inward A/c		1,000	—
Discount Allowed A/c		1,000	—
Discount Received A/c		—	1,000
		2,21,000	2,21,000

Illustration 28

The Balance Sheet of R. Furniture as on 31st March 2012 is given below:

Liabilities	Rs.	Assets	Rs.
Capital	1,00,000	Cash	42,000
General Reserves	19,000	Sundry Debtors	90,000
Sundry Creditors	25,000	Inventory	10,000
		Prepaid Rent	2,000
	1,44,000		1,44,000

Following is the summary of transactions that occurred during April 2012:

		Rs.
(a)	Collections from Debtors	88,000
(b)	Payments to Creditors	24,000
(c)	Acquisition of inventory on credit	80,000
(d)	Inventory costing Rs. 70,000 was sold on credit for	85,000
(e)	Recognition of Rent expenses for April	1,000
(f)	Wages paid in Cash for April	8,000

Required :

A. Prepare all ledger accounts after including opening balances as on 31st March 2012. (Journal entries are not required).

B. Prepare the Trial Balance as on 30th April 2012 from the ledger accounts.

[CFA]

Solution

In the books of R. Furniture

Cash A/c

Dr. Cr.

Date	Particulars	Amount	Date	Particulars	Amount
2012		Rs.	2012		Rs.
April 1	To Balance b/d	42,000	?	By S/Creditors A/c	24,000
			"	Wages A/c	8,000
"	S/ Debtors A/c	88,000	April 30	By Balance c/d	98,000
		1,30,000			1,30,000
2012					
May 1	To Balance b/d	98,000			

Sundry Debtors A/c

Dr. Cr.

Date	Particulars	Amount	Date	Particulars	Amount
2012		Rs.	2012		Rs.
April ?	To Balance b/d	90,000	?	By Cash A/c	88,000
	" Sales A/c	85,000	April 30	" Balance c/d	87,000
		1,75,000			1,75,000
2012					
May 1	To Balance b/d	87,000			

Sundry Creditors A/c

Dr. Cr.

Date	Particulars	Amount	Date	Particulars	Amount
2012		Rs.	2012		Rs.
?	To Cash A/c	24,000	April ?	By Balance b/d	25,000
April 30	" Balance c/d	81,000		" Purchases A/c	80,000
		1,05,000			1,05,000
			2012		
			May 1	To Balance b/d	81,000

Purchases A/c

Dr. Cr.

Date	Particulars	Amount	Date	Particulars	Amount
2012		Rs.	2012		Rs.
?	To S/ Creditors A/c	80,000	April 30	By Balance c/d	80,000
		80,000			80,000
2012					
May 1	To Balance b/d	80,000			

Sales A/c

Dr. Cr.

Date	Particulars	Amount	Date	Particulars	Amount
2012		Rs.	2012		Rs.
April 30	To Balance c/d	85,000	April ?	By Sundry Debtors A/c	85,000
		85,000			85,000
			2012		
			May 1	To Balance b/d	85,000

Inventory A/c

Dr. Cr.

Date	Particulars	Amount	Date	Particulars	Amount
2012		Rs.	2012		Rs.
April	To Balance b/d	10,000	April 30	By Balance c/d	10,000
		10,000			10,000
2012					
May 1	To Balance b/d	10,000			

Prepaid Rent A/c

Dr. Date	Particulars	Amount	Date	Particulars	Cr. Amount
2012		Rs.	2012		Rs.
April ?	To Balance b/d	2,000	April 30	By Rent A/c	1,000
			"	Balance c/d	1,000
		2,000			2,000
2012					
May 1	To Balance b/d	1,000			

Rent A/c

Dr. Date	Particulars	Amount	Date	Particulars	Cr. Amount
2012		Rs.	2012		Rs.
April 30	To Prepaid Rent	1,000	April 30	By Balance c/d	1,000
		1,000			1,000
2012					
May 1	To Balance b/d	1,000			

Capital A/c

Dr. Date	Particulars	Amount	Date	Particulars	Cr. Amount
2012		Rs.	2012		Rs.
April 30	To Balance c/d	1,00,000	April 1	By Balance b/d	1,00,000
		1,00,000			1,00,000
			2012		
			May 1	To Balance b/d	1,00,000

General Reserve A/c

Dr. Date	Particulars	Amount	Date	Particulars	Cr. Amount
2012		Rs.	2012		Rs.
April 30	To Balance c/d	19,000	April 1	By Balance b/d	19,000
		19,000			19,000
			2012		
			May 1	To Balance b/d	19,000

Wages A/c

Dr. Date	Particulars	Amount	Date	Particulars	Cr. Amount
		Rs.	2012		Rs.
?	To Cash A/c	8,000	April 30	By Balance c/d	8,000
		8,000			8,000
2012					
May 1	To Balance b/d	8,000			

Trial Balance
as at 30th April 2012

Heads of Accounts	L.F.	Debit	Credit
		Rs.	Rs.
Cash A/c		98,000	—
Sundry Debtors A/c		87,000	—
Sundry Creditors A/c		—	81,000
Purchase A/c		80,000	—
Sales A/c		—	85,000
Inventory A/c		10,000	—
Prepaid Rent A/c		1,000	—
Rent A/c		1,000	—
Capital A/c		—	1,00,000
General Reserve A/c		—	19,000
Wages A/c		8,000	—
		2,85,000	2,85,000

Treatment of Closing Stock

Usually, or in most cases, closing stock does not appear in Trial balance, as no separate account is opened for it. It reveals the balance of unsold goods out of purchase or opening stock. We know that, when goods are purchased, the entry is :

Purchase A/c Dr.
  To Cash A/c (in case of cash purchases)
or, To Creditors (in case of credit purchases)

But the closing stock will appear in Trial Balance only when the same is adjusted against purchase; in that case, the entry being

Closing Stock A/c Dr.
  To Purchases A/c

Illustration 29

From the following ledger accounts balances, prepare a Trial Balance for the year ended 31.12.2012:

	Rs.		Rs.
Capital A/c	40,000	Petty Cash	5,000
Current (Cr.) A/c	5,000	Depreciation	2,000
Sales	5,00,000	Cash at Bank	40,000
Adjusted Purchases	4,00,000	Stock at 31.12.2012	60,000
Salaries	12,000	Interest (Cr.)	5,000
Carriage Inward	2,000	Accrued Interest	2,000
Carriage Outward	3,000	Investment, in 5% Govt. Loan	10,000
Discount (Dr.)	5,000	Prov. for Bad and Doubtful Debts	3,000
Building	40,000	General Reserve	10,000
Expenses Outstanding	5,000	Bad Debts Recovered	1,000
Prepaid Insurance	1,000	Profit & Loss A/c 1.1.2012(Cr.)	10,000
Sales Ledger Balances	60,000	Loan A/c (Cr.)	33,000
Purchase Ledger Balances	30,000		

In the books of ... ...

Trial Balance as at 31st Dec. 2012

Heads of Accounts	*L.F.*	*Debit*	*Credit*
		Rs.	Rs.
Capital A/c		—	40,000
Current (Cr.) A/c		—	5,000
Sales A/c		—	5,00,000
Adjusted Purchases A/c		4,00,000	—
Salaries A/c		12,000	—
Carriage Inward A/c		2,000	—
Carriage Outward A/c		3,000	—
Discount (Dr.) A/c		5,000	—
Building A/c		40,000	—
Expenses Outstanding A/c		—	5,000
Prepaid Insurance A/c		1,000	—
Sales Ledger Balances		60,000	—
Purchase Ledger Balances		—	30,000
Petty Cash A/c		5,000	—
Depreciation A/c		2,000	—
Cash at Bank A/c		40,000	—
Stock at 31.12.2012		60,000	—
Interest (Cr.) A/c		—	5,000
Accrued Interest A/c		2,000	—
Investment, in 5% Govt. Loan A/c		10,000	—
Provision for Bad and Doubtful Debts A/c		—	3,000
General Reserve A/c		—	10,000
Bad Debts Recovered A/c		—	1,000
Profit & Loss A/c 1.1.2012 (Cr.)		—	10,000
Loan A/c (Cr.)		—	33,000
		6,42,000	6,42,000

(c) Correction of Wrong Trial Balance

Illustration 30

The following is the Trial Balance of R & Co. showing debit total of Rs. 3,18,200 and credit total of Rs. 3,76,200.

You are required to ascertain the correct total of Trial Balance after pointing out the errors causing the disagreement.

Trial Balançe
as on 31.12.2012

	Debit Rs.	Credit Rs.
Capital	—	1,00,000
Cash in Hand	1,200	—
Bills Payable	22,000	—
Bills Receivable	—	20,000
Purchases	1,20,000	—
Opening Stock	35,000	—
Creditors	24,000	—
Sales	—	2,00,200
Bad Debts Reserve	1,000	—
Debtors	—	50,000
Plant & Machinery	60,000	—
Furniture	15,000	—
Rent & Taxes	5,000	—
Drawings	5,000	—
Wages	10,000	—
Income-tax	—	6,000
Salaries	20,000	—
	3,18,200	3,76,200

Solution

The above Trial Balance can be redrafted under any of the following ways :

Method I

Trial Balance
as at 31st Dec. 2012

Heads of Accounts	*L.F.*	*Debit* Rs.	*Credit* Rs.
Capital A/c		—	1,00,000
Cash A/c		1,200	—
Bills Payable A/c		—	22,000
Bills Receivable A/c		20,000	—
Purchases A/c		1,20,000	—
Opening Stock		35,000	—
Creditors A/c		—	24,000
Sales A/c		—	2,00,200
Bad Debt Reserve A/c		—	1,000
Debtors A/c		50,000	—
Plant & Machinery A/c		60,000	—
Furniture A/c		15,000	—
Rent & Taxes A/c		5,000	—
Drawings A/c		5,000	—
Wages A/c		10,000	—
Income-tax A/c		6,000	—
Salaries A/c		20,000	—
		3,47,200	3,47,200

Method II

[Note : Under this method, only the wrong postings should be corrected.]

Correction of Trial Balance

	Debit Rs.	Credit Rs.
Total as per Trial Balance	3,18,200	3,76,200
Bills payable being credit balance, but shown as debit balance	– 22,000	+ 22,000
	2,96,200	3,98,200
Bills Receivable being debit balance, but shown as credit balance	+ 20,000	– 20,000
	3,16,200	3,78,200
Creditors being credit balance, but shown as debit balance	– 24,000	+ 24,000
	2,92,200	4,02,200
Bad Debts Reserve being a credit balance, but shown as debit balance	– 1,000	+ 1,000
	2,91,200	4,03,200
Debtors being debit balance, but shown as credit balance	+ 50,000	– 50,000
	3,41,200	3,53,200
Income-tax being debit balance, but shown as credit balance	+ 6,000	– 6,000
	3,47,200	3,47,200

Illustration 31

The Trial Balance of Sen Motor Repairing Works shows a total debit of Rs. 2,65,600 and a total credit Rs. 70,400.

After scrutiny the following facts are discovered :

Items	Correct Ledger Balance	Figures Appeared in Trial Balance	
Repairs	60,600	60,600	(debit side)
Bank Overdraft	5,000	5,000	(")
Plant	15,000	5,100	(")
Provision for Bad Debts	420	240	(")
Carriage Outward	4,500	5,400	(credit side)
Closing Stock (not adjusted)	83,140	83,140	(debit side)

Calculate the correct total of the Trial Balance.

Solution

	Debit Rs.	Credit Rs.
Total as per Trial Balance	2,65,600	70,400
Repairs being credit balance, but shown as debit balance	– 60,600	+ 60,600
	2,05,000	1,31,000
Bank Overdraft being credit balance, but shown as debit balance	– 5,000	+ 5,000
	2,00,000	1,36,000
Plant understated (15,000 – 5,100),	+ 9,900	—
	2,09,900	1,36,000
Provision for bad debts understated, being credit balance, but shown as debit balance	– 240	+ 420
	2,09,660	1,36,420
Carriage outward overstated, being debit balance, but shown as credit balance	+ 4,500	– 5,400
	2,14,160	1,31,020
Closing Stock (as it is not adjusted)	83,140	—
Correct Total of Trial Balance	1,31,020	1,31,020

Pre-Closing or Adjusted Trial Balance

Usually a trial balance is prepared before considering the adjustments on the principle that all debits are equal to all credits. But an adjusted trial balance is one which is prepared after considering the adjustments that are available at the end of the financial year. No doubt this trial balance supplies the convenient source of some information which becomes necessary in order to prepare a Final Account. The following illustration will, however, makė the principle clear.

Illustration 32

The following trial balance is presented by Mr. Munir Parekh. You are asked to prepare an Adjusted Trial Balance after taking into consideration the necessary adjustments and also show the necessary adjusting entries for the purpose :

	Rs.		Rs.
Opening Stock	10,000	Capital	50,000
Purchases	40,000	Sales	1,00,000
Wages	8,000	Sundry Creditors	30,000
Salaries	12,000	Bills Payable	20,000
Carriage	5,000		
Rent	7,000		
Insurance	3,000		
Repairs	3,000		
Interest	2,000		
Land and Building	30,000		
Plant and Machinery	20,000		
Furniture	10,000		
Bills Receivable	10,000		
Sundry Debtors	40,000		
	2,00,000		2,00,000

Additional Information :

(a) Closing Stock amounted to Rs. 25,000. (b) Outstanding Salaries and Wages were Rs. 5,000 and Rs. 3,000, respectively. (c) Insurance paid in advance amounted to Rs. 1,000. (d) Depreciate Plant and Machinery and Furniture @ Rs. 10% and 5%, respectively. (e) Goods costing Rs. 3,000 were taken by Mr. Parekh for his own use. (f) Sales include Rs. 1,000 worth of goods, i.e., cost price, taken by Mr. Parekh also for his own use. (g) Write-off Bad Debts amounting to Rs. 1,000 and make a provision for bad debts @ 5% on Sundry Debtors.

Solution

In the books of Mr. Munir Parekh

Journal

Date	Particulars		L.F.	Debit Rs.	Credit Rs.
	(a) Closing Stock A/c	Dr.		25,000	
	To Purchases A/c				25,000
	(Closing Stocks adjusted against purchase)				
	(b) Salaries A/c	Dr.		5,000	
	To Outstanding Salaries A/c				5,000
	(Outstanding Salaries adjusted)				
	Wages A/c Dr.			3,000	
	To Outstanding Wages A/c				3,000
	(Outstanding wages adjusted)				
	(c) Prepaid Insurance A/c	Dr.		1,000	
	To Insurance A/c				1,000
	(Prepaid Insurance adjusted)				
	(d) Depreciation A/c	Dr.		2,500	
	To Plant and Machinery A/c				2,000
	" Furniture A/c				500
	(Depreciation provided on various assets)				

Contd.

			Rs.	Rs.
(e)	Drawings A/c Dr. To Purchase A/c (Goods taken for own use, adjusted)		3,000	3,000
(f)	Sales A/c Dr. To Debtors A/c (Goods taken by the proprietor wrongly included in sales, now cancelled)		1,000	1,000
	Drawings A/c Dr. To Purchase A/c (Goods taken by the proprietor for his own use)		1,000	1,000
(g)	Bad Debts A/c Dr. To Sundry Debtors A/c (Amount written-off as Bad Debts)		1,000	1,000
	Bad Debts A/c Dr. To Provision of Bad Debts A/c (Provision of Bad Debts created @ 5% on Sundry debtors i.e., 40,000 – 1,000 = 39,000 × 5%)		1,950	1,950

Trial Balance (Adjusted)
as at ……

Heads of Accounts	*L.F.*	*Rs.*	*Rs.*
Opening Stock	…	10,000	—
Purchases (40,000 – 25,000 – 3,000 – 1,000)	…	11,000	—
Wages (8,000 + 3,000)	…	11,000	—
Salaries (12,000 + 5,000)	…	17,000	—
Carriage	…	5,000	—
Rent	…	7,000	—
Insurance (3,000 – 1,000)	…	2,000	—
Repairs	…	3,000	—
Interest	…	2,000	—
Land and Building	…	30,000	—
Plant and Machinery (20,000 – 2,000)	…	18,000	—
Furniture (10,000 – 500)	…	9,500	—
Bills Receivable	…	10,000	—
Sundry Debtors (40,000 – 1,000 – 1,000)	…	38,000	—
Capital	…	—	50,000
Sales (1,00,000 – 1,000)	…	—	99,000
Sundry Creditors	…	—	30,000
Bills Payable	…	—	20,000
Closing Stock	…	25,000	—
Outstanding Liabilities (5,000 + 3,000)	…		8,000
Prepaid Insurance	…	1,000	—
Depreciation (2,000 + 500)	…	2,500	—
Drawings (3,000 + 1,000)	…	4,000	—
Bad Debts (1,000 + 1,900)	…	2,900	—
Provision for Bad Debts	…	—	1,900
		2,08,900	2,08,900

Post-Closing Trial Balance

Consider the following illustration:

Illustration 33

From the following particulars of the 'Business Centre', prepare the Trading and Profit and Loss Account for the year ended 31st December 2012 after giving effect to the adjustments indicated below :

	Rs.		Rs.
Capital Account as at 1.1.2012	3,60,000	Wages	22,500
Drawings by the proprietor	50,000	Cash Discount Received	7,500
Purchases	10,52,500	Building	1,00,000
Rates and Taxes	12,500	Furniture and Fixtures	25,750

Contd.

	Rs.		Rs.
Salaries	50,000	Plant and Machinery	47,500
Lighting and Heating	10,000	Sundry Debtors	93,500
Insurance	3,000	4% Govt. Promissory Notes	
Advertisement	10,000	(Subscribed on 1.1.2012)	10,000
Bad Debts written-off	5,000	Sundry Creditors	52,500
Cash Discount Allowed	1,000	Sales	12,56,500
Sundry Expenses	1,750	Cash in hand	23,000
Opening Stock	55,000	Cash at bank	97,000
Postage and Telegram	6,500	Stock-in-trade at 31st December 2012	45,000

Adjustments :

(1) Provide Depreciation at 10 per cent on Machinery, $2\frac{1}{2}$ per cent on Building and at 5 per cent on Furniture.

(2) Provide $2\frac{1}{2}$ per cent on Debtors for doubtful debts.

(3) Purchase invoices aggregating Rs. 12,500 were omitted to be entered in the Purchase Day Book.

(4) Debtors include Rs. 2,500 due from the proprietor.

(5) An amount of Rs. 2,500 received in respect of a private loan advanced by the proprietor was wrongly credited to Sundry Debtors Account.

(6) Purchase invoices of the value of Rs. 37,500 were entered in the Purchase Day Book on 29th December 2012, but the goods in respect thereof were received on 3rd January next year.

(7) An amount of Rs. 1,750 received from a debtor was wrongly credited to sales account.

(8) The annual interest on Government Promissory Notes accrued due on 31st December 2012, but was collected only in next year.

Solution **[CA]**

Trading and Profit and Loss Account of the 'Business Centre'
for the year ended December 31, 20 12

Dr. *Particulars*		*Amount* Rs.	*Particulars*		Cr. *Amount* Rs.
To Opening Stock		55,000	By Sales	12,56,500	
" Purchase		10,27,500[1]	*Less* : Receipt		
" Wages		22,500	wrongly credited	1,750	12,54,750*
" Profit and Loss A/c					
" Gross Profit transferred		1,94,750	" Closing Stock		45,000
		12,99,750			12,99,750
To Rent and Taxes		12,500	By Trading A/c		
" Salaries		50,000	Gross Profit transferred		1,94,750
" Lighting and Heating		10,000	" Discount		7,500
" Insurance		3,000	" Interest on G.P. Notes		
" Advertisement		10,000	(Outstanding)		400
" Bad Debts		5,000			
" Provision for Doubtful Debts		2,294[2]			
" Discounts		1,000			
" Sundry Expenses		1,750			
" Postage and Telegrams		6,500			
" Depreciation :					
Building ($2\frac{1}{2}$%)	2,500				
Furniture & Fixture (5%)	1,288				

Contd.

* Since Debtors include Rs. 2,500 due from the proprietor which may be attributable to the withdrawal of goods by the owner for his personal use and such a withdrawal does not affect profit, as such, both the purchases and sales should be further reduced by Rs. 2,500 each.

		Rs.		Rs.
Plant and Machinery (10%)	4,750			
		8,538		
To Capital A/c Net Profit transferred		92,068		
		2,02,650		2,02,650

Working Notes :

		Rs.
1. ***Purchases*** : Already Given		10,52,500
Add : Invoices omitted		12,500
		10,65,000
Less : Invoice entered in the Purchases Day Book on 29th December 2012 but goods not yet received		37,500*
		10,27,500

			Rs.
2.	Prov. for Doubtful Debts		
	Sundry Debtors : Already given		93,500
Add :	Receipt of private loan wrongly credited to Debtors		2,500
			96,000
Less :	Receipt from debtor wrongly credited to Sales	1,750	
	Transfer to proprietor	2,500	
			4,250
			91,750
	Provision at $2\frac{1}{2}$ % on Rs. 91,750		2,294

After preparing Trading and Profit and Loss Account (i.e., after effecting all the adjustments and the final closure of all the nominal accounts), if remaining balances are extracted from the books and checked, the trial balance which is prepared is called post-closing (or post-clearing) trial balance. This is to distinguish from the one prepared before the adjusting and closing entries and is known as pre-closing and pre-adjusted trial balance.

The post closing trial balance of the said problem is presented:

'Business Centre'
Post-closing Trial Balance
as on 31st December 2012

	Debit	*Credit*
	Rs.	Rs.
Capital (after transfer of net profit and drawings etc.)		4,02,068
S. Creditors		65,000
Provision for Doubtful Debts		2,294
Building	97,500	
Furniture and Fixtures	24,462	
Plant and Machinery	42,750	
Stock	45,000	
Goods-in-transit	37,500	
Debtors	91,750	
4% G. P. Notes	10,000	
Cash	23,000	
Bank	97,000	
Outstanding Interest	400	
Total	4,69,362	4,69,362

Now, items pertaining to the real and personal accounts are carried forward to next year. Usually debit items are the assets owned by the business and credit items are the liabilities owed by the firm. The amount which is owing to creditors is an external (outside) liability whereas the sum (capital) belonging to the proprietor is an internal liability. Since the totals of the debit and credit items tally, the sums of the assets and liabilities also should agree. Accordingly, the assets (resources or properties) owned equate with the liabilities (sources or equities) incurred.

* It represents "Goods in Transit" to be shown in the assets side of the balance sheet.

The statement listing the 'post-closing trial balance' items as assets and liabilities (i.e., claims against the assets) is called a position statement (or Balance Sheet). As such, the aforesaid data would appear in the balance sheet which is presented:

'Business Centre'
Balance Sheet
as on 31st December 2012

Liabilities	*Rs.*	*Assets*	*Rs.*	*Rs.*
Capital	4,02,068	Building		97,500
Sundry Creditors	65,000	Plant and Machinery		42,750
		Furniture and Fixtures		24,462
		Goods-in-Transit		37,500
		Stock		45,000
		Debtors	91,750	
		Less : Prov. for Bad Debts	2,294	89,456
		4% G. P. Notes		10,000
		Cash		23,000
		Bank		97,000
		Outstanding Interest		400
	4,67,068			4,67,068

ASSIGNMENT MATERIALS
THEORETICAL
Multiple Choice Questions

1. A. Give the correct answer from the following:

(a) When an asset is purchased. Asset Account is:
(i) Debited; (ii) Credited; (iii) None of these

(b) When plants are purchased for resale, Plant Account is:
(i) Debited; (ii) Credited; (iii) None of these

(c) When Commission is received, Commission Account is:
(i) Credited; (ii) Debited; (iii) None of these

(d) When installation expenses are paid for Plant, Installation Expenses are :
(i) Debited; (ii) Credited; (iii) None of these

(e) When repairs are made, Repair Account is:
(i) Credited; (ii) Debited; (iii) None of these

(f) When Registration Expenses are incurred for purchasing a Plot of Land Registration Expense is:
(i) Debited; (ii) Credited; (iii) None of these

(g) When goods are taken over by the proprietor for his own use. Drawing Account is :
(i) Debited ; (ii) Credited; (iii) None of these

(h) When Travelling Expenses are paid, Travelling Expenses are:
(i) Debited ; (ii) Credited; (iii) None of these

(i) When Bad Debts are recovered, Bad Debts Recovery Account is:
(i) Credited; (ii) Debited; (iii) None of these

(j) When plants are sold, Plant Account is:
(i) Debited ; (ii) Credited; (iii) None of these

[Ans. (a) (i); (b) (iii); (c) (i); (d) (iii); (e) (ii); (f) (iii); (g) (i); (h) (i); (i) (i); (j) (ii)]

2. (a) Capital Rs. 30,000; Liabilities Rs. 10,000. Assets will be:
(i) Rs. 40,000 ; (ii) Rs. 20,000; (iii) None of these

(b) Capital Rs. 40,000; Profit Rs. 10,000; Drawings Rs. 12,000; Additional Capital Rs. 5,000. Assets will be:
(i) Rs. 63,000 ; (ii) Rs. 43,000; (iii) None of these

(c) Asset Rs. 5,000; Capital Rs. 40,000; Profit Rs. 15,000. Drawings will be:
(i) Rs. 5,000 ; (ii) Rs. 15,000; (iii) None of these

(d) Capital Rs. 50,000; Loss Rs. 10,000; Drawing Rs. 10,000. Assets will be:
(i) Rs. 40,000 ; (ii) Rs. 30,000; (iii) None of these

(e) Asset Rs. 60,000; Capital Rs. 30,000; Additional Capital Rs. 5,000; Drawing Rs. 10,000. Profit will be:
(i) Rs. 50,000 ; (ii) Rs. 35,000; (iii) None of these

[Ans. (a) (i); (b) (ii); (c) (i); (d) (ii); (e) (ii)]

3. (a) The process of recording transactions is called
(i) Journalising ; (ii) Posting; (iii) Casting.

(b) Compound Entry is related to:
(i) More than Two Accounts ; (ii) Two Accounts; (iii) Less than Two Accounts.

(c) Increase in assets means:
(i) Profit ; (ii) Loss; (iii) None of these.

(d) Decrease in assets means:
(i) Profit ; (ii) Loss; (iii) None of these.

(e) Increase in capital:
(i) Credit ; (ii) Debit; (iii) None of these.

(f) Increase in assets:
(i) Debit; (ii) Credit ; (iii) None of these.

(g) Simple Entry means where there is:
(i) one entry; (ii) two entry ; (iii) Compound Entry.

(h) Journal is called
(i) Original Book; (ii) Subsidiary Book ; (iii) Supplementary Book.

[Ans. (a) (i); (b) (i); (c) (i); (d) (ii); (e) (i); (f) (i); (g) (i); (h) (i)]

4. (a) The Golden Rule "what comes in is debit and what goes out is Credit" is applicable to:
(i) Personal Account; (ii) Real Account ; (iii) Nominal Account.

(b) Nominal Account relates to:
(i) Expenses/losses or income/gains; (ii) Assets and Liabilities; (iii) Customers, creditors etc.

(c) Real Account relates to:
(i) assets; (ii) expenses or losses ; (iii) customers, creditors etc.

(d) Personal Account relates to:
(i) assets and liabilities; (ii) expenses/losses ; (iii) customer/creditor.

(e) Under Double entry System, every transaction affects:
(i) debt and credit side of the same account; (ii) two accounts ; (iii) Same accounts in the opposite side.

[Ans. (a) (ii); (b) (i); (c) (i); (d) (iii); (e) (iii)]

Short-Answer Type Questions

5. How do you ascertain 'Debit' or 'Credit' for Purchase Account?
6. How do you ascertain 'Debit' or 'Credit' under Real Account?
7. How do you ascertain 'Debit' or 'Credit' under Nominal Account?
8. How do you ascertain 'Debit' or 'Credit' in case of Personal Account under Modern Approach?
9. How do you ascertain 'Debit' or 'Credit' in case of Real Account under Modern Approach?
10. How do you ascertain 'Debit' or 'Credit' in case of Nominal Account under Modern Approach?
11. Define **Debit** and **Credit**. How do you ascertain them?
12. What is the Golden Rule of Book-keeping? How do you ascertain Debit and Credit with the help of the Golden Rule?

13. What is the Traditional Approach for ascertaining **Debit and Credit?**
14. What is Journal? Discuss the various steps for recording transactions in journal.
15. What is journal? Discuss the various steps for subdivision of Journal.
    What are special Journals? What kinds of transaction are recorded in Journal? Discuss the limitations of Journals.
16. Write notes on:
    (a) Debit and Credit Notes: (b) Book of Original Entry; (c) Purchase Book and Sales Book.
17. What is a Trial Balance? What are its advantages?
18. What is Ledger? Discuss its application in Double Entry System of Book-keeping
19. Discuss the functions of Ledger. How many kinds of accounts are found in the Ledger?
20. Discuss the various entries which are to be passed through a journal even if we keep all subsidiary books.
21. (a) 'Every debit has a corresponding credit'. —Discuss.
    (b) 'Every transaction has a double aspect.' —Discuss.
22. What do you mean by Practical System of Book-keeping? State at least three of its advantages.
23. Why is Journal called the Book of Original Entry?
24. Mention the different types of errors.

Long-Answer type Questions

25. "Accounting Equation is the modern concept of Double Entry System."—Comment.
26. "Accounting Equation is applicable in all the Current Assets." —Justify.
27. Describe the fundamental accounting equation. How are the revenue and expense related to it?
28. How do you compute Accounting Equation? Explain it with the help of three examples.
29. What is Hybrid System of Accounting?
30. How do you convert Cash Basis of Accounting into Mercantile Basis of Accounting?
31. Explain the objectives and functions of a Trial Balance.
32. What are Pre-closing and Post-closing Trial Balance? Illustrate with an example.
33. Mention the errors which are not disclosed by a Trial balance.
34. Explain the Characteristics of a Trial Balance.
35. Mention the errors which are disclosed by a Trial Balance.
36. Mention the errors which affect the agreement of a Trial Balance.
37. Mention the errors which do not affect the agreement of Trial Balance.

PRACTICAL

Debit and Credit

1. Ascertain 'Debit' and 'Credit' from the following:

(i)	Sold goods for cash	(ii)	Sold goods on credit
(iii)	Sold goods to A for cash	(iv)	Sold a plant for cash
(v)	Paid salary to Mr. X	(vi)	Invested further capital
(vii)	Paid to Mr. Y	(viii)	Received interest
(ix)	Paid advertisement	(x)	Paid rent to landlord Mr. Z
(xi)	Bought goods from Y	(xii)	Bought goods from T for cash
(xiii)	Received loan from Mr. D	(xiv)	Received commission in cash
(xv)	Paid carriage	(xvi)	Paid carriage on goods sold
(xvii)	Bought a machine for cash	(xviii)	Sold furniture for cash
(xix)	Received dividend	(xx)	Bought goods for cash.

Accounting Equation

2. Prepare Accounting Entries from the following:
   (a) Commenced business with cash Rs. 60,000;
   (b) Prepaid Rent Rs. 500;
   (c) Purchase goods for cash Rs. 30,000; Credit Rs. 20,000;

(d) Sold goods for cash Rs. 30,000; Cost Price Rs. 20,000;
(e) Paid Salary Rs. 500 and outstanding Salary amounted to Rs. 100;
(f) Bought a TV for personal use Rs. 5,000.

[Ans. Assets Rs. 84,500 = Liabilities Rs. 20,100 + Capital Rs. 64,400]

3. Mr. X ltd. the following transactions:

(a) Commenced business with cash Rs. 50,000;
(b) Purchase goods for cash Rs. 20,000 and credit Rs. 30,000;
(c) Sold goods for cash Rs. 40,000 (Cost Price Rs. 30,000);
(d) Rent paid Rs. 500;
(e) Rent Outstanding Rs. 100;
(f) Bought Furniture for Rs. 5,000 on credit;
(g) Bought a TV for personal use Rs. 5,000;
(h) Purchased Building for cash Rs. 20,000.

Use accounting equations to show the effect of the above transactions of his assets; liabilities and capital and also show his Balance Sheet.

[Ans. Assets Rs. 89,500 = Liabilities Rs. 35,100 + Capital Rs. 54,400; Balance Sheet Rs. 89,500]

Cash And Accrual Basis

4. Ascertain the net profit of Mr. B. Banerjee for the year ended 31.12.2012, on Mercantile Basis, from the following particulars :

	Rs.
Net profit on cash basis	11,950
Fees outstanding on 31.12.2011	800
Fees outstanding on 31.12.2012	500
Expenses outstanding on 31.12.2012	600
Expenses outstanding on 31.12.2011	300
Expenses paid in advance on 31.12.2011	400
Expenses paid in advance on 31.12.2012	600
Fees received in advance on 31.12.2012	1,000

[Ans. Net Profit under Mercantile Basis Rs. 10,550]

5. Mr. Sinha, an Income-tax practitioner, furnishes the following information on his income and expenses for the year ended 31.3.2011 :

	Rs.
Fees received in cash	57,000
Fees accrued but not received	10,000
Salaries of staff paid	5,600
Salaries of staff due but not paid	800
Rent of his chamber paid	4,800
Rent of his chamber paid in advance	600
Sundry Expenses paid	300

Ascertain his net income (Profit) under (a) Cash Basis of Accounting; (b) Accrual Basis of Accounting.

[Ans. Net Income under Cash Basis Rs. 46,300; Net Income under Accrual Basis Rs. 56,100]

Journal

6. Pass journal entries in the books of Miss. Anindita Paul for the year ended 31st Dec. 2012:

Dec. 1. Started business with a capital of:
Cash Rs. 3,000; Bank Rs. 4,000; Plant Rs. 12,000; Creditors Rs. 4,000 and Debtors Rs. 8,000

3. Purchased a plant for Rs. 50,000, Cost of carriage Rs. 500; and installation expenses being paid for Rs. 1,500

4. Purchased furniture for resale from X Ltd. Rs. 3,000
5. Purchased furniture for office decoration Rs. 8,000
8. Sold furniture out of those meant for resale Rs. 4,000
10. Returned a part of furniture out of those meant for resale to X Ltd. for Rs. 400.
14. Goods drawn by the proprietor for her own use for Rs. 1,000
18. Goods distributed as free samples Rs. 500
19. Paid Rs. 4,000 into business Bank Account from private cash
22. A table purchased for Rs. 500 for the personal use of Miss Paul
25. Withdrawn cash from business for private use Rs. 1,000
27. Paid salary to Mr. X Rs. 3,000.
29. Paid advertisement to Anandabazar Patrika for Rs. 500.
30. Miss Paul encashed her Savings Deposit Certificates and deposited the amount into her business for Rs. 3,000
31. Life Insurance Premium paid by Miss Paul for Rs. 1,000.

7. Pass journal entries in respect of the following transactions in the books of Mr. Bakshi :

(i) Started business with a capital of Rs. 14,000 in cash
(ii) Opened a Bank Account for Rs. 12,000
(iii) Purchased Furniture for resale Rs. 1,000
(iv) Purchased Furniture for office decoration Rs. 500
(v) Sold furniture out of those meant for resale Rs. 1,500
(vi) Paid Rs. 1,000 into business Bank Account from private cash
(vii) Received cash from Mr. X as loan Rs. 1,000
(viii) Mr. X charged interest on loan Rs. 105
(ix) Bank collected dividend and credited to the account of Mr. Bakshi Rs. 700
(x) Purchased a signboard for advertisement purpose Rs. 300
(xi) Purchased three typewriters from Banerjee & Co. for resale @ Rs. 1,500
(xii) Returned one typewriter from Banerjee & Co. not being in good condition
(xiii) Issued a cheque to Banerjee & Co. for Rs. 3,000
(viv) Sold two typewriters out of those meant for resale Rs. 4,000
(xv) Withdrew cash from bank for personal use Rs. 1,000
(xvi) Paid Rent out of Personal cash for Rs. 3,000.

8. Journalise the following transactions :

(a) Received Rs. 1,500 from Mr. Y in full settlement of Rs. 1,600.
(b) Received Rs. 1,000 from Mr. Z after allowing him a discount of Rs. 100.
(c) Paid to Mr. D Rs. 490 in full settlement of Rs. 500.
(d) Paid to Mr. E Rs. 1,300 after receiving a discount of Rs. 200.
(e) Received Rs. 3,500 from Mr. H as first and final dividend from his official receiver against dues of Rs. 7,000

Ledger

9. Miss Suranjana furnished the following particulars as on 1st Jan. 2001 and you are asked to show the entries and open the ledger account and bring down their balances : Cash A/c Rs. 10,000; Plant A/c Rs. 8,000; Capital A/c Rs. 25,000; Debtors Rs. 7,000; Creditors Rs. 3,000; Cash at Bank Rs. 8,000.

Following transactions took place during the month 2001:

1. Bought goods for Cash Rs. 3,000;
2. Sold goods on Credit Rs. 8,000;
3. Paid salary Rs. 1,000;
4. Bought a New Plant for Rs. 5,000;
5. Further Capital invested in the business Rs. 10,000;
6. Paid rent by cheque Rs. 1,000;

7. Bought goods on Credit Rs. 2,000;
8. Deposite into Bank Rs. 3,000.

[Ans. Cash A/c Rs. 8,000, Plant A/c Rs. 13,000, Capital A/c Rs. 35,000, Debtors A/c Rs. 15,000, Creditors A/c Rs. 5,000, Cash at Bank Rs. 10,000, Purchase A/c Rs. 5,000, Sales A/c Rs. 8,000, Salary A/c Rs. 1,000, Rent A/c Rs. 1,000]

10. Sumana bought goods from Suparna valued Rs. 6,000 on 1.1.2012. On 15th January, she returned goods to the value of Rs. 500 as the goods were not according to sample. On 1st Feb. she issued a cheque for Rs. 3,000 to Suparna who presented the cheque to the bank but it was returned dishonoured. On the same day, Sumana paid Rs. 1,000 in Cash to Suparna and requested her to wait for one month. On 15th March Sumana became insolvent and only 50 paise in the rupee was relised from her estate as final dividend.

Show Suparna's Account in the books of Sumana and Sumana's Account in the books of Suparna.

[Ans. Bad Debts and Deficiency Rs. 2,250]

Trial Balance

11. From the following Ledger Accounts' balances prepare a Trial Balance of Sri G.M. Sinha for the year ended 31st Dec. 2011:

Purchases (adjusted) Rs. 8,000; Sales Rs. 25,000; Carriage Inwards Rs. 2,000; Capital Rs. 37,000; Drawings Rs. 5,000; Wages Rs. 4,000; Salaries Rs. 5,000; Plant and Machinery Rs. 12,000; Land and Building Rs. 7,000; Patent and Copyrights Rs. 4,000; Bad Debts Rs. 1,000; Depreciation on Plant and Machinery Rs. 1,000; Discount on Sales Rs. 1,000; Discount on Purchases Rs. 500; Bad Debts Rs. 2,000; Provision for Bad Debts Rs. 1,500; Trade Expenses Rs. 1,000; Prepaid Salaries Rs. 1,000; Outstanding Wages Rs. 1,000; Bills Receivable Rs. 4,000; Bills Payable Rs. 1,000; Sundry Debtors Rs. 8,000; Sundry Creditors Rs. 3,000; Sock (31.12.2011) Rs. 3,000.

[Ans. Total of Trial Balance Rs. 69,000]

12. From the following balances presented by Sri. Debashish Poddar, prepare a Trial Balance for the year ended 31st Dec. 2011:

Capital Rs. 1,15,000; Gross Profit Rs. 50,000; Drawings Rs. 8,000; Interest Received Rs. 10,000; Salaries Rs. 20,000; Insurance Rs. 5,000; Bad Debts Rs. 2,000; Sundry Debtors Rs. 20,000; Land and Building Rs. 40,000; Plant and Machinery Rs. 35,000; Furniture & Fittings Rs. 7,000; Bills Receivable Rs. 6,000; Investment Rs. 10,000; Provision for Bad Bebts Rs. 1,000; Creditors Rs. 39,000; Bills Payable Rs. 20,000; Loan on Mortgage at 10% p.a. Rs. 10,000; Outstanding Salary Rs. 5,000; Accrued Interest Rs. 1,000; Prepaid Insurance Rs. 1,000; Depreciation: Land and Building Rs. 4,000; On Furniture & Fittings Rs. 3,500, on Plant and Machinery Rs. 1,000; Outstanding Interest on Mortgage Rs. 500; Closing Stock Rs. 87,000.

[Ans. Total of Trial Balance Rs. 2,50,500]

[**Hint :** Closing stock will appear in Trial Balance. Gross profit shows a credit balance.]

13. The total of the debit side of the Trial Balance of a large boot and shoe repairing firm as at 31.12.2012 is Rs. 1,66,590 and that of the credit side is Rs. 42,470.

After several checking and rechecking the following mistakes are discovered:

Items of Accounts	*Correct Figures (as it should be)*	*Figure as it appears in the Trial Balance*
	Rs.	Rs.
Opening Stock	14,900	14,800
Repairs	61,780	61,780 (appears on the debit side)
Rent and Rates	2,160	2,400
Sundry Creditors	6,070	5,900
Sundry Debtors	8,060	8,310

Ascertain the correct total of the Trial Balance.

[CU BCom (Hons.)]

[Ans. Correct Total of Trial Balance Rs. 1,04,420]

CHAPTER 4

SUBSIDIARY BOOKS

Learning Objectives

Subdivisions of Journal

Cash Discount

Trade Discount

Subsidiary Books

1. *Purchase Day Book*
2. *Sales Day Book*
   —Application of Sales Tax
3. *Returns Inward Book*
   —Excise Duty
   —Credit Note
4. *Returns Outward Book*
   —Debit Note
5. *Bills Receivable Book*
6. *Bills Payable Book*

Subdivisions of Journal

Since there are numerous transactions in a business unit, it becomes necessary to use a number of subsidiary journals instead of a single journal although one journal is used for maintaining one particular class of transactions. That is why, in all business houses, a number of original entries for recording the different types of transactions are used.

Cash Book is the most important Day Book. It contains all cash transactions.

For further detail about the Cash Book, please, see Chapter 7.

Cash Book contains all cash transactions. Therefore, the following subsidiary books are maintained for credit and other types of transactions :

1. ***Purchase Day Book (meant for recording all credit purchases of goods)***
2. ***Sales Day Book (meant for recording all credit sales of goods)***
3. ***Returns Inward Book (meant for recording goods returned by the customers)***
4. ***Returns Outward Book (meant for recording goods returned to suppliers)***
5. ***Bills Receivable Book (meant for recording all transactions relating to Bills Receivable)***
6. ***Bills Payable Book (meant for recording all transactions relating to Bills Payable)***
7. ***Journal Proper (meant for recording those transactions which are not recorded in the above books. This part has separately been explained).***

Before explaining the above subsidiary books, we are going to discuss certains terms used in Subsidiary Books, viz., Cash Discount and Trade Discount—which are very important for the purpose.

Cash Discount

An amount which is allowed for the prompt settlement of a debt arising out of a sale within a specified time and calculated on a percentage basis is known as Cash Discount, i.e., it is always associated with actual payment. Cash discount taken or allowed are usually shown in an income statement as reduction from sales or purchases as financial expense or income on the principle that the prompt settlement of a receivable or payable is a prepayment, the 'normal' payment being at the end of a credit period. In either case, the receivables and payables are first stated in the accounts at their gross amounts and the discounts are recorded in separate accounts as they are taken (E. L. Kohler—*A Dictionary for Accountants)*. In short, cash discount is allowed by the firm when the payment is made by its customers (known as **Discount Allowed**) and cash discount is received when the payment is made by the firm to its creditors (known as **Discount Received**).

Trade Discount

It is also a deduction from the catalogue, list or published price, calculated on a certain percentage basis, which is allowed either by a wholesaler or a manufacturer to their retailers who can sell the goods at the published price. It is to be remembered in this respect that this discount is allowed irrespective of the fact whether the payment is made by cash or on credit. Therefore, ***actual price or net amount, i.e., after allowing trade discount, is to be recorded in the books of accounts.***

One point must be remembered—the same customer may take advantage of the trade discount and the cash discount.

Differences between Cash Discount and Trade Discount

Trade Discount	Cash Discount
1. Trade discount is given by the manufacturer or the wholesaler to a retailer and not to others.	1. Cash discount may be allowed by seller to any debtor.
2. The object of this discount is to help the retailer to earn some profit.	2. Cash discount actually encourages the debtors to pay within a specified period of time.

Contd.

3. It is not usually accounted for in the books since the net amount (i.e., after deducting discount) is shown.	3. This discount must be accounted for in the books since it is deducted from the gross selling price.
4. This discount is allowed only when there is sale—either Cash or Credit.	4. Cash discount is allowed only when there is cash receipt or cash payment including cheques.
5. It is usually given at the same rate which is applicable to all customers.	5. It varies from customer to customer depending on the time and period of payment.
6. It is calculated at a certain percentage on list/catalogue/published price.	6. It is calculated always on net amount payable.

Illustration 1

Trade Discount

Suppose, Rate of Trade Discount is @ 20%

		Rs.
Value of 10 lbs of tea @ Rs. 40 =	Rs.	400
Less : Trade discount @ 20%		80
Net amount payable		320

The customer, in this case, should pay Rs. 320 and not Rs. 400. Therefore, his account will be debited by Rs. 320 (in the books of seller) and sales account will also be credited by Rs. 320 (in the books of customer/purchaser). Trade discount amounting to Rs. 80 must not be recorded in the books of accounts at all.

Cash Discount

Suppose, rate of Cash Discount is @ 10%

	Rs.
Total amount	320
Less : Cash discount @ 10%	32
Net amount payable	288

In this case, although the customer should have to pay Rs. 320, he will pay only Rs. 288 since he is allowed a cash discount of Rs. 32 for timely payment, i.e., his total payment must be Rs. 288. This cash discount is a gain in the hands of the customer while this is a loss to the seller.

E. & O. E.

This is an abbreviated term which means **'Errors and Omissions Excepted.'** In other words, if there is any error in the invoice, which results in an under–or over-charge, the same has to be adjusted accordingly.

1. PURCHASE DAY BOOK

Purchase Day Book contains the transactions relating to credit purchase of goods, i.e., it keeps record about the details of credit purchase of goods which have been bought for the purpose of re-sale. It is also known as Bought Day Book, Purchase Journal, etc.

Entries are made from inward invoices received from the suppliers in this book. The entries are posted daily in detail to the Suppliers Account in the ledger. But the Purchase Day Book is totalled only at the end of a day, a week, a fortnight or a month and final total is ruled off and posted to the debit of Purchase Account in the Ledger. It should be remembered that purchase invoices received from different suppliers contain different numbers and, as such, they should again be numbered by the purchaser serially for future reference.

But before discussing the purchase Day Book, we are to explain the most significant aspect, i.e., the *'INVOICE'*.

Invoice

Needless to mention here that entries in the Purchase Day Book and Sales Day Book are made from the invoice. It is the bill of demand sent by the suppliers to the customers relating to goods supplied and the cost thereon. It contains full details relating to the amount of demand computed and the terms of payment, the names and addresses of the customers and suppliers to the contract of sale of goods, etc.

Specimen of an Invoice

INVOICE

Gram : 'Bit'	8/1 Chintamoni Das Lane
Phone : 2334-6403	26th Dec. 2011
M/s P. Bose & Co.	No. 808/11
25 Motisil Street	Bought of New Central Book Agency
Chennai 1	Publishers and Book sellers
	8/1 Chintamoni Das Lane, Kolkata 9
Terms 2%—90 days	
	Rs.
100 copies H. S. Practical Accounts @ Rs. 80 per copy	8,000
200 copies Practical Accounts Part I @ Rs. 100 per copy	20,000
100 copies Practical Accounts Part II @ Rs. 120 per copy	12,000
	40,000
Less : Trade Discount @ 20%	8,000
	32,000
Add : Packing Charges	500
	32,500
Per Eastern Railway (Madras Mail)	
Freight Paid	
	E.& O. E.
	A. Sen
	Manager

To sum up

Outward Invoice or, Sales Invoice or Sales Voucher is the **invoice issued by the supplier of goods sold by him on credit and to the related buyer who receives the goods—the invoice is called** ***Inward Invoice,*** or ***Purchase Invoice*** or ***Purchase Voucher.***

The ruling of a Purchase Day Book is presented :

Purchase Day Book

Date	*Particulars*	*Inward Invoice*	*L.F.*	*Details*	*Total*	*Remarks*
				Rs.	Rs.	

Explanation

(i) The 'Date' Column = It represents the date on which the transaction took place.

(ii) The 'Particulars' Column = This column includes the name of the sellers and particulars of goods purchased.

(iii) Inward 'Invoice' Column = It reveals the serial number of the Inward Invoice.

(iv) The 'L F.' Column = It informs the page number of the supplier's account in the Supplier's Ledger.

(v) The 'Details 'Column = It reveals the amount of goods purchased and the amount of trade discount, if any, and other discounts and incidental expenses, if any.

(vi) The 'Total' Column = This column represents the 'net' price of the goods, i.e., the amount which is receivable to the creditors after adjusting discounts/expenses, if any.

(vii) The 'Remarks' Column = This column contains any extra information or the rate of Trade Discount, etc.

Sometimes, the purchaser purchases different varieties of goods. For this purpose additional columns are to be used which is known as Columnar Purchase Day Book.

Illustration 2

From the following particulars of M/s B. Bros, prepare a Columnar Purchase Day Book :

2011 Jan. 5. Purchased 100 pieces of Silk Garments from Das & Sons @ Rs. 60 per piece (Invoice No. P/10) less Trade Discount @ 10%.

17. Purchased from Indian Silk House 300 yds of Silk @ Rs. 40 per yd (Invoice No. T/17) less Trade Discount @ $7\frac{1}{2}$%, Sales-tax @ 10%.

26. Purchased from Simla Woollen Stores, 50 pieces of Woollen Garments @ Rs. 80 per piece (Invoice No. G/26) less Trade Discount @ 5%, Carriage Rs. 150.

27. Purchased 100 pieces of Cotton Garments from Bashirhat Trading Corporation @ Rs. 20 per piece (Invoice No. Z/17) less Trade Discount @ 10%.

Solution

In the books of M/s B. Bros
Purchase Day Book

Date	*Particulars or name of the sellers and particulars of the goods purchased*	*Inward Invoice No.*	*L.F.*	*Details*	*Total amount*	*Silk Garments*	*Cotton Garments*	*Woollen Garments*	*Remark*
				Rs.	Rs.	Rs.	Rs.	Rs.	Rs.
2011 Jan. 5	**Das & Sons :** 100 pieces of Silk Garments @ Rs. 60 per piece	P/10		6,000					10% T.D.
	Less : Trade Discount @ 10%			600					
					5,400	5,400			
17	**Indian Silk House :** 300 yds of Silk @ Rs. 40 per yd.	T/17		12,000					
	Less : Trade Discount @ $7\frac{1}{2}$ %			900					$7\frac{1}{2}$ % T.D.
				11,100					
	Add : Sales-tax @ 10%			1,110					10% S.T.
					12,210	12,210			
26	**Simla Woollen Stores :** 50 pieces of Woollen Garments @ Rs. 80 per piece	G/26		4,000					
	Less : Trade Discount @ 5%			200					5% T.D.
				3,800					
	Add : Carriage			150					
					3,950			3,950	
27	**Bashirhat Trading Corporation :** 100 pieces of Cotton Garments @ Rs. 20 per piece	Z/17		2,000					10% T.D.
	Less : Trade Discount @ 10%			200					
					1,800		1,800		
	Total				23,360	17,610	1,800	3,950	

Posting the Purchase Day Book into the Ledger

Posting the Purchase Day Book will be made only when the transactions have already been recorded in the Purchase Day Book. They are posted to the respective ledgers after taking the following into consideration :

(a) At first, each and every entry will be posted to the credit side of the respective (i.e., individual) creditor's account in the creditors' ledger to make it up to-date; at the end of the day i.e., from this book the entries are daily posted in details to the Suppliers' Account.

(b) The grand total of the 'total' column is ruled—off and transferred to the debit of Purchase Account in General Ledger at the end of the month. The entry in that case will be :

Purchase A/c	Dr.
To Sundry Creditors Account	

The following illustration will make the principle clear :

Illustration 3

Compile a Columnar Purchase Day Book from the following particulars and post them into Ledger account :

2011 Dec.

5. Purchased from A. & Co. 5 meters of cloth at Rs. 20 per metre.
10. Purchased from B. Bakshi 25 woollen suits at Rs. 200 each and 40 meters ordinary silk at Rs. 10 per meter.
25. Purchased from C. & Co. 25 Silken Punjabis at Rs. 20 each and 20 meters serge at Rs. 20 per meters .
28. Purchased from B. Sen; 30 woollen suits at Rs. 200 each and 50 meters of silk at Rs. 10 per meter. Trade Discount @ 10%.

Solution

In the books of ....

Columnar Purchases Day Book

Date	*Particulars*	*Inward Invoice No.*	*L.F.*	*Details*	*Amount*	*Cloth*	*Garments*	*Remark*
				Rs.	Rs.	Rs.	Rs.	Rs.
2011								
Dec. 5	**A & Co.** 5 meter cloth @ Rs. 20 per meter				100	100		
10	**B. Bakshi** 25 Woollen suits @ Rs. 200 each				5,000		5,000	
	40 meter Silk @ Rs. 10 per meter				400	400		
25	**C. & Co.** 25 Silken Punjabi s @ Rs. 20 each				500		500	
	20 meters serge at Rs. 20 per meter				400	400		
28	**B. Sen** 30 Woollen suits @ Rs. 200			6,000				
	Less : Trade Discount @ 10%			600				
					5,400		5,400	10% T.D.
	50 meters of silk @ Rs. 10 per meter			500				

Contd.

					Rs.	Rs.	Rs.	Rs.	Rs.
	Less : Trade Discount @ 10%				50				
						450	450		
	Total					12,250	1,350	10,900	

Considering the above Purchases Day Book, we post them into the ledger in the following manner :

In the General Ledger

Purchase Account

Dr.									Cr.
Date	*Particulars*	*L. F.*	*V. N.*	*Amount*	*Date*	*Particulars*	*L. F.*	*V. N.*	*Amount*
2011				Rs.					Rs.
Dec. 31	To Sundry Creditors A/c			12,250		By			

Sundry Creditors Account

Dr									Cr.
Date	*Particulars*	*L. F.*	*V. N.*	*Amount*	*Date*	*Particulars*	*L. F.*	*V. N.*	*Amount*
				Rs.	2011				Rs.
	To				Dec. 31	By Purchase A/c			12,250

In the Creditors' Ledger

A & Co. Account

Dr.									Cr.
Date	*Particulars*	*L. F.*	*V. N.*	*Amount*	*Date*	*Particulars*	*L. F.*	*V. N.*	*Amount*
				Rs.	2011				Rs.
	To				Dec. 5.	By Purchase A/c			100

B Bakshi Account

Dr.									Cr.
Date	*Particulars*	*L. F.*	*V. N.*	*Amount*	*Date*	*Particulars*	*L. F.*	*V. N.*	*Amount*
				Rs.	2011				Rs.
	To				Dec. 10.	By Purchase A/c			5,400

C & Co. Account

Dr.								Cr.
Date	*Particulars*	*LF.*	*V. N.*	*Amount*	*Date*	*Particulars*	*L. F.*	*V. N.*	*Amount*
				Rs.	2011				Rs.
	To				Dec. 25.	By Purchase A/c			900

B. Sen Account

Dr.									Cr.
Date	*Particulars*	*L. F.*	*V. N.*	*Amount*	*Date*	*Particulars*	*L. F.*	*V. N.*	*Amount*
				Rs.	2011				Rs.
	To				Dec. 28.	By Purchase A/c			5,850

2. SALES DAY BOOK

This book contains the transactions relating to credit sale of goods, i.e., it keeps record about the details of only credit sale of goods. It is also known as Sold Day Book, Sales Journal etc. The Sales Day Book is written from the copies of outward invoices. The debit entries (the amount recoverable from customers) are posted individually, whereas credit to Sales Account is given at the end of a day, a week, a fortnight, a month etc. In the Sales Day Book, however, *Outward Invoice No.* is used. The specimen of such an invoice is almost same as it has been shown while explaining Purchase Day Book.

The ruling of a Sales Day Book, however, is presented below :

Sales Day Book

Date	*Particulars*	*Outward Invoice No.*	*L.F.*	*Details*	*Total*	*Remarks*
				Rs.	Rs.	

Explanation

(i) The 'Date' Column	=	It represents the date on which the transaction took place i.e., when invoice is prepared.
(ii) The 'Particulars' Column	=	This column includes the names of the purchasers and particulars of good sold.
(iii) The 'Outward Invoice' Column	=	It reveals the serial number of the Outward Invoice.
(iv) The 'L.F.' Column	=	It takes the page number of the customers' account in the Debtors' Ledger.
(v) The 'Details' Column	=	It contains the amount of goods sold and amount of trade discount, if allowed, or any incidental expences etc., if any.
(vi) The 'Total' Column	=	This column expresses the 'net' price of the goods, i.e., the amount which is recoverable from the customers after adjusting any discount/adjustments, if any.
(vii) The 'Remarks' Column	=	This column contains any extra information, viz., rate of trade discount, the rate of sales-tax, etc.

The following illustration will make the principle clear.

Illustration 4

From the following particulars of M/s Banerjee & Sons, prepare a Columnar Sales Day Book (viz., Tea, Coffee, Cocoa) :

2011 Jan. 2. Sold to Nag & Co. 100 lbs of Tea @ Rs. 10 per lb, less Trade Discount @ 10%.
7. Sold to Sen Bros. 200 lbs of Tea @ Rs. 12 per lb, less Trade Discount @ 5%.
12. Sold to Bhattacharyya & Co. 50 lbs of Coffee @ Rs. 60 per lb, Trade Discount @ 10%, packing charges Rs. 25.
20. Sold to Sur & Co. 60 lbs of Cocoa @ Rs. 10 per lb, Trade Discount @ 10%.
26. Sold to Dey & Sons, 100 lbs of Coffee @ Rs. 50 per lb, Trade Discount @ 10%.

Solution

In the books of Banerjee & Sons
Sales Day Book

Date	*Particulars or name of the Purchasers and Particulars of Goods Sold*	*Invoice No.*	*L.F.*	*Details*	*Total*	*Tea*	*Coffee*	*Cocoa*	*Remark*
				Rs.	Rs.	Rs.	Rs.	Rs.	
2011 Jan. 2	**Nag & Co.** 100 lbs of Tea @ Rs. 10 per lb			1,000					
	Less : Trade Discount @ 10%			100					10% T.D.
					900	900			
7	**Sen Bros.** 200 lbs of Tea @ Rs. 12 per lb			2,400					
	Less : Trade Discount @ 5%			120					5 % T.D.
					2,280	2,280			
12	**Bhattacharyya & Co.** 50 lbs of Coffee @ Rs. 60 per lb.			3,000					
	Less : Trade Discount @ 10%			300					10% T.D.
				2,700					
	Add : Packing charges			25					
					2,725		2,725		

Contd.

				Rs.	Rs.	Rs.	Rs.	Rs.	
20	Sur & Co. 60 lbs of Cocoa @ Rs. 10 per lb *Less* : Trade Discount @ 10%			600 60	540			540	10% T.D.
26	Dey & Sons 100 lbs of Coffee @ Rs. 50 per lb *Less* : Trade Discount @ 10%			5,000 500	4,500		4,500		10% T.D.
	Total				10,945	3,180	7,225	540	

Application of Sales Tax in Sales Day Book

We know that while selling an article, sales tax is taken from the customer on a fixed percentage basis on net selling price, i.e., after deducting trade discount. In other words, it is the duty of the seller to collect the amount of sales tax from the customer and deposit the same to the government periodically. A separate column is opened for the purpose and the total amount of such column is credited to Sales Tax Account.

Naturally, when the amount of such tax is paid by the seller to the government, the entry will be :

Sales Tax A/c Dr.
 To Cash/Bank A/c

Consequently, if any balance is left at the end of the year, the same is shown as a liability in the liabilities side of the Balance Sheet.

For the time being, amount of sales tax will be added to the amount of sales.[1]

Excise Duty

It is imposed on almost all the commodities that are produced or manufactured in India. However, those items on which the state governments impose excise duty are exempted from central excise duty. From accounting point of view, it should be remembered that excise duty is calculated on gross price/list price.[2]

Illustration 5

From the following particulars, prepare a Sales Day Book with a separate column for Sales-tax recovery :

2011 Jan. 4. Sold to X & Co. 30 chests of coffee @ Rs. 300 per chest, less 5% trade discount. Excise duty @ 5% extra.

6. Sold to Y & Co. 50 chests of coffee @ Rs. 150 per chest, less 10% trade discount, Excise duty @ 5% extra.

10. Sold to Z & Co. 100 chests of coffee @ Rs. 100 per chest, less 10% trade discount, Excise duty @ 5% extra.

Sales tax is charged @ 10% on the net prices in all cases.

Solution

In the books of ....

Sales Day Book

Date	*Particulars*	*L.F.*	*Gross Price*	*Trade Discount*	*Excise Duty*	*Net Price*	*Sales Tax*	*Total Amount*	*Remarks*
			Rs.	Rs.	Rs.	Rs.	Rs.	Rs.	Rs.
2011 Jan. 4	X & Co. 30 chests of Coffee @ Rs. 300 per chest		9,000	450	450	9,000	900	9,900.00	5% T.D. 5% E. D.

Contd.

---

[1] Sales tax is imposed not only on the sale of goods but also on certain transactions viz., (i) hirepurchase and lease transactions; (ii) transaction relating to contract, (iii) supply of foodstuff to hotel and restaurants.

[2] Excise Duties are of two types : (i) **specific** and (ii) **ad valorem**, A specific duty is determined on the basis of **quantity of goods manufactured** on the other hand, **ad valorem** duty is ascertained on the **basis of value/price of goods manufactured.**

				Rs.	Rs.	Rs.	Rs.	Rs.	Rs.	Rs.
	Trade Discount @ 5%									5% S. Tax
6	Y & Co									
	50 chests of Coffee @ Rs. 150 per chest			7,500	750	375	7,125	712·50	7,837·50	10% T.D. 5% E. D.
	Trade Discount @ 10%									10% S. Tax
10	Z & Co.									
	50 chest of Coffee @ Rs. 100 per chest			10,000	1,000	500	9,500	950	10,450·00	10% T.D. 5% E. D.
	Trade Discount @ 10%									10% S. Tax
				26,500	2,200	1,325	25,625	2,562·50	28,187·50	

Note : Excise Duty is calculated on *'Gross Price'* wheras sales-tax is calculated on *'Net Price'*.

Posting the Sales Day Book into the Ledger

The Sales Day Book is written from the copies of outward invoices. The debit entries relating to amounts recoverable from the customers are daily posted individually, whereas, credit to Sales Account is given at the end of a day, a week, a fortnight, a month, etc.

In short :

(a) Each and every entry will be posted to the debit side of the respective (i.e., individual) debtor's account in the debtors ledger at the end of the day ;

(b) The grand total of the 'Total' column is ruled off and transferred to the general ledger at the end of the month. The entries for this purpose will be :

Sundry Debtors A/c	Dr.
To Sales A/c	
" Sales Tax A/c (remains outstanding, if any)	

Illustration 6

Considering the figures from the previous illustration, show how you would post them into ledger.

Solution

In General Ledger

Dr. **Sundry Debtors Account** Cr.

Date	*Particulars*	*L. F.*	*V. N.*	*Amount*	*Date*	*Particulars*	*L. F.*	*V. N.*	*Amount*
2011				Rs.					Rs.
Jan. 31	To Sales A/c			25,625.00		By			
	" Sales Tax Payable A/c			2,562.50					

Dr. **Sales Account** Cr.

Date	*Particulars*	*L. F.*	*V. N.*	*Amount*	*Date*	*Particulars*	*L. F.*	*V. N.*	*Amount*
	To			Rs.	2011				Rs.
					Jan. 31	By Sundry Debtors A/c			25,625.00

Dr. **Sale Tax Payable Account** Cr.

Date	*Particulars*	*L. F.*	*V. N.*	*Amount*	*Date*	*Particulars*	*L. F.*	*V. N.*	*Amount*
	To			Rs.	2011				Rs.
					Jan. 31	By Sundry Debtors A/c			2,562·50

In the Debtors Ledger

Dr. **X & Co. Account** Cr.

Date	*Particulars*	*L. F.*	*V. N.*	*Amount*	*Date*	*Particulars*	*L. F.*	*V. N.*	*Amount*
2011				Rs.					Rs.
Jan. 4	To Sales A/c			9,000		By			
	" Sales Tax Payable A/c			900					

Dr. **Y & Co. Account** Cr.

Date	Particulars	L.F.	V.N.	Amount	Date	Particulars	L.F.	V.N.	Amount
2011				Rs.					Rs.
Jan. 6	To Sales A/c			7,125·00		By			
	" Sales Tax Payable A/c			712·50					

Dr. **Z & Co. Account** Cr.

Date	Particulars	L.F.	V.N.	Amount	Date	Particulars	L.F.	V.N.	Amount
2011				Rs.					Rs.
Jan. 10	To Sales A/c			9,500		By			
	" Sales Tax Payable A/c			950					

3. SALES RETURN BOOK

This book contains the transactions relating to goods that are returned by the customers for a number of reasons; e.g., not according to sample, or not up to the mark etc. It is also known as Returns Inward Book. In short, ***this book is used to record goods returned to us by our customers.***

Generally, when a customer returns goods to the suppliers, he issues a *Debit Note* for the value of the goods returned by him. Similarly, the supplier who receives those goods issues a *Credit Note.* However, the original credit note is sent to the customer concerned and the duplicate copy is kept in the file for future reference and contact. Before explaining the Sales Return Book, it becomes necessary to explain the term *Credit Notes* and its role.

Credit Note

It is nothing but a ***statement sent by one person to another person showing the amount credited to the account of the latter along with a brief explanation.*** The credit notes are used for sales return in order to intimate related abatement of the claims to the other party concerned. These credit notes are serially numbered and are similar to invoices although they are usually printed in red ink.

The specimen of a Credit Note is presented :

Credit Note

M/s P. Bose & Co. 55 College Street Kolkata 12		Date 13th April 2010 Cr. By Sen & Sons AH 40, Salt Lake Kolkata 54	
2010		Rs.	Rs.
April 13.	5 bags of cement @ Rs. 200 per bag as per invoice no. 316 dated 1st April 2010	1,000	
	Less : Discount @ 10%	100	
	Returned due to inferior quality		900
			E & O E **S. Sen** *Manager*

The outline of a Sales Return Book is presented :

Sales Return Book

Date	Particulars	Outward Invoice	L.F.	Details	Total	Remarks
				Rs.	Rs.	

Note : Here, the 'Remarks' Column is meant for return of goods, e.g., not according to sample, or due to inferior quality, etc.

Illustration 7

Enter the following transactions in Returns Inward Book :

2011, April 6. Returned by Shawl Kutir to us 3 shawls each costing Rs. 150, due to inferior quality. Credit Note No. 12/4.

8. Agartala Tailors returned to us 4 suits, each costing Rs. 250, on account of being not in accordance with their order. Credit Note No. 12/5.

21. Tripura Stores returned to us 6 dozen silk handkerchiefs, each dozen costing Rs. 60, being out of size. Credit Note No. 12/6

30. Udaipur Textiles returned to us 10 woollen trousers, each costing Rs. 250, being worn and sold. Credit Note No. 12/7.

Solution

In the books of ....

Returns Inward Book/Sales Return Book

Date	Particulars	Credit Note No.	L.F.	Details	Total	Remark
2011				Rs.	Rs.	
April	**Shawl Kutir**					
6	3 shawls @ Rs. 150 each	12/4		450		due to inferior quality
8	Agartala Tailors					
	4 suits @ Rs. 250 each	12/5		1,000		not in accordance with the order
21	**Tripura Stores**	12/6		360		out of size
	6 doz. handkerchiefs @ Rs. 60 each					
30	**Udaipur Textiles**					
	10 woollen trousers @ Rs. 250	12/7		2,500	4,310	being worn
					4,310	

Posting the Sales Return Book into the Ledger

When the Sales Return Book is properly recorded, they should be posted to the respective ledgers in the following manner :

(a) each and every entry must be entered to the credit side of the respective (i.e, individual) customers' account in the Debtors Ledger at the end of the day.

(b) the grand total of the *'Total'* column is transferred to the general ledger at the end of the month. The entries for such purpose will be :

Sales Return /Return Inward A/c	Dr.
To Sundry Debtors Account	

Illustration 8

Consider the previous illustration and post the transactions into the ledger.

Solution

In the General Ledger

Sales Return Account

Dr. *Cr.*

Date	*Particulars*	*L.F.*	*Amount*	*Date*	*Particulars*	*L.F.*	*Amount*
2011			Rs.				Rs.
April 30	To Sundry Debtors A/c		4,310		By		

Sundry Debtors Account

Dr. *Cr.*

Date	*Particulars*	*L.F.*	*Amount*	*Date*	*Particulars*	*L.F.*	*Amount*
			Rs.	2011			Rs.
	To			April 30	By Sales Return A/c		4,310

In the Debtors' Ledger

Dr. **Shawl Kutir** Cr.

Date	Particulars	L.F.	Amount	Date		Particulars	L.F.	Amount
			Rs.	2011				Rs.
	To			April 6	By	Sales Return A/c		450

Dr. **Agartala Tailors Account** Cr.

Date	Particulars	L.F.	Amount	Date		Particulars	L.F.	Amount
			Rs.	2011				Rs.
	To			April 8	By	Sales Return A/c		1,000

Dr. **Tripura Stores Account** Cr.

Date	Particulars	L.F.	Amount	Date		Particulars	L.F.	Amount
			Rs.	2011				Rs.
	To			April 21	By	Sales Return A/c		360

Dr. **Udaipur Textiles Account** Cr.

Date	Particulars	L.F.	Amount	Date		Particulars	L.F.	Amount
			Rs.	2011				Rs.
	To			April 30	By	Sales Return A/c		2,500

4. PURCHASES RETURN BOOK

This book records the transactions relating to goods that are returned by us to our creditors, e.g., goods broken in-transit, not according to sample, etc. It is also known as Returns Outward Book. Before explaining the Purchase Return Book, it becomes necessary to know the *'Debit Note'* and its role.

Debit Note

It is a simple statement sent by a person to another person showing the amount debited to the account of the latter along with a brief explanation. ***The debit notes are issued by a trader relating to purchases returns in order to put up his claim for abatement of his dues to the other party.*** Debit notes are serially numbered and are similar to invoices although they are usually printed in red ink.

Note : It is evident that if one party issues the debit note, the other party need not issue a credit note, and vice versa. The other party, of course, should adjust the account in his books accordingly.

The specimen of a *Debit Note* is given :

Debit Note

M/s Sen Bros.
22 Ram Mohun Sarani
Kolkata 700 009 — 4th Feb. 2011

Dr. to Das & Co.
122 Shyambazar Street
Kolkata 700 004

2011		Rs.	Rs.
Feb. 4.	20 Radio Sets purchased under your Invoice No. 394, dated 15th Jan. 2011, now returned, as the sets are not in working condition, @ Rs. 500 per set	10,000	
	Add : Freight	100	
			10,100
			10,100

E. & O.E.
B. Banerjee
Manager

The outline of a Purchase Return Book is presented :

Purchase Return Book

Date	Particulars	Debit Note	L.F.	Details	Total	Remarks
				Rs.	Rs.	

Note : In this case also, the 'Remarks column' is meant for the reasons for return of goods.

Illustration 9

Enter the following transactions in a Returns Inward Book/Purchase Return Book :

2011, Dec. 3. Returned to Basu & Co., Kolkata, 150 cases of defective articles valued @ Rs. 50 per case. Debit Note No. 04/4.

12. Das and Sons allowed us an allowance of Rs. 1,000 for retaining their goods of damaged condition sent to us as per our invoice No. Z/22, Debit Note No. 04/5.

18. We sent a Debit Note for Rs. 100 to Dey Bros. who overcharged the invoice through mistake. Debit Note No-04/6.

Solution

In the books of ....

Returns Outward Book/Purchases Return Book

Date	Particulars	Debit Note No.	L.F.	Details	Total	Remark
2011				Rs.	Rs.	
Dec. 3	**Basu & Co.**	04/4				
	150 cases of defective articles @ Rs. 50 per case			7,500		defective
12	**Das & Sons**	04/5				
	Allowance granted for retaining damaged goods as per our Invoice No. Z/22			1,000		damaged
18	**Dey Bros.**	04/6				
	Adjustment of overcharge			100		overcharged
					8,600	
	Total				8,600	

Posting the Purchases Return Book into Ledger

When the Purchases Return Book is properly maintained, the entries should be posted to the respective ledger from it in the following manner :

(a) each and every entry must be entered to the debit side of the respective (i.e., individual) account in the creditors ledger.

(b) the grand total of the 'Total' column is transferred to the general ledger at the end of the month. The entries for this purpose will be :

Sundry Creditors A/c	Dr.
To Purchases Return/Returns Outward A/c	

Illustration 10

Consider the previous illustration and post the transactions into ledgers :

Solution

In the General Ledger

Dr. **Purchases Return Account** Cr.

Date	Particulars	L.F.	Amount	Date	Particulars	L.F.	Amount
			Rs.	2011			Rs.
	To			Dec. 31	By Sundry Creditors A/c		8,600

Dr. **Sundry Creditors Account** Cr.

Date	Particulars	L.F.	Amount	Date	Particulars	L.F.	Amount
2011			Rs.				Rs.
Dec. 31	To Purchases Return A/c		8,600		By		

In the Creditors Ledger

Basu & Co. Account

Dr. Date	Particulars	L.F.	Amount	Date	Particulars	L.F.	Amount Cr.
2011			Rs.				Rs.
Dec. 3	To Purchases Return A/c		7,500		By		

Das & Sons Account

Dr. Date	Particulars	L.F.	Amount	Date	Particulars	L.F.	Amount Cr.
2011			Rs.				Rs.
Dec. 12	To Purchases Return A/c		1,000		By		

Dey Bros. Account

Dr. Date	Particulars	L.F.	Amount	Date	Particulars	L.F.	Amount Cr.
2011			Rs.				Rs.
Dec. 18	To Purchases Return A/c		100		By		

5. Bills Receivable Book*

Bills Receivable Book is a book where all bills received are recorded and therefrom posted directly to the credit of the respective customer's account. The total amounts of the bills so received during the period (either at the end of the week or month) is to be posted in one sum to the debit of Bills Receivable Account.

The usual form of Bills Receivable Book is presented :

Bills Receivable Book

No. of Bills	Date of Receipt of Bill	From whom	Name of Receiver	Name of Drawer	Name of Acceptor	Date of Bill	Due Date	L.F.	Amount of Bill	How disposed-off

* For further details, please see the chapter *Negotiable Instruments*.

Explanation

(1) No. of Bills	This column takes the serial number of bill which has been recorded.
(2) Date of Receipt	This column takes the actual date of the bill when the same is received from the customer.
(3) From Whom	This column records the name of the customer from whom the bill has been received.
(4) Name of 'Receiver'	This column is meant for recording the name from whom the bills has been received (sometimes bills are received from other than the drawee).
(5) Name of the Drawer	This column takes the name of the drawer, i.e., the creditor, of the bill.
(6) Name of the Acceptor	This column takes the name of the debtor customer or the acceptor of the bill.
(7) Date of Bills	This column takes the actual date of drawing a bill.
(8) Terms	It records the period of the bill e.g., 2 months, 3 months, etc.
(9) Due Date	This column takes the date on which the bill is matured for payment.
(10) L. F.	It contains the page number of the debtor's ledger.
(11) Amount of the bill	This column contains the amount/value of the bill.
(12) How disposed-off	The column expresses how the bill is paid, i.e., whether it was discounted by the bank or held till the date of maturity by the drawer.

6. BILLS PAYABLE BOOK*

This is a book where all the particulars relating to bills accepted are recorded and therefrom posted directly to the debit of the respective creditor's account. The total amounts of the bills so accepted during the period (either at the end of the week or month) is to be posted in one sum to the credit of Bills Payable Account.

The usual form of Bills Payable Book is presented :

Bills Payable Book

No. of Bills	Date of Acceptance	To whom given	Name of the Drawer	Name of the Payee	Where Payable	Date of Bill	Term	Due date	L.F.	Amount of the Bill	How disposed-off

* For further details, please see the chapter *'Negotiable Instruments'*

Explanation

(1) No. of Bills	This column takes the serial number of the bill which has been recovered.
(2) Date of Acceptance	This column takes the actual date of the bill when the same is accepted.
(3) To whom given	It records the name of the person to whom the bill is given.
(4) Name of the Drawer	This column takes the name of the drawer of the bill.
(5) Name of the Payee	This column takes the name of the bank where the bill is paid.
(6) Where Payable	This column records the name of bank where it is payable.
(7) Date of Bill	This column takes the actual date of drawing the bill.
(8) Terms	This column contains the period of the bill.
(9) Due Date	This column contains the date on which the bill is matured for payment.
(10) L. F.	It contains the page number of the creditors' ledger.
(11) Amount of the bill	This column contains the amount/value of the bill.
(12) How disposed-off	This column reveals how the bill is paid.

ASSIGNMENT MATERIALS

THEORETICAL

Multiple Choice Questions

1. (a) For recording Credit Purchase we use:

(i) Sales Day Book; (ii) Purchase Day Book; (iii) None of these

(b) For recording goods returned by customer we use:

(i) Return Inward Book; (ii) Returns Outward Book; (iii) None of these

(c) Sales Tax is calculated on:

(i) Gross Price; (ii) Net Price; (iii) List Price.

(d) Excise duty is calculated on :

(i) Gross Price; (ii) Net Price; (iii) List Price.

(e) Trade Discount is calculated on:

(i) List Price; (ii) Net Price; (iii) None of these.

(f) Cash Discount is calculated on :

(i) List Price; (ii) Catalogue Price; (iii) None of these.

(g) Debit Note is used for:

(i) Returns Outward Book; (ii) Returns Inward Book; (iii) None of these.

(h) Credit Note is used for:

(i) Returns Inward Book; (ii) Returns Outward Book; (iii) None of these.

(i) For recording Credit Sales, we use:

(i) Purchase Day Book; (ii) Sales Day Book; (iii) None of these.

(j) Carriage paid for selling good will be added to:

(i) Net Selling Price; (ii) Gross Price; (iii) None of these.

[Ans. (a) (ii); (b) (i); (c) (ii); (d) (i); (e) (i); (f) (iii); (g) (i); (h) (i); (i) (ii); (j) (i)]

Short Answer-Type Questions

2. Write notes on:

   (a) Debit Notes; (b) Credit Notes; (c) Purchases Day Book; (d) Sales Day Book.
3. What are Cash Discount and Trade Discount? Explain them with the help of an example.
4. Distinguish between Cash Discount and Trade Discount.
5. What is meant by 'Subdivision of Journal'?
6. What are Bills Receivable Book and Bills Payable Book?
7. State the functions of various types of Day Books separately.
8. Discuss the use and nature of Returns Inward Book and Returns Outward Book.

Long Answer-Type Questions

9. Distinguish between Trade Discount and Cash Discount.

   (a) Define Trade Discount and Cash Discount.

   (b) Distinguish between the two.

   (c) Can a particular trader enjoy both the discounts simultaneously?

PRACTICAL

1. **(a) Purchase Day Book**

Record the following transactions in an appropriate book of original entry and post them into suitable ledger accounts:

2011			Rs.
Dec.	4.	Purchased goods from Sen & Co.	6,000
		Less : Trade Discount @ 10%	—
"	8.	Purchased goods from Banerjee Bros.	8,000
		Less : Trade Discount @ $7\frac{1}{2}$%	—
		Packing Charges	250
"	17.	Brought goods from Mukherjee & Co.	10,000
		Allowed Trade Discount	1,000
		Excise Duty	500
		Containers and packing charges	150

[Ans. Total of Purchase Day Book Rs. 22,700]

2. Enter the following transactions of Sri Sen in a suitably ruled Purchase Day Book and post them into proper ledger accounts :

Date	*Name of the Suppliers*	*Bags of Sugar*	*Rate per bag*	*Trade Dis.*	*Invoice No.*	*Cost of packing and delivery charges*
2010			Rs.			Rs.
Nov. 1	Sib Sankar Gupta	20	100	@ 10%	1/25	105
5	Jiban Ghose	30	80	@ 5%	1/27	80
7	Saha Bros	50	120	—	1/30	150
9	Sib Sankar Gupta	10	100	@ 10%	1/31	75
15	Sen & Co.	25	110	@ $2\frac{1}{2}$ %	1/32	100
20	Dutta & Sons	30	100	—	1/33	110

[Ans. Total of Purchase Day Book Rs. 17,281.25]

(b) Sales Day Book

3. From the following particulars, prepare a Sales Day Book with a separate column for Sales Tax Recovery :

2011 Jan. 4. Sold to X & Co. 30 chests of Coffee @ Rs. 300 per chest, less 5% Trade Discount, Excise Duty @ 5% extra.

6. Sold to Y & Co. 50 chests of Tea @ of Rs. 150 per chest, less 10% Trade Discount, Excise Duty @ 5% extra.

10. Sold to Z & Co. 100 chests of Tea @ Rs. 100 per chest and 50 chests of Coffee @ Rs. 200 per chest, less 10% Trade Discount, Excise Duty @ 5% extra.

20. Sold to T & Co. 100 chests of Tea @ Rs. 100 per chest, less 10% Trade Discount.

25. Sold to P & Co. 50 chests of Coffee @ Rs. 200 per chest, less $12\frac{1}{2}$% Trade Discount, Excise duty @ 5% extra.

Sales Tax is charged @ 10% on the net price in all cases.

[Ans. Total of Sales Day Book Rs. 58,712·50; Sales-Tax Recovery Rs. 5,337·50]

4. Enter the following transactions in a suitably ruled Sales Day Book and post them into ledger accounts :

Date	Name of the Customers	Bags of Sugar	Invoice No.	Rate per bag	Trade Discount	Cost of Carriage	Excise
2011				Rs.		Rs.	
June. 5	Sen & Co.	100	C/320	100	10%	100	6%
9	Das & Co	50	C/321	110	$7\frac{1}{2}$%	110	6%
11	Bose & Co.	150	C/322	100	$2\frac{1}{2}$%	—	6%
15	Paul & Co.	200	C/323	110	10%	200	6%
20	Dutta & Co.	100	C/324	105	—	—	6%

Sales-tax is to be charged @ 10% on the net price in all cases.

[Ans. Total of Sales Day Book Rs. 69,523·02; Sales Tax Recovery Rs. 6,320·27]

(c) Returns Inward Book

5. Enter the following transactions in a suitable Returns Inward Book and post them into ledger:

2011 May 3. Returned by Basirhat Traders, 10 Woollen Shawls @ Rs. 150 each, originally sold at 10% discount.

8. Returned by Sat Lake Trading, 20 Cotton Shirts @ Rs. 50 each, originally sold at 5% discount.

9. Returned by Gariahat Store, 10 Woollen Shawls @ 200 each, originally sold at 5% discount.

18. Returned by Sen Bros., 2 doz. woollen garments @ Rs. 350 per doz., originally sold at 10% discount.

31. Returned by B & Co., 10 pieces cotton shorts @ Rs. 20 each, originally sold at 10% discount.

Hint : Make two columns—Shawls and Garments.

[Ans. Total of Returns Inward Book Rs. 5,010]

(d) Returns Outward Book

6 From the following particulars, compile a Returns Outward Book of M/s Dhar Trading :

2011 Jan. 2. Returned to S. Saha, 10 kg of Tea @ Rs. 50 per kg originally purchased at 10% trade discount.

4. Returned to B. Bhar, 5 kg of Coffee, @ Rs. 100 per kg, originally purchased at 5% trade discount.

8. Returned to M. Mehta, 25 kg of Tea @ Rs. 40 per kg originally purchased at 10% trade discount.

12. Returned to B. Bros, 15 kg Coffee @ Rs. 100 per kg originally purchased at 10% discount.

22. Returned to L. Laha, 10 kg of Tea @ Rs. 60 per kg originally purchased at 20% trade discount.

[Ans. Total of Returns Outward Book Rs. 3,655]

Hint : Make separate columns for Tea and Coffee.

(e) Bills Receivable Book

7. Enter the following bills in a Bills Receivable Book of M/s XYZ & Co. and post them into ledger for the month of September 1990 :

2011 Sept. 4. Received a bill from Mr. M. Das at 1 month after date for Rs. 500.

8. Received a bill from Mr. P. Rowl at 2 months' after date for Rs. 1,000.

17. Received a bill from Mr D. Dutta at 4 months' after date for Rs. 800.

22. Received a bill from H. Haba at 1 month after date for Rs. 1,000.

31. Discounted the bill of Mr. M. Das by S. B. I. and charged discount @ 10% p.a.

[Ans. Total of Bills Receivable Book Rs. 2,800]

(f) Bills Payable Book

8. The following bills have been acepted by Mr. Bhattacharyya for the month of October 2011. Enter the following transactions on his Bills Payable Book and post them into ledger :

2011 Oct. 4. Accepted a 2 months' bill drawn by Mr. A for Rs. 1,000.

9. Accepted a 3 months' bill drawn by Mr. B for Rs. 800.

15. Accepted a 4 months' bill drawn by Mr. D for Rs. 2,000.

18. Discharged the bill of Mr. A by cash payment.

[Ans. Total of Bills Payable Book Rs. 2,800]

CHAPTER 5

CAPITAL AND REVENUE TRANSACTIONS

Learning Objectives

Introduction

Capital Transactions

Revenue Transactions

Capital Expenditure

Revenue Expenditure

Deferred Revenue Expenditure

Differences—Capital Expenditure, Revenue Expenditure & Deferred Revenue Expenditure

Capitalised Expenditure

Non-Recurring Expenditure

Recurring Expenditure

Capital Receipts and Revenue Receipts

Capital Losses and Revenue Losses

Introduction

In order to ascertain the correct amount of profit for a period, proper differentiation between capital and revenue transactions is absolutely necessary. Because, if a capital expenditure is charged against profit, profit will be understated and, consequently, there will be erosion of capital. On the other hand, if revenue expenditure is treated as capital, the profit will be overstated. Thus, the proper difference must be accounted for while ascertaining business profit. Capital and revenue transactions may be compared with the tree and its fruits. Trees produce fruits which may be consumed, and more fruits will be grown if care is taken. Similarly, there will be no fruits if the trees are not properly preserved. So also is the case of Capital and Revenue transactions, i.e., Capital is the source of Revenue and Revenue is the product of Capital. To produce Revenue, Capital is invested; as the fruits make new trees so also Revenue creates new Capital.

It has already been highlighted above that transactions are classified into: (1) **Capital Transactions,** and (2) **Revenue Transactions.**

Capital Transactions

The transactions which provide benefits or supply services to the business unit *for more than one year or one operating cycle of the business* are known as Capital Transactions.

Revenue Transactions

The transactions which provide benefits or supply services to a business unit *for one accounting period only* are known as Revenue Transactions.

Transactions which relate to receipts are again subdivided into two:

(1) Capital Receipts, and (2) Revenue Receipts.

The whole classification can be depicted as:

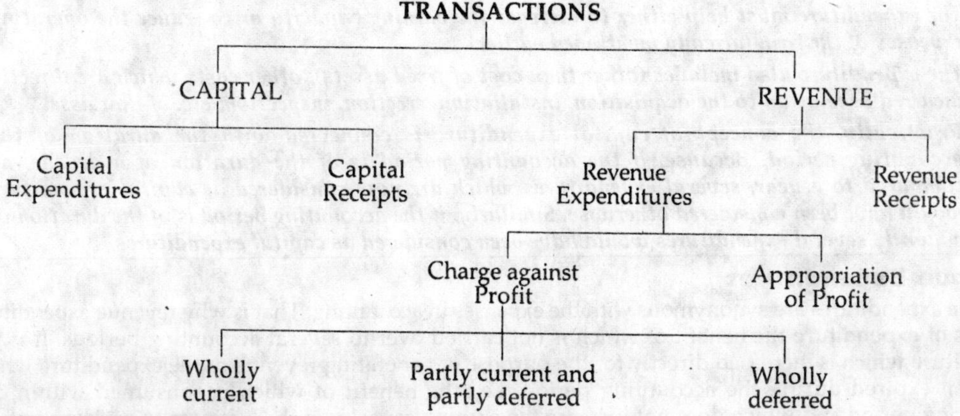

Capital Expenditure

According to E. L. Kohler, capital expenditure is an expenditure intended to benefit future period in contrast to a revenue expenditure which benefits a current period.[1] In other words, capital expenditure consists of those expenditures the benefits of which are carried over to several accounting periods or, in other words, the benefits of which are not consumed within one accounting period. It refers to that outlay which may result either in: (a) acquiring a long-term or fixed asset, e.g., Building, Machinery, etc., or (b) in providing such assets by:

(i) increasing its efficiency or capacity, e.g., substitution of a better part for the original one.

(ii) affecting economy in its operation, e.g., cost of replacing a petrol-driven engine by a diesel-driven engine.

Thus, capital expenditure is increased either in acquiring, extending or improving assets which are of permanent nature and also which increase the earning capacity of the business and also which are not acquired for sale.

---

1 Kohler, E. L., *Dictionary for Accountants*, Prentice-Hall of India Ltd., 1992, New Delhi, P. 74

Some Examples

(i) Expenditure resulting in the acquisition of fixed or long-living assets, e.g., Land, Building, Machinery, Furniture, Motor Car, Trade Mark, Patent Rights, etc.

(ii) Expenditure resulting in the extension or improvement of fixed assets, e.g., amount spent for increasing the seating accommodation in a cinema-hall.

(iii) Expenditure incurred for the purchase or erection of fixed assets, e.g., expenses to be incurred for erecting a plant.

(iv) Cost of overhauling secondhand machine.

(v) Expenditure incurred for acquiring the right to carry on business, e.g., Goodwill, Copyright, etc.

(vi) Expenditure incurred by remodelling and reconditioning an old plant or property.

(vii) Major repairs and replacement of plant—which result in increased efficiency.

(viii) Expenditure incurred for maintaining an asset into working condition.

At first, this type of expenditure is recorded in the books as an asset. Since the asset is used for the purpose of earning revenues in different accounting periods, a part of the said asset is consumed and becomes a revenue expenditure for the respective accounting periods by way of depreciation.

Characteristics of Capital Expenditure	
(a)	***The expenditure is incurred for the purpose of acquiring either a new fixed asset or to improve or to extend an existing asset, i.e., they must be assets.***
(b)	***The benefits to be derived from such expenditures must be of an enduring nature, i.e., they must not be fully consumed or used up in the accounting period in which it is incurred. These expenditures must not be consumed in one single year. Therefore, such benefits must be capable of repeated use, or, must be spread over a number of accounting years.***
(c)	***The expenditure must help either to increase the earning capacity or to reduce the operating expenses of the firm (already mentioned earlier).***
(d)	***The expenditure also includes (other than cost of fixed assets), other costs which are directly incurred in relation to the acquisition, installation, erection, inspection, etc. of that asset.***
	Practically, the concept of capital expenditure is connected with the duration of the accounting period. Because, if the accounting period is of the duration of a decade, as compared to a year, several expenditures which are now considered as capital expenditure would have been considered otherwise. Similarly, if the accounting period is of the duration of a month, several expenditures would have been considered as capital expenditures.

Revenue Expenditures

Revenue expenditures are synonymous with the expenses in accounting. That is why revenue expenditure consists of expenditure the benefit of which is not carried over to several accounting periods. It is the expenditure which is increased directly for the purpose of generating revenue or the expenditure which has been expired during the accounting period, i.e., the benefit of which is consumed within one accounting period and which does not increase the earning capacity of the business. According to E. L. Kohler: "An expenditure charged against operation: a term used to contrast with capital expenditure". It is also to be noted that the expenditure which is not even directly connected with the revenue generation process but the benefit of which has been fully consumed within the completed accounting period is also known as Revenue Expenditure (e.g., Rent of the office, i.e., expenses relating to office and administration, and selling and distribution).

This expenditure is practically incurred in order to maintain the existing earning capacity of the business and includes all expenses which arise in the normal course of the business. Examples are:

Direct production expenses and indirect operating expenses, e.g., cost of sales, office and administration expenses, selling and distribution expenses, financial expenses, upkeep of fixed assets, etc.

Characteristics of Revenue Expenditure	
(a)	***Small expenditures which are incurred for a fixed asset into working order, e.g., repairs, renewals etc.***
(b)	***Expenditures which are incurred for day-to-day business operations and the benefit of which will be consumed within one accounting year or less, i.e. any periodical cost, e.g., Rent, Salaries, Advertisements, etc.***
(c)	***Expenditures which are incurred on consumable items, e.g., stock of stationery.***
(d)	***Expenditures which are charged against profit***

Some More Examples

(i) Cost of goods purchased for resale;
(ii) Expenditures incurred in the normal course of the business, e.g., office and adminis-tration, selling and distribution expenses;
(iii) Expenditures incurred for maintaining the business, e.g., cost of stores consumed during production;
(iv) Obsolescence of fixed assets;
(v) Depreciation of fixed assets, loss on sale of assets, interest on loans taken for business finance, etc.;
(vi) Upkeep of fixed assets are—repairs, renewals, etc.

Deferred Revenue Expenditure

It is revenue expenditure and not a capital one. A revenue expenditure which is not treated as such on the ground that its benefit is not fully consumed or exhausted in the accounting period in which the same is incurred. In other words, a heavy revenue expenditure—the benefit of which may be extended over a number of years, and not for the current year only—is called Deferred Revenue Expenditure. Only a portion of the total expenditure is considered as revenue expenditure of each accounting period. As such, the balance of the expenditure is carried forward from one accounting period to the next accounting period and is shown in the assets side of the Balance Sheet as an asset.

For example, if a firm incurs Rs. 10,000 by way of advertisement for a period of 10 years, Rs. 1,000 (i.e., Rs. 10,000 × $\frac{1}{10}$) is to be charged against the Income Statement (Profit and Loss Account) as revenue expenditure, by way of advertisement for the current year and Rs. 9,000 will be carried forward in the Assets side of the Balance Sheet as Deferred Revenue Expenditure—since the benefit will accrue in the subsequent years.

Characteristics of Deferred Revenue Expenditure	
(a)	*It is neither a capital expenditure nor any ownership is exercised on it as an asset.*
(b)	*Any abnormal loss of exceptional nature may be treated.*
(c)	*As it presumes anticipated benefits, only the expired benefit is taken into consideration in the current accounting year.*
(d)	*The benefit of this expenditure may be consumed over a number of years, as such, proportionate amount is to be carried forward for these related years.*
(e)	*This expenditure is treated as an asset and shown in the Assets side of the Balance Sheet.*

Examples:

Preliminary Expenses, Brokerage and Underwriting Commissions, Research and Deve-lopment Expenses.

Deferred revenue expenditures comprise:

(i)	Expenditures wholly paid in advance	e.g., Telephone rental, which is payable entirely for the future period, i.e., no benefit accrues to the current year and, as such, the total amount is carried forward. It will appear in the Assets side of the Balance Sheet as prepaid item.
(ii)	Expenditures partly paid in advance	e.g., Insurance premium, which is payable partly for the current year and partly for the next year. This is allocated between the current and future period in proportion to their utilised and unutilised benefits. Utilised portion is charged to current year's Profit and Loss Account, and unutilised portion is shown as prepaid Insurance in the Assets side of the Balance Sheet.
(iii)	Abnormal Losses	Any loss of an exceptional nature, e.g., Loss arising from a fire in the non-insured assets, may not be written-off totally in current year's Profit and Loss Account; some portion may be spread over for two or three years as deferred revenue expenditure which is shown in the Assets side of the Balance Sheet, as Fictitious Assets, under the head *Miscellaneous Expenditures.*

AS 26, ***Intangible Assets***, contradicts the above concept. As per para 56, it states that expenditure is incurred to provide future economic benefits to an enterprise that can be recognised as an expense when it is incurred e.g., expenditure on scientific research is recognized as an expense when it is incurred. In short, the entire amount of the expenditure is treated as expense for the current year only and will not proportionately be transferred like deferred charge although the benefit will be enjoyed for a number of years.

Differences—Capital Expenditure, Revenue Expenditure and Deferred Revenue Expenditure

Capital Expenditure	Revenue Expenditure	Deferred Revenue Expenditure
1. Capital expenditure is meant for enduring benefit beyond the accounting year—lasts for a long time.	1. Revenue expenditure is the expenditure the benefit of which is consumed during the current year only—lasts only for the current year.	1. Deferred revenue expenditure is the expenditure the benefit of which is continued for more than one accounting period—lasts for more than one accounting period.
2. It represents unexpired cost, i.e., cost of benefit for use in future.	2. It represents expired cost.	2. —
3. It relates to the acquisition of fixed assets.	3. It relates only to the acquisition of current assets.	3. It relates to the heavy revenue expenditures.
4. It may be treated as a non-recurring expenditure.	4. It is treated as a recurring expenditure.	4. It is treated as a non-recurring expenditure.
5. It is debited to an asset Account	5. It is debited to an expense Account	5. —
6. It is a real Account	6. It is a nominal account	6. —
7. It appears in the Balance Sheet	7. It appears in Trading or Profit and Loss Account.	7. —
8. It helps to increase the earning capacity of the business and also reduces the operating cost.	8. It helps to earn existing revenues.	8. It ensures the application of modern concept of matching cost against revenue.
9. Capital expenditure is transfrable, i.e., it can be disposed-off and transferred for money or money's worth.	9. Revenue Expenditure is not transferable.	9. Deferred Revenue Expenditure is also not transferable.
10. It is associated with property right belonging to the entity.	10. In Revenue Expenditure there is no such right.	10. In Deferred Revenue Expenditure also, there is no such right.
11. It is not matched with capital Profit	11. It is matched with revenue profit	11. —

OTHER EXPENDITURES

Capitalised Expenditure

Expenditure is primarily of a revenue nature. But if the same is incurred for the purpose of acquiring an asset or increasing its value it is known as *Capitalised Expenditure.* According to E. L. Kohler: "an item of cost usually charged to Profit and Loss Account but because related to a period of construction, added to a capital asset account." Thus, they are revenue in nature but are incurred for acquiring an asset. That is, an item of cost usually charged to Profit and Loss Account, but, since it is related to a period of construction, the same is added to a capital-asset account. For instance, amount spent initially for repairing a secondhand machine is, no doubt, a revenue expenditure, but, as it is added to the cost of secondhand machine, it is capitalised.

Other Examples

(a) Carriage — Carriage paid for the acquisition of a plant or machine to be installed in the business is a capitalised expenditure.

(b) Installation Expenses — Installation expenses incurred for a plant is also a capitalised expenditure.

(c) Legal Expenses — Legal expenses (e.g., Registration Charges or layer's fees etc.) for the purchase of a land is also a capitalised expenditure.

(d) Materials and Wages — Materials and Wages which are used for the construction of an office/factory building is also a capitalised expenditure.

Characteristics of such expenditures

(a) They are related to original asset.

(b) The written-down value of the asset is increased by the amount of such expenditure.

Non-Recurring Expenditure

The expenditure incurred in an accounting period, the benefit of which is consumed or carried forward over a number of accounting periods, including the current year, is called a *Non-recurring Expenditure*. That is, such expenditures are known as Capital Expenditure.

It is interesting to note that, while valuing unsold stock in consignment account, non-recurring expense means the expenses which are incurred by consignee in transferring goods from the consignor's godown to the consignee's godown, viz., freight, customs duty, dock charges, insurance in-transit, loading and unloading expense, etc., i.e., expenses of consignee which are incurred only for once.

Recurring Expenditure

The expenditure incurred in an accounting period again and again, the benefits of which are consumed within the related accounting period, i.e., within the current year, are known as recurring expenditures since they are repetitive in nature, e.g., Salary, Rent, Wages etc. In short, they are revenue expenditure.

Of course, in consignment account, while valuing unsold stock, recurring expense means the expense which is incurred by the consignee again and again, e.g., godown rent, storage, advertisement—i.e., selling expenses.

Capital Receipts and Revenue Receipts

Like capital expenditure and revenue expenditure, there must be proper distinction between capital receipts and revenue receipts from the accounting point of view, otherwise the results of the operation from an income statement will be incorrect/wrong and the financial position of the firm which will be exhibited with the help of a Balance Sheet will be a misleading one. Thus, a clear distinction must be made between the two.

Capital Receipts

The amount of capital which is contributed by the owner—either in the form of cash or in various kinds of assets or any contribution made by others towards the business as capital. These receipts do not have any effect on the result of the operation of the business, i.e., the profit or loss for the corresponding years. In short, these are non-recurring receipts from the owner of the business or lender of money creating a liability.

Examples:

(i) By selling an asset which was acquired earlier and was not meant for resale;

(ii) Further capital introduced by the owners; and

(iii) A loan was taken by mortgaging any fixed asset, say, Land and Building.

> ***To sum up: Capital receipts include the amount received by the issue of shares, long term loans taken from a bank, i.e., the receipts which arise not from the ordinary or regular course of business.***

Revenue Receipts

Revenue receipts, on the other hand, comprise sale proceeds of merchandise together with other receipts related to business (viz., commission and discount received, dividend and subscription received, etc.), i.e., all the recurring incomes which a business earns during the normal course of its activities. They do not create any liability of the firm. In other words, they are recurring receipts, i.e., sale of goods or services during the normal course of the business and which help to produce the result of the firm for the current accounting period under consideration. They directly affect the result of the operation, i.e., profit or loss of the firm. These receipts are adjusted against revenue expenditure in order to find out the profit or loss of the firm.

Examples:

(i) Commission and Discount received; (ii) Dividend and Interest received on investment, etc.

Capital Profit and Revenue Profit

Like Capital Receipts and Revenue Receipts, there must also be a clear distinction between the two; otherwise, neither the Income Statement nor the Balance Sheet will produce faithful records.

Capital Profit

Capital Profits (of a company) arise from:

(i) Profits prior to incorporation; (ii) Premium received on the issue of shares; (iii) Profits made on the resale of forfeited shares; (iv) Redemption of debentures at a discount; and (v) Profit made on sale or revalue of a fixed asset.

These capital profits are transferred to Capital Reserve, i.e., capitalised. They may be set-off only against capital losses which may arise at a future date.

Revenue Profit

Revenue Profit is the profit which arises from the normal course of the business, i.e., the result of the operation (i.e., excess of revenue receipts over revenue expenditure) which is the primary objective of the business. This profit arises out of the sale of merchandise which a business deals in. In short, it may also be termed as 'Net Profit'.

Capital and Revenue Losses

We have distinguished capital profit and revenue profit in the earlier paragraph. Now we would like to distinguish the difference between capital losses and revenue losses. They affect the firm from different angles, e.g., revenue losses affect the result of the operation whereas capital losses alter the financial position of the business.

Capital Losses

Capital losses are the losses which arise from:

(i) the sale of fixed asset (i.e., market value of the asset is less than the written-down value of the asset) or, elimination/diminution of assets; (ii) issue of shares at a discount (when shares are issued for raising capital in settlement of a debt which is more than its book value); (iii) book value of debenture issued at par/at a discount and redeemed at a premium).

Capital losses are treated like capital profit. But it is interesting enough to state that capital losses arising out of selling of fixed assets are adjusted against Profit and Loss Account while calculating the net profit/loss of the firm but the other capital losses, stated above, are adjusted against capital profit and—if there is no capital profit—the same will be shown in the Assets side of the Balance Sheet as a fictitious asset and will be set-off against the revenue or profit over a few succeeding years.

Revenue Losses

Revenue losses are the losses that arise from the normal operational activities of the firm. In other words, when sale price of the merchandise is less than the cost of such merchandise. In short, it is the *'Net Loss'* (i.e., excess of debit over credit side of Income Statement/Profit and Loss Account). It arises from many factors, viz.

(i) when value of inventory has gone down (i.e., market price is less than cost price); (ii) when fixed expenditures are proportionately higher; (iii) when any abnormal loss arises; (iv) when the trend of sale is declining.

GENERAL ILLUSTRATIONS

Illustration 1

State whether the following are true or false:

(a) Overall expenses of secondhand machinery purchased are Revenue Expenditure.

(b) Legal fees to acquire property is Capital Expenditure.

(c) Amount spent as lawyer's fee to defend a suit claiming that the firm's factory site belonged to the plaintiff—is Capital Expenditure.

(d) Amount spent for the replacement of worn-out parts of a machine is Capital Expenditure.

(e) Expenses incurred on the repairs and whitewashing for the first time on purchase of an old building are Revenue Expenses.

(f) Expenses in connection with obtaining a licence for running a Cinema-hall is Capital Expenditure.

(g) Amount spent for the construction of temporary huts, which were necessary for the construction of the Cinema-hall and were demolished when the Cinema-hall was ready, is Capital Expenditure.

(h) Expenditure on making a few more Exits in a Cinema-hall to comply with Government orders is Capital Expenditure.

(i) Expenditure on heavy advertising to introduce a new product or to explore a new market is Capital Expenditure.

Solution

(a) False; (b) True; (c) True; (d) True; (e) True; (f) True; (g) True; (h) True; (i) False (i.e., Deferred Revenue Expenditure).

Illustration 2

State whether the following items of expenditure of a club are Capital or Revenue:

(i) Newspapers and Periodicals

(ii) Printing and Stationeries

(iii) Purchase of Books

(iv) Purchase of Land

(v) Legal expenses for acquisition of Land

(vi) Entertainment expenses

(vii) Depreciation on Furniture

(viii) Interest paid

(ix) Repairs to Building

(x) Cost of replacing a Billiard Table

(xi) Wages paid for installation of Plant

(xii) Entrance fees (at the date of admission only)

(xiii) Profit on Sale of Plant

(xiv) Preliminary Expenses

(xv) Advertisement to be utilised for 5 years Rs. 5,000.

Solution

(i) Revenue Expenditure : The benefit continues for one year only, i.e., it is a nominal account.

(ii) Revenue Expenditure : It is a nominal account and also the benefit lasts for one year only.

(iii) Capital Expenditure : It is a real account, and a fixed asset which will give us service for a long period.

(iv) Capital Expenditure : It is a real account, and a fixed asset as well, the benefit of which will continue for a long period.

(v) Capital Expenditure : It is a real account and it will increase the value of land, hence, value of land will be increased. Moreover, it is incidental to the acquisition of fixed assets.

(vi) Revenue Expenditure : It is a nominal account the benefit of which will last for one year only.

(vii) Revenue Expenditure : It is a nominal account showing the normal wear and tear due to use of the assets and value of assets is reduced.

(viii) Revenue Expenditure : It is a nominal account the benefit of which will last for one year only.

(ix) Revenue Expenditure : It is a nominal account and it is incurred for maintaining an existing fixed asset.

(x) Capital Expenditure : It is a real account. It is a fixed asset which will give us a long period of service.

(xi) Capital Expenditure : It will increase the value of plant which will give us service for a long period. It is incidental to the Plant and also will increase the earning capacity of the firm.

(xii) Capital Income : Since it is taken only once, i.e., at the time of entrance, it is a capital income.

(xiii) Capital Income : It is a capital profit.

(xiv) Deferred Revenue Expenditure : It is neither capital nor revenue expenditure but a deferred revenue expenditure. It is written-off over certain periods out of Profit and Loss Account.

(xv) Deferred Revenue Expenditure : A huge revenue expenditure, the benefit will be set-off against the profit over certain periods.

Illustration 3

Pass Journal entries for:

1. Purchased a Plant for Rs. 50,000, paid by a cheque, and installation expense being Rs. 1,000 and cost of carriage Rs. 500, paid by cash.
2. Purchased Furniture from Prabartak and Co. for Rs. 12,000, carriage paid Rs. 500.
3. Bought goods from X and Co. for cash Rs. 8,000, carriage paid Rs. 100.

Solution

In the Books of A Co. Ltd.
Journal

Date	*Particulars*		*L.F.*	*Debit*	*Credit*
?				Rs.	Rs.
	1. Plant A/c	Dr.		51,500[1]	
	To Bank A/c				50,000
	To Cash A/c				1,500
	(Bought a Plant by cheque and paid installation expenses and carriage paid in Cash)				
	2. Furniture A/c	Dr.		12,500[2]	
	To Prabartak and Co. A/c				12,000
	To Cash A/c				500
	(Bought furniture on credit and paid carriage in Cash)				
	3. Purchase A/c	Dr.		8,000[3]	
	To Cash A/c				8,000
	(Goods purchased for Cash)				
	Carriage Inwards A/c	Dr.		100	
	To Cash A/c				100
	(Carriage paid)				

Notes: 1. Installation expense and carriage paid for Plant are capital expenditure which are incidental to the acquisition of fixed asset, i.e., plant, and, hence, will be added with the value of Plant.

2. Similarly, carriage paid for furniture is also capital expenditure, as such, it will be added to the cost of furniture, i.e., it is incidental to the acquisition of fixed asset, viz., Furniture.

3. Carriage paid for purchasing goods is a revenue expenditure since goods are meant for re-sale purposes.

Illustration 4

State, with reasons, which of the following expenditures are Revenue and which are Capital:

(a) Purchase of Freehold Land.

(b) Registration expenses incurred for purchasing land.

(f) Expenses incurred for extension of factory shed.

(g) Repainting the factory building.

(c) Expenses incurred for making boundary wall.
(d) Cost of rebuilding damages by rain.
(e) Insurance premium paid for building.
(h) Cost of repairs to motor car.
(i) Cost of remodelling an old building.
(j) Cost of pucca water drain.

Solution

(a) Capital Expenditure : It is a fixed asset which will render service for a long period of time and also a real account.

(b) Capital Expenditure : It is incidental to the acquisition of fixed asset and will be added with the cost price of the land.

(c) Capital Expenditure : It is incurred in order to maintain the existing fixed asset, i.e., land.

(d) Revenue Expenditure : It does neither increase the book value of assets nor does it bring into existence a new fixed asset.

(e) Revenue Expenditure : It is a regular expenditure the benefit of which is consumed only in one year.

(f) Capital Expenditure : It is incurred in order to maintain the existing fixed assets and also added to the value of the assets. It is a real account.

(g) Revenue Expenditure : It is a regular expenditure incurred for maintaining the fixed asset the benefit of which is consumed within one year. It is a nominal account.

(h) Revenue Expenditure : It is incurred for running an existing fixed asset.

(i) Capital Expenditure : It will increase the value of an existing fixed asset the benefit of which gives a long period of service.

(j) Capital Expenditure : It is a real account the benefit of which will give a long period of service.

Illustration 5

Explain in short whether the following expenditures are Capital or Revenue:

(a) Rs. 5,000 incurred in defending a legal suit for breach of contract for supplying goods to the customers.
(b) Rs. 3,000 paid for expense relating to removing stock to another place for sale.
(c) Rs. 10,000 incurred for replacement of a worn-out plant although the plant is having a W.D.V. of Rs. 1,000, with no scrap value.
(d) Rs. 1,000 incurred for demolition of an old building.
(e) Purchased a delivery van for supplying goods amounted to Rs. 10,000.
(f) Research expenditure incurred for Rs. 20,000 for a new product although it was not successful.

Solution

(a) Revenue Expenditure : It is a regular expenditure. But it is related to a fixed asset, it would be treated as a capital expenditure.

(b) Revenue Expenditure : It is a regular expenditure incurred by the firm and, hence, revenue.

(c) Capital Expenditure : It is the acquisition Cost of fixed assets. The W.D.V. of the old Plant should be treated as a revenue loss.

(d) Revenue Expenditure : It will not increase the value of the assets. If the amount had been very large, it may have been treated as deferred revenue expenditure instead of revenue expenditure.

(e) Capital Expenditure : It is the acquisition of fixed assets.

(f) Revenue Expenditure : Since the research was not successful the entire amount should be treated as of revenue nature of a special type which would be set-off against profit for a number of years. If it had been successful it would have been treated as a capital expenditure although AS-26 contradicts this view.

Illustration 6

The following expenditures have been incurred by a company for its Plant and Machinery:

		Rs.
(i)	Cost price of second hand Plant	10,000
(ii)	Installation expenses paid	1,000
(iii)	Cost of carriage for the same	500
(iv)	Overhauling charges	1,500
(v)	Repairs: Ordinary	500
	Special for accidental damage	500
(vi)	Cost of setting-up and removal to another place	500

State whether these expenses are Capital or Revenue and also prepare the Plant Account.

Solution

(i) Capital Expenditure : It is the acquisition of fixed asset which will serve for a long period of time. It is a real account.

(ii) Capital Expenditure : It is incidental to the acquisition of fixed assets and will be added to the book value of assets.

(iii) Capital Expenditure : It is also incidental to the acquisition of fixed asset and will be added to the book value of Plant.

(iv) Capital Expenditure : It is also incidental to the acquisition of fixed asset, viz., Plant.

(v) (a) Ordinary:

Revenue Expenditure : It is a regular expense incurred for maintaining the assets due tonormal wear and tear.

Special for accidental damage : Capital Expenditure is incurred for the existing asset for its use.

(vi) Capital Expenditure : It is incidental to the acquisition of fixed assets.

Plant Account (Extract)

Dr. Cr.

Date	Particulars	Amount	Date	Particulars	Amount
?		Rs.	?		Rs.
	To Bank A/c —			By	
	Cost Price	10,000			
	" Bank Account				
	Installation Expenditure	1,000			
	Carriage	500			
	Overhauling Charges	1,500			
	Repairs (Special)	500			
	Setting-up Expenses	500			
		14,000			

Illustration 7

State, with reasons, whether the following expenditures are Capital or Revenue:

(a) Hire charges paid for a Motor Car.
(b) Cleaning and greasing of new machine.
(c) Purchase of Patent and Copyright.
(d) Legal fees paid to defend a title suit which proved to be unsuccessful.
(e) Fitting a new engine to a delivery van.
(f) Installation charges incurred relating to a new gas-fired boiler in a coalfield.
(g) Purchased a secondhand petrol-pump and cost of reinstallation expenses and repainting incurred for the purpose.
(h) Security deposit paid to CESC for taking electricity.

Solution

(a) Revenue Expenditure : It is a regular expenditure to run the organisation.

(b) Revenue Expenditure : It does not increase the value of the asset. It is simply incurred to run the machine for its normal use.

(c) Capital Expenditure : It is incurred for acquiring a right of an asset the benefit of which will be consumed for a number of years.

(d) Revenue Expenditure : It was incurred for the purpose of maintaining the ownership of a fixed asset which belongs to the firm.

(e) Capital Expenditure : It is the acquisition of fixed asset which is added to the existing fixed assets.

(f) Capital Expenditure : Since it will increase the earning capacity of the firm and incidental to the acquisition of assets, it is capital expenditure.

(g) Capital Expenditure : It is the acquisition of fixed assets, reinstallation expense and repainting expense which are incidental to the acquisition of asset and will be added to the cost.

(h) Capital Expenditure : It is a capital expenditure since the benefit will accrue for a number of years and help the firm for its normal use.

Illustration 8

State with reasons which of the following items are to be considered as Capital and which are Revenue:

1. Spent Rs. 20,000 for remodelling the factory and the value of factory enhanced by Rs. 15,000.
2. Wages paid for the installation of Machine amounted to Rs. 2,000 and cost of carriage for the same also amounted to Rs. 500.
3. An old machine costing Rs. 3,000 (or, W.D.V. Rs. 1,800) was sold for Rs. 1,000.
4. The cost of removal of stock from old factory to the new one amounted to Rs. 1,000.
5. The expenses incurred for whitewashing the factory building amounted to Rs. 4,000.
6. Purchase of Patent rights Rs. 4,000, and renewal fee for the next year Rs. 400.
7. Cost of repainting the factory building Rs. 800.
8. Compensation paid to a retrenched employee for loss of employment amounted to Rs. 2,000.
9. Purchase of new tyre for Rs. 2,000 for an old car.
10. Imported goods worth Rs. 20,000 confiscated by Customs authorities for non-disclosure of material facts.
11. Fees paid to a lawyer for drawing an agreement of lease for an immovable property amounted to Rs. 1,000.
12. Expenses incurred on research work for a particular product which ultimately did not produce any fruitful result amounted to Rs. 10,000.
13. Cost of conversion of gas plant to oil fuel plant for the generation of electricity amounted to Rs. 20,000.
14. Plant appearing in the book value Rs. 8,000 and stock valued at Rs. 4,000 were destroyed by fire, amount recovered from the Insurance Company for Rs. 10,000 and Rs. 5,000, respectively.
15. Incurred Rs. 4,000 in redecorating a cinema-hall and Rs. 12,000 in enhancing the sitting accommodation.
16. Fire insurance premium of Rs. 12,000 is paid on 30th Nov. for one year. The accounting date is 31st December.
17. A firm of builders spends Rs. 1,60,000 in purchasing a plot of land and erects office for its own use on a quarter of the site. The remaining land is used for building houses which are sold to the public.
18. A sum of Rs. 2,000 spent on a machine comprises Rs. 400 for replacement of worn-out parts and Rs. 1,600 for additions to new devices which enable the output to be doubled.
19. Visit of Sales Manager to U.K. total cost of which was Rs. 20,000, for promoting export sales—visit is quite successful.

Solution

1. Rs. 15,000 (by which the value of factory is enhanced) for remodelling is a capital expenditure since it will increase the earning capacity of the firm and Rs. 5,000 (i.e., Rs. 20,000 – Rs. 15,000) which is also incurred for remodelling is a revenue expenditure as it does not increase the earning capacity but for maintaining as a regular course of business.

2. Wages paid for the installation of machine amounting to Rs. 2,000 and carriage paid for the purpose amounting to Rs. 500 are capital expenditure since they all are incidental to the acquisition of fixed assets and its installation. Moreover, they will also increase the earning capacity.

3. The loss on sale of old machine amounting to Rs. 800 (i.e., Rs. 1,800 – Rs. 1,000) is a revenue loss since it represents under-provision for depreciation already made in the earlier years and the selling price—amounting to Rs. 1,000—is a capital receipt as it reveals the proceeds of a sale of fixed assets.

4. The cost of removal of Stock amounting to Rs. 1,000 is a revenue expenditure of special nature which may be written-off against the revenue of a number of years, i.e., like deferred revenue expenditure—since it does not increase the efficiency of the asset or earning capacity.

5. The expenses which are incurred for whitewashing the factory building amounted to Rs. 4,000 may be considered as a regular expenditure in order to maintain the factory and, as such, the same should be treated as revenue expenditure.

6. The cost of Patent Rights amounting to Rs. 4,000 is a capital expenditure since it is a fixed asset (more or less) by nature which helps in earning revenue over a period of few years. But the renewal fee is undoubtedly a revenue expenditure since it is designated to supply benefit only for one financial year, i.e., the current year.

7. Cost of repainting the factory building amounting to Rs. 800 may be considered as a regular expenditure in order to maintain the building and, as such, it must be treated as revenue expenditure. On the contrary, if this is done at the interval of a few years, the expense of such painting may be spread over the period over which the benefit is actually taken.

8. Compensation paid to a retrenched employee amounting to Rs. 2,000 may be treated as revenue expenditure of special type and non-recurring nature which will ultimately be written-off against Profit and Loss Account over a number of certain periods—considering it as deferred revenue expenditure. This is because compensation for loss of service is generally paid against the salary payable to the employee for the period of notice before retrenchment.

9. Purchase of a new tyre for an old car amounting to Rs. 2,000 is a revenue expenditure since it is nothing but a cost of replacement of a part of an existing fixed asset.

10. Imported goods amounting to Rs. 20,000—which were confiscated by Customs authorities for non-disclosure of material facts—is an abnormal revenue loss and non-recurring in nature, which are incurred in the regular course of the business. As such, it is better to treat the same as deferred revenue expenditure which may be written-off against the period of few years.

11. Fees paid to a lawyer for drafting an agreement of lease amounting to Rs. 1,000 is a capital expenditure since it is incidental to the acquisition of such lease which is a part of fixed asset.

12. Expenditure on scientific research, if it is fruitful, may be treated as capital expenditure. But, if the product did not result in a success the same should be treated as an expenditure of special nature which, again, should be written-off against the Profit and Loss Account over a number of years like deferred revenue expenditure.

13. In this case, the purpose of conversion is not known to us. It may happen for two purposes: (i) the said conversion may increase the efficiency of the plant, or (ii) the said conversion may arise since there is nonavailability of gas supply in the locality, or any other purpose. The former is a capital expenditure whereas the latter is a revenue expenditure—which is written-off against the revenue over a number of years by charging Profit and Loss Account.

14. The excess amounts which are realised from Insurance Company over the book value of Plant amounting to Rs. 2,000 (Rs. 10,000 – Rs. 8,000) is a capital profit since plant is an item of fixed asset while the excess amounts which are realised from the Insurance Company over the value of stock amounting to Rs. 1,000 (Rs. 5,000 – Rs. 4,000) is a revenue profit since stock is an item of current asset and which is meant for resale.

15. Redecoration of a cinema hall amounting to Rs. 4,000 is a revenue expenditure as it does not enhance the earning capacity. But if it is a substantially large amount, the same may be treated as a deferred revenue expenditure and may be spread over two to three years. But enhancement of sitting accommodation increases the earning capacity. As such, it should be capitalised.

16. Fire insurance premium is usually paid in advance and, as such, Rs. 1,200 would have been paid for the following period. As premium is paid on 30th Nov. and current year closes on 31st Dec., one month's premium amounting to Rs. 100 ($\frac{\text{Rs. } 1,200}{12} \times 1$) would be charged to revenue and the balance Rs. 1,100 (Rs. 1,200 – Rs. 100) would be carried forward as deferred revenue expenditure as 'Prepaid Insurance Premium' in the Assets side of the Balance Sheet.

17. Rs. 40,000 $(1,60,000 \times \frac{1}{4})$ which is incurred by the builders while erecting offices for use should be capitalised and the balance, i.e., Rs. 1,20,000 (Rs. 1,60,000 – Rs. 40,000) which is spent for constructing the building sold out to the public is a revenue expenditure.

18. Rs. 400, which is incurred by replacing worn-out parts, is a revenue charge since it is a routine expenditure for maintaining the existing earning capacity of the firm and Rs. 1,600, which is incurred for additions to a new device, is a capital expenditure since it results in an increase in the earning capacity.

19. Visit of sales manager to U.K. for promoting export sales is an expenditure in the nature of advertisement campaign. As the visit is found to be quite successful it is likely to render benefit for enhancing export sales over a number of years and, as such, it may be treated as deferred revenue expenditure and may be written-off against Profit and Loss Account over the related number of years.

ASSIGNMENT MATERIALS

THEORETICAL

Multiple Choice Questions

1. (a) Purchase of goods for ordinary course of business is a:
(i) Revenue Expenditure; (ii) Capital Expenditure; (iii) None of these.

(b) Prepaid Rent is a:
(i) Capital Expenditure; (ii) Revenue Expenditure; (iii) Deferred Revenue Expenditure.

(c) Carriage paid for purchasing a machine is a:
(i) Capital Expenditure; (ii) Revenue Expenditure; (iii) None of these.

(d) Cost of overhauling a secondhand plant is a:
(i) Revenue Expenditure; (ii) Capital Expenditure; (iii) None of these.

(e) Increasing the seating capacity in a Cinemahall is a:
(i) Capital Expenditure; (ii) Revenue Expenditure; (iii) None of these.

[Ans. (a) (i); (b) (iii); (c) (i); (d) (ii); (e) (i)]

Short Answer-Type Questions

2. How would you classify transactions into Capital and Revenue?
3. What do you mean by Capital Expenditure, Revenue Expenditure and Deferred Revenue Expenditure? Give two examples of each type.
4. Explain briefly the principles of determining Capital Expenditure and Revenue Expenditure.
5. How would you distinguish between Capital Expenditure and Revenue Expenditure?
6. Why is the distinction between 'Capital' and 'Revenue' of great importance in Accountancy?
7. Write short notes on:
(i) Recurring Expenditure. (ii) Non-Recurring Expenditure. (iii) Deferred Revenue Expenditure. (iv) Capitalised Expenditure.
8. Distinguish between:
(i) Capital Receipts and Capital Income. (ii) Revenue Receipts and Revenue Income.
(iii) Capital Loss and Revenue Loss.
9. Do you think that the distinction between Capital Expenditure and Revenue Expenditure is necessary in Accountancy? What are the disadvantages, if such distinction is not made?
10. Explain Deferred Revenue Expenses. How are they treated in accounts?
11. (a) How do you distinguish between Capital Expenditure and Revenue Expenditure?
(b) What are the principles for determining Capital Expenditure and Revenue Expenditure?
12. Write a short note on Deferred Revenue Expenditure.

Essay-Type Questions

13. How do you classify the transactions between capital and revenue?
14. Distinguish between:
    (a) Capital and Revenue Expenditure;
    (b) Capital and Revenue Receipts;
    (c) Recurring and Non-recurring Expenditure;
    (d) Revenue Expenditure and Deferred Revenue Expenditure.
15. Define Capital Receipts with suitable examples.
16. Why is it so necessary to distinguish expenditures into capital and revenue in accounting?
17. What problem will arise if we do not distinguish properly the receipts between capital and revenue?

PRACTICAL

1. X Ltd incurred the following *'legal expenses'*. You are asked to state which of the following expenditures are Capital and which are Revenue:
   (i) Legal expenses amounted to Rs. 1,000 incurred relating to income tax appeal.
   (ii) Legal expenses incurred for purchasing a plot of land amounted to Rs. 4,000.
   (iii) Legal expenses incurred for raising funds by the issue of equity shares amounted to Rs. 5,000.
   (iv) Legal expenses incurred against the action for infringement of trademarks amounted to Rs. 7,000.
   (v) Legal expenses incurred while defending a suit for breach of contract for the supply of goods to customers amounted to Rs. 3,500.
   (vi) Legal expenses paid for the recovery of bad debts amounted to Rs. 1,000.
   (vii) Legal expenses incurred for the concealment of material fact by the company amounted to Rs. 2,500.
2. From the following transactions relating to a Plant acquired by a firm, state whether each of the transactions is Capital or Revenue:
   (i) A secondhand plant was purchased for Rs. 50,000, incidental charges being Rs. 5,000.
   (ii) Cost of installation amounted to Rs. 3,000.
   (iii) Purchased different accessories for the plant amounted to Rs. 1,000.
   (iv) Due to short-circuit the plant was partly destroyed and repaired at a cost of Rs. 5,000.
   (v) Rs. 1,500 were paid to the operator who was injured by this plant.
   (vi) The operator's salary for the plant amounted to Rs. 2,000 p.m.
   (vii) The plant was sold for Rs. 45,000.
3. State with reasons whether the following items relating to a Sugar Mill Company are Capital or Revenue:
   (a) A motor truck costing Rs. 15,000 and standing in the books at Rs. 7,250 was sold for Rs. 12,000.
   (b) Rs. 20,000 received from an issue of further shares, the expenses of issue being Rs. 2,500.
   (c) Rs. 75,000 being cost of land purchased for agricultural farm and Rs. 450 paid for land revenue.
   (d) Rs. 1,50,000 paid for excise duty on sugar manufactured.
   (e) Rs. 50,000 invested in Government loan.
   (f) Rs. 60,000 spent on the construction of railway siding.

[Hints: (a) Capital, (b) Capital, (c) Capital, (d) Revenue, (e) Capital, (f) Capital]

4. Classify the following items between Capital and Revenue giving reasons for the same:
   (i) Rs. 5,000 spent towards additions to the machinery.
   (ii) Repairs for Rs. 1,000 necessitated by negligence.
   (iii) Rs. 500 spent to remove a worn-out part and replace it with a new one.
   (iv) Rs. 100 wages paid in connection with the erection of a new machinery.
   (v) Old machinery of book value of Rs. 7,500 worn-out, dismantled at a cost of Rs. 1,000 and scrap realised for Rs. 100.
   (vi) Secondhand motor car purchased for Rs. 10,000 and spent Rs. 1,000 for repairs immediately.
   (vii) Employees' State Insurance premium Rs. 660 paid.
   (viii) Insurance claim of Rs. 5,000 received from the Insurance Company for loss of goods by fire of Rs. 6,000.

[CA Entrance]

5. State with reasons whether the following are Capital or Revenue Expenditure:
   (i) Expenses incurred in connection with obtaining a license for starting the factory were Rs. 10,000.
   (ii) Rs. 1,000 paid for removal of stock to a new site.
   (iii) Rings and Pistons of an engine were changed at a cost of Rs. 5,000 to get fuel efficiency.
   (iv) Rs. 2,000 spent as lawyer's fee to defend a suit claiming that the firm's factory site belonged to the plaintiff. The suit was not successful.

[CA Entrance]

6. State with reasons whether the following are Capital or Revenue Expenditure:
   (i) Expenses incurred in connection with obtaining a license for starting the factory were Rs. 8,000.
   (ii) Rs. 1,500 paid for removal of stock to a new site.
   (iii) Rings and pistons of an engine were changed at a cost of Rs. 4,000 to get fuel efficiency.
   (iv) Rs. 2,500 spent as Lawyer's fee to defend a suit claiming that the firm's factory site belonged to the plaintiff. The suit was not successful.
   (v) Rs. 8,000 were spent on advertising the introduction of a new product in the market, the benefit of which will be effective during four years.
   (vi) A factory shed was constructed at a cost of Rs. 40,000. A sum of Rs. 4,000 had been incurred in the construction of temporary huts for storing building materials.

[CA Entrance—Adapted]

CHAPTER 6

ARITHMETIC OF ACCOUNTANCY

Learning Objectives

A. *Effect of Percentage of Cost Price and Selling Price*

B. *Computation of Managerial Remunerations, etc.*

C. *Effect of Ratio*

Meaning

In a career spanning more than four decades as a college lecturer and examiner in various public examinations in Accountancy, the author has learnt that one of the contributory causes of failure in examinations in the subject is the lack of ability to compute arithmetical calculations quickly and accurately. Simple arithmetical points should be developed by an accountancy student.

In this chapter, an attempt is made to deal with the calculations which are frequently required while working out problems that are set at the accountancy examinations which may create endless confusion and uncertainty among the students.

The students should realise that they can save a great deal of time if they work out calculations in a systematic manner and procedure.

A. Effect of Percentage On Cost Price And Selling Price

Profit can be expressed as a percentage either on *cost* or on *sales*.

We know

Selling Price	=	Cost Price	+	Profit
Cost Price	=	Selling Price	–	Profit

If percentage (%) of profit on cost is given, cost should be taken as Rs. 100.

For example, Profit is 25% on Cost Price

	Selling Price =	Profit +	Cost Price
	Rs.	Rs.	Rs.
	125	25	100
i.e.	$\frac{1}{5}$th	25	$\frac{1}{4}$th

$\therefore \quad \frac{1}{5}$th of S.P = $\frac{1}{4}$th of C.P.

or, 20% of S.P. = 25% of C.P.

Thus, if % of profit on Cost is given, *Cost price must be taken as Rs. 100.*

So,

(i) 25% of C.P. i.e. $\frac{25}{100}$ or $\frac{1}{4}$th is equal to $\frac{25}{125}$ or 20% or $\frac{1}{5}$th of S.P.

(ii) $33\frac{1}{3}$% of C.P. i.e. $\frac{33\frac{1}{3}}{100}$ or $\frac{1}{3}$rd is equal to $\frac{33\frac{1}{3}}{133\frac{1}{3}}$ or 25% or $\frac{1}{4}$th of S.P.

(iii) 50 % of C.P. i.e. $\frac{50}{100}$ or $\frac{1}{2}$ is equal to $\frac{50}{150}$ or $33\frac{1}{3}$% or $\frac{1}{3}$rd of S.P.

Illustration 1

Find out the cost price of an article which is sold for Rs. 2,000 at a profit of 25% on cost.

Solution

Let,

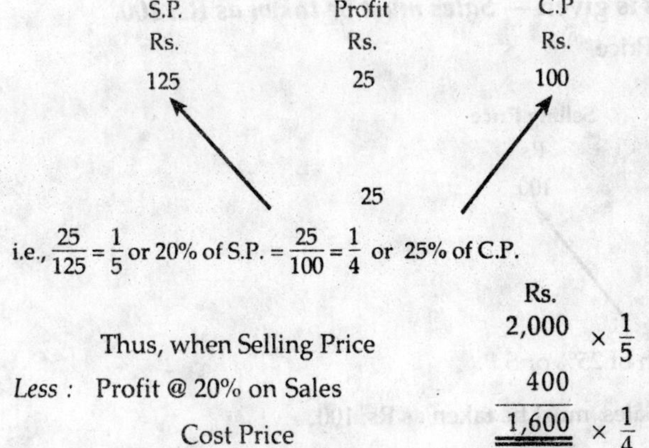

i.e., $\frac{25}{125} = \frac{1}{5}$ or 20% of S.P. = $\frac{25}{100} = \frac{1}{4}$ or 25% of C.P.

		Rs.	
	Thus, when Selling Price	2,000	$\times \frac{1}{5}$
Less :	Profit @ 20% on Sales	400	
	Cost Price	1,600	$\times \frac{1}{4}$

Alternatively

	S.P.	Profit	C.P.	
	Rs.	Rs.	Rs.	
	125	25	100	
When	2,000		$\frac{1,000 \times 2,000}{125}$	= Rs. 1,600.

Illustration 2

Find out the selling price of an article which was purchased for Rs. 3,000 but sold at a profit of $33\frac{1}{3}$% on Cost.

Let,

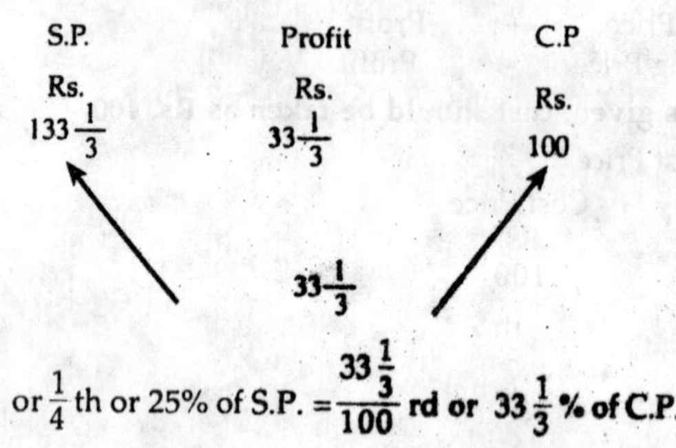

$\frac{33\frac{1}{3}}{133\frac{1}{3}}$ or $\frac{1}{4}$th or 25% of S.P. = $\frac{33\frac{1}{3}}{100}$ **rd or $33\frac{1}{3}$% of C.P.**

	Rs.	
Thus, when Cost Price	3,000	$\times \frac{1}{3}$
Add: Profit @ $33\frac{1}{3}$ % on Cost	1,000	
Selling Price	4,000	$\times \frac{1}{4}$

Alternatively

Cost Price	Profit	Selling Price
Rs.	Rs.	Rs.
100	$33\frac{1}{3}$	$133\frac{1}{3}$
3,000		$133\frac{1}{3} \times \frac{3,000}{100}$ = Rs. 4,000.

If percentage (%) of profit on Sales is given — *Sales must be taken as Rs. 100.*

For example — Profit is 25% of Selling Price.

Let,

Cost Price	Profit	Selling Price
Rs.	Rs.	Rs.
75	25	100

25

$\frac{25}{75}$ or, $\frac{1}{3}$ rd or $33\frac{1}{3}$ % C. P. = $\frac{25}{100}$ or $\frac{1}{4}$ th of 25% or S.P.

That is, if % of profit on Sales is given, Sales must be taken as Rs. 100.

So,

(i) 25% of S.P. i.e. $\frac{25}{100}$ or $\frac{1}{4}$ th is equal to $\frac{25}{75}$ or $33\frac{1}{3}$ or $\frac{1}{3}$ rd of C.P.

(ii) $33\frac{1}{3}$ % of S. P. i.e. $\frac{33\frac{1}{3}}{100}$ or $\frac{1}{3}$ rd is equal to $\frac{33\frac{1}{3}}{66\frac{2}{3}}$ or 50% or $\frac{1}{2}$ of C.P.

(iii) 50 % of S.P. i.e. $\frac{50}{100}$ or $\frac{1}{2}$ is equal to $\frac{50}{50}$ or 100% or 1 of C.P.

Illustration 3

Find out the Cost Price of an article which is sold for Rs. 2,000 at a profit of 25% on Sales.

Solution

Let,

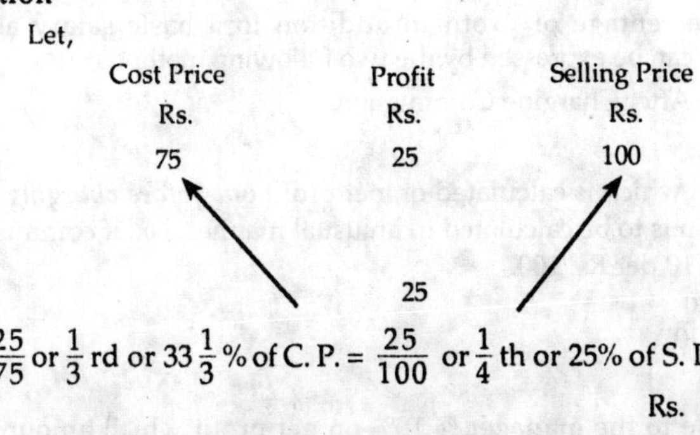

$\frac{25}{75}$ or $\frac{1}{3}$ rd or $33\frac{1}{3}$ % of C. P. = $\frac{25}{100}$ or $\frac{1}{4}$ th or 25% of S. P.

	Rs.	
Thus, when Selling Price	2,000	$\times \frac{1}{4}$
Less : Profit @ 25% on Sales	500	
Cost Price	1,500	$\times \frac{1}{3}$

Alternatively

	S.P.	Profit	C.P.
	Rs.	Rs.	Rs.
	100	25	75
When,	2,000		$75 \times \frac{2,000}{100}$ = Rs. 1,500

Illustration 4

Find out the selling price of an article which was purchased for Rs. 3,000 but sold at a profit of $33\frac{1}{3}$ % on sales.

Solution

Let,

C.P	Profit	S.P.
Rs.	Rs.	Rs.
$66\frac{2}{3}$	$33\frac{1}{3}$	100

$33\frac{1}{3}$

$\frac{33\frac{1}{3}}{66\frac{2}{3}}$ i.e., $\frac{1}{2}$ or 50% of C. P. = $\frac{33\frac{1}{3}}{100}$ $\frac{1}{3}$ rd or $33\frac{1}{3}$ % of S. P.

	Rs.	
Thus, when Cost Price	3,000	$\times \frac{1}{2}$
Add : Profit @ 50% on Cost	1,500	
Selling Price	4,500	$\times \frac{1}{3}$

Alternatively

	C.P.	Profit	S.P.
	Rs.	Rs.	Rs.
	$66\frac{2}{3}$	$33\frac{1}{3}$	100
When,	3,000		$\frac{100 \times 3,000}{66\frac{2}{3}}$ = Rs. 4,500.

B. Computation Of Managerial Remuneration, Commission Etc.

Usually, managers are paid at a certain percentage of profit in addition to a basic salary as his remuneration or commission. This commission can be expressed by the two following methods :

(i) Before Charging Commission. (ii) After Charging Commission.

(i) Before Charging Commission

If the commission is paid to the managers which is calculated on net profit *but before charging such commission* — in that case the said commission is to be calculated in an usual manner, i.e., if commission is @ 10% on net profit, commission will be Rs. 10 per Rs. 100.

Total commission will be = Net Profit $\times \frac{10}{100}$.

Illustration 5

Calculate the amount of Commission payable to the manager @ 10% on net profit which amounts to Rs. 1,100 before charging such commission.

Solution

Calculation of commission payable to the manager :

Commission = Net Profit (before charging commission) $\times \frac{10}{100}$

= Rs. 1,100 $\times \frac{10}{100}$

= Rs. 110.

Note : In this case actual net profit (i.e. net profit after charging commission) will be Rs. 990 (i.e. Rs. 1,100 – Rs. 110).

(ii) After Charging Commission

If the commission is paid to the manager which is calculated on net profit but *after charging such commission,* the said commission is to be calculated in the following manner :

If the rate of Commission is 10%.

Net Profit (after charging com.)	Profit	Profit before charging Net Profit
Rs.	Rs.	Rs.
100	10	110

i.e., manager is entitled to a commission of Rs. 10 per Rs. 110 and not on Rs. 100.

$\therefore$ His Commission = Net Profit (before charging com.) $\times \frac{10}{110}$

Alternatively

	Net Profit (before charging Com.)	Rs. 110	(i.e, Net Profit + Com.) = Total
Less :	@ $\frac{1}{11}$	10	100 + 10 = 110
	Net Profit	100 × 10 %	$\therefore$ Com = $\frac{10}{110} = \frac{1}{11}$.

Another Alternative

Commission may be calculated with the help of the following formula :

(a) In terms of fraction $\left(\text{i.e., } \frac{1}{4} \text{ or } \frac{1}{5} \text{ etc.}\right) \frac{\text{Rate}}{\text{Rate} + 1}$

For instance, if the manager is entitled to a commission @ $\frac{1}{4}$th of net profit, after charging such commission

i.e. $\dfrac{\frac{1}{4}}{\frac{1}{4}+1} = \dfrac{\frac{1}{4}}{\frac{5}{4}} = \frac{1}{4} \times \frac{4}{5} = \frac{1}{5}$

(b) In terms of Percentage (i.e. 10%, 20% etc.)

$$= \frac{\text{Rate}}{\text{Rate} + 100}$$

(If the Rate is 10%) $= \dfrac{10}{10 + 100} = \dfrac{10}{110} = \dfrac{1}{11}$

Illustration 6

Calculate the amount of commission payable to the manager @ 10% on net profit which amounts to Rs. 1,100 after charging such commission.

Solution

Calculation of commission payable to the manager :

Commission = Net Profit (before charging Com.) × $\frac{10}{110}$

= Rs. 1,100 × $\frac{10}{110}$

= Rs. 100

That is, Net Profit (before charging Com.) Rs. 1,100

Less : Commission @ $\frac{1}{11}$ 100

Net Profit after charging Commission 1,000 × 10% = 100

GENERAL ILLUSTRATIONS

Illustration 7

A is entitled to a commission made up of two parts : (a) 5% on sales, and (b) 10% on the excess of sales over cost of sales, such cost to include the total commissions payable.

Total Cost of goods (excluding Commission) Rs. 40,000

Sales $\left(\frac{3}{4}\text{th of the goods}\right)$ Rs. 48,000

Calculate the commission payable to A.

Solution

Calculation of Commission payable to A

(a) Commission = Sales × $\frac{5}{100}$ = Rs. 48,000 × $\frac{5}{100}$ = Rs. 2,400.

Cost of Sales = Rs. 40,000 × $\frac{3}{4}$ = Rs. 30,000

(b) Excess of Sales over Cost of Sales = Sales – Cost of Sales

= Rs. 48,000 – Rs. 30,000

= Rs. 18,000

Now, Commission @ 10% on Rs. 18,000 after charging such commission including the commission of Rs. 2,400 payable under (a) above.

Thus, Commission payable = Rs. 15,600 (Rs. 18,000 – Rs. 2,400) × $\frac{10}{110}$

= Rs. 1,418 (approx).

∴ Total Commission = Rs. 2,400 + Rs. 1,418 = Rs. 3,818.

Illustration 8

A manager is entitled to a commission at a certain percentage of net profit (such commission to be charged in arriving at the net profit).

The commission is to be allowed as the following rates :

First Rs. 10,000 of the net profit			Nil
Next Rs. 20,000	"	@	10%
Next Rs. 30,000	"	@	15%
Next Rs. 60,000	"	@	20%
Balance	"	@	30%

The net profit before charging the manager's commission is Rs. 1,45,000.
Compute the amount of commission payable to manager.

Solution

Calculation of commissions payable to manager :

			Commission Rs.		Total Net Profit considered Rs.
First Rs. 10,000 of the net profit			—		10,000
Next Rs. 20,000	"	@ 10%	2,000	(20,000 + 2,000)	22,000
Next Rs. 30,000	"	@ 15%	4,500	(30,000 + 4,500)	34,500
Next Rs. 60,000	"	@ 20%	12,000	(60,000 + 12,000)	72,000
∴ Total			18,500		1,38,500

Illustration 9

X and Y were appointed Office Manager and Factory Manager, respectively of ABC Ltd. in January 2012. Their terms of appointment included, amongst other things, the payment of commission on the following basis :

X—a commission of 5% of the net profit after charging commission of Y.
Y—a commission of 4% of the net profit after charging commission of X.
The Profit and Loss Account of 2012 disclosed a net profit of Rs. 10,00,000.
You are required to ascertain the commission payable to X and Y.

Solution

Let a be the commission payable to X and b be the commission payable to Y

Then according to given condition

$$a = \frac{5}{100} \times (10,00,000 - b) \quad \ldots \quad \ldots \quad (1)$$

$$b = \frac{4}{100} \times (10,00,000 - a) \quad \ldots \quad \ldots \quad (2)$$

From equation (1) we get

$$a = \frac{5}{100} \times (10,00,000 - b)$$

or $100a = 50,00,000 - 5b$

or $100a + 5b = 50,00,000 \quad \ldots \quad \ldots \quad (3)$

From equation (2) we get

$$b = \frac{4}{100} \times (10,00,000 - a)$$

or $100b = 40,00,000 - 4a$

or $4a + 100b = 40,00,000 \quad \ldots \quad \ldots \quad (4)$

Multiplying equation (4) by 25 we get

$100a + 2,500\,b = 10,00,00,000 \quad \ldots \quad \ldots \quad (5)$ Subtracting (3) from (5)

$-100a - 5b = -50,00,000 \quad \ldots \quad \ldots \quad (3)$

$2,495b = 9,50,00,000$

$$\therefore \quad b = \frac{9,50,00,000}{2,495} = 38,076$$

By putting the value of b in equation no. (1) we get

$$a = \frac{5}{100}(10,00,000 - 38,076).$$

or $a = \frac{1}{20} \times$ Rs. 9,61,924 = Rs. 48,096.

Therefore, commission payable to X is Rs. 48,096, and payable to Y is Rs. 38,076.

Illustration 10

The Board of Directors consists of one Managing Director and two other Directors in X Co. Ltd. The Managing Director is to get 5% commission on the profits after charging all commissions and the other Directors are to get 1% commission on the profits after charging all commissions. The profit of the company for the year 2012 is Rs. 10,60,000 before charging the commission of all Directors.

You are to ascertain the commission payable to the Managing Director and other Directors.

Solution

Commission is to be calculated on the same amount for both categories of Directors (i.e., after deducting their commission from the profit). So, commission to be paid to Directors = 5% + 1% = 6%.

Therefore, Total Commission payable = Rs. 10,60,000 × $\frac{6}{106}$ = 60,000

∴ Managing Director will get = Rs. 60,000 × $\frac{5}{6}$ = Rs. 50,000

Other two Directors will get = Rs. 60,000 × $\frac{1}{6}$ = Rs. 10,000

Alternative Approach

Let the total remuneration of the Managing Director be x. Then, the remuneration of the other two Directors will be = $\frac{1}{101}$ (10,60,000 – x)

$$\therefore \quad x = \frac{5}{105}\left\{ (10{,}60{,}000) - \frac{1}{101}(10{,}60{,}000 - x) \right\}$$

$$\text{or,} \quad x = \frac{1}{21}\left\{ \left(10{,}60{,}000 - 10{,}495 - \frac{1}{101}x\right) \right\}$$

$$\text{or,} \quad x = \frac{1}{21}\left(10{,}49{,}505 + \frac{1}{101}x\right)$$

or, $21x = 10{,}49{,}505 + \frac{1}{101}x$ (multiplying both sides by 21)

or, $101 \times 21x = 10{,}49{,}505 \times 101 + x$ (multiplying both sides by 101)

or, $2{,}121x = 10{,}60{,}00{,}000 + x$

∴ $2{,}120x = 10{,}60{,}00{,}000$

∴ $x = \frac{10{,}60{,}00{,}000}{2{,}120}$ = Rs. 50,000.

So, other two Directors will get

$\frac{1}{101}$ (10,60,000 – x)

or, $\frac{1}{101}$ (10,60,000 – 50,000)

or, $\frac{1}{101}$ × 10,10,000

= Rs. 10,000.

Illustration 11

In XYZ Co. Ltd. there are two wholetime Directors and three other parttime Directors. The wholetime Directors are entitled to commission @ 10% of the profit remaining after charging the commission of the parttime Directors. The parttime Directors are entitled to commission @ 1% of the profits after charging the commission of the wholetime Directors.

The net profit of the company before charging the commissions of all the Directors is Rs. 20,00,000.

You are asked to find out the total remuneration payable to the wholetime Directors and parttime Directors.

Solution

Let us assume the remuneration payable to wholetime Directors is x.

So, the remuneration payable to part time Directors is $\frac{1}{100}$ (Rs. 20,00,000 – x).

Therefore, the profit after paying the remuneration to parttime Directors will be

$$\text{Rs. } 20,00,000 - \frac{1}{100} (\text{Rs. } 20,00,000 - x)$$

Then, $x = \frac{10}{100} \left\{ 20,00,000 - \frac{1}{100} (20,00,000 - x) \right\}$

or, $x = \frac{1}{10} \left\{ 20,00,000 - \frac{1}{100} (20,00,000 - x) \right\}$

or, $10x = 20,00,000 - \frac{1}{100} (20,00,000 - x)$ (multiplying both sides by 10)

or, $1,000x = 20,00,00,000 - (20,00,000 - x)$ (" " " " 100)

or, $1,000x = 20,00,00,000 - 20,00,000 + x$

or, $999x = 20,00,00,000 - 20,00,000$

or, $999x = 19,80,00,000$

$\therefore \quad x = \frac{19,80,00,000}{999}$

= Rs. 2,00,000 (approx.)

i.e., Remuneration payable to wholetime Directors is Rs. 2,00,000.

So, remuneration payable to parttime Directors is :

$= \frac{1}{100}$ (Rs. 20,00,000 – Rs. 2,00,000)

$= \frac{1}{100} \times$ Rs. 18,00,000

= Rs. 18,000.

C. Effect of Ratio

Ratio is a fraction whose *numerator* is the antecedent and *denominator* the consequent. It is simply an expression of one number in terms of another. It may also be defined **as the *relationship or proportion* that one amount bears to another, the first number being the numerator and the latter the denominator.** It is also the relation of the latter to the earlier amount and computed by dividing the amount for the latter date or period by the amount of the earlier date or period.

Ratio may be expressed in different forms, such as :

(i) Pure Ratio, e.g. 2 : 1.

(ii) Ratio which refers to ratios ascertained with reference to time period— e.g. working capital turnover 3 times a year; and

(iii) Percentage e.g.— Net Profit is 20% of Sales (This aspect has already been explained in earlier paragraph)

This is, no doubt, a very important tool in Accounting.

Illustration 12

A and B are partners sharing profits and losses as 2 : 1. They admitted C as a partner with $\frac{1}{4}$th share in the business. They then admitted D as a partner with $\frac{1}{5}$th share in the business.

Find out the profit-sharing ratio after C's and D's admission, respectively.

Solution

After C's admission

Let the total share be 1.

$$1 - \frac{1}{4} = \frac{3}{4}$$

$$A = \frac{3}{4} \text{ of } \frac{2}{3} \text{ or } \frac{3}{4} \times \frac{2}{3} = \frac{6}{12}$$

$$B = \frac{3}{4} \text{ of } \frac{1}{3} \text{ or } \frac{3}{4} \times \frac{1}{3} = \frac{3}{12}$$

$C = \frac{1}{4} \left(\text{or } \frac{1 \times 3}{4 \times 3} \right) = \frac{3}{12}$ (multiplying both the numerator and the denominator by 3)

Thus, the profit-sharing ratio among A, B and C is = 6 : 3 : 3

or, 2 : 1 : 1

After D's admission

Let the total share be 1.

Then, $1 - \frac{1}{5} = \frac{4}{5}$ $A = \frac{4}{5}$ of $\frac{2}{4}$ or, $\frac{4}{5} \times \frac{2}{4} = \frac{8}{20}$ $B = \frac{4}{5}$ of $\frac{1}{4}$ or $\frac{4}{5} \times \frac{1}{4} = \frac{4}{20}$

$C = \frac{4}{5}$ of $\frac{1}{4}$ or $\frac{4}{5} \times \frac{1}{4} = \frac{4}{20}$. $D = \frac{1}{5}\left(\text{of } \frac{1 \times 4}{5 \times 4}\right) = \frac{4}{20}$ (multiplying both the numerator and denominator by 4).

Thus, the profit-sharing ratio among A, B, C and D is = 8 : 4 : 4 : 4 or 2 : 1 : 1 : 1.

Illustration 13

X, Y and Z start business in partnership. X puts in Rs. 20,000 for the whole year, Y puts Rs. 30,000 at first and increases it to Rs. 40,000 at the end of four months but withdraws Rs. 20,000 at the end of six months, while Z puts Rs. 40,000 at first but withdraws Rs. 10,000 at the end of nine months.

At the end of the year how should they divide a profit of Rs. 79,100 on the basis of effective capital employed by each partner ?

Solution

Effective Capital Employed

	Amounts Rs.	Months	Product Rs.	(i.e. for 1 month)
X	20,000	12	2,40,000	2,40,000
Y	30,000	12	3,60,000	
	10,000	8	(+) 80,000	
	20,000	6	(−) 1,20,000	
				3,20,000
Z	40,000	12	4,80,000	
	10,000	3	(−) 30,000	
				4,50,000

Average Capital Ratio :

X : Y : Z = Rs. 2,40,000 : Rs. 3,20,000 : Rs. 4,50,000

or 24 : 32 : 45 (Total 101)

Thus, A will get = Rs. $79,100 \times \frac{24}{101}$ = Rs. 18,796

B " " = Rs. $79,100 \times \frac{32}{101}$ = Rs. 25,061

C " " = Rs. $79,100 \times \frac{45}{101}$ = Rs. 35,243

Illustration 14

P and Q are partners sharing profits and losses as 4 : 1. They admit R into partnership for one-third $\left(\frac{1}{3}\right)$ share of profits; as between themselves, P and Q agree to share future profits and losses equally.

Find out the gaining-or sacrificing-ratio among the partners.

Solution :

Let the total share be 1.

Then, $1 - \frac{1}{3} = \frac{2}{3}$

P $\frac{2}{3} \times \frac{1}{2} = \frac{1}{3}$

Q $\frac{2}{3} \times \frac{1}{2} = \frac{1}{3}$

R $= \frac{1}{3}$ (i.e., P : Q : R = 1 : 1 : 1)

Now,

we can easily calculate the gaining-or sacrificing-ratios :

$$P = \frac{4}{5} - \frac{1}{3} = \frac{12-5}{15} = \frac{7}{15} \quad \textit{(sacrifices)}$$

$$Q = \frac{1}{5} - \frac{1}{3} = \frac{3-5}{15} = \frac{-2}{15} \quad \textit{(gains)}$$

$$R = \frac{1}{3}\left(\text{or } \frac{1 \times 5}{3 \times 5}\right) = \frac{-5}{15} \quad \textit{(gains)}$$

That is, the sacrifice which is made by P, i.e., $\frac{7}{15}$, is taken by Q and R by $\frac{2}{15}$ and $\frac{5}{15}$, respectively.

Thus, P sacrifices $\frac{7}{15}$

Q gains $\frac{2}{15}$

R gains $\frac{5}{15}$

ASSIGNMENT MATERIALS

PRACTICAL

Short Answer-Type Questions

1. What is the Cost Price of an article which is sold for Rs. 5,000 at a profit of $33\frac{1}{3}$% on Cost?

   [Ans. Rs. 3,750]

2. What is the Selling Price of an article which is purchased for Rs. 4,000 and sold at a profit of 20% on sales?

   [Ans. Rs. 5,000]

3. Find out the selling price of an article which was purchased for Rs. 12,000 but sold at a profit of 25% on sales.

   [Ans. Rs. 16,000]

4. Find out the cost price of an article which is sold for Rs. 10,000 at a profit of 20% on sales.

   [Ans. Rs. 8,000]

5. (a) Calculate amount of commission on net profit— Net Profit Rs. 11,000. Commission @ 10% on net profit before charging such commission.

   [Ans. Rs. 1,100]

   (b) Calculate the amount of commission if it is calculated @ 10% on net profit after charging such commission.

   [Ans. Rs. 1,000 (Rs. 11,000 × $\frac{10}{110}$)]

CHAPTER 7

CASH BOOK

Learning Objectives

Meaning

Cash Book is a Journalised Ledger

Similarities of Cash Book with Journals

Similarities of Cash Book with Ledger

Characteristics

Classification of Cash Book

1. *Cash Book as the Only Book of Original Entry*
2. *Single Column Cash Book*
3. *Double Column Cash Book*
4. *Triple Column Cash Book*
5. *Multicolumnar Cash Book*
6. *Miscellaneous:*
   - *(i) Cash Book with Two Bank Accounts*
   - *(ii) Cash Book with Missing Sales*
   - *(iii) Mini-Max Cash Book*
7. *Petty Cash Book*
   - *(i) Under Analytical System*
   - *(ii) Under Imprest System*

Meaning of Cash Book

The book which keeps records of all cash transactions, i.e., cash receipts and cash payments, is called a Cash Book. Its ruling is like a ledger account and it is divided into two sides, viz., debit and credit. All receipts are recorded on the debit side, whereas all payments are recorded on the credit side. Since it serves the function of a Cash Account, there is no necessity of opening such account in the ledger.

Cash Book is a book of original entry on the ground that all cash transactions are recorded first in it and thereafter recorded from the Cash Book to the various ledger accounts. It is also called a Ledger or Book of Final Entry, since all cash receipts are entered on the debit side, whereas all cash payments on the credit side, i.e., it is maintained under double entry principle. That is why ***Cash Book is both a subsidiary book and a main book.***

Cash Book is a Journalised Ledger

Frequently the question arises before us "Is Cash Book a Journal or a Ledger"? The answer is 'both', i.e., ***it serves both as a journal as well as a ledger***. That is why it is called ***'Journalised Ledger'***. It is journal in the sense that all cash transactions are recorded in a Cash Book together with narration and, as such, they are posted to the relevant accounts in the corresponding ledger. Similarly, Cash Book is a ledger in the sense that it serves both the purposes of Cash Book and bank accounts. In other words, no separate Cash Account is opened in the ledger if Cash Book is maintained. Thus, it can rightly be called that ***Cash Book is a journalised ledger.***

Moreover, the following points will highlight the above proposition :

Similarities of Cash Book with Journals

We find the following similarities :

(i) When Cash Book serves as the only book of original entry : (ii) As transactions are recorded here date-wise; (iii) As narrations are given like Journals; (iv) As it also contains ledger folio number like journal; and (v) As transactions are posted from the cash book to the relevant ledgers correspondingly.

Similarities of Cash Book with Ledger

We find the following similarities :

(i) Format of a Cash Book is like the format of a ledger : (i.e., it has two sides, **debit— in the left hand side, and credit — in the right hand side.** (ii) We also use 'To' and 'By' like ledgers. (iii) ***The Cash Book is the book of final entry*** as no separate Cash/Bank Account is opened. (iv) Balancing in Cash Book is done periodically like ledgers.

Characteristics of a Cash Book

The following are the primary characteristics of a Cash Book

(a) Cash Book records only cash transactions, i.e., all cash receipts and all cash payments.
(b) It can never show a credit balance, i.e., under no circumstances the credit side of the cash can exceed the debit side.
(c) All receipts are recorded on the debit side; all payments are recorded on the credit side.
(d) All cash transactions are recorded chronologically.
(e) It is a journalised ledger, i.e., it serves both as a journal as well as a ledger.
(f) In each side of the Cash Book, there must be five columns (in case of Single Column Cash Book, columns are increased in the Case of Double and Triple Column Cash Book by one or two, respectively) viz.,

(i) *Date* — This column contains the date-wise transactions, i.e., year, month and the date of the transaction.

(ii) *Particulars* — This column is used for writing the heads of accounts to be credited (on the debit side) and debited (on the credit side), respectively, together with the narration.

(iii) *Voucher No.* — We know that a voucher is a documentary evidence against a transaction. Vouchers are of two types, viz., Receipts Vouchers (for all transactions relating to receipts) and Payment Vouchers (for all transactions relating to payments). It always bears a serial number which is written in the column.

(iv) ***Ledger Folio*** — It is the page mark i.e., on which page of the ledger the concerned account is recorded. It helps to find out the required ledger quickly.

(v) ***Amount*** — This column contains the amount/figure of the transactions so made.

CASH BOOK— TYPES/CLASSIFICATION

The popular forms of Cash Book are :

1. ***Cash Book as an*** *only Book of Original Entry;*
2. ***Single Column or*** *Simple Cash Book;*
3. ***Double Column*** *Cash Book (i.e., Cash and Bank, or Cash and Discount Column);*
4. ***Three or Triple*** *Column Cash Book (i.e., Cash, Bank and Discount Columns);*
5. ***Multicolumnar*** *Cash Book, or Analytical Cash Book;*
6. ***Miscellaneous :***
   (i) Cash Book *with two Bank Accounts; (ii) Cash Book with Missing Sales; (iii) Mini-Max Cash* ***Book.***
7. ***Petty Cash Book***
   (i) Analytical System; and (ii) Imprest System.

1. Cash Book as the only Book of Original Entry

As soon as any transaction occurs, it is recorded on chronological basis in a book which is known as Book of Original Entry, it records all types of transactions, even if there are some credit transactions. It has already been mentioned earlier that only cash transactions are recorded in a Cash Book. But if Cash Book serves the above purposes it will be known as **'Cash Book as the only Book of Original Entry'.**

To sum up

For non-cash or credit transactions, however, there will be two entries in the Cash Book, ultimately, there will be no effect in cash balance. For example, if goods are purchased from X & Co. for Rs. 5,000 on credit, the entries under this type of Cash Book will be as under :

			Dr. Rs.	Cr. Rs.
(i)	*Purchase A/c*	*Dr.*	*5,000*	
	To Cash A/c			*5,000*
(ii)	*Cash A/c*	*Dr.*	*5,000*	
	To X & Co. A/c			*5,000*
	Although the original entry is :			
	Purchase A/c	*Dr.*	*5,000*	
	To X & Co. A/c			*5,000*

The following illustration will make the principle clear :

Illustration 1

From the following particulars write-up a Cash Book of Sri Amalesh Roy Choudhury, which serves as the only Book of Original Entry and balance it on 31st Dec. 2010 :

2010 Dec.		Rs.	2010 Dec.		Rs.
1	Started business with Cash	8,000	22	Sold goods for Cash	4,000
2	Sold goods for Cash	1,000	25	Goods Returned by Mr. D	400
4	Sold goods to Mr. X on credit	2,000	26	Purchased goods from Mr. H on credit	2,000
11	Purchased goods from Mr. Y on credit	2,500	27	Issued a Bills Payable to Mr. H	500
13	Paid Rent by Cheque	500	28	Goods returned to Mr. H	300
16	Paid to Mr. Y in Cash	2,400	30	Paid to Mr. H. by Cheque	1,100
	Received Discount	100		Received Discount	100
18	Sold goods to Mr. D on Credit	3,000	31	Purchased goods for Cash	800
19	Received a Bills Receivable from Mr. D	1,000			

Solution

In the books of Sri Amalesh Roy Choudhury
Cash Book
(as the only book of original entry)

Dr. *Cr.*

Date		Particulars	L.F.	Amount	Date		Particulars	L.F.	Amount
2010				Rs.	2010				Rs.
Dec. 1	To	Capital A/c. (Business started)		8,000	Dec. 4	By	Mr X A/c (Goods sold on Credit)		2,000
2	"	Sales A/c (Goods sold for Cash)		1,000	11	"	Purchase (Credit) A/c (Goods Purchased on Credit)		2,500
4	"	Sales (Credit) A/c (Goods sold to Mr. X)		2,000	13	"	Rent A/c (Paid by cheque)		500
11	"	Mr. Y A/c (Purchased goods on credit)		2,500	16	"	Y A/c (Paid to Y)		2,400
						"	Y A/c (Discount Received)		100
13	"	Bank A/c (Withdrawn by cheque)		500	18	"	D A/c (Goods sold on credit)		3,000
16	"	Discount Received A/c		100	19	"	Bills Receivable A/c (Bills received from D)		1,000
18	"	Sales (Credit) A/c (Goods sold to D on Credit)		3,000	25	"	Returns Inward A/c (Goods returned from D)		400
19	To	D A/c (Bills Received)		1,000	26	"	Purchase (credit) A/c (Goods purchased on credit)		2,000
22	"	Sales A/c (Goods sold for cash)		4,000	27	"	H A/c (Bills Received)		500
25	"	D A/c (Goods returned by D)		400	28	"	H A/c (Goods Returned)		300
26	"	H A/c (Purchased goods on credit)		2,000	30	"	H A/c (Cash paid)		1,100
27	"	Bills Payable A/c (Bills issued to H)		500		"	H A/c (Discount Received A/c)		100
28	"	Returns Outward A/c (Goods returned to H)		300	31	"	Purchase (Cash) A/c (Goods purchased for cash)		800
30	"	Bank A/c (Withdrawn by cheque)		1,100		"	Balance c/d		9,800
	"	Discount Received A/c		100					
				26,500					26,500

2. Single Column Cash Book

This is the simplest form of Cash Book which keeps records of all cash transactions and is used particularly by those firms who have no bank and discount transactions, i.e., it is used by small traders. All Cash Receipts are entered in the debit side and all Cash Payments on the credit side of this type of Cash Book. The difference between the debit side and credit side represents the balance, i.e., amount of cash in hand and the balance must be a debit one. When cash transactions are many and bank transactions (if any) are few, this Cash Book may conveniently be used.

This Cash Book records only cash transactions and, for bank transactions, a separate Bank Account is opened in the ledger where all transactions relating to 'cheques' are recorded. It should be remembered that the debit entries of the Cash Book relating to bank are posted in the credit side, and vice versa.

We know that Cash Book serves the function of a ledger. As such, the Cash aspect of double entry is complete when the same is recorded in cash book but for recording the other part of transactions the related account is to be posted only in one side; i.e., the entries on the debit side of Cash Book are posted to the credit side of the respective accounts. The Cash Book folio is written in the ledger while ledger folio in the Cash Book.

Consider the following illustration.

Illustration 2

From the following particulars, compile a Single Column Cash Book of Sri S. Saha and bring down the balance and post them into ledger accounts on 31st Dec. 2009:

2009			Rs.	2009			
Dec.	1	Balance in hand	3,000	Dec.	11	Received Rent from Mr. K	300
	3	Purchased goods for Cash	300		15	Received from Mr. Z on account	400
	4	Paid for Advertisement	50		21	Sold goods for Cash	500
	7	Further capital introduced	1,000		25	Paid to Creditors	900
	9	Purchased Furniture	500		31	Paid Salary	500
	10	Spent for private use	750				

Solution

In the books of S. Saha

Dr. **Cash Book (Single Column)** Cr.

Date		Particulars	V. N.	L. F.	Amount	Date		Particular	V. N.	L. F.	Amount
2009					Rs.	2009					Rs.
Dec. 1	To	Balance b/d			3,000	Dec. 3	By	Purchase A/c (Goods purchased for Cash)		40	300
7	"	Capital A/c (Fresh capital		8	1,000	4	"	Advertisement A/c (Advertisement paid)		36	50
11	"	Rent A/c (Rent Received)		17	300	9	"	Furniture A/c (Furniture Purchased)		80	500
13	"	Z A/c (Cash Received)		26	400	10	"	Drawings A/c (Spent for private use)		29	750
21	"	Sales A/c (Goods sold for Cash)		53	500	25	"	Creditors A/c (Cash paid to creditor)		63	900
						31	"	Salary A/c (Salary paid in Cash)		84	500
						31	"	Balance c/d			2,200
					5,200						5,200
2010											
Jan. 1	To	Balance b/d			2,200						

Dr. **Purchases Account** (Page 40) Cr.

Date	Particulars	L. F.	Amount	Date	Particulars	L. F.	Amount
2009			Rs.				Rs.
Dec. 3	To Cash A/c	CB 40	300				

Dr. **Advertisement Account** (Page 36) Cr.

Date	Particulars	L. F.	Amount	Date	Particulars	L. F.	Amount
2009			Rs.				Rs.
Dec. 4	To Cash A/c	CB 40	50				

Dr. **Capital Account** (Page 8) Cr.

Date	Particulars	L. F.	Amount	Date	Particulars	L. F.	Amount
2009			Rs.	2009			Rs.
				Dec. 7	By Cash A/c	CB 40	1,000

Dr. **Furniture Account** (Page 80) Cr.

Date	Particulars	L. F.	Amount	Date	Particulars	L. F.	Amount
2009			Rs.				Rs.
Dec. 9	To Cash A/c	CB 40	500				

Dr. **Drawings Account** (Page 29) Cr.

Date	Particulars	L. F.	Amount	Date	Particulars	L. F.	Amount
2009			Rs.				Rs.
Dec. 10	To Cash A/c	CB 40	750				

Dr. **Rent Account** (Page 17) Cr.

Date	Particulars	L. F.	Amount	Date	Particulars	L. F.	Amount
			Rs.	2009			Rs.
				Dec. 11	By Cash A/c	CB 40	300

Dr. **Z Account** (Page 26) Cr.

Date	Particulars	L. F.	Amount	Date	Particulars	L. F.	Amount
			Rs.	2009			Rs.
				Dec. 15	By Cash A/c	CB 40	400

Dr. **Sales Account** (Page 53) Cr.

Date	Particulars	L. F.	Amount	Date	Particulars	L. F.	Amount
			Rs.	2009			Rs.
				Dec. 21	By Cash A/c	CB 40	500

Dr. **Creditors Account** (Page 63) Cr.

Date	Particulars	L. F.	Amount	Date	Particulars	L. F.	Amount
2009			Rs.				Rs.
Dec. 25	To Cash A/c	CB 40	900				

Dr. **Salary Account** (Page 84) Cr.

Date	Particulars	L. F.	Amount	Date	Particulars	L. F.	Amount
2009			Rs.				Rs.
Dec. 31.	To Cash A/c	CB 40	500				

3. Double Column Cash Book

Where there are discounts or bank transactions, the Cash Book is maintained by one more column, viz., Discount or Bank, i.e., its ruling is similar to Single Column Cash Book except by one additional money column. This type of Cash Book maintains both Cash and Bank or Cash and Discount transactions side by side. The principles of banking transactions are, however, similar to cash transactions, i.e., all receipts on the debit side and all payments on the credit side. But, in the case of discount, discount received is recorded on the credit side of the book, whereas discount allowed is recorded on the debit side of the same. Cash and Bank columns are balanced, but discount columns are simply totalled.

Contra Transactions

Sometimes more ready money remains idle in cash box than the actual requirement, i.e., for cash payment. Such idle or surplus monies are deposited into bank. On the contrary, there may be a shortage of liquid cash in order to meet various payments; such shortage of cash may be compensated by withdrawing money from bank. Needless to mention that when cash is deposited into bank, bank balance is increased and cash balance is decreased. At the same time, when cash is withdrawn from bank, Cash balance is increased and bank balance is decreased. So, the entries for the two purposes will be :

(i) When Cash is deposited into Bank

Cash A/c Dr.
To Bank A/c

(ii) When Cash is withdrawn from Bank

Bank A/c Dr.
To Cash A/c

To Sum up

Thus, the transaction which affects Cash and Bank only is called a Contra Transaction or Contra Entry* and, hence, will appear in both sides of the Double Column Cash Book. In the first case (i.e., deposited Cash into Bank), To, Cash in Bank Column and By, Bank, in Cash Column, and vice versa. The letter 'C' should be used in L.F. column which stands for contra.

* If Double Column Cash Book is prepared by taking up the Cash and Discount Column, any transaction which affects Cash and Discount is also called Contra Transaction. Usually, the transactions which affect Cash and Bank are known as Contra Transactions.

Illustration 3

The following illustration will make the transactions clear :

2010			Rs.
Jan.	1	Balance in hand	4,000
		Balance at Bank	10,000
	3	Deposited cash into Bank	1,000
	4	Withdrew cash from Bank	3,000
	14	Received a cheque from Mr. D	1,000
	16	The above cheque was deposited into Bank	—
	19	Withdrew cash from bank for office use	1,000
	25	Deposited all cash in excess of Rs. 5,000 into the Bank	—
	30	Cashed for Mr. G and deposited into Bank	500
	31	Withdrew all cash from Bank in excess of Rs. 6,000.	

N. B. Narrations are not required.

From the above particulars of Miss Anindita, prepare a Cash book with Cash and Bank Column for the month of January 2010:

Solution

In the books of Miss Anindita
Cash Book (With Cash and Bank Column)
(Without Narration)

Dr. Cr.

Date	Particulars	L. F.	V. N.	Cash	Bank	Date	Particulars	L. F.	V. N.	Cash	Bank
2010				Rs.	Rs.	2010				Rs.	Rs.
Jan. 1	To Balance b/d	(C)		4,000	10,000	Jan. 3	By Bank A/c	(C)		1,000	
3	" Cash A/c	(C)			1,000	4	" Cash A/c	(C)			3,000
4	" Bank A/c	(C)		3,000		16	" Bank A/c	(C)		1,000	
14	" D. A/c			1,000		19	" Cash A/c	(C)			1,000
16	" Cash A/c	(C)			1,000	25	" Bank A/c	(C)		2,000	
19	" Bank A/c	(C)		1,000		30	" G A/c			500	
25	" Cash A/c (Rs. 9,000 – (Rs. 2,000 = Rs. 7,000 – Rs. 5,000)	(C)			2,000	31	" Cash A/c *(bal. fig.)*	(C)			4,500
							By Balance c/d			9,000	6,000
30	To G A/c				500						
31	" Bank A/c	(C)		4,500							
				13,500	14,500					13,500	14,500
Feb. 1	To Balance b/d			9,000	6,000						

Note : (C) stands for 'Contra'.

Treatment relating to 'Cheque' transactions

1. When a cheque is received and no further information is given at a later date about the same, it will be assumed that the said cheque has already been deposited into bank on the same day when it was received.

The entry will be :

Bank A/c Dr.
To Debtors/Party A/c

But if it is found that the said cheque has been deposited into bank at a subsequent date, the entry will be

(i) When the cheque is received
Cash A/c Dr.
To Debtors/Party A/c

(ii) When the same was deposited into bank at a subsequent date
Bank A/c Dr.
To Cash A/c
(i.e., a contra entry)

(iii) When the said cheque is dishonoured by the bank
Debtors/Party A/c Dr.
To Bank A/c

2. When a cheque is received but the same is endorsed to the creditors on the same day or at a later date the entry will be—

(i) When the cheque is received
Cash A/c Dr.
To Debtors/Party A/c

(ii) When endorsed to a creditor—
Creditors A/c Dr.
To Cash A/c
(i.e., the cheque is going out from cash box)

(iii) When the endorsed cheque is returned dishonoured
Debtors/Party A/c Dr.
To Creditors A/c
(There will be no effect in Cash book for the dishonour)

3. When a 'bearer' cheque is received from a customer

(i) On the day when it is received but not encashed or deposited into bank
The entry is
Cash A/c Dr.
To Debtors/Party A/c

(ii) When the said cheque is encashed over the bank counter
There will be no entry in the Cash Book since Cash Book has already been debited by it.

(iii) When the said cheque is deposited into bank
Bank A/c Dr.
To Cash A/c

(iv) When the bearer cheque is dishonoured—
Party/Debtors A/c Dr.
To Cash A/c

(v) When the 'bearer' cheque is endorsed to a Creditor
Creditor A/c Dr.
To Cash A/c

(vi) When the said 'bearer' cheque is dishonoured after endorsement
Party/Debtors A/c Dr.
To Creditors
(There will be no effect in Cash Book)

4. (i) When a cheque is issued to a creditor, the entry will be
Creditors/Party A/c Dr.
To Bank A/c

(ii) If the said cheque is dishonoured on any ground
Bank A/c Dr.
To Creditors/Party A/c

(iii) If the 'Stop Payment' order was served due to pick pocket or any other reason after issuing a cheque, entry will be
Bank A/c Dr.
To Creditors/Party A/c

The following illustration will solve the problems relating to 'cheque' transaction.

Illustration 4

Enter the following transactions in a suitable Cash Book of Miss. Sudipta Dutta with Cash and Bank Column for the month of March 2010 :

2010		Rs.
March 1	Balance in hand	**5,000**
	Balance at Bank	**15,500**
3	Issued a cheque to Mr. D for Salary	**1,000**
4	Received a cheque from Mr. P.	**500**
5	Issued a cheque for office use	**1,000**
7	Issued a cheque for private use	**500**

9	Received three cheques from Mr. A., Mr. B and Mr. C. for Rs. 500; Rs. 1,000 and Rs. 1,250, respectively	—
11	The first cheque was deposited into Bank The second cheque was endorsed to Mr. T. for goods purchased The third cheque was endorsed to Mr. Y for purchase of Furniture	
12	Received a 'bearer' cheque from Mr. R for	300
13	The above cheque was cashed at the Bank counter	—
14	Received another 'bearer' cheque from Mr. Z	500
15	The above cheque was dishonoured at the Bank counter	—
16	Received another 'bearer' cheque from Mr. P and endorsed it to Mr. K	700
17	Received a 'crossed' cheque from a customer and deposited into Bank	800
18	Received a cheque from Mr. S for	300
19	Deposited the cheque into the Bank	—
20	Mr. S's cheque returned dishonoured	—
21	Issued a cheque to Mr. L for	1,000
23	'Stop Payment' order was served to the Bank as the it pick-pocketed	—
24	Received a cheque from Mr. B for	1,000
25	The cheque received from Mr. B returned dishonoured at the counter and he paid cash in lieu of the cheque on next day	—
26	Received a cheque from Mr. Kar	500
27	Mr. Kar's cheque was endorsed to Mr. Das	—
28	Mr. Kar's cheque was returned dishonoured	—
29	Mr. Kar paid cash for the same	—
30	Issued a cheque to Mr. C, our creditor	—
31	Cheque issued to Mr. C returned dishonoured on technical grounds	750
"	Sold goods and received cash Rs. 300 and cheque Rs. 700	

N.B. Narrations are not required.

Solution

In the books of Miss Sudipta Dutta
Cash Book *(With Cash and Bank Column)*
(Without Narration)

Dr. Cr.

Date	Particulars	L. F.	V. N.	Cash	Bank	Date	Particulars	L. F.	V. N.	Cash	Bank
2010				Rs.	Rs.	2010				Rs.	Rs.
March	To Balance b/d			5,000	15,500	Mar. 3	By Salary A/c				1,000
4 "	P A/c				500	5 "	Cash A/c	(C)			1,000
5 "	Bank A/c	(C)		1,000		7 "	Drawing A/c				500
9 "	A. A/c			500		11 "	Bank A/c	(C)		500	
"	B A/c			1,000		"	T A/c			1,000	
"	C A/c			1,250		"	Y A/c			1,250	
11 "	Cash A/c	(C)			500	15 "	Z A/c			500	
12 "	R A/c			300		16 "	K A/c			700	
14 "	Z A/c	(C)		500		19 "	Bank A/c	(C)		300	
16 "	P A/c			700		20 "	S A/c				300
17 "	Customers A/c				800	21 "	L A/c				1,000
18 "	S A/c			300		25 "	B A/c			1,000	
19 "	Cash A/c	(C)			300	27 "	Das A/c			500	
23 "	L A/c				1,000	30 "	C A/c				750
24 "	B A/c			1,000		31 "	Balance c/d			8,100	15,500
25 "	B A/c			1,000							
26 "	Kar A/c			500							
29 "	Kar A/c			500							
31 "	C A/c				750						
"	Sales A/c			300	700						
				13,850	20,050					13,850	20,050
April 1	To Balance b/d			8,100	15,500						

Note : For 13th —There will be no entry in the Cash Book.
For 28th — There will be no effect in the Cash Book, the entry being—Mr. Kar's Account Debit and Mr. Das's Account Credit.

Application of Debit Card and Credit Card

Debit Cards

Debit cards are electronic plastic cards which are used as a substitute for cash and which helps to reduce the dependence for carrying cash and cheque. Debit cards are directly linked to the bank account of a cardholder. At present, it is used as on alternative mode of payment. As soon as a cardholder withdraws money from an ATM or uses the same for making necessary payments, the balance of his/her account is automatically reduced.* There are different types of debit cards : (i) On-line Card; (ii) Off-line Card; (iii) Prepaid Card; (iv) Electronic Purse Debit Card; (v) Others. Debit cards become more populer as they use the funds from the savings of the cardholders.

Benefits of Debit Card

The benefits of a Debit Card are:

(i) Debit Cards can be used for making online purchase and payment;
(ii) Debit cards do not charge high rate of interest;
(iii) Debit cards provide freedom from carrying cash/cheque at the time of travelling;
(iv) A person having poor credit status may also get a debit card.

At present, some of the banks issue debit cards:

e.g., City Bank, HSBC, Standard Chartered, American Express, Bank of America etc.

Credit Cards

Credit card is a financial instrument which allows the holder to pay for goods and services on credit and in lieu of cash. It is a plastic card with a magnetic strip containing data. Practically, credit card allows the cardholders to purchase goods and services immediately and settle the bill at a subsequent date for aggregated transactions. Immediately after receiving the card, the card holder can make purchases within the prescribed limit. The supplier of the goods and services can verify the validity of the card within a second. Each credit card contains a unique personal identification number (PIN) which is like a password which authenticates the card. The cardholder gets credit card statement at regular intervals which states all the purchase for which payments were made out of the card. The cardholder makes payment to the issuing authority at the due date. If default is made, interest is charged at a high rate on outstanding balances. There are different types of credit cards. viz., Gold Credit Cards, Business Credit Cards, Premium Credit Cards, etc. Some foreign Credit cards are : HSBC, American Express ANZ etc. Similarly, the major credit card suppliers in India are: HDFC, ICICI Bank, Axis Bank, SBI, Bank of Baroda, City Bank, American Express etc.

Accounting for Credit Cards

It is needless to say that sale through credit card is equivalent to cash sale to a seller or supplier of goods and services.

Entries in the Book of Seller

(i) ***For total sales made by credit-card***

Bank A/c	Dr.	—with the amount of total sale
To Sales A/c		

(ii) ***For payment of commission or fees***

Commission/Fees A/c	Dr.	—with the amount of Commission
To Bank A/c		

4. Three or Triple Column Cash Book

In order to incorporate Cash discounts which are allowed by the business to its customers, i.e., Cash Discount allowed and discount which are allowed by the suppliers to the business, i.e., Cash Discount received, Triple Column Cash Book is prepared by adding one additional Column with Double Column

* Debit cards allow customers to buy as per their requirements using funds directly debited from their accounts.

Cash Book. The debit Columns are separately used for Cash Book receipts and Discount Allowed whereas the credit Columns are used for Cash, Bank payments and Discount Received. In this context, it may be mentioned that each item of discount allowed is posted to the credit of respective customer's account in the sales ledger together with related cash receipts and each item of discount received is posted to the debit of respective supplier's accounts in the purchase ledger along with related Cash payments. At the end of each period (week or month) the discount columns are added up. *The discount columns must not be balanced.* The total amount of the debit side represents the total amount of discount allowed to customers and the total amount of the credit side represents the total amount of discount received by the business. Discount Allowed and Discount Received are posted in the general ledger accordingly.

Special Point for Cheque Transactions

Discount is allowed when payment is received by cheque and discount is received when payment is made to suppliers by cheque. Now, if the cheque is subsequently dishonoured, the discount should be written-back. When a cheque is dishonoured, the dishonoured entry is to be made in Cash Book but the entry for cancellation of Discount cannot be made through Cash Book since the same is made through general journal for the purpose.

Illustration 5

From the following transactions, show the necessary journal entries :

(i) Cash purchases of goods from P & Co. for Rs. 2,000, Less Cash Discount @ 20% and paid by cheque.

(ii) Cash Sales of goods to T & Co. for Rs. 10,000, Less Cash Discount @ 10% and the amount received by cheque.

(iii) The cheque which was received from T & Co. returned dishonoured due to lack of funds.

(iv) The cheque which was issued to P & Co. was dishonoured on technical grounds.

Solution

In the books of

Journal ....

Date	Particulars		L.F.	Debit	Credit
				Rs.	Rs.
?	Parchases A/c	Dr.		2,000	
	To Bank A/c				1,600
	" Discount Received A/c				400
	(Purchase of goods at a discount of 20% and paid by cheque)				
?	Bank A/c	Dr.		9,000	
	Discount Allowed A/c	Dr.		1,000	
	To Sales A/c				10,000
	(Sold goods at a discount of 10% and received a cheque)				
?	T & Co. A/c	Dr.		10,000	
	To Bank A/c				9,000
	" Discount Allowed A/c				1,000
	(Cheque dishonoured)				
?	Bank A/c	Dr.		1,600	
	Discount Received A/c	Dr.		400	
	To P & Co. A/c				2,000
	(Cheque dishonoured)				

Illustration 6

Enter the following transactions of Suparna Mukherjee in a Triple Column Cash Book and balance the book on 31st Dec. 2010:

2010			Rs.
Dec.	1	Cash in hand	4,000
		Cash at bank	10,000
	3	P settled his account for Rs. 800, Less 5% discount by cheque	—
	5	Issued a cheque to D in settlement of his account for Rs. 1,080 at a discount of Rs. 80	—

Contd.

2010		Rs.
6	Drew a cheque for purchases Rs. 1,000, Less 4% discount	—
8	Received a cheque from Y, a debtor, Rs. 800. Discount allowed Rs. 50.	
10	Received a cheque from T, a debtor, in full settlement of a debt for Rs. 1,000 *Less* 10% discount and the cheque is endorsed to R, a creditor, in settlement of a claim for Rs. 1,050.	—
12	Cash Stolen	500
15	Received a cheque for Rs. 4,500 in full settlement of the account of Z at a discount of 10% and deposited the same into Bank	—
20	Received a cheque from B for Rs. 450 (i.e., Rs. 500, *Less* Cash discount Rs. 50.)	—
22	B's cheque was dishonoured	
24	Received cheque for discount from G who was paid in full previously	50
25	Received a cheque from E in full settlement of his account for Rs. 400 and cashed the cheque over the counter	360
27	Settled by cheque to Mr. Dutta for Rs. 300 *Less* Cash discount @ 10%	—
28	Cheque given to Mr. Dutta returned dishonoured	—
31	Bought goods from B. Bose for Rs. 1,000, Less Trade Discount @ 10% and Cash Discount @ 5% —paid Rs. 100 in Cash and balance by cheque	—
"	Paid Cash Rs. 100 for Discount Allowed to K who paid the amount in full previously.	

N.B. Narrations are not required.

Solution

In the books of Suparna Mukherjee
Cash Book
(With Cash, Bank and Discount Columns)
(Without Narration)

Dr. *Cr.*

Date	*Particulars*	*L. F.*	*V. N.*	*Cash*	*Bank*	*Discount*	*Date*	*Particulars*	*L. F.*	*V. N.*	*Cash*	*Bank*	*Discount*
2010				Rs.	Rs.	Rs.	2010				Rs.	Rs.	Rs.
Dec. 1	To Balance b/d			4,000	10,000		Dec. 5	By D A/c				1,000	80
3	" P A/c				760	40	6	" Purchases A/c				960	40
8	" Y A/c				800	50	10	" R A/c			900		150
10	" T A/c			900		100	12	" P & L A/c			500		
15	" Z A/c				4,500	500		(Cash Stolen)					
20	" B A/c				450	50	22	" B A/c				450	50
24	" Dis. Received A/c	(C)			50		24	" Bank A/c	(C)				50
							27	" Dutta A/c				270	30
25	" E A/c			360		40	31	" B. Bose A/c			100	755	45
28	" Dutta A/c				270	30	"	" Dis. Allowed A/c	(C)		100		
31	" Cash A/c	(C)				100	"	" Balance c/d			3,660	13,395	
				5,260	16,830	910					5,260	16,830	445
2011													
Jan. 1	To Balance b/d			3,660	13,395	—							

5. Multicolumnar Cash Book

It is usually maintained by large business units. The receipts and payments sides of this book are divided into such columns which are frequently required. e.g., Cash Sales, which occur again and again—is posted in the 'Sales' column and, ultimately, the total of the sales column is posted to the credit side of sales account. In this way, all other heads of receipts and payments are recorded.

Consider the following illustration.

Illustration 7

From the following particulars prepare a Multi-Columnar Cash Book of 'Manasa Mandir' of Lake Town, with analytical columns of receipts : For Subscription, Donation, Interest and Dividends and

Miscellaneous receipts and payments : Rent and Lighting, Salaries and Wages, Charities, Kirtan expenses and Miscellaneous payments :

2009			Rs.				Rs.
Jan.	1.	Cash in hand	4,000	Jan.	21.	Paid salaries and wages	800
	2.	Subscription received	5,000		23.	Donation received	1,000
	5.	Donation received	1,000		24.	Kirtan expenses	2,000
	6.	Paid house rent	500		25.	Paid electric bill	300
	7.	Interest received from bank	100		30.	Paid hall rent	700
	10.	Dividend received	300			Received pranami	1,200
	15.	Paid to C. M's Relief Fund	500		31.	Paid for Matribhoga	2,000
	20.	Subscription received	700				

Solution

In the books of Manasa Mandir

Cash Book (Multicolumnar)

Dr. *Cr.*

Date	Particulars	V. N	Total	Subs-cription	Dona-tion	Int+ Div.	Mis Recp.	Date	Particulars	V. N	Total	Rent & Light	Salary & Wages	Cha-rities	Kirtan	Mis. Exp.
2009			Rs	Rs.	Rs.	Rs.	Rs.	2009			Rs.	Rs.	Rs.	Rs.	Rs.	Rs.
Jan.1	To Balance b/d		4,000					Jan. 6	By Rent A/c		500	500				
2	" Subscription A/c		5,000	5,000				15	" C..M. Relief Fund A/c		500			500		
5	" Donation A/c		1,000		1,000											
7	" Interest A/c		100			100		21	" Salary & Wages A/c		800		800			
10	" Dividend A/c		300			300										
20	" Subscription A/c		700	700				24	" Kirtan A/c		2,000				2,000	
23	" Donation A/c		1,000		1,000			25	" Electricity A/c		300	300				
30	" Pranami A/c		1,200				1,200	30	" Rent A/c		700	700				
								31	" Matri Bhoga A/c		2,000					2,000
									" Balance c/d		6,500					
			13,300	5,700	2,000	400	1,200				13,300	1,500	800	500	2,000	2,000
	To Balance b/d		6,500													

6. Miscellaneous

(i) Cash Book with Two bank Accounts

In this case, the principle of Double Column Cash Book is to be strictly followed. The only difference is that one additional amount column is to be opened for the purpose.

Try to understand the illustration that follows :

Illustration 8

Mr. X operates two bank accounts both of which are maintained in the Columnar Cash Book itself.

You are required to draw up a Cash Book with necessary columns and show how the following transactions relating to 28th February 2010 will appear therein to close the Cash Book for the day :

		Rs.	
(1)	Opening balances		
	Cash	150	
	National Bank	11,240	(Overdraft)
	Overseas Bank	35,460	

(2) Received a cheque for Rs. 1,250 in respect of sales for realising which the National Bank charged Rs. 2 and credited the balance.

(3) Purchased goods for Rs. 13,210 and a cheque issued on the Overseas Bank. The Bank charged Rs. 3 for collection of the cheque to the concerned party.

(4) Paid office expenses of Rs. 45 and Rs. 15 for stationery.

(5) Out of cash sales of Rs. 13,625 a sum of Rs. 10,000 was deposited in the National Bank.

(6) Credit purchases of Rs. 15,000 were made from Mr. Smith, who sent the documents relating to the goods through the Overseas Bank for 90% of their value. The Bank charged Rs. 115 for realising the documents.

(7) Withdrew Rs. 5,000 from the Overseas Bank.
(8) Deposited Rs. 5,000 in National Bank.
(9) A Bill Receivable for Rs. 10,000 was discounted with the Overseas Bank which charged 1% towards discounting.
(10) A Demand Draft was purchased for Rs. 3,000 from a bank after paying Rs. 2 towards their charges and paid to the Electric Supply Corporation as deposit.
(11) Interest of Rs. 122 and Rs. 50 was credited and debited, respectively, by the Overseas Bank and National Bank.
(12) An amount of Rs. 1,500 was withdrawn from the Overseas Bank and salaries paid to that extent.
(13) Manager's salary of Rs. 1,000 was paid by cheque drawn on the National Bank.
(14) Overseas Bank collected dividends of Rs. 1,250 and sent a credit note.
(15) An amount of Rs. 1,500 was transferred from the Overseas Bank to the National Bank.

N.B. Narrations are not required.

Solution

In the books of Mr. X

Dr. **Cash Book** *(with Cash and Two Bank Columns)* *Cr.*

Date	Particulars	L.F.	Cash	Bank: National	Bank: Overseas	Date	Particulars	L.F.	Cash	Bank: National	Bank: Overseas
2010			Rs.	Rs.	Rs.	2010			Rs.	Rs.	Rs.
Feb. 28	To Balance b/d		150		35,460	Feb. 28	By Balance b/f			11,240	
	" Sales A/c			1,250			" Bank Charges A/c			2	
	" Sales A/c		13,625				" Purchase [1] A/c				13,210
	" Cash A/c	(C)		10,000			" Office Exp. A/c		45		
	" Overseas Bank [3] A/c	(C)	5,000				" Stationery A/c		15		
							" National Bank A/c	(C)	10,000		
	" Cash A/c	(C)		5,000			" Purchases[2] A/c				13,500
	" B/R A/c			10,000			" Bank Charges A/c				115
	" Bank Int. A/c			122			" Cash A/c	(C)			5,000
	" Overseas Bank A/c	(C)	1,500				" National Bank	(C)	5,000		
	" Dividends A/c (Collected and credited by Bank)				1,250		" Discounting Charges A/c				100
							" Deposit with E.S. Corpn.[4]		3,000		
							" Bank Charges A/c		2		
	" Overseas Bank A/c	(C)		1,500			" Intt. on O/D			50	
							" Cash A/c				1,500
							" Salaries A/c		1,500		
							" Salaries A/c (Manager's Salary)			1,000	
							" National Bank A/c				1,500
							" Balance c/d		713	5,458	11,907
			20,275	17,750	46,832				20,275	17,750	46,832
2010											
Mar 1	To Balance b/d		713	5,458	11,907						

Note :

1. Bank charges paid by others is ignored since it is not related to Mr. X. 2. Only 90% of Rs. 15,000 i.e., Rs. 13,500 (Rs. 15,000 × $\frac{90}{100}$) is to be recorded. 3. Since all transactions are for the day, i.e., 28th, it is assumed that cash is withdrawn from Overseas Bank first and then the same is deposited into National Bank. 4. This transaction is not related to either National or Overseas Bank of Mr. X.

(ii) Cash Book with Missing Sales

Sometimes it is found that the credit side of cash book, i.e., the payments side, is greater than the debit side, i.e., the receipts side, which is practically impossible since it is not possible to make more payment than what is actually left in hand. In that case, the difference may be treated as the 'Missing Sales'.

Consider the following illustration:

Illustration 9

Mr. P is a retail trader. He enters details of his transactions in a diary. All his cash outlays are paid out of cash takings. At the end of each week he leaves Rs. 100 in the till and pays the balance into the Bank.

The following are the entries in his diary for the 1st week of August 2009 from Aug. 1 to Aug. 6. (Aug. 7 being a Sunday on which day his shop remains closed):

2009						Rs.
Aug.	1	Balance in till	100	4	Gave cheque for Rs. 350 to Mr. B for goods supplied by him in July 2009.	
		Balance at Bank	890			
	2	Bought goods for Cash	220	5	Took for personal expenses	100
	3	Received from Mr. S repay-ment of his loan, in Cash	60	6	Cashed Savings Deposit Certi-ficate Rs. 160, kept Rs. 60 for self and paid balance into till.	
	3	Bought goods on credit from Mr. W	480		Paid into Bank	480

Write-up Cash Book for the week and bring down the balances at the close of the business on Aug. 6.

N.B.: *Narrations are not required.*

In the books of Mr. P.

Cash Book *(with Cash and Bank columns)*

Dr.												Cr.
Date	*Particulars*	*L. F.*	*V. N.*	*Cash*	*Bank*	*Date*	*Particulars*	*L. F.*	*V. N.*	*Cash*	*Bank*	
2009 Aug.				Rs.	Rs.	2009 Aug.				Rs.	Rs.	
1	To Balance b/d			100	890	2	By Purchases A/c			220		
2	" Sales A/c[1]			120		4	" B A/c				350	
3	" S—Loan A/c			60		5	" Drawing A/c			100		
5	" Sales A/c[1]			40		6	" Drawings A/c			60		
6	" Saving Deposit Certificate[2]			160		6	" Bank A/c	(C)		480		
6	" Sales[1] A/c			480			" Balance c/d			100	1,020	
6	" Cash A/c	(C)			480							
				960	1,370					960	1,370	
Aug. 8	To Balance b/d			100	1,020							

Notes :

1. Total Cash balance on 1st Aug. was only Rs. 100, but total payments were Rs. 220. Therefore, it is assumed that the difference, Rs. 120 (i.e., Rs. 200 – Rs. 100) represents Cash sales. Same principle is also being followed in other dates, viz., on 5th Aug. and 6th Aug.
2. It has also been assumed that the Savings Deposit Certificate is the business property and, as such, when it is encashed, Cash is increased by the like amount leaving Rs. 60 for drawings. However, if it is assumed that the said Certificate is the property of the owner it will be treated as additional capital by Rs. 100 (160 – 60) i.e., after deducting Rs. 60 for Drawings.
3. Credit purchases of goods is ignored here, since it is a Double Column Cash Book and it has also been assumed that Cash Book does not serve as only Book of original entry.

(iii) Mini-Max Cash Book

This is nothing but the ordinary Double Column Cash Book (i.e., Cash Book with Cash and Bank columns) with the exception that if, in any day, Cash balance falls short by the minimum amount to be maintained in hand, the said shortage is to be compensated by withdrawing money from bank simply by passing a contra entry. On the contrary, if in any day Cash balance is found to be in excess of the maximum balance to be kept in hand, the said surplus of cash is to be deposited into bank by again passing a contra entry. And if, however, the balance lies between the minimum and the maximum balance, there will neither be any entry for withdrawals nor any entry for depositing money into bank, i.e., there will not be any entry for the purpose.

Illustration 10

From the following particulars, write-up a suitable Cash Book of Mr. P. Laha, for the 1st week of Dec. 2010, after taking into consideration the following :

			Rs.
(i)	On 1.12.2010	Balance in hand	300
		Balance at Bank	5,000

(ii) Cheque received and deposited into bank on the same day.

(iii) If the Cash in hand on any day be less than Rs. 200, necessary amount should be withdrawn from the bank to maintain the Cash in hand at Rs. 200, and if the Cash in hand in any day be more than Rs. 400, then the excess over Rs. 400 should be deposited into bank on that day.

Dec. 2010	*Receipts*	*Cash* Rs.	*Cheque* Rs.	*Payments*	*Cash* Rs.	*Cheque* Rs.
1.	Sales	200	1,000	Creditors	100	400
				Rent	300	200
2.	S. Sen	300		Wages	50	
	Sales	400	200	Drawings	100	150
				Stationery	50	
3.	—	—	—	Misc. Expenses	100	
4.	Sales	100	200	Drawings	250	100
6.	P. Roy	500	1,000	Banerjee	100	500
	Sales	100		Carriage	50	
7.	Sales	200		Expenses	350	100

N.B. Narrations are not required.

Solution

In the books of P. Laha

Cash Book *(with Cash and Bank Columns)*

Dr. *Cr.*

Date	*Particulars*	*L. F.*	*V. N.*	*Cash*	*Bank*	*Date*	*Particulars*	*L. F.*	*V. N.*	*Cash*	*Bank*
2010				Rs.	Rs.	2010				Rs.	Rs.
Dec. 1	To Balance b/d			300	5,000	Dec. 1	By Creditors			100	400
	" Sales A/c			200	1,000		" Rent A/c			300	200
	" Bank A/c	(C)		100[1]			" Cash A/c	(C)			100[1]
2	" S. Sen A/c			300		2	" Wages A/c			50	
	" Sales A/c			400	200		" Drawings A/c			100	150
	" Cash A/c	(C)			300[2]		" Stationery A/c			50	
4	" Sales A/c			100	200		" Bank A/c	(C)		300[2]	
	" Bank A/c	(C)		50[4]		3	" Misc. Exp. A/c			100[3]	
6	" P. Roy A/c			500	1,000	4	" Drawings A/c			250	100
	" Sales A/c			100			" Cash A/c	(C)			50[4]
	" Cash A/c	(C)			250[5]	6	" Banerjee A/c			100	500
7	" Sales A/c			200			" Carriage A/c			50	
							" Bank A/c	(C)		250[5]	
						7	" Expenses A/c			350	100
							" Balance c/d			250	6,350
				2,250	7,950					2,250	7,950
Dec. 8	To Balance b/d			250	6,350						

Notes : 1 and 3. The Cash balance on 1st Dec. falls short of Rs. 100 (i.e., Rs. 500 – 400) = 100) than the minimum amount of Rs. 200. That is why, Rs. 100 is to be withdrawn from the bank. Same principle is also applied on 3rd Dec.

2 and 4. The Cash balance on 2nd Dec. was found to be in excess by Rs. 300 (i.e., 900 – 200 = 700 than the maximum level of Rs. 400). That is why Rs. 300 is to be deposited into bank. Same principle is also applied on 4th Dec.

5 and 6. Since the balance on 5th and 6th Dec. lies between the minimum and maximum level of Rs. 200 and Rs. 400, respectively, there will be no entry, either for withdrawal or for any deposit.

7. Petty Cash Book

Small payments on account of conveyance, postage and telegrams, cartage, printing and stationery etc. are to be made daily. Now, if all such payments are incorporated in the general Cash Book, the same will simply be bulky and unwieldy. As a result, in order to avoid these difficulties, a Cash Book is opened which will incorporate all these day-to-day small payments under different heads of expenses. Such a Cash Book is termed 'Petty Cash Book'. To avoid individual posting, the petty expenses are classified into different heads of expenses, stated earlier. The ruling of such a book provides separate columns for each head of expense and totalled periodically, and debited to the respective expenses in the ledger. This Cash Book is prepared by the petty cashier and hence maintained by taking the advance from the General/Head/Chief Cashier and credited by these periodical totals.

This Cash Book may be maintained under two methods :

(i) **Imprest System**, (ii) **Analytical or Columnar System.**

(i) Imprest System of Petty Cash

Under this method, a certain sum is advanced to the Petty Cashier for a particular period, say, for a week, in order to meet the different petty expenses for the week. At the end of the week, the amount actually spent by the Petty Cashier is to be reimbursed by the general/head/chief cashier, to restore the sum advanced, in order to meet the expenses for the next week. In short, the sum which is given by the general/head/chief cashier is meant for making up the imprest amount. This system is known as Imprest System.

Advantages

The Imprest System of Petty Cash has the following advantags:

(i) Under this system, the Petty Cashier is not allowed to draw cash from the General Cashier as and when he desires and, as such, defalcation of Cash can be minimised since there is no unnecessary accumulation of Cash in his hand.

(ii) The Petty Cashier must satisfy about the expenses during the previous period to a responsible person and, hence, strict supervision and control over his activities is exercised.

(iii) The Petty Cashier is to keep the imprest amount of Cash which helps to check Petty Cash in hand as and when necessary.

(iv) Since the Petty Cashier must submit his account to the General Cashier before his further drawings, accounts are always kept up-to-date.

Illustration 11

Record the following transactions of Mr. A. Banerjee who keeps his Petty Cash Book under the Imprest System with several analytical columns (the imprest amount being Rs. 100) :

2010			Rs.	2010			Rs.
Feb.	1.	Cash in hand	30.00	Feb.	16.	Bought Stamps	4.50
		Received Cash to make up to Imprest			18.	Paid to Creditors	10.00
	3.	Purchased postage stamps	10.50		20.	Paid for a telegram	8.40
	4.	Paid Coolie-hire	7.40		21.	Paid for Office Exp.	7.50
	6.	Purchased paper and ink	6.00		22.	Paid for repairs of Typewriter	16.00
	9.	Paid Wages for clearing office room	10.00		25.	Paid bus fare	2.50
	12.	Paid Taxi fare	20.50		26.	Tiffin Expenses	6.00
	14.	Received from a Debtor	20.00		28.	Paid for Travelling	5.50

Solution

In the books of Sri A. Banerjee
Petty Cash Book (Under Imprest System)

Amount Received	*Date*		*Particulars*	*V. N.*	*Total Amount*	*Postage and Telegram*	*Stationery*	*Office Expenses*	*Travelling*	*Miscellaneous or Ledger Account*
Rs. P.	2010				Rs. P.	Rs. P	Rs. P	Rs. P.	Rs. P	Rs. P
30.00	Feb.	1	To Balance b/d							
70.00		"	Cash received							
		3	By Postage Stamps		10.50	10.50				

Contd.

Rs. P.	2010			Rs. P.	Rs. P	Rs. P	Rs. P.	Rs. P	Rs. P
	4 "	Coolie-hire		7.40					7.40
	6 "	Paper & Ink		6.00		6.00			
	7 "	Office Cleaner		10.00			10.00		
	12 "	Taxi-fare		20.50				20.50	
20.00	14 "	Debtors		—					
	16 "	Stamps		4.50	4.50				
	18 "	Creditors		10.00					10.00
	20 "	Telegram		8.40	8.40				
	21 "	Office Expenses		7.50			7.50		
	22 "	Repairs of Typewriter		16.00			16.00		
	25 "	Bus fare		2.50				2.50	
	26 "	Tiffin Expenses		6.00					6.00
	28 "	Travelling		5.50				5.50	
				114.80	23.40	6.00	33.50	28.50	23.40
	"	By Balance c/d		5.20					
120.00				120.00					
5.20	Mar. 1	To Balance b/d							

(ii) Analytical or Columnar Petty Cash Book

Under this system, an Analytical or Columnar form for various expenses are maintained, i.e., a separate column for each usual head of expense and a column for the total. This Cash Book helps the businessmen to know the information about the amount being spent on each head of petty expenses. It avoids the unnecessary labour that are used while posting each item of petty payment separately in the ledger. Thus, only the totals of various columns are posted in the general ledger.

Petty Cash Book—Its Nature

It may serve either as :

(a) A Subsidiary Book, (b) In the status of a separate Cash Book.

(a) As a subsidiary Book

Under this method, a statement of Petty Cash Expenses for the period is prepared by the Petty Cashier which is submitted by him to the General Cashier, who, after being satisfied, presents to the Petty Cashier the amount that has actually been spent at the beginning of the next period. Petty Cash Account in the ledger is debited and Cash Book is credited, when original advance is made to the Petty Cashier. As such, posting relating to expenses are made from the Petty Cash Book to the respective ledger accounts in the ledger, and the total expenses are credited to the Petty Cash Account. Thus, the debit balance of Petty Cash Account represents Petty Cash in hand which must be shown in the assets side of the Balance Sheet as a current asset. Consider the following illustration :

Illustration 12

Complete a Petty Cash Book (assuming that the Petty Cash Book is a Subsidiary book only) from the following particulars. Show also the ledger postings :

2010 Jan.	1	Received from General Cashier Rs. 300
	2	Paid for Stationery Expenses Rs. 20
		Paid for Postage & Telegrams Rs. 10
		Paid for office expenses Rs. 15
	4	Purchased paper and ink for Rs. 10
		Paid telephone bill of office Rs. 30
	5	Paid for tiffin to office peon Rs. 8
		Bought postage stamps for Rs. 15
	6	Bought Furniture for Rs. 80 and paid to Mr. X on account Rs. 20. Paid for Stationery Rs. 8
	7	Paid for Miscellaneous office expenses Rs. 10

Solution

In the books of ...
Petty Cash Book

Dr. Cr.

Amount	C.B. Folio	Date	Particulars	V. N.	Total	Stationery	Postage & Telegram	Office Expenses	Ledger Folio	Ledger Amount
Rs.		2010			Rs.	Rs.	Rs.	Rs.		Rs.
300	20	Jan. 1	To Cash		20	20				
		2	By Stationery		10		10			
		"	Postage & Telegram		15			15		
		"	Office exp.		10	10				
		4 "	Paper & ink		30			30		
		"	Telephone bill		8			8		
		5 "	Tiffin to peon		15		15			
		"	Postage Stamps		80				40	80
		6 "	Furniture		20				44	20
		"	X A/c		8	8				
		7 "	Misc. Exp.		10			10		
					226	(LF50) 38	25	63		100
			By Balance c/d		74					
300					300					
74		Jan. 8	To Balance b/d			LF-21	LF-22	LF-23		

Note : The unusual expenditures viz., Capital Expenditure or any other expenditure are to be passed through ledger Account Column, although each item should be posted individually but other expenses are posted with their total for the period.

Statement of Petty Cash Expenses
for the period from Jan. 1, 2010 to Jan. 7, 2010

		Rs.	Rs.
	Amount advanced to Petty Cashier		300
Less :	Petty Cash Expenses		
	Stationery	38	
	Postage and Telegram	25	
	Office Expenses	63	
	Ledger Accounts		
	Furniture	80	
	Mr. X	20	
			226
	Balance in hand		74

S/d Petty Cashier
7.1. 1989

Dr. **Cash Book** (Extracts) (Page 20) Cr.

Date	Particulars	J.F.	Amount	Date		Particulars	J.F.	Amount
				2010 Jan. 1	By	Petty Cash (advance to Petty Cashier)		Rs. 300

LEDGER

Dr. **Petty Cash Account** (Page 50) Cr.

Date	Particulars	J.F.	Amount	Date		Particulars	J.F.	Amount
2010 Jan. 1	To Cash A/c	20	Rs. 300	2010 Jan. 1	By	Sundries (as per Petty Cash Book)		Rs.

Dr. **Stationery Account** (Page 21) Cr.

Date	Particulars	J.F.	Amount	Date	Particulars	J.F.	Amount
2010 Jan. 7	To Petty Cash A/c	50	Rs. 38				Rs.

Dr. **Postage and Telegrams Account** (Page 22) Cr.

Date	Particulars	J.F.	Amount	Date	Particulars	J.F.	Amount
2010			Rs.				Rs.
Jan. 7	To Petty Cash A/c	50	25				

Dr. **Office Expenses Account** (page 23) Cr.

Date	Particulars	J.F.	Amount	Date	Particulars	J.F.	Amount
2010			Rs.				Rs.
Jan. 7	To Petty Cash A/c	50	63				

Dr. **Furniture Account** (Page 40) Cr.

Date	Particulars	J.F.	Amount	Date	Particulars	J.F.	Amount
2010			Rs.				Rs.
Jan. 7	To Petty Cash A/c	50	80				

Dr. **X Account** (Page 44) Cr.

Date	Particulars	J.F.	Amount	Date	Particulars	J.F.	Amount
2010			Rs.				Rs.
Jan. 7	To Petty Cash A/c	50	20				

Note : Here, the ledger folio of each account had been mentioned in the Petty Cash Book, as the posting has been made directly to the respective ledger accounts from the Petty Cash Book and, as such, Ledger Folio No. of the Petty Cash Book has been mentioned in each account.

On the contrary, if postings were made directly from the Cash Book, the Cash Book folio would have been mentioned in each account and, as such, there would have been no entry in the credit side of Petty Cash Book.

That is, in that case, the Cash Book as well as Petty Cash Book will be as follows :

Dr. **Cash Book** *(Extracts)* (Page 20) Cr.

Date	Particulars	J.F.	Amount	Date	Particulars	L.F.	Amount
2010			Rs.	2010			Rs.
				Jan. 1	By Petty Cash A/c	50	300
				Jan. 7	" Stationery	21	38
					" Postage & Telegram	22	25
					" Office Expenses	23	63
					" Furniture	40	80
					" X	44	20

Dr. **Petty Cash Account** (Page 50) Cr.

Date	Particulars	J.F.	Amount	Date	Particulars	J.F.	Amount
2010			Rs.				Rs.
Jan. 7	To Cash A/c	20	300				

(b) The Status of a Separate Cash Book

Under this method, Petty Cash Book is debited and Cash Book is credited — when original advance is made to the Petty Cashier. Moreover, the total disbursement, as usually recorded in Petty Cash Book, and also the total of the respective analytical columns, are posted to the respective ledger accounts—at the end of each period. Thus, the balance which is represented by a Petty Cash Book reveals the Petty Cash in hand, which must be shown in the assets side of the Balance Sheet.

Illustration 13

Take the data contained in Illustration 12 and prepare a Petty Cash Book, post the items into respective ledger accounts and restore the Petty Cashier to his original balance as on 8th Jan. 2010, assuming that Petty Cash Book maintains the status of a separate Cash Book.

Solution

In the Books of
Petty Cash Book

Dr. Cr.

Amount	C.B. Folio	Date	Particulars	V. N.	Total	Stationery	Postage & Telegram	Office Expenses	Ledger Folio	Ledger Amount
Rs.		2010			Rs.	Rs.	Rs.	Rs.		Rs.
300	20	Jan.	To Cash							
		2.	By Stationery		20	20				
			" Postage & Telegram		10		10			

Contd.

Rs.		2010			Rs.	Rs.	Rs.	Rs.		Rs.
			" Office expenses		15			15		
		4.	" Paper & ink		10	10				
			" Telephone bill		30			30		
		5.	" Tiffin to peon		8			8		
			" Postage Stamps		15		15			
		6.	" Furniture		80				40	80
			" X A/c		20				44	20
			" Stationery		8	8				
		7.	" Misc. Exp.		10			10		
					226	(LF50) 38	25	63		100
			By Balance c/d		74					
300					300	LF 21	LF 22	LF 23		
74			To Balance b/d							
226		8.	To Cash							

LEDGER

Dr. **Stationery Account** (Page No. 21) Cr.

Date	Particulars	J.F.	Amount	Date	Particulars	J.F.	Amount
2010			Rs.				Rs.
Jan. 7	To Petty Cash A/c	50	38				

Dr. **Postage and Telegrams Account** (Page No. 22) Cr.

Date	Particulars	J.F.	Amount	Date	Particulars	J.F.	Amount
2010			Rs.				Rs.
Jan. 7	To Petty Cash A/c	50	25				

Dr. **Other Expenses Account** (Page No. 23) Cr.

Date	Particulars	J.F.	Amount	Date	Particulars	J.F.	Amount
2010			Rs.				Rs.
Jan. 7	To Petty Cash A/c	50	63				

Dr. **Furniture Account** (Page No. 40) Cr.

Date	Particulars	J.F.	Amount	Date	Particulars	J.F.	Amount
2010			Rs.				Rs.
Jan. 7	To Petty Cash A/c	50	80				

Dr. **X Account** (Page No. 44) Cr.

Date	Particulars	J.F.	Amount	Date	Particulars	J.F.	Amount
1994			Rs.				Rs.
Jan. 7	To Petty Cash A/c	50	20				

GENERAL ILLUSTRATIONS

Illustration 14

Record the following transactions of Keshab Kabasi in the Cash Book and Journal. Only transactions not suitable for the Cash Book are to be taken to the Journal. Kabasi has an overdraft arrangement with the bank subject to a maximum limit of Rs. 5,000.

2000

April 1 Cash Balance brought forward Rs. 1,260.

1 Bank overdraft brought forward Rs. 3,600.

1 Advanced to Petty Cashier by cheque Rs. 500.

2 Received from Tarun Sen a cheque for Rs. 580 for goods sold in March 2000. Allowed him discount Rs. 20.

3 Received from Tanmay Roy Rs. 8,000. The amount was written-off as bad last year.

4 Paid cash into bank Rs. 1,500.

6 Sold goods to Tamal Baul for Rs. 4,000 subject to 10% trade discount and 5% discount for cash in 10 days

9 Received from Debesh Das, in full settlement of his account of Rs. 1,600. Somesh Bose's acceptance for Rs. 1,500
Discount the bill with the Banker for Rs. 1,450.

April 10 Consignment to Sharma & Co., Baroda—Goods worth Rs. 5,000.
10 Paid freight and insurance on the above Rs. 250
11 Tamal Baul gave a cheque in settlement of his account.
12 Paid Abir Bose by cheque Rs. 1,750, the balance of his account less Rs. 50 discount
15 Purchased goods from Sarit Sekhar for Rs. 3,000 and accepted a bill drawn by him for the amount. Paid carriage on purchase Rs. 150.
17 Drew cheque for office cash Rs. 500.
18 Purchased an office desk by cheque Rs. 1,870. Paid cartage thereon in cash Rs. 100.
20 Somesh Bose's acceptance returned dishonoured; noting charges paid by the Bank Rs. 20.
21 Debesh Das gave a cheque in full settlement of his account.
25 Goods of the value Rs. 1,800 insured with National Insurance Co. for Rs. 1,500 destroyed by fire.
The Insurance Co. accepted the claim and sent a cheque for the amount.
26 Purchased through bank Rs. 5,000, 8% Govt. Bonds at Rs. 95. Commission, stamps and fees Rs. 50.
27 Auctioned a typewriter, book value Rs. 500, for Rs. 700
28 Received from Haran Sur cheque for Rs. 600, in full settlement of account, Rs. 850, he (Haran Sur) being in financial difficulties.
30 Drew cheque for office cash raising the overdraft to the maximum permissible limit.

Solution **[CU BCom (Hon.) 2001]**

In the Books of Keshab Kabasi

Cash Book (with Cash, Bank and Discount Columns)

Dr. *Cr.*

Date	*Particulars*	*L. F.*	*Cash*	*Bank*	*Discount*	*Date*	*Particulars*	*L. F.*	*Cash*	*Bank*	*Discount*
2000			Rs.	Rs.	Rs.	2000			Rs.	Rs.	Rs.
Apr. 2	To Balance b/d		1,260			Apr. 1	By Balance b/d			3,600	
"	Tarun Sen A/c (Cheque received and discount allowed)			580	20	"	Petty Cash A/c (Cheque issued to petty cashier)			500	
3 "	Bad Debt Recovered A/c (Realised B/D)			800		4 "	Bank A/c (Cash deposited in to Bank)	(C)	1,500		
4 "	Cash A/c (Cash deposited into Bank)	(C)		1,500		10 "	Consignment A/c (Freight etc. paid on consignment)		250		
9 "	Bills Receivable A/c (Bill discounted)			1,450		12 "	Abir Bose A/c (Cheque issued and discount received)			1,750	50
11 "	Tamal Baul A/c (Cheq. received & discount allowed			3,420	180	15 "	Carriage Inwards A/c (Paid carriage on purchase)		150		
17 "	Bank A/c (Cash withdrawn for office use)	(c)	500			17 "	Cash A/c (Cash withdrawn for office use)	(C)		500	
21 "	Debesh Das A/c (Cheque received in full settlement)			1,620		18 "	Office Equipment A/c (Purchased office desk)			1,870	
25 "	Insurance Claim A/c (Cheque received against claim)			1,500		18 "	Office Equipment A/c (Carriage paid on desk)		100		
						20 "	Debesh Das A/c			1,520	

Contd.

2010			Rs.	Rs.	Rs.	2010			Rs.	Rs.	Rs.
27 "	Office Equipment A/c (Sale of old typewriter)		700				(Bills previously received from D. Das & discounted Dishonoured at a noting charge of Rs. 20)				
28 "	Haran Sur. A/c (Cheque received and discount allowed)			600	250	26 "	Investment in 8% Govt. Bound A/c (Total Payment for Inv. purchased)			4,800	
30 "	Bank A/c (Cash withdrawn for office use)	(C)	1,130			30 "	Cash A/c (Cash withdrawn for office)	(C)		1,130	
"	Balance c/d		—	5,000	—				2,390		
			4,390	15,670	450				4,390	15,670	50
May 1	To Balance b/d		2,390			May 1	To Balance b/d				5,000

Journal (Proper)

Date	Particulars	L.F.	Debit	Credit
2000			Rs.	Rs.
Apr. 6	Tamal Baul A/c Dr.		3,600	
	To Sales A/c			3,600
	(Goods valuing Rs. 4,000 sold out to T. Bose at a trade discount of 10%.)			
9	Bills Receivable A/c Dr.		1,500	
	Discount Allowed A/c Dr.		100	
	To Debesh Das A/c			1,600
	(S. Bose acceptance received from D. Das and discount allowed to him Rs. 100.)			
10	Consignment A/c Dr.		5,000	
	To Goods sent on Consignment A/c			5,000
	(Value of goods sent to Sharma & Co. on Consi-gnment basis.)			
15	Purchase A/c Dr.		3,000	
	To Sarit Sekhar A/c			3,000
	(Goods purchased from S. Sekhar on credit.)			
	Sarit Sekhar A/c Dr.		3,000	
	To Bills Payable A/c			3,000
	(Bill accepted in favour of S. Sekhar against goods purchased.)			
20	Debesh Das A/c Dr.		100	
	To Discount Allowed A/c			100
	(Discount previously allowed to D Das now disallowed and written-back on dishonour of his party's bill.)			
25	Stock Destroyed by Fire A/c Dr.		1,800	
	To Purchase/Trading A/c			1,800
	(Value of goods destroyed by fire.)			
	Insurance Claim A/c Dr.		1,500	
	Profit & Loss A/c Dr.		300	
	To Stock Destroyed by Fire A/c			1,800
	(An insurance claim accepted by the Insurance company against the loss of stock by fire and balance net loss charged to Profit & Loss A/c.)			
27	Office Equipment A/c Dr.		200	
	To Profit & Loss A/c			200
	(Profit on sale of old typewriter transferred to Profit & Loss A/c.)			

Working Notes :

1. On 6.4.2010, Goods sold to Tamal Baul for Rs. 4,000 at a trade discount of 10% i.e., Rs. 4,000– Rs. 400 = Rs. 3,600. Cash discount will be calculated @ 5% on Rs. 3,600 or Rs. 180 (Rs. 3,600 × 5%)

2. *On 20.4.2000 :*	*The entry will be*		
	Debesh Das A/c Dr.	1,620	
	To Bank A/c		1,500
	" Discount Allowed (Discount written back)		120
3. *On 25.4.2000 :*	*The entry being*		
	Goods Destroyed by Fire A/c Dr.	1,800	
	To Purchase A/ (Trading A/c)		1,800
	Bank A/c Dr.	1,500	
	Profit and Loss A/c Dr.	300	
	To Goods Destroyed by Fire		1,800

On 26.4.2000 : Purchase of 8% Govt. Bond = Principal + Expenses

$$= (\text{Rs. } 5{,}000 \times \frac{95}{100}) + \text{Rs. } 50 = \text{Rs. } 4{,}750 + \text{Rs. } 50$$

$$= \text{Rs. } 4{,}800$$

ASSIGNMENT MATERIALS
THEORETICAL

Multiple Choice Questions

1. (a) Cash Book always shows a—
   (i) Debit balance; (ii) Credit balance; (iii) Both
   (b) Cash Book is a—
   (i) Journal; (ii) Ledger; (iii) Journalised Ledger.
   (c) Cash Account shows—
   (i) Debit balance; (ii) Credit or Debit balance; (iii) Both
   (d) Cash sales are recorded in—
   (i) Cash Book; (ii) Sales Day Book; (iii) Journal.
   (e) A columnar Cash Book records—
   (i) all cash transactions only; (ii) both cash and bank transactions; (iii) all cash transactions excluding cash sales and cash purchases.
   (f) Petty cash Book is meant
   (i) for recording small expenditure to be paid in cash; (ii) for small day-to-day expenditure; (iii) for recording small expendirure and incomes.
   (g) Imprest system is used for—
   (i) Petty Cash Book; (ii) Cash Book; (iii) Day Book.
   (h) The Petty Cash Book is used for recording—
   (i) All cash payments; (ii) Petty cash payments; (iii) Petty cash receipts and payments.
   (i) The balance of Petty Cash Book is—
   (i) a liability; (ii) an asset; (iii) an expense.
   (j) Cash Discount is allowed on—
   (i) Cash Sales; (ii) Cash Purchase; (iii) Prompt payment.
   (k) Trade Discount is allowed
   (i) by a manufacturer to a trader; (ii) by a trader to a consumer; (iii) both.

[Ans. (a) (i); (b) (iii); (c) (i); (d) (i); (e) (ii); (f) (i); (g) (i); (h) (iii); (i) (ii); (j) (iii); (k) (i)]

Short Answer-Type Questions

2. What is a Cash Book? What purpose does it serve?
3. Discuss the various types of cash book maintained by a firm.
4. Why does a cash book always show a debit balance?
5. 'Cash Book is a journal as well as a ledger.'—Discuss.
6. When is a cash book called the only book of original entry?

Long Answer-Type Questions

7. What is a Double Column Cash Book? What are 'Contra Transactions'?
8. Discuss the treatment relating to 'cheque' transactions (at least three).
9. What is the Imprest System of Petty Cash? How do you prepare such a Cash Book?
10. Is there any difference between Imprest System of Petty Cash and Analytical System of Petty Cash? If so, discuss them.
11. Discuss the method of posting the Cash Book in the ledger.
12. What are the advantages of Imprest System of Petty Cash?
13. What is meant by the Imprest System of maintaining Petty Cash?
14. Define.
    (a) Imprest System of Petty Cash, (b) Analytical System of Petty Cash.
15. (i) Why is Cash Book called as a Journalised Ledger?

PRACTICAL

(a) Double Column Cash Book

1. From the following particulars, prepare a Double Column Cash Book :

2010			Rs.
Dec.	1	Cash in hand Rs. 1,000, Cash at Bank (Cr.)	5,000
	2	Gave a cheque to Petty Cashier for petty payment	100
	5	Received three cheques from Mr. T on account of Cash Sales, Rs. 300, Rs. 500 and Rs. 750, the 1st cheque being paid into Bank.	
	6	The second cheque is endorsed to Mr. P against purchase of goods and the third cheque is endorsed to Mr. G for his Salary.	
	8	Deposited Cash into Bank	150
	9.	Drew cheque for	
		Printing	50
		Personal expenses	150
		Payment to Mr. C	300
	11	Bank charges interest on overdraft	250
	12	Cashed for Mr. X and paid into Bank	300
	15	Received a cheque from Mr. K and endorsed the same to Mr. H for	500
	19	The above cheque returned dishonoured	
	22	Issued a cheque to Mr. C, our creditor, for	500
	23	Stopped the payment of the above cheque by advice to Bank.	
	25	Recovered Cash from customer Sri H. Bose and deposited into Bank on 26th morning for Rs. 300.	
	31	Withdrew for personal use	
		from Bank	1,000
		from Cash	500
		Paid Salary to Mr. X by cheque	350

[Ans. Cash Balance Rs. 50; Bank Balance (Cr.) Rs. 6,150]

[Hints : for 12 Dec.—the entry being—Bank A/c Dr. and Cash A/c Cr. for 19 Dec.—there will be no effect in Cash Book.]

2. Enter the following Cash and Bank transactions of Sri Sudhansu Talukder for the month of Dec. 2010. Prepare his Cash Book and bring down the balances :

2010			Rs.
Dec.	1	Balance in hand	3,500
		Balance at Bank	12,500
	4	Received two cheques	
		(i) from Cash Sales	750
		(ii) from Mr. N. Bose	1,000
	7	Endorsed the 1st cheque against purchase of goods. Endorsed the 2nd cheque against purchase of Furniture.	
	9	Received Rent from Mr. Das in cheque Rs. 500.	
	10	The above cheque was deposited into Bank.	
	15	Bank reported that the above cheque was dishonoured.	

Contd.

		Rs.
17	Received Cash Rs. 1,000 and a bearer cheque Rs. 300 (K. Sen) on account of sales.	
18	The above cheque was dishonoured at the Bank counter.	
20	Drew from Bank	
	for office use	1,000
	for private use	500
22	Deposited Cash into Bank	500
25	Customer directly deposited into our Bank Account	1,000
26	Discounted with the Bank a bill (of Rs. 400)	370
27	Paid Miscellaneous Expenses in Cash	750
31	Bank allowed Interest Rs. 700 and deducted Bank Charges Rs. 100	
	Issued a cheque to C for Commission Rs. 100.	

[Ans. Cash Balance Rs. 4,250; Bank Balance Rs. 13,370]
[Hints : for 17th—To, K. Sen in Cash Column; for 18th—By, K. Sen in Cash Column; for 26th—To, B/R, in Bank Column Rs. 370]

3. **From the following particulars, prepare a suitable Double Column Cash Book with Cash and Bank Column of Sri Sarkar, for the month of Oct. 2010 :**

2010			Rs.
Oct.	1	Balance in hand	3,000
		Bank Overdraft	1,500
		Admitted Mr. Bose as partner and received Cash from him as Capital 2,000	
	3	Mr. Sarkar sold his household Furniture for Rs. 1,000 and deposited into business Bank Account.	
	6	Cash drawing by Sarkar @ Rs. 1,200 p. m. Bose @ Rs. 600 p. m.	
	7	Issued a cheque to Mr. Kanjilal for Rs. 700.	
	8	'Stop Payment' order was served to the Bank as the same was pickpocketed.	
	9	Received a bearer cheque from Mr. B. for Rs. 100.	
	10	Endorsed the above cheque to Mr. C.	
	1	Received these cheques on account of Sales : (i) from K. Sen Rs. 300; (ii) from M. Sen Rs. 500; (iii) from D. Poddar Rs. 700 (bearer cheque)	
	17	Deposited K. Sen's cheque into Bank.	
		Endorsed M. Sen's cheque to P. Das for purchase of goods.	
		D. Poddar's cheque presented to the Bank counter and was dishonoured.	
	25	Received a fresh cheque from D. Poddar which was deposited into Bank.	
	31	Issued a cheque to the landlord Mr. Ray of Rs. 300.	

[Ans. Cash Balance Rs. 3,200; Bank Balance Rs. 200]
[Hints : for 3rd—To Capital, in Bank Column Rs. 1,000; for 8th—To Kanjilal, in Bank Column Rs. 700.]

4. **From the following particulars, write-up a suitable Cash Book of K & Co. and bring down the balances for the month of May 2010 :**

2010			Rs.
May	1	Balance at Bank of Baroda (overdraft)	6,000
	2	Drawn for office use	10,000
		Bought Furniture for Cash	3,200
	8	Paid Wages to staff	1,500
	10	Purchase made by cheque	2,500
	15	Paid to Sri Suresh on account	4,450
	20	Sold goods and received payment in Cash Rs. 8,500 and by cheque Rs. 12,500.	
	22	Deposited Cash into Bank	540
	25	Discounted with the Bank a B/R of Rs. 500 for Rs. 490.	
	26	Received a cheque from Y & Co.	7,800
	28	B/R of 25th May dishonoured.	
	30	Bank charged interest on overdraft Rs. 200 and Incidental Charges Rs. 25.	
	30	Drew for the private use of the proprietor from Bank in excess of Rs. 2,000.	

[Ans. Bank Balance Rs. 2,000; Cash Balance Rs. 8,810; Drawings Rs. 105]
[Hints : for 28th—By Debtors A/c in Bank Column Rs. 500.]

(b) Cash Book with two Bank Columns

5. Sri P operates two Bank Accounts both of which are maintained in the columnar Cash Book itself.

You are required to draw up a proforma of the Cash Book and show how the following transactions relating to 28th Feb. 2010 will appear therein and close the Cash Book for the day :

(i) Opening balance :

Cash	100	
State Bank	10,000	(o/d)
United Bank	30,000	

(ii) Received cheque for Rs. 1,000 in respect of sales for realising which State Bank charged Rs. 2 and credited the balance.

(iii) Purchased goods for Rs. 13,000 and a cheque issued on the United Bank.

(iv) Paid Office Expenses Rs. 45 and Rs. 15 for Stationery.

(v) Out of Cash sales of Rs. 13,000, a sum of Rs. 10,000 was deposited in the State Bank.

(vi) Credit purchases of Rs. 15,000 were made from Q who sent the documents relating to the goods through the United Bank for 90% of their values. The Bank charged Rs. 100 for realising the document.

(vii) Deposited Rs. 5,000 in State Bank.

(viii) A "B/R" for Rs. 10,000 was discounted with the United Bank, which charges 1% towards discounting.

(ix) Withdrew Rs. 5,000 from United Bank.

(x) A Demand Draft was purchased for Rs. 3,000 from a Bank after paying Rs. 2 towards charges.

[CU BCom (Hons.)]

[Ans. Cash in hand Rs. 38; Balance at State Bank Rs. 5,998; Balance at United Bank Rs. 8,300]

[Hints : for (vi) By Q's A/c in Bank Col. Rs. 13,500 $\left(15,000 \times \frac{90}{100}\right)$ and Rs. 100 for charges. for (x) by Demand Draft for Rs. 3,002.]

(c) Triple Column Cash Book

6. The following are the transactions of Mr. X, a sole trader, for the first week of October 2010:

2010. October

1 Received from Abdul by cheque Rs. 275, discount allowed to him Rs. 5.
Paid conveyance expenses Rs. 25 in cash.

3 Purchased furniture from Harumal and issued cheque for Rs. 900.
Paid postage expenses in cash Rs. 15.

4 Paid staff salaries by cash Rs. 600.
Withdrew from Bank Rs. 500.

5 Paid Rahul & Co. by cheque Rs. 1,980 in full settlement of their dues of Rs. 2,000.

7 Cheque in favour of Rahul & Co. returned not honoured since date was wrongly mentioned in the cheque. Issued a fresh cheque in their favour including Rs. 5 towards bank charges on cheque returned.

The following were the balances on October 1, 2010:

Cash	Rs.	738
Bank	Rs.	12,175

Write-up the Cash Book of Mr. X for the week showing Discount, Cash and Bank columns, balancing the Book on the 7th October.

[CA Entrance]

[Ans. Cash Balance Rs. 598; Bank Balance Rs. 9,065; Discount Allowed Rs. 5; Discount Received Rs. 20]

(d) Petty Cash Book

(i) Under Imprest System

7. From the undermentioned particulars, write-up the Petty Cash Book of A. Das kept under Imprest System and show how much will be paid to Petty Cashier on 8th Feb.:

2010			Rs.
Feb.	1	Cash in hand	1.70
		Cheque received from the Chief Cashier	48.30
	2	Purchased Postage Stamps	2.70
	3	Carriage on Goods	3.30
		Purchase of Ink & Paper	4.90
	4	Tram fare to office peon	.80
		Repairs to Typewriter	5.70
	5	Telegram to Chennai	3.80
		Taxi fare for the manager	5.10
	6	Purchased one small Office Table	13.50
		Tiffin Expenses	5.20
	7	Wages for clearing the office room	2.50

[Ans. Balance in hand Rs. 2.50, Reimbursement Rs. 47.50]

(ii) Under Analytical System :

8. At the start an advance of Rs. 50 is made for a Petty Cash Book on April 1, 2010.

The following are the items of expenditure during the month :

			Rs.
April	1	Purchase of Postage Stamps	3.75
	3	Paid Coolie-hire for goods bought	.50
April	8	Purchase of Stationery	.37
	10	Tiffin charges to a peon	.50
	15	Sending a Telegram to Chennai	1.87
	18	Purchased Ink	2.44
	20	Purchase of Postage Stamps	7.50
	21	Payment of book-binder's charges	7.12
	24	Purchase of Three Tumblers for office	1.12
	25	Repairs to Furniture	8.87
	28	Replacement of Electric bulbs	6.69
	29	Tram fare paid to office peon	4.19

Write-up a Petty Cash Book recording all the above payments.

[CU BCom]

[Ans. Petty Cash Balance Rs. 5.08]

(e) Missing Sales

9. Mr. M. carries on business in a small retail shop. He enters details of his transac-tions in a diary. All cash outlays are paid out of takings and other cash receipts and at the end of each week he leaves Rs. 150 in the shop cash and pays the balance into the bank.

	The entries for the first week of June 2010 are :	Rs.
1.	Balance in shop Cash Rs. 150 Bank	1,335
2.	Bought Goods for Cash	330
"	Received from Mr. A repayment of his Loan in Cash	90
3.	Bought Goods from Mr. B	720
"	Gave cheque for Rs. 525 to Mr. C for goods supplied	
4.	Gave wife Rs. 150 for household expenses	
"	Cashed Fixed Deposit Certificate Rs. 500	
	Kept Rs. 100 for self, paid balance into shop Cash	
5.	Paid into Bank	600
"	Gave Mr. D cheque for Rs. 450 in repayment of some liabilities	
6.	Cashed Rs. 120 for Mr. E and paid into Bank	
"	Bought Stationery for Cash	160
"	Gave cheque to Mr. B for goods bought this month, deducting Rs. 10 for discount	

Write-up the Cash Book for the week and bring down the balance at the close of the business on June 6.

[CU BCom (Hons.)]

[Ans. Cash Balance Rs. 150, Bank Balance Rs. 370]

CHAPTER 8

BANK RECONCILIATION STATEMENT

Bank Reconciliation Statement—its meaning

Meaning

Causes of Disagreement

Usefulness, Utility and Importance

Method of Preparation

A. Preparation of Bank Reconciliation Statement without Adjusting in Cash Book

- (a) *Taking Balance as per Cash Book*
- (b) *Taking Balance as per Pass Book*
- (c) *Taking overdraft as per Cash Book*
- (d) *Taking overdraft as per Pass Book*
- (e) *Where there are two Bank Accounts*

B. Preparation of Bank Reconciliation Statement with Adjustments in Cash Book

- (f) *With Amendments in Cash Book*
    - (a) *Where there is Favourable Balance*
    - (b) *Where there is Unfavourable Balance*
- (g) *Where there are Two Bank Accounts*
- (h) *Amendments of Cash Book after Reconciliation Statement*
    - (i) *Where Cash Book and Pass Book are given*
    - (ii) *Where the Books relate to the Same Period*
    - (iii) *When the Pass Book is given for the Succeeding Period*

Meaning

It has already been explained in an earlier chapter that when an individual or a firm deposits any money in a bank or withdraws money by issuing a cheque from a bank, he/it enters the transaction in the debit side of the bank column of the Cash Book for such deposits and credit side of the Cash Book (bank column) for such withdrawals. Similarly, bank also records such transactions in its book, i.e., it credits such account for deposit and debits such account for any withdrawals and at the same time, the bank issues a book to the account holder after incorporating of all such transactions—the bank Pass Book. Of course, in case of a Current Account, bank issues a statement instead of a pass book.

A specimen of a pass book or a statement is presented :

Mr. X in Savings/Current Account with
State Bank of India

Date		*Particulars*	*Cheque*	*Debit*	*Credit*	*Dr. or Cr.*	*Balance*
2010				Rs.	Rs.		Rs.
Jan. 1	By	Balance b/d				Cr.	10,000
2	To	Cash		1,000		Cr.	9,000
3	By	Cash			4,000	Cr.	13,000
6	By	Cheque			8,000	Cr.	21,000
20	To	Cheque	0241	5,000		Cr.	16,000
26	To	Cheque	0242	4,000		Cr.	12,000
30	By	Interest			400	Cr.	12,400

The students are advised to note that the debit side of the bank column of the Cash Book must be equal to the credit side of the bank pass book, and vice versa. That is

Cash Book	=	*Debit*	=	*Favourable balance*
Cash Book	=	*Credit*	=	*Unfavourable/Overdraft balance*
Pass Book	=	*Credit*	=	*Favourable balance*
Pass Book	=	*Debit*	=	*Unfavourable/Overdraft balance.*

Usually, for the above reasons, it may be expected that the bank balance shown by a Cash Book should tally with the balance shown by the Pass Book at a particular date. But in actual practice, it does not always so happen, due to the following causes of disagreement. The student should note that a Bank Reconciliation Statement may be started with any of the following balances :

Balance as per Cash Book (favourable)
Balance as per Cash Book (unfavourable/overdraft)
Balance as per Pass Book (favourable)
Balance as per Pass Book (unfavourabale/overdraft)

CAUSES OF DISAGREEMENT

The causes of disagreement arise from : (a) Timing, (b) Transactions, and (c) Errors :

(a) **Timing** : One of the causes of disagreement between the balance shown by the pass book and the balance shown by the cash book is the ***Timing factor***. For example, when a cheque is deposited into bank, the same is immediately recorded in the debit side of the cash book, but bank will credit only when the amount will be realised from that concerned party.

(b) **Transactions** : Another cause of disagreement between the two balances is the ***Transaction element***. There are certain transactions which the bank records in its book before recording the same by the business. For example, Interest credited by bank or bank charges debited by bank is recorded earlier in pass book and, as it is not known to the trader, these transactions are not recorded at all in his books for which disagreement arises.

(c) **Errors** : Another cause of disagreement is the ***Errors*** which may be committed either by the persons who has prepared the cash book or by the bank. For example, debit side of the cash book has been overcast or wrong debit or credit made by bank.

Some of the Common Causes of Disagreement are

(a) ***Cheques Deposited but not Credited***

When a person receives any cheque from his customer or any other source, he deposits the same into the bank. For this purpose, he debits bank account in Cash Book and credits, the customer's account. But, in practice, when the bank receives the cheque, it takes some time for its realisation. Between these times, the balance shown by Cash Book will be more than the balance shown by the Pass Book. Moreover, if the bank is unable to collect the cheque, or if the cheque returns dishonoured, the bank will not credit the concerned account. As such, there will be a difference between the balance shown as per Cash Book (which is more) and the balance shown by the Pass Book (which is less).

(b) ***Cheques Drawn/Issued but not Presented***

When a person issues/draws a cheque to his creditor or any other person, he credits Bank Account in the Cash Book and debits creditor's account. But, in reality, the creditor may not present that cheque to the bank immediately for payment. Usually, it takes some time. Between these times, the balance shown by the cash book will be less than the balance shown by the pass book. At the same time, if the creditor does not present the cheque into the bank, there will be a difference between the balance shown as per Cash Book (which is less) and the balance shown as per Pass Book (which is more).

(c) ***Dividend/Incomes (Insurance Claim, etc.) collected by Bank***

When Dividends or Incomes (i.e., Insurance Claims, etc.) are collected by the bank, the bank credits the concerned account immediately. In practice, it takes some time to inform its clients. Between these times, the balance shown by the Pass Book will be more than the balance shown by the Cash Book, since the transaction was not at all recorded in the Cash Book.

(d) ***Interest Credited by Bank not entered in Cash Book***

When the bank allows interest to its customers (usually monthly/quarterly/half-yearly/annually) it credits the customer's or client's account and informs its client at a latter date. Since it was not known to the trader the same was not at all recorded in the debit side of the Cash Book. Thus, between these times, the balance shown by the Pass Book (which is more) must not agree with the balance shown the Cash Book (which is less).

(e) ***Bank Charges not entered in Cash Book***

Usually, a bank charges some amount against the customer's/traders account for the services rendered by it or on account of incidental charges/collection charges, etc., and debits the concerned account in the Pass Book. Since it was not known to the trader, it was not at all recorded in the credit side of the Cash Book. Thus, between the two balances that shown by the Pass Book (which is less) must not agree with the balance shown by the Cash Book (which is more).

(f) ***Direct Deposit made by the Customers***

When a customer has directly deposited into the bank account, the bank credits the amount in the Pass Book and informs us at a latter date. Since it was not known to us, no entry was made in the debit side of our Cash Book and credit of customer's account. Thus, between these times, the balance shown by the Pass Book (which is more) must not agree with the balance shown by the Cash Book (which is less).

(g) ***Standing Instructions***

When standing instructions are given to the bank for the payment of insurance premium, Pay order, or payment of any expenses and paid by the bank accordingly it debits the concerned account and informs at a later date. Since it was not known to the trader, no entry for such expenses was made in the credit side of the Cash Book. Thus, between these periods, the balance shown by the Pass Book must not agree with the balance shown by the Cash Book.

(h) ***Errors***

If any error is committed by the Cash Book or by the Pass Book, the same will cause the differences between the two. For example :

(i) ***Debit side of the Cash Book is overcast/undercast***

If the debit side of the cash book is overcast the balance shown by the Cash Book will be more (of course, if there is a favourable balance) than the balance shown by the Pass Book. In case of undercasting, it will be reversed.

(ii) ***Wrong Debit/Credit made by bank***

If the bank wrongly debits or credits the accounts of the party, there must be a difference between the two balances also.

Usefulness Utility or Importance of Bank Reconciliation Statement

It has already been explained earlier that the balance shown by a Cash Book should tally with the balance shown by a Pass Book. Since the two balances do not happen to be equal due to the above causes of disagreement, it becomes necessary to prepare a reconciliation statement for the purpose of ascertaining the correct bank balance which is shown while preparing final accounts (i.e., Balance Sheet). This statement is very important to an accountant because the accountant must confirm that both the balances i.e., the balance shown by a Cash Book and the balance shown by a Pass Book is identical at a certain period and, needless to say, Bank Reconciliation Statement is a basis for such confirmation.

It also helps to detect any mistakes that have arisen both from the cash book as well as from the pass book. It also prevents fraud while recording transactions and it also expresses the reasons for any delay while collecting cheques.

Method of Preparation

It is to be noted that if the Cash Book balance is given, we are to find out the Pass Book balance. In that case, the only principle to be followed is to see what has been done by the Pass Book for each individual items—we are to follow it, i.e., if it is seen that the Pass Book balance has increased by that amount we will simply 'add' the amount, and vice versa. Similarly, if the Pass Book balance is given we are to find out the Cash Book balance. In that case, our duty would be just to follow it, i.e., if it is found that the Cash Book balance has increased by the amount, we will also 'add' the amount, and vice versa.

The above principle is also, however, applicable in the case of overdraft balances. That is, if overdraft as per Cash Book is given we are to ascertain the overdraft balance as per Pass Book. In that case, we are to consider the Pass Book balances, i.e., if it is seen that the overdraft balance of the Pass Book is increased, our duty will be to 'add' that amount in order to ascertain the overdraft balance shown by the Pass Book, and vice versa.

To Sum up

While preparing a Bank Reconciliation Statement we are to remember that if balance as per Cash Book is given, we are to find out the balance as per Pass Book. In that case, our duty is to follow the Pass Book, i.e., what is done by the Pass Book, we will do the same thing. In other words, if we find that the Pass Book balance has increased we will increase the same i.e., to be added to the item, and vice versa in the opposite case.

Same principle is to be followed in case of overdraft balances also.

Thus, the following procedure may be adopted while preparing a **Bank Reconciliation Statement:**

S.L.	Causes of Disagreement	What to do, if started from Cash Book		What to do, if started from Pass Book	
		Favourable Balance	Unfavourable or Overdraft	Favourable Balance	Unfavourable or Overdraft
1.	Cheque issued/drawn but not presented	Add	Less	Less	Add
2.	Cheque paid/deposited into Bank but not credited	Less	Add	Add	Less
3.	Direct deposit made by customers into bank not recorded in Cash Book	Add	Less	Less	Add
4.	Bank met a pay order as per standing instruction, not entered in Cash Book	Less	Add	Add	Less
5.	Bank collected dividend or any income but not recorded in Cash Book	Add	Less	Less	Add
6.	Bank charges debited in Pass Book but not recorded in Cash Book	Less	Add	Add	Less
7.	Bank charges interest on overdraft but not recorded in Cash Book	Does not arise	Add	Does not arise	Less
8.	Bank credited interest but not debited in Cash Book	Add	Does not arise	Less	Does not arise

Contd.

9.	Cheque deposited but dishonoured, not recorded in Cash Book	Less	Add	Add	Less
10.	Cheque issued and recorded in Cash Book as deposited into bank but the same was not deposited into bank	Less	Add	Add	Less
11.	Cheques issued but not recorded in Cash Book	Less	Add	Add	Less
12.	Interest on bank deposits recorded in Cash Book but not credited by the bank	Less	Does not arise	Add	Does not arise
13.	Interest on overdraft recorded in Cash Book but not debited in Pass Book	Does not arise	Less	Does not arise	Add

The proforma or specimen form of a Bank Reconciliation statement is presented :

Bank Reconciliations Statement
as at ....

		Rs.	Rs.
	Balance as per Cash Book		•••
Add :	Cheques issued but not presented for payment	•••	
	Interest credited by bank not recorded in Cash Book	•••	
	Dividend collected by bank not recorded in Cash Book	•••	
			•••
			•••
Less :	Cheques deposited but not credited	•••	
	Bank met a pay order not entered in Cash Book	•••	
	Debit side of the Cash Book was overcast	•••	
			•••
	Balance as per Pass Book		•••

Alternative Approach

Under this method the Bank Reconciliation statement is prepared in two columns, one for **'Debit'**, the other for **'Credit'**.

Rules :

(i) Write-up the balance either as per Cash Book or Pass Book in appropriate columns i.e., debit balance in debit column and credit balance in credit column.

(ii) Write the following types of items in the **debit** column:
   (a) Wrong or excess credit either in Pass Book or Cash Book
   (b) Transactions either not debited or debited short either in Pass Book or in Cash Book.

(iii) Write the following types of items in the **credit** column:
   (a) Wrong or excess debit either in Pass Book or in Cash Book
   (b) Transactions either not credited or credited short either in Pass Book or in Cash Book

Add both the columns and find out the difference between the two columns and put the difference in the smaller amount column, i.e., just like balancing of an account, to become equal. The difference represents bank balance as per other books.

Consider the specimen given :

Bank Reconciliations Statement
as at ....

	Debit	Credit
	Rs.	Rs.
Balance per Cash Book/Pass Book (Debit balance in Debit Column and Credit balance in Credit column)	•••	•••
Bank credited for Interest	•••	
Cheques issued but not presented	•••	
Direct deposit made by customer	•••	
Bank changes not entered in Cash Book		•••

Contd.

	Rs.	Rs.
Bank met a pay order not entered in Cash Book		•••
Cheques deposited but not credited		•••
Balance as per Cash Book/Pass Book		•••
Total	•••	•••

The following illustration will help us to understand the above two principles clearly:

Illustration 1

From the following information presented by Miss Amrita Ghosh, prepare a Bank Reconciliation Statement reconciling the bank balance as per Cash Book with the balance shown by the Pass Book for the month of 31st Dec. 2010.

(i) Balance as per Cash Book Rs. 40,000
(ii) Cheques issued but not presented Rs. 10,000
(iii) Cheques deposited but not credited Rs. 30,000
(iv) Interest credited by Bank not entered in Cash Book Rs. 5,000
(v) Bank charge debited in Pass Book Rs. 1,000
(vi) Direct deposit made by customer Rs. 26,000
(vii) Bank paid L.I. Premium not entered in Cash Book Rs. 5,000
(viii) Balance as per Pass Book Rs. 45,000

Solution

1. ***Under First Method***

Bank Reconciliation Statement
as at 31st Dec. 2010

		Rs.	Rs.
	Balance as per Cash Book		40,000
Add :	Cheques issued but not presented	10,000	
	Interest credited by bank not entered in Cash Book	5,000	
	Direct deposit made by customer	26,000	41,000
			81,000
Less :	Cheque deposited but not credited	30,000	
	Bank charged in Pass Book	1,000	
	Bank paid L.I.P. not entered in Cash Book	5,000	36,000
	Balance as per Pass Book		45,000

2. ***Under Alternative Method***

Bank Reconciliation Statement
as at ....

		Debit Rs.	Credit Rs.
	Balance as per Cash Book	40,000	
Add :	Cheques issued but not presented	10,000	
	Cheques deposited but not credited	—	30,000
	Interest credited by bank	5,000	—
	Bank charges debited by bank	—	1,000
	Direct deposit made by customer	26,000	—
	Bank paid L.I.P.	—	5,000
	Balance as per Pass Book	—	45,000
		81,000	81,000

Of the two methods stated above, the first one is easy and familiar, and, as such, the subsequent illustrations are solved under the First Method.

A. Preparation of Bank Reconciliation Statement without Adjusting in Cash Book, i.e., Ordinary

(a) Taking Balance as per Cash Book (Favourable) :

It has already been stated earlier while discussing the method of its preparation that, if Cash Book balance is given, we are to find out the Pass Book balance. In that case our duty is to see what has been done by the Pass Book for each individual item, we are to follow it, i.e., if it is seen that the Pass Book balance has increased by that amount, we will simply 'add' the amount, and vice versa.

Some of the items are given :

Add : (The items which will increase the Pass Book balance)

(i) Cheques issued but not presented for payment; (ii) Interest credited by bank but not recorded in Cash Book; (iii) Dividend collected by bank but not recorded in Cash Book; (iv) Debtors directly deposited into bank but not entered in Cash Book; (v) Bank Charges (postal) recorded twice in Cash Book; *Less :* (i) Cheques deposited but not credited by the bank; (ii) Debit side of the Cash Book was overcast; (iii) Credit side of the Cash Book was undercast; (iv) Dishonoured cheque appeared in the Pass Book but not entered in Cash Book; (v) Bank met a bill payable but not recorded in Cash Book.

Illustration 2

From the following particulars, prepare Bank Reconciliation Statement as at 31st Dec. 2010, showing the balance as per Pass Book as on that date:

		Rs.
(i)	Balance as per Cash Book (Dr.)	5,000
(ii)	Cheques issued to creditors but not presented	3,000
(iii)	Cheques deposited into bank but not credited by bank	8,000
(iv)	Interest credited by bank, but not entered in Cash Book	300
(v)	Bank charges debited by bank, not entered in Cash Book	100
(vi)	A customer directly deposited into our bank account but it was not recorded in Cash Book	9,000
(vii)	As per instruction, Bank met pay-order not recorded in Cash Book	1,000
(viii)	Bank wrongly debited in Pass Book	500

Solution

Bank Reconciliation Statement
as at 31st Dec. 2010

		Rs.	Rs.
	Balance as per Cash Book		5,000
Add :	Cheques issued but not presented	3,000	
	Interest credited by bank not recorded in Cash Book	300	
	Direct deposit made by customer not entered in Cash Book	9,000	12,300
			17,300
Less :	Cheque deposited into bank but not credited	8,000	
	Bank charges debited in Pass Book not in Cash Book	100	
	Bank met 'Pay Order' not entered in Cash Book	1,000	
	Wrong debit made by bank	500	9,600
	Balance as per Pass Book		7,700

Analysis and Interpretation

We are to remember the principles of preparing a Bank Reconciliation Statement. The principle is that if Cash Book balance is given we are to find out the Pass Book balance. In that case, what has been done by the Pass Book for each individual item, we are to follow it, i.e., if Pass book balance is increased, we will 'add' the amount, or vice versa in the opposite case. Consider one by one:

(i) When cheque was issued it was recorded on the credit side of the Cash Book so that the Cash Book balance was reduced. But the cheque was not presented to the Bank for payment. As such, the bank balance was more by that amount. Since bank balance was more, we are to increase. So it will be added.

(ii) Interest was credited by the bank. It means bank balance was increased as per Pass Book. So it will be added.

(iii) Bank charges were debited by the bank, i.e., bank balance was reduced. So it will be subtracted.

(iv) Due to this transaction bank balance was increased. So it will be added.

(v) When bank met pay order, it was debited, so bank balance as per Pass Book was reduced. So it will be subtracted.

(vi) Bank balance was reduced as a result of wrong debit. So it will be subtracted.

Illustration 3

From the following particulars prepare a Bank Reconciliation Statement for Sri Arindam Ghosh as at 31st March 2010:

		Rs.
(a)	Bank balance as per Cash Book	70,000
(b)	Cheques issued but presented after 31st March	10,000
(c)	Three chepues were issued for Rs. 5,000, Rs. 10,000 and Rs. 15,000, respectively, but the cheque for 10,000 was presented on 3rd April	
(d)	Cheque issued but not recorded in Cash Book	7,500
(e)	Cheques deposited but credited after 31st March	2,500
(f)	Three cheques were deposited for Rs. 10,000, Rs. 12,000 Rs. 16,000, respectively, but the cheque for Rs. 16,000 was credited on 2nd Aprils.	
(g)	Cheques deposited into Bank but not recorded in Cash Book	10,000
(h)	Debit side of the Cash Book was overcast by	5,000
(i)	Credit side of the Cash Book was undercast by	8,000
(j)	Bank Interest credited for Rs. 1,500 and debited by Interest Rs. 500 not recorded in Cash Book	10,000
(k)	Dividend collected by bank not recorded in Cash Book	10,000
(l)	A debtor directly deposited into Bank but not recorded in Cash Book	5,000
(m)	Rs. 10,000 in respect of dishonoured cheque appeared in the Pass Book but not in the Cash Book	
(n)	Bank met a Bill Payable of the firm for Rs. 15,000 on 30th March, under advice to the firm on 2nd April	
(o)	Bank's charges (postal) for a cheque book for Sri Ghose Rs. 50 were entered in the Cash Book twice	
(p)	A cheque for Rs. 500 drawn by Mr. Mukherjee had been charged to Sri Ghose account by error in March 2010.	

Solution

Bank Reconciliation Statement
as at 31st March. 2010

		Rs.	Rs.
	Bank Balance as per Cash Book		70,000
Add :	Cheques issued but not presented	10,000	
	Cheques issued but not presented	10,000	
	Cheques deposited into bank, but not recorded in Cash Book	10,000	
	Interest credited by Bank not recorded in Cash Book	1,500	
	Dividend collected by Bank not recorded in Cash Book	10,000	
	Debtors directly deposited into Bank, but not recorded in Cash Book	5,000	
	Bank's charges (postal) recorded twice in Cash Book	50	
			46,550
			1,16,550
Less :	Cheques issue but not recorded in Cash Book	7,500	
	Cheques deposited but not credited by the Bank	2,500	
	Cheques deposited but not credited by the Bank	16,000	
	Debit side of the Cash Book was overcast	5,000	
	Credit side of the Cash Book was undercast	8,000	
	Bank charges debited by Bank not recorded in Cash Book	500	
	Dishonoured cheques appeared in Pass Book but not entered in Cash Book	10,000	
	Bank met a Bills Payable, but not record in Cash Book	15,000	
	A cheque drawn by Mr. Mukherjee wrongly debited by Bank to Sri Ghosh A/c	500	
			65,000
	Bank Balance as per Pass Book		51,550

(b) Taking balance as per Pass Book (Favourable)

If balance as per Pass Book is given, our duty is to find out the balance as per Cash Book. In that case, our duty is to see what has been done by the Cash Book for each individual item we are to follow it, i.e., if it is found that the Cash Book balance has been increased by that amount, we will simply 'add' the amount, and vice versa.

Some of the items are given :

Add : (The items which will increase the Cash Book balance)

(i) Bank charges not recorded in Cash Book; (ii) Cheque deposited but not credited; (iii) Debit side of the Cash Book was overcast; (iv) Dishonoured cheque appeared in the Pass book but not entered in Cash Book; (v) Bank met a bill payable but not recorded in Cash Book.

Less : (i) Cheque received but not presented; (ii) Interest credited by bank not recorded in Cash Book; (iii) Dividend collected by bank but not recorded in Cash Book; (iv) Debtors directly deposited into bank not entered in Cash Book; (v) Bank charges (postal) recorded twice in Cash Book.

Illustration 4

From the following particulars, prepare a Bank Reconciliation Statement, showing the balance as per Cash Book on 31st March 2010 :

		Rs.
(a)	Balance as per Pass Book	8,000
(b)	Cheques deposited but not credited by the Bank	1,000
(c)	Cheques issued but not presented for payment	500
(d)	Cheques deposited into Bank without recording in Cash Book	600
(e)	Cheques issued to Creditors but not recorded in Cash Book	700
(f)	Dividend collected by Bank, not recorded in Cash Book	100
(g)	Debtors directly deposited into Bank but not recorded in Cash Book	2,000
(h)	Debit side of the Cash Book was undercast by	1,000
(i)	Bank charges debited in Pass Book, not recorded in Cash Book	50
(j)	Bank met a Bill Payable for Rs. 1,000 on 30.3.2010 under advice to the firm on 2.4.2010	—
(k)	A bill for Rs. 2,000 discounted for Rs. 1,900 returned dishonoured by Bank, noting charge being	10
(l)	A bill for Rs. 1,000 discounted with the Bank is entered in the Cash Book without recording the discounting charges	100

Solution

Bank Reconciliation Statement
as at 31st March 2010

		Amount Rs.	Amount Rs.
	Bank Balance as per Pass Book		8,000
Add :	Cheques deposited but not credited by the Bank	1,000	
	Cheques issued to creditors but not recorded in Cash Book	700	
	Bank charges debited in the Pass Book, but not entered in Cash Book	50	
	Bank met a Bill Payable, not recorded in Cash Book	1,000	
	Bills discounted and dishonoured, not entered in Cash Book	2,010	
	A bill discounted by the Bank without recording the discounting charges	100	4,860
			12,860
Less :	Cheques issued but not presented for payment	500	
	Cheques deposited into Bank without recording in Cash Book	600	
	Dividend collected by Bank, not recorded in Cash Book	100	
	Debtors directly deposited into Bank not recorded in Cash Book	2,000	
	Debit side of the Cash Book was undercast	1,000	4,200
	Bank Balance as per Cash Book		8,660

(c) Taking Overdraft as per Cash Book :

If overdraft as per Cash Book is given, our duty is to find out the overdraft balance as per Pass Book. In that case, we are to see what has been done by the Cash Book for each individual item; we are to follow it, i.e., if it is found that the Cash Book balance (Cr.) has increased by that amount, we will simply 'add' the amount, and vice versa. It is to be remembered that there will be no change in principle for overdraft balances.

Some of the items are given :

Add : (The items which will increase the Cash Book overdraft (Cr.) balance.)

(i) Cheques paid/deposited into bank but not credited; (ii) Bank met a pay order as per standing instruction, not entered in Cash Book; (iii) Bank charges debited in Pass Book, but not in Cash Book; (iv) Bank charges interest on overdraft but not recorded in Cash Book; (v) Cheques deposited and dishonoured but not recorded in Cash Book.

Less :

(i) Cheques issued/drawn but not presented; (ii) Direct deposit made by customers into bank not recorded in Cash Book; (iii) Bank collected dividend or any income not entered in Cash Book; (iv) Interest on overdraft recorded in Cash Book but not entered in Pass Book; (v) Credit side of the Cash Book was overcast.

Illustration 5

From the following particulars, prepare the Bank Reconciliation Statement :

		Rs.
(i)	Bank overdraft as per the Cash Book	16,200
(ii)	A cheque deposited as per Bank Statement but not recorded in the Cash book	700
(iii)	Debit side of the Bank Column cast short	100
(iv)	A cheque for Rs. 5,000 deposited but collection as per the Bank Statement	4,996
(v)	A party's cheque returned dishonoured as per the Bank Statement only	530
(vi)	Bills collected directly by the bank	3,500
(vii)	Bank charges recorded twice in the Cash Book	25
(viii)	A bill for Rs. 8,000 discounted for Rs. 7,960 returned dishonoured by the bank, noting charges being	15
(ix)	Cheques deposited but not yet collected by the bank	2,320
(x)	Cheques issued but not yet presented for encashment	1,250

Solution **[CU BCom (Hons.)]**

Bank Reconciliation Statement as at ......

			Amount Rs.	Amount Rs.
		Bank Overdraft per the Cash Book		16,200
Add :	(iv)	Cheque for Rs. 5,000 deposited but collection as per Bank Statement Rs. 4,996	4	
	(v)	Cheque returned dichonoured as per the Bank Statement not entered in Cash Book	530	
	(vii)	Bills for Rs. 8,000 discounted for Rs. 7,960 returned dishonoured by the bank, noting charges being Rs. 15	8,015	
	(ix)	Cheque deposited but not collected by bank	2,320	10,869
				27,069
Less :	(ii)	Cheque deposited but not recorded in the Cash Book	700	
	(iii)	Debit side of the bank column cash short	100	
	(vi)	Bills collected directly by the bank not entered in Cash Book	3,500	
	(vii)	Bank charges recorded twice in the Cash Book	25	
	(x)	Cheques issued but not presented for payment	1,250	5,575
		Bank overdraft as per the Pass Book		21,494

Illustration 6

On December 31, 2010, my Cash Book showed a bank overdraft of Rs. 49,350. On going through the bank Pass Book for reconciling the balance, I find the following :

Out of cheques drawn on Dec. 2010, those for Rs. 3,700 were cashed by the bankers on Jan. 2, 2011, and a crossed cheque for Rs. 750 was given to Judy, was returned by her and a bearer one was issued to her in lieu on Jan. 1, 2011.

Cash and cheques amounting to Rs. 3,400 were deposited in bank on Dec. 29, 2010 but cheques worth Rs. 1,300 were cleared by the bank on Jan. 1, 2011, and one cheque for Rs. 250 was returned by them as dishonoured on the latter date.

According to my standing orders, the bankers have, on Dec. 31, 2011, paid Rs. 320 as interest to my creditor, paid quarterly premium on my policy account to Rs. 160 and have paid a second call for Rs. 600 on shares held by me and lodged with the bankers for safe custody. They have also received Rs. 150 as dividend on my shares and recovered an Insurance claim of Rs. 800, their charges and commission on the above being Rs. 15. On receipt on information of the above transactions, I have passed necessary entries in my Cash Book on Jan. 1, 2011.

My bankers seem to have given me a wrong credit for Rs. 500 paid in by me in No. 2 account, and a wrong debit in respect of a cheque for Rs. 300 drawn against my No. 2 account.

Prepare a Reconciliation Statement as on Dec. 2010.

Solution

Bank Reconciliation Statement

as at 31st Dec. 2010

		Amount Rs.	*Amount* Rs.
	Overdraft as per Cash Book		49,350
Add :	Cheques deposited into bank but not credited (1,300 + 250)	1,550	
	Bank paid Interest Insurance premium and call money, not entered in Cash Book (320 + 160 + 600)	1,080	
	Wrong debit made by bank	300	2,930
			52,280
Less :	Cheques drawn but not cashed (3,700 + 750)	4,450	
	Bank received dividend and recovered Insurance claim, not entered in the Cash Book (150 + 800 – 15)	935	
	Wrong credit made by bank	500	
			5,885
	Overdraft as per Pass Book		46,395

Illustration 7

On checking P's Cash Book with the Bank Statement of his Current Account for the month of March 2010, you find:

(i) Cash Book showed an Overdraft of Rs. 4,500.

(ii) The payment side of the Cash Book has been undercast by Rs. 150.

(iii) A cheque of Rs. 750 drawn on Current Account has been shown as drawn on his Savings Account in the Cash Book.

(iv) Under instructions from Mr. P the Bank had transferred interest Rs. 900 from his Deposit Account to his Current Account on 3rd April 2010. This amount had, however, been recorded in the Cash book before 31st March 2010.

(v) Cheques amounting to Rs. 7,500 drawn and entered in the Cash Book had not been presented.

(vi) Cheques amounting to Rs. 6,000 sent to the bank for collection, though entered in the Cash Book, had not been credited by the Bank.

(vii) Bank Charges of Rs. 75 as per Bank Statement had not been taken in the Cash Book.

(viii) Dividends of Rs. 3,000 had been paid direct to the Bank and not entered in Cash Book.

(ix) A cheque issued to R for Rs. 200 was replaced when out of date, but it was entered in the Cash Book again and no other entry have been recorded. Both the cheques were also included in the total of cheques issued but not presented as shown above.

You are required to arrive at the balance, as it would appear in the bank statement as on 31st March 2010

Solution

Bank Reconciliation Statement
as at March 2010

		Amount Rs.	Amount Rs.
	Overdraft as per Cash Book		4,500
Add :	Payment side of the Cash Book has been undercast	150	
	Cheque drawn on Current A/c, wrongly drawn from Savings A/c	750	
	Interest on Deposit A/c transferred, not entered in Pass Book	900	
	Cheques Deposited but not credited	6,000	
	Bank charges not entered in Cash Book	75	
			7,875
			12,375
Less :	Cheques deposited but not credited	7,500	
	Dividend collected by bank and credited in Pass Book but not in Cash Book	3,000	
			10,500
	Overdraft as per Pass Book		1,875

Note : For item (ix) : There will be no effect in Bank Reconciliation Statement as the same has already been included in item (v).

Illustration 8

From the following particulars prepare a Bank Reconciliation Statement for Sri S. Sarkar as at 31st December 2010 :

(a) Bank Balance as per Cash Book (Cr.) — Rs. 610.
(b) Cheques issued but not presented—Rs. 3,000.
(c) Cheques deposited but not credited by bank—Rs. 2,500.
(d) A cheque drawn for Rs. 100 had been incorrectly entered as Rs. 10 in the Cash Book.
(e) A debtor directly deposited into Sarkar's Bank Account, but not recorded in Cash Book—Rs. 1,000.
(f) Credit side of the Cash Book (Bank Column) was undercast by Rs. 500.
(g) A cheque for Rs. 5,000 drawn by Mr. Banerjee has been charged to Sri Sarkar's account in error.
(h) Bank paid a Bill Payable for Rs. 1,450 but it was recorded in Cash Book as Rs. 1,540.
(i) The receipt column of the Cash Book has been over cast Rs. 1,000.
(j) Discount allowed Rs. 410 has been entered through mistake with the cheque in the Bank Column of the Cash Book.
(k) Pursuant to instruction dated 30th Dec. 2010, asking the banker to transfer Rs. 10,000 of Fixed Deposit Account; entry for this was made in the Cash Book but the Bank acted on Jan. 2011.
(l) The Bank debited the account for Rs. 500 being the amount of a cheque received from a customer and returned dishonoured but not entered in Cash Book.
(m) Cheque amounting to Rs. 300, though actually banked, was not entered in Cash Book.
(n) The bank pass Book shows a favourable balance of Rs. 3,780.

Solution

Bank Reconciliation Statement
as at 31st Dec. 2010

		Amount Rs.	Amount Rs.
	Bank Balance as per Cash Book (Cr.)		610
Add :	Cheques deposited but not credited by the Bank	2,500	
	Cheque drawn for Rs. 100 but recorded only Rs. 10 in the Cash Book	90	
	Credit side of the Cash book was undercast	500	
	Bank wrongly debited Sarker's Account	5,000	
	Receipt column of the Cash Book was overcast	1,000	
	Discount Allowed Rs. 410 has been entered through mistake with the cheque in the Bank column of the Cash Book	410	*Contd.*

		Rs.	Rs.
	Bank debited for a dishonoured cheque, not entered in Cash Book	500	
			10,000
			10,610
Less :	Cheques issued but not presented.	3,000	
	A debtor directly deposited into bank but not recorded in Cash Book	1,000	
	Bank paid Rs. 1,450 against a B/P, but recorded in Cash Book as Rs. 1,540	90	
	Transfer to Fixed Deposit Account not recorded in Pass Book	10,000	
	Cheques deposited but not recorded in Cash Book	300	
			14,390
	Bank Balance as per Pass Book (Cr.)		3,780[1]

Note : 1 In this case, it is found that the sum total of subtractions (Less) is more than the sum total of additions (Add) which indicates opposite balance, i.e., favourable although it was started with an unfavourable balance.

Illustration 9

On 30th November 2011, the Cash Book of Khagen Paul showed a debit balance on the current account with the Scottish Bank Ltd. of Rs. 56,200. The Bank Statement at that date showed a balance due to the bank of Rs. 55,360.

The following additional information has been obtained :

(a) The credit side of the Cash Book for June 2011 does not cross—add, the error being the over-statement of the bank drawn column by Rs. 2,370.

(b) A deposit receipt for Rs. 40,000 was uplifted on 1st October 2011 with interest thereon for Rs. 4,400. Rs. 30,000 was relodged on deposit receipt and the balance lodged in the current account. No entries have been made in the books in respect of these transactions.

(c) The Cash Book includes an entry for a cheque for Rs. 5,340 received from a customer in October 2011. The cheque was, however, post-dated and was still held by the cashier on 30th November 2011.

(d) No entries have been made in the Cash Book in respect of bond interest payments made by standing order amounting to Rs. 1,250 per month. The payments are due on the first of each month commencing on 1st April 2011 and all payments have been made on the due dates.

(e) A bill of exchange was received from a customer of Rs. 71,190 which was the balance due by the customer as shown by his sales ledger account. The bill was discounted with the bank, the sum of Rs. 63,000 being received and lodged in the current account. The cashier has entered the bill at its full value in the Cash Book.

(f) No entries have been made in the books in respect of bank overdraft interest and bank charges of Rs. 7,010 and Rs. 670, respectively, debited by the bank during the year, while amounts of Rs. 2,670 and Rs. 530, respectively, were accrued but unapplied as at 30th November 2011.

(g) Amounts totalling Rs. 48,870 received from customers by credit transfer during the year have not been recorded in the Cash Book.

(h) The following bank lodgements have been entered in the Cash Book as having been made prior to 1st December 2011 :

Pay-in-slip dated	Credited on bank statement	Amount of lodgement Rs.
29th November 2011	30th November 2011	1,66,210
30th November 2011	1st December 2011	1,31,570
1st December 2011	2nd December 2011	1,24,180

(i) Cheque payments amounting to Rs. 1,09,760 including cheques for Rs. 6,310 that were outstanding at 30th November 2010, had not been debited on the bank statement by 30th November 2011.

Prepare a Bank Reconciliation Statement at 30th November 2011.

Solution

Bank Reconciliation Statement
as at 30th November 2011

			Amount Rs.	Amount Rs.
		Balance as per the Cash Book		56,200
Add :	(a)	Overstatement in bank drawn column done by the Cash Book	2,370	
	(b)	Amount lodged in current account not recorded in the Cash Book (Rs. 40,000 – Rs. 4,400 + Rs. 30,000)	14,400	
	(g)	Credit transfer by customers not recorded in the Cash Book	48,870	
	(i)	Cheque issued but not presented	1,09,760	
				1,75,400
				2,31,600
Less :	(c)	Post-dated cheque recorded in the Cash Book but not deposited in the Bank	5,340	
	(d)	Payment of Interest recorded in the Cash Book (Rs. 1,250 × 8)	10,000	
	(e)	Bill amount wrongly entered in the Cash Book as Rs. 71,190 in place of Rs. 63,000	8,190	
	(f)	Interest on overdraft and Bank charges not recorded in the Cash Book (Rs. 7,010 + Rs. 670)	7,680	
	(h)	Cheque deposited but not credited by the Bank (Rs. 1,31,570 + Rs. 1,24,180)	2,55,750	
				2,86,960
		Overdraft as per Pass Book		55,360

(d) Taking Overdraft as per Pass Book

If overdraft as per Pass Book is given our duty is to find out the overdraft balance as per Cash Book. In that case, our duty is to see what has been done by the Cash Book for each individual item, we are to follow it, i.e., if it is found that the Cash Book balance (Cr.) has been increased by that amount, we will simply 'add' the amount, and vice versa.

Some of the items are :

Add : (The items which will increase the Pass book overdraft (Dr.) balances)

(i) Cheques issued/drawn but not presented; (ii) Direct deposit made by customers into bank but not recorded in Cash Book; (iii) Bank collected dividend or any other income but not entered in Cash Book; (iv) Interest on overdraft recorded in Cash Book but not in Pass Book; (v) Credit side of the Cash Book was overcast.

Less :

(i) Cheques paid/deposited into bank but not credited; (ii) Bank met a pay order, but not entered in Cash Book; (iii) Bank Charges debited in Pass Book but not enterned in Cash Book; (iv) Bank charges interest on overdraft but not entered in Cash Book; (v) Cheque deposited but dishonoured but not recorded in Cash Book.

Illustration 10

Prepare a Bank Reconciliation Statement from the following data as on 30.11.2011 :

(i) Balance as per Pass Book on 30.11.2011, overdrawn Rs. 9,204.

(ii) Cheques drawn on 30.11.2011 but not cleared till Dec. 2011, Rs. 3,225; Rs. 745 and Rs. 926.

(iii) Bank Overdraft interest charged on 28.11.2011, not entered in Cash Book Rs. 1,610.

(iv) Cheques received on 29.11.2011 entered in Cash Book but not deposited to Bank till 3rd December 2011, Rs. 11,322 and Rs. 1,730.

(v) Cheque received amounting to Rs. 35 entered in the Cash Book twice.

(vi) Bills Receivable due on 29.11.2011 was sent to Bank for collection on 28.11.2011, and was entered in Cash Book forthwith but the proceeds were not credited in Bank Pass Book till 3rd Dec. 2011, Rs. 2,980.

(vii) A periodic payment by Bank for Rs. 80 under standing instruction not entered in Cash Book.

(viii) Cheque deposited on 30th Nov. 2011 dishonoured but the entry, therefore, was not made in the Cash Book Rs. 1,890.

[ICWA]

Solution

Bank Reconciliation Statement

as at 30th Nov. 2011

		Amount	Amount
		Rs.	Rs.
	Overdraft Balance as per Pass Book (Dr.)		9,204
Add :	Cheques drawn but not cleared (Rs. 3,225 + Rs. 745 + Rs. 926)	4,896	4,896
			14,100
Less :	Interest on Bank overdraft not entered in Cash Book	1,610	
	Cheques received and entered in the Cash Books as deposited into Bank but actually not deposited till 3rd Dec. 2011. (Rs. 11,322 + Rs. 1,730)	13,052	
	Cheque received and entered in the Cash Book twice	35	
	Bills sent to Bank for collection but not credited till 3rd Dec. 2011	2,980	
	A periodic payment made by bank not entered in Cash Book	80	
	Cheques deposited and dishnoured but not entered in Cash Book	1,890	19,647
	Bank Balance as per Cash Book (Dr.)		5,547

Illustration 11

When comparing the Cash Book of Shri C. Basu, with the Bank Pass Book on 31.12.2011, you observed the following :

(i) The Bank Pass Book showed a Debit Balance of Rs. 15,000

(ii) The total of the credit side of the Cash Book on 25.12.2011 ought to have been Rs. 1,600 instead of Rs. 2,600 and the incorrect figure was brought forward.

(iii) Cheques issued amounted to Rs. 5,500 but of these only Rs. 5,000 were presented for payment within 31.12.2011.

(iv) A Debtor directly deposited into Basu's Bank Account on 25th Dec. but not recorded at all in the Cash Book Rs. 1,000.

(v) The credit balance of Cash Book on a particular day Rs. 3,200 was wrongly carried forward to the debit of the next folio.

(vi) Dividend collected by Bank, but not recorded in Cash Book Rs. 1,000, whereas Bank charges Interest on overdraft Rs. 300, also not recorded in Cash Book.

(vii) Bank paid Insurance premium Rs. 200, but recorded in Cash Book Rs. 20 only.

Prepare a Bank Reconciliation Statement.

Solution

Bank Reconciliation Statement

as at 31st December 2011

		Amount	Amount
		Rs.	Rs.
	Overdraft balance as per Pass Book (Dr.)		15,000
Add :	The total of the credit side of the Cash Book ought to have been Rs. 1,600 instead of Rs. 2,600 and the incorrect figure was brought forward (i.e., Rs. 2,600 – 1,600)	1,000	
	Cheque issued but not presented for payment (Rs. 5,500 – Rs. 5,000)	500	
	A debtor directly deposited into bank', but not, recorded in Cash Book	1,000	
	Dividend collected by bank but not recorded in Cash Book	1,000	3,500
			18,500
Less :	The credit balance of Cash Book of Rs. 3,200 was carried forward to the debit of the next folio (Rs. 3,200 × 2) (since it affects the Cash Book in Double amount)	6,400	
	Bank Charges not recorded in Cash Book	300	
	Bank paid Insurance premium Rs. 200 but Cash Book records only Rs. 20 (Rs. 200 – Rs. 20)	180	
			6,880
	Overdraft balance as per Cash Book (Cr.)		11,620

(e) Where there are Two Bank Accounts

Sometimes a business maintains two separate accounts either in a bank or in a different bank. Problem arises when there is inter-transfer of transaction between the two accounts or wrong posting of transactions in the two accounts. For example, a cheque is deposited into Bank Account No. I, but the same is credited by the bank in Account II, or vice-versa. Similarly, when a cheque is issued to a party from Account II, the same is wrongly posted in Account I by the bank or vice versa. In that case, we are to prepare two Bank Reconciliation Statements separately in order to find out the correct balance lying at the bank. These problems may arise if both the accounts are opened in a bank. But, if the accounts are opened in two different banks, the said problems may be avoided by the bank. But, in that case, the errors may be committed by the cashier or the persons who is responsible to prepare the Cash Book.

Illustration 12

Perfect Pvt. Ltd. has two accounts with Ever Bank Ltd. The accounts were known as Account I and Account II. As at Dec 31, 2011, the balance as per A/c books reflected the following :

Account I Rs. 1,25,000 Regular balance

Account II Rs. 1,11,250 Overdraft balance.

The accountant failed to tally the balances with the Pass Book and the following information was available:

(a) The Bank has charged Interest on Account II Rs. 11,375 and credited Interest on Account I Rs. 1,250. These were not recorded by the accountant.

(b) Rs. 12,500 drawn on Dec. 10, 2011 from Account I was recorded in the books of Account II.

(c) Bank charges of Rs. 150 and Rs. 1,125 for Account I and Account II were not recorded in the books.

(d) A deposit of Rs. 17,500 in Account I was wrongly entered in Account II in the books.

(e) Two cheques of Rs. 12,500 and Rs. 13,750 deposited in Account I, but entered in Account II in the books, were dishonoured. The entries for dishonoured cheques were entered correctly in Account II.

(f) Cheques issued for Rs. 1,50,000 and Rs. 15,000 from Accounts I and II, respectively, were, not presented until Jan. 5, 2011.

(g) Cheques deposited Rs. 1,25,000 and Rs. 1,17,500 in Accounts I and II, respectively, were credited by bank on Feb. 2, 2011.

You are required to prepare the Bank Reconciliation Statement for Accounts I and II.

Solution **[ICWA]**

Bank Reconciliation Statement—(Account-I)

as at 31st December 2011

		Amount Rs.	*Amount* Rs.
	Bank balance as per Cash Book		1,25,000
Add :	Interest earned but not recorded in Cash Book	1,250	
	A deposit made into Account I wrongly entered in Account II	17,500	
	Cheques deposited but not entered (Rs. 12,500 + Rs. 13,750)	26,250	
	Cheques issued but not presented for payment	1,50,000	1,95,000
			3,20,000
Less:	A withdrawal from Account I wrongly recorded in Account II	12,500	
	Bank charges debited in Pass Book but not entered in Cash Book	150	
	Cheques dishonoured but not recorded in Cash Book (Rs. 12,500 + Rs. 13,750).	26,250	
	Cheques deposited but not credited by the Bank	1,25,000	1,63,900
	Bank Balance as per Pass Book		1,56,100

Bank Reconciliation Statement—Account II

as at 31st December 2011

		Amount Rs.	*Amount* Rs.
	Overdraft balance as per Cash Book		1,11,250
Add :	Interest charged on overdraft but not entered in Cash Book	11,375	
	Bank charges debited by bank but not entered in Cash Book	1,125	*Contd.*

		Rs.	Rs.
	A deposit made with Account I Wrongly entered in Account II	17,500	
	Cheques deposited but not credited by the bank	1,17,500	1,47,500
			2,58,750
Less:	Withdrawal wrongly recorded	12,500	
	Cheque issued but not presented	15,000	
			27,500
	Overdraft balance as per Pass Book		2,31,250

B. Preparation of Bank Reconciliation Statement with Adjustments in Cash Book

We all know that the correct bank balance is necessary in order to ascertain the correct financial statements. Therefore, the Cash Book should be corrected or amended before preparing the Bank Reconciliation Statement. For this purpose, the Cash Book (bank column) will be amended which will contain the items either

(i) **Not recorded in Cash Book**

i.e., (i) Bank charges debited by bank, (ii) B/R or cheques dishonoured, (iii) Dividend collected by bank, (iv) Direct deposit made by customers, (v) Payment made by bank as per standing order.

(ii) **Any error made by Cash Book**

i.e., (i) Undercesting/overcasting in debit/credit side, (ii) Amount entered twice. (iii) Debit items in the credit side/credit items on the debit side.

Note : In short, the transactions which have already been recorded in cash book correctly will not appear any more in this amended Cash Book.

Naturally, we should ignore the transactions which had already been entered in Cash Book viz., (i) Cheques issued but not presented; (ii) Cheques deposited but not credited by the bank, (iii) Any error made by bank etc.

Having the correct balance from the amended Cash Book, a Bank Reconciliation Statement is prepared, which will include the remaining items viz.

(i) Cheques deposited into bank but not credited, (ii) Cheques issued but not credited, (iii) Any error committed by bank etc.

Note : **Adjustment or amendment of Cash Book is only possible provided the balance as per Cash Book is given (favourable or unfavorable).**

To sum-up

1. ***Open the Cash Book (Bank column) with the opening balance (i.e.,favourable balance on the debit side) (To Balance b/d) and unfavourable balance on the credit side (By Balance b/d), respectively.***
2. ***Adjust the necessary items (either which were not at all recorded in the Cash Book, or any error done by the Cash Book) accordingly after making necessary corrections in the Cash Book.***
3. ***Find out the balance of the Cash Book and bring down such balance.***
4. ***By taking that balance of the said amended Cash Book, prepare a Bank Reconciliation Statement. (It must be remembered here that those items which had already been recorded in the amended Cash Book will not appear any more in the Bank Reconciliation Statement.)***

(f) With Amendments in Cash Book

(a) Where there is a favourable balance

Illustration 13

On Dec. 31, 2011, the bank column of the Cash Book of P shows a debit balance of Rs. 922. On examination of the Cash Book and statement you find that :

(i) Cheques amounting to Rs. 1,260 issued before Dec. 31 and entered in Cash Book were not presented for payment till after that date.

(ii) Cheques amounting to Rs. 500 entered in the Cash Book as sent to bank on Dec. 31 were entered in the Bank Statement after that date.

(iii) A cheque from a Debtor for Rs. 146 had been dishonoured prior to Dec. 31 but no record appeared in the Cash Book.

(iv) A dividend warrant for Rs. 76 was paid direct to the bank and nothing appeared in Cash Book.
(v) Bank Interest and Charges amounting to Rs. 84 were not entered in the Cash Book but appeared in the Bank Statement.
(vi) There was no entry in the Cash Book for a club membership subscription Rs. 20 paid by banker's order in November 2011.
(vii) Bank's charges (postal) for a chèque book received by P of Rs. 2 was entered in the Cash Book twice.
(viii) A cheque for Rs. 54 drawn by Q had been charged to P's account in error.

Prepare a Bank Reconciliation Statement : (i) Without adjusting in Cash Book, and (ii) With adjustment in Cash Book, to bring down the correct balance and prepare a statement reconciling the correct Cash Book balance with the balance as per Bank Statement.

Solution

(i)

Bank Reconciliation Statement
as at 31st December 2011

		Amount Rs.	Amount Rs.
	Balance as per Cash Book		922
Add :	Cheques issued but not presented	1,260	
	Dividend collected by bank not entered in Cash Book	76	
	Bank Charges recorded twice in Cash Book	2	1,338
			2,260
Less :	Cheques sent to bank but not credited by bank	500	
	Cheques drawn by Q but charged to P's A/c in error by bank	54	
	Cheque received from a debtor returned dishonoured	146	
	Bank Interest and Charges not entered in Cash Book	84	
	Club membership subscription paid by bank but not recorded in Cash Book	20	804
	Balance as per Pass Book		1,456

(ii)

In the books of P
Cash Book *(Bank Column only)*

Dr. Date		Particulars	Amount	Cr. Date		Particulars	Amount
2011			Rs.	2011			Rs.
Dec. 31	To	Balance b/d	922	Dec. 31	By	Debtors A/c (Cheque dishonoured)	146
31	To	Dividend A/c	76	31	"	Bank Interest and Charges	84
31	"	Bank Charges A/c (cancellation of wrong entry)	2	31	"	Drawing (club membership subscription)	20
					"	Balance c/d	750
			1,000				1,000
2012							
Jan. 1	To	Balance b/d	750				

Bank Reconciliation Statement
as at 31st Dec. 2011

		Amount Rs.	Amount Rs.
	Bank Balance as per Cash Book (as amended) Dr.		750
Add :	Cheques issued but not presented for payment within 31st Dec. 2011	1,260	1,260
			2,010
Less :	Cheques sent to Bank but not credited by the Bank within 31st Dec. 2011	500	
	Cheques drawn by Q but charged to P's A/c in error by Bank	54	554
	Bank Balance as per Pass Book		1,456

Analysis and Interpretation

Items Nos.

(i) Since it has been recorded in the Cash Book, it will not appear in amended Cash Book, the same will appear in Bank Reconciliation Statement only.

(ii) It has also been recorded in the Cash Book. So the same will not appear in amended Cash Book, but will appear only in Bank Reconciliation Statement.

(iii) Since it has not been recorded in Cash Book, it will be recorded in amended Cash Book in the credit side. Debtors Account will be debited and Bank Account will be credited.

(iv) Since it has not been recorded in the Cash Book, it will be recorded in amended Cash Book. Thus an adjustment is required : Bank Account will be debited and Dividend Account will be credited.

(v) This item also requires adjustment since the same was not recorded in Cash Book. It will be recorded in the credit side of the Amended Cash Book. Bank Charges Account will be debited and Bank Account will be credited.

(vi) This item also requires adjustment since the same did not appear in Cash Book. It will be recorded in the credit side of the Amended Cash Book. Drawings Amount will be debited and Bank Account will be credited for the pupose.

(vii) This is an error, so it requires adjustment. Since it has been recorded twice in the credit side of the Cash Book, Rs. 2 should be written on the debit side of the amended Cash Book for correction.

(viii) This is an error committed by the Bank. So, it will appear in the Bank Reconciliation Statement. As Pass Book balance has been reduced, it will also be reduced i.e., it will be 'less'.

Note : ***It is interesting to note that the result of the Bank Reconciliation Statement must be the same whether it is prepared under : (i) Without adjustment in Cash Book, or (ii) With adjustment in Cash Book Methods.***

Illustration 14

When Sweetex Ltd. received its Bank Statement for the period ended 30th June 2011, this did not agree with the balance shown in the Cash Book of Rs. 2,972 in the Company's favour.

An examination of the Cash Book and Bank Statement disclosed:

(a) A deposit of Rs. 492 paid on 29th June 2011, had not been credited by the bank until 1st July 2011.

(b) Bank Charges amounting to Rs. 17 had not been entered in the Cash Book.

(c) A debit of Rs. 42 appeared on the Bank Statement for an unpaid cheque which had been returned marked *"out of date"*. The cheque had been re-dated by the customer of Sweetex Ltd. and paid into the Bank again on 3rd July 2011.

(d) A standing order for payment of an annual subscription amounting to Rs. 10 had not been entered in the Cash Book.

(e) On 25th June, the Managing Director had given the Cashier a cheque for Rs. 100 to pay into his personal account at the Bank. The Cashier had paid into the Company's account by mistake.

(f) On 27th June, two customers of Sweetex Ltd. had paid direct to the Company's Bank account Rs. 499 and Rs. 157, respectively, in payment for goods supplied. The advices were not received by the company until 1st July and were entered in the Cash Book under that date.

(g) On 30th March 2011, the company had entered into a hire-purchase agreement, to pay by banker's order a sum of Rs. 26 on the 10th day of each month, commencing from April. No entries had been made in the Cash Book.

(h) A cheque for Rs. 364, received from Mr. B and paid into the Bank, had been entered twice in the Cash Book.

(i) Cheques issued amounting to Rs. 4,672 had not been presented to the bank for payment until after 30th June 2011.

(j) A customer of the company who received a Cash discount of $2\frac{1}{2}$ % on his account of Rs. 200, paid the company a cheque on 10th June. The Cashier, in error, entered the gross amount in the bank column of the Cash Book.

After making the adjustments required by the foregoing, the Bank statement reconciled with the balance in the Cash Book.

You are required :

(i) To show the necessary adjustments in the Cash Book of Sweetext Ltd. bringing down the correct balance on 30th June 2011 (ii) To prepare a Bank Reconciliation Statement as on that date.

Solution

In the books of
Sweetex Ltd.
Cash Book (Bank Column only)

Dr. Cr.

Date	*Particulars*	*Amount*	*Date*	*Particulars*	*Amount*
2011		Rs.	2011		Rs.
June 30	To Balance b/d	2,972	June 30	By Bank Charges A/c	17
	" Debtors' A/c (direct deposit) (Rs. 499 + Rs. 157)	656		" Annual Subscription A/c	10
				" Hire-Purchase A/c Vendor (26 × 3)	78
				" B. A/c (Cheque wrongly debited twice)	364
				" Discount allowed A/c (Rs. 200 × $2\frac{1}{2}$ %)	5
				" Balance c/d	3,154
		3,628			3,628
July 1	To Balance c/d	3,154			

Note : There will be no entry in the amended Cash Book for the Managing Director's cheque which was wrongly deposited by the cashier on the assumption that the same was not recorded in Cash Book and, therefore, no amendment is necessary in Cash Book, only Rs. 100 to be added to Bank Reconciliation Statement.

Bank Reconciliation Statement
as at 30th June 2011

		Amount	*Amount*
		Rs.	Rs.
	Balance as per Cash Book (amended)		3,154
Add :	Cheque issued but not presented	4,672	
	Cheque issued for Managing Director, but not presented for payment	100	4,772
			7,926
Less :	Amount deposited but not credited by bank	492	
	Cheque returned out of date and re-deposited after re-dating	42	534
	Balance as per Pass Book		7,392

(b) Where there is an Unfavourable Balance

Illustration 15

On 30th June, 2011, Sri C. Chanda's Cash Book showed that he had an overdraft of Rs. 300 on his Current Account at the Bank.

On checking the Cash Book with the bank statement you find:

(1) Cheques drawn, amounting to Rs. 500, had been entered in the Cash Book but had not been presented.

(2) Cheques received, amounting to Rs. 400, had been entered in the Cash Book but had not been credited by the bank.

(3) On instructions from Sri C. Chanda the bank had transferred interest, Rs. 60 from his deposit account to his current account, recording the transfer on 5th July 2011. This amount had, however, been credited in the Cash Book as on 30th June 2011.

(4) Bank Charges, Rs. 35, shown in the statement had not been entered in the Cash Book.

(5) The payment side of the Cash Book had been undercast by Rs. 10.
(6) Dividends amounting to Rs. 200 had been paid direct to the bank and not entered in the Cash Book.
(7) A cheque, Rs. 50, drawn on deposit account had been shown in the Cash Book as drawn on current account.
(8) A cheque issued to Sri B. Banerjee for Rs. 25 was replaced when out of date. It was entered again in the Cash Book—no other entry being made. Both cheques were included in the total of unpresented cheques shown above.

You are required :

(a) To indicate the appropriate adjustments in the Cash Book, and (b) To prepare a statement reconciling the amended balance with that shown in the bank statement.

Solution **[ICWA]**

In the books of C. Chanda
Cash Book *(Bank Column only)*

Dr. Date	Particulars	Amount	Date	Particulars	Amount *Cr.*
2011		Rs.	2011		Rs.
June. 30	To Bank Interest A/c (Rs. 60 for cancellation wrong positng + Rs. 60 for correct one)	120	June. 30	By Balance b/d	300
	" Dividend A/c	200		" Bank Charges A/c	35
	" Error — cheque drawn Deposit A/c (written-back)	50		" Error—Undercasting	10
	" Error — Cheque issued Banerjee	25		" Balance c/d	50
		395			395
July 1	To Balance b/d	50			

Bank Reconciliation Statement
as at 30th June 2011

	Amount	Amount
	Rs.	Rs.
Balance as per Cash Book		50
Add : Cheque issued but not presented (500 – 25)	475	475
		525
Less ; Cheque paid in but not credited	400	
Bank Interest transferred from Deposit A/c	60	460
∴ Balance as per Pass Book		65

Illustration 16

The following is a summary of a Cash Book, as presented to you for the month of Dec. 2011 :

	Rs.		Rs.
Receipts	1,469	Balance b/d	761
Balance c/d	554	Payments	1,262
	2,023		2,023

All receipts are banked and payments made by cheque. On investigation you discover :

1. Bank Charge of Rs. 136, entered in the bank statement, had not been entered in the Cash Book.
2. Cheques drawn, amounting to Rs. 267, had not been presented to the bank for payment.
3. Cheques received, totalling Rs. 762, had been entered in the Cash Book and paid into Bank, but had not been credited by the Bank until Jan. 2012.
4. A cheque for Rs. 22 had been entered as a receipt in the Cash Book instead of as a payment.
5. A cheque for Rs. 25 had been debited by the Bank in error.
6. A cheque received for Rs. 80 had been returned by the Bank and marked *"No funds available"*. No adjustment had been made in the Cash Book.

7. All dividends receivable are credited directly to the Bank Account. During December, amount totalling Rs. 62 were credited by the Bank and no entries made in the Cash Book.
8. A Cheque drawn for Rs. 6 had been incorrectly entered in the Cash Book as Rs. 66.
9. The balance brought forward should have been Rs. 711.
10. The Bank statement as on 31st Dec. 2011 showed an Overdraft of Rs. 1,162.

You are required to :

(i) Show the adjustments required to the Cash Book; (ii) Prepare a Bank Reconciliation Statement as on 31.12.11.

Solution

In the books of … ……
Cash Book
(Bank Column only)

Dr. Cr.

Date	Particulars	Amount	Date	Particulars	Amount
2011		Rs.	2011		Rs.
Dec.	To Dividend A/c	62	Dec.	By Balance b/d	554
	" Creditors A/c (Cheque issued for Rs. 6 recorded as Rs. 66)	60		" Bank Charges A/c	136
	To Error— Wrong carry-forward (Rs. 761 – Rs. 711)	50		" Error— (Cheque issued but recorded as received 22 × 2)	44
	" Balance c/d	642		" Debtors A/c (Cheque returned)	80
		814			814
			2012 Jan. 1	By Balance b/d	642

Bank Reconciliation Statement
as at 31st Dec. 2011

	Amount	Amount
	Rs.	Rs.
Overdraft as per Cash Book (as amended)		642
Add : Cheque deposited but not credited	762	
Wrong debit made By bank	25	787
		1,429
Less : Cheque drawn but not presented	267	267
Overdraft as per Pass Book		1,162

Illustration 17

Cash Book of Shri Madhab for the month ending 31st December 2011

Dr. **Cash Book (Bank Column)** Cr.

Date	Particulars	Amount	Date	Particulars	Amount
2011		Rs.	2011		Rs.
Dec. 19	To Cash	54,000	Dec. 10	By Balance b/d	60,000
24	" Buddha	36,000	8	" Ram	3,000
.26	" Chaitanya	15,000	10	" Lakshman	600
11	" Balanced c/d	11,460	19	" Bharat	360
			24	" Satrughna	52,500
		1,16,460			1,16,460

On receipt of the Bank Statement on 31st December, 2011, Shri Madav collected the following information :

(a) Credit transfer not recorded in the Cash Book Rs. 300.
(b) Interest on Government Bond collected by the bank but not entered in Cash Book Rs. 1,620.
(c) Cheques for Rs. 20,000 deposited but the bank collected only Rs. 5,000
(d) Dividend collected by the bank directly but not intimated the same to Shri Madhab Rs. 1,500.
(e) Bank Charges recorded twice in the Cash Book Rs. 510.
(f) Interest on overdraft charged by the bank but not entered in the Cash Book Rs. 1,500.
(g) Cheques for Rs. 66,100 issued by the trader but presented to the bank for payment only Rs. 10,000.

You are asked to amend the Cash Book and prepare a Bank Reconciliation Statement from the above information.

Solution **[CU BCom (Hons.)—1999 Adapted]**

In the books of Shri Madhab
Cash Book (Bank Column)

Date	Particulars	L.F.	Amount	Date	Particulars	L.F.	Amount
2011			Rs.	2011			Rs.
Dec. 31	To Credit Transfer		300	Dec. 31	By Balance b/d (Overdraft balance)		11,460
	" Interest on Govt. Bond A/c (Collected by Bank)		1,620		" Interest on Bank Overdraft A/c		1,500
	" Dividend (Collected by Bank)		1,500				
	" Bank Charges A/c (For recording twice)		510				
	" Balance c/d (bal fig.)		9,030				
			12,960				12,960
				Dec. 31	By Balance b/d		9,030

Bank Reconciliation Statement
as at 31st Dec. 2011

		Amount
		Rs.
	Overdraft as per Cash Book (as amended)	9,030
Add :	Cheque deposited into Bank but not yet collected by Bank and credited in the Pass Book (20,000 – 5,000)	15,000
		24,030
Less :	Cheques issued to the parties but not yet presented to the Bank for payment/collection (66,100 – 10,000)	56,100
	Bank Balance as per Pass Book (Cr.)	(–) 32,070

(g) Where There are Two Bank Accounts

Illustration 18

Sri A. Basu maintains two separate banking accounts, one with Untied Bank of India and the other with State Bank of India. On 31st Dec. 2011, the bank balances as per statement of United Bank of India and State Bank of India were Rs. 2,556 and Rs. 2,548, respectively. But the bank balances in Basu's books on the date were Rs. 2,870 (Dr.) and Rs. 4,680 (Dr.), respectively.

On scrutiny of these records following information was ascertained :

(a) A cheque of Rs. 250 from Sri D. Roy which was directly remitted to the United Bank of India was not entered in Basu's book.
(b) A cheque of Rs. 700, drawn on State Bank of India and paid to S & Co. was entered in the United Bank of India account in Basu's Cash Book.
(c) Payment of Rs. 1,020, by United Bank of India to Life Insurance Corporation of India under a standing order, was not recorded in Basu's Cash Book.

(d) Cheque lodged but not credited—Rs. 212, for United Bank of India and Rs. 1,600, for State Bank of India.

(e) A cheque for Rs. 57 paid in State Bank of India was returned dishonoured but this was not recorded in Basu's Book.

(f) Bank charges of Rs. 32 and 45, for United Bank of India and State Bank of India, respectively, were not accounted for by Sri Basu.

(g) Rs. 350 recorded to be deposited into State Bank of India on 30th Dec. 2011, was actually credited by the bank on 4.1.2012.

(h) There were no unpresented cheques except one for Rs. 620 drawn on State Bank of India.

Ascertain actual bank balance of Sri Basu on 31.12.2011 and prepare a Bank Reconciliation Statement.

Solution **[CU BCom (Hons.) Adapted]**

In the Books of Sri A. Basu

Dr. **Cash Book (*Bank Column only*)** *Cr.*

Date	*Particulars*	*U.B.I.*	*S.B.I.*	*Date*	*Particulars*	*U.B.I.*	*S.B.I.*
2011		Rs.	Rs.	2011		Rs.	Rs.
Dec. 31	To Balance b/d	2,870	4,680	Dec. 31	By U.B.I. (Cheque wrongly entered in S.B.I.)		700
	D. Roy A/c (Cheque directly deposited)	250			By Drawings A/c (L.I.C. Premium)	1,020	
	To S. B. I. Cheque wrongly entered in S. B. I.	700			" Debtors A/c		57
					" Bank Charges A/c	32	45
					" Balance c/d	2,768	3,878
		3,820	4,680			3,820	4,680
2012							
Jan. 1	To Balance b/d	2,768	3,878				

Bank Reconciliation Statement

as at 31st Dec. 2011

	U. B. I.	S. B. I.
	Rs.	Rs.
Bank Balance as per Cash Book	2,768	3,878
Add : Cheque issued but not presented	—	620
	2,768	4,498
Less : Cheque deposited but not credited	212	1,600
	2,556	2,898
Amount deposited but not yet credited	—	350
Bank Balance as per Pass Book	2,556	2,548

(h) Amendments of Cash Book after Reconciliation Statement

It has already been pointed out earlier that if the balance (favourable or unfavourable) as per Cash Book is not given, it is not possible for us to prepare an amended Cash book. In that case our first duty is to prepare a Bank Reconciliation Statement taking the balances (favourable or unfavourable) as per Pass Book and to find out the balance as per Cash Book. When the balance as per Cash Book is known, we can easily prepare an amended Cash Book by taking up that Cash Book balance.

The following illustration will make the principle clear :

Illustration 19

S, a merchant, maintains two bank accounts, No. 1 account is for his business, No. 2 account is his private account.

On June 30, 2011 there was a balance of Rs. 890 standing to his credit in No. 1 account as per Pass Book.

It was discovered that :

(a) The receipt column of the Cash Book has been overcast by Rs. 1,000.

(b) Cheques amounting to Rs. 3,760, entered in the Cash Book as paid into the bank, have not yet been cleared.

(c) Cheques issued, amounting to Rs. 5,230, have not been presented.

(d) Discount allowed Rs. 110 has been entered through mistake with the cheque in the bank column of the Cash Book.

(e) A credit note of Rs. 290 received from bank in June 2011 has not yet been recorded in the Cash Book.

(f) A cheque of Rs. 100, originally issued in 2010, was replaced when out of date and entered again in the Cash Book, no other entry being made therein. It was still outstanding (and not out of date) on June 30, 2011. Both the cheques were included in the total unpresented cheques of Rs. 5,230.

(g) The bank has charged the No. 2 account with a cheque for Rs. 2,000 in error. This should have been charged to No. 1 account.

You are required to prepare a Bank Reconciliation Statement of No. 1. account and then to show the necessary adjustments in Cash Book in bringing down the correct balance of No. 1 Account on 1st July 2011.

[CU BCom (Hons.)]

Solution

Bank Reconciliation Statement
as at 30th June 2011

		Amount	Amount
		Rs.	Rs.
	Bank Balance as per Pass Book		890
Add :	Amount overcasting in the receipt side of the Cash Book	1,000	
	Cheques deposited but not yet credited.	3,760	
	Discount allowed but wrongly entered in the Bank col of the Cash Book	110	
			4,870
			5,760
Less :	Cheques issued but not presented for payment (Rs. 5,230 – 100)	5,130	
	Cheques issued and entered twice in the Cash Book	100	
	Cheques issued but wrongly charged by the bank in No. 2 Account	2,000	
	Account credited by the bank as per Credit Note but not entered in the Cash Book	290	
			7,520
	Overdraft as per Cash Book		1,760

Cash Book
(Bank Column of No. 1 Account)

Dr. Cr.

Date	Particulars	Amount	Date	Particulars	Amount
2011		Rs.	2011		Rs.
June 30	To Party A/c adjustment	100	June 30	By Balance b/d (As per B. R. S.)	1,760
	" Party A/c (Cancellation of extra entry)	290		" Error—Overcasting	1,000
	" Balance c/d	2,480		" Discount Allowed A/c	110
		2,870			2,870
			2011		
			July 1	By Balance b/d	2,480

Illustration 20

Alexander furnishes you with the following information and asks you to:

(i) Recorded the transactions in the cash book with bank column for Nov. 2011, and

(ii) Prepare reconciliation statements with State Bank of India as on 31st October, and 30th November 2011.

(a) On October 31, 2011 there was bank overdraft of Rs. 14,000 as per Cash Book and cash in hand of Rs. 7,500.

Bank statement as on that date showed cheques deposited but not yet realised of Rs. 40,000 while cheques issued but not presented for payment amounted to Rs. 60,000.

(b) During the month, customers paid Rs. 4,50,000 which were deposited into bank. Of these, cheques of Rs. 50,000 were deposited on 30th November 2011 and realised subsequently. The bank realised all the other cheques and charged Rs. 300 as collection expenses. These charges are to be entered in the Cash Book and not kept as reconciliation item.

(c) Cheques issued during the month totalled to Rs. 4,20,000. Bank statement showed that cheques presented for payment totalled to Rs. 4,50,000 only of which one cheque of Rs. 7,000 issued in October 2011 was returned on 5.11.2011 for want of Alexander's signature on the cheque. Alexander paid cash to the payee of the cheque and cancelled the cheque. The bank charged Rs. 25 for cheque return.

(d) Cheques presented for payment during the month included cash withdrawn from bank Rs. 15,000. 40% of this cash is handed over on various dates to the petty cashier while 50% is taken by Alexander for his personal use.

(e) Bank charged Rs. 100 for cheque book issued.

Solution **[ICWA]**

Cash Book

Dr. *Cr.*

Date	Particulars	Cash	Bank	Date	Particulars	Cash	Bank
2011		Rs.	Rs.	2011		Rs.	Rs.
Nov. 30	To Balance b/d	7,500	—	Nov. 30	By Balance b/d	—	14,000
"	Customers A/c	—	4,50,000	"	Bank Charges	—	300
"	Suppliers A/c	—	7,000	"	Cash A/c	—	15,000
"	Bank A/c	15,000	—	"	Suppliers A/c	7,000	4,05,000[1]
				"	Petty Cash A/c	6,000	—
				"	Drawings A/c	7,500	—
				"	Bank Charges A/c		
					cheque return	—	25
					Cheque book	—	100
				"	Balance c/d	2,000	22,575
		22,500	4,57,000			22,500	4,57,000

Reconciliation Statement with State Bank of India
as on 31st October 2011

		Rs.
	Overdraft as per Cash Book	14,000
Add :	Cheques deposited but not yet realised	40,000
		54,000
Less :	Cheques issue but not yet presented for payment	60,000
	Balance as per bank statement (Favourable)	6,000

Reconciliation Statement with State Bank of India
as on 30th November 2011

		Rs.
	Balance as per Cash Book	22,575
Add :	Cheques issued but not yet presented for payment (Rs. 60,000 + Rs. 4,20,000 – Rs. 4,50,000)	30,000
		52,575
Less :	Cheques deposited but not yet realised (Rs. 4,50,000 – Rs. 4,00,000)	50,000
	Balance as per bank statement	2,575

Working Note :

1. Total withdrawals amounted to Rs. 4,20,000 which include Rs. 15,000; So, Rs. 4,20,000 – Rs. 15,000 = 4,05,000 was paid to creditors.
2. Of the amount of Rs. 15,000, 40% of Rs. 15,000 was given to Petty Cashier, 50%, i.e., 7,500 taken for personal use, balance 10% or 1,500 remained in Cash in hand.

(I) Where Cash Book and Pass Book are given

Needless to mention that where both the books are presented we are to analyse the two books and pick out the respective items which produce the difference between the two balances. The method actually depends on the *periods* for which the information is given.

To Sum up

1. ***Compare the debit side items of the Cash Book with the credit side items of Pass Book and put tick mark son those items which have already been recorded in both the books. Now unticked items of the credit side of the Pass Book indicate 'amounts credited by the bank but not recorded in the Pass Book which need reconciliation'. Similarly, unticked items of the debit side of the Cash Book indicate 'Amounts deposited but not credited by the bank, which also need necessary reconciliation.'***
2. ***Similarly, compare the credit side items of the Cash Book with the debit side items of the Pass Book and put similar tick mark s on those items which have already been recorded in both the books. Now unticked credit sides items of the Cash Book indicate 'cheques issued but not presented for payment' which need reconciliation. At the same time, unticked items of the debit side of the Pass Book reveal 'Amounts debited by the bank but not recorded in Cash Book, which also need reconciliation'.***

Consider the following example :

Cash Book
(Bank Column)*(Extract)*

Dr. Cr.

Date		*Particulars*	*J. F.*	*Amount*	*Date*		*Particulars*	*L. F.*	*Amount*
2010				Rs.	2010				Rs.
Jan. 1	To	Balanced b/d		5,000	Jan. 2	By	X Ltd. A/c		1,000
5	"	Ram A/c		1,000	6	"	Ram A/c		1,000
9	"	S. Sen A/c		500	9	"	T. Ltd .A/c		1,500
15	"	P. Roy A/c		3,000	16	"	P. Roy A/c		3,000
20	"	A. Bose A/c		1,500	20	"	D. Bose A/c		500

Pass Book

Date		*Particulars*	*Cheques No.*	*Dr. Withdrawals*	*Cr. Deposits*	*Balance*
2010			Rs.	Rs.	Rs.	Rs.
Jan. 1	By	Balance b/d				5,000
2	To	X Ltd.		1,000		4,000
10	"	T Ltd.		1,500		2,500
"	By	S. Sen A/c			500	3,000
20	To	D. Bose A/c		500		2,500
22	"	A Bose A/c			1,500	4,000
23	"	Rent A/c		500		3,500
24	"	A. Roy A/c			1,000	4,500

Now, from the above, it is quite clear that, from the credit side of Cash Book, Ram A/c and P. Roy A/c for Rs. 1,000 and Rs. 3,000 were not ticked up, it means *'cheques issued but not presented'* and from the debit side of the Pass Book, only one item was unticked i.e., Rent A/c amounting to Rs. 500, it reveals, *'payment made by bank but not recorded in Cash Book'*.

Similarly, from the debit side of Cash Book it is found that two cheques received from Ram A/c and P. Roy A/c were deposited into bank but not credited by the bank for Rs. 4,000 (Rs. 1,000 + Rs. 3,000) i.e., *cheques deposited but not credited.* On the contrary, one item of a deposit in the Pass Book amounting to Rs. 500 was also not ticked up, i.e., *'direct deposit made by the customers not recorded in Cash Book'.*

3. ***Now after considering the above items we can easily prepare a Bank Reconciliation Statement in the usual manner and procedure.***

(i) Where the Books Relate to the Same Period

Under the circumstance, we are to find out such transactions which do not occur in both the books since they create the difference between the two books which require proper reconciliation.

Illustration 21

The following are the Cash Book and Bank Pass Book of Sri N for the month of April 2011:

Cash Book (Bank Column only)

Dr. *Cr.*

Date	Particulars	Amount	Date	Particulars	Amount
2011		Rs.	2011		Rs.
April 1	To Balance b/d	12,500	April 1	By Salaries Account (Cheque No. 183)	4,000
4	" Sales Account	8,000	6	" Purchase Account (Cheque No. 184)	3,200
8	" P. Account	1,500	11	" Machinery Account (Cheque No. 185)	6,000
13	" M. Account	3,400	15	By Omprokash Account (Cheque No. 186)	1,000
18	" Kamal Account	4,600	16	" Drawings Account (Cheque No. 187)	800
21	" Furniture Account	1,200	23	" K. Account (Cheque No. 188)	2,000
25	To Sales Account	3,800	27	" S. Account (Cheque No. 189)	1,000
30	" F. Account	3,000	30	" Printing Account (Cheque No. 190)	500
			30	" Balance c/d.	19,500
		38,000			38,000

Pass Book

Date	Particulars	Cheque Nos.	Dr. (Withdrawals)	Credit (Deposits)	Dr. or Cr.	Balance
2011			Rs.	Rs.		Rs.
April 1	By Balance b/d					12,500
2	To Cheque	183	4,000		Cr.	8,500
	By Cheque			8,000	Cr.	16,500
6	To Cheque	184	3,200		Cr.	13,300
10	By Cheque			1,500	Cr.	14,800
16	By Cheque			3,400	Cr.	18,200
17	To Cheque	187	800		Cr.	17,400
20	By Cheque			4,600	Cr.	22,000
24	" Cheque			3,800	Cr.	25,800
28	To Cheque	185	6,000		Cr.	19,800
28	" Cheque	189	1,000		Cr.	18,800
30	By Interest			100	Cr.	18,900
30	" Deposit (K. Sen)			3,000	Cr.	21,900
30	" Charges		10		Cr.	21,890

You are required to prepare a Bank Reconciliation Statement as at 30th April 2011.

Solution

Bank Reconciliation Statement
as at 30th April 2011

		Amount	Amount
		Rs.	Rs.
	Bank Balance as per Cash Book		19,500
Add :	Cheques issued but not presented	3,500	
	Direct deposit made by the customer, K. Sen	3,000	

Contd.

		Rs.	Rs.
	Interest credited by Bank, but not entered in Cash Book	100	
			6,600
			26,100
Less:	Cheques deposited but not credited (Rs. 1,200 + Rs. 3,000)	4,200	
	Bank Charges debited by Bank, but not entered in Cash Book	10	
			4,210
	Bank Balance as per Pass Book		21,890

Working Note :

1. ***Cheques issued but not presented*** : On 15.4.2011, Rs. 1,000, on 23.4.2011; Rs. 2,000 and on 30.4.2011 Rs. 500 (i.e., Rs. 1,000 + Rs. 2,000 + Rs. 500) Rs. 3,500. These cheques were issued but not presented to the bank, so as per Pass Book the balance was increased—it would be added.
2. ***Cheques deposited but not credited*** : On 21.4.2011 Rs. 1,200; on 30.4.2011, Rs. 3,000) (i.e., Rs. 1,200 + Rs. 3,000) 4,200. These cheques were deposited into bank but not credited. So as per Pass Book the balance was reduced,— it would be subtracted.
3. ***Direct deposit made by the customer*** (K. Sen) on 30.4.2011 increased the balance as per Pass Book—it would be added.
4. Same as Interest credited by bank on 31.4.2011.—Rs. 100.
5. Bank charges debited by bank not entered in Cash Book. on 30.4.2011 Rs. 10—Pass Book balance was reduced—it would be subtracted.

Illustration 22

You are given below the Cash Book (Bank column) and the Bank Statement which reveals that the bank balance as per Cash Book of Mr. T. Sinha for the month of January, 2011 did not agree with his bank balance as per Pass Book. You are asked to mention the reasons of disagreement and prepare a Bank Reconciliation Statement as on 31st January 2011

Dr. **Cash Book (Bank Column only)** *Cr.*

Date	*Particulars*	*Amount*	*Date*	*Particulars*	*Amount*
2011		Rs.	2011		Rs.
Jan. 1	To Balance b/d	5,780	Jan. 2	By J. K. Traders	3,500
" 3	" A. K. Roy	2,500	" 4	" Rent (Paid to H. Kar)	750
" 11	" S. Bros.	5,250	" 7	" B. Ghosh	1,200
" 16	" Cash	2,000	" 15	" French Motor Car Co.	2,450
" 20	" N. Singh	1,420	" 26	" Insurance Premium (Life Insurance Corpn.)	600
			" 31	" Balance c/f	8,450
		16,950			16,950

Bank Statement

Date	*Particulars*	*Dr. (Wthdrasals)*	*Cr. (Deposits)*	*Balance*
2011		Rs.	Rs.	Rs.
Jan. 1	To Balance b/f			5,780 (Cr.)
" 4	" A. K. Roy		2,500	8,280
" 4	" H. Kar (Rent)	750		7,530
" 6	" J. K. Traders	3,500		4,030
" 8	" Bank Charges	150		3,880
" 15	" S. Bros.		5,250	9,130
" 16	" Cash		2,000	11,130
" 16	" French Motor Car Co.	2,450		8,680
" 25	" Interest		120	8,800
" 31	" Dividend		600	9,400 (*Cr.*)

[CU BCom (Hons.)]

Solution

In the Books of Mr. T. Sinha

Statement showing the Reasons of Disagreement, between the entries in the Cash Book (Bank Column) and Bank Statement (Pass Book)

		Rs.
(i)	Cheque issued to B. Ghosh but not yet collected from Bank or presented to Bank for collection	1,200
(ii)	Cheque paid to Life Insurance Corporation as Insurance premium but not yet cashed	600
(iii)	Cheque received from N. Singh and deposited into Bank but not yet cleared and credited in the Bank Statement	1,420
(iv)	Bank Charges debited in the Bank Statement but not entered in the Cash Book	150
(v)	Interest credited in the Bank Statement but not entered and recorded in the Cash Book	120
(vi)	Dividend collected by Bank as per standing order but not entered in the Cash Book	600

Bank Reconciliation Statement
as at 31st January 2011

Particulars	*Amount* Rs.	*Amount* Rs.
Bank Balance as per Cash Book		8,450
Add : (i) Cheque issued but not collected from bank	1,200	
(ii) Life Insurance Premium paid by cheque but not encashed	600	
(iii) Interest credited in Bank Statement but not recorded in the Cash Book	120	
(iv) Dividend collected by the Bank as per standing order but not entered in the Cash Book	600	2,520
		10,970
Less : (i) Cheque received and deposited into the Bank but not credited in the Bank Statement	1,420	
Bank Charges debited in the Bank Statement but not entered in the Cash Book	150	1,570
Bank Balance as per Pass Book		9,400

Illustration 23

On 31st March 2009, Bank Account of Mr. Tandon Ltd. does not agree with the balance as shown by his Pass Book on that date. The entries in his Cash Book and Pass Book for the month of March disclosed the following :

Cash Book
(Bank Column only)

Dr. *Cr.*

Date		*Particulars*	*Amount*	*Date*		*Particulars*	*Amount*
2009			Rs.	2009			Rs.
March. 1	To	Balance b/d	16,190	March 4	By	L. I. C. Ltd. (Cheque No. 618769)	3,750
2	"	X Y Ltd.	6,100	13	"	Y Ltd. (Cheque No. 618770)	6,250
3	"	D M & Co.	9,500	15	"	D & Co. (Cheque No. 618771)	2,750
9	"	S. Ltd.	6,030	21	"	M. K. Ltd. (Cheque No. 618772)	930
20	"	D. M. & Co.	7,720	30	"	Q & Co. (Cheque No. 618773)	350
31	"	X Y Ltd.	600	31	"	C. S. Ltd. (Cheque No. 618774)	1,000
					"	Balance c/d	32,110
			47,140				47,140

Pass Book

Date	Particulars	Withdrawal	Deposit	Balance
		Rs.	Rs.	Rs.
March, 1	Balance			18,750 (Cr.)
3	Cheque No. 618768	2,560		16,190 "
6	X Y Ltd.	—	6,100	22,290 "
10	Ch. No. 618769	—	3,750	26,040 "
12	D. M & Co.	—	5,900	31,940 "
14	S. Ltd.	—	6,030	37,970 "
20	Ch. No. 618771	2,750	—	35,220 "
24	D M & Co.	—	7,720	42,940 "
26	Ch. No. 618772	390	—	42,550 "
29	Bank Charges	200	—	42,350 "
30	Ch. No. 618773	350	—	42,000 "
31	Balance		—	42,000 "

You are required to prepare a Bank Reconciliation Statement as at 31st March 2009 without preparing an amended Cash Book.

[ICWA]

Reasons for Disagreement

Working Notes:

1. on 4.3. 2009 : Cheque issued for Rs. 3,750 wrongly credited by the bank; now Rs. 7,500 (i.e., Rs. 3,750 × 2) will be added
2. on 31.3.2009 : Cheque issued Rs. 6,250 was not presented to the bank for payment.
3. on 21.3.2009 : Cheque issued for Rs. 930, wrongly debited by bank Rs. 390, now Rs. 540 (Rs. 930 – Rs. 390) to be added.
4. 31.3..2009 : Cheque issued but not presented Rs. 1,000 – to be added.
5. 8.3. 2009 : Deposited Rs. 9,500 into bank but bank wrongly credited Rs. 5,900 (i.e., (Rs. 9,500 – Rs. 5,900)—Rs. 3,600 to be deducted

29. 3. 2009 : Bank charges amounting to Rs. 200 not entered in Cash Book.
31. 3. 2009 : Debit side of the Cash Book was overcast by Rs. 1,000.
31. 3. 2009 : Cheque deposited but not credited by bank amounted to Rs. 600.

Solution

Bank Reconciliation Statement
as at 31st March 2009

		Amount	Amount
		Rs.	Rs.
	Balance as per Cash Book		32,110
Add :	Cheques (No. 618769) issued for Rs. 3,750 wrongly entered as a deposit in Pass Book	7,500	
	Cheque (No. 618770) issued but not presented	6,250	
	Cheque (No. 618774) issued but not presented	1,000	
	Cheque (No. 618772) issued to M. K. Ltd, for Rs. 930 wrongly shown in Pass Book as Rs. 390	540	15,290
			47,400
Less :	Rs. 9,500 shown as a deposit in cash book but credited by the bank as Rs. 5,900 (i.e., Rs. 9,500 – Rs. 5,900)	3,600	
	Bank Charges not entered in Cash Book	200	
	Debit side of the Cash Book overcast by	1,000	
	Cheque deposited for Rs. 600 but not credited	600	5,400
	Balance as per Pass Book		42,000

(ii) When the Pass Book is given for the Succeeding Period

Under the circumstances we are to find out such transactions which appear in both the books but not in the same month. (For example, Cash Book is given for the month of December 2010 whereas Pass Book is given for the month of January 2011.) Now, put tick marks on the transaction which appeared on the credit side of the Cash Book and recorded on the debit side of the Pass Book i.e., *'Cheques issued but not presented for payment within the month'* which need reconciliation. Again, put tick mark on the transactions which appeared on the debit side of the Cash Book and recorded on the credit side of the Pass Book, i.e., *'Cheques deposited but not credited by the bank'* need reconciliation and so on.

Now we can easily prepare the Bank Reconciliation Statement in the usual manner and procedure without any trouble. Consider the following illustration.

Illustration 24

Mr. P. K. Sen furnished the following partiulars:

In the books of P. K. Sen
Cash Book (Bank Column only)

Dr.			Cr.		
Date	Particulars	Amount	Date	Particulars	Amount
2010		Rs.	2010		Rs.
Dec.	To Balance b/d	1,000	Dec. 1	By Drawings	500
"	" D. C. Bhattacharyya	750	4	" K. Das	700
"	" A. Das Gupta	250	6	" Rent	450
"	" M. Sen	800	15	" P. K. Roy	650
"	" M. Mukherjee	2,500	20	" S. N. Bose	330
"	" Rajesh	1,700	25	" H. K. Roy	900
			30	" Wages & Salaries	770
			31	" Balance c/d	2,700
		7,000			7,000

Bank Pass Book
P. K. Sen in Account Current with Bank

Dr.			Cr.		
Date	*Particulars*	*Amount*	*Date*	*Particulars*	*Amount*
2011		Rs.	2011		Rs.
Jan. 2	To P. D. Roy	650	Jan. ?	By Bal. b/d	1,280
4	" K. Chandra	350	1	" M. Mukherjee	2,500
7	" S. N. Bose	330	4	" P. Pal	500
9	" H. K. Roy	900	5	" S. Sen	300
11	" D. K. Bose	470	9	" M. Sen	800

Prepare a Bank Reconciliation Statement as on 31st Dec. 2010.

Solution

Bank Reconciliation Statement
as at 31st Dec. 2010

	Amount	Amount
	Rs.	Rs.
Balance as per Cash Book		2,700
Add : Cheques issued but not presented :		
P. K. Roy	650	
S. N. Bose	330	
H. K. Roy	900	1,880
		4,580
Less : Cheques deposited but not credited :		
M. Mukherjee	2,500	
M. Sen	800	3,300
Balance as per Pass Book		1,280

GENERAL ILLUSTRATIONS

Illustration 25

On 31.3.2009 X Ltd. presented the following information where Profit and Loss Account showed a net profit of Rs. 60,000 and Bank Balance (Overhead) Rs. 25,000 out of total assets of Rs. 1,00,000. His balance as per Cash Book does not agree with the balance as per Pass Book. On investigation you found the following reasons:

(a) Standing Order — As per standing order, bank met the following payment although these were not recorded in Cash Book.

(i) Insurance Premium Rs. 3,000 (ii) Repayment of bank loan @ Rs. 1,000 p.m. (including Rs. 250 for interst); Telephone bill as per ECS Rs. 500 p.m.

(b) A cheque for Rs. 50 received from Mr. P entered in the credit side of the Cash Book had been wrongly recorded in the debit side as Rs. 5,000 as purchase of goods.

(c) Dividend received by bank amounting to Rs. 4,000 not entered in Cash Book

(d) Cheques deposited into bank but not credited by the bank amounting to Rs. 6,000.

(e) Cheques issued to creditors but not presented amounted to Rs. 1,000.

(f) Two cheques of Rs. 5,000 and Rs. 6,000 received from debtors were returned dishonourd, not entered in Cash Book

(g) The cheques were returned dishonoured for the following reasons.

  (i) Cheque amounting to Rs. 5,000 was not signed properly which should be honoured subsequently

  (ii) Cheque for Rs. 6,000 was dishonoured as the customer became insolvent.

Prepare (a) a Bank Reconciliation Statement as on 31.3.2009; and
(b) a statement showing the effect of the above on profit.

Solution

Bank Reconciliation Statement
as at 31st March 2009

			Amount Rs.	Amount Rs.
	Overdraft as per Cash Book			25,000
Add :	As per Standing Order, Bank paid the following expenses not entered in Cash Book :			
	Insurance Premium	3,000		
	Bank Loan (Rs. 1,000 × 12)	12,000		
	Telephone Bill (Rs. 500 × 12)	6,000	21,000	
	Cheque deposited but not credited by the bank		6,000	
	Cheque deposited into bank but returned dishonoured, not entered in Cash Book (Rs. 5,000 + Rs. 6,000)		11,000	38,000
				63,000
	Dividend Received by bank not entered in Cash Book		4,000	
Less :	Cheque issued but not present for payment		1,000	
	A cheque received from a Customer for Rs. 50 wrongly recorded Rs. 5,000 as purchase in the Credit side of the Cash Book		5,050	10,050
	Overdraft as per Pass Book			52,950

Effect on Profit

		Rs.	Rs.
	Profit from Profit & Loss A/c		60,000
	Increase in Profit		
Add :	Wrong debit made as cash purchase of goods	5,000	
	Divided Received	4,000	9,000
			69,000
Less :	**Decrease in profit**		
	Insurance Premium	3,000	
	Interest on Loan	250	
	Telephone Bill	6,000	
	Bad Debts	6,000	15,250
	Corrected Profit		53,750

Illustration 26

The Secretary of the Systematic Club has prepared the following draft Balance Sheet of the Club as on Sept. 30, 2011:

Balance Sheet

Dr. Liabilities		Amount Rs.	Assets		Amount Cr. Rs.
	Capital A/c :			Fixtures and Fittings	10,600
	Balance	14,300	Less :	Depreciation	1,000
Less :	Loss for the year	2,100			
		12,200			9,600
	Subscriptions in Advance	600		Stock	3,200
	Creditors	2,400		Debtors	1,400
				Balance at Bank	950
				Cash in hand	50
		15,200			15,200

You ascertain the following :

1. The amount of the loss was only on balancing figure as the books had been kept on a single entry basis.
2. The balance at bank was that shown by the bank statement at close of business on Sept. 30, 2011.
3. The following amounts has been paid into the bank on Sept. 30, 2011, but had not been credited by the bank :
   (i) Two cheques for Rs. 50, each of which had been cashed for members. One had been duly honoured but the other had been returned marked 'Refer to Drawer,' on being approached since, the member repaid Rs. 50 in cash.
   (ii) A member's subscription of Rs. 80 for the year 2011-12.
4. The following cheques had been drawn and despatched in Sept. but had not been presented until October :
   (i) Rs. 480, for bar supplies which had been delivered but had not been included in Stocks.
   (ii) Rs. 350, for an additional typewriter, received on Oct. 2.
   (iii) Rs. 100, bonus to the professional, included under creditors.
   (iv) Rs. 140, for fuel which had been included in the Stock figure, but not in the creditors. This cheque was dated Oct. 1.

You are required to prepare :

(1) A Bank Reconciliation Statement as at Sept. 30, 2011, and
(2) A revised Balance Sheet, as on that date, to give effect to the consequential adjustments, assuming that, otherwise, the items in the draft Balance Sheet were correct.

Solution

Bank Reconciliation Statement
as at 30th September 2011

	Amount Rs.	Amount Rs.
Balance as per Pass Book		950
Add : Amount paid into bank but not credited :		
(i) Cheques (Rs. 100 – Rs. 50 for dishonoured)	50	
(ii) Subscriptions	80	130
		1,080
Less : Cheques drawn but not presented :		
(i) Bar supplies	480	
(ii) Typewriter	350	
(iii) Bonus to professionals	100	930
Balance as per Cash Book		150

Note : Rs. 140 for fuel will not be taken into consideration since the same is dated Oct. 1.

Balance Sheet *as at 30th September 2011*

Liabilities	*Amount*	*Amount*	*Assets*	*Amount*	*Amount*
	Rs.	Rs.		Rs.	Rs.
Capital	14,300		Fixture & Fittings	10,600	
Less : Loss	2,140		*Less* : Depreciation	1,000	
		12,160			9,600
Subscription, Received in Advance (600 + 80)		680	Typewriter		350
			Stock (3,200 + 480)		3,680
Creditors			Debtors		1,400
(2,400 + 140 fuel – 100 bonus)		2,440	Cash at Bank		150
			Cash in hand		100
		15,280			15,280

ASSIGNMENT MATERIALS

THEORETICAL

1. **Fill in the blanks :**

(i) Bank balance as per Cash Book is Rs. 18,500; Rs. 4,500 is entered in Cash Book as paid into bank but not credited by the bank. The Pass Book Balance is Rs. ... ...

(ii) Bank balance as per Pass Book is Rs. 20,000. Dividends of Rs. 1,000 collected by Bank but entered in the Cash Book as Rs. 100. The Cash Book Bank balance is Rs. ... ...

(iii) Overdraft balance as per Pass Book is Rs. 8,500. A cheque of Rs. 3,450 issued but wrongly entered in the debit side of the Cash Book. The cheque is not yet presented for payment. Overdraft Bank balance as per Cash Book is Rs. ... ...

(iv) Overdraft Bank balance as shown by the Cash Book is Rs. 6,000. A cheque for Rs. 10,400 was deposited to Bank but omitted in the Cash Book. In the Pass Book the amount is wrongly entered in the withdrawal column. Overdraft balance as per Pass Book is Rs. ... ...

(v) Bank balance as per Cash Book is Rs. 7,800. Bank charges of Rs. 75 debited by Bank but not recorded in Cash Book. The Pass Book balance is Rs. ... ...

(vi) Bank balance as per Pass Book is Rs. 9,700. Cash withdrawn from Bank for Rs. 3,000 but recorded as Rs. 300 in the Cash Book. Bank balance as per Cash Book is Rs. ... ...

(vii) Overdraft balance as per Pass Book is Rs. 11,500. Interest on Overdraft Rs. 350 debited by Bank but not recorded in the Cash Book. Bank balance as per Cash Book is Rs. ....

(viii) Bank balance as per Cash Book is Rs. 570. Debit side of the Cash Book Bank column is overadded to the extent of Rs. 10,000. Overdraft balance as per Pass Book is Rs. ... ...

(Your answer in each case must be supported by workings in the form of plus or minus in brackets)

[Ans. (i) Cr. Rs. 14,000; (ii) Dr. Rs.19,100; (iii) Cr. or O/D Rs. 5,050; (iv) Dr. or O/D Rs. 16,400; (v) Dr. Rs. 12,400; (vi) Cr. Rs. 7,725; (vii) Cr. Rs. 11,150; (viii) Dr. or O/D Rs. 9,430]

Multiple Choice Questions

2. (a) If balance as per Cash Book is given, unrepresented cheques are:
(i) Added; (ii) Subtracted; (iii) No effect.

(b) If balance as per Pass Book is given, uncredited cheques are:
(i) Added; (ii) Subtracted; (iii) No effect.

(c) If overdraft as per Cash Book is given, direct deposit made by customer is:
(i) Added; (ii) Subtracted; (iii) No effect.

(d) If overdraft as per Pass Book is given, interest on overdraft is:
(i) Added; (ii) Subtracted; (iii) No effect.

(e) If overdraft as per Cash Book is given, overcasting in the Debit Side of the Cash Book is:
(i) Added; (ii) Subtracted; (iii) No effect.

[Ans. (a) Added; (b) Added; (c) Subtracted; (d) Subtracted; (e) Added]

Short Answer-Type Questions

3. What is a bank Reconciliation Statement? Why is it prepared?
4. Discuss the usefulness of a Bank Reconciliation statement.
5. Discuss at least five causes of disagreement between the balance shown by the Cash Book and the balance shown by the Pass Book.
6. What is an 'Amended Cash Book' in Bank Reconciliation Statement? Discuss the method of its correction.
7. Why and how is the Bank Reconciliation Statement prepared? Who prepares an Bank Reconciliation Statement?
8. Give any five causes of disagreement between the Cash Book and Pass Book balances.
9. Which two books will you consider while preparing a Bank Reconciliation Statement?
10. Why should the balance shown by the Cash Book agree with the balance shown by the Pass Book? Do they tally always? If not, why?
11. Briefly state the utility of a Bank Reconciliation Statement.

Essay or Long Answer-Type Questions

12. What do you mean by a Bank Reconciliation Statement?
13. (a) What are the main causes of difference between Bank Pass Book and Cash Book balances?
    (b) State the method that is used in business to reconcile bank account and cash account, if they differ from each other.
14. What is a Bank Reconciliation Statement? Discuss briefly its utility.
15. What is a Bank Reconciliation Statement? Why is this statement prepared? Mention five causes of disagreement between the Bank Balance as per Cash Book and Bank Balance as per Pass Book.
16. What is a Bank Reconciliation Statement? Discuss briefly its utility.

PRACTICAL

(a) Taking Balance as per Cash Book

1. On 31st Dec. 2005, the Bank column of the Cash Book of Mr. Gour Hari Khara, shows a debit balance of Rs. 3,500. On examination of the Cash Book and statement you find that :

(i) Mr. Khara had issued three cheques for Rs. 500, Rs. 750, Rs. 900 on 25th Dec. but the cheque for Rs. 500 was presented into the Bank on 3rd January 2005

(ii) Mr. Khara had deposited into his Bank Account on 26th Dec. cheques for Rs. 350, Rs. 550, Rs. 1,000 and Rs. 1,200. Of these, the cheque for Rs. 350 was credited by the Bank on 2nd January and the cheque for Rs. 1,000 was not credited at all.

(iii) A cheque for Rs. 100 drawn by Mr. Banerjee had been charged to Mr. Khara's account in error.

(iv) A cheque from a Debtor for Rs. 750 had been dishonoured prior to 31st December but no record appeared in the Cash Book.

(v) Bank's charges (postal) for a Cheque Book received by Mr. Khara. Rs. 5, was entered in the Cash Book twice.

(vi) Debit side of the Cash Book was undercast by Rs. 500.

(vii) Bills Receivable collected by Bank and credited in Pass Book for Rs. 700, not debited in Cash Book.

(viii) Interest credited by Bank, but not debited in Cash Book Rs. 700.

Prepare a Bank Reconciliation Statement as on 31.12.2005.

[Ans. Balance as per Pass Book Rs. 3,705]

2. The Cash Book of Mr. X shows Rs. 10,000 as the balance at Bank as on 31st Dec. 2011, but this does not agree with the balance as pr the Bank Pass Book n the same date.

On scrutiny you find the following discrepancies:

(i) A cheque issued for Rs, 500 issued but wrongly recorded in Cash Column.

(ii) The payment side of the Cash Book was undercast by Rs. 550.

(iii) The debit side of the Cash Book was overcast by Rs. 400.

(iv) One deposit amounting to Rs. 800 was recorded in the Cash Book as if there is no bank column.

(v) One outgoing cheque amounting to Rs. 400 was recorded twice in Cash Book.

(vi) The debit balance in the Cash Book on a particular day amounting to Rs. 750 was brought forward as a credit balance in the next day.

(vii) Dividend amounting to Rs. 500 collected by bank and subscription paid by bank amounting to Rs. 100, were not recorded in Cash Book.

(viii) Cheques totalling Rs. 8,000 were issued but the cheques totalling Rs. 3,500 were encashed in Jan. 2011.

(ix) Cheque issued for Rs. 1,000 were recorded in Cash Book as only Rs. 100.

[Ans. Balance as per Pass Book Rs. 13,450]

(b) Taking Balance as per Pass Book

3. From the following partiulars, prepare a Bank Reconciliation Statement showing the balance as Cash Book as on 31.3.2010 :

(i) The Bank Balance as per Pass Book showed a credit balance of Rs. 25,000.

(ii) Cheque received and sent to Bank without recording in Cash Book Rs. 3,000.

(iii) Three cheques for Rs. 1,000, Rs. 2,000 and Rs. 3,000 were issued on 26th March, but the cheque for Rs. 2,000 was presnted to the Bank for payment on 5th April.

(iv) A cheque for Rs. 2,500 which was received from a customer was entered in the Bank Column of the Cash Book, but the same was paid into Bank on 3rd April.

(v) Credit side of the Cash Book (Bank Col.) was overcast by Rs. 500.

(vi) Bank wrongly debited in Pass Book Rs. 1,000.

(vii) A bill for Rs. 2,000 discounted with the Bank is entered in the Cash Book without recording the discount charges of Rs. 200.

(viii) Bank Charges not adjusted in Cash Book Rs. 50.

[Ans. Balance as per Cash Book Rs. 23,250]

4. From the following particulars, prepare a Bank Reconciliation Statement as on 31st March 2010 : (i) Bank Balance as on 31st March 2010 as per Pass Book Rs. 15,200.

(ii) Bank Charges debited Rs. 130.

(iii) Cheques issued but not presented to Bank for payment Rs. 2,000.

(iv) Cheques deposited to Bank but not credited in the Pass Book Rs. 7,000.

(v) A cheques entered as a deposit in the Cash Book instead of a payment Rs. 220.

(vi) Rs. 364 paid into Bank had been entered twice in the Cash Book.

(vii) The receipt column of the Cash Book has been overcast by Rs. 1,000.

(viii) A cheque drawn for Rs. 9 had been incorrectly enter in the Cash Book as Rs. 99.

[Ans. Balance as per Cash Book Rs. 22,044]

(c) Taking Overdraft as per Cash Book

5. From the following particulars, prepare the Bank Reconciliation Statement :

	Rs.
Bank Overdraft as per Cash Book	1,62,000
A cheque deposited as per Bank Statement but not recorded in Cash Book	7,000
Debit side of the Bank Column cast short	1,000
A cheque for Rs. 5,000 deposited but collection as per Bank Statement	49,960
A party's cheque returned dishonoured as per Bank's Statement only	5,300
Bills collected directly by Bank	35,000
Bank's Charges recorded twice in Cash Book	250
A Bill for Rs. 80,000 discounted for Rs. 79,600 returned dishonoured by the Bank, noting charges being	150
Cheques deposited but not yet collected by Bank	23,200
Cheques issued but not yet presented for encashment	12,500

Indicate which of the items are to be adjusted in the books of accounts before preparation of the Balance Sheet.

[Ans. **Overdraft as per Pass Book Rs. 2,14,940]**

6. From the undermentioned particulars of a businessman prepare the Bank Reconciliation Statement as on 31st December 2010 :

(i) Bank overdraft as per Cash Book Rs. 1,410.

(ii) During the month, the total amount of cheques for Rs. 2,700 was deposited into Bank, but, out of those, one cheque for Rs. 480 was recorded in the Pass Book on 4th January.

(iii) During the month, cheques amounting to Rs. 3,470 were drawn in favour of creditors—of them one creditor for Rs. 1,440 encashed his cheque on 8th January, whereas the other for Rs. 660 has not encashed his cheque yet.

(iv) As per order the Bank on 28.12.2010 had paid out Rs. 400 to a creditor, but, by mistake the same has not yet been entered in the Cash Book.

(v) According to agreement, a debtor had deposited directly into the Bank Account Rs. 295, on 30.12.2010, but the same has not been recorded in the Cash Book.

(vi) In the month of December, the Bank, without any intimation, had debited the account of the businessman for Rs. 50 as Bank Charges and credited the same for Rs. 120 as interest for last year.

[Ans. Balance as per Pass Book (Cr.) Rs. 175]

(d) Overdraft as per Pass Book

7. From the following particulars prepare a Bank Reconciliation Statement for Sri Subhadeep Sarkar as at 31st Dec. 2004 :

(a) Bank Balance as per Pass Book (Dr.) Rs. 610.

(b) Cheques issued but not presented Rs. 3,000.

(c) Cheques deposited but not credited by Bank Rs. 2,500.

(d) A Debtor directly deposited into Sarkar's Bank Account, but not recorded in Cash Book, Rs. 1,000.

(e) Credit side of the Cash Book (Bank Column) was undercast by Rs. 500.

(f) A cheque drawn for Rs. 100 had been incorrectly entered in the Cash Book as Rs. 10.

(g) A cheque for Rs. 5,000 drawn by Mr Banerjee had been charged to Sri Sarkar's Account in error.

(h) Bank paid a Bill Payable for Rs. 1,450 but it was recorded in Cash Book as Rs. 1,540.

(i) The receipt column of the Cash Book has been overcast by Rs. 1,000.

(j) Discount Allowed Rs. 410 has been entered through mistake with the cheque in the Bank Column of the Cash Book.

(k) Pursuant to instruction dated 30th Dec. 2004, asking the Banker to transfer Rs. 1,000 to Fixed Deposit Account, entry for this was made in the Cash Book but the Bank acted on the instruction of 2nd Jan. 2005.

(l) The Bank debited the account for Rs. 500 being the amount of a cheque received from a customer and returned dishonoured but not entered in Cash Book.

(m) Cheques amounting to Rs. 300, though actually banked, were not entered in Cash Book.

[Ans. Balance as per Cash Book (Dr.) Rs. 4,000]

(e) Where there are two Bank Accounts

8. Mr Banker is having two Bank accounts (I and II) with INDIAN BANK. On 31st December 2011 his ledger shows a balance of Rs. 5,000 in Account I and an overdraft of Rs. 2,250 in Account II.

On verification of the Ledger entries with the respective Bank Statements, the following mistakes were found:

(a) A deposit of Rs. 15,000 made into Account I on 20th December, 2011 has been entered in the ledger in Account II.

(b) A withdrawal of Rs. 5,000 from Account I on 2nd November, 2011 has been entered in the ledger in Account II.

(c) Two cheques of Rs. 5,000 and Rs. 7,500 deposited in Account I on 1st December, 2011 (and entered in the book in Account II) have been dishonoured by the Banks. The entries for dishonour of these cheques have been entered in the books in Account II.

(d) Mr Banker has issued cheques on 29th December 2011 of Rs. 10,000 from Account I and for Rs. 1,000 from Account II. These cheques were not encashed till 2nd January 20012.

(e) Incidental charges of Rs. 10 and Rs. 25 charged in Accounts I and II, respectively, have not been entered in the books.

(f) Deposits of Rs. 5,000 and Rs. 3,500 made into the Accounts of I and II, respectively, on 30th December 2011 have not been given credit by Bank till 5th January 2012.

Prepare a Bank Reconciliation Statement as on 31st December 2011 for the above two accounts.
[Ans. Account I—Balance as per Pass Book Rs. 19,990, Account II—Overdraft as per Pass Book Rs. 14,775]

(f) With Amendments in Cash Book

(i) Where there is a favourable balance

9. According to the Cash book of A, there was a balance of Rs. 1,050 in favour on 30.6.2005 in his business Bank Account. However, according to the bank statement the account was overdrawn.

On investigation you find that:

(i) The receipts column of the Cash Book had been over-added by Rs. 1,100.

(ii) Cheques drawn and entered in Cash Book in June 2005, amounting to Rs. 1,670, were not presented until July 2005.

(iii) Discount received from a supplier of Rs. 100 had been included with the cheque entered in the bank column of the Cash Book in April 2005.

(iv) An amount of Rs. 750 paid directly into A's A/c by a customer, not entered in Cash Book.

(v) A cheque payment of Rs. 1,230 in April 2005, had been entered in the Cash Book as Rs. 1,320.

(vi) The Bank has charged the business account with a cheque for Rs. 2,200 in Feb.. 2005, which should have been passed through A's private account.

(vii) Bank charges of Rs. 80 at 31.12.04 and Rs. 100 at 30.6.05 has not yet been entered in the Cash Book.

(viii) Cheques to the value of Rs. 3,780 received from customers were recorded in the Cash Book on 28.6.2005 but not entered by the Bank until 2.7.2005

You are asked to prepare appropriate adjustments in Cash Book as at 30.6.05, and prepare a statement reconciling the adjusted Cash Book balance with the balance shown by the bank statement.
[Ans. Adjusted Cash Book Balance (Dr.) Rs. 70; Balance as per Pass Book (Dr.) Rs. 2,600]

(ii) Where there is unfavourable balance

10. From the following particulars find out adjusted Bank balance after rectification of errors in the Cash Book and then prepare Bank Reconciliation Statement of Iswar Prasad, a sole-trader, on 31.12.2005 :

	Rs.
Bank Overdraft as per Cash Book	73,300
Cheque deposited as per Bank Statement but not entered in the Cash Book	2,800
Cheque recorded as sent for collection but not sent to Bank	10,000
Credit side of Bank column in the Cash Book shows a shortcasting of Rs. 120. Premium on proprietor's L/P paid by Bank on standing advice as per Bank Statement	5,100
Bank charges recorded twice in the Cash Book	200
Cheques received and collected entered twice in the Cash Book	5,500
Cheque issued but dishonoured on technical ground as per Bank Statement	3,080
Bills collected by Bank directly as per Bank Statement	20,100
Cheques deposited Rs. 40,000 but collections against the same as per Bank Statement	39,900

[Ans. Adjusted Cash Book (Cr.) Rs. 57,840, Overdraft as per Pass Book Rs. 67,940]

11. Mr H's Cash Book, on 30th June 2010, showed a balance due to his Bank of Rs. 12,100 on his No. 1 Account.

On investigation you find :

(i) Cheques drawn amounting to Rs. 4,200 has not been presented to the Bank for payment.

(ii) Cheques of Rs. 3,600 entered in the Cash Book as paid into the Bank had not been credited by the Bank.

(iii) The receipts side of the Cash Book had been undercast by Rs. 1,000.

(iv) Bank charges of Rs. 10 and interest on overdraft of Rs. 450 entered on the Bank statement had been entered in the Cash Book.

(v) A cheque for Rs. 5,200 drawn on No. 1 Account had been charged by the Bank in error to the No. 2 Account.

(vi) A Dividend of Rs. 300 paid direct to the Bank has not been entered in the Cash Book.

(vii) A cheque for Rs. 1,000 paid into Bank had been dishonoured and shown as such by the Bank but no entry of dishonour had been made in the Cash Book.

(viii) A cheque drawn for Rs. 640 had been entered in Cash Book in error as Rs. 460.

(ix) A cheque for Rs. 420, drawn by another customer of the same name, had been charged to H's Bank account in error.

You are required :

(1) to show the appropriate adjustment to be made in the Cash Book, and

(2) to prepare a Bank Reconciliation Statement for No. 1 Account as on 30.6.96.

[Ans. Adjusted Cash Book Balance Rs. 12,440 (Cr.), Overdraft as per Pass Book Rs. 7,060]

Miscellaneous

12. Mr. Jones is having two accounts (A and B) with the Central Bank of India. On 31.12.1209, his Cash Book shows a balance of Rs. 5,000 in Account 'A' and an overdraft of Rs. 2,250 in Account 'B'. On verifying the Cash Book entries with the respective Bank Statement, the following mistakes were noticed :

(i) A deposit of Rs. 1,500 made into 'A' on 20.12.09 has been entered in the Cash Book in Account 'B'.

(ii) A withdrawal of Rs. 500 from Account 'A' on 2.12.09 has been entered in the Cash Book in Account 'B'.

(iii) Two cheques of Rs. 500 and Rs. 750 deposited in 'A' Account on 1.12.09 (and entered in the Cash Book in 'B' Account) have been dishonoured by the bankers. The entries for the dishonour of these cheques have been entered in the Cash Book in 'B' Account.

(iv) In the Accounts 'A' and 'B' Mr. Jones has issued, on 29.12.09, cheques for Rs. 10,000 Rs. 1,000, respectively, and these have not been cashed till 31.12.09

(v) Incidental charges of Rs. 10 and Rs. 25 charged in the Accounts 'A' and 'B', respectively, have not been entered in the Cash Book.

(vi) The bank has credited an Interest of Rs. 50 for Account 'A' and has charged Interest of Rs. 275 for Account 'B' which have not been recorded in the Cash Book.

(vii) The deposits of Rs. 5,000 and Rs. 3,500 made into the Accounts 'A' and 'B', both on 30.12.09, have not been given credit to by the bank till 31.12.09.

[Ans. Balance as per Cash Book Account I Rs. 11,040; Overdraft as per Pass Book Account II Rs. 6,050]

CHAPTER 9

JOURNAL PROPER

Learning Objectives

Types of Transactions recorded in Journal Proper

A. Credit Purchase and Credit Sale of Assets
B. Transfer Entries
C. Opening Entries
D. Closing Entries
E. Adjusting Entries

JOURNAL PROPER OR GENERAL JOURNAL

Meaning

It has already been highlighted in earlier chapters that credit transactions are recorded in different subsidiary/primary books of accounts according to their nature. For instance

For Credit Purchases	—	*In Purchase Day Book*
For Credit Sales	—	*In Sales Day Book*
For Purchases Return	—	*In Returns Outward Book*
For Sales Return	—	*In Returns Inward Book*
For Cash Transactions	—	*In Cash Book*

In other words, almost all the common transactions of a business are recorded in the above five primary books of accounts. But there are ***transactions which occasionally happen which are not recorded in the above primary books of accounts; they are recorded, however, in a special book, known as Journal Proper.*** That is, the transactions which are not recorded in the respective primary books of accounts are recorded in Journal Proper.

The following types of transactions are recorded in a Journal Proper :

A. Credit Purchase and Credit Sale of Assets

B. Transfer Entries

C. Opening Entries

D. Closing Entries

E. Adjusting Entries

F. Rectification of Errors

(This part has been explained in a separate chapter)

A. CREDIT PURCHASE AND CREDIT SALES OF ASSETS

When any asset is purchased or sold during the year on credit the same should not be passed through the Purchase Day Book or Sales Day Book since they are not common business transactions. However, they will be recorded in Journal Proper e.g., Sold a Plant on credit to Mr. X for Rs. 8,000.

Illustration 1

Show the entries from the following particulars :

(i) Purchased a Plant from Machinery & Co. for Rs. 4,000 on 3.12.2010 on credit. (ii) Sold one Furniture to Das & Co. for Rs. 8,000 on credit on 4.12.2010.

In the books of ....
Journal

Date	*Particulars*		*L.F.*	*Debit*	*Credit*
2010				Rs.	Rs.
Dec. 3	Plant A/c	Dr.		4,000	
	To Machinery & Co. A/c				4,000
	(Plant purchased on credit from Machinery & Co.)				
4	Das & Co. A/c	Dr.		8,000	
	To Furniture A/c				8,000
	(Old furniture sold on credit to Das & Co.)				

B. TRANSFER ENTRIES (i.e., Transfer from one Account to Another)

When any transfer is made from one account to another, it must pass through Journal Proper e.g., 50% of the profit is transferred to Reserve Fund.

Illustration 2

(i) Transfer from Ram's account to Rahim's account for Rs. 500. (ii) Transfer 50% of profits to the Reserve Fund, profits amounted to Rs. 10,000. (iii) Debtors included Rs. 1,000 due from Sri M. L. Das, whereas creditors included also Rs. 500 due to Sri Das; set-off the two accounts. (iv) Transfer from Purchase Account to Drawings Account Rs. 1,000. (v) Drawings of Rs. 2,000 is transferred to Capital A/c. (vi) Transfer Bad Debts of Rs. 200 to Reserve for Bad Debts A/c. (vii) Gross Profit of Rs. 20,000 is transferred to Profit and Loss A/c. (viii) Net Profit of Rs. 12,000 is transferred to Capital A/c.

Solution

In the books of ... ...
Journal

Date	Particulars		L.F.	Debit	Credit
?				Rs.	Rs.
(i)	Rahim A/c	Dr.		500	
	To Ram A/c				500
	(Transfer from Ram to Rahim)				
(ii)	Profit and Loss A/c	Dr.		5,000	
	To Reserve Fund A/c				5,000
	(Profit transferred to Reserve Fund)				
(iii)	M. L. Das (Creditors) A/c	Dr.		500	
	To M. L. Das (Debtors) A/c				500
	(Set-off made)				
(iv)	Drawings A/c	Dr.		1,000	
	To Purchases A/c				1,000
	(Drawings adjusted against purchases)				
(v)	Capital A/c	Dr.		2,000	
	To Drawings A/c				2,000
	(Balance of Drawings A/c transferred to adjust Capital Accounts)				
(vi)	Reserve for Bad Debts A/c	Dr.		200	
	To Bad Debts A/c				200
	(Balance of Bad Debts transferred to Reserve for Bad Debts A/c)				
(vii)	Trading A/c	Dr.		20,000	
	To Profit and Loss A/c				20,000
	(Gross Profit transferred)				
(viii)	Profit and Loss A/c	Dr.		12,000	
	To Capital A/c				12,000
	(Net Profit transferred)				

C. OPENING ENTRIES

When the assets and liabilities are transferred from the previous year to current year, the same is to be passed through journal proper. It is to be noted in this respect that all assets will be debited and all liabilities will be credited and the difference between the assets and liabilities will represent capital at the beginning of the year, e.g., Started business with a Capital of : Cash Rs. 1,000, Bank Rs. 3,000, Plant Rs. 10,000, Stock Rs. 4,000, Debtors Rs. 8,000 and Creditors Rs. 4,000. Hence, the capital is Rs. 22,000.

Illustration 3

Show the opening entry from the following particulars :

	Rs.
Cash at Bank	10,000
Cash in Hand	5,000
Plant & Machinery	6,000
Stock-in-trade	7,000
Sundry Debtors (including Reserve for Bad Debts Rs. 1,000)	10,000
Sundry Creditors	5,000
Bills Receivable	3,000
Bills Payable	1,000
Loan (Cr.)	1,000
Reserve (Cr.)	1,000

Solution

In the books of ... ...
Journal

Date	Particulars		L.F.	Dr. Amount	Cr. Amount
?				Rs.	Rs.
	Cash at Bank A/c	Dr.		10,000	
	Cash in hand A/c	Dr.		5,000	
	Plant & Machinery A/c	Dr.		6,000	

Contd.

Particulars		Rs.	Rs.
Stock-in-trade A/c	Dr.	7,000	
Sundry Debtors A/c	Dr.	10,000	
Bills Receivable A/c	Dr.	3,000	
To Reserve for Bad Debt			1,000
" Sundry Creditor			5,000
" Bills Payable			1,000
" Loan (Cr.)			1,000
" Reserve (Cr.)			1,000
" Capital *(bal. fig.)*			32,000
(Incorporation of the opening assets and liabilities as at ....)			

D. CLOSING ENTRIES

In order to ascertain the profit or loss for the year all the revenue accounts relating to incomes or expenditures are transferred to either Trading Account or Profit and Loss Account from which the gross profit and net profit are arrived at. The same is done with the help of journal proper, e.g., Trading Account to be debited by : Opening Stock, Purchases, Wages etc. and credited by Sales and Closing Stock,—the difference between the two sides will represent gross profit (if credit side is greater) or gross loss (if debit side is greater) as the case may be.

Illustration 4

The following are the balance in the books of Khaitan & Co. as on 31st Dec. 2011. Pass the Closing Entries :

	Rs.		Rs.
Opening Stock	20,000	Salaries	10,000
Purchases	70,000	Rent	7,000
Purchases Return	5,000	Insurance	1,000
Productive Wages	15,000	Discount Allowed	3,000
Non-productive Wages	6,000	Discount Received	2,000
Carriage Inward	3,000	Commission Received	5,000
Freight and Duty	5,000	Repairs	1,000
Sales	1,50,000	Depreciation	4,000
Carriage Outward	3,000	Interest Paid	3,000
Sales Return	2,000	Closing Stock	60,000

Solution

In the books ....
Journal

Date	*Particulars*		*L.F.*	*Debit*	*Credit*
2011				Rs.	Rs.
Dec. 31	Trading A/c	Dr.		1,15,000	
	To Opening Stock				20,000
	" Purchases				70,000
	" Productive Wages				15,000
	" Carriage Inwards				3,000
	" Freight and Duty				5,000
	" Sales Return				2,000
	(Transfer of balances for closing the latter accounts)				
	Sales A/c	Dr.		1,50,000	
	Purchases Return A/c	Dr.		5,000	
	Closing Stock A/c	Dr.		60,000	
	To Trading A/c				2,15,000
	(Transfer of balance for closing the former accounts)				
	Trading A/c	Dr.		1,00,000	
	To Profit and Loss A/c				1,00,000
	(Gross profit transferred)				

Contd.

			Rs.	Rs.
	Profit and Loss A/c		38,000	
	To Non-productive Wages			6,000
	" Carriage Outward			3,000
	" Salaries			10,000
	" Rent			7,000
	" Insurance			1,000
	" Discount Allowed			3,000
	" Repairs			1,000
	" Depreciation			4,000
	" Interest			3,000
	(Transfer of balances for closing the latter accounts)			
	Discount Reserved A/c	Dr.	2,000	
	Commission Received A/c	Dr.	5,000	
	To Profit and Loss A/c			7,000
	(Transfer of balance for closing the former accounts)			
	Profit and Loss A/c	Dr.	69,000	
	To Capital A/c			69,000
	(Net profit transferred)			

E. ADJUSTING ENTRIES

There are certain incomes and expenditures which are not recorded even at the closing date of accounts. If those incomes and expenditures are not taken into consideration, ascertainment of financial result (i.e., profit or loss) becomes impossible and, at the same time, will be incomplete as well as incorrect. That is why, in order to prepare the final accounts for a particular period or date, these adjustments (income/expenditure) are to be adjusted—since they affect profits or losses, assets and liabilities of a business i.e.,, the financial position as a whole.

Some of them along with their treatment in final accounts are discussed hereunder :

(a) Closing Stock

We know that closing stock is neither recorded in an account nor it is recorded in a Trial Balance. At the time of preparing Profit and Loss Account valuation of stock must be made for unsold goods since they affect profit. For this purpose closing stock should be valued at *Cost price or market price, whichever is less.* The entry will be :

Closing Stock A/c* Dr.
To Trading A/c

(* If the closing stock has already appeared in the Trial Balance (i.e., adjusted with purchases) the same will be shown as an asset in the asset side of the Balance Sheet).

(b) Outstanding/Unpaid Expenses

The expenses which are not paid during a particular accounting period must be taken into consideration while preparing Profit and Loss Account for the period. The entry will be :

Particular Expense A/c Dr.
To Outstanding Expenses A/c

But if the outstanding expenses have already appeared in the Trial Balance it means the same has already been adjusted and, as such, the amount which is shown in the credit side of a trial balance will appear only in the liability side of the Balance Sheet.

(c) Prepaid or Unexpired Expenses

The expenses which have been paid in advance is to be considered while preparing Profit and Loss Account, otherwise correct profit/loss cannot be ascertained. The entry will be :

Prepaid Expense A/c Dr.
To Particular Expenses A/c

But if the prepaid expenses account appear in the Trial Balance, the same has already been adjusted and, as such, it will simply appear in the asset side of the Balance Sheet.

(d) Income Received in Advance

The incomes which should not have been received but has already been received must be adjusted while preparing Profit and Loss Account for ascertaining correct financial position. The entry will be :

Particular Income A/c Dr.

To Income Received in Advance A/c

But, if the same appears in Trial Balance, no further adjustment is necessary, but it will appear in the liability side of the Balance Sheet.

(e) Accrued or Outstanding Income

The incomes which have already accrued but not yet received should also be considered at the time of preparing Profit and Loss Account. The entry is :

Accrued Income A/c Dr.

To Particular Income A/c

But if the same appears in the Trial Balance no further adjustment is necessary, the same will appear in the asset side of the Balance Sheet.

(f) Depreciation of Assets

Different fixed assets which are used by the business for the purpose of earning revenue are depreciated gradually. This depreciation charge must be taken into consideration while preparing Profit and Loss Account. The entry is :

Depreciation A/c Dr.

To Assets A/c

But if the depreciation appears in Trial Balance no further adjustment is required. The same will simply be debited to Profit and Loss Account. There will be no deduction from the asset in the asset side of the Balance Sheet since the same has already been done.

However, for making provision for depreciation, the entry will be :

Profit and Loss A/c Dr.

To Provision for Depreciation A/c

The amount of depreciation is to be added with the existing provision and the total provision must be shown in the liability side of the Balance Sheet, or as a deduction from the asset in the asset side of the Balance Sheet.

(g) Bad Debts, Provision for Bad Debts, Provision for Discount on Debtors and Creditors

Please see the relevant chapter that follows for details.

(h) Interest on Capital and Drawings

Sometimes interest is charged on the Capital contributed by the owners, i.e., interest on capital which is to be paid by the firm to its owners. The same must be adjusted before preparing Profit and Loss Account. The entry will be :

Interest on Capital A/c Dr.

To Capital/Current A/c

But if interest on Capital appears in the Trial Balance it will simply be debited by transferring to Profit and Loss Appropriation Account. In case of interest on drawings, which is charged by the business to its owners, the entry is :

Drawings/Capital A/c Dr.

To Interest on Drawings A/c

If it appears in the Trial Balance, it will be credited to Profit and Loss Appropriation Account and nothing will be adjusted against Drawings/Capital Accounts.

(i) Interest on Loan

If any amount is taken by way of loan and interest is charged on it which remains outstanding, the same must be considered while preparing Profit and Loss Account. The entry is :

Interest on Loan A/c Dr.

To Loan A/c

If, however, it appears in the Trial Balance no further adjustment is necessary, it will be debited to Profit and Loss Account.

(j) Treatment of Stock

(i) *Stock when lost by accident*

The value of stock which has been lost due to accident must be ascertained first.

The following entries are necessary before preparing the Profit and Loss Account :

(a) ***When stock is lost by accident, (say, fire) but not recovered from Insurance Co. :***

(i) Stock Destroyed by Fire A/c Dr.
To Trading A/c

(ii) Profit and Loss A/c Dr.
To Stock Destroyed by Fire A/c

(b) ***When stock is lost by fire, but the entire amount was recovered from Insurance Company :***

(i) Stock Destroyed by Fire A/c Dr.
To Trading A/c

(ii) Bank A/c Dr.
To Stock Destroyed by Fire A/c

If admitted by Insurance Co. :

(iii) Insurance Claims A/c Dr.
To Stock Destroyed by Fire A/c

(c) ***When stock is lost by fire but a portion was recovered from Insurance Co.***

(i) Stock Destroyed by Fire A/c Dr. (with the total amonut of loss)
To Trading A/c

(ii) Bank A/c Dr. (amount received from Insurance Co.)
P & L A/c Dr. (actual loss)
To Stock Destroyed by Fire A/c (total amount)

(d) ***When stock is used by the proprietor but not recorded :***

Sometimes a part of the goods/stock may be used by the proprietor for his own use. For this purpose the entry will be :

Drawings A/c Dr.
To Purchases/Opening Stock A/c

That is, in other words, the amount should be deducted from purchases or opening stock in Trading Account and the same also will be added with Drawings which is adjusted against Capital or Current Account.*

(e) ***When stock is used for private use and included in sales :***

For this purpose, the following entries are required to be passed

(a) Sales A/c Dr. (for cancellation)
To Debtors A/c

(b) Drawings A/c Dr. (for correct one)
To Purchases/Opening Stock

Thus, the amount should be deducted from Sales and Debtors, respectively, and, at the same time, it will be added with the drawings and will be deducted from purchases or opening stock.

(f) ***When stock is used as stationery :***

Sometimes a part of stock is being used as stationery. For this purpose, the entry will be :

Stationery A/c Dr.
To Purchases/Opening Stock.

Thus, the amount is to be deducted from purchases or opening stock and the same is to be closed by transferring to Profit and Loss Account by way of Stationery.

(g) ***When stock is distributed as free sample or free gift etc. :***

In this case, the entry will be :

Advertisement or Charity A/c Dr.
To Purchases/Opening Stock A/c

---

* When Fluctuating Capital Method is followed, Drawings will be deducted from Capital A/c while, in case of Fixed Capital Method, the same will be deducted from Current A/c.

That is, the amount should be deducted from Purchases or Opening Stock and the same is to be transferred to Profit and Loss Account by way of Advertisement/Charity.

(k) Income-tax

In case of Sole-Proprietorship business, it is a personal liability of the proprietor. Hence, if it appears in the Trial Balance, the same should be added with drawings.

But in case of partnership or any other business, income-tax is payable by the business. Thus, if it appears in the Trial Balance, the same should be debited to Profit and Loss Appropriation as a charge against appropriation of profit.

(l) Treatment of Purchases

(i) *When purchases are not passed through the books although the same are included in stock :*

(a) If it relates to the current financial year

We are to pass the usual entry; viz.

Purchases A/c Dr.
To Creditors/Suppliers A/c

(b) If it relates to the next year

It will simply be deducted from the closing stock.

(ii) *When purchases are recorded in the books but not included in stock (due to delayed delivery or any other reason) :*

For this purpose, simply a cancellation entry for purchases should be made (if it relates to the next period) by debiting Creditors or Suppliers Account and Crediting Purchase Account. Generally, the amount should be included with the value of closing stock on the ground that the same relates to the current financial year.

(iii) *When purchases are made for the current financial year but neither recorded at all in the books nor included in closing stock :*

In this case, we are to pass simply an usual entry as :

Purchases A/c Dr.
To Creditors/Suppliers A/c

Thus, it will be added with the amount of purchases as well as with the amount of creditors. Moreover, the same should also be included in the amount of closing stock.

(iv) *When purchases are made for private purpose but not passed through the books :*

There will be no entry in the books of the business if the proprietor wants to pay or assume a private liability. But in other cases the following entry should be passed

Drawings A/c Dr.
To Cash/Bank (for cash purchases)
" Creditors/Suppliers (for credit purchases)

Thus it will be added with the amount of Drawings and the same will be deducted from Cash or Bank or will be added with the amount of Creditors (for credit purchases only).

(v) *When assets are purchased but wrongly included with the amount of purchases :*

For this purpose, the following entry should be passed

Particular Asset A/c Dr.
To Purchases A/c

That is, value of asset should be increased and the same amount will be deducted from the purchases. It should be remembered that, if there is any depreciation on such asset, the same should also be computed on such enhanced value.

(m) Debtors which arise out of dishonoured cheques or discounted bills but not adjusted

The entry for this purpose will be

Debtors A/c Dr.
To Bank A/c

That is, the amount should be added with Debtors and the same should also be deducted from Bank Account. But out of those debtors, if any proves to be bad, the entry will be —

Bad Debts A/c Dr.

To Debtors A/c

i.e., Bad Debts to be transferred to Profit and Loss Account, the same also should be deducted from Debtors in the asset side of the Balance Sheet. If there is any provision for bad debts the same should be computed after adjusting the above bad debts.

(n) When revenue expenses are wrongly charged to Capital

Sometimes it may so happen that some revenue expenses viz., repairs and maintenance expenses etc, are charged wrongly to Capital i.e., Asset Account. For this purpose, the following entry should be passed

Particular Expenses A/c Dr.

To Particular Asset A/c

Expenses should be transferred to Profit and Loss Account and the same amount also should be deducted from the Particular Asset A/c. Depreciation, if any, should also be adjusted accordingly.

(o) When revenue expenses are capitalised

Sometimes some expenses which are related to assets should be capitalised although they are revenue in nature, viz., installation expenses. However, for this purpose, the following entry should be passed—

Particular Asset A/c Dr.

To Expenses A/c

Depreciation should be calculated for the increased value of such asset.

(p) When revenue expenses are treated as deferred one

Sometimes some revenue expenses may produce the services over a number of years, e.g., Advertisement Expenses. A proportionate amount should be charged to Profit and Loss Account every year and the balance (which is not transferred) is shown as an asset in the asset side of the Balance Sheet. Of course, if the adjustment states the amount which is not transferred to Profit and Loss Account, the entry will be

Deferred Expenses A/c Dr.

To Expenses A/c

And, in the next year

Expenses A/c Dr. } amount to be transfered to the

To Deferred Expenses A/c } year's Profit and Loss Account

and the balance is to be shown as an asset in the asset side of the Balance Sheet.

(q) When General Reserve or Reserve Fund is created

Since the creation of reserve is not a charge against profit, but an appropriation of profit, the entry will be

Profit and Loss Appropriation A/c Dr.

To General Reserve/Reserve Fund A/c

(r) Set-Off

Sometimes a person may be both a debtor and a creditor to the firm. In that case, the lower of the amount payable to and receivable from such person is to be set-off. The set-off amount is to be deducted both from the Debtors and from the Creditors in the Balance Sheet. The entry will be

Creditors (in Bought Ledger) A/c Dr.

To Debtors (in Sales Ledger) A/c

(s) Goods sent on approval

If goods are sent to the customer on Sale or Return basis, the same must not be treated as actual sale till the period is not expired. Thus, if goods are sent on approval basis, we pass the usual entry for credit sales. Naturally, if the goods are lying in the hands of the customer, awaiting approval, the following entries should be passed

(i) for cancellation of the original entry

Sales A/c Dr.

To Customer/Debtors A/c

(ii) For the inclusion of closing stock at cost

Closing Stock A/c Dr.

To Trading A/c

Illustration 5

Pass the necessary Adjusting Entries for the following :

(i) Closing Stock Rs. 10,000; (ii) Prepaid/Unexpired Insurance Rs. 1,500; (iii) Outstanding/Unpaid (or, due but not paid) Salary Rs. 3,000; (iv) Depreciate Plant by Rs. 1,000; (v) Interest accrued on investment Rs. 500; (vi) Commission received in advance Rs. 1,000; (vii) Rs. 500 due from S. Chakraborty, a customer, proved irrecoverable owing to his bankruptcy. (viii) Provision for Bad Debts is to be made @ 10% on Sundry Debtors which was Rs. 20,000; (ix) Provide Reserve for Discount on Debtors Rs. 30,000 and creditors Rs. 10,000 @ 10% and 5%, respectively; (x) Provide Interest on Capital Rs. 1,000 and on Drawings Rs. 250; (xi) Provide Interest on Loan @ 10% on Rs. 40,000; (xii) Included amongst the Debtors is Rs. 8,000 due from D and included amongst Creditors Rs. 5,000 due to him.

Solution

In the books ....
Journal

Date	*Particulars*		*L.F.*	*Debit*	*Credit*
?				Rs.	Rs.
(i)	Closing Stock A/c	Dr.		10,000	
	To Trading A/c				10,000
	(Closing Stock adjusted)				
(ii)	Prepaid Insurance A/c	Dr.		1,500	
	To Insurance A/c				1,500
	(Prepaid Insurance adjusted)				
(iii)	Salary A/c	Dr.		3,000	
	To Outstanding Salary				3,000
	(Outstanding Salary adjusted)				
(iv)	Depreciation A/c	Dr.		1,000	
	To Plant A/c				1,000
	(Depreciation on plant adjusted)				
(v)	Accrued Interest A/c	Dr.		500	
	To Interest A/c				500
	(Interest Accrued on Investment adjusted)				
(vi)	Commission A/c	Dr.		1,000	
	To Commission Received in Advance A/c				1,000
	(Commission received in advance adjusted)				
(vii)	Bad Debts A/c	Dr.		500	
	To S. Charkraborty (Debtors)				500
	(Bad Debts written-off adjusted)				
(viii)	Profit and Loss A/c	Dr.		2,000	
	To Provision for Bad Debts A/c				2,000
	(Provision for Bad Debt adjusted)				
(ix)	Profit and Loss A/c	Dr.		3,000	
	To Reserve for Discount on Debtors A/c				3,000
	(Reserve for discount on debtors adjusted)				
	Reserve for Discount on Creditors A/c	Dr.		500	
	To Profit and Loss A/c				500
	(Reserve for Discount on Creditors adjusted)				
(x)	Interest on Capital A/c	Dr.		1,000	
	To Capital A/c				1,000
	(Interest on capital adjusted)				
	Drawings/Capital A/c	Dr.		250	
	To Interest on Drawings A/c				250
	(Interest on drawings adjusted)				
(xi)	Interest on Loan A/c	Dr.		4,000	
	To Loan A/c				4,000
	(Interest on loan adjusted)				
(xii)	Sundry Creditors A/c	Dr.		5,000	
	To Sundry Debtors A/c				5,000
	(Set-off made between D (as creditor) and D (as debtor)				

GENERAL ILLUSTRATIONS

Illustration 6

From the following particulars presented by Sen Bros. pass the proper adjusting entries assuming that the business closes its accounts on 31st Dec. 2011:

(a) Closing Stock Cost price Rs. 5,000 Market price Rs. 3,000
(b) Goods valued Rs. 5,000 were destroyed by fire, not covered by Insurance at all.
(c) Goods valued Rs. 10,000 were destroyed by fire but Insurance Company admitted only 50% of the claim.
(d) Goods valued Rs. 5,000 destroyed by fire, but the Insurance Company admitted the claim in full.
(e) 50% of the goodwill is to be written-off. Value of goodwill was Rs. 10,000.

Solution

In the books of Sen Bros.
Journal

Date	*Particulars*		*L.F.*	*Debit*	*Credit*
2011				Rs.	Rs.
Dec. 31					
(a)	Closing Stock A/c	Dr.		3,000	
	To Trading A/c				3,000
	(Closing stock adjusted i.e., cost price or market price, whichever is lower)				
(b)	Stock Destroyed by Fire A/c	Dr.		5,000	
	To Trading A/c				5,000
	(Stock destroyed by fire adjusted)				
	Profit and Loss A/c	Dr.		5,000	
	To Stock Destroyed by Fire A/c				5,000
	(Loss of stock destroyed by fire charged to Profit and Loss Account)				
(c)	Stock Destroyed by Fire A/c	Dr.		10,000	
	To Trading A.c				10,000
	(Stock destroyed by Fire adjusted)				
	Admitted Insurance Claim A/c	Dr.		5,000	
	Profit and Loss A/c	Dr.		5,000	
	To Stock Destroyed by Fire A/c				10,000
	(50% of the stock lost by fire was admitted and the balance i.e., unrecoverable part, being a revenue charge, transferred to Profit and Loss Account)				
(d)	Stock Destroyed by Fire A/c	Dr.		5,000	
	To Trading A/c				5,000
	(Stock destroyed by fire adjusted)				
	Admitted Insurance Claim A/c	Dr.		5,000	
	To Stock Destroyed by Fire A/c				5,000
	(Amount recoverable from insurance co. for stock destroyed by fire)				
(e)	Profit and Loss A/c	Dr.		5,000	
	To Goodwill A/c				5,000
	(50% of goodwill to be written-off against Profit and Loss Account.)				

Illustration 7

Rent paid for the year ended 31st December 2011 amounted Rs. 12,000 which included Rs. 1,000 for 2010 and Rs. 700 for 2012. Moreover, in 2010, Rs. 800 was paid in advance by way of Rent and Outstanding Rent for the year ended 31st December 2011 amounted to Rs. 2,500. Show the necessary Ledger Accounts.

Dr. **Rent Account** *Cr.*

Date	*Particulars*	*Amount*	*Date*	*Particulars*	*Amount*
2011		Rs.	2011		Rs.
Jan. 1	To Prepaid Rent A/c	800	Jan. 1	By Outstanding Rent A/c	1,000
Jan. 1 to Dec. 31	" Bank A/c	12,000	Dec. 31	" Prepaid Rent A/c	700
Dec. 31	" Outstanding Rent A/c	2,500		" Profit and Loss A/c (bal. fig.)	13,600
		15,300			15,300

Dr. **Outstanding Rent Account** Cr.

Date		Particulars	Amount	Date		Particulars	Amount
2011			Rs.	2011			Rs.
Jan. 1	To	Rent A/c	1,000	Jan. 1	By	Balance b/d	1,000
Dec. 31	"	Balance c/d	2,500	Dec. 31	"	Rent A/c	2,500
			3,500				3,500

Dr. **Prepaid Rent Account** Cr.

Date		Particulars	Amount	Date		Particulars	Amount
2011			Rs.	2011			Rs.
Jan. 1	To	Balance b/d	800	Jan. 1	By	Rent A/c	800
	"	Rent A/c	700	Dec. 31	"	Balance c/d	700
			1,500				1,500

Alternative approach : i.e., (if "Above the Line or Below the Line" Method is followed)

Dr. **Rent Account** Cr.

Date		Particulars	Amount	Date		Particulars	Amount
2011			Rs.	2011			Rs.
Jan. 1	To	Balance b/d (prepaid)	800	Jan. 1	By	Balance b/d (outstanding)	1,000
Jan. 1 to Dec. 31	"	Bank A/c	12,000	Dec. 31	"	Profit & Loss A/c *(bal. fig.)*	13,600
Dec. 31	"	Outstanding Rent A/c	2,500		"	Balance c/d prepaid	700
			15,300				15,300
2012				2012			
Jan. 1	To	Balance b/d	700	Jan. 1	By	Balance b/d	2,500

Illustration 8

Accounts of a company, closed for the year, showed Net Profit Rs. 26,504, Gross Profit Rs. 74,319 and the Balance Sheet total was Rs. 2,15,824. It is now observed that the following were not taken into account :

(a) Goods costing Rs. 1,315 were distributed by way of free samples during the year : (b) Depreciation on fixed assets amounting to Rs. 4,591; (c) Outstanding salaries Rs. 1,200 and wages Rs. 720; (d) Prepaid insurance premium Rs. 250; (e) Wages Rs. 700 paid for installation of a machine were not taken out of wages account; (f) Cost of repairs to Building Rs. 500 was debited to the Building Account. What would be the (i) adjusted Net Profit, (ii) adjusted Gross Profit and (iii) Balance Sheet total?

[CU BCom (Hons.)]

Solution

In the books ....

Journal

		Gross Profit	*Net Profit*	*B/S Total*
		Rs.	Rs.	Rs.
Amounts as per Accounts		74,319	26,504	2,15,824
Goods distributed as free samples[1]	...	(+) 1,315	—	
Depreciation on fixed assets[2]	...	—	(–) 4,591	(–) 4,591
Outstanding Expenses :				
Wages	...	(–) 720	(–) 720	—
Salaries	...	—	(–) 1,200	—
Prepaid Insurance	...	—	(+) 250	(+) 250
Wages for installation of machine	...	(+) 700	(+) 700	(+) 700
Cost of repairs to Building	...	—	(–) 500	(–) 500
Correct Amounts		75,614	20,443	2,11,683

Notes :

1 Even if the item is not considered at all the profit shall be correct. As such, net profit—which was ascertained without considering the item—does not require any adjustment but gross profit ascertained was reduced by omission of the item. Hence, gross profit only requires necessary adjustment for the purpose.

2 Assumed that the figure for depreciation Rs. 4,591 has been arrived at after adjusting the installation expense in Machinery A/c (e) and elimination of repairing expense from Building A/c. (f).

Illustration 9

The Trial Balance of Mr. M has been agreed as at December 31, 1995.

How would you deal with the following items when making up the Final Accounts ? Note briefly the points involved :

(a) Insurance account Dr. Rs. 693. This is the balance after crediting a sum of Rs. 2,317 received in respect of a fire claim for stock destroyed by fire.

(b) Forfeited Shares Account Cr. Rs. 600. This is the balance remaining after the necessary entries have been passed in relation to 200 shares forfeited and reissued.

(c) Patents Dr. Rs. 20,000. This represents the total actual cost to date of patents. About half of the expenditure relates to patents which are admittedly valueless, but balance is considerably less than the value of remaining patents.

(d) Building Accounts Dr. Rs. 12,00,000. This represents actual expenditure on structures erected on land held on a lease which has 15 years to run.

[CU BCom (Hons.)]

Solution **In the books of Mr. M**

(a) The balance of Insurance Account shows a debit balance amounting to Rs. 693 which is the uncovered part of insurance of those goods which were destroyed by fire. This is a revenue loss which must be adjusted against Profit and Loss Account i.e., Profit and Loss Account should be debited and Stock Destroyed by Fire Account should be credited.

(b) The balance of Share Forfeiture Account, amounting to Rs. 600 after re-issuing all the forfeited shares, is a capital profit which must be transferred to capital reserve according to Companies Act, 1956. (Students are advised to see the Company Accounts for further details.) i.e., the entry will be — Forfeited Shares Account will be debited and Capital Reserve Account will be credited.

(c) It is needless to mention that 50% of the cost of the Patents (i.e., Rs. 20,000 × $\frac{50}{100}$) Rs. 10,000 should be written-off against Profit and Loss Account since the same becomes valueless, i.e., Profit and Loss Account should be debited by Rs. 10,000 and Patents Account should be credited by the same amount. But it is better to write-off the said amount, i.e., Rs. 10,000, after a number of years in order to show that the profit of a particular year must not be adversely affected, and, for the remaining half, the same should be shown as an asset at its cost price, irrespective of the market price, in the asset side of the Balance Sheet—as it is acquired for long-term use (as a fixed asset) and not for re-sale.

(d) Building is a fixed asset which was erected on a Leasehold land for a fixed period of time i.e., 15 years and, as such, the entire asset should be written-off against Profit and Loss Account over a period of 15 years, i.e., Rs. 12,00,000 × $\frac{1}{15}$ = Rs. 80,000 should be written-off against Profit and Loss Account every year i.e., Profit and Loss Account should be debited and Leasehold Building should be credited.

Illustration 10

A and B, partners in a firm, have prepared from the books of account the following Draft Balance Sheet as on 31st December 2011 :

	A Rs.	B Rs.	Rs.		Rs.	Rs.
Capital (1.1.2011)	20,100	10,000		Freehold Building (at cost)		12,000
Profit for the year	4,770	4,770		Plant and Machinery (at cost)	15,000	
	24,870	14,770		*Less :* Depreciation	7,000	
Less : Drawings	2,000	3,800				8,000
	22,870	10,970		Motor Vehicles (at cost)	8,000	
			33,840	*Less :* Depreciation	2,700	
Creditors			7,800			5,300

Contd.

	Rs.	Rs.	Rs.		Rs.	Rs.
Bank Overdraft			2,700	Stock		5,000
				Debtors		14,000
				Cash in hand		40
			44,340			44,340

During the course of your examination of the books you ascertain that adjustments are required for the following items :

(a) Freehold Buildings are shown at cost less Rs. 3,000 being the proceeds of the sale during the year of premises costing Rs. 3,500.

(b) Plant and Machinery having net book value of Rs. 215 had been scrapped during the year. The original cost was Rs. 615.

(c) Motor Vehicle licences for 12 months' period costing Rs. 100 had been written-off, but did not expire until 30th June 2012.

(d) Debt to the value of Rs. 521 were considered to be bad and a further Rs. 270 doubtful requiring 100% provision. Provision had previously been made for Rs. 500 doubtful debt.

(e) Stock included at a value of Rs. 1,870 had a net realisable value of only Rs. 1,300 and scrap material having a value of Rs. 330 had been omitted from the stock revaluation.

(f) The cashier has misappropriated Rs. 35.

(g) The Cash Book included payments amounting to Rs. 3,462, the cheques having been made out but not mailed to suppliers until 2012.

(h) Interest is to be allowed on Partners' Opening Capital Account balances less drawings during the year at 9%.

You are required to prepare :

(i) a statement of Profit and Loss adjustment for the period; and (ii) a revised Balance Sheet as on 31st Dec. 2011.

Solution

In the books of A and B
Statement of Profit and Loss Adjustment
for the year ended 31st Dec. 2011

		Rs.	Rs.
	Profit as per Draft Balance Sheet (4,770 + 4,770)		9,540
Add :	Motor Vehicle licence paid in advance	50	
	Provision for bad debts, no longer required (500 – 270)	230	
	Scrap materials omitted from the books	330	610
			10,150
Less :	Loss on sale of premises (Rs. 3,500 – 3,000)	500	
	Plant and Machinery (B. V.) scrapped during the year	215	
	Bad Debts written-off	521	
	Decrease in realisable value of stock (Rs. 1,870 – 1,300)	570	
	Misappropriation of Cash	35	1,841
	Adjusted Profit		8,309
Less :	Interest on Capital :		
	A @ 9% on Rs. 18,100 =	1,629	
	B @ 9% on Rs. 6,200 =	558	2,187
	Revised distribution of profit		6,122
		A = 6,122 × $\frac{1}{2}$ =	3,061
		B = 6,122 × $\frac{1}{2}$ =	3,061

Balance Sheet
as at 31st Dec. 2011

Liabilities	Rs.	Rs.	*Assets*	Rs.	Rs.
Capital			Freehold Building		
A	20,100		(12,000 – 500)		11,500
Add : Share of Profit	3,061		Plant and Machinery		
Add : Int. on Cap.	1,629		(15,000 – 615)	14,385	
	24,790		*Less :* Depreciation		
Less : Drawings	2,000		(7,000 – 400)	6,600	
		22,790			7,785
B	10,000		Motor Vehicles	8,000	
Add : Share of Profit	3,061		*Less :* Depreciation	2,700	
Add : Int. on Cap.	558				5,300
	13,619		Stock (5,000 + 330 – 570)		4,760
Less : Drawings	3,800		Debtors (14,000 + 500)	14,500	
Creditors		9,819	*Less :* Bad Debts	521	
(99,800 + 3,462)		11,262		13,979	
			Less : Prov. for Bad Debts	270	13,709
			Prepaid licence		50
			Cash at Bank (3,462 – 2,700)		762
			Cash in hand (40 – 35)		5
		43,871			43,871

ASSIGNMENT MATERIALS

THEORITICAL

Fill in the Blanks

1. Fill in the blanks :
   (a) For depreciation on plant; Depreciation Account is ....
   (b) For Bad Debts' Bad Debts Accounting is ....
   (c) For Outstanding Salary; Outstanding Salary Account is ....
   (d) For Closing Stock : Closing Stock Account is ....
   (e) For writing off Goodwill : Goodwill Account is ....
   (f) For Stock destroyed by fire : Stock Destroyed by Fire Account is ....
   (g) For goods used by proprietor : Drawing Account is ....
   (h) For Prepaid Insurance : Prepaid Insurance Account is ....

Short-Answer Type Questions

2. What is a Journal Proper? What kind of Transactions are passed through Journal Proper?
3. What is a Opening Entry? Explain it with the help of an example.
4. Write notes on :
   (a) Transfer Entry, (b) Closing Entry; (c) Adjusting Entry.
5. What do you mean by Adjusting Entry? Why are such entries made?
6. Distinguish between Outstanding Expenses and Prepaid Expenses.
7. Distinguish between Outstanding Income and Income Received in Advance.
8. Distinguish between :
   (a) Opening Entry and Closing Entry
   (b) Adjusting Entry and Closing Entry.
9. Has Journal Proper an effect on Profit? Explain.
10. What is the difference between Journal and Special Journal?

Long-Answer Type Questions

11. How do you treat the following: (a) Bad Debts; (b) Interest on Capital; (c) Interest on Drawings; (d) Deprecation on Asset?

12. What is the impact of Journal Proper while ascertaining net profit of a firm?
13. What is the impact of Adjusting Entry while ascertaining net profit of a firm?
14. What kind of transactions are passed through journal proper?
15. Discuss the role of different adjusting entries in accounts.

PRACTICAL

A. Credit Purchase and Credit Sale of Assets

1. Show the entries from the following particulars :

(i) Purchased a Plant from Machinery Co. Ltd. for Rs. 5,000 on 3. 12. 2011 on credit.
(ii) Sold old Furniture to M/s Das & Co. for Rs. 3,000 on credit on 10.12. 2011.
(iii) Purchased one Typewriter from H. M. T. for Rs. 4,000 paid as advance Rs. 1,000 only on 12.12. 2011.
(iv) Sold one Old Plant for Rs. 3,000 on credit to C. Chatterjee, written-down value was Rs. 4,250 (on 13.12.2011).
(v) Sold one old furniture on Credit (Book value Rs. 1,000, Depreciation already provided Rs. 600) for Rs. 800. to M/s Poddar & Co. (on 20.12. 2011).

B. Transfer Entries

2. Record the following Transfer Entries with proper narrations :

(a) Bad Debts written-off Rs. 800 to be adjusted against Provision for Bad Debts Account.
(b) Transfer from Jadav's A/c to Rahim's A/c for Rs. 800.
(c) Sales Returns of Rs. 500 to Sales Account.
(d) Purchase Returns of Rs. 250 to Purchase Account.
(e) Transfer 50% of the net profit to Reserve Fund; profit being Rs. 10,000.
(f) Drawings amounted to Rs. 1,200 transferred to Capital Account.
(g) Debtor included Rs. 1,000 due from Mr. X whereas creditors included Rs. 500 due to Mr. X. Set-off the accounts.

C. Opening Entries

3. X & Co. had the following balances as at 31st Dec. 2011. You are asked to show the opening entry at the beginning of 2011:

	Rs.		Rs.
Plant	10,000	Reserve Fund	5,000
Land	12,000	Outstanding Salary	3,000
Debtors	18,000	Prepaid Insurance	1,000
Stock	15,000	Furniture & Fittings	8,000
Creditors	5,000	Loan (taken)	3,000
Bills Receivable	8,000	Capital	50,000
Bills Payable	3,000		
Bank Overdraft	3,000		

4. Following are the ledger balances of Sri N. Payra as on 30. 6. 2010, the close of the accounting year. Which accounts will you close and how?

	Rs.		Rs.
Capital A/c	30,000	Wages A/c	3,000
Plant & Machinery A/c	10,000	Carriage Inward A/c	1,000
Drawings A/c	2,000	Carriage Outward A/c	2,000
Cash in hand	1,000	Discount Allowed A/c	1,000
Cash at Bank	10,000	Discount Received A/c	2,000
Opening Stock	5,000	Bad Debts A/c	1,000
Closing Stock	10,000	Provision for Bad Debts A/c	1,500
Purchases A/c	12,000	Furniture & Fittings A/c	5,000

Contd.

	Rs.		Rs.
Sales A/c	40,000	Bank Overdraft A/c	6,000
Returns Outward A/c	2,000	Sundry Debtors A/c	10,000
Returns Inward A/c	4,000	Sundry Creditors A/c	5,000
Interest Received A/c	1,000	Trade Expenses A/c	2,000
		Miscellaneous Expenses A/c	3,000

Hints : Capital A/c, Plant and Machinery A/c, Drawings A/c, Cash in hand, Cash at Bank, Furniture and Fittings, Bank Overdraft A/c, Sundry Debtors A/c and Sundry Creditors A/c are to be excluded.

(e) Adjusting Entries

5. Give journal entries to record the following :

(i) Interest on Savings Bank Account of Bank of India amounted to Rs. 500 has not been recorded in the books.

(ii) Cash discount is to be allowed to a customer on sales Rs. 1,00,000 less returns Rs. 10,000 @ 5%.

(iii) Bad debts previously written-off now recovered Rs. 500.

(iv) Rs. 1,000 is to be written-off against lease.

(v) Goods valued Rs. 1,000 were distributed by way of advertisement.

(vi) Write-off goodwill account which stood in the books Rs. 5,000.

(vii) Royalty received in advance Rs. 500.

(viii) Goods purchased but in-transit Rs. 4,000.

(ix) Commission amounting to Rs. 500 has been received in advance for work to be done in the next year.

(x) $\frac{1}{5}$ th of the Preliminary Expenses of Rs. 5,000 is to be written-off.

6. From the following particulars, pass the proper adjusting entries. The business closed its accounts on 31st Dec. 2010 :

(i) Provision for Doubtful Debts is to be made @ 5% on Sundry Debtors which was Rs. 15,000.

(ii) The advertisement expenses of Rs. 10,000 is to be spread over 5 years.

(iii) Goods-in-transit was valued at Rs. 8,000.

(iv) Rent for the next three months was received in advance, annual Rent being Rs. 1,200.

(v) Interest on Capital is to be provided @ 10% p.a. Capital being Rs. 20,000 as on 1.1.2010, further Capital was introduced on 30. 9. 2010. Rs. 5,000.

(vi) Interest on Drawings should be provided @ 10% p.a. (on an average 6 months), Drawings for the year amounted to Rs. 10,000.

7. Show necessary Journal entries in respect of the following :

(i) Closing Stock of Finished Goods (as at 31.12. 2010) Rs. 30,000.

(ii) Outstanding Salaries and Wages (as at 31.12. 2010) Rs. 10,000.

(iii) Depreciation on Plant and Machinery to be provided for the year ended 31. 12. 2010 Rs. 10,000.

(iv) Bad debts to be written-off to the extent of Rs. 300 and a Provision for doubtful debts to be created @ $2\frac{1}{2}$% (Total of Sundry Debtors being Rs. 30,000).

(v) Interest @ 15% p.a. has accrued on Investments of Rs. 20,000 (Interest is payable on 31st March and 30th September in each year and accounts are closed on 31st December every year).

(vi) Rent for the year 2010 was paid @ Rs. 300 p.m. only up to October 2010.

(vii) Insurance Premium of Rs. 600 was paid for the half year ended 31st March 2011 (Accounts being closed on 31st December 2011).

[BU B Com (Hons]

CHAPTER 10

RECTIFICATION OF ERRORS

Learning Objectives
Introduction
Types of Errors
—Clerical
—Errors of Omission
—Errors of Commission
—Errors of Duplication
—Compensating Errors
—Errors of Principle
Management of Errors
A. Prevention of Errors
B. Detection of Errors
C. Rectification of Errors
A. Before Preparing Trial Balance
—Double Sided Errors
—Single Sided Errors
B. After Preparing Trial Balance
—Double Sided Errors
—Single Sided Errors
C After Preparing Final Accounts
—Double Sided Errors
—Single Sided Errors

Introduction

At the time of preparing accounts errors may arise due to the innocence or carelessness of the persons who are engaged to prepare the accounts from the various transactions. Usually, the errors may occur innocently in accounts, but sometimes they are deliberately committed. Prevention and detection of errors are the major functions of the auditor although it is not an easy task. There are different types of errors. [Students are requested to see Chapter 3 for detailed explanation of Errors].

In the present study, however, we will highlight the different types of errors through a new outlook:

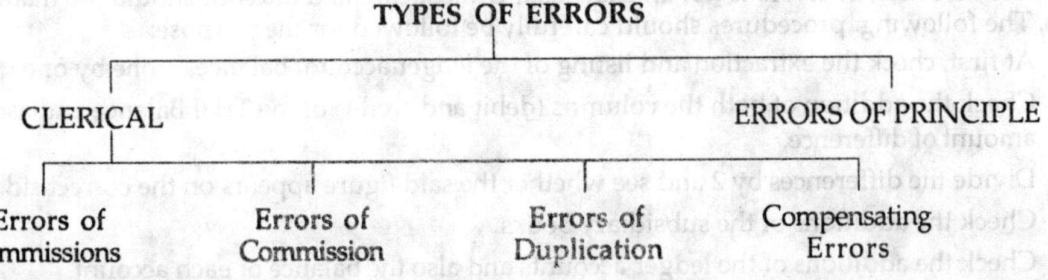

(a) **Clerical Errors**

These errors are committed by the persons who are preparing accounts or by the accountant or accounts clerks e.g., (i) Omission of a transactions wholly or partly; (ii) wrong posting from one page to another page; (iii) at the time of balancing accounts etc.

(i) **Errors of Omission**

These errors are committed by the accounts clerk. It means a transaction is not at all recorded in the books, or, the transactions are recorded in journal but omitted to be posted in the ledger although the omission may be honest or deliberate. It is not an easy task to detect this type of error as the Trial Balance is agreed.

(ii) **Errors of Commission**

These types of errors arise due to the negligence of the accounts clerk while recording transactions in the books of account, e.g., recording wrong entries, wrong posting and casting, or carry forward etc.

(iii) **Errors of Duplication**

These are also clerical errors and they occur when the same transaction is recorded twice in journal and posted into ledger therefrom. It is not so difficult to detect. Trial Balance will agree.

(iv) **Compensating Errors**

When one error is compensated or counter-balanced by an another error and consequently, the adverse effect of one debit or credit is neutralised by another debit on Credit. It may also happen when an undercasting of an account is counter-balanced by an overcasting of an another account.

(b) **Errors of Principle**

Errors of principle arise when a transaction is not recorded as per fundamental principles of accounting, e.g., wrong allocation of expenditure between capital and revenue, improper provision for depreciation or provision for bad and doubtful debts. If these errors are committed deliberately, it is very difficult to detect, ultimate object is to falsify and manipulate the accounts which affect the results of the operation and financial position.

Management of Errors

The entire management of errors may be performed with the help of the following:

A. **Prevention of Errors;**
B. **Detection of Errors; and**
C. **Rectification of Errors.**

A. Prevention of Errors

Errors may be avoided if proper prevention is made while preparing accounts. It is rightly said that ***"Prevention is better than cure"***. In order to avoid errors, the management should introduce effective internal control system. Sometimes errors are intentionally done by the management to window-dress the financial health of the enterprise which is against the principles of accounting. But the errors which are committed innocently, can be prevented as the innocent errors arise due to (a) inadequate knowledge of accounting; and (b) carelessness while preparing accounts.

The first one can be prevented if the accounts clerk or concerned employees are properly trained about the knowledge of accounting continuously. The second one is very difficult to prevent as preparing accounts depends on the human element to a great extent even after introducing computers in the field of accounting. The employees or the accounts clerks should be given a professional outlook so that careless should be reduced as far as possible.

B. Delection of Errors

No doubt detection of errors is not an easy task. Utmost care and attempt should be made to detect the errors. The following procedures should carefully be followed for the purpose:

(i) At first, check the extraction and listing of the ledger account balances—one by one.

(ii) Check the addition of both the columns (debit and credit) of the Trial Balance and ascertain the amount of difference.

(iii) Divide the differences by 2 and see whether the said figure appears on the correct side or not.

(iv) Check the additions of the subsidiary books.

(v) Check the additions of the ledger accounts and also the balance of each account.

(vi) Check the positing from subsidiary books to the ledger.

(vii) Check that balance of the account which is exactly equal to the difference of Trial Balance, if any.

(viii) Check the opening balances of all accounts—whether brought forward correctly or not.

(ix) Up to the level, if the errors are not even deleted, checking and re-checking must be done by other staff following the same principle.

(x) If the trial balance is still not agreed, checking should be started again from the journal and book of original entry—using tick mark (√) against each and every transaction.

C. Rectification of Errors

The error may again be sub-divided into:

(a) Single-Sided Error or, One-Sided Error; (b) Double-Sided Error.

Now, for the purpose of rectification of the errors the most important factor is the **time element**, i.e., ***when errors were actually detected :***

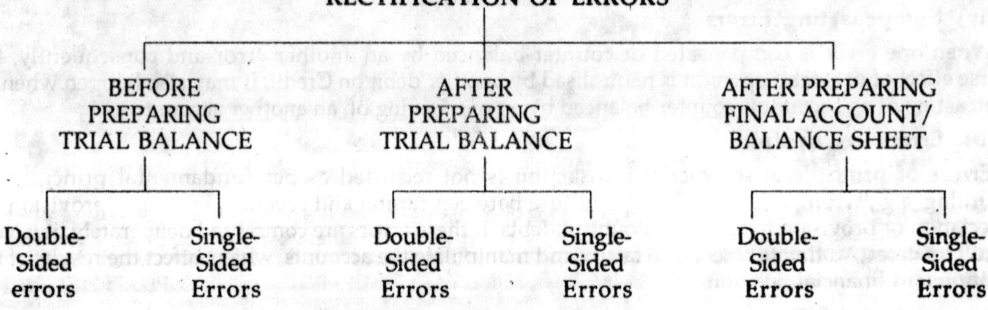

METHOD OF PREPARATION

A. BEFORE PREPARING TRIAL BALANCE

When the errors are detected before preparing the Trial Balance, i.e., before the accounts are closed, it becomes necessary to know the effect of each error in the accounts in the ledger:

The errors are of two types:

(1) Double-Sided Error; and (2) Single-Sided Error.

1. Double-Sided Error

For each double-sided error, the following principles should be carefully remembered:

(a) What was the correct entry? (b) What entry had been made? (c) Rectifying entry?

Illustration 1

Purchased a plant for Rs. 5,000 wrongly passed through Purchases Account.

Solution

Date	Particulars		L.F.	Debit	Credit	
				Rs.	Rs.	
	(a) Plant A/c	Dr.		5,000		Correct entry
	To Sales A/c				5,000	
	(b) Purchase A/c	Dr.		5,000		Entry made
	To Cash A/c				5,000	
	(c) Plant A/c	Dr.		5,000		Rectifying entry
	To Purchases A/c				5,000	

Illustration 2

Sold goods to Mr. X for Rs. 1,000, not recorded in the books.

Solution

Date	Particulars		L.F.	Debit	Credit	
				Rs.	Rs.	
	(a) X A/c	Dr.		1,000		Correct entry
	To Sales A/c				1,000	
	(b) Nil					
	(c) X A/c	Dr.		1,000		Rectifying entry
	To Sales A/c				1,000	

[**Note :** Here the original entry becomes the rectifying entry since it is an error of omission.]

Illustration 3

Paid salary to Mr. X for Rs. 1,000 wrongly recorded as Rs. 100 in the books of accounts.

Solution

Date	Particulars		L.F.	Debit	Credit	
				Rs.	Rs.	
	(a) Salary A/c	Dr.		1,000		Correct entry
	To Cash A/c				1,000	
	(b) Salary A/c	Dr.		100		Entry made
	To Cash A/c				100	
	(c) Salary A/c	Dr.		900		Rectifying entry
	To Cash A/c				900	

Illustration 4

Pass rectification entries for the following transactions assuming that they are debited before preparing Trial Balance:

(1) A builder's bill for Rs. 4,600 for the erection of a small shed was debited to Repairs Account.

(2) Repairs to plant, amounting to Rs. 900, has been charged to Plant and Machinery Account.

(3) Wages paid to the firm's workmen, for making certain additions to machinery, amounting to Rs. 340, were debited to Wages Account.

(4) A cheque for Rs. 750, received from S. Desai, was credited to the account of R. Ram.

(5) Goods to the value of Rs. 700, returned by X, were included in closing stock, but no entry was made in the books.

(6) Goods costing Rs. 2,000 were purchased for various members of the staff and the cost was included in Purchases. A similar amount was deducted from the salaries of the staff members concerned and the net payments to them debited to Salaries Account.

(7) A bill of exchange (received from Hari) for Rs. 3,000 had been returned by the Bank, with whom it had been discounted as dishonoured and had been credited to Bank Account and debited to Bills Receivable Account.

(8) Goods sold to Z for Rs. 475 have been wrongly entered in the Sales book as Rs. 745.

[CA (Entrance)—Adapted]

Solution

In the books of.........

Journal

Date	Particulars	L.F..	Debit Rs.	Credit Rs.
1.	Building A/c Dr. To Repairs A/c (Expenses for erecting small shed wrongly debited to repairs account instead of building account, now rectified.)		4,600	4,600
2.	Repairs A/c Dr. To Plant & Machinery A/c (Repairs made to Plant & Machinery has been wrongly charged to Plant & Machinery A/c, now rectified.)		900	900
3.	Plant & Machinery A/c Dr. To Wages A/c (Wages paid for addition to machinery had been wrongly debited to Wges A/c, now rectified.)		340	340
4.	R. Ram A/c Dr. To S. Desai A/c (Cheque received from S. Desai wrongly credited to R. Ram, now rectified.)		750	750
5.	Returns Inward A/c Dr. To X. A/c (Goods returned by X not recorded in the books at all, now rectified.)		700	700
6.	Salaries A/c Dr. To Purchase A/c (Goods purchase for staff members wrongly debited to Purchase A/c now rectified.)		2,000	2,000
7.	Hari A/c Dr. To Bills receivable A/c (Bill accepted by Hari was discounted but later dishonoured but wrongly debited to Bills Receivable A/c, now rectified.)		3,000	3,000
8.	Sales A/c (Rs. 745 – 475) Dr. To Z A/c (Sales to Z of Rs. 475, wrongly recorded in the sales book as Rs. 745, now rectified.)		270	270

2. Single-sided Errors

In this case, no entry is required but the relevant account is rectified by making the necessary posting (i.e., by debiting or crediting the affected account).

Illustration 5

Sales Account was cast short by Rs. 1,000.

Solution

The only correction is to be made in Sales Account in the following manner:

Dr. Sales A/c Cr.

	Rs.		Rs.
		By Error — Wrong Posting from X A/c	1,000

So, Sales Account should be credited by Rs. 1,000.

Illustration 6

Goods sold to Mr. X for Rs. 500, X A/c was wrongly credited by Rs. 50.

Solution

In this case, X A/c should be debited by Rs. 500, but his account was wrongly credited by Rs. 50. So, his account should be debited by Rs. 550 (500 + 50).

Dr. X A/c Cr.

	Rs.		Rs.
To Sales A/c	550	By Sales A/c —Errors	50

So, X's Account should be debited by Rs. 550.

Illustration 7

Returns Inward Book was recorded as Rs. 2,000, in place of Rs. 2,500.

Solution

It reveals that the Returns Inward Book was undercast by Rs. 500. This account must be debited by Rs. 500 more.

Dr. **Returns Inward A/c** *Cr.*

		Rs.		Rs.
To	Debtors A/c	2,000		
"	Debtors A/c—Error	500		

Thus, Returns Inward Account should be debited by Rs. 500.

Illustration 8

The following errors were committed by the accountant of M/s Das & Co.:

(a) Cash paid to Ram Rs. 520, was posted in his account as Rs. 250. (b) Sales Day Book was undercast by Rs. 1,000. (c) Purchase of Stationery Rs. 200 were not posted to the Stationery Account. (d) Goods returned by Mr. Banerjee Rs. 1,500, posted to his account from Returns Inward Book as Rs. 5,100. Rectify the above errors assuming that they were detected before preparation of Trial Balance.

Solution

In the Books of M/s Das & Co.

Journal

Date	*Particulars*	*L.F.*	*Debit*	*Credit*
			Rs.	Rs.
	(a) Ram will be debited with Rs. 270 (i.e., Rs. 520 – Rs. 250)			
	(b) Sales Account will be credited with Rs. 1,000			
	(c) Stationery Account will be debited with Rs. 200			
	(d) Banerjee's Account will be debited with Rs. 3,600 (i.e., Rs. 5,100 – Rs. 1,500)			

B. AFTER PREPARING TRIAL BALANCE BUT BEFORE PREPARING FINAL ACCOUNTS

If the errors are not detected at the time of preparing Trial Balance, difference will arise, which is transferred to a newly opened Suspense Account and the Trial Balance will automatically agree. If the errors are detected after preparing Trial Balance, the following procedure should carefully be followed:

(1) Double-sided Errors; and (2) Single-sided Errors.

(1) Double-sided Errors

The same principle will be followed here like before, preparing Trial Balances in case of double-sided errors, i.e.,

Step I What was the correct Entry?

Step II What entry (Wrong) had been made?

Step III Rectifing entry, it will be made in such a manner so that after cancelling Step I and Step III, Step I may appear.

Illustration 9

A machine was purchased but wrongly passed through the Purchases Account amounted to Rs. 4,000.

Solution

In this case, the relevant entries will be:

Date	*Particulars*		*L.F.*	*Debit*	*Credit*	
				Rs.	Rs.	
	(a) Machinery A/c	Dr.		4,000		Correct entry
	To Cash A/c				4,000	
	(b) Purchases A/c	Dr.		4,000		Entry made
	To Cash A/c				4,000	
	(c) Machinery A/c	Dr.		4,000		Rectifying entry
	To Purchases A/c				4,000	

Here, there is no error in Cash A/c, the only error is that instead of debiting Machinery A/c, Purchase A/c has been debited. Thus, the rectifying entry will be

Machinery A/c Dr.
To Purchases A/c

} In this case by cancelling (b) and (c) i.e., Purchase A/c Debit and Credit, original Entry stands.

Illustration 10

A plant was sold for Rs. 4,000 wrongly passed through Sales Account.

Solution

Date	Particulars	L.F.	Debit	Credit	
			Rs.	Rs.	
	(a) Cash A/c Dr. To Plant A/c		4,000	4,000	Correct Entry
	(b) Cash A/c Dr. To Sales A/c		4,000	4,000	Entry Made
	(c) Sales A/c Dr. To Plant A/c		4,000	4,000	Rectifying Entry

Illustration 11

Paid Salary to Mr X for Rs. 5,000 has wrongly been entered in Cash Book Rs. 500.

Solution

Date	Particulars	L.F.	Debit	Credit	
			Rs.	Rs.	
	(a) Salary A/c Dr. To Cash A/c		5,000	5,000	Correct Entry
	(b) Salary A/c Dr. To Cash A/c		500	500	Entry Made
	(c) Salary A/c Dr. To Cash A/c		4,500	4,500	Rectifying Entry

Illustration 12

Rectify the following errors, assuming that these were detected after preparing Trial Balance:

(i) Interest received Rs. 300 was credited to Commission Account.

(ii) Purchased Plant for Rs. 4,000, wrongly debited to Purchases Account.

(iii) Sold old Furniture for Rs. 800, wrongly credited to Sales Account.

(iv) Rs. 2,000, salary paid to Mr. B. Bose, stands debited to his Personal Account.

(v) Rs. 1,000, paid to B. Bros. against our acceptance, were debited to B. Bros. Account.

(vi) Purchase of goods for the consumption of the proprietor was debited to Purchases Account for Rs. 800.

(vii) A credit sale of Rs. 400 was posted from Sales Book to Sen & Co. instead of Das & Co.

(viii) Furniture worth Rs. 2,000, purchased for Cash, was debited to Repairs Account.

Solution

In the Books of ....
Journal

Date	Particulars	L.F.	Debit	Credit
			Rs.	Rs.
?	(i) Commission A/c Dr. To Interest A/c (Interest received but wrongly credited to Commission Account, now rectified)		300	300
	(ii) Plant A/c Dr. To Purchases A/c (Plant purchased but wrongly debited to Purchases Account, now rectified)		4,000	4,000

Contd.

			Rs.	Rs.
?				
(iii)	Sales A/c To Furniture (Old) A/c (Old Furniture sold but wrongly credited to Sales Account, now rectified)	Dr.	800	800
(iv)	Salary A/c To B. Bose A/c (Salary paid to B. Bose, wrongly debited to his account, now rectified)	Dr.	2,000	2,000
(v)	Bills Payable A/c To B. Bros A/c (Acceptance paid but wrongly debited to B. Bose's Account, now rectified)	Dr.	1,000	1,000
(vi)	Drawings A/c To Purchases A/c (Goods purchased for private consumption, wrongly debited to Purchases Account, now rectified)	Dr.	800	800
(vii)	Das & Co. A/c To Sen & Co. A/c (Goods sold to Das & Co. but wrongly debited to Sen & Co., now rectified)	Dr.	400	400
(viii)	Furniture A/c To Repairs A/c (Furniture purchased but wrongly debited to Repairs Account, now rectified)	Dr.	2,000	2,000

2. Single Sided Errors

If there is any single sided error, open the relevant account and pass the entry through Suspense Account.

Suspense Account

It is not usual to commit errors while preparing various books of accounts, i.e., certain types of errors may exist in books, e.g., clerical errors, errors of commission, etc. Now if the Trial Balance does not agree due to the existence of some errors in the books of account, final accounts of the firm cannot be prepared. It may take a long period to rectify all the errors. Thus, in order to prepare the final accounts, the difference so appeared is transferred to **Suspense Account or Difference in Books Account** to make the Trial Balance agree pending detection of error or errors. It is practically a temporary solution. When the error or errors are located and rectified the Suspense Account will automatically be closed. In short, the use of Suspense Account is primarily connected with the disagreement of Trial Balance. The Suspense Account will appear in the Balance Sheet. **If Suspense Account appears in the credit side of the Trial Balance the same will appear in the Liabilities side of the Balance Sheet, and vice versa in the opposite case.**

If the errors are detected before preparing Trial Balance, question of Suspense Account will not arise at all since all the ledger accounts are not closed. The concerned account can easily be rectified since the account is not balanced. But if the errors are detected after preparing Trial Balance. Suspense, Account must appear in the books as all the ledger accounts are closed.

Students should remember that at the time of preparing Suspense Account, at first we are to write the balance of Suspense Account. If Trial Balance shows excess credit, the balance will be written as "To, Difference in Books A/c" in debit side, and vice versa in the opposite case. If the opening balance of Suspense Account is not given after posting the rectifying entries, difference in any side of Suspense Account will be represented as the Opening Balance, and the same is written as "Difference in Books A/c" in the debit side if credit side is greater than the debit side, and vice versa.

The purpose of Suspense Account is:

(i) ***For the purpose of a disagreed Trial Balance***

If the Trial Balance does not agree, this account is used for the purpose. In other words, if the debit side of the Trial Balance is greater than the credit side, the Suspense Account is to be written on the credit side, so that both sides of the Trial Balance will be equal. At a subsequent date, when the errors are detected, the rectifying entries are duly passed and the Suspense Account will automatically be closed and vice-versa in the opposite case.

(ii) *For posting doubtful transactions*

Sometimes it may so happen that, for some reason or other, one transaction cannot accurately be recorded in the books. For example, we have received some goods valued Rs. 1,000 from some of our creditors, the names of the creditors are not known. In that case, we are to pass the following entry:

		Dr.	
(i) Purchases A/c	Dr.	1,000	
To Suspense A/c			1,000

At a subsequent date, when we will be able to know the name of the creditor, say Mr. Y, we will have to pass the following entry:

Suspense A/c	Dr.	1,000	
To Mr. Y A/c			1,000

So the Suspense A/c, which was opened temporarily, is then closed.

Illustration 13

Rectify the following errors, assuming that these were detected after preparing Trial Balance:

(i) Sales Day Book was overcast by Rs. 1,000. (ii) Purchase Day Book was undercast by Rs. 2,000. (iii) Discount allowed Rs. 300, not posted to Discount Account. (iv) A Debtor's balance of Rs. 800 was not included in Debtor's list. (v) A sale of Rs. 2,000 was posted in the ledger as Rs. 200. (vi) Discount allowed to customer for Rs. 100 was posted to the Discount Received Account. (vii) Goods sold to Mr. B for Rs. 700, wrongly credited to his account. (viii) Goods purchased from Mr. X for Rs. 900, wrongly debited to his Account. (ix) Returns Inward Book was overcast by Rs. 500. (x) Returns Outward Book was cast short by Rs. 300.

Solution

In the books of ....

Journal

Date	*Particulars*		*L.F.*	*Debit*	*Credit*
?				Rs.	Rs.
	(i) Sales A/c	Dr.		1,000	
	To Suspense A/c				1,000
	(Sales Day Book was overcast by Rs. 1,000, now rectified)				
	(ii) Purchases A/c	Dr.		2,000	
	To Suspense A/c				2,000
	(Purchase Day Book was undercast by Rs. 2,000, now rectified)				
	(iii) Discount Allowed A/c	Dr.		300	
	To Suspense A/c				300
	(Discount allowed to customer, not posted to the Discount Account, now rectified)				
	(iv) Debtors A/c	Dr.		800	
	To Suspense A/c				800
	(Debtor's balance was not included, now rectified)				
	(v) Suspense A/c	Dr.		1,800	
	To Sales A/c				1,800
	(Sales Account was credited by Rs. 200, instead of Rs. 2,000, now rectified)				
	(vi) Discount Allowed A/c	Dr.		100	
	Discount Received A/c	Dr.		100	
	To Suspense A/c				200
	(Discount allowed to customer but wrongly credited to Discount Received Account, now rectified)				
	(vii) B A/c	Dr.		1,400	
	To Suspense A/c				1,400
	(Goods sold to B but wrongly credited to his account, now rectified)				
	(viii) Suspense A/c	Dr.		1,800	
	To X A/c				1,800
	(Goods purchased from S, but wrongly debited to his account, now rectified)				
	(ix) Suspense A/c	Dr.		500	
	To Returns Inward A/c				500
	(Returns Inward Book was overcast short)				
	(x) Suspense A/c	Dr.		300	
	To Returns Outward A/c				300
	(Returns Outward Book was cast short.)				

Illustration 14

Mr. X could not agree the Trial Balance. He transferred to the Suspense Account Rs. 296, being excess of the debit side total. The following errors were subsequently discovered:

(i) Sales Day Book was overcast by Rs. 300. (ii) An amount of Rs. 55, received from Mr. Y, was posted to his account as Rs. 550. (iii) Purchases Return Book total on a folio was carried forward as Rs. 221, instead of Rs. 112. (iv) A cash sale of Rs. 1,235, duly entered in the Cash Book, but posted to Sales A/c as Rs. 235. (v) Rest of the difference was due to wrong total in Salaries A/c.

Show the entries to rectify the above errors and prepare Suspense Account.

Solution

In the books of Mr. X

Journal

Date	*Particulars*		*L.F.*	*Debit*	*Credit*
?				Rs.	Rs.
	(i) Sales A/c	Dr.		300	
	To Suspense A/c				300
	(Sales Book was overcast, now rectified)				
	(ii) Y A/c	Dr.		495	
	To Suspense A/c				495
	(Amount received from Y Rs. 55 wrongly recorded as Rs. 550, now rectified)				
	(iii) Returns Outward A/c	Dr.		109	
	To Suspense A/c				109
	(Total of purchase Returns Book was carried forward as Rs. 221, instead of Rs. 112, now rectified)				
	(iv) Suspense A/c	Dr.		1,000	
	To Sales A/c				1,000
	(Cash sales being Rs. 1,235, recorded only Rs. 235 in Sales A/c, now rectified)				
	(v) Suspense A/c	Dr.		200	
	To Salaries A/c				200
	(Salary A/c was overcast by Rs. 200, now rectified)				

Suspense A/c

Dr. *Date*	*Particulars*	*Amount*	*Date*	*Particulars*	*Amount* Cr.
		Rs.			Rs.
	To Sales A/c	1,000		By Difference in T. B.	296
	" Salaries A/c *(bal. fig.)*	200		" Sales A/c	300
				" Y A/c	495
				" Returns Outward A/c	109
		1,200			1,200

Workings Notes :

For (i) Rs. 55 received from Mr. Y but wrongly credited by Rs. 550 so, excess credit was made for Rs. 495 which should be debited.

(ii) Returns outward book was also credited by Rs. 109 in excess of the amount for which Returns outward account should be debited.

(iii) In this case sales, account should be credited by Rs. 1,235, but by mistake it was credited for Rs. 235 only. Now Rs. 1,000 should also be credited to Sales Account.

Mixed Problems

Preparation of corrected Trial Balance.Recatifying Entries and Supense A/c

Illustration 15

A novice bookkeeper drew up the following Trial Balance for the year ended 31st December 2011:

Heads of Accounts	*L.F.*	*Debit*	*Credit*
		Rs.	Rs.
Capital A/c		—	30,000
Drawings A/c		5,000	—
Purchases A/c		16,000	—
Sales A/c		—	45,000
Returns Inward A/c		—	3,000

Contd.

		Rs.	Rs.
Returns Outwards A/c		2,000	—
Carriage Inwards A/c		1,000	—
Carriage Outwards A/c		—	2,000
Bank Overdraft A/c		6,000	—
Provision for Bad Debts A/c		3,000	—
Discount Allowed A/c		—	1,000
Discount Received A/c		2,000	—
General Expenses A/c		5,000	—
Plant and Machinery A/c		10,000	—
Sundry Debtors A/c		8,000	—
Sundry Creditors A/c		—	5,000
Opening Stock A/c		4,000	—
Cash in Hand A/c		8,000	—
Dividend Received A/c		—	4,000
Goodwill A/c		17,000	—
		87,000	90,000

You are required to:

(i) Draw up a corrected Trial Balance after transfering the errors to Suspense Account.
(ii) Show the rectifying entries, after detecting the following; and
(iii) Show the Suspense Account:

(a) Sales Account was overcast by Rs. 4,500;
(b) Purchased a Plant for Rs. 2,000, wrongly debited to Purchase A/c;
(c) Discount Allowed to customer Rs. 3,000; not debited to Discount Account;
(d) Goods purchased from Sen for Rs. 1,500, wrongly debited to his account;
(e) Goods sold to Banerjee for Rs. 2,250, wrongly credited to him;
(f) Purchases Account was undercast by Rs. 6,000;
(g) Goods returned by customer for Rs. 1,000, wrongly passed through Returns Outward Account, although the personal account was correctly recorded;
(h) Wages paid for making a Furniture for Rs. 4,000, wrongly debited to Wages Account.

Solution

In the books of ....
Trial balance
as at 31st December 2011

Heads of Accounts	*L.F.*	*Debit*	*Credit*
		Rs.	Rs.
Capital A/c		—	30,000
Drawings A/c		5,000	—
Purchases A/c		16,000	—
Sales A/c		—	45,000
Returns Inwards A/c		3,000	—
Returns Outwards A/c		—	2,000
Carriage Inwards A/c		1,000	—
Carriage Outwards A/c		2,000	—
Bank Overdraft A/c		—	6,000
Provision for Bad Debts A/c		—	3,000
Discount Allowed A/c		1,000	—
Discount Received A/c		—	2,000
General Expenses A/c		5,000	—
Plant and Machinery A/c		10,000	—
Sundry Debtors A/c		8,000	—
Sundry Creditors A/c		—	5,000
Opening Stock A/c		4,000	—
Cash in hand A/c		8,000	—
Dividend Received A/c		—	4,000
Goodwill A/c		17,000	—
Suspense A/c (bal. Fig.)		17,000	—
		97,000	97,000

In the books of ....
Journal

Date		Particulars	L.F.	Debit	Credit
2011				Rs.	Rs.
Dec.	(a)	Sales A/c Dr.		4,500	
		To Suspense A/c			4,500
		(Sales amount was undercast, now rectified)			
	(b)	Plant A/c Dr.		2,000	
		To Purchases A/c			2,000
		(Purchased a Plant but wrongly passed through Purchases A/c, now rectified)			
	(c)	Discount Allowed A/c Dr.		3,000	
		To Suspense A/c			3,000
		(Discount allowed to customers, not debited to discount account, now rectified)			
	(d)	Suspense A/c Dr.		3,000	
		To Sen A/c			3,000
		(Goods purchased for Sen for Rs. 1,500, wrongly debited to his account, now rectified)			
	(e)	Banerjee A/c Dr.		4,500	
		To Suspense A/c			4,500
		(Goods sold to Banerjee for Rs. 2,250, wrongly credited to his account, now rectified)			
	(f)	Purchases A/c Dr.		6,000	
		To Suspense A/c			6,000
		(Purchases account was cast short)			
	(g)	Returns Inward A/c Dr.		1,000	
		Returns Outward A/c Dr.		1,000	
		To Suspense A/c			2,000
		(Goods returned by customer, wrongly passed through Returns Outward Book, now rectified)			
	(h)	Furniture A/c Dr.		4,000	
		To Wages A/c			4,000
		(Wages paid for making a furniture, wrongly debited to Wages A/c, now rectified)			

Suspense A/c

Dr.							Cr.
Date		Particulars	Amount	Date		Particulars	Amount
2011			Rs.	2008			Rs.
Dec. 31	To	Difference in Trial Balance (*bal. Fig.*)	17,000	Dec. 31	By	Sales A/c	4,500
	"	Sen A/c	3,000		"	Discount Allowed A/c	3,000
					"	Banerjee A/c	4,500
					"	Purchases A/c	6,000
					"	Returns Inwards A/c	1,000
					"	Returns Outwards A/c	1,000
			20,000				20,000

Note: **Items (b) and (h) do not affect the agreement of Trial Balance since they are double-sided errors.**

Illustration 16

A book-keeper finds the difference in the Trial Balance amounting to Rs. 1,000 and puts it in the Suspense Account.

Later on he detected the following errors:

(a) **Purchased goods from Ravi Rs. 15,000 but entered into Sales Book.**

(b) **Received one bill for Rs. 25,000 from Arun but recorded in Bills Payable Book.**

(c) **An item of Rs. 3,500 relating to prepaid rent account was omitted to be brought forward.**

(d) **An item of Rs. 2,000 in respect of purchase returns, had been wrongly entered in the Purchase Book.**

(e) **Rs. 25,000 paid to Harish against our acceptance was debited to Harish Account.**

(f) Bills received from Janaki for repairs done to plant Rs. 2,500 and plant supplied for Rs. 45,000 were entered in the Purchase Book as Rs. 46,000.

Give rectifying journal entries with full narration and prepare Suspense Accounts.

[CA Foundation, May 1998—Adapted]

Solution

In the books of ....

Journal

Date		*Particulars*		*L.F.*	*Debit*	*Credit*
?					Rs.	Rs.
Dec.	1.	Purchase A/c	Dr.		15,000	
		Sales A/c	Dr.		15,000	
		To Ravi A/c				30,000
		(Purchases were wrongly entered into Sales Book, now rectified.)				
	2.	Bills Receivable A/c	Dr.		25,000	
		Bills Payable A/c			25,000	
		To Suspense A/c				50,000
		(Wrong recording in Bills Payable Book instead of Bills Receivable book, now rectified.)				
	3.	Prepaid Rent A/c	Dr.		3,500	
		To Suspense A/c				3,500
		(Prepaid rent account was omitted to be brought forward, now rectified)				
	4.	Suspense A/c	Dr.		4,000	
		To Purchases A/c				2,000
		" Purchase Returns A/c				2,000
		(Purchase returns had been wrongly entered in the Purchase Book, now rectified.)				
	5.	Bills Payable A/c	Dr.		25,000	
		To Harish A/c				25,00
		(Wrong debit to Harish Account instead of Bills Payable Account, now rectified.)				
	6.	Repairs A/c	Dr.		2,500	
		Plant A/c	Dr.		45,000	
		To Purchases A/c				46,000
		" Suspense A/c				1,500
		(Wrong recording for repairs and cost of plant purchased in the Purchases Book, now rectified.)				

Dr. **Suspense A/c** Cr.

Date	*Particulars*	*Amount*	*Date*	*Particulars*	*Amount*
?		Rs.	?		Rs.
	To Difference in Trial Balance	1,000		By Prepaid Rent A/c	3,500
	" Purchase A/c	2,000		" Repairs to Radio A/c	1,500
	" Purchase Returns A/c	2,000			
		5,000			5,000

Workings Notes :

1. For (a) It has been assumed that as a result of wrong posting Sales Book and Debtors accounts are equally affected. If it is assumed that Ravi's account is correctly recorded, in that case Suspense Account will be credited in place of Ravi Account.
2. For (b) It has also been assumed that Bills Payable Account, and Arun's Account are equally affected. So, no Suspense Account will appear. Because

Original entry being		*Entry Made*		*Rectifing Entry*	
B/R A/c	Dr.	Arun A/c	Dr.	B/R A/c	Dr.
To Arun A/c		To B/P A/c		B/P A/c	Dr.
				To Arun A/c	

3. For (f) A bill (not B/R) is received for repairing of plant for Rs. 2,500 which should have been debited and plant purchased for Rs. 45,000, not debited to Plant A/c; instead of Purchase A/c was wrongly debited by Rs. 46,000, So Repairs A/c should be debited by Rs. 2,500, Plant A/c also should be debited by Rs. 45,000 and Purchase A/c should be credited for cancellation for Rs. 46,000 and the balance to be tranferred to Suspense A/c.

Effect of Rectifying Entries on Net Profit[1]

Net Profit of a firm will be affected by the items of nominal account. In other words, personal accounts or real accounts will not affect the net profit. At the same time, if a wrong debit is made for a nominal account in place of a correct debit of a nominal account, profit will not be affected. For example, if Rent Account is debited for Rs. 1,000 in place of Salary Account, profit will not be affected. Only the heads of account will be rectified and not the amount as both the accounts appear in the debit side of Profit and Loss Account.

The rectifying entry will be: Salary Account will be debited and Rent Account will be credited, i.e., profit will not be affected at all. On the other hand, if there is only one debit or credit in nominal accounts, profit will be affected. For example, if discount is allowed to Mr. X for Rs. 1,000 the usual entry is

Discount Allowed A/c	Dr.	1,000	
To Mr. X A/c			1,000

Now, if the Discount Allowed Account is not debited in Profit and Loss Account, profit will be affected by Rs. 1,000. Thus, only nominal accounts affect the net profit of a firm. Personal Accounts and Real Accounts do not have any bearing on net profits. Consider the illustrations that follow:

Illustration 17

Rectify the following errors by way of journal entries and work out their effect on the Profit and Loss Account of the concern:

(a) Returns Inwards Book for December was short-totalled by Rs. 100.
(b) Rs. 5,810, being cash paid to Hira Chand, was debited to Ram Chand as Rs. 5,010.
(c) Rs. 1,500 worth of furniture purchased on credit was debited to Purchases Account.
(d) A purchase made for Rs. 500 was posted to the Purchases Account as Rs. 50.
(e) Wages paid for the erection of machinery amounting to Rs. 700 was debited to Wages Account.
(f) Goods purchased for proprietor's use for Rs. 1,000 was debited to Purchases Account.
(g) A sum of Rs. 1,000 written-off from machinery had not been posted to Depreciation Account.
(h) Rs. 100 received from Raghu had been debited to Sunder.
(i) Rs. 1,150 received from Radhey Mohan was debited to his account.
(j) Purchase returns worth Rs. 980 to Shri Hari Kishan were not recorded in the books.

Solution

In the books of ....
Journal

Date	Particulars		L.F.	Debit	Credit
?				Rs.	Rs.
	(a) Returns Inward A/c	Dr.		100	
	To Suspense A/c				100
	(Return Inward book was undercast by Rs. 100, now rectified)				
	(b) Hira Chand A/c	Dr.		5,810	
	To Ram Chand A/c				5,010
	" Suspense A/c				800
	(Cash paid to Hira Rs. 5,810 was wrongly debited to Ram Chand A/c as Rs. 5,010, now rectified)				
	(c) Furniture A/c	Dr.		1,500	
	To Purchases A/c				1,500
	(Purchase of furniture was wrongly debited to Purchase A/c, now rectified)				
	(d) Purchases A/c	Dr.		450	
	To Suspense A/c				450
	(Purchase of Rs. 500 was wrongly posted as Rs. 50 to the Purchases A/c, now rectified)				
	(e) Machinery A/c	Dr.		700	
	To Wages A/c				700
	(Wages paid for erection of machinery was wrongly debited to Wages A/c, now rectified)				*Contd.*

1 This part has been discussed in detail in a subsequent paragraph,—Appiication of Profit and Loss Adjustment Account

?			Rs.	Rs.
	(f) Drawings A/c To Purchases A/c (Goods purchased for personal use wrongly debited to Purchases A/c, now rectified)	Dr.	1,000	1,000
	(g) Depreciation A/c To Suspense A/c (Depreciation on machinery was not posted to Depreciation A/c, now rectified)	Dr.	1,000	1,000
	(h) Suspense A/c To Sunder A/c " Raghu A/c (Cash received from Raghu wrongly debited to Sunder's A/c, now rectified)	Dr.	200	100 100
	(i) Suspense A/c To Radhey Mohan (Rs. 1,150 × 2) (Cash received from Radhey Mohan wrongly debited to his account, now rectified)	Dr.	2,300	2,300
	(j) Hari Kishan A/c To Purchases Return A/c (Purchases return to Hari Kishan were not recorded in the books, now rectified)	Dr.	980	980

Effect on Profit

	Increase Rs.	*Decrease* Rs.
(a)	—	100
(b) No effect	—	—
(c)	1,500	—
(d)	—	450
(e)	700	—
(f)	1,000	—
(g)	—	1,000
(h) No effect	—	—
(i) No effect	—	—
(j)	980	—
	4,180	1,550
Increase in Profit	—	2,630
	4,180	4,180

Illustration 18

X & Co. has produced a Trial Balance as on March 31, 2011 which does not balance, the difference of Rs. 1,760 being transferred to the Suspense Account.

An examination of the Company's books discloses the following errors:

(a) The Sales Day Book has been undercast by Rs. 800 and posted to the Debtors Control Account accordingly.

(b) Goods received from XYZ Limited on March 31, 2011 costing Rs. 9,690 have been included in stock but the invoice has not been received.

(c) Sales Account in the General Ledger has been credited with a credit note for Rs. 950 being trade-in allowance given on a company van. This amount had already been taken into account when dealing with the replacement in the Motor Van Account.

(d) An invoice from Joseph & Co. amounting Rs. 4,450 for goods purchased has been omitted from the Purchase Day Book and posted direct to Purchases Account in the General Ledger and Joseph & Co. Account in the Suppliers' Ledger but had not been included in the Suppliers' Ledger Control Account in the Trial Balance.

(e) Discount allowed for the month of March amounting to Rs. 1,740 has not been posted to Discount Allowed Account in the General Ledger.

(f) A cheque for Rs. 1,920 received from Jolly Limited, a debtor, has been posted directly to the Sales Account in the General Ledger.

You are required: (i) to give the journal entries, where necessary, to correct these errors, or, if no Journal entry is required, state how they will be corrected; (ii) to prepare a statement showing the effect the corrections would have on the company's profit for the year; and (iii) to prepare Suspense Account.

[ICWA]

Solution

Tutorial Note :

Under Self-Balancing System, Debtors' Control Account is opened in the General Ledger in place of Sundry Debtors Account, i.e., Debtors Control Account should be debited and Sales Account should be credited. Same principle is also applied in case of Creditors Ledger Control Account.

In the books of X & Co.
Journal

Date	Particulars		L.F.	Debit	Credit
2010				Rs.	Rs.
Mar. 31	(a) Debtors Contral A/c	Dr.		800	
	To Sales A/c				800
	(Sales Day Book was undercast, now rectified)				
	(b) No entry is required, simply Rs. 9,600 to be deducted from Stock				
	(c) Sales A/c	Dr.		950	
	To Suspense A/c				950
	(Trade-in-allowance credited to Sales A/c, now rectified)				
	(d) Suspense A/c	Dr.		4,450	
	To Creditors Ledger Control A/c				4,450
	(Credit purchased was not posted in the general ledger)				
	(e) Discount Allowed A/c	Dr.		1,740	
	To Suspense A/c				1,740
	(Discount allowed to customers not credited to Discount Account, now rectified)				
	(f) Sales A/c	Dr.		1,920	
	To Debtor's Control A/c				1,920
	(Cheque received wrongly credited to Sales Account, now rectified)				

Effect on Profit

		Increase	Decrease
		Rs.	Rs.
(a)		800	—
(b)	No effect	—	—
(c)		—	950
(d)	No effect	—	—
(e)		—	1,740
(f)		—	1,920
		800	4,610
	Decrease in Profit	3,810	—
		4,610	4,610

Suspense A/c

Dr.					Cr.
Date	Particulars	Rs.	Date	Particulars	Rs.
2010 Mar. 31	To Creditors Ledger Control A/c	4,450	2010 Mar. 31	By Difference in T. B.	1,760
				" Sales A/c	950
				" Discount Allowed A/c	1,740
		4,450			4,450

Illustration 19

The following errors were detected in the books of Hill Billy and Sons before preparing the final accounts for the year ended 30th June 2011:

(a) A builder's bill for Rs. 3,400 for the erection of a small shed was debited to Repairs Account.
(b) A cheque for Rs. 450 received from Prasad Singh and Co. was dishonoured and debited to Discount Account.
(c) Goods to the value of Rs. 370 returned by Banerjee and Co. were included in stock, but no entry was made in the books.
(d) Repairs to Plant amounting to Rs. 680 had been charged to Plant and Machinery Account.
(e) Wages paid to firm's own workmen for making certain additions to machinery amounting to Rs. 830 were posted to Wages Account.
(f) A sum of Rs. 200 drawn by the proprietor was debited to Travelling Expenses Account.

Give the journal entries necessary to correct these errors, and show the effect of these on the Gross Profit, the Net Profit, and the Balance Sheet total.

Which of these errors, if any, will cause disagreement of the Trial Balance?

Give reasons for your answer.

Solution

In the books of Hill Billy and Sons

Journal

Date	Particulars	L.F.	Debit	Credit
2011			Rs.	Rs.
Jan. 30	(a) Building A/c Dr.		3,400	
	To Repairs A/c			3,400
	(Erection of shed wrongly debited to Repairs Account, now rectified)			
	(b) Prasad Singh A/c Dr.		450	
	To Discount A/c			450
	(Cheque received and dishonoured but debited to Discount Account, now rectified)			
	(c) Returns Inward A/c Dr.		370	
	To Banerjee and Co. A/c			370
	(Good returned by Banerjee and Co. but not recorded at all in the books, now rectified)			
	(d) Repairs A/c Dr.		680	
	To Plant and Machinery A/c			680
	(Repairs made to Plant and Machinery wrongly debited to Plant and Machinery Account, now rectified)			
	(e) Machinery A/c Dr.		830	
	To Wages A/c			830
	(Wages paid for machinery, wrongly debited to Wages Account, now rectified)			
	(f) Drawings A/c Dr.		200	
	To Travelling Expenses A/c			200
	(Amount drawn by the proprietor, wrongly debited to Travelling Expenses Account, now rectified)			

Effect in Gross Profit, Net Profit and Balance Sheet

	Gross Profit	Net Pofit	Balance Sheet
	Rs.	Rs.	Rs.
1. (a)	—	(–) 3,400	+ 3,400
(b)	—	(–) 450	+ 450
(c)	(+) 370	—	(–) 370
(d)	—	+ 680	(–) 680
(e)	(–) 830	—	+ 830
(f)	—	(–) 200	+ 200

None of the above errors will affect the agreement of Trial Balance since both debit and credit are equally affected. There was no Suspense Account. Agreement of Trial Balance will be affected only when there will be a Suspense Account, i.e., here all are double-sided errors.

GENERAL ILLUSTRATIONS

Illustration 20

Rectify the following errors assuming that these are detected after the preparation of Trial Balance :

(a) A purchase of goods from Partha & Co. on the last day of the year was taken into stock but the Invoice was not passed through the Purchase Book, amounted to Rs. 3,000.

(b) Payment made for the cost of stamps and registration fees amounting to Rs. 5,200 of a new land was debited to Legal Charges Account, amounting to Rs. 2,500.

(c) A cheque received from an Insurance Co. amounting to Rs. 500, against goods destroyed by fire, was deposited by the proprietor into his own private bank account and the full value of the invoice was passed through the Purchase Book.

(d) A furniture, which stood in the books at Rs. 400, was sold for Rs. 250, in part exchange for a new furniture costing Rs. 2,250, and the net invoice, Rs. 2,000, was wrongly passed through the Purchase Book.

(e) Sale of goods on approval amounting to Rs. 500 was included in Sale Account although goods to the value of Rs. 100 was returned out of them. No entry was made for return and the returned goods were included into closing stock at the cost price of Rs. 80.

Solution

In the books of X & Co.
Journal

Date	*Particulars*		*L.F.*	*Debit* Rs.	*Credit* Rs.
(a)	Purchases A/c	Dr.		3,000	
	To Partha & Co. A/c				3,000
	(Goods purchased from Partha were taken into stock but not recorded in Purchase Book, now rectified.)				
(b)	Land A/c	Dr.		5,200	
	To Legal Charges A/c				2,500
	" Suspense A/c				2,700
	(Payment made for stamps and registration fees forRs. 5,200, but wrongly debited to legal charges byRs. 2,500, now rectified.)				
(c)	Drawings A/c	Dr.		500	
	To Purchases A/c				500
	(Cheque received from the Insurance Co. for goods destroyed by fire and the amount deposited into private bank account of the proprietor, but wrongly debited to Purchase A/c, now rectified.)				
(d)	Furniture A/c (Rs. 2,250 – 400)	Dr.		1,850	
	Loss on Sale of Furniture A/c	Dr.		150	
	To Purchase A/c				2,000
	(Purchase of a new furniture in exchange of an old one passed through the Purchase Book, now rectified.)				
(e)	Sales A/c	Dr.		100	
	To Customers A/c				100
	(Goods returned by customer out of goods sent on approval basis but not received, now rectified.)				

Working Notes :

1. For (a) Goods purchase and taken into stock but title was not transferred. So, we can treat the matter in two following wayes:
   Either — We can deduct the amount from the value of Closing Stock
   Or — We can write the usual entry, Purchase A/c Dr. and Partha & Co. A/c Credit.
2. For (b) It is a Capital expenditure, hence Land A/c should be debited for the correct amount of Rs. 5,200. Since legal charge (being a revenue expenditure) was debited for Rs. 2,500, the same should be credited for cancellation and excess amount should be credited to Suspense A/c.
3. For (c) Since the amount received from the Insurance a Company for goods destroyed by fire and the amount was deposited into private bank A/c, so Drawings A/c should be debited and Purchase A/c should be credited for cancellation.

4. For (d)

Value of Furniture	400	New Furniture Costing Rs.	2,250
Less : Exchange Value	250	*Less :* Exchange Value	250
Loss on Exchange	150	Net Payment	2,000

∴ Loss on Sale A/c will be debited by Rs. 150. Furniture A/c will be debited by Rs. 1,850 (i.e., 2,250 – Rs. 400) and Purchase A/c for Rs. 2,000 will be credited for Cancellation.

5. For (e) Only cancellation entry for goods return should be recorded i.e., Rs. 150. The entry will be

(a) Sales A/c Dr.
To Customer A/c

(b) Since the goods will be included with Closing Stock at cost, the entry is :
Closing Stock A/c Dr.
To Trading A/c
At cost i.e., Rs. 80

Illustration 21

The Trial Balance of S & Co., Chennai, did not tally as on 31.12.2011. The following errors were detected as a result of checking the books of accounts;

Pass the necessary journal entries to rectify the errors and find out the differences in the Trial Balance :

(a) Rs. 60 received from M & Co. on 31.12.2011, was entered in the Cash Book on 2nd Jan. 2012.
(b) The Returns Inward Book for December showed Rs. 200 less in totals.
(c) The purchase of a typewriter for Rs. 800 was entered in the Purchase Journal.
(d) Wages of workers engaged in construction of Building, amounting to Rs. 500, was debited to Wages Account.
(e) A purchase of Rs. 671 had been posted to the debit of suppliers Mr. D. Das as Rs. 617.
(f) Goods amounting to Rs. 100 had been returned by Mr. Shah and were taken into stock, but no entry was passed for the transaction.
(g) Rs. 2,000, paid for purchase of a Motor Cycle for Mr. S (proprietor), had been charged to Miscellaneous Expenses Account.
(h) A sale of Rs. 300, to Mr. A was credited to his account.
(i) A sale of Rs. 1,000 has been passed through Purchase Journal. The customer's account has, however, been correctly debited.

[ICWA—Adapted)

Solution

In the books of X & Co.
Journal

Date	Particulars	L.F.	Debit	Credit
2011			Rs.	Rs.
Dec. 3				
(a)	Cash A/c Dr.		60	
	To M & Co. A/c			60
	(Cash received from M & Co. on 31.12.2011 but wrongly recorded on 2.1.2012, now rectified.)			
(b)	Returns Inward A/c Dr.		200	
	To Suspense A/c			200
	(Returns Inward Book was cast short by Rs. 200, now rectified.)			
(c)	Office Equipment A/c Dr.		800	
	To Purchases A/c			800
	(Office equipment purchased, but wrongly debited to Purchase Account, now rectified.)			
(d)	Building A/c Dr.		500	
	To Wages A/c			500
	(Wages paid for the construction of building, but wrongly debited to Wages Account, now rectified.)			

Contd.

			Rs.	Rs.
(e)	Suspense A/c	Dr.	1,288	
	To Mr. D. Das A/c			1,288
	(Goods purchased from D. Das for Rs. 671, but wrongly debited to his account by Rs. 617, now rectified.)			
(f)	Returns Inward A/c	Dr.	100	
	To Shah A/c			100
	(Goods returned by Shah, but not recorded in the books, now rectified.)			
(g)	Drawing A/c	Dr.	2,000	
	To Miscellaneous Expenses A/c			2,000
	(Motor Cycle purchased for the proprietor, but wrongly debited to Miscellaneous Expenses Account, now rectified.)			
(h)	A. A/c	Dr.	600	
	To Suspense A/c			600
	(Goods sold to A., but wrongly credited to his account, now rectified.)			
(i)	Suspense A/c	Dr.	2,000	
	To Purchases A/c			1,000
	" Sales A/c			1,000
	(Goods sold to customers, but wrongly passed through the Purchases Account, now rectified.)			

Dr. **Suspense Account** Cr.

Date	Particulars	Rs.	Date	Particulars	Rs.
?	To Das A/c	1,288	?	By Difference in Trial Balance *(bal. fig.)*	2,488
	" Purchase A/c	1,000		" Returns Inward A/c	200
	" Sales A/c	1,000		" A. A/c	600
		3,288			3,288

Illustration 22

At 31st December 1999, the accountant of TTC & Co. has failed to balance his books of account. The difference has been carried to a Suspense Account. Subsequently, the following errors are discovered :

(a) The total of the Purchase Day Book for September has been posted in the Nominal Ledger as Rs. 3,850. The Day Book total is Rs. 3,580.

(b) Cash discounts allowed for the month of November Rs. 750, and discounts received Rs. 430 have been posted to the wrong sides of the Discount Account in the Ledger.

(c) A return of goods by a customer Rs. 150 has been posted to the debit side in the Sales Ledger.

(d) A book debt of Rs. 260 due by Sujay Sen has been omitted from the list of Sales Ledger balances.

(e) Cash drawings of the proprietor, amounting to Rs. 500, have not been posted to the ledger.

(f) An amount of Rs. 200, being insurance paid in advance in the previous year, had not been brought forward as an opening balance in the Insurance Account.

After the discovery and correction of the errors mentioned, the books balanced.

You are required to :

(i) Prepare and complete the Suspense Account showing the requisite corrective entries in it. (Journal entries are not required but the appropriate names of the opposite accounts should be written in the Suspense Account).

(ii) State the incorrect total of the credit column of the Trial Balance, given that the incorrect total of the debit column was Rs. 1,37,560.

Solution **[CU BCom. (Hons.) 2000]**

(i) **In the books of TTC & Co.**

Dr. **Suspense Account** Cr.

Date	Particulars	Rs.	Date	Particulars	Rs.
1999			1999		
Dec. 31	To Difference in Trial Balance *(bal. fig.)*	1,030	Dec. 31	By Discount Allowed A/c	640
				" Debtors A/c	260

Contd.

1999			Rs	1999			Rs.
Dec. 31	"	Purchase A/c	270	Dec. 31	"	Drawings A/c	500
	"	Customers A/c	300		"	Prepaid Insurance A/c	200
			1,600				1,600

Therefore, there was a difference in Trial Balance amounting to Rs. 1,030, by excess credit.

(ii) The incorrect total of credit side of the Trial Balance was Rs. 1,38,590 (i.e., Rs. 1,37,560 + Rs. 1,030).

Illustration 23

The following errors were discovered in the books of Mr. D affecting the year ended 31st March 2011. The difference was carried to a Suspense Account and the Trial Balance was agreed.

Give corrective journal entries :

(1) A cheque of Rs. 750, received for loss of stock by fire, had been deposited in the proprietor's private bank account.

(2) An item of purchase of Rs. 151 was entered in the Purchase Day Book as Rs. 15, and posted to the Supplier's A/c as Rs. 51.

(3) A Sales Return of Rs. 500, was not entered in the financial accounts though it was duly taken in the stock book.

(4) An amount of Rs. 300 was received in full settlement from a customer after he was allowed a discount of Rs. 50, but while writing the books, the amount received was entered in the Discount column and the Discount allowed was entered in the Amount column.

(5) Bills receivable from Mr. A of Rs. 1,000, was posted to the credit of Bills Payable Account and also credited to the Account of Mr. A.

Solution **[CA—Adapted]**

In the Books of Mr. D
Journal

Date	Particulars		L.F.	Debit Rs.	Credit Rs.
2011 March 31					
(1)	Drawings A/c	Dr.		750	
	To Purchases A/c[1]				750
	(Cheque received for loss of stock by fire deposited by the proprietor in the Private Bank A/c, now rectified.)				
(2)	Purchases A/c (151 – 15)	Dr.		136	
	To Supplier's A/c (151 – 51)				100
	" Suspense A/c				36
	(Purchase of Rs. 151 wrongly entered in the Purchase Day Book as Rs. 15, and posted to the Supplier's A/c as Rs. 51, now rectified.)				
(3)	Returns Inward A/c	Dr.		500	
	To Customer's A/c				500
	(Return of goods by customer as omitted to be recorded in the books, although included in stock, now rectified.)				
(4)	Cash A/c (300 – 50)	Dr.		250	
	To Discount Allowed A/c				250
	(Rs. 300, received from a customer after allowing a discount of Rs. 50, wrongly entered in the Cash Book as Rs. 300 in the discount column and Rs. 50 in the amount column, now rectified.)				
(5)	Bills Payable A/c	Dr.		1,000	
	Bills Receivable A/c	Dr.		1,000	
	To Suspense A/c				2,000
	(B/R received from A wrongly credited to B/P A/c although A's A/c was correctly recorded, now rectified.)				

Working Note :

1. For (1) It has been assumed that no adjustment entry was passed when the goods were lost by fire. Because, if it is assumed that the adjusting entry had already been passed in the books (i.e.,, Loss by Fire A/c Dr. and Purchase A/c Cr.), in that case, the rectifying entry will be :

Drawings A/c	Dr.	
To Loss by Fire A/c		

2. For (4)

The Correct entry was				Entry Made			
Cash A/c	Dr.	300		Cash A/c	Dr.	50	
Discount Allowed A/c	Dr.	50		Diacount Allowed	Dr.	300	
To Customer			350	To Customer			350

Illustration 24

You are presented with a Trial Balance of Saxena as on 30.6.2011, showing the credit is in excess by Rs. 415, which has been carried to Suspense Account.

On a close scrutiny of the books, the following errors are revealed :

(a) A cheque of Rs. 3,456 received from Sankar, after allowing him a discount of Rs. 46, was endorsed to Sharma in full settlement for Rs. 3,500. The cheque was finally dishonoured but no entries were passed in the books.

(b) Goods of the value of Rs. 230, returned by Swaminathan, were entered in the Purchase Day Book and posted therefrom to Swaika as Rs. 320.

(c) Bad Debts aggregating Rs. 505 written-off during the year in the Sales Ledger but were not recorded in the General Ledger.

(d) Bills for Rs. 750 received from Sureka for repairs done to machinery was entered in the Inward Invoice Book as Rs. 650.

(e) Goods worth Rs. 1,234 purchased from Saraf on 28.6.2011 had been entered in the Purchase Day Book and credited to him but were not delivered till 5th July 2011 taken by the purchases on 30.6.2011. The title of the goods was, however, passed on 28.6.2011.

(f) Rs. 79 paid for freight on machinery was debited to Freight Account as Rs. 97.

You are required to pass the necessary journal entries for correcting the above. **[ICWA]**

Solution

In the books of Saxena

Journal

Date	*Particulars*		*L.F.*	*Debit* Rs.	*Credit* Rs.
2011 June 30					
(a)	Sankar A/c	Dr.		3,502	
	Discount Received A/c	Dr.		44	
	To Sharma A/c				3,500
	" Discount Allowed A/c				46
	(Cheque received from Sankar was endorsed to Sharma after allowing discount Rs. 46 and it was dishonoured, now rectified.)				
(b)	Returns Inward A/c	Dr.		230	
	Swaika A/c	Dr.		320	
	To Purchases A/c				230
	" Swaminathan A/c				230
	" Suspense A/c				90
	(Goods returned by Swaminathan for Rs. 230, wrongly recorded in Purchase Day Book and credited to Swaika's Account Rs. 320, now rectified.)				
(c)	Bad Debts A/c	Dr.		505	
	To Suspense A/c				505
	(Bad debts written-off but not recorded, now rectified.)				
(d)	Repairs A/c	Dr.		750	
	To Purchases A/c				650
	" Sureka A/c				100
	(Repairs done for machinery for Rs. 750, wrongly recorded as Rs. 650 in Purchase A/c, now rectified.)				

Contd.

			Rs.	Rs.
(e)	Goods-in-transit A/c	Dr.	1,234	
	To Trading A/c			1,234
	(Goods were in-transit which were not considered, now rectified.)			
(f)	Machinery A/c	Dr.	79	
	Suspense A/c	Dr.	18	
	To Freight A/c			97
	(Amount paid for freight Rs. 79 on Machinery was wrongly debited to Freight Account Rs. 97, now rectified.)			

Workings :

1. For (a) : Correct Entry

(i)	Bank A/c	Dr.	3,456		When Received
	Discount Allowed A/c	Dr.	46		
	To Sankar A/c			3,502	
(ii)	Sharma A/c	Dr.	3,500		When Endorsed
	To Bank A/c			3,456	
	" Discount Received A/c			44	
(iii)	Sankar A/c	Dr.	3,502		When Dishonoured
	Discount Received A/c	Dr.	44		
	To Sharma A/c			3,500	
	" Discount Allowed A/c			46	

So, dishonoured entry will be the Rectifying Entry

2. For (b) : Correct Entry

(i)	Returns Inward A/c	Dr.	230	
	To Swaminathan A/c			230
(ii)	**Entry Made**			
	Purchase A/c	Dr.	230	
	To Swaika A/c			320
(iii)	**Rectifying Entry**			
	Returns Inward A/c	Dr.	230	
	Swaika A/c	Dr.	320	
	To Purchase A/c			230
	" Swaminathan			230
	" Suspense A/c			90

Preparation of Suspense Account and effect on Net Profit

Illustration 25

The book-keeper of a firm, having been unable to agree the Trial Balance, raises a Suspense Account. The following errors were discovered :

(a) The addition of the analysis column in the tabular purchase journal posted to goods purchased for Re-sale Account was found to be Rs. 150 short, though the addition of the total column was correct.

(b) Goods bought from a supplier, amounting to Rs. 77, had been posted to the credit of his account Rs. 770.

(c) A dishonoured bill of exchange, receivable for Rs. 1,600, returned to the firm's bank, had been credited to the Bank Account and debited to Bills Receivable Account. A cheque was received later from the customer for Rs. 1,600, and duly paid.

(d) An item of Rs. 80, entered in the Sale Return Book, had been posted to the debit of the customer who returned the goods.

(e) Sundry item of Plant sold, amounting to Rs. 3,000, had been entered in the Sales Day Book, the total of which book had been posted to the credit of Sales Account.

(f) An amount of Rs. 800, owing by a customer, had been omitted from the list of Sundry Debtors.

(g) Discount amounting to Rs. 30, allowed to a customer, had been duly entered in his account, but not posted to the Discount Account.

(h) An amount of Rs. 100, being rates treated as paid in advance in the previous year, had not been brought forward as a balance on the Rates Account.

(1) Show the Suspense Account; (2) Explain the effect of the corrections on the profit shown in the uncertified accounts.

[ICWA]

Solution

Dr. **Suspense Account** *Cr.*

Date	*Particulars*	Rs.	*Date*	*Particulars*	Rs.
?	To Difference in Trial Balance *(bal. fig.)*	1,613	?	By Goods Purchased for Re-sale A/c	150
				" Creditors A/c	693
				" Debtors A/c	800
"	Debtors A/c	160		" Discount Allowed A/c	30
				" Rates A/c	100
		1,773			1,773

Effect of correction on the profit :

			Increase in profit (+) Rs.	Decrease in profit (−) Rs.
Items :	(a)	... ...		150
	(b)	No effect	—	—
	(c)	No effect	—	—
	(d)	No effect	—	—
	(e)	... ...	—	3,000
	(f)	No effect	—	—
	(g)	... ...	—	30
	(h)	... ...	—	100
			Nil	3,280

Hence, profit will be reduced by Rs. 3,280.

Illustration 26

The Trial Balance of Mr. Careless did not agree and he opened a Suspense Account with the amount of difference. On scrutiny you find that :

(a) Rs. 800, spent on repairs of a furniture purchased second-hand so as to make it ready for use, was debited to Repairs Account for Rs. 80.

(b) Received a final dividend from one of our customers Mr. Z for Rs. 400, whose account had already been written-off as bad debt, was credited to a newly opened account in his name and the same was, however, included in the total amount of Sundry Creditors, which was Rs. 40,000.

(c) Of the total amount of Rs. 40,000 shown as above, as creditors, another item of Rs. 4,000 represents credits given to Y, a customer, when the payment against sales invoice was received. However, the invoice itself was not entered in the books, although a cash discount of 20% was allowed to him.

You are asked to show the rectifying entries using Suspense Account whenever necessary and ascertain the correct amount of the creditors.

Solution

In the books of Mr. Careless

Journal

Date	*Particulars*	*L.F.*	*Debit* Rs.	*Credit* Rs.
?	(a) Furniture A/c Dr.		800	
	To Repairs A/c			80
	" Suspense A/c			720
	(Repairs to furniture made Rs. 800, but wrongly debited to Repairs A/c as Rs. 80, now rectified.)			

Contd.

			Rs.	Rs.
(b)	Z A/c Dr. To Bad Debt Recovery A/c (Bad Debt recovered but wrongly credited to Debtors A/c, now rectified.)		400	400
(c)	(a) Y A/c Dr. To Sales A/c (Credit sales not recorded in the books, now rectified.)		5,000	5,000
	(b) Discount Allowed A/c Dr. To Y A/c (Discount allowed but not recorded in the books, now rectified.)		1,000	1,000

Workings Note :

For : (a) Repairs to Furniture is a capital expenditure but the same was wrongly treated as Revenue Expenditure.

(b) The dividend, which has been recovered from Mr. Z, should be credited to Bad Debts Recovery Account but it was wrongly credited to his account—thereby making him as if he is our creditor. As such, the creditors account proved to be incorrect and should have been rectified.

(c) Rs. 4,000, which was received, being 80% of the amount i.e., the sales value, will be (i.e., $\frac{100}{80} \times 4{,}000$) 5,000, and, consequently, the amount of discount @ 20% on Rs. 5,000 will be Rs. 1,000.

Amount of total creditors will be rectified as:

		Rs.
Creditors (as per list)		40,000
Less : Recovery of bad debt which was correctly credited to Creditors A/c	400	
Wrong credit being given to the customer without any debit for the same and wrongly credited to creditors	4,000	
		4,400
Correct total of Creditors		35,600

Illustration 27

How would you rectify the following errors discovered after the preparation of Trial Balance ?

(a) A cheque for Rs. 125, received as Insurance claim for loss of goods-in-transit at the time of import, was deposited by the proprietor into his private bank account. The full value of the invoice was passed through the Purchase Book.

(b) A purchase of Rs. 500 from A & Co. on the last day of the year was taken into stock, but the invoice was not passed through the Purchase Book.

(c) Sale of goods on approval amounting to Rs. 300 was included in Sales Account, out of which goods to the value of Rs. 125 were returned. No record of the return was made in the Books but the returned goods were included in the stock at their cost of Rs. 100.

(d) A typewriter which stood in the books at Rs. 200 was sold for Rs. 125, in part exchange for a new typewriter costing Rs. 1,125, and the next invoice of Rs. 1,000 was passed through the Purchase Book.

(e) 4% G. P. Notes of the face value of Rs. 5,000, purchased through Lakhotia at 96% ex. div., brokerage Rs. 25. Accrued Interest to date of purchase Rs. 130. The total payment of Rs. 4,955 stands debited in the books in the name of the broker Lakhotia.

[ICWA.—Adapted]

Solution

In the books of ... ...

Journal

Date	Particulars	L.F.	Debit	Credit
			Rs.	Rs.
(a)	Drawing A/c Dr. To Purchases A/c (Cheque received from the Insurance Co. and deposited into private bank account but recorded through purchase account, now rectified.)		125	125

Contd.

			Rs.	Rs.
(b)	Purchases A/c	Dr.	500	
	To A & Co. A/c			500
	(Goods purchased from A & Co. and taken into stock but not recorded in the books, now rectified.)			
(c)	Sales A/c Returns Inward A/c	Dr.	125	
	To Customer A/c			125
	(Goods returned by customers sent out on approval basis but not recorded in the books, now rectified.)			
(d)	Office Equipment (New) A/c	Dr.	1,125	
	Loss on Sale of Office Equipment A/c	Dr.	75	
	To Purchases A/c			1,000
	" Office Equipment (Old) A/c			200
	(A new typewriter was purchased by the exchange of old one, but wrongly passed through Purchase Account, now rectified.)			
(e)	Investment A/c (Rs. $5{,}000 \times \frac{96}{100} + 25$)	Dr.	4,825	
	Interest on Investment A/c (Accrued)	Dr.	130	
	To Lakhotia A/c			4,955
	(G. P. Notes purchased but wrongly debited to Lakhotia Account, now rectified.)			

Illustration 28

The Trial balance of S. Saha on 31st March 2011 did not agree. The difference was transferred to a Suspense Account and it was decided to proceed with the preparation of the draft accounts. The following errors were detected after the accounts were closed.

You are asked to:

(i) Calculate the original difference in Trial Balance; (ii) Show rectification entries; (iii) Prepare Suspense Account; (iv) Calculate the correct Gross Profit and Net Profit for the year although the Draft Accounts showed a Gross Profit of Rs. 51,752 and Net Profit of Rs. 18,248.

(a) Sales Day Book was cast short by Rs. 600 in Nov. 2010.

(b) Discount allowed to customer amounting to Rs. 92 had been posted wrongly to Discount Received Account as Rs. 128.

(c) Repairs made to Motor Car amounting to Rs. 240 had been debited to Motor Car Account.

(d) A new plant purchased for Rs. 10,000 had been debited to Purchase Account.

(e) Defective machine costing Rs. 248 returned to the suppliers had wrongly been recorded in the books as if goods were purchased.

(f) Wages of Rs. 138 incurred for making an almirah had wrongly been debited to Wages Account Rs. 192.

Solution

(i) **Original difference in Trial Balance is calculated as:**

S.L.	*Nature of Errors*	*Excess Debit*	*Excess Credit*
		Rs.	Rs.
(a)	Short credit to Sales A/c	600	—
(b)	Short debit to Discount Allowed	—	92
	Excess credit to Discount Received	—	128
(c)	No effect	—	—
(d)	No effect	—	—
(e)	No effect	—	—
(f)	Short debit to Furniture A/c	—	138
	Excess debit to Wages A/c	192	—
		792	358
	Difference in T. B. posted to the credit of Suspense A/c	—	434
		792	792

(ii) **Rectifying Entries:**

Journal

Date	Particulars		L.F.	Debit Rs.	Credit Rs.
2011 Mar. 31	(a) Suspense A/c	Dr.		600	
	To Sales A/c				600
	(Sales Day Book was cast short, now rectified)				
	(b) Discount Allowed A/c	Dr.		92	
	Discount Received A/c	Dr.		128	
	To Suspense A/c				220
	(Discount allowed to customer of Rs. 92 wrongly posted through Discount Received A/c Rs. 128, now rectified)				
	(c) Repairs A/c	Dr.		240	
	To Motor Car A/c				240
	(Repairs made to Motor Car, wrongly debited to Motor Car A/c, now rectified)				
	(d) Plant A/c	Dr.		10,000	
	To Purchases A/c				10,000
	(Purchase of Plant wrongly passed through Purchases A/c, now rectified)				
	(e) Machinery Suppliers A/c	Dr.		496	
	To Machinery A/c				248
	" Purchases A/c				248
	(Defective machinery returned to suppliers wrongly debited to Purchases A/c, now rectified)				
	(f) Furniture A/c	Dr.		138	
	Suspense A/c	Dr.		54	
	To Wages A/c				192
	(Wages paid for making a furniture for Rs. 138 wrongly debited to Wages A/c Rs. 192, now rectified)				

Since draft accounts are prepared, Sales Account will not be replaced by Profit and Loss Adjustment Account

(iii) **Suspense Account**

Dr. Cr.

Date	Particulars	Amount Rs.	Date	Particulars	Amount Rs.
	To Sales A/c	600		By Difference in Trial Balance	434
	" Wages A/c	54		" Discount Allowed A/c	92
				" Discount Received A/c	128
		654			654

(iv) (a) **Ascertainment of Correct Gross Profit**

		Addition Rs.	Subtraction Rs.
(a)	Increase in Sales	600	—
(d)	Reduction in Purchases	10,000	—
(e)	Reduction in Purchase	248	—
(f)	Reduction in Wages	192	—
		11,040	—

Thus, the gross profit will be increased by Rs. 11,040. So the true Gross Profit will be Rs. 62,792 (i.e., Rs. 51,752 + Rs. 11,040).

(b) Ascertainment of Correct Net Profit

		Addition Rs.	Subtraction Rs.
(b)	Increase in Discount Allowed	—	92
	Reduction in Discount Received	—	128
(c)	Increase in Repairs to Motor Car	—	240
		—	460

The Net Profit will be decreased by Rs. 460. So the true Net Profit will be Rs. 28,828 (i.e., Rs. 18,248 + Rs. 11,040 – Rs. 460).

C. AFTER PREPARING FINAL ACCOUNTS

If the errors are not detected even after repeated efforts the Final Accounts may be prepared by taking up the difference through Suspense Account. If Suspense Accounts shows a debit balance, the same will be shown in the Asset side of the Balance Sheet, and vice versa. This is done particularly when it is urgently needed. But in the next year, when errors are detected, the old books are revised and rectified. It should be remembered that rectification at this period should require careful consideration, since the errors of the earlier period may creep into other accounts.

When an error affects any asset or liability account the effect should continue, and, as such, they should be debited or credited for the purpose of rectification.

1. For Double-sided Errors

The following points should be carefully considered:

Step I ***All the nominal accounts (i.e., which are closed by transferring to Trading and Profit and Loss A/c or accounts which affect profit) are to be replaced by Profit and Loss Adjustment Account, and the same is closed by transferring to Capital Account.***

Step II ***Real and Personal Accounts have been carried forward to the next year accordingly; and***

Step III ***The Suspense Account, if any, also will be carried forward to the next year.***

It should be remembered here that the treatment will be the same as **after Trial Balance stated above**. In other words, the only difference here is that all the nominal accounts are to be replaced by Profit and Loss Adjustment Account.

Illustration 29

Purchased a plant for Rs. 5,000. Wrongly passed through Purchases Account.

Solution

The rectifying entry under the case will be:

		Rs.	Rs.
Plant A/c	Dr.	5,000	
To Profit and Loss Adjustment A/c			5,000

i.e., instead of crediting Purchases Account, Profit and Loss Adjustment Account should be credited since it affects profit.

Illustration 30

Rent Paid Rs. 1,000, wrongly passed through Insurance Account.

Solution

Here the rectifying entry will be:

			Rs.	Rs.
(i)	*If after Trial Balance:*			
	Rent A/c	Dr.	1,000	
	To Insurance A/c			1,000
(ii)	*If after Final Accounts:*			
	Profit and Loss Adjustment A/c	Dr.	1,000	
	To Profit and Loss Adjustment A/c			1,000

That is, debit is being replaced by another debit item, so there is no effect on profit. As such, no entry is required for the purpose.

2. For Single-sided Errors

Same principle should be followed here which is stated above under Double-Sided Error. The Suspense A/c, under this method, is to be carried forward to the next year.

Illustration 31

Sales Day Book was overcast by Rs. 1,000.

Solution

			Rs.	Rs.
(i)	In case of ***after Trial Balance:***			
	Sales A/c	Dr.	1,000	
	To **Suspense A/c**			1,000

(ii) In case of ***Afteer Final Accounts:***

		Dr.	Rs.	Rs.
Profit and Loss Adjustment A/c		Dr.	1,000	
To Suspense A/c				1,000

i.e., Any account which affects profit is to be replaced by transferring to Profit and Loss Adjustment Account.

Illustration 32

Purchased a Plant for Rs. 5,000, not debited to Plant Account.

Solution

		Rs.	Rs.
(i) In case of ***After Trial Balance:***			
Plant A/c	Dr.	5,000	
To Suspense A/c			5,000
(ii) In case of ***After Final Accounts:***			
Plant A/c	Dr.	5,000	
To Suspense A/c			5,000

i.e., There will be no difference between the two.

COMPARATIVE ANALYSIS OF ERRORS AT DIFFERENT TIMES AT A GLANCE

Illustration 33

The following errors committed by accountant of M/s Das & Co. :

(a) Cash paid to Ram Rs. 520, was posted to his account as Rs. 250.
(b) Sales Day Book was undercast by Rs. 1,000.
(c) Purchase of stationery Rs. 200, was not posted to the Stationery Account.
(d) Goods returned by M. Banerjee Rs. 1,500 posted to his account from Returns Inward Book as Rs. 5,100.
(e) Purchased goods from S. Talukdar for Rs. 1,000, was entered in the Purchase Day Book as Rs. 100.
(f) Rs. 500 paid for now furniture was charged to Office Expense Account.
(g) A Sale of Rs. 500 to P. K. Sen was passed through the Purchase Day Book.
(h) Salary paid to Mr. X—Rs. 500, wrongly debited to his Personal Account.

Rectify the above errors by suitable journal entries (without Narration) whenever necessary, assuming that they were detected :

(a) Before preparation of Trial Balance.
(b) After preparation of Trial Balance and taking the difference to a Suspense Account but before preparing Final Accounts.
(c) After preparation of Final Accounts.

N.B. Narrations are not required.

Solution

In the books of M/s Das & Co.
Journal ***(without narration)***

Before preparation of Trial Balance	After preparation of Trial Balance but before preparation of Final Accounts	Dr. Rs.	Cr. Rs.	After preparation of Final Accounts	Dr. Rs.	Cr. Rs.
(a) Ram A/c will be debited with Rs. 270 (i.e., 520 – 250)	(a) Ram A/c Dr. To Suspense A/c	270	 270	(a) Ram A/c Dr. To Suspense A/c	270	 270
(b) Sales Account will be credited with Rs. 1,000	(b) Suspense A/c Dr. To Sales A/c	1,000	 1,000	(b) Suspense A/c Dr. To Profit and Loss Adjustment A/c	1,000	 1,000
(c) Stationery Account will be debited with Rs. 200	(c) Stationery A/c Dr. To Suspense A/c	200	 200	(c) Profit and Loss Adjustment A/c Dr. To Suspense A/c	200	 200

Contd.

(d) Banerjee account will be debited with Rs. 3,600 (i.e., 5,100 – 1,500)	(d) Banerjee A/c Dr. 3,600 To Suspense A/c 3,600	(d) Banerjee A/c Dr. 3,600 To Suspense A/c 3,600
(e) Purchase A/c Dr. 900 To S. Talukdar A/c 900	(e) Purchase A/c Dr. 900 To S. Talukdar A/c 900	(e) Profit & Loss Adjustment A/c Dr. 900 To S. Talukdar A/c 900
(f) Office Furniture A/c Dr. 500 To Office Exp. A/c 500	(f) Office Fuirniture A/c Dr. 500 To Office Exp. A/c 500	(f) Office Furniture A/c Dr. 500 To Profit & Loss Adjustment A/c 500
(g) P. K. Sen A/c Dr. 1,000 To Purchases A/c 500 " Sales A/c 500	(g) P. K. Sen A/c Dr. 1,000 To Purchases A/c 500 " Sales A/c 500	(g) P. K. Sen A/c Dr. 1,000 To Profit & Loss Adjustment A/c 1,000
(h) Salary A/c Dr. 500 To X A/c 500	(h) Salary A/c Dr. 500 To X A/c 500	(h) Profit & Loss Adjustment A/c Dr. 500 To X A/c 500

Note : Balance of Profit and Loss Adjustment Account should be transferred to Capital Account.

Illustration 34

There was a difference in Trial Balance of Shri Subhayan Basu, a trader, on 31st December 1992 and the difference in books was carried to a Suspense Account and the books were closed. Subsequently, on going through the books, the following errors were located :

(a) Rs. 2,296 paid for repairs to Motor Car, was debited to Motor Car Account as Rs. 696.
(b) A sale of Rs. 1,400 to Jayanta Mukherjee entered in the Sales Book as Rs. 2,120.
(c) A cash discount of Rs. 800 received was entered in the Cash Book but was not posted in the ledger.
(d) Rs. 400 being purchase returns posted to the debit of Purchases Account.
(e) The purchase of a machine on 1st April 1992 for Rs. 24,000 was entered into the Purchases Book.
(f) While carrying forward total of one page in Nandan Das's Account, the amount of Rs. 1,000 was written on the credit side instead of the debit side.
(g) A cheque of Rs. 6,912 received from Mrs. Sankari Das (after allowing her a discount of Rs. 92) was endorsed to Pranab Ghosh in full settlement for Rs. 7,000. The cheque was finally dishonoured but no entries were passed in the books.

Give journal entries to rectify the above errors and prepare Suspense Account.

[CU BCom (Hons.) Adapted]

Solution

In the books of X & Co.
Journal

Date		Particulars	L.F.	Debit	Credit
1992				Rs.	Rs.
Dec. 31	(a)	Profit and Loss Adjustment Dr.		2,296	
		To Motor Car A/c			696
		" Suspense A/c			1,600
		(Repairs of motor car Rs. 2,296 wrongly debited to Motor Car A/c as Rs. 696, now rectified.)			
	(b)	Profit and Loss Adjustment A/c Dr.		720	
		To J. Mukherjee A/c			720
		(Sales of Rs. 1,400 entered in the sales book as Rs. 2,120, now rectified.)			
	(c)	Suspence A/c Dr.		800	
		To Profit and Loss Adjustment A/c			800
		(Cash discount received not entered in the ledger, now rectified.)			
	(d)	Suspense A/c Dr.		800	
		To Profit and Loss Adjustment A/c			800
		(Purchase return wrongly entered in the debit side of purchase A/c, now rectified.)			

Contd.

			Rs.	Rs.
(e)	Machinary A/c	Dr.	24,000	
	To Profit and Loss Adjustment A/c			24,000
	(Purchase of machinery wrongly entered through Purchase book, now rectified.)			
(f)	S. Debtors A/c (Nandan Das)	Dr.	2,000	
	To Suspense A/c	Dr.		2,000
	(Debit total wrongly entered in the credit side of a Debtor A/c, now rectified.)			
(g)	Mrs. Sankari Das A/c	Dr.	7,004	
	Profit & Loss Adjustment A/c	Dr.	88	
	To Pranab Ghosh A/c			7,000
	" Profit & Loss Adjustment A/c			92
	(Endorsed cheque dishonoured, not entered in the books, now recorded.)			

Dr. **Suspense Account** Cr.

Date	Particulars	J.F.	Rs.	Date	Particulars	J.F.	Rs.
1992 Dec. 31	To Difference in T. B.		2,000	1992 Dec. 31	By P & L Adustment A/c		1,600
"	" P & L Adustment A/c		800	"	" Sundry Debtors A/c		2,000
"	" P & L Adustment A/c		800				
			3,600				3,600

Illustration 35

After getting an agreed Trial Balance, the account of Mr. Sen Bros. drafted the Trading and Profit and Loss Account and Balance Sheet. The following errors were detected by the auditors :

(a) Rs. 2,500 received from the Insurance Company in full payment of the claim for loss of stock in transit, was deposited by the proprietor into his private bank account and was not recorded in business book.

(b) Goods purchased for Rs. 2,000 were included in stock, the invoice was not entered in the books.

(c) There were compensating errors in the books, namely :

(i) A payment of Rs. 300, as Commission to a Sales agent, had not been posted from the Cash Book.

(ii) Dividend received were undercast by Rs. 100.

(iii) Purchases amounting to Rs. 190 were not posted to the account of Suppliers from the Purchase Journal.

(iv) Debit side of the Customer's Account in the Sales Ledger was overcast by Rs. 10.

(d) Goods sold for Rs. 500 were returned by a customer, but no record of this return was made in the books although the returned goods were included in Stock at their cost of Rs. 380.

Show the journal entries, Suspense Account, Profit and Loss Adjustment A/c and the effect of these errors and summarise the alterations necessary in the originally drafted statements of Account.

Solution **[CU BCom (Hons.)]**

Effect of each of the above errors is to be noted :

(a) Drawings as well as profits are understated by Rs. 2,500. As such, Profit and Loss Adjustment A/c should be credited by Rs. 2,500, debiting Lost-in-Transit A/c.

The amount which has been recovered from Insurance Company should have been credited to Lost-in-Transit A/c but wrongly credited to private account of the proprieor.

(b) Here, profit is overstated by Rs. 2,000 since goods have been included with Stock, without passing any entry in the Purchase Day Book for the same. As such, Purchase A/c should be debited and Sundry Creditors A/c should be credited.

(c) Profit is overstated by Rs. 200 (Rs. 300 – 100). Sundry Creditors are understated by Rs. 190, whereas Sundry Debtors are overstated by Rs. 10.

(d) Sales as well as profit are overstated by Rs. 500, and Sundry Debtors are also overstated by Rs. 500.

In the books of M/s Sen Bros
Journal

Date		Particulars	L.F.	Debit	Credit
?				Rs.	Rs.
	(a)	Drawings A/c Dr.		2,500	
		To Profit and Loss Adjustment A/c			2,500
		(Insurance claim received on account of goods Lost-in-transit wrongly deposited by the proprietor into his private bank account, now rectified.)			
	(b)	Profit and Loss Adjustment A/c Dr.		2,000	
		To Sundry Creditors A/c			2,000
		(Purchase of goods on credit not recorded at all in the books, now rectified.)			
	(c)(i)	Profit and Loss Adjustment A/c Dr.		300	
		To Suspense A/c			300
		(Payment of Commission on Sales not recorded to Commission A/c, now rectified.)			
	(ii)	Suspense A/c Dr.		100	
		To Profit and Loss Adjustment A/c			100
		(Dividends were undercast, now rectified.)			
	(iii)	Suspense A/c Dr.		190	
		To Sundry Creditors A/c			190
		(Goods purchased on credit not credited to Creditors A/c, now rectified.			
	(iv)	Suspense A/c Dr.		10	
		To Sundry Debtors A/c			10
		(Sundry Debtors Account was overcast, now rectified.)			
	(d)	Profit and Loss Adjustment A/c Dr.		500	
		To Sundry Debtors A/c			500
		(Goods returned by customer not credited to Customers A/c, now rectified.)			
		Capital A/c Dr.		200	
		To Profit and Loss Adjustment A/c			200
		(Net Loss transferred to Capital A/c.)			

Dr. **Suspense Account** Cr.

Date	Particulars	Amount	Date	Particulars	Amount
?		Rs.	?		Rs.
	To P & L Adjustment A/c	100		By P & L Adjustment A/c	300
	" Sundry Creditors A/c	190			
	" Sundry Debtors A/c	10			
		300			300

Dr. **Profit and Loss Adjustment Account** Cr.

Date	Particulars	Amount	Date	Particulars	Amount
?		Rs.	?		Rs.
	To Sundry Creditors A/c	2,000		By Drawings A/c	2,500
	" Suspense A/c	300		" Suspense A/c	100
	" Sundry Debtors A/c	500		" Capital A/c — Loss *(Bal. Fig.)*	200
		2,800			2,800

Alterntively

Adjustments to be made in a summarised form as under :

Date	Particulars			L.F.	Debit	Credit
					Rs.	Rs.
	Drawings	(a) A/c	Dr.		2,500	
	Purchases	(b) A/c	Dr.		2,000	
	Commission	(c) A/c	Dr.		300	
	Sales	(d) A/c	Dr.		500	
	To Lost-in-Transit	(a) A/c				2,500
	" Sundry Creditors	(b) A/c				2,000
	" Dividend	(c) A/c				100
	" Sundry Creditors	(c) A/c				190
	" Sundry Debtors	(d) A/c				10
	" Sundry Creditors	(d) A/c				500
	(Adjustment made for various errors.)					

Note : The question, here, suggests that alteration may be made if necessary, although the final accounts has been prepared. As such, rectification in nominal account has been adjusted accordingly.

Illustration 36

After taking into consideration the closing stock of Rs. 4,000, the Profit and Loss Account of Mr. Z, for the year ended 31st Dec. 2011, showed a net profit of Rs. 2,000.

After scrutiny of the books of accounts the following information is obtained:

(1) Mr. Z took goods from the business for his own use amounting to Rs. 800, not recorded in the books.

(2) Purchase included Rs. 500, spent on purchasing a Furniture for his business.

(3) Sale of goods amounted to Rs. 1,000, sold and delivered in Dec., while the same was entered in Jan. 2012.

(4) Purchased goods for Rs. 1,200, had been entered in the books on 26th Dec. 2011, but the same was not included in stock.

(5) Closing Stock included a sum of Rs. 400, relating to goods purchased and invoiced on 29th Dec. 2011, but the same was recorded in the books in January 2012.

Calculate the adjusted net profit for the year ended 31st Dec. 2011, and ascertain the correct value of closing stock.

Solution

In order to ascertain the correct net profit, a Peofit, & Loss Adjustment Account may be prepared as:

Dr. **Profit and Loss Adjustment Account** *Cr.*

Date	Particulars	Rs.	Date	Particulars	Rs.
2011			2011		
Dec. 30	To Suppliers' A/c	400	Dec. 31	By Net Profit as per P & L A/c	2,000
	" Capital A/c			" Drawings A/c	800
	" Correct Net Profit for the year *(bal. fig.)*	5,100		" Furniture A/c	500
				" Closing Stock A/c	1,200
				" Customers A/c	1,000
		5,500			5,500

Note : It should be noted that entries (3) and (5) which are passed should be calculated in the next accounting period.

Correct Value of Closing Stock

		Rs.
	Closing stock already given (on 31.12.2011)	4,000
Plus :	Goods already included in purchases but not in closing stock	1,200
∴	Correct value of Closing Stock	5,200

Illustration 37

The Trial Balance of a concern has agreed but the following mistakes were discovered after the preparation of Final Account :

(i) No Adjustment entry was passed for an amount of Rs. 2,000 relating to outstanding rent. (ii) Purchase Book was overcast by Rs. 1,000. (iii) Rs. 4,000 depreciation of machinery had been omitted to be recorded in the books. (iv) Rs. 600 paid for Purchase of Stationery has been debited to Purchases Account. (v) Sales Book was overcast by Rs. 1,000. (vi) Rs. 5,000 received in respect of Book Debt had been credited to Sales Account.

Show the effect of the above errors in Profit and Loss Account and Balance Sheet.

Solution

Effect of Errors in Profit and Loss Account and Balance Sheet:

In Profit and Loss A/c	In Balance Sheet
(i) Profit was overcast by Rs. 2,000.	(i) So, Capital was overstated by Rs. 2,000 and outstanding liabilities was understated by Rs. 2,000.
(ii) G.P. was understated by Rs. 1,000, so also the net profit	(ii) Capital was understated by Rs. 1,000.
(iii) N.P. was overstated by Rs. 4,000.	(iii) Machinery was overstated by Rs. 4,000 and Capital was overstated by Rs. 4,000.
(iv) No effect on net profit.	(iv) No effect.
(v) G.P. and N.P. were overstated by Rs. 1,000.	(v) Capital was overstated by Rs. 1,000.
(vi) G.P. and N.P. were overstated by Rs. 5,000.	(vi) Capital and Sundry Debtors were overstated by Rs. 5,000.

THUS, THE EFFECT IN PROFIT

	(+)	(−)
(i) ...	2,000	
(ii) ...	—	1,000
(iii) ...	4,000	—
(iv) No effect	—	—
(v) ...	1,000	—
(vi) ...	5,000	—
	12,000	1,000

EFFECT IN BALANCE SHEET

	Assets	Liabilities
(i) ...		+ 2,000
(ii) ...		− 2,000
		− 1,000
(iii) ...	+ 4,000	+ 4,000
(iv) No effect	—	—
(v) ...		+ 1,000
(vi) ...	+ 5,000	+ 5,000
	9,000	9,000

Profit overstated by Rs. 11,000 (Rs. 12,000 – 1,000).

Illustration 38

The following errors were located in the books of Miss Gunjan Sen after the same were closed for the year ended 31st December 2011, and the Balance Sheet was prepared as on that date by showing the difference in Suspense Account :

(a) The Balance of Furniture account on 1.1.2011 was carried forward from previous year at Rs. 3,500, instead of Rs. 5,300. A Depreciation of 15% p.a. was charged on written-down value.

(b) A credit sale of Rs. 4,000 to Miss Piu Sen was correctly recorded in the Sales Day Book but was posted to the credit of Miss Sen, a Reserve for Doubtful Debt at 5% and also a Reserve for Discount on Debtors @ 10% were made in the books.

(c) Closing Stock was overvalued by Rs. 3,000.

(d) A plant was purchased on 1.7.2011 for Rs. 10,000. The payment was made from the private bank account of the proprietor. No entry was made. Depreciation to be provided @ 10% p.a.

Pass necessary rectification entries and close Suspense Account and Profit and Loss Adjustment Account.

Solution

Workings Notes :

(a) Furniture Account should be debited and depreciation should also be calculated @ 15% p.a. on Rs. 1,800 i.e., Rs. 270.

(b) Miss Piu's account should be debited by Rs. 8,000 (Rs. 4,000 × 2) and Reserve for Bad Debts to be calculated @ 5% on Rs. 8,000 i.e., Rs. 400. Similarly, reserve for discount on Debtors should also be calculated @ 10% on Rs. 7,600 (i.e., Rs. 8,000 – Rs. 400) i.e., Rs. 760.

(c) Capital Account and Opening Stock have been overstated.

(d) Plant amount should be debited and Capital amount should be credited. Depreciation should also be provided @ 10% p.a. for 6 months, i.e., Rs. 500.

In the books of Gunjan Sen

Journal

Date	Particulars		L.F.	Debit	Credit
2011				Rs.	Rs.
Dec. 31(a)	(i) Furniture A/c	Dr.		1,800	
	To Suspense A/c				1,800
	(Furniture account was carried forward wrongly, now rectified.)				
	(ii) Profit and Loss Adjustment A/c	Dr.		270	
	To Furniture A/c				270
	(Depreciation on furniture not provided for.)				
(b)	(i) Sundry Debtors A/c	Dr.		8,000	
	To Suspense A/c				8,000
	(Credit sale to customer wrongly credited to him, now rectified.)				
	(ii) Profit and Loss Adjustment A/c	Dr.		1,160	
	To Reserve for Bad Debt A/c				400
	" Reserve for Discount on Debtors A/c				760
	(Reserve for Bad Debts and reserve for discount on Debtors not provided for in the books, now rectified.)				
(c)	Profit and Loss Adjustment A/c	Dr.		3,000	
	To Opening Stock A/c				3,000
	(Closing Stock was overvalued.)				
(d)	(i) Plant A/c	Dr.		10,000	
	To Capital A/c				10,000
	(Plant purchased from private bank account i.e., additional capital.)				
	(ii) Profit and Loss Adjustment A/c	Dr.		500	
	To Plant A/c				500
	(Depreciation on plant not provided for.)				

Suspense Account

Dr. Cr.

Date	Particulars	Rs.	Date	Particulars	Rs.
2011 Dec. 31	To Differ. in T. B	9,800	2011 Dec. 31	By Fur. A/c	1,800
				" Sundry Debtors A/c	8,000
		9,800			9,800

Profit and Loss Adjustment Account

Dr. Cr.

Particulars	Rs.	Particulars	Rs.
To Fur. A/c	270	By Capital A/c *(bal. fig.)*	4,930
" R/B/Debts A/c	400		
" R/Dis./Debtors	760		
" Op. Stock	3,000		
" Plant A/c	500		
	4,930		4,930

Illustration 39

The following errors were discovered in the books of A. Slack on December 31, 2011. The difference in the Trial Balance had been entered in a Suspense Account and on correction of the errors the Suspense Account was eliminated :

(i) The total Purchase Day Book had been undercast by Rs. 100.

(ii) The discount column of the debit side of the Cash Book had been posted to the credit of Discount Received Account Rs. 20.

(iii) Rs. 76 for repairs of Motor Van had been taken to the Motor Van Account.

(iv) A cheque received from B. Quick Rs. 39, had been debited in the Cash Book, but the double entry had not been completed.

(v) The Returns Outward Book had been overcast by Rs. 50.

(vi) A cheque of Rs. 6,192 received from Mr. X (after allowing a discount of Rs. 92) was endorsed to Mr. Y in full settlement of Rs. 7,000. The cheque was finally dishonoured but no entries were passed in the book.

(a) Show by means of journal entries how these errors would be corrected in the books of A. Slack.

(b) Show the Suspense Account bringing out the original difference in books.

(c) The Final Accounts to December 31, 2011 has been prepared on the basis of the incorrect figure. The net profit disclosed by these accounts was Rs. 4,320.

Show your calculations which affect the net profit for the year.

[CU BCom (Hons.)—Adapted]

Solution

In the books of A. Slack
Journal

Date	*Particulars*		*L.F.*	*Debit*	*Credit*
2011				Rs.	Rs.
Dec. 31	(i) Profit and Loss Adjustment A/c	Dr.		100	
	To Suspense A/c				100
	(Purchase Day Book was undercast by Rs. 100, now rectified.)				
	(ii) Profit and Loss Adjustment A/c	Dr.		40	
	To Suspense A/c				40
	(Discount allowed Rs. 20 to customer wrongly credited to discount received account, now rectified.)				
	(iii) Profit and Loss Adjustment A/c	Dr.		76	
	To Motor Van A/c				76
	(Repairs made to Motor Van, but wrongly debited to Motor Van Account, now rectified.)				
	(iv) Suspense A/c	Dr.		39	
	To B. Quick A/c				39
	(Cheque received from B. Quick, not credited to his account, now rectified.)				
	(v) Profit and Loss Adjustment A/c	Dr.		50	
	To Suspense A/c				50
	(Returns Outward Book was overcast by Rs. 50, now rectified.)				
	(vi) X A/c	Dr.		6,284	
	Profit and Loss A/c (Dis. Recd.)	Dr.		808	
	To Y A/c				7,000
	" Profit and Loss Adjustment (Dis. All.) A/c				92
	(Cheque received and endorsed but dishonoured, now rectified.)				

Suspense Account

Dr.					*Cr.*
Date	*Particulars*	*Amount*	*Date*	*Particulars*	*Amount*
2011		Rs.	2011		Rs.
	To Difference in Trial Balance (*bal. fig.*)	151		By P & L Adjustment A/c	100
	" B. Quick A/c	39		" P & L Adjustment A/c	40
				" P & L Adjustment A/c	50
		190			190

Profit and Loss Adjustment Account

Dr.	Rs.		Cr. Rs.
To Suspense A/c	100	By Net Profit transferred	4,320
" Suspense A/c	40	" X A/c	92
" Motor Van A/c	76		
" Suspense A/c	50		
" Y A/c	808		
" Capital A/c (Adjusted Net Profit transferred)	3,338		
	4,412		4,412

Tutorial Note

In this case, the books were closed after creation of Suspense Account in the Trial Balance and subsequently the errors over detected. Thus, it becomes clear that errors are rectified after preparation of Final Account. As such, all nominal account should be replaced by Profit and Loss Adjustment Account.

Illustration 40

The undermentioned errors were discovered in the books of Mr. X, after the Profit and Loss Account had been prepared for the year ended 31st March 2011. The difference in Trial Balance was carried to Suspense Account in the Balance Sheet. Mr. X provided depreciation on Machinery at 10% p.a. and on Furniture at 5% p.a. A Reserve for Bad Debts was provided at 2% on outstanding debtors. Net profit for the year was transferred to Capital Account :

(a) A cheque received for Rs. 8,000 from a customer was not posted to ledger. The corresponding Sales Invoice was for Rs. 12,000, which had been wrongly passed through the Sales Day Book as Rs. 2,000.

(b) A machine purchased for Rs. 20,000 on 1st April 2011 was wrongly debited to Furniture Account.

(c) Sales included Rs. 25,000, for goods sold for cash on behalf of Mr. Y, Mr. X was entitled to a commission of 10% on sales plus expenses, for which no adjustment was made. His Trade Expenses include Rs. 1,500, as Selling Expenses in connection with the above sale.

(d) Some old furniture (Book value on 1st April 2011, Rs. 6,000) was disposed-off for Rs. 3,000 on 30th September 2011 but the proceeds had been wrongly credited to Sales Account.

(e) A Credit Sale for Rs. 5,000 had been passed twice through the Sales Day Book.

You are required to give the journal entries rectifying above errors.

[CA Adapted]

Solution

In the books of X
Journal

Date		Particulars		L.F.	Debit Rs.	Credit Rs.
2011 March 31	(a)	Customer (Rs. 12,000 – 2,000 – 8,000) A/c	Dr.		2,000	
		Suspense A/c	Dr.		8,000	
		To Profit & Loss Adjustment A/c (Rs. 12,000 – 2,000)				10,000
		(Sales were undercast by Rs. 10,000 (Rs. 12,000 – 2,000) andRs. 8,000, received from the customer not posted to his account, now rectified.)				
	(b)	Machinery A/c[1]	Dr.		18,000	
		Profit & Loss Adjustment A/c	Dr.		1,000	
		To Furniture A/c				19,000
		(Purchase of machinery wrongly debited to Furniture A/c, now rectified and depreciation adjusted accordingly.)				
	(c)	Profit & Loss Adjustment A/c[2]	Dr.		21,000	
		To Mr. Y				21,000
		(Consignment sale was treated as normal sale, commission receivable not accounted for and consignment expenses was treated as trade expenses and they were adjusted and rectified.)				

Contd.

2011				Rs.	Rs.
	(d)	Profit & Loss Adjustment A/c[3]	Dr.	5,700	
		To Furniture A/c			5,700
		(Sale of Furniture wrongly credited to Sales A/c, now rectified and loss on sale also adjusted accordingly.)			
	(e)	Profit & Loss Adjustment A/c	Dr.	5,000	
		To Customer A/c			5,000
		(Credit sale recorded twice in the books, now rectified.)			
	(f)	Provision for Doubtful Debts A/c[4]	Dr.	60	
		To Profit & Adjustment A/c			60
		(Provision for doubtful debts written-back.)			
	(g)	Mr. X's Capital A/c	Dr.	22,640	
		To Profit & Loss Adjustment A/c			22,640
		(Balance of Profit & Loss Adjustment A/c transferred to Mr. X's Capital.)			

Note :

1. Machinery purchased for Rs. 20,000 had been debited to Furniture Account and depreciation @ 5% had been charged accordingly. As such, Furniture A/c was debited by the net amount, i.e., Rs. 19,000 (Rs. 20,000 – 1,000) which is cancelled by crediting Furniture A/c. But Machinery Account should be debited with Rs. 18,000 (i.e., Rs. 20,000 – 2,000) at cost less depreciation. Thus, there is a shortage of Rs. 1,000 (Rs. 2,000 – 1,000) in provision for depreciation account for which Profit and Loss Adjustment Account should be debited.
2. Since consignment sale has been treated as normal sales, Profit and Loss Adjustment Account should be debited and credited to Y's Account. For commission receivable on sale amounting to Rs. 2,500, Y's A/c will be debited and Profit and Loss Adjustment Account should be credited. On the contrary, for expenses on consignment, (which has been included with trade expenses), Y's A/c will be debited and Profit and Loss Adjustment Account will be credited. Thus, net debit to Profit and Loss Adjustment Account will be Rs. 21,000 (i.e., Rs. 25,000 – 2,500 – 1,500).
3. Since the sale proceeds of furniture has been credited to Sales A/c, depreciation should be charged for full year on old furniture sold. As such, book value of furniture sold is Rs. 5,700 (i.e., Rs. 6,000 – 300), which should be credited to Furniture A/c. Profit and Loss Adjustment Account should be debited by Rs. 5,700, by the proceeds of furniture plus the loss on sale Rs. 2,700 (i.e., Rs. 3,000 – 300).
4. Amount of debtors has been reduced by Rs. 3,000 (Rs. 5,000 – Rs. 2,000), due to rectification entry of (a) and (e). Hence provision for bad debt should also be reduced by Rs. 60 (i.e., $3{,}000 \times \frac{2}{100}$).

GENERAL ILLUSTRATIONS

Illustration 41

Rectify the following errors in the books of Mr. Z assuming that these were detected after preparing Trial Balance :

(i) Sales included Rs. 5,000, for goods sold for cash out of goods consigned by Mr. X. Mr. Z is, however, entitled to a Commission of 20% on such sales and expenses incurred in this connection Rs. 50 which was already debited to Trade Expenses Account.

(ii) Sales of goods on 'Sale or Return' amounting to Rs. 500, was included in Sales Account, out of which goods to the value of Rs. 100 (cost Rs. 80), were not yet approved and the same was lying with customers on closing date.

(iii) Goods sold for Rs. 1,000 was returned by a customer but not recorded in the books, although the same were included in the Closing Stock at cost Rs. 750.

(iv) A credit sale of Rs. 1,600 to Mr. Y had been omitted to be recorded in the Sales Day Book. Again, when a cheque is received from him for Rs. 1,000 (as a part payment), his account has been credited in the Creditors Ledger.

(v) Out of the total amount of Rs. 40,000 shown as Debtors, a sum of Rs. 4,000, represents debit given to Mr. P, a supplier (when the payment was made against purchases). However, the invoice was not entered in the books. A Cash Discount of 20%, was allowed by the suppliers.

N. B. Narrations are not required.

Solution

In the books of Mr. Z

Journal *(without narration)*

Date	*Particulars*		*L.F.*	*Debit*	*Credit*
				Rs.	Rs.
(i)	Sales A/c	Dr.		5,000	
	To Trade Expenses A/c				200
	" Commission A/c				1,000
	" Consignor A/c				3,800
(ii)	Sales A/c	Dr.		800	
	To Sales or Return Suspense A/c				800
(iii)	Returns Inward A/c	Dr.		1,000	
	To Customers A/c				1,000
(iv) (a)	Y A/c (in Debtors Ledger)	Dr.		1,600	
	To Sales A/c				1,600
(b)	Y A/c (in Creditors Ledger)			1,000	
	To Y A/c (in Debtors Ledger)				1,000
(v) (a)	Purchase A/c	Dr.		5,000	
	To P (in Creditors Ledger) A/c (Rs. 4,000 $\times \frac{100}{80}$)				5,000
(b)	P A/c (in Creditors Ledger)	Dr.		5,000	
	To P A/c (in Debtors Ledger)				4,000
	" Discount Received A/c				1,000

Illustration 42

The books of accounts of A. Co. Ltd., for the year ending 31st March 2011, were closed with a difference in books carried forward. The following errors were detected subsequently:

(a) Returns Outwards Book was undercast by Rs. 100.

(b) Rs. 1,500, being the total of the Discount Column on the credit side of the Cash Book, was not posted.

(c) Rs. 6,000, being the cost of purchase of Office Furniture, was debited to Purchases Account.

(d) A credit sale of Rs. 760 was wrongly posted as Rs. 670 to the Customers' Account in the Sales Ledger.

(e) The Sales Account was understated by Rs. 10,000, being the carry-over mistake in the Sales Day Book.

(f) Closing Stock was overstated by Rs. 10,000, being casting error in the schedule of Inventory.

Pass rectification entries in the next year.

Prepare Suspense Account and state effect of the errors in determination of Net Profit of last year.

Solution

In the books of A Co. Ltd.

Journal

Date	*Particulars*		*L.F.*	*Debit*	*Credit*
2011				Rs.	Rs.
Mar. 31	(a) Suspense A/c	Dr.		100	
	To Profit and Loss Adjustment A/c				100
	(Returns Outward Book was undercast, now rectified)				
	(b) Suspense A/c	Dr.		1,500	
	To Profit and Loss Adjustment A/c				1,500
	(Discount received was not recorded, now rectified)				
	(c) Office Furniture A/c	Dr.		6,000	
	To Profit and Loss Adjustment A/c				6,000
	(Office Furniture purchased wrongly debited to Purchases Account, now rectified)				
	(d) Debtors' A/c	Dr.		90	
	To Suspense A/c				90
	(Debtors' Account was posted Rs. 670, in place of Rs. 760, now rectified)				

Contd.

2011			Rs.	Rs.
	(e) Suspense A/c To Profit and Loss A/c (Sales Account was undercast by Rs. 10,000, now rectified)	Dr.	10,000	10,000
	(f) Suspense A/c To Profit and Loss Adjustment A/c (Closing Stock was overstated, now rectified)	Dr.	10,000	10,000

Dr. **Suspense Account** Cr.

Date	Particulars	Amount	Date	Particulars	Amount
2011		Rs.	2011		Rs.
Mar. 31	To P & L Adjustment A/c	100	Mar. 31	By Difference in Trial Balance (bal. fig.)	21,510
	To P & L Adjustment A/c	1,500		By Debtors' A/c	90
	To P & L Adjustment A/c	10,000			
	To P & L Adjustment A/c	10,000			
		21,600			21,600

Effect on Profit

			Increase (+) Rs.	Decrease (–) Rs.
Item	(a)	... ...	—	100
	(b)	... ...	—	1,500
	(c)	... ...	—	6,000
	(d)	No effect	—	—
	(e)	... ...	—	10,000
	(f)	... ...	—	10,000
			Nil	27,600

∴ Profit will be reduced by Rs. 27,600.

Illustration 43

Following is the Balance Sheet of Mr. R. Roy and Co. for the year ended 31.12.2011, which was prepared on the basis of an unagreed Trial Balance. A Suspense Account was prepared for the difference in the Trial Balance.

Balance Sheet
as at 31.12.2011

	Rs.	Rs.		Rs.
Capital	50,000		Plant and Machinery	15,000
Add: Net Profit	15,000		Motor Vehicles	10,000
	65,000		Investments	5,000
Less: Drawings	10,000		Stock	10,000
		55,000	Debtors	8,000
Creditors		1,500	Cash at Bank	9,650
Loan		1,600	Suspense A/c	450
		58,100		58,100

The following errors were detected for the difference in the Trial Balance:

(i) Interest charged by bank, in Cash Book, not recorded in Interest Account—Rs. 100.

(ii) Sales Day Book was undercast by Rs. 500.

(iii) Purchased a Plant for Rs. 1,500, in cash, credited in Cash Book, but not recorded in Plant Account.

(iv) Received cash from Mr. Sen, our customer, for Rs. 300, recorded in Cash Book but the corresponding double entry was not made.

(v) Goods purchased from Mr. Biswas for Rs. 1,500, entered correctly in the Purchase Day Book, but credited to Biswas Account only Rs. 150.

(vi) Goods taken by the proprietor for Rs. 1,000, credited to Purchases Account but not recorded in Drawings Account.

You are required:

(a) To show the rectifying entries;
(b) To prepare the Suspense Account;
(c) To ascertain the correct Net Profit; and
(d) To prepare the correct Balance Sheet.

Solution

(a)

In the books of Mr. Roy Ltd.
Journal

Date	Particulars		L.F.	Debit Rs.	Credit Rs.
2011 Dec. 31	(i) Profit and Loss Adjustment A/c To Suspense A/c (Interest charged by bank but not debited to Interest A/c, rectified)	Dr.		100	100
	(ii) Suspense A/c To Profit and Loss Adjustment A/c (Sales Day Book was cast short)	Dr.		500	500
	(iii) Plant A/c To Suspense A/c (Plant purchased but not recorded in Plant A/c, now rectified)	Dr.		1,500	1,500
	(iv) Suspense A/c To Mr. Sen A/c (Received cash from customer, not credited to his account, now rectified)	Dr.		300	300
	(v) Suspense A/c To Biswas A/c (Goods purchased from Biswas for Rs. 1,500, but only Rs. 150 was credited to his account, now rectified)	Dr.		1,350	1,350
	(vi) Drawings A/c To Suspense A/c (Goods taken by the proprietor for his own use, not debited to Drawings A/c, now rectified)	Dr.		1,000	1,000

(b)

Suspense Account

Dr. Cr.

Date	Particulars	Rs.	Date	Particulars	Rs.
2011 Dec. 31	To Difference in T/B	450	2011 Dec. 31	By P & L Adjustment	100
	" P & L Adjustment A/c	500		" Plant A/c	1,500
	" Customer A/c	300		" Drawings A/c	1,000
	" Biswas A/c	1,350			
		2,600			2,600

(c)

Profit and Loss Adjustment Account

Dr. Cr.

	Rs.		Rs.
To Suspense A/c	100	By Balance b/d	15,000
" Balance c/d	15,400	" Suspense A/c	500
	15,500		15,500

(d)

Corrected Balance Sheet
as at 31st December 2011

Liabilities	Rs.	Rs.	Assets	Rs.
Capital	50,000		Plant and Machinery (15,000 + 1,500)	16,500
Add: Net Profit	15,400		Motor Vehicles	10,000
	65,400		Investment	5,000
Less: Drawings (10,000 + 1,000)	11,000		Stock	10,000
		54,400	Debtors (8,000 – 300)	7,700
Creditors (1,500 + 1,350)		2,850	Cash at Bank	9,650
Loan		1,600		
		58,850		58,850

Illustration 44

The following Balance Sheet was prepared by a novice on 31.12.1995:

Balance Sheet

Dr. Cr.

Liabilities	*Amount*	*Assets*	*Amount*
	Rs.		Rs.
Capital	98,500	Furniture and other Fixed Assets	59,500
Net Profit during the year	45,700	Stock	61,000
Loan	50,000	Debtors	38,190
Creditors	22,150	Fixed Deposits	25,750
Suspense A/c	2,110	Bank	19,820
		Drawings	14,200
	2,18,460		2,18,460

On close scrutiny the following errors were discovered :

(a) Closing stock was overvalued by Rs. 4,000.

(b) A sale of Rs. 2,300 was recorded in Sales Day Book as Rs. 3,200, though it was rightly posted in Sales Account.

(c) The total of one page of Purchase Day Book was carried forward as Rs. 3,800 instead of Rs. 8,300.

(d) Outstanding telephone bill of Rs. 510 was not recorded in the books.

(e) A collection of Rs. 2,000 from a customer was posted in the Creditors Account.

(f) Rent for one month Rs. 2,500 was recorded in the books as rent of the residential house of the proprietor.

(g) Some old furniture were purchased at Rs. 2,000 for resale but they were recorded in the books as fixed assets and depreciation was charged at 10% p.a.

(h) A Fixed Deposit of Rs. 5,000 matured and Rs. 7,500 was realised. But the entire amount was credited to Fixed Deposit Account.

Show necessary Journal entries to rectify the errors, prepare a Profit and Loss Adjustment Account and the Balance Sheet after the rectification.

[CU BCom (Hons.) 1995]

Solution

In the books of ......

Journal

Date	*Particulars*		*L.F.*	*Debit*	*Credit*
				Rs.	Rs.
(a)	Profit & Loss Adjustment A/c	Dr.		4,000	
	To Stock A/c				4,000
	(Rectification made for overvaluation of Closing Stock.)				
(b)	Suspense A/c	Dr.		900	
	To Sundry Debtors A/c (Rs. 3,200 – 2,300)				900
	(Sale of Rs. 2,300 posted to Debtors A/c as Rs. 3,200, now rectified.)				
(c)	Profit & Loss Adjustment A/c (Rs. 8,300 – 3,800)	Dr.		4,500	
	To Suspense A/c				4,500
	(Wrong carry forward in the Purchase Day Book, now rectified.)				
(d)	Profit & Loss Adjustment A/c	Dr.		510	
	To Outstanding Telephone Bill A/c				510
	(Outstanding telephone bill not provided, now rectified.)				
(e)	Sundry Creditors A/c	Dr.		2,000	
	To Sundry Debtors A/c				2,000
	(Collection from Debtors wrongly credited to Sundry Creditors A/c, now rectified.)				

Contd.

			Rs.	Rs.
(f)	Profit & Loss Adjustment A/c	Dr.	2,500	
	To Drawings A/c			2,500
	(Office Rent wrongly recorded as rent of residential house of proprietor, now rectified.)			
(g)	Stock A/c	Dr.	2,000	
	To Fixed Assets A/c			2,000
(i)	Fixed Assets A/c	Dr.	200	
	To Profit and Loss Adjustment A/c			200
(ii)	(Purchase of furniture for re-sale wrongly treated as a fixed asset and depreciation charged thereon, now rectified.)			
(h)	Fixed Deposit A/c	Dr.	2,500	
	To Profit & Loss Adjustment A/c (Int. on F. D. A/c)			2,500
	(Interest received on Fixed Deposit credited to Fixed Deposit A/c, now rectified.)			

Dr. Profit & Loss Adjustment Account Cr.

	Rs.		Rs.
To Stock A/c	4,000	By Net Profit (as per P/L)	45,700
" Suspense A/c	4,500	" Stock A/c	200
" Outstanding Telephone Bills A/c	510	" Fixed Deposit A/c	2,500
" Drawings A/c	2,500		
" Capital A/c (Correct Net Profit)	36,890		
	48,400		48,400

Balance Sheet
as at 31.12.95 (Corrected)

Liabilities		*Amount*	*Assets*	*Amount*
		Rs.		Rs.
Capital A/c	98,500		Furniture and Other Fixed Assets (Rs. 59,500 – 1,800)	57,700
Add : Profit (adjusted)	36,890			
	1,35,390		Stock (Rs. 61,000 – 4,000 + 2,000)	59,000
Less : Drawings	11,700	1,23,690	Sundry Debtors (Rs. 38,190 – 900 – 2,000)	35,290
Loan		55,000		
Sundry Creditors (Rs. 22,150 – 2,000)		20,150	Fixed Deposits (Rs. 25,750 + 2,500)	28,250
Outstanding Telephone Bill		510	Bank	19,820
Suspense A/c		5,710		
		2,00,060		2,00,060

Dr. Suspense Account Cr.

	Rs.		Rs.
To Sundry Debtors A/c	900	By Balance b/d	2,110
" Balance c/d	5,710	" Profit & Loss Adjustment A/c	4,500
	6,610		6,610

Notes:

1. It is interesting to note that after rectifying the errors, the Suspense Account did not agree, i.e., Suspense Account again shows a credit balance of Rs. 5,710. It means there are other undetected errors. Sinces all the errors are not yet rectified, the balance of Profit and Loss Adjustment does not exhibit the correct net profit although the same is transferred to Capital Account.
2. For item (b), Debtors Account wrongly debited by Rs. 900 (Rs. 3,200 – Rs. 2,300).
3. For items (g), Furniture purchased for re-sale wrongly debited to Fixed Assets Account and deprecation @ 10% p.a. on Rs. 2,000 will be Rs. 200 was charged accordingly. Now, they should be adjusted.

Illustration 45

The first draft of the final accounts of Ram Bros disclosed a net profit of Rs. 41,004, and a capital employed of Rs. 3,52,600, before providing for the manager's efficiency bonus, but including Rs. 8,928 (credit balance) for errors held in suspense.

Mr. M, the manager, receives a basic salary plus an annual bonus of Rs. 300, for every complete percentage point by which the net profit to capital employed percentage exceeds 10%. In this context, net profit before charging the manager's bonus, and capital employed is defined as fixed assets plus working capital. The bonus calculation is not carried out until the figures have been audited.

During the course of the audit it was discovered that :

(a) Discounts allowed Rs. 536 had been credited to Discount Received Account.

(b) The sale for cash, of some disused fixtures and fittings, which had been completely written-off in previous year, had been credited to Fixtures and Fittings Rs. 470.

(c) An amount of Rs. 380, owned by M & Co. for goods supplied, had been settled in contra against an amount of Rs. 850, owing to M & Co.; but the ledger entries had not yet been made.

(d) A glass canopy containing chemicals, which was kept in the warehouse, had sprung a leak. The resultant seepage had caused irreparable damage to stock valued at Rs. 800, but no account had yet been taken of this fact.

(e) Due to an oversight, credit sales for the last three days of the accounting year, amounting to Rs. 1,575, have been completely omitted from the Sales Day Book.

(f) In the Purchase Day Book, a sub-total of Rs. 27,183.54 had been carried forward as Rs. 37,183.54. Creditors, however, have been correctly posted.

(g) A credit sale invoice of Rs. 978 had been entered in the Sales Day Book as Rs. 789.

(h) A credit note from a supplier for Rs. 21, in respect of faulty goods, had not been posted.

(i) The proprietor of Ram Bros sometimes, for his convenience, abstracts cash from the till for personal purposes. During the year, this had amounted to Rs. 86. The book-keeper states that he has "reduced cash sales so that the cash book balances".

Required : (i) Necessary Journal entries to rectify the errors; (ii) recalculate the net profit and capital employed figures after the above errors have been corrected; (iii) calculate the manager's bonus; and (iv) open the Suspense Account and post the eliminating entries.

[CCA Adapted]

Solution

In the books of Ram Bros
Journal

Date		Particulars		L.F.	Debit Rs.	Credit Rs.
	(a)	Profit and Loss Adjustment A/c	Dr.		1,072	
		To Suspense A/c				1,072
		(Discount allowed Rs. 536 had been credited to Discount Received Account. Now rectified.)				
	(b)	Furniture & Fixture A/c	Dr.		470	
		To Profit & Loss Adjustment A/c				470
		(Sale of fully depreciated furniture wrongly credited to Furniture Account, now rectified.)				
	(c)	Sundry Creditors A/c	Dr.		380	
		To Sundry Debtors A/c				380
		(Mutual indebtedness set-off.)				
	(d)	Profit & Loss Adjustment A/c	Dr.		800	
		To Stock-in-trade A/c				800
		(Damaged stock has not been taken into account, now rectified.)				
	(e)	Sundry Debtors A/c	Dr.		1,575	
		To Profit & Loss Adjustment A/c				1,575
		(Credit sales omitted from Sales Day Book, now rectified.)				

Contd.

			Rs.	Rs.
(f)	Suspense A/c	Dr.	10,000	
	To Profit & Loss Adjustment A/c			10,000
	(Purchase Day Book was overcast by Rs. 10,000, now rectified.)			
(g)	Sundry Debtors A/c	Dr.	189	
	To Profit & Loss Adjustment A/c			189
	(Sales of Rs. 978 had been credited to Sales Day Book as Rs. 789, now rectified.)			
(h)	Sundry Creditors A/c	Dr.	21	
	To Profit & Loss Adjustment A/c			21
	(Credit note from supplier had not been posted, now rectified.)			
	Drawings A/c	Dr.	86	
	To Profit & Loss Adjustment A/c			86
	(Cash withdrawn by propritor)			

Dr. **Profit & Loss Adjustment Account** Cr.

		Rs.			Rs.
To	Suspense A/c	1,072	By	Balance b/d	41,004
"	Stock in Trade A/c	800	"	Furniture & Fixtures A/c	470
"	Capital A/c (bal. fig.)	51,473	"	Sundry Debtors A/c	1,575
				Suspense A/c	10,000
			"	Sundry Debtors A/c	189
			"	Sundry Creditors A/c	21
			"	Drawings A/c	86
		53,345			53,345

Capital Employed *(Revised)*

		Rs.	Rs.	Rs.
	Balance			3,52,600
Add :	Wrong Balance of Suspense A/c		8,928	
	Fixed Assets (F & F)		470	
	Current Assets (Net) :			
	Sundry Debtors	1,575		
	Sundry Debtors	189		
	Sundry Creditors	21		
		1,785		
Less :	Stock	800	985	
				10,383
				3,62,983

Calculation of Bonus

Return on Capital Employed $= \frac{\text{Rs. } 51,473}{\text{Rs. } 3,62,983} \times 100 = 14.2$ % and since it exceeds only by 4 whole %, bonus will be Rs. 1,200 (Rs. 300 × 4).

Dr. **Suspense Account** Cr.

Date	Particulars	Amount	Date	Particulars	Amount
?		Rs.	?		Rs.
	To P & L Adjustment A/c	10,000		By Balance b/d	8,928
				" P & L Adjustment A/c	1,072
		10,000			10,000

ASSIGNMENT MATERIALS
THEORETICAL

Objective-Type Questions

1. State whether the following statements are 'True' or 'False':
   (a) When the Trial Balance does not agree, the difference is transferred to Suspense Account.
   (b) Errors do not have any effect on profit.
   (c) Trial Balance cannot detect the compensation errors.

(d) Errors of omission does not affect Trial Balance.
(e) Errors of Principle affect Trial Balance.
(f) Double-sided errors mean when two accounts are affected.
(g) Suspense Account arises in case of Single-sided errors.
(h) When the errors are detected Suspense Account is automatically adjusted.
(i) If the errors are detected after the preparation of Trial Balance, any nominal account item is adjusted through Profit and Loss Adjustment Account.
(j) Suspense Account does not arise in case of errors detected before the preparation of Trial Balance.

[Ans. True: (a); (c); (d); (f); (g); (h); (i); (j). False: (b); (e)]

Multiple Choice Questions

2. (a) Double-sided errors arise when:
(i) Two Accounts are affected; (ii) When one account is affected; (iii) None of these.

(b) Compensating error arises when:
(i) One account is affected; (ii) One error is compensated with another; (iii) When two accounts are affected.

(c) The balance of Profit and Loss Adjustment Account is transferred to:
(i) Profit and Loss Account; (ii) Capital Account; (iii) Net Profit.

(d) The balance of Suspense Account is transferred to:
(i) Difference in Trial Balance; (ii) Trial Balance; (iii) None of these.

(e) Suspense Account arises when there is:
(i) Single-sided error; (ii) Double-sided error; (iii) Both.

(f) Question of Suspense Account does not arise, if the errors are detected:
(i) After the preparation of Trial Balance; (ii) Before the preparation of Trial Balance; (iii) After the preparation of Balance Sheet.

(g) Errors of Principle arise when:
(i) Wrong posting according to Accounting Principle; (ii) As per Trial Balance; (iii) As per ledger posting.

(h) Errors of Omission arise when:
(i) The transaction is not at all recorded in the books; (ii) The transaction is recorded in a wrong account; (iii) None of these.

(i) Profit and Loss Adjustment Account is to be opened:
(i) After the preparation of Trial Balance; (ii) After the preparation of Final Accounts; (iii) Before the preparation of Trial Balance.

(j) Rectification of Errors come under:
(i) Journal Proper; (ii) Adjusting Entries; (iii) Opening Entries.

[Ans. (a) (i); (b) (ii); (c) (ii); (d) (i); (e) (i); (f) (i); (g) (i); (h) (i); (i) (ii); (j) (i)]

Short Answer-Type Questions

3. What is Suspense Account?
4. Which errors are not detected by a Trial Balance?
5. Which errors can be detected by a Trial Balance?
6. What will you do if the Trial Balance does not agree?
7. Discuss the errors that affect the agreement of a Trial Balance.
8. What are Single-sided Errors? How do you rectify them?
9. What are Double-sided Errors? How do you rectify them?
10. What are Rectification Entries? Explain the method of correction.
11. Discuss the errors which do not effect the agreement of Trial Balance.
12. What is a Compensating Error? Explain it with the help of an example.
11. What are Errors of Principle? Explain with the help of an example.

14. What are Errors of Commission? Explain with the help of an example.
15. When do you open 'Difference in Book Account'?

Long Answer-Type Questions

16. Explain the effect of errors in profit.
17. Discuss the various kinds of errors with examples.
18. What is Suspense Account? Explain its effect.
19. If the errors are not rectified, will the profit be affected?

PRACTICAL

1. Double-sided Errors

2. Rectify the following errors from the following particulars (assumed these were detected after preparing Trial Balance):
   (i) The purchases of an Office Table costing Rs. 500 has been wrongly passed through the Invoice Book.
   (ii) Rs. 1,000, Salary paid to Mr. Bose, stands wrongly debited to his personal account.
   (iii) An amount of Rs. 500, withdrawn by the proprietor for personal use, has been wrongly debited to Trade Expenses Account.
   (iv) An amount of Rs. 250 received for Commission has been wrongly entered in the Cash Book as received for Interest.
   (v) Returns Inwards of Rs. 300 from P was not recorded in the books, although the goods were taken into stock.
   (vi) Rs. 1,000 paid to C. Bros. against our acceptance were debited to B. Bros.'s account.
   (vii) A credit sale of Rs. 325 was posted from Sales Book to credit of Sen and Co. instead of Das and Co.
   (viii) A purchase of goods from Roy and Co. for Rs. 900 was made, but the goods were in-transit.
   (ix) Purchase of Stationery for Rs. 105 was debited to Office Typewriter Account.
   (x) Repairs to Office Car Rs. 200 were debited to Car Account.
   (xi) Goods returned to Sri S. Sen for Rs. 150 were debited to R. Sen's Account.
   (xii) Furniture worth Rs. 1,000 purchased for cash was debited to Repairs Account.
   (xiii) Purchase of goods for the consumption of the proprietor was debited to Purchases Account for Rs. 800.
   (xiv) Wages and Materials paid for construction of a Garage debited to these two accounts, Rs. 300 and Rs. 400, respectively.
   (xv) A cheque returned by Bank as dishonoured debited to Discount Account for Rs. 550.

B. Single-sided Errors

2. Rectify the following errors assuming that these were detected after preparing Trial Balance:
   (i) Sales Day Book was overcast by Rs. 1,000.
   (ii) Sales Day Book was cast short by Rs. 300.
   (iii) Purchase Day Book was overcast by Rs. 500.
   (iv) Purchase Day Book was undercast by Rs. 175.
   (v) Discount Allowed Rs. 300 not posted to Discount Account.
   (vi) Returns Inwards Book was undercast by Rs. 400.
   (vii) Returns Outwards Book was overcast by Rs. 200.
   (viii) A Debtor's balance of Rs. 350 was not included in Debtors' list.
   (ix) Addition of the payment side of the Cash Book was short by Rs. 100.
   (x) A sale of Rs. 100 was posted in the ledger as Rs. 1,000.
3. Rectify the following errors:
   (i) Discount Allowed to Customer for Rs. 100 was posted to the Discount Received Account.
   (ii) Interest received Rs. 300 was debited to Interest Account.
   (iii) Goods sold to Mr. B for Rs. 700, wrongly debited to his Account.
   (iv) Goods returned by Mr. P for Rs. 200, wrongly debited to his Account.
   (v) Discount received Rs. 300 was debited to Discount Allowed Account.
   (vi) Goods purchased from Mr. X, for Rs. 900, wrongly debited to X's Account.

C. Mixed Problems (i.e., Both Double-sided and Single-sided Errors.

4. The under-mentioned errors could not be detected by the bookkeeper of G. D. Bose, a sole-trader:
   (i) The Sales Day Book was cast Rs. 500 short.
   (ii) The purchase of an Office Almirah for Rs. 450 was passed through the Purchases Day Book.
   (iii) The sale of goods worth Rs. 250 to B. Bose was credited to his account.
   (iv) Goods worth Rs. 350 taken by G. D. Bose were not debited to any account.
   (v) Purchase of Stationery for Rs. 50 was debited to Office Typewriter Account.

   The Trial Balance was agreed by keeping the difference in 'Suspense Account'.

   You are required to state:
   (a) What items would affect the agreement of the Trial Balance?
   (b) What was the amount in the 'Suspense Account'?

   Give corrective journal entries for rectification of the errors.

5. Following errors are detected after the preparation of Trial Balance and creation of a Suspense Account. Pass the entries necessary to correct them:
   (i) An invoice received from Ajit for Rs. 500 was posted to the debit of Ajit's account as Rs. 550.
   (ii) A sale of old Furniture for Rs. 300 was entered in Sales Day Book as Rs. 30.
   (iii) Rs. 600 paid for Salary was debited to Employees' Account.
   (iv) A Bills Payable, accepted for Rs. 450, was posted as Rs. 540 to the credit of Drawers' Account.
   (v) The Purchase Day Book was undercast by Rs. 300.

   Also show the Suspense Account.

6. Pass rectification entries for the following transactions:
   (i) Interest paid to Mr. A by cheque was wrongly entered into the cash column as interest received Rs. 1,250.
   (ii) Rs. 300 Salary paid to Mr. N stands wrongly debited to his personal account.
   (iii) Goods sold to Mr. R for Rs. 475 have been wrongly entered in the Sales Book as Rs. 745.
   (iv) An amount of Rs. 900 received for commission has been wrongly entered in the Cash Book as received on Dividend.
   (v) Discount Allowed by Mr. T of Rs. 60 on payment to him of Rs. 740 has not been entered in the books of accounts at all.

   Find out the difference in Trial Balance arising out of the above errors.

D. After Preparation of Final Accounts

7. A trader has balanced his Trial Balance by putting the difference of Rs. 310 in a debit of Suspense Account and has prepared a Trading and Profit and Loss Account and the Balance Sheet. On subsequent scrutiny the books disclosed several errors as detailed below:

   Rectify these errors and prepare Suspense Account:
   (a) A Sale of goods to X for Rs. 350 has been credited to his account.
   (b) Goods purchased from Y amounting Rs. 750 were entered in the Purchase Day Book but were omitted from Y's Account in the Creditor's Ledger.
   (c) An Office Typewriter purchased for Rs. 500 had been passed through the Purchases Account.
   (d) Goods returned to S. Sen, valued Rs. 75, were debited to P. Sen's Account.
   (e) Repairs to Office Car, valued Rs. 750, were debited to the Office Car Account.
   (f) Goods sold to R. Banerjee, valued Rs. 730, have been posted in his account as Rs. 370.

   [CA Entrance]

8. On 31st March 2011, while balancing the books of Shri Ramdoss, they did not agree. The difference in Trial Balance amounting to Rs. 783 was debited to Suspense Account. Later, the following errors were noticed:

   Give the journal entries for rectification and prepare the Suspense Account:
   (a) The total of Purchases Book of March 2011 has been undercast by Rs. 300.
   (b) Rs. 228 paid for repairing the machinery has been debited to Machinery Account.
   (c) The Sales Book has been overcast by Rs. 150.
   (d) The sales of Rs. 1,200 to Mr. David has been passed through Purchases Book.

(e) Cash Rs. 117 received from Shri M. Das, though entered in the Cash Book, has not been posted to Shri M. Das's Account.

(f) Goods returned by Mr. N. Navin Rs. 225 have been entered in the Returns Outwards Book. Mr. N. Navin's account is correctly posted.

[CA Entrance]

9. On preparing a Trial Balance on 31st December 2011, a trader finds that the credit balance exceeded the debit balance by Rs. 1,720 and he transferred this difference to 'Suspense Account' to agree the Trial Balance.

The following errors were subsequently discovered:

(i) Outstanding Salary of Rs. 3,000 had not been taken into account.

(ii) Returns Inwards Book was cast short by Rs. 500.

(iii) Rs. 300 owing by a customer had been omitted from the list of Sundry Debtors.

(iv) A Sale of Rs. 750 had been entered in the Sales Book as Rs. 570.

(v) Goods costing Rs. 800 were sent to a customer on Sale-or-Return basis for Rs. 1,000. These had been recorded in the books as actual sales but no information regarding their acceptance by the customer was received up to 31.12.2011.

(vi) Repairs made for Rs. 500, wrongly debited to Buildings Account.

(vii) Paid Cash Rs. 1,000 to Mr. Roy, wrongly credited to his account by Rs. 100.

Show the required Journal entries to rectify the errors.

10. An accountant, while balancing his books, found that there was a difference (excess credit) of Rs. 860 in the Trial Balance. The difference was placed in the Suspense Account and the books were closed.

The following errors were disclosed afterwards:

(a) Rs. 3,000 sale proceeds of old Machinery has been posted to Sales Account.

(b) Rs. 50, the price of goods purchased from Ram, had been shown on the credit side of his account as Rs. 500.

(c) Rs. 30, the discount allowed by Raziv, had been shown in his account but not posted to Discount Account.

(d) A sum of Rs. 640 owed by Mohan had not been included in the list of Debtors.

(e) Account of Sukh had been debited with Rs. 100 on account of goods returned by him.

Give journal entries to correct these errors and prepare the Suspense Account.

11. Rectify the following errors assuming that these were detected after the preparation of Trial Balance:

(i) A purchase of Rs. 69.00 from Parimal entered in the Purchases Day Book was debited to Parimal's Account as Rs. 60.50.

(ii) A sale of Rs. 300 to Mr. Sarkar was wrongly credited to his account.

(iii) An amount of Rs. 50 paid for Rent is posted twice in Rent Account.

(iv) The total of a Sales Day Book on a particular day was carried forward as Rs. 214 in place of Rs. 421.

(v) An item of purchase of Rs. 440 is entered in the Purchases Day Book as Rs. 44 and posted to the debit of Suppliers' Account as Rs. 40.

(vi) A sale of Furniture realised Rs.100, entered in the debit side of the Cash Book as Rs.10 and posted to the credit of Sales Account as Rs. 1,000.

(vii) A sale of goods to Mr. Roy for Rs. 500 has been wrongly passed through the Purchases Book.

(viii) A purchase of goods from Mr. Sen for Rs. 1,000 has been wrongly passed through the Sales Book.

(ix) Goods amounting to Rs. 400 have been returned by P. Sen and taken into stock, but no entry in respect thereof was made in the books.

(x) A credit purchase of Rs. 750 from Mr. S. N. Sen was debited to Plant Account and credited to Mr. N. S. Sen's Account as Rs. 100.

Show also the Suspense Account after preparation of the Final Account.

CHAPTER 11

BAD DEBTS, PROVISION FOR BAD DEBTS, PROVISION FOR DISCOUNT ON DEBTORS AND PROVISION FOR DISCOUNT ON CREDITORS

Introduction

We know that goods are sold for cash as well as for credit. In case of cash sales, cash is realised at the point of sale. So no problem arises on regarding the collection of the proceeds. But, in the case of credit sales, the problem arises regarding the collection of proceeds from customers as the proceeds are not collected at the point of sale. Because, the two transactions (viz., sale of proceeds, and actual realisation of cash) take place at two different dates.

Usually credit sales are recorded in Sales Day Book and subsequently they are posted to the general ledger after passing the following entry—

Sundry Debtors A/c Dr.
To Sales A/c

It is interesting to note that while preparing final accounts total amounts of sales (i.e., cash and credit) appear in the credit side of the Trading Account. That is why, in accounting, revenue is recognised at the point of sale and not at the time where the proceeds are collected. It has already been pointed out above that no problem practically arises in the case of cash sales. But in the case of credit sales, problems arise although goods are sold on credit to known customers. In real world situation, debts become irrecoverable for a number of reasons, viz., insolvency of the customer, unwillingness to pay, etc. Actually, it is not possible for the business to ascertain which debt will be proved bad or which one might be doubtful or which one may be considered as good.*

Bad Debts

It has been pointed out above that bad debts are the uncollectable and irrecoverable debt—either whole or in part—since the debtors cannot pay or the creditors find it impracticable to enforce payment. If it is definitely known that the amount recoverable from a debtor cannot be realised at all, the same may be treated as a business loss and it should be accounted for accordingly as an operating expense as it is a 'must' if the firm extends credit facilities to its customers whether known or unknown. According to GAAP (Generally Accepted Accounting Principles) revenues should be matched against the related expenses for the related year. Naturally, if the debt which become due to customers are not realised, the same may be treated as an expense and should also be matched against the revenue for that year. That is why the amount of bad debts may be transferred to Profit and Loss Account of that year when the goods were sold which, in other words, conform the principles of matching. But, in real-world situation, that is seldom followed as it is very difficult to reopen the account.

Consequence of Bad Debts—if not provided for in the books

If the amount of bad debts is not provided for in the books of account, the same will invite the following :

(i) If the amount of bad debt is not properly accounted for in the books in the related year, the profit of the year will be overstated and, at the same time, if the same is adjusted against the income of the succeeding year, the profit for such year will be understated, i.e., the principle is to adjust the amount of bad debt in the year in which it is related.

(ii) When goods are sold on credit, such sale is considered as an income while ascertaining the measurement of income for a period and which produces an asset, viz., debtors, which, again, appear on the asset side of the Balance Sheet of a firm. But, if a part of such sales is not realised or is proved to be irrecoverable, the same can no more be treated as an asset, rather, it becomes a loss to the firm and such losses must be accounted for, i.e., in the books, otherwise the principles of conservatism will be violated.

(iii) The effect of such bad debts will mislead the liquidity position as the amount of debtors (which is inclusive of bad debts) will be overstated.

For the reasons stated above, the accountants suggest the following against the bad debt losses against debtors, viz., (i) Actual amount of bad debts should be treated as a loss; and (ii) proper provision must be made against such bad debts.

Accounting Steps for Bad Debts

The following entries are to be passed in the books of the firm:

---

* Debts may be classified into :
(i) Good Debts — The debts which are sure to be realised are called Good Debts.
(ii) Doubtful Debts — The debts which may or may not be realised are called Doubtful Debts.
(iii) Bad Debts—The debts which cannot be realised at all are called Bad Debts or Unrealised Debts or Irrecoverable Debts.

(i) *When goods are sold on credit —*

Debtors/Customers A/c	Dr.		from Sales Day Book.
To Sales A/c			

(ii) *If Sundry Debtors Account is maintained in the general ledger, i.e., in lieu of individual customer's account —*

Sundry Debtors A/c	Dr.		With the amount of total credit sale.
To Sales A/c			

(iii) *When cash is realised from Debtors—*

Cash/Bank A/c	Dr.		With the amount of cash realised.
To Debtors A/c			

(iv) *For actual amount of bad debts (if there is no provision for bad debts) —*

Bad Debts A/c	Dr.		With the amount of actual bad debts.
To Sundry Debtors A/c			

(v) *When bad debt is transferred —*

Profit and Loss A/c	Dr.		With the actual amount.
To Bad Debts A/c			

(vi) *If there is an existing provision i.e., old reserve, for actual bad debts —*

Provision for Bad Debts A/c	Dr.		With the actual amount of bad debts.
To Bad Debts A/c			

Illustration 1

On 1.10.2010, X sold goods to Y for Rs. 5,000 on credit. On 15.10.2010, Y paid Rs. 4,000. On 1.12.2010, Y become insolvent, nothing was realised from his estates.

Show the entries, ledger accounts, Profit and Loss Account and Balance Sheet.

Solution

In the books of ....

Journal

Date	*Particulars*		*L.F.*	*Debit*	*Credit*
2010				Rs.	Rs.
Oct. 1	Y A/c	Dr.		5,000	
	To Sales A/c				5,000
	(Goods sold to Y on Credit)				
15	Cash A/c	Dr.		4,000	
	To Y A/c				4,000
	(Amount received from Y.)				
Dec. 1	Bad Debts A/c	Dr.		1,000	
	To Y A/c				1,000
	(Amount due to Y was proved bad.)				

Dr. **Y Account** *Cr.*

Date	*Particulars*	*Amount*	*Date*	*Particulars*	*Amount*
2010		Rs.	2010		Rs.
Oct. 1	To Sales A/c	5,000	Oct. 15	By Cash A/c	4,000
			Dec. 1	" Bad Debts A/c	1,000
		5,000			5,000

Dr. **Sales Account** *Cr.*

Date	*Particulars*	*Amount*	*Date*	*Particulars*	*Amount*
2010		Rs.	2010		Rs.
Dec. 31	To Balance c/d	5,000	Oct. 1	By Y A/c	5,000
		5,000			5,000

Dr. **Bad Debts Account** *Cr.*

Date	*Particulars*	*Amount*	*Date*	*Particulars*	*Amount*
2010		Rs.	2010		Rs.
Dec. 1	To Y A/c	1,000	Dec. 31	By Profit and Loss A/c	1,000
		1,000			1,000

Profit and Loss Account (Extracts)
for the Year ended Dec. 31, 2010

Dr. Particulars	Amount	Particulars	Amount Cr.
	Rs.		Rs.
To Bad Debts A/c	1,000		
	1,000		

Balance Sheet (Extracts)
as at Dec. 31, 2010

Dr. Liabilities	Amount	Assets		Amount Cr.
	Rs.			Rs.
		Debtors (Y)	1,000	
		Less : Bad Debts	1,000	Nil

Points to Remember

1. While preparing final accounts it must be remembered that Bad Debts will appear in the debit side of Profit and Loss Account as a loss and cannot be deducted from Sales Account in Trading Account.

To Sum up
For Final Accounts
Bad Debts :

(i) If only within the Trial Balance—

(a) If there is no old provision— *To be debited to Profit and Loss A/c*

(b) If there is any old provision— *To appear on the debit side of Provision for Bad Debts A/c*

(ii) If outside the Trial Balane — (i.e., in the adjustment)

(a) If there is no old provision *(a) To be debited to Profit & Loss A/c and* *(b) To be deducted from Sundry Debtors in the asset side of the Balance Sheet*

(b) If there is any old provision — *(a) Same as (i) (b) above*

Provision for Bad Debts

It has already been stated that book debts may be grouped into Good, Bad and Doubtful. Good debts are that part of the debts which are fully recoverable, whereas, bad debts are totally irrecoverable. But in between the two, doubtful debts remain, which may prove bad and which are to some extent unknown since the amount is not known. An estimate is made of the likely irrecoverable amount, depending on the past experience and the reports of the customers. This is recorded in the books as, *'Provision for Bad Debts' or 'Reserve for Doubtful Debts' or 'Provision for Bad and Doubtful Debts.'* It is calculated on the certain percentage on total doubtful debts (after adjustments of bad debts, if any). It is practically a loss of the current year, which is actually written-off in the next year. The provision is created by reducing the profit of the current year by debiting Profit and Loss Account.

It should be remembered that provision should be made in the period under review, relating to debts which may not be realised in future i.e., in the succeeding period which, in other words, is known as Provision for Bad Debts.* Provision for Doubtful Debts is usually calculated by a certain fixed percentage on Sundry Debtors (after deducting Bad Debts, if any.) It is created by debiting Profit and Loss Account and crediting Provision for Bad Debts Account and the credit balance of the latter is shown as a deduction from Sundry Debtors in the assets side of the Balance Sheet until and unless it is statutorily required to show the same on the liabilities side of the Balance Sheet.

There are three methods that are used to record the transactions relating to Bad Debts and Provision for Bad Debts Account.

* The word 'Provision' is designed to use such amounts which are set aside out of periodical profit or surplus in order to provide for or renewal of assets or for other known liabilities, which cannot be accurately ascertained/determined while preparing Balance Sheet, e.g., Provision for Bad Debts, Provision for Discount on Debtors, etc. But, in other cases, the work 'Reserve' should be used.

Accounting Steps for Provision for Bad Debts

FIRST METHOD

Under this method Bad Debts Account is debited to Profit and Loss Account directly at the begining of the first year and the new provision which is to be credited depends upon the old one. The entries for this purpose will be :

In the First Year

(a) *For Bad Debts —*

(i)	Bad Debts A/c	Dr.	With the amount of actual bad debts
	To Sundry Debtors A/c		
(ii)	*For transfering Bad Debts to Profit & Loss Account*		
	Profit and Loss A/c	Dr.	—Do—
	To Bad Debts A/c		
(b)	*For making Provisions for Bad Debts—*		
	Profit and Loss A/c	Dr.	With the amount of prov. for bad debts
	To Provision for Bad Debts A/c		

In the Second/Subsequent Year

(a) *For Bad Debts —*

(i)	Bad Debt A/c	Dr.	Actual amount of bad debts
	To Sundry Debtors A/c		
	For transferring Bad Debts to Profit and Loss Account—		
(ii)	Profit and Loss A/c	Dr.	Actual amount of bad debts
	To Bad Debts A/c		
(b)	*For making provision for Bad Debts—*		
(i)	*If closing provision is more than the opening provision—*		
	Profit and Loss A/c	Dr.	
	To Provision for Bad Debts A/c		
(ii)	*If closing provision is less than the opening provision —*		
	Provision for Bad Debts A/c	Dr.	
	To Profit and Loss A/c		

To Sum up

Bad Debts : ***To be transferred to Profit and Loss Account directly.***

Provision for Bad Debts : ***To be transferred to Profit and Loss Account with the amount of extra or excess provision.***

SECOND METHOD

Under this method, however, a *'Provision for Bad Debts Account'* is maintained by debiting Profit and Loss Account and actual amount of bad debts will be adjusted against the provision for bad debts so opened. The entries for this purpose will be :

In the First Year

(a) *For Bad Debts—*

(i)	Bad Debts A/c	Dr.	Actual amount of bad debts
	To Sundry Debtors A/c		
(ii)	*For transferring Bad Debts to Profit & Loss Account—*		Actual amount of bad debts
	Profit and Loss A/c	Dr.	—Do—
	To Bad Debts A/c		
(b)	*For Provisions for Bad Debts Account—*		
	Profit and Loss A/c	Dr.	With the amount of provision
	To Provision for Bad Debts A/c		

In the Second/Subsequent Year

(i)	Bad Debts A/c	Dr.	With the actual amount of bad debts
	To Sundry Debtors A/c		

(ii) *For Bad Debts —*

Provision for Bad Debts A/c Dr. To Bad Debts A/c	}	With the actual amount of bad debts

(b) Next year's provision is estimated which is carried forward and the extra or excess provisions are adjusted against the old provisions which are transferred to Profit and Loss Account. The entry will be :

(i) *If new provision is more than the old one :*

Profit and Loss A/c Dr. To Provision for Bad Debts A/c	}	With the amount of provision transferred

(ii) *If new provision is less than the old one :*

Provision for Bad Debts A/c Dr. To Profit and Loss A/c	}	With the amount of excess provision

Profit and Loss Account takes the following form :

Profit and Loss A/c (Extracts)
for the year ended

Dr.		Rs.	Rs.	Cr.	Rs.	Rs.
To	Bad Debts	* *				
Add :	New Reserve/ Provision required	* *				
		* *				
Less :	Old Reserve/ Existing Provision	* *				
			* *			

To Sum up

Bad Debts	:	***To be adjusted against Provision for Bad Debts Account.***
Provision for Bad Debts	:	***After adjusting the bad debts, extra or excess provision (against the old provision after comparing the old and new provisions) is transferred to Profit and Loss Account.***

THIRD METHOD

Under this method Provision for Bad Debts will be adjusted against bad debts, and the extra as excess provision—after comparing the old and new provisions—is transferred to Bad Debts Account, the balance being transferred to Profit and Loss Account.

(a) *For Bad Debts—*

Bad Debts A/c Dr. To Sundry Debtors A/c	}	With the actual amount of bad debts

(b) *Provision for Bad Debts will be adjusted against bad debts (old and new) at the end of the year—if old provisions is less than the new one :*

Profit and Loss A/c Dr. To Bad Debts A/c	}	Amount transferred to P & L A/c

In the opposite case, i.e., if old provision is more than the new one :

Bad Debts A/c Dr.
To Profit and Loss A/c

Of the three methods stated above, the Second Method is, perhaps, the best one.

To Sum up

Three Methods :

Method I :

Bad Debts :	***To be transferred to Profit and Loss Account directly.***
Provision for Bad Debts :	***To be transferred to Profit and Loss Account with the amount of extra or excess provision.***

Method II :

Bad Debts :	***To be adjusted against Provision for Bad Debts Account***
Provision for Bad Debts :	***After adjusting bad debts, extra or excess provision (against the old provision after comparing the old and new provisions) is transferred to Profit and Loss Account.***

Method III :

Provision for Bad Debts :	***To be adjusted against Bad Debts Account, the extra or excess provision (after comparing the old and new provisions) is transferred to Bad Debts Account, the balance is taken to Profit and Loss Account.***

The above three methods can better be understood with the help of the following illustration :

Illustration 2

From the following information, prepare the Bad Debts Account and Provision for Bad Debts Account under each of the above three methods :

		Rs.
1.1.2010	Provision for Doubtful Debts amounted to	2,000
31.12.2010	Bad Debts written–off during 2010	1,200
	Sundry Debtors	50,000
31.12.2011	Bad Debts written-off during 2011	1,000
	Sundry Debtors	40,000
	Provision for Doubtful Debts to be provided for @ 5% for 2010 and $2\frac{1}{2}$% for 2011.	

Show also how the relevant items would appear in the Profit and Loss Account and Balance Sheet for 2010 and 2011.

Solution

METHOD I

In the Books of ....

Bad Debts Account

Dr.					Cr.
Date	*Particulars*	*Amount*	*Date*	*Particulars*	*Amount*
2010		Rs.	2010		Rs.
Dec. 31	To Sundry Debtors A/c	1,200	Dec. 31	By Profit and Loss A/c	1,200
		1,200			1,200
2011 Dec. 31	To Sundry Debtors A/c	1,000	2011 Dec. 31	By Profit and Loss A/c	1,000
		1,000			1,000

Provision for Bad Debts Account

Dr.					Cr.
Date	*Particulars*	*Amount*	*Date*	*Particulars*	*Amount*
2010		Rs.	2010		Rs.
Dec. 31	To Balance c/d (5% on Rs. 50,000)	2,500	Jan. 1	By Balance b/d	2,000
			Dec. 31	" Profit and Loss A/c *(bal fig.)*	500
		2,500			2,500
2011	To Profit and Loss A/c *(bal. fig.)*	1,500	2011 Jan. 1	By Balance b/d	2,500
Dec. 31	" Balance c/d ($2\frac{1}{2}$% on Rs. 40,000)	1,000			
		2,500			2,500
			2012 Jan. 1	By Balance b/d	1,000

Profit and Loss Account (Extract)
for the year ended 31st Dec. 2010

Dr.					Cr.
	Rs.	Rs.			Rs.
To Bad Debts A/c		1,200			
To Provision for Bad Debt A/c					

Contd.

	Rs.	Rs.		Rs.
Prov. required	2,500			
Less : Existing Provision	2,000			
		500		

Profit and Loss Account (Extract)
for the year ended 31st Dec. 2011

Dr.		Rs.			Rs. Cr.
To Bad Debts A/c		1,000	By Provision for Bad Debts A/c		
			Prov. Existing	2,500	
			Less : Provision required	1,000	
					1,500

Balance Sheet (Extract)
as at 31st December 2010

Liabilities		Rs.	*Assets*		Rs.
			Sundry Debtors	50,000	
			Less : Provision for Bad Debts A/c	2,500	
					47,500

Balance Sheet (Extract)
as at 31st December 2011

Liabilities		Rs.	*Assets*		Rs.
			Sundry Debtors	40,000	
			Less : Provision for Bad Debts A/c	1,000	
					39,000

METHOD II

Solution

Bad Debts Account

Dr. *Date*	*Particulars*	*Amount*	*Date*	*Particulars*	*Amount* Cr.
2010		Rs.	2010		Rs.
Dec. 31	To Sundry Debtors A/c	1,200	Dec. 31	By Provision for Bad Debts A/c —Transfer	1,200
		1,200			1,200
2011			2011		
Dec. 31	To Sundry Debtors A/c	1,000	Dec. 31	By Provision for Bad Debts A/c —Transfer	1,000
		1,000			1,000

Provision for Bad Debts Account

Dr. *Date*	*Particulars*	*Amount*	*Date*	*Particulars*	*Amount* Cr.
2010		Rs.	2010		Rs.
Dec. 31	To Bad Debts A/c	1,200	Jan. 1	By Balance b/d	2,000
	" Balance c/d (@ 5% on Rs. 50,000)	2,500	Dec. 31	" Profit and Loss A/c *(further provision required)*	1,700
		3,700			3,700
2011			2011		
Dec. 31	To Bad Debts A/c	1,000	Jan. 1	By Balance b/d	2,500
	Profit and Loss A/c *(amount found in excess)*	500			
	To Balance c/d (@ $2\frac{1}{2}$% on Rs. 40,000)	1,000			
		2,500			2,500

Profit and Loss Account (Extracts)
for the year ended 31st Dec. 2010

Dr.		Rs.			Cr. Rs.
To Provision for Bad Debts A/c					
Provision required	2,500				
Add: Bad Debt	1,200				
	3,700				
Less: Existing Provision	2,000				
		1,700			

Profit and Loss Account (Extract)
for the year ended 31st Dec. 2011

Dr.		Rs.			Cr. Rs.
To Bad Debts A/c		1,000	By Provision for Bad Debts A/c		
			Existing Provision	2,500	
			Less: Provision required	1,000	
					1,500

***N.B.*: The Balance Sheet under this method will be similar to Method I stated above.**

METHOD III

Bad Debts Account

Dr. Date	Particulars	Amount Rs.	Date	Particulars	Cr. Amount Rs.
2010			2010		
Dec. 31	To Sundry Debtors A/c	1,200	Jan. 1	By Provision for Bad Debts A/c	2,000
	" Provision c/d (5% of Rs. 50,000)	2,500		" Profit and Loss A/c *(bal. fig.)*	1,700
		3,700			3,700
2011			2011		
Dec. 31	To Sundry Debtors A/c	1,000	Jan. 1	By Provision b/d	2,500
	" Profit and Loss A/c *(bal. fig.)*	500			
	" Provision c/d ($2\frac{1}{2}$ % on Rs. 40,000)	1,000			
		2,500			2,500

***N.B.*: The Profit and Loss Account and the Balance Sheet will be similar to Method I stated above.**

Illustration 3

The Bad Debts during the year 2008 amounted to Rs. 1,000. The Sundry Debtors as on 31.12.2008 were Rs. 25,000 and 5% Reserve for Doubtful Debts is required to be maintained. Bad Debts during 2009 amounted to Rs. 1,200. The Sundry Debtors as on 31.12.2009 were Rs. 40,000 and a reserve @ 6% is to be mantained at the end of 2009.

Show the entrie for 2008 and 2009 in the books of Mr. Arindam.

Solution

In the books of Mr. Arindam
Journal

Date	Particulars		L.F.	Debit Rs.	Credit Rs.
2008					
Dec. 31	Bad Debts A/c	Dr.		1,000	
	To Sundry Debtors A/c				1,000
	(Bad Debts written-off.)				
	Profit and Loss A/c	Dr.		1,000	
	To Bad Debts A/c				1,000
	(Bad Debts transferred to P & L A/c)				

Contd.

			Rs.	Rs.
2008 Dec. 31	Profit and Loss A/c	Dr.	1,250	
	To Provisions for Bad Debts A/c			1,250
	(A provision created @ 5% on Rs. 25,000 out of P & L A/c)			
2009 ?	Bad Debts A/c	Dr.	1,200	
	To Sundry Debtors A/c			1,200
	(Bad Debts written-off.)			
Dec. 31	Provision for Bad Debts A/c	Dr.	1,200	
	To Bad Debts A/c			1,200
	(Bad Bebts adjusted against the provisions.)			
"	Profit and Loss A/c	Dr.	2,350	
	To Provision for Bad Debts A/c			2,350
	(Furthr provisions created out of P & L A/c			

Further Provision = Bad Debts + New Provision – Old Provision
= Rs. 1,200 + Rs. 2,400 (6% on Rs. 40,000) – Rs. 1,250
= Rs. 2,350

Illustration 4

The Trial Balance of M/s Sen & Co., as on 31.3.2011, contained the following items: Reserve for Bad Debts Rs. 12,000; Bad Debts Rs. 8,000 and Sundry Debtors Rs. 1,00,000.

You are required to show the Provision for Bad Debts Account assuming that provision for Bad Debts to be created @ 2% on Debtors and further Bad Debts amounted to Rs. 5,000. M/s Sen & Co. closing its account on 31st March, every year.

Dr. **Provision/Reserve for Bad Debts Account** *Cr.*

Date		*Particulars*	*Amount*	*Date*		*Particulars*	*Amount*
2011			Rs.	2010			Rs.
March 31	To	Bad Debts A/c (Rs. 12,000 + Rs. 5,000)	17,000	Apr. 1	By	Balance b/d	12,000
	"	Balance c/d (2% on Rs. 1,00,000)	2,000	2011 March 31	"	Profit and Loss A/c (bal. fig.) —Further Provision to be created	7,000
			19,000				19,000

Working Notes:

1. The Bad Debts which are given in the Trial Balance has already been adjusted against Sundry Debtors.
2. The further Bad Debts amounting to Rs. 5,000 which are given in the adjustment should be adjusted against Sundry Debtors by passing the following entry

		Rs.	Rs.
Bad Debts A/c	Dr.	5,000	
To Sundry Debtors A/c			5,000

∴ Total Bad Debts will be Rs. 17,000 (Rs. 12,000 + Rs. 5,000)

3. The Reserve for Bad Debts which is given in the Trial Balance is the old provision or old reserve.
4. New Provision will be calculated on Rs. 2,00,000 i.e., on Closing Debtors = Rs. 2,000 (Rs. 1,00,000 × 2%)

Illustration 5

A provision for bad and doubtful debts, equal to 5 per cent of debtors, is created every year-end by a business concern. From the particulars given below write-up the Provision for Bad and Doubtful Debts Account for five consecutive years, assuming that accumulated bad debts are, for their necessary adjustments, transferred to the said provision account each year before the new provision is made for the next year.

Balance extracted from the Trial Balance	1st Year Rs.	2nd Year Rs.	3rd Year Rs.	4th Year Rs.	5th Year Rs.
Sundry Debtors	45,000	48,500	56,800	62,000	58,400
Bad Debts written-off	1,800	2,000	4,000	2,700	2,800
Closing Adjustments:	—	—	—	520	—
Bad Debts written-off	200	140	420	260	300

Balance of the 'Provision for Bad Debts and Doubtful Debts Account' at the beginning of the 1st year was Rs. 2,500.

Solution

In the books of ....

Provision for Bad Debts Account

Dr. *Cr.*

Date	Particulars	Amount	Date	Particulars	Amount
		Rs.			Rs.
Year I yr. End	To Bad Debts Account	1,800	Year I yr. Opening	By Balance b/d	2,500
	" Bad Debts Account	200		" P & L Accounts (bal. fig.)	1,740
	" Balance c/d (5% on Rs. 45,000 – Rs. 200)	2,240	End		
		4,240			4,240
Year II yr. End	To Bad Debts Account	2,000	Year II yr. Opening	By Balance b/d	2,240
	" Bad Debts Account	140		" P & L Account (bal. fig.)	2,318
	" Balance c/d (5% on Rs. 48,500 – Rs. 140)	2,418	End		
		4,558			4,558
Year III yr. End	To Bad Debts Account	4,000	Year III yr. Opening	By Balance b/d	2,418
	" Bad Debts Account	420		" P & L Account (bal. fig.)	4,821
	" Balance c/d (5% on Rs. 56,800 – Rs. 420)	2,819	End		
		7,239			7,239
Year IV yr. End	To Bad Debts Aceount	2,700	Year IV yr. Opening	By Balance b/d	2,819
	" Bad Debts Account	260		" P & L Account (bal. fig.)	3,228
	" Balance c/d (5% on Rs. 62,000 – Rs. 260)	3,087	End		
		6,047			6,047
Year V yr. End	To Bad Debts Account	2,800	Year V yr. Opening	By Balance b/d	3,087
	" Bad Debts Account	300		" P & L Account (bal. fig.)	2,918
	" Balance c/d (5% on Rs. 58,000 – Rs. 300)	2,905	End		
		6,005			6,005
			VI yr. Opening	By Balance b/d	2,905

Illustration 6

The following is the Trial Balance of Sen Brothers for the year ended 31st Dec. 2008:

	Dr. Rs.	Cr. Rs.
Sundry Debtors	12,000	—
Bad Debts	400	—
Provision for Bad Debts	—	200
Expenses	3,000	—
Gross Profit	—	8,000
Assets	8,000	—
Liabilities	—	2,800
Capital	—	12,400
	23,400	23,400

You are required to prepare Bad Debts Account, Provision for Bad Debts Account, Profit and Loss Accounts and Balance Sheet bearing in mind that provision should be made @ 5% on Sundry Debtors.

Solution

In the books of Sen Brothers

Bad Debts Account

Dr. Date	Particulars	Amount	Date	Particulars	Cr. Amount
2008		Rs.	2008		Rs.
Dec. 31	To Balance b/d	400	Dec. 31	By Prov. for Bad Debts A/c	400
		400			400

Provision for Bad Debts Account

Dr. Date	Particulars	Amount	Date	Particulars	Cr. Amount
2008		Rs.	2008		Rs.
Dec. 31	To Bad Debts A/c	400	Jan. 1	By Balance b/d	200
	" Balance c/d (5% on Rs. 12,000)	600		" Profit and Loss A/c (*bal. fig.*)	800
		1,000			1,000

Profit and Loss Account
for the year ended 31st Dec. 2008

Dr.	Rs.	Rs.	Cr.	Rs.
To Bad Debts A/c	400		By Trading A/c —Gross Profit	8,000
Add: New Reserve	600			
	1,000			
Less: Old Reserve	200			
		800		
To Expenses		3,000		
To Capital A/c—Net Profit		4,200		
		8,000		8,000

Balance Sheet
as at 31st Dec. 2008

Liabilities	Rs.	Rs.	Assets	Rs.	Rs.
Capital	12,400		Sundry Assets		8,000
Add: Net Profit	4,200		Sundry Debtors	12,000	
		16,600	*Less:* New Reserve	600	
Liabilities		2,800			11,400
		19,400			19,400

Illustration 7

Trial Balance as on 31st December 2011 of Sri Mazumdar contains the following items:

	Rs.
Reserve for Bad Debts	12,000
Bad Debts	8,000
Sundry Debtors	1,00,000

On equity it was ascertained that Debtors include

(a) Rs. 10,000 due from M & Co. (Creditors include Rs. 18,000 due to the same party;

(b) Rs. 5,000 due on account of sale of Furniture; and

(c) Bad Debts of Rs. 5,000

You are required to show Bad Debts Account, Reserve for Bad Debts Account bearing in mind that Provision for Bad Debts is to be created at 2% of Trade Debtors.

[CU BCom (Hons.)]

Solution

In the books of Mr. Mazundar

Bad Debts Account

Dr. Cr.

Date		Particulars	Amount	Date		Particulars	Amount
2011			Rs.	2011			Rs.
Dec. 31	To	Balance b/d	8,000	Dec. 31	By	Provision for Bad Debts A/c	13,000
Dec. 31	"	Sundry Debtors A/c	5,000				
			13,000				13,000

Provision for Bad Debts Account

Dr. Cr.

Date		Particulars	Amount	Date		Particulars	Amount
2011			Rs.	2011			Rs.
Dec. 31	To	Bad Debts A/c	13,000	Jan. 1	By	Balance b/d	12,000
	"	Balance c/d (2% on Rs. 80,000*)	1,600		"	Profit & Loss A/c (*bal. fig.* Further provision required.)	2,600
			14,600				14,600

*Amount of closing Debtors on which new provision is to be Created = Debtors-Set off – Sale of Furniture – Bad Debts

= Rs. 1,00,000 – Rs. 10,000 – Rs. 5,000 – Rs. 5,000

= Rs. 80,000

Illustration 8

Mr. Soumya furnished the following particulars:

	1.1.2010	1.1.2011
	Rs.	Rs.
Sales (90% Credit)	1,00,000	1,20,000
Cash received from Debtors	80,000	90,000
Discount Allowed	5,000	8,000
Returns Inward	3,000	2,000
Bad Debt Written-off	4,000	8,000
Transfer from Debtors and Creditors (Set-off)	—	5,000

Additional Information

(a) Provision for Bad Debts and Sundry Debtors as on 1.1.2010 were Rs. 1,500 and Rs. 30,000, respectively

(b) On 31.12.2010 Provision for Doubtful Debts is to be required @ 5% on Sundry Debtors after making a specific provision of Rs. 500 from Mr. Banerjee, a customer, who was declared insolvent.

(c) On 31.12.2011 Provision for Bad Debts is to be made @ 8% on Sundry Debtors.

Prepare Sundry Debtors Account and Provision for Bad Debts Account.

Solution

In the books of ....

Sundry Debtors Account

Dr. Cr.

Date		Particulars	Amount	Date		Particulars	Amount
20110			Rs.	2010			Rs.
Jan. 1	To	Balance b/d	30,000	?	By	Cash Received from Debtors) A/c	80,000
	"	(Credit) Sales A/c (90% of Rs. 1,00,000)	90,000		"	Discount Allowed A/c	5,000
					"	Returns Inward A/c	3,000
					"	Bad Debts A/c	4,000
				Dec. 31	"	Balance c/d	28,000
			1,20,000				1,20,000

			Rs.				Rs.
2011				2011			
Jan. 1	To	Balance b/d	28,000	?	By	Cash (Received from Debtors A/c	90,000
	"	Sales A/c (90%)	1,08,000		"	Discount Allowed A/c	8,000
					"	Returns Inward A/c	2,000
					"	Bad Debts A/c	8,000
					"	Sundry Creditors A/c (Set-off)	5,000
				Dec. 31	"	Balance c/d	23,000
			1,36,000				1,36,000

Dr. **Provision for Bad Debts Account** Cr.

Date		Particulars	Amount	Date		Particulars	Amount
2010			Rs.	2010			Rs.
Dec. 31	To	Balance c/d	1,875[1]	Jan. 1	By	Balance b/d	1,500
	"			2010 Dec. 31.	"	Profit & Loss A/c (bal. fig.) —Further provision to be made	375
			1,875				1,875
2011				2011			
Dec. 31	To	Profit & Loss A/c —Provision found in excess	35	Jan. 1	By	Balance b/d	1,875
	"	Balance c/d	1,840[2]				
			1,875				1,875

Working Notes:

(1) On 31.12.2010 Balance of Sundry Debtors were Rs. 28,000 of which a customer, Mr. Banerjee, became insolvent having an unpaid balance of Rs. 500. So provision should be made for doubtful debts @ 100% on Rs. 500 and on balance Rs. 27,500 (i.e., Rs. 28,000 – Rs. 500) @ 5%.

∴ Total provision for bad debt as on 31.12.2010 will be Rs. 500 + 5% of Rs. 27,500 = Rs. 500 + Rs. 1,375 = Rs. 1,875

(2) On 31.12.2011, the provision of bad debts will be simply (i.e., Rs. 23,000 × 8%) Rs. 1,840.

Provision for Bad Debts on Specific Debtors

Illustration 9

After examination of the Sales Ledger it was decided to make specific provision in the accounts for the year ended 31st March 2011 for the following doubtful debts:

X—Rs. 950, Y—Rs. 150, Z—Rs. 1,340, T—Rs. 690.

It was also decided to make a general provision of 5 per cent on the other debtors who, on 31st March 2010, amounted to Rs. 1,08,000.

No further business transactions were entered into with any of these debtors, but the Receivers of X and T sent final dividends of Rs. 300 and Rs. 420, respectively, and Z paid his debt in full.

On 31st March 2011 it was decided to maintain the provision against X's debt and to make further provisions for the following debts considered doubtful:

S—Rs. 650, P—Rs. 340; O—Rs. 510.

The other debtors amounted to Rs. 1,30,000 and it was required to make the general provision for doubtful debts equal to 5 per cent of these debts. You are required to show Bad Debts Account and Provision for Bad Debts Account.

Solution

In the books of ....

Dr. **Bad Debts Account** Cr.

Date		Particulars	Amount	Date		Particulars	Amount
2011			Rs.	2011			Rs.
March 31	To	Sundry Debtors A/c	920[1]	March 31	By	Provision for Bad Debts A/c	920
			920				920

Dr. **Provision for Bad Debts Account** Cr.

Date		Particulars	Amount	Date		Particulars	Amount
2011			Rs.	2010			Rs.
Mar. 31	To	Bad Debts A/c	920	April 1	By	Balance b/d	8,530[2]
	"	Balance c/d	8,150[3]	2011 Mar. 31	"	Profit & Loss A/c (*bal. fig.* —Further provision to be created.)	540
			9,070				9,070

Working Notes :

1. Bad Debts

		Rs.
X	(Rs. 950 – Rs. 300)	650
T	(Rs. 690 – 420)	270
		920

2. Opening Provision

	Rs.
X	950
Y	150
Z	1,340
T	690
General Provision (@ 5% on Rs. 1,08,000)	5,400
	8,530

3. Closing Provision

	Rs.
Y	150
S	650
P	340
Q	510
General Provision (@ 5% on Rs. 1,30,000)	6,500
	8,150

Provision for Discount on Debtors

Sometimes, in order to give some incentive to the customers for prompt payment, a cash discount is allowed to them which is treated as an expense of the firm and, consequently, the net realisable value of the debtors will be reduced. For allowing such a cash discount a provision is to be made on good debtors, i.e., the cash discount which is allowed to customer is to be made always on good debtors (i.e., after deducting bad debts and provision for bad debts). Thus, the discount which is allowed to customers of the period under review (for prompt payment) in the next period is known as Provision for Discount on Debtors.

Sometimes it becomes difficult to estimate how many customers will take the benefit of cash discount which, again, depends on the opportunity cost of liquid funds. In short, if the amount of cash discount is more than—or at least equal to—the opportunity cost, most of the customers may avail the benefit of cash discount. For this purpose, as estimate is to be prepared which is calculated by way of a certain percentage on the balance of outstanding debtors.

Care should be taken that such provision for discount on debtors be calculated after deducting the bad debts and the provision for bad debts for the current year from the book value of debtors. This provision is also to be made by debiting Profit and Loss Account of the current year which is actually adjusted in the next year. The actual amount of discount allowed will, however, be adjusted against the provisions.

Accounting Steps

Needless to mention that the accounting procedure is similar to the *'Provision for Bad Debts'*, already stated (Here Second Method is followed).

In the First Year

(a) *For Discount Allowed*

(i) Discount Account A/c To Sundry Debtors A/c	Dr.	Actual amount of discount allowed
(ii) *For transferring Discount Allowed to Profit and Loss A/c* Profit and Loss A/c To Discount Allowed A/c	Dr.	—do—

(b) *For Provision for Discount on Debtors*

Profit and Loss A/c To Provision for Discount on Debtors A/c	Dr.	With the amount of provision

In the Second/Subsequent Year

(a) *For Discount Allowed*

(i) Discount Account A/c Dr. — With the amount of discount allowed
  To Sundry Debtors A/c

(ii) *Provision for Discount on Debtors* — —do—
Provision for Discount on Debtors Dr.
  To Discount Allowed A/c

(b) Next year's provision is estimated which is carried forward and the extra or excess provisions are adjusted against the old provision which is transferred to Profit and Loss Account. The entry for this purpose will be:

(i) *If new provision is more than the old one:*
Profit and Loss A/c Dr. — With the amount of provision transferred
  To Provision for Discount on Debtors A/c

(ii) *If new provision is less than the old one:*
Provision for Discount on Debtors A/c Dr.
  To Profit and Loss A/c

Profit and Loss Account will take the following form:

Profit and Loss A/c (Extracts)
for the year ended ....

Dr.	Rs.			Cr. Rs.
To Discount Allowed	......			
Add: New Reserve/Provision required	......			
	......			
Less: Old Reserve/Existing Provision	......			
		......		

To sum-up

Discount Allowed : ***To be adjusted against Provision for Discount on Debtors.***

Provision for Discount on Debtors : ***After adjusting the bad debts, extra or excess provision (against the old provision after comparing the old and new provisions) is transferred to Profit and Loss Account.***

The following illustration will make the principle clear:

Illustration 10

The following figures appear in books of Mr. S. K. Dasgupta:

2008		Rs.
Jan. 1	Provision for Bad and Doubtful Debts	8,000
	Provision for Discount on Debtors	2,000
Dec. 31	Bad Debts written-off during the year	6,000
	Discount Allowed during the year	1,800
	Sundry Debtors (as per ledger)	51,000

Write-off further Bad Debts for Rs. 1,000. Make a provision for Discount on Debtors @ $2\frac{1}{2}$% and also make a provision for bad debts @ 5% on Debtors. Show the relevant accounts. Show how the items will appear in Profit and Loss Account and Balance Sheet.

Solution

In the books of Mr. S. K. Das Gupta
Journal

Date	*Particulars*		*L.F.*	*Debit* Rs.	*Credit* Rs.
2008 Dec. 31	Bad Debts A/c	Dr.		1,000	
	To Sundry Debtors A/c				1,000
	(Bad Debts Written-off)				

Contd.

2011			Rs.	Rs.
	Provision for Bad Debts A/c	Dr.	7,000	
	To Bad Debts A/c			7,000
	(Bad Debts Adjusted against Provision for Bad Debts.)			
	Profit & Loss A/c	Dr.	1,500	
	To Provision for Bad Debts A/c			1,500
	(Further proisions created out of P & L A/c)			
	Discount Allowed A/c	Dr.	1,000	
	To Sundry Debtors A/c			1,000
	(Discount allowed to Debtors.)			
	Provision for Discount on Debtors A/c	Dr.	1,800	
	To Discount Allowed A/c			1,800
	(Discount allowed adjusted against Provision foe Discount on Debtors A/c.)			
	Profit and Loss A/c	Dr.	1,988	
	To Provision for Discount on Debtors A/c			1,988
	(Further provision created out of P & L A/c)			

Dr. Provision for Bad Debts Account Cr.

Date	Particulars	Amount	Date	Particulars	Amount
2008		Rs.	2008		Rs.
Dec. 31	To Bad Debts A/c (6,000 + 1,000)	7,000	Jan. 1	By Balance b/d	8,000
	" Balance c/d	2,500[1]	Dec. 31	" Profit and Loss A/c (*bal. fig.*)	1,500
		9,500			9,500
			2009		
			Jan. 1	By Balance b/d	2,500

Dr. Provision for Discount on Debtors Account Cr.

Date	Particulars	Amount	Date	Particulars	Amount
2008		Rs.	2008		Rs.
Dec. 31	To Discount Allowed A/c	2,800	Jan. 1	By Balance b/d	2,000
	" Balance c/d	1,188[2]	Dec. 31	" Profit and Loss A/c (*bal. fig.*)	1,988
		3,988			3,988
			2009		
			Jan. 1	By Balance b/d	1,188

Dr. Bad Debts Account Cr.

Date	Particulars	Amount	Date	Particulars	Amount
2008		Rs.	2008		Rs.
Dec. 31	To Balance b/d	6,000	Dec. 31	By Provision for Bad Debts A/c	7,000
	" Sundry Debtors A/c	1,000			
		7,000			7,000

Dr. Discount Allowed Account Cr.

Date	Particulars	Amount	Date	Particulars	Amount
2008		Rs.	2008		Rs.
Dec. 31	To Balance b/d	1,800	Dec. 31	By Provision for Discount on Debtors A/c	2,800
	" Sundry Debtors A/c	1,000			
		2,800			2,800

Profit and Loss Account (Extracts)
for the year ended 31st Dec. 2008

Dr.	Rs.	Rs.		Cr. Rs.
To Provision for Bad Debts				
Prov. Required	2,500			
Add: Bad Debts	7,000			
	9,500			
Less: Existing Provision	8,000			
		1,500		
To Provision for Discount on Debtors				
Provision Required	1,188			
Add: Discount Allowed	2,800			
	3,988			
Less: Existing Provision	2,000			
		1988		

Balance Sheet (Extracts)
as at 31st December 2008

Liabilities	Rs.	*Assets*	Rs.	Rs.
		Sundry Debtors	51,000	
		Less: Bad Debts	1,000	
			50,000	
		Less: Prov. for Bad Debts @ 5%	2,500	
			47,500	
		Less: Prov. for Discount on Debtors @ $2\frac{1}{2}$%	1,188	
				46,312

Workings :

1. Closing balance of Provision for Bad Debts on 31.12.2008 will be on Rs. 50,000 (i.e., Rs. 51,000 – Further Bad Debts Rs. 1,000) @ 5%). So, the amount will be Rs. 2,500 (Rs. 50,000 × 5%)
2. Closing balance of Provision for Discount on Debtors on 31.12.2008 will be on Rs. 47,500 (i.e., Debtors – Bad Debts – Closing Balance of provision for bad debts on (Rs. 51,000 – Rs. 1,000 – Rs. 2,500) Rs. 47,500 @ $2\frac{1}{2}$% or; Rs. 1,188.

Provision for Discount on Creditors

The discount or rebate the trader expects to receive for prompt payment from creditors is to be adjusted by crediting the Profit and Loss Account since it is an anticipated profit. This is usually calculated on the basis of a certain percentage on creditors which actually depends on past experience of the trader. This provision is made by *debiting Provision for Discount on Creditors Account and crediting Profit and Loss Account of* the current year which is actually adjusted in the next year. The actual amount of discount received will, however, be adjusted against the provision. The provision is shown by way of a deduction from Sundry Creditors in the liabilities side of the Balance Sheet.

Accounting Steps

It is also needless to mention that accounting procedures are similar to Provision for Discount on Debtors *but the entries are converse.*

In the First Year

(a) *For Discount Received*

(i) Sundry Creditors A/c — Dr. — Actual amount of Discount Received
  To Discount Received A/c

(ii) *For transferring Discount Received to Profit and Loss A/c*
  Discount Received A/c — Dr. — —do—
  To Profit and Loss A/c

(b) *For Provision for Discount on Creditors*

Provision for Discount on Creditors A/c Dr. To Profit and Loss A/c		With the amount of Provision

In the Second/Subsequent Year

(a) *For Discount Received*

(i) Sundry Creditors A/c To Discount Received A/c	Dr.	With the amount of Discount Received
(ii) *Discount Received A/c* To Provision for Discount on Creditors A/c	Dr.	—do—

(b) Next year's provision is estimated which is carried forward and extra or excess provisions are adjusted against the old provision which is transferred to Profit and Loss Account. The entry, for this purpose, will be:

(i) *If new provision is more than the old one* Provision for Discount on Creditors A/c To Profit and Loss A/c	Dr.	With the amount of Provision Transferred
(ii) *If new provision is less than the old one* Profit and Loss A/c To Provision for Discount on Creditors A/c	Dr.	

Profit and Loss Account, however, will take the following form:

Profit and Loss Account (Extracts)
for the year ended ... .

Dr. Cr.

		Rs.	Rs.
	To Discount Received	......	
	Add: New Reserve/Provision required	......	
		......	
	Less: Old Reserve/Existing Provision	......	
			......

To sum-up

Discount Received : ***To be adjusted against Provision for Discount on Creditors.***

Provision for Discount on Creditors : ***After adjusting the discount received, extra or excess provision (against the old provision after comparing the old and new provisions) is transferred to Profit and Loss Account.***

The following illustration will make the principle clear:

Illustration 11

From the following particulars prepare the necessary accounts:

	Rs.
Provision for Discount on Creditors on 1.1.2008	2,000
Discount received during the year 2008	1,000
Sundry Creditors on 31.12.2008	60,000
Provision for Discount on Creditors to be made @ 5%	
Discount received during the year 2009	250
Sundry Creditors on 31.12.2009	20,000
Provision for Discount on Creditors to be made @ 5%	

Show also how they will appear in Profit and Loss Account and Balance Sheet.

Solution

Dr. **Discount Received Account** Cr.

Date	*Particulars*	*Amount*	*Date*	*Particulars*	*Amount*
2008		Rs.	2008		Rs.
Dec. 31	To Provision for Discount on Creditors A/c—Transfer	1,000	Dec. 31	By Sundry Creditors A/c	1,000
		1,000			1,000

Contd.

2009 Dec. 31	To	Provision for Discount on Creditors A/c—Transfer	250	2009 Dec. 31	By	Sundry Creditors	250
			250				250

Dr. **Provision for Discount on Creditors Account** Cr.

Date		Particulars	Amount	Date		Particulars	Amount
2008			Rs.	2008			Rs.
Jan. 1	To	Balance b/d	2,000	Dec. 31	By	Sundry Creditors	1,000
Dec. 31	"	Profit and Loss A/c (further provision required)	2,000		"	Balance c/d (5% on Rs. 60,000)	3,000
2009			4,000	2009			4,000
Jan. 1	To	Balance b/d	3,000	Dec. 31	By	Discount Received	250
					"	Profit and Loss A/c (provision found in excess)	1,750
					"	Balance c/d (5% on Rs. 20,000)	1,000
			3,000				3,000

Profit and Loss Account (Extracts)
for the year ended 31st Dec. 2008

	Rs.		Rs.	Rs.
		By Prov. for Discount on Creditors		
		Provision Required	3,000	
		Add: Discount Received	1,000	
			4,000	
		Less: Existing Provision	2,000	
				2,000

Dr. **Profit and Loss Account (Extracts)** Cr.
for the year ended 31st Dec. 2009

	Rs.	Rs.		Rs.
To Prov. for Disc. on Creditors			By Discount Received	250
Existing Provision	3,000			
Less: Provision Required	1,000			
		2,000		

Balance Sheet (Extracts)
as at 31st Dec. 2008

	Rs.	Rs.		Rs.
Sundry Creditors	60,000			
Less: Prov. for Discount on Creditors	3,000			
		57,000		

Balance Sheet (Extracts)
as at 31st Dec. 2009

	Rs.	Rs.		Rs.
Sundry Creditors	20,000			
Less: Prov. for Discount on Creditors	1,000			
		19,000		

Recovery of Bad Debts

Sometimes the debt which was written-off as bad previously may be recovered partially or wholly. Such a realised bad debt is known as *Bad Debt Recovered*. The amount is to be credited to Bad Debts Recovery Account. Since it is a clear profit, it is transferred to Profit and Loss Account in the year in which the same is recovered.

The following entries should be passed for the purpose:

(i) *For recovering bad debts:*

Cash/Bank A/c	Dr.	With the amount of bad debts recovered
To Bad Debts Recovery A/c		

(ii) *For transferring to Profit and Loss Account*

Bad Debts Recovery A/c	Dr.
To Profit and Loss Account	

(ii) If the Provision for Bad Debts Account is maintained and bad debts are adjusted against such provision. Bad Debts Reserve Account should be closed by transferring to Profit and Loss Account. So the entry will be:

Bad Debts Recovery A/c	Dr.
To Provision for Bad Debts A/c	

Illustration 12

On 31st Dec. 2008, Sundry Debtors and Provision for Bad Debts were Rs. 50,000 and Rs. 5,000, respectively. During the year 2009, Rs. 3,000 were bad and written-off. On 30th, an amount of Rs. 400 was received on account of a debt which was written-off as bad last year. On 31st Dec. 2009 the Debtors' list was verified and it was found that Sundry Debtors stood in the books as Rs. 40,000, out of which a customer, Mr. X, who owed Rs. 800, was to be written-off as bad. Prepare Bad Debts Account and Provision for Bad Debts Account, assuming that same percentage should be maintained for Provision for Bad Debts as it was on 31st Dec. 2008. Show also how the items will appear in Profit and Loss Account and the Balance Sheet.

Solution

In the books of ....

Bad Debts Account

Dr. | *Cr.*

Date	*Particulars*	*Amount*	*Date*	*Particulars*	*Amount*
2009		Rs.	2009		Rs.
Dec. 31	To Sundry Debtors	3,000	Dec. 31	By Prov. for Bad Debts A/c (*bal. fig.*)	3,800
	" X A/c	800			
		3,800			3,800

Provision for Bad Debts Account

Dr. | *Cr.*

Date	*Particulars*	*Amount*	*Date*	*Particulars*	*Amount*
2009		Rs.	2009		Rs.
Dec. 31	To Bad Debts A/c	3,800	Jan. 1	By Balance b/d	5,000
	" Balance c/d [10% on Rs. 39,200 (40,000 – 800)]	3,920	Dec. 31	" P & L A/c (*bal. fig.*)	2,720
		7,720			7,720

Profit and Loss Account (Extracts)

for the year ended 31st Dec. 2009

Dr. | *Cr.*

	Rs.			Rs.
To Provision for Bad Debts:			By Bad Debts Recovery A/c	400[1]
Provision Required	3,920			
Add: Bad Debts	3,800			
	7,720			
Less: Existing Provision	5,000	2,720		

Balance Sheet (Extracts)

as at 31st Dec. 2009

	Rs.		Rs.	Rs.
		Sundry Debtors	40,000	
		Less: Bad Debts	800	
			39,200	
		Less: Prov. for Bad Debts @ 10%	3,920	
				35,280

Notes:

1. Recovery of bad debts may be treated in the following manner

   Cash/Bank A/c Dr.

   To Bad Debts Recovery A/c

   Bad Debts Recovery A/c is to be transferred to Profit and Loss A/c directly by passing the following entry:

   Bad Debts Recovery A/c Dr.

   To Profit and Loss A/c

2. Percentage of Provision $\frac{\text{Rs. } 5,000}{\text{Rs. } 50,000} \times 100 = 10\%$

GENERAL ILLUSTRATIONS

Illustration 13

Banik and Co. is in business as a distributor of household goods on credit terms to a wide range of customers. The following balances were extracted from its ledger at 31st March 2000:

	Rs.
Sales	9,42,520
Debtors balance at 31.3.1999	98,412
Discount allowed	8,324
Cash received from debtors	8,76,940
Returns inward	30,510
Carriage outwards	5,760
Provision for doubtful debts as at 31.3.1999	6,876

Subsequent enquiries reveal the following information:

A cheque for Rs. 3,528 from Samar Som, a customer, has been returned by the bank marked 'refer to drawer'. Bad Debts totalling Rs. 8,536 are to be written-off, and the provision for doubtful debts is to be raised to 10% of debtors' balances at 31st March 2000.

On the last day of the year a cheque is received for Rs. 1,400 from the *Receiver* of Naresh Guha. This customer ceased to trade in January 1998 when he owed Banik and Co. Rs. 7,000 and the debt had been written-off as a bad debt in the year ended 31st March 1998. No entry in respect of this cheque has yet been made in the books.

Write-up the following accounts for the year ended 31st March 2000:

(a) Sundry Debtors Accounts.

(b) Provision for Doubtful Debts Account. **[CU BCom. (Hons.) 2001]**

Solution

In the books of Banik & Co.

Sundry Debtors Account

Dr. *Cr.*

Date	*Particulars*	*Amount*	*Date*	*Particulars*	*Amount*
1999		Rs.	2000		Rs.
Apr. 1	To Balance b/d	98,412	Mar. 31	By Cash A/c	8,76.940
2000				" Discount Allowed A/c	8,324
Mar. 31	" Sales A/c	9,42,520		" Returns Inward A/c	30,510
	" Carriage Out. A/c	5,760		" Bad Debts	8,536
	" Bank A/c			" Balance c/d	1,25,910
	—Cheque Dishonoured	3,528			
		10,50,220			10,50,220

Provision for Bad Debts Account

Dr. *Cr.*

Date	*Particulars*	*Amount*	*Date*	*Particulars*	*Amount*
2000		Rs.	2000		Rs.
Mar. 31	To Bad Debts A/c	8,536	Apr. 1	By Balance b/d	6,876
	" Balance c/d			" P & L A/c	14,251
	$\left(Rs.\ 1,25,910 \times \frac{10}{100}\right)$	12,591		*(bal. fig.)*	
		21,127			21,127

Notes : 1. Recovery of bad debt will appear in the credit side of Profit & Loss Account.
2. It has been assumed that the firm sends goods to its customers and the carriage which is paid is recovered from the customer concerned at a subsequent date.

Illustration 14

From the following particulars, prepare the necessary accounts:

	Rs.
Provision for Doubtful Debts on 1.1.2010	6,000
Provision for Discount on Debtors on 1.1.2010	2,000
Bad Debts written-off during the year 2010	4,000
Bad Debts Recovery Account (Cr.)	500
Discount allowed during the year 2010	1,500
Sundry Debtors on 31.12.2010.	1,20,000
Provision for Doubtful Debts to be provided for @ 10%	
Provision for Discount on Debtors to be provided for @ 5%	
Bad Debts written-off during the year 2010	1,250
Discount allowed during the year 2010	400
Sundry Debtors on 31.12.2010	40,000
Provision for Doubtful Debts to be provided for @ 10%,	
Provision for discount on Debtors to be provided for @ 5%.	

Solution

In the books of ....

Bad Debts Account

Dr. Cr.

Date	Particulars	Amount	Date	Particulars	Amount
2010		Rs.	2010		Rs.
Dec. 31	To Sundry Debtors A/c	4,000	Dec. 31	By Provision for Doubtful Debts A/c (transfer)	4,000
		4,000			4,000
2011			2010		
Dec. 31	To Sundry Debtors A/c	1,250	Dec. 31	By Provision for Doubtful Debts A/c (transfer)	1,250
		1,250			1,250

Provision for Doubtful Debts Account

Dr. Cr.

Date	Particulars	Amount	Date	Particulars	Amount
2010		Rs.	2010		Rs.
Dec. 31	To Bad Debts A/c	4,000	Jan. 1	By Balance b/d	6,000
	To Balance c/d (10% on Rs. 1,20,000)	12,000	Dec. 31	" Profit and Loss A/c (*further provision required*)	10,000
		16,000			16,000
2011			2011		
Dec. 31	To Bad Debts A/c	1,250	Jan. 1	By Balance b/d	12,000
	To P & L Account (Prov. found in excess)	6,750			
	To Balance c/d (10% on Rs. 40,000)	4,000			
		12,000			12,000

Discount Allowed Account

Dr. Cr.

Date	Particulars	Amount	Date	Particulars	Amount
2010		Rs.	2010		Rs.
Dec. 31	To Sundry Debtors A/c	1,500	Dec. 31	By Provision for Discount on Debtors A/c (transfer)	1,500
		1,500			1,500

2011		Rs.	2011			Rs.
Dec. 31	To Sundry Debtors A/c	400	Dec. 31	By	Provision for Discount on Debtors A/c —transfer	400
		400				400

Dr. **Provision for Discount on Debtors Account** Cr.

Date	Particulars	Amount	Date		Particulars	Amount
2010		Rs.	2010			Rs.
Dec. 31	To Disc. Allowed A/c	1,500	Jan. 1	By	Balance b/d	2,000
	" Balance c/d @ 5% on Rs. 1,08,000 (Rs. 1,20,000 – Rs. 12,000)	5,400	Dec. 31	"	Profit and Loss A/c *(further provision required)*	4,900
		6,900				6,900
2011			2011	By	Balance b/d	5,400
Dec. 31	To Disc. Allowed A/c	400				
	" Profit and Loss A/c *(prov. found in excess)*	3,200				
	" Balance c/d @ 5% on Rs. 36,000 (Rs. 40,000 – Rs. 4,000)	1,800				
		5,400				5,400

Dr. **Bad Debts Recovery Account** Cr.

Date	Particulars	Amount	Date		Particulars	Amount
2010		Rs.	2010			Rs.
Dec. 31	To Profit and Loss A/c	500		By	Cash A/c	500
		500				500

Illustration 15

A firm has the following balance on 1.1.2008:

		Rs.
(a)	Provision for Bad and Doubtful Debts	2,500
(b)	Provision for Discount on Debtors	1,200
(c)	Provision for Discount on Creditors	1,000

During the year, Bad Debts amounted to Rs. 2,000, Discounts allowed were Rs. 100 and Discount received were Rs. 200. During 2009, Bad Debts amounting to Rs. 1,000 were written-off while Discount allowed and received were Rs. 2,000, and Rs. 500, respectively.

Total Debtors on 31.12.2008 were Rs. 48,000, before writing-off Bad Debts but after allowing Discounts. On 31.12.2009, the amount was Rs. 17,000, after writing-off Bad Debts, but before allowing Discounts. Total Creditors on these two dates were Rs. 20,000, and Rs. 25,000, respectively.

It is the firm's policy to maintain a provision of 5% against Bad and Doubtful Debts and 2% for discount on Debtors and a provision of 3% for discount on Creditors.

Show the accounts relating to Provision on Debtors and Provision on Creditors for the years 2008 and 2009.

Solution **[ICWA]**

In the books of ....

Dr. **Bad Debts Account** Cr.

Date	Particulars	Amount	Date		Particulars	Amount
2008		Rs.	2008			Rs.
Dec. 31	To Sundry Debtors A/c	2,000	Dec. 31	By	Provision for Bad and Doubtful Debts A/c	2,000
		2,000				2,000
2009			2009			
Dec. 31	To Sundry Debtors A/c	1,000	Dec. 31	By	Provision for Bad and Doubtful Debts A/c	1,000
		1,000				1,000

Dr. **Provision for Bad and Doubtful Debts Account** Cr.

Date	Particulars	Amount	Date	Particulars	Amount
2008		Rs.	2008		Rs.
Dec. 31	To Bad Debts A/c	2,000	Jan. 1	By Balance b/d	2,500
	" Balance c/d 5% on Rs. 46,000 (48,000 – 2,000)	2,300	Dec. 31	" Profit and Loss Account *(bal. fig.)*	1,800
		4,300			4,300
2009			2009	By Balance b/d	2,300
Dec.	To Bad Debts A/c	1,000	Jan. 1		
	" Profit and Loss A/c *(bal. fig.)*	450			
	To Balance c/d 5% on Rs. 17,000	850			
		2,300			2,300
			2010		
			Jan. 1	By Balance b/d	750

Dr. **Discount Allowed Account** Cr.

Date	Particulars	Amount	Date	Particulars	Amount
2008		Rs.	2008		Rs.
Dec. 31	To Sundry Debtors A/c	100	Dec. 31	By Provision for Discount on Debtors A/c	100
		100			100
2009			2009		
Dec. 31	To Sundry Debtors A/c	2,000	Dec. 31	By Provision for Discount on Debtors A/c	2,000
		2,000			2,000

Dr. **Provision for Discount on Debtors Account** Cr.

Date	Particulars	Amount	Date	Particulars	Amount
2008		Rs.	2008		Rs.
Dec. 31	To Discount Allowed A/c	100	Jan. 1	By Balance b/d	1,200
	" Profit and Loss A/c *(bal. fig.)*	226			
	To Balance c/d 2% on Rs. 43,700 (48,000 – 2,000 – 2,300)	874			
		1,200			1,200
Dec. 31	To Discount Allowed A/c	2,000	2009		
	To Balance c/d 2% on Rs. 16,150 (17,000 – 850)	323	Jan. 1	By Balance b/d	874
			Dec. 31	By Profit and Loss A/c *(bal. fig.)*	1,449
		2,323			2,323
			2011		
			Jan. 1	By Balance b/d	285

Dr. **Discount Received Account** Cr.

Date	Particulars	Amount	Date	Particulars	Amount
2008		Rs.	2008		Rs.
Dec. 31	To Provision for Discount on Creditors A/c	200	Dec. 31	By Sundry Creditors A/c	200
		200			200
2009			2009		
Dec. 31	To Provision for Discount on Creditors A/c	500	Dec. 31	By Sundry Creditors A/c	500
		500			500

Provision for Discount on Creditors Account

Dr. Date	Particulars	Amount	Date	Particulars	Cr. Amount
		Rs.			Rs.
2008 Jan. 1	To Balance b/d	1,000	2008 Dec. 31	By Discount Received A/c	200
				" Profit and Loss A/c. (bal. fig.)	200
				" Balance c/d (3% on Rs. 20,000)	600
		1,000			1,000
		Rs.			Rs.
2009 Jan. 1	To Balance b/d	600	2009 Dec. 31	By Discount Received A/c	500
	" Profit and Loss A/c (Bal. fig.)	650		" Balance c/d (3% on Rs. 25,000)	750
		1,250			1,250
2010 Jan. 1	To Balance b/d	750			

Illustration 16

1. A trader maintained Provision for Doubtful Debts @ 5%, a Provision for Discount @ 2% on Debtors and Reserve for Discount @ 2% on Creditors which on 1.1.2010 stood at Rs. 1,500, Rs. 500 and Rs. 400, respectively. His balance on 31.12.2010 and on 31.12.2011 were :

	31.12.2010	31.12.2011
	Rs.	Rs.
Bad Debts written-off	1,800	300
Discount Allowed	600	200
Sundry Debtors	20,000	6,000
Discount Received	300	50
Sundry Creditors	15,000	10,000

Show necessary accounts in the Ledger. **[ICWA]**

Solution

In the books of ....

Bad Debts Account

Dr. Date	Particulars	Amount	Date	Particulars	Cr. Amount
		Rs.			Rs.
2010 Dec. 31	To Sundry Debtors A/c	1,800	2010 Dec. 31	By Prov. for Bad Debts A/c	1,800
		1,800			1,800
2011 Dec. 31	To Sundry Debtors A/c	300	2011 Dec. 31	By Prov. for Bad Debts A/c	300
		300			300

Discount Allowed Account

Dr. Date	Particulars	Amount	Date	Particulars	Cr. Amount
		Rs.			Rs.
2010 Dec. 31	To Sundry Debtors A/c	600	2010 Dec. 31	By Prov. for Discount on Debtors A/c	600
		600			600
2011 Dec. 31	" Sundry Debtors A/c	200	2011 Dec. 31	By Prov. for Discount on Debtors A/c	200
		200			200

Discount Received Account

Dr. Date	Particulars	Amount	Date	Particulars	Cr. Amount
		Rs.			Rs.
2010 Dec. 31	To Prov. for Discount on Creditors A/c	300	2010 Dec. 31	By Sundry Creditors A/c	300
		300			300

Date		Particulars	Amount	Date		Particulars	Amount
2011			Rs.	2011			Rs.
Dec.	To	Prov. for Discount on Creditors A/c	50	Dec. 31	By	Sundry Creditors A/c	50
			50				50

Dr. **Provision for Bad Debts Account** Cr.

Date		Particulars	Amount	Date		Particulars	Amount
2010			Rs.	2010			Rs.
Dec. 31	To	Bad Debts A/c *(provision found in excess)*	1,800	Jan. 1	By	Balance b/d	1,500
	"	Balance c/d	1,000	Dec. 31	"	Profit and Loss A/c *(further provision required)*	1,300
			2,800				2,800
2011				2011			
	To	Bad Debts A/c	300	Jan. 1	By	Balance b/d	1,000
Dec. 31	"	Profit and Loss A/c *(provision found in excess)*	400				
	"	Balance c/d	300				
			1,000				1,000

Dr. **Prov. for Discount on Debtors Account** Cr.

Date		Particulars	Amount	Date		Particulars	Amount
2010			Rs.	2010			Rs.
Dec. 31	To	Discount Allowed A/c	600	Jan. 1	By	Balance b/d	500
	"	Balance c/d (2% on Rs. 19,000)	380	Dec. 31	"	Profit and Loss A/c *(further provision required)*	480
			980				980
2011	To	Discount Allowed A/c	200	2011			
Dec. 31	"	Profit and Loss A/c *(provision found in excess)*	66	Jan. 1	By	Balance b/d	380
	"	Balance c/d (2% on Rs. 5,700)	114				
			380				380

Dr. **Prov. for Discount on Creditors Account** Cr.

Date		Particulars	Amount	Date		Particulars	Amount
2010			Rs.	2010			Rs.
Jan. 1	To	Balance b/d	400	Dec. 31	By	Discount Received A/c	300
Dec. 31	"	Profit and Loss A/c *(further provision required)*	200		"	Balance c/d (2% on Rs. 1,500)	300
			600				600
2011				2011			
Jan. 1	To	Balance b/d	300	Dec. 31	By	Discount received A/c	50
					"	Profit and Loss A/c (provision found in excess.)	50
					"	Balance c/d (2% on Rs. 10,000)	200
			300				300

Specific Debtors

Illustration 17

A Ltd. makes provision for doubtful debts at the end of each year against specific debtors. On 31.12.2009, the following debtors' balances were considered doubtful and provided for :

	Rs.
B	1,500
C.	400
D	250

Following are the particulars for the year ended 31.12.2010 :

(a) Bad Debts written-off :

	Rs.
B	1,200
E	300
P	200

(b) Amount realised against debts written-off in earlier years :

	Rs.
R	700
S	600
N	500

(c) Debts considered doubtful at the end of the year :

	Rs.
G	800
H	900
K	1,000

(d) Debtors considered doubtful at the commencement of the year 2010 were either realised or written-off as bad.

Write-up Provision for Doubtful Debts Account, Bad Debts Account, and the relevant amounts in the Profit and Loss Account for the year ended 31.12.2010.

[CU BCom (Hons.)]

Solution

In the books of A Ltd.

Provision for Doubtful Debts Account

Dr. *Cr.*

Date		*Particulars*	*Amount*	*Date*		*Particulars*	*Amount*
			Rs.				Rs.
2010				2009			
Dec. 31	To	Bad Debts A/c		Jan. 1	By	Balance b/d	2,150
		(Rs. 1,200+ Rs. 300 + Rs. 200)	1,700			(Rs. 150+ Rs. 400+ Rs. 250)	
	To	Balance c/d	2,700	Dec. 31	By	Profit and Loss A/c	2,250
		(Rs. 800 + Rs. 900 + Rs. 1,000)				*(Further provision required)*	
			4,400				4,400

Bad Debts Account

Dr. *Cr.*

Date		*Particulars*	*Amount*	*Date*		*Particulars*	*Amount*
2010			Rs.	2010			Rs.
Dec. 31	To	Sundry Debtors A/c	1,700	Dec. 31	By	Provision for Doubtful	1,700
		(B + E + P)				Debts A/c—transfer	
			1,700				1,700

Profit and Loss Account (Extracts)
for the year ended 31.12.2010

Dr. *Cr.*

	Rs.	Rs.		Rs.
To Prov. for Doubtful Debts :			By **Bad Debts recovered**	1,800
Bad Debts	1,700		**(Rs. 700 + Rs. 600 + Rs. 500)**	
Add : New Provision	2,700			
	4,400			
Less : Existing Provision	2,150			
(Old Reserve)		2,250		

Illustration 18

On 1.1.2011, the Bad and Doubtful Debts Reserve Account of a concern showed a balance of Rs. 60,000, and the Debtors amounted to Rs. 15,00,000. Out of these, during 2011, Debtors amounting to Rs. 10,75,000 paid in full, but the following debts proved bad or doubtful:

A (Rs. 20,000)—bad to full extent.

B (Rs. 40,000)—insolvent, estate expected to pay 50P in the rupee.

C (Rs. 12,000) — paid $33\frac{1}{3}$% in full settlement.

The remaining debts were considered somewhat doubtful on Dec. 31.

The following further debts become due during 2011 but remained outstanding on Dec. 31 :

D (Rs. 20,000)—expected to prove bad totally.

E (Rs. 80,000)—expected to prove 5% bad.

F (Rs. 6,40,000)—expected to prove 4% bad.

G (Rs. 4,00,000)—expected to prove bad to some extent.

H (Rs. 12,60,000)—expected to prove wholly good.

It was decided to write-off actual bad debts and to make a reserve of 5% on debts of unknown doubtful nature. Draw-up the Bad and Doubtful Debts Reserve Account and show the balance of the account as at Dec. 31, 2011.

Solution **[CU BCom (Hons.)]**

In the Books of ......

Bad and Doubtful Debts Reserve Account

Dr. *Cr.*

Date	Particulars	Amount	Date	Particulars	Amount
2011		Rs.	2011		Rs.
Dec. 31	To Bad Debts	28,000[1]	Jan. 1	By Balance b/d	60,000
"	Balance c/d	1,07,250[2]	Dec. 31	" Profit and Loss Account (*bal. fig.*)	75,250
		1,35,250			1,35,250
			2012		
			Jan. 1	By Balance b/d	1,07,250

Working :

1. **Bad Debts :**

	Rs.
Due to Mr. A— full amount	20,000
Due to Mr. C— (Rs. 12,000 × $\frac{2}{3}$)	8,000
	28,000

2. **New Provision to be made on 3.12.2011 :**

			Rs.
For Mr. B—(Rs. 40,000 × 50%)			20,000
Mr. D—(Rs. 20,000, expected to prove totally bad)			20,000
Mr. E—(Rs. 80,000 × 5%)			4,000
Mr. F—(Rs. 6,40,000 × 4%)			25,600
Others of unknown nature :			
Debtors on 1.1.2001		15,00,000	
Add : Debts due from G		4,00,000	
		19,00,000	
Less : Debtors paid to full :	10,75,000		
(already considered for A, B and C) (Rs. 20,000 + Rs. 40,000 + Rs. 12,000)	72,000	11,47,000	
	@ 5% on	7,53,000 =	37,650
			1,07,250

Illustration 19

The following balances were appearing in the books of X Ltd. as on 1.1.2011

		Rs.
(i)	Sundry Debtors (including Rs. 4,000 due from X)	48,000
(ii)	Sundry Creditors (including R. 3,000 due to X)	36,000
(iii)	Provision for Doubtful Debts	2,500

(iv) Provision for Discount on Debtors 1,200
(v) Provision for Discount on Creditors 500

No entry has been passed in the books to record the dishonour of two cheques of Rs. 1,000 and Rs. 1,500, respectively. These cheques were received from customers. First one is expected to be 75% bad and the second one is expected to be 50% bad.

A Provision for Doubtful Debts @ 5% on Debtors and @ 2% on Creditors are maintained.

Prepare the Provisions Accounts.

Solution

Before preparing the Provision Accounts, the following figures should be computed first :

(a) Closing Balance of Provision for Doubtful Debts:

			Rs.
	@ 5% on Rs. 45,000 (i.e., Rs. 48,000 – Rs. 3,000 Set-off)	=	2,250
Add :	75% of the 1st dishonoured cheque, i.e., Rs. 1,000 × $\frac{75}{100}$	=	750
Add :	50% of the 2nd dishonoured cheque (i.e., Rs. 1,500 × $\frac{50}{100}$)	=	750
			3,750

(b) Closing Balance of Provision for Discount on Debtors :

		Rs.
	Debtors Balance	48,000
Less :	Mutual Indebtedness	3,000
		45,000
Less :	Provision for Bad Debts @ 5%	2,250
		42,750
Less :	Provision for Discount on Debtors @ 2% on Rs. 42,750	855
		41,895

(c) Closing Balance of Provision for Discount on Creditors :

		Rs.
	Creditors' Balance	36,000
Less :	Mutual Indebtedness	3,000
		33,000
Less :	Provision for Discount on Creditors @ 2%	660
		32,340

Notes : Since the cheques have been dishonoured, no discount will be allowed, as such, no provision has been made on it.

In the books of X Ltd.

Provision for Bad Debts Account

Dr. Cr.

Date		*Particulars*	*Amount*	*Date*		*Particulars*	*Amount*
2011			Rs.	2011			Rs.
Dec. 31	To	Balance c/d [as per working Note (a)]	3,750	Jan. 1	By	Balance b/d	2,500
				Dec. 31	"	Profit and Loss Account *(bal. fig.)*	1,250
			3,750				3,750

Provision for Discount on Debtors Account

Dr. Cr.

Date		*Particulars*	*Amount*	*Date*		*Particulars*	*Amount*
2011			Rs.	2011			Rs.
Dec. 31	To	Profit and Loss A/c *(bal. fig.)*	345	Jan. 1	By	Balance b/d	1,200
	"	Balance c/d [as per working (b)]	855				
			1,200				1,200

Dr. **Provision for Discount on Creditors Account** Cr.

Date	Particulars	Amount	Date	Particulars	Amount
2011		Rs.	2011		Rs.
Jan. 1	To Balance b/d	500	Dec. 31	By Balance b/d [as per working (c)]	660
Dec. 31	" Profit and Loss A/c *(bal. fig.)*	160			
		660			660

Illustration 20

Sen Ltd. furnished the following particulars on 31st Dec. 2008:

	Rs.
Stock (on 1.1.2008)	24,000
Sundry Debtors (on 1.1.2008)	48,000
Sundry Creditors (on 1.1.2008)	40,000
Other transactions	
Purchases during the year (Purchases are made equally by cash and credit but cost of goods purchased on credit was more than cash purchase by $12\frac{1}{2}$%)	2,55,000
Payments to Creditors (after receiving a discout of 2%)	1,17,600
Receipts from Debtors (after allowing a discount of $2\frac{1}{2}$%)	1,75,500
Bills Receivable Discounted (@ 2%)	18,375
Endorsed bill dishonoured	1,200
Bills endorsed to creditors	6,000
Balances on 31.12.2008 :	
Bills Receivable	5,250
Stock	21,000

Other Information

Goods were sold at a profit of 50% on cost. Goods costing Rs. 8,000 were distributed as free sample. Bad Debts amounted to Rs. 1,700. More provision for bad debts @ 5% on debtors and provision for discount on Debtors and Creditors @ 3%. You are asked to prepare :

(a) Provision for Bad Debts Account; (b) Provision for Discount on Debtors Account; and (c) Provision for Discount on Creditors Account.

Solution

Before preparing the *'provisions'* account, we are to calculate the following components :

(a) Credit Purchases

	Rs.
Let the Cash Purchases be	100.0
∴ Credit purchases will be $12\frac{1}{2}$% more, i.e., (Rs. 100 + 12.5)	112.5

Purchase are made equally between cash and credit.

∴ Ratio of cash purchase and credit purchase are 100 : 112.5 or, 8 : 9.

	Rs.
So, cash purchases will be (Rs. 2,55,000 × $\frac{8}{17}$)	1,20,000
and, credit purchases will be (Rs. 2,55,000 × $\frac{9}{17}$)	1,35,000
	2,55,000

(b) Credit Sales

Since there is no cash sales, total sales represent all credit.

Cost of goods sold	=	Opening Stock + Purchase – Closing Stock – Goods used for Advertisement.
	=	Rs. 24,000 + Rs. 2,55,000 – Rs. 21,000 – Rs. 8,000
	=	Rs. 2,50,000
Add : G. P. @ 50% of Cost.	=	1,25,000
		Rs. 3,75,000

(c)

Bills Receivable A/c

Dr.	Rs.		Rs. Cr.
To Debtors A/c *(bal. fig.)*	30,000	By Bank A/c (98%)	18,375
		" Dis. @ 2%	375
		" Creditors A/c	6,000
		" Balance b/d	5,250
	30,000		30,000

(d)

Sundry Debtors A/c

Dr.	Rs.		Rs. Cr.
To Balance b/d	48,000	By Cash (@ 97 ½%)	1,75,500
" Sales	3,75,000	" Discount @ (2½%)	4,500
" Creditors A/c	1,200	" B/R A/c	30,000
		" B/D A/c	1,700
		" Balancee c/d	2,12,500
	4,24,200		4,24,200

(e)

Sundry Creditors Account

Dr.	Rs.		Rs. Cr.
To Cash (@ 98%)	1,17,600	By Balance b/d	33,000
" Discount (@ 2%)	2,400	" Debtors A/c	1,200
" Bills Receivable (Endorsed)	6,000	" Purchase A/c	1,35,000
" Balance c/d	43,200		
	1,69,200		1,69,200

In the books of X Ltd.

Provision for Bad Debts Account

Dr. Date	Particulars	Amount	Date	Particulars	Amount Cr.
		Rs.			Rs.
2008			2008		
Dec. 31	To Bad Debts A/c	1,700	Jan. 1	By Balance b/d (5% of Rs. 48,000)	2,400
"	Balance c/d (5% of Rs. 2,12,500)	10,625	Dec. 31	" Profit & Loss A/c *(bal. fig.)*	9,925
		12,325			12,325

Provision for Discount on Debtors Account

Dr. Date	Particulars	Amount	Date	Particulars	Amount Cr.
		Rs.			Rs.
1998			1998		
Dec. 31	To Discount Allowed A/c	4,500	Jan. 1	By Balance b/d (3% on (48,000 – 2,400))	1,368
"	Balance c/d (3% on (2,12,500 – 10,625)	6,056	Dec. 31	" Profit & Loss A/c *(bal. fig.)*	9,188
		10,556			10,556

Provision for Discount on Creditors Account

Dr. Date	Particulars	Amount	Date	Particulars	Amount Cr.
		Rs.			Rs.
2008			2008		
Jan. 1	To Balance b/d (3% on Rs. 33,000)	990	Dec. 31	By Discount Received A/c	2,400
"	" Profit and Loss A/c *(bal. fig.)*	2,706	"	Balance c/d (3% on Rs. 43,200)	1,296
		3,696			3,696

ASSIGNMENT MATERIALS

THEORETICAL

Multiple Choice Questions

1. (a) For Creating Provisions for Doubtful Debts, the Contra account is:
(i) Sundry Debtors, (ii) Trading Account, (iii) Profit and Loss A/c, (iv) None of these.

(b) Bad Debts arise when the amount due to debts is found to be:
(i) Recoverable, (ii) Irrecoverable, (iii) Recoverable at a subsequent date.

(c) Recovery of bad debts will be transferred to:
(i) Trading A/c, (ii) Profit and Loss A/c, (iii) Balance Sheet.

(d) Provision for bad debts is a charge:
(i) Against Profit; (ii) Against Appropriation of Profit; (iii) Sundry Debtors.

(e) Provision for Discount on Debtors is adjusted against:
(i) Sundry Debtors, (ii) Profit and Loss A/c, (iii) Balance Sheet.

(f) Purpose of creating Specific Reserve:
(i) Providing for Contingent Liability, (ii) Known Liability, (iii) Any unforeseen Liability.

(g) Capital Revenue is created out of:
(i) Profit on Sale of Asset, (ii) Profit on Sale of Goods, (iii) Revenue Income.

(h) Secret Reserve is created by:
(i) Undervaluing the Asset, (ii) Overvaluing the Asset, (iii) None of these.

[Ans. (a) (iii); (b) (ii); (c) (ii); (d) (i); (e) (ii); (f) (i); (g) (i); (h) (i)]

2. Ascertain the net amount to be debited or credited to Profit and Loss Account in the following cases:

	Bad Debts Rs.	Old Provisions Rs.	New Provisions Rs.	Closing Debtors Rs.
(i)	1,000	2,500	5%	50,000
(ii)	500	—	$2\frac{1}{2}$%	10,000
(iii)	—	2,000	10%	1,00,000
(iv)	2,500	1,500	5%	2,00,000
(v)	100	1,400	3%	30,000
(vi)	800	2,500	—	40,000
(vii)	3,000	8,000	10%	3,00,000

[Ans. (i) Rs. 1,000 (Dr.); (ii) Rs. 750 (Dr.); (iii) Rs. 8,000 (Dr.); (iv) Rs. 11,000 (Dr.); (v) Rs. 400 (Cr.); (vi) Rs. 1,700 (Cr.); (vii) Rs. 2,000 (Cr.)]

Short Answer-Type Questions

1. Define Bad Debts. How is it treated in the books of accounts?
2. What is the difference between Bad Debts and Provision for Bad Debts?
3. Why should we make Provision for Discount on Debtors and Creditors?
4. How does one treat recovery of bad debt in accounts?
5. Define Recovery of bad debts.
6. What are Bad Debts? Explain how provisions are created for such a contingency.
7. What do you understand by Bad Debts and Doubtful Debts?
8. Define:
(a) Good Debts; (b) Bad Debts; (c) Doubtful Debts.
9. Discuss the differences between Bad Debts and Provision for Bad Debts.
10. What is Recovery of Bad Debts? How do you deal with it in the Accounts?
11. Discuss the treatment of 'Provision for Discount on Debtors' and 'Provision for Discount on Creditors'.

Essay-Type Questions

12. 'Provision for depreciation must be provided for, but provision for bad debts may or may not be provided.'—Comment on this statement.
13. (a) Distinguish between Bad Debts, Provision for Doubtful Debts and Reserve for Bad Debts.
    (b) Bad Debts are directly adjusted against Sundry Debtors while provision for Doubtful Debts is shown as a deduction from Sundry Debtors figure—why?
14. Why is it necessary to create provision for Discount on Debtors?
15. (a) What do you mean by 'Bad Debts' and 'Doubtful Debts'?
    (b) How is bad debt accounted for?
    (c) State the differences between bad debts and doubtful debts.
16. Why is it necessary to create provision for Discount on Creditors?
17. What do you mean by recovery of bad debt? How is this accounted for?
18. (a) Distinguish between 'bad debts' and 'doubtful debts'. How are these treated in accounting?
    (b) Distinguish between Reserve and Provision for Doubtful Debt.

PRACTICAL

Bad Debts

1. On 10.6.2008, Saikat sold gods to Ram for Rs. 3,000. On 11.6.08 Ram paid by cheque only Rs. 1,000. On 20.6.08 Sailkat again sold goods to Ram valued Rs. 2,000. On the same day Ram paid Rs. 900. On 31.10.08 Ram became insolvent. Saikat realised only a dividend of 50 P in the rupee from his estate for the balance.

Show the entries in the books of Saikat.

[Ans. Bad Debts Rs. 1,550]

Provision for Bad Debts

2. From the following information prepare the Bad Debts Account and Provision for Bad Debts Account under each of the above three methods:

1.1.2004	Provision for Doubtful Debts amounted to	2,000
31.12.2004	Bad Debts written-off during 2004	1,200
	Sundry Debtors	50,000
31.12.2005	Bad Debts written-off during 2005	1,000
	Sundry Debtors	40,000

Provision for Doubtful Debts to be provided for @ 5% for 2004 and @ $2\frac{1}{2}$% for 2005.

Show also how the relevant items would appear in the Profit and Loss Account and Balance Sheet for 2004 and 2005.

[Ans. Transferred to P & L A/c in 2004 Rs. 1,700, = Provision found in excess Rs. 500]

3. Anirban Ltd. makes provision for bad debts at a varying percentage based on its outstanding debtors balance at the end of the year.

The data relating to consecutive three years appear before you as on 31st March:

	2002 Rs.	2003 Rs.	2004 Rs.
Provision for bad debts @	10%	15%	20%
Bad debts	2,000	1,000	5,000
Total Debtors at the end of the year	1,20,000	60,000	2,00,000

The Provision for bad debts at the beginning of 2002 amounts to Rs. 1,000.

You are required to:

(1) Show the Bad Debts Account and Provisions for Bad Debts Account for the consecutive three years and the resultant Profit and Loss Account and Balance Sheet.

(2) Assume also that a sum of Rs. 500 written-off as bad in 2002 was recovered subsequently in cash in 2003. How would you treat it in your books?

[Ans. Transferred to Profit & Loss A/c in 2002 Rs. 13,000; 2004; Rs. 36,000 and Provision found in excess Rs. 2,000 in 2003]

4. A's Balance Sheet as at 30th June 2009 included the following items in the list of current assets:

	Rs.	Rs.
Debtors	98,000	
Less: Provision for Bad Debts	2,450	
		95,550

At the end of the two following financial years the gross amount of Debtors (before deducting a provision) were

	2010	2011
At 30th June	Rs. 94,000	Rs. 1,02,000

On each of these dates there were Provision for Bad Debts calculated in the same percentage basis as at 30th June 2009.

The actual amount of Bad Debts written-off from Debtors accounts over these period were:

	2010	2011
For the year to 30th June	Rs. 2,600	Rs. 2,300

You are asked to show these transactions in A's ledger for the period from the 1st July 2009 to 31st June 2011.

[Ans. Provision required : 30.6.2010 Rs. 2,350; 30.6.2011 Rs. 2,550. Transferred to P & L A/c : 30.6.2010 Rs. 2,500; 30,06.2011 Rs. 2,500]

5. R. Singh a trader makes provision for Doubtful Debts at the end of each year against specific debtors. On 31.3.1997, the following debtors' balances were consider doubtful and provided for, B— Rs. 3,000; C—Rs. 800; D—Rs. 500.

Following are the particulars for the year ended 31st March 1998:

(i) Bad Debts Written off: B—Rs. 2,400; E–Rs. 500; P—Rs. 500.
(ii) Bad Debts Recovered : R—Rs. 1,400; S—Rs. 1,200; N—Rs. 1,000
(iii) Bad Debts considered doubtful at the end of the year: G—Rs. 1,600; H—Rs. 1,800; K—Rs. 2,000

Debts consider doubtful at the commencement of the year were either realised or written-off as Bad Debts.

Write-up Bad Debts Account and Provision for Doubtful Debts Account for the year ended 31st March 1998.

[ICWA (Inter) Dec. 1998]

[Ans. Transferred to P & L A/c Rs. 4,500]

Provision for Discount on Debtors

6. On 31.12.2000 the Trial Balance of G. Gupta contained the following ledger balances:

Reserve for Bad and Doubtful Debts Account (1.1.00) was Rs. 1,000.

Reserve for Discount on Debtors Account (1.1.00) was Rs. 750. Sundry Debtors Account was Rs. 40,400 (of the Debtors Rs. 400 are bad and should be written-off). Discount Allowed Rs. 300.

On 31.12.2001, the Sundry Debtors Account was Rs. 20,500 (of which Rs. 500 are bad and Discount Allowed Rs. 400 should be written-off). It is desired to maintain the Reserve for Bad and Doubtful Debts Account at 5% on Sundry Debtors and the Reserve for Discount on Debtors at $2\frac{1}{2}$%.

Show by means of ledger accounts how the Reserve for Bad and Doubtful Debts Account and the Reserve for Discount on Debtors Account will appear in the books of G. Gupta for the year 2000 and 2001 and bring down the balance on 1.1.2002.

[Ans. Yr. 2,000—Transferred to P & L A/c for Provision for Bad Debts Rs 1,400, —Transferred to P & L A/c for Reserve for Discount on debtors Rs. 525. 2001— Provision found in excess for Reserve for Bad Debts Rs. 500] —Provision found in excess for Reserve for Discount on Debtors Rs. 100]

7. A company maintains its Reserve for Bad Debts @ 5% and a Reserve for Discount on Debtors @ 2%. You are given the following details:

	2004	2005
	Rs.	Rs.
Bad Debts	800	1,500
Discount allowed	1,200	500
Recovery of Bad Debts written-off in earlier years	500	300

Sundry Debtors (before writing-off Bad Debts and discounts) amounted to Rs. 60,000 on 31st December 2004 and Rs. 42,000 on 31st December 2005.

On 1st January 2004, Reserve for Bad Debts and Reserve for Discount on Debtors had balances of Rs. 4,500 and Rs. 800, respectively.

Show the Reserve for Bad Debts Account and Reserve for Discount on Debtors Account for 2004 and 2005.

[Ans. 2004 Provisions found for excess for Reserve for Bad debts Rs. 850 2005 : Provisions required and transferred from p & L A/c Rs. 1,502 Transferred toP & L A/c Rs. 600 for Reserve for bad Debts Transferred to & P & L for reserve for Discount on Debtorsrs. 158]

8. On 1.1.2004 the Reserve for Doubtful Debts Account, in the books of S. Soman, stood at Rs. 1,200 and the Reserve for Discount on Debtors Account at Rs. 150.

On 31.12.2004, the Sundry Debtors were Rs. 20,400 of which Rs. 400 are bad and to be written-off. The Discount Allowed to Debtors during 2004 were Rs. 300.

On 31.12.2005, the Sundry Debtors were Rs. 10,100 of which Rs. 100 are bad and to be written-off. The Discount Allowed to Debtors during 2005 were Rs. 50.

On 31.12.2006, Sundry Debtors were Rs. 36,200 of which Rs. 200 are bad and are to be written-off. The Discount Allowed to Debtors during 2006 were Rs. 600.

It is desired to maintain a Reserve for Doubtful Debts at 5% on Sundry Debtors and a Reserve for Discount on Debtors at 2% on Debtors.

Show how the Reserve for Doubtful Debts Account and the Reserve for Discount on Debtors Account would appear in the ledger of S. Soman for the years 2004, 2005, and 2006, bringing down the balance on 1.1.2006.

[Ans. Transferred to P & L A/c for Reserve for Bad Debts 2004 Rs. 200; 2005 Rs. 400 (Excess) : 2006 Rs. 2,450; Transferred to P & L A/c for Reserve for Discount on Debtors : 2004 : Rs. 230; 2005 Rs. 140 (Excess); 2006 Rs. 1075]

Provision for Discount on Creditors

9. A company maintains its Reserve for Discount on Sundry Creditors @ 4%. On 1.4.2009 Reserve for discount on Sundry Creditors stood in the books for Rs. 9,500. On 31st March 2010 and 31st March 2011 Sundry Creditors (after adjustment of discount received) amounted to Rs. 1,30,000 and Rs. 1,80,000 respectively.

Discount received	Rs.
2009-10	4,500
2010-11	12,000

Show the Reserve for Discount on Sundry Creditors Account for 2009-10 and 2010-11.

[Ans. Provision required Rs. 5,200; Credit to P & L A/c Rs. 200 on 31.3.2010 On 31.3.2011, Provision required Rs. 7,200; Credit to P & L A/c Rs. 14,000]

Mixed

10. The Trial balance of a trader as on 31st March 2011 showed the following balances:

	Dr. Rs.	Cr. Rs.
Bad Debtors	2,000	—
Discount allowed	1,400	—
Discount received	—	950
Provision for Bad Debts	—	2,800
Provision for Discount on Debtors	—	1,596
Provision for Discount on Creditors	1,100	—
Sundry Debtors	60,500	—
Sundry Creditors	—	50,000

At the time of preparation of final accounts he decided:

(i) to write-off Rs. 500 as bad debts. (ii) to provide 5% for bad debts. (iii) to provide 3% for discount on debtors; and (iv) to provide $2\frac{1}{2}$% for Discount on creditors.

Write-up the important ledger accounts for the above.

[Ans. Provision required for Bad Debts Rs. 3,000; Transfer from P/L A/c Rs. 2,700. Provision required for Discount on Drs. Rs. 1,710; Transfer from P/L A/c Rs. 1,514. Provision required for Discount on Crs. Rs. 1,250; Transfer to P/L A/c Rs. 1,100.]

CHAPTER 12

RESERVES AND PROVISIONS

Learning Objectives

Reserves

Meaning

Importance

Provisions

Meaning

Difference between Reserves and Provisions

Types of Reserves

—Secret Reserves

—Meaning

—Method of Creating Secret Reserves

—Objects

—Danger or Objections to Secret Reserves

—Revenue Reserves

(i) General Reserves

—Contingent Reserves

—Free Reserves

—Objects of Creating General Reserves

(ii) Specific Reserves

—Dividend Equalisation Reserves

—Investments Fluctuation Reserves

—Debenture Redemption Reserves

—Purpose of Creating Specific Reserves

—Capital Reserve

—Creation of Capital Reserve

—Uses of Capital Reserve

—Differences between Revenue Reserves and Capital Reserves

RESERVES AND PROVISIONS

Reserves

'Reserve' means the part of profit which is set aside in order to meet any future uncertainties, i.e., that part of profit (revenue or capital) which is set aside to meet any unknown or known liability. It is an appropriation of profit and not a charge against profit. Financial position of the business is strengthened by it. It must be remembered that it is neither a liability nor a provision. In short, it implies that the amount which is set aside out of profit to cover any known or unknown liability or diminution in the value of assets in future (e.g., Sinking Fund to replace an asset). Examples of Reserves are: (i) General Reserve, and (ii) Dividend, Equalisation Reserve, Reserve for Expansions, etc.

(a) Importance

It has already been stated above that financial position of a firm is strengthened. It helps a firm in case of emergency need of funds, i.e., it helps a firm to tackle its financial problem particularly when the same has suffered from actual shortage of funds (i.e., liquid resource). There are many purposes of its creation out of profit. These are:

(i) to expand and develop; (ii) to repay liabilities; (iii) to replace an asset; (iv) to meet unforeseen liabilities; (v) to declare and pay a steady rate of dividend; (vi) to meet legal requirements (i.e., payment of Income Tax etc.); (vii) to make a better financial position.

Provisions

It means any amount written-off or retained by way of providing for depreciation, renewals or diminution in the value of assets or retained by way of providing for any known liability of which the amount cannot be determined with substantial accuracy. It is a charge against profit. In other words, it is an amount which is payable in future, i.e., it is a liability which a firm will have to pay. From accounting point of view it may be stated that if the amount relating to a liability is not certain an estimated amount is set aside against profit (i.e., by debiting Profit and Loss Appropriation Account). So, 'Provision' means an estimated amount to met an expense or loss in future which is not yet certain. (e.g., Provision for Taxations, Provision for Depreciations, Provisions for Doubtful Debts, Provision for Discount on Debtors, Provisions for Repairs and Renewals, etc.)

As per Companies Act, 1956, provision means any amount written-off or retained by way of providing for depreciations, renewals or diminution in value of assets, or retained by providing for any known liability of which the amount cannot be determined with substantial accuracy.

(b) Differences between 'Reserves' and 'Provisions'

The following points of distinction between Reserves and Provisions are to be noted:

Points of Distinction	Reserves	Provisions
1. *Purpose*	General Reserve is not created for any particular purpose.	Provisions are created for a particular purpose and must be used for that particular purpose only.
2. *Process of Creation*	It is created out of Profit and Loss Appropriation Account, i.e., if there is net loss, it can never be created, since it is a charge against appropriation of profit.	It is created out of Profit and Loss Account, i.e., charge against profit. Hence, it is created irrespective of profit or loss.
3. *Objects of Creation*	It is created for strengthening the financial position of a firm.	It is created to meet any contin-gent liability.
4. *Utilisation*	It can be used for the purpose of distributing dividend, i.e., in case of insufficient profit.	It cannot be utilised for the purpose of distributing dividend.
5. *For Taxation Purpose*	The amount of Reserve which will be added back to profit for ascertaining taxable income.	Only the amount which is reasonable will qualify for deduction.
6. *Treatment in Accounts*	It is shown as liability in the Liability side of the Balance Sheet under the head Reserves and Surplus.	It is shown as a deduction from the concerned item.

7. Creation	Whether reserve will be created or not depends on the owners or the directors.	It is compulsorily created.
8. Investment Purposes	A part of the Reserve may be invested outside the business.	Does not arise.

Types of Reserves

Reserves may be classified as under:

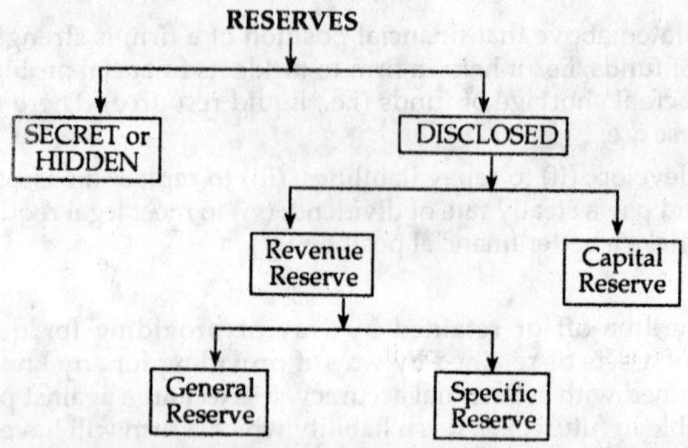

Secret Reserves or Hidden Reserves

Any Reserve which does not appear on the face of the Balance Sheet or which is not disclosed or if the amount cannot be ascertained by examining the Balance Sheet is called Hidden Reserve or Secret Reserve or Inner Reserve. It is created by understatement of Assets (e.g., undervaluation of Closing Stock) or overstatement of liabilities (e.g., fictitious names are included in the list of Creditors). It must be remembered that this Reserve is not disclosed in the face of the Balance Sheet.

Methods of Creating Secret Reserves

The different methods which are used for creating Secret Reserves are:

(i) By undervaluing the assets from Cost or Market Price. (ii) By providing excessive depreciation on Assets. (iii) By charging Capital Expenditure to Revenue Expenditure. (iv) By showing Contingent Liabilities as Real Liabilities. (v) By omitting Assets from the Balance Sheet. (vi) By making more reserve either for Reserve for Bad Debts or discount than what is required. (vii) By ignoring the permanent increase in the value of any asset. (viii) By undervaluing the value of Goodwill.

Objects of Creating Secret Reserves

The objects of creating Secret Reserves are:

This reserve is created in order to:

(i) Meet extraordinary losses without, however, disclosing to shareholders. (ii) Strengthen the financial condition. (iii) Avoid undesirable circumstances. (iv) Increase working capital for future needs. (v) Equalise the rate of dividend, i.e., to maintain uniform rate of dividend. (vi) Utilise the said reserve in case of need in future.

Danger or Objection to Secret Reserves

The Secret Reserve has the following disadvantages:

(i) The correct picture of the business cannot be exhibited. (ii) It misuses the Reserves. (iii) Goodwill of the firm may be damaged as a result of such reserve. (iv) Value of the Assets may go down in the market. (v) Shareholders are deprived from the share of profit. (vi) Possibility of misuse of Reserve. (vii) Possibility of arising crisis in the firm. (viii) Possibility of losing appropriate compensation.

Revenue Reserves

Revenue Reserves are created out of profits available for distribution of dividend. It represents undistributed profits. In other words, "It is that portion, or any detail thereof, of the net worth or total equity of an enterprise representing retained earnings available for withdrawal by proprietors."—Kohler.

Examples:

(i) General Reserve, (ii) Dividend Equalisation Reserve, (iii) Investment Fluctuation Reserve, (iv) Debenture Redemption Reserve.

Revenue Reserve is of two types: viz.,. (i) General Reserve, and (ii) Specific Reserve.

(i) **General Reserve:** When the entire amount of profits is not distributed by way of dividend but a certain portion of such profit (which arises out of normal trading activities of the business) is set aside to strengthen the financial conditions of the business, particularly for the purpose of working capital, it is called General Reserve.

This reserve is also termed as:

Contingent Reserve, Free Reserve (as they are not created for a specific purpose).

This reserve is not created to meet any contingent or specific liability. It is also called Undistributed Profit.

Objectives of Creating General Reserves

The objectives of creating a General Reserve are:

(i) It provides additional working capital.

(ii) It can meet any unforeseen losses or expenses.

(iii) Financial position is strengthened by it.

(iv) It equalises the rate of dividend by creating Dividend Equalisation Fund.

(v) It helps to increase the goodwill of the firm among creditors/outsiders.

(vi) It conceals additional profit.

It must be remembered that it is not compulsory to create this reserve out of profit. It is a source of internal financing. It is nothing but **Retained Profits** or known as **'Ploughing Back of Profit'**.

(ii) **Specific Reserve:** A Specific Reserve is created for some specific purpose and is utilised only for that purpose. It is also called **Provision**. This Reserve is created to provide for losses and contingencies which result in losses and are known or expected at the end of the year for making provisions for such contingencies which may happen at a future date.

It is a charge against Profit and not an appropriation of Profit. Thus, it is created out of Profit and Loss Account and not from Profit and Loss Appropriation Account. It must be remembered that this reserve must be created irrespective of profit or loss and this reserve must be provided before distribution of dividend.

Examples:

Dividend Equalisation Fund; Debenture Redemption Reserve; Capital Redemption Reserve; Development Rebate Reserve; etc.

Purpose of Creating Specific Reserves

The Specific Reserve is created for the following purposes:

(i) Providing for Depreciation on Fixed Asset:
Examples: Expenses for Depreciations, Repairs and Renewals, etc.

(ii) Providing for Contingent Liabilities:
Examples: Dispute cases.

(iii) Providing for Outstanding Expenses:
Examples: Outstanding Salaries; Wages; etc.

(iv) Providing for diminution in assets or increase in liabilities:
Examples: Bad and Doubtful Debts on Debtors, Dishonour of Bill Discounted, etc.

Capital Reserves

The reserve which is created out of capital profit is called Capital Reserve. This reserve is not available for distribution of dividend in cash, except under certain circumstances, i.e., this reserve represents capital items which are not free for distribution. This is why, as per Companies Act, 1956, Schedule VI, Part III, Capital Reserve must not include any amount regarded as free for distribution through Profit and Loss Account.

Creation of Capital Reserves

Capital Reserve is created out of the following (i.e., not out of Profit and Loss Appropriation Account):

(i) Profits Prior to Incorporation; (ii) Profits on Redemption of Debentures at a Discount; (iii) Profits on Sales of Fixed Assets; (iv) Profits on Revaluations of Fixed Assets; (v) Premium on issue of Shares and Debentures; (vi) Profit by Forfeiting Shares (i.e., Balance of Share Forfeiture Account); (vii) Profit made while purchasing a business (i.e., if net assets acquired are more than the purchase consideration); (viii) Profit earned by any means other than normal activities of the business.

Uses of Capital Reserves

It has already been stated above that this reserve cannot be used for the purpose of distributing dividend. This reserve can be adjusted against any capital loss.

It may also be:

(i) utilised for the purpose of issuing bonus shares, if the Article so provides;

(ii) utilised for writing-off various types of intangibles and fictitious assets, e.g., Goodwill.

Differences between Revenue Reserves and Capital Reserves

The significant points of difference are:

Revenue Reserve	Capital Reserve
1. Revenue Reserve is created out of current year's profit.	1. Capital Reserve is created out of (i) profits prior to incorporation, (ii) profit on sale of fixed asset, etc.
2. It is available for dividend.	2. It is not available for dividend.
3. It is used to meet any unforeseen losses or expenses.	3. It is used for writing-off various intangibles and fictitious assets.
4. It provides additional working capital.	4. It does not provide additional working capital.
5. It is not compulsory to create such reserve.	5. It is compulsory.

ASSIGNMENT MATERIALS

THEORETICAL

Multiple Choice Questions

1. (a) Provision is created for a

(i) Particular Purpose (ii) General purpose
(iii) Both purposes (iv) None of these

(b) Provision is created out of:

(i) P & L Appropriations A/c (ii) Profit and Loss A/c
(iii) Trading A/c (iv) None of these

(c) Provision is a charge against:

(i) Profit (ii) Appropriation of Profit
(iii) Both (iv) None of these

(d) Reserve is created out of:

(i) Trading A/c (ii) P & L Appropriation A/c
(iii) Profit and Loss A/c (iv) None of these

(e) Secret Reserve is created by:

(i) Showing Contingent liability as real liabilities (ii) Debiting Profit and Loss A/c
(iii) By debiting P & L Appropriation A/c (iv) None of these

(f) Object of creating Secret Reserve is :

(i) to meet extraordinary Losses (ii) to meet expenses
(iii) To meet any long-term liability (iv) None of these

(g) Object of creating General Reserve is:

(i) to meet any unforeseen losses (ii) tåo meet any known liability

(iii) to meet any unknown liability (iv) None of these

[Ans. (a) (i); (b) (ii); (c) (i); (d)(ii); (e)(i); (f) (i); (g) (i)]

Short Answer-Type Questions

1. (a) Distinguish between Reserves and Provisions.

   (b) Why is it necessary to create Provisions for Bad Debts?
2. What is the purpose of creating Reserve?
3. What are the different types of Reserves?
4. What is Hidden Reserve? How is it created?
5. What are the effects of creating Secret Reserve?
6. What is Capital Reserve?
7. Is maintenance of Secret Reserve legal?
8. Is there any difference between General Reserve and Specific Reserve?
9. What is Revenue Reserve?
10. Give two uses of Capital Reserve.

Long Answer-Type Questions

1. Distinguish between a Reserve and a Provision.
2. Discuss the method of creating Capital Reserve.
3. What is Capital Reserve? Give examples.
4. Discuss the accounting treatment of Reserve and Provision.
5. Distinguish between Revenue Reserve and Capital Reserve.
6. What is Capital Reserve? How is it created?
7. What is Specific Reserve? Mention the purpose of creating Specific Reserve.
8. What is Secret Reserve? What are the objects of creating Secret Reserve?
9. What is Revenue Reserve? How is it created? What are its purposes?
10. Explain the different types of Reserve with examples.

CHAPTER 13

ACCOUNTING FOR FIXED ASSETS AND ACCOUNTING FOR DEPRECIATION

Learning Objectives

ACCOUNTING FOR FIXED ASSETS

Introduction

Presentation of Fixed Assets as per Schedule VI of the Companies Act, 1956

Valuation of Fixed Assets

ACCOUNTING FOR DEPRECIATION

Introduction

Certain Terms

Nature of Depreciation

Causes of Depreciation

Characteristics of Depreciation

Objects and Necessity of Depreciation

Measurement of Depreciation

Consequences—if depreciation is not provided for

Procedure for calculating Depreciation

Depreciation to be calculated as per Income-Tax Act, 1961

Method of Depreciation

A. Methods Based on the Concept of Allocation of Expired Deferred Cost

—Fixed Instalment Method

—Diminishing Balance Method

—Sum of the year's Digit Method

—Working Hour Method

—Production Unit Method

—Mileage Method

B. Method Based on the Concept of Recovery and Maintenance of Capital

—Sinking Fund Method

—Annuity Method

—Insurance Policy Method

C. Special Methods

—Revaluation Method

—Depletion Method

—Compound Interest Method

—Inventory System of Depreciation

—Retirement Method

Profit and Loss on Disposal of Fixed Assets

Recording Exchange of Used Assets with new ones

Change in Method

—With Prospective Effect

—With Retrospective Effect

Objectives of Management about Depreciation Policy

Provision for Depreciation and the methods prescribed by the Companies Act

Depreciation Policy

Selecting Appropriate Method

General Illustration

AS 6, Depreciation Account (Revised)

Summary of AS 6

ACCOUNTING FOR FIXED ASSETS AND ACCOUNTING FOR DEPRECIATION

ACCOUNTING FOR FIXED ASSETS

Introduction

Every firm needs certain amount of fixed assets for their smooth operational activities. The primary objective for the acquisition of fixed assets is to earn revenue. Without fixed asset production function cannot be started. Certain amount of fixed assets are absolutely required for the proper functioning of a firm. No firm can survive without fixed assets.

However, in order to be a fixed one, an asset must satisfy the following three characteristics:

(i) ***the asset which has been acquired is not for resale;***

(ii) ***the asset must have a comparatively long life, i.e., it must not be converted into cash or consumed in the ordinary course of business within a period of one accounting cycle.***

(iii) ***the asset must help the process of production, supply of goods, and services.***

Fixed assets are use for the purpose of earning revenue over a long period of time. They are—more or less—permanent in nature. Sometimes they are also called Block, e.g., Land and Building, Plant and Machinery, Furniture and Fixtures, etc.

As per AS 10, fixed asset is an asset held with the intention of being used for the purpose of producing or providing goods or services and is not help for sale in the normal course of business.

Fixed assets are not consumed during the process of production or manufacture, rather, they are more or less permanent in nature. Cohen Committee of Company Law Amendment in England explained the fixed assets as "assets not held for sale or conversion into cash." According to the Statement on Auditing Practice (issued by ICAI)— A convenient working rule is to regard as fixed assets those acquired for the purpose of use in the business with the object of earning revenue and which are not intended for resale at a profit and conversion into cash in the ordinary course of business.

Presentation of Fixed Assets as per Schedule VI of the Companies Act, 1956[1]

As per Part I of Schedule VI of the Companies Act, 1956, the presentation of fixed assets in the Balance Sheet are:

(a) Goodwill; (b) Land; (c) Building;
(d) Leasehold; (e) Railway Siding; (f) Plant and Machinery;
(g) Furniture and Fittings; (h) Development of Property; (i) Patent, Trade Mark and Designs;
(j) Livestock; (k) Vehicles etc.

Alternative Approach for Presentation of Fixed Assets[2]

Fixed assets are shown as an application of funds, i.e., the assets are shown:

	Application of Funds	Current Year Rs.	Previous Year Rs.
	Fixed Assets		
	Gross Block	***	***
Less :	Depreciation	***	***
	Net Block	***	***

Disclosures

Fixed Assets are to be disclosed in the following manner:

(a) The expenditure on fixed assets should categorically be classified as: (i) Goodwill; (ii) Land; (iii) Building; (iv) Leasehold; (v) Railway siding; (vi) Plant and Machinery; (vii) Furniture and Fitting; (viii) Development of property; (ix) Patent, Trademarks and Designs; (x) Livestocks; and (xi) Vehicles etc.

(b) Under each head the original cost, the additions thereto and deductions therefor, during the year and the total depreciation written-off or provided up to the end of the year to be stated.

(c) In every case, where the original cost cannot be ascertained without unreasonable expenses or delay the valuation shown by the books shall be given. Such valuation shall be the net amount at which an asset stood in the company's books at the commencement of this Act after deducting the previous amount and, at the same time, where any such asset is sold, the amount of sale proceeds shall be shown as deduction.

1 For further details, the students are advised to see the chapter *Final Accounts of Companies* in this volume
2 This form has been followed by many companies

(d) Where sales have been written-off on a reduction of capital or a revaluation on assets, every Balance Sheet shall show the reduced figures with the date of reduction in place of original cost. Similarly, where sums have been added by writing-up the assets, every Balance Sheet shall show the increased figures with the date of increase in place of original cost.

(e) Each Balance Sheet for the first five years subsequent to the date of variation shall show also the amount of variation so made.

(f) Deprecation written-off or provided shall be allocated under different asset heads and deducted in arriving at the fixed assets value.

Valuation of Fixed Assets

As fixed assets are constantly used during the process of production its value gradually decreases due to normal wear and tear. That is why fixed assets should be valued at cost less depreciation. In other words, fixed assets are valued at original/historical cost minus total depreciation charged till the Balance Sheet date. So, these assets are valued as per "Going Concern Value/Historical Value/Token Value." The logic behind this principle is that these assets are acquired for the purpose of earning revenue and for smooth operation of the business during the process of production, and not for resale. Fluctuations in the value of fixed assets does not have any impact on the activities, i.e., for the purpose of earning revenue, and, as such, it does not affect the price of such assets. These assets are not valued as a saleable unit like others; rather, they should be valued from the standpoint of their utility towards the firm. However, the valuation of a fixed asset is an arbitrary one as the amount of depreciation is merely an estimate on which the value of fixed asset depends. For this purpose current replacement or realisable value should not be taken into consideration at the time of valuing the fixed assets. Thus, fixed assets should be valued at cost less depreciation written-off on a proper and consistent basis.

IND AS 16 : PROPERTY, PLANT AND EQUIPMENT

While discussing "Accounting for Fixed Asset", we must consider the appropriate Accounting Standard in this regard.

Definitions

The following terms are used in this standard with their meanings specified:

Carrying amount is the amount at which an asset is recognised after deducting any accumulated depreciation and accumulated impairment losses.

Cost is the amount of cash or cash equivalents paid or the fair value of the other consideration given to acquire an asset at the time of its acquisition or construction or, where applicable, the amount attributed to that asset when initially recognised in accordance with the specific requirements of other Indian Accounting Standards, e.g., Ind AS 102 Share-based Payment.

Depreciable amount is the cost of an asset, to other amount substituted for cost, less the residual value.

Depreciation is the systematic allocation of the depreciable amount of an asset over its useful life.

Entity-specific value is the present value of the cash flows an entity expects to arise from the continuing use of an asset, and from its disposal at the end of its useful life, or expects to incur when setting a liability.

Fair value is the amount for which an asset could be exchanged between knowledgeable willing parties in an arm's length transaction.

An impairment loss is the amount by which the carrying amount of an asset exceeds its recoverable amount.

Property, plant, and equipment are tangible items that :

(a) are held for use in the production or supply of goods or services, for rental to others, or for administrative purposes; and

(b) are expected to be used during more than one period.

Recoverable amount is the higher of an asset's fair value less costs to sell, and its value in use.

The residual value of an asset is the estimated amount that an entity would currently obtain from disposal of the asset, after deducting the estimated costs of disposal, if the asset was already of the age and in the condition expected at the end of its useful life.

Useful life is :

(a) the period over which an asset is expected to be available for use by an entity; or

(b) the number of production or similar units expected to be obtained from the asset by an entity.

Recognition

The cost of an item of property, plant and equipment shall be recognised as an asset if, and only if:

(a) it is probable that future economic benefits associated with the item will flow to the entity; and

(b) the cost of the item can be measured reliably.

ACCOUNTING FOR DEPRECIATION

Introduction

Generally, 'depreciation' means gradual decrease in the value of an asset which arises due to normal wear and tear, obsolescence etc. In short, **depreciation means the gradual diminution, loss or shrinkage in the utility value of an asset due to wear and tear in use, effluxion of time or obsolescence.** It represents a portion of the total cost of fixed asset which has expired and, as such, turned into expense in the process of its use during a particular accounting period. Practically, the payment which is made against the purchase of a fixed asset is an advance payment for an expense. Purchase of fixed asset represents claims to service which will gradually be expired in future. The fixed asset will gradually be consumed over a number of years after rendering services. In other words, the said claims to services (represented by fixed assets) gradually expire and turn into expense in the course of rendering services over a number of years. Hence, the portion of fixed assets (in the form of claims to services) consumed during a particular accounting period as a result of its use, is known as depreciation. Therefore, depreciation may be treated as an expense which also represents the flow-out of a portion of a fixed asset as a result of its use.

However, the definition of the Committee on Terminology of the American Institute of Certified Public Accountants (AICPA) on accounting terminology is used very widely. It states:

"Depreciation accounting is a system of accounting which aims to distribute the cost or other basic value of tangible capital assets, less salvage (if any), over the estimated useful life of the unit (which may be a group of assets) in a systematic and rational manner. It is a *process of allocation, not of valuation.* Depreciation for the year is the portion of the total charge under such a system that is allocated to the year. Although the allocation may properly take into account occurrences during the year, it is not intended to be the measurement of the effect of all such occurrences."

The above definition may be criticised as:

(i) It does not classify properly what is meant by systematic and rational manner. The word 'rational' may mean that it should reasonably be related to the expected benefits in any case.

(ii) This definition also does not indicate whether historical cost or any other kind of cost should be allocated.

(iii) Some accountants are of the opinion that depreciation is nothing but an arbitrary allocation of cost. As such, according to them, conventional methods allocate historical cost over a number of years arbitrarily.

The above criticisms may be overcome on the following grounds : Is there any possibility to identify how much an individual fixed asset contributes directly to earn revenue; if it would have, no doubt the conventional allocation method would have been considered a more, logical one. Since revenue is the result of the collective contributions of current and fixed assets, labour and other factors it is impossible to identify how much each of them contributes to the total pool. According to the cause-and-effect relation, allocation of fixed cost is not possible until the contribution of individual factors are ascertained. In that càse, conventional allocation method simply attempts to allocate the historical fixed cost throughout the period of its lifespan in a systematic and rational manner.

For every conventional allocation method there must be some presuppositions. For example, certain assumptions and approximations are made under each method on the relation between the market prices and the degree of their use, estimated scrap value, nature and type of repairs and maintenance etc.

The principle of allocation depends on various factors. For example, anticipated change in revenue, life of the asset, degree of uncertainty etc., which have important role in selecting the method of allocation, may be considered as the most appropriate and suitable ones, although all the said factors may not be treated equally. At the same time, all the assumptions are not equally applicable to all the assets. As such, a particular method should be adopted for an individual asset depending on the nature of the same instead of applying a general method.

Certain Useful Terms

Amortisation

Amortisation means the gradual extinguishment of any amount over a period of time. It is charged to write-off the intangible assets over its useful life (i.e., goodwill, patent, trademarks etc.). It is not applicable in case of fixed assets viz., leasehold premises, by way of depreciation. So, depreciation and amortisation are equivalent terms. The only difference which may be noted between the two is: depreciation is either credited directly to the asset or through provisions for depreciation/accumulated depreciation account, but amortisation is directly credited to the asset concerned. Amortisation is usually used for intangible assets whereas depreciation is used for fixed assets.

Dilapidation

The term 'Dilapidation' is used in case of leasehold properties. Usually, when a property is leased out, the landlord of the property can demand that the property must be returned to the landlord in the same condition when it was leased out after the expiry of the lease period. As a result, the leaseholders usually set aside a certain sum of money every year in order to provide for dilapidation which may be required at the time of returning the property to the original landlords. Naturally, the amount of dilapidation is added to the cost of such leased properties. It may be mentioned that depreciation is to be calculated on the total cost (i.e., the lease rent paid plus the amount provided for dilapidation).

Obsolescence

The loss in usefulness of an asset resulting from new invention, change in style, legislation or other causes having no physical relation to the object affected. Obsolescence may be classified as ordinary obsolescence or loss due to normal progress or development of industry. Extraordinary obsolescence, on the other hand, arises due to sudden unforeseen causes, i.e., unexpected style change, etc. Ordinary obsolescence is customarily included as a factor in determining depreciation rates to allow for gradual lessening of service life through factors other than physical wear and tear.

Depletion

There are some fixed assets which are wasting in nature and which lose their usefulness due to the extraction of raw materials from them, i.e., they get fully exhausted. These assets are termed as wasting assets, e.g., mines, quarries, oil-wells, etc. Actually, natural resources come under this category. The charge for depletion is made on the basis of consumption of the respective asset. These assets are quite different from other fixed assets like, Land, Building, Plant and Machinery, etc.

Replacement Cost of Assets

The primary objective of charging depreciation against Profit and Loss Account is to ascertain the correct cost of production as well as to determine the correct Net Profit. In other words, depreciation should be charged against Profit and Loss Account over the useful life of the assets, and, as such, depreciation is calculated on the basis of cost price of the assets. But at present this view has not been accepted by some professional people and academicians. According to them, as a result of changing price level, depreciation charged on historical cost basis does not

(i) show the correct amount of profit/income;

(ii) arrange accurate funds for replacement of assets as the amount of depreciations based on historical cost will be lower than the depreciation based on replacement cost;

(iii) exhibit the true/real value of the assets, i.e., the Balance Sheet does not exhibit the true and fair view of the financial position of a firm.

Thus, it is stated that depreciation should be provided on replacement cost basis—which is more realistic and logical and not on the basis of historical cost.

Nature of Depreciation

The nature of depreciation is enumerated :

(a) Diminution of Value

It has been highlighted above that **depreciation is considered as the diminution of value of a fixed asset which arises due to normal wear and tear, obsolescence, or the passage (effluxion) of time.** In the past, depreciation was considered as a reduction in the value of a fixed asset. But, at present, this theory, i.e., diminution in value, is not accepted on the following grounds :

Here, the term 'value' denotes different meanings and interpretations and, as such, it is a controversial term. Thus, when it is used in connection with depreciation, the meaning and the method of computation of depreciation change, which, in other words, provides a different result. Besides, the value so computed with the help of any method does not remain static throughout the period of the assets due to change in price level and other economic factors. As a result, this concept suffers from certain limitations in measuring the periodic depreciation. Since the term 'value' has only a subjective significance, this concept of value actually fails to convey the real significance of depreciation in the area of financial accounting. Thus, at present, the concept of depreciation as diminution of value is not recognised.

(b) **Allocation of Cost**

Depreciation is considered as an *allocation of cost* (which has already been pointed out) **of a fixed asset.** It may be regarded as a periodic charge or expense which is to be matched against the revenues earned. We all know that a fixed asset, having a long life, is acquired not for re-sale but for the purpose of use in a firm and such fixed asset has a specific number of years of useful life (excepting land).

Every fixed asset is used in the business for the purpose of earning revenue through the process of manufacturing or trading at a particular accounting period. Since the fixed asset renders services for the said period, it loses its proportional ability to render service in future as there is a flow-out of the fixed asset. This principle, however, is not applicable in case of a current asset which is consumed in full when the same is used in the business. But, in case of fixed assets, the services can be used without consuming it in full. As such, although the entire asset is used in the business operation for a particular period, only a portion of the same is consumed or exhausted. This consumption in the value of asset actually reduces the future service-rendering capacity of the asset. This reduction in the future service-rendering capacity of the asset may be due to either utilisation or obsolescence, or innovations, etc. But this reduction is not always exactly equal to the service rendered by it. As a result, this partial flow-out of a fixed asset is accounted for by way of an imputed transaction which is known as depreciation. It is needless to mention that, as the fixed asset has a long life and only a portion of its service-rendering capacity is consumed, the entire cost of the asset cannot be charged by way of depreciation against the revenues earned for a particular period. That is, only a part of the total cost of fixed asset should be charged against the revenues earned in each of the consecutive accounting periods throughout the life of the asset by way of depreciation. In other words, a part of the total cost of fixed asset should be allocated by way of depreciation to each accounting period, against the revenues earned in the respective periods.

At present, this concept (i.e., allocation of cost) is widely accepted. Under this concept, the cost of fixed asset is considered as deferred charge which should be written-off against revenues during the effective life of the asset. Therefore, the cost (i.e., historical cost) of the asset is spread over throughout the periods of its effective life in a proper way. Hence, **depreciation is considered as a part of the total historical cost of a fixed asset which is allocated against the respective revenues over the periods of its effective life.**

(c) **Expiration of Capital Outlay**

Depreciation may also be considered as an expiration of the capital outlay. When plant or machine is commissioned into use by a going concern in order to earn revenue, its usuable capacity gets exhausted continuously. The capital outlay consists of financial capital or cash invested in fixed asset (plant or machine) which is simultaneously expired by the amount of exhaustion of its usable capacity, as an outlay. Under this concept, depreciation is the measure of that portion of the capital outlay on the fixed assets which has expired. And, as such, the expired portion of the capital outlay must be charged against the revenue for recovery of capital for the period. It may be mentioned that this concept is practically similar to the concept (b) stated above, i.e., allocation of cost.

(d) **Diminution of Life**

It has been highlighted above that depreciation is based on allocation of cost and, hence, it may occur even when the value of the asset rises due to rise in prices. G. O. May identifies **depreciation as *diminution of the life* of the asset.** It is a different concept which is based on the process that a cost proportional to the expired life of the asset is charged against the revenue earned during each of the consecutive accounting periods, i.e., cost of the asset proportionate to its expired life is charged against the revenues earned. Practically, the concept is also similar to the concept of allocation of expired cost.

(e) **Maintenance of Capital**

Depreciation is frequently regarded as a means of maintenance of nominal capital which is invested in a fixed asset. Depreciation which is charged against revenues earned allows for the recovery of the entire historical cost of a fixed asset which is expired gradually over a number of years as a result of its use. In other words, the amount of capital which is invested for acquiring fixed assets and those which are consumed gradually in order to earn revenue for a number of years is again received back.

This is nothing but the maintenance of nominal capital invested in fixed assets. And, as such, it may be said that provision for depreciation on fixed assets on the basis of historical cost actually helps to maintain intact the nominal capital. But this method fails to maintain the real capital value of the assets if the price level rises and consequently identical fixed assets cannot be acquired with the same nominal capital which is created by the said provision for depreciation. Moreover, charging periodical depreciation on the basis of historical cost helps to maintain at least the nominal capital of the asset intact. But during the period of inflation, the maintenance of nominal capital does not indicate the maintenance of real capital since there will be an erosion in the purchasing power of money and, consequently, there will be an erosion of real capital. Therefore, when there is a fall in the purchasing power of money or prices rise as a result of inflation, the maintenance of real capital through the process of provision for depreciation on the basis of historical cost should not be considered for the purpose of maintaining the real capital. On the contrary, the higher current replacement cost for the same may be taken into consideration from one period to another. The depreciation of a particular period must be adjusted with the replacement cost and prevalent price level. If, however, there is a constant rise in price due to inflation—the total adjusted depreciation so calculated will fail to be equal to the total replacement cost of an identical fixed asset which is to be replaced in place of the existing asset at the end of its working life. Hence the adjusted depreciation should be further readjusted again for the purpose of replacement against the constant rise in price.

(f) Sources of Fund for Working Capital, or, Is Depreciation a Source of Fund?

Sometimes **depreciation is considered as a source of fund or a source of working capital.** It has been stated above that depreciation is an expense as expired cost. Like other business expenses, depreciation is charged against gross revenue of the period in which cost for fixed assets degenerates into expenses as expired cost. Nevertheless, an altogether different situation is believed to arise from charging depreciation to gross revenue as expenses as against the effect of charging other business expenses to the asset. This difference may be ascribed to the fact that whereas other business expenses are cash-consuming, depreciation—as business expense—is of non-cash variety. There is no inflow of cash or other liquid assets in respect of imputed expenses of depreciation. As a result, whereas charging of other business expenses to gross revenue goes to compensate the loss of cash that is spent in total by way of incurring these expenses but, apparently, it is not so in case of non-cash consuming expense as involved in charging depreciation to gross revenue. Here, the supposed loss of a portion of fixed assets—although not caused by any physical transfer of the same—is attained to be compensated or replaced by holding back an equivalent quantity of liquid resources out of gross revenue. As a result, there is an increase of fund, although the so-called cost of fixed assets actually stands exactly where it did in the past. This difference in consequence of charging depreciation to gross revenue on one hand and other business expenses is believed to be the process by which depreciation may serve as a source of working capital.

(g) Decline in Service Potential

The American Accounting Association Committee on Concepts and Standards defines depreciation as : **"any decline in the service potential of plant and other long term assets should be recognised in the account in periods in which such decline occurs ... . The service potential of assets may decline because of ... gradual or economic deterioration because of obsolescence or change in consumer demand."**[1]. According to this definition, the initial cost of an asset is assumed to represent the value of a storehouse of services that can be released over the life of the asset. Whenever a portion of these services expires through use or other causes, the quantity of service potential declines; and a portion of the cost of the asset should be transferred to an expense, another asset, or a loss account. This definition is a static concept since it is based on an allocation of cost to each quantity of potential service of the asset.

However, this definition is less static than the definition made by FASB (Financial Accounting Standard Board), since the latter recognises that the loss of service potential may be irregular and may be subject to many factors which cannot be foreseen when the asset is purchased. It assumes that the conditions anticipated at the time of purchase will continue without material change throughout the period of the asset.

According to the AAA Committee on Accounting Concepts and Standards—Long-lived assets also defined the term as an expiration of service potential of the asset. The Committee further stated that **depreciation must be based on the current cost of restoring the service potential consumed during the period.**[2] No doubt this definition is based on decline in the value of the asset.

Causes of Depreciation

The main causes of depreciation are:

(i) **Physical deterioration** (i.e., wear and tear); (ii) **Economic factors;** (iii) **Passage** (Effluxion) of **time** (i.e., time factors); and (iv) **Depletion** (i.e., exhaustion).

1 AAA Committee on Accounting Concepts and Standards, Accounting and Reporting Standards for Corporate Financial Statements and Preceding Statements and Supplements (AAA, 1957), pp. 4-6

2 Committee on Concepts and Standards—Long-Lived Assets, AAA, *"Accounting for Land, Building and Equipments"*, Supplementary Statement No. 1, Accounting Review 39 (July 1964), p. 696

(ii) *Physical deterioration* : It is caused by—(a) normal wear and tear resulting from use, (b) rust, rot, erosion etc. arising from exposure to wind, rain, sun and other climatic factors, and (c) careless handling of the assets when they are operated. These are known as depreciation by physical deterioration.

(iii) *Economic factors*: These factors prove the use of asset uneconomic although the same may be in good physical condition. These arise due to : (a) **obsolescence**—caused by invention of improved techniques or equipment; decline in demand (by change in customers' preference, taste etc.) for articles producible from the existing plant; (b) **inadequacy**—which refers to the termination of the use of an asset due to increase in the volume of activities.

(iv) *Passage (Effluxion) of time* : There are some fixed assets, e.g., lease, patents, licences, copyright etc. which lose their value simply with the passage of time. Even if such an asset is not used at all, it loses its working capacity over a particular period of time. And, as such, it should be written-off gradually during the entire period of its legal life in order to write it off fully by the end of the life. If any provision is made against this type of asset, the same is termed as provision for amortisation rather than provision for depreciation.

(v) *Depletion:* There are some fixed assets which are wasting in nature and which lose their usefulness due to the extraction of raw materials from them, i.e., they get fully exhausted. They are termed as wasting assets, e.g., mines, quarries, oil-wells etc. Actually, natural resources come under this category. The charge for depletion (provision for depletion) is made on the basis of consumption of the respective assets.

Characteristics of Depreciation

The important characteristics of depreciation are :

(i) Depreciation refers to a permanent/gradual and continuous decrease in the utility value of a fixed asset and it continues till the end of the useful life of the asset.

(ii) Depreciation is a charge against profit (i.e., revenue earned) for a particular accounting period.

(iii) Depreciation is always computed in a systematic and rational manner since it is not a sudden loss.

(iv) Depreciation is a process of allocation of expired cost and not of valuation of fixed assets.

(v) Whatever method for calculating depreciation is followed, the exact amount can never be calculated. It can simply be estimated.

(vi) Depreciation may be physical and functional.

(vii) The fundamental objects of depreciation are : to (a) maintain the nominal capital invested in fixed assets, and (b) allocate the expired portion of the cost of fixed assets against a number of accounting periods.

(viii) Depreciation is a must, i.e., it always takes place whether the asset is carefully handled or neglected, or it is a very costly one, etc.

(ix) If the market value of a fixed asset is fluctuating, the same does not affect the amount of depreciation so made on the respective assets.

(x) Depreciation is calculated in respect of fixed assets only, i.e., Plant and Machinery, Furniture, etc.

Objects of and Necessity for Providing Depreciation

The primary objects of and necessity for providing depreciation of fixed assets are:

(i) The primary object of providing depreciation is to find out the *correct cost of production*. We know when an asset is acquired for the purpose of using it in order to earn revenue, it is gradually consumed. It has already been pointed out earlier that the asset loses its value when it is used and such a decrease in value is like any other expense which must be debited to Profit and Loss Account before arriving at the divisible profits. This consumption of the fixed asset must be provided for every year during the life of the asset through depreciation accounting. In other words, the total cost of fixed assets will be charged against the cost of production or revenues among the accounting periods in which the asset was used. Since all the previous accounting periods took advantage of its use, it is fair that the Profit and Loss Account of these years must also be debited with the amount of such *expense* in order to arrive at the true net profit or loss for the year. Moreover, if depreciation is not provided, profits of the year will be inflated.

(ii) If the amount of depreciation is not provided in the books of account, the value of fixed assets will be shown at a higher value in the Balance Sheet than its real value, i.e., it will be overvalued. As such, this overvaluation of fixed asset *will not represent a true and fair view of the state of affairs* of the concern.

(iii) It has already been highlighted above that the object of providing for depreciation is to keep the *nominal capital* (invested in fixed assets) intact by distributing the loss in its value over a number of years when it is in use. Practically, the provision so made for depreciation of fixed assets help to recover the expired costs of such assets consumed for the purpose of earning revenue for a particular period. As a result of creating such a charge against the revenue by way of provision for depreciation the consumed capital will be recovered and the same will be retained within the business itself. On the contrary, if it is not done, maintenance of nominal capital invested in fixed assets will not be possible and, consequently, there will be a case for liquidation. At the same time, a part of the said capital will be returned to the owners in the form of dividend. This is the way the nominal capital is kept intact when an asset has been used for earning revenue—the reduction in the value of assets by its use has entered into the cost of production as an expense.

(iv) If the amount of depreciation of fixed assets is not provided for from period to period in the books of account, the said assets will be shown at their original costs which is higher than the real value, i.e., they will be shown at overvalued figure in the Balance Sheet. At the same time, a part of the capital had been returned to the shareholders in the form of profit/dividend without making provisions for replacing the capital. As such, the Balance Sheet will not present *a true and fair view of the state of affairs of a firm*. Thus, provision for depreciation should always be made against fixed assets.

(v) According to Sec. 205 of the Companies Act, 1956, provision for depreciation on fixed asset must be made before a company can distribute its profits/dividend. In the case of proprietary concern, it is not necessary to do so. But from a sound financial point of view, it is necessary to do so in order (a) to arrive at the real cost of production, (b) to arrive at true profit, (c) to show the correct state of affairs and to keep the capital intact, and (d) to make proper provision for the replacement of the assets.

Measurement of Depreciation

Measurement of depreciation is not an easy task. On the contrary, it is very difficult to calculate the exact amount of depreciation since they depend on a number of factors. Some of the factors are:

(i) The original cost of asset; (ii) The additions, if any, made to the assets during the year taking into consideration the date on which these additions were made; (iii) The expected amount of interest which could be earned if the sum spent in the acquisition of assets had been invested outside; (iv) The estimated efficiency life of the asset; (v) The scrap, break-up or the residual value of asset; (vi) Obsolescence, i.e., the chance of the asset going out of fashion; (vii) The working hours of the asset concerned; (viii) The repairs and renewals; (ix) The skill of the operators who handle the assets; and (x) The legal provisions (i.e., provision of the Companies Act, the Income Tax Act and others) relating to depreciation.

The above factors should be taken into consideration at the time of determining the amount of depreciation in such a way so as to see that a proper and reasonable estimate can be made against the amount of depreciations. It has already been stated above that the calculation of the exact amount of depreciation is not an easy task.

The same is due to:

(i) Estimation of the working life of the asset becomes practically impossible. Only the probable life of the asset can be estimated on the basis of past experience and on the advice of the technical experts.

(ii) Moreover, proper estimation of the scrap value of the asset in advance also becomes very difficult which will be realised in future.

(iii) Estimation of the risk of obsolescence is also not an easy task, i.e., it is very difficult to make an estimate.

(iv) Finally, it is not so easy to measure the use of the asset.

Consequences—if Depreciation is not provided for

Needless to mention here that if the amount of depreciation is not provided for, neither the Profit and Loss Account nor the Balance Sheet will exhibit the true financial position for the year. Ultimately:

(i) Profit will be overstated, i.e. Profit and Loss Account will show an incorrect amount of profit.

(ii) Value of the concerned asset will also be overstated which results in correction valuation shown in the Balance Sheet.

(iii) There will be a case of erosion of capital since dividend will be paid out of capital on the basis of incorrect determination of profit.

(iv) Periodic expenses which must include depreciation will be understated—that will show an excess profit.

(v) Cost of the production of the article will not be correct if the amount of depreciation is not included with indirect expenses.

(vi) Capital employed will be overstated as nothing is deducted from fixed assets by way of depreciation.

(vii) Violation of Companies Act—which states that a company must provide for depreciation before declaring dividends.

Procedure for Calculating Depreciation

The following procedure should carefully be followed:

(a) **If the specific date of purchase/acquisition of asset is given.**

Under the circumstances, no problem arises regarding the calculation of depreciation. In this case depreciation is to be calculated from the date of acquisition to the closing date of preparing accounts i.e., the end of the year. But special attention may be given when asset is acquired in the middle of a month, say on 20th May, in that case, it is better to ignore the month of May, i.e., from June to December (of course, if the firm uses calendar year) or 7 months. But if the asset is acquired on, say, 8th May in that case, period should be considered from May to December, i.e., 8 months. In short, depreciation should be calculated to the nearest whole month.

(b) **If the specific date of purchase/acquisition of asset is not given.**

Under the circumstances, depreciation should be calculated on an average of 6 months i.e., the mean of opening and closing value of the asset.

Depreciation to be Calculated as per Income-Tax Act, 1961

As per Income-Tax Act, 1961, depreciation of asset is calculated for the whole year irrespective of the date of acquisition i.e., even if the asset is acquired on 1st Dec. depreciation is to be calculated for 12 months.

Now, the different methods of depreciation may be classified as:

Methods of Depreciation

(a) **Methods based on the concept of expired deferred cost:** Under these methods, depreciation is considered as an allocation of expired deferred cost (already stated earlier in the present chapter) and their rates are ascertained either on the basis of time or on the basis of use.

(b) **Methods based on the concept of recovery and maintenance of capital:** Under these methods, depreciation is considered as means of recovering and maintaining capital outlay (which has already been incurred for the purpose of acquiring the fixed assets).

(c) **Special methods:** These methods are used for certain specific assets and they are particularly applicable for solving the problems that may arise in relation to depreciation.

METHODS OF DEPRECIATION

Methods of depreciation may be grouped under the following heads:

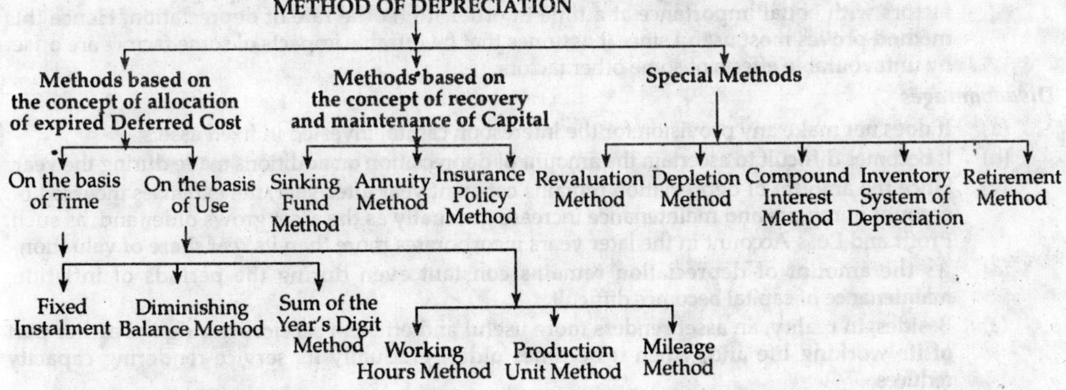

The above methods are discussed:

Fixed Instalment Method

Under this method, a fixed percentage of the original cost of the fixed assets *minus* scrap value is written-off every year till the end of its estimated life by way of depreciation.* That is, the amount charged as depreciation is calculated in the following manner:

* If the amount of depreciation is plotted on a graph it will form a straight line. That is why it is also called Straight Line Method.

Depreciation $\frac{C-S}{L}$, where

C— stands for cost of the fixed assets.

S— stands for the expected scrap value to be realised at the end of its effective life.

L— Estimated working or effective life of the fixed assets.

The amount of depreciation depends on the cost price of the asset, its scrap value and the estimated working life. This method is suitable for those assets whose working life can easily be estimated, i.e., period-based assets, e.g., Patent, or Leashold where the effective life of the asset is measured in a specific duration of time, regardless of the use or consumption of service from the asset.

Example :

A plant was purchased for Rs. 1,00,000 on 1.1.1995 and its estimated scrap value was Rs. 10,000, having an estimated life of 10 years. In that case, the amount of depreciation is calculated as:

$$\text{Depreciation} = \frac{\text{Cost Price of the Asset} - \text{Scrap Value}}{\text{Estimated life of the Asset}}$$

$$= \frac{\text{Rs. } 1,00,000 - \text{Rs. } 10,000}{10}$$

$$= \text{Rs. } 9,000$$

Practically, this method assumes that the benefit derived from—and the cost of expiration of—an asset is uniform throughout its effective life. Depreciation is considered a function of time and, at the same time, a certain or uniform portion of the depreciable cost is allocated to each accounting period. Use, age and efficiency factors are neglected in this case.

Advantages

(a) This method is very simple and easy to calculate.

(b) No cumbersome records of yearly output or usage hours are required, as such, the expiry of calendar period is more easily established than the output made on every depreciable item.

(c) Since longevity of patent or leasehold right etc. depends on the settlement of agreement, almost identical benefits may be derived from these assets throughout their lives. At the same time, as the longevity depends on the period of time, values of these assets gradually decrease with time at a fixed rate. Hence, Straight Line Method may be considered as the appropriate method in these cases.

(d) The life of the assets, their scrap value together with repairs and maintenance cost etc. cannot be accurately measured. As a result, any single method cannot incorporate all the relevant factors with equal importance at a time in order to fix the rate of depreciation. Hence this method proves most useful since it assumes that favourable impacts of some factors are offset by unfavourable effects of some other factors.

Disadvantages

(a) It does not make any provision for the interest on capital invested in fixed assets.

(b) It becomes difficult to ascertain the amount of depreciation on additions made during the year.

(c) Since the amount of depreciation remains constant year after year, the expenses incurred on account of repairs and maintenance increase gradually as the asset grows older and, as such, Profit and Loss Account in the later years incorporates more than its real share of valuation.

(d) As the amount of depreciation remains constant even during the periods of inflation, maintenance of capital becomes difficult.

(e) Besides, in reality, an asset renders more useful and efficient services during the earlier part of its working life and, when it becomes older, gradually its service-rendering capacity reduces.

(f) This method is not recognised by the Income-Tax authorities.

Under *Straight Line Method,* the amount of depreciations can be recorded into the following two methods, viz :

A. Direct Method

Under this method, depreciation is directly charged against the asset i.e., ***no provision for Depreciation Account is maintained.*** The same is done by debiting Depreciation Account and crediting the Asset, and the Depreciation Account is closed by transferring to Profit and Loss Account at the end of the year. Needless to mention here that the Asset Account will be shown at its written-down value, i.e., *cost less* *depreciation* at the end of the year. It is not possible to find out the total amount of depreciation and the cost prices of the asset under this method.

> ***To Sum up***
>
> ***The entries under this method will be***
>
> ***(i) For the amount of depreciation to be provided at the end of the year***
>
> ***Depreciation A/c Dr.***
> ***To Asset A/c*** } ***With the amount of depreciation***
>
> ***(ii) For transferring the amount of depreciation at the end of the year***
>
> ***Profit and Loss A/c Dr.***
> ***To Depreciation A/c*** } **With the amount of depreciation transferred**

Illustration 1

On 1.1.2010, a Plant was purchased for Rs. 1,00,000, installation expenses being Rs. 10,000. Its scrap value will be Rs. 10,000. Estimated life of the Plant was 10 years.

Find out the amount of depreciation under Straight Line Method and show the entries, Plant Account up to 31st Dec. 2011.

Show also the Depreciation Account, Profit and Loss Account and the Balance Sheet.

Annual Depreciation = Cost Price of the Asset – Scrap Value/Estimated life of the asset
= (Rs. 1,00,000 + Rs. 10,000) – Rs. 10,000/10
= Rs. 10,000

Solution

In the Books of ...
Journal

Date	*Particulars*		*L.F.*	*V.N.*	*Debit*	*Credit*
					Rs.	Rs.
2010 Jan. 1	Plant A/c	Dr.			1,10,000	
	To Bank A/c					1,10,000
	(Purchased a plant for Cash Rs. 1,00,000, Installation expenses being Rs. 10,000)					
Dec. 31	Depreciation A/c	Dr.			10,000	
	To Plant A/c					10,000
	(Depreciation on Plant charged)					
"	Profit and Loss A/c	Dr.			10,000	
	To Depreciation A/c					10,000
	(Depreciation transferred to Profit and Loss Account)					
2011 Dec. 31	Depreciation A/c	Dr.			10,000	
	To Plant A/c					10,000
	(Depreciation on Plant charged)					
"	Profit and Loss A/c	Dr.			10,000	
	To Depreciation A/c					10,000
	(Depreciation transferred to Profit and Loss A/c)					

In the Books of ...
Plant Account

Dr. Cr.

Date	*Particulars*	*Amount*	*Date*	*Particulars*	*Amount*
2010		Rs.	2010		Rs.
Jan. 1	To Bank A/c	1,00,000	Dec. 31	By Depreciation A/c	10,000
	" Bank A/c (–) Installation expenses	10,000		" Balance c/d	1,00,000
		1,10,000			1,10,000
2011			2011		
Jan. 1	To Balance b/d	1,00,000	Dec. 31	By Depreciation A/c	10,000
				" Balance c/d	90,000
		1,00,000			1,00,000

Depreciation Account

Dr. Cr.

Date	Particulars	Amount	Date	Particulars	Amount
2010		Rs.	2010		Rs.
Dec. 31	To Plant A/c	10,000	Dec. 31	By Profit and Loss A/c —Transferred	10,000
		10,000			10,000
2011			2011		
Dec. 31	To Plant A/c	10,000	Dec. 31	By Profit and Loss A/c —Transferred	10,000
		10,000			10,000

Profit and Loss Account (Extract) *for the year ended 31st December 2010*

Dr. Cr.

Date	Particulars	Amount	Date	Particulars	Amount
		Rs.			Rs.
	To Depreciation on Plant A/c	10,000			

Profit and Loss Account (Extract) *for the year ended 31st December 2011*

Dr. Cr.

Date	Particulars	Amount	Date	Particulars	Amount
		Rs.			Rs.
	To Depreciation on Plant A/c	10,000			

Balance Sheet (Extract) *as at 31st December 2010*

Liabilities	Rs.	Assets	Rs.	Rs.
		Plant	1,00,000	
		Less : Depreciation	10,000	
				1,00,000

Balance Sheet (Extract) *as at 31st December 2011*

Liabilities	Rs.	Assets	Rs.	Rs.
		Plant	1,10,000	
		Less : Depreciation	10,000	
				90,000

B. Indirect Method

Under this method, amount of depreciation is not charged to Asset Account like Direct Method. On the contrary, the amount of depreciation is debited to Depreciation Account and credited to *Provision for Depreciation Account* or *Accumulated Depreciation Account*, and not the Asset Account like earlier method viz, *where no Provision for Depreciation Account is maintained*. Accordingly, the amount of depreciation is transferred to Profit and Loss account of the end of the year, but the Asset Account will appear at cost and the accumulated depreciation is either shown as a deduction from the asset or the same may be shown as a liability in the liabilities side of the Balance Sheet. Needless to mention here that, under this method, the original cost of the asset can be known and the total amount of depreciation (up-to-date) can also be known from the Provision for Depreciation Account or Accumulated Depreciation Account so maintained as the balance of accumulated depreciation account gradually increases year after year. When the useful life of the asset is over, the provision for Depreciation Account is debited and Asset Account is credited; if any balance is left in the Asset Account, the same is transferred to the Profit and Loss Account in that year.

To Sum up

The entries under this method will be

(i) For the amount of depreciation to be provided at the end of the year

Depreciation A/c **Dr.** *To Provision for Depreciation A/c* *or, Accumulated Depreciation A/c*	*With the amount of depreciation*

(ii) For transferring the amount of depreciation at the end of the year		
Profit and Loss A/c ***Dr.***	}	***With the amount of depreciation***
To Depreciation A/c		***transferred***

Illustration 2

Consider the pervious Illustration No. 1 and show the entries, Plant Account, Depreciation Account, Provisions for Depreciation Account, Profit and Loss Account? and the Balance Sheet assuming that Provision for Depreciation Account is maintained.

Solution

In the Books of ...
Journal

Date	*Particulars*	*L.F.*	*V.N.*	*Debit*	*Credit*
2010				Rs.	Rs.
Jan. 1	Plant A/c Dr.			1,10,000	
	To Bank A/c				1,10,000
	(Purchased a plant for cash Rs.1,00,000, installation expenses being Rs. 10,000)				
Dec. 31	Depreciation A/c Dr.			10,000	
	To Provision for Depreciation A/c				10,000
	(Amount of depreciation provided for)				
"	Profit and Loss A/c Dr.			10,000	
	To Depreciation A/c				10,000
	(Amount of depreciation transferred to Profit and Loss A/c)				
2011	Depreciation A/c Dr.			10,000	
Dec. 31	To Provision for Depreciation A/c				10,000
	(Amount of depreciation provided for)				
"	Profit and Loss A/c Dr.			10,000	
	To Depreciation A/c				10,000
	(Amount of depreciation transferred to Profit and Loss A/c)				

Plant Account

Dr. Cr.

Date	*Particulars*	*Amount*	*Date*	*Particulars*	*Amount*
2010		Rs.	2010		Rs.
Jan. 1	To Bank A/c	1,10,000	Dec. 31	By Balance c/d	1,10,000
		1,10,000			1,10,000
2011			2011		
Jan. 1	To Balance b/d	1,10,000	Dec. 31	By Balance c/d	1,10,000
		1,10,000			1,10,000
2012					
Jan. 1	To Balance b/d	1,10,000			

Depreciation Account

Dr. Cr.

Date	*Particulars*	*Amount*	*Date*	*Particulars*	*Amount*
2010		Rs.	2010		Rs.
Dec. 31	To Provision for Depreciation A/c	10,000	Dec. 31	By Profit and Loss A/c —Transfer	10,000
		10,000			10,000
2011		Rs.	2011		Rs.
Dec. 31	To Provision for Depreciation A/c	10,000	Dec. 31	By Profit and Loss A/c —Transfer	10,000
		10,000			10,000

Provision for Depreciation Account

Dr.					Cr.
Date	Particulars	Amount	Date	Particulars	Amount
2010		Rs.	2010		Rs.
Dec. 31	To Balance c/d	10,000	Dec. 31	By Depreciation A/c	10,000
		10,000			10,000
2011			2011		
Dec. 31	To Balance c/d	20,000	Dec. 31	By Balance b/d	10,000
				" Depreciation A/c	10,000
		20,000			20,000
			2012		
			Jan. 1	To Balance b/d	20,000

Profit and Loss Account (Extract) *for the year ended 31st December 2010*

Dr.					Cr.
Date	Particulars	Amount	Date	Particulars	Amount
		Rs.			Rs.
	To Depreciation A/c	10,000		By	

Profit and Loss Account (Extract) *for the year ended 31st December 2011*

Dr.					Cr.
Date	Particulars	Amount	Date	Particulars	Amount
		Rs.			Rs.
	To Depreciation A/c	10,000		By	

Balance Sheet (Extract) *as at 31st December 2010*

Liabilities	Rs.	Assets	Rs.	Rs.
		Plant	1,10,000	
		Less : Prov. for Depreciation A/c	10,000*	
				1,00,000

* This may also be written on the liabilities side of the Balance Sheet.

Balance Sheet (Extract) *as at 31st December 2011*

Liabilities	Rs.	Assets	Rs.	Rs.
		Plant	1,10,000	
		Less : Prov. for Depreciation A/c	20,000	
				90,000

When Provision for Depreciation Account is maintained

Illustration 3

A plant, which originally costs and stands in the books on 1.1.2012 at Rs. 20,000, is sold for Rs. 12,000 on 30.6.2012. Rs. 7,500 was set aside by the firm by way of depreciation of the plant up to 31.12.1012. On 1.10.2012, a new plant is purchased for Rs. 25,000.

Show journal entries and ledger accounts assuming that the business closes its accounts on 31st December every year and provides for depreciation @ 10% on original cost.

Solution

In the Books of ...
Journal

Date	Particulars		Debit	Credit
2012			Rs.	Rs.
Jan. 1	Bank A/c	Dr.	12,000	
	To Plant A/c			12,000
	(Sale proceeds of old plant)			

Contd.

Date	Particulars		Dr. (Rs.)	Cr. (Rs.)
2012			Rs.	Rs.
June 30	Depreciation A/c	Dr.	1,000	
	To Provision for Depreciation A/c			1,000
	(Depreciation @ 10% on Plant sold up to 30th June)			
"	Provision for Depreciation A/c		8,500	
	To Plant A/c			8,500
	(Provision for Depreciation transferred)			
"	Plant A/c	Dr.	500	
	To Profit on Sale of Plant A/c			500
	(Profit made on Sale of Plant) i.e.,			
	(20,000 – 8,500 = 11,500 and 12,000 – 11,500 = 500)			
Oct. 1	Plant A/c	Dr.	25,000	
	To Bank A/c			25,000
	(New Plant purchased)			
Dec. 31	Depreciation A/c	Dr.	625	
	To Provision for Depreciation A/c			625
	(Depreciation provided on new plant for 3 months @ 10%)			
"	Profit and Loss A/c	Dr.	1,625	
	To Depreciation A/c			1,625
	(Depreciation transferred to P & L A/c)			
	Profit on Sale of Plant A/c	Dr.	500	
	To Profit and Loss A/c			500
	(Profit on sale transferred)			

Plant Account

Dr. Cr.

Date	*Particulars*	*Amount*	*Date*	*Particulars*	*Amount*
2012		Rs.	2012		Rs.
Jan. 1	To Balance b/d	20,000	June 30	By Bank A/c – Sale of Plant	12,000
June 30	" Profit on Sale on Plant A/c	500		" Prov. for Depreciation A/c	8,500
Oct. 1	" Bank A/c — Purchase	25,000	Dec. 31	" Balance c/d	25,000
		45,500			45,500
2013					
Jan. 1	To Balance b/d	25,000			

Provision for Depreciation Account

Dr. Cr.

Date	*Particulars*	*Amount*	*Date*	*Particulars*	*Amount*
2012		Rs.	2012		Rs.
June 30	To Plant A/c — Transfer	8,500	Jan. 1	By Balance b/d	7,500
Dec. 31	" Balance c/d	625	June 30	" Depreciation A/c	1,000
			Dec. 31	" Depreciation A/c	625
		9,125			9,125
			2013		
			Jan. 1	By Balance	625

Depreciation Account

Dr. Cr.

Date	*Particulars*	*Amount*	*Date*	*Particulars*	*Amount*
2012		Rs.	2012		Rs.
June 30	To Provision for Dep. A/c	1,000	Dec. 31	By Profit and Loss A/c —Transfer	
Dec. 31	" Prov. for Dep. A/c	625			1,625
		1,625			1,625

Diminishing Balance Method or Accelerated Depreciation Method

Under this method, a fixed percentage is written-off every year on the written-down value of the asset till the amount is reduced to its scrap value. Depreciation, under this method, is gradually diminished or decreased, i.e., depreciation is calculated at a fixed percentage on *reduced balance of the asset brought forward from the previous year*. As such, amount of depreciation becomes higher at the earlier periods and becomes gradually lower in the subsequent periods when repairs and maintenance charges increase gradually. This method is found suitable for Plant and Machinery, Furniture and Fixture, i.e., on those assets which have a longer life and which is difficult to estimate. However, this written-down value is calculated with the help of the following formula:

$$W = C\left(1 - \frac{r}{100}\right)^n$$

where, W, stands for written-down value;
C, the original cost;
r, the rate of Depreciation, and
n, the number of years' effective life.

For example, if the original cost of the asset is Rs. 1,00,000 the rate of depreciation is @ 10% and its effective life is 10 years, the written-down value of this asset will be :

$$W = C\left(1 - \frac{r}{100}\right)^n$$

$$= \text{Rs. } 1{,}00{,}000\left(1 - \frac{10}{100}\right)^{10}$$

$$= \text{Rs. } 387.42$$

Similarly, for the computation of the rate of depreciation the following formula may be applied :

$$D = 1 - \sqrt[n]{\frac{S}{C}}$$

where, D, the Depreciation;
n, number of years' effective life;
S, the Scrap value;
C, the Cost Price.

For example, if the Cost Price of an asset is Rs. 1,00,000, its scrap value is Rs. 20,000 and its effective life is 10 years, the rate of depreciation is calculated as :

$$D = 1 - \sqrt[n]{\frac{S}{C}}$$

$$= 1 - \sqrt[10]{\frac{\text{Rs. } 20{,}000}{\text{Rs. } 1{,}00{,}000}}$$

$$= \text{Rs. } 0.5528$$

Now, to sum up, the whole principle for calculating the amount of depreciation under Reducing Balance Method is outlined below with the help of the following example :
Let us suppose,

The cost price of a plant is Rs. 1,00,000, its rate of depreciation is @ 20%, its scrap value is Rs. 10,000, and effective life is 5 years.

Year	Cost Price/Written-down Value at the beginning of the year	Depreciation		Accumulated Depreciation	Written-down Value at the closing
	Rs.	Rs.		Rs.	Rs.
I	1,00,000	Rs. 1,00,000 $\frac{20}{100}$ =	20,000	20,000	80,000
II	80,000	Rs. 80,000 $\frac{20}{100}$ =	16,000	36,000	64,000
III	64,000	Rs. 1,64,000 $\frac{20}{100}$ =	12,800	48,800	51,200

IV	51,200	Rs. 51,200 $\frac{20}{100}$ =	10,240	59,040	40,960
V	40,960	Rs. 40,960 $\frac{20}{100}$ =	8,192	67,232	32,768

From the table presented above, it becomes clear that the Written-Down Value (WDV) of the plant at the end of its effective life is Rs. 32,768. Since its scrap value is only Rs. 10,000, loss on sale of plant will be Rs. 22,768 (i.e., Rs., 32,768 – Rs. 10,000).

This method, practically, recognises a broader view of the cost of the service of the asset as it relates to the amount of service provided each year.

Advantages

(a) The amount of depreciation decreases continuously with the gradual decrease in service potential of assets.

(b) We know that the earlier period of the working life of the asset would benefit more than that in the later periods, and, as such, the method of depreciation should reflect this trend. The same is possible under this method as it provides a large portion of the cost of the assets as an expense (by way of depreciation) in the earlier periods than in the later years.

(c) When additions are made to the assets, fresh calculations of depreciation are not necessary.

(d) This method is recognised by the Income-Tax authorities.

(e) Elimination of a major portion of cost in earlier years also minimises the impact of obsolescence.

Disadvantages

(a) It takes a very long time to reduce the asset to its scrap value until and unless the rate of depreciation is very high.

(b) It does not help to ascertain properly the cost of goods manufactured since the cost of production per unit of goods manufactured will be reduced as a result of reduced amount of depreciation.

(c) Calculation of depreciation is somewhat time-consuming. Moreover, it is impossible to reduce the book value to zero by continually applying a constant rate to the Written-down Value.

(d) This method puts too much emphasis on the historical cost.

Differences between Straight Line Method and Diminishing Balance Method

As per Straight Line Method, the Written-down Value of the asset over its useful life becomes nil, but under Diminishing Balance Method, there must have been some Written-down Value over its useful life since amount of depreciation gradually decreases year after year.

However, the points of distinction between the two are:

Straight Line Method	Diminishing Balance Method
1. Under this method amount of depreciation remains fixed year after year which is written-off.	1. Under this method amount of depreciation varies from year to year since it is calculated on Written-down Value.
2. Depreciation is calculated on the original cost of the asset.	2. Depreciation is calculated on the Written-down Value of the assets.
3. The Written-down Value of the asset over its useful life becomes nil since equal amount of depreciation is written-off for a fixed period.	3. The Written-down Value of the asset can never be nil over its useful life.
4. The effect of depreciation on profit remains same year after year since the amount is fixed.	4. The effect of depreciation on profit varies from year to year since the amount is variable.
5. In case of addition to assets, depreciation is calculated separately.	5. In case of addition, depreciation is not separately calculated since it is computed on total Written-down Value of the assets.
6. This method is mostly suitable for less costly assets, e.g., Furniture and Fixture, and which depreciates due to effluxion of time e.g., Patent, Trademarks, etc.	6. This method is suitable for costly assets viz., Plant and Machinery.
7. Usually a lower rate of percentage is to be taken into consideration for calculating the amount of depreciation.	7. Usually a higher rate of depreciation is taken into consideration since it is calculated on WDV.

Illustration 4

On 1.1.2008 a machine was purchased for Rs. 1,00,000. On 30.9.2010, a new machine was purchased for Rs. 20,000, installation expenses being Rs. 5,000.

Show the Machinery Account up to 31st Dec. 2011, assuming that the rate of depreciation was 10% on Reducing Balance Method.

Solution

In the Books of ...
Machinery Account

Dr. *Cr.*

Date	Particulars	Amount	Date	Particulars	Amount
2008		Rs.	2008		Rs.
Jan. 1	To Bank A/c	1,00,000	Dec. 31	By Depreciation A/c	10,000
			"	Balance c/d	90,000
		1,00,000			1,00,000
2009			2009		
Jan. 1	To Balance b/d	90,000	Dec. 31	By Depreciation A/c	9,000
			"	Balance c/d	81,000
		90,000			90,000
2010			2010		
Jan. 1	To Balance b/d	81,000	Dec. 31	By Depreciation A/c (8,100 + 625)	8,725
Sept. 30	" Bank A/c	20,000	"	Balance c/d	97,275
	" Bank A/c Installation Expenses	5,000			
		1,06,000			1,06,000
2011			2011		
Jan. 1	To Balance b/d	97,275	Dec. 31	By Depreciation A/c	9,728
			"	Balance c/d	87,547
2012		97,275			97,275
Jan. 1	To Balance b/d	87,547			

Sum of the Year's Digit Method ["Rule of 78"]

It is a variant of the Diminishing Balance Method. In this method also, amount of depreciation reduces constantly. It is applied to fairly long-living assets. Unlike the Reducing/Diminishing Balance Method, a constantly decreasing rate is applied on the original cost of the asset minus salvage value, if any. As such, the original book value will be zero as in Straight Line Method. The amount/rate of depreciation can easily be calculated.

It sums up the years in an asset's life span to be used as denominator and reverses the individual year numbers to be used as numerator. For example, if the cost price, salvage value and the estimated life of an asset are Rs. 90,000, Rs. 6,000 and 6 years, respectively, the denominator will be: 1 + 2 + 3 + 4 + 5 + 6 = 21. The numerators for the first to sixth year will be: 6, 5, 4, 3, 2, and 1, respectively. Here, the depreciable cost becomes Rs. 84,000 (Rs. 90,000 – 6,000).

The above principle can be illustrated with the help of the following table:

Year	Opening Book Value	Depreciable Cost	Rate	Depreciation Charge	Total Depreciation	Closing Book Value
	Rs.	Rs.		Rs.	Rs.	Rs.
1	90,000	84,000	$\frac{6}{21}$	24,000	24,000	66,000
2	66,000	84,000	$\frac{5}{21}$	20,000	44,000	46,000
3	46,000	84,000	$\frac{4}{21}$	16,000	60,000	30,000
4	30,000	84,000	$\frac{3}{21}$	12,000	72,000	18,000

Contd.

5	18,000	84,000	$\frac{2}{21}$	8,000	80,000	10,000
6	10,000	84,000	$\frac{1}{21}$	4,000	84,000	6,000

Sum of the year's digit can be computed with the help of the following formula:

$$S = \frac{n(n+1)}{2} \quad \text{where, } S = \text{Sum of years}$$

n = Number of years

or, the depreciation can also be computed by the following formula:

$$\textit{Depreciation} = \frac{\textit{No. of years of the remaining Life of the Asset}}{\textit{Total of the digits}} \times \textit{Amount to be written-off}$$

(Cost Price – Salvage Value)

To Sum up

This method is known as "Rule of 78" as the same is based on the sum of the digits 1 to 12. If it is used as a monthly basis and as there are 12 months in a year, the sum total of the months will be 78 (i.e., 1 + 2 + 3 + 4 ... + 12), of course if 1 is assigned to January, 2 for February, and so on.

Working Hours Method

Under this method, the life of the asset is estimated in terms of working hours and depreciation is charged on the basis of hours worked, i.e., the machine is used in terms of hours worked during the year.

Hourly rate is calculated on the basis of the following formula:

$$\textit{Hourly Rate} = \frac{\textit{Cost Price of the Asset} - \textit{Scrap Value}}{\textit{Estimated total number of hours of asset}}$$

$$\textit{Depreciation} = \textit{Total number of working hours used} \times \textit{Hourly Rate}$$

No doubt this method proves the best where it is possible to ascertain the estimated life of the asset in terms of working hours. At the same time, this method is also based on the sound principle of correct computation of depreciation on the basis of actual use.

But even this method is not free from snags for:

(i) It is not very easy to ascertain the estimated working hours of the asset, and (ii) the method of calculating the estimated working hours during a particular period is time-consuming and expensive.

Production Unit Method

Under this method, the total life of an asset is estimated in terms of the total number of units of goods which are expected to be manufactured by the machine till it becomes a scrap. The rate of depreciation per unit of goods manufactured is determined and the amount of depreciation is calculated on the basis of the rate multiplied by the number of units of goods for a particular period. Hence

$$\textit{Depreciation} = \frac{(\text{Cost Price} - \text{Scrap Value}) \times \text{No. of units of goods manufactured for a period}}{\text{Total number of units of goods expected to be manufactured during the entire life of the asset}}$$

This method is also not free from snags. Because, under this system, it is very difficult to ascertain the estimated total number of units of goods to be manufactured during the entire life of the asset.

Mileage Method

This method is particularly applicable to those assets the use of which can be measured in terms of miles (or, kilometres) and not in terms of time, e.g., a car, a bus, a motorcycle etc. The rate of depreciation per mile/kilometres run is determined and the amount of depreciation is calculated on the basis of the rate multiplied by the working distance covered by the vehicle for the period.

$$\textit{Hence, Depreciation} = \frac{(\text{Cost Price} - \text{Scrap Value}) \times \text{Miles or kms run for a period}}{\text{Total miles or kms expected to be run by a vehicle during the entire life of the asset}}$$

Sinking Fund Method

This method is also known as Depreciation Fund, Amortisation or Redemption Fund Method. Under this method, a certain amount is written-off every year by debiting Profit and Loss Account and crediting Depreciation/Sinking Fund Account during the estimated life of the asset The amount of depreciation is calculated on the basis of the depreciation fund table. The amount of depreciation is calculated in such a way that it will produce an equal amount—e.g., scrap value—if invested in outside securities every year with compound interest. When the life of the asset has expired the investments are sold in the market and the proceeds are utilised for the purpose of replacing by a new asset.

Amount of depreciation may be calculated with the help of the following:

$$\text{Depreciation} = \frac{1}{\frac{(1+r)^{n-1}}{r}}$$ where r stands for rate of interest, and n stands for number of years.

Sinking Fund Table

[Periodic deposit which will amount to Re. 1]

$$\left[\frac{1}{(1+i)^{n-1}}\right]$$

N	1%	2%	2.5%	3%	4%	5%	6%
1	1.0000	1.0000	1.0000	1.0000	1.0000	1.0000	1.0000
2	.4975	.4951	.4938	.4926	.4902	.4878	.4854
3	.3300	.3268	.3251	.3235	.3203	.3172	.3144
4	.2463	.2426	.2408	.2390	.2355	.2320	.2286
5	.1960	.1922	.1902	.1884	.1846	.1810	.1174
6	.1625	.1585	.1666	.1546	.1508	.1470	.1434
7	.1386	.1345	.1325	.1305	.1266	.1228	.1191
8	.1207	.1165	.1145	.1125	.1085	.1047	.1010
9	.1067	.1025	.1005	.0984	.0945	.0907	.0870
10	.0956	.0913	.0893	.0872	.0833	.0795	.0759
15	.0621	.0578	.0558	.0538	.0499	.0463	.0430
20	.0454	.0412	.0391	.0372	.0336	.0302	.0272
25	.0354	.0312	.0293	.0274	.0240	.0219	.0182

Advantages

(a) The primary advantage of this method is that a fund is created during the working life of an asset, which is equal to the depreciated value (Cost Price *minus* Scrap Value) of the same at the end of its effective life. Since the amount of depreciation is kept aside and invested in readily marketable securities, they are easily saleable, the process being utilised for the purpose of replacement of asset, i.e., ready cash is made available.

(b) Another advantage is that one can know at any time the original value of the asset since it is always shown in the Balance Sheet.

(c) One can also know the exact amount written-off in any year by comparing the Depreciation Fund Account for different years.

(d) This method is also useful if the asset is to be replaced when it becomes a scrap.

Disadvantages

(a) One cannot know whether the investment will be sold for a price which will be sufficient to replace the asset or not.

(b) The amount which is invested in securities is withdrawn for the business and, as such, working capital is reduced.

Accounting Entries

(a) ***At the end of 1st year***

For Annual Depreciation

(i) Depreciation A/c Dr.

To Sinking Fund A/c

(ii) Profit and Loss A/c Dr.

To Depreciation A/c

or, Direct Entry:
Profit and Loss A/c Dr.
To Sinking Fund A/c

(b) *For the Investment of Annual Depreciation*
Sinking Fund Investment A/c Dr.
To Bank A/c

At the Subsequent Years

(a) *For the Receipt of Interest of Sinking Fund Investment*
Bank A/c Dr.
To Interest on Investment A/c

(b) *For Transfer of Interest*
Interest on Investment A/c Dr.
To Sinking Fund A/c
or, Bank A/c Dr.
To Sinking Fund A/c

(c) *For Annual Depreciation*
Profit and Loss A/c Dr.
To Sinking Fund A/c

(d) *For the Investment of Annual Depreciation*
Sinking Fund Investment A/c Dr.
To Bank A/c (including interest)

Note: In the last year, of course, the entry (d) is not necessary since question of investment will not arise.

At the end of the Asset's life

(a) *For Sale of Investment*
Bank A/c Dr.
To Sinking Fund Investment A/c

(b) *For Transfer of Profit on Sale on Investment*
Sinking Fund Investment A/c Dr.
To Sinking Fund A/c
(in case of loss, the entry will be reserved)

(c) *For Sale of Old Asset as Scrap*
Bank A/c Dr.
To (Old) Asset A/c

(d) *For Transfer of Sinking Fund Account*
Sinking Fund A/c Dr.
To Asset A/c

Illustration 5

On 1.1.2005, a company purchased a machinery at a cost of Rs. 1,00,000. The machinery is expected to run for 5 years at the end of which the estimated scrap value is Rs. 25,000. In order to provide sufficient fund for the replacement of the machinery at the end of its life, it is decided to create a Sinking Fund and to invest the amount in gilt-edged securities yielding 4% interest. On 31.12.2009, the Machinery is sold-off as scrap for Rs. 15,000. On the same date investments are sold at Rs. 65,000. A Machinery is purchased on the following day for Rs. 90,000.

Show the Sinking Account, Sinking Fund Investment Account.

(Re. 0.1846 at 4% will yield Re. 1 in 5 years)

Solution

Sum Required	Annual Instalment
1	0.1846
(Rs. 1,00,000 – Rs. 25,000) = Rs. 75,000	$0.1846 \times \frac{75,000}{1}$ = Rs. 13,845

In the Books of ...

Sinking Fund Account

Dr. Cr.

Date	Particulars	Amount	Date	Particulars	Amount
2005		Rs.	2005		Rs.
Dec. 31	To Balance c/d	13,845	Dec. 31	By Profit and Loss A/c	13,845
		13,845			13,845
2006			2006		
Dec. 31	To Balance c/d	28,244	Jan. 1	By Balance b/d	13,845
				" Bank Interest	554
			Dec. 31	" Profit and Loss A/c	13,845
		28,244			28,244
2007			2007		
Dec. 31	To Balance c/d	43,219	Jan. 1	By Balance b/d	28,244
				" Bank Interest	1,130
			Dec. 31	" Profit and Loss A/c	13,845
		43,219			43,219
2008			2008		
Dec. 31	To Balance c/d	58,793	Jan. 1	By Balance b/d	43,219
				" Bank Interest	1,729
			Dec. 31	" Profit and Loss A/c	13,845
		58,793			58,793
2009			2009		
Dec. 31	To Machinery A/c (transfer)	81,197	Jan. 1	By Balance b/d	58,793
				" Bank Interest	2,352
			Dec. 31	" Profit and Loss A/c	13,845
				" Sinking Fund Investments	6,207
		81,197			81,197

Sinking Fund Investment Account

Dr. Cr.

Date	Particulars	Amount	Date	Particulars	Amount
2005		Rs.	2005		Rs.
Dec. 31	To Bank A/c	13,845	Dec. 31	By Balance c/d	13,845
		13,845			13,845
2006			2006		
Jan. 1	To Balance b/d	13,845	Dec. 31	By Balance c/d	28,244
Dec. 31	" Bank (554 + 13,845)	14,399			
		28,244			28,244
2007			2007		
Jan. 1	To Balance b/d	28,244	Dec. 31	By Balance c/d	43,219
Dec. 31	" Bank (1,130 + 13,845)	14,975			
		43,219			43,219
2008			2008		
Jan. 1	To Balance b/d	43,219	Dec. 31	By Balance c/d	58,793
Dec. 31	" Bank (1,729 + 13,845)	15,574			
		58,793			58,793
2009			2009		
Jan. 1	To Balance b/d	58,793	Dec. 31	By Bank A/c (Sale of Investment)	65,000
Dec. 31	" Sinking Fund A/c *(Profit on sale—bal. fig.)*	6,207			
		65,000			65,000

Annuity Method

Under this method, the money invested in the purchase of assets earns interest at a fixed rate which is debited to the asset account at reduced value and a fixed amount of depreciation is charged every year for the estimated life of the asset which is calculated as per Annuity Table and which, ultimately, will be reduced to its residual value or nil. The amount of depreciation remains constant but the interest will be gradually lesser. This method is found suitable where a large amount of money is invested for the acquisition of the asset and where the life of the asset is definite, i.e., lease. This method incorporates the interest lost on the capital which is invested and blocked in an asset and, thus, the said loss is already included with the cost of the asset by debiting the same in the asset account every year. As a result, the total amount of depreciation becomes higher than the original cost of the asset. Because, the total amount of depreciation includes not only the original cost of the asset but also the interest.

According to this method, the fund or money is left in the business for internal use and not invested in outside securities like Sinking Fund System. It is to be noted that the amount of depreciation remains constant but the amount of interest changes, i.e., it becomes gradually lesser.

Annuity Table

[Periodic payment required to amortise Re. 1 and interest]

$$\left[\frac{i}{1-\frac{1}{(1+1)^n}}\right]$$

Period—Years	3%	4%	5%	6%
1	1.0300	1.0400	1.0500	1.0600
2	.5226	.5302	.5378	.5454
3	.3535	.3603	.3672	.3741
4	.2690	.2755	.2820	.2885
5	.2184	.2246	.2310	.2374
6	.1846	.1908	.1907	.2034
7	.1605	.1666	.1728	.1791
8	.1425	.1485	.1547	.1610
9	.1284	.1345	.1407	.1470
10	.1172	.1233	.1295	.1359
15	.0838	.0899	.0963	.1030
20	.0672	.0736	.0802	.0872
25	.0574	.0640	.0710	.0782

Advantages

(a) It is to some extent scientific, since it recognises that the purchase of an asset is an investment in the business and charges interest on such investment.

(b) The depreciation, under this method, not only provides for recovery of invested capital but also arranges for collecting interest on uncovered capital, i.e., depreciation includes a part of capital *plus* interest on uncovered capital.

Disadvantages

(a) This method is not suitable where additions to assets are made from year to year—since calculations on the same is very difficult and complicated.

(b) The total consolidated cost of repairs and depreciation of an asset may not remain uniform from year to year.

(c) The asset is shown in the Balance Sheet at a figure which is higher than its actual cost.

Accounting Entries

Entries under this method are to be made for (i) Interest, and (ii) Depreciation.

(i) ***As regards Interest***

It is calculated on the debit balance of the Asset Account at the beginning of the period at the prescribed rate. The entry will be

Asset A/c Dr. Interest on Capital sunk in the assets.
To Interest A/c

(ii) *As regards Depreciation*

The amount of depreciation is to be found out from the Annuity Table (Depreciation). The entry will be

Depreciation A/c Dr. With the amount of depreciation.
To Asset A/c

Illustration 6

A Co. Ltd. has acquired a lease of a Cinema Building for a term of 5 years by payment of Rs. 40,000. It is proposed to depreciate the lease by the Annuity Method, charging 5% interest p.a.

Show the Ledger Accounts of the asset during the period of the lease.

Reference to the annuity table shows that the amount for Re. 1 for 5 years at 5% is Re. 0.230975.

Solution

Present Value	Annual Depreciation
1	0.230975
40,000	$0.230975 \times \frac{40,000}{1}$ = Rs. 9,239

In the Books of A Co. Ltd.
Lease Account

Dr. Cr.

Date	Particulars	Amount	Date	Particulars	Amount
I Year		Rs.	I Year		Rs.
Opening	To Bank A/c	40,000	End	By Depreciation A/c	9,239
End	" Interest A/c	2,000		" Balance c/d	32,761
		42,000			42,000
II Year		Rs.	II Year		Rs.
Opening	To Balance b/d	32,761	End	By Depreciation A/c	9,239
End	" Interest A/c	1,638		" Balance c/d	25,160
		34,399			34,399
III Year		Rs.	III Year		Rs.
Opening	To Balance b/d	25,160	End	By Depreciation A/c	9,239
End	" Interest A/c	1,258		" Balance c/d	17,179
		26,418			26,418
IV Year		Rs.	IV Year		Rs.
Opening	To Balance b/d	17,179	End	By Depreciation A/c	9,239
End	" Interest A/c	859		" Balance c/d	8,799
		18,038			18,038
V Year		Rs.	V Year		Rs.
Opening	To Balance b/d	8,799	End	By Depreciation A/c	9,239
End	" Interest A/c	440			
		9,239			9,239

Insurance Policy Method

According to this method, an insurance policy is taken on the life of the asset in such a way that, at the end of a fixed period, the insurance company will pay the sum assured and a new asset can easily be acquired by that amount. In short, an endowment insurance policy is taken on the estimated life of the asset in such a way that at the end of the stipulated life the insurance company will pay the assured sum by which the asset can easily be replaced.

This method is similar to the Sinking Fund Method with the exception that, under Sinking Fund Method, the annual instalment of depreciation shall be invested in outside securities whereas, under this method, an insurance policy is taken out and the premium on the policy is paid every year by debiting Profit and Loss Account by way of depreciation.

Advantages

(a) A liquid fund is created for the replacement of a new asset in place of an old one at the end of a stipulated period. As a result, the firms do not have any difficulty.

(b) Since there is no investment, problem of selection for the same does not arise, like Sinking Fund Method. Moreover, the firm is not to purchase securities every year for the purpose of investment and interest thereon.

(c) This method eliminates the risks that are involved in buying and selling securities because, at the end of the stipulated period, the insurance company will pay the stipulated amount by which the new asset can easily be replaced.

Disadvantages

(a) This method is found unsuitable where additions are made to assets during the period of its working life.

(b) This method is more expensive since the insurance company keeps its own margin.

Accounting Entries

In the first year and subsequent years

(i) *When premium paid at the beginning of the first year*

Depreciation Fund Policy A/c Dr.
To Bank A/c

(ii) *When depreciation provided at the end of the year*

Profit and Loss A/c Dr.
To Depreciation Fund A/c

In the last year (in addition to the above two entries)

(iii) *When amount received on maturity of policy*

Bank A/c Dr.
To Depreciation Fund Policy A/c

(iv) *When Profit is made on policy*

Depreciation Fund Policy A/c Dr.
To Depreciation Fund A/c

(v) *When Depreciation Fund Account is closed*

Depreciation Fund A/c Dr.
To Old Asset A/c

(vi) *When scrap-value realised on old asset*

Bank A/c Dr.
To Old Asset A/c

(vii) *When balance of old asset account is transferred*

Profit and Loss A/c Dr.
To Old Asset A/c (in case of loss on sale)

(viii) *When new asset is purchased*

New Asset A/c Dr.
To Bank A/c

Illustration 7

M/s AB & Co. purchased a machine for Rs. 1,000 which is expected to last 3 years only. They are informed that its scrap will realise Rs. 125. They decide to purchase an endowment policy for three years for a sum of Rs. 875. The annual premium is Rs. 275 and the rate of interest works out at 3% compound interest. The scrap of machine actually realised Rs. 110.

Show Depreciation Account, Depreciation Policy Account and Machinery Account for all the three years. Calculations may be made correct to the nearest rupee only.

Solution

In the Books of M/s AB & Co.
Depreciation Fund Account

Dr. *Cr.*

Date	*Particulars*	*Amount*	*Date*	*Particulars*	*Amount*
Year		Rs.	Year		Rs.
I (end)	To Balance c/d	283	I (end)	By Profit and Loss A/c	275
				" Depreciation Policy A/c	8
		283			283

Contd.

Date	Particulars	Amount	Date	Particulars	Amount
Year		Rs.	Year		Rs.
II (end)	To Balance c/d	575	II (Commencement)	By Balance b/d	283
				" Profit and Loss A/c	275
			(end)	" Depreciation Policy A/c	17
		575			575
Year			Year		
III (end)	To Machinery A/c	875	III (Commencement)	By Balance b/d	575
				" Profit and Loss A/c	275
			(end)	" Depreciation Policy A/c	25
		875			875

Depreciation Policy Account

Dr. Cr.

Date	Particulars	Amount	Date	Particulars	Amount
Year		Rs.	Year		Rs.
I (Commencement)	To Bank A/c	275	I (end)	By Balance c/d	283
(end)	" Depreciation Fund A/c	8			
		283			283
Year		Rs.	Year		Rs.
II (Commencement)	To Balance b/d	283	II (end)	By Balance c/d	575
	" Bank A/c	275			
(end)	" Depreciation Fund A/c	17			
		575			575
Year			Year		
III (Commencement)	To Balance b/d	575	III (end)	By Balance c/d	875
	" Bank A/c	275			
(end)	" Depreciation Fund A/c	25			
		875			875

Machinery Account

Dr. Cr.

Date	Particulars	Amount	Date	Particulars	Amount
Year		Rs.	Year		Rs.
I	To Bank A/c	1,000	I (end)	By Balance c/d	1,000
		1,000			1,000
II	To Balance b/d	1,000	II (end)	By Balance c/d	1,000
		1,000			1,000
III	To Balance b/d	1,000	III (end)	By Dep. Fund A/c	875
				" Bank A/c (Sales)	110
				" P & L A/c (Loss)	15
		1,000			1,000

Revaluation Method

Under this method, where the life of the asset is uncertain, depreciation cannot be calculated ordinarily, so the asset is revalued at the Balance Sheet date. Therefore, the difference between the book value of the asset and the revalued figures is considered as depreciation (appreciated value is not to be taken into account). The valuation should be under 'Going Concern' basis. This method is suitable for those assets whose estimated life is uncertain and depreciate rapidly, e.g., Livestock, Casks, Jars, Packages, Jigs, Trademarks, etc.

In other words, this method is applicable in the following cases where:

(i) the life of the asset cannot be estimated properly; (ii) the ordinary method and procedure of depreciation on mathematical basis cannot be applied; (iii) the asset has a very short and uncertain life; (iv) the asset is not fixed in nature; (v) the asset is not so significant to the business.

Under this method, the asset is submitted to an expert for proper valuation at the end of every year and fall in value of the asset is treated as depreciation which is debited to Profit and Loss Account by crediting the Asset Account. But, if there is any appreciation in the value of assets, it should be ignored or the same may be credited to a Reserve Account.

Illustration 8

A company manufactures loose tools for its own use. At the end of each year depreciation is charged on Revaluation Method. From the following particulars, show the Loose Tools Account:

Year ended 31.12.2009	—	Loose Tools manufactured	Rs. 5,000
		(Revalued on 31.12.2009 Rs. 4,100)	
Year ended 31.12.2010	—	Loose Tools manufactured	Rs. 2,700
		(Revalued on 31.12.2010 Rs. 5,700)	
Year ended 31.12.2011	—	Loose Tools manufactured	Rs. 1,000
		(Revalued on 31.12.2011 Rs. 6,000)	
Year ended 31.12.2012	—	Loose Tools manufactured	Rs. 1,500
		(Revalued on 31.12.2012 Rs. 5,100)	

The value as on 31.12.2012 is after considering the sale of loose tools of the book value of Rs. 1,200 (as on 31.12.2012) for Rs. 950.

[ICWA Inter, New]

Solution

In the Books of ...
Loose Tools Account

Dr. Cr.

Date		Particulars	Amount	Date		Particulars	Amount
2009			Rs.	2009			Rs.
	To	Cost of Production A/c Or, Bank A/c	5,000	Dec. 31	By	Depreciation A/c *(bal. fig.)*	900
					"	Balance c/d	4,100
			5,000				5,000
2010				2010			
Jan. 1	To	Balance b/d	4,100	Dec. 31	By	Depreciation A/c *(bal. fig.)*	1,100
Dec. 31	"	Cost of Production A/c	2,700		"	Balance c/d	5,700
			6,800				6,800
2011				2011			
Jan. 1	To	Balance b/d	5,700	Dec. 31	By	Depreciation A/c *(bal. fig.)*	700
Dec. 31	"	Cost of Production A/c	1,000		"	Balance c/d	6,000
			6,700				6,700
2012				2012			
Jan. 1	To	Balance b/d	6,000	Dec. 31	By	Bank A/c–Sale	950
Dec. 31	"	Cost of Production A/c	1,500		"	Profit and Loss A/c —Loss on Sale	250
					"	Depreciation A/c *(bal. fig.)*	1,200
					"	Balance c/d	5,100
			7,500				7,500

Depletion Method

This method is applicable in case of wasting assets, e.g., mines, quarries, oil-wells, etc. Under this method, depreciation is charged on the basis of output extracted in comparison with the estimated total contents of the mines. It is to be remembered that the total contents of the asset are first estimated in terms of tons, gallons etc. Thereafter, the total cost of the said asset is divided by the total units of contents in order to find out the rate of depreciation. Hence, amount of depreciation is calculated on the basis of quantity extracted for a particular year by multiplying the rate of depreciation so ascertained. The value of an wasting asset is reduced by the value of the deposits which have already been depleted every year. Naturally, when the asset is fully exhausted, the value of the asset will simply be nil.

Illustration 9

B. Collieries Ltd. acquired the lease right for 20 years of a mine on January 1, 2006, on a lump payment of Rs. 5,00,000. Estimated coal deposit was 20,00,000 tonnes, 75% of which, it is expected, could be raised within the lease period. The Lease Account was shown for 5 years charging depreciation under Straight Line Method. On 31st October 2011, the company decided to depreciate the lease under Depletion Method with retrospective effect from 1st January 2006. The annual raising were 20,000 tonnes in 2006; 30,000 tonnes in 2007; 1,00,000 tonnes in 2008 and 2,00,000 tonnes in each of the years 2009, 2010 and 2011.

Show Lease Account from 1st January 2006 to 31st December 2011, showing clearly your calculations.

Solution **[CU BCom (Hons)]**

In the Books of B. Collieries Ltd.

Lease Account

Dr. *Cr.*

Date	*Particulars*	*Amount*	*Date*	*Particulars*	*Amount*
2006		Rs.	2006		Rs.
Jan. 1	To Bank A/c	5,00,000	Dec. 31	By Depreciation A/c (Rs. 5,00,000 ÷ 20)	25,000
				" Balance c/d	4,75,000
		5,00,000			5,00,000
2007			2007		
Jan. 1	To Balance b/d	4,75,000	Dec. 31	By Depreciation A/c	25,000
				" Balance c/d	4,50,000
		4,75,000			4,75,000
2008			2008		
Jan. 1	To Balance b/d	4,50,000	Dec. 31	By Depreciation A/c	25,000
				" Balance c/d	4,25,000
		4,50,000			4,50,000
2009			2009		
Jan. 1	To Balance b/d	4,25,000	Dec. 31	By Depreciation A/c	25,000
				" Balance c/d	4,00,000
		4,25,000			4,25,000
2010			2010		
Jan. 1	To Balance b/d	4,00,000	Dec. 31	By Depreciation A/c	25,000
				" Balance c/d	3,75,000
		4,00,000			4,00,000
2011			2011		
Jan. 1	To Balance b/d	3,75,000	Dec. 31	By Depreciation[1]	66,667
				Profit and Loss A/c[2] —Depr. undercharged	58,333
				" Balance c/d	2,50,000
		3,75,000			3,75,000
2012					
Jan. 1	To Balance b/d	2,50,000			

Notes :

1. Total quantity of Coal 20,00,000 tonnes. Expected raising 15,00,000 (i.e., 20,00,000 × 75%). Depreciation per tonne will be Rs. $\frac{5,00,000}{15,00,000} = 33\frac{1}{3}$ paise, So, for 2011, Depreciation will be Rs. 66,667 (i.e., 20,00,000 × $33\frac{1}{3}$ paise)
2. Total depreciation from 2006 to 2010 amounted to Rs. 1,25,000 i.e., 25,000 × 5. Depreciation under new method will be — Total quantity raised, i.e., 5,50,000 + tonnes [20,000 + 30,000 + 1,00,000 + 4,00,000 (2,00,000 × 2)] × $33\frac{1}{3}$ paise = Rs. 1,83,333. Under-depreciation amounted to Rs. 58,333 (i.e., 1,83,333 – 1,25,000).

Compound Interest Method

This method is to some extent similar to the Sinking Fund Method and is generally applied in case of the electric supply company. Under this method, accumulated investments are made at a very low rate of compound interest which becomes equal to ninety per cent of the original cost of the asset. The balance ten per cent is considered as the scrap value for the same. In short, provision for depreciation should be made in such a way as investments, together with the accumulated compound interest, will be at least equal to ninety per cent of the original cost of the asset at the end of the effective life.

There are, however, two other methods which have developed recently in the accounting literature. They are:

(a) Double Declining Balance Method;

(b) Group or Composite Depreciation Method.

(a) Double Declining Balance Method

Under this method, depreciation is calculated at a rate which is higher than the Diminishing Balance Method (generally at a Double rate). Of course, in the USA, this rate cannot exceed Double of the straight line rate. The principle of this method can be illustrated with the help of the following:

Say, cost price of an asset is Rs. 20,000. Estimated life is 5 years and scrap value Rs. 1,000.

The rate of depreciation in this case will be $2 \times \frac{1}{5}$ or, $\frac{2}{5}$ or, 40%.

As such, depreciation for the first year will be $\left(\text{Rs. } 20{,}000 \times \frac{40}{100}\right)$ Rs. 8,000 and that of the second year will be 40% of (20,000 – 8,000) Rs. 12,000 i.e., Rs. 4,800. Similarly, in the third year it will be 40% of (20,000 – 8,000 – 4,800) Rs. 7,200 or Rs. 2,880. Depreciation for the following two years will be Rs. 1,728 and Rs. 1,037, respectively.

The above illustration can be presented better with the help of the following table:

Depreciation Schedule
Under Double Declining Balance Method

Year	Opening Balance	Depreciation	Depreciation Cumulative	Closing Balance
	Rs.	Rs.	Rs.	Rs.
1	20,000	8,000	8,000	12,000
2	12,000	4,800	2,800	7,000
3	7,200	2,880	15,680	4,320
4	4,320	1,728	17,408	2,592
5	2,592	1,037	18,445	1,555

Thus, the above table shows that asset account leaves a balance at the end of its effective life which may not be equal to its estimated scrap value. Scrap value was estimated at Rs. 1,000. The excess balance over the estimated scrap value, i.e., Rs. 555 (1,555 – 1,000), may be considered as the depreciation for the final year. Therefore, amount of depreciation for the last year (5th year) will be Rs. 1,592 (1,037 + 555), instead of Rs. 1,037.

(b) Group or Composite Depreciation Method

Usually, a firm is to possess numerous similar fixed assets (with approximately same unit costs and life expectancies) e.g., all fans, all meters etc. are treated together and depreciated collectively which is known as *'Group Depreciation'*. If dissimilar assets, like all chairs and typewriters, are so treated, say, under the head 'Office Equipment' and depreciated accordingly, the process is known as *Composite Depreciation*. Group or composite depreciation is generally applied to relatively low value assets where maintenance of individual records is costly. Under group or composite system, average life expectancy will determine the rate and amount of periodic depreciation and not on the basis of the individual life of an asset, although the individual life and the average life of the assets vary. This collective method proves no gain or loss since it recognises that loss on some asset will be offset by the profits on other assets. The rate of depreciation will remain constant and will accumulate accordingly.

In short, under this method, all tangible assets are considered as a single asset in a collective sense and, as such, only an Asset Account and Accumulated Depreciation Account are opened. It has already been pointed out above that since there is a single rate of depreciation on collective asset, separate accounts are not maintained. But, if there is any addition to asset or depletion of or transfer of an asset, i.e., if there is any change, the same must be incorporated. Any profit or loss so made on account of any change is also transferred to Profit and Loss Account. Depreciation is charged on the opening balance of the Single Asset Account at a fixed rate although the lives of the assets may not be the same. (The rate of depreciation is calculated on the average life of all the assets).

The above principle may be explained with the help of the following illustration:

Depreciation Schedule
Group or Composite Depreciation Method

Name and type of assets	Cost price of the assets	Scrap value	Total Depreciation	Estimated life	Annual depreciation (on the basis of Straight Line)
	Rs.	Rs.	Rs.		Rs.
P_1	7,500	1,500	6,000	6	1,000
P_2	5,500	1,500	4,000	4	1,000
P_3	3,400	400	3,000	2	1,500
P_4	1,250	250	1,000	4	250
P_5	2,350	350	2,000	8	250
	20,000	4,000	16,000		4000

It is evident from the table that the composite or average life is 4 years (16,000 ÷ 4,000), the total Written-down Value of all the assets is Rs. 16,000 and the amount of depreciation is Rs. 4,000.

Hence, the group or composite depreciation rate will be

$$\left(\frac{\text{Rs. } 4,000}{\text{Rs. } 20,000}\right) \times 100 = 20\%$$

Depreciation for the first year will be Rs. 4,000 as it is equal to the product of the composite rate of depreciation. Therefore, the aggregate of all the annual depreciations and the aggregates of the scrap value at the end of the year will be Rs. 16,000 and Rs. 4,000, respectively, which is equal to the purchase price of Rs. 20,000.

If there is any addition or alternation to the assets, i.e.,, if there is any change, the average or composite life of the remaining assets and the rate of composite depreciation should be changed accordingly.

This method is not free from snags. Where the real life of an asset is shorter than the composite life the entire amount of depreciation is actually not recovered (as in the case of asset P_3). In the opposite case (i.e., where the real life of an asset is higher than the composite life), the entire amount of depreciation is recovered before the expired period of the said asset (as in the case of P_1 and P_5). Therefore, earlier under-depreciation is adjusted with subsequent over-depreciation. The gain or loss which arises from the normal variation in the estimated life and the real life is not considered at all. Besides, minor errors or variation which usually occur throughout the life of the assets are not recognised.

Inventory System of Depreciation

This method is applicable to those assets whose value are small in comparison with other assets, e.g., loose tools. In other words, this method is very useful for those assets whose life cannot be ascertained with certainty, e.g., Livestock. Under this method, depreciation is computed as:

Depreciation = Cost of the asset in working conditions at the beginning of the year + Purchased during the year — Cost of the asset in working condition at the end of the year.

Illustration 10

On 1.1.2005, a firm has loose tools in working condition costing Rs. 4,000. It purchased loose tools during the year Rs. 5,000. At the end of the year it had loose tools in working condition Rs. 3,000 only.

Calculate the amount of depreciation.

Solution

Depreciation = Cost of the Assets (opening) + Purchases – Cost of the Assets (closing)
= Rs. 4,000 + Rs. 5,000 – Rs. 3,000
= Rs. 6,000.

The entry for this purpose will be as usual, viz:

Depreciation A/c Dr. }
To Assets A/c } with the amount of Depreciation

Retirement Method

Under this method, provision is made on the assets which are shortly to be retired. This is particularly applicable in the case of public utility concerns.

Illustration 11

Out of the total fixed asset account, which contains the cost of total 1,000 poles costing Rs. 500 each, 10 of them are replaced at a cost of Rs. 700 per pole. Residual value of each old pole is estimated at Rs. 50.

Show the entry and the amount of depreciation in this case.

Solution

Depreciation to be calculated as:

		Rs.
Cost of ten old poles @ Rs. 700	=	7,000
Less: Residual value (Rs. 50 × 10)	=	500
		6,500

Journal

Date	*Particulars*		*L.F.*	*Debit*	*Credit*
?				Rs.	Rs.
	Depreciation A/c	Dr.		6,500	
	Bank (Residual value of old poles) A/c	Dr.		500	
	To Bank A/c				7,000
	(Purchase of new poles and retirement of old poles are recorded in the books)				

PROFIT/LOSS ON DISPOSAL/SALE OF FIXED ASSETS

Sometimes an asset may be sold out before its useful life for a number of reasons (due to technological development, over-depreciation, etc.) including a part of some assets which will no longer be needed in future. Needless to mention that the Written-Down Value of the old asset may not be exactly equal to the sale prices for the same. That is, ***if the sale price is less than the Written-Down Value, there is a case of loss, and vice versa. This profit or loss on sale of asset is adjusted in the year of sale in Profit and Loss Account.*** AS 10, para 26, also corroborates this view. As per para 26 of AS 10, losses arising from the retirement or gains or losses arising from disposal of fixed assets which is carried at cost should be recognised in the profit and loss statement.

Accounting Treatment

The accounting treatment depends on the method for recording depreciation for this purpose. There are two methods:

(a) **Where no provision for depreciation account is maintained**

At first, Written-Down Value of the assets sold will be transferred to *'Assets Disposal Account'*.

The subsequent entries are:

(i) ***For transferring the WDV of assets to Assets Disposal A/c:***

Assets Disposal A/c Dr.
To Assets A/c

(ii) ***For sale proceeds:***

Bank A/c Dr.
To Assets Disposal A/c

(iii) ***For Current year's depreciation, if any:***

Depreciation (P & L A/c) A/c Dr.
To Assets Disposal A/c

(iv) ***For Profit on Sale of Assets Sold:***

Assets Disposal A/c Dr.
To Profit and Loss A/c

(v) *For Loss on Sale of Assets Sold:*
Profit and Loss A/c Dr.
To Assets Disposal A/c

Alternative Approach

Under the circumstances, all adjustments are to be passed through the Assets Account instead of opening or transferring for the same to Asset Disposal Account. The entries for the purpose will be:

(i) *For sale proceeds:*
Bank A/c Dr.
To Assets A/c

(ii) *For current year's depreciation, if any*
Depreciation (P & L) A/c Dr.
To Assets A/c

(iii) *For profit on sale (i.e., if sale price is more than WDV)*
Assets A/c Dr.
To Profit and Loss A/c (Profit on sale)

(iv) *For loss on sale (i.e., if sale price is less than WDV)*
Profit and Loss A/c (Loss on Sale) A/c Dr.
To Asset A/c

The following illustration will help us to understand the principle clearly:

Illustration 12

On 1.1.2008, the Plant Account showed a balance of Rs. 80,000. Out of the above, a Plant, whose book value was Rs. 10,000 on that date, was sold for Rs. 6,000 on 1.4.2009. On 1.10.2009, another plant was purchased for Rs. 20,000.

Show Journal Entries and the Plant Account up to 31st Dec. 2009 assuming that the business charges depreciation @ 10% p.a. on straight line method and closes its accounts on 31st December every year if no Provision for Depreciation Account is opened.

Statement of Depreciation

		Plant I	*Plant II*	*Plant III*	*Total Depreciation*
		Rs.	Rs.	Rs.	Rs.
01.01.2008	Book Value	70,000	10,000		
31.12.2008	Depreciation @ 10%	7,000	1,000		8,000
01.01.2009	WDV	63,000	9,000		
01.04.2009	Depreciation @ 10%		250		
01.04.2009	WDV		8,750		
	Sold for		6,000		
	Loss on Sale		2,750		
01.10.2009	Book Value			20,000	
31.12.2009	Depreciation @ 10%	7,000		500	7,750
01.01.2010	WDV	56,000		19,500	

Journal

Date	*Particulars*		*L.F.*	*Debit*	*Credit*
2008				Rs.	Rs.
Dec. 31	Depreciation A/c	Dr.		8,000	
	To Plant A/c				8,000
	(Depreciation charged on Plant @ 10%)				
	Profit and Loss A/c	Dr.		8,000	
	To Depreciation A/c				8,000
	(Depreciation transferred to Profit and Loss Account)				

Contd.

			Rs.	Rs.
2009	Plant Disposal A/c	Dr.	9,000	
	To Plant A/c			9,000
	(WDV of the plant sold transferred to Plant Disposal A/c)			
"	Bank A/c	Dr.	6,000	
	To Plant Disposal A/c			6,000
	(Sale proceeds of old plant)			
"	P & L (Depreciation) A/c	Dr.	250	
	To Plant Disposal A/c			250
	(Depreciation on asset sold)			
"	Profit and Loss A/c	Dr.	2,750	
	To Plant Disposal A/c			2,750
	(Loss on sale transferred)			
Dec. 31	Profit and Loss A/c	Dr.	7,500	
	To Depreciation A/c			7,500
	(Depreciation transferred to Profit and Loss Account)			

Plant Account

Dr. Cr.

Date	Particulars	Amount	Date		Particulars	Amount
2008		Rs.	2008			Rs.
Jan. 1	To Balance b/d	80,000	Dec. 31	By	Depreciation A/c	8,000
			Dec. 31	"	Balance c/d	72,000
		80,000				80,000
2009			2009			
Jan. 1	To Balance b/d	72,000	Apr. 1	By	Plant Disposal A/c	9,000
Oct. 1	" Bank A/c—Purchases	20,000	Dec. 31	"	Depreciation A/c	7,500
			"	"	Balance c/d	75,500
		92,000				92,000
2010						
Jan. 1	To Balance b/d	75,500				

Plant Disposal Account

Dr. Cr.

Date	Particulars	Amount	Date		Particulars	Amount
2009		Rs.	2009			Rs.
Apr. 1	To Plant A/c	9,000	Apr. 1	By	Bank A/c — Sale Proceeds	6,000
				"	P & L A/c — Depreciation	250
				"	P & L A/c — Loss on Sale	2,750
		9,000				9,000

Alternative Approach

In the Books of ...

Journal

Date	Particulars		L.F.	Debit	Credit
2008				Rs.	Rs.
Dec. 31	Depreciation A/c	Dr.		8,000	
	To Plant A/c				8,000
	(Depreciation charged on Plant @ 10%)				
	Profit and Loss A/c	Dr.		8,000	
	To Depreciation A/c				8,000
2009	Bank A/c	Dr.		6,000	
April 1	To Plant A/c				6,000
	(Sale proceeds of old plant)				

Contd.

2009			Rs.	Rs.
	Depreciation A/c	Dr.	250	
	To Plant A/c			250
	(Depreciation charged on plant sold for 3 months)			
	P & L A/c (Loss on Sale of Plant A/c)	Dr.	2,750	
	To Plant A/c			2,750
	(Loss on sale of plant)			
Oct. 1	Plant A/c	Dr.	20,000	
	To Bank A/c			20,000
	(New plant purchased)			
Dec. 31	Depreciation A/c	Dr.	7,500	
	To Plant A/c			7,500
	(Depreciation provided on plants)			
"	Profit and Loss A/c	Dr.	7,750	
	To Depreciation A/c			7,750
	(Depreciation transferred to Profit and Loss A/c)			

Plant Account

Dr. Cr.

Date	Particulars	Amount	Date	Particulars	Amount
2008		Rs.	2008		Rs.
Jan. 1	To Balance b/d	80,000	Dec. 31	By Depreciation A/c	8,000
				" Balance c/d	72,000
		80,000			80,000
2009			2009		
Jan. 1	To Balance b/d	72,000	Apr. 1	By Bank—Sale Proceeds	6,000
Oct. 1	" Bank A/c—Purchased	20,000		" Depreciation A/c	250
				" Loss on Sale of Plant	2,750
			Dec. 31	By Depreciation A/c	7,500
				" Balance c/d	75,500
		92,000			92,000
2010					
Jan. 1	To Balance b/d	75,500			

(b) Provision for Depreciation Account is maintained in case of Disposal of Assets

Under this method, the cost of the asset is transferred to a separate account known as *'Asset Disposal Account'* and, similarly, the amount of depreciation provided for the asset from the date of purchase to the date of sale must be transferred from the Provision for Depreciation Account to the *'Assets Disposal Account'*. The following entries are required for the purposes:

(i) ***For transferring the assets to Asset Disposal Account:***

Asset Disposal A/c Dr. } at original cost
 To Assets A/c

(ii) ***For transferring provisions for depreciation on disposal assets:***

Provision for Depreciation A/c Dr.
 To Asset Disposal A/c

(iii) ***For sale proceeds of disposed assets:***

Cash/Bank A/c Dr.
 To Asset Disposal A/c

(iv) ***For current year's depreciation:***

Depreciation A/c Dr.
 To Asset Disposal A/c

(v) ***For profit on sale of disposed assets:***

Asset Disposal A/c Dr.
 To Profit and Loss A/c

(vi) *For loss on sale of disposed assets:*

Profit and Loss A/c Dr.

To Asset Disposal A/c

Illustration 13

On 1.1.2005, X purchased 6 machines for Rs. 15,000 each. His accounting year ends on 31st Dec. Depreciation @ 10% on initial cost has been charged to Profit and Loss Account and credited to a separate *Depreciation Provision Account*.

On 1.1.2006, one machine was sold for Rs. 12,500 and, on 1.1.2007, a second machine was sold for Rs. 12,500. An improved model which costs Rs. 28,000 was purchased on 1st July 2006. The same rate of depreciation was decided for the new machine as well.

You are required to show:

(1) The Machinery Account, (2) The Machinery Disposal Account, and (3) The Provision for Depreciation Account.

Solution

In the Books of X

Machinery Account

Dr. *Cr.*

Date	*Particulars*	*Amount*	*Date*	*Particulars*	*Amount*
2005		Rs.	2005		Rs.
Jan. 1	To Bank A/c	90,000	Dec. 31	By Balance c/d	90,000
		90,000			90,000
2006			2006		
Jan. 1	To Balance b/d	90,000	Jan. 1	By Machinery Disposal A/c	15,000
July 1	" Bank A/c	28,000	Dec. 31	" Balance c/d	1,03,000
		1,18,000			1,18,000
2007			2007		
Jan. 1	To Balance b/d	1,03,000	Jan. 1	By Machinery Disposal A/c	15,000
			Dec. 31	" Balance c/d	88,000
		1,03,000			1,03,000
2008					
Jan. 1	To Balance b/d	88,000			

Note: Students are advised to know that at any time the balance in the ass•s account will always represent the cost of assets.

Machinery Disposal Account

Dr. *Cr.*

Date	*Particulars*	*Amount*	*Date*	*Particulars*	*Amount*
2006		Rs.	2006		Rs.
Jan. 1	To Machinery A/c	15,000	Jan. 1	By Prov. for Depreciation A/c	1,500
				" Bank—Sale	12,500
			Dec. 31	" Profit and Loss A/c —Loss	1,000
		15,000			15,000
2007			2007		
Jan. 1	To Machinery A/c	15,000	Jan. 1	By Prov. for Depr. A/c	3,000
Dec. 31	" P & L A/c (Profit)	500		" Bank— Sale	12,500
		15,500			15,500

Provision for Depreciation Account

Dr. *Cr.*

Date	*Particulars*	*Amount*	*Date*	*Particulars*	*Amount*
2005		Rs.	2005		Rs.
Jan. 1	To Balance c/d	9,000	Dec. 31	By Depreciation A/c	9,000
		9,000			9,000

Contd.

			Rs.				Rs.
2006				2006			
Jan. 1	To	Machinery Disposal A/c	1,500	Jan. 1	By	Balance b/d	9,000
Dec. 31	"	Balance c/d	16,400	Dec. 31	"	Depreciation A/c	8,900*
			17,900				17,900
2007				2007			
Jan. 1	To	Machinery Disposal A/c	3,000	Jan. 1	By	Balance b/d	16,400**
Dec. 31	"	Balance c/d	22,200	Dec. 31	"	Depreciation A/c	8,800
			25,200				25,200

			Rs.
*	@ 10% p.a. on Rs. 75,000 (Rs. 90,000 – Rs. 15,000)	=	7,500
	Add: @ 10% p.a. on Rs. 28,000 for 6 months	=	1,400
			8,900
**	@10% p.a. on Rs. 60,000 (Rs. 75,000 – Rs. 15,000)		6,000
	Add: @ 10% p.a. on Rs. 28,000		2,800
			8,800

RECORDING EXCHANGE OF USED ASSETS WITH NEW ONES

We all know that if a new asset is acquired in exchange for an old one which has already been used and depreciated accordingly, the firm has to pay only the difference in prices. In other words, the difference between the price of the new asset and the price of the old one is granted by the seller. The value of the old asset so exchanged is called **trade-in-allowance**—which is considered as a part of the price of the new asset acquired. Needless to mention that the price of the old asset so granted by the seller of the new asset may not be equal to the Written-Down Value of the old asset. In that case, profit on exchange or loss on exchange may arise, i.e., if the trade-in-allowance is more than WDV of the old asset, them there is a profit, and *vice versa*. Practically, principles should be different for profit or for loss so made on account of trading-in used assets for new one.

It is interesting enough that loss on such asset is recognised, but not the profit on such assets due to the two following facts:

(i) no revenue is actually realised by substituting a new asset in place of an old one;

(ii) if the payment is made for cash, discount, if any, is allowed from the catalogue price of the asset—the same is substituted by the prof so made on such asset.

The following example will help us to understand the principle clearly:

Illustration 14

X Ltd. acquired a plant at a cost of **Rs. 4,000**, accumulated depreciation up to the date was Rs. 3,200. This was exchanged with a new plant at a list price of Rs. 6,000 from Y Ltd. The payment for the new one consisted of a trade-in-allowance of Rs. 1,400 for the old one and the balance Rs. 4,600 to be paid in cash. The old plant could have been sold for cash Rs. 1,000.

Show the entries for recording the exchange of plants.

Solution

The Written-down Value of the old asset was Rs. 800 (Rs. 4,000 – Rs. 3,200).

The old plant could have been sold for Rs. 1,000 in the open market, but the same gave to the seller of the new one Rs. 1,400, giving a trade-in-allowance of Rs. 400 which may be considered as a reduction of the price from the new plant. In other words, the price for the new one is to be considered as Rs. 5,600 (i.e., Rs. 6,000 – Rs. 400).

It is to be remembered that for calculating the profit on exchange of the old one, Rs. 1,000 should be considered as the sale price. Thus, the profit is Rs. 200 (i.e., Rs. 4,000 – Rs. 3,200 = Rs. 800 as compared to Rs. 1,000). Now, the following entries are required for the purpose:

In the Books of X Ltd.
Journal *(without narration)*

Date	*Particulars*		*L.F.*	*Debit*	*Credit*
				Rs.	Rs.
(i)	*For sale of old plant:*				
	Provision for Depreciation A/c	Dr.		3,200	
	Y Ltd. A/c	Dr.		1,000	
	To Old Plant A/c				4,000
	To Profit and Loss A/c				200

Contd.

			Rs.	Rs.
(ii)	*For purchase of new plant:*			
	New Plant A/c	Dr.	5,600	
	To Y Ltd. A/c			1,000
	To Cash A/c			4,600
(iii)	Alternatively: Compound entry:			
	Provision for Depreciation A/c	Dr.	3,200	
	New Plant A/c	Dr.	5,600	
	To Old Plant A/c			4,000
	To Cash A/c			4,600
	To Profit and Loss A/c			200

Illustration 15

On 1.1.2008, X purchased a roasting machine for Rs. 60,000 and a grinding machine for Rs. 40,000. On 1.1.2009, he purchased one oil-expeller for Rs. 1,00,000. On 1.1.2010, the roasting machine got out of order and a new roaster was purchased, costing Rs. 1,20,000, after surrendering the old one and paying cash of Rs. 90,000. On 1.1.2011, the oil-expeller, purchased on 1.1.2009, was destroyed by fire and the insurance company paid Rs. 60,000 only.

Show Machinery Account for 2008, 2009, 2010 and 2011, charging depreciation @ 10% p.a. on the WDV method.

Solution

Statement of Depreciation

Particulars		*Roasting*	*Grinding*	*Oil-Expeller*	*New Roaster*	*Total Depreciation*
		Rs.	Rs.	Rs.	Rs.	Rs.
01.01.2008	Book Value	60,000	40,000			
31.12.2008	Dep. @ 10%	6,000	4,000			10,000
01.01.2009	WDV	54,000	36,000			
01.01.2009	Book Value			1,00,000		
31.12.2009	Dep. @ 10%	5,400	3,600	10,000		19,000
01.01.2010	WDV	48,600	32,400	90,000		
Less: Surrendered		48,600				
01.01.2010	Book Value				1,20,000	
31.12.2010	Dep. @ 10%		3,240	9,000	12,000	24,240
01.01.2011	WDV		29,160	81,000	1,08,000	
Less: Loss by Fire				81,000		
31.12.2011	Dep. @ 10%		2,916		10,800	13,716
01.01.2012	WDV		26,244		97,200	

∴ Trade-in-Allowance = Cost – Cash Payment
= Rs. 1,20,000 – Rs. 90,000
= Rs. 30,000.

So, Amount of Loss on exchange will be = WDV – Trade-in-Allowance
= Rs. 48,600 – Rs. 30,000
= Rs. 18,600.

Dr. **Machinery Account** *Cr.*

Date	*Particulars*	*Amount*	*Date*	*Particulars*	*Amount*
2008		Rs.	2008		Rs.
Jan. 1	To Bank A/c	1,00,000	Dec. 31	By Depreciation A/c	10,000
			"	Balance c/d	90,000
		1,00,000			1,00,000
2009			2009		
Jan. 1	To Balance b/d	90,000	Dec. 31	By Depreciation A/c	19,000
"	" Bank A/c	1,00,000	"	Balance c/d	1,71,000
		1,90,000			1,90,000

Date		Particulars	Amount	Date		Particulars	Amount
2010				2010			
Jan. 1	To	Balance b/d	1,71,000	Jan. 1	By	Vendor A/c (Trade-in-All)	30,000
"	"	Bank A/c	90,000		"	Profit & Loss A/c (Loss in Exchange)	18,600
	"	Trade-in-Allowance A/c	30,000	Dec. 31	"	Depreciation A/c	24,240
					"	Balance c/d	2,18,160
			2,91,000				2,91,000
2011				2011			
Jan. 1	To	Balance b/d	2,18,160	Jan. 1	By	Accidental Loss A/c —transferred	81,000
				Dec. 31	"	Depreciation A/c	13,716
					"	Balance c/d	1,23,444
			2,18,160				2,18,160
2012							
Jan. 1	To	Balance b/d	1,23,444				

Accidental Loss Account

Dr. Cr.

Date		Particulars	Amount	Date		Particulars	Amount
2005			Rs.	2005			Rs.
Jan. 1	To	Machinery A/c	81,000	Jan. 1	By	Insurance Claim A/c	60,000
					"	Profit & Loss A/c	21,000
			81,000				81,000

CHANGE IN METHOD

Sometimes it becomes necessary to change the method of depreciation for ascertaining more correct estimated amount of depreciation. As such, the estimated useful life on the residual value is drawn up and depreciation should also be computed on the revised value of such asset. **Logical view** — In our opinion :

"The depreciation method selected should be applied consistently from period to period. A change from one method of providing depreciation to another should be made only if the adoption of the new method is required by statute or for compliance with an accounting standard or if it is considered that the change would result in a more appropriate preparation or presentation of the financial statements of the enterprise. When such a change in the method of depreciation is made, depreciation should be recalculated in accordance with the new method from the date of the asset coming into use. The deficiency or surplus arising from retrospective recomputation of depreciation in accordance with the new method should be adjusted in the accounts in the year in which the method of depreciation is changed. In case the change in the method results in deficiency in depreciation in respect of past years, the deficiency should be charged in the statement of profit and loss. In case the change in the method results in surplus, the surplus should be credited to the statement of profit and loss, such a change should be treated as a change in accounting policy and its effect should be quantified and disclosed."

The change in method may be made possible in two ways:

(1) Without Retrospective Effect, i.e., with Prospective Effect, and

(2) With Retrospective Effect.

(1). Without Retrospective Effect

Under this method, *the change in method is to be taken into consideration for the rest of the useful life of the asset commencing from the year in which such change is effected and not from the beginning of the year.*

The following illustrations will make the above principles clear:

Illustration 16

A Ltd. purchase on 1.1.2007 a second-hand Plant for Rs. 30,000 and immediately spent Rs. 20,000 on overhauling it. On 1.7.2007, additional machinery costing Rs. 25,000 was purchased. On 1.7.2009, the Plant purchased on 1.1.2007 became obsolete and was sold for Rs. 10,000. On that date new machinery was purchased at a cost of Rs. 60,000.

Depreciation was provided for annually on 31st Dec. @ 10% p.a. on original cost of assets. In 2010, however, the company changed this method of providing for depreciation and adopted the method of writing-off 15% on diminishing value.

Show the Machinery Account as it would appear in the books of the company for the years 2007 to 2011 (both inclusive). **[CA]**

Solution

Statement of Depreciation

	Particulars	Plant I	Plant II	Plant III	Total Depreciation
		Rs.	Rs.	Rs.	Rs.
01.01.2007	Book Value	50,000			
01.07.2007	Book Value		25,000		
31.12.2007	Dep. @ 10%	5,000	1,250		6,250
01.01.2008	WDV	45,000	23,750		
31.12.2008	Dep. @ 10%	5,000	2,500		7,500
01.01.2009	WDV	40,000	21,250		
01.07.2009	Book Value			60,000	
	Dep. @ 10%	2,500			
	WDV	37,500			
	Sold for	10,000			
	Loss on Sale	27,500			
31.12.2009	Dep. @ 10%		2,500	3,000	8,000
01.01.2010	WDV		18,750	57,000	
31.12.2010	Dep. @ 15% (on R. B. Method)		2,813	8,550	11,363
01.01.2011	WDV		15,937	48,450	
31.12.2011	Dep. @ 15 %		2,390	7,268	9,658
01.01.2012	WDV		13,547	41,182	

Plant Account

Dr. *Cr.*

Date		Particulars	Amount	Date		Particulars	Amount
2007			Rs.	2007			Rs.
Jan. 1	To	Bank A/c	50,000	Dec. 31	By	Depreciation A/c	6,250
July 1	"	Bank A/c	25,000		"	Balance c/d	68,750
			75,000				75,000
2008				2008			
Jan. 1	To	Balance b/d	68,750	Dec. 31	By	Depreciation A/c	7,500
					"	Balance c/d	61,250
			68,750				68,750
2009				2009			
Jan. 1	To	Balance b/d	61,250	July 1	By	Depreciation A/c	2,500
July 1	"	Bank A/c	60,000		"	Bank (Sales) A/c	10,000
					"	Loss on Sale A/c	27,500
				Dec. 31	"	Depreciation A/c	5,500
					"	Balance c/d	75,750
			1,21,250				1,21,250
2010				2010			
Jan. 1	To	Balance b/d	75,750	Dec. 31	By	Depreciation A/c	11,363
					"	Balance c/d	64,387
			75,750				75,750

Contd.

Date	Particulars	Rs.	Date	Particulars	Rs.
2011			2011		
Jan. 1	To Balance b/d	64,387	Dec. 31	By Depreciation A/c	9,658
				" Balance c/d	54,729
		64,387			64,387
2012					
Jan. 1	To Balance b/d	54,729			

Illustration 17

A second-hand machine was purchased on 1.1.2007 for Rs. 4,00,000. Overhauling and installation expenses for the same machine amounted to Rs. 1,00,000. Another machine was purchased for Rs. 2,00,000 on 1.7.2007.

On 1.7.2009, the machine installed on 1.1.2007 was sold for Rs. 2,50,000. Dismantling charge for the machine sold on 1.7.2009 were Rs. 10,000. On the same date another machine was purchased for Rs. 8,00,000 and was commissioned on 30.9.2009. The company has adopted calendar year as its financial year. Under the existing practice, the company provides depreciation @ 10% p.a. on original cost. In 2010, it has been decided that depreciation will be charged on the diminishing balance @ 15% p.a. The change is not to be made with retrospective effect.

Show Plant Account from 2007 to 2011. Also show Sale of Asset Account. **[ICWA]**

Solution

Statement of Depreciation

	Particulars	*Machine I*	*Machine II*	*Machine III*	*Total Depreciation*
		Rs.	Rs.	Rs.	Rs.
1.1.2007	Book Value (including overhauling)	5,00,000			
1.7.2007	Book Value		2,00,000		
31.12.2007	Dep. @ 10%	50,000	10,000		60,000
1.1.2008	WDV	4,50,000	1,90,000		
31.12.2008	Dep. @ 10%	50,000	20,000		70,000
1.1.2009	WDV	4,00,000	1,70,000		
1.7.2009	Book Value			8,00,000	
	Dep. @ 10%	25,000			
	WDV	3,75,000			
	Add: Dismantling Ch.	10,000			
		3,85,000			
	Sold for	2,50,000			
	Loss on Sale	1,35,000			
31.12.2009	Dep. @ 10%		20,000	40,000	85,000
01.01.2010	WDV		1,50,000	7,60,000	
31.12.2010	Dep. @ 15%		22,500	1,14,000	1,36,500
01.01.2011	WDV		1,27,500	6,46,000	
31.12.2011	Dep. @ 15%		19,125	96,900	1,16,025
01.01.2012	WDV		1,08,375	5,49,100	

Machinery Account

Dr. *Cr.*

Date	*Particulars*	*Amount*	*Date*	*Particulars*	*Amount*
2007		Rs.	2007		Rs.
Jan. 1	To Bank A/c	4,00,000	Dec. 31	By Depreciation A/c	60,000
	" Bank A/c—Overhauling and Installation Exp.	1,00,000		" Balance c/d	6,40,000
July 1	" Bank A/c	2,00,000			
		7,00,000			7,00,000

2008				2008			
Jan. 1	To	Balance b/d	6,40,000	Dec. 31	By	Depreciation A/c	70,000
					"	Balance c/d	5,70,000
			6,40,000				6,40,000
2009				2009			
Jan. 1	To	Balance b/d	5,70,000	July 1	By	Sale of Asset	4,10,000
July 1	"	Bank A/c	8,00,000	Dec. 31	"	Depreciation A/c	60,000
	"	Bank (Dis. Ch.) A/c	10,000		"	Balance c/d	9,10,000
			13,80,000				13,80,000
2010				2010			
Jan. 1	To	Balance b/d	9,10,000	Dec. 31	By	Depreciation A/c	1,36,500
					"	Balance c/d	7,73,500
			9,10,000				9,10,000
2011				2011			
Jan. 1	To	Balance b/d	7,73,500	Dec. 31	By	Depreciation A/c	1,16,025
					"	Balance c/d	6,57,475
			7,73,500				7,73,500
2012							
Jan. 1	To	Balance b/d	6,57,475				

Dr. **Sale of Asset Account** Cr.

Date	Particulars	Amount	Date	Particulars	Amount
2009		Rs.	2009		Rs.
Jan. 1	To Machinery A/c	4,10,000	July 1	By Depreciation A/c	25,000
				" Bank (Sale) A/c	2,50,000
				" Profit and Loss A/c —Loss on Sale A/c	1,35,000
		4,10,000			4,10,000

(2) With Retrospective Effect

Under this method, ***the depreciation should be calculated from the beginning of the year in which the asset was acquired under changed/new method. The difference so made between the two methods—i.e., under-depreciation or over-depreciation—should be adjusted against Profit and Loss Account of the year in which the change takes place.*** In short, students are to calculate:

(i) Amount of depreciation under old method.
(ii) Amount of depreciation under new method.
(iii) Ascertain under—depreciation (if old value is less) or over-depreciation (if old value is more) which should be adjusted by passing the following:

Thus, (a) *For under-depreciation*

Profit and Loss A/c	Dr.	If old value is less
To Assets A/c		

(b) *For over-depreciation*

Asset A/c	Dr.	If old value is more
To Profit and Loss A/c		

(iv) Whatever will be the under-depreciation or over-depreciation the same should be adjustd in current year's Profit and Loss Account.
(v) New method should be followed subsequently from the date of change.

The following illustration will help us to understand the principle clearly:

Illustration 18

A company charges depreciation @ 10% p.a. on Written-Down Value (WDV) basis and its financial year is from April to March. It purchased a machine costing Rs. 10,00,000 on 1.4.2000. On 31.3.2004, the company decides to switch over to Straight Line Method of depreciation with retrospective effect from 1.4.2000.

What will be the journal entries to be passed by the company on 30.3.2004?

Solution

Depreciation as per Written-down Value Basis

		Rs.	Total Dep.
01.04.2000	Book Value	10,00,000	
31.03.2001	Dep. @ 10%	1,00,000	1,00,000
01.04.2001	WDV	9,00,000	
31.03.2002	Dep.	90,000	90,000
01.04.2002	WDV	8,10,000	
31.03.2003	Dep.	81,000	81,000
01.04.2003	WDV	7,29,000	2,71,000

Depreciation as per Straight Line Method

Since Straight Line Method of depreciation is followed, amount of depreciation per year will be @ Rs. 1,00,000 for 3 years i.e., Rs. 3,00,000.

∴ Depreciation under-charged = Dep. as per Straight Line Method – Dep. as per WDV Method
= Rs. 3,00,000 – Rs. 2,71,000 = Rs. 29,000

	Rs.
Depreciation for the year from 1.4.2003 to 31.3.2004 will be	1,00,000
Add: Dep. under-charged	29,000
Total Depreciation charged	1,29,000

The entry will be:

		Rs.	Rs.
Depreciation on Machinery A/c	Dr.	1,29,000	
To Machinery A/c	Dr.		1,29,000

Illustration 19

XYZ Ltd purchased an equipment on 1.4.2007, at a Cost of Rs. 10,00,000 and have charged depreciation as per Straight Line Method on 31.3.2008 and 31.3.2009 @ 20% p.a. On 31.3.2010 the company decides to switch-over to the Written-down Value Method with retrospective effect w.e.f. 1.4.2007.

How much depreciation should it charge on 31.3.2010?

Solution

Depreciation as per Straight Line Method

Depreciation @ 20% p.a. on Rs. 10,00,000 will be Rs. 2,00,000 p.a. from 1.4.2007 to 31.3.2009 = 2 years. Depreciation will be Rs. 2,00,000 × 2 = Rs. 4,00,000

Depreciation as per Written-down Value Method

		Rs.	Total Dep.
01.04.2007	Book Value	10,00,000	
31.03.2008	Dep. @ 20%	2,00,000	2,00,000
01.04.2008	WDV	8,00,000	
31.03.2009	Dep. @ 20%	1,60,000	1,60,000
01.04.2009	WDV	6,40,000	3,60,000

		Rs.
Depreciation overcharged	= Dep. as per Straight Line Method – Dep. as per WDV Method	
	= Rs. 4,00,000 – Rs. 3,60,000	
	= Rs. 40,000	
Depreciation for 31.3.2010	= (Rs. 10,00,000 – Rs. 4,00,000)	
	= Rs. 6,00,000 = 6,00,000 × 20% =	1,20,000
Less: Depreciation overcharged	=	40,000
To be charged on 31.3.2010		80,000

Change of method of charging depreciation from Diminishing Balance to Straight Line Method

Illustration 20

M/s Hot and Cold commenced business on 1st July 2007, when they purchased a new machinery at a cost of Rs. 8,00,000. On 1st Jan. 2009, they purchased another machinery for Rs. 6,00,000 and again on 1st Oct. 2011, machinery costing Rs. 15,00,000 was purchased. They adopted a policy of charging @ 20% p.a. on diminishing balance basis.

On 1st July 2011, they, however, changed the method of providing depreciation and adopted the method of writing-off the Machinery Account at 15% p.a. under Straight Line Method with retrospective effect from 1st July 2007, the adjustment being made in the accounts for the year ended 30th June 2012.

The depreciation has been charged on time basis.

You are required to calculate the difference in depreciation to be adjusted in the Machinery on 1st July 2011, and show the Machinery Account for the year ended 30th June 2012. **[ICWA]**

Solution

In the Books of M/s Hot and Cold

Machinery Account

Dr. Cr.

Date	*Particulars*	*Amount*	*Date*	*Particulars*	*Amount*
2011		Rs.	2012		Rs.
July 1	To Balance b/d	6,73,280[1]	June 30	By Depreciation A/c	3,78,750[3]
	" Profit and Loss A/c (Dep. overcharged)	21,720[2]		" Balance c/d	18,16,250
Oct. 1	" Bank (purchased) A/c	15,00,000			
		21,95,000			21,95,000
2012					
July 1	To Balance b/d	18,16,250			

Workings:

1. Book value of Machinery as on 1.7.2011 and the total amount of depreciation under Diminishing Balance Method up to 30.6.2011:

Depreciation under Diminishing Balance Method.

Statement of Depreciation

Particulars		*Machinery I*	*Machinery II*	*Total Depreciation*
		Rs.	Rs.	Rs.
1.7.2007	Book Value	8,00,000		
30.6.2008	Dep. @ 20%	1,60,000		1,60,000
1.7.2008	WDV	6,40,000		
1.1.2009	Book Value		6,00,000	
30.6.2009	Dep. @ 20%	1,28,000	60,000	1,88,000
1.7.2009	WDV	5,12,000	5,40,000	
30.6.2010	Dep. @ 20%	1,02,400	1,08,000	2,10,400
1.7.2010	WDV	4,09,600	4,32,000	
30.6.2011	Dep. @ 20%	81,920	86,400	1,68,320
		3,27,680	3,45,600	
		Rs.	6,73,280	7,26,720

2. **Depreciation Overcharged:**

Now, Depreciation under Straight Line Method:

		Rs.
On Rs. 8,00,000 @ 15% = 1,20,000 × 4 years (i.e., from 1.7.07 to 30.6.2011)	=	4,80,000
On Rs. 6,00,000 @ 15% = 90,000 × 2 years (i.e., from 1.1.09 to 30.6.2011)	=	2,25,000
		7,05,000

∴ Depreciation Overcharged = Reducing Balance basis – Straight Line basis
= Rs. 7,26,720 – Rs. 7,05,000
= Rs. 21,720

3. **Depreciation for the year:**

		Rs.
On Rs. 14,00,000 @ 15% for 1 year	=	2,10,000
On Rs. 15,00,000 @ 15% for 9 months	=	1,68,750
		3,78,750

Change in method from Diminishing Balance Method to Straight Line Method

Illustration 21

M/s Mill and Wright commenced business on 1st Jan. 2007, when they purchased plant and equipment for, Rs. 7,00,000. They adopted a policy of (i) charging depreciation at 15% p.a. on diminishing balance basis, and (ii) charging full year's depreciation on additions.

Over the years, their purchases of plants have been:

Date	Rs.
1.8.2008	1,50,000
30.9.2011	2,00,000

On 1.1.2011 it, was decided to change the method of rate of depreciation to 10% on Straight Line basis with retrospective effect from 1st Jan. 2007, the adjustment being made in accounts for the year ending 31st Dec. 2011.

Calculate the difference in depreciation to be adjusted in the Plant and Equipment Account on 1st Jan. 2011, and show the ledger account for the year 2011.

[CA Entrance]

Solution

Statement showing the difference in depreciation due to change in method

Particulars		*Book-value as per diminishing balance method @ 15%*	*Book-value as per proposed straight line method @ 10%*	*Depreciation @ 15% under diminishing balance method*	*Depreciation @ 10% on straight line method*
		Rs.	Rs.		Rs.
1.1.2007	Book Value	7,00,000	7,00,000		
31.12.2007	Depreciation	1,05,000	70,000	1,05,000	70,000
1.1.2008	WDV	5,95,000	6,30,000		
1.8.2008	Additions	1,50,000	1,50,000		
		7,45,000	7,80,000		
31.12.2008	Depreciation	1,11,750	85,000	1,11,750	85,000
1.1.2009	WDV	6,33,250	6,95,000		
31.12.2009	Depreciation	94,988	85,000	94,988	85,000
1.1.2010	WDV	5,38,262	6,10,000		
31.12.2010	Depreciation	80,739	85,000	80,739	85,000
1.1.2011	WDV	4,57,523	5,25,000	3,92,477	3,25,000

Difference of depreciation due to change in Method = Rs. 3,92,477 – Rs. 3,25,000 = Rs. 67,477, i.e., depreciation was overcharged by Rs. 67,477.

Dr. **Plant and Equipment Account** Cr.

Date	*Particulars*	*Amount*	*Date*	*Particulars*	*Amount*
2011		Rs.	2011		Rs.
July 1	To Balance b/d	4,57,523	Dec. 31	By Depreciation A/c	1,05,000*
	" Profit and Loss A/c (Dep. overcharged)	67,477		" Balance c/d	6,20,000
Sept. 10	" Bank A/c —Additions	2,00,000			
		7,25,000			7,25,000

* @ 10% on Rs. 7,00,000 + Rs. 1,50,000 + 2,00,000 = Rs. 1,05,000

Change in method of charging depreciation from Diminishing Balance Method to Straight Ling Method

Illustration 22

Ram Ltd., which depreciates its machinery at 10% p.a. on Diminishing Balance Method, had on 1st January 2011 Rs. 9,72,000 on the debit side of Machinery Account.

During the year 2011 machinery purchased on 1st January 2009 for Rs. 80,000 was sold for Rs. 45,000 on 1st July 2011 and a new machinery at a cost of Rs. 1,50,000 was purchased and installed on the same date, installation charges being Rs. 8,000.

The company wanted to change the method of depreciation from Diminishing Balance Method to Straight Line Method with effect from 1st January 2009. Difference of depreciation up to 31st December 2011.

Show Machinery Account. **[CA Foundation]**

Solution

In the Books of Ram Ltd.
Machinery Account

Dr. Date	Particulars	Amount	Date	Particulars	Cr. Amount
2011		Rs.	2011		Rs.
Jan. 1	To Balance b/d	9,72,000	July 30	By Bank A/c —Sale	45,000
July	" Bank A/c —Purchase	1,50,000		" Depreciation A/c $\left(Rs. 80,000 \times \frac{10}{100} \times \frac{6}{12}\right)$	4,000
	" Bank A/c —Installation Charges	8,000		" Profit and Loss A/c —Loss on Sale	15,000[1]
			Dec. 31	" Depreciation A/c	1,19,000[3]
				" Profit and Loss A/c —Dep. undercharged	12,000[2]
				" Balance c/d	9,34,000
		11,30,000			11,30,000

Workings :

1. Loss on Sale of Plant Sold

		Rs.
	Book Value	80,000
Less:	Dep. @ 10% for $2\frac{1}{2}$ years on Straight Line Method	20,000
	WDV on 1.7.2011	60,000
Less:	Sold for	45,000
∴	Loss on Sale	15,000

2. Depreciation Undercharged

		Rs.
	Book Value as on 1.1.2009 $\left(Rs. 80,000 \times \frac{100}{90} \times \frac{100}{90}\right)$	12,00,000
	Depreciation @ 10% for 2 years (i.e., 2009 & 2010) Rs. 1,20,000 × 2 =	2,40,000
Less :	Already charged as per Diminishing Balance Method— (Rs. 1,20,000 + Rs. 1,08,000)	2,28,000
	Depreciation undercharged	12,000

3. Depreciation for 2009

		Old Machine I		New Machine II
	On. 1.1.2009		On 1.7.2011 —B.V.	15,800
	Book Value	12,00,000	Dep. @ 10% for 6 months	7,900
Less :	Sold	80,000		
		11,20,000		
	Depreciation @ 10%	1,12,000		

∴ Total Depreciation Rs. 1,12,000 + Rs. 7,900 = Rs. 1,19,900.

Change in method of charging depreciations from Straight Line Method to Written-down Value Method

Illustration 23

A firm purchased on 1st January 1999 certain machinery for Rs. 9,70,000 and spent Rs. 30,000 on its erection. On 1st July 1999 additional machinery costing Rs. 5,00,000 was acquired. On 1st July 2001 the machinery purchased on 1st January 1999, having become obsolete, was auctioned for Rs. 4,00,000 and, on the same date, a new machine was purchased at a cost of Rs. 7,50,000.

Depreciation was provided for annually on 31st December @ 10% p.a. on the original cost of the asset. In 2002, however, the firm changed this method of providing depreciation and adopted the method of writing-off 20% p.a. on the written-down value with effect from 1st January 1999.

Show the Machinery Account as it would stand at the end of each year from 1999 to 2002.

[CU BCom (Hons.) 2003]

Solution

In the Books of Ram Ltd.
Machinery Account

Dr. | *Cr.*

Date	*Particulars*		*Amount*	*Date*	*Particulars*	*Amount*
1999			Rs.	1999		Rs.
Jan. 1	To Bank A/c:			Dec. 31	By Depreciation A/c	1,25,00
	Cost	9,70,000		"	" Balance c/d	13,75,000
	Erection charge	30,000	10,00,000			
July 1	" Bank A/c		5,00,000			
			15,00,000			15,00,000
2000				2000		
Jan. 1	To Balance b/d		13,75,000	Dec. 31	By Depreciation A/c	1,50,000
					" Balance c/d	12,25,000
			13,75,000			13,75,000
2001				2001		
Jan. 1	To Balance b/d		12,25,000	July 1	By Bank—Sale of Machine	4,00,000
July 1	" Bank A/c		7,50,000	July 1	" P & L A/c (Loss on Sale)	3,50,000
				Dec. 31.	" Depreciation A/c	1,37,500
				"	" Balance c/d	10,87,500
			19,75,000			19,75,000
2002				2002		
Dec. 31	To Balance b/d		10,87,500	Dec. 31	By Profit & Loss A/c	1,24,500
					" Dep. undercharged	
					" Depreciation A/c	1,92,600
					" Balance c/d	7,70,400
			10,87,500			10,87,500
2003						
Jan. 1	To Balance b/d		7,70,400			

Workings :

Depreciation under Straight Line Method

	Particulars	*Machine No. 1*	*Machine No. 2*	*Machine No. 3*	*Machine No. 4*
		Rs.	Rs.		Rs.
1.1.1999	Book Value (Rs. 9,70,000 + Rs. 30,000)	10,00,000			
1.7.1999	Book Value		5,00,000		1,25,000
31.11.1999	Depreciation @ 10%	1,00,000	25,000		
1.1.2000	WDV	9,00,000	4,75,000		
31.12.2000	Depreciation @ 10%	1,00,000	50,000		1,50,000
1.1.2001	WDV	8,00,000	4,25,000		
1.7..2001	Depreciation @ 10%	50,000			
1.7.2001	WDV	7,50,000			
	Sold for	4,00,000			
	Loss on Sale	3,50,000			
1.7.2001	Book Value			7,50,000	
31.12.2001	Depreciation		50,000	37,500	1,37,500
1.1.2002	WDV		3,75,000	7,12,500	

Note : For the machine which became obsolete and sold, question of adjustment does not arise. So, total deprecation charge for Machine No. 2 (Rs. 25,000 + Rs. 50,000 + Rs. 50,000) Rs. 1,25,000 and for Machine 3 for Rs. 37,500 only. Thus, total depreciation already charged under :

Straight Line Method for Machine No. 2 and Machine No. 3 were Rs. 1,62,500 (i.e., Rs. 1,25,000 + Rs. 37,500).

Depreciation under Diminishing Balance Method

(Since Machine No. 1 has already been sold, it has no effect and as such the same should be excluded.)

	Particulars	Machine No. 2	Machine No. 3	Total Depreciation
		Rs.		Rs.
1.7.1999	Book Value	5,00,000		
31.12.1999	Depreciation @ 10%	50,000		50,000
1.1.2000	WDV	4,50,000		90,000
31.12.2000	Depreciation @ 10%	90,000		
1.1.2000	WDV	3,60,000		
1.7.2001	Book Value		7,50,000	
31.12.2001	Depreciation @ 10%	72,000	75,000	1,47,000
1.1.2002	WDV	2,88,000	6,75,000	2,87,000
31.11.2002	Depreciation @ 10%	57,600	1,35,00	1,92,600
		2,30,400	5,40,000	

Depreciation Undercharged

		Rs.
	Depreciation as per Diminishing Balance Method	2,87,000
Less :	Depreciation already charged under Straight Line Method	1,62,500
	∴ Depreciation Undercharged	1,24,500

Objectives of Management about Depreciation Policy

The management has to consider the following objectives while framing a proper depreciation policy:

(i) To recover the cost of fixed assets before its effective life;

(ii) Creating funds to replace such asset in future;

(iii) To take the advantage of tax benefit;

(iv) To determine the correct profit which does not mean dividend paid out of capital;

(v) Following a uniform rate of return; and

(vi) Sometimes to create a source of fund for working capital.

Provision for Depreciation and the Methods prescribed by the Companies Act

At present the Companies Act makes depreciation a legal compulsion, i.e., according to Sec. 205, a company cannot declare and pay dividend for any financial year out of profit before charging depreciation. The Companies Act also lays down how the depreciation has to be worked out.

According to Sec. 205(2) of the Act, depreciation must be provided either:

(a) to the extent specified in Sec. 350[1]; or

(b) in respect of each items of depreciable asset, for such an amount which is arrived at by dividing 95% of the original cost thereof to the company by the specified period relating to such asset; or

(c) on any other basis which has been approved by the Central Government which has the effect of writing-off by way of depreciation 95% of the original cost to the company of each such depreciable asset on the expiry of the specified period; or

(d) as regards any other depreciable assets for which no rate of depreciation has been laid down by the Indian Income-tax Act, 1961, or the rules made thereunder, on such basis as may be approved by the Central Government by any general order published in the official gazette or by any special order in any particular case.

The Act also provided that when depreciation is provided for in the manner stated in (a), (b), (c) above, for any asset which is being sold, discarded, demolished or destroyed (before charging depreciation in full) the excess of WDV over its sale prices shall be written-off in the financial year.

Similarly, for clauses (b) and (c) stated above the specified period in respect of any depreciable asset shall mean the number of years at the end of which at least 95% of the original cost of that asset will have

1 Section 350 provides that depreciation shall be the amount calculated with reference to the Written-down Value of the asset as shown by the books of the company at the end of the financial year expiring at the commencement of this Act or immediately thereafter and at the end of each subsequent financial year, at the rate specified for the assets by the Indian Income-tax Act, 1961, and the rules made thereunder for the time being in force, as normal depreciation including therein extra and multiple shift allowances but not including therein any special, initial or other depreciation or any development rebate, whether allowed by that Act or those rules or otherwise

been provided for by way of depreciation if the depreciation was to be calculated according to Sec. 350 of the Companies Act.

Since there is a sharp rise in the rate of depreciation by the Income-tax Act, the companies find it extremely difficult to declare and pay dividend after charging depreciation. For this purpose, an amendment was proposed. After such amendment, depreciation should be calculated according to the prescribed rates which have been specified—the Schedule XIV of the Act as:

(i) Asset have been clarified as:
(a) Building; (b) Plant and Machinery; (c) Furniture and Fittings; (d) Ships.

(ii) Rates of depreciation have been prescribed only as by the following alternatives, viz.:
(a) Straight Line Method; and (b) Diminishing Balance Method.

(iii) In case of addition or sold/discarded/demolished etc., depreciation should be calculated on a *pro rata* basis.

(iv) Rate of depreciation for Double-Shift/Triple-Shift working have been applied only in case of Plant and Machinery.

The rates which have been specified in the Schedule XIV (some of them) are given:

Rates of Depreciation as per Companies Act, 1956 (Sec. 2058, Sec. 350)

(Schedule XIV)

	Single Shift		Double Shift		Triple Shift	
	WDV	SLM	WDV	SLM	WDV	SLM
1. (i) Building (Other than factory building)	5%	1.63%	—	—	—	—
(ii) Factory building	10%	3.34%	—	—	—	—
(iii) Purely Temporary Erection (No Extra Shift dep. is available)	100%	100%	—	—	—	—
2. Plant and Machinery (General rates)	13.41%	4.75%	20.87%	7.42%	27.82%	10.34%
3. Furniture and Fittings (General rate) (No Extra Shift dep. is available)	18.10%	6.33%	—	—	—	—
4. Ships (No extra shift dep. is available)	27.05%	10%	—	—	—	—

Depreciation Policy — from the standpoint of Management

It is known to us that a huge amount is blocked in fixed assets for acquiring modern machines. For the purpose of such acquisition, the management must take some concrete decisions. Thus, the policy must include:

(i) to select the appropriate method;
(ii) to review the current provision for depreciation—whether there is any under-provision for depreciation or over-provision for depreciation;
(iii) to evaluate the existing policy of depreciation from the standpoint of tax consideration;
(iv) to constitute a committee for depreciation taking engineers and accountants;
(v) to ascertain the proper amount of depreciation and its recording procedure; and
(vi) to disclose the policy of depreciation in the published annual report for the benefit of shareholders, outsiders etc.

Selecting Appropriate Method

The following factors should carefully be considered while selecting the appropriate method of depreciation for the assets :

(i) *Conservatism* : Whatever the method selected must be consistent, e.g., if Straight Line Method is followed for computing depreciation in the case of Plant and Machinery, the same must be consistent over the years. But different methods may be used for different types of assets.

(ii) *Considerations* : While selecting the appropriate method, the firm must be conservative not only from the standpoint of depreciation but also from the standpoint of estimated life of the asset and also its scrap value which are, practically, based on certain estimated information. In other words, the amount of depreciation will be computed in such a manner so that the profit of the firm is not adversely affected (because, in both the cases—whether under-depreciation or over-depreciation—profit is affected.)

(iii) *Services* : Assets provide more services in earlier years than the later years as their working capacity gradually decreases in subsequent years. Moreover, repairs and maintenance expenses are gradually increased. For this purpose, more depreciation should be charged on the earlier years than the later years (i.e., Reducing Balance Method should be adopted). On the contrary, if it is found that the assets produce equal service or repairs and maintenance expenses are almost equal. In that case, Straight Line Method may be advocated.

(iv) *Income-Tax* : For income-tax purpose, it is better to follow a particular method of depreciation.

(v) *Computation* : Instead of applying different rates for different types of assets, a single rate may be applied in all the assets irrespective of their 'caste and creed,' i.e., their nature, types, estimated life, scrap value etc.

(vi) *Reasons* : The value of the assets may be reduced due to :
(a) time (a fixed period, e.g., lease);
(b) extraction (when exhausted, e.g., mines); and
(c) usage (i.e., application, e.g., Plant and Machinery).

(vii) *Improvement in Technology* : An asset may become obsolete as a result of the technological improvement before its life.

(viii) *Prevailing law* : Sometimes the method and rate of depreciation have been determined and fixed by the prevailing law of the country, e.g., the rate and method of depreciation is to be fixed and followed as per Schedule XIV of the Companies Act for all limited companies in India.

From the discussion made so far, while selecting an appropriate method of depreciation, the above factors should clearly be considered with reasonable care and their respective importance on the assets concerned. The same should be done in such a manner that the costs should be matched with revenues and, as a result, the problems will be minimised.

GENERAL ILLUSTRATIONS

Change in method of charging depreciation from Diminishing Balance Method to Straight Line Method

Illustration 24

Y Ltd. maintained its Plant Account under Diminishing Balance Method since 1.1.2000. Balance of Plant Account as on 1.1.2003 was Rs. 36,450 after charging depreciation @ 10 p.a. under Diminishing Balance Method. On 1.7.2003 a new plant was purchased for Rs. 30,000. On 1.1.2004 the company decided to change the method of charging depreciation from Diminishing Balance Method to Straight Line Method, the rate of depreciation being 12% p.a. with retrospective effect from 1.1.2000. On 1.10.2004 another plant was purchased for Rs. 20,000.

Show the Plant Account for the year ended Dec. 31st 2003 and 2004.

Solution

Book Value of Plant as on 1.1.2000

$$= \text{Rs. } 36{,}450 \times \frac{100}{90} \times \frac{100}{90} \times \frac{100}{90} = \text{Rs. } 50{,}000$$

Statement of Depreciation
(Under Diminishing Balance Method)

Date	*Particulars*	*Plant I*	*Plant II*	*Total Depr.*
		Rs.	Rs.	Rs.
01.01.2000	Book Value.	50,000	—	
31.12.2000	Depreciation @ 10%	5,000		5,000
01.01.2001	WDV	45,000		
31.12.2001	Depreciation @ 10%	4,500		4,500
01.01.2002	WDV	40,500		
31.12.2002	Depreciation @ 10%	4,050		4,050
01.01.2003	WDV	36,450		
31.07.2003	Book Value		30,000	
31.12.2003	Depreciation @ 10%	3,645	1,500	5,145
01.01.2004	WDV	32,805	28,500	18,695

Depreciation under Straight Line Method

Depreciation @ 12% on Rs. 50,000 = Rs. 6,000 for 4 years will be Rs. 24,000 + Rs. 1,800 on addition, i.e., total will be Rs. 25,800.

Depreciation under-charged = Rs. 25,800 – Rs. 18,695 = Rs. 7,105.

Plant Account

Dr. Cr.

Date	Particulars	Amount	Date	Particulars	Amount
2003		Rs.	2003		Rs.
Jan. 1	To Balance b/d	36,450	Dec. 31	By Depreciation A/c (Rs. 3,645 + Rs. 1,500)	5,145
July 1	To Bank A/c—Purchase	30,000		By Balance c/d	61,305
		66,450			66,450
2004			2004		
Jan. 1	To Balance b/d	61,305	Jan. 1	By Profit and Loss A/c —Depreciation under-charged	7,105
Oct. 1	To Bank A/c—Purchase	20,000	Dec. 31	By Depreciation A/c (Rs. 6,000 + 3,600 + 600)	10,200
				By Balance c/d	64,000
		81,305			81,305

Ascertainment of Book-Value of various plants purchased at different dates

Illustration 25

The balance in the Machinery Account as on 31.12.2007 was Rs. 12,600 which was arrived at after charging depreciation on machinery at the 1st year @ 10%; 2nd year @ 20% p.a.; 3rd year @ 30% p.a., and 4th year @ 40% p.a. under Straight Line Method. The balance included a machinery purchased on 1.1.2005, the Written-down Value of which was Rs. 3,200; another machine was purchased on 1.4.2006, the Written-down Value of which was Rs. 4,900 and another machine was purchased on 1.7.2007, the Written-down Value of which was Rs. 4,500. All the machines were depreciated for full years irrespective of the date of purchase or sale.

Prepare Machinery Account for the years ending 2008 and 2009.

Workings :

1. **Book-Value of 1st Plant as on 1.1.2005**

   Depreciation already charged in 1st year, 2nd year and 3rd year, @ 10%, 20% and 30% = 60%

   ∴ Balance left 40% (100% – 60%) for 4th year, the value of which was Rs. 3,200.

   So, Book-Value as on 1.1.2005 = $\frac{\text{Rs. } 3,200}{40} \times 100$ = Rs. 8,000

2. **Book-Value of 2nd Plant as on 1.1.2006**

   Depreciation already charged in 1st year and 2nd year @ 10% and 20% = 30%

   Balance left 70% (100% – 30%), the value of which was Rs. 4,900

   So, Book-Value as on 1.1.2006 = $\frac{\text{Rs. } 4,900}{70} \times 100$ = Rs. 7,000

3. **Book-Value of 3rd Plant as on 1.1.2007**

   Depreciation already charged in 1st year @ 10%

   ∴ Balance left 90% (100% – 10%), the value of which was Rs. 4,500

   So, Book-Value as on 1.1.2007 = $\frac{\text{Rs. } 4,500}{90} \times 100$ = Rs. 5,000.

Statement of Depreciation

Date	Particulars	Machine I	Machine II	Machine III	Total Depreciation
		Rs.	Rs.	Rs.	Rs.
01.01.2005	Book Value	8,000			
31.12.2005	Depreciation	800			800
01.01.2006	WDV	7,200			

Contd.

		Rs.	Rs.	Rs.	Rs.
01.01.2006	Book Value		7,000		
31.12.2006	Depreciation	1,600	700		2,300
01.01.2007	WDV	5,600	6,300		
01.01.2007	Book Value			5,000	
31.12.2007	Depreciation	2,400	1,400	500	4,300
01.01.2008	WDV	3,200	4,900	4,500	
31.12.2008	Depreciation	3,200	2,100	1,000	6,300
01.01.2009	WDV	—	2,800	3,500	
31.12.2009	Depreciation	—	2,800	1,500	4,300
01.01.2010	WDV	—	—	2,000	

Dr. **Machinery Account** Cr.

Date	Particulars	Amount	Date	Particulars	Amount
2008		Rs.	2008		Rs.
Jan. 1	To Balance b/d		Dec. 31	By Depreciation A/c	6,300
	(Rs. 3,200 + 4,900 + 4,500)	12,600		" Balance c/d	6,300
		12,600			12,600
2009			2009		
Jan. 1	To Balance b/d	6,300	Dec. 31	By Depreciation A/c	4,300
				" Balance c/d	2,000
		6,300			6,300

Ascertainment of Opening Balance and Loss on Sale

Illustration 26

Prepare the Machinery Account in the books of Mr. X from 2006 to 2009. Balance of Machinery Account as on 1.1.2006 was Rs. 70,000 after charging depreciation @ 10% p.a. for the previous three years under Straight Line Method. On 1.10.2006, another machinery of Rs. 50,000 was purchased and paid installation expenses amounted to Rs. 10,000. On 1.7.2007, $\frac{2}{5}$th of the machinery purchased before 2006 was disposed-off at Rs. 22,000 and on 1.4.2008, the machinery purchased in the year 2006 was discarded. Assume the business closes its account on 31st Dec. every year and same rate of depreciation was charged for all the years.

Solution

In the Books of Mr. X

Dr. **Machinery Account** Cr.

Date	Particulars	Amount	Date	Particulars	Amount
2008		Rs.	2008		Rs.
Jan. 1	To Balance b/d	70,000	Dec. 31	By Depreciation A/c	11,500
Oct. 10	" Bank A/c			(Rs. 10,000* + Rs. 1,500)	
	—Purchase	60,000		" Balance c/d	1,18,500
		1,30,000			1,30,000
2007			2007		
Jan. 1	To Balance b/d	1,18,500	Dec. 31	By Depreciation A/c	2,000
				$\left(\text{Rs.}10{,}000 \times \frac{2}{3} \times \frac{6}{12}\right)$	
				" Bank A/c—Sale	22,000
			Dec. 31	" Depreciation A/c	12,000
				$\left(\text{Rs.}10{,}000 \times \frac{3}{5}\right)$ + Rs. 6,000	
				" Balance c/d	82,500
		1,18,500			1,18,500

Contd.

2008			Rs.	2008			Rs.
Jan. 1	To	Balance b/d	82,500	April 1	By	Depreciation A/c $\left(\text{Rs.}6{,}000\times\frac{3}{12}\right)$	1,500
					"	Profit and Loss A/c (Rs. 60,000 –1,500 – 6,000 – 1,500)	51,000
				Dec. 31	"	Depreciation A/c	6,000
					"	Balance c/d	24,000
			82,500				82,500

Workings:

1. ***Depreciation for 2006**

Depreciation @ 10% for 3 years already charged, so the balance left 70% (100% – 30%) the value of which was Rs. 70,000.

So, Cost Price was Rs. 70,000 × $\frac{100}{70}$ = Rs. 1,00,000;

Depreciation will be @ 10% on Rs. 1,00,000 = Rs. 10,000

2. **Sale of Machine**

In 2007, $\frac{2}{5}$th of Rs. 1,00,000 = Rs. 40,000 (i.e., depreciation @ 10% will be Rs. 4,000 per year)

Less:	Dep. of 4 years =	16,000
	WDV =	24,000
Less:	Dep. for 6 months =	2,000
	WDV =	22,000
Sold for =		22,000
No Peofir/No Loss		—

Plant destroyed by fire

Illustration 27

A company charges depreciation on Plant & Machinery under Reducing Balance System @ 15% p.a. On 1.4.2008 the balance in ledger stood at Rs. 4,60,000. The following particulars are given relating to Plant & Machinery during the 4 years ended 31.3.2012 :

Date	
1.9.2008	A machine purchased for Rs. 20,000 (installation expenses Rs. 1,000) on 1.5.2006 was fully destroyed in an accident.
1.7.2009	Purchased a new machine costing Rs. 50,000 (installation expenses Rs. 2,500). A sum of Rs. 30,000 was paid on the same date and the balance was paid in May 2010.
31.8.2010	Plant purchased on 1.4.2007 for Rs. 30,000 (installation expenses Rs. 1,500) was disposed-off for Rs. 36,000.
1.11.2011	Some old machinery (book-value on 1.4.2008 Rs. 10,000) were sold for Rs, 4,000.

Show the Plant & Machinery Account as would appear in the books of the company for the 4 years ended 31.3.2012 assuming depreciation is charged proportionately even if the asset is sold or destroyed.

[ICWA]

Solution

Statement of Depreciation

	Particulars	*Plant I*	*Plant II*	*Plant III*	*Plant IV*	*Plant V*	*Total Depr.*
		Rs.	Rs.	Rs.	Rs.	Rs.	Rs.
1.4.2008	WDV	4,44,604[2]	15,396[1]				
1.9.2008	Dep. @ 15%		962				
	Value of Plant Destroyed		14,434				

Contd.

		Rs.	Rs.	Rs.	Rs.	Rs.	Rs.
31.3.2009	Dep. @ 15%						67,653
	on Rs. 4,44,604	66,691					
1.4.2009	WDV	3,77,913					
1.7.2009	Book Value			52,500			
31.3.2010	Dep. @ 15%	56,687		5,906			62,593
1.4.2010	WDV	3,21,226		46,594			
	Less : Plant sold	19,345			19,345[3]		
		3,01,881					
31.8.2010	Depreciation @ 15%				1,209		
	WDV				18,136		
	Sold for				36,000		
	Profit on Sale				17,864		53,480
31.3.2011	Depreciation	45,282		6,989			
1.4.2011	WDV	2,56,599		39,605			
	Less : Plant Sold	6,141				6,141[4]	
		2,50,458					
1.11.2011	Depreciation @ 15%					537	
						5,604	
	Sold for					4,000	
	Loss on Sale					1,604	44,046
31.3.2012	Depreciation	37,569		5,940			
1.4.2012	WDV	2,12,889		33,665			

1. WDV of Plant Destroyed on 1.4.2008

		Rs.
1.5.2006	Cost	21,000
31.3.2007	Dep. @ 15%	2,887
1.4.2007	WDV	18,113
31.3.2008	Dep. @ 15% on WDV	2,717
1.4.2008	WDV	15,396

2. WDV of other Plant on 1.4.2008

	Rs.
1.4.2008—WDV	4,60,000
Less : Plant Destroyed	15,396
	4,44,604

3. WDV of Assets sold on 31.8.2010

		Rs.
	Cost 1.4.07	31,500
Less:	31.3.08 Dep.	4,725
		26,775
	31.3.09 Dep.	4,016
		22,759
	31.3.10 Dep.	3,414
	1.4.10 WDV	19,345

4. WDV of Assets sold on 1.11.2011

		Rs.
1.4.08	WDV	10,000
31.3.09	Dep.	1,500
1.4.09	WDV	8,500
31.3.10	Dep.	1,275
1.4.10	WDV	7,225
31.3.11	Dep.	1,084
1.4.11	WDV	6,141

In the Books of ...

Plant and Machinery Account

Dr. *Cr.*

Date	*Particulars*	*Amount*	*Date*	*Particulars*	*Amount*
2008		Rs.	2008		Rs.
Apr. 1	To Balance b/d	4,60,000	Sept. 1	By Depreciation A/c	962
				" Profit and Loss A/c —Destroyed plant	14,434
			2009		
			Mar. 31	" Depreciation A/c	66,691
				" Balance c/d	3,77,913
		4,60,000			4,60,000

Contd.

Date		Particulars	Rs.	Date		Particulars	Rs.
2009				2009			
Apr. 1	To	Balance b/d	3,77,913	March 31	By	Depreciation A/c	62,593
July 1	"	Bank A/c	32,500				
	"	Creditors A/c (50,000 – 30,000)	20,000		"	Balance c/d	3,67,820
			4,30,413				4,30,413
2010				2010			
Apr. 1	To	Balance b/d	3,67,820	Aug. 31	By	Bank A/c – Sale	36,000
Aug. 31	"	Profit on Loss A/c — Profit on Sale	17,864		"	Depreciation A/c	1,209
				2011			
				Mar. 31	"	Depreciation A/c	52,271
					"	Balance c/d	2,96,204
			3,85,684				3,85,684
2011				2011			
Apr. 1	To	Balance b/d	2,96,204	Nov. 1	By	Bank A/c – Sale	4,000
					"	Depreciation A/c	537
					"	Profit & Loss A/c —Loss on Sale	1,604
				2012			
				Mar. 31	"	Depreciation A/c	43,510
					"	Balance c/d	2,46,553
			2,96,204				2,96,204

Change of method of deprection and Plant destroyed by fire

Illustration 28

On 1.4.2002. X Ltd. acquired a new plant 'A' for Rs. 2,00,000 and further sum of Rs. 10,000 was spent for its installation. On 1.10.2003, another plant 'B' was purchased for Rs. 2,50,000.

In an accident on 31.12.2004, plant 'A' was destroyed. The scrap was sold for Rs. 20,000. On 15.1.2005, a used plant 'C' was purchased for Rs. 3,00,000 and a further sum of Rs. 45,000 was spent for its repairs and Rs. 5,000 on its erection.

The company had been providing for depreciation at 10% on.a straight line basis. It was the practice to provide depreciation for the full year on all acquisitions made at any time during the year and to ignore depreciation on any item sold or disposed of during the year. None of these assets was misused. The accounts are closed annually on 31st March.

It has now been decided to provide depreciation @ 20% under the diminishing balance method with retrospective effect in respect of existing items of plant and to make the necessary adjustment entries on 1.4.12006.

Required

(a) Determine the additional depreciation, if any, to be provided on account of the change in the method of depreciation; (b) Prepare the Plant Account and Accumulated Depreciation Account for all the years up to the financial year ending on 31st March 2006.

Solution

(a) Depreciation Under Straight Line Method

Statement of Depreciation

	Particulars	*Plant 'A'*	*Plant 'B'*	*Plant 'C'*	*Total Depreciation*
		Rs.	Rs.	Rs.	Rs.
1.4..2002	Book Value	2,10,000			
31.3..2003	Dep. @ 10%	21,000			21,000
1.4.2003	WDV	1,89,000			
1.10.2004	Book Value		2,50,000		
31.3.2004	Dep. @ 10%	21,000	25,000		46,000
1.4.2004	WDV	1,68,000	2,25,000		
31.12.2004	Sold for	20,000			
	Loss on Sale	1,48,000			

Contd.

Date	Particulars				
15.1.2005	Book Value			3,50,000	
31.3.2005	Dep. @ 10%		25,000	35,000	60,000
1.4.2005	WDV		2,00,000	3,15,000	
31.3..2006	Dep. @ 10%		25,000	35,000	60,000
1.4.2007	WDV		1,75,000	2,80,000	1,87,000
			Less : Depreciation 'A'		42,000
			Total Accumulated Depreciation		1,45,000

(b) Depreciation Under Diminishing Balance Method

Statement of Depreciation

	Particulars	*Plant 'B'*	*Plant 'C'*	*Total Depreciation*
		Rs.	Rs.	Rs.
1.10. 2003	Book Value	2,50,000		
31.3.2003	Dep. @ 20%	50,000		50,000
1.4.2004	WDV	2,00,000		
15.1.2005	Book Value		3,50,000	
31.3.2005	Dep. @ 20%	40,000	70,000	1,10,000
1.4.2005	WDV	1,60,000	2,80,000	
31.3.2006	Dep. @ 20%	32,000	56,000	88,000
1.4.2007	WDV	1,28,000	2,29,000	2,48,000

∴ Additional depreciation to be provided in 2006

= Rs. 2,48,000 – Rs. 1,45,000 = Rs. 1,03,000

Note : Since Provision for Depreciation Account is maintained, additional depreciation and sale of plant 'A' along with its depreciation, loss etc. are passed through Provision for Depreciation Account.

In the Books of X Ltd.

Plant Account

Dr. *Cr.*

Date		*Particulars*	*Amount*	*Date*		*Particulars*	*Amount*
2002			Rs.	2003			Rs.
Apr. 1	To	Bank A/c (Rs. 2,00,000 + Rs. 10,000)	2,10,000	Mar. 31	By	Balance c/d	2,10,000
			2,10,000				2,10,000
2003				2004			
Apr. 1	To	Balance b/d	2,10,000	Mar. 31	By	Balance c/d	4,60,000
Oct.1	"	Bank A/c	2,50,000				
			4,60,000				4,60,000
2004				2004			
Apr. 1	To	Balance b/d	4,60,000	Dec. 31	By	Plant Disposal A/c	2,10,000
2005				2005			
Jan. 15	"	Bank A/c (Rs. 3,00,000 + Rs. 50,000)	3,50,000	Mar. 31	"	Balance c/d	6,00,000
			8,10,000				8,10,000
2005				2006			
Apr. 1	To	Balance b/d	6,00,000	Mar. 31	By	Balance c/d	6,00,000
			6,00,000				6,00,000
2006							
Apr. 1	To	Balance b/d	6,00,000				

Provision for Depreciation Account

Dr. *Cr.*

Date		*Particulars*	*Amount*	*Date*		*Particulars*	*Amount*
2003			Rs.	2003			Rs.
Mar. 3	To	Balance c/d	21,000	Mar. 31	By	Depreciation A/c	21,000
			21,000				21,000

Contd.

2004		Rs.	Apr. 1	By	Balance b/d	21,000
Mar. 31	To	Balance c/d	67,000	2004		
			Mar. 31	"	Depreciation A/c	46,000
		67,000				67,000
Dec. 31	To Plant Disposal A/c	42,000	Apr. 1	By	Balance b/d	67,000
2005			2005			
Mar. 31	" Balance c/d	85,000	Mar. 31	"	Depreciation A/c	60,000
		1,27,000				1,27,000
2005			Apr. 1	By	Balance b/d	85,000
Mar. 31	To Balance c/d	1,45,000	2006			
			Mar. 31	"	Depreciation A/c	60,000
		1,45,000				1,45,000
			Apr. 1	"	By Balance b/d	1,45,000
				"	Profit and Loss (additional Depr.)	1,03,000

Dr. **Plant Disposal Account** Cr.

Date	Particulars	Amount	Date	Particulars	Amount
2004		Rs.	2004		Rs.
Dec. 31	To Plant A/c	2,10,000	Dec. 31	By Bank A/c —Sales	20,000
				" Prov. for Depreciation A/c	42,000
				" Profit & Loss A/c —Loss	1,48,000
		2,10,000			2,10,000

A Harder Problem

Illustration 29

A company writes-off 10% of the original cost of Plant and Machinery in every year till the whole cost of a particular piece of machinery is wiped-off. Full depreciation is written-off even if the machinery is in use for part of a year. Accounts are made up to 31st December.

On 1.1.2010, the balance in the Plant and Machinery Account was Rs. 1,95,150.

The original cost of various items in use are:

	Rs.
Items bought in 1999 or earlier	58,000
Items bought in 2000	31,000
Items bought in 2001	17,000
Items bought in 2002 or later	2,52,000
	3,58,000

During 2010 new plant was bought at a cost of Rs. 29,500 and one machine which had cost Rs. 5,500 in 1995 was sold for Rs. 350. During 2011 there were additions costing Rs. 18,000 and a machine which had cost Rs.7,000 in 2004 was sold for Rs. 1,500.

Write-up the Plant and Machinery Account for 2010 and 2011.

Solution **[CU BCom (Hons) & CA]**

Dr. **Plant and Machinery Account** Cr.

Date	Particulars	Amount	Date	Particulars	Amount
2010		Rs.	2010		Rs.
Jan. 1	To Balance b/d	1,95,150	?	By Bank A/c—Sale	350
	" Bank A/c	29,500	Dec. 31	" Depreciation A/c	29,850
Dec. 31	" Profit and Loss A/c —Profit on Sale	350		" Balance c/d	1,94,800
		2,25,000			2,25,000

Contd.

		Rs.			Rs.
2011			2011		
Jan. 1	To Balance b/d	1,94,800	?	By Bank A/c	1,500
	" Bank A/c	18,000	Dec. 31	" Depreciation A/c	29,950
	" Profit and Loss A/c — Profit and Sale	800		" Balance c/d	1,82,150
		2,13,600			2,13,600
2012					
Jan. 1	To Balance b/d	1,82,150			

Workings :

1. ***Profit on sale of Machinery in 2010 :***
   Written-down value of the machine is nil.
   So, the entire sale proceeds of Rs. 350 is the amount of profit.
2. ***Depreciation to be provided for in 2010***

	Rs.
Machinery purchased in 2001—on Rs. 17,000 @ 10%	1,700
Machinery purchased in 2002 or later on Rs. 2,52,000 @ 10%	25,200
Machinery purchased in 2010—on Rs. 29,500 @ 10%	2,950
	29,850

(No depreciation is be charged on 1999 on earlier year's machine, as they are already written-off.)

3. ***Profit on Machinery sold in 2011***

		Rs.
	Book Value	7,000
Less :	Depreciation @ 10% for 9 years	6,300
	WDV	700
	Sold for	1,500
∴	Profit on Sale	800

4. ***Depreciation to be provided for in 2011***

	Rs.
Machinery purchased in 2001 or later, on Rs. 2,52,000 @ 10%	25,200
Machinery purchased in 2010, on Rs. 29,500 @ 10%	2,950
Machinery purchased in 2011, on Rs. 18,000 @ 10%	1,800
	29,950

Adjustment for Profit or Loss on Sale of Assets

Illustration 30

A Ltd. Co. was charging depreciation on its Plant and Machinery on the Straight-Line Method at 10% p.a. since 2002. The directors decided in 2007 to change the method of providing depreciation to written-down value keeping the rate at 10%, retrospectively.

The following information were available from records:

	2002	2003	2004	2005	2006
	Rs.	Rs.	Rs.	Rs.	Rs.
Plant and Machinery purchased at cost	1,80,000	40,000	60,000	—	2,50,000
Plant and Machinery Sold—of cost price (as purchased in 2002)	—	5,000	8,000	—	—
Depreciation charged to P & L A/c	18,000	21,500	26,700	26,700	51,700
Actual sale proceeds of Plant and Machinery, as sold	—	4,000	7,200	—	

Depreciation is not charged on assets sold during the year.

You are required to compute the impact on the profit of the company pursuant to the change in method of computing depreciation and the Asset Account (at cost) and Depreciation Account; also the profit/loss on asset sold in the two methods of depreciation.

[ICWA]

Solution

In the Books of ...

Plant and Machinery Account

Dr. Cr.

Date		Particulars	Amount	Date		Particulars	Amount
2002			Rs.	2002			Rs.
?	To	Bank A/c—Purchase	1,80,000	?	By	Depreciation A/c	18,000
					"	Balance c/d	1,62,000
			1,80,000				1,80,000
2003				2003			
?	To	Balance b/d	1,62,000	?	By	Depreciation	19,750
	"	Bank A/c—Purchase	40,000		"	Bank A/c—Sale	4,000
					"	Loss on Sale A/c	500
					"	Balance c/d	1,77,750
			2,02,000				2,02,000
2004				2004			
?	To	Balance b/d	1,77,750	?	By	Bank A/c —Sale	7,200
	"	Bank A/c—Purchase	60,000		"	Depreciation	23,127
	"	Profit on Sale A/c	720		".	Balance c/d	2,08,143
			2,38,470				2,38,470
2005				2005			
?	To	Balance b/d	2,08,143	?	"	Depreciation A/c	20,814
					"	Balance c/d	1,87,329
			2,08,143				2,08,143
	To	Balance b/d	1,87,329		"	Depreciation A/c	43,733
	"	Bank A/c—Purchase	2,50,000		"	Balance c/d	3,93,596
			4,37,329				4,37,329

Workings :

Statement showing the impact of profit due to change in method :

Year	Depreciation under Straight Line Method	Depreciation under Reducing Balance Method	Net Adjustments
Rs.	Rs.	Rs.	Rs.
2002	18,000	18,000	—
2003	21,500	19,750	(–) 1,750
2004	26,700	23,127	(–) 3,573
2005	26,700	20,814	(–) 5,886
2006	51,700	43,733	(–) 7,967
			(–) 19,176

∴ **Profit will be increased by Rs. 19,176 due to change in method.**

At the same time, a further adjustment is also necessary for profit/loss on sale of assets :

Year	Profit/Loss Straight Line Method	Profit/Loss Reducing Balance Mehtod	Net Adjustments
Rs.	Rs.	Rs.	Rs.
2003	(–) 500	(+) 500	—
2004	(–) 800	(+) 720	(–) 80
			(–) 80

∴ **Profit will be reduced by Rs. 80.**

∴ **Net effect in profit rs. 19,096 (Rs. 19.176 – 80).**

Change in method of depreciation with restropective effect

Illustration 31

X Ltd. provides depreciation on its plant @ 10% on Reducing Balance Method. On 31.12.2008, it decides to adopt the Straight Line Method of charging depreciation instead of Reducing Balance Method with retrospective effect from 1st January 2005 although the rate of depreciation is same.

On 1.1.2008, the plant account stood in the books at Rs. 72,900. On 1.4.2008, X Ltd. sold a plant for Rs. 14,000 whose written-down value was Rs. 18,900 on 1.1.2005. On 1.9.2008, a new plant was also purchased for Rs. 45,000.

Show the Plant Account in the books of X Ltd. for the year 2008 only.

Solution

In the Books of X Ltd.

Plant Account

Dr. Cr.

Date	Particulars	Amount	Date	Particulars	Amount
2008		Rs.	2008		Rs.
Jan. 1	To Balance b/d	72,900	Apr. 1	By Depreciation A/c (on plant for 3 months)	344[2]
Apr. 1	" Profit on sale of Plant A/c	566[1]		" Bank A/c —Sale proceeds	14,000
Sept. 1	" Bank A/c —Purchase	45,000	Dec. 31	" Depreciation A/c	9,610[3]
				" Profit and Loss A/c	2,352[4]
				" Balance c/d	92,160
		1,18,466			1,18,466
2009					
Jan. 1	To Balance b/d	92,160			

Workings :

	Rs.
1. ***Book value as on 1.1.2005 of the original plant***	
$\left(\text{Rs. } 72{,}900 \times \frac{100}{90} \times \frac{100}{90} \times \frac{100}{90}\right)$	1,00,000
Less : Book value of plant on 1.1.2005 sold in 2008	18,900
Book value on 1.1.2005 for the balance plant	81,100

	Rs.
2. ***Profit on Sale of Machinery***	
Book value on 1.1.2005	18,900
Less : Depreciation for 2005 @ 10%	1,890
	17,010
Less : Depreciation for 2006 @ 10%	1,701
	15,309
Less : Depreciation for 2007 @ 10%	1,531
	13,778
Less : Depreciation for 2008 for 3 months $\left(1{,}378 \times \frac{5}{12}\right)$	344
	13,434
WDV on 1.4.2008 sold for	14,000
Profit on Sale	566

	Rs.
3. ***Depreciation for 2008***	
On Balance Plant on Rs. 81,100 @ 10%	8,110
On New Plant Purchased — $\left(\text{Rs. } 45{,}000 \times \frac{10}{100} \times \frac{4}{12}\right)$	1,500
	9,610
On Plant sold (for three months already calculated)	344
Total Depreciation	9,954

4. *Adjustment for additional depreciation due to change in method*

	Rs.
Depreciation on Rs. 81,100 @ 10% for 3 years under Straight, Line method (i.e., 8,110 × 3)	24,330

Depreciation already written-off under Diminishing Balance Method:

	Rs.	Rs.	
Book value on 1.1.2005	81,100		
Less : Depreciation for 2005	8,110	8,110	
	72,990		
Less : Depreciation for 2006	7,299	7,299	
	65,691		
Less : Depreciation for 2007	6,569	6,569	
			21,978
			2,352

Illustration 32

A company provides depreciation on Plant and Machinery as 20% p.a. on reducing balances. On 1st April 2010, the balance of the Plant and Machinery Account was Rs. 5,00,000. It was discovered in 2010-11 that :

(a) Rs. 25,000 being repairs to machinery incurred on 30th June 2008 had been capitalised.

(b) Rs. 50,000 being the cost of a generator purchased on 1st October 2007 had been written-off to stores.

Directors want to correct the mistakes while finalising the accounts for the year ended 31st March 2011.

A plant that cost Rs. 40,000 on 30th September 2009 was scrapped and replaced with a more sophisticated one on 31st December 2010 by spending Rs. 60,000. Scrap realised Rs. 10,000.

Prepare the Plant and Machinery Account as it would appear on 31st March 2011, after providing depreciation for that year.

Solution **[ICWA—Final]**

In the Books of ...
Plant and Machinery Account

Dr. *Cr.*

Date	*Particulars*	*Amount*	*Date*	*Particulars*	*Amount*
2010		Rs.	2011		Rs.
Apr. 1	To Balance b/d	5,00,000	Mar. 31	By Depreciation A/c (for 9 months on scrapped machine)	5,400[1]
Dec. 31	" Bank A/c	60,000		" Bank A/c—Sale	10,000
2011				" Profit & Loss A/c—Loss	20,600[2]
Mar. 31	" Profit and Loss A/c	11,800[4]		" Depreciation A/c	98,160[3]
				" Balance c/d	4,37,640
		5,71,800			5,71,800

Workings :

1. Depreciation on Rs. 36,000 (i.e., Rs. 40,000 – Rs. 4,000 $\times \frac{20}{100} \times \frac{9}{12}$ = Rs. 5,400.

2. Loss on Sale = Rs. 36,000 – Dep. Rs. 5,400 – Sale Price Rs. 10,000 = Rs. 20,600.

3.

	Rs.		Rs.
Cost of Generator (1.10.07)	50,000	Amount wrongly capitalised	25,000
Less : Dep. for 6 months	5,000	*Less :* Dep. for 9 months	3,750
WDV	45,000	WDV	21,250
Less : Depreciation	9,000	*Less :* Depreciation	4,250
	36,000		
Less : Depreciation	7,200		
WDV on 1.4.2010	28,800	WDV on 1.4.2010	17,000

		Rs.
Written-down value of P & M (before correction)		5,00,000
Less :	WDV Capitalised	17,000
		4,83,000
Add :	WDV of Generator	28,800
		5,11,800
Less :	WDV Plant Sold	36,000
		4,75,800

∴ Dep. for current year = on 4,75,800 × 20% ... 95,160

on 60,000 × 20% × $\frac{3}{12}$ = ... 3,000

98,160

4. Adjustment in Plant and Machinery account Rs. 11,800 (i.e., Rs. 28,800 – Rs. 17,000).

PROVISION FOR REPAIRS AND RENEWALS

Under this method, total amounts of repairs and renewals are estimated for the whole life of the asset and the same is added to its Capital Costs (minus scrap value) in order to produce a total or composite figure. Now this composite figure is then divided by the estimated life of the asset to find out the amount relating to repairs, renewals and depreciation which is to be charged to Profit and Loss Account every year. That is, Profit and Loss Account will be debited, and Provision for Depreciation and Repairs Account will be credited. and, for each and every year, actual amount of repairs and renewals is to be debited to the Provision Account and not the Profit and Loss Account.

The balance of Provision Account will reveal the net amount which will be set aside for depreciation and should, therefore, be equal to the difference of its cost price and its scrap value. Of course, the asset will become useless in the mean time. At the end of the working life of the asset, the Provision Account is closed by transferring the same to Asset Account.

But it should be remembered that if the asset account shows any balance due to incorrect estimation, the said balance is to be transferred to Profit and Loss Account.

Illustration 33

The following particulars are available from the books of a public company having a large fleet of transport vehicles :

	Rs.
Balance of Repairs and Renewals Reserve Account	20,000
as on 31st March 2011	1,15,000
Actual repair charges incurred during the year ended	
31st March 2011	75,000
31st March 2012	32,000

The company transfers annually a sum of Rs. 40,000 to the 'Repairs and Renewal Reserve A/c'.

Draw up the 'Repairs and Renewals Reserve A/c' for the years 2010-11 and 2011-12.

Solution **[CA]**

In the Books of ... Co. Ltd.

Dr. **Repairs and Renewals Reserve Account** *Cr.*

Date	*Particulars*	*Amount*	*Date*	*Particulars*	*Amount*
2011		Rs.	2010		Rs.
Mar. 31	To Repairs A/c	75,000	Apr. 1	By Balance b/d *(bal. fig.)*	1,50,000
"	Balance c/d	1,15,000	2011		
	(figure supplied)		Mar. 31	" Profit & Loss A/c	40,000
		1,90,000			1,90,000
2012			2012		
Mar. 31	To Repairs A/c	32,000	Apr. 1	By Balance b/d	1,15,000
"	Balance c/d	1,23,000	2012		
			Mar. 31	" Profit & Loss A/c	40,000
		1,55,000			1,55,000
			2012		
			Apr. 1	By Balance b/d	1,23,000

Illustration 34

A combined provision for depreciation and repairs and renewals was made every year at 15% of the original cost of machine purchased at Rs. 50,000. The 'Provision for Depreciation and Maintenance Account' that was opened for the purpose was, therefore, debited with the actual costs of repairs and renewals which were as stated below : Costs of Repairs and Renewals

Year 1 : Rs. 1,500; Year 2 : Rs. 1,600; Year 3 : Rs. 2,100; Year 4 : Rs. 3,000; Year 5 : Rs. 4,200.

At the end of the fifth year the machine was sold out at Rs. 20,000 after utilising a few of its minor parts valued at Rs. 4,000, in installing in its place a new machine purchased at Rs. 75,000. The resulting loss in the disposal of the old machine was debited to revenue.

Write-up 'Provision for Depreciation and Maintenance Account' for the five years and the 'Old and the New Machine Accounts' at the end.

Solution

In the Books of ...

Provision for Depreciation and Maintenance Account

Dr. Cr.

Date	Particulars	Amount	Date	Particulars	Amount
1st Year		Rs.	1st Year		Rs.
	To Repairs & Renewals A/c	1,500		By Profit & Loss A/c:	
	" Balance c/d	6,000		15% of 50,000	7,500
		7,500			7,500
2nd Year			2nd Year		
	To Repairs & Renewals A/c	1,600		By Balance b/d	6,000
	" Balance c/d	11,900		Profit & Loss A/c	7,500
		13,500			13,500
3rd Year			3rd Year		
	To Repairs & Renewals A/c	2,100		By Balance b/d	11,900
	" Balance c/d	17,300		Profit & Loss A/c	7,500
		19,400			19,400
4th Year			4th Year		
	To Repairs & Renewals A/c	3,000		By Balance b/d	17,300
	" Balance c/d	21,800		Profit & Loss A/c	7,500
		24,800			24,800
5th Year			5th Year		
	To Repairs & Renewals A/c	4,200		By Balance b/d	21,800
	" Old Machine A/c —transfer	25,100		Profit & Loss A/c	7,500
		29,300			29,300

Old Machine Account

Dr. Cr.

Date	Particulars	Amount	Date	Particulars	Amount
5th Year		Rs.	5th Year		Rs.
	To Balance b/d	50,000		By Bank A/c—(Sale proceeds)	20,000
				" New Machine A/c—(parts used in new machine)	4,000
				" Provision for Derpreciation and Maintenance A/c	25,100
				" Profit & Loss A/c *(bal. fig.)*	900
		50,000			50,000

New Machine Account

Dr. Cr.

Date	Particulars	Amount	Date	Particulars	Amount
5th Year		Rs.	5thYear		Rs.
	To Bank A/c	75,000		By Balance c/d	79,000
	" Old Machine A/c —parts used	4,000			
		79,000			79,000
6th Year					
	To Balance b/d	79,000			

IND AS 16, PROPERTY, PLANT AND EQUIPMENT

Depreciation

Some Important Provisions

43. Each part of an item of property, plant and equipment with a cost that is significant in relation to the total cost of the item shall be depreciated separately.

44. An entity allocates the amount initially recognised in respect of an item of property, plant and equipment to its significant parts and depreciates separately each such part. For example, it may be appropriate to depreciate separately the airframe and engines of an aircraft, whether owned or subject to a finance lease. Similarly, if an entity acquires property, plant and equipment subject to an operating lease in which it is the lessor, it may be appropriate to depreciate separately amounts reflected in the cost of that item that are attributable to favourable or unfavourable lease terms relative to market terms.

45. A significant part of an item of property, plant and equipment may have a useful life and a depreciation method that are the same as the useful life and the depreciation method of another significant part of that same item. Such parts may be grouped in determining the depreciation charge.

46. To the extent that an entity depreciates separately some parts of an item of property, plant and equipment, it also depreciates separately the remainder of the item. The remainder consists of the parts of the item that are individually not significant. If an entity has varying expectations for these parts, approximation techniques may be necessary to depreciate the remainder in a manner that faithfully represents the consumption pattern and/or useful life of its parts.

47. An entity may choose to depreciate separately the parts of an item that do not have a cost that is significant in relation to the total cost of the item.

48. The depreciation charge for each period shall be recognised in profit or loss unless it is included in the carrying amount of another asset.

49. The depreciation charge for a period is usually recognised in profit or loss. However, sometimes, the future economic benefits embodied in an asset are absorbed in producing other assets. In this case, the depreciation charge constitutes part of the cost of the other asset and is included in its carrying amount. For example, the depreciation of manufacturing plant and equipment is included in the costs of conversion of inventories (see Ind AS 2). Similarly, depreciation of property, plant and equipment used for development activities may be included in the cost of an intangible asset recognised in accordance with Ind AS 38 Intangible Assets.

Depreciable Amount and Depreciation Period

50. The depreciable amount of an asset shall be allocated on a systematic basis over its useful life.

51. The residual value and the useful life of an asset shall be reviewed at least at each financial year-end and, if expectations differ from previous estimates, the change(s) shall be accounted for as a change in an accounting estimate in accordance with Ind AS 8 *Accounting Policies, Changes in Accounting Estimates and Errors.*

52. Depreciation is recognised even if the fair value of the asset exceeds its carrying amount, as long as the asset's residual value does not exceed its carrying amount. Repair and maintenance of an asset do not negate the need to depreciate it.

53. The depreciable amount of an asset is determined after deducting its residual value. In practice, the residual value of an asset is often insignificant and therefore immaterial in the calculation of the depreciable amount.

54. The residual value of an asset may increase to an amount equal to or greater than the asset's carrying amount. If it does, the asset's depreciation charge is zero unless and until its residual value subsequently decreases to an amount below the asset's carrying amount.

55. Depreciation of an asset begins when it is available for use, i.e., when it is in the location and condition necessary for it to be capable of operating in the manner intended by management. Depreciation of an asset ceases at the earlier of the date that the asset is classified as held for sale (or included in a disposal group that is classified as held for sale) in accordance with Ind AS 105 and the date that the asset is derecognised. Therefore, depreciation does not cease when the asset becomes idle or is retired from active use unless the asset is fully depreciated. However, under usage methods of depreciation the depreciation charge can be zero while there is no production.

56. The future economic benefits embodied in an asset are consumed by an entity principally through its use. However, other factors, such as technical or commercial obsolescence and wear and tear while an asset remains idle, often result in the diminution of the economic benefits that might have been obtained

from the asset. Consequently, all the following factors are considered in determining the useful life of an asset :

(a) expected usage of the asset. Usage is assessed by reference to the asset's expected capacity or physical output.

(b) expected physical wear and tear, which depends on operational factors such as the number of shifts for which the asset is to be used and the repair and maintenance programme, and the care and maintenance of the asset while idle.

(c) technical or commercial obsolescence arising from changes or improvements in production, or from a change in the market demand for the product or service output of the asset.

(d) legal or similar limits on the use of the asset, such as the expiry dates of related leases.

57. The useful life of an asset is defined in terms of the asset's expected utility to the entity. The asset management policy of the entity may involve the disposal of assets after a specified time or after consumption of a specified proportion of the future economic benefits embodied in the asset. Therefore, the useful life of an asset may be shorter than its economic life. The estimation of the useful life of the asset is a matter of judgment based on the experience of the entity with similar assets.

58. Land and buildings are separable assets and are accounted for separately, even when they are acquired together. With some exceptions, such as quarries and sites used for landfill, land has an unlimited useful life and therefore is not depreciated. Buildings have a limited useful life and therefore are depreciable assets. An increase in the value of the land on which a building stands does not affect the determination of the depreciable amount of the building.

59. If the cost of land includes the costs of site dismantlement, removal and restoration, that portion of the land asset is depreciated over the period of benefits obtained by incurring those costs. In some cases, the land itself may have a limited useful life, in which case it is depreciated in a manner that reflects the benefits to be derived from it.

DEPRECIATION METHOD

60. The depreciation method used shall reflect the pattern in which the asset's future economic benefits are expected to be consumed by the entity.

61. The depreciation method applied to an asset shall be reviewed at least at each financial year-end and, if there has been a significant change in the expected pattern of consumption of the future economic benefits embodied in the asset, the method shall be changed to reflect the changed pattern. Such a change shall be accounted for as a change in an accounting estimate in accordance with Ind AS 8.

62. A variety of depreciation methods can be used to allocate the depreciable amount of an asset on a systematic basis over its useful life. These methods include the straightline method, the diminishing balance method, and the units of production method. Straight-line depreciation results in a constant charge over the useful life if the asset's residual value does not change. The diminishing balance method results in a decreasing charge over the useful life. The units of production method results in a charge based on the expected use or output. The entity selects the method that most closely reflects the expected pattern of consumption of the future economic benefits embodied in the asset. That method is applied consistently from period to period unless there is a change in the expected pattern of consumption of those future economic benefits.

ASSIGNMENT MATERIALS

THEORETICAL

Multiple Choice Questions

1. (a) Depreciation arises from—

(i) Obsolescence, (ii) fall in the value of money, (iii) physical wear and tear, (iv) fall in the market value of assets.

(b) Depreciation is the process of

(i) allocation, (ii) valuation, (iii) both valuation and allocation.

(c) Under Straight Line Method of depreciation, it

(i) remains fixed every year, (ii) increases every year, (iii) decreases every year.

(d) Object of depreciation is to

(i) find out true profit, (ii) provide funds for replacement, (iii) show the true financial position in the Balance Sheet.

(e) Under Diminishing Balance Method amount of depreciation gradually
(i) decreases, (ii) increases, (iii) remains fixed.

(f) Fix the amount of depreciation from the following
Cost price Rs. 10,000, Scrap value Rs. 1,000, Estimated life of 10 years:
(i) Rs. 800; (ii) 900; (iii) Rs. 1,100.

(g) Depreciation is provided on:
(i) Current Assets, (ii) Fixed Assets, (iii) Circulating Assets.

(h) Depreciation Amount is closed by transferring to
(i) Trading Account, (ii) Profit and Loss Account, (iii) Balance Sheet.

(i) If the amount of depreciation remains constant over the year, the method of depreciation is:
(i) Straight Line Method, (ii) Written-down Value Method, (iii) None of these.

[Ans. (a) (iii); (b) (i); (c) (i); (d) (i); (e) (i); (f) Rs. 900; (g) (ii); (h) (ii); (i) (i)]

Short Answer-Type Questions

1. What is depreciation? Discuss the different methods of depreciation.
2. Define Sinking Fund Method of depreciation. Can you explain for what kind of assets this method is particularly useful?
3. Distinguish between Straight Line Method and Diminishing Balance Method of depreciation.
4. Is depreciation a source of working capital?—Discuss.
5. Discuss the nature and causes of depreciation.
6. Explain the objects of and necessity for providing depreciation.
7. Distinguish with suitable examples between Straight Line (or Fixed Instalment) Method and Machine Hour Rate Method of Depreciation.
8. Why is it necessary to charge depreciation on Fixed Assets?
9. What factors should be considered for determining the amount of depreciation?
10. Discuss the basic factors on which the calculation of depreciation depends.
11. "Depreciation accounting is a process of allocation, not of valuation."—Discuss.
12. Suggest the suitable method of depreciation with proper reasons for the following accounts of a newly established firm—
(a) Plant and Machinery, (b) Land and Building, (c) Furniture and Fittings, (d) Leasehold Property, (e) Coal Mines, (f) Motor Truck, (g) Horse and Carts.
13. How do you treat the profit or loss on sale of assets?
14. What do you mean by "Decline in Service Potential"?
15. Define the following:
Amortisation, Depreciation, Obsolescence, WDV
16. Discuss the differences between Straight Line Method and Diminishing Balance Method of Depreciation.
17. (a) What do you mean by Depreciation?
(b) Why is it necessary to charge Depreciation?
(c) Distinguish between Straight Line Method and Diminishing Balance Method of Depreciation.

Essay-Type Questions

18. State the differences between fixed instalment and reducing balance methods of charging depreciation.
19. Is depreciation a source of internal capital? Give reasons.
20. What is depreciation? Why is it necessary to compute depreciation?
21. What are the reasons for charging depreciation on assets?

22. What is depreciation? Distinguish between straight-line method and diminishing balance method of depreciation.

23. What are the reasons for charging depreciation?

24. If the purchase price of an equipment is 'P', its salvage value is 'S', useful life is 'N' years, and the rates of Annual Depreciation is 'D' then establish the relationship between P, S, N and D for Straight Line Method and Written-down Value Method.

PRACTICAL

A. Straight Line Method

1. The following details regarding machinery are available from the books of Simco Engineers Limited:

(a) Balance as on 1.4.1993 Rs. 97,000 on Machinery Account.

(b) Bought new machinery on 1.10.1993 for Rs. 40,000.

(c) The opening balance includes Rs. 70,000 worth of machinery bought on 31.3.93.

(d) Incurred expenses on installation Rs. 8,000 on item (b).

(e) Sold machinery on 1.1.1994 for Rs. 32,000 (its original cost was Rs. 40,000 on 1.1.1990).

(f) More of depreciation in Fixed Instalment System @ 10% p.a. bearing in mind the dates of purchase and sale.

Show the Machinery A/c for the year 1st April 1993 to 31st March 1994.

[Ans. Depreciation 1993-94: 12,400 (10,000 + 2,400); Balance of Machinery A/c Rs. 1,08,600]

2. On 1st April 1996, Jute Traders' Association bought a machine at Rs. 80,000. The company had to pay Rs. 5,000 as its installation charges.

On July 1 of the same year another machine was bought at Rs. 1,00,000.

On 30th June 1998, the first machine was sold out for Rs. 65,000 to replace another new machine costing Rs. 1,00,000.

Show the Machinery Account as it would appear in the books of the company during all those years up to 31st December 1998 (from 1st April 1996) assuming that the books of account are closed on 31st December every year and depreciation is to be written-off @ 10% per annum on the original cost of these machines.

[Ans. Dep. for 1996, 1997, 1998 Rs. 11,375, Rs. 18,500, Rs. 19,250; Loss on Sale Rs. 875; Balance of Machinery Rs. 1,70,000]

B. Diminishing Balance Method

3. A Plant was purchased for Rs. 10,000 on 1.1.1988. On 1.4.1989 another Plant was purchased for Rs. 12,000 (including Rs. 2,000 for installation). On 1.10.1990 another Plant was also purchased for Rs. 20,000 by disposing-off the first Plant for Rs. 8,000. On 1.1.1991 another Plant was also purchased for Rs. 25,000 by disposing-off the 2nd Plant for Rs. 4,000 only.

Show the Plant Account up to 31.12.1991 assuming that the rate of depreciation is @ 10% on Reducing Balance Method.

[Ans. Profit on Sale Rs. 508; Loss on Sale Rs. 5,900; Balance of Plant A/c on 31.12.1991 Rs. 40,050]

4. On 1.1.1988 the Plant Account of the firm showed a balance of Rs. 1,00,000. On 1.7.1988 a part of the said Plant, whose book value on 1.1.1988 was Rs. 20,000, was sold at Rs. 8,000 in part exchange for a new Plant costing Rs. 17,000. The net invoice, however, amounting to Rs. 9,000, was passed through the Purchase Day Book. At the same time Rs. 1,000 incurred by way of installation of Plant was wrongly debited to Wages Account.

Show the necessary entries before preparing final accounts for the year ended 31st Dec. 1988 assuming that the rate of depreciation is @ 10% p.a. on Diminishing Balance Method.

Show also the Plant Account and Plant Disposal Account.

[Ans. Balance of Plant A/c Rs. 89,100]

5. A company, whose accounting year is the calendar year, purchased machinery on 1st April 2005 costing Rs. 30,000.

It further purchased a machine costing Rs. 20,000 on 1st October 2005 and another machine costing Rs. 10,000 on 1st July 2006.

On 1st January 2007, of the machinery which were purchased on 1st April 2005, one machine costing Rs. 10,000 became obsolete and was sold for Rs. 3,000.

Show how the Machinery Account would appear for all the three years in the books of the company after charging depreciation at 10% p.a. on Written-Down Value Method.

[CA Entrance]

[Ans. Balance of Machinery A/c Rs. 39,330; Loss on Sale Rs. 5,325; Dep. for 2007 Rs. 4,320]

6. The Machinery A/c of a factory showed a balance of Rs. 1,90,000 on 1st January 2009. Its accounts were made up on 31st December each year and depreciation is written-off at 10% under the Diminishing Balance Method.

On 1st June 2009, new machinery acquired at a cost of Rs. 28,000 and installation charges incurred in erecting the machine works out to Rs. 892 on the same date. On 1st June 2009, a machine, which had cost Rs. 6,000 on 1st January 2004, was sold for Rs. 750, another machine, which had cost Rs. 600 on 1st January 2005, was scrapped on the same date and it realised nothing.

Write-up Plant and Machinery Account for the year 2009, allowing the same rate of depreciation as in the past, calculating depreciation to the nearest multiple of a rupee.

[CA Entrance]

[Ans. Loss on Sale Rs. 2,645; Loss on Scrapping Rs. 377; Total Depreciation Rs. 20,291]

C. Change in Methods with Prospective Effect

7. A company purchased second-hand machinery on 1.1.2004 for Rs. 37,000 and immediately spent Rs. 3,000 on its erection. On 1.7.2005, it purchased another machine for Rs. 10,000 and, on 1.7.2006, it sold-off the first machine for Rs. 28,000 and bought another for Rs. 25,000. On 1.7.2007, the second machine was also sold-off for Rs. 2,000.

Depreciation was provided on the Machinery @ 10% p.a. on the original cost annually on 31st December. In 2006, however, the company changed the method of providing depreciation and adopted the Written-down Value Method, rate of depreciation being 15% p.a.

Give Machinery Account for the four years commencing from the acquisition of first machine.

[Ans. Depreciation for 2004 Rs. 4,000; Depreciation for 2005 Rs. 4,500; Depreciation for 2006 Rs. 5,700 (Loss on Sale Rs. 1,600); Depreciation for 2007 Rs. 4,073 (Loss on Sale Rs. 5,470); Balance of Machinery A/c as on 31.12.2007 Rs. 19,657]

8. A firm purchased on 1.1.2004 certain machinery for Rs. 58,200 and spent Rs. 1,800 on its erection. On 1.7.2004, additional machinery costing Rs. 20,000 was purchased. On 1.7.2006, the Machinery purchased on 1st January 1994, having become obsolete, was auctioned for Rs. 28,600 and on the same date fresh Machinery was purchased at a cost of Rs. 40,000.

Depreciation was provided for annually on 31st Dec. @ 10% on Written-down Value in 2007; however, the firm changed this method of providing depreciation and adopted the method of providing 5% p.a. depreciation on the original cost of the Machinery.

Give the Machinery Account as it would stand at the end of each year from 2004 to 2007.

[Ans. Depreciation 2004 Rs. 7,000; 2005 Rs. 7,300; 2006 Rs. 6,140 (Loss on Sale Rs. 17,570); 2007 Rs. 3,000]

D. Change in Methods with Retrospective Effect

9. W. Ltd. commenced business on 1.1.2007, when they purchased Plant and Equipments of Rs. 7,00,000. They adopted a policy of charging depreciation @ 15% p.a. on Diminishing Balance Method and to charge full year's depreciation on addition.

Over the years, their further purchases of Plant have been Rs. 1,50,000 on 1.8.2008 and Rs. 2,00,000 on 30.9.2010.

On 1.1.2011, it was decided to change the method and rate of depreciation to 10% on Straight Line Method with retrospective effect from 1.1.2007, the adjustment being made in accounts for the year ending 31st Dec. 2011.

Calculate the difference in depreciation to be adjusted in the Plant and Equipment Account on 1.1.2011 and show the Plant and Equipment Account for the year up to 31.12.2011.

[Ans. Balance of Plant and Equipment A/c Rs. 6,00,000 on 31.12.2011; Depreciation Overcharged Rs. 77,477]

10. Depreciation has been charged for the years 1990 to 1993 @ 10% on Reducing Balance Method on opening balance of each item of Plant and Machinery in use. The balance of Plant and Machinery

Account at the end of 31st Dec. 1993 was Rs. 54,000. There were no sales during these years; purchases were Rs. 16,800 in Sept. 1990 and Rs. 11,400 in Dec. 1992.

On 31st Dec. 1993, the management decided that the depreciation should be charged @ 20% on the same method but calculated on the closing balance of each year with retrospective effect from 1990.

Show the adjusting journal entry to be passed for giving effect to the revised basis.

[Ans. Additional Provision Required Rs. 21,161]

11. On 1.4.1987, a new plant was purchased by G. Ltd for Rs. 40,000 and a further sum of Rs. 2,000 was spent on its installation. On 1.10.1988, another plant was acquired for Rs. 25,000.

Due to an accident on 3.1.1990, the first Plant was totally destroyed and the remnants were sold for Rs. 1,000 only.

On 21st Jan. 2000, a second-hand Plant was purchased for Rs. 30,000 and a further sum of Rs. 5,000 was spent in bringing the same to use on and from 15.3.2000.

Depreciation has been provided at 10% on Straight Line Method. It was the practice to provide depreciation for full year on all acquisitions made at any time during any year and to ignore depreciation on any item sold or disposed of during the year. None of the assets were insured. The accounts are closed annually on 31st March.

It is now decided to follow the rate of 15% on Diminishing Balance Method with retrospective effect in respect of the existing items of Plant and to make the necessary adjustments on 31.3.2000.

Show the Plant Account, the Depreciation Provision Account for all the years up to 31.3.1990, and also Plant Disposal Account.

[CA]

[Ans. Balance of Plant A/c at 31.3.2000 Rs. 60,000; Loss on Disposal A/c Rs. 32,6000; Depreciation Provision for Change in method on 31.3.2000 Rs. 3,688]

Miscellaneous

12. Glass, Cutlery etc. : Balance on 1st January, 1998, Rs. 28,000. Glass, Cutlery, etc. : Purchased during the year Rs. 16,000. Depreciation is to be charged on the above assets as follows : $\frac{1}{5}$ of their values is to be written-off in the year of purchase and $\frac{2}{5}$ths in each of the next two years. Of the stock of glass, cutlery, etc. as on 1st January 1998 (Rs. 28,000) one-half was one year old and the other half two years old.

You are asked to find out the total depreciation to be charged to Profit & Loss Account for the year 1998 and to prepare the Glass, Cutlery etc. Account and Depreciation Account since 1996—assuming that the purchases were made on 1st January.

Also show the Balance Sheet as on 31.12.98 giving the above effect.

[CU BCom (Hons) 1999]

[Ans. Depreciation : 1996 Rs. 7,000; 1997 Rs. 17,500; 1998, Rs. 24,200; Balance of Glass, Cutlery on 31.12.1998 Rs. 19,800]

13. The net profit of a firm for 1989, 1990 and 1991 were Rs. 29,600, Rs. 31,550 and Rs. 31,870, respectively, calculating depreciation on a particular method on machinery and fixtures.

All the assets in question were acquired on 1st January 1989 for Rs. 1,28,000 (Machinery) and Rs. 25,600 (Fixtures and Fittings). The method of depreciation used was the Straight Line Method, assuming for the Machinery a working life of 8 years and scrap value of Rs. 10,000 and of the Fixtures and Fittings a working life of 12 years and scrap value of Rs. 4,000. The method proposed to be used now is the Reducing Balance Method (Machinery @ 25% p.a. and Fixtures and Fittings @ $12\frac{1}{2}$% p.a).

You are asked to re-calculate the net profits for 1989, 1990 and 1991.

Show also Journal entries to give effect to the above proposal on and from 31st December 1991.

[CU BCom (Hons)]

[Ans. P & L A/c (Dr.). Rs. 32,800; Machinery (Cr.) Rs. 29,750; Fixture & Fit tings (Cr.) Rs. 3,050]

Chapter 14

INVENTORY VALUATION

Learning Objectives

Introduction

Reasons for too much emphasis on Inventory Valuation

Cost Elements

Methods of Recording Inventory

Methods of Valuation of Inventory

A. Based on Historical Cost

—FIFO Method

—LIFO Method

—Average Cost Method

(i) Simple Average Cost

(ii) Weighted Average Cost

—Base Stock Method

Specific Identification Cost/Unit Cost/Actual Cost

—Standard Cost Method

—Inflated Cost Method

—Reverse Cost Method

—Replacement Cost Method

—Realisable Market Value Method

B. Cost or Market Price—whichever is Lower

—Net Realisable Value Basis

—Replacement Value Basis

C. Under Periodic Inventory System and Perpetual Inventory System

—Periodic Inventory System

—Perpetual Inventory System

Determining More Appropriate Method

Valuation under Cost Accounting Records Rules

Presentation of Inventory in Financial Statement

(i) As per the requirements of Schedule VI of the Companies Act

(ii) As per requirements of Indian Accounting Standard AS 2

AS 2— Valuation of Inventories

Introduction

The term 'Inventory' is used to designate the aggregate of terms of tangible property. They are either (i) held for sale in the ordinary course of business (i.e., stock-in-trade or saleable finished goods), or (ii) in the process of production for such sale (i.e., convertible work-in-progress), or (iii) to be currently consumed in the production of goods or services to be available for sale (i.e., consumable materials and supplies). Therefore, inventory means and includes :

1. Raw Materials; 2. Work-in-Progress; 3. Finished Goods, and 4. Consumable stores and spare parts.

However, the nature of the inventory depends on the type of operation carried out. For example, in case of a trading concern, inventory will comprise of only stock-in-trade or finished goods whereas, in case of a manufacturing concern, the same will comprise of the above four items.

Reasons for too much emphasis on Inventory Valuation

The following three seem to be the important reasons for too much emphasis on inventory valuation:

(i) Inventory constitutes the major bulk of current assets and it represents the major current assets investment. As such, its valuation should be made in such a way so that the profit or income is determined accurately and the Balance Sheet can exhibit a true and fair position at a particular date.

(ii) Since the inventory has direct impact on profit, proper determination of the latter depends on the proper valuation of the former. In other words, if closing inventory is undervalued, profit will be understated, or *vice versa*. Besides, if the ending inventory is overvalued and is shown in the Balance Sheet, the same amounts to a case of *'window-dressing'* which will exhibit a wrong picture about the liquidity position of a firm. Therefore, inventory should always be valued properly so that the short term liquidity must not suffer, i.e., creditors must not be misled. If inventory is valued properly, Balance Sheet will exhibit a true and fair view of the financial position of a firm.

(iii) The next one involves the fluctuations in commodity prices. It again seems to be greater appreciation of the effects of these changes on the individual firm and the business community as a whole. In the words of Paul, Garner S. : "It became common knowledge that the income of some enterprises for specific years was tremendously influenced by the accounting procedure adopted for handling the fluctuations in the market value of the inventory consumed in operations or sold. Many firms began to indicate in their published statements the income (or loss) before and after *'inventory adjustment'* as they called it. These adjustments were quickly impressed on the mind of the public with the result that increasing attention was devoted to the matter not only by accountants, but also by students of finance, banking credit, taxation and others."[1]

Cost Elements

The presentation of inventory in the annual financial statement on the basis of historical cost system of valuation is widely accepted although there are some other methods which are used for certain special cases.

Historical cost of inventories is the sum total of costs of purchases including cost of conversion and certain other costs which are incurred in order to be a finished product.

Cost of Purchases : It includes purchase price together with import duties, other purchase taxes, transport and handling cost, and any other costs which are directly attributable to prime cost after deducting rebate and discounts, etc.

Cost of Conversion : It includes cost of purchases plus the production overhead (both fixed and variable overhead) which are incurred during production. But certain other costs are to be excluded from the cost of conversion, e.g., waste material of exceptional amounts, cost of idle plant, etc.

Production Overhead : It relates to the cost of production other than the cost of direct materials and direct labours, e.g., indirect materials, indirect labours, factory expenses, etc.

Other Expenses : It includes costs which are necessary for the inventories in order to be a finished/marketable product, e.g., expenditure which are incurred in designing product for specific customers, etc.

Cost of Inventory as per AS 2, has been explained in a subsequent paragraph.

---

1 Paul, Garner S.—*Valuation of Inventories—Handbook of Modern Accountancy Theory*, Ed. by M. Backer, P. 306.

Methods of Recording Inventory

While preparing final accounts of a firm, inventories should properly be valued, otherwise, the financial result of the firm will mislead us. However, the inventories may be recorded in the books of the account (after its proper valuation before preparing final accounts) under the following methods :

Method I

If it is desired to adjust the amount of purchases made during this year, i.e., in order to reduce the amount of purchases, the following entry may be passed in the books :

(i) Closing Stock A/c Dr.
To Purchases A/c

Note : It is most important to note that if this entry is duly passed in the books, closing stock must appear in Trial Balance—the same will not appear in the credit side of the Trading Account, i.e., it will simply appear on the asset side of the Balance Sheet. Because, the purchases so made or adjusted here is known as *Adjusted Purchases.*

Method II

If it is decided to close the amount of purchases by transferring to Trading Account/ Manufacturing Account, the following entry may be passed :

(i) Closing Stock A/c Dr.
To Trading A/c

It should be remembered here that the above entry is based on the basis of the following concept :

Cost of Goods Sold = Opening Stock + Purchases* – Closing Stock

* In case of a manufacture, production:

Sometimes we can use the above equation in the following manner:

Cost of Goods Sold = Sales – Gross Profit.

METHODS OF VALUATION OF INVENTORY

A. Based on Historical Cost

Valuation of inventory is made on a conservative basis, i.e., expected profits are not to be considered whereas possible losses are to be provided for. As such, it is valued at the lowest of (i) historical cost; (ii) net realisable value, and (iii) replacement price/value.

The term 'cost' usually refers to designate the historical cost, i.e., outlay of cash or its equivalent in the acquisition of particular items of inventory. In other words, it is the sum total of the price paid along with all expenditures and charges directly or indirectly incurred in bringing inventory to its existing condition and location. Therefore, in case of materials and supplies, the price paid including freight and carriage represents their cost and sometimes a part of the storage expenditure is also included. In case of work-in-progress, however, cost represents sum total of direct material cost, direct wages and direct expenses including manufacturing and factory overhead. The elements making up cost of finished goods or stock-in-trade are incurred in bringing : (i) the purchase price of goods, stores, and in case of processed stock, materials used in manufacture, (ii) all direct expenditures (e.g., direct wages, cost of tools, design) incurred in bringing stock-in-trade to its existing condition and location; and (iii) indirect or overhead expenditure incidental to the class of stock-in-trade concerned.[1]

As the production and sales cycle is a continuous and repetitive process, costs which are incurred during an accounting period at different times in order to bring an article to its existing condition and location varies due to certain factors, viz., the seasonal effects, the efficiency of the workers, the attitude of management, etc. This variation, no doubt, creates the difficulty of identification of cost of inventories for the purpose of their valuation. Of course, the said difficulties may be overcome by certain arbitrary assumptions and, as such, different bases are generally adopted. Some of them are enumerated below :

(a) First-in-First-out (FIFO)

Under this method, materials which are received first are also issued first. In other words, the pricing of the issue of the first lot is done at the cost at which that lot was acquired. As such, the closing inventories are valued at latest purchase price and, thus, it will represent current condition as far as possible. That is, closing inventories are always out of the latest lots acquired or purchased or manufactured. The same leads to represent replacement price. This method is particularly applicable where prices do not fluctuate very frequently and the materials are not fast moving.

1 The Institute of Chartered Accountants of England & Wales—Recommendation 10, para 2.

Advantages :

(i) This method is *simple to understand* and easy to operate.

(ii) This method is also found to be more *suitable* where the *prices are fluctuating* very frequently and the materials are slow moving.

(iii) It is *a logical method* since it utilises those items of inventory which are acquired or purchased or manufactured first.

(iv) It is a very *useful method*, particularly when the *prices are falling.*

(v) As ending inventory consists of *recently purchased goods, closing stock valuation becomes almost equal to current market price.*

Disadvantages :

(i) At the time of rising prices, when lower costs are absorbed by production and higher costs are represented by closing stock, more working capital will be required in order to replace the stock.

(ii) If there are large number of purchases at different prices it will complicate the store ledger and increase the possibility of clerical errors.

(iii) Comparison between the two jobs becomes difficult if two similar jobs are charged with materials at different prices.

Illustration 1

In a factory, stores are issued and accounted for on FIFO method. If the stock of a particular material on 1st Jan. 2012 is 1,000 units valued at Rs. 5 per unit and the particulars of purchases and issues during the month of January 2012 are as follows, prepare a statement showing how the value of issues should be arrived at :

Dates				
Jan.	3	Purchases	200	units at Rs. 5.50
	9	Issues	1,000	units
	15	Purchases	1,400	units at Rs. 600
	17	Issues	1,000	units
	21	Purchases	800	units at Rs. 650
	23	Issues	1,000	units

Solution

Store Ledger Account
FIFO Method

Name of Material—
Specification—
Code No.—
Unit of Measurement—

Bill No.—
Location—

Folio No.—
Maximum level—
Minimum level—
Re-ordering level—

	Receipts				Issues				Balance			
Date	*G.R. No.*	*Quantity*	*Rate*	*Amount*	*S.R. No.*	*Quantity*	*Rate*	*Amount*	*Quantity*	*Rate*	*Amount*	*Remarks*
2012				Rs.				Rs.			Rs.	
Jan. 1									1,000	5	5,000	
3		200	5.5	1,100					1,000 200	5 5.5	5,000 1,100	
9						1,000	5	5,000	200	5.5	1,100	
15		1,400	6	8,400					200 1,400	5.5 6	1,100 8,400	
17						200 800	5.5 6	1,100 4,800	600	6	3,600	
21		800	6.5	5,200					600 800	6 6.5	3,600 5,200	
23						600 400	6 6.5	3,600 2,600	400	6.5	2,600	

(b) Last-in-First-Out (LIFO)

Under this method, it is assumed that the materials purchased are issued in the reverse order to FIFO, i.e., **the last receipt is the first issued or the latest lots of inventories are exhausted first.**.In short, inventories are valued *at earlier purchase prices.*

Advantages :

(i) This method is also *simple to understand* and *easy to operate.*

(ii) It *can easily be applied,* particularly when inventories *are not too large* and their prices are *fairly steady.*

(iii) The cost of materials which is charged to jobs represent more or less the current market price.

(iv) At the time of raising prices it makes *high charge to production.* As such, quantity of materials can easily be procured without requiring additional funds.

(v) This method, no doubt, gives a better result when *profit fluctuates during* the period of changing price level (inflation).

(vi) The effect of current market price is reflected in the cost of production and cost of goods sold as well.

(vii) Since inventories represent earlier low prices and, as such, there will be *no unrealised* profit in Profit and Loss Account under financial accounting.

Disadvantages :

(i) In condition of rising prices, the closing inventories will be undervalued, i.e., it will have no impact on the current market conditions.

(ii) At times of falling prices, this method will reveal a lower charge to production and a higher value of closing inventories which has no relation to the current replacement value.

(iii) Like FIFO method, if there are large number of purchases at different prices, possibility of clerical errors will increase.

(iv) Comparison of cost becomes unreliable if two jobs are charged at different prices.

Illustration 2

Consider Illustration 1, and follow LIFO Method:

Store Ledger Account
FIFO Method

Name of Material— | Folio No.—
Specification— | Maximum level—
Code No.— **Bill No.—** | Minimum level—
Unit of Measurement— **Location—** | Re-ordering level—

	Receipts				Issues				Balance			
Date	*G.R. No.*	*Quantity*	*Rate*	*Amount*	*S.R. No.*	*Quantity*	*Rate*	*Amount*	*Quantity*	*Rate*	*Amount*	*Remarks*
2012				Rs.				Rs.			Rs.	
Jan. 1									1,000	5	5,000	
3		200	5.5	1,100					1,000 200	5 5.5	5,000 1,100	
9						200 800	5.5 5	1,100 4,000	200	5	1,000	
15		1,400	6	8,400					200 1,400	5 6	1,000 8,400	
17						1,000	6	6,000	200 400	5 6	1,000 2,400	
21		800	6.5	5,200					200 400 800	5 6 6.5	1,000 2,400 5,200	
23						800 200	6.5 6	5,200 1,200	200 200	5 6	1,000 1,200	

(c) Average Cost Method

Under this method, all items in the stores are mixed up in such a way that consumption of materials or sale of finished goods cannot be recognised from any particular lot of purchases. As a result, closing inventories are valued at the average cost of all the lots acquired under each type during a particular period.

The average cost may be :

(i) Simple Average Cost; and (ii) Weighted Average Cost.

(i) Simple Average Cost

Under this method, average of different prices are only considered without having regard to the quantities involved. The simple average cost is calculated by adding the different prices and thereafter divided by the total number of purchases. This method is applicable where there is wide fluctuation in prices.

Illustration 3

Consider **Illustration 1**, and follow Simple Average Method:

Solution

Store Ledger Account
Simple Average Method

Name of Material—		Folio No.—
Specification—		Maximum level—
Code No.—	Bill No.—	Minimum level—
Unit of Measurement—	Location—	Re-ordering level—

	Receipts				Issues				Balance			
Date	*G.R. No.*	*Quantity*	*Rate*	*Amount*	*S.R. No.*	*Quantity*	*Rate*	*Amount*	*Quantity*	*Rate*	*Amount*	*Remarks*
2012				Rs.				Rs.			Rs.	
Jan. 1.									1,000	5	5,000	
Jan. 3		200	5.5	1,100					1,200	—	6,100	
9						1,000	5.25	5,250	200		850	
15		1,400	6	8,400					1,600	—	9,250	
17						1,000	5.75	5,750	600	—	3,500	
21		800	6.5	5,200					1,400	—	8,700	
23						1,000	6.25	6,250	400	—	2,450	

Notes :

1st Issue Price $= \dfrac{(\text{Rs. } 5 + \text{Rs. } 5.50)}{2}$ = Rs. 5.25. 2nd Issue Price $= \dfrac{(\text{Rs. } 5.50 + \text{Rs. } 6)}{2}$ = Rs. 5.75.

3rd Issue Price $= \dfrac{(\text{Rs. } 6 + \text{Rs. } 6.50)}{2}$ = Rs. 6.25

(ii) Weighted Average Method

Under this method, rate of average cost is calculated by taking into consideration both the prices and quantities acquired at such prices, i.e., the total value of materials in stock at the time of issue divided by the total quantity of materials in stock in order to find out the weighted average rate. It is superior than the ordinary Simple Average Method since it takes into account both the prices and the quantities. This method proves very useful where there is a heavy fluctuation in the prices of inventories as it tends to smooth out fluctuations in prices by taking the average cost of different lots acquired at different times. But, under this method, cost of goods sold does not represent the actual cost.

Advantages :

(i) This method is very useful in periods when there is wide fluctuation in prices of different inventory items, since it smoothens the effect of price fluctuation.

(ii) Possibility of clerical errors reduces until and unless purchases are made frequently.

(iii) The need of calculation of new issue prices arises only when new purchases are made.

Disadvantages :

(i) When frequent purchases are made, the work for calculation of rates becomes difficult.

(ii) The cost of materials is not charged out at actual cost and, hence, profit or loss will reveal a misleading result.

Illustration 4

Consider **Illustration 1**, and follow Weighted Average Method:

Store Ledger Account
Weighted Average Method

Name of Material— Folio No.—
Specification— Maximum level—
Code No.— **Bill No.—** Minimum level—
Unit of Measurement— **Location—** Re-ordering level—

	Receipts				Issues				Balance			
Date	*G.R. No.*	*Quantity*	*Rate*	*Amount*	*S.R. No.*	*Quantity*	*Rate*	*Amount*	*Quantity*	*Rate*	*Amount*	*Remarks*
2012				Rs.				Rs.			Rs.	
Jan. 1									1,000	5	5,000	
3		200	5.5	1,100					1,200	5.08	6,100	
9						1,000	5.08	5,080	200	5.08	1,020	
15		1,400	6	8,400					1,600	5.89	9,420*	
17						1,000	5.89	5,890	600	5.89	3,530	
21		800	6.5	5,200					1,400	6.24	8,730	
23						1,000	6.24	6,240	400	6.24	2,490	

* *Note* **: Due to fractions.**

(d) Base Stock Method

Under this method, it is assumed that every firm has to maintain a certain minimum amount of inventory (in the form of raw materials, work-in-progress and finished goods) throughout the year. The same will have to be maintained for meeting emergency needs, such as undue delay in supply of raw materials, excessive consumption. This minimum level of inventory goes by the name of Base Stock or Safety Stock. 'Base Stock' serves as the signal below which the inventory level of a firm is never allowed to fall. (Therefore, inventory, to the extent of 'Base Stock', though basically as a class falls within the category of current assets, assumes, for all practical purposes, the character of fixed assets.)

Generally, there may not be any wide variation between the volume of closing and opening inventory unless there is a remarkable change in the scale of operation and other factors. The 'Base Stock' level is usually created out of the first lot of the materials purchased or goods manufactured at the beginning of the period and, as such, it is valued at the cost price of the first lot. Therefore, under this method, closing inventories are generally taken to be equal to the 'Base Stock' level and, hence, they are valued at the values allotted to the respective 'Base Stock'. However, if there is any excess (over base stock level) the same should be valued either on the basis of FIFO or LIFO methods.

It should be remembered that this method is generally used with FIFO or LIFO method. There is, however, difference of opinion among the accountants as to the principles to be followed for valuation of inventories when this method is adopted. For example, Finney and Miller suggest that 'Base Stock' may be valued at *lowest cost experienced* and valuation of closing inventory (when it goes below base stock) 'should be made by deducting the value of the deficient quantity calculated at the current cost from the value of the normal quantity of base stock calculated at the base price'. Further, Yorston, Smyth and Brown suggest that 'the difference between the replacement price and the fixed price of the basic stock is deducted from the total value of the stock on hand computed at the basic price.' This method usually is operated either in conjunction with FIFO or LIFO method. It may be observed that the objective of pricing inventories on the basis of this method is to apply the current prices to issue. So, this objective will be fulfilled only when LIFO method is adopted as a method of calculation.[1]

Advantages :

(i) This method is simple to understand and easy to operate. (ii) This technique serves the valuation of closing stock easily. (iii) This method practically renders the profit and loss most conservative. (iv) It

1 Banerjee, B.—*Cost Accounting*—World Press (P) Ltd., 1981, P. 63.

is particularly applicable where a certain quantity of basic materials is needed in process for a long time.
(v) All the advantages of FIFO and LIFO method will also be applicable in this method.

Disadvantages :

(i) The disadvantages appearing in FIFO or LIFO may also apply to this method.

(ii) Sometimes 'Base Stock' may appear in Balance Sheet at most unreliable price and, as such, the owners/shareholders may be cheated.

(iii) Since 'Base Stock' is a part of stock of materials (i.e., a part of current assets) it can be treated as a fixed asset which appears at cost in the Balance Sheet.

Illustration 5

Consider **Illustration 1**, and follow Base Stock Method :

Solution

Store Ledger Account
Base Stock Method

Name of Material—		Folio No.—
Specification—		Maximum level—
Code No.—	**Bill No.—**	Minimum level—
Unit of Measurement—	**Location—**	Re-ordering level—

	Receipts				**Issues**				**Balance**			
Date	*G.R. No.*	*Quantity*	*Rate*	*Amount*	*S.R. No.*	*Quantity*	*Rate*	*Amount*	*Quantity*	*Rate*	*Amount*	*Remarks*
2012				Rs.				Rs.			Rs.	
Jan. 1									1,000	5	5,000	
3		200	5.5	1,100					100	5	500	
									900	5	4,500	
									200	5.5	1,100	
9						900	5	4,500	100	5	500	
						100	5.5	550	100	5.5	500	
15		1,400	6	8,400					100	5.	500	
									100	5.5	550	
									1,400	6	8,400	
17						100	5.5	550	100	5	500	
						900	6	5,400	500	6	3,000	
21		800	6.5	5,200					100	5	500	
									500	6	3,000	
									800	6.5	5,200	
23						500	6	3,000	100	5	500	
						500	6.5	3,250	300	6.5	1,950	

* 10% of 1,000 = 100 units are considered as Base Stock.

Illustration 6

A company started on 1.1.2011 purchased raw materials during 1994 as stated below :

Jan. 2	800	kg @ Rs. 62 per kg
Feb. 26	1,200	kg @ Rs. 57 per kg
April 13	2,500	kg @ Rs. 59 per kg
July 10	3,000	kg @ Rs. 56 per kg
Sept. 18	1,500	kg @ Rs. 60 per kg
Nov. 29	1,000	kg @ Rs. 65 per kg

While preparing its final accounts on 31st Dec. 2011 this company had 1,300 kg of raw materials in its godown. Calculate the value of closing stock of raw materials according to (i) First-In-First-Out basis; (ii) Last-in-First-Out basis, and (iii) Weighted Average basis.

[Delhi BCom (Hons.)]

Solution

(i) **Since the raw materials are valued at FIFO basis, the valuation of closing raw materials would be @ last two rates as :**

		Rs.
300	kg @ Rs. 60 =	18,000
1,000	kg @ Rs. 65 =	65,000
1,300		83,000

(ii) Since the raw materials are valued at LIFO basis the valuation of closing raw materials would be @ first two rates as:

		Rs.
800	kg @ Rs. 62 =	49,600
500	kg @ Rs. 57 =	28,500
1,300		78,100

(iii) Weighted Average basis :

Date	Quantity	Rate Rs.	Product Rs.
Jan. 2	800	62	49,600
Feb. 26	1,200	57	68,400
April 13	2,500	59	1,47,500
July 10	3,000	56	1,68,000
Sept. 18	1,500	60	90,000
Nov. 29	1,000	65	65,000
	10,000		5,88,500

∴ Weighted Average Prices = $\frac{\text{Rs. } 5{,}88{,}500}{\text{Rs. } 10{,}000}$ = Rs. 58.85

∴ Value of closing raw materials will be Rs. 76,505 (i.e., 1,300 × Rs. 58.85).

Specific Identification Cost/Unit Cost or Actual Cost

This method of valuation is adopted where each item of inventory and its actual cost is identifiable. It attributes certain specific costs to the identified items of inventory where each such item and its cost is identifiable. That is, this method of valuation can easily be applied where the closing inventory items can correctly be identified with specific lots. But this method suffers from the following limitations :

(i) Where there is bulk quantities of inventories, partly finished goods or finished goods, and where individual units of inventories lose their identity.

(ii) Where there is innumerable units of inventories, keeping records for each of them becomes expensive as well as time-consuming.

Other Methods of Valuation of Inventory —Other than those based on Historical Cost

Some of the important methods of valuation of inventory (other than those based on historical cost) are :

(a) Standard Cost Method; (b) Inflated Cost Method; (c) Reverse Cost Method; (d) Replacement Cost Method; and (e) Realisable Market Value Method.

(a) Standard Cost Method

Under this method, closing inventories are valued at pre-fixed standard rates. This method is found suitable where the manufacturing units are engaged in production on a large scale. But this method cannot reveal the true value of inventory when production is completed after passing through several processes or where manufactured products are of different varieties. At the same time, if there is a slight error in fixing the single standard rate, the same will affect the measure of all items of inventory.

Illustration 7

Consider **Illustration 1,** and follow Standard Price/Cost Method assuming that the Standard Price is fixed at Rs. 5.5 per unit.

Solution

Store Ledger Account
Standard Cost Price Method

Name of Material—
Specification—
Code No.—
Unit of Measurement—

Bill No.—
Location—

Folio No.—
Maximum level—
Minimum level—
Re-ordering level—

	Receipts				Issues				Balance			
Date	*G.R. No.*	*Quantity*	*Rate*	*Amount*	*S.R. No.*	*Quantity*	*Rate*	*Amount*	*Quantity*	*Rate*	*Amount*	*Remarks*
2012				Rs.				Rs.			Rs.	
Jan. 1									1,000	5	5,000	
3		200	5.5	1,100					1,200	—	6,100	
9						1,000	5.5	5,500	200	—	600	
15		1,400	6	8,400					1,600	—	9,000	
17						1,000	5.5	5,500	600	—	3,500	
21		800	6.5	5,200					1,400	—	8,700	
23						1,000	5.5	5,500	400	—	3,200	

(b) Inflated Cost Method

Under this method, closing inventories are valued at a cost per unit which is higher than the actual cost per unit to provide for the normal loss due to certain defects inherent in them, e.g., loss due to evaporation, shrinkage, etc.

(c) Reverse Cost Method

Under this method, inventories are valued at an estimated cost which is determined by deducting an amount equivalent to the normal profit margin and the estimated cost disposal from the current selling prices. This method is also referred to as 'Adjusted Selling Price'[1].

(d) Replacement Cost Method

Under this method, each closing item of inventory is valued at cost which is to be incurred for purchasing/procuring the said item from the open market on the date of valuation, i.e., they are valued at the replacement cost as on that date. This cost of replacement should be determined in relation on the current market price of similar items.

(e) Realisable Market Value Method

Under this method, each closing item of inventory is valued at its estimated net realisable value, i.e., prospective selling price less all prospective costs to be incurred in conditioning and selling the goods, may be adopted suitably for the purpose of valuation.

B. Cost OR Market Price, whichever is lower

The conventional method of valuation of inventories, of course, which is universally applicable at present is *'historical cost price or the market price/value—whichever is lower.'* The term 'market price/value' is used to designate the 'replacement price/value' and 'net realisable value'. As such, at present inventories are valued at the lowest of (i) historical cost, (ii) net realisable value, and (iii) replacement price/value. If this method is used as a method of valuation of inventories, Profit and Loss Account will automatically be adjusted when historical cost will be more than the net realisable or replacement value. However, market value is to be determined on two bases :

1. 'Net Realisable Value' Basis, and 2. 'Replacement Value' Basis.

(a) Net Realisable Value Basis ***(See AS 2 that follows in a subsequent paragraph)***

Under this concept, 'market prices/value' is considered as the 'net realisable value' which is equal to the estimated selling price in the ordinary course of business minus the cost of completion. This method of valuation of inventories is particularly followed where the inventories are damaged or partially obsolete. In this case, inventories are to be valued below the historical cost since the selling price of the same items will be reduced. As a result, historical cost for the items will not be realised and the difference will, however, be adjusted in Profit and Loss Account by writing down the inventories to the net realisable value. That is why value of inventories must not be shown at a higher figure than its expected

1 Recommendation 10, Para. 3, The Institute of Chartered Accountants of England & Wales.

realisable value in future. It should be remembered that the estimated realisable value must not be determined on the basis of temporary fluctuation of prices but on the basis of most reliable evidence.

(b) Replacement Value Basis

Under this concept, the market value is considered to be the current replacement cost which is equal to the current cost of acquisition—either by purchases or by production together with the incidental acquisition cost. This basis usually applies more appropriately to materials or purchased merchandise since calculation of replacement cost of work-in-progress or finished goods will not be an easy task. Current cost of each element of total cost of inventory will be determined. However, current cost of raw materials and labour should be determined (with tolerable precision) by incorporating current rate of wages and materials to be multiplied by actual quantity of material or labour related to finished or semi-finished product.

It may be noted that there is a difference between replacement value and realisable value. The former represents a sacrificial value whereas the latter represents a beneficial value. At the same time, historical cost represents a sacrificial value and realised value is beneficial value. Sometimes, market value on reproductive basis should be determined on the basis of market price of raw materials, labour and overheads.

However, the AICPA has approved certain limits for inventory valuation which have been stated by the Committee on Accounting Procedure, Bulletin 29, as under[1] :

'As used in the phrase *'lower of cost or market'* the term 'market' means current replacement cost (by purchase or by production, as the case may be) except that :

(i) Market should not exceed the net realisable value (i.e., estimated selling price in the ordinary course of business less reasonably predictable costs of completion and disposal), and

(ii) Market should not be less than net realisable value reduced by an allowance for 'an approximately normal profit margin'.

From the above, exception (ii) states not to reduce value until there is a clear apparent loss. The AICPA prefers to use 'market value' only to the 'replacement or reproduction value' and 'net realisable value' is treated as a separate item. But, the Institute of Chartered Accountants of England and Wales prefers to use 'lower of cost and net realisable value','at the lowest of cost, net realisable value and replacement including reproduction price' or 'at cost less provision to reduce to net realisable value'.

Therefore, after considering the recommendations of both the Institutes, valuation should be made on the basis of the lowest of the three (stated above), with one exception imposed by AICPA. That is, if market price is found to be so lower than the net realisable value less normal profit, the latter should be considered.

C. Under Periodic Inventory System and Under Perpetual Inventory System

Periodic Inventory System

Under this method stock-taking is usually done periodically, i.e., once or twice in a year. This method is particularly applicable where the materials are of small value and also for determining the physical movement of stock and its closing balance as on a particular date. Closing inventory is ascertained on the basis of physical counting and cost of goods is calculated on such basis at periodic intervals on the basis of the following (which has already been explained earlier while discussing the **Methods of Recording Inventory, Method II**) viz. :

Cost of Goods Sold = Opening Inventory + Purchases – Closing Inventory.

Accounting under this method is done as:

(a) Trading Account is debited with the opening inventory which was the closing one at the end of the last year.

(b) Trading Account is debited with the amount of purchases of inventory made during the year, i.e., purchase account is transferred to Trading Account.

(c) Trading Account is credited with the closing inventory (calculated on the basis of physical counting) by passing the usual entry, viz., closing Inventory Account is debited and Trading Account is credited.

(d) The difference between the two sides of Trading Account is known as Cost of Goods Sold.

1 Accounting Research Bulletin 29. The American Institute of Accountants, Statement 3.

Perpetual Inventory System

Perpetual inventory system is a system of records which is maintained by the controlling department. It reveals the physical movement of stocks and their current balance. Store balances are recorded whenever any receipt or issue is made, i.e., up-to-date recording is maintained. Under this method, an inventory account is opened which reveals the cost of goods sold during an accounting cycle whenever is required. A perpetual inventory system is usually checked by a programme of continuous stock taking. This system is intended as an aid to material control. In short, when the up-to-date record is maintained the balance shown by store ledger must agree with the physical balance. If any discrepancies arise, proper investigation must be made and a report will have to be submitted.

However, the following entries are required for the purpose :

(i) ***When inventory/stock is purchased :***

Stock/inventory A/c	Dr.		
To Cash/Bank A/c		(in case of cash purchase)	
To Creditors/Suppliers A/c		(in case of credit purchases)	

(ii) ***When inventory/stock is sold :***

Cash/Bank A/c	Dr.	(in case of cash sales)	with the amount of sales
Debtors/Customers A/c	Dr.	(in case of credit dates)	
To Sales A/c			

(iii) Cost of Goods Sold A/c	Dr.		with the amount of inventory
To Stock/Inventory A/c			

Illustration 8

From the following **data**, calculate the value of closing inventory according to "Last-in-First-out" Method on 31st March 2012 having an **opening balance** of 400 units @ Rs. 7.50 using : (i) Periodic Inventory System, (ii) Perpetual Inventory System :

	Purchases		Issues
March 5	600 Units @ Rs. 8.00 each	March 3	300 Units
March 15	500 Units @ Rs. 9.00 each	March 10	500 Units
March 25	400 Units @ Rs. 8.50 each	March 17	400 Units
March 30	300 Units @ Rs. 9.50 each	March 26	500 Units
		March 31	200 Units

Solution

(i) ***Under Periodic Inventory System :***

Total units purchased 1,800 units (600 + 500 + 400 + 300) but the opening balance in hand was 400 units. Thus, total quantity to be sold 2,200 (1,800 + 400) out of which no. of units were issued 1,900 (300 + 500 + 400 + 500 + 200). So, closing stock remains only 300 units (i.e., 2,200 – 1,900). The same will be valued @ Rs. 7.50 each. Thus, its value of 300 units will be Rs. 2,250 (i.e., 300 × Rs. 7.50).

(ii) ***Under Perpetual Inventory System :***

Store Ledger
LIFO basis—Perpetual

Date	Receipts G.R. No.	Quan-tity	Rate	Amount	Issues S.R. No.	Quan-tity	Rate	Amount	Balance Quan-tity	Rate	Amount
2012			Rs.	Rs.			Rs.	Rs.		Rs.	Rs.
Mar. 1									400	7.5	3,000
3						300	7.5	2,250	100	7.5	750
5		600	8	4,800					100	7.5	750
									600	8	4,800
10						500	8	4,000	100	7.5	750
									100	8	800
15		500	9	4,500					100	7.5	750
									100	8	800
									500	9	4,500

Contd.

2012		Rs.	Rs.			Rs.	Rs.		Rs.	Rs.
17					400	9	3,600	100	7.5	750
								100	8	800
								100	9	900
25	400	8.5	3,4 00					100	7.5	750
								100	8	800
								100	9	900
								400	8.5	3,400
26					400	8.5	3,400	100	7.5	750
					100	9	900	100	8	800
30	300	9.5	2,850					100	7.5	750
								100	8	800
								300	9.5	2,850
31					200	9.5	1,900	100	7.5	750
								100	8	800
								100	9.5	950
								300		2,500

Determining More Appropriate Method

The method of valuation of inventory discussed so far is suitable to specific circumstances, i.e., all methods are not applicable in all cases. The method which is most suitable to the specific case should be adopted. The Recommendations of the Institute of Chartered Accountants of England and Wales are helpful in this context. According to them 'No particular basis of valuation is suitable for all types of business but whatever the basis adopted, it should be applied consistently year after year'. But before applying the same, the following points should be considered :

(i) In what way does the product actually (physically) flow into production and sales, that is, the oldest units disposed off first, or the newest units disposed off first, or the items acquired at different times mixed together in such a way as to make them indistinguishable from the standpoint of disposal priority ?

(ii) Which method or methods have the tendency to 'smooth out' the reported periodic progress figures for the individual business firm ?

(iii) Which method provides the most conservative (lowest in amount) inventory figure for the end of period Balance Sheet ?

(iv) Which method provides the most useful type of cost of production and cost of sales figures for control and internal management purposes ?

(v) What method provides the most useful figure for the aid in determining selling prices in so far as selling prices may be influenced by expired costs and expenses ?

(vi) Which method comes closest to carrying out the concept of historical accounting ?

Some accountants prefer to use 'Unit Cost' or 'FIFO' method for valuation while others are favouring 'LIFO' method. The 'Average Cost' method may also be suggested by some other accountants.

In making a selection between FIFO and LIFO, it becomes necessary to decide first whether current costs should be applied to the inventory (under FIFO method) or the same should be matched against current revenues (under LIFO method). That is, FIFO method places emphasis on the Balance Sheet while LIFO method places emphasis on Profit and Loss Account. During periods of changing costs and prices, more meaningful statements of profits are produced if current costs are applied to current sales, thus achieving a better matching of costs and revenues.[1]

On the contrary, if LIFO method is followed, closing inventory will be valued at replacement price. Therefore, like FIFO, it does not lead to a misstatement of working capital position in the Balance Sheet. Although the LIFO advocates a more appropriate matching of costs against revenues—it is such an important objective as it offsets the 'incorrect' Balance Sheet results, the fact remains that, conceivably inventory qualities might eventually be priced at such 'old' costs as to produce a misstatement of working capital position that would be seriously misleading.[2]

1 Finney and Miller—*Principles of Accounting—Intermediate*—4th Edn., P. 363.

2 Recommendation 10, para 3, The Institute of Chartered Accountants of England and Wales

The average cost method may be applied during periods of price fluctuations and the same is most suitable where several production processes are involved in manufacturing concerns. However, whatever method a firm adopts, the same should be applied consistently year after year.

Valuation under Cost Accounting Records Rules

Under the Cost Accounting Record Rules, the actual cost of production of the articles to which the rules apply is to be arrived at. But, if there are joint products or multi-products or multi-process, proper allocation and accumulation of cost procedures are to be adopted in order to find out the actual cost of the products. If the Balance Sheet value of stock is different from the value which is determined in accordance with Cost Accounting Record Rules, a reconciliation statement is to be prepared between the financial accounts and the cost accounts which will reveal the difference in the valuation of stock and the reasons therefor. And, where a firm maintains cost records on the basis of standard cost, the records must indicate clearly the procedures followed in determining the cost of the product under such a system. The method which is adopted for adjusting the cost variances in working out the actual cost of the product must be indicated.

Cost records must indicate the method that is followed for ascertaining the cost of the work-in-progress and finished goods in order to show the elements of cost which are to be taken into account.

Presentation of Inventory in Financial Statements

Inventory can be presented in the financial statement under two headings:

(i) As per the requirement of Schedule VI of the Companies Act, 1956; and

(ii) As per the requirement of Indian Accounting Standard AS 2.

(i) As per the requirement of Schedule VI of the Companies Act

According to the requirement of Schedule VI of the Companies Act, 1956, inventories are shown under the head **'Current Assets, Loans & Advances'** as:

(a) Stores and spare parts; (b) Loose Tools; (c) Raw Materials; (d) Work-in-progress; and (e) Finished goods.

Mode of Valuation of the above must be disclosed except in the case of raw materials. Similarly, in the case of a manufacturing concern, the requirements of Profit and Loss Account require the disclosure of physical quantities of raw material consumed including the opening and closing stock of finished goods produced. In the case of a trading concern, however, opening and closing stock including the purchases made during the year must be split up into various categories relating to each class of goods, including their quantities so traded.

(ii) As per the requirements of Indian Accounting Standard AS 2

AS 2 : Valuation of Inventories

As per para 3, AS 2, Inventories are assets—(a) held for sale in the ordinary course of business; (b) in the process of production for such sale; or (c) in the form of materials or supplies to be consumed in the production process or in the rendering of services.

Cost of Inventories

The Cost of inventories should comprise all costs of purchases, costs of conversion and other costs incurred in bringing the inventories to their present location and condition.

In short,

Cost of Inventories	=	Cost of Purchase + Cost of Conversion + Other Costs (only to the extent that they are incurred in bringing the inventories to their present location and condition).

Cost Formula

14. ***The cost of inventories of items that are not ordinarily interchangeable and goods or services produced and segregated for specific projects should be assigned by specific identification of their individual costs.***

16. ***The cost of inventories, other than those dealt with in paragraph 14, should be assigned by using the first in, first-out (FIFO), or weighted average cost formula. The formula used should reflect the fairest possible approximation to the cost incurred in bringing the items of inventory to their present location and condition.***

Net Realisable Value

Net realisable value is the estimated selling price in the ordinary course of business less the estimated costs of completion and the estimated costs necessary to make the sale.

While ascertaining *Net Relisable Value*, the student must remember the following (as per AS 2)

20. The cost of inventories may not be recoverable if those inventories are damaged, if they have become wholly or partially obsolete, or if their selling prices have declined. The cost of inventories may also not be recoverable if the estimated costs of completion or the estimated costs necessary to make the sale have increased. The practice of writing down inventories below cost to net realisable value is consistent with the view that assets should not be carried in excess of amounts expected to be realised from their sale or use.

21. Inventories are usually written down to net realisable value on an item-by-item basis. In some circumstances, however, it may be appropriate to group similar or related items. This may be the case with items of inventory relating to the same product line that have similar purposes or end uses and are produced and marketed in the same geographical area and cannot be practicably evaluated separately from other items in that product line. It is not appropriate to write down inventories based on a classification of inventory, for example, finished goods, or all the inventories in a particular business segment.

22. Estimates of net realiable value are based on the most reliable evidence available at the time the estimates are made as to the amount the inventories are expected to realise. These estimates take into consideration fluctuations of price or cost directly relating to events occurring after the balance sheet date to the extent that such event confirms the conditions existing at the balance sheet date.

23. Estimates of net realisable value also take into consideration the purpose for which the inventory is held. For example, the net realisable value of the quantity of inventory held to satisfy firm sales or service contracts is based on the contract price. If the sales contracts are for less than the inventory quantities held, the net realisable value of the excess inventory is based on general selling prices. Contingent losses on firm sales contracts in excess of inventory quantities held and contingent losses on firm purchase contracts are dealt with in accordance with the principles enunciated in Accounting Standard (AS) 4, Contingencies and Events Occurring After the Balance Sheet Date.

24. Materials and other supplies held for use in the production of inventories are not written down below cost if the finished products in which they will be incorporated are expected to be sold at or above cost. However, when there has been decline in the price of materials and it is estimated that the cost of the finished products will exceed net realisable value, the materials are written down to net realisable value. In such circums-tances, the replacement cost of the materials may be the best available measure of their net realisable value.

25. An assessment is made of net realisable value as at each balance sheet date.

Illustration 9

How do you deal with the following?

On 31.3.2010, the Closing Stock of Sankha Ltd. includes 10,000 units @ Rs. 8 i.e., Rs. 80,000. But the current market price as on that date was @ Rs. 9 i.e., Rs. 90,000.

Solution

According to para 25, AS 2, **Valuation of Inventories**, an assessment is made of net realisable value as at each Balance Sheet date. Hence, the value of stock should be Rs. 90,000 i.e., @ Rs. 9 per unit.

Illustration 10

The following information presented by P Ltd. Ascertain the value of stock to be included in the Balance Sheet—

Cost Price of the certain stock amounted to Rs. 60,000, being obsolete, it can be used for production purposes after incurring Rs. 10,000, for modification. The same should be used as a by-product for an existing another product, the purchase price for the same amounted to Rs. 40,000.

Solution

Cost Price of the product (given) Rs. 60,000

Net Realisable value of the product (Rs. 40,000 – Rs. 10,000) = Rs. 30,000.

Hence, Rs. 30,000 should be treated as the value of stock for inclusion in Balance Sheet.

Illustration 11

The company deals in three products, A, B and C which are neither similar nor inter-changeable. At the time of closing of its account for the year ended 2002-03, this historical cost and net realisable value of the items of closing stock are determined as follows:

Items	Historical Cost (Rs. in lakhs)	Net Realisable Value (Rs. in lakhs)
A	40	28
B	32	32
C	16	24

What will be the value of Closing Stock?

[CA PE-II, May 2004]

Solution

According to para 5, AS 2 **Valuation of Inventories**, inventories would be valued as per the cost and net realisable value whichever is lower. Thus, inventories should be valued as per item-wise as under:

Items	Historical Cost (Rs. in Lakhs)	Net Realisable Value (Rs. in Lakhs)	Valuation of Closing Stock (Rs. in Lakhs)
A	40	28	28
B	32	32	32
C	16	24	16
	88	84	76

So, value of closing stock will be Rs. 76 lakhs.

Illustration 12

'Sonar Sansar' deals in old colour TVs. It has 4 TVs, the particulars of which are given below.

You are asked to compute the value of stock to be included in Balance Sheet for the year ended 3.3.2010:

TVs	Onida	Philips	EC	Sony	Total
	Rs.	Rs.	Rs.	Rs.	Rs.
Cost Price	10,000	20,000	35,000	50,000	1,15,000
Expenses incurred in bringing into saleable Condition	3,000	2,000	5,000	—	10,000
Net Realisable Value	18,000	30,000	36,000	55,000	1,39,000

Solution

As per para 5, AS 2 **Valuation of Inventories**, inventories would be valued at the lower of Cost or Net Realisable Value which are:

TVs	Onida	Philips	EC	Sony	Total (Value of Stock)
	Rs.	Rs.	Rs.	Rs.	Rs.
Cost Price (including Expenses)	13,000	22,000	40,000	50,000	1,25,000
Net Realisable Value	18,000	30,000	36,000	55,000	1,39,000
Value of Stock	13,000	22,000	36,000	50,000	1,21,000

∴ Value of stock to be included in the Balance Sheet would be Rs. 1,21,000 i.e., Lower of Cost Prices Rs. 1,25,000 and Net Realisable Value Rs. 1,21,000).

Illustration 13

The following particulars are presented by T Ltd. as on 31.3.2010.

Compute the value of stock as per AS 2.

		Rs.
Stock held by T. Ltd. :	Cost Price	10,550
	Net Realisable Value	11,500

The details of such stock were:

	Cost Price	**Net Realisable Value**
	Rs.	Rs.
Cotton	5,600	4,960
Woolen	3,450	4,540
Synthetic	1,500	2,000
	10,550	11,500

Solution

As per para, 21 AS 2, **Valuation of Inventories**, inventories are written-down to net realisable value on an item-by-item basis.

Valuation of Stock as per AS 2

	Cost Price	Net Realisable Value	Value of Stock
	Rs.	Rs.	Rs.
Cotton	5,600	4,960	4,960
Woollen	3,450	4,540	3,450
Synthetic	1,500	2,000	1,500
	10,550	11,500	9,910

Hence, value of stock will be taken as Rs. 9,910, as per AS 2.

Illustration 14

The total stock of Z Ltd., as on 31.3.2010, was Rs. 5,00,000 of which stock amounting to Rs. 31,000 was ascertained as per AS 2. Compute the value of stock as per AS 2 for inclusion in financial statement as on that date:

Type of Product	Cost of Materials	Production Expenses incurred	Selling and Distribution Expenses to be incurred	Estimated Selling Price
	Rs.	Rs.	Rs.	Rs.
P	10,000	2,000	1,000	15,000
S	5,000	—	500	4,500
T	12,000	3,000	2,000	18,000
	27,000	5,000	3,500	37,500

Solution

As per para 21, AS 2, **Valuation of Inventories**, inventories are usually written-down to net realisable value on item-by-item basis. Thus, value of stock will be computed as under:

Computations of Value of Stock as per AS 2

Product	Cost Price (Including Productive Expenses)	Net Realisable Value (Excluding Selling and Distribution Expenses from Selling Price)	Value of Stock (Lower of Cost Price or Net Realisable Value)
	Rs.	Rs.	Rs.
P	12,000 (Rs. 10,000 + Rs. 2,000)	14,000 (Rs. 15,000 – Rs. 1,000)	12,000
S	5,000	4,000 (Rs. 4,500 – Rs. 500)	4,000
T	15,000 (Rs. 12,000 + Rs. 3,000)	16,000 (Rs. 18,000 – Rs. 2,000)	15,000
			31,000

So, value of stock will be Rs. 31,000 for inclusion in the financial statement as per AS 2.

INVENTORY/STOCK TAKING

Usefulness

Generally, stocks are valued at the closing date of the financial year. But sometimes it may so happen that the value of stock has been ascertained on a certain date instead of valuing the same on the closing date of the financial year which may either be the succeeding or preceding date of the financial year. As a result, a reconciliation is to be made compulsory in order to ascertain the real position of stock.

In short, if stocks are valued at a certain date which is *after* the closing date of the financial year, the value of goods purchased, sold or returned are to be deducted in order to ascertain the value of the same between those two dates. On the contrary, if stocks are valued at a certain date which is *before* the closing date of the financial year, the above items will, however, be added.

Principles to be followed

(a) Goods are purchased and invoices are passed through the books in the same accounting period, so that the liability is also taken into consideration in the same accounting period as appropriate asset.

(b) Goods sold but not actually delivered should be included with sales for a particular accounting period but to be excluded from stock.

(c) Goods belonging to the business, although not in its physical possession, must be included with stocks.

Accounting Information

If stocks are valued at a date which is after the closing date of the financial year—in that case; the problems of a Stock Reconciliation will be as under :

		Rs.	Rs.
	Stock as on the date of accounting		* *
Add :	*Adjusted net sales*	* *	
	Goods sold but not recorded in the invoice	* *	
	Goods purchased but not yet received etc.	* *	
	Purchase returns, if any	* *	
	Goods-in-transit, if any	* *	
	Undercasting in Stock Sheet	* *	* *
Less :	*Adjusted Net Purchases*	* *	
	Goods purchased but not yet received	* *	
	Goods purchased but received earlier, etc.	* *	
	Goods held on consignment basis	* *	
	Overcasting in stock sheet	* *	
	Sales returns, if any	* *	* *
	Value of stock at the end of financial year		

If stocks are valued at a date which is before the date of the financial year the position will be reversed. In addition to above, if any error exists, viz., (i) undercasting or overcasting in the schedule of inventory, (ii) if there is any wrong addition or subtraction in the schedule of inventory, (iii) or any wrong carry forward in inventory schedule etc., the same must be rectified.

Sometimes it may so happen that, due to some unavoidable circumstances, it may not be possible to take stock on the closing date after the business hours. In that case, value of stock is considered either on the basis of closing date or on the basis of a few days earlier or later which is convenient to the management without making any disturbance in the normal activity. As such, the same stock should be valued after making some adjustments which are:

(i) When sales and stock taking rate are affected on the closing date, special attention must be given to see that goods which are sold but not delivered are not at all included with the stock as on that date.

(ii) It is needless to mention that if stock taking is done in any date after the closing date, the entire amount of sales (at cost or market price, whichever is less) must be added to the value of stock along with the returns outwards, if any. At the same time, goods purchased and received between the closing date and that date together with returns inward (at cost or market price, whichever is less) if any, are to be excluded while valuing stock.

A. When stocks are valued after the closing date of the financial year

Illustration 15

From the following information, ascertain the value of stock as on 31.3.1997:

	Rs.
Value of stock on 1.4.1996	70,000
Purchase during the period from 1.4.1996 to 31.3.1997	3,46,000
Manufacturing expense during the above period	70,000
Sales during the same period	5,22,000

At the time of valuing stock on 31.3.996 a sum of Rs. 6,000 was written-off a particular item which was originally purchased for Rs. 20,000 and was sold for Rs. 16,000. But for the above transactions the gross profit earned during the year was 25% on cost.

[CA Foundation, May 1998]

Solution

Statement of Valuation of Stock
as on 31st March 1997

		Rs.	Rs.
	Value of Stock on 1.4.1996		70,000
Add:	Purchase from 1.4.1996 to 31.3.1997		3,46,000
Add:	Manufacturing Expenses		70,000
			4,86,000
Loss:	Cost of Sales:		
	Sales	5,22,000	
Less:	Gross Profit	1,03,200[1]	4,18,800
	Value of stock as on 31.3.1997		67,200

Workings:

		Rs.
	Gross Profit on Normal Sales	
	i.e., Rs. 5,22,000 – Rs. 16,000 = Rs. 5,06,000 × $\frac{20}{100}$ =	1,01,200
Add:	Gross Profit on abnormal item	
	i.e., Rs. 16,000 – Rs. 14,000 (Rs. 20,000 – Rs. 6,000)	2,000
		1,03,200

Illustration 16

The Profit and Loss Account of Hanuman showed net profit of Rs. 60,000, after considering the closing stock of Rs. 37,500 on 31st March 1999. Subsequently the following information was obtained from scrutiny of the books:

(i) Purchases for the year included Rs. 1,500 paid for new electric fittings for the shop.

(ii) Hanuman gave away goods valued at Rs. 4,000 as free samples for which no entry was made in the books of accounts.

(iii) Invoices for goods amounting to Rs. 25,000 have been entered on 27th March 1999, but the goods were not included in stock.

(iv) In March 1999 goods of Rs. 20,000 sold and delivered were taken in the Sales for April 1999.

(v) Goods costing Rs. 7,500 were sent on sale or return in March 1999 at a margin of Profit of $33\frac{1}{3}$% on cost. Though approval was given in April 1999 these were taken as sales for March 1999.

Calculate the value of stock on 31st March 1999 and the adjusted Net Profit for the year ended on that date.

Solution **[CA Foundation, May 2000]**

(a) **Calculation of Value of Stock on 31st March 1999**

		Rs.
	Stock on 31st March 1999 (given)	37,500
Add:	Purchases of March 1999 not included in stock	25,000
	Goods lying with customers on approval basis	7,500
		70,00

(b) **Profit and Loss (Adjustment) Account**

Dr. *Cr.*

	Particulars	*Amount* Rs.		*Particulars*	*Amount* Rs.
To	Advertisement (samples)		By	Net Profit (given)	60,000
"	Sales (Goods approved in April to be taken as April sales: 7,500 + 2,500)	10,000	"	Electric fittings (wrongly included)	1,500
"	Adjusted Net Profit *(bal. fig.)*	1,04,000	"	Advertisement	4,000
			"	Stock (Purchases of March not included)	25,000
			"	Sales (March Sale wrongly taken as April sales)	20,000
			"	Stock (goods sent on approval not included)	7,500
		1,18,000			1,18,000

Illustration 17

A trader prepared his accounts on 31st March each year. Due to some unavovidable reasons, no stockt-king could be possible till 15th April 2002 on which date the total cost of goods in his godown came to Rs. 50,000. The followng facts were established between 31st March and 15th April 2002:

(i) Sales Rs. 41,000 (including cash sales Rs. 10,000).

(ii) Purchass Rs. 5,034 (including cash purchases Rs. 1,990)

(iii) Sales Return Rs. 1,000.

(iv) On 15th March, goods of the sale value of Rs. 10,000 were sent on sale or return basis to a customer, the period of approval being four weeks. He returned 40% of the goods on 10th April, approving the rest; the customer was billed on 16th April.

(v) The trader has also received goods costing Rs. 8,000 in March for sale on consignment basis; 20% of the goods has been sold by 31st March, and another 50% by the 15th April. These sales are not included in above sales.

Goods are sold by the trader at a profit of 20% on sales.

You are required to ascertain the vlue of Inventory as on 31st March 2002.

Solution

[PE-1 May 2003]

Statement of Valuation of Stock on 31st March 2002

		Rs.	Rs.
	Value of Stock as on 15th April 2002		50,000
Add:	Cost of sales from 31st March 2002 to 15th April 2002		
	Sales (Rs. 41,000 – Rs. 1,000)	40,000	
Less :	Gross Profit (20% of Rs. 40,000)	8,000	32,000
	Cost of goods sent on approval basis (80% of Rs. 6,000)		4,800
			86,800
Loss :	Purchases from 31st March 2002 to 15th April 2002	5,034	
	Unsold stock out of goods received on consignment basis (30% of Rs. 8,000)	2,400	
			7,434
	Value of Stock as on 31.3.2002		79,366

Illustration 18

Physical verification of stock in a business was done on 23rd June 2000. The value of the stock was Rs. 4,80,000. The following transactions took place between 23rd June and 30th June 2000:

(i) Out of the goods sent on consignment, goods at cost Rs. 24,000 were unsold.

(ii) Purchases of Rs. 40,000 were made out of which goods worth Rs. 16,000 were delivered on 5th July 2000.

(iii) Sales were Rs. 1,36,000, which include goods worth Rs. 32,000 sent on approval, Half of these goods were returned before 30th June 2000, but no information is available regarding the remaining goods.

(iv) Goods are sold at cost plus 25%. However, goods costing Rs. 24,000 had been sold for Rs. 12,000.

Determine the value of stock on 30th June 2000.

Solution

[CA Foundation, Nov. 2000]

Statement of Valuation of Stock on 30th June 2000

		Rs.	Rs.
	Value of Stock as on 23rd June 2000		4,80,000
Add:	Stock of consignment	24,000	
	Goods in transit	16,000	
	Purchases during the period from 23rd June 2000 to 30th June 2000 (40,000 – 16,000)	24,000	
	Cost of goods sent on approval (80% of Rs. 16,000)	12,800	76,800
			5,56,800

		Rs	Rs.
Less:	Cost of goods sold:		
	Sales (Rs. 1,36,000 – Rs. 16,000)	1,20,000	
Loss :	Gross Profit	9,600[1]	1,10,400
	Value of Stock as on 30th June 2000		4,46,400

Workings

		Rs.	Rs.
1.	**Calculation of Gross Profit on normal sales**		
	Actual sales		1,36,000
Less:	Abnormal sales	12,000	
	Return of goods sent on approval	16,000	28,000
			1,08,000
	Calculation of Gross Profit:		Rs.
	Gross profit on normal sales (Rs. 1,08,000 × 20%)		21,600
Less :	Loss on sale of (abnormal) goods (Rs. 24,000 – Rs. 12,000)		12,000
	Gross Profit		9,600

Illustration 19

X's financial year ends on the last Wednesday in September but actual stock is not taken until the following Saturday, when it is ascertained at Rs. 33,500. You find that:

(i) Sales are entered in the Sales Day Book on the same day as despatched and returns Inward in the Returns Books the day the goods are received back.

(ii) Purchases are entered in the Purchase Day Book as the invoice are received.

(iii) Purchases between Wednesday and Saturday, per Purchase Day Book, were Rs. 120, but of these, goods amounting to Rs. 40 were not received until after the stock was taken.

(iv) Sales between Wednesday and Saturday per Sales Day Book and Cash Sales were Rs. 1,720.

(v) Goods invoiced during September (prior to the last Wednesday) but not received until after Wednesday accounted to Rs. 100 of which Rs. 70 worth were received between Wednesday and Saturday.

(vi) Goods sold in the previous week Rs. 60 were returned on Monday but did not reach X until Thursday.

(vii) The rate of gross profit on sales is 25%

Ascertain the value of Stock at the end of the financial year, assuming that the market value is higher than cost and that the Purchases and Sales Day Books are not to be amended.

[CA Entrance —CU BCom (Hons.) 2008—Adapted]

Solution

Statement showing the Value of Stock as on ....

		Rs.	Rs.
	Value of Closing Stock as on Saturday		33,500
Less :	Goods purchased and received between Wednesday and Saturday	120	
Less :	Goods received after Saturday	40	80
			33,420
Add :	Cost of goods sold and despatched between Wednesday and Saturday	1,720	
Less :	Gross Profit (Rs. 1,720 × 25%)	430	1,290
			34,710
Less :	Goods returned by customers out of sales of the last year	60	
Less :	Gross Profit (Rs. 60 × 25%)	15	45
			34,665
Add :	Goods invoiced in September (already included in purchases of the last year) but not receive until Wednesday	100	
Less :	Goods invoiced and received between Wednesday and Saturday	70	30
	Value of Stock for inclusion in final accounts		34,695

Note: No entry is required for goods purchased of Rs. 2,000, which had been received prior to 31.3.2004 as it had already been adjusted.

Illustration 20

P made up his annual accounts to Nov. 30, 2011. All purchase and sale invoices and credit notes dated Nov. 2011 had been duly entered in the books, but all such documents dated Dec., 2011 had been treated as relating to the year commencing Dec. 1, 2011.

Stock was taken on Dec. 7, 2011, when the stock was found to be Rs. 3,94,800 valued at cost. The rate of Gross Profit earned was 30% on sale price. Further—

(a) Goods were received from suppliers during the five days from Dec. 1 to Dec. 5 (Dec. 6 was Sunday). The connected invoices dated Nov. 2011, amounted to Rs. 1,800 and those dated Dec. 2011 to Rs. 9,180.

(b) Sales and Sales returns for the period from Dec. 1 to Dec. 4, 2011 were, respectively, Rs. 12,600 and Rs. 1,440. The sales return did not include any item relating to supply between Dec. 1 and 5.

(c) The Stock included goods valued at Rs. 2,100 held by P on sale or return for which no entries had been made in the books.

(d) A sub-total of Rs. 27,600 on one of the Stock Sheet had been carried to the summary of Stock Sheet as Rs. 26,700.

(e) One Stock Sheet has been overcast by Rs. 3,000.

(f) One item of a number of articles costing Rs. 1,875 had been entered as Rs. 875.

Prepare a statement showing the value of the Stock to be included in the accounts on the 30th Nov. 2011.

Solution

Statement showing the Value of Stock
as on November 30, 2011

		Rs.	Rs.
	Stock on December 7, 2011		3,94,800
Less :	Goods received during the period 1st to 5th December, 2011 and, as such, included in stock but the same has not been included in the purchases of the last accounting year which was invoiced in December		9,180
			3,85,620
Add :	Cost of goods sold during the period 1st to 5th December 2011:		
	Sales	12,600	
Less :	Gross Profit @ 30%	3,780	8,820
			3,94,440
Less :	Cost of goods returned during the period 1st to 5th December 2011 (out of last accounting year's sales) :		
	Returns	1,440	
Less :	Gross Profit @ 30%	432	1,008
			3,93,432
Add :	Error in carry forward : Rs. (27,600 – 26,700)		900
			3,94,332
Less :	Overcasting in Stock Sheet		3,000
			3,91,332
Add :	Error which was in extending an item of Rs. 1,875 as Rs. 875 : Rs. (1,875 – 875)		1,000
			3,92,332
Less :	Goods held on sale or return		2,100
	Value of Stock on November 30, 2011 to be included in the accounts		3,90,232

Illustration 21

Sundaram closed his books of accounts on 31st March 2012, but due to certain difficulties, it was not possible for him to conduct physical stock taking on that date, physical stock was taken on 7th April when it was valued at Rs. 45,000. An examination of the records of inventories from 1st to 7th April revealed the following :

(a) Net sales during the period were Rs. 10,200. These goods were sold at the usual rate of gross profit of 15% on cost except goods which realised Rs. 1,200 on the basis of 20% profit on cost.

(b) Purchases during the period were Rs. 8,000 of which Rs. 1,000 worth of goods were delivered on 9th April only.

(c) Sales return during the period were Rs. 1,200 of which 50% were out of the sales at 20% gross profit mentioned above.

(d) On 5th April, Sundaram received certain goods costing Rs. 5,000 to be sold by him on consignment basis.

You are required to prepare a statement showing clearly the value of the stock, to be taken into account in Sundaram's final accounts for the year ended 31st March 2012.

Solution

Statement showing the Value of Stock
on 31st March 2012

		Rs.	Rs.	Rs.
	Stock as on 7th April			45,000
Add :	Cost of Goods Sold during April 1 to April 7	Rs.	Rs.	Rs.
	Gross Sales	9,000	1,200	
Less :	Sales Returns	600	600	
	Net Sales	8,400	600	
Less :	Gross Profit @ 15% on Cost i.e., $(8{,}400 \times \frac{15}{115})$	1,096	—	
	and @ $\frac{1}{6}$ of Rs. 600 (i.e., $\frac{1}{5}$ th of CP or $\frac{1}{6}$ th of SP)	—	100	
		7,304	500	7,804
				52,804
Less :	Goods purchased and actually received during April 1 to April 7	8,000		
Less :	Purchases : Goods not yet received	1,000		7,000
				45,804
Less :	Goods received on 5th April on consignment basis			5,000
	Value of Stock as on April 1, 2012			40,804

Illustration 22

Mr. Bepari closes his books of accounts on 30th June each year. In the year 2012, for some unavoidable reasons, he could not take his stock on 30th June and physical stock was taken only on 7th July 2012, and was valued at Rs. 11,250. Scrutiny of the inventories from 1st July to 7th July 2012 disclosed the following :

(i) Sales during the period amounted to Rs. 2,550. These goods were sold at usual rate of gross profit of 25% on cost except one sale of Rs. 300 which has been effected at a profit of 20% on cost.

(ii) Sales amounting to Rs. 625 made on 6th July has been delivered only on 9th July.

(iii) Purchases during the period were of Rs. 2,000 of which goods costing Rs. 1,750 were delivered on or before 7th July.

(iv) During this period sales returns amounted to Rs. 200 including Rs. 150 out of sales prior to 30th June 2012, at usual rate of 25% on cost.

(v) On 6th July Mr. Bepari received on consignment certain goods invoiced at Rs. 1,250 from Shri C to be sold on his behalf and at his risk.

(vi) Goods sent on Sale or Return and invoiced at Rs. 1,125 on 7th July were not included in the sales stated above.

Ascertain the value of stock on 30th June 2012. **[CA]**

Solution

Statement showing the value of Stock
as on 30th June 2012

		Rs.	Rs.
	Value of stock as taken on 7th July 2012		11,250
Add :	Cost of adjusted sales from 1st July 2012 :		
	Sales for the period	2,550	
	Less : Goods sold on 6th July but delivered on 9th July	625	
		1,925	
	Less : Sales at lesser than usual rate	300	
		1,625	
	Less : G.P. at 25% on cost or 20% on sales	325	1,300
			12,550
Add :	Cost of goods sold at lesser price ($\frac{100}{120}$ × Rs. 300)	250	
Add :	Cost of goods sent on Sale or Return ($\frac{100}{125}$ × Rs. 1,125)	900	1,150
			13,700
Less :	Goods received out of purchases during the period		
"	1st to 7th July	1,750	
	Cost of sales returns out of sales prior to 30th June ($\frac{100}{125}$ × Rs. 150)	120	
"	Cost of goods received on consignment basis	1,250	3,120
	Value of Stock on 30th June 2012		10,580

Illustration 23

C. S. Ltd., wholesalers, prepares accounts to 31st March each year. On 31st March 2012, their stock-taking expert was ill and the preparation of the physical inventory was delayed until 3rd April 2012. On that date the stock were ascertained and valued at cost and included in the accounts to March 2012 at Rs. 24,000

An examination of inventories and related financial records disclosed that, between 1st and 3rd April, 2012

(a) Sales totalled Rs. 4,000 (red wine Rs. 2,800 and white wine Rs. 1,200). The total included (i) Rs. 200 in respect of red wines which left the cellars on 29th March 2012, and (ii) Rs. 400 in respect of red wines not despatched until 12th April 2012. The rate of gross profit to sales was 40% for red wines and 30% for white wines.

(b) Returns from customers totalled Rs. 600 (red Rs. 400 and white Rs. 200).

(c) Purchases totalled Rs. 1,800 and included (i) Rs. 600 for wines received in March 2012, and (ii) Rs. 300 for wines received on 12th April 2012.

(d) Returns outward totalled Rs. 400. Other factors affecting the stock-taking were:

(e) The inadvertent omission from the accounts on 31st March 2011, and 2012 of stocks in foreign country costing Rs. 3,000.

(f) Arithmetical errors in the stock sheet on 3rd April 2012, resulting in an overvaluation of Rs. 280.

You are required to prepare a statement showing the correct amount of the stock, at cost, as on 31st March 2012.

Solution

Statement showing the Value of Stock
as at 31st March 2012

				Red wines	White wines
		Rs.	Rs.	Rs.	Rs.
	Value of Stock as on 3rd April 2012				24,000
Add :	Cost of adjusted sales between 1st and 3rd April				
	Total Sales	2,800	1,200		

Contd.

		Rs.	Rs.	Rs.	Rs.
Less :	Goods left in cellars	200			
		2,600			
Less :	Goods despatched after stock-taking	400			
		2,200			
Less :	Returns inward	400	200		
		1,800	1,000		
Less :	Gross profit @ 40% and 30%, respectively	720	300		
		1,080	700	1,780	
Less :	Omission in foreign country stock			3,000	
					4,780
					28,780
Less :	Adjusted purchased between 1st and 3rd April Purchases			1,800	
Less :	Goods received in March			600	
				1,200	
Less :	Goods received after 3rd April			300	
				900	
Less :	Returns outward			400	500
					28,280
Less :	Overvaluation of Stock				280
	Value of stock as on 31st March				28,000

B. When stocks are valued before the Closing date of the financial year

It has already been stated earlier that when stocks are valued before the date of the financial year, the treatment will be reversed. Moreover, if any error exists, the same must also be rectified accordingly. Consider the following illustrations one by one :

Illustration 24

A firm had to take complete stock on 21st June 2012, because of a deal for sale of business which fell through only at the later stage. As a result, stock was not again taken on 30th June 2012, when accounts were closed for the year. The stock on 21st June 2012 was Rs. 67,460. The following information is supplied to you regarding transactions in stock between 21st June and 30th June, 2012:

(1) Goods purchased from 21st June to 30th June amount to Rs. 4,820 out of which goods worth Rs. 1,900 were received on 2nd July 2012.

(2) Sales during the said period amounted to Rs. 16,800 including Rs. 3,600 for goods sent on approval, half of which was still returnable on 30th June 2012. The firm sells goods at cost plus 25%, but there was one lot of goods which had cost Rs. 2,800 but had to be sold for Rs. 1,200 due to damage caused by rain. The stock as on 21st June 2012 included these goods at cost.

(3) Unsold goods in the hand of a consignee on 30th June 2012, were valued at Rs. 3,200.

Prepare a statement showing the actual value of stock as on 30th June 2012 **[CA]**

Solution

Notes :

(1) It has been assumed that the ownership of the stock was not transferred. If it is assumed that the same had been transferred, in that case, the value of stock would be Rs. 61,640 (i.e., 59,740 + 1,900).

(2) It has also been assumed that the cost price of such goods has already been added on 21st June.

Statement showing the value of Stock *as on 30th June 2012*

		Rs.	Rs.
	Value of Stock as taken on 21st June 2012		67,460
Add :	Cost of goods purchased and received on or before 30th June :		
	Purchases	4,820	
Less :	Received on 2nd July	1,900	2,920
Add :	Cost of stock in the hands of the consignee on 30th June		3,200
			73,580
	Value of goods sold during the period 22nd June to 30th June :		

Contd.

		Rs.	Rs.
Less :	Sales	16,800	
Less :	Goods sent on 'sale on approval' and returnable after 30th June	1,800	
		15,000	
Less :	Gross Profit @ 20% on sale of normal goods of Rs. 13,800 (Rs. 1,5000 – 1,200)	2,760	12,240
			61,340
	Value of Stock on 30th June 2012		1,600
			59,740

Illustration 25

Moon Ltd. keeps no stock records, but a physical inventory of Stock is made at the end of quarter and the valuation is taken at Cost. The company's year ends on 30.9.08 and Draft Accounts have been prepared to that date. The Stock Inventory taken on 30.9.08 was, however, misled and you have been advised to value the Closing Stock as on 30.9.08, with the Stock figure as on 30.6.08 and some other information as available to you are :

(i) The Cost of Stock on 30.6.08 as shown by the inventory was Rs. 80,000.

(ii) On 30th June, Stock sheets showed the following discrepancies :

(a) A page total of Rs. 5,000 had been carried to the summary as Rs. 6,000.

(b) The total of a page had been undercast by Rs. 200.

(iii) Invoice of purchase entered in the Purchases Book during the months from July to September 2008 totalled Rs. 70,000. Of this, Rs. 3,000 related to goods received prior to 30th June 2008. Invoices entered in October 2008 relating to goods received on September 2008 totalled Rs. 4,000.

(iv) Sales invoiced to customers from July to September 2008 totalled Rs. 90,000. Of this, Rs. 5,000 related to goods despatched on or before 30.6.08. Goods despatched to customers before 30.9.08 but invoiced on October 2008 totalled Rs. 4,000.

(v) During the final quarter, credit notes at invoiced value of Rs. 1,000 had been issued to customers in respect of goods returned during that period.

(vi) The Gross margin earned by the company is 25% of cost.

You are required to prepare a statement showing the amount of stock at cost as on 30.9.2008.

Solution **[ICWA]**

Statement showing the Value of Stock
as on 30th September 2008

		Rs.	Rs.	Rs.
	Value of Stock on 30th June 2008			80,000
Add :	Undercasting in page total		200	
	Purchases :			
	July to September	70,000		
	Less : Goods received prior to 30th June	3,000		
		67,000		
	Add : Goods purchased before 30th June	4,000	71,000	71,200
				1,51,200
Less :	Sales:			
	July to September	90,000		
	Add : Goods sent before 30th Sept. but invoiced in Oct.	4,000		
		94,000		
	Less : Goods despatched before 30th June	5,000		
		89,000		
	Less : Goods returned	1,000		
		88,000		
	Less : G.P. @ 25% on Cost (or, 20% on sales)	17,600		
	Cost of sales		70,400	
	Wrong carry forward in page total		1,000	71,400
	Value of Closing Stock on 30th Sept. 2008			79,800

Illustration 26

Determine the value of stock to be taken for Balance Sheet as at 31st March 2012, from the following information :

The stock was physically verified on 23rd March 2012 and was valued at Rs. 6,00,000. Between 23rd March 2012 and 31st March 2012, the following transactions had taken place:

1. Purchase Rs. 50,000, of this, goods worth Rs. 20,000 were delivered on 5th April 2012.
2. Out of goods sent on consignment, goods worth Rs. 30,000 (at cost) were unsold.
3. Sales was of Rs. 1,70,000. This includes goods worth Rs. 40,000 sent on approval, half of these were returned before 31st March. As regards remaining, no intimation is received.
4. Normally firm sells goods on cost plus 25%. However, a lot of goods costing Rs. 30,000 was sold for Rs. 15,000.

Solution **[ICWA Adapted]**

Note : The problem deals with the problems of stock-taking at a date which is *before* the date of the financial year. So, the treatment will be reversed as again the stocks are valued at a date which is *after* the closing date of the financial year.

Statement showing the Value of Physical Stock
as on 31st March 2012

		Rs.	Rs.	Rs.
	Stock as on 23rd March 2012			6,00,000
Add :	Purchases between 23rd March to 31st March Rs. 50,000 – 20,000 =	30,000		
	In-Transit	20,000	50,000	
	Goods in the hands of consignee at Cost		30,000	
	Goods on Approval with customer at Cost :			
	Goods Sent	40,000		
Less :	$\frac{1}{2}$ returned before 31st March	20,000		
		20,000		
Less :	Gross Profit @ 20% on cost or 25% on sales	4,000	16,000	
				96,000
				6,96,000
Less :	Cost of sales between 23rd March and 31st March :			
	Goods Sold	1,70,000		
Less :	Sent on Approval	20,000		
		1,50,000		
Less :	Abnormal Sales	15,000		
		1,35,000		
Less :	Gross Profit @ 20% on Sales	27,000	1,08,000	
	Cost of Abnormal Sales		30,000	1,38,000
	Value of Stock as on 31st March 2012			5,58,000

ASSIGNMENT MATERIALS
THEORETICAL

Multiple Choice Questions

1. (a) Undervaluation of Closing Stock

(i) Increases gross profit (ii) Decreases gross profit
(iii) No effect (iv) None of these

(b) Overvaluation of Opening Stock

(i) Increases gross profit (ii) Decreases gross profit
(iii) No effect (iv) None of these

(c) FIFO method is followed in case of

(i) Falling in price (ii) Increase in price
(iii) Both (iv) None of these

(d) LIFO method is followed where

(i) Prices are increasing (ii) Prices are decreasing
(iii) Both (iv) None of these

(e) AS per AS 2, Closing Stock should be valued at

(i) Cost price or Net Realisable Value, whichever is higher. (ii) Cost Price or Net Realisable Value, whichever is lower
(iii) Both (iv) None of these

[Ans. (a) (ii); (b) (ii); (c) (i); (d) (i); (e) (ii).

Short Answer-Type Questions

1. State two advantages and two disadvantages of LIFO method.
2. What is Weighted Average Cost method?
3. What is the difference between FIFO and LIFO methods?
4. When do you follow LIFO method?
5. When do you follow FIFO method for valuation?
6. What is Average Cost method?
7. Which method will you follow when there is a fluctuation in the price of materials, and why?
8. State two advantages and two disadvantages of Weighted Average Cost.
9. Explain the logic behind the principles for valuing closing stock, cost price or market price, whichever is lower.
10. Define : (a) Cost Price (b) Net Realisable Value
11. What is Perpetual Inventory System?
12. Distinguish between Perpetual Inventory System and Periodic Inventory System.

Long Answer-Type Questions

1. Explain the different methods of valuation of Inventory.
2. Distinguish between FIFO & LIFO methods of valuation of Inventory.
3. What is Base Stock Method? What are its advantages.
4. Distinguish between Net Realisable value and Replacement value.
5. Explain Net Realisable value as per AS 2.
6. How do you reconcile stock?
7. Distinguish between FIFO and LIFO method of valuing inventory.
8. Explan the various methods of recording inventory.
9. Explain the merits and demerits of FIFO method.
10. Explain the merits and demerits of LIFO method.

PRACTICAL

1. T Ltd. conducts physical stock-taking every year at the end of the accounting year. Owing to certain difficulties, it was not possible for it to conduct physical stock-taking at the end of the accounting year ending 30th June 2010. Physical stock was taken on 8th July 2010 when it was valued at Rs. 34,500.

The following transactions took place during 1st July to 8th July 2010 :

1. Net sales during the period were Rs. 9,340. These goods were sold at the usual rate of gross profit of 25% on cost except goods which realised Rs. 840 on the basis of 20% profit on cost.
2. Purchase during the period were Rs. 7,500 of which Rs. 800 worth of goods were delivered to the company only on 10th July 2010.

3. Sales returns during the period were Rs. 1,500 of which 50% were out of the sales at 20% gross profit mentioned above.
4. On 5th July 2010, goods worth Rs. 4,000 were received, which were to be sold on consignment basis.

You are required to prepare a statement showing clearly the value of stock to be taken into account in T Ltd.'s final accounts for the year ended the 30th June, 2010.

[Ans. Value of Stock Rs. 30,075]

2. A firm prepares accounts annually up to 30th November and stock taking takes place in the following week-end. In the year 2010, stock taking commenced on 4th December when the value of stock on that date was found Rs. 25,000.

From the following information, you are required to ascertain the value of stock on 30th November 2010 :

1. The average rate of gross profit is 20% on sales.
2. Goods outward are entered in the Sales Day Book as on the day of despatch.
3. Goods inward are entered in the Purchases Day Book as on the date of the invoice.
4. Sales during the period 1st to 4th December, as shown by the Sales Day Book and the Cash Book, was Rs. 1,500.
5. Purchase during the same period as shown by the Purchase Day Book amounted to Rs. 1,200, but of these goods to the value of Rs. 200 were not received until 4th December.
6. Goods invoice during November and not received until December totalled Rs. 1,600. Of these, goods to the value of Rs. 1,000 were received during the period 1st to 4th December and Rs. 600 after 4th December.
7. In November, goods were sent to a customer on sale or return basis. The sale price was Rs. 1,000. The goods were still returned by customer on 30th November.

[CA]

[Ans. Value of Stock Rs. 26,600]

3. Mr. Vijay's financial year ends on 30th June 2007, but actual stock is not taken until the following 8th July 2007, when it is ascertained at Rs. 7,425.

You find that :

(a) Sales are entered in the sales book on the same day as despatched and returns inward in the returns inward book on the day the goods are received back.
(b) Purchases are entered in the Purchase Day Book as the invoices are received.
(c) Sales between 30th June 2007 and 8th July 2007 as per the Sales Day Book and Cash book are Rs. 8,600.
(d) Purchases between 30th June 2007 and 8th July 2007 as per the Purchase Day Book are Rs. 660, but of these goods amounting to Rs. 60 are not received until after the stock was taken.
(e) Goods invoiced during June (before 30th June), but not received until after 30th June amounted to Rs. 500 of which Rs. 350 worth are received between 30th June 2007 and 8th July 2007.
(f) Rate of gross profit is $33\frac{1}{3}$ % on cost.

Ascertain the value of Stock on 30th June 2007.

[Ans. Value of Stock Rs. 13,425]

4. Hans Ltd. keeps no running stock records but a physical inventory of stock is made at the end of each quarter and evaluated at cost. The company's year ends on 31st Sept. and draft accounts have been prepared on that date. The stock inventory taken on 31st Sept. 2012 was accidentally destroyed before the items had been evaluated, the closing stock figure used in the draft accounts being that shown by the inventory taken on 30th June 2012. The gross profit margin earned by the company is 25% of cost.

During the year they discovered:

a. The cost of the stock on 30th June 2012 as shown by the inventory was Rs. 40,525.
b. On 31st June 2012 stock sheets showed the following discrepancies :
   1. A page total of Rs. 5,059 had been carried to the summary as Rs. 5,509.

2. The total of a page undercast by Rs. 98.
3. 100 items which had a cost of Rs. 5 each had been taken at 25 paise each.

c. Invoice for purchases entered in Purchase Book during the month of July, August and Sept. 2012 totalled Rs. 38,560. Of this total, Rs. 2,800 related to goods received prior to 30th June 2012. Invoices entered in Oct. 2012 relating to goods received in Sept. 2012 totalled Rs. 3,700.

d. Sales invoiced to customers in July, Aug. and Sept. 2012 totalled Rs. 51,073. Of this total, Rs. 3,824 related to goods despatched to customers before 30th Sept. 2012 but invoices in Oct. 2012 totalled Rs. 5,241.

e. During the final quarter to the Co.'s year, credit notes at invoices value of Rs. 1,280 had been issued to customers in respect of goods returned during the period.

You are required to prepare a statement showing the amount of the stock at cost on 30th Sept. 2012.

[Ans. Value of Stock Rs. 39,140]

5. Krishna Udyog Ltd. makes up its accounts to December 31 each year. The company was unable to take stock by physical inventory till 14th January 2011 on which date the stock was valued at Rs. 1,85,000. It was, therefore, necessary to estimate the value of stock in hand as on December 31, 2010.

You ascertain the following facts regarding the period January 1 to January 14, 2012 :

(1) Purchase totalled Rs. 48,000 and included (i) Rs. 5,000 in respect of goods received in December 2010; (ii) Rs. 6,000 in respect of goods received on January 19, 2011; (iii) Rs. 2,000 in respect of goods received but returned to suppliers on January 7, 2011 for which no credit note has been received or passed through the books.

(2) Sales totalled Rs. 60,000 and included (i) Rs. 1,500 in respect of goods which left the warehouse on December 2010; (ii) Rs. 2,800 in respect of goods which were not despatchad until January 16, 2011; (iii) Rs. 750 in respect of goods invoiced and despatched on January 10, 2011, but returned by the customers on January 12 for which no credit note had been passed but which were, in fact, included in the stock taken on January 14, 2011.

(3) Other returns to suppliers totalled Rs. 1,400, and other returns by customers were Rs. 450.

(4) The rate of gross profit was 20% on the selling price with the exception of a isolated purchase on January 7, 2011 of 100 similar articles which had cost Rs. 11,000. Of these articles 50 were sold on January 7, 2011 for Rs. 6,500 and the remainder had been included at cost in the stock taken on January 14, 2011.

Prepare a statement showing the estimated value of stock on December 31, 2010 at cost.

[Ans. Value of Stock Rs. 1,91,500]

CHAPTER 15

REVENUE RECOGNITION

Learning Objectives

Introduction, Meaning

Recognition of Revenue

Measurement of Revenue

Accounting Standard—Ind AS 18

Expenses : Meaning

Measurement of Expenses

Recognition of Expenses

Balance Sheet as at 30th September 2011

Liabilities	Amount	Amount	Assets	Amount	Amount
	Rs.	Rs.		Rs.	Rs.
Capital	14,300		Fixture & Fittings	10,800	
[illegible]	[illegible]		Less : Depreciation	1,000	
		15,160			9,600
Subscription Received		680	Typewriter		[illegible]
in Advance (600 + 80)			Stock (3,200 + 480)		3,680
Creditors			Debtors		[illegible]
(2,400 + 140 fuel – 100 bonus)		2,440	Cash at Bank		150
			Cash in hand		
		15,280			15,280

ASSIGNMENT MATERIALS

THEORETICAL

1. **Fill in the blanks :**

(i) Bank balance as per Cash Book is Rs. 18,500; Rs. 4,500 is entered in Cash Book as paid into bank but not credited by the bank. The Pass Book Balance is Rs. ....

(ii) Bank balance as per Pass Book is Rs. 20,000. Dividends of Rs. 1,000 collected by Bank but entered in the Cash Book as Rs. 100. The Cash Book Bank balance is Rs. ....

(iii) Overdraft balance as per Pass Book is Rs. 8,500. A cheque of Rs. 3,450 is wrongly entered in the debit side of the Cash Book. The cheque is not yet presented for payment. Overdraft Bank balance as per Cash Book is Rs. ....

(iv) Overdraft Bank balance as shown by the Cash Book is Rs. 5,000. A cheque for Rs. 10,400 was deposited to Bank but omitted in the Cash Book. In the Pass Book the amount is wrongly entered in the withdrawal column. Overdraft balance as per Pass Book is Rs. ....

(v) Bank balance as per Cash Book is Rs. 7,800. Bank charges of Rs. 75 debited by Bank but not recorded in Cash Book. The Pass Book balance is Rs. ....

(vi) Bank balance as per Pass Book is Rs. 9,700. Cash withdrawn from Bank for Rs. 3,000 but recorded as Rs. 300 in the Cash Book. Bank balance as per Cash Book is Rs. ....

(vii) Overdraft balance as per Pass Book is Rs. 11,500. Interest on Overdraft Rs. 350 debited by Bank but not recorded in the Cash Book. Bank balance as per Cash Book is Rs. ....

(viii) Bank balance as per Cash Book is Rs. 570. Debit side of the Cash Book Bank column is overcasted to the extent of Rs. 10,000. Overdraft balance as per Pass Book is Rs. ....

(Your answer in each case must be supported by workings in the form of plus or minus in brackets)

[Ans. (i) Cr. Rs. 14,000; (ii) Dr. Rs. 19,100; (iii) Cr. or O/D. Rs. [illegible]; (iv) Dr. or O/D. Rs. [illegible]; (v) Dr. Rs. 12,400; (vi) Cr. Rs. 7,725; (vii) Cr. Rs. 11,150; (viii) Dr. or O/D Rs. [illegible]]

Multiple Choice Questions

2. (a) If balance as per Cash Book is given, unrepresented cheques are:

(i) Added; (ii) Subtracted; (iii) No effect.

(b) If balance as per Pass Book is given, uncredited cheques are:

(i) Added; (ii) Subtracted; (iii) No effect.

(c) If overdraft as per Cash Book is given, direct deposit made by customer is:

(i) Added; (ii) Subtracted; (iii) No effect.

(d) If overdraft as per Pass Book is given, Interest on overdraft is:

(i) Added; (ii) Subtracted; (iii) No effect.

(e) If overdraft as per Cash Book is given, overcasting in the Debit Side of the Cash Book is:

(i) Added; (ii) Subtracted; (iii) No effect.

[Ans. (a) Added; (b) Added; (c) Subtracted; (d) Subtracted; [illegible]

Introduction

It is actually very difficult to define the term 'revenue' since it is associated with specific accounting procedures. Certain types of value changes along with the rules for determining that change when revenue is reported. That is why, in accounting literature, the concept of revenue has not been clearly defined (as it is generally discussed in relation to its measurement and timing in the context of double entry principles). However, there are two approaches which are advocated in accounting literature regarding the concept of revenue: (1) the inflow of assets resulting from the operational activities of the business, and (2) the creation of goods and services and transfer of the same to the consumers or other producers, i.e., revenue is considered as an inflow of net assets and/or an outflow of goods and services.

According to Paton and Littleton, revenue is the product of the entity which refers to the goods and services created during a specific time span by an enterprise. American Accounting Association, Committee on Accounting Concepts and Standards, embraces the above ideas and defines : "Revenue ... is the monetary expression of the aggregate of products or services, transferred by an enterprise to its customers during a period of time"[1].

The operation of a business enterprise consists of a continuous process of repeated conversion of economic resources and their exchanges. Generally, these conversions and exchanges are made at higher values. In other words, the values realised or earned are higher than their respective values which are lost in exchanges and conversions.

As such, net assets of the business increase by the amount of excess values which are earned or realised.

Recognition of Revenue

Revenue is considered or recognised in accounting as having been earned on the date on which it is realised (even if the same is not received in cash within the said period). That is, it refers to the timing of its recognition in accounts. Because, earning of revenue and the receipt of cash for the same are not practically identical. On the contrary, they are totally different. Therefore, revenues accrued in the accounting period in which they are earned, i.e., revenues, are measured in accordance with the actual concept of accounting and, as such, the same is treated as theoretically realised though not practically realised/received in cash.

In determining whether a particular revenue should be recognised at a particular point of time, regard must be made to:

(i) the amount involved should be capable of being measured objectively;

(ii) it must earn revenue; and

(iii) the revenue must have been realised in the form of an asset or assets (usually cash or receivables) or by the extinction of a liability.2

Although the particular nature of the firm will determine the time of revenue recognition, the following criteria are widely used, in general, in order to determine the point of time:

(a) If the amount of revenue is ***ascertained with accuracy*** and the ***receipt of the same is certain,*** in that case, realisation of revenue may be recognised and may also be treated as earned in the books. However, in the opposite case, i.e., if the revenue cannot correctly be measured and, at the same time, the receipt of the same is uncertain, no revenue can be recognised as realised and, as such, must not be recorded as earned in the books. There will be an exception to the rule if there is a guaranteed market at a fixed price. Because the firm, in that case, is able to sell its products at a guaranteed price, e.g., rare metals.

(b) The commonly accepted evidence of realisation of revenue is the ***market transactions (i.e., the actual sale of goods or services)*** since there is an applied transaction with an outsider involving an exchange of the output for a money/monetary claim.

The accountants recognise revenue at such a stage due to:

(i) The expected selling price or the possibility of selling the output at a given rate is uncertain before the point of actual sale, particularly in case of a new product or a non-standardised product which, in other words, eludes the accountant of adequate evidence to justify the upward revision in the value of the product.

---

1 AAA Committee on Accounting Concepts and Standards, *Accounting and Reporting Standards for Corporate Financial Statements and Preceding Statements and Supplements* (AAA 1959), p. 5

2 Yorston, Smyth, Brown—*Advanced Accounting*—N. M. Tripathi Ltd., Mumbai, 1968, p. 20

(ii) Actual selling of goods and services constitute the significant step for the purpose of earning revenue.

It may so happen that the recognition of revenue is delayed, even when a sale has been made, due to some unusual circumstances prevailing in the business. As a result of this problem, the AICPA (Accounting Standard Division) has suggested some conditions for recognising the sales revenue:

(i) "The selling price should be substantially fixed at the date of the exchange of goods or services.

(ii) The buyer has either made full payment or has accepted a debt, the repayment of which is not to be postponed or deferred until the merchandise is resold by him.

(iii) The obligation to the seller by the buyer is to change in no way because of the loss of goods in the latter's custody.

(iv) The seller, in his part, must not have any significant obligation for future performance to bring about a resale of the merchandise sold by him to the buyer and held in the latter's custody.

(v) Further returns of the merchandise can be predicted with reasonable accuracy."

(c) If there are ***inflow of resources without supplying goods and services*** in an accounting period which will be supplied in a subsequent date or in an accounting period, the said inflows can never be treated as revenue earned in the accounting period when the same are actually received in cash. On the contrary, they should be considered as advance payment and must be shown in the liability side of the Balance Sheet in the particular accounting period when such payment is received. They should be considered as revenue realised when the goods and services will be provided in the future accounting period, e.g., subscription/rent received in advance.

It is evident from the foregoing discussions that the revenue is recognised as earned/realised at the point of actual sale of goods and services. However, this principle has some exceptions:

(i) **Revenue Recognition on Completion of Production:** If revenue is measured objectively prior to the date of exchange between the buyer and the seller, the revenue is recognised on the earlier date. In other words, if the business deals with standard products which are sold in an organised market at a price which can be determined at any point of time, e.g., gold mining—revenue is recognised in the accounting period in which the gold is mined and not in the period in which it is sold.

(ii) **Revenue Recognition before Completion of Production:** It is known to all that actual sale basis of the revenue recognition is not followed in case of long-term contracts. If the revenue is recognised only on the completion of the contract, recognition of revenue at the final point of sale would simply result in a highly distorted picture of income for the different accounting periods. In order to avoid such problems on the basis of progress of contract, the portion of the construction which has been completed and approved is revalued and, on that basis, a percentage to the ultimate contract price is recorded as a realised revenue even before the contract is completed.

(iii) **Non-recognition of Revenue in case of Doubt:** This method is particularly applicable where the sale transaction is deemed not to be adequate and, as a result, additional evidence in support of such transaction may be considered necessary. Sometimes, in a sale transaction, some conditions may be imposed which may express positive weakness for rendering the evidence of sale inadequate, in order to recognise the revenue. For example, in case of a hire-purchase transaction—where the purchaser has a right to cancel the contract and the seller has a right to repossess the asset. In this case, revenue is recognised only by the aggregate amount of instalment (which may have fallen due during the specific accounting period which have already been realised in cash or will be realised definitely).

(iv) **Revenue Recognition against Cash Payment:** This method is widely accepted by professional people who are engaged in professional services and maintain cash basis of accounting for the purpose of recognition of revenue. Here, the revenue is not recognised till the payment is received in cash. So, the revenue is treated as realised for the period only when the cash is received and not in the period where the services are actually supplied, although, for recognising revenue, it is practically impracticable.

Measurement of Revenue

Revenue is properly measured either by the exchange value of the product or services of the firm. This exchange value actually reveals the cash equivalent or the present discounted value of the money which is received from the revenue transaction. This may be similar to the price established in the transaction.

For this purpose, proper allowance must be made in order to wait for final collection. For example, a cash sale of Rs. 1,000 will produce a revenue of Rs. 1,000 but if the payment is made after a year, it produces a revenue which will be less than Rs. 1,000, since question of discount will appear in the latter case. If the waiting period is very short, naturally, the discount factor may be ignored.

The above criterion for the purpose of measurement of revenue relates to the present value of money or its equivalent which is finally received from the revenue transaction since all returns, trade discounts and other reductions are subtracted from the revenue so earned. Cash discounts and bad debt, if any, are also to be deducted.

It is to be noted that cash discounts are allowed to customers for two purposes: (i) to reduce the amount of bad debt losses, and (ii) to equate the money-value received within the discount period with the present discounted money value (which will be received under the granted credit terms at a later date). Practically, if the rate of cash discount was fixed rationally, the sellers would be less interested in whether they received the net amount or gross price minus certain amount of expected bad debt losses. In this context, cash discounts and expected bad debt losses are to some extent similar.

INDIAN ACCOUNTING STANDARD—IND AS 18 REVENUE

Definitions

7. The following terms are used in this Standard with the meanings specified :

   Revenue is the gross inflow of economic benefits during the period arising in the course of the ordinary activities of an entity when those inflows result in increases in equity, other than increases relating to contributions from equity participant.

   Fair value is the amount for which an asset could be exchanged, or a liability settled, between knowledgeable, willing parties in an arm's length transaction.

8. Revenue includes only the gross inflows of economic benefits received and receivable by the entity on its own account. Amounts collected on behalf of third parties such as sales taxes, goods and services taxes and value added taxes are not economic benefits which flow to the entity and do not result in increases in equity. Therefore, they are excluded from revenue. Similarly, in an agency relationship, the gross inflows of economic benefits include amounts collected on behalf of the principal and which do not result in increases in equity for the entity. The amounts collected on behalf of the principal are not revenue, instead, revenue is the amount of commission.

Measurement of Revenue

9. **Revenue shall be measured at the fair value of the consideration received or receivable.**[1]

10. The amount of revenue arising on a transaction is usually determined by agreement between the entity and the buyer or user of the asset. It is measured at the fair value of the consideration received or receivable taking into account the amount of any trade discounts and volume rebates allowed by the entity.

11. In most cases, the consideration is in the form of cash or cash equivalents and the amount of revenue is the amount of cash or cash equivalents received or receivable. However, when the inflow of cash or cash equivalents is deferred, the fair value of the consideration may be less than the nominal amount of cash received or receivable. For example, an entity may provide interest-free credit to the buyer or accept a note receivable bearing a below-market interest rate from the buyer as consideration for the sale of goods. When the arrangement effectively constitutes a financing transaction, the fair value of the consideration is determined by discounting all future receipts using an imputed rate of interest. The imputed rate of interest is the more clearly determinable of either :

    (a) the prevailing rate for a similar instrument of an issuer with a similar credit rating : or

    (b) a rate of interest that discounts the nominal amount of the instrument to the current cash sales price of the goods or services.

    The difference between the fair value and the nominal amount of the consideration is recognised as interest revenue in accordance with paragraphs 29 and 30 and in accordance with Ind AS 39.

---

1 See also Appendix A of this Standard : Revenue—Barter Transactions Involving Advertising Services

12. When goods or services are exchanged or swapped for goods or services which are of a similar nature and value, the exchange is not regarded as a transaction which generates revenue. This is often the case with commodities like oil or milk where suppliers exchange or swap inventories in various locations to fulfil demand on a timely basis in a particular location. When goods are sold or services are rendered in exchange for dissimilar goods or services, the exchang is regarded as a transaction which generates revenue. The revenue is measured at the fair value of the gôods or services received, adjusted by the amount of any cash or cash equivalents transferred. ***When the fair value of the goods or services received cannot be measured reliably, the revenue is measured at the fair value of the goods or services given up, adjusted by the amount of any cash or cash equivalents transferred.***

Identification of the Transaction

13. The recognition criteria in this Standard are usually applied separately to each transaction. However, in certain circumstances, it is necessary to apply the recognition criteria to the separately identifiable components of a single transaction in order to reflect the substance of the transaction. For example, when the selling price of a product includes an identifiable amount for subsequent servicing, that amount is deferred and recognised as revenue over the period during which the service is performed. Conversely, the recognition criteria are applied to two or more transactions together when they are linked in such a way that the commercial effect cannot be understood without reference to the series of transactions as a whole. For example, an entity may sell goods and, at the same time, enter into a separate agreement to repurchase the goods at a later date, thus negating the substantive effect of the transaction; in such a case, the two transactions are dealts with together.

Sale of Goods

14. Revenue from the sale of goods shall be recognised when all the following conditions have been satisfied :
    (a) the entity has transferred to the buyer the significant risks and regards of ownership of the goods;
    (b) the entity retains neither continuing managerial involvement to the degree usually associated with ownership nor effective control over the goods sold;
    (c) the amount of revenue can be measured reliably;
    (d) it is probable that the economic benefits associated with the transaction will flow to the entity; and
    (e) the costs incurred or to be incurred in respect of the transaction can be measured reliably.

15. The assessment of when an entity has transferred the significant risks and rewards of ownership to the buyer requires an examination of the circumstances of the transaction. In most cases, the transfer of the risks and rewards of ownership coincides with the transfer of the legal title or the passing of possession to the buyer. This is the case for most retail sales. In other cases, the transfer of risks and rewards of ownership occur at a different time from the transfer of legal title or the passing of possession.

16. If the entity retains significant risks of ownership, the transaction is not a sale and revenue is not recognised. An entity may retain a significant risk of ownership in a number of ways. Examples of situations in which the entity may retain the significant risks and rewards of ownership are :
    (a) When the entity retains an obligation for unsatisfactory performance not covered by normal warranty provisions;
    (b) when the receipt of the revenue from a particular sale is contingent on the derivation of revenue by the buyer from its sale of the goods;
    (c) When the goods are shipped subject to installation and the installation is a significant part of the contract which has not yet been completed by the entity; and
    (d) when the buyer has the right to rescind the purchase for a reason specified in the sales contract and the entity is uncertain about the probability of return.

17. If an entity retains only an insignificant risk of ownership, the transaction is a sale and revenue is recognised. For example, a seller may retain the legal title to the goods solely to protect the collectibility of the amount due. In such a case, if the entity has transferred the significant risks and rewards of ownership, the transaction is a sale and revenue is recognised. Another example of an entity retaining only an insignificant risk of ownership may

be a retail sale when a refund is offered if the customer is not satisfied. Revenue in such cases is recognised at the time of sale provided the seller can reliably estimate future returns and recognises a liability for returns based on previous experience and other relevant factors.

18. ***Revenue is recognised only when it is probable that the economic benefits associated with the transaction will flow to the entity. In some cases, this may not be probable until the consideration is received or until an uncertainty is removed.*** For example, it may be uncertain that a foreign governmental authority will grant permission to remit the consideration from a sale in a foreign country. When the permission is granted, the uncertainty is removed and revenue is recognised. However, when an uncertainty arises about the collectibility of an amount already included in revenue, the uncollectible amount or the amount in respect of which recovery has ceased to be probable is recognised as an expense, rather than as an adjustment of the amount of revenue originally recognised.

19. Revenue and expenses that relate to the same transaction or other event are recognised simultaneously, this process is commonly referred to as the matching of revenues and expenses. Expenses, including warranties and other costs, to be incurred after the shipment of the goods can normally be measured reliably when the other conditions for the recognition of revenue have been satisfied. However, revenue cannot be recognised when the expenses cannot be measured reliably; in such circumstances, any consideration already received for the sale of the goods is recognised as a liability.

Rendering of Services

20. When the outcome of a transaction involving the rendering of services can be estimated reliably, revenue associated with the transaction shall be recognised by reference to the stage of completion of the transaction at the end of the reporting period. The outcome of a transaction can be estimated reliably when all the following conditions are satisfied :

    (a) the amount of revenue can be measured reliably;

    (b) it is probable that the economic benefits associated with the transaction will flow to the entity;

    (c) the stage of completion of the transaction at the end of the reporting period can be measured reliably; and

    (d) the costs incurred for the transaction and the costs to complete the transaction can be measured reliably.[1]

21. The recognition of revenue by reference to the stage of completion of a transaction is often referred to as the percentage of completion method. Under this method, revenue is recognised in the accounting periods in which the services are rendered. The recognition of revenue on this basis provides useful information on the extent of service activity and performance during a period. Ind AS 11 also requires the recognition of revenue on this basis. The requirements of that Standard are generally applicable to the recognition of revenue and the associated expenses for a transaction involving the rendering of services.

22. Revenue is recognised only when it is probable that the economic benefits associated with the transaction will flow to the entity. However, when an uncertainty arises about the collectibility of an amount already included in revenue, the uncollectible amount, or the amount in respect of which recovery has ceased to be probable, is recognised as an expense, rather than as an adjustment of the amount of revenue originally recognised.

23. **An entity is generally able to make reliable estimates after it has agreed to the following with the other parties to the transaction :**

    (a) each party's enforceable rights regarding the service to be provided and received by the parties;

    (b) the consideration to be exchanged; and

    (c) the manner and terms of settlement.

    It is also usually necessary for the entity to have an effective internal financial budgeting and reporting system. The entity reviews and, when necessary, revises the estimates of revenue as

---

1 **See also Appendix A of this Standard : Revenue—Barter Transactions Involving Advertising Services, and Appendix B of Ind AS 17—Evaluating the Substance of Transactions Involving the Legal form of a Lease**

the service is performed. The need for such revisions does not necessarily indicate that the outcome of the transaction cannot be estimated reliably.

24. The stage of completion of a transaction may be determined by a variety of methods. An entity uses the method that measures reliably the services performed. Depending on the nature of the transaction, the methods may include :
   (a) surveys of work performed;
   (b) services performed to date as a percentage of total services to be performed; or
   (c) the proportion that costs incurred to date bear to the estimated total costs of the transaction. Only costs that reflect services performed to date are included in costs incurred to date. Only costs that reflect services performed or to be performed are included in the estimated total costs of the transaction.

   Progress payments advances received from customers often do not reflect the services performed.

25. For practical purposes, when services are performed by an indeterminate number of acts over a specified period of time, revenue is recognised on a straight-line basis over the specified period unless there is evidence that some other method better represents the stage of completion. When a specific act is much more significant than any other acts, the recognition of revenue is postponed until the significant act is executed.

26. When the outcome of the transaction involving the rendering of services cannot be estimated reliably, revenue shall be recognised only to the extent of the expenses recognised that are recoverable.

27. During the early stages of a transaction, it is often the case that the outcome of the transaction cannot be estimated reliably. Nevertheless, it may be probable that the entity will recover the transaction costs incurred. Therefore, revenue is recognised only to the extent of costs incurred that are expected to be recoverable. As the outcome of the transaction cannot be estimated reliably, no profit is rcognised.

28. When the outcome of a transaction cannot be estimated reliably and it is not probable that the costs incurred will be recovered, revenue is not recognised and the costs incurred are recognised as an expense. When the uncertainties that prevented the outcome of the contract being estimated reliably no longer exist, revenue is recognised in accordance with paragraph 20 rather than in accordance with paragraph 26.

Interest, Royalties and Dividends

29. Revenue arising from the use by others of entity assets yielding interest, royalties and dividends shall be recognised on the bases set out in paragraph 30 when :
   (a) it is probable that the economic benefits associated with the transaction will flow to the entity; and
   (b) the amount of the revenue can be measured reliably.

30. Revenue shall be recognised on the following bases :
   (a) interest shall be recognised using the effective interest method as set out in Ind AS 39;
   (b) royalties shall be recognised on an accrual basis in accordance with the substance of the relevant agreement; and
   (c) dividends shall be recognised when the shareholder's right to receive payment is established.

31. [Refer to Appendix no. 1]

32. When unpaid interest has accrued before the acquisition of an interest-bearing investment, the subsequent receipt of interest is allocated between pre-acquisition and post-acquisition periods; only the post-acquisition portion is recognised as revenue.

33. Royalties accrue in accordance with the terms of the relevant agreement and are usually recognised on that basis unless, having regard to the substance of the agreement, it is more appropriate to recognise revenue on some other systematic and rational basis.

34. Revenue is recognised only when it is probable that the economic benefits associated with the transaction will flow to the entity. However, when an uncertainty arises about the

collectibility of an amount already included in revenue, the uncollectible amount, or the amount in respect of which recovery has ceased to be probable, is recognised as an expense, rather than as an adjustment of the amount of revenue originally recognised.

GENERAL ILLUSTRATIONS

Illustration 1

When can revenue be recognised in the case of transaction of sale of goods?

[CA Inter, May 1998]

Solution

According to para 14, **Ind AS 18 Revenue**, revenue from the sale of goods shall be recognised when all the following conditions have been satisfied :

(a) the entity has transferred to the buyer the significant risks and rewards of ownership of the goods;

(b) the entity retains neither continuing managerial involvement to the degree usually associated with ownership nor effective control over the goods sold;

(c) the amount of revenue can be measured reliably;

(d) it is probable that the economic benefits associated with the transactions will flow to the entity; and

(e) the costs incurred or to be incurred in respect of the transaction can be measured reliably.

Illustration 2

X Ltd. has recognised Rs. 10 lakhs on accrual basis from dividends on units of mutual fund of the face value of Rs. 50 lakhs held by it as at the end of the financial year on 31st March 2003. The dividends on mutual funds were declared @ 20% on 15th June 2003. The dividend was proposed on 10th April 2003 by the declaring company.

Whether the treatment is as per the relevant Accounting Standard? [CA PE II, Nov. 2003]

Solution

As per para 30, **Ind AS 18**, dividends from investment in shares shall be recognised when the shoreholder's right to receive payment is established.

In the present case, the dividend was proposed on 10th April 2003, but the scheme was declared on 15th June 2003. Thus, it is quite clear that the right to receive payment is already established on 15th June 2003. So, income from dividend on units of mutual fund must be recognised by X Ltd. for the year ended 31st March 2004.

It may be mentioned here that the recognition of Rs. 10 lakhs under accrual basis in the year 2002-03 is not made as per AS 18.

Illustration 3

Arjun Ltd. sold farm equipments through its dealers. One of the conditions at the time of sale is payment of consideration in 14 days and, in the event of delay, interest is chargeable @ 15% p.a. The company has not realised interest from the dealers in the past. However, for the year ended 31.3.2006, it wants to recognise interest due on the balances due from dealers. The account is ascertained at Rs. 9 lakhs.

Decide whether the income by way of interest from dealers is eligible for recognition as per AS 18.

[CA PE II, May 2006]

Solution

As per para 18, **Ind AS 18**, revenue is recognised only when it is probable that the economic benefits associated with the transaction will flow to the entity. In some cases, this may not be probable until the consideration is received or until an uncertainty is removed. When an uncertainty arises about the collectibility of an amount already included in revenue, the uncollectible amount or the amount in respect of which recovery has ceased to be probable is recognised as an expense, rather than as an adjustment of the amount of revenue originally recognised.

However, in the present case, it has been found that the company did not realise the amount of interest in the past for delayed payment made by dealers. Thus, interest can be recognised only when the ultimate collection is made, or taken. Hence, in the present case, interest income is not to be considered as recognised-revenue.

Illustration 4

Y Co. Ltd. used certain resources of X Co. Ltd. In return X Co. Ltd. received Rs. 10 lakhs and Rs. 15 lakhs as interest and royalties, respectively, from Y Co. Ltd. during the year 2003-04.

You are required to state whether and on what basis these revenue can be recognised by X Co. Ltd.

[CA Final, May 1999]

Solution

As paras 30, 32, and 33, **Ind AS 18**, Revenue, interest shall be recognised using the effective interest method as set out in Ind AS 39. And, when unpaid interest was accrued before the acquisition of an interest bearing investments, the subsequent receipt of interest is allocated between pre-acquisition and post-acquisition periods; only the post-acquisition portion is recognied as revenue.

Similarly, as per paras 30 and 33, royalty shall be recognied on an accrual is basis in accordance with the substance of the relevant agreement and royalties accrue in accordance with the terms of the relevant agreement and are usually recognised on that basis unless, having regard to the substance of the agreement, it is more appropriate to recognise revenue on some other systematic and rational basis.

Illustration 5

Advise B Co. Ltd. about the treatment of the following in the final statement of accounts for the year ended 31st March 2004 : "As a result of a recently announced price revision granted by the Govt. of India w.e.f 1.7.2003, the company stands to receive Rs. 5,20,000 from its customers in respect of sales made in 2003-04." **[CA Final, Nov. 1993, May 1995]**

Solution

It becomes quite clear from the above question that as a result of price revision granted by the Govt. additional sales are to be made for Rs. 5,20,000 in 2003-04 although accounts are prepared for the year ended 31.3.2004.

As per para 18, **Ind AS 18,** when an uncertainty arises about the collectibility of an amount already included in the revenue, the uncollecitible amount or the amount in respect of which recovery has ceased to be probable is recognised as an expense, rather than as an adjustment of the amount of revenue originally recognised.

Thus, if there is no uncertainty as to the ultimate collection of Rs. 5,20,000, it should be recognised as revenue and may be treated accordingly in the financial statement for the period under 31.3.2004.

Illustration 6

Advise P. Co. Ltd. about the treatment of the following in the final statement of accounts for the year ended 31.3.2004: A claim lodged with the Railways in March 2001, for loss of goods of Rs. 2,00,000 had been passed for payment in March 2004, for Rs. 1,50,000. No entry was passed in the books of the company, where the claim was lodged. **[CA Final, May 2000]**

Solution

It becomes clear from the above statement that the accounts were prepared for the year ended 31.3.2004. The problem states that there was a loss amounting to Rs. 2,00,000 in 2000-01, which was lodged in March 2001 with the Railways. The problem further states that when the claim was lodged no entry was passed in the books of account. This corroborates **Ind AS 18** as it says : "revenue recognition is postponed if there is any uncertainty regarding its ultimates collection".

But Rs. 1,50,000 was settled for payment against the claim of Rs. 2,00,000 in March 2004. Needless to say that the revenue is recognised in the financial statement prepared for the period ended 31.3.2004 as it was passed for payment.

Illustration 7

How would you deal with the following in the annual accounts of a company for the year ended 31.3.2004? The Board of Directors decided on 31.3.2004 to increase the sale price of certain items retrospectively from 1.1.2004. In view of the price revisions w.e.f 1.1.2004, the company has to receive Rs. 15 lakhs from its customers in respect of sales made from 1.1.2004 to 31st March 2004 and the accountant cannot make up his mind whether to include Rs. 15 lakhs in the sales for 2003-04.

[CA Final, May 1996]

Solution

As per Para 18, **Ind AS 18**, revenue should be recognised only when there is no uncertainty about its ultimate collection. If any uncertainty regarding ultimate collection exists, revenue should not be recognised. As such, whether the said Rs. 15 lakhs will be treated as recognised depends upon its nature of certainty. If no uncertainty exists, the same should be treated as recognised revenue and, in the opposite case, it should be postponed.

Illustration 8

TVSM Co. has taken a transit insurance policy. Suddenly, in the year 2002-03, the percentage of accident has gone up to 7% and the company wants to recognise insurance claim as revenue in 2002-03, in accordance with relevant accounting standard. Do you agree? **[CA Final, May 2003]**

Solution

As per para 18 of **Ind AS 18, Revenue,** revenue is recognised only when it is probable that the economic benefits associated with the transaction will flow to the entity. In some cases, this may not be probable until the consideration is received or until an uncertainty is removed. If any uncertainty arises regarding the realisation of revenue, revenue cannot be recognised.

Thus, in this case, since there are uncertainties, revenue cannot be recognised.

Illustration 9

Bottom Ltd. entered into a sale deed for its immovable property before the end of the year. But registration was done with Registrar subsequent to Balance Sheet date. But before finalisation, is it possible to recognise the sale and the gain at the Balance Sheet date? Give your views with reasons.

[CA Final, Nov. 2005]

Solution

As per para, 14, **Ind AS 18, Revenue**, revenue from the sale of goods should be recognised when all the following conditions have been fulfilled—

(a) the entity has transferred to the buyer the significant risks and rewards of ownership of goods;

(b) the entity retains neither continuing managerial involvement to the degree usually associated with ownership nor effective control over the goods sold;

(c) the amount of revenue can be measured reliably;

(d) it is probable that the economic benefits associated with the transaction will flow to the entity; and

(e) the costs incurred or to be incurred in respect of the transaction can be measured reliably.

In the present case, sale of immovable property with a gain on such sale should be recognised at the Balance Sheet date although registration for such sale had been done subsequent to the Balance Sheet date. It may be mentioned here that registration cannot bring any uncertainty as it was nothing but a technical matter.

Illustration 10

SCL Ltd. sells agricultural products to dealers. One of the conditions of sale is that interest is payable at the rate of 2% p.m. for delayed payments. Percentage of interest recovery is only 10% on such overdue outstanding due to various reasons. During the year 2002-03, the company wants to recognise the entire interest receivable. Do you agree? **[CA Final, May 2003]**

Solution

As per para 18, **Ind AS 18,** Recognition of Revenue requires that revenue is measurable at the time of sale. Interests, royalties, dividends should be recognised as revenue only where there will not be any uncertainty regarding the ultimate collection. It may be appropriate to recognise revenue only when it is reasonably certain that ultimate collection will be made. When there is no uncertainty as to ultimate collection, revenue is recognised at the time of sale even though payments are made by instalment—para 9.2. In the present case, however, SC Ltd. cannot recognise the entire amount of interest as revenue.

Recovery of Interest @ 10% on outstanding balance is a mere estimate which is uncertain to ultimate collection.

EXPENSES

The term 'expenses' is a flow concept. It represents both favourable and unfavourable changes made in an accounting period. The favourable one represents revenue whereas the unfavourable one represents the expense. In short, the consumption or use of goods and services in order to earn revenue is the expense. Thus, Hendriksen opines : 'expenses are the using or consuming of goods and services in the process of obtaining revenues'.[1]

The American Accounting Association, Committee on Concepts and Standards, defines : 'Expense is the expired cost, directly or indirectly related to given fiscal period, of the flow of goods or services into the market and of related operations'. The primary objective of all costs is to earn revenue from the customers in exchange of goods and services produced by the firm at a given period. As such, the amount which is spent in anticipation of earning revenue, no doubt, constitute cost.

Needless to mention that ***all sacrifices are not expenses***. The sacrifices which are directly or indirectly related to the production are included with expenses. At the same time, such sacrifices are losses against which neither any benefit has been realised nor is there any chance of realising the same in future. Thus, the benefits which are received in excess of the sacrifices are incomes which are accrued to the proprietors.

Expenses are defined in terms of ***cost expirations or cost allocations frequently***. They are the structural model for the measurement of accounting income and they do not reflect real-world situations. Expense valuation in that context is a problem which differs from the definition of expense. Expenses are measured in terms of valuation of goods or services used or consumed, but the said measurement does not define it. Therefore, the difference between the two is that the measurement of an expense is based on cost and the definition of an expense is an activity or a process.

Measurement of Expense

The most common measurements of expense are :

(a) Historical Cost ; (b) Current Measurement (e.g., Replacement Cost); and (c) Opportunity Cost or Current Cash Equivalent.

(a) **Historical Cost***

The conventional method of measuring expenses is the historical cost concept measurement. The primary reason is that they are assumed to be verifiable since they represent cash outlays by the enterprise. They also represent the exchange value of goods and services while they were acquired by the firm.

Arguments for Historical Cost

(i) Under this method only, the expenses can be objectively determined and ascertained.

(ii) The measurement is verifiable since it is based on exchange prices.

(iii) Personal bias of the valuer is neglected here, so, manipulation of reports and statements may be avoided.

Arguments against Historical Cost

(i) It does not represent a relevant measurement of the goods and services used in order to meet the objectives of the external users of financial reports and statements.

(ii) It does not permit a separation of operating activity from gains and losses arising from favourable purchases and unpredictable price changes.

1 Hendriksen, E. S. — *Accounting Theory*, op. cit, p. 187

* It is actually the cash equivalent outlay for goods and services actually received. The historical costs are recorded in the books of accounts. The expired portions are known as 'expenses' and appear in the revenue/income statement whereas unexpired portions are known as 'assets' and appear in the Balance Sheet. It is very much significant in determining periodical net income and current financial position

(iii) The impact of price level changes between purchase of raw material and the sale of finished product is not recognised here.

(b) **Current Measurement** (e.g., Replacement Cost)[1].

Revenue is generally measured in terms of the current price received against the product sold. Therefore, the expenses matched should also be measured in terms of the current price of goods or services used or consumed. Because, income which arises from sale transaction is the excess of cash or claims received over the amount of the resources used. As such, the measurement of expenses in terms of current price has the advantages between the income which arises from the transactions and the gains or losses which arise from the holding of assets before the use. The gains and losses which occur before the use may arise either from price changes, or from deterioration, or from obsolescence, or other factors. At the same time, when the acquisition of goods and services before the use is necessary along with loss or deterioration, this reduction in value should be included in the measurement of expenses.

(c) **Opportunity Cost or Current Cash Equivalent**

Current price may be taken either from current liquidation/sale price or from a replacement cost. Current cash equivalent or a current liquidation/sale price is significant while measuring expenses since it expresses the opportunity cost of a firm for using such specific asset. Moreover, this measurement does not make any speculation about the future replacement. In other words, the liquidation price/current cash equivalent is particularly significant when there is a favourable market for purchase or sale for the item.

Recognition of Expenses

An expense is recognised for an accounting period provided there is :

(i) a direct relation with the revenue earned during that period, e.g., selling expenses and commissions which are incurred with cost of goods sold;

(ii) an indirect relation with revenue earned during that period, e.g., indirect operating expenses;

(iii) a measurable expiration of some assets which are not directly and/or indirectly related with revenue for the said period, e.g., losses which arise from pilferage/theft or accidents etc.

In short, the expenses will be recognised in a particular accounting period if they relate to :

(a) the direct cost of goods sold;

(b) the indirect cost of operating expenses; and

(c) the exceptional losses incurred, if any.

ASSIGNMENT MATERIALS

THEORETICAL

Multiple Choice Questions

1. (a) Revenue is recognised

(i) at the point of sale, (ii) after sales, (iii) before sales.

(b) Revenue relates to

(i) Interest, (ii) Royalties, (iii) Interest, Royalties, Dividend.

(c) Revenue Recognition is postponed when

(i) there is certainty, (ii) uncertainty exists, (iii) both.

---

1 It is the cost of replacing an asset at current market price. Replacement cost analysis is particularly applicable and useful where there is a plan for replacement of obsolete asset

(d) Royalty is earned

(i) on cost basis, (ii) accrual basis, (iii) hybrid basis.

(e) Interest is treated as recognised revenue on

(i) money properties, (ii) time properties, (iii) none of these.

[Ans. (a) (i); (b) (ii); (c) (ii); (d) (ii); (e) (ii)]

Short Answer-Type Questions

1. Define Revenue.
2. How do you recognise Revenue?
3. Define:
   (a) Sale of Goods, (b) Rendering of Services. **[CA Final—Adapted]**
4. Mention the effect of uncertainties on Revenue Recognition.
5. How are revenue accruing from Interest, Dividend and Royalties recognised?
6. Write notes on:
   (a) Proportionate Completion Period, (b) Completed Service Contract Method.
7. How do you treat Rendering of Services in Revenue Recognition?

Essay-Type Questions

1. What do you mean by Revenue?
2. How is Revenue recognised?
3. How do you treat the effect of Uncertainties in Revenue Recognition?
4. What do you mean by Rendering of Services? How is the same recognised as Revenue?
5. What do you mean by Sale of Goods? How is the same recognised as Revenue?
6. Write notes on "Effect of Uncertainties on Revenue Recognition". **[CA Final, May 1997]**
7. Discuss the principles behind the timing of Revenue Recognition. **[ICWA Final, Dec. 1994]**
8. What do you mean by Expense? How do you measure Expenses?
9. How do you recognise Expenses?
10. What do you mean by "Rendering of Services" as per Ind AS 18?

CHAPTER 16

NEGOTIABLE INSTRUMENTS

Learning Objectives

Meaning

Characteristics

Promissory Note

Essentials element of a Promissory Note

Bills of Exchange

Essential Elements of Bills of Exchange

Different Parties in a Bill of Exchange

Acceptance of Bills of Exchange

Holder and Holder in Due Course

—Holder

—Holder in Due Course

Dishonour of Bills of Exchange

Discounting of Bills

Endorsement of Bills

Retirement of Bills

Renewal of Bills

Accommodation Bills

Documentary Bills

Notary Public

Noting

Protest

Tenure, Days of Grace, and Date of Maturity

Difference between a Promissory Note and a Bill of Exchange

Cheque

Difference between a Bill of Exchange and Cheque

Bill Receivable Book

Bills Payable Book

Method of Accounting

(a) *Bills drawn and honoured at maturity*

(b) *Bills discounted by bank and honoured at maturity*

—*As a Contingent Liability*

—*Proportionate Discounting Charges*

—*Treatment of Discount*

(c) *Bills drawn and endorsed to creditors and honoured at maturity*

(d) *Bills drawn and sent to the bank for collection and honoured at maturity*

(e) *Advance by way of Security of Bills*

Dishonour of Bill

—*Noting Charges*

—*Successive Endorsement*

—*Insolvency of the drawee and its effect*

—*Provision against doubtful drawee*

Renewal of Bills

Retirement of Bill

Accommodation Bill

(a) *When the bill is drawn only for the accommodation of the drawer*

(b) *When there is only one bill, proceeds being shared by the parties*

(c) *When there are two bills of equal amount, proceeds being taken by each other*

(d) *For the accommodation of more than two parties*

NEGOTIABLE INSTRUMENTS

Meaning

'Negotiable' means transferable by delivery and 'instrument' means a written document by which a right is created in favour of some person(s). Thus, literally, it means 'a document transferable by delivery'. In other words, documents of a certain type which are used in commercial transactions and some monetary dealings are called Negotiable Instruments. In India, the said term is used in a restricted sense. According to Sec. 31(1) of The Negotiable Instruments Act, 1981, a Negotiable Instrument means a promissory note, bill of exchange, or cheque—payable either to order, or to bearer.

Thus, *in India, three kinds of instruments are recognised as Negotiable Instruments: Promissory Notes, Bills of Exchange and Cheques.*

Characteristics of Negotiable Instruments

A Negotiable Instrument has the following characteristics:

(a) It must be freely transferable; (b) Title of holder must be free from all defects; (c) Account must be recovered; (d) There are certain presumptions: (i) Consideration; (ii) Date; (iii) Time of acceptance; (iv) Time of transfer; (v) Order of endorsement; (vi) Stamp; (vii) Holder and holder in due course; and (vii) Proof of protest.

Promissory Note

According to Sec. 4 of the Negotiable Instruments Act, 'A promissory note is an instrument in writing containing an unconditional undertaking signed by the maker, to pay a certain sum of money only to, or to order, of a certain person, or to the bearer of the instrument'. The person who makes the promise is called the 'maker' and the person who gets the money is called the 'payee'.

Specimen of a Promissory Note

Rs. 10,000 — 1st April 2010, Kolkata

On demand I promise to pay Mr Sankha Das or order the sum of Rupees Ten Thousand only with interest @ 8% p. until payment, for value received.

Stamp — P Duta

Essential Elements of a Promissory Note

In order to be a valid one, a promissory note must fulfil the following requirements:

(a) The instrument must be in writing; (b) The instrument must be signed by its maker; (c) The instrument must contain a promise to pay; (d) The promise to pay must be conditional; (e) The marker of the instrument must be certain and definite; (f) It must be stamped; (g) The sum of money to be paid must be certain; (h) The payment must be in legal tender money of India; (i) The money must be payable to definite person according to his order; (j) The promissory note must be payable on demand or after a certain definite period of time.

Bills of Exchange

According to Sec. 5, of The Negotiable Instruments Act.: 'A Bill of exchange is an instrument in writing containing an unconditional order signed by *the maker, directing certain person to pay a certain sum of money only to, or to the order of, a certain person or to the bearer of the instrument'.*

Specimen of Bill of Exchange

Revenue Stamp — **Rs. 5,000.00** — 4 College Street, Kolkata 700 012, 8th of August 2000

At 90 days' sight pay this sole Bill of Exchange of Sri P. K. Das, or to his order, the sum of Rupees Five Thousand only for value received.

Contd.

To	Per Pro
NCBA & Co. Ltd.	M P & Co. Ltd.
54 Gariahat Road	S/d S. Sen
Kolkata 700 029	S/d K. Roy
	Secretary/Mg. Director

Essential Elements of Bills of Exchange

In order to be a valid one, a bill of exchange must fulfil the following requirements:

(a) The instrument must be in writing; (b) The instrument must be signed by the drawer; (c) The instrument must contain an *order to pay* which must be expressed as unconditional; (d) The drawee and the payee must be *certain and definite individuals;* (e) The amount of money to be paid must be certain; (f) The payment must be in the legal tender money of India; (g) The money must be payable to a definite person or according to his order; (h) It must be properly stamped; and (i) It may be made payable on demand, or after a definite period of time.

Different Parties in a Bill of Exchange

Drawer — The person who draws or makes the Bill, i.e., a creditor

Drawee — The person to whom the order is made, i.e., a debtor.

Payee — The person to whom the sum mentioned in the bill is payable

Draw in case of need — Sometimes the name of another person is mentioned as the person who will accept the bill if the original drawee does not accept it: such a person is called the 'Drawee in case of need'.

Acceptance of Bills of Exchange

When the drawee, after accepting the bill, plus his signature across the face of a bill of exchange, it is called acceptance, and, when accepted, the drawee becomes the acceptor. This acceptance is necessary for every bill transaction except the 'bill at sight'. This acceptance may be of two types:

General acceptance : When the drawee accepts the liability to pay the amount mentioned in the bill in full without, however, any condition or limitation, i.e., unconditional.

Qualified acceptance : When the drawee puts some condition(s) on the acceptance, i.e., conditional.

Holder and Holder in Due Course

Holder

According to Sec. 8 of The Negotiable Instrument Act, a holder is 'any person entitled in his own name to the possession thereof and to receive or recover the amount due thereon from the parties thereon'. That is, the person who is legally entitled to received the money due on the instrument is called the 'holder'.

Holder in Due Course

According to Sec. 9 of The Negotiable Instruments Act, the holder in due course is a particular kind of holder.

The holder of a Negotiable Instrument is called the holder in due course if he is satisfied of these conditions:

(i) He obtained the instrument for valuable consideration;
(ii) He became holder of the instrument;
(iii) He has no cause to believe that any defect existed in the title of the person from whom he derived his title.

Dishonour of Bills of Exchange

A bill may be said to be dishonoured in two ways:

(a) By non-acceptance; (b) By non-payment
(b) Dishonoured by non-acceptance—when the drawee does not accept the bill.
(c) Dishonoured by non-payment—when the drawee makes default in payment on due date.

Discounting of Bills

When the holder of bill wants to get the money before the due date, he can sell the bill to a bank against a small charge (known as discounting charge). Discounting charge is imposed by the bank at a fixed rate per cent p.a. from the date of discounting to the date of maturity.

Endorsement of Bills

Endorsement means signature of the holder made with the object of transferring the document. The person who endorses is called the 'endorsee', and one to whom it is endorsed is called the 'endorser'.

Retirement of Bills

When the drawee pays the bill before its due date, it is called retirement of a bill. The holders allow him a certain amount calculated at a certain rate per cent p.a. which is known as rebate, from the date of retirement to the date of maturity

Renewal of Bills

When the drawee of a bill is unable to meet the same on due date he may accept a fresh bill (of course, with the consent of the drawer), including interest, in place of the old bill, along with incidental expenses, if any, for some extended period—it is called renewal of bill.

Accommodation of Bills

An accommodation bill is one which has been signed by a person, as drawer, acceptor or endorser, without any consideration, for the purpose of assisting financial accommodation for one or more parties. The party accommodating is call the 'accommodation party' and the party accommodated is called he 'accommodated party'. In case of dishonour, no one can sue the other. It is also known as **Kite Bill.**

Documentary Bills

A documentary bill is one to which different shipping documents like Bill of Lading, Marine Insurance Policy, Railway Receipts, Invoices etc. are attached. A documentary bill may be of two types, viz, (a) Documents against Acceptance of bills or D/A bills, and (b) Documents against Payments of bills or D/P bills.

Notary Public

Notary public is an officer appointed by the Central or State Government to exercise the power and functions relating to noting and protesting of negotiable instrument for dishonour. Actually, 'Noting' authenticates the fact of dishonour. The fee which is paid in this respect is called 'Noting Charges'.

Noting

According to Sec. 99 of The Negotiable Instruments Act: 'When a promissory note or bill of exchange has been dishonored by non-acceptance or non-payment, the holder may cause such dishonour to be noted by a notary public up to the instrument, or upon a paper attached thereto or partly upon each of them. Such note must be made within a reasonable time after dishonour, and must specify the date of dishonour, the reasons, if any, assigned for such dishonour, or, if the instrument has not been expressly dishonoured, the reason why the holder treats it as dishonoured, and the noting charges'.

Protest

According to Sec. 100 of The Negotiable Instruments Act—'When a promissory note or bill of exchange has been dishonoured by non-acceptance or non-payment, the holder may, within a reasonable time, cause such dishonour to be noted and certified by a notary public. Such certificate is called 'Protest'.

Tenure, Days of Grace and Date of Maturity or Due Date of Bills

Tenure

The bill which is drawn may be payable at sight, on demand after sight, after date, etc. The period between the date of drawing the bill and the period on which it becomes due is called the Tenure of the Bill.

Days of Grace

A bill which is payable on demand becomes due immediately on presentation for payment. Similarly, a bill which is not payable on demand becomes due on the third day from the date of maturity. These three days are called *Days of Grace*. For example, if a bill is drawn on 1.1.2012 for 4 months, the due date or date of maturity will be 4.5.2012. The same can be computed as under:

Date of Drawing	1.1.2012
Add : Period/Tenure	4
	1.5 2012
Add: Days of Grace	3— —
Due Date/Date of Maturity	4.5.2012

Note : Here, **month means calendar month.**

Date of Maturity

If there is an *after date bill*, the period is to be counted from the *date of drawing the bill*, but when there is an *after sight bill*, the said period is to be counted from the *date of acceptance of the bill*. For example, if a bill is drawn on 28th January 2011, and is made payable at one month *after date*, the due date will be 3rd day after 28th Feb. i.e, 3 March 2011.

To Sum up:

(i) ***When the period of the bill is stated in days, the date of maturity will also be calculated in terms of days, i.e., excluding the date of transaction but including the date of payment.***

e.g., if a bill is drawn on 18th January 2011 for 60 days, the date of maturity will be 21st March 2011

(ii) ***If the period of the bill is stated in months, the date of maturity will also be calculated in terms of months neglecting, however, the number of days in a month.***

e.g., if a bill is drawn on 20th May 2011 for 3 months, the date of maturity will, naturally, be 23rd August 2011

(iii) ***When the date of maturity of a bill falls on a public holiday, the bill shall become due on the preceding business day and if the preceding day again falls on a public holiday, it will become due on the day preceding the previous day—Sec. 25.***

e.g., if the date of maturity of a bill falls on 15th August (Independence Day) it falls due on 14th August. But if 14th falls again on a public holiday, then 13th August will be considered as the date of maturity.

Illustration 1

Ascertain the due date of the following instruments:

(i) A promissory note, date 31st August 2012, payable 90 days after date;
(ii) A bill of exchange, date 15th March 2012, payable 4 months after date;
(iii) A bill of exchange dated 10th September 2012, accepted on 15th September, payable at 90 days after sight;
(iv) A bill of exchange, dated 1st April 2012, payable 4 months after date.

Solution

(i) 60 days from 31st August 2012 is 2nd December 2012:

	Days
September	30
October	31
	61
Period	– 90
∴ November	29
Add : Days of Grace	3

Due date will be 2nd December.

(ii) 4 month from 15th March 2012 will be 15th July 2012 and 3 days will be added as days of grace, i.e., 18th July 2012 i.e.

Date of Drawing	15—3—2012
Add: Tenure	—4—
	15—7—2012
Add: Days of Grace	3—0—0
Due Date	18—7—2012

(iii) It must be remembered that in case of **After Sight** bill, the period is counted from the date of acceptance of the bill. So 90 days from 15th Sept. 2012 will be 17th December 2012 which is calculated as:

	Days
September (30 – 15)	15
October	31

	Days
November	30
	76
Period	90
∴ December	14
Add : Days of Grace	3
Due Date	**17th December 2012**

(iv)		
	Date of Drawing	1—4—2012
	Tenure	4
		1—8—2012
	Add: Days of Grace	3—0—0
	Due Date	4—8—2012

Differences between a Promissory Notes and a Bill of Exchange

Point of Difference	Promissory Note	Bills of Exchange
1. *Number of parties*	1. There are two parties—the maker and the payee.	1. There are three parties—the drawer, the drawee, and the payee.
2. *Promise and Order*	2. In a promissory note, there is a promise to pay.	2. In a bill of exchange, there is an order to pay.
3. *Acceptance*	3. A promissory note is sighted by the person liable to pay and, as such, no acceptance is necessary.	3. A bill of exchange requires to be accepted by the drawee before it is binding upon him—except in certain cases.
4. *Liability*	4. Its maker is primarily liable.	4. Its drawer is liable only when the drawee does not accept or pay the amount due.
5. *Notice*	5. Notice of dishonour to the maker is not necessary in case of non-payment or non-acceptance of an instrument.	5. In this case, notice must be given to all persons liable to pay which is called the notice of dishonour.
6. *Protest*	6. In case of dishonour, protest is not necessary.	6. In case of dishonour, a foreign bill must be protested if it is necessary according to the law of the place where it is drawn.
7. *Relationship*	7. In this case, the maker stands in an immediate relationship to the payee.	7. In a bill of exchange, a drawer stands in an immediate relationship with the acceptor and not to the payee.

Cheque

According to Sec. 6 of The Negotiable Instruments Act.: 'A cheque is a bill of exchange drawn upon a specified banker and payable on demand'.

Essential features of a cheque

A cheque has the following features:

(a) A cheque must fulfil all the essential element of a bill of exchange; (b) It must be payable to bearer or to order but, in either case, it must be payable on demand; (c) The banker named pays it when it is presented for payment; (d) Bills and notes may be written entirely by hand; (e) The signature must tally with the specimen signature of the drawee kept in the bank; (f) A cheque must be dated; (g) A cheque drawn with a future date is valid but the same is payable on and after such specified date.

Differences between a Bill of Exchange and a Cheque

Bill of exchange	Cheque
1. A bill of exchange can be drawn upon any person including a bank.	1. A cheque can be drawn only upon a bank.
2. A bill of exchange requires acceptance.	2. A cheque does not require any acceptance.
3. The acceptor of a bill of exchange is allowed days of grace for 3 days after the date of maturity of the bill.	3. A cheque is always payable on demand.
4. A bill of exchange must be stamped (except in certain cases).	4. A cheque does not require any stamp.
5. The payment of a bill cannot be countermanded.	5. The payment of a cheque may be countermanded.
6. There is no provision for crossing a bill.	6. A cheque may be a crossed one.
7. The drawer of a bill of exchange is discharged from liability of bill if not presented to acceptor for payment at the due date.	7. The drawer of cheque is discharged from his liability only when he suffers the damages owing to delay in presenting the cheque for payment.
8. Notice of dishonour is necessary.	8. Notice of dishonour is not necessary.

Bills Receivable Book

Bill Receivable Book is a book where all bills which are received are recorded and therefrom posted directly to the credit of the respective customer's account. The total amounts of the bills so received during the period (either at the end of the week or month) is to be posted in on sum to the debit of Bills Receivable Account. The form from mof Bills Receivable Book (with imaginary figures) is:

Bills Receivable Book

No. of Bill	*Date of Receipt*	*From whom received*	*Name of Receiver*	*Name of Drawer*	*Where Pay-able*	*Date of Bill*	*Terms*	*Due date*	*L.F.*	*Amount of Bill*	*How disposed of*
1.	2009 Jan. 31	M. Sen	D. Das	P. Roy	State Bank of India, Kolkata	2009 Nov. 20	3 months	2009 23rd Feb.	8	1,000	Discounted on Jan. 31, 2009

Bills Payable Book

This is a book where all particulars relating to bills accepted are recorded and there from posted directly to the debit of respective creditor's account. The total amounts of the bills so accepted during the period (either at the end of the week or month) is to be posted in one sum to the credit of Bills Payable Account.

The usual form of Bills Payable Book (with imaginary figures) is:

No. of Bill	*Date of Acceptance*	*To whom given*	*Name of the Drawee*	*Name of the Payee*	*Where Payable*	*Date of Bill*	*Terms*	*Due Date*	*L.F.*	*Amount of the Bill*	*How disposed of*
1.	2009 March 4	A. Dutta	K. Sen	P. Kar	United Bank of India, Kolkata	2009 May 3	3 months	2009 Aug. 3	9	2,000	Paid on Aug. 6, 2009

METHOD OF ACCOUNTING

(a) Bills drawn and honoured at maturity

Under the circumstances, the drawer (i.e., creditor) can retain the bill with himself till due date if he is not in need of immediate cash. In other words, the acceptor/drawee will pay/honour the bill on due date. The following entries will be required for the purpose :

	Transaction	Entries in the books of Drawer	Entries in the books of Drawee
1.	When the bill is drawn by the drawer and accepted by drawee	Bills Receivable A/c Dr. To Drawee A/c	Drawer A/c Dr. To Bills Payable A/c
2.	When the bill is honoured at maturity	Cash/Bank A/c Dr. To Bill Receivable A/c (Only when the drawer retains the bill till due date and receives payment)	Bills Payable A/c Dr. To Cash/Bank A/c

Illustration 1

On 1.1.2011 X sold goods to Y on credit for Rs. 1,000 and drew a bill on Y for Rs. 1,000 for 2 months after date. Y accepted it on 3.1.2011 and returned to X. On maturity, the bill was duly honoured by Y. Show the entries.

Solution

In the books of X
Journal

Date	*Particulars*		*L.F.*	*Debit* Rs.	*Credit* Rs.
2011 Jan. 1	Y A/c To Sales A/c (Goods sold to Y on credit)	Dr.		1,000	1,000
Jan. 3	Bills Receivable A/c To Y A/c (Bills accepted by Y for 2 months)	Dr.		1,000	1,000
Mar. 4	Bank A/c To Bills Receivable A/c (Bills honoured at maturity)	Dr.		1,000	1,000

In the books of Y
Journal

Date	*Particulars*		*L.F.*	*Debit* Rs.	*Credit* Rs.
2011 Jan. 1	Purchases A/c To X A/c (Goods purchased on credit from X)	Dr.		1,000	1,000
Jan. 3	X A/c To Bills Payable A/c (Bills accepted for 2 months after date)	Dr.		1,000	1,000
Mar. 4	Bills Payable A/c To Bank A/c (Bills met on maturity)	Dr.		1,000	1,000

(b) Bills discounted by bank and honoured at maturity

We have already explained earlier that the drawer receives payment from the drawee only on the date of maturity. Sometimes it may so happen that he needs immediate cash. For this purpose, he may discount the bill to a bank and receives payment at the cost of a certain amount of discount, i.e., the bill is sold to the banker. In short, *right to get payment* is given to the banker. Thus, discount is the consideration for receiving payment in advance, i.e., before the date of maturity, and it is the difference between the bill value and the money so received. But bank will discount the bill and pay the drawer only when the drawer has agreed to pay the full value of the bill in case of default (by the drawee).

It may be mentioned that amount of discount depends on current interest rates and the unexpired period of the bill. Unexpired period is the difference (in periods) between the date of discounting of the bill and the date of maturity of the bill. Discount may be computed as:

$$\textit{Discounting of bill} = \textit{Face Value of the bill} \times \textit{Rate of Interest} \times \frac{\textit{Unexpired days/months of the bill}}{\textit{365 days or 12 months}}$$

In this respect it may further be explained that a bank usually discounts a bill provided the drawer has an account in the bank. Thus, instead of paying cash to the drawer, the bank makes credit to the account of the drawer with the net amount of the bill (i.e., face value *minus* discounting charges) which is termed as proceeds.

When a drawer discounts a bill with the bank he debits the bank column of the cash book by crediting Bills Receivable Account with the net amount and the discounting charge of the bill will be transferred to 'Discounting to the Bills Account' on the debit side. At the end of the year the amount of discount will be transferred to Profit and Loss Account like an expense.

On maturity, the bank will present the bill to the drawee for payment. If the payment is made, there will be no entry in the books of the drawer as he has taken the benefit from the bank. It may be noted in this respect that if a bill is drawn by the drawer, it is shown as a current asset in the asset side of the Balance Sheet in the books of the drawer. But if it is discounted nothing will appear in the Balance Sheet.

As a Contingent Liability

'Contingent liability for bills discounted' will arise only if due date of the bill falls due at the end of the accounting year. If a discounted bill is dishonoured at a subsequent date, no doubt the bank will debit the drawer's account with the full amount of the bill since it is nothing but a potential obligation of the drawer to pay in case of dishonour of bill.

In company accounts, 'contingent liability for bill discounted' is shown under the head 'Contingent Liabilities' at the footnote of the liabilities side of the Balance Sheet.

Proportionate Discount Charges

If the date of maturity of a bill falls on a date of a month within the accounting year, no problem relating to *discounting of bill* will arise. But problem arises when the date of maturity falls on a month of the next year, i.e., when the due date falls on two accounting periods. In that case, proportionate amount of discount will be charged to Profit and Loss Account. e.g., A bill drawn on 1st Nov. 2012 for Rs. 10,000 for 3 months. The bill was discounted by the bank on the same day @ 12% p.a. Therefore, the total amount of discount will be Rs. 300 (i.e., 10,000 $\times \frac{12}{100} \times \frac{3}{12}$). So $\frac{2}{3}$rd of Rs. 300 i.e., Rs. 200 will be transferred to Profit and Loss Account for the year ended 31st Dec. 2012.

Treatment of Discount in the Books of the Bank

The following entries are recorded in the books of the bank:

(a) ***When the bill is discounted***:

Bill Discounted A/c Dr.
  To Customer's Current A/c
  " Discounting on Bill A/c

(b) ***When amount is received from the drawee***:

Cash A/c Dr.
  To Bills Discounted A/c

But the entries in the books of Drawer and Drawee will be:

	Transactions	Entries in the books of Drawer	Entries in the books of Drawee
1.	When the bill is drawn	Bills Receivable A/c Dr. To Drawee A/c	Drawer A/c Dr. To Bills Payable A/c
2.	When the bill is discounted by the bank	Cash/Bank A/c Dr. Discount A/c Dr. To Bills Receivable A/c	—
3.	When the same is honoured at maturity	—	Bills Payable A/c Dr. To Cash/Bank A/c

The following illustration will make the principle clear:

Illustration 2

On 1.1.12011 H draws a three months' bill of Rs. 1,000 on P. The latter accepts and returns the same to the former on the same date. The bill was discounted with the U.B.I. @ 10% p.a. On due date the bill was honoured by payment.

You are required to give entries in the books of all the parties.

Solution

In the books of H
Journal

Date	Particulars		L.F.	Debit	Credit
2011				Rs.	Rs.
Jan. 1	Bill Receivable A/c	Dr.		1,000	
	To P A/c				1,000
	(Bill accepted by P for 3 months)				
	Bank A/c	Dr.		975	
	Discount on Bills A/c	Dr.		25 †	
	To Bills Receivable A/c				1,000
	(Bill discounted by bank at Rs. 975)				

† Amount of discount $= \text{Rs. } 1{,}000 \times \frac{10}{100} \times \frac{3}{12} = \text{Rs. } 25$

Alternative Approach (for discounting the bill):

			Rs.	Rs.
(a)	Bank A/c	Dr.	1,000	
	To Bill Receivable A/c			1,000
(b)	Discount on Bill A/c	Dr.	25	
	To Bank A/c			25

Because, in practice, as soon as a bill is discounted by the bank, the bank usually credits the customer's account with full value, without paying him in cash and debits the same account with the amount of discount. Again, the customer debits the amount in full while recording in the bank column of the Cash Book and credits for discount also in the bank column of the Cash Book.

In the books of P
Journal

Date	Particulars		L.F.	Debit	Credit
2011				Rs.	Rs.
Jan. 1	H A/c	Dr.		1,000	
	To Bills Payable A/c				1,000
	(Bill accepted for 3 months)				
Apr. 4	Bills Payable A/c	Dr.		1,000	
	To Bank A/c				1,000
	(Bill met on maturity)				

In the books of Bank
Journal

Date	Particulars		L.F.	Debit	Credit
2011				Rs.	Rs.
Jan. 1	Bill Discounted A/c	Dr.		1,000	
	To Discount on Bill A/c				25
	" H's Current A/c				975
	(H's bill discounted)				
Apr. 4	Cash A/c	Dr.		1,000	
	To Bill Discounted A/c				1,000
	(Received Cash on maturity of the discounted bill of H)				

(c) Bills drawn and endorsed to Creditors and honoured at maturity

Sometimes the drawer of a bill may purchase goods on credit from the creditors. In that case, instead of paying him in cash he may request to take the bill and endorses the same. Since a bill of exchange is a negotiable instrument, the drawer, thus, can transfer to any other party by physical delivery. Sometimes the drawer of a bill endorses the same to a creditor in settlement of a debt (either full or in part).* This is what is known as 'Endorsement of a Bill' (which we have already discussed above).

So, the drawer (who actually endorsed the bill) is called the *endorser* and to whom the bill is endorsed, i.e., the creditor, is called the *endorsee*. Thus, the original payee, i.e., the drawer, endorses the bill after putting his initial and passes it to the new payee, viz., the creditor.

* Usually the creditor takes it at its discounted value when the bill is actuallly taken by him.

The following entries are required in the books of the parties :

	Transactions	*In the books of Drawer*	*Entries in the books of Drawee*	*Entries in the books of Creditors*
1.	When the bill is drawn	Bills Receivable A/c Dr. To Drawee A/c	Drawer A/c Dr. To Bills Payable A/c	—
2.	When the bill is endorsed to creditors	Creditor's or, Endorsee's A/c Dr. To B/R A/c	—	B/R A/c Dr. To Drawer A/c
3.	When the bill is honoured at maturity	—	Bills Payable A/c Dr. To Cash/Bank A/c	Cash /Bank A/c Dr. To B/R A/c

Illustration 3

On. 1.4.2011 P draws a bill on Q for Rs. 800 for goods sold at 90 days after sight. Q accepts the bill on 5.4.2011. P, however, endorsed the bill to T in settlement of a debt of Rs. 850. On maturity the bill was duly honoured by Q. Show the entries in the books of all the parties.

Solution

In the books of P
Journal

Date	*Particulars*		*L.F.*	*Debit*	*Credit*
2010				Rs.	Rs.
April 1	Q A/c	Dr.		800	
	To Sales A/c				800
	(Good sold to Q on credit)				
5	Bills Receivable A/c	Dr.		800	
	To Q A/c				800
	(Bill accepted by Q for 90 days after sight)				
"	T A/c	Dr.		850	
	To Bills Receivable A/c				800
	" Discount Received A/c				50
	(Bills endorsed to T in settlement of a debt of Rs. 850)				

In the books of Q
Journal

Date	*Particulars*		*L.F.*	*Debit*	*Credit*
2011				Rs.	Rs.
April 1	Purchases A/c	Dr.		800	
	To P A/c				800
	(Goods purchased on credit from P)				
5	P A/c	Dr.		800	
	To Bills Payable A/c				800
	(Bill accepted for 90 days after sight)				
July 7	Bills Payable A/c	Dr.		800	
	To Bank A/c				800
	(Bill met at maturity)				

In the books of T
Journal

Date	*Particulars*		*L.F.*	*Debit*	*Credit*
2011				Rs.	Rs.
April 5	Bills Receivable A/c	Dr.		800	
	Discount Allowed	Dr.		50	
	To P A/c				850
	(Bill received from P in settlement of a debt of Rs. 850)				
July 7	Bank A/c	Dr.		800	
	To Bills Receivable A/c				800
	(Amount received on maturity)				

Notes :

1. When bill is draw 'after sight' period is counted from the date of acceptance of the bill.

2. Due date may be calculated as:

April (30 – 5) 25 + May 31 + June 30 = 86 days

Total number of days 90

∴ July = 90 – 86 = 4 days + Days of grace 3 = 7th July.

(d) Bills drawn and sent to the Bank for collection and honoured at maturity

This particularly arises when a business receives a large number of bills from its customers. Since it is very difficult to present the bills to different parties and at different due dates, the bills are sent to the bank for collection, i.e., as soon as the bills are received, they are sent to the bank. Bank will realise the amount from the different drawees and will credit the drawer's account at the cost of certain amount of charge. The instruction is given to the bank before due date so that bank may present the same after due date. For this purpose the drawer will open a new account in his book viz. *Bills for Collection Account*, and not the Bank Account since amount can only be realised after due date by the bank. Any balance left in *Bills for Collection Account* will reveal the amount of uncollected bills lying in the hands of the bank.

The following entries are required for the purpose :

	Transactions	In the books of Drawer	In the books of Drawee	In the books of bank
1	When the bill is drawn	B/R A/c Dr. To Drawee A/c	Drawer A/c Dr. To B/P A/c	—
2	When the bill is sent to the bank for collection	Bill for Collection A/c Dr. To B/R A/c	—	No entry
3	When the bill is honoured at maturity	Bank A/c Dr. Collection Charges A/c Dr. To Bill for Collection A/c	B/P A/c Dr. To Cash/Bank A/c	Cash /Bank A/c Dr. To Customer's Current A/c " Collection Charges A/c

The following illustration will make the principle clear:

Illustration 4

X drew a bill on 1.10.2011 for Rs. 3,000 on Y for 3 months. Y accepted the bill and returned it to X. X sent the bill to the bank for collection. After maturity X received an intimation from the bank that the bill was duly honoured by Y and bank charge Rs. 10 for collection. Show the entries in the books of X and Y.

Solution

In the books of X
Journal

Date	*Particulars*		*L.F.*	*Debit*	*Credit*
2011				Rs.	Rs.
Oct. 1	Bills Receivable A/c	Dr.		3,000	
	To Y A/c				3,000
	(Bill accepted by Y for 3 months)				
"	Bill for Collection A/c	Dr.		3,000	
	To Bills Receivable A/c				3,000
	(Bills sent to the bank for collection)				
2012					
Jan. 4	Bank A/c	Dr.		2,990	
	Bank Charges A/c	Dr.		10	
	To Bills for Collection A/c				3,000
	(Bill sent at maturity and amount received from bank after deducting bank charges)				

In the books of Y
Journal

Date	*Particulars*		*L.F.*	*Debit*	*Credit*
2011				Rs.	Rs.
Oct. 1	X A/c	Dr.		3,000	
	To Bills Payable A/c				3,000
	(Bills accepted for 3 months)				

Contd.

2012 Jan. 4	Bills Payable A/c Dr. To Bank A/c (Bill honoured at maturity)		3,000	3,000

In the books of Bank

Journal

Date	*Particulars*	*L.F.*	*Debit* Rs.	*Credit* Rs.
2011 Oct. 1.	No entry for receiving the bills			
2012 Jan. 4	Cash/Bank A/c Dr. To X's A/c " Collection Charges A/c (Bill honoured at maturity)		3,000	2,990 10

Illustration 5

On 1.5.2011 Jadu drew four bills of exchange on Madhu for Rs. 250, Rs. 500, Rs. 750 and Rs. 1,000 for 1 month, 2 months, 3 months, and 4 months, respectively. Madhu accepted the bills and returned to Jadu. Jadu endorsed the first bill to his creditor Sadhu. The second bill he sent to the bank for collection. He discounted the third bill by the bank at 12% p.a. He retained the fourth bill till due date. All the bills were duly honoured at maturity. Show the entries in the books of Jadu.

Solution

In the books of X

Journal

Date	*Particulars*	*L.F.*	*Debit* Rs.	*Credit* Rs.
2011 May 1	Bills Receivable A/c Dr.* To Madhu A/c (Bill accepted by Madhu for 1 month)		250	250
	Bill Receivable A/c Dr. To Madhu A/c (Bills accepted by Madhu for 2 months)		500	500
	Bill Receivable A/c Dr. To Madhu A/c (Bill accepted by Madhu for 3 months)		750	750
	Bills Receivable A/c Dr. To Madhu A/c (Bill accepted by Madhu for 4 months)		1,000	1,000
	Sadhu A/c Dr. To Bills Receivable A/c (First bill endorsed to creditor, Sadhu)		250	250
	Bills for Collection A/c Dr. To Bills Receivable A/c (Second bill sent to the bank for collection)		500	500
	Bank A/c Dr. Discount A/c Dr. To Bills Receivable A/c (Third bill discounted by Bank @ 12% p.a.)		727.50 22.50	750
July 4	Bank A/c Dr. To Bill for Collection A/c (Second bill honoured at maturity)		500	500
Sept. 4	Cash/Bank A/c Dr. To Bills Receivable A/c (Fourth bill honoured at maturity)		1,000	1,000

* When there are more than one bill and their dates of maturity also are different, it is better to make separate entries for each of them.

Successive endorsement

Illustration 6

On 1.1.2010 A drew a bill on B for Rs. 1,000 for 3 months. B accepted it and returned it to A. A endorsed the bill to C and C to D who discounted the bill for Rs. 975. At maturity the bill was duly honoured by B. Show the entries in the books of all the parties.

Solution

In the books of A
Journal

Date	Particulars		L.F.	Debit	Credit
2010				Rs.	Rs.
Jan. 1	Bills Receivable A/c	Dr.		1,000	
	To B A/c				1,000
	(Bill accepted by B for 3 months)				
"	C A/c	Dr.		1,000	
	To Bills Receivable A/c				1,000
	(Bills endorsed to C)				

In the books of B
Journal

Date	Particulars		L.F.	Debit	Credit
2010				Rs.	Rs.
Jan. 1	A A/c	Dr.		1,000	
	To Bills Payable A/c				1,000
	(Bill accepted for 3 months)				
April 4	Bills Payable A/c	Dr.		1,000	
	To Cash/Bank A/c				1,000
	(Bill honoured at maturity)				

In the books of C
Journal

Date	Particulars		L.F.	Debit	Credit
2010				Rs.	Rs.
Jan. 1	Bills Receivable A/c	Dr.		1,000	
	To A A/c				1,000
	(Bill receivable from A)				
"	D A/c	Dr.		1,000	
	To Bills Receivable A/c				1,000
	(Bill received from A and endorsed to D)				

In the books of D
Journal

Date	Particulars		L.F.	Debit	Credit
2010				Rs.	Rs.
Jan. 1	Bills Receivable A/c	Dr.		1,000	
	To C A/c				1,000
	(Bill receivable from C)				
"	Cash A/c	Dr.		975	
	Discount A/c	Dr.		25	
	To Bills Receivable A/c				1,000
	(Bill discounted by bank)				

In the books of Bank
Journal

Date	Particulars		L.F.	Debit	Credit
2011				Rs.	Rs.
Jan. 1	Bills Discounted A/c	Dr.		1,000	
	To D's Current A/c				975
	" Discount A/c				25
	(Bill discounted)				

Contd.

				Rs.	Rs.
April 4	Cash/Bank A/c To Bills Discounted A/c (Bill honoured at maturity)	Dr.		1,000	1,000

(e) Advance by way of Security of Bills

Sometimes the drawer of the bill, without discounting the bill, takes an advance from the banker as a loan by depositing the bill as a security. It belongs to the property of the drawer and, as such, it must be shown as an asset in the assets side of the Balance Sheet. The following entries are to be passed :

(i) ***Where the advance is taken by depositing the bill***

Bank A/c Dr.
  To Bill Receivable A/c
  To Advances on Bills A/c

Naturally, at the date of maturity, when the bill is presented by the bank for payment to the drawee, he honours it. It is needless to say that the bank will refund the excess or surplus amount, if any, after deducting the advance money together with interest and when the banker will inform the drawer that the bill was duly honoured by the drawee, he will pass the following entries :

(ii) ***For the bill collected by bankers***

Advances on Bill A/c Dr.
  To Bill Receivable A/c

(iii) ***For interest charged by banks***

Interest A/c Dr.
  To Advances on Bill A/c

(iv) ***For receiving the balance of proceeds***

Bank A/c Dr.
  To Advances on Bills A/c

The following illustration will make the principle clear :

Illustration 7

On 1.1.2011, A drew a bill on B for goods sold to him for Rs. 1,000 for 3 months. B accepted the bill and returned to A. A deposited the bill to the bank as security and took a loan for Rs. 800 at 12% p.a. The bill was duly honoured by B on due date. The banker remitted the balance of the proceeds after deducting the advances together with interest. Show the entries in the books of A.

Solution

In the books of A
Journal

Date	*Particulars*		*L.F.*	*Debit*	*Credit*
2011				Rs.	Rs.
Jan. 1	B A/c To Sales A/c (Goods sold to B on credit)	Dr.		1,000	1,000
	Bills Receivable A/c To B A/c (Bill drawn on B for 3 months)	Dr.		1,000	1,000
	Bank A/c To Advances on Bill A/c (Loan taken from bank at 12% p.a. on security of the bill)	Dr.		800	800
April 4	Advances on Bill A/c To Bills Receivable A/c (Bills collected by bank on maturity)	Dr.		1,000	1,000
"	Bank A/c Interest A/c To Advances on Bills A/c (Balance of the proceeds received from the bank after adjusting loan together with interest)	Dr. Dr.		176 24	200

Dishonour of Bills

A bill is said to be dishonoured when the drawee fails to pay or honour the bill on due date. It has already been explained that dishonour may be made in two ways (i) Dishonour by-non-acceptance; (ii) Dishonour by non-payment. It must be noted that while dishonour of bills, entries in the books of all the parties will be made in such a manner so that original entry will be cancelled and the original position of the respective parties will be stood in the books .

The following entries will be passed in the books of the parties:

Transactions	Entries in the books of Drawer		Entries in the books of Drawee	
When the bill is dishonoured	(a) *If retained till due date*			
	Drawee's A/c	Dr.	Bills Payable A/c	Dr.
	To Bills Receivable A/c		To Drawer A/c	
	(b) *If discounted by Bank*			
	Drawee's A/c	Dr.	—Do—	
	To Bank A/c			
	(c) *If endorsed to a Creditor*			
	Drawee's A/c	Dr.	—Do—	
	To Endorsee's or Creditors A/c			
	(d) *If sent to bank for collection*			
	Drawee's A/c	Dr.	—Do—	
	To Bill for Collection A/c			

Illustration 8

On 1.2.2012, J. Jadav received from K. Kadam three acceptances for Rs. 6,000, Rs. 8,000 and Rs. 10,000 for two months.

The first bill for Rs. 6,000 was endorsed to M. Mehata; the second bill for Rs. 8,000 was held till due date; and the third bill for Rs. 10,000 was discounted for Rs. 50 discount.

At maturity all the bills were dishonoured. Give the journal entries in the books of J. Jadav and the ledger accounts in the books of K. Kadam, in respect of these transactions.

Solution

In the books of J. Jadav

Journal

Date	*Particulars*		*L.F.*	*Debit* Rs.	*Credit* Rs.
2012 Feb. 1	Bills Receivable A/c	Dr.		6,000	
	To K. Kadam A/c				6,000
	(Bill drawn and accepted by J. Jadav for 2 months)				
"	Bills Receivable A/c	Dr.		8,000	
	To K.Kadam A/c				8,000
	(Bill drawn and accepted by J. Jadav for 2 months)				
"	Bills Receivable A/c	Dr.		10,000	
	To K. Kadam A/c				10,000
	(Bill drawn and accepted by J. Jadav for 2 months)				
"	M. Mehata A/c	Dr.		6,000	
	To Bills Receivable A/c				6,000
	(Bill for Rs. 6,000 endorsed to M. Mehata)				
"	Bank A/c	Dr.		9,950	
	Discount A/c	Dr.		50	
	To Bills Receivable A/c				10,000
	(Bill for Rs. 10,000 discounted by the Bank)				
April 4	K Kadam A/c	Dr.		6,000	
	To M. Mehata A/c				6,000
	(Bill endorsed to M. Mehata dishonoured byK. Kadam)				

Contd.

			Rs.	Rs.
2012 April 4	K. Kadam A/c	Dr.	8,000	
	To Bills Receivable A/c			8,000
	(Bill for Rs. 8,000 dishonoured by K. Kadam)			
"	K. Kadam A/c	Dr.	10,000	
	To Bank A/c			10,000
	(Bill discounted by bank dishonoured by K. Kadam)			

In the books of K. Kadam

Jadav Account

Dr.					Cr.
Date	Particulars	Amount	Date	Particulars	Amount
2012		Rs.	2012		Rs.
Feb. 1	To Bills Payable A/c	6,000	Feb. 1	By Balance b/d	24,000
	" Bills Payable A/c	8,000	April 4	" Bills Payable A/c	6,000
	" Bills Payable A/c	10,000		" Bills Payable A/c	8,000
"	" Balance c/d	24,000		" Bills Payable A/c	10,000
		48,000			48,000
				Balance b/d	24,000

Noting charges

When the drawee fails to pay/honour the bill on due date, the bill is said to be dishonoured and when a bill is dishonoured, the holder may cause such dishonour to be noted by a notary public upon the instrument. Such note must be made within a reasonable time after dishonour and also must specify the date of dishonour, the reason for it, and the notary charges. Notary public is an officer of State and/or Central Government to exercise the power and function relating to noting and protecting for dishonour of bill. The fee which is paid is called 'Noting Charge'. Actually the fees are to be paid by the drawee.

(a) ***When the drawer pays for the amount of Noting Charge***

Drawee A/c Dr.
To Cash/Bank A/c

(b) ***When the endorser pays for the amount of Noting Charge***

Drawee A/c Dr.
To Endorsee A/c

(c) ***When the bank pays for the amount of Noting Charge***

Drawee A/c Dr.
To Bank A/c

(a) When the bill is sent to the bank for collection and dishonoured, noting charges, in that case, are paid by the drawer.

For the amount of noting charges, there will be no separate entries in the books of drawer, or all other parties, only the amount of noting charges will be included with the dishonoured entry.

But in the books of drawee the entry will be

Noting Charges A/c Dr.
To Drawer A/c

Illustration 9

S. Sen and B. Banerjee have a number of transactions on bill of exchange between them. You are required to show the journal entries in their books in respect of the following transactions:

1.1.2011 : Sen draws a bill on Banerjee to Rs. 15,450 payable after a month, inclusive of interest at 3% p.m.

3.1.2011 : Sen discounts a bill for Rs. 25,000 drawn on 30.12.2010 with his bank, discounting charges being 15% p.a. the bill is payable on 3.2.2011.

4.1.2011 : Sen endorses the bill for Rs. 15,450 in favour of R. Ram towards accounts.

1.2.2011 : Banerjee pays the bill for Rs. 15,450.

7.2.2011 : The bill for Rs. 25,000 is returned by Sen's bankers as unpaid with their charges of Rs. 10.

[CA Entrance]

Solution

In the books of S. Sen
Journal

Date	Particulars		L.F.	Debit	Credit
2011				Rs.	Rs.
Jan. 1	Bills Receivable A/c	Dr.		15,450	
	To B. Banerjee A/c				15,000
	" Interest A/c $\left(15{,}450 \times \frac{3}{103}\right)$				450
	(Bill drawn and accepted for Rs. 15,000 plus interest at 3% p.m.)				
3	Bank A/c	Dr.		24,688	
	Discount A/c	Dr.		312	
	To Bills Receivable A/c				25,000
	(Bills discounted by bank at 15% p.a.) $\left(\text{Rs. } 25{,}000 \times \frac{15}{100} \times \frac{1}{12}\right)$				
4	R. Ram A/c	Dr.		15,450	
	To Bills Receivable A/c				15,450
	(Bill receivable from B. Banerjee endorsed to R. Ram)				
4	B. Banerjee A/c	Dr.		25,010	
	To Bank A/c				25,010
	(Bill which was discounted returned dishonoured)				

In the books of B. Banerjee
Journal

Date	Particulars		L.F.	Debit	Credit
2011				Rs.	Rs.
Jan. 1	S. Sen A/c	Dr.		15,000	
	Interest A/c	Dr.		450	
	To Bills Payable A/c				15,450
	(Bill accepted for 1 month including interest)				
Feb. 1	Bills Payable A/c	Dr.		15,450	
	To Bank A/c				15,450
	(Bill honoured at maturity)				
4	Bills Payable A/c	Dr.		25,000	
	Noting Charges A/c	Dr.		10	
	To S. Sen A/c				25,010
	(Bill dishonoured at maturity, noting charge being Rs. 10)				

Successive Endorsement

Illustration 10

Saurav purchased goods worth Rs. 1,000 from Ratul for which the latter drew a bill on the former, payable after one month. Saurav accepted it and returned it to Ratul. Ratul endorsed it to Subash, and Subash to Amit. Amit discounted the bill with State Bank of India at 6% p.a. On maturity, the bill was dishonoured, noting charge being Rs. 10. Show the entries in the books of all the parties including the books of State Bank of India.

Solution

In the books of Ratul
Journal

Date	Particulars		L.F.	Debit	Credit
2011				Rs.	Rs.
?	Surav A/c	Dr.		1,000	
	To Sales A/c				1,000
	(Goods sold to Saurav)				
?	Bills Receivable A/c	Dr.		1,000	
	To Saurav A/c				1,000
	(Bill drawn and accepted by Saurav for 1 month)				
?	Subash A/c	Dr.		1,000	
	To Bills Receivable A/c				1,000
	(Bill endorsed to Subash)				

Contd.

			Rs.	Rs.
	Saurav A/c Dr. To Subash A/c (Bill endorsed to Subash dishonoured by Saurav including noting charge of Rs. 10)		1,010	1,010

In the books of Saurav

Journal

Date	Particulars	L.F.	Debit	Credit
			Rs.	Rs.
?	Purchases A/c Dr. To Ratul A/c (Goods purchased from Ratul)		1,000	1,000
?	Ratul A/c Dr. To Bills Payable A/c (Bill accepted for 1 month)		1,000	1,000
?	Bills Payable A/c Dr. Noting Charge A/c Dr. To Ratul A/c (Bill dishonoured at maturity, noting charge being Rs. 10)		1,000 10	1,010

In the books of Subash

Journal

Date	Particulars	L.F.	Debit	Credit
			Rs.	Rs.
?	Bills Receivable A/c Dr. To Ratul A/c (Bill received from Ratul)		1,000	1,000
?	Amit A/c Dr. To Bills Receivable A/c (Bill received from Ratul endorsed to Amit)		1,000	1,000
?	Ratul A/c Dr. To Amit A/c (Bill endorsed to Amit dishonoured on maturity, noting charge being Rs. 10)		1,010	1,010

In the books of Amit

Journal

Date	Particulars	L.F.	Debit	Credit
			Rs.	Rs.
?	Bills Receivable A/c Dr. To Subash A/c (Bill received from Subash)		1,000	1,000
?	Bank A/c Dr. Discount A/c Dr. To Bills Receivable A/c (Bill received from Subash discounted by the Bank at 6% p.a.)		995 5	1,000
?	Subash A/c Dr. To Bank A/c (Bill received from Subash dishonoured, noting charge being Rs. 10)		1,010	1,010

In the books of State Bank of India

Journal

Date	Particulars	L.F.	Debit	Credit
			Rs.	Rs.
?	Bills Discounted A/c Dr. To Amit's Current A/c " Discount A/c (Amit's bill discounted which is due after 1 month)		1,000	995 5

Contd.

				Rs.	Rs.
?	Amit's Current A/c	Dr.		1,010	
	To Bills Discounted A/c				1,000
	" Cash A/c				10
	(Bill received from Amit dishonoured at maturity, noting charge being Rs. 10)				

Insolvency of the Drawee and its effect in the Books of Drawer

Generally, a person is said to be insolvent when he is unable to pay or settle his debts. In other words, a person is declared as insolvent provided his liabilities exceed assets, i.e., insolvency arises out of bankruptcy. Naturally, when a person becomes insolvent, his assets are sold by liquidator or offical receiver who pays the creditor in proportion to their dues out of assets realised which, in other words, goes by the name of 'Dividend' in accounting terminology and is expressed in terms of paise in the rupee (50 paise in the rupee). Needless to mention here that when the drawee becomes insolvent, the bill (which he accepted) is dishonoured. The following entries are required in the books of Drawer and Drawee:

	Transactions	*In the Books of Drawer*	*In the Books of Drawee*
1.	When the bill is dishonoured	Pass usual entry	Bills Payable A/c Dr. To Drawer A/c
2.	When the amount is received, say, 50% in the rupee	Cash/Bank A/c (50%) Dr. Bad Debts A/c (50%) Dr. To Drawee A/c	Drawer A/c Dr. To Cash/Bank A/c (50%) " Deficiency or, Amount Unpaid A/c (50%)

Illustration 11

On 1.1.2011 Raja accepted a bill drawn by Walia for Rs. 4,000 for 4 months. On the same date, Walia discounted the bill by the bank at 12% p.a. Just on the date of maturity, Raja became insolvent. A first and final dividend was realised from his official receiver @ 60 paise in the rupee. Show the entries in the books of both the parties.

Solution

In the books of Walia
Journal

Date	*Particulars*		*L.F.*	*Debit*	*Credit*
2011				Rs.	Rs.
Jan. 1	Bills Receivable A/c	Dr.		4,000	
	To Raja A/c				4,000
	(Bills drawn accepted by Raja for 4 months)				
"	Bank A/c	Dr.		3,840	
	Discount A/c	Dr.		160	
	To Bills Receivable A/c				4,000
	(Bills discounted by the bank at 12% p.a.)				
May 4	Raja A/c	Dr.		4,000	
	To Bank A/c				4,000
	(Bill dishonoured by Raja at maturity)				
"	Bank A/c	Dr.		2,400	
	Bad Debts A/c	Dr.		1,600	
	To Raja A/c				4,000
	(Amounts received from the official receiver of Raja @ 60 p. in the rupee).				

In the books of Raja
Journal

Date	*Particulars*		*L.F.*	*Debit*	*Credit*
2011				Rs.	Rs.
Jan. 1	Walia A/c	Dr.		4,000	
	To Bills Payable A/c				4,000
	(Bill accepted by Walia for 4 months)				

Contd.

Date	Particulars		L.F.	Debit	Credit
2011				Rs.	Rs.
May 4	Bills Payable A/c	Dr.		4,000	
	To Walia A/c				4,000
	(Bill dishonoured at maturity)				
"	Walia A/c	Dr.		4,000	
	To Bank A/c				2,400
	" Deficiency A/c				1,600
	(Amount paid to Walia @ 60 paise in the rupee and unpaid amount being transferred to Deficiency Account)				

Provision against Doubtful Drawees

From accounting point of view it is not necessary to create any provision against doubtful drawees, i.e., the bill is expected to be dishonoured. The reason is that when the bill is dishonoured the drawee will again be converted into debtors. But problem arises when the bill is discounted by the drawer at the end of the financial year when the bill has not matured for payment. At that time, if it is anticipated that a liability will be materialisied (i.e., if the drawee becomes insolvent) proper provision against such doubtful drawees must be made in the books of account.

In that case, we are to pass the usual entry which is followed while preparing final accounts. i.e.,

Profit and Loss A/c Dr.
To Provision for Bad Debts A/c

RENEWAL OF BILLS

It has already been explained earlier that when the drawee of a bill is unable to meet the same on due date, he may accept a fresh bill including interest in place of the old bill together with the incidental expenses, if any, for some extended period, the said bill is known as *renewal of bill*. In this case, if part payment is made, the value of the new bill will be the face value of the original bill plus interest on renewed bill minus the part payment so made. But ***if interest is paid in Cash, the same will not be included with the amount of fresh bill.***

The following entries are to be passed in the books of drawer and drawee :

Transactions	*Entries in the books of Drawer*	*Entries in the books of Drawee*
1. When the bill is dishonoured i.e., for cancellation	Usual entry	Bills Payable A/c Dr. To Drawer A/c
2. For interest on renewed period	Drawee A/c Dr. To Interest A/c	Interest A/c Dr. To Drawer A/c
If the interest is paid by Cash	Cash A/c Dr. To Interest A/c	Interest A/c Dr. To Cash A/c
3. For part payment in Cash	Cash/Bank A/c Dr. To Drawee A/c	Drawer A/c Dr. To Cash/Bank A/c
4. For fresh bill	Bills Receivable A/c Dr.* To Drawee A/c	Drawer A/c Dr. To Bills Payable A/c

* It includes the amount of interest. But if interest is paid in cash, it will not include the amount of interest.

The following illustration will make the principle clear:

Illustration 12

On 1.1.2012, X draws a bill at 3 months on Y for Rs. 2,000. Y accepts it. X immediately discounts the bill at 5% p.a. On 15.3.2012, Y being unable to meet the bill offers X Rs. 1,500 and requests him to draw on him another bill for 3 months for the balance including interest therein @ $7\frac{1}{2}$ %. X accepts the agreement and, on maturity, Y meets the bill.

Show the entries in the books of X and Y.

Solution

In the books of X
Journal

Date	*Particulars*		*L.F.*	*Debit*	*Credit*
2012				Rs.	Rs.
Jan. 1	Bills Receivable A/c	Dr.		2,000	
	To Y A/c				2,000
	(Bill accepted by Y for 3 months)				

Contd.

Date	Particulars		L.F.	Debit	Credit
2012				Rs.	Rs.
"	Bank A/c	Dr.		1,975	
	Discount A/c	Dr.		25	
	To Bills Receivable A/c				2,000
	(Bill discounted by the bank at 5% p.a.)				
Mar. 15	Y A/c	Dr.		2,000	
	To Bank A/c				2,000
	(Bill dishonoured by Y)				
"	Cash A/c	Dr.		1,500	
	To Y A/c				1,500
	(Cash received from Y as a part payment of the bill dishonoured)				
"	Y A/c	Dr.		9.37	
	To Interest A/c				9.37
	(Interest receivable from Y on Rs. 500 @ $7\frac{1}{2}$ p.a. for 3 months)				
"	Bills Receivable A/c	Dr.		509.37	
	To Y A/c				509.37
	(Fresh bill drawn for the balance including interest and accepted by Y for 3 months)				
June 18	Cash A/c	Dr.		509.37	
	To Bills Receivable A/c				509.37
	(Bill honoured at maturity)				

In the books of Y
Journal

Date	*Particulars*		*L.F.*	*Debit*	*Credit*
2012				Rs.	Rs.
Jan. 1	X A/c	Dr.		2,000.00	
	To Bills Payable A/c				2,000.00
	(Bill accepted by Y for 3 months)				
Mar. 15	Bills Payable A/c	Dr.		2,000.00	
	To X A/c				2,000.00
	(Bill discounted on maturity)				
"	X A/c	Dr.		1,500.00	
	To Cash A/c				1,500.00
	(Cash paid to X as a part payment of the bill dishonoured)				
"	Interest A/c	Dr.		9.37	
	To X A/c				9.37
	(Interest payable to X on Rs. 500 @ $7\frac{1}{2}$ % p.a. for 3 months)				
"	X A/c	Dr.		509.37	
	To Bills Payable A/c				509.37
	(Fresh bill accepted for the balance plus interest for 3 months)				
June 18	Bills Payable A/c	Dr.		509.37	
	To Cash A/c				509.37
	(Fresh bill honoured at maturity)				

Illustration 13

Short owes Slow Rs. 6,000 for which the former accepts a three months' bill drawn by the latter. Slow immediately discounts the bill with his banker, Strong Bank, at 12% p.a. On the due date the bill is dishonoured and Strong Bank pays Rs. 20 as noting charges.

Short pays Rs. 1,180 including interest of Rs. 200 and gives another bill at three months' for the balance. Slow endorses the bill to his creditor Slim in full settlement of his debts for Rs. 5,100. Slim discounts the bill with his banker Strong Bank who charges Rs. 40 as discount. Before maturity Short becomes bankrupt and first and final dividend of 20 paise in a rupee is realised from his estate.

Show the journal entries in the books of Slim and Strong Bank and the ledger account of Short in the books of Slow.

[ICWA]

Solution

In the books of Slim

Journal

Date	Particulars		L.F.	Debit	Credit
				Rs.	Rs.
?	Bills Receivable A/c	Dr.		5,040	
	Discount Allowed A/c	Dr.		60	
	To Slow A/c				5,100
	(Endorsed bill received from Slow in full settlement.)				
?	Bank A/c	Dr.		5,000	
	Discount A/c	Dr.		40	
	To Bills Receivable				5,040
	(Bill discounted by the bank)				
?	Slow A/c	Dr.		5,100	
	To Bank A/c				5,040
	" Discount Allowed A/c				60
	(Bill dishonoured at maturity.)				

In the books of Strong Bank

Journal

Date	Particulars		L.F.	Debit	Credit
				Rs.	Rs.
?	Bills Discounted A/c	Dr.		6,000	
	To Slow's Current A/c				5,820
	" Discount A/c				180
	(Bill discounted which is due for 3 months.)				
?	Noting Charges A/c	Dr.		20	
	To Cash A/c				20
	(Noting charges incurred for dishonour of the bill.)				
?	Slow's Current Account A/c	Dr.		6,020	
	To Bills Discounted A/c				6,000
	" Noting Charges A/c				20
	(Bill dishonoured, noting charges being Rs. 20.)				
?	Bills Discounted A/c	Dr.		5,040	
	To Slim's Current A/c				5,000
	" Discount A/c				40
	(Bill discounted which is due for 3 months.)				
?	Slim's Current A/c	Dr.		5,040	
	To Bills Discounted A/c				5,040
	(Bill dishonoured at maturity.)				

In the books of Slow

Short Account

Dr. Cr.

Date	Particculars	Amount	Date	Particulars	Amount	Amount
?		Rs.	?		Rs.	Rs.
	To Balance b/d	6,000		By Bills Receivable A/c		6,000
	" Strong Bank A/c	6,020		" Cash A/c		1,180
	" Interest A/c	200		" Bills Receivable		5,040
	" Slim A/c	5,040		" Cash Account (20%)	1,008	
				" Bad Debts A/c	4,032	5,040
		17,260				17,260

Illustration 14

Mr David draws two bills of exchange on 1.1.95 for Rs. 6,000 and Rs. 10,000. The bills of exchange for Rs. 6,000 is for two months while the bill of exchange for Rs. 10,000 is for three months. These bills are acepted by Mr. Thomas. On 4.3.95 Mr. Thomas requests Mr. David to renew the first bill with interest at 18% p.a. for a period of two months. Mr. David agrees to this prposal. On 20.3.95 Mr. Thomas retires the acceptance for Rs. 10,000, the interest rebate, i.e., discount, being Rs. 100. Before the due date of the renewed bill, Mr. Thomas become insolvent and only 50 paise in a rupee could be recovered from his estate.

You are to give the journal entries in the books of Mr. David.

[CA Foundation, Nov. 1995]

Solution

In the books of Mr. David

Journal

Date	Particulars		L.F.	Debit	Credit
1995				Rs.	Rs.
Jan. 1	Bills Receivable A/c	Dr.		6,000	
	To Mr. Thomas A/c				6,000
	(Bill drawn for 2 months.)				
?	Bills Receivable A/c	Dr.		10,000	
	To Mr. Thomas A/c				10,000
	(Bills drawn for 3 months)				
Mar. 4	Mr. Thomas A/c	Dr.		6,000	
	To Bills Receivable A/c				6,000
	(Bill dishonoured at maturity.)				
	Mr. Thomas A/c	Dr.		180	
	To Interest A/c				180
	(Interest receivable on fresh bill)				
	Bills Receivable A/c	Dr.		6,180	
	To Mr. Thomas A/c				6,180
	(Bill drawn for 2 months)				
" 20	Bank A/c	Dr.		9,900	
	Reabate Allowed A/c			100	
	To Bills Rceivable A/c				10,000
	(Bill retired at a rebate of Rs. 100.)				
May 7	Mr. Thomas A/c	Dr.		6,180	
	To Bills Receivable A/c				6,180
	(First bills dishonoured at maturity)				
?	Bank A/c	Dr.		3,090	
	To Bad Debts A/c			3,090	
	To Mr. Thomas A/c				6,180
	(50% of the amount realised from Thomas' estate as he became insolvent .)				

Illustration 15

Mr. P.C. Nag draws a three months' bill of exchange for Rs. 15,000 on his debtors Pranab Ghosh, who accepted it on 1st January 2005. P. C. Nag discounts the bill on 4th January with his bank, the discount rate being 10% per annum. On the due date the bill is dishonoured by Pranab Ghosh, the noting charges being Rs. 50. On 1st April, 2005 Pranab Ghosh makes an offer to P C. Nag to pay him Cash Rs. 5,000 on account and to settle the balance by agreeing to accept one bill of exchange for Rs. 6,000 at one month and the othe for the balance at three months, the latter including interest @ 12% p.a. for both the bills. P.C. Nag accepts the arrangements. The first bill is met on due date. But before maturity of the second bill Pranab Ghosh becomes insolvent and a dividend of 50 paise in the rupee is realised from his estate on 4th July 2005.

Show the Journal Entries in the books of P. C. Nag and Pranab Ghosh with narrations.

Solution **[CU BCom. (Hons.)]**

In the books of Mr. P.C.Nag

Journal

Date	Particulars		L.F.	Dr. Amount	Cr. Amount
2005				Rs.	Rs.
Jan. 1	Bills Receivable A/c	Dr.		15,000	
	To Pranab Ghosh A/c				15,000
	(Bill drawn on Pranab Ghosh and accepted by him)				
?	Bank A/c	Dr.		14,625	
	Discount on Bill A/c [$15,000 \times \frac{10}{100} \times \frac{3}{12}$]	Dr.		375	
	" Bill Receivable A/c				15,000
	(Bills discounted by bank @ 10% p.a. 3 months)				

Contd.

Date	Particulars		L.F.	Rs.	Rs.
2011					
Apr. 1	Pranab Ghosh A/c	Dr.		15,050	
	To Bank A/c				15,050
	(Bill dishonoured at maturity, noting charges being Rs. 50.)				
"	Cash A/c	Dr.		5,000	
	To Pranab Ghosh A/c				5,000
	(Cash received from Pranab Ghosh.)				
"	Pranab Ghosh A/c	Dr.		180[1]	
	To Interest A/c				180
	(Interest receivable from Pranab Ghosh @ 12% p.a.)				
"	Bills Receivable A/c (10,000 + 50 + 180)	Dr.		10,230	
	To Pranab Ghosh A/c				10,230
	(Fresh bills drawn and accepted by Pranab Ghosh)				
May 4	Bank A/c	Dr.		6,000	
	To Bills Receivable A/c				6,000
	(First renewed bill honoured at maturity)				
July 4	Pranab Ghosh A/c	Dr.		4,230	
	To Bill Receivable A/c				4,230
	(Second bills dishonoured at maturity.)				
"	Bank A/c	Dr.		2115	
	Bad Debts A/c	Dr.		2115	
	To Pranab Ghosh A/c				4,230[2]
	(50% of the dues from Pranab Ghosh received and the balance treated as Bad Debts.)				

In the books of Pranab Ghosh
Journal

Date	Particulars		L.F.	Dr. Amount	Cr. Amount
				Rs.	Rs.
2005					
Jan. 1	P. C. Nag A/c	Dr.		15,000	
	To Bills Payable A/c				15,000
	(Bill accepted for P. C. Nag.)				
Apr. 1	Bills Payable A/c	Dr.		15,000	
	Noting Charges A/c	Dr.		50	
	To P. C. Nag A/c				15,050
	(The Bill dishonoured and noting charges due)				
"	Interest A/c	Dr.		180	
	To P. C. Nag A/c				180
	(Interest Payable @12% p.a.)				
"	P. C. Nag A/c	Dr.		5,000	
	To Cash A/c				5,000
	(Cash paid to P. C. Nag)				
"	P. C. Nag A/c	Dr.		10,230	
	To Bills Payable A/c				10,230
	(Fresh bills accepted)				
May 4	Bills Payable A/c	Dr.		6,000	
	To Bank A/c				6,000
	(Bill honoured at maturity)				
July 4	Bills Payable A/c	Dr.		4,230	
	To P. C. Nag A/c				4,230
	(Bill dihonoured at maturity)				
"	P. C. Nag A/c	Dr.		4,230	
	To Bank A/c				2,115
	" Deficiency A/c				2,115
	(50% of dues paid)				

Workings

1. Interest is calculated as under

	Rs.
On Rs. 6,000 for 1 month @ 12% p.a. = Rs. 6,000 $\times \frac{12}{100} \times \frac{1}{12}$ =	60
On Rs. 4,000 for 3 months @ 12% p.a. = Rs. 4,000 $\times \frac{12}{100} \times \frac{3}{12}$ =	120
	180

2. **Pranab Ghosh A/c**

Dr. *Cr.*

Particulars	Rs.	Particulars		Rs.
To Balance b/d	15,000	By Bills Receivable A/c		15,000
" Bank A/c	15,050	" Cash A/c		5,000
" Interest A/c	180	" Bills Receivable A/c		10,230
" Bills Receivable A/c	4,230	Bank A/c	2,115	
		Bad Debts A/c	2,115	
		(bal. fig.)		4,230
	34,460			34,460

Illustration 17

On 1st January 1996 Debdas sold goods of the value of Rs. 2,000 to Debu on credit and drew a bill for three months for the same amount which Debu accepted on the same date. The Bill was discounted for Rs. 1,970. On the due date Debu notified his inability to meet the bill and requested Debdas to take it up and pay the noting charges of Rs. 15, which Debdas did. The following day Debu met his obligation with a bill at two months for the amount together with interest at 6% p.a. and paid cash for noting charges. When this bill became due, Debu paid cash Rs. 1,000 and accepted a fresh bill at 3 months for Rs. 1,050. Debu became insolvent before this last bill became due and a first and final dividend of 25 paise in the rupee was realised from his estate on 1st December 1996.

Pass entries in the books of Debdas to record the above transactions.

Solution **[CU BCom. (Hons.) 1997]**

In the books of Debdas

Journal

Date	Particulars		L.F.	Amount	Amount
2010				Rs.	Rs.
Jan. 1	Debu A/c	Dr.		2,000	
	To Sales A/c				2,000
	(Goods sold to Debu on credit)				
"	Bills Receivable A/c	Dr.		2,000	
	To Debu A/c				2,000
	(Bill of 3 months Received from Debu)				
"	Bank A/c	Dr.		1,970	
	Discount A/c	Dr.		30	
	To Bills Receivable A/c				2,000
	(Debu's acceptance of Rs. 2,000 discounted with the Bank at a discounting charge of Rs. 30)				
Apr. 4	Debu A/c	Dr.		2,015	
	To Bank A/c				2,015
	(Bill dishonoured at maturity, noting charg being Rs. 15)				
Apr. 5	Debu A/c	Dr.		20	
	To Interest A/c				20
	(Interest receivable from Debu @ 6% p.a. on dues of Rs. 2,000 for two months.)				
"	Bills Receivable A/c	Dr.		2,020	
	To Debu A/c				2,020
	(A bill of 2 months received from Debu)				

Contd.

Date	Particulars		Rs.	Rs.
	Cash A/c To Debu A/c (Cash received from Debu for the amount of noting charges)	Dr.	15	15
June 8	Debu A/c To Bills Receivable A/c (Debu's 2nd acceptance dishonoured.)	Dr.	2,020	2,020
"	Cash A/c To Debu A/c (Cash received from Debu as part payment)	Dr.	1,000	1,000
	Debu A/c To Interest A/c (Interest receivable from Debu on the balance due of Rs. 1,020)	Dr.	30	30
	Bills Receivable A/c To Debu A/c (A new bill of 3 months received from Debu with interest)	Dr.	1,050	1,050
Sep. 11	Debu A/c To Bills Receivable A/c (Debu's 3rd acceptance dishonoured.)	Dr.	1,050	1,050
Dec. 1	Bank A/c Bad Debts A/c To Debu A/c (First & Final dividend of 25% realised from the estate of Debu against dues of Rs. 1,050 and balance written-off as bad debts.)	Dr.	262.50 787.50	1,050

Workings :

1. Since cash is paid for noting charges, amount of the 2nd bill will be Rs. 2,000 + Interest on Rs. 2,000 @ 6% for two months, i.e., amount of interest will be Rs. 20. (Rs. 2,000 × $\frac{6}{100}$ × $\frac{2}{12}$).
   Hence, value of the 2nd bill will be Rs. 2,000 + Rs. 20 = 2,020.
2. When the 3rd bill was drawn the balance due by Debu was Rs. 2,020 – Rs. 1,000 = Rs. 1,020 but bill value was Rs. 1,050. Naturally, amount of interest was Rs. 1,050 – Rs. 1,020 = Rs. 30.
3. During insolvency balance due by Debu was Rs. 1,050. So, amount realised from Debu's estate as first and final dividend would be @ 25% on Rs. 1,050, i.e., Rs. 262.50. Thus, amount of bad debts will be Rs. 1,050 – Rs. 262.50 = Rs. 787.50 i.e., @ 75% of Rs. 1,050 which was written-off as bad debts.

Illustration 18

X draws a three months' bill of exchange for 3,000 on his debtor, Z, who accepts it on 1st January 2011. X discounts the bill on 4th January with his bankers, the discount rate being 6% per annum. On the due date the bill is dishonoured by Z, the charges for noting and expenses being Rs. 20. Z then makes an offer to X to pay him Rs. 1,000 in cash on account and to settle the balance by agreeing to accept one bill of exchange for Rs. 1,200 at one month and the other for the balance at three months, the latter including interest at 9% per annum for both the bills. X accepts the arrangement. The bill for Rs. 1,200 is met on the due date, but the other bill is dishonoured.

Show, in X's Ledger, accounts for Z and Bills Receivable Account and in Z's Ledger, accounts for X and Bills Payable.

[CU BCom (Hons.)]

Solution

In the books of X
Z Account

Dr. *Cr.*

Date		*Particulars*	*Amount*	*Date*		*Particulars*	*Amount*
2011			Rs.	2011			Rs.
Jan. 1	To	Balance b/d	3,000.00	Jan. 1	By	Bills Receivable A/c	3,000.00
Apr. 4	"	Bank (bill dishonoured and noting charges) A/c	3,020..00	Apr. 4	"	Bank A/c	1,000.00
"	"	Interest[1] A/c	27.45		"	Bills Receivable A/c (1,200 + 847.45)[2]	2,047.45
July 7	"	Bills Receivable A/c	847.45	July 7	"	Balance c/d	847.45
			6,894.90				6,894.90

Bills Receivable Account

Dr. Cr.

Date		Particulars	Amount	Date		Particulars	Amount
2011			Rs.	2011			Rs.
Jan.	1	To Z A/c	3,000.00	Jan.	4	By Bank[2] A/c	2,955.00
Apr.	4	" Z A/c	2,047.45	"	4	" Discount on Bills A/c	45.00
				May	4	" Bank (amount received on maturity) A/c	1,200.00
				July	7	" Z (bill dishonoured) A/c	847.45
			5,047.45				5,047.45

In Z's Ledger

X Account

Dr. Cr.

Date		Particulars	Amount	Date		Particulars	Amount
2011			Rs.	2011			Rs.
Jan.	1	To Bills Payable A/c	3,000.00	Jan.	1	By Balance b/d	3,000.00
"	4	" Bank A/c	1,000.00	Apr.	4	" Bills Payable A/c (bill honoured) A/c	3,000,00
Apr.	4	" Bills Payable A/c	2,047.45	"	4	" Noting Charges A/c	20.00
July	7	" Balance c/d	847.45	"	4	" Interest A/c	27.45
				July	7	" Bills Payable A/c	847.45
			6,894.90				6,894.90

Bills Payable Account

Dr. Cr.

Date		Particulars	Amount	Date		Particulars	Amount
2011			Rs.	2011			Rs.
Apr.	4	To X (bill dishonoured) A/c	3,000.00	Jan.	1	By X A/c	3,000.00
May	7	" Bank A/c	1,200.00	Jan.	1	" X A/c	2,047.45
July	7	" X (bill dishonoured) A/c	847.45				
			5,047.45				5,047.45

Workings :

[1]Calculation of interest :	Rs.
on Rs. 1,200 for 1 month	9.00
on Rs. 820 (i.e., Rs. 2,020 – Rs. 1,200) for 3 months	18.45
	27.45

[2]Amount of Second bill : Rs. (820 + 27.45) or Rs. 847.45.

Illustration 19

In the books of Arjun there was a balance of Rs. 13,000 due by Bheem on 31st March 1998, which was written-off as bad debt in closing of the books on that date. On 12th July, Bheem paid cash Rs. 12,000 in full and final settlement of his dues.

Further transaction took place between Arjun and Bheem as follows:

1998 Aug. 4 Arjun sold goods to Bheem valued to Rs. 25,000 which were paid by cheque Rs. 4,000 and a Bill of Exchange for Rs. 21,000 at one month. Arjun discounted the Bill of Exchange at the Bank for Rs. 20,900.

Sep. 7 Bheem's bill was dishonoured and Arjun was called upon to take it up. This he did by paying noting charges of Rs. 100.

Sept. 8 Bheem met his obligation for Rs. 21,000 with a bill at two months' for the same amount, paid cash for noting charges on the old bill and interest of Rs. 200 on the new bill.

Nov. 11 Bheem met his bill by paying cash Rs. 11,000 and accepted a fresh bill at 2 months' for Rs. 10,400 including interest.

Dec. 11 Bheem, having become insolvent, paid final dividend of 50 paise in the rupee.

Show Journal entries in the books of Arjun and necessary Ledger accounts in the books of Bheem.

[CU BCom (Hons.) 1999)]

In the books of Debdas

Journal

Date	Particulars		L.F.	Dr. Amount	Cr. Amount
1998				Rs.	Rs.
Mar. 13	Bad Debts A/c	Dr.		13,000	
	To Bheem A/c				13,000
	(Amount due from Bheem written-off as bad)				
July 12	Cash A/c	Dr.		12,000	
	To Bad Debts Recovery A/c				12,000
	(A portion of the amount already written-off as bad, now recovered)				
Aug. 4	Bheem A/c	Dr.		25,000	
	To Sales A/c				25,000
	(Goods sold on credit to Bheem)				
"	Bank A/c	Dr.		4,000	
	Bill Receivable A/c	Dr.		21,000	
	To Bheem A/c				25,000
	(Payment received by a cheque and by a bill accepted by Bheem for the balance				
"	Bank A/c	Dr.		20,900	
	Discount on Bill A/c	Dr.		100	
	To Bills Receivable A/c				21,000
	(The above bill discounted with bank immediately)				
Sept. 7	Bheem A/c	Dr.		21,000	
	To Bank A/c				21,000
	(Discounted bill dishonoured including noting chages)				
8	Bheem A/c	Dr.		200	
	To Interest Receivable A/c				200
	(Interest receivable from Bheem on renewal of the bill)				
8	Cash A/c	Dr.		300	
	Bill Receivable A/c			21,000	
	To Bheem A/c				21,300
	(Cash received from Bheem for interest and noting charges and a bill drawn on him—renewal of his earlier acceptance)				
Nov. 11	Bheem A/c	Dr.		21,000	
	To Bill Receivable A/c				21,000
	(Acceptance of Bheem retained but dishonored on maturity)				
"	Bheem A/c	Dr.		400	
	To Interest Receivable A/c				400
	(Interest receivable from Bheem on renewal of the bill)				
"	Cash A/c	Dr.		11,000	
	Bills Receivable A/c	Dr.		10,400	
	To Bheem A/c				21,400
	(Cash received from Bheém and an acceptance given by him for the balance amount inclusive of interest]				
Dec. 11.	Bheem A/c	Dr.		10,400	
	To Bill Receivable A/c				10,400
	(Accptance received from Bheem noted as dishonoured for his insolvency)				
"	Bank A/c	Dr.		5,200	
	Bad Debts A/c	Dr.		5,200	
	To Bheem A/c				10,400
	(Cash received @ 50% on dues by Bheem and the balance written-off as bad debts).				

In the books of Bheem
Arjun Account

Date		Particulars	Amount	Date		Particulars	Amount
1998			Rs.	1998			Rs.
July 12	To	Cash A/c	12,000	Apr. 1	By	Balance b/d	13,000
	"	Disc. Received A/c	1,000	Aug. 4	"	Purchases A/c	25,000
Aug. 4	"	Bank A/c	4,000		"	Bills Payabe A/c	21,000
	"	Bill Payable A/c	21,000	Sept. 7	"	Noting Charges A/c	100
Sept. 8	"	Cash A/c	300	8	"	Int. Payable A/c	200
	"	Bill Payable A/c	21,000	Nov. 11	"	Bills Payable A/c	21,000
Nov. 11	"	Cash A/c	11,000	"	"	Int. Payable A/c	400
	"	Bill Payable A/c	10,400	Dec. 11	"	Bills Payable A/c	10,400
Dec. 11	"	Cash A/c	5,200				
	"	Deficiency A/c	5,200				
			91,100				91,100

RETIREMENT OF BILL

Retirement of bill arises only when the drawee pays the bill before its due date. As such, the drawer allows him a certain amount of rebate/discount calculated at a certain rate per cent p.a. from the date of retirement to the date of maturity. Thus, the rebate/discount which is allowed by the drawer is an expense to him while the same is a gain to the drawee. Care should be taken while calculating the rebate or discount.

Because, ***discount/rebate will be calculated from the date of retirement to the date of maturity.***

The following entries are required to be passed in the books of drawer and drawee :

	Transactions	In the books of Drawer		In the books of Drawee	
1.	When the bill is drawn	Bills Receivable A/c	Dr.	Drawer A/c Dr.	
		To Drawee A/c		To Bills Payable A/c	
2.	When the bill is retired	Cash/Bank A/c	Dr.	Bills Payable A/c	Dr.
		Rebate Allowed A/c	Dr.	To Rebate Received A/c	
		To Bill Receivable A/c		" Cash/Bank A/c	

Illustration 20

A bought goods from B for 1,000 on credit. For this purpose, B drew a bill on A which was accepted by A on 1.10.2012 for the amount payable after three months. On 1.11.2012, A arranged to retire the bill at a rebate of 12% p.a. Show the entries in the books of B and A.

Solution

In the books of B
Journal

Date	Particulars		L.F.	Debit	Credit
2012				Rs.	Rs.
Oct. 1	A A/c	Dr.		1,000	
	To Sales A/c				1,000
	(Goods sold to A)				
"	Bill Receivable A/c	Dr.		1,000	
	To A A/c				1,000
	(Bill drawn which was accepted by A for 3 months)				
Nov. 1	Cash A/c	Dr.		979	
	Rebate Allowed A/c	Dr.		21	
	To Bills Receivable				1,000
	(Bill accepted by A retired under a rebate of 12% p.a.)				

Note: Rebate = Rs. $1{,}000 \times \frac{12}{100} \times \frac{65}{365}$ (from Nov. 1 to Jan. 4) = 21.36 p. (Say Rs. 21).

In the books of A
Journal

Date	Particulars		L.F.	Debit	Credit
2012				Rs.	Rs.
Oct. 1	Purchases A/c	Dr.		1,000	1,000
	To B A/c				
	(Goods purchased on credit)				

Contd.

Date	Particulars		L.F.	Debit	Credit
2012				Rs.	Rs.
"	B A/c	Dr.		1,000	
	To Bills Payable A/c				1,000
	(Bill accepted for 3 months)				
Nov. 1	Bills Payable A/c	Dr.		1,000	
	To Cash A/c				979
	" Rebate Received A/c				21
	(Bill retired under a rebate of 12% p.a)				

ACCOMMODATION BILL

An accommodation bill is one which has been signed by a person, as drawer, acceptor or endorser, without any consideration, for the purpose of assisting financial accommodation for one or more parties. The party accommodating is called the 'accommodation party' and the party accommodated is called the 'accommodated party'. In case of dishonour, no one can sue the other.

Thus, it is drawn for the purpose of assisting financial accommodation for one or more parties without any consideration. It should be remembered that an ordinary bill, i.e., trade bill, is drawn for some consideration. In other words, there must be a debtor and a creditor; creditor draws on a bill on debtor. But in case of an accommodation bill, there is no such consideration, that is why these bills are also termed as *'kite bills'* and in that case there is also no such debtor or creditor relationship.

The following are the differences between a *'Trade Bill'* and *'Accommodation Bill'*:

Trade Bill	Accommodation Bill
1. There must be a debtor-creditor relationship, i.e., the creditor draws the bill and the debtor accepts the bill.	1. No debtor-creditor relationship exists.
2. This bill is acknowledged as debt.	2. This bill cannot be acknowledged as debt.
3. This bill may or may not be discounted.	3. This bill must be discounted, otherwise, the basic purpose will not be served.
4. The drawer can take legal steps in case of dishonour of bill.	4. No legal step can be taken in case of dishonour of bill.
5. If this bill is discounted by the bank, the discounting charge is to be borne by the drawer.	5. The discounting charges are to be shared by both the parties according to the agreed ratio or equally or proportionate benefit.
6. This bill is drawn always for a valued consideration.	6. This bill is drawn not for a valued consideration.

There are three types of accommodation which are presented below one by one :

(1) **When the bill is drawn only for the accommodation of the drawer** *i.e., for the personal accommodation of the drawer.*

This particularly happens when one person is in urgent need of funds and he requests his friend to accept the bill for the purpose. Naturally, he will discount the bill immediately by the bank at the cost of certain amount of discount and he will take the proceeds. Just before the due date he will remit the money to the drawee so that he can easily honour the bill at the date of maturity.

Consider the following illustrations :

Case I — When the bill is honoured

Illustration 21

On 1.1.2012, Mr. X requested his friend Mr. Y to accept a bill drawn on him for Rs. 1,000 for 3 months. Mr. Y accepted the bill and returned to Mr. X. Mr. X immediately discounted the bill by the bank @ 12% p.a. At the date of maturity he remitted the money to Mr. Y who honoured the bill.

Show the entries in the books of Mr. X and Mr. Y.

Solution

In the books of Mr. X

Journal

Date	Particulars		L.F.	Debit	Credit
2012				Rs.	Rs.
Jan. 1	Bills Receivable A/c	Dr.		1,000	
	To Mr. Y A/c				1,000
	(Bill drawn on Mr. Y for 3 months for own accommodation)				
Jan. 1	Bank A/c	Dr.		970	
	Disount A/c	Dr.		30	
	To Bills Receivable A/c				1,000
	(Bill discounted by the bank @ 12% p.a. for 3 months)				

Contd.

Date	Particulars		L.F.	Debit	Credit
2012				Rs.	Rs.
Apr. 4	Mr. Y A/c	Dr.		1,000	
	To Cash A/c				1,000
	(Cash remitted to Mr. Y at maturity)				

In the books of Mr. Y

Journal

Date	Particulars		L.F.	Debit	Credit
1997				Rs.	Rs.
Jan. 1	Mr. X A/c	Dr.		1,000	
	To Bills Payable A/c				1,000
	(Bill accepted for 3 months for personal accommodation of Mr. X)				
April 4	Cash A/c	Dr.		1,000	
	To Mr. X A/c				1,000
	(Cash received from Mr. X at maturity)				
"	Bills Payable A/c	Dr.		1,000	
	To Cash A/c				1,000
	(Bill honoured at maturity)				

Case II — When the bill is dishonoured

Illustration 22

On 1.1.2o12 Ram, for his own accommodation, drew a bill on Rahim for Rs. 1,000 for 3 months. Rahim accepted the bill and returned to Ram. Ram discounted the bill by the bank @ 12% p.a. On maturity Ram failed to remit the money to Rahim and Rahim dishonoured the bill, noting charges being Rs. 10.

Show the entries in the books of both the parties.

Solution

In the books of Ram

Journal

Date	Particulars		L.F.	Debit	Credit
2012				Rs.	Rs.
Jan. 1	Bills Receivable A/c	Dr.		1,000	
	To Rahim A/c				1,000
	(Bill drawn on Rahim for 3 months for own accommodation.)				
"	Bank A/c	Dr.		970	
	Discount A/c	Dr.		30	
	To Bills Receivable A/c				1,000
	(Bill discounted by the bank @ 12% p.a.)				
April 4	Rahim A/c	Dr.		1,010	
	To Bank A/c				
	(Bill dishonoured at maturity, noting charges being Rs. 10)				1,010

In the books of Rahim

Journal

Date	Particulars		L.F.	Debit	Credit
1998				Rs.	Rs.
Jan. 1	Ram A/c	Dr.		1,000	
	To Bills Payable A/c				1,000
	(Bills accepted for 3 months for Ram's accommodation)				
April 4	Bills Payable A/c	Dr.		1,000	
	Nothing Charges A/c	Dr.		10	1,010
	To Ram A/c				
	(Bill dishonoured at maturity)				

There are two types of accommodation :

(2) When there is only one bill, proceeds being shared by the parties :

Under the circumstances, one party draws a bill on other who accepts it and returns to the former. The drawer discounts the bill and remits half (or as specified) the proceeds to the former. Just before the due date, he (drawer) remits the other half to the latter so that the latter (drawee) can honour the bill on due date. ***It should be mentioned here that accommodation bill must be discounted by the bank; otherwise no one will get the benefit of immediate cash at the cost of certain amount of discount.***

The following entries are to be recorded in the books of the drawer and drawee :

	Transactions	In the books of Drawer		In the books of Drawee	
1.	When the bill is drawn	Bills Receivable A/c To Drawee A/c	Dr.	Drawer A/c To Bills Payable A/c	Dr.
2.	For discounting of the bill	Cash/Bank A/c Discount A/c To Bills Receivable A/c	Dr. Dr.	—	
3.	For remitting proceeds	Drawee A/c To Cash/Bank A/c " Discount A/c ($\frac{1}{2}$)	Dr.	Cash/Bank A/c Discount A/c To Drawer A/c	Dr. Dr.
4.	For remitting the balance at the date of maturity	Drawee A/c To Cash/Bank A/c	Dr.	Cash/Bank A/c To Drawer A/c	Dr.
5.	When the bill is honoured at maturity	—		Bills Payable A/c To Cash/Bank A/c	Dr.

The following illustration will make the principles clear :

Illustration 23

For mutual accommodation, A draws a bill on B for Rs. 2,000 for 2 months. B accepts the bill and returns it to A. A discounts the bill by the bank for Rs. 1,950 and remits half the proceeds to B. Before maturity, A remits the balance to B and B honours the bill.

Show the entries in the books of A and B.

Solution

In the books of A
Journal

Date	Particulars		L.F.	Debit Rs.	Credit Rs.
?	Bills Receivable A/c To B A/c (Bills accepted by B for 2 months)	Dr.		2,000	 2,000
?	Bank A/c Discount A/c To Bill Receivable A/c (Bill discounted by the bank)	Dr. Dr.		1,950 50	 2,000
?	B A/c To Bank A/c " Discount A/c (Half the proceeds remitted to B)	Dr.		1,000	 975 25
?	B A/c To Bank A/c (Remaining half remitted to B)	Dr.		1,000	 1,000

In the books of B
Journal

Date	Particulars		L.F.	Debit Rs.	Credit Rs.
?	A A/c To Bills Payable A/c (Bill accepted for 2 months)	Dr.		2,000	 2,000
?	Bank A/c Discount A/c To A A/c (Half the proceeds received from A)	Dr. Dr.		975 25	 1,000
?	Bank A/c To A A/c (Remaining half received from B on due date)	Dr.		1,000	 1,000
?	Bills Payable A/c To Bank A/c (Bill honoured at maturity)	Dr.		2,000	 2,000

(3) When there are two bills of equal amount, proceeds being taken by each other, i.e., Reciprocal drawings of bills

Under the circumstances, both parties draw bills on each other. They will also discount bills by the bank separately and will keep the proceeds himself. At maturity, each party will honour other's bill.

The following entries are to be recorded in the books of drawer and drawee :

	Transactions	In the books of Drawer		In the books of Drawee	
1.	When the bill is drawn by the drawer	Bills Receivable A/c To Drawee A/c	Dr.	Drawer A/c To Bills Payable A/c	Dr.
2.	When the bill is discounted by the drawer	Cash/Bank A/c Discount A/c To Bills Receivable A/c	Dr. Dr.	—	
3.	When the bill is drawn by the original drawee	Drawee A/c To Bills Payable A/c	Dr.	Bills Receivable A/c To Drawer A/c	Dr.
4.	When the 2nd bill is discounted	—		Cash/Bank A/c Discount A/c To Bills Receivable A/c	Dr. Dr.
5.	When the bill is honoured at maturity	Bills Payable A/c To Cash/Bank A/c	Dr.	Bills Payable A/c To Cash/Bank A/c	Dr.

The following illustration will make the above principle clear :

Case I — When the bill is honoured

Illustration 24

On 1.1.2011 X and Y draw bills on each other at 3 months for Rs. 1,000 for their mutual accommodation. They discount each other's bill at 6% p.a. and, on maturity, each party honours his own acceptance.

Show the entries in the books of both the parties.

Solution

In the books of X
Journal

Date	Particulars		L.F.	Debit	Credit
2011				Rs.	Rs.
Jan. 1	Bills Receivable A/c To Y A/c (Bills accepted by Y for 3 months)	Dr.		1,000	1,000
"	Bank A/c Discount A/c Dr. To Bills Receivable A/c (Bill discounted by the bank @ 6% p.a.)	Dr.		985 15	1,000
"	Y A/c To Bills Payable A/c (Bill accepted for 3 months)	Dr.		1,000	1,000
April 4	Bills Payable A/c To Bank A/c (Bill honoured at maturity)	Dr.		1,000	1,000

In the books of Y
Journal

Date	Particulars		L.F.	Debit	Credit
2011				Rs.	Rs.
Jan. 1	X A/c To Bills Payable A/c (Bill accepted for 3 months)	Dr.		1,000	1,000
?	Bills Receivable A/c To X A/c (Bill drawn and accepted by X for 3 months)	Dr.		1,000	1,000
?	Bank A/c Discount A/c To Bills Receivable A/c (Bill discounted by the bank @ 6% p.a.)	Dr. Dr.		985 15	1,000

Contd.

			Rs.	Rs.
2011 April 4	Bills Payable A/c To Bank A/c (Bill honoured at maturity)	Dr.	1,000	1,000

Illustration 25

X draws a bill for Rs. 1,500 and Y accepts the same for mutual accommodation of both in the ratio 2 : 1. X discounts the same for Rs. 1,410 and remits $\frac{1}{3}$rd of the proceeds to Y. Before due date, Y draws another bill for Rs. 2,100 on X in order to provide funds to meet the bill. The second bill is discounted for Rs. 2,040 by Y and a sum of Rs. 360 is remitted to X after meeting the first bill. The second bill is duly met.

Show the entries in the books of X.

Solution

In the books of X
Journal

Date	*Particulars*		*L.F.*	*Debit* Rs.	*Credit* Rs.
?	Bills Receivable A/c To Y A/c (Bill accepted by Y)	Dr.		1,500	1,500
"	Bank A/c Discount A/c To Bills Receivable A/c (Bill discounted by bank)	Dr. Dr.		1,410 90	1,500
"	Y A/c To Bank A/c " Discount A/c ($\frac{1}{3}$rd proceeds remitted to Y)	Dr.		500	470 30
	Y A/c To Bills Payable A/c (Bill accepted)	Dr.		2,100	2,100
	Bank A/c Discount A/c To Y A/c (Proceeds received from Y)	Dr. Dr.		360 40[1]	400
	Bills Payable A/c To Bank A/c (Bill honoured at maturity)	Dr.		2,100	2,100
	Cash/Bank A/c To Y A/c (Amount received from Y against final settlement)	Dr.		700[2]	700

1. **Share of Discount :**

	Rs.
After discounting of the 1st bill X received	1,000
Add : Amount remitted by Y	360
	1,360
But the benefit enjoyed by Y (Rs. 2,040 – 1,360) is	680
∴ Ratio in which discount charges are to be borne by them	= 1,360 : 680 or 2 : 1

Hence, X will share Rs. $60 \times \frac{2}{3}$ = Rs. 40.

Alternatively

		Rs.
Total discount on both the bill		150
X's share of total discount Rs. $150 \times \frac{2}{3}$	=	100
Less : Discount of the 1st bill borne by A Rs. $90 \times \frac{2}{3}$	=	60
∴ Discount to be borne on 2nd bill	=	40

2. In order to ascertain the final settlement, Y's A/c is to be prepared in the books of X in the following manner:

Y Account

Dr.	Rs.		Cr. Rs.
To Bank A/c	470	By Bills Receivable A/c	1,500
" Discount A/c	30	" Bank A/c	360
" Bills Payable A/c	2,100	" Discount A/c	40
		" Cash A/c *(bal. fig.)*	700
	2,600		2,600

Case II—When the bill is dishonoured

Illustration 26

Arun and Anand were friends and in need of funds. On 1.1.93 Arun drew a bill for Rs. 2,00,000 for 3 months on Anand. On 4.1.93 Arun got the bill discounted at 10% p.a. and remitted half of the proceeds to Anand. On the due date, Anand could not meet the bill, instead, Arun accepted Anand's bill for Rs. 1,20,000 on 4.4.93 for two months. This was discounted by Anand at 12% p.a. Out of this Rs. 19,600 was paid to Arun after deducting Rs. 400 discounting charges. Due to financial crisis, Arun became insolvent and the bill drawn on him was dishonoured and his estate paid 50%. Days of grace for discount purposes may be ignored.

Give Journal entries in the books of Arun and prepare Anand's account in Arun's books and Arun's account in the books of Anand.

Solution **[CA Foundation, Dec. 1993]**

In the books of Arun

Journal

Date	*Particulars*		*L.F.*	*Debit* Rs.	*Credit* Rs.
1993					
Jan. 1	Bills Receivable A/c	Dr.		2,00,000	
	To Arun A/c				2,00,000
	(Bill drawn for 3 months)				
Jan. 4	Bank A/c	Dr.		1,95,000	
	Discount A/c	Dr.		5,000	2,00,000
	To Bill Receivable A/c				
	(Bills discounted with the bank at 10% p.a.)				
"	Anand A/c	Dr.		1,00,000	
	To Bank A/c				97,500
	" Discount A/c				2,500
	(Half of the proceeds remitted to Anand)				
Aug. 4	Anand A/c	Dr.		1,20,000	
	To Bills Payable A/c				1,20,000
	(Acceptance of 2 months' bill drawn by Anand)				
"	Bank A/c	Dr.		19,600	
	Discount on Bills A/c	Dr.		400	
	To Anand A/c				20,000
	(Proceeds received from Anand)				
June 7	Bills Payable A/c	Dr.		1,20,000	
	To Anand A/c				1,20,000
	(Bill dishonoured at maturity)				
"	Anand A/c	Dr.		1,20,000	
	To Bank A/c				60,000
	" Deficiency A/c				60,000
	(50% of amount due to Anand paid and balance transferred to deficiency account)				

In the books of Arun

Anand Account

Dr. *Date*	*Particulars*	*Amount*	*Date*	*Particulars*	Cr. *Amount*
1993		Rs.	1993		Rs.
Jan. 4	To Bank A/c	97,500	Jan. 1	By Bills Receivable A/c	2,00,000
	" Discount on Bills A/c	2,500		" Bank A/c	19,600
Apr. 4	" Bills Payable A/c	1,20,000	Apr. 4	" Discount on Bills A/c	400
	" Bank A/c	60,000	June 7	" Bills Payable A/c	1,20,000
	" Deficiency A/c	60,000			
		3,40,000			3,40,000

In the books of Anand

Arun Account

Dr. Cr.

Date	Particulars	Amount	Date	Particulars	Amount
1993		Rs.	1993		Rs.
Jan. 1	To Bills Payable A/c	2,00,000	Jan. 1	By Bank A/c	97,500
	" Bank A/c	19,600		" Discount on Bills A/c	2,500
April 4	" Discount on Bills A/c	400	April 1	" Bills Receivable A/c	1,20,000
June 7	" Bank A/c	1,20,000		" Bank A/c	60,000
				" Bad Debts A/c	60,000
		3,40,000			3,40,000

Illustration 27

Subham draws on Rajendra a bill for Rs. 45,000 on 1st Jan. 1998 for 3 months. Rajendra accepts the bill and sends it to Subham who gets it discounted for Rs. 44,100. Subham immediately remits Rs. 14,200 to Rajendara. On the due date Subham, being unable to remit the amount due, accepted a bill for Rs. 63,000 for 3 months which is discounted by Rajendra for Rs. 61,650. Rajendra sends Rs. 11,100 to Subham. On the due date Shubham becomes insolvent, his estate paying forty paise in the rupee.

Give Journal Entries in the books of Subham and Rajendra.

[CA Foundation, May 1999]

Solution

In the books of Arun

Journal

Date	Particulars		L.F.	Debit	Credit
1998				Rs.	Rs.
Jan. 1	Bills Receivable A/c	Dr.		45,000	
	To Rajendra A/c				45,000
	(Bill drawn for 3 months for mutual accommodation)				
"	Bank A/c	Dr.		44,100	
	Discount A/c	Dr.		900	
	To Bills Receivable A/c				45,000
	(Bill discounted for Rs. 44,100)				
"	Rajendra A/c	Dr.		15,000	
	To Bank A/c				14,200
	" Discount A/c				800
	(One-third of proceeds remitted to Rajendra)				
Sept. 4	Rajendra A/c	Dr.		63,000	
	To Bills Payable A/c				63,000
	(Acceptance given to Rajendra, for 3 months)				
"	Bank A/c	Dr.		11,100	
	Discount A/c	Dr.		900[1]	
	To Rajendra A/c				12,000
	(Amount received from Rajendra)				
Dec. 7	Bills Payable A/c	Dr.		63,000	
	To Rajendra A/c				63,000
	(Bills Dishonourd as Rajendra became insolvent)				
"	Rajendra A/c	Dr.		42,000	
	To Bank A/c				16,800
	" Deficiency A/c				25,200
	(Amount paid (40%) and balance credited to deficiency Account)				

In the books of Rajendra

Journal

Date	Particulars		L.F.	Debit	Credit
1998				Rs.	Rs.
Jan. 1	Subham A/c	Dr.		45,000	
	To Bills Payable A/c				45,000
	(Acceptance given for 3 months)				

Contd.

Date	Particulars			Rs.	Rs.
"	Bank A/c	Dr.		14,700	
	Discount A/c	Dr.		300	
	To Subham				15,000
	(One-third of the proceeds of bill received after discounting)				
Sept. 4	Bills Receivable A/c	Dr.		63,000	
	To Shubham A/c				63,000
	(Bills drawn for 3 months)				
"	Bank A/c	Dr.		61,650	
	Discount A/c	Dr.		1,350	
	To Bills Receivable A/c				63,000
	(Bills discounted by bank for Rs. 61,650))				
"	Bills Payable A/c	Dr.		45,000	
	To Bank A/c				45,000
	(Own acceptance due on this date met)				
"	Sudham A/c	Dr.		12,000	
	To Bank A/c	Dr.			11,100
	" Discount A/c				900[1]
	(Amount remitted to Shubham, after discounting)				
Dec. 7	Sudham A/c	Dr.		63,000	
	To Bank Account	Dr.			63,000
	(Shubham acceptance dishonoured as he became insolvent)				
"	Bank A/c	Dr.		16,800	
	Bad Debts A/c	Dr.		25,200	
	To Subham A/c				42,000
	(Amount realised @ 40 paise in the rupee from his estate)				

[1] **Share of Discount**

	Rs.
After discounting of the 1st bill X received	30,000
Add: Amount remitted by Rajendra	11,100
	41,100

But the benefit enjoyed by Rajendra
(61,650 − 41,100) = Rs. 20,550
i.e., Rs. 41,100 : Rs. 20,550
Or, 2 : 1.

Hence, Subham will bear = Rs. 1,350 × $\frac{2}{3}$ = Rs. 900

Illustration 28

For mutual accommodation of themselves, Samaresh and Animesh draw bills on each order. On 2.1.2012. Samaresh draws a bill on Animesh for Rs. 2,000 payable three months and on 3.1.2012, Animesh draws a bill on Samaresh for Rs. 1,000 payable at three months. As arranged, both the bills are immediately discounted at 5% p.a. and the proceeds are shared equally. On maturity of the first bill Animesh becomes insolvent and is unable to honour the bill. A dividend of 50 paise in the rupee is realised from his estate on 30th June 2012. Show the relevant accounts in the books of Samaresh who closes his books on 30th June 2012.

Solution

In the books of Samaresh

Animesh Account

Dr. Date	Particulars	Amount	Date	Particulars		Cr. Amount
2012		Rs.	2012			Rs.
Jan. 1	To Cash A/c	987.50	Jan. 2	By Bills Receivable A/c		2,000.00
	" Discount A/c	12.50		" Cash A/c		493.75
3	" Bills Payable A/c	1,000.00		" Discount A/c	Rs.	6.25
April 5	" Cash A/c	2,000.00	June 30	" Cash A/c	750.00	
	(B/R dishonoured)			" Bad Debts A/c	750.00	
						1,500.00
		4,000.00				4,000.00

Bills Receivable Account

Dr. Date	Particulars	Amount	Date	Particulars	Cr. Amount
2012		Rs.	2012		Rs.
Jan. 2	To Animesh A/c	2,000	Jan. 2	By Cash A/c	1,975
				" Discount A/c	25
		2,000			2,000

Dr. **Bills Payable Account** Cr.

Date	Particulars	Amount	Date	Particulars	Amount
2012		Rs.	2012		Rs.
April 6	To Cash A/c	1,000	Jan. 3	By Animesh A/c	1,000
		1,000			1,000

Dr. **Cash Account (Extracts)** Cr.

Date	Particulars	Amount	Date	Particulars	Amount
2012		Rs.	2012		Rs.
Jan. 1	To Bills Receivable A/c	1,975.00	Jan. 2	By Animesh A/c	987.50
3	" Animesh A/c	493.75	April 5	" Animesh A/c	2,000.00
June 30	" Animesh A/c	750.00	April 5	" Bills Payable A/c	1,000.00

Dr. **Discount Account** Cr.

Date	Particulars	Amount	Date	Particulars	Amount
2012		Rs.	2012		Rs.
Jan. 2	To B/R A/c	25.00	Jan. 2	By Animesh A/c	12.50
3	" Animesh A/c	6.25	June 30	" Profit and Loss A/c *(bal. fig.)*	18.75
		31.25			31.25

Illustration 29

X drew on 1.1.2012, and Y accepted, a bill for three months for Rs. 5,000. On 4.1.2012, X discounted the bill @ 6% p.a. and remitted half the proceeds to Y. On 1.2.2012, Y drew and X accepted a bill for three months for Rs. 2,000. On 4.2.2012, Y discounted the bill @ 6% p.a. and remitted half the proceeds to X. X and Y agreed to share discounts equally. At maturity, X met his acceptance, but Y failed to meet his and recourse was had to X. X drew and Y accepted a new bill at 3 months for the amount of original bill plus interest at 5% p.a. On 1.7.2012, Y became bankrupt. A first and final dividend of 50 paise in the rupee was paid on 31st October. Y obtained discharge on 5.12.2012 and agreed to pay X the unsatisfied balance of his account, this was paid on 19th Jan. 2013. Write-up Y's account in X's books and state how would you advise X to treat the balance in accounts when preparing his Balance Sheet on 31.12.2012. Make calculations in months.

Solution **[CU BCom (Hons.)]**

In the books of X

Dr. **Y Account** Cr.

Date	Particulars	Amount	Date	Particulars		Amount
2012		Rs.	2012			Rs.
Jan. 4	**To Bank A/c (half proceeds)**	2,462.50	Jan. 1	By Bills Receivable A/c		5,000.00
	" **Discount A/c (half share of disc.)**	37.50	Feb. 4	" Bank (half proc.) A/c		985.00
			"	" Discount A/c (half share of discount)		15.00
			Apr. 4	" Bills Receivable A/c		5,062.50
Feb. 1	" **Bills Payable A/c**	2,000.00	Oct. 31	" Bank (Div.) A/c	1,781.25	
April 4	" **Bank A/c (Bills dishonoured)**	5,000.00	"	" Bad Debts A/c	1,781.25	3,562.50
	" **Interest A/c** $\left(\text{Rs. } 5{,}000 \times \frac{5}{10} \times \frac{3}{12}\right)$	62.50				
July 1	" **Bills Receivable A/c**	5,062.50				
		14,625.00				14,625.00

Note : [**The unsatisfied amount on 31st Oct. 2012 is to be written-off as bad debts after having received the amount of final dividend. It will have no impact at the time of preparing the final accounts although Y has agreed to pay which is actually not enforceable in the eye of law. Therefore, the same will simply be written-back when it will actually be received.**]

Illustration 30

Rita, for mutual accommodation of, 2 : 1 with Mita, draws on the latter of Rs. 9,000 and Rs. 6,000 for 3 months and 4 months respectively on 5th March 1993. Both the bills were discounted with the bank on 8th March 1993 @ 12% p.a. interest. On due date of the first bill Rita endorsed Sita's acceptance of Rs. 6,200 to Mita in settlement of her share. This bill was discounted by Mita at a charge of Rs. 60. On due date of the second bill Mita wanted appropriate share from Rita but the latter was not in a position to give any fund. To settle the problem Rita issued a promissory note for 3 months in favour of Mita for the amount due plus interest at 15% p.a. Mita discounted it immediately for Rs. 3,920. This promissory note was dishonoured on the due date at a noting charge of Rs. 40. On the same day Mita collected from Rita Rs. 1,850 in cash of which Rs. 60 is towards interest and drew a new bill at two months for Rs. 2,400. However, on the due date of this bill, Rita became insolvent. On the 10th February 1994 Mita received a first dividend of 20% from the estate of Rita and 10 the March 1994 a second and final dividend of 50% from the estate of Rita through official receiver.

Show Mita's Account and Rita's Account in the books of Rita and Mita, respectively.

Solution **[CU BCom. (Hons.)1993]**

In the books of Rita

Dr. Mita Account Cr.

Date		Particulars	Amount	Date		Particulars	Amount
1993			Rs.	1993			Rs.
Mar. 8	To	Bank A/c (2,910 + 1,920)	4,830	Mar. 5	By	Bill Receivable A/c	9,000
	"	Discount on Bill A/c (90 + 80)	170		"	Bill Receivable A/c	6,000
June 8	"	Bill Receivable A/c (endorsement)	6,200	June 8	"	Discount A/c	200
July 8	"	Bills Payable A/c	4,000	Oct. 11	"	Bills Payable A/c	4,000
Oct. 11	"	Bills Payable A/c	2,400		"	Noting Charges A/c	40
"	"	Cash A/c	1,690		"	Interest A/c	50
Dec. 31	"	Balance c/d	2,400	Dec. 14	"	Bills Payable A/c	2,400
			21,690				21,690
1994				1994			
Feb. 10	To	Bank A/c (First dividend @ 20% of Rs. 2,400)	480	Jan. 1	By	Balance b/d	2,400
Mar. 10	"	Bank A/c (Final dividend @ 50% of Rs. 2,400)	1,200				
	"	Deficiency A/c (30% of 2,400)	720				
			2,400				2,400

In the books of Mita

Dr. Rita Account Cr.

Date		Particulars	Amount	Date		Particulars	Amount
1993			Rs.	1993			Rs.
Mar. 5	To	Bills Receivable A/c	15,000	Mar. 8	By	Bank A/c	4,830
June 8	"	Discount A/c (Note 2)	200	June 8	"	Discount on Bill A/c (Note 1)	170
Oct. 11.	"	Bank A/c (4,000 + 40)	4,040	July 7	"	Bills Receivable A/c	6,200
	"	Interest A/c (Note 3)	50		"	Bills Receivable A/c	4,000
Dec. 14	"	Bills Receivable A/c	2,400	Oct. 11	"	Cash A/c	1,690
					"	Bills Receivable A/c	2,400
					"	Balance c/d	2,400
1994			21,690	1994			21,690
Jan. 1	To	Balance b/d	2,400	Feb. 10	By	Bank A/c	480
					"	Bank A/c	1,200
				Mar. 10	"	Bad Debts A/c	720
			2,400				2,400

Workings :

1. Remittance by Rita to Mita on 8.3.1993

	1st Bill (Rs.)		2nd Bill (Rs.)		Total (Rs.)
Bill Value	9,000		6,000		15,000
Less : Discount @ 12%	270	$(9{,}000 \times \frac{12}{100} \times \frac{3}{12})$	240	$(6{,}000 \times \frac{12}{100} \times \frac{4}{12})$	510
Net Proceeds	8,730		5,760		14,490
Remittance : $\frac{1}{3}$ of Rs. 8,730 =	2,910	($\frac{1}{3}$ of Rs. 5,,760)	1,920		4,380
Discount : $\frac{1}{3}$ of Rs. 270 =	90	($\frac{1}{3}$ of Rs. 240)	80		170

2. Discount on Endorsement on 8.6.1993

$\frac{2}{3}$ of Rs. 9,000 = Rs. 6,000 to be sent by Rita to Mita

But Sita's acceptance which was endorsed was Rs. 6,200

∴ Amount of Discount

(Rs. 6,200 – Rs. 6,000) = Rs. 200.

3. Interest on 11.10.1993

Interest = **Amount due from Rita – Amount Paid by Rita**

Amount due from Rita		**Amount Paid by Rita**	
Promissory Note	4,000	Amount Paid	1,690
Add : Noting	40	*Add* : New Acceptance	2,400
	4,040		4,090

∴ Net Adjustment for Interest = Rs. 4,090 – Rs. 4,040 = Rs. 50

Accommodation-Cum-Renewal

Illustration 31

On 1st January 1994 Vinod drew and Pramod accepted a bill at three months for Rs. 2,000. On 4th January 1994 Vinod discounted the bill at his bank at 15% p.a. and remitted half the proceeds to Pramod. On 1st February 1994 Pramod drew and Vinod accepted a bill at four months for Rs. 1,500. On 4th February 1994 Pramod discounted the bill at 15% p.a. with his bank and remitted half the proceeds to Vinod. They both agreed to share the discount equally.

At maturity Vinod met his acceptance, but Promod dishonoured his and Vinod had to pay the bill. Vinod drew and Pramod accepted a new bill at three months for the original bill plus interest at 18% p.a. On 1st July 1994 Pramod became insolvent and only 50 paise in the rupee was received from him.

Record the above transactions in Vinod's Journal.

Solution **[CA Foundation, Nov. 1994]**

In the books of Vinod
Journal

Date	*Particulars*		*L.F.*	*Debit* Rs.	*Credit* Rs.
1994					
Jan. 1	Bills Receivable A/c	Dr.		2,000	
	To Pramod A/c				2,000
	(Bill drawn on Pramod accepted)				
4	Bank A/c	Dr.		1,925	
	Discount on Bill A/c	Dr.		75	
	To Bill Receivable A/c				2,000
	(Bill discounted with the bank at 15%)				
4	Pramod A/c	Dr.		1,000	
	To Bank A/c				962.50
	" Discount on Bills A/c				37.50
	(Half of proceeds remitted to Pramod)				
Feb. 1	Pramod A/c	Dr.		1,500	
	To Bills Payable A/c				1,500
	(Acceptance of bill drawn by Pramod)				

Contd.

Date	Particulars		Rs.	Rs.
4	Bank A/c	Dr.	712.50	
	Discount on Bills A/c	Dr.	37.50	
	To Pramod A/c			750
	(Half of the proceeds received)			
Apr. 4	Pramod A/c	Dr.	2,000	
	To Bank A/c			2,000
	(Bill dishonoured at maturity)			
4	Pramod A/c	Dr.	90	
	To Interest A/c			90
	(Interest receivable on Rs. 2,000 @ 18% for 3 months)			
4	Bill Receivable A/c	Dr.	2.090	
	To Pramod A/c			2,090
	(Fresh bill drawn on Pramod accepted)			
June 4	Bills Payable A/c	Dr.	1,500	
	To Bank A/c			1,500
	(Bill honoured on maturity)			
July 1	Promod A/c	Dr.	2,090	
	To Bills Receivable A/c			2,090
	(Bill accepted by Pramod dishonoured as he became insolvent)			
1	Bank A/c	Dr.	920	
	Bad Debts A/c	Dr.	920	
	To Pramod A/c			1,840
	(Amount received from his estate @ 50 paise and balance transferred to Bad Debts A/c)			

Dr. **Promod Account** Cr.

Date		Particulars	Amount	Date		Particulars		Amount
?			Rs.	?				Rs.
	To	Bank A/c	962.50		By	Bills Receivable A/c		2,000.00
	"	Discount on Bills A/c	37.50		"	Bank A/c		712.50
	"	Bills Payable A/c	1,500.00		"	Discount on Bills A/c		37.50
	"	Bank A/c	2,000.00		"	Bills Receivable A/c		2,090.00
	"	Interest A/c	90.00		"	Bank A/c		
	"	Bills Receivable A/c	2,090.00			(50% of amount due)	920.00	
					"	Bad Debts A/c	920.00	
								1,840.00
			6,680.00					6,680.00

(4) For the accommodation of more than two Parties —Receiprocal drawings of bill

Under the circumstances, each party draws more than one bill to other and all the bills will be discounted by the respective parties. Cousequntly, the total net proceeds (i.e., after deducting discounting charges) are shared among the parties in agreed ratio, so also the total amount of discounting charges. Naturally, just before the due date, each party will remit his share to other in order to honour the bill.

Illustration 32

X, Y, and Z drew and accepted bills for their mutual accommodation as:

X drew a bill on Y for Rs. 5,000

Y drew a bill on Z for Rs. 10,000

Z drew a bill on Y for Rs. 15,000

All the bills were discounted by the bank @ 10% and proceeds are shared equally.

Show the entries in the books of X, Y & Z assuming that all the bills were duly honoured by the respective parties.

Solution

The total amount of the bills were Rs. 30,000 (i.e., Rs. 5,000 + Rs. 10,000 + Rs. 15,000)

The total amount of discount @ 10% Rs. 3,000 (i.e., Rs. 30,000 $\times \frac{10}{100}$)

∴ Each party's share (Net) = Rs. 10,000 (i.e., Rs. 30,000 × $\frac{1}{3}$) – Rs. 1,000 (i.e., Rs. 3,000 × $\frac{1}{3}$)

= Rs. 9,000.

But each party must to pay Rs. 10,000.

After discounting of the bill X got Rs. 4,500, so he must get Rs. 4,500 from Z just to make his share equal.

Similarly, Y got Rs. 9,000, i.e., the exact amount of his share, Z got Rs. 13,500 after discounting and when Z remitted Rs. 4,500 to X, his shares became Rs. 9,000 which is nothing but equal to others.

Thus, before the date of maturity of the bill, X had to honour a bill for Rs. 15,000 for which he would get Rs. 5,000 from Y as he (Y) had to honour a bill for Rs. 5,000 but he took Rs. 10,000. As such, excess Rs. 5,000 he had to remit to X. But Y had the exact amount in order to honour the bill.

In the books of X

Journal

Date	Particulars		L.F.	Debit Rs.	Credit Rs.
?	Bills Receivable A/c	Dr.		5,000	
	To Y A/c				5,000
	(Bill drawn on Y for mutual accommodation)				
	Z A/c	Dr.		15,000	
	To Bills Payable A/c				15,000
	(Bill accepted for mutual accommodation)				
	Bank A/c	Dr.		4,500	
	Discount A/c	Dr.		500	
	To Bills Receivable A/c				5,000
	(Bill discounted by bank @ 10%)				
	Bank A/c	Dr.		4,500	
	Discount A/c Dr.			500	
	To Z A/c				5,000
	(Amount received from Z to make his share equal)				
	Bank A/c	Dr.		5,000	
	To Y A/c				5,000
	(Amount received from Z to honour the bill)				
	Y A/c	Dr.		10,000	
	To Z A/c				10,000
	(Adjustment made for settlement)				
	Bills Payable A/c	Dr.		15,000	
	To Bank A/c				15,000
	(Bill honoured at maturity)				

In the books of Y

Journal

Date	Particulars		L.F.	Debit Rs.	Credit Rs.
?	X A/c	Dr.		5,000	
	To Bills Payable A/c				5,000
	(Bill accepted for mutual accommodation)				
	Bills Receivable A/c	Dr.		10,000	
	To Z A/c				10,000
	(Bill drawn for mutual accommodation)				
	Bank A/c	Dr.		9,000	
	Discount A/c	Dr.		1,000	
	To Bills Receivable A/c				10,000
	(Bill discounted by the bank @ 10%)				
	X A/c	Dr.		5,000	
	To Bank A/c				5,000
	(Amount remitted to X)				

Contd.

	Particulars		L.F.	Debit	Credit
				Rs.	Rs.
	Z A/c	Dr.		10,000	
	To X A/c				10,000
	(Adjustment made for settlement)				
	Bills Payable A/c	Dr.		5,000	
	To Bank A/c				5,000
	(Bill honoured at maturity)				

In the books of Z
Journal

Date	Particulars		L.F.	Debit	Credit
?				Rs.	Rs.
	Y A/c	Dr.		10,000	
	To Bills Payable A/c				10,000
	(Bill accepted for mutual accommodation)				
	Bills Receivable A/c	Dr.		15,000	
	To X A/c				15,000
	(Bill drawn on X for mutual accommodation)				
	Bank A/c	Dr.		13,500	
	Discount A/c	Dr.		1,500	
	To Bills Receivable A/c				15,000
	(Bill discounted by bank)				
	X A/c	Dr.		5,000	
	To Bank A/c				4,500
	" Discount A/c				500
	(Amount remitted to X to make his share equal)				
	X A/c	Dr.		10,000	
	To Y A/c				10,000
	(Adjustment made for settlement)				
	Bills Payable A/c	Dr.		10,000	
	To Bank A/c				10,000
	(Bills honoured at maturity)				

Illustration 33

R considered the debt of S as irrecoverable and wrote-off that debt of Rs. 1,200 as bad on 2.3.2012. On 30.6.2012, S paid cash Rs. 1,000 to R in full settlement of the account and on the date further goods were sold to S invoiced at Rs. 3,120. S paid by a cheque of Rs. 1,000 and accepted a bill of exchange for the balance of Rs. 2,120 at 2 months. R discounted the bill at the bank for Rs. 2,040. The bill at maturity was returned to R as dishonoured, noting charge being Rs. 5. Next day S accepted a fresh bill at one month and paid cash for the noting charge and interest at 6%. A day before due date, S paid cash Rs. 640 and accepted another bill for the balance sum at 3 months. After a month, thereafter, S, having become insolvent paid a compensation of 50 p. in the rupee.

Show the entries in the books of R. **[BU BCom (Hons.)]**

Solution

In the books of R
Journal

Date	Particulars		L.F.	Debit	Credit
2012				Rs.	Rs.
March 2	Bad Debts A/c	Dr.		1,200.00	
	To S A/c				1,200.00
	(Amount due to S written-off as bad.)				
June 30	Bank A/c	Dr.		1,000.00	
	To Bad Debts Recovery A/c				1,000.00
	(Amount recovered from S written-off as bad.)				
"	S A/c	Dr.		3,120.00	
	To Sales A/c				3,120.00
	(Goods sold to S.)				

Contd.

			Rs.	Rs.
June 30	Bank A/c	Dr.	1,000.00	
	Bills Receivable A/c	Dr.	2,120.00	
	To S A/c			3,120.00
	(Cash and bill received from S)			
"	Bank A/c	Dr.	2,040.00	
	Discount A/c Dr.		80.00	
	To Bills Receivable A/c			2,120.00
	(Bill discounted by the bank)			
Sept. 3	S A/c	Dr.	2,125.00	
	To Bank A/c			2,125.00
	(Bill dishonoured by S, noting charge being Rs. 5)			
Sept. 4	S A/c	Dr.	10.60	
	To Interest A/c			10.60
	(Interest receivable from S on Rs. 2,120 @ 6% for 1 month)			
"	Bank A/c	Dr.	15.60	
	To S A/c			15.60
	(Cash received from, S for interest and noting charges)			
"	Bills Receivable A/c	Dr.	2,120.00	
	To S A/c			2,120.00
	(Fresh bill drawn and accepted by S)			
Oct. 7	S A/c	Dr.	2,120.00	
	To Bills Receivable A/c			2,120.00
	(Bill dishonoured on maturity)			
"	Bank A/c	Dr.	640.00	
	To S A/c			640.00
	(Cash received from S as part payment)			
"	Bills Receivable A/c	Dr.	1,480.00	
	To S A/c			1,480.00
	(Fresh bill drawn and accepted by S)			
Nov. 7	S A/c	Dr.	1,480.00	
	To Bills Receivable A/c			1,480.00
	(Bill dishonoured as S became insolvent)			
"	Bank A/c	Dr.	740.00	
	Bad Debts A/c	Dr.	740.00	
	To S A/c			1,480.00
	(Cash received from S @ 50 in the rupee and the balance proved bad)			

Illustration 34

K accepted on 1.4.2012 a bill for Rs. 10,000 drawn by his creditor, C, at three months. C immediately discounted the bill with his banker at 7% p.a. K failed to meet the bill in due time and at his request C renewed it for a further period of three months by adding 12% p.a. interest to the amount on K's furnishing security. K endorsed two of his customer's bill for Rs. 7,000 and Rs. 5,400 due on 20.8.2012 and 10.9.2012, respectively. C discounted all the three bills at 7% p.a. with the bankers, but on the due date the second customer's bill was dishonoured. On due date, K became bankrupt and only 20 paise in the rupee was realised from his estate.

Show the entries in the books of C. **[CA Adapted]**

Solution

In the books of C

Journal

Date	*Particulars*		*L.F.*	*Debit*	*Credit*
2012				Rs.	Rs.
April 1	Bills Receivable A/c	Dr.		10,000	
	To K A/c				10,000
	(Bill drawn and accepted by K for 3 months)				

Contd.

			Rs.	Rs.
April 1	Bank A/c	Dr.	9,825	
	Discount A/c Dr.		175	
	To Bills Receivable A/c			10,000
	(Bill discounted at 7% p.a. by the bank)			
July 4	K A/c	Dr.	10,000	
	To Bank A/c			10,000
	(Bill dishonoured by K at maturity)			
	K A/c	Dr.	300	
	To Interest A/c			300
	(Interest receivable from K on Rs. 10,000 @ 12% p.a. for 3 months)			
	Bills Receivable A/c	Dr.	22,700	
	To K A/c			22,700
	(First bill for Rs. 10,300 drawn and accepted by K and other two bills for Rs. 12,400 received as security)			
	Bank A/c	Dr.	22,386	
	Discount A/c Dr.		314*	
	To Bills Receivable A/c			22,700
	(Three bills discounted by the bank @ 7% p.a.)			
Sept. 10	K A/c	Dr.	5,400	
	To Bank A/c			5,400
	(Bill for Rs. 5,400 received as security dishonoured)			
Oct. 7	K A/c	Dr.	10,300	
	To Bank A/c			10,300
	(Bill dishonoured as K has become insolvent)			
Oct. 7	Bank A/c	Dr.	660	
	Bad Debts A/c	Dr.	2,640	
	To K A/c			3,300
	(Account realised from the official liquidation @ 20 paise in the rupee and the balance written-off as bad)			

* Calculation of discount to be charged by bank :

	Rs.
On Rs. 10,300 @ 7% for 3 months, from July 4 = Rs. 10,300 $\times \frac{7}{100} \times \frac{3}{12} =$	180.25
On Rs. 7,000 @ 7% for 47 days, from July 4 to Aug. 20 = Rs. 7,000 $\times \frac{7}{100} \times \frac{47}{365} =$	63.10
On Rs. 5,400 @ 7% for 68 days, from July 4 to Sept. 10 = Rs. 5,400 $\times \frac{7}{100} \times \frac{68}{365}$	70.42
	313.77 or Rs. 314.00

Illustration 35

On 1st January 2012 X owes Y Rs. 10,000 for which Y draws on X two bills for Rs. 4,000 and Rs. 6,000 payable after 3 months and 4 months, respectively. Both the bills were drawn on 1st January 2012. Y discounts both the bills with his bankers on 3rd January, at 12% p.a. Before the due date of the 1st bill, X requests Y to assist him by providing with Rs. 4,000 cash and drawing a 3rd bill on him (X) for the amount plus interest @ 12% p.a. for 3 months. Y agrees to this proposal and pays the money after discounting the third bill with his banker @ 12% p.a. A week before the 2nd bill for Rs. 6,000 falls due, X again asks Y to assist him by providing Rs. 5,000. Y, however, is not in a position to pay any cash but he arranges with X to draw on him (Y) two bills for Rs. 2,000 and Rs. 3,000 at 2 months and 3 months, respectively, from the due date of the 2nd bill (Rs. 6,000). Y accepts these two bills and X discounts them with his bankers at 12% p.a. and, assisted by the proceeds, duly meets the 2nd bill on the due date. Y fails to meet his own acceptances. On 10th June 2012 X becomes bankrupt, before meeting his third bill. On 1st September 2012, a first and final dividend of 50 paise in a rupee is received from X's estate.

Pass Journal entries and the accounts of X in the books of Y.

[CA Adapted]

Solution

In the books of Y
Journal

Date	Particulars		L.F.	Debit	Credit
2012				Rs.	Rs.
Jan. 1	Bills Receivable A/c	Dr.		10,000[1]	
	To X A/c				10,000
	(Bills drawn on X for Rs. 4,000 and 6,000 payable after 3 months and 4 months, respectively)				
Jan. 3	Bank A/c	Dr.		9,640	
	Discount A/c[1]	Dr.		360	
	To Bills Receivable A/c				10,000
	(Bills discounted with the banker @ 12% p.a.)				
April 3	X A/c	Dr.		4,000	
	To Cash A/c				4,000
	(Cash paid to X)				
	X A/c	Dr.		120	
"	To Interest A/c [2]				120
	(Interest on Rs. 4,000 @ 12% p.a. for 3 months debited to X)				
	Bills Receivable A/c	Dr.		4,120	
"	To X A/c				4,120
	(A new bill drawn on X for Rs. 4,000 plus interest, payable after 3 months)				
	Bank A/c	Dr.		3,996	
"	Discount A/c	Dr.		124	
	To Bills Receivable A/c				4,120
	(Bill discounted with the banker @ 12% p.a.)				
May 4	X A/c	Dr.		5,000	
	To Bills Payable A/c				5,000
	(Bills accepted for financing X for Rs. 2,000 and 3,000 payable after 2 and 3 months, respectively)				
July 6	X A/c	Dr.		4,120	
	To Bank A/c				4,120
	(Dishonour of 3rd bill)				
July 7	Bills Payable A/c	Dr.		2,000	
	To X A/c				2,000
	(Dishonour of our acceptance given to X)				
Aug. 7	Bills Payable A/c	Dr.		3,000	
	To X A/c				3,000
	(Dishonour of our acceptance at maturity)				
Sept. 1	Bank A/c	Dr.		2,060	
	Bad Debts A/c	Dr.		2,060	
	To X A/c				4,120
	(50 paise in a rupee received from the estate of X as final dividend)				

1. Two separate entries can also be passed.

X Account

Dr. Cr.

Date		Particulars	Rs.	Date		Particulars		Rs.
2012				2012				
Jan. 1	To	Balance b/d	10,000	Jan. 1	By	Bills Receivable A/c		10,000
Apr. 3	"	Cash A/c	4,000	Apr. 3	"	Bills Receivable A/c		4,120
Apr. 3	"	Interest A/c	120	July 7	"	Bills Payable A/c		2,000
May 4	"	Bills Payable A/c	5,000	Aug. 7	"	Bills Payable A/c		3,000
July 6	"	Bank A/c	4,120	Sep. 1	"	Bank A/c	2,060	
				" 1	"	Bad Debts A/c	2,060	4,120
			23,240					23,240

Workings :

1. *Calculation of Discount*

				Rs.
1st bill	=	Rs. 4,000 × $\frac{12}{100}$ × $\frac{3}{12}$	=	120
2nd bill	=	Rs. 6,000 × $\frac{12}{100}$ × $\frac{4}{12}$	=	240
				360
3rd bill	=	Rs. 4,120 × $\frac{12}{100}$ × $\frac{3}{12}$	=	124

2. *Calculation of Interest*

Interest = Rs. 4,000 × $\frac{12}{100}$ × $\frac{3}{12}$ = 120

Illustration 36

On 1.9.2012 Honest Dealers purchased goods valued at Rs.72,000 from Best Manufactures. They sold them to Nice Consumers for Rs. 1,00,000, and agreed to accept two bills of exchange of equal value payable on 1.3.2012, for the invoice amount plus interest at 10% p.a. Honest Dealers could only sell one of the bills on 30.9.2012 at a discount of 6% p.a. The bill was, however, endorsed to the suppliers, Best Manufactures, who agreed to take the bill on 30th Sept. 2012 at a discount 12% p.a. together with a cheque for the balance. Show, by journal entries, how all these transactions should be recorded in the books of Honest Dealers. State also how the bills will appear in the Balance Sheet as at 31.12.2012 indicating clearly any note that should appear here.

Solution **[CU BCom (Hons.)]**

In the books of Honest Dealers
Journal

Date		*Particulars*		*L.F.*	*Debit*	*Credit*
2012					Rs.	Rs.
Sept.	1	Purchases A/c	Dr.		72,000	
		To Best Manufactures A/c				72,000
		(Goods purchased on credit)				
"		Nice Consumers A/c	Dr.		1,00,000	
		To Sales A/c				1,00,000
		(Goods sold on credit)				
"		Nice Consumers A/c	Dr.		5,000	
		To Interest A/c				5,000
		(Interest receivable from Nice Consumers on Rs. 1,00,000 @ 10% for 6 months)				
"		Bills Receivable A/c	Dr.		1,05,000	
		To Nice Consumers A/c				1,05,000
		(Bill drawn which was accepted by Nice Consumers including interest)				
Sept.	30	Bank A/c	Dr.		51,187.50	
		Discount A/c	Dr.		1,312.50	
		To Bills Receivable A/c				52,500
		(One of the bills was discounted by the bank @ 6% p.a. for 5 months (i.e., for 30.9.76 to 1.3.77)				
"		Best Manufacturers A/c	Dr.		72,000	
		Discount A/c	Dr.		2,625	
		To Bills Receivable A/c				52,500
		" Bank A/c				22,125
		(Settlement is made with Best Manufacturers by endorsing the bill at a discount of 12% and the balance paid by a cheque)				

[*Note* : There is a contingent liability for bills discounted to the extent of Rs. 1,05,000 which will be shown as a footnote in the Balance Sheet of Honest Traders]

Illustration 37

Journalise each of the following bill transactions in the books of Tridib :

(a) Rao's acceptance for Rs. 8,600 which was endorsed over by Tridib to Naik in full settlement of Rs. 9,000 was dishonoured. Naik paid noting charge of Rs. 50.

(b) Tridib's acceptance to Dexit for Rs. 7,500 was fully discharged by Mehata's acceptance to Tridib for Rs. 7,000.

(c) Goel's acceptance for Rs. 8,000 which was discounted by Tridib for Rs. 7,950 was dishonoured. The noting charge incurred by the banker amounted to Rs. 50.

(d) Tridib's acceptance to Joshi for Rs. 6,000 was renewed by a cash payment of Rs. 2,450 and acceptance of a new bill for the balance, plus interest of Rs. 50.

Solution

In the books of Tridib
Journal

Date	*Particulars*		*L.F.*	*Debit*	*Credit*
?				Rs.	Rs.
(a)	Rao A/c	Dr.		8,650	
	Discount A/c	Dr.		400	
	To Naik A/c				9,050
	(Bill received from Rao for Rs. 8,600 endorsed to Naik for the full settlement of Rs. 9,000 was dishonored, noting charge being Rs. 50)				
(b)	Bills Payable A/c	Dr.		7,500	
	To Bills Receivable A/c				7,000
	" Discount A/c				500
	(Acceptance to Dexit for Rs. 7,500 was discharged by Mehata's acceptance for Rs. 7,000)				
(c)	Goel A/c	Dr.		8,050	
	To Bank A/c				8,050
	(Bill dishonoured, noting charge being Rs. 50)				
(d)	Bills Payable A/c	Dr.		6,000	
	To Joshi A/c				6,000
	(Bill dishonoured at maturity)				
	Interest A/c	Dr.		50	
	To Joshi A/c				50
	(Interest payable to Joshi for dishonour)				
	Joshi A/c	Dr.		6,050	
	To Cash A/c				2,450
	" Bills Payabale A/c				3,600
	(Cash paid to Joshi and a fresh bill accepted for the balance)				

Average Due Date-Cum--Bills of Exchange

Illustration 38

For Sales made to X from time to time, Y had drawn upon him trade bills payable as:

				Rs.
Date	14 the May	Due	22nd July	6,000
"	15th June	"	2nd Aug.	5,000
"	15th June	"	30th Aug.	7,000
"	17th June	"	10th Sept.	6,000

On 2nd July, as mutually agreed, he draws upon X two bills of exchange of equal sums payable on the average due date. 15 days before the date of payment X desired to retire one of the bills at 6% p.a. and extended the date of another by 30 days at the same rate of interest. It was agreed to, subject to the condition that the discount payable on retirement would be adjusted against the interest on three extended bills. The arrangement having been carried through, Y endorsed the second bill to Z, one of his creditors, in full discharge of his liability for Rs. 12,000. The bill was dishonoured on due date and on October 30, X's estate finally realised 50 paise in the rupee.

You are required to work out the average due date and show the working of X's A/c, Bills Receivable A/c and Z's A/c as would appear in the books of Y. (Interest may be calculated on the basis of 30 days for a month.)

[CA]

Solution

Calculation of Average Due Date
22nd July is taken as '0' date

Due date		No. of days from '0' date	Amount	Product
			Rs.	Rs.
July	22	0	6,000	0
Aug.	2	11	5,000	55,000
Aug.	30	39	7,000	2,73,000
Sept.	10	50	6,000	3,00,000
			24,000	6,28,000

Average number of days = $\frac{\text{Rs. } 6,28,000}{\text{Rs. } 24,000}$ = 26 days Average Due Date = July 22 + 26 days = Aug. 17.

In the books of Y
X Account

Dr. Cr.

Date			Particulars	Amount	Date			Particulars	Amount
?				Rs.					Rs.
		To	Sales A/c	24,000	May	14	By	Bills Receivable A/c	6,000
July	2	"	Bills Receivable A/c —replacement of old bill	24,000	June	15	"	Bills Receivable A/c	5,000
					June	15	"	Bills Receivable A/c	7,000
Aug.	17	"	Bills Receivable A/c —renewal of bills	12,000	June	17	"	Bills Receivable A/c	6,000
		"	Interest A/c 30 days	60	July	2	"	Bills Receivable A/c —2 bills of Rs. 12,000 each	24,000
Sep.	16	"	Z A/c —dishonour of bills	12,030	Aug.	2	"	Interest A/c — Rebate for 15 days	30
						17	"	Bills Receivable A/c	12,030
					Oct.	30	"	Cash A/c 6,015	
					"	"	"	Bad Debts A/c 6,015	12,030
				72,090					72,090

Bills Receivable Account

Dr. Cr.

Date			Particulars	Amount	Date			Particulars	Amount
June	14	To	X A/c	6,000	July	2	By	Y A/c — Replacement of bills	24,000
	15	"	X A/c	5,000					
	15	"	X A/c	7,000	Aug.	2	"	Cash A/c	12,000
	17	"	X A/c	6,000		17	"	X A/c —Replacement of bill	12,000
July	2	"	X A/c	24,000					
Aug.	17	"	X A/c	12,030	"	17	"	Z A/c	12,030
				60,030					60,030

Z Account

Dr. Cr.

Date			Particulars	Amount	Date			Particulars	Amount
Aug.	17	To	Bills Receivable A/c	12,030	?		By	Balance b/d	12,000[1]
Sep.	16	"	Bank A/c [2]	12,030	Aug.	17	"	Interest A/c	30
					Sept.	16	"	X A/c	12,030
				24,060					24,060

Notes : 1. Since the problem indicates that Z is a creditor of Rs. 12,000, it is nothing but an opening balance.

2. It is assumed that Y made the payment of outstanding balance. But if it is assumed that the payment is not made, the account will show a balance of Rs. 12,030.

Accommodation with three parties

Illustration 39

A, B and C, by mutual accommodation, drew the following bills for three months :

A drew on B for Rs. 15,000 and on C Rs. 12,000.

B drew on A for Rs. 18,000 and on C Rs. 30,000.

C drew on A for Rs. 24,000 and on B Rs. 12,000.

All the bills were discounted at 10 per cent on the bills and were shared equally. On due date, C became insolvent and only 40% of the amount due could be realised from his estate.

Show entries in the books of A and C assuming that A and B had sent the money due and paid their obligations.

Solution **[CA —Adapted]**

In the books of A

Journal

Date	Particulars		L.F.	Debit	Credit
				Rs.	Rs.
?	Bills Receivable A/c	Dr.		27,000	
	To B A/c				15,000
	" C A/c				12,000
	(Acceptances received from B and C)				
	B A/c	Dr.		18,000	
	C A/c	Dr.		24,000	
	To Bills Payable A/c				42,000
	(Acceptance issued in favour of B and C)				
	B A/c	Dr.		18,000	
	To C A/c				18,000
	(Net amount of acceptances exchanged between B and C)				
	Bank A/c	Dr.		26,325	
	Discount A/c	Dr.		675	
	To Bills Receivable A/c				27,000
	(Acceptances from B and C discounted at 10%)				
	Bank A/c	Dr.		9,750	
	Discount A/c	Dr.		250	
	To B A/c				10,000
	(Amount received from B to share proceeds equally)				
	C A/c	Dr.		1,000	
	To B A/c				1,000
	(Amount paid to C equally)				
	Bills Payable A/c	Dr.		42,000	
	To Bank A/c				42,000
	(Own acceptances met on due date)				
	C A/c	Dr.		42,000	
	To Bank A/c				12,000
	" B A/c				30,000
	(C's acceptances dishonoured)				
	Bank A/c	Dr.		14,800	
	B A/c	Dr.		11,100	
	Bad Debts A/c	Dr.		11,100	
	To C A/c				37,000
	(40% of the amount due from C received in cash; half the loss on account of C's insolvency to be borne by B, balance written-off as bad debt)				
	B A/c	Dr.		8,900	
	To Bank A/c				8,900
	(Amount paid to B in settlement of his account)				

Workings :

	Total	A	B	C
	Rs.	Rs.	Rs.	Rs.
Total bills received	1,11,000	27,000	48,000	36,000
Less : Discount @ 10% p.a.	2,775	675	1,200	900
	1,08,225	26,325	46,800	35,100
Share of A 36,075		+ 9,750		
Share of B 36,075			– 10,725	
Share of C 36,075				+ 975
Adjustment required in cash to equalise the proceeds of each		36,075	36,075	36,075
Discount to be debited or credited to equalise discount charges		+ 250	– 250	+ 25

In the books of C
Journal

Date	*Particulars*		*L.F.*	*Debit*	*Credit*
?				Rs.	Rs.
	Bills Receivable A/c	Dr.		36,000	
	To A A/c				24,000
	" B A/c				12,000
	(Acceptances received from A and C)				
	A A/c	Dr.		12,000	
	B A/c	Dr.		30,000	
	To Bills Payable A/c				42,000
	(Acceptances issued in favour of A and B)				
	B A/c	Dr.		3,000	
	To A A/c				3,000
	(Net amount of acceptances exchanged between A and B)				
	Bank A/c	Dr.		35,100	
	Discount A/c	Dr.		900	
	To Bills Receivable A/c				36,000
	(Acceptances from A and B discounted at 10 per cent)				
	Bank A/c	Dr.		975	
	Discount A/c	Dr.		25	
	To B A/c				1,000
	(Amount received from B to make proceeds equal)				
	A A/c	Dr.		10,000	
	To B A/c				10,000
	(Amount paid by B to A to make proceeds equal)				
	Bills Payable A/c	Dr.		42,000	
	To A A/c				12,000
	" B A/c				30,000
	(Dishonour of acceptance)				
	A A/c	Dr.		17,000	
	B A/c	Dr.		20,000	
	To Cash A/c				14,800
	" Deficiency A/c				22,200
	(Payment to A and B @ 40% in full settlement)				

ASSIGNMENT MATERIALS

THEORETICAL

Fill in the Blanks

1.(a) A bill of exchange is an .... in writing containing an .... order signed by the market.

(b) Different parties in a bill of exchange are .... , ...and ....

(c) There are two kinds of acceptance ....

(d) Th person who makes the promissory note is called the....................

(e) Accommodation bill is also known as ....

(f) If there is an 'After date bill' the date of maturity is to be counted from the date of .... of the bill.

(g) If there is an 'After Sight' bill, the date of maturity is to be counted from the date of .... of the bill.

(h) 'Bill after date' is same as ....

(i) Endorsement comes from the Latin word ....

(j) Dishonour is of two types viz. (i) .... (ii) ....

[Ans. (a) Instrument, unconditional; (b) Drawer, Drawee, Payee; (c) General Acceptance and Qualified Acceptance; (d) Maker; (e) Kite Bill; (f) Drawing; (g) Acceptance; (h) Time instrument; (i) Endorsement; (j) Non-acceptance and non-payment]

Multiple Choice Questions

2. (a) A bill is drawn on 1.1.2005 for 3 months, its maturity date will be

(i) 4.4.2005; (ii) 1.4.2005; (iii) 4.3.2005.

(b) A bill is drawn on 12.7.2005 for 1 month, its maturity date will be

(i) 14.8.2005; (ii) 16.8.2005; (iii) 15.8.2005.

(c) A bill is drawn on 1.1.2005 for 3 months 'after date' which was accepted by the drawer on 4.1.2005, its maturity date will be

(i) 4.4.2005; (ii) 7.4.2005; (iii) 1.4.2005.

(d) A bill is drawn on 7.4.2005 for 3 months, after sight' when it was accepted by the drawer on 8.4.2005; its maturity date will be

(i) 10.7.2005; (ii) 11.7.2005; (iii) 1.7.2005.

(e) A bill is drawn on 23.11.2005 for 2 months, its date of maturity will be

(i) 26.1.2005; (ii) 25.1.2005; (iii) 1.1.2005.

[Ans. (a) (i); (b) (i); (c) (i); (d) (ii); (e) (ii)]

Short Answer-Type Questions

3. Define Bill of Exchange. Discuss the essential elements of a Bill of Exchange.
4. Define the following:
   Holder, Holder in Due Course, Promissory Note. Accommodation of Bills.
5. What is 'Noting' and 'Protest'? Discuss the differences between a Promissory Note and a Bill of Exchange.
6. What is a Cheque? Distinguish between a Bill of Exchange and a Cheque.
7. What is a Discounting of Bill?
8. Define the following:
   Endorsement of Bill, Retirement of Bill, Renewal of Bill, Documentary Bill.
9. Distinguish between:
   (i) Bill of Exchange and Promissory Note;
   (ii) Discounting of Bills and Retirement of Bill;
   (iii) A Trade Bill and an Accommodation Bill;

(iv) An IOU and a Promissory Note;

(v) Retiring of Bill and Renewal of Bill;

10. Discuss the different parties in a Bill of Exchange;
11. What are the essential elements of Bill of Exchange;
12. What is 'Days of Grace'? How do you calculate it? Explain it with the help of example;
13. Discuss the essential features of cheque;
14. What are 'Bill Receivable Book' and 'Bills Payable Book'?
15. What do you understand by endorsement of bills? What are the different types of endorsement of a bill?
16. What is the consequence of dishonour of bill?
17. Who draws the Bill of Exchange?
18. Who makes a Promissory Note?
19. Who is the payee of Bill of Exchange and a Promissory Note?
20. Who bears the noting charges?

Long Answer-Type Questions

21. Distinguish between Bills of Exchange and Promissory Note.
22. Distinguish between Bills of Exchange and a Cheque.
23. Explain the essential features of a Bills of Exchange.
24. What is date of maturity? How do you calculate it?
25. What are Contingent Liabilities for Bill Discounted? Explain its effect on a bill transaction.
26. (a) What is Dishonour of Bill? When such a situation happens?

    (b) What is Subsequent Endorsement of a bill?
27. What is the effect in the books of the drawer when the drawee becomes insolvent?
28. What is Renewal of Bill? Explain the role of Drawer and drawee under such a situation.
29. What is a 'Kite' Bill? When is such a bill drawn ? What are its advantages?

PRACTICAL

(a) Dishonour of Bills

1. On 1.9.2012, X received from Y three bills of exchange for Rs. 700, Rs. 600 and Rs. 500 for 3 months, 2 months, and 1 month, respectively.

On 1.10.2012, the first bill was endorsed in favour of creditor, K. On the same date, the second bill was discounted through Bank at 5% and the last bill was retained until the due dates. On due dates, all the bills were dishonoured. Show the entries that would appear in the books of X.

2. Y owed money to S and hence accepted two bills each of Rs. 4,850 of three months' duration drawn on him by the latter on July 1, 2011. S endorsed one of the bills in favour of H on July 7, 2011. On the same date he discounted the other bill with his bank and received net proceeds of Rs. 4,675.

Y failed to meet both the bills on the due date. On 4th Oct. 2011, the bank debited the account of S with value of the second bill plus their charges of Rs. 20.

Y is adjudicated insolvent and his estate paid 60 paise in the rupee on 1st Nov. 2011.

Show the entries in the books of both Y and S.

3. Rahim owed Ram Rs. 70,000 for which he accepted a bill drawn on him by Ram payable after 3 months from 1-1-2011.

On the 4th Jan. the bill was discounted by the drawer with his bank for 95% value.

The bill was not met on the due date and the bank, therefore, debited the same to the drawer's account with Rs. 10 incidental charges and Rs. 40 overdue interest, on the 10th April.

The drawee settled the bill value together with cost on 11th April.

Pass Journal entries in the books of Rahim and Ram for the above transactions.

[CA Entrance]

4. Amarnath drew on Parker a bill of exchange for Rs. 1,00,000 on 1st Jan. 2012 payable after 3 months from 1st Jan. 2012, which Parker accepted. On 4th Jan. 2012 Amarnath discounted the bill with his bankers at 18% p.a. Parker failed to meet the bill on due date and the bill was returned to Amarnath

with bank charges Rs. 200 debited to him by the bank. Amarnath claimed the bill value plus bank charges from Parker. However, only 40% of the amount claimed could be recovered by Amarnath on 8th April 2012 as Parker was declared insolvent.

Pass Journal entries in the books of Amarnath and Parker for the above transactions.

[CA Entrance]

5. On 1.1.2012, K. sold goods to S valuing Rs. 6,000. On 4.1.2012 K received from S Rs. 2,000 and drew a bill payable 3 months after date for the balance. On the same date K endorsed the accepted bill to A for full settlement of a debt of Rs. 4,000. On due date, the bill was dishonoured and S having become insolvent met on 5th May 2011, 60% of his acceptance.

Give Journal entries in the books of K & S.

[Hints: Bad Debts Rs. 1600]

(b) Renewal of Bills

6. On 1st March 2012 X buys goods from Y valued Rs. 90,000. Instead of paying cash, she agrees to give Y a bill of exchange at four months, the amount of the bill to include interest at 6% p.a. On the due date X is able to find only Rs. 73,000 in cash and she arranges with Y for the retirement of the bill in consideration of this payment and a fresh bill for the balance plus Rs. 25 as interest. Give Journal entries and prepare Y's Account in the books of X.

7 On November 1, 2012 Richard draws a three months' bill of exchange for Rs. 60,000 on his debtor, Richardson, who accepts it on the same date. On 4th November 2012 Richard discounted the bill at his bank at 4% p.a. The bill, however, was dishonoured on maturity, the noting charges incurred Rs. 100. Richardson immediately makes an offer to Richard to pay him Rs. 20,100 in cash on account and to settle the balance agreeing to accept one bill of exchange for Rs. 24,000 at one month and the other for the balance at three months, the latter including interest @ 6% p.a. for both the bills.

Richard agreed to the proposal. The bill for Rs. 24,000 was duly met at maturity but the other bill was dishonoured on maturity. Show the Ledger Accounts in the books of Richard.

8. Q drew a bill of exchange on P for Rs. 4,000 on 1st May 2011 for three months. P returned the bill to Q after accepting it. Q discounted the bill at his bank for Rs. 3,900. Just before the due date P approached Q for renewal of the bill. Q agreed on condition that Rs. 1,000 plus interest on the balance at 6% p.a. for 3 months be paid in cash immediately and a new bill for 3 months be drawn for the remaining balance. These conditions were carried through. On 7th November 2011 P became insolvent and his estate paid 40 paise in a rupee in full settlement. Give Journal Entries in the books of P and Q.

[Hint: Interest Rs. 45; Bad Debts Rs. 1,800]

9. Patel received from one of his customers a bill at three months for Rs. 16,000. He discounted it on the same day at 10% p.a. with his bankers. On the date of maturity the bill was dishonoured and the Bank incurred noting charges of Rs. 80. However, the customer paid him Rs. 2,000 plus noting charges plus interest for three months amounting to Rs. 420 in Cash and accepted a fresh bill at three months for Rs. 14,000, being the balance amount due from him. Patel gave the second bill to Naren, one of his creditors. The second bill was duly honoured on due date. Record these transactions in the Journal of Patel.

10. On 1.1.2012 R supplied goods to P to the value of Rs. 9,000 and settled the account by means of three bills of exchange for Rs. 3,000 each, due, respectively, after two, three and four months. A week later R discounted the first bill with his banker at a discount of Rs. 60, he held the other bills.

The first two bills were paid at maturity. On the date of maturity of the third bill, P arranged to renew the bill paying Rs. 1,000 in cash and giving R a fresh bill for four months to cover the balance with interest @ 6% p.a. R discounted the bill for Rs. 1,920 and the bill was paid on maturity. Show the entries in the books of both the parties.

11. On 2nd January 2011 Tarun sold goods for Rs. 5,600 to Tapan on credit subject to a trade discount @ 10%. On 30th January, Tarun drew on Tapan a bill for the net amount due one month *after date.* Tapan accepted the bill on 2nd February and returned the same to Tarun. On 3rd February, Tarun discounted the bill @ 6% p.a. On the due date the bill was returned dishonoured with noting charge of Rs. 15. On 13th March, as per subsequent agreement, Tarun drew on Tapan a bill for Rs. 5,100 (including interest) for 2 months *after sight.* Tapan accepted the bill on 16th March and returned the same to Tarun. The bill was met on the due date (19th May 2011 was Sunday).

Show Journal Entries in the books of Tarun.

12. Ramaratan sold goods to Ahmed for Rs. 10,000 on 30th June 2011, for which the latter accepted 4 bills of Rs. 2,500 each drawn on him payable after 2, 4, 6, 8 months, respectively. Ramaratan retained the first bill. The second bill was sent by him for collection. The third bill was endorsed by him. The fourth bill was discounted by him with his bankers at a discount of 15% p.a.

The first bill was met on the due date. As regards the second bill, Ahmed met Ramaratan two days before the maturity date of the bill and paid him Rs. 1,000 and accepted a fresh bill for 30 days for the balance with interest of 18% p.a. This bill as well as the third bill were met by the drawer.

Ahmed was declared insolvent on 31st Dec. 2011 and, on the fourth bill becoming due, the Bank debited Ramaratan with his amount of the bill and charges of Rs. 250. It is ascertained by Ramaratan that the estate of Ahmed will not be in a position to meet the liabilities to an extent of more than 40%.

What will be the entries to be made in the books of Ramaratan to record the above transactions? Show these with narrations.

13. On 1.1.2012, P draws a 3 months' Bill of Exchange for Rs. 30,000 on his Debtor, Q, who accepts it on the same date and discounts the bill on 4.1.2012 with his bankers, the discount rate being 6% p.a.

On the due date, the bill is dishonoured, the noting charges being Rs. 200. Q immediately makes an offer to P to pay him Rs. 10,000 cash on account and to settle the balance by agreeing to accept one Bill of Exchange for Rs. 12,000 at one month and the other for the balance at three months, the latter including interest at 12% p.a. for both the bills. P accepts the arrangement. The bill for Rs. 12,000 is met on the due date but the other bill is dishonoured. Show Q's account and Bills Receivable Account in the books of P.

[ICWA]

14 On 1st January 2012, P draws a three months' bill of exchange for Rs. 30,000 on his Debtor, Q, who accepts it on the same date. P discounts the bill on 4th January 2012 with his bankers, the discount rate being 6% p.a.

On the due date, the bill is dishonoured, the noting charges being Rs. 200. Q immediately makes an offer to P to pay him Rs. 10,000 cash on account and to settle the balance by agreeing to accept one bill of exchange for Rs. 12,000 at one month and the other for the balance at three months', the latter including interest at 12% p.a. for both the bills.

P accepts the arrangement. The bill for Rs. 12,000 is met on the due date, but the other bill is dishonoured.

Show Q's Account and Bills Receivable Account in the books of P. [ICWA]

Accommodation Bills

15. Mitra, for the mutual and temporary accommodation of himself and Ghosh, draws upon the latter a bill of exchange at 3 months', for Rs. 6,000 dated 1.1.92. Mitra discounts the bill immediately at his banker, the rate of discount being 5% and hands half the proceeds to Ghosh.

Ghosh, for a similar puprose and at the same time, draws a bill at 3 months' on Mitra for Rs. 3,000. This he discounts at his banker at 5% and hands half the proceeds to Mitra. Ghosh becomes bankrupt on 31st March 1982, and a first and final dividend of 25 P. in the rupee is paid on his estate on 30.6.1992.

Write-up Ghosh's Account in Mitra's book. Assume, in each case, that one-half of the charge for discounting the bill is chargeable to Ghosh and one-half to Mitra.

16. For their mutual accommodation A accepted, on 1st March 2011, a bill drawn by B for Rs. 4,000 at three months'. This bill was discounted less Rs. 60 for discount and the proceeds were shared equally.

On the same day and for the same purpose A received an acceptance from B for Rs. 6,000 for three months'. This bill was discounted less Rs. 90 for discount and the proceeds were shared as two-thirds to A and one-third to B.

On 1st June 2011, A sent a cheque to B in full settlement of his account, but at maturity B became insolvent. His estate paid a dividend of 60 P. in the rupee on August 10, 2011.

Give Journal entries in the books of A and B.

17. For their mutual accommodation K. Kamat accepted, on 1.3.2012, a bill drawn on him by R. Ratnam for Rs. 4,000 for three months. This bill was discounted for Rs. 60 discount and the moiety was sent by Ratnam to Kamat.

On the same day, and for the same purpose, Kamat received an acceptance from Ratnam for Rs. 6,000 for three months. This bill was discounted for Rs. 90 discount and proceeds were shared as two-thirds to Kamat and one-third to Ratnam.

Before the due date, Kamat sent a cheque to Ratnam in full settlement of his account, but at maturity Ratnam became insolvent and his estate paid a dividend of 50 paise in the rupee.

Give the Journal entries in the books of K. Kamat and R. Ratnam. [CA]

18. Journalise the following in the books of Mr. Sen:

(i) Mr. Sen's acceptance to Mr. Ghosh for Rs. 2,000 discharged by cash payment of Rs. 1,000 and an acceptance of a new bill for the balance plus interest of Rs. 10.

(ii) Mr. Roy's acceptance for Rs. 4,000, which was endorsed over by Mr. Sen to Mr. Dutt, was dishonoured. Noting charges paid by Mr. Dutt was Rs. 20.

(iii) Mr. Sen endorsed over Rajib's acceptance to him in settlement of a Bill payable by him for Rs. 1,500 to Sanjib.

(iv) Mr. Sen retired before the due date his acceptance to D. Das for Rs. 600, rebate allowed being Rs. 10.

19. Enter the following transactions in the Bills Receivable Book of H. Bhagwan:

2011: Feb.	1	Drew on Gopikishan at 30 days' sight; Rs. 10,000 against sales.
	2	Drew on Ramanlal at 45 days' sight; Rs. 15,750 against sales.
		Drew on Gopikishan at 30 days' sight; Rs. 14,200 against sales.
	3	Drew on Ramanlal at 45 days' sight; Rs. 16,000 against sales.

On the 4th February all the above bills were discounted by Bhagwan with his Bank, the discount rates being :

(a) Rs. 15 per thousand in the case of 30 days' bills, and

(b) Rs. 22·50 per thousand in the case of 45 days' bills.

Fractions of thousand are treated as thousand for discount rate purposes.

Show also the entries in the books of Bhagwan in :

(i) The Bills Receivable A/c ; (ii) Gopikishan A/c, and (iii) Ramanlal A/c.

CHAPTER 17

AVERAGE DUE DATE AND ACCOUNT CURRENT

Learning Objectives

AVERAGE DUE DATE

Meaning

Types of Problem

1. *Where amount is lent in* ***various*** *instalments but repayment is made in* ***one instalment*** *only.*
2. *Where amount is lent in* ***one instalment*** *but repayment is made on* ***various instalments***

Date of Maturity and its calculation

Reciprocal Bills

Calculation of Interest

Method of calculation of Interest

ACCOUNT CURRENT

Meaning

Methods of Preparation

1. *Forward Method or Ordinary Method*
2. *Product Method*
3. *Backward/Époque Method*
4. *Red Ink Interest Method*

Where the rates of Interest are different

When sum of the product on the debit or credit side or both sides are in '—'

—When sum of the product on the credit side is '—'

—When sum of the production on the debit side is '—'

—When sum of the product on both sides is '—'.

AVERAGE DUE DATE

Meaning

Average Due date is the mean or equated date on which a single payment of an aggregate sum may be made in lieu of several payments due on different dates without, however, involving either party to suffer any loss of interest, i.e, the date on which the settlement takes place between the parties is known as Average or Mean Due Date.

This is particularly helpful in the settlement of the following types of accounts, viz.,:

(i) in case of accounts which are to be settled by a series of bills due on different dates ; (ii) in case of calculation of interest on drawings of partners; (iii) in case of piecemeal distribution of assets during partnership dissolution etc.; and (iv) in the case of settlement of accounts between a principal and an agent.

Types of Problems

Two types of problems may arise. They are :

(1) Where amount is lent in **various** instalments but repayment is made in **one** instalment only;

(2) Where amount is lent in **one** instalment but repayment is made in **various** instalments.

Method (1) : **Where amount is lent in various instalments but repayment is made in one instalment :**

Step 1. *Take up the starting date (preferably the earliest due date as '0' date or 'base date' or 'starting date');*

Step 2. *Calculate the number of days from '0' date to each of the remaining due dates;*

Step 3. *Multiply each amount by the respective number of days so calculated in order to get the product;*

Step 4. *Add up the total products separately;*

Step 5. *Divide the total products by the total amounts of the bills;*

Step 6. *Add up the number of days so calculated with '0' date in order to find out the Average or Mean Due Date.*

Date of Maturity and Calculations

If there is an *after date bill*, the period is to be counted from the *date of drawing the bill* but when there is any *after sight bill*, the said period is to be counted from the *date of acceptance of the bill*. For example, if a bill is drawn on 28th January 1996, and is made payble at one month after date, the due date will be 3rd day after 28th Feb. i.e., 2nd March 1996.

To Sum up

(i) ***When the period of the bill is stated in days, the date of maturity will also be calculated in terms of days i.e., excluding the date of transaction but including the date of payment.***

E.g. ***If a bill is drawn on 18th January 2012 for 60 days, the maturity will be 21st March 2012.***

(ii) ***If the period of the bill is stated in month, the date of maturity will also be calculated in terms of month neglecting, however, the number of days in a month.***

E.g. ***If a bill is drawn on 20th May, 2012 for 3 months, of date of maturity will, naturally, be 23rd August, 2012.***

(iii) ***What the date of maturity of a bill falls on 'emergent holiday' declared by the Government, the date of maturity will be the next working day.***

(iv) ***When the date of maturity of a bill falls on a public holiday, the bill shall become due on the next preceding business day and if the next preceding day again falls on a public holiday, it will become due on the day preceding the previous day—Sec. 25.***

E.g. ***If the date of maturity of a bill falls on 15th August (Independence day) it falls due on 14th August. But if 14th August falls again on a public holiday, the 13th August will be considered as the date of maturity.***

Illustration 1

Calculate Average Due date from the following information:

Date of the Bill		Term	Amount
August 10,	1994	3 months	6,000
October 23,	1994	60 days	5,000
December 4,	1994	2 months	4,000
January 14,	1994	60 days	2,000
March 8,	1994	2 months	3,000

[CA Foundation, Nov. 1995, Nov. 1997]

Solution

Computation of Average Due Date — '0' Date = 13.11.1994

Date of the Bill	Due Date	No. of days from '0' date	Amount Rs.	Product Rs.
10. 8. 1994	13.11.1994	0	6,000	0
23.10.1994	25.12.1994	42 (17 + 25)	5,000	2,10,000
4.12.1994	7. 2.1995	86 (17 + 31 + 31 + 7)	4,000	3,44,000
14.1.1995	18.3.1995	125 (17 + 31 + 31 + 28 + 18)	2,000	2,50,000
8.3.1995	11.5.1995	179 (17 + 31 + 31 + 28 + 31 + 30 + 11)	3,000	5,37,000
			20,000	13,41,000

$\therefore$ Average Number of Days $= \frac{\text{Rs. } 13,41,000}{\text{Rs. } 20,000} = .67$ days (approx)

So, Average Due Date will be = 13th Nov. 1994 + 67 days = 19.1.1995.

Working

Due date to be Calculated as under

Date of the Bill	Periods	Due Date (after adding 3 days for grace)
10. 8. 1994	3 months	13.11.1994
23.10.1994	60 days	25.12.1994 (8 + 30 + 22 + 3)
4.12.1994	2 months	7.2.1995
14.1.1995	60 days	18.3.1995 (17 + 28 + 15 + 3)
8.3.1995	2 months	11.5.1995

Illustration 2

Sardar sold goods to Teri as under:

Date of Invoice	Value of Goods Sold Rs.	Date of Invoice	Value of Goods Sold Rs.
7.5.2009	1,000	24.5.2009	1,500
15.5.2009	2,000	1.6.2009	4,000
18.5.2009	3,500	7.6.2009	3,000

The payments were agreed to be made by bill payable 2 months (60 days) from the date of invoice. However, Teri wanted to make all the payments on a single date.

Calculate the date on which such a payment could be made without loss of interest to either party.

Solution

Calculation of Average Due Date — '0' Date = 16.7.2009

Date of Invoice	Due Date	No. of days from '0' Date	Amount Rs.	Product Rs.
7.5.2009	6.7.2009		1,000	0
15.5.2009	14.7.2009	8	2,000	16,000
18.5.2009	17.7.2009	11	3,500	38,500
24.5.2009	23.7.2009	17	1,500	25,500
1.6 .2009	31.7.2009	25	4,000	1,00,000
7.6.2009	6.8.2009	31	3,000	93,000
			15,000	2,73,000

$$\text{Average Number of Days} = \frac{\text{Rs. } 2,73,000}{\text{Rs. } 15,000} = 18 \text{ days (approx.)}$$

∴ Average Due Date will be = 18 days from '0' date i.e., 16th July + 18 days = 3rd August 2009

Workings

Due dates to be Calculated as under

Date of Invoice	Period in Days	Due Date			May + June + July + Aug.	
7.5.2009	60	6.7.2009	(From 7.5.2009 + 60 days)	=	24 + 30 + 6 =	60 days
15.5.2009	60	14.7.2009	(From 15.5.2009 + 60 days)	=	16 + 30 + 14 =	60 days
18.5.2009	60	17.7.2009	(From 18.5.2009 + 60 days)	=	13 + 30 + 17 =	60 days
24.5.2009	60	23.7.2009	(From 24..5.2009 + 60 days)	=	7 + 30 + 23 =	60 days
1.6.2009	60	31.7.2009	(From 1.6..2009 + 60 days)	=	— 29 + 31 =	60 days
7.6.2009	60	6.8.2009	(From 7.6..2009 + 60 days)	=	— 23 + 31 + 6 =	60 days

Illustration 3

Ramkumar having accepted the following bills drawn by his creditor Prakash Chand, due on different dates, approached his creditor to cancel them all and allow him to accept a single bill for the payment of his entire liability on the average due date.

You are requested to ascertain the total amount of the bill and its due date.

Bill No.	*Date of Drawing*	*Date of Acceptance*	*Amount of the Bill* Rs.	*Tenure*	
(i)	16.2.2011	20.2.2011	8,000	90 days	after sight
(ii)	6.3.2011	6.3.2011	6,000	2 months	after sight
(iii)	24.5.2011	31.5.2011	2,000	4 months	after sight
(iv)	1.6.2011	1.6.2011	9,000	1 month	after sight

[ICWA —Adapted]

Solution

'0' Date = 9.5.2011

Computation of Average Due Date

Date of Drawing	Due Date	No. of days from '0' Date	Amount Rs.	Product Rs.
16.2.2011	24.5.2011	15	8,000	1,20,000
6.3.2011	9.5.2011	0	6,000	'0'
24.5.2011	3.9.2011	117 (22 + 30 + 31 + 31 + 3)	2,000	2,34,000
1.6..2011	4.7.2011	56 (22 + 30 + 4)	9,000	5,04,000
			25,000	8,58,000

$$\text{Average Number of Days} = \frac{\text{Rs. } 8,58,000}{\text{Rs. } 25,000} = 34 \text{ days (approx)}$$

∴ Average due date will be = 9th May + 34 days = 12th June.

Total amount of the bill = Rs. 25,000

Workings

Since all the bill are *'After Sight'* the period is to be computed from the *date of acceptance* of the bill.

Due Date to be Calculated as under

Date of Acceptance	Periods	Due Date (with days of grace)		Feb + March + April + May	
20.2.2011	90 days	24.5.2011	(From 20.2.2011+ 90 days) =	8 + 31 + 30 + 21 =	90 days
6.3.2011	2 months	9.5.2011			
31.5.2011	4 months	3.9.2011			
1.6.20ɪ1	1 month	4.7.2011			

Illustration 4

For goods sold, Nair draws the following bills on Ray who accepts the same as per terms :

Amount of the Bill Rs.	*Date of Drawing*	*Date of Acceptance*	*Tenure*
8,000	6.1.2011	9.1.2011	3 months after date
9,000	15.2.2011	18.2.2011	60 days after date
8,000	21.2.2011	21.2.2011	2 months
15,000	14.3.2011	17.3.2011	30 days after sight

On 18th March 2011 it is agreed that the above bills will be withdrawn and the acceptor will pay the whole amount in one lump-sum by a cheque 15 days ahead of average due date and for this a rebate of Rs. 1,000 will be allowed. Calculate the average due date, the amount and the due date of the cheque.

Solution

Computation of Averge Due Date **'0' Date = 9.4.2011**

Date of Drawings	*Due Date*	*No. of days from '0' date*	*Amount* Rs.	*Product* Rs.
6.1.2011	9.4.2011	0	8,000	0
15.2.2011	19.4.2011	10	9,000	90,000
21.2.2011	24.4.2011	15	8,000	1,20,000
14.3.2011	19.4.2011	10	15,000	1,50,000
			40,000	3,60,000

Average number of days = $\frac{\text{Rs. } 3,60,000}{\text{Rs. } 40,000}$ = 9 days

∴ Average Due Date = April 9 + 9 days = April 18th 2011.

Amount of cheque = Rs. 40,000 – Rs. 1,000 = Rs. 39,000

Due Date of the cheque = April 18th – 15 days = April 3, 2011

Workings

Due Dates to be Calculated as under

It must be remember that in case of **After Date** bill, date of maturity is to be calculated from the **date of drawing** of the bill but in case of **After Sight bill**, the date of maturity is to be calculated from the **date of acceptance** of the bill.

Date of Drawing	**Date of Acceptance**	**Period**	**Due Date**
6.1.2011	9.1.2011	3 months	9.4.2011
15.2.2011	18.2.2011	60 days	19.4.2011
21.2.2011	21.2.2011	2 months	24.4.2011
14.3.2011	17.3.2011	30 days	19.4.2011

Reciprocal Bills

Sometimes the two parties in a bill of exchange mutually agree to accept the reciprocal bills (i.e., each party draws and accepts, respectively). Under the circumstances, the Average Due Date Method can better be applied where there are different bills and different due dates. The method of calculation is same as above. But after calculating the respective Average Due Date (for both Bills Receivable and Bills Payable), find out the difference both in **amounts** and in **product** and average number of days may be ascertained by dividing the former by the latter. Then add up the days so calculated with the '0' date in order to find out the Average Due Date.

Consider the following illustration

Illustration 5

A.N.K. had the following bills receivable and bills payable against A.N.R.

Calculate the average due date when the payment can be made or received without any loss of interest to either party.

Notes : Holidays intervening in the period : 15 Aug., 16 Aug., 6th Sept. 2009.

Bills Receivable			Bills Payable		
Date	Amount	Tenure (Months)	Date	Amount	Tenure (Months)
	Rs.			Rs.	
1.6.2009	3,000	3	29.5.2009	2,000	2
5.6.2009	2,500	3	3.6.2009	3,000	3
9.6.2009	6,000	1	10.6.2009	6,000	2
12.6.2009	10,000	2	13.6.2009	9,000	2
20.6.2009	15,000	3	27.6.2009	13,000	1

[CA]

Solution

Calculation of Average Due Date

The date of maturity of the Bills Receivable (after adding 3 days as grace) by A.N.R. are : 4. 9. 2009; 8.9.2009; 12.7.2009; 14.8.2009 and 23.9.2009. And the date of maturity of the Bills Payable by A.N.R. are : 1.8.2009; 5.9.2009; 13.8.2009; 14.8.2009 and 30.7.2009. 12th July 2009 is taken as the '0' date.

(i) Bills Receivable against A.N.R. : **'0' Date = 12.7.2009**

Computation of Average Due Date

Due Date	No. of days from '0' date	Amount	Product
		Rs.	Rs.
(1)	(2)	(3)	(4)
	(J + A + S)	3,000	1,62,000
4.9.2009	54 (19 + 31 + 4)		
8.9.2009	58 (19 + 31 + 8)	2,500	1,45,000
12.7.2009	0	6,000	0
14.8.2009	33 (19 + 14)	10,000	3,30,000
23.9.2009	73 (19 + 31 + 23)	15,000	10,95,000
		36,500	17,32,000

(ii) Bills Payable against A.N.R. : **'0' Date = 12.7.2009**

Due Date	No. of days from '0' date	Amount	Product
1.8.2009	20 (19 + 1)	2,000	40,000
5.9.2009	55 (19 + 31 + 5)	3,000	1,65,000
13.8.2009	32 (19 + 13)	6,000	1,92,000
14.8.2009	33 (19 + 14)	9,000	2,97,000
30.7.2009	18 (18)	13,000	2,34,000
		33,000	9,28,000

Now adjustment for the Bill :

	Amount	Product
Total Bills Receivable against A.N.R.	36,500	17,32,000
Total Bills Payable against A.N.R.	33,000	9,28,000
	3,500	8,04,000

Average number of days $= \dfrac{\text{Rs. } 8,04,000}{\text{Rs. } 3,500} = 230$ days (approx.)

∴ Average due date will be = July 12,2009 + 230 days = Feb. 27, 2010.

Note : If the date of maturity of a bill falls due on a public holiday the maturity date will be just the next preceding business day, e.g., bill which matures on Aug. 15 becomes due on Aug. 14.

Calculation of Interest

The Average Due Date method of computation, practically, simplifies interest calculations. The interest may be calculated from the Average Due Date to the date of settlement of accounts instead of making separate calculation for each bill. The interest so calculated will neither affect the creditors nor the debtors, i.e., both the debtors and the creditors will not lose interest for the period.

Under the circumstances, the creditors/drawers will receive and debtors/drawees will pay the interest at the specified rate for the delayed period. This is particularly applicable while calculating interest on partners' drawing in case of partnership firms.

Method of Calculation

Step 1. At first calculate the Average Due Date in the usual way.
Step 2. Ascertain the difference between the so ascertained Average Due Date and the date of closing the books.
Step 3. Interest is calculated with the help of the following :

$$\text{Interest} = \text{Amount} \times \frac{\text{Rate of interest}}{100} \times \frac{\text{No. of months}}{12}$$

Consider the following illustration :

Illustration 6

Satyajit and Prosenjit are two partners of a firm. They have drawn the following amounts from the firm in the year ending 31st March 2012:

Satyajit		Rs.	*Prosenjit*		Rs.
2011 :	Date		2011:	Date	
	1st July	300		1st June	500
	30th Sept.	500		1st August	400
	1st Nov.	800			
2012 :	28th February	200	2012 :	1st February	400
				1st March	900

Interest at 6% is charged on all drawings.

Calculate interest chargeable under Average Due Date System. (Calculation to be made in months.) [ICWA]

Solution

(a) Calculation of Interest in case of Satyajit :

Computation of Average Due Date — **'0' Date = 1.7.2011**

Date	Date from '0' Date	No. of days from '0' date J + A + S	Amount Rs.	Product Rs.
1.7.2011	0		300	0
30.9.2011	91	(30 + 31 + 30 + 1)	500	45,500
1.11.2011	123	(30 + 31 + 30 + 31+ 1)	800	98,400
28.2.2012	242	(30 + 31 + 30 + 31 + 30 + 31 + 31 + 28)	200	48,400
			1,800	1,92,300

∴ Average number of days = $\frac{\text{Rs. 1,92,300}}{\text{Rs. 1,800}}$ = 107 days (approx.)

Average due date = July 1 + 107 days = 16th Oct. 2011.

Therefore, interest is chargeable from 16.10.2011 to 31.3.2012, i.e., $5\frac{1}{2}$ months.

$$= \text{Rs. } 1,800 \times \frac{6}{100} \times \frac{5\frac{1}{2}}{12} = \text{Rs. } 49.50$$

(b) Calculation of Interest in case of Prosenjit :

Computation of Average Due Date — **'0' Date = 1.6.2011**

Date	*No. of days from '0' date*		*Amount* Rs.	*Product* Rs.
1.6.2011	0		500	0
1.8.2011	61	(29 + 31 + 1)	400	24,400
1.2.2012	245	(29 + 31 + 31 + 30 + 31 + 30 + 31 + 31 + 1)	400	98,000
1.3.2012	273	(29 + 31 + 31 + 30 + 31 + 30 + 31 + 31 + 28 + 1)	900	2,45,700
			2,200	3,68,100

∴ Average number of days = $\frac{\text{Rs. 3,68,100}}{\text{Rs. 2,200}}$ = 167 days (approx.)

Average Due Date will be June 1 + 167 days = Nov. 16, 2011.

∴ Interest is chargeable from 16.11.2011 to 31.3.2012 = $4\frac{1}{2}$ months

Amount of interest will be = Rs. 2,200 × $\frac{6}{100} \times \frac{4\frac{1}{2}}{12}$ = Rs. 49.50.

In case of Mutual dealings between the parties

It frequently happens in real-world situation that an individual plays both the role of a debtor as well as a creditor, i.e., mutual dealings. For example. Mr. X purchases raw materials from Y and he sells finished products to him. Consequently, for settlement purpose, who owes the higher amount pays the differece to the other person together with interest for the balance.

The following steps should carefully be followed for the purpose :

Step I *Find out the Product of both receivable and payable in usual manner like ordinary average due date method.*

Step II *Find out the difference of the product.*

Step III *Find out the difference of the amounts.*

Step VI *Average Due Date = '0' date +* $\frac{\textit{Difference in Product}}{\textit{Difference in Amount}}$

Step V *For Calculation of Interest:*

$$= \textit{Balance of Amount} \times \frac{\textit{Rate of Interest}}{100} \times \frac{\textit{Settlement Date} - \textit{Average Due Date}}{\textit{365 days or 12 months}}$$

Illustration 7

Mr. Big purchased goods from Mr. Small as follows :

Rs. 4,000 to be paid on 6th January 2003

Rs. 2,000 to be paid on 3rd February 2003

Rs. 3,000 to be paid on 31st March 2003.

He also sold goods to Mr. Small as follows:

Rs. 1,500 to be paid on 10th January 2003

Rs. 2,500 to be paid on 15th February 2003

Rs. 1,000 to be paid on 21st March 2003.

Mr. Big settled the account on 21st April 2003

(a) Find out the average due date.

(b) Calculate the interest at 5% p.a. from the average due date to the date of settlement.

Solution

Calculation of Average Due Date

(a) *For Big's Purchases*

6th January 2003 is taken as the starting date or '0' date

Date of Transaction	Amount Rs.	No. of days from '0'date	Product Rs.
6.1.2003	4,000	0	0
3.2.2003	2,000	28	56,000
31.3.2003	3,000	84	2,52,000
	9,000		3,08,000

(b) *For Big's Sales*

Date of Transaction	Amount Rs.	No. of days from '0'date	Product Rs.
10.1.2003	1,500	40	6,000
15.2.2003	2,500	40	1,00,000
21.3.2003	1,000	74	74,000
	5,000		1,80,000

Now, the difference in Product is Rs. 1,28,000 (i.e., Rs. 3,08,000 – Rs. 1,80,000) and the difference in amount is Rs. 4,000 (i.e., Rs. 9,000 – Rs. 5,000).

No. of days from '0' date = $\frac{\text{Rs. 1,28,000}}{\text{Rs. 4,000}}$ = 32 days i.e., Average Due Date = 6.1.2003 + 32 days = 7.2.2003

Date if Settlement = 21.4.2003

Hence, No. of days from average due date to the date of settlement = 73 days

∴ Amount of interest will be Rs. 40 $\left(\text{i.e. Rs. } 4,000 \times \frac{73}{365} \times \frac{5}{100}\right)$

Method (2) Where amount is lent in one instalment but repayment is made by various instalments

This method is just the opposite of "Method (1) Stated above

Method of Calculation

Step 1.	*Calculate the number of days from the date of lending to the date of each repayment made.*
Step 2.	*Ascertain the sum of those days/months/years.*
Sept 3.	*Divide the sum so ascertained (in Step 2) by the number of instalments paid.*
Step 4.	*The result will be the number of days/months by which the Average Due Date falls from the date of taking such loans.*
	The same will be calculated with the help of the following:
	Average Due Date :

$$= \text{Date of taking loan} + \frac{\text{Sum of days/months/years from the date of lending to date of repayment of each instalment}}{\text{No. of instalments}}$$

Consider the following illustration :

Illustration 8

When repayment of loan is made by monthly instalments

X lent Rs. 3,000 to Y on 1st January 2012 to be repaid by 5 equal monthly instalments starting from 1st February subject to interest at 10% p.a. Y intends to repay the loan by single payment on average due date. Find out that date and total interest payable.

Solution

Average Due Date = Date of taking loan +

$$\frac{\text{Sum of days/months/years from the date of lending to the date of repayment of each instalment}}{\text{No. of instalments}}$$

$$= \text{Jan. } 1 + \frac{1+2+3+4+5}{5}$$

$= \text{Jan. } 1 + 3$ months

= April 1.

Alternatively, the same can also be calculated as : '0' Date = 1.1.2012

Computation of Average Due Date

Starting date	*Due Date*	*Amount*	*No. of months from Jan. 1*	*Product*
		Rs.		
(1)	(2)	(3)	(4)	(5)
Jan. 1 2012	Feb. 1 2012	600	1	600
Jan. 1 2012	March 1 2012	600	2	1,200
Jan. 1 2012	April 1 2012	600	3	1,800
Jan. 1 2012	May 1 2012	600	4	2,400
Jan. 1 2012	June 1 2012	600	5	3,000
		3,000		9,000

$$\text{Average} = \frac{\text{Rs. } 9,000}{\text{Rs. } 3,000} = 3 \text{ months}$$

∴ Average due date is 3 months from Jan. 1. i.e., Jan 1 + 3 months = April 1.

Interest chargeable @ 10% on Rs. 3,000 for 3 months (April 1 to June 1) should be calculated

That is, interest will be = Rs. $3,000 \times \frac{10}{100} \times \frac{3}{12}$ = Rs. 75.

GENERAL ILLUSTRATIONS

Illustration 9

X accepted the following bills drawn by his creditor Y :

Feb. 10 for Rs. 4,000 at 3 months.

March 15 for Rs. 5,000 at 3 months.

April 12 for Rs. 6,000 at 3 months.

May 8 for Rs. 5,000 at 5 months.

On 1st June it was decided that X would withdraw all such bills and he should accept on that day two bills, one for Rs. 12,000 due in 3 months and the other for the balance for 5 months.

Calculate the amount of the second bill after taking into consideration that rate of interest is @ 10% p.a. Ignore days of grace.

Solution **[CU BCom (Hons.) 2000—Adapted**

Take May 10 as '0' date; the following table is prepared on that basis :

Compution of Average Due Date **'0' Date = 1.5.2012**

Date of Drawing		*Periods*	*Due Date of the original bills*		*Amount*	*No. of days from '0' date*		*Product*
					Rs.			Rs.
Feb.	10	3	May	10	4,000	0		0
March	15	3	June	15	5,000	36	(21 + 15)	1,80,000
April	12	3	July	12	6,000	33	(21 + 12)	1,98,000
May	8	5	Oct.	8	5,000	151	(21 + 30 + 31 + 31 + 30 + 8)	7,55,000
					20,000			11,33,000

∴ Average number of days = Rs. 11,33,000/Rs. 20,000 = 57 days (approx.)

∴ The average due date will be May 10 + 57 days, i.e., July 6.

Due date of the new bills = Sept. 1 and Nov. 1 .

Calculation for interest @ 10% p.a. on—

			Rs.
Rs. 12,000	from July 6 to Sept. 1 i.e., for 57 days	$= \text{Rs. } 12,000 \times \frac{10}{100} \times \frac{57}{365}$	= 187
Rs. 8,000	from July 6 to Nov. 1. i.e., for 118 days	$= \text{Rs. } 8,000 \times \frac{10}{100} \times \frac{118}{365}$	= 259
20,000			446

Therefore, amount of second bill will be Rs. 8,000 for the principal + Rs. 446 for interest = Rs. 8,446.

Illustration 10

Mr. Netural purchased goods from Mr. Positive on two months' credit. The purchases were made on the following dates :

		Rs.			Rs.
(a)	3rd March 1991	750	(d)	5th June 1991	1,000
(b)	13th April 1991	500	(e)	20th July 1991	600
(c)	8th May 1991	700			

He wishes to pay the total amount of Rs. 3,500 on the basis of average due date.

(i) Find out the average due date. (ii) If he desires to make the whole payment on 22nd September 1991, what will be the amount of interest @ 10% p.a.?

Solution

Taking 6th May 1991 as the starting date or '0' date, the following table is prepared :

'0' Date = 6.5.1991

(i) Date of Purchase	Due Date from '0' date	No. of Days	Amount Rs.	Product Rs.
3.3.1991	6.5.1991	0	750	0
13.4.1991	16.6.1991	31	500	15,500
8.5.1991	11.7.1991	66	700	46,200
5.6.1991	8.8.1991	94	1,000	94,000
20.7.1991	23.9.1991	140	600	84,000
			3,550	2,39,700

$\therefore$ Average number of days $= \dfrac{\text{Rs. } 2{,}39{,}700}{\text{Rs. } 3{,}550} = 68$ days (approx.)

$\therefore$ Average due date will be 68 days from '0' date i.e., 6th May + 68 days = 13 July

(ii) If he pays the amount on 22nd September, he has to pay interest for 71 days (i.e., from 13th July to 22nd Sept.) @ 10% p.a. Total amount of interest will be Rs. 69.05 (Rs. 3,550 $\times \dfrac{10}{100} \times \dfrac{71}{365}$).

ACCOUNT CURRENT

Account Current is a statement sent by one party to another in the form of a ledger incorporating their transactions serially along with the interest due or payable to date supported by the memorandum columns for item-wise interest and the net balance will be recorded either in the debit or in the credit side of the account. The statement is headed with the names of both the parties, receiving or sending, the former prefixed and the latter suffixed to "......in Account Current with ....". Thus, if X renders the account current to Y, the heading will be "Y in Account Current with X", or *vice versa*.

But the students should remember:

While calculating the number of days the same will be computed from the date of transaction to the date of closing the account and not the date of the due date.

This is frequently used by the following parties :

(i) By a creditor and a debtor; (ii) By a principal and his agent; (iii) By a broker and his clients; (iv) By a banker and his agents; (v) By a head-office and its branch; (vi) By a consignor and a consignee.

Calculation of Interest

(i) FORWARD METHOD OR ORDINARY METHOD

Under this method, the period is computed from the due date of each transaction to the closing date of the statement. The opening date covers the entire period and the closing date, however, bears 'zero' period (i.e., bears zero interest). Interest is debited if interest charged is more than interest receivable, and *vice versa*. This method is not so helpful since interest is to be calculated for each transaction separately.

To Sum up

Method of Preparation

Step 1. *Write-up the heading of the account as per above instruction, (i.e. if X renders the account current to Y, the heading will be "Y in Account Current with X";*

Step 2. *Ruling of the account will be as under :*

Dr. *X in Account Current with Y* *Cr.*

Date	*Particulars*	*Amount* Rs.	*Days* Rs.	*Product*	*Date*	*Particulars*	*Amount*	*Days* Rs.	*Product* Rs.
	To					By			

Step 3. *Post the transactions accordingly like Cash Book;*

Step 4. *Ascertain the due date of each transaction up to period of closing the books of account;*

Step 5. *Calculate the number of days;*

Step 6. *Calculate the amount of interest;*

Step 7. *Then ascertain the balance of the interest column and post it in the 'amount' column of the greater interest side column;*

Step 8. *At last, ascertain the balance of the 'amount' column.*

The following illustration will help us to understand the said principles clearly :

Illustration 11

Show Account Current rendered by Y to X for the half-year ended 30th June 2012; consider interest @ 10% p.a. from the following particulars:

	Rs.
On 1.1.2012 X owes Y	200
On 1.3.2012 X remits cash to Y	60
On 1.4.2012 X purchased goods from Y	120
On 1.5.2012 X remits cash to Y	180

Solution

X in Account Current with Y
(Interest @ 10% on 30th June 2012)

Dr. Cr.

Date	Particulars	Month	Interest	Amount	Date	Particulars	Month	Interest	Amount
2012				Rs.	2012		Rs.		Rs.
Jan. 1	To Balance b/d	6	10	200	Mar. 1	By Cash A/c	4	2	60
Apr. 1	" Sales A/c	3	3	120	May 1	" Cash A/c	2	3	180
June 30	" Interest A/c —Contra	—	—	8	June 30	" Balance of Interest Contra	—	8	—
					June 30	" Balance c/d	—	—	88
			13	328				13	328
July 1.	To Balance b/d	—	—	88					

(ii) PRODUCT METHOD

Product method is the modification of the above method. Under this method, the period is computed from the last due date of the transaction to the next date of transaction as against the closing date of the statement and the amount of transaction is to be multiplied by the number of days so calculated in order to get the product. Interest is calculated on the balance (either debit or credit) of the product for one day and the interest so calculated will be recorded in the heavier side of the amount column.

To Sum up

Method of Preparation

Step 1. Write-up the heading of the account as stated earlier.

Step 2. Ruling of the account will be as under :

X in Account Current with Y

Dr. *Cr.*

Date	*Particulars*	*Amount*	*Days*	*Product*	*Date*	*Particulars*	*Amount*	*Days*	*Product*
			Rs.					Rs.	Rs.
	To					By			

Step 3. Post the transactions accordingly;

Step 4. Ascertain the due date of each transaction up to the period of closing the books;

Step 5. Calculate the number of days;

Step 6. Calculate the amount of product by multiplying the number of days with the amount and post it into 'Product' column;

Step 7. Ascertain the balance of the Product column;

Step 8. Calculate the amount of interest on the balance of the product

(i.e., Interest = $\frac{\text{Balance of the product}}{365} \times \frac{\text{Rate of Interest}}{100}$)

Step 9. Put the amount of interest on the amount column;

Step 10. Ascertain the balance of the amount column.

The following illustration will make the principle clear:

Illustration 12

From the following particulars make up an Account Current to be rendered by S. Dasgupta to A. Halder at 31st Dec. 2012 reckoning interest at 5% p. a. :

			Rs.
June	30	Balance owing by A. Halder	520
July	17	Goods sold to A. Halder	40
Aug.	1	Cash received from A. Halder	500
Aug.	19	Goods sold to A. Halder	720
Aug.	30	Goods sold to A. Halder	50
Sept.	1	Cash received from A. Halder	400
Sept.	1	Halder accepted Dasgupta's draft at 3 months' date for	300
Oct.	22	Goods bought from A. Halder	20
Nov.	12	Goods sold to A. Halder	14
Dec.	14	Cash received from A. Halder	50

[ICWA—Inter & Company Secretary Prel.—Adapted]

Solution

Dr. **A. Halder in Account Current with S. Dasgupta** *Cr.*

Date	*Particulars*	*Amount*	*Days Dec. 31*	*Product*	*Date*	*Particulars*	*Amount*	*Days Dec. 31*	*Product*
2012				Rs.	2012		Rs.		Rs.
July 1	To Balance b/d	520	184[1]	95,680	Aug. 1	By Cash A/c	500	152	76,000
17	" Sales A/c	40	167	6,680	Sept. 1	" Cash A/c	400	121	48,400
Aug. 19	" Sales A/c	720	134	96,480		" B/R A/c	300	121	36,300
30	" Sales A/c	50	123	6,150	Oct. 22	" Purchases A/c	20	70	1,400
Nov. 12	" Sales A/c	14	49	686	Dec. 14	" Cash A/c	50	17	850
Dec. 31	" Interest A/c	6	—		31	" Balance c/d	80		42,726
		1,350		2,05,676			1,350		2,05,676

[*Note* : Interest will be = Rs. 42,726 × $\frac{5}{100}$ × $\frac{1}{365}$ = Rs. 6 (approx.)]

Workings :

1. **Calculation of days :**

		July +	Aug. +	Sept. +	Oct. +	Nov. +	Dec.	=	Total Days
From	July 1 to Dec. 31 =	31 +	31 +	30 +	31 +	30 +	31	=	184
"	July 17 " " =	14 +	31 +	30 +	31 +	30 +	31	=	167
"	Aug. 1 " " =	0 +	30 +	30 +	31 +	30 +	31	=	152
"	Aug. 19 " " =	0 +	12 +	30 +	31 +	30 +	31	=	134
"	Aug. 30 " " =	0 +	1 +	30 +	31 +	30 +	31	=	123
"	Sept. 1 " " =	0 +	0 +	29 +	31 +	30 +	31	=	121
"	Oct. 22 " " =	0 +	0 +	0 +	9 +	30 +	31	=	70
"	Nov. 12 " " =	0 +	0 +	0 +	0 +	18 +	31	=	49
"	Dec. 14 " " =	0 +	0 +	0 +	0 +	0 +	17	=	17

(iii) BACKWARD/EPOQUE METHOD

The procedure is just the opposite of the Forward Method. Under this method, the period is calculated from the opening date of the statement to the due-date of each transaction. Since the starting date is considered as base, closing balance covers the entire period and the opening balance bears 'zero' period, i.e., no interest is calculated on the opening balance but the same is calculated on the closing balance (excluding interest). The amount of interest is to be recorded in the shorter side and, thereafter, the amount is balanced accordingly.

To Sum up

Method of Preparation

Step 1. Write up the heading of the account as stated earlier.

Step 2. Ruling of the account will be as under :

X in Account Current with Y

Dr.									*Cr.*
Date	*Particulars*	*Months*	*Product*	*Amount*	*Date*	*Particulars*	*Months*	*Product*	*Amount*
		Rs.	Rs.	Rs.				Rs.	Rs.
	To					By			

Step 3. Post the transactions accordingly.

Step 4. Ascertain the due date of each transaction.

Step 5. Calculate the number of days from the opening date to the due date of each transaction.

Step 6. Calculate the amount of product of each transaction by multiplying the number of days with the amount and post into 'Product' column.

Step 7. Ascertain the balance of the 'Amount' column and then multiply the same by the number of days/months for the entire period of the account.

Step 8. Ascertain the balance of the 'Product' column.

Step 9. Calculate the amount of interest on the balance of the said 'Product' column, and put the amount of interest on the 'Amount' column.

Step 10. Ascertain the balance of the 'Amount' column.

Consider the following illustration :

Illustration 13

A owes B on 1.1.2012 for Rs. 800. On 31.1.2012 he remits Cash to the extent of Rs. 80. On 31.3.2012, he remits a bill of exchange for Rs. 400 (8 months date). Reckoning interest @ 5% p.a., prepare an Account Current with Epoque Method to be rendered by B to A. Calculation to be made in terms of month; and ignore date of grace.

Solution

A in Account Current With B

Dr.									*Cr.*
Date	*Particulars*	*Month*	*Product*	*Amount*	*Date*	*Particulars*	*Month*	*Product*	*Amount*
2012			Rs.	Rs.	2012				Rs.
July 1	To Balance b/d			800.00	Jan. 31	By Cash A/c	1	80	80.00
June 30	" Balance of Product		6,400		Mar. 31	" Bills A/c Payable A/c (Due 30th Nov. 2012)	11 (Jan to Nov.)	4,400	400.00
June 30	" Interest on Balance of Rs. 6,400 for 1 month @ 5%			26.67	June 30	" Balance of amount (800–80–400) = 320 × 6 =	6	1,920	—
					June 30	" Balance c/d	—	—	346.67
			6,400	826.67				6,400	826.67

(iv) RED INK INTEREST METHOD

If the due date does not fall within the drawn-up date of the account current, the interest is to be ignored from the entry date to the closing date but interest from this closing date to the post due date is, however, to be added in the opposite side by contra entry. This is done by red ink simply to show that the interest belongs to the opposite side, i.e., the credit red ink products are added to the debits and debit red ink products are added to the credit.

Illustration 14

P. Banerjee had the following transactions with P. Sen :

2011			Rs.
Jan.	20	Sold goods to P. Sen.	280
March	2	Bought goods from P. Sen	150
	3	Accepted P. Sen's draft at 1 month due	120
April	11	Cash paid to P. Sen due end of May	100
	30	Goods sold to P. Sen	80
May	11	Bought goods from P. Sen	200
June	12	P. Banerjee drew a bill on P. Sen, this day, payable two months after date and this was duly accepted by P. Sen	210

Make out an Account Current to be rendered by P. Banerjee to P. Sen as at 30th June, bringing interest into account @ 10% p.a.

Solution

Dr. **P. Sen in Account Current with P. Banerjee** *Cr.*

Date	Due Date	Particulars	Amount	Days	Products	Date	Due Date	Particulars	Amount	Days	Products
2011	2011		Rs.		Rs.	2011	2011		Rs.		Rs.
Jan. 20	Jan. 20	To Sales A/c	280.00	161	45,080	Mar. 2	Mar. 2	By Purchase A/c	150.00	120	18,000
Mar. 3	Apr. 6	" B/P A/c	120.00	85	10,200	May 11	May 11	" Purchases A/c	200.00	50	10,000
Apr. 11	Apr. 11	" Cash A/c	100.00	80	8,000	June 11	Aug. 14	" B/R A/c	210.00	(–) 45	(–) 9,450
Apr. 30	May 31	" Sales A/c	80.00	30	2,400	June 30		" Balance of Products	—	—	47,130
June 30		" Interest on balance of product for one day @ 10%	12.91		—			" Balance c/d	32.91		
			592.91		65,680				592.91		65,680
July 1		To Balance b/d	32.91								

Notes : 1. Interest $= \text{Rs. } 47{,}130 \times \frac{10}{100} \times \frac{1}{365} = \text{Rs. } 12.91$ 2. Calculation of days is not shown.

Where rates of interest are different

Sometimes both parties agree to charge and to allow interest on debit and credit items of different rates of interest. In those cases, there will be no problem if interest table method is used in order to calculate interest since interest will have to be calculated at agreed different rates on debit as well as credit items. But if product method is used, any one of the following two methods may be adopted for the purpose :

(a) At first, ascertain the debit or credit totals of product columns and then calculate interest on debit and credit totals separately by their respective rates of interest. At last, enter the balance of the interest amounts in the principal amounts column on the larger interest side.

(b) At first, ascertain the debit and credit totals of product columns and then multiply the product totals by their respective rates of interest and find out their balance. Interest will have to be calculated for one day or for one month (i.e., $\frac{1}{365}$ or $\frac{1}{12}$) on the balance which will be recorded in the amount column on the larger product side.

Illustration 15

From the following particulars prepare an Account Current by A to B charging interest on debits @ 6% and on credits @ 4% p.a. 2011 :

2011			Rs.
Jan.	1	Balance due from B	600
	10	Sold goods to B	520
	17	B returned goods	125
Feb.	10	B paid by cheque	400
	14	B accepted A's draft for 1 month	300
April	29	Goods sold to B	615
May	15	Received Cash from B	700
June	5	B accepted A's bill for 3 months	500

Solution

B in Account Current with A

(as on June 30, 1997)

Dr. Cr.

Due Date	Particulars	Amount	Days to June 30	Product	Due Date	Particulars	Amount	Days to June 30	Product
2011		Rs.		Rs.	2011		Rs.		Rs.
Jan. 1	To Balance b/d	600	181	1,08,600	Jan. 1	By Sales Return A/c	125	164	20,500
10	" Sales A/c	520	171	88,920	Feb. 10	" Bank A/c	400	140	56,000
Apr. 29	" Sales A/c	615	62	38,130	Mar. 17	" B/R A/c	300	105	31,500
				2,35,650	May 15	" Cash A/c	700	46	32,200
	" Rate of Interest			× 6	Sept. 8	" B/R A/c	500	(–) 70	(–) 35,000
									1,05,200
				14,13,900		" Rate of Interest			× 4
									4,20,800
June 30	" Interest on Balance of products (9,93,100 × 1 365 ÷ 100)	27.21			June 30	By Balance of product			9,93,100
	" Balance c/d	262.79							
		2,025		14,13,900			2,025		14,13,900
					July 1	By Balance b/d	262.79		

* Calculation of days are not shown.

When sum of the product on the debit or credit side or both sides are in '–'.

Sometimes sum of the product on both the sides may be in '+', interest in that case is calculated on the difference and the same is put on the *larger* side of the product (which has already been shown in the earlier problem). But when the sum of the products on both the sides is in '–', interest is calculated on the difference but the same is put on *smaller* side and the other side is in '–', interest is calculated on the sum of *both the products* and the same is put on the '+' side of the product.

Consider the following illustrations one by one :

When sum of the product on the credit side is in '–'

Illustration 16

Show the Account Current rendered by X to Y for the half-year ended 30th June 2011.

Following are the transactions :

2011			Rs.
Jan.	1	Y owes X	4,000
Feb.	1	Y remits Cash	2,000
Mar.	15	X sold goods to Y (due on May 1)	6,000
	31	Y sends a bill (due on Oct. 1 including days of grace)	4,000
May	30	Y purchased goods (due on Aug. 31)	8,000

Interest is to be calculated @ 5% p.a.

Solution

Y in Account Current with X

Dr. Cr.

Due Date	Particulars	Amount	Months to June 30	Product	Due Date	Particulars	Amount	Months to June 30	Product
2011		Rs.		Rs.	2011		Rs.		Rs.
Jan. 1	To Balance b/d	4,000.00	6	(+) 24,000	Feb. 1	By Cash A/c	2,000.00	5	(+) 10,000
May 1	" Sales A/c	6,000.00	2	(+) 12,000	Oct. 1	" B/R A/c	4,000.00	(–) 3	(–) 12,000
Aug. 31	" Sales A/c	8,000.00	(–) 2	(–) 16,000	June 30	" Balance c/d	12,091.70		
June 30	" Interest A/c	91.70							
		18,091.70		(+) 20,000			18,091.70		(–) 2,000
July 1	To Balance b/d	12,091.70							

* Interest is to be calculated on Rs. 22,000 (i.e., 20,000 – (– 2,000) @ 5%) for one month which is (i.e., 22,000 × $\frac{5}{100}$ × $\frac{1}{12}$) Rs. 91.7 and the same is to be put on the debit side of the amount column.

• *When sum of the product on the debit side is in '–'*

Illustration 17

Show the Account Current from the following particulars to be rendered by B to A on 30th June 2011 assuming that the rate of interest is @ 5% p.a. and ignoring days of grace :

2011			Rs.
Jan.	1	A owes to B	2,000
Feb.	1	A remits Cash	1,000
Mar.	15	B sold goods to X (due on May 1)	4,000
	31	A sends a bill (due on Oct. 1)	1,000
May	30	A purchased goods (due on Aug. 31)	20,000

Solution

Dr. **A in Account Current with B** Cr.

Due Date	Particulars	Amount	Months to June 30	Product	Date	Particulars	Amount	Months to June 30	Product
2011		Rs.		Rs.	2011		Rs.		Rs.
Jan. 1	To Balance b/d	2,000.00	6	12,000	Feb. 1	By Cash A/c	1,000.00	5	5,000
May 1	" Sales A/c	4,000.00	2	8,000	Mar. 1	" B/R A/c	1,000.00	(–) 3	(–) 3,000
Apr. 1	" Sales A/c	20,000.00	(–) 2	(–) 40,000	June 30	" Interest A/c	91.70	—	—
					" "	" Balance c/d	23,908.30		
		26,000.00		(–) 20,000			26,000.00		(+) 2,000
July 1	To Balance b/d	23,908.30							

* Interest is to be calculated on Rs. 22,000 (i.e.,– Rs. 20,000 – (+) Rs. 2,000) @ 5% p.a. for one month, i.e., Rs. (Rs. 22,000 × $\frac{5}{100}$ × $\frac{1}{12}$ = 91.7) and is to be credited.

When sum of the product on both the sides is in '–'

Illustration 18

Prepare an Account Current to be received by B to A on 30th June 2011 considering rate of interest @ 5% p.a. from the given particulars :

2011			Rs.
Jan.	1	A owes to B	2,000
Feb.	1	A remits Cash	1,000
Mar.	15	B sold goods to X (due on May 1)	4,000
	31	A sends a bill (due on Oct. 1)	3,000
May	30	A purchased goods (due on Aug. 31)	20,000

Solution

Dr. **A in Account Current with B** Cr.

Due Date	Particulars	Amount	Months to June 30	Product	Date	Particulars	Amount	Months to June 30	Product
2011		Rs.		Rs.	2011		Rs.		Rs.
Jan. 1	To Balance b/d	2,000.00	6	12,000	Feb. 1	By Cash A/c	1,000.00	5	5,000
May 1	" Sales A/c	4,000.00	2	8,000	Mar.31	" B/R A/c	3,000.00	(–) 3	(–) 9,000
Apr. 1	" Sales A/c	20,000.00	(–) 2	(–) 40,000	June 30	" Interest A/c	66.97	—	—
					" "	" Balance c/d	21,933.03		
		26,000.00		(–) 20,000			26,000.00		(+) 4,000
July 1	To Balance b/d	21,933.03							

* Interest is to be calculated on the difference of the product i.e., Rs. 16,000 (20,000 – 4,000) @ 5% for 1 month i.e., (Rs. 16,000 × $\frac{5}{100}$ × $\frac{1}{12}$ = Rs. 66.97 and the same is to be credited.

ASSIGNMENT MATERIALS

THEORETICAL

Short Answer-Type Questions

1. What is Average Due Date? How do you calculate it?
2. What is 'Due Date'? How do you calculate it?
3. What is Date of Maturity? How do you calculate it?
4. What are Reciprocal Bills?
5. How do you calculate the interest in case of outstanding bill?
6. What is Account Current?
7. What is Forward Method in Account Current?
8. What is Red Ink Interest Method under Account Current?

Long Answer-Type Questions

9. What kind of problems are to be dealt with in Average Due Date?
10. What is Date of Maturity ? How do you calculate the same?
11. What are Reciprocal Bills? How do you treat the same in Average Due Date?
12. How do you treat the mutual dealings between the parties?
13. Distinguish between Forward Method and Backward Method in Account Current.
14. What is Red Ink Interest Method? How do you calculate the amount of interest under the said method?
15. How do you treat in account current when rates of interest are different?
16. What is Epoque Method? Explain it in full.

PRACTICAL

(a) Average Due Date

1. Calculate the date on which the total amount of the following bills of exchange may be paid by a single cheque without any loss to any one of the parties :

Date of the bill	Period of the bill	Amount
		Rs.
1.1.2012	2 months	250
15.1.2012	3 "	300
30.1.2012	2 "	600
2.2.2012	3 "	300
15.2.2012	2 "	400

[Ans. Average Due Date = 9th April 2012]

2. What is the average due date of the following instalments payable under the contract :

July 1	Rs.	3,200
July 1	Rs.	4,000
Aug. 1	Rs.	1,800
		9,000

Draw a bill to meet Rs. 9,000 with interest @ 5% thereon at 60 days from the average due date.

[Ans. Average Due Date = 27th June]

3. X sold goods to Y as detailed below :

Date of Invoice	Value of goods sold	Date of Invoice	Value of goods sold
05.05.2010	Rs. 3,000	26.05.2010	2,250
12.05.2010	Rs. 1,500	01.06.2010	2,000
19.05.2010	Rs. 3,500	03.06.2010	1,000

The payments were agreed to be made by bills payable 90 days from the respective dates of the invoice. However, Y wanted to arrange for payment of all the bills to be made on a single date.

Calculate the date on which such a payment could be made without loss of interest to either party.

[Ans. Average Due Date = 20th Aug. 2010] **[CA]**

(b) Account Current

4. From the following particulars prepare the Account Current to be rendered by Mr. T to Mr. S as on 31.8.2012. Interest must be calculated @ 10% p.a.

		Rs.
11.6.2012	Goods sent to S	1,020
15.6.2012	Cash received from S	500
20.6.2012	Goods sent to S	650
7.7.2012	Goods sent to S	700
8.8.2012	Cash received from S	1,000

[Ans. Interest Rs. 32 : Balance Due Rs. 902] **[CA]**

5. S had the following transactions with K :

2012			Rs.
Jan.	1	Balance due from K	1,000
Feb.	16	Purchased goods from him	6,000
"	28	Sold goods to him	10,000
March	16	Received a cheque	3,000
April	20	Sold him goods (Invoiced on May 3)	10,000
June	16	Purchased goods from him (Invoiced on July 16)	15,000
Sept.	23	Paid him cash	3,000
Oct.	24	Accepted his bill for 3 months	5,000
Nov.	26	Received his acceptance for 2 months	8,000

You are asked to prepare an Account Current of K completed up to Dec. 31 2012 as will appear in the books of S reckoning 5% interest on the balance due.

[Ans. Interest on balance of the product @ 5% Rs. 129 for 1 day; Balance b/d Rs. 2,871] **[CA]**

Note : Effective date of the transactions should always be taken into consideration.

6. ABC had the following transactions with PQR in 2012 :

			Rs.
Jan.	1	Balance due to PQR	600
April	1	Sold goods to PQR	1,600
June	16	Received PQR's acceptance at 3 months' date	800
Oct.	1	Purchased goods from PQR	1,400
Oct.	4	Received cash from PQR	400
Dec.	6	Paid cash to PQR	200

Prepare and close PQR Account in ABC's ledger calculating interest @ 5% p.a.

[Ans. Balance of Interest (Cr.) Rs. 2.90 p; Balance of Account (Cr.) Rs. 1,402.90 p] **[CU BCom]**

7. The following are the transactions that took place between X and Y during the period from 1st Jan. to 30th June 2012:

2012			Rs.
Jan.	1	Balance due to X	602
"	17	Goods sold by X to Y	884
Feb.	16	Goods sold by Y to X (Invoiced April 1)	1,296
"	18	Goods returned by X to Y (Out of goods purchased on Feb. 16)	112
March	24	Goods sold by Y to X (Invoiced May 1)	712
April	22	Bills drawn by Y on X at 3 months	300
April	29	Cash paid by X to Y	500
May	17	Goods sold by X to Y (Invoiced June 1)	542
June	22	Goods sold by Y to X (Aug. 1)	45

Draw up an Account Current up to June 30, 2012 to be rendered by X to Y charging interest @ 5% p.a.

[Ans. Balance of Interest (Dr.), Rs. 22; Balance of Account (Dr.) Rs. 498] **[CA]**

8. Following transactions took place between X and Y during the month of April 2012:

			Rs.
April	1	Amount payable X to Y	10,000
	7	Received acceptance of X by Y for 2 months	5,000
	10	Bills receivable (accepted by Y) on 7.2.2012 is honoured on this due date	10,000
	10	X sold goods to Y (invoice dated 10.5.2012)	7,500
	12	X received cheque from Y dated 15.5.2012	7,500
	15	Y sold goods to X (invoice dated 15.5.2012)	6,000
	20	X returned goods sold by Y (on 15.5.2012)	1,000
	20	Bills accepted by Y is dishonoured on this due date	5,000

You are required to make out an Account Current by Products Method to be rendered by X to Y as on 30.4.2012, taking interest into account @ 10% p.a.

[Ans. Balance of Interest (Dr.) Rs. 114; Balance of Account (Dr.) Rs. 2,386] **[ICWA]**

CHAPTER 18

CONSIGNMENT ACCOUNTS

Learning Objectives

Meaning

Differences between Consignment and Sale

Proforma Invoice

Account Sales

Books of Consignment

Deal Credere Commission and Del Credere Agent

Stock Valuation

Books of Consignee—Consignment Inwards

Discounting Charges of the Bill

Loss of Goods on Consignment

- *A. Normal Loss*
- *B. Abnormal Loss*

Shortage or Deficiency of Stock

Partial Return of Goods by the Consignee

Invoice Price Method

Stock and Trading Method

Invoice Price—Memorandum Column Method

Consignment between two countries with different foreign exchanges

Special/Overriding Commission

Advance from Consignee as Caution/Security Money

Rectification of Errors

Meaning

A consignment is the despatch of goods by its owner to his agent for the purpose of selling. The former is called the principal or consignor and the latter is called the agent or consignee. The goods so despatched or sent by the consignor is regarded as 'consignment outward' in the books of the consignor, whereas, the goods so received by the consignee is treated as 'consignment inward' in his books. The goods may be despatched either within the same country or abroad. The goods are sold by the consignee on behalf of the consignor against commission. That is, it is nothing but an agency relationship.

Differences between Consignment and Sale

The following points may be noted :

(a) According to the Sale of Goods Act, 1930, where the property in the goods is transferred from the seller to the buyer the contract is called a 'sale'. But in consignment, the ownership of the goods is not transferred from the consignor to the consignee.

(b) In actual sales, the purchaser can dispose of the goods according to his own choice and desire since he is the owner of such goods. But in consignment, the consignee cannot do so since he is not the owner of the goods, and, at the same time, he is bound to sell the same as prescribed by the consignor.

(c) In case of sale, risk is transferred from the seller to the buyer as soon as the transaction takes place. Therefore, any loss, if incurred, is to be borne by the purchaser. But, in case of consignment, loss is to be borne by the consignor and not by the consignee—since he is only the agent.

(d) In a contract of sale, the purchaser cannot return the goods to the seller, but, in consignment, the consignee can do so if he thinks that the goods are not marketable.

(e) In case of a sale there are two parties, viz., buyer and seller. But, in case of a consignment, there are three parties, viz., consignor, consignee and the buyer.

Proforma Invoice

When an invoice is sent to the consignee by the consignor stating the facts relating to the full particulars of the goods, number and/or quality, price, grade, weight, measurement, transport and other incidental expenses etc. at the time of despatching the goods, such invoice is called 'Proforma Invoice'. 'Proforma Invoice' is like ordinary invoice which is used at the time of normal buying and selling transactions. Practically, it gives an idea to the consignee about the price in which the goods will be disposed of. Generally, " proforma" invoice, which is charged by the consignor, includes a certain minimum amount of profit beyond which the consignee is not allowed to sell. Therefore, 'Proforma Invoice' price is always higher than the actual cost price. So, if goods are sent by the consignor on 'Proforma Invoice' price basis, an adjustment is to be made at the end of the period in order to ascertain the correct amount of profit.

Account Sales

When sales relating to consignment is completed or the time period fixed by the consignor expires, consignee sends a statement relating to the goods received, destroyed-in-transit, or in godown, if any, effected sales including selling expenses and commission, deducting the amount of advance remitted by him to the consignor and, finally, the amount due to the consignor, such a statement is known as 'Account Sales'.

Preparation of Account Sale

Illustration 1

On 1.1.2012, Hadaram consigned to Bokaram 1,000 bales of Cotton invoice at Rs. 1,000 per bale. Hadaram incurred expenses of Rs. 15,000. On 1.6.2012, an Account Sales was received from Bokaram which showed that the entire goods were sold for Rs. 15,00,000. His expenses were—Clearing Charges Rs. 10,000, Godown Rent Rs. 7,500, Other Expenses Rs. 15,500. He was entitled to a Commission @ 5% on sales and also entitled to Del Credere Commission @ $2\frac{1}{2}$ % on sales. He sent an advance for Rs. 7,00,000.

Make out an Account Sales assuming that Bokaram remitted a Bank Draft for the balance on 31st Aug. 2012.

Solution

Account Sales

	Rs.	Rs.	Rs.
Gross Sale Proceeds			15,00,000
Less : Expenses :			
Clearing Charges	10,000		
Godown Rent	7,500		
Other Expenses	15,500	33,000	

Contd.

		Rs.	Rs.	Rs.
Less :	*Commissions :*			
	Ordinary Commission @ 5% on Sales	75,000		
	Del Credere Commission @ $2\frac{1}{2}$% on Sales	37,500		
			1,12,500	
				1,45,500
				13,54,500
Less :	Advance remitted by Cash			7,00,000
	Net amount due remitted by a Bank Draft			6,54,500

E&OE

for S/d ....

Date 31st August 2012

Books of Consignor

Since it is not an usual or ordinary sale transaction two special accounts are opened in the books of the consignor, viz., (1) the Consignment Account, (2) the Goods Sent on Consignment Account. The Consignment Account is prepared in order to show the consignment transactions and the eventual result (i.e., profit or loss) on the consignment. Consignment Account is to some extent synonymous with Trading Account in the sense that all costs and expenses appear in the debit side while all incomes, i.e., Sales and Closing Stock, appear in the credit side. The balance represents either profit or loss on consignment which is ultimately transferred to Profit and Loss Account. It is to be remembered that the balance of the 'Goods Sent on Consignment Account' is transferred to either Trading Account or Purchase Account. In addition to the above two accounts, Consignee's Personal Account is also to be opened in order to know the final settlement.

Accounting Steps

Entries in the books of Consignor

(i)	***When goods are sent :***		
	Consignment A/c	Dr.	at cost price
	To Goods Sent on Consignment A/c		
(ii)	***When expenses are incurred by Consignor :***		
	Consignment A/c	Dr.	
	To Cash/Bank A/c (if paid)		
	" Creditors for Expenses (if unpaid)		
(iii)	***When any advance is received from Consignee :***		
	Cash/B/R/Draft A/c	Dr.	with the amount of advance
	To Consignee's Personal A/c		
(iv)	***When goods are sold by Consignee :***		
	Consignee's Personal A/c	Dr.	with the amount of total sales
	To Consignment A/c		
(v)	***When expenses are incurred by Consignee :***		
	Consignment A/c	Dr.	with the amount of expenses incurred by Consignee
	To Consignee's Personal A/c		
(vi)	***When commission is charged by Consignee :***		
	Consignment A/c	Dr.	with the amount of commission
	To Consignee's Personal A/c		
(vii)	***If there is any unsold stock :***		
	Unsold Stock A/c	Dr.	with the amount of unsold stock
	To Consignment A/c		
(viii) (a)	***For abnormal loss on Consignment :***		
	Abnormal Loss A/c	Dr.	with the amount of Loss
	To Consignment A/c		
(b)	***If covered by Insurance Company :***		
	Insurance Co. A/c	Dr.	Do
	To Abnormal Loss A/c		
(c)	***If not covered by Insurance Company :***		Do
	Profit and Loss A/c	Dr.	
	To Abnormal Loss A/c		

Contd.

(ix) ***For Profit on Consignment A/c :***

Consignment A/c Dr. } with the amount of profit
  To Profit and Loss A/c

In case of loss, however, the entry will be reversed.

(x) ***For transferring Goods Sent on Consignment Account at the end of the year :***

Goods Sent on Consignment A/c Dr.
  To Trading (if the consignor is a manufacturer)
  " Purchases A/c (if the consignor is a wholesaler)

In order to find out the correct profit from General Profit and Loss Account, the above closing entry is to be passed. If the consignor is a manufacturer, he prepares a Manufacturing Account and the total cost of goods manufactured is transferred to Trading Account. For the purpose, the entry is :

Trading A/c Dr.
  To Manufacturing A/c

Again, if a part of such manufactured goods is sent on consignment basis, the Trading Account must be credited with the amount of cost of such goods—otherwise the correct profit cannot be ascertained. On the other hand, if the consignor is a wholesaler, he debits purchases account as soon as he purchases goods and, naturally, if any goods are sent out of that purchase, on consignment basis, Purchases Account must be credited for the purpose (i.e., to be deducted from purchases). So, the amount of adjusted purchase should be transferred to General Profit and Loss Account and profit/loss from General Profit and Loss Account will show an incorrect result if the above adjustment is not accounted for properly.

Illustration 2

Ordinary

Hiralal of Kolkata consigned 200 chests of patent medicines of the value of Rs. 1,200 each to Hareram of Goa. The consignor incurred by way of freight, insurance and sundry expenses a sum of Rs. 3,500 on the consignment. Hareram sent an advance of Rs. 1,90,000 against the consignment. In due course, an Account Sales was received from Goa. It disclosed that the consignee's expenses in various accounts amounted to Rs. 2,500. The goods were sold for Rs. 2,400 per chest. The consignee charged Ordinary Commission at $2\frac{1}{2}$% and Del Credere Commission at $7\frac{1}{2}$% on gross sale proceeds. A Bank Draft for the balance due was received from the consignee along with the Account Sales.

You are required to show the Journal Entries, the Consignment to Goa Account, Goods Sent on Consignment Account and Hareram's Personal Account in the books of Hiralal of Kolkata.

Solution

In the books of Hiralal of Kolkata
Journal

Date	*Particulars*		*L.F.*	*Debit* Rs.	*Credit* Rs.
?	Consignment to Goa A/c	Dr.		2,40,000	
	To Goods sent on Consignment A/c				2,40,000
	(200 chests of Medicines @ Rs. 1,200 sent to Hareram of Goa.)				
	Consignment to Goa A/c	Dr.		3,500	
	To Bank A/c				3,500
	(Expenses incurred for consignment by the Consignor.)				
	Bank A/c	Dr.		1,90,000	
	To Hareram A/c				1,90,000
	(Advance received from Hareram.)				
	Consignment to Goa A/c	Dr.		2,500	
	To Hareram A/c				2,500
	(Expenses incurred by Hareram.)				
	Hareram A/c Dr.			4,80,000	
	To Consignment to Goa A/c				4,80,000
	(Medicines are sold @ Rs. 2,400)				
	Consignment to Goa A/c	Dr.		48,000	
	To Hareram A/c				48,000
	(Commission charged by the Consignee.)				

Contd.

		Rs.	Rs.
Bank A/c Dr. To Hareram A/c (Final remittance received.)	Dr.	2,39,500	2,39,500
Goods Sent on Consignment A/c Dr. To Trading/Purchases A/c (Goods sent on Consignment adjusted against purchases.)	Dr.	2,40,000	2,40,000
Consignment to Goa A/c Dr. To Profit and Loss A/c (Profit made on consignment.)	Dr.	1,86,000	1,86,000

Dr. **Consignment to Goa Account*** Cr.

Date	Particulars		Amount	Date	Particulars	Amount
?			Rs.	?		Rs.
	To Goods sent on Consignment A/c		2,40,000		By Hareram A/c— Sale Proceeds	4,80,000
	" Bank – Expenses		3,500			
	" Hareram A/c – Expenses		2,500			
	" Hareram A/c—					
	Or. Com.	12,000				
	Del Credere Com.	36,000	48,000			
	" Profit and Loss A/c Profit on Consignment Trans.		1,86,000			
			4,80,000			4,80,000

Dr. **Hareram Account** Cr.

Date	Particulars	Amount	Date	Particulars	Amount
?		Rs.	?		Rs.
	To Consignment to Goa A/c— Sale Proceeds	4,80,000		By Bank – Advance	1,90,000
				" Consignment to Goa A/c – Expenses	2,500
				" —Commission	48,000
				" Bank—*(bal. fig.)*	2,39,500
		4,80,000			4,80,000

Dr. **Goods Sent on Consignment Account** Cr.

Date	Particulars	Amount	Date	Particulars	Amount
?		Rs.	?		Rs.
	To Trading A/c or Purchase A/c—Transfer	2,40,000		By Consignment to Goa A/c	2,40,000
		2,40,000			2,40,000

Profit and Loss Account (Extract)
for the year ended

Dr.	Rs.	Cr.	Rs.
		By Consignment to Goa A/c	1,86,000

Del Credere Commission, Del Credere Agent and Bad Debts

Generally, the consignee is not liable to the consignor on account of bad debts arising out of credit sales made by him. But, sometimes, in order to reduce the risk of collection from customers on account of credit sales, consignor makes a contract with the consignee so that the former will allow an extra commission to the latter other than the ordinary commission simply to cover the risk of collection from customers on account of credit sales. Such extra commission is known as *'Del Credere Commission'*. The consignee, in this case, is called *'Del Credere Agent'*.

From the above discussion it is quite clear that whether the consignor or the consignee will bear the amount of bad debt losses depends on its Del Credere Commission.

---

* We can also write simply Consignment Account, or, Consignment Outward Account.

Needless to mention that—

(i) If no Del Credere Commission is not given— = the Consignor will bear the amount of bad debt losses

(ii) If Del Credere Commission is given— = the Consignee will bear the amount of bad debt losses.

To sum up, the following treatment should be made in the book of consignor and consignee for credit sales when Del Credere Commission is allowed and when Del Credere Commission is not allowed :

(a) *If Del Credere Commission is allowed*

In the Books of Consignor

Credit sales will be treated as Cash sales i.e., there will be no difference between Cash and Credit sales. As such, there will be no entry or adjustment for bad debts in the books of Consignor.

The following entries will be recorded :

(i) For credit Sales :

Consignee's Personal A/c Dr.
To Consignment A/c

(ii) For Bad Debts :

No entry.

(iii) For Commission (Ordinary + D.C.C.) :

Consignment A/c Dr.
To Consignee's Personal A/c

In the Books of Consignee

Bad debts will be written-off against Del Credere Commission and there will be no effect in Consignor's Account.

The following entries will be recorded :

(i) For credit Sales :

(a) Consignment Debtors A/c Dr.
To Consignor A/c

(ii) For Bad Debts :

Bad Debts A/c Dr.
To Consignment Debtors A/c

(iii) For Collection from debtors :

Cash /Bank A/c Dr.
To Consignment Debtors A/c

(iv) For Closing Bad Debts :

Commission Received A/c Dr.
To Bad Debts A/c

(v) For balance of Commission :

Commission Received A/c Dr.
To Profit and Loss A/c

(b) *If Del Credere Commission is not allowed*

In the Books of Consignor

(i) For Credit Sales :

Consignment Debtors A/c Dr.
To Consignment A/c

(ii) For Bad Debts :

Consignment A/c Dr.
To Consignment Debtors A/c

(iii) For collection from Customers :

Cash/Bank A/c Dr.
(If collected by Consignor)
To Consignment Debtors

For collection from customer by consignee :

Consignee's Personal A/c Dr.
To Consignment Debtors A/c

In the Books of Consignee

(i) For Credit Sales :

No entry

(ii) For Bad Debts :

No entry

(iii) For collection from customers :

Cash/Bank A/c Dr
To Consignor A/c

Treatment of Del Credere Commission

Illustration 3

X of Kolkata sent goods to Y of Mumbai valued Rs. 1,00,000. X incurred Rs. 10,000 for various expenses. He also received an advance from Y amounting to Rs. 30,000. He received an account sales which showed that the entire goods were sold for Rs. 1,50,000 (out of which credit sales amounted to Rs. 10,000). Y collected Rs. 8,000 from customers out of credit sales. Y incurred the following expenses: Clearing Charges Rs. 2,000, Godown Rent Rs. 1,000. He informed that Rs. 1,000 were totally bad and could not be recovered. He was also entitled to an Ordinary Commission @ 5% on Sales.

You are required to prepare in the books of X —(i) the Consignment to Mumbai Account. (ii) Goods Sent on Consignment Account. (iii) Y's Account, assuming that (1) *Del Credere Commission was given* @ $2\frac{1}{2}$ %, and (2) *Del Credere Commission was not given.*

Solution

(1)

In the books of X

Consignment to Mumbai Account

Dr. Date	Particulars		Amount	Date	Particulars	Cr. Amount
?			Rs.	?		Rs.
	To Goods sent on Consignment A/c		1,00,000		By Y A/c— Sale Proceeds	1,50,000
	" Bank – Expenses		10,000			
	" Y A/c—					
	Clearing Charges	2,000				
	Godown Rent	1,000	3,000			
	" Y A/c—					
	Commission	7,500				
	Del Credere Com.	3,750	11,250			
	" Profit and Loss A/c					
	" Profit on Consignment—Trans.		25,750			
			1,50,000			1,50,000

Y Account

Dr. Date	Particulars	Amount	Date	Particulars	Cr. Amount
?		Rs.	?		Rs.
	To Consignment to Mumbai A/c – Sale Proceeds	1,50,000		By Bank – Advance	30,000
				" Consignment to Mumbai A/c – Expenses	3,000
				" Mumbai A/c – Commission	11,250
				" Balance c/d	1,05,750
		1,50,000			1,50,000

Goods Sent on Consignment Account

Dr. Date	Particulars	Amount	Date	Particulars	Cr. Amount
?		Rs.	?		Rs.
	To Trading A/c—Transfer	1,00,000		By Consignment to Mumbai A/c	1,00,000
		1,00,000			1,00,000

Note : There will be no effect for bad debts since Del Credere Commission is given.

(2)

In the books of X

Consignment to Mumbai Account

Dr. Date	Particulars		Amount	Date	Particulars	Cr. Amount
?			Rs.	?		Rs.
	To Goods sent on Consignment A/c		1,00,000		By Y A/c— Sale Proceeds	1,40,000
	" Bank – Expenses		10,000		" Consignment Debtors A/c Credit Sales	10,000
	" Y A/c—					
	Clearing Charges	2,000				
	Godown Rent	1,000	3,000			
	" Y A/c—					
	Commission @ 5%		7,500			
	Consignment Debtors A/c—					
	Bad Debts		1,000			
	" Profit and Loss A/c					
	Profit on Consignment Transferred		28,500			
			1,50,000			1,50,000

Dr. **Y Account** Cr.

Date	Particulars	Amount	Date	Particulars	Amount
?		Rs.	?		Rs.
	To Consignment to Mumbai	1,40,000		By Bank—Advance	30,000
	" Cash Sale Proceeds			" Consignment to Mumbai	
	" Consignment Debtors			—Expenses	3,000
	—Cash Received	8,000		" Commission	7,500
				" Balance c/d	1,07,500
		1,48,000			1,48,000

Dr. **Consignment Debtors Account** Cr.

Date	Particulars	Amount	Date	Particulars	Amount
?		Rs.	?		Rs.
	To Consignment to Mumbai A/c			By Y A/c—Cash Received	8,000
	—Credit Sale	10,000		" Consignment to Mumbai A/c —Bad Debts	1,000
				" Balance c/d	1,000
		10,000			10,000

Goods Sent on Consignment Account will be same as above.

Stock Valuation

In order to prepare final accounts of the consignor, it becomes necessary to ascertain the value of unsold stock, if any, lying in the hands of consignee. Otherwise, the net result, i.e., true profit or loss, cannot be ascertained and that is why an adjustment is to be made in the Consignment Account bearing in mind the principles of valuations of stock, viz., **cost price or market price—whichever is less.** Usually, unsold stock is valued at cost to the consignor plus proportionate expenses incurred by him along with the proportionate non-recurring expenses of the Consignee+. Alternatively, total cost of goods plus total expenses incurred by Consignor plus total non-recurring expenses of consignee are to be added and value of stock will be on the basis of proportionate unsold goods. (There are accountants who prefer to value stock only at cost price ignoring all expenses altogether. There are others who consider all expenses irrespective of 'caste and creed', i.e., their nature. Similarly, there are some other experts who prefer to take only expenses incurred by consignor etc.). In the present study we have followed the first method.

The usual entry for this purpose will be

Stock on Consignment/Consignment Stock A/c Dr.

To Consignment A/c

Unsold Stock will appear in the assets side of the Balance Sheet.* However, if it is assumed that the Unsold Stock will realise at less than cost, the net realisable value (i.e., realisable value minus estimated expenses including consignee's commission) is to be considered for the purpose. And if net realisable value is found to be less than cost, the Stock must be written-down accordingly since it is based on the principles of conservatism) i.e., anticipated losses must be provided for in the books.

To sum up, the following method should carefully be considered while valuing Unsold Stock :

+ **Non-recurring Expenses :**

It includes those expenses which are incurred in transferring goods from the consignor's godown to consignee's godown, viz., Freight, Customs duty, Dock Charges, Insurance-in-transit, Loading and Unloading Expenses, etc., i.e., the expenses of Consignee which are incurred only for once.

Recurring Expenses :

It includes those expenses which are incurred by the consignee for the purpose of selling the goods, viz., Godown Rent, Storage, Advertisement etc., i.e., the expenses which are incurred again and again.

* **In the next year, the stock will be transferred to Consignment Account. The entry will be :**

Consignment A/c Dr.

To Stock of Consignment A/c

Ordinary Method

(a) Where Cost Price is less than Market Price

		Rs.
	Total Cost	* *
Add :	Expenses incurred by Consignor	* *
Add :	Non-recurring expenses incurred by Consignor	* *
		* *

Value of Stock $= \dfrac{\text{Value of total goods} \times \text{unsold units/cases}}{\text{Total number of units/cases}}$

Alternatively

	Proportionate Cost Price	* *
Add :	Proportionate expenses of Consignor	* *
Add :	Proportionate expenses of Consignee	* *
	Value of Unsold Stock	* *

(b) ***Where Cost Price is more than the Market Price***

Market price is to be considered as the value of Unsold Stock

(c) ***Where there is invoice price of goods***

		Rs.
	Total Cost	
Add :	Expenses incurred by Consignor	
Add :	Non-recurring expenses incurred by Consignee	
	Total invoice value of goods	

Value of Stock $= \dfrac{\text{Total Invoice Value} \times \text{unsold units}}{\text{Total no. of units}}$ * *

Stock Reserve/Suspense = Difference between Invoice Value of Unsold Stock and Cost Price of unsold stock * *

* *

After ascertaining the *cost price* or *market price* with the help of the above, the lower/smaller one is to be considered as the value of unsold stock.

Valuation of Unsold Stock

Illustration 4

S. Gupta of Mumbai sent 500 cases @ Rs. 150 each to M. K. Menon of Chennai Ex. S. S. Jala Puri to be sold on his account and at his risk for $7\frac{1}{2}$% Commission and $2\frac{1}{2}$% Del Credere Commission and incurred Rs. 5,500 expenses. Rs. 20,000 advance has been received. Sri Menon sent an Account Sale disclosing that 300 cases have been sold for Rs. 230 each and another 100 cases @ Rs. 220 each. He has incurred unloading expenses etc. Rs. 750 and Selling Expenses Rs. 1,000. He informed that Rs. 1,000 was proved bad since the customer became insolvent and another customer deducted Rs. 500 due to a dispute in quality of goods.

Prepare :

(1) Consignment to Channai A/c (2) M. K. Menon A/c. and
(3) Goods Sent on Consignment A/c (4) Stock on Consignment A/c
(5) Balance Sheet.

Solution

In the Books of S. Gupta
Consignment to Chennai Account

Dr. Cr.

Date	Particulars	Amount Rs.	Date	Particulars	Amount Rs.
?	To Goods Sent on Consig. A/c (500 × Rs. 150)	75,000	?	By M. K. Menon (Sale Proceeds) A/c (Rs. 300 × 230 = Rs. 69,000) (Rs. 100 × 220 = Rs. 22,000)	91,000
	" Bank Expenses	5,500			
	" M. K. Menon A/c—Exp.				

Contd.

Particulars		Rs.		Particulars	Rs.
Unloading Exp.	750		"	Stock on Consignment A/c	16,250[1]
Selling	1,000				
		1,750			
" M. K. Menon A/c – Commission					
Ordinary	6,825				
Del Credere	2,275				
		9,100			
" Disputed amount		500[2]			
" Profit & Loss A/c Profit on Consignment transferred		15,400			
		1,07,250			1,07,250

Workings :

1. **Valuation of Unsold Stock**

		Rs.
	Total Cost	75,000
Add :	Expenses of Consignor	5,500
Add :	Non-recurring Expenses of Consignee	750
	Cost Price of 500 cases	81,250

$\therefore$ Value of Unsold Stock $= \frac{\text{Rs. } 81,250 \times 100}{500}$

$=$ Rs. 16,250

2. The loss which arises due to dispute in quality of goods is to be borne by the Consignor and, as such, it is a charged against the Consignment.
3. There will be no treatment for bad debts in the books of Consignor since Del Credere Commission is given.

M. K. Menon Account

Date	Particulars	Amount	Date	Particulars	Amount
?		Rs.	?		Rs.
	To Consignment to Chennai A/c —Sale Proceeds	91,000		By Bank—Advance	20,000
				" Consignment to Chennai A/c	
				" —Expenses	1,750
				" —Commission	9,100
				" —Disputed amount	500
				" Balance c/d	59,650
		91,000			91,000

Dr. Cr.

Goods Sent on Consignment Account

Date	Particulars	Amount	Date	Particulars	Amount
?		Rs.	?		Rs.
	To Trading A/c —Transfer	75,000		By Consignment to Chennai A/c	75,000
		75,000			75,000

Dr. Cr.

Stock on Consignment Account

Date	Particulars	Amount	Date	Particulars	Amount
?		Rs.	?		Rs.
	To Consignment to Chennai A/c	16,250		By Balance c/d	16,250
		16,250			16,250

Balance Sheet (Extracts)
as at ....

Liabilities	Rs.	Assets	Rs.
		M. K. Menon A/c	59,650
		Stock on Consignment	16,250

Value of stock as per FIFO/LIFO Method

Illustration 5

Begun, the consignor, informed the following:

Stock with Consignee, Patal on 1.1.2010—500 Motors costing Rs. 1,000 each

1,200 Motors @ Rs. 1,500 were sent out during the year. Begun incurred: Freight and Insurance Rs. 24,000. Patial reported the following:

Clearing charges Rs. 48,000, Godown Rent and Advertisement Rs. 12,000.

He was entilled to a commission @ 10% on sales.

He sold 1,000 Motors @ Rs. 2,000 per Motor

He remitted a draft for the balance.

Prepare Consignment Account in a Columnar form and ascertain the value of stock as per (a) FIFO Method, (b) LIFO Method of valuation.

Solution

In the books of Begun
Consignment Account

Dr. Cr.

Date	Particulars	As per FIFO Rs.	As per LIFO Rs.	Date	Particulars	As per FIFO Rs.	As per LIFO Rs.
2010				2010			
Jan. 1	To Stock on Consignment A/c (500 × Rs. 1,000)	5,00,000	5,00,000	?	By Patal A/c —Sale Proceeds	20,00,000	20,00,000
	" Goods Sent on Consignment A/c (1,200 × Rs. 1,500)	18,00,000	18,00,000		" Unsold stock or Stock on Consignment A/c	10,92,000	8,12,000
	" Bank A/c —Freight & Insurance	24,000	24,000				
	" Patal's A/c —Clearing Charges	48,000	48,000				
	—Godown Rent & Adv.	12,000	12,000				
	—Commission	2,00,000	2,00,000				
	" Profit & Loss A/c						
	" Net Profit Transferred	5,08,000	2,28,000				
		30,92,000	28,12,000			30,92,000	28,12,000

Workings

(a) Value of stock as per FIFO Method

Since FIFO method is followed, all the closing stock should be **Valued at current purchase price (out of goods sent during the year)**

	Rs.
Total cost	18,00,000
Add : Consignor Exp.	24,000
Add : Consignee's Non-recurring Exp.	48,000
Cost Price of 1,200 motors =	18,72,000

$\therefore$ Value of 700 Motors = $\frac{700 \times \text{Rs. } 18,72,000}{1,200}$ = 10,92,000

(b) Valuation of stock as per LIFO method

Since LIFO method is followed closing stock should be valued as under:

	Rs.
500 Motors @ Rs. 1,000 =	5,00,000
200 Motors $\left(\frac{200 \times \text{Rs. } 18,72,000}{1,200}\right)$ =	3,12,000
700	8,12,000

When Market Price is less than the Cost Price

Illustration 6

Vandana Traders of Delhi purchased 10,000 sarees @ Rs. 100 per saree. Out of these 6,000 sarees were sent on consignment to National Traders of Jodhpur at the selling price of Rs. 120 per saree. The consignors paid Rs. 3,000 for packing and freight.

National Traders sold 5,000 sarees @ Rs. 125 per saree and incurred Rs. 1,000 for selling expenses and remitted Rs. 5,00,000 to Delhi on account. They are entitled to a commission of 5% on total sales plus a further of 25% commission on any surplus price realised over Rs. 120 per saree.

3,000 sarees were sold at Delhi @ Rs. 110 per saree.

Owing to fall in market price, the value of stock of saree in hand is to be reduced by 10%.

You are required to prepare (i) Consignment Account, and (ii) National Traders Account. (iii) Trading and Profit & Loss Account

Solution **[CA Foundation May 1996 —Adapted]**

In the books of Vandana Traders

Consignment to Jodhpur Account

Dr. Cr.

Date	Particulars	Amount	Date	Particulars	Amount
?		Rs.	?		Rs.
	To Goods sent on Consignment A/c			By National Traders A/c	
	(6,000 × Rs. 100)	6,00,000		—Sale proceeds	
	" Bank A/c			(5,000 × Rs. 125)	6,25,000
	—Packing and Freight	3,000		" Stock on Consignment A/c	85,500[2]
	" National Traders A/c				
	—Selling Expenses	1,000			
	—Commission	37,500[1]			
	Profit and Loss A/c				
	—Profit on cconsignment transferred	69,000			
		7,10,500			7,10,500

Notes :

1. 3,000 sarees, which were sold at Delhi @ Rs. 110 per saree, are not to be taken into considera-tion since it is not a consignment transaction and, hence, the same is excluded from Consignment Account.

2. Although the consignor purchased 10,000 sarees, only 6,000 sarees are related to consignment transaction, balance is not to be taken into Consignment Account at all.

National Traders Account

Dr. Cr.

Date	Particulars	Amount	Date	Particulars	Amount
?		Rs.	?		Rs.
	To Consignment to Jodhpur A/c			By Bank A/c	5,00,000
	—Sale Proceeds	6,25,000		—Advance	
				" Consignment to Jodhpur A/c	
				—Exp. & Com.	38,500
				" Balance c/d	86,500
		6,25,000			6,25,000

Trading Account and Profit and Loss Account *for the year ended ....*

Dr. Cr.

Date	Particulars	Amount	Date	Particulars	Amount
?		Rs.	?		Rs.
	To Purchase A/c			By Sales A/c	
	(10,000 × Rs. 100)	10,00,000		(3,000 × Rs. 110)	3,30,000
	" Gross Profit c/d	15,500		" Goods sent on Consigment A/c	6,00,000
				(6,000 × Rs. 100)	
				" Unsold Stock A/c	85,500
		10,15,500			10,15,500
	To Capital A/c			By Gross Profit b/d	15,500
	—Net Profit transferred	84,500		" Consig. to Jodhpur A/c	69,000
				—Profit	
		84,500			84,500

Workings :

1. Calculation of Commission payable to National Traders

		Rs.
	Total Sales @ Rs. 125	6,25,000
Less :	Sales over Rs. 120	6,00,000
	Surplus Price Realised	25,000
	@ 5% on total Sales Rs. 6,25,000 × 5%	31,250
Add :	25% on Rs. 25,000	6,250
		37,500

2. Valuation of Unsold Stock

Since market price has fallen by 10%, valuation of unsold stock on consignment will be calculated as :

		Rs.
	Total Cost (1,000 × Rs. 100) (without considering expenses)	1,00,000
Less :	10% Reduction	10,000
		90,000
Less :	Consigniee's Com. @ 5%	4,500
	Estimated Selling Price	85,500

Valuation of Unsold Stock

Illustration 7

K sold goods on behalf of V on consignment basis. On 1.1.2012, he had with him a stock of Rs. 20,000 on consignment.

K had instruction to sell the goods at cost plus 25% and was entitled to a commission of 4% on sales, in addition to 1% Del Credere Commission on total sales for guaranteeing collection of all the sales proceeds.

During the year ended 31.12.2012, Cash Sales were Rs. 1,20,000. Credit Sales Rs. 1,05,000 and K's expenses relating to the Consignment Rs. 3,000, being Salaries and Insurance. Bad Debts were Rs. 3,000 and Goods Sent on Consignment Rs. 2,00,000.

From the above, ascertain the Value of unsold stock only.

Solution

Valuation on Closing Stock

		Rs.
	Opening Stock	20,000
Add :	Goods sent on Consignment	2,00,000
		2,20,000
Less :	Cost of Goods Sold	
	(Rs. 2,25,000 × $\frac{100}{125}$) Closing Stock	1,80,000
		40,000

Books of Cosignee/Consignment Inwards

It has been stated above that the consignee is merely an agent and, as such, he is not liable to pay for the goods which he receives from the consignor. For this purpose, he does not make any entry for such receipts. But he maintains adequate records for these transactions, viz., expenses and his commissions and also for the purpose of settlement of accounts with the consignor. He opens the personal account of the consignor in order to record such consignment transactions.

The consignment is referred to as Consignment Outward (i.e., simple Consignment Account) when goods are sent by the consignor to the consignee. The same consignment is known as Consignment Inward when it is received by the consignee, i.e., it may be stated as the receipt of goods by consignee which are to be sold on a commission basis at the risk of the the consignor.

The following entries are to be recorded in the books of consignee :

(i) ***When goods are received on Consignment :***

No Entry

(ii) ***When expenses are incurred by him :***

Consignor's A/c Dr.
  To Cash/Bank A/c

(iii) ***For advance to Consignor : For sending remittance :***

Consignor's A/c Dr.
  To Cash/Bank/Bills Payable A/c (in case of acceptance of a bill)

(iv) ***For Cash Sales :***

Bank A/c Dr.

To Consignor's A/c

(v) ***For Credit Sales :***

Consignment Debtors A/c Dr.

To Consignor's A/c

(vi) ***For Commission receivable :***

Consignor's A/c Dr.

To Ordinary Commission A/c

" Del Credere Commission A/c

(vii) ***For collection of debt (against credit Sales) :***

Bank A/c Dr.

To Consignment Debtors A/c

(viii) ***For bad debts, if any :***

(a) If no Del Credere Commission is paid

Consignor's A/c Dr.

To Consignment Debtors A/c

(Bad Debts relating to Consignment Debtors)

(b) If Del Credere Commission is paid :

Bad Debts A/c Dr.

To Consignment Debtors A/c

(Here, bad debts relating to debtors will be adjusted against Del Credere Commission Account in order to find out the net effect for the purpose.) The entry will be :

Del Credere Commission A/c Dr.

To Bad Debts A/c

(ix) ***For final settlement :***

Consignor A/c Dr.

To Cash/Bank Draft etc.

(x) ***For Balance of Stock :***

No Entry

Preparation of accounts in the books of consignee and Del Credere Commission

Illustration 8

Take Illustration 3, and prepare the necessary accounts in the books of Y.

Solution

In the books of Y

Dr. **X Account** *Cr.*

Date	*Particulars*	*Amount*	*Date*	*Particulars*	*Amount*
?		Rs.	?		Rs.
	To Cash A/c—Advance	30,000		By Bank A/c	
	" Commission received A/c:			—Cash Sales	1,40,000
	" Ordinary Commission	7,500		" Consignment Debtors	
	" Del Credere Commission	3,750		—Credit Sale	10,000
	" Bank A/c—Expenses	3,000			
	" Balance c/d	1,05,750			
		1,50,000			1,50,000

Dr. **Consignment Debtors Account** *Cr.*

Date	*Particulars*	*Amount*	*Date*	*Particulars*	*Amount*
?		Rs.	?		Rs.
	To X A/c	10,000		By Bank A/c	8,000
				" Commission Received A/c	
				—Bad Debts	1,000
				" Balance c/d	1,000
		10,000			10,000

Dr. **Commission Received Account** Cr.

Date	Particulars	Amount	Date	Particulars	Amount
?		Rs.	?		Rs.
	To Consignment Debtors A/c —Bad Debts	1,000		By X A/c (Rs. 7,500 + Rs. 3,750)	11,250
	" Profit and Loss A/c —Transfer	10,250			
		11,250			11,250

(2) ***In the books of Y***

Dr. **X Account** Cr.

Date	Particulars	Amount	Date	Particulars	Amount
?		Rs.	?		Rs.
	To Cash A/c—Advance	30,000		By Bank A/c —Cash Sales	1,40,000
	" Commission Received A/c	7,500		" Bank A/c —Received from Debtors	8,000
	" Bank—Expenses A/c	3,000			
	" Balance c/d	1,07,500			
		1,48,000			1,48,000

Dr. **Commission Received Account** Cr.

Date	Particulars	Amount	Date	Particulars	Amount
?		Rs.	?		Rs.
	To Profit and Loss A/c —Transfer	7,500		By X A/c	7,500
		7,500			7,500

Illustration 9

X of Mumbai consigned 1,000 boxes of medicines costing Rs. 60 per box to Y of Kolkata. The agent sold 400 boxes at Rs. 80 per box for cash, 400 boxes at Rs. 82 per box on credit, and they took over the balance to their own stock at Rs. 82 per box. X paid Freight and Insurance Rs. 500 and Miscellaneous Expenses Rs. 200. He drew on Y at 3 months for Rs. 45,000 which was duly accepted by the latter. Expenses incurred by Y : Carriage Rs. 50, Octoroi Rs. 40, Selling Expenses 210. Y was entitled to a Commission @ 5% and 2% as Del Credere Commission on total gross sale proceeds. Y sent an Account sales to his principal showing as a deduction therefrom their commission and the various expenses incurred by him. A month later all the debtors except one who owed Rs. 200 paid Cash and Y remitted the amount due on consignment. Show the entries and the necessary accounts in the books of Y.

Solution

Journal

Date	Particulars		L.F.	Debit	Credit
?				Rs.	Rs.
(i)	X A/c	Dr.		300	
	To Bank A/c				300
	(Expenses incurred on consignment.)				
(ii)	X A/c	Dr.		45,000	
	To Bills Payable A/c				45,000
	(Bill accepted for consignment.)				
(iii)	Bank A/c	Dr.		32,000	
	Consignment Debtors A/c	Dr.		32,800	
	To X A/c				64,800
	(Cash and Credit sales on consignment.)				
(iv)	Purchase A/c	Dr.		16,400	
	To X A/c				16,400
	(Remaining Stock taken.)				

Contd.

			Rs.	Rs.
(v)	X A/c	Dr.	5,684	
	To Commission A/c			5,684
	(Commission on sale charged.)			
(vi)	Cash A/c	Dr.	32,600	
	Bad Debts A/c	Dr.	200	
	To Consignment Debtors A/c			32,800
	(Collection on consignment debtors.)			
(vii)	Commission A/c	Dr.	200	
	To Bad Debts A/c			200
	(Bad debts adjusted against commission.)			
(viii)	X A/c	Dr.	30,216	
	To Bank A/c			30,216
	(Final remittance to X.)			

Dr. **X Account** Cr.

Date	Particulars	Amount	Date	Particulars	Amount
?		Rs.	?		Rs.
	To Bank A/c Expenses	300		By Cash A/-Cash Sales	32,000
	" Commission A/c	5,684		" Consignment Debtors A/c	
	" B/P A/c	45,000		—Credit Sales	
	" Bank – Final settlement	30,216		—Stock Taken	32,800
	(bal. fig.)			" Purchases A/c	16,400
		81,200			81,200

Dr. **Consignment Debtors Account** Cr.

Date	Particulars	Amount	Date	Particulars	Amount
?		Rs.	?		Rs.
	To X A/c	32,800		By Cash A/c	32,600
				" Bad Debts A/c	200
		32,800			32,800

Dr. **Bad Debts Account** Cr.

Date	Particulars	Amount	Date	Particulars	Amount
?		Rs.	?		Rs.
	To Consignment Debtors A/c	200		By Commission A/c	200
		200			200

Dr. **Commission Account** Cr.

Date	Particulars	Amount	Date	Particulars	Amount
?		Rs.	?		Rs.
	To Bad Debts A/c	200		By X A/c	5,684
	" P & L A/c	5,484			
		5,684			5,684

Illustration 10

Auto Agencies have sold out the following goods on behalf of different parties for which they have incurred some expenses and are entitled to commission and reimbursement of expenses:

	Life Light	Sieac	Akriti
	Rs.	Rs.	Rs.
Stock in hand	8,000	12,000	12,000
Goods Received	20,000	30,000	36,000
Goods Sold	24,000	26,000	44,000
Expenses	600	400	800
Remittance	20,000	22,000	40,000
Commission @ 10%	10%	6%	5%

Prepare the Consignor's Account and Commission Account in the books of Auto Agencies.

[ICWA]

Solution

In the books of Auto Agencies

Consignor Account

Dr. Cr.

Date	Particulars	Amount Life Light	Amount Sieac	Amount Akriti	Date	Particulars	Amount Life Light	Amount Sieac	Amount Akriti
		Rs.	Rs.	Rs.			Rs.	Rs.	Rs.
?	To Bank A/c	600	400	800	?	By Bank A/c —Sale proceeds	24,000	26,000	44,000
	" Comm. A/c	2,400	1,560	2,200					
	" Bank A/c	20,000	22,000	40,000					
	" Balance c/d	1,000	2,040	1,000					
		24,000	26,000	44,000			24,000	26,000	44,000

Commission Account

Dr. Cr.

Date	Particulars	Amount Life Light	Amount Sieac	Amount Akriti	Date	Particulars	Amount Life Light	Amount Sieac	Amount Akriti
?		Rs.	Rs.	Rs.	?		Rs.	Rs.	Rs.
	To P & L A/c	2,400	1,560	2,200		By Consignor A/c	2,400	1,560	2,200
		2,400	1,560	2,200			2,400	1,560	2,200

Discounting Charges of the Bill

When the consignor receives a bill from the consignee either as an advance or as a final settlement, he may discount the bill by the bank. Now the question arises whether the discounting charges of the bill will be treated as an expense of the consignment or not. There are two schools of thought about it. Some accountants are of opinion that discounting charges **should be adjusted against the Consignment Account** (i.e., discounting charges should appear in the debit side of Consignment Account) as it is an expense relating to consignment.

Some other accountants are of opinion that discounting charges of the bill should be **treated as a financial charge,** hence, **it should be adjusted against Profit and Loss Account and not against Consignment.**

However, both the methods are correct. The students are advised to give a note whatever method they follow.

Loss of Goods on Consignment

Sometimes a part of the goods may be lost, destroyed or damaged either in-transit or in consignee's godown. Such loss can broadly be sub-divided into :

A. Normal Loss.

B. Abnormal Loss.

A. Normal Loss and its Treatment

Normal Loss is that loss which is unavoidable, inherent and which arises due to natural causes, e.g., leakage, evaporation, drying etc. None (i.e., consignor or consignee) can prevent it. Since normal loss is a part of the cost of goods no additional adjustment is required for this purpose. But at the time of calculating the value of unsold stock on consignment, the quantity of such loss (and not the amount) is to be simply deducted from the total quantity received by the consignee in good condition or quantities available for sale. Thus, the value of closing stock may be computed as under :

$$\textit{Value of Closing Stock} = \frac{\textit{Total value of goods sent} \times \textit{Unsold quantity}}{\textit{Net quantity received (i.e., after normal loss) by consignee in good condition}}$$

Treatment of Normal Loss

Illustration 11

Kashim informed you the following particulars of his transactions relating to goods consigned to Karim for the year ended 31.12.2012:

	Rs.
Goods Sent (10,000 kg)	1,00,000
Kashim's Expenses	10,000

Contd.

		Rs.
Karim's Expenses :		
Freight and Insurance	2,000	
Selling Expenses	5,000	7,000
Sold (8,000 kg) for		
Loss due to natural wastage (100 kg)		1,12,000
Commission @ 5% on gross sales		

You are asked to prepare the Consignment Account only, with detailed calculation of unsold stock in the books of Kashim.

Solution

In the books of Kashim
Consignment Account

Dr. Cr.

Date	Particulars		Amount	Date	Particulars	Amount
?			Rs.	?		Rs.
	To Goods Sent on Consignment A/c		1,00,000		By Karim A/c Sale Proceeds	1,12,000
	" Bank A/c Expenses		10,000		" Stock on Consignment	21,495[1]
	" Karim A/c					
	Freight and Ins.	2,000				
	Selling Exps.	5,000	7,000			
	" Karim A/c Commission @ 5%		5,600			
	" Profit & Loss A/c					
	" Profit on Consignment —Transferred		10,895			
			1,33,495			1,33,495

Workings :

	Valuation of Unsold Stock :	Rs.
	Total Costs	1,00,000
Add :	Consignor's Exp	10,000
	C.P. of 10,000 kg	1,00,000
Add.	Non-recurring Exp. of Karim :	2,000
	Value of (10,000 – 100) = 9,900 kg	1,12,000

Therefore,

$$\text{value of stock} = \frac{1,900 \times \text{Rs. } 1,12,000}{9,900} = \text{Rs. } 21,495$$

B. Abnormal Loss and its treatment

This loss may be incurred due to accident or negligence, e.g., theft, fire, riot, flood etc. They do not occur frequently. If there is any abnormal loss, the same should be adjusted before ascertaining the result of the consignment. The valuation is to be done like unsold stock on consignment. But, special attention must be given to allocate expenses which are incurred ***prior to loss and subsequent to loss.*** Sometimes, a part or full of such loss may be admitted by or recovered from the Insurance company and should be adjusted accordingly. For this purpose, the following entries are to be recorded :

Treatment of Abnormal Loss

Method I

(a) ***For abnormal Loss :***
Abnormal Loss A/c Dr.
To Consignment A/c

(b) ***If goods are insured and admitted or covered by Insurance Company :***
Insurance Co./Bank A/c Dr.
To Abnormal Loss A/c

(c) ***If goods are not insured :***
Profit and Loss A/c Dr.
To Abnormal Loss A/c

(d) ***For the balance (i.e., which is not covered/admitted by Insurance Co.) :***
Profit and Loss A/c Dr.
To Abnormal Loss A/c

Method II

(a) ***If goods are insured/covered by Insurance company :***
Insurance Company A/c Dr.
To Consignment A/c

(b) ***If goods are not insured/covered by Insurance Company :***
Profit and Loss A/c Dr.
To Consignment A/c

(c) ***For the balance (i.e., which is not covered/admitted by Insurance Company) :***
Profit and Loss A/c Dr.
To Consignment A/c

Treatment of Abnormal Loss in-Transit

Illustration 12

2,000 shirts were consigned by Bhagwan & Co. of Delhi to Shreyans of Tokyo at cost of Rs. 150 each. Bhagwan & Co. paid freight Rs. 20,000 and Insurance Rs. 3,000.

During the transit 200 shirts were totally damaged by fire. Shreyans took delivery of the remaining shirts and paid Rs. 28,800 on customs duty. Shreyans settled his account immediately. Nothing was recovered from the insurer for the damaged goods.

Shreyans had sent a bank draft to Bhagwan & Co. for Rs. 1,00,000 as advance payment. 1,600 shirts were sold by him at Rs. 200 each. Expenses incurred by Shreyans on godown rent and advertisement etc. amounted to Rs. 4,000. He is entitled to a commission of 5%.

One of the customers to whom the goods were sold on credit could not pay the cost of 10 shirts.

Prepare the Consignment Account, the account of Shreyans and Abnormal Loss Account in the books of Bhagwan & Co.

Solution

In the books of Bhagwan & Co.
Consignment to Tokyo Account

Dr. Cr.

Date	Particulars		Amount Rs.	Date	Particulars	Amount Rs.
?	To Goods sent on Consignment A/c (2,000 × Rs. 150)		3,00,000	?	By Shreyans A/c —Sale Proceeds (1,590 × Rs. 200)	3,18,000
	" Bank A/c —Freight	20,000			" Consignment Debtors A/c —Credit Sales (10 × Rs. 200)	2,000
	—Insurance	3,000	23,000		" Abnormal Loss A/c	32,300[1]
	" Shreyans A/c —Custom Duty	28,800			" Stock on Consignment A/c	35,500[1]
	—Godown Rent, Adv. etc.	4,000				
	—Commission @ 5% on total Sales	16,000	48,800			
	" Consignment Debtors A/c " Bad Debts		2,000			
	" Profit and Loss A/c " —Profit on Consignment Transferred		14,000			
			3,87,800			3,87,800

Shreyans Account

Dr. Cr.

Date	Particulars	Amount Rs.	Date	Particulars	Amount Rs.
?	To Consignment to Tokyo A/c —Sale Proceeds	3,18,000	?	By Bank Draft A/c —Advance	1,00,000
				" Consignment to Tokyo A/c —Expenses & Com.	48,800
				" Bank A/c —Final Settlement	1,69,200
		3,18,000			3,18,000

Dr. **Abnormal Loss Account** Cr.

Date	Particulars	Amount	Date	Particulars	Amount
?		Rs.	?		Rs.
	To Consignment to Tokyo A/c	32,300		By Profit and Loss A/c	32,300
		32,300			32,300

Workings :

1. **Valuation of Goods Lost-in-transit and Unsold Stock**

		Rs.
Total Cost		3,00,000
Add :	Consignor's Expences	23,000
	C. P. of 2,000 Shirts	3,23,000
Less : **Lost-in-Transit**		
$\left(\frac{\text{Rs. } 3{,}23{,}000 \times 200}{2{,}000}\right) =$		32,300
		2,90,700
Add : Non-recurring Expenses of Consignee		28,800
	C. P. of 1,800 Shirts	3,19,500

Note : Since Del Credere Com. is not given by the consignor to the consignee, amount of bad debts is to be charged against Consignment Account.

$$\therefore \text{ Value of Unsold Stock } = \frac{\text{Rs. } 3{,}19{,}500 \times 200}{1{,}800} = \text{Rs. } 35{,}500$$

Abnormal Loss with Salvage Value

Illustration 13

Ramesh consigned 2,000 MT of chemicals at a cost of Rs. 800 per MT to John. Ramesh paid freight and insurance charges of Rs. 20,000. Of the above, 500 MT of chemicals were destroyed by fire during transit. John cleared the balance of 1,500 MT of chemicals and sold 1,000 MT at an average price of Rs. 1,000 per MT. John incurred the following expenses: Godown rent Rs. 5,000, Insurance Rs. 3,000, Clearing Charges Rs. 4,500. Insurance claim received against fire Rs. 4,00,000 after admitting the salvage value of stock destroyed by fire at Rs. 10,000. John was entitled to a commission of 10% on sale proceeds. John sends the balance to Ramesh after adjusting his commission and expenses out of the sale proceeds.

Prepare a Consignment Account and John's Account and Abnormal Loss Account in the books of Ramesh.

[CA Foundation, June 1993—Adapted]

Solution

In the books of Ramesh

Dr. **Consignment Account** Cr.

Date	Particulars		Amount	Date	Particulars	Amount
?			Rs.	?		Rs.
	To Goods Sent on Consignment A/c		16,00,000		By John's A/c—Sales—1,000 MT	
	" Bank A/c—Freight & Insurance		20,000		@ Rs. 1,000 per MT	10,00,000
	" John's A/c—Commission				" Abnorml Loss A/c	3,95,000[1]
	@ 10% Rs. 10,00,000		1,00,000		Consignment Stock A/c	4,16,500[2]
	" John's A/c				– Cost of 500 MT	
	Godown Rent	5,000				
	Insurnce	3,000				
	Clearing Charges	4,500	12,500			
	" Profit & Loss A/c—					
	Profit on Consignment trans.		79,000			
			18,11,500			18,11,500

Dr. **John Account** Cr.

Date	Particulars		Amount	Date	Particulars			Amount
			Rs.					Rs.
?	To	Consignment A/c —Sale proceeds	10,00,000	?	By	Consignment A/c		
						Godown Rent	5,000	
						Insurance	3,000	
						Clearing Charges	4,500	12,500
					"	Consignment A/c Com.		1,00,000
					"	Bank A/c—Balance paid		8,87,500
			10,00,000					10,00,000

Dr. **Abnormal Loss Account** Cr.

Date	Particulars		Amount	Date	Particulars		Amount
			Rs.				Rs.
?	To	Consignment A/c	3,95,000	?	By	Bank A/c—Insurance Claim	4,00,000
	"	Profit & Loss A/c (bal fig.)	15,000		"	Bank A/c—Salvage Value	10,000
			4,10,000				4,10,000

Workings :

1. **Valuation of Goods Destroyed by Fire-in-Transit and Unsold Stock**

		Rs.
	Total Cost of 2,000 MT	16,00,000
Add :	Consignor's Expenses	20,000
		16,20,000
Less :	Lost-in-Transit	
	$(\frac{500}{2,000} \times$ Rs. 16,20,000)	4,05,000
	(Actual Loss Rs. 4,05,000 – Salvage Rs. 10,000) = 3,95,000[1]	12,15,,000
Add :	Non-recurring Expenses of Consignee	4,500
	Cost of 1,500 MT	12,19,500

2. Value of Unsold Stock = Rs. $\frac{12,19,500 \times 500MT}{1,500MT}$ = 4,06,500

Add : Salvage Value of Goods 10,000

4,16,500

Ascertainment of Sales and Abnormal Loss

Illustration 14

Messers NCBA were appointed agent by Sunrise Limited in 2000.

You are given the following particulars relating to the year 2010-11:

		Rs.
(i)	Cost of goods despatched by the Company on consignment	7,50,000
(ii)	Goods fully destroyed in Transit (original cost)	50,000
(iii)	Expenses incurred by the Company towards :	
	Freight	2,500
	Insurance	1,500
(iv)	Expenses incurred by M/s NCBA :	
	Landing & Clearing	1,500
	Godown Rent	1,000
	Transport Charges	1,000
	Advertisements	800
	Insurance	800
(v)	Advance remitted by the Agent	1,50,000
(vi)	Bills payable accepted	25,000
(vii)	Goods destroyed by fire (at original cost) in Agent's godown	35,000

Contd.

		Rs.
(viii)	Bad Debts	3,000
(ix)	Unsold stock with Agent at the close of the year (at original cost)	50,000
(x)	Insurance claim recovered by the Consignor towards loss by fire	48,000
(xi)	Insurance claim recovered by the Agent towards loss by fire	35,000

All sales were effected by the Agent at 25% on original cost. The Agent is entitled to a Commission of 10% on gross sales.

You are required to show the Consignor's Account (Sunrise Ltd.) as would appear in the Books of NCBA.

Solution

In the books of NCBA
Consignor's Account (Sunrise Ltd.)

Dr. *Cr.*

Date		*Particulars*	*Amount*	*Date*		*Particulars*	*Amount*
?			Rs.	?			Rs.
	To	Bank A/c			By	Bank A/c	
		Landing & Clearing	1,500			(Sales Proceeds)	7,68,750
		Godown Rent	1,000		"	Bank A/c	
		Transport Charges	1,000			(Insurance Claim)	35,000
		Advertisements	800				
		Insurance	800				
	"	Bank (Advance) A/c	1,50,000				
	"	Bills Payable A/c	25,000				
	"	Commission (10% on Rs. 7,68,750) A/c	76,875				
	"	Balance c/d	5,46,775				
			8,03,750				8,03,750

Workings :

	Calculation of Sales		Rs.
	Cost of Goods despatched		7,50,000
Less :	Goods fully destroyed in transit	50,000	
	Goods destroyed by fire	35,000	
	Unsold Stock	50,000	
			1,35,000
	Original Cost of Goods Sold		6,15,000
Add :	Profit at 25% of Original Cost		1,53,750
	Sales		7,68,750

Ascertainment of Good Sent on consignment Gross Sale Proceeds and provision, for repairs on damaged Unsold Stock

Illustration 15

Mr. Ashit requests you to prepare a Consignment Account for the year ended 30th June 2012 and for the purpose gives you the following information to ascertain the profit earned on consignment :

(i)	Agent's commission @ 5% on gross sales			20,000
(ii)	Cost of goods fully damaged in transit, insurance claim recovered Rs. 18,000			20,000
(iii)	Expenses incurred by the agent :			
	Godown Rent	Rs.	400	
	Landing & Clearing	Rs.	1,000	
	Advertisements	Rs.	200	
	Transport charges	Rs.	900	
	Selling expenses	Rs.	1,000	3,500
(iv)	Freight expenses incurred by Ashit			2,000
(v)	Cost of unsold stock lying with agent at the end of the year			60,000

All sales were effected by the agent at a profit of 25% on cost.

The agent reported that the rest of the goods were also partially damaged for which Rs. 5,200 may have to incur for reparing purpose.

Solution

In the Books of Mr. Ashit
Consignment Account

Dr. Cr.

Date	Particulars		Amount	Date	Particulars	Amount
			Rs.			Rs.
?	To Goods sent on Consig.A/c		4,00,000[2]	?	By Agent A/c —Sale proceeds	4,00,000[1]
	" Bank – Freight		2,000		" Abnormal Loss A/c	20,100[3]
	" Agents A/c :				" Consignment Stock A/c	60,600
	Godown Rent	400				
	Landing & Clearing	1,000				
	Advertisement	200				
	Transport Exps.	900				
	Selling Exps.	1,000	3,500			
	" Agents A/c :					
	" Commission		20,000			
	" Provision for Repair		5,200[4]			
	" Profit and Loss A/c —Profit on Consignment Trans.		50,000			
			4,80,700			4,80,700

Workings :

1. **Gross Sale Proceeds**

Agent's com @ 5% on Gross Sales which is equal to Rs. 20,000

∴ Gross Sale Proceeds Rs. 4,00,000 (i.e., Rs. 20,000 × $\frac{100}{5}$)

2. **Cost of Goods Sent on Consignment**

		Rs.
	Gross Sale Proceeds	4,00,000
Less :	G. P. @ 25% on Cost or, @ 20% on Sales	80,000
	Cost of goods sold	3,20,000
Add :	Cost of goods damaged	20,000
Add :	Cost of unsold stock	60,000
		4,00,000

3. **Value of Goods Damaged**

Cost of goods	20,000
Add : Proportionate Exp. $\left(\frac{Rs. 20,000 \times Rs. 2,000}{Rs. 4,00,000}\right)$	100
	20,100

4. **Value of Unsold Stock**

Cost of goods	60,000
Add : Proportionate Exp. of Consignor $\left(\frac{Rs. 60,000 \times Rs. 2,000}{Rs. 4,00,000}\right)$	300
Add : Proportional non-recurring Exp. of consignee $\frac{Rs. 60,000}{(Rs. 4,00,000 - 20,000)} \times Rs. 1,900$	300
	60,600

4. **Provision for repairs on Damaged Unsold Stock**

Sometimes it may so happen that damaged goods need some repairs. In this case Rs. 5,200 is expected to be incurred for damaged unsold stock. For that purpose, the following entries are required to be passed :

(1) *For making provision for repairs*

Consignment A/c	Dr.	5,200	
To Provision for Repairs A/c			5,200

(2) *When actual amount will be incurred—*

Provision for repairs A/c	Dr.		
To Cash/Bank A/c			

Note : If actual expenses for repairs is less than the 'Provisions for Expenses' in that case, excess amount to be adjusted against Profit and Loss Account/Consignment Account subsequently. But if actual expenses, for repairs is more than the **provision for repairs** in that case. Consignment Account should be debited for such excess amount.

Goods Lost for Consignee's Negligence

Illustration 16

P of Kolkata, consigned goods costing Rs. 1,60,000 to R of Mumbai. The terms of the consignment were :

(a) Consignee to get commission of 5% on cash sales and 4% on credit sales.

(b) Any goods taken by consignee himself or goods lost through consignee's negligence, shall be valued at cost plus $12\frac{1}{2}$ % and no commission will be allowed on them.

The expenses incurred by the consignor were :

Carriage and freight Rs. 6,720 and Insurance Rs. 3,440. The consignor received Rs. 50,000 as advance against the consignment. Account sales together with a draft for the balance due was received by the consignor showing the following position :

Goods costing Rs. 1,28,000 were sold for cash at Rs. 1,40,000 and on credit at Rs. 1,08,000. Goods costing Rs. 8,000 were taken by R and goods costing Rs. 4,000 were lost through R's negligence. The expenses incurred by R were : Advertisement Rs. 1,720; other selling expenses Rs. 1,080.

Show the ledger accounts in the books of P.

Solution

In the books of P

Consignment to Mumbai Account

Dr. Date	Particulars		Amount	Date	Particulars	Cr. Amount
?			Rs.	?		Rs.
	To Goods Sent on Consignment A/c		1,60,000		By R' A/c—	
	" Bank A/c —Expenses :				Cash Sales	1,40,000
	Carriage and Freight	6,720			" R A/c—	
	Insurance	3,440	10,160		Goods taken	9,000
	" R A/c—				(Rs. 8,000 + $12\frac{1}{2}$ % on Rs. 8,000)	
	Advertisement	1,720			" R A/c—	
	Selling Expenses	1,080	2,800		Goods lost for his negligence	4,500
	" R A/c—				(Rs. 4,000 + $12\frac{1}{2}$ % on Rs. 4,000)	
	Commission on Cash Sales	7,000			" Consignment Debtors :	
	Commission on Credit Sales	4,320	11,320		Credit Sales	1,08,000
	" Profit and Loss A/c				" Stock on Consignment A/c	21,270
	" Profit on Consignment —Transferred		98,490			
			2,82,770			2,82,770

R Account

Dr. Date	Particulars	Amount	Date	Particulars	Cr. Amount
?		Rs.	?		Rs.
	To Consign. to Mumbai A/c			By Bank-Advance	50,000
	—Cash Sales	1,40,000		" Consignment to Mumbai A/c	
	—Goods taken	9,000		—Expenses	2,800
	—Goods lost	4,500		—Commission	11,320
				" Bank (amount due)	89,380
		1,53,500			1,53,500

Goods Sent on Consignment Account

Dr. Date	Particulars	Amount	Date	Particulars	Cr. Amount
?		Rs.	?		Rs.
	To Trading A/c			By Consignment to Mumbai A/c	1,60,000
	—Transfer	1,60,000			
		1,60,000			1,60,000

Consignment Debtors Account

Date	Particulars	Amount	Date	Particulars	Amount
Dr.					Cr.
		Rs.			Rs.
?	To Consignment to Mumbai A/c	1,08,000	?	By Balance c/d	1,08,000
		1,08,000			1,08,000

Workings :

Valuation of Unsold Stock

		Rs.
	Total cost of goods	1,60,000
Add :	Consignor's Expenses	10,160
		1,70,160

$\therefore$ Value of Unsold Stock $= \frac{\text{Rs. } 20,000}{\text{Rs. } 1,60,000} \times \text{Rs. } 1,70,160$

$= \text{Rs. } 21,270$

Opening Stock, Closing Stock, Abnormal Loss and Sale of Damaged Goods

Illustration 17

Star Mills, Surat, sends regular consignments of Yarn to X who is the selling agent of the mill and is entitled to a commission of 10 paise per kg Yarn sold. This includes Del Credere commission.

Following further information is furnished to you :

On 1st July 2010, Stock of Yarn with the agent 20,000 kg costing Rs. 50,000.

During the year ended 30th June 2011:

Total quantity of Yarn sold 1,50,000 kg @ Rs. 3.75 per kg

(These include the opening stock of 20,000 kg)

Total quantity of yarn consigned 1,60,000 kg @ Rs. 3 per kg

Total remittance by the agent Rs. 5,10,000.

Railway freight paid by the agent Rs. 40,000.

Of the sales made, X could not collect Rs. 11,000 due to insolvency of the customer.

5,000 kg of Yarn were damaged in-transit by railway for which the agent recovered Rs. 6,000. The damaged goods were sold @ Rs. 1.50 per kg.

Show the following ledger accounts in the books of Star Mills Ltd. for the year ended 30th June 2011: (a) Consignment Account; (b) Goods Damaged-in-Transit; Account and (c) X Account.

Solution

In the books of Star Mills Ltd.

Consignment Account

Date	Particulars	Amount	Date	Particulars	Amount
Dr.					Cr.
2010		Rs.	2011		Rs.
July 1	To Stock on Consignment A/c	50,000	June 30	By X A/c	
2011				—Sale Proceeds (1,50,000 × Rs. 3.75)	5,62,500
June 30	" Goods Sent on Consignment A/c (1,60,000 × Rs. 3)	4,80,000		" Goods damaged in Transit A/c	15,000[1]
	" X A/c —Railway Freight	40,000		" Stock on Consignment A/c	81,452[2]
	" X A/c —Commission	15,000			
	" Profit & Loss A/c				
	" Profit on Consignment Transferred	73,952			
		6,58,952			6,58,952

Dr. **Goods Damaged in-Transit Account** Cr.

Date	Particulars	Amount	Date	Particulars	Amount
2011		Rs.	2011		Rs.
June 30	To Consignment A/c	15,000	June 30	By X A/c —Insurance claim	6,000
	" X A/c —Commission	500		" X A/c —Sale Proceeds	7,500
				" Profit & Loss A/c (*bal. fig.*)	2,000
		15,500			15,500

Dr. **X Account** Cr.

Date	Particulars	Amount	Date	Particulars	Amount
2011		Rs.	2011		Rs.
June 30	To Consignment A/c —Sale Proceeds	5,62,500	June 30	By Consignment A/c	
	" Goods damaged in-transit A/c —Sale Proceeds	7,500		" —Expenses	40,000
	" Insurance claim	6,000		—Commission	15,000
				" Goods damaged in transit A/c	500
				" Bank A/c	5,10,000
				" Balance c/d	10,500
		5,76,000			5,76,000

Notes :

1. Lost-in-transit = Rs. 4,80,000 × $\frac{5,000 \text{ kg}}{1,60,000\text{kg}}$ = Rs. 15,000

2. Value of Unsold Sitock = (Rs. 5,20,000 – Rs. 15,000) Rs. 5,05,000 × $\frac{25,000 \text{ kg}}{1,55,000 \text{ kg}}$ = Rs. 81,452.

Abnormal Loss and Normal Loss

Illustration 18

Lubrizols Ltd. of Mumbai consigned 1,000 barrels of lubricant oil costing Rs. 800 per barrel to Central Oil Co. of Kolkata on 1.1.2011. Lubrizols Ltd. paid Rs. 50,000 as freight and insurance. 25 barrels were destroyed on 7.1.2011 in-transit. The insurance claim was settled at Rs. 15,000 and was paid directly to the consignor.

Central Oil took delivery of the consignment on 19.1.2011 and accepted a bill drawn upon them by Lubrizols Ltd., for Rs. 5,00,000 for 3 months. On 31.3.2011, Central Oil reported as follows :

(i) 750 barrels were sold as Rs. 1,200 per barrel.

(ii) The other expenses were :

	Rs.
Clearing charges	11,250
Godown Rent	10,000
Wages	30,000
Printing, Stationery, Advertisement	20,000

(iii) 25 barrels of oil were lost due to leakage which is considered to be normal loss.

Central Oil Co. is entitled to a commission of 5% on all the sales effected by them. Central Oil Company paid the amount due in respect of the consignment on 31st March itself.

Show the Consignment Account, the account of Central Oil Co., and the Lost-in-Transit Account as they will appear in the books of Lubrizols Ltd.

[ICWA—Adapted]

Solution

In the Books of Lubrizols Ltd.

Dr. **Consignment to Kolkata Account** Cr.

Date	Particulars	Amount	Date	Particulars	Amount
2011		Rs.	2011		Rs.
Jan. 1	To Goods Sent on Consignment A/c (1,000 × Rs. 800)	8,00,000	Jan. 7	By Abnormal Loss A/c	21,250
			Mar. 31	" Central Oil Co.	

Contd.

Date		Particulars	Rs.	Rs.	Date		Particulars	Rs.
2011								
Mar. 31	"	Bank A/c—Expenses		50,000			—Sale Proceeds (750 × Rs. 1,200)	9,00,000
	"	Central Oil Co A/c				"	Stock on Consignment A/c	1,76,842
		Clearing Charge	11,250					
		Godown Rent	10,000					
		Wages	30,000					
		Printing etc.	20,000	71,250				
	"	Central Oil Co.— Commission @ 5%		45,000				
	"	Profit and Loss A/c —Profit on Consignment Transferred		1,31,842				
				10,98,092				10,98,092

Dr. **Central Oil Co. Ltd. Account** Cr.

Date		Particulars	Amount	Date		Particulars	Amount
2011			Rs.	2011			Rs.
Mar. 31	To	Consignment to Kolkata A/c —Sale Proceeds	9,00,000	Jan. 19	By	Bills Receivable A/c	5,00,000
				Mar. 31	"	Consignment to Cal A/c	
						—Expenses	71,250
						—Commission	45,000
					"	Bank (amount due)	2,83,750
			9,00,000				9,00,000

Dr. **Abnormal Loss Account** Cr.

Date		Particulars	Amount	Date		Particulars	Amount
2011			Rs.	2011			Rs.
Jan. 7	To	Consignment to Kolkata	21,250	Jan. 7	By	Bank-Insurance claim	15,000
				Mar. 31	"	Profit and Loss A/c (bal. fig.)	6,250
			21,250				21,250

Workings :

Valuation of Goods Lost-in-Transit and Unsold Stock

		Rs.
	Total Cost (1,000 × Rs. 800)	8,00,000
Add :	Consignor's exp	50,000
	Value of 1,000 barrels	8,50,000
Less :	Lost-in-transit $\left(25 \times \frac{\text{Rs. } 8,50,000}{1,000}\right)$	21,250
		8,28,750
Add :	Non-recurring expenses of Consignee	11,250
	Value of (1,000 – 25 – 25) = 950 kg	8,40,000

Therefore, Value of Stock $= 200 \times \frac{\text{Rs. } 8,40,000}{950}$ = Rs. 1,76,842 (app.)

Shortage or Deficiency of Stock

Some shortage or deficiency may arise in stock at consignee's godown while actual physical stock taking is being conducted by the consignee. For this purpose proper valuation must be made for such shortage for stock. Valuation should be made on the same basis as the value of unsold stock.

The following entries are to be passed in the books :

(i) Stock Deficiency A/c Dr.
  To Consignment A/c

(ii) Profit and Loss A/c Dr.
  To Stock Deficiency A/c

But if there is an agreement between the consignor and consignee that such shortage or deficiency must be made good by the consignee, in that case, Consignee's Personal Account should be debited.

Value of Stock Deficiency

Illustration 19

From the following particulars, show the entries in the books of Consignor:

Goods sent on Consignment 100 books @ Rs. 100.

Expenses incurred by consignor :		Expenses incurred by consignee :	
Freight	Rs. 2,000	Clearing	Rs. 2,000
Insurance	Rs. 1,000	Storage	Rs. 500

Consignee sold 82 books and he informed that a deficiency of 3 units disclosed by his actual physical stock taking.

Solution

Valuation of Unsold Stock

		Rs.
	Total Cost	10,000
Add :	Consignor's Expenses	3,000
Add :	Consignees non-recurring exp.	2,000
	Cost Price of 100 books	15,000

$\therefore$ Value of Stock = Rs. 15,000 × $\frac{15}{100}$ = Rs. 2,250

Value of Deficiency of Stock = Rs. 15,000 × $\frac{3}{100}$ = Rs. 450

Journal
(without narration)

Date	*Particulars*		*L.F.*	*Debit* Rs.	*Credit* Rs.
	Stock on Consignment A/c	Dr.		2,250	
	To Consignment A/c				2,250
	Stock Deficiency A/c	Dr.		450	
	To Consignment A/c				450
	Profit and Loss A/c	Dr.		450	
	To Stock Deficiency				450

Partial Return of the Goods by the Consignee

Sometimes a part of the goods are returned by the consignee to the consignor due to a number of reasons. In that case, the consignor passes the following entry :

Goods Sent on Consignment A/c Dr.
 To Consignment A/c

(i.e., the reverse entry of when goods are sent). Now, the problem arises about the expenses of such returned goods (whether paid by Consignor or Consignee) i.e., whether the same should be charged against the consignment or not. There are two schools of thought. Some say, the expenses should not be charged against the consignment since the expense of returning goods is not a charge against the consignment; as a whole, the same should be charged against Profit and Loss Account. Some others are of opinion that the expenses of returning goods relate to the consignment; as such, the same should be charged against Consignment Account. The latter method is followed in this volume. For this purpose, the consignor will pass the following entry :

Consignment A/c Dr.
 To Cash/Bank (if paid by Consignor)
 " Consignee's Personal A/c (if paid by Consignee)

Partial return of goods and abnormal loss

Illustration 20

On 1.4.2011, Mr. Doshi of Darjeeling consigned 2,000 kg of tea costing Rs. 60 per kg to Mr. Naik of Nagpur. Mr. Doshi incurred the following expenses: Freight Rs. 2,000; Insurance Rs. 400 and Sundry Expenses Rs. 600. During the year ended 31.3.2012, Mr. Naik incurred the following expenses; Freight Rs. 600; Godown Rent Rs. 500 and Carriage to godown Rs. 1,000.

On 1.12.2011, Mr Naik sold 1,200 kg of tea for cash at a profit of 25% on sales. On 15.12.2012, Mr. Naik returned 150 kg of tea, which was of poor quality to Mr. Doshi and paid return freight and carriage of Rs. 250. Out of the remaining tea, 200 kg being partially damaged, was valued at 30% less than cost. Mr. Naik charged his commission at 5% and the balance so far due from him to Mr. Doshi on 31.3.2012. Mr. Doshi closes his books every year on 31st March.

You are required to prepare the following accounts in the books of Mr. Doshi—(a) Consignment to Nagpur Accounts, (b) Goods Sent on Consignment Account, (c) Personal account of Mr. Naik.

Solution

In the books of Mr. Doshi

Consignment to Nagpur Account

Dr. *Cr.*

Date	*Particulars*	*Amount*	*Date*	*Particulars*	*Amount*
2011		Rs.	2011		Rs.
April 1	To Goods Sent on Consignment A/c (2,000 × Rs. 60)	1,20,000	Dec. 1	By Naik A/c Sale Proceeds	96,000
	" Bank-Expenses : Freight 2,000; Insurance 400; Sundry Expenses 600	3,000	Dec. 15	" Goods Sent on Consignment A/c Returned 150 kg @ Rs. 60	9,000
Dec. 15	" Naik A/c Returned Freight and Carriage	250	2012 Mar. 31	" Abnormal Loss A/c	4,420
2012 Mar. 31	" Naik A/c Freight 600; Godown Rent 500; Carriage to Godown 1,000	2,100		" Stock on Consignment A/c Good Quality 27,900; Damage 7,980	35,880
	" Nail A/c Commission @ 5% on Rs. 96,000	4,800			
	" Profit and Loss A/c " Profit on Consignment Transferred	15,150			
		1,45,300			1,45,300

Naik Account

Dr. *Cr.*

Date	*Particulars*	*Amount*	*Date*	*Particulars*	*Amount*
2011		Rs.	2011		Rs.
Dec. 1	To Consignment to Nagpur A/c	96,000	Dec. 15	By Consignment to Nagpur A/c Returned Freight and Carriage	250
			2012 Mar. 31	" Consignment to Nagpur A/c —Expenses A/c	2,100
				—Commission	4,800
				" Bank (amount due) A/c	88,850
		96,000			96,000

Goods Sent on Consignment Account

Dr. *Cr.*

Date	*Particulars*	*Amount*	*Date*	*Particulars*	*Amount*
2011		Rs.	2011		Rs.
Dec. 15	To Consignment to Nagpur A/c —Returned	9,000	April 1	By Consignment to Nagpur A/c	1,20,000
2012 Mar. 31	" Trading A/c –Transfer	1,11,000			
		1,20,000			1,20,000

Workings :

1. Calculation of Sale Proceeds

	Cost Price	Profit	Selling Price
	Rs.	Rs.	Rs.
	75	25	100
∴	(1,200 × Rs. 60) = Rs. 72,000		$\frac{100 \times \text{Rs. } 72{,}000}{75} = 96{,}000$

2. Valuation of Damaged Goods and Abnormal Loss Rs.

Cost of 200 kg damaged goods @ Rs. 60 12,000

3. Valuation of Unsold Stock Rs.

Cost of 450 kg good quality @ Rs. 60 27,000

Add : Proportionate expenses of consignor— $\left(Rs.3{,}000 \times \frac{200}{2{,}000}\right)$		300
Add : Proportionate non-recurring expenses of consignee $\left(Rs.1{,}000 \times \frac{200}{2{,}000}\right)$		100
		12,400
Less : Estimated value – (at cost-30%) (200 × Rs. 42 (60 – 30% of 60)	8,400	
Less : Commission @ 5% on Rs. 8,400	420	
		7,980
		4,420

Add: Proportionate expenses of consignor $\left(Rs.3{,}000 \times \frac{450}{2{,}000}\right)$	675
Add : Proportionate non-recurring expenses of consignee $\left(Rs.1{,}000 \times \frac{450}{2{,}000}\right)$	225
	27,900
Plus : Unsold,value of damaged goods	7,980
∴ Total value of Stock	35,880

Note : Freight is treated as recurring expenses.

INVOICE PRICE METHOD

Sometimes the consignor does not prefer to disclose the true profit that is earned on consignment for many reasons (viz., to avoid competition, to give the fair price of goods etc.). For the purpose, he sends goods at **proforma invoice price** to the consignee which is fixed after adding certain percentage on cost or on sale/invoice price so that the consignee will not be able to know the profit which is earned by the consignor in consignment transaction.

For example, the cost prices of goods sent, say, Rs. 10,000, if the rate of profit on cost is 25%, the invoice price [i.e., Cost Price + Profit (Loading)] will be Rs. 12,500 (or, Rs. 10,000 + Rs. 2,500).

It must be remembered that if there is any unsold stock or any abnormal loss, they are to be valued at invoice price. Needless to mention that proper adjustment must be made to eliminate such loading—either on unsold stock or on abnormal loss—in order to bring them at cost.

The following entries are to be passed in the books of the consignor :

(i)	*When goods are sent :*		
	Consignment A/c To Goods Sent on Consignment A/c	Dr.	with the amount of invoice price of goods sent
(ii)	*For expenses incurred by Consignor :*		
	Consignment A/c To Cash/Bank A/c	Dr.	with the amount of expenses
(iii)	*For advance received from consignee by way of :* Cash/Draft/Bill		
	Cash/Draft/B/R A/c To Consignee's Personal A/c	Dr.	with the amount of advance
(iv)	*For goods sold by Consignee :*		
	Consignee's Personal A/c To Consignment A/c	Dr.	with the amount of sale proceeds
(v)	*For expenses incurred by Consignee or Commission Charged by him :*		
	Consignment A/c To Consignment A/c	Dr.	with the amount of expenses and commission
(vi)	*For abnormal Loss :*		
	Abnormal Loss A/c To Consignment A/c	Dr.	with the invoice price of goods lost
(vii)	*If covered by insurance :*		
	Bank/Insurance Claim A/c	Dr.	with the amount of claim
	Consignment A/c	Dr.	with the amount of loading
	Profit and Loss a/c To Abnormal Loss A/c	Dr.	with the amount of actual loss

Contd.

(viii) ***For Closing Stock :***

Closing Stock/Stock on Consignment A/c Dr. To Consignment A/c	}	with the amount invoice price of stock

Adjustment to be made at the end of the year :

(ix) ***For bringing down the value of goods sent to it cost :***

Goods sent on Consignment A/c Dr. To Consignment A/c	}	with the amount of loading

(x) ***For stock on Consignment :***

Consignment A/c Dr. To Stock Reserve/Suspense A/c	}	with the amount of loading in stock

(xi) ***For Loading on abnormal loss :***

Consignment A/c Dr. To Abnormal Loss A/c	}	with the amount of loading on abnormal loss

(xii) ***For transfer of goods sent on Consignment A/c :***

Goods sent on Consignment A/c Dr. To Trading/Purchases A/c	}	Actual cost of goods sent

(xiii) ***For profit on consignment :***

Consignment A/c Dr. To Profit and Loss A/c	}	with the amount of profit

In the Case of Loss, the entry will be reversed

After adjusting the loading, the amount of Unsold Stock, and Stock Reserve Account will be carried forward to the next year in the opposite side, i.e., it will appear in the debit of the Consignment Account. But in Balance Sheet, the Stock Reserve will be deducted from the stock on consignment in the asset side of the Balance Sheet as :

Balance Sheet (Extract)
as at ....

	Assets	Rs.	Rs.
	Stock on Consignment	* * *	
	Less : Stock Reserve	* * *	
			* * *

Note : In the books of Consignee, there will be no special treatment for this purpose.

Illustration 21

X consigned goods to Y worth Rs. 30,000. This was made by adding 50% on cost. X paid Rs. 2,000 for freight and insurance. Y accepted a 3 months' bill drawn by X for Rs. 20,000. On arrival of the goods at the destination Y paid Rs. 2,000 as Godown Rent. An Account Sale was received which showed that they had sold $\frac{9}{10}$th of the goods for Rs. 35,000. The consignee was entitled to a commission of 10% on gross sale proceeds. Show the entries and necessary accounts in the books of X.

Solution

In the Books of X
Journal

Date	*Particulars*		*L.F.*	*Debit*	*Credit*
				Rs.	Rs.
	Consignment A/c	Dr.		30,000	
	To Goods Sent on Consignment A/c				30,000
	(Goods Sent on Consignment at invoice price to Y.)				
	Consignment A/c	Dr.		2,000	
	To Bank A/c				2,000
	(Expenses incurred by X.)				
	Bills Receivable A/c	Dr.		20,000	
	To Y A/c				20,000
	(Bills accepted by Y for 3 months.)				
	Cash/Bank A/c	Dr.		20,000	
	To Bills Receivable A/c				20,000
	(Bills honoured at maturity by Y.)				

Contd.

Particulars		Rs.	Rs.
Consignment A/c	Dr.	2,000	
To Y A/c			2,000
(Expenses incurred by Y on consignment.)			
Y A/c	Dr.	35,000	
To Consignment A/c			35,000
(Goods sold by Y.)			
Consignment A/c	Dr.	3,500	
To Y A/c			3,500
(Commission charged by X @ 10% on sales.)			
Stock on Consignment A/c	Dr.	3,200	
To Consignment A/c			3,200
(Value of stock in the hands of Y.)			
Goods Sent on Consignment A/c	Dr.	10,000	
To Consignment A/c			10,000
(Difference between invoice price and cost price adjusted.)			
Consignment A/c	Dr.	1,000	
To Stock Reserve A/c			1,000
(Difference between the invoice price and cost price of unsold stock adjusted.)			
Consignment A/c	Dr.	9,700	
To Profit and Loss A/c			9,700
(Profit on consignment transferred.)			
Goods Sent on Consignment A/c	Dr.	20,000	
To Trading A/c			20,000
(Cost price of Goods sent on Consignment transferred.)			

In the books of X

Consignment Account

Dr. *Cr.*

Date	Particulars	Amount	Date	Particulars	Amount
		Rs.			Rs.
?	To Goods sent on Consignment A/c	30,000	?	By Goods Sent on Consignment A/c (Loading)	10,000
	" Bank A/c Freight and Insurance	2,000		" Y A/c —Sale Proceeds	35,000
	" Y A/c —Godown Rent	2,000		" Stock on Consignment A/c	3,200
	" Y A/c —Commission	3,500			
	" Stock Suspense/Reserve A/c	1,000			
	" Profit and Loss A/c —Profit on Consignment Transferred	9,700			
		48,200			48,200

Y Account

Dr. *Cr.*

Date	Particulars	Amount	Date	Particulars	Amount
		Rs.			Rs.
?	To Consignment A/c —Sale Proceeds	35,000	?	By Bills Receivable A/c	20,000
				" Consignment A/c —Expenses	2,000
				—Commission	3,500
				" Balance c/d	9,500
		35,000			35,000

Goods Sent on Consignment Account

Dr. *Cr.*

Date	Particulars	Amount	Date	Particulars	Amount
		Rs.			Rs.
?	To Consignment A/c (Loading)	10,000	?	By Consignment A/c	30,000
	" Trading A/c—Transfer	20,000			
		30,000			30,000

Dr. **Consignment Stock Account** Cr.

Date	Particulars	Amount	Date	Particulars	Amount
?		Rs.	?		Rs.
	To Consignment A/c	3,200		By Balance c/d	3,200
		3,200			3,200

Dr. **Stock Reserve Account** Cr.

Date	Particulars	Amount	Date	Particulars	Amount
?		Rs.	?		Rs.
	To Balance c/d	1,000		By Consignment A/c	1,000
		1,000			1,000

Workings :

1. Cost Price = $\left(\dfrac{Rs.\,30,000 \times 100}{150}\right)$ = Rs. 20,000.

∴ Loading (Invoice Price – Cost Price) = Rs. 30,000 – Rs. 20,000 = Rs. 10,000.

2. Unsold Stock Rs. 3,200 (i.e., Rs. 30,000 + Rs. 2,000) $\times \dfrac{1}{10}$

3. Stock Reserve/Suspense = Rs. 10,000 $\times \dfrac{1}{10}$ = Rs. 1,000.

INVOICE PRICE – ALTERNATIVE METHOD, OR, STOCK AND TRADING METHOD

Under this method, the following accounts are to be opened :

(i) Consignment Stock Account

This account reveals the excess amount realised over invoice price and also indicates the amount of stock on hand at invoice price.

(ii) Goods Sent on Consignment Account

This account incorporates the actual goods which are transferred to Trading or Purchase Account after adjusting the loading on goods sent, i.e., it is almost similar to earlier method.

(iii) Consignment Stock Reserve Account

This account shows the amount of gross profit without, however, considering the amount of any expense. The proportionate loading on unsold stock will be carried forward to the next accounting period.

(iv) Consignment Trading Account

This account incorporates the amount of expenses and shows the profit or loss on consignment.

(v) Consignee's Personal Account

This account is similar to the earlier method, (i.e., it takes into account the amount of sales against which the advance received from consignee, if any, his expenses and commission, the balance left at the end) but in a different manner.

The following journal entries are required under the method :

(i) ***When goods are sent at invoice price :***

Consignment Stock A/c Dr.
To Goods Sent on Consignment A/c

(ii) ***When goods are sold :***

Consignee's Personal A/c Dr.
To Consignment Stock A/c

(iii) ***When expenses are incurred by Consignor :***

Consignment Trading A/c Dr.
To Bank A/c

(iv) ***When expenses are incurred by consignee and also commission charged by him :***

Consignment Trading A/c Dr.
To Consignee's Personal A/c

(v) ***For Abnormal Loss (at invoice price) :***

Abnormal Loss A/c Dr.
To Consignment Stock A/c

Contd.

(vi) *For proportionate expenses on such and abnormal loss :*

Abnormal Loss A/c Dr.
To Consignment Stock A/c

(vii) *At the end of the year :*

(a) *For the balance in goods sent on Consignment Account :*

Goods Sent on Consignment A/c Dr.
To Trading A/c or Purchases A/c

(b) *For loading on goods sent :*

Goods Sent on Consignment A/c Dr.
To Consignment Stock Reserve A/c

(c) *For loading on abnormal loss if any :*

Consignment Stock Reserve A/c Dr.
To Abnormal Loss A/c

(d) *For Unsold Stock on Consignment :*

It should be noted that the value of consignment stock at invoice price (without considering proportionate expenses) will, however, be brought down as a debit balance in the Consignment Stock Account and with this amount the Stock Account should automatically agree, if any difference arises, the same should be transferred to Consignment Stock Reserve Account. Consequently, if selling price is higher than the invoice price the entry will be :

Consignment Stock A/c Dr.
To Consignment Stock Reserve A/c

(e) *For loading on Unsold Stock :*

Needless to mention here that the difference between the invoice prices of stock and cost prices of stock (i.e., loading) will be brought down as a credit balance in Stock Reserve Account. And after considering the same, the difference in Stock Reserve Account will be transferred to Trading Account or Purchase Account. The entry for this purpose will be :

Consignment Stock Reserve A/c Dr.*
To Consignment Trading A/c

(* vice versa in the opposites case)

(f) Now, the proportionate expenses relating to stock will be carried forward as a debit balance in the Consignment Trading Account and after charging this, Consignment Trading Account will show a profit or loss on consignment which is to be transferred to Profit and Loss Account at the end.

Illustration 22

Taking the previous Illustration No. 21, prepare the necessary ledger accounts under Stock and Trading Method :

Solution

Consignment Stock Account

Dr. Date	Particulars	Amount	Date	Particulars	Cr. Amount
		Rs.			Rs.
?	To Goods Sent on Consignment A/c	30,000	?	By Y A/c	
	" Consignment Stock Reserve A/c	8,000		—Sale proceeds	35,000
				" Stock c/d	3,000
		38,000			38,000

Goods Sent on Consignment Account

Dr. Date	Particulars	Amount	Date	Particulars	Cr. Amount
		Rs.			Rs.
?	To Consignment Stock Resere A/c	10,000	?	By Consignment stock A/c	30,000
	" Trading A/c—Transfer	20,000			
		30,000			30,000

Dr. **Consignment Stock Reserve Account** Cr.

Date	Particulars	Amount	Date	Particulars	Amount
?		Rs.	?		Rs.
	To Consignment Trading A/c	17,000		By Goods Sent on Consignment A/c	10,000
	" Balance c/d	1,000		" Consignment Stock A/c	8,000
		18,000			18,000

Dr. **Consignment Trading Account** Cr.

Date	Particulars	Amount	Date	Particulars	Amount
?		Rs.	?		Rs.
	To Bank A/c—Expenses	2,000		By Consignment Stock Reserve A/c	17,000
	" Y A/c—Expenses	2,000		" Proportionate all Expenses c/d	200
	" Bank A/c	3,500			
	" Profit and Loss A/c	9,700			
	" Profit on Consignment—Trans.	—			
		17,200			17,200
	To Proportionate Exp. A/c b/d	200			

INVOICE PRICE—MEMORANDUM COLUMN METHOD

In this method, there must be two columns in each side of the Consignment Account viz., (i) Invoice Price, and (ii) Cost Price. Invoice price column represents total invoice price of goods consigned, sales and closing stock which, in other words, serves as a memorandum column and if the debit side of the invoice price column is greater than the credit side, there will be an apparent loss, and vice versa. Cost Price Column, on the other hand, reveals the profit or loss on consignment.

Illustration 23

Take the previous problem no. 21 and show the Consignment Account using memorandum columns.

Dr. **Consignment Account** Cr.

Date	Particulars	Amount Invoice Price	Amount Cost Price	Date	Particulars	Amount Invoice Price	Amount Cost Price
?		Rs.	Rs.	?		Rs.	Rs.
	To Goods Sent on Consignment A/c	30,000	20,000		By Y A/c —Sales Proceeds	35,000	35,000
	" Bank—Expenses.	2,000	2,000		" Stock on Consignment A/c	3,200	2,200
	" Y A/c—Expenses	2,000	2,000				
	" Y A/c Commission	3,500	3,500				
	" Profit and Loss A/c						
	" Profit on Consignment—Transferred	—	9,700				
	Apparent Profit *(bal. fig.)*	·700	—				
		38,200	37,200			38,200	37,200

Dr. **Goods Sent on Consignment Account** Cr.

Date	Particulars	Amount Invoice Price	Amount Cost Price	Date	Particulars	Amount Invoice Price	Amount Cost Price
?		Rs.	Rs.	?		Rs.	Rs.
	To Trading A/c	30,000	20,000		By Consignment A/c	30,000	20,000
		30,000	20,000			30,000	20,000

Miscellaneous

Ascertainment of 'Goods Sent on Consignment' Unsold Stock

Illustration 24

The account sales received from Agent disclosed that the total sales effected by him amounted to Rs. 4,50,000. This included Rs. 3,12,500 for sales made at Invoice Price which is cost plus 25% and the balance at 10% above the Invoice Price. He incurred expenses to the tune of Rs. 5,000 out of which a sum of Rs. 1,800 is recurring in nature. Forwarding expenses of the Consignor totalled Rs. 2,400. The Agent had remitted the balance due from him through Bank Draft after deducting the expenses, 5% commission on gross sales, Bad debts Rs. 850 & Bills payable accepted by him for Rs. 10,000. The value of unsold stock at original cost lying with the Agent as at the end of the year amounted to Rs. 50,000. You are required to prepare the Consignment Account and the Agent's Account in the Books of Consignor.

Solution

In the books of Consignor

Consignment Account

Dr. Cr.

Date	Particulars	Amount	Date	Particulars	Amount
?		Rs.	?		Rs.
	To Goods sent on consignment A/c (I. P.)	5,00,000[1]		By Agents A/c —Sale Proceeds	4,50,000
	" Bank A/c—Expenses	2,400		" Goods Sent on Consignment A/c (Loading)	1,00,000[2]
	" Agents A/c —Expenses — Recurring	1,800		" Unsold Stock A/c	63,200[4]
	—Non-recurring	3,200			
	—Commission	22,500			
	—Bad Debts	850			
	" Stock Suspense A/c	12,500			
	" Profit and loss A/c —Profit on Consignment Transferred	69,950[3]			
		6,13,200			6,13,200

Agents Account

Dr. Cr.

Date	Particulars	Amount	Date	Particulars	Amount
?		Rs.	?		Rs.
	To Consignment A/c —Sale Proceeds	4,50,000		By Consignment A/c —Expenses	5,000
				—Commission	22,500
				—Bad Debts	850
				" Bills Receivable A/c	10,000
				" Bank Draft A/c	4,11,650
		4,50,000			4,50,000

Workings :

1. **Invoice value of Goods Sent**

	Rs.		Rs.
Total Sales	4,50,000		
Less : Sales at Invoice Price (cost plus 25%)	3,12,500	=	3,12,500
∴ Sales : 10% above the Invoice price	1,37,500		
∴ Invoice Price ($\frac{100}{110}$ × Rs. 1,37,500)		=	1,25,000
Total Invoice Price of goods sold		=	4,37,500
∴ Total Cost Price of goods sold : ($\frac{100}{125}$ × Ps. 4,37,500)		=	3,50,000
Add : Cost price of Unsold Stock		=	50,000
∴ Total Cost Price of goods consigned			4,00,000

Contd.

Total Invoice price of goods consigned : $\frac{125}{100}$ × Rs. 4,000,00 = 5,00,000

2. ∴ **Total Loading** Rs. (5,00,000 – 4 ,00,000) = 1,00,000

3. **Stock Reserve** = $\frac{\text{Rs. 50,000 (costs)}}{\text{Rs. 4,00,000 (costs)}}$ × Rs. 1,00,000 i.e., $\frac{1}{8}$ th of Rs. 1,00,000 = Rs. 12,500

4. **Value of Unsold Stock at Invoice Price plus proportionate expenses :**

Invoice Price = Rs. (50,000 + 12,500)	=	62,500
Add : Proportionate Forwarding expenses : $\frac{1}{8}$ th of Rs. 2,400	=	300
Add : Proportionate non-recurring expenses of the Agent : $\frac{1}{8}$ th of R. 3,200	=	400
	=	63,200

Invoice Price—Abnormal Loss

Illustration 25

P Co. Ltd. of Kolkata despatched 1,000 radio sets costing Rs. 150 each to R of Mumbai on 25.3.2011. The following expenses were paid by the company on the consignment : Freight Rs. 7,500, Cartage Rs. 500, Insurance Rs. 2,000.

The Proforma Invoice Price to the agents was for Rs. 2,00,000 and the remuneration was fixed at 5% on gross sale proceeds. The agents accepted a bill for Rs. 50,000 drawn on them as an advance.

50 sets were stolen-in-transit to Mumbai and an insurance claim of Rs. 7,000 was received in final settlement. On 31.12.2011, the company received an Account Sales from the agents as under:

	Rs.	Rs.
Sales proceeds of 800 sets		1,60,000
Less : Clearing Charges	1,900	
Storage	3,100	
Commission	8,000	
Net Proceeds		13,000
		1,47,000

They remitted a Sight Draft for the balance after deducting the amount of the bill already accepted. Show the ledger accounts in the books of the Consignor.

Solution

In the books of P Co. Ltd.
Consignment to Mumbai Account

Dr. Cr.

Date	*Particulars*		*Amount* Rs.	*Date*	*Particulars*	*Amount* Rs.
2011				2011		
Mar. 25	To Goods Sent on Consignment A/c		2,00,000	Dec. 31	By Goods Sent on Consignment A/c —Loading	50,000
	" Bank A/c Expenses :				" R A/c	
	Freight	7,500			Sale Proceeds	1,60,000
	Cartage	500			" Lost-in-Transit A/c	10,500[1]
	Insurance	2,000	10,000		" Stock on Consignment A/c	31,800[1]
	" R A/c Expenses					
	Clearing Charges	1,900				
	Storage	3,100				
	Commission	8,000	13,000			
	" Lost-in-Transit A/c (Loading—50 × Rs. 50)		2,500			
	" Stock Reserve A/c		7,500[2]			
	" Profit and Loss Account —Profit on Consignment Transferred		19,300			
			2,52,300			2,52,300

R Account

Date	Particulars	Amount	Date	Particulars	Amount
2011		Rs.	2011		Rs.
Dec. 31	To Consignment to Mumbai A/c —Sale Proceeds	1,60,000	Mar. 25	By Bills Receivable A/c	50,000
			Dec. 31	" Consignment to Mumbai A/c —Expenses	13,000
				" Bank (amount due) A/c	97,000
		1,60,000			1,60,000

Goods Sent on Consignment Account

Date	Particulars	Amount	Date	Particulars	Amount
2011		Rs.	2011		Rs.
Dec. 31	To Consignment to Mumbai A/c —Loading	50,000	Mar. 25	By Consignment to Mumbai A/c	2,00,000
	" Trading A/c	1,50,000			
		2,00,000			2,00,000

Lost-in-Transit Account

Date	Particulars	Amount	Date	Particulars	Amount
2011		Rs.	2011		Rs.
Dec. 31	To Consignment to Mumbai A/c	10,500	Dec. 31	By Consignment A/c [Loading (50 × Rs. 50)]	2,500
				" Bank A/c—Insurance Company	7,000
				" P & L A/c—*(bal. fig.)*	1,000
		10,500			10,500

Workings :

1. **Valuation of Goods Lost-in-Transit and Unsold Stock**

	Rs.
Invoice price of 1,000 sets	2,00,000
Add : Consignor's expenses	10,000
I. P. of 1,000 sets	2,10,000
Less : Lost-in-transit $\left(\frac{30 \times 2,10,000}{1,000}\right)$	10,500
	1,99,500
Add : Non-recurring expenses of Consignee	1,900
Invoice Price of 950 sets	2,01,400

Value of Unsold Stock = $150 \times \frac{\text{Rs. } 2,01,400}{950}$ = Rs. 31,800

2. **Stock Reserve** = Loading per set Rs.

$\left(\frac{2,00,000}{1,000} = 200 - 150\ (C.P.) = Rs. 50\right)$

$\therefore$ 150 sets Rs. 50 = Rs. 7,500.

Invoice Price : Abnormal Loss, and valuation of Unsold Stock

Illustration 26

On 1st July 2010, Mantu of Chennai consigned goods of the value of Rs. 50,000 to Pandey of Patna. This was made by adding 25% on the cost. Mantu paid thereon Rs. 2,500 for freight and Rs. 1,500 for insurance. During transit one-tenth of the goods was totally destroyed by fire and a sum of Rs. 2,400 was realised from the Insurance Company.

On arrival of the goods, Pandey paid Rs. 1,800 as carriage to godown. During the year ended 30th June 2011, Pandey paid Rs. 3,600 for godown rent and Rs. 1,900 for selling expenses.

One-ninth of the remaining goods was again destroyed by fire in godown and nothing was recovered from Insurance Company.

On 1st June 2011, Pandey sold half the original goods for Rs. 30,000 and charged a commission of 5% on sales. On 30th June 2011, Pandey sent a Bank Draft to Mantu for the amount so far due from him.

You are required to prepare the following Ledger Accounts in the books of Mantu of Chennai for the year ended 30th June 2011 : (a) Consignment to Patna Account, (b) Goods Destroyed by Fire Account, and (c) Personal Account of Pandey.

Solution **[CU BCom (Hons.)—Adapted]**

In the books of Mantu of Chennai

Consignment to Patna Account

Dr. Cr.

Date		Particulars		Amount	Date		Particulars	Amount
2010				Rs.	2011			Rs.
July 1	To	Goods sent on Consignment A/c		50,000	June 30	By	Goods Sent on Consignment A/c (Loading)	10,000[2]
	"	Cash A/c :				"	Goods Destroyed by Fire A/c	5,400[1]
		Freight	2,500			"	Goods Destroyed by Fire A/c	5,600[1]
		Insurance	1,500	4,000		"	Consignment Stock A/c	16,800[1]
	"	Goods Destroyed by Fire A/c —Loading A/c		1,000		"	Pandey A/c —Sale Proceeds	30,000
2011 June 30	"	Pandey's A/c :						
		Carriage Inward	1,800					
		Godown Rent	3,600					
		Selling Exp.	1,900	7,300				
	"	Pandey's A/c : Commission on Sales (5% on Rs. 30,000)		1,500				
	"	Goods destroyed by Fire A/c —Loading		1,000				
	"	Consignment Stock Reserve A/c		3,000[3]				
				67,800				67,800

N.B. There is no normal profit or loss on Consignment.

Goods Destroyed by Fire Account

Dr. Cr.

Date		Particulars	Amount	Date		Particulars	Amount
2011			Rs.	2010			Rs.
July 1	To	Consignment to Patna A/c		July 1	By	Consignment to Patna A/c —Loading	1,000
		—In transit	5,400				1,000
2011 June 30		—In Godown	5,600	2011 June 30	"	Bank A/c—nsurance claim	2,400
					"	Profit & Loss A/c	6,600
			11,000				11,000

Pandey Account

Dr. Cr.

Date		Particulars	Amount	Date		Particulars	Amount
2011			Rs.	2011			Rs.
June 30	To	Consignment to Patna A/c —Sale Proceeds	30,000	June 1	By	Consignment to Patna A/c —Exp.	7,300
						—Com.	1,500
					"	Bank Draft A/c	21,200
			30,000				30,000

Workings :

1. **Valuation of Goods Destroyed by Fire and Unsold Stock**

		Rs.
	Total Invoice Price	50,000
Add :	Consignor Exps. (Rs. 2,500 + 1,500)	4,000
		54,000
Less :	Lost-in-Transit $\left(\frac{1}{10}th\right)$	5,400
	Goods Landed $\left(1-\frac{1}{10}\right) = \frac{9}{10}$ th	48,600

2. Loading = Rs. 50,000 × $\frac{25}{125}$ = Rs. 10,000

Contd.

Add : Consignee's Non-recurring Exps.	1,800
	50,400
Less : Value of goods destroyed by fire in godown $\left(\frac{1}{9} \text{ of Rs. } 50,400\right)$	5,,600
Value of $\frac{8}{10}$th	44,800

Value of Unsold Stock

$\frac{9}{10} - \left(\frac{1}{9} \text{ of } \frac{9}{10}\right) = \frac{9}{10} - \frac{1}{10} = \frac{8}{10}$ th;

Goods Sold $\frac{1}{2}$ i.e., remained in Stock $\frac{8}{10} - \frac{1}{2} = \frac{3}{10}$ th

∴ Value of Unsold Stock = Rs. 44,800 × $\frac{3}{10} \times \frac{10}{8}$ = Rs. 16,800

Loading on goods destroyed and Lost in-Transit = Rs. 10,000 × $\frac{1}{10}$ = Rs. 1,000

—Consignee's Godown = Rs. 10,000 × $\frac{1}{10}$ = Rs. 1,000.

3. **Loading on Closing Stock** = Rs. 10,000 × $\frac{3}{10}$ = Rs. 3,000.

Ascertainment of Goods Sent on Consignment, Invoice Price, Lost-in-Trainsit and unsold Stock

Illustration 27

The Account Sales of 1,200 Transistor sets received from Mr. S. Raman and sold on account of and at the risk of Sri Mr. Chopra, Kolkata :

		Rs.	Rs.
1,200 Transistor Sets @ Rs. 1,200			14,40,000
Less : Expenses :			
Unloading expenses	3,000		
Selling expenses	4,000		
Transport charges (non-recurring)	6,100		
Godown rent	6,000		
Advertisements	2,000	21,100	
Less : Commission :			
5% Ordinary Commission	72,000		
1% Del Credere Commission	14,400	86,400	1,07,500
			13,32,500
Less : Advance sent			2,50,000
Balance – Draft enclosed herewith			10,82,500

Stock in hand closing—100 Sets.

On further information received, you come to know that :

(i) Bad debts amounted to Rs. 2,400 against 2 sets.
(ii) 20% above the invoice price is the sale price which is equal to cost plus 50%.
(iii) Chopra incurred forwarding expenses @ Rs. 10/- per Set.
(iv) During transit 10 Sets became fully damaged in-transit and Chopra recovered from insurance the full amount of original cost.

You are required to prepare the Consignment Account, Goods Sent on Consignment Account and Lost-In-Transit Account in the books of Mr. Chopra.

Solution

Workings :

1. If Invoice price is Rs. 100; Sale price would be Rs. 120; Cost Price Rs. 80

Accordingly when sale price is Rs 1,200; Cost price is Rs. 800; Invoice price—Rs. 1,000

2. Total No. of Transistor sets Sent on consignment :

Sold	1,200 Sets
Damaged in-Transit	10 Sets
Unsold	100 Sets
	1,310 (Total)

3. Loading = Rs. 13,10,000 – Rs. 10,48,000 = Rs. 2,62,000

Cost = (1,310 × 800) = Rs. 10,48,000

Invoice Price = 1,310 × 1,000) = Rs. 13,10,000.

Workings

4. *Valuation of Sets Lost-in-Transit*	Rs.
Invoice-Price for 10 sets (10 × Rs. 1,000)	10,000
Add : Proportionate Expenses of Consignee (10 × Rs. 10)	100
	10,100

5. *Valuation of Unsold Stock*	Rs.
Invoice Price of 100 sets = (100 × Rs. 1,000)	1,00,000
Add : Proportionate Expenses of consignee (100 × Rs. 10)	1,000
Add : Non-receiving Expenses of Consignee $\left(\frac{\text{Rs. } 9{,}100 \times 100}{1{,}300}\right)$	700
	1,01,700

In the books of Mr. Chopra

Consignment Account

Dr. Date	Particulars		Amount Rs.	Date	Particulars	Cr. Amount Rs.
?	To Goods Sent on Consignment : (Invoice price)		13,10,000[2]	?	By S. Raman's Account : (Sale proceeds of 1,200 sets @ Rs.1,200)	14,40,000
	Bank (Freight) (1,310 × 10)		13,100		Goods Sent on Consignment A/c- (Loading)	2,62,000[3]
	S. Raman's A/c (Expenses)				Goods Lost-in-Transit A/c :	10,100[4]
	Unloading Exp.	3,000			Consignment Stock A/c	1,01,700[5]
	Selling Exp.	4,000				
	Transport Charges	6,100				
	Godown Rent	6,000				
	Advertisement	2,000	21,100			
	S. Raman's A/c (Commission)					
	5% Ordinary Commission		72,000			
	1% Del Credere Commission		14,400			
	Goods lost-in-Transit : (loading on Inv. Price (10 × 200)		2,000			
	Consignment Stock Reserve A/c (Loading 100 × 200)		20,000			
	Profit & Loss A/c Profit on Consignment Trans.		3,61,200			
			18,13,800			18,13,800

Goods Sent on Consignment Account

Dr. Date	Particulars	Amount Rs.	Date	Particulars	Cr. Amount Rs.
?	To Consignment Account: (Loading on Invoice Price)	2,62,000	?	By Consignment Account : (Invoice Price)	13,10,000
	Purchase/Trading A/c —Transfer	10,48,000			
		13,10,000			13,10,000

Goods-Lost-In-Transit Account

Dr. Date	Particulars	Amount Rs.	Date	Particulars	Cr. Amount Rs.
?	To Consignment A/c	10,100	?	By Consignment A/c (loading on invoice price)	2,000
				Bank A/c (Claim received) (10 × 800)	8,000
				Profit & Loss Account	100
		10,100			10,100

Illustration 28

P of Kolkata consigned goods Costing Rs. 45,000 to Q of Delhi. The invoice was made so as to show a profit of $33\frac{1}{3}$% on cost. P paid Rs. 300 as Carriage and Rs. 1,200 as Freight and Insurance. Goods costing Rs. 5,000 were destroyed while in-transit and the Insurance Company admitted the full claim.

In Delhi, Q paid Rs. 240 as Carriage Inward and Rs. 600 as Godown Rent. Two-third of the goods received by Q were sold by him. Q sent a cheque to P for the sale proceeds after deducting the expenses incurred by him and the commission due to him ordinary @ 5% and Del Credere @ $2\frac{1}{2}$%. Show the Consignment Account in P's ledger.

Solution

In the books of P
Consignment to Delhi Account

Dr. Date	Particulars		Amount	Date	Particulars	Amount Cr.
?			Rs.	?		Rs.
	To Goods Sent on Consignment A/c (Rs. 45,000 × $\frac{4}{3}$)		60,000		By Q A/c —Sale Proceeds	35,555[2]
	" Bank A/c :				" Goods Sent on Consignment A/c —Loading	15,000
	Carriage	300				
	Freight & Insurance	1,200	1,500		" Abnormal Loss A/c	6,833[1]
	" Q A/c				" Unsold Stock A/c	18,302[1]
	Carriage	240				
	Godown Rent	600	840			
	" Q A/c :					
	Commission	1,777				
	Del Credere Com.	889	2,666			
	" Abnormal Loss (Loading) A/c		1,667			
	" Stock Suspense A/c		4,444[3]			
	" Profit and Loss A/c —Profit on Consignment A/c Transferred		4,573			
			75,690			75,690

Workings :

1. **Valuation of Goods Lost-in-Transit and Unsold Stock :**

		Rs.
	Invoice price of goods sent	60,000
Add :	Consignor's Expenses	1,500
		61,500
Less :	Invoice value of goods lost-in-transit	
	Rs. 61,500 × $\frac{1}{9}$ (i.e., Rs. 5,000 / Rs. 45,000)	6,833
	Received in good condition by Q	54,667
Add :	Non-recurring expenses of Q	240
	Total invoice value of goods received	54,907

∴ Value of Closing Stock will be ($\frac{1}{3}$ × Rs. 54,907) = Rs. 18,302

2. **Calculation of Sales :**

		Rs.
	Cost of goods sent	45,000
Less :	Cost of goods lost-in-transit	5,000
∴	Cost of goods received by Q	40,000
	Invoice price of the above is Rs. (40,000 × $\frac{4}{3}$) =	53,333
	Hence, sales will be = Rs. (53,333 × $\frac{2}{3}$) =	35,555

3. **Stock Suspense to be calculated as under :**

	Total Loading is	15,000
Less :	Loading on Goods lost-in-transit (5,000 × $\frac{1}{3}$) =	1,667
		13,333

∴ Stock Suspense = Rs. 13,333 × $\frac{1}{3}$ = Rs. 4,444.

Illustration 29

Vikram Milk Foods Co. Ltd. of Vikrampur sent to Sunder Stores, Sonepur, 5,000 kg of Baby Food packed in 2,000 tins of net weight 1 kg and 6,000 packets of net weight $\frac{1}{2}$ kg for sale on consignment basis. The consignee's commission was fixed at 5% of sale proceeds.

The cost price and selling price of the product were :

	(Rs.)		(Rs.)
Cost Price 1 Kg tin	10	$\frac{1}{2}$ Kg packet	6
Selling Price	15		7

The consignment was booked on freight "To Pay" basis and freight charges came to 2% of selling value. One case containing 50, 1 kg tin was lost-in-transit and admitted a claim of Rs. 450.

At the end of the first half year, the following information is gathered from the "Account Sales" sent by the consignee.

(i) Sales Proceeds : 1,500 (1 Kg Tin); 4,000 ($\frac{1}{2}$ Kg. packet)

(ii) Store Rent and Insurance Rs. 600. Find out the closing stock on consignment.

Show the Consignment A/c and the Consignee's A/c in the books of Vikram Milk Foods Co. Ltd. assuming that the consignee has paid the amount due from them.

Solution

In the books of Vikram Milk Food Co. Ltd.

Consignment to Sonepuri Account

Dr. Cr.

Date	Particulars	Amount	Date	Particulars	Amount
?		Rs.	?		Rs.
	To Goods Sent on Consig. A/c —Invoice Price (2,000 × Rs. 15 + 6,000 × Rs. 7)	72,000		By Goods Sent on Consig. A/c —Loading : 2,000 × Rs. 5 (15 – 10) = 10,000; 6,000 × Re. 1 (7 – 6) = 6,000	16,000
	" Sunder Stores A/c —Freight @ 2% on Rs. 72,000	1,440		" Abnormal Loss A/c (50 × 15 = Rs. 750 + 2%)	765
	" Sunder Stores A/c —Store Rent, Insurance	600		" Sunder A/c —Sale Proceeds 1,500 × 15 = Rs. 22,500; 4,000 × 7 = Rs. 28,000	50,500
	" Abnormal Loss A/c —Loading (50 × Rs. 5)	250		" Unsold Stock A/c	21,165
	" Stock Reserve A/c	4,250			
	" Sunder Stores A/c —Comm. @ 5% on Rs. 50,500	2,525			
	" Profit and Loss A/c —Profit on Consignment A/c Transferred	7,365			
		88,430			88,430

Sunder Stores Account

Dr. Cr.

Date	Particulars	Amount	Date	Particulars	Amount
?		Rs.	?		Rs.
	To Consignment to Sonepur A/c —Sale proceeds	50,500		By Consignment to Sonepur A/c — Freight 1,440; — Store Rent 600; — Commission 2,525	4,565
				" Bank A/c	45,935
		50,500			50,500

Calculation of Unsold Stock

		1 kg Tins		$\frac{1}{2}$ kg Packets	
		Units	Value (Sales) Rs.	Units	Value (Sales) Rs.
	Goods sent	2,000	30,000	6,000	42,000
Less :	Loss-in-transit	50	750	—	—
		1,950	29,250	6,000	42,000

Contd.

			Rs.		Rs.
Less :	Goods sold	1,500	22,500	4,000	28,000
		450	6,750	2,000	14,000
Add :	Freight @ 2%		135		280
			6,885		14,280

∴ Total value of Stock = Rs. 21,165 (Rs. 6,885 + Rs. 14,280)

Calculation of Stock Reserve

(a) Unsold stock of 1 kg tins × (S. P. of 1 kg tin – C. P. of 1 kg tin) = 450 × Rs. 5 (15 – 10) = Rs. 2,250

(b) Unsold stock of $\frac{1}{2}$ kg packets × (S. P. of $\frac{1}{2}$ kg packets – C. P. of $\frac{1}{2}$ kg packets)

= 2,000 × Re. 1. (7 – 6) = Rs. 2,000

∴ Stock Reserve = Rs. (2,250 + 2,000) = Rs. 4,250.

Consignment between two countries with different foreign exchange

In this case, preparation of Consignment and other accounts are same. The only difference is that due to the exchange (e.g., between £ and Rs.), if there is any loss in exchange, the said loss should be transferred to Consignment Account. Thus, the entry will be :

Consignment A/c Dr.
To Consignee's Personal A/c For loss in exchange.

In the opposite case, the entry will be reversed.

Illustration 30

X, a Kolkata merchant, has an agent Y in New York, to whom he sends goods on consignment. On June 1, X consigned to Y 100 cases of silk garments which had cost Rs. 2,000 each. X paid duties etc. Rs. 3,000, freight Rs. 12,000 and insurance Rs. 4,000.

On September 30, Y sent X an Account Sales showing that he had 70 cases for 1,400 dollars each and that he had incurred the following expenses :

Landing charges 840 dollars.

Selling expenses 1,400 dollars.

Y's commission was at the rate of 200 dollars per case sold plus one-third of the excess of the sale proceeds less ordinary commission over 900 dollars per case. With the Account Sales a bank draft was enclosed for the balance due which was encashed by X at the rate of say, Rs. 7.95 per dollar, X closed his books on September 30. No further sales having been reported by Y.

Using a rate of rupees say 8 to a dollar, you are required to show the necessary accounts in the Books of X.

Solution

In the books of X

Consignment to New York Account

Dr. *Cr.*

Date	*Particulars*	$	*Amount* Rs.	*Date*	*Particulars*	$	*Amount* Rs.
?	To Goods sent on Consig. A/c		2,00,000	?	By Y A/c —Sale of 70 cases	98,000	7,84,000
	" Bank : Rs.				By Stock on Consignment A/c[3]		67,716
	Duties etc. 3,000						
	Freight 12,000						
	Insurance 4,000		19,000				
	" Y A/c :						
	Landing Charges	840	6,720				
	Selling Expenses	1,400	11,200				
	" Y A/c :						
	Ordinary Commission[1]	14,000	1,12,000				
	Extra Commission[2]	7,000	56,000				
	" Y A/c : —Loss on Exchange[4]		3,738				
	" Profit & Loss A/c —Profit on Consignment— Transferred		4,43,058				
			8,51,716				8,51,716

Dr. **Goods Sent on Consignment Account** Cr.

Date	Particulars	Amount	Date	Particulars	Amount
?		Rs.	?		Rs.
	To Trading A/c —Transfer	2,00,000		By Consignment to New York A/c	2,00,000
		2,00,000			2,00,000

Dr. **Y Account** Cr.

Date	Particulars	$	Amount Rs.	Date	Particulars	$	Amount Rs.
?	To Consignment to New York A/c	98,000	7,84,000	?	By Consignment to New York A/c :		
					Landing Charges	840	6,720
					Selling Expenses	1,400	11,200
					" Consignment to New York A/c :		
					Ord. Commission	14,000	1,12,000
					Extra Commission	7,000	56,000
					" Bank	74,760	5,94,342
					" Loss on Exchange A/c		3,738
		98,000	7,84,000			98,000	7,84,000

Notes : Ordinary Commission

1. Commission per box \$ 200. 70 boxes were sold.

   ∴ Total Commission $70 \times \$ 200 = \$ 14{,}000$

2. **Extra Commission :**

Less : Expected	\$	1,400 per box		
Selling price	\$	900		
	\$	500 × 70 boxes =	\$ 35,000	additional selling price
Less : Ordinary Commission			\$ 14,000	
			\$ 21,000	$\times \frac{1}{3}$ = Rs. 7,000 extra commission.

3. **Unsold Stock :**

	Rs.
Total Cost	2,00,000
Add : X's Expenses	19,000
Add : Non-recurring Expenses of Y	6,720
Cost Price of 100 boxes	2,25,720

∴ Unsold Stock = Rs. $(2{,}25{,}729 \times \frac{30}{100})$ = Rs. 67,716.

4. **Loss in Exchange :**

Bank draft was encashed. As a result of difference in exchange rate, for each \$ Rs. 7·95 instead of Rs. 8 i.e., a loss of (8·00 – 7·95) = ·05 was suffered.

∴ Total loss in exchange = Rs. 74,760 × ·05 = Rs. 3,738.

Special Commissions/Overriding Commission

Illustration 31

G. Cycles (P) Ltd. Hyderabad, sent 2,000 cycle dynamos costing Rs. 50 each for sale on Consignment basis to Ramoo of Vijaywada, subject to the following terms:

(1) Normal selling price per dynamo Rs. 60.

(2) Consignee's Commission to be calculated as:

(a) 5% Commission on normal selling price;

(b) 1% additional Commission if selling price is more than normal selling price; and

(c) $\frac{1}{2}$ % Del Credere Commission on total sales for guaranteeing collection of cerdit sales.

Ramoo reported sales as :

		Rs.
Cash Sales:	500 dynamos at Rs. 60 each	30,000
	200 dynamos at Rs. 75 each	15,000

Contd.

			Rs.	Rs.
Cash Sales:	400 dynamos at Rs. 75 each			30,000
	400 dynamos at Rs. 80 each			32,000
			Total	1,07,000

Ascertain the Commission due to Consignee.

Solution

		Rs.	Rs.
Commission due to Consignee:			
Normal Commission—@ 5% on total sales Rs. 90,000 (1,500 × 60)			4,500
Add : **Additional Commission:** 1% on the Surplus Price :			
(a) For 200 dynamos: Actual Selling Price	200 × 75 = 15,000		
Less : Normal Selling Price	200 × 60 = 12,000		
Surplus Price	3,000	× 1% = 30	
(b) For 400 dynamos : Actual Selling Price	400 × 75 = 30,000		
Less : Normal Selling Price	200 × 60 = 24,000		
	6,000	× 1% = 60	
(c) For 400 dynamos: Actual Selling Price	400 × 80 = 32,000		
Less : Normal Selling Price	400 × 60 = 24,000		
	8,000	× 1% = 80	170
Add : Del Credere Commission : $\frac{1}{2}$% on total sales i.e., on Rs. 1,07,000			535
Total Commission Payable			5,205

Computation of Special Commission

Illustration 32

X of Kolkata sent on 15.1.2012, a consignment of 500 bicycles costing Rs. 100 each. Expenses of Rs. 700 met by the consignor. Y of Mumbai spends Rs. 1,500 for clearance and the selling expenses were Rs. 10 per bicycle.

Y sold, on 5.4.2012, 300 bicycles @ Rs. 160 each and, again. on 20.6.2012, 150 bicycles @ Rs. 172 each.

Y was entitled to a commission of Rs. 25 per bicycle sold plus one-fourth of the amount by which the gross sale proceeds less total commission thereon exceeded a sum calculated @ Rs. 125 per bicycle sold. Y sent the amount due to X on 30.6.2012.

You are required to show the Consignment Account and Y's Account in the books of X. **(CA)**

Solution

Dr. **Consignment to Mumbai Account** *Cr.*

Date	*Particulars*	*Amount*	*Date*	*Particulars*	*Amount*
2012		Rs.	2012		Rs.
Jan. 15	To Goods Sent on Consignment A/c (500 × Rs. 100)	50,000	Apr. 5	By Y A/c —Sale Proceeds	
	" Bank A/c – Expenses	700		300 × Rs. 160 = Rs. 48,000	
	" Y A/c – Expenses			150 × Rs. 172 = Rs. 25,800	73,800
	Clearance 1,500				
	Selling (450 × Rs. 10) 4,500	6,000		" Stock on Consignment A/c $(50{,}000 + 700 + 1{,}500) \times \frac{50}{500}$	5,220

Contd.

Date	Particulars		Amount	Date	Particulars	Amount
2012			Rs.	2012		Rs.
June 30	To Y A/c Ord. Commission Spl. Com.	11,250 1,260	12,510[1]		By	
	" Profit and Loss A/c —Profit on Consignment Transferred		9,810			
			79,020			79,020

Dr. **Y Account** Cr.

Date	Particulars	Amount	Date	Particulars	Amount
2012		Rs.	2012		Rs.
Apr. 5	To Consignment Mumbai A/c —Sale Proceeds	73,800	Jan. 15	By Consignment Mumbai A/c —Expenses	6,000
			June 30	" —Commission	12,510
				" Bank A/c	55,290
		73,800			73,800

Note :

1. **Calculation of Commission :**

	Rs.
Ordinary Com. = 450 × Rs. 25	11,250
Add : Special Com. = $\frac{1}{5}$ [(Gross Sale Proceeds – Total Com.) – (450 × 125)]	
* $\frac{1}{5}$ [(Rs. 73,800 – Rs. 11,250) – (Rs. 56,250)]	
= $\frac{1}{5}$ (Rs. 62,500 – Rs. 56,250)	
= $\frac{1}{5}$ × Rs. 6,300	1,260
	12,510

(* It should be considered as 'after charging', as the total Commission is not known).

$$\left\{ \text{So}, \frac{\text{Rate}}{\text{Rate}+1} = \frac{\frac{1}{4}}{\frac{1}{4}+1} = \frac{\frac{1}{4}}{\frac{5}{4}} = \frac{1}{4} \times \frac{4}{5} = \frac{1}{5} \right\}$$

Computation of Overriding Commission

Illustration 33

X of Ahmedabad consigned goods to Y of Mumbai for sale at proforma invoice price or over. Y is entitled to a commission on sale at 5% on proforma invoice price and 25% of any surplus price realised.

Goods consigned by X to Y during the year ended 31.3.2012, cost X Rs. 20,900 and invoiced at Rs. 28,400. X paid Rs. 1,045 freight and received Rs. 10,000 as advance from Y. 80% of the goods were sold by Y for Rs. 26,000. Y remitted the balance of proceeds deducting his commission.

Write-up the Consignment Account in the books of X.

Solution

In the books of X

Dr. **Consignment to Mumbai Account** Cr.

Date	Particulars	Amount	Date	Particulars	Amount
2012		Rs.	2012		Rs.
Mar. 31	To Goods Sent on Consignment A/c	28,400	Mar. 31	By Goods Sent on Consignment A/c —Loading (28,400 – 20,900)	7,500
	" Bank A/c – Expenses on Freight	1,045		" Y Account— Sale Proceeds	26,000
	" Y Account – Commission	1,956[1]		" Stock on Consignment $\frac{1}{5}$ (28,400 + 1,045)	5,889
	" Stock Reserve $\left(7,500 \times \frac{1}{5}\right)$	1,500			
	" Profit and Loss A/c —Profit on Consignment Transferred	6,488			
		39,389			39,389

Workings :

1. **Calculation of Commission :**

		Rs.		Rs.
	Invoice value of goods sent	28,400	So, commission to be calculated @	1,136
	Invoice value of goods sold 80% of 28,400 i.e.,	22,720	5% on Rs. 22,720	
	Sale Proceeds	26,000	and @ 25% on Rs. 3,280	820
Less :	Invoice value of goods sold	22,720	Total commission payable to Y	1,956
	Surplus price	3,280		

Overriding Commissions, Abnormal Loss, Unsold Stock etc.

Illustration 34

Rahim of Kolkata consigned 100 cases of medicine costing Rs. 1,000 per case to Karim of Kanpur on 1.1.2011. The goods were sold at 25% above cost. Any deficiency in selling price was to be borne by Karim. Karim was, however, entitled to a special commission @ 25% of any surplus price realised. Karim was further entitled to an ordinary commission of 5% and Del Credere Commission of $2\frac{1}{2}$% on all sales.

Rahim incurred the following expenses :

	Rs.
Packing charges	6,000
Loading charges	1,000
Lorry hire	12,000
Railway freight	21,000

The cases were received by Karim on 15.1.2011. The account sales received from Karim on 30.6.2011 revealed the following :

40 cases sold on 21.3.2011 @ Rs. 1,500 per case, 30 cases sold on 24.5.2011 @ Rs. 1,200 per case, 10 cases sold on 15.6.2011 @ Rs. 1,300 per case. 5 cases of medicine were stolen by a dishonest employee. A compensation of Rs. 2,000 was realised from him. Karim incurred unloading charges of Rs. 2,000 and warehouse rent Rs. 3,000. Karim enclosed a bank draft for the balance due.

Write-up necessary accounts in the books of Rahim. **[CU BCom (Hons.)]**

Solution

In the books of Rahim

Consignment to Kanpur Account

Dr. Cr.

Date	Particulars		Amount Rs.	Date	Particulars		Amount Rs.
2011				2011			
Jan 1	To Goods sent on Consignment A/c 100 × Rs. 1,000		1,00,000	Mar. 21	By Karim A/c—sale proceeds : 40 × Rs. 1,500	60,000	
	" Bank A/c—Expenses :			May 24	30 × Rs. 1,200	36,000	
	Packing charges	6,000		June 15	10 × Rs. 1,300	13,000	1,09,000
	Loading charges	1,000			" Goods Stolen A/c		7,100
	Lorry Hire	12,000			" Consignment Stock		21,300
	Railway freight	21,000	40,000		" Profit & Loss A/c Loss on Consignment —Transferred		16,900
June 30	To Karim A/c—Expenses :						
	Unloading Charges	2,000					
	Warehouse Rent	3,000	5,000				
	" Karim A/c—Commission		9,300[1]				
			1,54,300				1,54,300

Karim (Consignee) Account

Dr. Cr.

Date	Particulars	Amount Rs.	Date	Particulars	Amount Rs.
2011			2011		
June 30	To Consignment to Kanpur A/c —Sale proceeds	1,09,000	June 30	By Consignment to Kanpur A/c —Expenses	5,000
	" Goods stolen—Compensation realised	2,000		—Commission	9,300
				" Bank *(bal. fig.)*	96,700
		1,11,000			1,11,000

Dr. **Goods Stolen Account** Cr.

Date	Particulars	Amount	Date	Particulars	Amount
2011		Rs.	2011		Rs.
June 30	To Consignment to Kanpur	7,100	June 30	By Karim A/c – Compensation realised	2,000
				" Profit & Loss A/c	5,100
		7,100			7,100

Working Notes :

1. **Calculation of Karim's Commission :**

	Rs.
$7\frac{1}{2}$ % of sale proceeds (Rs. 1,09,000)	8,175
25% of surplus realised :	
25% of 40 × (1,500 – 1,250)	2,500
25% of 10 × (1,300 – 1,250)	125
	10,800
Less : Deficiency in selling price 30 × 50 = (1,250 – 1,200)	1,500
	9,300

2. **Valuation of Goods Stolen and Unsold Stock :**

	Rs.
Cost of 100 cases @ Rs. 1,000	1,00,000
Add : Expenses (Rs. 40,000 + 2,000)	42,000
Value of 100 cases	1,42,000

Value of 5 cases stolen : $(\frac{5}{100} \times \text{Rs. } 1,42,000)$ = Rs. 7,100

Value of 15 cases unsold stock : $(\frac{15}{100} \times \text{Rs. } 1,42,000)$ = Rs. 21,300.

Invoice Price, Abnormal Loss, Special Commission etc.

Illustration 35

Rahim of Mumbai consigned to Raju of Chennai goods to be sold at invoice price which represented 125% of cost. Raju is entitled to a commission of 10% on sales at invoice price and 25% of any excess price realised over invoice price. The expenses of freight and insurance incurred by Rahim were Rs. 10,000. The account sales received by Mr. Rahim shows that Raju effected sales aggregating to Rs. 1,00,000 in respect of 75% of the consignment. Hs selling expenses to be reimbursed were Rs. 8,000. 10% of the consignment goods of the value of Rs. 12,500 were destroyed by fire at the Chennai godown and the insurance company paid Rs. 12,000 net of salvage. Raju remitted the balance in favour of Rahim.

Prepare Consignment Account and the Accout of Mr. Raju in the books of Mr. Rahim.

[CA Foundation, June 1994]

Solution

In the books of Rahim

Dr. **Consignment to Chennai Account** Cr.

Date	Particulars	Amount	Date	Particulars	Amount
?		Rs.	?		Rs.
	To Goods Sent on Consignment A/c	1,25,000[1]		By Raju A/c —Sale Proceeds	1,00,000
	" Bank A/c —Freight and Insurance	10,000		" Goods Sent on Consignment A/c —Loading	25.000[2]
	" Raju A/c —Selling Expenses	8,000		" Abnormal Loss A/c	13,500[3]
	" Raju A/c —Commission	10,938[4]		" Stock on Consignment A/c	20,250[3]
	" Stock Reserve A/c —Loading on Unsold Stock (@ 15% on Rs. 25,000)	3,750		" Profit and Loss A/c —Loss on Consignment Transferred	1,438
	" Abnormal Loss A/c —Loading @ 10% on Rs. 25,000)	2,500			
		1,60,188			1,60,188

Dr. **Raju Account** Cr.

Date	Particulars	Amount	Date	Particulars	Amount
?		Rs.	?		Rs.
	To Consignment to Chenni A/c —Sale proceeds	1,00,000		By Consignment to Chenni A/c —Selling Expenses	8,000
				—Commission	10,938
				" Bank *(bal. fig.)*	81,062
		1,00,000			1,00,000

Workings:

1. **Calculation showing the amount of Goods sent on consignment**
   Invoice value of goods destroyed by fire (10% of the Consignment) is Rs. 12,500

∴ The invoice value of whole goods sent on consignment will be Rs. 1,25,000 (i.e., Rs. 12,500 × $\frac{100}{10}$)

2. **Loading on goods sent**
   Loading = Rs. 1,25,000 × $\frac{25}{125}$ = Rs. 25,000

3. **Valuation of goods destroyed by fire and unsold stock**

	Rs.
Invoice Value of Goods sent	1,25,000
Add : Consignor's Expenses	10,000
	1,35,000
∴ **Invoice Value of Goods Destroyed**	
= 13,50,000 × 10%	13,500
Similarly, Invoice Value of Unsold Stock	
= Rs. 1,35,000 × $\frac{15}{100}$ = Rs.	20,250

4. **Commission Payable to Raju**

Sale Proceeds (75% of Goods)	1,00,000
Less : Invoice Value of goods sold (Rs. 1,25,000 × $\frac{75}{100}$)	93,750
	6,250
∴ Commission @ 10% on 93,750 =	9,375
Special Comm. @ 25% on 6,250 =	1,563
	10,938

Advance from Consignee as Caution/Security Money

Sometimes the consignor takes some advance from the consignee against the goods which are despatched for sale. The advance money so received will automatically be adjusted against the total dues for ascertaining the net amount payable to the consignor. The entire amount of advance money may be adjusted even if a part of goods are sold provided that such advance is not treated as a caution or security money. This is because if the advance is taken as a security deposit or caution money, that portion of the advance money which are related to the goods remaining unsold must not be adjusted but the same should be carried forward (See **Illustration 36** that follows). Needless to mention that advance may be given by the consignee by cash or by draft or by bill as :

The consignor and the consignee will pass the usual entries in their respective books, viz.,

In the books of consignor :		Similarly, in the books of consignee :	
Cash/B/R/Draft A/c	Dr.	Consignor A/c	Dr.
To Consignee's Personal A/c		To Cash/B/R/Draft A/c	

Treatment of Security Money taken as Advance

Illustration 36

X of Kolkata consignees goods to Y in Mumbai, for sale at invoice price or over. Y is entitled to a commission of 5% on invoice price and 25% of any surplus price realised. X draws on Y at 90 days' sight for 80% of the invoice price, and upon sale, Y remits the balance of proceeds, after deducting his commission by Sight Draft.

Goods consigned by X to Y in the year cost X Rs. 10,450, including freight and were invoiced at Rs. 14,200. Sales made by Y were Rs. 13,380 and goods in his hand unsold at 31st December, represented an invoice value of Rs. 3,460 (original cost, including freight Rs. 2,610). Sight drafts actually received by X from Y up to 31st December were Rs. 3,140. Others were in-transit.

Prepare the necessary ledger accounts in the books of X.

Solution

In the books of X

Consignment to Mumbai Account

Dr. *Cr.*

Date	*Particulars*	*Amount*	*Date*	*Particulars*	*Amount*
?		Rs.	?		Rs.
	To Goods sent on Consignment A/c	14,200		By Goods Sent on Consignment A/c —Loading	3,750
	" Y A/c Commission	1,197[1]		" Y A/c —Sale Proceeds	13,380
	" Stock Reserve (3,460 – 2,610)	850		" Unsold Stock A/c	3,460
	" Profit and Loss A/c Profit on Consignment —Transferred	4,343			
		20,590			20,590

Dr. **Y Account** Cr.

Date	Particulars	Amount	Date	Particulars	Amount
?		Rs.	?		Rs.
	To Consignment to Mumbai A/c —Sale Proceeds	13,380		By Bills Receivable A/c	11,360
	" Balance c/d (Rs. 3,460 × 80%)	2,768		" Consignment to Mumbai A/c —Commission	1,197
				" Cash A/c	3,140
				" Draft-in-transit *(bal. fig.)* A/c	451
		16,148			16,148

Dr. **Goods Sent on Consignment Account** Cr.

Date	Particulars	Amount	Date	Particulars	Amount
?		Rs.	?		Rs.
	To Consignment A/c —Loading	3,750		By Consignment A/c	14,200
	" Trading A/c *(bal. fig.)*	10,450			
		14,200			14,200

Workings :

1. **Calculation of Commission :**

		Rs.	
	Invoice Value of goods	14,200	
Less ;	Unsold goods	3,460	
	Invoice value of goods sold	10,740	
	Total Sale Proceeds		13,380
Less :	Invoice value of goods sold		10,740
	Surplus price		2,640

	Rs.
Therefore, Commission to be calculated @ 5% on Rs. 10,740 =	537
and @ 25% on Rs. 2,640 =	660
Total Commission payable	1,197

Normal loss, Abnormal loss, Invoice Price etc.

Illustration 37

X Ltd. of Mumbai consigned 5,000 liters of liquor to Y Ltd. of Kolkata on 1st February 2011. The goods are charged at a Proforma Invoice value of Rs. 2,00,000 including profit of 20% on invoice. X Ltd. paid Rs. 5,000 as freight and insurance charges. During transit 200 liters were destroyed for which the insurance company paid directly to the consignor Rs. 5,000 in full settlement of the claim.

On 25th February, Y Ltd. paid for carriage and clearing charges Rs. 3,100 and sent to the consignor a bank draft for Rs. 40,000 as advance. Other expenses paid by the consignee were godown rent Rs. 1,200 and salesman's salary Rs. 900. Y Ltd. were entitled to a commission of 4%, plus 2% del credere on sales.

Y Ltd. reported that 4,000 liters were sold at Rs. 1,65,000 and 50 liters were lost due to evaporation. A customer who bought liquor of Rs. 1,500 was able to pay 40%, of the amount due from him. Assuming that Y Ltd. paid the amount by a bank draft, show the Consignment Account and Y Ltd. Account in the books of the X Ltd. On the date of closing the accounts, market price of liquor was Rs. 33.50 per liter.

Solution

In the books of X Ltd.

Dr. **Consignment to Calcutta Account** Cr.

Date	Particulars	Amount	Date	Particulars	Amount
2011		Rs.	2011		Rs.
Feb. 1	To Goods Sent on Consignment A/c	2,00,000	Feb. 25	By Goods Sent on Consignment A/c —Loading (Rs. 2,00,000 × $\frac{20}{100}$)	40,000
	" Bank A/c —Freight and Insurance	5,000			
Feb. 25	" Y Ltd A/c				

Contd.

2011			Rs.	2011			Rs.
	To —Consignment	3,100			By Y Ltd A/c		
	—Godown Rent	1,200			—Sale Proceeds		1,65,000
	—Salesman Salary	900	5,200		" Abnormal Loss A/c		8,200[1]
	" Y Ltd A/c				" Stock on Consignment A/c		31,563[1]
	—Or. Com.	6,600					
	—Del Credere Com.	3,300	9,900				
	" Abnormal Loss A/c						
	—Loading ($40,000 \times \frac{200}{5,000}$)		1,600				
	Stock Reserve A/c		7,946[2]				
	" Profit and Loss A/c Profit on Consignment —Transferred		15,117				
			2,44,763				2,44,763

Dr. **Y Ltd. Account** Cr.

Date	Particulars	Amount	Date	Particulars	Amount
2011		Rs.	2011		Rs.
Feb. 25	To Consignment Calculate A/c —Sale Proceeds	1,65,000	Feb. 25	By Bank A/c —Advance	40,000
	" Balance c/d —Adj. of security money $\left(\frac{Rs. 40,000 \times 750\ lit}{3,000\ lit}\right)$	6,000		" Consignment to Calculate A/c	
				—Commission	9,900
				—Expenses	5,200
				" Bank A/c (*bal. fig.*)	1,15,900
		1,71,000			1,71,000

Workings :

1. **Valuation of Goods Lost-in-Transit and Unsold Stock**

		Rs.
	Total Invoice Price of the goods	2,00,000
Add :	Consignor's Expenses	5,000
	C.P. of 5,000 litres	2,05,000
Less :	Lost-in-Transit $\left(\frac{Rs. 2,05,000 \times 200\ lit}{5,000\ lit}\right)$	8,200
		1,96,800
Add :	Non-recurring expenses of Consignee	3,100
	C.P. of (5,000 – 200 – 50) = 4,750 litres	1,99,900

$\therefore$ Value of unsold Stock (IP.) = Rs. $\frac{1,99,900}{4,750} \times 750$

= Rs. 31,563

2. **Stock Reserve**

		Rs.
Value of Stock		31,563
Less : Market Price (750 lit × Rs. 33.50)	25,125	
Less : Com. @ 6%	1,508	23,617
		7,946

GENERAL ILLUSTRATIONS

Illustration 38

Tilak of Tatanagar consigned goods costing Rs. 2,00,000 to his agent Pulak of Patna. The invoice was made proforma so as to show a profit of 25% on cost. Tilak paid freight and insurance Rs. 4,000. Pulak sold part of the consignment for Rs. 1,76,000 at a uniform price of 10% over invoice price and spent Rs. 6,000 as warehousing charges and Rs. 2,000 as selling expenses. Pulak is entitled to a commission of 5% on sales and 20% on the net profit after charging commission on sales

Draw-up the Consignment Account in the books of Tilak.

[CU BCom (Hons.) 2000)]

Solution

In the books of Tilak
Consignment to Patna Account

Dr. Cr.

Date	Particulars		Amount	Date	Particulars	Amount
?			Rs.	?		Rs.
	To Goods Sent on Consignment A/c		2,50,000[1]		By Pulak A/c	
	" Bank A/c				—Sale Process	1,76,000
	—Freight and Insurance		4000		" Goods Sent on Consignment A/c	50,000[1]
	" Pulak A/c				" Stock on Consignment A/c	91,440[2]
	—Warehousing Exp.	6,000				
	—Selling Expenses	2,000	8,000			
	" Pulak A/c					
	—Commission	8,800				
	—Extra Com.	5,728[4]	14,528			
	" Stock Reserve A/c		18,000[3]			
	" Profit & Loss A/c					
	—Net Profit transferred		22,912			
			3,17,440			3,17,440

Working

1. **Computation of Invoice Price & Loading**

CP	Rs.	SP/IP
100	25	125

2,00,000 $\frac{125 \times 2,00,000}{100}$

= Rs. 2,50,000

∴ Loading = IP – CP

= Rs. 2,50,000 – Rs. 2,00,000

= Rs. 50,000

2. **Portion of Goods Sold**

Invoice Price of Goods Sold

$= \text{Rs. } 1,76,000 \times \frac{100}{110} = \text{Rs. } 1,60,000$

(Since, it was in excess over 10% of IP)

∴ Portion Sold $= \frac{\text{Invoice Price of Goods Sold}}{\text{Invoice Price of Goods Sent}}$

$= \frac{\text{Rs. } 1,60,000}{\text{Rs. } 2,50,000} = \frac{16}{25}$ portion of goods sold,

Value of Unsold Stock $= 1 - \frac{16}{25} = \frac{9}{25}$

Value of Unsold Stock

	Rs.
Total Invoice Price	2,50,000
Add : Exp. Insurred buy Consignor	4,000
: Non-recurring Exp. of Consignee	6,000
	2,60,000

Value of Unsold Stock $= \text{Rs. } 2,60,000 \times \frac{9}{25}$

= Rs. 91,440.

3. **Loading on Closing Stock**

$= \text{Rs. } 50,000 \times \frac{9}{25} = \text{Rs. } 18,000$

4. **Commission**

		Rs.
Ordinary commission (1,76,000 × 5%)		8,800
Extra Comm. :		
Credit total of consignment	3,17,440	
Less : Debit Total of Consignment A/c	2,88,800	
Net Profit (before extra Com.)	28,640	

So extra com. will be @ 20% on Rs. 28,640

Or Rs. 5,728 (28,640 × 20%)

(It is not a case of 20% of profit after charging such Commision.)

Invoice Price—Abnormal Loss, extra commission, claim received by consigne from Insurance Company etc.

Illustration 39

On 1st January 2012 Goods at an invoice value of Rs. 1,32,000 were consigned by Chowdhury & Co. of Kolkata to their agent Gupta and Co. of Allahabad at a proforma invoice of 20% profit on cost.

Freight paid by the consignor amounted to Rs. 5,000. Gupta & Co. was allowed 5% ordinary commission and 3% del credere commission on gross sales. They were also allowed 5% of the net profit as extra commission after charging such commission. Allahabad expenses were:

Landing and Clearing charges Rs. 1,020. Godown Insurance premium Rs. 2,500.

$\frac{3}{4}$th of the goods were sold at 25% Profit on Sales. $\frac{1}{10}$th of the balance of goods were destroyed by fire and a claim for Rs. 8,500 was settled by the Insurance Co.

Prepare Consignment Account, Gupta and Co. Account, Stock Destroyed Account, and Consignment Stock Account in the books of Chowdhury & Co.

Solution **[CU BCom (Hons.) 1993—Adapted]**

In the books Chowdhury and Co.

Consignment to Allahabad Account

Dr. *Cr.*

Date	*Particulars*		*Amount*	*Date*	*Particulars*	*Amount*
2012			Rs.	2012		Rs.
Jan. 1	To Goods Sent on Consignment A/c (invoice value of goods sent to Allahabad)		1,32,000	Jan. 1	By Goods Sent on Consignment A/c (Loading on goods sent)	22,000[2]
	" Bank A/c (Exp.)		5,000	?	" Gupta & Co. A/c (3/4th goods sold)	1,10,000[3]
	" Gupta and Co. A/c				" Stock Destroyed A/c	3,450[1]
	Landing	1,020			" Consignment Stock A/c	31,055[1]
	Godown	2,500				
	" Gupta and Co. A/c		3,520			
	" Ord. Com.		5,500			
	" Del Credere Com.		3,300			
	" Stock Reserve A/c (loading on Closing Stock)		4,950			
	" Abnormal Loss (loading)		550			
	" Gupta and Co. A/c					
	" Extra Commission		556[4]			
	" P & L A/c (Profit on Consignment) transferred		11,129			
			1,66,505			1,66,505

Gupta and Co. Account

Dr. *Cr.*

Date	*Particulars*	*Amount*	*Date*	*Particulars*	*Amount*
2012		Rs.	2012		Rs.
?	To Consignment to Allahabad A/c	1,10,000	?	By Consignment to Allahabad A/c (Exp.)	3,520
	" Insurance Claim A/c	8,500		" Consignment A/c Ord. Com.	5,500
				" Del Credere Com.	3,300
				" Extra Com.	556
				" Balance c/d	1,05,624
		1,18,500			1,18,500

Stock Destroyed Account

Dr. *Cr.*

Date	*Particulars*	*Amount*	*Date*	*Particulars*	*Amount*
2012		Rs.	2012		Rs.
?	To Consignment to Allahabad A/c	3,450	?	By Insurance Claim A/c	8,500
	" P & L A/c (profit)	5,600		" Consignment to Allahabad A/c—loading	550
		9,050			9,050

Consignment Stock Account

Dr. *Cr.*

Date	*Particulars*	*Amount*	*Date*	*Particulars*	*Amount*
2012		Rs.	2012		Rs.
?	To Consignment to Allahabad A/c	31,055	?	By Balance c/d	31,055

Workings :

1. **Valuation of Goods Destroyed by Fire and Unsold Stock**

		Rs.
	Total Invoice Price	1,32,000
Add :	Consignor's Expenses	5,000
Add :	Non-recurring Expenses of Consignee	1,020
		1,38,020

Unsold Stock $\left(1-\frac{3}{4}\right)=\frac{1}{4}$, $\frac{1}{10}$th of $\frac{1}{4}$ lost by fire i.e., $\frac{1}{10}\times\frac{1}{4}=\frac{1}{40}$ of the balance lost by fire and unsold stock.

$\left(\frac{1}{4}-\frac{1}{40}\right)=\frac{9}{40}$th.

Value of Stock = Rs. 1,38,020 $\times\frac{9}{40}$ = Rs. 31,055

Stock destroyed by fire = Rs. 1,38,020 $\times\frac{1}{40}$ = Rs. 3,450.

2. **Calculation of Loading**

I.P. = Rs. 1,32,000

Loading = Rs. (1,32,000 $\times\frac{20}{120}$) = Rs. 22,000

Cost Price = Rs. 1,32,000 – Rs. 22,000 = Rs. 1,10,000

3. **Calculation of Sales**

CP	Profit	SP
75	25	100

$\left(\text{Rs. }1,10,000\times\frac{3}{4}\right)$ = Rs. 82,500 $\qquad \frac{100\times 82,500}{75}$ = Rs. 1,10,000

4. **Extra Commission**

	Rs.	
Profit before charging commisions	11,685	(P+C) = Total
Less : Commission @ $\frac{5}{105}$ or $\frac{1}{21}$ =	556	(100 + 5) = 105; $C=\frac{5}{105}$
Net Profit	11,129	

Opening Stock, Closing Stock, Abnormal Loss, Cash Sales, Credit Sales, etc.

Illustration 40

Indra of Delhi sends a consignment of elegant electronic wall clocks to Barun of Kolkata and charges proforma invoice price so as to show a profit of 25% on cost. The agent received commission @ 5% on all sales plus 3% del credere commission on credit sales made by him.

Stock of goods with the agent at the beginning of the year—40 clocks at proforma invoice price Rs. 25,000.

During the year ended 31st December 2012, Indra had the following transactions with Barun :

(a) Proforma invoice price of 200 clocks consigned to Barun—Rs. 1,25,000.

(b) Railway charges and insurance on the consignment paid by Indra—Rs. 3,500.

(c) Advance received from Barun—Rs. 37,500.

(d) Sales made by Barun :

(i) 80 clocks for cash—Rs. 53,750.

(ii) 100 clocks on credit—Rs. 70,000.

(e) Selling expenses made by agent—Rs. 6,250 and discount allowed by him Rs. 2,500.

(f) 30 clocks were damaged by the railway for which Barun recovered Rs. 6,750. The damaged clocks were sold on cash by Barun at Rs. 5,750.

(g) Out of the clocks sold on credit, Rs. 5,000 was irrecoverable and considered bad by the agent.

(h) The agent remitted the balance due by him by a bank draft.

Show necessary Ledger Accounts in the books of Indra.

[CU BCom (Hons.)]

Solution

In the books of Indra

Consignment to Kolkata Account

Dr. *Cr.*

Date	Particulars	Amount	Date	Particulars	Amount
2012		Rs.	2012		Rs.
Jan. 1	To Stock of Consignment A/c (I.P. of 40 clocks)	25,000	Jan. 1	By Stock Reserves —Loading on Opening Stock (Rs. 25,000 × $\frac{25}{125}$)	5,000
Dec. 31	" Goods sent on Consign. A/c (I.P. of 200 clocks)	1,25,000	Dec. 31	" Goods Sent on Consign. A/c —Loading on goods sent (Rs. 1,25,000 × $\frac{25}{125}$)	25,000
	" Bank A/c —Railway Charges & Insurance	3,500			
	" Barun A/c —Selling Expenses	6,250			

Contd.

2012		Rs.	2012		Rs.
	To Barun A/c —Discount allowed adjusted	2,500		By Barun A/c —Cash Sales (80 clocks)	53,750
	" Barun A/c —Or. Com	6,188		—Credit Sales (100 clocks)	70,000
	—Del Credere Com.	2,100		" Abnormal Loss A/c	19,275
	" Stock Reserve A/c—Loading on Closing Stock (Rs. 25,000 × $\frac{30}{200}$)	3,750		" Unsold Stock A/c —30 clocks	19,275
	" Abnormal Loss A/c—Loading	3,750			
	" Profit and Loss A/c Profit on Consignment —Trransferred	14,262			
		1,92,300			1,92,300

Barun Account

Date	Particulars	Amount	Date	Particulars	Amount
2012		Rs.	2012		Rs.
Dec. 31	To Consignment to Kolkata A/c —Cash and Credit Sales	1,23,750	Dec. 31	By Bank A/c—Advance	37,500
	" Abnormal Loss A/c —Sale of Damaged goods	5,750		" Consignment A/c —Selling Expenses	6,250
	" Abnormal Loss A/c —Compensation recovered	6,750		" Consignment to Kolkata A/c —Discount Allowed Adjusted	2,500
				" Consignment A/c —Ordinary Com.	6,188
				—Del Credere Com.	2,100
				" Abnormal Loss A/c —Ordinary Com. (on Cash Sale of damaged goods i.e., 5% on Rs. 5,750)	287
				" Bank A/c—Bank Draft Received	81,425
		1,36,250			1,36,250

Abnormal Loss Account

Date	Particulars	Amount	Date	Particulars	Amount
2012		Rs.	2012		Rs.
Dec. 31	To Consignment to Kolkata A/c	19,275	Dec. 31	By Consig. to Kolkata A/c—Loading	3,750
	" Barun A/c —Ordinary Com. on sale of damaged goods	287		" Barun A/c—Claims recovered	6,750
				" Barun A/c —Sale of damaged goods	5,750
				" Profit and Loss A/c —Net loss transferred	3,312
		19,562			19,562

Goods Sent on Consignment Account

Date	Particulars	Amount	Date	Particulars	Amount
2012		Rs.	2012		Rs.
Dec. 31	To Consig. to Kolkata A/c—Loading	25,000	Dec. 31	By Consignment to Kolkata A/c —I.P. of goods sent	1,25,000
	" Trading A/c —Cost of goods sent	1,00,000			
		1,25,000			1,25,000

Consignment Stock Account

Date	Particulars	Amount	Date	Particulars	Amount
2012		Rs.	2012		Rs.
Jan. 1	To Balance b/d	25,000	Jan. 1	By Consignment to Kolkata A/c	25,000
Dec. 31	" Consignment to Kolkata A/c —I.P. of Closing Stock	19,275	Dec. 31	" Balance c/d	19,275
		44,275			44,275
2013					
Jan. 1	To Balance b/d	19,275			

Dr. **Stock Reserve Account** Cr.

Date	Particulars	Amount	Date	Particulars	Amount
2012		Rs.	2012		Rs.
Jan. 1	To Consignment to Kolkata A/c —Loading on Opening Stock	5,000	Jan. 1	By Balance b/d	5,000
Dec. 31	" Balance c/d	3,750	Dec. 31	" Consignment to Kolkata A/c —Loading on Closing stock	3,750
		8,750			8,750
			2013		
			Jan. 1	By Balance b/d	3,750

Workings :

1 FIFO method is followed for valuation of unsold stock. Quantity unsold = 40 + 200 – 80 – 100 – 30 = 30 clocks. So, closing stock includes goods of current year only. Thus, the value of closing stock will be calculated as under :

Valuation of Goods Lost-in-Transit and Unsold Stock

		Rs.
	Total Invoice Price	1,25,000
Add :	Consignor's Expenses	3,500
	I.P. of 200 clocks	1,28,500
Less :	Lost-in-transit $\left(\frac{Rs. 1,28,500 \times 30}{200}\right)$ =	19,275
		1,09,225
Add :	Non-recurring expenses of consignee	Nil
	I.P. of 170 clocks	1,09,225
	Value of unsold stock at I.P. = Rs. $\frac{1,09,225 \times 30}{170}$	= Rs. 19,275

2. Total Commission

	Rs.
Or. Com. on Rs. (53,750 + 70,000), i.e., Rs. $(1,23,750 \times \frac{5}{100})$ =	6,187
Del Credere Com. Rs. $(70,000 \times \frac{3}{100})$	2,100
	8,288

3. It has also been assumed that discount allowed has already been permitted by the consignor. So, it is a charge against the consignment.

Note : Since the clocks were damaged by the railways, it has been assured that these were lost during transit.

Goods-in-transit, Special Commission, Abnormal Loss, etc.

Illustration 41

On 1.10.2001 S. Mittal of Faridabad sent on consignment to S. Bros. of Kolkata 100 boxes of goods costing Rs. 1,200 each and incurred Rs. 4,600 as freight, Rs. 300 as cartage and Rs. 600 as insurance in consigning the goods.

S. Bros. accepted a bill on 12.10.2001 at 3 months for 60% of the normal selling price of goods as security money and S. Mittal discounted the bill on 15.11.2001 at a discount of 2% p.a. The normal selling price was cost plus 45%.

S. Bros. had incurred Rs. 1,500 as unloading charges; Rs. 700 as godown rent and Rs. 1,600 as selling expenses. He was entitled to a commission @ 6% on normal selling price plus 20% of any surplus over and above the normal selling price.

He reported that 3/5th of the goods received had been sold for Rs. 1,16,400 and 10 boxes of goods were damaged on account of bad packing which would be sold only for Rs. 725 per box. It was found that 10 boxes of goods were still in transit on 31.12.2001 when the accounts of the consignor were closed. The amount due to S. Mittal was remitted by a bank draft.

Prepare necessary accounts in the books of S. Mittal.

Solution **[CU BCom (Hons)—2002]**

In the books of S. Mittal

Dr. **Consignment to Kolkata Account** Cr.

Date	Particulars		Amount	Date	Particulars	Amount
2001			Rs.	2001		Rs.
Oct. 1	To Goods Sent on Consign. A/c (100 × Rs. 1,200)		1,20,000	Dec. 31	By S. Bros A/c—Sale of 54 boxes	1,16,400
	" Bank A/c				" Unsold Stock A/c	
	—Freight	4,600			—10 Damaged Goods	6,815
	—Cartage	300			—26 boxes in good condition	33,063[3]
	—Insurance	600			" Goods-in-Transit A/c —10 boxes	12,550[2]
			5,500			

Contd.

2001		Rs.	2001		Rs.
Dec. 31	To S. Bros A/c			By	
	—Unloading Charge 1,500				
	—Godown Rent 700				
	—Selling Expenses 1,600				
	—Commission 10,126[4]	13,926			
Dec. 31	" Profit and Loss A/c Profit on Consignment A/c —Transferred	29,402			
		1,68,828			1,68,828

Dr. **S. Bros. Account** Cr.

Date	Particulars	Amount	Date	Particulars	Amount
2011		Rs.	2011		Rs.
Dec. 31	To Consignment to Kolkata A/c —Sale Proceed	1,16,400	Oct. 12	By B/R (Advance)	1,04,400[6]
	" Balance c/d (26 X Rs. 1,740 + 10 × Rs. 725) × $\frac{60}{100}$	31,494	Dec. 31	" Consignment to Kolkata A/c —Expenses & Com.	13,926
				" Bank Draft (*bal. fig.*)	29,568
		1,47,894			1,47,894

Dr. **Goods Sent on Consignment Account** Cr.

Date	Particulars	Amount	Date	Particulars	Amount
2001		Rs.	2001		Rs.
Dec. 31	To Trading A/c —Transferred	1,20,000	Oct. 1	By Consignment to Kolkata A/c	1,20,000
		1,20,000			1,20,000

Workings

1. **Valuation of Damaged Goods and Unsold Stock**

			Rs.
	Cost Price of 10 boxes @ Rs. 1,200		12,000
Add :	Proportionate expenses of consignor = $\left(\frac{\text{Rs.}5,500 \times 10}{100}\right)$		550
Add :	Proportional Expense of consignee = $\left(1,500 \times \frac{10}{90}\right)$		167
			12,717
Less :	Estimated value of those damaged goods Estimated Value 10 × Rs. 725 =	7,250	
Less :	Consignee Com. @ 6%	435	6,815
	Abnormal Loss		5,902

2. **Value of 10 boxes which were still in Transit**

		Rs.
	Cost Price of @ Rs. 1,200	12,000
Add :	Proportionate expenses $\left(\frac{\text{Rs.}5,500 \times 10}{100}\right)$	550
		12,550

3 **Value of Unsold Stock**

	Details of goods sent :	Boxes
	Goods sent	100
Less :	Damaged in transit	10
		90
Less :	Sold $\left(90 \times \frac{3}{5}\right)$	54
		36
Less :	Still in transit	10
	Unsold Stock	26

4. **Commission**

		Rs.
Normal Commission (54 × Rs. 1,740) = Rs. 93,960 × $\frac{6}{100}$ =		5,638
Special Commission Sales	1,16,400	
Less : Normal selling price 54 units @ Rs. 1,740 (i.e., Rs. 1,200 + 45%)	93,960	
Surplus Price	22,440 × 20% =	4,488
		10,126

	Cost Price of 26 boxes @ Rs. 1,200 =	31,200
Add :	Proportionate expenses of consignor $\left(\frac{\text{Rs.}5{,}500 \times 26}{100}\right)$	1,430
Add :	Consignee's non-recurring expenses $\left(\frac{\text{Rs.}1{,}500 \times 26}{90}\right)$	433
		33,063

5. Discount charge of the bill is assumed to be a financial charge, hence, the same should be adjusted against Profit and Loss Account and not in Consignment Account.
6. **Advance from Consignee**
   60% of the normal selling price
   i.e., (Rs. 1,740 × 100) = Rs. $(1{,}74{,}000 \times \frac{60}{100})$ = Rs. 1,04,400.

Invoice Price—Abnormal Loss, Special Commision etc.

Illustration 42

Kolkata Ayurvedic Ltd. produces a bottle of " Drakharista " at a cost of Rs. 10 each. They appointed Chennai Medical Store of Chennai their agent on the terms that the agent would get commission @ 10% on invoice price of goods sold and an extra commission at 25% on any surplus price realised above invoice price.

On 1.7.1998, Kolkata Ayurvedic Ltd. sent 50 boxes of "Drakharista" each box containing 50 bottles at invoice price showing a profit of $33\frac{1}{3}$% on such invoice price. They spent Rs. 3,000 for freight and Rs. 2,000 for insurance. 5 boxes were totally destroyed in transit and insurance claim of Rs. 2,300 was realised from insurance company. The agent took delivery of the remaining goods and spent Rs. 2,000 for duty and Rs. 1,000 for freight to carry the goods to the rented godown. He also sent a bills of exchange for Rs. 20,000 payable after two months to the consignor as advance.

At the end of the year the agent reported that 40 boxes were sold at Rs. 18 per bottle and 1 box of goods were lost due to bad packing. This would be treated as normal loss. The agent remitted a bank draft for the net amount after deducting his commission, advance money, godown rent Rs. 800 and selling expenses Rs. 200.

On 1.1.99 Kolkata Ayurvedic Ltd. discounted the bill of Rs. 20,000 for Rs. 19,800. On 1.3.99 the bank informed that the bill was dishonoured. Kolkata Ayurvedic Ltd. demanded the entire amount along with an additional amount of Rs. 200 as interest. The Chennai agent sent a bank draft for the amount on 15.3.99.

You are asked to show the following accounts in the books of the consignor : **(a) Consignment to Chennai Account; (b) Chennai Medical Stores Account; (c) Consignment Stock Accounts; (d) Consignment Stock Destroyed Account; (e) Consignment Stock Reserve Account.**

Solution **[CU BCom (Hons.)—1995]**

In the books of Kolkata Ayurvedic
Consignment to Chennai Account

Dr. *Cr.*

Date		*Particulars*		*Amount*	*Date*		*Particulars*	*Amount*
1998				Rs.	1998			Rs.
July 1	To	Goods Sent on Consignment A/c		37,500[1]		By	Goods Sent on Consignment—Loading	12,500
	"	Bank A/c			Dec. 31	"	Consignment Stock Destroyed A/c	4,250[2]
		—Freight	3,000			"	Chennai Medical Store A/c —Sale Proceeds (40 × 50 × Rs. 18)	36,000
		—Insurance	2,000	5,000		"	Consignment Stock A/c	3,750[2]
Dec. 31	"	Chennai Medical Stores A/c						
		—Duty	2,000					
		—Freight	1,000					
		—Godown Rent	800					
		—Selling Expense	200	4,000				
	"	Chennai Medical Stores A/c —Commission		4,500[4]				
	"	Consignment Stock Destroyed A/c —Loading		1,250				
	"	Consignment Stock Reserve A/c —Loading on Closing Stock (Rs. 12,500 × $\frac{4}{50}$)		1,023[3]				

Contd.

			Rs.			Rs.
1998				1998		
Dec. 31	To	Profit and Loss A/c Profit on Consignment —Transferred	3,227		By	
			56,500			56,500

Chennai Medical Store Account

Dr. Date		Particulars	Amount	Date		Particulars	Cr. Amount
1998			Rs.	1998			Rs.
Dec. 31	To	Consignment to Chennai A/c —Sale Proceeds	36,000	Dec. 31	By	Bills Receivable A/c	20,000
					"	Consignment to Chennai A/c —Expenses —Commission	4,000 4,500
					"	Bank Draft A/c	7,500
			36,000				36,000
1999				1999			
Mar. 1	To	Bank A/c (B/R dishonored)	20,000	Mar. 15	By	Bank Draft A/c	20,200
	"	Interest A/c	200				
			20,200				20,200

Consignment Stock Account

Dr. Date		Particulars	Amount	Date		Particulars	Cr. Amount
1998			Rs.	1998			Rs.
Dec. 31	To	Consignment to Chennai A/c	3,750	Dec. 31	By	Balance c/d	3,750
			3,750				3,750

Consignment Stock Destroyed Account

Dr. Date		Particulars	Amount	Date		Particulars	Cr. Amount
1998			Rs.	1998			Rs.
Dec. 31	To	Consignment to Chennai A/c	4,250	Dec. 31	By	Consignment to Chennai (Loading) A/c	1,250
					"	Bank A/c Insurance Claims	2,300
					"	Profit and Loss A/c *(bal. fig.)*	700
			4,250				4,250

Consignment Stock Reserve Account

Dr. Date		Particulars	Amount	Date		Particulars	Cr. Amount
1998			Rs.	1998			Rs.
Dec. 31	To	Balance c/d	1,023	Dec. 31	By	Consignment to Chennai A/c Loading on Closing Stock	1,023
			1,023				1,023

Workings :

1. Invoice Value of Goods Sent

		Rs.
	Cost of goods sent 50 boxes @ Rs. 500 (i.e., Rs. 10 × 50 bottols)	25,000
Add :	Loading (50% of Cost or $33\frac{1}{3}$ % of I.P.)	12,500
	Invoice Price	37,500

2. Valuation of Goods Destroyed in-Transit and Unsold Stock :

	Invoice value of goods sent	37,500
Add :	Consignor's Expenses	5,000
		42,500
Less :	Lost-in-Transit $\left(\frac{\text{Rs. } 42,500 \times 5}{50}\right)$	4,250
		38,250

3. Closing Stock Reserve

	Rs.
Total Loading	12,500
Less : Loading on Abnormal Loss (Rs. $12,500 \times \frac{5}{50}$)	1,250
Loading on 49 bottles	11,250
∴ So Closing Stock Reserve for 4 bottles = Rs. $11,250 \times \frac{4}{44}$	1,023

4. Commission Payable to Chennai Medical Stores

Total Sales	36,000
Invoice Value of goods sold	30,000
Surplus Price	6,000

Contd.

		Rs.		Rs.
Add :	Non-recurring expenses of Consignee	3,000	Ordinary Commission @ 10% on Rs. 30,000 =	3,000
	(2,000 + 1,000)		Special Commission @ 25% on Rs. 6,000 =	1,500
	I. P. of (50 – 5 – 1) 44 boxes	41,250		4,500

∴ Invoice Value of Unsold Stock = Rs. $(41,250 \times \frac{4}{44})$ = Rs. 3,750.

Rectification of Errors

Sometimes some wrong entries are made in the books of consiginor. For example, consignment sales are treated as **Sales** for which necessary corrections should be made.

Some of the entries are recorded here.

When goods are sent at Invoice Price	Correct Entry	Entry Made
(a) When goods are sent	(i) Consignment A/c Dr To Goods Sent on Consignment A/c	(i) Consignies Personal A/c Dr. To Goods sent on Consignt. A/c/Sales A/c
(b) For loading on Goods Sent	(i) Goods sent on Consignment A/c Dr. To Consignment A/c	—
(c) For Closing Stock on Consignment	(i) Stock on Consignment A/c Dr. To Consignment A/c	—
(d) For Loading on Closing Stock	(i) Consignment A/c Dr. To Stock Suspense/Reserve A/c	—
(e) For Goods Sold	(i) Consignee's Personal A/c Dr. To Consignment A/c	(i) Bank A/c Dr. To Consignee's Personal A/c

When Goods are Sent at Cost Price

Under the circumstances, only 'loading entries' will not be recorded. Other entries will remain same as above.

Illustration 43

In the Sales Ledger of XY Goods Co. the following account appears:

Dr. **Ram** *Cr.*

Date	*Particulars*	*Amount*	*Date*	*Particulars*	*Amount*
2011		Rs.	2011		Rs.
May 10	To Goods	12,000	July 5	By Cash	5,000
	" Expenses	720	July 31	" Balance c/d	7,720
		12,720			12,720

Upon enquiry you find that the debit to Ram of Rs. 12,000 represented goods costing Rs. 10,000 delivered to him on the understanding that he will try to sell them in his own make, or otherwise return them. For this he is to be allowed a commission of 10 per cent on all sales effected, out of which he is to defray the expenses that he may incur.

On 31st July 2011, when XY Goods Co. made up their annual accounts, it informed that Ram has sold half the goods at the prices at which they were invoiced to him but is doubtful about his ability to sell the remaining. He, therefore, proposes to offer his customers a special trade discount of 20 per cent and to waive any further sales commission. To this, XY Goods Co. agreed and took this information into account when closing their books.

You are required :

(a) to show the necessary corrective entries in the firm's Journal;

(b) to set out the account of Ram as it will appear when the Journal entries have been posted; and

(c) to state clearly the resultant profit or loss on the matter.

Solution **(CA)**

From the problem, it becomes clear that the goods which were sent to Ram on consignment basis has wrongly been treated as sales. For the purpose, the following entries are required to be passed :

(a) **Journal**

Date	Particulars		L.F.	Debit	Credit
2011				Rs.	Rs.
July 31	Sales/Goods A/c	Dr.		12,000	
	Consignment to Ram A/c	Dr.		720	
	To Ram A/c				12,720
	(Cancellation of wrong entry and expenses of consignment transferred.)				
July 31	Consignment A/c	Dr.		12,000	
	To Goods Sent on Consignment A/c				12,000
	(Invoice Price of goods sent on consignment.)				
"	Ram A/c	Dr.		6,000	
	To Consignment A/c				6,000
	(Goods sold by Ram.)				
"	Consignment A/c	Dr.		600	
	To Ram A/c				600
	(Commission @ 10% payable to Ram.)				
"	Stock on Consignment A/c	Dr.		6,360	
	To Consignment A/c				6,360[1]
	(Stock on consignment at Invoice Price.)				
"	Consignment to Ram A/c	Dr.		600	
	To Ram A/c				600
	(Commission payable to Ram.)				
"	Profit and Loss A/c	Dr.		520	
	To Consignment A/c				520
	(Loss on Consignment transferred.)				
	Goods Sent on Consignment A/c	Dr.		2,000	
	To Consignment A/c				2,000
	(Loading on goods sent.)(2,000 + 1,000)				
	Consignment A/c	Dr.		1,560	
	To Stock Reserve A/c				1,560[2]
	(Loading on Closing Stock)				

(b) **Ram Account**

Dr. Cr.

Date	Particulars	Amount	Date	Particulars	Amount
2011		Rs.	2011		Rs.
July 31	To Balance b/d	7,720	July 31	By Sales A/c	12,000
	" Consignment to Ram A/c —Sale Proceeds	6,000		" Consignment to Ram A/c	
				—Expenses	720
				—Commission	600
				" Balance c/d	400
		13,720			13,720

(c) **In order to find out the resultant profit or loss the following consignment Account is prepared :**

Dr. **Consignment to Ram Account** Cr.

Date	Particulars	Amount	Date	Particulars	Amount
2011		Rs.	2011		Rs.
July 31	To Goods Sent on Consignment A/c	12,000	July 31	By Goods Sent on Consignment A/c	
	" Ram A/c —Expenses	720		—Loading	2,000
	" Ram A/c —Commission	600		" Ram A/c —Sale Proceeds	6,000
	" Stock Reserve A/c	1,560[2]		" Stock on Consignment A/c	6,360[1]
				" Profit and Loss A/c Loss on Consignment —Transferred	520
		14,880			14,880

Note :

Stock on Consignment

1. $\frac{1}{2}$ of Invoice Price (Rs. 12,000 + Rs. 720) = Rs. 6,360.

2. Value of $\frac{1}{2}$ of goods at Invoice Priice Rs. 6,360 – Market Price of such goods at 20% discount = (Rs. 6,000 – Rs. 1,200) = Rs. 4,800

∴ Stock Reserve = Rs. 6,360 – Rs. 4,800 = Rs. 1,560

Illustration 44

Rama consigned goods to Ravindran, his agent at New Delhi, at cost price of Rs. 40,000. Rama's account, at the end of the year, drew up the agent's account as under :

Ravindran Account

Dr. Date	Particulars	Rs.	Date	Particulars	Cr. Rs.
	To Goods	40,000		By Cash	24,000
	" Profit and Loss A/c	3,300		" Balance c/d	19,300
		43,300			43,300

Ravindran sold the goods for Rs. 45,000 which exceeded by Rs. 9,000 over invoice value. He collected Rs. 38,000 after allowing discount of Rs. 2,000 to customers. Bad debts come to Rs. 1,000 and his non-recurring expenses to Rs. 800. Ravindran was entitled to a 5% commission on cash collected. Balance of stock is to be valued at invoice price.

From the above information, draw the accounts of Ravindran, Consignment, and Consignment Debtors in the books of Rama.

Solution **[CU BCom (Hons.) 2001—Adapted]**

In the books of Rama

Consignment to New Delhi Account

Dr. Date	Particulars	Amount Rs.	Date	Particulars	Cr. Amount Rs.
?	To Goods Sent on Consignment A/c	40,000	?	By Consignment Debtors A/c (sales)	45,000
	" Consignment Debtors A/c (disc. & bad debts)	3,000		" Stock on Consignment A/c	4,080[2]
	" Ravindran A/c (expenses)	800			
	" Ravindran A/c (commission)	1,900			
	" Profit and Loss —Profit on Consignment transferred	3,380			
		49,080			49,080

Ravindran Account

Dr. Date	Particulars	Amount Rs.	Date	Particulars	Cr. Amount Rs.
?	To Balance b/d	19,300	?	By Goods (sales) A/c	40,000
	" Consignment Debtors A/c (received from Debtors)	38,000		" Profit & Loss A/c	3,300[1]
				" Conign. to New Delhi A/c (exp.)	800
				" Consign. to New Delhi A/c (commission)	1,900
				" Balance c/d	11,300
		57,300			57,300

Consignment Debtors Account

Dr. Date	Particulars	Amount Rs.	Date	Particulars	Cr. Amount Rs.
?	To Consignment to New Delhi A/c	45,000	?	By Ravindran A/c	38,000
				" Consignment to New Delhi A/c (discount and bad debts)	3,000
				" Balance c/d	4,000
		45,000			45,000

Workings :

1. **Profit has been reversed here.** 2. **Value of Closing Stock**

		Rs.
	Cost of Goods Sent	40,000
Less:	Cost of Good Sold (Rs. 45,000 – Rs. 9,000)	36,000
		4,000
Add:	Proportionate Non-recurring Expenses = $(\frac{\text{Rs. }4,000}{\text{Rs. }40,000} \times \text{Rs. }800)$	80
		4,080

ASSIGNMENT MATERIALS

THEORETICAL

Multiple Choice Questions

1. (a) Account sales is prepared by:
(i) Consignor; (ii) Consignee; (iii) Both; (iv) Non of these.

(b) Consignor is the:
(i) Agent; (ii) Principal; (iii) Both; (iv) None of these.

(c) When Del Credere Commission is not given :
Bad Debts to be borne by
(i) Consignor; (ii) Consignee; (iii) Both; (iv) None of these.

(d) When Del Credere Commission is given—
Bad Debts to be borne by
(i) Consignor; (ii) Consignee; (iii) Both; (iv) None of these.

(e) Stock of Consignment to be valued as:
(i) Cost Price; (ii) Market Price; (iii) Cost Price or Market Price whichever is lower; (iv) None of these.

(f) Del Credere Commission is given
(i) to increase sales; (ii) to send money; (iii) to Cover the risk of collection on account of credit sales ; (iv) None of these.

(g) Normal loss is—
(i) An inherent loss; (ii) Sudden loss; (iii) Unexpected loss ; (iv) None of these.

(h) Abnormal Loss happens
(i) due to accident (ii) natural wastage; (iii) both ; (iv) None of these

[Ans. (a) (ii); (b) (ii); (c) (i); (d) (ii); (e) (iii); (f) (iii); (g) (i); (h) (i)]

Short Answer-Type Questions

2. Write notes on:
(i) Del Credere Commission; (ii) Account Sales; (iii) Normal Loss ; (iv) Abnormal Loss; (v) Security Money.

3. Explain the terms:
(i) Consignment; (ii) Cosignor; (iii) Consignee; (iv) Loading and Unloading Expenses; (v) Consignment Inward; (vi) Consignment Outward Account.

4. Distinguish between:
(i) Consignment and Sales; (ii) Sale Price and Invoice Price; (iii) Invoice and Proforma Invoice ; (iv) Ordinary Commission and Del Credere Commission; (v) Recurring and Non-recurring Expenses.

5. Explain which of the following expenses incurred by consignee will be added to cost:
Freight and Insurance, Godown Rent, Advertisement, Selling Expenses, Carriage Inward, Clearing Charges, Storage.
State also which are known as non-recurring expenses.

6. Explain why the following items do not appear in the books of consignee:
(i) Goods received from the consignor, and (ii) Unsold stock in consignment.

7. Calculate the amount of commission from the following :
(a) Profit before charging commission amounted to Rs. 44,000. Commission to be calculated @ 10% of profit after charging such commission.

(b) Gross Sale Proceeds Rs. 1,00,000, consignors expenses Rs. 5,000, Ordinary commission Rs. 50,000, Special Commission @ $\frac{1}{8}$ the of net proceeds after charging such commissions.

(c) Y is entitled to a commission of Rs. 25 per bicycle sold plus $\frac{1}{4}$ of the amount by which the gross sale proceeds less total commission exceeded a sum calculated @ Rs. 125 per bicycle sold.

Total sale proceeds Rs. 73,800.

(d) B was entitled to a commission of 3% on invoice price and 20% of any surplus price realised. Cost of goods sent Rs. 24,000; Invoice at a profit of 25% on invoice Price; $\frac{4}{5}$th goods were sold for Rs. 30,000.

(e) Y is entitled to a commission on sales at 5% on proforma invoice price and 25% of any surplus price realised. Invoice value of goods .Rs. 28,400. 80% of the goods were sold for 26,000.

[Ans. (a) Rs. 4000; (b) Rs. 10,000; (c) Rs. 9,810; (d) Rs. 1,648, (e) Rs. 1956]

Essay-Type Question

8. Discuss the differences between Consignment and Sale.
9. How do you treat the unsold stock in Consignment Account? Illustrate your answer with the help of an example.
10. Discuss the treatment of Normal Loss and Abnormal Loss in Consignment Account.
11. How do you incorporate shortage or Deficiency of stock in Consignment Account?
12. What is an Account Sale? Explain it with the help of an illustration.
13. What is Del Credere Commission? How do you treat it in Consignment Account?
14. How do you value the stock on consignment?
15. What is Proforma Invoice Price? Explain it with the help of an illustration.
16. What is Consignment Inward Accooount and Who prepares it?
17. (a) Why is a consignee not treated a consignor's debtor?
    (b) What is 'Abnormal Loss' in Consignment Accounts?
18. What is Overriding Commission in Consignment Account?
19. Distinguish between recurring and non-recurring expenses related to consignment.

PRACTICAL

Stock Valuation

1. Mr. Shetty is a consignee agent for Electra Engineers Ltd., Mumbai, who manufactues transistors. Model P and Model T are the most popular models with fixed retail price of Rs. 200 and Rs. 250, respectively, on which the manufactures have a profit of 20% calculated on the sales price.

The consignment arrangement with Mr. Shetty provides for the following commission structure:

(i) Model P $2\frac{1}{2}$% on the S. P. (ii) Model T 4% on the S.P. On July 1998 stock with Mr. Shetty was 200 of Model T and 200 of Model P. During the half year ended 31.12.98 the transactions were:

	Model P	Model T
Goods sent to Mr. Shetty	2,000 Nos.	1,000 Nos.
Sales by Mr. Shetty	2,100 Nos.	900 Nos.

The consignment sent to Mr. Shetty costs Rs. 30,000.

Show the Consignment Account showing separately the computation of commission due and the value of closing stock in the books of Electra Engineers Ltd.

[CA Entrance]

[Ans. Profit on Consignment Rs. 83,500; Value of Unsold Stock Rs. 80,000]

Normal and Abnormal Loss

2. XYZ Ltd. consigns on 1.11.2005 1,000 tins of groundnut oil from Kolkata to a party Mr. X in Mumbai. Each tin costs Rs. 30 @ Rs. 3 per kg XYZ Ltd. pays Rs. 5,000 by way of freight and other expenses. During transit 25 tins were accidentally destroyed. Mr. X takes delivery on 15.11.2005 and accepts a bill for Rs. 20,000 drawn by XYZ Ltd. at 3 months. On 31.12.2005, Mr. X sold 800 tins @ Rs. 50 per tin and reports to XYZ Ltd. a theft of 35 tins. Mr. X had also paid Rs. 600 as clearing charges,

Rs. 1,000 as godown rent and Rs. 2,000 by way of labour charges and fire insurance. Mr. X is entitled to receive a commission of 5% plus 1% for Del Credere risk.

Show the important ledger accounts up to 31.12.2005 in the books of XYZ Ltd. assuming that Mr. X pays the dues by bank draft.

[Ans. Profit on Consignment Rs. 6,108; Abnormal Loss Rs. 876; Unsold Stock Rs. 4,986; Value of Stolen Goods Rs. 1,247]

3. Sri Mehta of Mumbai consigns 1,000 cases of goods costing Rs. 100 each to Sri Sundaram of Chennai. Sri Mehta pays the following expenses in connection with the consignment : carriage Rs. 1,000; freight Rs. 3,000; and loading charges Rs. 1,000.

Sri Sundaram sells 700 cases at Rs. 140 per case and incurs the following expenses: clearing charges Rs. 850; warehousing and storage Rs. 1,700; and packing and selling expenses Rs. 600. It is found that 50 cases have been lost in transit and 100 cases are still in transit. Sri Sundaram is entitled to a commission of 10% on gross sales.

Draw up Consignment Accont and Sundaram's Account in the books of Mehta.

[Ans. Profit on Consignment Rs. 11,700; Abnormal Loss Rs. 5,250; Unsold Stock Rs. 15,900; Stock-in-transit Rs. 10,500]

4. Bharat Petroleum consigned 1,00,000 litres of petrol to its agent at a cost Rs. 5·00 per litre. The agent is to sell petrol on behalf of the company only to the registered dealers at Rs. 5·50 per litre and he is entitled to a selling commission of 6%. Bharat Petroleum incurred the following expenses :

Loading Charges Rs. 5,000, Freight Rs. 10,000 and Insurance & Other Expenses Rs. 10,000.

10,000 litres of petrol were destroyed in-transit and the insurance company admitted the claim of Rs. 40,000. The agent actually received 89,500 litres only due to leakages which was treated as a normal loss.

The agent incurred the following expenses :

Clearing Charges Rs. 4,000. Storage Rs. 5,000.

The agent sold 84,500 litres at scheduled rate, deducted his commission and expenses. He sent a Sight Draft for the balance.

Show the necessary ledger accounts in the books of Bharat Petroleum.

[Ans. Loss on Consignment Rs. 18,015; Value of Stock Rs. 26,620; Value of Abnormal Loss Rs. 52,500]

Invoice Price

5. The Export Promotion Company of New Delhi consigned 300 bales of clothing to M/s John Adams in England, on 1. 10. 2012. The cost price was Rs. 600 per bale, but the proforma invoice price was made out at a figure so as to show a gross profit of 20% on sales. The consignee reported on 31. 12. 2012 that they had sold $\frac{2}{3}$rd of the consignment at a profit of 25% on sales and that they had incurred Rs. 2,000 by way of freight, duty and landing charges and Rs. 1,000 by way of Godown Rent, Salaries, exclusive of their Commission. The Consignor had earlier incurred Rs. 900 by way of expenses in despatching the goods. The Consignee is entitled to a commission of 5% on sales and to one-fourth share of profit after charging up both their commission and share of profit. On 1. 1. 2013, John Adams sent a bill for the amount so far due from them.

Show the necessary ledger accounts in the books of the Consignor. (CA)

[Ans. Profit on Consignment Rs. 23,254; Value of Stock Rs. 75,967; Consignee's Commission Rs. 8,000; Consignment Share of Profit Rs. 5,813]

6. Bharat Exporters Company of Kolkata consigned 400 bales of cotton goods to Sri M. Inam of Mysore on 1. 11. 2011. The cost price was Rs. 600 per bale but the consignment invoice was made out at a figure to show a gross profit of 20% on invoice price. Sri Inam reported on 31. 1. 2012 that he had sold $\frac{3}{4}$th of the consignment at a profit of 25% on sales and he had incurred Rs. 2,500 by way of freight and landing charges etc. and also Rs. 1,500 by way of godown rent etc. exclusive of his commission. Consignor spent Rs. 1,200 earlier as expenses in despatching the goods. Sri Inam was entitled to a commission of 5% on sales and 20% of the net proceeds as bonus after charging up both the commission and the bonus. On 1. 2. 2012, Sri Inam sent a Bank Draft for the amount so far due from him.

Show the necessary ledger accounts in the books of Bharat Exporters Company.

[CU BCom (Hons.].

[Ans. Profit on Consignment Rs. 6,392; Value of Stock Rs. 75,925; Commission & Bonus Rs. 12,000 + 37,333 = Rs. 49,333]

7. P sends goods on consignment to T at an invoice price of 25% on sales to be sold for as ordinary commission of 5% on gross sales plus a special commission of 20% on excess of sale proceeds less all commission over the invoice price. P sends 100 chests of medicines at an invoice price of Rs. 1,000 per chest and incurs Rs. 5,000 for expenses. T paid the following expenses : Clearing charges Rs. 4,500, Godown Rent and Selling Expenses Rs. 5,000. 10 chests were destroyed in-transit (not covered by insurance due to technical defect in policy). T sells 60 chests for Rs. 1,00,000 and sends a draft for the balance.

Show the necessary ledger accounts in the books of P.

[Ans. Profit on Consignment Rs. 33,166; Total Commission Rs. 10,834; Value of Stock Rs. 33,000; Value of Abnormal Loss Rs. 10,500]

8. Niresh consigns 1,000 bats costing Rs. 500 each to Swaroop for sales and incurs Rs. 4,000 towards freight and Rs. 1,000 for insurance. Swaroop was able to take delivery of 900 bats only and 100 bats were destroyed in transit. Insurance Co. admitted the claim and paid the same. Swaroop will be entitled to a commission of 5% on sales, 2% del credere commission on credit sales only. He will be entitled for additional commission of 25% of the excess if the sale price exceeds the cost price by more than 20%. Swaroop has spent Rs. 2,000 towards sales expenses. The sale account is :

500 bats at Rs. 600 per bat in cash.
200 bats at Rs. 700 per bat in credit.

Consignment debtors paid their dues except one customer, to whom 4 bats were sold for Rs. 2,800, could pay only Rs. 800.

Show Consignment Account, Consignment Debtors A/c, Swaroop A/c and commission calculation.

[CA—Entrance]

[Ans. Profit on Consignment Rs. 54,700; Value of Unsold Stock Rs. 1,01,000]

Miscellaneous

9. P. Tsai of Singapore is the agent for sewing machines manufactured by Jyoti Exports of Mumbai. A machine costs Rs. 300, the invoice price to P. Tsai is Rs. 400. P. Tsai is entitled to a commission of 15% of this price plus 40% of the excess realised over Rs. 400. He is also responsible for all expenses incurred by him but not for freight to Singapore or customs duty.

Jyoti Exports despatched 200 machines in January 2010, drawing on P. Tsai for Rs. 40,000 for 3 months. P. Tsai accepted the draft. Expenses paid by P. Tsai were :

Freight Rs. 4,000; Customs duty Rs. 2,000; Storage Rs. 1,000; Insurance Rs. 800.

At the end of March 2010, P. Tsai reported that he has sold 150 machines at an average price of Rs. 440. It was agreed then that P. Tsai would take over the remaining machines on his own account at landed cost plus 20%.

Prepare the following accounts in the books of M/s Jyoti Exports :

(a) Consignment A/c; (b) P. Tsai's A/c.

[Ans. Profit on Consignment Rs. 8,400; Value of Goods Taken Rs. 19,800; Commission Rs. 11,400]

10. On 15th September 2011, Abhijit, a merchant of Kolkata, sent a consignment of 100 cases of goods to Kalisankar, his agent in Mumbai. On 22nd September, Abhijit received Kalisankar's acceptance of a six months' bill of exchange for Rs. 10,000 drawn by Abhijit which was immediately discounted for Rs. 9,750. The goods had cost Abhijit Rs. 100 per case and carriage, freight and insurance paid by him on 30th September amounted in total to Rs. 250. During the voyage two cases of the consignment were completely destroyed by fire and on 25th November Abhijit received the appropriate compensation from the insurance company.

Abhijit's accounting year ended on 31st December 2011 and Kalisankar sent him an interim Account Sales made up-to-date. It disclosed that 60 cases had been sold for Rs. 125 each and landing charges and import duty together amounted to Rs. 960 and distribution expenses to Rs. 100. Commission at 5% on sales and $2\frac{1}{2}$% del credere Commission was charged.

On 31st March 2012, Abhijit received the final Account Sales showing that the remainder of the consignment had been sold for Rs. 140 per case, distribution charges amounting to Rs. 160 had been paid, and commission was deducted from the balance due to Abhijit.

You are required to show the accounts for the above transactions in the ledger of Abhijit.

[CU BCom (Hons.)]

[Ans. Profit on Consignment Rs. 998; Unsold Stock Rs. 4,267; Abnormal Loss Rs. 8,056]

11. On October 1st 2012, M consigned goods to the value of Rs. 1,00,000 to S incurring expenses for freight and insurance of Rs. 6,000. An Account Sales was received from S, who is entitled to a commission @ 5% on gross sales, made up to December 31st 2012, the end of M's accounting year, which showed that :

(i) 60% of goods had been sold for Rs. 80,000, but only Rs. 65,000 had been so far been received.

(ii) Expenses of Rs. 3,000 had been incurred in connection with the goods consigned and Rs. 2,000 in connection with the goods sold.

On January 15th 2012 M incurred bank charges of Rs. 100 in cashing the sight draft for the balance due, which accompanied the Account Sales from S.

A further Account Sales was received, made up to March 31st 2012 which showed that :

(a) The balance of goods had been sold for Rs. 55,000 and Selling Expenses of Rs. 1,500 had been incurred;

(b) All cash due had been received, except that a bad debt of Rs. 1,000 had been incurred.

On April 15th 2012, M incurred Bank charges of Rs. 80 in cashing the sight draft on the balance due, which accompanied the Account Sales from S.

Write-up the accounts in the books of M necessary to reflect the above transactions.

[Ans. Profit on Consignment Rs. 85,000 and Rs. 6,070; Unsold Stock Rs. 43,600]

12. On 1st April 2011 Shiva Oil Mills Ltd. of Patna consigned 550 tins of mustard oil to Tarama Traders of Kolkata. Each tin contains 15 kg of oil. The cost being Rs. 21 per kg.

Oil is to be sold $33\frac{1}{3}$% above cost under the following terms :

Tarama Traders is to be paid 3% commission and 2% del credere commission on sales on the basis of the price specified above. Any deficit in selling price is to be fully borne by Tarama Traders, while only 50% of any surplus price realised may be retained by Tarama Traders.

Shiva Oil Mills Ltd. incurred freight and insurance Rs. 3,300 in despatching the tins. 20 tins were stolen in transit and insurance company paid Rs. 5,500 to Shiva Oil Mills Ltd. as final settlement of the claim. Tarama Traders accepted a bill for 3 months drawn by Shiva Oil Mills Ltd. for Rs. 40,000 which was discounted by the latter at Rs. 39,600.

On 18. 12. 2011 Tarama Traders sent an Account Sales which showed that 50 tins were sold @ Rs. 29 per kg, 200 tins were sold @ Rs. 32 per kg and, from the remaining tins, 3,750 kg of oil were sold @ Rs. 34 per kg Tarama Traders paid Rs. 4,270 as clearing charges and Rs. 1,200 as selling expenses. 50 kg of oil were lost due to leakage which was considered as normal loss. Tarama Traders collected entire sale proceeds except Rs. 420 which became irrecoverable.

Show Consignment A/c in the Books of Shiva Oils Mills Ltd. and Shiva Oil Mills Ltd. A/c in the books of Tarama Traders.

[BU BCom (Hons.)]

[Ans. Profit on Consignment Rs. 49,033; Commission Rs. 28,125; Sales Rs. 2,45,250 ; Unsold Stock Rs. 8,828]

13. Roy Brothers of Kolkata sent goods costing Rs. 60,000 to Patel Brothers of Mumbai on 10th September 2011, on consignment basis. The invoice price was made by adding 25% to the cost. Roy Brothers of Kolkata paid the following expenses in connection with the despatched goods : Packing Rs. 350, carriage Rs. 550 and other expenses Rs. 960.

On 25th September 2011, after receiving goods, Patel Brothers paid Rs. 850 as freight and Rs. 450 as carriage for taking goods to their godown and forwarded a 3 months' Bill for Rs. 15,000 to Roy Brothers.

On 31st December 2011 Patel Brothers sent an Account sales to Roy Brothers. Roy Brothers of Kolkata came to know from the Account Sales that Patel Brothers had sold half of the goods at Rs. 40,000 in cash and Rs. 20,000 on credit out of which Rs. 7,000 had already been collected by Patel Brothers. The expenses deducted by Patel Brothers also include Rs. 450 for Fire Insurance. Patel Brothers were entitled to an ordinary commission of 5% and del credere commission of $2\frac{1}{2}$% on Gross Sales.

On April 30, 2012, a Second Account Sales was sent by Patel Brothers. It showed that half of the remaining goods were sold by Patel Brothers at Rs. 15,000 in cash and Rs. 10,000 on credit. Their expenses during the period were Rs. 250 for Fire Insurance and Rs. 150 for other expenses. The remaining goods could not be sold and were brought back by Roy Brothers on 31st August 2012, at a further cost of Rs. 1,000. These goods were damaged on the way and were valued at 40% below their cost price. Patel

Brothers remitted with each Account Sales the balance due from them and Roy Brothers close their books of accounts on 31st December each year. Patel Brothers were able to collect all the dues from the debtors till 31st December 2012, except Rs. 1,500 from a debtor, which was treated as bad debt.

Draw-up the Consignment Account, Patel Brothers' Personal Account; and Goods Sent on Consignment Account in the books of Roy Brothers of Kolkata.

[BU BCom (Hons.)]

[Ans. Profit on Consignment Rs. 23,470 (2011) Loss on Consignment Rs. 855 (2012), Unsold Stock Rs. 9,000 and Rs. 39,080 in 2011 and for 2012 respectively]

14. A sent to B, on consignment, goods costing Rs. 60,000 and incurred expenses totalling Rs. 3,000. Account Sales revealed that $\frac{3}{4}$ of the goods were sold at a profit of 20% on sales and that B's expenses amounted to Rs. 3,500 including Rs. 1,500 being the cost of a typewriter purchased for A's personal use. B is entitled to a Commission of 10% on sales. Towards the end of the year, B requested A to allows him to purchase, for his private use, goods costing Rs. 2,000 at a concessional price of Rs. 2,375 to which A consented on the condition that B would not charge Commission on this sale. A fire occurred in B's godown, destroying goods, original cost of which to A was Rs. 5,000, and a claim of Rs. 3,000 was settled with the insurance company. The terms of agreement between A and B provided that any loss caused by any accident at the Consignee's end shall be borne by them in equal proportion. The rest of the goods remained unsold. B had earlier sent an advance of Rs. 10,000 to A.

Show Consignment Account, Consignee's Account and Insurance Claim Account in the books of A.

[CA—Adapted]

[Ans. Profit on Consignment Rs. 3,292; Value of Stock Rs. 8,667; Value of Abnormal Loss Rs. 5,417]

15. Dinesh of Mumbai consigned medicines to Rao of Chennai costing Rs. 1,00,000. The invoice was made proforma so as to show a profit of 25% on cost. Dinesh paid Freight Insurance Rs. 2,000. Rao sold part of consignment for Rs. 88,000 at uniform price of 10% over invoice price and spent Rs. 3,000 as Warehousing Charges, Rs. 1,000 as Selling Expenses. Sri Rao is entitled to a commission of 5% on sales and 20% of the net profit after charging such commission on sales. Sri Rao paid the amount due by Bank Draft. Draw-up the Consignment Account and Rao's Account in the books of Dinesh.

(CA)

[Ans. Profit on Consignment Rs. 11,456; Value of Stock Rs. 45,720; Balance due to Rao remitted by Bank Draft Rs. 76,736]

16. Bhola consigned 40 machines to Ram on 1.1.2011 on the following terms :

(a) All machines were to be sold 20% above cost of Rs. 10,000. Any deficit in selling price is to be borne by Ram while Ram is to retain 50% of any surplus price realised.

(b) Ram is to be paid 3% commission and 2% Del Credere commission on all sales. Bhola incurred Freight Charges of Rs. 40,000 in consigning the machines. Ram sent an Account Sales which showed that—

10 machines	were	sold	for	Rs. 12,000	each.
5 "	"	"	"	Rs. 10,000	each.
15 "	"	"	"	Rs. 14,000	each.

Ram had incurred unloading charges of Rs. 4,000 and Selling Expenses of Rs. 6,000. He had collected the entire sale proceeds except Rs. 2,000, which had become a bad debt. Ram sent a Bank Draft for the net amount due to Bhola.

On 30.6.2012, Ram sent a further Account Sales disclosing : 10 machines were sold at Rs. 12,000 each. Selling expenses were Rs. 1,500.

He also sent a Draft for the net amount due. Bhola closes his books on 31st Dec. every year.

Show the necessary ledger accounts in the books of Bhola.

(CA)

[Ans. Commission Rs. 24,000; Profit on Consignment Rs. 17,000 (on 31.12.2011; Profit on Consignment Rs. 1,500 (on 31.12.2012).]

CHAPTER 19

GOODS ON APPROVAL OR ON SALE OR RETURN

Introduction

Sometimes a firm sends goods to its customers with the option—either to retain or to return the same within a stipulated period. This is known as 'Sale or Return' or 'Sale on Approval'. Therefore, dealing with such goods simply indicates a change in possession and not a transfer of ownership until and unless the customer sends his approval, or the stipulated period has expired. Such transactions during this period cannot be treated as a 'Sale', i.e., ownership remains in the hands of the owner. As a result, profit cannot accrue on those transactions.

Accounting Steps

The system of keeping records for 'Sale or Return' depends, however, on the number of transactions. The transactions may be divided into three distinct categories :

(a) Where transactions are very few in number; (b) Where transactions are moderately large in number; and (c) Where transactions are numerous.

(A) WHERE TRANSACTIONS ARE VERY FEW IN NUMBER

Since the transactions are very few, there is no necessity of maintaining a separate book for this purpose. As soon as the transaction takes place, it is treated as actual sales and recorded with the help of journal on that basis. In other words, transactions relating to sales or return are treated as actual sales which, from accounting point of view, is not justified.

Under this method, how the transactions relating to *Sale or Return* are recorded in the books of the seller are discussed hereunder :

Entries under this method :

In the books of Seller

	Transactions	*Current year*	*Subsequent year*
(a)	When goods are sent :	Debtors A/c Dr. To Sales A/c (at selling price)	Does not arise
(b)	If goods are returned :	Sales A/c or Returns Inward A/c Dr. To Debtors A/c (at selling price)	Debtors Suspense A/c Dr. To Debtors A/c (at selling price)
(c)	If goods are sold :	No entry	Debtors Suspense A/c Dr. To Sales A/c (at selling price)
(d)	If goods are sold at a higher price than the selling price :	Debtors A/c Dr. To Sales A/c (for excess amount)	Do
(e)	If goods are sold at a smaller price than the selling price :	Sales A/c Dr. To Debtors A/c (difference)	Debtors Suspense A/c Dr. (at selling price) To Sales A/c (actual selling price) To Debtors A/c (by which it was reduced)
(f)	If goods are lying in the hands of Customers at the end of the year :	(i) Sales A/c Dr. To Debtors Suspense A/c* OR " Sale or Return Suspense A/c (at selling price) (ii) Stock on Sale or Return A/c Dr. To Trading A/c	Does not arise (cost price or market price, whichever is lower)

* It is also known as Stock on Approval Account/Stock with Customers on Sale or Return/Stock with Customers Account etc.

Note : In Balance Sheet, Stock on Sale or Return will be added to Closing Stock.

Illustration 1

A trader sends goods to his customers on sale or return basis. The following transactions took place during the year 2012 :

			Rs.
July	10	Sent goods to customers on sale or return (basis at cost plus 25%)	40,000
	15	Goods returned by customers	10,000
Aug.	4	Received sales information from customers for goods valued at	20,000
Dec.	31	Goods with customer neither sold nor returned	10,000

Assuming that the trader records the transactions on ordinary sales basis and that the date of final accounts was 31st December, show the entries.

Solution

In the books of ....
Journal

Date	Particulars	L.F.	Debit	Credit
			Rs.	Rs.
?	Sundry Debtors A/c Dr.		40,000	
	To Sales A/c			40,000
	(Goods sent on Sale or Return basis and treated as Sales.)			
" 15	Returns Inward/Sales A/c Dr.		10,000	
	To Sundry Debtors A/c			10,000
	(Goods returned by customers.)			
Dec. 31	Sales A/c Dr.		10,000	
	To Debtors Suspense A/c			10,000
	(Goods sent on 'Sale or Return' basis and included in sales but not approved by the customers within 31st December, now adjusted.)			
	Stock with Customer on Sale or Return A/c (Rs. 10,000 × $\frac{100}{125}$) Dr.		8,000	
	To Trading A/c			8,000
	(Goods lying with customers (at cost) on 'Sale or Return' basis included in Stock.)			

Illustration 2

In preparing the final accounts of a company it is found that the amount of Sundry Debtors, Rs. 4,20,000, includes Rs. 40,000 worth of goods sent out on approval and debited to Customers' Accounts, in respect of which the time for returning the goods had not yet expired. There goods have been invoiced at $33\frac{1}{3}$ % above cost.

Show the Journal Entries to be passed in preparing the final accounts and also state the adjustments to be made in the final accounts.

Solution **[CU BCom (Hons)]**

In the books of ....
Journal

Date	Particulars	L.F.	Debit	Credit
			Rs.	Rs.
	Sales A/c Dr.		40,000	
	To Debtors Suspense A/c			40,000
	(Adjustment at the end of the period for goods sent on 'Sale or Return' basis but not yet approved by the customers.)			
	Stock on Approval A/c Dr.		30,000	
	To Trading A/c			30,000
	(Value of the goods sent on 'Sale or Return' basis now included in Stock (Rs. 40,000 – 25% of Rs. 40,000.)			

Balance Sheet *(Extracts) as at 31st ....*

	Assets	Rs.	Rs.
	Sundry Debtors	* *	
	Less : Debtors Suspense	40,000	
			* *
	Stock on Approval (at cost)		30,000

(B) WHERE TRANSACTIONS ARE MODERATELY LARGE IN NUMBER

This method is applicable where the transactions relating to 'Sale or Return' are moderately large in number, i.e. neither more nor less. Under this method, a separate 'Sale or Return' Day Book is maintained for recording this type of transactions from which Debtors Account and Sales Account are debited and credited, respectively, for some time.

Sale or Return Day Book

(1) Goods Sent out on Approval			(2) Goods Sold			(3) Goods Returned		(4) Balance
Date	*Particulars*	*Amount*	*Date*	*L.F.*	*Amount*	*Date*	*Amount*	*Amount*
		Rs.			Rs.		Rs.	Rs.

Note : Valuation of closing stock in hand should be made on the basis of Cost Price or Market Price, whichever is lower, and the following entry is required to be passed :

	Stock with Customers on Sale or Return A/c Dr.			
	To Trading A/c			

Illustration 3

P. Ltd. sends out the following goods to their customers during the month of Jan. 2012 on 'Sale or Return' basis :

2012			Rs.	2012		
Jan.	1	P. Dey	1,800	Jan.	10	All the goods retained
	9	A. Kar	700		12	All the goods returned
	16	M. Das	1,500		20	Goods retained Rs. 1,000 and returned Rs. 500
	20	N. Pal	900		22	Goods returned Rs. 400 and no intimation as to the balance
	25	P. Banerjee	600			No intimation received as yet nor the goods returned
	31	D. Chatterjee	750			Do

Show how the above transactions will be recorded in the books of the firm assuming that the transactions are ***moderately large*** in number.

Solution

In the books of P. Ltd.
Sale or Return Day Book

(1) Goods Sent out			(2) Goods Sold			(3) Goods Returned		(4) Balance
Date	*Particulars*	*Amount*	*Date*	*L.F.*	*Amount*	*Date*	*Amount*	*Amount*
2012		Rs.	2012		Rs.	2012	Rs.	Rs.
Jan. 1	P. Dey	1,800	Jan. 10		1,800	Jan. 12	700	—
9	A. Kar	700	20		1,000	20	500	—
16	M. Das	1,500				22		
20	N. Pal	900					400	500
25	P. Banerjee	600						600
31	D. Chatterjee	750						750
		6,250			2,800		1,600	1,850

∴ Value of Stock amounted to Rs. 1,850 and valuation should be made on the basis of Cost Price or Market Price, whichever is lower.

(C) WHERE THE TRANSACTIONS ARE NUMEROUS

This method is particularly applicable where the transactions relating to 'Sale or Return' are numerous and, as such, amounts involved by these transactions are also very high. Under this method, a separate set of books is maintained. They are :

(a) Sale or Return Day Book; (b) Sale or Return Journal; and (c) Sale or Return Ledger.

Rulings :

Sale or Return Day Book

Date	*Particulars*	*Sale or Return Ledger*	*Remarks*

Sale or Return Journal

Goods Sold					Goods Returned			
Date	Particulars	Sale or Return L.F. No.	Sales L.F. No.	Amount	Date	Particulars	Sale or Return L.F. No.	Amount
				Rs.				Rs.

Dr. **Sale or Return Ledger... Account** Cr.

Date	Particulars	Sale or Return D.B.	Amount	Date	Sale or Return D.B.	Amount
			Rs.			Rs.

Entries under this method

	Transactions	Sale or Return Book	General Ledger
(a)	If goods are sent :	Debtors A/c Dr. To Goods on Sale or Return A/c	—
(b)	If goods are returned :	Goods on Sale or Return A/c Dr. To Debtors A/c	—
(c)	If goods are sold :	Goods on Sale or Return A/c Dr. To Debtors A/c (for cancellation)	Debtor A/c Dr. To Sales A/c
(d)	If goods are lying in the hands of Customers at the end of the year :		Stock on Sale or Return A/c Dr. To Trading A/c (Cost price or market price, whichever is lower)

Illustration 4

From the previous illustration, show how the transactions will be recorded in the books of the firm assuming that the ***transactions are numerous.***

Solution

Sales or Return Day Book

Date		Particulars	Sale or Return Ledger Folio No.	Amount
2012				Rs.
Jan.	1	P. Dey	11	1,800
	9	A. Kar	12	700
	16	M. Das	13	1,500
	20	N. Pal	14	900
	25	P. Banerjee	15	600
	31	D. Chatterjee	16	750
				6,250
				S. or R.L.F. No. 1

Sale or Return Journal

Goods Sold					Goods Returned			
Date	Particulars	Sale or Return L.F. No.	Sales L.F. No.	Amount	Date	Particulars	Sale or Return L.F. No.	Amount
2012				Rs.	2012			Rs.
Jan. 10	P. Dey	11	50	1,800	Jan. 12	A. Kar	5	700
20	M. Das	13	45	1,000	20	M. Das	6	500
					22	N. Pal	7	400
				2,800				1,600
				G.L.F. No. S. Or Ret. L.F. No. 1				S. or Ret. L.F. No. 1

Sale or Return Ledger

Goods on Sale or Return Account

Date		Particulars	Amount	Date		Particulars	Amount
2012			Rs.	2012			Rs.
Jan. 31	To	Sundries (Sales)	2,800	Jan. 31	By	Sundries	6,250
"	"	Sundries (Return)	1,600				
"	"	Balance c/d	1,850				
			6,250				6,250
				Feb. 1	By	Balance b/d	1,850

P. Dey Account

Date		Particulars	Amount	Date		Particulars	Amount
2012			Rs.	2012			Rs.
Jan. 1	To	Goods on Sale or Return A/c	1,800	Jan. 10	By	Goods on Sale or Return A/c (Returns)	1,800
			1,800				1,800

A. Kar Account

Date		Particulars	Amount	Date		Particulars	Amount
2012			Rs.	2012			Rs.
Jan. 9	To	Goods on Sale or Return A/c	700	Jan. 12	By	Goods on Sale or Return A/c (Sales)	700
			700				700

M. Das Account

Date		Particulars	Amount	Date		Particulars	Amount
2012			Rs.	2012			Rs.
Jan. 16	To	Goods on Sale or Return A/c	1,500	Jan. 20	By	Goods on Sale or Return A/c (Sales)	1,000
					"	Goods on Sale or Return A/c (Returns)	500
			1,500				1,500

N. Pal Account

Date		Particulars	Amount	Date		Particulars	Amount
2012			Rs.	2012			Rs.
Jan. 20	To	Goods on Sale or Return A/c	900	Jan. 22	By	Goods on Sale or Return A/c (Returns)	400
				Jan. 31	"	Balance c/d	500
			900				900

P. Banerjee Account

Date		Particulars	Amount	Date		Particulars	Amount
2012			Rs.	2012			Rs.
Jan. 25	To	Goods on Sale or Return A/c	600	Jan. 31	By	Balance c/d	600
			600				600
Feb. 1	To	Balance b/d	600				

D. Chatterjee Account

Date		Particulars	Amount	Date		Particulars	Amount
2012			Rs.	2012			Rs.
Jan. 31	To	Goods on Sale or Return A/c	750	Jan. 31	By	Balance c/d	750
			750				750
Feb. 1	To	Balance b/d	750				

Dr. **Trial Balance** *as at 31st Jan. 2012* Cr.

Heads of Account	*L.F.*	*Debit*	*Credit*
		Rs.	*Rs.*
Goods on Sale or Return		—	1,850
N. Pal		500	—
P. Banerjee		600	—
D. Chatterjee		750	—
		1,850	1,850

GENERAL ILLUSTRATIONS

Illustration 5

A gas company sends out its gas stoves to dealers on "Sale or Return". All such transactions are, however, treated like actual sales and are passed through the Day Book. Just before the end of the financial year 100 stoves, which cost them Rs. 150 each, have been sent to a dealer on 'Sale or Return' and have been debited to his account at Rs. 200 each, out of which only 20 stoves are sold at Rs. 220 each.

Show the entries in the journal of the company to adjust these transactions for the purpose of preparing the final accounts for the year ended December 31, 2010.

Solution

Workings

1. **Total Invoice Price of goods not yet approved :**
   Number of unapproved goods = 100 – 20 = 80.
   So, total invoice price of goods not yet approved
   = 80 × Rs. 200 = Rs. 16,000.

2. **Difference between total accepted price and invoice price of unapproved goods :**
   Difference per gas stove = (Rs. 220 – 200) = Rs. 20
   Therefore, the difference is = 20 × Rs. 20 = Rs. 400.

3. **Cost price of goods not yet approved :**
   Cost price per stove = Rs. 150
   Number of unapproved goods = 80
   So, total cost price = Rs. 150 × 80 = Rs. 12,000

Solution

In the books of Gas Company
Journal

Date	*Particulars*		*L.F.*	*Debit*	*Credit*
2010				*Rs.*	*Rs.*
Dec. 31	Sales A/c	Dr.		16,000	
	To Debtors Suspense A/c				16,000
	(Cancellation of the entry for 80 stoves sent to the customers on Sale or Return basis and invoiced the same at Rs. 200 each which were not accepted.)				
	Sundry Debtors A/c	Dr.		400	
	To Sales A/c				400
	(Extra price of 20 stoves @ Rs. 20 (220 – 200 adjusted.)				
Dec. 31	Stock with Customers on Sale or Return A/c	Dr.		12,000	
	To Trading Account				12,000
	(Cost price of 80 stoves sent on Sale or Return basis which were lying in the hands of Customers.)				

Illustration 6

X Ltd. sends goods to their customers on 'Sale on Approval' basis. All such transactions are, however, treated as actual sales and passed through the Sale Day Book. The goods are invoiced at 25% on cost.

On Dec. 1, 2012, goods valuing Rs. 1,50,000 (invoice price) was sent to the customers for their approval. On Dec. 15, goods worth Rs. 20,000 were returned by the customers. On December 25, intimation was received that goods worth Rs. 1,00,000 has been accepted by the customers but at a reduced price of 10% which was agreed by the company. The customers could not yet decide anything about the rest of the goods.

(a) Show the entries for the month of December 1999, assuming that the company prepares its final accounts on Dec. 31 every year.

(b) Again, assume that Debtors Suspense Account balance carried forward from 2012 included an amount of Rs. 3,500 (invoice price) due from Y, a customer to whom goods were sent on 1st December 2012 on 'Sale or Return' basis. These goods were returned by Y on 6th Jan. 2013. The remaining goods were, however, accepted by all other customers by 15 Jan. 2013. Show the entries.

Solution

In the books of X Ltd.
Journal

Date	Particulars		L.F.	Debit	Credit
2012				Rs.	Rs.
Dec. 1	Sundry Debtors A/c	Dr.		1,50,000	
	To Sales A/c				1,50,000
	(Goods sent out on 'Sale or Return' basis.)				
15	Sales/Returns Inwards A/c	Dr.		20,000	
	To Sundry Debtors A/c				20,000
	(Goods returned by customers.)				
25	Sales A/c	Dr.		10,000	
	To Sundry Debtors A/c				10,000
	(Difference of the price of the goods accepted by customers at a reduced price of 10% (1,00,000 × 10%)				
31	Sale A/c	Dr.		30,000*	
	To Debtors Suspense A/c				30,000
	(Cancellation of the entry of 1st December now adjusted.)				
"	Stock with Customers on 'Sale or Return' A/c	Dr.		24,000†	
	To Trading A/c				24,000
	(Cost price of the goods lying unsold with the customers on Sale or Return basis on Dec. 31.2012 Rs. 30,000 × $\frac{100}{125}$).				

Notes : 1. No entry is required for goods which are approved by the customers.

*2. Invoice price of the approved goods are calculated as:

			Rs.
	Invoice Price of total goods sent		1,50,000
Less :	Approved goods	1,00,000	
	Returned	20,000	1,20,000
			30,000

† 3. ***Closing Stock (on 'Sale or Return' goods at Cost)***

	Invoice Price	30,000
Less :	Loading (Rs. 30,000 × $\frac{25}{125}$)	6,000
	Cost Price of Unapproved Goods	24,000

(b)

In the books of ......
Journal

Date	Particulars		L.F.	Debit	Credit
2013				Rs.	Rs.
Jan. 6	Debtors Suspense A/c	Dr.		3,500	
	To Sundry Debtors A/c				3,500
	(Invoice price of the goods sent on 'Sale or Return' basis to Y in 2012, but returned in 2013.)				
	Debtors Suspense A/c	Dr.		26,500	
	To Sales A/c				26,500
	(Goods sent on 'Sale or Return' basis in 2012, approved by the customer in 2013.)				

Illustration 7

B. S. sends out goods on approval to a few customers and included the same in Sales Account. On 31.3. 2012, the stock in hand amounted to Rs. 80,000 and the Sundry Debtors balance stood at Rs. 1,50,000 which included Rs. 10,000 for goods sent on approval against which no intimation was received during the year. These goods were sent out at 25% above cost and were sent to R Rs. 4,000 and B Rs. 6,000. On 20th April, B returned the goods and on 25th April R intimated of his intention to retain the goods. Make adjustment entries and show how these items will appear in the Balance Sheet on 31st March 2012, and show what entries would be made in April 2012.

[ICWA CU BCom (Hons)—Adapted]

Solution

In the books of B. S.
Journal

Date	Particulars		L.F.	Debit	Credit
2012				Rs.	Rs.
Mar. 31	Sales A/c	Dr.		10,000	
	To Debtors Suspense A/c				10,000
	(Cancellation of the entry for goods sent on 'Sale or Return' basis which were not accepted.)				
	Stock with Customers on Sale or Return A/c	Dr.		8,000	
	To Trading A/c				8,000
	(Cost price of goods sent on 'Sale or Return' basis and lying in the hands of customers.)				

Balance Sheet (Extract) as at 31st March 2012

Liabilities	Assets	Amount	Amount
		Rs.	Rs.
	Sundry Debtors	1,50,000	
	Less : Debtors Suspense	10,000	1,40,000
	Stock	80,000	
	Add : Stock on approval	8,000	
			88,000

Journal

Date	Particulars		L.F.	Debit	Credit
2012				Rs.	Rs.
Apr. 30	Debtors Suspense A/c	Dr.		6,000	
	To B A/c				6,000
	(Return of goods sent to B on approval in the last year.)				
	Debtors Suspense A/c	Dr.		4,000	
	To Sales A/c				4,000
	(Sale of goods sent on approval in the last year.)				

Illustration 8

On 1st November 2012, M/s Tinni & Tubai Traders sent goods valuing Rs. 1,50,000 at invoice price to the customers on sale or return basis. On 10th December, goods worth Rs. 40,000 were returned by the customers. On 23rd December, intimation was received that goods worth Rs. 80,000 has been accepted by the customers but at a reduced price of 5% which was agreed by the Traders. The customers could not yet decide anything about the rest of the goods.

Show the Journal entries in the books of M/s Tinni & Tubai Traders at the end of financial year 31.12.2012. The Tinni & Tubai Traders invoiced goods to their customers at 25% above cost.

[CU BCom (Hons.)]

Solution

Since we are to show the entries at the end of the year i.e., 31.12.2012, the previous entries, i.e., for 1.1. 2012 and 10.12.2012, are not shown.

Before making actual attempt for solution we are to assume that

(i) the usual entry for sending the goods has already been made (i.e., Debtors A/c Dr. and Sales A/c Credit.)

(ii) Similarly, when goods were retained the usual entry had also been made.

Workings :

	Rs.
Invoice value of goods remaining in Stock	
Invoice Price of goods sent :	

Contd.

		Rs.
	(Rs. 1,50,000 × $\frac{125}{100}$)	1,87,500
Less : Returned		40,000
		1,47,500
Less : Sold		80,000
∴	Stock (invoice Price)	67,500

∴ Cost Price of such Stock = Rs. 67,500 × $\frac{100}{125}$ = Rs. 54,000.

In the books of M/s Tinni & Tubai Traders

Journal

Date	*Particulars*	L.F.	*Debit*	*Credit*
2012			Rs.	Rs.
Dec. 31	Sales A/c Dr.		67,500	
	To Debtors Suspense A/c			67,500
	(Goods sent on 'Sale or Return' basis and included in Sales but not approved by customers within 31st December, now adjusted.)			
	Sales A/c Dr.		4,000	
	To Sundry Debtors A/c			4,000
	(Reduction in price of goods sent to customer on Sale or Approval @ 5% on Rs. 80,000)			
	Stock with Customer on Sale or Return A/c Dr.		54,000	
	To Trading A/c			54,000
	(Goods lying with customers (at cost) on Sale or Return basis included in stock.)			

Illustration 9

Automobiles Ltd. sent out motor cars on 'Sale or Return'. They maintained a separate set of books for this type of business. During the month of April 2012, they sent out motor cars on 'Sales or Return' as:

2012 April		Rs.	2012 April
2	Y & Co. Ltd.	10,000	7 Returned
16	X & Co. Ltd.	15,000	20 Retained
20	Y & Co. Ltd.	16,000	25 Returned
28	Y & Co. Ltd.	20,000	No intimation received as to approval and Car not yet returned.

Show Day Book.

Solution

In the books of Automobiles Ltd.

Sale or Return Journal

Goods Sent Out			*Goods Sold*			*Goods Returned*		*Balance*
Date	*Particulars*	*Amount*	*Date*	*L.F.*	*Amount*	*Date*	*Amount*	*Amount*
2012		Rs.	2012		Rs.	2012	Rs.	Rs.
Apr. 2	Y & Co.	10,000				Apr. 7	10,000	
16	X & Co.	15,000	Apr. 20		15,000			
20	Y & Co.	16,000				25	16,000	
28	Y & Co.	20,000						20,000
		61,000			15,000		26,000	20,000

Note : Balance of Sale or Return Day Book, i.e., Rs. 20,000, is to be treated as goods lying in the hands of customers at invoice price (at the time of preparing final accounts). And the valuation will be made on the basis of cost price or invoice price, whichever is lower. The entry for this purpose will be :

Stock with Customers on Sale or Return A/c Dr.
To Trading A/c

Illustration 10

From the following particulars, prepare accounts in Goods on Approval Ledger and General Ledger :

	Rs.
Goods Sent out on approval	1,00,000
Goods Returned	25,000
Goods Accepted	70,000
Opening balance on approval	10,000
Cash received from customers	45,000
Opening dues from approved parties for goods already accepted	5,000

Solution

Goods on Approval Ledger

Goods out on Approval Account
Or, Sale or Return Suspense Account

Dr. Cr.

Date	Particulars	Amount Rs.	Date	Particulars	Amount Rs.
?	To Approval Debtors Control A/c —Returns	25,000	?	By Balance b/d	10,000
	" Approval Debtors Control A/c —Sales	70,000		" Approval Debtors Control A/c	1,00,000
	" Balance c/d	15,000			
		1,10,000			1,10,000

Approval Debtors Control Account

Dr. Cr.

Date	Particulars	Amount Rs.	Date	Particulars	Amount Rs.
?	To Balance b/d	10,000	?	By Goods out on Approval A/c —Returns	25,000
	" Goods on Approval —A/c	1,00,000		" Goods out on Approval A/c —Sales	70,000
				" Balance c/d	15,000
		1,10,000			1,10,000

General Ledger

Sundry Debtors Account

Dr. Cr.

Date	Particulars	Amount Rs.	Date	Particulars	Amount Rs.
?	To Balance b/d	5,000	?	By Bank A/c	45,000
	" Sales A/c	70,000		" Balance c/d	30,000
		75,000			75,000

Sales Account

Dr. Cr.

Date	Particulars	Amount Rs.	Date	Particulars	Amount Rs.
?	To Trading A/c	70,000	?	By Sundry Debtors A/c	70,000
		70,000			70,000

Illustration 11

A firm sells goods on sale or return basis, customers having the choice of returning the goods within a month. During April 2012, the following are the details of the goods sent :

2012 April	Customers	Value Rs.	Proforma Invoice No.
2	A	10,000	004
4	B	18,000	007
16	C	25,000	023
20	D	8,000	032
24	E	21,000	041
28	F	30,000	049

Within the stipulated time A and C returned the goods while B, D and E signified that they have accepted the goods. Show the following accounts in the books of the firm : Sale on Approval Account and Customers for Sale on Approval Account as on 15th May 2012.

Solution **[CA, CU BCom (Hons.)]**

In the books of ... ...

Sale on Approval Account

Dr. Cr.

Date	*Particulars*	*Amount*	*Date*	*Particulars*	*Amount*
2012		Rs.	2012		Rs.
May 2	To Customers for Sale on Approval A/c —Returned by A	10,000	April 2	By Customers for Sale on Approval A/c A	10,000
4	" Sold to B	18,000	4	" B	18,000
15	" Returned by C	25,000	16	" C	25,000
	Sold to D	8,000	20	" D	8,000
	Sold to E	21,000	24	" E	21,000
31	" Balance c/d	30,000	28	" F	30,000
		1,12,000			1,12,000

Customers For Sale on Approval Account

Dr. Cr.

Date	*Particulars*	*Amount*	*Date*	*Particulars*	*Amount*
2012		Rs.	?		Rs.
April	To Sale on Approval A/c		May 2	By Sale on Approval A/c —Returned by A	10,000
2	A	10,000	4	—Sold to B	18,000
4	B	18,000	15	—Returned by C	25,000
16	C	25,000		— Sold to D	8,000
20	D	8,000		— Sold to E	21,000
24	E	21,000	31	" Balance c/d	30,000
28	F	30,000			
		1,12,000			1,12,000

ASSIGNMENT MATERIALS

THEORETICAL

1. What do you understand by "Goods on Approval or on Sale or Return"?
2. How do you maintain accounts in case of "Goods on Approval or on Sale or Return"?
3. Distinguish between Actual Sales and "Goods on Approval or on Sale or Return"?

PRACTICAL

1. A trader has credited certain items of 'Sales on Approval' aggregating Rs. 10,000 to Sales Account. Of these, goods to the value of Rs. 3,000 have been returned and taken in stock at Rs. 1,500 though record of return was omitted in accounts; and in respect of another parcel of 1,000 (cost being Rs. 500) the period of approval did not expire on the closing date.

Show adjustment and correcting entries in the books of the trader.

2. Electronics Ltd. sends out its Accounting Machines costing Rs. 200 each to their customers on 'Sale or Return' basis. All such transactions are, however, treated like actual sales and are passed through the Day Book. Just before the end of the financial year, i.e., on December 24, 2009, 300 such Accounting Machines were sent out at an invoice price of Rs. 280 each, out of which only 90 Accounting Machines are accepted by the customers at Rs. 250 each and, as to the rest, no report is forthcoming.

Show the Journal entries in the books of the company for the purpose of preparing the final accounts for the year ended December 31, 2009.

3. Banamali Das send out goods on approval to a few customers and includes the same in the Sales Account. On 31.3.2012, the Sundry Debtors balance stood at Rs. 1,00,000 which included Rs. 7,000 goods sent on approval against which no intimation was received during the year. These goods were sent out at 25% over and above cost price and were sent to Sudipta Dutta Rs. 4,000 and Anita Paul Rs. 3,000.

Sudipta Dutta sent intimation of acceptance on 30th April and Anita Paul returned the goods on 10th April 2012.

Make adjustment entries and show how these items will appear in the Balance Sheet on 31st March 2012. Show also the entries to be made during April 2012.

4. Automobiles Ltd. sent out motor cars on 'Sale or Return'. They maintained a separate set of books for this type of business.

During the month of April 2012, they sent out motor cars on 'Sale or Return' as:

2012			Rs.	2012		
April	2	Y & Co. Ltd.	10,000	Apr.	7	Returned
"	16	X & Co. Ltd.	15,000	"	20	Retained
"	20	Y & Co. Ltd.	16,000	"	25	Returned
"	28	Y & Co. Ltd.	20,000			No intimation received as to approval and Car not yet returned

Show Day Books and Ledger Accounts.

5. Manab Mukherjee sends goods on approval basis which are as follows :

Date		Customer's Name	Sale Price of Goods sent	Goods Accepted	Goods Returned
2012			Rs.	Rs.	Rs.
Jan.	8	Sumana	5,000	4,000	1,000
"	10	Suparna	3,000	—	3,000
"	15	Subarna	7,000	7,000	—
"	20	Suchetana	2,500	2,000	500
"	25	Sukanya	3,000	—	—
"	30	Sudeshna	4,000	—	—

Show how these transactions will be dealt with where books are kept on Double Entry System. Date of approval has not expired in all the cases.

6. Guha Traders sent out goods on sale or approval basis to customers and includes the same in Sales Account. On 31st December 2012, the Stock in hand amounted to Rs. 40,000 and the Sundry Debtors balance stood at Rs. 75,000 which included Rs. 5,000 being invoice value of goods sent on Sale or Return against which no intimation was received during the year. These goods were sent out at 25% above cost and were sent to S. Dutta — Rs. 2,000 and R. Mitra — Rs. 3,000.

Make necessary adjustment entries and show how these items will appear in the Balance Sheet on 31st December 2012.

[CU BCom (Hons)]

7. Messrs New Central Book Agency sent consignments of their publications to the following customers on 'Sale or Return' basis in the first week of April 2012:

		Rs.
(a)	Mr. Menon, Chennai	500
(b)	Mr. Narain, Chennai	200
(c)	Mr. Ramesh, Mumbai	300
(d)	Mr. Govind, Mumbai	1,000
(e)	Mr. Ghosh, Kolkata	450
(f)	Mr. Poddar, Kolkata	250

The letters to the customers mentioned that if the books were not approved by them, they should be returned within one month, failing which they would be treated as sold. By the end of that month, the customers from Chennai had retained the books while those from Kolkata had returned them in time. Mr. Govind of Mumbai had accepted one of the consignments of Rs. 700 but returned the others; and the time of approval had not yet expired for Mr. Ramesh. Show the entries in the 'Sale or Return' Day Books and the accounts of the Mumbai parties in the Personal Ledger.

8. Condensed Book Publishers sent consignments of their publications to the following customers on sale or return basis in the 1st week of April 2012 :

		Rs.			Rs.
(a)	Mr. Mohan, Chennai	500	(d)	Mr. Ramesh, Mumbai	3000
(b)	Mr. Narain, Chennai	200	(e)	Mr.Ghosh, Kolkata	450
(c)	Mr. Govind, Chennai	1,000	(f)	Mr. Poddar, Kolkata	250

The letters to the customers mentioned that if the books were not approved by them, they should be returned within one month, failing which they would be treated as sold.

By the end of that month, the customers from Mumbai had retained the books, while those from Kolkata had returned them in time. Mr Govind of Mumbai had accepted one of the consignments of Rs. 700, returned the others, and the time of approval had not yet expired for Mr. Ramesh.

Show the entries in the Sale or Return Day Books and the accounts of the Mumbai parties in the Personal Ledger.

CHAPTER 20

JOINT VENTURES

Learning Objectives

Meaning

Characteristics of Joint Venture

Differences between—

—Joint Venture and Consignment

—Joint Venture and Partnership

Methods of Accounting

A. Where separate set of Books is maintained

1. Buying and Selling Goods

2. Construction of Civil Works

3. Underwriting Shares.

B. Where no separate set of Books is maintained

Normal Loss and Abnormal Loss and their treatment

C. Where Memorandum Joint Venture Account is Opened

Normal and Abnormal Losses

Underwriting Shares

Valuation of Unsold Stock and Interim Settlement of Accounts

Treatment of Unsold Stock

Joint Ventures with more than two ventures

Joint Venture with Interest calculation on Investment

Consignment-cum-Joint Venture

(i) Conversion from a particular date; and

(ii) Conversion with retrospective effect

Meaning

When two or more persons undertake to get involved in a particular venture other than their normal business activities, for a temporary period to which they contribute capital and share profits or losses on some agreed ratio, it is called a joint venture. It ceases with the completion of the task undertaken. It is regarded as temporary partnership without a firm name.

Characteristics of Joint Venture

From the definition stated above, the following characteristics of a joint venture can be stated :

(i) It is a temporary partnership;

(ii) It ceases to exist as soon as the particular venture is completed;

(iii) No firm name is necessary;

(iv) It is for a particular venture;

(v) Primary purpose of a joint venture is to earn profit and share the same among the co-ventures at an agreed ratio—or equally if there is no agreement;

(vi) In joint venture, combination of capital and skill is possible. For example, one partner may provide capital, other partner provides the mechanical appliances or technical skills, a third one may be an expert in selling goods. As a result, the profit can be maximised;

(vii) No treatment is necessary for normal and abnormal loss of goods in a Joint Venture.

Differences between Joint Venture and Consignment

The following differences may be noted :

(a) Joint venture may be regarded as a temporary partnership whereas consignment is not similar to joint venture since the relationship between consignor and consignee is that of the principal and agent.

(b) In joint venture, the venturers contribute capital and share profits or losses according to the agreed ratio, whereas, in a consignment, the consignee does not contribute any capital and also does not take a profit or incur a loss. He is only entitled to a commission.

(c) In joint venture, each co-venturer can take part in management of the venture, whereas, in consignment, neither the consignor nor the consignee can take part in the other's business.

(d) A joint venture is governed by the Partnership Act but a consignment is governed by the law relating to Agency and between the parties to the contract.

(e) A joint venture is short-lived and as soon as the venture is closed, the liability of the venturers is discharged. But a consignment is not so short-lived and, may continue over a long period of time between the consignor and the consignee.

Differences between Joint Venture and Partnership

Although a joint venture is similar to a partnership firm in many respects, it differs from it in the following manner :

(a) A partnership has a firm name while a joint venture does not possess such a common name.

(b) A partnership is a continuing business which is not restricted to any particular venture. On the contrary, a joint venture is purely temporary in nature and the same is restricted to a particular venture.

(c) The persons who enter into joint venture are called co-venturers or joint-venturers while, in case of a partnership, such persons are called partners.

(d) In case of partnership, the partners have joint and several liabilities while, in case of a joint venture, the liability depends on the mode of contract, i.e., certain liabilities may be joint and certain others may be individual.

(e) Separate set of books is maintained in case of a partnership firm whereas the same is not a must in case of a joint venture.

(f) In a partnership firm, Accrual Basis of accounting is followed whereas, in a joint venture, Cash Basis of accounting is usually followed.

(g) Profit or loss is ascertained at the end of the year, i.e., annually, in case of partnership, while, in case of joint venture, profit or loss is ascertained on completion of each venture.

Methods of Accounting

The undermentioned methods are to be followed where joint venture transaction takes place :

A. **WHERE SEPARATE SET OF BOOKS IS MAINTAINED;**
B. **WHERE NO SEPARATE SET OF BOOKS IS MAINTAINED; AND**
C. **WHERE MEMORANDUM JOINT VENTURE ACCOUNT IS PREPARED.**

A. Where separate set of books is maintained

This method is particularly followed where there are large transactions, i.e.,,the venture is a large one and is continued for a comparatively long period. Accounts are prepared under double entry principle. Needless to mention here that, usually, the following three accounts are prepared under this method:

(i) Joint Venture Account; (ii) Joint Bank Account; and (iii) Venturer's Capital Account.

(i) Joint Venture Account

This account represents the result of the business, i.e., the profit or loss. It is like a Trading/Profit and Loss Account of a trading concern. This account is debited by the cost of goods, expenses, goods supplied by the venturers, etc. and is credited by sale proceeds, unsold stock (taken by the venturers) etc. and, if credit side of this account is greater than the debit side, the difference represents profit on joint venture and vice versa in the opposite case. The profit or loss so made is transferred to Venturer's Capital Account.

(ii) Joint Bank Account

It is like an ordinary Cash Book or Bank Account. All incomes including the capitals contributed by the venturers appear on the debit side of this account whereas all expenses of the venture appear on the credit side of this account including the final payments made to the venturers. The bank account is automatically closed, leaving no balance on either side.

(iii) Venturer's Capital Account

This is the capital account of the venturers relating to venture. This account is credited by the capital contributed by the venturers, goods supplied by them from their own stock, expenses made personally by them, etc., whereas this account is debited for any withdrawals or any assets taken from the venture. The profit or loss so made on venture is transferred to this account in profit-sharing ratio and this account is closed by cash payment from joint bank, and vice versa in the opposite case.

Entries under this method

(i) ***When capital is contributed by the venturers:***

Joint Bank A/c	Dr.	with the amount of capital contribution
To Venturer's Capital A/c		

(ii) ***When goods are purchased or expenses are incurred out of joint bank A/c:***

Joint Venture A/c	Dr.	with the amount of goods purchased or expenses incurred
To Joint Bank A/c		

(iii) ***When goods are sold:***

Joint Bank A/c	Dr.	with the amount of sale proceeds
To Joint Venture A/c		

(iv) ***When expenses incurred or materials supplied personally by any venturers:***

Joint Venture A/c	Dr.	with the amount contributed personally by any venturer
To Venturer's Capital A/c		

(v) ***When unsold stock or any sale proceeds are taken by any venturer:***

Venturer's Capital A/c	Dr.	with the amount of stock/ proceeds taken
To Joint Venture A/c		

(vi) ***When goods are purchased on credit on account of venture:***

Joint Venture A/c	Dr.	with the amount of goods purchased on credit
To Creditors A/c		

(vii) ***When payment is made to creditors :***

Creditors A/c Dr.
To Joint Bank A/c } payment made to creditors

(viii) ***When goods are sold on credit :***

Debtors A/c Dr.
To Joint Venture A/c } with the amount of credit sales

(ix) ***When cash is received from Debtors :***

Joint Bank A/c Dr.
To Debtors A/c } with the amount of cash received from debtors

(x) ***When certain amount is proved bad :***

Joint Venture A/c Dr.
To Sundry Debtors A/c } with the amount of bad debt

(xi) ***For profit on venture (i.e., if credit side is greater than the debit side) :***

Joint Venture A/c Dr.
To Venturer's Capital A/c } with the amount of profit on venture

(xii) ***For loss on venture (i.e., if debit side is greater than the credit side) :***

Venturer's Capital A/c Dr.
To Joint Venture A/c } with the amount of loss on venture

(xiii) ***When the final settlement is made to the venturers :***

Venturer's Capital A/c Dr.
To Joint Bank A/c } for final settlement

(xiv) ***When cash to be brought in by the venture for final settlement :***

Joint Bank A/c Dr. "
To Venturer's Capital A/c

After passing the above entries, the Capital Account of the Venturers and Joint Bank Account will automatically be closed.

It is important to note that joint venture transaction may be any one of the following three types under Separate Set of Books :

1. **Buying and Selling Goods;** 2. **Undertaking to construct Civil Works, like Building, Bridges etc.;** 3. **Underwriting Shares.**

1. Buying and Selling Goods

Joint Venture with buying and selling goods

Illustration 1

A and B entered into a Joint Venture sharing profits and losses in the ratio of 3 : 2. They opened a Joint Bank Account where A and B contributed Rs. 50,000 and Rs. 40,000, respectively, as capital.

A purchased goods for Rs. 30,000 and incurred Rs. 5,000 for expenses out of Joint Bank and he also supplied materials from his own stock for Rs. 3,000. He sold the entire goods for Rs. 50,000 and the money was deposited into Joint Bank. A received Rs. 5,000 from B.

B purchased goods for Rs. 25,000 and incurred Rs. 3,000 for various expenses out of Joint Bank. He sold all the goods for Rs. 44,000 except goods valued Rs. 2,000, which he took for his own use. The proceeds were also deposited into Joint Bank. Show the entries and write-up Joint Venture Account, Joint Bank Account, and the Capital Accounts of A and B.

Solution

In the books of Joint Venture
Journal

Date	*Particulars*		*L.F.*	*Debit*	*Credit*
?				Rs.	Rs.
	Joint Bank A/c	Dr.		90,000	
	To A's Capital A/c				50,000
	" B's Capital A/c				40,000
	(Capital contributed by A and B and opened a bank account.)				
	Joint Venture A/c	Dr.		35,000	
	To Bank A/c				35,000
	(Goods purchased and expenses incurred out of Joint Bank A/c)				

Contd.

Particulars		Rs.	Rs.
Joint Venture A/c	Dr.	3,000	
To A's Capital A/c			3,000
(Material supplied by A from his own stock)			
Joint Bank A/c		50,000	
To Joint Venture A/c			50,000
(Goods sold by A and proceeds were deposited into bank)			
A's Capital A/c	Dr.	5,000	
To B's Capital A/c			5,000
(Amount received by A from B.)			
Joint Venture A/c	Dr.	28,000	
To Joint Bank A/c			28,000
(Goods purchased and expenses incurred out of Joint Bank A/c)			
Joint Bank A/c	Dr.	44,000	
To Joint Venture A/c			44,000
(Goods sold by B and proceeds were deposited into Bank A/c)			
B's Capital A/c	Dr.	2,000	
To Joint Venture A/c			2,000
(Unsold stock taken by B)			
Joint Venture A/c	Dr.	30,000	
To A's Capital A/c			18,000
" B's Capital A/c			12,000
(Profit on Venture transferred to B's Capital A/c)			
A's Capital A/c	Dr.	66,000	
B's Capital A/c	Dr.	55,000	
To Joint Bank A/c			1,21,000
(Final settlement made)			

Dr. Joint Venture Account Cr.

Date	Particulars	Amount	Amount	Date	Particulars	Amount
?		Rs.	Rs.	?		Rs.
	To Joint Bank A/c :				By Joint Bank A/c :	
	Purchase of Goods	30,000			Sale Proceeds	50,000
	Expenses	5,000			" Joint Bank A/c :	
			35,000		Sale Proceeds	44,000
	To A's Capital A/c :				By B's Capital A/c :	
	Materials Supplied		3,000		Goods taken	2,000
	" Joint Bank A/c :					
	Purchase of Goods	25,000				
	Expenses	3,000				
			28,000			
	" Profit on Venture :					
	A's Capital A/c	18,000				
	B's Capital A/c	12,000				
			30,000			
			96,000			96,000

Dr. Joint Bank Account Cr.

Date	Particulars	Amount	Date	Particulars	Amount
?		Rs.	?		Rs.
	To A's Capital A/c	50,000		By Joint Venture A/c	35,000
	" B's Capital A/c	40,000		" Joint Venture A/c	28,000
	" Joint Venture A/c	50,000		" A's Capital A/c	66,000
	" Joint Venture A/c	44,000		" B's Capital A/c	55,000
				(final payments)	
		1,84,000			1,84,000

(Venture) Capital Account

Dr. *Cr.*

Date	Particulars	Amount A	Amount B	Date	Particulars	Amount A	Amount B
?		Rs.	Rs.	?		Rs.	Rs.
	To B's Capital A/c —Remittance	5,000	—		By Joint Bank A/c	50,000	40,000
	" Joint Venture A/c (goods taken)	—	2,000		" Joint Venture A/c	3,000	—
	" Joint Bank A/c (final payments) (*bal. fig.*)	66,000	55,000		" Joint Venture A/c (Share of Profit)	18,000	12,000
					" A's Capital A/c —Remittance	—	5,000
		71,000	57,000			71,000	57,000

Preparation of Balance Sheet

Illustration 2

Das and Krishnan entered into a joint venture sharing profits and losses as 3 : 2. They opened a Bank Account by depositing Rs. 40,000 each.

Das purchased 800 kgs of an item @ Rs. 60 and his expenses were Rs. 13,000. Krishnan purchased a second item of 10,000 kgs @ 2.10 and his expenses were Rs. 11,000. Expenses were met from private sources and purchases were paid for from Joint Bank Account.

Krishnan sold 600 kgs of the first item @ Rs. 100 and his selling expenses were Rs. 5,500. Das sold 8,000 kgs of the second item @ 5.00 and his selling expenses were Rs. 6,000. All the sale proceed were deposited in the Joint Bank Account and expenses were met from private sources.

Write-up necessary accounts in the books of the venture. Also prepare a Balance Sheet of the venture.

Solution

In the books of Joint Venture

Joint Venture Account

Dr. *Cr.*

Date	Particulars		Amount Rs.	Date	Particulars	Amount Rs.
?	To Joint Bank A/c : Purchases : 800 kgs @ Rs. 60		48,000	?	By Joint Bank A/c : Sale Proceed 600 kgs @ Rs. 100	60,000
	" Das's Capital A/c : Expenses on :				8,000 kgs. @ Rs. 5	40,000
	Purchases	13,000			" Unsold Stock :	
	Sales	6,000	19,000		(Rs. 48,000 + Rs. 13,000) × $\frac{200}{800}$ = 15,250	
					(Rs. 21,000 + Rs. 11,000) × $\frac{2,000}{10,000}$ = 6,400	21,650
	To Joint Bank A/c Purchases : 10,000 kgs @ Rs. 2.10		21,000			
	" Krishnan's Capital A/c : Expenses on :					
	Purchases	11,000				
	Sales	5,500	16,500			
	" Profit on Venture :					
	Das's Capital ($\frac{3}{5}$)	10,290				
	Krishnan's Capital ($\frac{2}{5}$)	6,860	17,150			
			1,21,650			1,21,650

Dr. **Joint Bank Account** Cr.

Date		Particulars	Amount	Date		Particulars	Amount
			Rs.				Rs.
?	To	Das's Capital A/c	40,000	?	By	Joint Venture A/c :	
		Krishnan's Capital A/c	40,000			Purchases	69,000
	"	Joint Venture A/c :				(Rs. 48,000 + Rs. 21,000)	
		Sale Proceeds	1,00,000		"	Balance c/d	1,11,000
		(Rs. 60,000 + Rs. 40,000)					
			1,80,000				1,80,000

Dr. **Capital Account** Cr.

Date		Particulars	Amount Das	Amount Krishnan	Date		Particulars	Amount Das	Amount Krishnan
			Rs.	Rs.				Rs.	Rs.
	To	Balance c/d	69,290	63,360		By	Joint Bank A/c	40,000	40,000
						"	Joint Venture A/c	19,000	16,500
						"	Joint Venture A/c	10,290	6,860
			69,290	63,360				69,290	63,360

Balance Sheet

Liabilities		Rs.	Assets	Rs.
Capital Accounts :			Cash at Bank	1,11,000
Das	69,290		Closing Stock	21,650
Krishnan	63,360			
		1,32,650		
		1,32,650		1,32,650

Insurance claim for abnormal loss, unsold stock taken by venturers etc.

Illustration 3

A and B entered into Joint Venture on 1.10.2008 for sale of specified goods paying Rs. 60,000 and Rs. 40,000, respectively, in a Joint Bank Account, sharing Profits and Losses in the ratio of 3 : 5. It was agreed that Jt. Bank Account is to be used for purchase and sale and each venture is to meet his Jt. Venture expenses out of private funds. Each venturer is to charge a commission @ 5% on sales made by him.

The transactions for the period ended 31.3.2009 were :

A purchased goods costing Rs. 40,000 and expenses in connection thereof amounted to Rs. 6,000. He sold 90% of these goods at 30% over the cost price and selling expenses amounted to Rs. 2,500.

B purchased goods costing Rs. 50,000 and expenses in connection thereof amounted to Rs. 6,500. He sold 80% of these goods at 25% over the cost price and selling expenses amounted to Rs. 3,000. $\frac{1}{5}$th of the remaining goods purchased by A was destroyed by fire on 28th February 2009 and Insurance Company admitted a claim for Rs. 2,000.

Write-up the Jt. Venture A/c, Jt. Bank A/c, Venturers' A/c.

[CU BCom (Hons.)]

Solution

In the books of A and B

Dr. **Joint Venture Account** Cr.

Date		Particulars	Amount	Date		Particulars	Amount
2009			Rs.	2009			Rs.
Mar. 31	To	Joint Bank A/c :		Mar. 31	By	Joint Bank A/c (Sales)	
		Cost of Goods (by A)	40,000		"	A	46,800[1]
		Cost of Goods (by B)	50,000			B	50,000[1]
	"	A A/c (Expenses) [6,000 + 2,500]	8,500		"	Joint Bank A/c	
	"	B A/c (Expenses) [6,500 + 3,000]	9,500			(Insurance claim)	2,000[2]
	"	A A/c (Commission)			"	A's Capital	
		[5% of 46,800]	2,340			(Stock taken over) A/c	5,617[3]

Contd.

2009		Rs.	2009		Rs.
	To B A/c (Commission) [5% of 50,000]	2,500		By B's Capital (Stock taken over) A/c	9,363
	Profit on Venture :				
	A's Capital 352				
	B's Capital 588	940			
		1,13,780			1,13,780

Dr. **Capital Account** Cr.

Date		Particulars	Amount A	Amount B	Date		Particulars	Amount A	Amount B
2009			Rs.	Rs.	2009			Rs.	Rs.
Mar. 31	To	Joint Venture A/c (Stock taken over)	5,617	9,363	Mar. 31	By	Joint Bank A/c	60,000	40,000
	"	Joint Bank A/c (Final settlement)	65,575	43,225		"	Joint Venture A/c (Expenses)	8,500	9,500
						"	Joint Venture A/c (Commission)	2,340	2,500
						"	Joint Venture A/c (Profit)	352	588
			71,192	52,588				71,192	52,588

Dr. **Joint Bank Account** Cr.

Date			Amount	Date			Amount
2009			Rs.	2009			Rs.
Mar. 31	To	A's Capital A/c	60,000	Mar. 31	By	Joint Venture A/c [40,000 + 50,000]	90,000
	"	B's Capital A/c	40,000		"	A's Capital A/c	65,575
	"	Joint Venture A/c [46,800 + 50,000]	96,800		"	B's Capital A/c	43,225
	"	Joint Venture A/c	2,000				
			1,98,800				1,98,800

Workings :

1. Calculation of Sales

Sales made by A :

	Rs.	Rs.
Cost of Goods Rs. 40,000 × 90% =	36,000	
Add : Profit @ 30%	10,800	
		46,800

Sales made by B :

	Rs.	Rs.
Cost of Goods Rs. 50,000 × 80% =	40,000	
Add : Profit @ 25%	10,000	
		50,000

2. Insurance Claim

Amount of insurance claim is recorded through Joint Bank Account. Thus, the entry is :

Joint Bank A/c Dr.
 To Joint Venture A/c

3. Unsold Stock taken over by A and B

Stock taken by A :	Rs.
Purchase of Goods	40,000
Add : Non-recurring Expenses	6,000
	46,000

Stock taken by B :	Rs.
Purchase of Goods	50,000
Add : Non-recurring Expenses	6,500
	56,500

∴ **10% of Rs. 46,000 = Rs. 4,600 out of which $\frac{1}{5}$th was lost.**

Thus, value of stock taken = Rs. 4,600 × $\frac{4}{5}$ = Rs. 3,680.

Stock = Rs. 56,500 × 20 %
= Rs. 11,300

∴ **Total stock both of A and B = Rs. 3,680 + Rs. 11,300**
= Rs. 14,980

∴ Value of stock taken by A = Rs. 14,980 × $\frac{3}{8}$ = Rs. 5,617

Value of stock taken by B = Rs. 14,980 × $\frac{5}{8}$ = Rs. 9,363

2. Construction of Civil Work

Construction contract, Caution money, Consideration paid by cash and shares, special Commission

Illustration 4

Dey, Das and Dutta entered into a joint venture to construct a building of a company for a consideration of Rs. 5,00,000. They shared profits or losses in the ratio 2 : 2 : 1. But, Dutta, being a civil engineer, was entitled to special commission @ 10% of the profits of venture after charging such commission. It was also agreed that each venturer was entitled to incur miscellaneous expenses to the maximum limit of Rs. 10,000 or the actual amount of such expenses, whichever is less. Miscellaneous expenses incurred by the venturers were Dey Rs. 6,000, Das Rs. 9,000 and Dutta Rs. 12,000.

They opened a joint bank account. The contributions of the ventures were : Dey Rs. 2,00,000; Das Rs. 1,50,000 and Dutta Rs. 1,00,000.

The actual expenses were: Materials Rs. 1,80,000; Wages Rs. 1,00,000; Plant and Machinery were supplied by Das from his own stock Rs. 50,000.

The building was completed and the company paid the agreed consideration subject to Rs. 50,000 as retention money, by cash Rs. 3,00,000 and the balance by the equity shares of the company of Rs. 100 each at an agreed value of Rs. 150. The ventures sold the shares in the market at Rs. 200 each.

The Plant and Machinery were taken over by Das at a valuation of Rs. 20,000, unsold materials were taken over by Dey for Rs. 15,000 and Dutta took up the retention money at Rs. 40,000.

Show the necessary ledger accounts in the books of the ventures.

Solution

In the books of Joint Venture

Dr. **Joint Venture Account** Cr.

Date	Particulars		Amount	Date	Particulars	Amount
?			Rs.	?		Rs.
	To Joint Bank A/c				By Joint Bank A/c —Contract Price	3,00,000
	Materials	1,80,000			" Bank A/c—Sale of Shares	2,00,000
	Wages	1,00,000	2,80,000		" Das's Capital A/c	
	" Das's Capital A/c —Plant & Machinery		50,000		—Plant & Machinery taken	20,000
	" Dey's Capital —Exp.		6,000		" Deys' Capital A/c —Materials taken	15,000
	" Das's Capital —Exp.		9,000		" Dutta's Capital A/c	
	" Dutta's Capital —Exp.		10,000		—Retention money taken	40,000
	" Dutta's Capital—Loss		20,000			
	" Profit on Venture:					
	Dey	80,000				
	Das	80,000				
	Dutta	40,000	2,00,000			
			5,75,000			5,75,000

Dr. **Joint Bank Account** Cr.

Date	Particulars	Amount	Date	Particulars	Amount
?		Rs.	?		Rs.
	To Dey's Capital A/c	2,00,000		By Joint Venture A/c	2,80,000
	" Das's Capital A/c	1,50,000		" Dey's Capital A/c	2,66,000
	" Dutta's Capital A/c	1,00,000		" Das's Capital A/c	2,74,000
	" Joint Venture A/c	3,00,000		" Dutta's Capital A/c	1,30,000
	" Joint Venture	2,00,000			
		9,50,000			9,50,000

Dr. **Capital Account** Cr.

Date	Particulars	Dey	Das	Dutta	Date	Particulars	Dey	Das	Dutta
?		Rs.	Rs.	Rs.	?		Rs.	Rs.	Rs.
	To Joint Venture A/c	20,000	15,000	40,000		By Joint Bank A/c	2,00,000	1,50,000	1,00,000
	" Joint Bank A/c					" Joint Venture	—	50,000	—

Contd.

?		Rs.	Rs.	Rs.	?		Rs.	Rs.	Rs.
	To —Final settlement	2,66,000	2,74,000	1,30,000		By Joint Venture	—	—	20,000
	—					" Joint Venture	6,000	9,000	10,000
						" Joint Venture —Profit	80,000	80,000	40,000
		2,86,000	2,89,000	1,70,000			2,86,000	2,89,000	1,70,000

Workings* 1. *Calculation of sale proceeds of equity shares :

	Rs.
Contract price	5,00,000
Less : Retention money	50,000
Less : Cash payment	4,50,000
Paid by shares	3,00,000
	1,50,000

∴ No. of shares = $\frac{\text{Rs. } 1,50,000}{150}$ = 1,000

Sales proceed = 1,000 × Rs. 200 = Rs. 2,,00,000

2. **Dutta's Commissions :**

Profit before charging Commission Rs. 2,20,000 (i.e., Rs. 5,75,000 – Rs. 3,55,000)

Dutta's Commission = $\frac{10}{110}$ × Rs. 2,20,000 = Rs. 20,,000

Preparation of Shares Account, Creditors Accounts

Illustration 5

X and Y are doing business separately as engineering contractors, They undertake jointly to build and instal new machinery for a company for a contract price of Rs. 1,34,000– Rs. 84,000 payable in instalments in cash and the balance as fully paid shares in the new company. A bank account is opened in joint name, X paying Rs. 45,000 and Y Rs. 20,000. They agree to share profits and losses in the proportion of 3/5 and 2/5, respectively. The transactions were :

	Rs.
Amount advanced to suppliers for supply of materials	52,000
Value of materials supplied by suppliers	89,000
Balance amount paid to suppliers in full and final settlement	35,500
Paid Wages	36,000
Materials purchased in Cash	2,500
Materials supplied by X from stock	9,250
Engineering consultant's fees paid	3,250
Value of stock lost by fire and not covered by Insurance	3,500

The contract was completed and price was duly received. X took all the shares at an agreed value of Rs. 47,000 and Y took the balance stock of materials worth Rs. 3,500 at an agreed value of Rs. 2,750.

Show the necessary ledger accounts assuming that separate set of books is maintained.

Solution **[ICWA Adapted]**

In the books of Joint Venture

Joint Venture Account

Dr. *Cr.*

Date	*Particulars*		*Amount*	*Date*	*Particulars*		*Amount*
?			Rs.	?			Rs.
	To Creditors A/c (Materials Supplied)		89,000		By Creditors A/c (Discount Received)		1,500
	" Joint Bank A/c :				(Rs. 89,000 – Rs. 52,000 – Rs. 35,500)		
	Wages	36,000			" Joint Bank A/c (Part Contract Price Received)		84,000
	Materials	2,500			" Shares A/c (Balance)		50,000
	Consultant's Fees	3,250	41,750		" Y's Capital A/c (Materials taken)		2,750
	" X's Capital A/c (Materials Supplied)		9,250		" Loss on Venture :		
					X's Capital A/c (3/5)	2,850	
	" Shares A/c (Loss in value)		3,000		Y's Capital A/c (2/5)	1,900	4,750
			1,43,000				1,43,000

Creditors Account

Dr. *Cr.*

Date	*Particulars*	*Amount*	*Date*	*Particulars*	*Amount*
?		Rs.	?		Rs.
	To Joint Bank A/c (Payment)	52,000		By Joint Venture A/c (Materials Supplied)	89,000
	" Joint Bank A/c (Payment)	35,500			
	" Joint Venture A/c (Discount)	1,500			
		89,000			89,000

Dr. **Joint Bank Account** Cr.

Date	Particulars	Amount	Date	Particulars		Amount
?		Rs.	?			Rs.
	To X's Capital A/c	45,000		By Creditors' A/c		52,000
	Y's Capital A/c	20,000		" Creditors' A/c		35,500
	" Joint Bank A/c (Part Contract Price)	84,000		" Joint Venture A/c :		
				Wages	36,000	
				Materials	2,500	
				Consultants' Fees	3,250	
						41,750
				" X's Capital A/c		4,400
				" Y's Capital A/c		15,350
		1,49,000				1,49,000

Dr. **Capital Account** Cr.

Date	Particulars	Amount X	Amount Y	Date	Particulars	Amount X	Amount Y
?		Rs.	Rs.	?		Rs.	Rs.
	To Joint Venture A/c (Materials taken)	—	2,750		By Joint Bank A/c	45,000	20,000
	" Shares A/c (Shares taken)	47,000	—		" Joint Venture A/c (Materials supplied)	9,250	—
	" Joint Venture A/c (Loss on Venture)	2,850	1,900				
	" Joint Bank A/c (Final payment) *(bal. fig.)*	4,400	15,350				
		54,250	20,000			54,250	20,000

Dr. **Shares Account** Cr.

Date	Particulars	Amount	Date	Particulars	Amount
?		Rs.	?		Rs.
	To Joint Venture A/c (Part Contract Price)	50,000		By X's Capital A/c (Share taken)	47,000
				" Joint Venture A/c (Loss in value)	3,000
		50,000			50,000

Note : There will be no effect for stock lost by fire.

Commission payable to venturer, unsold flat taken by venturer at a profit

Illustration 6

Ujjal and Sajjal started a joint venture to construct five flats in a building sharing profits and losses in the ratio of 3 : 2. The contract price of each flat was Rs. 90,000. Ujjal contributed Rs. 2,00,000 and Sajjal Rs. 1,40,000 and a bank account was opened in their names. Cost of raw material, wages, and other expenses amounted to Rs. 2,90,000, Rs. 35,000, and Rs. 5,000, respectively, and the architect's fee of 2% of the contract price were met from the Joint Bank Account. Ujjal supplied further raw materials costing Rs. 15,000 and Sajjal supplied a machine costing Rs. 5,000, Ujjal paid Rs. 3,000 for transport charges. Sajjal is entitled to a commission of 1% on the cost of raw materials used. Four of the flats were disposed-off at the contract price but the fifth one was not according to specification and, hence, could not be disposed-off. This flat was taken over by Ujjal at the cost of construction plus 5 p.c. profit. The unused raw materials and the machine were taken by Sajjal at Rs. 5,000 and Rs. 1,000, respectively.

Prepare Joint Venture Account, Joint Bank Accounts, Ujjal Account and Sajjal Account to close the venture.

Solution **[BU BCom (Hons.)]**

In the books of Ujjal and Sajjal

Dr. **Joint Venture Account** Cr.

Date	Particulars	Amount	Amount	Date	Particulars	Amount
?		Rs.	Rs.	?		Rs.
	To Joint Bank A/c				By Joint Bank A/c (Sale 4 flats @ Rs. 90,000)	3,60,000
	Materials	2,90,000			" Ujjal's Capital A/c :	74,760[2]
	Wages	35,000				

Contd.

Date	Particulars	Rs.	Rs.	Date	Particulars	Rs.
?		Rs.	Rs.	?		Rs.
	To Other Expenses	5,000			By —Flat taken	
	Architect's Fees	9,000			Sajjal's Capital A/c	
			3,39,000		— Stock taken	5,000
	" Ujjal's Capital A/c				—Machine taken	1,000
	Raw Materials	15,000				
	Transportation Charges	3,000[1]	18,000			
	" Sajjal's Capital A/c					
	Machine	5,000				
	Commission	3,000	8,000			
	" Profit on Venture :					
	Ujjal's Capital A/c ($\frac{3}{5}$)	45,456				
	Sajjal's Capital A/c ($\frac{2}{5}$)	30,304				
			75,760			
			4,40,760			4,40,760

Dr. **Joint Bank Account** Cr.

Date	Particulars	Amount	Date	Particulars	Amount
?		Rs.	?		Rs.
	To Ujjal's Capital A/c	2,00,000		By Joint Venture A/c	
	" Sajjal's Capital A/c	1,40,000		—Expenses	3,39,000
	" Joint Venture A/c	3,60,000		" Ujjal's Capital A/c	1,88,696
				" Sajjal's Capital A/c	1,72,304
		7,00,000			7,00,000

Dr. **Capital Account** Cr.

Date	Particulars	Amount Ujjal	Amount Sajjal	Date	Particulars	Amount Ujjal	Amount Sajjal
		Rs.	Rs.			Rs.	Rs.
	To Joint Venture A/c	74,760	6,000		By Joint Bank A/c	2,00,000	1,40,000
	" Joint Bank A/c				" Joint Venture A/c	15,000	5,000
	—Fixed payment	1,88,696	1,72,304		" Joint Venture A/c	3,000	3,000
					" Joint Venture A/c—Profit	45,456	30,304
		2,63,456	1,78,304			2,63,456	1,78,304

Workings

1. Calculation of Commission payable to Sajjal :

	Rs.
Materials purchased	2,90,000
Add : Supplied by Ujjal	15,000
	3,05,000
Less : Taken by Sajjal	5,000
Materials used	3,00,000
∴ Com. @ 1% on Rs. 3,00,000 = Rs.	3,000

2. Valuation of the Unsold Flat taken by Ujjal :

	Rs.
Materials Used	3,00,000
Wages	35,000
Other Expenses	5,000
Architect's Fees	9,000
Depreciation of Machines (5,000 – 1,000)	4,000
Transportation Charges	3,000
Total Cost of 5 flats	3,56,000
Cost of one flat Rs. $\frac{3,56,000}{5}$ = Rs.	71,200
Add : Profit @ 5%	3,560
	74,760

Underwriting of Shares

Illustration 7

Harun and Rasid entered into a Joint Venture to act as underwriters of a newly formed company which issued 50,000 shares of Rs. 10 each. The extent of underwriting was 80%. They opened a joint banking account by contributing Rs. 65,000 each. Public subscribed for 35,000 shares and the underwriters duly discharged their obligations in consideration of a commission of 5% which they received by cheque. Miscellaneous expenses amounting to Rs. 4,800 were met out of the joint banking account. Harun took 2,000 shares at Rs. 9 per share and Rasid took 2,500 shares at Rs. 9.50 per share. The rest of the shares were sold at Rs. 13 per share, brokerage being 0.50 per share. Profits on joint venture are to be shared equally. Prepare the following accounts in the books of the ventures:

(a) Joint Venture Account; (b) Joint Bank Account, and (c) Venturer's Accounts.

Solution **[CU BCom (Hons.)]**

In the books of Joint Venture of Harun and Rasid

Joint Venture Account

Dr. Cr.

Date		Particulars		Amount Rs.	Date		Particulars	Amount Rs.
?	To	Joint Bank A/c Cost of Shares		1,20,000[1]	?	By	Joint Bank A/c Commission received	20,000[2]
	"	Joint Bank A/c — Miscellaneous Expenses		4,800		"	Venturers A/c : — (Shares taken Over)	
	"	Profit on Venture					Harun (2,000 × Rs. 9)	18,000
		Harun	15,350				Rasid (2,500 × Rs. 9.50)	23,750
		Rasid	15,350	30,700			Joint Bank A/c (Sale of Shares—	93,750[3]
				1,55,500				1,55,500

Joint Bank Account

Dr. Cr.

Date		Particulars	Amount Rs.	Date		Particulars	Amount Rs.
?	To	Venturers A/c		?	By	Joint Venture A/c	1,20,000
		Harun	65,000		"	Joint Venture A/c	4,800
	"	Rasid	65,000		"	Venturers A/c	
	"	Joint renture A/c	20,000			(Final settlement)	
	"	Joint Venture A/c	93,750		"	Harun	62,350
					"	Rasid	56,600
			2,43,750				2,43,750

Venture Account

Dr. Cr.

Date		Particulars	Amount Harun Rs.	Amount Rasid Rs.	Date		Particulars	Amount Harun Rs.	Amount Rasid Rs.
	To	Joint Ventures A/c	18,000	23,,750		By	Joint Bank A/c	65,000	65,000
	"	Joint Bank A/c — Final settlement	62,350	56,600		"	Joint Venture A/c (Profit)	15,350	15,350
			80,350	80,350				80,350	80,350

Workings

1. **Purchase of Shares** No. of Shares

		No. of Shares
	Issue of Shares	50,000
Less :	Public Subscribed	35,000
	Shortfall	15,000

Since extent of underwriting is 80%

Purchase of Shares 80% of 15,000 = 12,000 shares

∴ Cost of Shares = 12,000 share × Rs. 10 = Rs. 1,20,000

2. **Commission received**

Commission will be computed on 80% of total guaranteed issue of shares i.e., on 50,000 shares × 80% = 40,000 shares

∴ Value of shares @ Rs. 10 = Rs. 4,00,000

Commission @ 5% on Rs. 4,00,000 = Rs. 20,000

3. **Sale Proceeds of Shares**

	Purchase of shares		12,000
Less :	Shares taken by		
	Harun	2,000 Shares	
	Rasid	2,500 Shares	
			4,500
	No. of Shares Sold		7,500

Sale Proceeds will be @ Rs. 12.50 (i.e., Rs. 13 – Re. 0.50) Rs. × 7,500 shares = Rs. 93,750

Miscellaneous

A Harder Problem

Illustration 8

Wadekar and Pataudi enter into a joint venture to develop some building sites and sell them on the understanding that the result of the venture would be shared in the ratio of 4 : 5 between them. It is also agreed that any cash investments they make in the venture would be entitled to interest at 10% per annum.

They chose a five bigha agricultural plot and purchased it for Rs. 60,000. They approached a nationalised bank which agreed to finance them to the extent of 80% of the cost at 16% interest p.a. The buying agreements were finalised on 1st July 2012, and the vendors were paid-off on the same day. Balance of purchase consideration and also the registration expenses, which came at 8%, were met by Wadekar out of his own resources.

Pataudi met the cost of preparation of the layout, advertisement etc. which was as under :

(a)	Levelling and engineering expenses paid to architect and town planner on 1.8.2012 at	Rs. 400	per cotta
(b)	Municipal fees paid on 1.9.2012 at	Rs. 250	per cotta
(c)	Advertisement expenses met on 1.10.2012	Rs. 15,000	
(d)	Entertainment expenses paid on 31.12.2012	Rs. 10,000	

Plots were advertised for sale in newspapers on 15.9.2012 and, on the basis of response, the entire area was dealt with as :

(i) 10% of the total area was left for roads and lanes.

(ii) 12 plots each of 3 cottas, $2\frac{1}{2}$ cottas, and $1\frac{1}{2}$ cottas were made.

(iii) The balance area was taken equally by Wadekar and Pataudi at cost.

(iv) $1\frac{1}{2}$ cotta plots carried a premium of 50%, $2\frac{1}{2}$ cotta plot a premium of 40% and 3 cotta plot at a premium of 25% over cost.

(v) Pataudi to receive 8% of the sale proceeds as management fees for his efforts.

The entire transactions were put through by 31st December 2012.

Show the Joint Venture Account and the Capital Accounts of co-venturers.

[1 bigha is equal to 20 cottas]

[CA Adapted]

Solution

In the books of Wadekar and Pataudi
Joint Venture Account[1]

Dr. *Cr.*

Date		*Particulars*	*Amount*	*Amount*	*Date*		*Particulars*	*Amount*	*Amount*
2012			Rs.	Rs.	2012			Rs.	Rs.
July 1.	To	Bank A/c—Cost of Land		48,000	Sept. 15	By	Bank A/c —Sale Proceeds[2]		
	"	Wadekar's Capital A/c :							
		Cost of Land	12,000				Rs. 6,450 × 12	77,400	
		Registration Expenses	4,800				Rs. 6,020 × 12	72,240	
				16,800			Rs. 3,870 × 12	46,440	
Aug. 1	"	Pataudi's Capital A/c :							1,96,080
					Sept. 15	"	Wadekar's Capital A/c [6]		
		Levelling & Engineering Exp.	40,000						
		Municipal Fees	25,000				—Cost of Land taken over		5,160

Contd.

2012		Rs.	Rs.	2012		Rs.	Rs.
Oct. 1.	To Advertisement Expenses	15,000			By Pataudi's Capital A/c [6] — Cost of Land taken over		5,160
Dec. 31.	Entertainment Expenses	10,000	90,000				
	To Pataudi's Capital A/c —Management Fees		15,686				
"	" Wadekar's Capital A/c —Interest @ 10% [3]		840				
	" Pataudis Capital A/c —Interest @ 10% [4]		2,875				
	" Bank Loan A/c —Interest @ 16% [5]		3,840				
	" Wadekar's Capital A/c —Share of Profit ($\frac{4}{9}$)	12,604					
"	" Pataudi's Capital A/c —Share of Profit ($\frac{5}{9}$)	15,755	28,359				
			2,06,400				2,06,400

Dr. **Wadekar's Capital Account** Cr.

Date	Particulars	Amount	Date	Particulars	Amount
2012		Rs.	2012		Rs.
Dec. 31	To Joint Venture A/c —Cost of Land taken over	5,160	July 1	By Bank A/c—Cost of Land	12,000
	" Bank A/c—Final payment	25,084		" Bank A/c—Registration Exp.	4,800
			Dec. 31	" Joint Venture A/c — Interest @ 10%	840
				" Joint Venture A/c —Share of Profit	12,604
		30,244			30,244

Dr. **Pataudi's Capital Account** Cr.

Date	Particulars	Amount	Date	Particulars	Amount
2012		Rs.	2012		Rs.
Dec. 31	To Joint Venture A/c —Cost of Land taken over	5,160	Aug. 1	By Bank A/c—Levelling & Engineering Expenses	40,000
	" Bank A/c—Final payment	1,19,156	Sept. 1	" Bank A/c—Municipal Fees	25,000
			Oct. 1	" Bank A/c—Advertisement	15,000
			Dec. 31	" Bank A/c—Entertainment Exp.	10,000
				" Joint Venture A/c —Management Fees	15,686
				" Joint Venture A/c —Interest @ 10%	2,875
				" Joint Venture A/c —Share of Profit	15,755
		1,24,316			1,24,316

The following accounts are presented before the students in order to understand the solution—although these accounts are not required :

Dr. **Bank Loan Account** *Cr.*

Date	Particulars	Amount	Date	Particulars	Amount
2012		Rs.	2012		Rs.
Dec. 31	To Bank A/c —Repayment	51,840	July 1	By Bank A/c	48,000
			Dec. 31	" Joint Venture A/c —Interest @ 16% for 6 months	3,840
		51,840			51,840

Dr. **Bank Account** *Cr.*

Date	Particulars	Amount	Date	Particulars	Amount
2012		Rs.	2012		Rs.
July 1	To Bank A/c—Loan A/c	48,000	Aug. 1	By Joint Venture A/c —Cost of Land	48,000
Dec. 31	" Joint Venture A/c —Sale proceeds	1,96,080	Dec. 31	" Bank Loan A/c —Repayment	51,840
				" Wadekar's Capital A/c —Repayment	25,084
				" Pataudi's Capital A/c —Repayment	1,19,156
		2,44,080			2,44,080

Notes :

1. Students are to note that although it is a Joint Venture Account it is like a Memorandum Joint Venture Account (although method of preparation is different) and not an ordinary Joint Venture Account.

2. Cost of total land amounted to Rs. 1,54,800 (i.e., Rs. 60,000 + Rs. 4,800 + Rs. 90,000). Since saleable land is only 90 cottas (100 – 10), cost of each cotta Rs. 1,720 (i.e., Rs. 1,54,800 ÷ 90). Thus, Cost of every 3 cottas = Rs. 5,160 (i.e., Rs. 1,720 × 3) + profit @ 25% i.e., Rs. 1,290 = Rs. 6,450 × 12 = Rs. 77,400.

Cost of every $2\frac{1}{2}$ cottas = Rs. 4,300 + 40% profit Rs. 1,720 = Rs. 6,020 × 12 = Rs. 72,240.

Cost of every $1\frac{1}{2}$ cottas = Rs. 2,580 + 50% profit Rs. 1,290 = Rs. 3,870 × 12 = Rs. 46,440.

3. On Rs. $16{,}800 \times \frac{10}{100} \times \frac{6}{12}$ = Rs. 840.

4. | | | Rs. |
|---|---|---|
| Interest on Rs. $40{,}000 \times \frac{10}{100} \times \frac{5}{12}$ | = | 1,667 |
| Interest on Rs. $25{,}000 \times \frac{10}{100} \times \frac{4}{12}$ | = | 833 |
| Interest on Rs. $15{,}000 \times \frac{10}{100} \times \frac{3}{12}$ | = | 375 |
| | Rs. | 2,875 |

5. On Rs. $48{,}000 \times \frac{16}{100} \times \frac{6}{12}$ = Rs. 3,840.

6. Unsold land 6 cottas, i.e., (100 – 10 = 90 less 84 cottas sold = 6 cottas unsold) each of the venturers took 3 cottas @ Rs. 1,720, i.e., Rs. 5,160.

B. Where no separate set of books is maintained

This method is applicable where the joint venture transactions are limited and the venturers reside at two different places. Under this method, each venturer will record his own transactions plus the transactions relating to co-venturers. In short, one venturer will prepare a Joint Venture Account and the other venturer's capital whereas the other venturer will prepare a Joint Venture Account and the capital of the other's, i.e., two accounts are prepared in each party ledger. For example, there are two venturers, A and B. So, A will prepare a Joint Venture Account and B's Capital Account in his book while B will also prepare a Joint Venture Account and A's Capital Account in his book.

(1) **Joint Venture Account :** It should be prepared like the previous one which reveals the result of the business i.e., profit/loss which, ultimately, will be transferred to venturers' capital. But in this case, one's own share of profit or loss should be transferred to his Profit or Loss Account but co-venturer's share of profit or loss should be transferred to his personal account.

(2) **Personal Account of the Co-venturers :** Since this is a personal account of the co-venturer, his account will be debited with the amount of goods purchased, expenses incurred, profit so earned, etc. and is credited with the amount of sale proceeds, unsold stock taken, etc. The balance of this account will go to either (1) the Balance Sheet, if it is so prepared, or (2) the same will represent the final payment of receipts and payments between the venturers.

Entries under this method :

Suppose there are two venturers, viz., A and B.

	In A's Journal		In B's Journal	
(i)	***If goods are supplied by A :***			
	Joint Venture A/c	Dr.	Joint Venture A/c	Dr.
	To Goods Sent to Joint Venture A/c		To A A/c	
(ii)	***If expenses are incurred by A :***			
	Joint Venture A/c	Dr.	*Joint Venture A/c*	*Dr.*
	To Bank A/c		*To A A/c*	
(iii)	***If commission is charged by A on Sales/ Purchase :***			
	Joint Venture A/c	Dr.	Joint Venture A/c	Dr.
	To Commission A/c		To A A/c	
(iv)	***If goods are sold by A :***			
	Bank A/c	Dr.	A A/c	Dr.
	To Joint Venture A/c		To Joint Venture A/c	
(v)	***If unsold goods are taken by A :***			
	Unsold Stock A/c	Dr.	A A/c	Dr.
	To Joint Venture A/c		To Joint Venture A/c	
(vi)	***If goods are supplied by B :***			
	Joint Venture A/c	Dr.	Joint Venture A/c	Dr.
	To B A/c		To Goods Sent to Joint Venture A/c	
(vii)	***If expenses are incurred by B :***			
	Joint Venture A/c	Dr.	Joint Venture A/c	Dr.
	To B A/c		To Bank A/c	
(viii)	***If commission is charged by B on sales :***			
	Joint Venture A/c	Dr.	Joint Venture A/c	Dr.
	To B A/c		To Commission A/c	
(ix)	***If goods are sold by B :***			
	B A/c	Dr.	Bank A/c	Dr.
	To Joint Venture A/c		To Joint Venture A/c	
(x)	***If unsold Stock is taken by B :***			
	B A/c	Dr.	Unsold Stock A/c	Dr.
	To Joint Venture A/c		To Joint Venture A/c	
(xi)	***For Profit on Venture :***			
	Joint Venture A/c	Dr.	Joint Venture A/c	Dr.
	To Profit and Loss A/c (A's share)		To A A/c (A's share)	
	" B A/c (B's share)		" Profit and Loss A/c (B's share)	
(xii)	***For Loss on Venture :***			
	Profit and Loss A/c	Dr.	*Profit and Loss A/c*	Dr.
	B's A/c	Dr.	A's A/c	Dr.
	To Joint Venture A/c		To Joint Venture A/c	

Prepartion of accounts in both the books of the Venturers

Illustration 9

A and B entered into a joint venture of undertaking the subscriptions at par of the entire share capital of the Copper Mines Ltd. consisting of 1,00,000 equity shares of Rs. 10 each and to pay all expenses upto allotment. The profits were to be shared by them in the ratio of 3 : 2. The consideration in return for this agreement was the allotment of 12,000 other shares of Rs. 10 each to be issued to them as fully paid. A provided the funds for registration fees Rs. 12,000, advertising expenses Rs. 11,000; expenses on printing and distribution of prospectus Rs. 7,500 and other printing and stationery expenses Rs. 2,000. B contributed towards payment of office rent Rs. 3,000, legal charges Rs. 13,450; salary to clerical staff Rs. 9,000 and other petty disbursements Rs. 1,750. The prospectus was issued and applications fell short of the issue by 15,000 shares. A took these over on joint account and paid for the same in full. The venturers received the 12,000 fully paid shares as underwriting commission. They sold the entire holding at Rs. 12.50 less. '50 paise brokerage per share. The net proceeds were received by A for 15,000 shares and B for 12,000 shares. Writes out the necessary accounts in the books of both the parties showing the adjustment.

[ICWA June 1996]

Solution

In the books of A

Joint Venture Account

Dr.							Cr.
Date		Particulars	Amount	Date		Particulars	Amount
?			Rs.	?			Rs.
	To	Bank A/c			By	Bank	
		Cost of Shares				(Sale of 15,000	
		(15,000 × Rs. 10) 1,50,000				shares @ Rs. 12)	1,80,000
		Registration 12,000			"	B's A/c	
		Advertisement 11,000				(Sale of 12,000	
		Printing etc. 7,500				shares @ Rs. 12)	1,44,000
		Printing & Stat. 2,000	1,82,500				
	"	B' A/c					
		Rent 3,000					
		Legal Exp. 13,750					
		Salary 9,000					
		Petty Disbursement 1,750	27,500				
	"	Profit on Venture					
		Profit &Loss A/c $\frac{3}{5}$ 68,400					
		B's A/c $\frac{2}{5}$ 45,600	1,14,000				
			3,24,000				3,24,000

B's Account

Dr.							Cr.
Date		Particulars	Amount	Date		Particulars	Amount
?			Rs.	?			Rs.
	To	Joint Venture A/c—			By	Joint Venture A/c	
		—Sale Proceeds	1,44,000			—Rent	3,000
						—Legal Expenses	13,750
						—Salaries	9,000
						—Petty Disbursement	1,750
					"	Share of Profit	45,600
					"	Bank A/c (Final Payment)	70,900
			1,44,000				1,44,000

In the books of B

Joint Venture Account

Dr.							Cr.
Date		Particulars	Amount	Date		Particulars	Amount
?			Rs.	?			Rs.
	To	A's A/c			By	A's A/c	
		—Cost of Shares 1,50,000				(Sale Proceeds)	1,80,000
		—Registration Exp. 12,000			"	Bank A/c	
		—Advertisement 11,000				(Sale Proceeds)	1,44,000
		—Printing etc. 7,500					
		—Printing & Stationery 2,000	1,82,500				
		Bank A/c					
		Rent 3,000					
		Legal Exp. 13,750					
		Salary 9,000					
		Petty Disbursement 1,750	27,500				

Contd.

Date	Particulars		Rs.	Date	Particulars	Rs.
?	To Profit on Venture			?	By	
	A's A/c $\frac{3}{5}$	68,400				
	Profit & Loss A/c $\frac{2}{5}$	45,600				
			1,14,000			
			3,24,000			3,24,000

A's Account

Dr. Cr.

Date	Particulars	Amount Rs.	Date	Particulars	Amount Rs.
?	To Joint Venture A/c (Sale Proceeds)	1,80,000	?	By Joint Venture A/c Cost of Shares	1,50,000
	" Bank A/c (Final Settlement)	70,900		" Registration Expenses	12,000
				" Advertisement	11,000
				" Printing & Stationery	7,500
				" Joint Venture A/c	2,000
				Share of Profit	68,400
		2,50,900			2,50,900

Unsold Stock taken by the Venturer at usual profit

Illustration 10

Das and Roy entered into a joint venture involving the buying and selling of old railway materials. The profit or loss was to be shared equally. The cost of the materials purchased was Rs. 42,500 which was paid by Das who drew a bill on Roy at a two months' demand of Rs. 30,000. The bill was discounted by Das at a cost of Rs. 240.

The transactions relating to the venture were (a) Das paid Rs. 300 for carriage, Rs. 500 for commission on sales and Rs. 200 for travelling expenses; (b) Roy paid Rs. 100 travelling expenses and Rs. 150 sundry expenses; (c) Sales made by Das amounted to Rs. 20,000; and (d) Sales made by Roy were Rs. 30,000.

Goods costing Rs. 1,000 and Rs. 1,500 (being unsold stock) were retained by Das and Roy, respectively, and these were charged to them at prices so as to show the same rate of gross profit as is made on the total sales (excluding these sales). Das was credited with a sum of Rs. 400 to cover the cost of warehousing and insurance. The expenses in connection with the bills were to be treated as a charge against the venture.

You are required to prepare Das's Capital Account and Joint Venture with Das Account in the books of Roy.

Solution **[CU BCom (Hons.) Adapted]**

In the books of Roy
Joint Venture with Das Account

Dr. Cr.

Date	Particulars	Rs.	Amount	Date	Particulars	Rs.	Amount Rs.
?	To Das's Capital A/c:			?	By Das's Capital A/c:		
	Purchase	42,500			Sale Proceeds		20,000
	Discounting Charge	240			" Das's Capital A/c:		
	Carriage	300			Goods taken over		1,250[1]
	Commission	500			" Bank A/c:		
	Travelling Expenses	200			Sale Proceeds		30,000
	Warehousing etc.	400					
			44,140		" Goods taken over		1,875[2]
	" Bank A/c:						
	Travelling Expenses	100					
	Sundry Expenses	150					
			250				
	" Profit on Venture:						
	Profit and Loss A/c	4,367					
	Das's Capital A/c	4,368					
			8,735				
			53,125				53,125

Dr. **Das's Capital Account** Cr.

Date	Particulars	Amount	Date	Particulars		Amount
?		Rs.	?		Rs.	Rs.
	To Joint Venture A/c : Sale Proceeds	20,000		By Joint Venture A/c : Purchase	42,500	
	" Joint Venture A/c : Goods taken over	1,250		Discounting Charges	240	
	To Bills Payable A/c	30,000		Carriage	300	
				By Commission	500	
				Travelling Expenses	200	
				Warehousing etc.	400	44,140
				" Joint Venture A/c : Share of Profit		4,368
				" Balance c/d		2,742
		51,250				51,250

Workings :

1 & 2 : **Unsold goods are taken over by Das and Roy at the following prices :**

Percentage of Profit

	Rs.	Rs.
Sales (Rs. 20,000 + Rs. 30,000)		50,000
Less : Cost of Goods	42,500	
Less : Unsold Stock (Rs. 1,000 + 1,500)	2,500	
		40,000
Gross Profit		10,000

Goods taken by	Das Rs.	Roy Rs.
Goods taken at cost	1,000	1,500
At a profit of 25%	250	375
	1,250	1,875

∴ Percentage of Gross Profit on Cost = $\frac{\text{Rs. } 10,000}{\text{Rs. } 40,000} \times 100 = 25\%$

Normal Loss, Abnormal Loss and their Treatment

Normal Loss : In the previous chapter, ***Consignment Accounts,*** we have explained in details the treatment of Normal Loss. There we found that there would be no separate treatment for normal loss. But while the value of ascertaining closing stock, ***it would simply be deducted from the total quantity of goods sent.*** Same principle also will be applied in case of Joint Venture. If there is no unsold stock, there will not be any treatment of normal loss but if there is any closing stock, the quantity of normal loss will be deducted from the total quantity of goods sent.

Abnormal Loss : We have also explained in the previous chapter, i.e., **in Consignment Account,** the treatment of Abnormal Loss. But in Joint Venture, there will not be any treatment of Abnormal Loss Account. But if any claim is received from the Insurance company, the same must be recorded in the books. In short, there will not any separate entry/ treatment for abnormal loss in Joint Venture.

Illustration 11

John and Ali entered into a Joint Venture agreeing to share profits and losses in the ratio of 3 : 2.

On 4.1.2011, Ali purchases goods costing Rs. 60,000 and spent Rs. 2,000 as expenses. On the same date he sent to John part of these goods costing Rs. 40,000.

On 7.2.2011, John sent Rs. 30,000 to Ali. On 10.2.2011, he purchased goods costing Rs. 50,000 and sent half of the goods to Ali. He paid Rs. 1,000 as carriage.

On 24.3.2011, Ali sold most of the goods in his possession for Rs. 55,000 and the remaining goods costing Rs. 3,000 were taken over by him at an agreed valuation of Rs. 4,000.

On 18.4.2011, John sold all the goods in his possession for Rs. 75,000 except some damaged goods costing Rs. 5,000 which was agreed to be written-off as unsaleable. His selling expenses amounted to Rs. 2,000. On 30.4.2011, the amount required to settle the accounts between John and Ali was paid by the appropriate party. Show the Joint Venture Account and John's Account in the books of Ali.

Solution

In the books of Ali

Joint Venture Account

Dr. Date		Particulars	Rs.	Amount Rs.	Date		Particulars	Cr. Amount Rs.
2011					2011			
Jan. 4	To	Bank A/c :			Mar. 24	By	Bank A/c :	
		Purchases	60,000				Sale Proceeds	55,000
		Expenses	2,000				Goods taken over	4,000
				62,000	April 18	"	John A/c:	
Feb. 10	"	John A/c :					Sale Proceeds	75,000
		Purchases	50,000					
		Expenses	1,000					
				51,000				
April 18	"	John A/c :						
		Selling Expenses		2,000				
April 30	"	Profit on Venture :						
		P & L A/c	7,600					
		John A/c	11,400					
				19,000				
				1,34,000				1,34,000

John Account

Dr. Date		Particulars	Amount Rs.	Date		Particulars	Cr. Amount Rs.
2011				2011			
April 18	To	Joint Venture A/c — Sale Proceeds	75,000	Feb. 7	By	Bank A/c — Advance	30,000
April 30	"	Bank A/c — Final payment	19,400	Feb. 10	"	Joint Venture A/c — Purchases & Expenses	51,000
				April 18	"	Joint Venture A/c — Selling Expenses	2,000
				April 30	"	Joint Venture A/c — Share of Profit	11,400
			94,400				94,400

N.B. :

1. There will be no entry for damaged goods.
2. There will also be no entry for some goods sent by Ali to John as the original purchase made by Ali recorded, same also when John sent goods to Ali.

Abnormal loss and Consequent insurance claim

Illustration 12

Arun and Balu entered into a Joint Venture to purchase, recondition and sell second hand cars. Arun purchased 100 cars during the period 1.1.99 to 30.6.99 at the following prices and paid for the same:

20 cars @ Rs. 15,000 each; 40 cars @ Rs. 25,000 each; 40 cars @ Rs. 55,000 each.

Balu during the same period reconditioned the cars by spending the following amounts:

Spare parts used Rs. 1,80,000; Painting Rs. 2,00,000; Air-conditioning 10 cars Rs. 3,00,000; Testing charges Rs. 20,000; Insurance Rs. 60,000; Labour charges Rs. 10,40,000.

Arun and Balu sold the cars, the details of which are:

	Sold by Arun	Balu
A. C. Cars	5	4
Non-A. C. Cars	35	46

A. C. cars were sold at Rs. 1,75,000 each. Non-A. C. cars were sold:

Arun	35 cars @ Rs. 1.25 lakhs each
Balu	35 cars @ Rs. 1,10 lakhs each
	11 cars @ Rs. 0.80 lakhs each

During testing one non-A. C. car met with an accident and the Insurance Company paid the actual cost as claim,

Prepare the Joint Venture Account and Account of Balu in the books of Arun.

[CA Foundation, Nov. 1999—Adapted]

Solution

In the books of Arun
Joint Venture Account

Dr. Cr.

Date	Particulars	Amount	Amount	Date	Particulars	Amount	Amount
?			Rs.	?			Rs.
	To Bank A/c (Cost of cars Purchased)		35,00,000[1]		By Bank A/c Sale Proceeds		52,50,000[2]
	" Balu (Reconditioning charges) :				" Balu A/c — Sale Proceeds		54,30,000[3]
	" Spare parts	1,80,000			" Insurance claim		50,000[4]
	" Painting	2,00,000			" Closing stock:		
	" Air-conditioning	3,00,000			" A. C. car	80,000	
	" Testing charges	20,000			" Non-A. C. car (8 × Rs. 50,000)	4,00,000	4,80,000
	" Insurance	60,000					
	" Labour charges	10,40,000	18,00,000				
	" Profit on Venture:						
	" P & L A/c $\frac{1}{2}$	29,55,000					
	" Balu $\frac{1}{2}$	29,55,000	59,10,000				
			1,12,10,000				1,12,10,000

Balu Account

Dr. Cr.

Date	Particulars	Amount	Date	Particulars	Amount
?		Rs.	?		Rs.
	To Joint Venture A/c —Sale Proceeds	54,30,000		By Joint Venture (Reconditioning Charges)	18,00,000
				Joint Venture A/c (Share of profit)	29,55,000
				Balance c/d	6,75,000
		54,30,000			54,30,000

Workings

		Rs.
1.	**Cost of Cars Purchased**	
	(20 car × Rs. 15,000) + (40 Cars × Rs. 25,000) + (40 Cars × Rs. 55,000)	35,00,000
2.	**Sales Proceeds**	
	Arun— (5 × Rs. 1,75,000) + (35 × Rs. 1,25,000)	52,50,000
	Balu— (4 × Rs. 1,75,000) + (35 × Rs. 1,10,000 + (11 × Rs. 80,000)	54,30,000
3.	**Closing Stock** (A. C. Cars + Non-A.C. Cars)	35,00,000
	Purchase Price	
Add :	Reconditioning Charges	15,00,000
		50,00,000
	Cost per Non-A.C. Car = Rs. 50,00,000 ÷ 100 and,	50,000
	cost of 10 A.C. Cars Rs. 30,00,000 ÷ 100	30,000
	∴ Total Cost for A.C. cars (50,000 + 30,000)	80,000

4. Actual cost per Non-A.C. car (calculated above) Rs. 50,000, which has been paid by the insurance company.

Ascertainment of Sales, computation for loss of goods damaged and special commission

Illustration 13

X and Y entered into a joint venture agreement to share the profits and losses in the ratio of 2 : 1. X supplied goods worth Rs. 60,000 to Y incurring expenses amounting to Rs. 2,000 for freight and insurance. During transit, goods costing Rs. 5,000 became damaged and a sum of Rs. 3,000 was recovered from the Insurance Company. Y reported that 90% of the remaining goods were sold at a profit of 30% on their original cost. Towards the end of the venture a fire occurred and, as a result, the balance stock lying unsold with Y was damaged. The goods were not insured and Y agreed to compensate X by paying in cash 80% of the aggregate of the original cost of such goods plus proportionate expenses incurred by X. Apart from joint venture share of profits, Y was also entitled, under the agreement, to a commission of 5% of the net profits of joint venture after charging such commission. Selling expenses incurred by Y totalled Rs. 1,000. Y had earlier remitted an advance of Rs. 10,000. Y duly paid the balance due to X by draft.

You are required to prepare in the books of X : (1) Joint Venture Account, (2) Y Account.

Solution

In the books of X

Joint Venture Account

Dr. Cr.

Date	*Particulars*	*Amount*	*Date*	*Particulars*	*Amount*
?		Rs.	?		Rs.
	To Goods Supplied	60,000		By Bank A/c — Received from Insurance Co.	3,000
	" Bank A/c —Freight & Insurance	2,000		" Y A/c — Sale Proceeds	64,350[1]
	" Y A/c —Selling Expenses	1,000		" Y A/c — Compensation for Loss	4,546
	" Y A/c — Commission	424			
	" Profit on Venture : P & L A/c — ($\frac{2}{3}$) = 5,648; Y A/c — ($\frac{1}{3}$) = 2,824	8,472			
		71,896			71,896

Y Account

Dr. Cr.

Date	*Particulars*	*Amount*	*Date*	*Particulars*	*Amount*
?		Rs.	?		Rs.
	To Joint Venture A/c — Sale Proceeds	64,350		By Bank A/c—Advance	10,000
	" Joint Venture A/c — Compensation for Loss	4,546		" Joint Venture A/c — Expenses	1,000
				— Commission	424
				— Share of Profit	2,824
				" Bank A/c —Final Payment	54,648
		68,896			68,896

Workings :

1. **Calculation of Sale Proceeds**

	Rs.
Cost of Goods	60,000
Less : Cost of Damaged Goods	5,000
	55,000
Less : Cost of Goods Unsold (55,000 × 10%)	5,500
Cost of Goods Sold	49,500
Add : Profit 30%	14,850
	64,350

2. **Calculation of Compensation for Loss of Goods Damaged**

	Rs.
Cost of Goods Damaged Unsold	5,500
Add : Proportionate Expenses $\left(\frac{2,000}{60,000} \times 5,500\right) =$	183
	5,683
Y will compensate @ 80% of Rs. 5,683 = $\left(i.e., \text{Rs. } 5,683 \times \frac{80}{100}\right)$	4,546

3. **Calculation of Commission Payable to Y**

Profit before charging Y's Commission = Rs. 8,896 (i.e., Rs. 71,896 – Rs. 63,000)

∴ Commission will be Rs. 424 $\left(\text{i.e., Rs. } 8,896 \times \frac{5}{105}\right)$

A Harder Problem

Illustration 14

Maganbhai of Rajkot and Ramanan of Chennai enter into a joint venture deciding to share profits and losses in the ratio of 3 : 2. Maganbhai purchases 3,000 kg of material A for Rs. 1,50,000 and sends it to Nana of Pune for processing. Maganbhai pays the transport cost amounting to Rs. 6,000. Ramanan purchases 2,000 kg of material B for Rs. 2,00,000 and send it to Nana of Pune for processing. The transport cost amounting to Rs. 10,000 is paid by Ramanan. Nana does the processing work and manufactures 4,800 units of finished product C. Nana prepares a "conversion cost" bill on the joint venture at 20 per unit. Maganbhai pays this bill. The goods are sent to Banerjee of Kolkata, the transport cost amounting to Rs. 18,000 being paid by Maganbhai. Banerjee sells 90% of the goods at Rs. 150 per unit. He takes over the balance goods at Rs. 120 per unit. After deducting his own commission @ 10% of sale proceeds, he remits the amount to Maganbhai. The co-venturers agree to settle the account, after retaining 30% of the profits for taxation on the income of association of persons.

You are required to show the ledger accounts in the books of Maganbhai. [CA]

Solution

In the books of Maganbhai

Joint Venture Account

Dr. Cr.

Date	Particulars	Rs.	Amount	Date	Particulars	Amount
?		Rs.	?			Rs.
	To Bank A/c				By Banerjee A/c	
	—Cost of Goods	1,50,000			—Sale Proceeds	6,48,000
	—Transport Cost	6,000			[4,800 – 480 = 4,320 × Rs. 150]	
	—Conversion Cost				" Banerjee A/c	57,600
	(4,800 × Rs. 20)	96,000			—Goods taken (480 × Rs. 120)	
	—Transport Cost	18,000	2,70,000			
	" Ramanan A/c					
	—Cost of Goods	2,00,000				
	—Transport Cost	10,000	2,10,000			
	" Banerjee A/c					
	—Commission @ 10% on Sales		64,800			
	" Net Profit c/d (before appropriation)		1,60,800			
			7,05,600			7,05,600
	To Prov. for Tax @ 30%		48,240		By Net Profit b/d	1,60,800
	" Profit on Venture :					
	P & L A/c	67,536				
	Ramanan A/c	45,024	1,12,560			
			1,60,800			1,60,800

Banerjee Account

Dr. Cr.

Date	Particulars	Amount	Date	Particulars	Amount
?		Rs.	?		Rs.
	To Joint Venture A/c —Sale Proceeds	6,48,000		By Joint Venture A/c —Commission	64,800
	" Joint Venture A/c —Goods taken	57,600		" Bank A/c —Final payment	6,40,800
		7,05,600			7,05,600

Ramanan Account

Dr. Cr.

Date	Particulars	Amount	Date	Particulars	Amount
?		Rs.	?		Rs.
	To Bank A/c *(bal. fig.)*	2,55,024		By Joint Venture A/c	
				—Cost of Goods	2,00,000
				—Expenses	10,000
				—Profit	45,024
		2,55,024			2,55,024

C. Where Memorandum Joint Venture Account is opened

This is practically the modified version of the second method stated above. The primary advantage of this method is that one partner will keep records of his own transactions and not the other in his own ledger. Each party must render to the other a complete statement of all transactions entered into by him for ascertaining profit or loss and these must then be combined into a *Memorandum Joint Venture Account.* Thus, under this method, the following accounts are to be opened :

(a) Memorandum Joint Venture Account; (b) Joint Venture with .... Account.

(a) **Memorandum Joint Venture Account**

This account is in the nature of a Profit and Loss Account, i.e., expenses on the debit side and incomes on the credit side, the difference represents profit or loss which are shared between the venturers. It is not a part of double entry system as it is a *Memorandum Account,* only the name of the respective venturers are to be recorded here. For example :

(i) ***If goods are supplied by A (venturer), the entry being :***

Memorandum Joint Venture A/c Dr.
 To A A/c

(ii) ***If Goods are sold by A :***

A A/c Dr.
 To Memorandum Joint Venture A/c

Same principle is to be followed in the case of other venturer, say, B.

(b) **Joint Venture with .... Account**

It is practically a personal account. The concerned venturer debits this account with all payments and goods supplied by him on behalf of the joint venture (e.g., cost of goods, expenses, material supplied etc.) and credits all incomes and unsold stock taken by him (if any). After incorporating the items the balance represents the final settlement between the venturers.

For example :

(i) ***If goods are supplied by or expenses are incurred by A (venture) in his book, the entry being :***

Joint Venture with .... Account Dr.
 To Bank/Goods Supplied A/c

(ii) ***If Goods are sold by A :***

Bank A/c Dr.
 To Joint Venture with .... Account

Same principle is to be applied in the case of other venturer, say B.

(iii) ***If Goods are taken by A :***

Drawings/Goods Taken A/c Dr.
 To Joint Venture with ...... A/c

(iv) ***For Share of Profit :***

Joint Venture with .... A/c Dr.
 To Profit and Loss A/c

[In the case of loss, it will be reversed]

(v) ***For final settlement :***

(i) ***If payment is made to other Venturer :***

Joint Venture with .... A/c Dr.
 To Bank A/c

(ii) ***If the amount is received from the other venturer :***

Bank A/c Dr.
 To Joint Venture with .... A/c

Illustration 15

Ravi and Suresh entered into a joint venture for purchase and sale of electronic goods, sharing profits and losses in the ratio of 3 : 2. They also agreed to receive 5% commission on their individual sales and the following information was extracted from the records :

July 1, 2012 : Ravi purchased goods worth Rs.1,90,000 financed to the extent of 90% out of his funds and balance by loan from his uncle Shyam.

August 1, 2012 : Ravi sent goods costing Rs. 1,70,000 to Suresh and paid Rs. 1,410 as freight. Suresh paid Rs.13,410 to Ravi.

October 1, 2012 : Suresh sold all the goods sent to him. Ravi paid the loan taken from his uncle, including interest of Rs. 350.

All sales, by either party, were made at a uniform profit of 40% above cost. On November 30, 2012, they decided to close the venture by transferring the balance of goods unsold, lying with Ravi at a cost of Rs. 9,000, to a wholesale dealer.

You are required to prepare the Memorandum Joint Venture Account, and Joint Venture with Ravi in the books of Suresh and Joint Venture with Suresh in the books of Ravi. They further disclosed that goods worth Rs. 4,000 were taken personally by Ravi at an agreed price of Rs. 5,000.

Solution **[ICWA]**

Memorandum Joint Venture Account

Dr. Date		Particulars	Rs.	Amount Rs.	Date		Particulars	Cr. Amount Rs.
2012					2012			
July 1	To	Ravi—Purchaser	1,71,000		Oct. 1	By	Suresh—Sale Proceeds (Rs. 1,70,000 + 40%)	2,38,000
		Loan—Purchaser	19,000	1,90,000	Nov. 30	"	Ravi—Stock taken	5,000
Aug. 1	"	Ravi—Freight		1,410		"	Ravi—Sale Proceeds (Rs. 1,90,000 – Rs. 1,70,000 – Rs. 9,000 – Rs. 4,000) = Rs. 7,000 + 40%	9,800
Oct. 1	"	Ravi—Interest on Loan		350				
	"	Suresh—Commission (@ 5% on Rs. 2,38,000)		11,900				
Nov. 30	"	Ravi—Commission (@ 5% on Rs. 9,800)		490	"	"	Stock— (Transferred to wholesale dealer)	9,000
"	"	Profit on Venture :						
		Ravi—($\frac{3}{5}$)	34,590					
		Suresh—($\frac{2}{5}$)	23,060	57,650				
				2,61,800				2,61,800

In the books of Ravi
Joint Venture with Suresh

Dr. Date		Particulars	Amount Rs.	Date		Particulars	Cr. Amount Rs.
2012				2012			
July 1	To	Bank A/c (Purchase of Goods)	1,90,000	Aug. 1	By	Cash A/c	13,410
Aug. 1	"	Bank A/c (freight)	1,410	Nov. 30	"	Stock taken	5,000
Oct. 1	"	Bank A/c (Interest on Loan)	350	"	"	Stock transferred to wholesale dealer	9,000
Nov. 30	"	Commission	490	"	"	Bank (Sale Proceeds) A/c	9,800
"	"	Share of Profit	34,590		"	Bank (Final settlement) A/c	1,89,630
			2,26,840				2,26,840

In the books of Suresh
Joint Venture with Ravi

Dr. Date		Particulars	Amount Rs.	Date		Particulars	Cr. Amount Rs.
2012				2012			
Oct. 1	To	Commission	11,900	Oct. 1	By	Bank (Sale Proceeds)	2,38,000
"	"	Cash A/c	13,410				
	"	Share of Profit	23,060				
Nov. 30	"	Bank (Final settlement)	1,89,630				
			2,38,000				2,38,000

Abnormal loss, Value of unsold stock etc.

Illustration 16

Aswin of Chennai and Gupta of Delhi entered into a joint venture on 1.4.2012 for the purpose of buying second-hand cars, reconditioning and selling them as Diesel-airconditioned. Aswin has agreed to buy second-hand cars and recondition them and fit diesel engines. Gupta has agreed to fix air-conditioners and sell them at Delhi. They have agreed to share the profits and losses equally and settle their accounts at the end of each year.

The following are the details of purchase, and expenses incurred by Aswin and Gupta during the year 1.4.2012 to 31.3.2013:

	Aswin Rs.	Gupta Rs.
Cost of 10 cars purchased at average price	5,00,000	
Reconditioning expenditure	45,000	
Cost of 10 diesel engines	30,000	

Contd.

	Rs.	Rs.
Labour charges	18,000	32,000
8 Air-conditioners purchased		4,00,000
Buying commission @ 5%	25,000	
Selling commission @ 5%		60,000
Sale value realised on sale of 8 cars		12,00,000
Expenses incurred		
Freight—local	10,000	8,000
Delhi	30,000	—
Rent—Office	10,000	10,000
—Garage	12,000	20,000
Insurance	16,000	20,000
Miscellaneous expenses	6,000	10,000

Gupta sent a cheque for Rs. 6,00,000 to Aswin on 1.3.2013. Of the balance of 2 cars, one car met with accident on the way to garage before reconditioning and the insurance company settled the claim at Rs. 30,000 as a total loss. The old petrol engines were sold @ Rs. 500 per engine and one diesel engine was sold at Rs. 3,000 by Aswin. All of them were sold before 31.3.2013. Aswin retained the balance one car as a non-airconditioned diesel car for his personal use which was priced at average cost.

Aswin/Gupta settled the balance due to/by them as on 31.3.2013 by sending a crossed cheque as the case may be *Prepare :*

(1) Memorandum Joint Venture Account. (2) Joint Venture Account with Gupta in the books of Aswin. (3) Joint Venture Account with Aswin in the books of Gupta.

Solution

In the books of Aswin and Gupta

Memorandum Joint Venture Account

Dr. *Cr.*

Date	*Particulars*		*Amount*	*Date*	*Particulars*	*Amount*
2013			Rs.	2013		Rs.
Mar. 31	To Aswin A/c			Mar. 31	By Gupta	
	Cost of Cars		5,00,000		—Sale Proceeds	12,00,000
	Reconditioning Exp.		45,000		" Aswin—	
	Cost of Diesel Engine		30,000		(Sale of Petrol	
	Labour Charges		18,000		Engine 9 × Rs. 500)	4,500
	Buying Com.		25,000		" Sale of Diesel Engine	3,000
	Freight — Local		10,000		" Insurance Claim	30,000[1]
	" — Delhi		30,000		" Car Taken	68,389[2]
	Rent—Office		10,000			
	—Garrage		12,000			
	Insurance		16,000			
	Misc. Exp.		6,000			
	Gupta A/c					
	Labour		32,000			
	Cost of Air-conditioner		4,00,000			
	Selling Com.		60,000			
	Expenses		8,000			
	Rent — Office		10,000			
	—Garage		20,000			
	Insurance		20,000			
	Mis. Exp.		10,000			
	Profit on Venture—					
	Aswin	21,945				
	Gupta	21,944				
			43,889			
			13,05,889			13,05,889

In the books of Aswin

Dr. **Joint Venture with Gupta** Cr.

Date	Particulars	Amount	Date	Particulars	Amount
2013		Rs.	2013		Rs.
Mar. 31	To Bank A/c :		Mar. 31	By Bank A/c—Advance	6,00,000
	" Cost of Car	5,00,000		Bank A/c —	
	" Reconditioning Exp.	45,000		" Sale of Petrol Engine	4,500
	" Cost of Diesel Engines	30,000		" Sale of Diesel Engine	3,000
	" Labour Charges	18,000		" Insurance Claim	30,000
	" Buying Com.	25,000		" Car taken	68,389
	" Freight—Local	10,000		" Bank A/c *(bal. fig.)*	18,056
	—Delhi	30,000			
	" Rent—Office	10,000			
	—Garage	12,000			
	" Insurance	16,000			
	" Misc. Expenses	6,000			
	" Share of Profit	21,945			
		7,23,945			7,23,945

In the books of Gupta

Dr. **Joint Venture with Aswin** Cr.

Date	Particulars	Amount	Date	Particulars	Amount
2013		Rs.	2013		Rs.
Mar. 31	To Bank A/c		Mar. 31	By Bank A/c	
	— Advance	6,00,000		— Sales Proceeds	12,00,000
	" Bank A/c—				
	Labour	32,000			
	Cost of Air-conditioners	4,00,000			
	Selling Commission	60,000			
	Expenses	8,000			
	Rent—Office	10,000			
	—Garrage	20,000			
	Insurance	20,000			
	Misc. Expenses	10,000			
	" Share of Profit	21,944			
	" Bank *(bal. fig.)*	18,056			
		12,00,000			12,00,000

Workings :

1. It has been assumed that Aswin has recovered the amount from the Insurance Company.
2. Cost of Car taken

			Rs.
Cost of one Car	Rs. 5,00,000	$\times \frac{1}{10} =$	50,000
Cost of one Diesel Engine	Rs. 30,000	$\times \frac{1}{10} =$	3,000
Local Freight Charges	Rs. 10,000	$\times \frac{1}{10} =$	1,000
Buying Commission	Rs. 25,000	$\times \frac{1}{10} =$	2,500
Reconditioning Expenses	Rs. 45,000	$\times \frac{1}{9} =$	5,000
Labour Charges	Rs. 18,000	$\times \frac{1}{9} =$	2,000
Office Rent	Rs. 10,000	$\times \frac{1}{9} =$	1,111
Garage Rent	Rs. 12,000	$\times \frac{1}{9} =$	1,333
Insurance	Rs. 16,000	$\times \frac{1}{9} =$	1,778
Misc. Exp.	Rs. 6,000	$\times \frac{1}{9} =$	667
			68,389

Illustration 17

Thread of Tatanagar and Needle of Nagpur entered into a Joint Venture to trade together in the buying and re-selling of cheap machinery. Profit or loss to be shared in the ratio of 2 : 3. Thread undertook to make the purchases and Needle to effect sales.

Needle remitted Rs. 75,000 to Thread towards the Joint Venture. Thread purchased machinery worth Rs. 60,000 and paid Rs. 28,500 for repairs, of these, $2\frac{1}{2}$ % as buying commission and Rs. 2,700 for other sundry expenses. He then sent all the machines purchased and repaired to Needle at Nagpur.

While taking delivery of the machinery at Nagpur, Needle incurred Rs. 4,500 towards Railway Freight and Rs. 2,100 towards Octroi. He sold part of the machinery for Rs. 1,05,000 and kept the remaining for himself at an agreed value of Rs. 22,500. Other expenses of Needle were:

(i) Godown rent Rs. 1,350, (ii) Insurance Rs. 1,680, (iii) Brokerage Rs. 2,490, and (iv) Miscellaneous Rs. 1,920. Both the parties decided to close the Venture at this stage.

You are to prepare Accounts for the Joint Venture to show how matters stood in each party's ledger and prepare a statement showing the result of the Venture.

Solution

In the books of Thread
Joint Venture with Needle

Dr. *Cr.*

Date	*Particulars*	*Amount*	*Amount*	*Date*	*Particulars*	*Amount*
?		Rs.	Rs.			Rs.
	To Bank A/c				By Bank A/c	75,000
	—Machinery	60,000			—Amount Received from Needle	
	—Repairs	28,500			" Cash A/c	26,004
	—Com.	1,500			— Final Settlement	
	—A's Expenses	2,700	92,700			
	" Share of Profit		8,304*			
			1,01,004			1,01,004

In the books of Needle
Joint Venture with Thread

Dr. *Cr.*

Date	*Particulars*		*Amount*	*Date*	*Particulars*	*Amount*
?		Rs.	Rs.	?		Rs.
	To Bank A/c				By Bank A/c	1,05,000
	—Amount remitted to Thread		75,000		—Sale Proceeds	
	—Bank A/c				" Purchases A/c	
	—Railway	4,500			—Machinery taken	22,500
	—Octroi	2,100				
	—Godown Rent	1,350				
	—Insurance	1,680				
	—Brokerage	2,490				
	—Misc. Exp.	1,920	14,040			
	" Share of Profit		12,456			
	" Cash A/c					
	—Final Settlement		26,004			
			1,27,500			1,27,500

* Settlement showing the result of these entries, i.e., the Profit of the Venture

			Rs.
	Total Credit Side :		
	Sale Proceeds		1,05,000
	Machinery retained by Needle		22,500
			1,27,500
Less:	Debit side :		
	Purchase & Exp. by Thread	92,700	
	Purchase & Exp. by Needle	14,040	
			1,06,740
		Profit	20,760

Thread— $20,760 \times \frac{2}{5} = 8,304$

Needle— $20,760 \times \frac{3}{5} = 12,456$

Ascertainment of Sales

Illustration 18

Bhim and Arjun entered into a joint venture for buying and selling plastic goods and agreed to share profits and losses in the ratio of 3 : 2.

On October 1, 2008, Bhim purchased goods at a cost of Rs. 60,000 and half of the goods were handed over to Arjun. On October 15, he again purchased goods worth Rs. 20,000. He incurred expenses Rs. 2,000.

On October 15, Arjun also made a purchase of Rs. 37,500 and, on the same day, he sent to Bhim goods worth Rs. 15,000. He incurred expenses of Rs. 900. On October 20, Bhim in, order to help Arjun, sent Rs. 16,000 to him. Both the parties sold goods at a profit of 25% on Sale.

On March 31, 2008, Bhim had unsold stock of goods of Rs. 12,500, of these, goods costing Rs. 5,000 were taken away by him and the remainder sold for Rs. 8,000. Arjun was able to sell away complete goods excepting goods costing Rs. 2,500 which were badly damaged and were treated as unsaleable. Rs. 3,000 owing to Bhim was unrecoverable and treated as joint loss.

On March 31, 2009 both the parties decided to close the books. You are required to prepare :

(a) The Joint Venture Account as it would appear in the books of Bhim recording his own transactions, and

(b) A Memorandum Joint Venture Account, showing the profits of the business.

Solution

In the books of Bhim
Joint Venture with Arjun A/c

Dr. Cr.

Date		Particulars	Amount	Date		Particulars		Amount
2008			Rs.	2009			Rs.	Rs.
Oct. 1	To	Purchases	60,000	Mar. 31	By	Sales	70,000	
						Less : Bad Debts	3,000	
15	"	Bank—Expenses	20,000	"				67,000
15	"	Bank—Advance	2,000	"	"	Purchases		
20	"	Cash A/c	16,000			—Stock taken over		5,000
2009				"	"	Sales A/c — Stock Sold		8,000
Mar. 31	"	Share of Profit	15,760	"	"	Bank-remittances received		33,760
			1,13,760					1,13,760

In the books of Bhim & Arjun
Memorandum Joint Venture A/c

Dr. Cr.

Date		Particulars		Amount	Date		Particulars	Amount
2009				Rs.	2009			Rs.
Oct. 1	To	Purchase :			Mar. 31	By	Sales :	
		Bhim		60,000			Bhim	70,000
		Bhim		20,000			Arjun	66,667
		Arjun		37,500			Bhim	8,000
15		Expenses :					Stock	
		Bhim		2,000			—Taken over by Bhim	5,000
		Arjun		900				
		Bad Debts incurred by Bhim		3,000				
2009								
Mar. 31	"	Profit on Venture						
		Bhim	Rs. 15,760					
		Arjun	Rs. 10,507					
				26,267				
				1,49,667				1,49,667

Workings : Computation of Sales

	Bhim	Arjun
	Rs.	Rs.
Purchases (60,000 + 20,000)	80,000	37,500
Add : Received from other party	15,000	30,000
	95,000	67,500

Contd.

	Rs.	Rs.
Less : Sent to other party	30,000	15,000
	65,000	52,500
Less : Stock	12,500	2,500
Cost of Goods Sold	52,500	50,000
Add : Profit at 25% on Sales i.e., $33\frac{1}{3}$ % on Cost	17,500	16,667
Sales	70,000	66,667

Abnormal Loss

Illustration 19

X and Y decided to work a joint venture for the sale of electric motors.

On 1st May 2012, X purchased 200 electric motors at Rs. 175 each and despatched 150 motors to Y incurring Rs. 1,000 as freight and insurance charges. 10 electric motors were damaged in transit. On 1st Feb. 2013, Rs. 500 were received by X from the insurance company, in full settlement of his claim. On 15th March 2013, X sold 50 electric motors at Rs. 225 each. He received Rs. 15,000 from Y on 1st April 2013.

On 15th May 2012, Y took delivery of the electric motors and incurred the following expenses:

Clearing Charges Rs. 170; Repair charges to electric motors damaged in-transit Rs. 300; Godown Rent for 3 months Rs. 600

He sold the electric motors as :

1.2.2013	10 damaged motors Rs. 170 each
	40 motors at Rs. 200 each
15.3.2013	20 motors at Rs. 315 each
1.4.2013	80 motors at Rs. 250 each

It is agreed that they are entitled to a commission of 10% on the respective sales effected by them; that the profits and losses shall be shared between X and Y in the ratio of 2 : 1. Y remits X the balance of amount due on 30th April 2013. You are required to show the Memorandum Joint Venture Account only. You are required to show the Memorandum Joint Venture Account only.

Solution

Dr. **Memorandum Joint Venture Account** Cr.

Date	Particulars	Rs.	Amount Rs.	Date	Particulars		Amount Rs.
2012				2013			
May 1	To X : Cost of Motors (200 × Rs. 175)		35,000	Mar. 15	By X : Sale of Motors (50 × Rs. 225)		11,250
"	" X : Freight and Insurance		1,000	Feb. 1	" Y : Sale of Motors		
May 15	" Y :				10 × Rs. 170 =	Rs. 1,700	
	Clearing Charge	170			40 × Rs. 200 =	Rs. 8,000	
	Repairs	300		Mar. 15	20 × Rs. 315 =	Rs. 6,300	
	Ground Rent	600			80 × Rs. 250 =	Rs. 20,000	
			1,070				36,000
Apr. 15	" X : Commission @ 10%		1,125	Apr. 1	" X : Insurance Claim		500
	" Y : Commission @ 10%		3,600				
" 30	" Profit on Venture :						
	X ($\frac{2}{3}$)	3,970					
	Y ($\frac{1}{3}$)	1,985	5,955				
			47,750				47,750

Illustration 20

On 2.5.2011, Satna of Patna and Suri of Puri entered into a joint venture to buy and sell dolls. They agree to share profit and losses as 3 : 2.

On 7.6.2011, Suri purchased 600 dolls at Rs. 52 each and sent 240 dolls to Satna incurring Rs. 3,700 as freight and insurance charges, 25 of such dolls were damaged in-transit and on 1.7.2011, he recovered a sum of Rs. 250 from insurance company. On 15.7.2011, Satna made a remittance of Rs. 7,050 to Suri.

On 26.7.2011, Satna purchased 300 dolls at Rs. 55 each and sent 100 dolls to Suri incurring Rs. 1,500 as freight and insurance charges.

On 14.8.2011, 18 damaged dolls were taken over by Satna for personal purposes at an agreed valuation of Rs. 25 each and distributed the remaining damaged dolls, free of cost, amongst their customers. On 11.11.2011, both Satna and Suri disposed of all the dolls in their possession at Rs. 60 each.

On 30.11.2011, the venture was closed and the accounts were settled by bank draft. You are required : (a) to prepare a Memorandum Joint Venture Account, and (b) to show the account in the books of Satna to record his own transactions.

Solution

Dr. **Memorandum Joint Venture Account** Cr.

Date		Particulars		Amount	Date		Particulars	Amount
2011				Rs.	2011			Rs.
June 7	To	Suri : Purchases (600 × Rs. 52)		31,200	July 1	By	Suri—Insurance Claim	250
		Freight and Insurance		3,700	Aug. 14		Satna : Damaged Dolls Taken over (18 × Rs. 25)	450
July 26	"	Satna : Purchases (300 × Rs. 55)		16,500	Nov. 11	"	Satna : Sales Proceeds (215 + 200 = 415 × Rs. 60)	24,900
		Freight and Insurance		1,500		"	Suri : (360 + 100 = 460 × Rs. 60)	27,600
Nov. 30	"	Profit on Venture :						
		Satna ($\frac{3}{5}$)	180					
		Suri ($\frac{2}{5}$)	120					
				300				
				53,200				53,200

Note : There will be no adjustment for the dolls which were distributed amongst the customers free of cost.

In the books of Satna

Dr. **Joint Venture with Suri** Cr.

Date		Particulars	Amount	Date		Particulars	Amount
2011			Rs.	2011			Rs.
July 15	To	Bank (Remittance)	7,050	Aug. 14	By	Dolls taken over	450
July 26	"	Cost of Dolls	16,500	Nov. 11	"	Bank — Sale Proceeds	24,900
		Freight and Insurance	1,500				
Nov. 30	"	Share of Profit	180				
Nov. "	"	Bank (Final Remittance)	120				
			25,350				25,350

Inter-transfer of Goods

Illustration 21

X and Y entered into a joint venture agreeing to share profits and losses in the ratio of 2 : 1.

On 1.5.2012, X purchased goods costing Rs. 7,200 and sent half of the goods to Y. On 15.6.2012, he purchased another lot of goods costing Rs. 2,400 and spent Rs. 240 as expenses.

On 20.6.2012, Y purchased goods costing Rs. 4,500 and on 25.6.2012, sent to X part of this goods costing Rs. 1,800 and paid Rs. 110 as carriage. On 2.7.2012, X made a remittance of Rs. 2,000 to Y.

Sales were made by both the venturers at a uniform price of $33\frac{1}{3}$ % above cost excluding expenses. Each venture was successful in collecting cash proceeds on sales effected by him except a sum of Rs. 400 owing to X and this was ultimately agreed to be written-off as a loss of the venture.

On 25.8.2012, unsold goods costing Rs. 1,500 were in the possession of X. Of these, goods costing Rs. 600 were taken over by him and the balance was sold for Rs. 1,000. Y disposed of the goods in his possession except some damaged goods costing Rs. 300 which it was agreed to be written-off as unsaleable. On 31.8.2012, the venture was closed and the amounts were settled by Bank Draft. You are required to prepare: (i) The Joint Venture Account as it would appear in the books of X recording his transactions in regard thereto. (ii) A Memorandum Joint Venture Account showing the net profit.

Solution

Memorandum Joint Venture Account

Dr. Date	Particulars		Amount	Date	Particulars		Cr. Amount
2012		Rs.	Rs.	2012		Rs.	Rs.
May 1	To Cost of Goods :			?	By Sale Proceeds*		
June 20	X	9,600			X	9,400[1]	
	Y	4,500			Y	800	
			14,100				17,400
	" Expenses :			Aug. 25	" X—Stock taken		600
	X	240					
	Y	110	350				
	" X—Bad Debts		400				
Aug. 31	" Profit on Venture :						
	X−($\frac{2}{3}$)	2,100					
	Y−($\frac{1}{3}$)	1,050					
			3,150				
			18,000				18,000

In the books of X
Joint Venture with Y

Dr. Date	Particulars	Amount	Date	Particulars	Cr. Amount
2011		Rs.	2011		Rs.
	To Bank A/c : Cost of Goods	7,200		By Bank A/c : Sale Proceeds (Rs. 8,400 + Rs. 1,000)	9,400
	" Bank A/c : Cost of Goods	2,400		" Purchases — Stock taken over	600
	" Bank A/c : Expenses	240		" Bank A/c (*Final remittance*) (*bal. fig.*)	4,340
	" Bank A/c : Remittance to Y	2,000			
	" Bad Debts A/c	400			
	" P & L A/c Share of Profit	2,100			
		14,340			14,340

1 Calculation of Sales :

		X	Y
		Rs.	Rs.
Cost of Goods (7,200 + 2,400)		9,600	4,500
Goods Sent by X to Y		− 3,600	+ 3,600
		6,000	8,100
	Rs.	Rs.	
Goods Sent by Y to X	+ 1,800	− 1,800	
	7,800	6,300	
Cost of Goods Unsold	− 1,500	− 1,300	∴ Total Sales (Rs. 9,400 + 8,000) = Rs. 17,400.
	6,300	6,000	
Profit @ $33\frac{1}{3}$% on Cost	+ 2,100	2,000	
	8,400	8,000	
Plus : Sales made by X	+ 1,000	—	
	9,400	8,000	

A Typical Problem

Illustration 22

A and B entered into a Joint Venture to trade in electronic devices. It was agreed that A would be entitled to a commission of 5% on gross sales of devices exported and the profits and losses of the venture be shared 4 : 3. The following transactions took place during 2011:

May 1 A purchased electronic devices at a cost of Rs. 1,94,600 paying Rs. 1,54,200 in cash and accepting a bill of exchange for the balance.

May 5	A sent to B electronic devices which had cost Rs. 84,200. B paid the carriage thereon Rs. 1,260 and paid Rs. 20,550 to A.
May 10	B purchased electronic devices at a cost of Rs. 76,710.
June 3	B paid the bill accepted by A.
June 15	B paid shipping charges and insurance costs of export sales amounting to Rs. 4,260 and inland carriage Rs. 3,040.
June 30	It was agreed to close down the joint venture by which time sales by A were Rs. 1,64,900 including exports of Rs. 1,24,000 and those of B Rs. 1,72,500 including exports of Rs. 42,600. A agreed to take over the remaining stock for Rs. 5,400.
June 28	A had been notified by a customer in Nepal that a device he had sold for Rs. 4,000 was being returned as faulty and he claimed a refund of the full price together with cost and damage of Rs. 1,110. It was agreed that A would forego his commission on the sale but that the loss be borne by the venturer. B agreed to pay Rs. 5,100 into a special bank account to enable A to settle the claim and that this amount should be provided in the Joint Venture Account as on 30th June. The final settlement between A and B was deferred until such time as the Nepal claim had been settled. On 30th September A settled the claim for Rs. 4,290 and paid the money of the special bank account. The returned electronic device was sold by A as scrap for Rs. 100 and he retained the proceeds. The special bank account was closed by payment out to A and B of the amount due to them. You are required to prepare (a) The Joint Venture Account in the books of both A and B, and (b) The Memorandum Joint Venture Account showing the position both at 30th June'2011 and at 30th September '2011.

Solution

In the books of A

Joint Venture with B Account

Dr. Cr.

Date		Particulars	Amount	Date		Particulars	Amount
2011			Rs.	2011			Rs.
May 1	To	Cash A/c (Purchase)	1,54,200	May 5	By	Cash A/c (Received from B)	20,550
	"	Bills Payable (")	40,400		"	Bills Payable (Paid by B)	40,400
June 30	"	Commission	8,130[2]	June 30	"	Cash A/c (Sales)	1,64,900
"	"	Balance c/d	28,520	"	"	Drawings A/c (Stock taken over)	5,400
			2,31,250				2,31,250
Sept. 30	To	Profit & Loss A/c (Share of Profit)	28,920	July 1	By	Balance b/d	28,520
				Sept. 30	"	Cash A/c (Sale of Scrap)	100
				"	"	Cash (Special Bank)	300
			28,920				28,920

In the books of B

Joint Venture with A Account

Dr. Cr.

Date		Particulars	Amount	Date		Particulars	Amount
2011			Rs.	2011			Rs.
May 5	To	Cash A/c —Paid to A	20,550	June 30	By	Cash A/c —Sales	1,72,500
	"	Cash A/c—Carriages	1,260				
10	"	Cash A/c—Purchases	76,710				
June 3	"	Cash A/c—A's acceptance paid	40,400				
15	"	Cash A/c : Shipping etc.	4,260				
		Inland Carriage	3,040				
28	"	Cash A/c — Special Bank	5,100[2]				
June 30	"	Balance c/d	21,180				
			1,72,500				1,72,500
Sept. 30	"	Profit & Loss A/c (Share of Profit)	21,690	July 1	By	Balance b/d	21,180
				Sept. 30	"	Cash A/c (Special Bank)	510
			21,690				21,690

Dr. **Memorandum joint Venture Account** Cr.

Date	Particulars		Amount	Date	Particulars		Amount
2011			Rs.	2011			Rs.
May 1	To Purchases :			June 30	By Sales :		
1	A	1,94,600			A	1,64,900	
10	B	76,710	2,71,310	"	B	1,72,500	3,37,400
June 30	To Commission —A		8,130	June 30	By Drawings —A		5,400
	" Carriage —B		1,260				
	" Shipping & Insurance —A		4,260				
	" Inland Carriage		3,040				
	" Cost and Damage		5,100				
"	" Net Profit c/d [Up to 30.6.2011]		49,700				
			3,42,800				3,42,800
Sept. 30	To Profit on Venture			July 1	By Net Profit b/d		49,700
	A $\left(\frac{4}{7}\right)$ =	28,920		Sept. 30	" Sale as Scrap		100
	B $\left(\frac{3}{7}\right)$ =	21,690)		"	" Over-provision for Cost & Damage [5,100 – 4,290]		810
			50,610				
			50,610				50,610

Workings :

1. Commission Payable to A

		Rs.
Sales (Export)	A :	1,24,000
	B :	42,600
		1,66,600
Less : Return of Goods		4,000
@ 5% = Rs. 8,130		1,62,600

2. Amount of to be calculated

		Rs.
	Received from Customer (Nepal)	4,290
Add :	To be brought in by A & B (Rs. 300 + 510)	810
		5,100
Less :	Payments to B	5,100

Underwriting Shares, unsold shares taken, Commission received etc.

Illustration 23

A and B enter into a joint venture for guaranteeing the subscription at par of 1,00,000 shares of Rs. 10 each of a Joint Stock Company. They agree to share profits and losses in the ratio of 2 : 3. The terms with the company are $4\frac{1}{2}$ % commission in cash and 6,000 shares of the company as fully paid-up.

The public took up 88,000 of the shares and the balance share of the guaranteed issue are taken up by A and B who provide cash equally. The commission in cash is taken by partners in the ratio of 4 : 5.

The entire shareholding of the joint venture is then sold through brokers—25% price of Rs. 9. 50% at a price of Rs. 8.75; 15% at a price of Rs. 8.50 and the remaining 10% are taken over by A and B equally at Rs. 8 per share. The sale proceeds of the shares are taken by the partners equally.

Prepare a Joint Venture Memorandum Account and the separate accounts of A and B in the books of B and A, respectively, showing the adjustment of the final balance between A and B.

Ignore interest and income-tax.

Solution

Dr. **Memorandum Joint Venture Account** Cr.

Date	Particulars		Amount	Date	Particulars	Amount
?			Rs.	?		Rs.
	To A (Cost of Shares)		60,000[1]		By A (Commission)	20,000[3]
	" B (Cost of Shares)		60,000		B (Commission)	25,000
	" Profit on Joint Venture				" A (Sale Proceeds)	71,100[2]
	A	32,640			B (Sale Proceeds)	71,100
	B	48,960			" A (Shares taken)	7,200[4]
			81,600		B (Shares taken)	7,200
			2,01,600			2,01,600

In the books of A
Joint Venture with B

Dr. Date	Particulars	Amount	Date	Particulars	Amount Cr.
?		Rs.	?		Rs.
	To Bank — Cost of Shares	60,000		By Bank — Commission	20,000
	" Share of Profit	32,640		Bank — Sale Proceeds	71,100
	" Bank —Final settlement	5,660		" Shares taken	7,200
		98,300			98,300

In the books of B
Joint Venture with A

Dr. Date	Particulars	Amount	Date	Particulars	Amount Cr.
2011		Rs.	2011		Rs.
	To Bank — Cost of Shares	60,000		By Bank — Commission	25,000
	" Share of Profit	48,960		Bank — Sale Proceeds	71,100
				" Shares taken	7,200
				" Bank — Final settlement	5,660
		1,08,960			1,08,960

Workings :

1. **Purchase of Shares** (1,00,000 – 88,000) = 12,000 @ Rs. 10 = Rs. 1,20,000 provided by A and B equally i.e., Rs. 60,000 each.

2. **Calculation of Sales**

	6,000	Shares taken as Commission
	12,000	shares purchased
Entire share-holding	**18,000**	

	Rs.	
25% of 18,000 = 4,500 shares	@ 9.00	= 40,500
50% of 18,000 = 9,000 "	@ 8.75	= 78,750
15% of 18,000 = 2,700 "	@ 8.50	= 22,950
		1,42,200

$\times \frac{1}{2}$ = Rs. 71,100 made by A and B each

3. **Commission in Cash** 1,00,000 Shares @ Rs. 10 = Rs. 10,00,000 × $4\frac{1}{2}$ % = Rs. 45,000 to be taken by A and B in the ratio 4 : 5.

4. **Unsold Shares taken equally by A and B** 10% of 18,000 = 1,800 shares @ Rs. 8.00 = Rs. 14,400 × $\frac{1}{2}$ = Rs. 7,200 each.

Valuation of Unsold Stock and Interim Settlement of Accounts between the Venturers

It is needless to mention that if the venturers desire to prepare the accounts before the completion of the venture, valuation of stock as on that date must be determined for ascertaining the result of the venture. The same will appear in the credit side of Joint Venture Account (if it is not taken over by any venturer). However, the valuation must be made according to the standard practice of valuation, i.e., cost price (cost price + proportionate non-recurring expenses) or market price, whichever is lower.

Treatment of Unsold Stock

In Memorandum Joint Venture Account

(i) Credit the Memorandum Joint Venture Account with the amount of unsold stock and bring down the same in the next accounting period, (ii) divide the same between the venturer in profit-sharing ratio or the specific ratio, if given (iii) each co-venturer will record in his own book the amount of his share of stock.

Illustration 24

On 1st June 2012, Pandey and Parker entered into a Joint Venture to consign goods to Parekh to be sold on their joint risk. They agreed to share profits and losses in the ratio of 3 : 2.

On 15th April 2012, Pandey consigned goods to the value of Rs. 36,000 and incurred expenses amounting to Rs. 3,000. On 31st July 2012, Parker also consigned goods to the value of Rs. 22,000 and incurred expenses amounting to Rs. 1,800. On 15th Nov. 2012, Parekh sold 80% of the total goods for Rs. 60,000 and remitted the proceeds to Pandey after deducting 5% commission on sales. On 31st Dec.

2012, on which date accounts were prepared, an interim settlement was effected between Pandey and Parker. On 15th August 2013 Parekh sold the remainder of the total goods for Rs. 8,000 and remitted the proceeds to Parker, less 5% commission on sales. On 31st Oct. 2013, a final settlement was effected between Pandey and Parker. You are required : (a) to show the account in the books of each co-venturer to record his own transactions, and (b) to prepare a Memorandum Joint Venture Account. **[ICWA]**

Solution

Memorandum Joint Venture Account

Dr. Cr.

Date		Particulars		Amount	Date		Particulars		Amount
2012				Rs.	2012				Rs.
Apr. 15	To	Pandey — Goods Supplied		36,000	Nov. 15	By	Parekh — Sale Proceeds		60,000
		Expenses		3,000	Dec. 31	"	Unsold Stock c/d		12,560
July 31	"	Parker — Goods Supplied		22,000			(36,000 + 3,000 + 22,000 +		
		Expenses		1,800			1,800) × 20%		
Nov. 15	"	Parekh's Commission		3,000					
Dec. 31	"	Profit on Venture :							
		Pandey	4,056						
		Parker	2,704						
				6,760					
				72,560					72,560
2013					2013				
Jan. 1	To	Unsold Stock b/d		12,560	Aug. 15	By	Parekh — Sale Proceeds		8,000
Aug. 15	"	Parekh's Commission		400	Oct. 31		Loss on Venture :		
							Pandey	2,976	
							Parker	1,984	
									4,960
				12,960					12,960

In the books of Pandey
Joint Venture with Parker

Dr. Cr.

Date		Particulars	Amount	Date		Particulars	Amount
2012			Rs.	2012			Rs.
Apr. 15	To	Goods Consigned	36,000	Nov. 15	By	Bank — Sale Proceeds	57,000
	"	Bank — Expenses	3,000			(60,000 — 3,000 Com.)	
Dec. 31	"	Share of Profit	4,056		"	Unsold Stock c/d	7,536
	"	Bank (Remittance)	21,480			$(12,560 \times \frac{3}{5})$	
			64,536				64,536
2013				2013			
Jan. 1	To	Unsold Stock b/d	7,536	Oct. 31	By	Share of Loss	2,976
					"	Bank *(bal. fig.)*	4,560
			7,536				7,536

In the books of Parker
Joint Venture with Pandey

Dr. Cr.

Date		Particulars	Amount	Date		Particulars	Amount
2012			Rs.	2012			Rs.
July 31	To	Goods Consigned	22,000	Dec. 31	By	Unsold Stock c/d	5,024
	"	Bank — Expenses	1,800			$(12,560 \times \frac{2}{5})$	
Dec. 31	"	Share of Profit	2,704		"	Bank (Remittance)	21,480
			26,504				26,504
2013				2013			
Jan. 1	To	Unsold Stock b/d	5,024	Aug. 15	By	Bank — Sale Proceeds	7,600
Oct. 31	"	Bank (Remittance)	4,560			(8,000 – 400)	
					"	Share of Loss	1,984
			9,584				9,584

Joint Venture with more than two ventures

Illustration 25

A, B, and C enter into Joint Venture sharing profits and losses in the ratio of 2 : 2 : 1. From the following information you are asked to prepare the necessary accounts in the books of the parties assuming that they maintain no separate set of books :

	A	B	C
	Rs.	Rs.	Rs.
Materials supplied	12,000	6,000	—
Expenses paid	3,000	2,000	1,000
Gross sale proceeds	—	20,000	10,000
Unsold stock taken over	—	2,000	500

Solution

In the books of A
Joint Venture Account

Dr. Cr.

Date	Particulars			Amount	Date	Particulars		Amount
?				Rs.	?			Rs.
	To Bank A/c :	Materials Purchased		12,000		By B A/c :	Sale Proceeds	20,000
		Expenses		3,000			Stock Taken	2,000
	" B A/c :	Materials Purchased		6,000		" C A/c :	Sale Proceeds	10,000
		Expenses		2,000			Stock Taken	500
	" C A/c :	Expenses		1,000				
	Profit :							
	B		3,400					
	C		1,700					
	P & L A/c		3,400	8,500				
				32,500				32,500

Co-venturers' Account

Dr. Cr.

Date	Particulars	Amount	Amount	Date	Particulars	Amount	Amount
?		Rs.	Rs.	?		Rs.	Rs.
	To Joint Venture A/c :				By Joint Venture A/c :		
	Sale Proceeds	20,000	10,000		Materials	6,000	—
	Stock Taken	2,000	500		Expenses	2,000	1,000
					" Share of Profit	3,400	1,700
					" Balance c/d	10,600	7,800
		22,000	10,500			22,000	10,500
	To Balance b/d	10,600	7,800				

In the books of B
Joint Venture Account

Dr. Cr.

Date	Particulars			Amount	Date	Particulars		Amount
?				Rs.	?			Rs.
	To Bank A/c	Materials Purchased		6,000		By Bank A/c :	Sale Proceeds	20,000
		Expenses		2,000			Stock Taken	2,000
	" A A/c :	Materials Purchased		12,000		" C A/c :	Sale Proceeds	10,000
		Expenses		3,000			Stock Taken	500
	" C A/c :	Expenses		1,000				
	Profit :							
	A		3,400					
	C		1,700					
	P & L A/c		3,400	8,500				
				32,500				32,500

Dr. **Co-venturers' Account** Cr.

Date	Particulars	Amount A	Amount C	Date	Particulars	Amount A	Amount C
		Rs.	Rs.			Rs.	Rs.
?	To Joint Venture A/c :			?	By Joint Venture A/c :		
	Sale Proceeds	—	10,000		Materials	12,000	—
	Stock Taken	—	500		Expenses	3,000	1,000
	" Balance b/d	18,400	—		" Share of Profit	3,400	1,700
					" Balance c/d	—	7,800
		18,400	10,500			18,400	10,500
	To Balance c/d	—	7,800		" Balance b/d	18,400	—

In the books of C

Dr. **Joint Venture Account** Cr.

Date	Particulars			Amount	Date	Particulars		Amount
?				Rs.	?			Rs.
	To Bank A/c :	Expenses		1,000		By Bank A/c :	Sale Proceeds	10,000
	" A A/c :	Materials Purchased		12,000			Stock Taken	500
		Expenses		3,000		" B A/c :	Sale Proceeds	20,000
	" B A/c :	Materials Purchased		6,000			Stock Taken	2,000
		Expenses		2,000				
	" Profit :							
	A		3,400					
	B		3,400					
	P & L A/c		1,700	8,500				
				32,500				32,500

Dr. **Co-venturers' Account** Cr.

Date	Particulars	Amount A	Amount B	Date	Particulars	Amount A	Amount B
		Rs.	Rs.			Rs.	Rs.
	To Joint Venture A/c :				By Joint Venture A/c :		
	Sale Proceeds	—	20,000		Materials	12,000	6,000
	Stock Taken	—	2,000		Expenses	3,000	2,000
	" Balance c/d	18,400	—		" Share of Profit	3,400	3,400
					" Balance c/d	—	10,600
		18,400	22,000			18,400	22,000
	To Balance b/d	—	10,600		" Balance b/d	18,400	—

JOINT VENTURE WITH INTEREST CALCULATION

Calculation of Interest on Investment

Illustration 26

Ashim and Anup entered into a joint venture to buy and sell second hand T. V. sets. They shared profits and losses equally. It was agreed that interest @ 10% would be provided for the amount invested by the venturers in the venture.

On 1.8.2001 Ashim purchased 6 T.V. sets for Rs. 36,000 and paid Rs. 3,300 to the mechanic for repairing. He sold all the T. V. sets for Rs. 47,500 on 15.9.01.

On 1.9.01 Anup purchased 3 T.V sets at a cost of Rs. 18,300 and incurred Rs. 2,100 for repairing. He sold 2 T. V. sets for Rs. 16,400 on 25.11.01. The venture was closed 30.11.2001 and the T. V. set still unsold was taken over by Anup at cost plus 8%.

Prepare Memorandum Joint Venture account and the account of "Joint Venture with Anup" in the books of Ashim.

[CU BCom (Hons.) 2002]

Solution

Memorandum Joint Venture Account

Dr. Cr.

Date		Particulars	Amount	Amount	Date		Particulars	Amount	Amount
2001			Rs.	Rs.	2001			Rs.	Rs.
Aug. 1	To	Ashim : Cost of T.V.	36,000		Sept. 15	By	Ashim : Sales		
		Repairs	3,300	39,300			Proceed		47,500
Sept. 1	"	Anup : Cost T.V.	18,300		Nov. 25	"	Anup : Sales		
		Repairs	2,100	20,400			Proceed		16,400
Nov. 30	"	Ashim : Interest	491		Nov. 30	"	Anup : T.V. Sets		
		Anup : Interest	510	1,001[1]			Taken Over		7,344[2]
	"	Profit on Venture							
	"	Ashim $\frac{1}{2}$	5,272						
		Anup $\frac{1}{2}$	5,271	10,543					
				71,244					71,244

In the books of Ashim
Joint Venture Account

Dr. Cr.

Date		Particulars		Amount	Date		Particulars	Amount
2001				Rs.	2001			Rs.
Aug. 1	To	Bank A/c :	Cost of TV	36,000	Sept. 15	By	Bank A/c :	47,500
			Repairs	3,300			—Sale Proceeds	
Nov. 30	"	Interest A/c		491				
	"	Share of Profit		5,272				
	"	Bank A/c *(bal. fig.)*						
		—Final Settlement		2,437				
				47,500				47,500

Workings :

1. **Interest on Investment for Ashim**

On 1.8.2001 Invested Rs. 39,600 which he received on 15.9.2001 out of sale proceeds of 47,500.

So, Interest will be calculated for $1\frac{1}{2}$ months (i.e., from 1.8.2001 to 15.9.2001) :

∴ Interest will be Rs. 491 $\left(\text{i.e., Rs. } 39,600 \times \frac{10}{100} \times \frac{1\frac{2}{2}}{12}\right)$

2. **Valuation of Unsold Stock taken by Anup**

	Rs.
Total Cost for 3 Set =	20,400
∴ For one set = Rs. 20,400 ÷ 3 =	6,800
Add : Profit @ 8%	544
	7,344

For Anup

On. 1.9.200 Invested Rs. 20,400 which he received in part of Rs. 16,400 on 25.11.2001 i.e., 2 months 25 days, say 3 months.

∴ Interest = Rs. 16,400 × $\frac{10}{100} \times \frac{3}{12}$ = Rs. 410

Rest (Rs. 20,400 – Rs. 16,400) Rs. 4,000

For 3 month—

Interest = Rs. 4,000 × $\frac{10}{100} \times \frac{3}{12}$ = Rs. 100

Rs. 510

Interest on Investment, brokerage, Valuation of at unsold stock etc.

Illustration 27

M of Chennai and C of Kolkata entered into a Joint Venture of purchase and sale of Jute and Cotton. They agreed to share profits and losses in the ratio 3 : 2 and also to be entitled to an interest of 10% p.a. (on monthly basis) on Capital invested by each of them.

The following transactions took place :

On 1st July 1995, M purchased 800 bales of Cotton @ Rs. 424 per bale, the brokerage being Rs. 12,800 and despatched to C incurring Rs. 6,400 as freight and insurance.

On 15th July 1995, C purchased 1,200 bales of Jute @ Rs. 192 per bale, brokerage being Rs. 8 per bale and despatched to M incurring Rs. 4,800 as freight and insurance.

On 1st August 1995, C sold 300 bales of Cotton @ Rs. 576 per bale, brokerage being Rs. 16 per bale.

On 1st September 1995, C sold 450 bales of Cotton @ Rs. 580 per bale, brokerage being Rs. 12 per bale.

On 15th August 1995, M sold 400 bales of Jute @ Rs. 288 per bale, brokerage being Rs. 8 per bale and on 15th September 1995, sold 700 bales of Jute @ Rs. 292 per bale brokerage being Rs. 4 per bale. Each partner took unsold stock in his hand at cost plus $12\frac{1}{2}$% on 30th September 1995, on which date venture was closed. Show a Memorandum Joint Venture Account and the Account of M in the books of C and the Account of C in the books of M.

Solution **[CU BCom (Hons.)1994)]**

In the books of M and C
Memorandum Joint Venturer Account

Dr. Cr.

Date	*Particulars*	*Amount*	*Date*	*Particulars*	*Amount*
1995		Rs.	*1995*		Rs.
July 1	To M– Cost of 800 bales of Cotton with brokerage (400 × Rs. 424) + 12,800)	3,52,000	July 1	By M– Sale of Jute excluding brokerage : 400 bales (400 × Rs. 280 (288 – 8) 1,12,000; 700 bales (700 × Rs. 288 (291 – 4) 2,01,600	3,13,600
July 15	" C– Cost of 1,200 bales of Jutes withbrokerage (1,200 × Rs. 192) + (1,200 × 8)	2,40,000	Aug. 1	" C– Sale of Cotton excluding brokerage: 300 bales (300 × Rs. 560 (576 – 16) 1,68,000; 450 bales (450 × Rs. 568 (580– 12) 2,55,600	4,23,600
	" M– Freight and Insurance charges	6,400		" M– 100 bales of Jute unsold stock taken over	22,950[1]
	" C– Freight and Insurance charges	4,800	Sept.1	" C– 50 bales of Cotton taken over	25,200[2]
	" M– Interest on Capital invested	8,026[3]			
	" C– Interest on Capital invested	2,680[3]			
	" Share of Prrofit : M– Rs. 1,71,444 × $\frac{3}{5}$ = 1,02,866; C– Rs. 1,71,444 × $\frac{2}{5}$ = 68,578	1,71,444			
		7,85,350			7,85,350

In the books of M
Joint Venture with C

Dr. Cr.

Date	*Particulars*	*Amount*	*Date*	*Particulars*	*Amount*
1995		Rs.	*1995*		Rs.
July 1	To Bank A/c —Cost of 800 bales of cotton @ Rs. 424 each 3,39,200; *Add* : Brokerage 12,800	3,52,000	July 1	By Bank A/c —Sale of 400 bales of cotton @ Rs. 288 each 1,15,200; *Less* : Brokerage @ Rs. 8 per bale 3,200	1,12,000
	" Bank A/c —Freight and Insurance	6,400		Bank A/c —Sale of 700 bales of June	
	" Interest A/c	8,026			*Contd.*

To Share of Profit	1,02,866	By @ Rs. 292 each	2,04,000	
		Less : Brokerage &		
		Rs. 4 per bale	2,800	2,01,600
		" Unsold stock—100 bales of Jute		22,950
		" Bank A/c—Final remittance		1,32,742
	4,69,292			4,69,292

In the books of C

Dr. **Joint Venture with M** *Cr.*

Date		*Particulars*		*Amount*	*Date*		*Particulars*		*Amount*
1995				Rs.	*1995*				Rs.
July	To	Bank A/c —Cost of 1,200 bales of Jute @ Rs. 192 each	2,30,400		July	By	Bank A/c —Sale of 300 bales of cotton @ Rs. 576 each	1,72,800	
		Add : Brokerage	9,600	2,40,000			*Less :* Brokerage Rs. 16 per bale	4,800	1,68,000
	"	Bank A/c— Freight & Insurance		4,800		"	Bank A/c —Sale of 450 bales of cotton @ Rs. 580 each	2,61,000	
	"	Interest		2,680			*Less :* Brokerage Rs. 12 per bale	5,400	2,55,600
	"	Share of Profit		68,578		"	Unsold Stock —50 bales of Cotton		25,200
	"	Bank A/c —Final settlement		1,32,742					
				4,48,800					4,48,800

Workings :

1. Valuations of Unsold Stock taken by the venturer

Unsold Jute held by M

	Rs.
Total quantity (1,200 – 400 – 700) 100 bales @ Rs. 192 =	19,200
Add : Proportionate brokerage (100 × Rs. 8)	800
Add : Proportionate Freight and Insurance (Rs. $4,800 \times \frac{100}{1200}$)	400
Value at Cost	20,400
Add : Profit @ $12\frac{1}{2}$ % on Cost i.e., on Rs. 20,400 =	2,550
	22,950

2. Unsold Stock held by C

	Rs.
Total quantity (800 – 300 – 450) 50 bales @ Rs. 424 =	21,200
Add : Proportionate Brokerage (Rs. $12,800 \times \frac{50}{800}$)	800
Add : Proportionate Freight & Insurance (Rs. $6,400 \times \frac{50}{800}$)	400
Valued at Cost	22,400
Add : Profit @ $12\frac{1}{2}$ % on Cost i.e., on Rs. 22,400 =	2,800
	25,200

3. Interest on Capital Invested

For M:	Rs.	**For C**	Rs.
On 1.7.1995 : M invested (Rs. 3,39,200 + Rs. 12,800 + Rs. 6,400)	3,58,400	on 15.7.1995, C Invested (2,40,000 + 4,800)	2,44,800
15.8.1995 : Amount already realised from sale proceeds	1,12,000	On 1.8.1995 : Amount already realised from sale proceed	1,68,000
	2,46,400		76,800
on 15.9.1995 : Amount again realised	2,01,600	On 1.9.1995 : Amount again realised	2,55,600
Since Final settlement was made on 30.9.1995,		**Interest will be calculated as**	Rs.
Interest will be calculated as :		On Rs. 2,44,800 for 1 month (from 1.7.95 to 1.8.95) (Rs. $2,44,800 \times \frac{10}{100} \times \frac{1}{12}$)	2.040
On Rs. 3,58,400 for 2 months (from 1.7.95 to 31.8.95 = (Rs. $3,58,400 \times \frac{10}{100} \times \frac{1}{12}$)	5,973	On Rs. 76,800 for 1 month (from 1.8.95 to 1.9.95) (Rs. $76,800 \times \frac{10}{100} \times \frac{1}{12}$)	640

Contd.

	Rs.		Rs.
On rs. 2,46,400 for 1 month (from 1.9.95 to 30.9.95) $= (\text{Rs. } 2{,}46{,}400 \times \frac{10}{100} \times \frac{1}{12}) =$	2,053		
∴ Total amount of Interest	8,026		2,680

CONSIGNMENT-CUM-JOINT VENTURE

Sometimes the consignee is not satisfied simply by taking the commission as agent of the consignor. He wants to take part in profit instead on having commission. In that case, he requests the consignor to continue the business on a joint venture basis and working as a partner. This conversion from Consignment to Joint Venture may be made :

(i) from a particular date with prospective effect, and

(ii) with restrospective effect.

(i) Conversion from a particular date with Prospective effect

Under the circumstances the following procedure should carefully be followed:

(a) Open a Consignment Account and Consignee's Personal Account in the usual manner and ascertain the profit or loss so made which is to be transferred to Profit and Loss Account up to the date of conversion. Also ascertain the Consignee's balance up to the date of conversion.

(b) Open a Joint Venture Account (Following Method II) by taking up the stock on consignment (in the debit side) in the usual manner and ascertain the profit and loss which is to be shared between the parties.

(c) Open also Consignee's Personal Account by taking up the balance and record all the transactions relating to the joint venture as we usually do.

(d) Settle the Accounts.

The following illustrations will help us to understand the above principles clearly :

From Consignment to Joint Venture

Illustration 28

Sri Menon sent goods to Sri Gupta to be sold on consignment basis @ 5% commission. Goods costing Rs. 4,00,000 were sent and Rs. 40,000 expenses were incurred. Sri Gupta had to incur Rs. 10,000 expenses for landing and 75% of the goods were sold out for Rs. 4,80,000. So Gupta sent the amount due from him with the Account sale but wanted to return the balance goods as he was not agreeable to carry on as a commission agent. He was, however, persuaded to continue to joint venture basis. For one-third project, Rs. 2,00,000 worth of goods were further despatched by Sri Menon. All the goods (except Rs. 20,000 which were taken over by Sri Gupta for the same amount) were sold out for Rs. 5,00,000. Sri Menon incurred Rs. 20,000 expenses and expenses of Sri Gupta amounted to Rs. 17,000. Show the necessary accounts in the books of both the parties.

Solution

In the books of Menon

Dr. **Consignment to Gupta Account** *Cr.*

Date	*Particulars*	*Amount*	*Date*	*Particulars*	*Amount*
?		Rs.	?		Rs.
	To Goods Sent on Consignment A/c	4,00,000		By Gupta A/c — Sale Proceeds	4,80,000
	" Bank A/c (Expenses)	40,000		" Stock of Consignment A/c	1,12,500
	" Gupta A/c— Landing Charges	10,000		$\frac{25}{100}$ (4,00,000 + 40,000 + 10,000)	
	" Commission @ 5%	24,000			
	" Profit on Consignment —Transferred to P & L A/c	1,18,500			
		5,92,500			5,92,500

Dr. **Joint Venture with Sri Gupta Account** Cr.

Date	Particulars		Amount	Date	Particulars	Amount
?			Rs.	?		Rs.
	To Consignment to Sri Gupta A/c		1,12,500		By Gupta — Sale Proceeds	5,00,000
	" Goods Supplied		2,00,000		Gupta — Goods taken	20,000
	" Expenses		20,000			
	" Gupta —Expenses		17,000			
	" Profit on Venture :					
	Profit and Loss A/c $\frac{2}{3}$	1,13,667				
	Gupta $\frac{1}{3}$	56,833				
			1,70,500			
			5,20,000			5,20,000

Dr. **Sri Gupta Account** Cr.

Date	Particulars	Amount	Date	Particulars	Amount
?		Rs.	?		Rs.
	To Consignment to Sri Gupta A/c — Sale Proceeds	4,80,000		By Consignment to Sri Gupta — Expenses	10,000
				Commission	24,000
				" Bank — Remittance	4,46,000
		4,80,000			4,80,000
	To Joint Venture — Sale Proceeds	5,00,000		By Joint Venture — Expenses	17,000
	" Joint Venture — Goods taken	20,000		" Joint Venture — Share of Profit	56,833
				" Bank — Remittance	4,46,167
		5,20,000			5,20,000

In the books of Sri Gupta

Dr. **Joint Venture with Sri Menon Account** Cr.

Date	Particulars		Amount	Date	Particulars	Amount
?			Rs.	?		Rs.
	To Menon : Stock on Consignments		1,12,500		By Bank — Sale Proceeds	5,00,000
	Goods Supplied		2,00,000		" Goods taken	20,000
	Expenses		20,000			
	To Bank : Expenses		17,000			
	" Profit on Venture :					
	Profit and Loss A/c	56,833				
	Menon	1,13,667				
			1,70,500			
			5,20,000			5,20,000

Dr. **Sri Menon Account** Cr.

Date	Particulars	Amount	Date	Particulars	Amount
?		Rs.	?		Rs.
	To Landing Charges	10,000		By Bank — Sale Proceeds	4,80,000
	" Commission @ 5%	24,000			
	" Bank — Remittance	4,46,000			
		4,80,000			4,80,000
	To Bank — Remittance	4,46,167		" Joint Venture —	
				Stock on Consignment	1,12,500
				Goods Supplied	2,00,000
				Expenses	20,000
				Share of Profit	1,13,667
		4,46,167			4,46,167

Illustration 29

Debashish Poddar of Kolkata sent to Satish Roy of Guwahati goods costing Rs. 50,000 to be sold on consignment basis. Debashish Poddar incurred Rs. 5,000 for various expenses. Satish Roy incurred freight and clearing charges Rs. 4,000. Three-fourth of the goods were sold for Rs. 80,000 and the consignee Mr. Roy was entitled to a commission of 10% on gross sales. The consignee Mr. Roy remitted the amount due from him to the consignor Mr. Poddar immediately after sale along with the Account Sales.

Thereafter, Mr. Roy expressed his desire to return the goods still lying unsold at his hand as he was not agreeable to carry on or commission agency basis. He was, however, persuaded to continue on joint venture basis sharing profits and losses as Debashish Poddar $\frac{2}{3}$ and Sanjib Roy $\frac{1}{3}$.

Debashish Poddar then despatched another lot of goods costing Rs. 20,000. All the goods in possession of Sri Roy were sold for Rs. 44,000. Sri Poddar incurred Rs. 4,000 for various expenses whereas Sri Roy incurred Rs. 2,000 for freight and miscellaneous expenses.

Show the accounts in the books of Debashish Poddar.

Solution

In the books of Debashish Poddar

Consignment to Satish Roy Account

Dr. Cr.

Date	Particulars		Amount	Date	Particulars	Amount
?			Rs.	?		Rs.
	To Goods Sent on Consign.A/c		50,000		By Satish Roy A/c: —Sale Proceeds	80,000
	" Bank A/c (Expenses)		5,000		" Joint Venture with Satish Roy: Unsold Stock transferred: $\frac{1}{4}$ × Rs. 59,000 (50,000 + 5,000 + 4,000)	14,750
	" Satish Roy A/c: Freight etc.	4,000				
	Commission @ 10%	8,000	12,000			
	" Profit and Loss A/c: Profit on Consignment trans.		27,750			
			94,750			94,750

Satish Roy (Consignee) Account

Dr. Cr.

Date	Particulars	Amount	Date	Particulars		Amount
?		Rs.	?			Rs.
	To Consign. to Satish Roy A/c: —Sale Proceeds	80,000		By Consign. to Satish Roy A/c: Freight	4,000	
				Commission	8,000	12,000
				" Bank A/c *(bal. fig.)*		68,000
		80,000				80,000

Joint Venture with Satish Roy Account

Dr. Cr.

Date	Particulars	Amount	Date	Particulars	Amount
?		Rs.	?		Rs.
	To Consignment to Satish Roy A/c: Unsold Stock transferred	14,750		By Balance c/d	40,917
	" Bank A/c: Cost of Goods Sent	20,000			
	" Bank A/c: Expenses	4,000			
	" Profit ($\frac{2}{3}$ × Rs. 3,250)*	2,167			
		40,917			40,917

*Note: The profit (i.e., Rs. 3,250) can be ascertained by preparing Memorandum Joint Venture Account, i.e., Rs. (44,000 – 14,750 – 20,000 – 4,000 – 2,000) = Rs. 3,250.

(ii) Conversion with retrospective effect

Under the circumstances, we are to prepare accounts both under consignment basis as well as under joint venture basis in order to find out the amounts due to the other party as commission in the prior arrangement; and as share of profit in the latter case. Needless to mention here that if the other party gets more under the joint venture arrangement, the following entry should be passed:

Profit and Loss A/c Dr.

To Co-venturer's Personal A/c

In the opposite case, the entry will be reversed.

The following steps should carefully be followed for the purpose :

(i) Open a consignment account in the usual manner;
(ii) Ascertain the amount due and received by the consignee under consignment agreement;
(iii) Open a Joint Venture Account (Method II or III) in the usual manner bearing in mind that both of them were in business under joint venture basis;
(iv) Ascertain the amount due as co-venturer ;
(v) For the amount of difference, the above principles should be followed.

The following illustration will help us to understand the principles clearly.

Consignment-cum-Joint Venture

Illustration 30

On 1st January 2012, Singh of Amritsar, a manufacturer of sports goods, sent a consignment of 100 cricket bats to Bose of Kolkata to be sold on a consignment basis at a commission of 20%, such commission to cover the consignee's expenses but not the freight charges of the goods to Kolkata. The cost of each bat is Rs. 100 but is invoiced to Bose at Rs. 150 each. A case containing 10 cricket bats was lost against which the consignor lodged a claim and collected from the insurance company Rs. 800.

The consignee paid Rs. 540 as freight charges and spent a further sum of Rs. 400 as sales expenses. Consignor's expenses amounted to Rs. 500. The consignee accepted a bill of exchange drawn by Singh for 3 months (beginning with the date of despatch) for Rs. 10,000 which was discounted at 6% p.a. with the bankers. Bose sold 75 bats at Rs. 200 each and on 30th June 2012 remitted the balance due from him.

After making up the accounts on 30th June 2012, the parties decide to convert their relationship to that of a joint venture on the terms that the cost of a bat would be taken at Rs. 150. Singh to get an interest of 8% p.a. on his investment and Bose to get a commission of 10% on sales. The co-venturers are to share profits and losses equally.

Prepare the necessary accounts in the books of Singh and indicate the adjustment Journal entry required on conversion of the terms of despatch. The workings should form a part of your answer.

Solution

In the books of Singh

Consignment of Kolkata Account

Dr. Cr.

Date		Particulars	Amount	Date		Particulars	Amount
2012			Rs.	2012			Rs.
Jan. 1	To	Goods Sent on Consignment A/c (100 × Rs. 150)	15,000	June 30	By	Bose A/c — Sale Proceeds	15,000
	"	Bank A/c — Expenses	500		"	Goods Sent on Consignment A/c — Loading	5,000
June 30	To	Bose A/c — Freight	540		By	Abnormal Loss A/c	1,550[1]
	"	Abnormal Loss A/c — Loading	500		"	Stock on Consignment A/c	2,415[1]
	"	Stock Reserve A/c —Load on Closing Stock	750				
	"	Bose A/c — Commission	3,000				
	"	Profit and Loss A/c — Profit on Consignment trans.	3,675				
			23,965				23,965

Bose Account

Dr. Cr.

Date		Particulars	Amount	Date		Particulars	Amount
2012			Rs.	2012			Rs.
June 30	To	Consignment to Kolkata A/c —Sale Proceeds	15,000	June 30	By	Bills Receivable A/c	10,000
					"	Consignment to Kolkata A/c — Freight	540
						— Commission	3,000
					"	Bank A/c — Final Settlement	1,460
			15,000				15,000

Memorandum Joint Venture Account

Dr. Date	Particulars		Amount	Date	Particulars		Amount Cr.
2012			Rs.	2012			Rs.
	To Singh : A/c				By Bose :		
	— Goods Sent	15,000			— Sales		15,000
	— Expenses	500		"	Singh :		
	— Interest	600[2]			—Insurance Claim		800
			16,100	"	Unsold Stock (15 bats)		2,415
"	Bose :						
	— Freight	540		"	Loss on Venture :		
	— S. Expenses	400			Singh	163	
	— Commission	1,500			Bose	162	
			2,440				325
			18,540				18,540

Adjusting Journal Entry for Conversion

In the books of Singh
Journal

Date	Particulars		Dr. Rs.	Cr. Rs.
2012 June 15	Bose A/c	Dr.	1,262[3]	
	To Profit and Loss A/c			1,262
	(Adjustment made under new arrangement, i.e., Rs. 3,000 – Rs. 1,738)			

Workings :

1. Valuation of Abnormal loss and Unused Stock

	Rs.	Rs.
Total Invoice Price of 100 bats	15,000	
Add : Consignor's Expenses	500	
	15,500	
Less : Abnormal Loss $\frac{15{,}500 \times 10}{100}$	1,550	
	13,950	
Add : Non-recurring Expenses of Consignee		540
I. P. of 90 bats		14,490

∴ Value of Unsold Stock $\frac{\text{Rs. } 14{,}490 \times 15}{90}$ = Rs. 2,415.

2. Calculation of Interest

$$\text{Rs. } 15{,}000 \times \frac{8}{100} \times \frac{6}{12} = \text{Rs. } 600$$

3. Adjustments

	Rs.	Rs.
Amounts already received by Bose as Com.		**3,000**
Less : **Amounts due by Bose under new arrangement as co-venturer :**		
Commission	1,500	
Add : Selling Expenses	400	
	1,900	
Less : Loss on Venture	162	
		1,738

Note:

While preparing joint venture, abnormal loss is not taken into consideration and, at the same time, no stock reserve is necessary for joint venture purposes.

GENERAL ILLUSTRATIONS

Underwriting of Shares

Illustration 31

A and B entered into a Joint Venture as equal partners and guaranteed, as underwriters, the subscription at par of 10,00,000 shares of Re. 1 each of Madan Ltd. and to pay all expenses up to allotment in consideration of Madan Ltd. issuing to them 30,000 other shares of Re. 1 each, fully paid up, and, paying Rs. 20,000 in cash.

A introduced cash into the business to meet the following expenses: Stamp charges and Registration fees etc.— Rs. 5,000; Advertising charges—Rs. 2,000.

B, introduced cash to meet the following expenses: Printing charges of documents—Rs. 4,000; Solicitor's charges-Rs. 2,500; Rent—Rs. 550.

Applications fell short of 10,00,000 shares by 40,000 shares. A took up those shares on joint account in terms of their agreement with Madan Ltd. and himself paid for those shares.

Finally, Madan Ltd. handed over the shares and the Cash to A and B in full payment of the underwriting commission as per agreement. The Cash thus received was taken over by B. Out of the total 70,000 shares received by the venturers, 55,000 shares were sold out for Rs. 50,000 and the proceeds were taken by A and the rest of the shares were taken up by B at an agreed value of Rs. 12,000.

Prepare Memorandum Joint Venture A/c including necessary accounts in the boos of both the parties assuming that they settled their accounts by payment of cash.

[CU BCom Part I (Hons.) 1998]

Solution

Dr. **Memorandum Joint Venture Account** Cr.

Date	Particulars		Amount	Date	Particulars	Amount
?			Rs.	?		Rs.
	To A—Stamp Charges and Registration Fees		5,000		By A—Commission Received	20,000
	" A—Advertising Charges		2,000		" B—Sale of shares	50,000
	" B-Printing Charges of Documents		4,000		" —Shares taken over	12,000
	" Solicitor's Charges (B)		2,500			
	" B—Rent		500			
	" A—Cost of shares (A) 40,000 Re. 1)		40,000			
	" Profit on Venture:					
	A $(\frac{1}{2})$	14,000				
	B $(\frac{1}{2})$	14,000	28,000			
			82,000			82,000

In the books of A

Dr. **Joint Venture with B** Cr.

Date	Particulars	Amount	Date	Particulars	Amount
?		Rs.	?		Rs.
	To Bank A/c			By Bank A/c	50,000
	" Stamp Charges & Registration Fees	5,000		" —Sale Proceeds of Shares Received	
	" Advertising Charges	2,000			
	" Cost of Shares	40,000		" Cash A/c (Balance Received)	11,000
	" Profit & Loss A/c (Profit)	14,000			
		61,000			61,000

In the books of B

Dr. **Joint Venture with A** Cr.

Date	Particulars	Amount	Date	Particulars	Amount
?		Rs.	?		Rs.
	To Bank A/c			By Bank A/c (Commission Received)	20,000
	" Printing Charges of Documents	4,000			
	" Solicitor's Charges	2,500		" Purchases A/c (Shares taken over)	12,000
	" Rent	500			
	" Profit and Loss A/c (Profit)	14,000			
	" Cash A/c (Balance remitted)	11,000			
		32,000			32,000

Underwriting of shares, Interest on bank Loan, etc.

Illustration 32

Gopal and Gopi, who are sharebrokers, agree to enter into a joint venture to underwrite 5,00,000 Equity shares of Rs. 10 each of a new floatation of X Ltd. X Ltd. agrees to allot them fully paid 4,000 shares in the company in consideration of the underwriting arrangement. The parties are to share profits and losses equally.

In connection with the venture Gopal paid printing and stationery Rs. 5,000, postage Rs. 1,000 and advertisement Rs. 3,000 while Gopi paid postage Rs. 750, solicitor's fees Rs. 3,500 and entertainment expenses Rs. 4,000. The public subscription was for 4,80,000 shares only and the underwriters were forced to take up the balance and pay for them. To enable themselves to do so, Gopal approached the New

Bank of India, which, on the security of the shares, advanced the required sum on 1st July 2002 at 15% interest per annum. The underwriters paid for the shares on the same day and were also allotted the 4,000 shares by X Ltd. as per agreement. The underwriters, through the bank, sold their entire holding in the market in equal lots and realised 90% of the face value for the first lot on 30th September and 85% for the second lot on 31st October 2002. The sale proceeds were applied in full discharge of the bank loan and accrued interest thereon on the same dates. Share transfer fees of Rs. 1,000 were met. You are required to show a Joint Venture Account only.

Solution

Dr. **Joint Venture Account** *Cr.*

Date	*Particulars*	*Amount*	*Date*	*Particulars*		*Amount*
		Rs.				Rs.
?	To Gopal : Printing and Stationery	5,000	?	By Sale of Shares		2,10,000[1]
	: Postage	1,000		" Loss on venture		
	: Advertisement	3,000		" Gopal	8,497	
	" Gopal : Postage	750		Gopi	8,497	16,994
	Solicitor's fees	3,500				
	Entertainment Exps.	4,000				
	Cost of Shares	2,00,000				
	Share Transfer Fees	1,000				
	" Interest on Bank Loan	8,744[2]				
		2,26,994				2,26,994

Workings :

1. **Sale of Shares**

	No. of Shares
Purchased	20,000
Received Commission	4,000
	24,000

∴ Sold equally in each lost 24,000 ÷ 2
= 12,000 Shares.

	Rs.
1st 12,000 × Rs. 9 (i.e., 90% of Rs. 10) =	1,08,000
2nd Lot 12,000 × Rs. 8.50 (i.e., 85% of 10) =	1,02,000
	2,10,000

2 **Interest on Bank Loan**

	Rs.
Total Loan for purchasing Shares	2,00,000
	Rs.
Interest (for July, Aug., Sept.) @ 15% $= \text{Rs. } 2{,}00{,}000 \times \frac{15}{100} \times \frac{3}{12} =$	7,500
Add : **Interest of Rest of Loan** Sale proceeds on 30th Sept. amount to (Rs. 1,08,000 – Rs. 7,500) 1,00,500 Rest loan (Rs. 2,00,000 – Rs. 1,00,500) Rs. 1,00,500 = Rs. 99,500 for 1 month $\therefore \text{Rs. } 99{,}500 \times \frac{15}{100} \times \frac{1}{12} =$	1,244
	8,744

ASSIGNMENT MATERIALS

THEORETICAL

Multiple Choice Questions

1. (a) **Joint Bank Account is opened where:**
(i) Separate set of book is maintained; (ii) No separate set of book is maintained; (iii) Where Memorandum Joint Venture account is opened.

(b) When goods are supplied by the co-venturers:
(i) Joint Venture Account will be debited; (ii) Venturer's Capital Account are to be debited; (iii) Purchase Account will be debited.

(c) When goods are purchased:
(i) Joint Venture Account is debited; (ii) Purchased Account is debited; (iii) Personal Account is debited.

(d) Joint Venture is a :
(i) Temporary Partnership; (ii) Permanent Partnership; (iii) None of these.

(e) In Joint Venture firm name is—
(i) Necessary; (ii) Not necessary; (iii) Both.

[Ans. (a) (i); (b) (i); (c) (i); (d) (i); (e) (ii).]

Short-Answer-Type Questions

2. What is underwriting of share? How do you treat the same in Joint Venture?
3. Mention any three differences between Joint Venture and Partnership.
4. Mention any four differences between Joint Venture and Consignment.
5. How do you treat abnormal loss in Joint Venture?
6. What is Consignment-cum-Joint Venture?
7. How do you treat unsold stock in Joint Venture?
8. Mention any five characteristies of Joint Venture.

Long-Answer-Type Question

9. Distinguish between Consignment and Joint Venture.
10. State the characteristies of Joint Venture.
11. Distinguish between Joint Venture and Partnership.
12. What is Memorandum Joint Venture Account? How is it prepared?
13. Discuss the role of normal loss and abnormal loss in Joint Venture.
14. What is Consignment-cum-Joint Venture? How is the conversion made?
15. How do you treat the value of unsold stock?

PRACTICAL

Where separates set of books is maintained

1. Mono and Anasua entered into a Joint Venture and agreed to share profits and losses in the ratio of 2 : 3. They opened a Joint Bank Account in which Mono and Anasua contributed Rs. 8,000 and Rs. 10,000, respectively.

They purchased 10 condemned television sets at Rs. 1,500 each. They met the reconditioning cost of Rs. 3,000 from the Joint Bank Account. Carriage and other expenses of Rs. 2,000 were borne by Anasua. Anasua received a cheque of Rs. 1,000 from Mono. Nine sets were sold @ Rs. 2,500 each and the rest was taken over by Ansasua at cost.

Prepare the Joint Venture Account, Joint Bank Account, and close the accounts of the ventures.

[Ans. Profit on Venture Rs. 4,500; Final payment to Mono Rs. 10,800, Anasua Rs. 11,700]

2. R and S undertook jointly to build a house for a company for an agreed price of Rs. 60,000 payable Rs. 45,000 in cash and the balance in fully paid shares of the company. A joint bank account was opened in their names into which R paid Rs. 15,000 and S paid Rs. 10,000. Profit-sharing ratio being 3 : 2.

From the following transactions prepare necessary accounts in the books of R and S:

Materials purchased Rs. 20,000, Wages paid Rs. 15,000. Materials supplied by R Rs. 3,000. Materials supplied by S Rs.2,500. Arrchitect's fees paid by S. Rs. 1,000.

The joint venture was closed 50% of the shares were sold at Rs. 8,000 and the balance were taken over by A and B equally at an agreed valuation of R. 4,000.

[Ans. Profit on Joint Venture Rs. 15,500]

3. Ram and Ravan are carrying on a business as contractors. They jointly taken up the work of constructing a building of Mr. Bose at an agreed price of Rs. 5,00,000, payable Rs. 3,00,000 in cash and Rs. 2,00,000 in fully paid shares of a Company. A bank account is opened in which Ram and Ravan paid Rs. 3,00,000 and Rs. 75,000, respectively.

The following costs were incurred in completing the construction: (a)Salary paid Rs. 1,00,000. (b) Materials purchased, Rs. 2,00,000. (c) Materials supplied by Ram from the stock of his own business, Rs. 50,000. (d) Engineer's fees paid by Ravan Rs. 10,000.

The contract price was duly received. The accounts of the venture were closed; Ram taking up all the shares at an agreed valuation of Rs. 1,70,000 and Ravan taking up the unused stock of materials at Rs. 15,000.

Prepare necessary accounts in the Ledger of the venture assuming that a separate set of books are maintained for this purpose and that the net result of the same is shared by Ram and Ravan in the ratio of 3 : 2.

[Ans. Profit on Joint Venture Rs. 1,25,000]

4. In 2012, A and B entered into a joint venture to product a publicity film for A Co. The contract price of the film was Rs. 1,50,000. On the same day, they opened a joint banking account towards which A contributed Rs. 50,000 and B contributed Rs. 30,000. A & Co. Ltd. made an advance payment of Rs. 25,000 in cash of which Rs. 13,000 were put into the joint banking account and the balance was taken by B for purchase of raw film. The expenses of the joint venture were as:

	Rs.	
Purchase of Raw film	60,000	(of which Rs. 15,000 were paid by A personally)
Remuneration of the artists	25,000	(of which Rs. 5,000 were paid by B personally)
Remuneration of technical staff	18,000	
Other production expenses	12,000	

Except Rs. 15,000 and Rs. 5,000 paid by A and B, respectively, as indicated above, all expenses were paid out of joint banking account.

The film was completed on 30.9.2012 and delivered to A & Co. Ltd. on the same day. The stock of unused raw film was valued at Rs. 10,000 and was taken over by A.

A & Co. Ltd. were not satisfied with the film and asked the producer to reduce the price. A and B agreed to accept 20% less than the contract price. On 30.10.2012, A & Co. Ltd. paid their dues. On 5.11.2012, the Joint Bank account was closed, and A and B were paid the balance standing to the credit of their accounts. They had agreed to share profit and loss in proportion to their initial contribution.

Show the ledger accounts recording all the above transactions in the books of the Joint Venture.

[Ans. Profit on Joint Venture Rs. 15,000]

5. B and W entered into a joint venture paying Rs. 3,000 and Rs. 5,000, respectively, in a Joint Bank Account and sharing profits and losses in the proportion of 3 : 2, respectively. It was agreed that the Joint Bank Account is to be used for purchase and sales while each venturer is to meet his joint venture expenses out of his private funds. Each venture is to charge commission at 5% on sales made by him.

The transactions for the year ended 31.12.2002 were:

B purchased 80 tonnes of wheat at Rs. 60 per tonnes and his expenses were Rs. 300. W sold 60 tonnes of that wheat at Rs. 75 and his expenses were Rs. 200.

W purchased 10 tonns of sugar for Rs. 2,100 and his expenses were Rs. 100. B sold 8 tonns of that sugar for Rs. 1,900 and his expenses were Rs. 150.

Write up the Joint Venture Account, Joint Bank Account and the Personal Accounts of the venturers for 2002. Also prepare the Balance Sheet as at 31.12.2002 for the joint venture.

[Ans. Profit on Joint Venture Rs. 245; Balaram Sheet Rs. 9,215]

Where no separate set of books is maintained

6. A and B enter into a joint ventue agreeing to share the profits and losses as $\frac{3}{4}$th and $\frac{1}{4}$th, repectively. On 1.1.2010, A sent Rs. 40,000 to B. B purchases several varieties of goods and sends them to A. The particulars of such purchases : 2,000 shirts @ Rs. 20 each—Rs. 40,000; 1,000 cotton trousers @ Rs. 10 each—Rs. 10,000; 400 track suits @ Rs. 20 each—Rs. 8,000. The expenses paid by B amounted to Rs. 400. A sold the first variety for Rs. 70,000, the second for Rs. 25,000 and the third for Rs. 10,000. His expenses were Rs. 1,000. Moreover, as per agreement. A is to receive a commission of 2% of the sales effected by him.

Show the Joint Venture Account and the Account of B in the books of A.

[Ans. Profit on Venture Rs. 43,500; Balance due from A to B Rs. 29,275]

Memorandum Joint Venture Account

7. Shipra of Siliguri and Balaram of Mumbai entered intp a joint venture with the object of buying and selling tea. Shipra agreed to arrange the purchase and Balaram to effect sales. They agreed to share profits and losses in the ratio of 2 : 1.

Shipra purchased 100 boxes of tea at Rs. 1,500 per box subject to 10% trade discount and paid freight Rs. 3,500 and insurance Rs. 500.

Balaram remitted Rs. 45,000 to Shipra towards joint venture. He took delivery of the goods at Mumbai and paid Rs. 350 for cartage. He sold 95 boxes of tea for Rs. 1,90,000 and kept 5 boxes for himself at an agreed value of Rs. 9,500. His other expenses were; godown rent Rs. 150 and insurance charges Rs. 75. They decided to settle their accounts by sending bank draft.

Prepae Memorandum Joint venture Account and the accounts as they would apper in the ledger of each of the two parties.

[Ans. Profit on Venture Rs. 59,925; Final payment by Balaram to Shipra Rs. 1,33,950]

8. B of Mumbaii and C of Kaalkata enter into a joint venture to consign scrap-iron to A of Agra, to be sold on their risk. They share profits or losses equally. A is entitled to a commission of 10% of the net proceeds after charging such commission.

B sends 50 tonnes serah-ironcosting Rs. 4,300 per tonne and pays freight and other expenses of Rs. 30,000, C sends 70 tonnes costing Rs. 5,000 per tonne and pays freight and other expenses of Rs. 40,000.

All the scraps are sold by A @ Rs. 10,000 per tonne and he pays selling expenses of Rs. 12,000. He remits Rs. 5,00,000 to B and the balance of the net proceeds to C by bank draft.

You are required (a) to show the account in the books of B and C to record their own transactions, and (b) to prepare a Memorandum Joint Venture Account.

[Ans. Profit on Venture Rs. 44,500; Final Payment made by B to C Rs. 32,500. Commission Rs. 1,08,000]

9. Success and Sincere agree to enter into a joint venture to buy and sell Television sets. Profits and Losses were to be divided as 2 : 1.

On 3rd May 2011, Success purchased three T. V. sets for Rs. 3,600, Rs. 4,100 and Rs. 4,400, respectively. He bought a special cabinet costing Rs. 800 which he fixed for one of the sets, the old cabinet was not re-useable. On 31st May 2011 he sold two of the sets for Rs. 4,500 each, paying the proceeds into his private bank account.

On 15th June 2011 he sold the other set for Rs. 5,000 which amount he paid over to Sincere who paid it into his bank account.

On 4th May 2011, Sincere purchased a T.V. set for Rs. 2,600, having incurred expenditure of Rs. 300 on repairing, sold it on 12th May 2011 for Rs. 3,500, paying the proceeds into his bank account. This set developed mechanical trouble and, on 25th May 2011, Sincere agreed to take the set back at a price of Rs. 2,800 which he paid out of his bank account. The set was still unsold at 30th June 2011 and it was agreed that Sincere should take it over for his personal use at a valuation of Rs. 2,700. Other expenses incurred by Success was Rs. 400 and by Sincere was Rs. 170.

Success paid into his bank net receipt of Rs. 200 in respect of commission given by the manufacturer.

On 1st July 2011, the sum required in full settlement as between Success and Sincere was paid by the party accountable.

You are required to prepare (a) Memorandum Joint Venture Account, and (b) the account of joint venture with Success as it would appear in the books of Sincere.

[Ans. Profit on Venture Rs. 1,230]

Underwriting Shares

10. M and N decided to work in partnership with the following scheme, agreeing to share profit as under : M$\frac{3}{4}$, N$\frac{1}{4}$.

They guaranteed the subscription at par of 10,00,000 shares of Re. 1 each in S. Ltd. and to pay all expenses up to allotment in consideration of S. Ltd. issuing to them 50,000 other shares of Re. 1 each, fully paid.

M and N introduced cash as :

		Rs.
M—	Stamp Charges etc.	4,000
	Advertising Charges	3,000
	Printing Charges etc.	3,000
N—	Rent	2,000
	Solicitor's Charges	3,000

Applications fell short of the 10,00,000 shares by 30,000 shares and N introduced Rs. 30,000 for the purchase of those shares. The guarantee having been fulfilled, S Ltd. handed over the venturers 50,000 shares. All their holdings were subsequently sold by the venturer, N receiving Rs. 18,000 and M

Rs. 50,000. Write-up necessary accounts in the books of both the parties on the presumption that Memorandum Joint Venture Account is opened for the purpose.

[Ans. Profit on Joint Venture Rs. 23,000]

11. X Ltd. is a finance company which argeed to take a half-interest in a syndicate formed to underwrite a public issue of 80,000 shares of Rs. 10 each at par in Y Ltd. The syndicate was to receive a commission on issue of $2\frac{1}{2}$% in cash, $2\frac{1}{2}$% in fully paid other shares in the company and to be responsible for all expenses connected with the issue up to the date of allotment.

Rs. 25,000 was advanced to the syndicate by X Ltd. towards the finance of the venture. Subscriptions were received from the public for 50,000 shares in Y Ltd. and the syndicate took up the balance. The syndicate incurred expenses in connection with the issue amounting to Rs. 7,900 and, in addition, were charged Rs. 1,500 by X Ltd. for clerical services supplied.

The shares belonging to the syndicate were sold (with the exception of 5,000 shares) at an average price of Rs. 9.50 per share; and, by agreement, X Ltd. took over the balance of 5,000 shares at Rs. 9 per share. You are asked to prepare an Account showing the Profit or Loss of the syndicate in connection with the venture, and to show, by means of Journal entries, how the transactions, so far as they affect X Ltd., would appear in that company's books.

[Ans. Profit on Venture Rs. 12,100; Balance due to the syndicate Rs. 12,450]

Miscellaneous

12. D of Delhi and B of Mumbai entered into joint venture for the purpose of buying and selling second-hand typewriters. B to make purchases and D to effect sales. The profit and loss was to be shared equally by D and B. A sum of Rs. 15,000 was remitted by D towards the venture.

B purchased 20 old typewriters for Rs. 15,000 and paid Rs. 9,000 for their reconditioning and sent them to Delhi. His other expenses were: buying commission Rs. 1,000; cartage Rs. 200, and other expenses Rs. 100.

D took delivery of the typewriters and paid Rs. 270 for octroi and Rs. 100 for cartage. He sold 12 typewriters at Rs. 2,200 each; 4 typewriters at Rs. 2,100 each and 3 typewriters at Rs. 2,000 each. He retained the remaining typewriter for his personal use at an agreed value of Rs. 1,500. His other expenses were: Insurance Rs. 250; Rent Rs. 400, Brokerage Rs. 1,200 and Miscellaneous expenses Rs. 200.

Each party's ledger contains a record of his own transactions on joint account.

Prepare a statement showing the result of the venture and the account of the venture in D's ledger as it will finally appear, assuming that the matter was finally settled between the parties.

[Ans. Profit on Joint Venture Rs. 43,580]

13. On 1st January 2012, Singh of Amritsar, a manufacturer of sports goods, sent a consignment of 100 Cricket bats to Bose of Kolkata to be sold on a consignment basis at a commission of 20%, such commission to cover the consignee's expenses but not the freight charges of the goods to Kolkata . The cost of each bat is Rs. 100 and invoiced to Bose at Rs. 150 each. A case containing 10 Cricket bats was lost against which the consignor lodged a claim and collected from the insurance company Rs. 800. The consignee paid Rs. 540 as freight charges and spent a further sum of Rs. 400 as sales expenses. The consignor's expenses amounted to Rs. 500. The consignee accepted a bill of exchange drawn by Singh for 3 months (being with the date of despatch) for Rs. 10,000 which was discounted at 6% p.a. with the bankers. Bose sold 75 bats at Rs. 200 each and on 30th June 2012 remitted the balance due from him.

After making up the accounts on 30th June 2012, the parties decide to convert their relationship to that of a Joint Venture on the terms that the cost of a bat would be taken at Rs. 150. Singh to get an interest at 8% p.a. on his investment and Bose to get a commission of 10% on sales. Ventures are to share profit & losses equally close the books of the firm.

[Ans. Profit on Consignment Rs. 3,675; Abnormal Loss Rs. 1,550; Unsold Stock Rs. 2,415; Stock Reserve for Consignment Rs. 750; Loss on Joint Venture Rs. 325]

CHAPTER 21

MANUFACTURING ACCOUNT AND ELEMENTS OF COST

Learning Objectives

Meaning

Analysis of Total Cost

—Direct Material

—Direct Labour

—Direct/Chargeable Expenses

—Overhead

—Production Overhead

—Office and Administration Overhead

—Selling and Distribution Overhead

Difference between Manufacturing Account and Trading Account

Manufacturing Profit

Unrealised Profit on Closing Stock

Elements of Cost/Cost Sheet

Objects of preparing Cost Sheet

Introduction

A manufacturing unit usually prepares its final accounts in the form of a Manufacturing Account, a Trading and Profit and Loss Account and a Balance Sheet at the end of a specified period. The purpose for which the Manufacturing Account is prepared is to ascertain the cost of product of the goods produced and/or manufactured. The expenses relating to the factory will be transferred to this account. Here, expenses are classified into two groups, viz., Direct or Chargeable, and Indirect or Factory. Direct Expenses constitute raw materials consumed, plus all direct expenses, the total of which represents Prime Cost. But Indirect Expenses, on the other hand, include all expenses relating to factory.

But before highlighting further about the Manufacturing Account, it becomes necessary to explain the analysis of total cost. Because, a part of total cost appears in the Manufacturing Account in the form of Prime Cost and Factory/Work Cost.

Analysis of Total Cost

The total cost of a product which is incidental to production, administration, selling and distribution, may be analysed as:

(a) **Direct Materials**
(b) **Direct Wages**
(c) **Direct/Chargeable Expenses**

} Constitute **Prime Cost**

(d) **Overhead :**

- (i) Production — i.e., Indirect — relating to factory expenses;
- (ii) Office and Administration; and
- (iii) Selling and Distribution.

Needless to mention here that, items (a), (b) and (c) constitute **Prime Cost**. With Prime Cost, if indirect expenses/factory expenses are added, we get ***Factory/Work Costs***. Similarly, with Factory Cost, if we add the Office and Administrative expenses, we get **Cost of Production**. In the same manner, if selling and distribution expenses are added to the cost of production, we get ***Total Cost or Cost of Sales.***

It is interesting to point out that the first two types of cost will appear in the Manufacturing Account (viz., Prime Cost and Factory Cost.) The other types of Cost (viz., Office and Administration, and Selling and Distribution) are associated with the total cost or Cost of Sales while preparing Cost Sheet. But all of them are discussed hereunder although the last two parts are required for the next part of our discussion. However, the above components of cost are described :

(a) Direct Materials

Direct materials are those materials which form a part of the product, the cost of which are entirely charged to prime cost, i.e., it is the material which can be charged directly to the cost of the product. However, the following groups of materials fall within this category :

(i) All materials which are specially purchased for a particular job; (ii) All materials acquired and requisitioned from the store for a particular product; (iii) Materials passing from one process to another; and (iv) Primary packing materials.

In short, it includes prime cost materials, processing materials, production materials, store materials etc. The following items will be added to the invoice price of the materials :

Import Duties, Dock charges, Transport of materials, Storing of materials; Cost of purchasing and Receiving materials; Cost of rectifying materials etc.

In this connection, it may be mentioned here that consumption of direct materials is calculated as :

		Rs.
	Raw Materials (Opening)	***
Add :	Purchases of Raw Materials	***
		***†
Less :	Raw Materials (Closing)	***
	Material Consumed	***

† Items like Carriage Inwards, Import Duty etc. may be added to this figure or may separately be shown.

(b) Direct Wages

Direct wages are paid for construction or composition or conformation or condition of the product produced by a firm. Direct labour (wages) cost can easily be identified with a particular product, process, job etc. and, as such, this can easily be charged. Direct labour cost includes cost for:

(i) Labourers engaged/employed on the actual production work of a particular product, e.g., machine operator.

(ii) Labourers specially engaged/employed for producing a particular product or rendering services e.g., foreman.

(iii) Labourers engaged/employed on the actual work of rendering a service, e.g.; driver in the case of transport services.

In addition to the above, the services of the following persons will be treated as Direct Wages; e.g., general labour, foremen, chargehands, shop clerks, etc.

It should be remembered that while considering the amount of direct wages, ***accrual basis of accounting should be considered***. In short, outstanding wages or prepaid wages, if any, should be adjusted accordingly.

(c) Direct Expenses

Direct expenses are those which are directly incurred on a specific cost unit, i.e., they can easily be charged directly. In other words, direct expenses include any expenditure other than direct materials or direct labour directly connected with prime cost. Such expenses are charged directly to the particular cost account as a part of the prime cost. They are also called chargeable expenses. Direct expenses include :

(i) Hire charges paid for special tools/equipment/plant for a particular production order on product;

(ii) Cost of special layout, designer drawings, patterns, etc., which are required for a specific work order or job, etc.;

(iii) Maintenance Cost of such (i) equipment;

(iv) Travelling expenses relating to the receipt of a specific job;

(v) Experimental cost relating to a specific project;

(vi) Royalties paid directly, etc.; and

(vii) Fees or remuneration paid to the architect/surveyors, etc. relating to the specific work order, etc.

(d) Overhead

The above three elements of cost constitute prime cost and all expenses other than the prime cost are known as overhead. In other words, overheads are all expenses other than direct expenses. It may be recalled that Prime Cost plus Production/Indirect/Factory overhead constitute Factory/Works Cost.

Overhead may be sub-divided into :

(i) Production Overhead; (ii) Office and Administration Overhead; and (iii) Selling and Distribution Overhead.

(i) Production Overhead

Production overhead takes all indirect expenditure which are incurred by a firm from the receipt of order to the despatch of the product after completion to the customers. It may be repeated again that any expenses which are not taken into account as direct are known as overhead. Production overhead is also called factory overhead or works overhead. Production overhead includes :

(i) Indirect Material; (ii) Indirect Wages; (iii) Rent, Rates and Insurance (other than Office and Administration and Selling and Distribution); (iv) Power; (v) Depreciation; and (vi) Miscellaneous/ Sundry expenses.

From the discussion made so far, the same is related to Manufacturing Account. The other parts of cost are related to cost sheet which are also discussed subsequently. Although the following overheads are not related to the Manufacturing Account, they are explaind below for the interest of preparing a cost sheet.

(ii) Office and Administration Overhead

Office and Administration overhead consists of all expenses which are incurred in the direct control and administration including accounting, secretarial and financial control of a firm. In other words, it relates to all indirect expenses which are incurred in relation to:

(i) direction, administration and control of operation; (ii) accounting, secretarial, financial, legal activities etc. (iii) formulation of basic policies.

Thus, Office and Administration overhead includes :

Expenses in running the general office (e.g., office rent, light, heat, salaries of staff, secretary, accountants etc., general manager, director, executives, bank charges, legal charges and miscellaneous fixed expenses.)

(iii) Selling and Distribution Overhead

The cost which is incurred in publicising and presenting to customers the product of the firm in attractive form at acceptable price along with the costs of all relevant research work, securing of order, delivery of the goods to the customers etc. is known as selling and distribution cost. It may be mentioned here that selling cost is that portion of selling overhead which is incurred in securing orders. It includes :

Salaries and Commission of sales, managers, travellers and agents, Godown Rent, Storage, training of salesmen, the cost of preparing tenders, technical advice to customers, etc.

Now we are going to highlight again the concept and application of Manufacturing Account.

A Manufacturing Account may be represented as under :

Items which appear in the debit side of a Manufacturing Account.

(i) Raw Materials consumed i.e., Raw Materials (opening) + Purchases of Raw Materials – Raw Materials (closing).

(ii) Direct Wages (i.e., Manufacturing Wages).

(iii) Chargeable Expenses (i.e., expenses relating to manufacture of goods).
The total of all the above three items are known as 'Prime Cost'.

(iv) Indirect/Factory Expenses (i.e., fuel, power, Indirect Wages, factory light, rent, etc);

(v) Work-in-Progress (opening) to be added;

(vi) Work-in-Progress (closing) should appear on the credit side (but it is customary to show the Work-in-Progress (closing) by way of a deduction from the total Indirect/Factory expenses).

The cost of production or cost of goods manufactured which will be ascertained from Manufacturing Account is to be transferred to Trading Account.

It has already been highlighted earlier that the Manufacturing Account is prepared in order to ascertain the cost of goods produced or manufactured. If the manufacturer desires to know the profit or loss on manufacture, this account will help him know whether it would be more profitable to manufacture the articles or purchase the same from outside. The manufacturing profit so ascertained is to be transferred to Profit and Loss Account.

The outline of a Manufacturing Account is presented :

Manufacturing Account
for the year ended ....

Dr. *Cr.*

	Particulars	*Amount*	*Amount*	*Particulars*	*Amount*
		Rs.	Rs.		Rs.
To	Raw Materials (Opening)	* *		By Trading Account	
Add :	Purchases of raw materials	* *		—transferred	* *
		* *			
Less :	Raw Materials (closing)	* *			
	Material Consumed		* *		
"	Direct Wages		* *		
"	Chargeable Expenses		* *		
	Prime Cost		* *		
	Indirect/Factory Expenses :				
	Fuel and Power	* *			
	Indirect Wages	* *			
	Factory light, rent				
	Insurance etc.	* *			
		* *			
Add :	Work-in-Progress (opening)	* *			
		* *			
Less :	Work-in-Progress (closing)	* *	* *		
	Factory/Works Cost		* *		* *

Illustration 1

From the following particulars presented by Mazumdar Bros. prepare a Manufacturing Account for the year ended 31.12.2011 :

	Rs.		Rs.
Opening Stock :		Factory Rent	4,000
Raw Materials	3,000	Repairs to Plant	2,000
Work-in-Progress	4,000	Repairs to Factory	1,000
Finished goods	8,000	Supervisor's Salary	8,000
Closing Stock :		Salaries of Works Staff	3,000
Raw Materials	1,000	Wages of Durwan	1,000
Work-in-Progress	5,000	Royalties on production	2,000
Finished goods	4,000	Works Manager's Salary	6,000
Purchases of Raw Materials	40,000		
Wages of Workers	20,000		
Light, Gas etc. (factory)	2,000		
Carriage Inwards	1,000		
Hire of Special Plant	2,000		

Solution

In the books of Mazumdar Bros.

Manufacturing Account *for the year ended 31st December 2011*

Dr. *Cr.*

Particulars	*Amount* Rs.	*Amount* Rs.	*Particulars*	*Amount* Rs.	*Amount* Rs.
To *Raw Materials consumed :*			By Trading A/c (Cost of production transferred)		93,000
Raw Materials (Opening)	3,000				
Purchases	40,000				
	43,000				
Less : Raw Materials (Closing)	1,000				
	42,000				
Add : Carriage Inwards	1,000				
		43,000			
Wages		20,000			
Chargeable Expenses :					
Hire of Special Plant	2,000				
Royalty on Production	2,000				
		4,000			
Prime Cost		67,000			
Factory Expenses :					
Light, Gas, etc.	2,000				
Factory Rent	4,000				
Repairs to Plant	2,000				
Repairs to Factory	1,000				
Supervisor's Salary	8,000				
Salary of Works Staff	3,000				
Wages of Durwan	1,000				
Works Manager's Salary	6,000				
	27,000				
Add : Work-in-Progress (Opening)	4,000				
	31,000				
Less : Work-in-Progress (Closing)	5,000				
		26,000			
Factory Cost		93,000			93,000

Note : Finished goods (both opening and closing) are not to be considered while preparing Manufacturing Account.

Differences between Manufacturing Account and Trading Account

Manufacturing Account	*Trading Account*
1. This account is prepared and maintained by a manufacturer.	1. This account is prepared and maintained by a trader.
2. It reveals the factory cost of goods produced or manufactured during the accounting period.	2. It reveals the result of the trained activities, i.e., gross profit or gross loss during the accounting period.
3. The balance of this account is transferred to Trading Account.	3. The balance of this account represents either gross profit or gross loss which is transferred to Profit and Loss Account.
4. Opening Stock and Closing Stock of finished goods are not at all considered while preparing this account.	4. This account incorporates both opening and closing stock of finished goods.
5. This account does not reveal the results of the manufacturing unit, i.e., profit or loss, until they are separately valued for such purposes.	5. It reveals the result of trading, i.e., profit or loss.

Note : Although the preparation of Trading Account has separately been highlighted in the subsequent chapter under the *"Final Accounts of Trading Concerns"*, the students are advised to consider the following subsequent problems after going through the said chapter.

Manufacturing Account and Trading Account

Illustration 2

From the following particulars, prepare a Manufacturing Account and a Trading Account for the year ended 31.12.2012:

	Rs.		Rs.
Raw Materials (1.1.2012)	12,000	Carriage Inwards	1,000
Work-in-Progress (1.1.2012)	8,000	Returns Outward	2,000
Finished goods (1.1.2012)	9,000	Royalty on Production	1,000
Purchase of Raw Materials	80,000	Purchases of Finished Goods	8,000
Direct Wages	10,000	Carriage on Finished Goods purchased	500
Indirect Wages	8,000	Fuel and Power	2,500
Sales	1,74,000	Repairs and Maintenance	1,500
Returns Inward	5,000		
Dep. of Factory Assets	4,000		
Raw Materials (31.12.2012)	6,000		
Work-in-Progress (31.12.2012)	2,500		
Finished Goods (31.12.2012)	5,000		

Goods are transferred from Production Dept. to Sales Dept. at cost *plus* 20%.

Adjustments :

(i) Outstanding Direct Wages amounted to Rs. 3,000 ; (ii) Prepaid Fuel and Power amounted to Rs. 500.

Solution

In the books of ....

Dr. **Manufacturing and Trading Account** *For the year ended 31st Dec. 2012* *Cr.*

	Particulars	Rs.	Rs.		*Particulars*	Rs.	Rs.
To	Raw Materials (opening)	12,000		By	Trading Account		1,44,000
	Add : Purchases	80,000			(cost of production)		
		92,000					
	Less : Raw Materials (closing)	6,000					
		86,000					
	Less : Returns Outward	2,000					
	Materials Consumed	84,000					

Contd.

		Rs.	Rs.		Rs.	Rs.
Direct wages	10,000					
Add : Outstanding	3,000					
		13,000				
" Carriage Inwards		1,000				
" Royalty on Production		1,000				
Prime Cost			99,000			
Factory Expenses :						
Indirect Wages		8,000				
Dep. on assets		4,000				
Fuel and Power	2,500					
Less : Prepaid	500					
		2,000				
Repairs & Maintenance		1,500				
		15,500				
Add : Work-in-Progress (opening)		8,000				
		23,500				
Less : Work-in-Progress (closing)		2,500				
			21,000			
Production Cost			1,20,000			
Factory Profit @ 20%			24,000			
			1,44,000			1,44,000
To Finished Goods (Opening)			9,000	By Sales	1,74,000	
" Cost of Production			1,44,000	*Less* : Returns Inward	5,000	
" Purchase of F.G.			8,000			1,69,000
" Carriage			500			
			1,61,500			
" *Less* : Finished Goods (closing)			5,000			
			1,56,500			
Mfg. Cost of goods sold						
Profit and Loss A/c (Gross Profit transferred)			12,500			
			1,69,000			1,69,000

Manufacturing Profit

It has always been explained earlier that the Manufacturing Account reveals the cost of goods produced or manufactured which should ultimately be transferred to Trading Account. But if it is desired by the firm to know the profit or loss on manufacture, the manufactured goods should separately be valued after adding certain percentage of profit—either on cost price or on sale price on arbitrary basis. The amount of profit will be added to factory cost and should be transferred to Trading Account. The profit or loss so made on manufactured goods is transferred to Profit and Loss Account. If this principle is adopted, the manufacturing department is used as a profit centre.

In short, the Manufacturing Account may be prepared under any one of the following techniques:

(i) **At Cost Price** — Which we have already explained earlier;

(ii) **At Selling Price** — At current selling price, the goods are transferred. It helps to take decision whether the manufacturing department will be closed down if it shows a loss or if the same goods can be procured from the open market at a reduced price.

(iii) **At cost plus certain fixed percentage** — It has been explained in the above paragraph.

Unrealised Profit on Closing Stock

The students must remember that in the case of (ii) and (iii), the profit shown by the manufacturing department must be transferred to Profit and Loss Account by passing the following entry :

Profit and Loss A/c Dr.
 To Stock Reserve A/c

That is, while making valuation of closing stock of finished goods the profit element which has already been included must be deducted from the value of Closing Stock.

The above three methods can be explained with the help of the following illustrations:

(ii) **At Selling Price**

Illustration 3

From the following particulars presented by a firm for the year ended 31st Dec. 2011; ascertain (i) Raw Material Consumed; (ii) Prime Cost; (iii) Works Cost; (iv) Gross Profit on manufacture, (v) Gross Profit on sales, (vi) Percentage of net profit on sales:

	Rs.		Rs.
Stock on 1.1.2011:		Office Salaries	8,000
Raw Materials	3,000	General Expenses	1,000
Manufactured goods	5,000	Repairs to Machinery	1,000
Purchases :		Depreciation on Plant and Machinery	4,000
Raw Materials	40,000	Travelling Expenses	2,000
Manufactured goods	18,000	Sales	1,35,000
Coal	3,000	Carriage Inwards :	
Factory Rent	5,000	Raw Materials	4,000
Manufacturing Salaries and Wages	16,000	Manufactured Goods	5,000
Carriage Outwards	3,000		
Office Rent	6,000		
Printing and Stationery	1,000		

Additional Information :

(i) Goods manufactured are supplied by the manufacturing department at current selling price of Rs. 90,000.

(ii) Stock as on 31st December 2011:

Raw Materials Rs. 1,000; Manufactured goods Rs. 8,000 (all are from the goods supplied by the manufacturing department).

(iii) Stock of finished goods as on 31st December 2011 were the goods that were purchased from the open market during the year.

Solution

In the books of the firm

Dr. **Manufacturing Account** *for the year ended 31st December 2011* Cr.

	Particulars	Amount Rs.	Amount Rs.		*Particulars*	Amount Rs.
To	Direct Materials :			By	Trading A/c	
"	Raw Materials (Opening)	3,000			—transferred	90,000
	Add : Purchases of Raw Materials	40,000				
		43,000				
	Less : Raw Materials (Closing)	1,000				
"	*Materials Consumed*		42,000			
"	Direct Labour : Manufacturing Salaries and Wages		16,000			
"	Direct Expenses : Carriage Inwards		4,000			
"	**Prime Cost**		62,000			
"	Factory Expenses :					
	Coal	3,000				
	Factory Rent	5,000				
	Repairs to Machinery	1,000				

Contd.

		Rs.	Rs.		Rs.
To	Depreciation on Plant and Machinery	4,000		By	
			13,000		
"	Factory Cost		75,000		
"	Manufacturing Profit		15,000		
			90,000		90,000

Dr. **Trading and Profit and Loss Account** *for the year ended 31st December 2011* Cr.

		Rs.	Rs.			Rs.
To	Manufacturing A/c		90,000	By	Sales	1,35,000
"	Opening Stock of finished goods		5,000			
"	Purchase of finished goods from open market		18,000			
			1,13,000			
"	*Less :* Closing Stock of finished goods		8,000			
"	Cost of goods sold		1,05,000			
"	Carriage Inward on manufactured goods		5,000			
"	Profit and Loss A/c—					
"	Gross Profit transferred		25,000			
			1,35,000			1,35,000
	Administration Expenses					
To	Office Rent		6,000	By	Trading A/c —Gross Profit	25,000
"	Printing and Stationery		1,000			
"	Office Salary		8,000			
"	General Expenses		1,000			
"	*Selling and Distribution Expenses*					
"	Travelling Expenses		2,000			
"	Carriage Outward		3,000			
"	Net Profit		4,000			
			25,000			25,000

Dr. **General Profit and Loss Account[2]** *for the year ended 31st December 2011* Cr.

		Rs.			Rs.
To	Provision for the unrealised profit on closing stock of finished goods	1,334[1]	By	Net Trading Profit	4,000
"	Net Profit	17,666	"	Manufactured Profit	15,000
		19,000			19,000

Workings :

1. **Provision for unrealised profit on closing stock of finished goods is calculated as :**

Percentage of gross profit on manufactured goods transferred

$$= \frac{\text{Gross Profit}}{\text{Manufactured goods transfered}} \times 100$$

$$= \frac{\text{Rs. } 15{,}000}{\text{Rs. } 90{,}000} \times 100$$

$$= 16.67\%$$

∴ Provision for Unrealised profit on Closing stock of manufactured goods = Rs. 8,000 × 16.67 = Rs. 1,334.

2. It is better to prepare this account. Alternatively, Manufacturing Profit and provisions for unrealised profit on closing stock of manufactured goods may also be adjusted in the Profit and Loss Account.

(iii) At Cost plus certain percentage of profit

Illustration 4

From the following particulars, prepare a Manufacturing Account for the year ended 31.3.2012:

On 1.4.2011	Rs.		Rs.
Raw Materials	6,000	Depreciation on :	
Work-in-Progress	5,000	Plant & Machinery	3,000
Stock of Stores (factory)	7,000	Loose Tools	2,000
Purchase of Raw Materials	60,000	Furniture (factory)	1,000
Purchase of Stores (factory)	15,000	On 31.3..2012	
Carriage Inwards	6,000	Raw Materials	9,000
Direct Wages	9,000	Work-in-Progress	6,000
Indirect Wages	5,000	Stock of Stores (factory)	5,000
Hire of Special Plant	1,000		
Factory Rent & Rates	9,000		
" Insurance	3,000		
" Lighting	2,000		
" Repairs & Renewals etc.	6,000		

Goods are transferred at a profit of 50% on transfer price.

Solution

In the books of ....

Dr. **Manufacturing Account** *for the year ended 31st March 2012* Cr.

Particulars	*Amount*	*Amount*	*Particulars*	*Amount*	*Amount*
	Rs.	Rs.		Rs.	Rs.
To Raw Materials (opening)	6,000		By Trading A/c		2,40,000
Add : Purchases	60,000		(transferred at cost		
	66,000		of production *plus* 100%)		
Less : Raw Materials (closing)	9,000				
" Material Consumed		57,000			
" Direct Wages		9,000			
" Carriage Inwards		6,000			
" Hire of special Plant		1,000			
Prime Cost		73,000			
" *Factory Expenses :*					
" Stock of Stores (opening)	7,000				
Add : Purchases	15,000				
	22,000				
Less : Stock of Stores (closing)	5,000				
	17,000				
" Indirect Wages	5,000				
" Factory Rent & Rates	9,000				
" Insurance	3,000				
" Lighting	2,000				
" Repairs etc.	6,000				
" Depreciation on :					
" Plant & Machinery	3,000				
" Loose Tools	2,000				
" Furniture (factory)	1,000				
	48,000				
Add : Work-in-Progress (opening)	5,000				
	53,000				
Less : Work-in-Progress (Closing)	6,000	47,000			
To Factory Cost		1,20,000			
" Profit and Loss A/c (Manufacturing profit transferred) (50% of Transfer Price or 100% of Cost Price)		1,20,000			
		2,40,000			2,40,000

Preparation of Manufacturing Account, Trading Account and Profit and Loss Account and Balance Sheet

Illustration 5

The following information is given to you from the books of a manufacturer in respect of the year ended 31st March 2012:

	Rs.		Rs.
Stock of Raw Materials (1.4.2011)	25,000	Electricity & Telephone	600
Freight — Inward	8,500	Selling Expenses	600
Freight — Outward	6,000	Miscellaneous Expenses	14,000
Wages — Direct	18,000	Stock of Raw Materials (31.3.2012)	2,000
Wages — Indirect	14,000	Stock of Finished Goods :	
Sales	4,18,000	Opening	30,000
Stationery	1,500	Closing	40,000
Travelling Expenses	5,000	Provision for doubtful debts	8,500
Salaries (H.O.)	26,000	Depreciation on plant	4,000
Factory Expenses	26,000	Depreciation on office	
Interest on loan paid	1,800	furniture and equipments	3,000
Returns Inward	5,000	Repairs to Plant and Machinery	4,650
Returns Outward	3,500	Scrap Sales	3,700
Power and Fuel	8,000	Purchases of Raw Materials	2,50,000
Coal Consumed	9,000		
Work-in-Progress (1-4-2011)	7,000		
Work-in-Progress (31-3-2012)	4,000		
Bank interest received	2,600		

Adjustments necessary for :

(i) Finished goods worth Rs. 5,000 were distributed as free samples.

(ii) A loan was obtained on 1st October 2011 for Rs. 50,000 carrying interest @ 10% p.a.

(iii) Bad debts to be written-off Rs. 750 and provision for doubtful debts to be maintained at Rs. 7,000.

(iv) Electricity and Telephone to be apportioned as Factory $\frac{3}{5}$th and office $\frac{2}{5}$th.

(v) A fire occurred destroying finished goods worth Rs. 15,000. Insurance Company admitted a claim of Rs. 12,000, not yet received.

(vi) Stock of stationery in hand (31.3.2012) Rs. 150.

You are required to prepare the Manufacturing Account and Trading Account and Profit and Loss Account for the year ended 31st March 2012.

Solution

In the books of the Manufacturer

Manufacturing Accounting *for the year ended 31st March 2012*

Dr. Cr.

	Particulars	*Amount*	*Amount*		*Particulars*	*Amount*	*Amount*
		Rs.	Rs.			Rs.	Rs.
To	Cost of Material consumed			By	Manufacturing cost of production transferred to trading account		3,44,550
"	Opening Stock	25,000					
	Add : Purchases	2,50,000					
	Add : Freight Inward	8,500					
		2,83,500					
	Less : Returns Outward	3,500					
		2,80,000					
	Less : Closing Stock	22,000	2,58,000				
"	Wages Direct		18,000				
"	**Prime Cost**		2,76,000				
"	*Indirect Exp.*						
	Wages Indirect	14,000					
	Factory Exp.	26,000					
	Power & Fuel	8,000					

Contd.

	Rs.	Rs.		Rs.	Rs.
To Coal Consumed	9,000		By		
Electricity & Telephone ($\frac{3}{5}$th of Rs. 6,000)	3,600				
Depreciation on :					
Plant & Machinery	4,000				
Repairs to Plant	4,650				
	69,250				
Less : Sale of Scrap	3,700				
	65,550				
Add : Opening Stock of W-I-P	7,000				
	72,550				
Less : Closing Stock of W-I-P	4,000				
		68,550			
		3,44,550			3,44,550

Dr. **Trading and Profit and Loss Account** *for the year ended 31st March 2012* Cr.

Particulars	*Amount* Rs.	*Amount* Rs.	*Particulars*	*Amount* Rs.	*Amount* Rs.
To Opening stock of finished goods		30,000	By Sales	4,18,000	
			Less : Returns Inward	5,000	
Manufacturing cost of Production b/f		3,44,550			4,13,000
" Profit & Loss A/c —Gross profit transferred		98,450	" Goods Distributed as free sample		5,000
			" Goods destroyed by fire		15,000
			" Closing stock of finished goods		40,000
		4,73,000			4,73,000
To Salaries		26,000	By Trading A/c —Gross Profit		98,450
" Electricity & Telephone ($\frac{2}{5}$th of Rs. 6,000)		2,400	" Bank interest received		2,600
" Stationery	1,500		" Provision for doubtful debts not required (Rs. 8,500 – 7,000)		1,500
Less : Stock-in-hand	150				
		1,350			
" Interest on loan	1,800				
Add : Outstanding (Rs. $50,000 \times \frac{6}{12} \times \frac{10}{100} - 1,800$)	700				
		2,500			
" Travelling Expenses		5,000			
" Selling Expenses		6,000			
" Bad Debts		750			
" Freight Outwards		6,000			
" Miscellaneous Expenses		14,000			
" Loss By Fire	15,000				
Less : Claim admitted by Insurance Co.	12,000				
		3,000			
" Depreciation on office furniture & equipments		3,000			
" Advertisements (Free sample)		5,000			
" Capital A/c Net Profit transferred		27,550			
		1,02,550			1,02,550

Treatment of Provision for Unrealised Profit on Opening Stock and Closing Stock

Illustration 6

Piu Sen of Salt Lake carries on business as a clothing manufacturer with two managers, Goonjan, who is responsible for the factory, and Chandrani, who is responsible for the sales department. Each manager is entitled to a commission of 20% of the net profit of his/her department before charging such commission.

Finished goods are transferred from the factory to the sales department at cost plus 20%.

Piu is to be credited with interest @ 8% p.a. of her fixed capital of which three-quarters is to be taken as being employed by the factory, and one-quarter by sales department.

The Trial Balance of the business as on 31st December 2012 was :

	Rs.		Rs.
Freehold factory at cost (including land Rs. 4,000)	20,000	Capital A/c— Piu	30,000
Factory Plant and Machinery at Cost	4,800	Provisions for Depreciation 31st December 2011:	
Travellers' Cars	2,600	Freehold Factory	1,920
Stock 31st December 2011:		Factory Plant and Machinery	1,600
Raw Materials at cost	6,800	Travellers' Car	1,200
Finished Goods at transferred value	2,520	Finished Goods Stock Provision December 31, 2011	420
Trade Debtors	3,600	Trade Creditors	4,200
Purchases of Raw Materials	36,600	Provision for Doubtful Debts	280
Wages and Salaries	19,800	Sales	72,000
Rates and Insurance (factory 1,160)	1,510		
Sundry Expenses (factory 1,100)	1,500		
Motor Expenses	400		
Balance at Bank	11,490		
	1,11,620		1,11,620

You are given the following further information:

(1) Stock on hand as on 31st December 2012 were as follows: Raw Materials at cost Rs. 8,400; Finished goods at transferred value Rs. 2,400.

(2) Wages and Salaries included:
Goonjan's salary Rs. 1,400; Chandrani's salary Rs. 1,500; Piu's drawing Rs. 2,400; Sales department wages and salaries Rs. 1,800. The balance represents direct wages.

(3) Provision is to be made for depreciation on freehold factory, plant and machinery and travellers' cars at 2%, 10% and 25%, respectively, calculated at cost.

(4) On 31st December 2012, Rs. 120 was owing for Sundry Expenses (sales departments) and rates paid in advance amounted to Rs. 260 (sales department Rs. 50).

(5) Of the Trade Debtors, Rs. 60, for which provision had previously been made, is to be written-off.

You are required to prepare:

(a) Accounts for the year ended 31st December 2012, showing (i) Prime cost; (ii) Factory cost of goods produced; (iii) Profit of the factory and of the sales department; and (iv) Appropriation of profit.

(b) The Balance Sheet as on that date.

[CA Eng. Adapted]

Solution

In the books of Miss Piu Sen

Dr. **Manufacturing and Trading and Profit and Loss Account** *for the year ended 31st December 2012* *Cr.*

Particulars	*Amount*	*Amount*	*Particulars*	*Amount*
	Rs.	Rs.		Rs.
To Raw Materials (opening)	6,800		By Trading A/c — transferred	64,500
Add: Purchases	36,600			
	43,400			
Less: Raw Materials (closing)	8,400			
Materials Consumed		35,000		
Direct wages		12,700		
Prime Cost		47,700		

Contd.

	Rs.	Rs.		Rs.
To *Factory Expenses*			By	
Salary—Manager	1,400			
Rates and Insurance (Rs. 1,160 – Rs. 210)	950			
Interest on Capital	1,800			
Sundry Expenses	1,100			
Depreciation on:				
Factory	320			
Plant and Machinery	480			
		6,050		
Factory Cost		53,750		
Factory Profit @ 20%		10,750		
		64,500		64,500
Finished Goods (opening)		2,520	By Sales	72,000
Manufacturing A/c —transferred		64,500		
		67,020		
Less: Finished Goods (closing)		2,400		
		64,620		
Profit and Loss A/c Gross Profit transferred		7,380		
		72,000		72,000
To *Selling and Distribution Expe.*			By Trading A/c	
Interest on Capital		600	" Gross Profit transferred	7,380
Salary—Manager		1,500	Provision for Bad Debt (no longer required)	60
Wages & Salaries		1,800		
Motor Expenses		400		
Bad Debts		60		
Rates and Insurance (Rs. 350 – Rs. 50)		300		
Sundry Expenses (Rs. 400 + Rs. 120)		520		
Depreciation on Travellers' Car		650		
Profit & Loss Appropriation A/c Profit on Sales Dept. transferred		1,610		
		7,440		7,440

Dr. **Profit and Loss Appropriation Account** *for the year ended 31st December 2012* *Cr.*

Particulars	*Amount* Rs.	*Particulars*	*Amount* Rs.
To Provision for unrealised profit on Closing Stock $\left(\text{Rs. }2,400 \times \frac{20}{120}\right)$	400[2]	By Manufacturing A/c —Manufacturing Profit	10,750
" Commission:		" Profit & Loss A/c —Sale Department	1,610
Goonjan $\left(\text{Rs. }10,750 \times \frac{20}{100}\right)$	2,150	" Provision for Unrealised Stock: on Opening Stock	420[1]
Chandrani $\left(\text{Rs. }1,610 \times \frac{20}{100}\right)$	322	$\left(\text{Rs. }2,520 \times \frac{20}{120}\right)$	
" Current A/c Net Profit transferred	9,908		
	12,780		12,780

Balance Sheet *as at 31st December 2012*

Liabilities	Rs.	Rs.	*Assets*	Rs.	Rs.
Capital A/c		30,000	Freehold Land & Building	20,000	
Current A/c:			*Less:* Depreciation	2,240	
Net Profit	9,908				17,760
Add: Interest on Capital	2,400		Plant and Machinery	4,800	
	12,308		*Less:* Depreciation	2,080	
Less: Drawings	2,400				2,720
		9,908	Motor Cars	2,600	
Trade Creditors		4,200	*Less:* Depreciation	1,850	750
Outstanding Liabilities:			Closing Stock:		
Managers' Com.:			Raw Material		8,400
Goonjan	2,150		Finished Goods		2,000
Chandrani	322		(Rs. 2,400 – Rs. 400)		
Sundry Expenses	120		Trade Debtors		3,320
		2,592	(Rs. 3,540 – Rs. 220)		
			Prepaid Expenses		260
			Balance at Bank		11,490
		46,700			46,700

Provision for Unrealised Profit on Stock is calculated as

∴ 1. Opening Stock Reserve $\left(\text{Rs. } 2,520 \times \frac{20}{120}\right)$ = Rs. 420 2. Closing Stock Reserve $\left(\text{Rs. } 2,400 \times \frac{20}{120}\right)$ = Rs. 400

ELEMENTS OF COST/COST SHEET

Cost sheet is a statement which presents detailed information relating to the various stages of cost, and it also shows the total cost of the product manufactured during a particular period of time. Thus, the cost sheet is prepared for a particular period of time, viz., monthly, quarterly, or yearly, etc..

It has already been explained earlier that a Manufacturing Accounts deals with cost relating to cost of goods manufactured, i.e., only Prime Cost and Factory Cost. If office and administration expenses (already explained in and earlier paragraph) are added to the costs, we get the cost of production. Similarly, if selling and distribution expenses (already explained earlier) are added to the cost of production, we get cost of goods sold or total cost.

Objects of preparing Cost Sheet

A cost sheet is prepared for :

(i) The total cost and cost per unit of the product can be ascertained;

(ii) It helps the management to fix up the selling price on the basis of the cost per unit of the product after charging certain percentage of profit on cost;

(iii) It also helps the management presenting a comparative study of current cost with the existing cost per unit;

(iv) After proper comparison the management may take the corrective measures;

(v) It helps the management while formulating suitable production policy;

(vi) It is very helpful to submit a price quotation for tenders; and

(vii) It also helps the management by supplying suitable information for management control.

Method of Preparation of a Cost Sheet

Step	***I***	=	***Prime Cost***	=	***Direct Material + Direct Labour + Direct Expenses***
Step	***II***	=	***Work Cost***	=	***Prime Cost + Factory/Indirect Expenses***
Step	***III***	=	***Cost of Production***	=	***Works Cost + Office and Administration Expenses***
Step	***IV***	=	***Total Cost***	=	***Cost of Production + Selling and Distribution Expenses***
			Profit	=	***Sales – Total Cost***

The above method can better be presented with the help of the following *Pro-forma Cost Sheet :*

Cost Sheet

Period ....

Unit Produced :

	Details	Total	Cost per Unit
	Rs.	Rs.	Rs.
Raw Materials (Opening)	* * *		
Add : Purchases of Raw Materials	* * *		
	* * *		
Less : Raw Materials (Closing)	* * *		
	* * *		
Less : Returns Outward	* * *		
	* * *		
Less : Abnormal Loss of Materials	* * *		
Material Consumed	* * *		
Direct Wages	* * *		
Direct Expenses/Chargeable Expenses	* * *		
Carriage Inward	* * *		
Hire of special plant	* * *		
PRIME COST		* * *	* * *
Indirect/Factory Expenses			
Indirect Wages	* * *		
Factory Expenses :			
" Rent and Rates and Taxes	* * *		
" Lighting andHeating	* * *		
" Fuel and Power	* * *		
Indirect Material	* * *		
Repairs to Plant	* * *		
Depreciation on Plant	* * *		
Loose Tools	* * *		
	* * *		
Less : Sale of Scrap	* * *		
	* * *		
Add : Work-in-Progress (Opening)	* * *		
	* * *		
Less : Work-in-Progress (Closing)	* * *		
		* * *	* * *
FACTORY COST/WORK COST/PRODUCTION COST		* * *	* * *
Office and Administrations Expenses/Overhead :			
Office Rent and Taxes	* * *		
Office, Salaries, Lighting, Insurance	* * *		
Establishment charges, Postage, Repairs	* * *		
Audit Fees, Legal Expenses	* * *		
Depreciation on Furniture Management Expenses etc.	* * *	* * *	* * *
		* * *	* * *
Add : Finished Goods (Opening)		* * *	
		* * *	
Less : Finished goods (Closing)		* * *	* * *
COST OF PRODUCTION OF GOODS SOLD		* * *	* * *
Selling and Distribution Expenses /Overheads :			
Godown Rent, Storage	* * *		
Advertisement, Carriage Outwards	* * *		
Selling Expenses and Commission	* * *		
Showrooms' Rent, Salesmen	* * *		
Salaries, Debt Collection Charges, etc.	* * *		
		* * *	* * *
TOTAL COST/COST OF GOODS SOLD		* * *	* * *
Profit (*bal. fig.*)		* * *	* * *
Sales		* * *	* * *

Preparation of Cost Sheet

Illustration 7

Product Ltd. requests you to prepare a statement showing the cost of goods sold, cost per unit and profit per unit of the product produced by them assuming that profit should be made @ 20% on sales :

	Rs.		Rs.
Raw Materials (1.1.2012)	30,000	Factory Rent	7,000
Raw Materials (31.12.2012)	35,000	Office Stationery	1,000
Purchases of Raw Materials	1,50,000	Office Lighting	3,000
Direct Wages :		Office Rent and Taxes	4,000
Paid	50,000	Office Salaries	10,000
Unpaid	5,000	Managerial Remuneration	3,000
Carriage Inwards	7,000	Dep. on Office Equipment	4,000
Fuel and Power	3,000	Sundry Office Expenses	1,000
Indirect Wages :		Salesmen's Salary and Expenses	2,000
Paid	15,000	Advertisement	1,500
Unpaid	10,000	Packing	2,500
Factory Lighting	5,000	Carriage Outwards	4,000
Factory Insurance	3,000	Sundry Selling and Distribution Expenses	3,000
Repairs on Factory Machines	6,000	Units Produced	10,000
Dep. on Factory Machines	5,000		

Solution

Cost Sheet

for the year ended 31st December 2012 (Units produced 10,000)

Dr. *Cr.*

	Particulars		*Amount*	*Amount*	*Per unit*
		Rs.	Rs.	Rs.	Rs.
	Raw Materials (1.1.2012)		30,000		
Add :	Purchase of Raw Materials		1,50,000		
			1,80,000		
Less :	Raw Materials (31.12.2012)		35,000		
	Material Consumed		1,45,000		
	Direct Wages :				
	Paid	50,000			
	Unpaid	5,000			
			55,000		
	Carriage Inward		7,000		
	PRIME COST			2,07,000	20.70
Indirect/Factory Expenses :					
	Fuel and Power		3,000		
	Indirect Wages				
	Paid	15,000			
	Unpaid	10,000			
			25,000		
	Factory Lighting		5,000		
	Factory Insurance		3,000		
	Factory Rent		7,000		
	Repairs on Factory Machines		6,000		
	Dep. on Factory Machines		5,000		
				54,000	5.40
	FACTORY COST			2,61,000	26.10
Office and Administrative Expenses :					
	Office Stationery		1,000		
	Office Lighting		3,000		
	Office Rent and Taxes		4,000		
	Office Salaries		10,000		
	Managerial Remuneration		3,000		
	Sundry Office Expenses		1,000		

Contd.

	Rs.	Rs.	Rs.	Rs.
Dep. on Office Equipment		4,000		
			26,000	2.60
COST OF PRODUCTION			2,87,000	28.70
Selling and Distribution Expenses :				
Salesmen's Salaries and Expenses		2,000		
Advertisement		1,500		
Packing		2,500		
Carriage Outwards		4,000		
Sundry Selling and Distribution Expenses		3,000		
COST OF GOODS SOLD			13,000	1.30
			3,00,000	30.00
Add : Profit (25% on Cost or 20% on Sales)			75,000	7.50
Selling Price			3,75,000	37.50

Preparation of Cost Sheet

Illustration 8

The Modern Manufacturing Company submits the following information on 31st March 2012 :

	Rs.	Rs.
Sales for the year		2,75,000
Inventories at the beginning :		
Finished Goods	7,000	
Work-in-Progress	4,000	
Raw Materials	3,000	14,000
Purchases of Materials		1,10,000
Direct Labour		65,000
Factory Overhead was 60% of the Direct labour cost—		
Other expenses for the year were :		
Selling expenses 10% of Sales		
Administrative expenses 5% of sales		
Inventories at the end :		
Finished Goods	8,000	
Work-in-Progress	6,000	
Raw Materials	4,000	

Prepare Statement of Cost.

Solution

[CA — Adapted]

In the books of
Modern Manufacturing Co.
Statement of Cost
for the year ended 31st March 2012

		Details Rs.	Total Rs.
	Raw Materials Consumed :		
	Raw Materials (Opening)	3,000	
Add :	**Purchases of Raw Materials**	1,10,000	
		1,13,000	
Less :	Raw Materials (Closing)	4,000	
		1,09,000	
	Direct Labour	65,000	
	Prime Cost		1,74,000
	Factory Overhead (60% of direct Labour) (Rs. 65,000 × $\frac{60}{100}$)		39,000
			2,13,000
Add :	Work in-Progress (Opening)		4,000
			2,17,000

Contd.

		Rs.	Rs.
Less :	Work-in-Progress (Closing)		6,000
	Factory Cost		2,11,000
	Administrative Expenses @ 5 % of Sales	13,750	
Add :	Finished goods (opening)	7,000	
		20,750	
Less :	Finished goods (closing)	8,000	
	Cost of Production		12,750
	Selling expenses @ 10% of Sales		2,23,750
	Total Cost/Cost of Sales		27,500
	Profit *(bal. fig.)*		2,51,250
			23,750
	Sales		2,75,000

ASSIGNMENT MATERIALS
THEORETICAL

Objective-Type Questions

1. State whether the following statement are 'True' or 'False':
   (a) Manufacturing Account is prepared by the Trader.
   (b) Prime Cost = Material Consumed + Direct Expense.
   (c) Material Consumed = Purchase of Materials – Opening Stock of Raw Materials + Closing Stock of Raw Materials.
   (d) Factory Cost = Prime Cost + Indirect Expenses.
   (e) Cost of Production = Factory Cost + Office and Administration Overhead.
   (f) Cost of Goods Sold = Cost of Production + Selling and Distribution Overhead.
   (g) Hire charges paid for a special plant is an example of direct expenses.
   (h) Sale of scrap is directly deducted from Prime Cost.
   (i) Total cost of Manufacturing Account is transferred to Trading Account.
   (j) Manufacturing Account includes only the cost of goods manufactured.

[Ans. True: (b); (d); (e); (f); (g); (i); (j). False: (a); (c); (h)]

Multiple Choice Questions

2.(a) Manufacturing Account includes all:
(i) Direct expenses; (ii) Indirect expenses; (iii) Both.

(b) Manufacturing profit is calculated on:
(i) Cost of goods manufactured; (ii) Cost of goods sold; (iii) None of these.

(c) Cost of Manufacturing Account is transferred to:
(i) Trading Account; (ii) Profit and Loss Account; (iii) Balance Sheet.

(d) Opening stock and closing stock of F.G. do not appear in:
(i) Manufacturing Account; (ii) Trading Account; (iii) Balance Sheet.

(e) All Indirect expenses are recorded in:
(i) Trading Account; (ii) Manufacturing Account; (iii) Balance Sheet.

[Ans. (a) (iii); (b) (i); (c) (i); (d) (i); (e) (ii)]

Short Answer-Type Questions

3 What is a Manufacturing Account?
4. Distinguish between a Manufacturing Account and a Trading Account.
5. What is the purpose of preparing a Manufacturing Account?
6. Mention two advantages of Manufacturing Account.
7. How do you prepare a Manufacturing Account?
8. What is the primary objective of preparing a Manufacturing Account?
9. How do you calculate Manufacturing Profit?
10. Discuss the various elements of Cost.

PRACTICAL

(a) *Preparation of Manufacturing Account*

1. B. Banerjee furnishes the following details relating to the year ended on 31st December 2011:

	1.1.2011	31.12.2011		31-12-2011
		Rs.		Rs.
Raw Materials	2,874	2,125	Factory Rent and Rates	4,244
Work-in-Progress	2,000	1,850	Wages — Production	35,000
Finished Goods	8,635	9,260	Repairs to Plant	1,975
Other Balances at 31st December 2011 :			Power	4,026
			Other manufacturing expenses	1,160
Purchases — Raw Materials		22,160	Office Rent	3,750
Carriage Inwards		966	Other Office expenses	1,418
Returns outward		814	Sales	99,000

Depreciation of Rs. 1,063 for the year is to be charged on plant and machinery.

You are required to prepare a Manufacturing Account and Trading Account, using the balances that are relevant, showing clearly :

(*a*) Cost of Raw Materials consumed; (*b*) Prime Cost of Goods produced; (*c*) Factory Cost of Finished Goods produced ; (*d*) Cost of Goods sold ; (*e*) Gross profit.

[Ans. (a) 23,061; (b) Rs. 58,061; (c) Rs. 70,679; (d) Rs. 70,054; (e) Rs. 28,946]

(b) When goods are transferred after adding certain percentages on Cost/Transfer Price

2. From the following particulars presented by Mr. Roy, prepare a Manufacturing Account for the year ended 31. 10. 2012, assuming that goods produced in the factory are transferred to Sales Department at a profit of 25% on transfer price :

On. 1. 9. 2011

	Rs.		Rs.
Raw Materials	10,000	Factory Rent & Taxes	6,000
Work-in-Progress	5,000	Factory Expenses	1,000
Purchase of Raw Materials	80,000	Depreciation on—	
Carriage Inwards	2,000	Plant & Machinery	2,000
Direct Wages	16,000	Factory Building	3,000
Indirect Wages	4,000	On 31. 10. 2012	
Royalty on Production	3,000	Raw Materials	9,000
Factory Lighting	2,000	Work-in-Progress	6,000
Factory Insurance	4,000		

[Ans. Cost of Production Rs. 1,23,000; Transfer Price Rs. 1,64,000]

[Hints :

(1) Royalty on Production is a chargeable expense. (2) 25% on Transfer Price is equal to $33\frac{1}{3}$ % on Cost Price.]

Statement of Cost of Goods Sold

3. From the following particulars prepare a statement showing the Cost of Goods Sold and the Profit or Loss :

	Rs.		Rs.
Raw Materials	30,000	Factory Rent & Taxes	3,000
Productive Wages	10,000	Power & Fuel	2,000
Direct Expenses	15,000	Salary of Works Manager	5,000
Carriage Inwards	1,000	Salary of General Manager	10,000
Carriage Outwards	2,000	Depreciation on :	
Salaries to sales staff	2,000	Factory assets	2,000
Distribution expenses	3,000	Office equipments	3,000
Advertisement	2,000	Repairs to factory assets	2,000
Godown Rent	3,000	Repairs to office assets	3,000

The total output was 5,000 units.

Units sold were 4,000 @ Rs. 25 per unit.

[Ans. Cost of 4,000 units Rs. 68,800; Cost of Goods Sold Rs. 80,800; Profit Rs. 19,200]

[*Hints :* Cost of production per unit = Rs 86,000 ÷ 5,000 = Rs. 17.20.

Therefore, cost of unsold 1,000 units = Rs.17.20 × 1,000 = Rs. 17,200.]

4. Nice Products Ltd. informs you the following particulars:

	Rs.
Direct Materials	1,00,000
Direct Labour	50,000
Factory expenses are 100% of direct labour.	
Office and Administrative expenses are 50% of works cost.	
Selling and distribution expenses are 25% of cost of production.	
Units produced	5,000

Ascertain the cost of goods sold, profit per unit; and also determine the total selling prices assuming that the rate of profit is 20% on total cost.

[Ans. Cost of Goods Sold Rs. 3,75,000; Profit per unit Rs. 15.00; Selling price Rs. 4,50,000]

Manufacturing Account and Trading Account

5. From the following Trial Balance, prepare the Manufacturing Account and the Trading Account of Sri Gautam Sanyal for year ended 12.1.2012:

Trial Balance

As at 31. 12. 2012

	Debit Rs.		Credit Rs.
Plant & Machinery	2,00,000	Capital	1,00,000
Furniture & Fixture	10,000	Sales	5,00,000
Purchase of Raw Materials	2,50,000	Creditors	50,000
Carriage Inwards	10,000	Bank Overdraft	50,000
Carriage Outwards	20,000	Loan	1,00,000
Wages	30,000		
Rates & Insurance (factory)	2,000		
Rent and Tax :			
Factory	5,000		
Office	10,000		
Salary of General Manager	20,000		
Salary of Works Manager	15,000		
Sundry Debtors	80,000		
Opening Stock :			
Raw Materials	40,000		
Finished goods	30,000		
Cash in hand	10,000		
Goodwill	68,000		
	8,00,000		*8,00,000*

Adjustments :

(i) Stock on 31. 12. 2012
Raw materials Rs. 50,000
Finished Goods Rs. 20,000

(ii) Depreciate—
Plant & Machinery @ 10% p. a.
Furniture & Fixture @ 20% p.a.

(iii) Salary of General Manager is to be allocated in the ratio 4 : 1 to office and factory, respectively.

(iv) Wages was paid in advance amounted to Rs. 5,000.

(v) Salary of Works Manager remain outstanding Rs. 3,000.

[Ans. Cost of Production Rs. 3,24,000; Gross Profit Rs. 1,66,000]

[**Hint** : Depreciation on Furniture & Fixture will be excluded]

Chapter 22

FINAL ACCOUNTS OF TRADING CONCERNS

Learning Objectives

Introduction

Trading Account

- *—How to prepare Trading Account*
- *—Items appearing in the debit side of Trading Account*
- *—Items appearing in the credit side of Trading Account*
- *—Gross Profit/Gross Loss*
- *—Cost of Goods Sold*
- *—Advantages*
- *—Information available from a Trading Account*
- *—Gross Profit Ratio*

Profit and Loss Account

- *—Items appearing in the debit side of Profit and Loss Account*
- *—Items appearing in the credit side of Profit and Loss Account*
- *—Method of Preparation*
  - *—Horizontal Form*
  - *—Vertical Form*
- *—Differences between*
  - *—Trading Account and Profit & Loss Account*
  - *—Gross Profit and Net Profit*

Profit and Loss Appropriation Account

Balance Sheet

- *—Introduction*
- *—Need/Functions of Balance Sheet*
- *—Limitations*
- *—Profit and Loss Account vs Balance Sheet*
- *—Methods of Preparation*

A. *Horizontal Form of Balance Sheet*
   - *(i) Rigidity Preference Method*
   - *(ii) Liquidity Preference Method*

B. *Vertical Form of Balance Sheet*

—Classification of Assets and Liabilities

Application of Indian Accounting Standards

Ind AS 1 : Preparation of Financial Statements (Disclosures of Accounting Policies)

Ind AS 2 : Inventory

Ind AS 10 : Events After the Reporting Date

Ind AS 18 : Revenue Recognition

Ind AS 38 : Intangible Assets

Some Important Adjustments

Methods of Preparation of Final Accounts

FINAL ACCOUNTS OF TRADING CONCERNS

When the trial balance has been prepared, our immediate task is to prepare the final accounts according to the sequence of accounting procedures. Financial accounts of a firm includes :

(i) The Trading Account; (ii) The Profit and Loss Account/Income Statement; and (iii) The Balance Sheet.

The first part, viz., the Trading Account and the Profit and Loss Account, presents the result of the operation during a definite period of time while the last part, viz., the Balance Sheet, presents us the financial position as a whole at a given date. Since the Trading and Profit and Loss Account are prepared in order to know the financial result for the business undertaking and the Balance Sheet is prepared for the financial position at the end of the accounting period, all of them are collectively called **Final Accounts.**

TRADING ACCOUNT

The purpose for which the Trading Account is prepared is primarily to ascertain the Gross Profit or Gross Loss. Gross Profit or Gross Loss is the difference between actual sale proceeds and the cost of goods sold [Gross Profit = Excess of sale proceeds over cost of goods sold and; Gross Loss = Excess of cost of goods sold over sale proceeds].

A Trading Account is prepared by a merchandising concern which purchases goods and sells the same during a particular accounting period. Gross Profit is a very important concept in accounting since percentage of gross profit on sales/turnover is an important indicator of business efficiency. It is also helpful for the purpose of making comparison—although the same may fluctuate from year to year. It should be remembered that the basis of calculation must be consistent. For this purpose, the required items should not vary from one year to another. The required items, of course, may vary from one business unit to other business unit, but, in general, those items which vary directly with the turnover and which form a part of the cost of the goods sold will appear in the Trading Account.

The purpose of Trading Account is not only to show the gross profit but also the percentage share of gross profit on sales—which is very significant for the purpose of making comparison with the past trading periods. Because, a comparative study of absolute figures as well as percentage share are highly significant and desirable in order to measure the progress of a business unit. This comparison will actually reveal the favourable and unfavourable points of the business units, along with some valuable information which are necessary for making future decisions, formulating policies, fixing-up prices, etc. It also helps to calculate the estimated value of stock which arises from Stock Destroyed by Fire.

How to prepare Trading Account?

It has already been presented above that a Trading Account shows the result of the undertaking either as a Gross Profit (if credit side is greater than the debit side) or Gross Loss (if debit side is greater than the credit side). That is why the presentation and the format of a Trading Account is very important. Although its form is like an ordinary account (i.e., "T"-shaped) it is quite different than the other accounts which are created from day-to-day transactions. ***This account is prepared at the end of the financial year; as such, it does not bear any date, or folio column like ordinary account.***

Items appearing in Debit Side of Trading Account

The discussion on the preparation of Trading Account will not be completed until we highlight the items which will appear in the Trading Account.

The following items will appear in the *debit side* of the Trading Account :

(a) Opening Stock

In the case of a new firm, there will not be any opening stock, because it is nothing but the closing stock of last year. Thus, opening stock, in the case of a manufacturing unit, is composed of : Raw Materials, Work-in-Progress, and Finished Goods. But in the case of a trading concern, the opening stock is composed of finished goods only. The amount of opening stock will be presented in the Trial Balance. However, it is an important item of Trading Account.

(b) Purchases

The next important item that appears in the debit side of the Trading Account is the amount of *'Purchases'* made during the year. It includes both cash and credit purchase of goods. But before ascertaining the amount of total purchases, the following precautions must be taken into consideration:

Adjustments Relating to Purchase

(i) To see that purchases do not include the amount of goods taken or purchased by the proprietor for his own use—if it is included, the following entries should be passed:

Drawings A/c Dr.
To Purchases A/c

(ii) To see that purchases do not include the cost of goods sent on consignment basis—if it is included, the following entries should be passed :

Goods Sent on Consignment A/c Dr.
To Purchases A/c

(iii) To see that purchases do not include any capital item/asset, e.g., plant—if it is included, the following entries should be passed :

Plant A/c Dr.
To Purchases A/c

(iv) To see that if goods are purchased and still in-transit, the following entries are passed or not :

Goods-in-transit A/c Dr.
To Creditors/Cash A/c

Same principle is also applied in case of stationery purchase.

But if the amount of such goods are already included with the amount of purchases and closing stock have been included accordingly—it should be treated as :

Either (i) Creditors A/c Dr.
To Purchases A/c } i.e., opposite entry

Or, (ii) the amount should simply be deducted from the closing stock.

(v) To see that purchases do not include the amount of goods either on account of consignment transaction or from hire-purchase transactions or transactions from **Goods Sent on 'Sale or Return'** basis,—if it is included, the following entries should be passed:

Goods Sent on Consignment/Hire-Purchase Goods/Sale or Return A/c Dr.
To Purchases A/c

(vi) To see also that purchases do not include any goods distributed as free samples—if it is included, the following entries should be passed :

Advertisement A/c Dr.
To Purchases A/c

(c) Returns Outward

If any goods are returned to the creditors, we know that the entries for such purpose is :

Creditors A/c Dr.
To Returns Outward A/c

Thus, it may be shown either as a deduction from the purchase in the debit side of Trading Account or it may be recorded in the credit side of the Trading Account. The amount of Returns Outward is shown in the credit side of the Trial Balance.

(d) Direct Expenses

Practically direct expenses, also known as chargeable expenses, are those expenses which are directly related to production or related to purchase of goods or the expenses which are incurred to convert the goods to saleable condition, i.e., which are directly connected with Prime Cost. Direct Expenses include: (i) Carriage Inward; (ii) Freight and Insurance; (iii) Direct Wages; (iv) Octroi, (v) Fuel; (vi) Lighting and Heating (vii) Import Duty, etc.

(For further details please see Chapter 19, **Manufacturing Account**)

Items appearing in the Credit Side of Trading Account

(a) Sales

Sales include cash and credit sales of goods which are taken from the trial balance. But care must be taken about the computation of net sales which will appear in the credit side of Trading Account.

Adjustments relating to Sales

For this purpose we must :

(i) see that sales must not include the sale of any fixed assets, say Furniture. If it is included, the following entries should be passed :

Sales A/c Dr.
To Furniture A/c*

(ii) see that sales must not include the sale of goods on account of consignment, hire-purchase or sale of goods on approval—if it is included, the following entries are required for the purpose :

Sales A/c Dr.
To Goods Sold on Sale or Return/
Consignment/Hire-Purchase Sales A/c.

(iii) see that sales must not include the amount of "goods sold but not yet despatched"—if it includes, the following entries should be passed :

Sales A/c Dr.
To Customer/Debtors A/c } At selling price

But the value of closing stock will be increased by the amount of cost of such goods.

It is interesting to note that sales should be taken when cash is realised from the customer. Because, in the case of credit sale, there is a time lag between the date of sale and actual realisation of cash. But, while calculating gross profit, both cash and credit sales are considered.

(b) Returns Inward

If any goods are returned by our customer the entries for this purpose is :

Returns Inward A/c Dr.
To Customer/Debtors A/c.

Thus, it may be shown either as deduction from the sales in the credit side of the Trading Account or it may be recorded in the debit side of the Trading Account. Returns Inward is shown in the debit side of the Trial Balance.

(c) Closing Stock

Closing stock is the value of the goods which remain unsold in the hands of the trader at the end of the year. In the case of a manufacturing concern, closing stock consists of : Raw Materials, Work-in-Progress, and Finished Goods. But in the case of a trading concern, closing stock includes only stock of finished goods. Care should be taken for the proper valuation of such goods. Valuation of closing stock should be made on the basis of **Cost Price or Market Price, whichever is lower.**

In addition to the above, if the closing stock has already been adjusted against purchases, the same will not appear at all in the Trading Account. The same will appear on the Assets side of the Balance Sheet only.

For further details please see Chapter 14, **Inventory Valuation.**

Gross Profit/Gross Loss

Needless to say that if the total of credit side of Trading Account is greater than the total debit side of Trading Account, the so-called difference is known as Gross Profit. In the opposite case, that is a Gross Loss, i.e., if total of debit side is greater than the total of credit side.

Entries for preparing a Trading Account

Journal entries are the **closing entries** which had already been highlighted in **Journal Proper,** *viz.* Chapter 9.

* If the asset is sold or exchanged at a loss, the loss will be charged against Profit and Loss Account. On the contrary, if the asset is sold at a profit, the profit will be transferred to Capital Reserve (being a capital profit).

(a) ***For the items that appear in the debit side :***

Trading A/c Dr.
To Opening Stock A/c
" Purchase (Net) A/c
" Wages A/c
" Carriage A/c
" Other Direct Expenses A/c

(b) ***For the items that appear in the credit side :***

Sales (Net) A/c Dr.
Closing Stock A/c Dr.
To Trading A/c

(c) ***For the Gross Profit (i.e., when credit side is greater than the debit side) :***

Trading A/c Dr.
To Profit and Loss A/c

(d) ***For Gross Loss (i.e., when debit side is greater than the credit side) :***

Profit and Loss A/c Dr.
To Trading A/c

Preparation of Trading Account

Trading Account can be prepared in two Ways :

(a) Horizontal form or 'T' form, and (b) Vertical form.

(a) Horizontal Form

Trading Account
for the year ended ...

Dr. *Cr.*

Particulars		*Amount* Rs.	*Particulars*	*Amount* Rs.
To Opening Stock		* * *	By Sales	* * *
" Purchases	* * *		*Less* : Returns Inward	* * *
Less : Returns Outward	* * *			
		* * *	" Closing Stock	* * *
" *Direct Expenses :*				
Wages		* * *		
Carriage Inward		* * *		
Freight and Ins.		* * *		
Octroi		* * *		
Fuel		* * *		
Lighting and Heating		* * *		
Import Duty		* * *		
Royalty in Prod.		* * *		
" P & L A/c		* * *		
Gross Profit (transferred)		* * *		
		* * *		

(b) Vertical Form

Sales	* * *	
Less : Returns Inwards	* * *	
		* * *
Less* : *Expenses & Cost		
Opening Stock	* * *	
Purchase (Less Return)	* * *	
Direct Expenses		
Wages	* * *	
Carriage Inwards	* * *	
Freight & Insurance	* * *	
Fuel	* * *	
Lighting & Heating	* * *	
Octroi	* * *	
Import Duty, etc.	* * *	
	* * *	
Less: Closing Stock	* * *	
	* * *	
Cost of Goods Sold	* * *	* * *
Gross Profit		* * *

It has already been explained in an earlier paragraph that the purpose of preparing a Trading Account is to ascertain the Gross Profit or Gross Loss at the end of a financial year. Gross Profit or Gross Loss so ascertained is the difference between *'Sales'* and ***Cost of Goods Sold***. So, it becomes necessary to know the above two items: viz., Sales and Cost of Goods Sold.

Sales : It is not a problem for us to compute the total amount of Sales. We can get it from the Trial Balance.

Cost of Goods Sold

Cost of Goods Sold is not the same as Cost of Goods Purchased. Cost of Goods Sold is computed as :

Either :

Cost of Goods Sold		*Rs.*
	Opening Stock	* * *
Add :	*Purchases**	* * *
		* * *
Less:	*Closing Stock*	* * *
		* * *

Or,

Cost of Goods Sold = Sales – Gross Profit

* Hence, the item Purchases includes not only the cost of goods purchased but also the direct expenses.

Thus, from the above it becomes clear that:

Sales = Cost of Goods Sold + Gross Profit

Or, **Gross Profit = Sales – Cost of Goods Sold**

Advantages of Trading Account

A profit-seeking concern or a trading concern may have the following advantages from a Trading Account:

(i) The Gross Profit or Gross Loss can easily be known from a Trading Account prepared at the end of the financial year.

(ii) The primary success or failure of the concern can be judged on the basis of the gross profit ratio on sales.

(iii) Stock turnover ratio can be computed from this account which helps to know the turnover of stock for the year.

(iv) A firm may change its purchasing policy in order to increase the Gross Profit or to reduce the Gross Loss which it gets from a Trading Account.

(v) Any adjustment relating to any item that appear in the Trading Account can be known.

(vi) Gross Profit Ratio helps us to ascertain the value of closing stock destroyed by fire which is very important for the purpose of calculating Insurance Claim.

(vii) Gross Profit Ratio can be computed for two years from the Trading Account which helps us to compare the financial performances for two consecutive years.

Information available from a Trading Account

The following information is available from a Trading Account:

(a) The percentage of Gross Profit on sales can easily be calculated and compared with that of the previous year or years in order to understand the progress or otherwise of the firm.

(b) For the variation of Gross Profit, information may be obtained as to whether the purchases that have been made or expenses which have been incurred are judicious or not.

(c) The opening and closing stock may be known and compared with the last year's level and also with the amount of purchases so made..

(d) It may also be known that anticipated percentage of profit has been earned or not; if not, the reasons thereof.

Illustration 1

From the following particulars, show the entries and prepare the Trading Account under (i) **Horizontal Form**, and (ii) **Vertical Form**, of Sri Debashish Poddar of Kolkata, for the year ended 31st December 2012 :

	Rs.		Rs.
Opening Stock	5,000	Cash discount on purchases	4,000
Credit purchases	40,000	Cash discount on sales	2,000

Contd.

	Rs.		Rs.
Cash purchases	30,000	Works Manager's salary	8,000
Returns Inwards	7,000	Gas, Fuel, etc.	2,000
Return Outwards	7,000	Supervisor's salary	6,000
Cash Sales	60,000	Wages	10,000
Credit Sale (gross)	45,000	Packing charges for goods sold	2,000
Carriage Inwards	3,000	Import Duties	3,000
Carriage on goods delivered	1,000	Export Duties	4,000
		Excise Duties	2,000

Adjustments

1. Closing Stock : Cost Price—Rs. 30,000, Market Price—Rs. 35,000.
2. Wages outstanding, Rs. 3,000, and wages paid in advance Rs. 1,000.
3. Mr. Poddar took goods worth Rs. 2,000 for his private use.
4. Stock destroyed by fire amounted to Rs. 5,000, not covered by Insurance.
5. Supervisor's salary is to be apportioned between factory and office in the ratio 2 : 1.
6. Wages paid for the construction of garage, wrongly debited to Wages Account—Rs. 1,000.
7. Goods costing Rs. 5,000 were sent to customer on 'Sale or Return' basis on 30th Dec. These were recorded as actual sales. The rate of Gross Profit was $\frac{1}{6}$ th of sales.

Solution

(i) **Horizontal Form**

In the Books of Sri Debashish Poddar

Journal

Date	*Particulars*	*L.F.*	*Debit*	*Credit*
2012			Rs.	Rs.
Dec. 31	Trading A/c Dr.		99,000	
	To Opening Stock A/c			5,000
	" Purchases (adjusted) A/c			61,000
	" Carriage Inwards A/c			3,000
	" Import Duties A/c			3,000
	" Excise Duty A/c			2,000
	" Works Manager's Salary A/c			8,000
	" Gas, Fuel etc. A/c			2,000
	" Supervisors' Salary A/c			4,000
	" Wages Adjusted A/c			11,000
	(Transferred to Trading A/c)			
	Sales (adjusted) A/c Dr.		92,000	
	Closing Stock (adjusted) A/c Dr.		40,000	
	To Trading A/c			1,32,000
	(Transferred to Trading A/c)			
	Trading A/c Dr.		33,000	
	To Profit and Loss A/c			33,000
	(Gross Profit transferred to Profit and Loss A/c)			

Trading Account

Dr. *for the year ended 31st December 2012* Cr.

Particulars	*Amount*	*Amount*	*Particulars*	*Amount*	*Amount*
	Rs.	Rs.		Rs.	Rs.
To Opening Stock		5,000	By Sales Credit	45,000	
" Purchases—Credit	40,000		*Less* : Return Inwards	7,000	
Less : Return Outwards	7,000			38,000	
	33,000		*Less* : Sales or Return		
Add : Cash Purchases	30,000		(Rs. 5,000 + 1,000)	6,000	
	63,000			32,000	

Contd.

	Rs.	Rs.		Rs.	Rs.
Less : Drawings	2,000		*Add* : Cash Sales	60,000	
		61,000			92,000
To Carriage Inwards		3,000	By Closing Stock	30,000	
" Import Duties		3,000	*Add* : Sale or Return	5,000	
" Excise Duties		2,000		35,000	
" Works Manager's Salary		8,000	*Add* : Stock Destroyed		
" Gas, Fuel, etc.		2,000	by Fire	5,000	
" Supervisor's Salary	6,000				40,000
Less : For office $\frac{1}{3}$	2,000	4,000			
" Wages	10,000				
Add : Outstanding	3,000				
	13,000				
Less : Prepaid	1,000				
	12,000				
Less : For Garage	1,000	11,000			
" Profit and Loss Account (Gross Profit transferred)		33,000			
		1,32,000			1,32,000

(ii) **Under Vertical Form**

		Rs.	Rs.
	Sales (adjusted)		92,000
Less:	***Cost and Expenses***		
	Opening Stock	5,000	
	Purchase (adjusted)	61,000	
	Carriage Inwards	3,000	
	Import Duties	3,000	
	Excise Duties	2,000	
	Works Manager's Salary	8,000	
	Gas, Fuel, etc.	2,000	
	Supervisor's Salary	4,000	
	Wages (adjusted)	11,000	
		99,000	
Less:	Closing Stock (adjusted)	40,000	
			59,000
	Gross Profit		33,000

Note : Carriage on goods delivered (i.e., Carriage Outwards), Packing Charges for Goods Sold, Export Duties, Cash Discount on Purchases, Cash Discount on Sales will not appear in the Trading Account.

Gross Profit Ratio

This is the ratio of gross profit on sales/turnover for a particular period which is expressed in terms of percentage with the help of the following :

Percentage of Gross Profit on Sales

$$\text{or Gross Profit Ratio} = \frac{\text{Gross Profit}}{\text{Sales (Net)}} \times 100$$

In other words, it indicates how much profit is earned on sale proceeds of each Rs. 100.

Analysis of changes in the rate of Gross Profit

If the rate of *gross profit increases* in the current financial year, in comparison with the previous year, the same may happen due to:

(a) Selling price has been increased without a corresponding increase in cost;

(b) Opening stock has been valued at a reduced price, although the same should have been valued at a higher price;

(c) There has been an omission relating to purchases of goods which was not accounted for;

(d) There has been an overcasting in sales invoice relating to goods sold;

(e) Closing Stock has been valued at a higher price although the same should have been valued at a lower price, etc.

On the contrary, if the rate of gross profit reduces, the same may happen due to :

(a) Selling price has been reduced without a corresponding reduction in cost price;

(b) Cost price of the goods has been increased without a corresponding increase in selling price;

(c) Opening Stock has been valued at a higher figure than what should have been done;

(d) Closing Stock has been valued at a lower figure than what should have been done;

(e) Goods purchased by the proprietor for his own use, wrongly included with the amount of purchases;

(f) There has been an omission in sales invoice; etc.

Illustration 2

Mr. X furnished the following particulars:

	31st Dec. 1999	31st Dec. 2000
	Rs.	Rs.
Sales	1,90,000	2,90,000
Purchases	1,00,000	1,30,000
Opening Stock	30,000	20,000
Closing Stock	20,000	40,000

From the above calculate:

(a) Gross Profit Ratio (Percentage of Gross Profit on sales; (b) Cost of Goods Sold; (c) Rate of Stock Turnover.

Solution

(a)

In the Books of Mr. X

Trading Account *for the year ended 31st Dec. ...*

Dr. Cr.

Particulars	*1999*	*2,000*	*Particulars*	*1999*	*2,000*
	Rs.	Rs.		Rs.	Rs.
To Opening Stock	30,000	20,000	By Sales	1,90,000	2,90,000
" Purchases	1,00,000	1,30,000	" Closing Stock	20,000	40,000
" P and L A/c (Gross Profit transferred)	80,000	1,80,000			
	2,10,000	3,30,000		2,10,000	3,30,000

∴ **Percentage of Gross Profit on Sales or Gross Profit Ratio**

1999 **2000**

$$= \frac{\text{Gross Profit}}{\text{Sales}} \times 100 \quad = \frac{\text{Rs. } 80{,}000}{\text{Rs. } 1{,}90{,}000} \times 100 \quad = \frac{\text{Rs. } 1{,}80{,}000}{\text{Rs. } 2{,}90{,}000} \times 100$$

$= 42.1\%$ $= 62.07\%$

(b) Cost of Goods Sold

	1999	2000
	Rs.	Rs.
Opening Stock	30,000	20,000
Add: Purchases	1,00,000	1,30,000
	1,30,000	1,50,000
Less: Closing Stock	20,000	40,000
	1,10,000	1,10,000

or, **Cost of Good Sold = Sales – Gross Profit**

For 1999 : Cost of Goods Sold = Rs. 1,90,000 – Rs. 80,000

= Rs. 1,10,000

For 2000 : Cost of Goods Sold = Rs. 2,90,000 – Rs. 1,80,000

= 1,10,000

(c) **Rate of Stock Turnover**

		1999	**2000**
$\frac{\text{Cost of Goods Sold}}{\text{Average Stock}}$	=	$\frac{\text{Rs. } 1,10,000}{\text{Rs. } 25,000}$	$\frac{\text{Rs. } 1,10,000}{\text{Rs. } 30,000}$
		= 4.4 times	= 3.7 times

Illustration 3

Mr. Banerjee's sales during 2009 were Rs. 10,000 more than purchases during the year. His Closing Stock was valued at Rs. 10,000. Rate of Gross Profit on Sales was @ 40%.

Draw up his Trading Account.

Solution

In the Books of Mr. Banerjee
Trading Account *for the year ended 31st Dec. 2009*

Dr. *Cr.*

		Rs.			Rs.
To	Purchases	40,000	By	Sales	50,000
"	Profit and Loss A/c (Gross Profit transferred)	20,000	"	Closing Stock	10,000
		60,000			60,000

Workings :

We know that Gross profit is the difference between the credit side and debit side of Trading A/c. Here, credit side is greater than the debit side by Rs. 20,000 (i.e., Closing Stock Rs. 10,000 and Sales figure is more than the purchase figure by Rs. 10,000) which is represented as gross profit. Now, the gross profit is 40% of sales.

$\therefore$ Amount of sales will be Rs. 50,000 $\left(\text{i.e., Rs. } 20,000 \times \frac{100}{40}\right)$. Purchase is less than sales by Rs. 10,000. So, amount of purchase will be Rs. 40,000 (i.e., Rs. 50,000 – Rs. 10,000).

PROFIT AND LOSS ACCOUNT

Taking the gross profit/gross loss from the Trading Account, our immediate task is to prepare the next account, viz., Profit and Loss Account. Since the balance of the Trading Account in form of gross profit or gross loss is transferred to Profit and Loss Account, it is used as a sub-section of Profit and Loss Account. This account reveals the net result of the business unit during an accounting period which is, ultimately, transferred to capital account in case of a sole-proprietorship firm or to Profit and Loss Appropriation Account in case of a partnership firm.

This account reveals the result of the operation of the business unit after incorporating the profit or loss on usual course of business, other capital gains and losses including the profit on sale of capital assets, but must not include any appropriation items, viz., provision for taxation, proposed dividend, transfer to reserve, etc. With the amount of gross profit/gross loss from the Trading Account, other non-operating and non-trading incomes and abnormal incomes and gains must be added on the credit side of this account. Similarly, all other expenses as shown by a Trial Balance (except the direct expenses which have been already charged to Trading Account) will appear on the debit side of this account. That is, all operating/trading expenses, administration and selling and distribution expenses, abnormal losses, financial expenses, etc. will appear on the debit side of this account.

> ***To Sum up***
>
> ***All the nominal accounts which are left after preparing a Trading Account are to be transferred to this account. This transfer, however, is to be made on the basis the double entry principle, i.e., all expenses and losses (i.e., office and administration, selling and distribution, all non-operating expenses, and abnormal losses) will appear on the debit side of this account and all incomes and gains (i.e., operating, non-operating, abnormal gains, etc.) will appear on the credit side of this account with the amount of gross profit or gross loss.***

It must also be remembered that after transferring the nominal accounts all other adjustments (i.e., outstanding or prepaid expenses, accrued incomes, incomes received in advance, depreciation on assets, etc.) are to be adjusted since this account reveals the net income after matching revenues against expenses under accrual basis of accounting. In short, all expenses—whether paid or unpaid—and all incomes—whether received or accrued—must be taken into consideration while preparing this account.

The difference between the two sides represent either the net profit or net loss of the firm (i.e., Net Profit = excess of credit side over debit side, and Net Loss = excess of debit side over credit side). In short, net profit reveals the excess of gross profit plus other incomes over all expenses and losses. The expenses which appear on the debit side of the Profit and Loss Account may be classified into :

(i) **Operating expenses**, and (ii) **Non-operating expenses**. They are further sub-divided into :

(a) Office and Administration including Maintenance expenses.

(b) Selling and Distribution including Financial expenses;

(c) Abnormal Losses.

Similarly, the incomes which appear on the credit side of the account may be divided into :

(i) **Operating Incomes**; and (ii) **Non-operating Incomes.**

They are also further sub-divided into :

(a) Gross Profit; (b) Revenue Incomes; (c) Non-trading/Non-operating Incomes; (d) Abnormal Gains, etc.

Thus, **the following items will appear on the debit side of Profit and Loss Account :**

(a) Office and Administration Expenses

These expenses are incurred for day-to-day operational and maintenance activities of the firm. It includes : Office Rent, Office Salaries, Office Lighting, Insurance, Postage and Telegram, Audit Fees, Stationery, Repairs and Renewals, Depreciation on : Office Building, Office Furniture, Office Machinery, etc.

(b) Selling and Distribution Expenses

These expenses are incurred for sales promotion and distribution of goods sold. It includes : Advertisement, Carriage Outward, Godown Rent, Storage, Salaries to Sales Staff, Selling Expenses and Commission on Sales, Bad Debts, Provision for Bad Debts, etc.

(c) Financial Expenses

These expenses are incurred for managing and supplying the sources of the finance necessary for the firm. It includes : Interest on Loan, Interest on Overdraft, Bank Charges, Bill Discounting, Discount Allowed, Interest on Deposits, etc. which may happen during the year.

(d) Abnormal Losses

All abnormal losses are charged against Profit and Loss Account. It includes : Stock destroyed by Fire, Goods Lost-in-Transit, Loss on Sale of Assets, etc.*

Items which will appear on the credit side of the Profit and Loss Account

(a) Gross Profit

The gross profit which is the balancing figure of Trading Account, and which is transferred to Profit and Loss Account.

(b) Revenue Incomes

These are incomes which arise in the ordinary course of the business, and which are the incomes for the period only. It includes : Commission Received, Discount Received, etc.

(c) Non-Trading/Non-operating Incomes

These are incomes that are received for non-operating activities of the firm, i.e., they do not affect normal operational activities. They include : Dividend Received, Interest on bank deposits, Income from sub-letting house property, etc.

(d) Abnormal Gains

These are incomes that are received out of capital gains during the period. They include : Profit on Sale of Investment, etc.

Entries (i.e., Closing Entries) for preparing a Profit and Loss Account

Needless to mention here also that journal entries are nothing but the *Closing Entries* which had already been explained in Chapter 9, **Journal Proper**.

---

* Care must be taken about the following expenses which must not appear in the Profit and Loss Account, viz.

(i) **Personal expenses of the proprietor;**

(ii) **Any kind of drawings—either in cash or in kind; and**

(iii) **Personal expenses of the proprietor paid by the firm; e.g., life insurance premium, income-tax etc.**

(iv) **Preliminary Expenses**

(a) *For the items that appear in the debit side :*

Profit and Loss A/c Dr.
  To Expenses and Losses A/c

(b) *For the items that appear in the credit side :*

(All) Incomes and Gains A/c Dr.
  To Profit and Loss A/c

(c) *For Net Profit (i.e., when credit side is greater than the debit side):*

Profit and Loss A/c Dr.
  To Capital A/c

(d) *For Net Loss (i.e., when debit side is greater than the credit side) :*

Capital A/c Dr.
  To Profit and Loss A/c

Methods of Preparation : Pofit & Loss Account can also be prepared under (i) Horizonal Form or 'T' Form, and (ii) Vertical Form.

(i) Under Horizontal Form

Profit and Loss Account
for the year ended ...

Dr. Expenditures	Rs.	Incomes Cr.	Rs.
To *Office and Administration Expenses*		By Trading A/c —Gross Profit transferred	* * *
" Office Rent, Rates and Taxes	* * *	" *Revenue Incomes :*	
" Office Salaries	* * *	Commission Received	* * *
" Office Lighting	* * *	Discount Received	* * *
" Insurance	* * *	By *Non-Trading/Non-Operating Incomes :*	
" Postage and Telegram	* * *	" Dividend Received	* * *
" Audit Fees	* * *	" Interest on Bank Deposits	* * *
" Stationery	* * *	" Income from Sub-letting House Property	* * *
" Repairs and Renewals	* * *	By *Abnormal Gains*	
" Depreciation on :		Profit on Sale of Investments	* * *
Office Building	* * *		
Office Furniture	* * *		
Office Machinery	* * *		
To *Selling and Distribution Expenses*			
" Advertisement	* * *		
" Carriage Outwards	* * *		
" Godown Rent	* * *		
" Storage	* * *		
" Selling Expenses	* * *		
" Salesmen's Salaries and Commission	* * *		
" Bad Debts	* * *		
" Provision for Bad Debts	* * *		
To *Financial Expenses*			
" Interest on Loan	* * *		
" Interest on Overdraft	* * *		
" Bank Charges	* * *		
" Bill Discounting	* * *		
" Discount Allowed	* * *		
" Interest on Debentures	* * *		
To *Abnormal Losses*			
" Stock Destroyed by Fire	* * *		
" Goods Lost-in-transit	* * *		
" Loss on Sale of Assets	* * *		
" Capital A/c (Net Profit transferred)	* * *		
	* * *		* * *

(ii) Under Vertical Form

Profit and Loss Account (in a short form)
In the year ended ...

			Rs.
	Gross Profit		* * *
Add:	Other Revenue Incomes	* * *	
	Non-Trading Incomes	* * *	
	Abnormal Gains	* * *	
			* * *
			* * *
Less:			
	Office and Administration Expenses	* * *	
	Selling and Distribution Expenses	* * *	
	Financial Expenses	* * *	
	Financial Losses	* * *	
			* * *
	Net Profit		* * *

Net Profit/Net Loss

Just like Gross Profit/Gross Loss, when the total of credit side of Profit and Loss Account is greater than the total of the debit side of Profit and Loss Account, the difference is known as Net Profit. In the opposite case, there is Net Loss.

Illustration 4

Prepare the Profit and Loss Account of M/s N. Das & Co. for the year ended 31st March 2012

	Rs.		Rs.
Gross Profit from Trading Account (for the year ended 31.3.2012)	80,000	Repairs and Renewals	3,000
Commission Received	5,000	Advertisement	5,000
Discount Received	3,000	Carriage Outwards	6,000
Bank Interest	7,000	Bad Debts	1,000
Dividend Received	5,000	Interest on Loan	3,000
Office Rent	8,000	Discount Allowed	2,000
Insurance	4,000	Loss on Sale of Assets	3,000
Salaries	10,000	Interest on Overdraft	1,000
Audit Fees	3,000	Bank Charges	1,000
Stationery	1,000	Profit on Sale of Investment	5,000

Solution

In the Books of M/s N. Das & Co.

Dr. **Profit and Loss Account** *for the year ended 31st Dec. 2012* *Cr.*

	Expenditures	Rs.		*Incomes*	Rs.
To	*Office and Administration Expenses*		By	Trading A/c	
"	Office Rent	8,000		—Gross Profit	80,000
"	Insurance	4,000		*Revenue Incomes*	
"	Salaries	10,000	"	Commission Received	5,000
"	Audit Fees	3,000	"	Discount Received	3,000
"	Stationery	1,000		*Non-Trading Income*	
"	Repair and Renewals	3,000	"	Bank Interest	7,000
	Selling and Distribution Expenses		"	Dividend Received	5,000
"	Advertisement	5,000		*Abnormal Gain*	
"	Carriage Outwards	6,000	"	Profit on Sale of Investment	5,000
"	Bad Debts	1,000			
	Financial Expenses				
"	Interest on Loan	3,000			
"	Discount Allowed	2,000			
"	Interest on Overdraft	1,000			

Contd.

		Rs.		Rs.
To	Bank Charges	1,000	By	
	Abnormal Loss			
"	Loss on Sale of Asset	3,000		
"	Capital A/c			
	—Net Profit Transferred	54,000		
		1,05,000		1,05,000

Differences between Trading Account and Profit and Loss Account

The differences between the Trading Account and the Profit and Loss Account may be summed up as:

Trading	Profit and Loss Account
1. The gross financial result of a firm can be known from a Trading Account.	1. The net financial result of a firm can be known from a Profit and Loss Account.
2. All direct expenses and incomes appear in a Trading Account.	2. All indirect expenses and incomes appear in a Profit and Loss Account.
3. The difference between the Debit side and the Credit side of Trading Account represents gross profit or gross loss.	3. The difference between the Debit side and the Credit side of a Profit and Loss Account represent net profit or net loss.
4. It is started by incorporating opening stock.	4. It is started by incorporating gross profit or gross loss.
5. Dividend cannot be declared and paid on the basis of gross profit.	5. Dividend is paid on the basis of net profit.
6. Gross Profit Ratio may be computed.	6. Net Profit Ratio is computed.
7. No financial decision can be taken on the basis of gross profit from a Trading Account.	7. Financial decision may be taken on the basis of net profit from a Profit and Loss Account.
8. Only information about the direct expenses and incomes is available.	8. Only information about these indirect expenses and incomes are available.
9. Income-Tax is not computed on the basis of gross profit.	9. Income-Tax is computed on the basis of net profit.

Differences between Gross Profit and Net Profit

The differences between the gross profit and the net profit may be outlined:

Gross Profit	Net Profit
1. The difference between the credit side and the debit side of Trading Account represents gross profit (i.e., if credit side is greater).	1. The difference between the credit side and the debit side of Profit and Loss Account represents net profit (i.e., if credit side is greater).
2. It is ascertained from a Trading Account.	2. It is ascertained from a Profit and Loss Account.
3. Gross profit is transferred to Profit and Loss Account.	3. Net profit is transferred to Capital Account.
4. Gross profit is the difference between direct incomes and direct expenses.	4. Net profit is the difference between indirect incomes and indirect expenses.
5. It presents the gross result of the business.	5. It presents the net result of the business.
6. It presents the gross profit ratio (i.e., percentage of gross profit on sales/turnover).	6. It present the net profit ratio (i.e., percentage of net profit on sales/turnover).
7. It is ascertained at first.	7. It is ascertained after ascertaining gross profit.

Profit and Loss Appropriation Account

It has been pointed out that, in case of a partnership firm, the profit arising from Profit and Loss Account is to be transferred to Profit and Loss Appropriation Account. Profit and Loss Appropriation Account is an account where those expenses are shown which are treated as *appropriation of profit*, e.g., Interest on Partners' Capital, Partners' Salaries, Partner's Commission, i.e., items relating to partners. In other words, Interest on Partners' Capital, Partners' Salaries, Partners' Commission will appear on the Debit side whereas Interest on Partners' Drawings, along with the profit which is coming from Profit and Loss Account, will appear on the Credit side of this account. The difference will represent the net distributable profit or loss which will be shared between the partners.

Note: A company also prepares a Profit and Loss Appropriation Account but in a different manner.

The following illustration will help to make the said principle clear:

Illustration 5

A, B and C are partners sharing profits and losses as 2 : 2 : 1.

Prepare a Profit and Loss Appropriation Account for the year ended 31.12.2008:

	Rs.
Net Profit from Profit and Loss Account	30,000
A and C are each entitled to a salary (yearly) of	5,000
B is entitled to a Commission @ 10% on the above net profit.	
Interest on Capital is to be charged @ 5% p.a. whereas	
Interest on Drawings @ 10% p.a. (for 6 months)	

Capital at the beginning of the year:

Capital	Drawings
A Rs. 40,000	A Rs. 4,000
B Rs. 20,000	B Rs. 2,000
C Rs. 10,000	C Rs. 1,000

Solution

In the Books of A, B and C

Dr. **Profit and Loss Appropriation Account** *for the year ended 31st December 2008* Cr.

Particulars	Rs.	Rs.	Particulars	Rs.	Rs.
To Interest on Capital			By Profit and Loss A/c		30,000
A	2,000		" Interest on Drawings		
B	1,000		A	200	
C	500		B	100	
		3,500	C	50	350
" Salary					
A	5,000				
C	5,000				
		10,000			
" Commission					
B		3,000			
Net Divisible Profit					
A	5,540				
B	5,540				
C	2,770	13,850			
		30,350			30,350

Balance Sheet

Since all the nominal accounts of a trial balance are closed by transferring either to Manufacturing Account or to Trading and Profit and Loss Account, there remains the personal and real accounts of the trial balance. Now, the Balance Sheet is prepared by taking up all the personal accounts (Capital and Drawings) and real accounts (Assets and Properties) together with the net result obtained from Profit and Loss Account showing the debit balance on the right hand side (called Assets side) and credit balance on the left hand side (called Liabilities side) in order to show the real financial position of a firm at a particular date. Thus, a Balance Sheet is not an account but it is a statement prepared from the balances of accounts. Practically, the balances do not transfer to the Balance Sheet but they simply remain in the accounts for appearing as the opening balance in the next year.

The left hand side (i.e., the Liabilities side) of the Balance Sheet represents the sources from which the funds of a firm have been obtained and the right hand side (i.e., the Assets side) of the Balance Sheet shows the ways in which these funds are used. Funds may be procured from the owners who invest resources and also from outsiders who advance resources in any other way which, in other words, presents a classification of source of funds into the proprietor's funds and external liabilities. At the same time, the uses of these funds express the property that a business unit has acquired, i.e., the Assets.

The Balance Sheet is a sophisticated report which serves as a valuable source of information to the users of financial statements, viz., the owners and outsiders. It presents in a summary form a picture—uncluttered by details—the financial position of the business at a particular date. It gives us a good idea about the financial position of a business unit if we analyse, scrutinise and interpret the assets and liabilities at a particular date.

Need/Functions of Balance Sheet

The functions of Balance Sheet are:

(i) A Balance Sheet exhibits the true financial position of a firm by showing the assets (i.e. resources) and liabilities (i.e., obligations) at a particular date to the owner as well as to the outsiders.

(ii) It helps the investor to know the earning capacity of the firm and the dividend pay-out ratio.

(iii) It also provides valuable information about the existence of the firm, after scrutinising some financial ratios, to the creditors and investors by which they can take proper decision(s).

(iv) It also highlights the financial strength of the firm to the creditors so that they can review the repaying capacity after analysing some ratios (e.g. Debt-Equity Ratio, Current Ratio etc.)

(v) A detailed financial position can be known if we analyse and scrutinise the assets and liabilities at a particular date.

From the above, it becomes clear that a Balance Sheet is a very important tool of financial statement to the users of accounting information; primarily to the creditors, investors, and the shareholders. But it must be remembered that a single Balance Sheet for a particular year is not at all sufficient for the purpose. The analysis of Balance Sheet will be significant and meaningful only when a comparative study (at least 5 years' data) can be made which will, no doubt, present valuable information.

Limitations of Balance Sheet

The Balance Sheet is not free from snags. Some of the limitations are:

(i) A Balance Sheet is prepared on the basis of historical cost and, as such, does not exhibit the current values. Thus, it fails to convey the true picture about the financial position desired by an analyst.

(ii) A Balance Sheet is prepared at the end of a particular period as per the requirements of the management when it shows a very favourable condition. This is particularly applicable in the case of seasonal firms.

(iii) Sometimes the historical cost of a Balance Sheet does not convey any fruitful information to some users of accounting information. The same may become useful with the application of ratio analysis.

(iv) Balance Sheet is affected by the accounting policies relating to: Inventory Valuation, Depreciation of Assets, Provision for Bad and Doubtful debts, etc. Thus it becomes necessary to disclose such policies.

(v) Sometimes a Balance Sheet cannot exhibit the real value of certain factors which are important to the business (e.g., skill, technical experience, etc.).

(vi) Sometimes a Balance Sheet is window-dressed —these mislead us.

(vii) Value of some current assets (e.g. Stock, Debtors, etc.) are valued on the basis of some estimates which may not always prove worthwhile in future. Thus, it does not convey the true financial position.

(viii) When there is inflationary situation or change in the purchasing power of money, a conventional Balance Sheet particularly misleads us since the assets purchased at various intervals are added up with the values which have already been changed.

(ix) Balance Sheet is prepared with a lot of schedule of assets and liabilities for various information. Still, that is not sufficient. A detailed list of such assets and liabilities are required for correct analysis and interpretation.

(x) A conventional financial report based on the conventional Balance Sheet is not able to throw light on Social Accounting which is the crying need of the day.

Profit and Loss Account vs Balance Sheet

The fundamental differences between the Profit and Loss Account and the Balance Sheet are :

Profit and Loss Account	Balance Sheet
1. A Profit & Loss Account presents the result of the undertaking at a particular date.	1. A Balance Sheet exhibits the financial position as a whole at a particular date.
2. It takes all the nominal accounts.	2. It takes all the real and personal accounts.
3. It is itself an account.	3. It is a statement.
4. All the nominal accounts are closed by transferring to Profit and Loss Account, i.e., these accounts do not exist.	4. Balance Sheet is prepared by taking the real and personal accounts and their balances are brought forward in the next year.
5. The difference in Profit and Loss Account represents net profit or net loss.	5. No such difference arises in the Balance Sheet.
6. The left hand side of Profit and Loss Account is the Expenditure side and right hand side is the Income side.	6. The left hand side of the Balance Sheet is known as Liabilities whereas the right hand side is called Assets side.

Format of Balance Sheet

The Balance Sheet can be portrayed into two following forms: viz. Horizontal Form or the Account Form, and Vertical Form or the Report Form. Again, under Horizontal Form, the Balance Sheet has two sides, viz., Assets (in the right hand side) and Liabilities (in the left hand side).[1]

A. Horizontal Form of Balance Sheet

This form of Balance Sheet is explained below with the help of Marshalling of Balance Sheet or Marshalling of Assets and Liabilities.

Marshalling of Assets and Liabilities

'Marshalling' means the sequence of Balance Sheet items, i.e., the Balance Sheet may be prepared either under (a) **Liquidity Preference Method**, or (b) **Permanence or Rigidity Preference Method**.

(a) **Liquidity Preference Method:** Under this method, the more liquid or current assets (Cash, Bank, Debtors, etc.) are listed at the top whereas the least liquid assets or fixed assets (Plant and Machinery, Land and Building etc.) are placed at the bottom of the Balance Sheet. In case of liabilities, however, the same principle is followed, i.e., more liquid liabilities (e.g., short-term creditors) are listed at the top and the least one at the bottom, and investments, if any, are placed in-between the two.

See the outline of a Balance Sheet prepared under Liquidity Preference Method:

Under Liquidity Preference Method
Balance Sheet as at ...

Liabilities	Rs.	*Assets*	Rs.
Current Liabilities:		Current Assets:	
Sundry Creditors		Cash	
Bills Payable		Cash at Bank	
Bank Overdraft		Bills Receivable	
Outstanding Expenses		Sundry Debtors	
Income Received in Advance		Prepaid Expenses	
Long-term Liabilities:		Accrued Income	
Loans on Mortgage		Stock-in-Trade	
Debentures		Investments (with details)	
Capital Accounts:		Fixed Assets:	
Current Accounts		Furniture	
Capital Accounts		Plant and Machinery	
		Land and Building	
		Goodwill	

(b) **Permanence or Rigidity Preference Method:** Under this method, the least liquid or fixed assets etc. (Plant and Machinery, Land and Building, etc.) are placed at the top of the Balance Sheet whereas the more liquid or current assets (Cash, Bank, Debtors, etc.) are listed at the bottom of the Balance Sheet (Investments, if any, are placed in-between the fixed assets and current assets). That is, it is

1 In USA it is reversed, i.e., assets are shown in the left hand side and liabilities are shown in the right hand side

just the opposite of the earlier method. In case of liabilities the same principle is followed. The outline of the Balance Sheet under Rigidity Preference Method is presented :

Under Permanence or Rigidity Preference Method

Balance Sheet as at ...

Liabilities	Rs.	*Assets*	Rs.
Capital Accounts:		Fixed Assets:	
Capital Accounts		Goodwill	
Current Accounts		Land and Building	
Long-term Liabilities:		Plant and Machinery	
Debentures		Furniture	
Loan on Mortgage		Investments (with details)	
Current Liabilities:		Current Assets:	
Bank Overdraft		Stock-in-Trade	
Sundry Creditors		Sundry Debtors	
Outstanding Expenses		Prepaid Expenses	
Income Received in Advance		Accrued Income	
Bills Payable		Bills Receivable	
		Cash	
		Cash at Bank	

Illustration 6

From the following particulars prepare a Balance Sheet as at 31.12.2008 (i) as per Rigidity Preference Method, (ii) Liquidity Preference method:

Capital (1.1.08) Rs. 50,000; Drawings Rs. 3,000; Net Profit for the year Rs. 15,000; Closing Stock Rs. 6,000; Loan on Mortgage Rs. 7,500; Bills Payable Rs. 2,500; Bills Receivable Rs. 4,000; Goodwill Rs. 6,000; Book-Debts Rs. 9,000; Creditors Rs. 3,000; Plant and Machinery Rs. 20,000; Investments Rs. 9,000; Cash in hand Rs. 1,000; Cash at Bank Rs. 3,000; Land and Building Rs. 17,000.

Solution

(i) Rigidity Preference Method:

In the Books of ...

Balance Sheet *as at 31st December 2008*

Liabilities	Rs.	Rs.	*Assets*	Rs.
Capital Account:			Fixed Assets :	
Capital	50,000		Goodwill	6,000
Add: Net Profit	15,000		Land and Building	17,000
	65,000		Plant and Machinery	20,000
Less: Drawings	3,000		Investment	9,000
		62,000		
Long-term Liabilities:			Current Assets :	
Loan on Mortgage		7,500	Closing Stock	6,000
Current Liabilities:			Bills Receivable	4,000
Bills Payable		2,500	Book-Debts	9,000
Creditors		3,000	Cash at Bank	3,000
			Cash in hand	1,000
		75,000		75,000

(ii) Liquidity Preference Method:

In the Books of ...

Balance Sheet *as at 31st December 2008*

Liabilities	Rs.	Rs.	*Assets*	Rs.
Current Liabilities:			Current Assets:	
Creditors		3,000	Cash in hand	1,000
Bills Payable		2,500	Cash at Bank	3,000
Long-term Liabilities:			Book-Debts	9,000
Loan on Mortgage		7,500	Bills Receivable	4,000

Contd.

	Rs.	Rs.		Rs.
Capital Account:			Closing Stock	6,000
Capital	50,000		Investments	9,000
Add: Net Profit	15,000		Fixed Assets:	
	65,000		Plant and Machinery	20,000
Less: Drawings	3,000		Land and Building	17,000
		62,000	Goodwill	6,000
		75,000		75,000

B. Vertical Form of Balance Sheet

Under this form, the Balance Sheet is presented in a statement form. No doubt this is more advantageous than the Horizontal Form. For this purpose, the Joint Stock Companies are using this method on a large scale. This method has the following advantages :

(i) This form of Balance Sheet can easily be understood by any person—since it is very simple to understand;

(ii) This method explains each component clearly, e.g., total fixed assets or total current assets, working capital. It also helps to understand the shareholders' fund, utilisation of resources etc.;

(iii) This form is also very useful for the purpose of making comparisons with the help of ratio analysis.

Outline of Vertical Form of Balance Sheet

In the Books of ...
Balance Sheet *as at ...*

		Rs.	Rs.
Fixed Assets:			
Goodwill		...	
Land and Building		...	
Plant and Machinery		...	
Furniture		...	
Investment		...	
			...
Current Assets:			
Stock-in-Trade		...	
Sundry Debtors		...	
Prepaid Expenses		...	
Accrued Income		...	
Bills Receivable		...	
Cash at Bank		...	
Cash in hand		...	
Current Liabilities:			
Sundry Creditors	...	...	
Bills Payable	...	...	
Bank Overdraft	...	...	
Outstanding Expenses	...	...	
Represented by Shareholders' Fund:		...	
Capital	...		
Reserves	...		
Long-Term Liabilities	...	...	
			...

The previous illustration is explained under Vertical or Report Form:

Balance Sheet *as at 31st December 2008*

	Rs.	Rs.
Fixed Assets:		
Goodwill	6,000	
Land and Building	17,000	
Plant and Machinery	20,000	
Investments	9,000	52,000

Contd.

		Rs.	Rs.
Current Assets:			
Closing Stock		6,000	
Book Debt		9,000	
Bills Receivable		4,000	
Cash at Bank		3,000	
Cash in hand		1,000	
		23,000	
Current Liabilities:			
Creditors	3,000		
Bills Payable	2,500		
		5,500	17,500
			69,500
Represented by Proprietor's Fund:			
Capital (Net)	47,000		
Profit	15,000	62,000	
Loan on Mortgage		7,500	
			69,500

The discussion on the Balance Sheet will not be completed if we do not highlight the two components of the Balance Sheet viz., the Asset and the Liabilities and their classification.

CLASSIFICATION OF ASSETS AND LIABILITIES

Classification of Assets

According to Professor G. D. Roy, the classification of assets is summarised as under:*

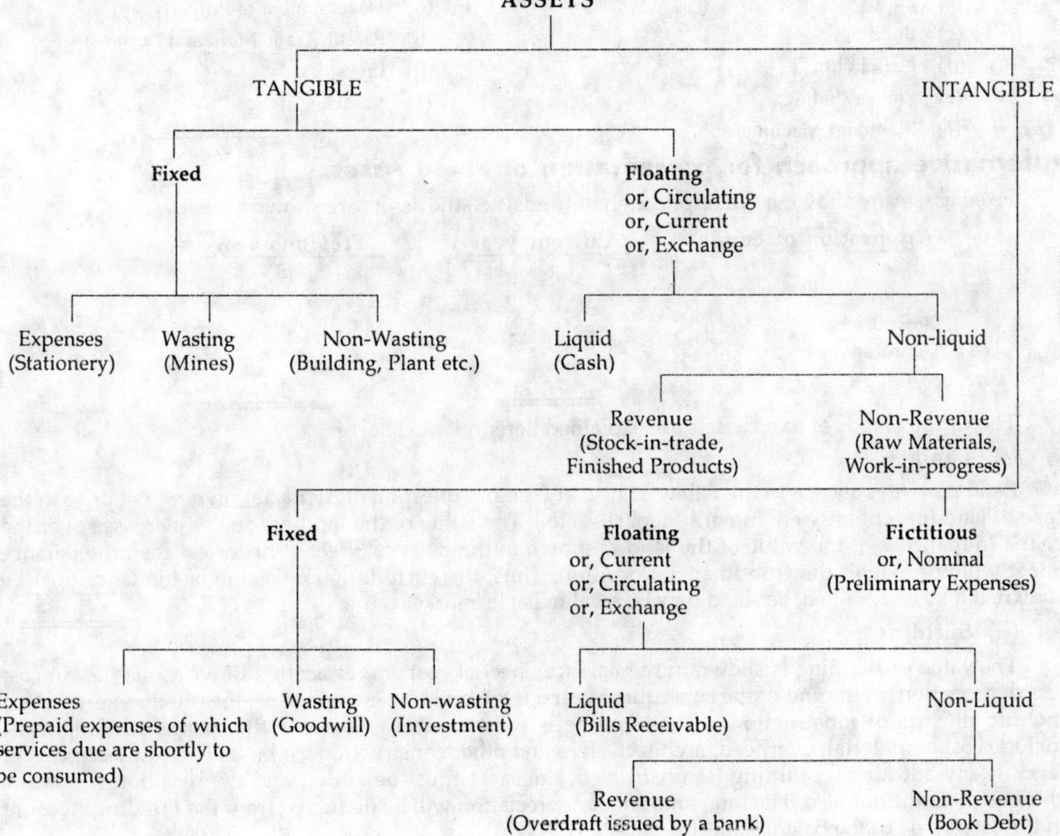

* Roy G. D.—*A Survey of Accounting Ideas*—Alpha Publishing Concern—1st ed., P. 39

Tangible Assets

The Capital Assets which have some physical existence are known as *Tangible Assets.*

They can, therefore, be seen, touched and felt, e.g., Plant and Machinery.

Intangible Assets

The Capital Assets which have no physical existence and whose value is limited by the rights and anticipated benefits that possession confers upon the owner is known as Intangible Assets. They cannot be seen or felt although they help to generate revenue in future—Goodwill, Patents, Trade Marks, etc.

Fixed Assets

In order to be a fixed one, an asset must satisfy the following three characteristics :

(i) the asset which has been acquired is not for re-sale;

(ii) the asset which has a comparatively long life, i.e., it must not be converted into cash or consumed in the ordinary course of business within a period of one accounting cycle;

(iii) the asset which helps the process of production, supply of goods and services.

Fixed assets are used for the purpose of earning revenue over a long period of time. They are more or less permanent in nature. Sometimes they are also called *Block*, e.g., Land and Building, Plant and Machinery, Furniture and Fixtures, etc.

Presentation of Fixed Assets as per Schedule VI of the Companies Act, 1956

As per Part I of Schedule VI of the Companies Act, 1956, the presentation of fixed assets in the Balance Sheet are :

(a) Goodwill;
(b) Land;
(c) Building;
(d) Leasehold;
(e) Railway Siding;
(f) Plant and Machinery;
(g) Furniture and Fittings;
(h) Development of Property;
(i) Patent, Trade Mark and Designs;
(j) Livestock;
(k) Vehicles; etc.

Alternative approach for presentation of Fixed Assets[1]

Fixed assets are shown as an application of funds, i.e., the assets are shown as below :

Application of Funds	Current year	Previous year
	Rs.	Rs.
Fixed Assets		
Gross Block	* * *	* * *
Less : Depreciation	* * *	* * *
Net Block	* * *	* * *

The various kinds of fixed assets are explained hereunder in short :

(i) Land

Land is always shown in the Balance Sheet at cost and question of depreciation does not arise in the case of land (except oil-well, mineral deposits, etc.). The value of the land gradually increases over the years. In that case, if the value of the land is shown in the Balance Sheet at historical cost, the Balance Sheet will not exhibit the true financial position. Thus, the current market value of the land must be shown. It may be revalued, i.e., land may be revalued at its market value.

(ii) Building

The value of Building is shown in the Balance Sheet at cost and at written-down value (i.e., at cost less depreciation) at the end of the subsequent years. If the building is purchased, the purchase price must include all costs of construction. If the building is constructed by the firm, the cost of building must include cost of material, overhead, architect's fees and other construction expenses in addition to cost of land. If any additional building is constructed, the same must be added and depreciation should be charged on additions also. The total amount of depreciation will be deducted from the Building Account in the assets side of the Balance Sheet.

---

1 This form has been followed by many companies

(iii) **Plant and Machinery**

Another item of fixed asset is the Plant and Machinery of the firm. It includes various classes and kinds of plants, machines, equipments, etc. which are frequently used for productive purposes and the total value of such plants and machines are shown in the assets side of the Balance Sheet at written-down value at the end of the period. If any addition is made, depreciation should also be charged on them. Care must be taken that installation expenses, cost of carriage and other necessary expenses for installation, if any, must be added with the cost price of the plant and machinery and depreciation should also be charged. Similarly, if any old machinery is sold or exchanged, the written-down value should be adjusted accordingly.

(iv) **Furniture and Fittings**

The above principle is equally applicable in the case of Furniture and Fittings. When the furniture is purchased, the same must be recorded at historical cost but the value of the furniture and fitting will be shown at written-down value at the end of the year. If any addition is made, the depreciation should also be charged on it. Similarly, if any old furniture is sold or replaced or exchanged with a new one, the profit or loss on sale must be adjusted after making necessary adjustment for depreciation.

Investment

The amount of investment in various kinds of securities are shown as assets in the asset side of the Balance Sheet. The value of the investment should be made at current market value and, as such, if current market value of such investment is more or less, the same must be adjusted accordingly at the end of the year in the Balance Sheet, otherwise the Balance Sheet will not exhibit the true financial position. Similarly, if any addition is made or a part of such investments are sold, the same must also be adjusted accordingly. It must also be remembered that investments are of two types: viz., (i) Long-term Investments, and (ii) Short-term Investments.

Long-term Investments are treated as fixed whereas Short-term Investments are treated as current assets (i.e., if the investment is made for one year or less).

Current/Fluctuating/Circulating Assets

An asset is termed current asset when it is acquired either for the purpose of selling or disposing-off after taking some required benefit through the process of manufacturing, or which constantly changes in form and contributes to transactions that take place with the operation of the business—although such asset does not continue for long in the same form. As for instance, cash is often parted with in exchange of goods or services or in repayment of a certain liability, say Creditor. Similarly, Debtors as asset yield place to cash on realisation, or stock-in-trade is replaced by cash or Debtors on its sale, the former in case of cash sales and the latter in case of credit sales. So, they are not only short-lived but also change their form and one type of asset can easily be converted into another, say Cash. Cash can be converted into Raw Materials, Raw Materials into Work-in-progress, Work-in-progress into Finished Products, and Finished Products into Debtors in case of credit sales, and Debtors into Cash. That is why they are also defined as *Circulating Assets.* Time required for ultimate conversion of any component of current assets into cash is normally taken to be one year or less.

Nowadays, this concept has suffered a bit of change. It is not essential that current assets should always be converted into cash immediately. It may also be lost or consumed. For example, when salaries and wages are paid in Cash, part of cash is consumed and it does not create any current asset through transformation directly. But when cash is received from Debtors, Debtors are not converted into Cash, Debtors here are not consumed but transformed or, rather, converted. The period of conversion in this case is reckoned to be one operating cycle of the business instead of one year, e.g., Inventories (including Raw Materials, Work-in-progress, Finished Goods), Debtors including receivables, Prepaid Expenses, Cash, Bank.

Current assets are arranged in the Balance Sheet in the following manner:

(i) Closing Stock (Inventories) : (a) Raw Materials, (b) Work-in-progress, (c) Finished Goods; (ii) Debtors; (iii) Bills Receivable; (iv) Prepaid Expenses; (v) Cash at Bank; (vi) Cash in hand; (vii) Advances (Short-term).

But, as per Schedule VI of the Companies Act, 1956, the arrangement order of current assets are :

Current Assets, Loans and Advances

A. **Current Assets**

Accrued Interest, Stores and Spares, Loose Tools, Stock-in-trade :
Raw Materials, Work-in-progress, Finished Goods.
Sundry Debtors; Cash at Bank; Cash in hand.

B. Loans and Advances

Loans to Subsidiaries, Partnership firms, Bills of Exchange etc.

The various kinds of current assets are :

(i) Closing Stock

Closing stock or inventories include : Raw Materials, Work-in-Progress, and Finished Goods. The most important and significant is the basis of valuation of inventiories. We know that the valuation of inventories may be made by various methods, viz., FIFO, LIFO, Simple Average, Weighted Average Method etc. The normal basis of valuations of inventories is the *Cost Price* or *Market Price*, whichever is less. For further details please see Chapter 14—**INVENTORY VALUATION** in this volume.

(ii) Sundry Debtors

Sundry Debtors, alternatively known as Book Debts or Accounts Receivable, are the collection of debts that are due from the customers. The amount of debtors which will be shown in the assets side of the Balance Sheet must be presented after deducting the amount of bad debts, provision for bad debts and also provision for discount on debtors (which is allowed for prompt payment on good debtors).

(iii) Bills Receivable

Bills Receivable is an instrument made by a customer to pay the amount due either at a specified date or on demand. The amount of such bill is shown as an asset in the assets side of the Balance Sheet at its face value. That is, if any interest is included with the amount of bill value (in case of renewal of bill), the same must be deducted.

(iv) Prepaid Expenses

Prepaid Expense is another item of current asset which appear on the assets side of the Balance Sheet. It is the short-term pre-payments made for the succeeding year and the same will be transferred to the expenses account for the succeeding year. Such amount is calculated on the basis of unexpired period.

(v) Cash at Bank

The amount lying at the bank is also an item of current assets. It must not include the fixed deposits, if any, made by the firm. In fact, the current account of the firm represents the amount of cash at bank which is shown as an asset in the assets side of the Balance Sheet.

(vi) Cash in Hand

This is the most liquid amount in the hands of a firm and shown as an asset in the assets side of the Balance Sheet.

(vii) Short-term Loans and Advances

Particularly, the temporary surplus fund of the business are invested in outside securities in the form of short-term loans and investments which appear in the assets side of the Balance Sheet. But the basis of valuation for such investments are : ***Cost Price or Market Price, whichever is less***, like inventories. For this purpose, profit or loss on realising such investment must be adjusted accordingly.

Liquid/Quick Assets

The current assets which can immediately (i.e., at short notice) be converted into cash with a little risk of loss about their realisable value, although their realisable value is almost certain, are liquid/quick assets. Liquid assets comprise all current assets minus Stock and Prepaid Expenses. Stock is excluded from the liquid assets on the ground that it is not converted into cash in the immediate future, so also the prepaid expenses., e.g., Debtors including Receivables, Cash, Bank.

Wasting Assets

The fixed assets which have a limited useful life and which, by nature, depreciate rapidly are termed wasting assets, i.e., an asset that diminishes in value by reason of—and commensurately with—the extraction or removal of a natural product, e.g., Mines, Oil, Ores—which it contains.

Fictitious Assets

These assets are nothing but the unwritten-off losses or non-recoupable costs. They are really not assets but are worthless items. They are not expected to realise any value or render any service in future. These assets are to be written-off against Profit and Loss Account as early as possible, e.g., Preliminary Expenses, Discount on Issue of Shares and Debentures, etc.

Contingent Assets

An asset, the existence, value and ownership of which depend upon the occurrence or non-occurrence of a specified event or upon the performance or non-performance of a specified act, i.e., these assets are those which have not become an asset but ***may*** become an asset on the happening of some event(s). These assets are not required to be disclosed in the Balance Sheet. Sometimes contingent assets grow out of contingent liabilities. That is, contingent liability which arises out of a contract for capital expenditure will give rise to an asset when the payment is made. Till the payment is made, the asset which is inferred by a contingent liability is treated as contingent assets, e.g., Sale agreement to acquire a property, Hire-Purchase transactions.

Classification of Liabilities

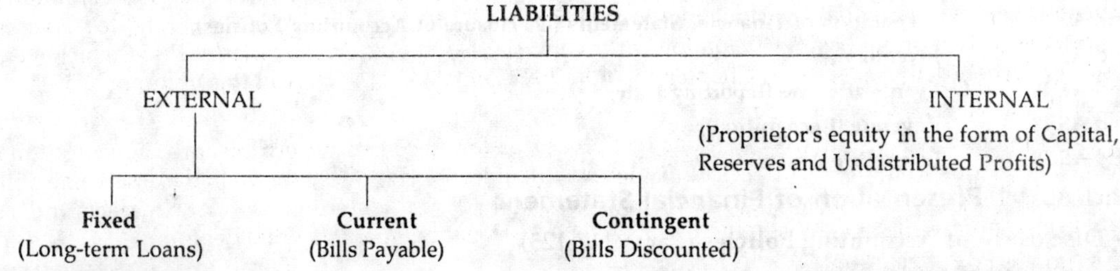

Fixed Liabilities

The liabilities which are repayable after a long period of time are known as Fixed Liabilities, i.e., they do not become due for payment in the ordinary course of the business within a relatively short period. In other words, liabilities which fall due after a comparatively long period is known as fixed or long term liabilities. Fixed liabilities are, therefore, those which are not repayable within one year of the Balance Sheet date or normal operating cycle of the business. But a closer examination would reveal that, towards the end of their lives, fixed liabilities also may be treated as current liabilities. Debentures are the typical example of this type of liability, e.g., Long-term loans, Debentures.

Current Liabilities

Current liabilities are those which are repayable or liquidated within a short-period of time by the use of either (i) existing resources of current assets; or (ii) by the creation of similar current liabilities. The short period concerned is used to refer to a period not exceeding one year from the Balance Sheet date or within an operating cycle of the business like current assets. Usually, the current liabilities are created for the purpose of the production cycle, e.g., Sundry Creditors, Bills Payables, Outstanding Expenses, like outstanding wages, salaries, commissions, including various kinds of outstanding taxes. It is interesting to note that there are other current liabilities what are not directly related with the production cycle, but related to business, e.g., instalment payment in case of asset acquired on hire-purchase and instalment basis. Thus, the current liabilities mean and include:

(i) Trade Creditors; (ii) Bills Payable; (iii) Outstanding Expenses; (iv) Provision for Tax Payables; (v) Bank Overdraft; (vi) Proposed Dividend; (vii) Deferred Revenue, and Advances from Customer.

Contingent Liabilities

It is an anticipated liability which has not matured or the amount has not been determined or the claim has not yet been acknowledged as debt, etc. In short, it is an obligation relating to a past transaction of other event or condition, that may arise in consequence of a future event now deemed possible but not probable, e.g., claim against company not acknowledged as debt. This liability is of two types : viz., (i) One type involves the incurring of a loss if it materialises, e.g., liability arising for bill discounted; (ii) Other type involves the acquisition of an asset, e.g., liability for calls on partly paid shares.

Contingent Liabilities are shown under the liabilities side of a Balance Sheet as a footnote, i.e., the amount will not appear in the money column.

Internal Liabilities

These represent the proprietors' equity, i.e., all those amounts which are entitled to the proprietor e.g., Capital, Reserve and Surplus, Undistributed Profit.

We know that the business has got a separate legal entity, i.e., it is quite different from its owner. When the owner invests money in the firm, it is nothing but a loan to the business. The business must repay the same. When it makes profit, it is added with capital, because, liability of the business increases. That is why both capital and profit are liability of the business.

But the liability which is taken by the business from outsiders, those are not considered as *capital*. They are outside or external liabilities. Only the liability to the owner is considered as *Capital* and, accordingly, the profit or loss so earned or suffered, is adjusted against the *Capital*, i.e., liability to the owner.

APPLICATION OF NEW INDIAN ACCOUNTING STANDARDS

Some important Accounting Standards (Ind ASs) are very relevant for the preparation of final accounts of a Trading Concern since some of them are mandatory:

We will highlight here the important aspects or summary of some Indian Accounting Standards :

Ind AS 1	:	**Preparation of Financial Statements (Disclosure of Accounting Policies);**
Ind AS 2	:	**Inventory;**
Ind AS 10	:	**Events after the Reporting Date;**
Ind AS 18	:	**Revenue (Recognition);**
Ind AS 38	:	**Intangible Assets.**

Ind AS 1: Presentation of Financial Statement

—Disclosure of Accounting Policies (Paras 117-125)

Summary of some of them—

117. An entity shall disclose in the summary of significant accounting policies :

(a) the measurement basis (or bases) used in preparing the financial statements, and

(b) the other accounting policies used that are relevant to an understanding of the financial statements.

121. An accounting policy may be significant because of the nature of the entity's operations even if amounts for current and prior periods are not material. It is also appropriate to disclose each significant accounting policy that is not specifically required by Ind ASs but the entity selects and applies in accordance with Ind AS 8 i.e., ***all significant accounting policies in the preparation and presentation of financial statements should be disclosed.***

122. An entity shall disclose, in the summary of significant accounting policies or other notes, that have the most significant effect on the amounts recognised in the financial statements.

125. An entity shall disclose information about the assumptions it makes about the future, and other major sources of estimation uncertainty at the end of the reporting period, that have a significant risk of resulting in a material adjustment to the carrying amounts of assets and liabilities within the next financial year.

Ind AS 2 : Valuation of Inventories

(This standard had already been explained in Chapter 14, **Inventory Valuation**)

Ind AS 10 : Events after the Reporting Dates (Paras 3-7)

The following terms are used in this Standard with the meanings specified :

3. ***Events after the reporting period*** are those events, favourable and unfavourable, that occur between the end of the reporting period and the date when the financial statements are approved by the Board of Directors in case of a company, and, by the corresponding approving authority in case of any other entity for issue. Two types of events can be identified :

(a) those that provide evidence of conditions that existed at the end of the reporting period (adjusting events after the reporting period); and

(b) those that are indicative of conditions that arose after the reporting period (non-adjusting events after the reporting period).

4. The process involved in approving the financial statements for issue will vary depending upon the management structure, statutory requirements and procedures followed in preparing and finalising the financial statements.

5. In some cases, an entity is required to submit its financial statements to its shareholders for approval after the financial statements have been approved by the Board for issue. In such cases, the financial statements are approved for issue on the date of approval by the Board, not the date when shareholders approved the financial statements.

6. In some cases, the management of an entity is required to issue its financial statements to a supervisory board (made up solely of non-executives) for approval. In such cases, the financial statements are approved for issue when the management approves them for issue to the supervisory Board.

7. Events after the reporting period include all events up to the date when the financial statements are approved for issue, even if those events occur after the public announcement of profit or of other selected financial information.

Illustration 7

The financial statements of Construction Ltd. for the year ended 31.3.2009 were considered and approved by the Board of Directors on 20.5.2009.

"The company was engaged in construction work involving Rs. 10 crores. In the course of execution of work a portion of factory shed under construction came crashing down on 30.5.2009. Fortunately there was no loss of life, but the company will have to rebuild the construction at an additional cost of Rs. 2 crores which cannot be recovered from the contractee."

How should this event be reported ?

[ICWA (Final Dec. 2001)—Adapted]

Solution

As per **Para 3, Ind AS 10, "Events After the Reporting Date"**—are those significant events, both favourable and unfavourable, that occur between the Balance Sheet date and the date on which the financial statements are approved by the Board of Directors in the case of a company, and, by the corresponding approving authority in case of any other entity.

However, in the present case, financial statements were prepared for the year ended 31.3.2009, the final statements were approved by the Board of Directors on 20.5.2009, and a portion of construction crashed down on 30.5.2009. The present unfavourable event is not an event which comes under "Events Occurring After Balance Sheet Date." As such, no adjustment is required against assets and liabilities and, at the same time, it does not require to disclose the matter in the financial statement. But as it is, no doubt, a material change which affects the financial position and which happened as a result of the event occurred after the Balance Sheet date, the same should be mentioned in the Directors' Report of the company.

Illustration 8

State how the amount of Loss due to fire will be dealt with in the financial statement.

On 7.1.2009, the Plant and Machinery of X Ltd. were badly damaged by fire which caused an estimated loss amounting to Rs. 10,00,000. It was estimated/expected that 50% of the amount might be recovered from the insurance company as it was insured (accounts closes on 31st Dec. every year).

Solution

The Plant and Machinery were destroyed by fire on 7.1.2009, i.e., after the closing of the books of account. The estimated loss was Rs. 10,00,000. It is quite clear that the fire broke out after the Balance Sheet date and did not affect the financial statements as on 31st Dec. 2008. Thus, as per **Ind AS 10**, the events that occur after the Balance Sheet date cannot be adjusted in the financial statements any more as it had no effect while preparing the financial statement for the period ended 31st Dec. 2008. But as per the disclosure of AS 10 the same must be informed to the appropriate authority.

Ind AS 18 : Revenue (Recognition)

(This Standard has already been explained in **Chapter 15—*Revenue Recognition***)

Ind AS 38 : Intangible Assets (Paras 68-71)

An intangible asset is an identifiable non-monetary asset without physical substance.

This Standard applies to, among other things, expenditure on advertising, training, start-up, research and development activities. Research and development activities are directed to the development of knowledge. Therefore, although these activities may result in an asset with physical substance (eg., a prototype), the physical element of the asset is secondary to its intangible component, i.e., the knowledge embodied in it.

68. Expenditure on an intangible item shall be recognised as an expense when it is incurred unless :

(a) it forms part of the cost of an intangible asset that meets the recognition criteria (see paragraphs 18-67); or

(b) **the item is acquired in a business combination and cannot be recognised as an intangible asset. If this is the case, it forms part of the amount recognised as goodwill at the acquisition date (see Ind AS 103).**

69. In some cases, expenditure is incurred to provide future economic benefits to an entity, but no intangible asset or other asset is acquired or created that can be recognised. In the case of the supply of goods, the entity recognises such expenditure as an expense when it has a right to access those goods in services. For example, expenditure on research is recognised as an expense when it is incurred except when it is acquired as part of a business combination. Other examples of expenditure that is recognised as an expense when it is incurred include :

(a) expenditure on start-up activities (i.e., start-up costs), unless this expenditure is included in the cost of an item of property, plant and equipment in acccordance with **Ind AS 16.** Start-up costs may consist of establishment costs such as legal and secretarial: costs incurred in establishing a legal entity, expenditure to open a new facility or business (i.e. pre-opening costs) or expenditures for starting new operations or launching new products or processes (i.e. pre-opening costs), or expenditures for starting new operations or launching new products or processes (i.e. pre-operating costs).

(b) expenditure on training activities.

(c) expenditure of advertising and promotional activities (including mail order catalogues).

(d) expenditure on relocating or reorganising part or all of an entity.

Paragraph 68 does not preclude an entity from recognising a prepayment as an asset shen payment for goods has been made in advance of the entity obtaining a right to access those goods. Similarly, paragraph 68 does not preclude an entity from recognising a prepayment as an asset when payment for services has been made in advance of the entity receiving those services.

Past expenses not to be recognised as an asset

Expenditure on an intangible item that was initially recognised as an expense shall not be recognised as part of the cost of an intangible asset at a later date.

SOME IMPORTANT ADJUSTMENTS

If there are any adjustments those are to be adjusted accordingly before ascertaining the net profit of the firm. (For further details, please see Chapter 9—**JOURNAL PROPER**—*Adjusting Entries*). Only certain adjustments are explained here in order to avoid repetition :

A. Outstanding Expenses

Outstanding expenses are those expenses which are not paid during the accounting period although they have become due for payment. The entry for this purpose is :

(Particular) Expense A/c Dr.
To Outstanding Expenses A/c

Consider the following example :

Salary paid for the year ended 31st December 1998 amounted to Rs. 11,000. But **Outstanding Salary** for the period was Rs. 1,000.

Show the Salary, Outstanding Salary, Profit and Loss Account and the Balance Sheet for the year ended 31st December 1998.

We are to pass the following entries :

		Rs.	Rs.
(i) ***For Salary Paid :*** Salary A/c	Dr.	11,000	
To Cash/Bank A/c			11,000
(ii) ***For Outstanding Salary :*** Salary A/c	Dr.	1,000	
To Outstanding Salary A/c			1,000

Salary A/c

Dr.	Rs.		Cr. Rs.
To Cash A/c	11,000	By Profit and Loss A/c — transferred	12,000
" Outstanding Salary A/c	1,000		
	12,000		12,000

Outstanding Salary A/c

Dr.	Rs.		Cr. Rs.
To Balance c/d	1,000	By Salary A/c	1,000
	1,000		1,000
		By Balance b/d	1,000

Profit and Loss A/c (Extract)
for the year ended 31st December 1998

Dr.	Rs.	Rs.		Cr. Rs.
To Salary	11,000		By	
Add : Outstanding Salary	1,000			
		12,000		

Balance Sheet (Extract)
as 31st December 1998

Liabilities	Rs.	*Assets*	Rs.
Outstanding Salary A/c	1,000		

Important Note

If the outstanding expenses have already appeared in the Trial Balance, it means the same has already been adjusted; as such, the amount which is shown in the credit side of a Trial Balance will appear only in the liability side of the Balance Sheet.

B. Prepaid Expenses

Prepaid expenses are those expenses which are paid in advance during the period although they are not yet due for payment. The entry for this purpose will be :

Prepaid Expenses A/c Dr.
To (Particular) Expenses A/c

Consider the following example :

Insurance paid for the year ended 31st March 1999 amounted to Rs. 6,000 out of which Rs. 500 was paid in advance for the year 2,000.

Show the Insurance Account, Prepaid Insurance Account, Profit and Loss Account, and the Balanc Sheet for the year ended 31st March 1999.

Solution

We are to pass the following entries :

		Rs.	Rs.
(i) ***For the Insurance paid :***			
Insurance A/c	Dr.	6,000	
To Cash/Bank A/c			6,000
(ii) ***For Prepaid Insurance :***			
Prepaid Insurance A/c	Dr.	500	
To Insurance A/c			500

Insurance A/c

Dr.	Rs.		Cr. Rs.
To Cash A/c	6,000	By Prepaid Insurance A/c	500
		" Profit and Loss A/c — Transferred	5,500
	6,000		6,000

Prepaid Insurance A/c

Dr.	Rs.		Cr. Rs.
To Insurance A/c	500	By Balance c/d	500
	500		500
To Balance b/d	500		

Profit and Loss A/c (Extract)
for the year ended 31st March 1999

Dr.	Rs.	Rs.		Cr. Rs.
To Insurance A/c	6,000		By	
Less : Prepaid Insurance	500			
		5,500		

Balance Sheet (Extract)
as at 31st March 1999

Liabilities	Rs.	*Assets*	Rs.
		Prepaid Insurance A/c	500

Important Note

If the amount of prepaid expenses appear in the Trial Balance, the same has already been adjusted and, as such, the same will appear only in the assets side of the Balance Sheet.

C. Accrued Incomes

The income which has already become due but not yet received within the accounting year is known as 'Accrued Income'. The entry for this purpose will be :

Accrued Income A/c Dr.
To (Particular)) Income A/c

Consider the following example :

Income received for the year ended 31st December 1998 amounted to Rs. 9,000. But accrued interest for the period amounted to Rs. 1,000.

Show the Interest Account, Accrued Interest Account, Profit and Loss Account and the Balance Sheet.

Solution

We are to pass the following entries :

		Rs.	Rs.
(i) ***For the Interest received :***			
Cash/Bank A/c	Dr.	9,000	
To Interest A/c			9,000
(ii) ***For Accrued Interest :***			
Accrued Interest A/c	Dr.	1,000	
To Interest A/c			1,000

Interest A/c

Dr.	Rs.		Cr. Rs.
To Profit & Loss A/c — transferred	10,000	By Cash A/c	9,000
		" Accrued Interest A/c	1,000
	10,000		10,000

Accrued Interest A/c

Dr.	Rs.		Cr. Rs.
To Interest A/c	1,000	By Balance c/d	1,000
	1,000		1,000
To Balance b/d	1,000		

Profit and Loss A/c (*Extract*)
for the year ended 31st Dec. 1998

Dr.		Cr.	Rs.	Rs.
		By Interest A/c	9,000	
		Add : Accrued Interest	1,000	
				10,000

Balance Sheet (*Extract*)
as at 31st Dec. 1998

Liabilities	Rs.	*Assets*	Rs.
		Accrued Interest A/c	1,000

Important Note

If the amount of accrued interest appears in the Trial Balance, no further adjustment is necessary, i.e., the same has already been adjusted and, as such, the same will appear only in the assets side of the Balance Sheet.

D. Incomes Received in Advance

The incomes which should not have been received but has already been received must be adjusted while preparing Profit and Loss Account, i.e., the incomes which have not become due but have already been received in advance during the year. The entry for the purpose will be:

(Particular) Income A/c Dr.
To Income Received in Advance A/c

Consider the following example :

Interest received during the year ended 31st December 1998 amounted to Rs. 5,000, out of which Rs. 1,000 was received in advance for the year 1999.

Show the Interest Account, Interest Received in Advance Account, Profit and Loss Account and the Balance Sheet.

Solution

We are to pass the following entries :

		Rs.	Rs.
(i) ***For the Interest Received :***			
Cash/Bank A/c	Dr.	5,000	
To Interest A/c			5,000
(ii) ***For interest received in advance :***			
Interest A/c	Dr.	1,000	
To Interest Received in Advance A/c			1,000

Dr. Interest A/c Cr.

	Rs.		Rs.
To Interest Received in Advance A/c	1,000	By Cash A/c	5,000
" P & L A/c — transferred	4,000		
	5,000		5,000

Dr. Interest Received in Advance A/c Cr.

	Rs.		Rs.
To Balance c/d	1,000	By Interest A/c	1,000
	1,000		1,000
		By Balance b/d	1,000

Profit and Loss A/c *(Extract)*
for the year ended 31st Dec. 1998

Dr.	Rs.		Rs.	Cr. Rs.
To		By Interest	5,000	
		Less : Interest Received in Advance	1,000	
			4,000	

Balance Sheet *(Extract)*
as at 31st Dec. 1998

Liabilities	Rs.	*Assets*	Rs.
Interest Received in Advance	1,000		

Important Note

If the amount of income received in advance appears in the Trial Balance, the same will only appear in the liabilities side of the Balance Sheet.

E. Depreciation of Assets

Different fixed assets which are used by the business for the purpose of earning revenue are depreciated gradually. This depreciation charge must be taken into consideration while preparing Profit and Loss Account. The entry is:

Depreciation A/c Dr.
 To Assets A/c

But if the depreciation appears in Trial Balance no further adjustment is required. The same will simply be debited to Profit and Loss Account. There will be no deduction from the asset in the Asset side of the Balance Sheet since the same has already been done.

However, for making provision for depreciation, the entry will be:

Profit and Loss A/c Dr.
 To Provision for Depreciation A/c

The amount of depreciation is to be added to the existing provision and the total provision must be shown in the Liability side of the Balance Sheet or as a deduction from the asset in the Asset side of the Balance Sheet.

The following example will make the principle clear:

Example

Trial Balance (Extract) *as on 31st Dec. ...*

	Rs.	Rs.
Plant and Machinery	1,00,000	

Additional Information

(i) Depreciate Plant and Machinery by 10% p.a.

Solution

Adjusting entries being:

		Rs.	Rs.
Depreciation A/c	Dr.	10,000	
To Plant and Machinery A/c			10,000

Effect in Final Accounts

Profit and Loss Account *(Extract)*
for the year ended ...

Dr.			Cr.
	Rs.		Rs.
To Depreciation on: Plant and Machinery	10,000		

Balance Sheet *(Extract)* as at

Liabilities	*Assets*	Rs.	Rs.
	Plant and Machinery	1,00,000	
	Less: Depreciation	10,000	
			90,000

F. Interest on Capital and Drawings: Sometimes interest is charged on the capital contributed by the owners, i.e., interest on capital which is to be paid by the firm to its owners. The same must be adjusted before preparing Profit and Loss Account.

The entry will be:

Interest on Capital A/c Dr.
  To Capital/Current A/c

But, if interest on capital appears in the Trial Balance, it will simply be debited by transferring to Profit and Loss Appropriation Account. In case of interest on drawings, which is charged by the business to its owners, the entry is:

Drawings/Capital A/c Dr.
  To Interest on Drawings A/c

If it appears in the Trial Balance, it will be credited to Profit and Loss Appropriation Account and nothing will be adjusted against Drawings/Capital Accounts.

G. Interest on Loan: If any amount is taken by way of loan, interest is charged on it, which remains outstanding. The same must be considered while preparing Profit and Loss Account. The entry is:

Interest on Loan A/c Dr.
  To Loan A/c

If, however, it appears in the Trial Balance, no further adjustment is necessary, it will be debited to Profit and Loss Account.

H. Treatment of Purchasesâ

(i) When Purchases are not passed through the books although the same are included in stock:

(a) ***If it relates to the current financial year***

We are to pass the usual entries, viz.

Purchases A/c Dr.
To Creditors/Suppliers A/c

(b) ***If it relates to the next year:***

It will simply be deducted from the closing stock.

(ii) When purchases are recorded in the books but not included in stock (due to delayed delivery or any other reasons):

For this purpose, simply a cancellation entry for purchases should be made (if it relates to the next period) by debiting Creditors or Suppliers' Account and Crediting Purchase Account. Generally, the amount should be included with the value of closing stock on the ground, that the same relates to the current financial year.

(iii) When purchases are made for the current financial year, but, neither recorded at all in the books nor included in closing stock:

In this case, we are to pass simply an usual entry as:

Purchases A/c Dr.
To Creditors/Suppliers A/c

Thus, it will be added to the amount of purchases, as well as with the amount of creditors. Moreover, the same should also be included in the amount of closing stock.

(iv) When purchases are made for private purchase but not passed through the books:

There will be no entry in the books of the business if the proprietor wants to pay or assume a private liability. But, in other case, the following entry should be passed:

Drawings A/c Dr.
To Cash/Bank (for cash purchases)
To Creditors/Suppliers (for credit purchases)

Thus, it will be added to the amount of Drawings and the same will be deducted from Cash or Bank or will be added to the amount of Creditors (for credit purchases only).

(v) When assets are purchased but wrongly included with the amount of purchase:

For this purpose the following entry should be passed:

Particular Asset A/c Dr.
To Purchases A/c

That is, value of asset should be increased and the same amount will be deducted from the purchases.

It should be remembered that, if there is any depreciation on such asset, the same should also be computed on such enhanced value.

I. Closing Stock

We know that closing stock is neither recorded in an account nor is it recorded in a Trial Balance. At the time of preparing Profit and Loss Account, valuation of stock must be made for unsold goods since they affect profit. For this purpose closing stock should be valued at Cost Price or Market Price, whichever is less.

The entry will be:

Closing Stock A/c Dr.
To Trading A/c

[If the closing stock has already appeared in the Trial Balance (i.e., adjusted with purchases) the same will be shown as an asset in the Asset side of the Balance Sheet.]

Treatment of Stock

4. Stock when lost by accident

The value of stock which has been lost due to accident must be ascertained first. The following entries are necessary before preparing the Profit and Loss Account:

(a) ***When stock is lost by accident (say, fire), but not recovered from Insurance Company :***

(i) Stock Destroyed by Fire A/c Dr.
To Trading A/c

(ii) Profit and Loss A/c Dr.
To Stock Destroyed by Fire A/c

(b) ***When stock is lost by fire, but the entire amount was recovered from Insurance Company:***

(i) Stock Destroyed by Fire A/c Dr.
To Trading A/c

(ii) Bank A/c Dr.
To Stock Destroyed by Fire A/c

If admitted by Insurance Co.:

(iii) Insurance Claims A/c Dr.
To Stock Destroyed by Fire A/c

(c) ***When stock is lost by fire but a portion was recovered from Insurance Company :***

(i) Stock Destroyed by Fire A/c Dr. (with the total amount of loss)
To Trading A/c

(ii) Bank A/c Dr. (amount received from Insurance Co.)
Profit and Loss A/c Dr. (actual loss)
To Stock Destroyed by Fire A/c (total amount)

B, When stock is used by the proprietor but not recorded

Sometimes a part of the goods/stock may be used by the proprietor for his own use. For this purpose the entry will be:

Drawings A/c Dr.
To Purchases/Opening Stock A/c

That is, in other words, the amount should be deducted from purchases or opening stock in Trading Account and the same also will be added with Drawings which is adjusted against Capital or Current Account.[1]

C. **When stock is used for private use and included in sales**

For this purpose, the following entries are required to be passed:

(a) Sales A/c Dr. (for cancellation)
To Debtors A/c

(b) Drawings A/c Dr. (for correct one)
To Purchases/Opening Stock A/c

Thus, the amount should be deducted from Sales and Debtors, respectively, at the same time; it will be added with the drawings and will be deducted from purchases or opening stock.

D. **When stock is used as stationery**

Sometimes a part of stock is being used as stationery. For this purpose, the entry will be:

Stationery A/c Dr.
To Purchases/Opening Stock A/c

Thus, the amount is to be deducted from purchases or opening stock and the same is to be closed by transferring to Profit and Loss Account by way of Stationery.

E. **When (opening) stock is distributed as free sample or free gift, etc.**

In this case, the entry will be:

Advertisement or Charity A/c Dr.
To Opening Stock A/c

That is, the amount should be deducted from Purchases or Opening Stock and the same is to be transferred to Profit and Loss Account by way of Advertisement/Charity.

Example

Mr X presented the following Trial Balance (Extracted) as on 31.3.2011 :

Trial Balance *(Extract)*
for the year ended 31.3.2011

Debit	Rs.	*Credit*	Rs.
Drawings	10,000	Sales	40,000
Opening Stock	5,000		
Debtors	25,000		
Stationery	5,000		
Advertisement	3,000		
Purchase	15,600		

Additional Information

(a) Closing Stock: Market Price Rs. 20,000; Cost Price Rs. 25,000.
(b) Stock destroyed by fire amounting to Rs. 5,000; only Rs. 4,000 were recovered from the Insurance Company.
(c) A part of opening stock was used by the proprietor—amounted to Rs. 1000.
(d) Stock used for private purpose wrongly included in sales—amounted to Rs. 3,000.
(e) A part of stock was used as Stationery—amounted to Rs. 500.
(f) A part of opening stock had been distributed as free sample for Rs. 1,000.

Show the effect of the above in final account, also show the adjusting entries.

---

[1] When Fluctuating Capital Method is followed, Drawings will be deducted from Capital A/c while, in case of Fixed Capital Method, the same Drawings will be deducted from Current A/c

Solution

In the Books of Mr. X

(a) Valuation of Closing Stock

Closing Stock should be valued as per cost price or market price, whichever is lower. In the present case, since market price of Rs. 20,000 is less than the Cost Price of Rs. 25,000, Rs. 20,000 should be considered as the value of Closing Stock. The entry being:

		Rs.	Rs.
Closing Stock A/c	Dr.	20,000	
To Trading A/c			20,000

Thus, Closing Stock will appear in the credit side of Trading Account and the same will also appear in the assets side of the Balance Sheet under the head **Current Assets.**

(b) Stock Destroyed by Fire

The usual entry being:

		Rs.	Rs.
Stock Destroyed by Fire A/c	Dr.	10,000	
To Trading A/c			10,000

Where a part is recovered from the Insurance Company

		Rs.	Rs.
Bank A/c	Dr.	4,000	
Profit and Loss A/c	Dr.	1,000	
To Stock Destroyed Fire A/c			5,000

Treatment in Final Account

Dr. **Trading A/c (Extract)** *for the year ended ...* Cr.

	Rs.		Rs.	Rs.
To		By Closing Stock	20,000	
		Add : Stock Destroyed	5,000	25,000

Profit & Loss A/c (Extract) for the year ended ...

	Rs.		Rs.
To Stock Destroyed by Fire A/c	1,000		

Balance Sheet (Extract) *as at ...*

		Assets	Rs.
		Bank —Received from Insurance Com.	4,000

(c) Opening Stock used by Proprietor. The entry being:

		Rs.	Rs.
Drawings A/c	Dr.	1,000	
To Opening Stock			1,000

Treatment in Final Account

Dr. **Trading A/c (Extract)** *for the year ended ...* Cr.

	Rs.		Rs.
To Opening Stock	5,000	By	
Less ; Drawings	1,000		
	4,000		

Balance Sheet (Extract) *as at ...*

Liabilities		Rs.	*Assets*	Rs.
Less : Drawing	10,000			
Add: Stock Used	1,000	11,000		

(c) Stock used for private use, wrongly included in Sales

In this case, two entries are required, one for cancellation of wrong entry and the other for rectifying entry. Thus :

			Rs.	Rs.
(i)	Sales A/c	Dr.	3,000	
	To Debtors A/c			3,000
(ii)	Drawings A/c	Dr.	3,000	
	To Stock A/c			3,000

Treatment in Final Account

Dr. ***Sales A/c (Extract)*** Cr.

	Rs.		Rs.	Rs.
To Debtors	3,000	By Balance b/d	40,000	

Dr. **Debtors A/c** Cr.

	Rs.		Rs.
To Balance b/d	25,000	By Sales A/c	3,000

Dr. *Drawings A/c* Cr.

	Rs.		Rs.
To Balance b/d	10,000	By	
" Stock A/c	3,000		

Treatment in Final Account

Dr. **Trading A/c** *for the year ended...* Cr.

	Rs.		Rs.
To Open. Stock	5,000	By Sales	40,000
Less : Drawings	3,000	*Less:* For	
	2,000	Cancella-tion entry	3,000
			37,000

Balance Sheet *as at ...*

		Rs.			Rs.
Less : Drawing	10,000		Debtors	25,000	
Add: Stock Used	3,000		*Less: Drawings*	3,000	
		13,000			22,000

(d) **Stock used as Stationery. The entry being:**

		Rs.	Rs.
Stationery A/c	Dr.	500	
To Opening Stock A/c			500

Treatment in Final Account

Dr. **Trading A/c (*Extract*)** *for the year ended ...* Cr.

	Rs.		Rs.
To Open. Stock	5,000	By	
Less : Stationery	500		
	4,500		

Dr. **P & L A/c (*Extract*)** *for the year ended ...* Cr.

Liabilities		Rs.	*Assets*	Rs.
To Stationery	5,000		By	
Add: Stock Used	500			
		5,500		

(e) **Stock Distributed as Free Sample. The entry being:**

		Rs.	Rs.
Advertisement A/c	Dr.	1,000	
To Opening Stock A/c			1,000

Treatment in Final Account

Dr. **Trading A/c (*Extract*)** *for the year ended ...* Cr.

	Rs.		Rs.
To Open. Stock	5,000	By	
Less : Free Sample	1,000		
	4,000		

Dr. **P & L A/c (*Extract*)** *for the year ended ...* Cr.

	Rs.		Rs.
To Advertisement	3,000	By	
***Add:* Stock as free sample**	1,000		
	4,000		

J. Manager's Commission on Net Profit: Sometimes the manager is given a special commission to be calculated on net profit in addition to his salary/remuneration in order to induce him to take more interest in the firm. Such commission is calculated on net profit. Since net profit is ascertained at the end of the year, so also is the manager's commission. That is why the amount remains outstanding at the end of the year. Thus, the adjustment is:

Manager's Commission A/c Dr.

To Outstanding Manager's Commission A/c

Methods of Calculation

It may be calculated in two ways:

(i) On profit before charging commission; (ii) On profit after charging commission.

(i) **On profit before charging commission:** Under the circumstances, the commission is directly calculated on net profits, i.e., on profit, before charging commission, in the following manner:

$$\textit{Manager's Commission} = \textit{Net Profit (before charging commission)} \times \frac{\textit{Rate}}{100}$$

Example

If net profit before charging commission is Rs. 11,000 and commission payable to manager is 10%, then the Manager's Commission will be:

$$\text{Rs. } 11{,}000 \times \frac{10}{100} = \text{Rs. } 1{,}100$$

(ii) **On profit after charging commission:** Under the circumstances the commission will be calculated on net profit after charging such commission, i.e., the manager is entitled to a commission on net profit which remains after charging his commission.

In that case, the commission is calculated as:

$$\text{Manager's Commission} = \text{Net Profit (before charging commission)} \times \frac{\text{Rate}}{\text{Rate} + 100}$$

Example

Taking the previous example, Manager's Commission will be:

$$\text{Manager's Commission} = \text{Rs. } 11{,}000 \times \frac{10}{10 + 100} = \text{Rs. } 11{,}000 \times \frac{10}{110} = \text{Rs. } 1{,}000.$$

Example

Compute the Commission for General Manager and Works Manager from the following information :

(1) General Manager is to be given commission at 10% after charging the commission of Works Manger and his own.

(2) Works Manager is to be given commission at 5% after charging the commission of General Manager and his own.

(3) Profit before charging General Manager's commission and Works Manager's commission were Rs. 11,500.

Solution

Profit before charging Commission amounted to Rs. 11,500. Since both the General Manager and Works Manager take commission @ 10% and 5%, respectively, after charging their respective commissions, total commission will be 15% (after charging such com.)—which means $\frac{15}{115}$ of the said profit.

Thus, General Manager will get $= \text{Rs.} 11{,}500 \times \frac{10}{115} = \text{Rs. } 1{,}000$

and, Works Manager will get $= \text{Rs. } 11{,}500 \times \frac{10}{115} = \text{Rs. } 500$

K. Goods Sent on Approval: If goods are sent to the customer on Sale or Return Basis, the same must not be treated as actual sale till the period is not expired. Thus, if goods are sent on approval basis, we pass the usual entry for credit sales. Naturally, if the goods are lying in the hands of the customer, awaiting approval, the following entries should be passed:

(i) *For cancellation of the original entry*

Sales A/c Dr.

To Customers/Debtors A/c

(ii) *For inclusion in Closing Stock at cost*

Closing Stock A/c Dr.

To Trading A/c

Example

Goods costing Rs. 5,000 were sent to a customer on **'Sale or Return Basis'** on 30th Dec. 2009. These were recorded as actual sales. The rate of gross profit was $\frac{1}{6}$th of sales (given) Rs. 50,000; Debtors were Rs. 40,000, value of Closing Stock amounted to Rs. 20,000.

Show the entries and treatment in Final Account.

Solution

(i) Rate of profit is $\frac{1}{6}$th of Sales i.e., $\frac{1}{5}$th of Cost.

So, Cost Price Rs. 5,000 + Profit Rs. 1,000 = Selling Price Rs. 6,000.

Thus, Rs. 6,000 to be deducted from Sales in Trading A/c and the same to be deducted from Sundry Debtors in Balance Sheet.

(ii) Rs. 5,000, i.e., the Cost Price to be added to Closing Stock. So, Closing Stock will be Rs. (30,000 + 5,000) = Rs. 35,000, both in Trading A/c and in the assets side of the Balance Sheet as well.

Thus, the entries will be

			Rs.	Rs.
(i)	Sales A/c	Dr.	6,000	
	To Debtors A/c			6,000
(ii)	Closing Stock A/c	Dr.	5,000	
	To Trading A/c (at Cost) A/c			5,000

Treatment in Final Account

Dr. *Trading A/c (Extract) for the year ended ...* Cr.

	Rs.	Rs.
By Sales	50,000	
Less : Sales or Return	6,000	44,000
" Closing Stock	20,000	
Add : Sale or Return	5,000	25,000

Balance Sheet (*Extract*) as at ...

	Rs.			Rs.
To		Stock		25,000
		Debtors	40,000	
		Less: Sale or Return	6,000	34,000

L. Set-Off: Sometimes a person may be considered both a debtor and a creditor to the firm. In that case, the lower of the amount—payable to and receivable from such person—is to be set-off. The set-off amount is to be deducted both from the Debtors and from the Creditors in the Balance Sheet. The entry will be:

Creditors (in Bought Ledger) A/c Dr.
To Debtors (in Sales Ledger) A/c

Example

Sundry Debtors include Rs. 5,000 due from Mr. Sen whereas Sundry Creditors included Rs. 2,000 due to Mr. Sen.

Show the entries and effect in final account.

Debtors and Creditors were Rs. 40,000, and Rs. 30,000, respectively.

Solution

The entry being

			Rs.	Rs.
(i)	Creditors A/c	Dr.	2,000	
	To Debtors A/c (the lower amount)			2,000

Balance Sheet (*Extract*) as at ...

Liabilities		Rs.	*Assets*		Rs.
Creditors	30,000		Debtors	40,000	
Less: Mutual Indebtedness	2,000	28,000	*Less:* Mutual Indebtedness	2,000	38,000

M. Debtors which arise out of dishonoured cheques or discounted bills but not adjusted

The entry for this purpose will be:

Debtors A/c Dr.
To Bank A/c

That is, the amount should be added to Debtors and the same should also be deducted from Bank Account. But, out of those debtors, **if any amount proves to be bad**, the entry will be

Bad Debts A/c Dr.
To Debtors A/c

i.e., Bad Debts to be transferred to Profit and Loss Account, the same also should be deducted from Debtors, in the Asset side of the Balance Sheet. If there is any provision for bad debts, the same should be ascertained after adjusting the above bad debts.

Example

Show the entries and their treatment in Final Account:

A cheque for Rs. 1,000 received from Mr X—which was deposited into bank but returned dishonoured—not entered in Cash Book. Mr X became insolvent. Nothing has been realised from his estate. Amount of Debtors and Cash at Bank were Rs. 20,000, Rs. 11,000, respectively :

The Rectification Entry being :

			Rs.	Rs.
(i)	X A/c	Dr.	1,,000	
	To Bank A/c			1,000
(ii)	Bad Debts A/c	Dr.	1,000	
	To X A/c			1,000

Treatment in Final Account

Dr. P & L A/c (*Extract*) *for the year ended* ... *Cr.*

	Rs.		Rs.	Rs.
To Bad Debts A/c	1,000			

Balance Sheet (*Extract*) as at ...

	Assets		Rs.
	Debtors	20,000	
	Add: Dishonoured Cheque	1,000	
		21,000	
	Less: B/D A/c	1,000	20,000
	Bank A/c	11,000	
	Less: Dishonoured Cheque	1,000	10,000

N. Income-Tax

In case of Sole Proprietorship Firm

In case of Sole Proprietorship firm, Income-tax is treated as **Drawings** as it is a personal liability of the proprietor. Income-tax cannot be considered as a business **expense** as it does not help to earn revenue like other nominal accounts. Thus, income-tax is paid by the owner. Since it is treated as drawings, the same will be deducted from the Capital Account. However, if it appears in the Trial Balance, the same should be added to Drawings. The entries to be recorded are:

(a) ***When Income-Tax paid***

(i) Income-Tax A/c Dr.
To Bank A/c

(b) ***When transferred to drawings***

(ii) Drawings A/c Dr.
To Income-Tax A/c

In case of Partnership Firm

Under the circumstances, income-tax is payable by the business. Thus, if it appears in the Trial Balance, the same should be debited to Profit and Loss Account as a charge against profit by passing the following entries:

(a) ***When charged against profit***

(i) Profit and Loss A/c Dr.
To Income-Tax

(b) When Income-tax is paid

(ii) Income-Tax A/c Dr.
To Bank A/c

O. *Advance Tax*

Like income-tax stated above, advance tax also will be treated as **"Drawings"**. Advance Tax is paid against the income which is assessed at a subsequent date. The same is paid by the owner. Advance tax is adjusted accordingly against the total amount of tax payable computed at a subsequent date. The entries are:

(a) ***When advance tax is paid***

(i) Advance Tax A/c Dr.
To Bank A/c

(b) ***When transfers to drawings***

(ii) Drawings A/c Dr.
To Advance Tax

P. *Sales Tax*

The seller collects the amount of sales tax from the customers and deposits the same to the Government. The seller should separately record that amount of Sales Tax and actual amount of sales in Sales Day Book. But usually, it is wrongly included in Sales.

The difference between the amount of Sales Tax collected from the Customers by the seller and the amount of Sale Tax paid to the Government is to be shown as a current liability as unpaid amount. The usual entries for Sales Tax are :

(i) *In case of Credit Sales*

Debtors A/c Dr.
To Sales A/c
" Sales Tax A/c

(ii) *In case of Cash Sales*

Cash A/c Dr.
To Sales A/c
" Sales Tax A/c

(iii) *When Sales Tax is included with Sales*

Sales A/c Dr.
To Sales Tax A/c

(iv) **When Sales Tax is paid to the Govt.**

Sales Tax A/c Dr.
To Bank A/c

Note : If there is any unpaid amount, the same is treated as current liability.

Example

Compute the amount of Sales Tax from the following :
Sales (including of Sales Tax @ 20%) Rs. 1,20,000
Sales Tax paid Rs. 15,000.

Solution

Sales are inclusive of Sales Tax. So, amount of Sales Tax will be (Rs. 1,20,000 × $\frac{20}{120}$) Rs. 20,000. ∴ Unpaid portion of Sales Tax is Rs. 5,000 (i.e., Rs. 20,000 – Rs. 15,000) which is to be shown as a current liability.

Q. MODVATable *Excise Duty on Purchases*[1]

Modified Value Added Tax (MODVAT) is a concept of Central Excise Law. It enables a manufacturer to avail credit of duty paid on notified eligible and duly paid inputs used in the manufacture of the notified dutiable final products and utilise such credit towards the payable of duty on any final products. It allows the manufacturer to get instant credit on and compute reimbursement of the excise duty paid on the components and raw materials, i.e., it avoids double taxation.

Entries for adjustable MODVATable excise duty are

(i) ***For adjustment of MODVATable excise duty on purchase***

MODVATable Credit Receivable A/c Dr.
To Purchases/Trading A/c

(ii) ***For excise duty paid on finished products***

Trading A/c Dr.
To Excise Duty A/c

Note : MODVATable Credit Receivable is deducted from Excise Duty Payable and net amount is to be paid by manufacturer.

R. When revenue expenses are wrongly charged to capital: Sometimes, it may so happen that some revenue expenses—viz., repairs and maintenance expenses etc.—are charged wrongly to capital, i.e., Asset Account. For this purpose, the following entry should be passed:

Particular Expenses A/c Dr.
To Particular Asset A/c

Expenses should be transferred to Profit and Loss Account and the same amount also should be deducted from the particular Asset A/c. Depreciation, if any, should also be adjusted accordingly.

S. When revenue expenses are capitalised: Sometimes, some expenses which are related to assets should be capitalised although they are revenue in nature, viz., installation expenses. However, for this purpose, the following entries should be passed:

Particular Asset A/c Dr.
To Expenses A/c

Depreciation should be calculated of the increased value of such asset.

1. In the budget for 2000-01, the then Finance Minister replaced the multiple MODVAT system by a Single Central Value Added Tax (CENVAT); the rate of which at present is 14% (from 2008-09)

T. Provident Fund

Usually employees' own contribution to Provident Fund is directly deducted from salary. Employers may also contribute some amount. Both employees' contribution and employer's contribution should be deposited with the Provident Fund authority. The entries being:

(i) ***For Employees' contributions which is deducted from salary***

Salary A/c Dr.
 To Bank (Net payment) A/c
 " Provident Fund Deduction A.c

(ii) ***For Employer's' Contribution***

Salary A/c Dr.
 To Contribution to Provident Fund A/c

(iii) ***When both the contribution of employees and employer are deposited***

Provident Fund Deduction A/c Dr.
Contribution to Provident Fund A/c
 To Bank A/c

U. Creation of General Reserve or Reserve Fund

Sometimes a part is transferred to General Reserve. Since the creation of Reserve is not a charge against profit, but an appropriation of profit, the entry will be :

Profit and Loss Appropriation A/c Dr.
 To General Reserve A/c

V. Stationery included in Stock

Sometimes stock of stationery is added to the Opening Stock/Closing Stock of Goods. We are to find out the actual amount of stationery consumed during the year which is charged against Profit and Loss account.

Example

Stock on 1.1.2011 Rs. 10,000 (inclusive of stock of stationery of Rs. 300)
Stock on 31.12.2011 Rs. 8,000 (inclusive of stock of stationery Rs. 50)
Creditors for Stationery on 1.1.2011. Rs. 200
Creditors for Sationery on 31.12.2011 Rs. 130
Stationery used by the proprietor for Rs. 100
Advances paid for stationery carried forward from 2010, Rs. 20
Advances paid for Stationery on 31.12.2011, Rs. 30
Amount paid for Stationery during the year 2011, Rs. 1,080
Ascertain the amount of Stationery to be consumed during the year.

Solution

Computation of Stationery to be consumed

		Rs.	Rs.
	Stock of Stationery on 1.1.2011		300
Add:	Paid for Stationery	1,080	
Less:	Payment made for last year	200	
		880	
Add:	Payment made last year but stationery received this year	20	
		900	
Add:	Creditors for Stationery on 31.12.2011	130	
		1,030	
Less:	Advance paid for Stationery to be received in next year	30	1,000
			1,300
Less:	Drawings		100
			1,200
Less:	Stock of Stationery on 31.12.2011		50
			1,150

W. Profit or Loss on Sale or Exchange of an Asset

Sometimes an asset may be sold out before its useful life for a number of reasons (due to technological development, over-depreciation etc.) including a part of some assets which will be no longer needed in future. The written-down value of the old asset may not be exactly equal to the sale prices for the same. That is, if the sale price is less than the written-down value, there is a case of loss, and *vice versa*. This profit or loss on sale of asset is adjusted in the year of sale in Profit and Loss Account. Same principle is also applicable in case of exchange of an asset.

Example

Show the entries and their effect in Final Account from the following particulars on 31.12.2012:

Furniture shown in Trial Balance Rs. 36,000.

Furniture appearing in the books on 1.1.2012 at Rs. 6,000 was disposed of on 30.6.2012 at Rs. 3,500 in part exchange for new furniture costing Rs. 5,000. A net invoice for Rs. 1,500 was passed through Purchase Day Book.

Solution

Loss on Sale of Furniture	Rs.	**Depreciation of Furniture**	Rs.
Book Value on 1.1.2012	6,000	On Old Furniture	
Less: Depreciation for 6 months @ 10%	300	(Rs. 36,000 – Rs. 6,000)	
WDV on 30.6.2012	5,700	30,000 × 10%	3,000
Less: Exchange for	3,500	On Furniture exchanged	300
Loss on Exchange	2,200	On New Furniture for 6 months	
		$\left(5{,}000 \times \frac{10\%}{100} \times \frac{6}{12}\right)$	250
			3,550

The entries are:

			Rs.	Rs.
(i)	*For Loss on Exchange*			
	Profit and Loss A/c	Dr.	2,200	
	To Furniture			2,200
	For Depreciation			
(ii)	Depreciation A/c	Dr.	3,550	
	To Furniture A/c			3,550
	For Purchase of New Furniture			
(iii)	Furniture A/c	Dr.	1,500	
	To Purchase A/c			1,500

X. On Consignment and Joint Venture Transactions

Example

Given below are the information and extract from the Trial Balance. Show how you will carry out the adjustments :

Trial Balance *as at 31st December 2012*

	Dr. Rs.	*Cr.* Rs.
Material Consumed	7,50,000	
Stock on 31.12.2012	1,00,000	
Suspense Account of S. Sen		40,000
Suspense Account of P. Sen	15,000	
Other balances		8,25,000
	8,65,000	8,65,000

Information

(i) Analysis of S. Sen's Account reveals that goods costing Rs. 60,000 were sent to him under consignment agreement. All the goods were sold except $\frac{1}{4}$ (which was valued at cost) for Rs. 1,00,000 against which a cheque of Rs. 40,000 only was received. No entry was passed except that of cheque received. Commission @ 1% is payable to S. Sen.

(ii) Similarly, a joint venture agreement was entered into with P. Sen for which an advance of Rs. 15,000 was made. It is now ascertained that the venture earned a profit of Rs. 10,000 of which the proprietor's share is $\frac{3}{5}$th.

Solution

For (a) ***For Consignment Transactions :***

The following entries are required for the purpose :

	Particulars		Dr. Rs.	Cr. Rs.
(i)	Consignment A/c	Dr.	60,000	
	To Goods Sent on Consignment			60,000
(ii)	***For Sale of Goods :***			
	S. Sen's Suspense A/c	Dr.	1,00,000	
	To Consignment A/c			1,00,000
(iii)	***For Commission on Sale @ 1%***			
	Consignment A/c	Dr.	1,000	
	To S. Sen's A/c			1,000
(iv)	***For Unsold Stock ($\frac{1}{4}$th) :***			
	Unsold Stock A/c	Dr.	15,000	
	To Consignment A/c			15,000

Dr. **Consignment Account** Cr.

Particulars	Amount Rs.	Particulars	Amount Rs.
To Goods Sent on Consignment A/c	60,000	By S. Sen's A/c —Sale proceeds	1,00,000
" S. Sen A/c (Com.)	1,000	" Unsold Stock A/c	15,000
" Profit and Loss A/c Net Profit transferred (will appear in the new Trial Balance)	54,000		
	1,15,000		1,15,000

Dr. **S. Sen's Suspense Account** Cr.

Particulars	Amount Rs.	Particulars	Amount Rs.
To Consignment A/c — Sale Proceeds	1,00,000	By Balance b/d	40,000
		" Consignment A/c — Commission	1,000
		" Balance c/d (will appear on the debit side of new Trial Balance)	59,000
	1,00,000		1,00,000

Dr. **Goods Sent on Consignment Account** Cr.

Particulars	Amount Rs.	Particulars	Amount Rs.
To Purchase/Material Consumed A/c — transferred	60,000	By Consignment A/c	60,000
	60,000		60,000

(b) **For Joint Venture Transactions**

The following entries are are required for the purpose :

	Particulars		Dr. Rs.	Cr. Rs.
(i)	For profit on Joint Venture @$\frac{3}{5}$ share, i.e., Rs. 10,000 × $\frac{3}{5}$ = Rs. 6,000.			
	P. Sen A/c	Dr.	6,000	
	To Profit and Loss A/c			6,000

Dr. **Profit on Joint Venture Account** Cr.

Particulars	Amount Rs.	Particulars	Amount Rs.
To Balance c/d (will appear in the credit side of new Trial Balance)	6,000	By Joint Venture A/c	6,000
	6,000		6,000

Dr. **P. Sen's Account** Cr.

Particulars	Amount	Particulars	Amount
	Rs.		Rs.
To Balance b/d	15,000	By Balance c/d	
" Profit and Loss A/c		(will appear in the debit side of	
— Profit on Joint Venture	6,000	the new Trial Balance)	21,000
	21,000		21,000

Dr. **Trial Balance (Adjusted/New)** *as at 31st December 2012* Cr.

	Rs.	Rs.		Rs.
Material Consumed	7,50,000		Profit on Consignment	54,000
Less : Goods Sent on Consignment	60,000		Profit on Joint Venture	6,000
		6,90,000	Other balance (given)	8,25,000
Stock on 31.12.2012	1,00,000			
Add : Closing Stock with Consignment	15,000	1,15,000		
S. Sen's Suspense A/c		59,000		
P. Sen's Suspense A/c		21,000		
		8,85,000		8,85,000

Method of Preparation of Final Accounts

Step I : ***Open all the three accounts at a time, i.e., Trading Account, Profit and Loss Account, and Balance Sheet at first using inner column and outer column in each case.***

Step II : ***Tick the accounts which relate to adjustment.***

Step III : ***Place all the accounts in their respective places, i.e., in Trading Account, Profit and Loss Account, and Balance Sheet and use inner column for Step II.***

Step IV: ***Consider the adjustments one by one by Double Entry Principle. (Remember that each adjustment has two-fold effect e.g., depreciation—it will appear in debit side of P & L A/c and will be deducted from the concerned asset account).***

Step V: ***Close the Trading Account at first and the result of Trading Account (whether Gross Profit or Gross Loss) will appear in Profit and—Loss Account. Then close the Profit & Loss Account which will exhibit either Net Profit or Net Loss which will be added to or subtracted from Capital Account in Balance sheet.***

Thereafter, add-up the total of Balance Sheet which must be equal.

Note : All the adjustments will have a two-fold effect, i.e., will be posted twice.

GENERAL ILLUSTRATIONS

Illustration 9

(Placement of various accounts in respective places)

From the following particulars presented by Mr. X prepare a Trial Balance and Trading and Profit and Loss A/c for the year ended 31.12.2009 and a Balance Sheet as on that date (If you find any difference in Trial Balance put the difference in Suspense A/c) :

	Rs.		Rs.
Capital	1,00,000	Purchases	2,50,000
Sales	9,00,000	Wages	25,000
Plant and Machinery	80,000	Purchase Returns	20,000
Opening Stock	30,000	Sales Returns	10,000
Land and Building	90,000	Furniture and Fixtures	30,000
Income Tax	10,000	Royalty on Production	20,000
Royalty on Sales	25,000	Goodwill	10,000
Patent	10,000	Investments	60,000
Sundry Debtors	1,60,000	Reserve for Discount on Debtors	8,000
Sundry Creditors	1,00,000	Bad Debts	10,000
Reserve for Discount on Creditors	3,000	Provision for Bad Debts	15,000
Interest (Cr.)	10,000	Bills Receivable	8,000
Bills Payable	5,000	Interest on Loan	5,000

Contd.

	Rs.		Rs.
Loan Taken	50,000	Drawings	60,000
Bank Overdraft	40,000	Cash in hand	5,000
Cash at Bank	15,000	Advertisement	10,000
Lease (10 years')	20,000	Discount Allowed	5,000
Repairs	3,000	Insurance	6,000
Discount Received	20,000	Salary	30,000
Rent	20,000	Carriage Outwards	3,000
Carriage Inwards	10,000		
Dividend Received	40,000		

Adjustment

Closing Stock Rs. 50,000.

Solution

Tutorial Note: This illustration will help the students to understand the placement of various ledger accounts in final account. It will help them as ready reference.

In the Books of Mr. X
Trial Balance *as at 31.12.2009*

Heads of Accounts	*Debit* Rs.	*Credit* Rs.
Capital		1,00,000
Sales		9,00,000
Plant and Machinery	80,000	
Opening Stock	30,000	
Purchases	2,50,000	
Wages	25,000	
Purchases Returns		20,000
Sales Returns	10,000	
Land and Building	90,000	
Furniture and Fixtures	30,000	
Income-Tax	10,000	
Royalty on Production	20,000	
Royalty on Sales	25,000	
Patent	10,000	
Sundry Debtors	1,60,000	
Reserve for Discount on Creditors	3,000	
Sundry Creditors		1,00,000
Interest (Cr.)		10,000
Bills Payable		5,000
Loan Taken		50,000
Bank Overdraft		40,000
Cash at Bank	15,000	
Lease (10 years')	20,000	
Repairs	3,000	
Carriage Inwards	10,000	
Discount Received		8,000
Rent	20,000	
Dividend Received		40,000
Goodwill	10,000	
Investments	60,000	
Reserve for Discount on Debtors		8,000
Bad Debts	10,000	
Provision for Bad Debts		15,000
Bills Receivable	8,000	
Interest on Loan	5,000	

Contd.

	Rs.	Rs.
Drawings	60,000	
Cash in hand	5,000	
Advertisement	10,000	
Discount Allowed	5,000	
Insurance	6,000	
Salary	30,000	
Carriage Outwards	3,000	
Suspense A/c	2,73,000	
	12,96,000	12,96,000

In the Books of Mr. X

Trading Account *for the year ended 31st Dec. 2009*

Dr. Particulars	Amount Rs.	Amount Rs.	Particulars *Cr.*	Amount Rs.	Amount Rs.
To Opening Stock		30,000	By Sales	9,00,000	
" Purchases	2,50,000		*Less:* Sales Returns	10,000	
Less: Returns Outwards	20,000				8,90,000
		2,30,000	" Closing Stock		50,000
" Wages		25,000			
" Royalty on Production		20,000			
" Carriage Inwards		10,000			
" Trading A/c (Gross Profit transferred)		6,25,000			
		9,40,000			9,40,000

Profit and Loss A/c *for the year ended 31st Dec. 2009*

Dr. Particulars	Amount Rs.	Particulars *Cr.*	Amount Rs.
To Royalty on Sales	25,000	By Trading A/c (Gross Profit)	6,25,000
" Reserve for Discount on Creditors	3,000	" Interest	10,000
" Repairs	3,000	" Discount Received	8,000
" Rent	20,000	" Dividend Received	40,000
" Bad Debts	10,000	" Reserve for Discount on Debtors	8,000
" Interest on Loan	5,000	" Provision for Bad Debts	15,000
" Advertisement	10,000		
" Discount Allowed	5,000		
" Insurance	6,000		
" Salary	30,000		
" Carriage Outwards	3,000		
" Write-off Lease	2,000		
" Capital A/c (Net Profit transferred)	5,84,000		
	7,06,000		7,06,000

Balance Sheet *as at 31st Dec. 2009*

Liabilities	Rs.	Rs.	Assets	Rs.	Rs.
Capital	1,00,000		Goodwill		10,000
Add: Net Profit	5,84,000		Patent		10,000
	6,84,000		Plant and Machinery		80,000
Less: Income-tax	10,000		Land and Building		90,000
	6,74,000		Furniture and Fixtures		30,000
Less: Drawings	60,000		Lease (10 years')	20,000	
		6,14,000	*Less:* Written-off	2,000	
Sundry Creditors		1,00,000			18,000

Contd.

	Rs.	Rs.		Rs.	Rs.
Bills Payable		5,000	Investment		60,000
Loan Taken		50,000	Closing Stock		50,000
Bank Overdraft		40,000	Sundry Debtors		1,60,000
			Bills Receivable		8,000
			Cash at Bank		15,000
			Cash in hand		5,000
			Suspense A/c		2,73,000
		8,09,000			8,09,000

Illustration 10

(Adjustments are given within the Trial Balance)

From the following Trial Balance presented by Mr. Y prepare a final account for the year ended 31st Dec. 2011:

Trial Balance *for the year ended 31st Dec. 2011*

Debit	Rs.	*Credit*	Rs.
Rent	5,000	Gross Profit	50,000
Bad Debt	5,000	Outstanding Rent	1,000
Drawings	20,000	Provisions for Bad Debts	8,000
Interest on Capital	15,000	Capital	1,50,000
Income-Tax	5,000	Interest on Drawings	2,000
Insurance	6,000	Income-Tax Refund	1,000
Prepaid Insurance	2,000	Loan	30,000
Plant and Machinery	80,000	Outstanding Audit Fees	3,000
Depreciation on Plant and Machinery	8,000	Commission	12,000
Interest on Loan	3,000	Commission Received in Advance	2,000
Debtors	25,000	Other Current Liabilities	15,000
Closing Stock	25,000	Interest	6,000
Investment	20,000		
Accrued Interest	1,000		
Goodwill	10,000		
Plant	5,000		
Suspense A/c	45,000		
	2,80,000		2,80,000

Solution

Special Note

1. All the adjustments are given in the trial balance. It means all adjusting entries have already been passed. Now, these accounts should be closed. Moreover, Gross Profit has been given, i.e., Trading Account has already been prepared. That is why closing stock has appeared in Trial Balance.

2. Since all the adjusting entries have been passed/recorded, they should now simply be closed, e.g., Depreciation on Plant and Machinery has already been deducted from Plant and Machinery Account by passing the following entry, i.e., Depreciation on P & M was debited and Plant and Machinery was credited. Now the same will appear only in Profit and Loss Account.

Solution

In the Books of Mr. Y

Profit and Loss A/c *for the year ended 31st Dec. 2011*

Dr. *Cr.*

Particulars	*Amount* Rs.		*Amount* Rs.	*Amount* Rs.
To Rent	5,000	By Trading A/c (G.P.)		50,000
" Bad Debts	5,000	" Reserve for Bad Debts		8,000
" Interest on Capital	15,000	" Interest on Drawings		2,000
" Insurance	6,000	" Income–Tax Refund		1,000
" Depreciation on P & M	8,000	" Commission		12,000
" Interest on Loan	3,000	" Interest		6,000
" Capital A/c (Net Profit transferred)	37,000			
	79,000			79,000

Balance Sheet *as at 31st Dec. 2011*

Liabilities	Rs.	Rs.	*Assets*	Rs.	Rs.
Capital	1,50,000		Goodwill		10,000
Add: Net Profit	37,000		Patent		5,000
	1,87,000		Plant and Machinery		80,000
Less: Drawings	20,000		Investments		20,000
	1,67,000		Closing Stock		25,000
Less: Income-Tax	5,000		Debtors		25,000
		1,62,000	Accured Interest		1,000
Outstanding Rent		1,000	Prepaid Insurance		2,000
Loan		30,000	Suspense A/c		45,000
Outstanding Audit Fee		3,000			
Commission Received in Advance		2,000			
Current Liabilities		15,000			
		2,13,000			2,13,000

Illustration 11

(With ordinary adjustments)

From the following particulars presented by Mr. Z, prepare a Trading and Profit and Loss A/c for year ended 31.12.2009 and a Balance Sheet as on that date:

Heads of Accounts	*Debit* Rs.	*Heads of Accounts*	*Credit* Rs.
Opening Stock	5,000	Capital	50,000
Purchases (less Returns)	25,000	Sales (less Returns)	50,000
Wages	10,000	Creditors	5,000
Rent	7,000	Loan @ 8%	10,000
Insurance	3,000	Bills Payable	3,000
Bad Debts	3,000	Bank Overdraft	6,500
Debtors	15,000	Provision for Bad Debts	500
Plant and Machinery	10,000	Dividend Received	5,000
Building	30,000		
Bank	10,000		
Cash	5,000		
Drawings	7,000		
	1,30,000		1,30,000

Additional Information

1. Closing Stock: Cost Price Rs. 18,000; Market Price Rs. 12,000. 2. Provide Outstanding Rent for Rs.1,000. 3. Insurance was paid in advance Rs. 500. 4. Provide Interest on Capital @ 5% p.a. and Interest on Drawings @ 10% p.a. (for six months). 5. Bad Debts amounted to Rs. 1,000, make a provision for Bad Debts @ 5% and for Discount on Debtors and also a provision @ 2.5% on creditors. 6. Stock destroyed by fire amounted to Rs. 5,000, covered by insurance Rs. 3,000. 7. The proprietor introduced Rs. 10,000 as capital on 1st July 2009. 8. Dividend Received after deduction of tax at source Rs. 1,000.

Solution

In the Books of Mr. Z

Dr. **Trading Account and Profit and Loss Account** *for the year ended on 31.12.2009* *Cr.*

Particulars	Rs.	*Amount* Rs.	*Particulars*	*Amount* Rs.	*Amount* Rs.
To Opening Stock		5,000	By Sales		50,000
" Purchases		25,000	" Closing Stock	12,000[1]	
" Wages		10,000	*Add:* Stock Destroyed by Fire	5,000	
" Profit and Loss A/c		27,000			17,000
(Gross Profit transferred)		67,000			67,000
To Rent	7,000		By Trading A/c (G.P.)		27,000
Add: Outstanding	1,000	8,000	" Interest on Drawings		350
" Insurance	3,000		Rs. 7,000 $\times \frac{10}{100} \times \frac{6}{12}$		

Contd.

	Rs.	Rs.		Rs.	Rs.
Less: Prepaid	500	2,500	By Reserve for Discount on		
" Bad Debts	3,000		Creditors		125
Add: Further Bad Debts	1,000	4,000	" Dividend Received	5,000	
" Reserve for Bad Debts			*Add:* Tax Deducted		
New Reserve	1,400		at source	1,000	
Less: Old Reserve	500	900			6,000[4]
" Interest on Loan		800			
" Interest on Capital		2,250[2]			
" Reserve for Disc. on Debtors		630			
" Stock Destroyed by Fire		2,000[3]			
" Capital A/c (Net Profit transferred)		12,395			
		33,475			33,475

Balance Sheet *as at 31st Dec. 2009*

Liabilities	*Amount* Rs.	*Amount* Rs.	*Assets*	*Amount* Rs.	*Amount* Rs.
Capital (40,000 + 10,000)	50,000		Plant and Machinery		10,000
Add: Interest on Capital	2,250		Building		30,000
	52,250		Closing Stock		12,000
Add: Net Profit	12,395		Insurance Claim		3,000
	64,645		Sundry Debtors	15,000	
Less: Drawings (7,000 + 350)	7,350		*Less:* Bad Debts	1,000	
		57,295		14,000	
Creditors	5,000		*Less:* Reserve for B/D	1,400	
Less: Reserve for Discount on Creditors	125	4,875		12,600	
			Less: Reserve for Disc.		
Loan	10,000		on Debtors	630	11,970
Add: Outstanding Interest	800	10,800	Advance Tax		1,000
Bills Payable		3,000	Prepaid Insurance		500
Bank Overdraft		6,500	Cash		10,000
Outstanding Rent		1,000	Bank		5,000
		83,470			83,470

Workings :

1. Valuation of Closing Stock

Closing Stock should be valued as per Cost Price or market price, whichever is lower. Since market price of Rs. 12,000 is less than the Cost Price of Rs. 18,000, so market price is considered.

3. Abnormal Loss

Stock destroyed by fire was Rs. 5,000, out of which Rs. 3,000 was covered by Insurance Company.

Thus, Rs. 5,000 to be added with the value of closing stock, Rs. 3,000 will appear in the assets side of the Balance Sheet and Rs. 2,000 (5,000 – Rs. 3,000) actual loss, will appear in debit side of P & L A/c.

2. Interest on Capital

Total capital as on 31.12.2009 was Rs. 50,000 of which Rs. 10,000 was introduced on 1st July 2009, i.e., Opening Capital was Rs. 40,000. So, interest on Capital to be calculated as

On Rs. 40,000 for full year @ 5% — Rs.

$= \text{Rs. } 40{,}000 \times \frac{5}{100} = 2{,}000$

on Rs. 10,000 for 6 months

$= \text{Rs. } 10{,}000 \times \frac{5}{100} \times \frac{6}{12} = 250$

2,250

4. Dividend Received

Total Dividend received = Dividend Received + Tax Deducted at Source

= Rs. 5,000 + Rs. 1,000

= Rs. 6,000

And, Rs. 1,000 will appear in the assets side of the Balance Sheet as 'Advance Tax'

Stock Valuations, Abnormal Loss, Provident Fund, Additions to plant, etc.

Illustration 12

From the following Trial Balance, prepare Trading and a Profit and Loss Account for the year ended 31.3.2012 and a Balance Sheet as on that date :

Heads of Accounts	*Debit*	*Heads of Accounts*	*Credit*
	Rs.		Rs.
Opening Stock	25,000	Capital	1,00,000
Purchases	70,000	Bank Loan (taken on 1.4.2011) @ 6%	20,000
Returns	3,000	Sales	2,00,000
Royalty on Production	7,000	Returns	5,000
Royalty on Sales	5,000	Reserve for Bad Debts	4,000
Wages	12,000	Commission	5,000
Carriage	8,000	Apprentice Premium (for 3 years)	15,000
Non-Productive Wages	5,000	Purchase Ledger Balance	40,000
Rent (11 months)	11,000	Reserve Fund	8,000
Insurance (paid up to 30.6.2012) (Annual Premium Rs. 4,000)	5,000	Interest on Fixed Deposit	1,000
Plant and Machinery	80,000	Provident Fund deducted from Salary	2,000
Goodwill	20,000		
Sales Ledger Balance	60,000		
Fixed Deposit (at 12% p.a. on 1.10.2011)	20,000		
Bad Debts	4,000		
Salaries	20,000		
Investments	5,000		
Income-Tax	5,000		
Drawings	20,000		
Lease (5 years')	10,000		
Sales Tax	5,000		
	4,00,000		4,00,000

Adjustments

1. Stock was not taken on 31.3.2012, but only on 7.4.2012. The transaction from 1.4.2012 to 7.4.2012 were: Sales Rs. 75,000; Purchases Rs. 20,000. The stock on 7.4.2012 was valued at Cost Rs. 10,000. Rate of Gross Profit was 20%.
2. Stock destroyed by fire for Rs. 10,000 covered by the Insurance Company in full.
3. Write-off $\frac{1}{4}$ Goodwill.
4. Write-off further Bad Debts for Rs. 4,000 and make a Provision for Bad Debts @ 5% on Debtors.
5. Goods distributed as free samples for Rs. 1,000.
6. Proprietor took goods for his own use for Rs. 5,000.
7. A Plant was purchased (not included above) on 1.10.2012 for Rs. 20,000 on credit from X Ltd., Installation Expenses Rs. 5,000 wrongly debited to Wages Account.
8. Goods sold on credit to Mr. X for Rs. 5,000 not recorded at all in the books.
9. Depreciate Plant @ 10% per annum.
10. Provide employer's share of Provident Fund Contribution Rs. 2,000.

Solution

In the Books of ...

Dr. **Trading Account and Profit & Loss Account** *for the year ended 31st March 2012* Cr.

Particulars	*Amount*	*Amount*	*Particulars*		*Amount*	*Amount*
	Rs.	Rs.			Rs.	Rs.
To Opening Stock		25,000	By Sales		2,00,000	
" Purchases	70,000		*Add:* Further Sales		5,000	
Less: Advertisement	1,000				2,05,000	
	69,000		*Less:* Sales Tax	5,000		
Less: Returns	5,000		*Add :* Returns	3,000	8,000	1,97,000
	64,000		Closing Stock		50,000	

Contd.

	Rs.	Rs.		Rs.	Rs.
Less: Drawings	5,000	59,000			
" Royalty on Production			*Add:* Stock Destroyed by Fire	10,000	60,000
" Wages	12,000				
Less: Installation Exp.	5,000	7,000			
" Carriage Inwards		8,000			
" Profit and Loss A/c (Gross Profit transferred)		1,51,000			
		2,57,000			2,57,000
To Royalty on Sales		5,000	By Trading A/c —Gross Profit		1,51,000
" Non-Productive Wages		5,000	" Reserve for Bad Debts (Old Reserve)	4,000	
" Rent	11,000		*Less:* New Reserve	3,050	950
Add: Outstanding	1,000	12,000			
To Insurance	5,000				
Less: Prepaid	1,000	4,000			
" Employer's Share of P.F.		2,000	" Commission		5,000
To Bad Debts		8,000			
" Written-off Lease		2,000	" Int. on Fixed Deposits	1,000	
" Written-off Goodwill		5,000	*Add:* Accrued	200	1,200
" Advertisement		1,000			
" Salary		20,000	" Apprentice Premium		5,000
" Interest on Bank Loan		1,200			
" Depreciation on Plant		8,625			
" Capital A/c (Net Profit transferred)		89,325			
		1,63,150			1,63,150

Balance Sheet *as at 31st March 2012*

Liabilities		Rs.	Rs.	*Assets*	Rs.	Rs.
Capital		1,00,000		Goodwill	20,000	
Add: Net Profit		89,325		*Less:* Written-off	5,000	15,000
		1,89,325		Plant and Machinery	80,000	
Less: Drawings	20,000			Addition	20,000	
Income-Tax	5,000			Installation	5,000	
Goods Taken	5,000				1,05,000	
		30,000	1,59,325	*Less:* Depreciation	8,625	
Reserve Fund			8,000	(8,000 + 625)		96,375
Creditors			40,000	Lease	10,000	
Bank Loan		20,000		*Less:* Written-off	2,000	8,000
Add: Outstanding Interest		1,200	21,200	Closing Stock		50,000
Outstanding Rent			1,000	Sundry Debtors	60,000	
Provident Fund				*Add:* Sale	5,000	
(Rs. 2,000 + Rs. 2,000)			4,000		65,000	
Apprentice Premium		15,000		*Less:* Bad Debts	4,000	
Less: $\frac{1}{3}$ of Current Year		5,000			61,000	
			10,000			
Creditors (X Ltd.) for Plant A/c			20,000	*Less* Provision for Bad Debts	3,050	57,950
				Investments		5,000
				Fixed Deposits	20,000	
				Add: Accrued	200	20,200
				Prepaid Insurance		1,000
				Insurance Claim		10,000
			2,63,525			2,63,525

Workings :

1. Valuation of Closing Stock

		Rs.
Stock as on 7.4.2012		10,000
Add: Cost of Goods Sold between 1.4.2012 and 7.4.2012		
Selling Price	75,000	
Less : Gross Profit @ 20% on Sales	15,000	
		60,000
		70,000
Less : Cost of Goods Purchased between 1.4.2012 and 7.4.2012		20,000
Closing Stock as on 31.3.2012		50,000

2 Stock Destroyed by Fire

Since entire amount was recovered from Insurance Company, there was no Loss of Stock.

3. Goods Distributed as Free Sample

It will be treated as advertisement. The entry will be: Advertisement A/c Debit and Purchase A/c Credit.

4. Employer's Contributors to Provident Fund

Since employer vcontributes equal amount, it will appear in the debit side of P & L A/c i.e., adjusted against P & L A/c. And Rs. 2000 + (Employer's Contribution) will appear in the liabilities side of Balance Sheet, i.e., Rs. 4,000.

5. Prepaid Insurance

Annual Insurance Rs. 4,000

Since one-quarter was paid in advance, it will be Rs. 4,000 × $\frac{1}{4}$ = 1,000

Mutual Indebtedness, Advertisement, Suspense Account, Cheque dishonoured, etc.

Illustration 13

The following Trial Balance has been prepared by Hava-Goba Brothers for the year ended on 31.3.2011. You are asked to prepare a Trading Account and Profit and Loss Account for the year ended 31.3.2011 and a Balance Sheet as on that date:

Heads of Accounts	Rs.	*Heads of Accounts*	Rs.
Drawings	30,000	Sales	3,00,000
Adjusted Purchase	1,20,000	Creditors	50,000
Lighting and Heating	20,000	Loan @ 12% from X (taken on 1.7.2010)	50,000
Wages	15,000	Provision for Bad Debts	15,000
Gas and Fuel	10,000	Reserve Fund	25,000
Factory Expenses	5,000	Bills Payable	5,000
Plant and Machinery	80,000	United Bank of India	10,000
Land and Building	60,000	Profit and Loss A/c (1.4.2010)	10,000
Sundry Debtors (including P. Sen's dishonoured cheque Rs. 2,000)	70,000	Miscellaneous Receipts	5,000
		Capital	2,00,000
		Interest on Investment	5,000
Bad Debts	10,000	Commission	15,000
Discount	5,000		
Salary	20,000		
Rent	16,000		
Interest on Loan	3,000		
Investment in Y Ltd.	40,000		
Cash at Bank	40,000		
Cash in hand	10,000		
Bills Receivable	30,000		
Insurance (including Premium of Rs.12,000 p.a. paid up to 30.6.2011)	15,000		
Advertisement Suspense A/c	25,000		
Loose Tools	25,000		
Closing Stock	41,000		
	6,90,000		6,90,000

Adjustments

1. Closing Stock of loose tools Rs. 20,000. 2. Lighting and Heating should be apportioned between factory and office in the ratio 3 : 1. 3. Write-off 1/2 of P. Sen's cheque. 4. Rent should be paid @ Rs. 1,500 per month. 5. Advertisement Suspense A/c is carried forward for four years. 6. A bill of Rs. 5,000 was returned dishonoured; not recorded in the books. 7 Interest due but not received Rs. 1,000. 8. Debtors

include Rs. 5,000 due from Mr. Das whereas Creditors include Rs. 8,000 due to Mr. Das. 9. Two cheques of Rs. 1,000 and Rs. 2,000 were returned dishonoured but not recorded. 10. Transfer 50% of the Net Profit to Reserve Fund.

Solution

In the Books of Hava-Goba Brothers

Dr. **Trading Account & Profit and Loss A/c** *for the year ended 31.3.2011* *Cr.*

Particulars		Amount	Particulars		Amount
		Rs.			Rs.
To Adjusted Purchase		1,20,000	By Sales		3,00,000
" Gas and Fuel		10,000			
" Wages		15,000			
" Factory Expenses		5,000			
" Factory Expenses		15,000			
" Profit and Loss A/c (Gross Profit transferred)		1,35,000			
		3,00,000			3,00,000
To Lighting and Heating	20,000		By Trading Account		1,35,000
Less: Factory 3/5	15,000		" Provisions for		
		5,000	Bad Debts		15,000
" Bad Debts		10,000	" Commission		15,000
" Discount		5,000	" Miscellaneous Receipt		5,000
" Salary		20,000			
" Rent	16,000		" Int. on Investment	5,000	
Add: Outstanding	2,000	18,000	*Add:* Accrued	1,000	
" Interest on Loan	3,000				6,000
Add: Outstanding	1,500	4,500			
" Insurance	15,000				
Less: Prepaid	3,000	12,000			
" Advertisement Suspense A/c		25,000			
" Write-off Loose Tools		5,000			
" Write-off P. Sen's Cheque		1,000			
" Reserve Fund		45,250			
" Capital (Net Profit transferred)		25,250			
		1,76,000			1,76,000

Balance Sheet *as at 31st March 2011*

Liabilities	Rs.	Rs.	*Assets*	Rs.	Rs.
Capital	2,00,000		Land and Building		60,000
Add: Profit for 2010	10,000		Plant and Machinery		80,000
Add: Net Profit	25,250		Loose Tools	25,000	
	2,35,250		*Less:* Written-off	5,000	20,000
Less: Drawings	30,000	2,05,250	Accrued Interest		1,000
Outstanding Rent		2,000	Investments		40,000
Bills Payable		5,000	Closing Stock		41,000
Creditors	50,000		Prepaid Insurance		3,000
Less: Set-off	5,000	45,000	Debtors	70,000	
Loan Taken	50,000		*Less:* $\frac{1}{2}$ of P. Sen's Cheque	1,000	
Add: Outstanding	1,500	51,500			
Reserve Fund	25,000			69,000	
Additions	45,250	70,250	*Add:* Dishonoured Bill	5,000	
United Bank of India		10,000		74,000	
			Less: Set-off	5,000	
				69,000	
			Add: Dishonourd Cheque	3,000	72,000

Contd.

	Rs.	Rs.		Rs.	Rs.
			Bills Receivable	30,000	
			Less: Dishonoured Bill	5,000	25,000
			Cash at Bank	40,000	
			Less: Dishonoured Cheque	3,000	37,000
			Cash in hand		10,000
		3,89,000			3,89,000

Workings :

1. Write-off Loose Tools

	Rs.
Loose Tools Purchased	25,000
Less: Stock of Loose tools	20,000
Written-off	5,000

2 Write-off P. Sen's Cheque

	Rs.
P. Sen's Cheque amounted to	2,000
Less: $\frac{1}{2}$ written-off as bad	1,000
	1,000

3. Dishonour of Bill

When a bill is dishonoured, the entry is

Debtors A/c Dr.
To B/R A/c

So, it will be added to debtors and will be subtracted from B/R.

4. Mutual Indebtedness/Set-off

Mr. Das is debtor as well a creditor. Thus, the lower amount of Rs. 5,000 will be deducted both from Debtors as well as from Creditors, the entry being

Creditors A/c Dr. 5,000
To Debtor A/c 5,000

5. Dishonour of Cheque

When a cheque is dishonoured, the entry is—

Debtors A/c Dr. 3,000
To Bank A/c 3,000

6. Transfer of Net Profit to Reserve Fund

Profit and Loss A/c Dr.
To Reserve Fund A/c

That is, 50% of net profit, i.e., Rs. 45,250, will appear in the debit side of P & L A/c and the same will also appear in the liabilities side of the Balance Sheet.

7. Advertisement Suspense Account

It is a case of deferred revenue expenditure. So, $\frac{4}{5}$ of Rs. 25,000, or Rs. 20,000, should be carried forward for next four years.

But, as per para 20, **Ind AS 38, *Intangible Assets,*** it should be treated as intangible assets and, hence, the entire amount should be charged to Profit and Loss Account. As per the said para, when it is probable that the future economic benefits that are attributable to the asset will flow to the enterprise and the cost of the asset can be measured reliably, it is treated as intangible assets. Thus, the entire amount of Rs. 25,000 should be debited to Profit and Loss Account.

Illustration 14

(Adjusting and rectifying entries)

From the following particulars presented by Mr. X, prepare a Trading Account and Profit and Loss Account for the year ended 31st Dec. 2012 and also show the adjusting and rectifying entries:

	Dr. Rs.		*Cr.* Rs.
Drawings	18,000	Capital	50,000
Plant and Machinery	50,000	Sales (less Returns)	2,00,000
Purchases	60,000	Creditors	20,000
Sundry Debtors	40,000	Bank Overdraft	10,000
Wages	10,000	Provision for Bad Debts	2,000
Carriage	3,000	Cash Credit	10,000
Salaries	7,000	Bills Payable	8,000
Rent	6,000		
Repairs	3,000		
Insurance	5,000		
Opening Stock	12,000		
Land and Building	40,000		
Furniture	10,000		
Discount	20,000		
Suspense A/c	16,000		
	3,00,000		3,00,000

Additional Information

(a) Closing Stock Rs. 30,000.
(b) Purchases include purchases of materials used for the construction of Building Rs. 5,000.
(c) Sales include sale of Furniture at a selling price of Rs. 1,000 (Book value Rs. 2,000).
(d) Wages include Rs. 3,000 incurred for the erection of a Machinery.
(e) The proprietor Mr. Banerjee took goods for his own use from the business amounted to Rs. 1,000.
(f) Purchased a Plant for Rs. 5,000, wrongly debited to Purchase Account.
(g) Rent included Rs. 1,000 paid for Mr. Banerjee's residential portion.
(h) Purchase of Stationery for Rs. 100 was debited to Repairs Account.
(i) A customer's cheque returned dishonoured, wrongly debited to Discount Account, Rs. 1,000.
(j) A sale of goods to a customer not debited to Customers A/c, Rs. 16,000.
(k) Stock destroyed by fire amounted to Rs. 10,000. Insurance Co. admitted only Rs. 8,000.

Solution

In the Books of Mr. X

Journal Entries *(Without Narration)*

			Rs.	Rs.	To do
?	(a) Closing Stock A/c	Dr.	30,000		To be shown in the Credit side of Trading A/c and in the Assets side of the Balance Sheet.
	To Trading A/c			30,000	
	(b) Building A/c	Dr.	5,000		To be deducted from Purchase and added to Building.
	To Purchase A/c			5,000	
	(c) Sales A/c	Dr.	1,000		To be deducted from Sales Rs. 1,000 and to be debited to Profit & Loss A/c Rs. 1,000 and to be deducted from Furniture Rs. 2,000
	Profit and Loss A/c	Dr.	1,000		
	To Furniture A/c			2,000	
	(d) Plant and Machinery A/c	Dr.	3,000		To be deducted from Wages and added to Machinery.
	To Wages A/c			3,000	
	(e) Drawings A/c	Dr.	1,000		To be deducted from Purchases and to be added to Drawings.
	To Purchases A/c			1,000	
	(f) Plant and Machinery A/c	Dr.	5,000		To be deducted from Purchases and added to Plant and Machinery.
	To Purchases A/c			5,000	
	(g) Drawings A/c	Dr.	1,000		To be deducted from Rent and added to Drawings.
	To Rent A/c			1,000	
	(h) Stationery A/c	Dr.	100		To be deducted from Repairs and to be debited to P and L A/c by way of Stationery.
	To Repairs A/c			100	
	(i) Debtors A/c	Dr.	1,000		To be deducted from Discount and added to Debtors.
	To Discount A/c			1,000	
	(j) Debtors A/c	Dr.	16,000		To be deducted from Suspense A/c and added to Debtors.
	To Suspense A/c			16,000	
	(k) Stock Destroyed by Fire A/c	Dr.	10,000		To be debited to Profit and Loss A/c by Rs. 2,000 and to be shown in the Assets side of the Balance Sheet by Rs. 8,000 and to be added to Closing Stock by Rs. 10,000.
	To Trading A/c			10,000	
	Insurance Claim A/c	Dr.	8,000		
	Profit and Loss A/c	Dr.	2,000		
	To Stock Destroyed by Fire A/c			10,000	

Dr. **Trading Account and Profit and Loss A/c** *for the year ended 31st Dec. 2012* Cr.

Particulars	*Amount* Rs.	*Amount* Rs.	*Particulars*	*Amount* Rs.	*Amount* Rs.
To Opening Stock		12,000	By Sales	2,00,000	
" Purchases	60,000		*Less:* Furniture	1,000	1,99,000
Less: Building	5,000		" Closing Stock	30,000	
	55,000		*Add:* Stock Destroyed		
Less: Drawings	1,000		by Fire	10,000	40,000
	54,000				
Less: Plant and Machinery	5,000	49,000			

Contd.

	Rs.	Rs.		Rs.	Rs.
To Wages	10,000				
Less: Plant and Machinery	3,000	7,000			
" Carriage		3,000			
" Profit and Loss A/c —Gross Profit transferred		1,68,000			
		2,39,000			2,39,000
To Salaries		7,000	By Trading A/c —Gross Profit transferred		1,68,000
" Rent	6,000		" Provision for Bad Debts		2,000
Less: Drawings	1,000	5,000			
" Repairs	3,000				
Less: Stationery	100	2,900			
" Insurance		5,000			
" Discount	20,000				
Less; Discount	1,000	19,000			
" Loss on Sale of Furniture		1,000			
" Stationery		100			
" Stock Destroyed by Fire		2,000			
" Capital A/c —Net Profit transferred		1,28,000			
		1,70,000			1,70,000

Balance Sheet *as at 31st Dec. 2012*

Liabilities		Rs.	Rs.	*Assets*	Rs.	Rs.
Capital		50,000		Plant and Machinery	50,000	
Add: Net Profit		1,28,000		*Add:* Wages	3,000	
		1,78,000			53,000	
Less: Drawings	18,000			Additions	5,000	58,000
Purchase	1,000			Land and Building	40,000	
Rent	1,000			Additions	5,000	45,000
		20,000	1,58,000	Furniture	10,000	
Creditors			20,000	*Less:* Sale of Furniture	2,000	8,000
Bank Overdraft			10,000	Closing Stock		30,000
Cash Credit			10,000	Sundry Debtors	40,000	
Bills Payable			8,000	*Add:* Discount	1,000	
					41,000	
				Add: Suspense A/c	16,000	57,000
				Suspense A/c	16,000	
				Less: Debtors	16,000	Nil
				Insurance Claim		8,000
			2,06,000			2,06,000

Illustration 15

Abnormal Loss, Manager's Commission, Sale or Return etc.

From the following particulars, prepare a Final Account of Mr. A for the year ended on 31.12.2009:

	Rs.		Rs.
Opening Stock	25,000	Capital	50,000
Purchases	80,000	Sales	2,00,000
Wages	20,000	Bank Loan at 12% p.a. (1.4.2009)	50,000
Interest on Bank Loan	3,000	Creditors	30,000
Deposits @ 10%	40,000	Commission	10,000
Plant and Machinery	60,000	Interest on Deposits	3,000
Land and Building	40,000	Provision for Bad Debts	4,000

Contd.

	Rs.		Rs.
Additions (1.7.2009)	10,000	Cash Credit	5,000
Debtors	65,000	Advance (Cr.)	33,000
Rent	5,000		
Salary	10,000		
Stationery	5,000		
Bad Debts	5,000		
Cash	5,000		
Bank	5,000		
Drawings	7,000		
	3,85,000		3,85,000

Adjustments

1. Commission received in advance amount to Rs. 1,000.
2. Purchase invoices of Rs. 1,000 were omitted from the book.
3. Goods purchased for Rs. 4,000 were received in Stock but no entry was made in the invoice book.
4. Provide Manager's Commission @ 10% on the Net Profit after charging such commissions.
5. Invoice of value of Rs. 4,000 were recorded in the Sales Book on 26 Dec. 09, but the goods were not despatched until 4th Jan. 2010 and were included in the Closing Stock.
6. Stationery worth Rs. 1,000 taken by the proprietor not recorded in the books.
7. Goods costing Rs. 5,000 were sent to a customer on sale or return basis; on 30th Dec. they were recorded as actual sales. The rate of Gross Profit was @ 1/6 of the sale.
8. Stock valued for Rs. 3,000 destroyed by fire; not covered by insurance.
9. Closing Stock amounted to Rs. 40,000.
10. Provide depreciation @ 10% on Land and Building p.a.

Solution

In the Books of Mr. A

Dr. *Trading Account and Profit and Loss Account for the year ended 31st Dec. 2009* Cr.

Particulars	*Amount*	*Amount*	*Particulars*	*Amount*	*Amount*
	Rs.	Rs.		Rs.	Rs.
To Opening Stock		25,000	By Sales	2,00,000	
" Purchases	80,000		*Less:* Sales Returns	6,000[4]	1,94,000
Add: Further Purchases	1,000[1]		Closing Stock	40,000	
	81,000		*Less:* Sales	4,000[2]	
Add: Purchases	4,000[3]	85,000		36,000	
" Wages		20,000	*Add:* Sales or Return	5,000	
" Profit & Loss A/c		1,08,000		41,000	
(Gross Profit transferred)			*Add:* Stock Destroyed by Fire	3,000	44,000
		2,38,000			2,38,000
" Interest on Loan	3,000		" Trading Account		1,08,000
Add: Outstanding	1,500	4,500	—Gross Profit		
" Rent		5,000	" Commission	10,000	
To Salary		10,000	*Less:* Advance Commission	1,000	9,000
" Stationery	5,000		By Interest on Deposits	3,000	
Less: Drawings	1,000	4,000	*Add:* Accrued Interest	1,000	4,000
" Bad Debts		5,000	" Prov. for Bad Debts		4,000
" Depreciation		4,500			
" Stock Destroyed by Fire		3,000			
" Manager's Commission		8,091[5]			
" Capital		80,909			
(Net Profit transferred)					
		1,25,000			1,25,000

Balance Sheet *as at 31st Dec. 2009*

Liabilities	Rs.	Rs.	*Assets*	Rs.	Rs.
Capital		50,000	Plant and Machinery		60,000
Add: Net Profit		80,909	Land and Building	40,000	
		1,30,909	Additions	10,000	
Less: Drawings	7,000			50,000	
Add: Stationery	1,000	8,000	*Less:* Depreciation		
		1,22,909	(4,000 + 500)	4,500	45,500
Creditors	30,000		Closing Stock	40,000	
Add: Further Purchase	1,000		*Less:* Goods Sold	4,000	
	31,000			36,000	
Add: Purchases	4,000	35,000	*Add:* Sale or Return	5,000	41,000
Commission Received in Advance		1,000	Debtors	65,000	
			Less: Sale or Return	6,000	59,000
Bank Loan	50,000		Deposits	40,000	
Add: Outstanding	1,500	51,500	*Add:* Accrued Interest	1,000	41,000
Cash Credits		5,000	Cash		5,000
Advances		33,000	Bank		5,000
Manager's Commission		8,091			
		2,56,500			2,56,500

Workings :

1. **Omission of Purchase**

(2) and (3) The entry being:

Purchase A/c Dr.
To Creditors A/c

(i.e., it will be added to purchases and will be added also to creditors.

2. **For item (v)**

Goods were sold but not despatched

Since the goods were not despatched the same should be deducted from Closing Stock.

3. **Stationery taken over, the entry being:**

Drawings A/c Dr.
To Stationery A/c

i.e., it will be added to Drawings and will be deducted from Stationery.

4. **For (vii) goods 'Sale or Return'**

(i) Rate of Profit is $\frac{1}{6}$th of Sales, i.e., $\frac{1}{5}$th of Cost.

So, Cost Price Rs. 5,000 + Profit Rs. 1,000 = Selling Price Rs. 6,000.

Thus, Rs. 6,000 to be deducted from Sales in Trading A/c, and the same to be deducted from Sundry Debtors in Balance Sheet.

(ii) Rs. 5,000, i.e. the Cost Price, to be added to Closing Stock. So, Closing Stock will be Rs. (30,000 + 5,000) = Rs. 35,000, both in Trading A/c and in the Assets side of the Balance Sheet as well.

5. **Manager's Commission**

		Rs.
Profit before charging Commission (Rs. 1,25,000 – Rs. 36,000)	=	89,000
Less : Manager's Commission $\frac{\text{Rate}}{\text{Rate} + 100} = \frac{10}{100 + 10} = \frac{10}{110} = \frac{1}{11} \times$ Rs. 89,000	=	8,091
		80,909

MODVAT Excise[1] Duty, Duty Drawback, Cash Subsidy, Prior Period Items, etc.

Illustration 16

The following Trial Balance was presented by Sri Soumya Banerjee for the year ended 31st March 2010. You are required to prepare a Trading Account, Profit and Loss Account for the year ended 31st March 2010, and a Balance Sheet as on that date.

[1] Although MODVAT had been replaced by CENVAT from 2008-09, its accounting effect is only shown

Debit	Rs.	Credit	Rs.
Opening Stock :		Capital	2,00,000
Raw Materials	20,000	Sales	4,00,000
Finished Goods	30,000	Purchases Return	10,000
Purchases	2,00,000	Duty Drawback	30,000
Sales Return	60,000	Cash Subsidy	
Octroi	5,000	(for purchase of raw materials)	1,000
Excise Duty	80,000	Sundry Creditors	80,000
Sales Tax	40,000	Cash Credit	29,000
Office Salaries	50,000		
MODVAT Credit Receivable	30,000		
Land and Buildings	80,000		
Plant and Machinery	30,000		
Furniture & Fittings	5,000		
Sundry Debtors	20,000		
Cash at Bank	4,000		
Drawings	40,000		
Wages	50,000		
Outstanding Expenses of 2008-09	6,000		
	7,50,000		7,50,000

Additional Information

(1) Closing Stock : Raw Materials Rs. 25,000; Finished Goods Rs. 85,000

(ii) Sales includes Sales Tax and Excise Duty Rs. 50,000 and Rs. 1,00,000, respectively.

(iii) Purchase include MODVATable Excise Duty of Rs. 50,000

Solution

In the Books of Sri Soumya Banerjee

Trading and Profit and Loss Account ***for the year ended on 31st Dec. 2009***

Dr. Cr.

	Particulars	Amount Rs.	Amount Rs.		Particulars	Amount Rs.	Amount Rs.
To	Opening Stock:			By	Sales	4,00,000	
	Raw Materials		20,000		*Less:* Returns Inward	60,000	
	Finished Goods		30,000			3,40,000	
"	Purchases	2,00,000			*Less:* Sale Tax	50,000	
	Less: Returns Outward	10,000				2,90,000	
		1,90,000			*Less:* Excise Duty	1,00,000	
	Less: MODVAT Credit Receivable	50,000					1,90,000
		1,40,000		"	Closing Stock:		
	Less: Duty Drawback	30,000			Raw Materials	25,000	
		1,10,000			Finished Goods	85,000	
	Less: Cash Subsidy	1,000					1,10,000
			1,09,000				
"	Octroi		5,000				
"	Wages		50,000				
"	Profit and Loss A/c —Gross Profit Transferred		86,000				
			3,00,000				3,00,000
To	Office Salaries		50,000	By	Trading A/c —Gross Profit		86,000
"	Prior Period Items —Office Expenses		6,000				
"	Captal A/c —Net Profit Transferred		30,000				
			86,000				86,000

Balance Sheet *as at 31st March 2010*

Liabilities	*Amount* Rs.	*Amount* Rs.	*Assets*	*Amount* Rs.	*Amount* Rs.
Capital	2,00,000		Land and Building		80,000
Add : Net Profit	30,000		Plant and Machinery		30,000
	2,30,000		Furniture and Fittings		5,000
Less: Drawings	40,000		Closing Stock		
		1,90,000	Raw Material	25,000	
Sundry Creditors		80,000	Finished Goods	85,000	1,10,000
Cash Credit		29,000	Debtors		20,000
Sales Tax Payable		10,000[2]	Cash at Bank		4,000
			Modvat Credit Receivable		60,000[1]
		3,09,000			3,09,000

Workings :

1. **MODVAT Credit Receivable**

		Rs.
Gross Excise Duty on Sales :		
Total	1,00,000	
Less: Already Paid	80,000	
		20,000
Total MODVAT Credit Receivable		
MODVAT Credit Receivable	30,000	
Add: MODVAT Excisable Duty	50,000	
		80,000
Less: Excise Duty adjusted against MODVAT Credit Receivable		20,000
MODVAT Credit receivable unadjusted against excise duty payable		60,000

∴ This MODVAT Credit Receivable will appear in the assets side of the Balance Sheet as liquid asset.

2. **Sales Tax Payable**

	Rs.
Total amount due	50,000
Less: Amount already paid	40,000
Outstanding Sales Tax	10,000

Final Accounts of Partnership Firm

The method of preparation of final accounts of a partnership firm is similar to the method of preparation of final accounts of a sole proprietorship firm. The only difference is that, in case of preparing final accounts of a partnership firm, a Profit and Loss Appropriation Account will have to be opened. Only the appropriation items (e.g., Partners' Salaries, and Commissions, Interest on Partners' Capital, Interest on Partners' Drawings transferred to Reserve etc.) will appear in that account. Net Profit or Net Loss should be distributed as per agreed ratio. This aspect has already been explained in an earlier paragraph.

Illustration 17

A and B are partners sharing profits in proportion to their Capitals. At the close of their financial year on 30th September 2011, the following balances stood to the credit of the partners :

Capital Accounts : A Rs. 20,000; B Rs. 5,000; Current Accounts : A Rs. 1,060; B Rs. 2,800.

The partnership deed provides :

(a) B shall be credited with a partnership salary of Rs. 1,000 per annum for running business.

(b) B shall be entitled to a commission of 10% of the Divisible Profit before charging such commission.

(c) Interest at 5% per annum to be allowed on Capital and Current Accounts.

(d) The partners' drawings were : A Rs. 10,000; B Rs. 3,000.

The Interest to be charged on such drawings were : A Rs. 330; B Rs. 80.

In addition to the entries necessary to record the above particulars the following balances were extracted from the books of the firm as on 30th September 2012 :

	Rs.		Rs.
Freehold Premises	15,000	Machinery and Plant—balance at the beginning	13,280
Sundry Creditors	24,150	Machinery—additions	1,560
Advertising	4,339	Motor Vans	900
Office Salaries	2,189	Factory Expenses paid in advance	70

Contd.

	Rs.		Rs.
Sundry Debtors	16,020	Cash at bank	2,841
Office Expenses	622	Cash in hand	31
Insurance	364	Mortgage on freehold premises at 6% per annum	10,000
Delivery Expenses	2,203	Office Furniture	300
Stock	21,069	Mortgage interest	450
Provision for Doubtful Debts—as on 30-9-2011	600	Patents	4,000
Trading Account Credit Balance	34,628		

You are required to prepare a Profit & Loss Account for the year ended 30th September 2012 and the Balance Sheet as on that date.

Given below are the additional information towards the preparation of the required Final Accounts:

(a) Depreciation to be provided as follows : Plant, old balance 10% per annum; Plant—additions (for full year) 25% per annum; Office Furniture 10% per annum; Patents 10% per annum; (b) Motor Vans are to be taken at Rs. 800 for the purpose of Final Accounts; (c) The Provision for Bad Debts is to be made up to 5% on Sundry Debtors; (d) Interest on the mortgage has been paid up to 30th June 2012; (e) The following amounts are to be carried forward to next year; Insurance Rs. 62, Advertising Rs. 878; (f) Office Salaries Rs. 69 were owing at the end of the year.

Solution

In the Books of A and B

Dr. **Profit and Loss Account** *for the year ended 30th September 2012* Cr.

Particulars	Amount Rs.	Amount Rs.	Particulars	Amount Rs.	Amount Rs.
To Office Salaries	2,189		By Gross Profit (Trading A/c— Credit Balance)		34,628
Add : Outstanding	69	2,258			
" Office Expenses		622			
" Insurance	364				
Less : Prepaid	62	302			
" Delivery Expenses		2,203			
" Advertising	4,339				
Less : Carried Forward	878	3,461			
" Provision for Bad Debts (5% of Rs. 16,020)	801				
Less : Old Reserve	600	201			
" Mortgage Interest	450				
Add : Outstanding (@ 6% on Rs. 10,000 for 3 months)	150	600			
" Depreciation on :					
Plant & Machinery[1]	1,718				
Office Furniture (10% on Rs. 300)	30				
Patents (10% on Rs. 4,000)	400				
Motor Vans (Rs. 900 – Rs. 800)	100	2,248			
" Profit and Loss Appropriation Account Net Profit c/d		22,733			
		34,628			34,628

Dr. **Profit and Loss Appropriation Account** *for the year ended 30th September 2012* Cr.

Particulars	Rs.	Amount Rs.	Particulars	Rs.	Amount Rs.
To Salary—B		1,000	By Profit and Loss A/c Net Profit b/d		22,733
" Interest on Capital[2]			Interest on Drawings :		
A :	1,000		A :	330	
B :	250	1,250	B :	80	410

Contd.

		Rs.		Rs.
To Interest on Current A/c (c)			By	
A :	53			
B :	140	193		
" Commission—B[4]		2,070		
" Divisible Profit[5]				
A :	14,904			
B :	3,726	18,630		
		23,143		23,143

Balance Sheet *as at 30th September 2012*

Liabilities	Rs.	Rs.	*Assets*	Rs.	Rs.
Capital Account :			*Fixed Assets :*		
A :	20,000		Freehold Premises		15,000
B :	5,000	25,000	Patents	4,000	
Current Accounts :			*Less* : Depreciation	400	3,600
A	1,060		Plant and Machinery	13,280	
Add : Interest on Capital	1,000		Additions during the year	1,560	
Interest on Current A/c	53			14,840	
Profit :	14,904		*Less* : Depreciation	1,718	13,122
	17,017		Motor Vans	900	
Less : Drawings	10,000		*Less* : Depreciation	100	800
	7,017		Office Furniture	300	
Less : Interest on Drawings	330	6,687	*Less* : Depreciation	30	270
B :	2,800		*Current Assets :*		
Add : Interest on Capital	250		Stock		21,069
Interest on Current A/c	140		Sundry Debtors	16,020	
Salary	1,000		*Less* : Provision for Bad Debts	801	15,219
Commission	2,070		Prepaid Factory Expenses		70
Profit	3,726		Prepaid Insurance		62
	9,986		Advertising Suspenses		878
Less : Drawings	3,000		Cash in hand		31
	6,986		Cash at Bank		2,841
Less : Interest on Drawings	80	6,906			
Mortgage on Freehold Premises	10,000				
Add : Interest Accrued	150	10,150			
Sundry Creditors		24,150			
Salaries Accrued		69			
		72,962			72,962

Workings :

(1) **Depreciation on Plant and Machinery**

			Rs.
Old balance : 10% on	Rs. 13,280	=	1,328
Additions : 25% on	Rs. 1,560	=	390
			1,718

(2) **Interest on Capital**

				Rs.
A :	5% on	Rs. 20,000	=	1,000
B :	5% on	Rs. 5,000	=	250
				1,250

(3) **Interest on Current Account**

A : 5% on	Rs. 1,060	=	53
B : 5% on	Rs. 2,800	=	140
			193

(4) **B's Commission**

Divisible Profit before charging commission :

Rs. (23,733 + 410) – Rs. (1,000 + 1,250 + 193)

= Rs. 23,143 – Rs. 2,443 = Rs. 20,700

∴ Commission = 10% of Rs. 20,700 = 2,070

(5) **Apportionment of Divisible Profit :**

Ratio of Capital of A and B = 20,000 : 5,000 = 4

∴ A's share of Profit = $\frac{4}{5}$th of Rs. 18,630 = 14,904

B's share of Profit = $\frac{1}{5}$th of Rs. 18,630 = 3,726

Preparation of Final Accounts under Cash Basis

We have already highlighted cash basis of accounting earlier in **Chapter 3**. It has already been mentioned there that cash basis of accounting is followed by the professional people, e.g., Doctors, Lawyers, Chartered Accountants etc. Actually, actual profit or loss cannot be ascertained if accounts are prepared under cash basis, as accrual items have direct bearing on Profit/Loss of a firm. Under this method, expenses or incomes are considered on Cash basis e.g., Salary paid Rs. 5,000. Outstanding Salary Rs. 1,000; Prepaid Salary Rs. 2,000.

If we want to ascertain the actual amount of payment of salary, it will be:

		Rs.
	Salary	5,000
Less:	Outstanding Salary	1,000
		4,000
Add:	Prepaid Salary	2,000
		6,000

Other expenses and incomes will be adjusted accordingly.

Illustration 18

Final Accounts under Cash Basis

Mr. Oswal maintains his accounts on Mercantile Basis. The following Trial Balance has been prepared from his books as at 31st March 2012 after making necessary adjustments for outstanding and accrued items as well as depreciation :

Trial Balance *as at 31st March 2012*

	Dr. Rs.	*Cr.* Rs.
Plant and Machinery	2,12,500	
Sundry Creditors		2,64,000
Sales		6,50,000
Purchases	4,20,000	
Salaries	40,000	
Prepaid Insurance	370	
Advance Rent	2,000	
Outstanding Salary		6,000
Advance Salary	2,500	
Electricity Charges	2,650	
Furniture and Fixtures	72,000	
Opening Stock	50,000	
Outstanding Electricity Charges		450
Insurance	1,200	
Rent	10,000	
Miscellaneous Expenses	14,000	
Cash in hand	3,000	
Investments	80,000	
Drawings	24,000	
Dividend from Investments		8,000
Accrued Dividend from Investments	1,500	
Depreciation on Plant and Machinery	37,500	
Depreciation on Furniture	8,000	
Capital Account		2,11,970
Telephone Charges	6,000	
Sundry Debtors	1,70,500	
Stationery and Printing	1,200	
Cash at Bank	65,000	
Interest on Loan	8,000	
Interest Due but not paid on Loan		1,500
Loan Account		90,000
	12,31,920	12,31,920

Additional Information

(i) Salaries include Rs. 10,000 towards renovation of Proprietor's residence.

(ii) Closing Stock amounted to Rs. 75,000.

Mr. Oswal, however, requests you to prepare a Trading and Profit & Loss Account for the year ended 31st March 2012 and a Balance Sheet as on that date following cash basis of accounting.

Solution

In the Books of Mr. Oswal

Dr. **Trading and Profit and Loss Account** *for the year ended 31st March 2012* Cr.

Particulars	*Amount* Rs.	*Amount* Rs.	*Particulars*	*Amount* Rs.	*Amount* Rs.
To Opening Stock		50,000	By Sales		6,50,000
" Purchases		4,20,000	" Closing Stock		75,000
" Profit & Loss A/c Gross Profit transferred		2,55,000			
		7,25,000			7,25,000
To Salaries	40,000		By Trading A/c —Gross Profit transferred		2,55,000
Less : Outstanding Salary	6,000		" Dividend from Investment	8,000	
	34,000		*Less* : Accrued	1,500	
Add : Advance Salary	2,500				6,500
	36,500				
Less : Renovation (Drawings)	10,000	26,500			
" Insurance	1,200				
Add : Prepaid	370	1,570			
" Rent	10,000				
Add : Advance Rent	2,000				
		12,000			
" Electricity Charges	2,650				
Less : Outstanding	450	2,200			
" Miscellaneous Expenses		14,000			
" Stationery & Printing		1,200			
" Interest on Loan	8,000				
Less : Outstanding	1,500	6,500			
" Telephone Charges		6,000			
" Depreciation :					
Plant & Machinery	37,500				
Furniture & Fixtures	8,000	45,500			
" Capital Account Net Profit transferred		1,46,030			
		2,61,500			2,61,500

Balance Sheet *as at 31st March 2012*

Liabilities	Rs.	Rs.	*Assets*	Rs.	Rs.
Capital Account	2,11,970		Plant and Machinery (at cost less depreciation)		2,12,500
Add : Net Profit during the year	1,46,030		Furniture & Fixtures (at cost less depreciation)		72,000
	3,58,000		Investments		80,000
Less : Drawings (Rs. 24,000 + 10,000)	34,000		Stock-in-Trade		75,000
		3,24,000	Debtors		1,70,500
Loan Account		90,000	Cash in hand		3,000
Sundry Creditors		2,64,000	Cash at Bank		65,000
		6,78,000			6,78,000

MISCELLANEOUS

Illustration 19

From the following particulars extracted from the books of Banerjee, prepare Trading and Profit and Loss Account and Balance Sheet as at 31st March 2010 after making the necessary adjustments :

	Rs.		Rs.
Banerjee's Capital A/c (Cr.)	54,050	Interest Received	725
Stock on 1.4.2009	23,400	Cash with Traders Banks Ltd.	4,000
Sales	1,44,800	Discount Received	1,495
Sales Return	4,300	Investment (at 5%) as on 1.4.2009	2,500
Purchases	1,21,550	Discount Allowed	3,770
Purchase Returns	2,900	General Expenses	1,960
Carriage Inwards	9,300	Audit Fees	350
Rent	2,850	Fire Insurance Premium	300
Salaries	4,650	Travelling Expenses	1,165
Sundry Debtors	12,000	Postage and Telegrams	435
Sundry Creditors	7,400	Cash on hand	190
Loan from Dena Bank Ltd. (at 12%)	10,000	Deposit at 10% as on 1.4.2009 (Dr.)	15,000
Interest paid	450	Drawings	5,000
Printing and Stationery	1,700	Furniture	900
Advertisement	5,600		

Adjustments

(1) Value of stock as on 31st March 2010 is Rs. 39,300. This includes goods returned by customers on 31st March 2010, to the value of Rs. 1,500, for which no entry has been passed in the books.

(2) Purchases include furniture purchased on 1.1.2010 for Rs. 1,000.

(3) Depreciation should be provided on the furniture at 10% @ p.a.

(4) The loan account from Dena Bank in the books of Banerjee appears as :

			Rs.				Rs.
31.3.2010	To	Balance c/d	10,000	1.4.2009	By	Balance b/d	5,000
				31.3.2010	"	Bank	5,000
			10,000				10,000

(5) Sundry Debtors include Rs. 2,000 due from Robert and Sundry Creditors include Rs. 1,000 due to him.

(6) Interest paid includes Rs. 300 paid to Dena Bank.

(7) Interest received represents Rs. 100 from the Sundry Debtors and the balance on investments and deposits.

(8) Provide for interest payable to Dena Bank and for interest receivable on investment and deposits.

(9) Make a provision for doubtful debts at 5% on the balance under "Sundry Debtors". No such provision need be made for the deposits. **[CA Foundation—Adapted]**

Solution

In the Books of Banerjee

Dr. **Trading and Profit and Loss Account** *for the year ended 31st March 2010* *Cr.*

Particulars	*Amount*	*Amount*	*Particulars*	*Amount*	*Amount*
	Rs.	Rs.		Rs.	Rs.
To Opening Stock		23,400	By Sales	1,44,800	
" Purchases	1,21,550		*Less :* Returns Inward	5,800	
Less : Returns Outward	2,900				1,39,000
	1,18,650		" Closing Stock		39,300
Less : Furniture Purchased	1,000	1,17,650			
" Carriage Inward		9,300			
" Profit and Loss A/c —Gross Profit transferred		27,950			
		1,78,300			1,78,300

	Rs.	Rs.		Rs.	Rs.
To Rent		2,850	By Trading A/c		
" Salaries		4,650	—Gross Profit		27,950
" Printing and Stationery		1,700	" Discount Received		1,495
" Advertisement		5,600	" Interest	725	
" Interest (Rs. 450 + 600 – 300)		750	*Add* : Accrued Interest	1,000	
" Discount Allowed		3,770			1,725
" Fire Insurance Premium		300			
" General Expenses		1,960			
" Travelling Expenses		1,165			
" Post and Telegram		435			
" Reserve for Bad Debts		475			
" Audit Fees		350			
" Depreciation on Furniture		115			
" Capital A/c					
(Net Profit transferred)		7,050			
		31,170			31,170

Balance Sheet *as at 31st March 2010*

Liabilities	Rs.	Rs.	*Assets*	Rs.	Rs.
Capital	54,050		Furniture	900	
Add : Net Profit	7,050		Additions	1,000	
	61,100			1,900	
Less : Drawings	5,000	56,100	*Less* : Depreciation	115[3]	1,785
Loan from Dena Bank		10,000	Deposits		15,000
Sundry Creditors	7,400		Investment		2,500
Less : Mutual Indebtedness	1,000	6,400	Closing Stock		39,300
Outstanding			Sundry Debtors	12,000	
Interest on Bank Loan		300[1]	*Less* : Returns	1,500	
				10,500	
			Less : Mutual Indebtedness	1,000	
				9,500	
			Less : Prov. for Bad Debts	475	9,025
			Accrued Interest on Investment & Deposits		1,000[2]
			Cash with Traders Bank		4,000
			Cash in hand		190
		72,800			72,800

Workings :

1. Outstanding Interest on Bank Loan

	Rs.
Interest per year Rs. $5,000 \times \frac{12}{100}$	600
Less : Already paid	300
Outstanding	300

2. Accrued Interest on Investments and Deposits

	Rs.
Annual Interest of Deposit = Rs. $15,000 \times \frac{10}{100}$	1,500
Add : Annual Interest on Investment = Rs. $2,500 \times \frac{5}{100}$	125
	1,625
Less : Interest Received (Rs. 725 – 100)	625
	1,000

Note **: Interest received from Debtors Rs. 100 has already been included with the Interest Account, so there will be no further treatment.**

3. Depreciation on Furniture @ 10%

	Rs.
On Rs. $900 \times \frac{10}{100}$	90
On Additions (1.1.2010 – 31.3.2011)	
Rs. $1,000 \times \frac{10}{100} \times \frac{3}{12}$	25
	115

Sale or Return basis, Commission of Works Manager and General Manager, etc.

Illustration 20

From the following balance and information for the year ended 31.12.2010, prepare the final accounts in the books of Miss Piu Sen :

Dr.	Rs.		*Cr.* Rs.
Plant and Machinery	18,000	Capital	60,000
Depreciation on P & M	2,000	Sales	2,49,000
Repairs to Plant	1,600	Bank Overdraft	13,800
Wages	28,000	Salaries Outstanding	2,000
Salaries	4,000	Bills Payable	3,000
Income-tax	500	Provision for Bad Debts	6,000
Cash	2,000	Discount on Purchases	4,000
Land	24,500	Creditors	23,300
Depreciation on Building	2,500		
Purchases less Returns	1,23,500		
Accrued Income	1,500		
Bills Receivable	30,000		
Bad Debts	1,000		
Debtors	35,000		
Opening Stock	37,000		
Building	50,000		
	3,61,100		3,61,100

Adjustments

1. Stock on 31.12.2010 :
   Market Price Rs. 40,000; Cost Price Rs. 30,000.
2. Write-off Rs. 3,000 bad debts and maintain a provision of 5% on Debtors.
3. Goods costing Rs. 5,000 were sent to a customer on 'Sale or Return Basis' on 30th December. These were recorded as actual sales. The rate of gross profit was $\frac{1}{6}$th of sale.
4. Rs. 1,200 paid as Rent of the office were debited to Landlord Account and were included in the list of Sundry Debtors.
5. General Manager is to be given Commission at 10% after charging the Commission of Works Manager and his own.
6. Works Manager is to be given Commission at 5% after charging the Commission of General Manager and his own.

[CA]

Solution

In the Books of Miss Piu Sen

Trading and Profit and Loss Account ***for the year ended 31st December 2010***

Dr. Particular	Amount Rs.	Amount Rs.	Particular	Amount Rs.	*Cr.* Amount Rs.
To Opening Stock		37,000	By Sales	2,49,000	
" Purchases (*Less* returns)		1,23,500	*Less* : Sale on Approval	6,000[1]	2,43,000
" Wages		28,000			
" Profit and Loss A/c —Gross Profit transferred		89,500	" Closing Stock	30,000[2]	
			Add : Cost of Unapproved Goods	5,000[1]	35,000
		2,78,000			2,78,000
To Salaries		4,000	By Trading A/c —Gross Profit		89,500
" Repairs to Plant		1,600			
" Rent		1,200[3]	" Provisions for Bad Debts		
" Depreciation on :					
Plant and Machinery	2,000		Old Prov .	6,000	
Building	2,500	4,500	*Less* : New Prov.	1,240	4,760

Contd.

	Rs.	Rs.		Rs.	Rs.
To Bad Debts	1,000		By Discount on Purchases		4,000
Add : Further Bad Debts	3,000	4,000			
" General Manager's Commission		7,214[4]			
" Works Manager's Commission		3,607[5]			
" Capital A/c —Net Profit transferred		72,139			
		98,260			98,260

Balance Sheet *as at 31st December 2010*

Liabilities	Rs.	Rs.	*Assets*	Rs.	Rs.
Capital	60,000		Land		24,500
Add : Net Profit	72,139		Buildings (WDV)		50,000
	1,32,139		Plant & Machinery (WDV)		18,000
Less : Income-tax	500	1,31,639	Stock (Rs. 30,000 + 5,000)		35,000
Sundry Creditors		23,300	Sundry Debtors	35,000	
Bank Overdraft		13,800	*Less* : Sale or Return	6,000	
Bills Payable		3,000		29,000	
Outstanding Liabilities			*Less* : Bad Debts	3,000	
for Salaries	2,000			26,000	
General Manager Com.	7,214		*Less* : Rent wrongly		
Works Manager's Com.	3,607		included	1,200	
		12,821		24,800	
			Less : Prov. for Bad Debts	1,240	23,560
			Bills Receivable		30,000
			Accrued Income		1,500
			Cash in hand		2,000
		1,84,560			1,84,560

Workings :

1. **For goods 'Sale or Return'**
   (i) **Rate of profit is $\frac{1}{6}$th of Sales, i.e., $\frac{1}{5}$ th of Cost.**
   So, Cost Price Rs. 5,000 + Profit Rs. 1,000 = Selling Price Rs. 6,000.
   Thus, Rs. 6,000 to be deducted from Sales in Trading A/c and the same to be deducted from Sundry Debtors in Balance Sheet.
   (ii) **Rs. 5,000, i.e., the Cost Price, to be added with Closing Stock. So, Closing Stock will be Rs. (30,000 + 5,000) = Rs. 35,000, both in Trading A/c and in the assets side of the Balance Sheet as well.**
2. **Closing Stock should be taken as *Cost Price or Market Price, whichever is less;* hence, Rs. 30,000 is to be considered as the value of unsold stock.**
3. **The entry being : Rent A/c Dr.**
   To Debtors A/c
   That is, Rs. 1,200 is to be deducted from Sundry Debtors in the asset side of the Balance Sheet and the same is also to be charged against Profit and Loss A/c.
4. **Profit before charging Commission amounted to Rs. 82,960. Since both the General Manager and Works Manager take commission @ 10% and 5%, respectively, after charging their respective commissions, so, total commission will be 15% (after charging such com.)—means $\frac{15}{115}$ of the said profit.**

   Thus, General Manager will get = Rs. $82,960 \times \frac{10}{115}$ = Rs. 7,214

   and, Works Manager will get = Rs. $82,960 \times \frac{5}{115}$ = Rs. 3,607.

***Undervaluation of Stock, Abnormal Loss, Provident Fund, Amortisation of Patent* etc.**

Illustration 21

From the following Trial Balance of Sri Sarbanga Sundar Sammadder prepare Trading and Profit and Loss Account for the year ending 31st December 1998 and a Balance Sheet as on that date after taking into consideration the necessary adjustments :

Heads of Account	Debit	Credit
	Rs.	Rs.
Capital and Drawings	10,200	95,000
Stock (1-1-98)	18,900	
Purchases and Sales	1,38,600	2,02,000
Printing and Stationery	2,600	
Debtors and Creditors	22,800	16,020
Freehold Premises	39,000	
Deposit with Shreyashi Das at 10% (since 30-6-98)	18,000	
Salaries (including advance Rs. 3,500)	28,200	
Returns	890	1,580
Provident Fund		6,550
Interest on Deposit with Shreyashi Das		450
Furniture and Fixture	8,600	
Trade Expenses	12,650	
Outstanding Trade Expenses		1,600
Provision for Doubtful Debts		2,200
Bad Debt recovered		700
Income Tax	7,900	
Bank Balance	6,950	
Cash in hand	6,310	
Patent Right	5,400	
Suspense A/c		900
	3,27,000	3,27,000

Adjustments

(i) Last year's closing stock was valued at 10% below cost. Sri Sammadder wants to revert to cost. Stock as on 31.12.98 was valued at Rs. 16,400 (at cost).

(ii) Goods costing Rs. 650 pilfered by a dishonest employee and furniture (book value on 1.1.98 Rs. 700) destroyed by an accidental fire on 31.12.98.

(iii) Sunanda Bhowmick is included in both debtors and creditors—the amount due from him is Rs. 430 and the amount due to him is Rs. 200.

(iv) New furniture costing Rs. 1,200 was purchased on 31.12.98 on credit but not yet recorded.

(v) Suspense A/c represents a cheque received from a debtor in full settlement of a claim for Rs. 1,000. The cheque was deposited into bank and duly collected also.

(vi) The employer's contribution to provident fund Rs. 1,240 is yet to be paid.

(vii) Write-off Rs. 400 as bad and maintain provision for doubtful debts @ 5% on debtors.

(viii) Depreciate all tangible fixed assets @ 10% p.a. Patent was acquired in 1997 and annual amortisation equal to 1/10th of the cost stated last year.

(ix) Creditors include suppliers of stationery Rs. 200. **[CU BCom (Hons) 1999]**

Solution

In the Books of Sri Sammadder

Trading and Profit & Loss Account *for the year ended 31st Dec. 1998*

Dr. Particulars	Amount	Amount	Cr. Particulars	Amount	Amount
	Rs.	Rs.		Rs.	Rs.
To Opening Stock		21,000	By Sales	2,02,000	
" Purchases	1,38,600		*Less* : Return Inwards	890	2,01,110
Less : Goods Pilferred	650		" Closing Stock		16,400
	1,37,950				
Less : Return Outward	1,580	1,36,370			
" Profit and Loss A/c —Gross Profit transferred		60,140			
		2,17,510			2,17,510
To Printing and Stationery		2,600	By Trading A/c		
" Salaries	28,200		" Gross Profit		60,140
Less : Advance	3,500	24,700	" Interest on Deposit with S. Das	450	
" Trade Expenses		12,650	*Add* : Accrued	450	900
" Discount Allowed		100			

Contd

		Rs.	Rs.			Rs.	Rs.
To	Abnormal Loss :			By	Bad Debt Recovery		700
	Goods Pilferred	650		"	Prov. for Bad Debts	2,200	
"	Furniture Destroyed (Rs. 700 – 70)	630	1,280		*Less :* New Reserve	1,060	
"	Depreciation :						1,140
	On Freehold Premises	3,900		"	Undervaluation of Opening Stock		2,100
	On Furniture	860					
	On Patent (Rs. 5,400 × $\frac{1}{9}$)	600	5,360				
"	Bad Debts		400				
"	Employer's Contribution to Provident Fund		1,240				
"	Capital A/c Net Profit transferred		16,650				
			64,980				64,980

Balance Sheet *as on 31st Dec. 1998*

Liabilities	Rs.	Rs.	*Assets*	Rs.	Rs.
Capital (1.1.98)	95,000		Freehold Premises	39,000	
Add : Net Profit	16,650		*Less* : Depreciation	3,900	35,100
	1,11,650		Furniture and Fixture	8,600	
Less : Drawings	10,200		*Less* : Destroyed	630	
	1,01,450			7,970	
Less : Income Tax	7,900		*Less* : Depreciation	860	
		93,550	*Add* : New Furniture	1,200	8,310
Sundry Creditors	16,020		Deposit with S. Das		18,000
Less : Suppliers of Stationery	200		Stock in Trade		16,400
	15,820		Sundry Debtors	22,800	
Less : Set-off	200		*Less* : Cheque received	1,000	
		15,620		21,800	
Suppliers of Stationery		200	*Less* : Set-off	200	
Suppliers of Furniture		1,200		21,600	
Provident Fund	6,550		*Less* : Bad Debts	400	
Add : Current year's Contribution	1,240			21,200	
		7,790	*Less* : Provision for B/Debt	1,060	20,140
Outstanding Trade Expenses		1,600	Patents	5,400	
			Less : Depreciation	600	4,800
			Prepaid Salary		3,500
			Accrued Interest		450
			Bank balance		6,950
			Cash in hand		6,310
		1,19,960			1,19,960

Workings :

For (i): Since last year's Closing Stock was undervalued, Opening Stock of Current year also was undervalued. So actual Value of Opening Stock will be =

$$\text{Rs. } 18,900 \times \frac{100}{90} = \text{Rs. } 21,000$$

For (ii): Abnormal Loss of Goods

Profit and Loss A/c Dr.	650	
To Purchase A/c		650

It includes in the determination of net profit or loss for the current periods. An alternative approach is to show such item in the statement of profit and loss after determining the current profit or loss. We have followed the first one here.

For (iii) The entry for this purpose will be:

		Rs.	Rs.
Suspense A/c	Dr.	900	
Discount Allowed A/c	Dr.	100	
To Debtors A/c			1,000

Abnormal Loss of Furniture

Book Value – Depreciation = Rs. 700 – 70 = Rs. 630 to appear in debit side of P & L A/c and also will be deducted from Furniture.

For (vi) : Employees' contribution is not paid i.e., the entry will be:

P & L A/c (Employees' Cont.)	Dr.	1,240	
To Outstanding PF Cont. A/c			1,240

It will be added to PF balance of Rs. 6,550, in the liability side of the Balance Sheet

For (viii) : Write-off/Depreciation on Patent

Rs. 5,400 is given after charging one year's depreciation of patent, which was Rs. 6,000 (i.e., 5,400 × $\frac{100}{90}$) in 1997.

∴ Dep. will be Rs. 600.

or, Rs. 5,400 × $\frac{1}{9}$ = Rs. 600

***Stock Valuation, Cash Embezzlement,* etc.**

Illustration 22

The following Trial Balance has been prepared by Sm. Bijolly Acharya as on 31.3.99:

Trial Balance *as on 31.3.99*

Heads of Accounts	*Debit*	*Credit*
	Rs.	Rs.
Capital and Drawings	3,600	90,400
Stock (1-4-98)	12,300	
Wages	16,400	
Plant and Machinery	34,000	
Sundry Debtors	13,160	1,000 (Advance)
Sundry Creditors		12,750
Purchases and Sales	52,300	99,150
Freehold Property	29,700	
Returns	320	540
Salaries	12,800	
Rent	2,400	
Outstanding Rent		200
Trade Expenses	2,060	
Furniture and Fixture	3,100	
Bad Debts	560	
Provision for Bad Debts		480
Patent and Trade Mark	4,100	
Electricity	1,290	
Loose Tools	1,510	
Advertisement Suspense	4,200	
Gas and Fuel	2,050	
Insurance	1,330	
Cash at Bank	5,200	
Cash in hand	2,140	
	2,04,520	2,04,520

Additional Information

(i) Stock was not taken on 31.3.99 but actually taken on 7.4.99 at Rs. 10,200. Transactions during the week ended 7.4.99 were : Sales—Rs. 12,800; Purchases—Rs. 8,100.

A uniform $16\frac{2}{3}$% profit is made on the selling price.

(ii) Rs. 510 received from a debtor, whose balance had been written-off as bad, was recorded as Cash Sale.

(iii) Private goods of Sm. Acharya costing Rs. 2,400 and sold for Rs. 2,880 was included in sales.

(iv) Advance from customers is entitled to 12% interest which is due for 2 months.

(v) Electricity expenses include a deposit of Rs. 600 to the W B State Electricity Board.

(vi) The effect of advertisement is expected to last for the coming two years also.

(vii) A furniture costing Rs. 1,600 purchased on 31.12.98 from M/s Assam Furniture Mart on Credit was omitted to be recorded.

(viii) Cash embezzled by a dishonest employee—Rs. 900.

(ix) Patent and Trade Mark is to be amortised in 10 equal instalments.

(x) Provision for Bad Debts is to be adjusted to 5% of Sundry Debtors. Loose Tools are valued at Rs. 1,020. Provide depreciation @ 10% on Plant and Machinery; @ 15% on Furniture.

You are required to prepare Trading and Profit and Loss Account for the year and a Balance Sheet as at the end of the year. **[CU BCom (Hons) 2000]**

Solution

In the Books of Bijolly Acharya

Trading and Profit & Loss Account *for the year ended 31st March 1999*

Dr. *Particulars*	*Amount* Rs.	*Amount* Rs.	*Particulars*	*Amount* Rs.	*Amount* Rs. Cr.
To Opening Stock		12,300	By Sales	99,150	
" Purchases	52,300		*Less* : Sale of private goods	2,880[3]	
Less : Returns Outward	540	51,760		96,270	
" Wages		16,400	*Less* : Bad Debts Recovery	510	
" Gas and Fuel		2,050		95,760	
" Profit and Loss A/c			*Less* : Returns Inward	320	
—Gross Profit		25,697			95,440
			" Closing Stock		12,767[1]
		1,08,207			1,08,207
To Salaries		12,800	By Trading A/c		
" Rent		2,400	" —Gross Profit		25,697
" Trade Expenses		2,060	" Bad Debt Recovery		510[2]
" Bad Debts		560	" Capital A/c		3,756
" Electricity (Less Deposit)		690[5]	(Net Loss)		
" Advertisement		4,200[6]			
" Insurance		1,330			
" Cash Embezzlement		900[7]			
" Dep. on Trade Marks		410			
" Loose Tools		490			
" P & M		3,400			
" Furniture		525			
" Prov. for Bad Debt (new)	658				
Less : Old Reserve	480	178			
" Int. Payable to Customers		20[4]			
		29,963			29,963

Balance Sheet *as at 31st March 1999*

Liabilities	Rs.	Rs.	*Assets*	Rs.	Rs.
Opening Capital	90,400		Freehold Property		29,700
Add : Private goods of			Plant and Machinery	34,000	
Sm. Acharya sold by firm	2,880		*Less* : Depreciation	3,400	30,600
	93,280		Furniture and Fixture	3,100	
Less : Drawings	3,600		*Add* : New Furniture	1,600	
	89,680			4,700	
Less : Net Loss	3,756		*Less* : Depreciation	525	4,175
		85,924	Patents and Trade Marks	4,100	
Sundry Creditors		12,750	*Less* : Depreciation	410	3,690
Advance from Debtors	1,000		Loose Tools	1,510	
Add : Interest due thereon	20[4]		*Less* : Depreciation	490	1,020
		1,020	Closing Stock		12,767
Outstanding Rent		200[4]	Sundry Debtors	13,160	
Creditors for furniture		1,600	*Less* : Prov. for Bad Debt	658	12,502
			Deposit with Elect. Board		600
			Cash at Bank		5,200
			Cash in hand	2,140	
			Less : Cash Embezzled	900	1,240
		1,01,494			1,01,494

Workings

1. Value of Closing Stock

		Rs.
Stock as on 7.4.1999		10,200
Add : Cost of Goods Sold		
Sales	12,800	
Less : Gross Profit @ $16\frac{2}{3}$ % =	2,133	
		10,667
		20,867
Less : Purchases		8,100
Value of Stock as on 31.3.1999		12,767

2. Recovery of Bad Debts

Rs. 510 which was received against bad debts should be treated as recovery of Bad Debt. But as it was wrongly credited to Sales A/c; the rectifying entry will be

Sales A/c	Dr.	510	
To B/D Recovery A/c			510

So, Rs. 510 to be deducted from Sales and the same will appear in the credit side of P & L A/c

3. Selling of Private Goods

Selling of private goods amounting to Rs. 2,880 to be deducted from Sales, and the same is added to Capital as further Capital. Cost price of Rs. 400 to be ignored as the goods do not belong to the business.

4. Interest Payable to Customer in Advance

On Rs. 1,000 $\times \frac{12}{100} \times \frac{2}{12}$ = Rs. 20

5. Deposit to Electric Supply

Electricity deposit of Rs. 600 is an asset and to be deducted from electricity charge (i.e., Electricity Charge – Electricity Deposit.)

= Rs. 1,290 – Rs. 600

= Rs. 690 (will appear in debit side of P & L A/c)

7. For embezzlement of Cash

Profit & Loss A/c	Dr.	900	
To Cash A/c			900

6. Advertisement Suspense

Since effect of advertisement is expected to continue for the next two years, it is a case of Deferred Revenue Expenditure. So $\frac{2}{3}$ of Rs. 4,200 is to be carried forward and should appear in the assets side of the Balance Sheet as an asset.

But as per paras 68 and 69, **Ind AS 38, Intangible Assets,** when it is probable that the future economic benefits that are attributable to the asset will flow to the enterprise and the cost of the asset can be measured reliably, it can be treated as intangibles assets. As such, the entire amount of Rs. 4,200 should be written-off against Profit and Loss A/c as intangible assets.

Loss on Exchange of Furniture, Dishonour of Cheque, etc.

Illustration 23

The following is the Trial Balance of M/s Roy Traders as at 31st December 1992 :

You are asked to prepare the Trading and Profit & Loss Account for the year ended 31st December 1992 and Balance Sheet as on that date:

	Dr. Rs.	*Cr.* Rs.
Roy's Capital		2,16,000
Stock as on 1st January '92	93,600	
Sales and Sales Returns	17,200	5,79,200
Purchase and Purchase Returns	4,86,200	11,600
Freight and Carriage	37,200	
Rent and Taxes	11,400	
Salaries and Wages	18,600	
Sundry Debtors	48,000	
Sundry Creditors		29,600
Bank Loan (at 12% p.a.)		40,000
Bank Interest on above	3,800	
Printing & Advertisement	20,200	
Income from Investments		500
Cash at Bank	23,000	
Discount Received		8,560

Contd.

	Rs.	Rs.
Investments	10,000	
Furniture and Fittings	13,600	
Discounts Paid	5,080	
General Expenses	7,820	
Audit Fees	1,400	
Insurance	1,200	
Travelling Expenses	4,660	
Postage and Telegram	1,740	
Cash in hand	20,760	
Fixed Deposit with State Bank of India	40,000	
Drawings	20,000	
	8,85,460	8,85,460

Additional Information

(a) Closing Stock as on 31.12.92 Rs. 1,57,200.

(b) Included amongst the Debtors is Rs. 6,000 from Mr. S. Naha; and included amongst the Creditors is Rs. 2,000 to Mr. S. Naha.

(c) The effect of advertisement being not yet expired, a quarter of the amount of "Printing and Advertisement" is to be carried forward to the next year.

(d) Provide 2% for Discount on Debtors and create a Provision for Bad and Doubtful Debts at 5% on Debtors.

(e) Depreciation of 10% is to be written-off Furniture and Fittings.

(f) Wage owing on 31st December 1992, Rs. 600; and Salaries owing Rs. 1,000.

(g) Insurance was paid in advance up to 31st March 1993.

(h) Furniture, which stood at Rs. 1,200 in the books on 1st January 1992, was disposed-off at Rs. 580 on 30th June '92 in part exchange for a new Furniture costing Rs. 1,040. The net amount payable Rs. 460 was passed through the Purchase Book by mistake.

(i) Two dishonoured cheques for Rs. 400 and Rs. 600, respectively, had not been entered in the Cash Book. The first for Rs. 400 is known to be bad. In the case of the second cheque for Rs. 600, it is expected that the Debtor would be in a position to pay a dividend of 60 paise in the rupee.

(j) Interest receivable from fixed deposit with State Bank of India @ 12% p.a. and provide for interest on bank loan for the whole year. (All Working Notes must be shown.)

[CU BCom (Hons) 1993]

Solution

In the Books of M/s Roy Traders

Dr. **Trading Account and Profit & Loss Account** *for the year ended 31st Dec. 1992* Cr.

Particulars	Amount	Amount	Particulars	Amount	Amount
	Rs.	Rs.		Rs.	Rs.
To Opening Stock		93,600	By Sales	5,79,200	
" Purchases	4,86,200		*Less:* Returns Inward	17,200	5,62,000
Less : Returns Outward	11,600		" Closing Stock		1,57,200
	4,74,600				
Less: Furniture Purchase	460	4,74,140			
" Freight & Cartage		37,200			
" Profit and Loss A/c —Gross Profit transferred		1,14,260			
		7,19,200			7,19,200
To Rent and Taxes		11,400	" Trading A/c —Gross Profit		1,14,260
" Salaries & Wages	18,600				
Add: Outstanding	1,600	20,200	" Discount Received		8,560
" Bank Interest	3,800		" Income from Investment		500
Add: Outstanding	1,000	4,800	" Accrued Interest		

Contd.

		Rs.	Rs.			Rs.	Rs.
To	Printing and Adv.		20,200[2]	By	on Fixed Deposit		4,800[6]
"	Discount Allowed		5,080				
"	General Expenses		7,820				
"	Audit Fees		1,400				
"	Insurance	1,200					
	Less : Prepaid	240	960				
"	Travelling Expenses		4,660				
"	Postage & Telegram		1,740				
"	Bad Debts (Dishonoured Cheque)		400				
"	Prov. for Bad Debts and Doubtful Debts		2,540				
"	Prov. for Discount on Debtors		874				
"	Depreciation on: Furniture & Fittings		1,352[4]				
"	Loss on Exchange of Furniture		560[3]				
"	Capital A/c —Net Profit Transferred		44,134				
"			1,28,120				1,28,120

Balance Sheet *as on 31st Dec. 1992*

Liabilities	*Amount* Rs.	*Amount* Rs.	*Assets*	*Amount* Rs.	*Amount* Rs.
Capital	2,16,000		Furniture	13,600	
Add: Net Profit	44,134		*Less:* Exchange	1,140	
	2,60,134			12,460	
Less : Drawings	20,000		Additions	1,040	
		2,40,134		13,500	
Sundry Creditors A/c	29,600		*Less:* Depreciation	1,352	12,148
Less: Wrong credit for Furniture	460		Investment		10,000
	29,140		F.D. With SBI		40,000
			Closing Stock		1,57,200
Less: Set-off	2,000[1]	27,140	Closing Stock	48,000	
Creditors for Furniture		460	*Less:* Set-off	2,000[1]	
12% Bank Loan	40,000			46,000	
Add: Outstanding Interest	1,000	41,000	*Less:* Cheque Dishonoured	1,000	
Outstanding Liabilities:				47,000	
Salary	1,000		*Less:* Bad Debts	400	
Wages	600			46,600	
		1,600	*Less:* Provision for Bad Debts	2,540	
				44,060	
			Less: Prov. for Bad Debts	874	43,186[5]
			Prepaid Insurance		240
			Accrued Interest on F.D.		4,800
			Cash at bank	23,000	
			Less: Dishonoured Cheque	1,000	22,000
			Cash in hand		20,760
		3,10,334			3,10,334

Workings :

1. **Mutual Indebtedness**

It is a case of mutual indebtedness. So the lower amount i.e., Rs. 2,000 to be deducted from debtors as well as from creditors as the entry is :

Creditors A/c Dr.	2,000	
To Debtors A/c		2,000

2. **Printing and Advertisement**

It is a case of deferred revenue expenditure, i.e., $\frac{1}{4}$ of Rs. 20,200 = Rs. 5,050 should be carried forward. But **Ind AS 38** contradicts this view. As per paras 68 and 69, expenditure on an intangible item shall be recognised as an expense when it is incurred, and para 69 states that expenditure is incurred to provide future economic benefits to an entity, but no intangible asset or other asset is acquired or created that can be recognised. Expenditure on advertising and promotional activities can be treated as intangible asset which must be charged against Profit and Loss Statement in full. So the entire amount of Rs. 20,200 is charged against P & L A/c.

3. **Loss on Exchange of Furniture & Fittings**

	Rs.
Book value of Furniture sold on 1.1.1992	1,200
Less: Depreciation for 6 months (Rs. 1,200 × $\frac{10}{100}$ × $\frac{6}{12}$)	60
WDV on 30.6.1992	1,140
Less : Sold for	580
∴ Loss on Exchange	560

4. **Total Depreciation on Furniture & Fittings**

	Rs.
On Rs. 1,040 × $\frac{10}{100}$ × $\frac{6}{12}$ =	52
On Rs. 1,200 (which was exchanged)	60
On Rs. 12,400 (i.e., Rs. 13,600 – Rs. 1,200) × $\frac{10}{100}$ =	1,240
	1,352

5. **Sundry Debtors**

Sundry Debtors	48,000
Less: Set-off	2,000
	46,000
Add: Cheque Dish. (400 + 600)	1,000
	47,000
Less: Bad Debts	400
	46,600
Less: Prov. for Bad Debts	2,540*
	44,060
Less: Prov. for Disc. on Debtors	874
	43,186

* 60% of Rs. 600 is expected to be realised i.e., 40% is of doubtful nature, and so full provision should be made. Balance of Sundry Debtors after writing-off bad debts is Rs. 46,600. Thus, total provision will be both on Specific Debtors + General Debtors, i.e., 40% of Rs. 600 + 5% on Rs. 46,000 = Rs. 240 + Rs. 2,300 = Rs. 2,540.

6. **Accrued Interest on Fixed Deposit**

It has been assumed that fixed deposit with SBI was made at the beginning of the year. So, 12 months' interest to be calculated

$$\text{Rs. } 40,000 \times \frac{12}{100} = \text{Rs. } 4,800.$$

Illustration 24

From the following balances and information prepare Trading and Profit and Loss Account of Mr. A. Sen for the year ended 31st December 2001 and a Balance Sheet as on that date :

Particulars	Rs.	*Particulars*	Rs.
Stock (1.1.01)	15,100	Sales	1,67,200
Purchases	94,500	Returns Outward	1,500
Wages	30,900	Provision for Doubtful Debts	3,200
Electricity	3,750	Sundry Creditors	35,600
Furniture	12,500	Capital	80,000
Machinery	18,000	Discount Received	1,280
Motor Car	10,240		
Fuel	3,180		
Rent @ Rs. 450 p.m.	4,050		
Printing and Stationery	5,200		
Fixed Deposit (at 10% p.a.)	25,000		
Sundry Debtors	42,000		
Discount Allowed	1,400		
Insurance Premium	4,800		
Telephone Charges	3,750		
Bad Debts	500		
Cash at Bank	11,300		
Cash in hand	2,610		
	2,88,780		2,88,780

Other Information

(i) Stock on 31.12.01 is Rs. 26,700. The stock includes goods returned by a customer on 31st December 2001 to the value of Rs. 2,200 for which no entry has been made.

(ii) Stock valuing Rs. 5,000 destroyed by fire. Rs. 500 realised through sale of damaged goods and Insurance company paid Rs. 3,000 only against the claim.

(iii) Mr. A. Sen has been providing for depreciation on Motor Car @ 20% under Diminishing Balance Method. Now, he wants to provide depreciation @ 6% under Straight Line Method with effect from 1.1.98 (the date of purchase of the Motor Car).

(iv) Mr. A. Sen's Bank has debited Rs. 150 in the Pass Book as clearing charge which has not been entered in the Cash Book.

(v) Creditors include a balance of Rs. 1,600 to the credit of S. Chand in respect of which it has been decided and settled with the party to pay only Rs. 1,000.

(vi) Provide depreciation on Machinery @ 15% and on Furniture @ 10% per annum.

(vii) A Debtor of Rs. 12,000 accepted a bill drawn by Mr. A. Sen.

(viii) Create a provision for doubtful debts at 5% on Sundry Debtors. **[CU BCom (Hons) 2002]**

Solution

In the Books of Mr. A. Sen

Dr. **Trading and Profit & Loss Account** *for the year ended 31st Dec. 2001* *Cr.*

Particulars	*Amount*	*Amount*	*Particulars*	*Amount*	*Amount*
	Rs.	Rs.		Rs.	Rs.
To Opening Stock		15,100	By Sales	1,67,200	
" Purchases	94,500		*Less* : Returns Inward	2,200[1]	
Less : Returns Outward	1,500	93,000		1,65,000	
" Wages		30,900	" *Less* : Sale of damaged goods	500	1,64,500
" Fuel		3,180			
" Profit and Loss A/c —Gross Profit transferred		54,020	" Closing Stock	26,700	
			Add : Stock destroyed by fire	5,000	31,700
		1,96,200			1,96,200
To Rent	4,050		By Trading A/c —Gross Profit		54,020
Add : Outstanding	1,350	5,400[1]			
" Electricity		3,750	" Discount Received		1,280
" Printing and Stationery		5,200	" Prov. for Bad Debts—		
" Discount Allowed		1,400	Old Reserve	3,200	
" Insurance		4,800	*Less* : New Reserve	1,390	1,810
" Telephone Charges		3,750	" Rebate Received from a creditor (Rs. 1,600 – 1,000)		600
" Bad Debts		500			
" Loss of Stock Destroyed by Fire (Rs. 5,000 – Rs. 500 – Rs. 3,000)		1,500[2]	" Depreciation on Motor Car overcharged		6,160[3]
" Bank Clearing Charges		150	" Accured Interest on Fixed Dep.		2,500
" Depreciation :					
Machinery @ 5%	2,700				
Motor Car @ 6%	1,200				
Furniture @ 10%	1,250	5,150			
" Capital A/c —Net Profit transferred		34,770			
		66,370			66,370

Balance Sheet *as on 31st Dec. 2001*

Liabilities	Rs.	Rs.	*Assets*	Rs.	Rs.
Capital :	80,000		Machinery	18,000	
Add : Net Profit	34,770		*Less* : Depreciation	2,700	15,300
		1,14,770	Furniture	12,500	
Sundry Creditors	35,600		*Less* : Depreciation	1,250	11,250
Less : Rebate from S. Chand	600		Motor Car	10,240	
(Rs. 1,600 – 1,000)		35,000			

Contd.

	Rs.	Rs.		Rs.	Rs.
Outstanding Rent		1,350	*Add,:* Depreciation Overcharged	6,160	
				16,400	
			Less : Depreciation (6% on Rs. 20,000)	1,200	15,200
			Fixed Deposit	25,000	
			Add : Accrued Interest	2,500	27,500
			Closing Stock		26,700
			Sundry Debtors	42,000	
			Less : Return Inwards not yet recorded	2,200[1]	
				39,800	
			Less : B/R Received	12,000	
				27,800	
			Less : R/B/Debts @ 5%	1,390	26,410
			Bills Receivable		12,000
			Cash at Bank	11,300	
			Add : Insurance Claim received by cheque	3,000	
				14,300	
			Less : Clearing Charges	150	14,150
			Cash in hand		2,610
		1,51,120			1,51,120

Workings :

1. Returns Inward

Goods returned by customer, not recorded at all for Rs. 2,200. It is an error of omission, only correct entry should be recorded as

Returns Inward A/c	Dr.	2,200	
To Debtors A/c			2,200

i.e., Rs. 2,200 to be deducted from Sales and the same amount should also be deducted from Debtors.

2. Loss on Stock Destroyed by Fire

	Rs.
Value of Stock Destroyed by Fire	5,000
Less: Damaged goods sold	500
	4,500
Less: Insurance claim received	3,000
Loss of Stock	1,500

3. Depreciation on Motor car overcharged

WDV on Motor Car as on 1.1.2001 or 31.12.2000 10,240

So, cost of Motor Car as on 1.1.1998 was

$$\text{Rs. } 10{,}240 \times \frac{100}{80} \times \frac{100}{80} \times \frac{100}{80} = \text{Rs. } 20{,}000 = \quad 20{,}000$$

Depreciation as per Reducing Balance Method

	Rs.	Total Dep. Rs.
1.1.1998 Book Value	20,000	
31.12. 98 Depreciation @ 20%	4,000	4,000
1.1.1999 WDV	16,000	
31.12. 99 Depreciation @ 20%	3,200	3,200
1.1.2000 WDV	12,800	
31.12. 2000 Depreciation @ 20%	2,560	2,560
1.1.2001 WDV	10,240	9,760

Depreciation under Straight-line Method

Depreciation @ 6% on Rs. 20,000

$$= \text{Rs. } 20{,}000 \times \frac{6}{100} = \text{Rs.} \quad 1{,}200$$

		Rs.
For	1998	1,200
	1999	1,200
	2000	1,200
		3,600

So, Depreciation Overcharged (Rs. 9,760 – Rs. 3,600) = Rs. 6,160.

The entry will be:

Motor car A/c	Dr.	6,160	
To Profit and Loss A/c			6,100

Goods sold but not despatched, Dishonour of Cheques and Bill Endorsed, Petty Cash, etc.

Illustration 25

The accountant of Mr. P. Sundaram, the sole-proprietor of a business, extracted the following Trial Balance as on 31st March 2002:

	Dr. Rs.	Cr. Rs.
Cash in hand	16,000	
Cash at bank	25,000	
Petty Cash	1,000	
Furniture & Fixture	10,000	
Plant and Machinery	50,000	
Capital		60,000
Drawings	10,000	
Insurance Charges	1,000	
Salaries	12,000	
Wages	5,000	
Sundry Debtors	22,000	
Stock-in-trade (as on 1.4.2001)	28,000	
Trade Mark Rights (10 years from 1.4.99)	32,000	
Rent & Rates	5,000	
Purchases	1,40,000	
Freight Inward	10,000	
Postage, Telegram & other Trade Expenses	5,000	
Bad Debts	1,000	
9% Loan taken from D. Kumaran (taken on 1.10.2001)		15,000
Interest on Loan	500	
Creditors		37,500
Bills Receivable	10,000	
Sale		2,60,000
Outstanding Liability for Expenses	1,000	
Petty Cash Expenses	3,000	
Bills Payable		15,000
	3,87,500	3,87,500

Adjustments

(i) Stock lying in godown as on 31.3.2002 Rs. 38,000.

(ii) Invoices of the value of Rs. 5,000 were recorded in Sales Book on 27.3.2002 but goods were not despatched until 5.4.2002, the cost of such goods was Rs. 4,000.

(iii) The Petty Cash balance represents the month-end account. As on 31.3.2002, the petty cashier had vouchers totalling to Rs. 400 for which he had not received reimbursement from the main cashier.

(iv) Rent and Rates of Rs. 1,000 relating to 2000–2001 had not been provided in that year but were paid in May 2001 by 'outstanding liability for expenses'.

(v) Bills receivable of Rs. 5,000 were endorsed in favour of creditors during the year 2001-2002. Of these bills, a bill for Rs. 2,000 was dishonoured but not recorded in the books. Other bills would mature in June 2002.

(vi) Two dishonoured cheques of Rs. 400 and Rs. 600, respectively, had not been entered in the Cash Book. The first cheque for Rs. 400 was known to be bad. In case of the second cheque, it was expected that the debtor would be in a position to pay only 50 paise in a rupee. For other debtors, provision for doubtful debts to be provided @ 5%.

(vii) Provide depreciation on all tangible fixed assets @ 10% p.a.

Prepare Trading & Profit & Loss A/c for the year ended 31st March 2002 and a Balance Sheet as on that date. **[CU BCom (Hons) 2003]**

Solution

In the Books of Mr. P. Sundaram

Dr. **Trading and Profit & Loss Account** *for the year ended 31st March 2002* *Cr.*

Particulars	*Amount* Rs.	*Amount* Rs.	*Particulars*	*Amount* Rs.	*Amount* Rs.
To Opening Stock		28,000	By Sales		2,60,000
" Purchases		1,40,000	Closing Stock	38,000	
Wages		5,000	*Less: Cost* Price of goods		
" Freight Inward		10,000	sold but not despatched	4,000[1]	
" Profit & Loss A/c —Gross Profit		1,11,000			34,000
		2,94,000			2,94,000

	Rs.	Rs.		Rs.	Rs.
To Salaries		12,000	By Trading A/c		
" Rent & Rates	5,000		—Gross Profit		1,11,000
Add : Out. for (2000–01)	1,000	6,000			
" Insurance Charges		1,000			
" Postage etc.		5,000			
" Bad Debts	1,000				
" *Add:* Further Bad Debts	400	1,400			
" Interest on Loan	500				
" *Add:* Outstanding Interest	175	675			
" Petty Cash Expenses		3,400[2]			
" Provi. for Doubtful Debts		1,500			
" Trade Marks written-off		4,000[6]			
" Depreciation on:					
Plant & Machinery	5,000				
On Furniture & Fixture	1,000	6,000			
Capital A/c					
—Net Profit Transferred		70,025			
		1,11,000			1,11,000

Balance Sheet *as on 31st March 2002*

Liabilities	Rs.	Rs.	*Assets*	Rs.	Rs.
Capital :			Plant & Machinery	50,000	
Opening Balance	60,000		*Less:* Depreciation	5,000	45,000
Add: Net Profit	70,025				
	1,30,025		Furniture	10,000	
Less ; Drawings	10,000	1,20,025	*Less* : Depreciation	1,000	9,000
0% Loan from D. Kumaran	15,000		Trade Marks	32,000	
Add: Outstanding Interest	175	15,175	*Less* : Amount written-off	4,000	28,000
Sundry Creditors	37,500		Stock (38,000 – 4,000)		34,000
Add: Bill receivable			Sundry Debtors	24,600[5]	
endorsed but dishonoured	2,000[4]		*Less:* Prov. for Doubtful Debts	1,500	23,100
		39,500	Bills Receivable		10,000
Bills Payable		15,000	Cash at Bank	25,000	
			Less: Dishonoured Cheques		
			(400 + 600)	1,000	24,000
			Cash in Hand		16,000
			Petty Cash		600[2]
		1,89,700			1,89,700

Workings:

1. **Goods sold but not despatched**

Goods sold for Rs. 5,000 and recorded in the books but not despatched within the period, so, these goods were included with Closing Stock, the cost price was Rs. 4,000. So Rs. 4,000 to be deducted from the Closing Stock.

2. **Petty Cash Expenses**

Total Petty Cash Expenses will be Rs. 3,000 + Rs. 400 = Rs. 3,400; i.e., Rs. 400 is still to be reimbursed.

Petty Cash Balance will be = Rs. 1,000 – Rs. 400 = Rs. 600.

3. **Rent and Rates of 2000-01**

It becomes clear that Rs. 1,000 was the outstanding rent and rates of 2000-01 which was paid in the current year by passing the following into

		Rs.	Rs.
Out. Rent & Rates A/c	Dr.	1,000	
To Bank A/c			1,000

4. **Endorsed Bill dishonoured**

When endorsed bill dishonoured, the entry is

Debtors A/c	Dr.	2,000	
To Creditors A/c			2,000

i.e., both the amount of debtors and creditors will increase by Rs. 2,000. The other bills which are not yet matured are treated as Contingent Liabilities, i.e., Rs. 5,000 – Rs. 2,000 = Rs. 3,000.

i.e. it is charged against P & L A/c of the current year as Prior Period items.

6. **Trade Marks**

Two years, viz., 2000-01, 2001-02, already written-off, so, balance left for 8 years—the value of which is Rs. 32,000. So, Full Value of Trade Marks = Rs. 32,000 × $\frac{10}{8}$ = Rs. 40,000 ∴ $\frac{1}{10}$th to be written-off, i.e.,

Rs. 40,000 × $\frac{1}{10}$ = Rs. 4,000.

5. **Computation of Closing Debtors and Provision for Bad Debts**

	Rs.
Debtors (as per T.B.)	22,000
Add: Endorsed Bill dishonoured	2,000
Add: Cheque dishonoured	600
	24,600

Provision for Bad Debts

Specific Provision	
for cheque disnonoured @ 50% of Rs. 600 =	300
General Provision	
5% of Rs. 24,000 (Rs. 24,600 – Rs. 600)	1,200
Total Provision	1,500

Exchange of Motor Vehicles, Distribution of Profit, etc.

Illustration 26

Nag, Paul and Sen are partners in a firm sharing profit and losses : Nag 2/5ths, Paul 2/5ths and Sen 1/5th. Sen's annual share of profit (including salary and interest) is to be a minimum of Rs. 28,000, any deficit being borne by the other two partners in their profit-sharing ratio. No interest is allowed or charged on partners' Current Accounts, but Fixed Capital Accounts carry interest at 6% p.a.

The firm's Trial Balance as on 31st March 2000 was as follows :

	Rs.		Rs.	Rs.
Freehold Premises at cost	1,26,000	Capital Accounts :		
Plant & Machinery at cost	1,12,000	Nag	1,12,000	
Motor Vehicles	33,600	Paul	84,000	
Purchases	6,32,000	Sen	42,000	2,38,000
Stock, 1st April 1999	1,00,800	Current Accounts, 1st April 1999 :		
Wages	64,800	Nag	25,200	
Salaries	1,25,600	Paul	8,400	33,600
Trade Expenses	8,400	Sales		10,49,200
Repairs	16,800	Creditors		58,800
Discount Allowed	3,360	Provision for Doubtful Debts,		
Office Expenses	50,400	1st April 1999 :		4,760
Carriage Inwards	8,680	Discount received		5,880
Insurance	19,600	Provision for Depreciation,		
Professional Charges	19,600	1st April 1999 :		
Debtors	95,200	Plant & Machinery		33,600
Bank Balance	11,200	Motor Vehicles		16,800
Current Account, 1st April 1999				
Sen	1,400			
Carriage Outwards	11,200			
	14,40,640			14,40,640

Additional Information

(a) Stock on hand on 31st March 2000 amounted to Rs. 95,720.

(b) Sales include Rs. 33,600 goods sent to Goon and Co. on consignment basis at cost plus 20%. The goods remained in their hands unsold on 31st March 2000.

(c) The following amounts have been drawn each month by the partners as salaries :
Nag—Rs. 500, Paul—Rs. 600, Sen—Rs. 300.
All these amounts have been debited to Salaries Account.

(d) Paul is to be debited with Rs. 3,500 for goods taken by him from stock for personal purpose.

(e) Nag is to be credited with Rs. 2,500 for travelling expenses incurred by him for the purpose of the firm.

(f) Repairs include an item of Rs. 8,000 for alteration to the office, which should be capitalised.

(g) Insurance includes a premium of Rs. 6,000 paid for the year ended 30th September 2000 and office expenses accrued amount to Rs. 4,200.

(h) A motor vehicle costing Rs. 12,600 had been purchased during the year against which Rs. 5,000 had been allowed on the sale of an old vehicle, the net amount Rs. 7,600 being debited to Purchases Account. The vehicle sold had cost Rs. 10,500 and had been written-down to Rs. 3,000.

(i) Depreciation on Plant & Machinery and Motor Vehicles is to be provided at the rate of 10% and 20% p.a., respectively, on the original cost (No depreciation on assets sold and full year's depreciation on assets purchased during the year is chargeable).

(j) A debt of Rs. 840 is to be written-off and the provision for doubtful debts is to be increased to Rs. 6,800.

Prepare a Trading and Profit & Loss Account for the year ended 31st March 2000, and a Balance Sheet as on that date. **[CU BCom (Hons) 2001]**

Solution

In the Books of Partnership Firm

Dr. **Trading and Profit & Loss Account** *for the year ended 31st March 2000* *Cr.*

Particulars	*Amount* Rs.	*Amount* Rs.	*Particulars*	*Amount* Rs.	*Amount* Rs.
To Opening Stock		1,00,800	By Sales	10,49,200	
" Purchases	6,32,000		*Less* : Goods sent on Consignment	33,600[1]	10,15,600
Less : Purchase of Motor Car	7,600				
	6,24,400				
Less : Paul drawing	3,500	6,20,900	" Stock on Consignment $(33{,}600 \times \frac{100}{120})$		28,000
" Wages		64,800			
" Carriage Inwards		8,680			
" Profit & Loss A/c Gross Profit transferred		3,44,140	" Closing Stock		95,720
		11,39,320			11,39,320
To Salaries	1,25,600		By Trading Account		
Less : Partners' Salary	16,800	1,08,800	" Gross Profit		3,44,140
" Trade Expenses		8,400	" Discount Received		5,880
" Repairs	16,800		" Profit on Sale of Motor Vehicle (Rs. 5,000 – 3,000)		2,000[2]
Less : Alteration to Office Expenses	8,000	8,800			
" Discount Allowed		3,360			
" Office Expenses	50,400				
Add : Accrued	4,200	54,600			
" Insurance	19,600				
Less : Prepaid (Rs. $6{,}000 \times \frac{6}{12}$)	3,000	16,600			
" Professional Charges		19,600[2]			
" Bad Debt		840			
" Prov. for B/D (31.3.2000)	6,800				
Less : Old Reserve	4,760	2,040			
" Travelling Expenses		2,500			
" Carriage Outwards		11,200			
" Dep. on Plant		11,200			
" Dep. on Motor Vehicles		7,140[2]			
" Net Profit c/d		96,940			
		3,52,020			3,52,020

	Rs.	Rs.		Rs.	Rs.
To Partners' Salaries			By Net Profit b/d		96,940
Nag : Rs. 500 × 12	6,000				
Paul : Rs. 600 × 12	7,200				
Sen : Rs. 300 × 12	3,600	16,800			
" Interest on Capital					
Nag : Rs. 1,12,000 × $\frac{6}{100}$	6,720				
Paul : Rs. 84,000 × $\frac{6}{100}$	5,040				
Sen : Rs. 42,000 × $\frac{6}{100}$	2,520	14,280			
" Share of Profit					
Nag	21,990				
Paul	21,990				
Sen	21,880[3]	65,860			
		96,940			96,940

Balance Sheet *as on 31st March 2000*

Liabilities	Rs.	Rs.	*Assets*	Rs.	Rs.
Capital Accounts :			Freehold Premises at Cost		1,26,000
Nag	1,12,000		Alteration to Office		8,000
Paul	84,000		Plant & Machinery at Cost		1,12,000
Sen	42,000	2,38,000	Motor Vehicles	33,600	
			Less : Exchanged	10,500	
				23,100	
Current Accounts :			*Add* : Purchases	12,600	35,700
Nag	56,410[2]		Debtors	95,200	
Paul	31,930		*Less* : Goods Sent on Consignment	33,600[1]	
Sen	23,000	1,11,340		61,600	
Creditors		58,800	*Less* : Bad Debts	840	
Prov. for Dep. on P & M	33,600			60,760	
Add : New Provision	11,200	44,800	*Less* : Provision for Bad Debts	6,800	53,960
Prov. for Dep. on Motor Vehicles	16,800		Stock in Trade		95,720
Less : Provision written-back	7,500		Stock with Consignee		28,000
	9,300		Prepaid Insurance		3,000
Add : New Provision	7,140	16,440	Bank Balance		11,200
Office Exp. outstanding		4,200			
		4,73,580			4,73,580

Workings :

1. **Goods sent on Consignment**

For goods sent on consignment the entry was wrongly passed

Debtors A/c Dr.
To Sales A/c

Now, the rectifying entry will be

Sales A/c	Dr.	33,600	
To Debtors A/c			33,600

i.e., Both Sales Account and Debtors Account are to be reduced by Rs. 33,600

Cost of Goods Sent

Cost of Goods Sent Rs. 28,000 (Rs. 33,600 – Rs. 5,600)

i.e., $(33,600 \times \frac{20}{120})$ will be credited to Trading Account.

2. **Profit on exchange of Motor Vehicle**

	Rs.
Exchange Price	5,000
Less: WDV Motor Vehicles sold	3,000
So, Profit on Exchange	2,000

Depreciation of Motor Vehicles

	Rs.
Closing Balance of Motor Vehicle Asset (Rs. 33,600 – Rs. 10,500 + Rs. 12,600)	35,700

∴ Dep. = Rs. 35,700 × 20% = Rs. 7,140

3. **Sen's share of profit** Rs.

Net Profit after charging Int. on Capital and Partners' Salary 65,860

Sen's share = Rs. 65,860 × $\frac{1}{5}$ = 13,172

But his share must not be less than Rs. 28,000 including int. on capital plus salary. Thus, his minimum profit should be (Rs. 28,000 – Rs. 3,600 – Rs. 2,520) Rs. 21,880. So, there is a deficit of Rs. 8,708 (i.e., Rs. 21,880 – Rs. 13,172) which must be compensated by Nag and Paul equally. So Nag and Paul will bear Rs. 4,354 each (i.e., Rs. 8,708 × $\frac{1}{2}$).

Nag's share of profit = Rs. 65,860 × $\frac{2}{5}$ = Rs. 26,344 – Rs. 4,354 = Rs. 21,990

Paul's share of profit = Rs. 65,860 × $\frac{2}{5}$ = Rs. 26,344 – Rs. 4,354 = Rs. 21,990

4.

Current Account

Dr. *Cr.*

	Nag	Paul	Sen		Nag	Paul	Sen
	Rs.	Rs.	Rs.		Rs.	Rs.	Rs.
To Balance b/d	—	—	1,400	By Balance b/d	25,200	8,400	—
" Drawings —goods taken	—	3,500	—	" Int. on Capital	6,720	5,040	2,520
" Balance c/d	56,410	31,930	23,000	" Share of Profit	21,990	21,990	21,880
				" Tr. Expenses	2,500	—	—
	56,410	35,430	24,400		56,410	35,430	24,400

Note : Since the partners already withdrew their salary which was included with the salary paid, the same will not be added to current account.

ON CONSIGNMENT AND JOINT VENTURE

***Abnormal Loss, Consignment Transactions, Suspense Account,* etc.**

Illustration 27

Following is the Trial Balance of Sri Rahul as at 31st December 1993. You are required to prepare the Trading and Profit and Loss Account for the year ended 31st December 1993 and the Balance Sheet as on that date after making necessary adjustments :

	Rs.		Rs.
Purchases	60,000	Sales	1,00,000
Sales Ledger Balance	30,400	Purchase Ledger Balance	24,400
Returns Inward	2,000	Discount Received	600
Discount Allowed	2,000	Returns Outward	2,400
Building	44,000	Capital	53,200
Depreciation on Building	2,000	Suspense A/c	2,000
Income-tax	2,000	Good sent on Consignment	5,000
Wages	4,000	Profit on Consignment	1,000
Salaries	6,000	Apprenticeship Premium (for the year ending 31.3.1994)	2,400
Consignment Stock (31.12.93)	1,200		
Stock-in-trade (1.1.93)	20,000	Provision for Bad Debts	2,000
Trade Expenses	4,000	Commission	1,600
Insurance	400		
Cash in hand and at Bank	12,600		
Deposit with Asha	4,000		
	1,94,600		1,94,600

Adjustments :

(i) Stock-in-trade on 31.12.93 was value at Rs. 20,000.

(ii) Stock valued at Rs. 4,000 was destroyed by fire on 25.12.93 for which Insurance Company admitted claim of Rs. 2,400 only.

(iii) Deposit with Asha was realised together with interest at 10% p.a. for 6 months and deposited the same into Fixed Deposit Account with Bank of India on 1.10.1993, bearing interest at 6% p.a. but no entry had since been made.

(iv) Out of purchases, goods of Rs. 4,000 was distributed as free sample.

(v) Suspense Account represents a cheque received from Bapi, a customer in settlement of Rs. 2,400 due from him. The cheque was duly deposited and credited by bank.

(vi) Maintain provision for bad debts @ 5% on Debtors and provision for discount @ 2% on both Debtors and Creditors.

[CU BCom (Hons) 1994]

Solution

In the Books of Rahul
Trading and Profit and Loss Account
for the year ended 31st December 1993

Dr. Cr.

Particulars	*Amount* Rs.	*Amount* Rs.	*Particulars*	*Amount* Rs.	*Amount* Rs.
To Opening Stock		20,000	By Sales	1,00,000	
" Purchases	60,000		*Less* : Returns Inwards	2,000	98,000
Less : Returns Outward	2,400		" Closing Stock	20,000	
	57,600		*Add* : Stock destroyed by fire	4,000	24,000
Less : Free Sample distributed	4,000				
	53,600				
Less : Goods sent on Consignment	5,000	48,600			
" Wages		4,000			
" Profit and Loss A/c —Gross Profit transferred		49,400			
		1,22,000			1,22,000
To Salaries		6,000	By Trading A/c —Gross Profit		49,400
" Trade Expenses		4,000	" Discount Received		600
" Insurance		400	" Commission		1,600
" Cost of Free Sample		4,000	" Profit on Consignment		1,000
" Discount Allowed	2,000		" Apprenticeship Premium	2,400	
Add : Allowed to Bapi	400[2]	2,400	*Less* : Received in Adv.	600[3]	1,800
" Depreciation on Building		2,000	" Prov. for Bad Debts : Old Provision	2,000	
" Stock destroyed by fire (Rs. 4,000 – Rs. 2,400)		1,600	*Less* : New Provision	1,400	600
" Provision for Discount on Debtors		532	" Accrued Interest of Fixed Deposit		63
" Capital A/c —Net Profit transferred		34,819	" Interest on Deposit with Asha		200[1]
			" Prov. for Discount on Creditors		488
		55,751			55,751

Balance Sheet *as at 31st December 1993*

Liabilities	Rs.	Rs.	*Assets*	Rs.	Rs.
Capital	53,200		Building		44,000
Add : Net Profit	34,819		Closing Stock	20,000	
	88,019		*Add* : Consignment Stock	1,200	21,200
Less : Income-Tax (Drawings)	2,000	86,019	Sundry Debtors	30,400	
Sundry Creditors	24,400		*Less* : Amount due from Bapi	2,400	
Less : Prov. for Discount on Creditors	488	23,912		28,000	
Apprenticeship Premium Received in Advance		600	*Less* : Prov. for Bad Debts	1,400	
				26,600	
			Less : Prov. for Discount on Debtors	532	26,068

Contd.

	Rs.	Rs.		Rs.	Rs.
			Insurance Claim		2,400
			Fixed Deposit	4,200	
			Add : Accrued Interest	63	4,263
			Cash in hand and at Bank		12,600
		1,10,531			1,10,531

Note : Sales Ledger Balance means Sundry Debtors and Purchase Ledger Balance means Sundry Creditors.

Workings :

1. **Interest on Fixed Deposit**

Interest received from Asha Rs. 4,000 $\times \frac{10}{100} \times \frac{6}{12}$ = Rs. 200, credited to P & L A/c.

Amount invested in Fixed Deposit on 1.10.98 = Rs. 4,000 + Rs. 200 = Rs. 4,200.

Accrud Interest on Fixed Deposit from 1.10.93 to 31.12.93 = Rs. 63 \B\B $\left(\text{i.e., Rs. } 4{,}200 \times \frac{6}{100} \times \frac{3}{12}\right)$

2. **Discount Allowed**

For Item (v), the Journal entry will be :

Suspense A/c	Dr.	2,000	
Discount Allowed A/c	Dr.	400	
To Bapi A/c			2,400

In short, the Suspense A/c will be eliminated and P & L A/c will be debited with Rs. 400 for discount allowed and Rs. 2,400 will be deducted from Debtors.

3. Apprenticeship Premium received in advance amounted to (1.1.1994 to 31.3.94) Rs. 2,400 $\times \frac{3}{12}$ = Rs. 600.

Consignment and Joint Venture transactions, Stock Valuation, Exchange of motor car, etc.

Illustration 28

The following Trial Balance has been extracted from the books of Mr. Agarwal as on 31. 3. 2011 :

Trial Balance as on 31.3.2011

		Dr. Rs.		*Cr.* Rs.
Purchases		6,80,000	Sales	8,38,200
Sundry Debtors		96,000	Capital Account	1,97,000
Drawings		36,000	Sundry Creditors	1,14,000
Bad Debts		2,000	Outstanding Salary	2,500
Furniture & Fixtures		81,000	Sale of Old Papers	1,500
Office Equipments		54,000	Bank Overdraft (UBI)	60,000
Salaries		24,000		
Advanced Salary		1,500		
Carriage Inward		6,500		
Miscellaneous Expenses		12,000		
Travelling Expenses		6,500		
Stationery & Printing		1,500		
Rent		18,000		
Electricity & Telephone		6,800		
Cash in hand		5,900		
Cash at Bank (SBI)		53,000		
Stock (1.4.2010)		50,000		
Repairs		7,500		
Motor Car		56,000		
Depreciation :				
Furniture	9,000			
Office Equipment	6,000			
		15,000		
		12,13,200		12,13,200

Additional Information

(i) Sales includes Rs. 60,000 towards goods sold for cash on account of a joint venture with Mr. Reddy who incurred Rs. 800 as forwarding expenses. The joint venture earned a profit of Rs. 15,000 to which Mr. Reddy is entitled to 60%.

(ii) Motor car account represents an old motor car which was replaced on 1.4.2010 by a new motor car costing Rs. 1,20,000 with an additional cash payment of Rs. 40,000 lying debited to Purchase Account.

(iii) UBI has allowed an overdraft limit against hypothecation of stocks keeping a margin of 20%. The present balance is the maximum as permitted by the Bank.

(iv) Sundry Debtors include Rs. 4,000 as due from Mr. Trivedi and Sundry Creditors include Rs. 7,000 as payable to him.

(v) On 31.3.2011 outstanding rent amounted to Rs. 6,000 and you are informed that 50% of the total rent is attributable towards Agarwal's residence.

(vi) Depreciation to be provided on motor car @ 20% (excluding sold item).

Mr. Agarwal requests you to prepare a Trading and Profit & Loss Account for the year ended 31.3.2011 and a Balance Sheet as on that date.

Solution

In the Books of Mr. Agarwal

Dr. **Trading and Profit and Loss Account** *for the year ended 31st March 2011* *Cr.*

	Particulars	*Amount* Rs.	*Amount* Rs.		*Particulars*	*Amount* Rs.	*Amount* Rs.
To	Opening Stock		50,000	By	Sales	8,38,200	
"	Purchases	6,80,000			*Less* : Sale on account		
	Less : Motor Car	40,000	6,40,000		of Joint Venture	60,000[1]	7,78,200
"	Carriage Inward		6,500				
"	Profit and Loss A/c			"	Closing Stock		75,000[3]
	—G. P. transferred		1,56,700				
			8,53,200				8,53,200
To	Salaries		24,000	By	Trading A/c		
"	Travelling Expenses		6,500		—G. P. transferred		1,56,700
"	Printing & Stationery		1,500	"	Sale of old papers		1,500
"	Electricity & Telephone		6,800	"	Profit on Joint Venture		
"	Rent	18,000			(40% of Rs. 15,000)		6,000[4]
	Add : Outstanding	6,000		"	Profit on replacement		
		24,000			of Motor Car		24,000
	Less : Drawings	12,000	12,000		[(Rs. 1,20,000 –		
"	Bad Debts		2,000		(Rs. 56,000 + 40,000)]		
"	Miscellaneous Exp.		12,000				
"	Repairs		7,500				
"	Depreciation on :						
	Furniture	9,000					
	Office Equipment	6,000					
	Motor Car						
	(20% on Rs. 1,20,000)	24,000[2]	39,000				
"	Capital A/c						
	—Net Profit transferred		76,900				
			1,88,200				1,88,200

Balance Sheet *as at 31st March 2011*

Liabilities	Rs.	Rs.	*Assets*	Rs.	Rs.
Capital A/c	1,97,000		Furniture & Fixtures	90,000	
Add : Net Profit	76,900		*Less* : Depreciation	9,000	
	2,73,900				81,000
Less : Drawings			Office Equipment	60,000	
(Rs. 36,000 + 12,000)	48,000		*Less* : Depreciation	6,000	54,000
		2,25,900	Motor Car	56,000	
Bank Overdraft		60,000	Additions	1,20,000	
Creditors	1,14,000			1,76,000	

Contd.

	Rs.	Rs.		Rs.	Rs.
Less : Due to Trivedi	4,000	1,10,000	*Less* : Sold	56,000	
Amount payable to Reddy		54,000		1,20,000	
(Rs. 60,000 – 6,000)			*Less* : Depreciation	24,000	96,000
Outstanding Liabilities :			Stock		75,000
Salary	2,500		Debtors	96,000	
Rent	6,000		*Less* : Due from Trivedi	4,000	92,000
		8,500	Cash		5,900
			Bank		53,000
			Prepaid Salary		1,500
		4,58,400			4,58,400

Workings :

1. Profit on Joint Venture

Since Joint Venture sales are included with general sales, Rs. 60,000 will be deducted from sales. So Sales A/c should be debited by Rs. 60,000.

Agarwal made a Joint Venture with Mr. Reddy in 40% and 60% profit-sharing ratio. As profit on Joint Venture is Rs. 15,000, Agarwal is entitled to 40% of Rs. 15,000 = Rs. 6,000 to be credited to P & L A/c balance (Rs. 60,000 – Rs. 6,000) Rs. 54,000 payable to Reddy. Thus, the entry being

		Dr.	Cr.
Sales A/c	Dr.	60,000	
To P & L A/c (Profit on Joint Ven.)			6,000
" Reddy A/c			54,000

2. Depreciation on Motor Car and Profit on sale and replacement of Motor Car

Depreciation

On new motor car of Rs. 1,20,000 @ 20% = Rs. 24,000

Profit on Replacement

Cost of New Motor Car		1,20,000
Less: Exchange Value	56,000	
Cash Payment	40,000	
		96,000
Profit on Replacement		24,000

3. Closing Stock

Maximum allowable limit of overdraft is subject to a margin of 20% of Stock.

∴ Overdraft which is given Rs. 60,000, that is equal to 80%

$$\text{So, Value of Closing Stock} = \text{Rs. } 60{,}000 \times \frac{100}{80} = \text{Rs. } 75{,}000$$

Illustration 29

Consignment and Joint Venture Transactions, Stock of Stationery, B/R Dishonoured, etc.

The following is the Trial Balance of Mr. Tendulkar as at 31.3.2011 :

	Rs.		Rs.
Stock (1.4.2010)	45,000	Sales	3,25,000
Purchases	2,40,000	Capital	1,30,000
Wages	10,000	Creditors	35,000
Salaries	15,000	Purchase Returns	3,000
Discount Allowed	3,000	Discount Received	2,300
Rent and Rates	2,000	Prov. for Doubtful Debts	1,500
Trade Expenses	15,000	Sale of Furniture	1,200
Sales Return	2,000	Consignor's balance (1.4.2010)	10,000
Furniture (1.4.2010)	18,000	Consignment Sale	20,000
Building	35,000		
Drawings	10,000		
Bank Current A/c	24,000		
Fixed Deposit Bank A/c	16,000		
Debtors	45,000		
Consignment Expenses paid	4,000		
Cash sent to Consignor	22,000		
Bills Receivable	10,000		
Cash	12,000		
	5,28,000		5,28,000

Prepare Trading and Profit and Loss Account for the year ended 31st March 2011 and a Balance Sheet as on that date after taking into account the following adjustments :

(a) Stock on 31.3.2011 Rs. 40,000.

(b) Opening Stock and Closing Stock include stock of stationery amounting to Rs. 200 and Rs. 150, respectively. Trade expenses include payment of stationery Rs. 1,800. Credit purchase of stationery for Rs. 450 recorded as ordinary purchase. Stationery of Rs. 300 is consumed by proprietor.

(c) Furniture, which stood in the books of Rs. 2,000 on 1.4.2010, was sold on 30.9.2010.

(d) Bills Receivable includes a dishonoured bill of Rs. 1,500 and debtors include an amount of Rs. 1,000 in respect of an insolvent customer whose estate is expected to realise only 50 paise in the rupee.

(e) Tendulkar received Rs. 15,000 from Kambli in respect of joint business with him. The sum received stood credited to Sundry Creditors. It is noted that a sum of Rs. 5,000 is due to Tendulkar as his share of profit from the business.

(f) During the year the proceeds of a matured fixed deposit amounting to Rs. 14,000 has been credited to Fixed Deposit Account. The original amount was Rs. 10,000.

(g) Provide depreciation on all fixed assets @ 10% p.a. and provide 5% for doubtful debts of unknown nature.

(h) Commission on Sale of Consignment is Rs. 1,000.

Solution

In the Books of Mr. Tendulkar

Dr. **Trading and Profit and Loss Account** *for the year ended 31st March 2011* *Cr.*

Particulars	*Amount*	*Amount*	*Particulars*	*Amount*	*Amount*
	Rs.	Rs.		Rs.	Rs.
To Opening Stock	45,000		By Sales	3,25,000	
Less : Stock of Stationery	200	44,800	*Less* : Returns Inward	2,000	
" Purchases	2,40,000				3,23,000
Less : Returns Outward	3,000		" Closing Stock	40,000	
	2,37,000		*Less* : Stock of Stationery	150	
Less : Stationery Purchased	450	2,36,550			39,850
" Wages		10,000			
" Profit and Loss A/c					
—Gross Profit transferred		71,500			
		3,62,850			3,62,850
To Salaries		15,000	By Trading A/c		
" Discount Allowed		3,000	—Gross Profit		71,500
" Rent and Rates		2,000	" Discount Received		2,300
" Trade Expenses	15,000		" Interest on		
Less : Stationery Purchased	1,800	13,200	Fixed Deposits		4,000[5]
" Stationery Consumed		2,000[1]	" Share of		
" Loss on Sale of Furniture		700[2]	Joint Venture		5,000[4]
" Prov. for Doubtful Debts :			" Commission on		
New Provision	2,825		Consignment		1,000
Less : Old Provision	1,500	1,325			
" Depreciation on :					
Furniture @ 10% on					
(Rs. 16,000 = 1,600 + 100)	1,700				
Building @ 10%	3,500	5,200			
" Capital A/c					
—Net Profit transferred		41,375			
		83,800			83,800

Balance Sheet *as at 31st March 2011*

Liabilities	Rs.	Rs.	*Assets*	Rs.	Rs.
Capital	1,30,000		Building	35,000	
Add : Net Profit	41,375		*Less* : Depreciation	3,500	31,500
	1,71,375		Furniture	18,000	
Less : Drawings 10,000			*Less* : Sold (B.V.)	2,000	
Stationery Taken 300				16,000	
	10,300		*Less* : Depreciation	1,600	14,400
		1,61,075	Closing Stock		39,850
Creditors	35,000		Stock of Stationery		150
Less : Share of Joint Venture			Debtors	45,000	
Profit	5,000		*Add* : Dishonoured Bill	1,500[3]	
		30,000		46,500	
Consignor's A/c		3,000[7]	*Less* : Prov. for Bad Debts	2,825[6]	43,675
			Bills Receivable	10,000	
			Less : Dishonoured Bill	1,500	8,500
			Fixed Deposit A/c	16,000	
			Add : Accrued Interest	4,000	20,000
			Bank Current A/c		24,000
			Cash		12,000
		1,94,075			1,94,075

Workings :

1. Stationery Consumed

	Rs.
Opening Stock	200
Add : Cash purchases	1,800
Add : Credit purchases	450
	2,450
Less : Taken by proprietor	300
	2,150
Less : Closing Stock	150
	2,000

Similarly

(i) Rs. 200 and Rs. 150 to be deducted from Opening Stock and Closing Stock, respectively.

(ii) Rs. 1,800 to be deducted from Trade Expenses Account.

(iii) Rs. 450 to be deducted from purchases.

(iv) Rs. 300 to be added to drawings.

2. Loss on Sale of Furniture

	Rs.
Book Value	2,000
Less : Depreciation @ 10% for 6 months	100
	1,900
Less : Sold for	1,200
Loss on Sale	700

4. Profit on Joint Venture

Tendulkars' share of Profit on Joint Venture amounting to Rs. 5,000 wrongly credited to Sundry Creditors Account. Rectifying entry will be

Creditors A/c Dr. 5,000
To P & L A/c (Profit on Joint Venture A/c) 5,000

So, Rs. 5,000 to be deducted from creditors, Rs. 5,000 to be credited to Profit and Loss A/c.

3. Dishonoured Bill

Rs. 1,500 to be added to Debtors and to be deducted from Bills Receivable. Specific provision for Doubtful Debts @ 50% of Rs. 1,000 = Rs. 500.

5. Interest : Interest to be credited to P & L A/c Rs. 4,000 (i.e., Rs. 14,000 – 10,000) and added to Fixed Deposit.

6. Provision for Bad Debts on general debtors (unknown nature) :

	Rs.	Rs.
Debtor's Balance (Rs. 45,000 + Rs. 1,500)	46,500	
General Provision @ 5% on Rs. 46,500 =		2,325
Add : Specific Provision (as per 3 above)		500
∴ Total Provision to be made		2,825

7. **Consignor A/c**

		Rs.			Rs.
To	Profit and Loss A/c		By	Balance b/d	10,000
	—Commission on Sale	1,000	"	Consignment Sale	20,000
"	Expenses on Consignment	4,000			
"	Cash paid to Consignor	22,000			
"	Balance c/d	3,000			
		30,000			30,000

Illustration 30

Undervaluation of Opening Stock, Exchange of Furniture, Dishonoured Cheque, etc.

Sri Tirthankar is in business as Stationery Merchant. He also acts as a selling agent of Sri Arjun and for this he is given a commission at the rate of 10% on sales.

From the following Trial Balance you are required to prepare Trading and Profit and Loss Account for the year ended 31st December 1995 and a Balance Sheet as on that date after taking into consideration the adjustments noted below :

Trial Balance
as on 31.12.1995

Debit Balances	Rs.	*Credit Balance*	Rs.
Furniture & Fittings	36,000	Sales	6,65,000
Opening Stock	80,000	Capital	1,90,000
Sundry Debtors	75,000	Sundry Creditors	60,000
Bills Receivable	40,000	Purchase Return	2,000
Cash at Bank	36,000	Discount Received	2,000
Cash in hand	10,000	Consignor's Balance (1. 1. 95)	30,000
Purchases	5,20,000		
Wages	5,000		
Salaries	25,000		
Sales Return	3,000		
Printing & Advertising	12,000		
Postage	4,500		
Discount Allowed	2,500		
Drawings	15,000		
Other Trade Expenses	10,000		
Cash sent to Consignor	75,000		
	9,49,000		9,49,000

Adjustments

(1) Stock on 31.12.95 valued at cost Rs. 64,000.

(2) The effect of advertising is expected to last for coming year also and, as such, half of Printing and Advertising is to be carried forward.

(3) A cheque of Rs. 5,000 received from a customer was returned dishonoured by Bank but the same has not been recorded in the books. The customer has become insolvent and 60% is expected to be realised from his estate.

(4) Furniture appearing in the books on 1.1.95 at Rs. 6,000 was disposed-off on 30.6.95 at Rs. 3,500 in part exchange for a new furniture costing Rs. 5,000. A net invoice for Rs. 1,500 was passed through Purchase Day Book.

(5) Provide depreciation on Furniture and Fittings @ 10% p.a.

(6) Sales include Rs. 75,000 for goods sold in cash on behalf of Sri Arjun. Trade expenses also include Rs. 4,000 as expenses in connection with this sale.

(7) Opening stock has been valued at 20% below cost but Final Accounts should be prepared by taking stock at cost.

[CU BCom (Hons) 1996]

Solution

In the Books of Sri Tirthankar (A Stationery Merchant)
Trading and Profit & Loss Account *for the year ended 31st Dec. 1995*

Dr. Particulars	Amount Rs.	Amount Rs.	Particulars	Amount Rs.	Amount Rs. *Cr.*
To Opening stock (at cost)		1,00,000	By Sales	6,65,000	
" Purchases	5,20,000		*Less* : Goods sold on behalf of consignor	75,000	
Less : Furniture Purchased	1,500			5,90,000	
	5,18,500		*Less* : Sales Return	3,000	
Less : Purchase Return	2,000	5,16,500			5,87,000
" Wages		5,000	" Closing stock		64,000
" Profit & Loss A/c —Gross Profit transferred		29,500			
		6,51,000			6,51,000
To Salaries		25,000	By Trading of —Gross Profit		29,500
" Printing & Advt.	12,000		" Discount Received		2,000
Less : Prepaid (half)	6,000	6,000	" Commission Receivable (on Consignment Sales)		7,500
" Postage		4,500	" Undervaluations of Opening stock		20,000[1]
" Discount Allowed		2,500			
" Trade Expenses	10,000				
Less : Expenses in connection with Consignment Sales	4,000	6,000			
" Bad and Doubtful Debts		2,000[2]			
" Loss on Exch. of Furniture		2,200[3]			
" Dep. on Furniture		3,550[4]			
" Capital a/c		7,250			
" Net Profit transferred					
		59,000			59,000

Balance Sheet *as on 31st Dec. 1995*

Liabilities	Rs.	Rs.	*Assets*	Rs.	Rs.
Opening Capital	1,90,000		Furniture & Fittings (old)	36,000	
Add : Net Profit	7,250		*Less* : Furniture Exchanged	6,000	
	1,97,250			30,000	
Less : Drawings	15,000		*Less* : Depreciation @ 10%	3,000	
		1,82,250		27,000	
Sundry Creditors		60,000	*Add* : New Furniture Purchased	5,000	
Consignor's Balance		18,500[4]		32,000	
			Less : Dep. for 6 months @ 10%	250	31,750
			Sundry Debtors	75,000	
			Add : Cheque Dishonoured	5,000	
				80,000	
			Less : Bad & Doubtful Debts	2,000[2]	78,000
			Bills Receivable		40,000
			Closing Stock		64,000
			Cash at Bank	36,000	
			Less : Cheque Dishonoured	5,000	31,000
			Cash in hand		10,000
			Advertising prepaid		6,000
		2,60,750			2,60,750

Workings :

1. **Undervaluation of Opening Stock**

Since Opening Stock was valued at 20% below cost, actual cost of Opening Stock will be Rs. 80,000 × $\frac{100}{80}$ = Rs. 1,00,000.

∴ Undervaluation of Stock = Rs. 20,000 (Rs. 1,00,000 – Rs. 80,000). So profit would be increased by Rs. 20,000.

As per **Ind AS 8, Prior Period Items** are normally included in determination of net profit or loss for the current period. An alternative approach is to show such items in the statement of P & L after determination of current net profit or loss. We have, however, followed the first one here.

2. **Reserve for Bad Debts**

Since 60% of the debtors are expected to realise from the insolvent customer, provision for bad debts to be made for 40% of the amount, i.e., Rs. 5,000 × 40% = Rs. 2,000. It is treated as specific provision.

3. **Loss on Exchange of Furniture and Depreciation**

	Rs.	**Depreciation on Furniture**	Rs.
Book Value on 1.1.1995 =	6,000	on old Furniture Rs. 30,000 × 10%	3,000
Less : Dep. for 6 months @ 10% =	300	on Furniture Exchange	300
W.D.V on 30.6.1995 =	5,700	on new Furniture for 6 months	250
Less : Exchange for	3,500		
∴ Loss on Exchange	2,200		3,550

4. **Consignor's A/c**

Dr.	Rs.		Cr. Rs.
To Cash A/c	75,000	By Balance b/d	30,000
" Expenses A/c	4,000	" Sales A/c	75,000
" Commission A/c	7,500		
" Balance c/d	18,500		
	1,05,000		1,05,000

Illustration 31

Consignment and Joint Venture transactions, Provision for Bad Debts on specific debtors and on general debtors, etc.

From the following Trial Balance of Sri Manab Gope and the additional information, prepare a Trading and Profit & Loss Account for the year ending on 31st December 1997 and a Balance Sheet as at that date :

	Rs.		Rs.
Materials Consumed	1,75,000	Capital	75,000
Stock on 31.12.97	37,500	Sales	3,00,000
Debtors	30,000	Creditors	25,000
Wages—Productive	45,000	Commission Received	1,500
Others	7,500	Special Rebate Received	2,000
Salaries	7,500	Suspense A/c : Sri Roy	27,500
Electric Charges	2,500		
Freight & Insurance on Purchases	1,500		
Delivery Charges	1,000		
Depreciation	5,000		
Commission Paid	1,000		
Special Rebate Allowed	1,000		
Plant and Machinery	32,500		
Furniture	6,500		
Land and Building	47,500		
Suspense A/c —Smt. Banerjee	10,000		
Drawings	7,500		
Cash in hand	2,000		
Cash at Bank	10,500		
	4,31,000		4,31,000

Additional Information

(a) Salary includes the Proprietor's Salary of Rs. 3,000 for the year.

(b) Suspense A/c of Sri Roy represents a cheque received from him against Sale-proceeds of Goods sent to him on consignment. Goods costing Rs. 32,500 were sent to him on consignment, 4/5th of the goods was sold by him for Rs. 45,000. He is entitled to a commission at 10% on sale proceeds. The only entry passed in this connection was for the cheque received from him.

(c) Suspense A/c for Smt. Banerjee represents an advance of Rs. 10,000 to her in connection with a Joint Venture agreement entered into with her for which she is to get 2/5th share of profit. It is ascertained that the venture has earned a profit of Rs. 7,500.

(d) The scrutiny of the Schedule of Debtors reveals :

(i) Rs. 7,500 fully realisable; (ii) Rs. 5,000—75% realisable; (iii) Rs. 2,500—50% realisable; (iv) Provision for Doubtful Debts has to be provided for at 5% on the balance besides the amount that may be required as above. **[CU BCom (Hons) 1998]**

Solution

In the Books of Sri Manab Gope

Dr. **Trading and Profit & Loss Account** *for the year ended 31st Dec. 1997* Cr.

Particulars	*Amount* Rs.	*Amount* Rs.	*Particulars*	*Amount* Rs.	*Amount* Rs.
To Materials Consumed		1,75,000	By Goods Sent on Consignment		32,500[1]
" Productive Wages		45,000	Sales		3,00,000
" Freight and Insurance on Purchases		1,500			
" P & L A/c (G P transferred)		1,11,000			
		3,32,500			3,32,500
To Non-productive Wages		7,500	By Trading A/c (G. P. transferred)		1,11,000
" Salaries	7,500		" Commission Received		1,500
Less : Proprietor's Salary	3,000	4,500	" Special Rebate Received		2,000
" Electric Charges		2,500	" Profit on Joint Venture		4,500
" Delivery Charges		1,000	" Profit on Consignment		14,500[2]
" Depreciation		5,000			
" Commission paid		1,000			
" Special Rebate allowed		1,000			
" Provision for D/Debts		3,250[5]			
" Capital A/c (Net profit transferred)		1,07,750			
		1,33,500			1,33,500

Balance Sheet *as on 31st Dec. 1997*

Liabilities	Rs.	Rs.	*Assets*	Rs.	Rs.
Capital	75,000		Land and Building		47,500
Add : Net Profit	1,07,750		Plant and Machinery		32,500
	1,82,750		Furniture		6,500
Less : Drawings	7,500		Stock (in hand)		37,500
	1,75,250		Consignment Stock		6,500
Less : Salary of Proprietor	3,000		Sundry Debtors	30,000	
		1,72,250	*Less* : Prov. for D/Debts	3,250[5]	26,750
Creditors		25,000	Consignee (Roy) A/c		13,000[3]
			Co-venturer (Banerjee) A/c		14,500[4]
			Cash at Bank		10,500
			Cash in hand		2,000
		1,97,250			1,97,250

Workings :

1. **It may also be deducted from the material consumed**
2. **Profit on Consignment**

Dr. **Consignment Account** Cr.

	Rs.		*Rs.*
To Goods Sent on Consignment	32,500	*By* Roy A/c—Sale Proceeds	45,000
" Roy A/c—Commission	4,500	" Unsold Stock (Rs. 32,500 × 1/5)	6,500
" Profit & Loss A/c —Profit on Consignment transferred	14,500		
	51,500		51,500

3. **Amount to be received from Consignee**

Sri Roy Account (Consignee)

Dr.		Rs.			Cr. Rs.
To	Consignment A/c —Sale Proceeds	45,000	By	Bank—Advance	27,500
			"	Consignment (Com.)	4,500
			"	Balance c/d	13,000
		45,000			45,000

4. **Amount to be received from Smt. Banerjee**

Smt. Banerjee Account

Dr.		Rs.			Cr. Rs.
To	Bank A/c—Advance	10,000	By	Balance c/d	14,500
"	Profit on Joint venture	4,500			
		14,500			14,500

5. **Provision for Bad Debts to be calculated as**

			Rs.
on Rs.	7,500		Nil
on Rs.	5,000	@ 25%	1,250
on Rs.	2,500	@ 50%	1,250
on Rs.	15,000	(balance) @ 5%	750
	30,000		3,250

ON ADVANCED LEVEL

Illustration 32

Shri D, a trader, has extracted the following Trial Balance from his books as on 31st March 2012 :

	Dr. Rs.	Cr. Rs.
Purchases	4,00,000	
Sundry Debtors	1,50,000	
Cash in hand	4,000	
Cash at Bank	8,000	
Rent, Rates and Taxes	3,000	
Insurance Premium	9,000	
Salaries	42,000	
Carriage Outwards	21,000	
Carriage Inwards	18,000	
Sundry Creditors		50,000
Claim Recoverable	5,000	
Advertisement Suspense	9,000	
Furniture and Fittings	23,000	
Deposit with Suppliers	6,000	
Office Equipments	10,000	
Bills Receivable	6,000	
Bad Debts	4,000	
Sales		5,50,000
Opening Stock	30,000	
Electricity Expenses	2,000	
Capital		1,50,000
	7,50,000	7,50,000

The following further information is provided :

(1) The purchase invoice of Rs. 15,000 received from a supplier has not been entered through oversight.

(2) The claims recoverable has been settled with the insurance company for Rs. 2,000.

(3) 50% of the advertising suspense is to be written-off this year.

(4) Depreciation is to be provided on straight-line method on furniture and fittings (original cost Rs. 30,000) and office equipments (original cost Rs. 15,000) at 5% per annum.

(5) Goods costing Rs. 5,000 were despatched on 29th March 2012. The sale, however, took place on 2nd April 2012, when an invoice of Rs. 7,500 was sent to the customer for approval.

(6) Insurance has been paid up to 30th June 2012.

(7) The deposit with the suppliers was made on 1st October 2011, and it carried interest at 12% per annum.

(8) Two bills receivable from customers for Rs. 700 and Rs. 1,300 were dishonoured on 30th March 2012.

(9) It appeared that doubtful debts amounted to Rs. 3,400.

(10) Physical stock of goods in hand on 31st March 2012, at cost was Rs. 1,00,000.

Prepare Profit and Loss Account for the year ended 31st March 2012 and a Balance Sheet as on that date. **[CA—Adapted]**

Solution

In the Books of Sri D

Dr. **Profit and Loss Account**[1] *for the year ended 31st March 2012* Cr.

Particulars	*Amount*	*Amount*	*Particulars*	*Amount*	*Amount*
	Rs.	Rs.		Rs.	Rs.
To Opening Stock		30,000	By Sales	5,50,000	
" Purchases	4,00,000		*Less:* Sale or Return	7,500[4]	5,42,500
Add : Omission of Purchases	15,000[1]	4,15,000	" Closing Stock	1,00,000	
" Carriage Inwards		18,000	*Add* : Goods despatched but not sold	5,000[4]	1,05,000
" Salaries		42,000	" Interest on Deposit		360[5]
" Rent, Rates and Taxes		3,000			
" Insurance Premium	9,000				
Less : Prepaid	2,250[7]	6,750			
" Carriage Outwards		21,000			
" Claim Written-off		3,000[2]			
" Advertisement		9,000[3]			
" Bad Debts		4,000			
" Electricity Expenses		2,000			
" Prov. for Bad Debts		3,400			
" Depreciation :					
On Furniture & Fittings @ 5% on Rs. 30,000	1,500				
On Office Equipments @ 5% on Rs. 15,000	750	2,250			
" Capital A/c (Net Profit transferred)		88,460			
		6,47,860			6,47,860

Dr. **Balance Sheet** *as on 31st March 2012* Cr.

Liabilities	Rs.	Rs.	*Assets*	Rs.	Rs.
Current Liabilities			*Current Assets*		
Sundry Creditors (Rs. 50,000 + Rs. 15,000[1])		65,000	Cash in hand		4,000
Capital Account			Cash at Bank (8,000 – 2,000)		6,000
Balance on 1.4.2011	1,50,000		Bills Receivable		6,000
Add : Net Profit for the year	88,460	2,38,460	Sundry Debtors		1,41,100[6]
			Deposit with Suppliers		6,000
			Accrued Interest on Deposit		360
			Prepaid Insurance		2,250
			Claim Recoverable		2,000[2]
			Closing Stock		1,05,000
			Fixed Assets :		
			Office Equipment	10,000	
			Less : Depreciation	750	9,250
			Furniture and Fittings	23,000	
			Less : Depreciation	1,500	21,500
		3,03,460			3,03,460

Workings :

1. Error of Omission

Goods purchased not recorded at all. Only the correct entry to be recorded, i.e.,

		Rs.	Rs.
Purchase A/c	Dr.	15,000	
To Creditors A/c			15,000

2. For claims recoverable

Claims revoverable against stock amounted to Rs. 5,000, Rs. 2,000 are reccoverable, So, balance Rs. 3,000 is a loss which should be transferred to P & L A/c, the entry being :

		Rs.	Rs.
Abnormal Loss A/c	Dr.	5,000	
To Trading A/c			5,000
Insurance Co. A/c	Dr.	2,000	
Profit and Loss A/c	Dr.	3,000	
To Abnormal Loss A/c			5,000

3. Advertisement Suspenses Account

Please refer to Illustration 30—it is a case of intangible asset which should be written-off in full aginst P & L A/c, Para 20, AS 26.

4. Sale on Return basis

for Cancellation of entry

		Rs.	Rs.
Sales A/c	Dr.	7,500	
To Debtors A/c			7,500

As it is a Closing Stock:

Closing Stock A/c	Dr.	5,000	
To Trading A/c			5,000

5. Interest on Deposit

Interest @ 12% for 6 months (i.e.,1.10.2011 to 31.3.2012)

on Rs. 6,000 = Rs. $6{,}000 \times \frac{12}{100} \times \frac{6}{12}$ = Rs. 360

6. Closing Debtors

	Rs.
Debtors at the beginning	1,50,000
Less: Sale or Return basis	7,500
	1,42,500
Add: Dishonoured Bills (Rs. 700 + Rs. 1,300)	2,000
	1,44,500
Less: Provision for Doubtful Debts	3,400
	1,41,100

7. Prepaid Insurance

Annual Premium 9,000

Paid up to 30.6.2012 i.e., 3 months,

was in advance i.e., Rs. $9{,}000 \times \frac{3}{12}$ = Rs. 2,250

Note : Since we are asked to prepare Profit and Loss Account, all items relating to Trading Account are passed through Profit and Loss Account.

Illustration 33

Exchange of Furniture, Hire-Purchase transaction, Change in Method of depreciation , etc.

Sri Z, retired Government Officer, who started a business in Kolkata a few years back, gives you the following Trial Balance relating to the year ending on 31st March 2012:

	Dr. Rs.		*Cr.* Rs.
Sundry Debtors	84,000	Sundry Creditors	38,000
Stock on 1.4.2011	40,000	Bills Payable	3,700
Stock on 31.3.2012	50,000	Capital	90,000
Machinery	56,000	Provision for Bad Debts	3,200
Furniture	8,500	Sales	6,76,000
Bills Receivable	4,900		
Building Rent	9,600		
Cash in hand	4,250		
Cash at Bank	17,394		
Drawings	11,000		
Salaries	18,910		
Bad Debts	1,200		
Purchases	4,45,000		
Printing Charges	2,300		
Postage	1,500		
Telephone	1,600		
Miscellaneous Expenses	41,806		
Insurance	2,040		
Travelling Expenses	7,900		
Suspense	3,000		
	8,10,900		8,10,900

Additional Information

(1) An old furniture stood at Rs. 1,200 in the books on 1st April 2012, was disposed-off at Rs. 580 on 30th September 2012 in part exchange for a new furniture costing Rs. 1,040. A net invoice of Rs. 460 was passed through the Purchase Day Book.

(2) Sales include Rs. 20,000 on hire-purchase sale. Hire-purchase sales prices are fixed after adding $33\frac{1}{3}$% on cost. 40% of the instalments have not fallen due as yet (Profit or Loss on hire-purchase sale should be shown in Profit and Loss Account).

(3) Suspense account represents money advanced to Sales Manager who was sent to Delhi in March 2012 for sales promotion. On returning to Kolkata he submitted a statement disclosing that Rs. 1,200 was incurred for travelling, Rs. 500 for legal expenses and Rs. 900 for miscellaneous expenses. The balance lying with him was yet to be refunded.

(4) Sri Z desires to change in the method of depreciation on machinery from Straight Line Method to Diminishing Balance Method with retrospective effect from April 2008 when the machinery were bought, and the difference is to be adjusted in the accounting year 2011-12. The rate of depreciation will, however, remain unchanged.

(5) Business is carried on in a rented house. The ground floor, being 50% of the accommodation, used for business. Sri Z lives with his family on the first floor.

(6) The bad debts for the year amounted to Rs. 2,000. Provision for doubtful debts to be increased by Rs. 800.

(7) Insurance premium includes Rs. 1,000 being premium of Z's personal policy and the balance of insurance covers a period up to 30th June 2012.

(8) Sundry Debtors include Rs. 5,100 due from Shri Ramkumar and Sundry Creditors include Rs. 6,300 due to Shri Ramkumar.

(9) Two cheques of Rs. 1,200 and Rs. 1,000 were returned dishonoured on 30th March 2012, but were not recorded in Cash Book.

(10) Depreciation on time basis is to be provided on machinery at 10% as instructed and on furniture at 5% on diminishing balance.

You are required to prepare a Trading and Profit & Loss Account for the year ended 31st March 2012 and a Balance Sheet (in Vertical Form) as on that date.

Solution

In the Books of Sri Z

Dr. **Trading and Profit & Loss Account** *for the year ended 31st March 2012* Cr.

Particulars	*Amount* Rs.	*Amount* Rs.	*Particulars*	*Amount* Rs.	*Amount* Rs.
To Opening Stock		40,000	By Sales	6,76,000	
" Purchase	4,45,000		*Less* : H. P. Sales	20,000	
Less : Sale of Furniture	460				6,56,000
	4,44,540				
Less : Cost of H.P. Sales[2]	15,000	4,29,540			
Profit and Loss A/c					
" Gross Profit transferred		1,86,460			
		6,56,000			6,56,000
To Building Rent	9,600		By Trading A/c		
Less : For personal			(Gross Profit		
living of Proprietor	4,800[6]	4,800	trasferred)		1,86,460
" Salaries		18,910	" Profit on H.P. Sales		3,000[3]
" Bad Debts	1,200		" Depreciation over-		
Add : Further Bad Debts	800	2,000	charged[4]		2,320[5]
" Printing Charges		2,300			
" Postage		1,500			
" Telephone		1,600			
" Misc. Expenses	41,806				
Add : Incurred by Sales Manager	900	42,706			
" Insurance	2,040				
Less : Personal L.I.P. of Proprietor	1,000				
	1,040				
Less : Prepaid	260	780			
" Travelling Expenses	7,900				

Contd.

		Rs.	Rs.		Rs.	Rs.
To	*Add* : Incurred by Sales Manager	1,200	9,100	By		
"	Legal Expenses		500			
"	Provision for Bad Debts:					
	New Provision	4,000				
	Less : Old Provision	3,200	800			
"	Loss on Exchange of Furniture		590[2]			
	Depreciation :					
	On Machinery	5,832				
	On Furniture	447[2]	6,279			
"	Capital A/c					
	Net Profit transferred		99,915			
			1,91,780			1,91,780

Balance Sheet *as on 31st March 2012*

	Cost Rs.	Depreciation Rs.	Rs.	Rs.	Rs.
Capital Account					
Balance on 1st April 2010				90,000	
Add : Net Profit for the year				99,915	1,89,915
Less : Drawings				11,000	
Add : Personal LIP				1,000	
Add : Rent for living accommodation				4,800	16,800
					1,73,115
Represented by					
Fixed Assets					
Machinery on 31st March 2012	56,000				
Add : Depreciation over-charged	2,320				
	58,320	5,832		52,488	
Furniture	8,500				
Less : Exchanged during the year	1,170				
	7,330				
Add : Additions during the year	1,040				
	8,370	447		7,923	60,411
Current Assets					
Stock in hand				50,000[1]	
Stock on Hire-Purchase			8,000		
Less : Stock Reserve			2,000[3]	6,000	
Sundry Debtors			84,000		
Less : Debtors on H P			8,000		
Add : Value of Dishonoured cheques (Rs. 1,200 + 1,000)			2,200		
			78,200		
Less : Bad Debts written-off			800		
			77,400		
Less : Mutual Indebtedness			5,100[7]		
			72,300		
Less : Provision for Bad Debts			4,000	68,300	
Bills Receivable				4,900	
Advances to Sales Manager				400[4]	
Prepaid Insurance				260	
Cash in hand				4,250	
Cash at Bank			17,394		
Less : Value of two Dishonoured Cheques			2,200	15,194	

Contd.

	Rs.	Rs.	Rs.
		1,49,304	
Current Liabilities			
Sundry Creditors	38,000		
Less : Mutual Indebtedness	5,100		
	32,900		
Bills Payable	3,700	36,600	
			1,12,704
			1,73,115

Workings :

1. Closing Stock

Since Closing Stock has appeared in Trial Balance, it means adjustment entry (Closing Stock A/c Dr. and Purchase A/c Cr.) had already passed. As such, Closing Stock will simply appear in the assets side of the Balance Sheet.

2. Loss on Exchange of Furniture and Depreciation on Furniture

	Rs.
Book Value on 1.4.2012	1,200
Less : Dep. for 6 months (1.4.2012 to 30.9.2012) @ 5% (Rs. 1,200 × $\frac{5}{100} \times \frac{6}{12}$)	30
WDV on 30.9.2012	1,170
Less : Exchange for	580
∴ Loss on exchange	590

Depreciation on Furniture		Rs.
Old Furniture (Rs. 8,500 – Rs. 1,200) Rs. 7,300 × 5%	=	365
On Furniture Exchange	=	30
On New Furniture for 6 months Rs. 1,040 × $\frac{5}{100} \times \frac{6}{12}$	=	52
		447

3. Hire-Purchase Transactions

H P Sales amount to Rs. 20,000 (included in sales) which has already been arrived at after adding $33\frac{1}{3}$% on cost. It will be 25% on Rs. 20,000 = Rs. 5,000.

Profit on H P Sales

Since 40% of the investment is not yet matured, so 60% of the same may be treated as profit on H. P. Sale, i.e., Rs. 5,000 × 60% = Rs. 3,000.

Stock Reserve

			Rs.
	H P Stock 40% of Rs. 20,000	=	8,000
Less:	Stock on Reserve @ 25% on Rs. 8,000	=	2,000
	H P Stock at Cost		6,000

4. Suspense Account

The details of Suspense Account

Dr. **Suspense A/c** *Cr.*

	Rs.		Rs.
To Balance b/d	3,000	By Travelling Exp.	1,200
		" Legal Exp.	500
		" Mis. Exp.	900
		" Balance c/d Left as Cash	400
	3,000		3,000

So Travelling Expenses, Legal Expenses, and Misc. Expenses will appear in the debit side of P & L A/c, balance Rs. 400 will appear in the assets side of the Balance Sheet as Advance to Sales Manager.

5. Depreciation Overcharged

Depreciation @ 10% for 3 years under Straight Line Method is 30%. So, balance left is 70%, which is equal to Rs. 56,000. So original Cost was Rs. 80,000 (i.e., Rs. 56,000 × $\frac{100}{70}$). Thus, depreciation @ 10% on Rs. 80,000; i.e., Rs. 8,000 for 3 years = Rs. 24,000 has already been charged.

So, depreciations under Straight Line Method = Rs. 24,000

Dep. under Reducing Balance Method		Rs.	Depreciation Rs.
	Cost Price	80,000	
Less :	Depreciation	8,000	8,000
	WDV	72,000	
Less :	Depreciation	7,200	7,200
	WDV	64,800	
Less :	Depreciation	6,480	6,480
		58,320	21,680

∴ Depreciation Overcharged = (24,000 – 21,680)
= Rs. 2,320

The entry is:	Rs.
To Profit and Loss A/c	2,320

But as per Para 21, **AS 6 Depreciations Accounting,** the excess or surplus should be credited to P & L A/c.

6. Rent Paid

Since 50% of the accommodation is used by the proprietor, the entry will be :

		Rs.	Rs.
Rent A/c	Dr.	4,800	
Drawings A/c	Dr.	4,800	
To Cash A/c			9,600

7. Mutual Indebtedness

Since Ramkumar is the debtor as well as the creditor, the lower amount will be set-off from both Sundry Debtors and Sundry Creditors, i.e., is 5,100

Illustration 34

R retired from a company and started a business in Chennai. On retirement he got Rs. 1,00,000 from his employer which he invested in his business on 1.4.2011. He got from Life Insurance Corporation Rs. 20,000 on the maturity of his policy which he also invested in his business. He draws Rs. 1,000 for his personal expenses every month from 30th April 2011.

The following figures are extracted from his books on 31st December 2011:

	Rs.		Rs.
Purchases	3,10,000	Bad Debts	2,000
Cartage	5,000	Sundry Debtors	45,000
Salaries and Wages	24,000	Bills Receivable	30,000
Electricity Charges	4,500	Cash in hand	8,997
Travelling	8,900	Sales	3,00,000
Telephone	4,300	Income from Personal Investments	20,000
Advertisement	10,000	Creditors	85,000
Repairs and Renewals	3,303	Bank Overdraft	80,000
Plant and Machinery	1,50,000	Building (Cr.)	10,000

You are requested to prepare a Trading and Profit & Loss Account of the business for the period ended 31st December 2011, and also the Balance Sheet as on that date after taking into consideration the following further information :

(1) Purchases include Rs. 10,000 representing the value of furniture purchased.
(2) Rs. 4,000 representing erection wages on plant and machinery are debited to salaries and wages.
(3) Electricity charges include Rs. 2,500 paid as deposits to Electric Supply Company. There are bills outstanding to the extent of Rs. 500.
(4) Advertisement includes Rs. 4,000 representing the cost of a neon sign.
(5) A dishonoured bill of Rs. 5,000 stands debited to the debtor. 50% thereof considered doubtful and has to be provided for accordingly.
(6) A debtor for Rs. 1,000 was declared insolvent on 30th December 2011, and it is expected that nothing would be recovered from his estate.
(7) Provide 5% discount on net realisable debtors.
(8) R received Rs. 25,000 in respect of a business with B. The sum received stood credited to Sundry Creditors. It is noted that a sum of Rs. 5,000 was due to R as his share of profit from that business.
(9) During the period there was a fire damaging stock costing Rs. 50,000. The damaged goods were sold for Rs. 20,000. This sum of Rs. 20,000 is included in sales. The insurance company paid Rs. 25,000 towards the loss of stock. The godown containing the stock was also damaged to the extent of Rs. 15,000, which has also been paid by the insurance company. The total amount received from the insurance company was credited to Building Account.
(10) The bank overdraft was given on the hypothecation of stock-in-trade. You are informed that the bank had a margin of $33\frac{1}{3}$ % and the overdraft balance on 31st December 2011 was the maximum which could have been drawn on the basis of this margin.
(11) The manager of the business is entitled to a commission of 5% on the gross profit.
(12) Provide 10% depreciation on plant and machinery and on furniture and fittings and 5% on building. Depreciation to be provided on closing balance. **[CA]**

Solution

In the Books of Sri R

Dr. **Trading and Profit & Loss Account** *for the year ended 31st December 2011* Cr.

Particulars	Amount Rs.	Amount Rs.	Particulars	Amount Rs.	Amount Rs.
To Purchases	3,10,000		By Sales	3,00,000	
Less : Purchase of Furniture	10,000	3,00,000	*Less* : Sales of damaged goods[1]	20,000	2,80,000
" Cartage		5,000	" Closing Stock[2]		1,20,000
" Profit and Loss A/c —Gross Profit Transferred		1,45,000	" Goods damaged by Fire[1]		50,000
		4,50,000			4,50,000
To Goods damaged by Fire[1]		5,000	By Trading A/c —Gross Profit		1,45,000
" Salaries & Wages	24,000		" Share of profit from business with B		5,000
Less : Wages for erection of machinery	4,000	20,000			
" Electric Charges	4,500				
Less : Deposit with E. S. Co.	2,500				
	2,000				
Add : Outstanding	500	2,500			
" Travelling		8,900			
" Telephones		4,300			
" Advertisement	10,000				
Less : Cost of Neon Sign	4,000	6,000			
" Repairs and Renewals		3,303			
" Bad Debts	2,000				
Add : Further Bad Debts written-off	1,000	3,000			
" Provision for Bad Debts[3]		2,500[3]			
" Provision for Discount on Debtors[4]		2,075[4]			
" Depreciation :					
On Plant & Machinery @ 10% on Rs. 1,54,000	11,550				
" On Furniture & Fixture @ 10% on Rs. 14,000	1,050				
On Building @ 5% on Rs. 15,000[5]	563	13,163			
" Manager's Commission		7,250			
" Capital A/c Net Profit transferred		72,009			
		1,50,000			1,50,000

Balance Sheet *as on 31st December 2011*

Liabilities	Rs.	Rs.	Assets	Rs.	Rs.
Current Liabilities			*Current Assets*		
Sundry Creditors		80,000[6]	Cash in hand		8,997
Outstanding Expenses :			Bills Receivable		30,000
Electricity Charges	500		Sundry Debtors	45,000	
Commission to Manager	7,250	7,750	*Less* : Bad Debts Written-off	1,000	
Secured Loan				44,000	
Bank Overdraft (Secured by hypothecation of Stock-in-trade)		80,000	*Less* : Provision for Bad Debts	2,500	
				41,500	
Capital Account			*Less* : Prov. for Discount	2,075	39,425
Introduced on 1.3.2011	1,20,000		Deposit with Electric Supply Co.		2,500
Add : Income from			Stock-in-trade		1,20,000

Contd.

	Rs.	Rs.		Rs.	Rs.
Personal investment	20,000		*Fixed Assets*		
Balance on 1.3.2011	1,40,000		Furniture & Fixture	10,000	
Add : Net Profit	72,009		*Add* : Cost of Neon Sign	4,000	
	2,12,009			14,000	
Less : Drawings	9,000		*Less* : Depreciation	1,050	12,950
		2,03,009	Plant & Machinery	1,50,000	
			Add : Cost of Erection	4,000	
				1,54,000	
			Less : Depreciation	11,550	1,42,450
			Buildings	15,000[5]	
			Less : Depreciation	563	14,437
		3,70,759			3,70,759

Workings :

1. It is better to open a Goods Destroyed by Fire A/c in the following manner :

Dr. **Goods Destroyed by Fire A/c** *Cr.*

	Rs.		Rs.
To Trading A/c	50,000	By Bank (Sales)	20,000
		" Bank (Ins. Co.)	25,000
		" P & L A/c (*bal. fig.*)	5,000
	50,000		50,000

Thus, Rs. 20,0000, which was received from sale of damaged good, should be deducted from Sales.

2. Since overdraft is available from the bank up to $\frac{2}{3}$ of closing stock, value of closing stock to be determined on the basis of overdraft, i.e., Rs. 80,000 $\times \frac{3}{2}$ = Rs. 1,20,000.
3. Provision should be made for bad debts @ 50% on dishonoured bills.
4. Provision should be made on debtors as usual.
5. Wrong credit made to Building A/c for Rs. 40,000 (i.e., Rs. 25,000 for goods destroyed and Rs. 15,000 for godown destroyed). From that amount, if Rs. 10,000 (i.e., Building A/c credit) is deducted, Rs. 30,000 opening balance will come out and thus Rs. 15,000 for goods destroyed, if deducted Rs. 15,000 will also come out.
6. Rs. 25,000 has been received from B which has already been credited. But. R's (owner's) claim to it amounts to Rs. 5,000 (no longer his credit) which should be deducted from creditors.

Illustration 35

Consignment and Joint Venture transaction, Sale or Return, etc.

From the following balances and accompanying adjustments of J. B. & Sons, prepare Trading Account and Profit and Loss Account for the year ended 31st December 2012, and a Balance Sheet as on the date:

	Rs.		Rs.
Plant & Machinery	10,000	Sales	2,00,000
Purchases Returns	90,000	Capital	80,000
Factory Building	50,000		
Wages	10,000	Interest on Income-tax paid in advance	400
Fuel and Power	2,000	Suspenses A/c of Chotilal	30,000
Commission paid to Purchase Manager	1,000	Interest received in advance	3,600
Insurance and Taxes	4,000	Creditors	15,000
Life Insurance	1,000		
Goodwill	30,000		
Debtors	70,000		
Bad Debts	1,000		
Income -tax advance payment	4,000		
Income-tax	10,000		
Cash and Bank	15,000		
Stock on 31st December 2012	20,000		
Suspense A/c of Motilal	10,000		
Commission paid in advance	1,000		
	3,29,000		3,29,000

Additional Information

(1) On investigation it was found that goods costing Rs. 40,000 were sent to Chotilal under consignment; $\frac{3}{4}$ths of the goods were sold by him for Rs. 60,000. Remaining stock was valued at cost. A cheque of Rs. 30,000 was received from Chotilal. Entry for cash received was passed and credited to his Suspense A/c. Commission of 5% on sale is payable to Chotilal.

(2) Similarly, a joint venture agreement was made with Motital for which an advance of Rs. 10,000 was entered. It is now ascertained that the venture earned a profit of Rs. 6,000 of which J. B. & Sons are entitled to get $\frac{2}{3}$rds share.

(3) Debtors included an amount due from Chandi Ram of Rs. 2,000 and creditors included amount due to him Rs. 3,000.

(4) Purchases included purchase of materials used for the building Rs. 2,000.

(5) During the year a new plant was erected and the firm's own men have spent thereon amounting to Rs. 200. The amount was included in Wages Account.

(6) Goods costing Rs. 600 (Sale price Rs. 900) were sent on approval on 28th December, and recorded as sale, but no consent had been received up to 31st December.

(7) Make provision for doubtful debts at 5% and depreciate plant at 10% and building at 5%

[CA—Adapted]

Solution

In the Books of J. B. & Sons

Trading and Profit and Loss Account *for the year ended 31st December 2012*

Dr. *Particulars*	Amount Rs.	Amount Rs.	*Particulars*	Amount Rs.	Amount Rs. Cr.
To Purchases	90,000		By Sales	2,00,000	
Less : Materials used for Building	2,000	88,000	*Less* : Sale on approval	900[3]	1,99,100
" Wages	10,000		" Goods sent on		
Less : For Erection	200	9,800	Consignment		40,000†
" Fuel and Power		2,000	" Stock with Customers		600[3]
" Commission to Purchase Manager		1,000	(Sent on approval)		
" Profit and Loss A/c		1,38,900			
—Gross Profit transferred					
		2,39,700			2,39,700
To Insurance and Taxes		4,000	By Trading A/c		
" Bad Debts		1,000	—Gross Profit transferred		1,38,900
" Provision for Bad Debts		3,355			
" Depreciation on :					
Building @ 5% (on Rs. 52,000)	2,600				
Machinery @ 10% (on Rs. 10,200)	1,020	3,620			
" General Profit & Loss A/c		1,26,925			
(Net Profit transferred)					
		1,38,900			1,38,900

General Profit and Loss Account

Dr. *Particulars*	Rs.	*Particulars*	Rs. Cr.
To Capital A/c		By Profit and Loss A/c	
—Net Profit transferred	1,57,925	—Profit of business	1,26,925
		" Joint Venture	
		—Profit from business	4,000[2]
		(Rs. 6,000 × $\frac{2}{3}$)	
		" Consignment A/c	
		—Profit from Consignment	27,000[1]
	1,57,925		1,57,925

† These may also be deducted from purchases

Balance Sheet *as at 31st December 2012*

Liabilities		Rs.	Rs.	*Assets*	Rs.	Rs.
Capital		80,000		Goodwill		30,000
Add : Net Profit		1,57,925		Building	52,000	
		2,37,925		*Less* : Depreciation	2,600	49,400
Drawings				Plant & Machinery	10,200	
Less : Income-tax	10,000			*Less* : Depreciation	1,020	9,180
Income-tax in advance	4,000			Commission paid in advance		1,000
				Motilal		14,000
Life Insurance Prem.	1,000			Chotilal (consignee)		27,000[1]
	15,000					
Less : Int. on Advance Income Tax	400			Stock		
				In shop	20,000	
		14,600		On approval	600	
			2,23,325	On consignment	10,000	30,600
Interest received in advance			3,600	Debtors	70,000	
Creditors		15,000		*Less* : Cancellation by approval	900	
Less : Mutual Indebtedness		2,000			69,100	
(Set-off)			13,000	*Less* : Mutual Indebtedness (Set-off)	2,000	
					67,100	
				Less : R/Bad—Debts @ 5%	3,355	63,745
				Cash at Bank		15,000
			2,39,925			2,39,925

Workings :

1. Profit on Consignment

In order to ascertain the profit on consignment, the Consignment A/c is to be opened and also the Consignee's A/c to know the balance.

Dr. **Consignment A/c** *Cr.*

	Rs.		Rs.
To Goods sent on Consignment	40,000	By Consignee's A/c —Sale Proceeds	60,000
" Consignee A/c Commission A/c	3,000	" Stock on Consignment	10,000
" General P & L A/c Profit on Consignment transferred	27,000		
	70,000		70,000

Dr. **Chotial A/c** *Cr.*

	Rs.		Rs.
To Consig. A/c —Sales	60,000	By Balance b/d (as per T.B.)	30,000
		" Consignment A/c Com.	3,000
		" Balance c/d	27,000
	60,000		60,000

2. Profit on Joint Venture

At first we are to prepare Motilal's Personal A/c and the profit earned on Joint Venture should be debited to his account since he had not yet been given back and will be added to the total profit.

Dr. **Motilal A/c** *Cr.*

	Rs.		Rs.
To Balance b/d (as per T.B.)	10,000	By Balance c/d	14,000
" Profit on Joint Venture	4,000		
	14,000		14,000

3. Goods Sent on Approval

Since Sales Account was wrongly credited, so, for cancellation, the entry will be :

(i) Sales A/c Dr. 900
  To Debtors A/c 900

(ii) For actual amount will be added to Closing Stock
  Closing Stock A/c Dr. 600
  To Trading A/c 600

Illustration 36

Mr. Jayanta Mukherjee is a dealer in fertilisers. He purchases some chemicals and mixes them to manufacture the fertilisers. He has prepared the following statements. He requests you to examine them, and prepare a Trading Account, Profit and Loss Account and the Balance Sheet, after taking into account the additional information :

Dr. **Trading and Profit and Loss Account** *for the year ended March 31, 2012* Cr.

	Rs.	Rs.		Rs.	Rs.
To Stock as on 31.3.2012		8,00,000	By Sales		5,00,000
" Purchases		8,00,000	" Creditors		10,00,000
" Expenses		7,00,000	" Stock as on 1.4.2011		2,00,000
			" Other Incomes		1,00,000
			" Net Loss		5,00,000
		23,00,000			23,00,000

Balance Sheet *as at 31st March 2012*

Liabilities	Rs.	Rs.	*Assets*	Rs.	Rs.
Capital on 1.4.2011	3,00,000		Debtors		2,50,000
Less : Loss	5,00,000	8,00,000	Cash		20,000
Loans taken on 1.4.2011 at 12%		1,00,000	Bank		80,000
Surplus (difference)		4,50,000	Closing Stock		10,00,000
		13,50,000			13,50,000

On enquiry the following further information is obtained :

(a) He is entitled to a rebate of 10% on the listed price of a chemical. The purchase during the year ending March 31, 2012 of the said chemical at the listed price included in the purchases amounted to Rs. 4,00,000.

(b) The details of the expenses are as under : Mixing wages—Rs. 2,00,000; Administration and selling expenses—Rs. 2,00,000; Mixing equipment purchased—Rs. 1,00,000; Construction of factory sheds—Rs. 1,00,000; Advance for raw materials—Rs. 1,00,000; Total = Rs. 7,00,000.

(c) A certain raw material was received on April 2, 2012, the invoice for which amounting to Rs. 1,00,000 is included in the purchases.

(d) A customer who purchased the goods for Rs. 1,00,000 has not taken delivery. The value of such stock was inadvertently included in the closing stock as on March 31, 2012.

(e) He had entered into a joint venture with Mr. Babu Ram. The sales made on account of the joint venture was included in the sales for Rs. 2,00,000. He had paid Rs. 1,00,000 for the purchase of raw materials. It has been included in the expenses. His share of profit in the venture was determined at Rs. 50,000. The amount paid for settling the account was wrongly debited to Debtors Account.

(f) Sums received for cash sales for Rs. 5,00,000 were included in the creditors.

(g) An invoice for Rs. 50,000 for the goods received on March 25, 2012 and included in the stock was received only on April 1, 2012.

(h) Other outstandings as on March 31, 2012 were : Erection of factory sheds—Rs. 50,000; Other expenses—Rs. 25,000.

(i) Provide depreciation at 5% on the factory sheds and at 10% on the equipment on the closing balance.

(j) The bank balance of Rs. 80,000 includes the encashments of his personal deposit of Rs. 50,000 with the bank. He had forgotten to credit his Capital Account with this amount.

Solution

In the Books of Mr. Jayanta Mukherjee

Dr. **Trading and Profit and Loss Account** *for the year ended 31st March 2012* Cr.

Particulars	*Amount* Rs.	*Amount* Rs.	*Particulars*	*Amount* Rs.	*Amount* Rs.
To Opening Stock		2,00,000	By Sales	5,00,000	
" Purchases	8,00,000		*Less* : J. V. Sales	2,00,000	
Add : Further Purchases	50,000[6]			3,00,000	
	8,50,000		*Add* : Credited to Creditors	5,00,000[5]	8,00,000
Less : Rebate Received @ 10% on Rs. 4,00,000	40,000[1]	8,10,000			
" Mixing Wages		2,00,000	" Closing Stock	7,00,000[3]	
" Profit & Loss A/c —Gross Profit transferred		3,90,000	*Add* : Goods-in-transit	1,00,000[2]	8,00,000
		16,00,000			16,00,000

To	Adm. & Selling Expenses	2,00,000		By	Trading A/c		
	Add : Outstanding	25,000	2,25,000		—Gross Profit		3,90,000
"	Interest on Loan		12,000	"	Profit from		
"	Depreciation on :				Joint Venture		50,000[4]
	Factory shed	7,500		"	Other Income		1,00,000
"	Mixing Equipment	10,000	17,500				
"	Capital A/c						
	—Net Profit transferred		2,85,500				
			5,40,000				5,40,000

Balance Sheet *as at 31st March 2012*

Liabilities	Rs.	Rs.	*Assets*	Rs.	Rs.
Capital	3,00,000		Factory shed	1,00,000	
Add : Further capital	50,000		*Add* : Additions	50,000	
Add : Net Profit	2,85,500	6,35,500		1,50,000	
Loan	1,00,000		*Less* : Depreciation	7,500	1,42,500
Add : Outstanding Interest	12,000	1,12,000	Mixing Equipment	1,00,000	
Creditors	10,00,000		*Less* : Depreciation	10,000	90,000
Less : Cash Sales	5,00,000[5]		Closing Stock		7,00,000
	5,00,000		Goods-in-Transit		1,00,000
Add : Credit Purchases	50,000[6]	5,50,000	Sundry Debtors		2,00,000
Outstanding Expenses		25,000	Rebate Receivable		40,000
Outstanding for Factory shed		50,000	Cash at Bank		80,000
			Cash in hand		20,000
		13,72,500			13,72,500

Workings :

1. Rebate Receivable

Rebate to be received @ 10% on listed Price on purchase of Rs. 4,00,000, i.e., 10% of Rs. 4,00,000 = Rs. 40,000, to be deducted from purchase and to be shown as an asset in the assets side of the Balance Sheet as Rebate Receivable

2. Goods-in-Transit

The raw materials which were received on 2nd April 2012 should be treated as Goods-in-transit. The entry will be :

Goods-in-transit A/c Dr.	1,00,000	
To Trading A/c		1,00,000

i.e., Rs. 1,00,000 will appear in the credit side of Trading Account and the same will also appear in the asset side of the Balance Sheet

3. Closing Stock

	Rs.
Stores as on 31.3.12	8,00,000
Less : Goods Sold but wrongly included a Closing Stock	1,00,000
	7,00,000

4. Profit on Joint Venture

	Rs.
Joint Venture Sale	2,00,000
Less: Cost of Goods Sold	1,00,000
	1,00,000

Jayanta Mukherjee's Share Rs. $1,00,000 \times \frac{1}{2}$ = Rs. 50,000

5. Cash Sales wrongly included in Creditors

The entry will be :

Creditors A/c Dr.	5,00,000	
To Sales		5,00,000

6. Omission of Purchase on 25.3.2012

The correct entry will be

Purchase A/c Dr.	50,000	
To Creditors A/c		50,000

7. Encashment of Personal deposit is treated as further Capital.

Illustration 37

Mr. X is the proprietor of a business. The following Trial Balance was prepared from its books on 31st March 2012 :

	Dr. Rs.	*Cr.* Rs.
Land and Building	40,000	
Purchases and Sales	2,81,700	4,68,100
Returns	2,500	3,700
Travelling Expenses	6,900	

Contd.

	Rs.	Rs.
Dividends		960
Printing & Stationery	1,600	
10% Bank Loan (no movement during the year)		40,000
Cash at Bank	30,790	
Discounts	1,800	1,200
Miscellaneous Expenses	18,620	
Debtors and Creditors	64,000	63,130
Postage	800	
Furniture	8,000	
Joint Venture Suspense A/c	800	
Bills Payable		2,600
Cash in hand	4,900	
Motor Car	16,000	
Investment (Market Value Rs. 15,000)	12,000	
Capital		80,000
Drawings	10,000	
Bills Receivable	4,800	
Stock on 31.3.2011	63.680	
Stock on 31.3.2012	45,000	
Interest on Bank Loan	3,000	
Salaries	22,000	
Entertainment Expenses	1,800	
Carriage Inward	3,000	
Advertisement	16,000	
	6,59,690	6,59,690

Additional Information

(1) Dividend received including preacquisition dividend Rs. 260.

(2) Salaries include payment to domestic servant Rs. 1,500.

(3) During the year 2011-12 a bill of Rs. 2,000 received from a customer and endorsed to a supplier was dishonoured but no effect was given in the books.

(4) Sales include a sum of Rs. 24,000 received on sale of goods on behalf of Y. The goods were sold at a profit of 20% on cost. X is entitled to a commission of 10% on sales, for which no entry has been made. X also incurred expenses Rs. 1,200 in this respect which was debited to entertainment expenses and which he had not been reimbrused.

(5) On 1.10.2011, X entered into a Joint Venture with Z on an equal profit-sharing basis. Z supplied goods costing Rs. 27,000 which were recorded through Purchase Day Book. X sold these goods at a gross profit of 25% on sales and included these in sales account. Z spent Rs. 1,200 in despatching the goods for which no entry was made. The Joint Venture Suspense account represented the expenses incurred by X.

(6) 75% of the advertisement expenses are to be carried forward.

(7) Two cheques of Rs. 2,000 and Rs. 3,000 were deposited into bank on 29.3.2012 but not cleared by the bank till 31.3.2012.

(8) A bad debt of Rs. 4,000 written-off in 2009-10 was realised in the current year @ 50%, but no entry was made.

(9) It has been decided to create a provision for doubtful debts at 5% and depreciate fixed assets by 10%.

Prepare Trading and Profit and Loss Account of Mr. X for the year ended 31st March 2012 and a Balance Sheet on that date.

Solution

In the Books of Mr. X

Dr. **Trading and Profit and Loss Account** *for the year ended 31st March 2012* Cr.

Particulars	*Amount* Rs.	*Amount* Rs.	*Particulars*	*Amount* Rs.	*Amount* Rs.
To Opening Stock		63,680	By Sales	4,68,100	
" Purchases	2,81,700		*Less* : Returns Inward	2,500	
Less : Cost of J.V. Goods	27,000[5]			4,65,600	
	2,54,700		*Less* : Consignment		
Less : Returns Outward	3,700	2,51,000	Sale	24,000[1]	
" Carriage Inward		3,000		4,41,600	
" Profit and Loss A/c			*Less* : J. V. Sale	36,000[5]	
—Gross Profit transferred		87,920			4,05,600
		4,05,600			4,05,600
To Salaries	22,000		By Trading A/c		
Less : Drawings			—Gross Profit		87,920
(Paid to domestic servant)	1,500[2]	20,500	" Discounts received		1,200
" Miscellanerous Expenses		18,620	" Bad Debt Recovery		2,000[3]
" Discount		1,800	" Commission		2,400[4]
" Travelling Expenses		6,900	(received as		
" Printing & Stationery		1,600	consignee)		
" Postage		800	" Share of J. V. Profit		3,500[5]
" Entertainment Exp.	1,800		" Dividend		
Less : Expenses for Y	1,200[4]	600	(Post-acquisition)		700[1]
" Interest on Bank Loan	3,000				
Add : Outstanding	1,000	4,000			
" Advertisement ($\frac{1}{4}$ th)		4,000			
" Prov. for Doubtful Debts		3,300			
" Depreciation on :					
" Land & Building @ 10%	4,000				
Furniture @ 10%	800				
Motor Car	1,600	6,400			
" Capital A/c					
—Net Profit transferred		29,200			
		97,720			97,720

Balance Sheet *as at 31st March 2012*

Liabilities		Rs.	Rs.	*Assets*	Rs.	Rs.
Capital		80,000		Land & Building	40,000	
Add : Net Profit		29,200		*Less* : Depreciation	4,000	36,000
		1,09,200		Furniture	8,000	
Less : Drawings	10,000			*Less* : Depreciation	800	7,200
Add : Salaries for				Motor Car	16,000	
domestic servant	1,500[2]			*Less* : Depreciation	1,600	14,400
		11,500	97,700	Investment		
Sundry Creditors		63,130		(M. V. Rs. 15,000)	12,000	
Less : Cost of Goods on J. V.		27,000[5]		*Less* : Pre-acq. Dividend	260[1]	11,740
		36,130		Closing Stock		45,000
Add : Dishonour of endorsed				Sundry Debtors	64,000	
bill		2,000[3]	38,130	*Add* : Dishonoured Bill	2,000[3]	
Bills Payable			2,600		66,000	
10% Bank Loan		40,000		*Less* : Prov. for Bad Debts	3,300	62,700
Add : Interest		1,000	41,000	Bills Receivable		4,800

Contd.

	Rs.	Rs.		Rs.	Rs.
Amount payable to Y		20,400[4]	Prepaid Advertisement		12,000[6]
Amount payable to Z		31,700[5]	Cash at Bank		
			(Rs. 30,790 + 2,000[8])		32,790
			Cash in hand		4,900
		2,31,530			2,31,530

Workings :

As per Adjustments

1. For Dividend

It must be remembered that preacquisition dividend means any dividend received to a period earlier than the current year. Here, the entry for this purpose will be :

(a) For dividend received :

Cash/Bank A/c Dr. } with the total amount of dividend.
To Dividend Received

This entry has already been made in the books, now the entry will be

(b) Dividend Received A/c Dr.
To Investment A/c (for pre-acquisition dividend)
" Profit and Loss A/c (for post-acquisition dividend)

Thus,

(i) Rs. 260 to be deducted from Investment A/c.

(ii) Rs. 700 (i.e., Rs. 960 – Rs. 260) to be credited to Profit and Loss Account as post-acquisition dividend, i.e., dividend received for the current year.

2. **The entry for this purpose is :**

Drawings A/c Dr.
To Salary A/c

Thus,
(i) Rs. 1,500 to be added to Drawings, and
(ii) Rs. 1,500 to be deducted from Salary.

3. **For Endorsd Bill Dishonoured**

The entry will be :

Debtors A/c Dr.
To Creditors A/c

Thus,
(i) Rs. 2,000 to be added to Debtors; and
(ii) Rs. 2,000 to be added to Creditors.

4. **For consignment transactions**

Here, Mr. Y is the owner or the consignor and Mr. X is the agent or the consignee. So, in the books of X, Y's A/c will be shown as :

Dr. **Y Account** *Cr.*

	Rs.		Rs.
To Cash A/c—Expenses	1,200	By Bank A/c	
" Commission A/c	2,400	—Sales	24,000
" Balance c/d	20,400		
	24,000		24,000

Thus,

(i) Rs. 1,200 to be deducted from Entertainment Expenses;

(ii) Rs. 2,400 to be credited to Profit and Loss A/c as commission received;

(iii) Rs. 24,000 to be deducted from sales; and

(iv) Rs. 20,400 to be shown as a liability in the liabilities side of the Balance Sheet.

5. **For Joint Venture Transactions**

(i) For goods supplied by Z wrongly included in purchase. So, the rectifying entry is :

Joint Venture A/c	Dr.	27,000	
To Purchases A/c			27,000

(ii) And the creditors' account is equaly affected. So, the entry will be :

Sundry Creditors A/c	Dr.	27,000	
To Z A/c			27,000

(iii) J. V. sales wrongly credited to X's Sale A/c :

Sales A/c	Dr.	36,000*	
To Joint Venture A/c			36,000

* Rs. 27,000 + $\frac{1}{3}$ rd of Rs. 27,000
= Rs. 27,000 + Rs. 9,000
= Rs. 36,000

(iv) For Expenses incurred by Z :

Joint Venture A/c	Dr.	1,200	
To Z A/c			1,200

(v) For expenses incurred by X :

Joint Venture A/c	Dr.	800	
To Joint Venture Suspense A/c			800

(vi) Prepare the following Joint Venture Account for ascertaining the profit :

Joint Venture A/c

Dr.			Rs.		Cr. Rs.
To Purchase A/c			27,000	By Sales A/c	36,000
" Z – Expenses			1,200		
" J.V. Suspense A/c			800		
" Profit on Venture :					
" Z	3,500				
P & L A/c	3,500		7,000		
			36,000		36,000

Thus,

(i) Rs. 36,000 to be deducted from sales;
(ii) Rs. 27,000 to be deducted from Purchases and also to be deducted from Creditors A/c;
(iii) Rs. 800, i.e., Joint Venture Suspense A/c, will be cancelled and closed;
(iv) Rs. 3,500 to be credited to P & L A/c as profit on joint venture; and
(v) Rs. 31,700 to be shown as a liability to Z in the liabilities side of the Balance Sheet. The amount can be found out if we prepare Z A/c as under (in the books of X) :

Z Account

Dr.	Rs.		Cr. Rs.
To Balance c/d	31,700	By Sundry Creditors A/c	27,000
		" J. V. A/c —Exp.	1,200
		" J. V. A/c —Profit	3,500
	31,700		31,700

6. Rs. 12,000 (i.e., Rs. 16,000 × $\frac{3}{4}$) to be carried forward i.e., ignoring AS 26
7. There will be no entry for the purpose as they do not affect the Cash Book balance of Mr. X.
8. 50% of Rs. 4,000,, i.e., Rs. 2,000, to be credited to P & L A/c; and Rs. 2,000 to be added to Cash at Bank.

ASSIGNMENT MATERIALS

THEORETICAL

Objective-Type Questions

1. State whether the following statements are 'True' or 'False':
   (a) Profit and Loss Account shows the net operating result of a business.
   (b) As per rigidity method, most liquid assets are shown at the top of the Balance Sheet.
   (c) Depreciation is an amortised expenditure.
   (d) Closing Stock should be valued at cost price or market price, whichever is higher.
   (e) Goodwill is an intangible asset.
   (f) Suspense Account is opened when the Trial Balance does not agree.
   (g) Cost of Goods Sold = Sales – Gross Profit.

(h) Recovery of Bad Debts credited to Debtors Account.
(i) Income-tax of a sole proprietor is treated as Drawing.
(j) The surplus of cash book is the net income.

[Ans. True: (a); (c); (e); (f); (g); (i). False: (b); (d); (h); (j)]

Multiple Choice Questions

2. (a) Gross Profit is transferred to :
(i) Trading Account; (ii) Profit and Loss Account; (iii) Balance Sheet.
(b) Net Profit is transferred to :
(i) Profit and Loss Account; (ii) Capital Account.
3. Distinguish between Trading Account and Profit and Loss Account.
4. Why is a Profit and Loss Appropriation Account necessary in a Partnership Firm?
5. Define :
(a) Gross Profit Ratio.
(b) Liquidity Preference Method and Rigidity Preference Method of preparing Balance Sheet.
6. Distinguish between:
(i) Trading Account and Manufacturing Account.
(ii) Profit and Loss Account and Profit and Loss Appropriation Account.
(iii) Liquidity Preference Method and Rigidity Preference Method.
(iv) Gross Profit and Net Profit.
7. (a) State the difference between 'Assets' and 'Liabilities'.
(b) Can the Profit and the Capital be treated as liabilities? If so, why?
8. Write a short note on Asset.
9. What information is available from a Balance Sheet?

Essay Answer Type Questions

10. (a) What is a Balance Sheet?
(b) Can a Balance Sheet exhibit the true financial condition of a business?
(c) Distinguish between assets and liabilities.
11. (a) What do you mean by assets?
(b) State the different classes of assets with illustrations.
12. (a) What do you mean by assets and liabilities?
(b) How are assets and liabilities classified?
(c) Define intangible assets. Give four examples.
13. (a) What is a Balance Sheet? What are the pieces of information available from it? Why does a Balance Sheet balance?
(b) What is the interrelationship between the Balance Sheet and the Profit and Loss Account?

PRACTICAL

1. Following ledger account balances, as at 31.12.2002, were ascertained from the books of Sri B. Roy :

Stock—1.1.02 Rs. 46,800; Sales Rs. 2,89,600; Purchases Rs. 2,45,300; Purchases Returns Rs. 8,000; Sales Returns Rs. 10,600; Carriage Inwards Rs. 16,600; Rent and Taxes Rs. 5,800; Salaries and Wages Rs. 9,200; Capital Rs. 1,00,000; Discount Received Rs. 2,280; Sundry Debtors; Rs. 34,300; Sundry Creditors Rs. 25,100; Loan at 6% Rs. 20,000; Interest paid Rs. 900 ; Printing and Advertising Rs. 4,800; Furniture & Fittings Rs. 11,600; Income from Investment Rs. 250; Cash at Bank Rs. 7,000; Discount Paid Rs. 3,910; Investment at Cost Rs. 5,000; General Expenses Rs. 7,540; Audit Fees Rs. 600; Insurance Rs. 720; Travelling Expenses Rs. 2,310; Postage and Telegram Rs. 380; Cash in hand Rs. 870; 7% Fixed Deposit with the Chartered Bank Rs. 32,000; Drawings Rs. 9,000; Stock 31.12.02 Rs. 76,800.

You are requested to prepare the Trading and Profit and Loss Account for the year 2002, and the Balance Sheet as on that date after taking into account the following information for adjustments :

(a) Two dishonoured cheques for Rs. 200 and Rs. 320, respectively, from customers X and Y had not been entered in the Cash Book. The first one for Rs. 200 is bad and irrecoverable. In the case of the second cheque for Rs. 320, it is expected that Y would pay a dividend of 75 P in the rupee.

(b) Private purchases amounting to Rs. 450 had been included and recorded in Purchase Day Book.
(c) Provide full year's interest payable and receivable for the Loans and Fixed Deposit.
(d) Depreciation @ 10% p.a. to be written-off against Furniture & Fittings.
(e) Stock destroyed by fire for Rs. 10,000, not covered by Insurance Company.
(f) Sundry Debtors include Rs. 5,000, due from Sri J. Sen whereas Sundry Creditors include also Rs. 2,000 due to Sri J. Sen.

[Ans. Gross Profit Rs. 65,550; Net Profit Rs. 22,420; Balance Sheet Rs. 1,66,370]

2. Prepare the final accounts from the following information:

Mr. Fox is the proprietor of a large business of Silk-piece goods. The following Trial Balance is prepared from his books as on 31st March 2005:

	Dr. Rs.		*Cr.* Rs.
Debit Balances		Stock (1.4.2004)	63,680
Land & Building	40,000	Interest on Bank Loan	3,000
Purchases	3,26,700	Salaries (including advance Rs. 1,500)	22,000
Returns Inward	2,500	Carriage Inwards	3,000
Travelling Expenses	6,900	Establishment Expenses	1,595
Printing & Stationery	1,600	Advertisement	16,000
Cash at Bank	30,795	*Credit Balances*	
Discount Allowed	1,800	Sales	4,68,100
Misc. Expenses	18,620	Income from Investments	990
Sundry Debtors	64,000	12% Bank Loan Secured on	
Postage	800	Fixed Assets	
Furniture	8,000	(no movements during the year)	40,000
Cash in hand	5,900	Mr. Fox's Capital A/c	80,000
Motor Car	16,000	Sundry Creditors	63,100
Investment		Bills Payable	2,600
(Market Value Rs. 14,000)	12,000	Returns Outward	3,700
Drawings	10,000	Discount Received	1,200
Bills Receivable	4,800		

The following further information was obtained :

(1) Stock as on 31.3.2005 was Rs. 1,20,000. (2) Sundry Debtors include a sum of Rs. 3,000 due from Mr. B. and Sundry Creditors include a sum of Rs. 4,000 due to Mr. B. (3) The Reserve for Doubtful Debts is to be maintained @ 10% on Sundry Debtors and Reserve for Discount on Debtors and Discount on Creditors are to be created @ 5%. (4) Bills Receivable include dishonoured bill for Rs. 600. (5) Stock worth Rs. 10,000 was destroyed by fire on 25.2.05 in respect of which the insurance company admits a claim for only Rs. 7,500. (6) The manager of Mr. Fox is entitled to a commission of 10% of Net Profit calculated after charging such commission. (7) $\frac{3}{4}$ths of the advertisement expenses are to be carried forward. (8) $2\frac{1}{2}$% of the Net Profit is to be transferred to Reserve Fund. (9) Depreciation is to be charged on (i) Land & Building @ $2\frac{1}{2}$ %, (ii) Furniture @ 10%, and (iii) Motor Car @ 20%.

[Ans. Gross Profit Rs. 2,05,920; Net Profit Rs. 1,21,880; Balance Sheet Rs. 3,05,563]

3. Hira and Manik are partners in a firm sharing profits and losses in the ratio of their opening capitals. Below is given their trial Balance as at 31st March 2005 :

Trial Balance as at 31st March 2005

	Rs.			Rs.
Plant & Machinery	50,000	Sales		2,40,000
Opening Stock	30,000	Discount		2,000
Purchases	80,000	Sundry Creditors		20,000
Freehold Land & Buildings	85,000	Bills Payable		10,750
Carriage Inwards	1,700	Hira Loan A/c		50,000
Carriage Outwards	2,500	Capital A/cs		
Wages	16,000	Hira	50,000	
Sundry Debtors	50,000	Manik	25,000	75,000
Salaries	12,000			*Contd.*

		Rs.		Rs.
Furniture		18,000		
Trade Expenses		6,000		
Returns Inwards		950		
Advertisement Suspense		12,500		
Discount		900		
Partners' Drawings				
Hira	3,000			
Manik	2,000	5,000		
Bills Receivable		20,000		
Insurance		1,200		
Bad Debts		1,000		
Cash at Bank		5,000		
		3,97,750		3,97,750

You are required to prepare the Trading and Profit and Loss Account of the firm for the year ended 31st March 2005 and the Balance Sheet as at that date after taking into consideration the following adjustments :

(i) Closing Stock Rs. 45,000.

(ii) Depreciate Plant @ 10% and Furniture @ 20%. Appreciate Freehold Land & Building to Rs. 90,000.

(iii) Bad Debt Reserve to be raised to $2\frac{1}{2}$ % on Sundry Debtors.

(iv) Advertisement Suspense A/c to be written-off against revenue over five years.

(v) Partners' Drawings are to bear interest at 10% p.a.—amounts were withdrawn at 31st December 2005.

(vi) Annual charge for Insurance is Rs. 1,000—the balance represents amount paid in advance.

(vii) Hira gave loan to the firm on 30th September 2004.

(viii) Manik was to be allowed a partnership salary of Rs. 250 per month.

(ix) The partners agree to contribute 50% of the distributable profit to the National Defence Fund.

[CU BCom (Hons)]

[Ans. Gross Profit Rs. 1,56,350; Net Profit Rs. 1,26,100; Balance Sheet Rs. 2,78,350]

4. Following is the Trial Balance of Mr. X, as at 31.12.2012. You are required to prepare the Trading and Profit & Loss Account for the year ended 31.12.2011 and the Balance Sheet as at the date :

	Rs.		Rs.
Purchase	30,000	Sales	50,000
Sales Ledger Balance	15,200	Purchases Ledge Balance	12,000
Return Inwards	1,000	Returns Outwards	1,200
Discount Allowed	1,000	Discount Received	300
Buildings	22,000	Capital	26,600
Depreciation on Building	1,000	Suspense A/c	1,000
Income-tax	1,000	Goods Sent on Consignment	2,500
Wages	2,000	Profit on Consignment	500
Salaries	3,000	Apprenticeship Premium (for the year ending 31.3.2012)	1,200
Consignment Stock (31.12.2011)	600		
Stock (1.1.2011)	10,000	Provision for Bad Debt	1,200
Trade Expenses	2,000	Commission Received	800
Insurance	200		
Cash in hand & at Bank	6,300		
Deposit with Sajal	2,000		
	97,300		97,300

Adjustments

(i) Stock on 31.12.2011 was valued at Rs. 10,000.

(ii) Stock valued at Rs. 2,000 was destroyed by fire on 25.12.2011, for which the Insurance Company admitted a claim of Rs. 1,200 only.

(iii) Deposit with Sajal was realised together with interest @ 10% p.a. for 6 months and deposited the same into Fixed Deposit Account with Bank of Burdwan on 1.10.2011, bearing interest @ 6% p.a. but no entry had since been made.

(iv) Out of purchases, goods of Rs. 2,000 were distributed as advertising matter.

(v) Suspense Account represents cheque received from Subir, as customer, in settlement of Rs. 1,200 due from him. The cheque was duly deposited into and credited by bank.

(vi) Maintain Provision for Bad Debts @ 5% on Debtors and Provision for Discount @ 2% on Debtors.

[Ans. Gross Profit Rs. 24,700; Net Profit Rs. 17,166; Balance Sheet Rs. 55,266]

5. The following is the Trial Balance of Mr. Mahesh & Sen on 31.12.2011. Prepare Trading and Profit and Loss Account for the year ended 2011 and a Balance Sheet as at 31.12.2011 from it:

	Dr. Rs.	*Cr.* Rs.
Purchases	1,80,000	
Opening Stock	10,000	
Salaries, Less P.F.	5,400	
P.F. remittance including Prop. contribution 50%	1,200	
Rent @ 250 p.m.	2,750	
Machinery	29,000	
Wages	3,000	
Furniture and Fittings	5,000	
Electricity	550	
Trade Expenses	1,500	
Debtors	10,500	
Interest on Loan	900	
Commission	200	
Buildings	30,000	
Sales		2,05,000
Loans (10% Int.)		10,000
Creditors		15,000
Capital		55,000
Drawings	5,000	
	2,85,000	2,85,000

On 1.1.2011, machinery worth Rs. 5,000 was sold for Rs. 4,000 and credited to Machinery Account. Wages include Rs. 1,000 paid for machinery erection charges. Purchases include cost of Moped Scooter for Rs. 5,000. Proprietor has taken goods costing Rs. 1,000 for which no entry had been made. Sundry Debtors include Rs. 500 which have become bad. Provide 10% reserve for the debts. Electricity outstanding Rs. 50. Goods costing Rs. 5,000 were destroyed by fire and insurance claim was received Rs. 4,000. Provide depreciation at 10% on Machinery, Furniture and Moped. Provide depreciation @ 5% on Building. Closing Stock amounted to Rs. 12,000.

[Ans. Gross Profit Rs. 36,000; Net Profit Rs. 14,200; Balance Sheet Rs. 88,600]

6. From the following Trial Balance and information, prepare Trading and Profit and Loss Account of Mr. Rishabh for the year ended 31st March 2011 and a Balance Sheet as on that date:

	Debit Rs.	*Credit* Rs.
Capital		1,00,000
Drawings	12,000	
Land and Buildings	90,000	
Plant and Machinery	20,000	
Furniture	5,000	
Sales		1,40,000
Returns Outward		4,000
Debtors	18,400	
Loan from Gajanand on 1.7.2010 @ 6% p.a.		30,000
Purchases	80,000	
Returns inward	5,000	
Carriages	10,000	
Sundry Expenses	600	
Printing and Stationery	500	
Insurance Expenses	1,000	

Contd.

	Rs.	Rs.
Provision for Bad and Doubtful Debts		1,000
Provision for Discount on Debtors		380
Bad Debts	400	
Profit on Textile Deptt.		10,000
Stock of General goods on 1.4.2010	21,300	
Salaries and Wages	18,500	
Creditors		12,000
Trade Expenses	800	
Stock of Textile Goods on 31.3.2011	8,000	
Cash at Bank	4,600	
Cash in hand	1,280	
	2,97,380	2,97,380

Information

(i) Stock of General Goods on 31.3.2011 valued of Rs. 27,300;

(ii) Fire occurred on 23rd March 2011 and Rs. 10,000 worth of general goods were destroyed. The Insurance Company accepted claim for Rs. 6,000 only and issued the claim money on 10th April 2011;

(iii) Bad Debts amounting to Rs. 400 are to be written-off. Provision for Bad and Doubtful Debts is to be made as 5% and for discount at 2% on Debtors. Make a provision of 2% on Creditors for discount;

(iv) Received Rs. 6,000 worth of goods on 27th March 2011 but the invoice of purchase was not recorded in Purchase Book;

(v) Rishabh took away goods worth Rs. 2,000 for personal use, but no record was made thereof.

(vi) Charge depreciation at 2% on Land and Buildings, 20% on Plant and Machinery, and 5% on Furniture;

(vii) Insurance prepaid amounts to Rs. 200.

[Ans. Gross Profit Rs. 61,000; Net Profit Rs. 38,098; Balance Sheet Rs. 1,73,088]

7. From the following Trial Balance of Sri Gopal Bhar prepare a Trading Account, and Profit and Loss Account for the year ended 31st Dec. 2011 and also a Balance Sheet as on that date :

	Dr. Rs.		*Cr.* Rs.
Drawings	10,000	Capital	1,00,000
Purchases (Less Returns Rs. 3,000 and including stationery purchased Rs. 4,000)	68,000	Sales (Less Returns of Rs. 5,000)	1,50,000
Opening Stock (including stock of stationery Rs. 1,000)	13,000	Interest on investment for 10 months	1,000
Wages (excluding outstanding wages amounted to Rs. 4,000)	16,000	Sundry Creditors (discount receivable @ 5%)	30,000
Salaries for 10 months	10,000	Loan @ 12% p.a. (taken on 1.1.2011)	20,000
Insurance for 15 months	3,000	Bank Overdraft	9,000
Interest on loan	2,000		
Investments	12,000		
Plant and Machinery (Subject to dep. @ 10% p.a.)	30,000		
Land and Building (Subject to dep. @ 20% p.a.)	80,000		
Bad Debts	5,000		
Rent for 3 quarters	6,000		
Sundry Debtors (including Bad Debts Rs. 5,000 and 90% considered good)	55,000		
	3,10,000		3,10,000

His Closing Stock was Rs. 34,000 (including stock of stationery Rs. 2,000).

[Ans. Gross Profit Rs. 86,000; Net Profit Rs. 26,900; Balance Sheet Rs. 1,82,800]

8. From the following particulars prepare the Trading and Profit and Loss Account for the year 2011 and Balance Sheet as on 31.12.2011 of Prem Niwas :

	Dr. Rs.	Cr. Rs.
Building	50,000	
Machinery	22,000	
Furniture	10,000	
Bank	9,000	
Cash	1,000	
Loans (since 1.1.2011)		30,000
Capital		52,000
Debtors/Creditors	50,000	40,000
Opening Stock	12,000	
Purchases/Returns	2,50,000	10,000
Sales Returns/Sales	12,000	3,22,000
Rent	6,000	
Establishment	16,000	
P. F. deducted from salaries		1,000
Interest (10%)	2,000	
Electricity	1,000	
Phone	1,000	
Commission	6,000	
Insurance Premium	1,000	
Bad Debts	2,000	
Bills Receivable	4,000	
	4,55,000	4,55,000

Provide depreciation on building @ 5%, Machinery @ 15% and Furniture @ 10%. Stock was not taken on 31.12.2011 but only on 7.1.2012. The transactions from 1.1.2012 to 7.1.2012 are : Sales Rs. 25,000, Purchases Rs. 15,000, Stock on 7.1.2012 Rs. 18,000 and the Gross Profit 20%. During the year machinery to the value of Rs. 10,000 was destroyed by fire and the insurance claim was settled at Rs. 8,000 and credited to Machinery Account. Also provide Employer's share of P. F. Rs. 1,000; Provision for bad debts at 5%; Commission to the manager @ 10% on net profit after providing the commission.

[Ans. Gross Profit Rs. 81,000; Net Profit Rs. 30,000; Balance Sheet Rs. 1,58,000]

9. The following Trial Balance relates to the business of Mr. Bapan as on 31st March 2012 :

	Rs.		Rs.
Purchases	5,20,000	Capital Account	1,20,000
Building	70,000	Sales	7,90,000
Machinery	90,000	Sundry Creditors	1,26,000
Travelling Expenses	4,200	Bills Payable	12,000
Printing Charges	1,800	Bank Loan (taken on 1.10.2011)	60,000
Miscellaneous Expenses	76,600	Discount Received	2,400
Consignment Account	84,000	Furniture Account (Credit Balance)	10,000
Sundry Debtors	80,000		
Bills Receivable	15,000		
Stock (1.4.2011)	92,000		
Salaries	18,900		
Cash in hand	1,600		
Cash at Bank	31,600		
Insurance	3,500		
Advertisements	6,000		
Discount Allowed	1,200		
Drawings	20,000		
Addition to Furniture (on 1.10.2011)	4,000		
	11,20,400		11,20,400

Additional Information

1. Miscellaneous expenses include Rs. 1,000 given to his son in connection to his education.
2. A fire occurred on 1st April 2011 and, as a result, a large part of the building worth Rs. 40,000 was destroyed. Furniture worth Rs. 5,000 was also destroyed. A sum of Rs. 30,000 was recovered from insurance and was credited to Furniture Account. It was observed that the policy of insurance did not cover furniture.

3. Consignment Account represents goods costing Rs. 80,000 sent on consignment and consignor's expenses thereon. The consignee sold $\frac{3}{4}$th of the goods at a profit of 20% on sales. He was allowed a commission of 4% on actual collections which amounted to Rs. 65,000. There was a Bad Debt of Rs. 1,500. None of the consignee's transactions has been entered in the books and no remittance was made by the consignee till date.
4. Purchases include Rs. 30,000 for new machinery acquired on 1st November 2011.
5. The value of stock at cost as on 31st March 2012 as per physical verification amounted to be charged with Rs. 4,800.
6. Depreciation is to be provided as :

on Building at	5% p.a.
on Machinery at	10% p.a.
on Furniture at	10% p.a.

7. Interest on Bank Loan to be provided at 12% p.a.
8. It is desired to show profit or loss on consignment in the Profit & Loss Account.

You are required to prepare the Trading and Profit & Loss Account for the year eneded 31st March 2012 and the Balance Sheet as on that date after taking into consideration the above-mentioned information.

[Ans. Gross Profit Rs. 2,72,000; Net Profit Rs. 1,38,800; Balance Sheet Rs. 4,39,400; Profit on Consignment Rs. 7,900; Stock on Consignment Rs. 21,000; Due from Consignee Rs. 70,900; Sales by Consignee = Rs. 80,000 × $\frac{3}{4} \times \frac{100}{80}$ = Rs. 75,000]

10. The books of a trader in tea show the following balances as on 31st March 2012 :

	Rs.		Rs.
Opening Stock	1,00,000	Furniture & Fittings	35,000
Purchases	4,00,000	Air-Conditioner	30,000
Salaries	80,000	Sundry Debtors	1,00,000
Building	95,000	Sundry Creditors	80,000
Cash in hand	2,000	Loan on Mortgage	70,000
Cash at Bank	1,35,000	Interest paid on above	3,000
Rent, Rates & Taxes	15,000	Prepaid Expenses	4,000
Insurance Premium	3,000	Drawings	18,000
Miscellaneous Receipts	10,000	Capital	2,80,000
Sales	7,20,000	Bill Payable	30,000
Cash Discount Allowed	4,750	Bank Charges	2,000
Bad Debts	3,250	Legal Charges	6,000
Repairs to Buildings	2,900	Motor Vehicles	80,000
Miscellaneous Expenses	8,700	Travelling & Conveyance	10,000
Advertisements	20,000	Commission to Sales Manager	32,400

The following further information was obtained :

(1) Closing Stock was valued at Rs. 55,000.

(2) Legal Charges include Rs. 5,000 for cost of stamps and registration of building acquired during the year.

(3) Purchases include 400 kg tea valued at Rs. 20,000 which were found totally spoiled. Insurance claim lodged in this respect is expected to realise Rs. 15,000.

(4) Travelling and conveyance include proprietor's personal travelling for which he is to be charged with Rs. 4,800.

(5) Loan on Mortgage bears interest at 12% p.a. with half-yearly interest. The loan was taken on 1st June 1989. One instalment of Rs. 10,000 was repaid on 1st December 1989.

(6) The Sales Manager is entitled to a commission of $7\frac{1}{2}$% on total sales. However, the actual bad debts are deductible from such commission entitlement.

(7) Debtors include
   (a) Rs. 10,000 due from M & Co. (Creditor include Rs. 18,000 due to the same party);
   (b) Rs. 5,000 due on account of sale of furniture; and
   (c) Bad debts of Rs. 2,000.

(8) Provision for bad debts is to be created at 2% of net trade debtors.

(9) Depreciation is chargeable on Buildings at $2\frac{1}{2}$%; on Furniture and Fittings at 10%, on Air-conditioner at 15% and on Motor Vehicles at 20%.

(10) Miscellaneous receipts represent sales proceeds of Furniture—written-down value of which was Rs. 12,000.

(11) Insurance Premium includes annual premium of Rs. 1,000 paid on a new policy on 1st October 2011.

(12) Bills Payable include a bill of Rs. 10,000 which fell due on 31st March 2012 and was paid by the Bank as per standing instruction. The bank charges in this connection amounted to Rs. 100.

(13) The balance as per Bank Statement as on 31st March 2012 was Rs. 1,29,900.

Prepare Trading and Profit & Loss Account for the year ended 31st March 2012 and a Balance Sheet as at that date from the above information.

[Ans. Gross Profit Rs. 2,95,000; Net Profit Rs. 57,318; Balance Sheet Rs. 4,95,440]

Chapter 23

ACCOUNTING FOR NON-TRADING CONCERNS

Learning Objectives

Introduction and definition

Receipts vs Incomes

Payments vs Expenditures

Receipts and Payments Account

—How to Prepare

—Features of Receipts and Payments Account

Difference between Receipts and Payments Account and Cash Book

Income and Expenditure Account

—How to prepare

—Features of Income and Expenditure Account

Difference between Income and Expenditure Account and Receipts and Payment Account

Difference between Income and Expenditure Account and Profit and Loss Account

Balance Sheet

Certain Items and their treatment—

A. Subscriptions
B. Life Membership Fees
C. Donations
D. Entrance Fees/Admission Fees
E. Legacies
F. Sale of Old Assets
G. Some Obsolete Items

Fund Accounting—Its peculiarities

Classification of Funds

Methods of Accounting:

A. Preparation of Income and Expenditure Account and a Balance Sheet from a given Trial Balance

B. Preparation of Income and Expenditure Account and a Balance Sheet from a Receipts and Payments Account

C. Preparation of Opening Balance Sheet and Closing Balance Sheet from a given Income and Expenditure Account and a Receipts and Payments Account.

D. Preparation of Receipts and Payment Account from a given Income and Expenditure Account and a Balance Sheet

Preparation of Bank Reconciliations Statement

Preparation of Restaurant and Bar Trading Account

Introduction

The concern which renders service to its members and/or society is called non-trading concern. It is of two type, viz.

(i) Profit-seeking Concern :	e.g., practising chartered accountants, solicitor's firms, practising physicians, consulting engineers, architects.
(ii) Non-profit-seeking Concern :	e.g., schools, colleges, charitable trusts, hospital recreation clubs, athletic and sports clubs, trade unions — which render valuable services to the society.

The first part of the present study, viz., Profit-seeking concerns, has been discussed in the previous Chapter viz. Chapter—21. Here, we are going to present the accounting system and procedure of non-profit seeking concerns. Sinc̃e the object of these concerns is not to earn profit, as such, they do not prepare the Trading and Profit and Loss Account like trading concerns. They, however are to maintain proper books of accounts in order to supply to the members necessary information as regards cash and bank balances and the financial position as well although same accounting principle is being followed as in case of trading concerns.

In order to prepare the final accounts, usually, a non-trading concern prepares :

(i) **Receipts and Payments Account**; (ii) **Income and Expenditure Account**; and (iii) **Balance Sheet**

Before discussing the above, we are to know the difference between (i) Receipts and Incomes; and (ii) Payments and Expenditure, which are discussed hereunder:

Receipts vs Incomes

'Receipts' mean total amount of cash received for the current year and 'Incomes' mean total income earned for the current year. The following illustration will make the principle clear :

Let us suppos Lake Town Association has 500 members. Each member pays @ Rs. 100 for the year 2006-07 out of which 30 members did not pay their membership subscriptions.

In this case, total 'Receipts' will be = 470 × Rs. 100 = Rs. 47,000 i.e., the actual amount of cash received for the year 2006-07. But total 'Income' will mean and include Rs. 50,000 (i.e., 500 × Rs. 100).

It is interesting to note that if all the members pay their subscriptions in full, i.e., if there is no outstanding subscription, total 'Receipts' and total 'Incomes' will become, equal i.e., Rs. 50,000. Thus, we can say that 'Receipts' and 'Incomes' may or may not be equal. The differences between the two can be enumerated as shown:

Receipts	*Incomes*
1. As soon as we receive any cash, the same may be considered as 'Receipt'.	1. The amount of cash for the current year only, is known as income, i.e. all cash received may or not be considered as income.
2. It may be in the form of both capital and revenue transaction.	2. It must be in the form of revenue transactions only.
3. It is not meant for a particular accounting year, i.e., it may be taken into account for any year— whether present, past or future, i.e., any kind of cash receipt.	3. It is exclusively meant for the current year only.
4. It is recorded in the debit side of the cash book.	4. It is recorded in the credit side of Income and Expenditure Account.
5. It does not help to ascertain the results of the operation—surplus/deficit—i.e., not considered while preparing the final accounts.	5. It helps to ascertain the result of the operation. i.e., surplus/deficit, i.e., it is considered while preparing the final accounts.
6. We can call it 'receipt' till the same is received in cash.	6. We can call it 'income' even though the same is not received in cash.

Payments vs Expenditures

'Payments' mean total amount of cash paid for the current year and 'Expenditures' mean total amount of expenses to be incurred for the current year only. The following illustration will help us to understand the above principle clearly.

Let us suppose, Lake Town Association pays its rent to the landlord @ Rs. 1,000 p.m. but did not pay the rent of the month of Dec. 2010. In this case, total payment will be Rs. 11,000 (i.e., Rs. 1,000 × 11). But, total expenditure will be Rs. 12,000 (i.e., Rs. 1,000 × 12). It is needless to mention here that if there is no outstanding rent, there will be no difference between the term 'Payments' and 'Expenditures'. Thus, it can again be stated that 'Payments' or 'Expenditures' may or may not be equal.

The differences between 'Payments' and 'Expenditures' are :

Payments	*Expenditures*
1. As soon as we pay any cash, the same may be considered as 'Payment'.	1. The amount of cash we pay (revenue) for the current year only is known as 'Expenditure', i.e., all cash payments may or may not be considered as 'Expenditure'.
2. It may be in the form of both capital and revenue transaction.	2. It must be in the form of revenue transactions only.
3. It is not meant for a particular accounting year, i.e., it may be taken into account for any year— whether present, past or future, i.e., any kind of cash payment.	3. It is exclusively meant for the current year only.
4. It is recorded in the credit side of the cash book.	4. It is recorded in the debit side of Income and Expenditure Account.
5. It does not help to ascertain the results of the operation i.e., surplus/deficit—i.e., not considered while preparing the final accounts.	5. It helps to ascertain the result of the operation, i.e., deficit/surplus, i.e., it is considered while preparing the final accounts.
6. We can call it 'payments' till the same is paid in cash.	6. We can call it Expenditure' even though the same is not paid in cash.

1. Receipts and Payments Account

It is simply a summary of Cash Book prepared under appropriate heads after proper classification and analysis. It starts every year with the opening balance of Cash and Bank and closes also with the closing balance of Cash and Bank. All receipts are entered into the debit side whereas all payments are entered on the credit side of the account. It is a real account. The primary object of preparing this account is to find out the opening and closing balances of Cash and Bank and to show the accounts that are related to Receipts and Payments under different heads for a particular period. It must be remembered that Receipts and Payments Accounts takes only the receipts relating to capital and revenue items including arrear incomes and pre-payments , but does not take any income or expenses outstanding at the beginning or at the end. Practically, this account is merely a summary of cash transactions under important heads.

Features of a Receipts and Payments Account

The features of a Receipts and Payments Account are:

(a) It is like a Cash Book.

(b) It includes both Capital and Revenue items.

(c) It ignores outstanding incomes or expenses.

(d) It starts with the opening balance of cash and closes with closing balance of cash.

(e) It follows cash basis of accounting.

(f) As it is a summary of cash book, receipts are shown on the debit side and payments on the credit side.

(g) The difference between the two sides represents the balance of cash and the sam e is carried forward.

How to prepare a Receipts and Payments Account

The following steps should carefully be followed while preparing a Receipts and Payments Account:

Step 1	*Take the opening balance of Cash and Bank balances and post them on the debit side.*
Step 2	*All receipts (i.e., both Capital and Revenue) are to be posted on the debit side one by one.*

Step 3	***All payments (i.e., both Capital and Revenue) are to be posted on the credit side one by one.***
Step 4	***Adjust all arrear incomes and prepayments, if any.***
Step 5	***Exclude all outstanding incomes and expenses***
Step 6	***Add the total of the debit side and find out the difference which represents closing balance of Cash /Bank and post the same on the credit side.***

Ruling :

Dr. Receipts and Payments Account *for the year ended* .... *Cr.*

			Rs.				Rs.
To	Balance b/d			By	Salaries		***
	Cash	***		"	Rent		***
	Bank	***		"	Insurance		***
			***	"	Purchase of Books		***
"	Entrance Fees		***	"	Purchase of Buildings		***
"	Donation		***	"	Investments		***
"	Subscription		***	"	Telephone Charges		***
"	Sale of Newspapers		***	"	Billiards Table		***
"	Hall Rent		***	"	Paper, Ink etc.		***
"	Proceeds of Lectures		***	"	Purchase of Furniture		***
"	Interest etc.		***	"	Outstanding Liability, etc.		***
				"	Balance c/d		
					Cash	***	
					Bank	***	***
			***				***

Differences between Receipts and Payments Account and Cash Book

The significant points of distinction between a Receipts and Payment and Cash Book are :

	Points of Distinction		*Receipts and Payments Account*	*Cash Book*
1.	*Concerns/ institution*	:	This account is prepared by non-trading concerns.	1. This is prepared by all trading concerns.
2.	*Period*	:	This account is prepared periodically, i.e., at the end of the year, being a summary of cash book.	2. This book is regularly maintained.
3.	*Date*	:	Transactions are not recorded date wise.	3. All transactions must be recorded date wise.
4.	*Ledger folio*	:	Ledger folio column is absent here.	4. A separate column is maintained for Ledger folio.
5.	*Side*	:	Left hand side is called receipts side and right hand side is called payments side.	5. Left hand side is called debit side and right hand side is called credit side.
6.	*Procedure*	:	Entries are recorded in a summarised form and classified under appropriate heads of incomes and expenditures.	6. No summarisation and classification are maintained here.

2. Income and Expenditure Account

An Income and Expenditure account is one which shows either the surplus or the deficit after incorporating all revenue items in order to ascertain the result of the concern. In short, all revenue expenditures (paid or not) and all revenue incomes (received or not) for a particular period are entered in the debit side and credit side of this account, respectively . It is a nominal account. It is similar to Profit and Loss account of a trading concern. Therefore, like Profit and Loss Account, incomes and expenses relating to a particular period are taken into consideration, i.e., outstanding expenses and incomes, depreciation etc. for the period are to be included in this account. In short, it is like a Profit and Loss Account prepared under accrual basis.

The sources of revenues of this type of organisation are: Subscription from members, Donation from members or distinguished guests or Grant from local authorities or Government, Entrance Fees from members, etc. ***The entire amount of such revenue incomes (i.e., capital receipts should be excluded. e.g., Entrance fees or Donation, if they are treated as capital, will not appear in this account) will appear on the credit side of this account under accrual basis.*** Similarly, the expenses or payments of this type of organisation include: Salaries, Rent, Insurance, Honorarium to Secretary, Bank Charges etc. i.e., all revenue expenditures will appear on the debit side of the account.

Features of an Income and Expenditure Account

The features of an Income and Expenditure Account are:

(a) It is like a Trading/Profit and Loss Account of a trading concern.

(b) It takes only revenue items.

(c) Incomes are recorded on the credit side and expenses are recorded on the debit side of the account.

(d) It follows mercantile or accrual basis of accounting.

(e) The difference between the two sides represents either surplus or deficit.

(f) It neither starts with cash nor closes with cash.

(g) It records all expenses whether paid or outstanding and all incomes whether received or accrued.

How to prepare an Income and Expenditure Account

The following steps should carefully be followed while preparing an Income and Expenditure Account from a Receipts and Payments Account:

Step 1. *Exclude the opening and closing balance of Cash and Bank balance.*

Step 2. *Exclude all capital receipts and capital payments, i.e., only revenue receipts will appear on the credit side (i.e., income side), whereas revenue expenditures on the debit side (i.e., expenditure side) on accrual basis.*

Step 3. *Consider the adjustment, if any—*

Depreciation on fixed assets or loss on sale of fixed assets = debit side (i.e., expenditure side). Profit/gains on sale of fixed assets = Credit side (i.e., income side).

Step 4. *Ascertain the difference which represents surplus (excess of income over expenditure) or deficit (excess of expenditure over income).*

Ruling

Dr. **Income and Expenditure Account** ***for the year ended ....*** ***Cr.***

Expenditures	Rs.	Rs.	*Incomes*	Rs.	Rs.
To Salaries	***		By Subscriptions	***	
Add: Outstanding	***		*Add:* Outstanding for the		
		***	current year	***	
" Rent		***	*Less:* Subscription	***	
" Insurance	***		received in Advance	***	
" *Less* : Prepaid	***				***
		***	" Proceeds of Lectures		***
" Telephone Charges		***	" Hall Rent		***
" Paper, Ink, etc.		***	" Interest	***	
" Depreciation on:		***	*Add:* Accrued Interest	***	
Land & Building	***				***
Furniture and Fitting	***		" Sale of Newspaper etc.		***
		***	" Deficit—Excess of		
" Surplus—Excess of			expenditure over income		
income over expenditure		***	(if any)		***
		***			***

Income : *In this particular context, income is said to accrue only when the same satisfies the following conditions:*
(a) It is of a recurring nature; and (b) It must not be earmarked for a particular use.

Expenditure : *It is useful only in the current year, i.e., there must not be any use out of it in the future period. If there is any deferred revenue expenditure, the same is not treated as expenditure*

Difference between Receipts and Payments Account and Income and Expenditure Account

Receipts and Payments Account	*Income and Expenditure Account*
1. It includes items pertaining to the preceding, current and succeeding years.	1. It includes the items of current year only and items relating to preceding or succeeding years are to be excluded.
2. It is like a Cash Book.	
3. It includes both capital and revenue items.	2. It is a Trading and Profit & Loss Account.
4. It is a real account.	3. It includes only revenue items.
5. It always starts with the opening balance of Cash and closes with the closing balance of Cash.	4. It is a nominal account. 5. It neither starts with Cash nor closes with Cash.
6. Since it is a summary of Cash Book, receipts are shown on the debit side and payments on the credit side....	6. Here, incomes are recorded on the credit side, and expenses on the debit side.
7. It ignores the outstanding incomes or expenses since it deals with the actual receipts and payments.	7. It records all expenses, whether paid or not; and all incomes, whether received or not.
8. The difference between the two sides represent closing balance of Cash and Bank (unless there is Bank Overdraft) and carried forward to the next years.	8. The difference between the two sides represents either surplus or deficit.
9. It adopts cash basis of accounting and suggests the absence of double entry and Balance Sheet.	9. It adopts mercantile basis of accounting and suggests the presence of double entry along with Balance Sheets.
10. It is not accompanied by any other statement.	10. It is accompanied by Balance Sheet.

Difference between Income and Expenditure Account and Profit and Loss Account

Although we know from the above discussion that Income and Expenditure Account reveals the same objects for a non-trading concern as the Profit and Loss Account of a trading concern, yet there are some significant point of distinctions :

Points of Distinction		Income and Expenditure Account	Profit and Loss Account
1. *Concerns/institutions*	:	Only the non-trading concerns prepare this account.	Only the trading concerns prepare this account.
2. *Object*	:	The primary object of this account is to ascertain the surplus or deficit of the concerns.	The primary object is to ascertain the net profit or net loss of the concerns.
3. *Method of preparation*	:	This account is prepared by taking the data from the Receipts and Payments Account.	This account is prepared from the data taken from a Trial Balance.
4. *Result*	:	The result or the balance of this account is treated as Deficit or Surplus.	The balance is termed as Net Profit or Net Loss.
5. *Use of surplus*	:	The surplus of non-trading concerns is not available for distribution among the members.	The net profit is added to capital and the owner may withdraw it.
6. *Source of revenue*		The source of revenue of a non-trading concern are subscriptions, donations etc. from the members and others.	The sources of revenue are: Sale proceeds of goods and services of the concerns.

3. **Balance Sheet**

The method of preparing a Balance Sheet of a non-trading concern is similar to the method of a trading concern. It contains the particular assets and liabilities including Capital or General fund. The surplus or deficit so ascertained from Income and Expenditure Account is transferred to the Capital Fund. But, if Capital Fund is not given, the same is to be computed by preparing the opening Balance Sheet of the concern which is nothing but the excess of assets over liabilities.

The proforma of a Balance Sheet of a non-trading concern is presented

Balance Sheet *as at..............*

Liabilities	Rs.	Rs.	*Assets*	Rs.	Rs.
Capital Fund	***		Fixed Assets	***	
Add: Surplus	***		*Less:* Depreciation	***	
Less; Deficit, if any	***				***
		***	Sports Equipment	***	
Entrance fees (if Capital)		***	*Less:* Depreciation	***	
Donation (*)		***			***
Subscription Received			Investments		***
in Advance	***		Stock of Sports Materials		***
Outstanding Liabilities for :			Accrued Interest		***
Salary, Rent, Expenses etc.	***		Outstanding Subscriptions		***
		***	Cash at Bank		***
			Cash in hand		***
		***			***

Sources of Income of a Non-Trading Concern and certain special Items and their treatment

The various sources of Income of a non-trading concern are:

(a) Subscriptions; (b) Life Membership Fees; (c) Donations; (d) Entrance Fees or Admissions Fees; (e) Legacies; (f) Sale of old Asset; (8) Some obsolete items.

These are explained one by one.

A. **Subscription and its Treatment**

In a non-trading concern, subscription, as an income, plays a very significant role. It is received not for the current year only. Moreover, some amount of subscriptions may be received in the current year which was due for the last year (i.e., previous year's subscriptions received in the current year). Similarly, some amount of subscription may also be received in the current year as an advance of the succeeding or next year (i.e., subscription received in advance). Sometimes, current year's subscription was received in the previous year (i.e., subscription received in advance in the previous year account), etc. In order to find out the correct amount of subscription which will be credited to Income and Expenditure Account, all the adjustments should be taken into consideration, Consider the following examples one by one:

Example (a) Compute the amount of subscription to be credited to Income and Expenditure Account for the year ended 31st Dec. 2010.

	Rs.
Subscriptions, Received during the year 2010	50,000
Outstanding subscription for 2009	5,000
Outstanding subscription for 2010	8,000

Solution

Amount of subscriptions to be credited to Income and Expenditure Account

		Rs.
	Subscriptions, Received in 2010	50,000
Less:	Outstanding subscription for 2009	5,000
		45,000
Add:	Outstanding subscription for 2010	8,000
		53,000

By Opening Subscription Account

Dr. *Subscription Account* **Cr.**

Date		Particulars	Amount	Date		Particulars	Amount
2010			Rs.	2010			Rs.
Jan. 1	To	Outstanding Subscriptions A/c	5,000	?	By	Bank A/c	50,000
Dec. 31	"	Income and Exp. A/c	53,000	Dec. 31	"	Outstanding* Subscription A/c	8,000
			58,000				58,000

(b) Compute the amount of subscription to be credited to Income and Expenditure Account for the year ended 31st Dec. 2010.

	Rs.
Subscriptions, Received during the year 2010	80,000
Outstanding subscription for 2009	3,000
Outstanding subscription for 2010	5,000
Subscription Received in Advance for 2011	1,000

Solution

Amount of Subscription to be Credited to Income and Expenditure Account

		Rs.
	Subscriptions, Received during 2010	80,000
Less:	Outstanding subscription for 2009	3,000
		77,000
Less:	Subscription Received in Advance for 2011 Rs. 1,00,000	1,000
		76,000
Add:	Outstanding Subscription 2010	5,000
		81,000

By Opening Subscription Account

Dr. *Subscription Account* **Cr.**

Date		Particulars	Amount	Date		Particulars	Amount
2010			Rs.	2010			Rs.
Jan. 1	To	Outstanding Subs. A/c	3,000	?	By	Bank A/c	80,000
Dec. 31	"	Subcription Returned in Advances for 2011	1,000	Dec. 31	"	Outstanding Subscription A/c	5,000
	"	Income and Exp. A/c	81,000				
			85,000				85,000

(c) Compute the amount of Subscriptions to be credited to Income and Expenditure Account for the year ended 31st Dec. 2010.

	1.1.2010	31.12.2010
Subscriptions, Received during the year 2010 Rs. 1,00,000	Rs.	Rs.
Subscription Outstanding	3,000	5,000
Subscription Received in Advance	1,000	3,000

Solution

Amount of Subscription to be Credited to Income and Expenditure Account

		Rs.
	Subscriptions, Received during 2010	1,00,000
Less:	Outstanding subscription on 1.1.2010	3,000
		97,000
Add:	Outstanding subscription on 31.12. 2010	5,000
		1,02,000
Add:	Subscription Received in Advance on 1.1.2010	1,000
		1,03,000
Less:	Subscription Received in Advance on 31.12. 2010	3,000
		1,00,000

By Opening Subscription Account

Dr. **Subscription Account** Cr.

Date		Particulars	Amount	Date		Particulars	Amount
2010			Rs.	2010			Rs.
Jan. 1	To	Outstanding Subs. A/c	3,000	Jan. 1	By	Subscription Received in Advance A/c	1,000
Dec. 31		Subscriptions Received in Advance for 2011	3,000		"	Bank A/c	1,00,000
	"	Income and Exp. A/c	1,00,000	Dec. 31		Outstanding Subs. A/c	5,000
			1,06,000				1,06,000

(d) Compute the amount of subscription to be credited to Income and Expenditure Account for the year ended 31st Dec. 2010.

Subscription Received in 2010 as :

	Rs.
2009	15,000
2010	90,000
2011	8,000
Subscription Outstanding in 2009	18,000
Subscription Outstanding in 2010	25,000
Subscription Received in Advance in 2009 for 2010	6,000
Subscription Received in Advance in 2009 for 2011	4,000

Solution

Amount of Subscription to be credited to Income and Expenditure Account

		Rs.
	Subscriptions Received in 2010	90,000
Add:	Subscription Outstanding in 2010	25,000
Add:	Subscription Received in Advance 2009 for 2010	6,000
		1,21,,000

By Opening Subscription Account

Dr. ***Subscription Account*** Cr.

Date		Particulars	Amount	Date		Particulars	Amount
2010			Rs.	2010			Rs.
Dec. 31	To	Income and Exp. A/c —Transfer	1,21,000	Jan. 1	By	Subscription Received in Advance A/c	6,000
				Dec. 31	"	Bank A/c	90,000
						Outstanding Subs. A/c	25,000
			1,21,000				1,21,000

Note: In this case, since information relating to subscription for 2010 has specifically been stated, subscription relating to the year 2009 and 2011 are not to be considered. On the contrary, if the total amount of subscriptions received (i.e., 15,000 + 90,000 + 8,000) Rs. 1,13,000, was given, in that case, we are to adjust the same accordingly.

(e) Compute the amount of subscription to be received which will appear in the credit side of Receipts and Payment Account for the year ended 31st Dec. 2010 :

(i) Subscription as per Income and Expenditure Account Rs. 2,000

(ii) Subscription for 2009 unpaid at 1.1.2010 Rs. 200, Rs. 180 of which was received in 2010

(iii) Subscription paid in advance at 1.1.2010 Rs. 50

(iv) Subscription paid in advance at 31.12.2010 Rs. 40

(v) Subscription for 2010 unpaid at 31.12. 2010 Rs. 70

Solution

Computations of Subscription Received during the year 2010 for preparing Receipts and Payments Account

		Rs.
	Subscription (as per Income and Expenditure Account)	2,000
Add:	Subscription outstanding at 1.1.2010 for 2009	200
Add:	Subscription paid in advance for 2011 received in 2010	40
		2,240

		Rs.	Rs.
Less:	Subscription paid in advance on 1.1.2010	50	
	Balance unpaid for 2009 Rs. (200 – 180)	20	
	Outstanding Subscription for 2010	70	
			140
			2,100

By Opening Subscription Account

Dr. *Subscription Account* *Cr.*

Date		*Particulars*	*Amount*	*Date*		*Particulars*	*Amount*
2010			Rs.	2010			Rs.
Jan. 31	To	Outstanding Sub. A/c	200	Jan. 1	By	Subscription Received in Advance A/c	50
Dec 31	"	Income and Expenditure A/c	2,000	Dec. 31	"	Balance unpaid for 2009 (Rs. 200 – Rs. 180)	20
	"	Subscription Received in Advance	40		"	Cash Received (bal. fig.)	2,100
						Outstanding Subs. A/c	70
			2,240				2,240

(f)

	Rs.
Subscription Income for 2012-13 as per Income & Expenditure Account	82,000
Advance Subscription received in 2011-12	4,000
Subscriptions outstanding at the end of 2012-13 (including 1,000/for 2011-12)	9,500
Advance Subscription received for 2013-14	2,000
Subscription written-off during 2012-13	500
Subscription receivable on 1.4.2012	5,000
Subscription collected (2012-13) by the Secretary but not deposited	1,000

Prepare a statement showing subscription received in 2012-13 as per Receipts & Payments account.

Solution

Computation of Subscriptions Received as per Receipts and Payment Account

		Rs.	Rs.
	Subscription Income for 2012-13 as per Income and Expenditure Account		82,000
Less:	Advance Subscription received in 2011-12	4,000	
	Outstanding Subscription 2012-13 (9,500 – 1,000)	8,500	
			12,500
			69,500
Add:	Outstanding Subscription collected (5,000 minus outstanding at the end of 2012-13) (Rs. 1,000, minus Rs. 500 written-off)	3,500	
Add:	Advance subscription received for 2013-14	2,000	
			5,500
			75,000
Less:	Subscriptions Collected but not deposited		1,000
	Subscription received as per Receipts & Payments account in 2012-13		74,000

(g) Salt Lake Club presented the following particulars:

Compute the amount of subscriptions to be received as per Receipts and Payment Account for the year ended 31st March 2010

	31.3.2009	31.3.2010
	Rs.	Rs.
Advance Subscription	1,500	1,000
Arrear Subscription	3,000	5,000

The Club had 300 members on 31.3.2010 as per Register of members. No fresh members were admitted during the year but 10 member left the Club on 1.10.2009. Subscription payable Rs. 15 per month.

Solution

Computation of Subscription to be received for Receipts and Payment Account

Subscription for the year 2009-10:

			Rs.
	Subscription from April 2009 to Sept. 2009 (310 × Rs. 15 × 6)		27,900
	Subscription from Oct. 2009 to March 2010 (300 × Rs. 15 × 6)		27,000
			54,900
Less:	Advance Subscription on 31.3.2009	1,500	
	Arrear Subscription as on 31.3.2010	5,000	6,500
			48,400
Add:	Advance Subscription as on 31.3.2010	1,000	
	Arrear Subscription as on 31.3.2009	3,000	4,000
	Amount to be appeared in Receipts and Payments A/c		52,400

B. Life Membership Fees

There are some members who prefer to pay a lump-sum amount instead of periodic payment for an estimated period of longevity which is credited to the capital fund or, credited to a special fund known as Life Membership Fund, since it is a capital receipt. Sometimes, a part of it may be transferred practically to subscription account, the balance, if any, is transferred to capital fund after the death of the member.

Example (a) **Young Star Club presents the following information :**

Life Membership fees received Rs. 10,000, Rs. 20,000 and Rs. 40,000 in 2009, 2010 and 2011 respectively. The policy of the club to take credit of the said fees in 20 years qually. Show the Life Membership Fund Account and the amount credited to Income and Expenditures for the three consequitive years.

In the books of Young Star Club

Life Membership Fund Account

Dr. *Cr.*

Date	*Particulars*	*Amount*	*Date*	*Particulars*	*Amount*
		Rs.			Rs.
2009	To Income and Exp. A/c		2009	By Bank A/c	10,000
	(Rs. 10,000 × $\frac{1}{20}$)	500			
	" Balance c/d	9,500			
		10,000			10,000
2010	To Income and Exp. A/c		2010	By Balance b/d	9,500
	(Rs. 500 + Rs. 1,000			" Bank A/c	20,000
	(20,000 × $\frac{1}{20}$)	1,500			
	" Balance c/d	28,000			
		29,500			29,500

Contd.

		Rs.			Rs.
2011	To Income and Exp. A/c (Rs. 500 + Rs. 1,000 + Rs. 2,000 (40,000 × $\frac{1}{20}$))	3,500	2011	By Balance b/d	28,000
	" Balance c/d	64,500		" Bank A/c	40,000
		68,000			68,000

Example

(b) Lake Town Association presents the following particulars from which you are asked to prepare the Life Membership Fund. Rate of Life Membership Fees was Rs. 1,200 since its inception, i.e., 1975. From 1.1.2005, the rate of Life Membership Fees was increased by Rs. 300. The particulars of the transaction relating to life membership are furnished below:

	No. of Members
Members joined before 29 years	45
Members joined with the last 29 years	90
	135

It is the policy of the club to take credit the Life Membership Fees within 30 years equally. In 2006, 5 new members admitted and one member who joined in 2001 expired. On 1.1.2006, the balance of Life Membership Fund was Rs. 75,500.

Solution

Dr. *Life Membership Fund Account* *Cr.*

Date	*Particulars*	*Amount* Rs.	*Date*	*Particulars*	*Amount* Rs.
?	To Capital Fund A/c	1,000[3]	2006	By Balanced b/d	75,500
2006	" Income and Expenditure A/c	3,810[4]	Jan. 1	" Bank A/c	
Dec. 31	" Balance c/d	78,190		(5 Members Rs. 1,500)	7,500
		83,000			83,000

Workings :

1. 45 members who joined before 29 years, Life Membership Fees so received from them, has already been credited to Income and Expenditure Account. So nothing is left. As such, Income and Expenditure account must not be credited any more against those members.
2. As per problem, rate of life membership fee was Rs. 1,200 till 31.12.2005. So, amount to be credited to Income and Expenditure Account every year per member will be Rs. 40 (i.e., Rs. $\frac{1,200}{30 \text{ years}}$).
3. The member (who expired) was joined in 2001 paid Rs. 1,200, of which Rs. 200 (i.e., from 2001 to 2005) or, @ Rs. 40 for 5 years, had already been credited to Income and Expenditure Account and balance Rs. 1,000 (i.e., 1,200 – Rs. 200) to be credited to Capital Fund Account.
4. Amount credited to Income and Expenditure Account

	Rs.
For (90 – 1) = 89 members who joined withen the last 29 years @ Rs. 40 =	3,560
For 5 new members = $\frac{\text{Rs. } 1,500}{30}$ = Rs. 50 × 5 =	250
	3,810

C. Donations

Since Donations are not periodic, the same should not be treated as income. Unless otherwise povided, these are to be shown in the liabilities side of the Balance Sheet (i.e., to be added with Capital Fund). If specific instruction is given in that case, the relevant revenue portion will appear in Income and Expenditure Account. Thus:

Specific Donations — It will be treated as capital receipts and, as such, will appear in the liabilities side of the Balance Sheet

General Donations — It should be treated as revenue items and will appear at the credit side of Income and Expenditure Account since no specific condition is imposed, particularly when the amount is small and will appear in the credit side of Income and Expenditure Account.

If any asset is donated, the same should be credited to the particular fund for which it is meant.

D. **Entrance Fees or Admission Fees**

It may be treated either as a revenue item or a capital one, depending on the nature, rules and bye-laws of the organisation. It may also be called admission fees. ***If the organisation collects fees from its members every year, the same is to be treated as a revenue item and it will appear on the credit side of Income and Expenditure Account, whereas, if it collects fees only for once from its members the same is treated as a capital item which will appear in the liabilities side of the Balance Sheet.*** However, a note on this point should be given at the end of the solution.

E. **Legacies**

It is received as per will of the deceased person and it is a kind of donation. The treatment will, however, be like donation, i.e., in the absence of any clear information it should be treated as a revenue item, provided the amount is small, and is to be treated as capital if the amount is large. However, in both cases, a note should be given at the end of the solution.

F. **Sale of Old Assets**

Since sale of old assets is not an income, the same will not appear in the Income and Expenditure Account, the same is to be deducted from the respective assets in the Balance Sheet. If any profit or loss arises out of that sale of asset, the same should be adjusted accordingly in the Income and Expenditure Account.

G. **Some Obsolete Items**

These items may be treated as revenue income and, hence, these should be recorded in the credit side of Income and Expenditure Account.

Fund Accounting—its peculiarities

These are:

(i) Since the non-trading organisations receive grants and contributions from Government and other organisations with restrictions, such organisations cannot use such funds according to their choice.

(ii) Separates set of books may be maintained for such funds.

(iii) If any legally restricted asset is taken from any organisation/anyone, it must maintain a separate restricted fund for the purpose.

Classification of Funds

(a) **Capital Fund/General Fund**

Since there is no capital account in case of non-trading concerns, the difference between the assets side and the liabilities side of the Balance Sheet represents capital fund which is built-up from revenue/surplus of every year. It is also known as General Fund.

(b) **Special Fund**

Special Funds are created for specific purposes in order to meet the requirements of the contributors. In short, this fund can never be utilised for general purposes.

(c) **Unrestricted Funds**

There is no restrictions of using or utilising this fund. i.e., no restriction is imposed.

(d) **Restricted Funds**

This is just like the special funds stated above, i.e., there are some restriction on their use. In short, as per the instructions of the contributors, these funds can be used.

(e) **Property/Fixed Assets Funds**

These funds are created for the purpose of acquisitions of fixed assets.

(f) **Building Funds**

These funds are created for the purpose of construction of the building of the organisation.

(g) **Endowment Funds**

It is like an income—generating investment. As per the instruction of the contributors, when the principal amount remains intact for indefinite period, and the interest which is earned on it can be expended for the purpose by organisation. It is a permanent source of income.

There are Certain other funds as well. They are Annuity Funds, Loan Fund, etc.

Method of Accounting

A. **Preparation of Income and Expenditure Account and a Balance Sheet from a given Trial Balance.**

B. **Preparation of Income and Expenditure Account and a Balance Sheet from a Receipts and Payments Account.**

C. **Preparation of opening Balance Sheet and closing Balance Sheet from a given Income and Expenditure Account and a Receipts and Payments Account.**

D. **Preparation of Receipts and Payments Account from a given Income and Expenditure Account and a Balance Sheet.**

These are discussed next one by one :

A. Preparation of Income and Expenditure Account and a Balance Sheet from a given Trial Balance

The method of preparation of an Income and Expenditure Account has already been explained earlier. It is similar to a Profit and Loss Account for a trading concern. However, the following points should carefully be considered for its preparation :

(i) ***All the current year's revenue incomes are to be posted on the credit side***

(ii) ***All the current year's revenue expenditures are to be posted on the debit side***

(iii) ***If the credit side is greater than the debit side, there will be a 'Surplus' or 'Excess' of income over expenditure, and vice versa in the opposite case***

(iv) ***The surplus or deficit so made is to be added or subtracted against the capital fund***

(v) ***All capital incomes or capital expenditures are to be posted in the Balance Sheet.***

The following illustration will help to understand the principle:

Preparation of Income and Expenditure Account from a Trial Balance

Illustration 1

From the following Trial Balance of Brahma Samaj Education Society as at 31st December 2012, prepare an Income and Expenditure Account and a Balance Sheet:

	Dr. Rs.	*Cr.* Rs.
Furniture and Fittings	12,500	
Additions	3,200	
Library Books	17,500	
Additions	4,300	
Buildings	2,75,000	
General Investment	1,50,000	
Investment Reserve Fund		15,000
Sundry Debtors and Creditors	5,000	14,500
Entrance Fees		15,200
Examination Fees		2,400
Subscription Received		20,000
Certificate Fees		500
Hire of Society's Hall		6,500
Interest on Investment		5,500
Sundry Receipts		600
Staff Salaries	10,200	
Printing & Stationery	1,000	
Taxes	800	
Examination Expenses	650	
Subscription of Periodicals	1,200	
Prize Trust Fund		
Prize Trust Investments	15,800	
Prize Trust Income		
Prize Awarded		
Prize Fund, Bank Balance		

Contd.

	Rs.	Rs.
Donation Received (to be capitalised)		18,000
General Expenses	375	
Capital Fund		3,89,150
Cash at Bank	5,500	
Cash in hand	300	
	5,04,000	5,04,000

The following further information is supplied to enable you to make the necessary adjustments:

	Rs.		Rs.
Subscriptions to be received	4,500	Staff Salaries Outstanding	1,800
Subscription received in Advance	500	Taxes paid in Advance	150
Interest on General Investments accrued	450		

Provide depreciation at the following rates on : Library Books 15% p.a. Furniture & Fittings 5% p.a. Buildings 1% p.a.

The market value of General Investments on 31st Dec. 2012 was Rs. 1,35,000. But you are not required to bring down the book value to this level.

Solution

In the books of Brahma Samaj Education Society

Income and Expenditure Account *for the year ended 31st December 2012*

Dr. *Cr.*

Expenditures	Rs.	Rs.	*Incomes*	Rs.	Rs.
To Staff Salaries	10,200		By Subscriptions	20,000	
Add : Outstanding	1,800	12,000	*Add* : Outstanding	4,500	
To Printing & Stationery		1,000		24,500	
" Taxes	800		*Less* : Received in Advance	500	
Less : Prepaid	150	650			24,000
" Examination Fees		650	" Entrance Fees		15,200
" Subscriptions & Periodicals		1,200	" Examination Fees		2,400
" General Expenses		375	" Certificate Fees		500
" Depreciation on :			" Hire of Society Hall		6,500
Library Books 15%	2,948		" Interest	5,500	
Furniture & Fittings 5%	705		*Add* : Accrued	450	5,950
Buildings 1%	2,750	6,403	" Sundry Receipts		600
" Surplus — Excess of Income over Expenditure		32,872			
		55,150			55,150

Balance Sheet *as at 31st March 2012*

Liabilities	Rs.	Rs.	*Assets*	Rs.	Rs.
Capital Fund :					
Balance	3,89,150		Building	2,75,000	
Donations	18,000		*Less* : Depreciation	2,750	2,72,250
urplus	32,872	4,40,022	Furniture	15,700	
Fund		16,250	*Less* : Depreciation	705	14,995
serve Fund		15,000	Books	21,800	
Sundry ries		1,800	*Less* : Depreciation	2,948	
d in					18,852
			Prize Trust Investment		15,800
		500	General Investment		1,50,000
		14,500	Sundry Debtors		5,000
			Accrued Interest		450
			Outstanding Subscriptions		4,500

Contd.

	Rs.	Rs.		Rs.	Rs.
			Prepaid Taxes		150
			Prize Trust Bank Balance		275
			Cash at Bank		5,500
			Cash in hand		300
		4,88,752			4,88,072

Note : Depreciation on additions to Library Books and Furniture has been calculated for 6 months.

B. Preparation of Income and Expenditure Account and a Balance Sheet from a Receipts and Payments Account

The method of preparation of Income and Expenditure Account is almost similar to the earlier methods. Under this method, the adjustments relating to outstanding revenue incomes or revenue expenditures, prepaid expenses or pre-received incomes, etc. are to be adjusted accordingly in this account under double entry principle after following the steps (i) and (ii) stated above. In other words, all the revenue items are to be taken from Receipts and Payments Account in order to prepare the Income and Expenditure Account. The rest of items, i.e., capital incomes or capital expenditures are to be posted in the Balance Sheet in the usual manner after incorporating the adjustment under double entry principle.

The following steps should carefully be followed :

(a) For preparing Income and Expenditure Account

Step 1	*Ignore opening and closing balance of Cash and Bank.*
Step 2	*Also ignore all Capital Receipts and Capital Payments items.*
Step 3	*Debit all revenue expenditure items one by one from Receipts and Payments Account and add outstanding expenses, if any, and deduct prepaid expenses, if any.*
Step 4	*Credit all revenue receipts items one by one from Receipts and Payments Account and add outstanding incomes, if any, and deduct incomes received in advance, if any.*
Step 5	*Debit further for adjustment items, like depreciation on assets, Loss on sale of fixed assets or investments, etc. Similarly, credit items like profit on sale of fixed assets, investments, etc.*
Step 6	*If the credit side of Income and Expenditure Account is greater than the debit side, there is a Surplus — Excess of income over expenditure, or vice versa in the opposite case.*

(b) For preparing Balance Sheet

Step 1	*Prepare the Opening Balance Sheet (if the Capital fund is not given) by taking all the opening assets (including Cash and Bank Balance) and post them on the assets side and opening liabilities, if any, on the liability side, the differences will represent the Capital Fund/General/Accumulated Fund.*
Step 2	*Post all fixed assets which appeared in the opening Balance Sheet (if not sold) with additions, if any, (which are given in the credit side of Receipts and Payments Account) or deduct sale of fixed assets; if any, after deducting the amount of depreciation, if any and also opening fixed liabilities (if not paid) along with the closing liabilities.*
Step 3	*Post closing balance of cash and bank balances.*
Step 4	*In order to find out the closing capital fund, add surplus or deduct deficit from the opening capital fund.*
Step 5	*Post all other closing assets and liabilities as per adjustments given.*

Stock of Stationery and its treatment

Illustration 2

Calculate what amount will be posted to Income and Expenditure Account for the year 50
December 2011:

300

1,080

(a) Amount paid for stationery during the year 2011
Stock of stationery in hand on 31st December 2011

(b) Stock of stationery in hand on 1.1.2011
Payment made for stationery during the year 2011

	Stock of stationery in hand on 31.12.2011	50
(c)	Stock of stationery on 1.1.2011	300
	Creditors for stationery outstanding on 1.1.2011	200
	Amount paid for stationery during the year	1,080
	Stock of stationery on 31.12.2011	50
(d)	Stock of stationery on 1.1.2011	300
	Creditors for stationery outstanding on 1.1.2011	200
	Amount paid for stationery during the year	1,080
	Stock of stationery on 31.12.2011	50
	Creditor for stationery outstanding on 31.12.2011	130
(e)	Creditor for stationery on 1. 1. 2011	200
	Amount paid for stationery during the year 2011	1,080
	Creditors for stationery on 31.12.2011	130
(f)	Stock of stationery on 1.1.2011	300
	Creditors for stationery on 1.1.2011	200
	Advances paid for stationery carried forward from 2010	20
	Amount paid for stationery during the year 2011	1,080
	Stock of stationery on 31.12.2011	50
	Creditors for stationery on 31.12.2011	130
	Advance paid for stationery on 31.12.2011	30

[Delhi, BCom (Hons.)]

Solution

The following amount will appear on the debit side of Income and Expenditure Account:

(a)

		Rs.	Rs.
	Amount paid for stationery		1,080
Less :	Stock of stationery (closing)		50
	Stationery used		1,030

(b)

		Rs.	Rs.
	Stock of stationery (opening)		300
Add :	Purchases		1,080
			1,380
Less :	Stock of stationery (closing)		50
	Stationery used		1,330

(c)

	Stock of stationery (opening)		300
Add :	Payments made	1,080	
Less :	Payment made for creditors of last year	200	
			880
			1,180
Less :	Stock of stationery (closing)		50
	Stationery used		1,130

(d)

	Stock of stationery (opening)		300
Add :	Payment made	1,080	
Less :	Payment made for creditors of last year	200	
		880	
Add :	Creditor for stationery (closing)	130	1,010
			1,310
Less :	Stock of stationery (closing)		50
	Stationery used		1,260

(e)

	Payments made		1,080
Less :	Paid for last year (opening)		200
			880
	Creditors for stationery (closing)		130
	Stationery used		1,010

(f)

	Stock of stationery (opening)		300
Add :	Payments made	1,080	
Less :	Payment for last year	200	
		880	
Add :	Payment made last year but stationery received this year	20	
		900	
Add :	Creditors for stationery (closing)	130	
		1,030	
Less :	Adv. payment made (closing) for stationery to be received next year	30	1,000
			1,300
Less :	Stock of stationery (closing)		50
	Stationery used		1,250

Preparation of Income and Expenditure Account and Balance Sheet

Illustration 3

Following is the Youngmen's Library Cash Account for the year ending 31.12.2012:

	Receipts	Rs.		*Payments*	Rs.
To	Balance b/d	4,500	By	Salaries and Wages	6,800
"	Admission Fees	3,500	"	Rent	8,250
"	Subscriptions	19,500	"	Investments	3,500
"	Lecture Hall Hire Charges	2,500	"	Stationery	1,250
"	Miscellaneous	350	"	Electric Charges	730
"	Interest on Investments	600	"	Books	6,000
			"	Outstanding Expenses	700
			"	Balance c/d	3,720
		30,950			30,950

You are required to prepare an Income and Expenditure Account for the year ended 31.12.2012, and make a Balance Sheet as at 31.12.2012. The following further information are also made available to you :

(a) On 31.12.2011, the library had the following assets also :
Furniture Rs. 5,500, Books valued at Rs. 45,000 and Investments at a cost of Rs. 20,000.

(b) Subscriptions realised in advance this year amounted to Rs. 600 and outstanding liabilities on 31.12.2012, for Salaries and Wages Rs. 1,200 and for Rent Rs. 750.

(c) 60% of the Admission Fees should be capitalised.

(d) Furniture and Library Books are to be depreciated at 6% and 10% p.a., respectively.

Solution

In the books of Youngmen's Library
Balance Sheet *as at 31st December 2011*

Liabilities	Rs.	*Assets*	Rs.
Outstanding Expenses	700	Furniture	5,500
Capital Fund *(bal. fig.)*	74,300	Books	45,000
		Investments	20,000
		Cash	4,500
	75,000		75,000

Income and Expenditure Account
for the year ended 31st December 2012

Dr. Cr.

	Expenditures	Rs.	Rs.		*Incomes*	Rs.	Rs.
To	Salary and Wages	6,800		By	Subscriptions	19,500	
	Add : Outstanding	1,200	8,000		*Less* : Advance	600	18,900
"	Rent	8,250		"	Lecture Hall Hire Charges		2,500
	Add : Outstanding	750	9,000	"	Mis. Receipts		350
"	Postage and Stationery		1,250	"	Interest on Investment		600
"	Electric Charges		730	"	Admission Fees	3,500	
"	Depreciation on :				*Less* : Capital 60%	2,100	1,400
	Furniture	330		"	Deficit—Excess of Expenditure over Income		
	* Books	4,800	5,130				
			24,110				

*Depreciation to be calculated as :

on Rs. 45,000 @ 10%	4,500
on Rs. 6,000 @ 10% for 6 months	300
	4,800

Balance Sheet *as at 31st December 2012*

Liabilities	Rs.	Rs.	*Assets*	Rs.	Rs.
Capital Fund :			Furniture	5,500	
Balance as on 1.1.1992	74,300		*Less* : Depreciation	330	
Add : Admission Fees	2,100				5,170
	76,400		Books	45,000	
Less : Deficit	360	76,040	Additions	6,000	
				51,000	
Subscriptions received in Advance		600	*Less* : Depreciation	4,800	46,200
Outstanding Expenses :			Investments (at cost)	20,000	
Salary and Wages	1,200		Additions	3,500	
Rent	750				23,500
		1,950	Cash		3,720
		78,590			78,590

Illustration 4

The analysis of the Cash Book of General Library, Basirhat, for the year 2012 showed :

Receipts	Rs.	*Payments*	Rs.
Subscription 2011	1,000	Salaries	15,000
2012	30,000	Printing and Stationery	1,000
2013	2,000	Electric Charges	500
Interest on Investments	1,000	Rent and Rates	2,000
Sale of old Furniture	500	Telephone Charges	1,200
Sale of old Newspaper	100	Advertisement	100
Hall Rent	4,000	Meeting Expenses	400
Special Fund Receipts	3,000	Insurance Premium	500
Admission Fees (40% to be Capitalised)	5,000	Purchase of Library Books	10,000
Donation (50% to be Capitalised)	10,000	Purchase of Furniture	6,000
Telephone Receipts	100	Special Fund Expenses	2,000
		Miscellaneous Expenses	11,300

Additional information

(a) The assets of the Library on 1st January 2012 were : Cash in hand Rs. 3,000; Cash at Bank Rs. 7,000; 8% G.P. Notes Rs. 40,000; Library Books Rs. 20,000; Furniture Rs. 6,000.

(b) Salaries include Rs. 2,000 for 2011 and Rs. 3,000 for 2013.

(c) Outstanding Liabilities on 31.12.2012 were : Rent and Tax Rs. 1,000; Audit Fees Rs. 500.

(d) Outstanding assets on 31.12.2012 were : Subscription Rs. 2,500; Bank Interest Rs. 500.

(e) Special Fund Balance (Cr.) on 1.1.2012 was Rs. 3,000.

(f) Depreciate Library Books @ 10% and Furniture @ 5%.

(g) On 31.12.2012, Cash in hand was Rs. 4,000 and the balancing figure of the Cash Book represents Cash at Bank as on 31.12.2012.

Additions were made at the middle of the year and Furniture was sold at the beginning of the year. Prepare ...ne and Expenditure Account for the year ended 31.12.2012 and a Balance Sheet as on that date.

In the books of General Library
Balance Sheet *as at 1st January 2012*

...*bilities*	Rs.	*Assets*	Rs.
Ou...	2,000	Furniture	6,000
Speci...	3,000	Library Books	20,000
Capital F...	72,000	8% G. P. Notes	40,000
		Subscription Receivable	1,000
		Bank	7,000
		Cash	3,000
	77,000		77,000

Dr. **Income and Expenditure Account** *for the year ended 31st December 2012* Cr.

Expenditures		Rs.	*Incomes*		Rs.
To Salaries		10,000[1]	By Subscription	30,000	
" Printing and Stationery		1,000	*Add* : Outstanding	2,500	
" Electric Charges		500			32,500
" Rent & Rates	2,000		" Interest on Investment	1,000	
Add : Outstanding	1,000	3,000	*Add* : Accrued	2,200	
" Audit Fees (Outstanding)		500			3,200
" Telephone Charges		1,200	" Sale of old Newspapers		100
" Advertisement		100	" Hall Rent		4,000
" Meeting Expenses		400	" Admission Fees		3,000
" Insurance		500	" Donation		5,000
" Miscellaneous Expenses		11,300	" Telephone Receipts		100
" Depreciation on :			" Bank Interest (Accrued)		500
Library Book	2,500[2]				
Furniture	425[3]	2,925			
" Surplus : Excess of Income over Expen.		16,975			
		48,400			48,400

Balance Sheet *as at 31st March 2012*

Liabilities	Rs.	Rs.	*Assets*	Rs.	Rs.
Capital Fund	72,000		Furniture	6,000	
Add : Admission Fees			*Less* : Sold	500	
Capitalised	2,000			5,500	
Donations Capitalised	5,000		Additions	6,000	
Surplus	16,975	95,975		11,500	
Special Fund	3,000		*Less* : Depreciation	425	11,075
Additions	3,000		Library Books	20,000	
	6,000		Additions	10,000	
Less : Expenses	2,000	4,000		30,000	
Subscription Received in adv.		2,000	*Less* : Depreciation	2,500	27,500
Outstanding Liabilities :			8% G. P. Notes		40,000
Rent & Tax	1,000		Subscription Receivable		2,500
Audit Fees	500		Accrued Interest (2,200 + 500)		2,700
		1,500	Pre-paid Salary		3,000
			Cash at Bank		12,700[4]
			Cash in hand		4,000
		1,03,475			1,03,475

Workings :

1. **Payment for Salaries**

	Rs.
Salaries Paid	15,000
Less: For Last year	2,000
	13,000
Less: Prepaid	3,000
	10,000

2. **Depreciation on Libray Books** Rs

on Rs. 20,000 × $\frac{10}{100}$ =

on Rs. 10,000 × $\frac{10}{100} \times \frac{6}{12}$ =

Contd.

4. **Balance at Bank**

	Rs.
Total debits of Receipts side of Receipts and Payment A/c	56,700
Less: Total Payments of Receipts and payment A/c =	40,000
	16,700
Less: Cash in hand	4,000
	12,700

5. **Depreciation on Furniture**

Bank Balance after Sale (Rs. 6,000 – 500)	Rs.
on Rs. 5,500 × $\frac{5}{100}$ =	275
on Rs. 6,000 × $\frac{5}{100} \times \frac{6}{12}$ =	150
	425

Illustration 5

A summary of receipts and payments of Medical Aid Society for the year ended 31.12.2012 is given :

	Receipts	Rs.		*Payments*	Rs.
To	Balance (1.1.2012)	7,000	By	Payment for Medicines	30,000
"	Subscription	50,000	"	Honorarium to Doctors	10,000
"	Donation Fees	14,500	"	Salaries	27,500
"	Interest on Investment @ 7% p.a.	7,000	"	Sundry Expenses	500
"	Charity Show proceeds	10,000	"	Equipment Purchased	15,000
			"	Charity Show Expenses	1,000
			"	Balance (31.12.2012)	4,500
		88,500			88,500

Additional information :	1.1.2012	31.12.2012
Subscriptions due	500	1,000
Subscriptions received in advance	1,000	500
Stock of medicines	10,000	15,000
Amount due to medicine supplier	8,000	12,000
Value of Equipments	21,000	30,000
Value of Buildings	40,000	38,000

You are required to prepare Income and Expenditure Account for the year ended 31st December 2012 and the Balance Sheet as on that date.

Solution

In the books of Medical Aid Society

Dr. **Income and Expenditure Account** *for the year ended 31st December 2012* Cr.

	Expenditures	Rs.	Rs.		*Incomes*	Rs.	Rs.
To	Medicines		29,000[2]	By	Subscriptions	50,000	
"	Honorarium to Doctors		10,000		*Add* : Adv. for 2012	1,000	
"	Salaries		27,500			51,000	
"	Sundry Expenses		500		*Add* : Outstanding for 2012	1,000	
"	Charity Show Expenses		1,000			52,000	
"	Depreciation on :				*Less* : Outstanding for 2011	500	
	Equipment	6,000[3]				51,500	
	Building	2,000			*Less* : Received in Advance for 2013	500	51,000[4]
			8,000	"	Interest on Investment		7,000
				"	Charity Show proceeds		10,000
				"	Deficit — Excess of Expenditure over Income		8,000
			76,000				76,000

Balance Sheet *as at 31st December 2012*

	Rs.	Rs.	*Assets*	Rs.	Rs.
Capital Fund	1,69,500[1]		Building	40,000	
Less : Deficit	8,000	1,61,500	*Less* : Depreciation	2,000	38,000

Contd.

	Rs.	Rs.		Rs.	Rs.
Donation		14,500	Equipment	21,000	
Subscription Received			Additions	15,000	
in Advance		500		36,000	
Creditors for Medicines		12,000	*Less* : Depreciation	6,000	30,000
			Stock of Medicines		15,000
			Investment		1,00,000
			Outstanding Subscription		1,000
			Cash		4,500
		1,88,500			1,88,500

Workings :

1. **Balance Sheet** *as at 1st January 2012*

Liabilities	Rs.	*Assets*	Rs.
Capital Fund *(bal. fig.)*	1,69,500	Building	40,000
Creditors for Medicines	8,000	Equipment	21,000
Subscription Received in Advance	1,000	Stock of Medicine	10,000
		Investment (Rs. $\frac{7,000 \times 100}{7}$)	1,00,000
		Outstanding Subscriptions	500
		Cash	7,000
	1,78,500		1,78,500

2. **Creditors for Medicine A/c**

Dr. *Cr.*

	Rs.		Rs.
To Bank A/c	30,000	By Balance b/d	8,000
" Balance c/d	12,000	" Purchases *(bal. fig.)*	34,000
	42,000		42,000

Medicines Consumed = Opening Stock + Purchases – Closing Stock
= Rs. 10,000 + Rs. 34,000 – Rs. 15,000
= Rs. 29,000.

3. **Equipment A/c**

Dr. *Cr.*

	Rs.		Rs.
To Balance b/d	21,000	By Income & Expenditure A/c —Dep. *(bal. fig.)*	6,000
" Bank — Purchases	15,000	" Balance c/d	30,000
	36,000		36,000

4. A Subscriptions Account may also be opened in the following manner :

Subscriptions A/c

Dr. *Cr.*

	Rs.		Rs.
To Outstanding Subscription for 2012	500	By Subscription Received in Advance for 2012	1,000
" Income & Expenditure A/c *(bal. fig.)*	51,000	" Bank A/c	50,000
" Subscription Received in Advance for 2013	500	" Outstanding Subscription for 2012	1,000
	52,000		52,000

Illustration 6

Given below is the Receipts and Payments Account of the Amusement Club for the year ended 31.12.2011:

Receipts		Rs.	*Payments*	Rs.
To Balance b/d			By Salary of Secretary	3,600
	Cash	60	" Honorarium	450
	Bank	3,000	" Wages	2,400

Contd.

		Rs.			Rs.
"	Subscriptions (including Rs. 150 for 2010)	9,000	"	Charities	2,000
"	Sale of old Furniture on 1-1-2011	750	"	Printing & Stationery	300
"	Sale of old Newspapers	50	"	Postage	100
"	Legacies	3,000	"	Rent & Taxes	1,200
"	Interest on Investment (Cost of Investment Rs. 20,000)	1,200	"	Upkeep of Land	500
"	Endowment Fund	10,000	"	Sports Materials	2,500
"	Proceeds of Concerts	800	"	Balance c/d	14,850
"	Advertisement in the Year-book	40			
		27,900			27,900

Current assets and liabilities as on 31.12.2010 and 31.12.2011 are:

	31.12.2010 Rs.	31.12.2011 Rs.
Subscription in Arrears	200	450
Subscription in Advance	300	600
Furniture	2,000	1,080

Depreciation was 10% on the Furniture left after selling a part of it. It was decided that half of Legacies may be capitalised. Prepare Income and Expenditure Account for the year ending 31.12.2011 and a Balance Sheet as on that date.

Solution

In the books of Amusement Club

Dr. **Income and Expenditure Account** *for the year ended 31st December 2011* Cr.

	Expenditure	Rs.	Rs.		*Incomes*	Rs.	Rs.
To	Salary		3,600	By	Subscriptions		8,950[1]
"	Honorarium		450	"	Sale of old Newspaper		50
"	Wages		2,400	"	Legacies	3,000	
"	Charities		2,000		*Less* : $\frac{1}{2}$ Capital	1,500	
"	Printing & Stationery		300				1,500
"	Postage		100	"	Interest on Investment		1,200
"	Rent & Taxes		1,200	"	Proceeds of Concerts		800
"	Upkeep of Land		500	"	Advertisement in the Year-book		40
"	Sports Materials		2,500	"	Deficit—Excess of Expenditure over Income		680
"	Depreciation on : Furniture		120				
	Loss on Sale of Furniture		50[2]				
			13,220				13,220

Balance Sheet *as at 1st January 2011*

Liabilities	Rs.	*Assets*	Rs.
Capital Fund *(bal. fig.)*	24,960	Furniture	2,000
Subscription received in Advance	300	Investment	20,000
		Outstanding Subscription	200
		Cash	60
		Bank	3,000
	25,260		25,260

Workings:

1. **Subscription**

	Rs.
Subscription Received	9,000
Less : For 2010	200
	8,800

2. **Loss on Sale of Furniture**

WDV of Furniture left is Rs. 1,080 which is 90% of cost (Rs. $\frac{1,080 \times 100}{90}$) Rs. 1,200

Add: Outstanding for 2011	450
	9,250
Add: Received in Adv. in 2010 for 2011	300
	9,550
Less: Received in Advance for 2012	600
	8,950

∴ Rs. 2,000 – Rs. 1,200 = Rs. 800 is the cost of Furniture Sold.

Loss on Sale = Cost Price – Sale Price
= Rs. 800 – Rs. 750
= Rs. 50

Balance Sheet *as at 31st December 2011*

Liabilities	Rs.	Rs.	*Assets*	Rs.	Rs.
Capital Fund	24,960		Furniture	2,000	
Less : Deficit	680		*Less* : Sold	800	
		24,280		1,200	
Endowment Fund		10,000	*Less* : Depreciation	120	1,080
Legacies		1,500	Investment		20,000
Subscription Received in Adv.		600	Outstanding Subscription (including Rs. 50 for 2010)		450
			Cash & Bank		14,850
		36,380			36,380

Preparation of Bank Reconciliation Statement for ascertaining Bank Balance as per Pass Book

Sometimes Receipts and Payments Account does not present the Cash and Bank balance (both opening and closing) figure. As it is not possible to prepare the Balance Sheet of the concern without taking the balance at bank, we are to prepare a Bank Reconciliation Statement to find out the opening and closing balance of Cash at Bank in the usual manner to incorporate the receipts and payment based on the Receipts and Payments Account and additional information supplied.

Illustration 7

Following is the summary of bank transactions of a club during the year 2012:

Receipts and Payments Accounts

Dr.	Rs.		*Cr.* Rs.
To Petty Cash in hand	1,500	By Rent	6,000
" Balance as per Pass Book	20,000	" Entertainment	8,000
" Subscriptions	25,000	" Advertisement (for 2011 Rs. 500)	2,000
" Entertainment	19,000	" Capital Expenditure	20,000
" Legacy	8,000	" Upkeep of Grounds	3,000
" Donation for Books	5,000	" Salary	15,000
" General Donation	5,000	" Bank Charges	300
		" Petty Expenses	800
		" Balance as per Pass Book	27,700
		" Petty Cash in hand	700
	83,500		83,500

Additional Information

	On 1.1.2012 Rs.	31.12.2012 Rs.
(i) Unrepresented cheques, being payment of Rent	1,000	50
(ii) Interest or fixed deposit of Rs. 1,00,000 not entered in the Pass Book	—	6,000
(iii) Entry in respect of bank charges was not passed through the Cash Book	—	300
(iv) A member deposited subscription for 2013 direct into bank, not passed through the cash book	—	200
(v) Cheques deposited for subscription but not cleared by the bank	8,000	6,000

You are required to prepare Income and Expenditure account for the year ended 31st December 2012 and a Balance Sheet as on that date.

Solution

In the books of ....

Balance Sheet *as at 1st January 2012*

Liabilities	Rs.	*Assets*	Rs.
Outstanding Advertisement	500	Fixed Deposit	1,00,000
Capital Fund (*bal. fig.*)	1,28,000	Cash at Bank (as per Cash Book)	27,000[1]
		Petty Cash	1,500
	1,28,500		1,28,500

1. Cash at Bank as per Cash Book (as on 1.1.2012) is ascertained as under :

Bank Reconciliation Statement
as at 1st Jan. 2012

		Rs.	Rs.
	Balance as per Pass Book		20,000
Add :	Cheque deposited but not credited (for Subscription)	8,000	8,000
			28,000
Less :	Cheque issued but not presented (for Rent)	1,000	1,000
	Balance as per Cash Book		27,000

Dr. **Income and Expenditure Account** *for the year ended 31st December 2012* *Cr.*

	Expenditures	Rs.	Rs.		*Incomes*	Rs.	Rs.
To	Rent (as per Pass Book)	6,000		By	Subscriptions		
	Add : Outstanding	500			(as per Pass Book,	25,000	
		6,500			*Less :* Collected for last year	8,000	
	Less : For last year	1,000	5,500			17,000	
"	Entertainment		8,000		*Add :* Outstanding	6,000	
"	Advertisement					23,000	
	(Rs. 2,000 – Rs. 500)		1,500		*Less :* Received in Advance	200	
"	Upkeep of Grounds		3,000				22,800
"	Bank Charges		300	"	Entertainment		19,000
"	Salary		15,000	"	General Donation		5,000
"	Petty Expenses		800	"	Interest on Deposits		6,000
"	Surplus—						
	Excess of Income over Expenditure		18,700				
			52,800				52,800

Balance Sheet *as at 31st December 2012*

Liabilities	Rs	Rs.	*Assets*	Rs.	Rs.
Capital Fund	1,28,000		Fixed Deposit		1,00,000
Add : Surplus	18,700	1,46,700	Capital Expenditure		20,000
Donation for Books		5,000	Cash at Bank		39,300[2]
Legacy		8,000	(as per Cash Book)		
Outstanding Bank Charges		300	Petty Cash		700
		1,60,000			1,60,000

2. Cash at Bank (as on 31.12.2012) is ascertained as:

Bank Reconciliation Statement *as at 31st December 2012*

		Rs.	Rs.
	Balance as per Pass Book		27,700
Add :	Cheque deposited but not credited (for Subscription)	6,000	
	Interest on fixed deposit not entered in Pass Book	6,000	

Contd.

	Rs.	Rs.
Bank Charges not entered in Cash Book	300	12,300
		40,000
Less : Cheque issued but not presented (for Rent)	500	
Cheque directly deposited into Bank	200	
		700
Balance as per Cash Book		39,300

Restaurant Trading and Bar Trading

Sometimes some clubs arrange for Restaurant and Bar facilities for members and outsiders. Under the circumstances, Restaurant Trading or Bar Trading Account is opened to ascertain the Restaurant or Bar profit, just like Trading Account which is opened in case of a trading concern. The Restaurant or Bar profit so ascertaine from Restaurant Trading or Bar Trading is transferred to Income and Expenditure Account as we transfer the Gross Profit from Trading Account to Profit and Loss Account in case of Trading concern. In other words, the method of preparing a Restaurant or Bar Trading Account is like the method of preparing a Trading Account.

Preparation of Restaurant Trading and Bar Trading

Illustration 8

The following summary of the Cash Book has been prepared by the treasurer of a club:

	Receipts	Rs.		*Payments*	Rs.
To	Balance b/d	4,740	By	Wages—Outdoor Staff	13,380
"	Subscriptions	29,720	"	Restaurant Purchase	50,400
"	Entrance Fees	3,200	"	Rent—18 months to July 30, 2012	7,500
"	Restaurant Receipts	56,800	"	Rates	2,200
"	Games Competition Receipts	13,640	"	Secretary's Salary	3,120
"	Due to Secretary for Petty Exp.	80	"	Lighting	7,700
			"	Competition Prizes	4,000
			"	Printing & Postage etc.	6,000
			"	Placed in Fixed Deposit	8,000
			"	Balance c/d	5,880
		1,08,180			1,08,180

On April 1, 2011, the club's assets were : Furniture Rs. 48,000, Restaurant stock Rs. 2,600, Stock of prizes Rs. 800, Rs. 5,200 was owing for supplies to the restaurant.

On March 31, 2012, the Restaurant stocks were Rs. 3,000 and prizes in hand were Rs. 500, while the club owed Rs. 5,600 for restaurant supplies.

It was also found that subscriptions unpaid at March 31, 2012, amounted to Rs. 1,000 and that the figure of Rs. 29,720 shown in the Cash Book included Rs. 700 in respect of previous year and Rs. 400 paid in advance for the following year.

Prepare an account showing the Profit or Loss made on the Restaurant and a General Income and Expenditure Account for the year ended 31.3.2012, together with a Balance Sheet as at that date, after writing 10% off the Furniture.

[CU BCom (Hons.)]

Solution

In the books of ....

Dr. **Restaurant Trading Account** *for the year ended 31st March 2012* Cr.

	Particulars		*Amount*		*Particulars*	*Amount*
		Rs.	Rs.			Rs.
To	Opening Stock		2,600	By	Restaurant Receipts	56,800
"	Purchases	50,400		"	Closing Stock	3,000
	Add : Outstanding for 31.3.2012	5,600				
		56,000				
	Less : Outstanding for 1.4.2011	5,200	50,800			
"	Income & Expenditure A/c (G. P. transferred)		6,400			
			59,800			59,800

Balance Sheet *as at 1st April 2011*

Liabilities	Rs.	*Assets*	Rs.
Accumulated Fund *(bal. fig.)*	50,390	Furniture and Equipment	48,000
Owing for supplies to Restaurant	5,200	Restaurant Stock	2,600
Outstanding Rent (Jan. to March 2011)	1,250	Stock of Prize	800
		Outstanding Subscriptions	700
		Cash and Bank	4,740
	56,840		56,840

Dr. **Income and Expenditure Account** *for the year ended 31st March 2012* Cr.

Expenditures	Rs.	*Incomes*	Rs.	Rs.
To Wages	13,380	By Subscriptions : Subscription		29,620[3]
" Rent	5,000[1]	" Games Competition Receipts		13,640
" Rates	2,200	" Restaurant Trading—		
" Lighting, Cleaning, Services	7,700	Gross Profit		6,400
" Competition Prize	4,300[2]			
" Secretary's Salary	3,120			
" Printing, Postage and Sundries	6,000			
" Dep. on Furniture and Equipment & 10%	4,800			
" Surplus—Excess of Income over Expenditure	3,160			
	49,660			49,660

Balance Sheet *as at 31st March 2012*

Liabilities	Rs.	Rs.	*Assets*	Rs.	Rs.
Accumulated Fund :			Furniture and Equipment	48,000	
Balance on 1.4.2011	50,390		*Less* : Depreciation	4,800	43,200
Add : Surplus	3,160	53,550	Restaurant Stock		3,000
Entrance Fees		3,200	Stock of Prize		500
Subscriptions received in Advance		400	Outstanding Subscriptions		1,000
Owing for supplies to Restaurant		5,600	Prepaid Rent		1,250
Outstanding Petty Expenses		80	Fixed Deposit with Bank		8,000
			Cash and Bank		5,880
		62,830			62,830

Workings :

1. **For Rent**

	Rs.
Rent paid	7,500
Less: Outstanding for last year	1,250
	6,250
Less: Prepaid for 3 months (Rs. 7,500 × $\frac{3}{18}$)	1,250
	5,000

2. **Expenditure for Competition Prize**

	Rs.
Opening Stock	800
Add: Purchase	4,000
	4,800
Less: Closing Stock	500
	4,300

3. **Subscription**

Subscription Received	29,720
Less: Outstanding for last year	700
	29,020
Add: Outstanding for 2012	1,000
	30,020
Less: Received in Advance for 2013	400
	29,620

Illustration 9

The Balances from the books of Cosmos Club on 31.1.2013 were extracted as follows:

	Rs.		Rs.
Furniture on 31.3.2013	840	Purchases for Restaurant	10,787
Furniture additions from 1.4.2012 to 31.3.2013	542	Purchases for Bar	8,224
Fixture & Fittings on 31.3.2012	292	Rent and Rates	3,490
Billiards Table and Accessories on 31.3.2012	890	Wages	6,234
China Glass, Cutlery and Linen on 31.3.2012	200	Postage and Telegram Expenses	1,799
Stock in Restaurant on 31.3.2012	357	Electricity Charges	1,758
Bar Stock on 31.3.2012	30	Sundry Expenses	1,349
Restaurant takings	16,168	Cash on hand on 31.3.2013	136
Bar takings	13,050	Cash at Bank on 31.3.2013	920
Billiards and Sundry Receipts	2,566	Bank Debtors	2,833
Subscription from Members	3,150	Sundry Deposits	749
Interest on Deposit	87	Sundry Creditors	1,785
		Capital Fund on 31.3.2012	4,624

You are required to prepare separate Trading Accounts for Restaurant and Bar and the Income & Expenditure Account for the year ended 31.3.2013 together with the Balance Sheet as on that date, after making adjustments for :

(a) Cost of food etc. to staff is estimated at Rs. 5,500 of which Rs. 5,000 is to be credited to Restaurant and Rs. 500 to Bar.

(b) Stocks on 31.3.2013 were Rs. 23 and Rs. 295 for Restaurant and Bar, respectively.

(c) Depreciation shall be provided at 10% for Furniture, Fixtures and Fittings, Billiards Table and Accessories.

(d) Subscriptions due on 31.3.2013 were Rs. 500 and Sundry Expenses Rs. 500 were outstanding on that date.

(e) One-half of China Glass, Cutlery and Linen on 31.3.2012 shall be written-off during the year ended on 31.3.2013.

Solution

In the books of Cosmos Club

Dr. **Bar Trading Account** *for the year ended 31st March 2013* Cr.

Particulars		*Amount*	*Particulars*	*Amount*
		Rs.		Rs.
To Opening Stock		30	By Sales	13,050
" Purchases	8,224		" Closing Stock	295
Less : Food to Staff	500	7,724		
" Income and Expenditure A/c —Profit transferred		5,591		
		13,345		13,345

Dr. **Restaurant Trading Account** *for the year ended 31st March 2013* Cr.

Particulars		*Amount*	*Particulars*	*Amount*
		Rs.		Rs.
To Opening Stock		357	By Sales	16,168
" Purchases	10,787		" Closing Stock	23
Less : Food to Staff	5,000	5,787		
" Income and Expenditure A/c —Profit transferred		10,047		
		16,191		16,191

Dr. **Income and Expenditure Account** *for the year ended 31st March 2013* Cr.

Expenditures	Rs.	Rs.	*Incomes*	Rs.	Rs.
To Wages		6,234	By Subscriptions	3,150	
" Rent and Rates		3,490	*Add* : Outstanding	500	
" Sundry Expenses	1,349				3,650
Add : Outstanding	500	1,849			*Contd.*

		Rs.	Rs.			Rs.	Rs.
To	Postage and Telegram		1,799	By	Billiards and Sundry Receipts		2,566
"	Electricity Charges		1,758	"	Interest on Deposits		87
"	Cost of Food to Staff :			"	Profit from Bar A/c		5,591
	Bar	500		"	Profit from Restaurant A/c		10,047
	Restaurant	5,000	5,500				
"	Depreciation on :						
	Billiards Table	89					
	Furniture	138					
	Fixture & Fittings	29					
	China Glass, Cutlery, Linen	100	356				
"	Surplus—Excess of Income over Expenditure		955				
			21,941				21,941

Balance Sheet *as at 31st March 2013*

Liabilities	Rs.	Rs.	*Assets*	Rs.	Rs.
Capital Fund	4,624		Billiards Table	890	
Add : Surplus	955		*Less :* Depreciation	89	801
		5,579	Furniture	840	
Sundry Creditors		1,785	Additions	542	
Outstanding Expenses		500		1,382	
			Less : Depreciation	138	1,244
			Fixture & Fittings	292	
			Less : Depreciation	29	263
			Glass, Cutlery etc.	200	
			Less : Depreciation	100	100
			Bar Stock		295
			Restaurant Stock		23
			Outstanding Subscription		500
			Sundry Debtors		749
			Bank Deposit		2,833
			Cash at Bank		920
			Cash in hand		136
		7,864			7,864

Bar Trading

Illustration 10

Salt Lake Club makes up its accounts to 31st December each year. On 31.12.2012, the cashier of the club absconded leaving behind no information on cash. An examination of the records showed that the books had not been written-up for a considerable time and it was decided to reconstruct the figures from 1.1.2012.

A summary of the Bank Account for the year showed that :

	Rs.		Rs.
Balance on 1.1.2012	420	Rent and Rates	460
Bank Deposits	42,610	Insurance	40
		Light and Heat	156
		Bar Purchases	35,067
		Telephone	59
		Cash Withdrawn	5,848
		Balance as on 31.12.2012	1,400
	43,030		43,030

The following information is also obtained :

(1) The bar-man places takings in the bank night safe on his way home for crediting to the club account. The duplicate paying-in-slips totalled Rs. 40,610 for the year. The treasurer had no access to bar takings.

(2) The receipt counterfoils for members' subscription totalled Rs. 3,050 for the year.

(3) A summary of expenditure for petty cash and wages revealed : Glasses, Crockery maintenance—
Rs. 1,310; Wages Rs. 2,650; Sundry Expenses Rs. 475.

(4) Outstanding or prepaid accounts were :

	31.12.2011	31.12.2012
Prepaid Rates (Rs.)	26	28
Outstanding Expenses (Rs.)	64	100

The bar stock on 1.1.2012 was Rs. 3,607 and on 31.12.2012 Rs. 2,916. Opening cash with the cashier at the beginning of the year 2012 was Rs. 35 only. Prepare Income and Expenditure Account of the club for the year ended 31st Deember 2012.

Solution

In the books of Salt Lake Club.

Bar Trading Account

Dr. Cr.

Particulars	Amount Rs.	Particulars	Amount Rs.
To Opening Stock	3,607	By Sales	40,610
" Purchases	65,067	" Closing Stock	2,916
" Income and Expenditure A/c —Profit transferred	4,852		
	43,526		43,526

Income and Expenditure Account *for the year ended 31st December 2012*

Dr. Cr.

Expenditures	Rs.	Rs.	Incomes	Rs.	Rs.
To Rent and Rates	460		By Subscriptions		3,050
Less : Prepaid for current year	28		" Bar Trading A/c —Bar Profit		4,852
	432				
Add : Prepaid in last year	26	458			
" Insurance		40			
" Light and Heat		156			
" Wages		2,650			
" Telephone Charges		59			
" Glass and Crockery Maintenance		1,310			
" Sundry Expenses	475				
Less : Outstanding for 2012	64				
	411				
Add : Outstanding for 2012	100	511			
" Defalcation of Cash		2,498[1]			
" Surplus—Excess of Income over Expenditure		220			
		7,902			7,902

Workings :

1. Cash defalcated by Cashier is ascertained as :

Cash A/c

Dr. Cr.

	Rs.		Rs.
To Balance b/d	35	By Glass, Crockery etc.	1,310
" Subscriptions	3,050	" Wages	2,650
" Bank (withdrawn from bank)	5,848	" Sundry Expenses	475
		" Bank (amount not deposited) (42,610 – 40,610)	2,000
		" Defalcation of Cash *(bal. fig.)*	2,498
	8,933		8,933

Miscellaneous

Preparation of Income and Expenditure Account and Balance Sheet

Illustration 11

The following is the Receipts and Payments Account of Sydney Club for the year ended 31st March 2012:

Receipts	Rs.	*Payments*	Rs.
Opening balance :		Salary	1,20,000
Cash	10,000	Creditors	15,20,000
Bank	3,850	Printing and Stationery	70,000
Subscription Receipts	2,02,750	Postage	40,000
Entrance Donation	1,00,000	Telephone and Telex	52,000
Interest Received	58,000	Repairs and Maintenance	48,000
Sale of Asset	8,000	Glass and Table Linen	12,000
Miscellaneous Income	9,000	Crockery and Cutlery	14,000
Receipts at :		Garden Upkeep	8,000
Coffee Room	10,70,000	Membership Fees	4,000
Wines & Spirits	5,10,000	Insurance	5,000
Swimming Pool	80,000	Electricity	28,000
Tennis Court	1,02,000	Closing balance :	
		Cash	8,000
		Bank	2,24,600
	21,53,600		21,53,600

The assets and liabilities as on 1.4.2011 were:

	Rs.		Rs.
Fixed Asset (Net)	5,00,000	Sundry Creditors	1,12,000
Stock	3,80,000	Subscription Received in Advance	15,000
Investment in 12% Govt. Securities	5,00,000	Entrance Donation received pending Membership	1,00,000
Outstanding Subscription	12,000		
Prepaid Insurance	1,000	Gratuity Fund	1,50,000

The following adjustments are to be made while drawing-up the accounts :

(i) Subscription received in advance as on 31.3.2012 was Rs. 18,000,

(ii) Outstanding Subscriptions as on 31.3.2012 was Rs. 7,000.

(iii) Outstanding Expenses are : Salaries Rs. 8,000; Electricity Rs. 15,000.

(iv) 50% of Entrance Donation was to be capitalised. There has been no pending membership as on 31st March 2012.

(v) The cost of assets sold net as on 1.4.2011 was Rs. 10,000.

(vi) Depreciation is to be provided @ 10% on assets.

(vii) A sum of Rs. 20,000 received in October 2011 as entrance donation from an applicant was to be refunded as he has not fulfilled the requisite membership qualification. The refund was made on 3.6.2012.

(viii) Purchases made during the year amounted to Rs. 15,00,000.

(ix) The value of Closing Stock was Rs. 2,10,000.

(x) The club, as a matter of policy, charge-off to Income and Expenditure Account all purchases made on account of crockery, cutlery glass and linen in the year of purchase.

You are required to prepare an Income and Expenditure account for the year ended 31st March 2012, and the Balance Sheet as on 31st March 2012 along with necessary workings.

[CA Foundation]

Solution

In the books of Sydney Club

Income and Expenditure Account *for the year ended 31st March 2012*

Dr. *Cr.*

Expenditures	Rs.	Rs.	*Incomes*	Rs.	Rs.
To Salary	1,20,000		By Subscription		1,94,750[1]
Add : Outstanding	8,000	1,28,000	" Entrance Donation		90,000[2]

Contd.

		Rs.	Rs.			Rs.	Rs.
To	Printing & Stationery		70,000	By	Interest	58,000	
"	Postage		40,000		*Add* : Accrued Interest	2,000	
"	Telephone & Telex		52,000				60,000
"	Repairs & Maintenance		48,000	"	Misc. Income		9,000
"	Glass etc.		12,000	"	Profit from operation		92,000[3]
"	Crockery, Cutlery		14,000	"	Deficit—		
"	Garden Upkeep		8,000		Excess of Expenditure		
"	Membership Fees		4,000		over Income		30,250
"	Insurance	5,000					
"	Paid in Advance last year	1,000	6,000				
"	Electricity	28,000					
	Add : Outstanding	15,000	43,000				
"	Loss on Sale of Assets (Rs. 10,000 – Rs. 8,000)		2,000				
"	Depreciation : @ 10% on Assets (5,00,000 – 10,000)		49,000				
			4,76,000				4,76,000

Balance Sheet *as at 31st March 2012*

Liabilities	Rs.	Rs.	*Assets*	Rs.	Rs.
Capital Fund	10,29,850[4]		Fixed Assets	5,00,000	
Less : Deficit	30,250	9,99,600	*Less* : Sold	10,000	
Entrance Donation		90,000		4,90,000	
Gratuity Fund		1,50,000	*Less* : Depreciation	49,000	
Creditors		92,000[5]			4,41,000
Subscription Received in Advance		18,000	Investment		5,00,000
			Closing Stock		2,10,000
Entrance Donation Refundable		20,000	Accrued Interest		2,000
			Outstanding Subscription		7,000
Outstanding Liabilities :			Cash at Bank		2,24,600
Salary	8,000		Cash in hand		8,000
Electricity	15,000	23,000			
		13,92,600			13,92,600

Workings :

1. ***Subscription Received***

		Rs.
	Subscription Received	2,02,750
Add :	Outstanding	7,000
		2,09,750
Less :	Outstanding for last year	12,000
		1,97,750
Less :	Received in Advance	18,000
		1,79,750
Add :	Received in Advance last year	15,000
		1,94,750

2. ***Entrance Donation Received***

		Rs.
	Entrance Donation	1,00,000
Less :	Received in Advance	1,00,000
		2,00,000
Less :	Transfer for Ineligible members	20,000
		1,80,000
Less :	Capital @ 50%	90,000
		90,000

3. ***Profit from operation***

	Rs.	Rs.
Receipts from operation :		
Coffee Room	10,70,000	
Wine & Spirits	5,10,000	

Contd.

		Rs.	Rs.
	Swimming Pool	80,000	
	Tennis Court	1,02,000	17,62,000
Less :	Expenses :		
	Opening Stock	3,80,000	
Add :	Purchases	15,00,000	
		18,80,000	
Less :	Closing Stock	2,10,000	16,70,000
			92,000

4. **Balance Sheet** *as at 1st April 2011*

Liabilities	Rs.	*Assets*	Rs.
Entrance Donation		Fixed Asset	5,00,000
Received in Advance	1,00,000	Investment	5,00,000
Gratuity Fund	1,50,000	Stock	3,80,000
Creditors	1,12,000	Prepaid Expense	1,000
Subscription Received in Advance	15,000	Outstanding Subscription	12,000
Capital Fund *(bal. fig.)*	10,29,850	Bank	3,850
		Cash	10,000
	14,06,850		14,06,850

5. **Creditors A/c**

Dr. *Cr.*

	Rs.		Rs.
To Bank	15,20,000	By Balance b/d	1,12,000
" Balance c/d	92,000	" Purchases	15,00,000
	16,12,000		16,12,000

Illustration 12

The Sportswriters' Club gives the following Receipts and Payments A/c for the year ended 31.3.2012 :

Receipts and Payments Account

Receipts	Rs.	*Payments*	Rs.
To Balance (b/d)	4,820	By Salaries	12,000
" Subscription	28,600	" Rent and Electricity	7,220
" Miscellaneous Income	700	" Library Books	1,000
" Interest on Fixed Deposit	2,000	" Magazines and Newspapers	2,172
		" Sundry Expenses	10,278
		" Sports Equipment	1,000
		" Balance (c/d)	2,450
	36,120		36,120

Figures of other assets and liabilities are:

	As at March 31 2011 Rs.	2012 Rs.
Salaries Outstanding	710	170
Outstanding Rent and Electricity	864	973
Outstanding for Magazines and Newspapers	226	340
Fixed Deposit (10%) with Bank	20,000	20,000
Interest Accrued thereon	500	500
Subscriptions Receivable	1,263	1,575
Prepaid Expenses	417	620
Furniture	9,600	
Sports Equipment	7,200	
Library Books	5,000	

The closing values of Furniture and Sports Equipment are to be determined after charging depreciation @ 10% and 20% p.a., respectively, inclusive of the additions, if any, during the year. The Club's library books are valued at the end of every year and the value at the end of March 31, 2012 was Rs. 5,250.

From the above information you are required to prepare:

(a) The Club's Opening Balance Sheet as at March 31, 2011.

(b) The Club's Income and Expenditure A/c for the year ended on that date; and

(c) The Club's Closing Balance Sheet as at March 31, 2012.

Solution

In the books of Sportswriters' Club

Balance Sheet *as at 31st March 2011*

Liabilities	Rs.	*Assets*	Rs.
Outstanding Expenses :		Furniture	9,600
Salaries	710	Sports Equipment	7,200
Rent & Electricity	864	Library Books	5,000
Magazines & Newspapers	226	Cash in hand and at Bank	4,820
Accumulated Fund	47,000	Fixed Deposit	20,000
(bal. fig.)		Interest accrued on Fixed Deposit	500
		Subscription Receivable	1,263
		Prepaid Expenses	417
	48,800		48,800

Dr. **Income and Expenditure Account** *for the year ended 31st March 2012* Cr.

Expenditures	*Amount* Rs.	*Incomes*	*Amount* Rs.
To Salaries	11,460[1]	By Subscription earned	28,912[5]
" Rent & Electricity	7,329[2]	" Interest on Fixed Deposit	2,000[6]
" Magazines & Newspapers	2,286[3]	" Miscellaneous Income	700
Sundry Expenses	10,075[4]	" Deficit — Excess of	
" Library Books (written-off)	750	Expenditure over Income	2,888
" Depreciation :			
(i) Furniture	960		
(ii) Sports Equipment	1,640		
	34,500		34,500

Balance Sheet *as at 31st March 2012*

Liabilities	Rs.	*Amount* Rs.	*Assets*	Rs.	*Amount* Rs.
Accumulated Fund	47,000		Furniture	9,600	
Less : Excess of Expenditure			*Less* : Depreciation	960	8,640
over Incomes	2,888		Sports Equipment	7,200	
		44,112	*Less* : Depreciation	1,640	
Outstanding Expenses :				5,560	
Salary	170		*Add* : Purchases	1,000	6,560
Rent & Electricity	973		Library Books	5,000	
Magazines & Newspapers	340		*Add* : Purchases	1,000	
		1,483		6,000	
			Less : Written-off	750	5,250
			Cash in hand and at Bank		2,450
			Fixed Deposit		20,000
			Interest accrued on Fixed Deposit		500
			Subscription Receivable		1,575
			Prepaid Expenses		620
		45,595			45,595

Workings:

1. Payment for Salaries

	Rs.
Salaries Paid	12,000
Add: Outstanding for 2012	170
	12,170
Less: Outstanding for 2011	710
	11,460

2. Payment for Rent and Electricity

	Rs.
Rent and Electricity Paid	7,220
Add: Outstanding for 2012	973
	8,193
Less: Outstanding for 2011	864
	7,329

3. Payment for Magazine and Newspaper

Amount Paid	2,172
Add: Outstanding for 2012	340
	2,512
Less : Outstanding for 2011	226
	2,286

4. Payment for Sundry Expenses

Sundry Expenses Paid	10,278
Less: Prepaid in 2012	620
	9,658
Add : Prepaid in 2011 for 2012	417
	10,075

5. Subscription to be Received

Subscription Received	28,600
Add: Outstanding for 2012	1,575
	30,175
Less: Outstanding for 2011	1,263
	28,912

6. Interest on Fixed Deposit

	Rs.
Interest Received	2,000
Add : Accrued for 2012	500
	2,500
Less : Accrued for 2011	500
	2,000

Illustration 13

'Citizens Club' was registered in a city and the accountant prepared the following Receipts and Payments Account for the year ended Oct. 31, 2012 and showed a deficit of Rs. 14,520 :

	Rs.		Rs.
Receipts :		Payments :	
Subscriptions	62,130	Premises	30,000
Fare Receipts	7,200	Honorarium to Secretary	12,000
Variety Show Receipts (net)	12,810	Rent	2,400
Interest	690	Rates and Taxes	3,780
Bar Collection	22,350	Printing and Stationery	1,410
Cash spent more	1,000	Sundry Expenses	5,350
	1,06,180	Wages	2,520
Deficit	14,520	Fair Expenses	7,170
		Bar Purchase — Payments	17,310
		Repairs	960
		New Car (*less* : proceeds of old Car Rs. 9,000)	37,800
	1,20,700		1,20,700

The additional information should be obtained :

	31.10.2011 Rs.	31.10.2012 Rs.
Cash in hand	450	—
Bank balance as per Pass Book	24,690	10,440
Cheques issued not presented for Sundry Expenses	270	90
Subscriptions due	3,600	2,940
Premises at Cost	87,000	1,17,000
Accumulated dep. on Premises	56,400	—
Car at Cost	36,570	46,800
Accumulated dep. on Car	30,870	—
Bar Stock	2,130	2,610
Creditors for Bar Purchases	1,770	1,770

Cash overspent represents honorarium to Secretary not withdrawn due to Cash deficit. His annual honorarium is Rs. 12,000. Depreciation on premises and car is to be provided at 5% and 20% on written-down value.

You are required to prepare the correct Receipts and Payments Account, Income and Expenditure Account and Balance Sheet as at Oct. 31, 2012.

[CA Foundation & ICWA]

Solution

In the books of Citizens Club

Receipts and Payments Account *for the year ended 31st October 2012*

Dr. Receipts	Rs.	Cr. Payments	Rs.
To Balance b/d	450	By Premises	30,000
" Bank (24,690 – 270)	24,420	" Honorarium to Secretary	11,000
" Subscription	62,130	" Rent	2,400
" Fair Receipts	7,200	" Rates and Taxes	3,780
" Variety Show Receipts	12,810	" Printing and Stationery	1,410
" Interest	690	" Sundry Expenses	5,350
" Bar Receipts	22,350	" Wages	2,520
		" Fair Expenses	7,170
		" Bar Purchases	17,310[1]
		" Repairs	960
		" New Car	37,800
		" Bank Balance (10,440 – 90)	10,350
	1,30,050		1,30,050

Income and Expenditure Account *for the year ended 31st October 2012*

Dr. Expenditures	Rs.	Rs.	Cr. Incomes	Rs.
To Honorarium to Secretary	11,000		By Subscriptions	61,470[4]
Add : Outstanding	1,000	12,000	" Fair Receipts	7,200
" Rent		2,400	" Variety Show Receipts	12,810
" Rates and Taxes		3,780	" Interest	690
" Printing and Stationery		1,410	" Profit on Sale of old Car	3,300[2]
" Sundry Expenses		5,350	" Bar Trading A/c	
" Wages		2,520	—Gross Profit	6,000
" Fair Expenses		7,170		
" Repairs		960		
" Depreciation on :				
Premises @ 5% on 60,600		3,030		
Car @ 20% on 46,800		9,360		
" Surplus—Excess of Income over Expenditure		43,490		
		91,470		91,470

Balance Sheet *as at 31st October 2012*

Liabilities	Rs.	Rs.	Assets	Rs.	Rs.
Capital Fund as on 1.11.2111	65,130[3]		Premises at Cost	1,17,000	
Add : Surplus	43,490		*Less* : Depreciation	59,430	57,570
		1,08,620	Car at Cost	46,800	
Creditors (for bar purchase)		1,290	*Less* : Depreciation	9,360	37,440
Secretary's Honorarium outstanding		1,000	Bar Stock		2,610
			Outstanding Subscription		2,940
			Cash at Bank (Rs. 10,400 – Rs. 90)		10,350
		1,10,910			1,10,910

Bar Trading Account

Dr. Particulars	Amount Rs.	Amount Rs.	Cr. Particulars	Amount Rs.
To Opening Stock		2,130	By Bar Receipts	22,350
" Bar Purchase	17,310[1]		" Closing Stock	2,610
Add: Creditors for 2012	1,290			
	18,600			

Contd.

	Rs.	Rs.		Rs.
Less : Creditors in 2011	1,770	16,830		
" Income and Expenditure A/c —Profit		6,000		
		24,960		24,960

Workings:

1. **Creditors for Bar Purchase A/c**

Dr. *Cr.*

	Rs.		Rs.
To Bank A/c	17,310	By Balance b/d	1,770
" Balance c/d	1,770	" Purchase (bal. fig.)	17,310
	19,080		19,080

2. **Profit on Sale of Old Car**

	Rs.
WDV of Old Car :	
Cost Price	36,570
Less: Accumulated Dep.	30,870
WDV	5,700
Less: Sold for	9,000
Profit on Sale	3,300

3. **Balance Sheet** *as at 1.1.2011*

Liabilities	Rs.	*Assets*	Rs.
Accumullated Dep. :		Premises	87,000
On Premises	56,400	Car	36,570
On Car	30,870		
Credit for Bar Purchase	1,770	Bank Stock	2,130
		Outstanding Sub.	3,600
Capital Fund *(bal. fig.)*	65,130	Cash at Bank ((24,690 – 270)	24,420
		Cash in hand	450
	1,54,170		1,54,170

4. **Subscription Received for 2012**

	Rs.
Subscription Received	62,130
Add: Outstanding Subscription for 2012	2,940
	65,070
Less: Outstanding for 2011	3,600
	61,470

A Comprehensive Problem

Illustration 14

On 31st March 2009 Writers Club, a cultural association, had the following assets and liabilities:

Dr. *Bar Trading Account* *Cr.*

Particulars	*Amount* Rs.	*Particulars*	*Amount* Rs.
Trust Fund	5,00,000	Cash	3,000
Accumulated Surplus in Income and Expenditure A/c	1,05,000	Canara Bank: Savings A/c	7,000
Membership Fee Received in Advance for 2009-10	10,000	Fixed Deposit	2,00,000
Outstanding Expenses	10,000	Investments in : Government Securities	3,00,000
		Fixed Assets	95,000
		Membership Fee receivable	15,000
		Prepaid Expenses	5,000
	6,25,000		6,25,000

The following is the Receipts and Payments Account for the year ended 31st March 2010:

Receipts		Rs.	*Payments*		Rs.
Opening Balance:			Administrative Expenses		1,25,000
Cash	3,000		Programme expenses including cost		
Savings with Canara Bank	7,000	10,000	of printing souvenir		2,75,000
Membership Fee received			Fixed Deposits with Canara Bank		1,25,000
up to 31.3.2009	14,000		Fixed Assets purchased		80,000
for 2009 – 2010	1,30,000		Investments in ICICI Bonds		3,00,000
for 2010 – 2011	16,000	1,80,000	Closing Balance:		
Sale of tickets—programme		25,000	Cash	2,700	
Advertisements in programme			Saving with Canara Bank	3,000	7,700

Contd.

		Rs.			Rs.
Souvenir		5,00,000			
Fixed Deposits with Canara Bank		75,000			
Interest on Bank A/c:					
Savings	700				
Fixed Deposit	22,000	22,700			
Amount received on maturity of Government security inclusive of interest Rs. 8,000 (Cost of 80,000)		1,00,000			
		9,12,700			9,12,700

The club informs you that:

(i) Membership fee due for 2009-2010 is Rs. 25,000; it includes Rs. 1,000 due from a member who has not yet paid also for 2008-2009; provision for irrecoverable membership is to be made in respect of this member.

(ii) Income receivable on 31.3.2010 on ICICI bond is Rs. 30,000 and on government securities is Rs. 24,000.

(iii) Prepaid expenses on 31.3.2010 amount to Rs. 7,000.

(iv) Outstanding expenses on 31.3.2000 amount to Rs. 8,000.

(v) Depreciation provision is to be Rs. 12,500.

(vi) Programme is an annual feature.

The club asks you to prepare

(a) Income and expenditure account for the year ended 31st March 2010.

(b) Balance Sheet as at 31st March 2010.

Solution

In the books of Writer Club

Dr. **Income and Expenditure Account** *for the year ended 31st March 2010* *Cr.*

Expenditures	Rs.	Rs.	*Incomes*	Rs.	Rs.
To Expenses	1,25,000		By Membership Fees	1,50,000	
Add : Prepaid (Opening)	5,000		" *Add:* Received in		
" *Add:* Outstanding	8,000		2008-09	10,000	
	1,38,000		*Add* : Outstanding for		
Less: Outstanding (Op.)	10,000		the Current Year	25,000	1,85,000
	1,28,000		" Interest:		
Less: Prepaid	7,000		Savings	700	
		1,21,000	Fixed Deposit	22,000	22,700
" Prov. for Doubtful			" Interest on Securities		
Members 2008-09			Govt. Received	8,000	
2009 – 10 (Rs. 1,000 +			*Add:* Accrued	24,000	
Rs. 1,000)		2,000	*Add:* ICICI Bond	30,000	62,000
" Depreciation		12,500	" Income from Programme		
" Programme Expenses		2,75,000	Advertisement	5,00,000	
" Surplus—			Sale of ticket	25,000	5,25,000
Excess of Income			" Profit on Sale of		
Over Expenditure		3,96,200	Govt. Securities		
			(Rs. 1,00,000 – Rs. 8,000		
			– Rs. 80,000)		12,000
		8,06,700			8,06,700

Balance Sheet *as at 31st March 2010*

Liabilities	Rs.	Rs.	*Assets*	Rs.	Rs.
Capital Fund	5,00,000		Fixed Assets	95,000	
Add : Sirplus from last year	1,05,000		Additions	80,000	
Add: Surplus from				1,75,000	
Current Year	3,96,200		*Less* : Depreciation	12,500	1,62,500
Gratuity Fund		10,01,200	Investment		
Fees Received in Advance		16,000	Govt. Securities	3,00,000	
Outstanding Expenses		8,000	*Less:* Sold	80,000	2,20,000
			ICICI Bond		3,00,000
			Accrued Interest—		
			Govt. Securities	24,000	
			ICICI Bonds	30,000	54,000
			Outstanding Subscription		
			2008-09	1,000	
			2009-10	25,000	
				26,000	
			Less : Provision for Doubtful Debts	2,000	24,000
			Prepaid Expenses		7,000
			Cash at Bank—		
			Savings	5,000	
			Fixed Deposit	2,00,000	
			Additions	1,25,000	
				3,30,000	
			Less: Matured	75,000	2,55,000
			Cash in hand		2,700
		10,25,200			10,25,200

Illustration 15

The following is the Receipts and Payments Account of Apollo Club in respect of the year ended 31st March 2013:

Dr. **Receipts and Payments Account** *for the year ended 31st March 2013* *Cr.*

		Receipts		Rs.			*Payments*	Rs.
1.4.2012	To	Balance b/d			31.3.2013	By	Salaries	3,000
		Cash in hand		2,000	"	"	Stationery	1,000
31.3.2013	"	Subscriptions :	Rs.		"	"	Rates & Taxes	300
		2011-12	3,000		"	"	Telephone Charges	1,500
		2012-13	4,000		"	"	8% Securities at par	5,000
		2013-14	1,000		"	"	Sundry Expenses	200
				8,000	"		Balance c/d	
"	"	Profit on Sports		3,000	"	"	Cash in hand	3,000
"	"	Interest on 8% Securities		1,000				
				14,000				14,000

The following additional facts are ascertained:

(a) There are 500 members, each paying an annual subscription of Rs. 10. Rs. 3,500 being in arrears for 2011-12 at the beginning of 2012-13. During 2011-12, subscriptions were paid in advance by 30 members for 2012-13.

(b) Stock of stationery at 31st March 2012 was Rs. 400 and at 31st March 2013 Rs. 500.

(c) At 31st March 2013, the Rates and Taxes were prepaid to the following 31st January, the yearly charge being Rs. 300.

(d) A quarter's charge for telephone is outstanding, the amount accrued being Rs. 300. The charges for each quarter is same both for 2011-12 and 2012-13.

(e) Sundry expense accruing at 31st March 2012 were Rs. 50 and at 31st March 2013 Rs. 60.

(f) At 31st March 2012, Building stood in the books at Rs. 30,000 and it is required to write-off depreciation at 10% p.a.

(g) Value of 8% Securities at 31st March 2012 was Rs. 15,000 which was purchased at that date at par, additional securities worth Rs. 5,000 are purchased on 31st March 2013.

You are required to prepare:

(i) An Income and Expenditure Account for the year ended 31st March 2013, and

(ii) A Balance Sheet as at that date.

Solution

In the Books of Apollo Club
Balance Sheet *as at 31st March 2012*

Liabilities	Rs.	*Assets*	Rs.
Capital Fund *(bal. fig.)*	50,200	Building	30,000
Subscriptions received in		8% Securities	15,000
advance (30 × Rs. 10)	300	Outstanding Subscription	3,500
Outstanding Telephone Charges	600[3]	Stock of Stationery	400
Outstanding Expenses	50	Prepaid Rates and Taxes $\left(300 \times \frac{10}{12}\right)$	250
		Cash in hand	2,000
	51,150		51,150

Dr. **Income and Expenditure Account** *for the year ended 31st March 2013* Cr.

	Expenditures	Rs.	Rs.		*Incomes*	Rs.	Rs.
To	Salaries		3,000	By	Subscriptions (500 × Rs. 10)		5,000
"	Stationery :		900[1]	"	Interest on Securities	1,000	
"	Rates and Taxes		300[2]		(@ 8% on Rs. 15,000)		
"	Telephone Charges (300 × 4)		1,200[3]		*Add* : Accrued Interest	200	1,200
	(1,500 + 300 – 1,200) = Rs. 600 outstanding for the previous year			"	Profits on Sports		3,000
"	Sundry Expenses		210[4]				
"	Depreciation on Building (10% on Rs. 30,000)		3,000				
"	Surplus — Excess of Income over Expenditure		590				
			9,200				9,200

Balance Sheet *as at 31st March 2013*

Liabilities	Rs.	Rs.	*Assets*	Rs.	Rs.
Capital Fund :			Building	30,000	
Balance as on 1.4.2012	50,200		*Less* : Depreciation	3,000	27,000
Add : Surplus	590		8% Securities	15,000	
		50,790	Additions	5,000	
Subscriptions received in Adv.		1,000		20,000	
Outstanding Telephone Charges		300	*Add* : Accrued Interest	200	20,200
Outstanding Expenses		60	Stock of Stationery		500
			Prepaid Rates and Taxes		250[5]
			Outstanding Subscriptions :		
			for 2011–12	500	
			2012–13 (470 × Rs.10 – 4,000)	700	1,200
			Cash in hand		3,000
		52,150			52,150

Workings:

1. **Stationery Consumed**

	Rs.
Opening Stock	400
Add: Purchases	1,000
	1,400
Less: Closing Stock	500
	900

2. **Rent and Taxes**

	Rs.
Rent and Taxes paid	300
Add: From previous year	250
	550
Less: Prepaid	250
	300

3. **Telephone Charges**

Annual telephone charges (Rs. 300 × 4)	1,200

Outstanding Telephone Charges for the Previous Year

Telephone Charges Paid	1,500
Add: Outstanding for 2012	300
	1,800
Less: Annual Charges	1,200
	600

4. **Sundry Expenses**

	Rs.
Add: Sundry Expenses Paid	200
Add: Outstanding for Current Year	60
	260
Less: Outstanding for Previous Year	50
	210

5. **Prepaid Rates and Taxes**

	Rs.
Rates and Tax paid up to the following January	300
i.e., 10 months (1.4.2012 to 31.1.2013) $= \text{Rs. } 300 \times \frac{10}{12} =$	230

Annual Charges being Rs. 300

C. Preparation of Opening and Closing Balance Sheet from a given Income and Expenditure Account and a Receipts and Payments Account

In order to prepare the opening Balance Sheet, the following steps should be followed :

(i) Take all the opening assets and liabilities which are given under the Income and Expenditure Account and the Receipts and Payments Account as adjustments, one by one, i.e., assets on the assets side of the opening Balance Sheet and liabilities on the liabilities side of the Balance Sheet.

(ii) Take the opening balance of Cash and Bank account from the Receipts and Payments Account which are represented by "To, Balance b/d".

(iii) The difference between the assets side of the Balance Sheet and the liabilities side represents opening capital or Capital Fund.

And,

In order to prepare the closing Balance Sheet, the following steps should be followed :

(i) Take all the opening fixed assets (if not sold/discarded/lost, etc.) with additions, if any (which we get from Receipts and Payments Accounts) after charging depreciation, if any, in the assets side of the Balance Sheet.

(ii) Take the closing liabilities including Capital Fund (which we get from the opening Balance Sheet) and other funds such as Donation, Entrance Fees etc., including all other current liabilities and outstanding expenses.

(iii) Compare each and every individual item of Income and Expenditure Account with the items shown by the Receipts and Payments Account for the same. For example, if Salary Account is shown by the Income and Expenditure Account as Rs. 1,000, and, if the same account is shown by the Receipts and Payments Account, as only Rs. 750, it means Rs. 250 remains outstanding which must be shown in the liability side of the closing Balance Sheet. Income and Expenditure Account takes only the revenue items for the current year only.

Consider the following :

Dr. **Income and Expenditure Account** *for the year ended 31st December 2008* Cr.

	Rs.		Rs.
To Salary A/c	1,000		

Dr. **Receipts and Payments A/c** *for the year ended 31st December 2008* Cr.

	Rs.		Rs.
		By Salary A/c	750

Balance Sheet (Closing) *as at 31st December 2008*

Liabilities	Rs.	*Assets*	Rs.
Outstanding Salary	250		

Again, if Receipts and Payments Account shows that the Salary paid is Rs. 1,200, it reveals that Rs. 200 has been paid in advance which will be shown in the assets side of the closing Balance Sheet under the head 'Prepaid Salary'. In the opposite case, i.e., in case of an income, it will be reversed. For example, if Interest Account is shown by the Income and as Expenditure Account as Rs. 1,000, and, if the same account is shown by the Receipts and Payments Account only Rs. 800, it indicates Rs. 200 is accrued which is shown in the assets side of the closing Balance Sheet. Consider the following :

Dr. **Income and Expenditure Account** *for the year ended 31st December 2008* Cr.

	Rs.		Rs.
		By Interest A/c	1,000

Dr. **Receipts and Payments A/c** *for the year ended 31st December 2008* Cr.

	Rs.		Rs.
To Interest A/c	800		

Balance Sheet *as at 31st December 2008*

Liabilities	Rs.	*Assets*	Rs.
		Accrued Interest	200

Again, if Receipts and Payments Account shows that the Interest Received amounts to Rs. 1,500, it reveals that Rs. 500 (i.e., Rs. 1,500 – Rs. 1,000) has been received as advance interest—which must be shown in the liability side of the closing Balance Sheet.

Moreover, there are certain items which are also to be adjusted, e.g., Depreciation of Assets, etc.

Illustration 16

The following particulars relate to Fast Sports Club :

Dr. **Income and Expenditure Account** *for the year ended 31st Dec. 2012* Cr.

	Rs.		Rs.
To Salaries	6,000	By Admission Fees	15,000
" Printing & Stationery	2,500	" Subscriptions	25,000
" Advertising	1,000	" Rent Receipts	4,800
" Insurance Charges	900		
" Electricity	500		
" Dep. on Sports Equipment	12,000		
" Surplus	21,900		
	44,800		44,800

Dr. **Receipts and Payments Account** *for the year ended 31st Dec. 2012* Cr.

		Rs.		Rs.
To Balance		5,000	By Salary (including advance)	7,500
" Admission fee			" Printing & Stationery	2,500
2011	2,500		" Advertising	1,000
2012	13,500	16,000	" Insurance	
" Subscription			(part for next year)	1,200
2011	1,000		" Electricity	500
2012	23,000		" Fixed Asset Purchased	20,000
2013	2,000	26,000	" Balance	17,900
" Rent		3,600		
		50,600		50,600

On 1.1.2012 th e club had the following assets : Land and Building Rs. 60,000; Sports Equipment Rs. 30,00; Furniture Rs. 4,500. Prepare Opening and Closing Balance Sheet.

Solution

In the books of Fast Sports Club
Balance Sheet *as at 31st Dec. 2011*

Liabilities	Rs.	*Assets*	Rs.
Capital Fund (*bal. fig.*)	1,06,600	Land and Building	60,000
		Sports Equipment	30,000
		Furniture	4,500
		Rent Receivable	3,600
		Adm. Fees Receivable	2,500
		Outstanding Subs.	1,000
		Cash and Bank	5,000
	1,06,600		1,06,600

Balance Sheet *as at 31st Dec. 2012*

Liabilities		Rs.	*Assets*		Rs.
Capital Fund	1,06,600		Land and Building		60,000
Add: Surplus	21,900		Sports Equipment	30,000	
		1,28,500	*Less:* Deprecation	12,000	18,000
Subscription Received in Adv.		2,000	Furniture		4,500
			Fixed Assets (other)		20,000
			Prepaid Insurance		300
			Prepaid Salary		1,500
			Rent Receivable		4,800
			Outstanding Suns.		2,000
			Outstanding Adm. Fee		1,500
			Cash and Bank		17,900
		1,30,500			1,30,500

Illustration 17

Chanditala Adult Education Society submits to you the following Receipts & Payments Account and Income & Expenditure Account for the year ended 31st March 2012 :

Receipts & Payments Account (2011-12)

Dr.		Rs.	Rs.		Cr. Rs.
To Balance b/d			450	By Printing Charges	75
" Interest :	2010-11	100		" Advertisement	141
	2011-12	150	250	" Salary to Staff (including Payment for 2010-11)	1,300
" Tuition Fees :	2011-12	1,000			
	2011-13	100	1,100	" Rent	520
" Entrance Fees :	2011-12		420	" Miscellaneous Expenses	110
" Membership Fees:				" Furniture Purchased	670
2010-11		300		" Balance c/d	1,374
2011-12		1,150			
2012-13		390			
			1,840		
" Miscellaneous Income			130		
			4,190		4,190

Income & Expenditure Account (2011-12)

Dr.	Rs.		Cr. Rs.
To Printing Charges	80	By Tuition Fees	1,100
" Advertisement	150	" Membership Fees	1,150
" Rent	600	" Miscellaneous Income	130
" Salary to Staff	1,200	" Interest	60
" Miscellaneous Expenses	110		
" Excess of Income over Expend.	400		
	2,540		2,540

You are asked to prepare the Balance Sheet of the Society as on 31st March 2011 and 31st March 2012.

Additional information

The Society has the following assets on 31st March 2011 :

Investments Rs. 4,000; Furniture Rs. 2,000: Liabrary Books Rs. 1,500.

[CU BCom (Hons.)]

Solution

In the books of Chanditala Adult Education Society

Balance Sheet *as at 31st March 2011*

Liabilities	Rs.	*Assets*	Rs.
Outstanding Salaries	100[1]	Furniture	2,000
Capital Fund (bal. fig.)	8,250	Investment	4,000
		Library Books	1,500
		Accrued Interest	100[3]
		Membership Fees Receivable	300[2]
		Cash	450
	8,350		8,350

Balance Sheet *as at 31st March 2012*

Liabilities	*Amount* Rs.	*Amount* Rs.	*Assets*	*Amount* Rs.	*Amount* Rs.
Capital Fund	8,250		Furniture	2,000	
Add: Surplus	400		Additions	670	
Add: Capitalisation of					2,670
Entrance Fees	420	9,070	Library Books		1,500
Incomes Received in Advance			Accrued Interest		
Tuition Fees	100		(Rs. 160 – Rs. 150)		10
Membership Fees	390	490	Tuition fees Receivable		
Outstanding Liabilities			(Rs. 1,100 – Rs. 1,000)		100
Printing (Rs. 80 – Rs. 75)	5		Cash		1,374
Rent (Rs. 600 – Rs. 520)	80		Investments		4,000
Advt. (Rs. 150 – Rs. 141)	9	94			
		9,654			9,654

Workings :

1. **Outstanding Salary**

	Rs.
Payments (including 2010 – 11)	1,300
Less: Payment as per Inc. & Exp. A/c	1,200
	100

2. **Membership Fees Receivable**
   Membership Fees for 2010-11 received in 2011-12
   So, amount for 2011-12 still receivable at the same rate i.e., Rs. 300.

3. **Accrued Interest**
   Same as Note. 2. i.e.,
   Interest Rs. 100 of 2010-11 received in in 2011-12, So amount for 2011-12 in still due at the same rate i.e., Rs. 100

Illustration 18

From the following accounts taken from the books of S. S. Hospital for the year ended 31st December 2012, you are required to prepare its opening i.e., as at 1st January 2012, and its closing i.e., as at 31st December 2012, Balance Sheets :

Dr. **Receipts and Payments Account** *Cr.*

	Receipts	Rs.		*Payments*	Rs.
To	Balance		By	Furniture Purchased	1,000
"	Cash	600	"	Investments Purchased	2,000
"	Bank	7,000	"	Surgery and Dispensary	1,500
"	Govt. Securities	1,80,000	"	Diet Expenses	2,500
"	Receipts :		"	Rent and Taxes	2,400
	Subscriptions	30,000	"	Insurance	500
	Donation	6,000	"	Office Expenses	1,200
	Interest	10,000	"	Salary	24,000
	Miscellaneous	500	"	Miscellaneous Expenses	200
			"	Closing balances :	
				Cash	1,800
				Bank	17,000
				Govt. Securities	1,80,000
		2,34,100			2,34,100

Dr. Income and Expenditure Account *for the year ended 31st December 2012* **Cr.**

Expenditures	Rs.	Rs.	Incomes	Rs.	Rs.
To Salary Paid	24,000		By Subscription Receipts	30,000	
Less : For 2011	1,500		*Add :* Outstanding	8,000	
	22,500			38,000	
Add : Outstanding	1,000	23,500	*Less :* For 2011	10,000	
" Diet Expenses		2,500			28,000
" Surgery & Dispensary		1,500	" Donation		6,000
" Rent and Taxes :			" Interest	10,000	
Paid	2,400		*Less :* For 2011	2,500	
Less : Paid for 2011	200			7,500	
	2,200		*Add :* Outstanding	2,500	
Add : Outstanding	250	2,450			10,000
" Insurance	500		" Miscellaneous Receipts		500
Less : Prepaid	100	400			
" Office Expenses		1,200			
" Misc. Expenses		200			
" Depreciation on :					
Building @ $2\frac{1}{2}$%		5,000			
Furniture @ 10%		400			
Investment @ 20%		1,200			
" Surplus —Excess of Income over Expenditure		6,150			
		44,500			44,500

Depreciation on all assets has been worked out for the full year. Value of Building is exclusive of the cost of land of the hospital amounting to Rs. 50,000. Govt. securities of the face value of Rs. 2,00,000 (cost Rs. 1,80,000) represent investment of the endowment fund of the hospital.

Solution

In the books of S. S. Hospital
Balance Sheet *as at 1st January 2012*

Liabilities	Rs.	Assets	Rs.
Endowment Fund	1,80,000	Land	50,000
Outstanding Expenses		Building	2,00,000
Salaries	1,500	Furniture (Rs. 4,000 – Rs. 1,000)	3,000
Rent	200	Investments (Rs. 6,000 – Rs. 2,000)	4,000
Capital Fund *(bal. fig.)*	2,75,400	Govt. Securities	1,80,000
		Accrued Interest	2,500
		Outstanding Subscription	10,000
		Cash at Bank	7,000
		Cash in hand	600
	4,57,100		4,57,100

Balance Sheet *as at 31st December 2012*

Liabilities	Rs.	Rs.	Assets	Rs.	Rs.
Capital Fund	2,75,400		Land & Building		50,000
Add : Surplus	6,150	2,81,550	Building	2,00,000	
Endowment Fund		1,80,000	*Less :* Depreciation	5,000	1,95,000
Outstanding Liabilities :			Furniture	3,000	
Salary	1,000		Additions	1,000	
Rent	250	1,250		4,000	
			Less : Depreciation	400	3,600

Contd.

	Rs.	Rs.		Rs.	Rs.
			Investments	4,000	
			Additions	2,000	
				6,000	
			Less : Depreciation	1,200	4,800
			Govt. Securities		1,80,000
			Accrued Interest		2,500
			Outstanding Subscription		8,000
			Prepaid Insurance		100
			Cash at Bank		17,000
			Cash in hand		1,800
		4,62,800			4,62,800

Note : Assume Furniture and Investments were purchased at the beginning of the year.

Illustration 19

The following are the items of Receipts and Payments of the Bengal Club as summarised from the books of accounts maintained by the Secretary :

Receipts		Rs.	*Payments*	Rs.
Opening Balance	(1.1.2011)	4,200	Manager's Salary	1,000
Entrance Fees	(2010)	1,000	Printing and Stationery	2,600
Do	(2011)	10,000	Advertising	1,800
Subscriptions	(2010)	600	Fire Insurance	1,200
Do	(2011)	15,000	Investments Purchased	20,000
Interest Received on Investments		3,000	Closing Balance 31.12.2011	7,600
Subscriptions	(2012)	400		
		34,200		34,200

It was ascertained from enquiry that the following represented a fair picture of the Income and Expenditure of the Club for the year 2011 for audit purpose:

Expenditures	Rs.	Rs.	*Incomes*	Rs.
Manager's Salary		1,500	Entrance Fees	10,500
Printing & Stationery	2,000		Subscription	15,600
Add : Accrued	400	2,400	Interest on Investments	4,000
Advertising (accrued nil)		1,600		
Audit Fees		500		
Fire Insurance		1,000		
Depreciation		4,940		
Excess of Income over Expenditure		18,160		
		30,100		30,100

You are required to prepare the Balance Sheet of the Club as on 31.12.2010. and 31.12.11, it being given that the values of the fixed assets as on 31.12.2010 were : Building Rs. 44,000, Cricket Equipment Rs. 25,000 and Furniture Rs. 4,000. The rates of depreciation are : Building 5%, Cricket Equipments 10%, Furniture 6%. You are entitled to make assumptions as may be justified.

[CU BCom (Hons.)]

Solution

In the books of Bengal Club
Balance Sheet *as at 31st December 2010*

Liabilities	Rs.	*Assets*	Rs.
Outstanding Liabilities :		Buildings	44,000
Advertisement (1,800 – 1,600)	200	Furniture	4,000
Printing and Stationery (2,600 – 2,000)	600	Cricket Equipment	25,000
Capital Fund	78,000	Entrance Fees in arrear	1,000
(bal. fig.)		Subscription in arrear	600
		Cash	4,200
	78,800		78,800

Balance Sheet *as at 31st December 2011*

Liabilities	Rs.	Rs.	*Assets*	Rs.	Rs.
Capital Fund :			Buildings	44,000	
Balance on 1.1.2011	78,000		*Less* : Depreciation 5%	2,200	41,800
Add : Excess of Income over Expenditure	18,160		Furniture	4,000	
			Less : Depreciation 6%	240	3,760
		96,160	Cricket Equipment	25,000	
Subscriptions Received in Advance		400	*Less* : Depreciation 10%	2,500	22,500
			Investments		20,000
Outstanding Liabilities :			Subscriptions in arrear (15,600 – 15,000)		600
Printing and Stationery		400	Entrance Fees in arrear (10,500 – 10,000)		500
Manager's Salary : (1,500 – 1,000)		500	Accrued Interest on Investments (4,000 – 3,000)		1,000
Audit Fees		500	Prepaid Insurance (1,200 – 1,000)		200
			Cash		7,600
		97,960			97,960

Note : Advertisement Expenses and Printing and Stationery, which were paid in excess over Income and Expenditure A/c, are assumed to be outstanding for the previous year.

D. Preparation of Receipts and Payments Account from a given Income and Expenditure Account and a Balance Sheet

It has already been stated earlier that Receipts and Payments Account is a summary of Cash Book. We have also explained the method of preparing a Receipts and Payments Account therein. But if both Income and Expenditure Account and the Opening Balance Sheet are given, we are to consider each and individual items, one by one. Consider the following example :

Balance Sheet (Extract) *as at 31st December 2012*

Liabilities	Rs.	*Assets*	Rs.
Outstanding Salary	700	Prepaid Insurance	5000
		Outstanding Subscription	1,000

Income and Expenditure Account *for the year ended 31st December 2012*

	Rs.		Rs.
Salary	6,000	Subscription	12,000
Insurance	3,000		

Adjustments :

(i) Salary outstanding for the year 2012 amounted to Rs. 1,000. (ii) Insurance Prepaid amounted to Rs. 800. (iii) Subscription outstanding for the year 2012 amounted to Rs. 3,000.

Solution

(i) Amount paid on account of salary in Receipts and Payments Account

		Rs.
	Salary	6,000
Less :	Outstanding for 2012	1,000
		5,000
Add :	Outstanding for 2011	700
		5,700

(ii) Amount paid on account of Insurance in Receipts and Payments Account

		Rs.
	Insurance	3,000
Add :	Prepaid Insurance for 2013	800
		3,800
Less :	Prepaid Insurance for 2012 paid in 2011	500
		3,300

(iii) Amount received on account of Subscriptions in Receipts and Payments Account

		Rs.
	Subscriptions	12,000
Less :	Outstanding for 2012	3,000
		9,000
Add :	Outstanding for 2011	1,000
		10,000

Illustration 20

The Income and Expenditure Account of the Repose Club is :

Dr. **Income and Expenditure Account** *for the year ended 31st December 2012* Cr.

	Expenditures	Rs.		*Incomes*	Rs.
To	Salaries	1,750	By	Subscriptions	2,000
"	General Expenses	500	"	Donations	1,050
"	Depreciation	300			
"	Excess of Income over Expenditure	500			
		3,050			3,050

Adjustments were made in respect of the following :

(1) Subscriptions for 2011 unpaid at 1st Jan. 2012, Rs. 200; Rs. 180 of which was received in 2012.

(2) Subscriptions paid in advance at 1.1.2012 Rs. 50.

(3) Subscriptions paid in advance at 31.12.2012 Rs. 40.

(4) Subscriptions for 2012 unpaid at 31.12.2012 Rs. 70.

(5) Sundry Assets at beginning of period Rs. 2,600, Sundry Assets after depreciation Rs. 2,700 at the end of period.

(6) Cash balance at 1st January 2012 Rs. 160.

Prepare Receipts and Payments Account.

Solution

In the books of Repose Club

Dr. **Receipts and Payments Account** *for the year ended 31st December 2012* Cr.

	Receipts	Rs.		*Payments*	Rs.
To	Balance b/d	160	By	Salaries	1,750
"	Donations	1,050	"	General Expenses	500
"	Subscriptions (cash received)*	2,100	"	Sundry Assets	400[2]
			"	Balance c/d	660
		3,310			3,310

Workings 1 :

Dr. **Subscription Account** Cr.

	Particulars	Rs.		*Particulars*	Rs.
To	Balance b/d	200	By	Balance b/d	50
"	Income & Expenditure A/c	2,000	"	Balance (unpaid for 2011)	
"	Balance (paid in advance to 2013) c/d	40		(200 – 180) c/d	20
			"	Cash Received *(bal. fig.)*	2,100
			"	Balance (unpaid for 2012) c/d	70
		2,240			2,240
To	Balance b/d :		By	Balance (b/d 2013)	40
	For 2011	20			
	For 2012	70			

Workings 2 :

Dr. **Sundry Assets Account** Cr.

	Particulars	Rs.		*Particulars*	Rs.
To	Balance b/d	2,600	By	Depreciation	300
"	Purchase A/c *(bal. fig.)*	400	"	Balance c/d	2,700
		3,000			3,000

Illustration 21

You are given :

(i) Income and Expenditure Account; (ii) Opening Balance Sheet; (iii) Closing Balance Sheet relating to the year 2012.

(i) **Income and Expenditure Account**

for the year ended 2012

Dr. *Expenditures*	Rs.	Rs.	*Incomes*	Cr. Rs.
To Salaries	1,100		By Subscriptions	800
Add : Outstanding	100	1,200	" Medical Fees	1,400
" Insurance	150			
Less : Prepaid	13	137		
" Medicines		600		
" Surplus		263		
		2,200		2,200

(ii) **(Opening) Balance Sheet** *as at ....*

Liabilities	Rs.	*Assets*	Rs.
Capital Fund	4,050	Medical Equipment	3,250
Outstanding Salary	100	Furniture	500
		Cash	300
		Outstanding Subscriptions	100
	4,150		4,150

(Closing) Balance Sheet *as at 2012*

Liabilities		Rs.	*Assets*		Rs.
Capital Fund :	4,050		Medical Equipment	3,250	
Add : Surplus	263	4,313	Additions		
					3,750
Donations		550	Investments		500
Outstanding Salary		100	Furniture		500
Subscription Received in advance		50	Prepaid Investment		13
			Cash		250
		5,013			5,013

Prepare from the above information the Receipts and Payments Account for 2012.

Solution

Receipts and Payments Accounts

Dr. *Receipts*	Rs.	*Payments*	Cr. Rs.
To Balance b/d	300	By Salaries (1,200 + 100 – 100)	1,200
" Subscription (800 + 100 + 50)	950	" Insurance (137 + 13)	150
" Medical Fees	1,400	" Medicines	600
" Donations	550	" Medical Equipment	500
		" Investment	500
		" Balance c/d	250
	3,200		3,200

Illustration 22

The Calcutta Cricket Club gives you the following information :

Income and Expenditure Account *for the year ended 31st December 2012*

Dr. *Expenditures*	Rs.	Rs.	*Incomes*	Rs.	Cr. Rs.
To Remuneration to Coach		4,500	By Donation & Subscriptions		25,500
" Wages		5,000	" Bar Room :		
" Rent		2,500	Receipts	3,000	
" Printing and Stationery		2,600	*Less* : Payments	2,500	500
" Repairs		4,500	" Interest on Savings A/c		500
" Honorarium to Secretary		6,000	" Proceeds of Club :		
" Depreciation			Night	8,800	
on Equipments		4,700	*Less* : Expenses	4,000	4,800
" Surplus		1,500			
		31,300			31,300

Dr. **Balance Sheet** *as at 31st December 2012* Cr.

31.12.10	*Liabilities*			31.12.10	*Assets*	
Rs.			Rs.	Rs.		Rs.
	Expenses Unpaid :			1,000	Cash in hand	500
1,000	Printing & Stationery		800	3,000	Cash at Bank	1,000
	Wages		2,000	20,300	Savings Bank	21,100
4,000	Honorarium (Secy.)		6,000	1,500	Outstanding Subscriptions	1,000
800	Subscriptions Received in Advance		300	8,000	Equipments	17,500
28,000	Capital Fund as on 31.12.2011	28,000				
	Entrance Fees	2,500				
	Surplus	1,500	32,000			
33,800			41,100	33,800		41,100

Prepare the Receipts and Payments Account of the Club for 2012.

[CU BCom (Hons.)]

Solution

In the books of Calcutta Cricket Club

Dr. **Receipts and Payments Account** *for the year ended 31st December 2012* Cr.

Receipts	Rs.	Rs.	*Payments*	Rs.	Rs.
To Balance b/d :			By Remuneration to Coach		4,500
Cash in hand		1,000	" Wages		3,000
Cash at Bank :			" Rent		2,500
Current Account	3,000		" Printing and Stationery		2,800
Savings Account	20,300	23,300	" Repairs		4,500
" Donation and Subscriptions		25,500	" Honorarium to Secretary		4,000
" Bar Room Receipts		3,000	" Bar Room Expenses		2,500
" Interest on Savings Account		500	" Night Club Expenses		4,000
" Proceeds of Night Club		8,800	" Purchase of Equipments		14,200
" Entrance Fees		2,500	" Balance c/d :		
			Cash in hand		500
			Cash at Bank :		
			Current Account	1,000	
			Saving Account	21,100	22,100
		64,600			64,600

Workings :

1. Donation and Subscriptions received in 2012

		Rs.
	As per Income & Expenditure A/c	25,500
Add :	Outstanding on 31.12.2011	1,500
		27,000
Add :	Received in Advance on 31.12.2011	300
		27,300
Less :	Outstanding on 31.12.2011	1,000
		26,300
Less :	Received in Advance on 31.12.2011	800
		25,500

2. Wages paid in 2012

	As per Income & Exp. Account	5,000
Less :	Outstanding on 31.12.2012	2,000
		3,000

3. Printing and Stationery paid in 2012 :

		Rs.
	As per Income & Expenditure Account	2,600
Less :	Outstanding on 31.12.2012	800
		1,800
Add :	Outstanding on 31.12.2012	1,000
		2,800

4. Honorarium to Secretary paid in 2012

	As per Income & Expenditure Account	6,000
Add :	Outstanding on 31.12.2011	4,000
		10,000
Less :	Outstanding on 31.12.2012	6,000
		4,000

5. Purchase of Equipment in 2012 :

	Equipment on 31.12.2012	17,500
Add :	Depreciation	4,700
		22,200
Less :	Opening Balance	8,000
		14,200

Illustration 23

The following is the Income and Expenditure Account of City Club for the year ended 31.12.2012:

		Rs.			Rs.
To	Salaries	15,750	By	Subscriptions	55,000
"	Stationery	1,250	"	Donations	7,500
"	Rates and Taxes	6,210	"	Profit on Annual Meet	16,000
"	Postage & Telephones	2,520	"	Sale of Journal	5,250
"	Sundry Expenses	8,210	"	Profit on sale of Billiard Table	1,410
"	Repairs	5,260			
"	Table Tennis Ball	1,200			
"	Expenses of Journal	2,510			
"	Affiliation Fee to main Club	500			
"	Electricity	6,250			
"	Water Charges	1,210			
"	Billiards Room Expenditure	2,460			
"	Depreciation on Sundry Assets	1,560			
"	Excess of Income over Expenditure	30,270			
		85,160			85,160

The following further information are available:

	1.1.2012 Rs.	31.12.2012 Rs.
Sundry Assets (Other than Cash Balance)	46,500	47,650
Outstanding Subscriptions	1,560	2,610
Advance Subscriptions	2,500	1,600
Expenses Outstanding :		
Stationery	150	210
Telephone bill	220	240
Electricity	125	225
Due towards Purchase of Billiard Balls	—	165
Office Bearer's Fund	3,465	4,260

The Billiards Table sold during the year was used for 6 months during the year and its book value was Rs. 10,240 as on 30.6.2012.

Cash in hand at the beginning was Rs. 1,750. The club is affiliated to the main Club. It has paid one year's Affiliation Fee in advance. Out of the donations, a sum of Rs. 1,000 announced at the Annual Meet was duly taken into account but had not been received till 31.12.2012.

All amounts received towards Office Bearers' Fund are credited to the Fund and the expenses amounting Rs. 2,785 were also charged to the Fund directly.

From the particulars stated above, prepare (1) Receipts and Payments Account for the year ended 31.12.2012 and (2) Balance Sheet as at 31.12.2012.

Solution

In the books of City Club
Balance Sheet *at 1st January 2012*

Liabilities	Rs.	*Assets*	Rs.
Capital Fund (*bal. fig.*)	43,350	Sundry Assets	46,500
Subscription Received in Advance	2,500	Outstanding Subscription	1,560
Outstanding Liabilities :		Cash	1,750
Stationery	150		
Telephone Bills	220		
Electricity	125		
Office Bearers' Fund	3,465		
	49,810		49,810

Dr. **Receipts and Payments Account** *for the year ended 31st December 2012* Cr.

	Receipts	Rs.		*Payments*	Rs.
To	Balance b/d	1,750	By	Salaries	15,750
"	Subscription Received	53,050[1]	"	Stationery	1,1900[4]
"	Donation	6,500[2]	"	Rates and Taxes	6,210
"	Profit on Annual Meet	16,000	"	Postage & Telephones etc.	2,500[5]
"	Sale of Journal	5,250	"	Sundry Expenses	8,210
"	Sale of Billiards Table	10,090[3]	"	Repairs	5,260
"	Office Bearers' Fund		"	Table Tennis Ball	1,200
	(4,260 – 3,456)	795	"	Expenses of Journal	2,510
			"	Affiliation Fees (500 + 500)	1,000
			"	Electricity	6,150[6]
			"	Water Charges	1,210
			"	Billiards Room Expenditure	2,295
				(2,460 – 165)	
			"	Purchase of Sundry Assets	11,390
			"	Balance c/d	28,560
		93,435			93,435

Balance Sheet *as at 1st December 2012*

Liabilities		Rs.	*Assets*	Rs.
Capital Fund	43,350		Sundry Assets	47,650
Add : Surplus	30,270	73,620	Outstanding Subscription	2,610
Subscription Received in Advance		1,600	Prepaid Affiliation Fees	500
Outstanding Liabilities :			Donation Accrued	1,000
Stationery		210	Cash	28,560
Telephone		240		
Electricity		225		
Billiard Ball		165		
Office Bearers' Fund		4,260		
		80,320		80,320

Workings :

	1. Subscription Received	Rs.
	Subacroption Received	55,000
Add :	Outstanding on 1.1.2012	1,560
		56,560
Less :	Outstanding on 31.12.2012	2,610
	On 31.12.2012	53,950
Add :	Subs. Received in Advance	1,600
		55,550
Less :	Sub. Received in Adv. on 1.1. 2012	2,500
	Subs. Actually Received	53,050

	2. Donation Received	Rs.
	Donations as per In. & Exp. A/c	7,500
Less :	Anouncced at the Annual Meet	1,000
		6,500

	3. Amount Realised on Sale of Bill and Table (Part of Sundry Assets)	
	Book-Value	10,240
Less:	Depreciation	1,560
		8,680
Add :	Profit on Sales	1,410
		10,090

	4. Payment for Stationery	Rs.
	Stationery (as per In. & Exp. A/c)	1,250
Less :	Outstanding on 31.12.2012	210
		1,040
Add:	Outstanding on 1.1.2012	150
		1,190

	5. Payment for Postage, Telephone etc.	Rs.
	P & T (as per In. & Exp. A/c)	2,520
Less :	Outstanding on 31.12.2012	240
		2,280
Add:	Outstanding on 1.1.2012	220
		2,500

	6. Payment for Electricity	Rs.
	Electricity (as per In. & Exp. A/c)	6,250
Less :	Outstanding on 31.12.2012	225
		6,025
Add:	Outstanding on 1.1.2012	125
		6,150

Preparation of Corrected Receipts and Payments Account

Illustration 24

The Receipts and Payments Account of Trustwell Club prepared on 31st March 2003 is :

Receipts and Payments Account

	Receipts	Rs.	*Amount* Rs.		*Payments*	*Amount* Rs.
To	Balance b/d		450	By	Expenses (including Payment for sports material Rs. 2,700)	6,300
"	Annual income from Sub.	4,590		"	Loss on Sale of Furniture (cost price Rs. 450)	180
	Add: Outstanding of last year received this year	180			Balance c/d	90,450
		4,770				
	Less: Prepaid of last year	90				
			4,680			
"	Other Fees		1,800			
"	Donation for Building		90,000			
			96,930			96,930

Additional Information

Trustwell Club had balances as on 1.4.2002:
Sports material Furniture Rs. 1,800; Investment at 5% Rs. 27,000;
Balance as on 31.3.2003: Subscription receivable Rs. 270;
Subscription received in advance Rs. 90;
Stock of sports material Rs. 1,800.

Do you agree with the above Receipts and Payments Account? If not, prepare correct Receipts and Payments Account and Income and Expenditure account for the year ended 31st March 2003 and the Balance Sheet on that date.

[CA PE I, May 2003]

Solution

In the books of Trustwell Club

Corrected Receipts and Payments Account *for the year ended 31st March 2003*

Date		*Receipts*	*Amount* Rs.	*Date*		*Payments*	*Amount* Rs.
	To	Balance b/d	450		By	Expenses (Rs. 6,300 – Rs. 2,700)	3,600
	"	Subscription	4,500[2]		"	Sports Material	2,700
	"	Other Fees	1,800		"	Balance c/d (Cash in hand and at Bank)	90,720
	"	Donation for Building	90,000				
	"	Sale of Furniture	270[3]				
			97,020				97,020

Income and Expenditure Account *for the year ended 31st March 2003*

Dr. Cr.

	Expenditure	Rs.		*Income*	Rs.
To	Sundry Expenses	3,600	By	Subscription	4,590
"	Consumption of Sports Materials	7,560[4]	"	Other Fees	1,800
"	Loss on Sale of Furniture	180	"	Interest on Investment 95% on Rs. 27,000)	1,350
			"	Deficit—Excess of Expenditure over Income	3,600
		11,340			11,340

Balance Sheet *as on 31st March 2003*

Liabilities	Rs.	Rs.	*Assets*	Rs.	Rs.
Capital Fund	36,000[1]		Furniture	1,800	
Less: Excess of Expenditure over Income	3,600	32,400	*Less:* Sold	450	1,350
			5% Investment		27,000
Building Fund		90,000	Interest Accrued on Investment		1,350

Contd.

	Rs.	Rs.		Rs.
Subscription Received in Advance		90	Sports Materials	1,800
			Subscription Receivable	270
			Cash in Hand and at Bank	90,720
		1,22,490		1,22,490

Workings :

1. **Balance Sheet** ***as on 1st April 2002***

Liabilities	Rs.	*Assets*	Rs.
Subscription Received in Advance	90	Furniture	1,800
Capital Fund (*bal. fig.*)	36,000	Investment	27,000
		Sports Material	6,660
		Subscription Receivable	180
		Cash in hand and at Bank	450
	36,090		36,090

2. **Subscription Received**

	Rs.
Subscription (Annual Income)	4,590
Less: Receivable as on 31.3.2003	270
	4,320
Add: Advance received for the year 2003-04	90
	4,410
Add: Receivable on 31.3.2002	180
	4,590
Less: Advance Received as on 31.3.2002	90
	4,500

3. **Sale of Furniture**

	Rs.
Cost of Furniture	450
Less: Loss on Sale	180
∴ Sale of furniture	270

4. **Consumption of Sports Material**

Consumption = Opening Stock + Purchase – Closing Stock

= Rs. 6,660 + Rs. 2,700 – Rs. 1,800

= Rs. 7,560

Illustration 25

The Income and Expenditure Account of the Mumbai Club for the year 2012 is :

		Rs.			Rs.
To	Salaries	1,20,000	By	Subscription	1,70,000
"	Printing & Stationery	6,000	"	Entrance Fees	4,000
"	Postage	500	"	Contribution of Dinner	36,000
"	Telephone	1,500			
"	General Expenses	12,000			
"	Interest and Bank Charges	5,500			
"	Audit Fees	2,500			
"	Annual Dinner Expenses	25,000			
"	Depreciation	7,000			
"	Surplus	30,000			
		2,10,000			2,10,000

The account has been prepared after the following adjustments:

	Rs.		Rs.
Subscription outstanding 31.12.2011	16,000	The club owned a building since 2011	1,90,000
Subscription outstanding 31.12.2012	18,000	The club had sports equipments on 31.12.2011 value at	52,000
Subscription received in advance on 31.12.2011	13,000	At the end of the year, after depreciation of Rs. 7,000, equipment amounted to	63,000
Subscription received in advance on 31.12.2012	8,400	In 2011 the club had raised a Bank Loan which is still unpaid	30,000
Salaries outstanding 31.12.2011	6,000		
Salaries outstanding 31.12.2012	8,000	Cash in hand on 31.12.2012	28,500
Audit Fees from 2011 paid during 2012	2,000	Audit Fees for 2012 not paid	2,500

Prepare the Receipts and Payments Account of the Club for 2012 and the Balance Sheet as on 31st December 2012. All workings should form part of your answer.

[CA]

Solution

In the books of Mumbai Club

Receipts and Payments Account *for the year ended 31st December 2012*

Dr.				Cr.
Receipts	Rs.		*Payments*	Rs.
To Balance b/d *(bal. fig.)*	13,600	By	Salaries	1,18,000[3]
" Subscription	1,63,400[2]	"	Printing & Stationery	6,000
" Entrance Fees	4,000	"	Postage	500
" Contribution of Dinner	36,000	"	Telephone	1,500
		"	General Expenses	12,000
		"	Audit Fees	2,000
		"	Annual Dinner Expenses	25,000
		"	Interest and Bank Charges	5,500
		"	Sports Equipments	18,000
		"	Balance c/d	28,500
	2,17,000			2,17,000

Balance Sheet *as at 31st December 2012*

Liabilities	Rs.	Rs.	*Assets*	Rs.	Rs.
Capital Fund	2,20,600[1]		Building		1,90,000
Add : Surplus	30,000	2,50,600	Sports Equipment		
Bank Loan		30,000	Opening Balance	52,000	
Creditors for Expenses			Additions	18,000[4]	
Salaries	8,000			70,000	
Audit Fees	2,500	10,500	*Less* : Depreciation	7,000	63,000
Subscription Received in Adv.		8,400	Cash in hand		28,500
			Subscription Due		18,000
		2,99,500			2,99,500

Workings :

1. **Balance Sheet** *as at 31st December 2011*

Liabilities	Rs.	*Assets*	Rs.
Capital Fund *(bal. fig.)*	2,20,600	Building	1,90,000
Bank Loan	30,000	Sports Equipment	52,000
Outstanding Salaries	6,000	Outstanding Subscription	16,000
Outstanding Audit Fees	2,000	Cash	13,600
Subscription Received in Advance	13,000		
	2,71,600		2,71,600

2. **Subscription Received**

	Rs.
Subscription (As per Income & Expenditure A/c)	1,70,000
Add : Outstanding on 31.12.2011	16,000
	1,86,000
Less : Outstanding for 2012	18,000
	1,68,000
Add : Received in Adv. for 2013	8,400
	1,76,400
Less : Received in Adv. for 2011	13,000
	1,63,400

3. **Salaries Paid**

	Rs.
Salaries (As per Income & Expenditure A/c)	1,20,000
Less : Outstanding for 2012	8,000
	1,12,000
Add : Outstanding for 2011	6,000
	1,18,000

4. **Purchase of Sports Equipment** (Rs. 63, 000 + Rs. 7,000 – Rs. 52,000) 18,000

GENERAL ILLUSTRATIONS

Preparation of Receipts and Payments Account, Income & Expenditure Account, and Balance Sheet, where Revenue Income and Actual Receipts are given.

Illustration 26

The following information were obtained from the books of Delhi Club as on 31.3.2012, at the end of the first year of the Club. You are required to prepare Receipts and Payments Account, Income and Expenditure Account for the year ended 31.3.2012 and a Balance Sheet as at 31.3.2012 on mercantile basis :

(i) Donations received for Building and Library Room Rs. 2,00,000

(ii) Other Revenue income and actual receipts.

	Revenue Income Rs.	Actual Receipts Rs.
Entrance Fees	17,000	17,000
Subscription	20,000	19,000
Locker Rents	600	600
Sundry Income	1,600	1,060
Refreshmnt Account	—	16,000

(ii) Other revenue expenditure and actual Payments:

	Revenue Expenditure Rs.	Actual Payments Rs.
Land (Cost Rs. 10,000)	—	10,000
Furniture (cost Rs. 1,46,000)	—	1,30,000
Salaries	5,000	4,800
Maintenance of playgrounds	2,000	1,000
Rent	8,000	8,000
Refreshment Account	—	8,000

Donations to the extent of Rs. 25,000 were utilised for the purchase of Liabrary Books, balance was still unutilised. In order to keep it safe, 9% Govt. Bonds of Rs. 1,60,000 we purchased on 31.3.2012. Remaining amount was put in the Bank on 31.3.2012 under Term Deposit. Depreciation at 10% p.a. was to be provided for the whole year on Furniture and Library Books.

[CA Foundation]

Solution

In the books of Delhi Club

Dr. **Receipts and Payments Account** *for the year ended 31st March 2012* Cr.

Receipts	Rs.	*Payments*	Rs.
To Entrance fees	17,000	By Land	10,000
" Subscription	19,000	" Furniture	1,30,000
" Locker rent	600	" Salaries	4,800
" Sundry Income	1,060	" Playground Maintenance	1,000
" Refreshment	16,000	" Rent	8,000
" Donations for Building and Library room	2,00,000	" Refreshment	8,000
" Balance c/d —Overdraft	1,08,140	" Library Books	25,000
		" 9% Govt. Bond.	1,60,000
		" Bank (Term Deposit)	15,000
	3,61,800		3,61,800

Dr. **Income and Expenditure Account** *for the year ended 31st March 2012* Cr.

Expenditure	Rs.	Rs.	*Income*	Rs.	Rs.
To Salaries	4,800		By Subscription	19,000	
Add: Outstanding	200	5,000	*Add: Outstanding*	1,000	20,000
" Playground maintenance	1,000		" Locker Rent		600
Add: Outstanding	1,000	2,000	" Sundry Income	1,060	
" Rent		8,000	—Add: *Outstanding*	540	1,600
" Depreciation on:			" Refreshment A/c		16,000
Furniture	14,600		" Deficit		
Library Books	2,500	17,100	Excess of Expenditure over Income		1,900
" Refreshment Expenses		8,000			
		40,100			40,100

Balance Sheet *as at 31st March 2012*

Liabilities	Rs.	Rs.	*Assets*	Rs.	Rs.
Capital Fund		—	Law		10,000
Entrance Fees		17,000	Furniture	1,46,000	
Donation for Buildig, Libray			*Less:* Depreciation	14,600	1,31,400
Room Fund		2,00,000	Library Books	25,000	
Creditors for Furniture		16,000[4]	*Less:* Depreciation	2,500	22,500
Outstanding Salaries		200	9% Govt. Bond		1,60,000
Outstanding Expenses for			Outstanding Subscriptions		1,000
Playground		1,000	Accrued Sundry Income		540
Bank overdraft		1,08,140	Bank Term Deposit		15,000
			Deficit		1,900
		3,42,340			3,42,340

Workings :

1. Since there was no capital fund Deficit is shown in the Assets side.
2. Donation received for Building and Library Room is treated as Capital item.
3. Since the investment in Govt. Bond has been made at the closing date of the year, no interest has accrued.
4. Creditors for Furniture = Furniture Purchased – Payments made
   = Rs. 1,46,000 – Rs. 1,30,000
   = Rs. 16,000.

Preparation of Receipts and Payments Account, and Income and Expenditure Account, and Balance Sheet from incomplete information

Illustration 27

Universal Brotherhood Club does not maintain complete double entry books of accounts. From the following details, prepare a Receipts and Payments Account and Income and Expenditure Account for the year ending 31st December 2012 and a Balance Sheet as on that date:

	1.1.2012	31.1.2012
	Rs.	Rs.
Outstanding Subscriptions	14,000	19,600
Advance Subscriptions	2,800	5,600
Outstanding salaries	1,400	700
Salary advance	—	700
Cash in hand and at Bank	14,000	?
5% investments	14,000	7,000
Furniture	2,800	1,400
Sports Goods	5,600	11,200

Subscriptions for the year amount to Rs. 70,000. Salaries paid Rs. 15,400. Face Value of Investments was Rs. 16,800. 50% of investments was sold at 80% of Face Value. Interest on investments left unsold was received Rs. 1,400 of Furniture and sold for Rs. 700 at the beginning of the year. Sports goods were purchased at th end of the year. Charge 20% depreciation on Sports goods and 10% on Furniture. Sports expenses amount to Rs. 14,000. Miscellaneous expenses are Rs. 4,200 and rent amounts to Rs. 8,400.

[CU BCom (Hons.)]

Solution

In the books of Universal Brotherhood Club

Dr. **Receipts and Payments Account** *for the ended 31st December 2012* *Cr.*

	Receipts	*Amount*		*Payments*	*Amount*
		Rs.			Rs.
To	Balance b/d		By	Salaries	15,400
	Cash in hand and at Bank	14,000	"	Furniture of Sports Goods	5,600
"	Subscription	67,200[2]	"	Sports Expenses	14,000
"	Sale of Investments	6,720	"	Miscellaneous Expenses	4,200
"	Sale of Furniture	700	"	Rent	8,400
"	Interest on Investment	420	"	Balance c/d cash in hand and at bank	41,440
		89,040			89,040

Dr. *Income and Expenditure Account for the year ended 31st December 2012* Cr.

Expenditure	Amount	Amount	Income	Amount	Amount
	Rs.	Rs.		Rs.	Rs.
To Salaries	15,400		By Subscription		70,000
Add: Out. for Current year	700		" Interest on Investment		420[5]
	16,100				
Less: Out. of last year	1,400				
	14,700				
Less: Paid in advance	700	14,000			
" Rent		8,400			
" Sports Expenses		14,000			
" Miscellaneous Expenses		4,200			
" Loss on Sale of Furniture		700[4]			
" Loss on Sale of Investment		280[3]			
" Depreciation (1,120 + 140)		1,260			
" Surplus—Excess of Income Over Expenditure		27,580			
		70,420			70,420

Balance Sheet as at 31st March 2012

Liabilities	Amount	Amount	Assets	Amount	Amount
	Rs.	Rs.		Rs.	Rs.
Capital Fund:			Furniture	1,400	
Opening Balance	46,200[1]		*Less:* Depreciation	140	1,260
Add: Surplus	27,580	73,780	Sports Goods (Rs. 5,600 + 5,600)	11,200	
Subscription Received in Adv.		5,600	*Less:* Dep. @ 20% of on 5,600	1,120	10,080
Salary Outstanding		700	5% Invest. (Face Value Rs. 8,400)		7,000
			Outstanding Subscriptions		19,600
			Salary Prepaid		700
			Cash in hand & Bank		41,440
		80,080			80,080

Workings :

1. In order to find out the **Capital Fund** we are to prepare the following opening Balance Sheet :

Balance sheet *as at 1.1.2012*

Liabilities	Rs.	*Assets*	Rs.
Capital Fund *(bal. fig.)*	46,200	Furniture	2,800
		5% Investments	14,000
Out. Salaries	1,400	Sports Goods	5,600
Sub. Received in Advance	2,800	Out. Subscription	14,000
		Cash and Bank	14,000
	50,400		50,400

2. **Subscription Received**

	Rs.
Amount received in Current year	70,000
Add: Last Year's outstanding received	14,000
Add: Sub. Received in Adv. for next year	5,600
	89,600
Less: Current year's outstanding	19,600
	70,000
Less : Advance received Last year	2,800
	67,200

3 **Loss on Sale of Investment**

		Rs.
Cost Price (50% of Rs. 14,000)		7,000
Less: Sale of Investment		
Face Value	16,800	
Less: Unsold 50%	8,400	
	8,400	
80% of 8,400		6,720
∴ Loss on Sale		280

4. **Loss on Sale of Furniture and Dep. there on**

	Rs.
Furniture	2,800
Less: Sold (1.1.2012)	1,400
	1,400
Less: Dep. @ of 10%	140
	1,260

Loss on Sale (Rs. 1,400 – Rs. 700) = Rs. 700

5. **Interest on Investment**

on 50% Face Valuue i.e., Rs. 8,400

Interest = Rs. 8,400 × 5% = Rs. 420

Illustration 28

The following is the Receipts and Payments Account of Barisha Recreation Club for the year ended 31st December 2012.

	Receipts	*Rs.*		*Payments*	*Rs.*
To	Cash in hand	500	By	Rent of Club House	1,300
"	Cash at Bank	6,000	"	Painting of Club House	700
"	Members Subscription—		"	Wages for Ground Maintenance	1,500
	Ordinary for 2011	100	"	General Expenses	1,300
	Ordinary for 2012	1,800	"	Electricity Charges	1,800
	Ordinary for 2013	200	"	Investment	10,000
	Life	2,000	"	Secretary's Honorarium	600
"	Sale of Tickets for Annual Exhibition	10,000	"	Annual Meeting Expenses	400
"	Sale of Refreshment	12,000	"	Sports Equipments	1,800
"	Interest on Investment	1,300	"	Purchase of Refreshment	5,500
"	Sale of Furniture		"	Printing & Stationery	500
	(Original cost on		"	Insurance	300
	1.1.2011 was Rs. 500)	100	"	Cash in hand	2,000
			"	Cash at Bank	6,300
		34,000			34,000

The following information are also available :

(a) On 31.12.2011 outstanding subscription for 2011 was Rs. 150.

(b) On 31.12.2011 advance subscription for 2012 was Rs. 50.

(c) On 31.12.2011 outstanding subscription for 2012 was Rs. 300.

(d) A Life Membership Scheme was introduced in 2011. Under the scheme, Life Membership subscription is Rs. 500 and it is to be apportioned to revenue 1/10th every year over a period of 10 years. Life Membership subscription totalling Rs. 2,500 were collected during 2011.

(e) On 31.12.2012 Investment was Rs. 20,000 and interest accrued on Investment on 31.12.2012 was Rs. 1,200.

(f) On 31.12.2011 Furniture costing Rs. 8,000 were purchased and it was decided to write-off depreciation on Furniture and Sports Equipments at 10% per annum on Cost.

(g) In 2011 a plot of land was purchased for Rs. 20,000 to constructed Club-house.

(h) Other assets and liabilities of the Club were:

	Stock of Refreshment	Insurance Prepaid	Rent Accrued	Credittors for Refreshment
	Rs.	Rs.	Rs.	Rs.
31.12.2011	1,900	70	200	400
31.12.2012	2,100	50	100	500

You are required to prepare an Income and Expenditure Account for the year ended 31.12.2012 and also a Balance Sheet as on that date.

[CU BCom (Hons.)]

Note: It is better for us if we prepare a **Refreshment Trading Account**. Alternatively, we can adjust all the items relating to refreshment transaction in Income and Expenditure Account directly.

We have followed the first one.

Dr. **Refreshment Trading Account** *Cr.*

	Particulars	*Amount*		*Particulars*	*Amount*
		Rs.			Rs.
To	Opening Stock of Refreshment	1,900	By	Sale of Refreshment	12,000
"	Purchase of Refreshment	5,600[1]	"	Closing Stock of Refreshment	2,100
"	Income and Expenditure A/c —Profit transferred	6,600			
		14,100			14,100

Dr. **Income and Expenditure Account** *for the year and 31st Dec. 2012* Cr.

Expenditures	*Amount*	*Amount*	*Incomes*	*Amount*	*Amount*
	Rs.	Rs.		Rs.	Rs.
To Rent o Club House		1,200[2]	By Subscription (Ordinary)		2,150[5]
" Printing of Club House		700	" Life Members Subscription		450[6]
" Wages for Ground maintenance		1,500	" Sale of ticket for Annual exhibition		10,000
" General Expenses		1,300	" Interest on Investment	1,300	
" Electric Changes		1,800	*Add:* Accrued Interest	1200	2,500
" Secretary's Honorarium		600	" Profit on sale of		
" Annual Meeting Expenses		400	Refreshment		6,600
" Loss on Sale of Furniture		350[3]			
" Printing & Stationery		500			
" Insurance Premium		320[4]			
" Depreciation on:					
Furniture	750				
Sports equipment	180	930			
" Surplus–Excess of Income over Expenditure		12,100			
		21,700			21,700

Balance Sheet *as at 31st Dec. 2012*

Liabilities	*Amount*	*Amount*	*Assets*	*Amount*	*Amount*
	Rs.	Rs.		Rs.	Rs.
Capital Fund			Land		20,000
Opening Balance	52,920[7]		Furniture (Rs. 8,000 – Rs. 800)	7,200	
Add: Surplus	12,100	65,020	*Less:* WDV of Furniture Sold		
Outstanding Rent		100	(Rs. 500 – Rs. 50)	450	
Creditors for Refreshment		500	*Less:* Depreciation @ 10% p.a.	6,750	
Life Members' Subscription		3,800	on Rs. 7,500 (8,000 – Rs. 500)	750	6,000
Subscription Received in			Sports Equipment	1,800	
Advance		200	*Less:* Dep. @ 10% p.a.	180	1,620
			Investment	20,000	
			Additions	10,000	30,000
			Accrued Interest		1,200
			Stock of Refreshment		2,100
			Prepaid Insurance		50
			Outstanding Subscription		
			For 2011 (Rs. 150 – Rs. 100)	50	
			For 2012	300	350
			Cash at Bank		6,300
			Cash in hand		2,000
		69,620			69,620

Workings :

1. **Purchase of Refreshment**

Dr. **Creditors for Refreshment A/c** Cr.

	Rs.		Rs.
To Bank	5,500	By Balance b/d	400
" Balance c/d	500	" Purchase *(bal. fig.)*	5,600
	6,000		6,000

2. **Rent of Club House**

Dr. **Rent of Club House A/c** Cr.

	Rs.		Rs.
To Bank	1,300	By Out. Rent	200
" Out. Rent	100	" Inc. & Exp. A/c	1,200
	1,400		1,400

3. **Loss on Sale of Furniture**

	Rs.
WDV of Furniture Sold (Rs. 500 – Rs. 50)	450
Less: Sold for	100
Loss on Sale	350

4. **Insurance Premium A/c**

Dr.		Rs.			Cr. Rs.
To	Prepaid Insurance	70	By	Inc. & Exp. Creditors A/c (bal. fig.)	320
"	Bank A/c	300	"	Prepaid Ins.	50
		370			370

5. **Subscription Received**

Subscription A/c

Dr.	Rs.		Cr. Rs.
To Income & Expenditure A/c	2,150	By Subscription Rec. in adv.	50
		" Bank A/c	1,800
		" Out. Sus.	300
	2,150		2,150

6. **Life Membership Subacription Received**

Life Membership Subscription A/c

Dr.	Rs.		Cr. Rs.
2011		2011	
To Inc. & Exp.	250	By Bank A/c	2,500
" Balance c/d	2,250		
	2,500		2,500
2012		2012	
To Inc. & Exp. (250 + 200)	450	By Balance b/d	2,250
" Balance c/d	3,800	" Bank	2,000
	4,250		4,250

7. **Capital as on 1.1.2012**

Balance Sheet *as at 1st Jan. 2012*

Liabilities	Rs.	*Assets*	Rs.
Outstanding rent	200	Land	20,000
Sub. Received in Advance (2012)	50	Furniture (8,000 – 800)	7,200
Creditors for Refreshment	400	Investment	20,000
Life Subscription (2,500 – 250)	2,250	Stock of Refreshment	1,900
Capital Fund *(bal. fig.)*	52,920	Prepaid Insurance	70
		Outstanding Subscription 2011	150
		Bank	6,000
		Cash	500
	55,820		55,820

Preparation of Bank Reconciliation Statement, Revised Balance Sheet to be prepared and accounts were maintained under Single Entry System.

Illustration 29

The Secretary of the Systematic Club had prepared the following draft Balance Sheet of the Club as at 30.9.2012 :

Liabilities	Rs.	Rs.	*Assets*	Rs.	Rs.
Capital Accounts			Fixtures & Fitting as on 30.9.2012	10,600	
Balance as on 30.9.2012	14,300		*Less:* Depreciation for the year	1,000	9,600
Less: Loss for the year	2,100	12,200	Stock		3,200
Subscriptions Received in Advance		600	Debtors		1,400
			Balance at bank		950
Creditors		2,400	Cash in hand		50
		15,200			15,200

You are to ascertain the:

(1) The amount of loss was only a balancing figure as the book had been kept on a single entry basis.

(2) The balance at Bank was that shown by the bank statement at the close of the business on 30.9.2012.

(3) The following amount had been paid into bank on 30.9.2012 but had not been credited by the bank:

(i) Two cheques of Rs. 50 each had been cashed for a member—one had since been duly honoured but the other had been returned marked 'refer to drawer' and, on being approached, the member repaid Rs. 50 in cash.

(4) The following cheques had been drawn in September but had not been presented until October:
- (i) Rs. 480 for bar supplies which had been delivered but had not been included in stock;
- (ii) Rs. 350 for an additional typewriter received on October;
- (iii) Rs. 100 as bonus to the professional included under the creditors;
- (iv) Rs. 140 for fuel which had been included in the stock figure but not in the creditors and this cheue was dated October 1.

You are also required to prepare:

(a) a Bank Reconciliation Statement as on 30.9.2012. (b) Revised Balance Sheet as on the date to give effect to the consequential adjustments.

Solution **[ICWA]**

In the books of Systematic Club

Bank Reconciliation Statement *as on 30th September, 2012*

		Rs.	Rs.
	Balance as per Pass Book		950
Add:	*Cheques paid into bank but not yet credited: (Rs. 100 – Rs. 50).*	50	
	Subscription Received from the member	80	130
			1,080
Less:	*Cheques issued but not presented:*		
	Cheque for Bar supplies	480	
	Cheque for Bonus to professionals	100	
	Cheque for Typewriter	350	930
	Balance as per Cash Book		150

Balance Sheet *as at 30th September 2012*

Liabilities		Rs.	*Assets*	Rs.
Capital	14,300		Furniture & Fittings	9,600
Less; Lossy for the year			Advance for Typewriter	350
(bal fig.)	2,140[4]		Stock	3,680[2]
		12,160	Debtors	1,400
Subscription Received in Advance		680[1]	Cash at Bank	150
Creditors		2,440[3]	Csh in hand (Rs. 50 + Rs. 50)	100
		15,280		15,280

Workings :

1. **Subscription Received in Advance**	Rs.
Subscription received in Advance (already given)	600
Add: Subscription deposited into bank but not Credited for the year 2012-13	80
	680

2. **Closing Stock**	Rs.
Stock (already given)	3,200
Add: Stock of Bar	480
	3,680

3. **Creditors**	
Creditors (given)	2,400
Add: Fuel	140
	2,540
Less: Bonus to Professional	100
	2,440

Note : Net Loss is considered as the balancing figure as the detected information is not given for ascertaining the correct amount of loss.

Illustration 30

Following is the Income and Expenditure Account of the United Club for the year ended on 30.6.2012 :

Dr. **Income and Expenditure Account** *for the year ended 30.6.2012* Cr.

		Rs.			Rs.
To	Salaries	15,750	By	Subscriptions	45,000
"	Stationery	1,250	"	Donations	7,500
"	Postage	800	"	Sales of Furniture (Profit)	1,000

Contd.

		Rs.			Rs.
"	Sundry Expenses	4,700	"	Govt. Grant	4,000
"	Repairs & Maintenance	3,600	"	Interest on Fixed Deposit	800
"	Sports Expenses	1,800			
"	Swimming Pool Expenses & Maintenance	2,000			
"	Affiliation Fee	500			
"	Electricity	3,250			
"	Billiards Room Expenses	1,250			
"	Periodicals	1,200			
"	Audit Fees	250			
"	Depreciation on :				
	Sports Equipments	1,000			
	Buildings	2,500			
	Furniture	450			
"	Surplus—being Excess of Income over Expenditure	18,000			
		58,300			58,300

The above account is prepared after considering the information mentioned below :

Particulars	As on 1.7.2011	As on 30.6.2012
	Rs.	Rs.
(1) Building	1,00,000	97,500
(2) Sports Ground	1,00,000	1,00,000[1]
(3) Sports Equipments	6,000	9,000
(4) Furniture	5,000	—
(5) Fixed Deposits in Bank	8,000	8,000
(6) Bank A/c—Savings Deposits	—	25,000
(7) Subscriptions Outstanding	5,000	2,000
(8) Subscriptions Received in Advance	3,000	1,000
(9) Stock of Stationery	250	500
(10) Audit Fees Outstanding	200	250
(11) Salaries Outstanding	500	1,000
(12) Affiliation Fee Paid in Advance	—	250

Cash in hand on 1.7.2011 was Rs. 1,250. New Furniture of Rs. 9,000 has been purchased on credit but not entered in books. Depreciation has been charged on this Furniture at 5%.

You are required to prepare :

(1) Receipts and Payments Statement for the year ended on 30.6.2012. (2) Balance Sheet as on 30.6.2012.

Solution

In the books of United Club
Receipts and Payments Account *for the year ended 30th June 2012*

Dr. Cr.

	Receipts	Rs.		Payments	Rs.
To	Balance b/d	1,250	By	Salaries	15,250[3]
"	Subscription	46,000[2]	"	Stationery	1,500[5]
"	Donations	7,500	"	Postage	800
"	Govt. Grant	4,000	"	Sports Equipment	4,000
"	Interest on Fixed Deposit	800	"	Sundry Expenses	4,700
"	Sale of Furniture	6,000[7]	"	Repairs and Maintenance	3,600
			"	Sports Expenses	1,800
			"	Swimming Pool Expenses	2,000
			"	Electricity	3,250
			"	Billiards Room Expenses	1,250
			"	Periodicals	1,200
			"	Audit Fees	200[4]
			"	Bank A/c— Savings Deposit	25,000
			"	Affiliation Fees	750
			"	Balance c/d	250
		65,550			65,550

Balance Sheet *as at 30th June 2012*

Liabilities	Rs.	Rs.	*Assets*	Rs.	Rs.
Capital Fund :			Building	1,00,000	
Balance as on 1.7.2011	2,21,800		*Less :* Depreciation	2,500	
Add : Surplus during the year	18,000				97,500
		2,39,800	Furniture	5,000	
Subscription Received in Adv.		1,000	Additions	9,000	
Outstanding Liabilities :				14,000	
Salaries	1,000		*Less :* Sold	5,000	
Audit Fees	250			9,000	
		1,250	*Less :* Depreciation	450	8,550
Creditors (for Furniture)		9,000	Sports Ground		1,00,000
			Sports Equipments	6,000[6]	
			Additions	4,000	
				10,000	
			Less : Depreciation	1,000	9,000
			Fixed Deposit		8,000
			Stock of Stationery		500
			Bank Account— Saving Deposit		25,000
			Outstanding Subscription		2,000
			Prepaid Affiliation Fees		250
			Cash in hand		250
		2,51,050			2,51,050

Workings :

1. **Balance Sheet** *as at July 1, 2011*

Liabilities	Rs.	Rs.	*Assets*	Rs.
Capital Fund *(bal. fig.)*		2,21,800	Building	1,00,000
Subscription Received in Advance		3,000	Sports Ground	1,00,000
Outstanding Liabilities for :			Sports Equipments	6,000
Audit Fees	200		Furniture	5,000
Salaries	500		Fixed Deposit at Bank	8,000
		700	Outstanding Subscription	5,000
			Stock of Stationery	250
			Cash in hand	1,250
		2,25,500		2,25,500

2. Subscription received during the year

		Rs.
Subscription as per Income & Expenditure Account		45,000
Less : Received on 1.7.2011 for the current year	3,000	
Outstanding for the current year	2,000	5,000
		40,000
Add : Subscription outstanding for 1.7.2011	5,000	
Subscription received in advance for the current year	1,000	6,000
		46,000

3. Payment of Salaries

	Rs.
Salaries as per Income and Expenditure Account	15,250
Less : Outstanding for the current year	1,000
	14,750
Add : Outstanding on 1.7.2011	500
	15,250

4. Payment of Audit Fees Rs.

Audit Fees as per Income &

5. Purchase of Stationery during the year

	Rs.
Stationery as per Income & Expenditure Account	1,250
Less : Stock on 1.7.2011	250
	1,000
Add : Stock on 1.7.2012	500
	1,500

6. Purchase of Sports Equipments Rs.

Sports Equipment on 30.6.2011 9,000

	Rs.		Rs.
Expenditure Account	250	*Add* : Depreciation	1,000
Add : Outstanding on 1.7.2011	200		10,000
	450	*Less* : Opening balance	6,000
Less : Outstanding for the current year	250		4,000
	200	**7. Sale of Furniture**	Rs.
		Furniture on 1.7.2011	5,000
		Add : Profit on Sale	1,000
			6,000

Illustration 31

From the following details and information pertaining to Agarwal Nursing Home, you are required to prepare an Income and Expenditure Account and the Balance Sheet as at 31st March 2012:

(a) The Nursing Home was started on 1st April 2009 with Rs. 1,50,000 as capital. For the years ended 31st March 2010 and 31st March 2010, a loss of Rs. 14,000 and a profit of Rs. 32,000 were made :

(b) The equipment installed in the Nursing Home was financed fully by the State Bank of India to the extent of Rs. 3,50,000. The loan taken on 1st April 2009 from the bank carries an interest of 16% p.a. on diminishing balances and the principal is to be repaid in ten equal half-yearly instalments due on 30th September and 31st March along with interest. The commitments up to 1st April 2011 have been discharged by the business.

(c) From the Nursing Home's daily patient register, you notice :

(i) Bills are raised on a weekly basis for payment by patients.
(ii) Bills raised up to 24th March 2012 are Rs. 11,45,500.
(iii) Bills yet to be raised for the last week are Rs. 23,500.

(d) All receipts are banked with the State Bank of India in a Current Account and all expenses, except Rs. 500 drawn every week for petty cash expenses, are met by cheques.

The following is the summary of bank transactions :

	Rs.		Rs.
Deposits :			
Received from Patients	11,30,000	Equipment Maintenance	30,000
Discounts received from Drug Manufacturers and Agents	12,000	Withdrawals by Partners	48,000
Withdrawals :		Rent for Premises	30,000
Salaries and Wages to Doctors and Other Staff	4,50,000		
Payments to Creditors for Drugs, etc.	3,75,000		
Purchase of Detergents	20,000		
Power and Lighting Bills	70,100		

The bank has debited the current account with the loan instalments and interest due on the specified dates. A sum of Rs. 2,700 has also been debited by the bank towards insurance premium on the fire risks against Machinery Cover on behalf of the insured.

(e) Balances as on 1st April 2011 :	Rs.	(f) Amounts due on 31st March 2012 :	Rs.
Sundry Creditors for Drugs and Medicines	25,000		
Salary due to Staff	30,000	Salary to Staff	55,000
Rent due for March 2011	2,500	Amounts due for Purchases made	18,000
Accounts Receivable	30,000	Rent due for March 2012	—
Furniture	1,80,000	Stock of Medicines	12,000
Stock of Medicines	23,000		
Cash Imprest	500		
Interest-free Loan taken from the Disabled Warriors' Society, Delhi	1,38,000		

The Nursing Home is run by a partnership consisting of Mr. and Mrs. Agarwal (both being doctors) who are entitled to a salary of Rs. 2,000 and Rs. 1,000 per month, respectively. Husband and wife share capital and profits and losses in the same ratio as their salary entitlements. Drawings over and above the salary entitlements to be transferred to capital accounts of the partners in the same ratio as capital. Depreciation on equipment to be charged at 10% on the straight-line method and on furniture at 15% of their book value.

Solution

In the books of Agarwal Nursing Home

Dr. **Income and Expenditure Account** *for the year ended 31st March 2012* Cr.

Expenditures	Rs.	Rs.	*Incomes*	Rs.	Rs.
To Salaries	4,50,000		By Billings		11,69,000[1]
Add : Outstanding	15,000		(Receipts from Patients)		
	4,65,000		" Discount Received		12,000
Less : Outstanding for last year	30,000	4,35,000			
" Salaries to Partners (Rs. 3,000 × 12)		36,000			
" Rent		30,000			
" Medicine Consumed :					
Opening Stock	23,000				
Add : Purchases	3,68,000[2]				
	3,91,000				
Less : Closing Stock	12,000	3,79,000			
" Power and Lighting		70,100			
" Detergents		20,000			
" Machinery Maintenance and Repairs		30,000			
" Interest on Loan		30,800[3]			
" Fire Insurance Premium		2,700			
" Petty Expenses (Rs. 500 × 52)		26,000			
" Depreciation :					
Furniture & Fittings	27,000				
Machinery & Equipments	35,000	62,000			
" Surplus — Excess of Income over Expenditure					
Mr. Agarwal	39,600				
Mrs. Agarwal	19,800	59,400			
		11,81,000			11,81,000

Balance Sheet *as at 31st March 2012*

Liabilities	Rs.	Rs.	*Assets*	Rs.	Rs.
Capital Accounts :			Machinery Equipments at Cost	3,50,000	
Mr. Agarwal	1,12,000		*Less* : Depreciation	1,05,000	
Add : Surples	39,600				2,45,000
	1,51,600		Furniture & Fittings at Cost	1,80,000	
Less : Drawings	8,000	1,43,600	*Less* : Prov. for Depreciation	27,000	
Mr. Agarwal Capital	56,000				1,53,000
Add : Surplus	19,800		Stock of Medicines		12,000
	75,800		Amounts Receivable (from Partners)		69,000[1]
Less : Drawings	4,000	71,800			
Loan taken from :			Cash at Bank		49,400[4]
State Bank of India		1,40,000	Cash in hand		500
Disabled Welfare Society		1,38,000			
Creditors for Medicines		18,000			
Outstanding Expenses :					
Rent	2,500				
Salary	15,000	17,500			
		5,28,900			5,28,900

Workings :

1. Accounts Receivable A/c

Dr.	Rs.		Rs. *Cr.*
To Balance b/d	30,000	By Bank A/c	11,30,000
" Income & Expenditure A/c *(bal. fig.)*	11,69,000	" Balance c/d	69,000
	11,99,000		11,99,000

2. Purchase of Medicine Sundry Creditors A/c

Dr.	Rs.		Rs. *Cr.*
To Bank	3,75,000	By Balance b/d	25,000
" Balance c/d	18,000	" Purchases *(bal. fig.)*	3,68,000
	3,93,000		3,93,000

3. **Interest on loan is to be calculated as :**

		Rs.
On Rs. 2,10,000 × $\frac{16}{100} \times \frac{6}{12}$	=	16,800
On Rs. 1,75,000 × $\frac{16}{100} \times \frac{6}{12}$	=	14,000
		30,800

4. Closing Cash and Bank is ascertained from the preparation of Bank Account as:

Bank A/c

Dr.	Rs.		Rs. *Cr.*
To Balance b/d	60,000	By Salaries & Wages	4,50,000
" Parties	11,30,000	" Sundry Creditors	3,75,000
" Discount Received	12,000	" Detergents	20,000
		" Power and Lighting	70,100
		" Machinery Maintenance and Repairs	30,000
		" Rent	30,000
		" Drawings of Partners	12,000
		" Partners' Salary	36,000
		" Payment of Loan (two installments)	70,000
		" Interest on Loan	30,800
		" Insurance Premium	2,700
		" Sundry Expenses	26,000
		" Balance c/d	49,400
	12,02,000		12,02,000

Balance Sheet *as at 31st March 2011*

Liabilities	Rs.	Rs.	*Assets*	Rs.	Rs.
Mr. Agarwal's Capital	1,12,000*		Machinery & Equipments at Cost	3,50,000	
Mrs. Agarwal	56,000	1,68,000	*Less :* Depreciation Provision	70,000	2,80,000
Loan from SBI		2,10,000	Furniture		1,80,000
Loan from Disabled Welfare Society		1,38,000	Stock of Medicine		23,000
Creditors		25,000	Account Receivable		30,000
Outstanding Liabilities :			Cash in hand		500
Rent	2,500		Cash at Bank *(bal. fig.)*		60,000
Salary	30,000	32,500			
		5,73,500			5,73,500

* Opening Capital is ascertained as :

		Rs.
	Capital as on 1.1.2009	1,50,000
Add :	Profit (2010-11)	32,000
		1,82,000
Less :	Loss (2009-10)	14,000
		1,68,000

Mr. Agarwal's share = Rs. 1,68,000 × $\frac{2}{3}$ = Rs. 1,12,000

Mrs. Agarwal's share = Rs. 1,68,000 × $\frac{1}{3}$ = Rs. 56,000

ASSIGNMENT MATERIALS

THEORETICAL

Fill in the Blanks

1. Fill in the blanks:

Case	Subscription Received	Outstanding subscription at the beginning	Outstanding subscription at the end	Subscription credited to Income & Expenditure Account
	Rs.	Rs.	Rs.	Rs.
(a)	30,000	5,000	8,000	?
(b)	?	1,000	3,000	10,000
(c)	40,000	?	5,000	44,000
(d)	50,000	10,000	?	40,000

[Ans.(a) Rs. 33,000; (b) Rs. 8,000; (c) Rs. 1,000; (d) Rs. Nil]

Short Answer-Type Questions

2. Define Receipts and Incomes.
3. Define Payments and Expenditures.
4. What is Receipts and Payments Account?
5. What is Income and Expenditure Account?
6. Mention the features of Receipts and Payment Account.
7. Distinguish between Receipts and Payment Account and Income and Expenditure Account (any five point).
8. What is Subscription? How do you treat it?
9. Define : (a) Outstanding Subscription, and (b) Subscriptions Received in Advance.
10. What are Life Membership Fees and Life Membership Fund?

Long Answer-Type Questions

11. Distinguish between (a) Receipts and Incomes; (b) Expenditures and Payments.
12. What is Receipts and Payment Account? How do you prepare it?
13. What is Income and Expenditure Account? What are it's features?
14. Distinguish between Receipts and Payment Account and Income and Expenditure Account.
15. Distinguish between Income and Expenditure Account and Profit and Loss Account.
16. Explain the various funds used in a non-trading concern.
17. Explain the various methods of accounting of a non-trading Concern.
18. What is subscription? Explain its treatment.
19. Distinguish between Receipts and Payment Account and Cash Book.
20. What are the sources of income of a non-trading organisation?

PRACTICAL

Computation of Subscription

1. The Receipts and Payments Account of a club for the year ended 31.12.97 showed a debit entry of Rs. 10,000 for subscriptions. From the information available, it is found that :

Subscriptions outstanding on 31.12.96 was Rs. 2,000. Subscriptions outstanding on 31.12.97 was Rs. 4,000. Subscriptions received in advance as on 31.12.96 was Rs. 3,000. Subscriptions received in advance as on 31.12.97 was Rs. 2,000.

Calculate the Income from Subscriptions for the year ending 31.12.97. **[ICWA]**

[Ans. Rs. 13,000]

2. The following information were obtained from the Secretary of the Crazy Jay Club:

	Rs.
Subscriptions received in 1998-99 as per Receipts and Payments A/c	89,000
Advance subscriptions received in 1997-98	5,000
Subscriptions outstanding at the end of 1998-99 (including Rs. 1,500 for 1997-98)	12,500

Contd.

	Rs.
Advance subscriptions received for 1998-99	3,000
Subscriptions written-off during 1998-99	600
Subscriptions receivable on 1.4.1998	8,400

Prepare a statement of account showing the subscription income for the year ending 31st March 1999, and show how the relevant items will appear in the Income & Expenditure Account for the year and in the Balance Sheet as at the end of the year.

[Ans. Subscriptions for 2008-09 on Accrual basis Rs. 95,700; Balance to be shown in the Balance Sheet : Liability side Rs. 3,000; Asset side 2007-2008 Rs. 1,500, and 2008-09 Rs. 11,000]

Preparation of Income and Expenditure Account and Balance Sheet.

3. From the following particulars relating to Sishu Mangal Charitable Hospital, prepare Income and Expenditure Account for the year ended 31st December 2004 :

Dr. **Receipts and Payments Account** *for the year ended 31st December 2004* *Cr.*

	Receipts	Rs.		*Payments*	Rs.
To	Balance b/d	7,130	By	Medicines	30,590
"	Subscriptions	47,996	"	Doctors' Honorarium	9,000
"	Donations	14,500	"	Salaries	27,500
"	Interest on Investments (@ 7% for full one year)	7,000	"	Petty Expenses	461
"	Proceeds from Charity Show	10,450	"	Equipment	15,000
			"	Expenses on Charity Show	750
			"	Balance c/d	3,775
		87,076			87,076

Additional Information

		1.1.04	31.12.04
(i)	Subscriptions due	200	240
(ii)	Subscriptions received in advance	64	100
(iii)	Stock medicines	8,810	9,740
(iv)	Estimated Value of Equipment	21,200	31,600
(v)	Buildings (cost, less depreciation)	40,000	38,000

[Ans. Deficit Rs. 8,521, Subscription for 2004 Rs. 48,000]

4. From the Receipts and Payments Account of Green Park Cricket Club you are asked to prepare an Income and Expenditure Account for the year ended on 31st December 2001 :

Dr. **Receipts and Payments Accounts** *for the year ended 31.12.01* *Cr.*

	Receipts	Rs.		*Payments*	Rs.
To	Balance b/d		By	Salaries	2,100
	Cash in hand	1,200	"	Rent	3,600
	Cash at Bank	3,400	"	Equipments	10,000
"	Subscriptions	24,500	"	Sports Expenses	4,700
"	Entrance Fees	3,000	"	Remuneration to coach	4,000
			"	Sundry Expenses	1,100
			"	Printing and Stationery	800
			"	Balance c/d	
				Cash in hand	1,700
				Cash at bank	4,100
		32,100			32,100

The following information are also available :

	31.12.2000 Rs.	31.12.2001 Rs.
Subscription Received in Advance	1,400	2,700
Outstanding Subscription	2,100	3,200
Outstanding Rent	600	300
Advance Salaries	1,200	900
Equipments	18,000	23,000

60% of the Entrance Fees is to be capitalised. Interest on Savings Bank Account for Rs. 280 has not been entered in the Cash Book. An old equipment (W.D.V. Rs. 8,000) was exchanged at an agreed price of Rs. 5,000 for a new equipment costing Rs. 15,000.

[Ans. Surplus Rs. 4,480]

5. The Receipts and Payments Account of Star Football Club for the year ended 31st March 2002 was as :

		Rs.			Rs.
To	Balance b/d	48,000	By	Purchase of Balls	80,000
"	Subscription Received	2,46,000	"	Tournament Fees	10,000
"	Interest	2,000	"	Affiliation Fees	2,000
"	Sale of Furniture	10,000	"	Rent of Playground	5,000
"	Donation for Club Buildings	60,000	"	Refreshment Expenses	4,000
			"	Travelling Expenses	30,000
			"	Investment Prepaid at Face Value	1,00,000
			"	Salary	12,000
			"	Miscellaneous Expenses	8,000
			"	Balance c/d	1,15,000
		3,66,000			3,66,000

Prepare the Club's Income and Expenditure Account for the year ended 31st March 2002 and the Balance Sheet as on that date after taking the following information into account :

(i) The subscription received included Rs. 10,000 outstanding subscription of the year 2000-01. Subscription for the year 2001-02 amounting to Rs. 16,000 was still outstanding from members. Some members have paid subscription for the year 2002-03 amounting to Rs. 8,000 which is included in the subscriptions received.

(ii) Interest accrued but not received Rs. 500.

(iii) The book value of Furniture sold was Rs. 14,000.

(iv) The rent of playground Rs. 6,000 and salary Rs. 5,000 of the year 2001-02 are still outstanding, and rent of playground of the year 2000-01 Rs. 1,000 has been paid during the year.

(v) There is a stock of balls with this club of Rs. 4,000 on 31st March 2002.

[Ans. Capital Fund Rs. 71,000; Surplus Rs. 85,800; Balance Sheet Rs. 2,35,800]

6. The following is the Receipts and Payments Account of the J. M. Club in respect of the year ending 31st March 1995:

Receipts	Rs.	Rs.	*Payments*	Rs.
1.1.1994			31.3.1995	
To Balance b/d		2,050	By Salaries	4,160
31. 3. 1995			" Stationery	800
" Subscriptions			" Rates and Taxes	1,200
1993-94	80		" Telephone	200
1994-95	4,220		" Investment in	
1995-96	160	4,460	Govt. Securities	2,500
" Profit on Sports Meeting		2,850	Sundry Expenses	1,850
" Interest on Investments		2,000	Balance c/d	900
" Sundry Receipts		250		
		11,610		11,610

The following additional facts are ascertained :

(a) Stock of Stationery on 1st April 1994 was Rs. 100 and on 31st March 1995 Rs. 180.

(b) Rates and Taxes were prepaid to the extent of Rs. 400.

(c) Telephone Charges outstanding amounts to Rs. 75.

(d) In 1993-94, subscription received in advance amounting to Rs. 200 for current year and Rs. 180 were due on 31st March 1995 for 1994-95.

(e) On 31st March 1994, the Building stood in the books at Rs. 20,000 and it is required to write-off depreciation at 5%. Investments at 31st March 1994 were Rs. 40,000.

You are required to prepare Income and Expenditure Account for the year ended 31st March 1995 and a Balance Sheet as at that date.

[Ans. Excess of Income over Expenditure Rs. 895; Balance Sheet Rs. 63,160]

7. Given below is the Receipts and Payments Account of Calcutta Amusement Club:

Receipts and Payments Account *for the year ended 31st Dec. 1994*

Receipts		Rs.	*Payments*		Rs.
Balance			Purchase of Land		10,000
Cash	100		Salary of Secretary		4,000
Bank	4,000	4,100	Honorarium		500
Subscription (including subscription for 1993 Rs. 500)		12,000	Wages		3,000
			Charities		3,000
Sale of old Furniture (on 1.1.1994)		800	Printing and Stationery		400
			Postages		100
Sale of old newspaper		100	Rent and Taxes		1,500
Legacies		4,000	Upkeep of Land		600
Interest on Investments (Cost of Investment Rs. 30,000)		1,500	Sports Materials		3,200
Endowment Fund Receipts		8,000	Balance		
Proceeds of concerts		1,000	Cash	600	
Advertisement in the Year Book		100	Bank	4,700	5,300
		31,600			31,600

Current assets and liabilities as on 31st Dec. 1993 and 1994 are :

	31.12.1993 Rs.	31.12.1994 Rs.
Subscription in arrear	500	600
Subscription in advance	500	800
Furniture	3,000	1,800

Depreciation was 10% p.a. on the Furniture left after selling a part of it.

It was decided that half of the legacies may be capitalised.

Prepare Income and Expenditure Account for the year ending 31st Dec. 1994 and a Balance Sheet as on that date.

[Ans. Excess of Income over Expenditure Rs. 3,000; Balance Sheet Rs. 50,900]

8. The following shows the position of the Calcutta Library as at 1.1.1992:

Liabilities	Rs.	*Assets*	Rs.
Capital Fund	1,50,000	Building	50,000
Outstanding Liabilities (for expenses)	5,000	Furniture	5,000
		Library	25,000
		Investments	50,000
		Outstanding Subscriptions	20,000
		Cash in hand	5,000
	1,55,000		1,55,000

An analysis of the Cash Book during the year gives the following particulars :

	Receipts	Rs.		*Payments*	Rs.
To	Subscriptions	75,000	By	Salaries	3,600
"	Donation	50,000	"	Purchase of Books	40,000
"	Interest on Investment	600	"	Rent and Taxes	3,600
"	Sale of Old Furniture	500	"	Outstanding Liabilities	5,000
"	Proceeds of Lectures	8,000	"	Insurance Premium	1,500
			"	Printing & Stationery	450
			"	Purchase of Furniture	7,500
			"	Sundry Expenses	450
			"	Investments	75,000
			"	Balance c/d	2,000

The following adjustments are required :

(a) Outstanding Subscriptions amounted to Rs. 15,000; (b) Outstanding Liabilities for Expenses Rs. 7,500; (c) Insurance Premium amounting to Rs. 300 was paid in advance; (d) Depreciate Building @ 5% p. a.; Library Books @ 10% p. a. and Investment @ 5% p. a. (Such depreciation is to be calculated on the opening balance of the assets.)

Prepare Income and Expenditure Account for the year ended 31.12.1992 and a Balance Sheet as on that date.

[CU BCom (Hons.)]

[Ans. Excess of Income over Expenditure Rs. 54,300; Balance Sheet Rs. 2,61,800]

Hint : [Donation to be treated as capital]

9. The following is the Receipts and Payments Account of Apollo Club in respect of the year to 31st March 1993:

Dr. **Receipts and Payments Account** *for the year ended* 31.3.1993 *Cr.*

Receipts		Rs.	*Payments*	Rs.
1.4.92			31.3.93	
To Balance b/f			By Salaries	3,000
Cash in hand		2,000	" Stationery	1,000
31.3.93			" Rates & Taxes	300.
To Subscriptions :			By Telephone Charges	1,500
1991-92	3,000		" 8% Securities at par	5,000
1992-93	4,000		" Sundry Expenses	200
1993-94	1,000	8,000	" Balance c/d	
" Profit on Sports		3,000	Cash in hand	3,000
" Interest on 8% Securities		1,000		
		14,000		14,000

The following additional facts are ascertained :

(a) There are 500 members, each paying an annual subscription of Rs. 10, Rs. 3,500 being in arrears for 1991-92 at the beginning of 1992-93. During 1991-92 subscription were paid in advance by 30 members for 1992-93.

(b) Stock of stationery at 31st March 1992, was Rs. 400 and at 31st March 1993, Rs. 500.

(c) At 31st March 1993, the Rates and Taxes were prepaid to the following 31st January, the yearly charge being Rs. 300.

(d) A quarter's charge for telephone is outstanding, the amount accrued being Rs. 300. The charges for each quarter is same for both 1991-92 and 1992-93.

(e) Sundry expenses accruing at 31st March 1992 were Rs. 50 and at 31st March 1993, Rs. 60.

(f) At 31st March 1992, Building stood in the books at Rs. 30,000 and it is required to write-off depreciation at 10% p.a.

(g) Value of 8% Securities at 31st March 1992 was Rs. 15,000 which was purchased at that date at par, Additional Securities worth Rs. 5,000 are purchased on 31st March 1993.

You are required to prepare :

(i) An Income and Expenditure Account for the year ended 31st March 1993, and

(ii) A Balance Sheet as at that date.

[Ans. Capital Fund Rs. 50,200; Surplus Rs. 590; Balance Sheet Rs. 52,150]

10. Following is the Receipts & Payments Account of X Club for the year ended 31.12.1997 :

Receipts	Rs.	Rs.	*Payments*	Rs.	Rs.
Balance b/d			Salaries		
Cash	2,000		Secretary	6,000	
Bank	12,000	14,000	Staff	5,000	11,000
Subscription			Canteen Expenses		12,000
For 1997	5,500		Miscellaneous Expenses		2,500
Do 1996	500		Construction of Building		15,000
Do 1998	400	6,400	Balance c/d		
Interest from Bank		1,000	Cash	1,300	
Sale proceeds of old newspapers		400	Bank	4,000	5,300
Sale of old Furniture		2,000			
Canteen collections		12,000			
Donation for Building Fund		10,000			
		45,800			45,800

With the additional information given below, prepare the Income and Expenditure Account for the year ended 31.12.1997 and the Balance Sheet as on that date :

		31.12.1996	31.12.1997
		Rs.	Rs.
(a)	Subscription Receivable	1,000	600
(b)	Subscription Received in Advance	200	400
(c)	Salary of Staff outstanding	1,000	2,000
(d)	Canteen expenses prepaid	1,000	1,500
(e)	Furniture at book value	14,000	?
(f)	Building	15,000	?
(g)	Fixed Deposit with Bank	10,000	10,000

(h) Book value of Furniture sold during the year 1997 was Rs. 3,500

(i) Charge depreciation on Furniture at 10% p.a. on the closing balance.

[Ans. Excess of Expenditure over Income Rs. 8,850; Balance Sheet Rs. 57,350 ; Capital Fund Rs. 53,800]

11. From the following particulars of Dadar Matunga Club, you are required to prepare an Income and Expenditure Account for the year ended 31.12.1992, and a Balance Sheet as on that date.

On 1.1.1992, the assets and liabilities were :

Land and Building Rs. 55,000; Furniture & Fixture Rs. 5,000; Subscriptions outstanding for 1991 Rs. 500; Stock of Consumable Stores Rs. 1,000; Stock of Cutlery and Crockery Rs. 2,000; Investments Rs. 1,00,000; Bank Fixed Deposit Rs. 4,500; Balance at Bank Rs. 1,000; Outstanding Creditors for Expenses : Salaries Rs. 400; Stationery & Printing Rs. 200; Subscription for 1992, received in advance Rs. 400. Income & Expenditure Account (Cr.) Rs. 10,500.

The cash transactions during the year :

Subscription received Rs. 17,600; Entrance Fees Rs. 5,000; Interest on Investment etc. Rs. 3,010; Sale of old Furniture Rs. 100; Sundry Sales Rs. 90; Dining room receipts Rs. 20,600; Fixed Deposit matured Rs. 4,500; Salaries Rs. 5,000; Purchase of Consumable Stores Rs. 15,000; Stationery & Printing Rs. 800; Placed in Fixed Deposit with Bank Rs. 11,500; Extension to Building Rs. 12,000; Sundry Expenses Rs. 1,200; Cutlery and Crockery purchased Rs. 1,000.

On 31.12.1992, the Stock of Consumable Stores was valued at Rs. 2,000; Subscription for 1993 Rs. 600 were received in advance; Subscription for 1992 Rs. 800 were outstanding. Depreciate Land & Building by Rs. 2,000, Cutlery and Crockery by Rs. 500 and Furniture and Fixture by Rs. 200. Salaries outstanding were Rs. 500. Half of the Entrance Fees are to be capitalised.

[Ans. Excess of Income over Expenditure Rs. 20,300; Balance Sheet Rs. 1,91,900; Capital Fund Rs. 1,57,500; Closing Cash Balance Rs. 5,400]]

12. The analysis of the Cash Book of General Library, Basirhat, for the year 1994 showed the following :

Receipts		Rs.	*Payments*	Rs.
Subscriptions	1993	1,000	Salaries	15,000
	1994	30,000	Printing and Stationery	1,000
	1995	2,000	Electric Charges	500
Interest on Investments		1,000	Rent and Rates	2,000
Sale of old Furniture		500	Telephone Charges	1,200
Sale of old Newspapers		100	Advertisement	100
Hall Rent		4,000	Meeting Expenses	400
Special Fund Receipts		3,000	Insurance Premium	500
Admission Fees			Purchase of Library Books	10,000
(40% to be capitalised)		5,000	Purchase of Furniture	6,000
Donation (50% to be capitalised)		10,000	Special Fund Expenses	2,000
Telephone Receipts		100	Misc. Expenses	1,300

Additional Information

(a) The assets of the Library on 1st January 1994 were : Cash in hand Rs. 3,000; Cash at Bank Rs. 7,000; 8% G. P. Notes Rs. 40,000; Library Books Rs. 20,000; Furniture Rs. 6,000.

(b) Salaries include Rs. 2,000 for 1993 and Rs. 3,000 for 1995.

(c) Outstanding Liabilities on 31.12.1994 were : Rent and Tax Rs. 1,000; Audit Fees Rs. 500.

(d) Outstanding assets on 31.12.1994 were: Subscription Rs. 2,500; Bank Interest Rs. 500.
(e) Special Fund Balance (Cr.) on 1.1.1994, was Rs. 3,000.
(f) Depreciate Library Books @ 10% and Furniture @ 5%.
(g) On 31.12.1994, Cash in hand was Rs. 4,000 and the balancing figure of the Cash Book represents Cash at Bank as on 31.12.1994.

Prepare an Income and Expenditure Account for the year ended 31.12.1994 and a Balance Sheet as on that date.

Note : Additions were made at the middle of the year and Furniture was sold at the beginning of the year.
[Ans. Excess of Income over Expenditure Rs. 26,825; Balance Sheet Rs. 1,13,325; Capital Fund Rs. 72,000]

Prepparation of Balance Sheet

13. The following particulars relate to Fast Sports Club:

Income and Expenditure Account *for the year ended 31.12.1989*

		Rs.			Rs.
To	Salary	6,000	By	AdmissionFees	15,000
"	Printing and Stationery	2,500	"	Subscription	25,000
"	Advertising	900	"	Rent Receivable	4,800
"	Insurance Charges	1,000			
"	Electricity Charges	500			
"	Depreciation on Sports Equipments	12,000			
"	Excess of Income over expenditure	21,900			
		44,800			44,800

Receipts and Payments Account *for the year ended 31.12.1989*

			Rs.			Rs.
To	Balance		5,000	By	Salary (including advance)	7,500
"	Admission Fees :			"	Printing and Stationery	2,500
	1988	2,500			Advertising	1,000
	1989	13,500	16,000	"	Insurance Charges (partly for next year)	1,200
"	Subscription :			"	Electricity	500
	1988	1,000		"	Purchase of Fixed Assets	20,000
	1989	23,000		"	Balance	17,900
	1990	2,000	26,000			
"	Rent		3,600			
			50,600			50,600

On 1.1.1989 the Club had the following assets :

	Rs.
Land and Building	60,000
Sports Equipments	30,000
Furniture	4,500

Prepare opening and closing Balance Sheets. [CA Entrance]

[Ans. Balance Sheet (1.1.1989) Rs. 1,03,000; Balance Sheet (31.12.1989) Rs. 1,26,900]

14. The following are the items of Receipts and Payments of the Bengal Club as summarised from the books of accounts maintained by the Secretary :

Receipts		Rs.	*Payments*	Rs.
Opening Balance	(1.1.91)	4,200	Manager's Salary	1,000
Entrance Fees	(1990)	1,000	Printing and Stationery	2,600
Do	(1991)	10,000	Advertising	1,800
Subscriptions (1990)		600	Fire Insurance	1,200
Do	(1991)	15,000	Investments Purchased	20,000
Interest Received on Investments		3,000	Closing Balance 31.12.91	7,600
Subscriptions (1992)		400		
		34,200		34,200

It was ascertained from enquiry that the following represented a fair picture of the Income and Expenditure of the Club for the year 1991 for audit purpose :

Expenditures	Rs.	Rs.	*Incomes*	Rs.
Manager's Salary		1,500	Entrance Fees	10,500
Printing & Stationery	2,000		Subscription	15,600
Add : Accrued	400	2,400	Interest on Investments	4,000
Advertising (accrued Nil)		1,600		
Audit Fees		500		
Fire Insurance		1,000		
Depreciation		4,940		
Excess of Income over Expenditure		18,160		
		30,100		30,100

You are required to prepare the Balance Sheet of the Club as on 31.12.90, and 31.12.91, it being given that the values of the Fixed Assets as on 31.12.90 were : Building Rs. 44,000, Cricket Equipment Rs. 25,000 and Furniture Rs. 4,000. The rates of depreciation are; Building 5%, Cricket Equipment 10%, Furniture 6%. You are entitled to make assumptions as may be justified.

[Ans. Total of Opening Balance Sheet Rs. 78,800; Capital Fund Rs. 78,000. Total of Closing Balance Sheet Rs. 97,960]

PREPARATION OF RECEIPTS AND PAYMENTS ACCOUNT

15. From the following Income and Expenditure Account of the J. Club, Nagpur, in respect of the year ended 31st Dec. 1994, and a Balance Sheet as on that date, you are required to prepare Receipts and Payments Account for the year ending 31st Dec. 1994 :

Receipts and Payments Account ***for the year ended 31.12.94***

		Rs.			Rs.
To	Rent	1,800	By	Subscription	6,750
"	Salaries	6,240	"	Dividend	3,000
"	Stationery	1,080	"	Misc. Receipts	4,650
"	Telephone	405			
"	Sundry Expenses	2,565			
"	Depreciation on Assets	1,500			
"	Excess of Income over Expenditure	810			
		14,400			14,400

Balance Sheet ***as at 31.12.1994***

	Rs.	Rs.		Rs.	Rs.
Capital Fund	93,600		Cash in hand		1,350
Add : Surplus	810		Investment	60,000	
		94,410	*Add* : Additions		
Subscription in advance		240	during the year	3,750	63,750
Outstanding telephone		105	Assets	30,000	
			Less : Depreciation	1,500	28,500
			Stock of Stationery		270
			Rent Prepaid		450
			Accrued Subscription		435
		94,755			94,755

You are informed that:

(i) Subscription of Rs. 135 was in arrear on 1st Jan. 1994. (ii) On 1.1.1994, Stock of Stationery was worth Rs. 150. (iii) On 1.1.1994 Rent Prepaid were Rs. 4. (iv) On 1.1.1994 Mis. Receipts outstanding were Rs. 210.

[Ans. Total of Receipts and Payments Account Rs. 17,205; Subscriptions Rs. 6,690]

16. From the following particulars relating to the Young Men's Association, make out Receipts and Payments Account for 1998 and a Balance Sheet as at 31st December 1998 :

Income and Expenditure Account for 1998

		Rs.			Rs.
To	Salaries	4,000	By	Subscription	9,400
"	Gardener's Wages	1,500	"	Interest	600

Contd.

		Rs.			Rs.
To	Rent	600	By	Entrance Fees	1,000
"	Periodicals	100	"	Donation	500
"	Travelling	100			
"	Printing and Stationery	150			
"	General Expenses	400			
"	Excess of Income over Expenditure	4,650			
		11,500			11,500

Note : 50% of Entrance Fees have been capitalised.

Balance Sheet *as at 31.12.97*

	Rs.		Rs.
General Fund	17,250	Furniture	4,000
Outstanding Expenses :		Sports Equipment	2,000
Printer's Bill	200	6% Investment (F.V. Rs. 10,000)	9,000
Salaries	300	Subscription Receivable	500
Rent	50	Interest Receivable	300
		Cash and Bank	2,000
	17,800		17,800

Other details on 31.12.98 :

6% Investment (F.V. Rs. 11,000) Rs. 9,800; Subscription due Rs. 900; Accrued interest Rs. 150; Salaries unpaid Rs. 200; Wages paid in advance Rs. 100; Printer's bill Rs. 40; Furniture at cost Rs. 4,500. Depreciation charges not considered in the above income statement. On furniture Rs. 200; On sports equipment Rs. 250.

[Ans. Total of Receipts and Payments A/c Rs. 14,250; Closing Cash Rs. 5,690; Balance Sheet Rs. 22,690]

17. Summary of Receipts and Payments of Bombay Medical Aid Society for the year ended 31.12.2000 are:

Opening Cash balance in hand Rs. 8,000, Subscription Rs. 50,000, Donation Rs. 15,000, Interest on Investments @ 9% p.a. Rs. 9,000. Payments for medicine supply Rs. 30,000. Honorarium to Doctors Rs. 10,000, Salaries Rs. 28,000, Sundry Expenses Rs. 1,000, Equipment purchase Rs. 15,000. Charity Show expenses Rs. 1,500, Charity Show collections Rs. 12,500.

Additional Information

	1.1.2000 Rs.	31.12.2000 Rs.
Subscription due	1,500	2,200
Subscription received in advance	1,200	700
Stock of medicine	10,000	15,000
Amount due for medicine supply	9,000	13,000
Value of equipment	21,000	30,000
Value of building	50,000	48,000

You are required to prepare Receipts and Payments Account and Income and Expenditure Account for the year ended 31.12.2000 and Balance sheet as on 31.12.2000.

[CA Foundation]

[Ans. : Closing Cash Balance Rs. 9,000; Surplus Rs. 10,200; Balance Sheet Rs. 2,04,200; Capital Fund Rs. 1,80,300; Donation is treated as revenue.]

On Bar Trading

18. The following is the Receipts and Payments Account of the Calcutta Sports Club for the year ended 31.12.2002:

	Receipts	Rs.		*Payments*	Rs.
To	Entrance Fees	10,000	By	Special Fund Expenses	2,200
"	Special Fund receipts (for Governor's party)	3,000	"	Purchase of Sports Materials	2,400
			"	Bar Purchases and Exp.	3,000
"	Subscription	4,400	"	Salaries	2,400
"	Interest on Securities	600	"	Printing & Stationery	910
"	Bar Receipts	2,600	"	Billiards Expenses	2,260
"	Misc. Receipts	550	"	Sundry Expenses	

Contd.

		Rs.			Rs.
To	Donation	58,000	By	(including Insurance Premium)	440
"	Billiards Fees	2,500	"	Furniture	3,000
			"	Land & Building	49,000
			"	Investment	12,000
			"	Bank balances	3,600
			"	Cash balances	440
		81,650			81,650

Subscription include Rs. 250 for the year 2003 and subscription in arrear amounted to Rs. 900. Interest accrued amounted to Rs. 240. Salaries unpaid for the year amounted to Rs. 350 and Insurance prepaid Rs. 60. Stock of Sport Materials and Bar Stock at the end of the year are valued at Rs. 1,500 and Rs. 800, respectively. Depreciate Furniture by 6% and Land and Building by 2. 50% of the Entrance Fees are to be treated as revenue and the whole amount of Donation is to capitalised.

Prepare an Income and Expenditure Account for the year ended 31.12.2002 and a Balance Sheet as on that date.

[Ans. Excess of Income over Expenditure Rs. 6,780; Balance Sheet Rs. 70,380]

19. The Receipts and Payments Account for 1992 of the C. Y.'s Indoor Recreation Club is :

	Receipts	Rs.		*Payments*	Rs.
To	Donation	4,000	By	Rent	9,000
"	Life Membership Fees	5,000	"	Salaries	11,500
"	Entrance Fees	2,500	"	Furniture	2,000
"	Subscription	6,750	"	Electricity	600
"	Bar Receipts	25,000	"	Bar Purchases	20,000
"	Journey Receipts	1,800	"	Journey Expenses	1,505
"	Billiards Fees	500	"	Telephone	370
"	Table Tennis Fees	250	"	Postage	120
"	Card room Receipts	125	"	Bank balance	1,430
"	Grant from Calcutta Corporation	1,000	"	Cash balance	400
		46,925			46,925

(a) Donation in entirety, $\frac{3}{4}$ of the Life Membership Fees and $\frac{1}{2}$ of the Entrance Fees are to be capitalised.

(b) Subscriptions received in advance are Rs. 250, and outstanding Rs. 1,000.

(c) Rs. 200 was unrealised on Journey Account.

(d) Rent was paid for three years in advance.

(e) Salaries include an advance of Rs. 500 and a sum of Rs. 1,000 remained unpaid as on 31st Dec. 1992.

(f) Furniture is to be depreciated by 6%.

(g) Bar Stock as at 31st Dec. amounted to Rs. 5,000.

(h) Telephone Rent had been paid up to March 1993.

You are required to draw up an Income and Expenditure Account for 1992 and also a Balance Sheet as on that date.

[Ans. Excess of Income over Expenditure Rs. 6,984; Balance Sheet Rs. 17,234]

CHAPTER 24

ACCOUNTS OF PROFESSIONAL MEN

Learning Objectives

Meaning

Requirements of Maintenance of Accounts under Income Tax Act, 1961

Maintenance of Accounts (Sec. 44AA)

Books of Accounts

Medical Profession

—Accounts of Doctors

Relation between the Accounts of Professional Persons and their Household Accounts

—Accounts of Chartered Accountants

—Accounts of Solicitors/Lawyers

Introduction

Professional men—Doctors, Lawyers, Accountants, etc.—*usually maintain and prepare their accounts on cash basis.* Since the number of credit transactions is very limited, Accrual system of accounting is neglected here as the same is more lengthy and elaborate. But if there are numerous credit transactions, accrual/mercantile system may be adopted. It may be mentioned, however, that if cash basis of accounting is followed, it does not mean that outstanding expenses, depreciation etc. are not incorporated. In that case, incomes are recorded on Cash system whereas expenses are recorded on accrual/mercantile system i.e., Mixed/Hybrid system of accounting is followed.

There are two purposes for which professional people maintain their accounts : viz., (i) to ensure that all incomes and expenditures are properly recorded, (ii) to ascertain the net professional income for a given period.

Separate accounts should be maintained for private and professional incomes and expenditures. That is, incomes and expenses, either professional or private, must not be mixed up with the other.

Since professional people like lawyers, accountants etc. are to use a large amount of clients' money, care should be taken in such a way as the clients' money and own money are not mixed up. For this purpose, a separate bank account may be opened and, at the same time, separate columns should also be made in the Cash Book for the said purposes. Similarly, they are also to make payments on behalf of the clients and, subsequently, the same is reimbursed by the clients. These payments must not be mixed up with the expenses of profession.

Usually, professional people prepare their bills after the completion of the work and send the same to their clients which, in other words, does not help to ascertain the results of their profession. For this purpose, value of incompleted work should be estimated and accounted for ascertaining the real result of the profession at the end of the accounting period. It has to be remembered that if Income and Expenditure Account is prepared under 'Hybrid System', fees received and receivable including the value of incompleted work are treated as income, whereas a provision is to be made which is equal to the total amount of accrued fees and value of work-in-progress as well.

The following accounts may be maintained :

(a) *Cash Book* : A Cash Book is maintained which will incorporate all receipts and all payments. Since the credit transactions are very few in number they may be noted temporarily in a memorandum book and, when the actual receipts or payments will be made, they are to be incorporated in Cash Book. An Abstract Cash Account is to be prepared after summarising the Cash Book at the end of a period, say, a year, which will exhibit the receipts and payments under appropriate heads for the year. An Analytical Cash Book, with a number of analysis columns in both sides, may also be prepared alternatively which will eliminate the necessity of preparing an annual summary of Cash Book.

(b) *Stock Book :* One or more Stock Books should also be prepared in order to keep records of the transactions relating to (i) goods that are purchased for re-sale, e.g., medicine (in the case of a doctor)—revenue expenditure. (ii) articles that are purchased for use and not for resale; e.g., Equipment and Apparatus, Furniture, —capital expenditure. Although these transactions are recorded in Cash Book as soon as they take place, they should also be recorded in a Stock Book which will reveal a permanent and continuous record from the beginning to the end. The Stock Book will include the information relating to date and description of articles purchased, names and addresses of suppliers, quantity, prices etc. Similarly, if any article is sold, lost or destroyed or consumed a note to that effect is to be recorded in the Stock Book so that accounting stock and physical stock may be compared.

(c) *Income and Expenditure Account* : An Income and Expenditure Account is prepared (like Profit and Loss Account of a trader) at the end of the year for ascertaining the net professional income, by taking the incomes and expenses from the Summarised Cash Book or Abstract Cash Account together with the opening and closing balances of stock from the Stock Book. But, if Cash Basis of accounting is followed, only the incomes or expenses which are received or paid in Cash are to be taken into consideration at the time of preparing an Income and Expenditure Account. Outstanding and prepaid expenses, accrued incomes or incomes received in advance are ignored. A Balance Sheet may also be prepared from the Summarised or Abstract Cash Book and the Stock Book for a particular period.

To sum up :

The following points should carefully be noted to solve the problems relating to professional men :

(i) ***At first, ascertain the professional and non-professional expenses and incomes.***

(ii) ***Secondly, distinguish between capital and revenue incomes and expenses like non-trading concerns.***

(iii) ***In order to ascertain the professional income, and Income and Expenditure Account (sometimes Profit and Loss Account) relating to profession is to be opened by considering only the professional revenue incomes and expenditures.***

(iv) ***The method of preparation of Income an Expenditure Account is similar to the method of preparation of Income and Expenditure Account of a non-trading concern, i.e., expenditure on the debit side and incomes on the credit side.***

(v) ***Make a provision @ 100% for incoming outstanding at the beginning and also at the closing.***

Requirements of Maintenance of Accounts under Income Tax Act, 1961

Maintenance of Accounts (Sec. 44AA)

According to Section 44AA of the Income Tax Act, 1961, every person carrying on legal, medical, engineering or architectural profession or the profession of accountancy or technical consultancy or interior decoration or any other profession notified by the Board shall keep and maintain such books of accounts and other documents as may enable the AO to compute his total income.

Books of Accounts

The person engaged in the notified profession are supposed to maintain the books of accounts and other documents specified below as per Rule 6F framed in this behalf by the CBDT :

(a) Cash Book; (b) A Journal; (c) A Ledger; (d) Carbon copies of machine number bills where such bills are issued by the persons; and (e) original bills for expenditure incurred by such persons.

Medical Profession

A person carrying on medical profession shall, in addition to the books of accounts and other documents specified above, keep and maintain :

(a) A daily register in Form 3C.

(b) An inventory as on the first and the last day of the previous year, of the stock of drugs, medicines and other consumable accessories used for the purpose of his profession.

ACCOUNTS OF DOCTORS

Generally, a medical practitioner/doctor maintains a diary where he enters details of his transactions relating to incomes (such as, fees collected, fees yet to be collected, profit/loss on sale of medicines (if owned by him) and expenses (such as establishment charges, conveyance, miscellaneous). The incomes are grouped and recorded in a daily multicolumnar Cash Book and expenses are also grouped and recorded in the same book. But, where takings are deposited into bank and the payments are made by cheque, the bank pass book and the counterfoil of the cheques will reveal the necessary particulars for the expenditures. Where two or more specialists joint and carry on the profession, an Analytical (Multicolumnar) Cash Book may be maintained in such a way as the total fees of various specialists may easily be calculated separately. But in case of a partnership (between two specialists) separate accounts will have to be maintained for different heads of incomes and expenses of the different departments. Generally, the partners would draw an allowance every month and the balance of net profit is to be distributed among them as per profit-sharing ratio.

The usual departments are :

General Physicians, Pathology, Pediatrics, Physiotherapy, Psychiatry, Ear, Nose, Throat, Ophthalmology, Radiology, etc.

Sometimes medicines are supplied free of cost to the consulting doctors as samples which may be included in the fees. In that case, expenditures will include only the purchase of medicine and not the price of samples. At the end of the period, stock of medicines and stores are to be adjusted in order to ascertain the cost of medicines and stores which are consumed.

From the above, it is clear that a medical practitioner generally maintains a diary for the details of his transactions. But the accounts are to be prepared in such a way that the same may be presented to the Income Tax Authorities. However, the following suggestions may be noted :

(a) *Diary :* A doctor should write the names and addresses of his patients including the fees that are collected from them. For accrued fees, separate records are to be maintained under the head "To be billed".

(b) *Cash Book :* All Cash receipts and all Cash payments are to be recorded in this book.

(c) *Stock Book :* It keeps records about the purchase, sale and consumption of medicines.

(d) *Bill Book :* It is prepared in duplicate. It reveals the particulars of treatment done or recommended and the amount charged for the purpose. The original copy will go to the patient concerned and the duplicate will be kept for official purposes.

(e) *Receipt Book :* As soon as the fees are received against accrued fees (i.e., 'To be billed') the same is recorded in this book. It is also prepared in duplicate. The original copy is handed over to the patient concerned after its payment.

(f) *Profit and Loss A/c :* It reveals the profit earned or loss suffered on sale of medicines.

Sometimes it becomes necessary to prepare a special Card Book for recording the case history of different patients, the treatment so recommended and the result thus obtained so far, which may be helpful to follow-up the treatment in future.

Heads of Incomes :

(i) Visiting and attending fees, (ii) Consultation fees, (iii) Hospital services, (iv) Operation charges, (v) Income from lectures, if any, (vi) Pathological examination, (vii) E.S.I. or Income from societies, etc., (viii) Income from sale of medicines, etc.

Heads of Expenditures

Expenditures can be grouped into two (a) Capital Expenditure, and (b) Revenue Expenditure.

(a) **Capital Expenditures**

(i) Surgical Plants—X-ray Machines, etc. (ii) Surgical Instruments, (iii) Furniture, (iv) Microscope (for pathological examinations), etc.

(b) **Revenue Expenditures**

(i) Drugs—antibiotics, sendatives anaesthetist etc. (ii) Materials—Cotton, Plaster, Gauge, etc. (iii) Hire charge of operation theatre (if the same does not belong to the doctor). (iv) General Overhead — Telephone, Motor Car Expenses, Salaries, Stationery, Postage, Periodicals, Repairs, Rent, etc.

Note : Some of the general overheads stated above may be apportioned between profession and household where such expenses serve both the purposes.

Illustration 1

Dr. H. Mukherjee, a medical practitioner, started his practice in 1990. On 1.1.2012 his position was:

Balance Sheet *as at 1st January 2012*

Liabilities	*Amount*	*Assets*	*Amount*
	Rs.		Rs.
Capital	71,000	Surgical Equipments	15,000
		Furniture	10,000
		Other Instruments	8,000
		Microscope	6,000
		Motor Car	12,000
		Cash in hand	4,000
		Cash at Bank	16,000
	71,000		71,000

During the year 2012

Receipts : Visiting fees Rs. 20,000; Consultation fees Rs. 8,000; Surgical operation Rs. 16,000; Receipts for Hospital Service Rs. 3,600; ESI Rs. 4,000; Lectures Rs. 3,000; Pathological examinations Rs. 4,000; Part-time Lectures in a Medical College Rs. 3,600; Sales of Drugs Rs. 10,000.

Payments : Purchase of Drugs Rs. 8,000; Salaries Rs. 4,000; Printing & Stationery Rs. 1,000; Newspaper and Periodicals Rs. 1,000; Insurance (against assets of the profession) Rs. 1,000; Miscellaneous Expenses Rs. 2,500; Telephone bill Rs. 3,000; Repairs Rs. 500; Electricity Rs. 1,200; Rent Rs. 4,800; Purchase of gauge, cotton, oils, etc. Rs. 8,000; Subscription to Medical Association Rs. 500; Motor Car expenses Rs. 3,600; Hire of operation theatre Rs. 4,000; Charges of anaesthetist Rs. 5,000; Drawings Rs. 24,000; Balance in hand—Cash Rs. 1,000; Balance at Bank ?

Additional information :

(i) Outstanding salary amounted to Rs. 3,000. (ii)Electricity, Rent and Motor Car expenses are to be apportioned between profession and household in 3 : 1. (iii) Salary include Rs. 1,000 paid to attendant who renders $\frac{1}{4}$ of his service to the household purpose. (iv) Insurance was paid out of household cash amounting to Rs. 1,000.

Prepare a Receipts and Payments Account, Income and Expenditure Account for the year ended 31st December 2012 and a Balance Sheet as on that date.

Solution

Dr. **Receipts and Payments Account** *for the year ended 31st December 2012* Cr.

	Receipts		Rs.		Payments		Rs.
To	Balance b/d :			By	Purchase of Drugs		8,000
	in hand	4,000		"	Salaries		4,000
	at Bank	16,000	20,000	"	Printing and Stationery		1,000
"	Visiting Fees		20,000	"	Newspapers & Periodicals		1,000
"	Consultation Fees		8,000	"	Insurance		1,000
"	Surgical Operation		16,000	"	Misc. Expenses		2,500
"	Receipts from Hospital Service		3,600	"	Telephone Bill		3,000
"	E. S. I. Service		4,000	"	Repairs		500
"	Lectures		3,000	"	Electricity		1,200
"	Pathological Examinations		4,000	"	Rent		4,800
"	Part-time Lectureship		3,600	"	Purchase of Gauge, Cotton, Oil etc.		8,000
"	Sale of Drugs		10,000	"	Subscription to Medical Association		500
				"	Motor Car Expenses		3,600
				"	Hire of Operation Theatre		4,000
				"	Charges of Anesthetist		5,000
				"	Drawings		24,000
				"	Balance c/d		
					in hand	1,000	
					at bank *(bal. fig.)*	19,100	20,100
			92,200				92,200

Dr. **Income and Expenditure Account** *for the year ended 31st December 2012* Cr.

	Expenditures	Rs.	Rs.		Incomes	Rs.
To	Purchase of Drugs		8,000	By	Visiting Fees	20,000
"	Salaries	4,000		"	Consulting Fees	8,000
	Add : Outstanding	3,000		"	Surgical Operation	16,000
		7,000		"	Income from Hospital Service	3,600
	Less : For Household			"	E.S.I. Services	4,000
	Services $\frac{1}{4}$ of Rs. 1,000	250	6,750	"	Lectures	3,000
				"	Pathological Examinations	4,000

Contd.

		Rs.	Rs.			Rs.
To	Printing & Stationery		1,000	By	Part-time Lecturership	3,600
"	Newspapers & Periodicals		1,000	"	Sale of Drugs	10,000
"	Insurance	1,000				
	Add : Payment out of Household Cash	1,000	2,000			
"	Misc. Expenses		2,500			
"	Telephone Bills		3,000			
"	Repairs		500			
"	Electricity	1,200				
	Less : For Household Service $\frac{1}{4}$	300	900			
"	Rent	4,800				
	Less : For Household Service $\frac{1}{4}$	1,200	3,600			
"	Purchase of Gauge, Cotton etc.		8,000			
"	Subscription to Medical Association		500			
"	Motor Car Expenses	3,600				
	Less : For Household Service $\frac{1}{4}$	900	2,700			
"	Hire of Operation Theatre		4,000			
"	Charges to Anaesthetist		5,000			
"	Surplus—Excess of Income over Expenditure		22,750			
			72,200			72,200

Balance Sheet *as at 31st December 2012*

Liabilities		Rs.	Rs.	*Assets*	Rs.
Capital as on 1.1.2012		71,000		Surgical Equipment	15,000
Add : Introduced during the year		1,000		Furniture	10,000
		72,000		Other Instruments	8,000
Add : Surplus		22,750		Microscope	6,000
		94,750		Motor Car	12,000
Less : Drawings	24,000			Cash in hand	1,000
Salary of Attendants	250			Cash at Bank	19,100
Rent	1,200				
Motor Car	900				
Electricity	300	26,650	68,100		
Outstanding Salary			3,000		
			71,100		71,100

Illustration 2

Sri R. Chaudhuri is a medical practitioner. He lives in a rented house consisting of four rooms, one of which is used as his chamber. His Receipts and Payments Account (recording all the cash transactions of his profession and household) for the year ended 31st March 2010, was :

Receipts	Rs.	*Payments*	Rs.
Cash in hand	500	Drugs Purchased	25,000
Cash at Bank	15,000	Ration	500
Fees Collected	25,000	Marketing and Milk	5,000
Drugs Sold	40,000	Entertainment to Family Guests	2,000
Interest on Household Investments	2,000	Other Household Expenses	5,000

Contd.

	Rs.		Rs.
		Rent	6,600
		Motor Car Expenses	2,000
		Salaries and Wages	6,000
		Telephone Expenses	1,000
		Television	6,000
		Life Insurance Premium	3,600
		Cash in hand	400
		Cash at Bank	19,400
	82,500		82,500

You are required to prepare, for the year ended 31st March 2010, a Profit and Loss Account and one Income and Expenditure Account, respectively, for the 'Profession' and 'Household' of Shri Chaudhuri after taking into consideration the following additional information :

(a) Rent of Rs. 600 for the month of March 2010 being outstanding.

(b) Electricity charges amounting to Rs. 600 and Educational expenses amounting to Rs. 1,000 were met by Shri Chaudhuri's wife but had not been reimbursed to her.

(c) $\frac{3}{4}$th of the following expenses related to Shri Chaudhuri's household:

Rent, Motor Car Expenses, Salaries and Wages, Electricity Charges, and Telephone.

(d) Stock of drugs Rs. 2,000.

(c) The entire profit of 'profession' was to be taken as revenue of the 'Household'.

Solution

Profit and Loss Account
for 'Profession' of Sri R. Chaudhuri *for the year ended 31st March 2010*

Dr. Cr.

Particulars	*Amount* Rs.	*Amount* Rs.	*Particulars*	*Amount* Rs.	*Amount* Rs.
To Purchase of Drugs	25,000		By Fees Collected		25,000
Less : Stock at end	2,000	23,000	" Sale of Drugs		40,000
" Rent	6,600				
Add : Outstanding	600				
	7,200				
Less : For Household	5,400	1,800			
" Motor Car Expenses	2,000				
Less : For Household	1,500	500			
" Salaries & Wages	6,000				
Less : For Household	4,500	1,500			
" Telephone Expenses	1,000				
Less : For Household	750	250			
" Electricity (Outstanding)[1]	600				
Less : For Household	450	150			
" Net Income transferred to Household Income and Expenditure Account		37,800			
		65,000			65,000

Income and Expenditure Account for 'Household' of Sri Chaudhuri
for the year ended 31st March 2010

Dr. Cr.

Expenditures	Rs.	Rs.	*Incomes*	Rs.	Rs.
To Ration		500	By Net Income from Profession		37,800
" Marketing and Milk		5,000	" Interest on Investments		2,000
" Entertainment to Family Guests		2,000			

Contd.

		Rs.	Rs.			Rs.	Rs.
To	Household Expenses		5,000	By			
"	Rent	6,600					
	Add : Outstanding	600					
		7,200					
	Less : For Profession	1,800	5,400				
"	Motor Car Expenses ($\frac{3}{4}$)		1,500				
"	Salaries and Wages ($\frac{3}{4}$)		4,500				
"	Telephone Expenses	1,000					
	Less : for Profession	250	750				
"	Life Insurance Premium		3,600				
"	Electricity (Outstanding)	600					
	Less : For Profession	150	450				
"	Education Expenses (Outstanding)[1]		1,000				
"	Surplus—transferred to Family Savings Account		10,100				
			39,800				39,800

Note :

1. Since this amount has been paid by Mrs. Choudhury from her own funds, it should be treated as outstanding expenses. When payment will be made to her, Outstanding Expenses A/c will be debited and Cash or Bank A/c will be credited.

Illustration 3

Dr. Talukdar, M.B.B.S., retired from the Dept. of Health, Govt. of West Bengal, on 31st December 2010. On 1st January 2011, he started private practice at his own residence with a capital of Rs. 40,000 from his own savings and Rs. 20,000 by way of loan from his friend at an interest of 12% p.a. He maintains his books on cash basis of accounting. On 31st December 2011 his Abstract Cash Account showed the following information :

Abstract Cash Account

	Rs.		Rs.
Own Capital	40,000	Surgical Instruments	20,000
Loan	20,000	Motor Car	25,000
Visiting Fees	30,000	Purchase of Medicine	20,000
Lectures	2,000	Motor Car Expenses	6,000
Pension from Govt. of West Bengal	8,000	Misc. Expenses	4,000
Sales by Prescription	40,000	Salaries	6,000
Income from Personal Savings	10,000	Rent	12,000
Receipt from Certificate and Reports	3,000	Household Expenses	10,000
Prize from Lottery	20,000	Household Furniture	6,000
		Interest on Loan	2,400
		Festival Expenses	2,000
		Electricity Expenses	3,000
		Cost of Magazines & Journals	1,000
		Telephone Expenses	2,400
		Books Purchased (Medical)	3,000
		Balance in hand	17,000
		Balance at Bank	33,200
	1,73,000		1,73,000

Additional Information

(a) $\frac{2}{3}$ of Rent and Electricity Expenses and $\frac{1}{3}$ of Motor Car expenses and Telephone Bill are to be treated as household expenses.

(b) Salaries include Rs. 2,000 to be paid to a person who devotes 50% of his working time for household work.

(c) Stock of Medicines amounted to Rs. 4,000 on 31st December 2011.

Prepare a Capital Account, an Income and Expenditure Account for the year ended 31st December 2011 and a Balance Sheet as at that date.

Solution

Income and Expenditure Account *for the year ended 31st December 2011*

Dr.					Cr.
Expenditures	Rs.	Rs.		*Incomes*	Rs.
To Purchase of Medicine	20,000		By	Visiting Fees	30,000
Less : Stock on 31.12.2011	4,000	16,000	"	Lecturership	2,000
" Motor Car Expenses $\frac{2}{3}$		4,000	"	Sales by Prescription	40,000
" Misc. Expenses		4,000	"	Received from Certificate & Reports	3,000
" Salaries	6,000				
Less : Household Work	1,000	5,000			
" Rent $\frac{1}{3}$		4,000			
" Interest on Loan		2,400			
" Electricity Expenses ($\frac{1}{3}$)		1,000			
" Cost of Magazines & Journals		1,000			
" Telephone ($\frac{2}{3}$)		1,600			
" Surplus— Excess of Income over Expenditures		36,000			
		75,000			75,000

Capital Account *for the year ended 31st December 2011*

Dr.				Cr.
Particulars	*Amount* Rs.		*Particulars*	*Amount* Rs.
To Motor Car Expenses ($\frac{1}{3}$)	2,000	By	Cash	40,000
" Salaries ($2{,}000 \times \frac{1}{2}$)	1,000	"	Pension from W.B. Govt.	8,000
" Rent ($12{,}000 \times \frac{2}{3}$)	8,000	"	Income from Personal Savings	10,000
" Household Expenses	10,000	"	Prize from Lottery	20,000
" Household Furniture	6,000	"	Surplus— Excess of Income over Expenditure	36,000
" Festival Expenses	2,000			
" Electricity Expenses ($\frac{2}{3}$)	2,000			
" Telephone ($\frac{1}{3}$)	800			
" Balance c/d	82,200			
	1,14,000			1,14,000

Note : Household expenses, which are paid out of business cash, are treated as drawings and, hence, debited to Capital Account. Similarly, personal incomes, which are paid into the business cash, are treated as additional capital and, hence, credited to Capital Account.

Balance Sheet *as at 31st December 2011*

Liabilities	*Rs.*	*Assets*	*Rs.*
Capital A/c	82,200	Surgical Instruments	20,000
Loan	20,000	Motor Car	25,000
		Stock of Medicines	4,000
		Books	3,000
		Cash in hand	17,000
		Cash at Bank	33,200
	1,02,200		1,02,200

Relation between the Accounts of Professional Persons and their Household Accounts

In order to ascertain the relationship between the accounts of different professional persons and their household accounts, two separate entities should be discussed, viz., (1) Household, and (2) Professional. Since, the non-professional incomes are included with the professional incomes of the professional persons in many cases, and non-professional expenses are also included with the professional expenses, accounts of both profession and household are not maintained properly. From the accounting point of view, these two separate entities should not be mixed up with each other. Because, the transactions which affect the profession have no such effect on household accounts; and the transactions which affect the household have no such similar effect on profession. But there may be certain transactions which may affect both the entities, e.g., in a doctor's profession, some drugs may be used for his own family members which are taken from his professional accounts, or some surgical equipments may be purchased for his professional activities but the payment is made from his household accounts. The former is treated as *'Drawings'* and the latter is treated as *'Additional Capital'* in the professional accounts.

It should be remembered that professional accounting is made in order to :

(i) ascertain the profit or loss of profession during the period;

(ii) ascertain the financial position of the profession as a whole at a particular date with the help of a Statement of Affairs or Balance Sheet.

Similarly, the household accounting is made in order to :

(iii) ascertain income from different sources including the income from profession;

(iv) ascertain the change in family's property at a particular period which may result in 'Savings' or 'Borrowings'.

An illustration is presented which will make the principle clear.

Illustration 4

A medical practitioner has his chamber housed in a part of his own residential building for which a 'notional' monthly rent may be fixed at Rs. 1,000.

From the information given below prepare, for the year ending 30.3.2012, a Profit and Loss Account and an Income and Expenditure Account, respectively, of the 'Profession' and 'Household' of the said Medical Practitioner.

The summary of the transactions during the year ended 31st March 2012 were:

(i) Medical fees earned Rs. 1,02,500; (ii) Received interest on investment (Household) Rs. 25,000; (iii) Cost of running and maintaining a Car Rs. 14,000; (iv) Durwan — Pay Rs. 3,600; Add : food given from household Rs. 1,460 = Rs. 5,060; (v) Gas and Electricity Rs. 2,400; (vi) Pay of Assistants (Profession) Rs. 24,000; (vii) Provision for depreciation—Household Rs. 17,500; Profession Rs. 2,500 = Rs. 20,000; (viii) Household expenses Rs. 28,540 (Rs. 30,000, less food for Durwan Rs. 1,460).

Additional Information

(a) Expenses against item nos. (iii), (iv) and (v) are to be allocated equally between 'Household and Profession'.

(b) The entire profit earned in the profession was drawn for household use.

(c) Income-tax to be ignored.

Solution **[CU BCom]**

Dr. **Profit and Loss Account (Profession)** *for the year ended 31st March 2012* *Cr.*

Expenditure	*Amount*	*Incomes*	*Amount*
	Rs.		Rs.
To Motor Car Expenses ($\frac{1}{2}$)	7,000	By Medical Fees	1,02,500
" Durwan Pay ($\frac{1}{2}$)	2,530		
" Gas & Electricity ($\frac{1}{2}$)	1,200		
" Pay to Assistants	24,000		
" Prov. for Depreciation	2,500		
" Rent for Chamber (1,000 × 12)	12,000		
" Net Income— Tr. to Income and Expenditure A/c —Household	53,270		
	1,02,500		1,02,500

Income and Expenditure Account (Household) *for the year ended 31st March 2012*

Dr. Expenditures	Rs.	Incomes	Cr. Rs.
To Motor Car Expenses ($\frac{1}{2}$)	7,000	By Profit and Loss A/c	53,270
" Durwan Pay ($\frac{1}{2}$)	2,530	(Net income from Profession)	
" Gas & Electricity ($\frac{1}{2}$)	1,200	" Rent (charged to Chamber)	12,000
" Prov. for Depreciation	17,500	" Interest on Investments	25,000
" Household Expenses (Net)	28,540		
" Surplus—			
Tr. to Family Fund	33,500		
	90,270		90,270

ACCOUNTS OF CHARTERED ACCOUNTANTS

Accounts require professional perfection when it is maintained strictly according to different principles and procedures. Generally, Chartered Accountants are engaged with the auditing work of different individuals and institutions. These professional accountants are members of the Institute of Chartered Accountants of India. In order to be a member of this Institute, each member has to pass the examination conducted by the Institute. The Institute issues a certificate to the successful candidates and they are known as Chartered Accountants.

These professional accountants prepare the accounts of their clients, advise their client's about the payment of income-tax etc. in addition to the auditing work and, in return, they take fees.

Generally, these professional persons maintain a Cash Book, a Bill Register, Client's Register, General Ledger etc. These books are prepared like books of original entry and ledger. They also prepare final accounts in the usual way in order to ascertain the result of the profession. Instead of preparing Trading and Profit and Loss Account, they prepare Income and Expenditure Account and also a Balance Sheet at the end of the period. Some accountants prepare their accounts under Cash System. But it is better to prepare accounts under Mercantile System.

Illustration 5

A and B are in partnership practising as Chartered Accountants under the name and style AB & Co. sharing profits and losses in the manner shown below. They close their accounts on 31st March every year. The following was their Balance Sheet as at 31st March 2011:

Balance Sheet *as at 31st March 2011*

Liabilities		Rs.	Assets		Rs.
Partners' Capital			Furniture		20,000
A	65,000		Office Machinery		15,000
B	40,000	1,05,000	Library Books		8,000
Audit Fees collected in advance			Car		60,000
(A's Client)		10,000	Outstanding Audit Fees :		
Liability for Salary		5,000	A's Client	30,000	
Provision against outstanding			B's Client	20,000	50,000
Audit Fees		50,000	Cash at Bank		15,000
			Cash in hand		2,000
		1,70,000			1,70,000

The following is the summary of their cash/bank transactions *for the year ended 31st March 2012 :*

Receipts	Rs.	Payments	Rs.
Opening :		Salary	2,60,000
Bank Balance	15,000	Car Expenses	35,000
Cash Balance	2,000	Travelling Expenses	21,000

Contd.

		Rs.			Rs.
Audit Fees			Printing & Stationery		18,000
A's Clients	2,80,000		Postage Expenses		3,000
B's Clients	1,80,000	4,60,000	Telephone		15,000
Fees for other Services			Subscription for Journals		7,000
A's Clients	50,000		Library Books		12,000
B's Clients	50,000	90,000	Fax Machine		16,000
Miscellaneous Incomes		4,000	Membership Fees		2,000
			Drawings :		
			A	72,000	
			B	60,000	1,32,000
			Cash at Bank		48,000
			Cash in hand		2,000
		5,71,000			5,71,000

The following further information are available :

1. Audit Fees receivable :
   A's Clients Rs. 30,000
   B's Clients Rs. 50,000
2. Audit Fees collected in advance
   B's Clients Rs. 20,000
3. Outstanding Liability for Salary on 31st March 2012 Rs. 20,000.
4. Depreciation to be provided on : Furniture @ 10%, Office Machinery @ 20%, Library Books @ 10% and Car @ 20%.
5. It has been agreed that 80% of audit fees and 40% of fees for other services should be transferred to Income and Expenditure Account in respect of each partner's account, the balance being credited directly to the capital accounts. Profits/Losses to be divided between A and B in the ratio of 2 : 1, respectively.

You are required to prepare Income and Expenditure Account for the year ended 31st March 2012 and a Balance Sheet as at 31st March 2012.

[CA Foundation]

Solution

In the books of A B & Co.

Dr. **Income and Expenditure Account** *for the year ended 31st March 2012* Cr.

Expenditures	Rs.	Rs.	*Incomes*	Rs.	Rs.
To Salary	2,60,000		By Audit Fees		3,60,000[1]
Less : Outstanding for last year	5,000		" Fees for Other Services		36,000[2]
	2,55,000		" Miscellaneous Income		4,000
Add : Outstanding for current year	20,000	2,75,000			
" Car Expenses		35,000			
" Travelling		21,000			
" Printing		18,000			
" Postage		3,000			
" Telephone		15,000			
" Subscription for Journal		7,000			
" Membership Fees		2,000			
" Depreciation on :					
Furniture	2,000				
Machinery	6,200				
Books	2,000				
Car	12,000	22,200			
" Capital A/c —Profit transferred					
A's Share	1,200				
B's Share	600	1,800			
		4,00,000			4,00,000

Balance Sheet *as at 31st March 2012*

Liabilities	Rs.	Rs.	*Assets*	Rs.	Rs.
Capital A/c			Machinery	15,000	
A	82,200		Additions	16,000	
B	36,600	1,18,800[3]		31,000	
Audit Fees collected in advance		20,000	*Less* : Depreciation	6,200	24,800
(B's Client)			Furniture	20,000	
Liability for Salary		20,000	*Less* : Depreciation	2,000	18,000
Provision for			Library Books	8,000	
Outstanding Audit Fees		80,000	Additions	12,000	
				20,000	
			Less : Depreciation	2,000	18,000
			Car	60,000	
			Less : Depreciation	12,000	48,000
			Accrued Audit Fees :		
			A's Client	30,000	
			B's Client	50,000	80,000
			Cash at Bank		48,000
			Cash in hand		2,000
		2,38,800			2,38,800

Workings :

1. Audit Fees transferred

	A Rs.	B Rs.	
Audit Fees already collected	2,80,000	1,80,000	
Add : Outstanding Fees on 31.3.2012	30,000	50,000	
	3,10,000	2,30,000	
Less : Outstanding on 31.3.2011	30,000	20,000	
	2,80,000	2,10,000	
Add : Received in advance for last year	10,000		
Less : Received in advance for next year	—	20,000	
	2,90,000	1,90,000	
Add : Provisions (opening balance)	30,000	20,000	
	3,20,000	2,10,000	
Less : Provisions (closing balance)	30,000	50,000	
	2,90,000	1,60,000	
80% transferred to Income & Expenditure A/c	2,32,000	1,28,000	= Rs. 3,60,000
20% transferred to Capital A/c	58,000	32,000	= Rs. 90,000
	2,90,000	1,60,000	Rs. 4,50,000

2. Fees for other services

	A Rs.	B Rs.
Already collected	50,000	40,000
40 % transferred to Income & Expenditure A/c	20,000	16,000
60% transferred to Capital A/c	30,000	24,000
	50,000	40,000

3. **Capital A/c**

Dr. *Cr.*

	A Rs.	B Rs.		A Rs.	B Rs.
To Drawings	72,000	60,000	By Balance b/d	65,000	40,000
Balance c/d	82,200	36,600	" Audit Fees	58,000	32,000
			" Fees for Other Services	30,000	24,000
			" Share of Profit	1,200	600
	1,54,200	96,600		1,54,200	96,600

Illustration 6

Anirban and Dipankar are in partnership as Chartered Accountants sharing profits and losses in the ratio of 3 : 2 after providing for a partnership salary of Rs. 10,000 p.a. to each partner.

Their Trial Balance as on 31st December 2012 was as follows :

	Dr. Rs.	Cr. Rs.
Capital :		
Anirban		40,000
Dipankar		30,000
Drawings :		
Anirban	12,000	
Dipankar	8,000	
Work-in-progress (1.1.2012)	9,000	
Sundry clients for Fees	20,000	
Fees Earned		1,10,000
Reserve against due from clients etc.		20,000
Deposits from client against expenses		12,000
Staff salary	18,000	
Office Furniture (1.1.2012)	10,000	
Office Equipment —do—	8,000	
Library —do—	20,000	
Building —do—	25,000	
Expenses (including Rs. 4,000 on behalf of clients)	20,000	
Bank		
Clients	25,000	
Office	41,000	
Creditors for expenses		4,000
	2,16,000	2,16,000

Additional Information

(i) The work-in-progress at the end of the year was Rs. 15,000.

(ii) Depreciate : Office Furniture and Office Equipment by 10 % p.a.
Library Books and Building by 5% p.a.

(iii) Each partner has his own car, but the firm to be charged with Rs. 2,500 p.a. in respect of each car for work on behalf of the firm.

(iv) The manager of the firm is entitled to a commission @ 10% on collection of fees from clients.

Prepare the final accounts of the firm as on 31st December 2012.

Solution

In the books of M/s Anirban & Dipankar

Income and Expenditure Account *for the year ended 31st December 2012*

Dr. *Cr.*

	Expenditures	Rs.	Rs.		*Incomes*	Rs.
To	Work-in-progress (opening)		9,000	By	Fees earned	1,10,000
"	Expenses	20,000		"	Work-in-progress (closing)	15,000
	Less : For Clients	4,000	16,000			
"	Staff Salary		18,000			
"	Car Expenses (2,500 × 2)		5,000			
"	Manager's Com. (@ 10% on Rs. 1,10,000)		11,000			
"	Depreciation on :					
	Office Furniture @ 10%	1,000				
	Office Equipment @ 10%	800				
	Library @ 5%	1,000				
	Building @ 5%	1,250	4,050			

Contd.

	Rs.	Rs.		Rs.
To Profit c/d (Mercantile Profit) transferred		61,950	By	
		1,25,000		1,25,000
" Salaries :			By Profit b/d (Mercantile Profit) transferred	61,950
Anirban	10,000			
Dipankar	10,000	20,000		
" Share of Profit :				
Anirban	25,170			
Dipankar	16,780	41,950		
		61,950		61,950

Dr. **Balance Sheet** *as at 31st December 2012* Cr.

Liabilities	Rs.	Rs.	*Assets*	Rs.	Rs.
Capital Accounts :			Office Furniture	10,000	
Anirban	40,000		*Less* : Depreciation	1,000	9,000
Add : Share of Profit	25,170		Office Equipment	8,000	
Car Expenses	2,500		*Less* : Depreciation	800	7,200
Salaries	10,000		Library	20,000	
	77,670		*Less* : Depreciation	1,000	19,000
Less : Drawings	12,000	65,670	Building	25,000	
Dipankar	30,000		*Less* : Depreciation	1,250	23,750
Add : Share of Profit	16,780		Sundry Clients for Fees		20,000
Car Expenses	2,500		Work-in-progress (closing)		15,000
Salaries	10,000		Bank :		
	59,280		Client	25,000	
Less : Drawings	8,000	51,280	Office	41,000	66,000
Creditors for Expenses		4,000			
Manager's Comm.		11,000			
Reserve Against Due from Clients		20,000			
Deposit from Clients	12,000				
Less : Expenses	4,000	8,000			
		1,59,950			1,59,950

ACCOUNTS OF SOLICITORS/LAWYERS

Persons who are engaged with legal affairs and maintain their livelihood from the same are known as 'Lawyers'. They are also called Advocates, Barristers, Solicitors, etc. Since lawyers receive and pay on behalf of themselves and their clients, separate accounts for 'Office' and 'Clients' are to be maintained. An extra column, viz., Clients' Column, is also to be opened in the Cash Book in order to record the Cash transactions on behalf of the clients. Besides if the clients' transactions are very large in number, a separate bank account may also be prepared for the purpose. Therefore, different columns are opened in Cash Book for receipts and payments for 'Clients' and 'Office'. Similarly, two columns are opened in clients' ledger for recording two kinds of transactions, viz., when cash is received from the clients for service rendered to them, and the transactions which are exclusively for them.

When cash is received from clients on behalf of them, the same is debited in Cash Book (clients' column) and credited to Personal Account (clients' column) in General Ledger. Similarly, when payment is made on behalf of clients, Clients' Disbursement Account is debited and Bank Account (clients' column) is credited. But, for transferring money from Clients' Accounts to Office Account, contra entry is to be passed in Cash Book. However, if Clients' Disbursement Account is opened, its balance must be equal to the balance shown in Bank Account (clients' column).

When jobs are completed, a bill is sent to the clients for accrued fees, which is known as *Profit Costs.* Clients' Accounts are debited for *Profit Costs and Bill for Costs* whereas Fees Account and Disbursement Account are credited, respectively, for the purpose.

Sometimes, petty expenses on behalf of clients (e.g., postage, travelling expense) are made for which neither Clients' Account nor Clients' Disbursement accounts are debited but they are passed through the particular expenses account. Afterwards, the same is transferred to Clients' Account (in clients' column) from the Expenses Account.

If any advance is received from the clients for expenses, the same is adjusted from Deposit Account to Clients' Disbursement Account. When settlement is made, Clients' Account is credited as against Bank in office column. When the lawyers make some payment on behalf of clients and if the same is re-imbursed by the clients, the same is credited to Clients' Disbursement Account. But if the same is wrongly credited to Clients' Deposit Account, a journal entry is required to be passed for transferring the same of Clients' Disbursement Account.

Generally, Clients' Account reveals the outstanding amount for *Profit Costs.* Since disbursement is adjusted by debiting Clients' Deposit Account and crediting Clients' Account, the balance in Disbursement Account will include the amount spent for which no bills have yet been served and the said balance must be reconciled with the outstanding balance in Disbursement Book.

The work which has not yet been completed should be recorded in the books by debiting Work-in-Progress Account and crediting Profit Costs or Income and Expenditure Account directly. If there is any opening work-in-progress, the same should also be transferred to Profit Cost or Income and Expenditure Account.

An Income and Expenditure Account is prepared under Hybrid System (i.e., income on Cash Basis and expenses on Mercantile Basis) in order to find out the net result of the profession and a Balance Sheet is also to be prepared on the same date for ascertaining the financial position.

Illustration 7

X was client of a lawyer. There was a Debit Balance of Rs. 500 on 1.1.2012 in his name in the clients' ledger of the lawyer. On 7.1.2012 a cheque of Rs. 800 was received (including Rs. 100 advances for expenses of another work). On 31.1.2012, Costs Day Book shows Rs. 600 as fees charged to him. On the same date Bills Delivered Book shows that Rs. 450 bills sent to him including Rs. 250 disbursement made. Out of Rs. 250 disbursement, Rs. 30 was in respect of miscellaneous expenses debited to office expenses account.

Show the necessary accounts and the Cash Book.

Solution

Dr. **Cash Book** *(Bank) (Includes)* *Cr.*

Date		*Office*	*Clients*	*Date*		*Office*	*Clients*
2012			Rs.	2012			Rs.
Jan. 1	To X	—	800	Jan. 7	By X-Transfer	—	600
31	" X-Transfer	600	—				

General Ledger

Dr. **Office Expenses Account** *(Includes)* *Cr.*

Date		*Office*	*Clients*	*Date*		*Office*	*Clients*
2012			Rs.	2012			Rs.
				Jan. 31	By Clients' Disbursement A/c —X	—	30

Dr. **Clients' Disbursement Account** *(Includes)* *Cr.*

Date	*Particulars*	*Amount*	*Date*	*Particulars*	*Amount*
2012		Rs.	2012		Rs.
Jan. 31	To Office Expenses A/c	30	Jan. 31	By Clients' Control A/c	250

Dr. **Costs Account** *(Includes)* *Cr.*

Date	*Particulars*	*Amount*	*Date*	*Particulars*	*Amount*
2012		Rs.	2012		Rs.
			Jan. 31	By Clients' Control A/c —X	600

Dr. **Clients' Control Accounts** *(Includes)* Cr.

Date		Particulars	Amount	Date		Particulars	Amount
2012			Rs.	2012			Rs.
Jan.	31	By Clients'		Jan.	31	By Bank (Transfer) A/c—X	600
	31	Disbursement A/c	250				
	"	Costs A/c	600				

Clients' Ledger

Dr. **X Account** Cr.

Date		Particulars	Office	Clients	Date		Particulars	Office	Clients
2012			Rs.	Rs.	2012			Rs.	Rs.
Jan.	1	To Balance b/d	500		Jan.	7	By Bank A/c	—	800
	31	" Bank A/c —Tr.	—	600		31	" Bank A/c —Tr.	600	—
	"	" Clients Disbursement A/c	—	250		31	" Balance c/d	500	50
	"	" Costs A/c	600	—					
			1,100	850				1,100	850

Illustration 8

The following Trial Balance is presented by Mr. T. C. Bhattacharya, an advocate, for the year ended 31st December 2012. You are asked to prepare an Income and Expenditure Account for the year ended 31st December and a Balance Sheet as at that date.

Dr.	Rs.		Cr. Rs.
Drawings	12,000	Capital	10,000
Furniture	10,000	Provision for Unrealised Profit	18,000
Salaries	7,000	Clients' Deposit A/c	13,000
Rent	4,000	Costs (Profit)	60,000
Work-in-Progress (Opening)	3,000		
Clients' Disbursement	4,000		
Office Expenses	6,000		
Clients' Control A/c—for Bills of cost delivered	15,000		
Bank (Clients)	15,000		
Library	8,000		
Bank (Office)	13,000		
Cash in hand	4,000		
	1,01,000		1,01,000

Additional information :

(a) Works not yet completed as on 31st December 2012 amounted to Rs. 4,000.

(b) Clients' Disbursement Account should be Rs. 5,000.

(c) Out of the balance of Disbursement Account, a sum of Rs. 800 has been paid and credited to Clients' Deposit Account.

(d) Depreciation is to be charged on Furniture @ 10% p.a. and on Library @ 20% p.a.

(e) He makes 100% provision for unrealised profit.

(f) The bills of costs sent to clients include an amount of small disbursement debited to the Office Expenses Account.

Solution

In the books of T. C. Bhattacharya

Dr. **Income and Expenditure Account** *for the year ended 31st December 2012* Cr.

Expenditures	Rs.	Rs.	Income	Rs.
To Work-in-Progress (Opening)		3,000	By Profit Cost	60,000
" Office Expenses	6,000		" Work-in-Progress—Closing	4,000
Less : for Clients (5,000 – 4,000)	1,000	5,000		
" Rent		4,000		
" Salaries		7,000		

Contd.

	Rs.	Rs.		Rs.
To Depreciation on :			By	
Furniture 10%	1,000			
Library 20%	1,600	2,600		
" Balance c/d		42,400		
		64,000		64,000
To Provision for unrealised Profit :			By Balance b/d	42,400
Clients' Control A/c			" Provision for Unrealised Profit	
—Bills not yet collected	15,000		—Opening	18,000
Work-in-Progress	4,000	19,000		
" Capital A/c—Net Profit Transferred		41,400		
		60,400		60,400

Balance Sheet *as at 31st December 2012*

Liabilities	Rs.	Rs.	*Assets*	Rs.	Rs.
Capital	10,000		Furniture	10,000	
Add : Net Profit	41,400		*Less* : Depreciation	1,000	9,000
	51,400		Library	8,000	
Less : Drawings	12,000	39,400	*Less* : Depreciation	1,600	6,400
Provision for Unrealised Profit		19,000			
Clients' Deposit A/c			Work-in-Progress		4,000
(13,000 – 800)		12,200	Clients' Control A/c		
			Bills of Cost		15,000
			Clients' Disbursement A/c		
			(4,000 + 1,000 – 800)		4,200
			Cash at Bank :		
			Client	15,000	
			Office	13,000	28,000
			Cash in hand		4,000
		70,600			70,600

Illustration 9

The cash transactions of Smt. Moumita Ghosh, a lawyer, for the year ended 31st March 1998, were :

(i) Purchase of law books Rs. 14,000; (ii) Cost of Stationery Rs. 700; (iii) Salary of : Assistant Rs. 16,800 and Driver Rs. 14,000; (iv) Electric Charges Rs. 2,450; (v) Rent of Chamber Rs. 31,500; (vi) Subscriptions to Bar Council Rs. 3,500; ; (vii) Life Insurance premium Rs. 22,050; (viii) Telephone charges Rs. 10,500; (ix) Cost of installation of telephone Rs. 7,000; (x) Marketing Rs. 52,500; (xi) Motor car expenses Rs. 42,000; (xii) Renewal of licence Rs. 2,450; (xiii) Cost of medicine and medical expenses Rs. 10,500; (xiv) Salary to typist Rs. 12,600; (xv) Cost of typewriting machine Rs. 17,500; (xvi) Cost of education to children Rs. 4,200. (xvii) Receipts from Rent of household properties Rs. 21,000; (xviii) Sale of old law books Rs. 1,750; (xix) Income for working as an official liquidator Rs. 35,000 (including Rs. 3,500 relating to last year). (xx) Fees collected Rs. 2,45,000.

Additional Information

(a) Depreciation on motor car (Cost Rs. 1,08,500) @ 15%; (b) Depreciation @ 10% on law books and type machine; (c) Income from fees accrued but not received Rs. 28,000; (d) Life insurance premium is paid for the year ending on 30th June 1998; (e) Income from the profession is to be treated as income of the family;

(f) Salary to Assistant stated above includes Rs. 2,100 paid to domestic servant; (g) 1/4 of following expenses are relating to the family of Smt. Ghosh—Telephone charges, Electric charges and expenses relating to motor car; (h) Arrear rent on household properties Rs. 4,200.

From the above information, prepare, for the year ending 31st March 1998, at Profit and Loss Account and an Income and Expenditure Account, respectively, of the profession and household of the said lawyer.

[CU BCom (Hons.) 1999]

Solution

In the books of Smt. Moumita Ghosh

Dr. **Profit & Loss A/c (for Profession)** *for the year ended on 31st March 1998* *Cr.*

	Expenditures		*Amount*		*Incomes*		*Amount*
			Rs.			Rs.	Rs.
To	Cost Stationery		700	By	Fees Collected	2,45,000	
"	Salary of Assistant		14,700[1]		*Add:* Fees Accrued	28,000	2,73,000
"	Salary of Driver for Profession		10,500[2]	"	Income for Working as Official Liquidator	35,000	
"	Electric Charges for Profession		1,837[3]		*Less:* Income for last year included	3,500	31,500
"	Rent of Chamber		31,500	"	Provision for Income as Official Liquidator for last year		3,500[8]
"	Subscription to Bar Council		3,500	"	Sale of old Law Books		1,750[9]
"	Tele. Charges for Profession		7,875[4]				
"	Motor Car Expenses for Prof.		31,500[5]				
"	Salary of Typist		12,600				
"	Depreciation:						
"	Motor Car	12,206[6]					
	Law Book (10%)	1,400					
	Type Machine (10%)	1,750	15,356				
"	Renewal of Licence Fees for Profession		1,838[7]				
"	Provision for Accrued Fees		28,000[8]				
"	Income & Expenditure A/c Profit/Income (Excess of Income over Expenditure) transferred to household		1,49,844				
			3,09,750				3,09,750

Dr. **Income & Expenditure Account (for Household)** *for the year ended on 31st March 1998* *Cr.*

	Expenditures	*Amount*		*Incomes*		*Amount*
		Rs.				Rs.
To	Salary of Domestic Servant	2,100	By	Profit/Income transferred from Professional P & L A/c		1,49,844
"	Salary of Driver for Household ($^1/_4$ × Rs. 14,000)	3,500	"	Rent from Household Properties	21,000	
"	Electric Charges for Household ($^1/_4$ × Rs. 2,450)	613		*Add:* Accrued Rent	4,200	25,200
"	Telephone Charges for Household ($^1/_4$ × Rs. 10,500)	2,625				
"	Marketing	52,500				
	Motor Car Expenses for Household ($^1/_4$ × Rs. 42,000)	10,500				
"	Cost of Medicines & Medical Expenses	10,500				
"	Cost of Education for Children	4,200				
"	Life Insurance Premium	16,538[10]				
"	Depreciation on Motor car for Household	4,069				
"	Renewal of Licence for Household ($^1/_4$ × Rs. 2,450)	612				
"	Surplus of household (Transferred to Capital Fund)	67,287				
		1,75,044				1,75,044

Note: Accrual basis of accounting is followed here although cash basis of accounting is usually followed by professional people.

Workings :

1. **Salary of Assistant** Rs.

Salary Paid (inclusive of Salary of Domestic Servant Rs. 2,100) 16,800

Less: Salary of Domestic Servant 2,100

14,700

2. **Drivers Salary (for profession)** Rs.

@ $^3/_4$th Salary Paid Rs. $(14,000 \times \frac{3}{4})$ = Rs. 10,500

3. **Electric Charges (for Profession)** Rs.

@ $^3/_4$ Electric Charges paid $(Rs. 2,450 \times \frac{3}{4})$ = 1,837

4. **Telephone Charges (for Profession)** Rs.

@ $^3/_4$th Tel. charges paid $(Rs. 10,500 \times \frac{3}{4})$ = 7,875

5. **Motor Car Expenses (for Profession)** Rs.

@ $^3/_4$ = Motor Car Exp. $(Rs. 42,000 \times \frac{3}{4})$ = 31,500

6. **Depreciation on Motor Car**

@ 15% on Rs. 1,08,500 = 16,275

Dep. (for profession) = $(Rs. 16,275 \times \frac{3}{4})$ = Rs. 12,206

7. **Renewal of Licence Fees** Rs.

@ $^3/_4$ Fees = Rs. 2,450 $\times \frac{3}{4}$ = 1,838

8. **Provision for Accrued Fees**

Since it is a profession, 100% provisions should be made for Accrued Fees of Rs. 28,000. Moreover provi sion should also be made for the last year against "Income as official liquidator of Rs. 3,500" and since this amount has already been realised in full, such provision created in the last year should be credited to Profit and Loss Account (for Profession)

9. **Sale of Law Books**

In the absence of information it has been assume that WDV of law book is nil So, the entire sale proceeds is taken as profit and credited to Profit & Loss Account (for Profession)

10. **Life Insurance Premium (for household)** Rs.

LIP paid 22,050

Less: Prepaid $(Rs. 22,050 \times \frac{3}{4})$ 5,512

16,538

ASSIGNMENT MATERIALS

THEORETICAL

1. What basis of accounting is followed by the professional men and why ?
2. Discuss the relationship between the accounts of professional persons and their household accounts.
3. How do you maintain the accounts of a medical practitioner ?
4. Define : (i) Clients' Account, (ii) Clients' Disbursement Account, and (iii) Work-in-Progress Account of a Lawyer.

PRACTICAL

(a) Accounting for Doctors

1. Dr. Ghosh is a medical practitioner. On 1st January 1988 he had the following assets in his profession: Equipments and Furniture Rs. 40,000; Telephone installation Rs. 3,000; Stock of medicines Rs. 2,000; and Cash in hand Rs. 7,000.

The following is the Receipts and Payments Account of the profession for the year ended 31st December 1988 :

Receipts	Rs.	*Payments*	Rs.
Cash in hand	7,000	Purchase of medicine	35,000
Consultation fees	41,000	Salary of Assistant	10,000
Fees from operations	10,000	Purchase of Motor Car	20,000
Income from lectures	5,000	Postage and stationery	700
Sale of medicines	40,000	Telephone charges	600
		Professional periodicals	300
		Purchase of equipments	10,000
		Motor Car expenses	1,500
		Subscription to I.M.A.	300
		Household drawings	12,000
		Travelling expenses	6,600
		Cash in hand	6,000
	1,03,000		1,03,000

After considering the following information, ascertain the net income from profession of Dr. Ghosh for the year ended 31st December 1988 and prepare a Balance Sheet of the same as at that date:

(i) Stock of medicines on 31. 12. 1988 was Rs. 3,000; (ii) Depreciate equipment and furniture by 5% p. a. ; (iii) Consultation fees accrued Rs. 6,000; (iv) Salary of Assistant due Rs. 2,000; (v) 50% of the services of Motor Car is enjoyed by the family of Dr. Ghosh; (vi) Rs. 2,000 was still payable to the suppliers of medicines; and (viii) Provide Rs. 5,000 for Income tax of the profession.

[Ans. Net Profit from P & L A/c Rs. 31,500, Capital Fund Rs. 52,000; Balance Sheet Rs. 85,750]

2. A, B and C are three doctors who are running a Polyclinic. D, E, F and G were then taken in as partners on payment of Rs. 10,000 by each of them as Goodwill and also Rs. 40,000 to be brought in by each of them as Capital. Goodwill is shared by the existing partners equally. Each of the original partners also contributed Rs. 40,000 by way of Capital. The terms of sharing profits or losses were as :

(i) 60% of the visiting fee is to go to the specialist concerned.

(ii) 40% of the chamber fee will be payable to the individual specialist.

(iii) 50% of the operation fees and fees for Pathological reports, X-rays and ECG will accrue in favour of the doctor concerned.

(iv) Balance of profit or loss is shared equally.

(v) The proportion of fees and charges accruing in favour of individual doctors are to be withdrawn then and there.

(vi) The receipts for the year after the admission of new partners are :

	Visiting Fees	Chamber Fees	Fees for Reports, Operation, etc.
	Rs.	Rs.	Rs.
General Practitioner	60,000	80,000	—
Gynaecologist	10,000	70,000	40,000
Cardiologist	—	40,000	30,000
Child Specialist	40,000	60,000	—
Pathologist	—	—	40,000
Radiologist	—	16,000	80,000
Dentist	—	10,000	60,000

(vii) Expenses for the year are as :

	Rs.	Rs.
Rent	31,000	
Light	5,000	
Nurses' Salary	12,000	
Attendants' Wages	6,000	
Telephones	8,200	
Printing and Stationery	2,000	
Medicines, Band-Aids, Injections etc.	4,000	
Depreciation:		
Furniture	2,000	
X-ray Machine	10,000	
ECG Equipments	4,000	
Dentist's Chairs	2,000	
Surgical Equipments	2,000	20,000

Prepare the Profit and Loss Account of the Polyclinic, also showing the final distribution of profit or loss among the partners.

All workings should form part of your answer.

[Ans. Net Profit (Surplus) Rs 5,47,800; Shares of General Practitioners Rs. 1,03,200; Gynaecologist Rs. 89,200; Cardiologist Rs. 66,200; Child Specialist Rs. 83,200; Pathologist Rs. 55,200; Radiologist Rs. 81,600; Dentist Rs. 69,200]

(c) Accounting for 'Chartered Accountants'

3. A and B are Chartered Accountants, practising independently at Chennai and Bangalore, respectively, and decide, with effect from 1/4/2010, to form a partnership in which each of them will have an equal share in profits and losses. They decide to bring into the firm all their assets and liabilities of their proprietary practices except the outstanding due on Government audit work done prior to 31st March 2010 which will be to the benefit of the individuals concerned. It was also decided that a sum of goodwill equivalent to $1\frac{1}{2}$ times the value of net assets taken over will be credited to the partners' accounts. Details of assets and liabilities as on 31st March 2010 were as :

Assets :

	Rs.	Rs.
Cash in hand/at bank	16,000	12,000
Fixed deposits (out of professional receipts)	40,000	26,000
Amounts billed and receivable	38,000	32,000
Bills still to be raised		
(including Rs. 24,000 due to A on Government audit work)	1,60,000	82,000
Office Furniture, Fixtures, Telephone lines etc.	31,000	18,000
Amounts due to articled and audit clerks towards stipends	8,400	12,000
Rent deposit	18,000	18,000
Rent due	1,500	1,500
Office salaries due	6,000	4,500
Expenses to be paid	800	—
For the year 2010-11, the analysis of Bank/Cash account revealed :		
Gross fees received		4,42,000
(including Rs. 18,000 due to A on Government audit work)		
Office expenses		18,800
Rent		36,000
Printing and Stationery		40,000
Stipends paid		60,000
Salaries to Staff		82,000
Interest on Fixed Deposits credited		6,600
Liabilities :		
Drawings :		
A		50,000
B		36,000
Other information : as on 31.3.2011		
Bills due by clients		1,44,000
Bills still to be raised on clients		60,000
Salaries due		9,600

There were no outstanding bills for collection as on 31/3/2011 that related to earlier years.

The partners decided that,, from 1st April 2011, they will adopt the Mercantile System of Accounts for all items except professional receipts which will be accounted on Cash Basis. Interest on Fixed Deposits is to be shared in the ratio of holdings at the time of formation of the firm. Depreciate Furniture, and Fixture at 10%.

You are required to prepare the Profit and Loss Account of the firm for the year ended 31st March 1991 and also a Balance Sheet as at that date.

All workings are to form part of your answer.

[Ans. Opening Capital A Rs. 5,11,750; B Rs. 2,81,000; Net Profit Rs. 2,07,400 : Share of A Rs. 1,03,700; B Rs. 1,03,700; Balance Sheet Total Rs. 9,48,350]

Accounting for a 'Lecturer' of a College

4. Mr. A. Banerjee is a lecturer of a college. He submits you his Receipts and Payments Account for the year ended 31.12.2012 :

Receipts and Payments Account

		Rs.			Rs.
To	Balance b/d	5,000	By	Rent	3,000
"	Salary from the College	21,000	"	Household Expenses	15,000
"	Salary from part-time lecturership	1,200	"	Life Insurance Premium	1,000
"	Examiner's Fees	1,500	"	Telephone Charges	1,800
"	Tuition Fees	4,000	"	Travelling	1,500
"	Visiting Lecturership (N. B. U.)	3,000	"	Books	1,000
"	Paper-setter's Fees	1,200	"	Tuition Fees of his son	900
			"	Drawings	1,100
			"	Purchase of Shares	3,000
			"	Balance c/d	8,600
		36,900			36,900

You are required to prepare an Income and Expenditure Account for the year ended 31.12.2012 and a Balance Sheet as on that date after taking into consideration the following :

(i) 40% of the travelling expenses and telephone expenses are related to his 'Profession'.

(ii) Depreciate Books @ 50% p. a.

[Ans. Surplus Rs. 27,080; Balance Sheet Rs. 12,100]

Accounting for Lawyer

5. The following is the Trial Balance as on 31.3.2010, extracted from the books of the solicitor, Mr. X. You are required to prepare a Profit and Loss Account for the year ended 31.3.1990 and also a Balance Sheet as on that date :

Trial Balance *as at 31st March 2010*

Debit Balances	Rs.	*Credit Balances*	Rs.
Drawings for the year	30,000	Capital	20,000
Furniture	6,000	Loan from Mrs. X (free of Interest)	10,000
Salaries	15,000	Provision for unrealised Profits	8,000
Rent	3,400	Clients' Deposit Account	11,000
Work-in-Progress (1.4.2009)	3,000	Liabilities for Expenses	3,000
Clients' Disbursements	3,600	Costs (Profits)	60,000
Miscellaneous Expenses	4,000		
Clients' Control Accounts for bills of cost rendered	20,000		
Library	15,000		
Bank (Clients)	10,950		
Bank (Office)	800		
Cash	250		
	1,12,000		1,12,000

(a) Work not yet completed on 31.3.2010 was Rs. 4,000.

(b) Although specific disbursements for clients are debited to Clients' Disbursements Account, at the time of making bills, certain expenses in condition to specific disbursements are charged in the bills out of Miscellaneous Expenses. From a scrutiny of the Disbursements Account, it appears that Rs. 3,800 had not been charged to clients.

(c) Out of the balance in Disbursements, Rs. 100 had been paid and credited to Clients' Deposit Accounts.

(d) Provision at 100% against unrealised profits has to be made.

(e) Furniture and Library to be depreciated by 20%.

[Ans. Net Profit from P & L A/c Rs. 18,600; Balance Sheet Rs. 56,500]

CHAPTER 25

ACCOUNTS FROM INCOMPLETE RECORDS

Learning Objectives

Introduction

Meaning

Salient Features of Single Entry System

Advantages

Disadvantages

Differences between Single Entry System and Double Entry System

Methods and Techniques

A. *Statement of Affairs Method*

B. *Conversion Method*

A. ***Statement of Affairs***

Statement of Affairs vs. Balance Sheet

Statement of Profit and Loss

How to prepare a Statement of Profit and Loss

B. ***Conversion Method***

Some Practical Hints

Applications of Single Entry in Partnership Firms

Introduction and Meaning

Under this system, a Cash Book is prepared which shows the receipts and payments of cash transactions and no other ledger is maintained except a rough book for recording transactions relating to personal accounts. It is actually called 'Pure Single Entry'. Under this method, real accounts and nominal accounts are not recognised. In short, these transactions are only recorded in Cash Book without, however, applying the principles of double entry. That is why it is said : 'The system which does not totally follow the principles of Double Entry System is called Single Entry System'.

For recording transactions relating to personal accounts, however, double entry system is followed, say, when cash is received from a customer—it is recorded in Cash Book first and, thereafter, in the personal account of the customer concerned, i.e., recorded in two places—like double entry basis.

Again, no entry is recorded in the books of accounts for any internal transactions, like depreciation on assets. Therefore, it may be said that Single Entry System is nothing but an admixture of Single Entry, Double Entry, and no entry.

According to R. N. Carter, Single Entry cannot be termed as a system, as it is not based on any scientific system like Double Entry System. For this purpose, Single Entry is nowadays known as *Preparation of accounts from incomplete records.*

Practically, this system is followed by those firms whose transactions are limited and, at the same time, who maintain only the essential records. There is no hard and fast rule for maintaining records under this system , i.e., it depends on the circumstances and the necessity of the firm.

Salient Features of Single Entry System

The salient features of Single Entry System are :

(i) This system is followed by a sole proprietorship firm or a partnership firm. The companies cannot follow this system.

(ii) Under this system, only one Cash Book is maintained which mixes up both the private and business transactions.

(iii) Usually personal accounts are recorded only, i.e., Real and Nominal accounts are ignored.

(iv) Lack of uniformity is noticed if accounts are kept under Single Entry basis.

(v) Profit or loss, under this system, can be ascertained but not the financial position as a whole.

(vi) Arithmetical accuracy of the account is not possible since Trial Balance cannot be prepared.

(vii) Practically, this system is the admixture of Single Entry, Double Entry and no entry.

Advantages of Single Entry System

(i) Since this system is very simple anyone can maintain it without any adequate knowledge of accounting.

(ii) Limited accounts are to be opened under this system since the transactions relating to personal accounts are recognised only and not the Real and Nominal accounts.

(iii) Since the number of books are limited, expenses related to the keeping of records are also very nominal.

(iv) In the case of accounting for an event, i.e., household, social and festival etc., it is very helpful.

Disadvantages of Single Entry System

(i) Arithmetical accuracy of the books of account is not possible since the Trial Balance cannot be prepared under this system.

(ii) It is also not possible to ascertain the correct amount of profit or loss of the firm—i.e., results from operation—since the nominal accounts are missing under this system.

(iii) Similarly, Balance Sheet cannot be prepared since the real accounts are not recognised. Therefore, the real financial position cannot be known at the end of the accounting period.

(iv) As arithmetical accuracy is not possible, possibility of committing fraud or manipulation is greater in comparison with Double Entry System.

(v) Any statistical information relating to the business or the comparison between the two firms or the interim accounts etc.—which help the management to take decision or to formulate policy in future—is not possible under this system.

(vi) Outsiders (e.g., Income-tax authorities, Bank etc.) do not rely on this system.

Differences between Single Entry System and Double Entry System

The following points are to be carefully noted :

Single Entry System	Double Entry System
1. Under this system, only personal accounts are taken into consideration. Real and Nominal accounts are ignored except cash account which is opened in some cases.	1. Under this system, Personal, Real and Nominal accounts are taken into consideration.
2. Under this method, Cash Book, Debtors and Creditors Ledgers are maintained ignoring the effect of personal transactions. Personal transactions are consolidated with business transactions.	2. Under this system Debtors and Creditors Ledger, Cash Book and General Ledgers are maintained for a complete transaction.
3. Detection of errors and arithmetical accuracy are not possible since trial balance is not prepared.	3. Detection of errors and arithmetical accuracy is possible since trial balance is prepared.
4. Under this system final account i.e., Trading and Profit and Loss Account and Balance Sheet cannot be prepared.	4. Under this system final account of the firm can be prepared easily.
5. This system is not based on scientific basis and, as such, this method is not accepted by some authorities, e.g., Income-tax Department.	5. Since this method is based on scientific basis, it is accepted by all.
6. This system is not based on fixed principles and, as such, it is not at all reliable.	6. This system is based on certain fixed principles and, as such, is reliable.
7. Financial position cannot be known accurately at the end of the period and financial ratios (which are very significant) cannot be computed.	7. Financial position can be known accurately at the end of the period, thus financial ratios can easily be computed.

The definition, merits and demerits of Single Entry System have been discussed in an earlier chapter. Now, its methods and techniques are discussed here in detail.

Methods and Techniques

Ascertainment of Profit or Loss

Profit or Loss can be ascertained by the following two methods if Single Entry System is followed :

A. Statement of Affairs Method/Increase in Net Worth Method;

B. Conversion Method.

A. Statement of Affairs/Increase in Net Worth Method

Profit is ascertained by comparing the capitals between two accounting periods, viz., capital at the beginning and capital at the closing, when double entry system is not followed. Here, capital represents the net assets of the business. Therefore, if closing capital is greater than the opening capital (or, if closing net assets are greater in comparison with the opening net assets), the difference will simply represent profit; and there will be a loss in the opposite case. Now, the net assets or the capitals—either at the beginning or at the closing—can be ascertained by preparing a Statement of Affairs as at the opening and also as at the closing date. But if there are any adjustments or any drawings, these are also to be accounted for.

Statement of Affairs

A Statement of Affairs is a summarised statement of financial position (i.e., a statement of assets and liabilities) at a particular date of a business which is very much similar to the Balance Sheet. Care should be taken for different adjustments, like depreciation on assets, outstanding and prepaid expenses etc. at the time of preparing a Statement of Affairs.

Statement of Affairs vs Balance Sheet

There are some fundamental differences between a Statement of Affairs and a Balance Sheet, although the former looks like the latter :

	Statement of Affairs		Balance Sheet
1.	A Statement of Affairs is not reliable or dependable since it is prepared on the basis of estimate, assumption, information etc., on values of different assets.	1.	Since Balance Sheet is based on double entry principle, it is very much reliable and dependable.
2.	Under Single Entry System, a Statement of Affairs is prepared by incorporating the assets on the right side and liabilities on the left. The difference represents capital, which is recorded on the liability side of the same in order to agree the two sides. Since it is agreed in an artificial manner, it can never be considered a reliable statement.	2.	Under Double Entry System, a trial balance is prepared which exhibits the accuracy of accounts. And, since Balance Sheet is prepared from a trial balance, it can safely be taken as reliable.
3.	Since the capital is shown as a balancing figure, assets do not become liabilities.	3.	Since there is a capital account, assets will always be equal to the liabilities.
4.	It is very difficult to locate the assets or liabilities if they are omitted from the books.	4.	It is very easy to locate the omission of any asset or liability, since the Balance Sheet will not agree.
5.	The assets appear in a Statement of Affairs as per valuation but the method of valuation is not shown (i.e., they are based on arbitrary basis).	5.	The assets and liabilities which are shown in a Balance Sheet may be taken as true and correct since the balances are arrived at after recording all the transactions.

Statement of Profit and Loss

Statement of Profit and Loss is to be prepared in order to find out the profit or loss so made during the year. In this statement, at first, the opening capital is to be deducted from the closing capital, thereafter, the drawings of the proprietor will have to be added and further capital, if any, will have to be deducted and the rest will represent profit or loss as the case may be. But, if there are any adjustments, those are also to be adjusted.

How to prepare a Statement of Profit or Loss

First Method

The following steps should carefully be considered while preparing a Statement of Profit or Loss :

Step 1.	***Ascertain the opening capital (if not given) by preparing an opening Statement of Affairs;***
Step 2.	***Ascertain the closing capital by preparing a closing Statement of Affairs;***
Step 3.	***Deduct the opening capital from the closing capital;***
Step 4.	***Deduct the amount of further capital, if any, and add the amount of drawing, if any;***
Step 5.	***Other adjustments, if any, are to be adjusted accordingly.***

The result will represent the net profit or loss of the business.

Ruling :

Statement of Profit and Loss *for the year ended ....*

		Rs.	Rs.
	Capital (at the end)	* *	* *
Less :	Capital (at the beginning)	* *	
			* *
Add :	Drawings		* *
			* *
Less :	Further Capital (if any)		* *
	Profit/Loss		* *

Contd.

		Rs.	Rs.
Less :	Adjustments, if any, say, Bad Debts, Depreciation etc.		* *
	Net Profit/Loss for the period		* *
Less :	Appropriation items : (i) Interest on partners' capital (ii) Partners' salaries etc.		* *
	Divisible Profit		* *

Second Method

Step 1. ***Open a Statement of Profit and Loss and post all the closing assets at book values on the right hand side and all the closing liabilities on the left hand side, the difference will represent closing capital which will be carried forward.***

Step 2. ***Add amount of drawings with closing capital in the right hand side and opening capital and further capital (if any) on the left hand side, the difference will represent gross profit which will be carried forward.***

Step 3. ***Post all the adjustments (which appear in the debit side of P & L A/c) on the left hand side, and interest on drawings, if any, on the right hand side, the difference will represent net profit.***

Statement of Profit and Loss
for the year ended (Closing) ......

	Rs.		*Rs.*
All the Closing Liabilities	* *	**All the Closing Assets (at book value)**	* *
Capital (Closing) c/d *(bal. fig.)*	* *		
	* *		* *
Capital (Opening)	* *		
Further Capital (if any)	* *	Capital b/d	* *
Gross Profit c/d	* *	Drawings	* *
	* *		* *
Adjustments : like,			
Bad Debts	* *	Gross Profit b/d	* *
Depreciation on Assets, etc.	* *		
Net Profit	* *		
	* *		* *

Final Statement of Affairs

After preparing the Statement of Profit and Loss, the Statement of Affairs as at closing date is to be prepared which is similar to the preparation of Balance Sheet. In short, all additions to fixed assets, depreciation on assets, bad debts, provision for bad debts etc. are to be taken into consideration.

Statement of Affairs *as at ....*

Liabilities		Rs.	Rs.	*Assets*	Rs.	Rs.
Capital (Opening)		* *		Plant and Machinery	* *	
Add : Further Capital		* *		*Less :* Depreciation	* *	
Add : Interest on Capital		* *				* *
Add : Net Profit		* *		Land and Building	* *	
		* *		*Less :* Depreciation	* *	
Less : Drawings	* *					* *
Interest on Drawings	* *			Other Fixed Assets		* *
		* *		Investments		* *
Other Closing Liabilities			* *	Closing Stock		* *
				Sundry Debtors	* *	
				Less : Prov. for Bad Debts	* *	
						* *
				Cash at bank		* *
				Cash in hand		* *
			* *			* *

Simple Illustration

Illustration 1

V. P. keeps his books in Single Entry System. On 1.1.2012 his position was as follows :

Sundry Creditors Rs. 20,000; Cash in hand Rs. 300; Cash at Bank Rs. 10,500; Sundry Debtors Rs. 40,000; Stock Rs. 10,000; Plant Rs. 20,000.

On 31.12.2012, the position was :

Sundry Creditors Rs. 35,000; Cash in hand 500; Cash at Bank Rs. 22,000; Sundry Debtors Rs. 49,000; Stock Rs. 12,000; Plant Rs. 45,000.

V. P. drew Rs. 500 at the end of every month. He introduced Rs. 25,000 by way of additional capital. Depreciate Plant at 10% and raise a reserve of $2\frac{1}{2}$% against Sundry Debtors. You are required to prepare a Statement of Profit and Loss for the year ended 31st Dec. 2012 and a Statement of Affairs as on that date.

Solution

Statement of Affairs *as at 1st January 2012*

Liabilities	Rs.	*Assets*	Rs.
Sundry Creditors	20,000	Stock	10,000
Capital or Net Assets *(bal. fig.)*	60,800	Sundry Debtors	40,000
		Cash at Bank	10,500
		Cash in hand	300
		Plant	20,000
	80,800		80,800

Statement of Affairs *as at 31st December 2012*

Liabilities	Rs.	*Assets*	Rs.
Sundry Creditors	35,000	Stock	12,000
Capital or Net Assets *(bal. fig.)*	93,500	Sundry Debtors	49,000
		Cash at bank	22,000
		Cash in hand	500
		Plant	45,000
	1,28,500		1,28,500

Statement of Profit and Loss *for the year ended 31st Dec. 2012*

		Rs.	Rs.
	Capital as on 31st Dec. 2012		93,500
Less :	Capital as on 1st Jan. 2012		60,800
			32,700
Add :	Drawings (Rs. 500 × 12)		6,000
			38,700
Less :	Additional Capital		25,000
			13,700
Less :	Provision for Bad Debts	1,225	
	Depreciation on Plant	3,250	4,475
	Net Profit during the year		9,225

Alternative Approach

Statement of Profit and Loss *for the year ended 31st Dec. 2012*

	Rs.		Rs.
Sundry Creditors	35,000	Stock	12,000
Capital (Closing) or Net Assets c/d	93,500	Sundry Debtors	49,000
		Cash at Bank	22,000
		Cash in hand	500
		Plant	45,000
	1,28,500		1,28,500

	Rs.		Rs.
Capital (in 1.1.2012)	60,800	Capital (Closing) b/d	93,500
Additional Capital	25,000	Drawings (Rs. 500 × 12)	6,000
Gross Profit c/d	13,700		
	99,500		99,500
Provision for Bad Debts @ $2\frac{1}{2}$%	1,225	Gross Profit b/d	13,700
Depreciation on Plant @ 10%	3,250[1]		
Net Profit	9,225		
	13,700		13,700

Note :

1. Depreciation on Plant :

	Rs.
On Rs. 20,000 × $\frac{10}{100}$	2,000
On Rs. 25,000 × $\frac{10}{100} \times \frac{6}{12}$	1,250
	3,250

It has been assumed that additions were made at the middle of the year.

Alternative Approach

Statement of Profit and Loss *for the year ended 31st Dec. 2012*

	Rs.		Rs.
Opening Assets Stock	10,000	*Closing Assets* Stock	12,000
Sundry Debtors	40,000	Sundry Debtors	49,000
Cash at Bank	10,500	Cash at Bank	22,000
Cash in hand	300	Cash in hand	500
Plant	20,000	Plant	45,000
Closing Liabilities		*Opening Liabilities*	
Sundry Creditors	35,000	Sundry Creditors	20,000
Excess of Closing Net Assets over Opening Net Assets c/d	32,700		
	1,48,500		1,48,500
Additional Capital	25,000	Excess of Closing Net Assets over Opening Net Assets b/d	32,700
Gross Profit c/d	13,700	Drawings	6,000
	38,700		38,700
Provision for Bad Debts	1,225	Gross Profit b/d	13,700
Depreciation on Plant	3,250		
Net Profit	9,225		
	13,700		13,700

Note : Of the three methods stated above, the second one is the best, and the same has been followed while solving subsequent problems.

Statement of Affair *as at 31st Dec. 2012*

Liabilities	Rs.	Rs.	*Assets*	Rs.	Rs.
Sundry Creditors		35,000	Stock		12,000
Capital (as 1.1.2012)	60,800		Sundry Debtors	49,000	
Add : Additional Capital	25,000		*Less :* Provision for Bad Debts	1,225	47,775
Add : Net Profit	9,225		Cash at Bank		22,000
	95,025		Cash in hand		500
Less : Drawings	6,000		Plant	45,000	
		89,025	*Less :* Depreciation	3,250	41,750
		1,24,025			1,24,025

Illustration 2

R had Rs. 3,00,000 in bank on 1st January 2009 when he started his business. He closed his accounts on 31st March 2010. His single entry books (in which he did not maintain any account for the bank) showed his position as follows :

	31.3.2009	31.3.2010
	Rs.	Rs.
Cash in hand	2,000	3,000
Stock in trade	19,000	29,000
Debtors	1,000	2,000
Creditors	5,000	3,000

On 1st February 2009, he began drawing Rs. 700 per month for his personal expenses from the Cash Book of the business. His account in the bank had the following entries :

	Deposits	Withdrawals
	Rs.	Rs.
1.1.2009	3,00,000	—
1.1.2009 to 31.3.2009	—	2,23,000
1.4.2009 to 31.3.2010	2,30,000	2,70,000

The above withdrawals included payments by cheques of Rs. 2,00,000 and Rs. 60,000, respectively, during the period 1st January 2009 to 31st March 2009 and from 1st April 2009 to 31st March 2010 for the purchase of machinery for the business. The deposits after 1st January 2009 consisted wholly of sale price received from customers by cheques. Draw up R's Statement of Affairs as at 31st March 2009 and 31st March 2010, respectively, and work out his profit or loss for the year ended 31st March 2010.

Solution

Statement of Affairs *as at 31st Dec. 2009*

Liabilities	Rs.	*Assets*	Rs.	Rs.
Capital *(bal. fig.)*	2,94,000	Machinery		2,00,000
Creditors	5,000	Stock		19,000
		Debtors		1,000
		Bank	3,00,000	
		Less : Withdrawals	2,23,000	77,000
		Cash in hand		2,000
	2,99,000			2,99,000

Statement of Profit and Loss *for the year ended 31st March 2010*

	Rs.		Rs.
Creditors	3,000	Machinery	2,60,000
Capital (Closing) c/d	3,28,000	Stock	29,000
		Debtors	2,000
		Bank	37,000*
		Cash in hand	3,000
	3,31,000		3,31,000
Capital—Opening	2,94,000	Capital b/d	3,28,000
Net Profit	42,400	Drawings (Rs. 700 × 12)	8,400
	3,36,400		3,36,400

Statement of Affairs *as at 31st March 2010*

Liabilities	Rs.	Rs.	*Assets*	Rs.
Capital	2,94,000		Machinery	2,60,000
Add : Net Profit	42,400		Stock	29,000
	3,36,400		Debtors	2,000
Less : Drawings	8,400	3,28,000	Bank	37,000
Creditors		3,000	Cash in hand	3,000
		3,31,000		3,31,000

* Closing balance = Opening Balance + Deposits – Withdrawals

= Rs. 77,000 + Rs. 2,30,000 – Rs. 2,70,000 = Rs. 37,000

Preparation of Statemcnt of Profit and Loss ascertainings Bank Balance

Illustration 3

On 1.1.2012 a trader starts a business with capital of Rs. 1,00,000 with which he opened a bank account. On the same day, he bought Furniture and Fittings for shop costing Rs. 4,800 and goods for trade costing Rs. 25,000.

On 31.12.2012 his stock in hand was valued at Rs. 29,000 and Fittings stood at Rs. 6,300. On that date his Book Debts amounted to Rs. 78,000 of which Rs. 1,200 was considered to be bad. Creditors amounted to Rs. 15,000. His balance as per Cash Book was Rs. 5,500. A cheque for Rs. 400 sent for deposit on Dec. 30 was not realised till after Dec. 31 and a cheque for Rs. 70, issued on Dec. 29, was not presented to bank till after Dec. 31. Bank charges for the year amounted to Rs. 50 but this was not known to the trader on Dec. 31. His drawings during the year amounted to Rs. 9,300. He had also taken for personal use goods from the shop valued at Rs. 1,500. Prepare a statement showing the trader's profit or loss during 2012.

[CU BCom (Hons.)]

Solution

In the Books of ......

Statement of Profit and Loss *for the year ended 31st December 2012*

	Rs.			Rs.
Creditors	15,000	Cash at Bank (5,500 – 50)		5,450
Capital (Closing) c/d	1,02,550	Stock		29,000
		Debtors (78,000 – 1,200)		76,800
		Furniture and Fittings		6,300
	1,17,550			1,17,550
Capital (on 1.1.2012)	1,00,000	Capital (Closing) b/d		1,02,550
Net Profit c/d	13,350	Drawings—		
		Cash	9,300	
		Goods	1,500	
				10,800
	1,13,350			1,13,350

Notes :

There will be no adjustment in Cash Book for :

(i) a cheque of Rs. 400 deposited into Bank; and (ii) a cheque of Rs. 70 issued but not presented.

These have already been recorded in Cash Book and amended Cash Book Balance is considered as the closing balance of Cash at Bank.

Preparation of Statement of Profit and Loss Statement of Affairs, Profit on Sale of Furniture

Illustration 4

Mr. A does not maintain complete double entry books of account. From the following details determine profit for the year and a Statement of Affairs as at the end of the year :

Rs. 1,000 (cost) Furniture was sold for Rs. 5,000 on 1.1.2012. 19% depreciation is to be charged on Furniture. Mr. A has drawn Rs. 1,000 p.m. Rs. 2,000 was invested by Mr. A in 2012 :

	1.1.2012	31.12.2012	
	Rs.	Rs.	
Stock	40,000	60,000	
Debtors	30,000	40,000	
Cash	2,000	1,000	
Bank	10,000	5,000	(overdraft)
Creditors	15,000	25,000	
Outstanding Expenses	5,000	8,000	
Furniture (cost)	3,000	2,000	

Bank Balance on 1.1.2012 is as per Cash Book, but the bank overdraft on 31.12.2012 is as per bank statement. Rs. 2,000 cheques drawn in Dec. 2012 have not been encashed within the year.

[CU BCom (Hons.)]

Solution

In the Books of A
Statement of Affairs *as at 1st Jan. 2012*

Liabilities	Rs.	*Assets*	Rs.
Creditors	15,000	Cash	2,000
Outstanding Expenses	5,000	Bank	10,000
Capital (on 1.1.2012)	65,000	Debtors	30,000
		Stock	40,000
		Furniture	3,000
	85,000		85,000

Statement of Profit and Loss *for the year ended 31st Dec. 2012*

	Rs.		Rs.
Creditors	25,000	Cash	1,000
Outstanding Expenses	8,000	Debtors	40,000
Bank Overdraft	7,000[1]	Stock	60,000
Capital (Closing) c/d	59,000	Furniture	2,000
			1,03,000
		Less : Profit on Sale of Furniture	4,000[3]
	99,000		99,000
Capital (on 1.1.2012)	65,000	Capital (Closing) b/d	59,000
Additional Capital	2,000	Drawings—	12,000
Gross Profit c/d	4,000	(Rs. 1,000 × 12)	
	71,000		71,000
Depreciation on Furniture	200[2]	Gross Profit b/d	4,000
@ 10% on Rs. 2,000		Profit on Sale of Furniture	4,000
Net Profit	7,800		
	8,000		8,000

Notes :

1. Closing Bank Overdraft will be Rs. (5,000 + 2,000) = Rs. 7,000.
2. Depreciation on Furniture will be @ 10% on Rs. 2,000 which was used throughout the year.
3. Profit on Sale of Furniture Rs. (5,000 – 1,000) = Rs. 4,000 is included in closing assets and, therefore, it is to be deducted in order to ascertain the correct trading profit, therefore, it will again be added with profit shown separately.

Statement of Affairs *as at 31st Dec. 2012*

Liabilities	Rs.	Rs.	*Assets*	Rs.	Rs.
Creditors		25,000	Cash		1,000
Outstanding Expenses		8,000	Debtors		40,000
Bank Overdraft		7,000	Stock		60,000
Capital (1.1.2012)	65,000		Furniture (on 1.1.2012)	3,000	
Add : Additional Capital	2,000		*Less* : Sold on 1.1.2012 at book value	1,000	
Add : Net Profit	7,800			2,000	
	74,800		*Less* : Depreciation	200	
Less : Drawings	12,000	62,800			1,800
		1,02,800			1,02,800

A Comprehensive illustration

Illustration 5

Sri Amitabha Sen keeps his books by Single Entry Method. His financial position as on 1.1.2012 and 31.12.2012 were :

	1.1.2012	31.12.2012
	Rs.	Rs.
Cash	5,000	8,000
Bank	10,000	18,000
Stock	8,000	12,000
Debtors	12,000	15,000
Creditors	5,000	6,000
Plant and Machinery	10,000	15,000
Furniture and Fittings	6,000	6,000

During the year Sri Sen had withdrawn Rs. 6,000 for his private purposes and he had used Rs. 500 worth of the stock of his business also for his private purposes. On 1.7.2012 he sold some of his household furniture for Rs. 2,000 and paid this into his business Bank Account.

You are asked to prepare a Statement of Profit and Loss for the year ended 31.12.2012 and a Statement of Affairs as at that date after taking the following into consideration :

(a) Provide interest on capital @ 5% p.a. and interest on drawings (only on cash drawings) @ 10% p.a. (on an average of 6 months);

(b) Depreciate Plant and Machinery @ 10% p.a. (assume additions were made on 1.7.2012) and Furniture @ 5% p.a.

(c) Stock (on 31.12.2012) was overvalued by Rs. 1,000.

(d) Make a provision for bad debts 5% on Sundry Debtors.

Solution

Since the Opening Capital is not given, we are to find it out by preparing Statement of Affairs as at 1.1.2012 which is :

Statement of Affairs *as at 1st Jan. 2012*

Liabilities	Rs.	*Assets*	Rs.
Creditors	5,000	Cash	5,000
Capital *(bal. fig.)*	46,000	Bank	10,000
		Stock	8,000
		Debtors	12,000
		Plant and Machinery	10,000
		Furniture and Fittings	6,000
	51,000		51,000

Statement of Profit and Loss *for the year ended 31st December 2012*

	Rs.			Rs.
Creditors	6,000	Cash		8,000
Capital *(bal. fig.)* on 31.12.2012	68,000	Bank		18,000
		Stock		12,000
		Debtors		15,000
		Plant and Machinery		15,000
		Furniture and Fittings		6,000
	74,000			74,000
Capital (on 1.1.2012)	46,000	Capital (on 31.12.2012)		68,000
Additional Capital	2,000	Drawings :		
Gross Profit c/d	26,500	Cash	6,000	
		Goods taken	500	6,500
	74,500			74,500
Depreciation on :		Gross Profit b/d		26,500
Plant and Machinery @ 10%	1,250[1]			
Furniture and Fittings @ 5%	300			
Overvaluation of Stock	1,000			
Reserve for Bad Debts	750			
Net Profit c/d	23,200			
	26,500			26,500
Interest on Capital	2,350	Net Profit b/d		23,200
Net Profit	21,150	Interest on Drawings		300[3]
	23,500			23,500

Statement of Affairs *as at 31st Dec. 2012*

Liabilities	Rs.	Rs.	Rs.	*Assets*	Rs.	Rs.
Capital		46,000		Cash		8,000
Additional Capital		2,000		Bank		18,000
Add : Interest on Capital		2,350		Stock	2,000	
Add : Net Profit		21,150		*Less* : Over-valuation	1,000	
		71,500				11,000
Less : Drawings	6,500			Debtors	15,000	
Interest	300			*Less* : Reserve for Bad Debts	750	
		6,800				14,250
			64,700	Plant and Machinery	15,000	
Creditors			6,000	*Less* : Depreciation	1,250	
						13,750
				Furniture and Fittings	6,000	
				Less : Depreciation	300	5,700
			70,700			70,700

Workings :

1. **Depreciation on Plant an Machinery**

	Rs.
on Rs. 10,000 $\times \frac{10}{100} =$	1,000
on Rs. 5,000 $\times \frac{10}{100} \times \frac{6}{12} =$	250
	1,250

2. **Interrest on Capital**

	Rs.
On Rs. 46,000 $\times \frac{5}{100} =$	2,300
on Rs. 2,000 $\times \frac{5}{100} \times \frac{6}{12} =$	50
	1,250

3. **Interest on Drawings**

on Rs. 6,000 $\times \frac{10}{100} \times \frac{6}{12} = 300$

Uncommon Problem

Illustration 6

Mr. Kothari does not keep complete records of his business but gives you the following information :

His assets on 31st March 2013 consisted of MachinerY Rs. 1,50,000; Furniture Rs. 60,000; Motor Car Rs. 40,000; Stock-in-trade Rs. 50,000; Debtors Rs. 80,000; Cash in hand Rs. 12,000 and Cash at Bank for Rs. 30,000; Creditors on that date amounted to Rs. 1,20,000.

On further information received, you come to know that :

On 1st October 2012 he purchased a new machinery costing Rs. 50,000.

Sales are made for cash as well as on credit. There is no cash purchase. He always sells his goods at cost plus 25%. Cash sales for the year 2012-13 were accounted for Rs. 80,000.

During the year 2012-13 collection from Debtors amounted to Rs. 5,00,000 and a sum of Rs. 4,25,000 was paid to creditors.

He obtained a Bank Loan for Rs. 50,000 on 1st February 2012. The entire amount was repaid in February 2013 with interest Rs. 2,500.

In November 2012 his Life Insurance Policy for Rs. 50,000 became mature and the same was invested in the business. His Drawing were Rs. 2,500 per month throughout the year.

On 1st April 2012 he had Rs. 1,500 as Cash in hand and balance at Bank for Rs. 40,000. Debtors and Creditors on that date amounted to Rs. 60,000 and Rs. 90,000, respectively.

Provide depreciation on Machinery @ 15% p.a. on Furniture @ 10% p.a. and on Motor Car @ 20% p.a.

Mr. Kothari requests you to prepare a Statement of Profit & Loss for the year ended 31st March 2013 **[ICWA]**

Solution

(a) **Ascertainment of Credit Sales**

In the Books of Mr. Kothari Total Debtors A/c

Dr.		Rs.	Cr.	Rs.
To	Balance b/d	60,000	By Bank	5,00,000
"	Credit Sales *(bal. fig.)*	5,20,000	" Balance c/d	80,000
		5,80,000		5,80,000

(b) **Ascertainment of Credit Purchases**

Total Creditors A/c

Dr.		Rs.	Cr.	Rs.
To	Bank	4,25,000	By Bal. b/d	90,000
"	Balance c/d	1,20,000	" Credit Purchases *(bal. fig.)*	4,55,000
		5,45,000		5,45,000

(c) **Ascertainment of Opening Stock**

∴ Total Sales = Credit Sales + Cash Sales
= Rs. 5,20,000 + Rs. 80,000
= Rs. 6,00,000

Cost of Goods Sold = Rs. $6,00,000 \times \frac{100}{125}$ = Rs. 4,80,000

		Rs.
	Stock-in-trade as at 1st April 2012	
	Cost of Goods Sold	4,80,000
Add :	Closing Stock	50,000
		5,30,000
Less :	Purchase	4,55,000
	Opening Stock	75,000

(d) **Allocation of Interest**

Total Interest from 1.2.2012 to 1.2.2013 amounted to Rs. 2,500

	Rs.
So, Outstanding Interest from 1.2.2012 to 31.3.2012 = Rs. $2,500 \times \frac{2}{12}$ =	417
Balance from 1.4.2012 to 1.2.2013 = Rs. $2,500 \times \frac{10}{12}$ =	2,083
	2,500

(e) Ascertainment of Opening and Closing Capital.

Balance Sheet

Liabilities	Opening Rs.	Closing Rs.	*Assets*	Opening Rs.	Closing Rs.
Creditors	90,000	1,20,000	Machinery	1,00,000	1,50,000
Bank Loan	50,000	—	Furniture	60,000	60,000
Outstanding Interest on Bank Loan	417		Motor Car	40,000	40,000
Capital *(bal. fig.)*	2,36,083	3,02,000	Stock	75,000	50,000
			Debtors	60,000	80,000
			Cash in hand	1,500	12,000
			Cash at Bank	40,000	30,000
	3,76,500	4,22,000		3,76,500	4,22,000

Statement of Profit and Loss ***for the year ended 31st March 2012***

		Rs.	Rs.
	Closing Capital		3,02,000
Less :	Opening Capital	2,36,083	
	Additional Capital	50,000	2,86,083
			15,917
Add :	Drawings		30,000
			45,917
Less :	Depreciation on :		
	(i) Machinery @ 15%	18,750	
	(ii) Furniture @ 10%	6,000	
	(iii) Motor Car @ 20%	8,000	32,750
	Net Profit for the year		13,167

Ascertainment of Profit

Illustration 7

The Balance Sheet of A as at 31.12.2007 and 2008 are set out below. He does not understand as to what has happened to the profit of Rs. 1,20,000 as disclosed by 2008 Balance Sheet as he does not find it in his bank balance.

Draw up a statement which will explain to him as to how the profit may be accounted for.

Liabilities	2007 Rs.	2008 Rs.	*Assets*	2007 Rs.	2008 Rs.
Capital (31.12.2007)	2,30,000	2,30,000	Cash at Bank	10,000	10,000
Add : Profit for 2008		1,20,000	Sundry Debtors	1,40,000	1,60,000
		3,50,000	Stock	60,000	1,00,000
Less : Drawings during 2008		24,000	Motor Vehicles	20,000	16,000
		3,26,000	Plant	1,60,000	1,40,000
Mortgage on Freehold Property	1,60,000	1,20,000	Freehold Property	2,00,000	2,00,000
Sundry Creditors	2,00,000	1,80,000			
	5,90,000	6,26,000		5,90,000	6,26,000

Solution **[CU BCom (Hons.)]**

(Increase in assets or decrease in liabilities = Profit)
(Decrease in assets or increase in liabilities = Loss)

Statement for Ascertaining Profit and Loss

		Rs.		Rs.	Rs.
Increase in Assets :					
Sundry Debtors	2008	1,60,000			
Less : Sundry Debtors	2007	1,40,000		20,000	
Stock	2008	1,00,000			
Less : Stock	2007	60,000		40,000	60,000
Add : ***Decrease in Liabilities :***					
Mortgage F. P.	2008	1,60,000			
Less : Mortgage F. P.	2007	1,20,000		40,000	
Creditors	2008	2,00,000			
Less : Creditors	2007	1,80,000			
				20,000	
					60,000
					1,20,000
Less : ***Decrease in Assets :***					
Motor Vehicle	2007	20,000			
Less : Motor Vehicle	2008	16,000		4,000	
Plant	2007	1,60,000			
Less : Plant	2008	1,40,000			
				20,000	
					24,000
			Net Increase in Assets		96,000
			Add : Drawings		24,000
			Profit for the year		1,20,000

Ascertainment of Missing Figures

Illustration 8

The following balances are available from the books of Mr. Chakladar as on 31st March 2012 and 31st March 2013 :

	31.3.2012 Rs.	31.3.2013 Rs.
Furniture & Fixtures (at cost, less depreciation)	81,000	81,900
Stock-in-trade	50,000	75,000
Sundry Creditors	1,20,000	40,000
Sundry Debtors	85,000	52,000
Office Equipments (at cost, less depreciation)	54,000	48,600
Cash & Bank	60,000	5,000

Additional Information :

(i) His drawings were : 2011-12 Rs. 25,000
2012-13 Rs. 30,000

(ii) His total sales for 2012-2013 amounted to Rs. 6,00,000. Total cash sales figure is not readily available. He always sales his goods at cost plus 25%.

(iii) Payments to creditors in 2012-13 included Rs. 12,000 paid from his private Bank Account. There is no cash purchase.

(iv) Sundry Debtors on 31.3.93 includes a wrong credit of Rs. 20,000 as insurance claim received towards goods costing Rs. 25,000 destroyed by fire, and a further sum of Rs, 2,000 as recovered from a customer whose account was written-off in 2011-12.

(v) During the year goods costing Rs. 6,000 were distributed as free samples. Discounts allowed to debtors Rs. 12,000 and discounts received Rs. 8,000.

(vi) Depreciation is charged @ 10% on Furniture & Office Equipments. Mr. Chakladar requests you to prepare a Trading Account and Profit & Loss Account for the year ended 31st March 2013.

Solution **[ICWA (New)]**

Mr. Chakladar

Dr. **Trading and Profit &Loss Account** *for the year ended 31st March 2013* Cr.

	Particulars		Rs.		*Particulars*	Rs.
To	Opening Stock		50,000	By	Sales	6,00,000
"	Purchases (balancing figures)		5,36,000	"	Goods distributed as per sample	6,000
"	Gross Profit (i.e., 20% on turnover) on 25% on Cost.		1,20,000	"	Goods destroyed by fire	25,000
				"	Closing Stock	75,000
			7,06,000			7,06,000
To	Expenses (balance figure)		40,000	By	Gross Profit	1,20,000
"	Loss of Stock by Fire (25,000 – 20,000)		5,000	"	Bad Debt Recovery	2,000
"	Advertisement (free sample)		6,000	"	Discount Received	8,000
"	Discount Allowed		12,000			
"	Depreciation :					
	Furniture	9,100				
	Office Equipments	5,400	14,500			
"	Capital Account : —Net Profit transferred		52,500[2]			
			1,30,000			1,30,000

Workings :

1. **Balance Sheet** *as at ....*

Liabilities	31.3.2012	31.3.2013	*Assets*	31.3.2012	31.3.2013
	Rs.	Rs.		Rs.	Rs.
Creditors	1,20,000	40,000	Furniture & Fixture	81,000	81,900
Capital A/c *(bal. fig.)*	2,10,000	2,44,500	Office Equipment	54,000	48,600
			Stock	50,000	75,000
			Debtors	85,000	74,000*
			Cash at Bank	60,000	5,000
	3,30,000	2,84,500		3,30,000	2,84,500

* Rs. 52,000 + Rs. 20,000 claims received + Rs. 2,000 recovery of Bad Debts

2. **Ascertainment of Net Profit**

		Rs.
	Capital (as on 31.3.2013)	2,44,500
Less :	Capital (as on 31.3.2012)	2,10,000
		34,500
Add :	Drawings	30,000
		64,500
Less :	Further Capital	12,000
		52,500

Application of Single Entry System in Partnership Firms

The principles of preparing a Statement of Profit and Loss in case of a partnership firm is similar to sole-proprietorship business, only the appropriation items are to be separately shown after ascertaining the profit before appropriation, i.e., interest on capital, partners' salaries, and commission etc. will appear in the left hand side and interest on partners' drawings will appear in the right hand side, the difference will represent net profit which will be divided between/among partners in their profit-sharing ratio. However, for preparing Statement of Affairs, the principle is also the same. Only the capital accounts of the partners are to be separately shown.

Note : In preparing Statement of Profit and Loss the difference will represent closing Combined Capitals which will be carried forward.

Illustration 9

Kusum and Putul are partners in a firm sharing profits and losses as Kusum $\frac{3}{5}$ and Putul $\frac{2}{5}$. They keep their books on Single Entry System.

On 1.1.2012 the following Statement of Affairs was extracted from their books :

Liabilities		Rs.	*Assets*	Rs.
Sundry Creditors		30,000	Plant	30,000
Kusum—Loan A/c		25,000	Stock	20,000
Capital Account			Sundry Debtors	35,000
Kusum	25,000		Cash at Bank	15,000
Putul	20,000			
		45,000		
		1,00,000		1,00,000

On 31.12.2012, the assets and liabilities were:

Plant Rs. 50,000; Stock Rs. 30,000; Debtors Rs. 40,000; Cash Rs. 20,000; Creditors Rs. 20,000; Kusum Loan A/c Rs. 25,000, Drawing—Kusum Rs. 6,000 and Putul Rs. 4,000.

You are required to prepare a Profit and Loss Statement for the year ended 31.12.2012, and a Statement of Affairs as at that date after taking into consideration the following additional information :

(i) Plant to be depreciated by 10%; (ii) Stock is to be reduced to Rs, 25,000; (iii) A Reserve for Bad Debts to be raised @ $2\frac{1}{2}$% on Debtors; (iv) Interest on partners' capital is to be allowed @ 5% p.a. and @ 10% on drawings. (v) Allow interest on Kusum's Loan @ 6% p.a.

Solution

Statement of Profit and Loss *for the year ended 31st Dec. 2012*

	Rs.		Rs.
Creditors	20,000	Plant	50,000
Kusum's Loan	25,000	Stock	30,000
Combined Capital *(bal. fig.)* c/d		Debtors	40,000
(on 31.12.2012)	95,000	Cash	20,000
	1,40,000		1,40,000
Capital on 1.1.2012 :		Combined Capital (on 31.12.2012) b/d	95,000
Kusum	25,000	Drawings :	
Putul	20,000	Kusum	6,000
Gross Profit c/d	60,000	Putul	4,000
	1,05,000		1,05,000
Depreciation on Plant	4,000	Gross Profit b/d	60,000
Stock	5,000		
Reserve for Bad Debts	1,000		
Interest on Kusum's Loan	1,500		
Net Profit c/d	48,500		
	60,000		60,000

Contd.

		Rs.			Rs.
Interest on Capital :			Net Profit b/d		48,500
Kusum	1,250		Interest on Drawings :		
Putul	1,000		Kusum	300	
		2,250	Putul	200	
Share of Profit :					500
Kusum	28,050				
Putul	18,700				
		46,750			
		49,000			49,000

Statement of Affairs *as at 31st Dec. 2012*

Liabilities		Rs.	Rs.	*Assets*	Rs.	Rs.
Capital :				Plant	50,000	
Kusum (Opening)		25,000		*Less :* Depreciation	4,000	
Add : Interest on Capital		1,250				46,000
Add : Net Profit		28,050		Stock	30,000	
		54,300		*Less :* Reduction	5,000	
Less : Drawings	6,000					25,000
Interest	300			Debtors	40,000	
		6,300		*Less :* Reserve for Bad Debts	1,000	
			48,000			39,000
Capital :				Cash		20,000
Putul (Opening)		20,000				
Add : Interest on Capital		1,000				
Add : Net Profit		18,700				
		39,700				
Less : Drawings	4,000					
Interest	200					
		4,200	35,500			
Kusum : Loan		25,000				
Add : Interest on Loan		1,500	26,500			
Creditors			20,000			
			1,30,000			1,30,000

Note : Interest on Drawings should be charged on an average for 6 months.

Where a partner having deficit balance in Current Account

Illustration 10

A, B, and C were in partnership, and, towards the end of 2011, most of their books and records were destroyed by fire. The Balance Sheet as at 31.12.2011 was as follows :

Liabilities	Rs.	Rs.	*Assets*	Rs.
Creditors		11,000	Cash at Bank	4,800
Capital Accounts :			Debtors	7,200
A	9,000		Stock	13,000
B	6,000		Machinery & Plant	2,880
C	3,000		Fixtures & Fittings	1,200
		18,000	Advance Payments	70
Current Accounts :			Current Account :	
A	290		C	340
B	200			
		490		
		29,490		29,490

The partners' drawings during 2012 were A Rs. 2,800; B Rs. 2,000; C Rs. 1,300. On 31.12.2012 Cash at Bank was Rs. 6,400; Debtors Rs. 8,050; Stock Rs. 11,800; Advance Payments Rs. 50; Creditors

Rs. 12,080. Machinery is to be depreciated at 10% p.a. and Fixture & Fittings at $7\frac{1}{2}$% p.a. 5% interest is to be allowed on capital, and partners share profits in the respective proportions of $\frac{1}{2}$, $\frac{1}{3}$ and $\frac{1}{6}$.

You are required to prepare a statement showing the net trading profit for the year 2012 and the division of the same between the partners, together with the Balance Sheet as at 31.12.2012.

Solution

In the Books of A, B, and C

Statement of Profit and Loss *for the year ended 31st Dec. 2012*

	Rs.	Rs.		Rs.	Rs.
Creditors		12,080	Cash at Bank		6,400
Combined Capital (on 31.12.2012) c/d		18,300	Debtors		8,050
			Stock		11,800
			Advance Payments		50
			Machinery and Plant		2,880
			Fixtures and Fittings		1,200
		30,380			30,380
Capital (Opening)			Combined Capitals (on 31.12.2012) b/d		18,300
A	9,000		Current A/c		340
B	6,000		C		
C	3,000	18,000			
Current (Opening) A/c			Drawings		
A	290		A	2,800	
B	200	490	B	2,000	
			C	1,300	6,100
Gross Profit c/d		6,250			
		24,740			24,740
Depreciation on :			Gross Profit b/d		6,250
Machinery and Plant	288				
Fixture and Fittings	90	378			
Net Profit c/d		5,872			
		6,250			6,250
Interest on Capital			Net Profit b/d		5,872
A	450				
B	300				
C	150	900			
Share of Profit :					
A $\frac{1}{2}$	2,486				
B $\frac{1}{3}$	1,657				
C $\frac{1}{6}$	829	4,972			
		5,872			5,872

Balance Sheet *as at 31st Dec. 2012*

Liabilities	Rs.	Rs.	*Assets*	Rs.	Rs.
Creditors		12,080	Cash at Bank		6,400
Current A/cs—			Debtors		8,050
A	290		Stock		11,800
Add : Interest	450		Machinery & Plant	2,880	
Share of Profit	2,486		*Less :* Depreciation	288	
	3,226				2,592
Less : Drawings	2,800		Fixtures & Furniture	1,200	
		426	*Less :* Depreciation	90	
B	200				1,110
Add : Interest	300		Advance Payments		50

Contd.

	Rs.	Rs.		Rs.	Rs.
Share of Profit	1,657		Current A/c—		
	2,157		C	340	
Less : Drawings	2,000		*Add :* Drawings	1,300	
		157		1,640	
Capital A/cs—			*Less :* Interest 150		
A	9,000		Share of Profit 829		
B	6,000			979	
C	3,000	18,000			661
		30,663			30,663

GENERAL ILLUSTRATIONS

A. Comprehensive and harder illustration

Illustration 11

A and B started business on January 1, 2012 with Rs. 50,000 as capital, contributed equally; but the profit-sharing ratio was 3 : 2. Their drawings were Rs. 300 and Rs. 200 p.m., respectively. They had kept no account except the following information :

	31-12-2012	31-12-2013
	Rs.	Rs.
Machinery at Cost	20,000	25,000
Stock-in-trade	30,000	30,000
Debtors	50,000	60,000
Cash	2,000	500
Creditors	30,000	20,000
Outstanding Expenses	4,000	3,000
Bank Balance (as per Pass Book)	6,000	8,000

Provision is to be made for depreciation at 10% on the cost of machinery as at the end of each year. Debtors on 31.12.2012 include Rs. 5,000 for goods sent out on consignment at 25 per cent above cost, and the goods were not sold until 2013. A cheque for Rs. 1,000 had been deposited on 31.12.2012 but was credited on 2.1.2013. Cheque for Rs. 2,000 issued on 26.12.2013 was presented on 3.1.2014. A cheque for Rs. 1,000 was directly deposited by a customer on 27.12.13. A cheque for Rs. 500 deposited in December 2013 was dishonoured but no adjustment for these were made. Determine the profits for 2012 and 2013 and draw up a Balance Sheet as at 31st December 2013.

Solution

In the Books of A and B
Statement of Profit and Loss *as at 31st Dec. 2012*

	Rs.		Rs.
Creditors	30,000	Cash	2,000
Outstanding Expenses	4,000	Bank (6,000 + 1,000)	7,000
Combined Capital (on 31.12.2012) *(bal. fig.)* c/d	74,000	Debtors (50,000 – 5,000)	45,000
		Stock (30,000 + $\frac{4}{5}$ of 5,000)	34,000
		Plant and Machinery	20,000
	1,08,000		1,08,000
Combined Capital (opening)	50,000	Capital (on 31.12.2012) b/d	74,000
Gross Profit c/d	30,000	Drawings	
		A = 300 × 12	3,600
		B = 200 × 12	2,400
	80,000		80,000
Depreciation on Plant and Machinery	2,000	Gross Profit b/d	30,000
Net Profit c/d	28,000		
	30,000		30,000

		Rs.		Rs.
Share of Profit			Net Profit b/d	28,000
A $\frac{3}{5}$	16,800			
B $\frac{2}{5}$	11,200			
		28,000		
		28,000		28,000

Statement of Profit and Loss *for the year ended 21st December 2013*

		Rs.			Rs.
Creditors		20,000	Cash		500
Outstanding Expenses		3,000	Bank (8,000 – 2,000)		6,000
Combined Capital (on 31.12.2013)			Debtors (60,000 – 1,000 + 500)		59,500
(bal. fig.) c/d		98,000	Stock		30,000
			Plant and Machinery		25,000
		1,21,000			1,21,000
Combined Capital (Opening)		74,000	Capital (on 31.12.2013) b/d		98,000
Gross Profit c/d		30,000	Drawings		
			A =	300 × 12	3,600
			B =	200 × 12	2,400
		1,04,000			1,04,000
Depreciation on Plant and Machinery		2,500	Gross Profit b/d		30,000
Net Profit c/d		27,500			
		30,000			30,000
Share of Profit :			Net Profit b/d		27,500
A = $\frac{3}{5}$	16,500				
B = $\frac{2}{5}$	11,000				
		27,500			
		27,500			27,500

Balance Sheet *as at 31st Dec. 2013*

Liabilities	Rs.	Rs.	*Assets*	Rs.	Rs.
Creditors		20,000	Cash		500
Outstanding Expenses		3,000	Bank		6,000
Capital :			Debtors		59,500
A (Opening)	25,000		Stock		30,000
Add : Net Profit for 2012			Plant and Machinery		
and 2013 (16,800 + 16,500)	33,300		at Cost	25,000	
	58,300		*Less* : Depreciation		
Less : Drawings for			(2,000 + 2,500)	4,500	
2012-13 (3,600 + 3,600)	7,200	51,100			20,500
Capital :					
B (Opening)	25,000				
Add : Net Profit for 2012 and 2013					
(11,200 + 11,000)	22,200				
	47,200				
Less : Drawings for					
2012 and 2013 (2,400 + 2,400)	4,800	42,400			
		1,16,500			1,16,500

Notes :

1. Since debtors for 2012 include Rs. 5,000 for goods sent on consignments, debtors has been reduced by Rs. 5,000 and, at the same time, Closing Stock has been increased by Rs. 4,000 B (i.e., at cost 5,000 × $\frac{4}{5}$).

2. Bank balance for 2012 has also been increased by Rs. 1,000 since the cheque has been deposited into bank although the same was not credited by bank until after that date.

3. Similarly, since the amount of Rs. 2,000 was issued but not presented the same has been deducted from the Bank balance for 2013.

4. Debtors for 2013 has been reduced by Rs. 1,000 as one of the customers directly deposited into bank. Bank balance for the same period already includes such amount.

5. Debtors for 2013 has also been increased since one cheque received from customer amounting to Rs. 500 has been dishonoured. Bank balance, however, is not affected since the amount had already been adjusted on that date.

Ascertainment of Profit for various years

Illustration 12

Raja kept his book by Single Entry. His Statement of Affairs as on 31st Dec. 2007 was as follows :

Liabilities	Rs.	*Assets*	Rs.
Creditors	9,600	Premises	1,400
Raja's capital	15,600	Stock	4,000
		Debtors	3,000
		Cash and Bank	4,200
	25,200		12,600

He took Proja into partnership as on 1st Jan. 2008. Proja is to pay a premium of Rs. 1,800 out of his share of profit (including interest) exceeding Rs. 1,500 p.a. over which he was not authorised to draw. Proja brought Rs. 3,000 as his capital on 1st Jan. 2008. The profits were to be decided between Raja and Proja in the ratio of 2 : 1. Interest was to be allowed @ 5% p.a. on the opening balance of capital each year. Raja's drawings were : Rs. 3,600, Rs. 3,240, and Rs. 3,480 for 2008, 2009 and 2010, respectively, and Proja drew Rs. 1,500 each year. The assets and liabilities were (exclusive of capital) on 31st Dec. 2008, 2009, and 2010 :

	2008	2009	2010
	Rs.	Rs.	Rs.
Assets	30,000	29,700	34,200
Liabilities	10,500	9,000	9,600

Amounts due from Proja to Raja in respect of premium were to be transferred from his Capital Account to Raja's Capital Account. You are required to prepare the Capital Accounts of the partners.

Solution

In the Books of Raja and Proja
Capital Account

Dr. Cr.

Date	*Particulars*	*Raja*	*Proja*	*Date*	*Particulars*	*Raja*	*Proja*
2008		Rs.	Rs.	2008		Rs.	Rs.
Dec. 31	To Drawings	3,600	1,500	Jan. 1	By Balance b/d	15,600	—
	" Raja	—	340		" Cash	—	3,000
"	" Balance c/d	16,500	3,000	Dec. 31	" Interest	780	150
					" Profit	3,380	1,690
					" Proja	340	—
		20,100	4,840			20,100	4,840
2009				2009			
Dec. 31	To Drawings	3,240	1,500	Jan. 1	By Balance b/d	16,500	3,000
	" Raja	—	305	Dec. 31	" Interest	825	150
	" Balance c/d	17,700	3,000		" Profit	3,310	1,655
					" Proja	305	
		20,940	4,805			20,940	4,805

Contd.

2010		Rs.	Rs.	2010		Rs.	Rs.
Dec. 31	To Drawings	3,480	1,500	Jan. 1	By Balance b/d	17,700	3,000
"	Raja	—	1,155	Dec. 31	" Interest	885	150
"	Balance c/d	21,490	3,110		" Profit	5,230	2,615
					" Proja	1,155	—
		24,970	5,765			24,970	5,765
				2011			
				Jan. 1	By Balance b/d	21,490	3,110

Workings:

Statement of Affairs *as on 31st Dec.*

Liabilities	2008	2009	2010	*Assets*	2008	2009	2010
	Rs.	Rs.	Rs.		Rs.	Rs.	Rs.
Capital	10,500	9,000	9,600	Assets	30,000	29,700	34,200
(*Less : Drawings*)							
Raja (15,600 – 3,600)	12,000						
Proja (3,000 – 1,500)	1,500						
Raja (16,500 – 3,240)		13,260					
Proja (3,000 – 1,500)		1,500					
Raja (17,700 – 3,480)			14,220				
Proja (3,000 – 1,500)			1,500				
Profit *(bal. fig.)*	6,000	5,940	8,880				
	30,000	29,700	34,200		30,000	29,700	34,200

Division of Profit

For 2008

	Rs.	Rs.
Interest on Capital :		
Raja @ 5% on Rs. 15,600 =	780	
Proja @ 5% on Rs. 3,000 =	150	930
Share of Profit :		
Raja $\frac{2}{3}$	3,380	
Proja $\frac{1}{3}$	1,690	
		5,070
		6,000

For 2009

	Rs.	Rs.
Interest on Capital :		
Raja @ 5% on Rs. 16,500	825	
Proja @ 5% on Rs. 3,000	150	975
Share of Profit :		
Raja $\frac{2}{3}$	3,310	
Proja $\frac{1}{3}$	1,655	
		4,965
		5,940

For 2010

	Rs.	
Interest on Capital :		
Raja @ 5% on Rs. 17,700	885	
Proja @ 5% on Rs. 3,000	150	1,035
Share of Profit :		
Raja $\frac{2}{3}$	5,230	
Proja $\frac{1}{3}$	2,615	
		7,845
		8,880

Illustration 13

X, Y, and Z are in partnership sharing profits and losses in the proportion of 3 : 2 : 1.

Their Balance Sheet as on 1st Jan. 2012 was :

Liabilities		Rs.	*Assets*		Rs.
Capital :			Goodwill		30,000
X	30,000		Buildings		40,000
Y	20,000		Machinery		30,700
Z	15,000		Furniture		2,000
		65,000	Stock-in-trade		14,000
Reserve		24,000	Sundry Debtors	22,800	
Sundry Creditors		32,300	*Less :* Doubtful Debts	1,600	
Bank Overdraft		20,100			21,200
			Cash in hand		3,500
		1,41,400			1,41,400

On 31st Dec. 2012, Sundry Debtors Rs. 16,700; Sundry Creditors Rs. 45,700; Bank Overdraft Rs. 25,800; Closing Stock Rs. 9,300 and Cash in hand Rs. 4,200. Interest on Bank Overdraft amounting to Rs. 600 has not been accounted for. During the year, X has brought in Capital Rs. 5,000; and Y and Z had withdrawn Rs. 3,000 and Rs. 4,000, respectively. A claim for damages relating to an earlier period was settled at Rs. 6,200 and was adjusted against Reserve.

You are required to prepare :

(1) A Statement of Profit or Loss made by the firm after charging 5% depreciation on Building and Machinery reducing the Reserve for Doubtful Debts to Rs. 1,000 and allowing interest on capital at 6% p.a. on opening balance. (2) Balance Sheet of the firm as on 31st Dec. 2012.

Solution

In the Books of X, Y and Z

Statement of Profit and Loss *for the year ended 31st Dec. 2012*

	Rs.	Rs.		Rs.	Rs.
Sundry Creditors		45,700	Goodwill		30,000
Overdraft		25,800	Building		40,000
Outstanding Interest		600	Machinery		30,700
Capital (on 31.12. 2012)			Furniture		2,000
(bal. fig.) c/d		60,800	Stock		9,300
			Debtors		16,700
			Cash		4,200
		1,32,900			1,32,900
Capital (on 1.1.2012) :			Capital (on 31.12.2012) b/d		60,800
X	30,000		Drawings :		
Y	20,000		Y	3,000	
Z	15,000	65,000	Z	4,000	7,000
Reserve		24,000	Payment for earlier years		
Additional Capital—X		5,000	(not provided as liability)		6,200[1]
			Gross Loss c/d		20,000
		94,000			94,000
Gross Loss b/d		20,000	Net Loss c/d		24,535
Provision for Bad Debt		1,000[2]			
Depreciation on :					
Building	2,000				
Machinery	1,535	3,535			
		24,535			24,535
Net Loss b/d		24,535	Share of Loss :		
Interest on Capital :			X $\frac{3}{6}$	14,218	

Contd.

	Rs.	Rs.		Rs.	Rs.
X	1,800		Y $\frac{2}{6}$	9,478	
Y	1,200				
Z	900		Z $\frac{1}{6}$	4,739	
		3,900[3]			28,435
		28,435			28,435

Balance Sheet[4] as at 31st Dec. 2012

Liabilities	Rs.	Rs.	*Assets*	Rs.	Rs.
Capitals :			Goodwill		30,000
X		22,582[1]	Building	40,000	
Y		8,722[2]	Less : Depreciation	2,000	38,000
Z		7,161[3]	Machinery	30,700	
Reserve (24,000 – 6,200)		17,800	*Less* : Depreciation	1,535	29,165
Creditors		45,700	Furniture		2,000
Bank Overdraft	25,800		Stock		9,300
Add : Outstanding Interest	600		Debtors	16,700	
		26,400	Less : Prov. for B/Debts	1,000	15,700
			Cash		4,200
		1,28,365			1,28,365

Workings :

1. **Capital A/c**

Dr. *Cr.*

Particulars	X	Y	Z	*Particulars*	X	Y	Z
	Rs.	Rs.	Rs.			Rs.	Rs.
To Share of Loss	14,218	9,478	4,739	By Balance b/d	30,000	20,000	15,000
" Drawings		3,000	4,000	" Bank	5,000	—	
" Balance c/d	22,582	8,722	7,161	" Interest on Capital	1,800	1,200	900
	36,800	21,200	15,900		36,800	21,200	15,900

Notes

2. If the payment was not made, closing net assets would have been greater, and that is why the same is added.
3. It is needless to mention that, in Single Entry, no Reserve for Bad Debt Account is maintained. As such, necessary reserve for each year is to be created in the current year. Thus the same net profit may be brought about by the correct valuation of Debtors after deducting Rs. 1,000 by way of provision from the closing assets in the Balance Sheet.
4. It has been assumed that interest on capital should be provided even if there is a loss and it has also been assumed that additions and withdrawals are made at the end of the year.
5. This is nothing but a Statement of Affairs.

B. Conversion Method

When profit or loss is ascertained by preparing Trading Account and Profit and Loss Account, i.e., Under Double Entry System, it becomes necessary to convert Single Entry into Double Entry. The same may be done either permanently or temporarily.

(a) **If conversion is made permanently**, the following procedure should be adopted :

(i) *Prepare a Statement of Affairs :*

In order to find out the Opening Capital, a Statement of Affairs is to be prepared at the opening date. Naturally, an opening journal entry is to be passed :

Individual Assets A/c Dr.
 To Individual Liabilities A/c
 " Capital A/c *(bal. fig.)*

It is to be remembered in this context that Cash and Bank balances must tally with the Cash/Bank balances (at the date of opening) or, amounts of debtors and creditors must tally with the individual accounts of debtors and creditors etc.

(ii) *Scrutinise Cash Book :*

The Cash Book should be prepared and scrutinised thoroughly—even if the opening and closing balances are given—in order to find out the missing figures, viz., missing sales, drawings, etc. At the same time, if Petty Cash Book is maintained, the same should also be verified and respective amounts should be posted to the various accounts.

(iii) *Prepare other Subsidiary Books :*

The periodical totals of different subsidiary books, viz., Purchase Day Book, Sales Day Book, Bill Book, etc. should be posted to the respective impersonal accounts.

If Petty Cash Book is maintained the monthly analysis will have to be made to the various accounts for expenses and the total to be credited to Petty Cash Account.

(iv) *Check up Personal Accounts :*

The respective personal accounts relating to debtors and creditors should be scrutinised in order to see whether they have been properly recorded.

(b) **If conversion is made temporarily,** the following procedure should be adopted :

(i) *Prepare a Statement Affairs :*

Just to find out the opening capital, a Statement of Affairs as at the opening date is to be prepared. At the same time, opening balance of Cash, Bank, Debtors etc., may not be given in that problem; in the case, the respective accounts are to be prepared to find out the missing figures.

(ii) *Prepare a Cash Book :*

In order to ascertain the missing sales or amount of drawings, a Cash Book is to be prepared even if the opening and closing balances of the same are given.

(iii) *Prepare :*

(a) Total Debtors Account, (b) Total Creditors Account, (c) Bills Receivable Account, and (d) Bills Payable Account, in order to find out the credit sales and credit purchases during the year.

Some Practical Hints

We should remember that the principle of conversion of Single Entry into Double Entry may be of an infinite variety. As such, the solution to practical problems is beset with a number of difficult points which are, in practice, quite puzzling and confusing. We are going to discuss some of them in addition to the discussions that we have made so far for the calculation of sales (cash and credit), purchases (cash and credits), and opening capital.

(a) ***Ascertainement of Sales where cash record is not satisfactory***

Sometimes, cash record which is presented is not found to be reliable and, as such, it is really difficult to know the amount of total sales. In that case, we are to calculate estimated sales by calculating cost of goods sold and adding thereto the estimated gross profit in the following manner :

Cost of Goods Sold :

		Rs.
	Opening Stock	* *
Add :	Purchases	* *
Less :	Closing Stock	* *
		* *

Estimated Sales = Cost of Goods Sold + Estimated Gross Profit

Or, Cost of Goods Sold = Sales – Gross Profit

On the contrary, if sales and the rate of gross profit are given, we can easily calculate the amount of cost of goods sold which will actually help us to find out either opening stock, or closing stock, or purchases.

(b) ***Ascertainment of Closing Stock and Rate of Gross Profit***

Sometimes opening stock, purchases and sales are given but closing stock and rate of gross profit are not given. In that case, our duty is to prepare Combined Trading Account for two or more years in order to find out the rate of gross profit, of course if other relevant information is given.

(c) *Ascertainment of Cash and Bank Balances*

We know that most of the firms maintain a correct record of Cash and Bank transactions, as such, the summary may be made :

	Rs.		
(a) Receipts from Customers	* *	(a)	Payment to Creditors
(b) Cash Sales	* *	(b)	Cash Purchases
(c) Misc. Receipts	* *	(c)	Drawings
		(d)	Salaries and Expenses
		(e)	Misc. Expenses

Although the Cash or Bank summary is given, there may be some missing figures, viz., *Opening or Closing Balance of Cash or Bank, Receipts from Debtors, Payments to Creditors, Cash Purchases, Cash Sales, Drawings etc.* For this purpose, columnar Cash Book should be prepared and all the known figures should be posted and missing items should be the *balancing figure.* If a combined Cash and Bank balance is given, either cash or bank may be ascertained first and, thereafter, the other by the difference between the combined figure and the figure so calculated.

Again, the cash column may be complete first in order to get the missing *contra* figure and then only to complete the bank column with the help of that figure, or vice versa. However, if the separate Cash and Bank transactions are not given, a combined Cash and Bank Account will have to be prepared for the purpose. But if closing combined cash and bank balance is given, and if closing cash or bank balance is given, the other can simply be deducted from such combined figure so presented.

To Sum up

Step 1. Prepare a opening Statement of Affairs/opening Balance Sheet in order to find out the opening capital (if not given).

Step 2. Open Bills Receivable and Bills Payable Account to find out acceptance received and issued or to find out closing balances for the same.

Step 3. Open Total Debtors and Total Creditors Account in order to find out credit sales and credit purchases and/or closing/opening balance for the same.

Step 4. Open a Double Column Cash Book in order to find out any missing information about Cash Sales/Drawings/Cash Defalcation or closing balances for the same.

Step 5. Consider the adjustments given under Double Entry Principles.

Step 6. Now prepare Trading Account, Profit and Loss Account and the Balance Sheet in the usual manner.

Ascertaintment of Missing Figures, Credit Purchase, Credit Sales

Illustration 14

From the following particulars presented by Mr. Lal Kamal Singh, you are asked to prepare :

(i) Total Debtors Account; (ii) Total Creditors Account; (iii) Bills Receivable Account; (iv) Bills Payable Account and also ascertain total Purchases and Total Sales.

On 1.1.2012 :

	Rs.		Rs.
Total Debtors amounted to	30,000	Total Bills Receivable amounted to	12,000
" Creditors amounted to	10,000	" Bills Payable amounted to	4,000

Transaction during the year :

Cash received from Debtors	20,000
Discount allowed to Debtors	5,000
Bad Debts written-off	2,500
Returns Inward	4,000
Cash Sales	14,000
Cash Purchases	6,000
Cash received against Bills Receivable	9,000
Cash paid to Suppliers	8,000
(including a payment of Rs. 500 for purchasing a machine)	

Contd.

	Rs.
Cash paid against Bills Payable	2,500
Discount received from suppliers	500
Returns Outward	1,000
Bills Payable dishonoured	500

On 31.12.2012 :

Total	Debtors amounted to	50,000	Total	Bills Receivable amounted to	15,000
"	Creditors amounted to	20,000	"	Bills Payable amounted to	7,000

Solution

In the books of Mr. Lal Kamal Singh

Dr. **Bills Payable Account** Cr.

Particulars	Rs.	Particulars	Rs.
To	2,500	By Balance b/d	4,000
" (for dishonour)	500	" Total Creditors (bal. fig.)	6,000
" Balance c/d	7,000		
	10,000		10,000

Dr. **Total Creditors Account** Cr.

Particulars	Rs.	Particulars	Rs.
To Cash	7,500	By Balance b/d	10,000
" Discount Received	500	" B/P	500
" Returns Outward	1,000	" Credit Purchases (bal. fig.)	24,500
" B/P	6,000		
" Balance c/d	20,000		
	35,000		35,000

Dr. **Bills Receivable Account** Cr.

Particulars	Rs.	Particulars	Rs.
To Balance b/d	12,000	By Cash	9,000
" Total Debtors A/c (bal. fig.)	12,000	" Balance c/d	15,000
	24,000		24,000

Dr. **Total Debtors Account** Cr.

Particulars	Rs.	Particulars	Rs.
To Balance b/d	30,000	By Cash	20,000
" Total Debtors A/c (bal. fig.)	63,500	" Discount Allowed	5,000
		" B/R	12,000
		" Bad Debts	2,500
		" Returns Inward	4,000
		" Balance c/d	50,000
	93,500		93,500

Workings :

Total Purchase = Credit Purchase + Cash Purchasing
= Rs. 24,500 + Rs. 6,000
= Rs. 30,500

Total Sales = Credit Sales + Cash Sales
= Rs. 63,500 + Rs. 14,000
= Rs. 77,500

2. Purchase of a Machine for Rs. 500 will be excluded.

Preparation of Final Accounts

Illustration 15

You are given :

(a) The Balance Sheet of A on 1st April 2011. (b) The Cash transaction for the year up to 31st March 2012. (c) A summary of the remaining transactions for the year up to 31st March 2012 :

(a)

	Rs.		Rs.
Bank Overdraft	500	Cash in hand	70
Sundry Creditors	3,600	Bills Receivable	2,500
Bills Payable	1,600	Sundry Debtors	3,900
Capital	20,000	Stock of Goods	7,530
		Plant and Machinery	4,700
		Land and Building	7,000
	25,700		25,700

(b)

		Rs.				Rs.
To	Balance b/d	70	By	Balance b/d (Bank Overdraft)		500
"	Receipts from Debtors	29,000	"	Salaries		4,900
"	Bills Receivable	10,000	"	Wages		1,580
"	Cash Sales	3,700	"	Bills Payable		14,300
			"	Payment to Creditors		14,700
			"	Office Expenses		800
			"	Drawings		4,500
			"	Investment at par (9% G.P. Notes on 1.10.2011)		1,000
			"	Balance on 31.3.2012 :		
				Cash	40	
				Bank	450	490
		42,770				42,770

(c)

	Rs.		Rs.
Sales (Credit)	40,700	Bills Receivable Received	10,900
Discount to Customers	200	Bills Payable Issued	15,000
Purchases	30,000	Stock of Goods on 31.3.2012	5,300
Discount Received	100		

Provide for doubtful debts at 5% on debtors outstanding.

Provide for depreciation on Plant and Machinery at 5% and on Land and Building @ $2\frac{1}{2}$. Prepare the Trading and Profit and Loss Account for the year ended 31st March 2012, and Balance Sheet as on that date.

Solution

Dr. **Bills Receivable Account** Cr.

		Rs.			Rs.
To	Balance b/d	2,500	By	Cash A/c	10,000
"	Debtors A/c	10,900	"	Balance c/d	3,400
		13,400			13,400

Dr. **Total Debtors Account** Cr.

		Rs.			Rs.
To	Balance b/d	3,900	By	Cash A/c	29,000
"	Sales A/c	40,700	"	B/R A/c	10,900
			"	Discount Allowed A/c	200
			"	Balance c/d	4,500
		44,600			44,600

Dr. **Bills Payable Account** Cr.

		Rs.			Rs.
To	Cash A/c	14,300	By	Balance b/d	1,600
"	Balance c/d	2,300	"	Creditors A/c	15,000
		16,600			16,600

Dr. **Total Creditors Account** Cr.

		Rs.			Rs.
To	Cash A/c	14,700	By	Balance b/d	3,600
"	B/P A/c	15,000	"	Purchase A/c	30,000
"	Discount Received A/c	100			
"	Balance c/d	3,800			
		33,600			33,600

Dr. **Trading and Profit and Loss Account** *for the year ended 31st March 2012* Cr.

	Particulars	*Amount* Rs.		*Particulars*		*Amount* Rs.
To	Opening Stock	7,530	By	Sales		
"	Purchases	30,000		Cash	3,700	
"	Wages	1,580		Credit	40,700	
"	Profit and Loss A/c					44,400
	—Gross Profit transferred	10,590	"	Closing Stock		5,300
		49,700				49,700

Contd.

		Rs.			Rs.
To	Salaries	4,900	By	Trading A/c —Gross Profit	10,590
"	Office Expenses	800	"	Discount Received	100
"	Discount Allowed	200	"	Accrued Interest	45[3]
"	Reserve for Doubtful Debts	225[1]			
"	Depreciation on :				
	Plant and Machinery	235[2]			
	Land and building	175[2]			
"	Capital A/c — Net Profit transferred	4,200			
		10,735			10,735

Balance Sheet *as at 31st March 2012*

Liabilities	Rs.	Rs.	*Assets*	Rs.	Rs.
Capital	20,000		Plant and Machinery	4,700	
Add : Net Profit	4,200		*Less :* Depreciation	235	4,465
	24,200		Land and Building	7,000	
Less: Drawings	4,500		*Less :* Depreciation	175	6,825
		19,700	Investments		1,000
Bills Payable		2,300	Closing Stock		5,300
Sundry Creditors		3,800	Sundry Debtors	4,500	
			Less : Reserve for Bad Debts	225	4,275
			Bills Receivable		3,400
			Accrued Interest		45
			Cash at Bank		450
			Cash in hand		40
		25,800			25,800

Workings :

1. **Reserve for Doubtful Debts** Rs.
   (Reserve for bad debts should be calculated on Closing Balance of Debtors
   Debtors Rs. 4,500 × 5% 225

2. **Depreciation on Plant and Machinery** Rs.
   Plant & Machinery = Rs. 4,700 × 5% = 235
   Land & Building = Rs. 7,000 × $2\frac{1}{2}$% = 125

3. **Accrued Interest** Rs.
   Rs. 1,000 × $\frac{9}{12} \times \frac{6}{12}$ = 45

Illustration 16

Mr. Roy commenced business as a cloth merchant on 1.1.2012, with a capital of Rs. 10,000. On the same day he purchased Furniture and Fittings for cash Rs. 3,000.

From the following particulars obtained from his books kept by Single Entry, you are asked to prepare a Trading and Profit and Loss Account for the year ended 31.12.2012, and a Balance Sheet as on that date :

	Rs.		Rs.
Sales (inclusive of cash Rs. 7,000)	17,000	**Salaries to Staff**	2,000
Purchases (inclusive of cash Rs. 4,000)	15,000	**Bad Debts written-off**	500
Roy's Drawings	1,200	**Business Expenses**	700

Mr. Roy took cloth worth Rs. 500 from the shop for private use and paid Rs. 200 to his son, but omitted to record these transactions in his books. On 31.12.2012, his Sundry Debtors were Rs. 5,200 and Sundry Creditors Rs. 3,600. Stock in hand on 31.12.2012 was Rs. 6,500.

Solution

In the books of Mr. Roy

Dr. **Trading and Profit and Loss Account** *for the year ended 31st Dec. 2012* Cr.

	Rs.	Rs.		Rs.	Rs.
To Purchases :			By Sales :		
Cash	4,000		Cash	7,000	

Contd.

Particulars	Rs.	Rs.	Particulars	Rs.	Rs.
Credit	11,000		Credit	10,000[1]	
	15,000				17,000
Less : Drawings	500	14,500	" Closing Stock		6,500
" Profit and Loss A/c Gross Profit transferred		9,000			
		23,500			23,500
To Salaries		2,000	By Trading A/c		
" Business Expenses		700	" Gross Profit —transferred		9,000
" Bad Debts		500			
" Capital A/c Net Profit—transferred		5,800			
		9,000			9,000

Balance Sheet *as at 31st Dec. 2012*

Liabilities	Rs.	Rs.	*Assets*	Rs.
Capital	10,000		Furniture	3,000
Add : Net Profit	5,800		Debtors	5,200
	15,800		Closing Stock	6,500
Less : Drawings	1,900[3]	13,900	Cash	2,800[4]
Sundry Creditors		3,600		
		17,500		17,500

Workings :

1. **Total Debtors Account**

Dr. *Cr.*

	Rs.		Rs.
To Sales (Credit)	10,000	By Cash Received *(bal. fig.)*	4,300
		" Bad Debts	500
		" Balance c/d	5,200
	10,000		10,000

2. **Total Creditors Account**

Dr. *Cr.*

	Rs.		Rs.
To Cash —paid *(bal. fig.)*	7,400	By Purchases (Credit)	11,000
" Balance c/d	3,600		
	11,000		11,000

3. **Drawings Account**

Dr. *Cr.*

	Rs.		Rs.
To Cash —paid to son	200	By Balance c/d	1,900
" Purchase —goods taken	500		
" Cash	1,200		
	11,000		11,000

4. **Cash Book**

Dr. *Cr.*

	Rs.		Rs.
To Capital	10,000	By Purchases	4,000
" Sundry Debtors	4,300	" Drawings	1,200
		" Drawings—paid to son	200
" Sales	7,000	" Salaries	2,000
		" Business Expenses	700
		" Furniture	3,000
		" Creditors	7,400[2]
		" Balance c/d	2,800
	21,300		21,300

Illustration 17

Mr. X does not maintain regular books but keeps only Memoranda for his transactions. He furnishes the following information from the memoranda for the year ended 30.9.2012 :

		Rs.
(i)	Total collections from Debtors (in Cash)	15,000
(ii)	Cash sales (as gathered from Sales Invoice)	9,600
(iii)	The abstract of the Bank Account for the year ended 30.9.2012 is :	

	Rs.		Rs.
Cash Deposits out of Collections	23,955	Overdraft as on 1.10.2011	2,400
		Interest and Bank Charges	45
		Personal Drawings	1,200
		Salaries to Staff	5,100
		General Expenses	4,755
		Payment to Creditors	9,000
		Balance on 30.9.2012	1,455
	23,955		23,955

(iv) Other Balances as on 1.10.2011 are :

	Rs.		Rs.
Stock	5,400	Building	9,000
Debtors	13,200	Creditors	4,800
Furniture	600	Cash in hand	50

(v) He purchased one old scooter for Rs. 600 on 1.7.2012.

(vi) Besides the cash balance with the cashier, the following are the other balances as on 30.9.2012 : Stock Rs. 6,120; Debtors Rs. 18,000; Creditors Rs. 3,300.

Prepare the Profit and Loss Account for the year ended 30.9.2012 and the Balance Sheet as on that date after providing for depreciation @ 10% p.a. on all fixed asset.

[CU BCom (Hons.) Adapted]

Solution

In the books of Mr. X
Trading and Profit and Loss Account
for the year ended 30th Sept. 2012

Dr. *Cr.*

Particulars		*Amount* Rs.	*Particulars*		*Amount* Rs.
To Opening Stock		5,400	By Sales—		
" Purchases		7,500[3]	Cash	9,600	
" Profit and Loss A/c			Credit	19,800[2]	29,400
Gross Profit transferred		22,620	" Closing Stock		6,120
		35,520			35,520
To Interest and Bank Charges		45	By Trading A/c		
" Salaries to Staff		5,100	Gross Profit transferred		22,620
" General Expenses		4,755			
To Depreciation on :					
Furniture	60				
Building	900				
Scooter (3 months)	15	975			
" Capital A/c					
Net Profit transferred		11,745			
		22,620			22,620

Balance Sheet *as at 30th Sept. 2012*

Liabilities	Rs.	Rs.	*Assets*	Rs.	Rs.
Capital	21,050[1]		Building	9,000	
Add : Net Profit	11,745		*Less :* Depreciation	900	8,100
	32,795		Furniture	600	
Less : Drawings	1,200		*Less :* Depreciation	60	540
		31,595	Scooter	600	
Creditors		3,300	*Less :* Depreciation	15	585
			Stock		6,120
			Debtors		18,000
			Cash at Bank		1,455
			Cash in hand		95[4]
		34,895			34,895

Workings :

1. Computation of Capital

Dr. **Balance Sheet** *as at 1st Oct. 2011* Cr.

Liabilities	Rs.	*Assets*	Rs.
Creditors	4,800	Cash	50
Bank Overdraft	2,400	Debtors	13,200
Capital *(bal. fig.)*	21,050	Stock	5,400
		Furniture	600
		Building	9,000
	28,250		28,250

2 Computation of Credit Sales

Dr. **Total Debtors Account** Cr.

	Rs.		Rs.
To Balance b/d	13,200	By Cash	15,000
" Sales *(bal. fig.)*	19,800	" Balance c/d	18,000
	33,000		33,000

3. Computation of Credit Purchases

Dr. **Total Creditors Account** Cr.

	Rs.		Rs.
To Bank	9,000	By Balance b/d	4,800
" Balance c/d	3,300	" Purchases *(bal. fig.)*	7,500
	12,300		12,300

4. Ascertainment of Closing Cash

Dr. **Cash Account** Cr.

	Rs.		Rs.
To Balance b/d	50	By Bank	23,955
" Debtors	15,000	" Scooter	600
" Sales	9,600	" Balance c/d	95
	24,650		24,650

Some Missing Figures

Illustration 18

On 1.1.2013 Mr. S. Sen commenced business. He did not maintain proper books of account. At the end of the year following information was obtained after going through the records:

(i) All cash received on Cash Sales was banked after keeping Rs. 1,000 per month for petty expenses and after withholding monthly drawings of Rs. 500

(ii) Counterfoils of pay-in-slips revealed the following deposits: Capital contributed by Mr. Sen —Rs. 1,00,000; Balance of Cash Sales—Rs. 78,000; Collection from Debtors—Rs. 1,00,000.

(iii) Counterfoils of cheques revealed the following payments : Payments to Creditors—Rs. 1,50,000; Payments of Salary—Rs. 35,000; Purchase of Furniture—Rs. 10,000.

(iv) Sale were effected at a uniform rate of trading Profit at 25% on Sales.

(v) Discount allowed Rs. 2,000, Discount received R. 3,000 and Bad Debts Rs. 1,000, Conveyance Rs. 2,000 and Rent Rs. 2,200.

(vi) Petty Cash expenses were: Postage Rs. 200. Stationery Rs. 1,000.

(vii) On 31.12.2013 amount due by Debtors Rs. 10,000 and amount owing to creditors were Rs. 20,000.

You are required to prepare Trading and Profit & Loss Account for the year ended 31.12.2013 and a Balance Sheet as on that date.

Solution

In the books of Mr. S. Sen

Dr. **Trading and Profit and Loss Account** *for the year ended 31st Dec. 2013* Cr.

Particulars	*Amount* Rs.	*Particulars*		*Amount* Rs.
To Purchases	1,73,000[2]	By Sales—		
" Profit and Loss A/c	52,250[4]	Cash	96,000[1]	
" Gross Profit transferred		Credit	1,13,000[3]	
				2,09,000
		" Closing Stock (Bal. Fig.)		16,250[4]
	2,25,250			2,25,250
To Discount Allowed	2,000	By Trading A/c		
" Bad Debts	1,000	– Gross Profit		52,250
" Salaries	35,000	" Discount Received		3,000

Contd.

		Rs.		Rs.
To	Postages	200	By	
"	Stationery	1,000		
"	Conveyance	2,000		
"	Rent	2,200		
"	Capital A/c – Net Profit	11,850		
		55,250		55,250

Balance Sheet *as at 31st Dec. 2013*

Liabilities	Rs.	*Amount* Rs.	*Assets*	*Amount* Rs.
Capital	1,00,000		Furniture	10,000
Add: Net Profit	11,850		Stock	16,250
	1,11,850		Sundry Debtors	10,000
Less: Drawings (Rs. 500 × 12)	6,000	1,05,850	Cash at Bank	83,000[5]
Sundry Creditors		20,000	Petty Cash	6,600[6]
		1,25,850		1,25,850

Workings :

1. Ascertainment of Cash Sales

Dr. *Cash A/c* *Cr.*

	Rs.		Rs.
To Cash Sales *(bal. fig.)*	96,000	By Bank A/c	78,000
		" Petty Cash	12,000
		" Drawings	6,000
	96,000		96,000

2. Ascertainment of Credit Purchases

Dr. **Creditors A/c** *Cr.*

	Rs.		Rs.
To Bank A/c	1,50,00	By Balance b/d	—
" Discount Received	3,000	" Purchase *(bal. fig.)*	1,73,000
" Balance c/d	20,000		
	1,73,000		1,73,000

3. Ascertainment of Credit Sales

Dr. *Debtors A/c* *Cr.*

	Rs.		Rs.
To Balance b/d	—	By Bank A/c	1,00,000
" Sales *(bal. fig.)*	1,13,000	" Discount Allowed	2,000
		" Bad Debts	1,000
		" Balance c/d	10,000
	1,13,000		1,13,000

4. Ascertainment of Gross Profit A/c

Gross Profit is 25% of Total Sales
(i.e. Rs. 96,000 + Rs. 1,13,000) Rs. 2,09,000 × 25%
= Rs. 52,250
Add : Closing Stock will be the balance figure in Trading Account
Since the business was started on 1.1.2014 there will not be any Opening Stock.

5. Ascertainment of Balance at Bank

Dr. *Bank A/c* *Cr.*

	Rs.		Rs.
To Capital A/c	1,00,000	By Credit A/c	1,50,000
" Cash (Contra Entry)	78,000	" Furniture	10,000
" Debtors	1,00,000	" Salary	35,000
		" Balance c/d	83,000
	2,78,000		2,78,000

6. Ascertainment of Petty Cash A/c

Dr. *Cr.*

	Rs.		Rs.
To Cash A/c	12,000	By Postage	200
		" Stationery	1,000
		" Conveyance	2,000
		" Rent	2,200
		" Balance c/d	6,600
	12,000		12,000

Illustration 19

From the following information obtained from Mr. X, a trader, who does not keep proper accounts, prepare a Trading and Profit and Loss Account for the year ended 31st March 2012 and the Balance Sheet as on that date :

(a) Withdrawal as per pass book :

	Rs.		Rs.
Rent, Rates, Taxes and Insurance	12,000	X's Drawings	10,000
Furniture Purchased on 1.4.2011	2,000	Paid for Purchases	50,000
Printing Charges	1,000	Salaries	8,000
Advertisement Expenses	1,000	Wages	8,000
Postage and Telegrams	1,000		

(b) Balance at Bank on 31.3.2012 was Rs. 3,000.

(c) Stock on 1.4.2011 was Rs. 24,000 and Stock on 31st March 2012 was Rs. 4,000 less than of stock on 1.4.2011. Out of stock on 1.4.2011, spoiled stocks were sold for Rs. 2,000 which were not deposited into Bank Account.

(d) Payment for purchases included Rs. 4,000 for last year's purchases. Rs. 1,000 of previous year's purchases is still unpaid on 31.3.2012. Current year's list of unpaid invoices not ticked off in purchase register amounted to Rs. 5,000.

(e) Collections for sale were Rs. 1,00,000 which includes Rs. 12,000 in respect of previous year's sale. Balance of unticked bills of last year's sale still amounted to Rs. 8,000 on 31st March 2012. Unticked bills of the current year totalled up to Rs. 20,000.

(f) Salaries Rs. 500 and wages Rs. 500 were outstanding on 31st March 2012.

(g) Furniture on 31.3.2011 amounts to Rs. 6,000 and machinery on the same date were Rs. 50,000.

(h) Prepaid Insurance on 31.3.2012 amounted to Rs. 400.

(i) Depreciation at 10% p.a. shall be provided on Furniture and at 25% p.a. on Machinery.

He maintained purchases and sales registers and items are ticked off on collection or payments. All collections are deposited and payments are all in cheques. Petty expenses Rs. 1,000 were paid out of his drawings. All purchases and sales were made on credit basis. **[CA]**

Solution

In the books of Mr. X

Trading and Profit and Loss Account *for the year ended 31st March 2012*

Dr. *Cr.*

Particulars		*Amount* Rs.	*Particulars*		*Amount* Rs.
To Opening Stock		24,000	By Sales	1,08,000	
" Purchases		51,000	*Add* : Spoiled Goods Sold	2,000	1,10,000
" Wages	8,000		" Closing Stock		20,000
Add : Outstanding	500	8,500			
" Profit and Loss A/c —Gross Profit transferred		46,500			
		1,30,000			1,30,000
To Rent A/c	12,000		By Trading A/c —Gross Profit		46,500
Less : Prepaid	400	11,600			
" Printing		1,000			
" Advertisement		1,000			
" Postage and Telegram		1,000			
" Salaries	8,000				
Add : Outstanding	500	8,500			
" Petty Expenses		1,000			
" Depreciation on : Machinery @ 25%	12,500				
" Furniture @ 10%	800	13,300			
" Capital A/c —Net Profit transferred		9,100			
		46,500			46,500

Balance Sheet *as at 31st March 2012*

Liabilities	Rs.	Rs.	*Assets*	Rs.	Rs.
Capital	91,000		Machinery	50,000	
Add : Net Profit	9,100		*Less* : Depreciation	12,500	37,500
	1,00,100				
Less : Drawings	11,000	89,100	Furniture	6,000	
			Additions	2,000	
Creditors		6,000		8,000	
Outstanding Liabilities :			*Less* : Depreciation	800	7,200

Contd.

	Rs.	Rs.		Rs.	Rs.
Wages	500				
Salaries	500		Closing Stock		20,000
		1,000	Debtors		28,000
			Prepaid Rent etc.		400
			Cash at Bank		3,000
		96,100			96,100

Workings :

Total Debtors Account

Dr.	Rs.	Cr.	Rs.
To Balance b/d (12,000 + 8,000)	20,000	By Bank A/c	1,00,000
" Sales *(bal. fig.)*	1,08,000	" Balance c/d (8,000 + 20,000)	28,000
	1,28,000		1,28,000

Total Creditors Account

Dr.	Rs.	Cr.	Rs.
To Bank A/c	50,000	By Balance b/d (4,000 + 1,000)	5,000
" Balance c/d (1,000 + 5,000)	6,000	" Purchases A/c *(bal. fig.)*	51,000
	56,000		56,000

Balance Sheet
as at 1st April 2011

Liabilities	Rs.	*Assets*	Rs.
Bank Overdraft	4,000	Machinery	50,000
Creditors	5,000	Furniture	6,000
Capital *(bal. fig.)*	91,000	Stock	24,000
		Debtors	20,000
	1,00,000		1,00,000

Drawings Account

Dr.	Rs.	Cr.	Rs.
To Bank A/c	10,000	By Petty Expenses A/c	1,000
" Sales A/c —Spoiled goods	2,000	" Balance c/d	11,000
	12,000		12,000

Bank Account

Dr.	Rs.	Cr.	Rs.
To Debtors A/c	1,00,000	By Balance b/d *(bal. fig.)*	4,000
		" Rent etc.	12,000
		" Furniture	2,000
		" Printing	1,000
		" Advertisement	1,000
		" Postage and Telegram	1,000
		" Drawings	10,000
		" Creditors	50,000
		" Salaries	8,000
		" Wages	8,000
		" Balance c/d	3,000
	1,00,000		1,00,000

GENERAL ILLUSTRATIONS

Ascertainment of some missing figures and preparation of final accounts

Illustration 20

Mr. Reddy does not maintain complete records of his business but gives you the following information :

	31st March 2012 Rs.	31st March 2011 Rs.
Machinery	2,00,000	1,50,000
Sundry Creditors	86,000	?
Sundry Debtors	?	93,000
Stock-in-trade	70,000	50,000
Cash in hand	2,600	1,500
Furniture	27,000	30,000
Cash at bank	15,600	18,700

His cash transactions for the year ended 31st March 2012 included the following (besides certain other items) :

	Rs.		Rs.
Payments to Creditors	4,10,000	Cash Purchases	1,30,000
Cash Sales (25% of total Sales)	1,70,000	Collection from Debtors	5,27,000
Business Expenses	82,000	Withdrawn for Household Expenses	30,000

He maintains a uniform rate of gross profit of 25% on turnover. Outstanding Business expenses on 31st March 2012 amounted to Rs. 5,000. Addition of new machinery was made on October 1, 2011. Some old furniture (Book value Rs. 6,000) was sold during the year and the proceeds stands credited to Furniture Account. Provide depreciation on Machinery @ 15% p.a. and on Furniture @ 10% p.a. (excluding sold item).

Mr. Reddy requests you to prepare a Trading and Profit and Loss Account for the year ended 31st March 2012 and a Balance Sheet as on that date.

[ICWA]

Solution

Memorandum Trading Account *for the year ended 31st March 2012*

Dr.		Rs.	Cr.		Rs.
To Opening Stock		50,000	By Sales		
" Purchase *(bal. fig.)*			Cash	1,70,000	
Cash	1,30,000		Credit	5,10,000	
Credit	4,00,000				6,80,000[1]
		5,30,000[3]	" Closing Stock		70,000
" Gross Profit c/d		1,70,000[2]			
		7,50,000			7,50,000

Sundry Debtors Account

Dr.	Rs.	Cr.	Rs.
To Balance b/d	93,000	By Cash	5,27,000
" Sales	5,10,000	" Balance c/d *(bal. fig.)*	76,000
	6,03,000		6,03,000

Sundry Creditors Account

Dr.	Rs.	Cr.	Rs.
To Cash	4,10,000	By Balance b/d *(bal. fig.)*	96,000
" Balance c/d *(bal. fig.)*	86,000	" Purchases	4,00,000
	4,96,000		4,96,000

Balance Sheet *as at 1st April 2011*

Liabilities	Rs.	*Assets*	Rs.
Creditors	96,000	Machinery	1,50,000
Capital *(bal. fig.)*	2,47,200	Furniture	30,000
		Debtors	93,000
		Stock	50,000
		Bank	18,700
		Cash	1,500
	3,43,200		3,43,200

Profit and Loss Account *for the year ended 31st March 2012*

Dr.		Rs.	Cr.	Rs.
To Busi. Exp.	82,000		By Gross Profit b/d	1,70,000
" *Add* : Outstanding	5,000	87,000		
To Loss on Sale of Furniture		3,000[4]		
" Depreciation on :				
Machinery (22,500 + 3,750)		26,250		
Furniture		2,400		
Capital A/c—Net Profit transferred		51,350		
		1,70,000		1,70,000

Balance Sheet *as at 31st Dec. 2012*

Liabilities	Rs.	Rs.	*Assets*	Rs.	Rs.
Capital	2,47,200		Machinery	1,50,000	
Add : Net Profit	51,350		Additions	50,000	
	2,98,550			2,00,000	
Less : Drawings	30,000		*Less* : Depreciation	26,250	1,73,750
		2,68,550	Furniture	30,000	
Creditors		86,000	*Less* : Old	6,000	
Outstanding Exp.		5,000		24,000	
			Less : Depreciation	2,400	21,600
			Stock		70,000
			Debtors		76,000
			Bank		15,600
			Cash		2,600
		3,59,550			3,59,550

Workings :

1. **Computation of Sales** **Rs.**

Cash Sales = 25% of Total Sales which is 1,70,000

∴ Total Sales will be

(Rs. 1,70,000 × $\frac{100}{25}$) = 6,80,000

So Credit Sales = Total Sales – Cash Sales

= Rs. 6,80,000 – Rs. 1,70,000

= Rs. 5,10,000

2. Gross Profit

Gross Profit is 25% on Sales

i.e. Rs. 6,80,000 × 25% = **Rs. 1,70,000**

3. **Total Purchases**

Total Purchase = Sales + Closing Stock – Opening Stock – Gross Profit

= Rs. 6,80,000 + Rs. 70,000 – Rs. 50,000 – Rs. 1,70,000

= Rs. 5,30,000

Credit Purchase = Total Purchase – Cash Purchase

= Rs. 5,30,000 – Rs. 1,30,000

= Rs. 4,00,000

4. **Loss on Sale of Furniture**

Dr. **Furniture A/c** *Cr.*

	Rs.		Rs.
To Balance b/d	30,000	By Bank – Sale	3,000
		" Loss on Sales (6,000 – 3,000)	3,000
		" Dep. on Rs. 24,000	2,400
		" Bal. c/d	21,600
	30,000		30,000

Ascertainment of Total Sales, Opening Capital etc.

Illustration 21

Doll and Dolly are in partnership sharing profits and losses equally. They keep their books by Single Entry System. No ready figures are available for total sales but they maintain a steady gross profit rate of 25% on sales.

An abstract of their cash transactions for the year ended 30th June 2012 is :

Receipts	Rs.	*Payments*	Rs.
Cash in hand	10,800	Salaries	22,000
Receipts from Customers	2,70,000	Rent	4,400
Cash Sales	32,000	Advertising	1,800
		Printing	1,600
		General Exenses	19,100
		Payment to Trade Creditors	2,24,000
		Doll's Drawings	4,000
		Cash in hand	35,900
	3,12,800		3,12,800

The following balances are available from their books as on 30th June 2011 and 30th June 2012 :

	as on 30.6.2011	as on 30.6.2012
Stock-in-trade	44,000	50,000
Sundry Debtors	?	70,000
Sundry Creditors	46,800	37,000
Furniture	6,000	?

Other information :

(a) Discount allowed Rs. 2,800; (b) Discount earned Rs. 2,400; (c) Outstanding Printing Rs. 500; (d) Capital of Doll as on 30th June 2011 was Rs. 4,000 more than Capital of Dolly; (e) Provide depreciation on Furniture @ 10% p.a.

From the above, you are required to prepare :

(i) The Trading and Profit and Loss Account for the year ended 30th June 2012, and,

(ii) The Balance Sheet as on that date, in the books of Doll and Dolly.

[ICWA]

Solution

Dr. **Sundry Creditors Account** Cr.

	Rs.		Rs.
To Cash	2,24,000	By Balance b/d	46,800
" Discount Received	2,400	" Purchases *(bal. fig.)*	2,16,600
" Balance c/d	37,000		
	2,63,400		2,63,400

Dr. **Sundry Debtors Account** Cr.

	Rs.		Rs.
To Balance b/d *(bal. fig.)*	94,000	By Cash	2,70,000
		" Discount Allowed	2,800
" Sales	2,48,800	" Balance c/d	70,000
	3,42,800		3,42,800

Balance Sheet *as at 30th June 2011*

Liabilities	Rs.	Rs.	*Assets*	Rs.
Sundry Creditors		46,800	Furniture	6,000
Capital *(bal. fig.)*[2]			Stock	44,000
Doll	56,000		Debtors	94,000
Dolly	52,000	1,08,000	Cash	10,800
		1,54,800		1,54,800

Dr. **Trading and Profit and Loss Account** *for the year ended 30th June 2012* Cr.

Particulars	*Amount* Rs.	*Amount* Rs.	*Particulars*	*Amount* Rs.	*Amount* Rs.
To Opening Stock		44,000	By Sales :		
" Purchases (Credit)		2,16,600	Cash	32,000	
" Profit and Loss A/c			Credit	2,48,800	
Gross Profit transferred		70,200			2,80,800
			" Closing Stock		50,000
		3,30,800			3,30,800
To Salaries		22,000	By Trading A/c		
" Rent		4,400	Gross Profit transferred		70,200
" Advertising		1,800	" Discount Received		2,400
" Discount Allowed		2,800			
" General Expenses		19,100			
" Printing	1,600				
Add : Outstanding	500	2,100			
" Dep. on Furniture @ 10% on Rs. 6,000		600			
" Capital A/c—Net Profit					
Doll	9,900				
Dolly	9,900	19,800			
		72,600			72,600

Balance Sheet *as at 30th June 1994*

Liabilities	Rs.	Rs.	Assets	Rs.	Rs.
Capital :			Furniture	6,000	
Doll	56,000		*Less* : Depreciation	600	5,400
Add : Net Profit	9,900		Closing Stock		50,000
	65,900		Sundry Debtors		70,000
Less : Drawings	4,000	61,900	Cash in hand		35,900
Dolly	52,000				
Add : Net Profit	9,900	61,900			
Sundry Creditors		37,000			
Outstanding Printing		500			
		1,61,300			1,61,300

Workings ;

1. Calculation of Cash and Credit Sales

	Rs.
Opening Stock	44,000
Add : Purchases	2,16,600
	2,60,600
Less : Closing Stock	50,000
Cost of Goods Sold	2,10,600
Add : Gross Profit (@$\frac{1}{3}$rd of Cost)	70,200
Total Sales	2,80,800

Since Cash Sales is Rs. 32,000, Credit Sales will be Rs. 2,48,800, i.e. (Rs. 2,80,800 – Rs. 32,000).

2. Capital of Doll and Dolly

	Rs.
Total Capital	1,08,000
Less : Differences	4,000
	1,04,000

$\therefore$ Doll — 1,04,000 × $\frac{1}{2}$ = 52,000 + 4,000 = Rs. 56,000

Dolly — 1,04,000 × $\frac{1}{2}$ = Rs. 52,000

Ascertainment of some missing figures

Illustration 22

You are required to prepare Trading and Profit and Loss Account for the year ended 31st Dec. 2012 and a Balance Sheet as on 31.12.2012, from the following information :

Assets and Liabilities	1.1.2012	31.12.2012
	Rs.	Rs.
Creditors	15,770	12,400
Expenses Outstanding	600	330
Sundry Assets	11,610	12,040
Stock	8,040	11,120
Cash in hand and at Bank	6,960	8,080
Debtors	?	17,870

Details of the year's transactions are :

	Rs.		Rs.
Cash and Discount credited to Debtors	64,000	Receipts from Debtors (paid into Bank)	62,500
Returns from Debtors	1,450	Cash Purchases	1,030
Bad Debts	420	Expenses paid by cash	9,570
Sales—Cash and Credit	71,810	Drawings by cheque	430
Discount allowed by Creditors	700	Purchase of Machinery by cheque	3,180
Returns to Creditors	400	Cash payments into Bank	5,000
Capital introduced (paid into Bank)	8,500	Withdrawn from Bank into cash	9,240
		Cash in hand at end	1,200
		Payment to Creditors by cheque	60,270

Solution

Trading and Profit and Loss Account *for the year ended 31st Dec. 2012*

Dr. Particulars	Rs.	Rs.	Particulars	Rs.	Cr. Rs.
To Opening Stock		8,040	By Sales :		
" Purchases :			Cash	4,600[1]	
Cash	1,030		Credit	67,210[2]	
Credit	58,000[3]			71,810	
	59,030		*Less :* Returns	1,450	
Less : Returns	400				70,360
		58,630	By Closing Stock		11,120
To Profit and Loss A/c Gross Profit transferred		14,810			
		81,480			81,480
To Discount Allowed		1,500	By Trading A/c —Gross Profit transferred		14,810
" Bad Debts		420	" Discount Received		700
" General Expenses (9,570 + 330 – 600)		9,300			
" Depreciation		2,750			
" Capital A/c —Net Profit transferred		1,540			
		15,510			15,510

Balance Sheet *as at 31st Dec. 2012*

Liabilities		Rs.	Assets		Rs.
Capital	26,770[4]		Sundry Assets	11,610	
Additional Capital	8,500		Additions	3,180	
Add : Net Profit	1,540			14,790	
	36,810		*Less :* Depreciation	2,750[5]	
Less : Drawings	430				12,040
		36,380	Stock		11,120
Sundry Creditors		12,400	Debtors		17,870
Outstanding Expenses		330	Cash in hand		1,200
			Cash at Bank		6,880
		49,110			49,110

Workings :

1. **Ascertainment of Cash Sale**

Cash Book

Dr.	Cash Rs.	Bank Rs.		Cash Rs.	Cr. Bank Rs.
To Balance b/d	2,960	4,000	By Purchases	1,030	
" Capital		8,500	" Expenses	9,570	
" Debtors		62,500	" Plant & Machinery		3,180
" Bank (c)	9,240		" Drawings		430
" Cash (c)		5,000	" Creditors		60,270
" Sales *(bal. fig.)*	4,600		" Cash (c)		9,240
			" Bank (c)	5,000	
			" Balance c/d	1,200	6,880
	16,800	80,000		16,800	80,000

Notes :

Closing balance of Bank :
Rs. 8,080 – Rs. 1,200 (cash balance (cl.) already given) = Rs. 6,880.

Opening balance of Bank :
Rs. 80,000 – Rs. 76,000 (8,500 + 62,500 + 5,000) = Rs. 4,000

Opening balance of Cash will be Rs. 6,960 – Rs. 4,000 = Rs. 2,960.

2. **Ascertainment of Closing Debtors**

Total Debtors Account

Dr.	Rs.		Cr. Rs.
To Balance b/d (bal. fig.)	16,530	By Cash	62,500
		" Discount Allowed	1,500
" Sales (Credit) (71,810 – 4,600)	67,210	" Returns Inward	1,450
		" Bad Debts	420
		" Balance c/d	17,870
	83,740		83,740

3. **Ascertainment of Credit Purchase**

Total Creditors Account

Dr.	Rs.		Cr. Rs.
To Bank	60,270	By Balance	15,770
" Discount Received	700	" Purchases (Credit)	58,000
" Returns Outward	400		
" Balance c/d	12,400		
	73,770		73,770

4 **Ascertainment of Opening Capital**

Balance Sheet
as at 1st Jan. 2012

Liabilities	Rs.	*Assets*	Rs.
Sundry Creditors	15,770	Sundry Assets	11,610
Outstanding Expenses	600	Stock	8,040
Capital *(bal. fig.)*	26,770	Sundry Debtors	16,530
		Cash in hand	2,960
		Cash at Bank	4,000
	43,140		43,140

5. **Depreciation** = Opening bal. + Additions – Closing balance
= Rs. 11,610 + Rs. 3,180 – Rs. 12,040
= Rs. 2,750

Cash-lost by fire

Illustration 23

A fire in the office of Pioneer Trading Ltd. occurred in the evening of 31st March 1997, as a result of which the Cash, Bank and the Nominal Ledger kept in the cupboard were completely destroyed. The cash box containing cash representing the day's taking for 31st March 1997 was also destroyed. The Insurance Company concerned requests you to ascertain the amount of cash lost in the fire accident.

The Balance Sheet of the Company as at 31st December 1996 was as follows:

	Rs.			Rs.
Share Capital	60,000	Office Furniture (at Cost)	14,616	
Reserve and Balance of P & L A/c	85,028	*Less:* Depreciation	7,204	7,412
Trade Creditors	14,140	Stock-in-Trade (at Cost)		75,742
Dividend Unpaid	6,000	Trade Debtors		71,212
		Cash at Bank		10,802
	1,65,168			1,65,168

From the records and documents saved from the accident, the following information was obtained:

Balance on 31st March 1997;

Trade Debtors Rs. 1,19,612; Trade Creditors Rs. 31,610; Bank Balance after adjusting outstanding Rs. 14,822.

Transactions from 1st January to 31st March 1997 were:

Cash and Credit Sales, less Returns Rs. 8,21,154.

Miscellaneous Expenses Rs. 2,03,124;
Wages and Salaries Rs. 90,634;
Office Furniture purchased Rs. 1,300
Dividend paid Rs. 6,000;
Goods purchased on credit Rs. 4,69,212.
Depreciation provided on Furniture Rs. 360;
All receipts have been banked excepts those for 31st March 1997,
Stock-in trade on 31st March 1997 (valued at cost) was Rs. 53,816.

Required : (i) A Statement showing the Computation of the amount of cash lost in the fire accident; and (ii) Trading and Profit & Loss Account for three months ending 31st March 1997 and a Balance Sheet as at that date.

[CU BCom (Hons.) 1998]

Solution

(i) **Statement showing the Computation of Cash Lost by fire.**

		Rs.
	Cash in hand (on 1.1.1997)	Nil
Add:	Cash Received (out of Cash sales and Cash Received from Debtors) up to 31.3.1997	7,72,754[1]
		7,72,754
Less:	Cash deposited into bank up to 31.3.1997	7,56,820[3]
	Cash balance should remain in cash box but it was lost by fire on 31.3.1997	15,934

In the books of Pioneer Trading Ltd.

Dr. **Trading and Profit and Loss Account** *for the year ended 31st Dec. 1997* Cr.

Particulars	*Amount*	*Particulars*	*Amount*
	Rs.		Rs.
To Opening Stock	75,742	By Sales :	8,21,154
" Purchases :	4,69,212	" Closing Stock	53,816
" Wages & Salaries	90,634		
" Profit & Loss A/c —Gross Profit transferred	2,39,382		
	8,74,970		8,74,970
To Miscellaneous Expenses	2,03,124	By Trading A/c —Gross Profit	2,39,382
" Depreciation on Furniture	360		
—Net Profit	35,898		
	2,39,382		2,39,382

Balance Sheet* *as at 31st Dec. 1997*

Liabilities	*Rs.*	*Rs.*	*Assets*	*Rs.*	*Rs.*
Share Capital			**Fixed Assets**		
Reserves & Surplus		60,000	Furniture at Cost	14,616	
Balance	85,028		Additions	1,300	
Profit & Loss	35,898	1,20,926		15,916	
Secured Loans		Nil	*Less:* Depreciation up to date		
Unsecured Loans		Nil	(7,204 + 360)	7,564	8,352
Current Liabilities & Provisions			**Investment**		Nil
Sundry Creditors		31,610	**Current Assets, Loans and Advances**		

Contd.

	Rs.	Rs.		Rs.	Rs.
			Closing Stock		53,816
			Debtors		1,19,612
			Cash at bank		14,822
			Outstanding Insurance		
			Claim for Cash Lost		15,934
		2,12,536			2,12,536

* Since it is a Company, Balance Sheet has been prepared as per Schedule VI of the Companies Act.

Workings :

1. **Total Debtors Account**

Dr.	Rs.		Cr. Rs.
To Bal. b/d	71,212	By Cash (from Sales and from debtors) (bal. fig.)	7,72,754
" Sales (Cash and Credit Sales Less return)	8,21,154	" Balance c/d	1,19,612
	8,92,366		8,92,366

2. **Total Creditors Account**

Dr.	Rs.		Cr. Rs.
To Bank A/c (bal. fig.)	4,51,742	By Bal. b/d	14,140
" Balance c/d	31,610	" Purchase	4,69,212
	4,83,352		4,83,352

3. **Bank A/c**

Dr.	Rs.		Cr. Rs.
To Balance b/d	10,802	By Creditors	4,51,742
" Cash		" Mis. Exp.	2,03,124
" Deposited in to Bank (bal fig.)	7,56,820	" Wages o& Salaries	90,634
		" Furniture	1,300
		" Dividend	6,000
		" Balance c/d	14,822
	7,67,622		7,67,622

4. **Treatment of Cash Lost by Fire**

Either

Since the Insurance Co. has required to ascertain the claim, the amount of cash lost by firm should not be treated as a loss, hence, the same should be treated as an outstanding income.

Or, The amount of Cash lost can be adjusted against P & L A/c. When the Insurance Co. will be the same, Bank A/c will be debited and P & L A/c will be credited as a prior perioditem.

We have followed here the first alternative.

Cash absconded by cashier

Illustration 24

The following is the Balance Sheet of the retail business of Srinivas as at 31st December 1998:

Liabilities	Rs.	*Assets*	Rs.
Sri Srinivas's Capital	1,00,000	Furniture	10,000
Liabilities for Goods	20,500	Stock	70,000
Rent	1,000	Debtors	25,000
		Cash at bank	14,500
		Cash in hand	2,000
	1,21,500		1,21,500

You are furnished with the following information:

(1) Sri Srinivas sells his goods at a profit of 20% on sales.

(2) Goods are sold for cash and credit. Credit customers pay by cheques only.

(3) Payments for purchases are always made by cheques.

(4) It is the practice of Sri Srinivas to send to the bank every weekend the collections of the week after paying every week salary of Rs. 300 to the clerk, Sundry expenses of Rs. 50 and personal expense Rs. 100.

Analysis of the bank Passbook for the 13 weeks period ending 31st March 1999 disclosed the following:

	Rs.		Rs.
Payments to creditors	75,000	The following are the balances on	
Payments of rent up to 31.3.99	4,000	31st March 1999 :	
Amounts deposited into the bank	1,25,000	Stock	40,000
(include Rs. 30,000 received from		Debtors	30,000
debtors by cheques)		Creditors for goods	36,500

On the evening of 31st March, 1999 the Cashier absconded with the available cash in the cash box. There was no cash deposit in the week ended on that date. You are required to prepare a statement showing the amount of cash defalcated by the Cashier and also a Profit & Loss Account for the period ended 31st March 1999 and a Balance Sheet as on that date.

[CA Inter, May 1999]

Solution

Statement showing the amount of cash defalcated by the Cashier

		Rs.	Rs.
Cash balance as on 1.1.99			2,000
Add: Cash sales			1,16,250[3]
			1,18,250
Less :	Salary to clerk (Rs. 300 × 13)	3,900	
	Sundry expenses (Rs. 50 × 13)	650	
	Drawing of Sri Srinivas (Rs. 100 × 13)	1,300	
	Deposit into bank (Rs. 1,25,000 – Rs. 30,000)	95,000	
			1,00,850
	Cash balances as on 31.3.99 which has been defalcated by cashier		17,400

In the books of Sri Srinivas

Dr. **Trading and Profit and Loss Account** *for the 13 week period ended 31st March 1999* Cr.

Particulars	*Amount*	*Particulars*	*Amount*	*Amount*
	Rs.		Rs.	Rs.
To Opening Stock	70,000	By Sales :		
" Purchases :	91,000[2]	" Cash	1,16,250[3]	
" Profit & Loss A/c		Credit	35,000[1]	
—Gross Profit transferred	30,250			1,51,250[1]
		" Closing Stock		40,000
	1,91,250			1,91,250
To Salaries	3,900	By Trading A/c		30,250
" Rent (Rs. 4,000 – Rs. 1,000)	3,000	—Gross Profit		
" Sundry expenses	650			
" Defalcation of Cash	17,400			
Capital A/c				
—Net Profit transferred	5,300			
	30,250			30,250

Balance Sheet *as at 31st March 1999*

Liabilities	Rs.	Rs.	*Assets*	Rs.
Capital as on 1.1.99	1,00,000		Furniture	10,000
Add: Net Profit	5,300		Stock	40,000
	1,05,300		Debtors	30,000
Less : Drawings	1,300	1,04,000	Cash at Bank	*60,500*[5]
Liabilities for Goods		36,500		
		1,40,500		1,40,500

Workings :

Total Debtors A/c

Dr.	Rs.		Cr. Rs.
To Bal. b/d	25,000	By Bank A/c	30,000
" Sales		" Balance c/d	30,000
—Credit	35,000		
(bal. fig.)			
	60,000		60,000

Total Creditors A/c

Dr.	Rs.		Cr. Rs.
To Bank A/c	75,000	By Balance c/d	20,500
" Bal. c/d	36,500	" Purchase A/c	91,000
		(bal. fig.)	
	1,11,500		1,11,500

3. Cash Sales = Total Sales – Credit Sales
= Rs. 1,51,250 – Rs. 35,000
= Rs. 1,16,250

4. Calculation of Total Sales

	Rs.
Opening Stock	70,000
Add : Purchase	91,000
	1,61,000
Less: Closing Stock	40,000
	1,21,000
Add: Gross Profit (25% of C.P. or 20% on S.P.)	30,250
∴ Total Sales	1,51,250

Bank A/c

Dr.	Rs.		Cr. Rs.
To Balance b/d	14,500	By Creditors A/c	75,000
" Debtors A/c	30,000	" Rent A/c	4,000
" Cash A/c		" Balance c/d	60,500
(1,25,000 – Rs. 30,000)	95,000		
	1,39,500		1,39,500

Ascertainment of missing figures

Illustration 25

The following balances are available from the books of Arjun Chatterjee, a small trader, as on 31st December 1994 and 1995 :

	31.12.94 Rs.	31.12.95 Rs.
Building	60,000	60,000
Equipments	1,20,000	1,34,000
Furniture	10,000	10,000
Debtors	?	48,000
Creditors	32,000	?
Stock	?	34,000
Bank Loan	20,000	16,000
Cash	32,000	22,000

The transactions of Arjun Chatterjee during the year ended 31st December 1995 were:

	Rs.		Rs.
Collection from Debtors	1,86,000	Expenses	20,000
Payment to Creditors	1,22,000	Sale of one equipment (Book Value Rs. 10,000)	6,000
Cash Purchases	32,000	Drawings	20,000

Cash sales amounted to 10% of total sales. Credit sales amounted to Rs. 1,80,000. Credit purchases were 80% of total purchases. Arjun Chatterjee sells goods at cost plus $33\frac{1}{3}$%. His suppliers allowed him discount Rs. 2,000. Equipments and Furniture are to be depreciated by 10% per annum and Building by 2%. You are required to prepare the Trading and Profit and Loss Account of Arjun Chatterjee for the year ended 31st December 1995 and a Balance Sheet as on that date.

[CU BCom (Hons.)1996]

Solution

In books of Arjun Chatterjee
Trading and Profit and Loss Account *for the year ended 31st December 1995*

Dr. Particulars	Amount Rs.	Amount Rs.	Particulars Cr.	Amount Rs.	Amount Rs.
To Opening Stock		24,000[3]	By Sales : Cash	20,000[1]	
" Purchases : Cash	32,000[2]		Credit	1,80,000[4]	2,00,000
Credit	1,28,000[5]	1,60,000	" Closing Stock		34,000
" Profit & Loss A/c —Gross Profit transferred		50,000			
		2,34,000			2,34,000
To Expenses		20,000	By Trading A/c —Gross Profit		50,000
" Loss on Sale of Equipment		3,500	" Discount received		2,000
" Dep. on Building		1,200			
" Dep. on Furniture		1,000			
" Dep. on Equipments		12,700			
" Capital A/c Net Profit transferred		13,600			
		52,000			52,000

Balance Sheet *as at 31st December 1995*

Dr. Liabilities	Rs.	Rs.	Assets Cr.	Rs.	Rs.
Opening Capital	2,48,000[8]		Buildings	60,000	
Add : Net Profit	13,600		*Less* : Depreciation	1,200	
	2,61,600				58,800
Less : Drawings	20,000		Equipments (old + new)	1,34,000	
		2,41,600	*Less* : Deprciation (old + new)	12,200[7]	1,21,800
Creditors		36,000	Furniture	10,000	
Bank Loan		16,000	*Less* : Depreciation	1,000	9,000
			Debtors		48,000
			Stock		34,000
			Cash		22,000
		2,93,600			2,93,600

Workings :

1. Computation of **Cash Sales** = 10% of Total Sales, So, Credit Sales = 90% of Total Sales.

   $\therefore$ Amount of Cash Sales = $\frac{10}{90}$ of Credit Sales, i.e., Rs. 1,80,000 × $\frac{10}{90}$ = Rs. 20,000.

   Total Sales = Rs. 20,000 + Rs. 1,80,000 = Rs. 2,00,000.

2. Computation of **Credit Purchase** = 80% of Total Purchase. So, Cash Purchase = 20% of Total Purchase.

   $\therefore$ Credit Purchase is $\frac{80}{20}$ of Cash Purchase i.e., Rs. 32,000 × $\frac{80}{20}$ = Rs. 1,28,000.

   Total Purchase = Rs. 32,000 + Rs. 1,28,000 = Rs. 1,60,000.

3. Computation of **Opening Stock** = Cost of Goods Sold + Closing Stock – Purchases.

   $$\left[\begin{array}{l}\text{Cost of Good Sold} = \text{Sales} - \text{Gross Profit} \\ = \text{Rs. } 2{,}00{,}000 - \dfrac{33\frac{1}{3}}{133\frac{1}{3}} \text{ of Rs. } 2{,}00{,}000 \\ = \text{Rs.} 2{,}00{,}000 - \text{Rs.} 50{,}000 \\ = \text{Rs.} 1{,}50{,}000\end{array}\right]$$

   = Rs. 1,50,000 + Rs. 34,000 – Rs. 1,60,000
   = Rs. 24,000.

4. **Ascertainment of Opening Debtors**

Total Debtors Account

Dr.	Rs.		*Cr.* Rs.
To Balance b/d (*bal. fig.*)	54,000	By Cash	1,86,000
" Credit Sales	1,80,000	" Bal. b/d	48,000
	2,34,000		2,34,000

5. **Ascertainment of Credit Purchases**

Total Creditors Account

Dr.	Rs.		*Cr.* Rs.
To Cash	1,22,000	By Bal. b/d	32,000
" Discount Received	2,000	" Credit Purchases	1,28,000
" Balance c/d	36,000		
	1,60,000		1,60,000

6. **Loss on Sale of Equipment**

	Rs.
Book Value	10,000
Less : Depreciation for 6 months	500
	9,500
Less : Sold for	6,000
∴ Loss on Sales	3,500

7. **Depreciation on Equipment**

	Rs.
Old = Rs. 1,10,000 × 10% =	11,000
New = (Rs. 1,34,000 – Rs. 1,10,000) $= \text{Rs. } 24{,}000 \times \frac{10}{100} \times \frac{6}{12} =$	1,200
Sold Rs. $10{,}000 \times \frac{10}{100} \times \frac{6}{12} =$	500
	12,700

(Assume purchase and sale of equipment were made at the middle of the year)

8. **Ascertainment of Opening Capital**

Balance Sheet *as on 31st December 1995*

Liabilities	Rs.	*Assets*	Rs.
Capital (*bal. fig.*)	2,48,000	Buildings	60,000
Creditors	32,000	Equipment	1,20,000
Bank Loan	20,000	Furniture	10,000
		Debtors	54,000
		Stock	24,000
		Cash	32,000
	3,00,000		3,00,000

Illustration 26

Following are the particulars of Arpita & Co. :

(i) Assets and Liabilities

	1.1.95 Rs.	31.12.95 Rs.
Furniture	36,000	38,100
Stock	48,000	42,000
Sundry Debtors	96,000	—
Sundry Creditors	66,000	90,000
Prepaid Expenses	3,600	4,200
Outstanding Expenses	12,000	10,800
Cash in hand and at Bank	7,200	3,750

(ii) Cash transactions during the year 1995 :

Receipts from Debtors (after allowing $2\frac{1}{2}$% discount)	3,51,000
Bills Receivable discounted (discounted at an average rate of 2%)	36,750
Paid to Creditors (discount at 2%)	2,35,200
Freight Inwards	18,000
Drawings	42,000
Furniture purchased	6,000
4% Investment purchased at Rs. 96 (on 1.7.95)	57,600
Expenses including Salaries	87,000
Miscellaneous Receipts	3,000

(iii) During the year, Bills Receivable received were Rs. 60,000, Rs. 12,000 of which were endorsed in favour of creditors. Of the latter, a bill for Rs. 2,400 was dishonoured.

(iv) Goods costing Rs. 5,400 were used as advertising materials.

(v) Goods are invariably sold to show a profit of 50% on cost.

(vi) Difference in Cash Book, if any, is to be treated as drawings or introduction of capital by the proprietor.

(vii) Provision @ $2\frac{1}{2}$% on Debtors for Doubtful Debts to be provided for.

Prepare Trading and Profit & Loss Account for the year ended 31.12.95 and a Balance Sheet as on that date.

[CU BCom (Hons.)]

Solution

Workings :

1. Calculation of Credit Purchases

Creditors Account

Dr.		Rs.		Cr.	Rs.
To	Bank A/c (98%)	2,35,200	By	Balance b/d	66,000
"	Discount Received A/c (Rs. 2,35,200 × $\frac{2}{98}$)	4,800	"	Debtors A/c — Endorsed bill dishonoured	2,400
"	Bills Receivable A/c — Endorsed	12,000	"	Purchases A/c (*bal. fig.*)	2,73,600
"	Balance c/d	90,000			
		3,42,000			3,42,000

2. Calculation of Credit Sales (assume all sales are made for credit)

Cost of Goods Sold

		Rs.
	Opening Stock	48,000
Add :	Purchase (Net) (2,73,600 – 5,400)	2,68,200
		3,16,200
Add :	Freight	18,000
		3,34,200
Less :	Closing Stock	**42,000**
	Cost of Goods Sold	**2,92,200**
Add :	Profit @ 50% of Cost	**1,46,100**
	Sales	4,38,300

3. Bills Receivable Account

Dr.		Rs.		Cr.	Rs.
To	Debtors A/c	60,000	By	Creditors A/c —Endorsed	12,000
			"	Bank A/c (98%)	36,750
			"	Discount $(36,750 \times \frac{2}{98})$	750
			"	Balance c/d	10,500
		60,000			60,000

4. Debtors Account

Dr.		Rs.		Cr.	Rs.
To	Balance b/d	96,000	By	Bank A/c ($97\frac{1}{2}$ %)	3,51,000
"	Sales A/c	4,38,300	"	Discount Allowed A/c ($2\frac{1}{2}$ %)	9,000
"	Creditors A/c —Endorsed Bills Dishonoured	2,400	"	B/R	60,000
			"	Balance c/d	1,16,700
		5,36,700			5,36,700

5. Cash Account

Dr.		Rs.		Cr.	Rs.
To	Balance b/d	7,200	By	Furniture A/c	6,000
"	Debtors A/c	3,51,000	"	Investment A/c	57,600
"	B/R A/c	36,750	"	Expenses A/c	87,000
"	Misc. Receipts A/c	3,000	"	Creditors A/c	2,35,200
"	Capital A/c (*bal. fig.*)	51,600	"	Freight A/c	18,000
			"	Drawings A/c	42,000
			"	Balance c/d	3,750
		4,49,550			4,49,550

6. Balance Sheet *as at Jan. 1, 1995*

Liabilities	Rs.	*Assets*	Rs.
Outstanding Exp.	12,000	Furniture	36,000
S. Creditors	66,000	Stock	48,000
Capital (*bal. fig.*)	1,12,800	S. Debtors	96,000
		Prepaid Exp.	3,600
		Cash and Bank	7,200
	1,90,800		1,90,800

7. **Expenses for 1995**

		Rs.
	Expenses paid	87,000
Add :	Outstanding for 1995	10,800
Add :	Prepaid in 1994	3,600
		1,01,400
Less :	Prepaid for 1996	4,200
		97,200
Less :	Outstanding of 1994	12,000
		85,200

8. **Depreciation on Furniture**

		Rs.
	Opening Balance	36,000
	Additions	6,000
		42,000
Less :	Closing Balance	38,100
	∴ Depreciation	3,900

9. **Interest on Investments** Rs.

Face Value (Rs. 57,600 × $\frac{100}{96}$) = 60,000

∴ Accrued Interest

$= \text{Rs. } 60{,}000 \times \frac{4}{100} \times \frac{6}{12}$

= Rs. 1,200.

In the books of Arpita & Co.

Trading and Profit & Loss Account *for the year ended 31st December 1995*

Dr. *Particulars*	*Amount* Rs.	*Amount* Rs.	*Particulars*	*Cr.* *Amount* Rs.
To Opening Stock		48,000	By Sales	4,38,300
" Purchases	2,73,600		" Closing Stock	42,000
Less : Goods used for advertisements	5,400	2,68,200		
" Freight Inward		18,000		
" Profit & Loss A/c —Gross Profit transferred		1,46,100		
		4,80,300		4,80,300
To Expenses (including Salaries)		85,200	By Trading A/c —Gross Profit transferred	1,46,100
" Advertisements		5,400	" Accrued Interest	1,200
" Discount Allowed		9,000	" Discount Received	4,800
" Depreciation on Furniture		3,900	" Miscellaneous Receipts	3,000
" Discount on Bill		750		
" Provision for Bad Debts		2,918		
" Capital A/c —Net Profit transferred		47,932		
		1,55,100		1,55,100

Balance Sheet *as at 31st Dec. 1995*

Liabilities	Rs.	Rs.	*Assets*	Rs.	Rs.
Outstanding Expenses		10,800	Cash in hand and at Bank		3,750
Sundry Creditors		90,000	Prepaid Expenses		4,200
Capital	1,12,800		Accrued Interest		1,200
Add : Net Profit	47,932		Sundry Debtors	1,16,700	
Further Capital	51,600		*Less :* Provision for Bad Debts	2,918	1,13,782
	2,12,332		Bills Receivable		10,500
Less : Drawings	42,000	1,70,332	Stock		42,000
			4% Investments at Cost (Nominal Value 60,000)		57,600
			Furniture		38,100
		2,71,132			2,71,132

Illustration 27

K. Azad, who is in business as a wholesaler in sunflower oil, is a client of your accounting firm. You are required to draw up his final accounts for the year ended 31.3.1996.

From the files, you pick up his Balance Sheet as at 31.3.1995 reading as below:

Balance Sheet *as at 31.3.1995*

Liabilities	Rs.	*Assets*	Rs.	Rs.
K Azad's Capital	1,50,000	Cash and Bank Balances		75,000
Creditors for Oil Purchases	2,00,000	Debtors		1,60,000
12% Security Deposit from		Stock of Oil (125 tins)		1,25,000
Customers	50,000	Furniture	30,000	
Creditors for Expenses:		*Less:* Depreciation	3,000	27,000
Rent	6,000	Rent Advance		12,000
Salaries	4,000	Electricity Deposit		1,000
Commission	20,000	3-Wheeler Tempo Van	40,000	
		Less: Depreciation	10,000	
				30,000
	4,30,000			4,30,000

A Summary of the rough Cash Book of K. Azad for the year ended 31.3.1996 is as below:

Cash and Bank Summary

	Rs.		Rs.
Receipts			
Cash Sales	5,26,500		
Collections from Debtors	26,27,500		
Payments			
Landlord	79,000	Personal Income-tax	50,000
Salaries	48,000	Transfer on 1.1.95 to 12% Fixed Deposit	6,00,000
Miscellaneous Office Expenses	12,000	Creditors for Oil, Supplies	24,00,000
Commission	20,000		

A security of the other records gives you the following information :

(i) During the year oil was purchase at 250 tins per month basis at a unit cost of Rs. 1,000. 5 tins were damaged in transit in respect of which insurance claim has been preferred. The surveyors have since approved the claim at 80%. The damaged ones were sold for Rs. 1,500 which is included in the cash sales. One tin has been used up for personal consumption. Total number of tins sold during the year was 3,000 at a unit price of Rs. 1,750.

(ii) Rent until 30.9.95 was Rs. 6,000 per month and was increased thereafter by Rs. 1,000 per month. Additional advance rent of Rs. 2,000 was paid and this is included in the figure of payments to landlord.

(iii) Provide depreciation at 10% and 25% of WDV of furniture and tempo van, respectively.

(iv) It is further noticed that a customer has paid Rs. 10,000 on 31.3.96 as security deposit by cash. One of the staffs has defalcated. The claim against the Insurance Company is pending.

You are requested to prepare final accounts for the year ended 31.3.96.

[CA Inter May 1996]

Solution

In the books of K. Azad

Trading and Profit & Loss Account *for the year ended 31st March 1996*

Dr. *Particulars*		*Amount* Rs.	*Particulars*		Cr. *Amount* Rs.
To Opening Stock		1,25,000	By Sales		52,50,000
" Purchases	30,00,000		" Closing Stock	1,19,000[2]	
Less: Drawings	1,000	29,99,000	*Add:* Goods damaged	5,000	1,24,000
" Profit an Loss A/c —Gross Profit transferred		22,50,000			
		53,74,000			53,74,000

Contd.

		Rs.	Rs.			Rs.
To	Salaries (48,,000 – 4,000)		44,000	By	Trading A/c —Gross Profit	22,50,000
"	Misc. Office Expenses		12,000	"	Profit on goods damaged	500[1]
"	Commission (20,000 – 20,000)		—	"	Accrued Interest	36,000
"	Rent (Rs. 6,000 × 6 + Rs. 7,000 × 6)		78,000			
"	Interest on Security Deposit		6,000			
"	Loss of Deposit		10,000			
"	Depreciation on:					
	Tempo	7,500				
	Furniture	2,700				
			10,200			
"	Capital A/c —Net Profit transferred		21,26,300			
			22,86,500			22,86,500

Balance Sheet *as at 31st March, 1996*

Liabilities	Rs.	Rs.	*Assets*	Rs.	Rs.
Capital	1,50,000		Furniture	27,000	
Add: Net Profit	21,26,300		*Less Depreciation*	2,700	
	22,76,300				24,300
Less: Drawings			Tempo	30,000	
(50,0000 + 1,000)	51,000		*Less Depreciation*	7,500	
		22,25,300			22,500
Security Deposit	60,000		Fixed Deposit		6,00,000
Add: Interessst	6,000		Closing Stock		1,19,000
		66,000	Accrued Interest		36,000
Creditors		8,00,000[4]	Debtors		22,11,500[3]
Outstanding Rent		7,000	Electricity Deposit		1,000
			Prepaid Rent (12,000 + 2,000)		14,000
			Insurance Claim		4,000
			Cash at Bank		66,000[5]
		30,98,300			30,98,300

Workings :

1. **Profit on Damaged Goods**

	Rs.
Cost of Goods (5 × Rs. 1,000)	5,000
Less ; Insurance Claim @ 80%	4,000
	1,000
Less : Sale of Damaged Goods	1,500
∴ Profit	500

2. **Valuation of Closing Stock**

	Tins	Rate	Amount Rs.
Opening Stock	125	1,000	1,25,000
Add: Purchase	3,000	1,000	30,00,000
			31,25,000
Less: Damaged	5	1,000	5,000
			31,20,000
Less: Drawings	1	1,000	1,000
			31,19,000
Less: Cost of Sales	3, 000	1,000	30,00,000
∴ Closing Stock	119	1,000	1,19,000

3. **Debtors as on 31.3.1996**

		Rs.
Opening Balance		1,60,000
Add : Credit Sales :		
Total Sales (3,000 × Rs. 1,750)	52,,50,000	
Less : Cash Sales (5,26,500 – 1,500)	5,25,000	
		47,25,000
		48,85,000
Less : Cash Received		26,73,500
		22,11,500

4. **Creditors as on 31.3.1996**

Dr. **Total Creditors A/c** *Cr.*

To Cash	24,00,000	By Bal. b/d	2,00,000
" Bal. c/d	8,00,000	" Purchase	30,00,000
	32,00,000		32,00,000

5. **Cash and Bank as on 31.3.1996**

Cash and Bank A/c

Dr.		Rs.			Rs. Cr.
To	Balance b/d	75,000	By	Sales A/c	48,000
"	Sales A/c	5,25,000	"	Rent A/c	79,000
		26,73,500	"	Commission A/c	20,000
"	Security Deposit A/c	10,000	"	Misc. off. Exp. A/c	12,000
"	Sales (Damage Goods)	1,500	"	Drawings A/c	50,000
			"	Creditors A/c	24,00,000
			"	Fixed Deposit A/c	6,00,000
			"	P & L A/c	10,000
			"	Balanced	66,000
		32,85,000			32,85,000

A harder Problems

Illustration 28

The following is the Balance Sheet of Sanjoy, a small trader as on 31.3.1996 : *(Figs. in 000 rupees)*

Liabilities	Rs.	*Assets*	Rs.
Capital	200	Fixed Asset	145
Creditors	50	Stock	40
		Debtors	50
		Cash in hand	5
		Cash at Bank	10
	250		250

A fire destroyed the accounting records as well as the closing cash of the trader on 31.3.1997. However, the following informations was available:

(a) Debtors and Creditors on 31.3.1997 showed an increase of 20% as compared to 31.3.1996; (b) Credit Period : Debtors 1 month; Creditors 2 months. (c) Stock was maintained at the same level throughout the year. (d) Cash Sales constituted 20% of total sales. (e) All purchase were for credit only. (f) Current Ratio as on 31.3.1997 was exactly 2. (g) Total expenses excluding depreciation for the year amounted to Rs. 2,50,000. (h) Depreciation was provided at 10% on the closing value of fixed assets (i) Bank and Cash transactions:

(1) Payment to Creditors included Rs. 50,000 by cash. (2) Receipts from Debtors included Rs. 5,90,000 by way of cheque. (3) Cash deposited into bank Rs. 1,20,000; (4) Personal drawings from bank Rs. 50,000; (5) Fixed asset purchased and paid by cheque Rs. 2,25,000

You are required to preparee: (a) The Trading and Profit and Loss Account of Sanjoy for the year ended 31.3.1997; and (b) a Balance Sheet as on that date. For your exercise assume cash destroyed by fire is written-off in Profit and Loss Account.

Solution

In the books of Sanjoy
Trading and Profit and Loss Account
for the year ended 31st March 1997 (–000)

Dr. *Particulars*		*Amount* Rs.	*Particulars*			*Amount* Rs. Cr.
To	Opening Stock	40	By	Sales :		
"	Purchase	360^3		Cash	180	
"	Profit and Loss A/c		"	Stock	720^2	
	—Gross Profit Transferred	540				900
			"	Closing Stock		40
		940				940

Contd.

		Rs.			Rs.
To	Expenses	250[1]	By	Trading A/c	
"	Depreciation	37		—Gross Profit	540
"	Cash destroyed by fire	10			
"	Capital A/c	243			
	—Net Profit Transferred				
		540			540

Balance Sheet *as at 31st March 1997* *('000)*

Liabilities	Rs.	Rs.	*Assets*	Rs.	Rs.
Capital	200		Fixed Asset	145	
Add : Net Profit	243		Additions	225	
	443			370	
Less : Drawings	50		*Less* : Depreciation	37	333
		393	*Current Assets*		
Creditors		60	Closing Stock	40	
			Debtors	60	
			Cash at Bank	20[4]	120
		453			453

Workings :

1. **Ascertainment of Cash deposited into bank and expenses paid**

Dr. **Cash and Bank A/c** *Cr.*

		Cash	Bank			Cash	Bank
To		Rs.	Rs.	By		Rs.	Rs.
		5	10	"	Creditors	50	300
"	Sales	180	—	"	Bank(C)	120	—
"	Debtors	120	590	"	Drawings		50
"	Cash (c)		120	"	Assets		225
				"	Expenses	125	125
				"	Cash deposited	10	*(bal. fig.)*
					(Bal. fig.)		
				"	Bal. c/d	—	20
		305	720			305	720

2. **Computation of Sales**

Debtors balance (Opening) Rs. 50

∴ Debtors Closing balance (opening + 20% increase = Rs. 50 + Rs. 10 = Rs. 60

Since debtors are 1 month Sales, so, p.a. sales will be 60×12 = Rs. 720 which is 80% of total sales.

So, total sales will be Rs. $720 \times \frac{100}{80}$ = Rs. 900

∴ Cash sales Rs. $900 \times 20\%$ = Rs. 180

Credit sales = Rs. $900 \times 80\%$ = Rs. 720

3. **Calculation of Purchases**

Dr. **Total Creditors A/c** *Cr.*

		Rs.			Rs.
To	Cash	50	By	Bal. b/d	
"	Bank	300	"	Purchase	50
"	Bal. c/d			(60×6)	360
	(50 + 20%)	60			
		410			410

4. **Closing bank balance**

Total Current Assets = Rs. 60×2 = 120

Bank = Current Assets – Stock – Debtors
= 120 – Rs. 40 – Rs. 60
= Rs. 20

Illustration 29

On 1.4.2011, Mr. Silgardo bought for Rs. 50,000 a business whose assets and liabilities are shown below. The business carried on its operations in a rented shop from which it sold cosmetics and confectioneries. The business did not keep double entry account, but you are provided with the following information :

(i) Balance Sheet of the company as on 31st March 2011:

Liabilities	Rs.	*Assets*	Rs.
		Fixed Assets	
Capital A/c	50,000	Furniture and Fittings at cost	30,000
Profit and Loss A/c	10,500	*Current Assets*	
Creditors :		Stock at cost :	
Cosmetics	2,500	Cosmetics	5,000
Confectionery	2,000	Confectionery	3,000
Outstanding Rent	500	Sundry Debtors :	
		Confectionery	500
		Prepaid :	
		Rates and Insurance	2,500
		Balance with Bank	23,500
		Cash in hand	1,000
	65,500		65,500

(ii) Analysis of bank statements for the year ended 31st March 2012:

Paid in :	Rs.
Cash	2,45,000
Withdrawn for :	
Purchases of Cosmetics	1,00,000
Purchases of Confectionery	1,10,000
Repairs	4,000
Rent	6,000
Rates and Insurance	10,000
Electricity	4,000
Mr. Silgardo	15,000

(iii) The following were paid is cash.

	Rs.
Salaries	15,000
Confectionery Purchase	1,500
Trade Expenses	1,250
Cosmetics Purchases	5,000

(iv) Mr. Silgardo had taken from the shop cosmetics for his own consumption and paid into the till the cost price of Rs. 4,550.

(iv) Mr. Silgardo had taken from the shop cosmetics for his own consumption and paid into the till the cost price of Rs. 4,550.

(v) The following are the gross profit percentage with reference to sales :

Cosmetic	9%
Confectionery	30%

(vi) On 31st March 2012, there were :

	Stocks at cost	Debtors/Prepayments and Cash	Liabilities
	Rs.	Rs.	Rs.
Cosmetics	4,850	—	2,000
Confectionery	3,500	1,000	3,000
Rent	—	—	500
Rates and Insurance	—	2,750	—
Cash in hand	—	250	—
Accountancy/Audit Fees	—	—	2,000

(vii) Mr. Silgardo has instructed you to regard any shortage in cash as being due to accounts withdrawn by him.

You are required to prepare : (a) The Trading and Profit and Loss Account for the year ended March 31, 1994, showing separately the gross profit from (i) cosmetics, and (ii) confectionery. (b) The Balance Sheet as at 31st March 2012. (c) Total Debtors and Total Creditors Account, and; (d) An account in columnar form for Cash and Bank transactions.

[CA]

Solution

Before preparing the Trading and Profit and Loss Account and also the Balance Sheet, we are to prepare the Total Debtors Account, Total Creditors Account and a Double Column Cash Book and also the amount of sales which are as under :

Total Debtors Account

Dr. Cr.

	Cosmetics	Confectionery		Cosmetics	Confectionery
	Rs.	Rs.		Rs.	Rs.
To Balance b/d	—	500	By Cash A/c	1,10,000	1,59,500
" Sales	1,10,000	1,60,000	" Balance c/d *(bal. fig.)*	—	1,000
	1,10,000	1,60,500		1,10,000	1,60,500

Total Creditors Account

Dr. Cr.

	Cosmetics	Confectionery		Cosmetics	Confectionery
	Rs.	Rs.		Rs.	Rs.
To Cash A/c	5,000	1,500	By Balance b/d	2,500	2,000
" Bank a/c	1,00,000	1,10,000	" Purchases *(bal. fig.)*	1,04,500	1,12,500
" Balance c/d	2,000	3,000			
	1,07,000	1,14,500		1,07,000	1,14,500

Cash Book (with Cash and Bank Columns)

Dr. Cr.

Particulars	Cash	Bank	*Particulars*	Cash	Bank
	Rs.	Rs.		Rs.	Rs.
To Balance b/d	1,000	23,500	By Bank (c)	2,45,000	
" Sales	4,550		" Creditors A/c :		
" Debtors A/c			Cosmetics	5,000	1,00,000
Cosmetics	1,10,000		Confectionery	1,500	1,10,000
" Confectionery	1,59,500		" Repair		4,000
" Cash (c)		2,45,000	" Rent		6,000
			" Electricity		4,000
			" Drawings		15,000
			" Rates and Insurance		10,000
			" Expenses	1,250	
			" Salaries	15,000	
			" Drawings *(bal. fig.)*	7,050	
			" Balance c/d	250	19,500
	2,75,050	2,68,500		2,75,050	2,68,500

Calculation of Sales :

	Cosmetics		Confectionery	
	Rs.	Rs.		Rs.
Opening Stock		5,000		3,000
Add : Purchases		1,04,500		1,12,500
		1,09,500		1,15,500
Less : Closing Stock	4,850		3,500	
Sales (at cost)	4,550	9,400	—	3,500
Cost of Goods Sold		1,00,100		1,12,000
Add : Gross Profit @ $\frac{9}{91}$ in cosmetics		9,900		
@ $\frac{30}{70}$ in confectionery				48,000
		1,10,000		1,60,000

Profit and Loss Account *for the year ended 31st March 2012*

Dr. Particulars	Amount Rs.	Amount Rs.	Particulars	Amount Rs.	*Cr.* Amount Rs.
To Repairs		4,000	By Trading A/c		
" Electricity		4,000	—Gross Profit		
" Expenses		1,250	Cosmetics	9,900	
" Audit fees		2,000	Confectionery	48,000	
" Rent	6,000				57,900
Add : Outstanding	500				
	6,500				
Less : Outstanding in last year	500	6,000			
Rates and Insurance	10,000				
Less : Prepaid	2,750				
	7,250				
Add : Paid in last year	2,500	9,750			
" Salaries		15,000			
Capital A/c					
Net Profit transferred		15,900			
		57,900			57,900

Balance Sheet *as at 31st March 2012*

Liabilities	Rs.	Rs.	Assets	Rs.	Rs.
Capital :			Furniture and Fittings		30,000
(Rs. 50,000 + 10,500)	60,500		Closing Stock :		
Add : Net Profit	15,900		Cosmetics		4,850
	76,400		Confectionery		3,500
Less : Drawings (Rs. 15,000 + 7,050)	22,050	54,350	Sundry Debtors :		
Creditors :			Confectionery		1,000
Cosmetics	2,000		Prepaid Expenses		2,750
Confectionery	3,000	5,000	Cash at Bank		19,500
Outstanding Rent		500	Cash in hand		250
Outstanding Audit Fees		2,000			
		61,850			61,850

Illustration 30

A and B are Chartered Accountants practicing independently at Chennai and Bangalore, respectively, and decide, with effect from 1.4.22010, to form a partnership in which each of them will have an equal share in profits and losses. They decide to bring into the firm all their assets and liabilities of there proprietary practices except the outstanding dues on government audit work done prior to 31st March 2010, which will be to the benefit of the individuals concerned. It was also decided that a sum of goodwill, equivalent to $1\frac{1}{2}$ times the value of net assets taken over, will be credited to the partners' account. Details of assets and liabilities as on 31st March 2010 were as under :

	A Rs.	B Rs.
Cash in hand and at Bank	16,000	12,000
Fixed Deposits (out of professional receipts)	40,000	26,000
Amounts billed and receivable	38,000	32,000
Bills still to be raised		
(including Rs. 24,000 due to A on Govt. audit work)	1,60,000	82,000
Office Furniture, Fixtures, Telephone Lines etc.	31,000	18,000
Amounts due to articled and audit clerks towards stipends	8,400	12,000
Rent Deposits	18,000	18,000
Rent due	1,500	1,500
Office Salaries due	6,000	4,500
Expenses to be paid	800	—

For the year 2010-11 the analysis of bank/cash account revealed :

	Rs.
Gross Fees received (including Rs. 18,000 due to A on Govt. audit work)	4,42,000
Office Expenses	18,800
Rent	36,000
Printing and Stationery	40,000
Stipends paid	60,000
Salaries to Staff	82,000
Interest on Fixed Deposit credited	6,600
Drawings :	
A	50,000
B	36,000
Other information : as on 31.1.2011	
Bills due by clients	1,44,000
Bills still to be raised on clients	60,000
Salaries due	9,600

There were no outstanding bills for collection as on 31.3.2011 that referred to earlier years.

The partners decided that from 1.4.2010, they will adopt the Mercantile System of Account for all items except professional receipts which will be accounted on Cash Basis. Interest on Fixed Deposits is to be shared in the ratio of holding at the time of formation of the firm. Depreciate Furniture & Fixtures at 10%. You are required to prepare the Profit and Loss Account of the firm for the year ended 31st March 2011 and also a Balance Sheet as at that date. All workings are to form, part of your answer.

Solution

Before preparing the Profit and Loss Account and the Balance Sheet, the following workings are to be calculated :

Dr. **Cash Book** *(Cash and Bank consolidated)* *Cr.*

		Rs.			Rs.
To	Balance b/d	28,000	By	Office Expenses	18,800
"	Fees	4,42,000	"	Rent	36,000
"	Interest on Fixed Deposit	6,600	"	Printing and Stationery	40,000
			"	Stipends	60,000
			"	Salaries	82,000
			"	Drawings : A	50,000
				B	36,000
			"	Balance c/d *(bal. fig.)*	1,53,800
		4,76,600			4,76,600

Calculation of Goodwill

		A		B
Net Assets		Rs.		Rs.
Cash/Bank		16,000		12,000
Fixed Deposits		40,000		26,000
Debtors (Bills received but due)		38,000		32,000
" (Bills still to be received)		1,36,000		82,000
Office Furniture, Fittings & Telephone		31,000		18,000
Rent Deposits		18,000		18,000
		2,79,000		1,88,000
Less :				
Liabilities	Rs.		Rs.	
Stipends due	8,400		12,000	
Rent due	1,500		1,500	
Salaries due	6,000		4,500	
Office Expenses due	800		—	
		16,700		18,000
Net Assets		2,62,300		1,70,000

∴ Value of Goodwill will be $1\frac{1}{2}$ times of Net Assets = Rs. 3,93,450 Rs. 2,55,000

(i.e., Rs. 2,62,300 × $1\frac{1}{2}$) (i.e., Rs. 1,70,000 × $1\frac{1}{2}$)

Balance Sheet *as at 1st April 2011*

Liabilities	A Rs.	B Rs.	*Assets*	A Rs.	B Rs.
Capital *(bal. fig.)*	5,11,750	2,81,000	Cash/Bank	16,000	12,000
Outstanding Liabilities			Fixed Deposits	40,000	26,000
Stipends	8,400	12,000	Debtors (Bills received but due)	38,000	32,000
Rent	1,500	1,500	Debtors (Bills still to be received)	1,36,000	82,000
Salaries	6,000	4,500	Office Furniture etc.	31,000	18,000
Office Expenses	800	—	Rent Deposits	18,000	18,000
			Goodwill	3,93,450	2,55,000
				6,72,450	4,43,000
			Less : Sundry Debtors	1,44,000*	1,44,000
	5,28,450	2,99,000		5,28,450	2,99,000

Note : Since the partners decide to follow Mercantile System of Accounting from 1.4.2010, except Professional Fees, Cash Basis of Accounting was followed. As such, Outstanding Fees will not appear in Balance Sheet.

* As on 31.3.2010 :

Debtors billed and receivable	(Rs. 38,000 + Rs. 32,000)	=	Rs.	70,000
Add : Bill still to be received	(Rs. 1,36,000 + Rs. 82,000)	=	Rs.	2,18,000
			Rs.	2,88,000 ÷ 2
				= Rs. 1,44,000 each

In the books of A & B

Profit and Loss Account *for the year ended 31st March 2011*

Dr. Cr.

Particulars	Rs.	Rs.	*Particulars*	Rs.	Rs.
To Office Expenses	18,800		By Fees	4,42,000	
Less : For last year	800	18,000	*Less :* A's Fees on		
" Rent	36,000		Govt. Work	18,000	
Less : For last year	3,000	33,000			4,24,000
" Printing & Stationery		40,000			
" Stipends	60,000				
Less : For last year	20,400	39,600			
To Salaries	82,000				
Add : Outstanding for the Current Year	9,600				
	91,600				
Less : For the last year	10,500	81,100			
" Depreciation on : Furniture, Fixtures etc.		4,900			
" Capital A/c Net Profit transferred					
A	1,03,700				
B	1,03,700	2,07,400			
		4,24,000			4,24,000

Balance Sheet *as at 31st March 2011*

Liabilities	Rs.	Rs.	*Assets*	Rs.	Rs.
Capital :			Goodwill		6,48,450
A—Balance	5,11,750		(3,93,450 + 2,55,000)		
Add : Net Profit	1,03,700		Furniture, Fixture etc.	49,000	
Add : Fees	18,000		*Less :* Depreciation	4,900	44,100

Contd.

	Rs.	Rs.		Rs.	Rs.
Add : Interest on Fixed Deposit (20 : 13)	4,000		Fixed Deposits (40,000 + 26,000)		66,000
	6,37,450				
Less : Drawings	50,000	5,87,450	Rent Deposits (18,000 + 18,000)		36,000
B—Balance	2,81,000		Cash/Bank		1,53,800
Add : Net Profit	1,03,700				
Add : Int. on Fixed Deposit	2,600				
	3,87,300				
Less : Drawings	36,000	3,51,300			
Outstanding Salaries		9,600			
		9,48,350			9,48,350

Illustration 31

Miss. Anita Paul started a business as a provision merchant on 1.1.2012. She opened a Bank Account for the business with Rs. 25,000 and immediately spent Rs. 12,500 on Fixtures and Fittings. The only records kept were of cash sales which amounted in 2012 to Rs. 37,500 and in 2012 to Rs. 45,000. There were no credit sales. The following facts were ascertained :

(a) All expenses of the business had been met by cheques, and an analysis of the Bank Pass Book showed the following payments in the two years :

	Rs.
Purchases (of which Rs. 37,000 related to 2012)	63,750
Rent and Rates	5,100
Salaries	11,000
Advertising	1,400
Other Expenses	2,880

(b) The value of the Stock on 31.12.2013 was Rs. 15,000. No Stock was taken on 31.12.2012, but a uniform rate of Gross Profit may be assumed.

(c) Liabilities outstanding at 31.12.2013 were :

	Rs.
Purchases	7,500
Advertising	500
Other Expenses (Light, Heat, Telephone etc.)	170

(d) Amounts paid in advance at 31st Dec. 2013 were :

Rates	100
Other Expenses (Insurance)	50

(e) All business expenses arose equally in the two periods.

(f) Goods were taken from Stock for private consumption, the estimated cost being Rs. 500 in 2012 and Rs. 750 in 2013.

(g) Private Drawings amounting to Rs. 6,620 were met out of Cash Receipts and the balance was banked.

(h) Private income of Rs. 2,250 had been paid into the Bank.

The Fixtures and Fittings are to be written-off over 10 years in equal instalments.

On the basis of the foregoing information you are required to prepare :

(1) Trading and Profit and Loss Account for the years 2012 and 2013.

(2) Balance Sheet at 31.12.2013.

[CA Final]

Solution

In the books of Miss Anita Paul

Dr. **Trading Account and Profit and Loss Account** *for the year ended 31st Dec. ...* Cr.

Particulars	2012	2013	*Particulars*	2012	2013
	Rs.	Rs.		Rs.	Rs.
To Opening Stock	—	11,500	By Sales	37,500	45,000
" Purchases			" Closing Stock	11,500	15,000
Less : Drawings			*(bal. fig.)*		
(37,000 – 500)	36,500				
(34,250 – 750)		33,500			
" Profit and Loss A/c					
Gross Profit transferred	12,500	15,000			
(@ $33\frac{1}{3}$ % on Sales)					
	49,000	60,000		49,000	60,000
To Salaries	5,500	5,500	By Trading A/c		
" Advertising	950	950	Gross Profit		
" Rent and Rates	2,500	2,500	transferred	12,500	15,000
" Other Expenses					
(2,880 + 170 – 50) ÷ 2	1,500	1,500			
" Depreciation on :					
Furniture and Fittings	1,250	1,250			
" Capital A/c					
Net Profit transferred	800	3,300			
	12,500	15,000		12,500	15,000

Balance Sheet *as at 31st Dec. 2013*

Liabilities		*Amount*	*Amount*	*Assets*	*Amount*	*Amount*
		Rs.	Rs.		Rs.	Rs.
Capital		25,000		Furniture and Fittings	12,500	
Additional Capital		2,250		*Less* : Depreciation	2,500	
Add : Net Profit (92 + 93)		4,100				10,000
		31,350		Stock		15,000
Less : Drawings				Prepaid Expenses :		
Cash	6,620			Rates	100	
Goods				Insurance	50	
(500 + 750)	1,250					150
		7,870	23,480	Cash at Bank		6,500
Outstanding Expenses :						
Advertising		500				
Other Expenses		170	670			
Creditors			7,500			
			31,650			31,650

Workings :

1. **Calculation of Gross Profit Ratio on sales for the purpose of ascertaining the value of stock at 31.12.2012 :**

		Rs.	Rs.
	Sales		
	2012	37,500	
	2013	45,000	
			82,500
Add :	Closing Stock—2013		15,000
			97,500
Less :	Purchases	63,750	
Add :	Credit Purchases	7,500	
		71,250	
Less :	Drawings (500 + 750)	1,250	
			70,000
	Gross Profit		27,500

∴ Percentage of Gross Profit on Sales =

$$\frac{\text{Rs. } 27,500}{\text{Rs. } 82,500} \times 100 = 33\frac{1}{3}\%$$

Dr. **Bank A/c (for 2012 and 2013)** Cr.

		Rs.			Rs.
To	Capital	25,000	By	Fixtures and Fittings	12,500
"	Sales (82,500 – 6,620)	75,880	"	Purchases	63,750
"	Additional Capital	2,250	"	Rent and Rates	5,100
			"	Salaries	11,000
			"	Advertising	1,400
			"	Expenses	2,880
			"	Balance c/d	6,500
		1,03,130			1,03,130

Illustration 32

Subhadeep Sarker is an importer of fancy goods, operating from rented premises, which is on lease of Rs. 500 p.m. He prepares his accounts as on 31st December every year.

On night of December 31, 2013, all his books and records were destroyed in a fire.

The following was his summarised financial position as on 31st December 2012 :

	Rs.	Rs.	Rs.
Fixed Assets :			
Motor Car		6,500	
Furniture		10,000	16,500
Working Capital :			
Current Assets :			
Stock-in-trade (at Cost)	2,00,500		
Debtors	24,000		
Prepaid Rates	500		
Balance at Bank	27,060		
Cash in hand	590	2,52,650	
Less : Current Liabilities :			
Creditors (after adjustment of rebate due)	1,10,200		
Accrued Rent	1,000		
Due for Hire-Purchase Instalment	2,790		
		1,13,990	
Capital Amount			1,38,660
Net Asset			1,55,160

The following further information is also available :

(a) Subhadeep buys goods for re-sale only from one manufacturer in Japan, who allows a rebate of 3% of the goods purchased by him in excess of Rs. 5,00,000 in a calendar year. The rebate due for the year ended 31st December 2013 was Rs. 12,480.

(b) All goods are sold at a standard gross profit margin of 40% on selling price. Any rebate due is to be ignored for the purpose.

(c) Stock at cost on 31.12.2013 amounted to Rs. 90,200.

(d) Weekly cash expenses out of cash sales (before depositing the same into the bank) have been :

	Rs.
Drawings	250
Carriage Outward	450
Petrol	40
Sundries	20

(e) His bank statements for the year reveal the following information :

	Rs.		Rs.
Paid for purchase of goods	10,10,500	Hire-Purchases Instalments (final payments)	3,040
Car Expenses	3,680	Salaries	1,02,460
Rent	6,500	General Expenses	2,56,020
Rates for the year ended 31.3.2011	2,800	Drawings	37,060
Rebate from Japan for the year ended 31.12.2012	9,800	Balance as on 31st December	2,41,800

(f) Depreciation of Motor Car and Furniture is to be provided @ 20% and 10%, respectively.

You are required to prepare Subhadeep's Trading and Profit and Loss Account for the year ended on 31st December 2013, and a Balance Sheet as on that date.

Solution

Trading and Profit & Loss Account *for the year ended 31st December 2013*

Dr. Particulars	Amount Rs.	Amount Rs.	Particulars	Amount Rs.	Amount Rs. *Cr.*
To Opening Stock		2,00,500	By Sales :		
" Purchases		9,16,000[1]	Cash	39,520	
" Profit and Loss A/c			Credit	16,70,980	
Gross Profit transferred		6,84,200			17,10,500[2]
			" Closing Stock		90,200
		18,00,700			18,00,700
To General Expenses	1,56,020		By Trading A/c		
Add : Sundry Expenses	1,040	1,57,060	Gross Profit		
" Salaries		1,02,460	transferred		6,84,200
" Rent	6,500		" Rebate on Purchases		12,480
Less : Paid for last year	1,000				
	5,500				
Add : Outstanding	500	6,000			
" Rates	2,800				
Add : Prepaid in last year	500				
	3,300				
Less : Prepaid ($\frac{1}{4}$th)	700	2,600			
" Car Expenses	3,680				
Add : Cost of Petrol	2,080				
		5,760			
" Carriage Outwards		23,400			
" H. P. Interest		250			
[Rs. 3,040 – 2,790]					
To Depreciation :					
On Car	1,300				
On Furniture	1,000	2,300			
" Capital A/c					
Net Profit transferred		3,96,850			
		6,96,680			6,96,680

Balance Sheet *as at 31st Dec. 2013*

Liabilities	Rs.	Rs.	Assets	Rs.	Rs.
Capital Account			Motor Car	6,500	
Balance on 1.1.2012	1,55,160		*Less* : Depreciation	1,300	
Add : Net Profit for the year	3,96,850				5,200
	5,52,010		Furniture	10,000	
Less : Drawings	50,060		*Less* : Depreciation	1,000	
		5,01,950			9,000
Supplier Account		13,020[3]	Stock-in-trade		90,200
(After adjustment of Rebate)			Sundry Debtors		1,67,900[4]
Outstanding Rent		500	Prepaid Rates		700
			Balance at Bank		2,41,800[6]
			Cash in hand		670[5]
		5,15,470			5,15,470

Workings :

1. Calculation of Purchases

Purchases Rs. 5,00,000 + (Rs. 12,480 × $\frac{100}{3}$) = Rs. 5,00,000 + Rs. 4,16,000 = Rs. 9,16,000

2. Calculation of Sales

		Rs.
	Cost of Goods Sold :	
	Opening Stock	2,00,500
Add :	Purchases	9,16,000
		11,16,500
Less :	Closing Stock	90,200
	Cost of Goods Sold	10,26,300
Add :	Gross Profit	
	(Rs. 10,26,300 × $\frac{40}{60}$)	6,84,200
	Total Sales	17,10,500

3. Total Creditors A/c

Dr.	Rs.		Cr. Rs.
To Bank	10,10,500	By Balance b/d	1,10,200
" Rebate (2013)	12,480	" Purchases	9,16,000
" Balance c/d *(bal. fig.)*	13,020	" Bank (Rebate—2012)	9,800
	10,36,000		10,36,000

4. Total Debtors A/c

Dr.	Rs.		Cr. Rs.
To Balance b/d	24,000	By Cash Received	15,27,080
" Sales [17,10,500 – 39,520 (760 × 52)]	16,70,980	" Bal. c/d *(bal. fig.)*	1,67,900
	16,94,980		16,94,980

5. Cash Account

Dr.	Rs.		Cr. Rs.
To Balance b/d	590	By Drawings	13,000
" Sales	39,520	" Carriage Outwards	23,400
" Total Debtors A/c *(bal. fig.)*	15,27,080	By Cash Expenses	2,080
		" Sundries	1,040
		" Bank	15,27,000
		" Balance c/d	670
	15,67,190		15,67,190

6. Bank Account

Dr.	Rs.		Cr. Rs.
To Bal.b/d	27,060	By Creditors	10,10,500
" Rebate	9,800	" Drawings	37,060
" Cash *(bal. fig.)*	15,27,000	" Car Exp.	3,680
		" Rent	6,500
		" Rates	2,800
		" H.P. Inst.	3,040
		" Salaries	1,02,460
		" General Exp.	1,56,020
		" Balance c/d	2,41,800
	15,63,860		15,63,860

Weekly Expenses Rs. 760 (i.e., Rs. 250 + Rs. 450 + Rs. 40 + Rs. 20) × 52 = Rs. 39,520.

ASSIGNMENT MATERIALS

THEORETICAL

Short-Answer Type Questions

1. What is Single Entry System?
2. Mention the features of Single Entry System.
3. Give at least fourpoints on the advantages of Single Entry System.
4. Mention the disadvantages of Single Entry System.
5. Distinguish between Single Entry System and Double Entry System (5 points).
6. What is Statement of Profit and Loss? How will you prepare it?
7. What is Statement of Affairs?
8. How will you convert Single Entry into Double Entry?
9. How isa partnership firm maintained under Single Entry system?
10. How do you ascertain capital under Single Entry System?

Long-Answer Type Questions

11. Distinguish between Statement of Affairs and Balance Sheet.
12. How will you convert Single Entry System into Double Entry System?
13. Discuss the merits and demerits of Single Entry System.
14. What is Single Entry? What are its salient features?
15. Distinguish between Single Entry System and Double Entry System.
16. What is Statement of Profit and Loss? How will you prepare it?
17. What is Statement of Affairs? How will you prepare it?
18. Is Single Entry System is dependable? Explain its shortcomings.
19. What is Single Entry System? How do you maintain accounts under Single Entry?
20. Mentions the advantages and disadvantages of Single Entry System.

PRACTICAL

Statement of Affairs Method

1. Rajen could not maintain proper books of accounts. The following balances are provided to you.

	31.12.1994	31.12.1995
	Rs.	Rs.
Cash in hand	10,800	15,800
Bank Overdraft	20,000	15,000
Stock-in-trade	22,000	27,000
Sundry Debtors	15,000	21,000
Sundry Creditors	9,000	6,000
Bills Receivable	7,000	9,000
Bills Payable	4,000	3,000
Furniture and Fittings	2,500	2,500
Land and Buildings	25,000	25,000

Drawings during the year were Rs. 18,000 in cash and Rs. 2,000 in goods. Depreciation is to be calculated on Land and Buildings @ 2% p. a. and on Furniture and Fittings at 10% p.a. Of the Debtors Rs. 500 is bad. Provision for Bad Debt is to be made at 5% and provision at $2\frac{1}{2}$ % on Bills Receivable is also to be made. You are asked to prepare : (i) a Statement of Profit or Loss for the year ended 31.12.1995; and (ii) a Statement of Affairs as at that date.

[Ans. Net Profit Rs. 44,500; Statement of Affairs Rs. 97,800]

2. Following is the Statement of Affairs of M/s T, B, and S as on 1.1.1992 :

Liabilities	Rs.	*Assets*	Rs.
Sundry Creditors	9,000	Cash	500
Bills Payable	3,200	Stock	9,700
Capital Accounts :		Sundry Debtors	18,000
T	18,000	Plant & Machinery	12,000
B	12,000	Capital Account :	
		S	2,000
	42,200		42,200

During 1992, T and B withdrew Rs. 600 and Rs. 500 per month, respectively. On 31.12.1992, their assets and liabilities were as follows : Cash Rs. 1,380; Stock Rs. 10,200; Sundry Debtors Rs. 11,600; Plant & Machinery Rs. 12,000; Sundry Creditors Rs. 6,000; Bills Payable Rs. 1,180. You are to prepare the Statement of Affairs as on 31.12.1992, after considering the following information :

(a) Depreciation is to be charged @ 5% on Plant & Machinery.

(b) Partners are entitled to interest on capital @ 5% and partner having debit balance in capital account is to pay interest @ 5% also.

(c) T, B, and S share profits and losses in the ratio of 5 : 3 : 2, respectively.

[Ans. Profit Rs. 11,200; Statement of Affairs Rs. 34,580]

3. X and Y are partners in a firm sharing profits and losses as X 60% and Y 40%. Their Statement of Affairs as at 31.3.1992 is :

Liabilities		Rs.	*Assets*	Rs.
Creditors		20,000	Plant	40,000
X's Loan A/c		20,000	Land & Building	20,000
Capital			Stock	30,000
X	50,000		Debtors	20,000
Y	30,000	80,000	Cash	10,000
		1,20,000		1,20,000

The partners keep their books by Single Entry System. On 31.3.1993, the position of the business was as follows : Plant Rs. 50,000; Land & Building Rs. 20,000; Stock Rs. 40,000; Debtors Rs. 25,000; Creditors Rs. 25,000; Cash Rs. 20,000. You are required to ascertain the amount of the firm's profit or loss for the year ended 31.3.1993 and a Statement of Affairs as on that date after taking the following into consideration :

(i) Depreciate Plant @ 10% p.a. including additions.

(ii) On 1.10.1993, X increased his loan by Rs. 10,000 in order to pay for additional machinery which was installed on the same day.

(iii) Interest on loan is to be allowed @ 6% p.a.

(iv) During the year X and Y drew Rs. 12,000 and Rs. 9,000, respectively.

(v) Provide interest on capital @ 5% p.a. and interest on drawings @ 10% p.a. (on an average for 6 months).

[Ans. Profit Rs. 32,450; Statement of Affairs Rs. 1,50,750]

Conversion Method

4. The following is a summary of the Bank Account of Sri Debashish Poddar, a trader, for the year 2010 :

Bank Summary

	Rs.		Rs.
Balance, 1st Jan. 2010	5,140	Payment to Trade Creditors	1,87,860
Cash Sales and Receipts on account of Credit Sales	2,43,720	General Expenses	16,970
Balance, 31st Dec. 2010	1,180	Rent and Rates	7,710
		Drawings	37,500
	2,50,040		2,50,040

All business takings had been paid into the bank except Rs. 21,180, out of which Poddar paid Wages amounting to Rs. 12,800. He retained Rs. 8,380 for private purpose.

The following information is obtained from the books :

	31.12.2010	31.12.2010
	Rs.	Rs.
Stock-in-trade	24,300	31,500
Creditors (goods)	19,450	17,090
Debtors (goods)	22,400	26,900
Amount owing to a customer who had overpaid his account	600	—
Rates paid in advance	420	450
Creditors for general expenses	810	1,340
Furniture and Fittings	10,000	10,000

Discount received from Trade Creditors during 1986 amounted to Rs. 1,500. No discounts were allowed to customers.

The amount due to the customers who overpaid his account was set-off against sales to him in 2009.

You are required :

(a) to ascertain the balance of Poddar's capital account as at 31 Dec. 2009, and

(b) to prepare a Trading and Profit and Loss Account for the year 2010 and a Balance Sheet as on 31st Dec. 2010. Ignore depreciation on Fixed Assets.

[Ans. Gross Profit Rs. 90,200; Net Profit Rs. 53,720; Balance Sheet Rs. 68,850]

5. Mr. Chambal keeps his books on Single Entry System.

You are required to prepare his Trading and Profit and Loss Account for the year ended 31st March 1982 from the following information and also to show the Balance Sheet as on that date :

(a) A scrutiny of various ledger accounts reveals the following :

	As on 1.4.2011	As on 31.3.2012
	Rs.	Rs.
Stock in hand	4,500	6,000
Sundry Debtors	24,000	27,000
Sundry Creditors	15,000	12,500
Furniture	6,000	8,000
Machinery	30,000	30,000
Bills Receivable	20,000	21,000
Bills Payable	16,500	14,500
Reserve for Bad and Doubtful Debts	1,200	1,350

(b) An analysis of the bank statements for the year ended 31st March 2012 is as follows :

Receipts	Rs.	*Payments*	Rs.
Sundry Debtors	68,000	Balance b/d (as on 1.4.2012)	6,000
Cash Sales	24,400	Sundry Creditors	40,000
Bills Receivable	7,800	Cash Purchases	16,000
(proceeds of a B/R for		Interest on Bank o/d	500
Rs. 8,000 on discounting)		Salaries	7,500
		Insurance	3,000
		General Charges	2,500
		Rent and Taxes	1,000
		Drawings	4,000
		Carriage Inward	2,500
		Freight and Duty	1,500
		Furniture	2,000
		Bills Payable	12,000
		Balance c/d	1,700
	1,00,200		1,00,200

(c) There was a bad debt of Rs. 400 which was written-off.

(d) He had allowed Rs. 450 as discount and earned Rs. 300 as discount.

(e) He also owed Rs. 1,500 for expenses.

(f) Depreciation has to be provided at 5% on Machinery and 10% on Furniture p.a. for full year.

(g) Interest on Capital is to be allowed at 5% p.a.

[Ans. Gross Profit Rs. 38,950; Net Profit Rs. 17,460; Balance Sheet Rs. 90,050]

6. P is a small trader. He maintains no books but only an account with a bank in which all takings are lodged after meeting business expenses and his personal drawings and in which all payments for business purchases were passed through.

You are required to ascertain his trading result for the year ended 31.3.1984 and Balance Sheet as on that date from the following information :

(1) The bank statement shows deposits during the year of Rs. 12,020 and withdrawals of Rs. 11,850.

(2) The Assets and Liabilities on 31.3.1984 were : Stock Rs. 1,100; Book Debts Rs. 1,150; Bank balance Rs. 320; Furniture Rs. 2,000; and Trade Creditors Rs. 400.

(3) In the absence of reliable information, estimates are supplied on the following matters :

(a) The Stock and Book Debts have each increased by Rs. 100 during the year. There was no purchase or sale of furniture during the year.

(b) The trade creditors were Rs. 200 on 1.4.1983.

(c) During the year personal expenses amounted to Rs. 800 and business expenses Rs. 700.

[Ans. Gross Profit Rs. 1,670; Net Profit Rs. 970; Balance Sheet Rs. 4,570]

7. F. William inherited a small retail business which was valued for probate at Rs. 862, made up of Rs. 430 for the Goodwill, Fixture & Fittings, Rs. 120 for the Stock-in-trade, and Rs. 312 balance at bank.

He decided to operate the business himself and began trading in a rented shop on April 1, 2012, having arranged for the balance at bank to be transferred to an account in his name.

He lived in two rooms over the shop. The only books which he kept was a notebook to record amounts owing by customers. Cash outgoing by the business and his personal drawings were paid from till, surplus cash being paid into the bank at regular intervals. All purchases of goods were paid for by cheque.

The following is an analysis of his bank account for the year ended 31.3.2013 :

Banked	Rs.	Cheques drawn	Rs.
Cheques from customers for credit sales	240	Suppliers for goods	2,060
Sales of personal savings certificates	100	Furniture	124
Other bankings	2,068	Rent (9 months 4.2012 to 31.12.2012)	90
		Fire Insurance (12 months to May 31, 2013)	24
		Heat and Light	47
		Cash Register	50
	2,408		2,395

On March 2013, Stock-in-trade valued at cost was Rs. 186; amounts owing by customers were Rs. 68 and owing to suppliers Rs. 130. There were also owing for Heat and Light Rs. 13 and bonus to his assistant Rs. 4. Disbursement from the till for the 52 weeks were estimated at per week : Shop expenses Rs. 2; Wages Rs. 4; and Personal Drawings Rs. 5. Cash in hand on March 31, 2013 was Rs. 6. Rent, Fire Insurance and Heat and Light were assumed to be 80% for the shop and 20% for the dwelling.

You are required : (a) to prepare an estimated Trading and Profit and Loss Account for the year ended 31.3.2013, and a Balance Sheet as on that date.

[Ans. Gross Profit Rs. 830; Net Profit Rs. 354; Balance Sheet Rs. 1,193]

8. Nanimadhab started a grocery business on 1st January, 20, with a capital of Rs. 10,000. He spent Rs. 1,500 on furniture and fixtures in cash. He maintains his books on single entry.

Following figures are extracted from his books :

	Rs.
Sales (inclusive of cash sales Rs. 8,000)	20,000
Purchases (Inclusive of cash purchases Rs. 2,500)	12,000
Bad Debts written-off	750
Business expenses	1,050

Nanimadhab used groceries worth Rs. 1,500 and took Rs. 13,000 in cash for personal use. On 31st December, 2000, his Sundry Debtors were Rs. 1,250 and Sundry Creditors Rs. 1,500. Stock in hand on 31st December 2000 was Rs. 1,500.

Prepare a Trading and Profit and Loss Account for the year ended on 31st December 2000 and a Balance Sheet as on that date after writing-off 10% depreciation on furniture and fixtures.

[CU BCom (Hons.)]

[Ans. Gross Profit Rs. 11,000; Net Profit Rs. 9,050; Balance Sheet Rs. 6,050]

9. X does not maintain proper books of account. From the following information, prepare Trading and Profit and Loss Account for the year ended December 31, 2006 and Balance Sheet as on that date:

Assets and Liabilities	On 31.12.2005 Rs.	On 31.12.2006 Rs.
Debtors	9,000	12,500
Stock	4,900	6,600
Furniture	500	750
Creditors	3,000	2,250
Analysis of other transactions:		
Cash collected from Debtors	30,400	
Cash paid to Creditors	22,000	
Salaries	6,000	
Rent	750	
Office Expenses	900	
Drawings	1,500	
Fresh Capital introduced	1,000	
Cash Sales	750	
Cash Purchases	2,500	
Discount Received	350	
Discount Allowed	150	
Return Inward	500	
Return Outward	400	
Bad Debts	100	

He had Rs. 2,500 cash at the beginning of the year.

[CU BCom (Hons.)

[Ans. Gross Profit Rs. 12,500; Net Profit Rs. 4,250; Balance Sheet Rs. 20,600]

10. A retail tradesman asks you to prepare accounts of his business for the year ended 31.12.2002 and, on investigation, you find that while records of business takings and payments have been kept, they have not been reconciled with cash in hand. From time to time, cash had been paid into banking account and cheques thereon have been drawn both for business and private purposes.

From the following information obtained from the records and from your client, prepare the Trading and Profit and Loss Account for the year ended 31.12.2002, and the Balance Sheet as at that date.

During the year cash amounting to Rs. 1,000 was stolen from the safe. No record had been kept of amounts taken from cash for personal expenses and a difference in cash amounting to Rs. 365 is treated as private expenses:

	Rs.
Cash paid into bank	7,500
Private dividends paid into bank	100
Private payments out of bank	1,300
Business payments out of bank	6,100
Cash takings (Sales)	12,500
Payments for goods by cash and cheque	8,000
Wages	2,000
Delivery expenses	350
Rent and Rates	100
Lighting	50
General Expenses	230

The assets and liabilities at the beginning and at the end of the period are :

	Opening Rs.	Closing Rs.
Stock	1,000	750
Bank balance	400	600
Cash in hand	15	20
Debtors	700	1,000
Creditors	1,365	1,500
Investments	2,500	2,500

[CU BCom Adv. (Hons.)]

[Ans. Gross Profit Rs. 3,365; Net Profit Rs. 1,685; Balance Sheet Rs.. 4,870]

11. The following is the Balance Sheet of Sri Raman as on 30.6.2001 :

Liabilities	Rs.	*Assets*	Rs.
Capital	96,000	Building	65,000
Creditors	62,000	Furniture	10,000
Loan	30,000	Motor Car	18,000
		Stock	40,000
		Debtors	34,000
		Cash in hand	4,000
		Cash at Bank	17,000
	1,88,000		1,88,000

A fire occurred in the evening of 30.6.2012 in the premises of the trader, destroying all books and records. The cashier had absconded with the available cash in the cash box. Sri Raman gives you the following information :

(a) His sales for the year were 20% higher than the previous year's. He sells his goods at cost plus 25%. 20% of the total sales were made for cash. There were no cash purchases.

(b) From 1.7.2011, stock level was raised to Rs. 60,000 and maintained at that level throughout the year.

(c) Collection from Debtors amounted to Rs. 2,80,000 of which Rs. 70,000 were received in cash. Business expenses amounted to Rs. 40,000 of which Rs. 10,000 was outstanding on 30.6.2012, and Rs. 12,000 was paid by cheque.

(d) Analysis of the Pass Book revealed the following :

	Rs.		Rs.
Payments to Creditors	2,75,000	Cash deposited into bank	1,43,000
Personal Drawings	15,000	Cash withdrawn from bank for office use	24,000

(e) Gross profit as per last year's audited accounts was Rs. 60,000.

(f) Provide depreciation on Building and Furniture at 5% and Motor Car at 20%.

(g) The amount defalcated by the cashier may be treated as recoverable from him.

Prepare a Trading Account, Profit and Loss Account for the year ended 30.6.2012 and a Balance Sheet as on that date.

[Ans. Gross Profit Rs. 72,000; Net Profit Rs. 24,650; Balance Sheet Rs. 2,40,650]

12. Sumana Mazumdar commenced business in a retail shop on July 1st 2012, in premises for which she paid a Rent of Rs. 200 p.m. The shop occupied the ground floor and she used the upper storey for residential purposes. It is agreed that one-third of all expenditure on Rent, Rates and Insurance is attributable to such residential portion.

The only records she kept apart from her bank statements were files of receipted suppliers' statements and unpaid invoices for goods purchased, together with a note book in which she recorded sales on credit to special customers who paid her by cheque. Cash received from cash sales was paid into the till out of which Sumana Mazumdar paid certain amounts, of which she kept a rough record and she made weekly bankings out of the balance in the till. She paid all suppliers for goods purchased by cheque.

An analysis of the bank statements for the six months ended December 31, 2012, was as follows :

	Rs.		Rs.
Capital	4,000	Shop Fixtures & Fitting	2,000
Loan (interest-free)	2,000	Household Furniture	1,800
Suppliers cheque for goods returned	280	Suppliers for goods purchased	9,840
Special Customers	300	Rent	1,000
Deposits of other collections	11,930	Rates	300
		Heat and Light	180
		Insurance	200
		Closing balance	3,190
	18,510		18,510

Sumana Mazumdar estimates that the total amounts paid out of the till before making the weekly bankings for the six months were :

Drawings Rs. 2,000; Salaries and Wages Rs. 1,400; and Sundry Shop expenses Rs. 800.

It is also ascertained that as on December 31, 2012 :

(a) Stocks, correctly taken at cost, were : Goods Rs. 1,720; Fuel Rs. 120.

(b) The balance in the till was Rs. 260, including a post-dated cheque for Rs. 150 cashed for a customer.

(c) The Cash paid to the Bank included Rs. 300 from a sale of surplus shop fittings.

(d) The insurance premium covered the year to June 30th 1993, and the Rates for the period of nine months to March 31, 2013.

(e) Suppliers' unpaid invoices amounted to Rs. 2,240 and there was Rs. 80 owing for Light.

You are required to prepare Sumana Mazumdar's Balance Sheet as on 31.12.2012, and the Trading and Profit and Loss Account for the half-year ended as on that date.

[Ans. Gross Profit Rs. 6,170; Net Profit Rs. 2,970; Balance Sheet Rs. 7,190]

13. Sadhan Paul, a trader, has not kept a full set of books. The following is a summary of his bank statement for the year 2013 :

	Rs.		Rs.
Amount credited by Bank	1,21,950	Balance, Dec. 31, 2012	1,350
		Trade Creditors	1,06,400
		Rent and Taxes	2,800
		Drawings	3,650
		General Expenses	5,250
		Customer Cheques dishonoured	1,800
		Balance Dec. 31, 2013	700
	1,21,950		1,21,950

You ascertain the following information :

(i) All the dishonoured cheques were re-presented and all were honoured during the year, with the exception of a cheque for Rs. 110, received from Subhadeep Sarkar, which was again dishonoured and was, therefore, included twice in the amount of Rs. 1,800. The debt from Subhadeep Sarkar is to be regarded as irrecoverable.

(ii) Cheques drawn in favour of Trade Creditors, but not presented, were Rs. 1,400 on Dec. 31, 2012 and Rs. 2,250 on Dec. 31, 2013. All these cheques were presented in due course.

(iii) Trading receipts consisted partly of Cheques, and partly of Cash. Out of the Cash takings in 2013, Sadhan Paul paid Wages Rs. 11,450, retained Rs. 14,300 for private expenses, and, for the convenience of certain friends, cashed their Cheques amounting to Rs. 3,100. These cheques and all trading receipts, not applied as above, were paid into Bank.

(iv) Discount received from Trade Creditors in 2013 were Rs. 3,000.

(v) Stocks were valued at Rs. 12,000 on Dec. 31, 1992, and at Rs. 14,500 on Dec. 31, 2013. Trade Debtors and Trade Creditors were Rs. 4,800 and Rs. 10,600, respectively, on Dec. 31, 2012 and Rs. 5,100 (excluding Subhadeep Sarkar's Rs. 110) and Rs. 9,700, respectively, on Dec. 31, 2013. Accrued Expenses amounted to Rs. 360 on Dec. 31, 2012 and to Rs. 480 a year later.

You are required to prepare :

(a) a revised summary of Sadhan Paul's Bank Account for the year 2013.

(b) the Trading and Profit and Loss Account for the year 2013, and
(c) the Balance Sheet as on Dec. 31, 2013. Ignore depreciation of Fixed Assets and taxation.

[Ans. Gross Profit Rs. 29,700; Net Profit Rs. 24,420; Balance Sheet Rs. 19,740]

14. The following is the Balance Sheet of the retail business of Mr. Padamsi as on 31st December 1005 :

Liabilities	Rs.	*Assets*	Rs.
Mr. Padamsi's Capital	1,25,000	Furniture and Fixture	25,000
Creditors for goods	30,000	Stock	75,000
Outstanding Expenses (Rent)	1,000	Sundry Debtors	20,000
		Cash at Bank	35,000
		Cash in hand	1,000
	1,56,000		1,56,000

You are furnished with the following information :

1. Mr. Padamsi always sells his goods at a profit of 25% on sales.
2. Goods are sold for cash and credit. Credit customers pay by cheque only.
3. Payments for purchase are always made by cheque.
4. It is Mr. Padamsi's practice to bank his taking at the end of every week after paying the weekly expenses., viz. Salaries to clerks Rs. 250, Sundry Expenses Rs. 50 and Personal expenses Rs. 100.

Analysis of the bank pass book for the period ended 31.3.2006 disclose the following :

	Rs.
Payments to Creditors	75,000
Payment of Rent	4,000

Amount remitted to the bank Rs. 1,35,000 (including cheques for Rs. 10,000 received from customers to whom the goods were sold on credit).

The following are the balances as on 31.3.1996 :

	Rs.
Stock	32,500
Creditors for Goods	32,500
Sundry Debtors	30,000

In the evening of 31.5.2006, the cashier absconded with the available cash in the Cash Book.

You are required to prepare a statement showing the amount of cash defalcated by the cashier and also a Profit and Loss Account for the year ended 31st March 2006 and a Balance Sheet as on that date.

[Cash Sales Rs. 1,40,000; Gross Profit Rs. 40,000; Net Profit Rs. 22,300; Balance Sheet Rs. 1,78,500; Cash defalcated Rs. 10,800]

15. You are required to prepare Trading and Profit and Loss Account for the year ended 31.12.2005 and the Balance Sheet as at that date in respect of Mr. A's business from the following information:

(a) The Assets and Liabilities as on 31.12.2005 were:

	As on 31.12.2004 Rs.	As on 31.12.2005 Rs.
Bank Balance	Not available	20,000
Sundry Debtors	15,000	16,000
Sundry Creditors	5,000	8,000
Stock-in-trade	15,000	20,000
Fixed Assets	30,000	30,000

(b) Sundry Debtors as on 31.12.2005 include Bad Debts of Rs. 1,000.
(c) Fixed assets include property rented out for which Rent of Rs. 500 was received for the year and utilised for personal use.
(d) Repairs to premises amount of Rs. 600 which remained unpaid as on 31.12.2005.
(e) All sales receipts were banked after meeting business expenses of Rs. 5,000 and personal expenses of Rs. 3,000.
(f) All business payments were made by cheques.
(g) Cash purchases and cash sales amounted to Rs. 1,000 and Rs. 2,000, respectively.
(h) His account with bankers reveals that withdrawals amounted to Rs. 70,000 an deposits Rs. 90,000 for the years.

[Ans. Gross Profit Rs. 31,000; Net Profit Rs. 24,900; Balance Sheet Rs. 85,000]

CHAPTER 26

SELF BALANCING SYSTEM AND SECTIONAL BALANCING SYSTEM

Learning Objectives

Introduction and Meaning

Preparation of Trial Balance

Entries for Sales/Debtors Ledger

Entries for Purchasers/Creditors Ledger

Advantages of Self-Balancing System

Contra Transactions

Preparation of Debtors Ledger Adjustment Account

Preparation of Creditors Ledger Adjustment Account

Transfer Entries

Preparation of Debtors and Creditors Ledger Adjustment Account

Preparation of Two Debtors Ledger

Sectional Balancing System

Contra Transactions

Rectification of Errors

Introduction

A self-balancing ledger is one whose balances, when extracted, form a complete trial balance. In other words, each ledger is self-balancing. Under this system, each ledger is maintained under double entry principle, i.e., the principle of double entry is completed within the ledger itself. Naturally, the ledger which contains a double entry is also provided with a corresponding credit entry, and vice versa. This is done with the help of an account, viz., General Ledger Adjustment Account (to be maintained in Debtors and Creditors Ledgers), and also two other accounts, viz., Debtors/Sales Ledger Adjustment Account and Creditors/Purchases Ledger Adjustment Account (to be maintained in General Ledger). Thus, these aforesaid three accounts are to be maintained under self-balancing system. Therefore, the three ledgers have the following accounts :

(1) *Sales/Debtors Sold Ledger deals with :* (i) *accounts relating to trade debtors; and* (ii) *General Ledger Adjustment Account.*

(2) *Purchases/Creditors Bought Ledger deals with :* (i) *accounts relating to trade creditors; and* (ii) *General Ledger Adjustment Account.*

(3) *General/Nominal Ledger deals with :* *accounts relating to nominal, real and personal (other than trade debtors and trade creditors stated above); Debtors Ledger Adjustment Account and Creditors Ledger Adjustment Account.*

Preparation of Trial Balance

Under **Self-Balancing System** a trial balance can be prepared by taking the balance from the above three ledgers. If a trial balance is prepared from a single ledger that will not be balanced. In other words, a trial balance may be prepared simply by taking the balance from Debtors Ledger (i.e., only the debtors' balance) and no credit balance correspondingly, or, by simply taking the credit balances from Creditors Ledger (i.e., only the creditor's balances), it becomes very difficult to detect the errors, if any, if not the trial balance agrees automatically. It has been stated above that the system by which each ledger is automatically balanced is known as Self-Balancing Ledger. Under this system the scrutiny of ledger which does not balance is practically limited. To make the ledger balance, we know, a separate account is opened for such discrepancy under this system which is known as the Adjustment Account.

Entries for Sales/Debtors Ledger

Under self-balancing system, two types of entries are to be passed, one is usual double entry and the other self-balancing entry. As soon as the transaction takes place, the usual double entry is to be passed by debiting one account and crediting the other, i.e., one account relates to Debtors Ledger and the other relates to General Ledger. But the self-balancing entries are made for the adjustment account. For this purpose, the entries are made with the periodical totals of Sales Day Book, Returns Inward Book, Bills Receivable Book together with journal and sales ledger column of the cash book. For example, when goods are sold on credit, the usual entry is :

Individual Customer A/c Dr.
  To Sales A/c

But, under self-balancing system, the entry will be :

Debtors Ledger Adjustment A/c (in General Ledger) Dr.
  To General Ledger Adjustment A/c (in Debtors Ledger)

Thus, accounts relating to debtors will be passed through the Debtors Ledger Adjustment Account and all other corresponding items are passed through General Ledger, i.e., if Debtors Ledger Adjustment Account is debited General Ledger Adjustment Account is to be credited, and vice versa.

The following statement will make the principle clear :

Entries for the transactions relating to Trade Debtors

Transactions	*Usual Entry*	*Self-Balancing Entry*
1. For Credit Sales	Individual Customers A/c Dr. (in Debtors Ledger) To Sales A/c (in General Ledger)	Debtors Ledger Adjustment A/c Dr. (in General Ledger) To General Adjustment A/c (in Debtors Ledger)
2. For Cash/Cheques received from customers	Cash A/c Dr. (in General Ledger) To Individual Customers A/c (in Debtors Ledger)	General Ledger Adjustment A/c Dr. (in Debtors Ledger) To Debtors Ledger Adjustment A/c (in General Ledger)

Transactions	Usual Entry	Self-Balancing Entry
3. For Discount Allowed or allowances to customers	Discount Allowed A/c Dr. or, Allowances A/c Dr. (in General Ledger) To Individual Customers A/c (in Debtors Ledger)	Do
4. For Bad Debts	Bad Debts A/c Dr. (in General Ledger) To Individual Customers A/c (in Debtors Ledger)	Do
5. For Bills Receivable received from customers	Bills Receivable A/c Dr. (in General Ledger) To Individual Customers A/c (in Debtors Ledger)	Do
6. For Returns Inward	Returns Inward A/c Dr. (in General Ledger) To Individual Customers A/c (in Debtors Ledger)	Do
7. For Bills/Cheques Received/Dishonored	Individual Customers A/c Dr. (in Debtors Ledger) To Bills Receivable/Bank A/c (in General Ledger)	Debtors Ledger Adjustment A/c Dr. (in General Ledger) To General Ledger Adjustment A/c (in Debtors Ledger)
8. For interest on Customer's overdue account or cost of carriage charged to Customers	Individual Customers A/c Dr. (in Debtors Ledger) To Interest/Charges A/c (in General Ledger)	Do

In General Ledger

Debtors Ledger Adjustment Account

Dr. Cr.

Date		Particulars	Amount	Date		Particulars	Amount
2012			Rs.	2010			Rs.
Jan. 1	To	Balance b/d		Jan. 1	By	Balance b/d *(if any)*	
	"	General Ledger Adjustment A/c :			"	General Ledger	* *
		Credit Sales	* *			Adjustment A/c :	
Dec. 31	"	Carriage and Sundry Charges			"	Cash/Cheques received	* *
		debited to customer—			"	Bad Debts	* *
	"	Bills Receivable Dishonoured	* *		"	Returns Inward	* *
	"	Cheque Received and Dishonored	* *		"	Discount Allowed	* *
	"	Interest and Charges etc.	* *		"	Other Allowances	* *
	"	Refund-Cash paid to customers	* *		"	Bills Receivable	* *
	"	B/R discounted and dishonoured	* *		"	Transfer to or from	
	"	B/R endorsed and dishonoured	* *			other Ledgers	* *
		Interest charged to overdue account			"	Balance c/d	* *
	"	Balance c/d *(if any)*	* *				
			* *				* *

In the Debtors Ledger

General Ledger Adjustment Account

Dr. Cr.

Date		Particulars	Amount	Date		Particulars	Amount
2012			Rs.	2012			Rs.
Jan. 1	To	Balance b/d (if any)	***	Jan. 1	By	Balance b/d	***
	"	Debtors/Sold Ledger			"	Debtors/Sold Ledger	
		Adjustment A/c	***			Adjustment A/c—	

Contd.

2012		Rs.	2012		Rs.
	To —Cost and Cheque Received	***		By Debtors/Sold Ledger Adjustment A/c—	
	—Bad Debts	***		" Carrying and Sundry Charges	***
	—Returns Inward	***		" Bills Receivable Dishonoured	***
	—Discount Allowed	***		" Cheque Rec. and Dishonoured	***
	—Other Allowances	***		" Interest and Charges	***
	—Bills Receivable	***		" Refund-cash paid to Customers	***
	—Transfer to or from other Ledger	***		" B/R Discounted and Dishonoured	
	" Balance C/d	***		" B/R endorsed and Dishonoured	***
				" Interest Charges on Overdue A/c	
				" Balance c/d (if any)	***
		***			***

***Note :** One particular point is to be noted, i.e., self-balancing entries will only be made for those transactions which affect two ledgers. Naturally, if a transaction occurs which affects the same ledger (in both sides), say, general ledger, no entry is to be required. For example, Cash Sales, which actually affect two sides of general ledger, is not to be recorded. For the same reason, Provision/Reserve for bad debts, Recovery of bad debts. Trade Discount, Bills Receivable discounted or matured etc. will not appear at all.*

Entries for Purchases/Creditors Ledger

The same principle is, however, applied in the case of Creditors Ledger, i.e., the usual double entry function is to be maintained. In short, two types of entries—one relates to Creditors Ledger and the other relates to general ledger—are to be passed. Similarly, self-balancing entries are made for adjustment accounts. The entries are made with the periodical totals of Purchase Day Book, Returns Outward Book, Bills Payable Book and Journal together with purchase ledger column of Cash Book.

For example, when goods are purchased on credit, the usual entry is :

Purchase A/c Dr.
To Suppliers A/c

But, under self-balancing system, the entry will be :

General Ledger Adjustment A/c
(in Creditors Ledger)
To Creditors Ledger Adjustment A/c
(in General Ledger)

The following statement will make the principle clear :

Entries for the transactions relating to Trade Creditors

Transactions	*Usual Entry*	*Self-Balancing Entry*
1. For Credit Purchases	Purchase A/c Dr. (in General Ledger) To Creditors A/c (in Creditors Ledger)	General Ledger Adjustment A/c Dr. (in Creditors Ledger) To Creditors Ledger Adjustment A/c (in General Ledger)
2. For Cash Paid to Creditors	Creditors A/c Dr. (in Creditors Ledger) To Cash A/c (in General Ledger)	Creditors Ledger Adjustment A/c Dr. (in General Ledger) To General Ledger Adjustment A/c (in Creditors Ledger)
3. For Discount Received from Creditors	Creditors A/c Dr. (in Creditors Ledger) To Discount Received A/c (in General Ledger)	Do

Contd.

Transactions	*Usual Entry*	*Self-Balancing Entry*
4. For Bills Accepted in favour of Creditors	Creditors A/c Dr. (in Creditors Ledger) To Bills Payable A/c (in General Ledger)	Do
5. For Purchases Return	Creditors A/c Dr. (in Creditors Ledger) To Returns Outward A/c (in General Ledger)	Do
6. For Bills Payable Dishonoured	Bills Payable A/c Dr. (in General Ledger) To Creditors A/c (in Creditors Ledger)	General Ledger Adjustment A/c Dr. (in Creditors Ledger) To Creditors Ledger Adjustment A/c (in General Ledger)
7. For Interest and Charges charged by Creditors	Interest/Charges A/c Dr. (in General Ledger) To Creditors A/c (in Creditors Ledger)	Do

In General Ledger

Creditors Ledger Adjustment Account

Dr. *Cr.*

Date		*Particulars*	*Rs.*	*Date*		*Particulars*	*Rs.*
2012 Jan. 1	To	Balance b/d (*if any*)	* *	2012 Jan. 1	By	Balance b/d	* *
	"	General Ledger Adjustment Account :			"	General Ledger Adjustment Account :	
Dec. 31		Cash Paid	* *	Dec. 31		Credit Purchases	* *
		Bills Payable Accepted	* *			Bills Payable Dishonoured	* *
		Discount Received	* *			Interest and Charges	* *
		Returns Outward	* *		"	Balance c/d (*if any*)	* *
	"	Balance c/d	* *				
			* *				* *

In the Creditors Ledger

General Ledger Adjustment Account

Dr. *Cr.*

Date		*Particulars*	*Amount*	*Date*		*Particulars*	*Amount*
2012			Rs.	2012			Rs.
Jan. 1	To	Balance b/d	***	Jan. 1	By	Balance b/d (if any)	***
Dec. 31	"	Creditors/Bought Ledger Adjustment A/c		Dec. 31	"	Creditors/Bought Ledger Adjustment A/c—	
		—Credit Purchase	***		"	Cash paid	***
		—Bills Payable Dishonoured	***			Bills Payable Accepted	***
		—Interest and Charges	***		"	Discount Received	***
	"	Balance c/d (if any)	***		"	Returns Outward	***
					"	Balance c/d	***
			***				***

Note : Accounts relating to Creditors will be passed through the Creditors Ledger Adjustment Account and all other corresponding items are passed through General Ledger Adjustment Accounts, i.e., if Creditors Ledger Adjustment Account is credited, General Ledger Adjustment Account is to be debited, and vice versa.

Besides, another point which is to be noted is that no adjustment entry is required for the transactions which do not affect the two ledgers, viz., General Ledger and Creditors Ledger, e.g., Cash Purchase. For the same reasons, Provision for Discount on Creditors, Bills Payable matured etc. will not appear under this system.

Advantages of Self-Balancing System

(a) Errors can be detected and localised quickly and only the connected ledger can be checked without checking the other ledgers. Thus, it saves time, money and labour and, therefore, delay in balancing is minimised.

(b) This system is, perhaps, the best one for detecting frauds and errors relating to accounts committed by the clerks. In addition, if the trial balance does not agree for a particular ledger, the clerk who has prepared that ledger will be responsible. As a result, this system distinguishes efficient employees from inefficient ones.

(c) A complete trial balance can be compiled by taking the debtors and creditors balances or by taking the general ledger balances which facilitate the preparation of both the interim accounts and the final accounts without abstracting the individual personal ledger balances.

(d) Since this system provides sub-division of work among the different employees, work can be done quickly.

(e) A private ledger may be prepared in order to keep the confidential information relating to the proprietor's capital, reserves, profit etc., which is kept by the proprietor or by his trustworthy person and the balances of such ledgers are incorporated in the trial balance.

(f) By taking the balances from Debtors Ledger Adjustment Account and Creditors Ledger Adjustment Account recorded at the end of the general ledger, management may be informed about the amounts owing to or by the business and the necessary decision can be taken for the purpose.

(a) Preparation of Debtors/Sales Ledger Adjustment Account

Illustration 1

From the following particulars, prepare the Debtors Ledger Adjustment Account as it would appear in the General Ledger and General Ledger Adjustment Account as it would appear in the Debtors Ledger, for the year ended 31.12.2012 and show also the adjusting journal entries :

Jan. 1, 2012	Rs.	Dec. 31, 2012	Rs.
Balance of Debtors	10,000	Discount Allowed	6,000
Dec. 31st Credit Sales	1,50,000	Bills Receivable received	9,000
Cash Received from Debtors	65,000	Bills Receivable dishonoured	1,000
Bad Debts written-off	1,000	Allowances to customers	2,000
Returns Inward	2,000	Int. charged on dishonoured bills	500
		Int. on customers' overdue account	1,000

Solution

In the books of ....

Total Debtors Account

Dr. *Cr.*

Date	Particulars	Amount	Date	Particulars	Amount
2012 Jan. 1	To Balance b/d	10,000	2012 Dec. 31	By Cash	65,000
	" Sales	1,50,000		" Bad Debts	1,000
Dec. 31	" Bills Dischonoured	1,000		" Returns Inward	2,000
	" Interest charged	500		" Discount Allowed	6,000
	" Interest on customers' overdue account	1,000		" Bills Receivable	9,000
				" Allowances	2,000
				" Balance c/d	77,500
		1,62,500			1,62,500
2013 Jan. 1	To Balance b/d	77,500			

In the books of ....

Journal

Date	Particulars		L.F.	Debit	Credit
2012				Rs.	Rs.
Dec. 31.	Debtors Ledger Adjustment A/c (In General Ledger)	Dr.		1,52,500	
	To General Ledger Adjustment A/c (In Debtors Ledger)				1,52,500
	Various items debited to debtors during the month as :				
	Credit Sales	1,50,000			
	Bills Dishonoured	1,000			
	Interest charged	500			
	Interest on Customer's Overdue A/c	1,000			
		1,52,500			

Contd.

		Rs.	Rs.
General Ledger Adjustment A/c (in Debtors Ledger) Dr.		85,000	
To Debtors Ledger Adjustment A/c (In General Ledger)			85,000
Various items credited to Debtors during the month as :			
Cash	65,000		
Bad Debts	1,000		
Returns Inward	2,000		
Discount Allowed	6,000		
Bills Receivable	9,000		
Allowances	2,000		
	85,000		

In the General Ledger

Debtors Ledger Adjustment Account

Dr. Cr.

Date	Particulars	Amount	Date	Particulars	Amount
2012		Rs.	2012		Rs.
Jan. 1	To Balance b/d		Dec. 31	By General Ledger Adjustment A/c :	
Dec. 31	" General Ledger Adjustment A/c :	10,000		Cash	65,000
	Credit Sales	1,50,000		Bad Debts	1,000
	Bills Dishonoured	1,000		Returns Inward	2,000
	Interest charged	500		Discount Allowed	6,000
	Interest on customers' overdue account	1,000		Bills Receivable	9,000
				Allowances	2,000
				" Balance c/d	77,500
		1,62,500			1,62,500
2013					
Jan. 1	To Balance b/d	77,500			

In the Debtors Ledger

General Ledger Adjustment Account

Dr. Cr.

Date	Particulars	Amount	Date	Particulars	Amount
2012		Rs.	2012		Rs.
Jan. 1	To Debtors Ledger Adjustment A/c:		Jan. 1	By Balance b/d	10,000
	Cash	65,000	Dec. 31	" Debtors ledger Adjustment A/c:	
	Bad Debts	1,000		Credit Sales	1,50,000
	Returns Inward	2,000		Bills Dishonoured	1,000
	Discount Allowed	6,000		Interest Charged	500
	Bills Receivable	9,000		Interest on customers' overdue account	1,000
	Allowances	2,000			
	Balance c/d	77,500			
		1,62,500			1,62,500
2012			2012		
Jan. 1			Jan. 1	By Balance b/d	77,500

Where Individual debtors ledger is maintained

Illustration 2

Samaresh keeps his ledger on self-balancing system. From the following particulars, you are required to write up the individual Debtors' Account and the General Ledger Adjustment Account (in Sales ledger during the month of January 2012) :

(i) Individual Debtor's balances on 1.1.2012 :

A Rs. 1,530; B Rs. 1,620; C Rs. 1;890 and D Rs. 1,170.

(ii) Transactions during the month :

Jan. 2. Sold goods to A Rs. 1,710;
9. Received from B on account Rs. 300;
11. Received from A Rs. 1,500 in full settlement of his balance on 1.1.20...
12. Sold goods to B Rs. 600;
14. B returned goods which were damaged in-transit amounting to Rs. 180;
18. Received from C Rs. 1,800 and allowed him discount Rs. 90;
19. Received from A, a bill of exchange for Rs. 1,200 accepted by X payable on 25th Jan.;
22. Received from B Rs. 900;
25. A's bill returned dishonoured;
28. D became insolvent and 30 paise in the rupee was received from his estate in full and final settlement;
30. Sold goods to C Rs. 1,020.

[ICWA]

Solution

In the books of Samaresh
In Sales Ledger
General Ledger Adjustment Account

Dr. *Cr.*

Date		Particulars	Amount	Date		Particulars	Amount
2012			Rs.	2012			Rs.
Jan. 31	To	Sales Ledger Adj. A/c		Jan. 1	By	Balance b/d	6,210[1]
		Cash	4,851[3]	Jan. 31	"	Sales Ledger Adj. A/c—	
		Dis. Allowed	120[4]			Sales	3,330[2]
		Returns Inward	180[5]			B/R Dishonoured	1,200[7]
		B/R	1,200[7]				
		Bad Debts	819[6]				
	"	Balance c/d	3,570[8]				
			10,740				10,740
				Feb. 1	By	Balance b/d	3,570

A Account

Dr. *Cr.*

Date		Particulars	Amount	Date		Particulars	Amount
2012			Rs.	2012			Rs.
Jan. 1	To	Balance b/d	1,530	Jan. 11	By	Cash	1,500
" 2	"	Sales	1,710	" "	"	Dis. Allowed	30
" 25	"	B/R Dishonoured	1,200	" 19	"	B/R	1,200
				" 31	"	Balance c/d	1,710
			4,440				4,440

B Account

Dr. *Cr.*

Date		Particulars	Amount	Date		Particulars	Amount
2012			Rs.	2012			Rs.
Jan. 1	To	Balance b/d	1,620	Jan. 9	By	Balance b/d	300
" 12	"	Sales	600	" 14	"	Returns Inward	180
				" 22	"	Cash	900
				" 31	"	Balance c/d	840
			2,220				2,220

C Account

Dr. *Cr.*

Date		Particulars	Amount	Date		Particulars	Amount
2012			Rs.	2012			Rs.
Jan. 1	To	Balance b/d	1,890	Jan. 18	By	Cash	1,800
" 31	"	Sales	1,020	" "	"	Dis. Allowed	90
				" 31	"	Balance c/d	1,020
			2,910				2,910

Dr. **D Account** Cr.

Date	Particulars	Amount	Date	Particulars	Amount
2012		Rs.	2012		Rs.
Jan. 1	To Balance b/d	1,170	Jan. 28	By Cash	351
			"	Bad Debts	819
		1,170			1,170

Trial Balance
as at 31st Jan. 2012

Dr. Heads of Accounts	Dr.	Cr.
	Rs.	Rs.
A. Account	1,710	
B Account	840	
C. Account	1.020	
General Ledger Adjustment Account		3,570
	3,570	3,570

Workings :

(1) Total Debtor's balance as on 1.1.2012 = A + B + C + D = Rs. 1,530 + 1,620 + 1,890 + 1,170 = Rs. 6,210

(2) Total Sales = A + B + C = Rs. 1,710 + 600 + 1,020 = Rs. 3,330

(3) Total Cash Received = A + B + C + D = Rs. 300 + 1,500 + 1,800 + 900 + 351 = Rs. 4,851

(4) Total Discount Allowed = A + C = Rs. 30 + 90 = Rs. 120

(5) Returns Inward = B Rs. 180

(6) Bad Debts = D Rs. 819

(7) B/R Dishonoured = A Rs. 1,200

(h) Total Debtor's balance as on 31st Jan. 2012 = A + B + C = Rs. 1,710 + 840 + 1,020 = Rs. 3,570.

Contra Transactions/Adverse Balance

We all know that Debtors Ledger shows a debit balance and Creditors Ledger shows a credit balance. But sometimes it may so happen that the respective ledger show the opposite balances, i.e., Debtors Ledger shows a credit balance and Creditors Ledger shows a debit balance. Credit balance in Debtors Ledger may appear due to advance taken from Customer, Allowance made to Customer for defective articles after settlement etc. Whereas debit balance in Creditors Ledger may appear due to excess payment made to creditors, goods returned to creditors after settlement of accounts etc. Naturally, these contra balances—although they are small in amounts—are to be adjusted in adjustment accounts. It is to be remembered in this respect that ***debit balance in one ledger must not be set-off against the credit balance of another ledger.***

Illustration 3

From the following information prepare (1) Debtors Ledger Adjustment Account in the General Ledger, and (2) General Ledger Adjustment Account in the Debtors Ledger :

	Rs.			Rs.
Opening balance of Sundry Debtors	40,000	(Dr.)	Bad Debts	3,000
	2,000	(Cr.)	Bills Receivable Received	20,000
Cash and cheques receipts	1,60,000		Bills Receivable Discounted	2,000
Credit sales as per Sales Day Book	2,00,000		Provision for Bad Debts	2,000
Discount Allowed	6,000		Closing credit balance of Sundry Debtors	6,000
Returns Inward	4,000		Trans. from Debtors Ledger to Creditors Ledger	1,000
			Trans. from Creditors Ledger to Debtors Ledger	1,200

[ICWA]

Solution

In the General Ledger

Debtors Ledger Adjustment Account

Dr. *Cr.*

Date	Particulars	Amount	Date	Particulars	Amount
?		Rs.	?		Rs.
	To Balance b/d	40,000		By Balance b/d	2,000
	" General Ledger Adjustment A/c :			" General Ledger Adjustment A/c :	
	Credit Sales	2,00,000		Cash and Cheques	1,60,000
	" Balance c/d	6,000		Returns Inward	4,000
				Discount Allowed	6,000
				Bad Debts	3,000
				Bills Receivable	20,000
				Transfer to Cr. Ledger	1,000
				Transfer from Creditors to Debtors Ledger	1,200
				" Balance c/d	48,800
		2,46,000			2,46,000
?	To Balance b/d	48,800	?	By Balance b/d	6,000

In the Debtors Ledger

General Ledger Adjustment Account

Dr. *Cr.*

Date	Particulars	Amount	Date	Particulars	Amount
?		Rs.	?		Rs.
	To Balance b/d	2,000		By Balance b/d	40,000
	" Debtors Ledger Adjustment A/c :			" Debtors Ledger Adjustment A/c :	
	Cash and Cheques	1,60,000		Credit Sales	2,00,000
	Returns Inward	4,000		" Balance c/d	6,000
	Discount Allowed	6,000			
	Bad Debts	3,000			
	Bills Receivable	20,000			
	Transfer to Creditors Ledger	1,000			
	Transfer form Creditors to Debtors Ledger	1,200			
	" Balance c/d	48,800			
		2,46,000			2,46,000
?	To Balance b/d	6,000	?	By Balance b/d	48,800

Illustration 4

Write-up the Sales Ledger Adjustment Account as it would appear in the General Ledger from the following particulars :

		Rs.		Rs.
Opening balance of Debtors	(Dr.)	25,200	Bad Debts previously written-off now recovered	600
Do	(Cr.)	800	Allowances	840
Sales		62,400	Bills Receivable	2,600
Returns		6,340	Bills Dishonoured	1,000
Cash Received		40,100	Trade Discount	300
Discount Allowed		2,600	Transfer from Bought Ledger	2,400
Bad Debts written-off		7,420	Closing balances of Debtors (Dr.)	27,980
Reserve for Bad Debts		11,000	Do (Cr.)	2,480

[CU BCom (Hons.)]

Solution

In the General Ledger
Sales Ledger Adjustment Account

Dr. *Cr.*

Date		*Particulars*	*Amount*	*Date*		*Particulars*	*Amount*
?			Rs.	?			Rs.
	To	Balance b/d	25,200		By	Balance b/d	800
	"	General Ledger Adjustment A/c :			"	General Ledger Adjustment A/c :	
		Sales	62,400			Returns	6,340
		Bills Dishonoured	1,000			Discount Allowed	2,600
	"	Balance c/d	2,480			Cash	40,100
						Bad Debts	7,420
						Allowances	840
						Bills Receivable	2,600
						Transfer	2,400
					By	Balance c/d	27,980
			91,080				91,080
	To	Balanced b/d	27,980		By	Balance b/d	2,480

Notes : 1. Trade discount is not to be considered on the assumption that net sales figure is given.
2. Reserve for Bad Debts and Bad Debts previously written-off now recovered are excluded since these are not connected with Debtors.
4. Since both the opening and closing balances are given, Sales Ledger Adjustment Account is closed automatically.

Preparation of Debtors Ledger Adjustment Account having a continuous Credit balance

Illustration 5

Mr. Pallab Pynne deals in readymade garments. He sells his goods at 25% less than the catalogue price. He furnished details of his transactions for the consecutive three months to be started from April 2012. You are asked to prepare Debtors Ledger Adjustment Account for the months of April, May and June, 2012.

		April	May	June
		Rs.	Rs.	Rs.
Debtors Balance (on 1.4.2011)	Dr.	1,00,000		
	Cr.	3,000		
Credit Sales at catalogue Price		10,00,000	12,00,000	16,00,000
Discount Allowed		20,000	25,000	40,000
Cash Received from Customers		6,00,000	8,00,000	12,00,000
Returns Inwards at catalogue Price		20,000	40,000	60,000
Credit balance at the end of the month		1,000	4,000	3,000

Solution

In the General Ledger
Debtors Ledger Adjustment Account

Dr. *Cr.*

Date		*Particulars*	*Amount*	*Date*		*Particulars*	*Amount*
2012			Rs.	2012			Rs.
April 1	To	Balance b/d	1,00,000	April 1	By	Balance b/d	3,000
"	"	General Ledger Adjustment A/c		30	"	General Ledger Adj . A/c	
30		—Sales (Rs. 10,00,000 – 25%)	7,50,000			—Discount Allowed	20,000
	"	Balance c/d	1,000			—Cash Received	6,00,000
						—Returns Inward (Rs. 20,000 – 25%)	16,000
					"	Balance c/d	2,12,000
			8,51,000				8,51,000

Contd.

2012		Rs.	2012		Rs.
May 1	To Balance b/d	2,12,000	May 1	By Balance b/d	1,000
31	" General Ledger Adjustment A/c		31	" General Ledger Adj. A/c	
	—Sales (Rs. 12,00,000 – 25%)	9,00,000		—Discount Allowed	25,000
	" Balance c/d	4,000		—Cash Received	8,00,000
				—Returns Inwards	30,000
				(Rs. 40,000 – 25%)	
			30	" Balance c/d	2,60,000
		11,16,000			11,16,000
June 1	To Balance b/d	2,60,000	June 1	By Balance b/d	4,000
30	" General Ledger Adjustment A/c			" General Ledger Adj. A/c	
	—Sales (Rs. 16,00,000 – 25%)	12,00,000		—Discount Allowed	40,000
	" Balance c/d	3,000		—Cash Received	12,00,000
				—Returns Inward	45,000
				(Rs.. 60,000 – 25%)	
				" Balance c/d	1,74,000
		14,63,000			14,63,000

Where individual debtors position is given

Illustration 6

The following is a summarised analysis of the accounts of the outstanding debtors of a firm at the date of the annual closing as appearing on one of their ledgers :

Debtors	*Goods Sold during the year*	*Goods returned during the year*	*Cash and cheque received during the year*	*Discount allowed during the year*	*Bills of Exchange received during the year*
	Rs.	Rs.	Rs.	Rs.	Rs.
A	2,763	—	1,500	—	1,000
B	6,514	23	3,200	130	3,500
C	3,987	15	2,000	40	2,200
D	5,762	—	4,100	—	—
E	9,385	117	6,300	93	3,500
F	8,426	—	5,900	—	2,300
G	4,931	82	2,200	49	3,800

There was an outstanding balance of the debtors to the extent of Rs. 3,985 at the beginning of the year. Out of the above receipts, a bill for Rs. 700 given by B was dishonoured and the charges amounted to Rs. 5. Show how you would proceed to agree the Trial balance according to Self-Balancing System.

Solution

In the General Ledger
Debtors Ledger Adjustment Account

Dr. Cr.

Date	*Particulars*	*Amount* Rs.	*Date*	*Particulars*	*Amount* Rs.
?	To Balance b/d	3,985	?	By General Ledger Adj. A/c :	
	" General Ledger Adj. A/c :			Cash and Cheque	25,200
	Sales	41,768		Discount Allowed	312
	Bills Dishonoured	700		Bills Receivable	16,300
	Charges	5		Returns Inward	237
				" Balance c/d	4,409
		46,458			46,458
	To Balance b/d	4,409			

In the Debtors Ledger
General Ledger Adjustment Account

Dr. Cr.

Date	*Particulars*	*Amount* Rs.	*Date*	*Particulars*	*Amount* Rs.
?	To Debtors Ledger Adj. A/c :		?	By Balance b/d	3,985
	Cash and Cheque	25,200		" Debtors Ledger Adj. A/c :	
	Discount Allowed	312		Sales	41,768

Contd.

?			Rs.	?			Rs.
	To	Bills Receivable	16,300		By	Bills Dishonoured	700
		Returns Inward	237			Charges	5
	"	Balance c/d	4,409				
			46,458				46,458
					By	Balance b/d	4,409

Workings :

Debtors	*Goods Sold during the year*	*Goods returned during the year*	*Cash and cheque received during the year*	*Discount allowed during the year*	*Bills of Exchange received during the year*
	Rs.	*Rs.*	*Rs.*	*Rs.*	*Rs.*
A	2,763	—	1,500	—	1,000
B	6,514	23	3,200	130	3,500
C	3,987	15	2,000	40	2,200
D	5,762	—	4,100	—	—
E	9,385	117	6,300	93	3,500
F	8,426	—	5,900	—	2,300
G	4,931	82	2,200	49	3,800
	41,768	237	25,200	312	16,300

Comprehensive problem relating to Debtors Ledger

Illustration 7

From the following particulars, prepare the Debtors Ledger Adjustment Account as it would appear in the General Ledger for the year ended 30th June 2012 :

		Rs.			*Rs.*
Sundry Debtors (on 1.7.2011)	(Dr.)	80,000	Bills Receivable dishonoured		12,000
	(Cr.)	4,000	Bills Receivable discounted		4,000
Sales (including Cash Sales of Rs. 20,000)		1,20,000	Bills Receivable endorsed		11,000
Cash received from Debtors		60,000	Bills Receivable honoured at maturity		4,000
Returns Inward		10,000	Bills Receivable renewed		3,000
Discount and rebate allowed to Debtors		6,000	Interest on bills renewed		100
Allowances to customers on goods damaged-in-transit		4,000	Bills Receivable as endorsed dishonoured		1,000
Bad Debts written-off		8,000	Discount allowed but later on disallowed		1,000
Provision for Bad Debts		12,000	Carriage charged to customers		2,000
Provision for Discount on Debtors		2,000	Transfer from Debtors Ledger to Creditors Ledger		12,000
Bad Debts previously written-off, now recovered		10,000	Transfer from Creditors Ledger to Debtors Ledger		14,000
Interest on customers' overdue account		2,000	Sundry Debtors (on 30.6.2012)	Cr.	6,000
Trade Discount		1,000	Do	Dr.	55,100

In the General Ledger

Debtors Ledger Adjustment Account

Dr. *Cr.*

Date		*Particulars*	*Amount*	*Date*		*Particulars*	*Amount*
2011			Rs.	2011			Rs.
July 1	To	Balance b/d	80,000	July 1	By	Balance b/d	4,000
2012				2012			
June 30	"	General Ledger Adjustment A/c :		June 30	"	General Ledger Adjustment A/c :	
	"	Sales	1,00,000		"	Cash Received	60,000
	"	Interest	2,000		"	Returns Inward	10,000
	"	Bills Dishonoured	12,000		"	Discount and Rebate	6,000
	"	Interest	100		"	Allowances	4,000
	"	B/R endorsed				Bad Debts	8,000

Contd.

		Rs.				Rs.
	To Dishonoured	1,000		By	Bills Receivable	28,000
	Discount disallowed	1,000			Bills Receivable (renewed)	3,000
	Carriage	2,000			Transfer—	
	" Balance c/d	6,000			Debtors to Creditors	12,000
					Creditors to Debtors	14,000
				"	Balance c/d	55,100
		2,04,100				2,04,100
2012			2012			
July 1	To Balance b/d	55,100	July 1	By	Balance b/d	6,000

Dr. **Bills Receivable Account** Cr.

Date	Particulars	Amount	Date	Particulars	Amount
2012		Rs.	2012		Rs.
June 30	To Debtors A/c	3,000	June 30	By Debtors A/c	12,000
	" Debtors A/c *(bal. fig.)*	28,000		" Cash/Bank A/c	4,000
				" Creditors A/c	11,000
				" Cash A/c	4,000
		31,000			31,000

Notes : 1. Cash Sales will not appear in Debtors Ledger Adjustment Account.

2. Provision for Bad Debts and Provision for Discount on Debtors have no connection with Debtors Ledger, hence they will be excluded.

3. Recovery of Bad Debts will also be excluded.

4. Trade Discount is not to be recorded at all on the assumption that Net Sales are given.

5. Bills Receivable discounted, Bills Receivable endorsed and Bills Receivable honoured at maturity will not appear in Debtors Ledger Adjustment Account as they are not related to debtors.

A Typical Problem

Illustration 8

Mr. Mrinal Sen maintains his ledgers on self-balancing system. The transactions from January 1 to April 30, 2012 are given below. You are required to prepare the General Ledger Adjustment Account as will appear in Debtors Ledger:

(1) Opening Balance (January 1, 2012) :
Debtors Ledger Rs. 76,000

(2) Cash Sales Rs. 12,000 (being 10% of total sales).

(3) Collection from Customers (other than collections on Bills Receivable) amounted to Rs. 1,10,000 which included:

(a) A sum of Rs. 3,000 realised from the estate of an insolvent customer (at 0.60 P. per rupee).

(b) Rs. 6,500 received from a customer as advance for sale.

(c) Rs. 4,000 received from a debtor after adjustment of an advance of Rs. 2,000 made in December 2011.

(d) Rs. 1,250 received from a party whose account was written-off in earlier years.

(4) Interest charged to customers on overdue account Rs. 2,600.

(5) Bills Receivable drawn during the period Rs. 18,500.

(6) Bills Receivable collected during the period Rs. 10,600 (including Rs. 5,900) collected on Bills Receivable drawn during November and December 2011.

(7) Bills Receivable dishonoured on maturity Rs. 1,700.

(8) Bills Receivable endorsed to suppliers Rs. 6,000. Out of which Bills Receivable for Rs. 2,000 was discounted by Creditors at 5% duly met at maturity. Bills Receivable for Rs. 3,000 was dishonoured on maturity (noting charge being Rs. 20) and Bills Receivable amounting to Rs. 1,000 will mature in May 2012.

(9) Returns Inward Rs. 11,600.

(10) Transfer from Creditors Ledger to Debtors Ledger Rs. 6,900.

[CA]

Solution

In the Debtors Ledger

General Ledger Adjustment Account

Dr. Cr.

Date		Particulars	Amount	Date		Particulars	Amount
2012			Rs.	2012			Rs.
Jan. 1	To	Balance b/d	2,000[1]	Jan. 1	By	Balance b/d (Rs. 76,000 + Rs. 2,000)	78,000[4]
Apr. 30	"	Debtors Ledger Adjustment A/c :		Apr. 30	"	Debtors Ledger Adjustment A/c :	
		Cash Received	1,08,750[2]			Sales	
	"	Bad Debts	2,000[3]			(Rs. 12,000 × $\frac{90}{10}$)	1,08,000[5]
	"	Bills Receivable	18,500		"	Interest	2,600
	"	Returns Inward	11,600		"	B/R Dishonoured	1,700
	"	Transfer from Creditors Ledger	6,900		"	B/R Dishonoured (endorsed including noting charges)	3,020
	"	Balance c/d	50,070		"	Balance c/d	6,500[6]
			1,99,820				1,99,820
2012				2012			
May 1	To	Balance b/d	6,500	May 1	By	Balance b/d	50,070

Workings :

1. This amount reveals the advance balance, i.e., credit balance in Debtors Ledger and Debit Balance in General Ledger.

2. **Cash Received**

	Rs.
Collection from Customers	1,10,000
Less: Recovery of bad debts included therein	1,250
	1,08,750

3. **Bad Debts**

60% of debts were realised i.e., Rs. 3,000, So, for 40% of bad debts, the amount will be (Rs. 3,000 × $\frac{40}{60}$) = Rs. 2,000

4. **Debtors balance**

As on 1.1.2012	76,000
Add ; Advance balance	2,000
	78,000

5. **Sales**

Cash Sales is 10% which is equal to Rs. 12,000

∴ Credit sale is 90% = Rs. 12,000 × $\frac{90}{10}$ = Rs. 1,08,000

6. **Advance Balance**

as on 30.4.2012 Rs. 6,500 which was taken as advance is carried forward.

Preparation of Creditors Ledger Adjustment Account

Illustration 9

From the following particulars, prepare a Creditors Ledger Adjustment Account as it would appear in the General Ledger and show also the adjusting journal entries :

	Rs.		Rs.
Opening balance of Creditors	20,000	Bills payable issued during the year	5,000
Cash purchases	5,000	Bills payable matured	2,000
Credit purchases	45,000	Bills payable dishonored	500
Cash paid to suppliers	25,000	Bills payable renewed	200
Returns Outward	3,000	Interest on Bills payable renewed	20
Trade Discount	1,000	Sundry charges paid for	
Discount received from suppliers	3,000	dishonour of Bills payable	5

Solution

Total Creditors Account

Date	Dr. Particulars	Amount	Date	Cr. Particulars	Amount
?		Rs.	?		Rs.
	To Cash	25,000		By Balance b/d	20,000
	" Returns Outwards	3,000		" Purchases	45,000
	" Discount Received	3,000		" Bills Payable Dishonored	500
	" Bills payable	5,000		" Interest	20
	" Bills payable (Renewed)	200		" Charges	5
	" Balance c/d	29,325			
		65,525			65,525
				By Balance b/d	29,325

In the books of.........
Journal

Date	Particulars		L.F.	Debit	Credit
?				Rs.	Rs.
	General Ledger Adjustment A/c (In Creditors Ledger)) Dr.			45,525	
	To Creditors Ledger Adjustment A/c (In General Ledger)				45,525
	Various items credited to Creditors during the month as :				
	Purchases	45,000			
	Bills Payable Dishonoured	500			
	Interest	20			
	Charges	5			
		45,525			
	Creditors Ledger Adjustment A/c (in General Ledger) Dr.			36,200	
	To General Ledger Adjustment A/c (In Creditors Ledger)				36,200
	Various items debited to Creditors during the month as :				
	Cash	25,000			
	Returns Outward	3,000			
	Discount Receivable	3,000			
	Bills Payable	5,000			
	Bills Payable (Renewed)	200			
		36,200			

In the General Ledger
Creditors Ledger Adjustment Account

Date	Dr. Particulars	Amount	Date	Cr. Particulars	Amount
?		Rs.	?		Rs.
	To General Ledger Adjustment A/c :			By Balance b/d	20,000
	Cash	25,000		General Ledger Adjustment A/c :	
	Returns Outward	3,000		Purchase	45,000
	Discount Received	3,000		Bills Payable (Renewed)	500
	Bills Payable	5,000		Interest	20
	Bills Payable (Renewed)	200		Charges	5
	" Balance c/d	29,325			
		65,525			65,525
			?	By Balance b/d	29,325

Notes : 1. The following items will not appear in Creditors Ledger Adjustment Account as they do not have any bearing on it:

(i) Cash Purchases; (ii) Trade Discount; (iii) Bills Payable matured.

Preparation of Individual creditors ledger, Trial Balance, General Ledger Adjustment Account and Creditors Ledger Adjustment Account.

Illustration 10

From the following particulars, prepare individual Creditors Account, General Ledger Adjustment Account, Creditors Ledger Adjustment A/c (In the General Ledger) and a Trial Balance as on Dec. 1,2012. Balance of creditors are: X Rs. 6,000; R Rs. 4,000; Y Rs. 8,000; A Rs. 7,000; P Rs. 5,000; B Rs. 3,000 and Q Rs. 4,000.

Date	
2012 Dec.	
1.	Purchased from Mr. X for Rs. 2,000
2.	Paid Rs. 1,600 to Mr. X; Discount Allowed by him Rs. 400 and accepted a bill for Rs. 3,000
13.	Paid Rs. 4,000 to Mr. R towards the purchase made in Nov. 2011 in full
13.	Paid advance to Mr. Y Rs. 3,000
14.	Purchased goods from Mr. A Rs. 4,000
25.	Returned goods worth Rs. 1,000 to Mr. A
26.	Settled the balance due to Mr. A at a discount of 10% by cheque
27.	Goods purchased from Mr. Y for Rs. 2,500 against the advance paid on 13th
28.	Paid to Mr. P in full settlement of Rs. 3,000 against a debt of Rs. 4,000
30.	Purchased from B Rs. 2,000, paid Rs. 1,500 and received discount amounting to Rs. 500
31.	Goods returned to Q Rs. 750. The goods were originally purchased for cash in Oct. 4,000.

Solution **[CA]**

In the Creditors Ledger

X Account

Dr. Cr.

Date		Particulars	Amount	Date		Particulars	Amount
2012			Rs.	2012			Rs.
Dec. 2	To	Bank A/c	1,600	Dec. 1	By	Balance b/d	6,000
	"	Discount Received A/c	400	2	"	Purchase	2,000
	"	Bills Payable A/c	3,000				
	"	Balance c/d	3,000				
			8,000				8,000

R Account

Dr. Cr.

Date		Particulars	Amount	Date		Particulars	Amount
2012			Rs.	2012			Rs.
Dec. 13	To	Bank A/c	4,000	Dec. 1	By	Balance b/d	4,000
			4,000				4,000

Y Account

Dr. Cr.

Date		Particulars	Amount	Date		Particulars	Amount
2012			Rs.	2012			Rs.
Dec. 31	To	Bank A/c	3,000	Dec. 27	By	Balance b/d	8,000
	"	Balance c/d	7,500		"	Purchase	2,500
			10,500				10,500

A Account

Dr. Cr.

Date		Particulars	Amount	Date		Particulars	Amount
2012			Rs.	2012			Rs.
Dec. 25	To	Returns Outward A/c	1,000	Dec. 1	By	Balance b/d	7,000
26	"	Bank A/c	9,000	Dec. 14	"	Purchase	4,000
	"	Balance c/d	1,000				
			11,000				11,000

P Account

Date	Particulars	Amount	Date	Particulars	Amount
2012		Rs.	2012		Rs.
Dec. 28	To Bank A/c	3,000	Dec. 1	By Balance b/d	5,000
	" Discount Received A/c	1,000			
	" Balance c/d	1,000			
		5,000			5,000

B Account

Date	Particulars	Amount	Date	Particulars	Amount
2012		Rs.	2012		Rs.
Dec. 28	To Bank A/c	1,500	Dec. 1	By Balance b/d	3,000
	" Discount Received A/c	500	Dec. 30	" Purchase	2,000
	" Balance c/d	3,000			
		5,000			5,000

Q Account

Date	Particulars	Amount	Date	Particulars	Amount
2012		Rs.	2012		Rs.
Dec. 31	To Returns Outward A/c	750	Dec. 1	By Balance b/d	4,000
	" Balance c/d	3,250			
		4,000			4,000

Trial Balance

as at 31st Dec. 2012

Heads of Account	Debit	Credit
	Rs.	Rs.
X Account		3,000
Y Account		7,500
P Account		1,000
B Account		3,000
Q Account		3,250
General Ledger Adjustment Account	17,750	
	17,750	17,750

General/Nominal Ledger Adjustment Account

Date	Particulars	Amount	Date	Particulars	Amount
2012		Rs.	2012		Rs.
Dec. 1	To Balance b/d	37,000[1]	De. 31	By Creditors/Bought Ledger Adjustment A/c	
31	" Creditors/Broght Ledger Adjustment A/c			—Bank	22,100[3]
	—Credit Purchase	10,500[2]		—Discount Receiived	2,900[4]
				—Bills Payable	3,000[6]
				—Returns Outwards	1,750[5]
				" Balance c/d	17,750
		47,500			47,500

In the General Ledger

Creditors Ledger Adjustmeent Account

Date	Particulars	Amount	Date	Particulars	Amount
2012		Rs.	2012		Rs.
Dec.	To General Ledger Adj. A/c		Dec. 1	By Balance b/d	37,000
	—Bank	22,100	Dec. 31	" General Ledger Adj. A/c	

Contd.

2012		Rs.	2012		Rs.
	—Discount Received	2,900		—Credit Purchase	10,500
	—Bills Payable	3,000			
	—Returns Outward	1,750			
"	Balance c/d	17,750			
		47,500			47,500

Workings :

1. Total Creditors Balance as on 1.12.2012

	Rs.
X—	6,000
R—	4,000
Y—	8,000
A—	7,000
P—	5,000
B—	3,000
Q—	4,000
	37,000

2. Credit Purchase

	Rs.
1.12.2012—X	2,000
14.12.2012—A	4,000
27.12.2012—Y	2,500
30.12.2012—B	2,000
	10,500

3. Payment to Creditors

	Rs.
2.12.2012—X	1,600
13.12.2012—R	4,000
13.12.2012—Y	3,000
26.12.2012—A	9,000
28.12.2012—P	3,000
30.12.2012—B	1,500
	22,100

4. Discount Received

	Rs.
2.12.2012—X	400
26.12.2012—A	1,000
28.12.2012—P	1,000
30.12.2012—B	500
	2,900

5. Returns Outward

	Rs.
25.12.2012—A	1,000
31.12.2012—Q	750
	1,750

6. Bills Payable

	Rs.
2.12.2012—X	3,000
	3,000

Various items of creditors are given

Illustration 11

From the following particulars, prepare the Creditors Ledger Adjustment Account as it would appear in General Ledger and General Ledger Adjustment Account as it would appear in Creditors Ledger for the year ended 31st March 2012 :

		Rs.			Rs.
Sundry Creditors (on 1.4.2011)	*Cr.*	60,000	Bills Payable issued during the year		8,000
Do	*Dr.*	2,000	Bills Payable matured		1,000
Purchases (including Cash Purchases Rs. 10,000)		70,000	Bills Payable dishonoured		2,000
Returns Outward		10,000	Bills Payable renewed		1,000
Cash and Cheques paid to Creditors		30,000	Interest on Bills Payable renewed		50
Discount allowed by Creditors		6,000	Sundry Charges paid for dishonour of Bills Payable		50
Trade Discount		1,000	Total of set-off in Debtors Ledger		4,000
Price Reduction allowed on damaged goods		2,000	Sundry Creditors (on 31.3.2012)	*Dr.*	1,000
Bills receivable endorsed to Creditors		5,000	Do	*Cr.*	55,100

Solution

In the General Ledger
Creditors Ledger Adjustment Account

Dr. *Cr.*

Date		*Particulars*	*Amount*	*Date*		*Particulars*	*Amount*
2011			Rs.	2011			Rs.
April 1	To	Balance b/d	2,000	April 1	By	Balance b/d	60,000
2012				2012			
Mar. 31	"	General Ledger Adjustment A/c :		Mar. 31	"	General Ledger Adjustment A/c :	
		Returns Outward	10,000			Purchase	60,000
		Cash and Cheque	30,000			Bills Payable Dishonoured	2,000
		Discount Received	6,000			Interest	50

Contd.

Date		Particulars	Amount	Date		Particulars	Amount
2011			Rs.	2012			Rs.
		Allowances	2,000			Sundry Charges	50
		Bills Receivable	5,000		"	Balance c/d	1,000
		Bills Payable	8,000				
		Bills Payable (renewed)	1,000				
		Transfer	4,000				
	"	Balance c/d	55,100				
			1,23,100				1,23,100
2012 April 1	To	Balance b/d	1,000	2012 April 1	By	Balance b/d	55,100

In the Creditors Ledger
General Ledger Adjustment Account

Dr. Cr.

Date		*Particulars*	*Amount*	*Date*		*Particulars*	*Amount*
2011			Rs.	2011			Rs.
April 1	To	Balance b/d	60,000	April 1	By	Balance b/d	2,000
2012 Mar. 31	"	Creditors Ledger Adjustment A/c :		2012 Mar. 31	"	Creditors Ledger Adjustment A/c :	
		Purchases	60,000			Returns Outward	10,000
		Bills Payable dishonoured	2,000			Cash and Cheque	30,000
		Interest	50			Discount Received	6,000
		Sundry Charges	50			Allowances	2,000
	"	Balance c/d	1,000			Bills Receivable	5,000
						Bills Payable	8,000
						Bills Payable (renewed)	1,000
						Transfer	4,000
					"	Balance c/d	55,100
			1,23,100				1,23,100
2012 April 1	To	Balance b/d	55,100	2012 April 1	By	Balance b/d	1,000

Notes : 1. Cash purchases will not appear in Creditors Ledger.

2. Bills Payable matured will also not affect Creditors Ledger.

Transfer Entries

Sometimes it may so happen that a person becomes a debtor as well as a creditor of a firm, i.e., the firm sells goods of a person from whom goods are also purchased. Therefore, his name appears in the list of both debtors and creditors. In order to make settlement of accounts, smaller amount between the two is to be deducted both from debtors and creditors. The usual entry for this purpose is : Creditors Account debit and Debtors Account credit. Since the transaction affects the two ledger, viz., Debtor and Creditors, the two corresponding General Ledger are also to be affected, e.g., Debtors include Rs. 400 due from X whereas creditors include Rs. 300 due to X.

The usual transfer entry is:

		Dr.	Cr.
(i).	X (in Creditors Ledger) A/c Dr.	300	
	To X (in Debtors Ledger)		300

But, under self-balancing systems, the entry will be:

		Dr.	Cr.
(i)	Creditors Ledger Adjustment A/c Dr.	300	
	To General Ledger Adjustment A/c		300
(ii)	General Ledger Adjustment A/c Dr.	300	
	To Debtors Ledger Adjustment A/c		300
or, (i)	Creditors Ledger Adjustment A/c Dr.	300	
	To Debtors Ledger Adjustment A/c		300

> ***Note :*** *The transfer entry will always be the same whether the transfer is made from Debtors to Creditors or from Creditors to Debtors. But if the transfer is made only from one account to another in the same ledger, an adjusting entry is needed in order to correct the adjustment accounts together with the transfer entry.*

Illustration 12

(a) The books of Banerjee & Co. show :

(i) A sum of Rs. 10,000 due from Mukherjee & Co. in the Sales Ledger, and;

(ii) A sum of Rs. 2,500 due to Mukherjee & Co. in the Purchase Ledger.

Pass the transfer entries under self-balancing system.

Solution

In the books of Banerjee & Co.
Journal (without narration)

Date	Particulars		L.F.	Debit	Credit
				Rs.	Rs.
(a)	Mukherjee & Co. A/c (in the Purchase Ledger) To Mukherjee & Co. A/c (in the Sales Ledger)	Dr.		2,500	2,500
(b)	Purchase Ledger Adjustment A/c (in the General Ledger) To General Ledger Adjustment A/c (in the Purchase Ledger)	Dr.		2,500	2,500
(c)	General Ledger Adjustment A/c (in the Sales Ledger) To Sales Ledger Adjustment A/c (in the General Ledger)	Dr.		2,500	2,500

(b) Big Ltd. has two Debtors Ledger (A-L and M-Z) in use in the self-balancing system. Miss Barnali Das, a customer whose account shows a debit balance of Rs. 3,000 in the (A-L) Debtor's Ledger, marries Mr. Subash Sen and her account is required to be transferred to the (M-Z) Debtor's Ledger. Pass the transfer entries.

Solution

In the books of Big Ltd.
Journal (without narration)

Date	Particulars		L.F.	Debit	Credit
				Rs.	Rs.
(a)	Mrs. Sen A/c Dr. (in M-Z Debtors Ledger) To (Miss. Das A/c in A-L Debtors Ledger)			3,000	3,000
(b)	M-Z Debtors Ledger Adjustment A/c (in General Ledger) To General Ledeger Adjustment A/c (in M-Z Debtors Ledger)	Dr.		3,000	3,000
(c)	General Ledger Adjustment A/c (in A-L Debtors Ledger) To A-L Debtors Ledger Adjustment A/c (in General Ledger)	Dr.		3,000	3,000

Preparation of Debtors Ledger Adjustment and Creditors Ledger Adjustment Account

Illustration 13

Ess Bee Ltd. has three Ledgers in use, viz., a Debtors Ledger, a Creditors Ledger and a Nominal Ledger which are all kept on the system of Self-Balancing. From the following particulars, prepare (i) the Debtors Ledger Adjustment Account, and (ii) Creditors Ledger Adjustment Account in the Nominal Ledger.

	Rs.		Rs.
Jan. 1, 2012		June 30, 2012	
Balance of Sundry Debtors	32,000	Bills Payable accepted	3,000
Balance of Sundry Creditors	37,000	Bills Receivable received	6,000
30.6.2012		Returns Inward	1,750
Credit Purchases	9,000	Returns Outward	1,200
Credit Sales	19,600	Rebate allowed to Creditors	550
Cash Sales	1,500	Rebate allowed by Creditors	300
Paid to Creditors	19,750	Provision for Doubtful Debts	320
Discount allowed by them	650	Bad Debts	900
Cash received from Debtors	15,600	Bills Receivable dishonoured	750
Discount allowed by them	400		

[ICWA]

Solution

In the Nominal Ledger
Debtors Ledger Adjustment Account

Dr. *Cr.*

Date		*Particulars*	*Amount*	*Date*		*Particulars*	*Amount*
2012			Rs.	2012			Rs.
Jan. 1	To	balance b/d	32,000	June 30	By	Nominal Ledger Adjustment A/c :	
June 30	"	Nominal Ledger Adjustment A/c :				Cash Received	15,600
		Sales	19,600			Discount Allowed	400
		Bills Receivable Dishonored	750			Bills Receivable	6,000
						Returns Inward	1,750
						Rebate Allowed	550
						Bad Debts	900
					"	Balance c/d	27,150
			52,350				52,350
2012							
July 1	To	Balance b/d	27,150				

In the Nominal Ledger
Creditors Ledger Adjustment Account

Dr. *Cr.*

Date		*Particulars*	*Amount*	*Date*		*Particulars*	*Amount*
2012			Rs.	2012			Rs.
June 30	To	Nominal Ledger Adjustment A/c :		Jan. 1	By	Balance b/d	37,000
		Cash paid	19,750	June 30	"	Nominal Ledger Adjustment A/c	
		Bills Payable	3,000			Purchases	9,000
		Discount Received	650				
		Returns Outward	1,200				
		Rebate Received	300				
	"	Balance c/d	21,100				
			46,000				46,000
				2012			
				July 1	By	Balance b/d	21,100

Note : Cash Sale and Provision for bad debts will not appear in Debtors Ledger.

Illustration 14

K. Hassan has three ledgers in use— a Sales Ledger, a Bought Ledger and a Nominal Ledger all of which are kept in Self-Balancing System. From the following particulars prepare Sales Ledger Adjustment A/c in the General Ledger and Nominal Ledger Adjustment A/c in the Bought Ledger :

	Rs.		Rs.
2011, April 1		Credit Balance transferred from Bought Ledger to Sales Ledger	85
Balance of Sundry Creditors (*Dr.*)	150	Cheques dishonoured	500
Balance of Sundry Creditors (*Cr.*)	4,500	B/R endorsed to supplier (All these bills were duly honoured)	300
Balance of Debtors (*Cr.*)	250	B/R dishonoured and fresh Bills drawn with interest of Rs. 200	1,200
Balance of Debtors (*Dr.*)	8,700	Cash paid to suppliers	25,000
20.11, 31 March		Allowances to customers	100
Credit Purchase	45,000	Allowances Recovered	150
B/R drawn on customers (excluding bills renewed)	3,000	Bad Debts written-off	150
B/P Accepted	2,000	Bad Debts Revenue	500
Sales (including Cash Sales of Rs. 5,000)	60,000	Credit Balance transferred from Sales Ledger to Bought Ledger	100
Return Outward	1,500	Purchase Ledger Balance (*Dr.*)	48
Interest on Customers overdue account for payment	300	Sales Ledger Balance (*Cr.*)	112
Sales Return	450		
Cash and Cheques received from customers	32,000		

[CU BCom(Hons.)]

Solution

In the General Ledger
Sales Ledger Adjustment Account

Dr. *Cr.*

Date	*Particulars*	*Amount*	*Date*	*Particulars*	*Amount*
2011		Rs.	2012		Rs.
April 1	To Balance b/d	8,700	Jan. 1	By Balance b/d	250
2012			2012		
Mar. 31	" General Ledger Adjustment A/c :		Mar. 31	" General Ledger Adjustment A/c :	
	Sales (Rs. 60,000 – 5,000)	55,000		Bills Receivable	3,000
	Bank (Cheques dishonoured)	500		Bill Receivable (Renewal)	1,200
	Bill Receivable (dishonored)	1,000		Sales Return	450
	Interest on Overdue Accounts	300		Cash & cheques Received	32,000
	Interest charged on dishonoured bill	200		Transfer (from Bought Ledger)	85
	Transfer (to Bought Ledger)	100		Allowances	100
"	" Balance c/d	112		Bad Debts	150
				" Balance c/d (*bal. fig.*)	28,677
		65,912			65,912
April 1	To Balance b/d	28,677	April 1	By Balance b/d	112

In the bought Ledger
Nominal Ledger Adjustment Account

Dr. *Cr.*

Date	*Particulars*	*Amount*	*Date*	*Particulars*	*Amount*
2011		Rs.	2011		Rs.
April 1	To Balance b/d	4,500	April 1	By Balance b/d	150
2012			2012		
Mar. 31	" Bought Ledger Adjustment A/c :		Mar. 31	" Bought Ledger Adjustment A/c :	
	Credit Purchase	45,000		Bills Payable (accepted)	2,000
	Transfer from Sales Ledger	100		Returns Outward	1,500
				Transfer to Sales Ledger	85
				Bills Receivable (Endorsed)	300
				Cash Paid	25,000
				Allowance Received	150
"	Balance c/d	84		By Balance c/d (*bal. fig.*)	20,499
		49,684			49,684
April 1	To Balance b/d	20,499	April 1	By Balance b/d	84

Notes :

1. For the transfer of credit balance from Sales Ledger to Bought Ledger for Rs. 100 the entry being :
   Debtors Ledger Adjustment A/c Dr. Rs. 100
   To Creditors Ledger adjustment Rs. 100
   i.e., both debtors as well as creditors balance are increased as Sundry Debtors show a debit balance having a corresponding credit balance which is transferred.
2. Similarly, for the transfer of credit balance from Bought ledger to Sales for Rs. 85. i.e., in both ledgers, the entry being:
   Creditors Ledger Adjustment A/c Dr. Rs. 85
   To Debtors Ledger Adjustment A/c Rs. 85
   i.e., both creditors as well as debtors balances are reduced as Sundry Creditors show a credit balance having a corresponding debit balance.
3. Bad Debt Reserve will not appear in Debtors Ledger Adjustment Account.

Illustration 15

From the following particulars, prepare a Debtors Ledger Adjustment Account and Creditor's Ledger Adjustment Account as they would appear in the General Ledger:

		Rs.			Rs.
Jan. 1, 2012			Bad debts previously written-off now recovered		1,000
Balance of Debtors Ledger	–(Dr.)	40,000			
Balance of Debtors Ledger	–(Cr.)	1,000	Bills Receivable received		5,000
Balance of Creditors Ledger	–(Cr.)	20,000	Bills Receivable dishonoured		1,000
Balance of Creditors Ledger	–(Dr.)	700	Dishonoured cheques included in total cash received from Debtors		750
Dec. 31, 2012 Credit purchases		12,000	Cash discount which has been allowed on dishonoured cheques (above)		50
Credit sales		60,000			
Cash received from Debtors		45,000	Refunded to Debtors against Credit balances		100
Discount allowed to Debtors		4,000	Transfer from Purchase Ledger		1,000
Cash paid to Creditors		15,000	Balance of Debtors Ledger	(Cr.)	800
Discount received from Creditors		1,000	Balance of Debtors Ledger	(Dr.)	?
Bad Debts written-off		500	Balance of Creditors Ledger	(Dr.)	500
			Balance of Creditors Ledger	(Cr.)	?

Solution

In the General Ledger
Debtors Ledger Adjustment Account

Dr. Cr.

Date		Particulars	Amount	Date		Particulars	Amount
2012			Rs.	2012			Rs.
Jan. 1	To	Balance b/d	40,000	Jan. 1	By	Balance b/d	1,000
Dec. 31	"	General Ledger Adjustment A/c :		Dec. 31	"	General Ledger Adjustment A/c :	
		Sales	60,000			Cash	45,000
		Bills Received Dishonoured	1,000			Discount Allowed	4,000
		Dishonoured Cheques	750			Bad Debts	500
		Discount disallowed	50			Bills Receivable	5,000
		Cash (Refunded)	100			Transfer	1,000
	"	Balance c/d	800		"	Balance c/d	46,200
			1,02,700				1,02,700
2013				2013			
Jan. 1	To	Balance b/d	46,200	Jan. 1	By	Balance b/d	800

In the General Ledger
Creditors Ledger Adjustment Account

Dr. Cr.

Date		Particulars	Amount	Date		Particulars	Amount
2012			Rs.	2012			Rs.
Jan. 1	To	Balance b/d	700	Jan. 1	By	Balance b/d	20,000
Dec. 31	"	General Ledger		Dec. 31	"	General Ledger	

Contd.

Date	Particulars	Rs.	Date	Particulars	Rs.
2011		Rs.	2012		Rs.
	Adjustment A/c :			Adjustment A/c :	
	Cash	15,000		Purchases	12,000
	Discount Received	1,000	"	Balance c/d	500
	Transfer	1,000			
"	Balance c/d	14,800			
		32,500			32,500
2013			2013		
Jan. 1	To Balance b/d	500	Jan. 1	By Balance b/d	14,800

Illustration 16

On examining the books of Bombay Ltd. you ascertain that on 1st Jan. 2012, the Debtors' Ledger balances were Rs. 40,120 debit and Rs. 285 credit and the Creditors' Ledger balances on the same date are Rs. 31, 175 credit and Rs. 525 debit.

For the year ended 31st Dec. 2012, the following particulars are available :

	Rs.
Cash received from Debtors	2,76,060
Returns Outward	2,675
Bad Debts written-off	1,630
Sales	3,18,640
Bills Received	20,285
Returns Inward	5,010
Purchases	1,99,870
Bills Dishonoured	1,315
Cash paid to creditors	1,86,535
Discount Allowed	11,640
Cash received in respect of debit balance in Creditor's Ledger	525
Allowances of Customers on goods damaged in transit	1,060
Discount Received	7,375
Cash received in respect of debit previously written-off as bad	370
Amount due from Customers as shown by Debtor's Ledger, set-off against amount due to the same company as shown by Creditor's Ledger	2,170

On 31st Dec. 2012, there was no credit balance in the debtor's ledger except those outstanding on 1st Jan. 2012 and no debit balance in the Creditors Ledger.

You are required to prepare necessary adjustments accounts in the General Ledger recording the above transactions, bringing down the balances on 31st Dec. 2012.

[CU BCom (Hons.) New]

Solution

In the General Ledger
Debtors Ledger Adjustment Account

Dr. | *Cr.*

Date	*Particulars*	*Amount*	*Date*	*Particulars*	*Amount*
2012		Rs.	2012		Rs.
Jan. 1	To Balance b/d	40,120	Jan. 1	By Balance b/d	285
Dec. 31	" General Ledger Adjustment A/c :		Dec. 31	" General Ledger Adjustment A/c :	
	Sales	3,18,640		Cash	2,76,060
	Bills Receivable Dishonoured	1,315		Bad Debts	1,630
	" Balance c/d	285		Bills Receivable	20,285
				Returns Inward	5,010
				Discount Allowed	11,640
				Allowances	1,060
				Transfer	2,170
			"	Balance c/d	42,220
		3,60,360			3,60,360
2013			2013		
Jan. 1	To Balance b/d	42,220	Jan. 1	By Balance b/d	285

In the General Ledger
Creditors Ledger Adjustment Account

Dr. Date		Particulars	Amount	Date		Particulars	Cr. Amount
2012			Rs.	2012			Rs.
Jan. 1	To	Balance b/d	525	Jan. 1	By	Balance b/d	31,175
Dec. 31	"	General Ledger Adjustment A/c :		Dec. 31	"	General Ledger Adjustment A/c :	
		Cash	1,86,535			Purchase	1,99,870
		Returns Outward	2,675			Cash	525
		Discount Received	7,375				
		Transfer	2,170				
	"	Balance c/d	32,290				
			2,31,570				2,31,570
				2013			
				Jan. 1	By	Balance b/d	32,290

Notes:

1. For Cash Received in Respect of debit balance in Creditors Ledger, the entry is:
   Cash (General Ledger Adjustment A/c) Dr.
   To Creditors (Creditors Ledger Adjustment A/c)
   i.e., Creditors Ledger Adjustment Account will be credited by Rs. 525.
2. Credit balance in Debtors Ledger at the end was nothing but the opening Credit balance i.e., Rs. 285 and there was no debit balance of creditors Ledger at end of the year.

Illustration 17

From the following particulars, which have been extracted from the book of G & Co., for the year ended 31.1.2010, prepare General Ledger Adjustment Account in the Creditors Ledger and Debtors Ledger Adjustment Account in the General Ledger :

		Rs.		Rs.
Debtors balance (1.1.2010)	Dr.	20,000	Bills Receivable received	3,000
	Cr.	300	Bills Receivable endorsed	800
Creditors balance (1.1.2010)	Dr.	200	Bills Receivable as endorsed dishonoured	300
	Cr.	15,000	Bills Receivable discounted	1,400
Purchases (including Cash Rs. 4,000)		12,000	Bills Receivable dishonoured	400
Sales (including Cash Rs. 6,000)		25,000	Interest charged on dishonoured bills	30
Cash paid to suppliers in full settlement of claims of Rs. 9,000		8,500	Transfer from one ledger to another ledger	600
			Returns (Cr.)	700
Cash received from customers in full settlement of claims of Rs. 15,000		14,100	Debtors balance (31.12.2010) Cr.	450
			Creditors balance (31.12.2010) Dr.	10,870
Bills Payable accepted (including renewals)		2,000		
Bills Payable withdrawn upon renewals		500		
Interest on Bills Payable renewed		20		

[ICWA]

Solution

In the Creditors Ledger
General Ledger Adjustment Account

Dr. Date		Particulars	Amount	Date		Particulars	Cr. Amount
2010			Rs.	2010			Rs.
Jan. 1	To	Balance b/d	15,000	Jan. 1	By	Balance b/d	200
Dec. 31	"	Creditors Ledger Adjustment A/c :		Dec. 31	"	Creditors Ledger Adjustment A/c :	
		Purchases	8,000			Cash	8,500
		Bills Payable Withdrawn	500			Discount Received (9,000 – 8,500)	500
		Bills Receivable					

Contd.

			Rs.				Rs.
2010				2010			
	To	Dishonoured (as endorsed)	300		By	Returns Outward	700
		Interest	20			Bills Payable	2,000
	"	Balance c/d	350			Bills Receivable (endorsed)	800
						Transfer	600
					"	Balance c/d	10,870
			24,170				24,170
2011				2011			
Jan. 1	To	Balance b/d	10,870	Jan. 1	By	Balance b/d	350

In the General Ledger

Debtors Ledger Adjustment Account

Dr. Cr.

Date		Particulars	Amount	Date		Particulars	Amount
2010			Rs.	2010			Rs.
Jan. 1	To	Balance b/d	20,000	Jan. 1	By	Balance b/d	300
Dec. 31	"	General Ledger Adjustment A/c :		Dec. 31	"	General Ledger Adjustment A/c :	
		Sales	19,000			Cash	14,100
		B/R endorsed Dishonoured	300			Discount Allowed (15,000 – 14,100)	900
		Bills Dishonoured	400			Bills Receivable	3,000
		Interest	30			Transfer	600
	"	Balance c/d	450		"	Balance c/d	21,280
			40,180				40,180
2011				2011			
Jan. 1	To	Balance b/d	21,280	Jan. 1	By	Balance b/d	450

Illustration 18

Mr. Self-reliant maintains his books on Self-Balancing Ledger. From the following particulars, prepare General Ledger Adjustment Account in (a) Bought Ledger and (b) Sold Ledger :

1.11.2012	Rs.		Rs.
Bought Ledger — Debit Balance	700	Cash collected form Debtors	83,000
Bought Ledger— Credit Balance	30,640	Cash paid to Creditors	57,500
Sold Ledger — Debit Balance	66,930	Discount Allowed	650
Sold Ledger—Credit Balance	1,865	Discount Received	320
Transactions during the month of November 2012 :		Interest Charged to Debtors	592
Sales	1,35,000	Bills Receivable Received	10,000
Credit Sales	1,16,000	Bills Payable accepted	8,000
Purchases—Credit	72,700	Bills Receivable Dishonoured	2,500
Purchases—Cash	11,800	Notary Charges debited to Party's A/c	10
Sales Returns (out of Credit sales)	500	Cash paid to Customers	137
Provision for Bad and Doubtful Debts	270	30.11.2012	
Bad Debts written-off	1,000	Bought Ledger—Debit Balance	980
Amount received against B/D written-off last year	600	Sold Ledger—Credit Balance	266
Purchases Returns (out of Credit Purchase)	2,500		

[ICWA]

Solution

In Bought (Creditors) Ledger

General Ledger Adjustment Account

Dr. Cr.

Date		Particulars	Amount	Date		Particulars	Amount
2012			Rs.	2012			Rs.
Nov. 1	To	Balance b/d	30,640	Nov. 1	By	Balance b/d	700
" 30	"	Creditors Ledger Adjustment A/c		30	"	Creditors Ledger Adjustment A/c :	
		Purchases	72,700			Cash Paid	57,500

Contd.

			Rs.				Rs.
	"	Balance c/d	980			Purchase Returns	2,500
						Discount Received	320
						Bills Payable	8,000
					"	Balance c/d	35,300
			1,04,320				1,04,320
Dec. 1	To	Balance b/d	35,300	Dec. 1	By	Balance b/d	980

In Sold (Debtors) Ledger

General Ledger Adjustment Account

Dr. *Cr.*

Date		*Particulars*	*Amount*	*Date*		*Particulars*	*Amount*
2012			Rs.	2012			Rs.
Nov. 1	To	Balance b/d	1,865	Nov. 1	By	Balance b/d	66,930
30	"	Debtors Ledger Adjustment A/c :		30	"	Debtors Ledger Adjustment A/c :	
		Sales Returns	500			Sales	1,16,000
		Bad Debts	1,000			Interest Charges	592
		Cash Received	83,000			Bills Receivable Dishonoured	2,500
		Discount Allowed	650			Notary Charges	10
		Bills Receivable	10,000			Cash paid	137
	"	Balance c/d	89,420		"	Balance c/d	266
			1,86,435				1,86,435
Dec. 1	To	Balance b/d	266	Dec. 1	By	Balance b/d	89,420

Note : There will be no treatment for (i) Provision for Bad and Doubtful Debts and (ii) Recovery of Bad Debts in Debtors Ledger.

Illustration 19

The following information is available from the books of the trader for the period 1st Jan. to 31st March 2012 :

(1) Total Sales amounted to Rs. 60,000 including the sale of old furniture for Rs. 1,200 (book value is Rs. 3,500). The total cash sales were 80% less than total credit sales.

(2) Cash collection from Debtors amounted to 60% of the aggregated of the opening Debtors and Credit sales for the period. Discount allowed to them amounted to Rs. 2,600.

(3) Bills Receivable drawn during the period totalled Rs. 6,000 of which bills amounting to Rs. 3,000 were endorsed in favour of suppliers. Out of these endorsed bills, a Bill receivable for Rs. 600 was dishonoured for non-payment, as the party became insolvent and his estate realised nothing.

(4) Cheques received from customer of Rs. 6,000 were dishonored; a sum of Rs. 500 is irrecoverable.

(5) Bad Debts written-off in the earlier year realised Rs. 2,500.

(6) Sundry Debtors on 1st January stood at Rs. 40,000.

You are required to show the Debtors Ledger Adjustment Account in the General Ledger.

[CA]

Solution

In the General Ledger

Debtors Ledger Adjustment Account

Dr. *Cr.*

Date		*Particulars*	*Amount*	*Date*		*Particulars*	*Amount*
2012			Rs.	2012			Rs.
Jan. 1	To	Balance b/d	40,000	Jan. 1	By	General Ledger Adjustment A/c :	
Mar. 31	"	General Ledger Adjustment A/c :		Mar. 31		Cash	53,400[2]
		Sales	49,000[1]			Discount Allowed	2,600

Contd.

		Rs.			Rs.
	Bills Dishonoured	600		Bills Receivable	6,000
	Cheque Dishonoured	6,000		Bad Debts	1,100
			"	Balance c/d	32,500
		95,600			95,600

Workings :

1. **Computation of Credit Sales**

As per question Cash sales were 80% less than Credit Sales. So, if credit sales are Rs. 100 Cash Sales will be Rs. 20: Total Sales (Cash + Credit) will be Rs. 120. Total Sales (Rs. 60,000 – Rs. 1,200) = Rs. 58,800 :

$\therefore$ Amount of Credit sales will be $\frac{\text{Rs. } 58,800 \times 100}{120}$ = Rs. 49,000.

2. **Cash Received**

Cash received is 60% of opening Debtors plus Credit Sales i.e. Rs. 40,000 + Rs. 49,000 = Rs. 89,000.

Cash Received = Rs. 89,000 $\times \frac{60}{100}$ = Rs. 53,400.

PREPARATION OF TWO DEBTORS LEDGER

Sometimes a firm may maintain more than one Debtors and/or Creditors Ledger, particularly where it has a large number of debtors and/or Creditors. The division of such Ledger may be either :

(i) On the basis of ***Alphabetical*** :

e.g., (a) Debtors A to H
(b) Debtors I to P
(c) Debtors Q to Z

(ii) On the basis of ***Geographical*** location :

e.g., (a) Debtors—Southern Part
(b) Debtors —Eastern Part
(c) Debtors —Western Part
(d) Debtors —Northern Part

The method and procedure of preparing such ledgers is similar to the method discussed above. That is, in the General Ledger, for each group of Ledger, a separate Debtors Ledger Adjustment Account is to be opened and each Debtors Ledger must maintain a General Ledger Adjustment Account. Needless to mention here that it becomes necessary to prepare the Books of Original Entry in columnar form if Debtors Ledger is sub-divided into various alphabetical or geographical order.

The following illustration will help us to make the above principle clear.

Two Debtors Ledger

Illustration 20

In order to facilitate the balancing of his books a businessman divides his sales ledger alphabetically into two sections (A-M and N-Z, respectively), each being Self-Balancing Ledger by means of an adjustment account in the Private Ledger. On 1.4.2011, these accounts showed the following balances :

	Dr.	*Cr.*
	Rs.	Rs.
A-M Adjustment A/c	65,680	2,250
N-Z Adjustment A/c	47,860	583

The following is an analysis of the transactions affecting the ledger during the period ending 31.3.2011, as extracted from the books of accounts :

	A-M	N-Z
	Rs.	Rs.
Credit Sales	5,15,620	4,22,315
Return	10,216	6,713
Cash Received	4,20,500	3,75,020

Contd.

	Rs.	Rs.
Cash received in respect of accounts already written-off as bad included in the above	1,420	590
Discount Allowed	5,620	4,075
Bills of Exchange received	30,500	9,400
Bills of Exchange dishonoured	5,000	2,000
Bad Debts written-off	4,120	5,780

During the period Miss Davar, a customer, whose account then showed a debit balance of Rs. 1,250, married Mr. Shroff and her account was, therefore, transferred in the other Ledger. On 31.3.2012 the total credit balances standing in the A-M Ledger amounted to Rs. 6,250 and in the N-Z ledger to Rs. 4,250.

Write-up the two adjustment accounts bringing down the balances.

Solutio

In the Nominal Ledger

Debtors Ledger Adjustment Account

Dr. Cr.

Date	Particulars	Amount A-M	Amount N-Z	Date	Particulars	Amount A-M	Amount N-Z
2011		Rs.	Rs.	2011		Rs.	Rs.
April 1	To Balance b/d	65,680	47,860	April 1	By Balance c/d	2,250	583
2012				2012			
Mar. 31	" General Ledger Adjustment A/c :			Mar. 31	" General Ledger Adjustment A/c :		
	Sales	5,15,620	4,22,315		Returns	10,216	6,713
	Bad Debts recovery (for cancellation)	1,420	590		Cash	4,20,500	3,75,020
	Bills Dishonoured	5,000	2,000		Discounts	5,620	4,075
	Transfer	—	1,250		Bills Receivable	30,500	9,400
	" Balance c/d	6,250	4,250		Bad Debts	4,120	5,780
					Transfer	1,250	—
					" Balance c/d	1,19,514	76,694
		5,93,970	4,78,265			5,93,970	4,78,265
April 1	To Balance b/d	1,19,514	76,694	April 1	By Balance b/d	6,250	4,250

In A-M Debtors Ledger

General Ledger Adjustment Account

Dr. Cr.

Date	Particulars	Amount	Date	Particulars	Amount
2011		Rs.	2011		Rs.
April 1	To Balance b/d	2,250	April 1	By Balance b/d	65,680
2012			2012		
Mar. 31	" Debtors Ledger Adjustment A/c :		Mar. 31	" Debtors Ledger Adjustment A/c :	
	Returns	10,216		Sales	5,15,620
	Cash	4,20,500		Bad Debts recovery *(for cancellation)*	1,420
	Discounts	5,620		Bills Dishonoured	5,000
	Bills Receivable	30,500		" Balance c/d	6,250
	Bad Debts	4,120			
	Transfer	1,250			
	" Balance c/d	1,19,514			
		5,93,970			5,93,970
April 1	To Balance b/d	6,250	April 1	By Balance b/d	1,19,514

In N-Z Debtors Ledger

General Ledger Adjustment Account

Dr. Cr.

Date	Particulars	Amount	Date	Particulars	Amount
2011		Rs.	2011		Rs.
April 1	To Balance b/d	583	April 1	By Balance b/d	47,860

Contd.

2011			Rs.	2011			Rs.
Mar. 31	"	Debtors Ledger Adjustment A/c :		Mar. 31	"	Debtors Ledger Adjustment A/c :	
		Returns	6,713			Sales	4,22,315
		Cash	3,75,020			Bad Debts Recovery (for cancellation)	590
		Discounts	4,075			Bills Dishonoured	2,000
		Bills Receivable	9,400			Transfer	1,250
		Bad Debts	5,780		"	Balance c/d	4,250
		Transfer	76,694				
	"	Balance c/d					
			4,78,265				4,78,265
April 1	To	Balance b/d	4,250	April 1	By	Balance b/d	76,694

Note : Since Miss Davar (A-M) ledger, married Mr. Shroff, (N-Z) Ledger, there will simply be a transfer entry i.e.

		Rs.	Rs.
(N-Z) Debtors Ledger Adjustment A/c	Dr.	1,250	
To (A-M) Debtors Ledger Adjustment A/c			1,250

SECTIONAL BALANCING SYSTEM

Although 'self-balancing' and 'sectional balancing' are synonymously used, there are still some differences between the two. Under self-balancing, all the ledgers are self-balanced whereas, under sectional balancing, only general ledger is made self-balancing. For this reason, a control account is maintained in the general ledger for each of the purchases and sales ledger. These are called **Purchase Ledger Control Account** or **Total Creditors Account** and **Sales Ledger Control Account** or **Total Debtors Account.** Since these control accounts represent in total the opposite aspect of corresponding entries, the correctness of the posting of the individual accounts of the two ledgers can be made possible. The balance of Total Debtors Account should always be equal to the balance of the individual balances of customers account on a particular day. If this is so, the sales ledger may be considered as correct. Same principle is, however, applicable in the case of Total Creditors Account.

At the end of each month the total of Sales Day Book will be debited to **'Total Debtors Account'** and **'Sales Account'** is credited in the general ledger. At the same time, all the credit items (viz., Cash Received from Debtors, Discount Allowed, Bad Debts, Bills Receivable etc.,) are credited to *'Total Debtors Account'* and respective accounts are correspondingly debited.

Same principle is also to be applied while preparing **'Total Creditors Account'** in the opposite manner. In short, at the end of each month, the total of Purchase Day Book will be credited to **'Total Creditors Account'** and **'Purchases Account'** is debited in the General Ledger. At the same time, all the debit items (viz., Cash paid to Creditors, Discount Received, Returns Outward, Bills Payable etc.) are debited to **'Total Creditors Account'** and respective accounts are correspondingly credited.

Thus, the individual customer's account is debited in the **'Debtors Ledger'** whereas Cash Received, Discount Allowed, Bill Receivable etc. are credited. At the same time, individual creditor's account is credited with credit purchases in the **'Creditors Ledger'** whereas Cash Paid, Discount Received, Bills Payable etc. are debited. So the correctness of the posting of the individual accounts of the two ledgers can be made possible (i.e., total of individual customers accounts must be equal to the total of **'Total Debtors Account'**.

The entries are recorded in the following manner :

(a) **For Total Debtors**

Original Entry	*Debtors Ledger*	*General Ledger*
1. For Sales Day Book, Bills Receivable Dishonoured, Interest and Charges etc.	Individual Customer's Account is debited	Total Debtors A/c Dr. To Sales A/c " B/R Dishonoured A/c " Interest and Charges A/c

Contd.

2. For, Cash Receipts, Discount Allowed, Returns Inward, Bad Debts, Bills Receivable etc.	Individual Customer's Account is credited	Cash A/c Dr. Discount Allowed A/c Dr. Returns Inward A/c Dr. Bad Debts A/c Dr. Bills Receivable A/c Dr. To Total Debtors A/c
(b) **For Total Creditors** For Purchase Day Book, Interest and Charges, etc.	Individual Creditor's Account is credited	Purchase A/c Dr. Interest and Charges A/c Dr. To Total Creditor's A/c
For Cash Payment, Discount Received, Returns Outward, Bills Payable etc.	Individual Creditor's Account is debited	Total Creditor's A/c Dr. To Cash A/c " Discount Received A/c " Returns Outward A/c " Bills Payable A/c

The outline of **'Total Debtors Account'** and **'Total Creditors Account' is presented :**

Total Debtors Account

Dr. Cr.

Date	*Particulars*	*Rs.*	*Date*	*Particulars*	*Rs.*
	To Balance b/d	* * *		By Balance b/d (*if any*)	* * *
	" Credit Sales	* * *		" Cash/Cheque received	* * *
	" B/R dishonored	* * *		" Discount Allowed	* * *
	" Interest and Charges	* * *		" Bad Debts	* * *
	" Cash paid to Debtors	* * *		" Returns Inward	* * *
	Balance c/d (*if any*)	* * *		" Bills Receivable	* * *
				" Transfer	* * *
				Balance c/d	
		* * *			* * *

Total Creditors Account

Dr. Cr.

Date	*Particulars*	*Rs.*	*Date*	*Particulars*	*Rs.*
	To Balance b/d (*if any*)	* * *		By Balance b/d	* * *
	" Cash and Cheque paid	* * *		" Purchases	* * *
	" Discount Received	* * *		" B/P Dishonoured	* * *
	" Bills Payable	* * *		" Balance c/d (*if any*)	* * *
	" Returns Outward	* * *			
	" Transfer	* * *			
	" Balance c/d	* * *			
		* * *			* * *

Self-Balancing System vs Sectional Balancing System

Self-Balancing System	*Sectional Balancing System*
1. It is possible to prepare separate Trial Balance at the end of each separate Ledger.	1. It is possible to prepare a Trial Balance in the General Ledger only.
2. Under this method, Debtors Ledger, Creditors Ledger and the General Ledger are separately balanced.	2. Only the General Ledger is balanced.
3. Adjustment accounts are prepared on the basis of Double Entry Principle.	3. Only the General Ledger maintains Debtors Account and Creditors Account. No adjustment accounts are necessary.

Contra Transactions/Advance Balance

Like Self-balancing Ledger, if there is any contra transaction, i.e., if Total Debtors Account shows a credit balance or Total Creditor's Accounts show a debit balance, the same may be treated accordingly like Self-Balancing Ledger. In short, in Total Debtors Account — By Balance b/d (for opening balance) and in Total Creditors Account — To balance b/d (for opening balance) are to be recorded. The reasons for such a temporary balance has already been explained earlier.

The following illustration will highlight the above principle :

Illustration 21

The following Balance Sheet is presented by Mr. Visal on 1st April 2012 :

Balance sheet
as at April 1, 2012

Liabilities	*Rs.*	*Assets*	*Rs.*
Capital	2,00,000	Plant and Machinery	40,000
Total Creditors	40,000	Land and Building	80,000
		Stock	40,000
		Total Debtors	50,000
		Cash at Bank	20,000
		Cash in hand	10,000
	2,40,000		2,40,000

List of Debtors
A Rs. 30,000; B Rs. 15,000 and C Rs. 5,000.

List of Creditors
P Rs. 20,000; Q Rs. 12,000 and R Rs. 8,000.

You are requested to enter the following transactions of Mr. Visal (assuming that he keeps his Books under Sectional Balancing System) in proper books, post them into ledger and also prepare a Trial Balance for General Ledger as on 30th April 2012 :

April 1		Rs.	April		Rs.
1	Sold goods to C	20,000	14	Paid to Q by cash	5,000
2	Bought goods from R	12,000	17	Paid Rent by cheque	3,000
4	Received a cheque from C	10,000	18	Paid Wages by Cash	8,000
6	Bought goods from P	8,000	20	Sold goods to B	20,000
8	Paid to R by cash	7,000	22	Sold goods to A	25,000
9	Paid to P by cheque	10,000	28	Received from B in cash	16,000
12	Bought goods from Q	8,000	30	Received a cheque from A	20,000

Solution

Purchase Day Book

Date	*Name of the Creditor*	*Outward Invoice*	*L.F.*	*Details*	*Total*	*Remarks*
2012				Rs.	Rs.	
April 2	R			12,000	12,000	
6	P			8,000	8,000	
12	Q			8,000	8,000	
					28,000	

The entry :

		Rs.	Rs.
In the General Ledger			
Purchase A/c	Dr.	28,000	
To Total Creditors A/c			28,000

Sales Day Book

Date	*Name of the Customer*	*Inward Invoice*	*L.F.*	*Details*	*Total*	*Remarks*
2012				Rs.	Rs.	
April 1	C			20,000	20,000	
20	B			20,000	20,000	
22	A			25,000	25,000	
					65,000	

The entry :

		Rs.	Rs.
In the General Ledger			
Total Debtors A/c	Dr.	65,000	
To Sales A/c			65,000

Cash Book (with Cash and Bank Columns)

Dr. Cr.

Date	Particulars	L.F	Cash	Bank	Date	Particulars	L.F.	Cash	Bank
2012			Rs.	Rs.	2012			Rs.	Rs.
Apr. 1	To Balance b/d		10,000	20,000	Apr. 1	By R A/c		7,000	
4	" C A/c		—	10,000	9	" P A/c			10,000
28	" B A/c		16,000	—	14	" Q A/c		5,000	
31	" A A/c		—	20,000	17	" Rent A/c			3,000
					18	" Wages A/c		8,000	
					30	" Balance c/d		6,000	37,000
			26,000	50,000				26,000	50,000

In the General Ledger

Plant and Machinery Account

Dr. Cr.

Date	Particulars	L.F.	Amount	Date	Particulars	L.F.	Amount
2012			Rs.	2012			Rs.
Apr. 1	To Balance b/d		40,000	Apr. 30	By Balance c/d		40,000
			40,000				40,000

Land and Building Account

Dr. Cr.

Date	Particulars	L.F.	Amount	Date	Particulars	L.F.	Amount
2012			Rs.	2012			Rs.
Apr. 1	To Balance b/d		80,000	Apr. 30	By Balance c/d		80,000
			80,000				80,000

Stock Account

Dr. Cr.

Date	Particulars	L.F.	Amount	Date	Particulars	L.F.	Amount
2012			Rs.	2012			Rs.
Apr. 1	To Balance b/d		40,000	Apr. 30	By Balance c/d		40,000
			40,000				40,000

Total Debtors Account

Dr. Cr.

Date	Particulars	L.F.	Amount	Date	Particulars	L.F.	Amount
2012			Rs.	2012			Rs.
Apr. 1	To Balance b/d		50,000	Apr. 4	By Bank (C)		10,000
30	" Sales A/c		65,000	28	" Cash (B)		16,000
				31	" Bank (A)		20,000
					" Balance c/d		69,000
			1,15,000				1,15,000

Total Creditors Account

Dr. Cr.

Date	Particulars	L.F.	Amount	Date	Particulars	L.F.	Amount
2012			Rs.	2012			Rs.
Apr. 8	By Cash (R)		7,000	Apr. 1	To Balance b/d		40,000
9	" Bank (P)		10,000	30	" Purchase A/c		28,000
14	" Cash (Q)		5,000				
30	" Balance c/d		46,000				
			68,000				68,000

Capital Account

Dr. Date	Particulars	L.F.	Amount	Date	Particulars	L.F.	Cr. Amount
2012			Rs.	2012			Rs.
Apr. 30	To Balance c/d		2,00,000	Apr. 1	By Balance b/d		2,00,000
			2,00,000				2,00,000

Purchases Account

Dr. Date	Particulars	L.F.	Amount	Date	Particulars	L.F.	Cr. Amount
2012			Rs.	2012			Rs.
Apr. 30	To Total Creditors A/c		28,000	Apr. 30	By Balance c/d		28,000
			28,000				28,000

Sales Account

Dr. Date	Particulars	L.F.	Amount	Date	Particulars	L.F.	Cr. Amount
2012			Rs.	2012			Rs.
Apr. 30	To Balance c/d		65,000	Apr. 30	By Total Debtors A/c		65,000
			65,000				65,000

Rent Account

Dr. Date	Particulars	L.F.	Amount	Date	Particulars	L.F.	Cr. Amount
2012			Rs.	2012			Rs.
Apr. 17	To Bank A/c		3,000	Apr. 30	By Balance c/d		3,000
			3,000				3,000

Wages Account

Dr. Date	Particulars	L.F.	Amount	Date	Particulars	L.F.	Cr. Amount
2012			Rs.	2012			Rs.
Apr. 18	To Cash A/c		8,000	Apr. 30	By Balance c/d		8,000
			8,000				8,000

Trial Balance
as at April 30, 2012

Head of Account	L.F.	Debit	Credit
		Rs.	Rs.
Plant and Machinery A/c		40,000	—
Land and Building A/c		80,000	—
Stock A/c		40,000	—
Cash A/c		6,000	—
Bank A/c		37,000	—
Total Debtors A/c		69,000	—
Total Creditors A/c		—	46,000
Capital A/c		—	2,00,000
Purchase A/c		28,000	—
Sales A/c		—	65,000
Rent A/c		3,000	—
Wages A/c		8,000	—
		3,11,000	3,11,000

In the Debtors Ledger
A Account

Dr. Date	Particulars	L.F.	Amount	Date	Particulars	L.F.	Cr. Amount
2012			Rs.	2012			Rs.
Apr. 1	To Balance b/d		30,000	Apr. 30	By Bank A/c		20,000
22	" Sales A/c		25,000		" Balance c/d		35,000
			55,000				55,000

B Account

Dr. Cr.

Date		Particulars	L.F.	Amount	Date		Particulars	L.F.	Amount
				Rs.					Rs.
2012					2012				
Apr. 1	To	Balance b/d		15,000	Apr. 28	By	Cash A/c		16,000
20	"	Sales A/c		20,000	30	"	Balance c/d		19,000
				35,000					35,000

C Account

Dr. Cr.

Date		Particulars	L.F.	Amount	Date		Particulars	L.F.	Amount
				Rs.					Rs.
2012					2012				
Apr. 1	To	Balance c/d		5,000	Apr. 4	By	Cash A/c		10,000
20	"	Sales A/c		20,000	30	"	Balance c/d		15,000
				25,000					25,000

In the Creditors Ledger

P Account

Dr. Cr.

Date		Particulars	L.F.	Amount	Date		Particulars	L.F.	Amount
				Rs.					Rs.
2012					2012				
Apr. 9	To	Bank A/c		10,000	Apr. 1	By	Balance b/d		20,000
30	"	Balance c/d		18,000	6	"	Purchases A/c		8,000
				28,000					28,000

Q Account

Dr. Cr.

Date		Particulars	L.F.	Amount	Date		Particulars	L.F.	Amount
				Rs.					Rs.
2012					2012				
Apr. 14	To	Cash A/c		5,000	Apr. 1	By	Balance b/d		12,000
30	"	Balance c/d		15,000	2	"	Purchase A/c		8,000
				20,000					20,000

R Account

Dr. Cr.

Date		Particulars	L.F.	Amount	Date		Particulars	L.F.	Amount
				Rs.					Rs.
2012					2012				
Apr. 8	To	Cash A/c		7,000	Apr. 1	By	Balance b/d		8,000
30	"	Balance c/d		13,000	2	"	Purchase A/c		12,000
				20,000					20,000

Verification

		Rs.			Rs.
Total Debtors =	A	35,000	Total Creditors =	P	18,000
	B	19,000		Q	15,000
	C	15,000		R	13,000
		69,000			46,000

Illustration 22

From the following figures, prepare Total Debtors Account and Total Creditors Account for the year ended 31st December 2012 :

	Rs.		Rs.
Debtors on 1st January 2012	36,400	Discount received from creditors	8,500
Creditors on 1st January 2012	26,900	Bills Receivable endorsed to creditors	25,000
Sales (including cash sales Rs. 18,500)	3,01,600	Bills Payable given to creditors	48,000
Sales Returns	2,100	Endorsed bills dishonoured	5,000
Purchases	2,19,000	Noting charges charged from debtors	10
Purchases Returns	5,000	Provision made for bad and doubtful debts	3,800
Cash received from debtors (including Rs. 2,000 against a debt previously written-off)	2,49,500	Provision made for discount on debtors	300
		Provision made for discount on creditors	150

	Rs.		Rs.
Discount allowed to Debtors	4,050	Credit balance in Sold Ledger on 31st December 2012	2,100
Bills receivable received from Debtors	42,000		
Bad Debts written-off	2,500	Debit balance in Bought Ledger on 31st December 2012	1,600
Cash paid to Creditors	1,44,600		
Transfer from Bought Ledger to Sales Ledger	3,200		

Solution

Dr. **Total Debtors or Debtors Control Account** *Cr.*

Date		*Particulars*	*Amount*	*Date*		*Particulars*	*Amount*
2012			Rs.	2012			Rs.
Jan. 1	To	Balance b/d	36,400	Dec. 31	By	Sales Returns	2,100
Dec. 31	"	Sales (3,01,600 – 18,500)	2,83,100		"	Cash	2,47,500
	"	Total Creditors A/c (Endorsed B/R dishonoured)	5,000		"	Discount Allowed	4,050
	"	Cash (noting charges)	10		"	Bills Receivable	42,000
	"	Balance c/d	2,100		"	Bad Debts	2,500
					"	Transfer from Bought Ledger	3,200
					"	Balanced c/d	25,260
			3,26,610				3,26,610
2013				2013			
Jan. 1	By	Balance b/d	25,260	Jan. 1	By	Balance b/d	2,100

Dr. **Total Creditors or Creditors Control Account** *Cr.*

Date		*Particulars*	*Amount*	*Date*		*Particulars*	*Amount*
2012			Rs.	2012			Rs.
Dec. 31	To	Purchases Return	5,000	Jan. 1	By	Balance b/d	26,900
	"	Cash	1,44,600	Dec. 31	"	Purchases	2,19,000
	"	Transfer to Sales Ledger	3,200		"	Total Debtors A/c (Endorsed bill dishonoured)	5,000
	"	Discount Received	8,500		"	Balance c/d	1,600
	"	Bills Receivable	25,000				
	"	Bills Payable	48,000				
	"	Balance c/d	18,200				
			2,52,500				2,52,500
2013				2013			
July 1	By	Balance b/d	1,600	July 1	By	Balance b/d	18,200

Note : There will be no entry for Bad Debts recovered, Provisions made for Doubtful Debts, Discount on Debtors and Discount on Creditors.

Illustration 23

The following details were extracted from the books of a Company for the six months ended 31.3.2010 :

	Rs.		Rs.
Debtors balances total 1.10.2009	1,927	Purchase returns	182
Suppliers balances total 1.10.2009	1,215	Interest charged to Debtors	5
Cash paid to Suppliers	7,613	Debtors cheques dishonoured	76
Cash received from Debtors	12,993	Discount allowed	356
Purchases	8,849	Bills Payable accepted (including renewals)	891
Discounts received	56	Bills Payable withdrawn upon renewal	200
Bad Debts written-off	286	Interest on Bills payable renewed	3
Sales returns	93	Sales	13,308

The total of the Balances extracted from the Trade Ledgers on 31.3.2010, were

Sold Ledger Rs. 1,808 Bought Ledger Rs. 1,290

Prepare Total Debtors Account and Creditors Account from the details given above and show whether the balances agree with balances per schedule as extracted from the Trade Ledgers as on 31.3.2010.

Solution

Total Debtors Account

Dr. Date	Particulars	Amount	Date	Particulars	Cr. Amount
2009		Rs.	2010		Rs.
Oct. 1	To Balance b/d	1,927	Mar. 31	By Cash	12,993
2010				" Bad Debt	56
Mar. 31	" Sales	13,308		" Discount Allowed	356
	" Bank (cheque dishonoured)	76		" Returns Inward	93
	" Interest	5		" Balance c/d	1,818
		15,316			15,316

Total Creditors Account

Dr. Date	Particulars	Amount	Date	Particulars	Cr. Amount
2010		Rs.	2009		Rs.
Mar. 31	To Cash	7,613	Oct. 1	By Balance b/d	1,215
	" Returns Outward	182	2010	" Purchases	8,849
	" Bills Payable	891	Mar. 31	" Bills Payable (Renewal)	200
	" Discount Received	286		" Interest	3
	" Balance c/d	1,295			
		10,267			10,267

	Rs.		Rs.
Debtors balance as per schedule	1,808	whereas, Creditors balance as per schedule	1,290
Debtor balance as per Total Account	1,818	Creditors balance as per Total Account	1,295
Difference	10	Difference	5

Thus, the total accounts do not agree with the balance as per schedule.

Illustration 24

Total Accounts are employed in the business of Elite & Co. in relation to the Sales Ledger of X and Y. The following are the material details :

		X	Y
		Rs.	Rs.
Opening Balance	Dr.	12,500	31,000
	Cr.	300	—
Sales as per Sales Day Book		31,200	43,100
Returns as per Returns Day Book		3,170	2,050
Cash received as per Cash Book		20,050	51,200
Discount Allowed as per Cash Book		1,300	2,700
Bad Debts written-off as per journal		3,710	4,250
Provision for Bad Debts as per journal		5,000	6,000
Bad Debts, previously written-off now received as per Cash Book		300	—
Allowances as per Allowance Book		420	370
Bills Receivable as per Bills Book		1,300	—
Bills dishonoured as per Cash Book		500	—
Cash Sales		2,000	—
Closing Credit Balance		720	210

The transfer journal contains a correcting entry in respect of Rs. 1,200 sales which had been entered in error on X ledger analysis column in the Sales Day Book instead of in the Y ledger analysis column, although the item had been posted to the correct ledger account in Y ledger.

Prepare Total Debtors Accounts.

Solution

Debtors Control Account

Dr.							Cr.
Date	Particulars	Amount X	Amount Y	Date	Particulars	Amount X	Amount Y
		Rs.	Rs.			Rs.	Rs.
	To Balance b/d	12,500	31,000		By Balance b/d	300	—
	Sales	31,200	43,100		Returns	3,170	2,050
	Bills Dishonoured	500	—		Cash	20,050	51,200
	Transfer	—	1,200		Discount	1,300	2,700
	" Balance c/d	720	210		Bad Debts	3,710	4,250
					Allowances	420	370
					Bills Receivable	1,300	—
					Transfer	1,200	—
					" Balance c/d	13,470	14,940
		44,920	75,510			44,920	75,510
	To Balance b/d	13,470	14,940		By Balance b/d	720	210

RECTIFICATION OF ERRORS

Rectification of errors has already been discussed earlier in **Chapter 10 in present volume.** The same method and technique may be exercised here also. The only exception from that procedure is that we are to see whether or not the error (i) ***affects the total of subsidiary books and/or,*** (ii) ***relates to a transfer of account from one Ledger to another.***

Under the former, if the error affects purchase or sales ledger, the same may be rectified by making a self-balancing entry in addition to the usual rectifying entry. This is due to the fact that when the total of subsidiary book is wrong, the corresponding adjustment accounts are also affected accordingly. Needless to say, if the said error does not affect the total, no additional self-balancing entry is required.

For instance, if Purchase Day Book is undercast, the wrong total of the same will affect (i) Purchase Account, and (ii) Creditors Ledger Adjustment Account in General Ledger), and, also (iii) General Ledger Adjustment Account (in Creditors Ledger). Thus, the same will be rectified as :

(i) Normal rectifying entry for correcting purchase account—

Purchase A/c Dr.
To Suspense A/c

(ii) For correcting adjustment accounts under self-balancing system—

General Ledger Adjustment A/c Dr.
(in C.L.A.)
To Creditors Ledger Adjustment A/c
(in G.L.A.)

But if goods are purchased from Mr. A for Rs. 1,000 which has been posted as Rs. 100 only, the same error does not affect the total of purchase book and, as such, the above seconed entry (ii) is not required to be passed. Only the following entries are to be recorded —

Suspense A/c Dr. 900
To A A/c 900

Again, if there is any error which relates to the transfer of an account from one ledger to another in addition to usual rectifying entries, two more journal entries are needed.

Thus, the whole procedure may be summed up as :

(a) At first, correct the error in the usual manner;

(b) Secondly, to see whether the said error affects the total of subsidiary book or not.
If it affects—one additional entry is required.
If it does not affect —no entry is required.

(c) For transfer (from one ledger to another), necessary self-balancing entries are required.

Illustration 25

Rectify the following errors under self-balancing system :

(a) Sales Book was undercast by Rs. 100.

(b) Goods sold to Mr. X for Rs. 1,000 was recorded in the books as Rs. 100.

(c) Goods purchased from Mr. B for Rs. 500 was posted to C's account only, Rs. 50.

(d) Debit balance of Rs. 100 in P's Account in sales ledger was set-off against his account in the Creditors Ledger.

(e) Purchased a Plant for Rs. 4,000, passed through the invoice book.

Solution

In the books of ....

Journal

Date		Particulars		L.F.	Debit	Credit
					Rs.	Rs.
(a)	(i)	Suspense A/c	Dr.		100	
		To Sales A/c				100
		(It rectifies the Sales A/c)				
	(ii)	Debtors Ledger Adjustment A/c (In General Ledger)	Dr.		100	
		To General Ledger Adjustment A/c (In Debtors Ledger)				100
		(Sales book was undercast)				
(b)	(i)	Mr. X A/c	Dr.		900	
		To Sales A/c				900
		(It rectifies the undercasting)				
	(ii)	Debtors Ledger Adjustment A/c (In General Ledger)	Dr.		900	
		To General Ledger Adjustment A/c (In Debtors Ledger)				900
		(Undercasting affects the total)				
(c)	(i)	Suspense A/c	Dr.		450	
		C's A/c	Dr.		50	
		To B's A/c				500
		(Since it does not affect the total, 2nd type of entry is not needed. Only C's and B's accounts are to be corrected.)				
(d)	(i)	P (in C.L.A.) A/c	Dr.		100	
		To P (in D.L.A.) A/c				100
		(It makes the transfer effective)				
	(ii)	Creditors Ledger Adjustment A/c (In General Ledger)	Dr.		100	
		To General Ledger Adjustment A/c (in Creditors Ledger)				100
	(iii)	General Ledger Adjustment A/c (In Debtors Ledger)	Dr.		100	
		To Debtors Ledger Adjustment A/c (In General Ledger)				100
		(Transfer from one Ledger to another affects both the ledger and, as such, 2nd type of entries are needed.)				
(e)	(i)	Plant A/c	Dr.		4,000	
		To Purchase A/c				4,000
		(Purchase of Plant wrongly debited to Purchase A/c, now rectified)				
	(ii)	Party A/c (In Creditors Ledger)	Dr.		4,000	
		To Party A/c (In General Ledger)				4,000
		(It closes the suppliers account in Creditors Ledger and re-opens his account in General Ledger.)				

Contd.

			Rs.	Rs.
(iii)	Creditors Leger Adjustment A/c (In General Ledger)	Dr.	4,000	
	To General Ledger Adjustment A/c (In Creditors Ledger)			4,000
	(It cancels the old entry)			

Illustration 26

The net balance of the Sales Ledger Control Acount (Rs. 53,837) of a trader, as on Dec. 2012, does not tally with the total of the balances of the Sales Ledger Accounts.

The following errors are subsequently discovered and the necessary adjustments balanced the books :

(1) Debit Balance in the Sales Ledger to the total of Rs. 1,768 has not been included in the list of sales leger balances.

(2) A bad debt of Rs. 372 written-off in the Sales Ledger has not been entered in the Control Account or debited to Bad Debts Account.

(3) Discount of Rs. 415 allowed to a customer had been duly entered in the books. It had subsequently been disallowed and debited to the customer's acount but entered in the discount received column of the Cash Book.

(4) Rs. 693 has been transferred from a customer's account in the Sales Ledger to his account in the Purchase Ledger, but no entry had been made in the Control Account.

Draft the necesary adjustment entries in the Journal and show the adjustments in the Sales Ledger Control Account.

Solution **[CU BCom (Hons.)]**

In the books of ....
Journal

Date	*Particulars*		*L.F.*	*Debit* Rs.	*Credit* Rs.
2012 Dec. 31					
(1)	Rs. 1,768 should be included with sales ledger balances, and it will not affect Control Account			—	
(2)	Bad Debts A/c	Dr.		372	
	To Sales Ledger Control A/c				372
	(Bad debts written-off without recording Bad Debts Account and also not recorded in general ledger, now rectified.)				
(3) (i)	Discount Received A/c	Dr.		415	
	To Purchases Ledger Control A/c				415
(ii)	Sales Ledger Control A/c	Dr.		415	
	To Discount Allowed A/c				415
	(Cancellation of discount previously allowed which was wrongly entered in Discount Received account, now rectified.)				
(4)	Purchase Ledger Control A/c	Dr.		693	
	To Sales Ledger Control A/c				693
	(Transfer of a customer's balance from sales ledger to his account in the purchase ledger, not recorded, now rectified.)				

In General Ledger
Sales Ledger Control Account

Dr. Cr.

Date	*Particulars*	*Amount* Rs.	*Date*	*Particulars*	*Amount* Rs.
2012			2012		
July 1	To Balance b/d	53,837	July 1	By Bad Debts	372
Dec. 31	" Discount Allowed A/c	415	Dec. 31	" Purchase Ledger Control A/c	693
				" Balance c/d	53,187
		54,252			54,252
2013					
January	To Balance b/d	53,187			

Illustration 27

The balance on the Sales Ledger Control Account of Robin & Co. on September 30, 2012, amounted to Rs. 3,800, which did not agree with the net total of the list of sales ledger balance on that date.

Errors were found and the appropriate adjustments when made balanced the books. The errors were :

(a) Debit balance in the sales ledger amounting to Rs. 103 had been omitted from the list of balances.

(b) A Bad Debt amounting to Rs. 400 had been written-off in the sales ledger, but had not been posted to the Bad Debts Account, or entered in the Control Account.

(c) An item of goods sold to S. for Rs. 250 had been entered once in the Day Book but posted to his account twice.

(d) Rs. 25 Discount Allowed to W had been correctly recorded and posted in the books. This sum had been subsequently disallowed, debited to W's account, and entered in the discount received column of the Cash Book.

(e) No entry had been made in the Control Account in respect of the transfer of a debit of Rs. 70 from Q's Account in the Sales Ledger to his account in the Purchase Ledger.

(f) The Discount Allowed column in the Cash Book had been undercast by Rs. 140.

You are required to give the journal entries, where necessary, to rectify these errors, indicating whether or not any control accounts is affected, and to make necessary adjustments in the Sales Ledger Control Account bringing down the balance.

[CU BCom (Hons.)]

Solution

In the books of ....
Journal

Date	Particulars		L.F.	Debit Rs.	Credit Rs.
2012 Sept. 30					
(a)	Rs. 103 should be added with Sales Ledger balances and it will not affect Control Account.)				
(b)	Bad Debts A/c	Dr.		400	
	To Sales Ledger Control A/c				400
	(Bad Debts written-off without recording in general ledger, now rectified.)				
(c)	S's Account should be credited by Rs. 250.			—	—
	It will not affect Control Account.				
(d) (i)	Discount Received A/c	Dr.		25	
	To Purchases Ledger Control A/c				25
(ii)	Sales Ledger Control A/c	Dr.		25	
	To Discount Allowed A/c				25
	(Cancellation of discount previously allowed, which was wrongly treated as discount received, now rectified.)				
(e)	Purchase Ledger Control A/c	Dr.		70	
	To Sales Ledger Control A/c				70
	(Transfer of debit of Q's Account to Purchase Ledger, not recorded, now rectified.)				
(f)	Discount Allowed A/c	Dr.		140	
	To Sales Ledger Control A/c				140
	(Discount allowed account undercast, now rectified.)				

In General Ledger
Sales Ledger Control Account

Dr. Cr.

Date	Particulars	Amount Rs.	Date	Particulars	Amount Rs.
2011 Oct. 1	To Balance b/d	3,800	2012 Sept. 30	By Bad Debts A/c	400
2012 Sept. 30	" Discount Allowed A/c	25		" Purchases Ledger Control A/c	70
				" Discount Allowed, A/c	140
				" Balance c/d	3,215
		3,825			3,825
Oct. 1	To Balance b/d	3,215			

GENERAL ILLUSTRATIONS

Illustration 28

Prepare the General Ledger Adjustment Accounts as will appear in the Debtors and Debtors Ledger Adjustment Account in General Ledger and General Ledger Adjustment in Creditors Account Ledger and Creditors Ledger Adjustment Account in General Ledger from the balance on 1.4.2011 :

	Dr. Rs.	*Cr.* Rs.
Debtors Ledger	47,200	240
Creditors Ledger	280	26,300

Trans. for the year ended 31.3.2012	Rs.		Rs.
Total Sales	1,20,000	Bills Receivable Dishonoured	1,500
Cash Sales	8,100	Bills Receivables Discount	5,000
Total Purchases	89,500	Bills Receivable Endorsed to Creditors	4,000
Credit Purchase	67,000	Endorse Bills Dishonoured	1,000
Creditors paid-off (in full settlement of Rs. 40,000)	39,500	Bad Debts written-off (after deducting Bad Debts Recovered Rs. 300)	2,200
Received from Debtors (In full settlement of Rs. 59,000)	58,200	Provision from Doubtful Debts	550
		Transfer from Debtors' Ledger to Creditors' Ledger	1,100
Returns from Debtors	2,600	Transfer from Creditors' Ledger to Debtors' Ledger	1,900
Returns to Creditors	1,800	Balances on 31.3.2012	
Bills Accepted for Creditors	5,500	Debtors Ledger (Cr.)	380
Bills Payable Matured	8,000	Creditors : Ledger (Dr.)	420
Bills Accepted by Customer	20,100		

Solution

In Debtors' Ledger
General Ledger Adjustment Account

Dr. *Cr.*

Date	*Particulars*	*Amount*	*Date*	*Particulars*	*Amount*
		Rs.			Rs.
2011 April 1	To Balance b/d	240	2011 April 1	By Balance b/d	47,200
2012 Mar. 31	" Debtor's Ledger Adjustment Account		2012 Mar. 31	Debtors' Ledger Adjustment Account	
	Bank	58,200		Sales (on credit)	1,12,000
	Discount Allowed	800		Bills Receivable Dishonoured	1,500
	Returns	2,600		Endorse Bills Receivable Dishonoured	1,000
	Bills Receivable	20,100			
	Bad Debts written-off	2,500			
	Transfer	1,100			
	Transfer	1,900			
	By Balance c/d	74,640		By Balance c/d	380
		1,62,080			1,62,080

In General Ledger
Debtors Ledger Adjustment Account

Dr. *Cr.*

Date	*Particulars*	*Amount*	*Date*	*Particulars*	*Amount*
		Rs.			Rs.
2011 Apr.1	To Balance b/d	47,200	2011 Apr. 1	By Balance b/d	240
2012 Mar. 31	" General Ledger Adj. A/c		2012 Mar. 31	" General Ledger Adj. A/c	
	Sales (on Credit)	1,12,000		Bank	58,200
	B/R Dishonoured	1,500		Discount Allowed	800
	Endorsed Bill Receivable dishonoured	1,000		Returns Inward	2,600
				Bills Receivable	20,100
	By Balance c/d	380		Bad Debts written-off (Rs. 2,200 + Rs. 300)	2,500
				Transfer	1,100
				Transfer	1,900
				" Balance c/d	74,640
		1,62,080			1,62,080

In Creditors Ledger
General Ledger Adjustment Account

Dr. Cr.

Date	Particulars	Amount	Date	Particulars	Amount
2011		Rs.	2011		Rs.
Apr. 1	To Balance b/d	26,300	Jan. 11	By Balance b/d	280
2012			2012		
Mar. 31	To Creditors' Ledger Adjustment Account :		Mar. 31	" Creditors' Ledger Adjustment Account :	
	Purchases	67,000		Bank	39,500
	Endorsed Bills Receivable dishonoured	1,000		Discount Received	500
	Balance c/d	420		Returns	1,800
				Bills Payable	5,500
				Bills Receivable endorsed	4,000
				Transfer	1,,100
				Transfer	1,900
				Balance c/d	40,140
		94,720			94,720

In the General Ledger
Creditors Ledger Adjustment Account

Dr. Cr.

Date	Particulars	Amount	Date	Particulars	Amount
2011		Rs.	2011		Rs.
Apr. 1	To Balance c/d	280	Apr. 1	By Balance b/d	26,300
2012			2012		
Mar. 31	" General Ledger Adj. A/c		Mar. 31	" General Ledger Adj. A/c :	
	Bank	39,500		Purchases	67,000
	Discount Received	500		Endorsed B/R Dis.	1,000
	Returns Outward	1,800		By Balance c/d	420
	Bills Payable	5,500			
	B/R Endorsed	4,000			
	Transfer	1,100			
	Transfer	1,900			
	By Balance c/d	40,140			
		97,420			97,420

Workings:

1. The following items will neither affect Debtors Ledger nor Creditors Ledger as these do not have any bearing on them :

(i) Cash Sales; (ii) Bills Payable matured, (ii) Bills Receivable Discounted; (iv) Bad Debt recovered; and (v) Provision for Doubtful Debts.

2. **Discount Received**

Out of Rs. 40,000, creditors were paid for Rs..39,500

3. **Discount Allowed**

Out of Rs. 59,000. Cash received Rs. 58,200 i.e., Discount Allowed Rs. 59,000 – Rs. 58,200 = Rs. 800

∴ Discount Received : Rs. 40,000 – Rs. 39,500 = Rs. 500

Special Note

In the present problems, both the opening balance as well as the closing balance of both debtors and creditors are given, accounts are closed automatically having no difference in any side.

On Consignment Transactions

Illustration 29

From the following particulars prepare the General Ledger Adjustment Account as it would appear in Consignment of Delhi Enterprise assuming that the commission is payable @ 10% on sales:

		Mumbai	Kolkata	Kanpore	Chennai	Lucknow	Patna
2012		Rs,	Rs.	Rs.	Rs.	Rs.	Rs.
Jan. 1	Balance of Consignment Stock	50,000	60,000	50,000	70,000	20,000	20,000
Dec. 31	Goods sent on Consignment	2,00,000	3,00,000	4,00,000	2,00,000	1,00,000	1,50,000
"	Expenses Incurred	10,000	20,000	10,000	5,000	10,000	15,000
"	Sale of Consignment	4,00,000	5,00,000	6,00,000	3,00,000	2,00,000	2,50,000
"	Stock of Consignment	—	—	10,000	15,000	10,000	20,000

Commission in each case is 10% on sales.

Solution

In the Consignment Ledger
General Ledger Adjustment Account

Dr. Cr.

Date	Particulars	Amount	Date	Particulars	Amount
2012		Rs.	2012		Rs.
Dec. 3	To Sales	22,50,000	Jan 1	By Consignment Stock	2,70,000
	" Consignment Stock	55,000	Dec. 31	" Goods sent on Cons.	13,50,000
				" Expenses	70,000
				" Commission	2,25,000
				" Balance c/d (Profit)	2,90,000*
		23,05,000			23,05,000

* The total profit made on consignment is equal to the balance of General Ledger Adjustment Account.

Workings :

Before passing the General Ledger Adjusment Account, we are to commpute the following :

		Mumbai	+	Kolkata	+	Kanpore	+	Chennai	+	Lucknow	+	Patna	Total
		Rs.		Rs.		Rs.		Rs.		Rs.		Rs.	Rs.
Consignment Stock (Opening)	=	50,000	+	60,000	+	50,000	+	70,000	+	20,000	+	20,000	2,70,000
Goods Sent on Cons.	=	2,00,000	+	3,00,000	+	4,00,000	+	2,00,000	+	1,00,000	+	1,50,000	13,50,000
Expenses	=	10,000	+	20,000	+	10,000	+	5,000	+	10,000	+	15,000	70,000
Sales	=	4,00,000	+	5,00,000	+	6,00,000	+	3,00,000	+	2,00,000	+	2,50,000	22,50,000
Cons. Stock (closing)	=	0	+	0	+	10,000	+	15,000	+	10,000	+	20,000	55,000

Reconciliation of Balances

Illustration 30

The net total balances extracted from purchases ledger of Pradip Das, on 31st March 2010, amounted to Rs. 12,560 which did not agree with the balance on the Purchase Ledger Control Account.

The audit recalled the following errors and when the appropriate adjustments had been made for these, the books balance:

(a) A debit balance of Rs. 40 in the Purchase Ledger had been recorded as a credit balance.

(b) H had been debited for goods returned to him Rs. 90 and no other entry had been made.

(c) The Purchase Day Book had been overcast by Rs. 100.

(d) Credit balance on the Purchase Ledger amounting to Rs. 480 and the debit balance amounting to Rs. 24 had been omitted from the list of balances.

(e) A payment of Rs. 8 to for a cash purchase of goods had been recorded in the Petty Cash Book and posted to his account in the Purchase Ledger, no other entry having been made.

(f) The transfer of Rs. 120 from Z's account in the Sales Ledger to the credit of his account in the Purchase Ledger had not been entered in the Control Account.

You are required to prepare:

(1) A statement reconciling the original net balances extracted from the purchase ledger with the corrected balance on the Purchase Ledger Control Account, and

(2) The Purchase Ledger Control Account showing the balance just before the correction of the errors an the necessary adjustments thereon.

Solution

Reconciliation Statement

		Rs.	Rs.
	Net total balance in Purchase Ledger		12,500
Add:	Credit balance omitted		480
			13,040
Less:	Debit balance incorrectly recorded as credit balance	80	
	Debit balance omitted	24	104
			12,936

Balance as per General Ledger Control
Purchase Ledger Control Account

Dr. Cr.

		Rs.			Rs.
To	Returns	90	By	Balance b/d *(bal. fig.)*	13,014
"	Overcasting in Day Book	100	"	Sales Ledger Control A/c	120
"	Cash	8			
"	Balance c/d	12,936			
		13,134			13,134

Illustration 31

The details of the balances owed by customers were as follows as on 1st April 2012:

	Rs.
X	15,000
Y (6% considered to be bad; adequate provision maintained)	21,000
Z	18,000
Of the Customers	3,56,000
	4,10,000
Less: Advance by P	20,000
	3,90,000

Sales during the month amounted to Rs. 5,55,000 including a cash sales of Rs. 1,14,000; of the credit sales Rs. 26,000 was to P. X returned goods to the extent of Rs. 6,000 and sent a bill receivable for the balance. A sum of Rs. 4,500 was received from Y and the balance was written-off. On instructions from B, Z's balance was transferred to Y's account in the creditors ledger. The acceptance of X was dishonoured and noting charges were Rs. 150. D sent an advance of Rs. 18,000 for supply of goods. Out of the amount due from "Other Customers" on 1st April, 2012 Rs. 2,73,000 was rceived; the customers had earned $2\frac{1}{2}$% discount on the amount paid. Similarly, out of the sale in April, a sum of Rs. 97,500 has been received, earning discount at same rate.

Q, who owed Rs. 11,000, and H, who owed Rs. 8,000, turned doubtful; a provision of 50% of the amounts due was created. Other debts were considered all good.

Prepare Total Debtors Account for April 2012.

Solution

In the General Ledger
Creditors Ledger Adjustment Account

Dr. Cr.

Date		Particulars	Amount	Date		Particulars	Amount
2012			Rs.	2012			Rs.
Apr. 1	To	Balance b/d (15,000 + 21,000 + 18,000 + 3,56,000)	4,10,000	Apr. 1	By	Balance b/d —Advanced by P	20,000
April, 30	"	Sales (credit A/c (5,55,000 – 1,14,000)	4,41,000	Apr. 30	"	Cash A/c	3,93,000[1]
	"	Bills Receivable A/c —Dishonoured	9,000		"	Discount Allowed A/c	9,500[2]
	"	Cash A/c—Noting Charges	150		"	Bad Debts (21,000 – 4,500)	16,500
	"	Balance c/d —D	18,000		"	Returns Inwards A/c —by X	6,000
					"	Bills Receivable A/c —by X	9,000
					"	Transfer —Z balance	18,000
					"	Balance c/d	4,06,150
			8,78,150				8,78,150
May, I	To	Balance b/d	4,06,150	May 1	By	Balance b/d	18,000

Workings :

1. **Amount received from Customer**

		Rs.
	From Y	4,500
	D (advance)	18,000
Add:	Ex-sale before April 1	2,73,000

2. **Discount Allowed**

@ $2\frac{1}{2}$% on net, i.e. $97\frac{1}{2}$ $(100 - 2\frac{1}{2})$.

So, on Rs. 3,70,500 (2,73,000 + 97,500)

Ex-sale during April	97,500
	3,93,000

$$= \text{Rs. } 3{,}70{,}500 \times \frac{2\frac{1}{2}}{97\frac{1}{2}}$$

$$= \text{Rs. } 9{,}500$$

ASSIGNMENT MATERIALS

THEORETICAL

Short-Answer Type Questions

1. What is Self Balancing Ledger? Mention its advantages.
2. What are Transfer entries? How do you treat them?
3. What are Contra transactions?
4. What is Sectional Balancing System?
5. How do you prepare Trial Balance under Self-Balancing System?
6. How do you prepare two Debtors Ledger?
7. Define : General Ledger Adjuustment Account, Debtors Ledger Adjustment Account, Creditors Ledger Adjustment Account.
8. What are rectification of errors?

Long-Answer Type Questions

9. Distinguish between Self-Balancing System and Sectional Balancing System.
10. How do you rectify errors under Self-Balancing System?
11. How do you prepare two debtors ledger?
12. What are Contra transactions? Explain with the help of an example.
13. What are the advantage of Self-Balancing System?
14. What is Sectional Balancing System? How do you treat it?
15. Why do a Debtors Ledger Adjustment Account and a Creditors Ledger Adjustment Account show as opposite balance?

PRACTICAL

A. Preparationnn Debtors Leger Adjustment Account

1. The following details were extracted from the Books of Mr. Abu for the period ended 31st December 2012 :

2012 Jan. 1

Dec. 31	Rs.		Rs.
Sales Ledger Balances	12,400	Cheques dishonoured	100
Provision for Doubtful Debts	1,000	B/R as endorsed dishonoured	120
Sales (including cash sales Rs. 4,000)	23,000	Bills Receivable discounted	500
Cash received from customers	18,500	Bad Debts written-off	50
Bills Receivable received	3,000	Interest charged to customers	10
Returns from customers	380	Bad Debts previously written-off recovered	60
Bills endorsed	480		
Bills dishonoured	300	Transfer from Bought Ledger	150
		Sundry charges debited to customers	20

Prepare the necessary Adjustment Account.

[Ans. Debtors Ledger Adjustment A/c (Dr.) Rs. 9,870]

2. From the following particulars, prepare Adjustment Account for the year ended 30.5.2012, as it would appear in the General Ledger under Self-balancing System :

	Rs.
Debit balance in Debtors account as on 30.6.2011	5,500
Credit " " " " "	500
Credit sales	40,000
Recoveries during the year	25,000
Refunds during the year	500
Bills Receivable received	10,000

Contd.

	Rs.
Credit Notes issued for goods returned	1,000
Bills Receivable dishonoured	1,500
Cash discount allowed	300
Bad debts written-off	800
Transfer and other adjustments to the debit of Debtors Account	400
Transfer and other adjustments to the credit of Debtors Account	200

[Ans. Debtors Ledger Adjustment A/c (Dr.) Rs. 10,100]

3. From the following particulars, prepare Sales Ledger Adjustment Account in General Ledger :

		Rs.
1st Jan. 2012 :		
	Sales ledger balance	37,500
	Provision for Doubtful Debts	2,500
31st Jan. 2012 :		
	Sales during the month	75,000
	Cash received from customers	65,800
	Returns from customers	550
	Bills accepted by customers	3,200
	Cheques received from customers	3,150
	Bills dishonoured	800
31st Jan. 2012 :		
	Cheques dishonoured	250
	Bad debts written off	450
	Bad debts previously written-off recovered	80
	Bills accepted by customers renewed	200
		Rs.
	Interest charged on Bills renewed	5
	Carriage charged to customers	120
	Cash discount allowed	1,300
	Cash paid to customers, received by mistake	130

(*Note* : Renewed bill of Rs. 205 included in Rs. 3,200.)

[Ans. Sales Ledger Adjustment A/c (Dr.) Rs. 39,355]

Hints : Provision for doubtful debts; Bad debts previously written-off recovered; will not appear in Sales Ledger Adjustment A/c; Rs. 130 will appear in debit side of the D. L. Adjustment A/c for cash paid to customers, received by mistake.

4. From the following details extracted from the books of Suparna Ltd. for the year ended March 31, 2012, prepare Sales Ledger Adjustment Account as it would appear in the General Ledger:

		Rs.
Sales ledger balance as on 1.4.2012	(Dr.)	45,256
" " " " "	(Cr.)	156
Provision for Bad Debts		5,000
Total sales during the period		1,40,856
Cash sales during the period		15,200
Cash received from customers		1,56,215
Bills Receivable		11,250
Bills Dishonoured		1,270
Bad Debts written-off		1,000
Interest on overdue account		500
Cash discount allowed		150
Bad debts previously written-off now recovered		465
Returns from customers		726
Bills Receivable endorsed		2,000
Bills Receivable discounted		1,000

Goods to the value of Rs. 1,550 were returned by a customer for which fresh goods were issued. Though a credit note was issued for the return of the goods, the sales invoice was, inadvertently, not prepared for the issue of fresh goods.

[Ans. Debtors Ledger Adjustment A/c (Dr.) Rs. 4,735]

Hints : 1. Total Credit Sales = Total Sales – Cash Sales = Rs. 1,40,856 – Rs. 15,200 = Rs. 1,25,656.

2. Bills Receivable endorsed and Bills Receivable discounted have no connection with Debtors' Ledger, hence will be excluded.

5. Jolly Parai of Lake Town sold goods to the following customers viz., Manisha, Chandrani, Goonjan, Sujaya and Sohini. She keeps her ledgers under self-balancing system. She furnishes the following particulars for the year 2005 relating to her customers :

	Manisha	Chandrani	Goonjan	Sujaya	Sohini
	Rs.	Rs.	Rs.	Rs.	Rs.
Opening balance	1,000	—	2,000	500	1,500
Credit Sales	10,000	9,000	12,000	8,000	9,500
Cash Received	6,000	7,000	8,000	4,000	3,000
Discount Allowed	1,000	—	500	—	1,000
Goods Returned	500	500	1,000	1,500	—
B/R received	—	1,000	—	500	2,000
B/R dishonoured	—	—	—	500	1,000

You are required to show the Debtors Ledger Adjustment Account in the Nominal Ledger and respective customer's account and General Ledger Adjustment Account in Debtors Ledger.

Show also the Trial Balance under self-balancing system.

[Ans. Debtors Ledger Adjustment A/c (Dr.) Rs. 17,500]

B. Preparation of Creditors/Purchase Ledger Adjustment Account

6. X Co. Ltd. have three Ledgers — Debtors' Ledger, Creditors' Ledger and General Ledger — which are all kept under self-balancing system. From the following particulars prepare the relevant adjustment accounts that would appear in each of the Ledgers :

		Rs.			Rs.
Debtors' balance on 1.1.2010	(Dr.)	15,000	Bills Payable accepted		4,000
	(Cr.)	1,000	Bills Receivable drawn		7,500
Creditors' balance on 1.1.2010	(Dr.)	600	Bills Receivable dishonoured		2,000
	(Cr.)	12,800	Bills Receivable discounted		1,500
Purchases (including cash Rs. 1,500)		36,000	Bills Receivable endorsed		4,300
Sales (including cash Rs. 3,000)		75,000	B/R as endorsed dishonoured		1,000
Cash paid to Creditors		21,000	Bad Debt		800
Collection from Debtors		62,000	Provision for Bad Debt		1,100
Discount Allowed		260	Transfer from Debtors' Ledger to		
Discount Received		320	Creditors' Ledger		500
Returns Inward		2,400	Debtors' balance on 31.12.2010	(Cr.)	300
Returns Outward		1,600	Creditors' balance on 31.12.2010	(Dr.)	200

[CU BCom (Hons.)]

[Ans. Debtors' Ledger Adjustment A/c (Dr.) Rs. 25,840, Creditors' Ledger Adjustment A/c (Cr.) Rs. 16,180]

C. Preparation of Debtors Ledger Adustment Account and Creditors Ledger Adjustment Account.

7. Indian Radicals Ltd. has three ledgers — Debtors' Ledger, Creditors' Ledger and General Ledger — which are kept under self-balancing system. From the following particulars, prepare the relevant adjustment accounts that would appear in each of the Ledgers :

	Rs.		Rs.
Debtors' Ledger Balance on 1.1.10 (Dr.)	16,000	Acceptance matured	5,000
Debtors' Ledger Balance on 1.1.10 (Cr.)	2,000	Acceptance dishonoured	3,000
Creditors' Ledger Balance on 1.1.10 (Dr.)	1,800	Acceptance renewed	2,000
Creditors' Ledger Balance on 1.1.10 (Cr.)	14,000	Interest on renewal of Bills	500
Purchases (Including Cash Purchase Rs. 2,000)	36,500	Sundry charges for dishonoured B/P	100
		Bills Receivable drawn	10,000
Sales (Including Cash Sales Rs. 8,000)	80,000	Bills Receivable dishonoured	2,500
Cash Paid to Creditors	21,000	Bills Receivable discounted	4,000
Collection from Debtors	62,000	Bills Receivable endorsed	4,500
Discount Allowed	300	B/R as endorsed dishonoured	1,000
Discount Received	400	Bad Debts	400
Returns Inward	2,500	Provision for Doubtful Debts	1,500
Returns Outward	1,500	Transfer from Debtors' Ledger to	500
Bills Payable accepted (including renewal bills and interest thereon)	14,000	Creditors' Ledger	
		Debtors' Ledger Balance on 31.12.2010 (Cr.)	1,300

Contd.

	Rs.		Rs.
		Creditors' Ledger Balance on 31.12.2010 (Dr.)	1,200
		Transfer from Creditors' Ledger to Debtors' Ledger	700

[Ans. Debtors' Ledger Adjustment A/c (Dr. Balance on 31.12.1995) Rs. 14,400; Creditors' Ledger Adjustment A/c (Cr. Balance on 31.12.1995) Rs. 11,900]

8. From the following particulars, prepare Debtors Ledger Control Account and Suppliers Ledger Control Account as they would appear in the General Ledger of E. L. Ltd. for the year ended 31st March 2010 :

		Rs.		Rs.
Debtors Ledger balance on 1.4.2010	(Dr.)	40,120	Bad debts written-off	1,630
	(Cr.)	570	Cash received in respect of debts previously written-off as bad	590
Suppliers Ledger balance on 1.4.2010	(Cr.)	31,175		
	(Dr.)	1,050	Allowances to customers on goods damaged in-transit	2,120
Sales		3,18,640		
Purchases		1,99,870	Discount Received	7,375
Cash received from Debtors		2,76,060	Bills Receivable received	20,285
Cash paid to Creditors		1,26,535	Bills Receivable dishonoured	1,315
Discount allowed		11,640	Bills Payable accepted	60,000
Bills Payable matured during the year		49,000	Cash received in respect of debit balance in Suppliers Ledger	1,050
Returns Inward		5,010		
Returns Outward		2,675	Amount due from Debtors adjusted against the amount due to them in the Suppliers ledger	2,170

On 31.3.2011, there were no credit balance in the Debtors' Ledger, except those outstanding on 1st April 2010, and no debit balances in the Suppliers Ledger.

[Ans. Debtors Ledger Control A/c (Dr.) Rs. 41,160 (Cr.) Rs. 570 Creditors Ledger Control A/c (Cr.) Rs. 32,290]

9. There are three Self-balancing Ledgers in use in a business, viz., a Purchase Ledger, a Sales Ledger and a General Ledger. From the following particulars write-up the necessary Adjustment Accounts as they would appear in the General Ledger :

	Rs.		Rs.
Debtors' balance in General Ledger Adjustment A/c (Cr.)	50,000	Accepted Bills Receivable during the year	5,000
Creditors' balance in General Ledger Adjustment A/c (Dr.)	35,000	Bills Receivable dishonoured	100
		Int. charged from dishonoured bills	10
Credit Sales during the year	42,000	Trade discount during the year	800
Cash Sales during the year	15,000	Creditors paid-off during the year	25,000
Credit Purchases during the year	30,000	Received through bank from Debtors	30,000
Cash Purchases during the year	12,000	Discount allowed to the business	300
Discount allowed by the business	400	Bad Debts	500
Returns Inward	1,000	Transfer from one ledger to another	200
Returns Outward	600	Prov. for Bad and Doubtful Debts	1,000
Accepted Bills Payable during the year	4,000	Bad Debts previously written-off recovered	100

Goods of the sales value of Rs. 300 were returned by a customer for which fresh goods were issued. Though a credit note was issued for the return of goods the sales invoice was inadvertently not prepared for the issue of fresh goods.

[Ans. Debtors Ledger Adjustment Account (Dr.) Rs. 55,310; Creditors Ledger Adjustment Account (Cr.) Rs. 34,900]

Hints :

1. Cash Sales, Trade Discount, Provision for Bad and Doubtful Debts and Bad Debts previously writte-off recovered—will be excluded from the Debtors Ledger Adjustment A/c.
2. Cash purchases will not appear in Creditors Ledger Adjustment A/c.
3. Rs. 300 to be added with credit sales for fresh issue of goods.

10. On 1.1.2012 Manisha started business with the following assets and liabilities :

Liabilities		Rs.	*Assets*		Rs.
Creditors :			Cash		1,000
A	500		Bank		3,000
B	1,500		Stock		5,000
C	3,000	5,000	Bills Receivable		3,000
			Debtors :		
Bills Payable		2,000	X	1,000	
			Y	2,500	
Capital		23,000	Z	4,500	
					8,000
					10,000
		30,000			30,000

Following transactions took place during Jan. 2012 :

1. On 4.1.2012 : B/R accepted by Y for Rs. 1,000 returned dishonoured.
2. On 8.1.2012 : X was declared insolvent, only 50 p in the rupee was realised from his estate.
3. On 17.1.2012 : Z renewed his acceptance for Rs. 500 plus interest Rs. 50 for 3 months.
4. On 26.1.2012 : Renewed our acceptance to C for Rs. 1,050 (Rs. 50 for interest).

You are requested to show the entries :

(1) Under ordinary system. (2) Under Self-balancing system.

D. Preparation of Total Debtors Account or Debtors Control Account and Total Creditors Account or Creditors Control Account

11. From the books of X Ltd., you ascertain that on 1st June 2012 the Debtors' Ledger balance was Rs. 40,000 and Suppliers' Ledger balance on the same date was Rs. 31,155.

The following particulars are available for the year ended 31st Dec. 2012 :

	Rs.		Rs.
Sales	3,18,700	Return Inwards	5,000
Purchases	1,99,800	Return Outwards	2,600
Cash received from debtors	2,76,000	Bad Debts	1,600
Cash paid to creditors	1,26,500	Cash received in respect of debts	
Discount allowed	11,600	previously written-off as bad	600
Bills payable matured during the year	49,000	Discount received	7,300
Bills receivable received	20,300	Bills payable accepted	60,000
Bills receivable dishonoured	1,300		

From the above particulars you are required to show the Debtors' Ledger Control Account and Suppliers' Ledger Control Account as they would appear in the General Ledger of X Ltd. for the year ended 31st Dec. 2012.

[CU BCom (Hons.)]

[Ans. Debtors Ledger Control A/c (Dr.) Rs. 45,500; Creditors Ledger Control A/c (Cr.) Rs. 34,555]

12. From the following figures, prepare Total Debtors Account and Total Creditors Account for the year ended 31st December 2012 :

	Rs.		Rs.
Debtors on 1st January 2003	36,400	Discount received from creditors	8,500
Creditors on 1st January 2003	26,900	Bills Receivable endorsed to creditors	25,000
Sales (including cash sales Rs. 18,500)	3,01,600	Bills Payable given to creditors	48,000
Sales returns	2,100	Endorsed bills dishonoured	5,000
Purchases	2,19,000	Noting charges charged from debtors	10
Purchases returns	5,000	Provision made for bad and doubtful debts	3,800
Cash received from debtors (including Rs. 2,000 against a debt previously written-off)	2,49,500	Provision made for discount on debtors	300
		Provision made for discount on creditors	150
Discount allowed to debtors	4,050	Credit balance in Sold Ledger on	
Bills Receivable received from debtors	42,000	31st December 2003	2,100
Bad Debts written-off	2,500	Debit balance in Bought Ledger on	
Cash paid to creditors	1,44,600	31st December 2003	1,600
Transfer from Bought Ledger to Sales Ledger	3,200		

[Ans. Debtors' balance (Dr.) Rs. 25,260, (Cr.) Rs. 2,100; Creditors' balance (Dr.) Rs. 1,600, (Cr.) Rs. 18,200]

CHAPTER 27

INSURANCE CLAIMS

A. LOSS OF STOCK

Learning Objectives

Introduction

Computation of Claim for Loss of Stock

(a) Computation of Value of Stock at the date of fire

Procedure for Calculation

Gross Profit Ratio

(b) Computation of Actual Claim

Average Clause

Treatment of Abnormal Items of Goods

Accounting Entries in the books of insured for fire claims

B. LOSS OF PROFIT

Introduction

Indemnity Under Policy

Some Important Terms—

—Standing Charges

—Increased Cost of Working

—Indemnity

—Indemnity Period

—Gross Profit

—Standard Turnover

—Annual Turnover

—Averages

—Savings in Insured Standing Charges

Procedure for Ascertaining Claim

Average Clause

Workmen's Compensation Insurance and Group Gratuity Insurance

A. LOSS OF STOCK

Introduction

Claims in respect of assets, viz., Building, Machinery, Plant etc. are based on the value of these assets ifthe same are insured against fire or any other hazard. But difficulty arises, particularly in case of stock for which no account appears in the books. If the 'Stock Book' is maintained for the purpose, claims can be ascertained for loss of stock easily. Because, the value of stock which is recorded in the 'Stock Book' immediately before the fire takes place is to be compensated. On the other hand, if the 'Stock Book' is not maintained, value of stock destroyed by fire will be estimated on the basis of quantity and price of the same as shown by the different documents, papers and certain other information.

The following information is required in order to prepare a claim for loss of stock against the Insurance Company :

(i) Value of closing stock (shown as per last Balance Sheet); (ii) Amount of current purchases up to the date of fire; (iii) Amount of sales for the same period; (iv) Average rate of gross profit earned in the past years, i.e., the trend to gross profit; and (v) Salvaged value of stock.

Although, with the above information, the estimated value of stock destroyed by fire can be ascertained, the same, however, depends upon certain other factors which are :

(i) Whether the same method of valuation of stock is followed or not; (ii) Exact terms of policy; and (iii) Any other factor which affect the past gross profit, e.g., any exceptional rise in sale price.

Computation of Claim for Loss of Stock

We know that ascertainment of claim against any fixed asset is quite simple. But ascertainment of claim against stock at the date of fire is not so simple as there are different methods for its valuation and the value of stock is seldom stable—rather it always fluctuates. That is why exact amount of stock which was lost due to fire (or any other abnormal reason) cannot be ascertained correctly. However, it involves two following steps:

(a) Computation of value of stock at the date of fire;
(b) Computation of actual claim to be lodged.

(a) Computation of value of stock at the date of fire

At first we are to prepare a Memorandum or Estimated Trading Account in the usual manner from the next date of the last accounting period to the date of fire. Now, if the rate of gross profit is not given we are to ascertain if from the previous year's Trading Account on the assumption that the same rate of gross profit is maintained in the succeeding years. However the proforma of Memorandum Trading Account is given :

Memorandum Trading Account (from the 1st day of current year to the date of fire)

	Particulars	*Amount*		*Particulars*	*Amount*
To	Opening Stock	***	By	Sales (Less Returns)	***
"	Purchase (less Returns)	***	"	Closing Stock (balancing figure)	***
"	Other expenses (which usually appear in the debit side of Trading Account e.g., wages, carriage Inwards, etc.)	***			
"	Gross Profit (Percentage on sales)	***			
		***			***

Thus, the value of closing stock at the date of fire will be the balancing figure that appears from the Trading Account.

Procedure for Calculation

In short, the following procedure should, however, be applied for the purpose of ascertaining the value of stock destroyed by fire :

Step (i) Calculate the rate of gross profit on sales, gross profit ratio on the basis of last accounting year or on the basis of last few years after adjusting abnormal items, if any.

Step (ii) Prepare a Trading Account .

Therefore, abnormal items appearing in the Trading Account will be excluded for ascertaining the average rate of gross profit in the past years.

Generally, value of stock destroyed by fire can be ascertained with help of the following formula :

Value of stock destroyed = Opening Stock + Purchases up to the date of fire – Cost of goods sold (i.e., Sale Price – Gross Profit).

Gross Profit Ratio

The student should remember that gross profit is the key factor while calculating stock destroyed by fire. Gross profit should always be calculated of the basis of sales. If the gross profit ratio is not given, the same can be computed as :

$$\text{Gross Profit Ratio} = \frac{\text{Gross Profit}}{\text{Sales}} \times 100$$

The rate/ratio of gross profit is the average of ratios obtained in the last few year's, say, 2, 3 or 5 years. But if it is found that there is a continuous fall in the rate of gross profit from year to year, avoid that rate of gross profit. In that case, it is better to make an estimated rate of gross profit based on the *available information*. For example, if the G.P. ratios for 4 years has been 50%, 40%, 30%, and 20%, respectively, in the 5th year the same should be considered only at 10%. But, on the other hand, if there is a constant increase in the rate of gross profit, an average may be taken. Care should be taken particularly when there is an abnormal situation (which unduly inflates or deflates the amount of gross profit) and the said year should be excluded while calculating the average. But if the previous year's opening and closing stock are affected due to such abnormal situations those are to be adjusted accordingly before calculating the correct rate of gross profit.

(b) Computation of Actual Claim

From the above discussion, it becomes clear that value of stock at the date of fire will be the balancing figure comes from the Trading Account. But, the said amount cannot be claimed. In other words, if there is any salvaged value of stock, the same should be deducted from the value of stock destroyed in order to ascertain the amount of claim for stock lost by fire.

To Sum up

Amount of Claim for Loss of Stock

	Rs.
Value of closing stock at the date of Fire (as per Memorandum Trading Account)	* * *
Less : Stock/Goods Salvaged[1]	* * *
∴ Amount of Claim/Actual Loss	* * *

Note :

1. ***It must be remembered that the amount of claim should be limited to the amount of actual loss even though the insured value of actual goods is higher.***
2. ***If value of stock at the date of fire exceeds the amount of the insured value, the amount of claim is to be limited after applying the Average Clause.***

Illustration 1

A fire occurred at the premises of a trader on May 31, 2012, destroying a great part of his stock. On Jan. 1, 2012, appeared in the books at Rs. 60,000. The value of the Stock salvaged was Rs. 13,500. The Gross Profit on Sales was 30% and Sales amounted to Rs. 1,53,000 from January to date of fire, while for the same period the purchases amounted to Rs. 1,03,500. Prepare a statement of claim for submission to the Insurance Company.

[1] Sometimes a part of stock may be saved from the fire, i.e., the entire stock may not be destroyed by fire. These stocks are known as Salvaged Stock.

Solution

In the books of ...

Trading Account *for the period Jan. 1 to May 31,2012*

Dr. Particulars	Amount	Particulars	*Cr.* Amount
	Rs.		Rs.
To Opening Stock	60,000	By Sales	1,53,000
" Purchases	1,03,500	" Closing Stock *(bal. fig.)*	56,400
" Profit & Loss A/c	45,900		
" Gross Profit transferred (30% of Rs. 1,53,000)			
	2,09,400		2,09,400

	Rs.
Amount of Claim = Value of Stock as on May 31st	56,400
Less : Stock Salvaged	13,500
	42,900

Amount of Claim = Value of Stock at the date of Fire – Stock Salvaged = Rs. 56,400 – Rs. 13,500 = Rs. 42,900

Illustration 2

The premises of a trading firm caught fire on 31st October 2009 and the stock was damaged. The firm had made up accounts to 31st Dec. each year and on 31st Dec. 2008 the stock at cost was Rs. 13,000 as against Rs. 9,000 on 31st Dec. 2007.

Purchase from 1st Jan. 2009 to the date of fire were Rs. 35,000 as against Rs. 52,750 for the full year 2008, and the corresponding sales figure were Rs. 49,000 and Rs. 65,000, respectively. You are given the following further information :

(i) In April 2009, goods which cost Rs. 1,000 were given away for advertising purposes, no entries being made in the books.

(ii) During 2009, a clerk had misappropriated unrecorded cash sales. It is estimated that the defalcation averaged Rs. 20 per week from 1st Jan. 2009 until the clerk was dismissed on 21st May 2009.

(iii) The rate of gross profit is constant.

From the above information make estimated value of the stock in hand at the date of fire.

Solution

In the books of...

Memorandum Trading Account *for the period Jan. 1, 2009 to Oct. 31st, 2009*

Dr. Particulars	Amount	Amount	Particulars	*Cr.* Amount
	Rs.	Rs.		Rs.
To Opening Stock		13,000	By Sales	49,000
" Purchases	35,000		" Cash Sales (Stolen)	400
Less : Advertisement	1,000	34,000	" Closing Stock *(bal. fig.)*	9,850
" Profit & Loss A/c				
" Gross Profit (25% on sales*) transferred		12,250		
		59,250		59,250

Workings :

Percentage of gross profit on sales is based on 2008 figures shown below —

*** Trading Account** *for the period Jan. 1 2008 to Dec. 31st, 2008*

Dr. Particulars	Amount	Particulars	*Cr.* Amount
	Rs.		Rs.
To Opening Stock	9,000	By Sales	65,000
" Purchases	52,750	" Closing Stock	13,000
" Profit and Loss A/c			
" Gross Profit transferred (i.e., @ 25% on Sales)	16,250		
	78,000		78,000

$$\text{Percentage of G.P. on Sales} = \frac{\text{Rs. } 16,250}{\text{Rs. } 65,000} \times 100 = 25\%$$

Illustration 3

Fire occurred in the premises of A & Company on 1st Sept. 2009 and Stock of the value of Rs. 1,01,000 was salvaged and the business books and records were saved.

The following information was obtained :

	Rs.		Rs.
Purchase for the year ended 31.3.2009	7,00,000	Sales from 1.3.2009 to 1.9.2009	3,60,000
Sales for year ended 31.3.2009	11,00,000	Stock on 31.3.2008	3,00,000
Purchases from 1.3.2009 to 1.9.2009	2,40,000	Stock on 31.3.2009	3,40,000

Further information is also given that the Stock on 31.3.2009 was overvalued by Rs. 20,000.

Calculate the amount of the claim to be presented to the Insurance Company in respect of losses. Rate of Gross Profit is to be based on the year ended 31.3.2009.

Solution

In the books of A & Co.

Dr. **Memorandum Trading Account** *for the period April 1, 2009 to Sept. 1, 2009* Cr.

Particulars	*Amount*	*Particulars*	*Amount*
	Rs.		Rs.
To Opening Stock (at cost)	3,20,000	By Sales (3,60,000 × $\frac{5}{6}$)	3,00,000
" Purchases (Rs. 2,40,000 × $\frac{5}{6}$)	2,00,000	" Closing Stock *(bal. fig.)*	3,34,540
Profit and Loss A/c			
" Gross Profit transferred (38.18% on Rs. 3,00,000)	1,14,540		
	6,34,540		6,34,540

Amount of Claim = Value of Stock at the date of fire – Stock Salvaged

= Rs. 3,34,540 – Rs. 1,01,000 = Rs. 2,33,540

Workings :

In the books of A & Co.

Dr. **Trading Account** *for the year ended 31st March 2009* Cr.

Particulars	*Amount*	*Particulars*	*Amount*
	Rs.		Rs.
To Opening Stock	3,00,000	By Sales	11,00,000
" Purchases	7,00,000	" Closing Stock	
Profit and Loss A/c	4,20,000	(at cost i.e., 3,40,000 – 20,000)	3,20,000
" Gross Profit Transferred			
	14,20,000		14,20,000

Percentage/Rate of Gross Profit on Sales = $\frac{\text{Rs. } 4,20,000}{\text{Rs. } 11,00,000} \times 100$ = 38.18% (App.)

Note : Since purchases and sales include for March 2009, therefore $\frac{1}{6}$ of them are to be eliminated.

Illustration 4

There is a fire in godown of SPARK Ltd. on 1.7.2010, stock worth Rs. 30,000 was saved. The goods were insured and fully covered.

(i) An average gross profit of 20% on sale is maintained by the company.

(ii) The stock is valued at 10% above cost.

The purchases and sales for first 6 months of the year were Rs. 2,10,000 and Rs. 4,50,000, respectively; stock on January 1, 2010 was Rs. 1,48,500. The wages for that period amounted to Rs. 90,000. Find out the cost of the stock burnt.

(iii) Goods sold on approval but lost by fire Rs. 5,000.

[CU BCom (Hons.)—Adapted]

Solution

In the books of SPARK Ltd.

Dr. **Memorandum Trading Account** *for the 6 months ended 30th June 2010* Cr.

Particulars	*Amount*	*Particulars*	*Amount*
	Rs.		Rs.
To Opening Stock (Rs. 1,48,500 × $\frac{100}{110}$)	1,35,000	By Sales	4,50,000
" Purchases	2,10,000	" Closing Stock *(bal. fig.)*	75,000
" Wages	90,000		
" Profit and Loss A/c —Gross Profit transferred (@ 20% on Rs. 4,50,000)	90,000		
	5,25,000		5,25,000

∴ *Amount of Claim* = ***Value of Stock at the date of fire – Stock Salvaged + Sold on approval but lost***
= ***Rs. 75,000 – Rs. 30,000 + Rs. 5,000 = Rs. 50,000.***

Note : It has been assumed that while calculating gross profit in past year, correct valuation of stock was made.

Illustration 5

A fire broke out in the warehouse of Mercantile Traders Ltd. on 30th September 2013. The company desires to file a claim with the insurance company for loss of stock and gives you the following information to enable you to prepare a statement showing the amount to be claimed :

(a) The last accounts of the company were prepared on 31st December 2012

	Rs.		Rs.
(b) Sundry Debtors on 31.12.2012	40,000	(e) Stock on 31.12.2012	15,000
(c) Sundry Debtors on 30.9.2013	30,000	(f) Purchases from 1.1.2013 to 30.9.2013	1,25,000
(d) Cash received from Debtors	1,44,000	(g) Rate of Gross Profit to cost of sales	25%

Solution

In the books of Mercantile Traders Ltd.

Dr. **Sundry Debtors Account** Cr.

Date	*Particulars*	*Amount*	*Date*	*Particulars*	*Amount*
2013		Rs.	2013		Rs.
Jan. 1	To Balance b/d	40,000	Sept. 30	By Bank A/c	1,44,000
Sept. 30	" Sales *(bal fig.)*	1,34,000		" Balance c/d	30,000
		1,74,000			1,74,000

Dr. **MemorandumTrading Account** *for the period from 1.1.2013 to 30.9.2013* Cr.

Particulars	*Amount*	*Particulars*	*Amount*
	Rs.		Rs.
To Opening Stock	15,000	By Sales (as ascertained)	1,34,000
" Purchase	1,25,000	" Closing Stock *(bal. fig.)*	32,800
Profit and Loss A/c " Gross Profit transferred —@ 20% on Rs. 1,34,000	26,800		
	1,66,800		1,66,800

Amount of claim will be Rs. 32,800

Note : G.P. is 25% on cost **OR** 20% on sales.

Illustration 6

Chiranjib Das is a small wholesaler of fancy goods. On 30th September 2012, a fire occurred at his warehouse and the greater portion of his stock was destroyed. The value of stock salvaged was agreed at Rs. 550.

The books were saved and the following is an extract from his last accounts for the year ended 31st March 2012 :

Dr. **Trading Account** Cr.

	Particulars	Amount		Particulars	Amount
		Rs.			Rs.
To	Opening Stock	34,240	By	Sales	98,000
"	Purchases	78,470	"	Closing Stock	29,410
"	Gross Profit	14,700			
		1,27,410			1,27,410

The stock was fully insured against fire risk. Trade creditors on 31st March 2012 amounted to Rs. 12,304. Sales for the period to 30th September 2012 were Rs. 54,600 and payments made for purchases amounted to R. 44,008. On 30th September 2012 creditors were Rs. 11,056 You are required to prepare a statement showing the amount which G should claim from the insurance company for loss of stock.

Solution

Percentage of G.P. on Sales = $\frac{\text{Rs. } 14{,}700}{\text{Rs. } 98{,}000} \times 100 = 15\%$

In the books of Chiranjib Das
Sundry Creditors Account

Dr. Cr.

Date		Particulars	Amount	Date		Particulars	Amount
2012			Rs.	2012			Rs.
Sept. 30	To	Bank A/c	44,008	April 1	By	Balance b/d	12,304
	"	Balance c/d	11,056	Sept. 30	"	Purchases *(bal. fig.)*	42,760
			55,064				55,064

Dr. **Menorandum Trading Account** *for the period from 1st April to 30th Sept. 2012* Cr.

	Particulars	Amount		Particulars	Amount
		Rs.			Rs.
To	Opening Stock	29,410	By	Sales	54,600
"	Purchases *(as ascertained)*	42,760		Closing Stock	
	Profit and Loss A/c			*(balancing fig.)*	25,760
"	Gross Profit transferred				
	—@ 15% on Rs. 54,600	8,190			
		80,360			80,360

Amount of claim : = ***Value of Stock at the date of Fire – Stock Salvaged***

= ***Rs. 25,760 – Rs. 550 = Rs. 25,210***

Illustration 7

On 30th July 2011, the godown and business premises of a merchant were affected by fire and from accounting records salvaged, the following information is made available to you :

	Rs.		Rs.
Stock of goods at cost on 1.4.2010	1,00,000	Sales for the same period	6,00,000
Stock of goods at 10% lower than cost as on 31.3.2011	1,08,000	Purchase less returns for the period from 1.4.20011 to 20.7.2011	1,40,000
Purchase of goods for the year from 1.4.2010 to 31.3.2011	4,20,000	Sales less returns for the above period	3,10,000

Sales up to 20th July 2011 included Rs. 40,000 for which goods had not been despatched. Purchases up to 20th July 2011 did not include Rs. 20,000 for which purchase invoice had not been received from suppliers, though goods have been received at the godown.

Goods salvaged from the accident were worth Rs. 12,000 and these were handed over to the insured.

Ascertain the value of the claim for cost of goods/stock which could be preferred on the insurer.

Solution

Dr. **Memorandum Trading Account** *(from 1.4.2011 to 20.7.2011)* Cr.

Particulars	*Amount*	*Particulars*	*Amount*
	Rs.		Rs.
To Opening Stock	1,20,000	By Sales	
" Purchases		(Rs. 3,10,000 – Rs. 40,000)	2,70,000
(Rs. 1,40,000 + Rs. 20,000)	1,60,000	" Closing Stock	1,00,000
" Profit and Loss A/c		— Destroyed *(bal. fig.)*	
Gross Profit (@ $33\frac{1}{3}$ % on Sales)	90,000		
Transferred			
	3,70,000		3,70,000

∴ **Amount of Claim** = Closing Stock – Stock Salvaged = Rs. 1,00,000 – Rs. 12,000 = Rs. 88,000

Workings :

In order to find out the rate of gross pofit in the year 2010-11, the following Trading Account is to be prepared :

Dr. **Trading Account** *for the year ended 31st March 2011* Cr.

Particulars	*Amount*	*Particulars*	*Amount*
	Rs.		Rs.
To Opening Stock	1,00,000	By Sales	6,00,000
" Purchases	4,20,000	" Closing Stock	
" Profit and Loss			
Gross Profit *(bal. fig.)*	2,00,000	(Rs. 1,08,000 × $\frac{100}{90}$)	1,20,000
transferred			
	7,20,000		7,20,000

$$\therefore \text{ Percentage of G. P. on Sales} = \frac{\text{Rs. } 2,00,000}{\text{Rs.} 6,00,000} \times 100$$

$$= 33\frac{1}{3}\ \%$$

Illustration 8

A fire occurred on 15th Sept. 2012 in the premises of X Co. Ltd. From the following figures, calculate the amount of claim to be lodged with the Insurance Company for loss of Stock :

	Rs.		Rs.
Stock at cost as on 1.1.2011	20,000	Purchases from 1.1.2012 to 15.9.2012	88,000
Stock at cost on 1.1.2012	30,000	Sales 2011	60,000
Purchases 2011	40,000	Sales from 1.1.2012 to 15.9.2012	1,05,000

During the current year cost of purchases have risen by 10% above last year's level. Selling price has gone up by 5%. Salvage value of Stocks after fire was Rs. 2,000.

Solution

Dr. **Memorandum Trading Account** *from 1st January 2012 to 15th September 2012* Cr.

Particulars	*Actual*	*Last year*	*Particulars*	*Actual*	*Last year*
	Rs.	Rs.		Rs.	Rs.
To Opening Stock	30,000	30,000	By Sales	1,05,000	1,00,000
" Purchases	88,000	80,000	" Closing Stock	66,000	60,000
" Profit and Loss A/c			*(bal. fig.)*		
Gross Profit	53,000	50,000			
transferred					
	1,71,000	1,60,000		1,71,000	1,60,000

Workings :

Closing Stock of the last year will be Rs. 66,000 i.e., Rs. 60,000 + 10% (on F.I.F.O. basis)

Amount of claim will be = Value of stock at the date of fire – Salvaged Stock

= Rs. 66,000 – Rs. 2,000 = Rs. 64,000.

Dr. **Trading Account** *for the year ended 31st December 2011* Cr.

Particulars	*Amount*	*Particulars*	*Amount*
	Rs.		Rs.
To Opening Stock	20,000	By Sales	60,000
" Purchases	40,000	" Closing Stock	30,000
Profit and Loss A/c			
" Gross Profit transferred	30,000		
	90,000		90,000

$$\text{Percentage of Gross Profit on Sales} = \frac{\text{Rs. } 30{,}000}{\text{Rs. } 60{,}000} \times 100 = 50\%$$

Illustration 9

The godown of Miss Anindita Pal was destroyed by fire on 1st June 2009 when the goods in stock were insured for Rs. 30,000. The following particulars are available :

Balance Sheet (Extracts) *as at 31st Dec., 2008*

	Rs.		Rs.
Creditors (for goods supplied)	10,000	Stock (including goods held by agent Rs. 1,000)	18,000
		Debtors	35,000

Transactions up to 31st May 2009 include

	Rs.		Rs.
Cash Received from Debtors	1,70,000	Cash paid to Creditors	1,10,000
Bad debts written-off	1,750	Discount Received	500

Balances on 31st May 2009 :

Debtors	35,000
Creditors	15,000

Additional Information

(i) Debtors (on 31.5.2009) included an amount owing from the agent from sales to date Rs. 2,000, less 10% commission and his expenses amounting to Rs. 50. on 31.5.2009—the agent still held the said goods valued at Rs. 1,800 (at selling price).

(ii) Sales (total) for the period includes Rs. 800 for goods which have the selling price reduced by 50% and also Rs. 3,000 reduced by 25%.

(iii) The normal mark up is 50% on cost and, except the above, all sales can be assumed to be at the full selling price.

(iv) All the goods were destroyed and there was no salvage value of the goods.

Calculate the amount of claim.

Solution

In the books of Miss Anindita Pal

Dr. **Debtors Account** Cr.

Date	*Particulars*	*Amount*	*Date*	*Particulars*	*Amount*
2009		Rs.	2009		Rs.
Jan. 1	To Balance b/d	35,000	May 31	By Cash Received	1,70,000
May 31	" Sales *(bal. fig.)*	1,70,000		" Bad Debts	1,750[1]
				" Balance c/d (excluding owing from agents) (i.e., 35,000 – 1,750[1])	33,250
		2,05,000			2,05,000

Dr. **Creditors Account** Cr.

Date	Particulars	Amount	Date	Particulars	Amount
2009		Rs.	2009		Rs.
May 31	To Cash paid	1,10,000	Jan. 1	By Balance b/d	10,000
	" Discount Received	500	May, 31	" Purchases	
	" Balance c/d	15,000		(bal. fig.)	1,15,500
		1,25,500			1,25,500

Dr. **Godown Stock Account** Cr.

Particulars	Amount	Particulars	Amount
	Rs.		Rs.
To Balance b/d (18,000 – 1,000)	17,000	By Cost of goods Sold	1,14,534[2]
" Purchases		" Stock at agents	1,533[3]
(as per Creditors A/c)	1,15,500	" Stock Destroyed by fire *(bal. fig.)*	16,433
	1,32,500		1,32,500

Workings :

So, amount of claim to be lodged for Rs. 16,433.

1. ***Amounts owing from agents***

		Rs.
Sales		2,000
Less		
Commission @ 10% =	200	
Expenses	50	250
		1,750

2. ***Cost of Goods Sold***

Sales	Normal Selling Price	Cost ($\frac{2}{3}$ of S.P.)
Rs.	*Rs.*	*Rs.*
800	1,600	1,067
3,000	4,000 $(3,000 \times \frac{100}{75})$	2,667
1,66,200 *(bal. fig.)*	—	1,10,800
1,70,000		1,14,534

3. ***Stock at agent's hand***

Sales	Cost	
Rs.	*Rs.*	
2,000	1,333	(i.e., $2,000 \times \frac{2}{3}$)
—	1,200	$(1,800 \times \frac{2}{3})$
	2,533	
Less :	1,000	(i.e., in agent's hand at the beginning)
	1,533	Stock at cost to agent's hand

Average Clause

Fire insurance is a contract of indemnity. As a result, the owner of goods/stocks cannot claim more than the amount of actual loss sustained by fire. Under the circumstances, if the goods and/or assets are insured at a price which is either equal or more than the actual amount, the Insurance Company is liable to pay to the owner only the actual amount of loss sustained by fire and not more than that by way of compensation. In order to maintain the interest of the Insurance Company from ***'Under-Insurance'***, a condition is imposed what is known as ***Average Clause*** in the fire insurance policy. In this case, the Insurance Company is not liable to pay to the owner of goods the full amount of compensation for the loss of stock/assets sustained by fire. In other words, if the property/goods is under-insured, the insurer shall bear only that proportion of actual loss as his insurance bears to the actual value of property at the time of loss. Thus, the same can be ascertained with the help of the following :

$$\textit{Amount of Claim} = \textit{Actual Loss} \times \frac{\textit{Amount of Policy}}{\textit{Value of Stock at the date of Fire}}$$

For example, value of stock at the date of fire Rs. 10,000 and it was insured for Rs. 8,000. Amount of loss is Rs. 5,000. Therefore, amount of compensation will be made as :

$$\text{Claim} = \text{Rs. } 5{,}000 \times \frac{\text{Rs. } 8{,}000}{\text{Rs. } 10{,}000} = \text{Rs. } 4{,}000.$$

Note: ***Average Clause will be applicable only when the amount of policy is given in the problem and the amount of policy is less than the value of stock destroyed by fire or value of stock is more than the amount of claim.***

Illustration 10

Shymalesh took out a fire policy containing an Average Clause covering his stock for Rs. 30,000. His practice was to fix his selling price at cost plus $33\frac{1}{3}$%. He closes his books of 30th June every year. On 31.3.2008 a fire occurred at his premises and destroyed his stock. The salvaged stock was worth Rs. 12,000. During the period of 9 months preceding the fire his Purchase amounted to Rs. 1,22,000 and Sales Rs. 1,68,000. His stock at 1.7.2007 was valued at Rs. 40,000. You are required to prepare a statement showing the amount of claim.

Solution

In the books of Shymalesh

Dr. **Memorandum Trading Account** *for the period from 1st July 2007 to 31st March 2008* Cr.

Particulars	*Amount* Rs.	*Particulars*	*Amount* Rs.
To Opening Stock	40,000	By Sales A/c	1,68,000
" Purchases	1,22,000	" Closing Stock (*bal. fig.*)	36,000
" Profit & Loss A/c	42,000		
" Gross Profit transferred (@ 25% on Sale) (i.e., $33\frac{1}{3}$ % on Cost)			
	2,04,000		2,04,000

Amount of Claim

		Rs.
	Value of Closing Stock	36,000
Less :	Stock Salvaged	12,000
	Actual Loss of Stock/Amount of claim	24,000

In the present problem, question of Average Clause will be applied since amount of stock at the date of fire (i.e., Rs. 36,000) is more than the policy amount of Rs. 30,000, as under :

$$\therefore \quad \textit{Net Claim} = \textit{Loss of Stock} \times \frac{\textit{Policy Value}}{\textit{Value of Stock at the date of fire}} = \text{Rs. } 24{,}000 \times \frac{\text{Rs. } 30{,}000}{\text{Rs. } 36{,}000} = \text{Rs. } 20{,}000$$

Illustration 11

The godown of Purple Ltd. caught fire on 31.3.1999. As a result stock of goods in the godown of the company were gutted. Goods worth Rs. 41,360 could, however, be saved from the accident.

The following particulars are supplied to you :

	Rs.		Rs.
Stock on 1st January 1999	60,000	Sales to the date of fire	1,80,000
Purchases to the date of fire	2,60,000	Commission paid on purchases to the Purchase Manager	2%
Carriage paid on purchases	1,600	Average Gross profit on sales	$33\frac{1}{3}$ %

The Company had a fire policy of Rs. 1,60,000 covering its stock of goods in the godown. The policy is subject to Average Clause.

You are to ascertain (i) total loss of stock; and (ii) the amount of insurance claim to be made.

[CU BCom (Hons.) 2001 & 2008]

Solution

In the books of Purple Ltd.

Dr. **Memorandum Trading Account** *for the period from 1.1.1999 to 31.3.1999* Cr.

Particulars	Amount	Particulars	Amount
	Rs.		Rs.
To Opening Stock	60,000	By Sales	1,80,000
" Purchases	2,60,000	" Closing Stock *(bal. fig.)*	2,06,800
" Carriage	1,600		
" Commissions on Purchase (to Purchase Manager) (2% on Rs. 2,60,000)	5,200		
" Gross Profit (@ $33\frac{1}{3}$ % on sales)	60,000		
	3,86,800		3,86,800

Amount of claim to be lodged = Value of stock at the date of fire – Stock Salvaged

= Rs. 2,06,800 – Rs. 41,360 = Rs. 1,65,440

Since, the value of Stock is more than the Insurance policy, average clause should be applied as :

$$\textit{Amount of Claim} = \textit{Actual Loss} \times \frac{\textit{Amount of Policy}}{\textit{Value of stock destroyed}}$$

$$= \text{Rs. } 1,65,440 \times \frac{\text{Rs. } 1,60,000}{\text{Rs. } 2,06,800} = \text{Rs. } 1,28,000.$$

Illustration 12

A fire occurred in the premises of Sri Garib Dass on 1.4.2013 and a considerable part of the stock was destroyed. The stock salvaged was Rs. 56,000. Sri Dass had taken a fire insurance policy for Rs. 3,42,000 to cover the loss of stock by fire.

You are required to ascertain the insurance claim which the company should claim from the insurance company for the loss of stock by the fire. The following particulars are available :

	Rs.		Rs.
Purchases for the year 2012	18,76,000	Stock on 1.1.2012	2,88,000
Sales for the year 2012	23,20,000	Stock on 31.12.2012	4,84,000
Purchases from 1.1.2013 to 1.4.2013	3,64,000	Wages paid during the year 2012	2,00,000
Sales from 1.1.2013 to 1.4.2013	4,80,000	Wages paid during 1.1.2013 to 1.4.2013	36,000

Sri Dass had in June 2012 consigned goods worth Rs. 1,00,000 which, unfortunately, were lost in an accident. Since there was no insurance cover taken, the loss had to be borne by him in full.

Stocks at the end of each year for and till the end of calendar year 2011 had been valued at cost less 10%. From 2012, however, there was a change in the valuation of closing stock which was ascertained by adding 10% to its costs.

[CA]

Solution

In order to find out the rate of gross profit on sales for the year 2012, the following Trading Account is to be prepared for the same year as :

Trading Account

Dr. *for the year ended 31st Dec. 2012* Cr.

Particulars	Amount	Particulars	Amount
	Rs.		Rs.
To Opening Stock $\left(Rs. 2,88,000 \times \frac{100}{90}\right)$	3,20,000	By Sales	23,20,000
		" Stock lost by Accident	1,00,000
		" Closing Stock $\left(Rs. 4,84,000 \times \frac{100}{110}\right)$	4,40,000
" Purchases	18,76,000		
" Wages	2,00,000		

Contd.

	Rs.		Rs.
" Profit and Loss A/c Gross Profit *(bal. fig.)* transferred	4,64,000		
	28,60,000		28,60,000

$\therefore$ Rate of Gross Profit on Sales $= \frac{\text{Rs. } 4,64,000}{\text{Rs. } 23,20,000} \times 100 = 20\%$

Dr. **Trading Account** *for the period (from 1.1.2013 to 1.4.2013)* Cr.

Particulars	*Amount*	*Particulars*	*Amount*
	Rs.		Rs.
To Opening Stock	4,40,000	By Sales	4,80,000
" Purchases	3,64,000	" Closing Stock	
" Wages	36,000	—*(balancing fig.)*	4,56,000
" Profit and Loss A/c Gross Profit (@ 20% on Sales) transferred	96,000		
	9,36,000		9,36,000

Amount of Claim = Stock Destroyed – Salvaged

= Rs. 4,56,000 – Rs. 56,000
= Rs. 4,00,000

As the average clause is applicable (since the policy amount is less than the value of stock destroyed) here, the amount of claim will be :

$$\textit{Net Claim} = \textit{Loss of Stock} \times \frac{\textit{Amount of Policy}}{\textit{Stock at the date of fire}}$$

$$= \text{Rs. } 4,00,000 \times \frac{\text{Rs. } 3,42,000}{\text{Rs. } 4,56,000} = \text{Rs. } 3,00,000$$

Illustration 13

From the following figures, calculate the amount of claim for Loss of Stock with the Insurance Company : Date of fire 30th June 2009

	Rs.		Rs.
Stock at Cost on 1st January 2008	1,35,000	Purchases from 1st January 2009 to 30th June 2009	8,00,000
Stock at Cost on 1st January 2009	1,50,000	Sales during 2008	12,00,000
Purchases during 2008	9,15,000	Sales from 1st Jan 2009 to 30th June 2009	9,90,000

You are informed that :

(a) In 2009 the Cost of Purchases have risen by 20% above the level prevailing in 2008.
(b) In 2009 the Selling Prices have gone up by 10% over the level prevailing in 2008.
(c) Salvage Value of Stock Rs. 20,000.
(d) Fire Insurance Policy for Rs. 1,48,750 to cover the loss of stock by fire.

Solution **[CU BCom (Hons.)]**

Dr. **Memorandum Trading Account** *for the period from 1st Jan. 2009 to 30th June 2009* Cr.

Particulars	*Actual*	*At Last year rate*	*Particulars*	*Actual*	*At Last year rate*
	Rs.	Rs.		Rs.	Rs.
To Opening Stock	1,50,000	1,50,000	By Sales	9,90,000	9,00,000[2]
" Purchases	8,00,000	6,66,667[1]	" Closing Stock *(bal. fig.)*	1,70,000[4]	1,41,667
" Profit and Loss A/c Gross Profit c/d transferred	2,10,000	2,25,000[3]			
	11,60,000	10,41,667		11,60,000	10,41,667

Loss of Stock = Value of stock at the date of fire – Stock salvaged = Rs. 1,70,000 – Rs. 20,000
= Rs. 1,50,000

Since the policy amount is less than the value of stock destroyed, average clause is to be applied as under

$$\text{Net Claim} = \text{Loss of Stock} \times \frac{\text{Policy Value}}{\text{Value of Stock at the date of fire}} = \text{Rs. } 1{,}50{,}000 \times \frac{\text{Rs. } 1{,}48{,}750}{\text{Rs. } 1{,}70{,}000} = \text{Rs. } 1{,}31{,}250$$

Workings :

Dr. **Trading Account** *for the year ended 31st December 2008* Cr.

Particulars	Amount	Particulars	Amount
	Rs.		Rs.
To Opening Stock	1,35,000	By Sales	12,00,000
" Purchases A/c	9,15,000	" Closing Stock	1,50,000
" Profit and Loss A/c Gross Profit transferred	3,00,000		
	13,50,000		13,50,000

1. Percentage of Gross Profit on Sales

$$= \frac{\text{Rs. } 3{,}00{,}000}{\text{Rs. } 12{,}00{,}000} \times 100 = 25\%$$

$$= \text{Rs. } 8{,}00{,}000 \times \frac{100}{120} = \text{Rs. } 6{,}66{,}667$$

2. Purchase of 2009 at the price level of 2007

$$\text{Sales} = 9{,}90{,}000 \times \frac{100}{110} = \text{Rs. } 9{,}00{,}000$$

3. Gross Profit = 25% of Sales

$$= \text{Rs. } 9{,}90{,}000 \times \frac{25}{100} = \text{Rs. } 2{,}25{,}000$$

4. Closing Stock at Current Price

= Rs. 1,41,667 + 20% = Rs. 1,70,000

Treatment of Abnormal Item of Goods

It has been pointed out above that Abnormal Item of Goods, if any, should be excluded at the time of preparing Trading Account. Therefore, value of such goods which affect opening stock or purchase are to be deducted. Similarly, if any abnormal item of sale is included with sales, the same is also to be excluded.

As a result, the (Memorandum) Trading Account will disclose the stock of normal line of goods at the date of fire. Therefore, the unsold value of abnormal item of goods are to be added with the normal stock in order to ascertain the total value of stock. It is better, for this purpose, to prepare the (Memorandum) Trading Account in two columns, viz., Columnar Trading Account showing the Normal and Abnormal items of goods .

Illustration 14

A fire occurred in the godown of A Ltd. on 9th March 2010, destroying the entire Stock. The books and records were saved from which the following particulars were ascertained :

	Rs.		Rs.
Sales for the year 2009	10,01,000	Purchases for the period 1.1.2010 to 8.3.2010	1,25,000
Sales for the period 1.1.2010 to 8.3.2010	3,00,000	Stock on 1.1.2009	3,31,100
Purchases for the year 2009	8,00,000	Stock on 31.12.2009	3,85,000

The company has been following the practice of valuing the Stock of goods at actual cost plus 10%. Included in the Stock on 1.1.2009 were some shop-soiled goods which originally cost Rs. 2,000, but were valued at Rs. 1,100. These goods were sold during the year 2009 for Rs. 1,000. Subject to these, the rate of Gross Profit and the basis of valuation of Stock were uniform.

You are required to ascertain the value of the Stock destroyed.

Solution

In the books of A Ltd.

Dr. **Memorandum Trading Account** *for the period from Jan. 1, 2010 to March 8,2010* Cr.

Particulars	Amount	Particulars	Amount
	Rs.		Rs.
To Opening Stock	3,50,000	By Sales	3,00,000
" Purchases	1,25,000	" Closing Stock *(bal. fig.)*	2,50,000
" Profit and Loss A/c	75,000		

Contd.

	Rs.		Rs.
* Gross Profit transferred (@ 25% on Rs. 3,00,000)			
	5,50,000		5,50,000

∴ Value of Stock destroyed Rs. 2,50,000.

Workings :

* In order to find out the rate of gross profit the following Trading Account is to be prepared :

Dr. **Trading Account** *for the year ended 31st Dec. 2009* *Cr.*

Particulars	*Amount* Rs.	*Amount* Rs.	*Particulars*	*Amount* Rs.	*Amount* Rs.
To Opening Stock	3,31,100		By Sales	10,01,000	
Less : Shop-soiled goods	1,100		*Less* : Sale of shop-soiled goods	1,000	
	3,30,000				10,00,000
Less : Profit @ $\frac{1}{11}$ (i.e., $\frac{10}{110}$)	30,000	3,00,000	" Closing Stock		3,50,000
" Purchases		8,00,000			
" Profit and Loss A/c Gross Profit transferred *(bal fig.)*		2,50,000			
		13,50,000			13,50,000

∴ Rate of Gross Profit on Sale = $\frac{\text{Rs. } 2,50,000}{\text{Rs. } 10,00,000} \times 100 = 25\%$

Illustration 15

On 30th June 2010 accidental fire destroyed a major part of the stocks in the godown of Jay Associates. Stocks costing Rs. 30,000 could be salvaged but not their stores ledgers. A fire insurance policy was in force under which the sum insured was Rs. 3,50,000. From available records, the following information was retrieved :

(i) Total of sales invoices during the period April-June amounted to Rs. 30,20,000. An analysis showed that goods of the value of Rs. 3,00,000 had been returned by the customers before the date of the fire.

(ii) Opening stock on 1.4.2010 was Rs. 2,20,000 including stocks of value of Rs. 20,000 being lower of cost and net value subsequently realised.

(iii) Purchases between 1.4.2010 and 30.6.2010 were Rs. 21,00,000.

(iv) Normal gross profit rate was $33\frac{1}{3}$% on sales.

(v) A sum of Rs. 30,000 was incurred by way of fire fighting expenses on the day of the fire.

Prepare a statement showing the insurance claim recoverable.

[CA Inter Nov. 1996]

Solution

In the books of Jay Associates

Dr. **Memorandum Trading Account** *for the period from April 1, 2010 to 30th June 2010* *Cr.*

Particulars	*Amount* Rs.	*Amount* Rs.	*Particulars*	*Amount* Rs.	*Amount* Rs.
To Opening Stock	2,20,000		By Sales	30,20,000	
Less : Abnormal Items	20,000	2,00,000	*Less :* Returns	3,00,000	
" Purchases		21,00,000		27,20,000	
" Profit and Loss A/c			*Less :* Abnormal Items	20,000	27,00,000
— Gross Profit transferred (@ $33\frac{1}{3}$% on Rs. 27,00,000)		9,00,000	" Closing Stock *(bal. fig.)*		5,00,000
		32,00,000			32,00,000

Amount of Claim = Value of Stock at the date of fire – Stock Salvaged + Fire Figting Expences
= Rs. 5,00,000 – Rs. 30,000 + Rs. 30,000 = Rs. 5,00,000

Since value of Stock is more than the policy value of Rs. 3,50,000, principle of Average Clause should be applied as :

Net Claim = *Loss of Stock* × $\frac{\textit{Policy Value}}{\textit{Value of Sock at the date of fire}}$

= Rs. 5,00,000 × $\frac{\text{Rs. 3,50,000}}{\text{5,00,000}}$ = Rs. 3,50,000

Note : If the amount of fire fighting expenses are not added to the value of closing stock, the amount of loss will be Rs. 4,70,000, and, consequently, amount of claim also will be reduced.

Illustration 16

On 1.4.2012 the godown of Hindustan Ltd. was destroyed by fire. From the books of account, the following particulars are gathered :

	Rs.		Rs.
Stock at cost on 1.1.2011	27,570	Sales during 2011	3,51,000
Stock as per Balance Sheet on 31.12.2011	51,120	Sales from 1.1.2012 to 31.3.2012	91,500
Purchases during 2011	2,71,350	Value of goods salvaged	6,300
Purchases from 1.1.2012 to 31.3.2012	75,000		

Goods of which original cost was Rs. 3,600 has been valued at Rs. 1,500 on 31st Dec. 2011. These were sold in March 2012 for Rs. 2,700. Except this transaction, the rate of gross profit had remained constant. On 31st March 2012 goods worth Rs. 15,000 had been received by the godown-keeper, but had not been entered in the purchase account. Calculate the value of goods destroyed by fire.

[CA]

Solution

Dr. **Memorandum Trading Account** *(from 1.1.2012 to 31.3.2012)* Cr.

Particulars	*Amount*	*Particulars*	*Amount*
	Rs.		Rs.
To Opening Stock	49,620	By Sales (Rs. 91,500 – Rs. 2,700)	88,800
" Purchases	75,000	" Closing Stock	
" Gross Profit @ 30% on Sales	26,640	*(bal. fig.)*	62,460
	1,51,260		1,51,260

Amount of Claim : = Stock at he date of fire + Unrecorded purchases – Stock Salvaged
= Rs. 62,460 + Rs. 15,000 – Rs. 6,300 = Rs. 71,160.

Workings :

The Trading Account for 2011 is to be prepared to find out the rate of gross profit on sales :

Dr. **Trading Account** *for the year ended 31st December 2011* Cr.

Particulars	*Amount*	*Particulars*	*Amount*
	Rs.		Rs.
To Opening Stock	27,570	By Sales	3,51,000
" Purchases		" Closing Stock	
(Rs. 2,71,350 – Rs. 3,600)	2,67,750	(Rs. 51,120 – Rs. 1,500)	49,620
" Gross Profit *(bal. fig.)*	1,05,300		
	4,00,620		4,00,620

∴ Percentage of G. P. on sales = $\frac{\text{Rs. 1,05,300}}{\text{Rs. 3,51,000}}$ × 100 = 30%

Illustration 17

On 30.9.2012, the Stock of Fred Perry was lost in a fire accident. From the available records the following information is made available to you to enable you to prepare a statement of claim on the insurer :

	Rs.		Rs.
Stock at cost on 1.4.2011	37,500	Sales less returns for the year ended 313.2012	3,15,000
Stock at cost on 31.3.2012	52,000	Purchases less returns up to 30.9.2012	1,45,000
Purchases less returns for the year ended 31.3.2012	2,53,750	Sales less returns up to 30.9.2012	1,84,050

In valuing the Stock on 31.3.2012, due to obsolescence 50% of the value of the Stock which originally cost Rs. 6,000 had been written-off. In May 2012, three-fourth of these Stocks had been sold at 90% of original cost and it is now expected that the balance of the obsolete Stock would also realise the same price. Subject to the above, Gross Profit had remained uniform throughout. Stock to the value of Rs. 7,200 was salvaged.

Solution **[CA]**

In the books of Fred Parry

Memorandum Trading Accoun *from 1st April to 30 September 2012*

Dr. *Particulars*	*Normal items*	*Abnormal items*	*Particulars*	*Normal items*	*Abnormal items* Cr.
	Rs.	Rs.		Rs.	Rs.
To Opening Stock	49,000	6,000	By Sales	1,80,000	4,050[1]
" Purchases	1,45,000	—	" Loss		600
" Profit and Loss A/c Gross Profit transferred (25% on normal sales)	45,000	—	" Closing Stock	59,000	1,350[2]
	2,39,000	6,000		2,39,000	6,000

Amount of Claim : = Closing Stock : Normal Items + Abnormal Items – Stock Salvaged

= Rs. 59,000 + Rs. 1,350 – Rs. 7,200 = Rs. 53,150.

Workings :

In the books of Fred Parry Trading Account *for the year ended 31st March 2012*

Dr. *Particulars*	*Amount*	*Amount*	*Particulars*	*Amount*	*Amount* Cr.
	Rs.	Rs.		Rs.	Rs.
To Opening Stock		37,500	By Sales		3,15,000
" Purchases	2,53,750		" Closing Stock	52,000	
Less ; Cost of Obsolete items	6,000	2,47,750	*Less :* Obsolete items (6,000 – 3,000)	3,000	49,000
" Profit and Loss A/c Gross Profit transferred		78,750			
		3,64,000			3,64,000

Precentage of Gross profit on Sales = $\frac{\text{Rs. } 78,750}{\text{Rs. } 3,15,000} \times 100 = 25\%$

Note : 1. Sales : Rs. 6,000 × $\frac{3}{4}$ = Rs. 4,500 × $\frac{90}{100}$ = Rs. 4,050 2. Stock : Rs. 1,500 × $\frac{90}{100}$ = Rs. 1,350

Illustration 18

On 1.7.2010 a fire took place in the Godown of Chiranjib Das which destroyed all Stocks. Calculate the amount of insurance claim for stock from the following details :

	Rs.		Rs.
Sales in 2010	2,00,000	Stock as on 1.1.2012	2,70,000
Gross profit in 2010	60,000	Purchases from 1.1.2012 to 30.6.2012	4,00,000
Sales in 2011	3,00,000	Sales from 1.1.2012 to 30.6.2012	7,20,000
Gross Profit in 2011	60,000		

The following are also to be taken into consideration :

1. Stocks as on 31.12.1011 has been undervalued by 10%.

2. A stock-taking conducted in March 2012 has revealed that Stock costing Rs. 80,000 were lying in a damaged condition. 50% of these Stocks have been sold in May 2012 at 50% of cost and the balance are expected to be sold at 40% of cost.

Solution

In the books of Chiranjib Das

Dr. **Memorandum Trading Account** *for the period ended 30th June 2012* Cr.

	Particulars	*Normal Items*	*Other Items*		*Particulars*	*Normal Items*	*Other Items*
		Rs.	Rs.			Rs.	Rs.
To	Opening Stock	2,20,000	80,000	By	Sales	7,00,000	20,000[1]
"	Purchases	4,00,000	—	"	Gross Loss (bal. fig.)		44,000
"	Profit and Loss A/c Gross Profit transferred (@ 30% on Normal sales)	2,10,000	—	"	Closing Stock (bal. fig.)	1,30,000	16,000[2]
		8,30,000	80,000			8,30,000	80,000

Rate of Gross Profit in 2011 :

		Rs.
	Gross Profit	60,000
Add :	Increased value of Stock : (Rs. 2,70,000 × $\frac{10}{90}$)	30,000
		90,000

∴ Percentage of Gross profit on Sales is 30% ($\frac{\text{Rs. } 90,000}{\text{Rs. } 3,00,000}$ × 100)

Workings :

1. **Sales for other items :**

Rs. 80,000 × $\frac{50}{100}$ = 40,000 × $\frac{50}{100}$ = Rs. 20,000

2. **Closing Stock for other items :**

Rs. 80,000 × $\frac{50}{100}$ = Rs. 40,000 × $\frac{40}{100}$ = Rs. 16,000

∴ **Amount of Claim** (1,30,000 + 16,000) = Rs. 1,46,000

Illustration 19

Paul & Co. suffered a loss of stock due to fire on 16.8.93. From the following information prepare a statement showing claim for the loss to be submitted :

	Rs.		Rs.
Stock at cost 1.1.1992	73,500	Sales less returns for the year ended on 31.12.1992	4,87,000
Stock at cost 31.12.1992	79,600	Purchases less turn from 1.1.1993 to 16.8.1993	1,62,000
Purchase less returns for the year ended on 31.12.1992	3,98,000	Sales less returns from 1.1.1993 to 16.8.1993	2,31,200

In valuing stock for Balance Sheet at 31st December 1992 Rs. 2,300 had been written off certain stock which was a poor selling line, having cost Rs. 6,900. A portion of these goods was sold in March 1993 at a loss of Rs. 300 on the original cost of Rs. 3,500. The remainder of this stock was now estimated to be worth the original cost. Subject to the above exception gross profit had remained at a uniform rate throughout. The company had a fire policy of Rs. 43,500 covering its stock of goods in the godown. The policy is subject to Average Clause. The stock salvaged from fire was valued at Rs. 6,000.

[CU BCom (Hons.) 1994]

Solution

In the books of Paul & Co.

Dr. **Memorandum Trading Account** *for the period from 1st Jan to 16th Aug. 1993* Cr.

	Particulars	*Normal Items*	*Abnormal Items*		*Particulars*	*Normal Items*	*Abnormal Items*
		Rs.	Rs.			Rs.	Rs.
To	Opening Stock	75,000	6,900	By	Sales	2,28,000	3,200
"	Purchase	1,62,000	—	"	Loss	—	300
"	Gross Profit (20%[1] on Sales)	45,600		"	Closing Stock	54,600	3,400
		2,82,600	6,900			2,82,600	6,900

Amount of Claim

		Rs.
	Value of Stock (Normal)	54,600
Add :	Value of Stock (Abnormal)	3,400
		58,000
Less :	Stock Salvaged	6,000
		52,000

Since insurance policy was only for Rs. 43,500 which is lower than the amount of claim, principles of Average Clause to be applied as :

$$\therefore \text{ Net Claim} = \text{Loss of Stock} \times \frac{\text{Policy Value}}{\text{Value of Stock at the date of fire}} = \text{Rs. } 52{,}000 \times \frac{\text{Rs. } 43{,}500}{\text{Rs. } 58{,}000}$$

$$= \text{Rs. } 39{,}000$$

Workings :

Dr. **Trading Account** *for the year ended 31st Dec. 1992* Cr.

Particulars	*Amount*	*Particulars*	*Amount*
	Rs.		Rs.
To Opening Stock	73,500	By Sales	4,87,000
" Purchases	3,98,000	" Closing Stock :	
" Gross Profit	97,400	" Normal Items (79,600 – 4,600[2])	75,000
		Abnormal Items	6,900
	5,68,900		5,68,900

1 Percentage of Gross Profit on Sales $= \frac{\text{Rs. } 97{,}400}{4{,}87{,}000} \times 100 = 20\%$

2. Abnormal Items = Rs. 6,900 – Rs. 2,300 = Rs. 4,600

Illustration 20

A fire occured in the premise of Shymalesh & Co. on 15.5.99 causing destruction of large part of the stock. The firm had taken a fire insurance policy for Rs. 5,47,200 to cover the loss of stock by fire. From the records saved the following particulars were ascertained:

	Rs.		Rs.
Purchases for the year 1998	30,01,600	Stock on 31st December 1998	7,74,400
Sales for the year 1998	37,12,000	Wages paid during 1998	3,20,000
Purchases from 1st January 1999 to 15th May 1999	5,82,400	Wages paid during 1st January 1999 to 15th May 1999	57,600
Sales from 1st January 1999 to 15th May 1999	7,68,000	Stock Salvaged was	89,600
Stocks on 1st January 1998	4,60,800		

In 1998 some goods were destroyed by fire. The cost of such goods was Rs. 1,60,000. These goods were not covered by any insurance policy. In valuing the stock on 31st December 1998 stocks costing Rs. 34,000 were found to be poor selling line and Rs. 6,000 in relation to such stock were written off. A portion of these goods (original cost Rs. 5,000) were sold in April 1999 at a loss of Rs. 1,000 on original cost. The remainder of this stock was now estimated to be worth the original cost. Subject to the above exception, gross profit has remained at a uniform rate throughout. You are required to ascertain the insurance claim available to the firm.

[CU BCom (Hons.) 2000]

Solution

In the Books of Shymalesh & Co.

Dr. **Memorandum Trading Account** *for the period from 1st Jan. to 15th May 1999* Cr.

Particulars	*Normal Items*	*Abnormal Items*	*Particulars*	*Normal Items*	*Abnormal Items*
	Rs.	Rs.		Rs.	Rs.
To Opening Stock	7,46,400	34,000	By Sales	7,64,000[1]	4,000
" Purchase	5,82,400	—	" Loss *(bal. fig.)*	—	1,000
" Wages	57,600	—	" Closing stock *(bal. fig.)*	8,01,463	29,000
" Gross Profit (@ 23.4375[2]) on Rs. 7,64,000)	1,79,063	—			
	15,65,463	34,000		15,65,463	34,000

Amount of Claim = Value of Stock – Stock Salvaged
= (Rs. 8,01,463 + Rs. 29,000) – Rs. 89,600 = Rs. 7,40,863.

Since, policy amount is less than the amount of Claim, Average clause to be applied, i.e.,

$$\text{Net Claim} = \text{Loss of Stock} \times \frac{\text{Policy Value}}{\text{Stock destroyed at the date of fire}}$$

$$= \text{Rs. } 7{,}40{,}863 \times \frac{\text{Rs. } 5{,}47{,}200}{\text{Rs. } 8{,}30{,}463} = \text{Rs. } 4{,}88{,}162$$

Workings :

1. Sales Rs. 7,68,000 inclusive of Rs. 4,000 (i.e., Rs. 5,000 – Rs. 1,000) treated as abnormal sales.
2.

Dr. **Trading Account** *for the year ended 31st Dec. 2011* Cr.

Particulars	*Amount*	*Particulars*	*Amount*
	Rs.		Rs.
To Opening Stock	4,60,800	By Sales	37,12,000
" Purchases	30,01,600	" Abnormal Loss (not covered. by Ins.)	1,60,000
" Wages	3,20,000	" Closing Stock :	
" Gross Profit	8,70,000	Normal Item (7,74,400 – 28,000)	7,46,400
		Abnormal Items	34,000
	46,52,400		46,52,400

$$\textbf{Percentage of G.P. on sales} = \frac{8{,}70{,}000}{\text{Rs. } 37{,}12{,}000} \times 100 = 23.4375\%$$

Illustration 21

Victory Co. suffered a loss of stock due to fire on 31.3.2011. From the following information prepare a statement showing claim for the loss to be submitted :

	Rs.		Rs.
Stock on 1.1.2010	76,800	Closing Stock on 31.12.2010	63,600
Purchase during the year 2010	3,20,000	Purchase from 1.1.2011 to 31.3.2011	1,08,000
Sales during the year 2010	4,05,200	Sales from 1.1.2011 to 31.3. 2.011	1,22,800

An item of goods purchased in 2009 at a cost of Rs. 20,000 was valued at Rs. 12,000 on 31.12.2009. Half of these goods were sold during 2010 for Rs. 5,200 and the remaining stock was valued at Rs. 4,800 on 31.12.2010. One-fourth of the original stock was sold for Rs. 2,800 in February 2011 and the remaining stock was valued at 60% of the original cost. With the exception of this item, the rate of gross profit remained stationary. The stock salvaged was estimated at Rs. 24,000. There was an Average Clause in the insurance policy which was for Rs. 30,000.

[CU BCom (Hons.)]

Solution

In the books of Victory Co.

Dr. **Memorandum Trading Account** *for the period from 1st Jan. 2011 to 31st March 2011* Cr.

Particulars	*Normal Items*	*Abnormal Items*	*Particulars*	*Normal Items*	*Abnormal Items*
	Rs.	Rs.		Rs.	Rs.
To Opening Stock (Rs. 63,600 – Rs. 4,800)	58,800	10,000	By Sales (Rs. 1,22,800 – Rs. 2,800)	1,20,000	2,800
" Purchases	1,08,000		" Loss (*bal. fig.*)	—	4,200
" Profit and Loss A/c Gross Profit transferred (@ 18.5% on Rs. 1,20,000)	22,200		" Closing Stock : Normal Items (*bal. fig.*)	69,000	—
			" Abnormal Items $(\text{Rs. } 20{,}000 \times \frac{60}{100}) \times \frac{1}{4}$	—	3,000
	1,89,000	10,000		1,89,000	10,000

Amount of Claim = Value of Stock at the date of Fire + Value of Abnormal Items – Stock Salvaged
= Rs. 69,000 + Rs. 3,000 – Rs. 24,000 = Rs. 48,000

Since policy amount (Rs. 30,000) is less than the value of stock destroyed, principle of Average Clause should be applied as :

$$\text{Net Claim} = \textit{Actual Loss} \times \frac{\textit{Policy Value}}{\textit{Value of stock at the date of fire}}$$

$$= \text{Rs. } 48{,}000 \times \frac{\text{Rs. } 30{,}000}{\text{Rs. } 72{,}000} = \text{Rs. } 20{,}000.$$

Workings :

* In order to find out the rate of gross profit on sales, the following Trading Account is prepared :

Dr. **Trading Account** *for the year ended 31st Dec. 2010* Cr.

Particulars	Normal Items	Abnormal Items	Particulars	Normal Items	Abnormal Items
	Rs.	Rs.		Rs.	Rs.
To Opening Stock			By Sales		
(Rs. 76,800 – Rs. 12,000)	64,800	20,000	(Rs.4,05,200 – Rs. 5,200)	4,00,000	5,200
" Purchases	3,20,000		" Loss	—	4,800
" Profit and Loss A/c			" Closing Stock :		
Gross Profit transferred	74,000		Normal Items		
			(Rs. 63,600 – Rs. 4,800)	58,800	—
			" Abnormal Items	—	10,000
	4,58,800	20,000		4,58,800	20,000

$\therefore$ Rate of Gross Profit $= \dfrac{74,000}{\text{Rs. } 4,00,000} \times 100 = 18.5\,\%$

Illustration 22

On 16th August 2012, a fire occurred in the godown of Ganges Jute Mill and the godown was destroyed. From the following information prepare a statement showing the claim to be lodged to the Insurance Company :

	Rs.		Rs.
Stock on 1st January 2011	36,000	Sales for the year ended 31st December 2011	2,03,400
Wages paid—2011	6,000	Closing Stock on 31st December 2011	32,000
(out of that Rs. 1,000 paid for construction of a stage for performing a cultural programme by the Staff Recreation Club of Jute Mill)		Purchases from 1st January 2012 to 16th August 2012	74,000
		Sales from 1st January 2012 to 16th August 2012	82,600
Carriage Inward – 2011	3,000		
Purchases for the year ended 31st December 2011	1,42,000		

An item of stock purchased in 2010 at a cost of Rs. 10,000 was valued at Rs. 6,000 on 31st December 2010. Half of this Stock was sold in 2011 for Rs. 3,400; the remaining stock was valued at Rs. 2,000 on 31st December 2011. One-fourth of the original stock was sold in April, 2012 for Rs. 2,600. The remaining stock was considered to be worth 40% of its original cost. Stock of the value of Rs. 15,000 was salvaged. The amount of the Policy was for Rs. 42,000. There was an Average Clause in the Policy.

[CU BCom (Hons.)1998]

Solution

In the books of Ganges Jute Mill

Dr. **MemorandumTrading Account** *for the period from Jan. 1, 2012 to 16th Aug. 2012* Cr.

Particulars	Normal Items	Abnormal Items	Particulars	Normal Items	Abnormal Items
	Rs.	Rs.		Rs.	Rs.
To Opening Stock	30,000	5,000	By Sales		
" Purchases	74,000		(Rs. 82,600 – 2,600)	80,000	2,600
" Wages	2,606[2]		" Loss— (bal. fig.)		1,500
" Carriage Inwards	1,563		" Closing Stock :		
" Profit on Sale of			Normal Items		
Abnormal Items	—	100	*(bal. fig.)*	48,169	—
Profit and Loss A/c			Abnormal items		
Gross Profit transferred :			(Rs. 10,000 $\times \frac{40}{100} \times \frac{1}{4}$)		1,000
Normal Items					
(@ 25% on 80,000)	20,000				
	1,28,169	5,100		1,28,169	5,100

∴ **Amount of Claim**

		Rs.
	Estimated value of closing stock at the date of fire	48,169
Add :	Value of Abnormal Items	1,000
		49,169
Less :	Stock Salvaged	15,000
		34,169

But, as the policy amount (i.e., Rs. 42,000) is less than the valuing stock at the date of fire (i.e., Rs. 49,169), we are to apply the Average Clause as under :

$$\text{Net Claim} = \text{Actual Loss} \times \frac{\text{Policy Value}}{\text{Value of Stock at the date of fire}} = \text{Rs. } 34{,}169 \times \frac{\text{Rs. } 42{,}000}{\text{Rs. } 49{,}169} = \text{Rs. } 29{,}187$$

Workings :

In order to find out the rate of gross profit on sales, the following Trading Account is prepared :

Dr. **Trading Account** *for the year ended* **31st** *Dec. 2011* Cr.

	Particulars	Normal Items	Abnormal Items		Particulars	Normal Items	Abnormal Items
		Rs.	Rs.			Rs.	Rs.
To	Opening Stock (Rs. 36,000 – Rs. 6,000)	30,000	10,000	By	Sales (Rs. 2,03,400 – Rs. 3,400)	2,00,000	3,400
"	Purchases	1,42,000		"	Loss *(bal. fig.)*		1,600
"	Wages (6,000 – Non-productive Rs. 1,000)	5,000		"	Closing Stock Normal Items : (Rs. 32,000 – Rs. 2,000)	30,000	—
"	Carriage Inwards	3,000		"	Abnormal Items	—	5,000
	Profit and Loss A/c Gross Profit transferred	50,000					
		2,30,000	10,000			2,30,000	10,000

$$\therefore \quad \text{Rate of Gross Profit on Normal Items on Sales} = \frac{\text{Rs. } 50{,}000}{\text{Rs. } 2{,}00{,}000} \times 100 = 40\%$$

Notes :

1. It has been assumed that the rate of gross profit on sales in 2012 for fixing up the selling price is same.
2. It has also been assumed that Wages and Carriage Inwards (i.e., direct charges) are proportionaty increased in terms of purchase as in 2011.

   So, amount of Wages will be = Rs. 2,606 (i.e., $\frac{\text{Rs. } 74{,}000}{\text{Rs. } 1{,}42{,}000} \times \text{Rs. } 5{,}000$)

   and, amount of Carriage Inwards will be = Rs. 1,563 (i.e $\frac{\text{Rs. } 74{,}000}{1{,}42{,}000} \times \text{Rs. } 3{,}000$)
3. Cost of abnormal item is 10,000, $\frac{1}{4}$ th of which i.e., 2,500 was sold for Rs. 2,600 i.e., Profit on abnormal item = Rs. 100 (2,600 – 2,500)

ACCOUNTING ENTRIES IN THE BOOKS OF INSURED FOR FIRE CLAIMS

On admission of the claim

(i) *Admission of claims relating to 'Loss of Fixed Assets' :*

Insurance Company A/c Dr.
 To Fixed Assets

[any profit/loss made on such fixed assets should be transferred to Profit and Loss Account]

In case of profit

Fixed Assets A/c Dr.
 To Profit and Loss A/c

[In case of loss, the entry will be reversed.]

Contd.

(ii) *Admission of claims relating to 'Loss of Stock'*

Two types of Stock Losses can be found out, viz.

(a) Stock Destroyed — where goods are totally lost

(b) Stock Damaged — where goods are not totally lost but damaged by fire and not possible to sell at normal selling price.

Entries for the amount admitted :

(a) Insurance Co. A/c Dr.
To Stock Destroyed A/c
" Stock Damaged A/c

(b) ***For actual cost of stock lost :***
Stock Destroyed A/c Dr.
Stock Damaged A/c Dr.
To Trading A/c

(c) ***For the sale of damaged goods, if any,***
Bank A/c Dr.
To Stock Damaged A/c
(If there is any profit or loss, the same will be transferred to Profit and Loss Account)

(iii) *Admission of claims relating to 'Loss of Profit'**

(a) Insurance Company A/c Dr.
To Profit and Loss A/c } — amount relating to current year.

(b) ***On receipt of money from Insurance Co.***
Bank A/c Dr.
To Insurance Co. A/c

* It has been explained in details in the next part of the present chapter.

Illustration 23

A fire occurred on 21st May 2010, in the factory of M/s AB Traders. The following particulars are obtained as regards the costs and book value of various assets affected by fire, the amount claimed and admitted by XY Insurance Co. Ltd. :

	Book Value	*Claimed*	*Admitted*
	Rs.	*Rs.*	*Rs.*
Buildings	50,000	60,000	45,000
Plant and Machinery	70,000	75,000	60,000
Fittings	12,000	15,000	13,500
Stock Damaged	28,000	30,000	17,000
Stock Destroyed	45,000	50,000	40,000
Loss of Profit	—	55,000	37,000
Fire Expenses	—	1,200	1,200

The Buildings, Plants and Machinery and Fittings were completely destroyed by fire and most of the stock lying in a godown adjacent to the factory was also destroyed. The damaged goods saved were sold for Rs. 13,000. The claim admitted for loss of profit was Rs. 9,000 in respect of the profit for the remaining portion of the year ended 30th Sept. 2010 and Rs. 28,000 for 6 months thereafter when a new factory was built. The actual fire expenses incurred were Rs. 1,200. The Insurance Co. paid the amount for all claims on 27th Sept. 2010. Make Journal entries in the book of M/s AB Traders to record the above particulars including the Cash Book entries (without narration).

Solution

In the books of M/s AB Traders

Journal

Date	*Particulars*	*L.F.*	*Debit*	*Credit*
			Rs.	*Rs.*
2010 Sept. 30	XY Insurance Co Ltd. A/c Dr.		2,13,700	
	To Building A/c			45,000
	" Plant and Machinery A/c			60,000
	" Fittings A/c			13,500
	" Stock Damaged A/c .			17,000

Contd.

2010			Rs.	Rs.
Sept. 30	To Stock Destroyed A/c			40,000
	" Profit and Loss A/c			9,000
	" Profit and Loss Suspense A/c			28,000*
	" Fire Expenses A/c			1,200
	Stock Damaged A/c	Dr.	28,000	
	Stock Destroyed A/c	Dr.	45,000	
	To Trading A/c			73,000
	Bank A/c	Dr.	13,000	
	To Stock Damaged A/c			13,000
	Stock Damaged A/c	Dr.	2,000	
	To Profit and Loss A/c			2,000
	Profit and Loss A/c	Dr.	5,000	
	To Stock Destroyed A/c			5,000
	Profit and Loss A/c	Dr.	15,000	
	To Building A/c			5,000
	" Plant and Machinery A/c			10,000
	Fittings A/c	Dr.	1,500	
	To Profit and Loss A/c			1,500
	Fire Expenses A/c	Dr.	1,200	
	To Bank A/c			1,200
	Bank A/c	Dr.	2,13,700	
	To XY Insurance Co. A/c			2,13,700

* This will be credited to P & L A/c in this year. Net loss of fixed asset will be Rs. 13,500 (i.e., 15,000 – 1,500).

GENERAL ILLUSTRATIONS

Illustration 24

The premises of P were destroyed by fire on 30.6.2012. The following figures, however, were collected from various sources. Prepare a statement of claim in respect of the loss of stock for submission to the Fire Insurance Company. The firm closes its books on 31st December, every year.

Details	*2009*	*2010*	*2011*	*30.6.2012*
	Rs.	*Rs.*	*Rs.*	*Rs.*
Opening Stock	20,000	22,000	11,800	34,020
Purchases *less* returns	1,60,000	1,45,000	1,70,000	35,000
Sales *less* returns	2,00,000	1,98,500	1,87,500	26,000
Freight (Inwards)	5,000	3,000	5,000	1,000
Freight (Outwards)	6,000	7,000	3,000	250

In 2009, while valuing closing stock, a slow-moving item costing Rs. 5,000 was valued at Rs. 4,000. This was sold for Rs. 4,500 in 2010, an item costing Rs. 6,000 was wrongly valued at Rs. 7,000. This was sold for Rs. 5,500 in 2011, a slow-moving item, costing Rs. 12,000 was valued at Rs. 10,000; 50% of which was sold before 30.6.2011 for Rs. 6,000. The value of salvage was Rs. 8,000.

[CA Final]

Solution

In the books of P
Trading Account for the year ended...

Dr. Cr.

Particulars	*2009*	*2010*	*2011*		*Particulars*	*2009*	*2010*	*2011*
	Rs.	Rs.	Rs.			Rs.	Rs.	Rs.
To Opening Stock	20,000	22,000	11,800	By	Sales	2,00,000	1,98,500	1,87,500
Less : Abnormal item		4,000	7,000		*Less* : Abnormal items		4,500	5,500
		18,000	4,800				1,94,000	1,82,000
To Purchase	1,60,000	1,45,000	1,70,000	"	Closing Stock	23,000	10,800	36,020
" Freight (Inwards)	5,000	3,000	5,000					
" Gross Profit	38,000	38,800	38,220					
	2,23,000	2,04,800	2,18,020			2,23,000	2,04,800	2,18,020

Percentage of Gross Profit on Sales —

$$2009: \frac{38,000}{2,00,000} \times 100 = 19\%; \quad 2010: \frac{38,800}{1,94,000} \times 100 = 20\%; \quad 2011: \frac{38,220}{1,82,000} \times 100 = 21\%$$

$$\therefore \quad \text{Average} = \frac{19 + 20 + 21}{3} = 20\%$$

Workings :

	2009 Rs.	2010 Rs.	2011 Rs.
Adjusted Closing Stock			
Already given	22,000	11,800	34,020
Add : Undervaluation	1,000	—	2,000
Less : Overvaluation	—	1,000	—
	23,000	10,800	36,020

Dr. **Trading Account** *for the period from 1st Jan. 2012 to 30th June 2012* Cr.

Particulars	*Amount* Rs.	*Particulars*	*Amount* Rs.
To Opening Stock at cost	36,020	By Sales	26,000
Less : Cost of slow moving item	12,000	*Less* : Sales of slow moving item	6,000
	24,020		20,000
" Purchases	35,000	" Closing Stock *(bal. fig.)*	44,020
" Freight (Inwards)	1,000		
Profit and Loss A/c Gross Profit transferred (20% on 20,000)	4,000		
	64,020		64,020

Amount of Claim :

	Rs.
Estimated stock as per above Trading A/c	44,020
Add : 50% of the cost of slow-moving item not yet sold	6,000
	50,020
Less : Stock salvaged	8,000
Claim	42,020

Note : Although there is a declining trend in sales the rate of gross profit has increased progressively. As a result the rate of G.P. for 2011 (i.e., 21%) could safely be used as the basis for computing the claim instead of the average rate of 20%.

Illustration 25

The factory premises of Toy company were engulfed in fire on 31st March 2012, as a result of which a major part of stock burnt to ashes. The stock was covered by policy for Rs. 1,00,000, subject to Average Clause.

The records at the office revealed the following information :

1. (a) The Company sold goods to dealers on one month credit at dealer's price which is catalogue price less 15%. A cash discount is allowed @ 5% for immediate payment.
   (b) The goods are also sold to agents at catalogue price less 10% against cash payment.
   (c) Goods are sent to branches at catalogue price.
   (d) Catalogue price is cost + 100%.
2. The sale/despatch during the period up to date of fire is—
   (a) Sale to Dealer Rs. 3,40,000 (without Cash Discount)
   (b) Sale to Dealer Rs. 3,23,000 (Net of Cash Discount)
   (c) Sale to Agent Rs. 90,000
   (d) Despatch to branches Rs. 3,00,000.
3. Stock on 1.1.2012 was Rs. 2,50,000 at catalogue price. Purchases at cost from 1.1.2012 to 31st March, 2012 Rs. 6,25,000.
4. Salvaged Stock valued at Rs. 45,000.

Compute the amount of claim to be lodged. **[ICWA Final]**

Solution

In the books of Toy Company

Let the Cost price be Rs. 100.

Catalogue price will be Rs. 200 (i.e., Rs. 100 + 100%)

Agents' Price will be Rs. 180 (i.e., Rs. 200 – 10%)

Dealers' Price will be Rs. 170 (i.e., Rs. 200 – 15%)

Dealers' Price when cash discount is allowed will be Rs. 161.50 (i.e., dealers' price – 5% on Rs. 161.50).

Ascertainment of Loss of Stock

			Rs.
	Opening Stock (Rs. 2,50,000 × 50%)		1,25,000
Add :	Purchases		6,25,000
			7,50,000
Less :	Cost of Goods Sent :	Rs.	
	(i) To Dealers Rs. 3,40,000 × $\frac{100}{170}$ =	2,00,000	
	(ii) To Agents Rs. 90,000 × $\frac{100}{180}$ =	50,000	
	(iii) To Branches Rs. 3,00,000 × $\frac{100}{200}$ =	1,50,000	
	(iv) To Dealers (enjoying Cash Discount) Rs. 3,23,000 × $\frac{100}{161.50}$ =	2,00,000	6,00,000
	Closing Stock at Cost		1,50,000
	Less : Salvaged Stock		45,000
	∴ Loss of Stock		1,05,000

So, claims to be lodged after applying Average Clause : as policy value is less than the loss of stock

$$\text{Net claim} = \text{Loss of Stock} \times \frac{\text{Policy Value}}{\text{Stock at the date of fire}}$$

$$= \text{Rs. } 1,05,000 \times \frac{\text{Rs. } 1,00,000}{\text{Rs. } 1,50,000} = \text{Rs. } 70,000$$

Illustration 26

A fire occurred in the premises of M/s Fireprone Co. on 30th May 2012. From the following particulars, relating to the period from 1.1.2012 to 30.5.2012, you are required to ascertain the amount of claim to be filed with the insurance company for the loss of stock :

		Rs.
1.	Stock as per Balance Sheet as at 31st Dec. 2011	99,000
2.	Purchases (including purchase of Machinery costing Rs. 30,000)	1,70,000
3.	Wages (including wages for the installation of Machinery Rs. 3,000)	50,000
4.	Sales (including goods sold on approval basis amounting to Rs. 49,500. No confirmation has been received in respect of $\frac{2}{3}$ of such goods sold on approval basis.)	2,75,000
5.	Sales value of goods drawn by partners	15,000
6.	Cost of goods sent to consignee on 15th May 2012, lying unsold with them	16,500
7.	Sales value of goods distributed as free samples	1,500

The average rate of gross profit had been 20% in the past. The selling price had been increased by 20% with effect from 1.1.2012.

For valuing the stocks for the Balance Sheet as at 31st Dec. 2011, Rs. 1,000 had been written-off in respect of a slow moving item, the cost of which was Rs. 5,000. A portion of those goods were sold at a loss of Rs. 500 on the original cost of Rs. 2,500. The remainder of the stock was now estimated to be worth the original cost.

Subject to the above exceptions, the gross profit had remained at a uniform rate throughout.

The value of goods salvaged was estimated at Rs. 25,000.

The concern had taken an insurance policy for Rs. 60,000 which was subject to the average clause.

Solution **[ICWA Final (New)]**

In the books of M/s Fireprone Co. Ltd.

Memorandum Trading Account *for the period from 1.1.2012 to 30.5.2012*

Dr. *Particulars*		Normal Items	Abnormal Items	Cr. *Particulars*	Normal Items	Abnormal Items
		Rs.	Rs.		Rs.	Rs.
To Opening Stock		95,000	5,000	By Sales	2,40,000[1]	2,000
" Purchases	1,70,000			" Closing Stock lying with customers on approval	22,000[2]	—
Less : Machinery	30,000			" Loss		500
	1,40,000			" Closing Stock *(bal. fig.)*	72,500	2,500
Less : Goods sent to Consignor	16,500					
	1,23,500					
Less : Drawings	10,000[3]					
	1,13,500					
Less : Advertisement	1,000[4]					
		1,12,500	—			
" Wages (50,000 – 3,000)		47,000	—			
" Gross Profit (@ $33\frac{1}{3}$ % on Sales)		80,000				
		3,34,500	5,000		3,34,500	5,000

Amount of Claims = Value of Stock at the date of fire + Value of Abnormal Items – Stock Salvaged

= Rs. 72,500 + Rs. 2,500 – Rs. 25,000 = Rs. 50,000.

Claims after applying Average Clause = *Loss of Stock* × $\frac{\textit{Value of Policy}}{\textit{Closing Stock}}$ = Rs. 50,000 × $\frac{\text{Rs. } 60,000}{\text{Rs. } 75,000}$ = Rs. 40,000.

Workings :

1. Normal Sales

	Rs.
Total Sales	2,75,000
Less: Sold on approval (Rs. 49,500 × $\frac{2}{3}$)	33,000
	2.42,000
Less : Abnormal Items (Slow moving)	2,000
	2,40,000

2. Goods Sold on Approval

	Rs.
Goods Sold on approval (Rs. 49,500 × $\frac{2}{3}$) =	33,000
Less : Gross Profit @ $33\frac{1}{3}$ %	11,000
	22,000

3. Drawing by Partners

Goods taken	15,000
Less : Gross Profit @ $33\frac{1}{3}$ %	5,000
	10,000

4. Goods Distributed as free sample i.e., Adv.

	Rs.
Goods distributed (SP)	1,500
Less : Gross Profit @ $33\frac{1}{3}$ %	500
	1,000

5. Rate of Old Gross Profit

Old G.P. Ratio is 20%

6. Revised Gross Profit

	Rs.
Selling Price = Rs. 100 + Rs. 20	120
Cost Price (No change) (Rs. 100 – Rs. 20)	80
Profit	40

∴ Gross Profit Ratio = $\frac{40}{120} = \frac{1}{3}$ or $33\frac{1}{3}$ %

ASSIGNMENT MATERIALS

THEORETICAL

Multiple Choice Questions

1. (a) Stock destroyed by fire is —

(i) Normal Loss; (ii) Abnormal Loss; (iii) Both; (iv) None of these

(b) G. P. Ratio is equal to:

(i) $\frac{GP}{Sales} \times 100$ (ii) $\frac{Sales}{GP} \times 100$ (iii) $\frac{Purchase}{GP} \times 100$ (iv) $\frac{GP}{Purchase} \times 100$

(c) Stock salvaged is to be:

(i) Added to Closing Stock (ii) Subtracted from Closing stock (iii) No effect (iv) None of these

(d) Average clause is applicable when—

(i) Policy value is more than actual claims; (ii) Policy value is less than actual claim, (iii) In case of both (iv) None of these

(e) If value of stock at the date of fire exceeds the amount of insured value the amount of claim is limited :

(i) After applying average clause; (ii) Before applying average clause; (iii) No effect (iv) None of these.

[Ans. (a) (ii); (b) (ii); (c) (ii); ((d) (ii); (e) (i)]

Short-Answer Type Question

2. How do you calculate the Value of Stock at the date of fire?
3. What is G.P. Ratio? What does it convey?
4. How do you compute the Value of Stock and how do you treat the same in the books?
5. What is Average Clause?
6. How do you treat Abnormal Items of goods, Insurance Claims for Loss of Stock?
7. When do you apply Average Clause? Give an example.
8. States the effect of G.P. Ratio in valuing Closing Stock?

Long or Essay-Answer Type Questions

9. Discuss the procedure of calculation of the amount of claim for loss for stock destroyed by fire.
10. Discuss the treatment of abnormal items of goods with an example.
11. How do you calculate G.P. Ratio? State its effect while calculating abnormal loss of stock.
12. What is average clause? How do you ascertain the amount of Net Claim?
13. What are abnormal items of goods?
14. How do you compute the actual amount of claim?
15. Explain the entries for claims in the books of insured for the claims.

PRACTICAL

1. A merchant's godown caught fire on Nov. 3, 2012, at night causting serious damage to Stock. The following information is obtained from the books and records salvaged :

	Rs.
Stock at cost on 31.12.2010	45,000
Stock at cost on 31.12.2011	50,000
Purchases during 2011	4,75,000
Sales from January 1 to Nov. 3, 2012	4,00,000
Purchases from January 1 to Nov. 3, 2012	4,40,000
Sales during 2011	5,87,500

In June 2012, shopsoiled goods of the cost price of Rs. 2,000 were thrown away as valueless.

Assuming that the rate of Gross Profit on Sales has been the same in 2012 as in 2011, estimate the value of the Stock in the godown at the time of fire and a statement of claim for submission to the Insurance company.

[Ans. Amount of claim Rs. 1,68,000, Rate of Gross Profit on Sales @ 20%]

2. On 31.5.2012, the Premises and Stock of a firm were totally destroyed by fire, the books of account, however, being saved. In order to make a claim on their fire policy they ask your advice and you are able to obtain the following information. The Stock on hand has always been valued at 5% below cost :

	2009	2010	2011	2012
	Rs.	Rs.	Rs.	Rs.
Opening Stock	22,800	30,400	36,100	39,900
Purchases less returns	91,000	1,10,000	1,20,000	41,000
Sales less returns	1,40,000	1,70,000	1,86,000	75,000
Wages	28,400	31,200	34,200	12,000
Closing Stock	30,400	36,100	39,900	—

Prepare a statement for submission to the Insurance Company in support of your claim for loss of Stock.

[Ans. Amount of Claim Rs. 35,000]

3. Fire occurred in the premises of A. & Company on 1st Sept. 2012 and Stock of the value of Rs. 1,01,000 was salvaged and the business books and records were saved.

The following information was obtained :

	Rs.
Purchases for the year ended 31.3.2012	7,00,000
Sales for year ended 31.3.2012	11,00,000
Purchases from 1.3.2012 to 1.9.2012	2,40,000
Sales from 1.3.2012 to 1.9.2012	3,60,000
Stock on 31.3.2011	3,00,000
Stock on 31.3.2012	3,40,000

Further information is also given that the Stock on 31.3.2012 was overvalued by Rs. 20,000.

Calculate the amount of the claim to be presented to the Insurance Company inrespective of losses. Rate of Gross Profit is to be based on the year ended 31.3.2012.

[CU BCom (Hons.)]

[Ans. Rate of Gross Profit 38.18% (App.); Amount of Claim Rs. 2,33,540 (Value of Stock Rs. 3,34,540)]

4. A fire occurred on April 15, 2013, and destroyed the business premises of D. & Co. The books of accounts and Stock amounting to Rs. 1,80,000 were saved and the following information was rendered available from the books :

	Sales	Gross Profit
	Rs.	Rs.
Year ending Dec. 31, 2008	86,00,000	21,50,000
Year ending Dec. 31, 2009	71,00,000	21,30,000
Year ending Dec. 31, 2010	60,00,000	20,00,000
Year ending Dec. 31, 2011	55,00,000	18,70,000
Year ending Dec. 31, 2012	48,00,000	16,00,000

The Stock on Dec. 31, 2012, was valued at Rs. 9,70,000. The Purchase, Sales and production wages from Jan. 1, 2013 to April 14, 2013 were ascertained at Rs. 7,50,000, Rs. 15,90,000 and Rs. 3,00,000, respectively.

You are to prepare a statement in support of your claim against the Insurance Company together with any comments you may feel necessary to make.

[Ans. Amount of Claim Rs. 7,80,000]

5. The godown of Purple Ltd. caught fire on 15th June 2013. Records saved from fire showed the following particulars :

	Rs.
Stock at cost 1st January 2012	60,000
Stock at cost 31st December 2012	88,000
Purchases less Returns for the year 2012	5,68,000
Sales less Returns for the year 2012	7,20,000
Purchases less Returns from 1st January to 15th June 2013	1,80,000
Sales less Returns from 1st January to 15th June 2013	2,46,000

Gross Profit had remained at uniform rate. The stocks salvaged were worth Rs. 7,200 and they were retained by Purple Ltd.

The godown was insured. Show the amount of the claim.

[Ans. Rate of G.P. on Sales 25%; Amount of Claim Rs. 76,300] **[CU BCom (Hons.)]**

6. On 20th July 2011 the godown and business premises of a merchant were affected by fire and from accounting records, stock salvaged Rs. 12,000. The following information are supplied :

	Rs.
Stock of goods at cost on 1.4.2010	1,00,000
Stock of goods at 10% lower than cost as on 31.3.2011	1,08,000
Purchase of goods for the year from 1.4.2010 to 31.3.2011	4,20,000
Sales for the same period	6,00,000
Purchase less returns for the period from 1.4.2011 to 20.7.2011	1,40,000
Sales less returns for the above period	3,10,000

Sales up to 20th July 2011 included Rs. 40,000 for which goods had not been despatched. Purchases up to 20th July, 2011 did not include Rs. 20,000 for which purchase invoice had not been received from suppliers, though goods have been received at the godown.

Goods salvaged from the accident were worth Rs. 12,000 and these were handed over to the insured. Ascertain the value of the claim for cost of goods/stock which could be preferred on the insurer.

[CA]

[Ans. Value of stock at the date of fire Rs. 1,00,000. Amount of claim Rs. 88,000. Ratio of Gross Profit @ $33\frac{1}{3}$%]

7. On 17.6.2013, due to a fire in the warehouse of Sri Basanta Patra, the greater part of the Stocks were destroyed. The business books and records were saved, and the Stocks of the value of Rs. 2,820 was salvaged. The following particulars were ascertained :

	Rs.
Stock at cost as on 31.3.2012	14,400
Stock, as per Balance Sheet, as on 31.3.2013	15,700
Purchases for the year ended 31.3.2013	30,600
Sales for year ended 31.3.2013	50,000
Purchases from 1.4.2013 to 17.6.2013	12,500
Sales from 1.4.2013 to 17.6.2013	17,800

In valuing the Stock as on 31.3.2013, Rs. 300 was written-off a particular line of goods which were originally purchased at Rs. 600 and actually sold in April 2013 for Rs. 500. Excepting this transaction, the G. P. ratio remains the same.

You are required to calculate the amount of claim to be presented to the Insurance Company in respect of Stocks destroyed by fire.

[Ans. Insurance Claim for Loss of Stock Rs. 15,346; Rate of G.P. on Sales 42%]

8. The premises of a company were destroyed by fire on 15.6.2013. The records, however, were saved wherefrom the following particulars were available :

	Rs.
Stock at cost on 1.1.2012	30,000
Stock at cost on 31.12.2012	40,000
Purchases less returns for the year ended 31.12.2012	2,00,000
Sales less returns for the year ended 31.12.2012	2,50,000
Purchases less returns from 1.1.2013 to 15.6.2013	85,000
Sales less returns from 1.1.2013 to 15.6.2013	1,20,000

Rs. 2,500 had been written-off certain Stock, which was a poor selling line, while valuing the Stock for Balance Sheet as at 31.12.2012. The cost of such Stock was Rs. 4,000. A portion of this Stock was sold in March 2013 at a loss of Rs. 500 on the original cost of Rs. 2,000. The balance of this Stock was now estimated to be worth the original cost. Excepting the above, the Gross Profit had remained at an uniform rate throughout. The stock saved was Rs. 5,000.

You are required to ascertain the amount of loss on Stock which was to be claimed from the Insurance Company.

[Ans. Amount of Claim Rs. 31,625]

9. On 15th June 2009, the business house of Maneka & Co. was destroyed by fire. The following particulars are given to you :

	Rs.
Stock at Cost, 1st January 2008	4,41,000
Stock at Cost, 31st December 2008	4,77,600
Purchases, less returns, year ended 31st December 2008	23,88,000
Sales, less returns, year ended 31st December 2008	29,22,000
Purchases, less returns, 1st January 2009 to 15th June 2009	9,72,000
Sales, less returns, 1st January 2009 to 15th June 2009	13,87,200

In valuing stock for Balance Sheet at 31st December 2008, Rs. 13,800 had been written-off. There was a certain stock which was a poor selling line, having cost Rs. 41,400. A portion of these goods was sold in March 2009 at a loss of Rs. 1,500 on the original cost of Rs. 20,700. The remainder of this stock was now estimated to be worth the original cost. Subject to the above exception, gross profit had remained at a uniform rate throughout.

The stock salvaged from fire was valued at Rs. 34,800.

You are to ascertain the amount of claim to be placed with the fire insurance company concerned.

[CU BCom (Hons.)]

[Ans. Rate of Gross Profit 20%, Value of Closing Stock on 31.12.2008 Rs. 4,91,400. Value of Opening Stock on 1.1.2008 Rs. 4,91,400 – Rs. 41,400 = Rs. 4,50,000. Value of Closing Stock on 15.6.2008 Rs. 3,27,600. Claim Rs. 3,13,500]

B. LOSS OF PROFIT

Introduction

At present it is very common for a firm to protect its assets by insurance against damages caused by fire, floods etc. Practically, the loss which is sustained as a result of such fire or floods is not confined only to material damages but the same affect the firm as a whole. In short, after the fire, it may be found that the turnover of the business has declined owing to lack of raw materials, inability to manufacture or any other reason. On the other hand, expenses of the business may also increase.

We know that an ordinary fire policy is designed to make good "capital" losses due to assets being wholly or partly destroyed. However, it is apparent that the loss to a business in the event of a severe fire involves far more than the actual loss of capital assets. This is because the business will be restricted in its trading operations, and reduced turnover which results in a loss of net profit. At the same time, the greater part of the ordinary working cost will continue and this may prove a considerable drain on the finance of the firm and could result in its winding-up. As a result, insurance companies encourage businessmen to protect themselves against these losses by taking out policies for *'Loss of Profit'*. A pre-requisite to any form of loss of profit insurance is that the insured's property (i.e., Building, Plants etc.) is insured also against material loss.[1]

Indemnity under Policy

Subject to (i) fire, (ii) lightning and (iii) Explosion — the insurance company would indeminify the insured against :

(i) Loss of Net Profit,[2] following a reduction in turnover or output;

(ii) Payment of standing charges; and

(iii) Increased cost of working (which is necessary to avoid or diminish reduced turnover).

Some Important Terms

Standing Charges

It includes fixed charges which continue irrespective of reduction in turnover. It is just the opposite of variable charges which fluctuate with the turnover. Some of the examples :

(a) Wages and Salaries of permanent staff and employees;

(b) Rent, Rates and Taxes and Insurance;

(c) Directors' fees and Auditors' fees;

(d) Depreciation of fixed assets; and

(e) Sundry Standing charges restricted to 5% of the total of specified insured standing charges.

Note : It is to be noted in this respect that under loss of profit insurance ***gross profit means net profit plus insured standing charges.*** For this purpose standing charges which are meant for insurance and which are not should be properly distinguished.

Increased Cost of Working

It includes the ***additional expenditures which are incurred reasonable in order to avoid the reduction in turnover, i.e., the expenditures which have taken place during the indemnity period as a result to the damage.*** In short, unreasonable expenditure are to be excluded. For example, premises taken temporarily on hire to carry on production.

The same can be computed with the help of :

(a) Ascertain the proportionate increased cost of working only when all insured standing charges are not covered by the policy. The same is obtained by multiplying increased cost of working with the proportion of insured gross profit to actual gross profit :

Thus, Proportionate increased cost of working

$$= \frac{\text{Net Profit + Insured Standing Charges}}{\text{Net Profit + All Insurable Standing Charges}} \times \text{Increased Cost of Working}$$

(b) Limit this proportionate cost to the sum ascertained after applying the insured gross profit rate (adjusted) to the reduction in sales avoided.

That is, the lower of the two will be accepted.

Indemnity

The amount of compensation is the difference between the actual profit earned after the damage and the profit which should have been earned if the damage had not been occured.

Indemnity Period

This is the period that commences at the date of damage and ends not later than the stated number of months thereafter. In short, it is the period from the date of damage/hazard up to the date when the business begins its normal functions, subject to the number of days or months mentioned in the policy (as the period of indemnity). The term is selected by the proposer and should be sufficient to extend over the

---

1 Yorston, Smyth and Brown — *Advanced Accounting* — N. M. Tripathy (P) Ltd., 1968, P. 287.

2 Net profit referred to here is the ordinary net profit of the business as disclosed by the Revenue Statement and thus excludes capital receipts and payments — *Ibid.*

full period of any likely interruption.[†1] The period can be anywhere between 3 and 6 months. It is not needed for the policy to cover the entire indemnity period but what is required is that at the date of fire which leads complete or partial cessation of activity the policy must be in force.

The turnover for the 12 months immediately preceding the date of damage.

Gross Profit

It has already been stated earlier that *gross profit means net profit plus insured standing charges.* In case of loss, the amount would be insured—standing charges minus such a proportion of any net trading loss as the amount of the insured standing charges bears to the whole of the standing charges of this business.[3]

Rate of Gross Profit

It is the percentage of gross profit earned on the turnover during the financial year immediately preceding the date of damage.

Turnover

It is the amount paid or payable to the insured for goods sold, delivered and services.

Standard Turnover

It is the turnover during the period of 12 months immediately preceding the date of the damage which corresponds with the indemnity period. It may be explained with the help of the following example :

(i) Fire accident happened on 1st July 2000;

(ii) Indemnity period 5 months (from 1st July 2000 to 30th Nov. 2000);

(iii) Standard Turnover will be the amount which corresponds from 1st July to 30th Nov. 1999.

Annual Turnover

It is the turnover during the period of 12 months immediately before the date of damages.

Short Sales/Reduction in Turnover

When standard turnover exceeds the actual turnover during the period of interruption the same is known as ***Short Sales or Reduction in Turnover,*** i.e., the difference between the standard turnover and the actual turnover. Consider the following example :

(i) Standard Turnover from 1.7.1999 to 30th Nov. 1999 amounted to Rs. 2,00,000;

(ii) An adjustment of 20% should be made in respect of upward trend in turnover;

(iii) Actual sales during indemnity period (i.e., from 1st Duly 2000 to 30th Nov. 2000) amounted to Rs. 60,000.

Solution

Short Sales

		Rs.
	Standard Turnover (for 1.7.1999 to 30.11.1999)	2,00,000
Add :	20% Increase	40,000
		2,40,000
Less :	Actual sales during indemnity period	60,000
	∴ Short Sales	1,80,000

Averages

All forms of profits insurance are subject to average. **If the turnover is increased, the sum insured should also be increased, otherwise it will be a case of under-insurance. This will also be a under-insurance if** all standing charges are not covered by the policy.

---

†1 Risks not covered— The following items are not covered by the loss of profit policy— (i) third party liability due to damage, (ii) loss of goodwill, (iii) depreciation of stock, (iv) bad debts. (v) loss of credit etc.

3 *Ibid*

Savings in Insured Standing Charges

Generally, a provision is made for a *Savings in Insured Standing Charges* during the indemnity period and the same is to be deducted from the claim as well. It means that the amount of expense which may not be incurred as a result of the damage. The said amount, if any, must be deducted from the loss so assessed. It should be remembed in this respect that savings must be made during the period of indemnity and must be in respect of insured standing charges.

Procedure for Ascertaining Claim

Step 1 **Ascertain the amount of short sales/shortage in turnover (i.e., excess of standard sales over actual sales during interruption). Apply the rate of gross profit on short sales.**

Step 2 **Ascertain the increased cost of working and add it. If all standing charges are not insured, the claim in respect of increased cost of working must be reduced proportionately with the help of the formula :**

$$\text{Claim} = \frac{\text{Net Profit} + \text{Insured Standing Charges}}{\text{Net Profit} + \text{All Standing Charges}} \times \text{Increased cost of working}$$

But the claim in respect of increased cost of working must not exceed the sum produced by applying the rate of gross profit to the amount of reduction in turnover.

Step 3 **Deduct the amount of saving in the insured standing charges during the period of indemnity.**

Step 4 **Apply the test of 'Average Clause' to the sum so ascertained as :**

$$\therefore \text{Net Claim} = \text{Loss of Profit} \times \frac{\text{Amount of Policy}}{\text{Gross Profit on Annual Sales}}$$

Average clause

Needless to mention that the loss of profit so calculated is subject to the average clause (already discussed in short). It can be applied only when the amount of the policy is less than the gross profit :

$$\text{Claim} = \text{Loss of Profit} \times \frac{\text{Amount of Policy}}{\text{Gross Profit that may have been earned by the sales for 12 months ending on the date of fire (adjusted)}}$$

Illustration 27

From the following particulars prepare a claim for loss of profits under the Consequential Loss Policy.

Date of fire : June 30, 2006
Period of indemnity : Six months

	Rs.
Sum Insured	50,000
Turnover for the year ended June 30, 2006	2,00,000
Net Profit for the accounting year ending March 31, 2006	12,500
Standing charges for the accounting year ending March 31, 2006	28,500
Turnover for the year ending March 31, 2006	1,98,000
Turnover for the indemnity period from 01.07.2006 to 31.12.2006	56,000
Turnover for the period from 01.07.2005 to 31.12.2005	1,10,000

The turnover of the year 2006-07 had shown a tendency of increase of 10% over the turnover of the preceding year.

[CU BCom (Hons.) 2007]

Solution

Short Sales

		Rs.
(a)	Standard Turnover (from 1.7.05 to 31.12.05)	1,10,000
	Add: 10% Increase in 2006-07	11,000
		1,21,000
	Less : Actual Sales	56,000
		65,000

(b) **Rate of Gross Profit on Sales**

$$= \frac{\text{Net Profit + Insured Standing Charges}}{\text{Sales}} \times 100 = \frac{\text{Rs. } 12{,}500 + \text{Rs. } 28{,}500}{\text{Rs. } 1{,}98{,}000} \times 100 = \mathbf{20.70\%}$$

(c) **Gross Claim**

		Rs.
	Gross Profit on Short Sales = Rs. 65,000 × 20.70% =	13,460
Add :	Increased Cost of Workings	Nil
		13,460
Less :	Saving in Standing Chrges	Nil
	Amount of Gross Claim	13,460

Note : As the amount of insurance policy is more than the amount of gross claim, so gross claim to be lodged with Insurance Company

Illustration 28

From the following information, finalise the claims under a Loss of Profit Policy :

	Rs.		Rs.
Sales in 2001	1,00,000	(All insured) Standing charges in 2004	7,280
Sales in 2002	1,20,000	Date of dislocation by fire—1.1.2005	
Sales in 2003	1,44,000	Period of dislocation — 3 months	
Sales in 2004	1,72,800	Sales from 1.1.2004 – 31.3.2004	43,200
Net Profit in 2004	10,000	Sales from 1.1.2005 – 31.3.2005	11,840
		Indemnity period — 9 months	
		Policy value	50,000

There was no reduction in standing charges during the dislocation period, nor were there any additional costs.

Solution

Dr. **Memorandum Profit and Loss Account** Cr.

	Particulars	Amount Rs.		Particulars	Amount Rs.
To	Insured Standing Charges	7,280	By	Sales *(bal. fig.)*	17,280
"	Net Profit	10,000			
		17,280			17,280

$$\text{Percentage of Gross Profit on Sales} = \frac{\text{Rs. } 17{,}280}{\text{Rs. } 1{,}72{,}800} \times 100 = 10\%$$

(Since entire amount of sale proceeds represent gross profit).

∴ Amount of Short Sales :

	Rs.
Sales from 1.1.2004 to 31.3.2004	43,200
Add : 20% increase (since it shows from trend analysis)	8,640
	51,840
Less : (from 1.1.2005 to 31.3.2005)	11,840
Short Sales	40,000

∴ Amount of Claim will be Rs. 4,000 (Rs. 40,000 × $\frac{10}{100}$ (% of G.P. on sales)

Illustration 29

From the following information, you are required to work out the claim under the Loss of Profit insurance policy :

(1) Cover — Gross Profit Rs. 1,00,000. (2) Indemnity period— six months. (3) Damage— due to a fire accident on 28th December – accounting year ends on 31st December. (4) Net Profit plus all standing charges in prior accounting year Rs. 1,50,000. (5) Standing Charges uninsured Rs. 25,000. (6) Turnover of the last accounting year was Rs. 5,00,000, the rate of Gross Profit being 25%. (7) The annual turnover, namely, the turnover for 12th months immediately preceding the fire, Rs. 5,20,000. (8) As a consequence of fire, there was a reduction in certain insured standing charges at the rate of Rs. 25,000 p.a. (9) The

standard turnover was Rs. 2,60,000. (10) Increased cost of working during the period of indemnity were Rs. 20,000. (11) Turnover during the period of indemnity was Rs. 1,00,000 and, out of this turnover of Rs. 80,000 was maintained due to increased cost of working.

Solution

Short Sales :

		Rs.
	Standard turnover	2,60,000
Less :	Actual Turnover during indemnity period	1,00,000
		1,60,000

			Rs.
∴	Loss on Short Sales @ 25% i.e., Rs. 1,60,000 × $\frac{25}{100}$ =		40,000
	(being the rate of Gross Profit on sales)		
Add :	Increased Cost of Working :		
	Actual amount	20,000	
	Gross Profit @ 25% on Annual Turnover (Rs. 5,20,000 × $\frac{25}{100}$)	1,30,000	
	Gross Profit plus Uninsured Standing (Rs. 1,30,000 + Rs. 25,000 = 1,55,000)		
∴	Claim $\left(\text{Rs. } 20{,}000 \times \frac{\text{Rs. } 1{,}30{,}000}{\text{Rs. } 1{,}55{,}000}\right)$ =		16,774
			56,774
Less :	Saving in Standing Charges for 6 months		12,500
			44,274

$$\textit{Amount of claim} = \textit{Gross Claim} \times \frac{\textit{Sum Assured}}{\textit{Gross Profit on Adjusted Annual Turnover}}$$

$$= \text{Rs. } 44{,}274 \times \frac{\text{Rs. } 1{,}00{,}000}{\text{Rs. } 1{,}30{,}000 \text{ (25\% of Rs. } 5{,}20{,}000)}$$

$$= \text{Rs. } 34{,}057$$

Illustration 30

From the following claim, compute a consequential loss claim :

Financial year ends on 31st December, turnover Rs. 2,00,000

Indemnity period — 6 months

Period of interruption — 1st July to 31st October

Net Profit Rs. 18,000

Standing charges Rs. 42,000, out of which Rs. 10,000 have not been insured

Sum assured Rs. 50,000

Standard Turnover Rs. 65,000

Turnover in the period of interruption — Rs. 25,000 out of which Rs. 6,000 was from a rented place Rs. 600 p.m.

Annual turnover is Rs. 2,40,000

Saving in Standing Charges Rs. 4,725 p.a.

Date of fire – night 30th June.

It was agreed between insurer and the insured that the business trends would lead to an increase of 10% in the turnover.

[CA]

Solution

Short Sales = Standard Sales – Actual Sales during indemnity period
= Rs. 71,500 (Rs. 65,000 + 10% increase) – Rs. 25,000
= Rs. 46,500

	Rs.
Gross Profit on short sales @ Rs. 25%[1] = Rs. 46,500 × $\frac{25}{100}$ =	11,625
Add : Increased Cost of Working	1,500[2]
	13,125
Less : Savings in Standing Charges (Rs. 4,725 ÷ 3)	1,575
Gross Claim	11,550

∴ Amount of Claim = $\frac{\text{Rs. } 11,550 \times \text{Rs. } 50,000}{\text{Rs. } 66,000}$

= Rs. 8,750

Workings :

1. ***Rate of Gross Profit on Sales :***

Gross Profit = Net Profit + Insured standing charges
= Rs. 18,000 + Rs. 32,000
= Rs. 50,000

Turnover Rs. 2,00,000

∴ Percentage of Gross Profit on Turnover $\frac{\text{Rs. } 50,000}{\text{Rs. } 2,00,000} \times 100 = 25\%$

2. ***Cost of Working :***

Least of the following :

(a) Rent of Premises × $\frac{\text{Gross Profit}}{\text{Gross Profit + Uninsured Charges}}$

= Rs. 2,400 × $\frac{\text{Rs. } 50,000}{\text{Rs. } 50,000 + \text{Rs. } 10,000}$

= Rs. 2,000

(b) Or, 25% on additional sales i.e., Rs. 6,000 × $\frac{25}{100}$ = Rs. 1,500

So, Rs. 1,500 is to be considered.

Illustration 31

On September 1, 2010 a serious fire occurred at the premises of B. Ltd., and interrupted their business activities until December 31, 2010, when normal trading conditions were reestablished. B Ltd. is insured under loss of profit policy for Rs. 42,000, the period of indemnity being six months.

You ascertain the following information :

(a) The Net Profit for the year ended December 31, 2009 was Rs. 20,000;

(b) The annual insurable standing charges amounted to Rs. 30,000 of which Rs. 2,000 were not included in the definition of insured standing charges under the policy;

(c) The additional cost of working in order to mitigate the damage caused by the fire amounted to Rs. 3,600 and, but for this expenditure, the business would have had to shut down;

(d) The savings in insured standing charges in consequence of the firm amounted to Rs. 1,500;

(e) The turnover for the periods of four months ended April 30, August 31, and December 31 in each of the years 2009 and 2010 was :

2009	Rs. 65,000	Rs. 80,000	Rs. 95,000
2010	Rs. 70,000	Rs. 80,000	Rs. 15,000

You are required to compute the relevant claim under the terms of the Loss of Profit policy.

Solution

1. ***Rate of Gross Profit on Sales*** = $\frac{\text{Net Profit + Insured Standing Charges}}{\text{Sales}}$

$\frac{\text{Rs. } 20,000 + \text{Rs. } 28,000\ (30,000 - 2,000)}{\text{Rs. } 2,40,000\ (65,000 + 80,000 + 95,000)} \times 100 = 20\%$

2. ***Short Sales :***

	Rs.
Standard Turnover	95,000
Less : Actual Turnover during interruption	15,000
	80,000

Loss of Profit on Short Sales Rs. 16,000 (i.e., Rs. 80,000 × $\frac{20}{100}$)

3. *Gross Claim :*

		Rs.
	Loss of Profit on short sales	16,000
Add :	Increased cost of workings (subject to limit)	3,000*
		19,000
Less :	Savings in Standing Charges	1,500
	Gross Claim	17,500

4. *Amount of Claim :*

$= \text{Rs. } 17{,}500 \times \frac{\text{Rs. } 42{,}000}{\text{Rs. } 49{,}000 \text{ (20\% of Rs. } 95{,}000 + 70{,}000 + \text{Rs. } 80{,}000)}$

$=$ Rs. 15,000

* Actual amount is Rs. 3,600. But the same must not exceed the following two :

(i) $\frac{\text{Net Profit + Insured Standing Charges}}{\text{N.P. + All Standing Charges}} \times$ Increased Cost of Working

$= \frac{\text{Rs. } 48{,}000}{\text{Rs. } 50{,}000} \times \text{Rs. } 3{,}600 = \text{Rs. } 3{,}456$

(ii) 20% on Turnover = 15,000 × 20% = Rs. 3,000

Therefore, Rs. 3,000 is to be considered.

Illustration 32

A fire occurred on 1st July 2010 in the premises of A. Ltd. and business was practically disorganised up to 30th November 2010. From the books of account, the following information was extracted :

		Rs.			Rs.
(1)	Actual turnover from 1st July 2010 to November 2010	60,000	(5)	Turnover for the last financial year	5,00,000
(2)	Turnover from 1st July to 30th November 2009	2,00,000	(6)	Turnover for the year ending 30th June 2010	5,50,000
(3)	Net Profit for the last financial year	90,000	(7)	Total Standing Charges for the year	72,000
(4)	Insured Standing Charges for the last financial year	60,000			

The company incurred additional expenses amounting to Rs. 9,000 which reduced the loss in turnover. There was also a savings during the indemnity period of Rs. 2,486.

The company holds a 'Loss of Profit' policy for Rs. 1,65,000 having an indemnity period for 6 months. There has been a considerable increase in trade and it has been agreed that an adjustment of 20% be made in respect of upward trend in turnover.

Compute claim under 'Loss of Profit Insurance'.

[CA]

Solution

			Rs.
	Short Sales :		
	Standard Turnover (from 1.7.2009 to 30.11.2009)		2,00,000
Add :	Increase @ 20%		40,000
			2,40,000
Less :	Actual Sales during indemnity period (i.e., from 1.7.2010 to 30.11.2010)		60,000
			1,80,000
∴	Gross Profit @ 30% on Short Sales		54,000
	Additional Expenses :		
	Least of the following :		
	(a) Actual amount	9,000	
	(b) Gross Profit on additional sales @ 30% $(\text{Rs. } 60{,}000 \times \frac{30}{100})$	18,000	

	Rs.
(c) $\frac{\text{Net Profit + Insured Standing Charges}}{\text{Net Profit + All Standing Charges}} \times$ Additional Expenses	
$\frac{\text{Rs. 1,98,000}}{\text{Rs. 2,10,000}} \times$ Rs. 9,000 = 8,486	8,486
	62,486
Less : Saving in Expenses	2,486
	60,000

Net Claim = Amount of Claim × $\frac{\text{Amount of Policy}}{\text{G.P. on Annual Adjusted Turnover}}$

= Rs. 60,000 × $\frac{\text{1,65,000}}{\text{Rs. 1,98,000}}$ = Rs. 50,000

Note :

1. Rate of Gross Profit : $\frac{\text{Rs. 1,50,000}}{\text{Rs. 5,00,000}} \times 100 = 30\%$ 2. 30% on Rs. 6,60,000 (i.e., Rs. 5,50,000 + 20%).

Illustration 33

The premises of a company were partly destroyed by fire which took place on 1st March 2012 and as a result of which the business was disorganised from 1st March to 31st July 2011. Accounts are closed on 31st December every year. The company is insured under a Loss of Profit policy for Rs. 7,50,000. The period of indemnity specified in the policy is 6 months. From the following information, you are required to compute the amount of claim under the Loss of Profit policy :

	Rs.		Rs.
Turnover for the year 2011	40,00,000	Annual turnover for the year immediately preceding the fire, i.e., from	
Net Profit for the year 2011	2,40,000		
Insured Standing Charges	4,80,000	from 30.3.2011 to 29.2.2012	44,00,000
Uninsured Standing Charges	80,000	Increased cost of working	1,50,000
Turnover during the period of dislocation, i.e., from 1.3.2012 to 31.7.2012	8,00,000	Saving in insured Standing Charges	30,000
Standard turnover for the corresponding period in the preceding year i.e., from 1.3.2011 to 31.7.2011	20,00,000	Reduction in turnover avoided through increase in working cost	4,00,000

Owing to reasons acceptable to the insurer the 'Special Circumstances Clause' stipulate for :

(a) Increase of turnover (Standard and Annual) by 10%;

(b) Increase in the rate of Gross Profit by 2%.

Solution

		Rs.
(a) **Loss of Turnover/Short Sales during dislocation :**		
Standard Turnover of the preceding period (i.e., from 1.3.2011 to 31.7.2011)		20,00,000
Add : 10% increase		2,00,000
		22,00,000
Less : Actual Turnover during dislocation		8,00,000
	Short Sales	14,00,000
* Gross Profit @ 20% on Rs. 14,00,000		2,80,000
*Add :*** Increased Cost of working		80,000
		3,60,000
Less : Savings in Insured Standing Charges		30,000
		3,30,000

∴ **Application of Average Clause** = Amount of Claim × $\frac{\text{Amount of Policy}}{\text{G.P. on Annual (Adjusted) Turnover}}$

= Rs. 3,30,000 × $\frac{\text{Rs. 7,50,000}}{\text{Rs. 9,68,000}}$ = Rs. 2,55,680

G.P. on Annual Adjusted Turnover = Rs. 22,00,000 + 22,00,000

= Rs. 44,00,000 + Rs. 10% increase

= Rs. 44,00,000 + Rs. 4,40,000

= Rs. 48,40,000 × 20%
= Rs. 9,68,000)

* G.P. Ratio = $\frac{\text{Net Profit + Insured Standing Charges}}{\text{Sales}}$

= $\frac{2,40,000 + \text{Rs. } 4,80,000}{\text{Rs. } 40,00,000}$ = 18% + 2% increase = 20%

** Increased Cost of Working;
Least of the following :

(a) 20% on Rs. 4,00,000 (Saving in Liability) = Rs. 80,000

(b) $\frac{\text{Net Profit + Insured Standing Charges}}{\text{Net Profit + All Insurable Standing Charges}}$ × Increased Cost of Working

Or, $\frac{\text{Rs. } 2,40,000 + \text{Rs. } 4,80,000}{\text{Rs. } 2,40,000 + 5,60,000}$ × Rs. 1,50,000

= Rs. 1,35,000

∴ Rs. 80,000 is to be taken into consideration.

Illustration 34

A Loss of Profit Policy was taken for Rs. 80,000. Fire occurred on 15th March 2009. Indemnity period was for three months. Net profit for 2008 year ending on 31st Dec. was Rs. 56,000 and standing charges (all insured) amounted to Rs. 49,600. Determine insurance claims from the following details available from quarterly sales tax returns :

	2006	*2007*	*2008*	*2009*
	Rs.	*Rs.*	*Rs.*	*Rs.*
From 1st June to 31st March	1,20,000	1,30,000	1,42,000	1,30,000
From 1st April to 30th June	80,000	90,000	1,00,000	40,000
From 1st July to 30th Sept.	1,00,000	1,10,000	1,20,000	1,00,000
From 1st Oct. to 31st Dec.	1,36,000	1,50,000	1,66,000	1,60,000

Sales from 16.3.2008 to 31.3.2008 were Rs. 28,000
" " 16.3.2009 to 31.3.2009 " Rs. Nil
" " 16.6.2008 to 31.6.2008 " Rs. 24,000 and
" " 16.6.2009 to 31.6.2009 " Rs. 6,000

[CA]

Solution

Short Sales = Standard Sales[1] – Actual Sales during indemnity period
= 1,14,400 (i.e., Rs. 1,04,000 + 10%[3]) – Rs. 34,000[2]
= Rs. 80,400.

1. ***Standard Sales*** = Sales from 16.3.2008 to 31.3.2008 + Sales from 1.4.2008 to 15.6.2008 – Sales from 16,6,2008 to 30.6.2008
= Rs. 28,000 + Rs. 1,00,000 – Rs. 24,000
= Rs. 1,04,000.

2. ***Actual Sales*** = Sales from 16.3.2009 to 15.6.2009 + Sales from 1.4.2009 to 30.6.2009 – Sales from 16.6.2009 to 30.6.2099
= Rs. Nil + Rs. 40,000 – R. 6,000
= Rs. 34,000

3. ***Percentage of Increasing trend in Sales :***

Total Sales for 2006 (Rs. 1,20,000 + Rs. 80,000 + Rs. 1,00,000 + Rs. 1,36,000) = Rs. 4,36,000
" " " 2007 (Rs. 1,30,000 + Rs. 90,000 + Rs. 1,10,000 + Rs. 1,50,000) = Rs. 4,80,000
" " " 2008 (Rs. 1,42,000 + Rs. 1,00,000 + Rs. 1,20,000 + Rs. 1,66,000) = Rs. 5,28,000

Now, Percentage of Increase in Sales in 2007 over 2006 = $\frac{\text{Rs. } 44,000}{\text{Rs. } 4,36,000}$ × 100 = 10%

Percentage of Increase in Sales in 2008 over 2007 = $\frac{\text{Rs. } 48,000}{\text{Rs. } 4,80,000}$ × 100 = 10%

∴ Average Rate is $\frac{10\% + 10\%}{2}$ = 10%

Application of Average Clause = *Amount of Claim* × $\frac{\textit{Amount of Policy}}{\textit{G.P. on Annual (Adjusted) Turnover}}$

= Rs. 16,080 × $\frac{\text{Rs. 80,000}}{\text{Rs. 1,19,680}^*}$

= Rs. 10,749 (approx).

Calculation of G. P. on Annual Adjusted) Turnover :

	Rs.
Sales from 16.3.2008 to 31.3.2008	28,000
Sales from 1.4.2008 to 30.6.2008	1,00,000
Sales from 1.7.2008 to 30.9.2008	1,20,000
Sales from 1.10.2008 to 31.12.2008	1,66,000
Add : 1.1.2009 to 15.3.2009	1,30,000
	5,44,000
Add : 10% Increase	54,400
Adjusted Sales	5,98,400

∴ G. P. on Adjusted Sales = Rs. 5,98,400 × 20% = Rs. 1,19,680.

GENERAL ILLUSTRATIONS

Loss of Stock and consequent Loss of Profit

Illustration 35

S and M Ltd. give the following Trading and Profit and Loss Account for the year ended 31st December 2011 :

Trading and Profit and Loss Account
for the year ended 31st December 2011

Particulars	*Amount*	*Particulars*	*Amount*
	Rs.		**Rs.**
To Opening Stock	50,000	By Sales	8,00,000
" Purchases	3,00,000	" Closing Stock	70,000
" Wages (Rs. 20,000 for skilled workers)	1,60,000		
" Manufacturing Expenses	1,20,000		
" Gross Profit	2,40,000		
	8,70,000		8,70,000
" Office Administration Expenses	60,000	" Gross Profit	2,40,000
" Advertising	20,000		
" Selling Expenses (fixed)	40,000		
" Commission on Sales	48,000		
" Carriage Outwards	16,000		
" Net Profit	56,000		
	2,40,000		2,40,000

The company had taken out policies both against loss of stock and against loss of profit, the amounts being Rs. 80,000 and Rs. 1,72,000. Fire occured on 1st May 2012 and, as a result of which, sales were seriously affected for the period of 4 months. You are given the following further information :

(a) Purchases, wages and other manufacturing expenses for the first 4 months of 2012 were Rs. 1,00,000; Rs. 50,000 and Rs. 36,000, respectively.

(b) Sales for the same period were Rs. 2,40,000.

(c) Other sales figure were as follows :

	Rs.
From 1.1.22011 to 30.4.2011	3,00,000
" 1.5.2011 to 31.8.2011	3,60,000
" 1.5.2012 to 31.8.2012	60,000

(d) Due to rise in wages net profit during 2012 was expected to decline by 2% on sales.

(e) Additional expenses incurred during the period after fire amounted to Rs. 1,40,000. The amount of the policy included Rs. 1,20,000 for expenses leaving Rs. 20,000 uncovered. Ascertain the claim for stock and for loss of profit.

[CA]

Solution

A. Claim for Loss of Stock

Dr. **Trading Account** *for the period from 1st Jan. to 1st May 2012* Cr.

Particulars	Amount	Particulars	Amount
	Rs.		Rs.
To Opening Stock	70,000	By Sales	3,00,000
" Purchases	1,00,000	" Closing Stock *(bal. fig.)*	23,200
" Wages	50,000		
" Manufacturing Expenses	36,000		
" Gross Profit @ 28%[1]* on Sales	67,200		
	3,23,200		3,23,200

Claim for Loss of stock will be Rs. 80,000 (i.e., the amount of policy and not more).

1. G.P. of 2011 = $\frac{\text{Rs. } 2{,}40{,}000}{\text{Rs. } 8{,}00{,}000} \times 100$ = 30% – 2% decrease = 28%

B. Loss of Profit

Short Sales = Standard Sales – Actual Sales during indemnity period
= Rs. 2,88,000[1] – Rs. 60,000
= 2,28,000

		Rs.	Rs.
1.	Sales from 1.5.2011 to 31.8.2011	3,60,000	
	Less : 20% reduction in 2012 over 2011 $\left(\frac{\text{Rs. } 60{,}000}{\text{Rs. } 3{,}00{,}000} \times 100\right)$	72,000	
		2,88,000	

	Rs.		Rs.
Gross Profit on Short Sales = Rs. 2,28,000 × 20%[2]			45,600
Add : Increased Cost of Workings :			
Least of the following	Rs.		
(i) Actual Amount	1,40,000	=	(ii)
G. P. by additional sales Rs. 60,000 × 20%			
(iii) Addl. Exp. × $\frac{\text{G. P.}}{\text{G.P. + Uninsured Charges}}$	12,000	=	12,000
= Rs. 1,40,000 × $\frac{\text{Rs. } 1{,}18{,}400^3}{\text{Rs. } 1{,}38{,}400}$	1,19,769	=	
	Amount of Claim		57,600

Note : Application of Average Clause will not arise here as the policy amount (i.e., Rs. 1,72,000) is higher than the Gross Profit (i.e., Rs. 1,18,400).

Workings :

2. **Percentage of G. P. on Sales for 20011 : G.P.** = N. P + Insured Standing Charges
= Rs. 56,000 + Rs. 1,20,000
= Rs. 1,76,000

∴ G. P. Ratio = $\frac{\text{Rs. } 1{,}76{,}000}{\text{Rs. } 8{,}00{,}000} \times 100$ = 22% – 2% decrease for wages
= 20%

3. **G.P. (Adjusted) on Annual Turnover :**
Sales (1.1.2011 to 31.12.2011) + (1.1.2012 to 30.4.2012) = Rs. 8,00,000 + Rs. 2,40,000
= Rs. 10,40,000 *Contd.*

Less : From 1.1.2011 to 30.4.2011	=	Rs.	3,00,000
			7,40,000
Less : Reduced by 20%			1,48,000
			5,92,000
∴ G.P. = Rs. 5,92,000 × 20%	=	Rs.	1,18,400

Loss of Stock and Consiquently Loss of Profit

Illustration 36

Sony Ltd.'s Trading and Profit and Loss Account for the year ended 31st Dec. 2011 were as :

Trading and Profit and Loss Account *for the year ended 31st December 2011*

Particulars	*Amount*	*Particulars*	*Amount*
	Rs.		Rs.
To Opening Stock	20,000	By Sales	10,00,000
" Purchases	6,50,000	" Closing Stock	90,000
" Manufacturing Exp.	1,70,000		
" Gross Profit	2,50,000		
	10,90,000		10,90,000
To Administrative Expenses	80,000	By Gross Profit	2,50,000
" Selling Expenses	20,000		
" Finance Charges	1,00,000		
" Net Profit	50,000		
	2,50,000		2,50,000

The company had taken out a fire policy for Rs. 3,00,000 and a Loss of Profit Policy for Rs. 1,00,000 having an indemnity period of 6 months. A fire occurred on 1.4.2012 at the premises and the entire stock were gutted with nil salvage value. The net quarter sales, i.e., 1.4.2012 to 30.6.2012, was severely affected. The following are the other information :

	Rs.		Rs.
Sales during the period 1.1.2012 to 31.3.2012	2,50,000	Sale during the period 1.4.2012 to 30.6.2012	87,500
Purchase during the period 1.1.2012 to 31.3.2012	3,00,000	Standing charges insured	50,000
Manufacturing Expenses 1.1.2012 to 31.3.2012	70,000	Actual expenses incurred after fire	60,000

The general trend of the industry shows an increase of sale by 75% and decrease in G. P. by 5% due to increased costs. Ascertain the claims for loss stock and loss of profits.

Solution

A. Loss of Stock

In the books of Sony Ltd.
Trading Account
(from 1.1.2012 to 31.3.2012)

Dr. *Cr.*

Particulars	*Amount*	*Particulars*	*Amount*
	Rs.		Rs.
To Opening Stock	90,000	By Sales	2,50,000
" Purchases	3,00,000	" Closing Stock *(bal. fig.)*	2,60,000
" Manufacturing Expenses	70,000		
" Gross Profit (25% – 5% = 20% on Sales)	50,000		
	5,10,000		5,10,000

∴ Amount of claim for stock lost by fire is Rs. 2,60,000.

B. Loss of Profit

Short Sales = Standard Sales – Actual Sales during indemnity period

= Rs. 3,00,000[1] – Rs. 87,500 = Rs. 2,12,500

Gross Profit on Short Sales : G. P. = Net Profit + Insured Standing Charges

= Rs. 50,000 + Rs. 50,000 = Rs. 1,00,000

Contd.

$\therefore$ G.P. Ratio = $\frac{\text{Rs. } 1,00,000}{\text{Rs. } 10,00,000} \times 100$ = 10% – 5% for decreasing trend = 5%

		Rs.
So, G. P. on short sale = Rs. 2,12,500 × 5% =		10,625
Add : Increased Cost of Workings :		
Least of the following	Rs.	
(i) Actual Amount	= 60,000	
(ii) G. P. on Additional Sales Rs. 87,500 × 5%	= 4,375	
(iii) Addl. Exp. × $\frac{\text{G. P.}}{\text{G.P. + Uninsured Standing Charges}}$		
= Rs. 60,000 × $\frac{\text{Rs. } 55,000^2}{\text{Rs. } 1,85,000 \text{ (i.e., Rs. } 55,000 + 1,30,000)^3}$	= 17,838	4,375
Amount of Claim		15,000

Thus : **Amount of Total Claim :**

	Rs.
For Loss of Stock	2,60,000
For Loss of Profit	15,000
	2,75,000

Workings :

1. **Standard Sales**

		Rs.
Sales (1.1.2012 to 31.3.2012)	Rs. 2,50,000 × $\frac{100}{115}$ =	2,17,391
Sales (remaining 3 quarters of 2011)	(Rs. 10,00,000 – 2,17,391) =	7,82,609
$\therefore$ Per quarter average sales (1.4.2012 to 30.6.2012)		2,60,870 (i.e., 7,82,609 × 1/3)
Add : 15% increase	$\left(2,60,870 \times \frac{15}{100}\right)$ =	39,130
		3,00,000

2. **G.P on Adjusted Annual Turnover**

	Rs.
Turnover (from 1.4.2011 to 31.12.2011)	7,39,130
Add : Turnover (from 1.1.2012 to 31.3.2012) (including increasing effect)	2,50,000
	9,89,130
Add : 15% increase (only on Rs. 7,39,130)	1,10,870
	11,00,000

G. P. = Rs. 11,00,000 × 5% = Rs. 55,000

3. **Standing charges are :**

	Rs.
Administrative Exp.	80,000
Plus : Finance Charges	1,00,000
	1,80,000
Less : Insured Standing Ch.	50,000
$\therefore$ Uninsured Standing Charges	1,30,000

AMOUNT OF POLICY

One is to take out a policy for an adequate sum. Because then, in case of fire, he will not have to suffer any loss. And, as such, the sum which is to be insured is the net trading profit (i.e., G.P.) plus fixed expenses (including skilled labourers' wages) since they are rarely retrenched. Of course, unskilled labourers will be retrenched if there is no work. Similarly, advertising etc. are to be carried on, and, hence, these are to be treated as fixed expenses.

Illustration 37

From the following Trading and Profit and Loss Account of P Ltd. for the year ended 30th June 2012 compute the sum for insurance under a Loss of Profits Policy. It is desired that all standing charges be issued.

P. Ltd.

Dr. **Trading and Profit and Loss Account** *for the year ended 31st December 2012* Cr.

Particulars		*Amount*	*Particulars*	*Amount*
		Rs.		Rs.
To Opening Stock		1,00,000	By Sales	4,50,000
" Purchases		2,50,000	" Closing Stock	1,25,000
" Wages :				
Unskilled	10,000			
Unskilled	3,000	40,000		
" Gross Profit c/d		1,85,000		
		5,75,000		5,75,000
To Salaries (10% variable)		39,000	By Gross Profit b/d	1,85,000
" Interest on Debentures		3,000	" Interest on Investment	5,000
" Rates and Taxes		6,000		
" Light and Power		1,250		
" Insurance		2,000		
" Subscriptions		250		
" Legal Expenses (regarding Sales)		1,500		
" Advertising		1,500		
" General Expenses (40% Valuable)		7,500		
" Discount Allowed		7,500		
" Commission on Sales		12,500		
" Dep. on Building		15,000		
" Rent		7,500		
" Audit Fees		750		
" Director's Fees		10,000		
" Net Profit		74,750		
		1,90,000		1,90,000

[CA Final]

Solution

Amount of Loss of Profit Policy

		Rs.	Rs.
	Net Profit (Less Interest on Investment) i.e., Rs. 74,750 – Rs. 5,000		69,750
Add :	*Fixed Expenses*	Rs.	
	Skilled Labour	10,000	
	Salaries (90%)	35,100	
	Int. on Debentures	3,000	
	Rates and Taxes	6,000	
	Insurance	2,000	
	Subscriptions	250	
	Advertising	1,500	
	General Expenes (60%)	4,500	
	Dep. on Building	15,000	
	Rent	7,500	
	Audit Fees	750	
	Directors' fees	10,000	95,600
	Amount to be insured		1,65,350

Workmen's Compensation Insurance and Group Gratuity insurance

The type of policies cover the compensation which has to be paid for injuries or occupational diseases during the course of the work. Under Workmen's Compensation Act, policies may be taken to cover up the liability payable to workmen. Actually, the policy is granted on the basis of wage bills of the past period. Since premiums are payable in advance, the same must be computed on the basis of past periods' wages. When actual figures for the current year are available, the premium which are paid are adjusted accordingly. If premium is paid, Insurance Suspense Account should be debited. At the end of the year, when 'exact amount of premium due' will be calculated — Insurance Premium Account will be debited and Insurance Suspense Account should be credited and the balance of Insurance Suspense Account, if any, will be carried forward for a cash adjustment. Similarly, if any claim arises, the insured will pay to his workmen and, subsequently, he will recover the amount from the insurer. That is why, when payment is made—Insurance Company Account should be debited.

Apolicy may also be taken for the payment of gratuity. The amount of premium depends on the basis of salaries, wages, year of employment etc.

Illustration 38

On 1st April 2011, P Ltd., whose financial year ends on 30th June, took out an insurance policy with Z Co. Ltd., to cover against liability to workmen. The premium is payable @ 1% on wages paid. Adjustments for premium were to be made on 7th April of the following year. In October 2011, Rs. 3,750 had to be paid by way of compensation. The actual wages were as follows :

		Rs.
From :	1.4.2010 to 31.3.2011	1,00,000
"	1.4.2011 to 30.6.2011	22,500
"	1.7.2011 to 31.3.2012	67,500
"	1.4.2012 to 30.6.2012	27,500

Show the entries in the books of P Ltd. bearing in mind that the Insurance Company raised the rate of premium to $1\frac{1}{2}$% with effect from 1st April 2012.

Solution

In the books of P Ltd.
Journal

Date	Particulars		L.F.	Debit	Credit
2011				Rs.	Rs.
April 1	Workmen's Compensation Insurance Suspense A/c	Dr.		1,000	
	To Bank A/c				1,000
	(Provisional premium paid @ 1% on Rs. 1,00,000).				
June 30	Workmen's Compensation Insurance A/c	Dr.		225	
	To Workmen's Compensation Insurance Suspense A/c				225
	(Paid on wages @ 1% on Rs. 22,500 for 3 months ending June 30, 2011)				
October	Insurance Co. A/c	Dr.		3,750	
	To Bank A/c				3,750
	(Payment made to workmen against claims).				
	Bank A/c	Dr.		3,750	
	To Insurance Co. A/c				3,750
	(Amount received from Insurance Co.)				
2012 April 1	Workmen's Compensation Insurance A/c	Dr.		1,350	
	To Bank A/c				1,350
	Provisional premium paid @ $1\frac{1}{2}$% on Rs. 9,000).				

Contd.

2012			Rs.	Rs.
" 7	Bank A/c	Dr.	100	
	To Workmen's Compensation Insurance Suspense A/c			100
	(Refund of premium, to be calculated as :			
		Rs.		
	Premium paid	1,000		
	Less : Actual premium due @ 1% on Rs. 9,000)	900		
		100		
June 30	Workmen's Compensation Insurance a/c	Dr.	1,088	
	To Workmen's Compensation Insurance Suspense A/c			1,088
	(Premium chargeable to P & L (for 30.6.2012) to be calculated as :			
		Rs.		
	@ 1% on Rs. 67,500 =	675		
	@ $1\frac{1}{2}$ % on Rs. 27,500 =	413		
		1,088		

ASSIGNMENT MATERIALS

THEORETICAL

Multiple Choice Questions

1. (a) Standing Charges mean—

    (i) Fixed Charges (ii) Variable Charges (iii) Both iv) None of these

    (b) Short Sales mean—

    (i) Standard Sales exceeds actual sales (ii) Actual sales exceeds Standard Sales (iii) Both (iv) None of these

    (c) Net Claim is equal to:

    (i) Loss of Profit × $\frac{\text{Gross Profit}}{\text{Amount of Policy}}$ (ii) Loss of Profit × $\frac{\text{Amount of Policy}}{\text{G P on Short Sales}}$

    (iii) Loss of Profit × $\frac{\text{GP + Interest Cost}}{\text{GP on Short Sales.}}$ (v) None of these

    (d) Inncreased Cost of Working means when—

    (i) Additional expenditure incurred (ii) Expenditure incurred during indemnity period (iii) Fixed Cost incurred (iv) None of these.

    (e) Standard Turnover means—

    (i) Turnover immediately preceeding the date of damage ((ii) Turnover for damage period (iii) Both (iv) None of these

[Ans. (a) (i); (b) (i); (c) (ii); (d) (ii); (e) (i)]

Short-Answer Type Questions

2. Define : (a) Increased Cost of Working; (d) Short Sales
3. What is Indemnity Period?
4. What is Savings in Standing Changes?
5. What do you mean by Reduction in Turnover?
6. How do you ascertain the claim for Loss of Profit?

PRACTICAL

1. A firm has decided to arange for a Loss of Profit insurance and you are required to realise the sum to be assured on a full insurance basis from the following figures for the last financial year. It is anticipated that for the current financial year, turnover will increase by 10% and that all standing (fixed expenses) will remain unchanged :

	Rs.	Rs.
Total variable expenses		21,00,000
Fixed expenses :		
Wages and Salaries to skilled employees and salaries to Adm. staff	3,00,000	
Depreciation on all fixed assets	1,00,000	
Insurance Premiums	10,000	
Audit fees	4,000	
Directors' fees	4,000	
Travelling expenses (including motor car expenses)	40,000	
Postages, Cables and Telephones	3,000	
Trade Subscriptions	1,000	
Rent, Rates and Taxcs	30,000	4,92,000
Non-operating Income		50,000
Net Profit		4,08,000

[Ans. Amount of Claim Rs. 9,35,000]

2. Fire occurred in the premises of X. Co. Ltd. on 31st May 2009. The company had a Loss of Profit policy of Rs. 12,000. Sales from 1st May 2008 to 30th April 2009 were Rs. 1,00,000; similarly the sales from 1st May 2008 to 31st August 2008, being Rs. 30,000. During the indemnity period, which lasted 4 months, sales were Rs. 4,000. The company closed its accounts on 31st Dec.

The Profit and Loss Account for 2008 is given below :

Profit and Loss Account *for 2008*

Dr.		Rs.			Cr. Rs.
To	Opening Stock	10,000	By	Sales	95,000
"	Purchases	60,000	"	Closing Stock	5,000
"	Manufacturing Expenses	6,700			
"	Valuable Selling Expenses	9,050			
"	Fixed Expenses	7,250			
"	Net Profit	7,000			
		1,00,000			1,00,000

Comparing the sales of the first four months of 2009 with those of the 2008, it was found that sales were 20% higher in 2009. Determine the loss of profit.

[Ans. Loss of Profit Rs. 4,800]

3. In the dislocation period of 4 months covered by a consequential loss of policy of Rs. 24,000, a sale of Rs. 16,000 was obtained out of which Rs. 6,400 sale was received from another premises hired for this period, at a rent of Rs. 160 p.m. on temporary basis. However, there was saving in insured standing charges during this period at Rs. 960 p.a.

Sale in the same period of last year amounted to Rs. 48,000 and upward trend of 10% in business was expected in the current year. Sale of twelve months' immediately preceding fire was Rs. 1,60,000.

The following information is available from last year's Profit and Loss Account : Sales Rs. 1,44,000; Net Profit Rs. 16,000; Standing charges (out of which Rs. 3,200 is uninsured) Rs. 16,000.

Calculate the amount of claim under consequential loss policy.

[Ans. Amount of Claim Rs. 35,000]

4. (a) Bright Ltd. has a 'Loss of Profit' insurance policy of Rs. 12,60,000. The period of indemnity is three months. A fire occurred on 31st March 2009. The following information is available :

Sales	Rs.
for the year ended 31st December 2008	42,00,000
for the period from 1st April 2008 to 31st March 2009	48,00,000
for the period from 1st April 2009 to 30th June 2008	10,80,000
for the period from 1st April 2009 to 30th June 2009	72,000
Standing charges for 2008	9,60,000
Profit for 2008	3,00,000
Savings in standing charges because of fire	30,000
Additional expenses to reduce loss of turnover	60,000

Assuming no adjustment has to be made for the upward trend in turnover, compute the claim to be made on the insurance company.

(b) A trader took out a fire policy containing an average clause covering his stock for Rs. 15,000. His practice was to base his selling price at cost plus $31\frac{1}{3}$%.

He closes his books on 30th June every year.

On 31st March 2008, a fire occurred at his premises and destroyed his stock. The salvaged stock was Rs. 6,000. During the period of 9 months preceding the fire, his purchases amounted to Rs. 61,000 and sales to Rs. 84,000. His stock at 1st July 2009 was valued at Rs. 20,000.

You are required to prepare a statement showing the amount of claim.]

[Ans. (a) Amount of Claim Rs. 2,57,250; (b) Amount Claim for Loss of Stock Rs. 10,000]

5. On 31.12.2012 a fire damaged the Buildings of B Ltd., resulting in a disruption of the company's business, until 31.3.2013. The company is insured under a Loss of Profit policy for Rs. 2,70,000 with a six months' period of indemnity.

The company's accounts for its financial year ended 31.10.2012, showed :

Turnover	Rs. 10,00,000	Net Profit	Rs. 1,00,000

The Standing Charges, covered by the insurance policy, is Rs. 30,00,000. This figure was debited in the accounts for the year.

The turnover for the twelve months ended 31.12.2012 was Rs. 8,00,000; during the period of disruption it was Rs. 1,00,000, whereas during the corresponding three months' period in the preceding year it was Rs. 1,80,000.

A sum of Rs. 25,000 was expended to mitigate the effect of the loss but there was no savings in standing charges as a result of the fire. The policy indemnified the company against the Loss of Gross Profit due to— (a) the reduction in turnover; (b) increase in cost of working.

Draft the claim to be submitted to the Insurance Company.

[Ans. Amount of Claim Rs. 48,094]

CHAPTER 28

PARTNERSHIP ACCOUNTS

Learning Objectives

Introduction

Deed of Partnership

Partnership and Co-ownership

Registration of Partnership

Non-Registration

Effect of Registration

Registration—its Advantages

Rules applicable where there is no agreement

Rights and Duties of Partners

Types of Partners

Implied authority of a Partner

Implied authority by Statute-Limitation

A. APPROPRIATION OF PROFIT

Certain other points

— *Partners' Salaries, Commission etc.*

— *Interest on Drawings*

— *Interest on Capital*

— *Interest on Partners, Loan*

— *Partners' Capital Accounts*

— *Fluctuating Capital Method*

— *Fixed Capital Method*

Profit and Loss Appropriation Account and Distribution of Profit

Rectification of wrong Distribution of Profits or Adjustment of Net Profit of Prior Period.

Guaranteed Partnership

Employee admitted as a partner with retrospective effect

Conversion from Cash basis to Accrual basis

B. ADMISSION OF A NEW PARTNER

1. Regarding Profit-Sharing Ratio
2. Regarding Revaluation of Assets and Liabilities
3. Regarding Accumulated Profits/Losses, and/or Reserves and Surplus
4. Regarding Adjustments for Goodwill

Goodwill

—Classification

—Need for Valuation

—Factors affecting the value of Goodwill

—Methods of Valuation of Non-Purchased Goodwill

(a) **Years' purchase of Average Profit Method**

(b) **Years' purchase of Weighted Average Method**

(c) **Capitalisation Method**

(d) **Annuity Method**

(e) **Superprofit Method**

Treatment for Goodwill in Case of Admission of a New Partner

A. **Premium Method**

B. **Revaluation Method**

C. **Memorandum Revaluation Method**

Hidden or Inferred Goodwill

Illustration

5. **Regarding Adjustment of Capital, or Proportionate Capital Contribution**

General Illustrations

C. RETIREMENT OF A PARTNER

Introduction

Computation of Ratio

1. **Regarding Revaluation of Assets and Liabilities**
2. **Regarding Undistributed Profits and Reserves**
3. **Regarding Goodwill**

Retiring Partner's Total Claim

Right to Share of Profits after Retirement

General Illustrations

D. RETIREMENT-CUM-ADMISSION

Introduction

Memorandum Revaluation Account

Illustrations

E. CHANGE IN PROFIT-SHARING RATIO

Introduction

Illustrations

Change in Profit-Sharing Ratio during an accounting period

F. AMALGAMATION OF FIRMS

Introduction

1. **When two sole traders decide to form a partnership**
   —Purchase Consideration
   —Illustration
2. **When two existing partnership firms amalgamate and form a new firm**
3. **When an existing partnership firm takes a sole proprietorship business**
4. **When an existing partnership firm takes another partnership firm**

G. DEATH OF A PARTNERS

Introduction

Ascertainment of deceased Partner's claims

Disposal of Deceased Partner's Share

Ascertainment of the deceased partner's share of profit

Life Insurance Policy and its treatment

(i) Joint Life Policy

(ii) Individual Policy

General Illustrations

Carrying on the business without final settlement of deceased partner's account

Miscellaneous

Problem on Annuity

Introduction

According to Sec. 4 of the Indian Partnership Act, Partnership means "the relationship between persons who have agreed to share profits of a business carried on by all or any of them acting for all." And persons who have entered into partnership with one another are called individually 'partners' and collectively 'a firm'; and the name under which their business is carried on is called the 'firm name'. Accordingly, the essential features of partnership are :

(i) Contract—i.e., An agreement entered into by all its partners.

(ii) Business—i.e., A lawful business.

(iii) Profit Sharing—i.e., Sharing of profits or losses of the business.

(iv) Mutual Agency—i.e., The business is carried on by all or any of them acting for all.

(v) An association of two or more persons—i.e., the number of persons constituting a partnership must not exceed 10 in the case of a banking business and 20 in other business.

Partnership Agreement/Deed of Partnership

Partnership arises not from status but from contracts, which may be either verbal or written. The written contract between or among the partners is known as deed or agreement or articles of partnership and includes :

(a) Names and addresses of the firm and partners and the duration of the partnership; (b) Amount of capital to be contributed by each partner and the amount of drawings, to be taken at the end of the month or year; (c) Interest on capital and interest on loan given by the partners and also the interest on drawings, if any, and the rate of such interests; (d) Proportion of division of profits or losses; (e) Rights and duties of partners as between themselves; (f) When and how a new partner is to be admitted or an old partner is to be retired; (g) Method of valuation of goodwill in the case of admission, retirement, or death of a partner; (h) Methods of keeping accounts and audit; (i) The bank where the money should be deposited and the authority for signing cheques and other documents; (j) Rights, duties and liabilities of the partners; (k) In case of dispute, how the settlements are to be made between or among the partners.

Partnership and Co-ownership

The following points of difference between the two may be noted :

(i) Partnership arises from contract whereas co-ownership may arise either from contract or from the operation of law or from status. (ii) No partner can transfer his rights and interests without the consent of all other partners. But, in case of co-ownership, such consent is not required at all. (iii) In partnership, there is an implied authority, whereas no such implied authority exists in case of co-ownership. (iv) A partner can exercise lien on the property of the firm but such lien cannot be exercised in case of co-ownership. (v) A partner cannot claim division of partnership property in specie while a co-ownership can force such division. (vi) A partnership firm involves community of profit or loss but co-ownership does not. (vii) A partnership firm leads to business activities for the purpose of making profit. These are irrelevant to a co-ownership. (viii) A partner has a lien on the partnership assets for money spent by him for the partnership whereas a co-owner has no such lien.

Registration of Partnership

In order to carry on business, registration is not compulsory in case of a partnership firm. But an unregistered firm suffers from some disabilities and, as such, it is better to make the firm registered. According to Sections 56-71, the registration of a firm may be made at any time by sending by post or delivering to the **Registrar of Firms** of the locality a statement in the prescribed form and accompanied by appropriates fees stating the following particulars.

(i) the firm name; (ii) the place or principal place of business; (iii) the names of any other places where the firm carries on business; (iv) the dates of joining of each partner; (v) the full name and permanent address of each partner; and (vi) duration of the firm.

Non-Registration

When the partnership deed is prepared, the firm should be registered. Although registration of firm is not compulsory a non-registered firm is subjected to certain disabilities, e.g.,

(i) the firm cannot enforce its claim against any third party for recovering a debt, exceeding Rs. 100.

(ii) a partner cannot sue for enforcing his rights against any of his co-partners or against the firm.

Thus, the necessity for registration arises due to the fact that it safeguards the legitimates rights and obligations of the partners concerned when dispute or disagreement arises. But it should be remembered that non-registration does not preclude a third party to sue the firm or its partners and, as such, the partners may sue for the :

(a dissolution of the firm; (b) accounts after dissolution; (c) realisation of assets after dissolution.

The registration can be effected at any time, even at the time of the suit or even after a suit has been filed by the firm, which may be withdrawn and filed again after dissolution.

Registration : Its Advantages

The following advantages may be stated if the firm is registered :

(i) Registration of a firm will enable the firm to enforce its claim against third parties in a court of law. (ii) It will enable a partner to enforce his claim either against his co-partners or against third parties. (iii) It also safeguards third parties against fraud or misrepresentation done by a partner of a firm. (iv) By being registered an incoming partner empowers himself for dues against his fellow partners without relaying on their good faith.

Rules applicable where there is no Agreement

The following rules are applicable in the absence of Agreement :

(i) No partner is entitled to earn an interest on his capital; (ii) No partner is entitled to receive any salary from the firm; (iii) No interest on drawings is to be charged; (iv) Interest on partners' loan is to be charged @ 6% p.a. only; (v) Profits or losses should be divided equally.

Rights and Duties of Partners

The rights and duties of partners are of two types,viz :

(a) Mandatory;

(b) Subject to agreements among others.

(a) **Mandatory Rights and Duties**

The mandatory right and duties, however, can neither be changed nor be contracted out by agreement between the partners. The following are the mandatory rights and duties :

(i) *To carry on to the greatest common advantages*

According to Sec. 9 of the Indian Partnership Act, partners are bound to carry on the business of the firm to the greatest common advantages.

(ii) *To be just and faithful*

According to the same section, partners are bound to be just and faithful to each other.

(iii) *To render true accounts and full information*

Sec. 9 states that partners are bound to render true accounts and full information of all things affecting the firm to any partner or his legal representative.

(iv) *To indemnity*

Accounting to Sec. 10 every partner shall indemnify the firm for any loss caused to it by his fraud in the conduct of the business of the firm.

(b) **Subject to agreements among others**

Right of a Partners

To sum up, a partner has the following rights :

(i) A partner has a right to participate in the conduct of the business — Sec. 12(a). (ii) A partner shall have right to give his opinion on all matters of the firm—Sec. 12(c). (iii) A partner has a right to have access to and to inspect and copy and of the books of the firm—Sec. 12(d). (iv) Partners are entitled to share equally in the profit earned by them—Sec. 13(b). (v) A partner is entitled to earn an interest on loan given to the firm, in addition to his Capital, @ 6% p.a.—Sec. 13(d). (v) Every partner is entitled to use the property which is exclusively for the purpose of the business—Section 15. (vii) Every partner is the agent of other. He has implied authority to bind the firm by his own act in the conduct of the business of the firm—Sec. 18 and 19. (viii) A partner is entitled to dissolve the firm under certain conditions of Section 43, 44.

Types of Partners

Partners can be claimed as

(a) **Active partner**

The partner who contributes capital to the business on agreed terms and conditions and takes active part in the management of the business is called Active Partner.

(b) **Dormant Partner**

The partner who is not known to the outsiders as a partner but possesses real interest in the business and shares in the profits of the firm is called Dormant Partner.

(c) **Sleeping Partner**

The partner who does not take active part in the management but contributes capital and takes shares profit is known as Sleeping Partner.

(d) **'Holding out' partner or partner by Estoppel**

The partner who represents himself as a partner under the "doctrine of holding out" is called partner by Estoppel. It means that although he is not really a partner, he is deemed to be so in the eye of law.

(e) **Minor Partner**

Minor partner is not a partner. He is admitted to take the benefits of the firm. He is also entitled to share profits and he has a right to inspect books. He is not personally liable for the debts of the firm.

(f) **Secret Partner**

The partner who takes active part in the management of the business like active partner but prefers to work behind the scene just like a dormant partner is called Secret Partner.

(g) **Working Partner**

The partner who works in the firm due to certain qualifications and possesses real control over the management of the firm is known as Working Partner.

(h) **Incoming Partner**

The partner who joins in an established firm and who is exempted from all liabilities arising before his admission in called Incoming Partner. He may have to pay some premium to the old partners for his access to a well-established firm.

(i) **Retiring Partner**

The partner who has retired from the firm but is liable for all the obligations that are incurred before his retirement is known as Retiring Partner.

Implied Authority of a Partner

This type of authority may be derived by either of the following :

(i) Usage; (ii) Custom of Trade; (iii) Conduct of the partners; and (iv) Statute.

Implied authority by statute

Sec. 19(1) lays down that the act of a partner which is done to carry on, in the usual way, business of the kind carried on by the firm, binds that firm. The authority of a partner to bind the firm is conferred by this Section and is called his *Implied Authority*. However, the Indian Partnership Act, 1932, does not present any list of implied authority as an agent of the firm, but gives a list of limitations on the partners' implied authority to bind the firm which are :

Limitations

In the absence of usage or customs of trade to the contrary, the implied authority does not empower him to :

(i) submit a dispute relating to the business of the firm to arbitration; (ii) open a banking account on behalf of the firm in his name; (iii) compromise or relinquish any claim or portion of a claim by the firm; (iv) withdraw a suit or proceeding filed on behalf of the firm; (v) admit any liability in a suit or proceeding against the firm; (vi) acquire immovable property on behalf of the firm; (vii) transfer immovable property belonging to the firm; and (viii) enter into partnership on behalf of the firm.

A. APPROPRIATION OF PROFIT

Needless to mention that the profits of a partnership firm may either be appropriated, as such, or partly by way of interest on capital, salary, commission, etc.; and partly by way of profit. The mode of appropriation, of course, depends on the partnership agreement. In the absence of agreement, however, Section 13 of the Indian Partnership Act is to be applied which states that :

(i) No partner is entitled to earn any interest on capital contributd by him—i.e., interest on capital—Nil.

(ii) No partner is also entitled to any salary or commission, i.e., salary and commission—Nil;

(iii) Interest on loan advanced by any partner over and above his capital contributions, i.e.,—interest on loan.

(iv) Profits or losses should be divided equally

Certain Other Points

Partners' Salaries, Commissions etc.

Sometimes it may so happen that some partners devote more time or possess better skills and experience in comparison with his fellow partners. As a result, they should be allowed a special compensation either in the form of Salary or in the form of commission—which are not treated as business expenses but division of profits. As such, these should be adjusted in the appropriation section of the Profit and Loss Account. The entry for this purpose will be :

Profit and Loss Appropriation A/c Dr.
To Partners' Salaries A/c
" Partners' Commission A/c

It should be remembered that, in the absence of agreement no partner is entitled to receive any salary or commission—Sec. 32. If the partnership deed so provides, in that case only, partners are entitled case.

Interest on Drawings

Sometimes interest is charged on the partners' drawings; of course, if the partnership deed so provides, i.e., if there is an agreement between/among the partners about it. This method is particularly applicable where there is no stated dates or limits fixed for the drawings of the partner or where the amounts of drawings are unequal. Since it is not a business income like other revenue income (i.e., commission, discount etc.), it should be adjusted in the appropriation section of the Profit and Loss Account. It may be mentioned in this respect that interest on drawings should be calculated at a fixed rate from the date of drawings to the date of closing the accounts. Interest on drawings should be charged only when the drawings are taken in anticipation of profit and not against partners' salaries, partners' commission or interest on capital if the partners are allowed to withdraw the same as per partnership deed. The entry for interest or drawings will be :

(i) Interest on Partners' Drawings A/c Dr.
To Profit and Loss Appropriation A/c
(ii) Partners' Capital Current A/c Dr.
To Interest on Drawings A/c

Method of Calculation for Interest on Partners' Drawings

Example 1

In order to explain the method of calculation for interest on drawings, let us consider the following example :

There are four partners X, Y, Z, & P. X withdrew Rs. 1,000 at the beginning of each month, Y withdrew Rs. 1,000 at the end of each month and Z withdrew Rs. 1,000 at the middle of each month, P withdrew Rs. 12,000 (such drawings spread over throughout the year). Interest on drawings should be provided @ 10% p.a. (Accounting Period is January to December).

Now, consider the cases one by one :

Case I

When X withdrew Rs. 1,000 p.m. at the beginning of each month, interest for the first month should be calculated for 12 months, for the second month's interest should be calculated for 11 month and so on.

Thus, the interest on X's drawings is calculated as:

Months	*Period*	*Amount* Rs.	*Product (i.e., for 1 month)* Rs.
1st January	12	1,000	12,000
1st February	11	1,000	11,000
1st March	10	1,000	10,000
1st April	9	1,000	9,000
1st May	8	1,000	8,000
1st June	7	1,000	7,000
1st July	6	1,000	6,000
1st August	5	1,000	5,000
1st September	4	1,000	4,000
1st October	3	1,000	3,000
1st November	2	1,000	2,000
1st December	1	1,000	1,000
			78,000

Therefore, interest on X's drawings will be Rs. $78,000 \times \frac{10}{100} \times \frac{1}{12} =$ Rs. 650.

Case II

When Y withdrew Rs. 1,000 p.m. at the end of each month, interest for the first month should be calculated for 11 months, for the second month interest should be calculated for 10 months, and so on.

Thus, the interest on Y's drawings is calculated as:

Months	*Period*	*Amount* Rs.	*Product (i.e., for 1 month)* Rs.
31st January	11	1,000	11,000
28th February	10	1,000	10,000
31st March	9	1,000	9,000
30th April	8	1,000	8,000
31st May	7	1,000	7,000
30th June	6	1,000	6,000
31st July	5	1,000	5,000
31st August	4	1,000	4,000
30th September	3	1,000	3,000
31st October	2	1,000	2,000
30th November	1	1,000	1,000
31st December	0	1,000	0
			66,000

∴ Interest on Y's drawings will be Rs. $66{,}000 \times \frac{10}{100} \times \frac{1}{12}$ = Rs. 550.

Case III

When Z withdrew Rs. 1,000 p.m. at the middle of each month, interest for the first month should be calculated for $11\frac{1}{2}$ months, for the second months, interest should be calculated for $10\frac{1}{2}$ month, and so on.

Thus, the interest on Z's drawings is calculated as:

Months	*Period*	*Amount* Rs.	*Product (i.e., for 1 month)* Rs.
15th January	$11\frac{1}{2}$	1,000	11,500
15th February	$10\frac{1}{2}$	1,000	10,500
15th March	$9\frac{1}{2}$	1,000	9,500
15th April	$8\frac{1}{2}$	1,000	8,500
15th May	$7\frac{1}{2}$	1,000	7,500
15th June	$6\frac{1}{2}$	1,000	6,500
15th July	$5\frac{1}{2}$	1,000	5,500
15th August	$4\frac{1}{2}$	1,000	4,500
15th September	$3\frac{1}{2}$	1,000	3,500
15th October	$2\frac{1}{2}$	1,000	2,500
15th November	$1\frac{1}{2}$	1,000	1,500
15th December	$\frac{1}{2}$	1,000	500
			72,000

∴ Interest on Z's drawings will be Rs. $72{,}000 \times \frac{10}{100} \times \frac{1}{12}$ = Rs. 600.

Case IV

When P withdrew Rs. 12,000 throughout the year and such drawings are spread out evenly throughout the year, interest on such drawings should be calculated on an average for 6 months.

So, Interest on P's drawings = Rs. $12{,}000 \times \frac{10}{100} \times \frac{6}{12}$ = Rs. 600.

Alternative Approach

(a) *If drawings are taken at a fixed amount at the beginning of each month—Interest on drawings should be calculated for $6\frac{1}{2}$ months at the agreed rate p.a.*

(b) *If the drawings are taken at a fixed amount at the end of each month—Interest on drawings should be calculated for $5\frac{1}{2}$ months at the agreed rate p.a.*

(c) *If the drawings are taken at a fixed amount at the middle of each month—Interest on drawings should be calculated for 6 months at the agreed rate p.a.*

(d) *If drawings are taken evenly through out the year-interest on drawings is to be calculated on an average for 6 months at the agreed rate p.a.*

(e) *If the specific date of drawings is not given—Interest on drawings is to be calculated on an average for 6 months at the agreed rate p.a.*

Solution

Case I : Interest on Drawings $= \text{Rs. } 1{,}000 \times \frac{10}{100} \times 6\frac{1}{2}$ month = Rs. 650

Case II : Interest on Drawings $= \text{Rs. } 1{,}000 \times \frac{10}{100} \times 5\frac{1}{2}$ month = Rs. 550

Case III : Interest on Drawings $= \text{Rs. } 1{,}000 \times \frac{10}{100} \times 6$ month = Rs. 600

Case IV : Interest on Drawings $= \text{Rs. } 1{,}000 \times \frac{10}{100} \times 6$ month = Rs. 600

Interest on Capital

It has already been stated above that interest on partner's capital is not allowed unless the partnership deed so provides, i.e., there must be a definite provision in the partnership deed about it. Because, it is nothing but a division of a part of profit according to capital ratio which is particularly allowed when disproportionate capitals are contributed by partners and the same is followed just to compensate the partner who has contributed relatively more capital. When interest on capital is not charged, the real division of the profit will not be affected, provided the capital ratio and the profit-sharing ratio are equal, or the ratios of both capital and profit are the same. Interest on capital is to be calculated on the basis of effective utilisation of time i.e., after adjusting additional capital or any withdrawal.

But if the partnership deed provides for interest on capital but does not stipulate the effect in case of loss, no such interest on capital is allowed. ***As interest on partners' capital is taken as profit-sharing device and not as a business expense, like Salary and Wages, it must be shown in the appropriation part of the Profit and Loss Account.*** Interest on capital should always be calculated on time basis after considering the additional capital and withdrawal of capital, if any. Special attention must be given between the drawings in anticipation of profits and those of withdrawals of capital.

That is why ***interest on capital is considered as an appropriation of profit and not a charge against profit.*** The entry for this purpose will be :

Profit and Loss Appropriation A/c Dr.
  To Partners' Capital Account

It must be remembered that ***an interest on capital is a charge against appropriation of profit, the same is chargeable to the extent of available surplus (profit) only. Of course, it may be waived by the partners (i.e., if the Partnership Deed so provides). In such a case, the resultant losses, after charging interest on Capital, must be borne by the partners as per profit-sharing ratio.***

The following example will make the above principle clear:

A and B are partners sharing profits and losses in the ratio 2 : 1. Their capitals were : A Rs. 1,00,000; B Rs. 50,000. Interest on Capital should be provided @ 5% on capital. The net profit before charging interest on capital amounted to Rs. 6,000.

In this case, interest on Capital would be Rs. 7,500 (Rs. 5,000 + Rs. 2,500). But as the profit was Rs. 6,000 only the same will be distributed between A and B in 2 : 1 i.e., Rs. 4,000 and Rs. 2,000 only.

The Profit and Loss Appropriation Account will be represented as :

Dr. **Profit and Loss Appropriation Account** *Cr.*

Particulars		*Amount* Rs.	*Particulars*	*Amount* Rs.
To Interest on Capital			By Profit and Loss A/c	
A	4,000		—Net Profit	6,000
B	2,000			
		6,000		
		6,000		6,000

But, if the Partnership Deed so provides and the partners waive the limitation, the Profit and Loss Appropriation Account will be:

Dr. **Profit and Loss Appropriation Account** *Cr.*

Particulars		Amount		Particulars		Amount
		Rs.				Rs.
To Interest on Capital				By Profit and Loss A/c		
A	5,000			—Net Profit		6,000
B	2,500			" Net Loss		
		7,500		A	1,000	
				B	500	1,500
		7,500				7,500

Interest on Partners' Loan

It has already been stated earlier that even if there is no agreement between/among the partners, interest on partners' loan must be provided for @ 6% p.a. But if there is any prescribed rate for it, the same rate should be maintained.

Interest on Loan may be treated in the two following ways :

(i) ***As a charge against appropriation of profit***

There are some accountants who prefer to use interest on partners' loan as a charge against appropriation of profit since it is nothing but a part of appropriated profits. That is, interest on loan should be shown in the appropriation section of Profit and Loss Account. Moreover, Income Tax Act does not allow it as a business expense. The entry is :

Profit and Loss Appropriation A/c Dr.
  To Interest on Partners' Loan A/c

(ii) ***As a charge against profit***

There are some accountants who prefer to use interest on loan as a charge against profit like other business expenses since loan constitutes the liability of a partnership business and, as such, any interest paid on it is a business expense. Thus, the same should be adjusted against Profit and Loss Account and not in the appropriation section of Profit and Loss Account.

Profit and Loss A/c Dr.
  To Interest on Partners' Loan A/c

It should be noted that interest on partners' loan must be transferred to partners' Current Account, i.e., neither in Capital nor in Loan Account.

Partners' Capital Accounts

As per Partnership Deed, each partner may have to bring Capital from his private sources at the time of formation of a partnership firm. The following points are to be noted :

(i) Partners may contribute capital not only in cash but also in the form of other assets;

(ii) Capital should be contributed by each partner as per Partnership Deed or agreed ratio or sometimes as per profit-sharing ratio, i.e., it may not always be equal;

(iii) Sometimes, the ratio of capital may be changed by the partners, e.g., change in the profit-sharing ratio, admission, retirement etc.

(iv) Sometimes, a partner (being an expert) may not contribute any physical capital to the business. His specialised knowledge and experience may be counted.

(v) If a partner brings in any liability, the net asset will be treated as his capital (i.e., Total Assets – Total Liabilities), e.g., A and B were in partnership sharing profits or losses in the ratio 3 : 2. They took C into partnership for which he brought the following :

Cash Rs. 5,000, Bank Rs. 8,000, Plant Rs. 20,000, Stock Rs. 12,000, and Creditors Rs. 3,000.

The entries will be :

Cash A/c	Dr. 5,000	
Bank A/c	Dr. 8,000	
Plant A/c	Dr. 20,000	
Stock A/c	Dr. 12,000	
To Creditors A/c		3,000
" Capital A/c (*bal. fig.*)		42,000

In a partnership firm, generally, capital and current accounts or capital and drawings accounts are to be opened. Capital accounts may be prepared under the following two methods : viz.

(a) ***Fluctuating Capital Method***; and (b) ***Fixed Capital Method.***

Under the former, capital account is prepared by taking the opening balance of capital plus all other necessary adjustments (i.e., drawings, interest on capital, interest on drawings, partners' salaries and commission, share of profit, etc.)

Under the latter (i.e., Fixed Capital Method), the Capital Account of the partner remains fixed, and, naturally, no entry is required to be passed for sharing profits, drawings or any other adjustments, like interest on capital, interest on drawings, partners' salaries and commission etc. In short, capital account will show the same result year after year from the very beginning except for additional capital to be introduced by the partners. A separate current account is to be opened where all the necessary adjustments including drawings, interest on drawings etc. are to be adjusted. However, at the end of the year, when the account is to be closed, it will either show a debit or a credit balance—which will ultimately be transferred to the assets or liabilities side of the Balance Sheet.

The outline of Capital Accounts under *Fluctuating Capital Method* is presented as under (assuming that there are two partners A and B) :

Dr. **Capital A/c** Cr.

Date	*Particulars*	*A*	*B*	*Date*	*Particulars*	*A*	*B*
		Rs.	Rs.			Rs.	Rs.
	To Drawings	* * *	* * *		By Balance b/d	* * *	* * *
	" Interest on Drawings	* * *	* * *		" Interest on Capital	* * *	* * *
	" Balance c/d	* * *	* * *		" Salary	* * *	* * *
					" Commissions	* * *	* * *
					" Share of Profit	* * *	* * *
					By Balance b/d	* * *	* * *

The outline of Capital Account and Current Account under *Fixed Capital Method* are presented below :

Dr. **Capital A/c** *Cr.*

Date	*Particulars*	*A*	*B*	*Date*	*Particulars*	*A*	*B*
		Rs.	Rs.			Rs.	Rs.
	To Balance c/d	* * *	* * *		By Balance b/d	* * *	* * *
					By Balance b/d	* * *	* * *

Dr. **Current Account** *Cr.*

Date	*Particulars*	*A*	*B*	*Date*	*Particulars*	*A*	*B*
		Rs.	Rs.			Rs.	Rs.
	To Balance b/d (if any)	* * *	* * *		By Balance b/d	* * *	* * *
	To Drawings	* * *	* * *		" Interest on Capital	* * *	* * *
	" Interest on Drawings	* * *	* * *		" Salary	* * *	* * *
	" Balance c/d	* * *	* * *		" Commissions	* * *	* * *
					" Share of Profit	* * *	* * *
					" Interest on Loan	* * *	* * *
					By Balance b/d	* * *	* * *

Illustration 1

Prepare the Capital Accounts of the partners from the following particulars, assuming that (i) Fluctuating Capital Method is followed; (ii) Fixed Capital Method is followed :

	Piu		*Gunjan*	
	Rs.		Rs.	
Capital Account (as on 1.1.1998)	50,000		40,000	
Current Account (")	1,000	(Cr.)	1,000	(Dr.)
Drawings	5,000		4,000	
Partners' Salaries	6,000		4,000	
Partners' Commission	—		5,000	
Share of Profit	12,000		8,000	
Interest on Partners' Loan	1,000		—	
Interest on Capital	5,000		4,000	
Interest on Drawings	250		200	

Solution

(i) ***Under Fluctuating Capital Method***

Dr. **Capital Account** Cr.

Date	Particulars	Piu	Gunjan	Date	Particulars	Piu	Gunjan
		Rs.	Rs.			Rs.	Rs.
	To Drawings	5,000	4,000		By Balance b/d	50,000	40,000
	" Interest on Drawings	250	200		" Interest on Capital A/c	5,000	4,000
	To Balance c/d	67,750	56,800		By Salaries A/c	6,000	4,000
					" Commissions	—	5,000
					" Share of Profit	12,000	8,000
		73,000	61,000			73,000	61,000
					By Balance b/d	67,750	56,800

(ii) ***Under Fixed Capital Method***

Dr. **Capital A/c** Cr.

Date	Particulars	Piu	Gunjan	Date	Particulars	Piu	Gunjan
		Rs.	Rs.			Rs.	Rs.
	To Balance c/d	50,000	40,000		By Balance b/d	50,000	40,000
		50,000	40,000			50,000	40,000
					By Balance b/d	50,000	40,000

Dr. **Current Account** Cr.

Date	Particulars	Piu	Gunjan	Date	Particulars	Piu	Gunjan
		Rs.	Rs.			Rs.	Rs.
	To Balance b/d	—	1,000		By Balance b/d	1,000	—
	To Drawings	5,000	4,000		" Interest on Capital	5,000	4,000
	" Interest on Drawings	250	200		" Interest on Loan	1,000	—
	" Balance c/d	19,750	15,800		" Salary	6,000	4,000
					" Commission	—	5,000
					" Share of Profit	12,000	8,000
		25,000	21,000			25,000	21,000
					By Balance b/d	19,750	15,800

Profit and Loss Appropriation Account and Distribution of Net Profit

A Profit and Loss Appropriation Account is prepared by incorporating the net profit or net loss from Profit and Loss Account. The same is credited with the profit coming from Profit and Loss Account and interest on drawings of the partners and debited with interest on capital of the partners, partners' salaries and commission etc. After transferring a certain sum (usually on percentage basis) to Reserve Fund, if any, the balance of the net distributable profit is to be allocated/distributed between or among the partners according to their profit-sharing ratio. The account is an essential part of Partnership firms. It may be remembered in this respect that any amount payable to a partner e.g., Interest on Capital, Partners' Salaries and Commission etc. (except Rent Payable to partners) are to be charged as an appropriation of profit.

The mode of appropriation, of course, depends on the partnership agreement. In the absence of agreement, however, Sec. 13 of the Indian Partnership Act is to be applied which states that :

(a) No partner is entitled to earn any interest on capital contributed by him and no interest on drawings is to be charged; (b) No partner is entitled to any salary or commission; (c) Interest on partner's loan will be @ 6% p.a.; (d) Profit or loss should be divided equally.

The outline of a Profit and Loss Appropriation Account is given below (assume there are two partners) :

Dr. **Profit and Loss Appropriation Account** *for the year ended ...* Cr.

Particulars	Amount	Amount	Particulars	Amount	Amount
	Rs.	Rs.		Rs.	Rs.
To Interest on Capital			By Profit and Loss A/c		* * *
A	* * *		—Net Profit		
B	* * *		" Interest on		
		* * *	Drawings A/c		*Contd.*

		Rs.	Rs.		Rs.	Rs.
"	Salaries			A	* * *	
	A	* * *		B	* * *	
	B	* * *				* * *
			* * *			
"	Commission					
	A	* * *				
	B	* * *				
			* * *			
"	Reserve Fund		* * *			
	Net Divisible Profit					
	A	* * *				
	B	* * *	* * *			

Interest on Capital, Interest on Drawings, Commision before charging and after charging profit, transfer to Reserve Fund etc.

Illustration 2

X, Y, and Z are in partnership with capitals of Rs. 50,000; Rs. 30,000 and Rs. 20,000, respectively. Their drawings are : X Rs. 10,000, Y Rs. 5,000 and Z Rs. 5,000. Their partnership deed provides that :

(a) Interest on partners' capital should also be provided @ 5% p.a.; (b) Interest on partners' drawings should also be provided @ 10% p.a.; (c) The partners are entitled to a partnership salary of Rs. 2,000 each p.a.; (d) X is entitled to a commission @ 10% on the profit before charging the above provisions ; (e) Y is entitled to a commission @ 10% on net profit (after charging the above provisions) after charging his commission. (f) 25% of the net profit (after charging all the above provisions) should be transferred to Reserve Fund. (g) Of the net divisible profits, X is entitled to 50% of the 1st Rs. 20,000, Y to 40 % and Z to 10%, over that amount profits are shared equally.

X introducing Rs. 40,000 to the firm as loan at the beginning of the year.

Profit for the year amounted to Rs. 60,000.

From the above particulars, prepare Profit and Loss Appropriation Account and Partners' Capital Accounts undern (i) Fluctuating Capital Method and (ii) Fixed Capital Method.

Solution

In the books of X, Y, and Z

Profit and Loss Appropriation Account *for the year ended ...*

Dr. Cr.

Particulars	Amount Rs.	Amount Rs.	Amount Rs.	Particulars	Amount Rs.	Amount Rs.
To Interest on Capital :				By Profit and Loss A/c		
X		2,500		— Profit		60,000
Y		1,500		" Interest on Drawings		
Z		1,000	5,000	X	500	
" Salaries :				Y	250	
X		2,000		Z	250	1,000
Y		2,000				
Z		2,000	6,000			
" Commission :						
X		6,000				
Y		4,000	10,000			
" Reserve Fund		10,000				
" Share of Profit :						
X	13,333					
Y	11,333					
Z	5,334	30,000				
			40,000			
			61,000			61,000

Working Notes :

1. Commission to Y :

   Profit before charging Y's commission Rs. 61,000 – 5,000 – 6,000 – 6,000 = Rs. 44,000.

2. **Transfer to Reserve Fund**

   Y's commission will be Rs. 44,000 × $\frac{10}{110}$ = Rs. 4,000.

   Profit after charging Y's commission Rs. 40,000 (44,000 – 4,000)

   ∴ Reserve Fund will be Rs. 10,000 $\left(40,000 \times \frac{25}{100}\right)$

3. **Share of profit to be transferred to the Partners' Capital Accounts :**

   Net Distributable Profit Rs. 30,000 (40,000 – 10,000)

X = 50% of	Rs. 20,000	= Rs.	10,000	+ Rs.	3,333	(i.e., 10,000 × $\frac{1}{3}$)	= Rs. 13,333
Y = 40% of	Rs. 20,000	= Rs.	8,000	+ Rs.	3,333	"	= Rs. 11,333
Z = 10% of	Rs. 20,000	= Rs.	2,000	+ Rs.	3,334	"	= Rs. 5,334
			20,000		10,000		30,000

4. If the specific dates of drawings are not given, interest on drawings should be calculated on an average for 6 months.
5. It is assumed that interest on partners' loan is a charge against profit, hence should be adjusted against Profit and Loss Account.

(i) Fluctuating Capital Method

Dr. **Capital Account** Cr.

Date	Particulars	X	Y	Z	Date	Particulars	X	Y	Z
		Rs.	Rs.	Rs.			Rs.	Rs.	Rs.
	To Drawings	10,000	5,000	5,000		By Balance b/d	50,000	30,000	20,000
	" Interest on Drawings	500	250	250		" Interest on Cap.	2,500	1,500	1,000
	" Balance c/d	63,333	43,583	23,084		" Commission	6,000	4,000	—
						" Share of Profit	13,333	11,333	5,334
						" Salaries	2,000	2,000	2,000
		73,833	48,833	28,334			73,833	48,833	28,334
						By Balance b/d	63,333	43,583	23,084

(ii) Fixed Capital Method

Dr. **Capital Account** Cr.

Date	Particulars	X	Y	Z	Date	Particulars	X	Y	Z
		Rs.	Rs.	Rs.			Rs.	Rs.	Rs.
	To Balance c/d	50,000	30,000	20,000		By Balance b/d	50,000	30,000	20,000
		50,000	30,000	20,000			50,000	30,000	20,000
						By Balance b/d	50,000	30,000	20,000

Dr. **Current Account** Cr.

Date	Particulars	X	Y	Z	Date	Particulars	X	Y	Z
		Rs.	Rs.	Rs.			Rs.	Rs.	Rs.
	To Drawings	10,000	5,000	5,000		By Interest on Cap.	2,500	1,500	1,000
	" Interest on Drawings	500	250	250		" Salaries	2,000	2,000	2,000
	" Balance c/d	15,733	13,583	3,084		" Commission	6,000	4,000	—
						" Interest on Loan	2,400	—	—
						" Share of Profit	13,333	11,333	5,334
		26,233	18,833	8,334			26,233	18,833	8,334
						By Balance b/d	15,733	13,583	3,084

Drawings at different dates

Illustration 3

From the following information, prepare :

1. The Profit and Loss Appropriation Account of P, Q, and R for the year ended 31.12.2008.
2. The Capital and Current Accounts of Partners :

Partners	Capital (1.1.2008)	Current (1.1.2008)	Drawings (31.12.2008)
P	Rs. 6,000	Rs. 2,000 (Cr.)	Rs. 4,000
Q	Rs. 10,000	Rs. 1,000 (Cr.)	Rs. 4,800
R	Rs. 16,000	Rs. 1,000 (Cr.)	Rs. 4,800

(i) Interest is credited @ 6% p.a. on capital and is charged on drawings at the same rate. Interest is neither credited nor charged on the balances of current accounts.

(ii) Each partner took at the end of each quarter 25% of his drawings.

(iii) P and Q were to be credited with salaries of Rs. 2,400 and Rs. 1,600 p.a., respectively.

(iv) On 1.7.2008, P paid in an additional Rs. 2,000 as capital and R withdrew Rs. 2,000 from capital.

(v) The net profit before charging interest on capital and partners' salaries and before interest on drawings had been credited was Rs. 19,600.

(vi) Profit and Losses shared among P, Q and R were 5 : 4 : 3 respectively.

Solution

In the books of P, Q, and R

Dr. **Profit and Loss Appropriation Account** *for the year ended 31st December 2008* Cr.

Particulars	Rs.	Rs.	Particulars	Rs.	Rs.
To Interest on Capital :			By Profit and Loss A/c		19,600
P	420		—Net Profit		
Q	600		" Interest on Drawings		
R	900		P	90*	
		1,920	Q	108	
" Salary			R	108	
P	2,400				306
Q	1,600				
		4,000			
" Share of Profit					
P	5,828				
Q	4,662				
R	3,496				
		13,986			
		19,906			19,906

* For P :	Rs.	For Q & R :	Rs.
On Rs. 1,000 @ 6% p.a. for 9 months	45	On Rs. 1,200 @ 6% p.a. for 9 months	54
" " " " " 6 "	30	" " " " " 6 "	36
" " " " " 3 "	15	" " " " " 3 "	18
	90		108

Dr. **Capital Account** Cr.

Date	Particulars	P	Q	R	Date	Particulars	P	Q	R
2008		Rs.	Rs.	Rs.	2008		Rs.	Rs.	Rs.
July 1	To Bank A/c	—	—	2,000	Jan. 1	By Balance b/d	6,000	10,000	16,000
Dec. 31	" Balance c/d	8,000	10,000	14,000	July 1	" Bank A/c	2,000	—	—
		8,000	10,000	16,000			8,000	10,000	16,000

Dr. **Current Account** Cr.

Date	Particulars	P	Q	R	Date	Particulars	P	Q	R
2008		Rs.	Rs.	Rs.	2008		Rs.	Rs.	Rs.
Mar. 31	To Drawings A/c	1,000	1,200	1,200	Jan. 1	By Balance b/d	2,000	1,000	1,000
June 30	" Drawings A/c	1,000	1,200	1,200	Dec. 31	" Interest on			
Sept. 30	" Drawings A/c	1,000	1,200	1,200		Capital A/c	420	600	900
Dec. 31	" Drawings A/c	1,000	1,200	1,200		" Salary A/c	2,400	1,600	—
	" Interest on					" Share of			
	Drawings A/c	90	108	108		Profit	5,828	4,662	3,496
	" Balance c/d	6,558	2,954	488					
		10,648	7,862	5,396			10,648	7,862	5,396

Remuneration Payable to Partners under Personal Agreement

Illustration 4

A and B are in partnership and decide to admit C, the manager, as the third partner on and from 1.1.2012.

Interest is to be allowed at 5% p.a. on Partners' Capital, Capitals; A Rs. 50,000, B Rs. 30,000 and C Rs. 10,000.

C is credited with a salary of Rs. 500 p.m., Rs. 200 of which is to be debited to A; Rs. 100 to B and Rs. 200 to the firm. After providing for interest on capital the profits are to be divided in proportion of 5 : 3 : 2. The partners' drawings on which no interest is to be charged at the rate of Rs. 600, Rs. 500 and Rs. 500 p.m. of A, B and C, respectively. The profit for the year ended 31.12.2012 amounts to Rs. 50,000 before making any of the above adjustments.

Draw-up the Current Account of the partners in the ledger, giving effect to the above adjustments and showing the amount of cash each partner is entitled to at the end of the year.

Solution

In the books of A, B, and C

Dr. **Profit and Loss Appropriation Account** ***for the year ended 31st Dec. 2012*** Cr.

Particulars	Rs.	Rs.	Particulars	Rs.
To Interest on Capital :			By Profit and Loss A/c	
A	2,500		—Net Profit	50,000
B	1,500			
C	500	4,500		
" Salary :				
C		2,400		
" Share of profit :				
A $\frac{5}{10}$	21,550			
B $\frac{3}{10}$	12,930			
C $\frac{2}{10}$	8,620			
		43,100		
		50,000		50,000

Dr. **Current Account** Cr.

Particulars	A	B	C	Particulars	A	B	C
	Rs.	Rs.	Rs.		Rs.	Rs.	Rs.
To C's Capital	2,400	1,200	—	By Interest on Cap.	2,500	1,500	500
" Drawings	7,200	6,000	6,000	" Salary	—	—	2,400
" Balance c/d	14,450	7,230	9,120	" A's Capital	—	—	2,400
				" B's Capital	—	—	1,200
				" Share of Profit	21,550	12,930	8,620
	24,050	14,430	15,120		24,050	14,430	15,120
				By Balance b/d	14,450	7,230	9,120

Notes : Salary already paid by A and B to C is a private agreement, and, hence, will not be adjusted in their Current Accounts, but unpaid portion must be passed through Current Account. The salary which is paid by the firm, however, is to be recorded in Profit and Loss Appropriation Account.

When there is no Partnership Agreement

Illustration 5

Ram, Rahim and Karim are partners in a Firm. They have no agreement in respect of profit sharing ratio, interest on capital, interest on loan advanced by partners and remuneration payable to partners. In the matter of distribution of profit they have put forward the following claims:

(i) Ram, who has contributed maximum capital, demands interest on capital at 10% p.a. and share of profit in the capital ratio. But Rahim and Karim do not agree.

(ii) Rahim has devoted full time for running the business and demands salary at the rate of Rs. 500 p.m. But Ram and Karim do not agree.

(iii) Karim demands interest on loan of Rs. 2,000 advanced by him at the market rate of interest which is 12% p.a.

How shall you settle the dispute and prepare P & L Appropriation A/c in that light transferring 10% of the divisible profit to Reserve Fund? Net profit before taking into account any of the above claims amount to Rs. 45,000 at the end of the 1st year of their business.

[CU BCom (Hons.)]

Solution

Since there were no partnership agreement among the partners, Ram, Rahim, and Karim, Sec. 13 of the Indian Partnership Act should be followed which states that :

(i) In the absence of agreement, no partner is allowed to have any interest on capital contributed by him.—hence, the claim (in respect of interest on capital) which is made by Ram is not allowed or accepted.

(ii) In the absence of agreement, no partner is allowed to draw any partnership salary—hence, the claim (in respect of salary) which is made by Rahim is not accepted or allowed.

(iii) In the absence of agreement, interest on loan is allowed @ 6% p.a. i.e., if any partner advances any amount by way of loan in addition to his capital,hence, Karim's claim (in respect of interest on loan @ 12%) is not accepted or allowed, only 6% p.a. should be considered by way of interest on loan.

(iv) In the absence of agreement, profits or losses should be distributed among the partners equally—hence the claim which is demanded by Ram for his larger contribution on capital is not accepted or allowed.

On the basis of the above, the Profit and Loss Appropriation amount is drawn up :

Dr. **Profit and Loss Appropriation Account** ***for the year ended ...*** **Cr.**

Particulars	Rs.	Rs.	*Particulars*	Rs.
To Interest on Loan			By Profit and Loss A/c	
—Karim @ 6% on Rs.. 2,000		120	—Net Profit	45,000
" Reserve Fund A/c				
@ 10% Rs. 44,880		4,488		
" Share of Profit				
Ram $\frac{1}{3}$	13,464			
Rahim $\frac{1}{3}$	13,464			
Karim $\frac{1}{3}$	13,464			
		40,392		
		45,000		45,000

Ascertainment of opening capital and preparation of P & L Appropriation Account and Capital Account at a subsequent date

Illustration 6

A, B, and C formed a partnership business in 2001. They did not have any Partneship Deed. From the year 2003, they agreed upon on the following :

(a) Partners will share profits or losses equally. (b) Partners will get interest on capital @ 6% p.a. (c) 'A' will get a salary @ Rs. 1,000 p.m.

A, B, and C started the business contributing capital Rs. 10,000; Rs. 15,000, Rs. 20,000 respectively. They did not maintain any proper books of accounts. Only the records of assets and liabilities to outsiders were maintained by them. The assets and outside liabilities were:

	31.12.2001	*31.12.2002*
	Rs.	Rs.
Sundry Creditors	35,000	20,000
Furniture and Fixture	50,000	50,000
Stock	30,000	45,000
Sundry Debtors	25,000	30,000
Casth in hand and at Bank	20,000	25,000

They decided to prepare accounts as per Partnership Deed and charge depreciation on Furniture and Fixtures @ 10% p.a. on straight line basis w.e.f. 2001. Show Profit and Loss Appropriation Account and Partners Capital Account for 2001 and 2002.

Solution **[CU BCom (Hons.) 2004]**

Special Note

Profit and Loss Appropriation Account can be prepared only if profit before appropriation is given. Since in this problem it is not given, we are to find out the profit before appropriation for the years 2001 and 2002 by the preparation of Statement of Affairs for both the years (as applied in case of single Entry System). In other words, profit before appropriation will be the difference between closing capital and opening capital and after adjusting depreciation on furniture and fixtures. Only then we can prepare Profit and Loss Appropriation Account for 2001 and 2002. So, we are to ascertain the opening and closing capital at first as under :

Statement of Affairs *for the year ended 2001 and 2002*

Liabilities	*2001*	*2002*	*Assets*	*2001*	*2002*
	Rs..	Rs.		Rs.	Rs.
Sundry Creditors	35,000	20,000	Furniture & Fixture	50,000	50,000
Capital *(bal. fig.)*	90,000	1,30,000	Stock	30,000	45,000
			Sundry Debtors	25,000	25,000
			Cash in hand and at Bank	20,000	25,000
	1,25,000	1,50,000		1,25,000	1,50,000

Ascertaintment of Profit before Appropriation for 2001 and 2002.

	Rs.	Rs.	Rs.	Rs.
Closing Capital		90,000		1,30,000
Less : Opening Capital for 2001 :				
A	10,000			
B	15,000			
C	20,000			
		45,000		
			90,000	
Opening Capital for 2002				90,000
(Closing Çapital of 2001)				
Trading Profit		45,000		40,000
Less : Depreciation on Furniture and Fixture				
@ 10% on Rs. 50,000		5,000		5,000
Net Profit before appropriation		40,000		35,000

In the books of A, B and C

Dr. **Profit and Loss Appropriation Account** *for the year ended 31st Dec. 2001* *Cr.*

Particulars	*Amount*	*Amount*	*Paticulars*	*Amount*
	Rs.	Rs.		Rs.
To Partners' Salary		12,000	By Profit and Loss A/c	40,000
—A (1,000 × 12)			—Net Profit	*Contd.*

	Rs.	Rs.		Rs.
" Interest on Capital @ 6%				
A (on Rs. 10,000)	600			
B (on Rs. 15,000)	900			
C (on Rs. 20.000)	1,200			
		2,700		
" Share of Profit				
A $\frac{1}{3}$	8,433			
B $\frac{1}{3}$	8,433			
C $\frac{1}{3}$	8,433			
		25,300		
		40,000		40,000

Dr. ***Partners' Capital Accounts*** Cr.

Date	Particulars	A	B	C	Date	Particulars	A	B	C
		Rs.	Rs.	Rs.			Rs.	Rs.	Rs.
2001					2001				
Dec. 31	To Balance c/d	31,033	24,333	29,634	Jan. 1	By Bank A/c			
						" Capital	10,000	15,000	20,000
					Dec. 31	" Salary	12,000	—	—
						" Int, on Capital	600	900	1,200
						" Share of Profit	8,433	8,433	8,434
		31,033	24,333	29,634			31,033	24,333	29,634
2002					2002				
Dec. 31	To Balance c/d	50,862	31,760	37,378	Jan. 1	By Balance b/d	31,033	24,333	29,634
					Dec. 31	" Salary	12,000	—	—
						" Int. on Capital	1,862	1,460	1,778
						" Share of Profit	5,967	5,967	5,966
		50,862	31,760	37,378			50,862	31,760	37,378

Different calculations for Interest on Drawings, Salary written back, calculation of partners commission

Illustration 7

Ted, Phil and Gordon are in partnership sharing profits two-fifths, two-fifths, and one-fifth, and throughout the half year ended 31 December 2011 their capital accounts have remained unchanged at Rs. 60,000, Rs. 40,000 and Rs. 30,000, respectively.

Their current account balances on 1 July 2011 were : Phil Rs. 8,550 (Dr.); Gordon Rs. 6,550 (Dr); Ted Rs. 12,000 (Cr.)

During 2011, Ted withdrew Rs, 200 at the beginning of each month, Gordon withdrew Rs. 400 at the end of each month, while Phil withdrew Rs. 1,800 during the period of six months.

Their Partnership Deed provides that :

(a) Partners are allowed interest on capital @ 5% p.a.

(b) Partners are allowed or charged interest on current account balance @ 4% p.a.

(c) Interest on drawings @ 6% p.a.

(d) Gordon is entitled to a salary of Rs. 500 per month.

(e) Ted is entitled to a commission of 5% of the correct net profit of the firm.

(f) Phil is entitled to a commission of 5% of the correct net profit of the firm after charging such commission.

During the half year ended 2011, the net profit of the firm was Rs. 2,07,000 afte charging Gordon's salary which had been debited to Wages and Salaries Account.

You are required to prepare the Profit and Loss Appropriation Account of the firm only.

Solution

In the books of the firm

Dr. **Profit and Loss Appropriation A/c** *for the half year ended 31st Dec. 2011* Cr.

Particulars	*Amount* Rs.	Rs.	*Particulars*	*Amount* Rs.	Rs.
To Interest on Capital :			By P & L A/c :		
Ted	1,500		" Net Profit		2,07,000
Phil	1,000		" Interest on Drawings :		
Gordon	750	3,250	Ted	42	
			Phil	54	
" Interest on Current A/c :			Gordon	60	156[1]
Ted		240			
Salary (Rs. 500 × 6)		3,000	" Interest on Current A/c :		
Gordn			Phil	171	
" Commissions :			Gordon	131	302
—Ted		10,198[2]			
—Phil		9,227[3]	" Gordon's Salary written-back		3,000[4]
Share of Profit :					
Ted $\frac{2}{5}$	73,817				
Phil $\frac{2}{5}$	73,817				
Gordon $\frac{1}{5}$	36,909	1,84,543			
		2,10,458			2,10,458

Dr. *Current A/c* Cr.

Date	*Particulars*	*Ted* Rs.	*Phil* Rs.	*Gordon* Rs.	*Date*	*Particulars*	*Ted* Rs.	*Phil* Rs.	*Gordon* Rs.
2001					2001				
July 1	To Balance b/d	8,550	6,550	—	July 1	By Balance b/d	—	—	12,000
	" Interst on Drawings	42	54	60	Dec. 31	" Interest on Capital	1,500	1,000	750
	" Interest on Current A/c	—	171	131		" Interest on Current A/c	240	—	—
Dec. 31	To Salary	—	—	3,000	Dec. 31	" Salary	—	—	3,000
"	" Balance c/d	77,163	77,269	49,468	"	" Commission	10,198	9,227	—
						" Share of Profit	73,817	73,817	36,909
		85,755	84,044	52,659			85,755	84,044	52,659

Workings :

1. **Computation of Interest on Drawings :**

Month	*Ted* *Drawings*	*Months*	*Product*	*Gordon* *Drawings*	*Months*	*Product*
	Rs.		Rs.	Rs.	Rs.	Rs.
July	200	6	1,200	400	5	2,000
Aug.	200	5	1,000	400	4	1,600
Sept.	200	4	800	400	3	1,200
Oct.	200	3	600	400	2	800
Nov.	200	2	400	400	1	400
Dec.	200	1	200	400	0	0
			4,200			6,000

∴ Interest on drawings for Ted on Rs. 4,200 for one month @ 6% p.a.

$= \text{Rs. } 4,200 \times \frac{6}{100} \times \frac{1}{6} = \text{Rs. } 42.$

Interest on Drawings for Phil

$\text{on Rs. } 1,800 \times \frac{6}{100} \times \frac{6}{12} = \text{Rs. } 54$

2. **Ted's Commission**

Profit before charging Ted's com. (Rs. 2,10,458 – Rs. 3,250 – Rs. 240 – Rs. 3,000) — Rs. 2,03,968

∴ Ted's Com. @ 5% on

$\text{Rs. } 2,03,968 \times \frac{5}{100} =$ Rs. 10,198

Interst on Drawings for Gordon on Rs. 6,000 for one month @ 6% p.a.

$= \text{Rs. } 6,000 \times \frac{6}{100} \times \frac{1}{6} = \text{Rs. } 60$

3. **Phil's Commission**

Profit before charging Phil's Com. (Rs. 2,03,968 – Rs. 10,198) = Rs.1,93,770

Less : Phil's Com. @ $\frac{5}{105}$ or $\frac{1}{21} \times \text{Rs. } 1,93,770$ — 9,227

1,84,543

4. **Salary written-back**

Since net profit was given after charging Gordon's Salary, Gordon's Salary should be written -back. So, it will appear at both sides of Profit and Loss Appropriation Account i.e., profit was given after charging salary.

Adjustment of Profit

Illustration 8

X , Y, and Z are partners in a firm sharing profits and losses in the ratio of 2 : 1 : 1. It is agreed that interest on capital will be allowed @ 5% p.a. and interest on drawings will be charged @ 4% p.a. (No interest will be charged or allowed on Current Accounts).

The following are the particulars of the Capital, Current and Drawings Account of the partners :

	X	Y	Z	
	Rs.	Rs.	Rs.	
Capital A/c (1.1.2012)	75,000	40,000	30,000	
Current A/c (1.1.2012)	10,000	5,000	5,000	(Dr.)
Drawings	15,000	10,000	10,000	
Interest on Drawings (2012)	500	190	350	

The draft accounts for 2012 showed a net profit of Rs. 60,000 before taking into account interest on capital and drawings subject to the following adjustments :

(a) Life Insurance premium of X amounting to Rs. 1,000 paid by the firm on 1.10.2012 has been charged to Miscellaneous Expenditure A/c.

(b) Repairs to Machinery amounting to Rs. 10,000 has been debited to Plant Account and depreciation thereon charged @ 20%.

(c) Travelling expenses of Rs. 3,000 of Y for the pleasure trip to UK paid by the firm on 30.6.2012, has been debited to Travelling Expenses Account.

Prepare the Profit and Loss Appropriation Account for the year ended 31.12.2012, and Current Accounts of partners for the year.

Solution

Dr. **Profit and Loss Appropriation Account** *for the year ended 31st Dec. 2012* *Cr.*

Particulars	Amount Rs.	Amount Rs.	Particulars	Amount Rs.	Amount Rs.
To Interest on Capital :			By Profit and Loss A/c —Profit (as adjusted)		56,000
X	3,750		" Interest on Drawings :		
Y	2,000		X	510	
Z	1,500	7,250	Y	250	
" Share of Profit :			Z	350	1,110
X $\frac{2}{4}$	24,930				
Y $\frac{1}{4}$	12,465				
Z $\frac{1}{4}$	12,465	49,860			
		57,110			57,110

Dr. **Current Account** Cr.

Date	Particulars	X	Y	Z	Date	Particulars	X	Y	Z
2012		Rs.	Rs.	Rs.	2012		Rs.	Rs.	Rs.
Jan. 1	To Balance b/d	—	—	5,000	Jan. 1	By Balance b/d	10,000	5,000	—
Dec. 31	" Drawings	16,000	13,000	10,000	Dec. 31	" Interest on Cap.	3,750	2,000	1,500
	" Interest on Drawings	510	250	350		" Share of Profit	24,930	12,465	12,465
	Balance c/d	22,170	6,215	—		" Balance c/d	—	—	1,385
		38,680	19,465	15,350			38,680	19,465	15,350
	Balance b/d	—	—	1,385		Balance b/d	22,170	6,215	—

Workings :

Adjustment of Net Profit :

	Rs.	Rs.
1. Net Profit		60,000
Less : Repairs to machinery		10,000
		50,000
Add : Premium paid on X's life policy	1,000	
Travelling Expenses of Y	3,000	
Depreciation overcharged @ 20% on Rs. 10,000	2,000	6,000
		56,000

2. **Interest on Drawings :**

Rs. 510 for X, i.e., $\left(\text{Rs. } 500 + \text{Rs. } 1,000 \times \frac{4}{100} \times \frac{3}{12}\right)$

Rs. 250 for Y, i.e., $\left(\text{Rs. } 190 + \text{Rs. } 3,000 \times \frac{4}{100} \times \frac{6}{12}\right)$

Ascertainment of Opening Capital and Correct Net Profit

Miscellaneous

Illustration 9

Accountancy and Management are two partners sharing profits and losses in the ratio of 3 : 2. On 31.12.01 their Capital Accounts stood at Rs. 55,000 and Rs. 45,000 after distribution of net profit of Rs. 15,000 and due consideration of drawings of the partners for Rs. 6,000 and Rs. 4,000, respectively. After closing the books the following discrepancies were discovered :

(i) An item in the inventory was valued at Rs. 12,800 but had a realisable value of Rs. 8,300;

(ii) Rs. 2,400 paid for insurance premium for the year ending on 31.3.02 had been debited to Profit and Loss A/c;

(iii) Interest on capital at 5% on partners' capital as at the beginning of the year and interest on drawings of partners at 8% p.a. were left out of consideration.

Ascertain the correct net profit of the firm and redistribute the profit by preparing a Profit & Loss Appropriation A/c and determine the balance of Partner's Capital A/c.

Solution **[CU BCom (Hons.) 2002]**

Calculation of Correct Net Profit

		Rs.
	Net Profit as per P & L Appropriation A/c	15,000
Add :	Prepaid insurance $\left(\text{Rs. } 2,400 \times \frac{3}{12}\right)$	600
		15,600
Less :	Over-valuation of closing stock (Rs. 12,800 – 8,300)	4,500
	Correct Net Profit	11,100

Dr. **Profit and Loss Appropriation Account** *for the year ended 31st Dec. 2001* Cr.

Particulars	Amount	Amount	Particulars	Amount	Amount
	Rs.	Rs.		Rs.	Rs.
To Interest on Capital :			By Profit and Loss A/c (Net Profit)		11,100
A	2,600		" Interest on Drawings :		
B	2,150	4,750[2]	A	240	
			B	160	400[3]

Contd.

		Rs.	Rs.			Rs.	Rs.
"	Share of Profit :						
	A : Rs. $6{,}750 \times \frac{3}{5}$	4,050					
	B : Rs. $6{,}750 \times \frac{2}{5}$	2,700					
			6,750				
			11,500				11,500

Dr. **Partners' Capital Account** Cr.

Date	Particulars	A	B	Date	Particulars	A	B
2001		Rs.	Rs.	2001		Rs.	Rs.
Jan. 1	To Drawings	6,000	4,000	Jan. 1	By Balance b/d	52,000	45,000
Dec. 31	" Interest on Drawings	240	260	Dec. 31	" Interest on Capital	2,600	2,150
	Balance c/d	52,410	43,590		" Share of Profit	4,050	2,700
		58,650	47,850			58,650	47,850

Workings :

1. In order to find out the Opening Capital :

Dr. **Partners' Capital Account** Cr.

Date	Particulars	A	B	Date	Particulars	A	B
2002		Rs.	Rs.	2002		Rs.	Rs.
Dec. 31	To Drawings	6,000	4,000	Jan. 1	**By Balance b/d**	52,000	43,000
	" Balance c/d	55,000	45,000		**" Share of Profit**	9,000	6,000
		61,000	49,000			61,000	49,000

Workings :

2. **Interest on Capital**

	Rs.
A : Rs. $52{,}000 \times \frac{5}{100} =$	**2,600**
B : Rs. $43{,}000 \times \frac{5}{100} =$	**2,150**
	4,750

3. **Interest on Drawings**

	Rs.
A : Rs. $6{,}000 \times \frac{8}{100} \times \frac{6}{12} =$	**240**
B : Rs. $4{,}000 \times \frac{8}{100} \times \frac{6}{12} =$	**160**
	400

Illustration 10

On 1.1.2005, X decided to make his friend Y a partner in his firm. The balance to the credit of X on that day was Rs. 30,000. Y had a cash balance of Rs. 2,000 only which he introduced as capital in the business. He also agreed to pay a sum of Rs. 2,000 as goodwill by four equal annual instalments and to limit his drawings to Rs. 1,800 p.a., being his salary, until the balance of his capital account will accumulate to Rs. 12,000.

X was entitled to an annual salary of Rs. 2,400 and Y Rs. 1,800, interest on capital was to be provided @ 6% p.a. The balance of the profit were to be divided : X $\frac{3}{4}$ and Y $\frac{1}{4}$.

Profits for 5 years before the adjustments of interest and salaries were :

2005 — Rs. 10,000; 2006 — Rs. 12,000; 2007 — Rs. 9,000; 2008 — Rs. 8,400; 2009 — Rs. 15,600.

X drew his salary in full every year and the balance of his current account was transferred to his capital account at the end of each year. X was to be credited with interest on his initial capital only.

Prepare Y's Capital and Current Accounts for 5 years.

Solution

Dr. **Y's Capital Account** Cr.

Date	Particulars	Amount	Date	Particulars	Date
2005		Rs.	2005		Rs.
Dec. 31	To Balance c/d	2,590	Jan. 1	By Bank A/c	2,000
			Dec. 31	" Current A/c	590
		2,590			2,590

Contd.

Date	Particulars	Amount	Date	Particulars	Amount
2006			2006		
Dec. 31	To Balance c/d	3,708	Jan. 1	By Balance b/d	2,590
			Dec. 31	" Current A/c	1,118
		3,708			3,708
2007			2007		
Dec. 31	To Balance c/d	4,124	Jan. 1	By Balance b/d	3,708
			Dec. 31	" Current A/c	416
		4,124			4,124
2008			2008		
Dec. 31	To Balance c/d	4,410	Jan. 1	By Balance b/d	4,124
			Dec. 31	" Current A/c	286
		4,410			4,410
2009			2009		
Dec. 31	To Balance c/d	7,008	Jan. 1	By Balance b/d	4,410
			Dec. 31	" Current A/c	2,598
		7,008			7,008
			2010		
			Jan. 1	By Balance b/d	7,008

Dr. **Y's Current Account** Cr.

Date	*Particulars*	*Amount*	*Date*	*Particulars*	*Amount*
2005		Rs.	2005		
Dec. 31	To Bank (Salary)	1,800	Dec. 31	By Salary	1,800
	" X's Capital (Goodwill)	500		" Interest on Capital	120
	" Capital A/c	590		" Share of Profit	970*
		2,890			2,890
2006			2006		
Dec. 31	To Bank (Salary)	1,800	Dec. 31	By Salary	1,800
	" X's Capital (Goodwill)	500		" Interest on Capital	156
	" Capital A/c	1,118		" Share of Profit	1,462
		3,418			3,418
2007			2007		
Dec. 31	To Bank (Salary)	1,800	Dec. 31	By Salary	1,800
	" X's Capital (Goodwill)	500		" Interest on Capital	222
	" Capital A/c	416		" Share of Profit	694
		2,716			2,716
2008			2008		
Dec. 31	To Bank (Salary)	1,800	Dec. 31	By Salary	1,800
	" X's Capital (Goodwill)	500		" Interest on Capital	248
	" Capital A/c	286		" Share of Profit	538
		2,586			2,586
2009			2009		
Dec. 31	To Bank (Salary)	1,800	Dec. 31	By Salary	1,800
	" Capital A/c	2,598		" Interest on Capital	264
				" Share of Profit	2,334
		4,398			4,398

Workings :

Computation of Share of Profit

Years		**2005-**	**2006**	**2007**	**2008**	**2009**
		Rs	Rs	Rs.	Rs.	Rs.
Profit (Given)		10,000	12,000	9,000	8,400	15,600
Less : Salary						
X	2,400					
Y	1,800					
		4,200	4,200	4,200	4,200	4,200
		5,800	7,800	4,800	4,200	11,400

Contd.

		Rs		Rs		Rs.		Rs.		Rs.
Less : Interest on Capital										
X (Fixed)	1 800		1,800		1,800		1,800		1,800	
Y	120		156		222		248		264	
		1,920		1,956		2,022		2,048		2,064
Divisible Profit		3,880		5,844		2,778		2,152		9,336
Y's share @ $\frac{1}{4}$ =		970		1,462		694		538		2,334

Illustration 11

Sukhi and Dukhi are partners and, on Dec. 31, 2011, the capital account of the partnership firm was Rs. 84,000 out of which Rs. 56,000 was of Sukhi and Rs. 28,000 of Dukhi. Profits and Losses were shared in the ratio of 2 : 1 and drawings of the partners also were in the same proportion. On 31st Dec. 2012, the position of the firm was as under : (i) The total combined capital was Rs. 98,600. (ii) Dukhi had drawn Rs. 1,200 in excess of agreed proportion. (iii) Dukhi had to be credited with Rs. 2,000 as special salary as per agreement.(iv) Interest on capital was provided @ 5% p.a.

You are asked to prepare a statement showing how the capital of Rs. 98,600 will be divided between the two partners.

Solution

Statement showing the allocation of Partners' Capital :

	Sukhi Rs.	Dukhi Rs.	Total Rs.
Capital (as on 31.12.2011)	56,000	28,000	
Interest on Capital	2,800	1,400	
Salary	—	2,000	
	58,800	31,400	
Less : Excess Drawings	—	1,200	
Capital before Profits	58,800	30,200	89,000
Add : Profits (Rs. 98,600 – Rs. 89,000) Rs. 9,600 (in 2 : 1)	6,400	3,200	9,600
Capital (as on 31.12.2012)	65,200	33,400	98,600

Determination of Profit-sharing Ratio on the basis of Effective Capital Employed

Illustration 12

X, Y, and Z commence a business in partnership. X puts in Rs. 20,000 for the whole year. Y introduces Rs. 30,000 at first and increases it to Rs. 40,000 at the end of four months but withdraws Rs. 10,000 at the end of eight months. Z brings in Rs. 50,000 at first, but withdraws Rs. 15,000 at the end of six months. Interest on capital should be charged @ 5% p.a. on partners' capital (as per agreement).

At the end of the year they make a profit of Rs. 60,000 (before charging interest on capital).

Show how the partners should divide this amount on basis of effective capital employed by each partner.

Solution

Calculation of profit-sharing ratio on the basis of effective capital employed and also interest on Capital :

Partner	Amount Rs.	Month	Product (i.e., for 1 month) Rs.	Interest on capital Rs.
X	20,000	12	2,40,000	$2,40,000 \times \frac{5}{100} \times \frac{1}{12}$ = Rs. 1,000
Y	30,000	12	3,60,000	
	10,000	8	(+) 80,000	
			4,40,000	
	10,000	4	(–) 40,000	
				$4,00,000 \times \frac{5}{100} \times \frac{1}{12}$ = Rs. 1,667
Z	50,000	12	6,00,000	
	15,000	6	(–) 90,000	
				$5,10,000 \times \frac{5}{100} \times \frac{1}{12}$ = Rs. 2,125

∴ Profit-sharing Ratio = X : Y : Z = Rs. 2,40,000 : Rs. 4,00,000 : Rs. 5,10,000

= 24 : 40 : 51

Profit and Loss Appropriation Account *for the year ended ...*

Dr. Particulars	Amount Rs.	Amount Rs.	Particulars	Cr. Amount Rs.
To Interest on Capital :			By Profit and Loss A/c	60,000
X	1,000			
Y	1,667			
Z	2,125			
		4,792		
" Share of Profit :				
X	11,522			
Y	19,202			
Z	24,484			
		55,208		
		60,000		60,000

RECTIFICATION OF WRONG DISTRIBUTION OF PROFITS OR ADJUSTMENT OF NET PROFIT OF PRIOR PERIOD

Sometimes some mistakes relating to distribution of profits or accounting treatment may be discovered after the accounts have been closed for a certain period. In order to amend it, adjustments may be made after writing-back the profit which was wrongly distributed and, thereafter, a fresh distribution should be made on the correct basis through the Profit and Loss Appropriation (Adjustment) Account.

Alternatively, each partner's share of profit on correct basis as well as on wrong basis should be made and the difference may be adjusted simply by means of a journal entry, i.e., through capital transfer. This is particularly applicable when the partners desire not to alter the signed Balance Sheet.

Illustration 13

A, B, C, and D are equal partners. On 1st January 2012, their Capital Accounts stood as :

A—Rs. 8,000; B—Rs. 12,000; C—Rs.20,000; D—Rs.40,000

After the accounts for 2012 have been prepared, it is discovered that interest on capital at 5% p.a., as agreed upon, has not been credited to the Partner's Capital Accounts before distribution of profits. Instead of altering the signed Balance Sheet, it is decided to make an adjusting entry, at the beginning of the next year. Give the adjusting journal entry.

Solution

Statements showing the Adjustments

Partners	Interest on Capital not charged Rs.	Taken as profit	Adjustment Rs.
A	+ 400	$-1,000\ (\frac{1}{4})$	− 600
B	+ 600	$-1,000\ (\frac{1}{4})$	− 400
C	+ 1,000	$-1,000\ (\frac{1}{4})$	—
D	+ 2,000	$-1,000\ (\frac{1}{4})$	+ 1,000
	4,000	4,000	—

Journal

Date	Particulars		L.F.	Debit Rs.	Credit Rs.
2013 Jan. 1	A's Current A/c	Dr.		600	
	B's Current A/c	Dr.		400	
	To D's Current A/c				1,000
	(Interest on Capital not charged, now adjusted)				

Note : Since the interest on capital was not charged, profit was increased by the total amount of interest (which was Rs. 4,000) and taken by the partners in their profit-sharing ratio (i.e., equally). ***Therefore, Rs. 4,000 should be written-back.***

Rectification of Errors

Illustration 14

The net trading profit of ABC & Co. for the year ended 31st December 2012 was Rs. 30,000 and the same was distributed amongst the partners A, B, and C in their agreed ratio of $\frac{3}{5}$ ths, $\frac{1}{5}$ th and $\frac{1}{5}$ th, respectively. It was subsequently discovered that the undermentioned transactions were not passed through the account :

(i) Interest on capital @ 5% p.a.; (ii) Interest on drawings amounting to A Rs. 350, B Rs. 250, and C Rs. 150; (iii) Partners' salary to A Rs. 5,000 and C Rs. 750; (iv) An agreed commission of Rs. 3,000 payable to A arising out of a special transaction of the firm. The Capital Accounts of the partners are A Rs. 50,000, B Rs. 40,000, and C Rs. 30,000.

You are asked to pass necessary entries to rectify the position and show the Partners' Current Accounts incorporating the above items.

Solution

In the books of ABC & Co.
Journal

Date	*Particulars*		*L.F.*	*Debit*	*Credit*
2012				Rs.	Rs.
Dec. 31	A's Current A/c	Dr.		18,000	
	B's Current A/c	Dr.		6,000	
	C's Current A/c	Dr.		6,000	
	To Profit and Loss Adjustment A/c				30,000
	(Profit which was credited to partners written-back)				
	Profit and Loss Adjustment A/c Dr.			14,750	
	To Interest on Capital A/c :				
	A 2,500				
	B 2,000				
	C 1,500				6,000
	" Salary to Partners :				
	A 5,000				
	C 750				5,750
	" Commission : A				3,000
	(Interest on Capital, Partners' Salary and Commission charged to Profit and Loss Adjustment A/c)				
	Interest on Capital A/c	Dr.		6,000	
	Salary to Partner A/c	Dr.		5,750	
	Commission to A A/c	Dr.		3,000	
	To A's Current A/c (2,500 + 5,000 + 3,000)				10,500
	" B's Current A/c				2,000
	" C's Current A/c (1,500 + 750)				2,250
	(Interest on Capital, Salary and Commission adjusted)				
	Interest on Drawings A/c	Dr.		750	
	A 350				
	B 250				
	C 150				750
	To Profit and Loss Adjustment A/c				
	(Interest on partners' drawings charged to Profit and Loss Adjustment A/c)				
	A's Current A/c	Dr.		350	
	B's Current A/c	Dr.		250	
	C's Current A/c	Dr.		150	
	To Interest on Drawings A/c				750
	(Interest on drawings adjusted)				
	Profit and Loss Adjustment A/c	Dr.		16,000[1]	
	To A's Current A/c				9,600
	" B's Current A/c				3,200
	" C's Current A/c				3,200
	(Profit distributed amongst the partners)				

Dr. **Current Account** Cr.

Date	Particulars	A	B	C	Date	Particulars	A	B	C
		Rs.	Rs.	Rs.			Rs.	Rs.	Rs.
	To Share of Profit					By Balance b/d	18,000	6,000	6,000
	—written-back	18,000	6,000	6,000		" Interest on Cap.	2,500	2,000	1,500
	" Interest on					" Salary	5,000	—	750
	Drawings	350	250	150		" Commission	3,000	—	—
	" Balance c/d	19,750	4,950	5,300		" Share of Profit	9,600	3,200	3,200
		38,100	11,200	11,450			38,100	11,200	11,450
						By Balance b/d	19,750	4,950	5,300

Workings :

1 In order to find out the distribution profit the following Profit and Loss Adjustment Account should be prepared.

Dr. **Profit and Loss Adjustment Account** *for the year ended 31st Dec. 2012* Cr.

Particulars	Amount	Amount	Particulars		Amount
	Rs.	Rs.			Rs.
To Interest on Capital :			By A's Current A/c	18,000	
A	2,500		B's Current A/c	6,000	
B	2,000		C's Current A/c	6,000	
C	1,500		(Wrong profit written-back)		30,000
		6,000	" Interest on Drawings		
" Partners' Salaries			A	350	
A	5,000		B	250	
C	750		C	150	
		5,750			750
" Commission —					
A		3,000			
" Share of Profit :					
A's Current A/c	9,600				
B's Current A/c	3,200				
C's Current A/c	3,200				
		16,000			
		30,750			30,750

Illustration 15

S, T, and Q were partners sharing profits in the proportion of 3 : 2 : 1. Their capitals on 31st Dec. 2011 stood at Rs. 45,000, Rs. 15,000, and Rs. 15,500, respectively, after adjustments of net profit Rs. 18,000 for the year ending that date and drawings of Rs. 6,000, Rs. 4,000, and Rs. 2,000, respectively. It was discovered, however, that, while ascertaining the profits, the accountant did not take into consideration the following matters :

1. Interest at 6% p.a. on capital as on Jan. 2011.
2. Q was entitled to a salary of Rs. 2,000 p.a. of which Rs. 490 was unpaid.
3. Till 31st Dec. 2010 partners were sharing profits equally and that goodwill was valued at Rs. 12,000 on the date of reallocation of profits but adjustment was omitted in the capital accounts of the partners involved. It was decided to raised Goodwill Account in the books.
4. A loan of Rs. 5,000 from T was brought-forward from 2010 carrying interest at 8% p.a, and was merged into his capital on July 1, 2011. No interest on loan was, however, charged to Profit and Loss Account.

You are required to work out a Profit and Loss Adjustment Account and show the Journal entries necessary for readjustments of Capital Accounts and the revised Capital Accounts of partners, assuming that all their dues are to be adjusted in the Capital Accounts.

[CA]

Solution

Ascertainment of Opening Capital Balances

	S	T	Q
Capital at the end (31.12.2011)	45,000	15,000	15,500
Less : Profit of Rs. 18,000 distributed in the ratio 3 : 2 : 1	9,000	6,000	3,000
	36,000	9,000	12,500
Add : Drawings during the period	6,000	4,000	2,000
	42,000	13,000	14,500
Add : Goodwill raised in the books	4,000	4,000	4,000
	46,000	17,000	18,500
Less : Loan of Rs. 5,000 from T merged on 1.7.2011	—	5,000	—
Opening Capital of the partners (1.1.2011)	46,000	12,000	18,500

Dr. **Profit and Loss Adjustment Account** *for the year ended 31st Dec. 2011* Cr.

Particulars	*Amount* Rs.	*Amount* Rs.	*Particulars*	*Amount* Rs.	*Amount* Rs.
To Interest on Capital A/c :			By Profit and Loss A/c		
S	2,760		(Net Profit)		18,000
T	720				
Q	1,110	4,590			
" Partners' Salary A/c—Q		490			
" Partners' Loan A/c					
T (8% on Rs. 5,000 of 6 months)		200			
" Share of Profit A/c :					
S	6,360				
T	4,240				
Q	2,120	12,720			
		18,000			18,000

Statement showing the required Adjustments

Particulars	*P & L Adj. A/c* Dr.	Cr.	*S's Capital* Dr.	Cr.	*T's Capital* Dr.	Cr.	*Q's Capital* Dr.	Cr.
For Interest on Capital to be paid	4,590			2,760		720		1,110
For Unpaid Salary to Q	490							490
For Interest on Loan to T	200					200		
For Sharing of Profit	12,720			6,360		4,240		2,120
For Sharing of the above Losses in the ratio 3 : 2 : 1		18,000	9,000		6,000		3,000	
Total (Rs.)	18,000	18,000	9,000	9,120	6,000	5,160	3,000	3,720
Net Effect			(Cr.) 120		(Dr.) 840		(Cr.) 720	

Journal

Date	Particulars		L.F.	Debit Rs.	Credit Rs.
?	Goodwill A/c	Dr.		12,000	
	To S's Capital A/c				4,000
	" T's Capital A/c				4,000
	" Q's Capital A/c				4,000
	(Amount of Goodwill raised in the books)				
	T's Capital A/c	Dr.		840	
	To S's Capital A/c				120
	" Q's Capital A/c				720
	(Adjustment made among the partners)				

Dr. **Capital Account (Revised)** Cr.

Date	Particulars	S	T	Q	Date	Particulars	S	T	Q
		Rs.	Rs.	Rs.			Rs.	Rs.	Rs.
	To S's Capital A/c	—	120	—		By Balance b/d	45,000	15,000	15,500
	T's Capital A/c	—	720	—		" Goodwill A/c	4,000	4,000	4,000
	" Balance c/d	49,120	18,160	20,220		" T's Capital A/c	120	—	720
		49,120	19,000	20,220			49,120	19,000	20,220

Illustration 16

Below is the Profit and Loss Appropriation Account of X and Y for the year ended 31st March 2012 :

	Rs.		Rs.
To Interest on Capital :		By Net Profit	40,000
X—8% on Rs. 40,000	3,200	" Interest on Drawings :	
Y—8% on Rs. 30,000	2,400	X—6% on Rs. 8,000	240
By Salary		Y—6% on Rs. 6,000	180
X	4,800	(Calculated on average method)	
" Share of Profit :			
X $\frac{1}{2}$	15,010		
Y $\frac{1}{2}$	15,010		
	40,420		40,420

The entries were duly passed in the books but the following discrepancies were subsequently discovered.

(i) Interest on capital should have been allowed at 6% and that on drawings should have been charged at 8% p.a.

(ii) X was not entitled to get any salary but Y was entitled to get a monthly salary of Rs. 250.

(iii) Profit should have been shared in opening capital ratio.

You are required to redistribute the profit correctly. **[ICWA Adapted]**

Solution

In the books of X and Y

Dr. **Profit and Loss Adjustment Account** for the year ended 31st March 2012 Cr.

Particulars	Amount	Amount	Particulars	Amount	Amount
	Rs.	Rs.		Rs.	Rs.
To Interest on Capital @ 6% p.a. :			By X's Capital A/c — Amount already received written-back		22,770[1]
X	2,400				
Y	1,800	4,200	" Y's Capital A/c		
" Salary : Y		3,000	— Amount already received written-back		17,230
" Share of Profit :			" Interest on Drawings @ 8% :		
X $\frac{4}{7}$	19,063		X	320	
Y $\frac{3}{7}$	14,297				
		33,360	Y	240	560
		40,560			40,560

Workings :

1. X's Capital (Amount to be written-back) = Interest + Salary + Profit − Interest on Drawings
= 3,200 + 4,800 + 15,010 − 240
= Rs. 22,770.

Y's Capital (") = 2,400 + Nil + 15,010 − 180
= Rs. 17,230.

Illustration 17

The summarised Capital Accounts of the partners of M/s Kay and Kay appear as :

Dr. **Capital Accounts (Revised)** *Cr.*

Date	Particulars	Kamal	Kumar	Keerti	Date	Particulars	Kamal	Kumar	Keerti
2011		Rs.	Rs.	Rs.	2011		Rs.	Rs.	Rs.
Dec. 31	To Drawings	12,000	12,000	12,000	Dec. 31	By Balance b/d	20,000	30,000	40,000
	" Balance c/d	23,000	33,000	43,000		31.12.2011			
						Share of Profit	15,000	15,000	15,000
		35,000	45,000	55,000			35,000	45,000	55,000

On January 1, 2012, it is agreed that the following would be effective, retrospectively, from January 1, 2011 :

(1) Kamal shall be entitled to a salary of Rs. 750 p.m.

(2) Interest shall be allowed on partners' capitals at 5% on the opening balances.

(3) Profits shall be shared in proportion to opening balance in capital account.

(4) Keerti's share of profit exclusive of interest on his capital shall not fall below Rs. 15,000, the deficit, if any, being contributed by Kamal out of his share.

You are required to show entries in the capital accounts on January 1, 2012 to give effect to the above arrangement

Solution

Workings :

		Rs.
Net Profit		45,000
Less : Interest on Capital :		
Kamal	1,000	
Kumar	1,500	
Keerti	2,000	
	4,500	
Kamal's Salary (750 × 12) =	9,000	
		13,500
Distributable Profit		31,500

Kumar's Share $= 31{,}500 \times \frac{3}{9} = 10{,}500$ $= 10{,}500$

Keerti's Share $= 31{,}500 \times \frac{4}{9} = 14{,}000 + 1{,}000$ $= 15{,}000$

Kamal's Share $= 31{,}500 \times \frac{2}{9} = 7{,}000 - 1{,}000$ $= 6{,}000$

	Salary	+	Interest	+	Profit	=	Total	–	Wrong Profit	=	Net Adjustment
Kamal =	9,000	+	1,000	+	6,000	=	16,000	–	15,000	=	1,000 (Cr.)
Kumar =	—	+	1,500	+	10,500	=	12,000	–	15,000	=	3,000 (Dr.)
Keerti =	—	+	2,000	+	15,000	=	17,000	–	15,000	=	2,000 (Cr.)

In the books of M/s Kay and Kay

Journal

Date	Particulars	L.F.	Dr.	Cr.
2012			Rs.	Rs.
Jan. 1	Kumar's Capital A/c Dr.		3,000	
	To Kamal's Capital A/c			1,000
	" Keerti's Capital A/c			2,000
	(Adjustments made in the books)			

Illustration 18

A, B, and C were partners during the three years ended 31.12.2012, sharing profits and losses as follows :

	A	B	C
2010	$\frac{1}{2}$	$\frac{1}{4}$	$\frac{1}{4}$
2011	$\frac{2}{3}$	$\frac{1}{6}$	$\frac{1}{6}$
2012	$\frac{3}{4}$	$\frac{1}{8}$	$\frac{1}{8}$

On 1st January 2013, it was discovered that interest on capital @ 6% p.a. was not credited to each partner in respect of past three years, the partners' capitals on 1.1.2010 being as follows : A Rs. 10,000; B Rs. 5,000; C Rs. 5,000. Assume that net trading result were: 2010 Rs. 15,000 (Profit); 2011 Rs. 4,500 (Loss); 2012 Rs. 6,000 (Profit). Show the journal entry.

Solution

It is quite clear that interest on capital had not been paid for the last three years :

Interest Payable to Partners per year Rs. 1,200 (A Rs. 600; B Rs. 300 and C Rs. 300)

As such, total amount due to them for 3 years = Rs. 1,200 × 3 = Rs. 3,600.

[i.e., A (Rs. 600 × 3) + B (Rs. 300 × 3) + C (Rs. 300 × 3)]

The same amount they received by way of profit. That is, as per profit-sharing ratio, they received :

Ratio	Total	A Rs.	B Rs.	C Rs.
2010 2 : 1 : 1	1,200	600	300	300
2011 4 : 1 : 1	1,200*	800	200	200
2012 6 : 1 : 1	1,200	900	150	150
Total Amount received	3,600	2,300	650	650
Less : They should have received	3,600	1,800	900	900
Net Effect		(–) 500	(+) 250	(+) 250

In the books of A, B, and C

Journal

Date	*Particulars*		L.F.	*Dr.* Rs.	*Cr.* Rs.
?	A's Current A/c	Dr.		500	
	To B's Current A/c				250
	" C's Current A/c				250
	(Interest on Capital not charged for 3 years, now adjusted.)				

*** In this year, total loss made by the firm amounted to Rs. 4,500. If interest on capital has been charged, the loss actually would have been to Rs. 4,500 + Rs. 1,200 = Rs. 5,700 which should be distributed among A, B and C in 4 : 1 : 1. But, as interest on capital was not charged, Rs. 4,500 has been distributed instead of Rs. 5,700. So indirect profit amounted to Rs. 1,200 (5,700 – 4,500).**

GUARANTEED PARTNERSHIP

On the admission of a new partner, the old partners may give a guarantee that he (the new partner) shall receive a certain minimum amount, should the normal share to which he is entitled fall short of a stipulated amount. Usually, the old partners undertake this obligation although, in some cases, only one of such partners may himself assume responsibility. The partnership deed should state clearly and unambiguously this guarantee clause.

The problem on this issue may be divided into the following groups :

(i) ***When the guaranteed minimum is borne by all the remaining partners :***

Under this clause, the share of each partner should be computed first without considering guaranteed clause. If the guaranteed partner's share falls short of the stipulated minimum amount, the same deficiency must be compensated by other existing partners as per profit-sharing ratio.

(ii) ***When the guaranteed minimum is borne by one partner only :***

Under this agreement, the guaranteed partner is given his minimum amount. That is, if there is any shortfall, the same deficiency must be compensated by such partner who has given such guarantee. Other remaining partners' share will not be affected at all.

Minimum Profit guaranteed to a partner by all other existing partners

Illustration 19

A and B were in partnership sharing profits and losses in the ratio of 3 : 2. In appreciation of the services of their clerk, C—who was in receipt of a salary of Rs. 2,400 p.a. and a commission of 5% on the net profit after charging such salary and commission—they took him into partnership as from 1st April 2012, giving him one-eighth share of profits.

The agreement provided that any excess over his former remuneration to which C becomes entitled will be borne by A and B in the ratio of 2 : 3.

The profit for the year ended 31st March amounted to Rs. 44,400.

Prepare statement showing the distribution of the profit amongst all the partners.

Solution :

C's share of profit as a Partner :

	Rs.
Profit Rs. 44,400 × $\frac{1}{8}$	5,550
	5,550

C's share as a Manager :

	Rs.
Salary	2,400
Commission (Rs. 44,400 – Rs. 2,400) × $\frac{5}{105}$	2,000
	4,400

Therefore, excess Rs. 1,150 (i.e., Rs. 5,550 – Rs. 4,400) is to be borne by A and B in the ratio of 2 : 3.

A—Rs. 1,150 × $\frac{2}{5}$ = Rs. 460. B—Rs. 1,150 × $\frac{3}{5}$ = Rs. 690.

		Rs.		Rs.
	Now, total profit for the year	44,400	A gets = Rs. 40,000 × $\frac{3}{5}$ = Rs. 24,000 – Rs. 460 =	23,540
Less :	C's share as a manager	4,400	B gets = Rs. 40,000 × $\frac{2}{5}$ = Rs. 16,000 – Rs. 690 =	15,310
	Divisible Profit	40,000	C gets	5,550

Minimum profit guaranteed to a partner by another partner.

Illustration 20

Gold, Silver, and Copper entered into partnership on 1.1.2012 sharing profits and losses in the ratio 2 : 2 : 1. Gold, however, personally guaranteed that Copper's share of profits, after charging interest on capital @ 5% p.a., would not be less than Rs. 8,000 in any year. The capitals were : A Rs. 50,000, B Rs. 30,000, and C Rs. 20,000. The profit for the year ended 31st Dec. 2012 amounted to Rs. 35,000.

Show the Profit and Loss Appropriation Account.

Solution

In the books of Gold, Silver, and Copper

Dr. **Profit and Loss Appropriation Account** *for the year ended 31st Dec. 2012* Cr.

Particulars	*Amount* Rs.	*Amount* Rs.	*Particulars*	*Amount* Rs.	*Amount* Rs.
To Interest on Capital :			By Profit and Loss A/c —Net Profit		35,000
Gold	2,500				
Silver	1,500				
Copper	1,000	5,000			
" Balance c/d		30,000			
		35,000			35,000
To Share of Profit :			By Balance b/d		30,000
Gold 30,000 × $\frac{2}{5}$ =	12,000				
Less : Adjustment for Guarantee	2,000				
		10,000			
" Silver 30,000 × $\frac{2}{5}$ =		12,000			
Copper 30,000 × $\frac{1}{5}$ =	6,000				
Add : Adjustment for Guarantee	2,000	8,000			
		30,000			30,000

Illustration 21

X and Y were in partnership sharing profits and losses in the ratio 3 : 1. They took Z into partnership on a monthly salary of Rs. 800 and 10% of the profits after charging salary and such 10% profit or $\frac{1}{5}$th share of profits, whichever is higher. Should the latter exceed the former, the excess is to be borne by X. The profits for the year ended 31st Dec. 2012 amounted to Rs. 1,05,600. Show the distribution of profit among the partners.

Solution

(i) Z's share under the former agreement

	Rs.
Salary @ Rs. 800 × 12 =	9,600
Add : Share of Profit	9,600
Total	19,200

(ii) Z's share under the latter agreement

	Rs.
$\frac{1}{5}$th Share of Profit	
Profit	1,05,600
Add : Salary (no more to be paid)	9,600
	1,15,200

Z's share = Rs. 1,15,200 × $\frac{1}{5}$ = Rs. 23,040 and excess Rs. 23,040 – Rs. 19,200 = Rs. 3,840 to be borne by X. Thus, division of profit between X and Y are :

	Rs.
Profit for the year	1,05,600
Less : Z's share of profit under first alternative	9,600
to be shared between X and Y	96,000

	Rs.
X's share = Rs. 96,000 × $\frac{3}{4}$ =	72,000
Less : Z's guaranteed share	3,840
	68,160
Y's share = Rs. 96,000 × $\frac{1}{4}$ =	Rs. 24,000

Illustration 22

X, Y and his son Z were partners in the firm M/s X and Y. On 1.4.2011, G, the manager, was admitted as a partner. Profits and losses in new partnership were to be shared in ratio of 4 : 3 : 2 : 1.

G has previously been paid a salary of Rs. 1,200 p.a. and a commission of 2% of the profit after charging his salary and commission. It was agreed that, for the first year of the new partnership, any excess of his share of the profit over the sum he would have earned had he remained manager increased by Rs. 700, should be charged to X's share of profit.

On considering the draft accounts for the year ended 31st March 2012, the partners agreed to the following adjustments :

(a) To provide for bonus of Rs. 5,500 to staff;

(b) That X's son T, an employee of the partnership, should receive an additional bonus of Rs. 250 chargeable against his father's share of profit; and

(c) That Rs. 500 of Y's share of profit should be credited to his son Z.

The profit for the year ended 31.3.2012, before making above adjustments, amounted to Rs. 31,400. Show the Profit and Loss Appropriation Account.

Solution

In the books of X, Y , Z, and G

Dr. **Profit and Loss Appropriation Account** *for the year ended 31.3.2012* Cr.

	Particulars	*Amount* Rs.	*Amount* Rs.		*Particulars*	*Amount* Rs.	*Amount* Rs.
To	Bonus to Staff		5,500	By	Profit and Loss A/c —Net Profit		31,400
"	Share of Profits :						
	X $\frac{4}{10}$	10,360					
	Y $\frac{3}{10}$	7,770					
	Z $\frac{2}{10}$	5,180					

Contd.

		Rs.	Rs.			Rs.	Rs.
	G $\frac{1}{10}$	2,590					
			25,900				
			31,400				31,400
To	Bonus—T		250[3]	By	X's Capital A/c[1] (250 + 98)		348
"	Z's Capital A/c		500[2]	"	Y's Capital A/c[2]		500
"	Y's Capital A/c	59					
"	Z's Capital A/c	39	98				
			848				848

Workings :

1. Paid to T Rs. 250 + Rs. 98 to G, which is calculated as:

		Rs.
G gets		2,590
Less : As a Manager	1,200	
Plus : Com. (Rs. 30,200 × $\frac{2}{102}$)	592	1,792
Additional Amount		798
Less : Statutory Amount		700
		98

2. Paid to Z Rs. 500 (as per agreement) from Y' share.
3. Rs. 98 (additional amount of G) to be apportioned between Y and Z in the ratio of 3 : 2 since they have suffered a loss as a result to the primary distribution

Employee Admitted as a Partner with Retrospective Effect

We know that an employee of a firm may be admitted as a partner with retrospective effect, i.e., from an earlier date. In that case, accounts of the old partners together with the accounts of the new partner should be ascertained for each of the preceding years from which he is considered as a partner. Similarly, his share should also be ascertained for those years as an employee, i.e., how much he had already taken as an employee. Now if it is found that his share of profit as a partner becomes more than his share as an employee for all the years, the excess must be credited to his current account and old partners' current account must be debited as per profit-sharing ratio for the purpose.

On the contrary, in the opposite case, his current account will be debited and old partner's current account should be credited according to profit-sharing ratio. But if there is an agreement among the partners that new partner's share must not be less than what he had already received as an employee, the so-called deficit may be ignored or may not be considered.

Illustration 23

A and B commenced business on 1.7.2010 as partners with capitals of Rs. 1,20,000 and Rs. 80,000, respectively. The capitals remain fixed and carry interest at 7% p.a. Profits are to be shared in proportion to their capitals.

They appointed C as their manager on 1.7.2010 at a salary of Rs. 4,800 p.a. plus a bonus of 5% of the profits which, subject to this bonus and interest on capital, would be divisible between the partners. C has to deposit on 1.7.2010, Rs. 40,000 as security carrying interest at 8% p.a.

In July 2013, it was settled that C should be treated as a partner from 1st July 2010. It was agreed that he would be entitled to one-sixth of the profits and his security deposit would be treated as his capital carrying interest at 7% p.a. instead of the 8% he had received. It was further agreed that this new arrangement should not result in reducing C's share for any of these year, than he had already received under the original agreement and terms of his appointement.

The profits before charging for C's bonus and interest on capital on giving effect to the new arrangement were: (a) for the year ended 30th June 2011 Rs. 30,000; (b) or the year ended 30th June 2012 Rs. 58,000; (c) for the year ended 30th June 2013 Rs. 83,000.

Show the necessary journal entries to give effect to the new arrangement with explanatory computations.

[CU BCom (Hons.)]

C's share under the old arrangement :

Solution

Workings :

	2010-11	20111-12	2012-13
	Rs.	Rs.	Rs.
Salary	4,800	4,800	4,800
Interest on his deposit @ 8% on Rs. 40,000	3,200	3,200	3,200
Bonus @ 5% on profits :			
i.e., Rs. (30,000 – 14,000) (int. on Capital)	800	—	—
i.e., Rs. (58,000 – 14,000) (")	—	2,200	—
i.e., Rs. (83,000 – 14,000) (")	—	—	3,450
	8,800	10,200	11,450
C's share under the new arrangement :			
Interest on deposit @ 7% on Rs. 40,000	2,800	2,800	2,800
Share of Profit :			
$\frac{1}{6}$ × Rs. 21,200*	3,533	—	—
$\frac{1}{6}$ × Rs. 49,200	—	8,200	—
$\frac{1}{6}$ × Rs. 74,200	—	—	12,367
	6,333	11,000	15,167
Less : C's share under the old arrangement	8,800	10,200	11,450
(Total Rs. 4,517)	Nil	800	3,717
***Profit under new arrangement :**			
Profit (after charging salary and interest on deposit but before charging interest on capital.)	30,000	58,000	83,000
Add : Salary (not to be paid to C)	4,800	4,800	4,800
Add : 8% Interest on deposits	3,200	3,200	3,200
	38,000	66,000	91,000
Less : Interest on Capital @ 7% (Rs. 8,400 + Rs. 5,600 + Rs. 2,800)	16,800	16,800	16,800
	21,200	49,200	74,200

Journal

Date	Particulars		L.F.	Debit	Credit
?				Rs.	Rs.
	A's Current A/c	Dr.		2,710	
	B's Current A/c	Dr.		1,807	
	To C's Current A/c				4,517
	(Adjustment made among the partners. i.e., 800 + Rs. 3,717)				

Illustration 24

C and D had been in partnership for three years, sharing profits and losses in proportion to their capitals, which had not changed during the period, and were Rs. 1,00,000 and Rs. 50,000, respectively. At the end of the third year (31.12.2009) they agree to admit their manager E into partnership as from the beginning of the partnership. E had been in receipt of a salary of Rs. 3,500 p.a. during the period, and had Rs. 30,000 on loan to the firm since its inception, upon which he had received 6% p.a. interest.

The Profit and Loss Account of the firm had shown the following results after charging partners' interest upon capitals at 5% p.a., and E's salary and the interest upon his loan :

2007 Profit Rs. 25,700; 2008 Loss Rs. 4,216; 2009 Profit Rs. 17,600

The terms upon which E was to be admitted a partner were that he should have a salary of Rs. 2,500 p.a. and one-sixth interest in the business as from 1st January 2007 and that his loan should be treated as his capital, upon which he should receive the same rate of interest like C and D. C and D's ratio as between themselves should remain unaltered.

You are required to adjust the results of each of the three years and to show how they should be divided in accordance with the arrangement.

Solution

Determination and division of profit, under new arrangement, may be computed as under :

		Rs.	Rs.		Rs.
2007 :	Profit		25,700	Distribution :	
	Add : Interest to E		300	C $\frac{10}{18} \times 27{,}000$	15,000
	Salary to E		1,000	D $\frac{5}{18} \times 27{,}000$	7,500
				E $\frac{3}{18} \times 27{,}000$	4,500
			27,000		27,000
2008 :	Loss		4,216	C $\frac{10}{18} \times 2{,}916$	1,620
	Less : Interest to E	300		D $\frac{5}{18} \times 2{,}916$	810
	Salary to E	1,000	1,300	E $\frac{3}{18} \times 2{,}916$	486
			2,916		2,916
2009 :	Profit		17,600	C $\frac{10}{18} \times 18{,}900$	10,500
	Add : Interest to E		300	D $\frac{5}{18} \times 18{,}900$	5,250
	Salary to E		1,000	E $\frac{3}{18} \times 18{,}900$	3,150
			18,900		18,900

		Rs.
From the above, E will receive :	2007	4,500
	2009	3,150
		7,650
Less : Loss in 2008	486	
Interest 300 × 3	900	
Salary 1,000 × 3	3,000	4,386
Net amount to E		3,264

Journal

Date	*Particulars*		*L.F.*	*Debit* Rs.	*Credit* Rs.
?	C's Current A/c	Dr. $\left(\frac{2}{3}\right)$		2,176	
	D's Current A/c	Dr. $\left(\frac{1}{3}\right)$		1,088	
	To E's Current A/c				3,264

CONVERSION FROM CASH BASIS TO ACCRUAL BASIS

We have already highlighted 'Cash Basis' and 'Accrual Basis' of accounting in detail earlier in Chapter 1. We have also explained therein the procedure for conversion from 'Cash Basis' to 'Accrual Basis' of accounting. However, in the present study, we are going to discuss the effect of such accountings in a partnership business.

We know that often professional people—doctors, engineers, lawyers, accountants etc.—form a partnership business and they usually follow cash basis of accounting, ignoring altogether outstanding and prepaid items thereof. They may also maintain their accounts under 'Accrual Basis' (where all outstanding and prepaid items are considered, or 'Hybrid' basis (where incomes are under cash basis and expenses are under accrual basis). But none of the above methods incorporate the following items :

(a) Debtors, including prepayments for capital and revenue expenditure; (b) Creditors, including advance payments by clients; (c) Bad Debts and Depreciation, etc.

No doubt omission of the above items create secret or undisclosed assets and liabilities and, as such, affect profit or loss. As a result, it becomes necessary to convert the existing Cash Basis into Accrual Basis by incorporating the unrecorded assets and liabilities at their present value. If assets exceed the liabilities, the said excess is to be credited to partners' capital in profit-sharing ratio, and vice versa in the opposite case.

Illustration 25

X, Y, and Z resolve to carry their legal practices as partners sharing profits and losses in the ratio 3 : 2 : 1. Up to 31st Dec. 1988, it has been the practice of the firm to ignore debtors, creditors and incompleted work. Now, it is desired, with effect from Jan. 1989, to convert the existing practice into the Accrual Basis. The figures of unrecorded items on that date are Debtors Rs. 5,000; Creditors Rs. 500, and incompleted works Rs. 6,000.

You are asked to adjust the concerned accounts.

Solution

Needless to mention here that the adjustments would be effected by incorporating the ignored assets and liabilities since the assets exceed the liabilities by Rs. 10,500 (i.e., 6,000 + 5,000 – 500). For this purpose, partners' capital accounts should be credited by 3 : 2 : 1.

Thus, the single journal entry will be :

Journal

Date	*Particulars*		*L.F.*	*Debit*	*Credit*
?				Rs.	Rs.
	Debtors A/c	Dr.		5,000	
	Incompleted Works A/c	Dr.		6,000	
	To Creditors A/c				500
	" X's Capital A/c				5,250
	" Y's Capital A/c				3,500
	" Z's Capital A/c				1,750
	(Debtors, incompleted works and creditors are adjusted.)				

When conversion is made with retrospective effect, past profits of the preceding years are recast and the net effect (increase or decrease) is to be recorded—either individually or aggregately. The former is not desirable as it requires the rebalancing of the partners' capital and other accounts for each preceding year. But the latter alternative requires simply an adjustment of accounts with the overall net result only in the year of decision for the change and, thus, the said net result will reveal an ultimate result (profit or loss) which must be shown by a corresponding increase or decrease in assets and liabilities. The necessary adjustments must be made by debiting or crediting the partners' capital or current accounts according to profit-sharing ratio.

Illustration 26

A, B, and C start to carry on partnership business on 1st Jan. 2006 as legal practitioners sharings profits and losses in 3 : 2 : 1. In determining the profits as at 31st Dec., the practice of the firm is to treat income and expenditure under cash basis.

On 1.1.2009 it is agreed to apply accrual method of income also so as to prepare their Income and Expenditure Account according to full Mercantile System with effect from 2006 :

Year	*Profit*	*Outstanding Income*
2006	50,000	10,000
2007	70,000	16,000
2008	1,00,000	24,000

Show the adjustments and the journal entries as at 1st Jan. 2009.

Solution

Workings :

Statement showing the profit under full Mercantile Accounting System :

	2006	2007	2008	Total
	Rs.	Rs.	Rs.	Rs.
(A) Profits (on the existing practice)	50,000	70,000	1,00,000	2,20,000
Add : Outstanding Income as at 31st Dec.	10,000	16,000	24,000	50,000
	60,000	86,000	1,24,000	2,70,000
Less : Outstanding Income as on 1st Jan.	—	10,000	16,000	26,000
(B) Profit on Mercantile System	60,000	76,000	1,08,000	2,44,000
(C) Excess of Profits on Mercantile System (B – A)	10,000	6,000	8,000	24,000

Thus, the journal entries will be :

Journal

Date	Particulars		L.F.	Debit	Credit
?				Rs.	Rs.
	Outstanding Income A/c	Dr.		24,000	
	To A's Capital A/c				12,000
	" B's Capital A/c				8,000
	" C's Capital A/c				4,000
	(Outstanding incomes recorded as profit transferred to partners' capital account 3 : 2 : 1)				

Illustration 27

X, Y, and Z are partners in a Chartered Accountants' firm on 1st Jan. 2006 sharing profits and losses in 3 : 2 : 1. They maintain their accounts under cash basis. Partners' Salaries are : X Rs. 6,000, Y Rs. 4,000, and Z Rs. 2,000 p.a. Moreover, Z's share is guaranteed to a fixed minimum of Rs. 6,000 (including his salary).

In 2009, they however, decide to change the accounting method, i.e., from Cash Basis to Mercantile Basis, with restrospective effect. The particulars are :

Year	Profit (on cash basis before charging Partners' Salary)	Outstanding expenses on 31st Dec.	Fees earned but not received on 31st Dec.
	Rs.	Rs.	Rs.
2006	20,000	5,000	4,000
2007	24,000	4,000	6,000
2008	48,000	3,000	5,000

You are asked to show a Single journal entry after incorporating such change in the books.

Solution :

Workings :

A. **Statement showing Profit calculated under Mercantile Basis**

		2006	2007	2008
		Rs.	Rs.	Rs.
	Profit on Cash Basis	20,000	24,000	48,000
Less :	Outstanding Expenses on 31st Dec.	5,000	4,000	3,000
		15,000	20,000	45,000
Add :	Outstanding on 1st Jan.		5,000	4,000
		15,000	25,000	49,000
Add :	Accrued Fees on 31st Dec.	4,000	6,000	5,000
		19,000	31,000	54,000
Less :	Accrued Fees on 1st Jan.		4,000	6,000
	Profit on Mercantile Basis	19,000	27,000	48,000

B. **Share of Profit under Cash Basis**

			Total	X	Y	Z
2006			Rs.	Rs.	Rs.	Rs.
		Profit	20,000	—	—	—
	Less :	Salary	12,000	6,000	4,000	2,000
			8,000			
	Less :	Z's guaranteed minimum (6,000 – 2,000)	4,000	—	—	4,000
		Balance to X and Y (3 : 2)	4,000	2,400	1,600	—
2007			Total	X	Y	Z
		Profit	24,000	—	—	—
	Less :	Salary	12,000	6,000	4,000	2,000
			12,000			
	Less :	Z's guaranteed minimum	4,000	—	—	4,000
		Balance to X and Y (3 : 2)	8,000	4,800	3,200	—
2008						
		Profit	48,000			
		Salary	12,000	6,000	4,000	2,000
		Balance to X, Y, and Z is 3 : 2 : 1	36,000	18,000	12,000	6,000
		Total		43,200	28,800	20,000

C. **Share of Profit under Mercantile Basis**

2006					
	Profit	19,000	—	—	—
	Less : Salary	12,000	6,000	4,000	2,000
		7,000			
	Less : Z's guaranteed minimum	4,000	—	—	4,000
	Balance to X and Y (3 : 2)	3,000	1,800	1,200	—
2007					
	Profit	27,000	—	—	—
	Less : Salary	12,000	6,000	4,000	2,000
		15,000			
	Less Z's guaranteed minimum	4,000	—	—	4,000
	Balance to X and Y (3 : 2)	11,000	6,600	4,400	—
2008					
	Profit	48,000	—	—	—
	Less : Salary	12,000	6,000	4,000	2,000
	Balance to X, Y, and Z (3 : 2 : 1)	36,000	18,000	12,000	6,000
			44,400	29,600	20,000
	Net Adjustments (B – C)		1,200	800	Nil

Journal

Date	*Particulars*		*L.F.*	*Debit*	*Credit*
2009				Rs.	Rs.
Jan. 1	Accrued Fees A/c	Dr.		5,000	
	To Outstanding Expenses A/c				3,000
	" X's Capital A/c				1,200
	" Y's Capital A/c				800
	(Adjustments made for change in accounting method)				

GENERAL ILLUSTRATIONS

A comprehensive illustration

Illustration 28

A, B, and C are partners in X & Co. boot-dealers. The firm controls three shops and each partner undertakes the management of one of these; C, in addition, manages a Repair Department.

The profits of each department are subject to a charge for interest at 7.5% p.a. on loan and partners' capital employed. The profits of the Repair department are, in addition, chargeable with a salary of : Rs. 4,000 p.a. in favour of C.

The profits, subject to interest and salary as stated, are apportionable thus :

Repair Department : allocable to shops in proportion to their respective shares in the turnover of this department.

Shop : including transfer from repair department, 90% to individual partners taking control of each, respectively; 10% to a general pool.

General Pool : A $\frac{1}{2}$, B $\frac{1}{3}$, and C $\frac{1}{6}$.

For the year ended 2008, Repairs Department shows profits prior to charge for interest and salary of Rs. 4,000 Rs. 8,250. Turnover of this department with shops has been A Rs. 55,000; B Rs. 30,000; C Rs. 15,000. For the same period, profits of shops prior to charge for interest are A Rs. 64,000; B Rs. 56,050, and C Rs. 42,000.

Interest has been paid on loans of Rs. 1,00,000 and the partners are entitled to interest on their capital A Rs. 1,00,000; B Rs. 70,000; C Rs. 50,000. Loan and Partners Capital employed by A shop Rs. 1,40,000; B Shop Rs. 90,000; C Shop Rs. 60,000 and Repair Department Rs. 30,000.

Prepare for the year 2008 accounts showing allocation of interest and appropriation of profits.

Solution

In the books of A, B and C

Profit and Loss Appropriation Account *for the year ended 31st Dec. 2008*

Dr. Particulars	Shop A Rs.	Shop B Rs.	Shop C Rs.	Particulars Cr.	Shop A Rs.	Shop B Rs.	Shop C Rs.
To Interest on Capital				By Profit and Loss A/c —Net Profit	64,000	56,050	42,000
Shop A— 7.5% of 1,40,000	10,500			" Repairs Department A/c			
Shop B— 7.5% of 90,000		6,750		Shop A— 55% of 2,000	1,100		
Shop C— 7.5% of 60,000			4,500	Shop B— 30% of 2,000		600	
" Balance c/d	54,600	49,900	37,800	Shop C— 15% of 2,000			300
	65,100	56,650	42,300		65,100	56,650	42,300
To Capital A/c				By Balance b/d	54,600	49,900	37,800
A—90% of 54,600	49,140						
B—90% of 49,900		44,910					
C—90% of 37,800			34,020				
" General Pool A/c @ 10%	5,460	4,990	3,780				
	54,600	49,900	37,800		54,600	49,900	37,800

Repairs Department Account

Dr. Particulars	Amount Rs.	Particulars Cr.	Amount Rs.
To Interest on Capital and Loan A/c (7.5% of 30,000)	2,250	By Profit and Loss A/c	8,250
" Salary A/c C	4,000		
" Profit and Loss Appropriation A/c			
Shop A	1,100		
Shop B	600		
Shop C	300		
	8,250		8,250

Interest on Capital and Loan Account

Dr. Particulars	Amount Rs.	Particulars Cr.	Amount Rs.
To Capital A/c (7.5% of Rs. 1,00,000)	7,500	By Profit and Loss Appropriation A/c	
" Capital A/c		Shop A	10,500
A (7.5% of 1,00,000)	7,500	Shop B	6,750
B (7.5% of Rs. 70,000)	5,250	Shop C	4,500
C (7.5% of Rs. 50,000)	3,750	" Repairs Department A/c	2,250
	24,000		24,000

General Pool Account

Dr. Particulars	Amount Rs.	Particulars Cr.	Amount Rs.
To Capital A/c:		By Profit and Loss Appropriation A/c	
A $\frac{1}{2}$	7,115	Shop A	5,460
B $\frac{1}{3}$	4,743	Shop B	4,990
C $\frac{1}{6}$	2,372	Shop C	3,780
	14,230		14,230

Cross-Guarantee

Illustration 29

Jolly and Manisha were partner of a stationery shop sharing profits and loss in the ratio of 3 : 2. Munny, who had been running a similar business, requested Jolly and Manisha to form a new partnership to which all of them agreed on the following conditions :

(i) Profits and losses should be divided in the ratio of 3 : 2 : 1.

(ii) Jolly and Manisha guaranteed to the effect that Munny's share of profit would not be lower than Rs. 45,000 p.a.

(iii) Munny guaranteed that gross fees earned by her for partnership business shall be at least equal to her average gross fees of the preceding three years when she was doing business on her own.

Her average gross fees were Rs. 75,000. The profit of the new partnership for the first accounting year ended on 31st March 2012 was Rs. 2,25,000, and the gross fees earned by Munny for the firm were Rs. 48,000.

Show the distribution of the above profit in a Profit and Loss Appropriation Account for the year ended 31st March 2012.

Solution

In the books of Jolly, Manisha and Munny

Dr. **Profit and Loss Appropriation Account** *for the year ended 31st March 2012* Cr.

Particulars		*Amount* Rs.	*Particulars*	*Amount* Rs.
To Share of Profit :			By Profit and Loss A/c —Net Profit	2,25,000
Jolly	1,24,200		" Munny's Capital A/c	27,000[1]
Manisha	82,800			
Munny	45,000			
		2,52,000[2]		
		2,52,000		2,52,000

Workings :

1. Gross fees earned by Munny was in a deficit of Rs. 27,000 (i.e., Rs. 75,000 – Rs. 48,000) which should be compensated by her out of her capital account.

2. Munny's actual share of profit—Rs. 2,52,000 × $\frac{1}{6}$ = Rs. 42,000. Since the guaranteed amount is Rs. 45,000, deficit Rs. 3,000 to be compensated by Jolly and Manisha is 3 : 2. i.e., Jolly will compensate Rs. 3,000 × $\frac{3}{5}$ = Rs. 1,800 and Manisha Rs. 1,200. Net distributable profit will be computed as :

∴ Jolly = Rs. 2,52,000 × $\frac{3}{6}$ = Rs. 1,26,000 – Rs. 1,800 = Rs. 1,24,200

Manisha = Rs. 2,52,000 × $\frac{2}{6}$ = Rs. 84,000 – Rs. 1,200 = Rs. 82,800

Munny = Rs. 2,52,000 × $\frac{1}{6}$ = Rs. 42,000 + Rs. 1,800 + Rs. 1,200 = Rs. 45,000

Illustration 30

A, B, and C are partners, managing the business at Kolkata, Mumbai and Chennai branches, respectively. The terms of agreement are :

1. A sum of Rs. 600 p.m. to be charged against the branch profits as salary to the managing partner.
2. The profits and losses, after charging salary, are to be shared in the following manner :
   (a) The managing partner of each branch has to be paid 50% of the additional profits in excess of 20% return on average capital employed at the branch; and
   (b) The balance of the profits to be pooled for division in the ratio 4 : 3 : 3.
3. Interest on capital to be charged @ 8% p.a. and on Current Account (including overdrawals) @ 6% p.a., both on the opening balances.

The following information, made available for the year 2012, to enable you to prepare the statement of distribution of profits among the partners :

(a) Drawings in addition to salary from the respective branches : A— Rs. 15,000; B— Rs. Nil; C— Rs. 22,000.

(b) Balance on Capital and Current Accounts at the beginning of the year were :
Capital Accounts : A— Rs. 90,000; B— Rs. 84,000; C— Rs. 48,000.
Current Account : A— Rs. 12,,000 (Dr.) ; B— Rs. 7,500 (Cr.); C— Rs. 5,000 (Dr.).

4. Assets and Liabilities at the close of the year at the branches were :

	Kolkata Rs.	Mumbai Rs.	Chennai Rs.
Fixed Assets	30,000	48,000	36,000
Stock	25,000	18,000	15,000
Sundry Debtors	48,000	36,000	32,000
Cash and Bank	2,000	1,800	2,200
Sundry Creditors	18,000	12,000	10,000
Outstanding Expenses	1,800	1,200	1,000

5. During the year, fixed assets remained constant; current assets increased by 20% and Sundry Creditors by 10%.

Solution

Statement showing the Calculation of Average Capital Employed and Normal Profit

	Kolkata Rs.	Rs.	Mumbai Rs.	Rs.	Chennai Rs.	Rs.
Closing Capital Employed						
Fixed Asset	30,000		48,000		36,000	
Current Assets (Stock + Debtors + Cash & Bank)	75,000		55,800		49,200	
		1,05,000		1,03,800		85,200
Less : Current Liabilities (Creditors + Out. Exp.)		19,800		13,200		11,000
(a) Capital Employed		85,200		90,600		74,200
Opening Capital Employed						
Fixed Assets	30,000		48,000		36,000	
Current Assets (Closing × $\frac{100}{120}$)	62,500		46,500		41,000	
	92,500		94,500		77,000	
Less : Current Liabilities (Closing × $\frac{100}{120}$)	18,000		12,000		10,000	
(b) Capital Employed		74,500		82,500		67,000
Increase in Capital		10,700		8,100		7,200
Add : Drawings & Salary		22,200		7,200		29,200
(c) Profit		32,900		15,300		36,400
Average Capital Employed ($\frac{a+b}{2}$)		79,850		86,550		70,600
(d) Normal Profit @ 20% on Capital Employed		15,970		17,310		14,120
Increase in profit (c – d)		16,930		—		22,280
Managing partner's share @ 50%		8,465		—		11,140

Profit and Loss Appropriation Account *for the year ended 31st Dec. 2012*

Dr. Particulars	Kolkata Rs.	Mumbai Rs.	Chennai Rs.	Particulars	Kolkata Rs.	Mumbai Rs.	Cr. Chennai Rs.
To Salary				By Profit & Loss A/c —Net Profit	32,900	15,300	36,400
A	7,200						
B		7,200					
C			7,200				
" Share of extra Profit							
A	8,465						
C			11,140				
" Balance c/d	17,235	8,100	18,060				
	32,900	15,300	36,400		32,900	15,300	36,400

Contd

		Rs.			Rs.
To Interest on Current A/c—B @ 6%		450	By Balance b/d		
" Interest on Capital @ 8%			Kolkata		17,235
A		7,200	Mumbai		8,100
B		6,720	Chennai		18,060
C		3,840	" Interest on Current A/c		
" Share of Profit			A @ 6%		720
A	10,482		C @ 6%		300
B	7,862				
C	7,861				
		26,205			
		44,415			44,415

ASSIGNMENT MATERIALS

THEORETICAL

Short-Answer Type Questions

1. Distinguish between 'Fluctuating Capital' and 'Fixed Capital'.
2. What is Deed of Partnership? Distinguish between Partnership and Co-partnership.
3. How is interest on drawing calculated where there are several withdrawals at unequal intervals ?
4. Discuss the effect of Non-registration of a partnership firm.
5. What is a Profit and Loss Appropriation Account? Why is it so prepared ?
6. Discuss the treatment of Interest on Partners' Loan in partnership accounting.
7. Why do we open Current Account?
8. Distinguish between Capital Account and the Current Account of the partners.
9. Discuss the Rights and Duties of the partners. What is Implied Authority of a partner?
10. How do you treat the following in the books of the firm :
    (i) Interest on Capital ; (ii) Interest on Drawing, and (iii) Interest on Loan ?
11. (a) In the absence of a partnership deed, how would you decide the following :
    (i) Interest on Partners' Capital ; (ii) Interest on Partners' Drawings; (iii) Partners' Salaries; (iv) Partners' Commission; (v) Interest on Partners' Loan; (vi) Profit-sharing ratio?
12. A and B entered into a partnership having no Partnership Deed. Will the following claims made by A and B be legally enforceable:
    (i) A claims that interest on capital should be charged @ 12% p.a. B does not agree.
    (ii) B claims that interest on loan should be charged @ 15% p.a. A does not agree.
    (iii) B claims that interest on drawings should be calculated @ 12% p.a. A does not agree.
    (iv) A claims that profit should be shared between them according to capital ratio. B does not agree?
    (v) A claims that he should draw a salary of Rs. 6,000 p.a. being an active partner B does not agree?

Long-Answer Type Questions

13. What is Deed of Partnership?
14. Distinguish between Partnership and Co-partnership.
15. Is registration of partnership compulsory? Discuss the effects of non-registration of firms.
16. Explain the rules that are applicable where there is no partnership agreement.
17. Explain the implied authority of a partner.
18. Explain the Rights and Duties of partners.
19. Discuss the different types of partners.
20. How do you calculate the interest on drawings? Explain with the help of an example.
21. Distinguish between fluctuating capital and fixed capital in a partnership firm.
22. What is Profit and Loss Appropriation Account? How do you prepare it?
23. How do you treat interest on capital? Explain it in details.
24. How do you treat in accountwhen an employee is admitted in a firm?
25. How do you convert cash basis of accounting into accrual basis of accounting in case of a partnership firm?

PRACTICAL

1. A and B are partners in a firm sharing profits and losses of A $\frac{3}{4}$ths and B $\frac{1}{4}$th. The Profit and Loss Account of the firm for the year ended 31.3.2009 shows a net profit of Rs. 75,000.

You are required to prepare the Profit and Loss Appropriation Account by taking into consideration the undermentioned information :

(i) The Partners' Capital Account A Rs. 40,000; B Rs. 30,000. Interest on capital is to be calculated at 5% p.a. (ii) The Current Accounts of partners : A Rs. 15,000 (Cr.); B Rs. 10,000 (Cr.). (iii) Partners' drawing amounted to A Rs. 10,000; B. Rs. 7,500. Interest on drawings was to be charged at 10% p.a. at an average of 6 months. (iv) Partners' salaries A Rs. 6,000; B Rs. 4,500. (v) A's Loan A/c Rs. 25,000 (the loan was taken two years back). Give the Partners' Current Account also.

[Ans. Net Divisible Profit Rs. 60,375; Share of Profit; A Rs. 45,281; B Rs. 15,094; Closing balances of Current Account; A Rs. 59,281, B Rs. 23,219]

2. A, B, and C are partners sharing Profits and Losses in the proportion of 4 : 3 : 2.

During 2004 their Fixed Capital and Drawings (including salaries) :

Partners	Fixed Capital	Drawing including Salaries
	Rs.	Rs.
A	2,40,000	24,000
B	1,60,000	18,000
C	1,00,000	15,000

Each partner is entitled to a salary of Rs. 1,000 p.m. and interest @ 5% on the capital.

At the middle of the year A made an advance of Rs. 1,00,000 to the firm bearing interest at 6% p.a. The net profit for the year stood at Rs. 1,09,000 before charging interest on capital and loan but after charging partners' salaries.

Prepare the Partners' Current Account.

[Ans. Net Distributable Profit Rs. 81,000; A Rs. 36,000; B Rs. 27,000 and C Rs. 18,000; Balance of Current A/c (Cr.) : A Rs. 39,000, B Rs. 29,000 and C Rs. 20,000]

3. Rana, Saikat and Ram are partners with capitals of Rs. 1,00,000; Rs. 60,000 and Rs. 40,000, respectively. Their partnership deed provides that :

(i) Interest on partners' capital should be provided @ 5% p.a.;

(ii) Interest on partners drawings should be provided @ 10% p.a. (Drawings : Rana Rs. 10,000; Saikat Rs. 6,000 and Ram Rs. 4,000)

(iii) The partners are entitled to a partnership salary of Rs. 5,000 each p.a.

(iv) Rana is entitled to a commission @ 10% on the profit before charging the above provisions.

(v) Ram is entitled to a commision @ 10% on the net profit (after charging the above provisions) after charging his commission.

(vi) 25% of the net profit (after charging all the above provisions) should be transferred to Reserve Fund.

(vii) Partners will share profits or losses in the ratio of their capital,

The profit for the year ended 31.12.2005 amounted to Rs. 60,000.

You are required to prepare the Profit and Loss Appropriation Account and the Partners' Capital Accounts.

[Ans. Net Distributable Profit Rs. 20,455, Transferred to Reserve Fund Rs. 6,818; Share of Profit : Rana Rs. 10,228, Saikat Rs. 6,136, Ram Rs. 4,091, Ram's Com. Rs. 2,727; Closing balances of Capital A/c : Rana Rs. 1,15,728, Saikat Rs. 67,836, Ram Rs. 49,618]

4. M/s P, R, & Z are in partnership and on 1.4.2011; their respective capital was Rs. 80,000, Rs. 55,000 and Rs. 31,800. R and Z are entitled to draw salary of Rs. 5,000 and Rs. 4,000 per annum, respectively, before division of profits. Interest is allowed on capital @ 10%. p.a. and is not charged on drawings. Of the net profit first Rs. 20,000 is divided in the ratio of 40 : 35 : 25 among P, R and Z, respectively. Balance profit is shared equally.

The profit for the year ended 31.3.2012, after debiting partners' Salaries but before charging interest on Capital, was Rs. 46,340 and the partners had drawn Rs. 16,000 each for personal expenses.

Prepare Profit & Loss Appropriation Account and Partners' Capital Accounts for the year ended 31.3.2012.

[Ans. Share of Profit : P Rs. 11,220; R Rs. 10,220; Z Rs. 8,220; Closing balance of Capital A/c : P Rs. 83,220; R Rs. 59,720; Z Rs. 31,220]

5. King, Queen, and Prince are partners sharing profit and loss in proportion of 4 : 3 : 2. Prepare the Partners' Capital and Current Acccounts, as also the Profit and Loss Appropriation Account for the year ending 31.3.2011:

Detail available for :	King Rs.	Queen Rs.	Prince Rs
Capital as on 1.4.2010	60,000	90,000	1,50,000
Drawing during the year (including Salaries)	16,000	10,800	11,600
Salary Allowed p.m.	500	400	300
Interest on Capital @	10%	10%	10%
Interest on Drawing	500	300	400

Net Profit for the year after charging partners' salaries but before making other appropriations amounted to Rs. 82,206.

[Ans. Net Divisible Profit : Rs. 53,406; Balance of Current : King Rs. 19,236; Queen Rs. 20,502; Prince Rs. 18,468]

6. Ripa, Rani, and Rima are three partners in a firm. According to their partnership deed, the partners are entitled to draw Rs. 700 per month. On 1st day of every month Ripa, Rani, and Rima drew Rs. 700, Rs. 600, and Rs. 500, respectively. Interest on capitals and interest on drawings are fixed at 8% and 10%, respectively. Profit during the year 2004 was Rs. 75,500. Out of which Rs. 20,000 is to be transferred to General Reserve. Rani and Rima are entitled to receive salary of Rs. 3,000 and 4,500 p.a., respectiely, and Ripa is entitled to receive commission at 10% on net distributable profit after charging such commission . On 1st January 2004 the balances of their Capital Accounts were Rs. 50,000, Rs. 40,000, and Rs. 35,000, respectively.

You are required to show Profit and Loss Appropriation Account for the year ended 31st December 2004 and the Capital Account of partners in the books of the firm.

[Ans. Profit Rs. 35,609; Com. Rs. 3,561; Balance Divisible for Capital A/c : Ripa Rs. 60,576; Rani Rs. 50,480; Rima Rs. 47,844]

7. Below is the Profit and Loss Appropriation Account of A & Co. for the year ended 31.12.2012 :

			Rs.			Rs.
To	Interest on Capital :			By	Net profit	50,000
	X 6% on Rs. 50,000		3,000	"	Interest on Drawings :	
	Y 6% on Rs. 30,000		1,800		X 5% on Rs. 12,000	600
"	Partners' Salary :				Y 5% on Rs. 10,000	500
	X		3,600			
"	Share of Profits :					
	X	Rs. 25,620				
	Y	Rs. 17,080				
			42,700			
			51,100			51,100

The entries were duly passed in the books but the following discrepancies were subsequently discovered :

(1) Interest on capital should be charged at 5% and that on drawings at 6% p.a.

(2) X was not entitled to any partnership salary but Y was entitled to a salary of Rs. 200 p.m. not yet drawn by him.

(3) Profits to be shared in capital ratio.

(4) A loan of Rs. 10,000 stood in the books in the name of A carrying 6% interest p.a.

Pass journal entries to set these right.

[Ans. X's Current A/c (Dr.) Rs. 1,592; Y's Current A/c (Cr.) Rs. 1,592]

8. Ashok and Bimal are partners in a firm, commencing business on 1st July 2010 with capitals of Rs. 90,000 and Rs. 60,000, respectively. The capitals remain fixed and profits are shared in proportion to their capitals—which carry interest at 5% p.a. They appointed Chandipada, their manager, on 1.7.2010 at a salary of Rs. 300 p.m. plus a bonus of 5% of the profits which—subject to this charge and interest on capital would be divisible between Ashoke and Bimal. On 1.7.2010, Chandipada deposited Rs. 30,000, carrying interest at 6% p.a. In July 2013, it was agreed that Chandipada should be treated as a partner from 1.7.2010, entitling him to one-sixth of the profits but his deposits would carry 5% interest instead of 6% he had received. It was further arranged that in any case, however, Chandipada's share for any past year should not be less than what he had received under the original terms.

The profits before providing for Chandipada's bonus and interest on capital or giving effect to the new arrangements were : 2010-11 Rs. 24,000; 2011-12 Rs. 42,000; 2012-13 Rs. 60,000.

Show by single journal entry, with detailed explanatory narration, the adjustments necessary for the new arrangements.

[CU BCom (Hons.)]

[Ans. Asoke's Current A/c (Dr.) Rs. 2,190; Bimal's Current A/c (Dr.) Rs. 1,460; Chandipada's Current A/c (Cr.) Rs. 3,650]

9. Ram and Rahim are in partnership sharing profits and losses in the ratio of 3 : 2. As Ram, on account of his advancing years, feels he cannot work as hard as before, the chief clerk of the firm, Ratan, is admitted as a partner with effect from 1st January 2012, and becomes entitled to $\frac{1}{10}$ th of the net profits and nothing else, the mutual ratio between Ram and Rahim remaining unaltered.

Before becoming a partner, Ratan was getting a salary of Rs. 500 p.m. together with a commission of 4% on the net profits after deducting his salary and commission.

It is provided in the partnership deed that the share of Ratan's profits as a partner—in excess of the amount to which he would have been entitled if he had continued as the chief clerk—should be taken out of Ram's share of profits.

The net profit for the year ended Dec. 31, 2012, amounted to Rs. 1,10,000.

Draw up the ledger accounts for the net profit showing the distribution amongst the partners.

[Ans. Ram Rs. 59,000; Rahim Rs. 40,000; Ratan Rs. 11,000]

10. Kalyani & Ranu commenced business on 1st July 2010 as partners with capitals of Rs. 1,80,000 and Rs. 1,20,000, respectively. The capitals remain fixed and carry interest @ 10% p.a. Profits and Losses are to be shared in proportion to their capitals.

They appointed Anita as their manager on 1st July 2010 at a salary of Rs. 9,600 p.a. plus a bonus of 5% of the profits after charging such bonus and interest on capital. Anita had to deposit on 1st July 2010 Rs. 80,000 as security carrying interest at 12% p.a.

In June 2013 it was settled that Anita should be treated as a partner from the commencement of the business. It was agreed that she would be entitled to $\frac{1}{5}$th of the profits and her security deposit would be treated as her capital carrying interest at 10% p.a. instead of the 12% she had received. It was further agreed that this new arrangement should not result in Anita's share for any of these years being less than she had already received under the original agreement and terms of her appointment.

The Profits before charging Anita's bonus and interest on capital of partners for giving effect to the new arrangement were : (a) for the year 2010-11 Rs. 60,000; (b) for the year 2011-12 Rs. 1,20,000; (c) for the year 2012-13 Rs. 1,60,000.

Show by a single Journal entry how to give effect to the new arrangement with explanatory computations.

[CU BCom (Hons.)]

[Ans. Kalyani (Dr.) Rs. 5,882; Ranu (Dr.) Rs. 3,922; Anita (Cr.) Rs. 9,804]

11. The firm A, B, and C has existed for some years, Profits being shared as 2/5, 2/5 and 1/5, respectively. C, however, feels that this arrangement has not been satisfactory to him and requires to be placed on same basis as regards profits as A and B. He further wants that this arrangement shall apply

not only to future profits but also, retrospectively, to the profits of the past three years which were Rs. 26,000, Rs. 22,100 and Rs. 25,805, respectiveely. A and B have no objection to this. They further agree that in making such adjustment regards should be had to Rs. 6,500 value of goods which had been charged to profits but which actually were taken privately by B and Rs. 3,900 of office equipment for which no Asset Account had been opened in the books but charged to the Profit and Loss Account. Plant and Machinery of the firm had not been depreciated over past years and it was estimated that the total of the amounts which should have been written-off was Rs. 9,035. It was further agreed that, after adjustment, the Capital Accounts were to be equalised without, however, increasing or reducing the total capital of the firm.

Show the Adjustment Account and the Capital Accounts of the partners after giving effect to the above agreement, assuming that immediately after the distribution of last year's profits, Capital Accounts stood: A—Rs. 52,000; B—Rs. 39,000; C—Rs. 27,430.

[Ans. Net Distributable Profits Rs. 75,270; Closing Balance of Capital A/c A, B, and C Rs. 37,765 each; Cash to be withdrawn by A Rs. 9,763 and to be brought in by B and C Rs. 9,737 and Rs. 26]

12. Mehra & Ratnam are in partnership with capital of Rs. 28,000 and Rs. 14,000, respectively, sharing profits and losses as 2 : 1. Interest on Capital @ 5% p.a. and salary Rs. 2,800 p.a. to Ratnam are available.

Due to ill-health, Mehra ceased to take active part in the business with effect from 1.1.2012 and the following terms were agreed upon :

(i) That the manager, Jahar, shall be taken as a partner with a Capital of Rs. 5,000, he being entitled to a Salary of Rs. 5,250 p.a., the excess over Rs. 2,800 (the salary received by him as manager) to be borne by Mehra personally.

(ii) That Ratnam shall get a Salary of Rs. 3,500 p.a.

(iii) That Jahar shall be entitled to one-tenth share of Profits and Losses after charging interest on capital and partners' salaries.

(iv) That interest on capital shall be allowed @ 5% p.a. The net profit for the year ended 31.12.2012 was Rs. 22,400 before charging interest on capital and partners' salaries.

You are required to show the division of profits for the year 2012 between the partners.

[Ans. Jahar's Share Rs. 1,130; Ratnam's Share Rs. 4,125, and Mehra's Share Rs. 6,045]

13. A and B were in partnership sharing Profits and Losses in the ratio of 3 : 2. While drawing up their Annual Accounts it had been their practice to ignore accrued income and outstanding expense. Under a new partnership agreement entered into on 1st January 2010 they decided to share the profits earned in any year on the following bases :

Up to Rs. 25,000—Equally. Excess over Rs. 25,000—A $\frac{2}{3}$ rd, B $\frac{1}{3}$ rd

At the end of 2012 it was discovered that although they were sharing the profits as per the new agreement they continued to draw the Annual Accounts on the old basis. It was agreed that necessary correcting entries should be put through in December 2012. The relevant figures are extracted as:

	2009 Rs.	2010 Rs.	2011 Rs.	2012 Rs.
Profits already shared as on 31st December :	—	21,000	23,000	31,000
Accured Income	2,000	3,500	5,000	2,500
Outstanding Expenses	500	1,000.	1,300	300

You are required to give the necessary entries to correct the partners' accounts showing your workings, assuming that the books of accounts were duly closed at the end of each year.

[ICWA]

[Ans. Net Effect 2009 Profit Rs. 1,500 divided @ 3 : 2; 2010 Profit Rs. 1,000 equally; 2011 Profit Rs. 1,200 equally;2012 Loss Rs. 1,500 divided @ 2 : 1; Overall Net Credit to A Rs. 1,000 and B Rs. 1,200]

B. ADMISSION OF A NEW PARTNER

When an existing firm needs more finance for extension and development and/or technical skill, it appoints a new partner, of course with the consent of all the partners. But there are 'certain' adjustments which are to be adjusted at the time of admission of a new partner. The adjustments are :

1. Regarding Profit-Sharing Ratio;
2. Regarding Revaluation of Assets and Liabilities;
3. Regarding Accumulated Profits/Losses and/or, Reserves and Surplus;
4. Regarding Adjustment for Goodwill;
5. Regarding Adjustment in Capital, i.e., Proportionate Capital Contribution.

1. Regarding Profit-sharing Ratio

It is needless to mention that when a new partner is admitted, he is entitled to share some future profits of the firm as per agreement. Naturally, the old partners sacrifice the same from the their combined shares. The new partner may have such share even either from only one partner or from all. However, it must be remembered that, ***unless otherwise stated, the profit-sharing ratio between/among the old partners will remain unaltered/unaffected.***

Consider the following examples one by one :

Example 1

A and B are partners sharing profits and losses in the ratio of 3 : 2. They take C into partnership for $\frac{1}{4}$ share in the business. Calculate the future profits-sharing ratio.

Solution

Calculation showing Future Profit-sharing Ratio

$1-\frac{1}{4}=\frac{3}{4}$ Now, A gets $=\frac{3}{4}\times\frac{3}{5}=\frac{9}{20}$; B gets $=\frac{3}{4}\times\frac{2}{5}=\frac{6}{20}$; C gets $\frac{1}{4}=\frac{5}{20}$

Sacrificing Ratio : $\therefore$ A : B : C = 9 : 6 : 5.

Example 2

A and B are partners sharing profits and losses in the ratio of 3 : 2. They take C into partnership. The new profit-sharing ratio is 4 : 3 : 2 among A, B, and C. Calculate the sacrificing ratio.

Solution

Students are to remember that when both the old ratio and the new ratio will be given, they are to compute the sacrificing ratio—

The same is computed as :

$A=\frac{3}{5}-\frac{4}{9}=\frac{27-20}{45}=\frac{7}{45}$ (sacrifices) $B=\frac{2}{5}-\frac{3}{9}=\frac{18-15}{45}=\frac{3}{45}$ (sacrifices)

$C=\frac{7}{45}+\frac{3}{45}=\frac{10}{45}$ (gains) So, the sacrificing ratio between A and B is 7 : 3.

Example 3

A and B are partners sharing profits and losses in the ratio of 7 : 5. They take C into partnership. C is given $\frac{1}{6}$th share which he acquires $\frac{1}{24}$ from A and $\frac{1}{8}$th from B.

Calculate the furture profit-sharing ratio and also the sacrificing ratio.

Solution

Computation of Profit-sharing Ratio :

$A=\frac{7}{12}-\frac{1}{24}=\frac{14-1}{24}=\frac{13}{24}$

$B=\frac{5}{12}-\frac{1}{8}=\frac{10-3}{24}=\frac{7}{24}$

$C=\frac{1}{24}+\frac{1}{8}=\frac{1+3}{24}=\frac{4}{24}$

$\therefore$ Future profit-sharing ratio is : A : B : C = 13 : 7 : 4.

Sacrificing Ratio :

A sacrifices $\frac{1}{24}$

B sacrifices $\frac{1}{8}$

$\therefore$ Sacrificing Ratio is 1 : 3.

Example 4

A and B are in partnership sharing profits and losses in the ratio of 4 : 1. They take C into partnership for $\frac{1}{3}$ share of the profits between themselves. A and B agree to share furture profits and losses equally. Calculate the (a) future profit-sharing ratio; (b) sacrificing/gaining ratio.

Solution

(a) **Future Profit-sharing Ratio**

Since, C is given $\frac{1}{3}$rd profit, the remaining $\frac{2}{3}$ is taken by A and B equally, i.e., $\frac{1}{3}$rd each, so, the future profit-sharing ratio is equal, i.e., A : B : C = 1 : 1 : 1.

(b) **Sacrificing/Gaining Ratio**

$A = \frac{4}{5} - \frac{1}{3} = \frac{12-5}{15} = \frac{7}{15}$ (sacrifices) $\quad B = \frac{1}{5} - \frac{1}{3} = \frac{3-5}{15} = \frac{(-)2}{15}$ (gains)

$C = \frac{1}{3} = \frac{5}{15}$ (gains)

Here, A sacrifices alone $\frac{7}{15}$th from his share, out of which C takes $\frac{5}{15}$ and B takes $\frac{2}{15}$, i.e., B gains by $\frac{2}{15}$th.

2. Regarding Revaluation of Assets and Liabilities

It becomes necessary to revalue the assets and liabilities of the firm at the time of admission of a new partner in order to ascertain their true values; i.e., current market value of the assets should be ascertained, or some liabilities may be forgone the benefit of which will be enjoyed by the old partners, e.g., value of land may be appreciated, value of plant may be depreciated, some amount may be written-off as bad against some debtors, or stock may be undervalued or overvalued etc. It is needless to mention here that whatever the benefits arising from such revaluation of assets or liabilities will be enjoyed by the old partners. Similarly, in the opposite case, i.e., if there is any loss, the same is also to be suffered by the existing/old partners. The new partner will neither share the benefit nor will suffer for the loss.

In order to incorporate the revised values of assets and liabilities, **a Revaluation Account** or **Profit and Loss Adjustment Account** is to be opened for the purpose. This account will incorporate all such changes that are made in various assets and liabilities. The result of this account will show either a profit or a loss which will be transferred to old partners' Capital Account or Current Account in the old profit-sharing ratio.

The object of revaluation of assets and liabilities is to show the correct or current market values of assets and liabilities which will exhibit the current financial position at the time of admission of a partner. It is quite natural that the benefits or losses should be shared by the existing/old partners who are really responsible.

In this context, it is very relevant to refer **Ind AS 16 Property, Plant and Equipment**, paras 39-41, —which state :

39. "If an asset's carrying amount is increased as a result of revaluation the increase shall be recognised in other comprehensive income and accumulated in equity under the heading of **Revaluation Surplus**. However, the increase shall be recognised in profit or loss to the extent that it reverses a revaluation decrease of the same asset previously recognised in profit or loss."

40. "If an asset's carrying amount is decreased as a result of revaluation, the decrease shall be recognised in profit or loss. However, the decrease shall be recognised in other comprehensive income to the extent of any credit balance existing in the revaluation surplus in respect of that asset. The decrease recognised in other comprehensive income reduces the amount accumulated in equity under the heading of Revaluation Surplus."

41. "The revaluation surplus included in equity in respect of an item of **Property, Plant and Equipment** may be transferred directly to retain earnings when the asset is derecognised. This may involve transferring the whole of the surplus when the asset is retained or disposed of. However, some of the surplus may be transferred as the asset is used by the entity. In such a case, the amount of the surplus transferred would be the difference between depreciation based on the revalued carrying amount of the asset and depreciation based on the asset's original cost. Transfers from revaluation surplus to retain earnings are not made through profit or loss."

As per Partnership : Both the increase in net book value of fixed assets and the decrease in the net book value of fixed assets is credited and debited, respectively, to Revaluation Account. The profit or loss on revaluation is transferred to Partners' Capital Account.

However, the result of both the treatments is ultimately the same, i.e., they will be transferred to Partners' Capital Account.

***While solving the subsequent problems, we have used Revaluation Account for incorporating the net increase or net decrease in value of fixed assets in place of Revaluation Surplus Account which has been suggested by* Ind AS 16.**

Accounting Entries

(a) ***When revised values are to be shown***

The entries are

(a) ***When the value of the assets are increased***

Assets A/c	Dr.	only the increased value
To Revaluation A/c		

(b) ***When the value of the assets are reduced***

Revaluation A/c	Dr.	only the decreased value
To Assets A/c		

(c) ***When the value of liabilities are increased***

Revaluation A/c	Dr.	only the increased value
To Liabilities A/c		

(d) ***When the value of the liabilities are reduced***

Liabilities A/c	Dr.	only the decreased value
To Revaluation A/c		

(e) (i) ***For profit on Revaluation***

Revaluation A/c	Dr.
To Old Partners' Capital A/c	

(ii) ***For loss on Revaluation***

Old Partners' Capital A/c	Dr.
To Revaluation A/c	

Now, the above entries depend upon two conditions :

(a) When *Revalued Figures* of assets and liabilities are shown in the Balance Sheet.

(b) When *Original Figures* of assets and liabilities were shown in the Balance Sheet.

Illustration 1

(a) When revalued figures are shown

A and B were in partnership sharing profits and losses in the ratio of 3 : 2. Their Balance Sheet as on 30.6.2012 was :

Balance Sheet ***as at 30th June 2012***

	Rs.	Rs.		Rs.	Rs.
Capital Accounts :			Plant and Machinery		40,000
A	60,000		Land and Buildings		30,000
B	40,000		Furniture		10,000
		1,00,000	Stock		20,000
Creditors		30,000	Debtors	25,000	
			Less : Provision	2,500	22,500
			Cash		7,500
		1,30,000			1,30,000

They want to take C into partnership. But the following adjustments are to be incorporated :

(a) C pays Rs. 30,000 as capital for $\frac{1}{5}$th share in the business.

(b) The value of Plant and Machinery should be increased by 20% whereas the value of Land and Building should be reduced to Rs. 25,000.

(c) Certain investments amounting to Rs. 8,000 (not included in the above Balance Sheet) should be brought into account.

(d) The provision for doubtful debts should be increased to Rs. 5,000.

(e) An item of Rs. 1,000 included in Sundry Creditors is not likely to be claimed.

Give the necessary Journal entries to incorporate the above arrangements and prepare Revaluations Account, Partners' Capital Accounts and the revised Balance Sheet.

Solution

In the Books of A, B, and C
Journal

Date	Particulars		L.F.	Debit	Credit
1012				Rs.	Rs.
June 30	Cash A/c	Dr.		30,000	
	To C's Capital A/c				30,000
	(Cash brought in by C as capital)				
June 30	Plant and Machinery A/c	Dr.		8,000	
	Investment A/c	Dr.		8,000	
	Creditors' A/c	Dr.		1,000	
	To Revaluation A/c				17,000
	(Value of Plant and Machinery and Investment increased and value of Creditors decreased)				
	Revaluation A/c	Dr.		7,500	
	To Land and Building A/c				5,000
	" Provision for Doubtful Debts A/c				2,500
	(Value of the assets decreased on revaluation)				
	Revaluation A/c	Dr.		9,500	
	To A's Capital A/c				5,700
	" B's Capital A/c				3,800
	(Profit on revaluation transferred to capital accounts)				

Revaluation Account

Dr. Cr.

Particulars		Amount	Particulars	Amount
	Rs.	Rs.		Rs.
To Land and Building A/c		5,000	By Plant and Machinery A/c	8,000
" Provisions for Bad Debts A/c		2,500	Investments A/c	8,000
" Profit on Revaluation :			Creditors A/c	1,000
A $\frac{3}{5}$	5,700			
B $\frac{2}{5}$	3,800			
		9,500		
		17,000		17,000

Capital Account

Dr. Cr.

Particulars	A	B	C	Particulars	A	B	C
	Rs.	Rs.	Rs.		Rs.	Rs.	Rs.
To Balance c/d	65,700	43,800	30,000	By Balance b/d	60,000	40,000	—
				" Cash A/c	—	—	30,000
				" Revaluation A/c — Profit	5,700	3,800	—
	65,700	43,800	30,000		65,700	43,800	30,000
				By Balance b/d	65,700	43,800	30,000

Balance Sheet *as at 30th June 2012*

Liabilities		Amount	Assets		Amount
	Rs.	Rs.		Rs.	Rs.
Capital Accounts			Plant and Machinery		48,000
A	65,700		Land and Building		25,000
B	43,800		Furniture		10,000
C	30,000		Investments		8,000
		1,39,500	Stock		20,000
Creditors		29,000	Debtors	25,000	
			Less : Provision for Bad Debts	5,000	20,000
			Cash		37,500
		1,68,500			1,68,500

(b) When original values only shown, or when revised values are not to be recorded

Sometimes it is desired by the partners, including the new partner, that the revised values of assets and liabilities should not be shown in the new Balance Sheet, i.e., all such entries which are passed through Revaluation Account are reversed. For that purpose, we are to open a ***Memorandum Revaluation Account***. For instance, if Revaluation Account is debited and Plant Account is credited (for decreased value of Plant), in that case, the reverse entry will be to debit Plant Account and credit Revaluation Account. ***The Memorandum Revaluation Account is closed by transferring to Partners' Capital Accounts (including new partners) in new profit-sharing ratios.***

Illustration 2

Considering the previous problem, if the partners desire not to show the revalued figures of assets and liabilities, i.e., assets and liabilities are shown at old values, the Revaluation Account will be as under :

Solution

Dr. **Memorandum Revaluation Account** Cr.

Particulars	Rs.	Amount Rs.	Particulars	Rs.	Amount Rs.
To Land and Building A/c		5,000	By Plant and Machinery A/c		8,000
" Provision for Bad Debts A/c		2,500	" Investments A/c		8,000
" Profit on Revaluation :			" Creditors A/c		1,000
A $\frac{3}{5}$	5,700				
B $\frac{2}{5}$	3,800	9,500			
		17,000			17,000
To *Reversal of Items*			By *Reversal of Items*		
Plant and Machinery	8,000		Land and Building	5,000	
Investments	8,000		Prov. for Bad Debts	2,500	
Creditors	1,000				7,500
		17,000	" **Profit on Revaluation (Written-back)**		
			A $\frac{12}{25} \times 9,500 =$	4,560	
			B $\frac{8}{25} \times 9,500 =$	3,040	
			C $\frac{5}{25} \times 9,500 =$	1,900	9,500
		17,000			17,000

Dr. **Capital Account** Cr.

Particulars	A Rs.	B Rs.	C Rs.	Particulars	A Rs.	B Rs.	C Rs.
To Revaluation A/c — Profit written-back	4,560	3,040	1,900	By Balance b/d	60,000	40,000	—
" Balance c/d	61,140	40,760	28,100	" Cash	—	—	30,000
				" Revaluation A/c —Profit	5,700	3,800	—
	65,700	43,800	30,000		65,700	43.800	30,000
				By Balance b/d	61,140	40,760	28,100

Balance Sheet *as at 30th June 2012*

Liabilities	Rs.	Rs.	Assets	Rs.	Rs.
Capital :			Plant and Machinery		40,000
A	61,140		Land and Building		30,000
B	40,760		Furniture		10,000
C	28,100		Stock		20,000
		1,30,000	Debtors	25,000	
Creditors		30,000	*Less* : Provision	2,500	22,500
			Cash (7,500 + 30,000)		37,500
		1,60,000			1,60,000

Notes

1. From the above, it is quite clear that, except cash, no other assets and liabilities are changed, i.e., they remain at their original/book value.
2. The new profit-sharing ratio is calculated as :

$$1-\frac{1}{5}=\frac{4}{5} \qquad A=\frac{4}{5}\times\frac{3}{5}=\frac{12}{25};\ B=\frac{4}{5}\times\frac{2}{5}=\frac{8}{25};\ C=\frac{1}{5}=\frac{5}{25}$$

Thus, the ratio is : A : B : C = 12 : 8 : 5.

Illustration 3

M and S are partners sharing profits and losses in the proportion of $\frac{2}{3}$ and $\frac{1}{3}$. Their Balance Sheet as at 31.3.2012 stands as:

Liabilities	Rs.	Rs.	*Assets*	Rs.
Sundry Creditors		44,000	Cash at Bank	17,000
Capital Accounts :			Sundry Debtors	15,000
M	30,000		Bills Receivable	4,000
S	20,000		Stock	25,000
		50,000	Furniture and Fixture	3,000
			Land and Building	30,000
		94,000		94,000

R is admitted to partnership with effect from 1st April on the following terms :

(a) That he brings in Rs. 15,000 as his capital for $\frac{1}{4}$th share and pays Rs. 6,000 for goodwill, half of which is to be withdrawn by M and S;
(b) That there is likely to be a claim against the firm for damages for which a provision to the extent of Rs. 1,500 is to be made;
(c) That a bill for Rs. 300 for electric charges had been omitted to be accounted. It should, therefore, now be provided for;
(d) That the stock is to be reduced to Rs. 24,000 and Furniture and Fixtures by Rs. 500;
(e) That 5% Reserve for Bad and Doubtful Debts to be created;
(f) The value of Land and Building is to be appreciated by 20%;
(g) That included in the Sundry Creditors is an item of Rs. 1,200 which is not to be paid and, therefore, has to be written-back; and unrecorded creditors amounted to Rs. 500;
(h) That the profit-sharing ratio of the old firm will not change;
(i) A contingent liabiliy of Rs. 1,000 not included in the above Balance Sheet had to be paid for.

You are required to show the necessary accounts and the Balance Sheet of the new firm.

Solution

In the Books of M, S, and R
Revaluation Account

Dr. Cr.

	Particulars	Rs.	*Amount* Rs.		*Particulars*	*Amount* Rs.
To	Bank A/c (Contingent Liabilities)		1,000			
"	Provision for Damages		1,500	By	Land and Building	6,000
"	Outstanding Electric Bill		300	"	Sundry Creditors	1,200
"	Stock		1,000			
"	Furniture and Fixtures		500			
"	Reserve for Bad Debts		750			
To	Unrecorded Creditors		500			
"	Profit on Revaluation :					
	M $\frac{2}{3}$	1,100				
	S $\frac{1}{3}$	550	1,650			
			7,200			7,200

Dr. **Capital Account** Cr.

Particulars	M	S	R	Particulars	M	S	R
	Rs.	Rs.	Rs.		Rs.	Rs.	Rs.
To Bank (Goodwill withdrawn)	2,000	1,000	—	By Balance b/d	30,000	20,000	—
" Balance c/d	33,100	21,550	15,000	" Goodwill	4,000	2,000	—
				" Revaluation	1,100	550	—
				" Bank	—	—	15,000
	35,100	22,550	15,000		35,100	22,550	15,000
				By Balance b/d	33,100	21,550	15,000

Balance Sheet *as at 1st April 2012*

Liabilities	Rs.	Rs.	Assets	Rs.
Capital Account :			Land and Building (Rs. 30,000 + 6,000)	36,000
M	33,100		Furniture and Fixtures (Rs. 3,000 – Rs. 1,000)	2,000
S	21,550		Stock (Rs. 25,000 – Rs. 2,000)	23,000
R	15,000		Sundry Debtors (Rs. 15,000 – Rs. 750)	14,250
		69,650	Bills Receivable	4,000
Creditors (Rs. 44,000 – Rs. 1,200)		42,800	Cash at Bank	35,000
Outstanding Electric Bill		300	(Rs. 17,000 + Rs. 15,000 + Rs. 6,000 – Rs. 3,000)	
Provision for Damages		1,500		
		1,14,250		1,14,250

3. Regarding Accumulated Profits/Losses, and/or Reserves and Surplus

All accumulated profits (e.g., reserves, credit balance of Profit and Loss Account etc.) and losses (e.g., debit balance of Profit and Loss Account etc.) or and other surpluses, must be transferred to Capital Account or Current Account of the old partners as per old profit-sharing ratio before the admission of a new partner since these do not belong to the new partner.*

The following Journal entries are required to be passed for the purposes :

(a) *For accumulated Profits*

(i) General Reserve A/c Dr.
Profit and Loss (Cr.) A/c Dr.
Any other Accumulated Reserve A/c Dr.
To Old Partners' Capital A/c (as per old ratio)

(ii) *For accumulated Losses*
Old Partners' Capital A/c Dr.
To Accumulated Losses A/c (as per old ratio)

Sometimes the amount of General Reserve is to be shown at *Original Values.* In that case, the following entries are required to be passed :

(i) *For transferring the General Reserve to the Old Partners' Capital Account as per old ratio*
General Reserve A/c Dr.
To Old Partners' Capital A/c

(ii) *For maintaining at its Original Values*
All Partners' Capital A/c Dr. (as per new ratio)
(Including new partner)
To General Reserve A/c

Illustration 4

P, Q, and R were in partnership sharing profits and losses in the ratio 2 : 2 : 1. On 1st Jan. 2012, their Balance Sheet stood as:

* Students are to remember that Reserve and Surplus will always be transferred to Old Partners' Capital Account as per old ratio even if no information is given in the question

Balance Sheet *as at 1st Jan. 2012*

Liabilities		Rs.	*Assets*	Rs.
Capital :			Plant and Machinery	30,000
P	30,000		Land and Building	17,000
Q	20,000		Machinery Replacement Investment	7,000
R	10,000		Investment (M. V. Rs. 3,500)	4,000
		60,000	Stock	10,000
General Reserve		4,000	Debtors	5,000
Machinery Replacement Fund		8,000	Cash and Bank	7,000
Investment Fluctuation Fund		7,000		
Creditors		1,000		
		80,000		80,000

(a) Show the entry if S is admitted as a partner for $\frac{1}{4}$th share. (b) Show also if General Reserve is shown at its Original Value.

Solution

At the time of S's admission, all the accumulated profits should be closed with the help of the following entries :

Journal

Date	*Particulars*		*L.F.*	*Debit*	*Credit*
2012				Rs.	Rs.
Jan. 1	General Reserve A/c	Dr.		4,000	
	Investment Fluctuation Fund A/c	Dr.		6,500	
	(7,000 – 500)				
	To P's Capital A/c				4,200
	" Q's Capital A/c				4,200
	" R's Capital A/c				2,100
	(Accumulated profits are distributed in 2 : 2 : 1)				

Notes :

1. **Machinery Replacement Fund is an accumulated depreciation, as such, the same must not be divided among the partners.**
2. **Only balance of Investment Fluctuation Fund (i.e, after adjusting loss on investment) is divided.**

(b) Now, if only the General Reserve from the above illustration is to be shown at its *Original Value* in the Balance Sheet, the following entry is necessary for the purpose :

Journal

Date	*Particulars*		*L.F.*	*Debit*	*Credit*
2012				Rs.	Rs.
Jan1	P's Capital A/c	Dr.		1,200*	
	Q's Capital A/c	Dr.		1,200	
	R's Capital A/c	Dr.		600	
	S's Capital A/c	Dr.		1,000	
	To General Reserve A/c				4,000
	(Reserve shown at its original value)				

New Profit-sharing Ratio

$1 - \frac{1}{4} = \frac{3}{4}$ $P = \frac{3}{4} \times \frac{2}{5} = \frac{6}{20}$; $Q = \frac{3}{4} \times \frac{2}{5} = \frac{6}{20}$; $R = \frac{3}{4} \times \frac{1}{5} = \frac{3}{20}$; $S = \frac{1}{4} = \frac{5}{20}$

$\therefore$ P : Q : R : S = 6 : 6 : 3 : 5

Sometimes a part of a General Reserve is to be adjusted against Reserve for Bad and Doubtful Debts. In that case, the following entries are to be passed :

General Reserve A/c Dr.
To Reserve for Bad and Doubtful Debts A/c (only the affected account)
" Old Partners' Capital A/c (balance left as per old ratio)

Sometimes a part of the General Reserve is withdrawn by the old partners. In that case, the following entries are required :

(a) ***For transferring the General Reserve***

General Reserve A/c Dr. } Full amount as per old ratio
To Old Partners' Capital A/c

(b) *For withdrawing a part of the General Reserve by the old partners*

Old Partners' Capital A/c ... Dr.		Only the amount withdrawn
To Bank A/c		

Now, consider the following illustration :

Illustration 5

K and L are two partners sharing profits and losses in the ratio of 5 : 3. Their Balance Sheet as at 30th June 2010 is :

Liabilities	Rs.	Rs.	*Assets*	Rs.	Rs.
Creditors		30,000	Furniture		40,000
General Reserve		14,000	Patent		10,000
Capital Account :			Debtors	44,000	
K	40,000		*Less* : Reserve for Bad Debts	5,000	
L	50,000	90,000			39,000
			Stock		20,000
			Cash in hand		25,000
		1,34,000			1,34,000

On 1st July 2010, they take M into partnership. M brings Rs. 25,000 as his capital. The new profit-sharing ratio of K, L and M is 2 : 4 : 1. A Reserve for Bad Debts is created at 5%. General Reserve appears in the books of the new firm at its original figure.

Show the necessary Journal entries for General Reserve and Reserve for Bad Debts only.

Solution

In the Books of K, L, M
Journal

Date	*Particulars*		*L.F.*	*Debit*	*Credit*
2010				Rs.	Rs.
July 1	General Reserve A/c	Dr.		14,000	
	To K's Capital A/c				8,750
	" L's Capital A/c				5,250
	(Reserve credited to Old Partners' Capital Accounts in 5 : 3)				
	K's Capital A/c	Dr.		4,000	
	L's Capital A/c	Dr.		8,000	
	M's Capital A/c	Dr.		2,000	
	To General Reserve A/c				14,000
	(Reserve shown at its original value)				
	Reserve for Bad Debts A/c	Dr.		2,800	
	To Revaluation A/c				2,800
	(Excess provision written-back)				

4. Regarding Adjustments for Goodwill

Goodwill

Goodwill is an asset which has countless definitions. Accountants, Economists, Engineers and the Courts have defined goodwill in a number of ways from their respective angles. As such, they have suggested different methods for its nature and valuation. No doubt it is an *intangible real asset* and not a fictitious one. 'It is perhaps the most intangible of intangibles'.

Goodwill is a valuable asset if the concern is profitable; on the other hand, it is valueless if the concern is a losing one. Therefore, it can be stated that goodwill is the value of representative of the firms, judged in respect of its earning capacity. However, some of the definitions are discussed :

> 'What is goodwill ? It is a thing very easy to describe, very difficult to define. It is the benefit and advantages of the good name, reputation in connection with a business. It is the attractive force which brings in customers. It is the one thing which distinguishes an old established business from a new business at its first start'.—*Lord Macnaghten*
>
> 'When a man pays for goodwill he pays for something which places him in the position of being able to earn more money than he would be able to do by his own unaided efforts'. *Prof. Dicksee*
>
> 'Goodwill is the present value of a firm's anticipated *excess earnings*'. —*Dr. Canning*

Of the three definitions stated above, the last one is widely accepted by the Courts and by the Accountants as well. Here, the word *excess* indicates some special hints as to its valuation which, perhaps, is equal to earning attributable to rate of return on tangible and intangible assets (with the exception of goodwill) in excess of normal rate of return earned by the representative firms in the same industry. In short, the *excess* reveals the difference between the actual profit earned minus the normal rate of return on capital employed. In other words, Goodwill is the present value of expected future income in excess of a normal return on the investments in tangible assets or the excess of the price paid for a business as a whole over the book value, or over the computed value of all tangible net assets purchased. It is a real asset but intangible—since it has no physical existence.

Classification

P. D. Leake has classified goodwill as :

(i) *Dog-Goodwill* : Dogs are attached to the persons and, hence, such customers lead to personal goodwill which is not transferable.

(ii) *Cat-Goodwill* : Since cats prefer the person of the old home, similarly, such customers give rise to *locality goodwill.*

(iii) *Rat-Goodwill* : The other variety of customer has attachment neither to the person nor to the place which—in other words—known as *fugitive goodwill.*

Other Classifications

(a) Purchased/Acquired Goodwill

Purchased goodwill arises when a firm purchases another firm and ***when payment is made in excess of net assets acquired*** for that purpose—such excess payment is known as Purchased Goodwill.

Moreover, Goodwill, in general, is recorded in the books only when some consideration in money or money's worth has been paid for it. Whenever a business is acquired for a price (payable either in cash or in shares) which is in excess of the value of the net asssets of the business taken over the excess is termed as Goodwill. Goodwill arises from business connections, trade name or reputation of an enterprise, or from other intangible benefits enjoyed by an enterprise.

As a matter of financial prudence goodwill is written-off over a period. However, many enterprises do not write-off goodwill and retain it as an asset.

Moreover, Goodwill arising on amalgamation represents a payment made in anticipation of future income and it is appropriate to treat it as an asset to be amortised to income on a systematic basis over its useful life. Due to the nature of goodwill it is frequently difficult to estimate its useful life with reasonable certainty. Such estimation is, however, made on a prudent basis. Accordingly, it is considered appropriate to amortise goodwill over a period not exceeding 5 years unless a somewhat longer period can be justified.

(b) Inherent/Latent Goodwill

It is practically the reputation of a firm which has been acquired by the business over a period of time. It is not purchased for cash consideration. That is why it is not recorded in the books of accounts like Purchased Goodwill. This type of goodwill depends on a number of factors, viz., supplying goods and services of reasonable price to the society etc. Accountants are not concerned about it.

Inherent/Internally Generated Tangible Assets

As per **Ind AS 38**

Para 48. ***Internally generated goodwill should not be recognised as an asset.***

Para 49. In some cases, expenditure is incurred to generate future economic benefits, but it does not result in the creation of an intangible asset that meets the recognition criteria in this statement. Such expenditure is often described as contributing to internally generated goodwill. ***Internally generated goodwill is not recognised as an asset because it is not an identifiable resource controlled by the enterprise that can be measured realiably at cost.***

Para 50. Difference between the market value of an enterprise and the carrying amount of its identifiable net assets at any point in time may be due to a range of factors that affect the value of the enterprise. However, such difference cannot be considered to represent the cost of intangible assets controlled by the enterprise.

Need for Valuation

Valuation of goodwill may be made due to any one of the following reasons :

(a) ***In the case of a Sole Proprietorship Firm :***

(i) If the firm is sold to another person; (ii) If it takes any person as a partner; and (iii) If it is converted into a company.

(b) ***In the case of a Partnership Firm :***

(i) If any new partner is taken; (ii) If any old partner retires from the firm; (iii) If there is any change in profit-sharing ratio among the partners; (iv) If any partner dies; (v) If different partnership firms are amalgamated;.(vi) If any firm is sold; and (vii) If any firm is converted into a company.

(c) ***In the case of a Company :***

(i) If the goodwill has already been written-off in the past but value of the same is to be recorded further in the books of accounts;

(ii) If an existing company is being taken with or amalgamated with another existing company;

(iii) If the Stock Exchange Quotation of the value of shares of the Company is not available in order to compute gift tax, wealth tax etc.; and

(iv) If the shares are valued on the basis of instrinsic values, market value or fair value method.

Factors affecting the value of Goodwill

(a) *Locational factor*

If the firm is centrally located or located in a very prominent place, it can attract more customers resulting in an increase in turnover. Therefore, locational factor should always be considered while ascertaining the value of goodwill.

(b) *Time factor*

Time dimension is another factor which influences the value of goodwill. The comparatively old firm will enjoy more commercial reputation than the other one since the old one is better known to its customers although both of them may have the same locational advantages.

(c) *Nature of business*

This is another factor which also influences the value of goodwill which includes :

(i) The nature of goods; (ii) Risk involved; (iii) Monopolistic nature of business; (iv) Benefits of patents and trademarks; and (v) Easy access of raw materials, etc.

(d) *Capital required*

More buyers may be interested to purchase a business which requires comparatively small amount of capital but rate of earning profit is high and consequently rise the value of goodwill. On the contrary, the business which required large amount of capital but the rate of earning profit is comparatively less, no buyer will be interested to have the business and, hence, goodwill of the said firm is pulled down.

(e) *Trend of profit*

Value of goodwill may also be affected due to the fluctuation in the amount of profit (i.e., on the basis of rate of return). If the trend of profit is always rising, no doubt, value of goodwill will be high, and vice versa.

(f) *Efficiency of management*

The efficient management may also help to increase the value of goodwill by increasing profits through proper planned production, distribution and services. Therefore, in order to ascertain the value of goodwill, it must be noted that such efficiency in management must not be stopped.

(g) *Other factors*

There are certain other factors which directly or indirectly affect the value of goodwill :

(i) Condition of the money market; (ii) Possibility of competition; (iii) Government Policy; and (iv) Peace and security in the country.

Methods of Valuation of Non-Purchased Goodwill

Although the methods of valuation of goodwill is normally mentioned in the partnership deed, the valuation of the same is not an easy task. There are different methods for its valuation :

(a) Years' purchase of Average Profit Method

Under this method, the average profit of the last few years is ascertained first, and thereafter, the same is multiplied by an agreed number in order to find out the value of goodwill :

Average Profit = $\dfrac{\textit{Total profits for all the years}}{\textit{Number of years}}$

Value of Goodwill = *Average Profit × Years' purchase*

Illustration 6

A, B, and C are partners in a firm. They share profits and losses in the ratio of 3 : 2 : 1. The partnership deed provides that on the retirement of a partner, goodwill shall be calculated on the basis of 5 years' purchase of the average net profits for the preceding 8 years. C retires from the business on 31.12.2013. The net profits for the last 8 years are as follows : 2006 Rs. 6,000; 2007 Rs. 12,000; 2008 Rs. 20,000; 2009 Rs. 16,000; 2010 Rs. 25,000; 2011 Rs. 30,000; 2012 Rs. 36,000 and 2013 Rs. 31,000.

Compute the value of the goodwill of the firm.

Solution

Average Profits of the last 8 years

$$= \frac{\text{Rs. } 6{,}000 + \text{Rs. } 12{,}000 + \text{Rs. } 20{,}000 + \text{Rs. } 16{,}000 + \text{Rs. } 25{,}000 + \text{Rs. } 30{,}000 + \text{Rs. } 36{,}000 + \text{Rs. } 31{,}000}{8}$$

= Rs. 22,000

∴ Value of Goodwill = Rs. 22,000 × 5 = Rs. 1,10,000.

(b) **Years' purchase of Weighted Average Method**

Under this method, the profit of the past few years is multiplied by respective weights for ascertaining 'product'. Later, the total product is to be divided by the total weights in order to find out the value of goodwill.

Weighted Average Profit = $\dfrac{\textit{Product (Profit × Weights)}}{\textit{Total Weights}}$

Value of Goodwill = *Weighted Average Profit × Years' Purchase*

Illustration 7

The profit of S. Ltd. for the last 4 years were :

2005 Rs. 12,000; 2006 Rs. 15,000; 2007 Rs. 16,000, and 2008 Rs. 20,000.

Compute the value of goodwill of S. Ltd. on the basis of 3 years' purchase of weighted average after assigning weights 1, 2, 3 and 4 serially to the profits.

Solution

Year	Annual Profits'	Weights	Product (Profit × Weight)
	Rs.	Rs.	Rs.
2005	12,000	1	12,000
2006	15,000	2	30,000
2007	16,000	3	48,000
2008	20,000	4	80,000
		10	1,70,000

Weighted average of 4 years' profit = $\dfrac{\text{Rs. } 1{,}70{,}000}{10}$ = 17,000 ∴ Value of Goodwill = Rs. 17,000 × 3 = Rs. 51,000.

(c) **Capitalisation Method**

Under this method, the capitalised value of goodwill is ascertained on the basis of some minimum expected yield. Thereafter, the value of net tangible assets is deducted from the capitalised value of profit in order to get the value of goodwill.

Capitalised Value of Profit = $\dfrac{\textbf{\textit{Profit (adjusted)}}}{\textbf{\textit{Normal rate of Return}}} \times 100$

Value of Goodwill = Capitalised Value of Profit – Net Tangible Assets.

Illustration 8

P is desirous of selling his business to T. The former has earned profit in the past of Rs. 1,60,000 p.a. It is considered that such average profit fairly represents the profit likely to be earned in the future, except that—

(i) Chemist's fees Rs. 10,000 charged against such profits will not be payable by T as he is himself an able chemist and can work as such.

(ii) Rent at Rs. 30,000 p.a. which had been paid by P will not be a charge in future since T owns his own premises and can supply the accommodation necessary for the staff and equipment. The value is estimated at Rs. 1,50,000.

The value of the Net Tangible Assets of the business at the proposed date of sale was Rs. 19,00,000, and it was considered that a reasonable return on capital invested, for the type of business in question was 8%. The profits of the business of P would in no way be affected by the sale of the business to T and goodwill existed and was to be paid for on the basis that P's business was a continuing enterprise. Calculate the value of goodwill.

Solution

	Rs.	Rs.
Average Net Profit		1,60,000
Add : Chemist's Fees	10,000	
Rent	30,000	40,000
Maintainable Profit		2,00,000

Capitalised Value of Future Profit @ 8% = $\frac{\text{Rs. } 2,00,000}{8} \times 100$ = Rs. 25,00,000.

	Rs.
Capitalised Value of Future Profit	25,00,000
Less : Net Tangible Assets	19,00,000
∴ Value of Goodwill	6,00,000

(d) Annuity Method

Under this method, the value of goodwill is calculated on the basis of the following formula :

$$\textit{Value of Goodwill } V = \frac{a}{i}\left\{1 - \frac{1}{(1+i)^n}\right\}$$

where V = *Present value of the annuity;*
a = *Annual Superprofit;*
n = *Number of years; and*
i = *Rate of interest.*

Illustration 9

From the following particulars, compute the value of goodwill under "Annuity Method' :

Superprofit Rs. 10,000; Number of years over which superprofit is to be paid 5 Rate per cent per annum 5%

Solution

$$V = \frac{a}{i}\left\{1 - \frac{1}{(1+i)^n}\right\} \text{ or, } V = \frac{\text{Rs. } 10,000}{.05}\left\{1 - \frac{1}{(1+.05)^5}\right\}$$

where a = 10,000
i = 5% or 0.5
n = 5.

or, V = Rs. 43,260 or, say, Rs. 43,300.

(e) Superprofit Method

Superprofit represents the difference between the average profit earned by the business and the normal profit (on this basis of normal rate of return for representative firms in the industry) i.e., the firm's anticipated excess earnings. As such, if there is no anticipated excess earning over normal earnings, there will be no goodwill. This method of calculating goodwill depends on :

(i) Normal rate of return of the representative firms; (ii) Value of capital employed/Average capital employed; and (iii) Estimated future profit, i.e., the average profit of the last few years.

Superprofit = Average Profit (Adjusted) – Normal Profit

Value of Goodwill = Superprofit × Years' Purchase

The students should remember that the *number of years' purchase of goodwill* differs from firm to firm and industry to industry. Needless to mention that one or two years' purchase should be taken into consideration if the retiring partner of a business was the main source of success. It should also be remembered that *three to five years' purchase* is usually taken. Of course, a large number of years' purchase may be considered if the superprofit itself is found to be large. If there is a declining trend in superprofit, one or two years' purchase may be considered.

Illustration 10

From the following information, calculate value of Goodwill :

(i) Average capital employed in the business Rs. 6,00,000. (ii) Net Trading profits of the firm for the past three years were Rs. 1,07,600, Rs. 90,700, and Rs. 1,12,500. (iii) Rate of interest expected from capital having regard to the risk involved 12%. (iv) Fair remuneration to the partners for their services Rs. 12,000 p.a. (v) Sundry Assets of the firm Rs. 7,45,762, Current Liabilities Rs. 31,329.

Solution

Average Profit = $\frac{\text{Rs. } 1{,}07{,}600 + \text{Rs. } 90{,}700 + \text{Rs. } 1{,}12{,}500}{3}$ = Rs. 1,03,600.

Expected Future Profit = Rs. 1,03,600 – Rs. 12,000 (fair remuneration) = Rs. 91,600

Net Profit = Capital Employed × Normal Rate of Return (%)

Normal Profit = Rs. 6,00,000 × 12% = Rs. 6,00,000 × $\frac{12}{100}$ = Rs. 72,000

∴ Superprofit = Average Profit – Normal Profit

= Rs. 91,600 – Rs. 72,00 = Rs. 19,600

Value of Goodwill = Superprofit × Number of years = Rs. 19,600 × 3 = Rs. 58,800.

TREATMENT FOR GOODWILL IN CASE OF ADMISSION OF A NEW PARTNER

The following three methods that are followed for the adjustment of goodwill which are :

A. Premium Method; B. Revaluation Method; and C. Memorandum Revaluation Method.

A. Premium Method

This method is particularly followed when the new partner brings cash for goodwill and the same is shared by the old partners at their sacrificing ratio (i.e., the ratio at which they have surrendered part of their profits to the new partner) or at their old profit-sharing ratio itself where the profit-sharing ratio between the partners remains same.

However, the entry for this purpose will be :

(a) **When Goodwill is received in cash and retained in the business :**

(i) Bank A/c Dr. To Goodwill A/c		Amount of goodwill to be brought in by the new partner.
(ii) Goodwill A/c Dr. To Old Partners' Capital A/c		As per sacrificing ratio.
Or, (i) Bank A/c Dr. To Old Partners' Capital A/c		As per sacrificing ratio.

Illustration 11

X and Y are partners in a firm sharing profits and losses as X 75% and Y 25%. Their capital accounts as on 1.1.2010, were X Rs. 50,000 and Y Rs. 40,000. They admit Z as a partner for $\frac{1}{5}$th share of future profits of the firm. Z introduces Rs. 40,000, of which Rs. 20,000 was to be considered as premium for goodwill.

You are asked to record the above transactions in the books of the firm and show also the future profit-sharing ratio.

Solution

In the books of X, Y, and Z
Journal

Date	Particulars	L.F.	Debit	Credit
2010			Rs.	Rs.
Jan. 1	Bank A/c Dr.		40,000	
	To Z's Capital A/c			20,000
	" Goodwill A/c			20,000
	(Cash brought in by Z towards the premium for goodwill and capital)			
	Goodwill A/c Dr.		20,000	
	To X's Capital A/c			15,000
	" Y's Capital A/c			5,000
	(Premium brought by Z credited to X's and Y's Capital Account in the ratio of 3 : 1)			

Alternatively : for Goodwill

Bank A/c	Dr.	20,000	
To X's Capital A/c			15,000
" Y's Capital A/c			5,000

Future profit-sharing ratio :

$1 - \frac{1}{5} = \frac{4}{5}$ $X = \frac{4}{5} \times \frac{3}{4} = \frac{12}{20}$; $Y = \frac{4}{5} \times \frac{1}{4} = \frac{4}{20}$; $Z \frac{1}{5} = \frac{4}{20}$ $\therefore$ X : Y : Z :: 12 : 4 : 4 or, 3 : 1 : 1.

Undervaluation of Goodwill and Sacrificing Ratio

Illustration 12

X and Y are partners sharing profits and losses as 5 : 3. They take Z into partnership and the new profit- sharing ratio being 4 : 3 : 3. Book value of goodwill is Rs. 12,000. But the agreed value of goodwill is Rs. 22,000. Show the entries.

Solution

In the books of X, Y, and Z
Journal

Date	Particulars		L.F.	Debit Rs.	Credit Rs.
?	Bank A/c	Dr.		3,000	
	To Goodwill A/c				3,000
	(Premium for goodwill to be brought in by Z)				
	Goodwill A/c	Dr.		3,000	
	To X's Capital A/c				2,250
	" Y's Capital A/c				750
	(Goodwill to be credited to X and Y's capital accounts in the ratio of 3 : 1)				

Workings :

	Rs.
Agreed value of Goodwill	22,000
Book Value	12,000
So, undervaluation is	10,000

Now, Z is to bring Rs. 3,000 (Rs. 10,000 × $\frac{3}{10}$) which is to be taken over by X and Y in the sacrificing ratio of 9 : 3 or 3 : 1.

Sacrificing Ratio is to be calculated as:

$X = \frac{5}{8} - \frac{4}{10} = \frac{25-16}{40} = \frac{9}{40}$ (sacrifices) $Y = \frac{3}{8} - \frac{3}{10} = \frac{15-12}{40} = \frac{3}{40}$ (sacrifices)

$Z = \frac{9}{40} + \frac{3}{40} = \frac{12}{40} = \frac{3}{10}$ (gains)

Illustration 13

Dog and Cat are in partnership sharing profits and losses in the ratio 3 : 2. They admit Rat into partnership, the new ratio being 3 : 2 : 1. Goodwill is valued at Rs. 18,000. Rat contributed Rs. 23,000 towards his capital and also premium for goodwill.

Solution

In the books of Dog, Cat, and Rat
Journal

Date	Particulars		L.F.	Debit Rs.	Credit Rs.
?	Bank A/c	Dr.		23,000	
	To Goodwill A/c				3,000
	" Rat's Capital A/c				20,000
	(Premium for goodwill to be brought in by Rat.)				
	Goodwill A/c	Dr.		3,000	
	To Dog's Capital A/c				1,800
	" Cat's Capital A/c				1,200
	(Goodwill to be credited to Dog and Cat's capital accounts in the sacrificing ratio of 3 : 2.)				

Working Notes :

Agreed value of goodwill is Rs. 18,000 which is to be considered as the undervaluation of goodwill on the assumption that the book value of goodwill is nil. So, Rat is to bring Rs. 3,000 (i.e., 18,000 × $\frac{1}{6}$) as the premium for goodwill. Hence, his capital will be Rs. 20,000 (Rs. 23,000 – Rs. 3,000). The sacrificing ratio will be 3 : 2.

(b) When the goodwill is received in cash and withdrawn by old partners in part or full :

(i)	Bank A/c To Goodwill A/c	Dr.	Amount to be brought in by new partner.
(ii)	Goodwill A/c To Old Partners' Capital A/c	Dr.	As per sacrificing ratio.
Or, (i)	Bank A/c To Old Partners' Capital A/c	Dr.	As per sacrificing ratio.
(ii)	Old Partners' Capital A/c To Bank A/c	Dr.	To the extent of withdrawal.

The following illustration will make the principle clear :

Illustration 14

A, B, and C are in partnership sharing profits equally. On Dec. 31, 2012, their capital accounts were as follows : A Rs. 15,000, B Rs. 10,000, and C Rs. 5,000. On January 1, 2013, they admitted D as an equal partner, he agreed to bring in Rs. 4,000 as capital and to pay the old partners Rs. 3,000 for goodwill. Each of the partners was to leave one-half of his share of goodwill in the business and withdraw the other half. Show the entries.

Solution

In the books of A, B, C, and D
Journal Entries

Date	Particulars		L.F.	Debit	Credit
2013				Rs.	Rs.
Jan. 1	Bank A/c	Dr.		7,000	
	To D's Capital A/c				4,000
	" Goodwill A/c				3,000
	(Cash brought in by D as capital and goodwill)				
Jan. 1	Goodwill A/c	Dr.		3,000	
	To A's Capital A/c				1,000
	" B's Capital A/c				1,000
	" C's Capital A/c				1,000
	(Premium brought in by D credited to A, B, and C's Capital Accounts.)				
	A's Capital A/c	Dr.		500	
	B's Capital A/c	Dr.		500	
	C's Capital A/c	Dr.		500	
	To Bank A/c				1,500
	(Half of the premium to be withdrawn by the partners.)				

(c) When the amount of Goodwill is paid privately

Under the circumstances, there will be no entry in the books of the firm as it is neither a business transaction nor it affects the firms.

When Premium for Goodwill paid Privately

Illustration 15

A and B are partners sharing profits and losses in the ratio of 2 : 1. They take C as a partner for $\frac{1}{5}$th share. The goodwill accounts appears in the books at its full value Rs. 15,000. C is to pay proportionate amount as premium for goodwill which he pays to A and B privately.

Solution

There will be no entry for private payment made for goodwill to A and B. Although the new partner is paying premium for goodwill which appears in the books at its full value, the goodwill account should be written back to the old partners' capital account in old ratio :

Journal

Date	Particulars		L.F.	Debit	Credit
				Rs.	Rs.
?	A's Capital A/c	Dr.		10,000	
	B's Capital A/c	Dr.		5,000	
	To Goodwill A/c				15,000
	(Goodwill account written-back to the old partners' capital account in old ratio.)				

B. Revaluation Method

This method is applicable particularly

(a) **When the partner is unable to pay any amount in cash for goodwill, but a goodwill account is raised in the books at its full value.** The entry being

(i) Goodwill A/c Dr.
To Old Partners' Capital A/c } By the amount of goodwill at its full value.

(Under this method, goodwill must be shown in the assets side of the Balance Sheet.)

Now, if goodwill account is alrady raised in the books, the difference between this value and the value already raised in the Balance Sheet is to be credited to old partners.

But **AS 26 Intangible Assets** contradicts this view. As per AS 26, goodwill should be recorded only when there is some consideration for money or money's worth i.e., amount paid for acquisition of a firm (i.e., Purchased Goodwill). Thus, an adjustment may be made by debiting new partners capital account and crediting old partners' capital account (in sacrificing ratio). Consider the following illustration.

Illustration 16

X and Y are partners sharing profits and losses in the ratio 3 : 2. They admitted Z into partnership for $\frac{1}{4}$th share of profits in the business for which Z had to bring Rs. 20,000 as capital. Z was unable to pay anything for goodwill but a goodwill account was raised in the books for Rs. 15,000. Show the entries.

Solution

Journal Entries

Date	Particulars		L.F.	Debit	Credit
				Rs.	Rs.
	Bank A/c	Dr.		20,000	
	To Z's Capital A/c				20,000
	(Capital introduced by Z)				
	Goodwill A/c	Dr.		15,000	
	To X's Capital A/c				9,000
	" Y's Capital A/c				6,000
	(Goodwill account was raised in the books by crediting X's and Y's capital accounts in the ratio 3 : 2.)				

(b) **When the new partner brings a portion of goodwill**

Under the circumstances, the goodwill account is to be raised in the books for the remaining portion.

Illustration 17

A, B, and C are partners sharing profits and losses as to A — half; B — one-third; and C — one-sixth. As from 1.1.2011 they agreed to admit D into partnership for one sixth share in profits and losses, which he acquired equally from A and B and he agreed to bring in Rs. 2,00,000 for his capital and Rs. 1,00,000 as premium for goodwill. D paid in his capital money but in respect of premium for goodwill he could bring in only Rs. 50,000 and in regard to the unpaid amount, he agreed to the raising of goodwill account in the books of the new firms as would be appropriate in the circumstances.

You are required to : (i) give the Journal entries to carry out the above arrangements; (ii) calculate the new profit-sharing ratio of the partners.

Solution

(i)

In the books of A, B, and C
Journal

Date	Particulars		L.F.	Debit	Credit
2011				Rs.	Rs.
Jan. 1	Bank A/c	Dr.		2,50,000	
	To D's Capital A/c				2,00,000
	" Goodwill A/c				50,000
	(Capital and goodwill to be brought in by D in Cash.)				

Contd.

			Rs.	Rs.
2011 Jan. 1	Goodwill A/c Dr.		50,000	
	To A's Capital A/c			25,000
	" B's Capital A/c			25,000
	(Goodwill to be credited to A and B's capital accounts equally.)			
	Goodwill A/c Dr.		3,00,000*	
	To A's Capital A/c			1,50,000
	" B's Capital A/c			1,50,000
	(Goodwill account is raised in the books and credited to A and B's capital accounts equally.)			

For $\frac{1}{6}$th share D should bring Rs. 1,00,000, but he paid only Rs. 50,000, for the balance amount goodwill to be raised for Rs. 3,00,000 $\left(\text{Rs. } 50,000 \times \frac{6}{1}\right)$

(ii) New Profit-sharing Ratio

A $\frac{1}{2} - \frac{1}{12} = \frac{6-1}{12} = \frac{5}{12}$ C $\frac{1}{6} = \frac{2}{12}$

B $\frac{1}{3} - \frac{1}{12} = \frac{4-1}{12} = \frac{3}{12}$ D $\frac{1}{12} + \frac{1}{12} = \frac{2}{12}$ (i.e., $\frac{1}{6}$)

∴ **A : B : C : D = 5 : 3 : 2 : 2.** ∴ **Sacrificing Ratio is 1 : 1**

(c) When Goodwill Account is raised in the books and subsequently written-off :

(i) *For raising goodwill*
Goodwill A/c Dr. } At full value
To Old Partner's' Capital A/c
(To be distributed in old profit sharing ratio))

(ii) *For written-off*
All Partner's' Capital A/c Dr. } New Ratio
To Goodwill A/c

Consider the following :

Illustration 18

X and Y are partners in a firm sharing profits and losses in the ratio of 3 : 2. They take Mr. Z into the firm for $\frac{1}{3}$rd share in the business for which he is to pay Rs. 40,000 as premium for goodwill. But Z is unable to pay anything for goodwill. They decide to raise the amount of goodwill and subsequently written-off. As between X and Y they decide to share future profits and losses equally. Show the entries.

Solution

In the books of the firm
Journal

Date	*Particulars*	*L.F.*	*Debit*	*Credit*
			Rs.	Rs.
	Goodwill A/c Dr.		1,20,000	
	To X's Capital A/c			72,000
	" Y's Capital A/c			48,000
	(Goodwill raised at full value $\left(\text{Rs. } 40,000 \times \frac{3}{1}\right)$			
	X's Capital A/c Dr.		40,000	
	Y's Capital A/c Dr.		40,000	
	Z's Capital A/c Dr.		40,000	
	To Goodwill A/c			1,20,000
	(Goodwill written-off in new ratio immediately)			
	Alternative Approach			
	Z's Capital A/c Dr.		40,000*	
	To X's Capital A/c			32,000
	" Y's Capital A/c			8,000
	(Adjustment made for goodwill)			

* **Ajustment for Goodwill**

		X	Y	Z
		Rs.	Rs.	Rs.
Goodwill before admission	(3 : 2)	72,000	48,000	—
Less : Goodwill Written off	(1 : 1 : 1)	40,000	40,000	40,000
		32,000	8,000	(–) 40,000

(d) When new partner is temporarily incapable of paying premium but a Loan Account is raised against his name

Under the circumstances, a loan is granted to the new partner which is shown in the assets side of the Balance Sheet. The following entries are required for the purpose :

When Loan A/c is granted

(i) Loan to New Partner's Capital A/c Dr. To Goodwill A/c	}	with the amount of goodwill
(ii) ***When the goodwill is transferred :*** Goodwill A/c Dr. To Old Partners' Capital A/c	}	at sacrificing ratio

Illustration 19

P, Q, and R are partners. They share profits in the ratio 3 : 2 : 1. On 1.1.2012, their capital accounts had credit balance of Rs. 15,000, Rs. 10,000, and Rs. 5,000, respectively. On the same date, they admitted T as partner with one-fourth share of the business on his paying Rs. 10,000 as capital. As T was unable to bring any further sum towards the payment of premium for Goodwill (full value Rs. 6,000), it was decided to grant him a loan bearing interest at 6% p.a. and the old partners would be credited with their shares in it. Show necessary entries in the books of the firm on the assumption—(a) that the amount of loan was granted to T, and (b) that no loan was granted to T, but a Goodwill Account was raised in the books.

Solution

In the books of P, Q, R, and T
Journal

Date	*Particulars*	*L.F.*	*Debit*	*Credit*
2012			Rs.	Rs.
Jan. 1	Bank A/c Dr.		10,000	
	To T's Capital A/c			10,000
	(Capital introduced by T.)			
(a)	Loan to T A/c Dr.		1,500	
	To Goodwill A/c ($6,000 \times \frac{1}{4}$)			1,500
	(Goodwill to be adjusted by granting loan to T Account.)			
	Goodwill A/c Dr.		1,500	
	To P's Capital A/c			750
	" Q's Capital A/c			500
	" R's Capital A/c			250
	(Goodwill to be credited to P, Q, and R's Capital Account in the ratio of 3 : 2 : 1)			
(b)	Goodwill A/c Dr.		6,000	
	To P's Capital A/c			3,000
	" Q's Capital A/c			2,000
	" R's Capital A/c			1,000
	(Goodwill account was raised in the books at full value and credited to Old Partners' Capital Accounts in the ratio of 3 : 2 : 1)			

C. Memorandum Revaluation Method

Under this method, the value of goodwill is raised first as per Revaluation Method stated above and thereafter write-off among all the partners (including the new partner) by debiting their capital accounts by the new profit-sharing ratio i.e., ***goodwill account is raised and immediately written-off.***

(a) Goodwill raised, and written off

This part has already been stated in earlier paragraph.

(b) When any liability is transferred

Sometimes the new partner pays off any liability (say, Bank Overdraft) of the old firm which may be considered as the premiums for goodwill. The following entries are required for the purpose :

When liability (say, Bank Overdraft) is transferred

(i)	Bank Overdraft A/c To Goodwill A/c	Dr.	As per profit-sharing or sacrificing ratio
(ii)	Goodwill A/c To Old Partners' Capital A/c	Dr.	with the amount of Bank Overdraft.

Consider the following illustration :

Illustration 20

A and B were partners sharing profits and losses equally. They admitted C into partnership for $\frac{1}{4}$ share of profits. C brought Rs. 20,000 as capital. He was also to pay the Bank Overdraft of the firm amounting to Rs. 10,000. Show the entries.

Solution

In the books of A, B, and C
Journal

			Rs.	Rs.
?	Bank A/c	Dr.	20,000	
	To C's Capital A/c			20,000
	(Capital introduced by C)			
	Bank Overdraft A/c	Dr.	10,000	
	To Goodwill A/c			10,000
	(Bank overdraft paid by C)			
	Goodwill A/c	Dr.	10,000	
	To A/s Capital A/c			5,000
	" B's Capital A/c			5,000
	(Goodwill to be credited to A and B's capital accounts equally)			

Hidden or Inferred Goodwill

When the value of goodwill is computed on the basis of capital which is contributed by the new partners and his share of profit in the firm, it is called hidden or inferred goodwill. This particularly happens when (i) the partners do not desire to disclose the value of goodwill in the books of the accounts and (ii) the new partner does not bring cash separetly for his share of goodwill. In short, it is related to profit sharing ratio and the capital.

Illustration 21

X and Y were partners in a firm. They shared profits and losses in the ratio of 2 : 1. Their capitals were Rs. 1,00,000 and Rs. 50,000, respectively. They took Z into partnership for $\frac{1}{5}$th share of profit. Z brought Rs. 40,000 as capital. Ascertain the value of goodwill.

Solution

Value of Goodwill

Since Z brought Rs. 40,000 for his $\frac{1}{5}$th share, to total capital of the firm should have been Rs. 2,00,000 $\left(\text{i.e. Rs. } 40,000 \times \frac{5}{1}\right)$. The capital of X and Y should be (Rs. 2,00,000 – Rs. 40,000) Rs. 1,60,000. But their combined capitals were Rs. 1,50,000 (i.e., Rs. 1,00,000 and Rs. 50,000). So, hidden goodwill would be Rs. 10,000; (i.e., Rs. 1,60,000 – Rs. 1,50,000).

Miscellaneous Problems on Goodwill

Illustration 22

X and Y were partners in a firm having capitals were Rs. 80,000 and Rs. 1,20,000, respectively. They took Z into partnership on the following conditions :

(a) If Z acquires 25% share for a consideration of Rs. 80,000.
(b) If Z acquires 40% share for a consideration of Rs. 1,33,333.
(c) If Z desires to acquire 50% share, how much should he contribute?

Show the entries.

In the books of the firm
Journal

Date	Particulars		L.F.	Debit	Credit
				Rs.	Rs.
?	Bank A/c	Dr.		80,000	
	To Z's Capital A/c				50,000
	" Goodwill A/c				30,000
	(Capital and goodwill brought in by Z)				
	Goodwill A/c	Dr.		30,000	
	To X's Capital A/c.			15,000	
	" Y's Capital A/c			15,000	
	(Goodwill Credited to old partners.)				25,000
	X's Capital A/c (Rs. 15,000 + Rs. 20,000)	Dr.		35,000	
	Y's Capital A/c (Rs. 15,000 + Rs. 30,000)	Dr.		45,000	
	To Bank A/c				80,000
	(Goodwill and 25% of capital withdrawn by X & Y.))				
	Bank A/c	Dr.		1,33,333	
	To Z's Capital A/c				1,33,333
	(Capital brought in by Z)				
	Bank A/c	Dr.		2,00,000	
	To Z's Capital A/c				2,00,0(
	(Capital brought in by Z)				

Working Notes :

(a) The total capital of X and Y were Rs. 2,00,000 (Rs. 80,000 + Rs. 1,20,000) So, Z should bring in for his 25% share Rs. 50,000 (Rs. 2,00,000 × 25%). As he contributes Rs. 80,000, Balance Rs. 30,000 (Rs. 80,000 – Rs. 50,000) is treated as premium for goodwill. Moreover, X and Y will withdrawn 25% of their respective capital together with the premium for goodwill.

(b) Since Z's share is 40%, 60% remains in the hands of X and Y against their capital of Rs. 2,00,000. So, Z should bring Rs. 2,00,000 × $\frac{40}{60}$ = Rs. 1,33,333 i.e., Z pays exact amount neither more nor less against his capital contribution.

(c) Z acquires 50% share i.e., 50% to be shared by X and Y for their combined capital of Rs. 2,00,000. As such, Z should also contribute Rs. 2,00,000.

Illustration 23

P and Q are partners in a firm sharing profits and losses in the ratio of 3 : 2. They admit R as a partner on 1.1.97 on the basis of his buying $\frac{1}{5}$ of P's share and $\frac{1}{6}$ of Q's share. On 1.1.99 they permit R to purchase a further $\frac{1}{10}$ of their remaining shares. How much did R pay each of the others on each occassion for goodwill, assuming that the goodwill of the firm was Rs. 30,000 on the first occasion and Rs. 40,000 on the second? What is the ultimate share of each partner in the business?

[CU BCom (Hons.)2000]

Solution

(i) Calculation of Sacrificing ratio on 1.1.1997 and distribution of Premium for Goodwill brought in by R:

P sacrifices = $\frac{3}{5} \times \frac{1}{5} = \frac{3}{25}$ Q sacrifices = $\frac{2}{5} \times \frac{1}{6} = \frac{2}{30}$

So, sacrificing-ratio between P and Q = $\frac{3}{25} : \frac{2}{30}$ or, $\frac{18}{150} : \frac{10}{150}$ or, 9 : 5.

R's total share of Profit = $\frac{3}{25} + \frac{2}{30} = \frac{18+10}{150} = \frac{28}{150} = \frac{14}{75}$.

Value of goodwill Rs. 30,000.

R should bring for $\frac{14}{75}$ of Rs. 30,000 = Rs. 5,600, which should be taken over by P and Q in sacrificing-ratio of 9 : 5.

$\therefore$ P will get Rs. 5,600 $\times \frac{9}{14}$ = Rs. 3,600

Q will get Rs. 5,600 $\times \frac{5}{14}$ = Rs. 2,000

New Profit-sharing Ratio

$P = \frac{3}{5} - \frac{3}{25} = \frac{15-3}{25} = \frac{12}{25}$ $Q = \frac{2}{5} - \frac{2}{30} = \frac{12-2}{30} = \frac{10}{30}$

$R = \frac{3}{25} + \frac{2}{30} = \frac{18+10}{150} = \frac{28}{150}$

$\therefore$ $P:Q:R = \frac{12}{25}:\frac{10}{30}:\frac{28}{150}$ Or, 72 : 50 : 28 or, 36 : 25 : 14

(ii) Calculation of Sacrificing-ratio on 1.1.1999 and distribution of Premium for goodwill brought in by R :

P sacrifices = $\frac{36}{75} \times \frac{1}{10} = \frac{36}{750}$ Q sacrifices = $\frac{25}{75} \times \frac{1}{10} = \frac{25}{750}$

$\therefore$ **Sacrificing-ratio is 36 : 25.**

Thus, total share of profit received by R on 1.1.1999

$= \frac{36}{750} + \frac{25}{750} = \frac{61}{750}$

Value of Goodwill Rs. 40,000

R should bring Rs. 40,000 $\times \frac{61}{750}$ = Rs. 3,253 which should be taken over by P and Q in sacrificıng ratio of 36 : 25.

P will get = Rs. 3,253 $\times \frac{36}{61}$ = Rs. 1,920. Q will get = Rs. 3,253 $\times \frac{25}{61}$ = Rs. 1,333.

Thus, the new profit-sharing ratio among P, Q and R as on 1.1.1999 will be :

$P = \frac{36}{75} - \frac{36}{750} = \frac{360-36}{750} = \frac{324}{750}$ $Q = \frac{25}{75} - \frac{25}{750} = \frac{250-25}{750} = \frac{225}{750}$

$R = \frac{14}{75} + \frac{61}{750} = \frac{140-61}{750} = \frac{201}{750}$ $\therefore$ 324 : 225 : 201.

or. 108 : 75 : 67.

Illustration 24

(a) X and Y are partners sharing profits and losses in the ratio 5 : 3. They admit Z into partnership and the new ratio being 3 : 2 : 1. Z brings Rs. 6,000 as premium for goodwill. Goodwill Account appears at its full value in the books.

Solution

Working Notes :

If Z brings $\frac{1}{6}$ share Rs. 6,000 as goodwill, then the full value of goodwill will be Rs. 36,000 (Rs. 6,000 $\times \frac{6}{1}$) which will have to be brought in the books. Therefore, before crediting the premium to X and Y, goodwill should be written-back to them in the ratio of 5 : 3 for Rs. 36,000.

Thereafter, the goodwill which is to be brought by Z is to be taken by X and Y in the sacrificing ratio, i.e., 3 : 1.

In the books of X, Y, and Z
Journal

Date	*Particulars*		*L.F.*	*Debit*	*Credit*
				Rs.	Rs.
?	X's Capital A/c	Dr.		22,500	
	Y's Capital A/c	Dr.		13,500	
	To Goodwill A/c				36,000
	(Goodwill written-back to X and Y in the ratio 5 : 3.)				
	Bank A/c	Dr.		6,000	
	To Goodwill A/c				6,000
	(Goodwill to be brought in by Z.)				
	Goodwill A/c	Dr.		6,000	
	To X's Capital A/c				4,500
	" Y's Capital A/c				1,500
	(Premium for goodwill brought in by Z credited to X and Y's capital account in the sacrificing ratio 3 : 1.)				

(b) A, B, and C are partners in a firm sharing profits and losses in 3 : 1 : 1. They admit D as a partner and the new profits and losses ratio of A, B, C, and D becomes 4 : 3 : 2 : 1. D brings Rs. 30,000 as premium for goodwill. Draft the Journal entries showing the appropriation of the premium for goodwill.

Solution

Sacrificing ratio should be calculated first in the following way :

$$A = \frac{3}{5} - \frac{4}{10} = \frac{6-4}{10} = \frac{2}{10} \quad \text{(sacrifices)}$$

$$B = \frac{1}{5} - \frac{3}{10} = \frac{2-3}{10} = \frac{-1}{10} \quad \text{(gains)}$$

$$C = \frac{1}{5} - \frac{2}{10} = \frac{2-2}{10} = \frac{0}{10} \quad (-)$$

$$D = \frac{1}{10} = \frac{1}{10} \quad \text{(gains)}$$

Thus, entire goodwill is to be credited to A's Capital,, and B is also to pay the proportionate amount to A for gaining ratio i.e., Rs. 30,000 (Rs. 30,000 × $\frac{1}{10}$ × $\frac{10}{1}$).

In the books of X, Y, and Z

Journal

Date	Particulars		L.F.	Debit	Credit
?				Rs.	Rs.
	Bank A/c	Dr.		30,000	
	To A's Capital A/c				30,000
	(Goodwill brought in by D, credited to A's Capital A/c.)				
	B's Capital A/c	Dr.		30,000	
	To A's Capital A/c				30,000
	(Adjustment made for goodwill.)				

Illustration 25

P and Q are in partnership, sharing profits and losses as 4 : 1. They admit R into the firm, R paying a premium of Rs. 30,000 for $\frac{1}{3}$rd share of the profits, as between themselves P and Q agree to share future profits and losses equally. Draft Journal entry showing the appropriation of premium money.

[CU BCom (Hons.)]

Solution

Workings :

Sacrificing-ratio should be calculated first before crediting the premium for goodwill to the old partners. The same may be computed as:

$$P = \frac{4}{5} - \frac{1}{3} = \frac{12-5}{15} = \frac{7}{15} \quad \text{(sacrifices)} \qquad Q = \frac{1}{5} - \frac{1}{3} = \frac{3-5}{15} = \frac{-2}{15} \quad \text{(gains)}$$

$$R = \frac{1}{3} = \frac{5}{15} \quad \text{(gains)}$$

Since, P sacrifices alone from his own share, the entire goodwill of Rs. 30,000 is to be credited to his Capital Account.

Similarly, Q is also to pay the proportionate amount of Rs. 12,000 (i.e., Rs. 30,000 × $\frac{2}{15}$ × $\frac{3}{1}$) to P for the benefit received from P. The entries will be:

Journal

Date	Particulars		L.F.	Debit	Credit
				Rs.	Rs.
?	Bank A/c	Dr.		30,000	
	To Goodwill A/c				30,000
	(Premium for goodwill to be brought in by R.)				
	Goodwill A/c	Dr.		30,000	
	To P's Capital A/c				30,000
	(Goodwill to be credited to P's Capital A/c.)				
	Q's Capital A/c	Dr.		12,000	
	To P's Capital A/c				12,000
	(Adjustment made for goodwill.)				

Illustration 26

X and Y are in partnership sharing profits and losses as 3 : 2. They admit Z into the firm, Z paying a premium of Rs. 36,000 for $\frac{1}{6}$th share of the profits. As between themselves, X and Y agree to share future profits and losses equally. Draft Journal entries showing the appropriation of premium money.

Solution

Future Profit-sharing Ratio

$$1 - \frac{1}{6} = \frac{5}{6}$$

$$X \quad \frac{5}{6} \times \frac{1}{2} = \frac{5}{12}, \; Y \, \frac{5}{6} \times \frac{1}{2} = \frac{5}{12}, \; Z \, \frac{1}{6} = \frac{2}{12},$$

Ratio = X : Y : Z : : 5 : 5 : 2.

Now : Sacrificing Ratio

$$X \quad \frac{3}{5} - \frac{5}{12} = \frac{36-25}{60} = \frac{11}{60} \quad \text{(sacrifices)}$$

$$Y \quad \frac{2}{5} - \frac{5}{12} = \frac{24-25}{60} = \frac{-1}{60} \quad \text{(gains)}$$

$$Z \quad \frac{1}{6} = \frac{10}{60} \quad \text{(gains)}$$

Therefore, the entire goodwill is to be credited to X's capital account and, at the same time, Y is also to pay the proportionate amount to X = Rs. 3,600 (i.e., 36,000 × $\frac{1}{60} \times \frac{60}{10}$).

The consolidated entry will be :

			Rs.	Rs.
?	Bank A/c Dr.		36,000	
	Y's Capital A/c Dr.		3,600	
	To X's Capital A/c			39,600
	(Goodwill brought in by Z credited to X's capital account and the adjustment made for goodwill against Y's capital account.)			

Illustration 27

Amal and Bimal are partners, sharing profits and losses in the ratio of 2 : 3. Charu is admitted as partner on 1.1.2012 and he pays into the firm cash Rs. 9,000 of which Rs. 3,000 is to be premium on his admission to a quarter share, the ratio between Amal and Bimal to be 1 : 2.

Charu also brings into the business his own Goodwill to be run as a separate unit and the profit-sharing ratio to be Amal, Bimal, and Charu 2 : 3 : 5. The Goodwill is agreed at Rs. 4,800. Show the entries required to give effect to the above arrangement (for both the units separately.)

[CU BCom (Hons.)]

Solution

Working Notes :

1. Goodwill should be taken by Amal and Bimal in 3 : 2 i.e., Rs. 1,800 and Rs. 1,200, respectively, and
2. Amal's capital account should be debited by Rs. 960 ($\frac{2}{10}$ × Rs. 4,800) and Bimal's capital account should also be debited by Rs. 1,440 ($\frac{3}{10}$ × Rs. 4,800) and Charu's capital account should be credited by Rs. 2,400 (Rs. 960 + Rs. 1,440).

Sacrificing Ratio

$$\text{Amal} = \frac{2}{5} - \frac{1}{4} = \frac{8-5}{20} = \frac{3}{20} \quad \text{(sacrifices)} \qquad \text{Bimal} = \frac{3}{5} - \frac{2}{4} = \frac{12-10}{20} = \frac{2}{20} \quad \text{(sacrifices)}$$

$$\text{Charu} = \frac{3}{20} + \frac{2}{20} = \frac{5}{20} \quad \text{(gains)}$$

Hence, the sacrificing ratio is 3 : 2.

Journal

Date	*Particulars*	*L.F.*	*Dr.*	*Cr.*
2012			Rs.	Rs.
Jan. 1	Bank A/c Dr.		9,000	
	To Charu's Capital A/c			6,000
	" Goodwill A/c			3,000
	(Capital and goodwill to be brought in by Charu)			

Contd.

Date	Particulars		L.F.	Debit	Credit
2012				Rs.	Rs.
	Goodwill A/c	Dr.		3,000	
	To Amal's Capital A/c				1,800
	" Bimal's Capital A/c				1,200
	(Goodwill to be credited to Amal and Bimal's capital accounts in 3 : 2.)				
	Amal's Capital A/c	Dr.		960	
	Bimal's Capital A/c	Dr.		1,440	
	To Charu's Capital A/c				2,400
	(Adjustment made for goodwill.)				

Illustration 28

P, Q, and R were in partnership sharing profits and losses in the ratio of 2 : 2 : 1. They took S and T into partnership, the profit-sharing ratio being 5 : 4 : 3 : 2 : 1. S brought Rs. 14,000 for his share of goodwill but T was unable to pay anything for goodwill. Both the partners introduced Rs. 30,000 as capital. Show the entries assuming that no goodwill account was raised in the books.

Solution

In the books of the firm
Journal

Date	*Particulars*		*L.F.*	*Debit*	*Credit*
?				Rs.	Rs.
	Bank A/c	Dr.		74,000	
	To S's Capital A/c				30,000
	" T's Capital A/c				30,000
	" Goodwill A/c				14,000
	(Capital brought in by S and T, in addition, S brought the amount of goodwill.)				
	Goodwill A/c	Dr.		14,000	
	T's Capital A/c	Dr.		7,000	
	To P's Capital A/c				7,000
	" Q's Capital A/c				14,000
	(Adjustment made for goodwill.)				

Workings :

S brought Rs. 14,000 for his share of goodwill for $\frac{2}{15}$ share. So full value of goodwill Rs. 1,05,000 (i.e., Rs. 14,000 × $\frac{15}{2}$).

Goodwill distribution before admission

		P	Q	R	S	T
		Rs.	Rs.	Rs.	Rs.	Rs.
Total Rs. 1,05,000 (P : Q : R in 2 : 2 : 1)	=	42,000	42,000	21,000	—	—
Goodwill distribution after admission (P : Q : R : S : T in 5 : 4 : 3 : 2 : 1)	=	35,000	28,000	21,000	14,000	7,000
Sacrificing		(–) 7,000	(–) 14,000	—	—	—
Gains		—	—	—	(+) 14,000	(+) 7,000

Illustration 29

Show the entries under each of the following conditions in the books of the firm :

(a) A and B are partners sharing profits and losses in the ratio of 3 : 2. They admit C into partnership, C paying a premium of Rs. 2,000 for $\frac{1}{4}$th share of profits. No goodwill account appears in the books. They withdraw the amount of goodwill.

(b) X and Y are partners sharing profits and losses in the ratio of 3 : 2. They admit Z into partnership, Z paying a premium of Rs. 2,000 for $\frac{1}{4}$th share of profit. The new ratio is 3 : 3 : 2. Goodwill account appears in the books at Rs. 2,000. It was decided that goodwill should continue to appear in the books at Rs. 1,600.

(c) A and B are partners sharing profits and losses in the ratio of 4 : 1. They take C into partnership for $\frac{1}{3}$rd interest in the business. C brings Rs. 20,000 as capital but he was unable to pay anything for goodwill but a goodwill account is raised in the books for Rs. 5,000.

(d) P and Q are partners sharing profits equally. They admit R into partnership, R paying only Rs. 2,000 for premium out of his share of premium of Rs. 3,600 for $\frac{1}{4}$th share of profits. Goodwill account appears in the books at Rs. 12,000. The partners decide not to show goodwill account in the books.

(e) X and Y are partners. The capital amount of X and Y show a credit balance of Rs. 32,000 and Rs. 24,000. They admit Z as a partner for $\frac{1}{4}$th share. Z brings Rs. 32,000 as his share of capital.

(f) X, Y are partners sharing profits and losses in the ratio of 3 : 2. They take Z into partnership for $\frac{3}{7}$th profit ($\frac{2}{7}$th from X and $\frac{1}{7}$ from Y) and brings Rs. 6,000 as premium out of his share of Rs. 7,200. Goodwill account does not appear in the books of X and Y but the new firm decides that goodwill should appear in the books at Rs. 3,500.

Solution

In the books of the Firm
Journal

Date	Particulars		L.F.	Debit	Credit
				Rs.	Rs.
?	(a) Bank A/c	Dr.		2,000	
	To Goodwill A/c				2,000
	(Goodwill brought in by C.)				
	Goodwill A/c	Dr.		2,000	
	To A's Capital A/c				1,200
	" B's Capital A/c				800
	(Goodwill credited to old partners.)				
	X's Capital A/c	Dr.		1,200	
	Y's Capital A/c	Dr.		800	
	To Bank A/c				2,000
	(Goodwill withdrawn by X and Y.)				
	(b) X's Capital A/c	Dr.		1,200	
	Y's Capital A/c	Dr.		800	
	To Goodwill A/c				2,000
	(Goodwill written-off before admission.)				
	Bank A/c	Dr.		2,000	
	To Goodwill A/c				2,000
	(Goodwill brought in by Z.)				
	Goodwill A/c	Dr.		2,000	
	To X's Capital A/c				1,800
	" Y's Capital A/c				200
	(Goodwill credited to X's and Y's Capital Account as per sacrificing ratio (9 : 1) since the new ratio is given).				
	Goodwill A/c	Dr.		1,600	
	To X's Capital A/c				600
	" Y's Capital A/c				600
	" Z's Capital A/c				400
	(Goodwill raised in the books)				
	(c) Bank A/c	Dr.		20,000	
	To C's Capital A/c				20,000
	(Capital brought in by C.)				
	Goodwill A/c	Dr.		5,000	
	To A's Capital A/c				4,000
	" B's Capital A/c				1,000
	(Goodwill ratio in the books.)				

Contd.

Particulars		Rs.	Rs.
(d) Goodwill A/c	Dr.	2,400	
To P's Capital A/c			1,200
" Q's Capital A/c			1,200
(Goodwill raised at its face value i.e., Rs. 3,600 × 4 = 14,400 – Rs. 12,000)			
Bank A/c	Dr.	2,000	
To R's Capital A/c			2,000
(Amount brought in by R credited to his capital account.)			
P's Capital A/c	Dr.	5,400	
Q's Capital A/c	Dr.	5,400	
R's Capital A/c	Dr.	3,600	
To Goodwill A/c			14,400
(Goodwill written-off in the new ratio of 3 : 3 : 2*)			
(e) Bank A/c	Dr.	32,000	
To Z's Capital A/c			32,000
(Capital brought in by Z)			
Goodwill A/c	Dr.	40,000	
To X's Capital A/c			20,000
" Y's Capital A/c			20,000
(Goodwill should be inferred since total capital should have been Rs. 1,28,000 (i.e., Rs. 32,000 × $\frac{4}{1}$), but after admission total capital would be Rs. 88,000 (Rs. 32,000 + Rs. 24,000 + Rs. 32,000), the difference Rs. 40,000 Rs. 1,28,000 – Rs. 88,000) being treated as goodwill)			
(f) Goodwill A/c	Dr.	16,800	
To X's Capital A/c			10,080
" Y's Capital A/c			6,720
(Goodwill raised at its full value)			
X's Capital A/c	Dr.	4,180	
Y's Capital A/c	Dr.	3,420	
Z's Capital A/c	Dr.	5,700	
To Goodwill A/c			13,300
(Goodwill written-off in new ratio i.e., 11 : 9 : 15)			
Bank A/c	Dr.	6,000	
To Z's Capital A/c			6,000
(Goodwill brought in by Z.)			

* Future Profit-sharing Ratio

$1 - \frac{1}{4} = \frac{3}{4}$

$P = \frac{3}{4} \times \frac{1}{2} = \frac{3}{8}$ $\qquad Q = \frac{3}{4} \times \frac{1}{2} = \frac{3}{8}$

$R = \frac{1}{4} = \frac{2}{8}$

∴ P : Q : R = 3 : 3 : 2.

Illustration 30

A and B are equal partners. Their Balance Sheet as on 31.12.2012 stood as:

Liabilities		Rs.	*Assets*	Rs.
Creditors		3,000	Cash at Bank	2,000
Reserve		3,000	Bills Receivable	4,000
Capital Accounts :			Books Debts	6,000
A	9,000		Stock	4,000
B	7,000		Furniture	2,000
		16,000	Goodwill	4,000
		22,000		22,000

They admit C as a new partner with $\frac{1}{4}$ share in the business on condition that he brings in Rs. 4,000, as his capital. C also brings in Rs. 2,000, as premium for Goodwill. A and B, as between themselves, are to share profits and losses in the same ratio as before.

Pass the necessary Journal entries on the assumption that (i) if the partners decided to maintain Goodwill Account at its full value, (ii) they decide that Goodwill Account is to be maintained at its original value, and (iii) they decide to write-off the Goodwill Account from their books.

Show the adjusted Balance Sheet (preferably a columnar one) under each circumstance.

Solution

Workings :

		Rs.
	Total value of Goodwill Rs. 2,000 × $\frac{4}{1}$ =	8,000
Less :	Already raised in the books	4,000
	Undervaluation	4,000

(i) **In the first case :**

Rs. 4,000 to be debited to goodwill account in order to maintain at its full value and, therefore, the premium brought in by C will be credited to his own capital account.

(ii) **In the second case :**

Undervaluation goodwill is Rs. 4,000; and $\frac{1}{4}$th of Rs. 4,000 i.e., Rs. 1,000, to be credited to the old partners' capital account equally and balance Rs. 1,000 (since C brings Rs. 2,000, as premium) to be credited to his own capital account.

(iii) In the third case :

The existing goodwill (which is given in the Balance Sheet) will be wiped-off or written-back to old partners and the premium which is brought in by C will be credited to Old Partners' Capital Accounts.

Solution

In the books of A, B, and C

Journal

Date	*Particulars*		*L.F.*	*Debit* Rs.	*Credit* Rs.
2012 Dec. 31	Bank A/c	Dr.		4,000	
	To C's Capital A/c				4,000
	(Capital introduced by C.)				
	General Reserve A/c	Dr.		3,000	
	To A's Capital A/c				1,500
	" B's Capital A/c				1,500
	(General Reserve credited to old partners' capital accounts.)				
(i)	Goodwill A/c	Dr.		4,000	
	To A's Capital A/c				2,000
	" B's Capital A/c				2,000
	(Goodwill to be raised at its full value and credited to old partners' capital accounts.)				
	Bank A/c	Dr.		2,000	
	To C's Capital A/c				2,000
	(Premium brought in by C, credited to his own capital account.)				
(ii)	Bank A/c	Dr.		2,000	
	To A's Capital A/c				500
	" B's Capital A/c				500
	" C's Capital A/c				1,000
	(Premium to be brought in by C credited to the old partners' capital account to the extent of true premium equally and the balance to be credited to C's capital account.)				
(iii)	A's Capital A/c	Dr.		2,000	
	B's Capital A/c	Dr.		2,000	
	To Goodwill A/c				4,000
	(Existing goodwill written-back to old partners' capital accounts.)				
	Bank A/c	Dr.		2,000	
	To A's Capital A/c				1,000
	" B's Capital A/c				1,000
	(Premium brought in by C credited to old partners' capital accounts equally.)				

Balance Sheet *as at 31st Dec. 2012*

Liabilities	(i)	(ii)	(iii)	Assets	(i)	(ii)	(iii)
	Rs.	Rs.	Rs.		Rs.	Rs.	Rs.
Creditors	3,000	3,000	3,000	Cash	8,000	8,000	8,000
Capital Accounts :				Bills Receivable	4,000	4,000	4,000
A	12,500	11,000	9,500	Book Debts	6,000	6,000	6,000
B	10,500	9,000	7,500	Stock	4,000	4,000	4,000
C	6,000	5,000	4,000	Furniture	2,000	2,000	2,000
				Goodwill	8,000	4,000	—
	32,000	28,000	24,000		32,000	28,000	24,000

Value of Goodwill on the basis of Capitalisation of Profit

Illustration 31

A and B were partners sharing profits and losses in the ratio 3 : 2 and on 31.12.2012, the firm's book revealed the following particulars :

Liabilities	Rs.	Rs.	Assets	Rs.
Capital Account :			Plant and Machinery	20,000
A	30,000		Land and Building	15,000
B	20,000		Stock	15,000
		50,000	Debtors	9,000
Sundry Creditors		15,000	Bills Receivable	6,000
Bills Payable		10,000	Cash and Bank	10,000
		75,000		75,000

On 1.1.2013, they agreed to admit C into partnership on the following conditions :

(a) A Goodwill Account is to be raised in the books on the basis of capitalisation of profits @ 10% of the average profits of the last 5 years which were :

2008 Rs. 5,500; 2009 Rs. 7,000; 2010 Rs. 9,000; 2011 Rs. 12,500; 2012 Rs. 16,000.

(b) C is to get $\frac{1}{5}$th share of profits and is to contribute proportionate capital. He brings the following assets :

Goodwill Rs. 9,000; Stock Rs. 6,000 and the balance in Cash.

(c) Plant and Machinery are to be increased by Rs. 5,000 and Stock is to be reduced by 20%.

(d) Capital Accounts of the old partners are to be adjusted according to profit-sharing ratio.

Show the entries and the opening Balance Sheet of the new firm.

Solution

1. **Value of Goodwill**

					Rs.
	Average profit of the last 5 years	=	$\frac{\text{Rs. }(5{,}500 + 7{,}000 + 9{,}000 + 12{,}500 + 16{,}000)}{5}$		
		=	10,000		
∴	Capitalised Value	=	$\frac{(\text{Rs. }10{,}000 \times 100)}{10}$	=	1,00,000
Less :	Opening Capitals				
	A			30,000	
	B			20,000	
				50,000	
Add :	Profit on Revaluation (Rs. 5,000 – 3,000)			2,000	
					52,000
					48,000

In the books of A, B, and C
Journal

Date	Particulars		L.F.	Debit	Credit
2013				Rs.	Rs.
Jan. 1	Goodwill A/c	Dr.		48,000	
	To A's Capital A/c				28,800
	" B's Capital A/c				19,200
	(Goodwill raised in the books.)				
	Revaluation A/c	Dr.		3,000	
	To Stock A/c				3,000
	(Value of stock reduced.)				
	Plant and Machinery A/c	Dr.		5,000	
	To Revaluation A/c				5,000
	(Value of plant and machinery increased.)				
	Revaluation A/c	Dr.		2,000	
	To A's Capital A/c				1,200
	" B's Capital A/c				800
	(Profit on revaluation transferred.)				
	Goodwill A/c	Dr.		9,000	
	Stock A/c	Dr.		6,000	
	Cash *(bal. fig.)* A/c	Dr.		10,000[1]	
	To C's Capital A/c				25,000
	(Various assets brought in by C as capital.)				

Balance Sheet
as at 1st Jan. 2013

Liabilities	Rs.	Rs.	*Assets*	Rs.
Capital			Goodwill (48,000 + 9,000)	57,000
A	60,000		Plant and Machinery	25,000
B	40,000		(20,000 + 5,000)	
C	25,000		Land and Building	15,000
		1,25,000	Stock (15,000 – 3,000 + 6,000)	18,000
Creditors		15,000	Debtors	9,000
Bills Payable		10,000	Bills Receivable	6,000
			Cash at Bank (10,000 + 10,000)	20,000
		1,50,000		1,50,000

Note :

1. **Proportionate Capital of C.**

Combined Capital of A and B Rs. 1,00,000 (60,000 + 40,000) for $\frac{4}{5}$th share.

Therefore, C's Capital will be = Rs. 1,00,000 × $\frac{5}{4}$ × $\frac{1}{5}$ = Rs. 25,000.

5. Regarding Adjustment of Capital, or Proportionate Capital Contribution

Under this method, total capital of the firm should be computed first on the basis of the new partner's profit-sharing ratio and his capital. Then ascertain old partners' capital on the basis of their new profit-sharing ratio. At last, compare their capital with their existing capital (after adjusting all adjustments) and excess, if any, is to be withdrawn or deficit, if any, is to brought in by the respective partners, or the same may be adjusted against Current Account, of the partners or against the Loan account as per agreement.

Illustration 32

X any Y were in partnership sharing profits and losses in the ratio 3 : 2. They take Z into partnership. Z takes from X $\frac{1}{5}$ and from Y $\frac{1}{10}$. After one year X and Y again allow Z to acquire further $\frac{1}{10}$th of their remaining shares.

Ascertain how much should Z pay to X and Y on each occasion on account of goodwill assuming that the goodwill of the firm amounted to Rs. 50,000 on the first occasion and Rs. 1,00,000 in the next.

Show also the profit-sharing ratio.

Solution

On admission —

Z acquires : from X $\frac{1}{5}$th of $\frac{3}{5}$ i.e., $\frac{1}{5} \times \frac{3}{5} = \frac{3}{25}$ from Y $\frac{1}{10}$ th of $\frac{2}{5}$ i.e., $\frac{1}{10} \times \frac{2}{5} = \frac{2}{50}$

As such, he will have to pay to :

X Rs. 50,000 × $\frac{3}{25}$ = Rs. 6,000

Y Rs. 50,000 × $\frac{2}{50}$ = Rs. 2,000

He also acquires subsequently from :

X $\frac{1}{10}$th of $\left(\frac{3}{5} - \frac{3}{25}\right)$ or $\frac{1}{10}$ of $\frac{12}{25}$ or $\frac{1}{10} \times \frac{12}{25} = \frac{12}{250}$

Y $\frac{1}{10}$th of $\left(\frac{2}{5} - \frac{2}{50}\right)$ or $\frac{1}{10}$ of $\frac{18}{50}$ or $\frac{1}{10} \times \frac{18}{50} = \frac{18}{500}$

As such, he will have to pay to :

X Rs. 1,00,000 × $\frac{12}{250}$ = Rs. 4,800

Y Rs. 1,00,000 × $\frac{18}{500}$ = Rs. 3,600

Profit-sharing Ratio

1st Part X $= \frac{3}{5} - \frac{3}{25} = \frac{15 - 3}{25} = \frac{12}{25}$

Y $= \frac{2}{5} - \frac{2}{50} = \frac{20 - 2}{50} = \frac{18}{50}$

Z $= \frac{3}{25} + \frac{2}{50} = \frac{6 + 2}{50} = \frac{8}{50}$

or, X : Y : Z = 24 : 18 : 8 = 12 : 9 : 4

2nd Part X $= \frac{24}{50} - \frac{12}{250} = \frac{120 - 12}{250} = \frac{108}{250}$

Y $= \frac{18}{50} - \frac{18}{500} = \frac{180 - 18}{500} = \frac{162}{500}$

Z $= \frac{8}{50} + \frac{12}{250} + \frac{18}{500} = \frac{80 + 24 + 18}{500}$

$= \frac{122}{500}$

or, X : Y : Z = 216 : 162 : 122 = 108 : 81 : 61

Illustration 33

X, Y, and Z are partners sharing profits and losses as 4 : 3 : 2. For any change in partnership goodwill is to be valued at $2\frac{1}{2}$ times the average profits for 4 years but no goodwill account is to be raised.

The profits are :

2009 Rs. 50,000; 2010 Rs. 60,000; 2011 Rs. 56,000; 2012 Rs. 86,000

On 31st Dec. 2012, Y and Z each acquires from X an additional $\frac{1}{9}$th share in the firms.

On 1st Jan. 2013, X's son P is admitted as a partner. His share is to be $\frac{1}{7}$th of which a proportion calculated to produce Rs. 5,500 p.a. on the basis of profit, is ceded to him by his father; balance is to be purchased from Y and Z in proportion to their share immediately prior to P's admission.

Show the present ratio and also pass Journal entries. **[CU BCom (Hons.)]**

Solution

In the books of X, Y, and Z
Journal

Date	*Particulars*		*L.F.*	*Debit*	*Credit*
				Rs.	Rs.
2012 Dec. 1	Y's Capital A/c	Dr.		17,500	
	Z's Capital A/c	Dr.		17,500	
	To X's Capital A/c				35,000
	(Adjustment made for goodwill due to change in profit-sharing ratio.)				
2013 Jan. 1	P's Capital A/c	Dr.		8,750	
	To Y's Capital A/c				5,000
	" Z's Capital A/c				3,750
	(Adjustment of goodwill on P's admission)				

Workings :

1. **Valuation of Goodwill**

		Rs.
Profits for	2009	50,000
	2010	60,000
	2011	56,000
	2012	86,000
		2,52,000

Average Profit = $\frac{\text{Rs. } 2,52,000}{4}$ = Rs. 63,000

∴ Value of Goodwill = Rs. 63,000 × $2\frac{1}{2}$ = Rs. 1,57,500

2. Profit-sharing Ratio : X : Y : Z = 4 : 3 : 2 or, $\frac{4}{9}, \frac{3}{9}$, and $\frac{2}{9}$. Since, X ceded $\frac{1}{9}$ th to Y and $\frac{1}{9}$ th to Z, the new ratio will be = $X = \frac{2}{9}\left(\frac{4}{9} - \frac{1}{9} - \frac{1}{9}\right)$; $Y = \frac{4}{9}\left(\frac{3}{9} + \frac{1}{9}\right)$; $Z = \frac{3}{9}\left(\frac{2}{9} + \frac{1}{9}\right)$.

Premium payable to X by Y and Z for their respective $\frac{1}{9}$ th share will be Rs. 17,500 (i.e., Rs. 1,57,500 × $\frac{1}{9}$). Since no Goodwill Account is raised Y and Z's capital accounts will be debited and X's capital account will be credited.

3. P's share in the new firm (as agreed) is $\frac{1}{7}$. Thus, Rs. 63,000 × $\frac{1}{7}$ = Rs. 9,000.

Out of Rs. 9,000, he obtained from his father X Rs. 5,500, and the balance of Rs. 3,500 (i.e., 9,000 – 5,500) is to be purchased from Y and Z which they sell as per their profit-sharing ratio :

∴ Y sells = Rs. 3,500 × $\frac{4}{7}$ = Rs. 2,000 Z sells = Rs. 3,500 × $\frac{3}{7}$ = Rs. 1,500

Thus, the new profit-sharing ratio will be:

Partner	Present Share (in terms of profit)	Profits ceded to P	Balance of Share (in terms of profit)
	Rs.	Rs.	Rs.
X	14,000	5,500	8,500
Y	28,000	2,000	26,000
Z	21,000	1,500	19,500
	63,000	9,000	

∴ The new profit-sharing ratio will be : X : Y : Z : P = Rs. 8,500 : Rs. 26,000 : Rs. 19,500 : Rs. 9,000

= 17 : 52 : 39 : 18.

P will have to pay for goodwill (since goodwill is $2\frac{1}{2}$ times of average profit.)

To Y Rs. 2,000 × $2\frac{1}{2}$ = Rs. 5,000. To Z Rs. 1,500 × $2\frac{1}{2}$ = Rs. 3,750.

Illustration 34

A and B are partners in a firm sharing profits and losses in the ratio of 4 : 1. Their Balance Sheet as on 31st March 2012 is :

Liabilities	Rs.	Rs.	*Assets*	Rs.
Capital A/c			Furniture	20,000
A	25,000		Stock	40,000
B	65,000		Bills Receivable	10,000
		90,000	Debtors	30,000
Reserve		20,000	Cash at Bank	40,000
Creditors		25,000		
Bills Payable		5,000		
		1,40,000		1,40,000

They agreed to take C as a partner with effect from 1st April 2012 on the following terms :

(a) A, B, and C will share profits and losses in the ratio of 5 : 3 : 2.

(b) C will bring Rs. 20,000 as premium for goodwill and Rs. 30,000 as capital.

(c) Half of the Reserve is to be withdrawn by the partners.

(d) The assets will be revalued as follows :

Furniture Rs. 30,000; Stock Rs. 39,500; Debtors Rs. 28,500

(e) A creditor for Rs. 12,000 has agreed to forgo his claim by Rs. 2,000.

(f) After making the above adjustments, the Capital Accounts of A and B should be adjusted on the basis of C's capital, by bringing cash or withdrawing cash, as the case may be.

Pass necessary Journal entries without narration and prepare the Balance Sheet of the new firm as on 1st April 2012.

Solution

In the books of A, B, & C
Journal *(without Narration)*

Date	Particulars		L.F.	Debit	Credit
2012				Rs.	Rs.
April 1	Furniture A/c	Dr.		10,000	
	Creditors A/c	Dr.		2,000	
	To Revaluation A/c				12,000
	Revaluation A/c	Dr.		2,000	
	To Stock				500
	" Provision for Bad Debts				1,500
	Revaluation A/c	Dr.		10,000	
	To A's Capital A/c				8,000
	" B's Capital A/c				2,000
	Reserve A/c	Dr.		20,000	
	To A's Capital A/c				16,000
	" B's Capital A/c				4,000
	Bank A/c	Dr.		50,000	
	To Goodwill A/c				20,000
	" C's Capital A/c				30,000
	Goodwill A/c	Dr.		20,000	
	To A's Capital A/c				20,000
	A's Capital A/c	Dr.		10,000	
	To B's Capital A/c				10,000
	A's Capital A/c	Dr.		8,000	
	B's Capital A/c	Dr.		2,000	
	To Bank A/c				10,000
	Bank A/c	Dr.		4,000	
	To A's Capital A/c				4,000
	B's Capital A/c	Dr.		14,000	
	To Bank A/c				14,000

Balance Sheet *as at 1st April 2012*

Liabilities	Rs.	Rs.	Assets	Rs.	Rs.
Capital A/c			Furniture		30,000
A	75,000		Stock		39,500
B	45,000		Bills Receivable		10,000
C	30,000		Debtors	30,000	
		1,50,000	*Less :* Provision for		
Creditors		23,000	Bad Debts	1,500	
Bills Payable		5,000			28,500
			Cash at Bank (40,000 + 50,000 – 10,000 + 4,000 – 14,000)		70,000
		1,78,000			1,78,000

Workings :

Dr. **Partners' Capital Account** *Cr.*

		A	B	C			A	B	C
		Rs.	Rs.	Rs.			Rs.	Rs.	Rs.
To	A's Capital A/c	—	10,000	—	By	Balance b/d	25,000	65,000	—
"	Bank	8,000	2,000	—	"	Revaluation	8,000	2,000	—
"	Bank *(bal. fig.)*	—	14,000	—	"	Reserve	16,000	4,000	—
"	Balance c/d	75,000	45,000	30,000	"	Goodwill	20,000	—	—
					"	B's Capital	10,000	—	—
					"	Bank	—	—	30,000
					"	Bank *(bal. fig.)*	4,000	—	—
		83,000	71,000	30,000			83,000	71,000	30,000

C's brings for $\frac{2}{10}$ = Rs. 30,000

$\therefore$ A should bring for $\frac{5}{10} = \left(\text{Rs. } 30,000 \times \frac{10}{2} \times \frac{5}{10}\right)$ = Rs. 75,000

Similarly, B's Capital = $\left(\text{Rs. } 30,000 \times \frac{10}{2} \times \frac{3}{10}\right)$ = Rs. 45,000

B will have to pay Rs. 10,000 for Goodwill (Rs. 20,000 $\times \frac{10}{2} \times \frac{1}{10}$).

Sacrificing Ratio :

$A = \frac{4}{5} - \frac{5}{10} = \frac{8-5}{10} = \frac{3}{10}$ (sacrifices)

$B = \frac{1}{5} - \frac{3}{10} = \frac{2-3}{10} = (-)\ \frac{1}{10}$ (gains)

Illustration 35

The following is the Balance Sheet of A and B as at March 31, 2007. C is admitted as a partner on the that date when the position of A and B was as:

Liabilities	Rs.	*Assets*	Rs.
A's Capital A/c	10,000	Debtors	11,000
B's Capital A/c	8,000	Land and Building	8,000
Creditors	12,000	Plant and Machinery	10,000
General Resrve	16,000	Stock of Goods	12,000
Workmen's Compensation Fund	4,000	Cash and Bank Balance	9,000
	50,000		50,000

A and B shared profits in the proportion of 3 : 2. The following terms of admission are agreed upon :

(a) Revaluation of Assets : Land and Building Rs. 18,000 and Stock of Goods Rs. 16,000.

(b) The liability on Workmen's Compensation Fund is determined at Rs. 2,000.

(c) C brought in as his share of goodwill Rs. 10,000 in cash.

(d) C was to bring further cash as would make his capital equal to 20% of the combined capitals of partners A and B after above revaluation and adjustments are carried out.

(e) The future profit-sharing proportions are : A : B C : = 2 : 2 : 1

Prepare the new Balance Shet of the firm and the Capital Accounts of the partners.

[CU BCom (Hons.) 2008]

Solution

Dr. **Partners' Capital Account** *Cr.*

Particulars	A	B	C		*Particulars*	A	B	C
	Rs.	Rs.	Rs.			Rs.	Rs.	Rs.
To Balance c/d	39,200	20,800	12,000	By	Balance b/d	10,000	8,000	—
				"	Goodwill	10,000	—	—
				"	General Reserve	9,600	6,400	—
				"	Revaluation on —Procit	9,600	6,400	—
				"	Bank			12,000
	39,200	20,800	12,000			39,200	20,800	12,000

Balance Sheet *as at 1st April 2007*

Liabilities	Rs.	Rs.	*Assets*	Rs.	Rs.
Capital A/c			Land and Building (Rs. 8,000 + Rs. 10,000)		18,000
A	39,200				
B	20,800		Plant & Machinery		10,000
C	12,000		Stock (Rs. 12,000 + Rs. 4,000)		16,000
		72,000	Debtors		11,000
Creditors		12,000	Cash at Bank (Rs. 9,000 + Rs. 10,000, Rs. 12,000)		31,000
Workmen's Compensation Fund (Rs. 4,000 – Rs. 2,000)		2,000			
		86,000			86,000

Workings :

1. Allocation of Goodwill

Sacrificing Ratio = Old Ratio – New Ratio

$A = \frac{3}{5} - \frac{2}{5} = \frac{1}{5}$; *(Sacrifices)*

$B = \frac{2}{5} - \frac{2}{5} = 0$ –

$C = \quad = \frac{1}{5}$ *(Gains)*

As A sacrificing alone, so, A will get the entire amount of Goodwill brought in by C.

2. Revaluation Account

Dr *Particulars*		*Amount* Rs.	*Particulars*	Cr. *Amount* Rs.
To Profit on Revaluation			By Land & Building	10,000
A	9,600		" Stock	4,000
B	6,400		" Workmen's	
		16,000	Comp. Fund	2,000
		16,000		16,000

3. Capital brought in by C

Adjusted Capital of A and B are ((Rs. 39,200 + Rs. 20,800) = Rs. 60,000

So, C should bring 20% of Rs. 60,000 i.e., Rs. 12,000

New Partner brings various assets as Capital and Proportionate Capital

Illustration 36

The Balance Sheet of A and B, a partnership firm, as at 31.12.2004, is:

Liabilities	Rs.	Rs.	*Assets*	Rs.	Rs.
Capital A/c			*Fixed Assets :*		
A	12,000		Goodwill	12,000	
B	24,000		Land & Building	14,400	
		36,000	Furniture & Fixture	1,200	
Current Account					27,600
A	14,400		*Current Assets*		
B	9,600		Stock	25,200	
		24,000	Debtors	4,200	
Sundry Creditors		6,000			29,400
Bank Overdraft		3,000	C's Loan		12,000
		69,000			69,000

A and B share profits and losses as 1 : 2. The partners agree to admit C as a third partner from 1st Jan. 2004.

The assets are revalued as:

Goodwill Rs. 18,000; Land and Building Rs. 30,000; Furniture of Fixture Rs. 6,000.

C brings in the following assets into partnership :

Goodwill Rs. 6,000; Furniture & Fixtures Rs. 1,800, Stock Rs. 13,800.

Profits in the new firm are to be shared equally by the three partners and the Capital and Current Accounts are to be adjusted as to be equal. For this purpose, additional cash should be brought in or excess to be withdrawn by the partners concerned.

Draft the necessary journal entries and prepare the Capital Accounts and Current Accounts of the three partners and the opening Balance Sheet of the new firm showing the amount of cash, if any, which each partner may have to provide.

[CU BCom(Hons.) 2005]

Solution

In the books of the firm

Journal

Date	*Particulars*		*L.F.*	*Debit* Rs.	*Credit* Rs.
?	Goodwill A/c	Dr.		6,000	
	Furniture A/c	Dr.		1,800	
	Stock A/c	Dr.		13,800	
	To C's Capital A/c				21,600
	(Sundry assets brought in by C as capital)				

Contd.

	Particulars		Rs.	Rs.
	Goodwill A/c	Dr.	6,000	
	Land & Building A/c	Dr.	15,600	
	Furniture & Fixture A/c	Dr.	4,800	
	To Revaluation A/c			26,400
	(Value of assets increased on revaluation)			
	Revaluation A/c	Dr.	26,400	
	To A's Capital A/c			8,800
	" B's Capital A/c			17,600
	(Profit on revluation transferred)			
	B's Capital A/c	Dr.	2,400	
	To B's Current A/c			2,400
	(Excess amount is B's Capital Account transferred to B's Current Account)			
	A's Current A/c	Dr.	9,600	
	To A's Capital A/c			9,600
	(Deficit in A's Capital Account transferred from A's Current Account)			
	Bank A/c	Dr.	45,600	
	To A's Current A/c			16,000
	" C's Current A/c			29,600
	(Cash brought in by A and C to make their current account equal to that of B's)			

Dr. **Revaluation Account** **Cr.**

Particulars		Amount	Particulars	Amount
	Rs.	Rs.		Rs.
To Profit on Revalution			By Goodwill A/c	6,000
A	8,800		" Land & Building A/c	15,600
B	17,600		" Furniture & Fixture A/c	4,800
		26,400		
		26,400		26,400

Dr. **Bank Account** **Cr.**

Particulars	Amount	Particulars	Amount
	Rs.		Rs.
To A's Current A/c	16,000	By Balance b/d	3,000
" C's Current A/c	29,600	" Balance c/d	42,600
	45,600		45,600

Dr. **Capital Account** **Cr.**

Particulars	A	B	C	Particulars	A	B	C
	Rs.	Rs.	Rs.		Rs.	Rs.	Rs.
To B's Current A/c	—	2,400	—	By Balance b/d	12,000	24,000	—
" Balance c/d	21,600	21,600	21,600	" Sundry Assets A/c			21,600
				" A's Current A/c	9,600	—	—
	21,600	24,000	21,600		21,600	24,000	21,600

Dr. **Current Account** **Cr.**

Particulars	A	B	C	Particulars	A	B	C
	Rs.	Rs.	Rs.		Rs.	Rs.	Rs.
To A's Capital A/c	9,600	—	—	By Balance b/d	14,400	9,600	—
" Balance c/d	29,600	29,600	29,600	" Revaluation A/c —Profit	8,800	17,600	—
				" B's Capital A/c	—	2,400	—
				" Bank A/c	16,000	—	29,600
	39,200	29,600	29,600		39,200	29,600	29,600

Balance Sheet *as at 1st April 2004*

Liabilities	Rs.	Rs.	*Assets*	Rs.
Capital A/c			**Fixed Asset**	
A	21,600		Goodwill (Rs. 18,000 + Rs. 6,000)	24,000
B	21,600		Land & Building (Rs. 14,400 + Rs. 15,600)	30,000
C	21,600		Furniture & Fixture	7,800
		64,800	(Rs. 1,200 + Rs. 4,800 + Rs. 1,800)	
Current A/c			**Current Assets**	
A	29,600		Stock (Rs. 25,200 + Rs. 13,800)	39,000
B	29,600		Sundry Debtors	4,200
C	29,600		C's Loan A/c	12,000
		88,800	Bank	42,600
Sundry Creditors		6,000		
		1,59,600		1,59,600

Notes :

1. Since Current Account of the partners are given, it has been assumed that the fixed capital method has been followed, as such, profit on revaluation is transferrd to Partners' Current Account in place of Partners' Capital Account.
2. As profit-sharing ratio is equal, Capital Account and Current Account also will be equal i.e., is proportion to C, the new partner.
3. It has been also assumed that C has a separate business of his own. C brought the assets from his separate business.

GENERAL ILLUSTRATIONS

Illustration 37

On 31st March 2010, the Balance Sheet of M/s P. R. & S sharing profits and losses in the ratio of 6 : 5 : 3, stood as follows :

Balance Sheet *as at 31st March, 2010*

Liabilities		Rs.	*Assets*	Rs.
Sundry Creditors		37,800	Cash	3,780
Bills Payable		12,600	Sundry Debtors	52,920
General Reserve		21,000	Stock	58,800
Capital Accounts :	P	70,800	Furniture	14,700
	R	59,700	Land and Buildings	90,300
	S	29,100	Goodwill	10,500
		2,31,000		2,31,000

They agree to admit Q into partnership giving him $\frac{1}{8}$th share, on 1.4.2010 on the following terms :

(1) Furniture be depreciated by Rs. 1,840.
(2) Stock shall be valued 10% less than the balance shet value.
(3) A provision of Rs. 2,640 be made for outstanding repair bill.
(4) The value of land and buildings having appreciated be brought up to Rs. 1,19,700.
(5) Value of Goodwill be brought up to Rs. 28,140.
(6) Q should bring in cash Rs. 29,400 as his capital

After making the above adjustments the capital accounts of the old partners be adjusted on the basis of proportion of Q's Capital to his share in the business by bringing in or taking out cash.

You are required to prepare Revaluation Account, Capital Accounts of Partners, Cash Account and Balance Sheet as on 1.4.2010 after Q's admission.

Solution **[CA Foundation]**

In the books of P, R, S & Q

Revaluation Account

Dr. *Cr.*

Date	Particulars		Amount	Date	Particulars	Amount
2010			Rs.	2010		Rs.
April 1	To Furniture A/c		1,840	April 1	By Land and Building A/c	29,400
	" Stock A/c		5,880			
	" Repairs Payable A/c		2,640			
	" Capital A/c :					
	Profit on Revaluation transferred					
	P	8,160				
	R	6,800				
	S	4,080	19,040			
			29,400			29,400

Dr. **Capital Account** Cr.

Date	Particulars	P Rs.	R Rs.	S Rs.	Q Rs.	Date	Particulars	P Rs.	R Rs.	S Rs.	Q Rs.
	To Cash A/c (bal. fig.)	7,320	6,800	—	—		By Balance b/d	70,800	59,700	29,100	—
	" Bakabce c/d	88,200	73,500	44,100	29,400		" General Reserve A/c	9,000	7,500	4,500	—
							" Goodwill A/c	7,560	6,300	3,780	—
							" Revaluation A/c	8,160	6,800	4,080	—
							" Cash A/c (bal. fig.)	—	—	2,640	29,400
		95,520	80,300	44,100	29,400			95,520	80,300	44,100	29,400

Dr. **Cash Account** Cr.

Date	Particulars	Amount Rs.	Date	Particulars	Amount Rs.
2010 April 1	To Balance b/d	3,780	2010 April 1	By P's Capital A/c	7,320
	" Q's Capital A/c	29,400		" R's Capital A/c	6,800
	" S/s Capital A/c	2,640		" Balance c/d	21,700
		35,820			35,820

Balance Sheet *as at 1st April, 2010*

Liabilities		Rs.	Assets	Rs.
Capital Accounts :			Goodwill	28,140
P	88,200		Land and Buildings	1,19,700
R	73,500		Furniture	12,860
S	44,100		Stock	52,920
Q	29,400	2,35,200	Sundry Debtors	52,920
Bills Payable		12,600	Cash	21,700
Sundry Creditors		37,800		
Outstanding Repairs		2,640		
		2,88,240		2,88,240

Workings :

1. Future Profit-sharing ratio and Sacrificing Ratio :

$$1-\frac{1}{8}=\frac{7}{8}$$

$$P=\frac{7}{8}\times\frac{6}{14}=\frac{42}{112}$$

$$R=\frac{7}{8}\times\frac{5}{14}=\frac{35}{112}$$

$$S=\frac{7}{8}\times\frac{3}{14}=\frac{21}{112}$$

$$Q=\frac{1}{8}=\frac{\mathbf{14}}{\mathbf{112}}$$

Hence, Future Profit-sharing ratio

P : R : Q = 42 : 35 : 21 : 14

or, 6 : 5 : 3 : 2

Sacrificing ratio

$$P=\frac{6}{14}-\frac{42}{112}=\frac{48-42}{112}=\frac{6}{112}\text{ (Sacrifices)}$$

$$R=\frac{5}{14}-\frac{35}{112}=\frac{40-35}{112}=\frac{5}{112}\text{ (Sacrifices)}$$

$$S=\frac{3}{14}-\frac{21}{112}=\frac{24-21}{112}=\frac{3}{112}\text{ (Sacrifices)}$$

∴ Sacrificing ratio = P : R : S = 6 : 5 : 3.

2. Proportionate Capital

If Q brings for $\frac{14}{112}$ = Rs. 29,400

P should bring for $\frac{42}{112}$ = Rs. $29,400\times\frac{42}{112}\times\frac{112}{14}$

= Rs. 88,200

R should bring for $\frac{35}{112}$ = Rs. $29,400\times\frac{35}{112}\times\frac{112}{14}$

= Rs. 73,500

S should bring for $\frac{21}{112}$ = Rs. $29,400\times\frac{21}{112}\times\frac{112}{14}$

= Rs. 44,100

The entry for goodwill being:

		Dr.	
Goodwill A/c		Dr.	
(Rs. 28,140 – Rs. 10,500)		Rs. 17,640	
	To P's Capital A/c		Rs. 7,560
	" R's Capital A/c		6,300
	" S's Capital A/c		3,780

Illustration 38

Gopal and Govind are partners sharing profits and losses in the ratio 60 : 40. The firm's Balance Sheet as on 31.3.2012 was :

Liabilities	Rs.	*Assets*	Rs.
Capitals Accounts :		Fixed Assets	3,00,000
Gopal	1,20,000	Investments	50,000
Govind	80,000	Current Assets	2,00,000
Long-term Loans	2,00,000	Loans and Advances	1,00,000
Current Liabilities	2,50,000		
	6,50,000		6,50,000

Due to financial difficulties, they have decided to admit Guru as a partner in the firm from 1.4.2012 on the following terms :

Guru will be paid 40% of the profits.

Guru will bring in Cash Rs. 1,00,000 as capital.

It is agreed that goodwill of the firm will be valued at 2 years' purchase of 3 years' normal average profits of the firm and Guru will bring in Cash as his share of goodwill. It was also decided that the partners will not withdraw their share of goodwill nor will the goodwills appear in the books of account.

The profits of the previous three years were as follows :

For the year ended 31.3.2010 Profit Rs. 20,000 (includes insurance claims received of Rs. 40,000).

For the year ended 31.3.2011, Loss Rs. 80,000 (includes Voluntary Retirement Compensation paid Rs. 1,10,000).

For the year ended 31.3.2012 Profit Rs. 1,05,000 (includes a profit of Rs. 25,000 on the sale of assets.) It was decided to revalue the assets on 31.3.2012 as :

Fixed Asset (Net) Rs. 4,00,000; Investments Nil; Current Assets Rs. 1,80,000; Loans and Advances Rs. 1,00,000;

The new profit-sharing ratio after the admission of Guru was 35 : 25 : 40.

Pass Journal entries on admission, showed goodwill calculation and prepare Revaluation Account, Partners' Capital Accounts and Balance Sheet as on 1.4.2012, after the admission of Guru.

[CA Foundation]

Solution

Calculation of Goodwill

	31.3.2010	31.3.2011	31.3.2012
	Rs.	Rs.	Rs.
Profit/Loss for the year	20,000	(–) 80,000	1,05,000
Add/Less : Abnormal Items	(–) 40,000	1,10,000	(–) 25,000
	(–) 20,000	30,000	80,000

$$\text{Average Profit} = \frac{(-)\text{ Rs. } 20{,}000 + \text{Rs. } 30{,}000 + \text{Rs. } 80{,}000}{3} = \text{Rs. } 30{,}000$$

Value of Goodwill = Average Profit × 2 years' purchase

= Rs. 30,000 × 2

= Rs. 60,000.

Value of Goodwill to be brought in by Guru = Rs. 60,000 × 40% = Rs. 24,000.

The goodwill will be distributed between the old partners as per sacrificing ratio :

Gopal $= \frac{3}{5} - \frac{7}{20} = \frac{12-7}{20} = \frac{5}{20}$ (sacrifices)

Govind $= \frac{2}{5} - \frac{5}{20} = \frac{8-5}{20} = \frac{3}{20}$ (")

Guru $= \frac{5}{20} + \frac{3}{20} = \frac{8}{20}$ (gains)

Thus,

Gopal will get = Rs. 24,000 × $\frac{5}{8}$ = Rs. 15,000

Govind will get = Rs. 24,000 × $\frac{3}{8}$ = Rs. 9,000.

In the books of the firm
Journal

Date	Particulars		L.F.	Debit	Credit
2012				Rs.	Rs.
April 1	Bank A/c	Dr.		1,24,000	
	To Guru's Capital A/c				1,00,000
	" Goodwill A/c				24,000
	(Capital and goodwill to be brought in by Guru in Cash.)				
	Goodwill A/c	Dr.		24,000	
	To Gopal's Capital A/c				15,000
	" Govind's Capital A/c				9,000
	(Goodwill credited to old partners as per sacrificing ratio.)				
	Revaluation A/c	Dr.		70,000	
	To Investments A/c				50,000
	" Current Assets A/c				20,000
	(Value of investments and Current Assets reduced on revaluation.)				
	Fixed Assets A/c	Dr.		1,00,000	
	To Revaluation A/c				1,00,000
	(Value of fixed assets increased on revaluation.)				
	Revaluation A/c	Dr.		30,000	
	To Gopal's Capital A/c				18,000
	" Govinda's Capital A/c				12,000
	(Profit on revaluation transferred to old partners' capital account.)				

Revaluation Account

Dr. Cr.

Particulars		Amount	Particulars	Amount
		Rs.		Rs.
To Investment A/c		50,000	By Fixed Assets A/c	1,00,000
" Current Assets A/c		20,000		
" Profit on Revaluation :				
Gopal	18,000			
Govind	12,000			
		30,000		
		1,00,000		1,00,000

Capital Account

Dr. Cr.

Particulars	Gopal	Govind	Guru	Particulars	Gopal	Govind	Guru
	Rs.	Rs.	Rs.		Rs.	Rs.	Rs.
To Balance c/d	1,53,000	1,01,000	1,00,000	By Balance b/d	1,20,000	80,000	—
				" Bank A/c	—	—	1,00,000
				" Goodwill A/c	15,000	9,000	—
				" Revaluation A/c —Profit	18,000	12,000	—
	1,53,000	1,01,000	1,00,000		1,53,000	1,01,000	1,00,000

Balance Sheet *as at 31st April 2012*

Liabilities		Rs.	Assets	Rs.
Capital Accounts :			Fixed Asset	4,00,000
Gopal	1,53,000		Investment	Nil
Govind	1,01,000		Current Assets	
Guru	1,00,000		(1,80,000 + 1,24,000)	3,04,000
		3,54,000	Loans and Advances	1,00,000
Long-term Loan		2,00,000		
Current Liabilities		2,50,000		
		8,04,000		8,04,000

Illustration 39

X, Y, and Z are partners sharing profits and losses in the ratio of 3 : 2 : 1. A is admitted as a partner on 31.12.2008 for an equal share and he is to bring Rs. 30,000 as Capital.

The Balance Sheet of the firm is :

Liabilities		Rs.	*Assets*	Rs.
Capital :			Land and Building	40,000
X	40,000		Plant and Machinery	30,000
Y	40,000		Furniture and Fixture	20,000
Z	30,000		Stock	15,000
		1,10,000	Debtors	20,000
Creditors		27,000	Bills Receivable	12,000
Bank Overdraft		10,000	Cash and Bank	10,000
		1,47,000		1,47,000

A is admitted after considering the following adjustments :

(i) The value of goodwill is Rs. 24,000.

(ii) Make a provision for bad debts @ 5% on Debtors.

(iii) Out of the creditors a sum of Rs. 10,000 is owing to A.

(iv) Expenses on revaluation amounted to Rs. 2,000 paid by X.

(v) Bills valued Rs. 4,000 were discounted by the bank out of which a bill for Rs. 1,000 was dishonoured on 31.12.2008, but not entered in the books, although the due date of the other discounted bills fall in Jan. 2009.

(vi) Advertisement expenses of Rs. 1,000 is to be carried forward to the next accounting period.

(vii) During 2088, part of the furniture was sold for Rs. 5,000 (Book value Rs. 8,000), W.D.V. Rs. 7,000. The proceeds due wrongly credited to Sales Account.

(viii) Life Insurance Premium amounting to Rs. 2,010 for Y wrongly debited to P & L A/c.

Show the Revaluation Account, Capital Account and the Balance Sheet.

Solution

In the books of the firm

Revaluation Account

Dr. *Cr.*

Particulars	*Amount*	*Particulars*		*Amount*
	Rs.			Rs.
To X's Capital A/c—Exps.	2,000	By Y's Capital A/c		2,010
" Provision for Bad Debts on Rs. 21,000	1,050	" Advertisement Suspense A/c		1,000
" Furniture A/c	8,000	" Loss on Revaluation :		
		X	4,020	
		Y	2,680	
		Z	1,340	
				8,040
	11,050			11,050

Partners' Capital Account

Dr. *Cr.*

Particulars	X	Y	Z	A	*Particulars*	X	Y	Z	A
	Rs.	Rs.	Rs.	Rs.		Rs.	Rs.	Rs.	Rs.
To Revaluation A/c	—	2,010	—	—	By Balance b/d	40,000	40,000	30,000	—
" Revaluation A/c					" Bank A/c	—	—	—	20,000
—Loss	4,020	2,680	1,340	—	" Goodwill A/c	12,000	8,000	4,000	—
" Balance c/d	49,980	43,310	32,660	30,000	" Creditors A/c	—	—	—	10,000
					" Revaluation A/c	2,000	—	—	—
	54,000	48,000	34,000	30,000		54,000	48,000	34,000	30,000

Balance Sheet *as at 31st Dec. 2008*

Liabilities		Rs.	*Assets*		Rs.
Capital :			Goodwill		24,000
X	49,980		Land and Building		40,000
Y	43,310		Plant and Machinery		30,000
Z	32,660		Furniture and Fixture		12,000
A	30,000		Stock		15,000
		1,55,950	Debtors	21,000	
Creditors		17,000	*Less* : Prov. for Bad Debts	1,050	
Bills Payable		10,000			19,950
			Bills Receivable		12,000
			Advertisement Suspense A/c		1,000
			Cash and Bank		29,000
			(20,000 + 10,000 − 1,000)		
		1,82,950			1,82,950

Note : Contingent liabilities for bill discounted will be Rs. 3,000.

Illustration 40

A, B, and C are partners in a firm of accountants who maintain accounts on a cash basis sharing profits and losses in the ratio of 2 : 3 : 1.

Their Balance Sheet as on March 31, 2012, on which date D is admitted as a partner, is :

Liabilities	Rs.	*Assets*	Rs.
B Capital	35,000	Furniture	10,000
C Capital	22,000	Motor Car	20,000
		Cash at Bank	18,000
		A Capital	9,000
	57,000		57,000

D is given $\frac{1}{4}$ share of the profits and losses in the firm and the profit and loss sharing ratio as between the other partners remains as before. The following adjustments are to be made prior to D's admission :

(a) the motor car is taken over by B at a value of Rs. 25,000.

(b) The furniture is revalued at Rs. 18,000.

(c) Goodwill Account is raised in the books at Rs. 50,000. It is agreed among A, B, and C that C is interested in goodwill only up to a value of Rs. 30,000.

(d) Fees billed but not realised Rs. 11,000 are brought into account.

(e) Expenses incurred but not paid, Rs. 3,000 are provided for.

D brings in Rs. 20,000 in cash as his capital contribution. He is also to be credited with Rs. 20,000 for having agreed to amalgamate his separate practice as Chartered Accountant with this firm.

Pass necessary Journal entries and prepare the Balance Sheet of the firm after D's admission.

Solution

In the books of the firm
Journal

Date	*Particulars*		*L.F.*	*Debit* Rs.	*Credit* Rs.
2012					
April 1	Bank A/c	Dr.		20,000	
	Goodwill A/c	Dr.		20,000	
	To D's Capital A/c				40,000
	(Capital and Goodwill to be brought in by D.)				
	Goodwill A/c	Dr.		50,000[1]	
	To A's Capital A/c				18,000
	" B's Capital A/c				27,000
	" C's Capital A/c				5,000
	(Value of Goodwill raised in the books.)				

Contd.

		Rs.	Rs.
B's Capital A/c	Dr.	25,000	
To Motor Car A/c			20,000
" Revaluation A/c			5,000
(Motor Car taken by B at increased valued.)			
Furniture A/c	Dr.	8,000	
Accrued Fees A/c	Dr.	11,000	
To Revaluation A/c			19,000
(Value of Furniture increased and Accrued Fees brought into account.)			
Revaluation A/c	Dr.	3,000	
To Creditors for Expenses A/c			3,000
(Outstanding expenses provide for.)			
Revaluation A/c	Dr.	21,000	
To A's Capital A/c			7,000
" B's Capital A/c			10,500
" C's Capital A/c			3,500
(Profit on revaluation transferred.)			

Dr. **Capital Account** Cr.

Particulars	A Rs.	B Rs.	C Rs.	D Rs.	*Particulars*	A Rs.	B Rs.	C Rs.	D Rs.
To Balance b/d	9,000	—	—	—	By Balance b/d	—	35,000	22,000	—
" Motor Car A/c	—	20,000	—	—	" Goodwill A/c	18,000	27,000	5,000	—
" Revaluation A/c	—	5,000	—	—	" Bank A/c	—	—	—	20,000
" Balance c/d	16,000	47,500	30,500	40,000	" Goodwill A/c	—	—	—	20,000
					" Revaluation A/c —Profit	7,000	10,500	3,500	—
	25,000	72,500	30,500	40,000		25,000	72,500	30,500	40,000

Balance Sheet *as at* **31st Dec. 2012**

Liabilities		Rs.	*Assets*	Rs.
Capital :			Goodwill (50,000 + 20,000)	70,000
A	16,000		Furniture (10,000 + 8,000)	18,000
B	47,500		Accrued Fees	11,000
C	30,500		Cash at Bank (18,000 + 20,000)	38,000
D	40,000	1,34,000		
Creditors for Expenses		3,000		
		1,37,000		1,37,000

Workings :

1. **Distribution of Goodwill**

	Rs.	A Rs.	B Rs.	C Rs.
Goodwill to the extent of (in the old ratio i.e., 2 : 3 : 1)	30,000	10,000	15,000	5,000
And, the balance i.e., in the ratio of 2 : 3 between A and B	20,000	8,000	12,000	
	50,000	18,000	27,000	5,000

Illustration 41

Ranu and Mili are partners in a firm sharing Profits and Loses in the ratio of $\frac{2}{3}$ and $\frac{1}{3}$.

The Balance Sheet of the firm on 31st December 1995 was :

Liabilities	Rs.	Rs.	*Assets*		Rs.
Creditors		7,000	Goodwill		4,980
Investment Provision		2,000	Investments		25,000
General Reserve		10,500	Stock		15,000
Workmen's Compensation Fund		6,000	Debtors	20,000	
Capitals Accounts :			*Less* : Provision	2,500	
Ranu	30,000				17,500
Mili	24,500		Bills Receivable		12,500
		54,500	Bank		5,020
		80,000			80,000

On the above date Manisha is admitted for $\frac{2}{5}$th share in the profits or losses of the firm.

Following revaluations were made at the time of admission :

(a) Manisha is required to bring in Rs. 50,000 as Capital.
(b) Her Goodwill was calculated at Rs. 12,000.
(c) Ranu and Mili had purchased a Machinery on hire-purchase system for Rs. 15,000 of which only Rs. 500 are to be paid. Both Machinery and unpaid liability did not appear in the Balance Sheet.
(d) There was a Joint Life Policy on the livces of Ranu and Mili for Rs. 75,000. Surrender value of the policy on the date of admission amounted to Rs. 12,000.
(e) Accrued incomes not appearing in the books were Rs. 500.
(f) Markt value of Investments is Rs. 23,900.
(g) Claim on account of compensation is estimated as Rs. 750.
(h) Sikha, an old customer, whose account was written-off as bad, has promised to pay Rs. 1,750 in settlement of her full claim.
(i) Provision for doubtful debts is required at Rs. 3,000.

Prepare Revaluation Account, Partners' Capital Account and Opening Balance Sheet after admission of Manisha. **[CU BCom (Hons.) 1996)]**

Solution

In the books of Ranu, Milli and Manisha

Revaluation Account

Dr. Particulars	Rs.	Amount Rs.	Particulars	Cr. Amount Rs.
To Machine Suppliers' A/c		500	By Sikha (Debtors) A/c	1,750
" Prov. for Doubtful Debts (Rs. 3,000 – Rs. 2,500)		500	" Machinery A/c —Purchased on H.P. Adjusted	15,000
" Capital A/c —Profit on Revaluation			" Joint Life Policy A/c —Surrender value of JLP raised	12,000
Ranu – $\frac{2}{3}$ =	22,933		" Accrued Income A/c —Unrecorded	500
Milli – $\frac{1}{3}$ =	11,467	34,400	" Workmen's Compensation Fund A/c (Rs. 6,000 – Rs. 750)	5,250
			" Provision for Investment A/c	900
		35,400		35,400

Capital Accounts

Dr. Particulars	Ranu Rs.	Milli Rs.	Manisha Rs.	Particulars	Ranu Rs.	Milli Rs.	Cr. Manisha Rs.
To Balance c/d	76,613	47,807	50,000	By Balance b/d	30,000	24,500	—
				" General Reserve	7,000	3,500	—
				" Revaluation A/c —Profit	22,933	11,467	
				" Bank A/c	—	—	50,000
				" Goodwill	16,680	8,340[1]	—
	76,613	47,807	50,000		76,613	47,807	50,000

Balance Sheet *as at 31st Dec. 1996*

Liabilities	Rs.	Rs.	Assets	Rs.	Rs.
Capitals :			Goodwill (Rs. 4,980 + 25,020)		30,000
Ranu	76,613		Machinery		15,000
Milli	47,807		Investment (Cost)		25,000
Manisha	50,000		Joint Life Policy		12,000
		1,74,420	Stock		15,000
Creditors		7,000	Debtors	20,000	
Provisions for Investment (Rs. 2,000 – 900)		1,100	*Less* : Prov. for Bad Debt	3,000	
Machine Suppliers		500		17,000	
Workmen's Compensation Fund (Rs. 6,000 – 5,250)		750	*Add* : Recovery of Bad Debts	1,750	18,750
			Bills Receivable		12,500
			Accrued Income		500
			Bank (Rs. 5,020 + 50,000)		55,020
		1,83,770			1,83,770

Workings :

1. Manisha is admitted for $\frac{2}{5}$th share for which she had to bring Rs. 12,000 as her share of goodwill. So, full value of goodwill will be Rs. 30,000 (i.e., Rs. 12,000 $\times \frac{5}{2}$). Assume Manisha did not bring her share of goodwill in cash. So, goodwill account should be raised at its full value i.e., Rs. 30,000. But already raised in the books Rs. 4,980. So, Amount to be raised for goodwill Rs. 25,020 (i.e., Rs. 30,000 – Rs. 4,980).
2. Surrender value of Joint Life Policy is assumed to be raised at its full value and not written-off.
3. Cost of Invstment is Rs. 25,000 and their market value Rs. 23,900). So, provision for Invstment should be maintained for Rs. 1,100 (Rs. 25,000 – Rs. 23,900) But there was an old provision for Rs. 2,000. Thus, Provisions for Investmnt to be reduced by Rs. 900 (Rs. 2,000 – Rs. 1,100).
4. Since Sikha, an old customer, promised to pay Rs. 1,750 out of debts already written-off, the same may be treated as:

Sikha (Debtors) A/c Dr.	1,750	
Or, Bad Debts Recovery A/c Dr.		
To Revaluation A/c		1,750

Illustration 42

Rain and Storm are partner in a firm sharing profits and losses as 3 : 2. Their Balance Sheet on 31st December, 2000 stands as under :

Liabilities	Rs.	Rs.	*Assets*		Rs.
Creditors		35,000	Cash		4,000
Capitals Accounts :			Debtors	22,000	
Rain	40,000		*Less* : Provision for Bad Debts	2,000	
Storm	20,000				20,000
		60,000	Stock		18,000
			Machinery		20,000
			Land and Building		33,000
		95,000			95,000

On 1st January 2001 they agree to take Dust as a partner on the following conditions :

(i) The goodwill of the firm shall be valued at Rs. 23,750 and Dust shall pay his share of goodwill in cash.

(ii) Dust shall contribute Rs. 15,000 as his share of capital.

(iii) Land and Building shall be valued at Rs. 42,000, Machinery shall be depreciated by Rs. 5,000. Provision for bad debts shall be raised to Rs. 3,000 and another provision shall be made for a probable liability for damages amounting to Rs. 1,300.

(iv) The profit and loss sharing ratio shall be so adjusted that, between Rain and Storm, the former ratio is maintained, while between Storm and Dust there shall be the same ratio as between Rain and Storm.

(v) The capital shall be adjusted (without disturbing the ultimate total capital) so as to correspond with the new ratio, the excess or deficit being transferred to their respective Current Accounts.

Show Journal entries to give effect to the above arrangements and prepare the Opening Balance Sheet of the new firm.

[CU BCom (Hons.) 2001]

Solution

In the books of the firm
Journal

Date	*Particulars*		*L.F.*	*Debit* Rs.	*Credit* Rs.
2001					
Jan. 1	Cash A/c	Dr.		20,000	
	To Goodwill A/c				5,000
	" Dust Capital A/c				15,000
	(Cash brought in by Dust, the new partner, as premium for goodwill and Capital.)				
	Goodwill A/c	Dr.		5,000	
	To Rain Capital A/c				3,000
	" Storm Capital A/c				2,000
	(Premium of goodwill distributed between old partners in their sacrificing-ratio 3 : 2)				

Contd.

Particulars		Rs.	Rs.
Land & Building A/c	Dr.	9,000	
To Revaluation A/c			9,000
(Value of L & B increased.)			
Revaluation A/c	Dr.	7,300	
To Machinery A/c			5,000
" Prov. for B/D A/c			1,000
" Prov for liability for damages A/c			1,300
(Value of machine depréciated, prov. for B/D increased and prov. for liability for damages created.)			
Revaluation A/c	Dr.	1,700	
To Rain Capital A/c			1,020
" Storm Capital A/c			680
(Profit on revaluation transferred)			
Rain Capital A/c	Dr.	5,320	
To Rain Current A/c			5,320
(Rain's excess capital transferred to his Current Account)			
Storm Current A/c	Dr.	3,120	
Dust Current A/c	Dr.	2,200	
To Storm Capital A/c			3,120
" Dust Capital A/c			2,200
(Deficit of Capital Account transferred to Current Account.)			

Balance Sheet *as at 1st January 2001*

Liabilities	Rs.	Rs.	*Assets*	Rs.	Rs.
Capitals :			Land and Building		42,000
Rain	38,700		Plant and Machinery	20,000	
Storm	25,800		*Less* : Depreciationst	5,000	
Dust	17,200				15,000
		81,700	Stock		18,000
Current Account :			Debtors	22,000	
Rain		5,320	*Less* : Prov. for Bad Debt	3,000	
Provision for Damages		1,300			19,000
Creditors		35,000	Cash (Rs. 4,000 + Rs. 5,000 + Rs. 15,000)		24,000
			Current Account :		
			Stork		3,120
			Dust		2,200
		1,23,320			1,23,320

Workings :

1. **Net Profit-Sharing Ratio**

Storm : dust = 3 : 2 = 2 : x (say) as, $x = \frac{4}{3}$

Thus, the new ratio among Rain, Storm and Dust becomes = $3 : 2 : \frac{4}{3}$

Or, 9 : 6 : 4; Or , Rain $\frac{9}{19}$; Storm $\frac{6}{19}$ and dust $\frac{4}{19}$

So, the sacrificing-ratio will be :

$$\text{Rain} = \frac{3}{5} - \frac{9}{19} = \frac{57-45}{95} = \frac{12}{95} \text{ (sacrifices)}$$

$$\text{Storm} = \frac{2}{5} - \frac{6}{19} = \frac{38-30}{95} = \frac{8}{95} \text{ (sacrifices)}$$

So, the sacrificing-ratio is 12 : 8 or 3 : 2.

2. Total capital of the new firm will be **Rs. 81,700 (i.e., Rain Rs. 40,000 + Storm Rs. 20,000 + Profit on Rev. Rs. 1,700 + Goodwill Rs. 5,000 + Dust's Capital Rs. 15,000). Accordingly, the Capital Balance of the partner's will be :**

$$\text{Rain} = \text{Rs. } 81,700 \times \frac{9}{19} = \text{Rs. } 38,700$$

$$\text{Storm} = \text{Rs. } 81,700 \times \frac{6}{19} = \text{Rs. } 25,800$$

$$\text{Dust} = \text{Rs. } 81,700 \times \frac{4}{19} = \text{Rs. } 17,200$$

Dr. **Capital Account** Cr.

Particulars	Rain	Storm	Dust	Particulars	Rain	Storm	Dust
	Rs.	Rs.	Rs.		Rs.	Rs.	Rs.
To Rain Current A/c (bal. fig.)	5,320	—	—	By Balance b/d	40,000	20,000	—
" Balance c/d	38,700	25,800	17,200	" Bank			15,000
				" Goodwill	3,000	2,000	—
				" Revaluation A/c—Profit	1,020	680	—
				" Storm's Current A/c	—	3,120	—
				" Dust Current A/c	—	—	2,200
	44,020	25,800	17,200		44,020	25,800	17,200

Illustration 43

Quick and Slow are partners in a firm sharing profits and losses in the ratio of 3 : 2. The Balance Sheet of the firm as on 31st March 2013 was :

Liabilities	Rs.	Rs.	Assets	Rs.
Current Accounts			Furniture and Fixtures	60,000
Quick	1,20,000		Office Equipments	30,000
Slow	77,000		Motor Car	75,000
		1,97,000	Stock	50,000
General Reserve		30,000	Sundry Debtors	90,000
Sundry Creditors		96,000	Cash at Bank	18,000
		3,23,000		3,23,000

Smooth was admitted as a new partner with effect from 1st April 2013 and it was agreed that he would bring some private furniture worth Rs. 10,000 and private stock costing Rs. 8,000 and in addition, contribute Rs. 50,000 cash towards capital.

He would also bring proportionate share of goodwill which is to be valued at two years' purchase of the average profits of the last three years.

The profits of the last three years were : 2012-13 Rs. 52,000; 2011-12 Rs. 32,000; 2010-11 Rs. 28,000.

However, on a checking of the past records, it was noticed that on 1.4.2011 a new furniture costing Rs. 8,000 was purchased but wrongly debited to revenue, and in 2012–13 a purchase invoice for Rs. 4,000 dated 25.3.2013 has been omitted in the books. The firm charges depreciation on Furniture @ 10% p.a.

Your calculation of goodwill is to be made on the basis of correct profits.

On revaluation, value of Stock is to be reduced by 5% and Motor car is worth Rs. 85,000.

Smooth duly paid the required amount for goodwill and cash towards capital.

It was decided that the future profits of the firm would be shared as Quick 50%, Slow 30% and Smooth 20%. Assuming the above-mentioned arrangements were duly carried out, show the Capital Accounts of the partners and the Balance Sheet of the firm after Smooth's admission.

[ICWA]

Solution

Dr. **Capital Account** Cr.

Particulars	Quick	Slow	Smooth	Particulars	Quick	Slow	Smooth
	Rs.	Rs.	Rs.		Rs.	Rs.	Rs.
To Balance c/d	1,51,620	1,00,624	68,000	By Balance b/d	1,20,000	77,000	—
				" General Reserve	18,000	12,000	—
				" Revaluation A/c — Profit	4,500	3,000	—
				" Goodwill A/c (as sacrificing ratio is 1 : 1)	7,632	7,632	—
				" Furniture	—	—	10,000
				" Stock	—	—	8,000
				" Bank	—	—	50,000
				" Advertisement (for Profit)	1,488	992	—
	1,51,620	1,00,624	68,000		1,51,620	1,00,624	68,000

Balance Sheet *as at April 1, 2013*

Liabilities	Rs.	Rs.	*Assets*	Rs.	Rs.
Capital Accounts :			Furniture and Fittings	60,000	
Quick	1,51,620		*Add :* Brought in by Smooth	10,000	
Slow	1,00,624			70,000	
Smooth	68,000		*Add :* For Rectification	6,480	
		3,20,244			76,480
Sundry Creditors			Office Equipment		30,000
(Rs. 96,000 + Rs. 4,000)		1,00,000	Motor Car		85,000
			Stock	50,000	
			Add : Brought in by Smooth	8,000	
				58,000	
			Less : Revaluation	2,500	
					55,500
			Sundry Debtors		90,000
			Bank (18,000 + 50,000 + 15,264)		83,264
		4,20,244			4,20,244

Workings :

1. **Calculation of Goodwill**

Year	Profit Rs.	Adjustment	Correct Profit Rs.
2010—11	28,000	—	28,000
2011—12	32,000	+ 8,000 (New furniture)	39,200
		− 800 (Dep.)	
2012—13	52,000	− 4,000 (Purchase omitted)	47,280
		− 720 (Dep. on new furniture)	
		For 3 years	1,14,480

∴ Value of Goodwill Rs. 1,14,480 ÷ 3 = Rs. 38,160 × 2 = Rs. 76,320.

Smooth should bring Rs. 76,320 × 20% = Rs. 15,264.

2. **Adjusted Profit**

Furniture and Fixture A/c Dr. 6,480 (8,000 – 800 – 720)

To	Creditors	4,000
"	Quick's Capital A/c	1,488
"	Slow's Capital A/c	992

3. **Profit on Revaluations**

Motor Car – Stock = Rs. 10,000 – Rs. 2,500 = Rs. 7,500.

Illustration 44

Sen and Paul were partners sharing profits and losses in the ratio of 3 : 2. Their Balance Sheet as on 31.12.2010 stood as :

Liabilities		Rs.	*Assets*		Rs.
Capital :			Land and Building		14,000
Sen	32,000		Plant and Machinery		18,000
Paul	14,000		Stock		14,000
		46,000	Debtors	10,000	
Reserve		4,000	*Less :* Provision	2,000	
Creditors		6,000			8,000
			Cash and Bank		2,000
		56,000			56,000

On 1.1.2010, they took Saha in the firm on the following conditions :

(i) Saha was given $\frac{1}{5}$th interest in the business for which he had to pay **proportionate amount** as premium for goodwill. Sen and Das sacrified in 4 : 1.

(ii) Value of the goodwill was estimated at Rs. 18,400.

(iii) Revaluation of assets and other information were :
Land and Building to be increased to Rs. 18,000; Plant and Machinery to be reduced by Rs. 8,800. Debtors were considered good. The unsold stock lying with the consignee valued at Rs. 15,200 which should be brought into books.

(iv) The total capital of the new firm was agreed to be Rs. 80,000. Capital accounts of the partner will be in proportion to the new profit-sharing ratio for which additional capital should be brought in or excess to be withdrawn by partner concerned. Show the Revaluation Account, Capital Account and the Balance Sheet.

Solution

Proportionate amount of premium for goodwill to be brought in by Saha = Rs. 18,400 × $\frac{1}{5}$ = Rs. 3,680.

The amount of goodwill to be credited to Sen and Paul's Capital as per sacrificing ratio i.e., 4 : 1.

So, Sen will get Rs. 3,680 × $\frac{4}{5}$ = Rs. 2,944

Paul will get Rs. 3,680 × $\frac{1}{5}$ = Rs. 736

Future profit-sharing ratio or the new ratio :

Saha gets $\frac{1}{5}$ which is sacrificied by Sen and Paul in 4 : 1.

i.e., Sen sacrificies $\frac{4}{5}$ of $\frac{1}{5} = \frac{4}{25}$

Paul sacrifices $\frac{1}{5}$ of $\frac{1}{5} = \frac{1}{25}$

So, Sen's new share = $\frac{3}{5} - \frac{4}{25} = \frac{15-4}{25} = \frac{11}{25}$

Paul's new share = $\frac{2}{5} - \frac{1}{25} = \frac{10-1}{25} = \frac{9}{25}$

∴ New ratio—Sen : Paul : Saha = 11 : 9 : 5.

Revaluation Account

Dr. Cr.

Particulars		Rs.	Particulars	Rs.
To Plant and Machinery A/c		8,800	By Land and Building A/c	4,000
" Profit on Revaluation:			" Stock A/c	15,200
Sen $\frac{3}{5}$	7,440		" Provision for Bad Debt A/c —Written-back	2,000
Paul $\frac{2}{5}$	4,960			
		12,400		
		21,200		21,200

Capital Account

Dr. Cr.

Particulars	Sen Rs.	Paul Rs.	Saha Rs.	Particulars	Sen Rs.	Paul Rs.	Saha Rs.
To Bank A/c *(bal. fig.)*	9,584	—	—	By Balance b/d	32,000	14,000	—
" Balance c/d	35,200	28,800	16,000	" Bank A/c	—	—	16,000*
				" Reserve A/c	2,400	1,600	—
				By Revaluation A/c —Profit	7,440	4,960	—
				" Goodwill A/c	2,944	736	—
				" Bank A/c *(bal. fig.)*	—	7,504	—
	44,784	28,800	16,000		44,784	28,800	16,000

Balance Sheet *as at 1st April 2011*

Liabilities		Rs.	Assets	Rs.
Capital Account :			Land and Building (Rs. 14,000 + Rs. 4,000)	18,000
Sen	35,200		Maintained Machinery (Rs. 18,000 – Rs. 8,800)	9,200
Paul	28,800		Stock (Rs. 14,000 + Rs. 15,200)	29,200
Saha	16,000		Debtors	10,000
		80,000	Cash and Bank	
Creditors		6,000	(Rs. 2,000 + Rs. 16,000 + Rs. 7,504 + Rs. 3,680 – Rs, 9,584)	19,600
		86,000		86,000

***Proportionate Capitals :**

Total Capital of the new firm is Rs. 80,000

∴ Sen's share = Rs. 80,000 × $\frac{11}{25}$ = Rs. 35,200

Paul's share = Rs. 80,000 × $\frac{9}{25}$ = Rs. 28,800

Saha's share = Rs. 80,000 × $\frac{5}{25}$ = Rs. 16,000.

So, Sen will withdraw = Rs. 44,784 – Rs. 35,200 = Rs. 9,584

Paul will bring = Rs. 28,800 – Rs. 21,296 = Rs. 7,504

Illustration 45

A and B are partners in a firm sharing profits and losses in the ratio 3 : 2. Their Balance Sheet as on 31.12.2010 stood as:

Liabilities	Rs.	Rs.	*Assets*	Rs.	Rs.
Sundry Creditors		20,000	Goodwill		12,000
Capital Account			Cash in hand		15,000
A	12,000		Sundry Debtors	21,000	
B	30,000		*Less :* Reserve for		
		42,000	Bad Debts	1,000	
					20,000
			Stock-in-trade		10,750
			Fixture and Fittings		250
			Profit and Loss Account		4,000
		62,000			62,000

On 1.1.2011 they admit C as a partner on the following terms :

(a) The new profit-sharing ratio of A, B, and C becomes 5 : 3 : 2.

(b) Agreed value of Goodwill is Rs. 20,000 and C brings the necessary premium for Goodwill in cash, half of which is retained in the business. Book value of Goodwill should remain undisturbed.

(c) The Reserve for bad debts is to be raised to 10% of Sundry Debtors.

(d) Stock-in-trade is to be revalued at Rs. 12,000 but the effect is not to be shown in the books.

(e) Fixture and Fittings are to be reduced to Rs. 150.

(f) C should bring further sum in cash in order to make his capital equal to $\frac{1}{5}$th of the combined adjusted capital of A and B.

Show the necessary Journal entries and the Capital Accounts of the partners and also prepare the Balance Sheet of the new firm as at 1.1.2011.

Solution

In the books of A, B, and C
Journal

Date	*Particulars*		L.F.	*Debit*	*Credit*
2011				Rs.	Rs.
Jan. 1	Bank A/c	Dr.		9,420	
	To C's Capital A/c				7,820
	" Goodwill A/c				1,600
	(Goodwill and capital to be brought in by C in cash.)				
	Goodwill A/c	Dr.		1,600	
	To A's Capital A/c				800
	" B's Capital A/c				800
	(Goodwill to be credited to A and B's capital account in sacrificing ratio.)				
	A's Capital A/c	Dr.		400	
	B's Capital A/c	Dr.		400	
	To Bank A/c				800
	(Half of the goodwill to be withdrawn.)				
	A's Capital A/c	Dr.		2,400	
	B's Capital A/c	Dr.		1,600	
	To Profit and Loss A/c				4,000
	(Debit balance of P & L A/c transferred to A and B's capital in 3 : 2.)				

Contd.

		Rs.	Rs.
Profit and Loss Adjustment A/c	Dr.	1,200	
To Reserve for Bad Debts A/c			1,100
" Fixture and Fittings A/c			100
(Value of assets is reduced on revaluation before C's admission.)			
A's Capital A/c	Dr.	720	
B's Capital A/c	Dr.	480	
To Profit and Loss Adjustment A/c			1,200
(Loss on revaluation transferred to A and B's capital in 3 : 2.)			
C's Capital A/c	Dr.	250	
To A's Capital A/c			125
" B's Capital A/c			125
(Effect of stock on revaluation adjusted on C's admission.)			

Dr. **Capital Account** Cr.

Particulars	A	B	C	Particulars	A	B	C
	Rs.	Rs.	Rs.		Rs.	Rs.	Rs.
To Profit and Loss A/c —Loss	2,400	1,600	—	By Balance b/d	12,000	30,000	—
To Profit and Loss Adj. A/c—Loss	720	480	—	" Bank	—	—	7,820
" A's Capital	—	—	125	By Goodwill	800	800	—
B's Capital	—	—	125	" C's Capital	125	125	—
" Bank (Withdraw of Goodwill)	400	400					
" Balance c/d	9,405	28,445	7,570				
	12,925	30,925	7,820		12,925	30,925	7,820
				By Balance b/d	9,405	28,445	7,570

Balance Sheet *as at 1st Jan. 2011*

Liabilities	Rs.	Rs.	Assets	Rs.	Rs.
Capital :			Goodwill		12,000
A	9,405		Cash (Rs. 15,000 + Rs. 9,420 – Rs. 800)		23,620
B	28,445		Sundry Debtors	21,000	
C	7,570	45,420	*Less :* Prov. for Bad Debts	2,100	18,900
Sundry Creditors		20,000	Stock		10,750
			Furniture and Fixtures (Rs. 250 – Rs. 100)		150
		65,420			65,420

Workings :

1. Goodwill to be brought in by C

	Rs.
Agreed value of Goodwill	20,000
Less : as per Balance Sheet	12,000
Undervaluation	8,000

$\therefore$ C is to bring Rs. $8{,}000 \times \frac{1}{5} = 1{,}600$.

Sacrificing Ratio :

A $\frac{3}{5} - \frac{5}{10} = \frac{6-5}{10} = \frac{1}{10}$ (sacrifices)

B $\frac{2}{5} - \frac{3}{10} = \frac{4-3}{10} = \frac{1}{10}$ (sacrifices)

C $\frac{1}{10} + \frac{1}{10} = \frac{2}{10}$ (gains)

$\therefore$ Goodwill to be shared between A and B equally, i.e., (1 : 1).

2. Adjustments for increased value of Stock

Since the increased value of stock is not to be shown in the books, the effect of the same will be :

Increased value of stock Rs. 1,250 (Rs. 12,000 – Rs. 10,750)

	Credit Rs.	Debit Rs.	Net Effect Rs.
A	750 $\left(\frac{2}{5}\right)$	625 $\left(\frac{5}{10}\right)$	125 (Cr.)
B	500 $\left(\frac{2}{5}\right)$	375 $\left(\frac{3}{10}\right)$	125 (Cr.)
A	—	250 $\left(\frac{2}{10}\right)$	250 (Dr.)

3. Capital to be brought in By C

Existing capital of A and B			42,000
Less : P & L A/c (Dr.)		4,000	
Loss on Revaluation		1,200	5,200
			36,800
Add :	Premium brought in by C 1,600 × $\frac{1}{2}$	800	
	Stock revalued	250	1,050
			37,850

∴ C is to bring : Rs. 37,850 × $\frac{1}{5}$ = Rs. 7,570 + Rs. 250 (for stock) = Rs. 7,820.

Illustration 46

On 1.1.2012, A and B, who were trading in partnership, sharing $\frac{7}{12}$th and $\frac{5}{12}$th, respectively, take in C, giving him $\frac{1}{6}$th share, over and above his capital. C brings in Rs. 96,000 as his Goodwill for the $\frac{1}{6}$th share which he has acquired $\frac{1}{24}$th from A and $\frac{1}{6}$th from B. The cash brought in by C as his capital as well as for his share in Goodwill is credited in one separate account in his personal name.

On 31.12.2012, their Trial Balance stood as :

	Rs.		Rs.
Machinery	6,00,000	A's Capital	3,36,000
Furniture	40,000	B's Capital	2,40,000
Stock	1,20,000	C's Account (personal)	2,24,000
Debtors	2,00,000	Creditors	48,000
A's Drawings	32,000	Current year's Profit	2,32,000
B's Drawings	52,000		
C's Drawings	8,000		
Cash in hand	28,000		
	10,80,000		10,80,000

Interest on drawings is to be ignored but interest on capital account is to be allowed at 5% p.a. after the necessary adjustments therein as regards the Goodwill in cash brought in by C.

Prepare the Balance Sheet of the firm as on 31.12.2012, showing full details in the Capital Accounts of the three partners.

Solution

1. Sacrificing Ratio

A sacrifices $\frac{1}{24}$

B sacrifices $\frac{1}{8}$

∴ Sacrificing ratio is 1 : 3

Hence, Goodwill should be credited to A and B's capital account in 1 : 3.

2. Future Profit-sharing Ratio

$$A = \frac{7}{12} - \frac{1}{24} = \frac{14-1}{24} = \frac{13}{14}$$

$$B = \frac{5}{12} - \frac{1}{8} = \frac{10-3}{24} = \frac{7}{24}$$

$$C = \frac{1}{6} = \frac{4}{24}$$

∴ A : B : C = 13 : 7 : 4.

A will be credited by Rs. 24,000 $\left(96,000 \times \frac{1}{4}\right)$ B will be credited by Rs. 72,000 $\left(96,000 \times \frac{3}{4}\right)$

Dr. **Capital Account** Cr.

Particulars	A Rs.	B Rs.	C Rs.	Particulars	A Rs.	B Rs.	C Rs.
2012 Jan. 1				2012 Jan. 1			
To Balance c/d	3,60,000	3,12,000	1,28,000	By Balance b/d	3,36,000	2,40,000	—
				" Goodwill	24,000	72,000	—
				" Bank	—	—	1,28,000
	3,60,000	3,12,000	1,28,000		3,60,000	3,12,000	1,28,000
Dec. 31				Jan. 1			
To Drawings	32,000	52,000	8,000	By Balance b/d	3,60,000	3,12,000	1,28,000
To Balance c/d	4,50,000	3,31,600	1,58,400	Dec. 31			
				By Interest on Capital	18,000	15,600	6,400
				" Share of Profit	1,04,000	56,000	32,000
	4,82,000	3,83,600	1,66,400		4,82,000	3,83,600	1,66,400

Dr. **Profit and Loss Appropriation Account** *for the year ended 31st Dec. 2012* Cr.

	Rs.	Rs.		Rs.
To Interest on Capital :			By Profit and Loss A/c —Trading Profit	2,32,000
A	18,000			
B	15,600			
C	6,400	40,000		
" Net Profit :				
A $\frac{13}{24}$	1,04,000			
B $\frac{7}{24}$	56,000			
C $\frac{4}{24}$	32,000	1,92,000		
		2,32,000		2,32,000

Balance Sheet *as at 31st Dec. 2012*

Liabilities	Rs.	Rs.	Assets	Rs.	Rs.
Capital Accounts :			Machinery		6,00,000
A	4,50,000		Furniture		40,000
B	3,31,600		Stock		1,20,000
C	1,58,400	9,40,000	Debtors		2,00,000
Creditors		48,000	Cash in hand		28,000
		9,88,000			9,88,000

Illustration 47

X and Y were trading in partnership sharing profits and losses in the ratio of 7 : 5. On 1.1.2012, they admitted Z into partnership on the following terms :

Z was to have $\frac{1}{6}$th share which he purchased $\frac{1}{8}$th from X and $\frac{1}{24}$th from Y paying Rs. 20,000 for that share of Goodwill. Z also brought Rs. 25,000 as his capital into the firm. It was further agreed theirt Machinery should be reduced by 10% and that Investments should be reduced to their market value of Rs. 8,000.

The Balance Sheet of the old firm at 31.12.2011, was :

Liabilities	Rs.	Rs.	Assets	Rs.
Creditors		16,000	Machinery	20,000
Capital Accounts :			Furniture	4,000
X	25,000		Investment at Cost	12,000
Y	25,000		Stock	10,000
		50,000	Debtors	6,000
			Cash at Bank	14,000
		66,000		66,000

Interest on drawing is to be ignored but interest on capitals is to be allowed at 5% p.a. The profits of the new firm for the year ended 31.12.2012 amounted to Rs. 52,450 before charging interest on capitals. Drawings of the partners during the year were : X Rs. 16,325, Y Rs. 13,875 and Z Rs. 3,250.

You are required to show the Capital Account and prepare the Balance Sheet as at 31.12.2012.

Solution

In the books of X, Y, and Z
Capital Account

Dr. Particulars	X Rs.	Y Rs.	Z Rs.	Particulars *Cr.*	X Rs.	Y Rs.	Z Rs.
To Revaluation A/c—Loss	3,500	2,500[1]	—	By Balance b/d	25,000	25,000	—
" Balance c/d	36,500	27,500	25,000[3]	" Bank —Premium	15,000	5,000[2]	—
				" Bank	—	—	25,000
	40,000	30,000	25,000		40,000	30,000	25,000
To Drawings A/c	16,325	13,875	3,250	By Balance b/d	36,500	27,500	25,000
" Balance c/d	44,000	33,000	31,000	" Interest on Capital	1,825	1,375	1,250
				" Share of Profit	22,000	18,000	8,000[4]
	60,325	46,875	34,250		60,325	46,875	34,250
				By Balance b/d	44,000	33,000	31,000

Balance Sheet *as at 31st Dec. 2012*

Liabilities	Rs.	Rs.	*Assets*	Rs.
Capital			Machinery (20,000 – 2,000)	18,000
X	44,000		Furniture	4,000
Y	33,000		Investment (12,000 – 4,000)	8,000
Z	31,000		Stock	10,000
		1,08,000	Debtors	6,000
Creditors		16,000	Cash at Bank	78,000[5]
		1,24,000		1,24,000

Workings :

1.

Revaluation Account

Dr.	Rs.		*Cr.* Rs.
To Machinery	2,000	By Capital A/c —Loss on Revaluation	
" Investments	4,000	X 3,500	
		Y 2,500	6,000
	6,000		6,000

2. Goodwill should be distributed as per sacrificing ratio, i.e., $\frac{1}{8} : \frac{1}{24}$ or 3 : 1.

X's share = Rs. 20,000 × $\frac{3}{4}$ = Rs. 15,000

Y's share = Rs. 20,000 × $\frac{1}{4}$ = Rs. 5,000

3. Since there is interest on capital, it is better to carry forward this balance of capital account and, thereafter, interest on capital should be charged.

4. **Profit and Loss Appropriation Account**
for the year ended 31st Dec. 2012

Dr.		Rs.		*Cr.* Rs.
To Int. on Cap.			By P & L A/c —Net Profit	52,450
X	1,825			
Y	1,375			
Z	1,250	4,450		

5.

Bank A/c

Dr.	Rs.			*Cr.* Rs.
To Balance b/d	14,000	By Drawings		
" Goodwill	20,000	X	16,325	
" Z's Capital	25,000	Y	13,875	
" Profit (i.e., increase in Cash)	52,450	Z	3,250	33,450
		" Balance c/d		78,000
	1,11,450			1,11,450

Contd.

		Rs.		Rs.
To Share of Profit				
X $\frac{11}{24}$	22,000			
Y $\frac{9}{24}$	18,000			
Z $\frac{4}{24}$	8,000	48,000		
		52,450		52,450

Illustration 48

Lalkamal and Subhash are partners in a concern sharing profits and losses in proportion to capital. Their Balance Sheet as at 31.3.2012 was :

Liabilities	Rs.	Rs.	Assets	Rs.
Creditors		5,100	Machinery	26,000
Capital Accounts :			Furniture	2,000
Lalkamal	24,000		Stock	1,500
Subhash	12,000		Debtors	8,500
		36,000	Cash	3,100
		41,100		41,100

On 1.4.2012, they agreed to admit Rabin on payment of Rs. 10,000 cash as capital. The following agreements were also agreed to :

(1) Goodwill of the old firm to be valued at Rs. 6,000.

(2) Rabin to receive $\frac{1}{5}$th of the future profits.

(3) Lalkamal and Subhash are to share profits in proportion to their original capital.

They carried on business for 6 months and made a divisible profit of Rs. 9,000.

On 30.9.2012, the ledger balances were : Machinery Rs. 35,500; Furniture Rs. 2,480; Stock Rs. 7,520; Debtors Rs. 9,440; Creditors Rs. 4,140 and Cash ?

Apportion profits and prepare Balance Sheet of the new firm as at 30.9.2012.

Solution **[CA]**

In the books of Lalkamal, Subhash and Rabin
Capital Account

Dr. Cr.

Particulars	Lalkamal Rs.	Subhash Rs.	Rabin Rs.	Particulars	Lalkamal Rs.	Subhash Rs.	Rabin Rs.
To Balance c/d	28,000	14,000	10,000	By Balance b/d	24,000	12,000	—
				" Goodwill	4,000	2,000	—
				" Bank	—	—	10,000
	28,000	14,000	10,000		28,000	14,000	10,000
To Balance c/d	32,800	16,400	11,800	By Balance b/d	28,000	14,000	10,000
				" Share of Profit	4,800	2,400	1,800
	32,800	16,400	11,800		32,800	16,400	11,800

Balance Sheet *as at 30th Sept. 2012*

Liabilities	Rs.	Rs.	Assets	Rs.	Rs.
Capital Account :			Goodwill		6,000
Lalkamal	32,800		Machinery		35,500
Subhash	16,400		Furniture		2,480
Rabin	11,800		Stock		7,520
		61,000	Debtors		9,440
Creditors		4,140	Cash *(bal. fig.)*		4,200*
		65,140			65,140

* The same can also be ascertained by preparing Bank/Cash Account

Cash Account

Dr.		Rs.			Rs. Cr.
To	Balance b/d	3,100	By	Creditors (5,100 – 4,140)	960
"	Rabin's Capital	10,000	"	Machinery (35,500 – 26,000)	9,500
"	Net Profit	9,000	"	Furniture (2,480 – 2,000)	480
			"	Stock (7,520 – 1,500)	6,020
			"	Debtors (9,440 – 8,500)	940
			"	Balance c/d	4,200
		22,100			22,100

Illustration 49

A and B were partners sharing profits and losses equally. Their Balance Sheet as on 31st December 2012 was :

Liabilities	Rs.	Assets	Rs.
Capital Accounts :		Premises	30,000
A	60,000	Furniture	14,000
B	70,000	Stock	74,000
Creditors	30,000	Debtors	24,000
		Cash at Bank	18,000
	1,60,000		1,60,000

On 1.1.2013 they decided to admit C as a partner on the following conditions :

1. C should pay Rs. 60,000 as capital for being entitled to $\frac{1}{3}$rd share of profits. The remaining profits are to be shared by the old partners equally.
2. Stock to be valued at Rs. 70,000 and Premises to be taken at 95% of book values.
3. After the conclusion of the first trading year, a Goodwill Account should be raised at three times of the net profit of that year in excess of Rs. 30,100. Such Goodwill should be divided between A and B in the ratio of their sacrifices in favour of C.

Transactions during the year ended 31st December 2013 were :

	Rs.
Purchases	5,30,000
Sales	6,00,000
Payments for Purchases at 98% in full settlement	4,80,200
Collection from Debtors [after allowing 5% against a prompt payment of dues Rs. 40,000]	3,38,000
Sundry Expenses	18,000
Administration Expenses	60,000
Drawings of Partners	
A	5,000
B	4,000
C	3,000

On 31.12.2013 Stock was Rs. 1,20,000. Depreciation was to provided on Furniture Rs. 900.

C contributed sufficient cash to make his capital proportionate to his share of profit after Goodwill was calculated and given effect. You are required to prepare : (a). The amended Balance Sheet of the firm on 1.1.2013. (b). The Balance Sheet of the firm on 31.12.2013 after giving effect to the required adjustments.

[CA Adapted]

Solution

In the books of firm

Revaluation Account

Dr. Particulars	Rs.	Particulars		Rs. Cr.
To Stock A/c	4,000	By Loss on Revaluation		
" Premises A/c	1,500	A	2,750	
		B	2,750	5,500
	5,500			5,500

Dr. **Capital Account (as on 1.1.2013)** Cr.

Particulars	A Rs.	B Rs.	C Rs.	Particulars	A Rs.	B Rs.	C Rs.
To Revaluation A/c —Loss	2,750	2,750	—	By Balance b/d	60,000	70,000	—
" Balance c/d	57,250	67,250	60,000	" Bank A/c	—	—	60,000
	60,000	70,000	60,000		60,000	70,000	60,000

Balance Sheet *(Amended) as at 1st Jan. 2013*

Liabilities	Rs.	Assets	Rs.
Capital Accounts			
A	57,250	Premises (30,000 – 1,500)	28,500
B	67,250	Furniture	14,000
C	60,000	Stock (74,000 – 4,000)	70,000
Creditors	30,000	Debtors	24,000
		Bank (18,000 + 60,000)	78,000
	2,14,500		2,14,500

Dr. **Trading and Profit and Loss Account** *for year ended 31st Dec. 2013* Cr.

Particulars		Rs.	Particulars	Rs.
To Opening Stock		70,000	By Sales	6,00,000
" Purchases		5,30,000	" Closing Stock	1,20,000
" Profit and Loss A/c —Gross Profit transferred		1,20,000		
		7,20,000		7,20,000
To Sundry Expenses		18,000	By Trading A/c —Gross Profit	1,20,000
" Administrative Expenses		60,000	" Discount Received (98% = Rs. 4,80,200) [2% = Rs. 4,80,200 × $\frac{2}{98}$]	9,800
" Discount Allowed @ 5% on Rs. 40,000		2,000		
" Depreciation on Furniture		900		
" Share of Profit				
A	16,300			
B	16,300			
C	16,300	48,900		
		1,29,800		1,29,800

Dr. **Capital Account** Cr.

Particulars	A Rs.	B Rs.	C Rs.	Particulars	A Rs.	B Rs.	C Rs.
To Drawings	5,000	4,000	3,000	By Balance b/d	57,250	67,250	60,000
" Balance c/d	96,750	1,07,750	1,02,250[2]	" Share of Profit	16,300	16,300	16,300
				" Goodwill	28,200[1]	28,200	—
				" Bank *(bal. fig.)*	—	—	28,950
	1,01,750	1,11,750	1,05,250		1,01,750	1,11,750	1,05,250

Balance Sheet *as at 31st Dec. 2013*

Liabilities		Rs.	Assets		Rs.
Capital Account			Goodwill		56,400
A	96,750		Premises		28,500
B	1,07,750		Furniture	14,000	
C	1,02,250		*Less :* Depreciation	900	
		3,06,750			13,100
Creditors		70,000[4]	Stock		1,20,000
Bank Overdraft		1,25,250[5]	Debtors		2,84,000[3]
		5,02,000			5,02,000

1. **Valuation of Goodwill**

	Rs.
Net Profit	48,900
Less : Excess over	30,100
	18,800 × 3 = Rs. 56,400 to be shared between A and B in 1 : 1 (as per sacrificing ratio)

2. **Closing Capital of C**

Adjusted Capital of A and B for $\frac{2}{3}$ share = Rs. 2,04,500 (i.e., Rs. 96,750 + Rs. 1,07,750).

So for $\frac{1}{3}$ share C will have to bring Rs. 1,02,250 (i.e., Rs. 2,04,500 × $\frac{1}{3}$ × $\frac{3}{2}$)

3.

Dr. **Debtors A/c** Cr.

	Rs.		Rs.
To Balance b/d	24,000	By Cash	3,38,000
" Sales	6,00,000	" Discount Allowed	2,000
		" Balance c/d	2,84,000
	6,24,000		6,24,000

4.

Dr. **Creditors A/c** Cr.

	Rs.		Rs.
To Cash	4,80,200	By Balance b/d	30,000
" Discount Received	9,800	" Purchases	5,30,000
" Balance c/d	70,000		
	5,60,000		5,60,000

5.

Dr. **Bank A/c** Cr.

	Rs.			Rs.
To Balance b/d	78,000	By Creditors A/c		4,80,200
" Debtors A/c	3,38,000	" Expenses A/c (60,000 + 18,000)		78,000
" C's Capital	28,950	" Drawings		
" Balance c/d	1,25,250	A	5,000	
		B	4,000	
		C	3,000	12,000
	5,70,200			5,70,200

Illustration 50

X and Y are partners in a business started in 2001, sharing profits and losses in the ratio of 5 : 4. After the accounts for the calendar year 2004 were made up and their proportionate shares taken note of in their individual accounts, they decide to share profits and losses equally, restrospectively, for and from the year 2004. It was also discovered that in ascertaining the results in prior years certain adjustments, details of which are given below, had not been noticed :

	2001	2002	2003	2004
	Rs.	Rs.	Rs.	Rs.
Profits as per accounts	72,000	78,000	90,000	1,08,000
Incomes not taken into account	5,400	4,500	3,600	6,300
Expenses not provided for	9,000	6,000	10,800	7,200

On 31st December 2003, Reserves stood at Rs. 54,000. Capitals of X and Y Rs. 1,26,000 and Rs. 96,000, respectively, on 31st December 2004. On 1.1.2005, Z was decided to be admitted as a partner and was allotted $\frac{1}{5}$th share. Goodwill was decided to be ascertained by capitalising at 20% the average profits of the immediate two preceding years before admission. Z would bring in proportionate capitals. Capitals of X and Y are to be equal, the difference to be adjusted in their current accounts.

Profits for 2005 were Rs. 1,26,000. Drawings of X, Y, and Z for the year were Rs. 54,000; Rs. 48,000, and Rs. 18,000, respectively.

Incomes not taken into account are received in subsequent year. Expenses not provided for are paid in subsequent years.

Prepare Capital and Current Accounts of the partners for 2005.

Solution

In the books of X, Y, & Z

Dr. **Capital Account** Cr.

Particulars	X	Y	Z	*Particulars*	X	Y	Z
	Rs.	Rs.	Rs.		Rs.	Rs.	Rs.
To P& L Adjustment A/c (Profit)	60,000	48,000	—	By Balance b/d	1,26,000	96,000	—
				" Reserves	30,000	24,000	—

Contd.

	X Rs.	Y Rs.	Z Rs.		X Rs.	Y Rs.	Z Rs.
" P.& L Adjustment A/c (Net Outstandiang (Expenses)	4,000	3,200	—	" P & L A/c Adjustment A/c (Profit)	57,150	57,150[1]	—
To Balance c/d	1,49,150	1,25,950	—				
	2,13,150	1,77,150			2,13,150	1,77,150	
To Current A/c (bal. fig.)	61,250	38,050	—	By Balance b/d	1,49,150	1,25,950	—
" Balance c/d	1,98,600	1,98,600	99,300[3]	" Goodwill	1,10,700	1,10,700[2]	—
				" Bank	—	—	99,300
	2,59,850	2,36,650	99,300		2,59,850	2,36,650	99,300

Current Account

Dr. Cr.

Particulars	X Rs.	Y Rs.	Z Rs.	Particulars	X Rs.	Y Rs.	Z Rs.
To Drawings	54,000	48,000	18,000	By Capital A/c	61,250	38,050	—
" Balance c/d	57,650	40,450	7,200	" P & L A/c (Profit)	50,400	50,400	25,200
	1,11,650	88,450	25,200		1,11,650	88,450	25,200

Workings:

1. **Profit and Loss Adjustment A/c** *for the year ended 2004*

Dr. Cr.

Particulars	Rs.	Rs.	Particulars	Rs.
To Outstanding Expenses (for 2004)		7,200	By Capital A/c Net outstanding expenses for (2003)	7,200
" Capital A/c Net Profit			" Capital A/c : X & Y	1,08,000
X	57,150		" Accrued Income (for 2004)	6,300
Y	57,150	1,14,300		
		1,21,500		1,21,500

2. **Calculation of Adjusted Profit for 2003 and 2004 for the purpose of computing Goodwill :**

	2003 Rs.	2004 Rs.
Profit (given)	90,000	1,08,000
Add : Previous year's Outstanding Expenses	(+) 6,000	(+) 10,800
	96,000	1,18,800
Add : Current year's Accrued Incomes	+ 3,600	+ 6,300
	99,600	1,25,100
Less : Current year's Outstanding Exps.	(–) 10,800	(–) 7,200
	88,800	1,17,900
Less : Previous year's Accrued Incomes	(–) 4,500	(–) 3,600
	84,300	1,14,300

∴ Average Profit for 2003 and 2004 = Rs. 99,300 $\left(\dfrac{\text{Rs. } 84,300 + \text{Rs. } 1,14,300}{2}\right)$

∴ Capitalised Value of Profit = $\dfrac{\text{Profit}}{\text{Normal Rate of Return}} \times 100 = \dfrac{\text{Rs. } 99,300}{20} \times 100$

Capitalised Value/Net Tangible Assets	=	Rs.	4,96,500
Less : Capital of X & Y		Rs.	2,75,100
∴ Value of Goodwill		Rs.	2,21,400

3. Total Capital Rs. 4,96,500 will be divided among X, Y, and Z in 2 : 2 : 1, i.e., Rs. 1,98,600, Rs. 1,98,600, and Rs. 99,300, respectively.

Illustration 51

A and P were carrying on business in partnership since 2010. Their Balance Sheet as on 31st March 2011 was:

Liabilities		Rs.	*Assets*	Rs.
Capital			Goodwill	4,000
A	39,700		Motor Cars	16,500
P	21,300		Furniture and Fixtures	6,200
		61,000	Stock	29,400
Profit and Loss A/c		9,000	Debtors	39,600
Creditors		26,700	Cash at Bank	2,300
Bills Payable		1,500	Cash in hand	200
		98,200		98,200

On 1st April 2011, they decided to admit B as a partner on the following conditions :

(a) B will receive $\frac{1}{5}$th of the further profits (after charging interest on capital @ 5%) subject to a minimum of Rs. 6,000 p.a. Any deficiency in his share of profits is to be met from A's share.

(b) The goodwill of the firm is fixed at Rs. 8,000.

(c) An independent valuation revealed that motor cars are worth Rs. 19,000, while the value of Furniture is only Rs. 5,700, Rs. 1,500 of the Debtors are likely to become bad.

(d) B was to bring in capital equal to $\frac{1}{5}$th of the capitals of A and P arrived at after giving effect to the foregoing consideration.

(e) It was decided to restore goodwill to its original value.

During the year ended 31st March 2012, the firm earned a profit of Rs. 30,000 (before charging interest on Capital).

You are required to :

(i) Show Journal entries in respect of transactions taking place at the time of B's admission.

(ii) Show the Balance Sheet immediately after B's admission.

(iii) Show the Profit and Loss Appropriation Account for the year ended 31st March 2012, assuming that adjustments in respect of guaranteed profits are to be made through the Profit and Loss Appropriation Account.

Solution

In the books of the Firm

(i) **Journal**

			Rs.	Rs.
2011 April 1				
	(a) Goodwill A/c	Dr.	4,000	
	To A's Capital A/c			2,000
	" B's Capital A/c			2,000
	(Value of goodwill is raised in the book.)			
	(b) Revaluation A/c	Dr.	2,000	
	To Furniture and Fixtures A/c			500
	" Provision for Bad Debts A/c			1,500
	(Value of asset decreased on revaluation.)			
	(c) Motor Car A/c	Dr.	2,500	
	To Revaluation A/c			2,500
	(Value of asset increased on revaluation.)			
	(d) Revaluation A/c	Dr.	500	
	To A's Capital A/c			250
	" P's Capital A/c			250
	(Profit on revaluation transferred.)			
	(e) Profit and Loss A/c	Dr.	9,000	
	To A's Capital A/c			4,500
	" P's Capital A/c			4,500
	(Undistributed profit transferred.)			

Contd.

		Rs.	Rs.
(f) Bank A/c	Dr.	14,900	
To B's Capital A/c			14,900[1]
(Cash brought in by B as Capital.)			
(g) A's Capital A/c	Dr.	1,600	
P's Capital A/c	Dr.	1,600	
B's Capital A/c	Dr.	800	
To Goodwill A/c			4,000[2]
(Value of goodwill to the extent of Rs. 4,000 written-off.)			

(ii) **Balance Sheet** *as at 1st April 2011*

Liabilities	Rs.	Rs.	*Assets*	Rs.	Rs.
Capital :			Goodwill		4,000
A	44,850		Motor Cars	16,500	
B	26,450		*Add :* Appreciation	2,500	
C	14,100				19,000
		85,400	Furniture	6,200	
Creditors		26,700	*Less :* Written-off	500	
Bills Payable		1,500			5,700
			Stock		29,400
			Debtors	39,600	
			Less : Prov. for Bad Debts	1,500	
					38,100
			Cash at Bank		17,200
			(2,300 + 14,900)		
			Cash in hand		200
		1,13,600			1,13,600

(iii) **Profit and Loss Appropriation Account** *for the year ended 31st March 2012*

Dr. *Cr.*

Particulars	*Amount* Rs.	*Amount* Rs.	*Particulars*	*Amount* Rs.	*Amount* Rs.
To Interest on Capital :			By Profit and Loss A/c —Net Profit		30,000
A	2,242.5				
P	1,322.5				
B	705.0				
		4,270			
" B's Capital A/c —guaranteed Profits		6,000			
" Balance c/d		19,730			
		30,000			30,000
To A's Capital $\frac{1}{2}$	10,292		By Balance b/d		19,730
" P's Capital $\frac{1}{2}$	10,292		" A's Capital A/c (guaranteed share)		854[3]
		20,584[4]			
		20,584			20,584

Workings :

1. Capital to be brought in by B

		Rs.
	A and P's Combined Capital	61,000
Add :	Goodwill	4,000
Add :	Profit on Revaluation	500
Add :	Profit and Loss A/c (balance)	9,000
	Adjusted Capital	74,500

$74,500 \times \frac{1}{5}$ = Rs. Rs. 14,900 to be brought in by B.

2. Future Profit-sharing Ratio

$$1 - \frac{1}{5} = \frac{4}{5}$$

$$A = \frac{4}{5} \times \frac{1}{2} = \frac{4}{10}$$

$$P = \frac{4}{5} \times \frac{1}{2} = \frac{4}{10}$$

$$B = \frac{1}{2} = \frac{2}{10} \quad \therefore \quad A : P : B = 4 : 4 : 2$$

or = 2 : 2 : 1.

Share of Goodwill $4{,}000 \times \frac{2}{5}$ = 1,600 by A

$4{,}000 \times \frac{2}{5}$ = 1,600 by P

$4{,}000 \times \frac{1}{5}$ = 800 by B.

3. Guaranteed amount to be borne by A

		Rs.
	Profit	30,000
Less :	Interest on Capitals	4,270
	Divisible Profit	25,730

B's share = Rs. $25{,}730 \times \frac{1}{5}$ = 5,146.

But his guaranteed minimum is Rs. 6,000. Therefore, the deficit Rs. 854 (i.e., 6,000 – 5,146) to be borne by A.

4. Distribution of Profit between A and B

A = Rs. $25{,}730 \times \frac{2}{5}$ = Rs. 10,292 P = Rs. $25{,}730 \times \frac{2}{5}$ = Rs. 10,292

Less : Deficiency borne by him for B 854

Rs. 9,438

Continuous Change in Ratio without Goodwill Adjustment

Illustration 52

X was carrying a sole proprietorship business since 2000. He took Y into partnership on 1.1.2004, the profit-sharing ratio being 3 : 2. Goodwill of the firm amounted to Rs. 10,000.

On 1.1.2005, they took Z into partnership, new profit-sharing ratio being 3 : 2 : 1. Value of the goodwill now worth was Rs. 15,000.

On 1.1.2006, they also took A into partnership, new profit-sharing ratio being 4 : 3 : 2 : 1. Value of goodwill now worth was Rs. 18,000.

On 1.1.2007, Z retired and they took B into partnership, new profit-sharing ratio being 6 : 4 : 3 : 2. Goodwill on that date was agreed at Rs. 25,000.

Ascertain the amount payable to or receivable by the partners on account of goodwill which had not been raised in the books at all nor any premium actually was received from any partner for the purpose.

Solution

Statement showing the effect of raising and writing-back of Goodwill

Date	*Ratio*	*Total*	X	Y	Z	A	B
		Rs.	Rs.	Rs.	Rs.	Rs.	Rs.
1.1.2004	Credit in old ratio 1 : Nil	+ 10,000	+ 10,000	—	—	—	—
	Debit in new ratio (3 : 2)	– 10,000	– 6,000	– 4,000	—	—	—
1.1.2005	Credit in old ratio (3 : 2)	+ 15,000	+ 9,000	+ 6,000	—	—	—
	Debit in new ratio (3 : 2 : 1)	– 15,000	– 7,500	– 5,000	– 2,500	—	—
1.1.2006	Credit in old ratio (3 : 2 : 1)	+ 18,000	+ 9,000	+ 6,000	+ 3,000	—	—
	Debit in new ratio (4 : 3 : 2 : 1)	– 18,000	– 7,200	– 5,400	– 3,600	– 1,800	—
1.1.2007	Credit in old ratio (4 : 3 : 2 : 1)	+ 20,000	+ 8,000	+ 6,000	+ 4,000	+ 2,000	—
	Debit in new ratio (6 : 4 : 3 : 2)	– 20,000	– 8,000	– 5,333	—	– 4,000	– 2,667
		+ 68,000	+ 36,000	+ 18,000	+ 7,000	+ 2,000	—
	Net Amount Payable	– 63,000	– 28,700	– 19,733	– 6,100	– 5,800	– 2,667
	or Receivable	—	+ 7,300	– 1,733	+ 900	– 3,800	– 2,667

In the books of the firm
Journal

2007			Dr.	Cr.
Jan. 1			Rs.	Rs.
	Y's Capital A/c	Dr.	1,733	
	A's Capital A/c	Dr.	3,800	
	B's Capital A/c	Dr.	2,667	
	To X Capital A/c			7,300
	" Z Capital A/c			900
	(Adjustment for goodwill made on different dates.)			

Illustration 53

P, Q, and R were on partnership terms sharing profits and losses in the ratio of 6 : 3 : 1. They decided to take S into partnership with effect from April 1, 2008 on the following terms and conditions :

(i) S is to bring in his proportionate share of goodwill in cash. Goodwill is not to be brought into the books but necessary adjustments are to be made in the Old Partners' Capital Accounts.

(ii) Goodwill to be valued at 60% of the average annual profits of the previous three or four years, whichever is the higher.

(iii) The average profits for the purpose of goodwill for the past years were :
Year ending March 31, 2008 Rs. 48,000; Year ending March 31, 2007 Rs. 30,300;
Year ending March 31, 2006 Rs. 31,200; Year ending March 31, 2005 Rs. 42,200.

(iv) The new profit-sharing ratio between P, Q, R, and S will be 3 : 3 : 3 : 1.

(v) S should bring in Rs. 20,000 as capital.

(vi) The new partner is to receive an annual salary of Rs. 12,000 in addition to his share of profit. R personally guaranteed that the aggregate of salary and share of profit of the new patner shall not be less than Rs. 25,000 p.a.

The draft accounts for the year ending March 31, 2009, showed a profit of Rs. 1,32,800 before taking into account the salary of S.

Show the Journal entries (including cash entries) passed at the time of admission of the partner and also the distribution of the net profit for the year ending March 31, 2009, between the partners. **[CA]**

Solution

Computation of Goodwill

Average Profit of last 4 years

$$= \frac{\text{Rs. } 42,200 + \text{Rs. } 31,200 + \text{Rs. } 30,300 + \text{Rs. } 48,000}{4}$$

$$= \text{Rs. } \frac{1,51,700}{4}$$

$= \text{Rs. } 37,925$

Average Profit of last 3 years

$$= \frac{\text{Rs. } 31,200 + \text{Rs. } 30,300 + \text{Rs. } 48,000}{3}$$

$$= \frac{\text{Rs. } 1,09,500}{3}$$

$= \text{Rs. } 36,500$

So, Last 4 years' average is higher, which should be considered.

$$\text{Goodwill} = \text{Rs. } 37,925 \times \frac{60}{100} = \text{Rs. } 22,755 \qquad \therefore \text{ S's share} = \text{Rs. } 22,755 \times \frac{1}{10} = \text{Rs. } 2,275.$$

Sacrificing Ratio

Since old and new (i.e., after admission) ratios are given we are to find out the sacrificing ratio as :

$P = \frac{6}{10} - \frac{3}{10} = \frac{3}{10}$ (sacrifices) $\qquad R = \frac{1}{10} - \frac{3}{10} = \frac{2}{10}$ (gains)

$Q = \frac{3}{10} - \frac{3}{10} = 0 \qquad S = \frac{1}{10} = \frac{1}{10}$ (gains)

So, the entire amount of goodwill should be credited to P's Capital Account only. At the same time, R also will pay proportionately to P for his gaing ratio Rs. 4,550 $\left(\text{i.e., Rs. } 2,275 \times \frac{2}{10} \times \frac{10}{1}\right)$.

Journal

Date	Particulars		L.F.	Debit	Credit
2008				Rs.	Rs.
April 1	Bank A/c	Dr.		22,275	
	To S's Capital A/c				20,000
	" Goodwill A/c				2,275
	(Capital and goodwill to be brought in by S.)				

Contd.

		Rs.	Rs.
Goodwill A/c	Dr.	2,275	
To P's Capital A/c			2,275
(Goodwill credited to P's Capital Account as per sacrificing ratio)			
R's Capital A/c	Dr.	4,500	
To P's Capital A/c			4,500
(Capital transfer made for goodwill adjustment.)			

- **Distribution of Profit** : It is better for us if we prepare a Profit and Loss Appropriation Account for the purpose :

Profit and Loss Appropriation Account *for the year ended 31st March 2009*

Dr.		Rs.		*Cr.* Rs.
To Salary S		12,000	By Profit and Loss A/c —Net Profit	1,32,800
" Share of Profit				
P $\frac{3}{10}$ =	= 36,240			
Q $\frac{3}{10}$	= 36,240			
R $\frac{3}{10}$ (36,240 – 920)	= 35,320			
S $\frac{1}{10}$ (12,080 + 920)	= 13,000			
		1,20,800		
		1,32,800		1,32,800

Since S's share must not be less than Rs. 25,000, with salary, so his share of profit must be Rs. 13,000. As he gets Rs. 12,080, balance Rs. 920 to be compensated by R to S.

Illustration 54

The following is the Balance Sheet of M/s A and B as on 31st March 2009 :

Liabilities	Rs.	*Assets*	Rs.
		Land and Building	50,000
Capitals :		Stock	30,000
A	40,000	Debtors	20,000
B	50,000	Investment (6% Debentures in X Ltd.)	20,000
A's Loan A/c	10,000	Cash	10,000
General Reserve	10,000		
Liabilities	20,000		
	1,30,000		1,30,000

It was agreed that Mr. C is to be admitted for a fifth share in the futute profit from 1st April 2009. He is required to contribute cash towards goodwill and Rs. 10,000 towards capital.

The following further information is furnished :

(i) The partners A and B shared the profits in the ratio 3 : 2.

(ii) Mr. A was receiving a salary of Rs. 500 p.m. from the very inception of the firm in 2003 in addition to share of profit.

(iii) The further profit ratio between A, B, and C will be Rs. 3 : 1 : 1. Mr. A will not get any salary after admission of Mr. C.

(iv) (a) The goodwill of the firm shall be determined on the basis of 2 years' purchase of the average profits from business of the last 5 years. The particulars of the profits are : Year ended 31st March 2005—Rs. 20,000 (profit); 2006—Rs. 10,000 (loss); 2007—Rs. 20,000 (profit); 2008 —Rs. 25,000 (profit); 2009 — Rs. 30,000 (profit).
The above profits and losses are after charging the salary of Mr. A. The profits of the year ended 31st March 2005 included an extraneous profit of Rs. 30,000 and the loss of the year ended 31st March 2006 was on account of loss by strike to the extent of Rs. 20,000.

(b) It was agreed that the value of the goodwill of the firm shall appear in the books of the firm.

(v) The trading profit before depreciation for the year ended 31st March 2010 was Rs. 40,000.

(vi) The liabilities as on 31st March 2009 included a sum of Rs. 10,000 due to contractors in respect of the construction of the building. This bill was settled in full on 31st December 2009 on a payment of Rs. 8,000.

(vii) The partners had each drawn Rs. 1,000 p.m. as Drawings.

(viii) The value of other Assets and Liabilities as on 31st March 2010 was : Building (before depreciation) Rs. 60,000; Stock Rs. 40,000; Debtors Nil; Investments Rs. 20,000; Liabilities Nil.

(ix) Provide Depreciation @ 5% on Land and Building on the Closing Balance and Interest @ 6% on A's loan.

Prepare the Profit and Loss Account for the year ended 31st March 2010, Capital Account, and the Balance Sheet as on that date.

Solution

In the books of M/s A, B, and C
Profit and Loss Account *for the year ended 31st March 2010*

Dr. *Particulars*		Amount Rs.	*Particulars*	Amount Rs. Cr.
To Interest on A's Loan A/c @ 6%		600	By Trading A/c —Trading Profit	40,000
" Depreciation on Building		3,000	" Interest on Debentures A/c	1,200
" Share of Profit				
A	22,560			
B	7,520			
C	7,520	37,600		
		41,200		41,200

Capital Account

Dr. *Particulars*	A Rs.	B Rs.	C Rs.	*Particulars*	A Rs.	B Rs.	C Rs. Cr.
To Drawings A/c	12,000	12,000	12,000	By Balance b/d	40,000	50,000	—
" Balance c/d	80,320	65,360	13,440	" Goodwill A/c	23,760	15,840[1]	—
				By General Reserve A/c	6,000	4,000	—
				" Profit and Loss A/c —Profit	22,560	7,520	7,520
				" Bank A/c (i.e., Rs. 10,000 + 7,920)	—	—	17,920
	92,320	77,360	25,440		92,320	77,360	25,440

Balance Sheet *as at 31st March 2010*

Liabilities		Rs.	*Assets*	Rs.
Capitals :			Goodwill	39,600
A	80,320		Land and Building (Rs. 60,000 – Rs. 3,000)	57,000[2]
B	65,360		Investments	20,000
C	14,40	1,59,120	Stock	40,000
A's Loan A/c	10,000		Cash	13,120[3]
Add : Interest	600	10,600		
		1,69,720		1,69,720

Workings :

1. Computation of Goodwill

	2005 Rs.	2006 Rs.	2007 Rs.	2008 Rs.	2009 Rs.
Profit (as per P & L A/c)	20,000	– 10,000	20,000	25,000	30,000
Abnormal Items (adjusted)	– 30,000	20,000	—	—	—
	(–) 10,000	10,000			
Add : A's Salary	6,000	6,000	6,000	6,000	6,000
	– 4,000	16,000	26,000	31,000	36,000

Contd.

	Rs.	Rs.	Rs.	Rs.	Rs.
Less : Debenture Interest (being non-operating income)	– 1,200	– 1,200	– 1,200	– 1,200	– 1,200
Adjusted Net Profit	(–) 5,200	14,800	24,800	29,800	34,800

Thus, the Average Profit $= \dfrac{(-)\ 5{,}200 + \text{Rs. } 14{,}800 + \text{Rs. } 24{,}800 + \text{Rs. } 29{,}800 + \text{Rs. } 34{,}800}{5}$

= Rs. 19,800

Value of Goodwill = Rs. 19,800 × 2 = Rs. 39,600 ∴ C's Share of Goodwill = Rs. 39,600 × $\frac{1}{5}$ = Rs. 7,920

Notes :

Since the profit on settlement of building contractor's liability Rs. 2,000 (i.e., Rs. 10,000 – Rs. 8,000) is a non-operating income, as such, the same is not considered here; the same should be credited to Building Account.

2.

Dr. **Land and Building A/c** *Cr.*

	Rs.		Rs.
To Balance b/d	50,000	By Liabilities A/c	2,000
" Cash A/c *(bal. fig.)*	12,000	" Balance c/d	60,000
	62,000		62,000

3.

Dr. **Cash A/c** *Cr.*

	Rs.		Rs.
To Balance b/d	10,000	By Drawings A/c	36,000
" Interest on Investment	1,200	" Land and Buildings	12,000
" Debtors A/c	20,000	" Purchase A/c (40,000 – 30,000)	10,000
" Trading and Profit	40,000*	" Contractor's Liability	18,000
" C's Capital	17,920	" Balance c/d	13,120
	89,120		89,120

* It has been assumed that profit is the result of increase in Cash.

ASSIGNMENT MATERIALS

THEORETICAL

Short Answer-Type Questions

1. What is goodwill? Discuss under what circumstances valuation of goodwill is necessary.
2. Discuss the various methods of valuation of goodwill.
3. What is Superprofit Method ?
4. Discuss the various treatments of goodwill in the case of admission of a partner.
5. Define goodwill. Discuss the various methods of calculating goodwill.
6. Discuss briefly any three methods of valuation of goodwill with the help of an example.
7. What is Memorandum Revaluation Account?
   When is it necessary to open it ? Is there any difference between a Revaluation Account and Memorandum Revaluation Account?
8. What is Revaluation Account? Why is it so prepared ?
9. Explain why General Reserve is distributed amongst the old partners before a new partner is admitted.
10. What is Proportionate Capital of the partners? How do you ascertain it ?

Long Answer-Type Questions

11. How do you compute goodwill when a new partner is admitted ?
12. Explain the different classes of goodwill with an example from each class.
13. How do you treate undistributed Reserves/Profit in case of admission of partner?
14. Mention the factors that affect the value of goodwill.
15. What is Superprofit Method of Goodwill?
16. What is Hidden Goodwill? How do you calculates it?
17. What is Goodwill? How do you ascertain its value at the time of admission of a firm?
18. What is Memorandum Revaluation Account? When is such account opened?
19. Why do we value goodwill?

PRACTICAL

1. A and B are partners in a firm sharing profits and losses in 7 : 3. Their Balance Sheet as on 31.3.2005 is :

		Rs.			Rs.
Sundry Creditors		40,000	Cash in hand		36,000
Bank Overdraft		20,000	Sundry Debtors	Rs. 46,000	
Reserve		10,000	*Less :* Provision for Doubtful Debts	Rs. 2,000	
Capital Accounts :					44,000
A	Rs. 50,000				
B	Rs. 40,000		Furniture		30,000
		90,000	Stock-in-Trade		50,000
		1,60,000			1,60,000

On 1..2005, C joins the firm as third partner for 1/4th shares of the future profit or loss on the following terms and conditions :

(a) Goodwill is valued at Rs. 40,000 and C is to bring the necessary amount in Cash as Premium for Goodwill;

(b) 20% of the Reserve is to remain as a Provision against Bad and Doubtful Debts;

(c) Stock-in-trade is to be reduced by 40% and Furniture is to be reduced to 40%;

(d) A is to pay off the Bank Overdraft;

(e) C is to introduce Rs. 30,000 as his share of Capital to which amount other partners' capital shall have to be adjusted.

Show the necessary Journal entries to carry out the above transactions and prepare an amended Balance Sheet of the firm immediately after C has become a partner.

[Ans. (a) Loss on Revaluation Rs. 38,000, A will bring in Rs. 7,000, Total of Balance Sheet Rs. 1,60,000]

2. The Balance Sheet of Acharya and Agrawal as on 31.12.2012 was as follows :

Liabilities	Rs.	*Assets*	Rs.
Creditors	6,000	Stock	25,200
Bank Overdraft	3,000	Debtors	16,000
Acharya's Capital	12,000	Amin's Loan A/c	12,200
Agrawal's Capital	24,000	Furniture	1,200
Acharya's Current A/c	14,400	Land and Building	14,400
Agrawal's Current A/c	9,600		
	69,000		69,000

The partners shared profits and losses in the ratio of 1 : 2. They agreed to admit Amin as a partner from 1.1.2013 on the following terms :

(1) The assets and liabilities were revalued as under :

(a) Land and Building at Rs. 32,500; (b) Furniture Rs. 6,000; (c) Stock to be written-down by Rs. 2,200; (d) A reserve was to be created for doubtful debts at 5% on Sundry Debtors; (e) Creditors include Rs. 500 which were no more a liability.

(2) Amin, doing his own business, brought following assets and liabilities into partnership; Furniture Rs. 1,800; Investments Rs. 4,500; Stock Rs. 20,800; Sundry Creditors Rs. 5,500.

(3) The profits and losses of the new firm were to be shared equally by the partners.

(4) Amin was to bring Rs. 6,000 as his share of Goodwill in cash.

(5) Loan to Amin to be converted into his Current Account.

(6) Bank Overdraft was to be repaid.

(7) Acharya and Agrawal were to keep their respective capitals equal to that of Amin. Any surplus or deficit was to be adjusted through their respective Current Accounts.

You are required to prepare the entries and the opening Balance Sheet of the new firm.

[Ans. Profit Rs. 20,400, Capital Account Rs. 21,600 each, Current Account Acharya Rs. 11,600 (Cr.), Agrawal Rs. 31,600 (Cr.) Amin Rs. 12,200 (Dr.), Total of Balance Sheet Rs. 1,19,000]

3. X and Y are partners sharing profits and losses in proportions to their capital. Their Balance Sheet as at 31st March 2012 is given below :

Liabilities	Rs.	Assets	Rs.
Creditors	9,000	Freehold Premises	10,000
Bills Payable	6,000	Plant and Machinery	3,500
General Reserve	2,100	Furniture	1,750
Capital Accounts :		Office Equipments	550
X	20,000	Stock	14,100
Y	15,000	Bills Receivable	3,060
		Debtors	17,500
		Bank	1,590
		Cash	50
	52,100		52,100

On 1.4.2012, they admit Z on the following terms :

(1) Z to bring in Rs. 10,000 as capital and to pay Rs. 3,500 for goodwill and he will get $\frac{1}{4}$th share in profit;

(2) Reserve for Bad Debts to be raised on Debtors at 2%;

(3) Stock to be written-down by 5%;

(4) Freehold Premises to be revalued at Rs. 11,400, Plant and Machinery at Rs. 2,800, Furniture at Rs. 1,540, and Office Equipments at Rs. 495;

(5) Partners agreed that the values of the assets and liabilities are to remain the same, and, as such, there should be no change in their book values as a result of the above-mentioned adjustments.

You are required to make necessary adjustments in the Capital Accounts of the partners and show the Balance Sheet of the new firm.

[Ans. Closing Balance of Capital Account : X Rs. 22,212, Y Rs. 16,658, and Z Rs. 9,630; Total of Balance Sheet Rs. 65,600]

4. Ram and Sugriva were partners in a firm. They shared profits and losses in the ratio of 3 : 2. The following was their Balance Sheet as at 31st Dec. 2010 :

Balance Sheet *as at 31st December 2010*

Liabilities		Rs.	*Assets*	Rs.
Capital A/cs :			Goodwill	20,000
Ram	1,00,000		Plant	45,000
Sugriva	75,000		Furniture and Fittings	12,500
		1,75,000	Investments (at Cost)	25,000
Creditors		85,000	Stock	57,500
Bills Payable		5,000	Bills Receivable	10,000
			Debtors	55,000
			Cash in hand and at Bank	40,000
		2,65,000		2,65,000

On 1st January 2011 they agreed to admit Bibhishan as a partner on the following terms :

(a) The new profit-sharing ratio shall be Ram 2/5th, Sugriva 2/5th and Bibhishan 1/5th;

(b) Bibhishan is to bring his capital of Rs. 50,000 in Cash and to pay his share of Goodwill in the firm. Goodwill for this purpose is to be valued at 2 years' purchase of the average of the previous 4 years' profits.

The profits for the previous 4 years are :

2007	Rs. 25,000	2009	Rs. 25,000
2008	Rs. 22,500	2010	Rs. 27,500

(c) The other assets are to be revalued as:

Plant	Rs. 52,500	Stock	Rs. 63,000
Furniture and Fittings	Rs. 10,000	Debtors	Rs. 50,000
Investments	Rs. 22,000		

It was decided that for the purpose of Balance Sheet the values of assets except cash shall remain unchanged.

You are required to pass necessary Journal entries recording the above transactions and to prepare the opening Balance Sheet of the new firm.

[Ans. Balance of Capital A/c : Ram Rs. 1,06,500, Sugriva Rs. 75,000; Bibhishan Rs. 49,500, Total of Balance Sheet Rs. 3,21,000]

5. X and Y were in partnership sharing profits and losses as $\frac{2}{3}$ and $\frac{1}{3}$. As from 1st October 2010, they agreed to take Z as a new partner. The new partner will have $\frac{1}{6}$th share, the old partners agreeing

to share equally as between them in the new firm. Z brings in Rs. 50,000 as Capital and Rs. 4,000 as his share of goodwill to be retained in the firm.

The following is the Balance Sheet of the old firm as on 30th September 2010 :

Liabilities		Rs.	*Assets*	Rs.
Capital Accounts			Cash	7,000
X	62,500		Stock	50,000
Y	37,500		Debtors	30,000
		1,00,000	Plant	25,000
Creditors		50,000	Investments	38,000
		1,50,000		1,50,000

The following revaluations are agreed upon :
Stock Rs. 55,000; Plant Rs. 20,000; Investments Rs. 35,000;
Debtors subject to Reserve for Bad Debts of 5%;
It is further agreed that X alone is to be charged with any loss arising from the above.

The profits after depreciation of Plant @ 5% p.a for the year ended 30th September 2011 was Rs. 1,20,000 and the Drawings of the partners were : X Rs. 40,000, Y Rs. 40,000 and Z Rs. 10,000.

You are required to Journalise the opening adjustments and draw up the Balance Sheet as on 30th September 2011.

[Ans. Closing Balance of Capital Accounts : X Rs. 74,000, Y Rs. 45,500, and Z Rs. 60,000; Total of Balance Sheet Rs. 1,79,500]

6. Barnali and Sudipa are partners in a firm sharing profits and losses in the ratio of 2 : 1. Their Balance Sheet as on 31.2012 was :

Liabilities	Rs.	*Assets*		Rs.
Creditors	1,400	Bank		1,004
Investment Provision	400	Bills Receivable		2,500
Workmen's Compensation Fund	1,200	Debtors	4,000	
General Reserve	2,100	*Less* : Provision	500	3,500
Capital Account :		Stock		3,000
Barnali	6,000	Investment		5,000
Sudipa	4,900	Goodwill		996
	16,000			16,000

On the above date, Debjani is admitted for $\frac{2}{5}$th share in the profits and losses of the firm.

Following revaluations were made at the time of admission :

(a) Accrued incomes not appearing in the books Rs. 100.
(b) Market value of Investments is Rs. 4,500.
(c) Claim on account of workmen's compensation is estimated at Rs. 150.
(d) Provision for doubtful debts is required at Rs. 600.
(e) X, an old customer, whose account was written-off as bad, has promised to pay Rs. 350 in settlement of his full claim.
(f) The firm has purchased Machinery on Hire-Purchase System for Rs. 3,000 of which only Rs. 100 is to be paid. Both Machinery and unpaid liability did not appear in the Balance Sheet. There was a Joint Life Policy on the lives of Barnali and Sudipa for Rs. 15,000. Surrender value of the policy on the date of admission amounted to Rs. 2,400. It was decided to record this as an asset of the new firm.
(g) Debjani is required to bring in cash Rs. 10,000 as capital. Her share of Goodwill was calculated at Rs. 2,400. Full value of Goodwill is to be raised in the books.

You are required to prepare the Capital Accounts of the partners and the opening Balance Sheet of the new firm after the admission of Debjani.

[Ans. Profit on Revaluation Rs. 6,600, Closing Balance of Capital Account—Barnali Rs. 15,136, Sudipa Rs. 9,468, and Debjani Rs. 10,000, Total of Balance Sheet Rs. 36,754]

7. Marigold and Rose were in partnership sharing profits and losses as two-third and one-third. As from 1st October 2011 they agreed to take Jasmine as a new partner. The new partner will have one-sixth share, the old partners agreeing to share equally as between them in the new firm. Jasmine brings in Rs. 50,000 as capital and Rs. 4,000 as his share of goodwill to be retained in the firm.

The following is the Balance Sheet of the old firm as on 30th September 2012 :

Liabilities		Rs.	*Assets*	Rs.
Capital A/cs :			Cash	7,000
Marigold	62,500		Debtors	30,000
Rose	37,500		Stock	50,000
		1,00,000	Plant	25,000
Creditors		50,000	Investments	38,000
		1,50,000		1,50,000

The following revaluation is agreed upon :

Stock Rs. 55,00; PlantRs. 20,000; Investments Rs. 35,000

Debtors : Subject to reserve for bad debts of 5%.

It is further agreed that Marigold alone is to be charged with any loss arising from the above.

The profits, after depreciating Plant @ 5% p.a. for the year ended 30th September 2013, was Rs. 1,20,000 and the drawings of the partners were :

Marigold Rs. 40,000; Rose Rs. 40,000; Jasmine Rs. 10,000

You are required to Journalise the opening adjustments and draw up the Balance Sheet as on 30th September 2013.

[Ans. Total of Balance Sheet Rs. 2,29,500]

8. G, J, and M were in partnership sharing profits and losses : G six-tenths, J three-tenths, and M one-tenth.

The partnership deed provided :

(1) Interest at the rate of six per cent p.a. shall be allowed on fixed capital accounts. No interest shall be allowed on current accounts but eight per cent per annum is to be charged on any debit balance at the commencement of the year.

(2) Goodwill shall be valued at eighty per cent of the average annual profits of the previous three or four years, whichever is lower.

The following are the particulars of partners' accounts :

	Fixed Capital as on 31.12.2010	Balance on Current Account on 31.12.2010
	Rs.	Rs.
G	18,000	5,000 (Cr.)
J	9,000	1,000 (Cr.)
M	3,000	1,200 (Cr.)

The partners agreed to take T into partnership as on 1st January 2011, and on that day he introduced Rs. 3,500 in cash which included his fixed capital of Rs. 3,000. He is to receive a salary of Rs. 1,500 p.a. in addition to his share of profits. G personally guaranteed that the aggregate of T's salary and share of profit shall not be less than Rs. 3,000 per annum.

Profit-sharing ratios are to be G three-tenths, J three-tenths, M three-tenths, and T one-tenth.

Agreed profits for goodwill purposes for the past four years are :

	Rs.		Rs.
2010	16,337	2008	10,758
2009	10,255	2007	14,164

No account for goodwill is to be maintained in the books, adjusting entries for transactions between the partners being made in their current accounts.

The draft accounts for the year ended 31st December 2011, before taking into account T's salary or interest on partners' accounts, show a profit of Rs. 17,640. Partners' drawings during the year are : G Rs. 6,320, J Rs. 4,900, M Rs. 4,900, and T including salary Rs. 2,193.

You are required to prepare :

(a) A statement showing the division of profit for the year ended 31st December 2011, and

(b) The partners' current accounts for the year ended 31st December 2011, recording therein the entries necessary upon T's admission as a partner.

[CA]

[Ans. Balance of Current Account on 1.1.91 M Rs. 792, T Rs. 496,Value of Goodwill Rs. 9,9€0; Interest on Debit of Current A/c M Rs. 63, T Rs. 40, Net Devisible Profit Rs. 14,263; N sacrifices Rs.74. Balance of Current A/c : G Rs. 6,953 (Cr.), J 8, 919 (Cr.), M Rs. 1,296 (Dr.), T Rs. 45 (Cr.)]

C. RETIREMENT OF A PARTNER

An existing partner may retire from a firm due to many factors, e.g., old age, difference of opinion with other partners, better business prospect, etc. According to Sec. 32(1) of the Indian Partnership Act, a partner may retire (a) with the consent of all other partners; (b) in accordance with an express agreement by the partners; or, (c) where the partnership is at will—by giving notice in writing to all the partners of his intention to retire[1].

When a partner decides to retire from a partnership firm, two problems may arise, viz.:

(a) Amount payable to retiring partner and the procedure of computation of the retiring partner's interest; and

(b) the payment made to the retiring partner for the amount due.

But before highlighting the above, we are to compute the ratios under various methods in the case of Retirement of Partner.

These are explained below in details.

Calculation of Ratio and its various methods and treatment in accounting in case of Retirement of a Partner

Usually, when a partner retires from a firm, the existing partners take their share in various forms as under:

(a) When no fresh agreement is made among the existing partners

Under the circumstances, it is usually assumed that they will share the future profits as before and the same is done by eliminating the retiring partner's share. Consider the following illustration.

Example 1

A, B, and C were in partnership sharing profits and losses in the ratio of 3 : 2 : 1. B retires. Calculate the new profit-sharing ratio.

Solution

Old ratio = A : B : C = 3 : 2 : 1

New ratio will be = A : C = 3 : 1.

Or, A $= \frac{3}{4}$ B $= \frac{1}{4}$.

(b) When the existing partners acquire the share of the retiring partner

Under the circumstances, the new profit-sharing ratio will be computed after adding to their old ratio by which they have acquired.

Example 2

A, B and C were in partnership sharing profits and losses in the ratio of 3 : 2 : 1. B retires and his share is taken up by A and C in 2 : 1. Calculate the new profit-sharing ratio.

Solution

Old ratio = A : B : C = 3 : 2 : 1

Since A is taking $\frac{2}{3}$ rd of B's share,

i.e., A takes $\frac{2}{3}$ of $\frac{2}{6}$ or $\frac{4}{18}$.

∴ A's new share $= \frac{3}{6} + \frac{4}{18} = \frac{13}{18}$

Similarly, C is taking $\frac{1}{3}$ rd of B's share, i.e.,

C takes $\frac{1}{3}$ of $\frac{2}{6}$ or $\frac{2}{18}$

∴ C's new share C $= \frac{1}{6} + \frac{2}{18} = \frac{5}{18}$

Thus, the new ratio between A and C $= \frac{13}{18} : \frac{5}{18}$ or 13 : 5.

(c) In case of gaining ratio

Like admission of a partner, gaining ratio is computed by deducting the old share from his new share. This is particularly useful for the purpose of allocating goodwill. It may, again, be of the two following types:

(i) When the relative ratios remain unchanged between the existing partners

1 Saha Roy, H. K.—*Business and Economic Law*, New Central Book Agency (P) Ltd, 1990, p. 384

The following illustration will make the principle clear :

Example 3

A, B, and C were in partnership sharing profits and losses in the ratio of 3 : 2 : 1. C retires.

Calculate the gaining ratio as well as the new profit-sharing ratio.

Solution :

Old ratio = A : B : C = 3 : 2 : 1.

New ratio between A and B will be 3 : 2 or $\frac{3}{5}$ and $\frac{2}{5}$. In other words, C's share of $\frac{1}{6}$th is taken over by A and B in the same proportion i.e., 3 : 2.

Thus, the gaining ratio will be :

$A = \frac{3}{5} - \frac{3}{6} = \frac{18-15}{30} = \frac{3}{30}$ (gains) $\quad B = \frac{2}{5} - \frac{2}{6} = \frac{12-10}{30} = \frac{2}{30}$ (gains)

$C = $ sacrifices $\frac{3}{30} + \frac{2}{30} = \frac{5}{30}$ or $\frac{1}{6}$ (sacrifices)

Thus, the gaining ratio is 3 : 2.

(ii) **When the gaining ratio changes between the existing partners**

The following example will make the principle clear :

Example 4

A, B, and C were in partnership sharing profits and losses in the ratio of 3 : 2 : 1. C retired. His share was taken by A and B in 2 : 1. Calculate the gaining ratio and new profit-sharing ratio.

Solution

Old ratio = A : B : C = 3 : 2 : 1.

Now, A gains $\frac{2}{3}$ of $\frac{1}{6} = \frac{2}{18}$ from C $\quad$ Similarly, B gains $\frac{1}{3}$ of $\frac{1}{6} = \frac{1}{18}$ from C

So, his new ratio will be $\frac{3}{6} + \frac{2}{18} = \frac{11}{18}$ $\quad$ and—his new ratio will be $= \frac{2}{6} + \frac{1}{18} = \frac{7}{18}$

Thus, the new ratio between A and B is 11 : 7.

(iii) **When the existing partners take certain part of retiring partner's share**

Consider the following example.

Example 5

A, B, and C were in partnership sharing profits and losses in the ratio of 3 : 2 : 1. A retired. B and C take $\frac{4}{5}$th share of A in 2 : 3. Calculate the gaining ratio and the new profit-sharing ratio.

Solution

Old ratio = A : B : C = 3 : 2 : 1.

So A's share is $\frac{3}{6}$.

Now, B and C take $\frac{4}{5}$th of $\frac{3}{6} = \frac{4}{5} \times \frac{3}{6} = \frac{12}{30}$ $\quad$ B takes $\frac{2}{5}$th of $\frac{12}{30} = \frac{2}{5} \times \frac{12}{30} = \frac{24}{150}$

C takes $\frac{3}{5}$th of $\frac{12}{30} = \frac{3}{5} \times \frac{12}{30} = \frac{36}{150}$ $\quad$ B's new share, now, will be $= \frac{2}{6} + \frac{24}{150} = \frac{74}{150}$

So, C's new share will be $= \frac{1}{6} + \frac{36}{150} = \frac{61}{150}$

∴ The new ratio between B and C = 74 : 61.

[Proof : A's share left $\frac{1}{5}$th of $\frac{3}{6} = \frac{1}{5} \times \frac{3}{6} = \frac{3}{30}$ or $\frac{15}{150}$]

(iv) **When the retiring partner's share is taken by only one existing partner**

Consider the following example.

Example 6

A, B, and C were in partnership sharing profits and losses and takes them in the ratio of 3 : 2 : 1. C retired. His share was taken by A alone. Calculate the new profit-sharing ratio.

Solution

Old ratio = A : B : C = 3 : 2 : 1.

Since A takes entire share of C, his new ratio will be : $\frac{3}{6} + \frac{1}{6} = \frac{4}{6}$.

Thus, A gets $\frac{4}{6}$, B gets $\frac{2}{6}$ (unchanged). New ratio between A and B = 4 : 2 or 2 : 1.

Miscellaneous

Example 7

A, B, C, and D were in partnership sharing profits and losses in the ratio of 4 : 3 : 2 : 1. A retired. B, C, and D share the future profits and losses equally. Calculates the gaining ratio.

Solution

Old ratio = A : B : C : D = 4 : 3 : 2 : 1.

New ratio B : C : D = 1 : 1 : 1.

Thus, the gaining ratio is calculated as:

$B = \frac{3}{10} - \frac{1}{3} = \frac{9-10}{30} = \frac{(-)1}{30}$ (gains) $D = \frac{1}{10} - \frac{1}{3} = \frac{3-10}{30} = \frac{(-)7}{30}$ (gains)

$C = \frac{2}{10} - \frac{1}{3} = \frac{6-10}{30} = \frac{(-)4}{30}$ (gains) $A = \frac{1}{30} + \frac{4}{30} + \frac{7}{30} = \frac{12}{30}$ or $\frac{4}{10}$ (sacrifices)

So, the gaining ratio is 1 : 4 : 7. in the case of B, C, and D, respectively.

Like admission of a partner, there are certain adjustments which are to be made while retirement of a partner. They are :

1. Regarding Revaluation of Assets and Liabilities. 2. Regarding Undistributed Profits and Reserves, and 3. Regarding Goodwill.

1. Regarding Revaluation of Assets and Liabilities

(i) ***When revalued figures of assets and liabilities appear in the Balance Sheet***

Like admission of a new partner, when a partner retires from a firm, value of assets and liabilities are revalued at the date of retirement. Because, any profit or loss made on account of revaluation of assets and liabilities must be credited or debited to the retiring partner's capital account. The entry for the purpose is the same as we have done in the case of admission of a new partner. In other words, when the value of the assets are increased, or value of the liabilities are decreased, corresponding assets or liabilities account will be debited to the extent of increased value—and Revaluation Account will be credited. Similarly, in the opposite case, i.e., if the value of the assets are reduced or value of liabilities increased—Revaluation Account will be debited and corresponding assets or liabilities account will be credited to the extent of decreased value. The profit or loss revaluation so made will be transferred to the Partners' Capital Account in the old profit-sharing ratio.

As per Ind AS 16

39. "If an asset's carrying amount is increased as a result of revaluation the increase shall be recognised in other comprehensive income and accumulated in equity under the heading of **Revaluation Surplus.** However the increase shall be recognised in profit or loss to the extent that it reverses a revaluation decrease of the same asset previously recognised in profit or loss."

40. "If an asset's carrying amount is decreased as a result of revaluation, the decrease shall be recognised in profit or loss. However, the decrease shall be recognised in other comprehensive income to the extent of any credit balance existing in the revaluation surplus in respect of that asset. The decrease recognised in other comprehensive income reduces the amount accumulated in equity under the heading of **Revaluation Surplus.**"

41. "The revaluation surplus included in equity in respect of an item of **Property, Plant and Equipment** may be transferred directly to retained earnings when the asset is derecognised. This may involve transferring the whole of the surplus when the asset is retained or disposed of. However, some of the surplus may be transferred as the asset is used by the entity. In such a case, the amount of the surplus transferred would be the difference between depreciation based on the revalued carrying amount of the asset and depreciation based on the asset's original cost. Transfers from revaluation surplus to retained earnings are not made through profit or loss."

As per Partnership

Both the increase in net book value of fixed assets and decrease in the book value of fixed assets are credited and debited, respectively, to Revaluation Account in place of Revaluation Reserve Account (as per **Ind AS 16**). The profit or loss on revaluation is transferred to Partnership Capital Account.

However, the result in both the cases is the same, i.e., they will ultimately be transferred to Partners' Capital Account.

While solving the subsequent problems we have used Revaluation Account for incorporating the increase or decrease of fixed assets/other assets in place of Revaluation Reserve Account (As per Ind AS 16).

(ii) ***When revalued figures of assets and liabilities do not appear in the Balance Sheet***

Under the circumstances we are to open a ***Memorandum Revaluation Account*** like admission of a partner which we have explained earlier. In other words, original profit or loss or revaluation will be transferred to all partners' capital accounts—including retiring partner—in their old ratio. The same profit or loss, on revaluation, will be written-back to the existing partners' capital account only in the new ratio after adjusting the *'Reversal of Items'*. Thus, the increased or decreased values of assets and liabilities are adjusted accordingly. The following example will make the principles clear :

Illustration 1

A, B, and C were in partnership sharing profits and losses in the ratio 2 : 2 : 1. Their Balance Sheet as at 31.12.2012 stood as :

Balance Sheet *as at* **31st Dec. 2012**

Liabilities		Rs.	*Assets*	Rs.
Capital :			Plant and Machinery	40,000
A	60,000		Land and Building	50,000
B	40,000		Stock	30,000
C	30,000		Debtors	20,000
		1,30,000	Cash and Bank	10,000
General Reserve		10,000		
Creditors		10,000		
		1,50,000		1,50,000

B retired from the firm on 1st Jan. 2013 on the following conditions :

(i) Stock should be taken at Rs. 50,000. (ii) Land and Building and Plant and Machinery should be depreciated by 10% and 20%, respectively. (iii) B should be paid in full for which A and C would bring Rs. 20,000 each.

Show the Revaluation Account, Capital Account and the resultant Balance Sheet at the date of B's retirement assuming that ***the partners desire not to alter the book value of assets and liabilities.***

Solution

In the Books of A, B, and C

Memorandum Revaluation Account

Dr. Particulars		Amount Rs.	Particulars *Cr.*		Amount Rs.
To Land and Building A/c		5,000	By Stock A/c		20,000
" Plant and Machinery A/c		8,000			
" Profit on Revaluation :					
A	2,800				
B	2,800				
C	1,400				
		7,000			
		20,000			20,000
To **Reversal of Items**		20,000	By **Reversal of Items**		13,000
			" Profit Written-back		
			A $\frac{2}{3}$	4,667	
			C $\frac{1}{3}$	2,333	
					7,000
		20,000			20,000

Dr. **Capital Account** Cr.

Particulars	A Rs.	B Rs.	C Rs.	Particulars	A Rs.	B Rs.	C Rs.
To Revaluation A/c				By Balance b/d	60,000	40,000	30,000
—Profit				" Revaluation A/c			
Written-back	4,667	—	2,333	—Profit	2,800	2,800	1,400
" Reserve A/c	6,667	—	3,333	" Reserve A/c	4,000	4,000	2,000
" Bank A/c	—	46,800	—	" Bank A/c	20,000	—	20,000
" Balance c/d	75,466	—	47,734				
	86,800	46,800	53,400		86,800	46,800	53,400

Balance Sheet (after B's retirement) *as at 1st Jan. 2013*

Liabilities		Rs.	Assets	Rs.
Capital A/c			Plant and Machinery	40,000
A	75,466		Land and Building	50,000
C	47,734		Stock	30,000
		1,23,200	Debtors	20,000
General Reserve		10,000	Cash and Bank	
Creditors		10,000	(Rs. 10,000 + Rs. 20,000 + Rs. 20,000 – Rs. 46,800)	3,200
		1,43,200		1,43,200

2. Regarding Undistributed Profits and Reserves

Needless to mention here that at the date of retirement of a partner, if there is any undistributed profits/reserves or losses, the same will be transferred to all partners' capital account (including retiring partner) in the old profit-sharing ratio. For this purposes, the following entries are required :

(i) ***For Undistributed Profit/Reserves***

Profit/Reserve A/c Dr.	}	in the old ratio
To Partners' Capital A/c		

(ii) **For Undistributed Losses**

All Partners' Capital A/c Dr.	}	in the old ratio
To Profit and Loss A/c		

3. Regarding Goodwill

The goodwill is to be computed as per Partnership Deed. But, in absence of the same, any one of the following methods may be taken into consideration :

(a) When Goodwill is raised at its full value

When goodwill is raised in the books at its full value, Goodwill Account will be debited at its full value and corresponding Partners' Capital Accounts will be credited at their old profit-sharing ratio (in this case Goodwill Account must be shown in the asset side of the Balance Sheet).

In short, the entry will be :

(i) Goodwill A/c Dr.	}	at full value in profit-sharing ratio
To All Partners' Capital A/c (including retiring partners)		

(b) When Goodwill is raised at its full value and then written-off immediately

In that case, a Goodwill Account is to be debited at its full value and Partners' Capital Account (including retiring partner's) will be credited as per profit-sharing ratio. Thereafter, Existing Partners' Capital Accounts will be debited as per new profit-sharing ratio and Goodwill Account will be credited in order to write-off from the books (in this case Goodwill Account must not be shown in the asset side of the Balance Sheet).

Thus, the following entries are required to be passed :

(i) Goodwill A/c Dr.	}	at full value as per old profit-sharing ratio
To All Partners' Capital A/c (including retiring partner's)		
(ii) Existing Partners' Capital A/c Dr.	}	as per new ratio
To Goodwill A/c		

(c) When Goodwill is raised with the share of retiring partner only

In that case, only Goodwill Account is debited with the amount of retiring partner's share and retiring partner's capital account is credited (in this case, Goodwill Account must be shown in the asset side of the Balance Sheet).

So, the entry will be :

(i) Goodwill A/c	Dr.	with the amount of retiring partner's share
To Retiring Partner's Capital A/c		

(d) When Goodwill is raised with the share of retiring partner and then written-off, i.e., capital transfer

In that case, Existing Partners' Capital Account as per gaining ratio will be debited and retiring partner's Capital Account will be credited by the amount of retiring partner's share of goodwill (in this case, Goodwill Account must not be shown in the assets side of the Balance Sheet).

Thus, the entry will be :

(i) Existing Partners' Capital A/c	Dr.	only by the amount of retiring partner's share in gaining ratio
To Retiring Partner's Capital A/c		

But, in this context, it is very important to refer **Ind AS 38**, *Para 36* which states :

Goodwill should be recorded in the books only when some consideration in money or money's worth has been paid for it. Whenever a business is acquired for price (payable in cash or in shares or otherwise) which is in excess of the value of the net asset of the business taken over, the excess should be termed as 'goodwill'.

In other words, As per Ind AS 38, only Purchased Goodwill should be recorded. Thus, non-purchased or internally generated goodwill should be adjusted against Partners' Capital Accounts or Partner's Current Account.

So, **Ind AS 38**, contradicts the raising of Goodwill.

Illustration 2

A, B, and C are partners, their capitals being A Rs. 20,000, B Rs. 15,000, and C Rs. 10,000. They share profits or losses in the ratio of 3 : 2 : 1.

On 1.1.2010, C retires, the Goodwill is valued at Rs. 24,000.

Show the entries under each of the following conditions :

(a) If Goodwill account is raised and written-off; (b) If Goodwill account is not raised in the books, or if only the retiring partner's share of goodwill is to be recorded; (c) Goodwill account is raised with the share of retiring partner's only.

Solution

In the Books of A, B, and C
Journal

2010			Rs.	Rs.
Jan. 1	(a) (i) Goodwill A/c	Dr.	24,000	
	To A's Capital A/c			12,000
	" B's Capital A/c			8,000
	" C's Capital A/c			4,000
	(Goodwill account is raised in the books on C's retirement and credited to capital accounts in 3 : 2 : 1)			
	(ii) A's Capital A/c	Dr.	14,400	
	B's Capital A/c	Dr.	9,600	
	To Goodwill A/c			24,000
	(Value of goodwill raised and written-off on C's retirement against the remaining partners in 3 : 2)			
	(b) (i) Goodwill A/c	Dr.	4,000	
	To C's Capital A/c ($24,000 \times \frac{1}{6}$)			4,000
	(C's share of goodwill is raised on his retirement)			
	(ii) A's Capital A/c	Dr.	2,400	
	B's Capital A/c	Dr.	1,600	
	To Goodwill A/c			4,000
	(C's share of goodwill to be written-off between A and B's Capital is 3 : 2)			

Contd.

			Rs.	Rs.
	or, A's Capital A/c	Dr.	2,400	
	B's Capital A/c	Dr.	1,600	
	To C's Capital A/c			4,000
	(Adjustment made for goodwill on C's retirement against A and B's capital accounts in 3 : 2.)			
(c)	A's Capital A/c	Dr.	2,400	
	B's Capital A/c	Dr.	1,600	
	To C's Capital A/c			4,000
	(Goodwill account is raised in the books with the retiring partner's share.)			

Illustration 3

Retiring Partner's Total Claim

The partnership deed must be observed for the purpose of ascertaining the amount due to the retiring partner. In the absence of any specific agreement, however, the amount will include :

(i) Balance of his Capital and Current Account; (ii) his share of goodwill in the firm; (iii) his share of profit or loss on revaluation of assets and liabilities; (iv) his share of profit in undistributed profits or losses, if any; (v) his salary, interest on capital or drawings till the date of retirement; (vi) his share of profit till the date of retirement (less drawings).

Payment made to the retiring/outgoing partner for the amount due

The amount due to the retiring/outgoing partners may be made by any one of the following manner :

A. **Lump sum basis :**

(i) ***The amount may be paid off immediately from business cash in Lump Sum. The entrtes for this purpose will be :***

Retiring Partner's Capital A/c Dr.
To Cash/Bank A/c

Consider the following illustration

Illustration 4

P, Q, and R were in partnership sharing profits and losses equally. They had taken a Joint Life Policy of the face value of Rs. 18,000. Surrender value was Rs. 3,000. On 1.1.2003, P retired when the firm's Balance Sheet was :

Liabilities	Rs.	Rs.	*Assets*	Rs.
Capital Accounts :			Land and Building	4,200
P	8,000		Plant and Machinery	6,980
Q	6,800		Debtors	8,915
R	7,800		Investment	8,000
		22,600	Cash	7,433
Reserve Fund		6,000		
Creditors		6,928		
		35,528		35,528

According to Partnership Deed assets were agreed to be revalued on P's retirement as : Land and Building Rs. 5,800, Plant and Machinery Rs. 6,564, Investments Rs. 8,400.

Besides, Goodwill was then valued at Rs. 9,600. P accepted the investments at their revalued figure in part payment of his dues. Q paid in Rs. 4,000 as further capital and P was paid-off the balance of his account.

Prepare the Revaluation Account, Partners' Capital Account and the revised Balance Sheet of Q and R (assuming that the Goodwill Account is not to be raised in the books and the Joint Life Policy was also not to appear in the Balance Sheet).

Solution

Value of Goodwill Rs. 9,600, P's share of Goodwill $= \text{Rs. } 9{,}600 \times \frac{1}{3} = \text{Rs. } 3{,}200$.

In the books of P, Q, and R

Dr. **Revaluation Account** Cr.

Particulars	Rs.	*Amount* Rs.	*Particulars*	*Amount* Rs.
To Plant and Machinery		416	By Land and Building	1,600

Contd.

	Rs.	Rs.		Rs.
Capital A/c :			By Investments	400
Profit on Revaluation :				
P $\frac{1}{3}$	528			
Q $\frac{1}{3}$	528			
R $\frac{1}{3}$	528	1,584		
		2,000		2,000

Capital Account

Dr. Cr.

Particulars	P Rs.	Q Rs.	R Rs.	Particulars	P Rs.	Q Rs.	R Rs.
To P's Capital—		1,600	1,600	By Balance b/d	8,000	6,800	7,800
" Investments	8,400	—	—	" Rev.—Profit	528	528	528
" Bank (final Payment)	6,328	—	—	" Q's Capital	1,600	—	—
" P's Capital	—	500	500	" R's Capital	1,600	—	—
" Balance c/d	—	11,228	8,228	" Reserve Fund	2,000	2,000	2,000
				" Q's Capital	500	—	—
				" R's Capital	500	—	—
				" Bank	—	4,000	—
	14,728	13,328	10,328		14,728	13,328	10,328
				By Balance b/d	—	11,228	8,228

Balance Sheet *as at* **1st** *Jan.* **2003**

Liabilities	Rs.	Rs.	Assets	Rs.
Capital Accounts			Land and Building	5,800
Q	11,228		(Rs. 4,200 + Rs. 1,600)	
R	8,228		Plant and Machinery	6,564
		19,456	(Rs. 6,980 – Rs. 416)	
Creditors		6,928	Debtors	8,915
			Cash and Bank	5,105
			(Rs. 7,433 + Rs. 4,000 – Rs. 6,328)	
		26,384		26,384

Note :

P's share on surrender value of Joint Life Policy amounted to Rs. (3,000 × $\frac{1}{3}$) Rs. 1,000, it is to be debited to Q and R equally, since the same must not be shown in Balance Sheet.

B. Instalment basis

The amount due to him may be transferred to a Loan Account which is to be paid gradually with interest i.e., by instalments.

(a) ***For transferring to Loan Account:***
Retiring Partner's Capital A/c Dr.
To Retiring Partner's Loan A/c

(b) ***For the amount of Interest***
Interest A/c Dr.
To Retiring Partner's Loan A/c

(c) ***For the payment of instalment:***
Retiring Partner's Capital A/c Dr.
To Cash/Bank A/c

Illustration 5

A, B, and C were in partnership till 31st Dec. 2007 when C retired from partnership. The amount due to him after necessary adjustments arising in connection with such retirement was Rs. 1,00,000. At the request of the other partners he agreed to leave the amount with the new firm as loan on the following terms and conditions :

(i) Repayment of loan to be made at the end of each year by annual instalments representing 40% of future annual profit after charging salary of Rs. 7,500 p.a. to each partner.

(ii) Interest @ 5% p.a. calculated on the balance outstanding at the beginning of the year to be credited but such interest will not be taken into account for calculation of 40% stated above.

Profit before charging partners' salaries were : 2008 Rs. 15,000; 2009 Rs. 1,03,125; 2010 Rs. 1,11,875; 2011 Rs. 1,15,000; 2012 Rs. 1,43,250.

You are required to show C's Loan Account for all these years as it would appear in the books for the firm.

Solution

Workings :

Calculations of yearly instalment to be paid

	2008	2009	2010	2011	2012
	Rs.	Rs.	Rs.	Rs.	Rs.
Profit (before charging Salaries)	15,000	1,03,125	1,11,875	1,15,000	1,43,250
Less : Partners' Salaries @ Rs. 15,000	15,000	15,000	15,000	15,000	15,000
	—	88,125	96,875	1,00,000	1,28,250
Amount available for repayment of loan @ 40% for above	Nil	35,250	38,750	40,000	51,300

In the books of the firm

C's Loan Account

Dr. *Cr.*

Date	*Particulars*	*Amount*	*Date*	*Particulars*	*Amount*
2008		Rs.	2008		Rs.
Dec. 31	To Balance c/d	1,05,000	Jan. 1	By C's Capital	1,00,000
			Dec. 31	" Interest @ 5%	5,000
		1,05,000			1,05,000
2009			2009		
Dec. 31	To Bank	35,250	Jan. 1	By Balance b/d	1,05,000
	" Balance c/d	75,000	Dec. 31	" Interest @ 5%	5,250
		1,10,250			1,10,250
2010			2010		
Dec. 31	To Bank	38,750	Jan. 1	By Balance b/d	75,000
	" Balance c/d	40,000	Dec. 31	" Interest @ 5%	3,750
		78,750			78,750
2011			2011		
Dec. 31	To Bank	40,000	Jan. 1	By Balance b/d	40,000
	" Balance c/d	2,000	Dec. 31	" Interest @ 5%	2,000
		42,000			42,000
2012			2012		
Dec. 31	To Bank	2,100[1]	Jan. 1	By Balance b/d	2,000
			Dec. 31	" Interest @ 5%	100
		2,100			2,100

Notes : Only the unpaid balance with interest to be paid (i.e., Rs. 2,000 + Rs. 100) = Rs. 2,100; although the amount availabl e was Rs. 51,300.

C. Payment made Privately/or, made through firm

Existing partners may purchase out the retiring partner's share for which the payment may be made by the two following ways :

(a) ***If payment is made privately:***

Retiring Partner]s Capital A/c Dr.
 To Existing Partners' Capital A/c

(b) ***If payment is made through firm :***

Cash/Bank A/c Dr.
 To Existing Partners' Capital A/c
Retiring Partner's Capital A/c Dr.
 To Cash/Bank A/c

Right to Share of Profits after Retirement

If after retirement or death of one partner the continuing partners carry on the business of the firm with the property of the firm (without any final settlement of accounts) the ***outgoing partner*** (or the legal representative of the deceased partner) ***is entitled to get share of profits*** or 6% p.a. of his share of property of the firm at their option. Sec. 37 of the Indian Partnership Act provides : "where any member of a firm has died or otherwise ceased to be partner and the surviving or continuing partners carry on the business of the firm with the property of the firm without any final settlement of accounts as between them and the outgoing partner or his estate, then, in the absence of a contract to the contrary, the outgoing partner or his estate is entitled at the option of himself or his representatives to such share of the profits made since he ceased to be a partner as may be attributable to the use of his share of the property of the firm of to interest @ 6% p.a. on the amount of his share in the property of the firm." In order to find out the share of profit of the retiring partner, under the circumstances, the following steps are to be followed:

Step I : Ascertain the amount of average profit of the last year

Step II : Compute the amount of profit for such period or proportionate basis as :

$$= \textit{Average Profit} \times \frac{\textit{Period}}{12}$$

Step III : Ascertain the retiring partner's share of profit on the figure computed under Step II

Note : The share of profit so ascertained should be transferred to Profit and Loss Suspense Account by passing the following entry :

Profit and Loss Suspense A/c Dr.
To Retiring Partner's Capital A/c

Note : Since it is not the actual profit, i.e., merely an estimated figure, it is better to transfer the same to the Profit and Loss Suspense Account.

Illustration 6

X, Y, and Z were in partnership sharing profits and losses equally. Z retired on 31st March 2009. The Balance Sheet of the firm on 31st Dec. 2008 stood as :

Balance Sheet *as at 31st Dec. 2008*

	Rs.	Rs.		Rs.
Capital :			Goodwill	21,000
X	30,000		Land and Building	40,000
Y	20,000		Investment (at cost)	8,000
Z	10,000		Stock	12,000
		60,000	Debtors	15,000
General Reserve		9,000	Cash and Bank	7,000
Investment Fluctuation Fund		2,000		
Reserve for Doubtful Debts		1,000		
Creditors		31,000		
		1,03,000		1,03,000

On the date of retirement it was found that :

(i) Land and Building be valued at Rs. 60,000.

(ii) Investment be valued at Rs. 7,500.

(iii) Stock be valued at Rs. 10,500.

(iv) Goodwill be valued at one year's purchase of the average profit of the past 5 years which were : 2004 — Rs. 10,000; 2005 — Rs. 11,000; 2006 — Rs. 8,000; 22007 — Rs. 12,000, and 2008 — Rs. 19,000.

(v) Z's share of profit to the date of retirement be calculated on the basis of average profit of the preceding three years.

You are required to : (1) show Journal entries, (without narration), (2) C's Capital Account, and (3) the Balance Sheet.

Solution

(a) **Calculation of Goodwill**

$$\text{Average Profit} = \frac{\text{Rs. } 10{,}000 + \text{Rs. } 11{,}000 + \text{Rs. } 8{,}000 + 12{,}000 + \text{Rs. } 19{,}000}{5}$$

$$= \text{Rs. } \frac{60{,}000}{5} = \text{Rs. } 12{,}000$$

Value of Goodwill Rs. 12,000 × 1 = Rs. 12,000

Thus, there is a fall in the value of Goodwill amounting to Rs. 9,000 (i.e., Rs. 21,000 – Rs. 12,000).

(b) Calculation of Z's share of profit at the date of retirement

Average Profit of last three years $= \dfrac{\text{Rs. } 8{,}000 + \text{Rs. } 12{,}000 + \text{Rs. } 19{,}000}{3}$

$= \text{Rs. } 13{,}000$

Profit for 3 months (i.e., Jan. to March) on that basis $= \text{Rs. } 13{,}000 \times \dfrac{3}{12} = \text{Rs. } 3{,}250$

Z's share $= \text{Rs. } 3{,}250 \times \dfrac{1}{3} = \text{Rs. } 1{,}083$

In the books of X, Y, and Z
Journal
(without narrations)

Date	Particulars		L.F.	Debit	Credit
2009				Rs.	Rs.
March 31	X's Capital A/c	Dr.		3,000	
	Y's Capital A/c	Dr.		3,000	
	Z's Capital A/c	Dr.		3,000	
	To Goodwill A/c				9,000
	Profit and Loss Suspense A/c	Dr.		1,083	
	To Z's Capital A/c				1,083
	Land and Building A/c	Dr.		20,000	
	Reserve for Doubtful Debts A/c	Dr.		1,000	
	Investment Fluctuation A/c	Dr.		1,500	
	To Revaluation A/c				22,500
March 31	Revaluation A/c	Dr.		1,500	
	To Stock A/c				1,500
	Revaluation A/c	Dr.		21,000	
	To X's Capital A/c				7,000
	" Y's Capital A/c				7,000
	" Z's Capital A/c				7,000
	General Reserve A/c	Dr.		9,000	
	To X's Capital A/c				3,000
	" Y's Capital A/c				3,000
	" Z's Capital A/c				3,000
	Z's Capital A/c	Dr.		18,083	
	To Z's Loan A/c				18,083

Z's Capital Account

Dr. Cr.

Particulars	Amount	Particulars	Amount
	Rs.		Rs.
To Goodwill A/c	3,000	By Balance b/d	10,000
" Z's Loan A/c —Transfer	18,083	" Profit and Loss A/c	1,083
		" Revaluation A/c —Profit	7,000
		" General Reserve	3,000
	21,083		21,083

Balance Sheet *as at 31st March 2009*

Liabilities	Rs.	Assets	Rs.	Rs.
Capital :		Goodwill (21,000 – 9,000)		12,000
X (30,000 + 7,000 + 3,000 – 3,000)	37,000	Land and Building		60,000
Y (20,000 + 7,000 + 3,000 – 3,000)	27,000	Investment (at cost)	8,000	
Z's Loan A/c	18,083	*Less* : Reserve	500	
Creditors	31,000			7,500
		Stock		10,500
		Debtors		15,000
		Cash and Bank		7,000
		Profit and Loss Suspense A/c		1,083
	1,13,083			1,13,083

Notes :

1. **As all debtors are considered good, reserve for bad and doubtful debts is not required; as such, the same should be transferred to Revaluation Account.**

2. Market value of Investment has gone down by Rs. 500 (i.e., 8,000 – 7,500) which must be adjusted against Investment Fluctuation Reserve and the balance of the said account should be transferred to Revaluation Account.
3. If goodwill account is to be written-off the same shall be transferred to existing partners' capital account in the new ratio.

GENERAL ILLUSTRATIONS

Illustration 7

A, B, and C are partners in a firm. They shared profits and losses in the ratio of 3 : 2 : 1. On 1.4.2012, B retired and on that date Balance Sheet of the firm was :

Liabilities	Rs.	*Assets*	Rs.
Capital Accounts		Land and Building	2,50,000
A	3,40,000	Plant and Machinery	3,00,000
B	2,20,000	Investment	50,000
C	1,90,000	Stock	1,80,000
Sundry Creditors	1,60,000	Bills Receivable	20,000
Bills Payable	50,000	Sundry Debtors	1,00,000
		Cash at Bank	60,000
	9,60,000		9,60,000

(i) A and C decided to continue in partnership and share future profits and losses in the ratio of $\frac{5}{8}$th and $\frac{3}{8}$th, respectively.

(ii) The Goodwill of the firm was valued at two years' purchase based on the average of the last three years' profits. The profits of the last three years were :

2010-11	Profit	Rs. 2,48,000
2011-12	Loss	Rs. 36,000
2012-13	Profit	Rs. 1,48,000

It was decided that B's share of goodwill be adjusted in the Capital Accounts of A and C. (No goodwill account is to be raised in the books of the firms.)

(iii) Stock and Land and Building are to be depreciated by 10% and Plant and Machinery to be increased by 10%.

(iv) 5% is to be provided for doubtful debts on Sundry Debtors and provision is to be made for Rs. 12,000 for outstanding legal expenses.

(v) Amount due to B was transferred to his Loan A/c.

Show Profit and Loss Adjustment Account, Capital Account and the Balance Sheet after B's retirement.

Solution

B's share of Goodwill to be calculated as :

$$\text{Average Profit} = \frac{2,48,000 - \text{Rs. } 36,000 + \text{Rs. } 1,48,000}{3}$$

Value of Goodwill = Rs. 1,20,000 × 2 = Rs. 2,40,000.

$\therefore$ B's share = Rs. 2,40,000 × $\frac{2}{6}$ = Rs. 80,000

So, Rs. 80,000 should be divided between A and C's capital in the following gaining ratio :

$$A = \frac{3}{6} - \frac{5}{8} = \frac{12-15}{24} = \frac{-3}{24} \text{ (gains)} \qquad B = \frac{3}{24} + \frac{5}{24} = \frac{8}{24} = \frac{1}{3} \text{ (sacrifices)}$$

$$C = \frac{1}{6} - \frac{3}{8} = \frac{4-9}{24} = \frac{-5}{24} \text{ (gains)}$$

$\therefore$ The gaining ratio is 3 : 5, and the amount of B's share of Goodwill is to be adjusted in the following manner :

A's Capital A/c should be debited by Rs. 30,000 (i.e., 80,000 × $\frac{3}{8}$).

B's Capital A/c should be debited by Rs. 50,000 (i.e., 80,000 × $\frac{5}{8}$).

Profit and Loss Adjustment Account

Dr. Particulars	Amount	Particulars		Cr. Amount
	Rs.			Rs.
To Stock	18,000	To Plant and Machinery		30,000
" Building	25,000	" Capital A/c		
" R/B/ Debts	5,000	" Loss on Revaluation :		
" Prov. for Outstanding Legal Fees	12,000	A	15,000	
		B	10,000	
		C	3,000	30,000
	60,000			60,000

Capital Account

Dr. Particulars	A	B	C	Particulars	A	B	Cr. C
	Rs.	Rs.	Rs.		Rs.	Rs.	Rs.
To Profit and Loss Adjustment (Loss)	15,000	10,000	5,000	By Balance b/d	3,40,000	2,20,000	1,90,000
" B's Capital (Goodwill)	30,000	—	50,000	" A's Capital A/c	—	30,000	—
To B's Loan A/c — Transfer	—	2,90,000	—	" B's Capital A/c	—	50,000	—
" Balance c/d	2,95,000	—	1,35,000				
	3,40,000	3,00,000	1,90,000		3,40,000	3,00,000	1,90,000

Balance Sheet *as at April 1, 2012*

Liabilities	Rs.	Rs.	*Assets*	Rs.	Rs.
Capital A/c			Land and Building		2,25,000
A	2,95,000		(Rs. 2,50,000 – Rs. 25,000)		
C	1,35,000		Plant and Machinery		3,30,000
		4,30,000	(Rs. 3,00,000 + Rs. 30,000)		
B's Loan A/c		2,90,000	Investments		50,000
Creditors		1,60,000	Stock		1,62,000
Bills Payable		50,000	(Rs. 1,80,000 – Rs. 18,000)		
Outstanding Legal Expenses		12,000	Bills Receivable		20,000
			Sundry Debtors	1,00,000	
			Less : R/B/Debts	5,000	
					95,000
			Cash at Bank		60,000
		9,42,000			9,42,000

Illustration 8

On 31.3.2009, the Balance Sheet of M/s Ram, Rahul, and Rohit, sharing profits and losses in proportion to their capital, stood as :

	Rs.		Rs.
Capital Accounts :		Land and Building	2,00,000
Ram	3,00,000	Machinery	2,00,000
Rahul	2,00,000	Closing Stock	1,00,000
Rohit	1,00,000	Sundry Debtors	2,00,000
Sundry Creditors	2,00,000	Cash and Bank	1,00,000
	8,00,000		8,00,000

On 31.3.2009 Ram desired to retire from the firm and the remaining partners decided to carry on. It was agreed to revalue the assets and liabilities on that date on the following basis :

(i) Land and Building be appreciated by 30%

(ii) Machinery be depreciated by 20%

(iii) Closing Stock to be valued at Rs. 80,000

(iv) Provision for bad debts be made at 5%.

(v) Old credit balance of Sundry Creditors Rs. 10,000 be written-back.

(vi) Joint Life Policy of the partners surrendered and Cash obtained Rs. 60,000.

(vii) Goodwill of the firm be valued at Rs. 1,80,000 and Ram's share of goodwill be adjusted in the accounts of Rahul and Rohit who share the future profits equally. No goodwill account being raised.

(viii) The total capital of the firm is to be the same as before retirement. Individual capital be in their profit-sharing ratio.

(ix) Amount due to Ram is to be settled on the following basis :

50% on retirement and the balance 50% within one year.

Prepare Revaluation Account, Capital Accounts of partners, Cash Account and Balance Sheet as on 1.4.2009 of M/s Rahul and Rohit.

[CA Foundation]

Solution

In the books of the firm

Revaluation Account

Dr. *Cr.*

	Particulars		*Amount*		*Particulars*	*Amount*
			Rs.			Rs.
To	Machinery A/c		40,000	By	Land and Building A/c	60,000
"	Closing Stock A/c		20,000	"	Sundry Creditors A/c	10,000
"	Provision for Bad Debts A/c		10,000	"	Cash and Bank A/c	
"	Capital A/c :				—Surrender of J. L. Policy	60,000
"	Profit on Revaluation :					
	Ram	30,000				
	Rahul	20,000				
	Rohit	10,000				
			60,000			
			1,30,000			1,30,000

Capital Account

Dr. *Cr.*

Particulars	Ram	Rahul	Rohit	*Particulars*	Ram	Rahul	Rohit
	Rs.	Rs.	Rs.		Rs.	Rs.	Rs.
To Ram's A/c				By Balance b/d	3,00,000	2,00,000	1,00,000
—Goodwill	—	30,000	60,000	" Revaluation A/c			
" Bank A/c (50%)	2,10,000	—	—	—Profit	30,000	20,000	10,000
" Ram's Loan A/c	2,10,000	—	—	" Rahul's Capital A/c	30,000[1]	—	—
" Balance c/d	—	3,00,000	3,00,000	" Rohit's Capital A/c	60,000	—	—
				" Cash & Bank A/c			
				—Cash brought in	—	1,10,000	2,50,000
	4,20,000	3,30,000	3,60,000		4,20,000	3,30,000	3,60,000

Cash and Bank A/c

Dr. *Cr.*

	Particulars	*Amount*		*Particulars*	*Amount*
		Rs.			Rs.
To	Balance b/d	1,00,000	By	Ram's Capital A/c	2,10,000
"	Revaluation A/c		"	Balance c/d	3,10,000
	—J. L. Policy Surrendered	60,000			
"	Rahul's Capital A/c	1,10,000			
"	Rohit's Capital A/c	2,50,000			
		5,20,000			5,20,000

Balance Sheet *as at 1st April 2009*

Liabilities		Rs.	*Assets*		Rs.
Capital A/c :			Land and Building		2,60,000
Rahul	3,00,000		Machinery		1,60,000
Rohit	3,00,000		Closing Stock		80,000
		6,00,000	Sundry Debtors	2,00,000	
Ram's Loan A/c		2,10,000	*Less* : Prov. for Bad Debts	10,000	
Sundry Creditors		1,90,000			1,90,000
			Cash and Bank		3,10,000
		10,00,000			10,00,000

Workings :

1. **Ram's share of Goodwill at the date of retirement**

Total value of Goodwill = Rs. 1,80,000

Ram's Share of Goodwill = Rs. 1,80,000 × $\frac{1}{2}$ = Rs. 90,000

to be taken by Rahul and Rohit as per gaining ratio which is computed as :

Rahul $= \frac{1}{2} - \frac{1}{3} = \frac{3-2}{6} = \frac{1}{6}$ (gains) So, Rahul will bear = Rs. 90,000 × $\frac{1}{3}$ = Rs. 30,000

Rohit $= \frac{1}{2} - \frac{1}{6} = \frac{3-1}{6} = \frac{2}{6}$ (gains) Rohit will bear = Rs. 90,000 × $\frac{2}{3}$ = Rs. 60,000

∴ Gaining ratio is 1 : 2.

Illustration 9

A, B and C were in partnership sharing profits and losses in the proportions of 5 : 4: 3. The Balance Sheet of the firm as on 31st March 1998 was:

Liabilities		Rs.	*Assets*	Rs.
Capital	A	1,35,930	Goodwill	40,000
	B	95,120	Furniture	8,200
	C	61,170	Stock	1,57,300
Sundry Creditors		41,690	Sundry Debtors	93,500
			Cash	34,910
		3,33,910		3,33,910

A had been suffering from ill-health and gave notice that he wished to retire. An agreement was, therefore, entered into as on 31st March 1998, the terms of which are :

(i) The Profit and Loss account for the year ended 31st March 1998, which showed a net profit of Rs. 48,000, was to be re-opened. B was to be credited with Rs. 4,000 as bonus, in consideration of the extra work which had devolved upon him during the year. The profit-sharing ratio was to be revised as from 1st April 1997 to 3 : 4 : 4.

(ii) Goodwill was to be valued at two years' purchase of the average Profits of the preceeding five years. The Fixtures were to be valued by an independent valuer. A provision of 2% was to be made for doubtful debts and the remaining assets were to be taken at their book values.

The valuations arising out of the above agreement were Goodwill Rs. 56,800 and Fixtures Rs. 10,980.

B and C agreed, as between themselves, to continue the business, sharing profits in the ratio of 3 : 2 and decided to eliminate Goodwill from the Balance Sheet, to retain the Fixtures on the books at the revised value, and to increase the provision for doubtful debts to 6%.

You are required to submit the journal entries necessary to give effect to the above arrangements and to draw-up the capital account of the partners after carrying out all adjusting entries as stated above.

[CA Foundation May 1998]

Solution

In the books of A, B and C
Journal

Date	*Particulars*		*L.F.*	*Debit*	*Credit*
1998				Rs.	Rs.
March 31	A's Capital A/c	Dr.		20,000	
	B's Capital A/c	Dr.		16,000	
	C's Capital A/c	Dr.		12,000	
	To Profit and Loss Adjustment A/c				48,000
	(Profit written-back)				
	Profit and Loss Adjustment A/c	Dr.		4,000	
	To B's Capital A/c				4,000
	(Bonus credited to B's Capital A/c)				

Contd.

Particulars		Rs.	Rs.
Profit and Loss adjustment A/c	Dr.	44,000	
To A's Capital A/c			12,000
" B's Capital A/c			16,000
" C's Capital A/c			16,000
(Profit distributed in new ratio.)			
Revaluation A/c	Dr.	1,870	
To Provision for Bad Debts A/c			1,870
(Provisions made for bad debts)			
Goodwill A/c	Dr.	16,800	
Fixture A/c	Dr.	2,780	
To Revaluation A/c			19,580
(value of asset increased)			
Revaluation A/c	Dr.	17,710	
To A's Capital A/c			4,830
" B's Capital A/c			6,440
" C's Capital A/c			6,440
(Profit on revaluations transferred.)			
A's Capital A/c	Dr.	1,32,760	
To A's Loan A/c			1,32,760
(Amount due to A transferred to his Loan A/c)			
B's Capital A/c	Dr.	34,080	
C's Capital A/c	Dr.	22,720	
To Goodwill A/c			56,800
(Goodwill written-off.)			
B's Capital A/c	Dr.	2,244	
C's Capital A/c	Dr.	1,496	
To Provision for Bad Debts A/c			3,740
(Provisions for Bad Debts to be raised.)			

Dr. **Capital Account** Cr.

Particulars	A	B	C	*Particulars*	A	B	C
	Rs.	Rs.	Rs.		Rs.	Rs.	Rs.
To Profit and Loss Adjustment A/c	20,000	16,000	12,000	By Balance b/d	1,35,930	95,120	61,170
" Loan A/c	1,32,760	—	—	" P and L Adjustment A/c	—	4,000	—
" Goodwill A/c	—	34,080	22,720	" P and L A/c Adjustment A/c	12,000	16,000	16,000
" Prov. for Bad Debts A/c	—	2,244	1,496	" Revaluation on A/c —Profit	4,830	6,440	6,440
" Balance c/d	—	69,236	47,394				
	1,52,760	1,21,560	83,610		1,52,760	1,21,560	83,610

Illustration 10

Atin, Bratin and Jatin are partners in a firm sharing profits and losses in the ratio of 2 : 2 : 1. Their Balance Sheet as at 31.12.01 is :

Balance Sheet *ast at 31st Dec. 2001*

Liabilities		Rs.	*Assets*		Rs.
Capital Accounts :			Land and Building		72,000
Atin	65,600		Machinery		35,500
Bratin	43,700		Furniture		10,400
Jatin	32,200	1,41,500	Motor Car		18,000
General Reserve		22,000	Stock		19,800
Creditors		18,000	Sundry Debtors	23,700	
			Less: Provision for Bad Debt	1,500	22,200
			Cash at Bank		3,600
		1,81,500			1,81,500

Bratin retires on 31.12.2001 but Atin and Jatin continue in partnership sharing profits in the ratio of 3 : 2. The terms of retirement provide :

(a) Goodwill is to be valued at 2 years' purchase of the average annual profits of the last three years but it should not be shown in the books. The profits of the last three years are : 1998—Rs. 12,100; 1999—Rs. 8,480; 2000—Rs. 10,920.

(b) The value of Land & Building is to be appreciated by 20%, Machinery is to be valued at Rs. 32,000 and Provision for Doubtful Debts to be maintained at Rs. 1,800.

(c) A furniture costing Rs. 3,000 purchased on 1.7.2000 but was debited to Purchases Account. This asset is to be taken into account charging depreciation @ 10% p.a. under Straight Line Method.

(d) Annual insurance premium of Rs. 2,400 paid on 1.4.01 has been entirely charged to Profit and Loss Account.

(e) Bratin will take over the Motor Car at Rs. 16,000 and a Bank Loan of Rs. 50,000 is to be arranged for the balance amount payable to him on his retirement.

(f) The capital of the new firm will be readjusted by bringing in or paying of cash so that the capital of Atin and Jatin be in the new profit-sharing ratio.

Prepare Revaluation Account, Capital Account of partners and the Balance Sheet of the new firm.

[CU BCom (Hons.) 2002]

Solution

In the books of firm
Revaluation Account

Dr. | | | | | *Cr.*

Particulars		*Amount*	*Particulars*	*Amount*
		Rs.		Rs.
To Machinery A/c		3,500	By Land and Building A/c	14,400
" Provision for D/Debts		300	" Furniture A/c (written-back)	2,550
" Motor Car A/c		2,000	" Prepaid Insurance A/c	600
" Partners' Capital A/c : Profit on Revaluation				
A	4,700			
B	4,700			
J	2,350	11,750		
		17,550		17,550

Capital Account

Dr. | | | | | | | *Cr.*

Particulars	Atin	Bratin	Jatin	*Particulars*	Atin	Bratin	Jatin
	Rs.	Rs.	Rs.		Rs.	Rs.	Rs.
To Bratin's Capital A/c	4,580	—	4,580	By Balance b/d	65,600	43,700	32,200
" Bank A/c (*bal. fig.*)	9,186	50,360		" General Reserve A/c	8,800	8,800	4,400
" Motor Car A/c		16,000		" Revaluation A/c —Profit	4,700	4,700	2,350
" Balance c/d	65,334	—	43,556	" Atin's Capital A/c	—	4,580	—
				" Jatin's Capital A/c	—	4,580	—
				" Bank A/c (*bal. fig.*)	—	—	9,186
	79,100	66,360	48,136		79,100	66,360	48,136

Balance Sheet *as at 1st Jan. 2002*

Liabilities	Rs.	Rs.	*Assets*		Rs.
Capital A/c :			Land and Building A/c (Rs. 72,000 + Rs. 14,400)		86,400
Atin	65,334		Machinery (Rs. 35,500 – Rs. 3,500)		32,000
Jatin	43,556		Furniture (Rs. 10,400 + Rs. 2,550)		12,950
		1,08,890	Stock		19,800
Creditors		18,000	Sundry Debtors	23,700	
Bank Loan		50,000	*Less* : Prov. for Bad Debts	1,800	21,900
			Cash at Bank (Rs. 3,600 + Rs. 50,000 – Rs. 50,360)		3,240
			Prepaid Insurance		600
		1,76,890			1,76,890

Workings :

1. Value of Furniture written-back Rs. 3,000 – (Rs. 3,000 × $\frac{10}{100}$ × $\frac{18}{12}$) = Rs. 3,000 – Rs. 450 = Rs. 2,550.

2. **B's share of Goodwill**

		Rs.	Rs.
Profit for	1998		12,100
	1999		8,480
	2000	10,920	
Add ; Purchase of Furniture		3,000	
		13,920	
Less: Dep. on Furniture for 6 months		150	
			13,770
			34,350

3. **Gaining Ratio** =

Atin = $\frac{3}{5} - \frac{2}{5} = \frac{1}{5}$

Jatin = $\frac{2}{5} - \frac{1}{5} = \frac{1}{5}$

So gaing Ratio is 1 : 1.

∴ B's share of Goodwill

= Rs. 22,900 × $\frac{2}{5}$ = Rs. 9,160 to be Compensated by Atin and Jatin in the gaining ratio of 1 : 1

∴ *Average Profit* = $\frac{\text{Rs. } 34,350}{3}$ = 11,450 So, Value of Goodwill = Rs. 11,450 × 2 years' Purchase = Rs. 22,900.

4. **Closing Capital of Atin and Jatin**

Combined adjusted Capital of Atin and Jatin =

Atin Rs. (65,600 + 8,800 + 4,700 – 4,580) =	74,520
Jatin Rs. (32,200 + 4,400 + 2,350 – 4,580) =	34,370
Combined Capital	1,08,890

Now, this Capital will be in proportion to Profit-sharing Ratio i.e., 3 : 2

So, Atin's Capital will be Rs. 1,08,890 × $\frac{3}{5}$ = Rs. 65,334

Jatins Capital will be Rs. 1,08,890 × $\frac{2}{5}$ = Rs. 43,556

Illustration 11

The Balance Sheet of X, Y and Z who are sharing profits in proportion to their capital, stood as follows on March 31, 2005:

Liabilities	Rs.	Rs.	*Assets*	Rs.	Rs.
Capital Accounts :			Land and Buildings		25,000
X	20,000		Plant and Machinery		8,500
Y	15,000		Stock		8,000
Z	10,000		Debtors	5,000	
		45,000	*Less: Provision*	100	
Creditors		6,900			4,900
			Cash at Bank		5,500
		51,900			51,900

Y retired on the above date and the following was agreed upon :

(a) That Stock be depreciated by 6%

(b) That the Provision for Doubtful Debts be brought up to 5% on Debtors.

(c) That the Land and Buildings be appreciated by 20%.

(d) That a provision of Rs. 770 be made in respect of outstanding legal charges.

(e) That the Goodwill of the entire firm be fixed at Rs. 10,800 and Y's share of it be adjusted into the accounts of X and Z who are going to share future profits in the ratio of 5 : 3.

(f) That the assets and liabilities (except Cash at Bank) were to appear in the Balance Sheet at their old figures.

(g) That the entire capital of the firm as newly constituted be fixed at Rs. 28,000 between X and Z in the proportion of 5 : 3 (actual cash to be brought in as paid off, as the case may be).

Show the Balance Sheet after Y's retirement.

[CU BCom (Hons.) 2006]

Solution

In the books of the firm
Balance Sheet *as at* **31st March 2005**

Liabilities		Rs.	*Assets*		Rs.
Capital Accounts :			Land and Buildings		25,000
X	17,500		Plant and Machinery		8,500
Z	10,500	28,000	Stock		8,000
Y's Loan A/c		19,800	Debtors	5,000	
Creditors		6,900	*Less* : Prov. for Bad Debts	100	4,900
			Cash at Bank (Rs. 5,500 + Rs. 2,800)		8,300
		54,700			54,700

Note ; Since assets and liabilities will appear in the Balance Sheet at their old figure, Memorandum Revaluation Account should be opened.

Workings :

1. **Gaining Ratio**

$$X = \frac{5}{8} - \frac{4}{9} = \frac{45-32}{72} = \frac{13}{72}$$

$$Y = \frac{3}{8} - \frac{2}{9} = \frac{27-16}{72} = \frac{11}{71}$$

Hence, gaining ratio = 13 : 11

$\therefore$ Y's share of goodwill = Rs. 10,800 $\times \frac{3}{9}$

= Rs. 3,600

The entry being :

X's Capital A/c Dr.	1,950	
Z's Capital A/c Dr.	1,650	
To Y's Capital A/c		3,600
(In gaining ratio)		

Dr. ***Memorandum Revaluation Account*** *Cr.*

		Rs.			Rs.
To Under valuation of Stock		480	By Overvaluation of Land & Building		5,000
" Prov. for Bad Debts (Rs. 250 – Rs. 100)		150			
" Prov. for Legal Exp.		770			
" Profit on Rev. :					
X	1,600				
Y	1,200				
Z	800	3,600			
		5,000			5,000
To *Reversal of Items*			By *Reversal of Items*		
" Over valuation of Land & Building		5,000	" Undervaluation of Stock		480
			" Prov. for Bad Debts		150
			" Prov. for Legal Charges		770
			" Capital A/c Profit to be written-back		
			X – $\frac{5}{8}$	2,250	
			Y – $\frac{3}{8}$	1,350	3,600
		5,000			5,000

Dr. **Capital Account** *Cr.*

Particulars	X	Y	Z	*Particulars*	X	Y	Z
	Rs.	Rs.	Rs.		Rs.	Rs.	Rs.
To Memo. Revat. A/c	2,250	—	1,350	By Balance b/d	20,000	15,000	10,000
" Y's Capital A/c	1,950	—	1,650	" Revaluation A/c			

Contd.

	X Rs.	Y Rs.	Z Rs.		X Rs.	Y Rs.	Z Rs.
" Y's Loan A/c	—	19,800	—	—Profit	1,600	1,200	800
" Balance c/d	17,500*	—	10,500	" X' Capital	—	1,950	—
				Y's Capital A/c	—	1,650	—
				" Bank A/c *(bal. fig.)*	100	—	2,700
	21,700	19,800	13,500		21,700	19,800	13,500

* Total Capital = Rs. 28,000 in 5 : 3 , i.e. X Rs. 17,500; Y Rs. 10,500

Illustration 12

X, Y, and Z were in partnership sharing profits and losses as $\frac{1}{2}, \frac{1}{4}$, and $\frac{1}{4}$, respectively. It was agreed that interest should be allowed @ 10% p.a. on partners' Capital Accounts and charged @ 8% p.a. on their drawings. No interest was to be allowed or charged on Current Accounts.

The following are the particulars of their Capital Accounts, Current Accounts and Drawings (as shown by the Draft Accounts) :

	Capital Accounts balance on 1.1.2012 Rs.	Current Accounts balance on 1.1.2012 Rs.	Drawings for the year to 31st December Rs.	Interest on Drawings Rs.
X	1,50,000 (Cr.)	20,000 (Cr.)	30,000	2,000
Y	80,000 (Cr.)	10,000 (Cr.)	20,000	760
Z	60,000 (Cr.)	10,000 (Dr.)	20,000	1,400

The draft accounts for the year to 31st December 2012 showed a net profit of Rs. 1,20,000 before taking into account interest on partners' Capital Account balances and drawings.

The audit of the draft accounts revealed the following errors :

(i) The rent of X's private house, amounting to Rs. 1,500 and paid on 31st December 2012, had been included in rent charged in Profit and Loss Account.

(ii) Repairs amounting to Rs. 20,000 had been treated as addition to machinery, depreciation on which had been charged @ 20%.

(iii) The premium, amounting to Rs. 6,000 on Y's Life Insurance Policy, are paid on 30th June 2012, had been included in insurance charges in the Profit and Loss Account.

Z retired from the partnership on 31st December 2012 and agreed to leave the amount due to him from firm as a loan repayable by agreed instalments. X and Y agreed to continue in partnership sharing profits and losses as $\frac{2}{3}$ and $\frac{1}{3}$.

In ascertaining the amount due to Z from the firm and for the purpose of the new partnership, it was agreed to make the following adjustments :

(i) Goodwill to be valued at Rs. 1,44,000 but no account for goodwill to be raised in the books.

(ii) The value of freehold premises to be increased by Rs. 12,000.

(iii) Reserve for Bad Debts Rs. 12,000.

You are required to prepare (a) The Profit and Loss Appropriation Account for the year ended 31st December 2012, making all the necessary adjustments for the errors revealed; and (b) Partners' Capital and Current Accounts (in columnar form) for the year ended 31st December 2012, incorporating the adjustments on Z's retirement.

[CA]

Solution

Adjusted Net Profit

			Rs.
	Net Profit		1,20,000
Less :	Repairs to Machinery		20,000
			1,00,000
Add :	Premium paid on Y's life policy	6,000	
	Depreciation overcharged @ 20%	4,000	
	Rent of X	1,500	
			11,500
			1,11,500

Dr. **Profit and Loss Appropriation Account** *for the year ended 31st December 2012* Cr.

Particulars		Amount Rs.	Particulars		Amount Rs.
To Interest on Capital :			By Profit and Loss A/c		
X	15,000		—Net Profit as calculated above		1,11,500
Y	8,000		" Interest on Drawings :		
Z	6,000	29,000	X	2,000	
" Capital A/c:			Y (760 + 240)	1,000	
Share of Profit :			Z	1,400	4,400
X	43,450				
Y	21,725				
Z	21,725	86,900			
		1,15,900			1,15,900

Dr. **Capital Account** Cr.

Particulars	X Rs.	Y Rs.	Z Rs.	Particulars	X Rs.	Y Rs.	Z Rs.
To Z's Capital A/c	24,000	12,000	—	By Balance b/d	1,50,000	80,000	60,000
" Z's Current A/c	—	—	6,675	" X's Capital A/c	—	—	24,000
" Z's Loan A/c	—	—	99,325	" Y's Capital A/c	—	—	12,000
" Balance c/d	1,46,000	78,000	—	" Freehold Premises	20,000	10,000	10,000
	1,70,000	90,000	1,06,000		1,70,000	90,000	1,06,000

Dr. **Current Account** Cr.

Particulars	X Rs.	Y Rs.	Z Rs.	Particulars	X Rs.	Y Rs.	Z Rs.
To Balance b/d	—	—	10,000	By Balance b/d	20,000	10,000	—
" Drawings A/c	30,000	20,000	20,000	" Int. on Capital A/c	15,000	8,000	6,000
" House Rent	1,500	—	—	" Share of Profit	43,450	21,725	21,725
" Drawings (LIC)	—	6,000	—	" Z's Capital A/c			
" R/B/Debts	6,000	3,000	3,000	—Transfer	—	—	6,675
" Interest on Drawings	2,000	1,000	1,400				
" Balance c/d	38,950	9,725	—				
	78,450	39,725	34,400		78,450	39,725	34,400

Illustration 13

The Balance Sheet of X, Y, and Z, who are sharing profits and losses in the ratio of 4 : 3 : 2, respectively, stood as follows on 31st Dec. 2012 :

	Rs.	Rs.		Rs.	Rs.
Sundry Creditors		4,140	Cash at Bank		3,300
Capital Accounts :			Sundry Debtors	3,045	
X	12,000		*Less :* Provision	105	
Y	9,000				2,940
Z	6,000		Stock		4,800
		27,000	Plant and Machinery		5,100
			Land and Building		15,000
		31,140			31,140

Y having given notice to retire from the firm, the following adjustments in the books of the firm were agreed upon :

(a) The Land and Building be appreciated by 10%; (b) The provision for bad debts is no longer necessary; (c) That the stock be appreciated by 20%; (d) That adjustments be made in the accounts to rectify a mistake previously made whereby Y was credited in excess by Rs. 810 while X and Z were debited in excess by Rs. 420 and Rs. 390, respectively; (e) That the goodwill of the firm be fixed at Rs. 5,400 and Y's share of the same be adjusted to that of X and Z who are going to share in future profits in the ratio of 2 : 1; (f) That the entire capital of the firm, as newly constituted, will be readjusted by bringing in or paying of cash so that the future capital of X and Z be in the ratio of 2 : 1.

Pass Journal entries and prepare the Balance Sheet of the new firm showing Y's balance as loan.

Solution

In the books of X, Y, and Z
Journal

Date	*Particulars*		*L.F.*	*Debit*	*Credit*
2012				Rs.	Rs.
Dec. 31	X's Capital A/c	Dr.		1,200	
	Z's Capital A/c	Dr.		600	
	To Y's Capital A/c				1,800
	(Y's share of goodwill $(5{,}400 \times \frac{3}{9})$ to be debited to X and Z's Capital is 2 : 1.)				
	Y's Capital A/c	Dr.		810	
	To X's Capital A/c				420
	" Z's Capital A/c				390
	(Adjustment made in capital accounts to rectify the previous mistakes.)				
	Land and Building A/c	Dr.		1,500	
	Provision for Bad Debts A/c	Dr.		105	
	Stock A/c	Dr.		960	
	To Revaluation A/c				2,565
	(Adjustment made and assets revalued on Y's retirement.)				
	Revaluation A/c	Dr.		2,565	
	To X's Capital A/c				1,140
	" Y's Capital A/c				855
	" Z's Capital A/c				570
	(Profit on revaluation transferred.)				
	Cash A/c	Dr.		120	
	To X's Capital A/c				120
	(Cash to be brought in by X.)				
	Z's Capital A/c	Dr.		120	
	To Cash A/c				120
	(Amount withdrawn by Z.)				
	Y's Capital A/c	Dr.		10,845	
	To Y's Loan A/c				10,845
	(Balance of Y's Capital transferred to Y's Loan A/c.)				

Balance Sheet *as at 31st Dec. 2012*

Liabilities	Rs.	*Assets*	Rs.
Sundry Creditors	4,140	Cash at Bank	3,300
Y's Loan A/c	10,845	Sundry Debtors	3,045
Capital Accounts :		Stock	5,760
X (12,000 – 1,200 + 420 + 1,140 + 120)	12,480	Plant and Machinery	5,100
Z (6,000 – 600 + 390 + 570 – 120)	6,240	Land and Building	16,500
	33,705		33,705

Notes :

The capital accounts of the partners before adjustment were Rs. 27,000 and after adjustment Rs. 29,565 (i.e., 27,000 + 2,565). Out of which, Rs. 10,845 is due to Y which is transferred to his loan account and balance Rs. 18,720 (i.e., 29,565 – 10,845) to be divided between X and Y in 2 : 1. Thus, X brings Rs. 120 and Z withdraw Rs. 120 for this purpose.

Illustration 14

Ajoy, Bikash, and Kamal were partners sharing profits and losses in the ratio of 3 : 2 : 1. Their Balance Sheet as on 31.3.1998 stood as :

Liabilities		Rs.	*Assets*		Rs.
Sundry Creditors		12,500	Cash at Bank		1,500
General Reserve		18,000	Debtors 15,000		
Capital Accounts :			*Less* : Reserved for Bad Debts	1,500	
Ajoy	40,000				13,500
Bikash	21,000		Stock		12,500
Kamal	20,000		Jt. Life Policy		8,000
		81,000	Office Equipments		14,000
			Furniture		12,000
			Buildings		50,000
		1,11,500			1,11,500

Bikash retired on 1.4.98 subject to the following conditions :

(i) A typewriter purchased on 1.10.97 for Rs. 2,000, debited to Office Expenses A/c, is to be brought into account charging depreciation at the rate of 10% p.a.

(ii) Building revalued at Rs. 75,000. Furniture is to be written-down by Rs. 2,000 and stock is reduced to Rs. 10,000.

(iii) Reserve for Bad Debts is to be calculated @ 5% on Debtors.

(iv) Goodwill of the firm is valued at Rs. 18,000. But no Goodwill A/c is to be raised.

(v) Life Policy is to be shown at surrender value. The surrender value is Rs. 7,500.

(vi) Amount due to Bikash is to be transferred to Loan A/c.

(vii) Ajoy and Kamal will share profits & losses in the ratio 2 : 1 and their capitals are to be adjusted in the Profit-sharing Ratio.

You are required to prepare : Revaluation A/c, Partners' Capital A/c and Balance Sheet immediately after retirement.

[CU BCom (Hons.)]

Solution

In the books of Ajoy, Bikash, and Kamal
Revaluation Account

Dr. *Cr.*

Particulars		*Amount*	*Particulars*	*Amount*
		Rs.		Rs.
To Furniture A/c		2,000	By Office Equipment A/c	1,900[1]
" Stock A/c		2,500	" Building A/c	25,000
" Joint Life Policy A/c		500	" Reserve for Bad Debts A/c (Rs. 1,500 – Rs. 750)	750
To Capital A/c : Profit on Revaluation :				
Ajay	11,325			
Bikash	7,550			
Kamal	3,775	22,650		
		27,650		27,650

Capital Account

Dr. *Cr.*

Particulars	Ajoy	Bikash	Kamal	*Particulars*	Ajoy	Bikash	Kamal
	Rs.	Rs.	Rs.		Rs.	Rs.	Rs.
To Bikash's Loan A/c	—	40,550	—	By Balance b/d	40,000	21,000	20,000
" Bikash's Capital	3,000	—	3,000	" Revaluation A/c —Profit	11,325	7,550	3,775
" Bank A/c *(bal. fig.)*	3,258	—	—	" General Reserve A/c	9,000	6,000	3,000
" Balance c/d	54,067	—	27,033	" Ajoy Capital A/c	—	3,000[2]	—
				" Kamal Capital A/c	—	3,000	—
				" Bank A/c *(bal. fig.)*	—	—	3,258
	60,325	40,550	30,033		60,325	40,550	30,033

Balance Sheet *as at 1st April 1998*

Liabilities		Rs.	*Assets*		Rs.
Capital Accounts :-			Building		75,000
Ajoy	54,067		Furniture		10,000
Kamal	27,033		Office Equipment		15,900
		81,100	Joint Life Policy		7,500
Bikash's Loan A/c		40,550	Stock		10,000
Sundry Creditors		12,500	Debtors	15,000	
			Less : Reserve for Bad Debts	750	14,250
			Cash at Bank (Rs. 1,500 + Rs. 3,258 – Rs. 3,258)		1,500
		1,34,150			1,34,150

Workings :

	Rs.
1. **Typewriter purchased on 1.10.1997**	2,000
Less : Depreciation @ 10% for 6 months (1.10.97 to 31.3.98) $\left(\text{Rs. } 2{,}000 \times \frac{10}{100} \times \frac{6}{12}\right)$ =	100
W. D. V.	1,900

The rectifying entry :

		Dr.	Cr.
Office Equipment (Typewriters) A/c	Dr.	1,900	
To Revaluation A/c (Office Expenses)			1,900

2. **Sharing Goodwill**

Bikash's share of Goodwill Rs. 6,000 (i.e., Rs. 18,000 × $\frac{2}{6}$) will be taken by Ajoy and Kamal in the following gaining ratio :

Old Ratio = Ajoy : Bikash : Kamal = 3 : 2 : 1.

New Ratio := Ajoy : Kamal = 2 : 1.

∴ Ajoy gains $= \frac{2}{3} - \frac{3}{6} = \frac{4-3}{6} = \frac{1}{6}$

Kamal gains $= \frac{1}{3} - \frac{1}{6} = \frac{2-1}{6} = \frac{1}{6}$

∴ Gaining ratio is 1 : 1

3. **Closing balance of Capital Account of Ajoy and Kamal**

Ajoy's Capital Balance = Rs. 40,000 + Rs. 11,325 + Rs. 9,000 – Rs. 3,000 =	57,325
Kamal's Capital Balance = Rs. 20,000 + Rs. 3,775 + Rs. 3,000 – Rs. 3,000 =	23,775
	81,100

This closing capital balance will be in proportion to profit-sharing ratio i.e., 2 : 1

So, Ajoy's capital balance will be Rs. 81,100 × $\frac{2}{3}$ = Rs. 54,067

Kamal's capital balance will be Rs. 81,100 × $\frac{1}{3}$ = Rs. 27,033.

Illustration 15

X, Y, and Z were partners sharing profits and losses as 4 : 3 : 1. On 1.4.1995 their capitals were Rs. 15,000, Rs. 15,000, and Rs. 10,000, respectively. The Partnership Deed contained :

1. Interest on Capital would be provided @ 10% p.a.
2. In case of retirement, the goodwill would be valued at 2 years' purchase of the average distributable profits of the preceding 5 years.
3. The profit of the retiring partner to the date of retirement would be estimated on the basis of the average distributable profit of the last 3 years.
4. The firm would effect a Joint Life Policy for Rs. 30,000 whose premium would be charged as a business expense.

X retired from the firm on 1.10.95. The surrender value of the policy as on that date was ascertained as Rs. 8,000. Drawings of the partners up to that date were X Rs. 3,000; Y Rs. 2,000, and Z Rs. 1,000. The annual net profits after charging interest on capital and joint life policy premium were :

1990-91 Rs. 8,000; 1991-92 Rs. 8,800; 1992-93 Rs. 7,200; 1993-94 Rs. 9,500; 1994-95 Rs. 10,000.

X's final claims regarding revenue accounts were met out of the assets of the business and the rest was paid out of cash brought in by Y and Z in such proportions as to set their capital balances equated to their shares of profits.

Show the Partners' Capital Accounts. **[CA]**

Solution

1. Value of Goodwill

Average Profit $= \frac{\text{Rs. } 8{,}000 + \text{Rs. } 8{,}800 + \text{Rs. } 7{,}200 + \text{Rs. } 9{,}500 + \text{Rs. } 10{,}000}{5}$

= Rs. 8,700

∴ Value of Goodwill = Average Profit × 3 years'

= Rs. 8,700 × 2

= Rs. 17,400

X's share of Goodwill = Rs. 17,400 × $\frac{4}{8}$ = Rs. 8,700.

2. Profit up to the date of retirement

Last 3 years' annual average profit $= \frac{\text{Rs. } 7{,}200 + \text{Rs. } 9{,}500 + \text{Rs. } 10{,}000}{3}$

= Rs. 8,900

(In between 1.4.95 and 1.10.95) = Rs. 8,900 × $\frac{6}{12}$ = Rs. 4,450

∴ X's share = Rs. 4,450 × $\frac{4}{8}$ = Rs. 2,225.

3. X's total claims on Retirement

	on Revenue Account Rs.	Rest Rs.	Total Rs.
Capital		15,000	15,000
Share of Goodwill Rs. 17,400 × $\frac{4}{8}$		8,700	8,700
Interest on Capital for 6 months	750	—	750
Share of Profit	2,225	—	2,225
Share of J. L. Policy (Rs. 8,000 × $\frac{4}{8}$)	4,000	—	4,000
	6,975	23,700	30,675
Less: Drawings	3,000	—	3,000
	3,975	23,700	27,675

4. X's claims on the following to be adjusted against Y and Z's capital as per profit-sharing ratio i.e. 3 : 1. Goodwill Rs. 8,700 + J. L. Policy Rs. 4,000 + Share of Profit Rs. 2,225 = Rs. 14,925. So Y's capital account to be debited by Rs. 11,194 (i.e. Rs. 14,925 × $\frac{3}{4}$) and Z's capital account to be debited by Rs. 3,731 (i.e. Rs. 14,925 × $\frac{1}{4}$).

5. Adjustment of Y and Z's Capital as per Profit-sharing Ratio.

	Rs.
(i) Y's Capital (after adjustment 4 above) Rs. 15,000 – Rs. 11,194 ±	3,806
Less : Drawings	2,000
	1,806

	Rs.
(ii) Z's Capital (after adjustment 4 above) Rs. 10,000 – Rs. 3,731 =	6,269
Less : Drawings	1,000
	5,269

(iii) Thus, amount payable to X

	Rs.
Rest	23,700
Add : From Y	1,806
From Z	5,269
	30,775

6. Closing Balance of Capital Account of Y and Z

Y = Rs. 30,775 × $\frac{3}{4}$ = Rs. 23,081 and Z = Rs. 30,775 × $\frac{1}{4}$ = Rs. 7,694.

Dr. **Capital Account** Cr.

	Particulars	A	B	C		Particulars	A	B	C
		Rs.	Rs.	Rs.			Rs.	Rs.	Rs.
To	Capital A/c	—	11,194	3,731	By	Balance b/d	15,000	15,000	10,000
"	Drawings A/c	3,000	2,000	1,000	"	Interest on Capital A/c	750	—	—
"	Bank A/c	27,675	—	—					

Contd.

	Rs.	Rs.	Rs.		Rs.	Rs.	Rs.
To Balance c/d	—	23,081	7,694	By Y's Capital A/c	11,194	—	—
				" Z's Capital A/c	3,731	—	—
				" Bank A/c (bal. fig.)	—	21,275	2,425
	30,675	36,275	12,425		30,675	36,275	12,425

Illustration 16

A, B, and C were in partnership sharing profits and losses in the ratio 3 : 2 : 1. Their Balance Sheet as on 31.03.2007 was :

Liabilities	Rs.	*Assets*	Rs.
Capital A	60,000	Machinery	80,000
Capital B	50,000	Furniture	15,000
Capital C	40,000	Motor Car	30,000
Sundry Creditors	72,000	Stock	50,000
Bank Loan	30,000	Sundry Debtors	60,000
Other Liabilities	20,000	Cash at Bank	37,000
	2,72,000		2,72,000

A retired on 1.4.2007 and the partnership deed provided, *inter alia,* that, in the event of admission, retirement, or death of a partner, the assets and liabilities are to be revalued and that goodwill of the firm is to be computed on the basis of 2 years' purchase of the correct profit of the last 4 years.

It is discovered that the accounts required adjustments owing to certain mistakes in earlier years. On 1.10.2004, repairs to machinery for Rs. 6,000 had been wrongly debited to Machinery Accounts; and on 1.4.2005, a piece of furniture, whose book value was Rs. 2,000, was disposed off for Rs. 800 but the proceeds were wrongly credited to Sales Account. The partners had been charging depreciation on all fixed assets at 10% p.a. on the reducing balance system on a time basis.

Profits for the last four years without adjusting the above mentioned mistakes were:

2003-04 Rs. 20,000; 2004-05 Rs. 24,000; 2005-06 Rs. 32,000; 2006-07 Rs. 36,000.

Revaluation on the date of retirement was : Machinery Rs. 90,000; Furniture Rs. 10,000; Motor Car Rs. 22,000.

B and C decided to share future profits, after A's retirement, in the ratio of 3 : 2. It was further agreed that the retiring partner shall be credited with his due proportion of goodwill, without raising a Goodwill Account in the books.

A is to be paid 50% of the amount due to him on retirement immediately and the balance is to be transferred to his Loan Account carrying interest at 6% p.a. B and C are to bring necessary cash (in their new ratio) subject to the condition that a cash balance of Rs. 20,000 is to be maintained as working capital.

Show the Capital Accounts of the partners and the Balance Sheet of the firm after all the above-mentioned transactions have been carried out. Ignore fractions.

(All working should form part of your answer.)

[CA]

Solution

In the books of A, B, and C

Dr. **Revaluation Account** *Cr.*

Particulars	*Amount*	*Particulars*		*Amount*
	Rs.			Rs.
To Motor Car A/c	8,000	By Machinery A/c		10,000
" Furniture A/c	5,000	" Capital A/c		
		Loss on Revaluation :		
		A	1,500	
		B	1,000	
		C	500	
				3,000
	13,000			13,000

Dr. **Capital Account** Cr.

	Particulars	A	B	C		Particulars	A	B	C
		Rs.	Rs.	Rs.			Rs.	Rs.	Rs.
To	A's Capital A/c	—	14,101	12,339	By	Balance b/d	60,000	50,000	40,000
"	Revaluation A/c				"	B's Capital A/c	14,101[1]	—	—
	—Loss	1,500	1,000	500	"	C's Capital A/c	12,339	—	—
"	Bank A/c	42,470	—	—	"	Bank A/c	—	15,282	10,188
"	A's Loan A/c	42,470	—	—					
"	Balance c/d	—	50,181	37,349					
		86,440	65,282	50,188			86,440	65,282	50,188

Balance Sheet *as at 1st April 2007*

Liabilities		Rs.	Assets	Rs.
Capital A/c :				
B	50,181		Machinery	90,000
C	37,349	87,530	Furniture	10,000
Bank Loan A/c		30,000	Motor Car	22,000
A's Loan A/c		42,470	Stock	50,000
Sundry Creditors		72,000	Sundry Debtors	60,000
Other Liabilities		20,000	Cash at Bank	20,000
		2,52,000		2,52,000

Workings :

1. Computation of Goodwill and its adjustment

Calculation showing the adjusted Net Profit :

	2003-04	2004-05	2005-06	2006-07
	Rs.	Rs.	Rs.	Rs.
Profit (before adjustment)	20,000	24,000	32,000	36,000
Less : Repairs wrongly capitalised	—	− 6,000	—	—
Add : Depreciation on above	—	+ 300	+ 570	+ 513
Less : Sales wrongly credited	—	—	− 800	—
Less : Net loss on sale of Furniture unrecorded (2,000 − 800)	—	—	− 1,200	—
Add : Depreciation on Furniture wrongly charged	—	—	+ 200	+ 180
	20,000	18,300	30,770	36,693

$\therefore$ Average Profit $= \dfrac{\text{Rs. } 20{,}000 + \text{Rs. } 18{,}300 + \text{Rs. } 30{,}770 + \text{Rs. } 36{,}693}{4} = \text{Rs. } \dfrac{1{,}05{,}763}{4} = \text{Rs. } 26{,}440$

Value of Goodwill = Rs. 26,440 × 2 = Rs. 52,880

Entries for Goodwill

			Dr.	Cr.	
(i)	Goodwill A/c	Dr.	52,880		
	To A's Capital A/c			26,440	in 3 : 2 : 1
	" B's Capital A/c			17,627	
	" C's Capital A/c			8,813	
(ii)	B's Capital A/c	Dr.	31,728		in 3 : 2
	C's Capital A/c	Dr.	21,152		
	To Goodwill A/c			52,880	

$\therefore$ A gets Rs. 26,440. Out of which B will pay Rs. 14,101 (i.e., 31,728 − Rs. 17,627) and C will pay Rs. 12,339 (i.e., Rs. 21,152 − Rs. 8,813).

2. **Cash to be brought in by B and C**

Dr. **Bank A/c** Cr.

			Rs.			Rs.
To	Balance b/d		37,000	By	A's Capital A/c	42,470
"	B's Capital A/c $\left(\frac{3}{5}\right)$	15,282		"	Balance c/d (To be maintained)	20,000
"	C's Capital A/c $\left(\frac{2}{5}\right)$	10,188	25,470			
	(bal. fig.)					
			62,470			62,470

Illustration 17

Compass, Cone, and Circle are in partnership sharing profits and losses in the ratio of 3 : 2 : 1. The Balance Sheet of the firm as on 31st Dec. 2011 was :

Liabilities		Rs.	*Assets*		Rs.
Capital Accounts :			Machinery (at Cost)	50,000	
Compass	40,000		*Less* : Provision for Depreciation	8,000	
Cone	60,000				42,000
Circle	20,000		Furniture		1,000
		1,20,000	Sundry Debtors	80,000	
Reserve		30,000	*Less* : Prov. for Doubtful Debts	3,000	77,000
Sundry Creditors		60,000	Stocks		50,000
			Cash at Bank		40,000
		2,10,000			2,10,000

On 31st March, Cone retired and Compass and Circle continued in partnership, sharing profits and losses in the ratio of 3 : 2. It was agreed that adjustments were to be made in the Balance Sheet as on 31st March 2012, in respect of the following :

(a) The Machinery was to be revalued at Rs. 45,000; (b) The stock was to be reduced by 2%; (c) The Furniture was to be reduced to Rs. 600; (d) The provision for doubtful debts would be Rs. 4,000; (e) A provision of Rs. 300 was to be made for outstanding expenses.

The partnership agreement provided that, on the retirement of a partner, goodwill was to be valued at Rs. 24,000 and Cone's share of the same was to be adjusted into the accounts of Compass and Circle. The profit up to the date of retirement was estimated at Rs. 18,000.

Cone was to be paid off in full, Compass and Circle were to bring such an amount in cash so as to make their capital in proportion to the new profit-sharing ratio, subject to the condition that a cash balance of Rs. 20,000 was to be maintained as working capital.

Pass the necessary Journal entries to give effect to the above arrangements and prepare the Partners' Capital Accounts on 31st March 2012.

Solution

In the books of Compass, Cone, and Circle
Journal

Date	Particulars		L.F.	Dr. Amount Rs.	Cr. Amount Rs.
2012 March 31	Reserve A/c	Dr.		30,000	
	To Compass's Capital A/c				15,000
	" Cone's Capital A/c				10,000
	" Circle's Capital A/c				5,000
	(Reserve transferred to the capital accounts of the partners in 3 : 2 : 1)				
	Machinery A/c	Dr.		3,000	
	To Revaluation A/c				3,000
	(Value of the machinery increased on Cone's retirement)				
	Revaluation A/c	Dr.		2,700	
	To Stock A/c				1,000
	" Furniture A/c				400
	" Provision for Bad Debts A/c				1,000
	" Outstanding Expenses A/c				300
	(Value of the assets reduced Cn cone's retirement)				
	Revaluation A/c	Dr.		300	
	To Compass's Capital A/c				150
	" Cone's Capital A/c				100
	" Circle's Capital A/c				50
	(Profit on revaluation transferred to the capital accounts of the partners)				
	Compass's Capital A/c	Dr.		2,400	
	Circle's Capital A/c	Dr.		5,600	
	To Cone's Capital A/c				8,000[1]
	(Cone's share of goodwill to be adjusted against remaining partners' capital accounts in the gaining ratio of 3 : 7)				

Contd.

Particulars		Rs.	Rs.
Profit and Loss (Suspense) A/c	Dr.	18,000	
To Compass's Capital A/c			9,000
" Cone's Capital A/c			6,000
" Circle's Capital A/c			3,000
(Estimated profit transferred to the capital accounts of the partners.)			
Cone's Capital A/c	Dr.	84,100	
To Bank A/c			84,100
(Payment is made to Cone on his retirement.)			
Bank A/c	Dr.	46,100[2]	
To Compass's Capital A/c			16,430
" Circle's Capital A/c			29,670
(Cash to be brought in by Compass and Circle as per agreement.)			

Dr. **Capital Account** Cr.

Particulars	Compass Rs.	Cone Rs.	Circle Rs.	Particulars	Compass Rs.	Cone Rs.	Circle Rs.
To Cone's Capital	2,400		5,600	By Balance b/d	40,000	60,000	20,000
" Bank (*bal. fig.*)	—	84,100	—	" Reserve	15,000	10,000	5,000
" Balance c/d	78,180	—	52,120[3]	" Revaluation —Profit	150	100	50
				" Share of Profit	9,000	6,000	3,000
				" Compass's Capital	—	2,400	—
				" Circle's Capital	—	5,600	—
				" Bank (*bal. fig.*)	16,430	—	29,670
	80,580	84,100	57,720		80,580	84,100	57,720
				" Balance b/d	78,180	—	52,120

Working Notes :

1. **Total Value of Goodwill Rs. 24,000.**

∴ Cone's share of Goodwill = $24,000 \times \frac{2}{6}$ = 8,000 to be adjusted against Compass's and Circle's capital in 3 : 7.

Computation of ratio :

Compass $= \frac{3}{5} - \frac{3}{6} = \frac{3}{30}$ (gain) Circle $= \frac{2}{5} - \frac{1}{6} = \frac{7}{30}$ (gain)

2. **Bank A/c**

Dr. Cr.

	Rs.		Rs.
To Balance b/d	40,000	By Cone's Capital	84,100
" Profit—increase in Cash	18,000	" Balance c/d (to be maintained)	20,000
" Compass and Circle's Capital (*bal. fig.*)	46,100		
	1,04,100		1,04,100

3. **Total adjusted capitals of Compass and Cone**

	Rs.
Compass's Capital :	
(40,000 + 15,000 + 150 + 9,000 − 2,400)	61,750
Circle's Capital :	
(20,000 + 5,000 + 50 + 3,000 − 5,600)	22,450
Plus : Total Cash to be brought in	46,100
	1,30,300

Combined adjusted capitals

	Rs.
∴ Compass's Capital = $1,30,300 \times \frac{3}{5}$	= 78,180
Circle's Capital = $1,30,300 \times \frac{2}{5}$	= 52,120

Illustration 18

Apte, Gupte, and Sathe are partners in a firm profit sharing ratio as 4 : 3 : 3. Their Balance Sheet as at 31.12.2013 was :

Liabilities		Rs.	Assets		Rs.
Sundry Creditors		60,000	Cash in hand		32,000
Reserve		10,000	Debtors	70,000	
Capital Accounts :			*Less* : Provision for Bad Debts	2,000	
Apte	40,000				68,000
Gupte	30,000		Stock		50,000
Sathe	60,000		Furniture		20,000
		1,30,000	Machinery		30,000
		2,00,000			2,00,000

Gupte retires on 30.9.2014, and Apte and Sathe carry on the business in their old ratio. On retirement, the following provisions apply :

(a) Goodwill is to be valued at two years' purchase of average profit for last three completed years and the period up to the date of retirement but no goodwill account is to be raised.

(b) Value of Stock is to be increased by Rs. 7,000 and Furniture is to be reduced to Rs. 7,000. Provision for Bad Debts is not needed.

(c) Retiring partner's share is to be purchased by the existing partners in their profit-sharing ratio, payments to be made privately.

Profit for the last three years are as follows :

Rs.

Year ending 31.12.2011 Rs. 36,000; Year ending 31.12.2012 Rs. 21,000; Year ending 31.12.2013 Rs. 28,000.

Profit up to the date of retirement is estimated at Rs. 20,000.

Show the Journal entries to give effect to the above arrangements and prepare the Balance Sheet of the new firm following the retirement of Gupte.

Solution

Gupte's share of Goodwill to be calculated as :

Average Profit :

Year ending 31.12.11	36,000
" " 31.12.12	21,000
" " 31.12.13	28,000
And, Profit up to the date of retirement (30.9.14)	20,000
	1,05,000

$\therefore$ For $3\frac{3}{4}$ years

Value of Goodwull = Rs. 1,05,000 $\times \frac{4}{15} \times 2$

= Rs. 56,000.

And, Gupte's share of Goodwill Rs. 56,000 $\times \frac{3}{10}$

= Rs. 16,800.

In the books of Gupte and Sathe

Journal

Date	Particulars		L.F.	Dr. Amount Rs.	Cr. Amount Rs.
	Apte's Capital A/c	Dr.		9,600	
	Sathe's Capital A/c	Dr.		7,200	
	To Gupte's Capital A/c				16,800
	(Adjustment made for goodwill on Gupte's retirement against Apte and Sathe's accounts in 4 : 3.)				
	Reserve A/c	Dr.		10,000	
	To Apte's Capital A/c				4,000
	" Gupte's Capital A/c				3,000
	" Sathe's Capital A/c				3,000
	(Reserve credited to partners' capital accounts on Gupte's retirement.)				

Contd.

Particulars		Rs.	Rs.
Stock A/c	Dr.	7,000	
Provision for Bad Debts A/c	Dr.	2,000	
To Revaluation A/c			9,000
(Value of stock increased and provision for Bad Debts to be written-back on Gupte's retirement.)			
Revaluation A/c	Dr.	13,000	
To Furniture A/c			13,000
(Value of Furniture reduced on Gupte's retirement.)			
Apte's Capital A/c	Dr.	1,600	
Gupte's Capital A/c	Dr.	1,200	
Sathe's Capital A/c	Dr.	1,200	
To Revaluation A/c			4,000
(Loss on revaluation to be transferred to partners' capital accounts in 4 : 3 : 3.)			
Profit and Loss Suspense A/c	Dr.	6,000	
To Gupte's Capital A/c			6,000
(Gupte's share of profit up to the date of retirement transferred to his capital accounts.)			
Gupte's Capital A/c	Dr.	54,600	
To Apte's Capital A/c			31,200
" Sathe's Capital A/c			23,400
(Gupte's share acquired by Apte and Sathe in the profi-sharing ratio, payments to be made privately.)			

Capital Accounts

Dr. Cr.

Particulars	Apte	Gupte	Sathe	Particulars	Apte	Gupte	Sathe
	Rs.	Rs.	Rs.		Rs.	Rs.	Rs.
To Gupte's Capital	9,600	—	7,200	By Balance b/d	40,000	30,000	60,000
" Revaluation	1,600	1,200	1,200	" Apte's Capital	—	9,600	—
" Apte's Capital	—	31,200	—	" Sathe's Capital	—	7,200	—
" Sathe's Capital	—	23,400	—	" Reserve	4,000	3,000	3,000
" Balance c/d	64,000	—	78,000	" P & L Suspenses	—	6,000	—
				" Gupte's Capital	31,200	—	23,400
	75,200	55,800	86,400		75,200	55,800	86,400
				By Balance b/d	64,000	—	87,000

Balance Sheet *as at 30th Sept. 2014*

Liabilities		Rs.	Assets	Rs.
Capital Accounts :			Machinery	30,000
Apte	64,000		Furniture	7,000
Sathe	78,000		Stock	57,000
		1,42,000	Debtors	70,000
Creditors		60,000	Cash in hand	32,000
			Profit and Loss Suspense A/c	6,000
		2,02,000		2,02,000

Note :

Gupte's share of profit up to the date of his retirement has been credited to him against P & L Suspense Account which will ultimately be transferred to P & L Appropriation Account at the end of the year. But if the profit-sharing ratio between the existing partners changes, the entire amount of estimated profit should be credited to all partners' capital accounts.

Illustration 19

The following is the Balance Sheet of A, B, and C who were partners as on 31.3.2013 :

Balance Sheet *as at 31.3.2013*

Liabilities	Rs.	Assets	Rs.
A's Capital	33,600	Plant and Machinery	49,000
B's Capital	25,200	Furniture and Fittings	4,800
C's Capital	12,000	Stock-in-trade	22,800
Sundry Creditors	12,000	Sundry Debtors	21,600
15% Mortgage Loan	16,600	Cash in Band	1,000
		Cash at bank	200
	99,400		99,400

They share profits and losses in the ratio of 2 : 2 : 1. On 1.4.2013 C retired from the firm and claimed his share of secret reserve/profit arising out of the following :

(a) During the year ended 31.3.2013 purchase of machinery at a cost of Rs. 10,000 was charged to Purchase Account, the erection charges of Rs. 600 being charged to Machinery Repairs Account. (Depreciation is to be charged at 10% p.a.).

(b) Rs. 600 received from Mr. X on 30.3.2013 towards rent of the property sub-let was credited to his personal account instead of the Rent Account so as to reduce his debit balance from Rs. 1,000 to Rs. 400 debit on 31.3.2013.

(c) Interest on mortgage loan was paid in advance up to 31.5.2013, and the whole amount was charged to Interest Account during the year ended 31.3.2013.

After rectifying the above errors, it was mutually decided :

(i) The goodwill of the firm be valued at five times the average profits of the last three years. Such profits should be correct profits and not the book profits. The book profits for the last three financial years were : 2010-11—Rs. 18,380; 2011-12—Rs. 32,000; 2012-13—Rs. 7,471.

(ii) Plant and Machinery to be depreciated by 10% and Provision for Bad and Doubtful Debts be made at 5% on Sundry Debtors.

(iii) The goodwill should not appear in the books.

(iv) There is a liability for Rs. 501 for bills discounted. This has to be accounted for.

(v) C should be paid half of his dues in cash which shall be brought in by A and B in their profit-sharing proportion and the other half shall be left in the business as C's loan fetching an interest of 18% p.a.

Prepare Profit and Loss Adjustment Account, Revaluation Account, Capital Accounts of the partners and the Balance Sheet of A and B after C's retirement.

Solution **[CA]**

In the books of A, B, and C

Profit and Loss Adjustment Account

Dr. *Cr.*

	Particulars		*Amount*		*Particulars*	*Amount*
			Rs.			Rs.
To	Depreciation on P & M (Rs. 10,600 × 10%)		1,060	By	Plant and Machinery A/c (10,000 + 600)	10,600
"	Capital A/c —adjusted profit distributed			"	X's A/c (Rent received)	600
	A	4,222		"	Interest on Loan on Mortgage (Rs. 16,600 × $\frac{15}{100}$ × $\frac{2}{12}$)	415
	B	4,222				
	C	2,111				
			10,555			
			11,615			11,615

Revaluation Account

Dr. *Cr.*

	Particulars	*Amount*		*Particulars*		*Amount*
		Rs.				Rs.
To	Depreciation on P & M @ 10% (on 49,000 + 10,600 – 1,060) = 58,540	5,854	By	Capital A/c —Loss on Revaluation transferred		
"	Provision for Bad Debts	1,110		A	2,986	
"	Prov. for Bills Discounted	501		B	2,986	
				C	1,493	
						7,465
		7,465				7,465

Capital Accounts

Dr. *Cr.*

	Particulars	A	B	C		*Particulars*	A	B	C
		Rs.	Rs.	Rs.			Rs.	Rs.	Rs.
To	C's Capital A/c	11,401	11,401	—	By	Balance b/d	33,600	25,200	12,000
"	Revaluation A/c —Loss	2,986	2,986	1,493	"	A's Capital A/c	—	—	11,401*
"	Bank ($\frac{1}{2}$) A/c	—	—	17,710	"	B's Capital A/c	—	—	11,401
"	C's Loan A/c	—	—	17,710	"	Profit and Loss Adjustment A/c	4,222	4,222	2,111
"	Balance c/d	32,290	23,890		"	Bank A/c	8,855	8,855	—
		46,677	38,277	36,913			46,677	38,277	36,913

Balance Sheet *as at 31st April 2013*

Liabilities		Rs.	*Assets*		Rs.
Capital A/c			Plant and Machinery (58,540 – 5,854)		52,686
A	32,290		Furniture and Fittings		4,800
B	23,890		Stock-in-trade		22,800
		56,180	Sundry Debtors	22,200	
15% Loan on Mortgage		16,600	(Including Rs. 600 for Rent from X)		
C's Loan A/c		17,710	*Less :* Provision for Bad Debts	1,110	
Outstanding Liabilities for bills discounted		501			21,090
Sundry Creditors		12,000	Prepaid Interest on Mortgage		415
			Cash in hand		1,000
			Cash at Bank		200
			(200 + 8,855 + 8,855 – 17,710)		
		1,02,991			1,02,991

* C's share of Goodwill is calculated as:

$$\text{Average Profit} = \frac{(\text{Rs. } 18{,}380 + \text{Rs. } 32{,}000 + \text{Rs. } 18{,}026)}{3} = \text{Rs. } 22{,}802.$$

Value of Goodwill Rs. 1,14,010 (i.e., Rs. 22,802 × 5).

C's share = Rs. 1,14,010 × $\frac{1}{5}$ = Rs. 22,802 which must be compensated by A and B equally, i.e., Rs. 11,401 each.

Illustration 20

R, K, and C have carried on business as drapers for 20 years. On 30th June 2011 their Balance Sheet was:

Liabilities		Rs.	*Assets*	Rs.
Bank Overdraft		20,000	Plant and Machinery	32,000
Creditors for Supplies		30,000	Premises	50,000
Creditors for Expenses		18,000	Sundry Debtors	48,000
Capital Accounts (fixed)			Stock-in-trade	40,000
R	30,000		Cash and Bank Balances	8,000
K	20,000			
C	20,000	70,000		
Current Accounts				
R	16,000			
C	24,000			
		40,000		
		1,78,000		1,78,000

The profits and losses were shared in the ratio of fixed capitals on 30th June 2011. The partners agreed that due to old age R would retire from the firm when its goodwill will be valued and proportionate share credited to R. It was also decided that premises appearing in the books at cost would be valued at their market value of Rs. 80,000 and allotted to R in satisfaction of his dues. Any excess or deficit would be settled in cash. It was also agreed that stock-in-trade and debtors would be taken at 90% of the book value and an unrecorded liability of bonus of Rs. 10,000 to staff brought into books. Goodwill of the firm was to be taken at Rs. 70,000.

After R's retirement, the business was carried on by K and C sharing profits and losses equally till 30th Sept. 2011. The firm had made a net profit of Rs. 30,000 after crediting each partner's capital account with Rs. 500 p.m. as salary. No drawings were made by the partners in the quarter.

K and C now find that they cannot continue the business and decide to sell it to a private limited company as and from Oct. 2011. The company is to take over the entire business for a consideration of Rs. 90,000 which the vendors agree to take 40% in 14% Secured Debentures and the balance in cash to enable the company to pay the vendors and also leave it with a working capital of Rs. 20,000; the company made issue of equity shares of Rs. 10 each at par.

Show the Balance Sheet of the company after the takeover of the business of K and C.

[CA]

Solution

R's share of goodwill will be Rs. 30,000 (i.e., Rs. 70,000 × $\frac{3}{7}$) which is to be compensated by K and C equally or Rs. 15,000 each.

Dr. **Revaluation Account** *Cr.*

Particulars		*Amount*	*Particulars*	*Amount*
		Rs.		Rs.
To Stock @ 10%		4,000	By Premises	30,000
" Debtors @ 10%		4,800		
" Bonus to Staff		10,000		
" Capital A/c				
—Profit in Revaluation				
R	4,800			
K	3,200			
C	3,200			
		11,200		
		30,000		30,000

Dr. **Capital Accounts** *Cr.*

Particulars	R	K	C	*Particulars*	R	K	C
	Rs.	Rs.	Rs.		Rs.	Rs.	Rs.
To R's Capital A/c	—	15,000	15,000	By Balance b/d	30,000	20,000	20,000
" Premises	80,000	—	—	" Current A/c	16,000	—	24,000
" Cash	800	—	—	" K's Capital A/c	15,000	—	—
" Balance c/d	—	8,200	32,200	" C's Capital A/c	15,000	—	—
				" Revaluation A/c			
				—Profit	4,800	3,200	3,200
	80,800	23,200	47,200		80,800	23,200	47,200

In the books of the Company
Balance Sheet *(after R's retirement)*

Liabilities	Rs.	*Assets*	Rs.
Capital—		Plant and Machinery	32,000
K	8,200	Debtors	43,200
C	32,200	Stock-in-trade	36,000
Bank Overdraft	20,000	Cash	7,200
Creditors for Goods	30,000		
Creditors for Expenses	28,000		
	1,18,400		1,18,400

Dr. **Profit and Loss Appropriation Account** *for the period Sept. 30, 2011* *Cr.*

		Rs.		Rs.
To Salary			By Net Profit	30,000
K	1,500		Partners' Salary—	
C	1,500		—written-back	
		3,000	K 500 × 3 = 1,500	
" Share of Profit			C 500 × 3 = 1,500	3,000
K	15,000			
C	15,000			
		30,000		
		33,000		33,000

Balance Sheet *as at Sept. 30, 2011*

Liabilities	Rs.	*Assets*	Rs.
Capital :		Plant and Machinery	32,000
K (8,200 + 15,000)	23,200	Debtors	43,200
C (32,200 + 15,000)	47,200	Stock-in-trade	36,000
Bank Overdraft	20,000	Cash	7,200
Creditors for Goods	30,000	Increase in Assets (i.e., profit)	30,000
Creditors for Expenses	28,000		
	1,48,400		1,48,400

Notes :

Calculation of the value of goodwill paid by the company :

(Total Fixed Assets + Total Current Assets
– Total Current Liabilities)
= Rs. 1,48,400 – Rs. 78,000 + Rs. 3,000 = Rs. 73,400.
∴ Purchase Consideration – Total Net Assets
= Goodwill = Rs. 90,000 – Rs. 73,400 = Rs. 16,600.

Payment of Purchase Consideration :

by Cash Rs. 90,000 × 60% = Rs. 54,000
by Debenture (balance) = Rs. 36,000.
Total cash required = Rs. 54,000 + Rs. 20,000
(Working Capital) = Rs. 74,000.
∴ Equity shares to be issued : 7,400 @ Rs. 10.

Balance Sheet *as at Oct. 1, 2011*

Liabilities	Rs.	*Assets*	Rs.
Authorised Capital		*Fixed Assets*	
Issued and Paid-up :		Goodwill	16,600
7,400 Equity Shares of Rs. 10 each		Plant and Machinery	32,000
fully paid (of these, 5,400 paid for		*Investments*	—
consideration other than cash)	74,000	*Net Current Assets :*	
Reserve & Surplus	—	Cash	20,000
Secured Loan	—	Others	41,400
Unsecured Loan		*Misc. Expenditure*	—
14% Debenture	36,000		
Current Liabilities & Provisions			
	1,10,000		1,10,000

Illustration 21

A, B, and C are partners sharing profits and losses in the ratio of 3 : 3 : 4. The Balance Sheet as on 31.12.2012 is :

Liabilities	*Rs.*	*Assets*	*Rs.*
Sundry Creditors	12,000	Cash at Bank	3,000
Bills Payable	18,000	Bills Receivable	11,000
6% Mortgage Loan	17,000	Stock	25,000
Capital Accounts		Sundry Debtors	20,000
(A Rs. 50,000; B Rs. 45,000; C 65,000)	1,60,000	Furniture	5,000
General Reserve	10,000	Plant and Machinery	40,000
		Land and Building	1,13,000
	2,17,000		2,17,000

The firm earned profits as follows for the past five years : 2008 —Rs. 14,000; 2009 —Rs. 16,500; 2010 — Rs. 15,000; 2011 — Rs. 15,000 and 2012— Rs. 15,800.

On December 31, 2012, C retired from partnership and, in order to ascertain the amount due to C, the accounts of 2012 were verified and the following mistakes were detected :

(i) A bill receivable for Rs. 1,000 which was dishonoured and became irrecoverable was not taken into consideration while preparing the final accounts.

(ii) An amount of Rs. 200 paid for the rent of the house occupied by C was wrongly debited to the Rent Account of the firm.

(iii) Goods worth Rs. 1,500 given by B to the firm were not taken into account.

(iv) An outstanding bill for Rs. 500 towards electricity was not paid and the same was not adjusted while preparing the final accounts.

(v) Purchase of Machinery of July 1, 2012 at a cost of Rs. 9,500 was wrongly treated as the Purchase Account and the expenses of Rs. 500 incurred towards erection of the Machinery were charged to the Machinery Repairs Account. Depreciation on the Machinery Account was charged at 10% p.a.

The partners agreed to rectify the mistakes noted above and the following adjustments were made to settle the accounts of C :

(i) The provision was made at 5% on Sundry Debtors; (ii) Stock was revalued at Rs. 21,925; (iii) Plant and Machinery were depreciated by 15%; (iv) Land and building were appreciated by 20%; (v) Sundry creditors for Rs. 2,900 will not rank; (vi) Goodwill of the firm should be ascertained at three times the Average Profit of the last five years. The Goodwill Account should not appear in the books. Goodwill of C should be shared by A and B; (vii) The Capital of C should be purchased by A and B in the ratio of 3 : 2; (viii) Since C was in urgent need of Rs. 50,000, the partners are required to make payment to him in cash in their new profit-loss sharing ratio and the balance of C's capital will be treated as loan; and (ix) The partners are also required to adjust their capitals in cash in proportion to their new profit-loss sharing ratio.

You are required to prepare the Profit and Loss Adjustment Account, Revaluation Account, Capital Accounts of the partners, and also the Balance Sheet after the retirement of C. **[CA]**

Solution

In the books of A, B, and C

Profit and Loss Adjustment Account

Dr. Particulars		Amount	Particulars	Cr. Amount
		Rs.		Rs.
To Bills Receivable A/c		1,000	By C's Capital A/c—Rent	200
" B's Capital A/c—Goods given		1,500	" Plant and Machinery A/c (Rs. 9,500 + Rs. 500) .	10,000
" Outstanding Electricity A/c		500		
" Plant and Machinery A/c —Depreciation		500		
" Capital A/c :				
A	2,010			
B	2,010			
C	2,680	6,700		
		10,200		10,200

Revaluation Account

Dr. Particulars		Amount	Particulars	Cr. Amount
		Rs.		Rs.
To Provision for Sundry Debtors A/c		1,000	By Land and Building A/c	22,600
" Stock A/c		3,075	" Sundry Creditors A/c	2,900
" Plant and Machinery A/c		7,425[4]		
" Capital A/c				
A	4,200			
B	4,200			
C	5,600	14,000		
		25,500		25,500

Capital Account

Dr. Particulars	A	B	C	Particulars	A	B	Cr. C
	Rs.	Rs.	Rs.		Rs.	Rs.	Rs.
To Profit & Loss Adj. A/c	—	—	200	By Balance b/d	50,000	45,000	65,000
" C's Capital A/c	11,952	7,968	—	" Profit & Loss Adj. —Profit A/c	2,010	2,010	2,680
" Bank A/c	—	—	50,000	" Revaluation A/c — Profit	4,200	4,200	5,600
" C's Loan A/c	—	—	47,000	" General Reserve A/c	3,000	3,000	4,000
" Bank A/c (bal. fig.)	—	4,042	—	" P & L Adj. A/c	—	1,500	—
" Balance c/d	78,300[3]	66,700	—	" A's Capital A/c	—	—	11,952[1]
				" B's Capital A/c	—	—	7,968
				" Bank A/c (Payable to C in 27 : 23)	27,000	23,000	—
				" Bank A/c (bal. fig.)	4,042	—	—
	90,252	78,710	97,200		90,252	78,710	97,200

Balance Sheet *as at 31st Dec. 2012*

Liabilities		Rs.	Assets		Rs.
Capital Accounts :			Plant and Machinery		42,075
A	78,300		Land and Building		1,35,600
B	66,700	1,45,000	Furniture		5,000
			Stock		21,925
C's Loan A/c		47,000	Sundry Debtors	20,000	
6% Mortgage Loan A/c		17,000	*Less* : Reserve for Bad Debts	1,000	19,000
Bills Payable		18,000	Bills Receivable		10,000
Sundry Creditors		9,100	Cash and Bank		3,000
Outstanding Electricity		500			
		2,36,600			2,36,600

Workings :

1. **Computation of Goodwill and its adjustment**

		Rs.
	Total profits for 5 years (Rs. 14,000 + Rs. 16,500 + Rs. 15,000 + Rs. 15,000 + Rs. 15,800)	76,300
Add :	Profit as per P & L Adjustment A/c	6,700
		83,000

$\therefore$ Average Profit $= \frac{\text{Rs. } 83,000}{5} = \text{Rs. } 16,600$

$\therefore$ Value of Goodwill = Average Profit × 3 years' purchase
= Rs. 16,600 × 3
= Rs. 49,800

C's share of Goodwill Rs. 19,920 (i.e., Rs. 49,800 × $\frac{4}{10}$) to be taken by A and B in 3 : 2. So, A's Share = Rs. 11,952 (i.e., Rs. 19,920 × $\frac{3}{5}$ (and B's share Rs. 7,968 (i.e., 19,920 × $\frac{2}{5}$). The entry for the purpose will be :

		Rs.	Rs.
A's Capital A/c	Dr.	11,952	
B's Capital A/c	Dr.	7,968	
To C's Capital A/c			19,920

2. **New Profit-sharing Ratio**

C's share $\frac{4}{10}$ is taken by A and B in 3 : 2.

So, A takes $= \frac{4}{10} \times \frac{3}{5} = \frac{12}{50}$

B takes $= \frac{4}{10} \times \frac{2}{5} = \frac{8}{50}$

$\therefore$ A's total share $= \frac{3}{10} + \frac{12}{50} = \frac{15 + 12}{50} = \frac{27}{50}$

B's total share $= \frac{3}{10} + \frac{8}{50} = \frac{15 + 8}{50} = \frac{23}{50}$

$\therefore$ A : B = 27 : 23.

3. **Adjustments to be made in A's and B's Capital Accounts**

Combined Adjusted Capitals of A and B :

		Rs.
A =	(Rs. 50,000 + Rs. 3,000 + Rs. 2,010 + Rs. 4,200 + Rs. 27,000 – Rs. 11,952) =	74,258
B =	(Rs. 45,000 + Rs. 3,000 + Rs. 2,010 + Rs. 4,200 + Rs. 1,500 + Rs. 23,000 – Rs. 7,968) =	70,742
	Combined Adjusted Capital	1,45,000

This balance will be in proportion to 27 : 23 between A and B.

$\therefore$ A's closing balance will be = Rs. 1,45,000 × $\frac{27}{50}$ = Rs. 78,300

B's closing balance will be = Rs. 1,45,000 × $\frac{23}{50}$ = Rs. 66,700

4. **Depreciation on Plant**

Value of Plant (after rectification)

= (Rs. 40,000 + Rs. 9,000 + Rs. 500 + Rs. 500 – Dep. Rs. 500) Rs. 49,500 × $\frac{15}{100}$ = Rs. 7,425.

ASSIGNMENT MATERIALS

THEORETICAL

Short Answer-Type Question

1. How is the profit-sharing ratio of the existing partners determined at the time of retirement of a partner?
2. Write notes on :
   Gaining Ratio; Revaluation of Assets and Liabilities; Joint Life Policy; Surrender Value.
3. How do you settle the accounts of a retiring partner?
4. Discuss how you would incorporate the effect of increase or decrease in assets and liabilities through Revaluation Account at the time of retirement of a partner.

Essay-Type Questions

1. Discuss the methods of computation of a retiring partner's share in the firm.
2. How is the payment made to the retiring partner for the amount due?
3. Discuss the treatment of Goodwill at the time of retirement of a partner.
4. Why are the assets and liabilities revalued at the time of retirement of a partner?
5. Why is it considered necessary to revalue the assets on the retirement of a partner?
6. Should the retiring partner not be paid fully immediately on retirement? How should his account be shown in subsequent Balance Sheet?
7. What are the adjustments required on retirement of a partner from a firm?
8. What is Goodwill? Discuss the various modes of treatment of Goodwill on the retirement of a partner.
9. Discuss, with the help of an illustration, the differences between the *Sacrificing Ratio* and *Gaining Ratio*.
10. What do you mean by Reserve and Accumulated Profit or Loss of a firm? How do you treat them at the time of retirement of a partner?

PRACTICAL

Calculate the future profit-sharing ratio/new ratio and the gaining ratio:

1. P, Q and R were in partnership sharing profits and losses in the ratio of 3 ; 2 : 1. Q retires. Calculate the new ratio.

   [Ans. 3 : 1]

2. Calculate the new profit--sharing ratio :

   X, Y and Z were in partnership sharing profits and losses in the ratio $\frac{1}{2}, \frac{3}{10}, \frac{1}{5}$. Y retired. Y's share was taken over by X and Z in 2 : 1.

   [Ans. 7 : 3]

3. Calculate the gaining ratio :

   A B and C were in partnership sharing profits and losses in the ratio 3: 2 : 1. B retired. A and C decided to share future profits in the ratio of $\frac{5}{8}$ and $\frac{3}{8}$.

   [Ans. 3 : 5]

4. A, B, C, and D were in partnership sharing profits and losses in the ratio of 4 ; 3 : 2 : 1. A retired. B, C, and D, decided to share the future profit and losses equally. Calculate the gaining ratio.

   [Ans. 1 : 4 : 7]

5. X, Y, and Z were in partnership sharing profits and losses in the ratio 4 : 3 : 1. Y retired. Y sold his share of profit to X and Z for Rs. 16,200 – Rs. 7,200 being paid by X and Rs. 9,000 paid by Z. The profit for the year after B's retirement was Rs. 21,000. Calculate the gaining ratio.

   [Ans. 4 : 5]

6. P, Q, and R, were partners sharing profits and losses in the ratio of P $\frac{5}{10}$, and R $\frac{2}{10}$. They had taken out a joint life policy of the face value of Rs. 20,000. On 31st December 2001 its surrender value was Rs. 4,000. On this date the Balance Sheet of the firm stood as:

Liabilities		Rs.	*Assets*	Rs.
Sundry Creditors		5,300	Fixed Assets	25,000
Expenses Outstanding		700	Stock	11,000
Reserve		3,000	Book Debts	9,000
Capitals:			Cash at Bank	2,000
P	20,000			
Q	10,000			
R	8,000			
		38,000		
		47,000		47,000

On this date Q decided to retire and, for this purpose, (i) Goodwill was valued at Rs. 15,000; (ii) Fixed Assets were valued at Rs. 30,000, and (iii) Stock was considered as worth Rs. 10,000.

Q was to be paid through cash brought in by P and R in such a way as to make their capitals proportionate to their new profit-sharing ratio which was to be P $\frac{3}{5}$ and R $\frac{2}{5}$. Goodwill was to be passed through books without raising a goodwill account; the joint life policy was also not to appear in the Balance Sheet.

[Ans. Closing Balance of Capital A/c; P Rs. 27,000; Q Rs. 18,000; Q's Loan A/c Rs. 17,800. Total of Balance Sheet Rs. 51,000]

7. X, Y and Z are partners in a firm sharing profits and losses as 3 ; 2 : 1, respectively. The Balance Sheet of the firm as on 31st December 2005 was:

Balance Sheet *as at 31.12.2005*

Liabilities		*Amount*	*Assets*		*Amount*
	Rs.	Rs.			Rs.
Capital Accounts :			Factory Building		60,000
X	45,000		Machinery		25,000
Y	30,000		Furniture		15,000
X	25,000		Stock		20,000
		1,00,000	Debtors	15,000	
General Reserve		24,000	*Less* : Provision for		
Sundry Creditors		14,000	Doubtful Debt	500	14,500
			Cash in hand		3,500
		1,38,000			1,38,000

Y retired from the business on the same date and X and Z continued in partnership sharing Profits and Losses in the ratio 3 : 1, subjects to the following adjustments:

(a) Goodwill valued Rs. 18,000 is not be raised in the book. (b) Factory Building to be appreciated by Rs. 10,000 and Stock to be appreciated by 5% (c) Machinery and Furniture to be depreciated by 10%. (d) The Provision for Doubtful Debts to be raised to Rs. 1,000. (e) A provision of Rs. 600 to be made for Outstanding Expenses. (f) A typewriter costing Rs. 3,600 was purchased on 1.10.2005 but not recorded in the book.

X and Z are to bring in cash in their profit-sharing ratio to pay off Y's dues on retirement and leave a sum of Rs. 7,500 as working capital.

Prepare Revaluation Accounts and the New Balance Sheet of the firm.

[Ans. Profit on Revaluation Rs. 9,500, Closing Capital Balances: X Rs. 95,625 and Z Rs. 41,875; Y is to be paid Rs. 47,167; Cash to be brought in by X Rs. 38,857 and Z Rs. 12,792; Total of Balance Sheet Rs. 1,52,100]

8. X, Y and Z are partners sharing profits and losses in the ratio of 3 : 2 : 1. On 31.12.2000, Z retires. On that date the capital accounts of the partners showed credit balance of X Rs. 20,000, Y Rs. 15,000 and Z Rs. 10,000.

It was provided in the partnership deed that, in the case of retirement, the retiring partner shall be entitled to a share of the goodwill of the firm to be calculated on the average of the last three years' profit and that the payment of the capital and share of goodwill to be retiring partners shall be made by annual instalments of Rs. 4,000 each, interest being calculated @ 5% on the unpaid balances.

The profits for the years 1998, 1999 and 2000 were Rs. 8,000; Rs. 9,000 and Rs. 10,000, respectively. The first instalment was paid on 31.12.2001

Show, Z's Loan Account until the payment of the whole amount due to him was made.

[Ans. Z's Loan A/c Rs. 11,500]

9. Singh, Pandey, and Gupta are partners in a firm sharing profits and losses in the ratio of 3 : 2 : 1. The Balance Sheet of their business as on 31.3.2006 is :

Balance Sheet *as on 31.3.2006*

Liabilities	Rs.	*Assets*	Rs.
Capital Accounts :		Machinery	40,000
Singh	50,000	Furniture	20,000
Pandey	40,000	Motor Car	30,000
Gupta	30,000	Stock	25,000
General Reserve	12,000	Debtors	75,000
Creditors	60,000	Cash	2,000
	1,92,000		1,92,000

Singh retired with effect from 1.4.2006. Goodwill of the firm was valued at Rs. 24,000. On revaluation, Machinery and Furniture are to be appreciated by 10%. Debtors include Rs. 1,500 as Bad and Doubtful and are to be written-off. Value of stocks to be reduced to Rs. 23,000. Creditors include Rs. 800 as no more payable.

It was decided that due effect to be given to the retiring partner's capital account as his share of goodwill without raising any goodwill account. Pandey and Gupta are to share the future profits in equal proportion. Amounts payable to Singh is to be treated as loan to the firm.

You are required to prepare the Revaluation Account, Capital Accounts of the partners, and the Balance Sheet of the firm after Singh's retirement.

[Ans. Singh's Loan A/c Rs. 69,650; Closing Balance Capital A/c : Pandey Rs. 41,100; Gupta Rs. 24,550]

10. The following is the Balance Sheet as at 31.12.2012 of Chinu, Dinu, and Minu who are in partnership for a fixed term and shared profits and losses in the proportion of $\frac{1}{2}$, $\frac{1}{3}$, and $\frac{1}{6}$, respectively.

	Rs.	Rs.		Rs.
Capital Accounts :			Goodwill	8,000
Chinu	14,000		Plant and Machinery	14,000
Dinu	11,000		Stock	6,125
Minu	5,000		Debtors	9,815
		30,000	Cash at Bank	750
Creditors		8,690		
		38,690		38,690

Dinu retired on 1.1.2013, Chinu and Minu continued the business retaining all the assets at the values shown in the above Balance Sheet except that the Goodwill was agreed to be valued at Rs. 6,000 only and Plant and Machinery at Rs. 11,500. Under the Partnership agreement, any partner retiring otherwise than by death—bound himself to pay to the remaining partners a compensation equal to half of his share of the Goodwill (the remaining partners to divide this in their profit-sharing ratio) and to leave the balance of his capital accounts as loan to the firm to be paid-off at the firm's option at any time within three years.

Set out the necessary Ledger accounts showing the above transactions and a Balance Sheet showing the position immediately after Dinu's withdrawal from business, assuming Minu has brought in an additional capital of Rs. 10,000 of which Rs. 5,000 has been paid over to Dinu.

[Ans. Amount due to Dinu Rs. 3,500; Closing Balance of Capital Accounts : Chinu Rs. 12,500; Minu Rs. 14,500; Total of Balance Sheet Rs. 39,190]

11. X, Y and Z were carrying on business in partnership sharing profits and losses in proportion of 4 : 3 : 2. Their Balance sheet on 31.12.2012 stood as :

Liabilities		Rs.	*Assets*		Rs.
Sundry Creditors		20,700	Cash at bank		16,500
Capital Accounts :			Sundry Debtors	15,000	
X	60,000		*Less* : Reserve	300	
Y	45,000				14,700
X	30,000		Stock		24,000
		1,35,000	Plant and Machinery		25,500
			Land and Building		75,000
		1,55,700			1,55,700

Y retired from the business on the same date and the following adjustments of the assets and liabilities had been agreed upon before ascertaining amount payable by the firm to Y :

(a) That the Reserve for Doubtful Debts be brought up to 5% in debtors:

(b) Land and Building be appreciated by Rs. 1,750

(c) Provision of Rs. 2,000 be made in respect of outstanding audit fees.

(d) The goodwill of the firm be fixed at Rs. 32,400 and Y's share of the same be adjusted into the accounts of X and Z, who decided to continue the business sharing profits and losses in proportion of 5 : 3.

(e) Capital of the new firm be fixed at Rs. 84,000 between X and Z in proportion to their new profit-sharing ratio and actual cash be brought in by or paid-off to the continuing partners, as the case and may be.

(f) Y agreed to leave the amount due to him by the firm as loan to the new firm carrying interest at 6% p.a.

Show necessary accounts and the Balance Sheet of the new firm following retirement of Y.

[Ans. Y's Loan A/c Rs. 55,567; Total of Balance Sheet Rs. 1,62,267]

12. The following is the Balance Sheet of A, B, and C who were partners on 31.12.2012 :

Liabilities	Rs.	*Assets*	Rs.
A's Capital	33,600	Plant and Machinery	49,000
B's Capital	25,200	Furniture	4,800
C's Capital	12,600	Stock	22,800
Sundry Creditors	12,000	Sundry Debtors	21,600
5% Mortgage	16,000	Cash	1,200
	99,400		99,400

They share profits and losses in the ratio of 2 : 2 : 1. On 1.1.2013, C retired from the business and claimed his share in secret reserve/profit arising out of the following :

(1) During the year 2012, purchase of Machinery at a cost of Rs. 5,000 was charged to Purchase Account, the installation charges of Rs. 300 to erect the Machinery being charged to Machinery Repairs Account (Depreciation is to be charged at 10%).

(2) Rs. 1,200 received form Mr. Carefree towards rent of property sublet was credited to his Personal Account, instead of rent account so as to reduce his debit balance from Rs. 1,600 to Rs. 400.

(3) Interest on Mortgage loan was paid in advance up to 31.12.2013, and the whole amount was charged to Interest Account in 2012.

After rectifying the above errors, it was mutually decided that :

(a) The Goodwill of the firm be valued at two times the average profit of the last three years. Such profits should be the correct profits and not the book profits.

The book profits for the last three year were:

2010 Rs. 13,830; 2011 Rs. 32,000; 2012 Rs. 12,020

(b) Machinery be further depreciated by 10% and the provision for bad debts be made at 5% on debtors.

(c) The Goodwill Account should not appear in the books.

(d) There is a liability for Rs. 483 for bills discounted. This should be provided for.

(e) C should be paid half his dues in cash which shall be brought in by A and B in their profit-sharing proportion and the other half shall be left in the business as C's loan fetching 6% interest.

Pass necessary journal entries to give effect to the above and show C's Capital Account, Profit and Loss Adjustment Account, and the Balance Sheet of A and B after C's retirement.

[Ans. C's Loan Account Rs. 10,290. Total of Balance Sheet Rs. 99,683]

D. RETIREMENT-CUM-ADMISSION

The treatment of admission of a partner and the retirement of a partner separately. Now, we are to deal with the combined change or simultaneous retirement and admission. It should be stated that there is actually no deviation from the principle governing admission or retirement. Only two sets of transactions are to be recorded at the same time.

Memorandum Revaluation Account

When the partners decide not to show the changed values of assets and liabilities in the books of accounts, a Memorandum Revaluation Account is to be opened for this purpose[1]. The first part of this account is similar to the ordinary Revaluation Account, i.e., profits or losses are to be shared among the partners in their profit-sharing ratio. The second part of this account deals with the reversed entries and the profits or losses are transferred to the existing partners' Capital Account (i.e., profits/losses to be written-back) as per new profit-sharing ratio.

Illustration 1

A, B, and C are in partnership sharing profits and losses in the ratio 2 : 2 : 1. On 31.12.2012, the firm's Balance Sheet stands as:

Liabilities	Rs.	Rs.	*Assets*	Rs.
Capital Accounts			Sundry Assets	55,000
A	30,000		Bank	15,000
B	20,000			
C	10,000			
		60,000		
Sundry Creditors		10,000		
		70,000		70,000

On that date, C decides to retire. The value of goodwill is agreed to be Rs. 15,000 and Sundry Assets are taken to have increased in value by Rs. 25,000.

On C's retirement, D is admitted as a partner. He pays no premium for goodwill but brings in Rs. 15,000 as capital. Profits and losses are to be shared in the ratio of 4 : 3 : 3.

Show capital accounts and draw up two Balance Sheets (one after C's retirement and the other after D's admission). Assume that the goodwill account is to be wiped-off from the books and restore the Sundry assets at its original value.

[CU BCom (Hons.)]

Solution

In the books of A, B, C, and D
Memorandum Revaluation Account

Dr. Cr.

Particulars	Rs.	*Amount* Rs.	*Particulars*	Rs.	*Amount* Rs.
To Profit on Revaluation :			By Increase in Assets :		
A $\frac{2}{5}$	16,000		Sundry Assets		25,000
B $\frac{2}{5}$	16,000		Goodwill		15,000
C $\frac{1}{5}$	8,000	40,000			
		40,000			40,000
To Reversal of items		40,000	By Profit to be written-back :		
			A $\frac{4}{10}$	16,000	
			B $\frac{3}{10}$	12,000	
			D $\frac{3}{10}$	12,000	40,000
		40,000			40,000

1 It has already been highlighted earlier in the case of '*Admission of a Partner.*'

Dr. **Capital Account** Cr.

Particulars	A Rs.	B Rs.	C Rs.	Particulars	A Rs.	B Rs.	C Rs.
To C's Loan A/c		—	18,000	By Balance b/d	30,000	20,000	10,000
" Balance c/d	46,000	36,000	—	" Revaluation Profit	16,000	16,000	8,000
	46,000	36,000	18,000		46,000	36,000	18,000
				" Balance b/d	46,000	36,000	—

Balance Sheet (after C's retirement) as at 31st Dec. 2012

Liabilities	Rs.	Rs.	Assets	Rs.
Capital Accounts :			Sundry Assets (Rs. 55,000 + Rs. 25,000)	80,000
A	46,000		Goodwill	15,000
B	36,000		Bank	15,000
		82,000		
C's Loan A/c		18,000		
Sundry Creditors		10,000		
		1,10,000		1,10,000

Dr. **Capital Account** Cr.

Particulars	A Rs.	B Rs.	D Rs.	Particulars	A Rs.	B Rs.	D Rs.
To Revaluation —Profit written-back	16,000	12,000	12,000	By Balance b/d	46,000	36,000	—
" Balance c/d	30,000	24,000	3,000	" Bank	—	—	15,000
	46,000	36,000	15,000		46,000	36,000	15,000
				By Balance b/d	30,000	24,000	3,000

Balance Sheet (*after D's admission*) *as at 31st Dec. 2012*

Liabilities	Rs.	Rs.	Assets	Rs.
Capital Accounts :			Sundry Assets (Rs. 80,000 – Rs. 25,000)	55,000
A	30,000		Bank (Rs. 15,000 + Rs. 15,000)	30,000
B	24,000			
D	3,000			
		57,000		
C's Loan A/c		18,000		
Sundry Creditors		10,000		
		85,000		85,000

Illustration 2

Anil, Bimal, and Charu are partners sharing profits and losses in the proportion of 3 : 2 : 1. Following is the Balance Sheet as at 31.12.2012 :

Liabilities	Rs.	Rs.	Assets	Rs.
Capital :			Goodwill	10,000
Anil	65,000		Sundry Debtors	61,400
Bimal	38,000		Sundry Assets	1,48,000
Charu	28,000			
		1,31,000		
General Reserve		38,400		
Sundry Creditors		50,000		
		2,19,400		2,19,400

Charu desires to retire from the firm on 1.1.2013. In terms of agreement, Goodwill is to be revalued at Rs. 50,000, Sundry Debtors at Rs. 41,400 and other Sundry Assets at Rs. 1,50,000. The amount payable to the retired partner is for the present to be treated as loan with 5% interest. On the same day, i.e., on 1.1.2013, Dinen is admitted as a partner on payment of Rs. 32,000. Profits and losses are henceforth to be shared as 4 : 3 : 2 among Anil, Bimal, and Dinen. No alteration is to be made in the book value of the assets other than cash brought in by Dinen and the General Reserve.

Draw up the final Balance Sheet as at 1.1.2013, on the above basis after the admission of Dinen.

[CU BCom (Hons.)]

Solution

Dr. **Memorandum Revaluation Account** *Cr.*

Particulars		*Amount*	*Particulars*		*Amount*
	Rs.	Rs.			Rs.
To Sundry Debtors		20,000	By Goodwill		40,000
" Profit :			" Sundry Assets		2,000
Anil	11,000				
Bimal	7,333				
Charu	3,667	22,000			
		42,000			42,000
To *Reversal of items*		42,000	By *Reversal of items*		20,000
			" Profit on revaluation to be written-back :		
			Anil	9,778	
			Bimal	7,333	
			Dinen	4,889	22,000
		42,000			42,000

Dr. **Capital Accounts** *Cr.*

Particulars	Anil	Bimal	Charu	Dinen	*Particulars*	Anil	Bimal	Charu	Dinen
	Rs.	Rs.	Rs.	Rs.		Rs.	Rs.	Rs.	Rs.
To Revaluation —Profit written-back	9,778	7,333	—	4,889	By Balance b/d	65,000	38,000	28,000	—
" Charu's Loan	—	—	38,067	—	" Bank	—	—	—	32,000
" Balance c/d	85,422	50,800	—	27,111	" Revaluation —Profit	11,000	7,333	3,667	—
					" Reserve	19,200	12,800	6,400	—
	95,200	58,133	38,067	32,000		95,200	58,133	38,067	32,000
					By Balance b/d	85,422	50,800	—	27,111

Balance Sheet *as at 1st Jan. 2013*

Liabilities	Rs.	Rs.	*Assets*	Rs.
Capital Accounts :			Goodwill	10,000
Anil	85,422		Sundry Assets	1,48,000
Bimal	50,800		Sundry Debtors	61,400
Dinen	27,111	1,63,333	Cash	32,000
Charu's Loan		38,067		
Sundry Creditors		50,000		
		2,51,400		2,51,400

Illustration 3

Nimu and Simu are in partnership as equal partners. Nimu, by agreement, retires and his son, Ganu, joins the firm on the basis that he would get one-third share of the profit.

The balances of books of M/s Nimu and Simu were :

	Rs.	Rs.
Goodwill	24,000	
Bank	16,000	
Debtors	6,000	
Stock	52,000	
Creditors		12,000
Capital Accounts :		
Nimu		46,000
Simu		40,000
	98,000	98,000

Goodwill is agreed at Rs. 60,000 and written-up, accordingly. Sufficient money is to be introduced so as to enable Nimu to be paid-off and leave Rs. 8,000 in bank. Simu and Ganu are to provide such sum as to make their capital proportionate to their share of profit. Nimu agrees to contribute from his capital half of the amount Ganu has to provide. Assuming the agreement was carried out, show the entries required and prepare the Balance Sheet of the firm of M/s Simu and Ganu.

[ICWA]

Solution

Workings:

(a) Capital of the new firm will be

	Rs.
Goodwill	60,000
Bank (to be retained)	8,000
Debtors	6,000
Stock	52,000
	1,26,000
Less: Creditors	12,000
	1,14,000
∴ Simu Rs. $1,14,000 \times \frac{2}{3}$	76,000
Ganu Rs. $1,14,000 \times \frac{1}{3}$	38,000

(b) Amount to be brought in by Simu

		Rs.
Simu's Capital should be		76,000
Less: Already stands	40,000	
Profit on Rev. on Goodwill $(36,000 \times \frac{1}{2})$	18,000	
		58,000
Amount to be brought in		18,000

(c) Amount to be brought in by Ganu

Ganu's Capital should be	38,000
Less: $\frac{1}{2}$ of Rs. 38,000 to be contributed by his father	19,000
Amount to be brought in	19,000

(d) Amount to be paid to Nimu

Nimu's Capital	46,000
Add: Profit on Rev. of Goodwill $\left(36,000 \times \frac{1}{2}\right)$	18,000
	64,000
Less: Contributed to his son, Ganu	19,000
Amount to be paid-off	45,000

In the books of Nimu, Simu, and Ganu
Journal

Date	*Particulars*		*L. F.*	*Debit* Rs.	*Credit* Rs.
	Goodwill A/c	Dr.		36,000	
	To Nimu's Capital A/c				18,000
	" Simu's Capital A/c				18,000
	(Value of goodwill increased and credited to old partners' capital accounts.)				
	Bank A/c	Dr.		37,000	
	To Simu's Capital A/c				18,000
	" Ganu's Capital A/c				19,000
	(Cash to be brought in by Simu and Ganu.)				
	Nimu's Capital A/c	Dr.		45,000	
	To Bank A/c				45,000
	(Amount paid to Nimu on his retirement.)				

Balance Sheet *as at ......*

Liabilities	Rs.	Rs.	*Assets*	Rs.
Capital Accounts:			Goodwill	60,000
Simu	76,000		Debtors	6,000
Ganu	38,000		Stock	52,000
		1,14,000	Bank	8,000
Creditors		12,000		
		1,26,000		1,26,000

Illustration 4

P and Q were working in partnership sharing profits equally. On 31.12.2012 P decided to retire and in his place it was decided that R, his son, would be admitted as partner from 1.1.2013 and his share in profits will be one-third.

The Balance Sheet of the firm as on 31.12.2012, was as follows :

Liabilities	Rs.	*Assets*	Rs.
Sundry Creditors	14,700	Goodwill	15,000
Capitals :		Land and Building	40,050
P	54,300	Motor Car	12,000
Q	48,000	Furniture	9,300
		Sundry Debtors	24,150
		Cash at Bank	16,500
	1,17,000		1,17,000

It was further decided:

(a) The Goodwill should be raised to Rs. 20,000; (b) The Motor Car would be taken over by P at its book value; (c) The value of Land and Building would be increased by Rs. 8,280; (d) Q and R would introduce sufficient capital to pay off P to leave thereafter a sum of Rs. 7,350 as working capital in a manner that the capitals of the new partners will be in proportion to their profits-sharing ratio; (e) The capital payable by R was to be gifted to him by his father; (f) The new partners decided not to show Goodwill as an asset. The above arrangements were duly complied with. Show the partners' Capital Accounts, Cash Account and Balance Sheet

Solution

Workings :

Capital accounts of the new firm will be

Land and Building (40,050 + 8,280)	48,330	$Q = \frac{2}{3} \times 74{,}430 = \text{Rs. } 49{,}620$
Furniture	9,300	$R = \frac{1}{3} \times 74{,}430 = \text{Rs. } 24{,}810$
Sundry Debtors	24,150	
Cash and Bank	7,350	
	89,130	
Less : Creditors	14,700	
	74,430	

In the books of P, Q, and R

Revaluation Account

Dr. *Particulars*		*Amount* Rs.	*Particulars*	Cr. *Amount* Rs.
To Profit on Revaluation :			By Land and Building	8,280
P $\frac{1}{2}$	4,140			
Q $\frac{1}{2}$	4,140	8,280		
		8,280		8,280

Capital Account

Dr. *Particulars*	P Rs.	Q Rs.	R Rs.	*Particulars*	P Rs.	Q Rs.	Cr. R Rs.
To Goodwill	—	13,333	6,667	By Balance b/d	54,300	48,000	—
" Motor Car	12,000	—	—	" Goodwill	2,500	2,500	—
" R's Capital	24,810	—	—	" Revaluation —Profit	4,140	4,140	—
" Bank *(bal. fig.)*	24,130	—	—	" P's Capital	—	—	24,810
" Balance c/d	—	49,620	24,810	" Bank *(bal. fig.)*	—	8,313	6,667
	60,940	62,953	31,477		60,940	62,953	31,477
				By Balance b/d	—	49,620	24,810

Dr. **Bank Account** Cr.

Particulars	Amount	Particulars	Amount
	Rs.		Rs.
To Balance b/d	16,500	By P's Capital	24,130
" Q's Capital	8,313	" Balance c/d	7,350
" R's Capital	6,667		
	31,480		31,480
To Balance b/d	7,350		

Balance Sheet *as at 1st Jan. 2013*

Liabilities	Rs.	Rs.	Assets	Rs.
Capital			Land and Building	48,330
Q	49,620		Furniture	9,300
R	24,810		Sundry Debtors	24,150
		74,430	Cash and Bank	7,350
Sundry Creditors		14,700		
		89,130		89,130

Illustration 5

X, Y, and Z are partners sharing profits and losses in the proportion to 3 : 2 : 2, respectively. The Balance Sheet of the firm as on 1.1.2011 was:

Liabilities	Rs.	Rs.	Assets	Rs.
Capital Accounts :			Plant and Machinery	36,000
X	50,000		Furniture	14,000
Y	40,000		Stock	56,000
Z	35,000		Sundry Debtors	48,000
		1,25,000	Cash at Bank	9,000
Bank Overdraft		10,000		
Sundry Creditors		28,000		
		1,63,000		1,63,000

X retired on 1.1.2011, on which date R is admitted as a new partner. For the purpose of adjusting the rights as between on partners, goodwill to be valued at Rs. 42,000 and Sundry Debtors and Stock to be reduced by Rs. 8,000 and to Rs. 50,000, respectively. X is to receive Rs. 22,000 in cash on the date of retirement and the balance due to him is to remain as loan at 8% p.a. Repayment of loan to be made at the end of each year by annual instalments representing 25% of the future profit before charging interest on loan.

R is to bring in Rs. 50,000 in cash as his capital on the date of admission. The new partners are to share profits and losses equally after paying the interest on X's loan.

The net profit for the year ended 31st Dec. 2011, is Rs. 32,000 before taking into account the instalment payable to X.

You are required to show : (a) Profit and Loss Appropriation Account for the year ended 31st Dec. 2011. (b) Capital Accounts of the new partners; and (c) X's Loan Account as on 31st Dec. 2011.

Solution

In the books of X, Y, Z, and R

Dr. **Revaluation Account** Cr.

Particulars	Rs.	Amount	Particulars	Amount
		Rs.		Rs.
To Provision for Bad Debts		8,000	By Goodwill	42,000
" Stock		6,000		
" Share of Profit :				
X $\frac{3}{7}$	12,000			
Y $\frac{2}{7}$	8,000			
Z $\frac{2}{7}$	8,000			
		28,000		
		42,000		42,000

Capital Account

Dr. Particulars	X	Y	Z	Cr. Particulars	X	Y	Z
	Rs.	Rs.	Rs.		Rs.	Rs.	Rs.
To Bank—Repayment	22,000	—	—	By Balance b/d	50,000	40,000	35,000
" X's Loan A/c	40,000	—	—	" Revaluation —Profit	12,000	8,000	8,000
" Balance c/d	—	48,000	43,000				
	62,000	48,000	43,000		62,000	48,000	43,000
				By Balance b/d	—	48,000	43,000

Profit and Loss Appropriation Account *for the year ended 31st Dec. 2011*

Dr. Particulars	Rs.	Amount Rs.	Cr. Particulars	Amount Rs.
To Loan Redemption Fund A/c (25% of Rs. 32,000)		8,000	By Profit and Loss A/c —Net Profit	32,000
Share of Profit :				
Y $\frac{1}{3}$	8,000			
Z $\frac{1}{3}$	8,000			
R $\frac{1}{3}$	8,000	24,000		
		32,000		32,000

Capital Account

Dr. Particulars	Y	Z	R	Cr. Particulars	Y	Z	R
	Rs.	Rs.	Rs.		Rs.	Rs.	Rs.
To Balance c/d	56,000	51,000	58,000	By Balance b/d	48,000	43,000	—
				" Bank	—	—	50,000
				" Share Profit	8,000	8,000	8,000
	56,000	51,000	58,000		56,000	51,000	58,000
				By Balance b/d	56,000	51,000	58,000

X's Loan Account (8%)

Dr.	Particulars	Amount		Particulars	Cr. Amount
		Rs.	2011		Rs.
2011 Dec. 31	To Bank	8,000	Jan 1	By X's Capital A/c	40,000
	Balance c/d	35,200	Dec. 31	" Interest	3,200
		43,200			43,200
			2012 Jan 1	By Balance b/d	35,200

Illustration 6

A, B, and C were partners in a business and shared profits in the proportion of $\frac{1}{2} : \frac{1}{3} : \frac{1}{6}$, respectively. On 31st Dec. 2012, the Balance Sheet of their business was :

Liabilities	Rs.	Rs.	Assets	Rs.
Creditors		3,000	Goodwill	10,000
Capital Accounts :			Sundry Assets	12,000
A	14,000		Cash at Bank	11,000
B	10,000			
C	6,000	30,000		
		33,000		33,000

On 1st Jan. 2013, the following changes took place :

(i) C retired from the business and his share valued at Rs. 8,000 was taken over by A and B who paid the former in their profit-sharing proportions, from their personal sources.

(ii) D was then introduced in the business as a $\frac{1}{6}$th partner on condition that a further sum of Rs. 6,000 was allowed to be credited to A and B in their respective proportions, and that he contributed such a sum as would make his capital equal to $\frac{1}{4}$th of the total capital of A and B after all the above adjustments.

(iii) The new firm was converted into a limited company which took on the whole of the assets (except cash) for a consideration of Rs. 34,000, payable in fully paid shares of Rs. 10 each.

The bank balance of the firm was utilised in payment to creditors and the partners.

You are required to show the capital accounts of all the partners, giving effect to the above transactions.

Solution

In the books of A, B, C, and D
Capital Account

Dr. Cr.

Particulars	A	B	C	D	Particulars	A	B	C	D
	Rs.	Rs.	Rs.	Rs.		Rs.	Rs.	Rs.	Rs.
To C's Cap. A/c	1,200	800	—	—	By Balance b/d	14,000	10,000	6,000	—
" Bank	—	—	8,000	—	" A's Cap. A/c	—	—	1,200	—
" Shares	17,000	11,330	—	5,670	" B's Cap. A/c	—	—	800	—
" Bank (final payment)	7,200	5,470	—	4,330	" Bank—to pay-off C	4,800	3,200	—	—
					" Goodwill	3,600	2,400	—	—
					" Profit on realisation	3,000	2,000	—	1,000
					" Bank—Capital	—	—	—	9,000
	25,400	17,600	8,000	10,000		25,400	17,600	8,000	10,000

Working Notes :

1. Goodwill to be paid to C by A and B in their profits-sharing ratio

Goodwill Rs. 2,000 (Rs. 8,000 – Rs. 6,000) :

A is to pay = Rs. 2,000 × $\frac{3}{5}$ = Rs. 1,200.

B is to pay = Rs. 2,000 × $\frac{2}{5}$ = Rs. 800.

2. Capital to be brought in by D

Combined adjusted capitals of A and B are :

	Rs.
A = Rs. (14,000 + 4,800 + 3,600 – 1,200)	21,200
B = Rs. (10,000 + 3,200 + 2,400 – 800)	14,800
	36,000

∴ D is to bring $\left(\text{Rs. } 36,000 \times \frac{1}{4}\right)$ = Rs. 9,000 as his capital.

3. **Shares received by the partners will be distributed in profit-sharing ratio so that their interest will not be affected in the company.**

4. **Calculation of profit on realisation**

		Rs.	Rs.
Purchase Price			34,000
Less :	Assets taken :		
	Sundry Assets	12,000	
	Goodwill	16,000	
			28,000
	Profit		6,000

to be shared between A, B, and D in 3 : 2 : 1.

5. **Amount paid to C Rs. 8,000 which is to be brought in by A and B in 3 : 2.**

Illustration 7

Durga and Kali were working in partnership sharing profits equally. On 31st December 1997 Durga decided to retire and in her place it was decided that Lakshmi, her daughter, would be admitted as partner from January, 1, 1998, and her share in profits will be one-third.

The Balance Sheet of the firm as on December 31, 1997 was:

Liabilities	Rs.	*Assets*	Rs.
Sundry Creditors	22,050	Goodwill	22,500
Capital :		Land & Buildings	60,075
Durga	81,450	Motor Car	18,000
Kali	72,000	Furniture	13,950
		Sundry Debtors	36,225
		Cash & Bank Balances	24,750
	1,75,500		1,75,500

It was further decided :

(a) The Goodwill should be raised to Rs. 30,000. (b) The Motor Car would be taken over by Durga at its Book Value. (c) The Value of Land and Buildings would be increased by Rs. 12,420. (d) Kali and Lakshmi would introduced sufficient Capital to pay off Durg and to leave thereafter a sum of Rs. 11,025 as working capital in a manner that the capitals of the new partners will be in proportion to their profit-sharing ratio. (e) The capital payable by Lakshmi was to be gifted to her by her mother. (f) The new partners decided not to show Goodwill as an asset.

The partners introduce the Capital on 10.1.1998. Show Capital Account, Cash Account and the Balance Sheet.

[CU BCom (Hons.)1999]

Solution

In the Books of the firm

Capital Account

Dr. Particulars	Durga Rs.	Kali Rs.	Lakshmi Rs.	Particulars	Durga Rs.	Kali Rs.	Lakshmi *Cr.* Rs.
To Motor Car A/c	18,000	—	—	By Balance b/d	81,450	72,000	—
" Goodwill A/c	—	20,000[4]	10,000	" Goodwill A/c	3,750[4]	3,750	—
" Lakshmi's Capital A/c	47,215	—	—	" Rev. A/c —Land & Building	6,210	6,210	—
" Cash A/c —Final settlement *(bal. fig.)*	26,195[3]	—	—	" Durgas' Capital A/c	—	—	47,215[2]
" Balance c/d	—	74,430[1]	37,215	" Cash A/c *(bal. fig.)*	—	12,470	—
	91,410	94,430	47,215		91,410	94,430	47,215

Cash Account

Dr. Particulars	Amount Rs.	Particulars	*Cr.* Amount Rs.
To Balance b/d	24,750	By Durgas' Capital A/c	26,195
" Kalis' Capital A/c	12,470	" Balance c/d	11,025
	37,220		37,220

Balance Sheet *as at 1st Jan. 1998*

Liabilities		Rs.	*Assets*	Rs.
Capital Accounts			Land and Building	
Kali	74,430		(Rs. 60,075 + Rs. 12,420)	72,495
Lakshmi	37,215		Furniture	13,950
		1,11,645	Sundry Debtors	36,225
Sundry Creditors		22,050	Cash and Bank	11,025
		1,33,695		1,33,695

Workings:

1. Capital of Kali and Lakshmi (i.e., total Capital of the new firm

	Rs.
Land and Building	72,495
Furniture	13,950
Sundry Debtors	36,225
Cash	11,025
	1,33,695
Less: Creditors	22,050
	1,11,645

∴ Kali — Rs. 1,11,645 × $\frac{2}{3}$ 74,430

Lakshmi — 1,11,645 × $\frac{1}{3}$ 37,215

(Rs. 37,215 + Rs. 10,000 + Rs. 10,000 for Goodwill) Rs. 47,215

2. **The entire Capital of Lakshmi is to be to gifted by her mother from her own share; the entry will be :**

Durgas' Capital A/c Dr.	37,215	
To Lakshmi's Capital A/c		37,215

3. **Durgas' total claim to the firm was Rs. 91,410 of which she took Motor Car for Rs. 18,000; gifted her daughter Lakshmi Rs. 37,215, and balance she was paid off for Rs. 26,195.**

4. **For Goodwill**

In order to raise goodwill to Rs. 30,000 the following entry to be :

Goodwill A/c Dr.	7,500	
To Durga's Cap.		3,750
" Kali's Cap. A/c		3,750

For Written-off

Kali's Capital A/c Dr.	20,000	
Lakshmi Capital A/c Dr.	10,000	
To Goodwill A/c		30,000

Illustration 8

Dowell & Co. is a partnership firm with partners Mr. A, Mr. B and Mr. C, sharing profits and losses in the ratio of 10 : 6 : 4. The Balance Sheet of the firm as at 31st March 1996 is :

Liabilities		Rs.	*Assets*	Rs.
Capital :			Land	10,000
Mr. A	80,000		Buildings	2,00,000
Mr. B	20,000		Plant and Machinery	1,30,000
Mr. C	30,000		Furniture	43,000
		1,30,000	Investments	12,000
Reserves (Unappropriated profit)		20,000	Stock	1,30,000
Long Term Debt		3,00,000	Debtors	1,39,000
Bank Overdraft		44,000		
Trade Creditors		1,70,000		
		6,64,000		6,64,000

It was mutually agreed that Mr. B will retire from partnership and in his place Mr. D will be admitted as a partner with effect from 1st April 1996.

(i) Goodwill is to be valued at Rs. 1 lakh but the same will not appear as an asset in the books of the reconstituted firm.

(ii) Buildings and plant and machinery are to be depreciated by 5 percent and 20 percent, respectively. Investments are to be taken over by the retiring partner at Rs. 15,000. Provision of 20 percent is to be made on debtors to cover doubtful debts.

(iii) In the reconstituted firm, the total capital will be Rs. 2 lakhs which will be contributed by Mr. A, Mr. C and Mr. D in their new profit sharing ratio, which is 2 : 2 : 1.

(iv) The surplus funds, if any, will be used for repaying the Bank Overdraft.

(v) The amount due to the retiring partner shall be transferred to his loan account.

You are to prepare : (a) Revaluation A/c; (b) Partners' Capital Accounts; (c) Bank Account; and (d) Balance Sheet of the reconstituted firm as on 1st April 1996.

[CA Foundation Nov. 1996]

Solution

In the books of A, B and C

Revaluation Account

Dr. Particulars	Amount	Particulars		Amount Cr.
	Rs.			Rs.
To Building A/c	10,000	By Investment A/c		3,000
" Plant and Machinery A/c	26,000	" Capital A/c		
" Prov. for Bad Debts A/c	27,800	—Loss on Revaluation		
		A	30,400	
		B	18,240	
		C	12,160	60,800
	63,800			63,800

Capital Account

Dr. Particulars	A	B	C	D	Particulars	A	B	C	D Cr.
	Rs.	Rs.	Rs.	Rs.		Rs.	Rs.	Rs.	Rs.
To Reva. A/c —Loss	30,400	18,240	12,160	—	By Balance b/d	80,000	20,000	30,000	—
					" Reserve A/c	10,000	6,000	4,000	—
" Goodwill A/c	40,000	—	40,000	20,000	" Goodwill A/c	50,000	30,000	20,000	—
" Inv. A/c	—	15,000	—	—	" Bank A/c (*bal. fig.*)	10,400	—	78,160	60,000
" B's Loan A/c	—	22,760	—	—					
" Balance c/d	80,000	—	80,000	40,000					
	1,50,400	56,000	1,32,160	60,000		1,50,400	56,000	1,32,160	60,000

Bank Account

Dr. Particulars	Amount	Particulars	Amount Cr.
	Rs.		Rs.
To A's Capital A/c	10,400	By Balance b/d	44,000
" B's Capital A/c	78,160	" Balance c/d	1,04,560
" D's Capital A/c	60,000		
	1,48,560		1,48,560

Balance Sheet *as at 1st April 1996*

Liabilities	Rs.	Rs.	Assets	Rs.	Rs.
Capital Account			Land		10,000
A	80,000		Building		1,90,000
B	80,000		Plant and Machinery		1,04,000
C	40,000		Furniture		43,000
		2,00,000	Stock		1,30,000
Long-Term debts		3,00,000	Debtors	1,39,000	
Trade Creditors		1,70,000	*Less :* Res./Bad Debts	27,800	
B's Loan A/c		22,760			1,11,200
			Bank		1,04,560
		6,92,760			6,92,760

Illustration 9

Avinash, Basuda Ltd. and Chinmoy Ltd. were in partnership sharing profits and losses in the ratio of 9 : 4 ; 2. Basuda Ltd. retired from the partnership on 31st March 1998, when the firm's balance sheet was:

Particulars		Amount	Particulars	Amount
		Rs.		Rs.
Sundry Creditors		600	Cash and Bank	284
Capital Accounts:			Sundry Debtors	400
Avinash	2,700		Stock	800
Basuda Ltd.	1,200		Furniture	266
Chinmoy Ltd.	600		Plant	850
		4,500	Land and Building	2,500
		5,100		5,100

Basuda Ltd.'s share in goodwill and capital was acquired by Avinash and Chinmoy Ltd. in the ratio of 1 : 3, the continuing partners bringing in the necessary finance to pay off Basuda Ltd. The partnership deed provides that on retirement or admission of a partner, the goodwill of the firm is to be valued at three times the average annual profits of the firm for the four years ended on the date of retirement or admission. The profits of the firm during the four years ended 31st March 1998 in thousands of rupees were : 1994-95 Rs. 450, 1995-96 Rs. 250; 1996-97 Rs. 600; and 1997-98 Rs. 700.

The deed further provided that goodwill account is not to appear in the books of accounts at all.

The continuing partner agreed that with effect from 1st April 1998, Ghanashyam, son of Avinash is to be admitted as a partner with 25% share of profits.

Avinash gifts to Ghanashyam, by transfer from his capital account, an amount sufficient to cover up 12.5% of capital and goodwill requirement. The balance 12.5% of capital and goodwill requirement is purchased by Ghanashyam from Avinash and Chinmoy Ltd. in the ratio of 2 : 1.

The firm asks you to : (i) Prepare a statement showing the continuing partners' share; (ii) Pass journal entries including for bank transactions; and (iii) Prepare the balance sheet of the firm after Ghanashyam's admission.

[CA Inter, May 1998; CU BCom (Hons.) 2009 Adapted]

Solution

(i) **Statement showing the continuing Partner's Share**

Avinsh $= \frac{9}{15} + \frac{1}{15} = \frac{10}{15} - \frac{1}{8} - \frac{2}{24} = \frac{11}{24}$

Basuda Ltd. $= \frac{4}{15} - \frac{1}{15}$ (to Avinash) $- \frac{3}{15}$ (to Chinmoy)

Chinmoy Ltd. $= \frac{2}{15} + \frac{3}{15} = \frac{5}{15} - \frac{1}{24} = \frac{7}{24}$

Add: Purchase from Avinash $= \frac{2}{3} \times \frac{1}{8} = \frac{2}{24}$

Purchase from Chinmoy $= \frac{1}{3} \times \frac{1}{8} = \frac{1}{24}$

$\therefore \frac{1}{8} + \frac{2}{24} + \frac{1}{24} = \frac{6}{24}$

After Ghanashyam's Admission :

Gift by Avinash $\frac{12.5}{100} = \frac{1}{8}$

	Avinash		Chinmoy		Ghanashyam
$\therefore$	$\frac{11}{24}$	:	$\frac{7}{24}$	:	$\frac{6}{24}$
Or	11	:	7	:	6.

(ii) **In the book of the firm**

Journal

Date	Particulars		L.F.	Dr. Rs.	Cr. Rs.
1998 March 31st	Avinash's Capital A/c	Dr.		7,50,000	
	To Ghyanshyam's Capital				7,50,000
	(Gift made by Avinash to Ghyanshyam's)				
	Avinash 's Capital A/c	Dr.		1,00,000	
	Chinmoy Ltd. capital A/c	Dr.		3,00,000	
	To Basuda Ltd. A/c				4,00,000
	(Adjustment made for goodwill)				
	Bank A/c	Dr.		31,00,000	
	To Avinash 's Capital A/c				7,75,000
	" Chinmoy Ltd. A/c				13,87,500
	" Ghanashyam Capital A/c				9,37,500
	(Capital brought in)				
	Basuda Ltd. Capital A/c	Dr.		16,00,000	
	To Bank A/c				16,00,000
	(Final payment made)				
	Ghahashyam Capital A/c			1,87,500	
	To Avinash's Capital A/c				1,25,000
	" Chinmoy's Capital A/c				62,500
	(Adjustment made for goodwill)				

(iii) **Capital Account**

Particulars	Avinash	Basuda Ltd.	Chinmoy Ltd.	Ghana-shyam	Particulars	Avinash	Basuda Ltd.	Chinmoy Ltd.	Ghana-shyam
	Rs.	Rs.	Rs.	Rs.		Rs.	Rs.	Rs.	Rs.
To Basuda Ltd.	1,00,000	—	3,00,000	—	By Bal. (b/d)	27,00,000	12,00,000	6,00,000	—
" Avinash	—	—	—	1,25,000	" Avinash	—	1,00,000	—	—
" Chinmoy Ltd.	—	—	—	62,500	" Chinmoy Ltd.	—	3,00,000	—	—
" Ghanashyam	7,50,000	—	—	—	" Avinash	—	—	—	7,50,000
" Bank (bal. fig.)	—	16,00,000	—	—	" Ghanashyam	1,25,000	—	62,500	—
" Balance c/d	27,50,000	—	17,50,000	15,00,000	" Bank (bal. fig.)	7,75,000	—	13,87,500	9,37,500
	36,00,000	16,00,000	20,50,000	16,87,500		36,00,000	16,00,000	20,50,000	16,87,500

Balance Sheet *as at 1st April 1998*

Liabilities	Amount	Assets	Amount
	Rs.		Rs.
Capital Account		Land and Building	25,00,000
Avinash	27,50,000	Plant	8,50,000
Chinmoy Ltd.	17,50,000	Furniture	2,66,000
Ghanashyam	15,00,000	Stock	8,00,000
Creditors	6,00,000	Debtors	4,00,000
		Cash & Bank (2,84,000 + 31,00,000 – 16,00,000)	17,84,000
	66,00,000		66,00,000

Workings :

1. **Adjustment of Goodwill on Retirement**

Valuation of goodwill $\frac{(\text{Rs. } 4{,}50{,}000 + \text{Rs. } 2{,}50{,}000 + \text{Rs. } 6{,}00{,}000 + \text{Rs. } 7{,}00{,}000)}{4}$

Average Profit = Rs. 5,00,000

Value of goodwill Rs. 5,00,000 × 3 years' purchases = Rs. 15,00,000

Basuda Ltd. share = Rs. 15,00,000 × $\frac{4}{15}$ = Rs. 4,00,000

The entry will be:

Avinash A/c	Dr.	1,00,000	
Chinmoy Ltd. A/c	Dr.	3,00,000	
To Basuda Ltd.			4,00,000

2. **Balance of Capital Account**

Basuda Ltd. balance amounted to Rs. 16,00,000 for the $\frac{4}{15}$th share. Thus, the total capital balance will be Rs. 60,00,000 (i.e., 16,00,000 × $\frac{15}{4}$)

Hence, partners' share will be :

Avinash Rs. 60,00,000 × $\frac{11}{24}$ = Rs. 27,50,000

Chinmoy Ltd. Rs. 60,00,000 × $\frac{7}{24}$ = Rs. 17,50,000

Ghanashyam Rs. 60,00,000 × $\frac{6}{24}$ = Rs. 15,00,000

As per question, gifted by Avinash to Ghanashyam Rs. 15,00,000 × $\frac{1}{2}$ = Rs. 7,50,000.

The entry will be :

Avinash Capital A/c	Dr.	7,50,000	
To Ghanashyam Capital A/c			7,50,000

3. **Adjustments made for Goodwill on Admission**

Ghanashyam's share of Goodwill Rs. 15,00,000 × $\frac{1}{4}$ = Rs. 3,75,000

Out of which Gifted by Avinash Rs. 3,75,000 × $\frac{1}{2}$ Rs. 1,87,500

Balnce for Avinash and Chinoy in 2 : 1 = 1,87,500 × $\frac{2}{3}$ = Rs. 1,25,000

and Rs. 1,87,500 × $\frac{1}{3}$ = Rs. 62,500.

The entry will be :

		Rs.	Rs.
Ghanbashyam's Capital A/c	Dr.	1,87,500	
To Avinash Capital A/c			1,25,300
" Chinmoy Ltd. A/c			62,500

Illustration 10

Ashima, Chandrani and Chaitali, all engineers, are equal partners in "Ladies' Own Ltd." On 31.12.1994 Ashima retired due to old age and on next day her daughter Rupa, also an engineer, joined the firm. The new profit-sharing ratio was decided to be Chandrani $\frac{2}{5}$ths, Chaitali $\frac{2}{5}$ths and Rupa $\frac{1}{5}$th.

Balance Sheet as on 31.12.94 was :

Liabilities	*Rs.*	*Assets*	*Rs.*
Capital :		Furniture	10,000
Ashima	20,000	Books	5,000
Chandrani	20,000	Joint Life Policy	19,000
Chaitali	19,000	Cash	8,000
Creditors	2,500	Equipments	20,000
Outstanding Expenses	500		
	62,000		62,000

You have been given the following information :

(a) Up to 31.12.94 the accounts were prepared on cash basis, but on and from 1.1.95, it was decided to change the method to accrual basis and on that day Ashima was credited with Rs. 7,500 as her share of accrued fees, the other two partners were also credited with their shares in equal ratio.

(b) Ashima was also credited with Rs. 7,000 as her share of goodwill. But it was decided not to open goodwill account.

(c) On revaluation the value of Furniture was increased by Rs. 3,000, Books by Rs. 2,000, and Equipments by Rs. 7,000.

(d) Ashima agreed to takeover the Joint Life Policy at its book value.

(e) Rupa contributed Rs. 6,000 in cash as her share of goodwill.

(f) The balance in Ashima's capital account after all the adjustments should be treated as Rupa's capital contribution. It was further decided that the Capital Account balances of Chandrani and Chaitali should be so adjusted as to make capital of all the three partners equal to Profit-sharing ratio keeping Rupas's Capital fixed and for that purpose any deficiency should be brought in cash or any surplus to be transferred to Current Account.

(g) The following were the transactions during the year ending on 31.12.1995 after Rupa's admission : Consultancy fees for supervision works in different organisations amounting to Rs. 59,600 (net) were deposited into Bank after the following payments (i) Salaries Rs. 16,000 (ii) Rent Rs. 13,000 (iii) Miscellaneous Expenses Rs. 7,200 (iv) Drawings—Chandrani Rs. 6,000, Chaitali Rs. 4,000, and Rupa Rs. 3,600.

On 31.12.95 fees accrued Rs. 14,000 and rent outstanding was Rs. 1,000. Two motor cars of Chandrani and Chaitali were taken over by the firm at Rs. 30,000 and Rs. 25,000, respectively, on 30.6.95. Depreciation is to be charged on Furniture, Books, Equipments, and Motor Cars @ 10% p.a.

You are asked to prepare (i) Balance Sheet and Revaluation Account on 1.1.95; (ii) Profit and Loss Account for the year ended 31.12.95; and (iii) Balance Sheet on 31.12.1995.

[CU BCom (Hons.) 1995]

Solution

It is a contradictory problem. Because, it states that up to 31.12.1994 accounts were kept on cash basis but Balance Sheet on that date contained outstanding expenses.

In the books of the firm
Revaluation Account

Dr. Cr.

Particulars		*Rs.*	*Particulars*	*Rs.*
To Capital A/c :			By Furniture A/c	3,000
Profit on Revaluation			" Books A/c	2,000
Ashima	4,000		" Equipments A/c	7,000
Chandrani	4,000			
Chaitali	4,000			
		12,000		
		12,000		12,000

Capital Account

Dr. Particulars	Ashima	Chandrani	Chaitali	Rupa	Cr. Particulars	Ashima	Chandrani	Chaitali	Rupa
	Rs.	Rs.	Rs.	Rs.		Rs.	Rs.	Rs.	Rs.
To Ashima's Capital A/c	—	3,500	3,500	—	By Balance b/d	20,000	20,000	19,000	—
" J. L. Policy A/c	19,000	—	—	—	" Accrued Fees A/c	7,500	7,500	7,500	—
" Rupa's Capital A/c *(bal. fig.)*	19,500	—	—	—	" Revaluation A/c—Profit	4,000	4,000	4,000	—
" Balance c/d	—	39,000	39,000	19,500[1]	" Chaitali Cap. A/c	3,500	—	—	—
					" Chandrani Cap. A/c	3,500	—	—	—
					" Ashima Cap. A/c	—	—	—	19,500
					" Goodwill A/c	—	3,000	3,000	—
					" Cash A/c *(bal. fig.)*	—	8,000	9,000	—
	38,500	42,500	42,500	19,500		38,500	42,500	42,500	19,500

Balance Sheet *as at 1st Jan. 1995*

Liabilities		Rs.	Assets	Rs.
Capitals :			Furniture	13,000
Chandrani	39,000		Books	7,000
Chaitali	39,000		Equipments	27,000
Rupa	19,500		Accrued Fees	22,500
		97,500	Cash (Rs. 8,000 + Rs. 6,000 + Rs. 8,000	
Creditors		2,500	Rs. 9,000)	31,000
Outstanding Expenses		500		
		1,00,500		1,00,500

Profit and Loss Account *for the year ended 31st December 1995*

Dr.		Rs.	Cr.	Rs.
To Salary		16,000	By Fees Receivable A/c	1,00,900[2]
" Rent	13,000			
Add : Outstanding for 95	1,000			
		14,000		
" Misc. Expenses	7,200			
Less : Outstanding for 94	500			
		6,700		
" Depreciation		7,450[3]		
" Net Profit c/d		56,750		
		1,00,900		1,00,900
To Share of Profit :			By Net Profit b/d	56,750
Chandrani $\frac{2}{5}$	22,700			
Chaitali $\frac{2}{5}$	22,700			
Rupa $\frac{1}{5}$	11,350			
		56,750		
		56,750		56,750

Dr. **Capital Account** Cr.

	Particulars	Chand-rani	Chaitali	Rupa		Particulars	Chand-rani	Chaitali	Rupa
		Rs.	Rs.	Rs.			Rs.	Rs.	Rs.
To	Drawings A/c	6,000	4,000	3,600	By	Balance b/d	39,000	39,000	19,500
"	Balance c/d	85,700	82,700	27,250	"	Motor Car A/c	30,000	25,000	—
					"	Share of Profit A/c	22,700	22,700	11,350
		91,700	86,700	30,850			91,700	86,700	30,850

Balance Sheet *as at 31st Dec. 1995*

Liabilities		Rs.	Assets	Rs.
Capital Accounts :			Furniture (13,000 – 1,300)	11,700
Chandrani	85,700		Books (7,000 – 700)	6,300
Chaitali	82,700		Equipment (27,000 – 2,700)	24,300
Rupa	27,250		Motor Car (55,000 – 2,750)	52,250
		1,95,650	Accrued Fees	14,000
Outstanding Expenses		1,000	Cash	31,000
Sundry Creditors		2,500	Bank (net fees deposited)	59,600
		1,99,150		1,99,150

Workings :

1. After Ashima's retirement, gaining ratio between Chandrani and Chaitali is equal i.e., 1 : 1 (or Chandrani $= \frac{2}{5} - \frac{1}{3} = \frac{1}{15}$ and Chaitali $= \frac{2}{5} - \frac{1}{3} = \frac{1}{15}$). And, Rupa's Capital for $\frac{1}{5}$ share Rs. 19,500 so, Chandrani and Chaitali's share for $\frac{2}{5}$ Rs. 39,000 each.
2. Fees Receivable = Rs. 59,600 + Rs. 36,200 + Rs. 13,600 + Rs. 14,000 – Rs. 22,500 = Rs. 1,00,900.
3. Depreciation on :

		Rs.
Furniture	13,000 × 10%	1,300
Equipment	27,000 × 10%	2,700
Books	7,000 × 10%	700
Motor Car	$55{,}000 \times 10\% \times \frac{6}{12}$	2,750
		7,450

Illustration 11

Ardeshir, Burjor and Cawasji are partners of M/s Evergreen & Co. sharing profits and losses in the ratio of 3 : 3 : 2.Their Balance Sheet as on 30th September 2012 was :

	Rs.	Rs.
Fixed Assets		
Cost	3,00,000	
Less : Depreciation	1,80,000	1,20,000
Investment : Cost (Market Value Rs. 2,00,000)		80,000
Working Capital		3,00,000
		5,00,000
Finance by		
Loans from : Dorab	1,50,000	
Engineer	1,00,000	2,50,000
Reserves		1,00,000
Capitals : Bujor (Cr.)	2,00,000	
Cawasji (Cr.)	1,00,000	
	3,00,000	
Less : Ardeshir (Dr.)	1,50,000	1,50,000
		5,00,000

On that day Ardeshir retired from business. Burjor and Cawasji decided to admit Dorab as a partner and Engineer, who was a minor, to benefits of partnership. Burjor, Casasji, Dorab and Engineer are to share profits in the ratio of 3 : 3 : 2 : 2.

For the purpose of the above retirement-cum-admission it is decided that :

(a) Goodwill of the firm to be valued at Rs. 2,00,000. However, no account is to appear for goodwill. Treatment for goodwill in relation to minor is to be deferred to the date when he opts to be a partner on attaining majority, when the value of goodwill will be deemed, for this purpose, to remain unchanged at Rs. 2,00,000.

(b) Ardeshir takes over :

(i) Building (cost Rs. 1,00,000, written-down value Rs. 35,000) for Rs. 75,000.

(ii) Investments (cost Rs. 10,000) of their market value of Rs. 5,000.

(c) The continuing partners take over the remaining assets at their book values, except investments, which are taken over at their market values.

(d) Loans are to be transferred to capital accounts.

(e) The amount due to/from Ardeshir is to be settled by cheque immediately.

You are required to prepare : (a) the Revaluation/Adjustment Account; (b) the Capital Accounts; and (c) the Balance Sheet of the firm after giving effect to the above points of agreement.

Solution :

(a)

In the books of M/s Evergreen & Co.

Revaluation Account

Dr. *Cr.*

Particulars		Rs.	*Particulars*	Rs.
To Investment (which was taken over by Ardeshir)		5,000	By Building A/c	40,000
" Capital A/c			" Investment A/c (Rs. 1,95,000 – Rs. 70,000)	1,25,000
Profit on Revaluation :				
Ardeshir	60,000			
Burjor	60,000			
Cawasji	40,000			
		1,60,000		
		1,65,000		1,65,000

Capital Account

Dr. *Cr.*

Particulrs	*Ardeshir*	*Burjor*	*Cawasji*	*Dorab*	*Engineer*	*Particulars*	*Ardeshir*	*Burjor*	*Cawasji*	*Dorab*	*Engineer*
	Rs.	Rs.	Rs.	Rs.	Rs.		Rs.	Rs.	Rs.	Rs.	Rs.
To Balance b/d	1,50,000	—	—	—	—	By Balance b/d	—	2,00,000	1,00,000	—	—
" Ardeshir	—	—	25,000	50,000	—	" Cawasji A/c	25,000	—	—	—	—
To Building A/c	75,000	—	—	—	—	By Dorab A/c (Goodwill)	50,000	—	—	—	—
" Investment A/c	5,000	—	—	—	—	" Revaluation A/c —Profit	60,000	60,000	40,000	—	—
" Balance c/d	—	2,97,500	1,40,000	1,00,000	1,00,000	" Reserve A/c	37,500	37,500	25,000	—	—
						" Loans A/c	—	—	—	1,50,000	1,00,000
						" Bank (bal.fig.)	57,500	—	—	—	—
	2,30,000	2,97,500	1,65,000	1,50,000	1,00,000		2,30,000	2,97,500	1,65,000	1,50,000	1,00,000

Balance Sheet *as at Sept. 30,2012*

Liabilities	Rs.	Rs.	*Assets*	Rs.	Rs.
Capital A/c :			Fixed Asset	2,00,000	
Burjor	2,97,500		*Less :* Depreciation	1,15,000	
Cawasji	1,40,000				85,000
Dorab	1,00,000		Investments		1,95,000
Engineer	1,00,000		Working Capital		3,57,500
		6,37,500			
		6,37,500			6,37,500

Workings :

		Rs.			Rs.
1.	**Fixed Assets**		2.	**Provision for Depreciation**	
	Balance b/d	3,00,000		Opening Balance	1,80,000
	Add : Profit on Rev.			*Less* : Transfer from asset taken over	
	(75,000 – 35,000)	40,000		to be adjusted	65,000
		3,40,000			1,15,000
	Less : Prov. for Dep.	65,000			
		2,75,000			
	Less : Ardeshir (taken over)	75,000			
		2,00,000			

ASSIGNMENT MATERIALS

PRACTICAL

1. X and Y were two partners sharing profits and losses equally. On 30. 6. 2006, X decides to retire. His son Z was admitted as a partner with $\frac{1}{3}$rd share in the future profits.

The Balance Sheet of the firm as on 30. 6. 2006 was :

	Rs.	Rs.		Rs.
Capital :			Goodwill	75,000
X	2,67,500		Land and Building	2,00,000
Y	2,36,000		Motor Car	60,000
		5,03,500	Furniture	47,500
Reserve		8,000	Debtors	1,20,000
Creditors		73,500	Cash	82,500
		5,85,000		5,85,000

It was further decided that (a) Goodwill would be raised to Rs. 1,05,000, (b) Value of Land and Building would be increased by Rs. 46,000, (c) Provision for Bad Debts would be created @ $2\frac{1}{2}$ % on debtors.

X took motor Car at book value. Y and Z introduced sufficient capital to pay X and leave thereafter a sum of Rs. 36,750 as liquid cash in the firm. They introduced cash in such a manner that their capitals in the new firm stood in the proportion of their profit-sharing ratio. The partners decided not to show goodwill as asset Partners introduced or took back cash on 1. 7. 2006.

Prepare the necessary accounts and the Balance Sheet of the firm.

[Ans. Total of Balance Sheet Rs. 4,47,250; Capital of the new firm Rs. 3,73,700; Cash brought in by Y Rs. 42,666; and by Z Rs. 1,59,584; Paid to X Rs. 2,48,000]

2. Laurel and Hardy were carrying on the business as equal partners. It was agreed that Laurel should retire from the firm on 31.3.2013, and his son, Charlie, should join from 1.4.2013, and should be entitled to one-third of the profits of the partnership.

The Balance Sheet of the firm on 31.3.2013 was as follows :

Liabilities	Rs.	Rs.	*Assets*	Rs.
Creditors		9,800	Cash at Bank	11,000
Capital :			Debtors	16,100
Laurel	34,000		Furniture	14,200
Hardy	28,200		Building	20,700
		62,200	Goodwill	10,000
		72,000		72,000

On 31.3.2013, Goodwill was valued at Rs. 22,000 and Building at Rs. 24,000. It was agreed that enough money should be introduced to enable Laurel to be paid out and leave Rs. 10,000 by way of

working capital. Hardy and Charlie were to provide such sums as would make their capitals proportionate to their share of profits. Laurel agreed to make a personal loan to Charlie by transfer from his capital account half of the amounts which Charlie had to provide.

Hardy and Charlie paid in cash due from them on 1.4.2013, and the amount due to Laurel was paid out on the same day.

[Ans. Cash to be bought in by Hardy Rs. 15,150 and by Charlie Rs. 12,750, Cash to be paid to Laurel Rs. 28,900]

3. Hing and Ting were carrying on business as equal partners. On 1.4.1985, they agreed that Ting would retire from partnership with effect from 30.6.1985 and his son Chhat would join the firm as a partner with effect from 1.7.1985 with a fourth share of the profits of the firm.

The Balance Sheet of the firm as on 30.6.1985, is:

Liabilities	Rs.	Rs.	*Assets*	Rs.
Capital :			Plant and Machinery	25,000
Hing	30,400		Furniture and Fixtures	10,000
Ting	24,400		Stock-in-trade	12,000
		54,800	Sundry Debtors	8,800
Sundry Creditors		8,400	Cash at Bank	5,950
			Cash in hand	1,450
		63,200		63,200

The agreement contained the following further provisions :

(a) Goodwill shall be valued at Rs. 15,000 and shall be raised in the books of the firm.

(b) The Plant and Machinery, and Furniture and Fixtures shall be revalued at Rs. 27,500 and Rs. 8,500, respectively.

(c) Stock shall be reduced to its market value of Rs. 11,020.

(d) A Reserve for Bad and Doubtful Debts @ $2\frac{1}{2}$ % shall be raised against Sundry Debtors.

(e) The existing Cash and Bank balance shall be maintained.

(f) Chhat's capital shall be in proportion to his profit-sharing ratio.

(g) One-third of the capital to be contributed by Chhat would be transferred to him by his father and the balance should be brought in by him in cash.

(h) Hing would also bring in or withdraw any amount in order to make his capital proportionate to his profit-sharing ratio.

(i) Ting would be paid his dues in cash in full settlement.

Show the journal entries necessary to give effect to the above arrangements and draw the Balance Sheet after reconstitution.

[Ans. Ting transferred to Chhat Rs. 5,800 and he is to be paid in Cash; Rs. 26,000. Hing is to bring Cash Rs. 14,400 and Chhat Rs. 11,600; Total of Balance Sheet Rs. 78,000]

4. M, A and V were in partnership sharing profits and losses in the ratio 3 : 2 : 1. Their Balance Sheet as on 31st March 1994 was:

Balance Sheet
as on 31st March 1994

Liabilities		Rs.	*Assets*		Rs.
Capitals :			Cash in hand		2,600
M	5,000		Trade Debtors	17,900	
A	8,000		*Less* : Provision	1,000	
V	9,000				16,900
		22,000	Plant and Machinery		17,000
Trade Creditors		10,700	Furniture and Fixtures		3,000
Workmen's Accident Compensation Fund		5,000			
General Reserve		1,800			
		39,500			39,500

Vikram retired on this date. It was agreed that :

(a) Plant and Machinery to be revalued at Rs. 19,400, Provision on Debtors be kept at Rs. 1,900 and Liability for Workmen's Accident Compensation was decided at Rs. 2,300.

(b) V should get, apart from other amounts due to him, his shares in Goodwill Rs. 4,000. Partners decided not to show Goodwill Account in the books.

(c) The total amount payable to V was brought by M and A in their profit-sharing ratio.

Immediately after this, they admitted P as a partner on his bringing Rs. 8,000 as share in Goodwill and Rs. 14,000 as Capital. It was agreed that M, A, and P will hereafter share the profits and losses equally.

You are required to prepare—(i) Revaluation Account, (ii) Partners' Capital Accounts and (iii) Balance Sheet after all adjustments are carried out.

[Ans. Paid to V Rs. 14,000; Balance of Capital A/c : M Rs. 20,400; A Rs. 15,600; P Rs. 14,000; Total of Balance Sheet Rs. 63,000]

5. The Balance Sheet of A, B, and C who were in partnership sharing profits and losses in the ratio of 3 : 2 : 1, respectively, was as follows on 30.6.1992 :

	Rs.		Rs.
Sundry Creditors	12,800	Goodwill	50,000
Loan from D	14,600	Machinery	30,000
Capital Accounts :		Stock	16,500
A	50,620	Sundry Debtors	18,900
B	40,530	Cash in hand	1,200
C	13,830	Cash at Bank	15,780
	1,32,380		1,32,380

B retires from the partnership. A dissolution deed is drawn up by the partners as on 30.6.1982, the terms of which were :

(a) The Profit and Loss Account of the year which showed a profit of Rs. 15,000 was to be reworked. C was to be allowed remuneration of Rs. 3,000 for extra work done by him. A's account had been credited with interest at 6% p.a. on his capital of Rs. 45,000. The rate of interest was to be reduced to 4%. Machinery was to be further depreciated by Rs. 3,550. No interest had been allowed to D for the past several years. His account is to be credited with simple interest at 5% p.a. for three years.

(b) Goodwill of the firm was to be valued at Rs. 72,000 and the profit-sharing basis was to be revised as from 1.7.1981 in the proportion of 2 : 2 : 1.

(c) B is to take over the loan of D subject to a discount of 5% to which D agrees. B is to be paid Rs. 10,000 in cash on retirement and the balance to equal instalments with interest at 6% p.a.

(d) A and B continue in business taking Y into partnership giving him $\frac{1}{4}$th share in the business. Y brings Rs. 12,000 in cash. He is unable to contribute anything towards Goodwill. However, he agrees to his account being debited for his proportionate share.

Show the entries. **[CA]**

6. A and B are equal partners. A, by agreement, retires and C joins the firm on the basis of one-third share of profits on 1.1.2010. The balances of the books as on 31.12.2009 were :

	Dr. Rs.	Cr. Rs.
Goodwill	10,000	
Fixed Assets—at cost	1,20,000	
Current Assets :		
Stock	60,000	
Debtors	40,000	
Bank Balance	8,000	
Creditors		20,000
Provision for Depreciation		12,000
Capital Accounts :		
A		1,04,000
B		1,02,000
	2,38,000	2,38,000

Goodwill and Fixed Assets valued at Rs. 30,000 and Rs. 1,40,000, respectively, and it was agreed to be written-up accordingly before admission of C as partner. Sufficient money is to be introduced so as to enable A to be paid-off and leave Rs. 5,000 cash at Bank; B and C are to provide such sum as to make their capitals proportionate to their share of profit. Assuming the agreement was carried out, show the Journal entries required and prepare the Balance Sheet after admission of C.

[Ans. Capital of the new firm Rs. 2,55,000; Cash brought in by B Rs. 42,000 and C Rs. 85,000; Paid to A Rs. 1,30,000; Total of Balance Sheet Rs. 2,75,000]

7. Ram & Co. is a partnership firm with the partners A, B, and C sharing profits and losses in the ratio of 5 : 3 : 2. The Balance Sheet of the firm as on 30th June 2012 is :

Liabilities	Rs.	*Assets*	Rs.
Capital :		Land and Buildings	2,10,000
A	80,000	Plant and Machinery	1,30,000
B	20,000	Fixture and Fittings	40,000
C	30,000	Investments	12,000
Reserve	20,000	Stock	1,26,000
Long-term Loan	3,00,000	Debtors	1,39,000
Bank Overdraft	44,000		
Trade Creditors	1,63,000		
	6,57,000		6,57,000

It was mutually agreed that B will retire from partnership and in his place D will be admitted as a partner with effect from 1st July 2012. For this purpose, this following agreements are to be made :

(a) Goodwill is to be valued at Rs. 1,00,000 but the same will not appear as an asset in the books of the reconstituted firm.

(b) Land and Building and Plant and Machinery are to be depreciated by 10% and 5%, respectively. Investments are to be taken over by the retiring partner at Rs. 15,000. Provision of 20% is to be made as debtors to cover doubtful debt.

(c) In the reconstituted firm, the total capital will be Rs. 2,00,000 which will be contributed by A, C, and D in this new profit-sharing ratio which is 2 : 2 : 1.

(d) The surplus fund, if any, will be used for repaying the Bank Overdraft.

(e) The amount due to retiring partner shall be transferred to his Loan A/c.

You are requested to prepare (1) Revaluation Account, (2) Partners' Capital Account, (3) Bank Account, and (4) Balance Sheet of the reconstituted firm on 1st July 2012.

[Ans. B's Loan A/c Rs. 25,310; Closing Balance of Capital A/c A Rs. 80,000; C Rs. 80,000, D Rs. 40,000; Total of Balance Sheet Rs 6,88,310]

8. G and M were working in partnership sharing profits and losses equally. On 31.3.1979, G decided to retire and in his place it was decided that K would be admitted as a partner from 1.4.1979 and his share in the profits will be $\frac{1}{3}$. The Balance Sheet of the firm as on 31.3.2009 was :

Liabilities		Rs.	*Assets*	Rs.
Sundry Creditors		36,750	Goodwill	37,500
Capitals :			Land and Building	1,00,125
G	1,35,750		Motor Cars	30,000
M	1,20,000		Furniture	23,250
		2,55,750	Sundry Debtors	60,375
			Cash at Bank	41,250
		2,92,500		2,92,500

It was further decided:

(1) The Goodwill should be raised to Rs. 52,500.

(2) The value of Land and Building would be increased by Rs. 20,700.

(3) G should take Motor Car at book value.

(4) M and K would introduce sufficient capital to pay G and leave thereafter a sum of Rs. 18,375 as working cash in a manner that the capital of the new partners will be in the proportion to their profit-sharing ratio.

(5) The capital payable by K was to be gifted to him by G.

(6) The partners decided not to show Goodwill as asset.

(7) The partners introduced cash on 1.4.1979.

Prepare Profit and Loss Adjustment Account, Partners' Capital Accounts and Cash Account.

[Ans. Profit on Revaluation (including the appreciated value of Goodwill) Rs. 35,700; Amount Paid to G Rs. 44,075; Cash to be brought in by M Rs. 21,200]

E. CHANGE IN PROFIT-SHARING RATIO

Sometimes, it becomes necessary to change the profit-sharing ratio among the partners in a partnership firm. Naturally, due to the change in profit-sharing ratio one or more partners may acquire extra share sacrificed by other or others. Therefore, necessary adjustments are to be made for this purpose on the same principle as in the case of admission of a partner for over-under valuation of asset and liabilities, goodwill, Life Insurance Policy, accumulated profits and losses etc. As a result, if there is a change in profit-sharing ratio, the said profits or losses are to be adjusted either by preparing a Memorandum Revaluation Account or by preparing a Statement.

Illustration 1

The following is the Balance Sheet of A, B, and C as at 31.12.2011. The partners agree that from 1.1.2012, they will share profits and losses in the ratio of 4 : 3 : 3, instead of their old ratio 3 : 2 : 1.

Balance Sheet *as on 31.12.2011*

Liabilities	Rs.	Rs.	*Assets*	Rs.
Capital			Goodwill	30,000
A	50,000		Land and Building	40,000
B	40,000		Plant and Machinery	20,000
C	30,000		Sundry Debtors	25,000
		1,20,000	Stock	15,000
General Reserve		12,000	Cash and Bank	20,000
Sundry Creditors		18,000		
		1,50,000		1,50,000

The assets of the firm were revalued as :

Goodwill Rs. 40,000; Land and Building Rs. 50,000; Plant and Machinery Rs. 15,000; Stock Rs. 12,000; Sundry Debtors at book values.

Show by means of a single Journal entry the adjustments to be made on the occasion of the change in profit-sharing ratio, if the partners decide not to alter the figures of the assets or reserve in the books.

Solution :

In the books of A, B, and C

Memorandum Revaluation Account *for the year ended 31st Dec. 2012*

Dr. *Decrease in Assets*	Rs.	Rs.	Cr. *Increase in Assets*	Rs.	Rs.
To Plant and Machinery		5,000	By Goodwill		10,000
" Stock		3,000	" Land and Building		10,000
" Profit on Revaluation :			" Reserve		12,000
A $\frac{3}{6}$	12,000				
B $\frac{2}{6}$	8,000				
C $\frac{1}{6}$	4,000				
		24,000			
		32,000			32,000
To *Reversal of items*		20,000	By *Reversal of items*		8,000
" Reserve		12,000	" Profit written-back :		
			A $\frac{4}{10}$	9,600	
			B $\frac{3}{10}$	7,200	
			C $\frac{3}{10}$	7,200	
					24,000
		32,000			32,000

Net Adjustment :

	Credit Rs.	Debit Rs.	Net Adjustment Rs.	
A's Capital	12,000	9,600	2,400	(Cr.)
B's Capital	8,000	7,200	800	(Cr.)
C's Capital	4,000	7,200	3,200	(Dr.)

In the books of A, B, and C
Journal

Date	Particulars	L.F.	Debit Rs.	Credit Rs.
	C's Capital A/c Dr.		3,200	
	To A's Capital A/c			2,400
	" B's Capital A/c			800
	(Adjustment for revaluation of asset without changing the book value of the same changed in new profit-sharing ratio.)			

Illustration 2

Raju, Shashtri, and Tanka are partners in a firm, sharing profits and losses in the ratio of 5 : 3 : 2. Their Balance Sheet, as on 31st March 2012, stood as :

Balance Sheet

Liabilities	Rs.	Rs.	Assets	Rs.	Rs.
Sundry Creditors		25,000	Cash at Bank		10,000
General Reserve		20,000	Sundry Debtors	22,000	
Shashtri's Loan Account		15,000	*Less* : Reserve for Bad Debts	2,000	
Capital Accounts :					20,000
Raju	25,000		Furniture		10,000
Shashtri	10,000		Plant and Machinery		35,000
Tanka	5,000	40,000	Stock		25,000
		1,00,000			1,00,000

From 1st April 2012, the partners decided to change their profit-sharing ratio as 2 : 1 : 2 instead of their former ratio of 5 : 3 : 2 and for that purpose the following adjustments were agreed upon :

(i) The reserve for bad debt was to be raised to 10%.
(ii) Furniture was to be appreciated by Rs. 5,200.

They did not, however, want to alter the book values of the assets and reserves but record the change by passing one single Journal entry.

The Profit and Loss Account of the firm for the year ended 31st March 2013 showed a net profit of Rs. 22,900. You are required :

(a) to show the single Journal entry adjusting the partners' capital as on 1st April 2012, and
(b) to prepare the Profit and Loss Appropriation Account for the year ended 31st March 2013 after taking into consideration the following adjustments : (i) Interest on Capital at 5% p.a.; (ii) Interest on Shashtri's loan; and (iii) Transfer 25% of the divisible profit to the Reserve Fund after charging such Reserve.

Solution

(a)

In the books of Raju, Shashtri, and Tanka
Memorandum Revaluation Account
for the year ended 31st March, 2012

Dr. Cr.

Particulars	Rs.	Rs.	Particulars	Rs.	Rs.
To Reserve for Bad Debts		200	By Furniture		5,200
To Profit on Revaluation :			" General Reserve		20,000
Raju $\frac{5}{10}$	12,500				
Shashtri $\frac{3}{10}$	7,500				
Tanka $\frac{2}{10}$	5,000	25,000			
		25,200			25,200

Contd.

		Rs.				Rs.
To	*Reversal of items*	5,200	By	*Reversal of items*		200
"	General Reserve	20,000	"	Profit written-back		
				Raju $\frac{2}{5}$	10,000	
				Shashtri $\frac{1}{5}$	5,000	
				Tanka $\frac{2}{5}$	10,000	25,000
		25,200				25,200

Net Adjustments

	Credit	Debit	Net Adjustments	
	Rs.	Rs.	Rs.	
Raju	12,500	10,000	2,500	(Cr.)
Shashtri	7,500	5,000	2,500	(Cr.)
Tanka	5,000	10,000	5,000	(Dr.)

Journal

Date	*Particulars*	*L.F.*	*Debit* Rs.	*Credit* Rs.
	Tanka's Capital A/c Dr.		5,000	
	To Raju's Capital A/c			2,500
	" Shashtri's Capital A/c			2,500
	(Adjustment made for revaluation of asset without changing book values of the same changed in new profit-sharing ratio.)			

(b)

Dr. **Profit and Loss Appropriation Account** *for the year ended 31st March 2013* *Cr.*

Particulars	Rs.	*Amount* Rs.	*Particulars*	*Amount* Rs.
To Interest on Capital :			By Profit and Loss A/c —Net Profit	22,900
Raju @ 5% on (25,000 + 2,500)	1,375			
Shashtri @ 5% on (10,000 + 2,500)	625	2,000		
" Interest on Loan : Shashtri @ 6%		900		
" Reserve Fund @ 25%		4,000		
" Divisible Profit				
Raju $\frac{2}{5}$	6,400			
Shashtri $\frac{1}{5}$	3,200			
Tanka $\frac{2}{5}$	6,400	16,000		
		22,900		22,900

Note : Interest on Tanka's Capital Account will be nil, since his capital balance is also nil (5,000 – 5,000)

Illustration 3

Vishal, Sudip, and Arup are partners in a firm sharing profits and losses as 8 : 5 : 3. Their Balance Sheet as at 31st Dec. 1998 was as follows :

	Rs.		Rs.
Sundry Creditors	1,50,000	Cash	40,000
General Reserve	80,000	Bills Receivable	50,000
Partners' Loan A/c :		Sundry Debtors	60,000
Vishal	40,000	Stock	1,20,000
Sudip	30,000	Fixed Asset	2,80,000
Partners' Capital A/c :			
Vishal	1,00,000		
Sudip	80,000		
Arup	70,000		
	5,50,000		5,50,000

From 1st Jan. 1999, they agree to alter their profit-sharing ratio 5 : 6 : 5. It is also decided that :

(a) the fixed asset should be valued at Rs. 3,31,000.
(b) a provision of 5% on Sundry Debtors is made for doubtful debts.
(c) the goodwill of the firm at this date be valued at 3 years' purchase of the average net profits of the last five years before charging insurance premium; and the stock to be reduced to Rs. 1,12,000.

There is a joint life insurance policy for Rs. 2,00,000 for which an annual premium of Rs. 10,000 is paid, the premium being charged to Profit and Loss Account. The surrender value of the policy on 31st Dec. 1998 was Rs. 78,000.

The net profits of the firm for the last 5 years were Rs. 14,000; Rs. 17,000; Rs. 20,000; Rs. 22,000; and Rs. 27,000. Goodwill and Surrender Value of the joint life policy was not to appear in the books.

Draft Journal entries necessary to adjust the capital accounts of the partners and prepare the revised Balance Sheet.

[CA Foundation Adapted]

Solution

In the books of the firm
Journal

Date	Particulars		L.F.	Debit Rs.	Credit Rs.
1999 Jan. 1	General Reserve A/c	Dr.		80,000	
	To Vishal Capital A/c				40,000
	" Sudip's Capital A/c				25,000
	" Arup's Capital A/c				15,000
	(General Reserve transferred to Partners' Capital Account.)				
	Revaluation A/c	Dr.		11,000	
	To Stock A/c				8,000
	" Prov. for Bad Debts A/c				3,000
	(Value of stock reduced and provisions made for bad debts.)				
	Fixed Asset A/c	Dr.		51,000	
	To Revaluation A/c				51,000
	(Value of fixed assets increased.)				
	Revaluation A/c	Dr.		40,000	
	To Vishal's Capital A/c				20,000
	" Sudip's Capital A/c				12,500
	" Arup's Capital A/c				7,500
	(Profit on revaluation transferred.)				
	Sudip's Capital A/c	Dr.		10,500	
	Arup's Capital A/c	Dr.		21,000	
	To Vishal's Capital A/c				31,500
	(Adjustment made for goodwill and Joint Life Policy.)				

Although Capital Accounts are not wanted the same is prepared as under for preparing the Balance Sheet.

Dr. **Capital Account** Cr.

Particulars	Vishal Rs.	Sudip Rs.	Arup Rs.	Particulars	Vishal Rs.	Sudip Rs.	Arup Rs.
To Vishal's Capital A/c	—	10,500	21,000	By Balance b/d	1,00,000	80,000	70,000
" Balance c/d	1,91,500	1,07,000	71,500	" Revaluation A/c —Profit	20,000	12,500	7,500
				" General Reserved A/c	40,000	25,000	15,000
				" Sudip's Capital A/c	10,500	—	—
				Arup's Capital A/c	21,000	—	—
	1,91,500	1,17,500	92,500		1,91,500	1,17,500	92,500

Balance Sheet *as at 1st January 1999*

Liabilities	Rs.	Rs.	*Assets*	Rs.	Rs.
Capital A/c :			Fixed Assets		3,31,000
Vishal	1,91,500		Stock		1,12,000
Sudip	1,07,000		Sundry Debtors	60,000	
Arup	71,500	3,70,000	*Less* : Reserve for Bad Debts	3,000	
Partners' Loan A/c :					57,000
Vishal	40,000		Bills Receivable		50,000
Sudip	30,000	70,000	Cash		40,000
Sundry Creditors		1,50,000			
		5,90,000			5,90,000

Workings :

1. **Adjustments made for Goodwill and Joint Life Policy**

	Rs.
Average Profit = $\frac{14,000 + \text{Rs. } 17,000 + \text{Rs. } 20,000 + \text{Rs. } 22,000 + \text{Rs. } 27,000}{5}$	20,000
Add : Insurance Premium (p.a.)	10,000
Profit before charging insurance premium	30,000

∴ Value of Goodwill
= Average Profit × 3 years' purchase
= Rs. 30,000 × 3
= Rs. 90,000

	Rs.
Value of Goodill =	90,000
Add : Surrender Value of J. L. Policy	78,000
	1,68,000

Net Effect

	Vishal Rs.	Sudip Rs.	Arup Rs.
Profit Rs. 1,68,000 (in old ratio i.e., 8 : 5 : 3)	84,000	52,500	31,500
Profit Rs. 1,68,000 (in new ratio i.e., 5 : 6 : 5)	52,500	63,000	52,500
Net Effect	31,500 (Cr.)	10,500 (Dr.)	21,000 (Dr.)

Change in Profit-Sharing Ratio during an accounting period

When the profit sharing ratio among the partners changes, the profit of the firm should be divided between/among the partners on the basis of such changes i.e., prior to change and after such change, usually on the basis of time. For example, the profit sharing ratio of A. B and C from 1st January to 30th June was 3 : 2 : 1, but from 1st July it changed to 1 : 1 : 1. Thus, profit should be divided into two parts prior to change i.e., for 6 months and after change, i.e., also for 6 months.

Consider the following illustration.

Illustration 4

A B and C were in partnership sharing profits and losses in the ratio 2 : 2 : 1. They furnished the following particulars:

Dr. **Trading and Profit and Loss Account** *for the year ended 31st December 2010* *Cr.*

Particulars	Rs.	*Amount* Rs.	*Particulars*	*Amount* Rs.
To Purchases		40,000	By Sales	1,50,000
" Other Direct Expenses		10,000	" Closing Stock	20,000
" Gross Profit		1,20,000		
		1,70,000		1,70,000
To Depreciation		5,000	By Gross Profit	1,20,000
" Misc. Expenses		15,000		
" Net Profit		1,00,000		
		1,20,000		1,20,000

From 1st January 2010, the partner dicided that A would get a salary Rs. 1,000 p.m. and profit should be distributed in the ratio 5 : 3 : 2. Sales were made evenly throughout the year.

Show the Profit and Loss Appropriation Account for the year ended 31st December 2010.

Solution

Profit and Loss Appropriation Account *for the year ended 31st December 2010*

Dr. Particulars	1.1.2010 to 30.6.2010	1,7,2010 to 31.12.2010	Particulars	1.1.2010 to 30.6.2010	1,7,2010 to 31.12.2010 Cr.
	Rs.	Rs.		Rs.	Rs.
To Salary			By Net Profit	50,000	50,000
A		6,000			
" Share of Profit					
A	20,000	22,000			
B	20,000	13,200			
C	10,000	8,800			
	50,000	50,000		50,000	50,000

Illustration 5

X and Y were in partnership sharing profits and losses in the ratio of 3 : 2. As per Partnership Deed partners were entitled to an interest on capital @ 1o% p.a. and interest on drawings @ 5% p.a. (on total drawings) and X was entitled to a partnership salary of Rs. 5,000 p.m.

From 1.1.2010, the agreement was changed. The changed deed provided that X's salary would be reduced to Rs. 400 p.m. and Y also would get a salary of Rs. 400 p.m. Profit share ratio was 4 : 1. Other things will be same. The accounting period was from 1st April to 31st March. The particulars were:

Net Profit from P & L A/c Rs. 60,000; Capital A/c : A Rs. 20,000, B Rs. 40,000; Current Account : A Rs. 5,000; B Rs. 8,000; Drawings A Rs. 12,000; B Rs. 16,000.

You are requested to prepare : (a) Profit and Loss Appropriation Account and the Current Account of the partners for the period ended 31st March 2010.

Solution

In the books of the firm

Profit and Loss Appropriation Account *for the year ended 31st March 2010*

Dr. Particulars	April to December	January to March	Particulars	April to December	January to March Cr.
	Rs.	Rs.		Rs.	Rs.
To Interest on Capital :			By Net Profit	45,000	15,000
X	1,500	500	(Time ratio 3 : 1)		
Y	3,000	1,000	" Interest on Drawings :		
" Salary :			X	450	150
X	4,500	1,200	Y	600	200
Y	—	1,200			
" Share of Profit :					
X	22,230	9,160			
Y	14,820	2,290			
	46,050	30,310		46,050	30,310

Current Account

Dr. Particulars	X	Y	Particulars	X	Y Cr.
	Rs.	Rs.		Rs.	Rs.
To Drawings	12,000	16,000	By Balance c/d	5,000	8,000
" Interest on Drawings	600	800	" Interest on Capital	2,000	4,000
" Balance c/d	31,490	13,510	" Salary	5,700	1,200
			" Share of Profit	31,390	17,110
	44,090	30,310		44,090	30,310

Workings :

1. **Interest on Capital**

	X	Y
	Rs.	Rs.
@ 10% on Rs. 20,000 on X on Y Rs. 40,000	2,000	4,000
April to December	1,500	3,000
January to March	500	1,000
	2,000	4,000

2. **Interest on Drawings**

	X	Y
	Rs	Rs.
@ 5% on Rs. 12,000 on b/d on Y Rs. 16,000	600	800
April to December	450	600
January to March	150	200
	600	800

3. Partner's Salary

	X	Y
	Rs.	Rs.
On X — @ 500 × 9	4,500	—
400 × 3	1,200	400 × 3 = 1,200
	1,200	1,200

F. AMALGAMATION OF FIRMS

When two or more sole traders or firms carrying on business of a similar nature decide to amalgamate to avoid cut-throat competition and to secure internal and external economies of large scale production etc., the same is called amalgamation of firms. In short, it indicates winding up of two or more existing firms and a new firm is formed to take over their business. As a result of the amalgamation, the old partners of the old firms become the partners of the new firm.

Amalgamation of partnership may be made possible:

1. **When two sole traders decide to form a partnership;**
2. **When two existing partnership firms amalgamate and form a new firm;**
3. **When an existing partnership takes a sole proprietorship business; and**
4. **When an existing partnership firm takes another partnership firm.**

Case 1

When two sole traders decide to form a partnership

Under the circumstances, the existing set of books are closed and a new set of accounts is opened for recording all transactions including assets and liabilities.

Steps to be followed

The following entries are to be passed in order to close the books of the old firm :

(i) A Realisation Account is to be prepared in order to incorporate the change in the value of assets and liabilities like admission of a partner. The profits or losses of Revaluation Account are to be transferred to Partners' Capital Account in profit-sharing ratio.

(ii) All undistributed reserves or profits or losses (appearing in Balance Sheet) are to be transferred to Partners' Capital Accounts.

(iii) The assets and liabilities which are not taken over by the new firm are to be transferred to Partners' Capital Account in the Capital Ratio.

(iv) The Capital Accounts of the partners are to be adjusted as per agreement of amalgamation.

(v) The following entries to be passed for all assets and liabilities which are taken over by new firm :

Purchase Consideration

Purchase considerations usually is computed on the basis of Net Asset i.e., Total Asset takenover minus liabilities taken over or Net Asset = Asset taken over – liabilities taken over.

Accounting Entries

(a) ***For transferring Sundry Assets***

Realisation A/c To Sundry Assets A/c (With the exception of Cash and Bank i.e., if not taken over by the new firm)	Dr.	at Balance Sheet Values.

(b) ***For transferring Sundry Liabilities***

Sundry Liabilities A/c To Realisation A/c	Dr.	at Balance Sheet Values.

(c) ***For the amount of Purchase consideration***

New Firm A/c To Realisation A/c	Dr.	with the amount of Puchase Consideration

(d) ***For the amount of Purchase consideration***

Capital in the New Firm A/c To New Firm A/c	Dr.	with the amount of Puchase Consideration

(e) ***If any asset is taken over by the proprietor***

Capital A/c To Realisation A/c	Dr.	at Balance Sheet Values.

Particulars		Remarks
(f) ***If any unrecorded asset is recorded***		
Asset A/c	Dr.	at Specific Values
To Capital A/c		
(g) ***If any unrecorded asset is sold***		
Bank A/c	Dr.	Do
To Asset A/c		
(h) ***If any asset is not taken over by the new firm but sold by the old firm***		
Bank A/c	Dr.	at Selling Price
To Realisation A/c		
(i) ***If any liabilityis not taken over by the new firm***		
Liabilities A/c	Dr.	at Balance Sheet Values
To Bank A/c		
(j) ***If any unrecorded liability is recorded***		
Capital A/c	Dr.	at Specific Values.
To Liabilities A/c		
(k) ***If any unrecorded liability is paid***		
Liabilities A/c	Dr.	Do
To Bank A/c		
(l) ***For realisation expenses***		
Realisation A/c	Dr.	with the amount of Realisation Expenss
To Bank A/c		
(m) ***For any accumulated profit or reserve***		
Profit and Loss A/c	Dr.	at Balance Sheet Values
Reserve A/c		
To Capital A/c		
(n) ***For any accumulated losses***		
Capital A/c	Dr.	at Balance Sheet Values
To Profit and Loss A/c		
(o) ***For profit on realisation***		
Realisation A/c	Dr.	with Profit on Realisation
To Capital A/c		
(p) ***For loss on realisation***		
Capital A/c	Dr.	with Loss on Realisation.
To Realisation A/c		
(q) ***For final settlement of account***		
Capital A/c	Dr.	For Final Settlement
To Capital in the new firm A/c		

Entries in the books of New Firm

Particulars		Remarks
(a) ***When assets and liabilities are taken over***		
Asset A/c	Dr.	—value of asset taken
Goodwill A/c	Dr.	—(difference i.e. if credit total is more)
To Liabilities A/c		—value of liabilities taken
" Capital A/c		—purchase consideration
" Capital ReserveA/c		—difference (if debit total is more)

Illustration 1

The following Balance Sheets were presented by Mr. X and Mr. Y, two sole traders, on 31st March 2010:

Balance Sheet *as at 31st March 2010*

Liabilities	X	Y	*Assets*	X	Y
	Rs.	Rs.		Rs.	Rs.
Capital	1,60,000	80,000	Fixed Assets	1,00,000	50,000
Creditors	30,000	20,000	Investments	10,000	5,000
Bills Payable	10,000	15,000	Stock	40,000	30,000
			Debrors	20,000	10,000
			Cash and Bank	30,000	20,000
	2,00,000	1,15,000		2,00,000	1,15,000

They formed a partnership firm under the title M/s X and Y from 1.4.2010 under the following conditions:

(a) Asset to be revalued as : Fixed assets to be appreciated by 20% (b) Investment were taken at book value (c) Stock to be reduced by 20%; (d) A provision to be made (@ 10% on Debtors for X and @ 20% of Y.

(b) The capital of the partnership firm would be Rs. 2,00,000 to be contributed by X and Y is 3 : 2.

(c) Realisation expenses amount to Rs. 2,000 for X and Rs. 1,000 for Y.

Show the entries in the books of X and Y and the Opening Balance Sheet of the new firm.

Solution :

1. Calculation of Purchase Consideration

Net Asset

	X	Y
	Rs.	Rs.
Fixed assets (10% increase)	1,20,000	60,000
Investment (at book value)	10,000	5,000
Stock (20% decrease)	32,000	24,000
Debtors (10% for X and 20% for Y)	18,000	8,000
Cash and Bank (Rs. 30,000 – Rs. 2,000) (Rs.20,000 – Rs. 1,000)	28,000	19,000
	2,08,000	1,16,000
Less : **Liabilities**		
Creditors	30,000	20,000
Bills Payable	10,000	15,000
	40,000	35,000
Net Assets	1,68,000	81,000

2. Capital as per agreement

	X	Y
Rs. 2,00,000 (in 3 : 2)	1,50,000	50,000
Less : Net Assets	1,68,000	81,000
Cash to be brought in	(–) 18,000	—
Cash to be withdrawn	—	(–) 31,000

In the books of X

Journal

Date	*Particulars*		L.F.	*Debit*	*Credit*
2010				Rs.	Rs.
April 1	Realisation A/c	Dr.		1,98,000	
	To Fixed Asset A/c				1,00,000
	" Investment A/c				10,000
	" Stock A/c				40,000
	" Debtors A/c				20,000
	" Bank A/c (30,000 – Exp. Rs. 2,000)				28,000
	(Transfer of asset to Realisation A/c)				
	Creditors A/c	Dr.		30,000	
	Bills Payable A/c	Dr.		10,000	
	To Realisation A/c				40,000
	(Transfer of liabilities to Realisation A/c)				
	X and Y A/c	Dr.		1,68,000	
	To Realisation A/c				1,68,000
	(Purchase consideration receivable A/c)				

Contd.

Date	Particulars		L.F.	Debit Rs.	Credit Rs.
	Realisation A/c	Dr.		2,000	
	To Bank A/c				2,000
	(Expenses of realisation paid)				
	Realisation A/c	Dr.		8,000	
	To Capital A/c				8,000
	(Profit on realisation transferred)				
	Capital in X and Y A/c	Dr.		1,68,000	
	To X and Y A/c				1,68,000
	(Settlement of purchase consideration)				
	Capital A/c	Dr.		1,68,000	
	To Capital in X and Y A/c				1,68,000
	(Final settlement to close the account)				

In the books of Y
Journal

Date	Particulars		L.F.	Debit Rs.	Credit Rs.
2010 April 1	Realisation A/c	Dr.		1,14,000	
	To Fixed Asset A/c				50,000
	" Investment A/c				5,000
	" Stock A/c				30,000
	" Debtors A/c				10,000
	" Cash and Bank A/c				19,000
	(Transfer of assets to Realisation A/c)				
	Creditors A/c	Dr.		20,000	
	Bills Payable A/c	Dr.		15,000	
	To Realisation A/c				35,000
	(Transfer of liabilities to Realisation A/c)				
	X and Y A/c	Dr.		81,000	
	To Realisation A/c				81,000
	(Purchase consideration receivable A/c)				
	Realisation A/c	Dr.		1,000	
	To Bank A/c				1,000
	(Expenses of realisation paid)				
	Realisation A/c	Dr.		1,000	
	To Capital A/c				1,000
	(Profit on realisation transferred)				
	Capital in X and Y A/c	Dr.		81,000	
	To X and Y A/c				81,000
	(Settlement of purchase consideration)				
	Capital A/c	Dr.		81,000	
	To Capital in X and Y A/c				81,000
	(Final settlement to close the account)				

Balance Sheet of the New Firm *as on 1st April, 2010*

Liabilities	Amount Rs.	Amount Rs.	Assets	Amount Rs.
Capital			Fixed Assets (Rs. 1,20,000 + Rs. 60,000)	1,80,000
X	1,50,000		Investment (Rs. 10,000 + Rs. 5,000)	15,000
Y	50,000		Stock (Rs. 32,000 + Rs. 24,000	56,000
		2,00,000	Debtors (Rs. 18,000 + Rs. 8,000)	26,000
Creditors (Rs. 30,000 + Rs. 20,000)		50,000		
Bills Payable (Rs. 10,000 + Rs. 15,000)		25,000		
Bank Overdraft		2,000[1]		
		2,77,000		2,77,000

Workings ;

1.

Bank A/c

Dr. Particulars	Rs.	Particulars	Cr. Rs.
To Balance b/d (Rs. 28,000 + Rs. 19,000)	47,000	By X's Capital A/c	18,000
" Balance c/d	2,090	" Y's Capital A/c	31,000
	49,090		49,090

Illustration 2

Mr. X and Mr. Y have been trading individually as Cardboard Box Manufacturers. They agree to enter into a partnership and to carry on their former business under the style of Messrs Water, Fall & Co., w.e.f. 1.1.2012. It is agreed :

(1) that each partner shall have a fixed capital of Rs. 10,000; (2) that X's stock is to be brought in at Rs. 3,250, and Y's stock at Rs. 2,750 as per valuation; (3) that the reserves for bad debts are to be increased to 6% on the debtors; (4) that Y is to dispose off his office furniture and fixtures to the best advantage; and (5) that any deficiency on the net assets brought in is to be paid into the firm's Bank Account.

The Balance Sheet of Mr X as at 31.12.2011 were :

Liabilities	Rs.	*Assets*		Rs.
Sundry Creditors	1,810	Office Furniture and Fixtures		350
Capital A/c	10,625	Plant and Machinery		5,000
		Stock		3,400
		Sundry Debtors	2,750	
		Less : Reserve for Bad Debts	120	
				2,630
		Cash at Bank		980
		Cash in hand		75
	12,435			12,435

The Balance Sheet of Mr. Y as at 31.12.2011 were :

Liabilities	Rs.	*Assets*		Rs.
Sundry Creditors	2,102	Office Furniture and Fixtures		200
Capital A/c	10,133	Plant and Machinery		5,500
		Stock		2,800
		Sundry Debtors	3,025	
		Less : Reserve for Bad Debts	100	
				2,925
		Cash at Bank		765
		Cash in hand		45
	12,235			12,235

Give the Journal entries necessary to adjust each **trader's books prior to amalgamation** and also draw the Balance Sheet of X, Y & Co., as at 1.1.2012.

Solution

In the books of Mr. X
Journal

Date	*Particulars*		L.F.	*Debit* Rs.	*Credit* Rs.
2012 Jan. 1	Capital A/c	Dr.		195	
	To Reserve for Bad Debts A/c				45
	" Stock A/c				150
	(Value of assets reduced and debited to Capital Account.)				
	Capital A/c	Dr.		430	
	To Bank A/c				430
	(Excess cash withdrawn.)				

In the books of Y
Journal

Date	Particulars		L.F.	Debit	Credit
2012				Rs.	Rs.
Jan. 1	Capital A/c	Dr.		331	
	To Reserve for Bad Debts A/c				50
	" Stock A/c				81
	" Furniture and Fixture A/c				200
	(Value of assets reduced and debited to Capital Account.)				
	Bank A/c	Dr.		198	
	To Capital A/c				198
	(Additional Capital brought in.)				

Balance Sheet as at 1st Jan. 2012

Liabilities		Rs.	Assets		Rs.
Capital Accounts			**Fixed Asset**		
X	10,000		Plant and Machinery		10,500
Y	10,000	20,000	Furniture and Fixtures		350
			Current Assets		
Current Liabilities			Stock		6,000
Sundry Creditors		3,912	Sundry Debtors	5,775	
			Less : Prov. for Bad Debts	346	
					5,429
			Cash at Bank		1,513*
			Cash in hand		120
		23,912			23,912

Workings :

Capital Account

Dr. *Cr.*

Particulars	X	Y	Particulars	X	Y
	Rs.	Rs.		Rs.	Rs.
To Sundry Asset A/c	195	331	By Balance b/d	10,625	10,133
" Bank A/c *(bal. fig.)*	430		" Bank A/c		
" Balance b/d	10,000	10,000	*(bal. fig.)*	—	198
	10,625	10,331		10,625	10,331

*** Bank Account**

Dr. *Cr.*

	Rs.		Rs.
To Balance b/d		By X's Capital A/c	430
(Rs. 980 + Rs. 765)	1,745	" Balance c/d	1,513
" Y's Capital A/c	198		
	1,943		1,943

Case 2

When two existing partnership firms amalgamate and form a new firm

Under the circumstances, the books of the old firm are to be closed by transferring to Realisation Account where all assets and liabilities are transferred.

The entries are similar to Case 1, stated above

Illustration 3

The Balance Sheet of Messrs 'A & B' and Messrs 'C & D' as on 31.12.2012 were :

Liabilities	'A & B'	'C & D'	Assets	'A & B'	'C & D'
	Rs.	Rs.		Rs.	Rs.
Capitals :			Land	10,000	12,000
A	10,000		Machinery	7,000	8,000
B	10,000		Furniture	3,000	3,500

Contd.

	Rs.	Rs.		Rs.	Rs.
C		10,000	Debtors	6,000	8,500
D		10,000	Stock	8,000	10,000
Creditors	15,000	10,000	Cash and Bank	3,000	1,000
Loan		10,000			
Outstanding Expenses	2,000	3,000			
	37,000	43,000		37,000	43,000

The two firms decide to amalgamate and form into A, B, C, D and Co. with effect from 1.1.2013. Partners would share profits and losses equally between themselves as they were doing prior to amalgamation and they agreed to following revaluation of assets and liabilities :

	'A & B'	'C & D'
	Rs.	Rs.
Land	10,000	10,000
Machinery	7,000	8,000
Furniture	2,500	2,500
Debtors	5,500	7,000
Stock	8,000	8,000
Outstanding Expenses	2,000	3,500

In addition to the above it was decided :

(i) that the new firm would not take over the loan of 'C & D';

(ii) that the Goodwill of 'A & B' and 'C & D' were valued at Rs. 10,000 and Rs. 5,000, respectively, in the first instant but for the purpose of the Balance Sheet of the new firm, the combined Goodwill would be valued at Rs. 12,000; and

(iii) that the reconstructed capitals of the partners would be Rs. 14,000 each, partners introducing cash, if necessary.

You are required to show :

(a) the entries in the books of 'A & B' and 'C & D'.

(b) the entries and the opening Balance Sheet of the new firm.

[CA]

Solution

Calculation of Purchase Consideration

Net Asset

			A & B		C & D
			Rs.		Rs.
	Land		10,000		10,000
	Machinery		7,000		8,000
	Furniture		2,500		2,500
	Debtors		5,500		7,000
	Stock		8,000		8,000
	Goodwill		10,000		5,000
			43,000		40,500
Less :	Creditors	15,000		10,000	
	Outstanding Expenses	2,000		3,500	
			17,000		13,500
	Purchase Consideration		26,000		27,000

In the books of 'A & B'

Journal

Date	*Particulars*		*L.F.*	*Debit*	*Credit*
				Rs.	Rs.
?	Realisation A/c	Dr.		37,000	
	To Land A/c				10,000
	" Machinery A/c				7,000
	" Furniture A/c				3,000
	" Debtors A/c				6,000
	" Stpcl A/c				8,000
	" Cash & Bank a/c				3,000
	(Transfer of amount to Realisation A/c)				

Contd.

Particulars		Rs.	Rs.
Creditors A/c	Dr.	15,000	
Outstanding Expenss A/c	Dr.	2,000	
To Realisation A/c			17,000
(Transfer of liabilities to Realisation A/c.)			
A B C D & Co. A/c	Dr.	26,000	
To Realisation A/c			26,000
(Purchase consideration receivable.)			
Realisation A/c	Dr.	6,000	
To A's Capital A/c			3,000
" B's Capital A/c			3,000
(Profit on realisation transfered.)			
Capital in A B C D A/c	Dr.	26,000	
To A's Capital A/c			13,000
" B's Capital A/c			13,000
(Settlement of purchase consideration.)			
A's Capital A/c	Dr.	13,000	
B's Capital A/c	Dr.	13,000	
To Capital in A B C D A/c			26,000
(Final settlement made.)			

Importment Information

The problem can be solved in an alternative manner. Instead of using Realisation Account we may open Revaluation Account. Naturally, only the changed value of assets and liabilities are to be incorporated just like admission or retirement of a partner.

Use of Revaluation Account

Practically, Revaluation Account is used when the assets are remained in the same firm after revaluation is made. Consequently, profit or loss on revaluation as a result of such changes in assets and liabilities are transferred to Partners' Capital Account.

Use of Realisation Account

Realisation Account is opened when the assets are not in the hands of the same firm after revaluation is made. Consequently, when the firm is dissolved or sold it is better to use Realisation Account i.e., when the old firm does not exist.

In case of amalgamation of firms, it is, in our opinion, better to use Revaluation Account in place of Realisation Account. Thus, we are solving the subsequent problems using Revaluation Account. Entries will to som e extent be different than the earlier method.

Alternative Approach using Revaluation Account

In the books of 'A & B'

Journal

Date	Particulars		L.F.	Debit Rs.	Credit Rs.
2012 Dec. 31	Revaluation A/c	Dr.		1,000	
	To Furniture A/c				500
	" Provision for Bad Debts A/c				500
	(Value of the assets decreased.)				
	A's Capital A/c	Dr.		500	
	B's Capital A/c	Dr.		500	
	To Revaluation A/c				1,000
	(Loss on revaluation transferred to capital accounts.)				
	Goodwill A/c	Dr.		10,000	
	To A's Capital A/c				5,000
	" B's Capital A/c				5,000
	(Goodwill raised in the books on amalgamation.)				

Contd.

Date	Particulars		L.F.	Rs.	Rs.
	M/s A, B, C, and D A/c	Dr.		46,500	
	To Goodwill A/c				10,000
	" Land A/c				10,000
	" Furniture A/c				2,500
	" Machinery A/c				7,000
	" Debtors A/c				6,000
	" Stock A/c				8,000
	" Cash at Bank A/c				3,000
	(Assets are taken over by the new firm.)				
	Provision for Bad Debts A/c	Dr.		500	
	Creditors A/c	Dr.		15,000	
	Outstanding Expenses A/c	Dr.		2,000	
	To M/s A, B, C, and D A/c				17,500
	(Liabilities are taken over by the new firm.)				
	A's Capital A/c	Dr.		14,500	
	B's Capital A/c	Dr.		14,500	
	To M/s A, B, C, and D A/c				29,000
	(Transfer of capital to the new firm.)				

In the books of 'C and D'
Journal

Date	Particulars		L.F.	Debit Rs.	Credit Rs.
2012 Dec. 31	Revaluation A/c	Dr.		7,000	
	To Land A/c				2,000
	" Furniture A/c				1,000
	" Provision for Bad Debts A/c				1,500
	" Stock A/c				2,000
	" Outstanding Expenses A/c				500
	(Value of the assets decreased and outstanding expenses increased.)				
	C's Capital A/c	Dr.		3,500	
	D's Capital A/c			3,500	
	To Revaluation A/c				7,000
	(Loss on revaluation transferred to capital accounts.)				
	Goodwill A/c Dr.			5,000	
	To C's Capital A/c				2,500
	" D's Capital A/c				2,500
	(Goodwill raised in the books on amalgamation.)				
	Loan A/c	Dr.		10,000	
	To C's Capital A/c				5,000
	" D's Capital A/c				5,000
	(Loan not taken over by the new firm and hence adjusted against C and D's Capital account in *their capital ratio.*)				
	M/s A, B, C, and D A/c	Dr.		43,000	
	To Goodwill A/c				5,000
	" Land A/c				10,000
	" Machinery A/c				8,000
	" Furniture A/c				2,500
	" Debtors A/c				8,500
	" Stock A/c				8,000
	" Cash at Bank A/c				1,000
	(Assets are taken over.)				

Contd.

Particulars		Rs.	Rs.
Provision for Bad Debts A/c	Dr.	1,500	
Creditors A/c	Dr.	10,000	
Outstanding Expenses A/c	Dr.	3,500	
To M/s A, B, C, and D A/c			15,000
(Liabilities are taken over.)			
C's Capital A/c	Dr.	14,000	
D's Capital A/c	Dr.	14,000	
To M/s A, B, C, and D A/c			28,000
(Transfer of capital to the new firm.)			

In the books of M/s A, B, C, and D

Journal

Date	Particulars			L.F.	Debit	Credit
					Rs.	Rs.
2012						
Dec. 31	Goodwill A/c	(10,000 + 5,000)	Dr.		15,000	
	Land A/c	(10,000 + 10,000)	Dr.		20,000	
	Machinery A/c	(8,000 + 7,000)	Dr.		15,000	
	Furniture A/c	(2,500 + 2,500)	Dr.		5,000	
	Debtors A/c	(6,000 + 8,500)	Dr.		14,500	
	Stock A/c	(8,000 + 8,000)	Dr.		16,000	
	Cash and Bank A/c	(3,000 + 1,000)	Dr.		4,000	
	To Provision for Bad Debts A/c	(500 + 1,500)				2,000
	" Creditors A/c	(15,000 + 10,000)				25,000
	" Outstanding Expenses A/c	(2,000 + 3,500)				5,500
	" A's Capital A/c					14,500
	" B's Capital A/c					14,500
	" C's Capital A/c					14,000
	" D's Capital A/c					14,000
	(Incorporations of various assets and liabilities.)					
	A's Capital A/c		Dr.		750	
	B's Capital A/c		Dr.		750	
	C's Capital A/c		Dr.		750	
	D's Capital A/c		Dr.		750	
	To Goodwill A/c					3,000
	(Value of goodwill distributed to partners' capital accounts in profit-sharing ratio.)					
	Bank A/c		Dr.		2,000	
	To A's Capital A/c					250
	" B's Capital A/c					250
	" C's Capital A/c					750
	" D's Capital A/c					750
	(Cash brought in by the partners to make up Rs. 14,000.)					

Balance Sheet *as at 31st Dec. 2012*

Liabilities		Rs.	Assets		Rs.
Capital Accounts :			*Fixed Assets*		
A	14,000		Goodwill		12,000
B	14,000		Land		20,000
C	14,000		Machinery		15,000
D	14,000		Furniture		5,000
		56,000	*Current Assets*		
Current Liabilities			Stock		16,000
Creditors		25,000	Debtors	14,500	
Outstanding Expenses		5,500	*Less* : Provision for Bad Debts	2,000	
					12,500
			Cash and Bank (4,000 + 2,000)		6,000
		86,500			86,500

Illustration 4

X and Y are partners of X & Co. sharing profits and losses in the ratio of 3 : 1 and Y and Z are partners of Y & Co. sharing profits and losses in the ratio of 2 : 1.

On 31st March 2013, they decide to amalgamate and form a new firm M/s XYZ & Co. wherein X, Y, & Z would be partners sharing profits and losses in the ratio of 3 : 2 : 1.

The Balance Sheets of the two firms on the above date were:

Liabilities	*X & Co.* Rs.	*Y & Co.* Rs.	*Assets*	*X & Co.* Rs.	*Y & Co.* Rs.
Capital			Fixed Assets		
X	4,80,000	—	Building	1,00,000	—
Y	3,20,000	4,00,000	Machinery	3,00,000	3,20,000
Z	—	2,00,000	Furniture	40,000	12,000
Reserves	1,00,000	3,00,000	Current Assets		
Creditors	2,40,000	2,32,000	Stock	2,40,000	2,80,000
Due to X & Co.	—	2,00,000	Debtors	3,20,000	4,00,000
Bank Loan	1,60,000	—	Cash at Bank	60,000	1,80,000
			Cash in hand	40,000	20,000
			Due from Y & Co.	2,00,000	—
			Advances	—	1,20,000
	13,00,000	13,32,000		13,00,000	13,32,000

The amalgamated firm took over the business on the following terms :

(a) Building of X & Co. was valued at Rs. 2,00,000.

(b) Machinery of X & Co. was valued of 4,50,000 and that of Y & Co. at Rs. 4,00,000.

(c) Goodwill value of X & Co Rs. 1,00,000 and Y & Co. Rs. 82,000 but the same will not appear in the book of XYZ & Co.

(d) Partners of the new firm will bring necessary cash to pay other partners to adjust their capitals according to the profit-sharing ratio.

Show Journal entries in the books of Mr. XYZ & Co. and prepare the Balance Sheet as on 31.3.2013. **[CA]**

Solution

In the books of M/s XYZ & Co.
Calculation of Purchase Consideration

		X & Co. Rs.		*Y & Co.* Rs.
Goodwill		1,00,000		82,000
Building		2,00,000		—
Machinery		4,50,000		4,00,000
Furniture		40,000		12,000
Stock		2,40,000		2,80,000
Debtors		3,20,000		4,00,000
Cash at Bank		60,000		1,80,000
Cash in hand		40,000		20,000
Due from Y & Co.		2,00,000		—
Advances		—		1,20,000
		16,50,000		14,94,000
Less : *Current Liabilities*				
Creditors	2,40,000		2,32,000	
Due to X & Co.	—		2,00,000	
Bank Loan	1,60,000		—	
		4,00,000		4,32,000
Purchase Consideration		10,50,000		10,62,000

Thus, the combined capital of M/s XYZ & Co. will be Rs. 23,12,000 (i.e., Rs. 12,50,000 + Rs. 10,62,000) – Rs. 1,82,000 for goodwill since it will not appear in the books = Rs. 21,30,000 among X, Y, and Z in 3 : 2 : 1 or Rs. 10,65,000, Rs. 7,10,000, and Rs. 3,55,000, respectively.

Journal

Date	Particulars		L.F.	Debit	Credit
				Rs.	Rs.
2013					
March 31	Goodwill A/c	Dr.		1,00,000	
	Building A/c	Dr.		2,00,000	
	Machinery A/c	Dr.		4,50,000	
	Furniture A/c	Dr.		40,000	
	Stock A/c	Dr.		2,40,000	
	Debtors A/c	Dr.		3,20,000	
	Cash at Bank A/c	Dr.		60,000	
	Cash in hand A/c	Dr.		40,000	
	Due from Y & Co. A/c	Dr.		2,00,000	
	To Creditors A/c				2,40,000
	" Bank Loan A/c				1,60,000
	" X & Y's Capital A/c				12,50,000
	(Assets and liabilities of X & Co. taken over.)				
	Goodwill A/c Dr.			82,000	
	Machinery A/c	Dr.		4,00,000	
	Furniture A/c	Dr.		12,000	
	Stock A/c	Dr.		2,80,000	
	Debtors A/c	Dr.		4,00,000	
	Cash at Bank A/c	Dr.		1,80,000	
	Cash in hand A/c	Dr.		20,000	
	Advance A/c	Dr.		1,20,000	
	To Creditors A/c				2,32,000
	" Due to X & Co. A/c				2,00,000
	" Y & X's Capital A/c				10,62,000
	(Assets and liabilities of Y & Co. taken over.)				
	Due to X & Co. A/c	Dr.		2,00,000	
	To Due from Y & Co. A/c				2,00,000
	(Mutual indebtedness set-off.)				
	X's Capital A/c	Dr.		91,000	
	Y's Capital A/c	Dr.		60,667	
	Z's Capital A/c	Dr.		30,333	
	To Goodwill A/c				1,82,000
	(Goodwill written-off and already adjusted against Capital A/c.)				

Balance Sheet *as at 31st March 2013*

Liabilities	Rs.	Assets	Rs.
Capital A/c :		Building	2,00,000
X	10,65,000	Machinery	8,50,000
Y	7,10,000	Furniture	52,000
X	3,55,000	Advance	1,20,000
Creditors	4,72,000	Stock	5,20,000
Bank Loan	1,60,000	Debtors	7,20,000
		Cash at Bank	2,40,000
		Cash in hand	60,000
	27,62,000		27,62,000

Illustration 5

B and S are partners of S & Co., sharing profits and losses in the ratio of 3 : 1. S and T are partners of T & Co. sharing profits and losses in the ratio of 2 : 1. On 31.10.2012, they decided to amalgamate and form a new firm M/s BST & Co. wherein B, S, and T would be partners sharing profits and losses in the ratio of 3 : 2 : 1.

The Balance Sheets on the date were :

Liabilities	*S & Co.*	*T & Co.*	*Assets*	*S & Co.*	*T & Co.*
	Rs.	Rs.		Rs.	Rs.
Due to T & Co.	40,000	—	Cash in hand	10,000	5,000
Due to S & Co.	—	50,000	Cash at Bank	15,000	20,000
Other Creditor	60,000	58,000	Due from T & Co.	50,000	—
Reserve	25,000	50,000	Due from S & Co.	—	30,000
Capital			Other Debtors	80,000	1,00,000
B	1,20,000	—	Stock	60,000	70,000
S	80,000	1,00,000	Furniture	10,000	3,000
T	—	50,000	Vehicles	—	80,000
			Machinery	75,000	—
			Buildings	25,000	—
	3,25,000	3,08,000		3,25,000	3,08,000

The amalgamated firm took over the business on the following terms :

(a) Goodwill of S & Co. was worth Rs. 60,000 and that of T & Co. Rs. 50,000. Goodwill Account was not to be opened in the books of the new firm, the adjustments being recorded through capital accounts of the partners.

(b) Building, Machinery, and Vehicles were taken over at Rs. 50,000, Rs. 90,000, and Rs. 1,00,000, respectively.

(c) Provision for doubtful debts has to be carried forward at Rs. 4,000 in respect of debtors of S & Co. and Rs. 5,000 in respect of debtors of T & Co.

You are required to :

(i) Compute the adjustment necessary for goodwill.

(ii) Pass the Journal entries in the books of BST & Co., assuming that excess/deficit capitals (taking T's Capital as base) with reference to share in profits are to be transferred to current accounts.

Solution

In the books of B S T & Co.
Journal

Date	*Particulars*		*L.F.*	*Debit*	*Credit*
2012				Rs.	Rs.
Oct. 31	Cash A/c	Dr.		10,000	
	Bank A/c	Dr.		15,000	
	T & Co.'s A/c	Dr.		50,000	
	Sundry Debtors A/c	Dr.		80,000	
	Stock A/c	Dr.		60,000	
	Furniture A/c	Dr.		10,000	
	Machinery A/c	Dr.		90,000	
	Building A/c	Dr.		50,000	
	To Provision for Doubtful Debts A/c				4,000
	" S & Co. A/c				40,000
	" Sundry Creditors A/c				60,000
	" B's Capital A/c				1,65,750
	" S's Capital A/c				95,250
	(Assets and liabilities of S & Co. taken over.)				
	Cash A/c	Dr.		5,000	
	Bank A/c	Dr.		20,000	
	S & Co.'s A/c	Dr.		30,000	
	Sundry Debtors A/c	Dr.		1,00,000	
	Stock A/c	Dr.		70,000	
	Furniture A/c	Dr.		3,000	
	Vehicles A/c	Dr.		1,00,000	
	To Provision for Doubtful Debts A/c				5,000
	" S & Co. A/c				50,000
	" Sundry Creditors A/c				58,000
	" S's Capital A/c				1,43,333
	" T's Capital A/c				71,667
	(Assets and liabilities of T & Co. taken over.)				

Contd.

			Rs.	Rs.
2012				
Oct. 31	B's Capital A/c	Dr.	10,000	
	T's Capital A/c	Dr.	1,666	
	To S's Capital A/c			11,666
	(Adjustment made for Goodwill.)			
	S & Co.'s A/c	Dr.	50,000	
	To T & Co.'s A/c			50,000
	(Mutual indebtedness of S & Co. and T & Co. cancelled.)			
	B's Current A/c	Dr.	54,253	
	To B's Capital A/c			54,253
	(Amount credited to B's Capital A/c to bring capital in profit-sharing ratio.)			
	S's Capital A/c	Dr.	1,10,247	
	S's Current A/c			1,10,247
	(Excess Capital transferred to current account to bring capital in profit-sharing ratio.)			

Workings :

1. **Computation of adjustment for goodwill**

	Raised in old ratio				Written-off in new ratio		Net Effectt	
	S & Co.	T & Co.	Total					
	Rs.	Rs.	Rs.		Rs.		Rs.	
B	45,000	—	45,000	Cr.	55,000	Dr.	10,000	Dr.
S	15,000	33,333	48,333	Cr.	36,667	Dr.	11,666	Cr.
T	—	16,667	16,667	Cr.	18,333	Dr.	1,666	Dr.
	60,000	50,000	1,10,000		1,10,000			

2. **Capital in the new firm**

		B	S	T
	Rs.	Rs.	Rs.	Rs.
Balance as taken over :	S & Co.	1,65,750	95,250	—
	T & Co.	—	1,43,333	71,667
		1,65,750	2,38,583	71,667
Adjustment for Goodwill		– 10,000	+ 11,666	– 1,666
		1,55,750	2,50,249	70,001
Capital in the new ratio, taking T's Capital as the basis		2,10,003	1,40,002	70,001
		54,253 Dr.	1,10,247 Cr.	Nil

Illustration 6

Following were the Balance Sheets of both the firms as on Dec. 31, 2012 :

M/s A and B and M/s C and D *as on December 31, 2012*

Liabilities	*A & B*	*C & D*	*Assets*	*A & B*	*C & D*
	Rs.	Rs.		Rs.	Rs.
Trade Creditors	20,000	10,000	Cash	15,000	12,000
Bills Payable	5,000	—	Investments	10,000	8,000
Bank Overdraft	2,000	10,000	Debtors Rs. 10,000		
A's Loan	6,000	—	*Less* : Provision Rs. 1,000		
Capitals :				9,000	4,000
A	35,000	—	Furniture	12,000	6,000
B	22,000	—	Premises	30,000	—
C	—	36,000	Land	—	50,000
D	—	20,000	Machinery	15,000	—
General Reserve	8,000	3,000	Goodwill	9,000	—
Investment Fluctuation Fund	2,000	1,000			
	1,00,000	80,000		1,00,000	80,000

The two firms decided to amalgamate their business on 1st Jan. 2013. For this purpose, it was decided that the new firm shall not take furniture of both the firms and shall take over investment at 10% depreciation, Land at Rs. 80,000; Premises at. Rs. 45,000; Machine at Rs. 9,000. New firm agreed to take over only trade liabilities of both the firms are to pay Rs. 12,000 to each firm for goodwill. Unrecorded typewriter with C and D, valued at Rs. 800, was not taken over by the new firm. The Capital of the new firm was agreed at Rs. 1,60,000 to be divided among partners equally.

You are required to pass Journal entries and prepare Balance Sheet of the new firm.

Solution

In the books of M/s A and B
Journal

Date	Particulars		L.F.	Debit	Credit
2018				Rs.	Rs.
Jan. 1	Premises A/c	Dr.		15,000	
	Goodwill A/c Dr.			3,000	
	To Revaluation A/c				18,000
	(Value of the assets increased.)				
	Revaluation A/c	Dr.		6,000	
	To Machinery A/c				6,000
	(Value of Machine reduced.)				
	Revaluation A/c	Dr.		12,000	
	To A's Capital A/c				6,000
	" B's Capital A/c				6,000
	(Profit on revaluation transferred.)				
	Investment Fluctuation Fund A/c	Dr.		1,000	
	To Investment A/c				1,000
	(Decreased value of investment adjusted against fund.)				
	Investment Fluctuation Fund A/c	Dr.		1,000	
	General Reserve A/c	Dr.		8,000	
	To A's Capital A/c				4,500
	" B's Capital A/c				4,500
	(Accumulated profits/reserves transferred.)				
	Bank Overdraft A/c	Dr.		2,000	
	A's Loan A/c	Dr.		6,000	
	To Bank A/c				8,000
	(Liabilities paid off.)				
	A's Capital A/c	Dr.		6,000	
	B's Capital A/c	Dr.		6,000	
	To Furniture A/c				12,000
	(Furniture, not taken over, transferred to Capital Account.)				
	New Firm A/c	Dr.		92,000	
	To Goodwill A/c				12,000
	" Machinery A/c				9,000
	" Premises A/c				45,000
	" Investment A/c				9,000
	" Debtors A/c				10,000
	" Bank A/c				7,000
	(Asset taken over at market value.)				
	Sundry Creditors A/c	Dr.		20,000	
	Bills Payable A/c	Dr.		5,000	
	Prov. for Doubtful Debts A/c	Dr.		1,000	
	To New Firm A/c				26,000
	(Liability taken over.)				
	A's Capital A/c	Dr.		39,500	
	B's Capital A/c	Dr.		26,500	
	To New Firm A/c				66,000
	(Capital account and new firm account are closed.)				

In the books of M/s C & D
Journal

Date	Particulars		L.F.	Debit Rs.	Credit Rs.
2018					
Jan. 1	Goodwill A/c Dr.			12,000	
	Land A/c	Dr.		30,000	
	Typewriter A/c	Dr.		800	
	To Revaluation A/c				42,800
	(Value assets increased.)				
	Revaluation A/c	Dr.		42,800	
	To C's Capital A/c				21,400
	" D's Capital A/c				21,400
	(Profit on revaluation transferred.)				
	Investment Fluctuation Fund A/c	Dr.		800	
	To Investment A/c				800
	(Decreased value of investment adjusted against fund.)				
	Investment Fluctuation Fund A/c	Dr.		200	
	General Reserve A/c	Dr.		3,000	
	To C's Capital A/c				1,600
	" D's Capital A/c				1,600
	(Accumulated profits/reserves transferred.)				
	Bank Overdraft A/c	Dr.		10,000	
	To C's Capital A/c				5,000
	" D's Capital A/c				5,000
	(Liabilities not taken over transferred to capital accounts.)				
	C's Capital A/c	Dr.		3,400	
	D's Capital A/c	Dr.		3,400	
	To Typewriter A/c				800
	" Furniture A/c				6,000
	(Asset not taken over, transferred to capital accounts.)				
	New Firm A/c	Dr.		1,15,200	
	To Goodwill A/c				12,000
	" Land A/c				80,000
	" Investments A/c				7,200
	" Debtors A/c				8,000
	" Bank A/c				8,000
	(Assets taken over at market value.)				
	Sundry Creditors A/c	Dr.		10,000	
	To New Firm A/c				10,000
	(Liabilities taken over.)				
	C's Capital A/c	Dr.		60,600	
	D's Capital A/c	Dr.		44,600	
	To New Firm A/c				1,05,200
	(Capital accounts and new firm account are closed.)				

In the books of the New Firm
Journal

Date	Particulars		L.F.	Debit Rs.	Credit Rs.
2013					
Jan. 1	Goodwill A/c	Dr.		12,000	
	Machinery A/c	Dr.		9,000	
	Premises A/c	Dr.		45,000	
	Investment A/c	Dr.		9,000	
	Debtors A/c	Dr.		10,000	
	Bank A/c	Dr.		7,000	
	To Sundry Creditors A/c				20,000
	" Bills Payable A/c				5,000
	" Prov. for Doubtful Debts A/c				1,000
	" A's Capital A/c				39,500
	" B's Capital A/c				26,500
	(Asset and liabilities are incorporated.)				

Contd.

Date	Particulars		Rs.	Rs.
2013 Jan. 1	Goodwill A/c	Dr.	12,000	
	Land A/c	Dr.	80,000	
	Investment A/c	Dr.	7,200	
	Debtors A/c	Dr.	8,000	
	Bank A/c	Dr.	8,000	
	To Sundry Creditors A/c			10,000
	" C's Capital A/c			60,600
	" D's Capital A/c			44,600
	(Asset and liabilities are incorporated.)			
	A's Current A/c	Dr.	500	
	B's Current A/c	Dr.	13,500	
	To A's Capital A/c			500
	" B's Capital A/c			13,500
	(Deficit of Rs. 40,000 transferred to current account.)			
	C's Capital A/c	Dr.	20,600	
	D's Capital A/c	Dr.	4,600	
	To C's Current A/c			20,600
	" D's Current A/c			4,600
	(Surplus of Rs. 40,000 transferred to current account.)			

Balance Sheet *as at 1st Jan. 2013*

Liabilities	Rs.	Rs.	*Assets*	Rs.	Rs.
Capital Accounts :			Goodwill		24,000
A	40,000		Land		80,000
B	40,000		Premises		45,000
C	40,000		Machinery		9,000
D	40,000		Investment		16,200
		1,60,000	Debtors	18,000	
Current Accounts :			*Less* : Prov. for Doubtful Debts	1,000	
C	20,600				17,000
D	4,600		Bank		15,000
		25,200	Current A/c		
Bills Payable		5,000	A	500	
Sundry Creditors		30,000	B	13,500	
					14,000
		2,20,200			2,20,200

Note : 1. Liabilities which were not taken over transferred to capital account as there was insufficient bank balance.

Case 3

When an existing partnership firm takes a sole proprietorship business

Under the circumstances, the sole proprietorship firm is dissolved and compensated by a share of the partnership firm. Needless to say that the assets and liabilities of the sole proprietorship firms are taken over by the partnership firm at agreed values, usually based on market value.

The methods of closing accounts are same like earlier ones. However, they are :

(i) Value of goodwill is to be debited and partners' Capital account is to be credited as per old profit-sharing ratio.

(ii) The assets and liabilities of the firm are to be revalued and any profit or loss on revaluation is to be transferred to partners' capital account as per old profit-sharing ratio.

(iii) Accumulated reserves/profit is to be closed by transferring to partners' capital account as per old profit–sharing ratio.

(iv) The assets and liabilities of the sole proprietorship firm are added with the existing assets and liabilities of the partnership firm.

(v) The capital of the new partner viz., the sole proprietorship, must be equal to the agreed purchase consideration.

(vi) If the amount of purchase consideration exceeds net asset i.e., total assets minus liabilities taken over, the difference represents *Goodwill* and, in the opposites case, ***Capital Reserve.***

The following illustration will make the principle clear :

Illustration 7

On 31st Dec. 2011, the Balance Sheet of the partners X and Y sharing in proportion to their capitals, and the sole-trader Z are:

	Partners X & Y	*Sole-trader Z*		*Partners X & Y*	*Sole-trader Z*
	Rs.	Rs.		Rs.	Rs.
Capitals :			Goodwill	—	4,000
X	30,000	20,000	Building	50,000	—
Y	10,000	—	Stock	20,000	30,000
Creditors	52,000	26,000	Bills Receivable	10,000	10,000
Loan	—	10,000	Debtors	8,000	12,000
			Cash	4,000	—
	92,000	56,000		92,000	56,000

The partners resolve to admit Z as a partner and allow him to merge his business as with that of the partnership on the following terms :

(i) that X, Y, and Z would share profits and losses in the ratio of their capitals in the reconstituted partnership after all adjustments have given effect to;

(ii) the Building is to be appreciated by Rs. 30,000 and make a provision for bad debt @ 5% on debtors;

(iii) the goodwill of the partnership is to be put at Rs. 20,000 and of the sole-trader at Rs. 3,000, both being brought into books; and

(iv) stock is to be taken at Rs. 18,400, and Rs. 33,600, respectively, of the firm and the sole-traders.

Assuming that these have been duly carried out on Jan. 1, 2012, make necessary Journal entries and prepare the new Balance Sheet after amalgamation.

Solution

In the books of the firm

Journal

Date	*Particulars*		*L.F.*	*Debit*	*Credit*
				Rs.	Rs.
2011 Dec. 31	Goodwill A/c	Dr.		20,000	
	To X's Capital A/c				15,000
	" Y's Capital A/c				5,000
	(Goodwill Account is raised in the books.)				
	Building A/c	Dr.		30,000	
	To Revaluation A/c				30,000
	(Value of Building increased.)				
	Revaluation A/c	Dr.		2,000	
	To Stock A/c				1,600
	" Provision for Bad Debts A/c				400
	(Value of various assets reduced.)				
	Revaluation A/c	Dr.		28,000	
	To X's Capital A/c				21,000
	" Y's Capital A/c				7,000
	(Value of various assets reduced.)				
	Goodwill A/c	Dr.		3,000	
	Stock A/c	Dr.		33,600	
	Bills Receivable A/c	Dr.		10,000	
	Debtors A/c	Dr.		12,000	
	To Provision for Bad Debt A/c				600
	" Creditors A/c				26,000
	" Loan A/c				10,000
	" Z's Capital A/c *(bal. fig.)*				22,000
	(Incorporation of new partner's assets and liabilities.)				

Balance Sheet (after amalgamation)
as at 1st Jan. 2012

Liabilities	Rs.	*Assets*		Rs.
Capitals		Goodwill (20,000 + 3,000)		23,000
X (30,000 + 15,000 + 21,000)	66,000	Building		80,000
Y (10,000 + 5,000 + 7,000)	22,000	Stock (18,400 + 33,600)		52,000
Z	22,000	Bills Receivable (10,000 + 10,000)		20,000
Loan	10,000	Debtors (8,000 + 12,000)	20,000	
Creditors (52,000 + 26,000)	78,000	*Less* : Prov. for Bad Debts	1,000	
				19,000
		Cash		4,000
	1,98,000			1,98,000

Case 4

When an existing partnership firm takes another partnership firm

Under the circumstances, the books of the old firm are to be closed. The method, and procedure also same as explained earlier. For this purpose, the purchase consideration which is given is to be shared between the selling firm as per their share of the old firm. Naturally, any accumulated profit/reserve is transferred to the partners' capital account of the selling firms as per their old profit-sharing ratio. However, the capital accounts of the new partners (from the selling firm) are credited with their net assets.

The following illustration will make the principle clear :

Illustration 8

Following are the Balance Sheets of M/s AB and M/s CD as on 31.12.2012 :

Liabilities	*M/s AB*	*M/s CD*	*Assets*	*M/s AB*	*M/s CD*
	Rs.	Rs.		Rs.	Rs.
Capital A/c			Plant	30,000	20,000
A	40,000	—	Land	10,000	8,000
B	20,000	—	Investments		8,000
C		30,000	Stock	20,000	12,000
D		15,000	Debtors	10,000	10,000
Overdraft	8,000	—	Cash	10,000	2,000
Creditors	12,000	15,000			
	80,000	60,000		80,000	60,000

M/s AB absorbs M/s CD under the following conditions :

(i) The assets of M/s CD are revalued as: Plant at book value less 20%, Land at Rs. 20,000; Stock at Rs. 8,000; (ii) Investment were directly sold in the open market for Rs. 10,000. (iii) Goodwill to be taken at Rs. 10,000.

Similarly, the following adjustments are also to be made for M/s AB :

(i) Goodwill to be taken at Rs. 15,000; (ii) Other assets were revalued as:

Depreciate Plant by 10%; Value of Land to be increased by 20%; Stock to be taken at Rs. 16,000; Overdraft was repaid. Close the books of M/s CD and show the entries and the Balance Sheet in the books of M/s AB.

Solution

In the books of M/s CD
Journal

Date	*Particulars*		*L.F.*	*Debit*	*Credit*
2012				Rs.	Rs.
Dec. 31	**Revaluation A/c**	Dr.		8,000	
	To Plant A/c				4,000
	" Stock A/c				4,000
	(Value of asset reduced and adjusted on amalgamations)				
Dec. 31	Land A/c	Dr.		12,000	
	Investment A/c	Dr.		2,000	
	To Revaluation A/c				14,000
	(Value of asset increased and adjusted on amalgamation.)				

Contd.

Date	Particulars		L.F.	Debit Rs.	Credit Rs.
2012	Revaluation A/c	Dr.		6,000	
	To C's Capital A/c				3,000
	" D's Capital A/c				3,000
	(Profit on revaluation transferred.)				
	Goodwill A/c Dr.			10,000	
	To C's Capital A/c				5,000
	" D's Capital A/c				5,000
	(Value of goodwill raised.)				
	Bank A/c	Dr.		10,000	
	To Investments A/c				10,000
	(Investment sold in the open market.)				
	C's Capital A/c	Dr.		5,000	
	D's Capital A/c	Dr.		5,000	
	To Bank A/c				10,000
	(Proceeds of investment taken be C and D.)				
	M/s. AB A/c	Dr.		66,000	
	To Plant A/c				16,000
	" Land A/c				20,000
	" Stock A/c				8,000
	" Debtors A/c				10,000
	" Cash A/c				2,000
	" Goodwill A/c				10,000
	(Assets taken over by M/s AB.)				
	Creditors A/c	Dr.		15,000	
	To M/s AB A/c				15,000
	(Liabilities taken over by M/s. AB.)				
	C's Capital A/c	Dr.		33,000	
	D's Capital A/c	Dr.		18,000	
	To M/s AB A/c				51,000
	(Capital accounts of C and D transferred.)				

In the books of AB

Journal

Date	Particulars		L.F.	Debit	Credit
2012				Rs.	Rs.
Dec. 31	Revaluation A/c	Dr.		7,000	
	To Plant A/c				3,000
	" Stock A/c				4,000
	(Value of assets reduced and adjusted on amalgamation.)				
	Land A/c	Dr.		2,000	
	To Revaluation A/c				2,000
	(Value of assets increased and adjusted on amalgamation.)				
	A's Capital A/c	Dr.		2,500	
	B's Capital A/c	Dr.		2,500	
	To Revaluation A/c				5,000
	(Loss on revaluation transferred.)				
	Bank Overdraft A/c	Dr.		8,000	
	To Cash A/c				8,000
	(Bank overdraft repaid.)				
	Goodwill A/c	Dr.		15,000	
	To A's Capital A/c				7,500
	" B's Capital A/c				7,500
	(Value of goodwill raised in the books.)				
	Plant A/c	Dr.		16,000	
	Land A/c	Dr.		20,000	
	Stock A/c	Dr.		8,000	
	Debtors A/c	Dr.		10,000	
	Cash A/c	Dr.		2,000	
	Goodwill A/c	Dr.		10,000	
	To Creditors A/c				15,000
	" C's Capital A/c				33,000
	" D's Capital A/c				18,000
	(Incorporation of various assets and liabilities were made on amalgamation.)				

Dr. Capital Account Cr.

Particulars	A Rs.	B Rs.	Particulars	A Rs.	B Rs.
To Revaluation A/c —Loss	2,500	2,500	By Balance b/d	40,000	20,000
" Balance c/d	45,000	25,000	" Goodwill A/c	7,500	7,500
	47,500	27,500		47,500	27,500

Balance Sheet *as at 31st Dec. 2012*

Liabilities	Rs.	Rs.	Assets	Rs.
Capital A/cs :			Goodwill	25,000
A	45,000		Plant (Rs. 27,000 + Rs. 16,000)	43,000
B	25,000		Land (Rs. 20,000 + Rs. 12,000)	32,000
C	33,000		Stock (Rs. 8,000 + Rs. 16,000)	24,000
D	18,000	1,21,000	Debtors (Rs. 10,000 + Rs. 10,000)	20,000
Creditors		27,000	Cash (Rs. 2,000 + Rs. 2,000)	4,000
		1,48,000		1,48,000

ASSIGNMENT MATERIALS

THEORETICAL

1. What is Amalgamation of Firms?
   Under what circumstances one firm wants to amalgamate with any other?
2. How many kinds of amalgamation do you find in accounting?
3. Discuss the procedure of accounting in amalgamation.
4. Distinguish between : (a) Amalgamation of firms, and (b) Dissolution of firms.

PRACTICAL

1. X and Y are two sole-traders. Their Balance Sheet as on 1.1.2012 are:

X's Balance Sheet *as at 1st Jan. 2012*

Liabilities	Rs.	Assets	Rs.
Sundry Creditors	10,000	Plant and Machinery	8,000
Das Bank Ltd.	5,000	Stock-in-trade	10,000
Capital Account	15,000	Sundry Debtors	12,000
	30,000		30,000

Y's Balance Sheet *as at 1st Jan. 2012*

Liabilities	Rs.	Assets	Rs.
Sundry Creditors	8,000	Plant and Machfinery	10,000
Capital Account	20,000	Stock-in-trade	5,000
		Sundry Debtors	11,000
		Cash at Bank	2,000
	28,000		28,000

They agree to amalgamate their business as on 1.1.2012. The following revaluations were to be made: (a) Plant and Machinery were to be reduced by 10%. (b) Stock-in-trade was to be reduced in case of X by 20% and in case of Y by 10%. (c) A reserve of $2\frac{1}{2}$% is to be raised against Sundry Debtors. (d) Each partner is to be credited with Goodwill of Rs. 5,000. (e) The Bank Overdraft of X is to be paid-off by him.

You are required to give the journal entries for recording the above transactions in the books of X and Y. Give also the amalgamatred Balance Sheet of the partners as on 1.1.2012

[Ans : Total of Amalgamated Balance Sheet Rs. 86,500]

2. A and B carry on independent business in provisions and their positions as at 30 September are reflected in the Balance Sheets given:

	A Rs.	B Rs.
Stock-in-trade	1,70,000	98,000
Sundry Debtors	89,000	37,000

Contd.

	Rs.	Rs.
Cash at Bank	13,000	7,500
Cash in hand	987	234
Furniture and Fixtures	2,750	1,766
Investment	513	—
	2,76,250	1,44,500
Represented by		
Sundry Creditors for		
Purchases	1,10,000	47,000
Expenses	750	2,500
Bills Payable	12,500	—
Capital Account	1,53,000	95,000
	2,76,250	1,44,500

Both of them want to form a partnership firm from 1 October 2012 on the following understanding :

(a) The capital of the partnership would be Rs. 3 lakhs which would be contributed by them in the ratio 2 : 1.

(b) The assets of the individual businesses would be vaulted by C at which values, the firm will take them over and the value would be adjusted against the contribution due by A and B.

(c) C gave his valuation report as: Business of A : Stock-in-trade to be written-down by 15% and a portion of Sundry Debtors amounting to Rs. 9,000 estimated unrealisable not to be assumed by the firm; furniture and fixtures to be valued at Rs. 2,000 and investments to be taken at market value of 1,000.

Assets of B : Stocks to be written-up by 10% and Sundry Debtors to be admitted at 85% of their value; rest of the assets to be assumed at their book value.

(d) The firm is not to assume any creditors other than the dues on account of purchases made.

Prepare the opening Balance Sheet of the firm.

[CA]

[Ans. A introduces Rs. 68,513 and B withdraws Rs. 1,750; B/S Total Rs. 4,57,000]

3. Two partnership firms, carrying on business under the styles of Black and Co. and White and Co., respectively, decide to amalgamate into Grey and Co. with effect from 1 April 2012.

The respective Balance Sheets as on 31st March 2012 are :

Black & Co.
Balance Sheet *as on 31st March 2012*

	Rs.		Rs.
B's Capital Account	19,000	Plant and Machinery	10,000
Sundry Creditors	10,000	Stock-in-trade	20,000
Bank Overdraft	15,000	Sundry Debtors	10,000
		A's Capital A/c	4,000
	44,000		44,000

A and B share profits and losses in the proportion of 1 : 2.

White & Co.
Balance Sheet *as on 31st March 2012*

	Rs.		Rs.
X's Capital Account	10,000	Goodwill	10,000
Y's Capital Account	2,000	Stock-in-trade	5,000
Sundry Creditors	28,000	Sundry Debtors	10,000
		Cash in hand	6,000
		Cash at Bank	9,000
	40,000		40,000

X and Y share profits and losses equally.

Further information given :

(1) All fixed assets are to be devalued by 20%

(2) All stock-in-trade is to be appreciated by 50%.

(3) Black and Co. owes Rs. 5,000 to White and Co., as on 31st March 2012. The debt is settled at Rs. 2,000.

(4) Goodwill is to be ignored for the amalgamation.

(5) The fixed capital accounts in the new firm are to be Mr. A Rs. 2,000; Mr. B Rs. 3,000; Mr. X Rs. 1,000; Mr. D Rs. 4,000.

(6) B takes over the bank overdraft on Black & Co. and gifts to Mr. A the amount of money to be brought in by Mr. A to make up his capital contribution.

(7) X is paid off in cash from White & Co. and Y brings in sufficient cash to make up his required capital contribution.

Pass journal entries to close the books of both the firms as on 31 March, 2012

[Ans. Profit on Revaluation; Black and Co. Rs. 11,000; Loss on Revaluation; White & Co. Rs. 10.500]

4. A and B are in partnership sharing profits and losses equally and C is trading alone in the same line. On 1.1.2012, they decided to amalgamate the two businesses and to form a new firm M/s ABC & Co., wherein A, B and C would be partners sharing profits and losses equally.

Their Balance Sheets on that date are :

Liabilities	A & B Rs.	C Rs.	*Assets*	A & B Rs.	C Rs.
Capitals :			Land & Buildings	5,000	6,000
X	8,000	—	Machinery	3,500	4,000
Y	6,000	—	Furniture	1,500	1,750
C		10,000	Investments	8,500	—
Creditors	7,500	5,000	Stock	4,000	5,000
Loan	—	5,000	Debtors	8,000	4,250
Outstanding Expenses	1,000	1,500	Bank	2,000	500
	22,500	21,500		22,500	21,500

For the purpose of amalgamation, assets and liabilities are revalued as :

	A & B Rs.	C Rs.
Land & Buildings	5,000	5,000
Machinery	3,500	4,000
Furniture	1,250	1,250
Debtors	2,750	3,500
Stock	4,000	4,000
Outstanding Expenses	2,000	1,750

In addition to the above it is decided :

(i) that the new firm will not take over investments of A & B and loan of C.

(ii) that the Goodwill of A & B and C will be valued at Rs. 5,000 and Rs. 2,500, respectively, in the first instance, but for the purpose of the Balance Sheet of new firm, the combined Goodwill will be valued at Rs. 6,000.

(iii) that the reconstructed capital of partners should be Rs. 7,500 each, any excess or deficit will be transferred to their respective current accounts.

You are required to show :

(a) The journal entries to close the books of A & B.

(b) The journal entries to open the books of M/s ABC & Co., and

(c) The balance Sheet of the new firm.

[C U BCom (Hons.)]

[Ans. Loss on Revaluation Rs. 1,500 (A & B); Transferred to A's Capital A/c Rs. 8,000; B Rs. 6,000; Balance Sheet Rs. 44,750]

G. DEATH OF A PARTNER

Death of a partner dissolves the partnership but the surviving partners generally carry on the business by purchasing the deceased's share. Under the circumstances, the problems that may arise are similar to the problems stated earlier at the time of retirement of partner, with some difference. In short, in the case of a retirement of a partner, his share is transferred to his loan account (if not paid in cash immediately after his retirement) whereas, in the case of death of a partner, deceased partner's share (including a share of profit and goodwill) is transferred to his executor's account (i.e., Executors or Administrators or Personal or legal Representatives of deceased).

Ascertainment of deceased Partner's claims

The total claims of the deceased partners is computed as :

(i) Balance of Capital Account as per Balance Sheet (adjust the current account of the deceased partner, if any;

(ii) *Add :* *his share of Goodwill;*
(iii) *Add :* *his share of accumulated profits/reserves;*
(iv) *Add :* *his share of profit on revaluation;*
or, Less : *his share of loss on revaluation;*
(v) *Add :* *his share of Joint Life Policy;*
(vi) *Add :* *his share of profit up to the date of his death.*

We have already explained in details from (i) to (iv) & (vi) while discussing Retirement of Partners (in the previous chapter). Now we will only highlight (v) i.e., share of Joint Life Policy.

Before that we are presenting Disposal of Deceased Partner's Share and the computation of his profit.

Disposal of Deceased Partner's Share

Practically, that depends on the terms of agreement amongst the partners. The Partnership Deed may contain certain special provisions in order to determine the deceased partner's share and the mode of payment as well in a specialised manner. As such, the repayment may be made in either of the following manner:

(a) *Lump Sum Payment Method :* When the firm has sufficient funds to pay-off the total claims of the deceased partner's share, i.e., payment made in cash immediately, it is known as Lump Sum Payment Method. In other words, deceased partner's representative account will be debited and Bank account will be credited.

(b) *Instalment Payment Method :* When the firm is not in a position to pay off the total claims of the deceased partner due to insufficient funds, in that case, the total claim is first to be transferred to loan account and payment may be made either half-yearly or yearly as per terms after charging the interest on the unpaid balance, i.e., payment is made against unpaid balance plus interest.

This is made again in the following two procedures :

(i) **Decreasing Payment Method :**

Under this method, the total amount due is divided by a number of equal instalments and the instalment amount plus interest is paid accordingly.

(ii) **Equal Payment Method:**

Under this method, the total amount due is divided by a number of equal instalments in such a manner that the amount after including interest should always be equal.

(c) *Annuity Method :* Under this method an annuity is paid for a specified number of years to the deceased partner's legal representatives. The total claim is transferred to 'Annuity Suspense Account.' The interest at a certain rate on the unpaid balance is credited and the annuity payments are debited. Any surplus or deficit in this account after the final annuity payment will be shared among the existing partners in their profit-sharing ratio.

Ascertainment of the deceased partner's share of profit

Practically, it becomes possible to calculate the deceased partner's share of profit till the date of his death only when the final accounts of the firm is prepared up to the period of death. In actual practice, the same is neither possible nor practicable. However, the profit may be computed as per any one of the following methods :

(a) Time basis

Under this basis, profit can be divided between two periods, viz.

(i) beginning of the period to the date of death of the partner; and

(ii) from the period/date of death to the end of the period.

The following example will help us to make the principles clear :

Example

P, Q, and R were in partnership sharing profit and losses in the ratio of 3 : 2 : 1. R died on 1st April 1996, the profit for the period ended 31st Dec. 1996 were Rs. 96,000.

Ascertain the share of profit of the deceased partner.

Solution :

Profit for the year Rs. 96,000.

Profit for 1.1.1996 to 1.4.1996 i.e, for 3 months will be = Rs. 96,000 × $\frac{3}{12}$ = Rs. 24,000.

R's share of profit = Rs. 24,000 × $\frac{1}{6}$ = Rs. 4,000.

(b) Sales/Turnover basis

Under this basis, the share of profit of the deceased partner up to the date of his death can be ascertained on the basis of Sales/Turnover.

The following example will make the principle clear :

Example

P, Q, and R were in partnership sharing profits and losses in the ratio 2 : 2 : 1. R died on 1st April 1996. Turnover for the period 1996 amounted to Rs. 5,00,000, out of which turnover amounted to Rs. 1,25,000 for the period from 1st Jan. 1996 to 1st April 1996. The profit for the year amounted to Rs. 50,000. Calculates R's share of profit.

Solution

Proportionate profit up to the date of death is calculated as = $\frac{\text{Rs. } 1,25,000}{\text{Rs. } 5,00,000}$ × Rs. 50,000.

= Rs. 12,500

∴ R's share of profit = Rs. 12,500 × $\frac{1}{5}$ = Rs. 2,500.

Life Insurance Policy and its treatment

The disposal of the amount of life insurance policy may create a problem on the death of a partner. The object of the policy is to facilitate the repayment of the amount due to the legal representatives of the deceased partner. Therefore, if any partner dies after making a policy, his dues may be cleared out of the policy money realised from the insurance company without, however, disturbing the liquid sources of the firm. One point to be noted in this respect is that the amount realised on maturity is a partnership asset and any profit or loss out of this policy is to be shared among the partners in profit-sharing ratio (including the deceased partner). Life Insurance policy is of two types, viz.

(i) Joint Life Policy; and (ii) Individual Policy.

(i) Joint Life Policy

Accounting Steps

(1) When premium paid is treated as expense

Under this method, premium which is paid on the policy is charged in Profit and Loss Account every year and amount realised from the insurance company either on the surrender of policy or on the death of a partner is divided among the partners in profit-sharing ratio.

Entries

(a)	***When the premium is paid :***		
	Insurance Premium A/c	Dr.	With the amount of premium
	To Bank A/c		
(b)	***At the end of the year :***		
	Profit and Loss A/c	Dr.	Do.
	To Insurance Premium A/c		
(c)	***When the policy matures :***		
	Bank A/c	Dr.	With the amount received on maturity of the policy
	To Life Policy A/c		
(d)	***When the amount is divided among the partners :***		
	Life Policy A/c	Dr.	Do.
	To Partners' Capital A/c		

(2) When premium paid is treated as an asset

Under this method, the premium which is paid is debited of Life Policy Account. The same is reduced to its surrender value by a corresponding debit to Profit and Loss Account. And the amount of Life Policy Account which is in excess of its surrender value is treated as a loss and, hence, charged to Profit and Loss Account at the end of the year. Therefore, the balance of the Life Policy Account is treated as an asset and the amount which is received from the insurance company on maturity (in excess of its surrender value) will represent the net income and the same will be divided among the partners in profit-sharing ratio.

The entries for this purpose are :

(a)	***When premium is paid :***		
	Life Policy A/c	Dr.	With the amount of premium paid
	To Bank A/c		
(b)	***At the end of the year :***		
	Profit and Loss A/c	Dr.	Excess of life policy over its surrender value
	To Life Policy A/c		
(c)	***When policy matures :***		
	Bank A/c	Dr.	With the amount realised on maturity
	To Life Policy A/c		
(d)	***When net income of policy is distributed among the partners :***		
	Life Policy A/c	Dr.	Amount received minus surrender value
	To Partners' Capital A/c		

(3) When Life Policy Reserve Account is maintained

This method is nothing but the combined method of (1) and (2) stated above. Under this method, Profit and Loss Account is debited with the amount of premium paid and Life Policy Account is shown as an asset in the Balance Sheet as its surrender value. The entries are :

(a)	***When premium is paid :***		
	Life Policy A/c	Dr.	With the amount of premium paid
	To Bank A/c		
(b)	***At the end of the year :***		
(i)	Profit and Loss A/c	Dr.	Do.
	To Life Policy Reserve A/c		
(ii)	Life Policy Reserve A/c	Dr.	Excess of life policy over its surrender value
	To Life Policy A/c		

Now, Life Policy Account is shown as an asset in Life Policy Reserve Account at its surrender value in the liability side of the Balance Sheet.

(iii)	***When policy matures :***		
	Bank A/c	Dr.	With the amount received on maturity
	To Life Policy A/c		

(iv) ***When balance of Life Policy Reserve A/c is transferred to Life Policy A/c :***

Life Policy Reserve A/c	Dr.	Balance of Life Policy reserve
To Life Policy A/c		

(v) ***When Life Policy is distributed among partners :***

Life Policy A/c	Dr.	With net income
To Partner's Capital A/c		

Illustration 1

A, B, and C are partners sharing profits and losses in the ratio of 2 : 1 : 1. They took out a Joint Life Policy for Rs. 60,000 on 1st January 2009, for the purpose of providing funds for repayment of their shares of capital and goodwill in the event of death. The annual premium of Rs. 2,500 was payable on 1st February each year and the last premium was paid on 1st February 2012, B died on 10th March 2012, and policy money was received on 30th April 2012.

The surrender values of the policy as on 31st December each year were:

2009 Nil; 2010 Rs. 500; and 2011 Rs. 800.

Show the necessary account and Balance Sheet (as on 31st December each year) on assumptions:

(a) That the insurance premium is charged every year to the Profit and Loss Account of the firm as business expense;

(b) That insurance premium is debited to Joint Life Policy Account but an adjustment is made through the Profit and Loss Account each year to bring the Policy to its surrender value; and

(c) That a sum equal to the annual insurance premium is charged to Profit and Loss Appropriation Account each year and credited to Joint Life Policy Reserve Account through which the adjustment is made to bring the Policy to its surrender value.

Solution

Under Method (1)

In the books of A, B, and C

Joint Life Policy Account

Dr. Cr.

Date	Particulars	Amount Rs.	Date	Particulars	Amount Rs.
2012 April 30	To Capital Account —Profit transferred		2012 April 30	By Bank— Policy Money Received	60,000
	A $\frac{2}{4}$	30,000			
	B $\frac{1}{4}$	15,000			
	C $\frac{1}{4}$	15,000			
		60,000			60,000

Under Method (2)

Joint Life Policy Account

Dr. Cr.

Date	Particulars	Amount Rs.	Date	Particulars	Amount Rs.
2009 Feb. 1	To Bank A/c—Premium paid	2,500	2009 Dec. 31	By Profit and Loss A/c	2,500
		2,500			2,500
2010 Feb. 1	To Bank A/c—Premium paid	2,500	2010 Dec. 31	By Profit and Loss A/c	2,000
			"	Balance c/d	500
		2,500			2,500
2011 Jan. 1.	To Balance b/d	500	2011 Dec.31	By Profit and Loss A/c	2,200
Jan. 1	Bank A/c—Premium paid	2,500	"	" Balance c/d	800
		3,000			3,000

Contd.

			Rs.				Rs.
2012				2012			
Jan. 1	To	Balance b/d	800	April, 30	By	Bank A/c —Policy Money Received	60,000
Feb. 1	"	Bank—Premium paid	2,500				
April 31	"	Capital Accounts —Profit transferred					
		A $\frac{2}{4}$	28,350				
		B $\frac{1}{4}$	14,175				
		C $\frac{1}{4}$	14,175				
			60,000				60,000

***Under Method* (3)**

Joint Life Policy Account

Dr. *Cr.*

Date		*Particulars*	*Amount*	*Date*		*Particulars*	*Amount*
2009			Rs.	2009			Rs.
Feb. 1	To	Bank A/c—Premium paid	2,500	Dec. 31	By	Joint Life Policy Reserve A/c	2,500
			2,500				2,500
2010				2010			
Feb. 1	To	Bank A/c—Premium paid	2,500	Dec. 31	By	Joint Life Policy Reserve A/c	2,000
					"	Balance c/d	500
			2,500				2,500
2011				2011			
Jan. 1	To	Balance b/d	500	Dec. 31	By	Joint Life Policy Reserve A/c	2,200
Feb. 1	"	Bank A/c—Premium paid	2,500		"	Balance c/d	800
			3,000				3,000
2012				2012			
Jan. 1	To	Balance b/d	800	April 30	By	Bank—Policy Money Received	60,000
Feb. 1	"	Bank A/c—Premium paid	2,500		"	Joint Policy Reserve A/c—Balance transferred	800
April 30	"	Capital Accounts —Profit transferred					
		A	28,750				
		B	14,375				
		C	14,375				
			60,800				60,800

Illustration 2

M/s X, Y, and Z, who share profits and losses in the ratio of 3 : 2 : 2, arranged for a Joint Life Policy of the partners of Rs. 50,000 from 5.3.2007 in order to provide for the repayment of the deceased partner's share. The annual premium of Rs. 1,000 is debited to the Joint Life Policy Account. The premia were paid on 5th March on every year and the last of such premium was paid in 2,010.

The surrender values of the policy in the various years are : 2007 — Nil; 2008 — Rs. 100; 2009 — Rs. 250. A died on 14.4.2010 and the policy amount was secured in full on 30.4.2010.

Show the Joint Life Policy Account and the Joint Policy Reserve Account assuming that the Accounts were closed on 30th April every year.

[CA—Adapted]

Solution :

In the books of M/s X, Y, & Z
Joint Life Policy Account

Dr. *Cr.*

Date		*Particulars*	*Amount*	*Date*		*Particulars*	*Amount*
2007			Rs.	2007			Rs.
March 5	To	Bank A/c Premium	1,000	April 30	By	Joint Life Policy Reserve A/c	1,000
			1,000				1,000

Contd.

Date	Particulars	Rs.	Date	Particulars	Rs.
2008 March 3	To Bank A/c—Premium	1,000	2008 April 30	By Joint Life Policy Reserve A/c	900
				" Balance c/d	100
		1,000			1,000
2008 May 1	To Balance b/d	100	2009 April 30	By Joint Life Policy Reserve A/c	850
2009 March 3	" Bank A/c—Premium	1,000		" Balance c/d	250
		1,100			1,100
2009 May 1	To Balance b/d	250	2010 April 30	By Bank A/c Amount Received	50,000
2010 March 5	" Bank A/c—Premium	1,000			
April 30	" Joint Life Policy Reserve A/c	48,750			
		50,000			50,000

Joint Life Policy Reserve Account

Dr. Date	Particulars	Amount Rs.	Date	Particulars	Amount Rs. Cr.
2007 April 30	To Joint Life Policy A/c	1,000	2007 April 30	By Profit and Loss Appropriation A/c	1,000
		1,000			1,000
2008 April 30	To Joint Life Policy A/c	900	2008 April 30	By Profit and Loss Appropriation A/c	1,000
"	" Balance c/d	100			
		1,000			1,000
2009 April 30	To Joint Life Policy A/c	850	2008 May 1	By Balance b/d	100
"	" Balance c/d	250	2009 April 30	" Appropriation A/c	1,000
		1,100			1,100
2010 April 30	To Capital A/c		2009 May 1	By Balance b/d	250
	X 21,000		2010 April 30	" Joint Life Policy A/c	48,750
	Y 14,000				
	Z 14,000	49,000			
		49,000			49,000

(ii) Individual Policy

Sometimes, the partners may take individual policies instead of taking a Joint Life Policy. However, the treatment is same like Joint Life Policy. Under the circumstances, if a partner dies, his policy will mature and the insurers would pay the amount for which the deceased partner was insured. Needless to mention here that the legal representations of the deceased partner is entitled to receive the proportional amount of the policy matured together with the surrender value of the other policies on the lives of other partners who are surving.

The following illustration will make the above principle clear :

Illustration 3

P, Q, and R were partners sharing profits and losses in the ratio of 2 : 2 : 1. Policies taken by the individual partners, P, Q, and R, on their respective lives were Rs. 20,000, Rs. 16,000, and Rs. 32,000. The premium on such policies was charged against Profit and Loss Account. R died on 31st Dec. 2008. The surrender values were @ 20% of the amount of policies on that date.

Show the entries.

Solution

In the present problem, as the amount of premium was paid out of business, i.e., charged against Profit and Loss Account, policy did not appear in the Balance Sheet. As such, the entire amount so received on the death of R should be treated as profit. At the same time, the surrender values of the remaining surviving partners should also be treated as profit on that date since life policies were worth their surrender values and assets side of the Balance Sheet did not contain such values to that extent.

The entries for the purpose are:

Journal

Date	Particulars		L.F.	Debit	Credit
				Rs.	Rs.
2008 Dec. 31	Bank A/c	Dr.		32,000	
	To Profit and Loss Adjustment A/c				32,000
	(Amount received from the insurer on R's life.)				
	P's Life Policy A/c	Dr.		4,000	
	Q's Life Policy A/c	Dr.		3,200	
	To Profit and Loss Adjustment A/c				7,200
	(Surrender values of the policies of P and Q are recorded in the books.)				
	Profit and Loss Adjustment A/c	Dr.		39,200	
	To P's Capital A/c				15,680
	" Q's Capital A/c				15,680
	" R's Capital A/c				7,840
	(Profit on revaluation and realisation of policies transferred to Partners' Capital Accounts.)				

GENERAL ILLUSTRATIONS

Illustration 4

A, B and C carried on business in partnership, profits being divisible in the ratio of 3 : 2 : 1. The books on 31st December 2012 showed their capitals to be Rs. 5,200, Rs. 2,500 and Rs. 1,500.

On 28th February 2013 A died and you are instructed to prepare an account for presentation to his legal representatives having regard to the following facts :

(a) The firm had insured the partners' lives severally : A's for Rs. 4,500; B's for Rs. 2,400 and C's for Rs. 1,200.
Premia were charged to Profit and Loss Account. The surrender value of each policy on 28th February 2013, amounted in each case to one-fourth of the sum assured.

(b) Capital carried interest at 5% per annum.

(c) A's Drawings from 1st January 2013 to the date of his death amounted to Rs. 600.

(d) A's share of profits for portion of the current financial year for which he lived was to be taken at a sum calculated on the average of the last three years' profits. Goodwill is to be valued at 2 years' purchase of the average profits of the last three years. The annual profits were Rs. 1,450, Rs. 3,700 andRs. 4,300, respectively.

Show the account of the Executors of A and Journalise the entries affecting it.

Solution

Workings—A's claims on :

(1) Joint Life Policies :

A's policy : 3/6 of Rs. 4,500 or Rs. 2,250

B's and C's policies :

Surrender value : 1/4 of Rs. (2,400 + 1,200) or Rs. 900

∴ A's share: 3/6 of Rs. 900 or Rs. 450.

(2) Interest on Capital :

Interest on A's capital for 2 months : $\text{Rs. } 5{,}200 \times \frac{5}{100} \times \frac{2}{12}$ or Rs. 43.

(3) Share of Profit :

A's share of profit for 2 months on the basis of average of last 3 years :

Average Profit : $\frac{1,450 + 3,700 + 4,300}{3}$ or Rs. 3,150

Profit for 2 months : 2/12 of Rs. 3,150 or Rs. 525

∴ A's share : Rs. 525 × $\frac{3}{6}$ = Rs. 263.

(4) Goodwill

A's share of Goodwill :

Value of Goodwill at 2 years' purchase of average profit : 2 × 3,150 or Rs. 6,300

∴ A's share : Rs. 6,300 × $\frac{3}{6}$ = Rs. 3,150.

In the books of A, B, and C
Journal

Date	*Particulars*		*L.F.*	*Debit*	*Credit*
2013				Rs.	Rs.
Feb. 28	A's Capital A/c	Dr.		5,200	
	To Executors A/c				5,200
	(Balance standing in A's capital transferred)				
	Life Policy A/c [1]	Dr.		2,250	
	To Executors of A				2,250
	(A's share in the policy on his own life)				
	B's Capital A/c	Dr.		300	
	C's Capital A/c	Dr.		150	
	To Executors of A				450
	(A's share in the surrender value of the policies on the lives of B and C adjusted to the capital of B and C)[2]				
	Interest on Capital A/c	Dr.		43	
	To Executors of A				43
	(Interest on A's capital for 2 months up to the date of his death)				
	Profit and Loss Suspense A/c	Dr.		263	
	To Executors of A				263
	(A's share of profit on the basis of the average of last three years.)				
	B's Capital A/c	Dr.		2,100	
	C's Capital A/c	Dr.		1,050	
	To Executors of A				3,150
	(A's share of Goodwill adjusted against capitals of B and C)[2]				
	Executors of A	Dr.		600	
	To A's Drawings A/c				600
	(Balance standing in A's Drawings A/c transferred)				

Notes : 1. It has been assumed that the amount due on the life policy of A has not yet been received from the Insurance Company.

2. Since there is no change, A's share on Life Policy as well as in goodwill is to be borne by B and C in 2 : 1.

Executor's of A's Account

Dr.					Cr.
1	*Particulars*	*Amount*	*Date*	*Particulars*	*Amount*
2003		Rs.	2013		Rs.
Feb. 28	To A's Drawings A/c	600	Feb. 28	By A's Capital A/c	5,200
	" Balance c/d	10,756		" Joint Life Policy A/c	2,250
				" Interest on Capital A/c	43
				" Profit and Loss Suspense A/c	263
				" B's and C's Capital A/c —Goodwill	3,150
				" B and C's Capital A/c —Share of surrender value of B and C's policies	450
		11,356			11,356

Illustration 5

You are given the Balance Sheet of M/s Arun & Co. as on 31.12.2011 consisting of three partners —Mr. P, Mr. Q and Mr. R. They share profits and losses equally.

Balance Sheet of M/s Arun & Co.
as on 31.12.2011

Liabilities	Rs.	Assets	Rs.
Capital :		Plant and Machinery	11,825
P	5,000	Furniture	3,000
Q	8,000	Stock	9,250
R	7,000	Debtor	10,270
Creditors	5,000	Cash	5,655
6% Loan	15,000		
	40,000		40,000

R died on 1.1.2012, the following information is available :

(a) Rs. 1,130 received from Mr. Y as rent was credited to his personal account. He has already a debit balance for other transactions.

(b) Machine Costing Rs. 3,000 purchased on 27.12.2011 was debited to purchase account. Erection charges of Rs. 500 was charged to Repairs Account.

(c) A sum of Rs. 1,204, being interest, was paid in advance but the entire amount was charged to Profit and Loss Account in 2011.

(d) Machinery is valued at 20% below the book value after adjustment for (b) above.

(e) Debtors are estimated to be worth 95% of book value.

(f) Goodwill is to be valued at 3 years' purchase of the average profit of the years 2009, 2010 and 2011 and no goodwill account is to be raised.

(g) Profit for the years 2009 and 2010 were Rs. 9,000 and Rs. 10,000, respectively. Profit for the year 2011, subject to the adjustments (a), (b) and (c) above, was Rs. 6,921.

One-half of the dues to the deceased partner are to be met immediately by continuing partners in their profit-sharing ratio. Balance will continue as loan with 12% interest p.a. in the name of the executor of the deceased partner.

Show necessary accounts and Balance Sheet of the firm after one-half of the dues are paid.

[CA—Adapted and ICWA]

Solution

In the books of P, Q, and R
Profit and Loss Adjustment Account

Dr. Particulars		Amount Rs.	Particulars	Cr. Amount Rs.
To Plant and Machinery @ 20% on (11,825 + 3,000 + 500)		3,065	By Rent A/c (Debtors)	1,130
" Reserve for Bad Debts @ 5% on (10,270 + 1,130)		570	" Purchase (Plant and Machinery)	3,000
" Profit :			" Repairs A/c (Plant and Machinery)	500
P	733		" Prepaid Interest	1,204
Q	733			
R	733	2,199		
		5,834		5,834

Capital Account

Dr. Particulars	P Rs.	Q Rs.	R Rs.	Particulars	P Rs.	Q Rs.	Cr. R Rs.
To R's Capital A/c	5,292	5,293	—	By Balance b/d	5,000	8,000	7,000
" Bank A/c	—	—	9,159	" Profit and Loss Adjustment A/c	733	733	733
" R's Executor's A/c	—	—	9,159	" P & L A/c	—	—	10,585
" Balance c/d	5,021	8,019	—	" Bank	4,580	4,579	—
	10,313	13,312	18,318		10,313	13,312	18,318

Balance Sheet *as at Jan. 1, 2012*

Liabilities	Rs.	*Assets*		Rs.
Capital Accounts :		Plant and Machinery	11,825	
P	5,021	Additions	3,500	
Q	8,019		15,325	
R's Executor's A/c	9,159	*Less* : Depreciation	3,065	
Creditors	5,000			12,260
6% Loan A/c	15,000	Furniture		3,000
		Stock		9,250
		Debtors	10,270	
		Add : Rent	1,130	
			11,400	
		Less : Reserve for Bad Debts	570	
				10,830
		Prepaid Interest		1,204
		Bank		5,655
	42,199			42,199

Workings :

1. **R's Share of Goodwill :**

Average Profit $= \dfrac{\text{Rs. } 9{,}000 + \text{Rs. } 10{,}000 + \text{Rs. } 12{,}755}{3}$ (Rs. 6,921 + Rs. 5,834)

= Rs. 10,585

Value of Goodwill = Rs. 10,585 × 3 = Rs. 31,755

R's Share $= \dfrac{\text{Rs. } 31{,}755}{3}$ = Rs. 10,585 to be compensated by P & Q equally, i.e., Rs. 5,292 and Rs. 5,290, respectively.

Illustration 6

A, B and C were partners sharing profits and losses in the ratio of 3 : 2 : 1. On 1.7.2002, they contributed Rs. 15,000, Rs. 12,000 and Rs. 9,000, respectively, as fixed capital carrying interest at 5% p.a. They draw on account Rs. 400, Rs. 300 and Rs. 250 each month. On 30th June 2006, Y died, and it was settled with his legal representatives that they would be entitled to receive the following sums now :

(a) Y's Capital; (b) any undrawn balance of his share of profits, and (c) his share of goodwill which was to be valued at three years' purchase of the average profit of the last four years.

It appears that final accounts had never been prepared during all these years. The records revealed the following assets and liabilities as on 30th June 2006 :

Assets: Bank Rs. 7,500; Stock Rs. 36,000; Debtors Rs. 26,000; Building Rs. 35,500; Furniture Rs. 3,000; Machinery Rs. 15,000.

Liabilities: Loans and Deposits Rs. 25,000; Creditors Rs. 38,000. A and C introduced further Capital to pay-off the legal representatives of Y.

Show necessary accounts and the Balance Sheet of A and C as on 1st July 2006.

Solution **[CU MCom.]**

In the books of the firm

Statement of Profit and Loss *for the year ended 30th June 2006*

Liabilities	Rs.	*Assets*	Rs.
Loans and Deposits	25,000	Bank	7,500
Creditors	38,000	Stock	36,000
Capital *(bal. fig.)* c/d	60,000	Debtors	26,000
		Building	35,500
		Furniture	3,000
		Machinery	15,000
	1,23,000		1,23,000

Contd.

		Rs.		Rs.
Capital (Opening) :			Capital b/d	60,000
A	15,000		Drawings :	
B	12,000		A (Rs. 400 × 12 × 4) = Rs. 19,200	
C	9,000		B (Rs. 300 × 12 × 4) = Rs. 14,400	
		36,000	C (Rs. 250 × 12 × 4) = Rs. 12,000	
Gross Profit c/d		69,600		45,600
		1,05,600		1,05,600
Net Profit c/d		69,600	Gross Profit b/d	69,600
		69,600		69,600
Interest on Capital :			Net Profit b/d	69,600
A (Rs. 750 × 4)	3,000			
B (Rs. 600 × 4)	2,400			
C (Rs. 450 × 4)	1,800			
		7,200		
Share of Profit :				
A	31,200			
B	20,800			
C	10,400			
		62,400		
		69,600		69,600

Current Account

Dr. Particulars	A	B	C	Particulars	A	B	C Cr.
	Rs.	Rs.	Rs.		Rs.	Rs.	Rs.
To Bank A/c—Drawings	19,200	14,400	12,000	By Interest on Capital	3,000	2,400	1,800
" Executors of B A/c —Transfer	—	26,200	—	" P & L App. Suspense A/c —Share of Profit	31,200	20,800	10,400
" Balance c/d	41,100	—	8,900	" Goodwill	26,100	17,400	8,700[1]
	60,300	40,600	20,900		60,300	40,600	20,900

Capital Account

Dr. Particulars	A	B	C	Particulars	A	B	C Cr.
	Rs.	Rs.	Rs.		Rs.	Rs.	Rs.
To Executors of B A/c—Transfer	—	12,000	—	By Balance b/d	15,000	12,000	9,000
" Balance c/d	43,650	—	18,550	" Bank	28,650	—	9,550[3]
	43,650	12,000	18,550		43,650	12,000	18,550

Executors of Y Account

Dr.	Rs.		Cr. Rs.
To Bank A/c	38,200	By Y's Capital A/c	12,000
		" Y's Current A/c	26,200
	38,200		38,200

Balance Sheet *as at 1st July 2006*

Liabilities	Rs.	Rs.	Assets	Rs.
Loans and Deposits		25,000	Bank	7,500
Creditors		38,000	Stock	36,000
Capital Account :			Debtors	26,000

Contd.

A	43,650		Building	35,500
C	18,550	62,200	Furniture	3,000
			Machinery	15,000
Current Account :			Goodwill	52,200
A	41,100			
C	8,900	50,000		
		1,75,200		1,75,200

Notes :

1. Total profit for 4 years (before charging interest on capital) amounted to Rs. 69,600.

∴ Value of Goodwill $\frac{\text{Rs. } 69{,}600}{4}$ = Rs. 17,400 × 3 = Rs. 52,200.

2. Total payment to the executor of Y amounted to Rs. 38,200 which has been brought in by A and C in 3 : 1.

Illustration 7

A, B and C are partners sharing profits and losses at 5 : 3 : 2. A dies. The Balance Sheet as at the end of last year was :

Liabilities	Rs.	*Assets*	Rs.
Capital Account :		Land	1,00,000
A	2,00,000	Machinery	1,00,000
B	1,50,000	Debtors	3,00,000
C	1,00,000	Stock	2,00,000
Reserve	50,000	Cash at Bank	50,000
Creditors	2,50,000		
	7,50,000		7,50,000

Profit up to the date of death is estimated at Rs. 90,000 without considering any depreciation. One joint life policy of Rs. 1,50,000 (without profit) was taken in the last year. Premium of Rs. 10,000 was written-off to Profit and Loss Account. Each of the current assets (including Cash and Bank) is estimated to have gone up by 20%, creditors have increased by Rs. 20,000. Goodwill is to be calculated at 2 years' purchase of average profit of the three years.

The profits were : Rs. 90,000, Rs. 1,00,000, Rs. 1,10,000.

Dues to the deceased partner's representatives were to be settled on receipt of Insurance claim to the extent possible. Balance was to carry 10% interest from date of death and was to be paid after one year. Machinery was valued at Rs. 80,000. Prepare necessary accounts and a draft estimated Balance Sheet immediately after retirement.

Solution

In the books of A, B, and C

Revaluation Account

Dr. Cr.

	Particulars	*Amount* Rs.		*Particulars*	*Amountt* Rs.
To	Creditors	20,000	By	Debtors (3,00,000 × 20%)	60,000
"	Machinery	20,000	"	Stock (2,00,000 × 20%)	40,000
"	Profit and Loss Appropriation A/c	70,000	"	Cash and Bank (50,000 × 20%)	10,000
		1,10,000			1,10,000

* Calculation of Goodwill—

Average Profit = $\frac{\text{Rs. } 90{,}000 + \text{Rs. } 1{,}00{,}000 + \text{Rs. } 1{,}10{,}000}{3}$

= Rs. 1,00,000

Goodwill = Rs. 1,00,000 × 2 = Rs. 2,00,000.

A's share of goodwill = Rs. 2,00,000 × $\frac{5}{10}$ = Rs. 1,00,000 to be compensated by B and C in 3 : 2 i.e., Rs. 60,000 and Rs. 40,000 respectively

Dr. **Profit and Loss Appropriation Account** Cr.

Particulars	Rs.	Amount Rs.	Particulars	Amountt Rs.
To Share of Profit :			By Revaluation A/c (Profit)	70,000
A $\frac{5}{10}$	1,35,000		" Joint Life Policy	1,50,000
B $\frac{3}{10}$	81,000		" Reserve	50,000
C $\frac{2}{10}$	54,000			
		2,70,000		
		2,70,000		3,70,000

Balance Sheet *(immediately after A's death)*

Liabilities	Rs.	Rs.	Assets	Rs.
Capital Accounts :			Land	1,00,000
B (1,50,000 + 81,000 – 60,000)		1.71,000	Machinery	80,000
C (1,00,000 + 54,000 – 40,000)		1,14,000	Debtors	3,60,000
A's Executors A/c			Stock	2,40,000
(2,00,000 + 1,35,000 + 1,00,000)		4,35,000	Joint Life Policy	1,50,000
Creditors		2,70,000	Cash and Bank	60,000
		9,90,000		9,90,000

Carrying on the business without final settlement of deceased partner's account

Usually, the right of outgoing or deceased partner terminates at the date of his retirement or death but if the continuing or existing partners continue the business without any final settlement of the accounts as between the firm and outgoing partner or the legal representatives of the deceased partner, in the absence of agreement to the contrary, the outgoing partner or the legal representatives of the deceased is entitled (by Sec. 37 of the Indian Partnership Act) at his choice, to interest @ 6% p.a. on the amount due from the date of retirement or death to the date of payment or to that portion of profit which has been earned by the firm by that unpaid amount. Following problem will make the principle clear.

Illustration 8

A, B and C were in partnership sharing profits and losses in the ratio of 2 : 2 : 1. Their capital as on 1st Jan. 2007 were Rs. 1,00,000, Rs. 50,000 and Rs. 25,000, respectively. On 1st July 2007, C died. His representative agreed that :

(i) Goodwill of the firm be valued at Rs. 40,000. (No goodwill account appears in the Balance Sheet on 1.1.2007). (ii) Fixed assets be written-down by Rs. 10,000. (iii) During 2007, the firm earned a profit of Rs. 50,000. (iv) Drawings of the partners were :

	Up to 1st July 2007 Rs.	After 1st July 2007 Rs.
A	8,000	10,000
B	8,000	10,000
C	4,000	—

Prepare the Profit and Loss Appropriation Account, and the Capital Accounts of the partners for the year.

Solution

Dr. **Profit and Loss Appropriation Account** Cr.

Particulars	Amount Up to 1st July Rs.	Amount After 1st July Rs.	Particulars	Amount Up to 1st July Rs.	Amount After 1st July Rs.
To C's Representative's A/c	—	3,810	Net Profit	25,000	25,000
Share of Profit					
A	10,000	10,595			
B	10,000	10,595			
C	5,000	—			
	25,000	25,000		25,000	25,000

Capital Account

Dr. Cr.

Date	Particulars	A	B	C	Date	Particulars	A	B	C
2007		Rs.	Rs.	Rs.	2007		Rs.	Rs.	Rs.
July 1	To Drawings	8,000	8,000	4,000	Jan. 1	By Balance b/d	1,00,000	50,000	25,000
"	P & L Adjustment A/c	4,000	4,000	2,000	July 1	" P & L App. —Share of Prof.	10,000	10,000	5,000
	To C's Representation A/c	—	—	32,000		By Goodwill	16,000	16,000	8,000
"	Balance c/d	1,14,000	64,000	—					
		1,26,000	76,000	38,000			1,26,000	76,000	38,000
July 1	To Drawings	10,000	10,000	—	July 1	By Balance	1,14,000	64,000	—
"	Balance c/d	1,14,595	64,595	—		" P & L App. A/c —Share of Profit	10,595	10,595	—
		1,24,595	74,595	—			1,24,595	74,595	—

Note : 1. Proportion of profit belongs to C's representatives is calculated as:

$$\frac{\text{Rs. } 32{,}000}{\text{Rs. } 2{,}10{,}000} \times \text{Rs. } 25{,}000 = \text{Rs. } 3{,}810 \text{ (app.)}.$$

Illustration 9

The following was the Balance Sheet of A, B, and C who shared profits and Losses in the ratio of 1 : 2 : 2 as on 31st December 2010 :

Liabilities	Rs.	*Assets*	Rs.
Sundry Creditors	10,000	Debtors	25,000
Capital :		Machinery	20,000
A	10,000	Buildings	30,000
B	20,000	Stock	10,000
C	20,000	Cash at Bank	5,000
General Reserve	5,000	Investments	10,000
Investment Fluctuation Fund	3,000		
Bad Debts Reserve	2,000		
Bank Loan	30,000		
	1,00,000		1,00,000

C died on 31st March 2011. His account is to be settled under the following terms :

Goodwill is to be calculated at the rate of 2 years' purchase on the basis of the average of 5 years profit or loss. Profit for January to March 2011 is to be calculated proportionately on the average profit of 3 years. The profits were : 2006 Rs. 3,000, 2007 Rs. 7,000, 2008 Rs. 10,000, 2009 Rs. 14,000, 2010 loss Rs. 12,000. During 2010 a moped costing Rs. 4,000 was purchased and debited to Travelling Expenses Account on which depreciation is to be calculated @ 25%. Other values agreed on assets are : Stock Rs. 12,000, Building Rs. 35,000, Machinery Rs. 25,000 and Investments Rs. 8,000. Debtors are considered good.

Prepare new Balance Sheet of the firm, necessary Journal entries and Ledger Accounts of the partners.

Solution

[CA Foundation, May 2000 & CA Adapted]

In the books of A, B, & C

Journal

Date	*Particulars*		*L.F.*	*Debit*	*Credit*
2011				Rs.	Rs.
March 31	Stock A/c	Dr.		2,000	
	Buildings A/c	Dr.		5,000	
	Machinery A/c	Dr.		5,000	
	Moped A/c [4,000 – Depr. 1,000]	Dr.		3,000	
	To Revaluation A/c				15,000
	(Value of assets increased on revaluation)				

Contd.

Date	Particulars		Rs.	Rs.
2011 Mar. 31	Revaluation A/c	Dr.	2,000	
	To Investments A/c			2,000
	Revaluation A/c	Dr.	13,000	
	To A's Capital A/c			2,600
	" B's Capital A/c			5,200
	" C's apital A/c			5,200
	(Profit on revaluation transferred.)			
Mar. 31	General Reserve A/c	Dr.	5,000	
	Investment Fluctuation Fund A/c	Dr.	3,000	
	Bad Debts Reserve A/c	Dr.	2,000	
	To A's CapitalA/c			2,000
	" B's Capital A/c			4,000
	" C's Capital A/c			4,000
	(Transfer of Reserves etc. to Partners' Capitals in 1 : 2 : 2)			
"	Profit and Loss Suspense A/c	Dr.	500	
	To C's Capital A/c			500
	(Estimated share of Profit till his date of death transferred to the deceased partner's Capital Account)			
"	C's Capital A/c	Dr.	27,700	
	To C's Executors A/c			27,700
	(Total dues to the deceased partner transferred to his Executor's A/c)			

Capital Accounts

Dr. Cr.

Date	Particulars	A	B	C	Date	Particulars	A	B	C
2011		Rs.	Rs.	Rs.	2011		Rs.	Rs.	Rs.
Mar. 31	To C's Cap. A/c	1,333	2,667		Jan. 1	By Balance b/d	10,000	20,000	20,000
	" C's Executors A/c (Balance transferred)	—	—	33,700		" Revaluation A/c	2,600	5,200	5,200
	" Balance c/f	13,267	26,533	—	Mar. 31	" Sundry Reserves A/c	2,000	4,000	4,000
						" A's Cap. A/c	—	—	1,333
						" B's Cap. A/c	—	—	2,667
						" Profit & Loss Suspense A/c	—	—	500[2]
		14,600	29,200	33,700			14,600	29,200	33,700

Balance Sheet *as on 31st March 2011*

Dr. Cr.

Liabilities	Rs.	Rs.	Assets	Rs.	Rs.
Capitals :			Buildings		35,000
A	13,267		Machinery		25,000
B	26,533		Moped (cost *less* depreciation)		3,000
		39,800	Investments		8,000
C's Executor's A/c		33,700	Stock		12,000
Bank Loan		30,000	Debtors		25,000
Sundry Creditors		10,000	Bank		5,000
			Profit and Loss Suspense A/c		500
		1,13,500			1,13,500

Workings :

1. Computation of Goodwill

$$\text{Average Profit} = \frac{\text{Rs. } 3{,}000 + \text{Rs. } 7{,}000 + \text{Rs. } 10{,}000 + \text{Rs. } 14{,}000 - \text{Rs. } 9{,}000^{*}}{5}$$

= Rs. 5,000

∴ Goodwill = Rs. 5,000 × 2 (years' purchase) = Rs. 10,000.

∴ C's share of goodwill = Rs. 10,000 × $\frac{2}{5}$ = Rs. 4,000 to be compensated by A & B in 1: 2, i.e., Rs, 1,333 and Rs. 2,667, respectively.

	Rs.
Loss for 2010	12,000
Less : Cost of Moped wrongly charged	4,000
	8,000
Add : Dep. on Moped @ 25% of 4,000 =	1,000
	9,000

2. **Deceased Partners' share of Profit till the date of his death**

Average Profit (last 3 years) $= \frac{\text{Rs. } 10,000 + \text{Rs. } 14,000 - \text{Rs. } 9,000}{3} = \text{Rs. } 5,000$

∴ Estimated Profit for 3 months $= \text{Rs. } 5,000 \times \frac{3}{12} = \text{Rs. } 1,250$

So, C's share = Rs. 500 (i.e., Rs. $1,250 \times \frac{2}{5}$).

MISCELLANEOUS

Illustration 10

Haba, Goba, Boba were partners sharing profits and losses in the ratio 2 : 1 : 1. It was provided in the partnership deed that in the event of retirement/death of a partner he/his legal representatives would be paid :

(i) The balance in the Capital Account.

(ii) His share of goodwill of the firm valued at two years' purchases of normal average profits (after charging interest on fixed capital) for the last three years to 31st Dec. preceding the retirement on death.

(iii) His share of profits from the beginning of the accounting year to the date of retirement or death, which shall be taken on proportionate basis of profits of the previous year as increased by 25%.

(iv) Interest on Fixed Capital at 10% p.a. though payable to the partners will not be payable in the year of death or retirement.

(v) All the assets are to be revalued on the date of retirement or death and the profit and loss be debited/credited to the capital accounts in the profit-sharing ratio.

Haba died on 30th Sept. 2013. The books of account are closed on calendar year basis from 1st Jan. to 31st Dec.

The balance in the fixed capital accounts as on 1st Jan. 2013, were Haba Rs. 10,000, Goba Rs. 5,000 and Boba Rs. 5,000. The balance in the Current Accounts as on 1.1.2013 were Haba Rs. 20,000, Goba Rs. 10,000 and Boba Rs. 7,000. Drawings of Haba till 30th Sept. 2013 were Rs. 10,000. The profits of the firm before charging interest on Capital for the calendar years 2010, 2011 and 2012 were Rs. 1,00,000, Rs. 1,20,000 and Rs. 1,50,000, respectively. The profits include the following abnormal items of credit :

	2010	2011	2012
	Rs.	Rs.	Rs.
Profit on sale of assets	5,000	7,000	10,000
Insurance claim received	3,000	—	12,000

The firm has taken out of joint life policy for Rs. 1,00,000. Besides, the partners had severally insured their lives for Rs. 50,000 each, the premium in respect there of being charged to the Profit and Loss Account. The surrender value of the policies were 30% of the face value. On 30.6.2013 the firm received notice from the insurance company that the insurance premium in respect of a fire policy had been under charged to the extent of Rs. 6,000 in the year 2012 and the firm has to pay immediately. The revaluation of the assets indicate an upward revision in value of assets to the extent of Rs. 20,000.

Prepare an account showing the amount due to Haba's legal representatives as on 30.9.2013 along with necessary workings.

Solution

In the books of Haba, Goba, and Boba
Executors of Haba Account

Dr. Cr.

Date	Particulars	Amount	Date	Particulars	Amount
2013		Rs.	2013		Rs.
Sept. 30	To Balance c/d	2,91,031	Sept. 30	By Haba's Capital A/c	20,000[1]
				" Haba's Current A/c	2,71,031
		2,91,031			2,91,031

Workings :

1.

Haba's Capital Account

Dr. Cr.

Date		Particulars	Amount	Date		Particulars	Amount
2013			Rs.	2013			Rs.
Sept. 30	To	Executors of Haba A/c —Transfer	20,000	Jan. 1	By	Balance b/d	10,000
					"	Profit on Revaluation of Assets	10,000*
			20,000				20,000

Profit on Revaluation :

	Rs.
* Upward revision in the value of assets	20,000

∴ Haba's share of profit @$\frac{2}{4}$ = Rs. 20,000 × $\frac{2}{4}$ = Rs. 10,000. Usually, this item is transferred to Current Asset, but the same is transferred to Capital account as per requirement of the question, vide, No. (v).

Haba's Current Account

Dr. Cr.

Date		Particulars	Amount	Date		Particulars	Amount
2013			Rs.	2013			Rs.
Sept. 30	To	Drawings A/c	10,000	Jan. 1	By	Balance b/d	20,000
	"	Insurance Premium —Undercharged (Rs. 6,000 × $\frac{2}{4}$)	3,000	Sept. 30	"	Goodwill A/c	1,07,000[2]
					"	Share of Profit	67,031[3]
					"	Joint Life Policy	90,000[4]
	"	Executors of Haba A/c —Transfer	2,71,031				
			2,84,031				2,84,031

2. **Computation of Goodwill and Haba's share of Goodwill**

Adjusted Profit

	2010		2011		2012	
		Rs.		Rs.		Rs.
Profit (as per P & L A/c)		1,00,000		1,20,000		1,50,000
Less : Interest on Capital @ 10% =	2,000		2,000		2,000	
Abnormal Items :						
Profit on Sale of Assets	5,000		7,000		10,000	
Received from Insurance Co.	3,000		—		12,000	
Undercharged Insurance Premium	—		—		6,000	
		10,000		9,000		30,000
		90,000		1,11,000		1,20,000

∴ Average Profit = $\frac{\text{Rs. 90,000 + Rs. 1,11,000 + Rs. 1,20,000}}{3}$ = Rs. 1,07,000

∴ Value of Goodwill = Rs. 1,07,000 × 2 = Rs. 2,14,000 Haba's share of Goodwill = Rs. 2,14,000 × $\frac{2}{4}$ = Rs. 1,07,000.

3. **Haba's share of Profit**

		Rs.	Rs.
	Profit for 2012		1,50,000
Less :	Interest on Capital (excluding Haba's)	1,000	
	Undercharged Insurance Premium	6,000	7,000
			1,43,000
Add :	Increased by 2013		35,750
	Estimated Profit for 2013		1,78,750

Estimated Profit up to 30.9.2013 = Rs. 1,34,062 (i.e., 1,78,750 × $\frac{9}{12}$).

∴ Haba's share = (Rs. 1,34,062 × $\frac{2}{4}$) Rs. 67,031.

4. Haba's share of Joint Life Policy

		Rs.
	Joint Life policy (F.V.)	1,00,000
	Maturity Value of individual policy	50,000
Add :	Surrender value (30% of face value)	30,000
		1,80,000

∴ Haba's share = Rs. 1,80,000 × $\frac{2}{4}$ = Rs. 90,000.

Illustration 11

Firm ABC consisted of 3 partners, A, B and C sharing profits and losses in the ratio 5 : 3 : 2, respectively. The partner A died on February 20, 2009, Profit and Loss Account for the period up to date of death and Balance Sheet as on that date were prepared. The Balance Sheet as on that date was :

Balance Sheet

Liabilities	Rs.	Rs.	*Assets*	Rs.
Capital Accounts :			Land & Building	6,000
A	12,000		Machinery	35,000
B	16,000		Furniture	6,000
C	12,000		Stock	9,000
		40,000	Debtors	15,000
Loan from A		5,000	Bank	3,000
Current A/c ; (A Rs. 3,500; B Rs. 2,100, C Rs. 1,400)		7,000		
Creditors		22,000		
		74,000		74,000

In addition to the assets shown above, the firm had 3 life policies in the name of each partner, for insured value of Rs. 20,000 each, the premiums of which were charged to Profit and Loss Account.

According to the partnership deed, on death of partner, the assets and liabilities are to be revalued by a valuer. The revalued figures were :

(1) Land & Building Rs. 21,000; Machinery Rs. 45,000; Debtors are subject to a provision for doubtful debts at 10% and Furniture at Rs. 7,000:

(2) Provision for taxation to be created for Rs. 1,500.

(3) Death-claim for policy in the name of A will be realised in full and the surrender values of the other 2 policies were Rs. 7,500 each.

The business will be continued by B and C, henceforth sharing profits and losses equally. The net balance due to A is transferred to a Loan Account, which will be paid off later.

Show Capital Account, Revaluation Account and the new Balance Sheet of the firm.

Solution

In the books of A, B, and C

Revaluation Account

Dr. | *Cr.*

Particulars	Rs.	*Amount* Rs.	Particulars	*Amount* Rs.
To Reserve for Bad Bebts		1,500	By Land of Building	15,000
" Provision for Taxation		1,500	" Machinery	10,000
" Profit on Revaluation :			" Furniture	1,000
A $\frac{5}{10}$	11,500			
B $\frac{3}{10}$	6,900			
C $\frac{2}{10}$	4,600			
		23,000		
		26,000		26,000

Capital Account

Dr. | *Cr.*

Particulars	A Rs.	B Rs.	C Rs.	*Particulars*	A Rs.	B Rs.	C Rs.
To A's Executors A/c	41,000	—	—	By Balance b/d	12,000	16,000	12,000
" Balance c/d	—	33,400	23,600	" Revaluation A/c —Profit	11,500	6,900	4,600
				" Insurance Claim A/c	17,500	10,500	7,000
	41,000	33,400	23,600		41,000	33,400	23,600
				By Balance b/d	—	33,400	23,600

Dr. **A's Executors Account** Cr.

Particulars	Rs.	Amount Rs.	Particulars	Amount Rs.
To Balance c/d		49,500	By A's Capital A/c	41,000
			" Currents A/c	3,500
			" Loan A/c	5,000
		49,500		49,500

Dr. **Insurance Claim Account** Cr.

Particulars	Rs.	Amount Rs.	Particulars	Amount Rs.
To Capital Accounts :			By Bank :	
A	17,500		Claim of A's policy	20,000
B	10,500		Surrender of B and C's Policy	15,000
C	7,000		(7,500 × 2)	
		35,000		
		35,000		35,000

Balance Sheet *as at ....*

Liabilities	Rs.	Rs.	Assets	Rs.	Rs.
Capital Accounts :			Land and Buildings		21,000
B	33,400		Machinery		45,000
C	23,600	57,000	Furniture		7,000
Currennt A/c			Stock		9,000
B	2,100		Debtors	15,000	
C	1,400	3,500	*Less*: Reserve for Bad Debts	1,500	13,500
Loan from A's Estate		49,500	Bank (3,000 + 35,000)		38,000
Creditors		22,000			
Provision for Taxation		1,500			
		1,33,500			1,33,500

Illustration 12

Ravindra Singh, Sundaram, and Telewani were partners sharing profits and losses in the proportion of 1/2, 1/3 and 1/6, respectively. Telewani expired on 31st May 2005.

Partnership agreement provided that :

(a) Interest on fixed capital to be allowed at 12% p.a.

(b) Telewani to be credited with salary of Rs. 18,000 p.a.

(c) On the death of any of the partners, his heir will receive, in addition to balance in the fixed, capital and current account :

(i) Salary and interest on capital.

(ii) Share of proportionate profit from last Balance Sheet to the date of death based on annual average profits of last 3 years (after interest on capital and salary to partner).

(iii) Share of goodwill calculated at twice the average profits of last 3 years (before interest on capital and salary to partner).

(iv) Share of profit on joint assurance policy.

Following further information is available :

(A) Fixed capitals on 31.3.2005 :

Ravindra Singh Rs. 3,00,000; Sundaram Rs. 2,00,000; Telewani Rs. 1,00,000.

(B) Current Accounts (credit) on 31.3.2005 :

Ravindra Singh Rs. 50,000; Sundaram Rs. 10,000; Telewani Rs. 20,000.

(C) Joint Life Policy Rs. 1,00,000.

(D) There is no change in capital and current accounts since 31.3.2005.

(E) Joint Life Policy realised Rs. 1,50,000/- (on 15.6.2005 amount due to Telewani paid on receipt of policy amount).

(F) Profits (before interest and salary) were :

2004-05 Rs. 1,24,000; 2003-04 Rs. 1,20,000; 2002-03 Rs. 80,000; 2001-02 Rs.1,30,000.

(G) The firm closes its books on 31st March, Ravindra Singh and Sundaram decided to continue the firm and to raise goodwill.

Show the following accounts in the books of the firm relating to the above transactions :

(a) Current Accounts of Partners, (b) Profit and Loss Adjustment A/c, and (c) Heir of Telewani's Loan A/c.

[ICWA]

Solution

Workings :

Valuation of Goodwill and Telewani's share thereon :

$$\text{Average Profit} = \frac{\text{Rs. } 1{,}24{,}000 + \text{Rs. } 1{,}20{,}000 + \text{Rs. } 80{,}{,}000}{3}$$

$$= \text{Rs. } 1{,}08{,}000$$

And, Value of Goodwill = Rs. 1,08,000 × 2 = Rs. 2,16,000.

Telewani's Share of Goodwill = Rs. 2,16,000 × $\frac{1}{6}$ = 36,000.

(The entry for the purpose will be :

Ravindra's Current A/c Dr.	21,600	
Sundaram's Current A/c Dr.	14,400	
To Telewani's Current A/c		36,000)

Calculation of Profit to be credited to Telewani's Current Account

Average Profit (from the above) Rs. 1,08,000

∴ Proportionate profits for 2 months = Rs. 1,08,000 × $\frac{2}{12}$ = Rs. 18,000.

		Rs.
So, Proportionate profit for 2 months (before charging interest on Capital and Salary)		18,000
Less : Interest on Capital	Rs.	
Ravinder	6,000 $(3{,}00{,}000 \times \frac{12}{100} \times \frac{2}{12})$	
Sundaram	4,000 $(2{,}00{,}000 \times \frac{12}{100} \times \frac{2}{12})$	
Telewani	2,000 $(1{,}00{,}000 \times \frac{12}{100} \times \frac{2}{12})$	
	12,000	
Partners' Salary : Telewani 1,500 × 2 =	3,000	
		15,000
		3,000

∴ Telewani's share = Rs. 3,000 × $\frac{1}{6}$ = Rs. 500.

Dr. **Profit and Loss Adjustment Account** Cr.

Particulars	Amount Rs.	Amount Rs.	Particulars	Amount Rs.
To Current A/c :			By Joint Life Policy Profit (1,50,000 – 1,00,000)	50,000
Ravinder	25,000			
Sundaram	16,667			
Telewani	8,333			
		50,000		
		50,000		50,000

Particulars		Rs.	Particulars	Rs.
To Telewani's Current A/c :			By Balance c/d	15,500
Profit	500			
Salary	3,000			
Interest	2,000			
		5,500		
" Ravinder's Current A/c — Interest		6,000		
" Sundaram's Current A/c — Interest		4,000		
		15,500		15,500

Current Account

Dr. Particulars	Ravinder Rs.	Sundaram Rs.	Telewani Rs.	Particulars	Ravinder Rs.	Sundaram Rs.	Telewani Rs. Cr.
To Telewani Current A/c	21,600	14,400	—	By Balance b/d	50,000	10,000	20,000
" Heir of Telewani's Loan A/c	—	—	69,833	" P & L Adj. A/c (J.L.P.)	25,000	16,667	8,333
" Balance c/d	59,400	16,267	—	" Ravinder's Current A/c	—	—	21,600
				" Sundaram's Current A/c	—	—	14,400
				" P & L Adj. A/c : Profit	—	—	500
				Salary	—	—	3,000
				Interest	6,000	4,000	2,000
	81,000	30,667	69,833		81,000	30,667	69,833

Heir of Telewani's Loan Account

Dr. Particulars	Amount Rs.	Particulars	Amount Rs. Cr.
To Bank A/c	1,69,833	By Telewani's Capital A/c	1,00,000
		" Telewani's Current A/c	69,833
	1,69,833		1,69,833

Illustration 13

Basu, Chatterjee and Saxena were in partnership sharing profits $\frac{3}{6}$, $\frac{2}{6}$ and $\frac{1}{6}$, respectively. There was no provision in the agreement for interest on capital/drawings.

Basu died on 31st Dec. 2007 and on that date the partners balance were :

Current A/c : Basu Rs. 29,000 (Cr.); Chatterjee Rs. 20,000 (Cr.); Saxena Rs. 5,000 (Dr.); Capital A/c : Basu Rs. 60,000 (Cr.); Chatterjee Rs. 40,000 (Cr.); Saxena Rs. 20,000 (Cr.).

By the partnership agreement the sum due to Basu's estate was required to be paid within a period of 3 years, and minimum instalment of Rs. 20,000, each were to be paid, the first such instalment falling due immediately after death and the subsequent instalments at held yearly interval thereafter. Interest @ 5% p.a. was to be credited half-yearly.

In ascertaining his share, goodwill (not recorded in the books) was to be valued at Rs. 60,000 and the assets, excluding the joint endowment Assurance Policy mentioned below, were valued at Rs. 36,000 in excess of the book value.

No goodwill account was raised and no alternation was made to the book values of fixed assets. The Joint Assurance Policy shown in the books at Rs. 20,000 matured on 1.1.2008, realising Rs. 26,000; payment of Rs. 20,000 each were made to Basu's estate on 1.1.2008, 30.6.2008, and 31.12.2008. Chatterjee and Saxena continued trading on the same terms as previously and the net profit for the year 31.12.2008 (before charging the interest due to Basu's estate) amounted to Rs. 32,000. During that period the partners' drawings were : Chatterjee Rs. 15,000 and Saxena Rs. 8,000.

On 1.1.2009, the partnership was dissolved, an offer to purchase the business as a going concern for Rs. 1,40,000 being accepted on that day. A cheque for that sum was received on 15.3.2009.

The balance due to Basu's estate, including interest, was paid on 30.6.2009, and on that day Chatterjee and Saxena received the sums due to them.

You are required to write up the partners' capital and current account from 1.1.2008 closing them on 30.6.2009. Show also the accounts of the executors of Basu.

Solution

In the books of the Firm
Current Account

Dr. Date	Particulars	Basu	Chatterjee	Saxena	Date	Particulars	Basu	Chatterjee	Saxena Cr.
2008		Rs.	Rs.	Rs.	2008		Rs.	Rs.	Rs.
Jan. 1	To Balance b/d	—	—	5,000	Jan. 1	By Balance b/d	29,000	20,000	—
	" Goodwill A/c	—	40,000	20,000		" Joint Life Policy A/c	3,000	2,000	1,000
	" Reval. A/c —Profit written-back	—	24,000	12,000		Goodwill A/c	30,000	20,000	10,000
	" Capital A/c —Transfer	80,000	—	—		" Reval. A/c —Profit	18,000	12,000	6,000
						" Balance c/d	—	10,000	20,000
		80,000	64,000	37,000			80,000	64,000	37,000
2008					2008				
Jan. 1	To Balance b/d	—	10,000	20,000	Dec. 31	By Profit and Loss A/c	—	17,617	8,808[1]
Dec. 31	" Drawings A/c	—	15,000	8,000		" Balance c/d	—	7,383	19,192
		—	25,000	28,000			—	25,000	28,000
2009					2009				
Jan. 1	To Balance b/d	—	7,383	19,192	June 30	By Realisation A/c	—	12,573	6,287[2]
	" Capital A/c —Transfer	—	5,190	—		" Capital A/c —Transfer	—	—	12,905
		—	12,573	19,192			—	12,573	19,192

Capital Account

Dr. Date	Particulars	Basu	Chatterjee	Saxena	Date	Particulars	Basu	Chatterjee	Saxena Cr.
2008		Rs.	Rs.	Rs.	2008		Rs.	Rs.	Rs.
Jan. 1	To Executor's A/c	1,40,000	—	—	Jan. 1	By Balance b/d	60,000	40,000	20,000
	" Balance c/d	—	40,000	20,000		" Current A/c —Transfer	80,000	—	—
		1,40,000	40,000	20,000			1,40,000	40,000	20,000
2008									
Dec. 31	To Balance c/d	—	40,000	20,000	Jan. 1	By Balance b/d	—	40,000	20,000
		—	40,000	20,000			—	40,000	20,000
2009					2009				
June 30	To Current A/c	—	—	12,905	Jan. 1	By Balance b/d	—	40,000	20,000
	" Bank A/c	—	45,190	7,095	June 30	" Current A/c	—	5,190	—
		—	45,190	20,000			—	45,190	20,000

Basu's Executor's Account

Dr. Date	Particulars	Amount	Date	Particulars	Amount Cr.
2008		Rs.	2008		Rs.
Jan 1	To Bank A/c	20,000	Jan. 1	By Basu's Capital A/c	1,40,000
	" Balance c/d	1,20,000			
		1,40,000			1,40,000
2009			2009		
June 30	To Bank A/c	20,000	Jan. 1	By Balance b/d	1,20,000
	" Balance c/d	1,03,000	June 30	" Interest A/c (5% on Rs. 1,20,000 × $\frac{6}{12}$)	3,000
		1,23,000			1,23,000

			Rs.				Rs.
Dec. 31	To	Bank A/c	20,000	July 1	By	Balance b/d	1,03,000
	"	Balance c/d	85,575	Dec. 31	"	Interest A/c (5% on Rs. 1,03,000 × $\frac{6}{12}$)	2,575
			1,05,575				1,05,575
2009				2009			
June 30	To	Bank A/c	87,715	Jan. 1	By	Balance b/d	85,575
				June 30	"	Interest A/c (5% on Rs. 85,575 × $\frac{6}{12}$)	2,140
			87,715				87,715

Workings :

Computation of Net Distributable Profit

			Rs.
1.	Profits (given) (before charging interest)		32,000
	Less : Interest to Basu's executor :		
	On 30.6.2008	3,000	
	on 31.12.2008	2,575	5,575
			26,425

Chatterjee gets = Rs. 26,425 × $\frac{2}{3}$ = Rs. 17,617, and

Saxena gets = Rs. 26,425 × $\frac{1}{3}$ = Rs. 8,808.

2. **Profit on Realisation :**

In order to find out the Profit on Realisation, we are to prepare the following Balance Sheet and then the Realisation Account :

Balance Sheet

as at 31st Dec. 2009

Liabilities	*Rs.*	*Assets*	*Rs.*
Capital :		Current A/c :	
Chatterjee	40,000	Chatterjee	7,383
Saxena	20,000	Saxena	19,192
Basu's Executors	85,575	Sundry Assets *(bal. fig.)*	1,19,000
	1,45,575		1,45,575

Dr. **Realisation Account** *Cr.*

		Rs.			Rs.
To	Sundry Assets A/c	1,19,000	By	Bank A/c —Sale of Business	1,40,000
"	Profit on Realisation	21,000			
		1,40,000			1,40,000

From the profit on realisation i.e., Rs. 21,000, Rs. 2,140 to deducted as interest to executors of Basu and the balance Rs. 18,860 (i.e., Rs. 21,000 – Rs. 2,140) will be distributed between Chatterjee and Saxena in 2 : 1. So, Chatterjee will get Rs. 12,573, Saxena will get Rs. 6,287.

Illustration 14

X, Y and Z were in partnership sharing profits and losses in the ratio 2 : 2 : 1. Their Balance Sheet as on 31st Dec. 2009 stood as :

Particulars	*Amount*	*Particulars*	*Amount*
	Rs.		Rs.
Capital A/c :		Fixed Asset	40,000
X	25,000	Current Asset (including Cash at Bank Rs. 25,000)	45,000
Y	20,000		
Z	15,000		
Reserve	10,000		
Loans	10,000		
Creditors	5,000		
	85,000		85,000

X died on 31st March 2010. As per Partnership Deed, goodwill is to be computed on the basis of 3 times the average profit of the past 5 years.

Profit 2006 Rs. 15,000; 2007 Rs. 20,000; 2008 Rs. 25,000; 2009 Rs. 12,000 and 2010 Rs. 28,000. The existing partners and the excutors of A decided that profit of the deceased partner from 1.1.2013 to 31.3.2013, may be considered on the basis of profit of the last year. Executors were immediately paid Rs. 10,000 and the balance to be paid by $\frac{4}{5}$ annual instalment with interest @ 10% p.a.

Show X's Capital account and Executors of X Account.

Solution

1. **X's Share of Goodwill**

$$\text{Average Profit} = \frac{\text{Rs. } 15,000 + \text{Rs. } 20,000 + 25,000 + \text{Rs. } 12,000 + \text{Rs. } 28,000}{5}$$

Goodwill = Rs. 20,000 × 3 = Rs. 60,000; X's Share of Goodwill = Rs. 60,000 × $\frac{2}{5}$ = Rs. 24,000 to be taken by Y and Z in 2 : 1, i.e., Y = Rs. 24,000 × $\frac{2}{3}$ = Rs. 16,000; Z = Rs. 24,000 × $\frac{1}{3}$ =Rs. 8,000

2. **X's Share of Profit (from 1.1.2013 to 31.3.2013)**

Profit for 2012 (last year) Rs. 28,000 for 12 months

∴ For 3 months = R. 28,000 × $\frac{3}{12}$ = Rs. 7,000 credited to X's Capital Account by debiting Profit and Loss Suspense Account

In the books of the firm

X's Capital Account

Dr. Particulars	Amount	Cr. Particulars	Amount
	Rs.		Rs.
To Bank A/c	10,000	By Balance b/d	25,000
By X's Executor's A/c	50,000	To Reserve	4,000
		" Y's Capital A/c	16,000
		' Z's Capital A/c	8,000
		" Profit & Loss Suspense A/c	7,000
	60,000		60,000

X's Executor's Account

Dr. Date	Particulars	Amount	Date	Cr. Particulars	Amount
2010		Rs.	2010		Rs.
Dec. 31	To Balance c/d	50,000	March 31	By A's Capital A/c	50,000
		50,000			50,000
2011			2011		
March 31	To Bank A/c (Rs. 12,500 + Rs. 5,000)	17,500	Jan. 1	By Balance b/d	50,000
Dec. 31	" Balance c/d	37,500	March 31	" Interest @ 10%	5,000
		55,000			55,000
2012			2012		
March 31	To Bank A/c (Rs. 12,500 + Rs. 3,750)	16,250	Jan. 1	By Balance b/d	37,500
Dec. 31	" Balance c/d	25,000	March 31	" Interest @ 10%	3,750
		41,250			41,250
2013			2013		
March 31	To Bank A/c (Rs. 12,500 + Rs. 2,500)	15,000	Jan. 1	By Balance b/d	25,000
Dec. 31	" Balance c/d	12,500	March 31	" Interest @ 10%	2,500
		27,500			27,500
2014			2014		
March 31	To Bank	13,250	Jan. 1	By Balance b/d	12,500
			March 31	" Interest @ 10%	1,250
		13,250			13,250

Illustration 15

The following is the Balance Sheet of the firm of ABC as on 31.12.2013 :

Their profit-sharing ratio is 3 : 2 : 1:

Capital & Liabilities		Rs.	Assets	Rs.
Capital A/cs:			Fixed Assets	40,000
A		16,000	Sundry debtors	32,000
B		12,000	Insurance policy on	
C		10,000	Joint Life of Partners	6,000
Capital A/cs:			Stock	24,000
A		4,000	Bank	9,000
B		3,000	Cash	3,000
C		1,000		
Reserve		18,000		
P & L A/c	6,000			
Profit of the year	14,000	20,000		
Creditors		20,000		
Bank O/D		10,000		
		1,14,000		1,14,000

B died on 31.3.2014. His account has to be settled and paid. For the year 2014, proportionate profit of 2013 is to be taken into account. For 2013, a debt of Rs. 2,000 has to be adjusted. Goodwill has to be calculated 3 times of the four years' average profits. A policy is taken on the joint life of partners for Rs. 35,000 and the annual premium of Rs. 2,000 has to be paid on Feb. 1 every year. The profits for 2012 Rs. 16,000, 2011 Rs. 20,000 and 2010 is Rs. 12,000. Goodwill Account need not be kept in the accounts. Calculate the amount payable to B's heirs.

Show necessary ledger accounts of all partners and other detailed calculations:

Solution

In the books of the firm

Current Account

Dr. Particulars	A Rs.	B Rs.	C Rs.	Cr. Particulars	A Rs.	B Rs.	C Rs.
To Current A/c (Goodwill)	11,250	—	3,750	By Balance b/d	4,000	3,000	1,000
" B's Capital A/c	—	40,000	—	" Reserve A/c	9,000	6,000	3,000
" Balance c/d	24,250	—	7,750	" Profit & Loss A/c	9,000	6,000	3,000
				" Joint Life Policy A/c	13,500	9,000	4,500
				" A's Current A/c	—	11,250	—
				" C's Current A/c	—	3,750	—
				" Profit & Loss Suspense A/c	—	1,000	—
	35,500	40,000	11,500		35,500	40,000	11,500

Capital Account

Dr. Particulars	A Rs.	B Rs.	C Rs.	Cr. Particulars	A Rs.	B Rs.	C Rs.
To B's Execution's A/c	—	52,000	—	By Balance b/d	16,000	12,000	10,000
" Balance c/d	16,000	—	10,000	" B's Current A/c	—	40,000	—
	16,000	52,,000	10,000		16,000	52,000	10,000

B's Executor's Account

Dr. Particulars	Amount Rs.	Cr. Particulars	Amount Rs.
To Balance c/d	52,000	By B's Capital A/c	52,000
	52,000		52,000

Workings :

1. **Computation of Goodwill**

Average Profit = $\frac{\text{Rs. } 16{,}000 + \text{Rs. } 20{,}000 + \text{Rs. } 12{,}000 + \text{Rs. } 12{,}000 \text{ (Rs. } 14{,}000 - \text{Rs. } 2{,}000)}{4}$

= Rs. 15,000

Value of goodwill = Rs. 15,000 × 3 years' Purchase = Rs. 45,000

B's share of goodwill = Rs. 45,000 × $\frac{2}{6}$ = Rs. 15,000.

Gaining ratio between A and C = 3 : 1

A is to bear Rs. 15,,000 × $\frac{3}{4}$ = Rs. 11,250

B is to bear Rs. 15,000 × $\frac{1}{4}$ = Rs. 3,750

Note : Goodwill Account to be adjusted against Current Account as per AS 10 and AS 26, the entry being :

A's Current A/c	Dr.	11,250	
`C's Current A/c	Dr.	3,750	
To B's Current A/c			15,000

2. **Joint Life policy**

	Rs.
Joint life Policy (matured values)	33,000
Less : Value already appeared	6,000
	27,000

∴ To be credited to Partners' Current A/c in 3 : 2 : 1.

3. **Proportionate Profit for 3 Months**

Since the accounts were not settled on 31.12.2013, Profit for 3 months (from 1.1.2014-31.3.2014) to be credited to B's Current Account as

	Rs.
Current year's Profit (Rs. 14,000 – Rs. 2,000)	12,000

For 3 months = Rs. 12,000 × $\frac{3}{12}$ = Rs. 3,000

C's share = Rs. 3,000 × $\frac{2}{6}$ = Rs. 1,000 to be transferred to Profit and Loss Suspense Account.

Illustration 16

A, B and C were partners of a firm sharing profit and losses in the ratio of 3 : 4 : 3. The Balance Sheet of the firm, as at 31st March 1998, was:

Particulars		*Amount* Rs.	*Particulars*		*Amount* Rs.
Capital Accounts :			Fixed Asset		1,0,000
A	48,000		Current Asset		
B	64,000		Stock	30,000	
C	48,000	1,60,000	Debtors	60,000	
Reserve		20,000	Cash and Bank	30,000	
Creditors		40,000			1,20,000
		2,20,000			2,20,000

The firm had taken a Joint Life Policy for Rs. 1,00,000; the premium periodically paid was charged to Profit and Loss Account. Partner C died on 30th September 1998. It was agreed between the surviving partners and the legal representatives of C that:

(i) Goodwill of the firm will be taken at Rs. 60,000. (ii) Fixed Assets will be written-down by Rs. 20,000. (iii) In lieu of Profits, C should be paid at the rate of 25% per annum on his capital as on 31st March 1998. Policy money was received and the legal heirs were paid-off. The profits for the year ended 31st March 1999, after, charging depreciation of Rs. 10,000 (depreciation up to 30th September was agreed to be Rs. 6,000), were Rs. 48,000. Partners' Drawings Accounts show balances as : A Rs. 18,000 (drawn evenly over the year); B Rs. 24,000 (drawn evenly over the year); C (up to date of death) Rs. 20,000. On the basis of the above figures, please indicate the entitlement of the legal heirs of C, assuming that they had not been paid anything other than the share in the Joint Life Policy.

Solution **[CA Inter, Nov. 2000]**

Computation of entitlement of total claim of legal heirs ofC

(1) Profits for the half year ended 31st March 1999

		Rs.
	Profits for the year ended 31st March 1999 (after depreciation)	48,000
Add:	Depreciation	10,000
	Profits before depreciation	58,000

		Rs.
	Profits for the first half-year (assumed : spread evenly through out at the year)	29,000
Less :	Depreciation for the first 6 months	6,000
∴	Profits for the first of the half year (after depreciation).	23,000
	Profits for the second half (i.e., 1st October 1998 to 31st March 1999)	29,000
Less:	Depreciation for the next 6 months	4,000
	Profits for the second half year (after depreciation)	25,000

(2) Capital Accounts of Partners as on 30th September 1998

Capital Account

Dr. *Cr.*

Particulars	A	B	C	*Particulars*	A	B	C
	Rs.	Rs.	Rs.		Rs.	Rs.	Rs.
To Fixed Assets (loss on revaluation)	6,000	8,000	6,000	By Balance b/d	48,000	64,000	48,000
" Drawings A/c	9,000	12,000	20,000	" Reserve	6,000	8,000	6,,000
" C's Executor's A/c	—	—	52,000	" Goodwill	18,000	24,000	18,000
" Balance c/d	57,000	76,000	—	" P & L Appropriation A/c Rs. 48,000 @ 25% for 6 months)	—	—	6,000
	72,000	96,000	78,000		72,000	96,000	78,000

(3) As per Section 37 of the Indian Partnership Act

In the absence of any agreement, the representatives of the deceased partner can receive at their option interest at the rate of 6% per annum or the share of profit earned for the amount due. But if any specific rate is mentioned in the agreement, that rate of interest should have been followed. Since, in the present problems, the legal heirs of C have not been paid (except the share of G L P), the representatives of C may opt for:

Either,

(i) Interest on Rs. 52,000 for 6 months @ 6% p.a. = Rs. 1,560

Or,

(ii) Profit earned out of unsettled capital (in the second half year ended 31st March 1999)

$$\text{Rs. } 25{,}000 \times \frac{\text{Rs. } 52{,}000}{\text{Rs. } 57{,}000 + \text{Rs. } 76{,}000 + \text{Rs. } 52{,}000} = \text{Rs. } 7{,}027 \text{ (approx.)}$$

So, it should be quite justified to accept the second alternative since it is higher.

Illustration 17

A, B, and C were trading in partnership sharing profits and losses in the proportion of 4 : 3 : 3. The Trial Balance of the firm as on 31st Dec. 2012, subject to final adjustment, were:

	Dr.	*Cr.*
	Rs.	Rs.
Capital and Current/Drawings Accounts		
A	24,000	1,50,000
B	36,000	75,000
C	36,000	90,000
Land & Building	1,20,000	
Furniture & Fixture	22,500	
Stock	1,87,500	
Debtors	30,000	
Bank	60,000	
Creditors		45,000
Profit for the year before charging Interest		1,56,000
	5,16,000	5,16,000

C died on 30.6.2012. The partnership deed provided that:

(1) Interest was to be credit on capital accounts of the partners at 10% p.a. on the balance at the beginning of the year.

(2) On the death of a partner, (i) goodwill was to be valued at 3 years' purchase of average annual profits of three years up to the date of death, after deducing interest on Capital employed at 8% p.a. and a fair remuneration for each of the partners, (ii) Fixed assets were to be valued by an independent valuer and all other assets and liabilities to be taken at book values (3) wherever necessary, profit or loss should be apportioned on a time basis. (4) the amount due to the deceased partner's estate was to receive interest @ 12% p.a. from the date of death until paid.

You are ascertained that (a) Profit for the 3 years before charging partners' interest were: 2009 Rs. 1,68,000; 2010 Rs. 1,89,000; 2011 Rs. 1,80,000; (b) The independent valuation at the date of death revalued : Land & Building Rs. 1,50,000; Furniture & Fixture Rs. 15,000; (c) A fair remuneration for each of the partners would be Rs. 37,500 p.a. and that the capital employed in the business to be taken as Rs. 3,90,000 throughout. It was agreed among the partners that (i) Goodwill was not to be shown as an asset of the firm as on 31.12.2012. Therefore, adjustments for goodwill was to be made in Capital Accounts; (ii) A and B would share equally from the date of death of C; (iv) Depreciation on revised value of asset would be ignored. You are required to prepare (a) Partners' Capital Account and Current Accounts, and (b) the Balance Sheet of the firm as on 31.12.2012.

[CA—Modified]

Solution

In the books of the firm

Capital Account

Dr. Particulars	A	B	C	Particulars	A	B	C *Cr.*
	Rs.	Rs.	Rs.		Rs.	Rs.	Rs.
To C's Capital A/c —Goodwill	9,990	19,980	—	By Balance b/d	1,50,000	75,000	90,000
" C's Current A/c	—	—	12,825	" Revaluation Profit	9,000	6,750	6,750
" C's Executors A/c	—	—	1,13,895	" A's Capital A/c	—	—	9,990
" Balance c/d	1,49,010	61,770	—	" B's Capital A/c	—	—	19,980
	1,59,000	81,750	1,26,720		1,59,000	81,750	1,26,720

Current Account

Dr. Particulars	A	B	C	Particulars	A	B	C *Cr.*
	Rs.	Rs.	Rs.		Rs.	Rs.	Rs.
To Balance b/d	24,000	36,000	36,000	By Interest of Capital	15,000	7,500	4,500
" Balance c/d	45,858	20,133	—	" P & L App. A/c —Share of Profit (Jan to June)	24,900	18,675	18,675
				(July to Dec.)	29,958	29,958	—
				" C's Capital A/c —Transferred	—	—	12,825
	69,856	56,133	36,000		69,858	56,133	36,000

Balance Sheet *as at 31st Dec. 2012*

Particulars		Amount	Particulars	Amount
		Rs.		Rs.
Capital A/c :			Land and Building	1,50,000
A	1,49,010		Furniture & Fixture	15,000
B	61,770	2,10,780	Stock	1,87,500
Current A/c			Debtors	30,000
A	45,858		Cash at Bank	60,000
B	20,133	65,991		
C's Executor's A/c		1,20,729		
Creditors		45,000		
		4,42,500		4,42,500

Workings :

1. **Profit and Loss Appropriation Account**

Dr. Particulars	1.1.2012 To 30.6.2012	1.7.2012 To 31.12.2012	Particulars	1.1.2012 To 30.6.2012	1.7.2012 To 31.12.2012 Cr.
	Rs.	Rs.		Rs.	Rs.
To Int. on Cap. A/c			By P & L A/c	78,000	78,000
A	7,500	7,500	—Time basis		
B	3,750	3,750			
C	4,500	—			
" Interest on C's Executor's Loan A/c	—	6,834			
" Current A/c					
" Share of Profit					
A	24,900	29,958			
B	18,675	29,958			
C	18,675	—			
	78,000	78,000		78,000	78,000

Revaluation Account

Dr. Liabilities		Rs.	Assets	Rs. Cr.
To Furniture & Fixture		7,500	By Land & Buildings	30,000
" Capital A/c Share of Profit				
A	9,000			
B	6,750			
C	6,750	22,500		
		30,000		30,000

C's Executors Account

Dr.	Rs.		Rs. Cr.
To Balance c/d	1,20,729	By C's Capital A/c	1,13,895
		" Interest on Loan A/c	6,834
	1,20,729		1,20,729

4. **Adjustments for Goodwill**

Average Profit

		Rs.
2009-10	= $(\frac{1}{2} \times$ Rs. $1{,}68{,}000 + \frac{1}{2} \times 1{,}89{,}000)$	1,78,500
2010-11	= $(\frac{1}{2} \times$ Rs. $1{,}89{,}000 + \frac{1}{2} \times 1{,}80{,}000)$	1,84,500
2011-12	= $(\frac{1}{2} \times$ Rs. $1{,}80{,}000 + \frac{1}{2} \times 1{,}56{,}000)$	1,68,000
		5,31,000

∴ Average Profit $\frac{\text{Rs. } 5{,}31{,}000}{3}$ = Rs.	1,77,000
Less : Interest on Capital Employed (8% on Rs. 3,90,000)	31,200
	1,45,800
Less: Fair remuneration to Partners (Rs. 37,500 × 3)	1,12,500
	33,300

Value of Goodwill = Rs.33,300 × 3 years' purchase = Rs. 99,900.

C's share of Goodwill = Rs. 99,900 × $\frac{3}{10}$ = Rs. 29,970, to be Compensated by A and B by their gaining ratio of 1 : 2

i.e., Rs. 29,970 × $\frac{1}{3}$ = Rs. 9,990, and Rs. 29,970 × $\frac{2}{3}$ = Rs. 19,980 respectively .

Illustration 18

X and Y have been in partnership business for some years sharing profits in the proportions of $\frac{3}{5}$th, and $\frac{2}{5}$th, respectively, after salary entitlements of Rs. 8,000 and Rs. 12,000 p.a., respectively. Accounts are made up to 30th June each year.

Their partnership agreement provides, on the death of partner, for (i) revaluations of the firms' assets — net gain or loss to be dealt with in the capital accounts in the profit-sharing ratio, (ii) the amount due to a deceased partner's personal representatives to be the amount standing to the credit of his capital account, including salary and profits to date of death, less drawings on account, (iii) Rs. 10,000 to be paid immediately and the balance one year after death, and (iv) an annuity of Rs. 6,000 payable half-yearly in arrears to a deceased partner's widow.

X died on 31st Dec. 2009 when the lease of the partnership premises were deemed to be worth Rs. 40,000, Goodwill Rs. 25,000 and all other assets at their book values. Non-profit life assurance policies had been taken out of each partner's policy being debited to him. X's life was insured for Rs. 50,000 and Y's for Rs. 30,000. The surrender value of the policy on Y's life on 31st Dec. 2009 was Rs. 2,200 and the benefit thereof was assigned to him at that value by X's personal representatives.

On 31st March 2010, Z was taken into partnership by Y on terms that he should (i) introduce Rs. 25,000 as partnership capital, and (ii) receive $\frac{1}{5}$th share of profits, after charging the anunity to X's widow, with no provisions for partner's salaries.

Profits or losses are assumed to accrue evenly throughout a year. The partnership Trial Balance as on 30th June 2010 was:

	Rs.	Rs.
Lease	15,000	
Stock on 30.6.2010	65,000	
Gross Trading Profit (for the year ended 30.6.2010)		1,82,000
Office Salaries and Expenses	82,000	
Life Assurance Policy Premium :		
on X's life, paid Nov. 2009	650	
on Y's life, paid May 2010	250	
Cash from Life Assurance Policy on X's life		50,000
Annuity to X's widow, paid 30.6.2010	3,000	
Balance at Bank	61,000	
Capital Accounts on 30.6.2009 :		
X		37,000
Y		12,900
Sundry Debtors	33,000	
Sundry Creditors		41,000
Cash paid in by Z		25,000
Cash paid to personal representatives of X	10,000	
Partners' Drawings :		
X	27,000	
Y	46,000	
Z	5,000	
	3,47,900	3,47,900

You are required to prepare :

(a) the partnership Balance Sheet as on 30.6.2010, and (b) the capital accounts of the partners and the account of the personal representatives of X, covering the year ended 30.6.2010.

Solution **[CA Final, England —Adapted]**

(a)

In the books of Y and Z
Balance Sheet *as at* **30th June 2000**

Liabilities	Rs.	Rs.	*Assets*	Rs.	Rs.
Capitals Accounts :			*Fixed Assets*		
Y	98,100		Goodwill	25,000	
Z	24,700	1,22,800	Lease	40,000	65,000
Executor of X		60,200	*Current Assets*		
Creditors		41,000	Stock	65,000	
			Debtors	33,000	
			Bank	61,000	1,59,000
		2,24,000			2,24,000

(b)

Capital Account

Dr. Particulars	X Rs.	Y Rs.	Z Rs.	Particulars Cr.	X Rs.	Y Rs.	Z Rs.
To LIC Premium :				By Balance b/d	37,000	12,900	—
On X	—	650	—	" Revaluation A/c			—
On Y	—	250	—	—Profit	30,000	20,000[1]	—
" Drawings A/c	27,000	46,000	5,000	" Salaries (up to 31.12.2009)	4,000	6,000	—
" Executor of X A/c	68,000	—	—	" Profit (up to 31.12.2009)	24,000	16,000[2]	—
" Executor of X A/c : (Life Policy)	—	2,200[1]		By Bank A/c —X's Policy	—	50,000	—
To Balance c/d		98,100	24,700	" Bank A/c	—	—	25,000
				" Profit (up to 31.3.2010)	—	23,500	—
				" Profit (1.4.2000—30.6.2010)		18,800	4,700
	95,000	1,47,200	29,700		95,000	1,47,200	29,700

Note :

Since the policy is assigned to Y, : the entry will be :

Y's Capital A/c Dr.
 To Executor of X

Executor of X Account

Dr. Particulars	Amount Rs.	Particulars Cr.	Amount Rs.
To Bank A/c	10,000	By X's Capital A/c	68,000
" Balance c/d	60,200	" Y's Capital A/c	2,200
	70,200		70,200

Workings :

1. **Revaluation Account.**

Dr. Particulars		Amount Rs.	Particulars Cr.	Amount Rs.
To Capital A/c : Profit on Revalution			By Goodwill A/c	25,000*
X $\frac{3}{5}$	30,000		" Lease (Rs. 40,000 – Rs. 15,000)	25,000
Y $\frac{2}{5}$	20,000			
		50,000		
		50,000		50,000

* It may also be passed through capital account directly.

2. **Computation and Distribution of Profit**

	Rs.
Gross Profit	1,82,000
Less : Operating Expenses i.e., Salaries and Expenses	82,000
	1,00,000

		Rs.
(a) Now, Profit for the 6 months ended 31.12.2010		50,000
Less : Partners' Salaries :		
X	4,000	
Y	6,000	10,000
Divisible Profit		40,000

$\therefore$ X gets = Rs. 40,000 × $\frac{3}{5}$ = Rs. 24,000

Y gets = Rs. 40,000 × $\frac{2}{5}$ = Rs. 16,000

(b) Profit for the period 1.1.2010 to 31.3.2010

	Rs.	
(Rs. 1,00,000 × $\frac{3}{12}$)	25,000	∴ Y gets = Rs. 23,500 × $\frac{4}{5}$ = Rs. 18,800
Less : Amount payable to X	1,500	Z gets = Rs. 23,500 × $\frac{1}{5}$ = Rs. 4,700.
	23,500	

Illustration 19

P, Q, and R were in partnership as solicitors sharing profits and losses in the ratio of 3 : 2 : 1, respectively. The following is a summary of the partnership Balance Sheet as on Dec. 31, 2011 :

Liabilities	Rs.	Rs.	*Assets*	Rs.
Capital Accounts			Assurance Policy for Rs. 1,20,000	
P	68,000		Premiums paid to date	90,000
Q	47,800		Other Assets	82,800
R	22,000		Bank Balance (Clients' Account)	25,000
		1,37,800		
Loan Account : A		20,000		
Sundry Creditors		15,000		
Clients' Balances		25,000		
		1,97,800		1,97,800

No separate Drawings Accounts were kept. P and Q were each entitled to a salary at the rate of Rs. 6,000 per annum. Interest at the rate of 5 per cent per annum was allowed on the capital balances at the beginning of the year, but no interest was charged on drawings.

P died on 30 September 2012 and the amount of Rs. 1,20,000 receivable under the assurance policy was collected in due course, no further premiums having been paid or fallen due since 31 December 2011.

The partnership agreement provided, *inter alia*, that, on the death of a partner :

(1) Interest at the rate of 20 per cent per annum on the balance of the deceased partner's capital account at the date of the last balance sheet should be allowed from that date to the date of death in lieu of his rateable share of profits for that period.

(2) The amount due to deceased partner's estate should be treated as a loan carrying interest (chargeable to the Profit and Loss Account) at the rate of 6 per cent per annum from the date of death and should be paid in four equal instalments, the first to be paid within two months of his death, the second, third and fourth instalment half-yearly from the date of his death.

In accordance with other terms of the agreement, the goodwill of the partnership was valued at Rs. 84,000 and the assets as on 31 December 2011, other than the balance at bank or clients' account and the assurance policy, were revalued at Rs. 1,15,800. P is to be credited with his share of the goodwill and surplus on revaluation of assets without raising a goodwill account or adjusting the assets in the books.

The profit for the year ended 31 December 2012, before charging partners' salaries, loan interest or interest on capital, amounted to Rs. 54,640. Partners' drawings during 2012 amounted to :

P Rs. 35,650; Q Rs. 19,870; R Rs. 9,940.

The first payment, with interest due, was made on 30 November 2012 to P's estate.

Q and R agreed to continue the partnership on the same terms as before after taking over, in the ratio in which they shared profits. P lapsed share in the partnership. You are required to give :

(1) The Profit and Loss Appropriation Account for 2012; and

(2) Partners' Capital and Loan Account showing the balances due to the remaining partners and the sum due to P's executors on 31 December 2012.

Solution :

(1)

In the books of the Firm

Profit and Loss Appropriation Account *for the year ended 31st Dec. 2012*

Dr. Cr.

Particulars	*Amount*	*Particulars*	*Amount*
	Rs.		Rs.
To Salary : P (9 months)	4,500	By Profit and Loss A/c	54,640
Q	6,000	—Net Profit	

Contd.

			Rs.		Rs.
"	Interest on P's Loan (9 months)		900		
"	Executors of P (Interest)		1,980[1]		
"	Interest of Capital :				
	P (9 months)	2,550			
	Q	2,390			
	R	1,100	6,040		
"	P's Share of Profit		10,200[2]		
"	Divisible Profit				
	Q	16,680			
	R	8,340	25,020		
			54,640		54,640

Executor of P Account

Dr. Date		Particulars	Amount	Date		Particulars	Cr. Amount
2012			Rs.	2012			Rs.
Nov. 30	To	Bank A/c	37,440	Oct. 1	To	Capital A/c	1,44,000
Dec. 31	"	Balance c/d	1,08,540	Nov. 30	"	P & L App. A/c—Interest	1,440
				Dec. 31	"	P & L App. A/c —Interest Accrued	540
			1,45,980				1,45,980

Capital Account

Dr. Particulars	P	Q	R	Particulars	P	Q	Cr. R
	Rs.	Rs.	Rs.		Rs.	Rs.	Rs.
To Drawings A/c	35,650	19,870	9,940	By Balance b/d	68,000	47,800	22,000
" P's Capital A/c —Revaluation of Assets	—	11,000	5,500	" Interest on Capital	2,550	2,390	1,100
" P's Capital A/c —Goodwill	—	28,000	14,000	" Salaries	4,500	6,000	—
" P's Capital Executors A/c —Transfer	1,44,000	—	—	" Joint Life Policy	15,000	10,000	5,000[3]
" Balance c/d	—	24,000	7,000	" Q's Capital	11,000	—	—
				" R's Capital	5,500	—	—
				" Q's Capital	28,000	—	—
				" R's Capital	14,000	—	—
				" A's Loan A/c (with Interest)	20,900	—	—
				" Profit and Loss App. A/c —Profit	10,200	16,680	8,340
	1,79,650	82,870	36,440		1,79,650	82,870	36,440

Workings :

1. Interest on P's loan is calculated as

		Rs.
	Balance of Capital Account	1,44,000
Add :	Interest @ 6% for 2 months (Rs. 1,44,000 $\times \frac{6}{100} \times \frac{2}{12}$)	1,440
		1,45,440
Less :	Amount paid on 30, Nov. : Rs. 1,44,000 $\times \frac{1}{4}$ = Rs. 36,000 + Rs. 1,440 =	37,440
		1,08,000

∴ Interest on Rs. 1,08,000 for 1 month (from 1.12.2012 to 31.12.2012) Rs. 1,08,000 $\times \frac{6}{100} \times \frac{1}{12}$ = Rs. 540

∴ Total Interest = Rs. 1,440 + Rs. 540 = Rs. 1,980.

2. P's share of Profit

P's Capital on 1.1.2012 Rs. 68,000

20% on Rs. 68,000 for 9 months

= Rs. 68,000 $\times \frac{20}{100} \times \frac{9}{12}$ = Rs. 10,200

3. Joint Life Policy

		Rs.
	Amount received from the Insurance Company	1,20,000
Less :	Balance as per Balance Sheet on 31.12.2011	90,000
		30,000

∴ Rs. 30,000 to be credited to Partners' Capital Account in 3 : 2 : 1.

4. **Revaluation of Assets**

		Rs.
	Revalued Price	1,15,800
Less :	Book Value	82,800
	Profit on Revaluation	33,000

and P's share

$= \text{Rs. } 33,000 \times \frac{1}{2} = \text{Rs. } 16,500$

Thus, the entry being :

Q's Capital A/c	Dr.	11,000	
R's Capital A/c	Dr.	5,500	
To P's Capital A/c			16,500

Problem on Annuity

Illustration 20

X, Y and Z were in partnership sharing profits and losses in the ratio 2 : 2 : 1. X died on 1st June 2007, the Partnership Deed provided for the payment of an annuity of Rs. 4,000 p.a. together with interest @ 6% p.a. on yearly balances to the widow of the deceased partner. When X died, total amount payable was Rs. 40,000. First annuity was paid on 31st Dec. 2007. After securing the fourth instalment on 31st Dec. 2000, X's widow also died.

Prepare the necessary divisions of the amount.

Solution

X's Capital Account

Dr. Date	Particulars	Amount Rs.	Date	Particulars	Cr. Amount Rs.
2007 June 1	To X's Widow's Annuity Suspense A/c —Transfer	40,000	2007 June 1	By Balance b/d	40,000
		40,000			40,000

X's Widow's Annuity Suspense Account

Dr. Date	Particulars		Amount Rs.	Date	Particulars	Cr. Amount Rs.
2007 Dec. 31	To Bank (4,000 + 1,200)		5,200	2007 June 1	By A's Capital A/c	40,000
	" Balance c/d		36,000		" Interest	1,200
			41,200			41,200
2008 Dec. 31	To Bank (4,000 + 2,160)		6,160	2008 Jan. 1	By Balance b/d	36,000
	" Balance c/d		32,000	Dec. 31	" Interest	2,160
			38,160			38,160
2009 Dec. 31	To Bank (4,000 + 1,920)		5,920	2009 Jan. 1	By Balance b/d	32,000
	" Balance c/d		28,000	Dec. 31	" Interest	1,920
			33,920			33,920
2010 Dec. 31	To Bank (4,000 + 1,680)		5,680	2010 Jan. 1	By Balance b/d	28,000
	" Balance transferred to Capital A/c			Dec. 31	" Interest	1,680
	Y	16,000				
	Z	8,000				
			24,000			
			29,680			29,680

Admission and Death

Illustration 21

Sen and Chatterjee were partners sharing profits and losses as 3 : 2. They admitted Roy as third partner with effect from 1.1.2008, the new profit-sharing ratio being 5 : 3 : 2. They again took Ghosh as their fourth partner as on 1.1.2009, the new profit-sharing ratio being 9 : 5 : 4 : 2. On 1.1.2010, Bose was taken in as their fifth partner, the profit-sharing ratio now being agreed at 7 : 4 : 3 : 3 : 3. Chatterjee died on 1.1.2011 and you are requested to estimate the values of his share of goodwill, which had never been raised in the books of account, nor was any premium received from any entrant.

On enquiry you find that the respective values of the goodwill of the firm were :

Date	1.1.2008	1.1.2009	1.1.2010	1.1.2011
Value (Rs.)	4,000	6,000	8,000	12,000

Estimate the amount payable to the legal representatives of Chatterjee and state how such amount would be contributed by the continuing partners, provided they do not raise any goodwill account in the books and agree to share profits from 1.1.2011 on the following basis : Sen 40%; Roy 25%; Ghosh 20%; and Bose 15%.

[CU MCom]

Solution

In the books of the firm
Journal

			L.F.	Dr. Rs.	Cr. Rs.
(i) 2008 Jan. 1	Goodwill A/c	Dr.		4,000	
	To Sen's Capital A/c				2,400
	" Chatterjee's Capital A/c				1,600
	(Old ratio 3 : 2, new ratio 5 : 3 : 2.)				
(ii)	Sen's Capital A/c	Dr.		2,000	
	Chatterjee's Capital A/c	Dr.		1,200	
	Roy's Capital A/c	Dr.		800	
	To Goodwill A/c				4,000
	(Since Roy is admitted for $\frac{2}{10}$th share, value of goodwill at that time was Rs. 4,000. Hence, the same was raised in old ratio and written-off in new ratio.)				
(iii)	*When Ghosh was admitted :*				
2009 Jan. 1	Goodwill A/c	Dr.		6,000	
	To Sen's Capital A/c				3,000
	" Chatterjee's Capital A/c				1,800
	" Roy's Capital A/c				1,200
	(Goodwill raised old ratio i.e., 5 : 3 : 2, new ratio being 9 : 5 : 4 : 2.)				
(iv)	Sens's Capital A/c	Dr.		2,700	
	Chatterjee's Capital A/c	Dr.		1,500	
	Roy's Capital A/c	Dr.		1,200	
	Ghose's Capital A/c	Dr.		600	
	To Goodwill A/c				6,000
	(Goodwill written-off in new ratio.)				
(v)	*When Bose was admitted :*				
2010 Jan. 1	Goodwill A/c	Dr.		8,000	
	To Sen's Capital A/c				3,600
	" Chatterjee's Capital A/c				2,000
	" Roy's Capital A/c				1,600
	" Ghosh's Capital A/c				800
	(Goodwill raised in old ratio i.e., 9 : 5 : 4 : 2, new ratio being 7 : 4 :3 : 3: 3.)				
(vi)	Sen's Capital A/c	Dr.		2,800	
	Chaterjee's Capital A/c	Dr.		1,600	
	Roy's Capital A/c	Dr.		1,200	
	Ghosh's Capital A/c	Dr.		1,200	
	Bose's Capital A/c	Dr.		1,200	
	To Goodwill A/c				8,000
	(Goodwill written-off in new ratio.)				

Contd.

			Rs.	Rs.
(vii) 2011 Jan. 1	Goodwill A/c	Dr.	12,000	
	To Sen's Capital A/c			4,200
	" Chatterjee's Capital A/c			2,400
	" Roy's Capital A/c			1,800
	" Ghosh's Capital A/c			1,800
	" Bose's Capital A/c			1,800
	(Goodwill raised in old ratio.)			
(viii)	Sen's Capital A/c	Dr.	4,800*	
	Roy's Capital A/c	Dr.	3,000	
	Ghosh's Capital A/c	Dr.	2,400	
	Bose's Capital A/c	Dr.	1,800	
	To Goodwill A/c			12,000
	(Goodwill written-off in new ratio.)			

* Chatterjee died on 1.1.2011.
Old ratio was : 7 : 4 : 3 : 3 : 3.
New ratio being :
Sen 40%; Roy 25%; Ghosh 20%; and Bose 15%.
Net effect of the transaction.

Goodwill	Sen		Chatterjee		Roy		Ghosh		Bose	
	Dr.	Cr.	Dr.	Cr.	Dr.	Cr.	Dr.	Cr.	Dr.	Cr.
(1) on 1.1.2008										
(a)	—	2,400	—	1,600	—	—	—	—	—	—
(b)	2,000	—	1,200	—	800	—	—	—	—	—
(2) on 1.1.2009										
(a)	—	3,000	—	1,800	—	1,200	—	—	—	—
(b)	2,700	—	1,500	—	1,200	—	600	—	—	—
(3) on 1.1.2010										
(a)	—	3,600	—	2,000	—	1,600	—	800	—	—
(b)	2,800	—	1,600	—	1,200	—	1,200	—	1,200	—
(4) on 1.1.2011										
(a)	—	4,200	—	2,400	—	1,800	—	1,800	—	1,800
(b)	4,800	—	—	—	3,000	—	2,400	—	1,800	—
Total	12,300	13,200	4,300	7,800	6,200	4,600	4,200	2,600	3,000	1,800
Balance	900	—	3,500	—	—	1,600	—	1,600	—	1,200
	13,200	13,200	7,800	7,800	6,200	6,200	4,200	4,200	3,000	3,000

The entry will be :

Roy's Capital A/c	Dr.	1,600	
Ghosh's Capital A/c	Dr.	1,600	
Bose's Capital A/c	Dr.	1,200	
To Sen's Capital A/c			900
" Chatterjee's Capital A/c			3,500

Comments

From the above, it becomes clear that Sen's Capital must be credited by Rs. 900 Chatterjee legal representative will be entitled only Rs. 3,500. On the contrary, Roy, Ghosh, and Bose will have to be brought in Rs. 1,600, Rs. 1,600 and Rs. 1,200, respectively.

ASSIGNMENT MATERIALS

THEORETICAL

Short-Type Answer Questions

1. How do you ascertain the claims of a deceased partner?
2. Define : Annuity Method of Payment, Instalment Payment Method; Lump Sum Payment Method.
3. What is Joint Life Policy?
4. How do you ascertain the share of profit of a deceased partner?
5. How do you treat an individual policy?
6. How do you treat the share of profit of a deceased partner when the final settlement of accounts is not made?

Long-Type Answer Questions

7. How do you ascertain the total claims of deceased partner?
8. How do you dispose off the share of Deceased Partner?
9. What are the different methods that are used to settle the claims of a deceased partner?
10. How do you ascertain the share of profit of a deceased partner? Discuss also the circumstances on which final settlement of accounts is not made?

PRACTICAL

1. On 31st December 2011, the Balance Sheet of A, B, and C was :

	Rs.		Rs.
Sundry Creditors	15,000	Buildings	16,000
Reserve Fund	16,000	Investments	15,000
Capital :		Debtors	15,000
A	15,000	Bills Receivable	6,000
B	10,000	Stock	12,000
C	10,000	Cash at Bank	2,000
	66,000		66,000

The partnership deed provided that the profits will be shared in 2 : 1 : 1 and that, in the event of death of a partner, his executors will be entitled to be paid out :

(a) The capital to his credit at the date of last Balance Sheet; (b) His proportion of reserves at the date of last Balance Sheet; (c) His proportion of profits to the date of death based on the average profits on the last three completed years; and (d) By way of goodwill, his proportion of the total profits for the three preceding years without raising goodwill account.

The net profits for the last three years were : 2009 Rs. 16,000; 2010 Rs. 16,600; 2011 Rs. 15,400.

C died on 1st April 1992. He had withdrawn Rs. 4,000 to the date of his death. The Investments were sold at par and C's executors were paid-off.

Show the necessary Ledger accounts and the Balance Sheet of the surviving partners A and B.

[Ans. Value of Goodwill Rs. 48,000; C's Share of Profit Rs. 1,000; Amount paid to C's Executors Rs. 23,000]

2. A, B, and C were in partnership sharing profits equally. C died on 31st March 2012. The Balance Sheet of the firm as at 31st December 2011 was as follows :

Liabilities		Rs.	*Assets*	Rs.
Sundry Creditors		15,600	Cash in hand & at Bank	4,000
General Reserve		6,000	Debtors	18,000
Investment Fluctuation Fund		2,100	Stock	28,000
Reserve for Doubtful Debts		1,800	Investments (at cost)	8,000
Capital :			Freehold Property	30,000
A	30,000		Goodwill	13,500
B	25,000			
C	21,000			
		76,000		
		1,01,500		1,01,500

On the date of death it was found that :

(a) Freehold Property was worth Rs. 57,000; (b) Debtors were all good; (c) Stock was valued at Rs. 25,000; (d) Investments were valued at Rs. 7,500 and were taken over by A at that value; (e) A liability for workmen's compensation for Rs. 3,000 was to be provided for; (f) Goodwill was to be valued at one year's purchase of average profits of last 5 years; (g) C's share of profit up to the date of death was to be calculated on the basis of last year's profit.

The profit of the last five years were :

2007 Rs. 11,500; 2008 Rs. 12,500; 2009 Rs. 8,000; 2010 Rs. 10,000; and 2011 Rs. 12,000.

Prepare (i) Capital Account of C, and (ii) Balance Sheet of the remaining partners.

[Ans.Value of Goodwill Rs. 10,800; Paid to C's Executors Rs. 31,234; Total of Balance Sheet Rs. 1,15,800 (after considering Rs. 1,000 as profit on suspense)]

4. Rabi, Shahi and Tara in partnership sharing profits and losses in the proportions of 6 : 5 : 4. They take out a Joint Life Assurance Policy for Rs. 2,00,000 so that the funds required to pay-off the dues of a partner on his death may be available without presenting any financial difficulty to the firm. The annual premium on the policy is Rs. 7,500, and this is treated as a business expense. Accounts are closed annually on 31st Dec.

The Partnership Deed provides that the representatives of a deceased partner are entitled to (i) the deceased partner's capital appearing in the last Balance Sheet; (ii) interest on capital at 6% p.a. of the date of his death; (iii) his share of profits calculated till the date of his death or the average of the last three years' profits after inclusion of the policy premium as business expense; and (iv) share of Goodwill calculated at two years' purchase on the average of the last three years' profit before inclusion of the policy premium as a business expense.

Shashi died on 1.4.2006. His drawings in 2006 amounted to Rs. 3,000. His capital shown in the 2005 Balance Sheet was Rs. 80,000.

The profits for the years 2003, 2004 and 2005, after inclusion of the policy premium as a business expense, amounted to Rs. 65,000; Rs. 64,000 and Rs. 69,000 respectively.

Draw-up Shashi's account to show the amount due to his estate from the firm.

[Ans. Amount transferred to executor of Shashi Rs. 1,93,367]

5. Jaga, Bag and Khaga a partners in a firm sharing profit and losses in the ratio of 2 : 2 : 1, respectively. Their Balance Sheet as on 31.12.1998 was as follows:

Liabilities		Rs.	*Assets*	Rs.
Creditors		50,000	Cash at Bank	10,000
Capital Accounts:			Debtors	80,000
Jaga	50,000		Stock	45,000
Baga	40,000		Plant	15,000
Khaga	10,000	1,00,000		
		1,50,000		1,50,000

Jaga dies on 31.3.1999; partnership deed provides, inter alia, that in the event of death of a partner:

(i) The share of the deceased partner's capital shall be taken at the figure as at the date of last financial accounts and his share of profits will be added on the basis of the proportionate average profits of three previous years.

(ii) Goodwill of the firm will be taken at 2 years' purchase of the average profit of the three previous years.

The whole amount due to the deceased was to be transferred to a Loan Account started in the name of the executors and payable to them in two half-yearly instalments with 6% interest on the unpaid balance. The first instalment is payable forthwith. The profits of three previous years were Rs. 20,0000, Rs. 18,000 and Rs. 22,000, respectively.

You are required to ascertain the amount payable to the deceased partner's executors and close the Executor's Loan Account.

[Ans. Amount transferred to executor of Jaga Rs. 68,000]

6. It was provided under the partnership agreement among Naresh, Mahesh and Paresh that, in the event of the death of a partner, the survivors would have to purchase his share in the firm on the following terms :

(a) Deceased's share of Goodwill to be taken at three years' purchase of his share of profit on average of previous four years; and

(b) Total amount due to his representatives to be paid by survivors in four equal and half-yearly instalments commencing at 6 months after the date of death with 5% interest on outstanding dues.

The shared profits and losses in proportion of 9 : 4 : 3, and accounts were drawn up each year at 30th June.

Naresh died on 31.12.1998, and their capital accounts on that date were Naresh Rs. 10,800, Mahesh Rs. 6,400 and Paresh Rs. 3,600. Naresh's current acount on 31.12.1998 after crediting his share of profit to that date, however, showed a debit of Rs. 960.

Firm's profit for the year ended on 30.6.1995 Rs. 35,200; 30.6.1996 Rs. 28,160; 30.6.1997 Rs. 24,080; 30.6.1998 Rs. 8,704.

Show the relevant ledger accounts in the books of the firm recording half-yearly payments to Naresh's estate by the surviving partners.

[CU BCom (Hons.)]

[Ans. Amount transferred to executor of Naresh Rs. 50,400]

7. The following is the Balance Sheet of a firm consisting of three partners X, Y, and Z, sharing profits in the ratio of 4 : 3 : 1 :

Balance Sheet
as on 31.12.2005

		Rs.		Rs.
Creditors		1,20,000	Bank	50,000
Capital Accounts			Joint Survivorship Policy	32,000
X	1,00,000		Property and Assets	2,28,000
Y	70,000			
Z	20,000			
		1,90,000		
		3,10,000		3,10,000

On 1.1.2006 P was admitted as a partner entitling him to $\frac{1}{5}$th share of the profits. P paid Rs. 30,000 on account of capital and also Rs. 20,000 as his share of Goodwill (the latter sum to remain in the business).

On 30.6.2006, X died. The Joint Survivorship Policy realised Rs. 50,000. The share of the deceased partner in the Goodwill of the firm was determined at Rs. 36,000. The Profit and Loss Account for the period ending 30.12.2006 disclosed a profit of Rs. 45,000.

The surviving partners carried on the business, ratio of profit, inter se, remaining unchanged. Net Profit—before charging interest on Y's loan for the period from 1.7.2006 to 31.12.2006—amounted to Rs. 33,000.

Drawings of the partners:

	X	Y	Z	P
	Rs.	Rs.	Rs.	Rs.
For 6 months up to 30.6.2006	13,000	10,000	4,000	7,500
For 6 months up to 30.12.2006	—	8,000	5,000	7,000

A sum of Rs. 50,000 was advance by Y as loan to facilitate payment in full, on 1.12.2006, of the deceased partners's share.

Show the Partners' Capital Account and draft the Balance Sheet as at 31.12.2006.

The balance of 'Creditors' and 'Property and Asset' as on 31.12.2006, were Rs. 1,17,000 and Rs. 2,37,000, respectively.

[Ans. Amount paid to executor of X Rs. 1,70,335; Total of Balance Sheet Rs. 2,78,165]

8. The following figures were extracted from the Account Books of Vimal & Co., partnership firm having partners Mr. Anil and Mr. Bimal, who were sharing profits and losses in equal ratio as on 31st March 1987 :

	Dr. Rs.	Cr. Rs.
Mr. Anil's Capital Account		46,000
Mr. Bimal's Capital Account		26,000
Mr. Anil's Drawings Account	9,000	
Mr. Bimal's Drawings Account	7,000	
Gross Profit		33,600
Salaries	15,000	
Rent, rates and taxes	4,000	
Other overheads	4,000	
Discount received		400
Fixed assets	65,000	
Current assets	2,000	
	1,06,000	1,06,000

The partnership deed provides that :

(a) Interest at 5% p.a. is to be allowed on capitals, but no interest is to be charged on drawings (from 1-1-87 to 31-3-87) (b) On the death of a partner the surviving partners shall pay out the interest on the deceased partner. (c) The deceased partner shall be entitled to his share of goodwill of the firm calculated at two and half years' purchase of the average profits of the preceding three years' profit prior to the death of apparent. (d) Assets are to be taken at their book value on the date of death.

Mr. Anil died on 31st March 1987.

The profits of the preceding three years ending on 31-12-1984, 31-12-1985, and 31-12-1986, respectively, were Rs. 30,000, Rs. 25,000, and Rs. 35,000. The accounts were closed on 31st Dec. each year.

Prepare the Profit and Loss Account and the account to be produced to the executors of Mr. Anil showing the amount due to his estate.

[CA Entrance]

[Ans. Net Profit Rs. 11,000; Amount paid to Anil's Executor's A/c Rs. 80,125]

9. For some years X has been carrying on partnership business with a capital of Rs. 77,500 and his accounts are closed annually to 31st March.

On 1st April 1987 Y joined him as a partner with $\frac{1}{3}$rd interest in the profit and goodwill. Y introduced a sum of Rs. 40,000 on account of capital and it was agreed that X be credited with goodwill of Rs. 22,500.

The deed of partnership provided, *inter alia*, : (a) Capital and Current Accounts be kept separately. (b) Drawings be X Rs. 3,600 per month, Y Rs. 2,000 per month including salary as mentioned below; (c) Y be allowed salary of Rs. 6,000 per annum; (d) Interest be allowed on capitals at 5% per annum.

On the death of a partner, executors be entitled to : (a) Balance of capital and current accounts; (b) Interest on capital and salary up to the date of death; (c) Accruing share of profits to be based on the profits for the completed year immediately preceding the date of death; (d) Share of goodwill, the value of which is to be calculated at two years' purchase of the average profits (after charging interest on capital and partners' salary) for 3 completed years immediately preceding the date of death.

Profits before charging interest on capital and partners' salaries were as given hereunder: year ending 31st March 1988 Rs. 67,000; year ending 31st March 1989 Rs. 70,000; and year ending 31st March 1990 Rs. 77,000.

On 30th September 1989, Y introduced additional capital of Rs. 16,000.

Y died on 30th June 1990. It was ascertained that, up to 31st March 1990, he had drawn the amount as mentioned in (b) above and from 1st April 1990 to the date of death his drawings had been Rs. 5,500.

Prepare : (i) Profit and Loss Appropriation Account for each of the three years ending 31st March 1988, 1989, and 1990. (ii) Y's Capital and current accounts to show respective balances on 31st March 1990. (iii) A chart showing computation of the amount due to the executor of the deceased as on 30th June 1990.

[CA]

[Ans. Profit for 3 years Rs. 54,000; Rs. 57,000; and Rs. 63,600; Amount paid to Executors of Y Rs. 99,867. Increased value of Goodwill Rs. 93,900]

10. Jaswant, Kanji, and Chiranji were partners in the firm of Fire Works Company, their profit-sharing proportion being 4, 3, and 2, respectively. Their Balance Sheet, as at 30th June 1987, on which date Jaswant died, is:

Liabilities		Rs.	*Assets*	Rs.
Bank Overdraft		5,000	Cash	1,000
Creditors		2,000	Debtors	10,000
Workmen's Accident Fund		9,000	Stock	16,000
Partners' Current Accounts :			Motor Car	2,000
J	7,000		Furniture	1,000
K	4,000		Plant and Machinery	20,000
C	3,000		Land and Factory	30,000
		14,000		
Partners' Capital Accounts :				
J	20,000			
K	20,000			
C	10,000			
		50,000		
		80,000		80,000

The partnership agreement provided that, on the death of a partner :

(i) the firm shall be continued by the other partners; (ii) goodwill to be computed on the basis of two years' profits on the average of the three preceding accounting years; (iii) fixed and floating assets to be revalued; and (iv) the amount ascertained to be due to the deceased partner's legal representatives to be treated as loan to the firm and one-third of the amount plus interest at 6% per annum on the balance outstanding, to be paid on 30th June each year until fully repaid.

The profits of three preceding accounting years, which ended on 31st March each year, were Rs. 30,000, Rs. 45,000, and Rs. 60,000, respectively. On revaluation, as at 30th June 1997 the amounts for Land and Factory, Plant and Machinery, Furniture, Motor Car, and Stock came to Rs. 60,000; Rs. 80,000; Rs. 3,000; Rs. 5,000; and Rs. 21,000, respectively, whilst the Debtors were considered good at the book figure less 10% Reserve—for doubtful debts.

You are asked to give effect to the foregoing in the books of the firm and to prepare :

(a) Revaluation Account; (b) Revised Balance Sheet as at 30.6.97; and (c) The Legal Representatives' Loan Account for the three years ended 30.6.97 (calculations to be made to the nearest rupee)

[CA]

[Ans. Amount paid to Executor Rs. 1,15,000; Total of Balance Sheet Rs. 1,79,000]

Some exciting gifts are up for grabs with this book!!

FINANCIAL ACCOUNTING

VOLUME I

Dr S Kr Paul and Prof. Chandrani Paul

DEAR READERS

By now you must have gone through this book in the entirety. So we invite your assessment on this title with absolute impartiality and candid observations. After all, we publishers blindly depend on your benchmarking. Friends, please fill up the open spaces below with CAPITAL LETTERS. You may add some extra sheets of paper if the space provided is not sufficient for you.

i. What are the important topics of your syllabus which are not adequately covered in this book?

ii. In which chapters and on what topics the treatment of the subject-matter by the author is not satisfactory and why?

iii. Have you come across the typos, factual inaccuracies, inconsistencies, and other forms of mistakes in the book? If yes, then please specify the mistakes and page numbers.

iv. Name top three books on the same subject, which, in your consideration, are better than this book. Could you provide some reasons?

Your 1st Preference: ....

Your 2nd Preference: ....

Your 3rd Preference: ....

v. Any suggestion to improve the quality of illustrations, diagrams, etc.?

vi. How did you like the cover design? Any suggestion on colours?

vii. Suggestions for further improvement of production-standard:

viii. Who recommended you this book:

☐ Teacher ☐ Friend ☐ Parents ☐ Bookseller ☐ Librarian

ix. Name of the person who has recommended:

Designation: ....

Address: ....

Phone No.: ....

e-mail: ....

x. Name and address of the bookseller from whom you have purchased this book:

....

....

....

xi. Name and address of the library where you would like to find the book:

....

....

xii. Name and address of your institution (Please mention the University or Board):

....

....

xiii. Your name, e-mail, and complete postal address:

....

....

....

xiv. A few other titles published by us that you would like to read:

....

....

The best assessment will be rewarded half-yearly. The award will be in the form of our publications, as decided by the Editorial and Marketing Operations Division, amounting to Rs. 1000/- (Rupees one thousand) only.

....

Please mail the filled up coupon at your earliest to :

Editorial & Marketing Operations Division

NEW CENTRAL BOOK AGENCY (P) Ltd

8/1 Chintamoni Das Lane, Kolkata 700 009

West Bengal, INDIA

Phone + Fax: 033 + 2241 8411, 2241 8573, 2241 9094

e-mail: ncbapvtltd@eth.net, ncba@cal2.vsnl.net.in

Website: www.centralgroup.com